BUSINESS

LAW

BUSINESS LAW

ARTHUR R. MILLER
Harvard University

THOMAS L. GOSSMAN
Western Michigan University

Illustrations Developed by
GERALD W. STONE, JR.
RALPH T. BYRNS

SCOTT, FORESMAN/LITTLE, BROWN HIGHER EDUCATION
A Division of Scott, Foresman and Company
Glenview, Illinois   London, England

Library of Congress Cataloging-in-Publication Data

Miller, Arthur Raphael
  Business law.

  1. Commercial law—United States. 2. Industrial laws
and legislation—United States. 3. Business enterprises
—United States. 4. Business law—United States.
I. Gossman, Thomas L.   II. Title.
KF889.M52 1990   346.73′07   89-24335
ISBN 0-673-38413-6   347.3067

123456 - RRN - 949392919089

Preface

Business Law is a comprehensive text with cases, designed for use in a course required of business and accounting majors. It can be used in one- or two-term courses offered at the sophomore or junior level. It thoroughly covers the legal environment, commercial law, and the regulatory environment, and includes all topics tested in the business law section of the CPA exam.

The text grew out of our years of teaching law and business students around the country. As we evaluated the texts available for the undergraduate business law course we became convinced that there was a need for a new book that could provide a broad-based overview of the entire field. Many of the most popular texts were in fourth, fifth, or greater editions and had established areas of emphasis. While they were updated in each edition, they were still designed for courses as they were taught ten or fifteen years ago. We have therefore developed a text of broad scope that offers greater flexibility for today's instructors.

Today's business law students are usually committed to pursuing careers in management or accounting, and they need exposure to all areas of the law that could be of professional significance. So rather than offering exhaustive detail in selected areas, we decided our text should convey the fundamental reasoning embodied in business law. We have aimed for scope and clarity, and trust that students and teachers alike will find *Business Law* a valuable resource for current courses and future reference.

The approach we have taken emphasizes sound explication of the fundamentals and examination of numerous legal questions that face businesses in the 1990s. Particular aspects of our book have been designed to encourage critical thinking, and we have presented material in a way that allows individual instructors true flexibility in tailoring lectures and discussions to stress topics of the most value to their students.

APPROACH

This text is built on a *theory approach* that stresses the evolution of the law and legal reasoning. Historical perspectives and numerous examples encourage students to appreciate the varied aspects of particular legal questions; the consistent emphasis on theory allows them to understand the sources as well as applications of the law. Classic and contemporary cases complement the textual presentation and provide students with further opportunities to apply concepts and abstract rules.

We have concentrated on clearly explaining key points and providing useful concrete examples. Our carefully edited case excerpts illustrate ideas and challenge readers to apply their understanding. We believe our approach leaves ample room for individual teachers to expand upon important points and otherwise adapt the text to suit a range of classroom needs.

TEXT ORGANIZATION

Business Law employs a fairly standard organization that reflects common course designs. It begins by examining the legal environment, proceeds to cover topics in business and commercial law, and concludes with sections on the regulatory environment and several special topics. The scope of coverage in the text's ten parts differs from that of other books in some important ways that reflect our theory approach.

For example, we cover contracts in seven chapters (Part II) rather than the usual ten or eleven, because we organize topics of legality, writing, and form along with capacity in chapters on voidable and unenforceable contracts. Part V, Credit and Secured Transactions, offers expanded coverage of security interests and suretyship that lays the groundwork for later chapters on property. The property unit (Part VI) includes both traditional chapters and the challenging topic of intellectual property and computers. We have also included trusts and estates in this unit, emphasizing how these property-related concepts can affect contemporary business.

Part VII contains four chapters on agency law. We fully examine liability in the agency context in order to prepare students for a deeper understanding of business organizations, which are covered in Part VIII. We have included a full chapter on foreign corporations in Part VIII to offer readers insight into the important area of interstate operations. Finally, Part IX on government regulation contains two thorough chapters on antitrust law that show historical developments as well as current rules, and three chapters on employment-related law. Insurance, accounts' liability, and international law are addressed in Part X of the text.

CHAPTER HIGHLIGHTS

Part I, The Legal Environment of Business, begins with a chapter on ethics and the law that compares and contrasts the two systems of reasoning. Chapter 1 also illustrates the basic role ethical considerations play in the formulation of American law. It can be assigned at any point in the course when issues of business ethics arise, because it clearly reveals the ethical underpinnings of legal remedies as they apply to commerce.

Part I also includes a basic chapter introducing the law, a chapter on courts and procedure, and a single chapter on torts and crimes. It concludes with a straightforward chapter on constitutional law that fully rounds out the introduction to the American legal system.

Part II, the Common Law of Contracts, is organized to reflect the steps in formation and discharge. Chapter 9, Voidable Contracts, addresses issues of capacity and genuineness of as-

sent and includes a substantial section on minors. Chapter 10, Unenforceable Contracts, covers issues of legality, then handles concepts of writing and form in the context of the Statute of Frauds.

Chapter 13, Introduction to Sales, opens Part III with a historical perspective on the Uniform Commercial Code and ties sales concepts to the preceding unit on contracts. This chapter also thoroughly covers applications of UCC Article 2. Other chapters in Part III cover basic concepts of sales and warranties; Chapter 16 includes discussion of consumer protection.

Continuing with law under the UCC, Part IV on commmercial paper addresses negotiability, negotiation, and holder in due course in two carefully constructed chapters. Chapter 19 then covers liability and discharge; Chapter 20 examines banks and their relationships with customers and contains a special section on electronic funds transfers.

Part V, Credit and Secured Transactions, begins with two chapters on security interests. Chapter 21 discusses them in the context of personal property, while Chapter 22 addresses real property. Suretyship is given special treatment in Chapter 23, and the unit concludes with coverage of bankruptcy.

Property issues receive comprehensive coverage in Part VI. Chapter 25 covers personal property and bailments; Chapters 26 and 27 cover real property interests, transfer, and encumbrance. These two chapters offer in-depth treatment and key cases relating to leasehold estates, nonpossessory interests, marketable title, land contracts, deeds, and mortgages.

Chapter 28, Intellectual Property and Computers, begins with a detailed discussion of patents, copyrights, trademarks, and trade secrets, emphasizing their relevance in contemporary business practice. The chapter then looks at computer-related issues in property and constitutional contexts, and concludes by briefly tying these issues to contracts, torts, and criminal law.

The property unit is completed by Chapter 29 on trusts and Chapter 30 on decedents' estates. We have carefully emphasized how the protection and transfer of property in these contexts can be related to business operations. We include these topics in the property unit in order to provide continuity for students; however, these chapters may be assigned later as they are in many courses.

The four chapters in Part VII on agency provide a very firm foundation for understanding business organizations and later chapters on employment-related law. Chapter 31 fully defines the formation and nature of the agency relationship. Contract liability is the focus of Chapter 32; tort and criminal liability are covered in Chapter 33. Many of the issues often addressed in discussions of business ethics are examined in these chapters, and their relevance to today's students is clear. Part VII concludes with a chapter on duties and termination. Throughout the agency unit, we take appropriate opportunities to relate agency concepts to topics covered earlier in the text, thus offering truly comprehensive treatment of this important area.

Our business organization unit, Part VIII, contains eleven chapters in a traditional sequence. Following an introductory chapter that succinctly defines and compares the basic types of organization, three chapters are devoted to partnerships; one chapter focuses on limited partnerships; and five chapters examine corporations. We take a special look in Chapters 41 and 42 at corporate financing and shareholder liability, and follow this with a complete chapter on merger, acquisition, and dissolution. Chapter 44 provides detailed coverage of foreign corporations with a number of cases addressing relevant issues in interstate commerce. Part VIII concludes with a chapter on franchising and cooperatives, topics of particular interest to many business students.

Part IX, Government Regulation, focuses on American law as it is made and policed. We have consistently used historical perspectives to illustrate how government and the law have intertwined and evolved as business activities have expanded and changed. Chapter 46 introduces administrative agencies and their role in rulemaking and adjudication. Chapter 47 focuses on securities regulation, while Chapters 48 and 49

examine antitrust law, showing how it has evolved in the United States and its contemporary influence on businesses.

We include three chapters on labor and employment law, again because of the important role these concepts play in contemporary business. Chapter 50 looks at labor-management relations as the law has evolved to regulate them. Chapter 51 focuses on collective bargaining and various types of concerted action. Chapter 52, Employment Law, offers detailed coverage of such areas as safety, discrimination, and sexual harrassment.

The chapters in Part X focus on three "special topics." Chapter 53 covers insurance; Chapter 54 looks specifically at accountants' professional liability; and Chapter 55 addresses issues in international law. Chapter 55 ties previously covered concepts to international operations, and also looks at common concerns such as foreign distributors, foreign manufacturing facilities, expropriation, and licensing abroad.

PEDAGOGICAL FEATURES

Throughout the development of *Business Law* we have worked to create a text that is eminently readable. In addition to striving for crisp, clear prose we have developed a number of features that can help students understand and apply fundamental theories, concepts, and rules. Foremost among these is the presentation of cases in every chapter, yet other learning aids also greatly enhance the text's effectiveness.

Cases

The case decisions excerpted in *Business Law* have been carefully chosen with instructional flexibility in mind. Cases of great historical significance are included when appropriate, as they are in virtually all business law texts. We have also chosen to include many "classic" cases that will be familiar to most instructors; these cases show how the law has evolved while illlustrating rules discussed in the text. When applicable, we present several cases that show how a rule has been interpreted in different contexts or at different times. Numerous contemporary cases allow students to apply concepts to today's business issues. Overall, our approach encourages instructors to rely on the text for basic case illustrations and elaborate with additional cases as they wish.

Each case excerpt is preceded by a succinct explanation of the facts before the court and the disposition of the case at trial and on appeal. Following the edited text of the decision, we pose two or three questions to the student. These questions are not only designed to help the reader grasp the main point of the decision, they are also intended to provoke thought and discussion. Often a question will ask the student to extend the application of a rule to a slightly different factual situation, or to relate the case to two or more broad areas of the law. The case questions prod students to form opinions and view the decision from several perspectives.

Textual Examples

We have found in teaching (and in writing this book) that one can rarely offer students too many examples. Every concept and rule in this text is complemented by at least one concrete example that encourages the reader to "work through" an application of the law. In many chapters, we develop an example as we develop the concept presentation so that students can see how the law may apply to different aspects of the same situation. Particularly in complex areas such as sales, commercial paper, and property, the examples also help students pace their reading so that they have time to grasp important details.

Illustrations and Tables

In keeping with our overall pedagogical approach we have included diagrams and tables that summarize and organize key concepts. In Parts I and II, for example, the text is periodically broken up by tables that briefly define and categorize terms that will be fundamental to later discussions. Some diagrams offer visual summaries of steps in formation of legal relationships, while others show how different areas of the law may come to bear on a given situation. Still other illustrations augment the text with data that tie the law to contemporary business.

Other Chapter Features

Each chapter opens with a brief outline to help students plan their reading. Headings and subheadings are used liberally within the chapters to further organize and break up the narrative. Key terms are printed in bold where they are defined, and Latin terms are fully explained.

Chapters conclude with a narrative summary of key ideas that also lends perspective to the chapter as a whole. Key terms and concepts are listed in order of appearance to aid students in preparing for tests. An average of ten problems are offered at the end of each chapter to further encourage students to apply what they have learned. Most of these problems are based on actual cases, and the citations for them are provided in the *Instructor's Manual*.

Glossary and Appendixes

A thorough glossary is indispensable in a business law text that will probably be used as a reference for students' later work, and we have provided one. It includes many "terms of art" as well as all of the key terms in the text.

Most business law texts include appendixes that reproduce the United States Constitution and key portions of the UCC, for example. We have expanded our list of appendixes to include excerpts from major acts discussed at length in the text.

Our first appendix is on how to read and brief a case. It can be assigned early in the course for students who may be uncomfortable or unfamiliar with legal references. We then present the United States Constitution and the Uniform Commercial Code. Other appendixes provide relevant excerpts of the Uniform Partnership Act, the Uniform Limited Partnership Act, the Revised Uniform Limited Partnership Act, the Model Business Corporation Act, the Sherman and Clayton Acts, the Federal Trade Commission Act, the Robinson-Patman Act, the Foreign Corrupt Practices Act, and the National Labor Relations Act. It is our hope that these appendixes will help students appreciate the evolution of business law as well as make the text easier for them to use.

TEXT SUPPLEMENTS

Business Law is accompanied by a range of ancillary materials for use by instructors and students. They are specifically designed to enhance teaching and learning in a variety of course structures.

INSTRUCTOR'S MANUAL Written by Thomas Gossman and carefully designed to support the text, this helpful resource includes chapter outlines, chapter objectives, case synopses, and answers to all end of chapter problems from the text.

TEST BANK A comprehensive bank of over 3000 questions includes multiple choice, true/false, and short answer questions. Each question is coded according to the level of difficulty (easy, medium, hard) and includes a page reference to the main text where the information being tested is covered.

TESTMASTER COMPUTERIZED TEST BANK Available to qualified adopters of the text (for use with IBM PC's and compatibles), this computerized version of the test bank allows the instructor the flexibility of adding, editing, or deleting individual questions as well as creating different versions of the same test by means of a scramble option.

STUDENT STUDY GUIDE Created by Thomas Gossman to function as an interactive learning device, each chapter of this unique supplement includes a concept overview, chapter focus discussion, content outline, point of the case discussion, key terms and concepts drill, and a mastery quiz that includes approximately 30 questions per chapter that have purposely been designed to reflect the format of the Test Bank.

ACKNOWLEDGMENTS

Business Law grew out of our teaching experience, but it also developed over years of writing, rewriting, and painstaking refinement that have resulted in the combination of narrative, cases, and pedagogical aids we believe is superior to other texts available today. The manuscript was reviewed in several drafts by experienced business law teachers from a full range of two- and four-year institutions. We consulted people with expertise in specific areas of the law as well as seasoned instructors who could tell us what would or would not work in their classrooms. Our reviewers and editors provided almost endless feedback concerning the organization, clarity, and accuracy of the text, and the final product you see has therefore benefited from extensive developmental attention.

We offer our thanks to the following reviewers who devoted a great deal of time reading and advising us concerning the manuscript. Their comments and suggestions were of great help in improving this book.

- Thomas M. Apke, California State University, Fullerton
- Stanley R. Berkowitz, Northeastern University (Boston)
- Harvey R. Boller, Loyola University of Chicago
- William H. Daughtrey, Jr., Virginia Commonwealth University
- Alex Devience, Jr., DePaul University
- Debra Dobray, Southern Methodist University
- Larry L. Foster, Central State University
- John W. Gergacz, The University of Kansas
- Susan F. Grady, University of Massachusetts, Amherst
- Frances J. Hill, University of Wisconsin, Whitewater
- Janine S. Hiller, Virginia Polytechnic Institute and State University

- Michael E. Howard, The University of Iowa
- Richard J. Hunter, Jr., Seton Hall University
- James M. Jackman, Oklahoma State University
- Bryce Jones, Northeast Missouri State University
- Deborah Kemp, Louisiana State University
- Carey H. Kirk, University of Northern Iowa
- Gene A. Marsh, The University of Alabama, Tuscaloosa
- John W. McGee, Southwest Texas State University
- Daniel McLoughlin, San Francisco State University
- Leo C. Moerson, The George Washington University
- Alan Moggio, Illinois Central College
- James Molloy, University of Wisconsin, Whitewater
- Charles E. Moran, West Valley College
- W. Alfred Mukatis, Oregon State University
- Ross D. Petty, Babson College
- John F. Roake, Community College of San Mateo
- Ira B. Sprotzer, Rider College
- Larry D. Strate, University of Nevada, Las Vegas
- Gola E. Waters, Southern Illinois University at Carbondale
- Edward L. Welsh, Phoenix College
- Donald A. Wiesner, University of Miami

We offer a special thanks to Ms. Karen Star, Western Michigan University, who worked diligently and so cheerfully for so many months typing, revising, and correcting the manuscript.

We also wish to acknowledge the contribution of Gerald Stone and Ralph Byrns, two experienced and successful textbook authors, who developed our illustration program. Their contributions to the final draft helped us further refine our approach and certainly have enhanced the usefulness of the text.

Arthur R. Miller
Thomas L. Gossman

Brief table of contents

Table of contents

APPENDIX

BUSINESS
LAW

PART I

The Legal

Environment of

Business

An understanding of law and the legal system is essential to us in both our personal and business lives. Prior to embarking on a study of relevant substantive law, however, it is important to understand the underlying environment of the American legal system. Thus, Part I of this book addresses the legal environment. Chapter 1 discusses the relationship between ethics and law as an important basis for examining the nature and foundations of law, which it treated in Chapter 2. In turn, Chapter 3 examines the process by which legal rights and legal obligations are enforced through the court system. Chapter 4 treats two areas of substantive law—tort law and criminal law. Finally, Chapter 5 addresses the issue of constitutional law, which has a foundational impact on all areas of American law. A thorough grounding in the subject matter of these first five chapters is important as an aid to acquiring a clear understanding of the law.

1

Chapter | 1

Ethics and the Law

_____

_____

_____

_____

UNDERSTANDING THE SUBJECT OF ETHICS

Is it surprising that the first chapter of a business law book is devoted to a discussion of ethics? It shouldn't be, because ethics, law, and business are inextricably interwoven. In terms of the subject of this book, in a society such as ours, business could not function responsibly without both a legal and an ethical framework. So read on, because this chapter is of special importance.

Ethics is more than just a matter for philosophical debate. A clear understanding of certain broad ethical principles will facilitate the understanding of law and the process of legal reasoning immeasurably. This chapter is designed to help achieve that understanding.

Many law textbooks designed primarily for business students include a chapter on ethics. Most, however, deal with ethics in terms of right versus wrong and good versus bad in the process of decision making, and present cases illustrating ethical and unethical decisions by business managers and boards of directors. We have decided not to present that kind of material. Instead, this chapter approaches the subject of ethics as a study of how ethics affects the law, and how law affects ethics. This relationship between law and ethics should be thought of as an aid to understanding law and to predicting the legal ramifications of decisions that may be required in one's business and personal life.

The Rebirth of Concern for Ethics

Ethics, although hardly a new field, had received comparatively little attention for many years when it experienced a rebirth in the 1970s. The reason most often cited was the Watergate scandal. National attention was focused suddenly and intensely for several months on the "crimes" of the Nixon administration. The seriousness of the ethical breaches was viewed as directly related to the power and importance of those involved. Although the world was condemning the burglary and bugging of the Democratic National Headquarters by a handful of presidential aides and the coverup by the president, stories of murder, rape, kidnapping, burglary, and industrial espionage went virtually unnoticed. Why? Perhaps because the integrity of the nation's executive branch was at stake, and the confidence of many of its citizens in the principles of our society and government was shaken.

In addition to Watergate, the 1970s saw an increased concern about ethics in the business sector. In 1973, the Equity Funding Corporation of America collapsed, exposing a multibillion dollar business fraud. When the facts came out, they showed that this apparently successfull corporation was built on a foundation of falsified statements and phony business records. During the same decade, partially because of an inflationary economy, many large corporations ceased doing business, revealing many underfunded pension plans. Compounding the difficulties caused by the general unemployment resulting from the adverse economy, the dreams of countless retired and soon-to-be-retired workers simply vanished. Even with Congress's enactment of the Employees Retirement Income Security Act of 1974, the effects of underfunded pension plans have continued.

Although these and other stories of ethical crises in the 1970s seem to have faded into history, the 1980s saw the rise of new problems such as unfriendly corporate takeovers and insider trading, causing continued public concern over the ethics of business. Not surprisingly, corporate America has become more conscious of public opinion and the need to demonstrate business's ethical responsibility. The problem is that there appears to be great confusion and lack of agreement concerning the scope of the subject of ethics, what constitutes ethical behavior, and the relationship between ethics and the law.

What Is Ethics?

Most dictionaries define *ethics* by partial listings of its characteristics or concerns. For example, dictionaries include such generalized concepts as "honesty," "truth," and "justice." But ethics is more than these. **Ethics** is a branch of philosophy that addresses each person's relationships with every other person. Thus stated, you can see that ethics is extremely encompassing and very vague.

Adding to the lack of precision is the widely held thought that ethics is completely personal and subjective. That is, what is ethical is simply a matter of individual opinion. This is partially, but not wholly, true. We find almost total uniformity of opinion regarding many ethical questions. Virtually all societies, from the very beginning, have considered such acts as murder, rape, robbery, and incest to be wrong, and have punished people for these acts accordingly. Any deviation from certain standards of human behavior almost universally has been considered unacceptable.

The Relationship between Ethics and Law

Ethics both provides a basis for developing the law and arises out of and reflects the law. For purposes of this discussion, *law* may be defined as "a set of norms conceived by society for its own regulation." The objective of law is the governance of human conduct in the best interests of the particular social unit that makes the law. Therefore, law itself may be considered a kind of ethical system (regulating people's relationships with each other), differing from others only in that it is enforced by official power. Proceeding from this premise, four highly related questions are worth considering: (1) Is what is legal always ethical? (2) Is what is illegal always unethical? (3) Is what is ethical always legal? (4) Is what is unethical always illegal?

The Theory of Two Ethics

In order to answer the questions just posed, it is necessary to take a closer look at what is meant by "ethics." Most philosophers agree that there are two standards of ethics—*community (societal) ethics* and *personal (individual) ethics*. **Community ethics** comprehend the rules set down as minimum requirements for ethical conduct by members of society—for example, the "thou shalt nots" of the Bible. Compliance with the rules of civil and criminal law also falls into this category. These are minimum standards established by society for its own regulation.

The breach of any law constitutes both a legal and an ethical (moral) wrong. All agree that illegal conduct is not ethical conduct. However, there may be disagreement as to whether (1) the rule was broken, and (2) if so, whether unusual circumstances make breaking the law more ethical than complying with it. Many of these disagreements end up in the courts for resolution. The answers to these questions should become clearer as the category of personal ethics is considered.

Personal ethics refers to conduct that aspires to a higher standard of behavior than the minimums established by community ethics. The two bodies of ethics must be distinguished. Theoretically there should be little or no disagreement on the content of community ethics, since they are formulated by a consensus of community opinion. (In reality, there often is disagreement.) In contrast, personal ethics are highly subjective and, as the name implies, personal. Generally speaking, the two are clearly distinguishable by asking

whether particular conduct would be condemned by the community or if we would only be admired for conducting ourselves in a different way. If we would be condemned, the act is a breach of community ethics, and if we only would be admired for conducting ourselves in a different way, it is a breach of personal ethics not to pursue that course of behavior.

A particular situation may call both bodies of ethics into play. In some cases, community ethics may be violated in order to comply with personal ethics, and the overall result is considered, at least by most, to be "good." That is true of the civil rights activists who violated segregation statutes and trespass laws to achieve equal treatment for minority groups in the 1950s and 1960s. Deciding when this is appropriate poses a dilemma, and it raises three new questions: (1) Under what circumstances should community ethics be sacrificed for personal ethics? (For example, under

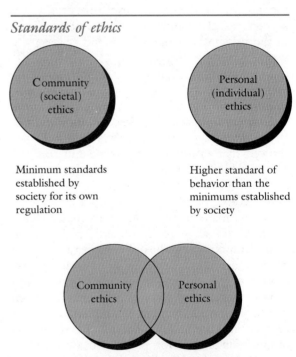

Standards of ethics

Community (societal) ethics

Personal (individual) ethics

Minimum standards established by society for its own regulation

Higher standard of behavior than the minimums established by society

Community ethics

Personal ethics

The two are not, however, mutually exclusive; each acts and in turn is acted upon by the other.

what driving conditions, and to what extent, might a person feel compelled by personal ethics to violate a speed law in order to rush an injured or sick passenger to a hospital?) (2) At what point must the law be ignored in order to achieve justice (fundamental fairness)? (3) When that point is reached, do we say that violating community ethics is not unethical, or do we say that it is justified and only less unethical than the alternative? To answer this last question probably serves no useful purpose, since it merely is theoretical. However, the first two must be answered in order for a legal system to function properly.

Law and Justice

Lawyers, judges, and courts face these first two questions in considering every case. Many of the cases in which they are involved make membership in the legal profession worthwhile. People face these questions daily in the conduct of their lives. Part of the problem is that **justice** (fundamental fairness) is a continuum, but legal principles are set at points along that continuum. Compare telling time by a sundial or an analog watch (one with continuously sweeping hands) to telling time by a digital watch. In theory, the analog timepiece (justice) always is accurate, not just at 12:01 and 12:02, but at all points in between. The digital timepiece (law), on the other hand, can be accurate only at specific, predetermined points—it registers either 12:01 or 12:02, but nothing in between.

Law sometimes is criticized as not serving justice. Certainly law applied inflexibly, without regard to justice or to the circumstances of a particular situation, is likely to yield results that are less than completely satisfactory. The job of lawyers and judges is to use the rules of law as tools for seeking a just result in every case. To some extent this is what is meant by applying "legislative intent" and "the spirit of the law." Unfortunately this utopian objective cannot be achieved in every case because our legal system is less than perfect.

For our society to remain civilized, we must obey the law and thereby comply with community ethics. But for many people that is only a beginning in certain situations. They feel obligated to follow an altered course in order to obey personal ethics. For example, suppose Alfred parks his car in a 30-minute parking zone, intending to remain there for two hours. In order to be in strict compliance with the law and community ethics, Alfred might return to his car at 30-minute intervals, drive it out onto the street, then immediately pull back into the parking space. A higher personal ethic, however, would require that Alfred move his car to another location to permit others an opportunity to park, which was the reason for the law. Suppose, however, this was a slow time for parking in the area, plenty of comparable spaces were available, and Alfred needed to remain in the space more than 30 minutes in order to help a sick friend. Might these facts change Alfred's duty under the law, community ethics, or personal ethics?

CONFLICTS BETWEEN LAW AND ETHICS

Elements of the Conflict

Conflicts between the law and ethical values are inevitable. This is true for two basic reasons. First, law is the creation of society, but ethics, to a great extent, is individual (personal ethics rather than only community ethics). We each hold our own ethical values, some of which are in common with those held by a majority of society, and some of which are not. Second, ethical values can change in an instant, but changing the law typically is a long and laborious process.

In a few instances, legislators and courts may decide to establish or retain a statute or a judicial precedent that is inconsistent with the ethical values of a majority of society, substituting their judgments about ethics or good social policy for those of their constituents. In many instances this occurs in highly emotional contexts such as abortion, school prayer, and the death penalty. Not surprisingly, this deviation is thought by many to be an imperfection of a representative democracy, which, they think, always should follow the will of the majority. On the other hand, this departure from the democratic ideal may be "morally right" according to some higher value, or even constitutionally mandated by provisions designed to protect the rights of minorities against the will of the majority.

Factors In Decision Making

When law and ethical values conflict, a choice must be made. However, the choice of either may bring condemnation and possibly sanctions from advocates of the other. This "Catch 22" situation virtually is impossible to avoid. Therefore, decisions ideally should be made to reap the greatest possible benefits at the least possible cost. Of particular importance is how our actions will be viewed by others.

Suppose Alan, a poor person, is dying of a fatal blood disease for which a cure has been discovered by Dr. Benson. The cost of the medicine is $2000. Alan tries his best, but is able to obtain only $400. He offers to give Dr. Benson the $400 if Dr. Benson will let him have the medicine and extend credit for the remainder. Dr. Benson refuses. Suppose, in the alternative: (1) Alan begs for money on the street in violation of an ordinance prohibiting public begging; (2) Alan breaks into Dr. Benson's office and steals the medicine; (3) Alan burglarizes Carr's home and steals the remaining $1600; or (4) Alan robs Davidson at gunpoint and takes $1600. Under which of these circumstances is Alan "most wrong"? Would it make any difference if it were Alan's brother, child, or friend who needed the medicine?

In all of these cases, Alan is violating the law and will be subject to some condemnation for that. Therefore, Alan also is guilty morally from the perspective of community ethics. However, if Alan chooses to do nothing and obey the law,

would he be guilty of a greater wrong? Presumably obeying the law might be more acceptable if it were Alan, rather than his brother, child, or friend, who was dying. Conversely, to what degree should Alan be condemned if he chose to act on the "instinct" for self-preservation?

Which option should Alan choose? From a legal viewpoint, the possibilities probably are listed in ascending order of legal seriousness, assuming that begging is less serious than burglary, that the burglary of a business is less serious than the burglary of a home, and that burglary is less serious than armed robbery.

From an ethical viewpoint, the same probably is true, but not entirely for the same reasons. Begging, perhaps, is not viewed as immoral under the circumstances of our story, except that it involves a breach of community ethics. Also, burglarizing Dr. Benson is preferred over involving parties who played no part in the creation of the problem, such as Carr and Davidson. In these circumstances, Alan will be faced not with determining which alternative is "right," but which is the "least wrong."

Sometimes we face legal/ethical conflicts of a second type. The law may mandate positive action, requiring that an individual do something he or she considers immoral. For example, under Nazi leadership, many Germans were obliged to participate, one way or another, in the extermination of millions of Jews. This was considered so offensive to generally held ethical beliefs that it was almost universally condemned, and compliance with Nazi law was considered a violation of "natural law." Following World War II, many participants in the holocaust were convicted of "crimes against humanity" by an international tribunal. Thus, Nazi laws presented Germans with two choices, both of which proved to be criminal. Certainly, practical considerations affected an individual's choice. Taking the ethical route of disobeying German law was likely to lead to immediate and dire consequences at the hands of the Nazi regime. Obeying German law, however, undoubtedly seemed safer because punishment for violating natural law was remote and uncertain, since most Germans believed their nation would not be defeated in the war and never anticipated a war-crimes tribunal being established. Thus, selection of the "ethical" alternative of refusing to participate in the holocaust required a high degree of moral commitment and courage on the part of the person involved.

A third type of conflict is presented when the law operates in an unethical fashion against the decision maker. For example, should minority group members have complied with the various laws fostering racial discrimination that existed prior to the Civil Rights Act of 1964? Black civil rights activists were faced with the choice of obeying these discriminatory laws or violating them to vindicate ethical values. Compliance by an individual presumably would have had little impact in perpetuating the perceived evil, and violating the law would have had little impact in eliminating it. However, the collective pursuit, by a substantial number of people, of what has come to be called civil disobedience, might, and apparently did, have an impact. The important question, though, is did the end justify the means? Would the result have been achieved as well by a more orderly process for changing the law? (Realistically, of course, at the very least it would have taken far longer for the normal legal process to achieve any semblance of racial equality.) The ultimate question, of course, is even if you believe disobedience to the law was proper in the civil rights context, when else does the end justify what means? Should a journalist, for example, trespass or break into an office to get information for a story about corruption on the theory that the public disclosure of evil justifies the criminal behavior?

A fourth and final type of ethical conflict occurs when the law permits, but does not require, particular action that an individual feels to be immoral. An example of this type of conflict is the Surpeme Court's decision giving women a legal right to an elective abortion. One who objects to the law on ethical grounds need not exercise the right and therefore remains personally untouched by it, although he or she may feel compelled to oppose it. In this type of conflict, the "moral" alternative generally can be followed without violating the law. Therefore, those who do violate the law in pursuit of the ethical result, for instance by bombing abortion clinics, ordinarily are more subject to condemnation from both a legal and an ethical perspective.

What can be concluded from all of this? Only that there inevitably are conflicts between law and ethics in many contexts. Situations may occur that even require, or at least encourage, an ultimate choice of which law to violate, rather than a choice of whether to violate. In all conflicts, however, individual ideals and societal ethical values become compelling forces.

It is important to understand that both law and ethics are factors in decision making. Sometimes they militate toward the same result, as in the case of the law and community ethics, or when personal ethics dictate that the greatest good can be done only by obeying the law. Sometimes they point to different results, and that is when personal ethics always are involved. However, it may be stated broadly that societal ethics ultimately are translated into law, at least if they are maintained for an appreciable period of time, but that is not true for personal ethics. The latter give rise to the most frequent and serious conflicts with the law, and therefore pose the most difficult choices for personal action.

Ethical conflicts

Conflict	Example
Undertaking unethical actions due to personal circumstances	Stealing money to obtain life-saving medicine
Being forced to undertake an action that is considered immoral	Executing a person against your will
Law operates in an unethical fashion	Internment of Japanese-Americans during World War II
Law permits immoral action	Various experiments performed on animals

ELEMENTS OF LEGAL AND ETHICAL GUILT

Although it seems impossible to establish absolute rules for determining which ethical values supervene which rules of law and vice versa, two factors appear fundamental in determining the degree of guilt associated with particular actions. These factors are intent and motive.

Intent (or voluntariness) is essential to moral guilt. No one should be condemned as unethical for any act that truly is involuntary. The same may be said of criminal guilt under the law. All crimes involve some degree of intent. On the other hand, although motive relates to the degree of ethical condemnation associated with certain conduct, it is not considered a factor in determining criminal guilt. It may be relevant, however, in assessing the kind and degree of punishment to be meted out.

In criminal law, in addition to being an essential element of criminal behavior, the type, or degree, of intent influences the degree of guilt and ultimately the degree of punishment. For example, suppose Amis kills Brinker under each of the following circumstances:

1. They are admiring the scenery from the edge of the Grand Canyon and Amis has his arm across Brinker's shoulders. Amis experiences an involuntary muscle spasm that causes his arm to come forward, pushing Brinker over the side.
2. Amis, while insane, incapable of knowing what he is doing, imagines Brinker is trying to harm him, and stabs her with a knife from a nearby table.
3. Amis, while intoxicated, incapable of knowing what he is doing, stabs Brinker as in the immediately preceding example.
4. Amis and Brinker are arguing and, during the argument, Brinker makes highly offensive statements about the moral character of Amis's mother in a loud tone of voice at a family gathering. Amis, in a fit of fury, grabs a knife and stabs Brinker to death.
5. In the immediately preceding example, assume Amis does nothing until the next day, when he waits in an alley for Brinker to pass by on her way home from work, forces Brinker into the alley, and stabs her.

In the *first* case Amis's act was totally involuntary, and Amis is neither ethically nor legally liable if the facts are shown to be as stated. The same is true in the *second* case; although the stabbing was voluntary and was intentionally done in one sense, Amis still will not be held criminally responsible for an act he could not control. In the *third* case, although Amis's state of mind was the same as in the second case, ethical and legal guilt will be attached to his act because his intoxication ("insanity") was self-induced. Also it is likely that his actions will be regarded as involving a higher degree of moral guilt than legal guilt. The *fourth* case involves an even higher degree of legal guilt because the intent is clear and the act, itself, was voluntary in the full sense of the term. Morally, Amis's guilt may be higher than in the third case, but perhaps it is merely the same. The question is whether Amis's moral guilt is greater because he acted in the heat of passion than when he voluntarily became intoxicated, knowing that he would not be in full control of his faculties. In the *fifth* case, Amis clearly is the most guilty, both morally and legally. The clarity of the premeditation—Amis's thinking about and calculating his actions—makes a great difference in both categories.

As previously mentioned, the element of motivation plays no real part in establishing the degree of offense in criminal law. However, it is an important factor in ethical guilt. Earlier in this chapter examples were given in which Alan obtained medicine to cure a fatal illness by several methods. In all of the cases, whether he acted to get the cure for himself or for someone else, the legal guilt was the same. However, less ethical guilt probably was attached when he acted to save the life of another rather than his own life. In addition, his punishment under the law probably would be less in that situation. It seems, therefore, that as intent is important to law, motive is important to ethics.

REGULATION OF ETHICAL STANDARDS

Ethical Decision Making

Ethical standards that have not been translated into law are regulated primarily by the unofficial sanction of social condemnation. Often that is enough. In some ways these social sanctions are a more positive regulating force than legal sanctions. They involve less formal procedure, and therefore their impact can be swifter and more certain. If an individual values community opinion, for either social or economic reasons, then the force of social condemnation may be persuasive in his or her decision about how to act. Under many circumstances, reliance on ethical standards can provide a viable alternative to legal regulation. In other situations, however, such as criminal conduct or when social condemnation is ineffective, regulation by official sanction is necessary.

Most people decide what course of action to pursue in a given situation by the rational process of weighing and balancing the potential benefits and repercussions of each possibility. The more attractive the benefits of socially undesirable activity, the greater the need for regulation by law. Social condemnation seems to become ineffective more quickly than legal punishment as the stakes get higher.

Legal sanctions typically are imposed to preserve free competition in the marketplace. Examples are found in the antitrust and securities laws. Legal sanctions also are available to regulate conduct that may cause great harm to others. Some examples of this are rules governing fiduciary relationships (relationships of high trust and confidence), controversies among family members and others in special relationships recognized by the common law, certain dealings under the Uniform

Commercial Code, and people providing various professional services. Let us look in more detail at some of these examples of legal regulation of ethical standards.

Competition in the Marketplace

Free enterprise is the basis for the economic system in the United States. In order for the economy to function properly, competition in the marketplace must be free and fair. History has demonstrated that completely unregulated competition falls prey to many disabling forces: artificial barriers are erected to prevent the entry of new competition; although the system works properly only when buyers are fully informed concerning their choices, the necessary information may be withheld; and some sellers will compete unfairly by refusing to account for external costs to society generated by their enterprises.

Antitrust law is the primary legal vehicle to prevent barriers to marketplace entry. Fair trade practice acts, securities laws, consumer rights legislation, and statutes regulating debtor/creditor relations deal with imperfect buyer knowledge. Environmental law, labor law, and food and drug regulations force sellers to account appropriately for the costs they impose on society.

Fiduciary Relationships

A **fiduciary relationship** may be defined as one involving the highest duty of trust and confidence. The fiduciary concept is understood most easily as an exception to the usual rule that most relationships are presumed by the law to be at arm's length—they are "adversarial." In conducting business, parties usually are expected to look out for themselves. One party to a transaction should not think that the other will be generous and act in anyone's best interests but his or her own. This works well in the vast majority of cases, but there are situations in which the arm's-length assumption is counterproductive or operates unfairly. It is in many of these contexts that a fiduciary duty is imposed.

Two common fiduciary relationships are those between a trustee and the beneficiaries of a trust, and between an executor or administrator of an estate and the beneficiaries of that estate (or, more technically, the probate court). The party who is under the fiduciary duty is expected, and legally required, to act only in the best interests of the one to whom the duty is owed—to act as that person reasonably would act in his or her own behalf under the circumstances. If this duty is violated, the law provides a remedy of damages for any injuries caused and, in some cases, criminal penalties as well.

Family and Other Special Relationships

Even in the absence of specific statutes, the law recognizes the need for ethical conduct in some situations. First, these may involve relationships that permit one person to take advantage of another who is justifiably trusting. These are situations in which the relationship of the parties naturally involves trust, such as that among family members and possibly even close friends, al-

though the latter presents special difficulties. Second, they may involve circumstances in which one person is incapable of dealing at "arm's length" with the other because he or she has been lulled into a false sense of security by the latter. Finally, the common law traditionally has imposed fiduciary duties on any person who undertakes certain kinds of employment.

Undue influence, which is the use of psychological or emotional pressure, or the use of one's position, is the theory most commonly used in seeking redress of unethical or unlawful behavior in relationships of the first and second types. Family relationships are the most common circumstances involved in undue influence cases. Courts traditionally have been predisposed to finding the "adversary" concept inapplicable in the family situation when there has been sharp dealing by a family member or when disputes arise over unusual gifts. This especially is true when the party doing the giving is old or in a state of dependency. Although the same may be true in cases of close personal relationships, these ordinarily involve a higher degree of proof, as the following case illustrates.

EATON v. SONTAG
387 A.2d 33 (Me. 1978)

This was an action by Russell C. Eaton and Evelyn M. Eaton (Plaintiffs/Appellees) against Frederick Sontag and Marie Sontag (Defendants/Appellants) to recover overdue installments on a note executed by Defendants to secure the price of a campground they purchased from Plaintiffs. Defendants counterclaimed for fraud in the sale. Among other things, Defendants contended that the rule of *caveat emptor*—or buyer beware—should not apply to the transaction because of the friendship between themselves and Plaintiffs for fifteen years. Defendants contended that this friendship raised the transaction between them to one of a confidential nature and imposed upon Plaintiffs a duty of disclosure beyond that required in ordinary transactions.

The trial court found for Plaintiffs on the complaint and also on Defendants' counterclaim, and Defendants appealed. Affirmed.

DUFRESNE, Active Retired Justice.

The expression "confidential relation" characterizing the status of persons *inter se* has a comprehensive meaning and application . . . and may vary in reference to the particular relationship involved, but it has not been construed to include the relationship of vendor and vendee or seller and purchaser merely because the parties to the transaction had known each other for some time and both or either were favorably impressed with the other.

The evidence here fails to disclose any particular dependence of one party upon the other's judgment for business transactions during their acquaintanceship of fifteen years. That one had developed a reliance on the other in a business way does not appear in this case. The Sontags did not act precipitously. Their first encounter with the plaintiff's offer of sale was negative. They took time for deliberation of the proposal. They had full opportunity for disinterested consultation before reaching their decision to purchase the campground. That the parties believed in their mutual honesty, sincerity and truthfulness on account of their social intercourse is not sufficient to consitute a confidential relationship as the term implies in the law of undue influence vitiating contracts.

Questions

1. Would the decision in this case have been different if the plaintiff had been a member of the defendant's family? What if the Sontags had not taken time for disinterested consultation?

2. What kinds of facts would show that there was sufficient justifiable reliance on a friend so that the law should declare a fiduciary relationship?

Close personal relationships of the type involved in the Eaton case are those that develop naturally over a substantial period of time. Because each of us is involved with many friends, and we frequently do business with them, the courts are hesitant to find undue influence. Not only is finding an appropriate point at which a friendship should be impressed with a fiduciary duty difficult at best, to impose it too freely would create an air of uncertainty in too many ordinary transactions. On the other hand, courts are not reluctant to act when a supposed friendship apparently has been procured by one party for the purpose of taking advantage of another. Compare the Eaton case with *Syester v. Banta* in Chapter 9, in which a handsome young dance instructor, working for an Arthur Murray dance studio, befriended a recently-widowed elderly lady apparently for the purpose of selling her several thousand dollars worth of dancing lessons. Should the law treat their's as a fiduciary relationship?

Finally, there are relationships long considered to involve a high degree of trust and confidence. Commonly understood as within this group are those of attorney-client, doctor-patient, and minister-counselee. In addition, however, the common law has recognized the duty of an employee to keep confidential the trade secrets of an employer. Also, and very broadly, Anglo-American law has imposed a very high ethical duty on every agent in all dealings concerning his or her principal. The agent's duty is discussed more fully in Chapter 31.

The Uniform Commercial Code

Today much of the law of contracts and other common law areas, insofar as they relate to comerical transactions, have been codified in the **Uniform Commercial Code (UCC)**. The UCC is a special uniform statute that has been adopted in all states (with some minor variations). In addition to codifying the common law, however, the code also has added certain rules that, in effect, enforce ethical standards in selected circumstances. Some examples are: Section 2–103(b), imposing a duty of good faith on all transactions involving the sale of goods; Section 2–205, establishing firm offers; and Section 2–302, empowering courts to handle unconscionable agreements and clauses. Of particular importance is the last section.

Prior to the enactment of UCC Section 2–302, with limited exceptions, courts of law had no general power to deal with "unfair" contracts, other than to enforce them if they met the legal requirements for valid and enforceable contracts. However, under Section 2–302, they now are empowered to refuse to enforce unfair, or unconscionable, contracts and clauses. **Unconscionable contracts** are those that are so one-sided they shock the ordinary conscience, and usually have been procured by someone with a dominant bargaining position over the other contracting party. Courts thus may do as they deem appropriate to ensure that the parties are treated fairly, including

---

Overview of the Uniform Commercial Code

UCC (first drafted 1944–1950 and published as "1952 Official Text"), enforces ethical standards in business activities

Major subdivisions:

Article	Subdivision
1	General Provisions
2	Sales (including Article 2A, leases of personal property)
3	Commercial Paper
4	Bank Deposits and Collections
5	Letters of Credit
6	Bulk Transfers
7	Warehouse Receipts, Bills of Lading, and Other Documents of Title
8	Investment Securities
9	Secured Transactions; Sales of Accounts and Chattel Paper
10	Effective Date and Repealer

---

refusing to enforce the contract, enforcing it without the unconscionable portion, or reforming it to make it fair. In doing so courts are allowed to enforce generally accepted standards of good faith and fair dealing. Other provisions of the UCC have a similar effect. Many of these are discussed in the next two parts of this book, which deal with the common law of contracts, and sales and the Uniform Commercial Code

Professional Ethics

Professions generally are identified by educational requirements and state licensing of their members. Also, professions usually are characterized by having codes of ethical conduct. These codes are highly developed in some professions such as law, medicine, and public accounting. Also, they typically are enforced by independent, quasi-public associations such as state bar or medical associations and the American Institute of Certified Public Accountants. In order to practice a profession, it often is necessary to be a member of one of these professional associations. For example, Michigan law requires membership in the Michigan State Bar Association in order to practice law in Michigan. This is known as an "integrated bar." In Indiana, membership in the Indiana State Bar Association is optional, just as membership in the American Bar Association is not required of any attorney. Nevertheless, all of these organizations seek to enforce ethical conduct in one way or another.

Does complying with professional standards of conduct mean only complying with the law? For the most part, yes. The duties of an attorney to respect personal confidences and to avoid conflicts of interest in representing clients always have been part of proper professional behavior, and also part of the broad concept of "fiduciary duty" required of all agents, as discussed in Chapter 31. However, in some cases, professional associations seek to impose standards of behavior not otherwise required by law.

On the other hand, for years, attorneys were restricted by the Canons of Professional Ethics from most forms of advertising and from charging fees below schedules set out by their professional associations. Enforcement of these standards now has been prohibited by the Supreme Court as violating public policy—the antitrust law in the case of fees, and the freedom to engage in commercial speech in the case of advertising. However, the general practice of direct solicitation of individual clients still is prohibited by bar associations. Thus, although most businesses and many professionals have a virtually unlimited right to solicit customers and clients, attorneys do not. Nor are attorneys allowed to "support and maintain" clients during the life of their cases because doing so stirs up litigation, sometimes needlessly, which is thought to be very unprofessional and burdensome for the courts. These ethical standards are over and above what the law generally requires of others, and their violation may result in a lawyer losing his or her license to practice. Proceedings for suspension and revocation of a license are illustrated by the following case.

IN RE DAGGS
384 Mich. 729, 187 N.W.2d 227 (1971)

LeRoy Daggs (Respondent/Appellant), a member of the State Bar of Michigan, undertook to represent a client in a divorce proceeding. He was paid a partial fee of $150 in September 1968, and thereafter he filed a complaint and obtained a preliminary injunction and order for attorney fees. In January 1970 the suit was dismissed for lack of progress. A grievance was filed with the State Bar, charging him with abandoning his client. Respondent's principal justification was that he had not been paid his full attorney fee as agreed.

A hearing panel ordered suspension of Respondent's privilege to practice law in Michigan for six months. Respondent petitioned for review by the Grievance Board, which affirmed in all respects but reduced the period of suspension to three months. Respondent then petitioned for review by the Supreme Court of Michigan. Order of the Grievance Board affirmed.

PER CURIAM.

Once a lawyer accepts retainer to represent a client he is obliged to exert his best efforts wholeheartedly to advance the client's legitimate interests with fidelity and diligence until he is relieved of that obligation either by his client or the court. The failure of a client to pay for his services does not relieve a lawyer of his duty to perform them completely and on time, save only when relieved as above.

Thus crediting fully Respondent's version of the transaction here involved his failure to prevent dismissal of the suit for lack of progress under the circumstances he describes is a violation of Canon 21 and misconduct warranting discipline under Rule 14.

In urging that the sanction imposed is too severe, Respondent argues that it is highly penal and that the complainant will receive no reparation for the grievance. He says that there was no misrepresentation, misappropriation, or misuse of funds involved and that the sanction simply permits a disgruntled client to vent her spleen and satisfy her real anger against her husband which she could not do because of her own failure to pay the required fee.

This brings into sharp focus the real purpose of these proceedings. Whatever the motive of the complainant in invoking the grievance procedure, the responsibility of our profession is to provide a fair and full method of ascertaining the validity of the complaint and imposing such sanction on a lawyer's conduct as may be warranted in the public interest. In this procedure we are not concerned with enforcing the rights of the individuals involved. The civil courts are provided for that. Rather here we seek to make sure that all of us who hold ourselves out to the public as counsellors and agents in the administration of Justice will so conduct ourselves as to merit the trust imposed in us.

We are satisfied from our examination of the record and consideration of the arguments that the discipline imposed is appropriate.

Conscious that every dereliction of our professional brothers diminishes us all we affirm the order of discipline in this case.

Respondent shall pay to the State Bar of Michigan the costs of this review.

Questions

1. Why should an attorney be held to higher standards than others who provide services of various kinds?
2. Under what circumstances should an attorney be permitted to discontinue serving a client?

Business Ethics

Unlike discrete groups of professionals, the business world has no formal code of ethics. Although recognized standards of conduct exist, their violation is controlled primarily by the "market sanction"—people may refuse to do business with a dishonest merchant. Undoubtedly this unofficial sanction works reasonably well, but, as history shows, it is far from completely effective. Industry groups such as automobile dealers associations, business associations such as chambers of commerce, and consumer organizations provide some additional control, but their sanctions are unofficial, and compliance is voluntary.

Ethical standards normally have been imposed on the business community by virtue of the law's recognition of the rules discussed previously in this chapter, some of which are part of the common law, and others the creation of the Uniform Commercial Code and other statutes. The standard pattern is for the law to react to correct an ethical problem that has become obvious in the marketplace. At the turn of this century, predatory practices led to the antitrust laws; the investment community's excessive speculation that produced the stock-market crash led to the securities laws in the 1930s; and concern about product safety and fair treatment of buyers led to the enactment of consumer protection statutes in the 1960s and 1970s. This pattern of ethical failures producing socially damaging consequences, followed by a corrective repsonse by the legal system, is bound to continue in the future.

There is evidence that the business community has become convinced about the importance of its ethical environment. A good illustration of the contemporary attention to business ethics is Congress's enactment of the Foreign Corrupt Practices Act in 1977. Its provisions sought to eliminate the problem of bribery of foreign officials by American businesses, and has the effect of imposing certain legally enforced ethical standards on foreign business transactions. Prior to the act, United States courts had no jurisdiction to punish the bribery of foreign officials by American businesses. In addition, there was general disagreement as to whether bribe payments might be considered legitimate business expenses and, thus, deductible on the income tax returns of the payers. American business contended that these payments were a way of commercial activities in foreign countries and had to be made in order to be competitive in these markets. Nevertheless, Congress determined that the failure of American business to act according to ethical standards necessitated enforcement by law.

Finally, there is considerable evidence that business ethics has come front and center in the preparation of this country's future business leaders. Only in recent years has business management been perceived as another profession having special educational needs. With the increasing complexity of the commercial world, the need for managers specifically educated and trained in the operation of the modern business enterprise also has increased. Schools of business at the undergraduate and graduate levels have begun to provide the needed education and training with an eye to the professional status of their graduates, part of which addresses the need for ethical standards of behavior. In addition, the American Assembly of Collegiate Schools of Business regards the teaching of ethics as a factor in evaluating candidates for accreditation. Whether or not ethics education really becomes a requirement for accreditation, it already has become an important element of many academic programs.

SUMMARY

In basic terms, ethics is a branch of philosophy that focuses on the individual's relationship with others. Although ethics frequently is thought of as entirely personal, in fact there is general, and sometimes unanimous, agreement on moral principles. A system of ethics both gives rise to law and is created by law. What society considers to be "right" often is reflected by society's laws, and law may be a molder of public opinion after the fact.

There are two general categories of ethics—community ethics and personal ethics. The former includes minimum standards, on which there is much agreement, and also embraces the duty to obey the law. The latter comprehends "higher duties," those that set one apart from the mass as a person of high moral principles—someone to be admired. It is in this latter context that ethics are the most personal. The relationship of these principles to law often is difficult, in that law focuses on precise points of permissible human behavior, and ethics is a flowing continuum of behavior that can be highly subjective.

Conflicts between law and ethics are inevitable, partly because law usually reflects the ethical consensus of society, which may be quite different from the ethical values of any given individual. When the two conflict in a particular case, decision making may become extremely difficult. Community ethics urges all to obey the law, but personal ethics may not. When the latter become significantly involved, the pressure on an individual to deviate from community ethics may become more intense.

The degree of guilt associated with alternative actions typically is determined by assessing two factors, motive and intent. Ethical guilt regards intent as a requirement, and the degree of guilt is assessed according to motive. On the other hand, the degree of legal guilt is assessed according to the actor's intent, and motive governs only the decision of what punishment is appropriate.

Although ethical standards are regulated primarily by the unofficial sanction of social condemnation, to some extent they also are enforced by law. We find this in the common law in the form of rules allowing the avoidance of obligations and transfers of property procured by undue influence, and in rules imposing fiduciary duties in some relationships such as trusts, decedents' estates, and various agency relationships. The Uniform Commerical Code has introduced additional elements of fairness to many business transactions. It has sought to allow courts more latitude to tailor remedies to the facts of each commercial case.

The regulation of the ethical standards of some professional practitioners has been accepted for sometime. In many cases these regulations have had the force of law. They respond to a perceived need for higher standards of conduct by those who are licensed by the state and whose professional activities may affect the public interest significantly.

The general business community's ethics have not yet been formulated, or regulated, to the same extent as the ethics of many professions. To the extent that they are regulated at all, most regulation of ethical standards in the general business sector comes by way of law, in particular by such statues as the Uniform Commercial Code, antitrust laws, and various consumer laws. This may change in the future given the fact that business management recently has begun to be considered as a profession, and there is a growing feeling that ethical standards are of great importance to a healthy business environment.

KEY TERMS AND CONCEPTS

ethics
community ethics
personal ethics
justice
fiduciary relationship
undue influence
caveat emptor
Uniform Commercial Code (UCC)
unconscionable contracts
professional ethics

PROBLEMS

1. Are all violations of the law also breaches of ethics?

2. Geary was employed by United States Steel, but there was no contract requiring Geary to remain, or requiring United States Steel to continue employing him, for any particular time. Geary believed one of United States Steel's products had not been tested sufficiently and constituted a danger to people using it. He informed his supervisor, on more than one occasion, and finally was told to "follow directions." In spite of this warning, he continued to voice his concern to his supervisor and other management employees. As a result of his persistence, the product was withdrawn from the market, but Geary also was fired. He sued United States Steel for wrongful discharge. Should he succeed in getting a judgment for damages?

3. The complainants, a group of migrant workers, contracted with the defendant, the owner of a migrant labor camp. They were to supply labor at a relatively low rate of compensation. After they came to the camp, however, they were worked very hard, were not permitted to leave the camp, and were threatened and subjected to physical abuse if they attempted to do so. On one occasion, the complainants slipped away from the camp. When the defendant located them, they were beaten, thrown into a bus, and taken back to camp against their wills. When they finally were rescued, the defendant was charged with kidnapping and slavery. The defendant contended that the complainants were under a contractual duty to supply services, that his actions were only protecting his rights under the contract, and that the facts did not constitute slavery. Should the defendant be convicted?

4. Jim and Alice were married and lived a comfortable life. Jim was a factory manager and Alice, who decided to take a sabbatical from her law practice, managed the household. After two years of marriage, Alice learned she was pregnant. She decided to have an abortion because she did not want to be a mother, but Jim objected. Assuming Alice was six weeks pregnant, consider the relative rights of Alice, Jim, and the fetus.

5. Mary, an eleven-year-old child, was born with a malformed left arm and leg. As she grew, she became increasingly more conscious of her useless arm, and constantly was taunted by other children and stared at whenever she went out. As a result, Mary wanted the arm amputated. However, her mother objected, fearing for her child's life. She wanted to wait until Mary was older, and more mature, before allowing her to make the decision. Mary, by a next friend (an adult representative, commonly a parent or guardian), petitioned the court to order the amputation. Should the wishes of Mary or her mother prevail?

Chapter | 2

Introduction to Law

_____

_____

_____

_____

OUTLINE

THE IMPORTANCE OF STUDYING LAW

Law surrounds us every day of our lives. Any failure to comply with the mandates of law may subject the violator not only to moral condemnation but to the possibility of adverse consequences imposed by our legal system.

Because it is ubiquitous, law cannot be ignored. It must be taken into account in every action we take. We cannot feel safe in our activities and prosper from them unless the law is recognized, understood, and accommodated. Ignorance of the law excuses no one. It is not a defense to the commission of a crime, nor does it protect us against the claim of another individual.

These principles particularly are true of anyone in the business world. If you should enter that universe, your activities will be governed by a vast array of legal doctrines, statutes, regulations, and case decisions. You will be expected to follow the law, and therefore it behooves you to know something about the law. Although ignorance of the law is no excuse, none of us really can know every principle and procedure of our complex legal system by heart. That expectation would be unrealistic, even of an attorney or a judge. However, if you are in business, you may be expected to be acquainted with the law to a degree that enables you to steer clear of its prohibitions and its pitfalls. In other words, although businesspeople cannot know every detail of the law, they can and should understand it sufficiently to know the legal implications of their decisions and to seek professional help when approaching an area of danger.

This, then, is the reason we, as responsible members of society, should have some understanding of the law. Practicing preventive medicine is better than the best cure; the same can be said for preventive law.

DEFINITIONS AND CONCEPTS OF LAW

Law may have as many definitions as it has persons seeking to define it. According to *Black's Law Dictionary, law* is "That which is laid down, ordained, or established. A rule or method according to which phenomena or actions coexist or follow each other. That which must be obeyed and followed by citizens, subject to sanctions or legal consequences, is a law." Although this definition undeniably is a good one, it says little more than that law is a rule that must be followed in order to avoid some kind of retribution. It says nothing of the true nature or the fabric of law, nor anything about its source. The definition ignores the variations in human thought, and the truth that law is both contemporaneous in its regula-

The rise in litigation, 1960–1986

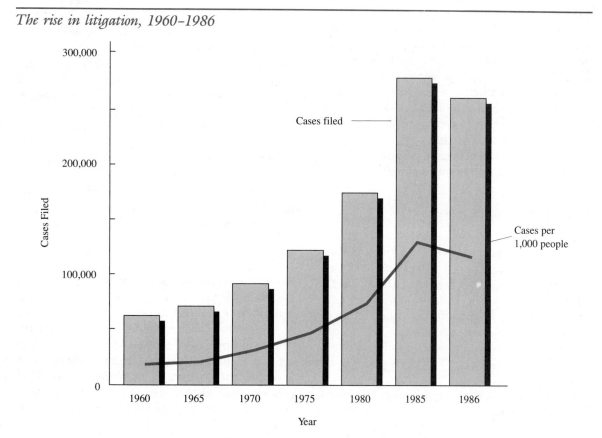

tion and a predictor of the future. The study of law, then, must focus on more than a mere definition.

The Natural Law School

There are those who believe that, ideally, all human conduct should conform to a set of laws that is founded on preordained "right." According to these philosophers, God, and not man, is the giver of all law, and the law is revealed through proper human conduct. This would make **natural law** the ultimate source of all law, and the basis for justice. Although most legal scholars today do not recognize natural law as "the law," its effect on jurisprudence is evident in history, ongoing, and profound. Natural law is the foundation of the Magna Charta, and its principles found voice in the Declaration of Independence and the Constitution of the United States, by such words as "We hold these truths to be self-evident, that all men are created equal, that they are endowed by their Creator with certain inalienable rights . . ." It was largely in recognition of a principle of natural law that Nazi "war criminals" were tried and punished following World War II. Their actions were found to abridge a "higher law" even though they were in accordance with the "law" of Germany at the time. They were convicted of "crimes against humanity."

The Historical School

The adherents of this school view law as having been developed by society over the course of time. It stands in opposition to what became known, especially in the 1960s and the 1970s, as the "situation ethic." The historical school emphasizes the stability of certain rules, while the situationists say, in essence, that the law has no past and no future—only a "now." Loosely translated, the situation ethic says, "If it feels good at the moment, do it."

The historical school occupies some common ground with the advocates of natural law. Natural law adherents believe law is absolute and unchanging, and the followers of the historical school advocate that the best law is that which has been tested by the generations and has continued to be an accepted part of the system.

Legal Positivism

Thomas Hobbes, a late-sixteenth-, early-seventeenth-century English philosopher, generally is recognized as the founder of this school. Legal positivists say that law flows from legitimate governmental authority; law is the result of some authorized process, and without government there is no law. In effect, then, law is what ever legitimate government authority says it is.

The Theory of Power

Also headed by Hobbes, this school views all law as arising from power. Its followers believe that, right or wrong, law is what those who have the power to enforce their will say it is. They emphasize the aspect of enforcement, without recognizing the compelling nature of ethics, or any notion of voluntary compliance. The theory of power is taken one step further by the school of economic determinism, which theorizes that all power is derived from wealth. Wealth and power, then, combined to form the basis for the writings of Karl Marx, who advocated the equal distribution of wealth, which would create an equal distribution of power, which, in turn, would result in an equal distribution of justice.

Legal Realism

Legal realism involves a combination of the philosophies of the historical school and legal positivism. Legal realists believe that law is given by society for the purpose of controlling the actions of its members, to the end that society may achieve its needs. They believe that a rule of law is good only if it serves those needs. Under **legal realism,** law always should be dynamic, constantly changing to conform to the needs of each

Concepts of law

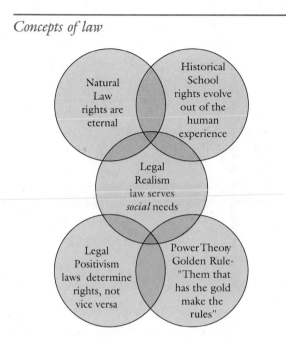

particular social unit. Also, within a single social unit, law must change as the needs of society change. Under this philosophy, although law remains relatively stable; it should change only when it is demonstrated that the needs of society have changed. Law is not seen as a preordained, unchanging truth.

SOURCES OF LAW

Although there may be differences of opinion as to the nature of law, and its bases, all agree that law must originate somewhere. Once in existence, it then may find its way to society by one of a number of vehicles. These intermediate vehicles are called "sources" of law. Law in the United States is derived from four primary sources and one secondary source.

Constitutions

In the United States, there are fifty-one separate and distinct legal systems—the federal and one for each of the fifty states (although in some senses, the legal regime of the District of Columbia represents a fifty-second system). Territories of the United States, such as Puerto Rico and the Virgin Islands, operate under the federal constitution. The powers of all these governments are derived from these written constitutions, and in order to be valid, every governmental action and every law must be grounded on some constitutional power of the governmental unit that seeks to do or to impose it. This requirement seeks to protect the rights of people from abuse by an arbitrary wielding of governmental power.

Legislative Enactments

Often when the term *law* is used, we think first of legislative enactments, particularly statutes. However, legislative enactments are not law in the true meaning of the term, but are only sources of law. Legislative enactments, called **statutes** on the state and federal levels and **ordinances** on the local level (city, township, county), are valuable predictors of what the law will be when a court decides a dispute. They provide a degree of stability in any area of law in which they are enacted.

Executive Orders and Administrative Rules

Just as the enactments of the legislative branch of a government provide a source of law, so it is with the work product of the executive branch. Executive sources may be divided into two classifications, executive orders and administrative rules.

The president of the United States, and the governors of the states, are empowered by their respective constitutions, and sometimes by legislative enactments, to mandate certain actions by means of **executive orders,** which have substantially the same force as legislative enactments. For example, during 1971, in an attempt to slow the spiral of inflation, President Nixon promulgated Executive Order No. 11615, which placed a temporary "freeze" on prices, rents, wages, and salaries. While in place, this executive order had the effect of law.

Especially during this century, solutions to problems have been sought increasingly through the use of administrative agencies. These agencies are given certain regulatory powers by the legislative body (Congress on the federal level). Within the power granted to it by the legislature, an agency will promulgate (draw up and publish) **administrative rules,** which are enactments similar in effect to statutes enacted by Congress or a state legislature, police compliance with them, and act as judge over controversies arising under them. For example, the Occupational Safety and Health Administration (OSHA) devises rules governing the duties of employers in providing for safety in the workplace. These rules have the same force as statutes, providing an additional source of law. The details of administrative agency procedures are discussed in Chapter 44.

Judicial Case Law

More than simply a source of law, **case law** (decisions of courts) may be regarded as "The Law." In "The Path of the Law," published in 1897, Justice Oliver Wendell Holmes wrote, "The prophecies of what courts will do in fact, and nothing more pretentious, are what I mean by law." Under this view, a statute, an ordinance, an executive order, or an administrative rule, although a predictor of law, is not law, and never was, if it is found to be unconstitutional or otherwise in excess of the powers of the governmental unit that promulgated it. Even "law" as established by a case decision may be overturned by a later case decision or by a legitimate enactment of a legislative body. In fact, as applied to similar factual situations, "the law" is what the court says it is in each case. This seems to leave law hanging in an uncertain state, with no continuity in space and time—it appears to have reference to a particular situation. Although this view is substantially correct, it is not entirely so in effect. Great predictability and stability in the system are provided by legislation and by the doctrine of *stare decisis,* which gives a judicial decision effect beyond the particular case in which it was rendered.

Hierarchies of legality

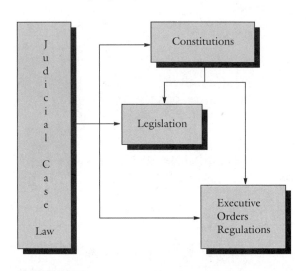

Other Sources

Occasionally, a court may be faced with a **case of first impression** *(res nova).* This is a dispute involving a question of law not dealt with by any of the other sources of law in the jurisdiction. The court must decide what rule of law should be adopted. In addition to looking at similar cases in surrounding and important jurisdictions, a court may resort to unofficial treatises written by legal scholars. Examples of such treatises by acknowledged legal scholars are Prosser on Torts, Corbin on Contracts, and the various Restatements of the Law, written under the auspices of the American Law Institute. Although not binding on a court, these writings provide a source of expert advice as to what the law should be. As such, they may be persuasive in cases of first impression.

CLASSIFICATIONS OF LAW

Sometimes it seems to the beginning student that law is a shapeless mass of rules. In fact, law can be separated into categories of related principles. An understanding of these categories can help the student begin to see just what "the law" really "looks" like. The following are some useful, general classifications. As their descriptions will show, they are merely guidelines and there is considerable overlap among them.

Substantive and Procedural

The term **substantive law** refers to that part of the law that creates, defines, and regulates rights and repsonsibilities. For example, if I own a piece of property, the nature of the property right, and the rights and duties involved in that ownership, are created and defined by rules of substantive law. If you run over someone with your automobile, substantive law defines the circumstances under which you will be liable to pay damages to that person.

Procedural law (sometimes called *adjective law*) prescribes the method of enforcing the rights and responsibilities that are created by substantive law, and prescribes the method of obtaining redress for any invasion of those substantive rules. Such matters as filing requirements, rights to a jury, and the rules of evidence are some of the important aspects of procedural law.

Public and Private

Public law is the branch of law that is concerned with the government in its political or sovereign capacity. Most of it is concerned with the relationship between individuals and the government. Examples of public law are criminal law and procedure, constitutional law, and administrative law, although these hardly exhaust the list.

Private law, then, refers to the remainder of the law—the part that governs rights and duties between individuals, including organizations. Examples of private law are contract law, tort law, property law, and domestic relations law. Of course, it should be recognized that a government may act as a "person" and become liable or have rights under private law. This occurs, for example, when the government enters into a contract, commits a tort, or owns property.

Criminal and Civil

Criminal law is the body of law established for the protection of all citizens collectively against the lawless acts of individuals. It prohibits certain acts considered offensive to society, and establishes punishment for violations.

Civil law, as the term is used here, refers to the part of American law that establishes rights between persons (citizens), and provides for the redress of the violation of private and civil rights. It sometimes is used as the equivalent of private law.

In order to avoid confusion later, it might be noted that the term **Civil Law** (capital C, capital L) may refer to the legal system of many countries of the world, especially in Europe and South America, and should be contrasted to Common Law, which is the name given to the legal system of the United States, England, and many independent nations that formerly were part of the British Empire.

Common Law and Equity

The term **common law** often is used to refer to the part of law established by judicial decisions rather than statutes. It also may be used to refer to a legal system founded in England in the middle of the thirteenth century—**Common Law** (capital C, capital L). Also, however, the term is used to refer to that part of civil law (small c, small l) that awards the remedy of money damages, when appropriate, as opposed to **equity,** which primarily awards other remedies, such as an injunction or specific performance of a contract. Remedies at law and in equity are discussed more fully in Chapters 4 and 12.

LAW DEFINED

As discussed at the beginning of this chapter, the term *law* has been defined many ways, in order to suit many different purposes. Although an examination of these variations is helpful in putting the foundations of law into perspective, it also is necessary to select a more generally acceptable definition to establish a structure for the task of learning the specifics of law. One definition has been offered by Frederick Maitland, an English scholar, who defined **law** as "a set of norms, conceived by society, for its own regulation." This definition, although brief, seems complete in all general respects, and points particularly to certain matters concerning law that merit further discussion.

"A Set of Norms"

The first part of Maitland's definition addresses the very important proposition that law is not a collection of absolutes; it consists of norms. This is one factor that differentiates the term *law* as used in the social sciences from the term as it is used in the physical sciences. In the physical sciences, *law* refers to something fixed and unchanging. A violation of a physical law results in a relatively fixed and predictable consequence. For example, consider the law of gravity. The law of gravity cannot be defied, it only can be broken or accommodated. If one were to be so foolish as to step off the top of a ten-story building, the consequences could be predicted with great certainty. Of course, if the person were equipped with a parachute, the normal consequences could be avoided by accommodating the law.

Consider, then, a person who is driving 45 m.p.h. in a 30 m.p.h. zone. Is he violating the law? He is certainly violating a legislative enactment (statute or ordinance). Thus, if he is charged (cited by a police officer, for example), and the prosecuting attorney elects to prosecute, and he is convicted in a court, then he may be punished for having violated the law. Suppose, however, that the driver is rushing a seriously injured person to a hospital, it is two o'clock in the morning, the road is straight, the weather is clear and dry, and there is no one else on the highway except a police officer. What is the chance that he will be charged, tried, and convicted? Probably, the necessary steps will be short-circuited at some point, not because he will "get a break" but because the police officer, the prosecuting attorney, or the court will decide that what the driver was doing was not what society intended to prohibit by enacting the statute or ordinance establishing the speed limit.

It is worth noting that, in the previous example, before it is finally determined that the law has been violated, all three branches of the government were involved—the *legislative,* by passing a statute or ordinance prohibiting a particular act, the *executive,* by bringing and pressing charges, and the *judicial,* by a trial leading to a judgment of a court. Therefore, it truly may be said that "the law" is what the court says it is in each particular situation. This process is necessary because law is not an absolute rule, but only a "norm."

"Conceived by Society"

In the social sciences, the source of all law is a social unit. In the absence of a society, there are only physical laws such as "survival of the fittest." Presumably social units came about because individuals grew tired of existing under a system limited to physical laws. Societies, then, were formed for the purpose of combining individual strengths into one strong unit, which made possible the establishment of social laws, originally for the primary purpose of mutual aid and protection. From this beginning, as societies grew and prospered, more laws were promulgated (established) to achieve various objectives that were considered socially desirable. Some protected the person, such as tort and criminal law. Others created and protected property rights, social institutions, and even moral values, such as contract law and domestic relations law. Still others sought to create, or to preserve, basic freedoms, such as the Bill of Rights.

Because law flows from the authority of social units, law necessarily changes from unit to unit and from time to time. For example, the laws of the United States are different, in many respects, from the laws of Mexico, and the laws of Mexico are different from the laws of any other country. Within the United States, laws may vary from state to state. Even within a particular state, county, township, and municipal laws vary.

In addition, the laws of each social unit will change with time. For example, federal law, as it concerned civil rights, changed markedly in 1964 with the passage of the Civil Rights Act. Thereafter, most states also changed their laws on the subject. These changes manifest a change in the attitudes of the lawgivers—the social units.

"For Its Own Regulation"

The purpose of all law is, of course, the regulation of society. This regulation may relate to any of a number of needs—personal safety, security of property rights, establishment and protection of social institutions, and any other needs society may wish to promote. Also as stated previously, without society there is no law. By the same token, without law there is no society. Every so-

cial unit must have a structure, and must exercise its power in the form of mandates supporting its survival, or else there is only survival of the fittest.

LAW AND JUSTICE

If a legal system could function perfectly, law and justice would coincide. Law, in theory, should form a framework for directing the actions of all of humankind to achieve the goal of social justice. Of course, the ultimate question, in any particular situation, as to what constitutes social justice is determined by ethics, not law. This should be clear from the discussion in Chapter 1, which you are encouraged to review in light of the preceding material. It also should be clear that courts have the power to see that justice is done, or to thwart it by unfair interpretation of the evidence or the law. This is illustrated in a humorous way by the case presented in the reprint of an article from *Res Gestae* (Journal of the Indiana State Bar Association).

A CASE OF STATUTORY CONSTRUCTION or IS A PONY, FORTUITOUSLY SADDLED WITH A FEATHER PILLOW, A "SMALL BIRD" WITHIN THE MEANING OF THE ONTARIO SMALL BIRDS ACT?

By
Paul H. Buchanan, Jr.

An Indian named Fred Ojibway was riding his pony through Queen's Park one day. Being impoverished Fred sat astride this pony on a downy pillow due to the unfortunate fact his saddle was in hock. The pony broke his leg. Following current Indian custom Fred then shot the pony "to relieve it of its awkwardness." Fred was charged with having breached the Small Birds Act, R.S.O. 1960, 724, s. 2, which made it an offense for anyone to maim, injure or kill small birds, and subject to a fine not in excess of two hundred dollars.

The learned magistrate acquitted the accused, holding as might be expected, that he had killed his pony and not a small bird.

The crown's appeal was allowed in an opinion which must be the ultimate in tongue-in-cheek judicial wit.

Blue, J., first pointed to Section 1 of the Small Birds Act which defined a bird as a "two-legged animal covered with feathers" and immediately observed that "there can be no doubt that this case is covered by this section."

In reaching this conclusion he referred to several ingenious arguments of counsel, such as the suggestion that a pony is not in fact a bird. The issue, he said, was not whether the animal in question is a bird or not in fact, but whether it is one in law. "Statutory interpretation," he continued, "has forced many a horse to eat bird seed for the rest of his life."

Patiently examining other "ingenious" arguments of counsel for the accused, the court disposed of them one by one. In response to the argument that the neighing noise emitted by the animal could not be produced by a bird, the court logically replied that a bird is no less a bird because it is silent. Equally logically disposed of were the iron shoes found on the animal which would disqualify it from being a bird. Blue, J., commented that how an animal dresses is of no concern to the court.

As to the more serious contention that the statutory definition contemplated a two-legged animal with feathers the court reasoned the statute created a standard for a minimum number of legs (two) and further noted it did not specify that the animal be "naturally covered" with feathers.

"Therefore, a horse with feathers on its back must be deemed for the purposes of the Act to be a bird and *a fortiori* a pony with feathers on its back is a small bird. (The court had previously disposed of the comparative size of birds and horses by noting that the word "small" referred to the length of the Small Birds Act and further that the accused was not charged under the Large Birds Act, R.S.O. 1960, c. 725.)

Apparently stung by counsel's query that, "If the pillow had been removed prior to the shooting would the animal still be a bird?" Blue, J., scornfully replied: "Is a bird any less a bird without its feathers?"

Regina v. Ojibway, 8 Criminal Law Quarterly 137 (Toronto, 1965).

It was a question of statutory construction.

Although some principles of legal justice, properly applied, are of value in lending predictability to the legal system, if carried beyond reasonable limits, legal justice may result in social injustice. The reverse, however, also is true. A court, in reaching its decision, should seek a proper combination of the two. This, perhaps, was accomplished in the following case, in which the predictability so necessary to society was preserved, but probably social justice was then achieved by the punishment handed down.

REGINA v. DUDLEY & STEPHENS
14 Q.B.D. 273 (1884)

Dudley (the master), Stephens (the mate), Parker (the cabin boy), and Brooks (an able-bodied seaman) were together in an open boat at sea following the shipwreck of the yacht, Mignonette. They were without food or water for eighteen days, except for a small turtle and some rainwater. On the eighteenth day, Dudley and Stephens proposed to Brooks that Parker be killed for food or all would die. Brooks rejected the proposal. On the twentieth day, Dudley killed Parker. Stephens consented, Brooks did not. All three, however, ate Parker for the next four days until their rescue. Had they not done so, they probably would not have lived long enough to be rescued. Parker, being the weakest of the group, probably would have been the first to perish.

Dudley and Stephens were jointly indicted for murdering Parker, and a jury found them guilty. The question at bar was whether the facts constituted murder.

LORD COLERIDGE, C. J.

Now it is admitted that the deliberate killing of this unoffending and unresisting boy was clearly murder, unless the killing can be justified by some well-recognized excuse admitted by law. It is further admitted that there was in this case no such excuse unless the killing was justified by what had been called "necessity." But the temptation to the act which existed here was not what the law has ever called necessity. Nor is this to be regretted. Though law and morality are not the same, and many things may be immoral which are not necessarily illegal, the absolute divorce of law from morality would be of fatal consequence; and such divorce would follow if the temptation to murder in this case were to be held by law an absolute defense of it. It is not so. To preserve one's life is, generally speaking, a duty, but it may be the plainest and the highest duty to sacrifice it. . . . It is not correct, therefore, to say that there is any absolute or unqualified necessity to preserve one's life. . . . It is not needful to point out the awful danger of admitting the principle which has been contended for. Who is to be the judge of this sort of necessity? By what measure is the comparative value of lives to be measured? Is it to be strength, or intellect, or what? . . . In this case the weakest, the youngest, the most unresisting was chosen. Was it more necessary to kill him than one of the grown men? The answer must be "No." It is not suggested that in this particular case the deeds were devilish; but it is quite plain that such a principle once admitted might be made the legal cloak for unbridled passion and atrocious crime. There is no safe path for judges to tread but to ascertain the law to the best of their ability and declare it according to their judgment; and, if in any case the law appears to be too severe on individuals, to leave it to the Sovereign to exercise the prerogative of mercy which the construction has entrusted to the hands fittest to dispense it. It must not be supposed that in refusing to admit temptation to be an excuse for crime it is forgotten how terrible the temptation was; how awful the suffering; how hard in such trials to keep the judgment straight and the conduct pure. We are often compelled to set up standards we cannot reach ourselves, and to lay down rules which we could not ourselves satisfy. But as man has no right to declare temptation to be an excuse though he might himself have yielded to it, nor allow compassion for the criminal to change or weaken in any manner the legal definition of the crime. It is, therefore, our duty to declare the prisoner's act was willful murder, and that the facts stated in the verdict are no legal justification. (NOTE: Queen Victoria later commuted the death sentence imposed on Dudley and Stephens to six months' imprisonment.)

Questions

1. Remembering the discussion in Chapter 1, what parts were played in this case by the elements of voluntariness (intent) and motive?

2. Should the judge in this case, instead of the queen, have commuted the sentences?

EVOLUTION OF THE LAW

Origin

Although "survival of the fittest" is thought by many to be the most basic law, that reference to "law," as previously discussed, is not really "law" as the term is used here. In fact, it really describes the absence of law. The first real laws probably were established by primitive societies in the form of customs and taboos. Although customs were quite informal, they were, we assume, rigidly enforced. Taboos were mostly (or entirely) of religious origin. These customs and taboos formed the framework within which early societies functioned, achieving many of the same benefits, and suffering from many of the same fallibilities, as modern laws.

Early Codes

A **code** may be defined as a collection of laws set down in written form, as opposed to the customs and taboos discussed above, which were largely informal. One of the earliest codes, familiar to most of us, is the Ten Commandments. Although often not thought of as sectarian (as opposed to religious) laws, the Ten Commandments form the foundation of Hebrew law, and to some extent the foundation of two modern legal systems— Common Law and Civil Law.

Of earlier origin, and more closely conforming to our notion of law, was the Code of Hammurabi. In about 1950 B.C., Hammurabi, King of Babylon, ordered that his laws be carved into the sides of stone columns for all to read, apparently feeling that some notice of crimes was necessary for the fair administration of law—an idea we still

cherish. In the sense it is used here, codification is found in all modern democratic legal systems.

Greek Law

Early Greek Law was democratic in character, but was not based on a code. Instead, it was founded on a philosophy of law and justice; the teachings of such philosophers as Aristotle, Socrates, and Plato were influential. It was as much a system of ethics as of law. Those who drafted our Declaration of Independence and our federal Constitution were schooled in Greek philosophy. This had a profound effect on those documents, and on the Revolutionary War.

Roman Law

Roman Law was much like the Greek, being both democratic and based on the teachings of philosophers. It developed in the Forum, which was a public meeting place, and was unique in its use of a lay jury to decide questions of both law and fact. (In our legal system, the lay jury decides only questions of fact, leaving questions of law to be decided by the judge.) Advocates such as Cicero, an attorney of his time, were all-important in the actual trial of cases under the Roman system. Advice was given by lesser advisors, called "jurisconsults." The culmination of Roman Law was codification in the Justinian Code of A.D. 520. As will become apparent, the Justinian Code continues to have a profound effect on law today.

Canon (Ecclesiastical) Law

This is a system of law, including separate courts, existing alongside the civil law system, with the Pope as its head. It had a profound effect in Europe between A.D. 400 and A.D. 1600. Of course, the Canon Law system provided the law governing church affairs and a forum for settling disputes arising under these laws. In addition, however, ecclesiastical courts provided an alternative to secular courts for settling disputes arising under the civil law system. The secular courts of the day were administered by petty nobles, and were considered by most to be weak, prejudiced, arbitrary, and nonprogressive. Canon Law provided a foundation for much of today's international and probate law, and, to a large extent, for our moral code. It might be noted that most other religions have tribunals that administer their laws.

Guild Systems

In addition to the system of Canon Law, other private dispute-resolution systems have contributed significantly to the development of law as we know it today. For centuries various trades and occupations—for example, printers, goldsmiths, and painters—were controlled by associations known as guilds. These guilds created and enforced rights and duties among their members. Our present maritime law is based on law developed by one such system to govern seamen. Of perhaps greater importance, however, was the Law Merchant, which was adopted by England as part of its Common Law and later was brought over to the United States. The Law Merchant became the foundation of our commerical law, providing much of the basis for the modern Uniform Commerical Code, particularly those portions concerning the sale of goods and the handling of commerical paper.

MODERN LEGAL SYSTEMS

Three major legal systems exist today—Islamic Law, Civil (Romanesque) Law, and Common

(Anglican) Law. Although the law of the countries of the world varies a great deal, most are based, primarily at least, on one of these systems.

Islamic

The Islamic system, so important in Moslem countries today, originated in about A.D. 600, in Arabia. It is founded on the Koran, the Moslem holy book, and the teachings of Mohammed (Al-Hadith). The Islamic system is characterized by the fact that it does not distinguish between law and morals, and there is no separation of church and state.

Civil (Romanesque) Law

The Civil Law system is the basis for the law of most of Europe, South America, some parts of Asia, the Province of Quebec in Canada, and the state of Louisiana in the United States. Its origin is found in the Justinian Code. Scholars trained in Roman Law became disgruntled with the Justinian Code, which was to be followed literally with no discussion of the merits of its provisions. Even the writing of legal treatises on the law was forbidden. Some of these scholars traveled to England to be educated under the Common Law, which was based on case decisions and encouraged discussion by way of treatises and commentaries. As these scholars traveled home through Europe, they spread a legal philosophy that was a mixture of the pure Roman Law (code) and Common Law (cases and discussion). As a result, the Civil (Romanesque) Law was born. The Civil Law, culminating in the adoption of the Napoleonic Code (the first part being the Civil Code of 1804) is a code-based system, modified by case decisions.

Common Law

The Common Law, or Anglican Law, is the system originating in England that is the basis for the United States legal system (except Louisiana). Its development began with William the Conqueror in 1066, and it was significantly developed by Henry II in 1154, becoming firmly established by the early thirteenth century. The term *Common Law* is used to distinguish it from the previous system of "shire" or "manorial" law. Under the earlier system, characteristic of the feudal period in England, each landowner was, in essence, a government with its own set of laws. A person traveling across England, therefore, would have been likely to pass through several quite diverse legal systems, each with its own petty courts. This was eliminated when the king's law was made "common" to all of England.

The most distinguishing characteristic of the Common Law is that it is founded on case law rather than on statutes, or a code system. As time passed, case law was supplemented by Acts of Parliament. This is the law that was brought to the United States and still serves as the basis for our law. Even today, courts feel bound by English common law until it is changed either by subsequent case decisions or by statute, and any statute that appears to change the common law is strictly construed so as to preserve the principles of judicially declared law.

THE RISE OF EQUITY

The concept of equity will be encountered in many of the remaining chapters of this book. It is necessary to have an appreciation of equity in order to understand the basis for certain remedies that might be available in the event of a breach of duty. Although in the lay sense of the term we often consider *equity* to mean simply "fairness" or "justice," it is more than that in the legal sense. Equity is a subsystem of the Common Law. It was born of a need to remedy some of the flaws in the Common Law system in order to achieve justice in situations in which the law was inadequate. In that sense, its roots do lie in concepts of fairness.

Two major sources of problems with the early Common Law were that the courts functioned according to a "writ system," and the remedy

available for most wrongs was limited to money damages. Frequently, one or both of these was found inadequate to achieve justice in a particular case. Under the writ system, the right to access to the courts was by purchasing a writ. Although a number of possible writs were available, it was necessary that the factual situation of the complainant's case fit neatly into one of the existing "pigeonholes." If not, no action was available in the law courts. If an injured party inadvertently purchased the wrong writ, he had no action unless he went back and purchased the correct one. Writs were expensive, and used writs had no trade-in value.

Even if the correct writ was purchased, and relief was available, money damages might not be an adequate remedy. For example, if Audrey promised to sell Britte an heirloom that had been in Britte's family for 600 years, and then breached her agreement, what good would a money-damage judgment do? The item, being one of a kind, could not be replaced on the open market, no matter how much money was granted in damages.

In order to avoid these limitations on the "law courts," subjects began pleading directly to the king for relief, which he sometimes granted—at least in cases of considerable importance, and if the applicant was a prominent or powerful person. Soon these pleas increased in number and the king referred them to his chancellor. As the numbers of pleas increased, the chancellors were designated a separate court (Court of Chancery), and they handled these pleas on a regular basis. The rules were, however, that the Chancery Court would consider a case only if the remedy of the "law courts" was nonexistent or inadequate, and then only if a special remedy—other than money—was necessary to achieve justice. There were other limitations. It was required that one who came to the court had to do so with "clean hands," and that he who asked for equity had to do equity, again reflecting the notion of fairness. Of the remedies granted by the equity courts, the most common were the injunction in tort cases and specific performance in breach-of-contract cases.

THE AMERICAN LEGAL SYSTEM

The legal system of the United States developed from these Common Law roots. The founders of our nation brought both the "law" and the "equity" aspects of the Common Law. Eventually the two were combined into one court system, and today, by statute, distinctions between law and equity have been abolished in almost all states. Both types of actions are tried in the same courts, and are handled by the same judges. Ordinarily, both legal and equitable forms of relief may be sought in the same lawsuit. Regardless of this merger of law and equity, however, some of the original procedural distinctions remain, and still are important in the processing of lawsuits.

Peculiarities of the American Legal System

In a number of respects, our legal system is completely unique. In others our institutions are shared with only a few other countries in the world.

Our concept of "separation of powers" within the government is a characteristic that may well have occurred first in the minds of our forbearers. Their experiences in England and other parts of Europe under the power of a monolithic monarchy led them to distribute the government's power among three separate, and constitutionally distinct, branches—the legislative, the executive, and the judicial. The basic function of each branch as a source of law was discussed earlier in this chapter.

Also unique to our system is the establishment of a strong central government with the states retaining certain powers. This was not always so, however. Our first constitution, ratified in 1781, established a "confederation" in which the central government was weak and most powers were retained by the states. Parochial attitudes made this system unworkable, and we were not really a nation united. For that reason, although empowered only to make certain amendments to the Articles of Confederation, those who drafted the second United States Constitution in 1787 went further and actually changed the entire governmental form to a "federation" (or federal form), with major powers vested in the central government. All powers not granted to the federal government, however, were retained by the states. The distribution of powers between the national government and the states has been the subject of, or has been involved in, more cases before the Supreme Court than any other constitutional principle.

As a result of the retention of powers by the states, the court system in the United States actually is made up of fifty-two separate and distinct systems—the federal, and those of the fifty states and the District of Columbia. (The courts of the territories of the United States are part of the federal court system.) There is very little interrelationship among these, although some cases may be heard in either state or federal courts, and some appeals from state-court decisions may be taken to the United States Supreme Court. The jurisdiction of the various courts is discussed more fully in Chapter 3.

A fourth distinctive characteristic of our legal system is that courts have the power to hold legislation unconstitutional. This is one of the reasons that courts may be fairly viewed as givers of law as well as sources of law. This characteristic is not completely unique to our system, but only a few other nations have it. For example, courts in West Germany and Australia have this power. In France, the constitutionality of legislation is determined by a Constitutional Council, which is not part of the judicial system.

Stare decisis also characterizes our system, as it does others based on the common law. The idea of *stare decisis* is that a decision in one case should be taken as **precedent** (a model) and guide the decisions in subsequent cases with the same, or similar, factual situations.

The federal court system

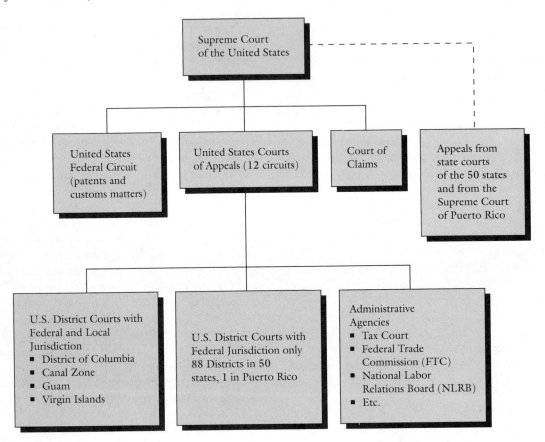

Stare Decisis

Literally translated, **stare decisis** means "to abide by decided cases." It provides a stabilizing influence in case law similar to that provided by statutes in statutory systems. But it is important to have some sense of which courts are bound by an earlier case and to what extent.

As previously discussed, there are fifty-two separate and distinct court systems in the United States. Each has its own jurisdiction (power to hear a case). Therefore, for the most part, the decisions of one court are binding only on the courts within the same system. That means a deci-

sion of a state court in Texas is not binding on the courts of any other state. It also would not be binding on the federal courts, except the federal courts sitting in Texas deciding cases under its "diversity of citizenship" jurisdiction (discussed in Chapter 3). Then that federal court is constrained to follow Texas precedents. Also, another state's court may decide that Texas law is applicable and governs a particular case before it, and similarly would be constrained to follow Texas precedents. Finally, decisions of the United States Supreme Court are binding on all federal and state courts

A typical state court system

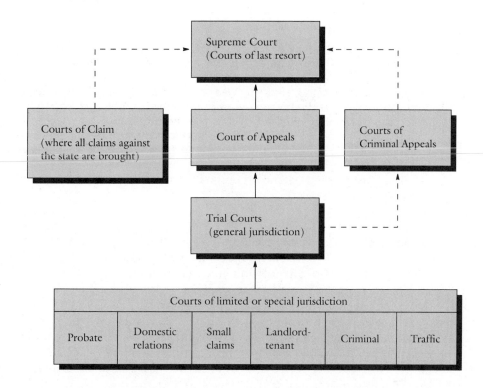

whenever their pronouncements are relevant.

Within a single judicial system, the decisions of any particular court are binding only on courts below the level of the court making them. However, the court rendering the decision also feels an obligation to be consistent, and will continue to follow the precedent until there is a good reason to overturn it. For example, as we will discuss in Chapter 3, the federal court system is made up of the Supreme Court at the top and the thirteen circuit courts of appeals on the next level down, under which are numerous trial courts (most notably district courts in each of the states). A decision of the Fifth Circuit Court of Appeals on an issue of federal law would be binding only on the district courts, particularly those geographically within that circuit, and other inferior courts. That decision probably would be followed by the Fifth Circuit Court in future rulings and would have some influence on other circuit courts (although it could be ignored by them), but could be fully reviewed by the Supreme Court. Decisions of trial courts generally are not published in official reports and are not binding as precedent on any other court. This is the reason that almost all cases presented in this book will be decisions of appellate, not trial, courts.

Because of the stabilizing effect of case precedent, which provides a measure of predictability to those who rely on the law, courts ordinarily stand by precedents until they are absolutely convinced that the rule no longer has merit. As illustrated by the following case, sometimes they stand by it too long.

FLAGIELLO v. PENNSYLVANIA HOSPITAL
417 Pa.486, 208 A.2d 193 (1965)

This was an action by Mary C. Flagiello and her husband Thomas Flagiello (Plaintiffs/Appellants) against Pennsylvania Hospital and two of its employees (Defendants), alleging trespass. Plaintiff, Mary C. Flagiello, while a patient in Pennsylvania Hospital, allegedly was caused to fall because of the negligence of two employees of the hospital. As a result, she sustained pain and suffering, her earning power was impaired, and further hospitalization was necessitated. The hospital defended on the ground that it was an institution engaged in a charitable enterprise and as such, was insulated from liability for negligence by the doctrine of charitable immunity.

The court granted Defendant Hospital's motion for judgment on the pleadings and Plaintiffs appealed. Reversed.

MUSMANNO, Justice.

Whatever Mrs. Flagiello received in the Pennsylvania Hospital was not bestowed on her gratuitously. She paid $24.50 a day for the services she was to receive. . . .

Thus, as a matter of integrity in nomenclature it must be stated that, although the hospitals here under discussion are known as charitable hospitals, it does not follow that they offer their services through the operation of charity. While in no way detracting from the contributions which these estimable institutions do make toward the alleviation and cure of the ills of mankind, a proper appraisement of the issue on appeal impels the candid statement that hospitals do receive payment for that contribution, and where a hospital is compensated for services rendered, it cannot, if language is to mirror reality, truly be called a charity hospital. . . .

Whatever the law may have been regarding charitable institutions in the past, it does not meet the conditions of today. Charitable enterprises are no longer housed in ramshackle wooden structures. They are not mere storm shelters to succor the traveler and temporarily refuge those stricken in a common disaster. Hospitals today are growing into mighty edifices in brick, stone, glass and marble. Many of them maintain large staffs, they use the best equipment that science can devise, they utilize the most modern methods in devoting themselves to the noblest purpose of man, that of helping one's stricken brother. But they do all this on a business basis, submitting invoices for services rendered—and properly so. . . .

Each court which has upheld the immunity rule has relied for its authority on a previous decision or decisions, scarcely ever placing the subject for study on the table of self-asserting justice. Thus one pursues the citations retrospectively to see how so strange a doctrine of exemption ever became engrafted on to the negligence law of Pennsylvania, which is not unknown for the common sense which permeates it, as well as the technological exactness which generally underlies it. Despite the claims of the supporters of the immunity rule that it is an ancient one, it did not really break through the crust of Pennsylvania's jurisprudence until 1888 in the case of Fire Insurance Patrol v. Boyd [Pa.]. . . .

In that case, Justice Paxson said that the charitable immunity rule "is hoary with antiquity and prevails alike in this country and in England." In support of this assertion he cited the case of Feoffees of Heriot's Hospital v. Ross, [Eng.] . . . decided in 1846, which had rested on Duncan v. Findlater, [Eng.]. . . .

Speaking for the English Court, Lord Cottenham had pronounced in both cases that:

> To give damages out of a trust fund would not be to apply it to those objects whom the author of the fund had in view, but would be to divert it to a completely different purpose.

Apart from the fact that this statement was made in 1839 and therefore could lay no claim, in 1888, to "antiquity," it was extraneous to the question as to whether a person injured through a tort committed by a charitable institution could recover against the institution. But even if it be assumed that the question bore some relationship to the problem under consideration in Fire Insurance Patrol v. Boyd . . . Lord Cottenham's pronouncement had been repudiated in 1866 in Mersey Docks Trustees v. Gibbs, [Eng.] . . . and what was said in 1861 in Holiday v. St. Leonard, [Eng.] . . . on the same subject was overruled in 1871 by the case of Foreman v. Mayor of Canterbury, [Eng.]. . . . Thus, the doctrine expounded in Fire Insurance Patrol v. Boyd, which depended on Feoffees, as authority, was, in fact, not the law in England in 1888. . . .

In arguing for retention of the immunity doctrine, its adherents never inquire whether the doctrine is grounded in "good morals and sound law." . . . They are content to refer to previous decisions of this court, and of other courts, as if yesteryear could do no wrong and as if the hand of the past must forever clutch the helm of the present. No attempt is ever made by the advocates of the immunity doctrine to justify in moral law and fair dealing a doctrine which deprives an injured person of a forum guaranteed to all others. . . .

If havoc and financial chaos were inevitably to follow the abrogation of the immunity doctrine, as the advocates for its retention insist, this would certainly have become apparent in the states where that doctrine is no longer a defense. But neither the defendant hospital nor the Hospital Association of Pennsylvania has submitted any evidence of catastrophe in the States where charitable hospitals are tortiously liable. Moreover, in a country based on the principle of equal justice for all, how can Pennsylvania deny to hospital patients the universally recognized right of compensation for injuries illegally inflicted? . . .

A rule that has become insolvent has no place in the active market of current enterprise. When a rule offends against reason, when it is at odds with every precept of natural justice, and when it cannot be defended on its own merits, but has to depend alone on a discredited genealogy, courts not only possess the inherent power to repudiate, but, indeed, it is required, by the very nature of judicial function, to abolish such a rule. . . .

Of course, the precedents here recalled do not justify a light and casual treatment of the doctrine of *stare decisis* but they proclaim unequivocally that where justice demands, reason dictates, equality enjoins and fair play decrees a change in judge-made law, courts will not lack in determination to establish that change. We, therefore, . . . hold that the hospital's liability must be governed by the same principles of law as apply to other employers.

Questions

1. To what extent did the Flagiello Court consider English cases to be binding precedent to be followed in American courts?

2. Why did the Flagiello Court refuse to apply the doctrine of charitable immunity? Was it bad law in its origin, or has something changed in the meantime?

Perhaps it is now becoming clear why the study of judicial cases is important. Cases provide an important source of law, and in many situations are the only source. In addition, the study of cases enables us to see how rules of law are applied to different factual situations in order to reach judicial decisions. To study rules of law in a vacuum is like studying the physical properties of a machine, such as an automobile, without ever learning how it works or what to do with its parts.

In order to study cases effectively, certain procedures should be followed. First, you should learn how go to a library and locate a case on a subject that interest you. Then you should learn how to read a case, mastering the art of determining what points should be extracted from the opinion, and why. Finally you should learn how to write a synopsis of the case that can be reviewed later. This final step is called "briefing," and the abstract of the case is referred to as a "brief." Now, you should refer to Appendix A and study the material on reading and briefing a case.

SUMMARY

Because law surrounds us in both our business and personal lives, an understanding of the legal system is necessary to an understanding of the very environment in which we live. It helps us to avoid legal conflicts by alerting us to what kinds of conduct may subject us to legal consequences such as a lawsuit.

This chapter has tried to help develop an understanding of what law is and how it was derived, and that the legal system in the United States is only one possible system among many. Although we may believe ours is the best system, we can justify such a belief only if we have some acquaintance with other systems and consider the characteristics, the advantages, and the disadvantages of each.

The classifications of law presented in this chapter should be studied carefully. By classifying law, we begin to develop a common language that will facilitate our studies. Also it enables us to look more deeply into the nature of law, and to develop some basis for analyzing the application of law to factual situations.

KEY TERMS AND CONCEPTS

natural law
legal realism
statute
ordinance
executive order
administrative rule
law
case of first impression
substantive law
procedural law
criminal law
civil law

Civil Law
common law
Common Law
equity
code
merger of law and equity
precedent
stare decisis

PROBLEMS

1. In this chapter, *law* is defined as "a set of norms, conceived by society, for its own regulation," which is only one of many possible definitions. To which of the schools of thought presented in this chapter would you ascribe this definition—Natural Law, the Historical School, the Theory of Power, or Legal Realism?

2. According to which constitutional power, if any, may a state legislature enact a statute requiring that a motorist must wear an approved seat belt while operating an automobile? What about requiring passengers to do the same? What about requiring those who operate or ride on a motorcycle or motor scooter to wear an approved helmet?

3. Problems concerning medical malpractice insurance have been widely discussed since the early 1970s. They focused primarily on the size of verdicts in malpractice lawsuits, the rise in premiums that resulted, the reality that this caused a significant rise in the cost of medical care for everyone, and the fear that, in some cases, these verdicts would make it impossible for doctors to practice their profession. In response, the Illinois legislature enacted legislation limiting recoveries in medical malpractice cases to a maximum of $500,000. Was the act constitutional?

4. Because of the principle of "separation of powers" in the Constitution, care must be exercised in determining the proper course of action when members of different branches of the government attempt to exercise conflicting powers.

This was the case when President Nixon sought to withhold certain tape recordings of White House conversations that had taken place during his administration when they were requested by Congress during the Watergate investigation. President Nixon asserted the principle of executive privilege. Should the president be allowed to withhold the tapes on this ground?

5. American Discounts, Inc., through its agents, caused to be published a list of prices for their goods, comparing them to the prices for the same goods being charged by the Kelly Co. The prices quoted as those of Kelly were exaggerated, and Kelly sued for violation of the Lanham (Trademark) Act, which prohibits the fraudulent use of the trademarks of another. Kelly contended that it also was intended to protect against violations of the type concerned in this case or, in essence, all deceptive practices involving the goods of a competitor. Should Kelly's suit be successful?

6. The Missouri legislature enacted a statute providing that in eminent domain cases, the landowner whose property was to be taken would be served with notice, and if the eminent domain notice was not objected to within 20 days, any question concerning the propriety of the taking would be waived. A jury of six then would establish a fair price after a hearing limited to that one issue. Barker was served with such a notice and did not object within the statutory period. He then filed suit against St. Louis County, the taker, claiming that he should not be deprived of his right to due process by silence and inaction. Should the statute be found unconstitutional?

7. Briney owned a house that for some time had stood unoccupied. It was her parents' home prior to their deaths. During a period of several months, the house was burglarized on numerous occasions, and furnishings were stolen, many of which were antiques. There seemed no way to secure the house from trespass, so Briney, aggravated by the thefts, set a "spring-gun"—a shotgun aimed just below one of the windows, rigged to go off whenever a wire attached to the trigger was tripped. One night, Katko crawled through the window, admittedly to steal antiques. The spring-gun fired and the charge shattered Katko's leg. Katko sued Briney for his injuries. Should Briney be held liable?

8.   The Uniform Commerical Code (with some state modification) has been enacted into law by all states and the District of Columbia. Can it be said, therefore, that it is "federal law"? Explain.

9.   Davis, Smith, Carson, and Phillips found themselves occupying a life boat together, at sea, following a shipwreck. After floating for several days, they encountered a storm. The boat, which was made for only two passengers, threatened to sink. It was decided that one of them had to be sacrificed for the good of the others. There was no real likelihood of rescue, or that the storm would let up in the near future. Phillips was the weakest and most likely to die anyway, so he was elected by Davis and Smith. Carson refused to take part and Phillips was not consulted. At what seemed to be the final moment, Davis and Smith killed Phillips and threw him overboard. The others were rescued 21 days later. It is agreed that if the action had not been taken, all would have died. Should they be found criminally liable for what they did? If so, to what extent should they be punished?

Chapter | 3

Courts and Procedure

INTRODUCTION

A basic understanding of the courts in the United States and the procedure by which they operate is a necessary step in understanding the legal system. This chapter will explore the structure of the court system, detail the route a lawsuit may take, and briefly touch on available remedies or legal relief. In addition, alternative methods of dispute resolution will be discussed.

AN OVERVIEW OF COURT PROCEDURE

Procedure is the body of rules that governs or provides the framework for the judicial process. The judicial process, in turn, guides the operation of courts in determining legal controversies.

When looking at legal decisions it is important to keep in mind the following points. (1) The judicial process deals not with abstract questions of hypothetical situations but with actual controversies between real people. (2) The system's primary objective is the resolution of these controversies. (3) This resolution proceeds according to standards of general application, not arbitrarily. (4) These standards are applied in a proceeding that follows a fixed format set out by a system of rules known as procedure.

A distinctive element of civil lawsuits in the United States is the **adversary system**. Under-

39

standing this element is central to understanding procedure. It means that the responsibility for beginning suit, for shaping the issues to be decided, and for producing evidence rests almost entirely on the parties to the controversy; the court takes a relatively small active part. Although the adversary system is not the only possible approach to dispute resolution, it remains a significant element of American judicial systems. In recent times there has been a trend toward increasing the affirmative involvement of judges. Nonetheless, it cannot be questioned that in the United States, the primary responsibility for and control over almost all phases of a lawsuit continue to reside in the parties involved.

When one reflects on the fact that the adversary system means victory may turn on considerations other than those of the just merits of the case, such as who has a better lawyer, there is reason to believe we have permitted it to take an exaggerated place in our judicial scheme. But the system remains, and its presence colors every facet of the law.

THE COURT SYSTEM

Each of the fifty states and the District of Columbia has its own judicial system. In addition there is a separate federal court system, as well as courts for each of the United States territories and possessions. The potential availability of more than one court in which to litigate a given dispute poses various tactical considerations that must be explored in choosing between a federal and state court and between different state courts. For example, an attorney might prefer a federal court to a state court because he believes that federal judges and juries are of a higher caliber than their state counterparts; conversely, a lawyer may prefer a state court if she expects a state judge or jury to be more sympathetic to her client and her case because it is of local significance. Finally, many attorneys simply are more experienced and comfortable at litigating in one court or the other. Each of these, and other complex tactical concerns, must be evaluated in light of the various

rules and statutes governing access to each court system. As a general proposition, most businesses, particularly the larger ones, prefer to litigate in the federal courts because they believe state courts and local juries have an antibusiness bias.

The existence of separate state and federal court systems is unique to the United States. This **dual court structure** is a result of the federal system of government embodied in the United States Constitution. The states and the federal government have separate powers. Thus, each court system operates independently under its own grant of power. The tactical considerations described in the previous paragraph are one result of these parallel court systems. In many substantive areas of the law, state and federal courts overlap in their powers to hear and resolve disputes—their jurisdiction is said to be *concurrent*. However, there are also some contexts in which an issue may be heard and decided by only one of the two—their jurisdiction is said to be *exclusive*. Controversies of merely local or statewide interest such as contracts, torts, property disputes, and most commercial matters generally are left to the state courts to resolve. Nationwide concerns such as patents, bankruptcy, and foreign relations may be restricted by Congress to being litigated in the federal courts. As a result, many aspects of interstate business fall within the jurisdiction of the federal courts.

Most judicial systems in the United States began as two-tiered structures made up of a trial tribunal and one court of review. Some state systems remain so today, but the federal and most state judicial systems are now three tiered, composed of a trial court, a court of intermediate appellate review that is final for most cases, and a court of last resort that is empowered to determine whether it will hear a particular case. Although the names of the specific courts may vary, their basic functions are comparable.

On the state level, the courts of **original jurisdiction** (courts in which cases are instituted and tried) usually consist of one set of general jurisdiction courts and several sets of special jurisdiction courts. The courts of **general jurisdiction** are organized into geographical districts comprising one or more counties. These courts hear cases of many kinds and are competent to grant every kind of relief. Generally, to sue in a general jurisdiction court, the plaintiff must have a claim for more than a certain amount, typically several thousand dollars. The courts of **special jurisdiction** include municipal courts, which hear less important matters; justice-of-the-peace courts, which hear very minor matters; and specialized tribunals such as probate courts, which hear cases involving decedents' estates, competency, and a variety of other matters.

We will use the federal structure to illustrate the function of a court system. The federal trial courts (courts of original jurisdiction) are called United States District Courts. There are ninety-one judicial districts in the nation, each having its own court. Every state, as well as the District of Columbia, has at least one judicial district, and many larger states have two, three, or even four. The decision to divide a particular state into more than one judicial district depends on population, geography, and caseload.

The federal district courts exercise general trial jurisdiction. Thus, they act as the initial tribunal for almost all cases, civil and criminal, that are permitted to enter the federal court system. Both a federal district court and the state trial courts may have authority to hear a particular case so that litigants can choose whether to sue in state or federal court.

A losing litigant in a federal court generally may appeal a final decision to the United States Court of Appeals for the circuit in which the district court is located. At present there are eleven numbered circuits; each consists of anywhere from three to ten states and territories. In addition, there is a court of appeals for the District of Columbia, which hears appeals from the federal district court there, and one for the Federal Circuit, which handles appeals from various specialized federal tribunals such as the Court of Claims (thus there are thirteen circuits in all).

Each court of appeals has four or more judges who usually sit in panels of three to review the cases before them. Appeals from federal administrative agencies often are subject to initial judicial review by a court of appeals as well.

At the apex of the federal court system is the Supreme Court of the United States, composed of nine justices. The justices, appointed by the president, are appointed for life, on good behavior, and must be confirmed by the Senate. Unless disqualified or ill, all justices participate in each decision of the Court.

Only a few types of cases may be appealed automatically—at the request of the losing party—to the Supreme Court; the rest are selected by the Court as a matter of discretion, which is exercised by the Court's decision to grant a **Writ of Certiorari** (permission to appeal). Cases come from the United States Courts of Appeals or the highest courts of the states. It is important to note that the Supreme Court not only reviews the decisions of the federal courts, but also reviews decisions of the state courts that involve issues of federal law. The Supreme Court also has limited original (trial) jurisdiction in certain special cases, such as suits between states.

Although, as already indicated, most states have three tiers of courts like the federal system, there is some difference in the role performed by the highest state court. In some states, appeals as a matter of right, rather than by permission, are even more limited than in the case of the United States Supreme Court. For example, in California almost all appeals to the highest state court are discretionary. This restriction allows a state supreme court to manage its caseload and to choose cases that will provide some needed clarification in the law or that involve issues or facts of such public significance that the court deems its decision necessary. Litigants disappointed in the trial court have to be content with a full review by the intermediate appellate court. At the other end of the spectrum are states such as New York, in which appeals as a matter of right to the state's highest court occur in many cases.

THE STEPS IN A LAWSUIT

The first step in a lawsuit is a matter of human dynamics. Lawsuits do not begin themselves; someone must decide to sue someone else. If that decision is made intelligently, the person choosing to sue must weigh several matters, among which three are basic: (1) Does the law provide any relief for such an injury? (2) If relief were granted, would it be worth the time, trouble, and expense of suing? (3) Would the relief be adequate in light of the other practical problems created by bringing a lawsuit?

A potential litigant obviously feels aggrieved or he would not be thinking of suing. But before going to court he must consider whether the grievance is one for which the law furnishes relief. There are a great many hurts that the law will not address. Someone loses his girlfriend to a wealthier suitor, or is offended by the garish paint on his neighbor's house. The law provides no remedies for these injuries, and litigation would be a wasteful exercise.

Then, and perhaps most important of all, the potential litigant must consider whether what is won will be worth the time, the effort, and the expense of going to court, and she must evaluate the options other than suit, including settlement, arbitration, and letting matters rest. Most frequently, the relief will be a judgment for damages. If this is true, she must decide if her injury is one for which a monetary payment will be satisfactory relief and whether the amount likely to be awarded will be sufficient.

Assuming money damages will be adequate, will the litigant be able to collect a judgment? Will he end with enough to pay his lawyer and the other litigation expenses that will be incurred? Even when the court may grant specific relief—for example, an order directing the opposing party to do something or to stop doing something—will compliance by the defendant be possible and worthwhile? The litigant also should consider whether there are risks not directly tied to the suit: Will he antagonize people whose goodwill he needs? Will the action publicize an error of judgment on his part or open his private affairs to public review? Only after he has resolved these and other questions will the prospective plaintiff be ready to embark on litigation. Let us now consider those steps in the light of a hypothetical case:

> *Andrea, walking along a sidewalk in front of a warehouse, was struck and seriously injured by a barrel dropped by Boris. On inquiry, Andrea found that the warehouse was owned by Carmen and that Boris apparently had been in Carmen's employ. Boris was without substantial assets and a judgment against him promised little material reward. But Carmen was wealthy, and Andrea was advised that if she could establish that Boris had been working for Carmen and had been negligent, she could then recover from Carmen. Andrea decided to sue Carmen for $100,000.*

Note that Andrea, the person bringing the suit, is the **plaintiff**; Carmen, the person being sued, is the **defendant**.

Determining a Proper Court

Andrea initially must decide in what court she will be able to bring the action. She probably will have some choice, but it will be a limited one. This is because the court selected must have **subject-matter jurisdiction** (that is, the constitution and statutes under which the court operates must have conferred upon it power to decide this type of case).

Andrea probably will bring suit in a state court because the subject-matter jurisdiction of the federal courts is limited. Federal courts' subject-matter jurisdiction extends to many, but not all, cases involving federal law, and to certain cases, like Andrea's, that do not involve federal law but in which there is what is called **diversity of citizenship** (the parties are citizens of different states or one of them is a citizen of a foreign country) and the required *amount in controversy* (more than $50,000) is at stake. Diversity cases do not have to be brought in the federal courts; the state courts also are competent to hear them. Thus, if Carmen and Andrea are citizens of different states, Andrea may bring her action for $100,000 in a federal or a state court. Indeed, in these

Elements of a lawsuit

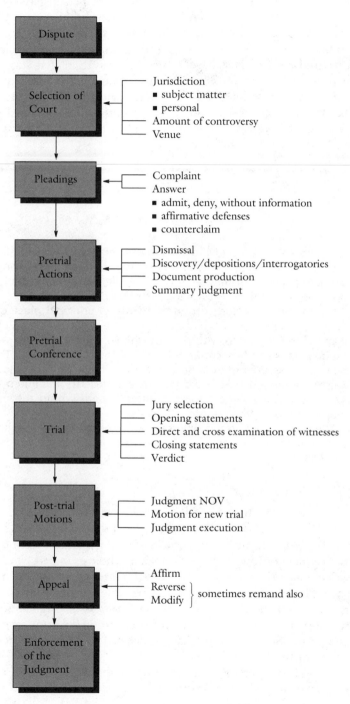

Dispute

Selection of Court
— Jurisdiction
  ■ subject matter
  ■ personal
— Amount of controversy
— Venue

Pleadings
— Complaint
  Answer
  ■ admit, deny, without information
  ■ affirmative defenses
  ■ counterclaim

Pretrial Actions
— Dismissal
— Discovery/depositions/interrogatories
— Document production
— Summary judgment

Pretrial Conference

Trial
— Jury selection
— Opening statements
— Direct and cross examination of witnesses
— Closing statements
— Verdict

Post-trial Motions
— Judgment NOV
— Motion for new trial
— Judgment execution

Appeal
— Affirm
— Reverse } sometimes remand also
— Modify

Enforcement of the Judgment

circumstances, if Andrea sued Carmen in a state court, Carmen (if she were not from the state) would have the option to *remove* the action from the state court in which it was commenced to the federal district court in that state.

The court selected by Andrea also must have **personal jurisdiction** over the defendant. That court, whether state or federal, must be one in which Carmen can be required to appear and defend the action. This generally means that Carmen must reside or be found in the state in which

the court is located. However, notions of jurisdiction over the person have been expanding in recent decades. In this case, if Carmen is not present in Andrea's state, but the accident occurred there, Andrea probably will be able to bring the action using a statute in that state allowing Andrea to reach out and grab Carmen wherever she is (called a **long-arm-jurisdiction** statute). In the following case, the court obtained jurisdiction over the defendant by using such a statute.

ANDERSEN v. NATIONAL PRESTO INDUSTRIES, INC.
257 Iowa 911, 135 N.W.2d 639 (1965)

This was an action by Dolores Andersen (Plaintiff/Appellant) against National Presto Industries, Inc. (Presto) and Gold Bond Stamp Company of Iowa (Defendants/Appellees) for injuries suffered while using an allegedly defective coffee pot manufactured by Presto and distributed by Gold Bond.

Presto was a foreign corporation with its principal place of business in Eau Claire, Wisconsin. Presto had no registered agent in Iowa. Pursuant to statute, Plaintiff served Presto with process (the complaint and the summons) by filing the papers with the secretary of state of the state of Iowa. The coffee pot had been purchased from Gold Bond Stamps in Iowa, and the injury occurred there. Presto contended that it did not have sufficient "minimum connection" with Iowa to be considered "doing business" there within the meaning of Iowa's long-arm jurisdiction statute.

The trial court entered judgment sustaining Presto's special appearance and challenge to jurisdiction of the Iowa courts, and Plaintiff appealed. Reversed and remanded.

THOMPSON, Justice.

In attempting to obtain jurisdiction the plaintiff followed section 617.3, code of 1962, I.C.A., as amended by chapter 325 of the Acts of the 60th General Assembly. So far as pertinent, this section now reads: "If a foreign corporation makes a contract with a resident of Iowa to be performed in whole or in part by either party in Iowa, *or if such foreign corporation commits a tort in whole or in part in Iowa against a resident of Iowa,* such acts shall be deemed to be doing business in Iowa by such foreign corporation for the purpose of service of process or original notice on such foreign corporation under this Act, and, if the corporation does not have a registered agent or agents in the State of Iowa, shall be deemed to constitute the appointment of the secretary of the state of Iowa." . . .

"The place of wrong is in the state where the last event necessary to make an actor liable for an alleged tort takes place." The significance of this rule is pointed up in

Price v. State Highway Commission . . . in this language: "Generally speaking and without undertaking in the least an all inclusive definition, a tort has a meaning somewhat similar to wrong and is an unlawful act injurious to another independent of contract." . . . We must assume that the legislature, in wording section 617.3 as it has now done, had in mind an actionable tort, rather than an act which by itself, without resulting injury, would not give a basis for recovery. It is also of considerable importance that the statute says "in whole or in part". It is not a strained or illogical conclusion that the legislature had in mind the exact situation here present, where the negligence occurred in another state, but the injury was inflicted in Iowa. In this situation, adopting what we think is the proper definition of a tort as related to the remedy contemplated by the statute, we think the tort was committed "in part" in Iowa. . . .

The defendant, and some of the authorities, place some emphasis upon the inconvenience caused to a non-resident defendant by being compelled to defend a suit in another state. We have pointed out above the greatly expanded means of communication and travel now available, both as to convenience and time. It also appears that the argument is one which is equally cogent in support of the plaintiff's position. If it is inconvenient and expensive to the defendant to go to another state to defend, it is equally so for the plaintiff to prosecute. There is much justice in a holding which places the burden of inconvenience and expense upon the tort feasor which puts its defective product upon the market in another state and so injures an innocent user, rather than upon the injured party. Convenience or the lack thereof is not in any event a good test for determining jurisdiction; but so far as it has any weight here, the argument is at least as available to the plaintiff as to the defendant.

The defendant urges that section 617.3 provides an extraordinary method of obtaining jurisdiction, and there must be clear and complete compliance with it. This is true; but we are not pointed to any deviation from the exact procedures required by the statute, and the defendant does not claim they were not literally followed. Its contention is based upon the two points stated in Division I above. These have been answered.

The ruling and judgment of the trial court is reversed, and the cause remanded for further proceedings in conformity with this opinion.

Questions

1. What is the rationale for a court's power to exercise long-arm jurisdiction?
2. In the Andersen case, suppose the plaintiff had purchased the defective appliance in Iowa, had been a resident of Illinois, and was injured while using it in Indiana. Which state(s) would have long-arm jurisdiction to reach the defendant? Why?

If personal jurisdiction cannot be attained over Carmen of Andrea's choosing, but she owns property in that state (for example, she owns the warehouse or has a bank account), she may be subject to suit anyway based on the attachment or seizure of that property, but the ability to collect the judgment will be limited to the value of the property.

Not every court that has jurisdiction over the subject matter and jurisdiction over the person will agree to hear a case. It also is necessary that an action be brought in a court located in a place that has some relationship with the lawsuit. Although every court in Andrea's state could assert personal jurisdiction over Carmen if she was within its boundaries, that state's statutes typically will provide that the case should be brought in a court in a district that includes the county in which either Andrea or Carmen lives or where the claim arose. The courts in these counties are said to have proper **venue**, which simply is the set of rules that allocate or assign cases to the different courts within a judicial system.

Jurisdiction over the subject matter is jealously guarded by the courts, and cannot be waived by the parties. If Andrea and Carmen are both citizens of the same state, a federal court will refuse to hear the action even if both want that court to hear it. Jurisdiction over the person and the rules determining the proper venue of the lawsuit essentially are protections for the defendant, who may waive them if he or she wishes to do so.

Commencing the Action

After the court has been selected, Andrea must give notice to Carmen that a lawsuit is under way, and invoke the court's power over her by **service of process**. Process typically consists of a **summons**, which directs the defendant to appear and defend under penalty of a **default judgment** (unless the defendant answers the summons, a judgment will be entered against her). Service of process usually is achieved by personal delivery to the defendant, or the summons is left at her home, sometimes by a public official such as a sheriff or a United States marshal. If Carmen lives in another state, but the circumstances are such that a court in Andrea's state may assert jurisdiction over her, the summons may be delivered to her by some other technique, such as sending the papers by registered mail and delivering the summons to her agent in Andrea's state. If Carmen cannot be located, service by publication in a newspaper for a certain length of time may be allowed. However,

this last kind of service is valid in only a limited range of cases. The United States Supreme Court repeatedly has emphasized that service must be reasonably calculated to bring the action to the defendant's notice, and from this perspective service by newspaper publication is marginal at best.

The Pleadings

Along with the summons, Andrea usually will serve on Carmen the first of the **pleadings**, a document commonly known as the **complaint**. This is a written statement that will contain Andrea's claim against Carmen. The elements of a complaint are: (1) an assertion of the court's jurisdiction to hear the case; (2) a statement showing that the plaintiff has a legal grievance and is entitled to a remedy; and (3) an identification of the remedy the plaintiff is seeking. Court systems vary greatly in the detail required in the pleadings, depending on which of three purposes the pleadings are expected to serve.

First, the system may require that the pleadings furnish a basis for identifying and separating the legal and factual contentions involved in the dispute so that the legal issues may be disposed of at an early stage. This objective would be served effectively in our case only if the pleadings set forth exactly what Boris's job required him to do. It would be served inadequately if the complaint only stated that "Boris was working for Carmen."

Second, the pleadings may be intended to establish, in advance, what the pleader proposes to prove at trial so that his or her opponent will know what arguments he or she must prepare to meet. If this objective is regarded as important, it will not be enough for the complaint to state only that "Boris was negligent," or that "Andrea suffered serious bodily injuries." It must describe Boris's act of negligence and describe Andrea's injuries with a fair amount of detail.

Third, the pleadings may be intended to give each party only a general notion of the opponent's contentions, in which event the system would rely upon subsequent stages of the lawsuit to identify the legal and factual contentions of the parties and to enable each to prepare to meet the opponent's case.

Obviously each of the first two objectives is desirable. It is a waste of everyone's time to try lawsuits when the underlying claim simply will not be recognized as legally sufficient, and it is only fair that a person called upon to defend a judicial proceeding should know what he or she is alleged to have done. Moreover, if fully pursued, either the first or second objective requires that the parties adhere to the position taken in the pleadings. They will not be allowed to introduce evidence in conflict with the pleadings or to change them. To the extent that amendments to the pleadings are permitted, the underlying objectives of the pleadings will be lost.

Over time the third objective has come to the fore in American procedure. Liberal discovery procedures have lessened the necessity for the early identification of the particular legal and factual allegations of the parties. This in turn has softened the insistence on extensive detail in the initial pleading stages of an action—a requirement that often demanded too much precision too early in the case. A minimal complaint containing the three elements discussed above generally will suffice in most courts today.

Following the service of Andrea's complaint, Carmen must respond either by filing an answer or by making a motion. She may challenge the sufficiency of the complaint and seek to end the case by a **motion to dismiss**, which is a request that the judge throw the case out of court without a trial on the merits. This motion may challenge the court's jurisdiction over the subject matter or Carmen's person, or the service of process. It also may be a *motion to dismiss for failure to state a cause of action* (historically known as a **demurrer**) that the law recognizes as actionable. For the purpose of this motion, the facts alleged in the complaint are accepted as true, and the court considers whether, on this assumption, the plaintiff has shown that he or she may be entitled to legal relief.

A motion to dismiss for failure to state a cause of action will be granted if the court determines that the plaintiff has failed to plead a **prima facie** (legally sufficient) case. There are three general situations in which this might occur. First, the complaint clearly may show that the injury is one for which the law furnishes no relief—for example, when a plaintiff simply alleges that "the defendant has made faces at me." Second, the plaintiff may have failed to include an allegation on a necessary part of the case; for example, Andrea might have alleged the accident, her injuries, and Boris's negligence, and have forgotten to allege that Boris worked for Carmen. Third, the complaint may be so general or so confused that the court finds it does not give adequate notice of what the plaintiff's claim is; this would be true, for example, of a complaint in which Andrea merely said, "Carmen injured me and owes me $100,000." The extent to which motions to dismiss will be granted on the second and third grounds will vary with the amount of detail a particular system requires of its pleadings. Ordinarily, if the motion is granted, the plaintiff is given an opportunity to amend the complaint and correct the defect.

If the motion to dismiss is denied, or if none is filed, then Carmen must file a response to the plaintiff's complaint called the **answer** in which she must admit or deny the allegations made by Andrea in the complaint. Moreover, if Carmen wishes to rely on certain contentions called **affirmative defenses** (new matters that would constitute defenses even if the allegations of the complaint were true)—for example, that Andrea's own negligence caused the accident, or that the accident happened too long ago to be sued upon now—she must plead them in the answer. If Carmen's answer only denies the allegations in the complaint, and she does not specifically invoke one or more of the affirmative defenses, she will not be permitted to rely on any of these defenses at trial. There may be further pleadings, but the tendency today is to close the pleadings after the answer and move on toward trial. There is one major exception: if Carmen has a claim against Andrea, most systems allow Carmen to plead this claim as a **counterclaim** as part of her answer. This is in essence a complaint by Carmen, and Andrea will have to respond to it.

The original action between Andrea and Carmen may expand in terms of the number of parties, and this can occur during the pleading stage. For example, although Andrea decided not to sue Boris, Carmen, the defendant, might bring Boris into the action, asking that Boris be held liable for whatever amount she may be found to owe to Andrea, since Carmen's liability depends on Boris's conduct having been at fault. Carmen will decide whether or not to do this based on a number of practical concerns, including the effect Boris's presence will have on the original suit. For example, will it arouse juror sympathy for a working person and prejudice Andrea?

Dismissal and Judgment Before Trial

One of the basic difficulties with attempting to resolve cases at the pleading stage is that the allegations of the parties must be accepted as true for the purpose of ruling on a motion to dismiss. The pleading stage is not a stage to resolve questions of fact—resolving questions of fact is the reason for having a trial. In some cases it will be possible to supplement the pleadings with additional information to show that an issue that is decisive of the case can be resolved without a trial or that there is absolutely no merit to the plaintiff's claim or the defendant's answer. This is done by a motion for **summary judgment**, which, if successful, will end the case. The additional information, usually in the form of an **affidavit** (a sworn statement) or material generated by the discovery process, distinguishes a motion to dismiss, which is based solely on the pleadings, from a motion for summary judgment. This motion can be supported by demonstrating that the crucial issue inevitably will have to be resolved in the moving party's favor at trial because the opposing party will be unable to produce any persuasive evidence

in support of his or her position on the issue. For example, suppose Carmen's position is that prior to the action she had fired Boris, but that Boris had snuck into the warehouse shortly before the accident and had thrown the barrel off the roof. On the face of the pleadings, we only have an allegation that Boris was Carmen's employee and a denial of that allegation; thus the pleadings present a question of who is right that cannot be resolved at this stage, and a trial is required.

Now, suppose Carmen moves for summary judgment, accompanying her motion with sworn statements from two witnesses that she had fired Boris, and that she had told the warehouse manager not to let Boris in the warehouse. The burden is now on Andrea to show that the issue of Boris's continued employment is genuine. A simple assertion by her that this is not so is not enough; after all, she has no personal knowledge of the facts. If Andrea cannot produce evidence that Boris was acting as Carmen's employee, summary judgment will be entered against her and the case will end.

It should be noted that in ruling on a motion for summary judgment, the judge does not decide who is telling the truth. If Andrea presents an affidavit of a witness who says he overheard Carmen firing Boris and then telling him that this was all a scam and that Boris should sneak into the warehouse and continue to work for her, summary judgment will not be appropriate even though the judge is convinced Andrea's witness is lying. That is to be determined at trial.

Discovery

In our discussion of the objectives of pleading, we noted that many of today's procedural systems do not regard the pleadings as the appropriate vehicle for requiring the parties to reveal the facts in order to prepare for trial. The procedure primarily charged with this function is pretrial **discovery**. This is a generic term for several methods of obtaining information from an opposing party or from witnesses.

The most significant discovery device is the taking of **depositions** of parties and witnesses. In this procedure, the person whose deposition is being taken is sworn in by a court officer and questioned by lawyers for each side, through direct and cross-examination, and his or her responses are recorded. The device is useful for finding information relevant to the case, including unearthing leads to other witnesses or documents; it also is useful for impeaching a witness who attempts to change his or her story at the trial. In our hypothetical case, the two parties almost certainly will want depositions taken of each other, as well as of Boris. The depositions of Andrea and Carmen will be particularly important because anything said will be treated as an admission; that is, it can be used by their adversaries as evidence at trial. Also, a deposition of a nonparty witness who is unavailable to appear at the trial may be used in place of live testimony.

Another device especially adapted to probing the content of an opponent's case is **written interrogatories** (sets of written questions to be answered under oath and in writing), which usually may be addressed only to a party in a suit. (One reason Andrea might join Boris as a defendant with Carmen or why Carmen might try to add Boris is that interrogatories can only be used against parties to the actions—not mere witnesses.) These interrogatories are answered by the party with counsel's aid, so the responses will not be as spontaneous as they are in a deposition. Nevertheless, interrogatories require the person asked the questions to supply information that is not carried in his or her head, but which he or she can get. Interrogatories are much less expensive for the party using them than depositions because they require less formality.

Other discovery devices include *orders for the production of documents*, such as the safety records of Carmen's warehouse, and *requests for admissions*, which will remove uncontested issues from the case and therefore eliminate unnecessary testimony and other evidence. A particularly useful device for Carmen will be a court order directing Andrea to submit to a *physical examination* by a physician of Carmen's choice to determine the real extent of her injuries.

The availability of discovery, which has become broad in scope and use throughout the country, has affected the philosophy of the pleadings. It enables parties to learn all relevant information and prepare for trial better than the pleadings ever did. When broad discovery is allowed, the initial stages of a lawsuit can be more flexible regarding pleading, since discovery provides several useful devices for obtaining information, thereby reducing the significance of the pleadings substantially. In addition, the availability of discovery does much to make summary judgment a viable and fair procedure.

Pretrial Conferences

In the federal courts and in some state courts there may be one or more **pretrial conferences**. These are meetings between the lawyers for both sides and the judge, and usually are held in the judge's chambers. The purpose is to identify the disputed issues and structure the course of the trial so that it runs smoothly and without surprises. In many cases the judge will suggest that the parties consider settlement if he or she feels that a trial would be wasteful or inefficient in the particular action. In many federal courts complicated cases are subjected to a series of these meetings, which start shortly after the case is filed.

Setting the Case for Trial

After discovery is completed, and if the case has not been terminated by dismissal, summary judgment, or settlement, it must be set for trial. Typically, either party may file a *note of issue*, at which time the case will be given a number and placed on a *trial calendar*. These calendars have become extremely long in many courts, and it may be several years before the case is called for trial, especially if a jury trial has been requested.

Jury Selection

In most damage actions the parties have a right to have the facts determined by a jury. This right is assured in the federal courts by the Seventh Amendment to the U.S. Constitution and is protected in most states by corresponding state constitutional provisions.

If there is a right to a trial by jury, either party may assert it, but if neither wishes to do so the judge will try the facts as well as the law. Because of a historical division between actions at law and suits in equity, there are many civil actions in which neither party has a right to jury trial; these include most cases in which the plaintiff wants an order directing or prohibiting specified conduct (an injunction) by the defendant rather than a judgment for money damages. An injunction is an *equitable remedy*. (Remedies will be discussed in more detail later in this chapter.)

If there is a right to a jury, and a jury has been demanded, the first order of business at trial will be to impanel the jurors. A large number of people selected at random from voting lists, tax rolls, or street directories, are ordered to report to the courthouse for jury duty. As the following case illustrates, although prospective jurors may be identified initially by a variety of methods, the selection of those who actually will serve in all cases must be random.

THIEL v. SOUTHERN PACIFIC COMPANY
328 U.S. 217, 66 S.Ct. 984 (1945)

This was an action by Thiel (Plaintiff/Petitioner) against Southern Pacific Company (Defendant/Respondent) for injuries suffered when he jumped from the window of a moving train. Defendant moved the trial to the federal district court on diversity of citizenship.

Plaintiff objected to the composition of the trial jury as being unrepresentative of the citizens of the district (mostly business executives and those having an employer's point of view), and moved to strike the panel. This motion was denied and after judgment was rendered for Defendant after trial, Plaintiff appealed the denial of his motion, among other things. The Circuit Court of Appeals affirmed, and the case came to the Supreme Court on *certiorari*. Reversed.

MURPHY, Justice.

The American tradition of trial by jury, considered in connection with either criminal or civil proceedings, necessarily contemplates an impartial jury drawn from a cross-section of the community. This does not mean, of course, that every jury must contain representatives of all the economic, social, religious, racial, political and geographical groups of the community; frequently such complete representation would be impossible. But it does mean that prospective jurors shall be selected by court officials without systematic and intentional exclusion of any of these groups. Recognition must be given to the fact that those eligible for jury service are to be found in every stratum of society. Jury competence is an individual rather than a group or class matter. This fact lies at the very heart of the jury system. To disregard it is to open the door to class distinctions and discriminations which are abhorrent to the democratic ideals of trial by jury.

The choice of the means by which unlawful distinctions and discriminations are to be avoided rests largely in the sound discretion of the trial courts and their officers. This discretion, of course, must be guided by pertinent statutory provisions. So far as federal jurors are concerned, they must be chosen "without reference to party affiliations," . . . and citizens cannot be disqualified "on account of race, color, or previous condition or servitude." . . . In addition, jurors must be returned from such parts of the district as the court may direct "so as to be most favorable to an impartial trial, and so as not to incur an unnecessary expense, or unduly burden the citizens of any part of the district with such service." . . . For the most part, of course, the qualifications and exemptions in regard to federal jurors are to be determined by the laws of the state where the federal court is located. . . . A state law creating an unlawful qualification, however, is not binding and should not be utilized in selecting federal jurors. . . .

The undisputed evidence in this case demonstrates a failure to abide by the proper rules and principles of jury selection. Both the clerk of the court and the jury commissioner testified that they deliberately and intentionally excluded from the jury lists all persons who work for a daily wage. They generally used the city directory as the source of names of prospective jurors. In the words of the clerk, "If I see in the directory the name of John Jones and it says he is a longshoreman, I do not put his name in, because I have found by experience that man will not serve as a juror, and I will not get people who will qualify. The minute that a juror is called into court on a venire [an order to appear for jury service] and says he is working for $10 a day and cannot afford to work for four, the Judge has never made one of these men serve, and so in order to avoid putting names of people in who I know won't qualify as jurors in this court, I do leave them out. . . . Where I thought the designation indicated that they were day laborers, I mean they were people who were compensated solely when they were working by the day, I leave them out." The jury commissioner corroborated this testimony, adding that he purposely excluded "all the iron craft, bricklayers, carpenters, and machinists" because in the past "those men came into court and offered that [financial hardship] as an excuse, and the judge usually let them go." The evidence indicated, however, that laborers who were paid weekly or monthly wages were placed on the jury lists, as well as the wives of daily wage earners.

It was further admitted that business men and their wives constituted at least 50% of the jury lists, although both the clerk and the commissioner denied that they consciously chose according to wealth or occupation. Thus the admitted discrimination was limited to those who worked for a daily wage, many of whom might suffer financial loss by serving on juries at the rate of $4 a day and would be excused for that reason.

This exclusion of all those who earn a daily wage cannot be justified by federal or state law. Certainly nothing in the federal statutes warrants such an exclusion. And the California statutes are equally devoid of justification for the practice. . . .

It is clear that a federal judge would be justified in excusing a daily wage earner for whom jury service would entail an undue financial hardship. But that fact cannot support the complete exclusion of all daily wage earners regardless of whether there is actual hardship involved. Here there was no effort, no intention, to determine in advance which individual members of the daily wage earning class would suffer an undue hardship by serving on a jury at the rate of $4 a day. All were systematically and automatically excluded. . . .

It follows that we cannot sanction the method by which the jury panel was formed in this case. The trial court should have granted petitioner's motion to strike the panel. That conclusion requires us to reverse the judgment below in the exercise of our power of supervision over the administration of justice in the federal courts.

Questions

1. To what extent is a party in a case entitled to have a jury of his or her "peers"?
2. Would it be proper under this decision if jurors were selected from a list taken from a roll of real estate owners in the district?

From the initial group, prospective jurors will be questioned by a proceeding called *voir dire*—usually by the judge but sometimes by the lawyers—about their possible biases. If someone called has prior knowledge of the case or is a personal friend of one of the parties, he or she probably will be *challenged for cause* and excused. If there is not enough reason to persuade the judge to excuse a juror for cause, then an attorney who feels that the particular juror may be prejudiced against his or her client may exercise one of a small number of **peremptory challenges** allowed, for which no reason need be given. Finally, a panel of twelve, or in recent years, and more likely, a panel of fewer than twelve, jurors will be selected. (Many courts now use six-member juries.)

Structure of the Trial

After the jurors have been sworn, the plaintiff's lawyer will make an **opening statement**, in which he will describe for the jury what the case is about, what his contentions are, and how he will prove them. The defendant's lawyer also may make an opening statement at this time, or may reserve the right to do so until she is ready to present her own case. Following the opening statement, the plaintiff's lawyer calls his witnesses one by one. Each witness is first questioned by the lawyer who called that witness—this is the **direct examination**. Then the lawyer for the other side has the opportunity to question the witness—this is the **cross examination**. These may be followed by *re-direct* and *re-cross* examination. Even further stages of questioning are possible. The judge maintains control over the length and tenor of the examination, and in particular will see to it that the stages beyond cross-examination are not prolonged.

Just as the primary responsibility for introducing evidence is placed on the lawyers, so too is the responsibility for objecting to evidence thought to be inadmissible under the rules of evidence. For example, testimony may be objectionable because it is **hearsay**; that is, it repeats what someone else has said for the purpose of proving the truth of what was said. (The best evidence of that is the testimony of the person who actually said it.) The judge will not raise this issue, however. It is up to the opposing counsel to object, and then the judge must rule on the objection. This kind of issue will recur continually throughout the trial, and the judge must be prepared to make instantaneous rulings so the trial can proceed with dispatch. This is why evidentiary rulings are a major source of errors raised on appeal by the losing party. If the judge rules a witness's answer inadmissible, she will instruct the jury to disregard it. (But realistically, can a juror who has heard the evidence really drive it from his or her mind?)

Documents, pictures, and other tangible items may be put into evidence, but unless their admissability has been stipulated in advance, they must be introduced through witnesses. For example, if Andrea's lawyer has had pictures taken of the accident scene and wishes to present them to the jury, he will call the photographer as a witness, have him testify that he took the pictures of the scene, and then show them to the photographer to identify them as the pictures he took. This is known as *laying the proper foundation* for the evidence. Once this is done, the photos may be introduced into evidence.

When the plaintiff's attorney has called all of his witnesses and their examinations are over, the plaintiff will *rest*. At this point, the defendant's lawyer may ask for *dismissal of the suit* on the ground that the plaintiff has not established a case. That means that the plaintiff has not introduced enough evidence to permit the jury to find in her favor. If the motion is denied, the defendant may rest if she believes that the jury will agree with her, but this is very risky. In almost all cases the defendant's attorney will proceed to pre-

sent witnesses of her own by way of defense. This requires going through the same process of direct and cross-examination. When the defendant has rested, the plaintiff may present new evidence to counter the defendant's presentation. This is called **rebuttal**. This procedure will continue until both sides rest. Again, the judge will maintain control over the process to prevent protraction of the trial.

When both sides have rested, either or both may move for a directed verdict claiming that there is no genuine dispute for the jury to decide. If that motion is granted, the case is decided by the judge and the jury is excused. If the motion is denied, the case must be submitted to the jury. The following case illustrates the reasoning of a court in determining to grant a directed verdict.

PERRINO v. D.C. TRANSIT SYSTEM, INC.
218 A.2d 519 (D.C.App., 1966)

This was an action by Linda Perrino (Plaintiff/Appellant) against D.C. Transit System, Inc. (Defendant/Appellee) for injuries sustained when she attempted to step aboard Defendant's bus. The trial court judge directed a verdict for Defendant and Plaintiff appealed. Affirmed.

CAYTON, Judge.

Plaintiff brought this action charging that she was injured as a result of a bus driver's negligence in stopping beyond a bus stop and so near a sewer that in attempting to board the bus she slipped and fell. At the close of her case the trial court granted a defense motion for directed verdict, and this appeal followed.

From testimony and photographs the following facts were developed. Plaintiff was waiting for a bus at a stop on Connecticut Avenue north of Tilden Street. The bus stopped south of and beyond the marked stop, about two and one-half feet away from the curb, opposite a catch basin or sewer opening. At that point the street has the usual incline toward the sewer opening. Plaintiff, being short (the record states 59 inches), was unable to step from the curb onto the bus; she reached unsuccessfully for the boarding handle, "couldn't seem to reach" the step, her right foot scraped the entrance step, and she fell to the ground. It was a clear, bright day.

We think a directed verdict was proper. Viewing the evidence in a light most favorable to plaintiff, the showing was not sufficient to make out a prima facie case. It left to speculation the initial question as to what caused the fall; it did not come close to establishing whether plaintiff fell because she was attempting, for one of her height, too long a step from the curb to the bus, or from the inclined street level to the bus, or for some other reason.

Nor was there proof of negligence on the part of the bus operator. Stopping a bus two and one half feet from a curb on an inclined portion of a street does not in itself constitute negligence. . . . This is also the rule as to stopping at a point not designated as a bus stop. . . .

We think it is clear that plaintiff in this case presented no evidence to support a verdict in her favor under the established law of this jurisdiction.

Questions

1. Under what circumstances should a court direct a verdict in favor of one of the parties?
2. Does a directed verdict deprive the losing party of his or her right to a jury trial? Why or why not?

Submitting the Case to the Jury

At the end of the trial the lawyers will make their final or **closing arguments** to the jury. They will review the evidence from their respective points of view, and may suggest how the jury should weigh certain items and resolve specific issues, but it is improper for the lawyers to discuss a matter that has been excluded or never raised during the trial itself. In other words, the lawyers are arguing and persuading, not testifying as witnesses. However, as illustrated by the following closing argument by a plaintiff's attorney, the outcome of a case very well may be altered by the content of the argument and how well it is presented.

SENATOR VEST'S TRIBUTE TO A DOG

A boy and his dog were crossing Defendant's property one day, apparently trespassing against the express warnings of Defendant, who then shot and killed the dog in retaliation. A lawsuit was filed by the boy's parents, and Senator Vest was asked to help with the trial. The case was particularly difficult in that, at the time, dogs were not considered "property," but were treated as similar to wild animals. After a lengthy trial, Senator Vest approached the jury and made the following closing argument:

Gentlemen of the Jury: The best friend a man has in the world may turn against him and become his enemy. His son or daughter that he has reared with loving care may prove ungrateful. Those who are nearest and dearest to us, those whom we trust with our happiness and our good name, may become traitors to their faith. The money that a man has he may lose. It flies away from him, perhaps when he needs it most. A man's reputation may be sacrificed in a moment of ill-considered action. The people who are prone to fall on their knees to do us honor when success is with us may be the first to throw the stone of malice when failure settles its clouds upon our heads.

The one absolutely unselfish friend that man can have in this selfish world, the one that never deserts him, the one that never proves ungrateful or treacherous, is his dog. A man's dog stands by him in prosperity and poverty, in health and sickness. He will sleep on the cold ground, when the wintry winds blow and the snow drives fiercely, if only he may be near his master's side. He will kiss the hand that has no food to offer; he will lick the wounds and sores that come in encounter with the roughness of the world. He guards the sleep of his pauper master, as if he were a prince. When all other friends desert, he remains. When riches take wings and reputation falls to pieces, he is as constant in his love as the sun in its journey through the heavens.

If fortune drives the master forth an outcast in the world, friendless and homeless, the faithful dog asks no higher privilege than that of accompanying him, to guard against danger, to fight his enemies, and when the last scene of all comes, and death takes the master in its embrace, and his body is laid away in the cold ground, no matter if all other friends pursue their way, there by the graveside will the noble dog be found, his head between his paws, his eyes sad, but open in watchfulness, faithful and true even in death.

Senator Vest sat down. He had spoken in a low voice, without gesture. When he finished, it is reported, the judge and jury were wiping their eyes. Although Plaintiff had asked for $200 in damages, the jury awarded $500.

The judge and the lawyers will confer out of the jury's hearing with regard to the content of the judge's **charge to the jury**, which contains his instructions to the jury. The judge's charge will summarize the facts and issues, tell the jury about the substantive law the jury must apply on each issue, give general information on determining the credibility of witnesses, and state who has the **burden of proof** on each issue of fact. The burden of proof in a civil case ordinarily requires that one party prove his or her contention on a given issue by a preponderance of the evidence (more than 50-50). What the burden means is that if a juror is unable to resolve an issue in his or her mind, he or she should decide that issue against the party who has the burden.

Each lawyer may propose instructions to the jury, but the judge has the duty to determine how to charge the jury on the basic aspects of the case. If a party's attorney has neither requested a particular instruction nor objected to the judge's charge, however, he or she usually will not be permitted to claim, on appeal, that the charge was erroneous.

Following the charge, the jury retires to deliberate and render its **verdict**. To reach their verdict, or decision, the jurors determine the facts and apply the law the judge has described to them to those facts. The jury decides who prevails and the amount of damages if the winning party is a claimant. Traditionally, only a unanimous jury verdict has been effective. In many states, and by consent of the parties in the federal courts, a nonunanimous verdict by the jurors is permitted in a civil action. If the minimum number of jurors required for a verdict are unable to agree, the jury is said to be *hung*, and a new trial with a different jury is required, unless, as is common, the parties settle.

Post-Trial Motions

After the jury has returned its verdict, but before judgment is entered, the losing party will have an opportunity to make certain post-trial motions. There may be a motion for a *judgment notwithstanding the verdict* (commonly called a **judgment n.o.v.**). This motion raises the same question as the directed verdict motion. The losing party also may move for a *new trial*. There are many grounds for this motion, including assertions that the judge erred in admitting or excluding certain evidence, that the charge to the jury was defective, that the attorneys, parties, or jurors have been guilty of some form of misconduct, or that the verdict is against the clear weight of the evidence—that is, it's just plain wrong.

The Judgment and Enforcement

The **judgment** is the final and formal resolution of the lawsuit. Judgment may be rendered on default when the defendant does not appear, or after motions dismissing or terminating the case, or after a trial on the merits. The judgment may be in the form of an award of money to the plaintiff, a declaration of rights between parties (a declaratory judgment), specific recovery of property, or an order requiring or prohibiting some future activity (an injunction). When the defendant has prevailed, the judgment may simply state that the plaintiff takes nothing by her complaint.

If a judgment states that the plaintiff shall recover a sum of money from the defendant, and the defendant does not pay, the plaintiff will have to undertake new legal proceedings to enforce the judgment. *Execution* is a common method of forcing the losing party to pay (satisfy) a monetary judgment. A **writ of execution** is issued by the court commanding an officer—usually the sheriff—to seize property of the losing party and sell it at auction to satisfy the plaintiff's judgment. Any of the defendant's money or property in the hands of a third person, such as wages or a bank account, may be taken by *garnishment*. When a plaintiff's judgment takes the form of an injunction (typically called the *decree*) and the defendant fails to obey, he or she may be held in *contempt of court* and punished by fine or imprisonment.

Appeal

Every judicial system provides for review of a trial court's decisions by an appellate court. Generally a party has the right to **appeal** any judgment to at least one higher court. When the system contains two levels of appellate courts, you may recall that review at the highest level occurs only at the discretion of that court except in certain classes of cases.

The party who petitions for an appeal is known as the appellant or petitioner. The opposing party is known as the appellee or respondent. The record on appeal will contain the pleadings, a *transcript of the trial* (the court reporter's verbatim record of the trial), and the orders and rulings relevant to the appeal. The parties present their arguments to the appellate court by written **briefs** that set out their legal arguments, and in most cases by *oral argument*. The appellate court may review any ruling of law by the trial judge, although frequently the scope of its review will be limited. There also are constitutional limits to the review of a jury's verdict, but even when a judge has sat without a jury, an appellate court rarely will re-examine a question of fact, because a cold printed appellate record does not convey the nuances of what the judge or jury observed at trial, notably the demeanor of the witnesses.

The appellate court has the power to *affirm*, *reverse*, or *modify* the trial court's judgment. If it reverses, it may order a particular judgment to be entered or it may **remand** (send back) the case to the trial court for a new trial or proceedings not inconsistent with its decision. Appeals always are heard by more than one judge. The decision of an appellate court usually is accompanied by a written opinion, signed by one of the judges. Concurring and dissenting opinions may be filed by the other judges. The opinions of a court are designed to set forth the reasons for a decision and to furnish guidance to lower courts, lawyers, and the public.

A NOTE ON REMEDIES

The remedies that may be obtained in a modern civil action should be viewed principally as a part of the substantive law: contract law, tort law, commercial law, and labor law, for example. Yet because the goal of a lawsuit is a remedy and the means of securing it is through a lawsuit, there is a close connection between remedies and procedure. The range of available remedies in a case may be limited by the manner in which the plaintiff has pleaded; conversely, certain procedural aspects of the case, such as whether it is tried by a judge or jury, may be determined by the remedy sought.

The most important types of relief a court may award in a civil action fall into three categories: declarative, specific, and compensatory. *Compensatory relief* calls for a judgment that the defendant pay the plaintiff a certain sum of money. Damages can be computed in a variety of ways and the difference in amount that could be collected under different theories might be considerable. There are significant differences in the processes of measuring the damages sustained in losing 100 shares of IBM stock, your arm, your reputation, or your peace of mind. Although it frequently is said that damages are recoverable only if they can be measured with a reasonable degree of certainty, this rule has come to require little more than a demonstration of whatever is feasible in the particular situation. For example, in comparatively recent years, the courts have begun to recognize that one whose spouse is injured wrongfully may be entitled to damages for the loss of sexual attentions. The fertile minds of lawyers never cease in the quest for damages for new immeasurables.

Specific relief generally consists of an order directing or forbidding certain conduct. The defendant may be commanded to return a watch taken from a plaintiff or to stop operating a pig farm in a residential neighborhood. Obviously, specific relief is not possible in all cases. For example, specific relief cannot cure Andrea in our hypothetical case; specific relief will be given only if damages would be inadequate. The reason for this is that there is a burden on the court in ordering and supervising performance of a decree of specific relief that is avoided if a simple judgment for money damages is entered.

Declaratory relief simply involves a court defining the rights and duties of the parties in a specific legal context. For example, a person may believe a contract is not valid and that he is under no obligation to perform it. Before acting on this belief the person may want a court to declare whether he is under a duty to perform so he will not suffer damages should he prove to be mistaken. This type of relief is not common, and its availability often is limited by statute.

There is a final point to be considered in evaluating the adequacy of any judicial remedy: how much of it will be consumed by the expenses of litigation? The modest costs awarded to a successful plaintiff, in most cases, will not reimburse her for her lawyer's fee or for many other of the substantial costs of a suit, such as the expense of investigation or the fees of expert witnesses. All these costs are borne by the litigant and usually are not reflected in the compensatory damages. Moreover, in most personal-injury actions the plaintiff's cost of recovery will be significantly affected because the attorney will receive a percentage, typically one-third, of the plaintiff's judgment. Of course, if the plaintiff fails to recover, the lawyer receives nothing other than his or her expenses.

ALTERNATIVE METHODS OF DISPUTE RESOLUTION

According to many thinkers we are experiencing a litigation explosion. We have heard the same complaint for decades. However, in recent years more attention has been focused on doing something about the problems of expense, delay, and questionable lawyer practices caused by overburdened courts. Among the solutions suggested and used to an increasingly greater extent are mediation, fact finding, and arbitration.

Mediation and Fact Finding

Traditionally, mediation and fact finding have been used mostly in the context of labor disputes. **Mediation** involves the use of a go-between—a mediator—whose job is to encourage settlement by the parties. The mediator does this as a dispas-

*Civil cases filed in United States Federal Courts
(for twelve month periods ending June 30)*

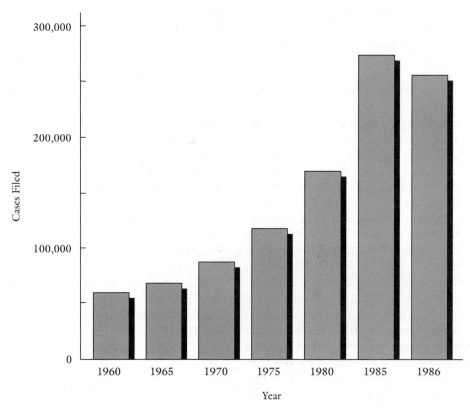

sionate third party who may discuss the issues with the parties, transmit offers and counteroffers between them, and sometimes make suggestions for settlement. Unlike a judge, however, a mediator makes no decisions that bind the parties.

Fact finding may be done as a part of mediation or as a separate step in the settlement process. A fact finder will be appointed by the parties to investigate the dispute and issue a report setting out the issues and the contentions of the parties. This report may be submitted with our without recommendations. Again, however, as with mediation, the fact finder's decisions do not bind the parties.

Although used primarily in the labor context, mediation, and even fact finding, can be at least temporary alternatives to litigation in any number of settings, such as disputes between a landlord and a tenant, a debtor and a creditor, or a husband and a wife who are contemplating separation or dissolution of their marriage. Indeed, mediation does not lead to findings that bind the parties, but it may be worth attempting in an effort to settle disputes of any kind. If nothing comes of the effort the court system is still an option, and the parties have not foreclosed any rights by giving mediation a chance.

Arbitration

Arbitration is by far the most broadly used alternative method of dispute resolution. It is a private system that uses impartial experts rather than judges. Although it is nonjudicial, the procedures

Total cases filed with American Arbitration Association

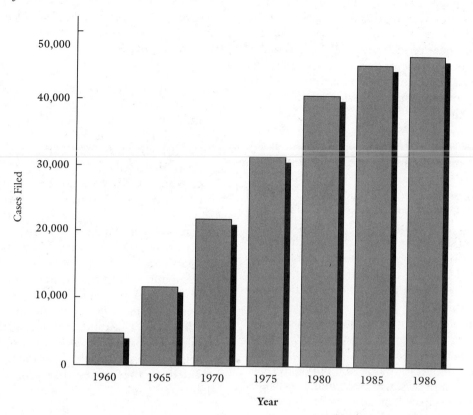

used and the results achieved are very similar to those in a lawsuit. For that reason, early attempts at arbitration met with little success and were almost uniformly invalidated by the courts as attempts to usurp judicial powers. Arbitration statutes, which now have been enacted by Congress and by state legislatures, have eliminated this challenge.

In most cases arbitration is voluntary, and an agreement between the parties provides that any dispute arising out of their relationship will be submitted to arbitration instead of the courts. However, there are some notable exceptions.

State laws governing, and in some cases compelling, arbitration are found (1) in statutes specifically relating to industrial dispute resolution, (2) in commercial arbitration statutes, and (3) in state labor relations acts, frequently similar to the National Labor Relations Act. Some states, such as Pennsylvania, have been experimenting with compulsory arbitration in civil cases involving smaller claims, ordinarily ranging between $5000 and $25,000, depending upon the jurisdiction. These experiments have been meeting with considerable success. Arbitration under federal statutes is voluntary for the most part. However, it may be compelled in certain circumstances, limited to the Railway Labor Act and to certain wartime industrial disputes.

When arbitration is voluntary, the process may be structured and limited in any manner agreeable to the parties because the arbitrator's powers are derived wholly from the consent of the parties. In the usual case, an arbitrator will be appointed by the parties, will conduct a trial-like proceeding, will decide questions both of law and of fact, and will make a final decision that will be binding on the parties. In most cases this decision will be entered on court records and will be given the force and effect of a court decision. However, the parties may agree to any other procedures, including an agreement that the arbitrator's findings will not be binding.

ADVANTAGES OF ARBITRATION. As an alternative to judicial dispute resolution, arbitration has a number of advantages: (1) as noted previously, it may be structured and limited in any manner agreeable to the parties; (2) it is less expensive and time consuming; (3) nontechnical language is used; (4) nontechnical procedures are followed; (5) remedies are more flexible than those provided by the court system; (6) hearings are private; and (7) future conflicts may be minimized by arbitration.

The time and costs involved in arbitration vary according to the type of hearing the parties choose. This may range from a private, informal hearing before one arbitrator to a public, formal hearing with attorneys, witnesses, and a verbatim record before a panel of arbitrators. Although attorneys and a legally trained arbitrator may be used, there is no requirement, and ordinarily no practical necessity, for either.

Bringing a case to arbitration affords the parties an opportunity to select an arbitrator who, in addition to being familiar with the law, is an expert concerning the matter to be arbitrated. Such an arbitrator is better equipped to understand the facts presented, is less dependant on expert witnesses to develop the facts, and is able to be flexible and to tailor a remedy to the particular circumstances of each case.

Because arbitration involves a private process, ordinarily the parties and the arbitrator are the only people in attendance. The public is rarely concerned or present. This helps to keep the atmosphere informal, which often aids the parties in presenting their cases. Ideally, the mood during arbitration is more conciliatory than adversary. In any event, however, the fact that the parties have agreed to arbitration, and have proceeded informally toward settlement of their dispute, often results in a mutual respect that lessens the chances of future disputes.

WHO MAY BE AN ARBITRATOR? An arbitrator may be anyone agreeable to the parties. It is important only that the person chosen be neutral and familiar with the arbitration process. It is desirable, however, that the arbitrator is also a person with some expertise in the area that is the subject of the conflict.

The American Arbitration Association (AAA) is a private organization that maintains a register of qualified people who are willing to serve as arbitrators. Upon request, the AAA will submit a list of candidates to the parties, who may choose an arbitrator agreeable to both of them. The AAA might submit a list of five names, and the parties would then rank the candidates one to five, with one being the most desirable and five being the least desirable. The candidate having the lowest combined total would be chosen as arbitrator. For example, suppose that when the candidates were submitted to the parties they ranked them as follows:

Candidate	Party A	Party B		Total
Adams	3	1	=	4
Baker	5	3	=	8
Calhoon	1	2	=	3
Davis	4	5	=	9
Ellis	2	4	=	6

Calhoon would be appointed because he or she is the most desirable (or the least offensive) to both parties.

THE AWARD. At the conclusion of the arbitration hearing, the arbitrator will reach a decision that is called an **award**. Ordinarily the award is binding on the parties and is final. Arbitration statutes typically require that arbitration awards be placed on public record within a period of time set by the statute, perhaps 30 days, at which time an award becomes enforceable to the same extent as a court judgment.

Generally, the right to appeal an arbitrator's award is severely limited. Courts give broad discretion to arbitrators to determine both questions of law and questions of fact, and to fashion appropriate remedies. However, as the following case illustrates, an arbitrator does not have full judicial power and is not permitted unlimited discretion.

GARRITY v. LYLE STUART, INC.
40 N.Y.2d 354, 353 N.E.2d 793 (1976)

Joan Garrity (Petitioner/Respondent) was the author of two books published by Lyle Stuart, Inc. (Defendant/Appellant). When a disagreement arose, Plaintiff sought arbitration pursuant to an arbitration clause in the publication contracts. Defendant objected to the proceedings and walked out. Thereafter, upon hearing Plaintiff's case, the arbitrator entered an award granting her $45,000 compensatory damages and $7500 punitive damages, although the arbitration clause in the contract made no mention of punitive damages.

Upon Plaintiff's application for confirmation of the arbitration award, the New York Supreme Court confirmed the order over Defendant's objection that the arbitrator had no power to grant punitive damages. Affirmed except as to the order for punitive damages.

BREITEL, Chief Justice.

Arbitrators generally are not bound by principles of substantive law or rules of evidence, and thus error of law or fact will not justify vacatur [overturning] of an award. . . . It is also true that arbitrators generally are free to fashion the remedy appropriate to the wrong, if they find one, but an authentic remedy is compensatory and measured by the harm caused and how it may be corrected. . . . These broad principles are tolerable so long as arbitrators are not thereby empowered to ride roughshod over strong policies in the law which control coercive private conduct and confine to the State and its courts the infliction of punitive sanctions on wrongdoers.

The court will vacate an award enforcing an illegal agreement or one violative of public policy. . . . Since enforcement of an award of punitive damages as a purely private remedy would violate public policy, an arbitrator's award which imposes punitive damages, even though agreed upon by the parties, should be vacated. . . .

Matter of Associated Gen. Contrs., N.Y. State Chapter (Savin Bros.) [citations omitted] is inapposite. That case did not involve an award of punitive damages. Instead, the court permitted the enforcement of an arbitration award of treble liquidated damages, amounting to a penalty, assessed however in accordance with the express terms of a trade association membership agreement. The court held that the public policy against permitting the awarding of penalties was not of "such magnitude as to call for judicial intrusion" (p. 959). In the instant case, however, there was no provision in the agreements permitting arbitrators to award liquidated damages or penalties. Indeed, the subject apparently had never ever been considered.

The prohibition against an arbitrator awarding punitive damages is based on strong public policy indeed. At law, on the civil side, in the absence of statute, punitive damages are available only in a limited number of instances. . . . It is a social exemplary "remedy", not a private compensatory remedy.

GABRIELLI, Judge (dissenting). . . . Arbitrators are entitled to "do justice. It has been said that, short of 'complete irrationality', they may fashion the law to fit the facts before them." . . . The award made here was neither irrational nor unjust. Indeed, defendant has not denied that its actions were designed to harass and intimidate plaintiff, as she claimed and the arbitrators obviously concluded. Hence, the award was within the power vested in the arbitrator.

Questions

1. What circumstances may entitle a court to set aside an arbitrator's award?
2. Under what circumstances may an arbitrator properly award punitive damages?

SUMMARY

Disputes and controversies do not exist in a vacuum. They occur within a specific context. The legal system is an important element that helps to shape this context. Therefore, we should remember that a clear understanding of any controversy requires some knowledge of the nature and character of the legal system and the procedural rules that govern it.

The court system is the mechanism for the resolution of legal and factual questions. Procedure is the process that guides a controversy through the court system to a resolution. Pleadings initiate the process. Discovery uncovers relevant information and clarifies what issues are in dispute. Then there are a number of motions that can be made that may resolve the controversy before trial. If the case is not settled or dismissed, a trial is the legal system's method of deciding what happened and who should prevail.

There are additional considerations when dealing with jury trial. The jury-selection process and the judge's charge to the jury are two examples. Despite the fact that jury trials are expensive and often slow, a jury provides a sense of public involvement in the administration of the legal system.

The right to appeal is a crucial element of the judicial process. A court of review is necessary to correct any mistakes or abuses that may have occurred at the trial level.

Remedies, whether at law for monetary damages or in equity for some specific decree, are the methods of carrying out the decisions of the courts and society as to how a controversy should be resolved and an injury rectified. The legal system and the judicial process act as a constant backdrop against which economic arrangements exist, decisions are made, and controversies are resolved.

Disputes also may be resolved by resort to nonjudicial means, such as mediation, fact finding, or arbitration. Mediation and fact finding are used most commonly in the resolution of labor disputes. Arbitration, however, is becoming increasingly more common in other contexts.

Arbitration usually is voluntary and involves the appointment of a person, or a panel, agreeable to the parties, who will decide the controversy in a manner similar to a judge. Generally arbitration procedures are less formal than those used in trying a lawsuit, and the atmosphere is more relaxed. At the conclusion of the arbitration hearing the arbitrator will make a decision, called an award, that will be binding on the parties unless they have agreed otherwise. The right to appeal an arbitration award is severely limited. Because the process of arbitration is private and informal, arbitration has become an attractive alternative to the court system in settling disputes—it is a quicker, simpler, and less expensive process.

KEY TERMS AND CONCEPTS

procedure
adversary system
dual court structure
original jurisdiction
general jurisdiction
special jurisdiction
writ of *certiorari*
plaintiff
defendant
subject-matter jurisdiction
diversity of citizenship
personal jurisdiction
long-arm jurisdiction
venue
service of process
summons
default judgment
pleadings
complaint
motion to dismiss
demurrer
prima facie
answer
affirmative defense
counterclaim
summary judgment
affidavit
discovery
deposition
written interrogatories
pretrial conference
peremptory challenge
opening statement
direct examination
cross examination
hearsay
rebuttal
closing argument
charge to the jury
burden of proof
verdict

judgment n.o.v.
judgment
writ of execution
appeal
brief
remand
mediation
fact finding
arbitration

PROBLEMS

1. The state of Ohio filed suit against Wyandotte Chemicals Corp., alleging that the defendant's dumping of mercury into streams that flowed into Lake Erie constituted a nuisance. The plaintiff alleged that Wyandotte's acts resulted in injury to the lake's water, vegetation, fish, and other wildlife. The action was filed originally in the Supreme Court of the United States. Did Ohio choose the proper court?

2. In *Thiel v. Southern Pacific Co.*, presented in this chapter, the court overturned the method of jury selection on the ground that it discriminated against those who worked for a wage. Should the court also have provided for other procedures to ensure a jury of "peers"? For example, should a minority person be tried before a jury of minorities, a case of a woman tried before a jury of women, and that of a wage earner before a jury of wage earners?

3. What is "hearsay" testimony, and why is it ordinarily not permitted as evidence in a trial?

4. What is the difference between an affidavit and a deposition? For what purposes may a deposition be used?

5. Nolan, a charity patient at a hospital, was injured by the negligence of one of the hospital's employees. Nolan filed suit. The case was subsequent to the case of *Flagiello v. Pennsylvania Hospital*, presented in Chapter 2. The hospital claimed the defense of charitable immunity, contending that Flagiello did away with the doctrine only insofar as cases concerned paying patients. Is the hospital correct?

6. Foreign Imports, Inc., a car dealer, sold a Volkswagen to Klippen. The car was equipped with defective seat belt equipment and, as a result, Klippen was injured in an accident. Klippen sued the manufacturer, Volkswagenwerk, A.G. of Germany in the courts of Alaska, where the sale and accident had occurred. The defendant contended it was not subject to the jurisdiction of the Alaska courts because it did not business, nor was it otherwise present, in Alaska. It sold its cars to an American distributor that sold them to Foreign Imports, Inc. under German contracts and did not own or control Foreign Imports, Inc. Did the Alaska courts have jurisdiction?

7. In a case involving a jury, what is the function of the judge? What is the function of the jury?

8. What are the purposes of discovery in the pretrial stage of a lawsuit?

9. At what points during a lawsuit may the court dismiss the suit? On what grounds should dismissal be ordered at each point?

Chapter 4

Torts and Crimes

CLASSIFICATIONS OF LIABILITY

The sources of legal liability may be classified as criminal or civil. In addition, civil liability may be subdivided further into tort liability and contract liability. Beginning with the premise that *all* liability under the law arises from a breach of duty, criminal liability may be distinguished from civil liability by considering to whom the duty is owed. Criminal liability arises from a breach of duty to society as a whole, and civil liability from a breach of duty to one or more individuals or entities within society. For example, the operation of an automobile at a high rate of speed, in a reckless manner, is a **crime** because it threatens all of society. If, while being driven in such a manner, the automobile strikes and injures a person, the act also becomes a **tort**, because of the breach of duty to a particular individual. Although most

Sources of legal liability

torts are also crimes, the reverse is not true. One who commits a breach of duty that is both criminal and tortious is subject to being held liable for both, in separate legal proceedings. In the criminal prosecution, the "state" will seek punishment in the hope of deterring the offender, and others by his example, from committing the same kind of wrong. In the civil action, the injured party ordinarily will seek damages to compensate for the personal loss he or she has suffered, although other remedies also are possible.

In the example of the automobile accident, the wrong against the injured person was a civil wrong, but why is it classified as a tort? As previously noted, all civil wrongs may be classified as either torts or breaches of contract. Just as we distinguished crimes from civil wrongs by considering to whom the duty was owed, we may distinguish torts from breaches of contract by looking at the source of a civil duty. A tort arises from the breach of a duty imposed on us by the legal system (society), and breach of contract from a duty an individual voluntarily assumes. For example, the driver committed a tort by injuring the innocent pedestrian, but we may assume that at no time had the driver agreed not to run over the person. Instead, the duty not to do so was imposed by law. On the other hand, suppose A contracts to sell his car to B for $500, and then fails to deliver it as promised. A has breached the duty to give up the car, and B has a cause of action for breach of contract. The duty breached did not

exist until A voluntarily assumed it by making a contractual promise.

TORT LAW

CLASSIFICATION OF TORTS

Torts may be classified according to the mental state of the defendant required for their commission. These range from intentional misconduct at one extreme to liability without fault on the other.

Intentional Torts

A tort is considered intentional if the wrongdoer either intended to cause an injury or intended to cause the act that caused an injury. For example, suppose Adler is driving down the street and sees Bronski in the intersection, attempting to cross. As a joke, she decides to graze Bronski with the fender of her car, and does so. By the most unusual of circumstances, the contact causes Bronski to fall and injure himself. Adler has committed an **intentional tort**. Although Adler may not have intended to injure Bronski, she did intend to bump him lightly (the act that caused the injury). That is all that is required for liability.

Negligence

The tort of negligence involves a lesser degree of mental involvement than does an intentional tort. It does not require an intent to injure, or even an intent to do the act that causes an injury. Instead, **negligence** arises when a person simply acts unreasonably under the circumstances. If, in the example, Adler had struck Bronski with her automobile because she was driving too fast, or was not in control of the car so as to avoid the accident, then the tort would be one of negligence. Adler did not intend the injury, or even the act that caused the injury (hitting Bronski with the automobile). Although Adler may have intended to drive too fast, driving too fast was not the cause of Bronski's injury. Instead, it was the cause of the cause.

Strict (Absolute) Liability

Under some circumstances, the law may impose tort liability on a person even though he has done nothing wrong. The law simply dictates that when a person engages in certain kinds of activity, he becomes the insurer of the safety of others. His conduct is neither intentional wrongdoing nor negligence, but he is liable without any fault at all. **Strict liability** is imposed simply to induce those who engage in certain activities that are unusually dangerous, such as the use of explosives or the keeping of wild animals, to exercise all possible caution (more than just reasonable care) to prevent injuries.

TWO THEORIES OF RECOVERY

A **trespass** action is brought to recover money damages for an injury to a person or property. It is an action "at law," and may be the underlying theory of recovery for an intentional tort, negligence, or an injury sustained in circumstances in which the law will impose strict liability. Although money damages are ordinarily an adequate remedy, they clearly are not adequate when an injury only has been threatened, or when an injury has occurred and there is sufficient evidence that the tortious conduct that led to the injury will be continued.

A **nuisance** action is brought seeking relief against a threatened or a continuing tort. Traditionally it is an action "in equity," seeking some relief other than, or in addition to, money damages. In tort law, that relief normally is an *injunction* (a court order either requiring that something be done, such as removing debris from the plaintiff's property, or that something not be done, such as polluting a stream, as is necessary under the particular circumstances before the court). As with trespass actions, the underlying tort may be intentional, negligent, or under strict liability.

Modern rules of procedure in most jurisdictions permit a single action to be brought under both theories—trespass and nuisance. One judge (or judge and jury) sitting as a court of law, may award money damages for the plaintiff's injuries, and then, sitting as a court of equity, the same judge may grant an injunction against the offensive conduct in the future.

INTENTIONAL TORTS GENERALLY

Intentional torts may be considered individually, or be classified in groups according to the rights affected. One useful classification model separates them according to whether they affect real estate, personal property, or some aspect of the person.

Trespass to Real Estate

As used in the context of tort classification (as opposed to the relief sought) the term *trespass* may be defined as "entering, or causing something to enter, the property of another without permission or privilege." Therefore, any unwarranted interference with another's real estate interests may constitute a trespass. The interference may concern someone else's title to real estate, or right to possession, or both. Accordingly, one who trespasses on real estate belonging to Johnson, but in the possession of Burch under a valid lease, commits a trespass against both. This would be true even if Burch did not actually have a lease but was in exclusive possession of the property only by permission of Johnson.

It is not necessary, in the case of an intentional trespass, that the property be physically injured or somehow reduced in value. The simple interference of the trespasser with either the title or the right to possession entitles the injured party to relief. Of course, without a real injury, only nominal damages and costs would be awarded.

At common law, real property was defined as including the earth's crust and all things permanently attached thereto or used peculiarly therewith. It also was considered to include everything, in a pie-shaped wedge, down to the center of the earth and everything above to "the heavens." The precise limits on real estate ownership are discussed more fully in Chapter 26.

Trespass to Personal Property

When the term *trespass* is used, it typically evokes an image of walking on someone's land without permission. However, that is only one kind of invasion that is actionable as a trespass. Land is not the only interest that can be trespassed against, nor is an invasion of the physical thing necessary. The property involved may be personal property as well as real estate, and even may be intangible, such as one's right to peace of mind or a good reputation.

Trespasses to personal property fall into two general categories—injury to personal property and conversion. An injury may be some physical alteration or the actual destruction of the property. It even may arise as a result of some verbal disparagement of the property (an action akin to defamation). Illustrations of trespass causing injury to personal property would be: Adano kicks the fender of Baxter's car, causing a dent; Adano sets fire to Baxter's car, totally destroying it; or Adano starts a rumor that Baxter's product, for example a computer, is overpriced and so unreliable as to be worthless. Carried to an extreme, the latter allegation may be just as injurious or destructive as any physical invasion.

Conversion of property occurs when one person exercises unlawful dominion and control over another's property. Its central element is an unlawful interference with the owner's right to title and exclusive possession. So, if Abe took Bo's hat from a hatrack and left with it, Abe would be guilty of conversion. This is true even if Abe took the hat by accident, with no intention of depriving Bo of it, and even if he did no physical harm to the hat. The interference with Bo's right to title and exclusive possession constitutes the tort. It is an intentional tort because Abe intended to take the hat, regardless of his motives. Although con-

version usually involves tangible property, it may occur in connection with intangibles such as ideas and artistic creations. The theoretical basis for common law and statutory copyright and patent violations is conversion. The creator has a property right in his or her mental creativity that may be converted, even though the product is intangible.

Trespass to the Person

In a legal sense, a person has a property right in his or her own body, and in other aspects of the person, including peace of mind, reputation, and certain relationships. The invasion of any of these may constitute a trespass.

Battery is a tort arising from an unprivileged touching of another person—any touching, whether or not physical harm or injury is caused. It should be understood, however, that not every touching is a battery. Two people on a date generally consent to some touching, and consent will be upheld within limits. Also, certain types of touching may be consented to by participating in sports activities, but ordinarily even voluntary participation in a breach of peace, such as an ordinary fight, is not considered valid consent. A touching also may be privileged by social convention, as when one shakes the hand of an acquaintance as a greeting. Finally, the law may imply consent, as when a person enters a public area, such as a store or crowded elevator. Again, however, the touching must be within the limits of the privilege or consent.

Assault, which ordinarily accompanies a battery, is a separate tort. It occurs when one person places another in reasonable fear of an impending battery. The threat must be real and under circumstances that make the possibility of the battery immediate. In addition, most states require that the intent must be posed by someone capable of inflicting it. If Ajax called Barb on the telephone and threatened to punch her in the nose, no immediate battery would be feared, and therefore no assault would occur. However, it is possible that continuing such conduct might result in the tort of intentional infliction of mental distress. However, a threat or a series of threats by someone incapable of carrying out the battery would be unlikely to constitute either tort.

Although criminal law conclusively presumes that an assault accompanies every battery, this is not true in tort law. If Ajax were to sneak up behind Barb and hit her on the head with a club, the action would be a battery but not an assault, since Barb never was put in fear. This is reasonable since tort law primarily seeks to protect the individual. But because it seeks to protect society, criminal law would find Ajax's conduct a threat to society in spite of Barb's personal lack of apprehension.

Defamation

The tort of **defamation** involves holding another person up to public ridicule or scorn. Therefore, to charge that someone is a crook, or that he has a noxious, antisocial disease, or that he has been convicted of a crime involving moral turpitude may constitute defamation (as may some lesser charges). If this is done in writing, it is called **libel**, and if done orally, it is called **slander**.

In all cases, the defamatory statement must be "published"—it must be communicated to a third party without permission or privilege. Therefore, making a charge in a private conversation between the speaker and the one about whom it is made would not constitute defamation. Neither would the communication by a physician to the Department of Health, concerning his diagnosis of certain communicable diseases discovered while examining one of his patients, because disclosure is required by law.

Truth is a defense under tort law, although not under criminal law. Again this is because of the different interests to be protected. However, in some situations, speaking the literal truth, such as saying "Ali told me that Baxter is a child molester," is not a defense. Even if true, the statement may be only a second publication of a defamatory statement. That Ali, in fact, did make the statement is no defense.

Injuries to Relationships

The alienation of some relationships, such as that between a husband and wife or between family members, may constitute a trespass. Although not universally recognized (because of the hesitance of the courts to interfere unduly in private affairs) injuries to relationships add to the possibility of an injury to property.

Closely resembling a cause of action based on interference with such a relationship is one based on the infliction of mental distress. Historically, the law refused to grant relief for the infliction of mental distress without an accompanying physical impact. The problem was the perceived inability of the courts to detect, or to measure, the mental trauma alone. The same may be said for alienating relationships. However, just as modern courts have changed their position regarding mental distress, there is reason to believe that they will do the same regarding relationships.

INTENTIONAL BUSINESS TORTS

Having described torts in general terms, further discussion of certain torts peculiarly related to business is in order. Some of the torts already described will be covered briefly. Others, not previously mentioned, will be discussed in greater detail. In all cases, however, the theories discussed earlier are applicable.

Fraud

The term **fraud** may be defined very generally as "a procuring by deception," although this definition will be refined further in this discussion. Fraud may fall into one of two general classifications—fraud in the execution or fraud in the inducement.

Classification of intentional torts

General	**Business**

1) Trespass to real estate	1) Fraud
	    a) in the execution
	    b) in the inducement

2) Trespass to personal property
    a) injury
    b) conversion
	2) Defamation

3) Trespass to person
    a) battery
    b) assault
    c) defamation
        i) libel
        ii) slander
	3) False Imprisonment

4) Injuries to relationships	4) Intentional infliction of mental distress 5) Trademark, patent, and copyright infringement 6) Interference with economic relations

Fraud in the execution contemplates circumstances in which a person may be caused to sign a legal document without any reason to understand the nature of the document he or she is signing. For example, suppose a celebrity is signing autographs and signs a piece of paper on which a procurer later writes in a contract, or perhaps a negotiable promissory note. Since the words of contract were added after the signature, it is clear that the celebrity had no intent to enter into the contract and was not negligent. Therefore, the signature was secured by fraud in the execution—a circumstance akin to forgery. Assuming the circumstances are proven, the signature is without force or effect.

The more common type of fraud, however, is fraud in the inducement, called *deceit* in tort law. In this situation, the person intends to agree to a certain obligation, but his or her willingness to do so was induced, or procured, by fraud. **Deceit** requires the proof of five elements: (1) there was a misrepresentation of material fact, (2) knowingly made, (3) with intent to defraud, (4) justifiable reliance on the part of the person deceived, and (5) a resulting injury.

The first element requires that the misrepresented fact be of sufficient importance that had the victim known the truth, he or she might not

have agreed to the obligation. Also, the misrepresentation must be of a fact (ordinarily not of an opinion) and it must be in relation to the past or the present (ordinarily not to the future). However, a false statement as to a present belief or intention, such as "I will put the money to cover the check in my account by the end of the day" may satisfy this requirement. Also, some statements made by experts, or a forecast by one who purports to have the ability to make accurate forecasts, may be actionable.

The statement also must be made with knowledge of its falsity, and with the intent to defraud the victim. An innocent statement, although it may be the ground for rescinding a contract, is not the basis for an action in deceit. The same is true of a statement the speaker knows is untrue, but on which the speaker has no reason to know the victim may rely. For example, in a casual conversation Angus tells Birdie that he would give $1000 for Cook's red Ford. In reliance on Angus's statement, Birdie buys the car from Cook for $700, expecting to sell it to Angus. Unless Angus should have realized Birdie would take such action in reliance on his statement, Angus would not be liable for deceit.

The victim must justifiably rely on the misrepresentation, which means that the reliance must be reasonable under the circumstances. The latter part of this requirement has been made easier to prove today, since the decline of the doctrine of *caveat emptor* ("let the buyer beware").

Finally, an injury must result. Without an injury, or at least some kind of detrimental interference with the plaintiff's rights, no tort results. Again, however, this element is not required if a misrepresentation action is brought for rescission of a contract rather than tort damages for fraud.

Defamation

The tort of defamation, which was discussed earlier, may have important implications in the business setting. In this environment, the false statement may involve a product or a company. If it causes injury, it may be actionable under such names as trade libel or disparagement. There is yet another legal risk that arises from the use of information, even when it is entirely accurate. Because many businesses, and professionals such as physicians, attorneys, and accountants, accumulate a great deal of personal information about customers, patients, and clients, and occasionally are requested to release some of this information to third parties, the possibility of defamation has increased. Also, although truth is a defense to a charge of defamation, it is not a defense in an action based on a tort related to defamation, invasion of privacy.

False Imprisonment

The tort of false imprisonment is committed when one person unlawfully deprives another of his or her freedom of movement. This may occur from the use of official force, as when one person, without just cause, procures the arrest of another. However, it also occurs in the event that a storekeeper, without just cause, restrains a customer from leaving her store because she suspects shoplifting. The same is true when a doctor prevents a patient from leaving his office because the patient has not paid his bill. Similar to the rule in assault cases, if the person does not know he or she is restrained, there is no tort of false imprisonment. For example, a guest in a hotel is locked in her room by the hotel manager. If the door is locked after she goes to sleep, and is unlocked the next morning before she awakens, no tort has been committed.

Intentional Infliction of Mental Distress

As discussed earlier, unjustifiable interference with another's peace of mind may constitute a tort. Under modern law, this is true even in the absence of a physical impact. There need be no proof of actual physical injury or loss if the act was wanton and willful and designed to cause mental distress. Injury will be assumed. This tortious misconduct sometimes has been labeled the new tort of "outrage." For example, consider the case of the pathologist who obtained the family's consent for an autopsy, assuring the family that the deceased would look "natural" at the funeral. In fact, the scalp and facial tissue were removed and, when the autopsy was completed, the scalp and facial tissue simply were placed back on the skull, but not secured. When the coffin was opened, in the presence of the family, some of the pieces of tissue had not remained in place. A less gruesome, but also shocking, case involved a woman who was the only passenger on a city bus. In a flight of fancy, the bus driver made a left turn up a railroad track. Although he managed to steer the bus off the track just in time to avoid a head-on collision with an oncoming train, the passenger was so frightened that she required rest, rehabilitation, and psychiatric therapy for an extended period of time.

Trademark, Patent, and Copyright Infringement

These rights are protected primarily by federal and state statutes, but they also are protected by common law. Although trademarks may be registered, and their unauthorized use will constitute a tort, registration is not required for a cause of action. It is an unfair method of competition when one company uses signs, names, or packaging of goods in a way that is calculated to confuse consumers, leading them to believe that its goods or services are those of a competitor.

Patent and copyright infringements are similar. These rights belong to the inventor or the author of an artistic creation. The wrongful appropriation of these rights constitutes a tort. The usual remedy is an injunction against further infringement, and damages for any loss sustained by the owner. Copyrights and patents are discussed more fully in Chapter 28.

Interference with Economic Relations

This is a general category of torts that includes the separate business torts of (1) disparagement of goods, (2) slander of title, (3) interference with contractual relations, and (4) interference with prospective business advantage. All of these may be included under the even broader heading of unfair methods of competition.

Interference with contractual relations involves the wrongful inducement of a breach of contract. However, not every breach induced by another is actionable. The key to liability is motive. For example, suppose a customer succeeds in convincing a store owner to discharge an employee because he felt that he had been treated rudely by that employee. Probably no liability will attach to the customer's conduct, even if it is later determined that his perception of the employee's conduct was inaccurate. However, to seek the wrongful discharge of an employee in order to take over her job might well be found tortious. In addition to motive, a court also will attempt to balance the competing interests of the parties involved—in this case, the right of the employee to be secure in her employment and the right of the customer to be treated in a courteous manner.

Interference with prospective business advantage sounds like an action to recover for a loss that is speculative at best, but that is not the case.

Although the advantage alleged to have been lost is prospective, and therefore is not as certain as a present contractual right, the crux of this tort is the use of wrongful means. As long as the value of the prospective advantage is reasonably certain, the use of means such as fraud, violence, intimidation, or bribery is considered tortious, and recovery will be allowed for the value of the advantage that might have been gained.

NEGLIGENCE

As discussed previously, commission of the tort of negligence involves mental involvement substantially less than that required for an intentional tort. Rather than an intention to cause an injury, negligence merely requires conduct that is unreasonable under the circumstances. Generally the proof of three elements is required: (1) a negligent act, (2) proximate cause, and (3) an injury.

Negligent Act

This element generally is defined as conduct that falls below an objective standard of behavior described as the degree of care that would be exercised by "a reasonable person of ordinary prudence under the same or similar circumstances." This does not necessarily mean a person is expected to act with the utmost consideration for the rights of others, sacrificing his or her own legitimate interests. Neither does it mean that one may pursue his or her own interests with abandon. Consider the following case. Although the opinion is written in a humorous style, it effectively states the considerations involved.

Three elements of negligence

To prove negligence three elements are generally required:

1) A negligent act
2) Proximate cause
   Foreseeability
   Zone of danger test
3) Injury

CORDAS et al. v. PEERLESS TRANSP. CO. et al.
27 N.Y.S.2d 198 (City Court of N.Y. 1941)

This was an action by Mary Cordas and others (Plaintiffs) against Peerless Transportation Co. and others (Defendants) to recover damages for injuries sustained by Mary Cordas when struck, while on the sidewalk, by a cab abandoned by Defendant's driver. The facts are found in the decision of the court. Defendant's motion to dismiss Plaintiff's complaint was granted.

CARLIN, Justice.

This case presents the ordinary man—that problem child of the law—in a most bizarre setting. As a lowly chauffeur in defendant's employ he became in a trice the protagonist in a breath-bating drama with a denouement almost tragic. It appears that a man, whose identity it would be indelicate to divulge was feloniously relieved of his portable goods by two nondescript highwaymen in an alley near 26th Street and Third Avenue, Manhattan; they induced him to relinquish his possessions by a strong argument ad hominem couched in the convincing cant of the criminal and pressed at the point of a most persuasive pistol. Laden with their loot, but not thereby impeded, they took an abrupt departure and he, shuffling off the coil of that discretion which enmeshed him in the alley, quickly gave chase through 26th Street toward 2d Avenue, whither they were resorting "with expedition swift as thought" for most obvious reasons. Somewhere on that thoroughfare of escape they indulged the stratagem of separation ostensibly to disconcert their pursuer and allay the ardor of his pursuit. He then centered on for capture the man with the pistol whom he saw board defendant's taxicab, which quickly veered south toward 25th Street on 2d Avenue. . . . The chauffeur apprehensive of certain dissolution from either Scylla, the pursuers, or Charybdis the pursued, quickly threw his car out of first speed in which he was proceeding, pulled on the emergency, jammed on his brakes and, although he thinks the motor was still running, swung open the door to his left and jumped out of his car. He confesses that the only act that smacked of intelligence was that by which he jammed the brakes in order to throw off balance the hold-up man who was half-standing and half-sitting with his pistol menacingly poised. Thus abandoning his car and passenger the chauffeur sped toward 26th Street and then turned to look; he saw the cab proceeding south toward 24th Street where it mounted the sidewalk. The plaintiff-mother and her two infant children were there injured by the cab. . . . Fortunately the injuries sustained were comparatively slight. Negligence has been variously defined but the common legal acceptation is the failure to exercise that care and caution which a reasonable and prudent person ordinarily would exercise under like conditions or circumstances. . . . "Negligence is 'not absolute or intrinsic,' but 'is always relevant to some circumstances of time, place or person.'" . . . The learned attorney for the plaintiffs concedes that the chauffeur acted in an emergency but claims a right to recovery upon the following proposition taken verbatim from his brief: "It is respectfully submitted that the value of the interests of the public at large to be immune from being injured by a dangerous instrumentality such as a car unattended while in motion is very superior to the right of a driver of a motor vehicle to abandon same while it is motion even when acting under the belief that his life is in danger and by abandoning same he will save his life". To hold thus under the facts adduced herein would be tantamount to a repeal by implication of the primal law of nature. . . . "The law in this state does not hold one in an emergency to the exercise of that mature judgment required of him under circumstances where he has an opportunity for deliberate action. He is not required to exercise unerring judgment, which would be expected of him, were he not confronted with an emergency requiring prompt action". . . . The chauffeur—the ordinary man in this case—acted in a split second in a most harrowing experience. To call him negligent would be to brand him coward; the court does not do so in spite of what those swaggering heroes, "whose valor plucks dead lions by the beard", may bluster to the contrary. The court is loathe to see the plaintiffs go without recovery even though their damages were slight, but cannot hold the defendant liable upon the facts adduced at the trial.

Questions

1.   To what extent may the decision in this case have been colored by the fact that the plaintiff was only injured rather than killed?
2.   Would the decision have been different if the defendant had failed to throw the transmission out of gear and put on the emergency brake?

Proximate Cause

Proximate cause may be defined as an unbroken chain of events leading from the negligent act to a resulting injury. It requires that the negligent act was the direct cause, or the cause of a cause, or some more remote link. However, there must be a link. For example, suppose that while speeding down a city street, Amy loses control of her car, strikes a second car, and the second car is pushed onto Bess's lawn, knocking down one of Bess's trees, which falls on Bess's house. Amy's negligence was the direct cause of the collision with the second car, and is linked in an unbroken chain of events to the injury to Bess's house. Therefore, Amy is liable to Bess for damages in the amount of the injury Bess has suffered.

Foreseeability

Although in most cases the rule of proximate cause is sufficient to limit properly the extent of liability for a negligent act, it occasionally may result in an injustice if left unrestricted. Among the first cases to bring this to the attention of the courts were cases involving fires set by railroad locomotives in the days of the wood-burning engines. A spark would set a fire along the track, and the fire would set another fire, which would set another fire, and so on. In justice, to what extent should the railroad be liable? Indefinitely? Such problems have caused the courts to adopt "foreseeability" as a limit on proximate cause. The rule, then, is that only injuries that reasonably were foreseeable at the time of the negligence should be compensable in a negligence action. Consider the case of the driver who was involved in a rather noisy collision with another automobile. The plaintiff, sitting in an open window on an upper story of a hotel some distance down the street became so interested in watching the accident that he fell out of the window and was injured. The court held that his injury was not foreseeable. However, the rule of foreseeability does not require that the negligent party foresee every detail of the result as the following case illustrates.

CITY OF ABILENE v. FILLMON
342 S.W.2d 227, Texas (1960)

This was an action by Ava N. Fillmon (Plaintiff/Appellee) against the City of Abilene, Texas (Defendant/Appellant) for damages for injuries sustained when she fell over a ridge of dirt in an alley. The ridge had been left by Defendant's employees in connection with the laying of some pipe. At the time of the injury, Plaintiff was fleeing from wasps she encountered while attempting to paint her back fence.

From a judgment for Plaintiff in the amount of $4650, Defendant appealed. Affirmed.

COLLINS, Justice.

Appellant City of Abilene particularly contends that the evidence does not support the finding that its negligence was the proximate cause of appellee's injury because of the absence of the element of foreseeability. Appellant urges that it should not be required to have foreseen that a band of stinging wasps would cause appellee to take sudden flight and fall over the ridge and injure herself. We cannot agree with this contention. The rule of foreseeability as applied to the law of negligence and proximate cause does not require anticipation of the full details of an accident. As stated in 65 C.J.S. Negligence Section 109, pages 670,671,672:

> . . . In order to render a negligent act or omission the proximate cause of the injury, it is sufficient if the wrongdoer by the exercise of ordinary or reasonable care could reasonably have foreseen or anticipated that a generally dangerous result, or some injury, or an injury of the same general nature as, or similar to, that which actually occurred, might occur.

The facts of the instant case are somewhat comparable to those in the case of Alice, Wade City & C.C. Telephone Company v. Billingsley. . . . In the cited case the plaintiff sued the telephone company alleging that it had negligently erected and maintained one of its poles in the traveled portion of a street; that plaintiff's wife drove a horse and buggy along the street and as the buggy was passing the telephone pole the horse threw its head to one side to drive away a fly, which caused a wheel of the buggy to collide with the telephone pole thereby throwing plaintiff's wife to the ground and injuring her. The appellate court affirmed the judgment in favor of the plaintiff and held against the defendant's contention that the action of the horse or of the fly in bothering the horse was the proximate cause of the plaintiff's injuries rather than the location of the telephone pole. In discussing the question the court stated as follows: "If it required both agencies to produce the result, or if both contributed thereto as concurrent forces, the presence and assistance of one will not exculpate the other, because it would still be the efficient cause of the injury. The intermediate cause must supersede the original wrongful act or omission, and be sufficient of itself to stand as the cause of the plaintiff's injury, to relieve the original wrongdoer from liability."

In the instant case there was ample evidence to the effect that the ridge was an efficient and moving cause of appellee's fall and injury. The attack of the wasps merely furnished the occasion or reason for appellee to move away from the fence. The attack by the wasps was not the sole cause of Mrs. Fillmon's fall and injury. It was only a concurring cause of the accident. Appellant's points urging that absence and insufficiency of the evidence to support the finding of the jury that its negligence was the proximate cause of appellee's injury are overruled.

Questions

1. What rule do we derive from this case as a standard for determining what kinds of results may be foreseeable as the consequences of a particular act?

2. If the plaintiff had not fallen over the pile of dirt, but it had caused her to change her course into the path of an oncoming car, would the defendant have been liable for those injuries?

Zone Of Danger Test

Another element that seems to aid courts in judging foreseeability is the "zone of danger test." This test requires that even remote injuries resulting from negligence still may be considered within the limits of foreseeability if there is some element connecting the injury to the incident in addition to geographical nearness. For example, in one case, a driver, who was operating his automobile at a high rate of speed, lost control and narrowly missed hitting some school children in a school crosswalk. A bystander became so frightened for the safety of the children that she fainted, sustaining an injury. The court held her injury was not within the limits of foreseeability. In another case, however, a driver, also speeding, narrowly missed hitting a child who had run into the street chasing a ball. His mother, seeing the child's danger, lost her balance and fell down some steps in front of her house and was injured. The court allowed a recovery. Although these cases simply may be inconsistent, the difference seems to be that the reaction of the mother was more understandable than the similar reaction of the bystander.

Injury

Compensable injuries proximately resulting from an act of negligence may take a wide variety of forms. The loss is usually economic, such as wages, or a loss of property, or even an interference with some property right that doesn't involve actual physical injury to the property. But the injury also may be to the person or psyche of the plaintiff. The usual remedy is money damages, but an injunction is possible if it can be shown that a person is likely to continue a course of negligence that endangers another person.

STRICT (ABSOLUTE) LIABILITY

Strict liability is a legal concept that encompasses liability of a defendant for injuries caused to a plaintiff even though the defendant did nothing wrong. That is, she neither intended the injury or the behavior that causes the injury, nor acted in an unreasonable manner. Strict liability is imposed in situations involving activities that may present an extraordinary danger to the public, such as the vending of food, drugs, and cosmetics that may be adulterated, or activities that may be considered ultrahazardous, such as the use of explosives, the demolition of buildings, or the keeping of wild or dangerous animals. In reading the following case, note the court's analysis of the factors leading it to conclude that the activity was ultrahazardous and therefore the rule of absolute liability should apply.

LUTHRINGER v. MOORE et al.
31 Cal.2d 489, 190 P.2d 1 (1948)

This was an action by Albert L. Luthringer (Plaintiff/Respondent) against a number of defendants, including R. L. Moore individually and doing business as Orchard Supply Company, and Sacramento Medico-Dental Building Company, for damages for personal injuries that resulted when Plaintiff breathed hydrocyanic acid gas being used by Defendant Moore to fumigate the basement of a building adjoining the building in which Plaintiff was employed. The buildings were owned by Defendant, Sacramento Medico-Dental Building Company, who had employed Moore to do the work. From a judgment in favor of Plaintiff, Defendant Moore appealed. Affirmed.

CARTER, Justice.

Defendant Moore was engaged to exterminate cockroaches and other vermin in the basement under the restaurant and that part under the dress shop. He made his preparations and released hydrocyanic acid gas in those rooms about midnight on November 16, 1943. Plaintiff, an employee of Flynn in the latter's pharmacy, in the course of his employment, arrived at the pharmacy about 8:45 a.m. on November 17, 1943, with the purpose of opening the store. . . . After entering the store he proceeded to a small mezzanine floor to put on his working clothes. Feeling ill he returned to the main floor and lost consciousness. He was discovered in that condition by Flynn's bookkeeper who arrived at the pharmacy between 9:15 and 9:30 a.m. Plaintiff was removed from the store, treated by the firemen of the city with a resuscitator and taken to the hospital where he received medical attention. He was found suffering from hydrocyanic acid gas poisoning and his injuries are from that source. . . .

It appears that the question of whether the case is a proper one for imposing absolute or strict liability is one of law for the court. . . .

Turning to the question of whether absolute or strict liability is appropriate in the instant case, we find that according to witness Bell (a man engaged in the pest control business), there are only three operators licensed to use lethal gas in pest control in Sacramento. And in regard to the nature of hydrocyanic acid gas he testified:

"Q. Do you know whether hydrocyanic acid gas is a poisonous gas or a lethal gas? A. It definitely is."

"Q. By lethal, you mean it is deadly, or causes death? A. That's right." . . .

"Q. How about the quantities of it that are required to cause death to animals or human beings? A. Minimum amount would be about 300 parts per million, would be a lethal dosage."

"Q. The amount to 300 parts by volume. A. Yes, sir."

"Q. That amount would be lethal to human beings? A. That is correct."

"Q. Do you know how long a time would be required? A. It would take very little time with that amount."

"Q. Can you tell us what the physical characteristics of hydrocyanic acid gas are? A. It is a little lighter-than-air gas; a very highly penetrative gas; susceptible to moisture quite a bit, it will follow moisture; it is noninflammable; the flashpoint is very low so that it can be used without much hazard of fire." . . .

"Q. I think you said the gas was very penetrative? A. Definitely."

"Q. What do you mean by that? A. That is one of the advantages of the gas; why they use it in fumigation. It will penetrate behind baseboards, cracks and crevices that we couldn't get at with any type of liquid insecticide. It will go through mattresses, chesterfields, furniture, some types of porous walls." . . .

"Q. Is it difficult to keep that gas confined? A. Yes, because of the fact it will penetrate you have to be careful to keep it in a definite area." . . .

"Q. In the ordinary operation, if you go in and seal up so that you consider it is adequately sealed, you still have some leakage of gas, or not? A. You will have some, yes, sir, unless it is very well built building." . . .

It has been said: "One who carries on an ultrahazardous activity is liable to another whose person, land or chattels the actor should recognize as likely to be harmed by the unpreventable miscarriage of the activity for harm resulting thereto from that which makes the activity ultrahazardous, although the utmost care is exercised to prevent the harm. . . . An activity is ultrahazardous if it (a) necessarily involves a risk of serious harm to the person, land or chattels of others which cannot be eliminated by the exercise of the utmost care, and (b) is not a matter of common usage." . . .

The above quoted evidence shows that the use of gas under the circumstances presented a hazardous activity; that it is perilous and likely to cause injury even though the utmost care is used; that defendant Moore knew or should have known that injury might result; and that the use of it under these circumstances is not a matter of "common usage" within the meaning of the term. The judgment against the defendant Moore is affirmed.

Questions

1. What might the defendant-exterminator do in the future to avoid strict liability for injuries such as these?

2. In what way does the application of strict liability in cases such as this benefit the public?

Other than certain areas of strict liability declared by statute, such as the drug statutes of a number of states, it is up to the courts to decide whether to apply this theory of liability. As noted above, there are some areas of general agreement. Beyond these, a court ordinarily will impose strict liability only in circumstances in which it feels that the public cannot adequately be protected by holding people only to the exercise of reasonable care, and therefore the law must encourage people engaging in these kinds of activities to exercise extreme care. In order to eliminate the problem of deciding whether to apply strict liability, one jurist, in a dissenting opinion disagreeing with the court's use of the rule, tendered that liability should rest on ordinary negligence, but the notion of what is reasonable care should be adjusted according to the degree and the gravity of the hazard involved in each case.

FACTORS ALTERING TORT LIABILITY

Defenses

The two most common defenses in cases involving intentional torts are permission and privilege. Permission may be most important in cases involving trespass, assault, and battery, as well as in those involving invasion of privacy or defamation. As discussed previously, two people on a date may be found to have consented to some touching. Also, by consenting to an examination or other medical procedure, a person may permit touching, even touching of a relatively serious nature, such as surgery. Likewise, information about a person may be released at that person's request.

Privilege also will operate as a defense. For example, even a homicide may be privileged under appropriate circumstances such as self-defense. A trespass to real estate may be privileged by custom (a stranger's coming to the door to ask for directions), or by law (a wayfarer seeking refuge from the rain in an abandoned outbuilding).

In negligence cases, the traditional defenses are assumption of risk and contributory negligence. Assumption of risk is a defense founded on the proposition that one who knows of certain risks attendant to a course of conduct should not be entitled to damages if he or she is injured by one of those known risks. For example, a person who uses explosives must assume his own responsibility if he is injured by one of the normal, known dangers they create.

The defense of contributory negligence is used to defeat a cause of action by proving that although the defendant was negligent and caused injury to the plaintiff, the plaintiff also was negligent, and that negligence contributed to his or her own injuries. For example, suppose it is proven that the defendant was driving his car at an excessive rate of speed, which caused him to run over and injure the plaintiff, a pedestrian. However, it also is proven that the plaintiff failed to look carefully before entering the crosswalk and, thus, negligently contributed to her own injuries. The plaintiff's cause of action is defeated totally, and she will not be entitled to collect from the defendant, regardless of the degree to which the negligence of each contributed to the injuries.

Recognizing the injustice caused by the contributory negligence rule, a number of states have replaced the defense of contributory negligence with that of comparative negligence (sometimes called "comparative rectitude"). This defense provides that if both parties' negligence contributed to the injuries, each should pay for those injuries in the same proportion as his negligence contributed to them. Therefore, in the previous example, if the driver was found to have contributed 75 percent to the injuries, and the pedestrian 25 percent, the driver would have to pay for 75 percent of the pedestrian's injuries and 75 percent of his own, and the pedestrian would have to pay 25 percent of the driver's injuries and 25 percent of her own. A few states apply a modified version of comparative negligence. In those states, the plaintiff's negligence does not affect his recovery unless it is found to have been 50 percent or more of the cause. Then, the plaintiff's cause of action is completely defeated in a manner similar to the rule of contributory negligence.

No-Fault Statutes

All states have one or more statutes creating liability under certain circumstances regardless of who was at fault in causing the injuries. A leading example is Workers' Compensation. When an employee is injured in the course of employment, these statutes require that a predetermined amount of compensation be paid for those injuries, by the employer, regardless of whether the employer was at fault in any way. In essence,

States with no fault auto insurance

= No Fault

Source: Western Insurance Information Service, phone conversation 3/9/89.

under this no-fault system, the employee gives up his or her right to bring a tort action for negligence against the employer, and the employer gives up his or her right to defend by use of any of the traditional common law defenses. Many states also have enacted no-fault statutes concerning automobile accidents. This was done to reduce the number of tort actions brought before the courts by eliminating suits in "fender bender" cases. Each driver is required to carry insurance, which pays for his or her own injuries in such cases.

Governmental (Sovereign) Immunity

Governmental units, federal, state, and local, are immune from tort suits unless they grant permission to be sued. This doctrine originated with the concept that "the king could do no wrong," but finds more modern support in the idea that when the government is sued, all citizens must bear the costs, yet the citizens are not able to defend their rights personally. However, governmental immunity protects governmental units only in situations in which the injuries were in connection with some traditional governmental function. Thus it does not cover the activities of governmental corporations, such as the Tennessee Valley Authority, or activities such as the operation of concession stands in public parks. Also, although the government itself may not be sued, the same is not always true of governmental officials who, in many cases, are not protected. Further, it should be noted that most governments have given permission for suits of various kinds, by statutes such as the Federal Tort Claims Act. Finally, although the doctrine of governmental immunity protects the government against tort suits, it does not extend to suits for breach of contract.

Charitable Immunity

Similar to governmental immunity, the doctrine of charitable immunity protects nonprofit organi-

zations, such as hospitals and private schools, from liability for torts. This doctrine originated to protect contributions, given for the purpose of supporting "good works," from being diverted into private hands by way of tort claims. This idea, however, seems to have outlived its usefulness, as discussed in Chapter 2, in *Flagiello v. Pennsylvania Hospital*. Today, it is recognized in only six jurisdictions, and it is fair to assume that it soon will be extinct.

Minors and Incapacitated Persons

Under the law of contracts, minors, insane persons, and incompetent persons ordinarily cannot bind themselves to obligations. Contracts entered into by these people usually are voidable or void. The same is not true under tort law, however. Such persons ordinarily are liable for torts they commit. Perhaps this difference in theories is logical and is supportable on the ground that in cases of tort, the injured party is usually an involuntary and innocent participant, but in contract cases he or she has voluntarily assumed an obligation and a relationship. Therefore, under tort law, it is more reasonable to shift the consequences of an injury.

Minors, however, do present some special considerations in tort law. Although minors of any age may be held liable for intentional torts such as assault and battery, those under the age of seven typically are presumed incapable of negligence. Between the ages of seven and fourteen, the law traditionally has applied a special standard for negligence. In this age range, the conduct of minors has been judged against the standard of another minor "of like age and understanding." After the age of fourteen, the "reasonable person" standard is applied. Consider the rationale of the court in the following case involving a minor's tort liability and the extent of the parents' liability.

ELLIS v. D'ANGELO et al.
116 Cal.App.2d 310, 253 P.2d 675 (1953)

This was an action by Ellis, a baby-sitter (Plaintiff/Appellant) against Salvatore D'Angelo, a four-year-old child, and his parents (Defendants/Appellants) for damages for injuries sustained when she was pushed to the floor by Salvatore. Her complaint was brought on three counts: (1) for intentional battery, (2) for negligence, and (3) against the parents for negligent failure to warn her of the child's habit of violently attacking people.

The trial court granted Defendants' demurrer to all three counts in the complaint. Plaintiff appealed. Reversed as to the first and third counts.

DOOLING, Justice.

[After reviewing a number of cases, and authorities on torts, including Prosser and Cooley, the court continued its analysis.] From these authorities and the cases which they cite it may be concluded generally that an infant is liable for his torts even though he lacks the mental development and capacity to recognize the wrongfulness of his conduct so long as he has the mental capacity to have the state of mind necessary to the commission of the particular tort with which he is charged. Thus as between a battery and negligent injury an infant may have the capacity to intend the violent contact which is essential to the commission of battery when the same infant would be incapable of realizing that his heedless conduct might foreseeably lead to injury to another which is the essential capacity of mind to create liability for negligence. . . .

In a case involving the question of the liability of an infant for his negligent conduct the court in Hoyt v. Rosenberg, 80 Cal.App.2d 500 at pages 506–507, 182 P.2d 234, at page 238,173 A.L.R. 883, said: "While the question as to whether a minor has been negligent in certain circumstances is ordinarily one of fact for the jury, an affirmative finding thereon . . . must conform to and be in accordance with the established rule that a minor is expected to use, not the quantum of care expected of an adult, but only that degree or amount of care which is ordinarily used by children of the same age under similar circumstances." . . .

So far as the count charging the infant defendant with negligence is concerned the question presented to the court is whether as a matter of common knowledge we can say that a child four years of age lacks the mental capacity to realize that his conduct which is not intended to bring harm to another may nevertheless be reasonably expected to bring about that result. In the absence of compelling judicial authority to the contrary in the courts of this state we are satisfied that a four year old child does not possess this mental capacity. . . .

When it comes to the count charging battery a very different question is presented. We certainly cannot say that a four-year-old child is incapable of intending the violent or the harmful striking of another. Whether a four-year-old child had such intent presents a fact question; and in view of section 41 of the Civil Code which makes the recognition of the wrongful character of the tort immaterial so far as the liability for compensatory damages is concerned, we must hold that the count charging battery states a cause of action.

The third count is without question sufficient to state a cause of action against the defendant parents. It alleges that these defendants employed plaintiff for the first time to act as baby-sitter for their son, that the son "habitually engaged in violently attacking and throwing himself forcibly and violently against other people, and violently shoving and knocking them, all of which said defendant parents knew," that said "parents negligently and carelessly failed to warn plaintiff of said child's said traits and disposition and negligently and carelessly failed to inform plaintiff that said child habitually indulged in such violent and furious attacks on others," and that shortly after plaintiff entered on her duties in the home the child attacked her to her resultant injury.

While it is the rule in California, as it is generally at the common law, that there is no vicarious liability on a parent for the torts of a child there is "another rule of law relating to the torts of minors which is somewhat in the nature of an exception, and that is that a parent may become liable for an injury caused by the child, where the parent's negligence made it possible for the child to cause the injury complained of, and probable that it would do so."

Questions

1. Is it anomalous that a child four years old cannot act unreasonably but can act with intent?

2. Would the public interest be better served if the parents of a minor child were liable for the child's torts in all cases?

Family Members

The rights of immediate family members to sue each other always has been severely restricted. For example, a suit by a child against his parents for "not raising him properly," or failing to provide a good education, would not be entertained by a court. Courts also resist actions by a spouse, or an unemancipated child, for injuries caused by the negligence of a spouse, a parent, or children. One reason for this is that courts refuse to interfere with ordinary family relations. In addition, allowing negligence actions could invite insurance fraud. This, however, would not pertain in many cases of intentional trespass, such as assault and battery, sexual misconduct, or conversion of property. Obviously, every person is entitled to reasonable protection from other family members and in contemporary society many intrafamily torts raise serious questions of public policy relating to child and spouse abuse.

STATUTORY LIABILITY UNDER RICO

In 1970, Congress enacted the Racketeer Influenced and Corrupt Organizations Act (RICO) as an amendment to the Organized Crime Control Act. RICO makes it an offense for anyone to acquire or maintain an interest in a business that affects interstate commerce by the use of a pattern of racketeering activity, including mail fraud, bribery, and embezzlement. Although the act originally was intended to control criminal activity in the business sector, as its title implies—perhaps primarily organized crime—its actual application has been much broader. Today, the lawsuits under RICO make up a disproportionate percentage of all the cases filed in federal courts, and its use has been extended to many types of commercial activities that one would not normally think of as part of a criminal pattern or organized crime.

In order to solicit the public's help in controlling crime, RICO provides that private lawsuits may be brought by anyone affected by its proscribed activities. If a lawsuit is successful, the plaintiff is awarded treble damages (the amount of actual damages multiplied by three), together with reasonable attorney fees. Under the act, two violations within a ten-year period, regardless of criminal conviction, constitute a "pattern of racketeering activity."

Since 1985, lawsuits under RICO have increased to a level causing alarm in the business and professional communities. In that year the Supreme Court refused to limit the act, stating that limitations should be addressed by Congress. This position was echoed in January 1989 by two federal appeals courts.

RICO's provisions have been applied to accountants, banks, securities brokers, and other businesses and professionals. Most of these lawsuits have involved fraud, particularly securities fraud, and few have addressed the kind of criminal activity apparently contemplated by Congress when RICO was enacted. As a result Congress is under pressure from a variety of sources, including a consortium of business and labor leaders, to rewrite the act to state more precisely the kinds of activity to be prohibited. Until the act is changed, its treble-damage provisions may be used in almost any case involving the use of the mail, or any other means of interstate communications, when fraud may be alleged.

REMEDIES

Damages

The most common remedies for tort injuries are money damages, which may be either compensatory or punitive (exemplary). **Compensatory damages** are those awarded to reimburse a party for injuries. They may be awarded for a loss of property, a loss of an expectation such as future wages, expenses incurred because of the injury, and for certain intangibles such as pain and suffering or the loss of consortium between spouses. However, compensatory damages may not be awarded for all injuries—only those that ordinarily may be expected to flow from the particular injury.

Punitive damages are awarded for the purpose of punishing a wrongdoer. They may be awarded in cases involving torts committed with malicious intent—for the express purpose of causing an injury, or otherwise with an evil mind. It is in this area that tort law and criminal law overlap. Punitive damages sometimes are authorized by statute, occasionally in a predetermined amount. An example is the provision for treble damages (compensatory damages multiplied by three) found in RICO. Otherwise, the court decides whether to award punitive damages, and the amount is established by the judge or jury according to what is felt necessary to punish the defendant for misconduct and to deter such conduct in the future. Punitive damages are awarded especially frequently in cases in which the defendant indicates a willingness to pay compensatory damages and continue the wrongful conduct.

Injunction

An **injunction** is a court order that something be done (mandatory) or not be done (prohibitory). In appropriate cases, an injunction even may be awarded without the participation of the person against whom it is granted—an *ex parte* proceeding. In these cases and others requiring the court to act relatively quickly, for example in deciding what to do with perishable goods, the injunction frequently is called a **temporary restraining order** or "TRO." The order is granted, and later a full hearing is held to determine whether to dissolve the order or to make it permanent. The violation of an injunction will subject the violator to having to appear and "show cause" why he or she should not be held in contempt of court, and possibly fined and/or imprisoned. As the following case illustrates, this is true even if it is later determined that the injunction should not have been granted in the first place.

WALKER et al v. CITY OF BIRMINGHAM
388 U.S. 307, 87 S.Ct. 1903, 18 L.Ed.2d 1210 (1967)

This action was brought to the Supreme Court on a petition for a Writ of *Certiorari* of a finding of contempt of court.

The city of Birmingham applied for an injunction restraining 139 individuals and two organizations (Defendants among them) from holding a civil rights demonstration. It was alleged that the expected demonstration would be in violation of several city ordinances. A temporary injunction was granted, and each of the petitioners (Walker and others) was served with copies or given notice of the injunction but chose to violate it. During the contempt proceeding that ensued, the trial court refused to consider Petitioners' evidence that both the ordinances alleged to have been offended and the injunction were so vague, and violative of their right of freedom of speech, as to be unconstitutional.

From judgments of conviction for contempt of court, Petitioners appealed. The judgment of the trial court was affirmed by the Supreme Court of Alabama, and again by the Supreme Court of the United States.

STEWART, Mr. Justice.

The Supreme Court of Alabama . . . declined to consider the petitioners' constitutional attacks upon the injunction and the underlying Birmingham parade ordinance:

> It is to be remembered that petitioners are charged with violating a temporary injunction. We are not reviewing a denial of a motion to dissolve or discharge a temporary injunction. Petitioners did not file any motion to vacate the temporary injunction until after the Friday and Sunday parades. Instead, petitioners deliberately defied the order of the court and did engage in and incite others to engage in mass street parades without a permit. . . .
>
> "We hold that the circuit court had the duty and authority, in the first instance, to determine the validity of the ordinance, and, until the decision of the circuit court is reversed for error by orderly review, either by the circuit court or a higher court, the orders of the circuit court based on its decision are to be respected and disobedience of them is contempt of its lawful authority, to be punished. Howat v. State of Kansas . . .

Howat v. State of Kansas . . . was decided by this Court almost 50 years ago. That was a case in which people had been punished by a Kansas trial court for refusing to obey an antistrike injunction issued under the state industrial relations act. They had claimed a right to disobey the court's order upon the ground that the state statute and the injunction based upon it were invalid under the Federal Constitution. The Supreme Court of Kansas had affirmed the judgment, holding that the trial court "had general power to issue injunctions in equity, and that even if its exercise of the power was erroneous, the injunction was not void, and the defendants were precluded from attacking it in this collateral proceeding . . . that, if the injunction was erroneous, jurisdiction was not thereby forfeited, that the error was subject to correction only by the ordinary method of appeal, and disobedience to the order constituted contempt." 258 U.S., at 189, 42 S.Ct. at 280.

This Court, in dismissing the writ of error, not only unanimously accepted but fully approved the validity of the rule of state law upon which the judgment of the Kansas court was grounded:

An injunction duly issuing out of a court of general jurisdiction with equity powers, upon pleadings properly invoking its action, and served upon persons made parties therein and within the jurisdiction, must be obeyed by them, however erroneous the action of the court may be, even if the error be in the assumption of the validity of a seeming, but void law going to the merits of the case. It is for the court of first instance to determine the question of the validity of the law, and until its decision is reversed for error by orderly review, either by itself or by a higher court, its orders based on its decision are to be respected, and disobedience of them is contempt of its lawful authority, to be punished. 258 U.S., at 189–190, 42 SCt., at 280.

The rule of state law accepted and approved in Howat v. State of Kansas is consistent with the rule of law followed by the federal courts. In the present case, however, we are asked to hold that this rule of law, upon which the Alabama courts relied, was constitutionally impermissible. We are asked to say that the Constitution compelled Alabama to allow the petitioners to violate this injunction, to organize and engage in these mass street parades and demonstrations, without any previous effort on their part to have the injunction dissolved or modified, or any attempt to secure a parade permit in accordance with its terms. Whatever the limits of Howat v. State of Kansas, we cannot accept the petitioners' contentions in the circumstances of this case.

Questions

1. Would the defendants in this case have been liable if the proceeding that led to the issuance of the injunction had not been conducted legally?

2. Under what circumstances may a person lawfully ignore a valid court order?

CRIMINAL LAW

CLASSIFICATION OF CRIMES

According to Seriousness

Crimes may be classified, according to seriousness, as treason, felonies, misdemeanors, and ordinance violations. Treason is considered a separate crime because it is an offense established by the Constitution of the United Sates, not by statute.

Treason is defined in Article 3, Section 3, clause 1, as follows: "Treason against the United States, shall consist only in levying war against them, or in adhering to their enemies, giving them aid and comfort." The crux of this crime may be found in an overt attempt to overthrow the government by someone owing the government allegiance. The attempt must be an overt act, more than merely thinking about, or planning, such activities. However, by statute Congress has created related, but lesser, crimes such as espionage, sedition, and conspiracy.

A **felony** is a crime for which the penalty may be death or imprisonment in a state or federal prison. Felonies are the most serious of the statutory crimes, and include such offenses as murder, arson, burglary, robbery, rape, and kidnapping. Felonies ordinarily are punishable by a substantial fine and imprisonment for a period longer than one year.

All other crimes, other than ordinance violations, are classified as **misdemeanors**, which are punishable by a fine, a jail term, or both. This is a jail term, not a prison term, and the period ordinarily is for one year or less. Some states, such as Michigan, have two classes of misdemeanors, the more serious of which may be punishable by a longer jail term, such as two years.

Ordinance violations, such as municipal traffic offenses, are in a separate category, although there is some disagreement whether an ordinance violation is a distinct offense or only another type of misdemeanor. Also, some jurisdictions have decriminalized these offenses, making them civil infractions. By doing so, the necessity of providing a court-appointed attorney may be avoided, and the prosecutor's burden of proof may be reduced. An ordinance is a legislative enactment of a governmental unit below the state level, such as a county, township, or city, as opposed to a statute.

According to Nature

Crimes also may be classified as *malum in se* and *malum prohibitum*. Crimes ***malum in se*** involve activities considered wrong because they are in violation of accepted notions of justice, morals, or natural law. Included would be murder, theft, and incest. There is almost unanimous agreement among civilized societies about these wrongs. Offenses ***malum prohibitum*** are those considered wrong only because laws have been enacted prohibiting the behavior. For example, there may be nothing inherently wrong with parking one's automobile in an area along a public roadway, but it may be made illegal by legislative enactment. Crimes *malum in se* tend to be more enduring, and vary less from social unit to social unit, and from time to time, than those that are *malum prohibitum*.

ELEMENTS OF A CRIME

Every crime consists of three elements: (1) a criminal act, (2) criminal intent, and (3) a concurrence of the act and the intent.

Act

A court has no power or authority to render criminal an act that has not been legislatively defined. All criminal acts must be defined as such by statute or ordinance. This is true no matter how horrible or unthinkable an act may be, and is in sharp contrast to the courts' power in civil cases to create new causes of action. This rule is a part of our system of jurisprudence in the United States and is justified on the ground of protecting citizens against the unlimited, arbitrary arm of the judiciary.

Classification of crimes by seriousness (in descending order)

Crime	Definition	Example
Treason	Attempt by overt act to overthrow the government to which the offender owes allegiance	Giving military secrets to enemy during time of war.
Felony	Crime for which punishment by federal law may be death or imprisonment for more than one year	Murder, rape, armed robbery
Misdemeanor	Crime less serious than a felony for which punishment may only be a fine or jail term	Shoplifting, speeding, intoxication
Ordinance violation	Violation of a municipal regulation	Parking ticket

Intent

Criminal intent, also called **mens rea**, is a key element of every crime. It is not the purpose of criminal law to compensate an individual for his or her injuries, but to prevent injuries, and threats of injury, to society and its members. This protection is sought by the imposition of penalties for criminal wrongs, directed toward altering the workings of the mind, with almost no focus on the effects of the act itself.

In criminal law, one is presumed to have intended the natural and probable consequences of his or her acts. Therefore, one who fires a gun at the windows of a passing train, and causes the death of a passenger in the train, will be held to have intended the homicide.

Concurrence of Act and Intent

Without the concurrence of the criminal intent and the criminal act, no crime can be committed. For example, suppose Helen came to Bob's house for the purpose of killing Bob. After waiting for a time, Helen changed her mind and went back to her car to start home. When she pulled from her parking space, Bob suddenly stepped in her path. Before Helen had a chance to react, she ran over and killed Bob. There would be no crime. Although intent and the act were in close proximity, they did not exist at the same time.

On the other hand, suppose Gus shot Bob nine times, intending to kill him. He then loaded Bob into the trunk of his car and drove him across the state line and, in the second state, believing Bob was dead, dumped the body into the river. Evidence later established that Bob died not from the shots, but from drowning after he was thrown into the river. Is Gus guilty of murder? In the first state, he intended to kill Bob but did not, and in the second he did not intend to kill him but did. In a similar case one court held, correctly, that murder was committed in the second state, holding that Gus's intent to kill Bob was a "continuing intent" that followed him through the intended act of disposing of the body.

BUSINESS CRIMES AND CORPORATE RESPONSIBILITY

Generally

By far the great majority of crimes are not business related. However, in recent years attention has been focused increasingly on criminal activity in the business sector, and much is being written concerning "white-collar crime" and "corporate crime." In addition, the attitude of the law seems to be shifting toward increasingly imposing more vicarious liability on corporations for crimes committed by their employees and agents.

Under common law principles, it has been considered contrary to the theory of criminal liability to impute to an employer an evil mind because of an employees' evil mind. Thus, courts and legislatures have resisted finding vicarious liability for crimes. This has been because of the emphasis in criminal law on the intent factor, discussed previously. Apparently for reasons of public policy, and because of a perceived increase in the need to protect society from criminal activity by employees who use their employer's businesses as vehicles for perpetuating crimes, that position has been eroding steadily.

Scope of Liability

Liability for business-related crimes may fall into any one of three categories. First, an officer, agent, or other employee who commits a criminal act will be liable as an individual. The fact that the crime may have been committed in the course and scope of his or her employment, or even under the direction and control of the employer, is of no consequence. The person who commits a crime always is liable.

Second, an agent or employee also may be liable for crimes he or she did not commit personally. Entering into a conspiracy, or acting as an accessory before or after the fact, or as an accomplice of another person who commits a crime, is sufficient to create liability. In addition to being culpable for any separate crime he or she actually commits (for example, being a conspirator), the agent or employee also will be liable for the ultimate crime committed by the other person. For example, a supervisor who instructs another employee to commit an antitrust violation—or, after a violation was committed, knowingly conceals evidence of the violation—can be prosecuted under this theory.

Third, someone who is responsible for personally overseeing parts of a business's operations, and thus the employees' work, may be liable for the criminal misconduct of those employees. Although essentially unknown at common law, this theory of criminal liability, known as the **responsible share doctrine**, is becoming increasingly more important. Its application is found especially in connection with federal regulatory acts (those administered by a federal agency). The leading case on the subject follows. Carefully note the court's reasoning.

UNITED STATES v. PARK
421 U.S. 658, 95 S.Ct. 1903 (1975)

John R. Park (Defendant/Respondent) was the president of Acme Markets, Inc., a large national food chain. Among his other duties, delegated to other employees, he was responsible for seeing that food offered for sale by Acme was sanitary. In April 1970, he was notified by letter from the Food and Drug Administration (FDA) that the conditions in two of Acme's warehouses were unsanitary because of rodent contamination. During two later examinations of the company's Baltimore warehouse, in 1971 and 1972, the FDA inspector found further evidence of rodent infestation, and the respondent was notified on each occasion, but the problem continued. Thereafter, Acme Markets, Inc. and Mr. Park were charged with violating Section 301(K) of the Food, Drug, and Cosmetic Act. Respondent defended on the ground that he was not "personally involved in the violation."

Acme Markets, Inc. pleaded guilty. Respondent Park was convicted, but the judgment was reversed by the Circuit Court of Appeals. That decision was then reversed by the Supreme Court, thus reinstating the conviction.

BURGER, Mr. Chief Justice.

The rule that corporate employees who have "a responsible share in the furtherance of the transaction which the statute outlaws" are subject to the criminal provisions of the Act was not formulated in a vacuum. . . . Cases under the Federal Food and Drugs Act of 1906 reflected the view both that knowledge or intent were not required to be proved in prosecutions under its criminal provisions, and that responsible corporate agents could be subjected to the liability thereby imposed. . . . Moreover, the principle had been recognized that a corporate agent, through whose act, default, or omission the corporation committed a crime, was himself guilty individually of that crime. The principle had been applied whether or not the crime required "consciousness of wrongdoing," and it had been applied not only to those corporate agents who themselves committed the criminal act, but also to those who by virtue of their managerial positions or other similar relation to the actor could be deemed responsible for its commission.

In the latter class of cases, the liability of managerial officers did not depend on their knowledge of, or personal participation in, the act made criminal by the statute.

Rather, where the statute under which they were prosecuted dispensed with "consciousness of wrongdoing," an omission or failure to act was deemed a sufficient basis for a responsible corporate agent's liability. It was enough in such cases that, by virtue of the relationship he bore to the corporation, the agent had the power to prevent the act complained of.

[United States v. Dotterweich] . . . and the cases which have followed reveal that in providing sanctions which reach and touch the individuals who execute the corporate mission—and this is by no means necessarily confined to a single corporate agent or employee—the Act imposes not only a positive duty to seek out and remedy violations when they occur but also, and primarily, a duty to implement measures that will insure that violations will not occur. The requirements of foresight and vigilance imposed on responsible corporate agents are beyond question demanding, and perhaps onerous, but they are no more stringent than the public has a right to expect of those who voluntarily assume positions of authority in business enterprises whose services and products affect the health and well-being of the public that supports them. . . .

The Act does not, as we observed in *Dotterweich*, make criminal liability turn on "awareness of some wrongdoing" or "conscious fraud." The duty imposed on Congress on responsible corporate agents is, we emphasize, one that requires the highest standard of foresight and vigilance, but the Act, in its criminal aspect, does not require that which is objectively impossible. The theory upon which responsible corporate agents are held criminally accountable for "causing" violations of the Act permits a claim that a defendant was "powerless" to prevent or correct the violation to "be raised defensively at a trial on the merits." United States v. Wiesenfeld Warehouse Co., 376 U.S. 86, 91, 84 S.Ct. 559, 563, 11 L.Ed 2d 536 (1964). If such a claim is made, the defendant has the burden of coming forward with evidence, but this does not alter the Government's ultimate burden of proving beyond a reasonable doubt the defendant's guilt, including his power, in light of the duty imposed by the Act, to prevent or correct the prohibited condition. Congress has seen fit to enforce the accountability of responsible corporate agents dealing with products which may affect the health of consumers by penal sanctions cast in rigorous terms, and the obligation of the courts is to give them effect so long as they do not violate the Constitution.

We cannot agree with the Court of Appeals that it was incumbent upon the District Court to instruct the jury that the Government had the burden of establishing "wrongful action" in the sense in which the Court of Appeals used that phrase. The concept of a "responsible relationship" to, or a "responsible share" in, a violation of the Act indeed imports some measure of blameworthiness; but it is equally clear that the Government establishes a prima facie case when it introduces evidence sufficient to warrant a finding by the trier of the facts that the defendant had, by reason of his position in the corporation, responsibility and authority either to prevent in the first instance, or promptly to correct, the violation complained of, and that he failed to do so. The failure thus to fulfill the duty imposed by the interaction of the corporate agent's authority and the statute furnishes a sufficient causal link. The considerations which prompted the imposition of this duty, and the scope of the duty, provide the measure of culpability.

Questions

1. How does "responsible share" liability in cases such as this relate to the requirement of criminal intent?

2. To come under the doctrine of responsible share, what degree of control or responsibility must a defendant have over the instrumentality of the crime?

SPECIFIC BUSINESS CRIMES

Although, theoretically, any crime may be committed in a business environment, some are more peculiar to the business context than others. These generally involve the misappropriation of property, the misuse of power obtained because of the business, or failure to comply with regulatory rules. The crimes discussed here are representative of the more important classifications, but are by no means exhaustive of the possibilities.

Fraud

The crime of fraud is the same as the tort of fraud, except that criminal, not civil, intent must be involved, and the burden of proof is different ("beyond a reasonable doubt" rather than "by a preponderance of the evidence"). In the business context, the most common fraud prosecutions occur on the federal level and concern violations of the mail and wire fraud statutes. The mail fraud statute is violated if the mail is used for the pur-

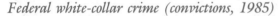

Federal white-collar crime (convictions, 1985)

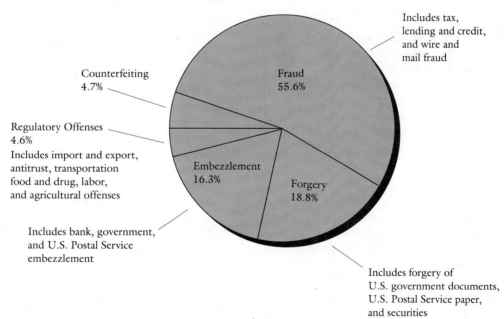

Counterfeiting
4.7%

Regulatory Offenses
4.6%
Includes import and export, antitrust, transportation food and drug, labor, and agricultural offenses

Includes bank, government, and U.S. Postal Service embezzlement

Embezzlement
16.3%

Fraud
55.6%

Includes tax, lending and credit, and wire and mail fraud

Forgery
18.8%

Includes forgery of U.S. government documents, U.S. Postal Service paper, and securities

Source: Bureau of Justice Statistics, Special Report on White Collar Crime, September 1987.

pose of fraud, regardless of whether the particular fraud committed is criminal or civil, or whether the federal government has jurisdiction over the fraud itself. It is the *use of the mail* to commit *any* fraud that is the violation.

Embezzlement

Although included within the broad definition of *theft* (conversion of the property of another with the intent to deprive the owner of the property permanently), embezzlement is the most common form of the crime in the business environment. **Embezzlement** is theft (misappropriation) by someone already in lawful possession of the property of another. Other forms of theft, such as burglary, robbery, and obtaining by false pretenses, involve an unlawful taking. The crime of embezzlement frequently is business related simply because employees are almost always in possession of some property of the employer.

Computer Crimes

With the "computer age" has come a whole new, fertile field for criminal activity. The possibilities include the use of computers in perpetrating fraud, the misuse of computerized databases, the theft of commercial computer services, and the theft of software. These offenses are discussed thoroughly in Chapter 28.

Conspiracy

As previously discussed, conspiracy is a crime that frequently may subject a business superior to criminal liability for acts of his or her subordinates. **Conspiracy** is found in the agreement of two or more persons to commit an unlawful act in the future—for example, an agreement to violate the antitrust laws. The agreement itself is the violation, regardless of whether the agreed-upon act is performed.

Obstruction of Justice

The various federal statutes creating this offense effectively prohibit all types of interferences with federal investigations and proceedings. Prohibited acts include everything from destruction of corporate records to direct threats and bribery of legal participants such as witnesses and jurors.

The basic federal statute on this subject was amended in 1982 to delete reference to interferences with witnesses; at the same time Congress enacted the Victim and Witness Protection Act of 1982, extending the coverage of obstruction offenses. This statute aims directly at the mental element, making the proscribed conduct punishable regardless of whether proceedings have been, or are intended to be, instituted and regardless of whether the evidence interfered with would be admissible in a proceeding. The statute seems to indicate increased federal attention to conduct that might interfere with the administration of justice, from the initial stage of proposing and enacting statutes and administrative rules, through the trial, and then to prevent retaliation after proceedings have been completed. Of particular interest to businesses may be the provisions concerning alteration and destruction of business records.

Foreign Corrupt Practices Act

Prior to the passage of the **Foreign Corrupt Practices Act** in 1977, bribery of foreign officials by United States domestic corporations was considered by many to be an ordinary part of doing business abroad. Indeed, these payments commonly were deducted as legitimate expenses on the income tax returns of the corporations involved. In addition, the payments were not disclosed to investors under the theory that they were not "material"; the Securities and Exchange Commission (SEC) disagreed.

The Foreign Corrupt Practices Act is enforced jointly by the SEC and the Department of Justice.

Its provisions apply to all domestic corporations regardless of whether they are registered with the SEC. Corrupt payments (bribery) of foreign public officials, a foreign political party or its officials, or a candidate for foreign political office are prohibited. The giving of gifts, which is customary in many foreign countries, is not prohibited, however. The difference between a gift and a corrupt payment is determined by the intent of the parties. If the paying party knows, or has reason to know, that the effect is or will be to cause the other party to change position with regard to whether the party making the payment will get or retain business, then it is not a gift.

Liability under the act extends to all who knowingly make or acquiesce to the making of a corrupt payment. This includes a corporation itself.

Securities Laws

A number of federal statutes and a mass of agency regulations provide a great variety of potential violations of the law in the area of securities transactions in addition to the Foreign Corrupt Practices Act. The violation of any of these is considered a civil infraction. In addition, all of the statutes except the Securities Investor Protection Act of 1970 provide criminal penalties. Most of these are *felonies,* so, their importance cannot be overstated. Any knowing or willful violation may result in *both* civil and criminal liability, imposed on both the actor and the corporation. The most familiar and most widely publicized violations in recent years have related to "insider trading."

Tax Crimes

The Watergate Investigation of 1973 spawned many statutory and regulatory changes, one of which was the Foreign Corrupt Practices Act, and another the increased focus on tax crimes. Bribes paid to foreign officials frequently were concealed, except that they were deducted (illegally)

as ordinary business expenses. The same was true of domestic bribes and other corrupt payments here at home. In addition to these problems, concern was focused on inaccurate corporate statements and transactions concealed by the use of foreign bank accounts. Since 1973, the Internal Revenue Service has investigated these areas more vigorously; enforcement has increased, and new statutes and regulations have been enacted. Perhaps even more important, however, is that the service's ability to investigate and pursue violations has been increased significantly by the Supreme Court decision in *U.S. v. Arthur Young & Co.,* 465 U.S. 805, 104 S.Ct. 1497 (1984), holding that an auditor's working papers are subject to subpoena by the Internal Revenue Service.

SUMMARY

An action, or sometimes even inaction, can create liability if it breaches some duty. If the duty is one owed to society as a whole, the breach will be considered criminal. If the duty is one owed to an individual, the breach will be a civil one. Criminal liability results in prosecution and punishment by way of a fine and/or imprisonment. Civil liability, on the other hand, may result in a private lawsuit and compensation, ordinarily by way of money damages.

Tort law recognizes three general classifications of torts—intentional, negligence, and absolute liability. The violation of a wide variety of rights may be the basis for tort liability. These may be in real estate, personal property, a person's body, a person's reputation, or even in less tangible things such as peace of mind, privacy, or marital relations.

Liability for intentional torts rests on a wrongdoer's intent to create an injury or to cause an act that results in an injury. Negligence involves a lesser degree of mental wrong. It results when someone has directly or proximately caused an injury by acting unreasonably under the circumstances. Absolute liability does not involve fault at all, but arises from the concept that one who enters into certain kinds of activities should be required to ensure the safety of all those who might be affected by the conduct. If any injury results from the activity, the actor should be liable as a matter of public policy rather than fault.

Criminal liability is always based on some wrongful intent, coinciding with an act that has been declared, by statute, to be unlawful. In degrees of seriousness, crimes may be broadly classified as treason, felonies, misdemeanors, and ordinance violations. Crimes of the first two types are punishable by death or imprisonment in a federal or state prison; those of the last two categories are punishable by a fine and/or confinement in a county or city jail.

Some crimes often are business related. These include theft (especially embezzlement), computer crimes, fraud, conspiracy, obstruction of justice, violations of the Foreign Corrupt Practices Act, and many crimes related to tax law. In every case, the individual who commits the crime is liable. However, the punishment of businesses for crimes committed by agents and employees is becoming increasingly more common. Commercial entities ordinarily were not vicariously liable for crimes in the past because the criminal law requires an evil mind. Today that has changed, and is continuing to change at a rapid pace. Businesses now are well advised to exercise close control over their personnel, especially in areas in which there is a significant possibility of criminal wrongdoing by their agents and employees.

KEY TERMS AND CONCEPTS

crime
tort
intentional tort
negligence
strict liability
trespass
nuisance
conversion
battery
assault
defamation
libel
slander
fraud
deceit
compensatory damages
punitive damages
injunction
ex parte
temporary restraining order
treason
felony
misdemeanor
malum in se
malum prohibitum
mens rea
responsible share doctrine
embezzlement
conspiracy
obstruction of justice
Foreign Corrupt Practices Act

PROBLEMS

1. Mrs. Dailey and her son, Timmy, who was 5 years and 9 months old, were invited to a backyard picnic at the home of Mrs. Garratt, an elderly neighbor. At one point in the afternoon Timmy, who enjoyed playing pranks, saw that Mrs. Garratt was about to sit down and playfully pulled the chair out from under her. Mrs. Garratt fell and was injured. She sued Timmy for damages for battery. In view of Timmy's age and the fact that he intended only to play a joke and not to injure Mrs. Garratt, should Mrs. Garratt recover? What if she sued Timmy's mother?

2. Williams, the plaintiff's decedent, was frightened one day when confronted by an armed convict who had escaped from custody at a nearby minimum-security prison. Being frightened so severely caused a brain hemorrhage that caused death. The convict, at the time, was being held for a "toy pistol" robbery and had a relatively good record while in custody. The plaintiff sued the state for negligence in causing the death by failing to act reasonably to see that its prisoner did not escape. Should a recovery be granted?

3.   The plaintiff, while crossing a street, was run down by an automobile driven by the defendant. Because of the defendant's negligence, the plaintiff suffered severe head injuries. The trial court granted damages in an amount to cover the injuries, including an amount awarded because of the possibility of epilepsy in the future, which the evidence showed she probably would suffer. Was the awarding of this last element of damages proper?

4.   Carter, a 5-year-old child, was bitten by a pet coyote that his neighbor kept on a rope in his yard. The coyote had been the family pet for two years and had never bitten anyone or indicated that he might. Children from the neighborhood regularly played with him. Should Carter be awarded damages against the neighbor for his injuries?

5.   During the summer, unrest in an area of Minneapolis along Plymouth Avenue resulted in rioting and looting. Property damage was great and the plaintiffs, fearing further injury to their business, asked the Minneapolis police for protection. They were assured that extra officers were being assigned to the area and would be there until the rioting was over. Nevertheless, the police were inadequate and the plaintiffs' business was burned to the ground the following night. Some years before, the state legislature had eliminated the defense of sovereign immunity, which previously had protected governmental units from liability in tort. The plaintiffs sued the city for negligence in failing to protect their property adequately. Should the city be held liable?

6.   While driving his car one evening, Archer narrowly escaped injury when he encountered a number of cattle wandering along the highway. He stopped and saw that they had come through a hole in the fence of a nearby pasture. Archer began rounding them up and, as he was driving them back across the highway near a curve, the plaintiff came around the curve and collided with the cattle. The plaintiff sued Archer, charging negligence in trying to take the cattle across the highway at a blind curve. Archer defended on the ground that he was not responsible for the cattle being there and was only a volunteer, trying to help so no one would be injured. Should Archer be liable for the plaintiff's injuries?

7.   Adams and Baker, in a disagreement over who was the better fighter, began fist fighting on the street in front of the Good Times Saloon. During the combat, Adams hit Baker in the jaw, causing him to fall back, knocking a bystander, Casey, into the path of a passing car. Baker's jaw was broken and Casey was killed. Should Adams be liable criminally or in tort for the injury to Baker and the death of Casey?

8.   Morrison lent his computer to Nolan, who have it to her secretary, Olsen, to use in typing a number of letters for Nolan. Without permission, Parsons took the computer from Olsen's desk and concealed it for the purpose of selling it later. What crime has Parsons committed? What if Olsen had concealed it for the same purpose?

9.   In Indiana, following the deaths of three people riding in a Pinto, Ford Motor Co. was charged with negligent homicide. The grounds of the charge involved negligence by the defendant in failing to recall the Pinto even though it knew, through its officers and directors, that the design of the Pinto was dangerous and the deaths were the direct result of that design flaw. Previously, a court in California had awarded damages against Ford in a tort action involving the same flaw. Should Ford Motor Co. be found guilty?

10.   Frequently a single act may be both a tort and a crime, but because the objectives of tort law and criminal law are different, this is not always true. State how these objectives differ. Also, give an example of an act that is a tort but not a crime, and an act that is a crime but not a tort.

Constitutional Law

PURPOSES OF CONSTITUTIONS

One of the special characteristics of government in the United States is that all official power is derived from written constitutions. Perhaps for most people, the word *constitution* is equated with the federal government. However, each of the fifty states also has a constitution. For the most part, these state constitutions follow the pattern of the federal constitution, and the theory behind constitutional forms of government is the same— to secure the people from the unlimited, arbitrary, and potentially abusive power of government. But **constitutions** do have other purposes, including creating and organizing the government, as well as defining the powers of each of the branches and placing limitations on those powers.

FRAMING OF THE UNITED STATES CONSTITUTION

In the years following the American Revolution, which separated us from England, there was no

United States government; there was only a grouping of contiguous land masses that had been colonies. After the American Revolution or War of Independence, each colony went about the business of establishing its own government, and each claimed **sovereignty** (independent and supreme governmental authority).

The Articles of Confederation

This first attempt at framing a constitutional central government might be characterized as an exercise in paranoia. The process began soon after independence was declared and, two years later, in July 1778, the Continental Congress adopted the Articles of Confederation. Although the document was ratified quickly by eleven states, Delaware and Maryland held out, and the Articles did not come into effect until March 1781.

The Articles of Confederation provided for a weak central government with almost no power. The states retained their sovereign powers and remained independent, with a very loose association among themselves. The only manifestation of a central government was Congress; there was no executive and no national court. Although Congress had powers concerning foreign relations, treaties, and war, it lacked one very important power, which proved fatal—the power to tax. The achievement of confederation policies was at the mercy of the states. Also, there was no provision to change this, or anything else in the Articles of Confederation, except by the unanimous vote of the states. These and other problems of the new confederation became apparent, and pressure to change began even before the Articles of Confederation were ratified.

In addition to the inability to raise operating revenue by taxing, another very important power was withheld from Congress—the power to regulate commerce among the states. This, together with the fact that each state retained the power to enact and enforce its own laws without limitation, prevented the formation of any real union among the states. Trading monopolies developed, and interstate trade and commerce were severely hampered. The problems were similar to those experienced in England some 500 years earlier, prior to the establishment of the Common Law. It was mostly because of these problems that the federal Constitution finally was drafted and adopted.

The Federal Constitution

In September 1786, representatives of five states met at Annapolis and resolved to recommend to the state legislatures that delegates be sent to convene and resolve the problems inherent in the Articles of Confederation. This recommendation was adopted by Congress the following February, and in May 1787, the delegates of twelve states (Rhode Island refused to participate) began to convene in Philadelphia, forming what later became known as the Constitutional Convention.

Although the delegates to the convention originally were sent to revise the Articles of Confederation, in fact they drafted an entirely new document and ultimately created and empowered an entirely new government. After resolving the conflict as to how states would be represented by creating bicameral Congress—the upper house (Senate) to be composed of two members elected from each state and the lower house (House of Representatives) to be apportioned according to each state's population (the "Great Compromise")—the new Constitution was adopted and ratified. The union of the states was changed from a confederation to a federation, and a strong central government was born. Still, the federal government was created as a government of "delegated powers," with all powers not expressly given to the federal government being reserved by the states. It is in this form that the Constitution endures today. Since 1787, changes in the Constitution have come only by way of amendment, although many would say they have come by way of court interpretation as well.

FUNDAMENTAL PRINCIPLES OF THE CONSTITUTION

The United States Constitution is a complex document. It is divided into seven articles and twenty-six amendments. The first three articles establish the structure of the government and specify the powers of its three branches—Article I, The Legislative Branch; Article II, The Executive Branch; and Article III, The Judicial Branch. Article IV provides for Relations Among States, Article V provides the Method of Amendment, Article VI provides for the Supremacy of United States Law, and Article VII provides for the Method of Ratification of the Constitution. The first ten amendments, known collectively as the Bill of Rights, were adopted soon after the original Constitution, and the other sixteen were adopted over the next 180 years. An Amendment 27, the Equal Rights Amendment, was proposed on March 22, 1972, but was not ratified by the required number of states.

The Constitution incorporates a number of simple and fundamental principles, each of which contributes to the creation of a form of government that has endured, and served the nation well, for over 200 years. The following principles universally are considered to be among the most important.

Consent of the Governed

The concept that a government should exist, both in form and in power, only with the consent of those it governs was a new concept to almost everyone at the time our Constitution was written. However, its importance in the minds of those who drafted the Constitution cannot be overstated. The first words in the Preamble, "We the people . . . ," clearly established this. Some eighty years later, in the Gettysburg Address, President Lincoln reaffirmed that ours was a government "of the people. . . ." The concept remains true today. Under the Constitution, the United States government was created by consent, its powers were granted to it by the people, it operates through representatives chosen by free election, and it will continue only as long as the governed continue to consent.

Limitation of Powers

Philosophically, the most important purpose of the Constitution is its limitation on official power, and undoubtedly that was the part that most occupied the thoughts of its framers. Remember that those who participated in the Constitutional Convention had recent, personal experience with the monolithic monarchies of England and the rest of western Europe. For the most part, they undoubtedly considered these experiences disappointing. The "Crown" was supreme and its power was unfettered. The first order of business, then, in framing a United States Constitution was to ensure that a single individual would not possess all governmental power, and that the authority granted to the new government would be limited to those that required administration by a central power.

Separation of Powers

The fear of unfettered power caused the "founding fathers" to divide (separate) the power of the central government among three branches, granting legislative power to Congress, administrative power to the executive branch, and judicial power to the judicial branch. These branches were designed to operate separately, each without interference from the others, except for the system of checks and balances that ties them together. The constitutional powers of each branch were intended to be exercised by that branch only, without usurpation, and without delegation. As the discussion of administrative law in Chapter 44 will indicate, the prohibition against delegation is not complete.

Checks and Balances

Even with the separation of powers, those who drafted the Constitution were not entirely confident that there could be no abuse of govern-

Checks and balances in the three branches of government

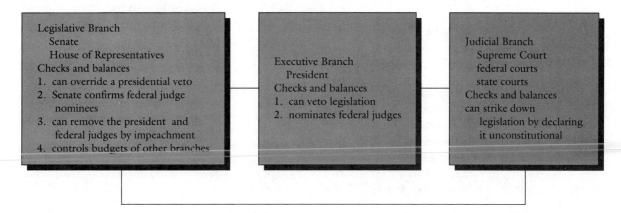

Legislative Branch
    Senate
        House of Representatives
Checks and balances
1. can override a presidential veto
2. Senate confirms federal judge
        nominees
3. can remove the president and
        federal judges by impeachment
4. controls budgets of other branches

Executive Branch
    President
Checks and balances
1. can veto legislation
2. nominates federal judges

Judicial Branch
    Supreme Court
        federal courts
        state courts
Checks and balances
can strike down
        legislation by declaring
        it unconstitutional

mental power. In addition, they built into the Constitution certain provisions by which each branch would have some limited control over the others. That is, each branch would have a check on the powers of the other two, and total governmental power would be balanced among the three branches. This, perhaps, is evidenced most clearly by the rights of the branches with regard to legislation.

Congress may enact legislation, but the statute may be vetoed by the president or held unconstitutional by the courts. Of course, Congress may vote to override any presidential veto and can overcome a court decision holding legislation unconstitutional by passing new legislation that avoids the problem the court felt was fatal. Other checks and balances include the fact that judges of the federal courts are selected by the president with the advice and consent of the Senate, and Congress has the power to remove the president and federal judges from office by impeachment.

Federalism

A further division of governmental power was accomplished by adopting a federal concept. Under **federalism**, the central government is one of **enumerated powers**, which means that the government has only those powers expressly granted

to it by the Constitution. The remaining powers are reserved to the states. Thus, the federal government has certain exclusive powers, such as regulating interstate commerce, coining money, and controlling bankruptcies. The states retain certain exclusive powers, such as controlling purely intrastate commerce, directing the disposition of property located within their respective borders (except that which is federally owned), and regulating marriage and divorce. Other powers, such as taxation, are shared by the states and the federal government. Although we commonly refer to the United States government as "the federal government," more accurately the federal government of the United States consists of the central government, the states, and state subdivisions.

The Republic

Although the United States frequently is referred to as a *democracy*, in fact it is a **republic**. True democracy means a "town-hall" method of governing. All of the people vote on every issue. Democracy is an ideal concept, but it is workable only in small units, and certainly not in a society as large as ours. Therefore, in order to have a say in the detailed operation of the government, citizens elect representatives who act for them in these matters. However, because of the devotion people have to the ideal of democracy, we often refer to our system as a *representative democracy*.

JUDICIAL INTERPRETATION

The constitutional role of the Supreme Court has long been the subject of heated debate. Exactly what it originally was intended to be is unclear. The ambiguity is because, more often than not, the powers granted in the Constitution are broad and general; their precise limits are unclear. Also, by nature, the English language is not precise. What is clear, however, is that in 1803, in *Marbury v. Madison*, the Supreme Court rightfully or wrongfully assumed the power to interpret the Constitution, and that prerogative has been retained to this day. Chief Justice John Marshall, speaking for the whole Court, without dissent or separate opinion (which previously had been the custom of the Court), declared that the Constitution was not intended to be a "solemn mocker." It means what it says, it is the supreme law of the land, and the Supreme Court is its interpreter.

In 1970, Senator Sam J. Ervin, Jr., and United States Attorney General Ramsey Clark debated the issue of the Supreme Court's power to interpret the Constitution at the Madison Hotel in Washington, D.C. Senator Ervin vigorously argued that the Supreme Court was intended to be a tribunal that decided disputes, not a policymaker, and that, constitutionally, the making of policy was limited to the people by constitutional amendment, and to the legislative branch by legislative act. He stated:

> Those who champion or seek to justify the activism of the Warren Court assert with glibness that the Constitution is a living document which the Court must interpret with flexibility. When they say the Constitution is a living document, they really mean that the Constitution is dead, and that activist justices as its executors may dispose of its remains as they please. I submit that the Constitution is, indeed, a living document, its words are binding on those who pledge themselves by oath or affirmation to support it.

Attorney General Clark, just as vigorously, argued that the Supreme Court should "interpret" the Constitution according to the times, and that its words should not be given a single meaning regardless of changes in society's needs and circumstances. He stated:

> We demean the Constitution of the United States by this endless Metaphysical debate over 'strict construction.' There are constitutional issues to be faced, perhaps even constitutional crises. They will require all the vision and courage we can muster. The false notion that men who wrote those words 183 years ago—a distant age—could foresee the unforeseeable, or that we can look back and in words alone, or from their intent in the context of 1787, divine the author's precise meaning as applied to current facts is contrary to all human experience. . . .
>
> . . . The crises which we face today, the great constitutional questions which are put to the Supreme Court for resolution are far more difficult. Mass society, urban poverty, racism, vast industry, huge labor unions, tall skyscrapers, automobiles, jet aircraft, television, nuclear energy, environmental pollution, mass assemblies and protests, and the interdependence of nations and individuals create issues undreamed of in the philosophies of the Founding Fathers.
>
> The Constitution guides by general principle—a light that recognizes the existence of change. By its very nature it must embody a whole theory in a quick phrase—to regulate commerce—the general welfare—due process of law—the equal protection of the laws. . . . If it were to be specific, it could not be a constitution nor hope to maintain a theory and framework of government with general powers and limitations.

QUESTIONS FOR THOUGHT. In assessing the merits and the demerits of the two conflicting theories of Senator Ervin and Attorney General Clark, consider: (1) How do *interpretation, adjudication,* and *policy-making* differ? (2) Is the method of amendment provided for in the Constitution really a sufficient vehicle for changing the Constitution? (3) Should Supreme Court justices—nonelected public officials—be empowered to change the meaning of the Constitution?

THE COMMERCE CLAUSE

Of all of Congress's powers, the most comprehensive in terms of business regulation is the **Commerce Clause**, Article I, Section 8, Clause 3: *"The Congress shall have the power . . . To regulate commerce with foreign Nations: and among the several States; and with Indian Tribes."* During the first forty years after the Constitution was adopted, little attention was paid to this provision, although it undoubtedly was considered one of the most important by the framers. Then, in 1842, the Supreme Court was called upon to define "commerce among the several states" in *Gibbons v. Ogden.*

GIBBONS v. OGDEN
22 U.S. 9, 6 L.Ed. 23 (1824)

This was an action by Aaron Ogden (Plaintiff/Respondent) against Thomas Gibbons (Defendant/Appellant) for an order enjoining Gibbons from operating his steamboats between New Jersey and the city of New York. The ground for his request was that Ogden was the assignee of an exclusive right to navigate the waters in question. The exclusive right originally was granted to Robert R. Livingston and Robert Fulton by several acts of the legislature of the state of New York. The validity of the assignment was not in question. However, Defendant challenged the constitutionality of the acts of the legislature in granting these exclusive rights given Congress's power to regulate commerce.

The New York Court of Chancery granted a preliminary injunction, which it made permanent after a hearing. That decree was affirmed by the Court for the Trial of Impeachments and the Correction of Errors. The Supreme Court reversed with an order to dismiss the Plaintiff's action.

MARSHALL, Chief Justice.

. . . The subject to be regulated is commerce; and our constitution being, as was aptly said at the bar, one of enumeration, and not of definition, to ascertain the extent of the power it becomes necessary to settle the meaning of the word. The counsel for the appellee would limit it to traffic, to buying and selling, or the interchange of commodities, and do not admit that it comprehends navigation. This would restrict a general term, applicable to many objects, to one of its significations. Commerce, undoubtedly, is traffic, but it is something more; it is intercourse. It describes the commercial intercourse between nations, and parts of nations, in all its branches, and is regulated by prescribing rules for carrying on that intercourse. The mind can scarcely conceive a system for regulating commerce between nations, which shall exclude all laws concerning navigation, which shall be silent on the admission of the vessels of the one nation into the ports of the other, and be confined to prescribing rules for the conduct of individuals, in the actual employment of buying and selling, or of barter.

If commerce does not include navigation, the government of the Union has no direct power over that subject, and can make no law prescribing what shall constitute American vessels, or requiring that they shall be navigated by American seamen. Yet this power has been exercised from the commencement of the government, has been exercised with the consent of all, and has been understood by all to be a commercial regulation. All America understands, and has uniformly understood, the word "commerce" to comprehend navigation. . . .

It has, we believe, been universally admitted that these words [of the Commerce Clause, "with foreign nations, and among the several states, and with the Indian tribes"] comprehend every species of commercial intercourse between the United States and foreign nations. No sort of trade can be carried on between this country and any other, to which this power does not extend. It has been truly said, that commerce, as the word is used in the constitution, is a unit, every part of which is indicated by the term.

If this be the admitted meaning of the word, in its application to foreign nations, it must carry the same meaning throughout the sentence, and remain a unit, unless there be some plain intelligible cause which alters it.

The subject to which the power is next applied, is to commerce "among the several states." The word "among" means intermingled with. A thing which is among others, is intermingled with them. Commerce among the states cannot stop at the external boundary line of each state, but may be introduced into the interior.

It is not intended to say that these words comprehend that commerce which is completely internal, which is carried on between man and man in a state, or between different parts of the same state, and which does not extend to or affect other states. Such a power would be inconvenient, and is certainly unnecessary. . . .

But it has been urged with great earnestness, that although the power of Congress to regulate commerce with foreign nations, and among the several states, be co-extensive with the subject itself, and have no other limits than are prescribed in the constitution, yet the states may severally exercise the same power within their respective jurisdictions. In support of this argument, it is said that they possessed it as an inseparable attribute of sovereignty, before the formation of the constitution, and still retain it, except so far as they have surrendered it by that instrument; that this principle results from the nature of the government, and is secured by the tenth amendment; that an affirmative grant of power is not exclusive, unless in its own nature it be such that the continued exercise of it by the former possessor is inconsistent with the grant, and that this is not of that description. . . .

In discussing the question, whether this power is still in the states, in the case under consideration, we may dismiss from it the inquiry, whether it is surrendered by the mere grant of Congress, or is retained until Congress shall exercise the power. We may dismiss that inquiry, because it has been exercised, and the regulations which Congress deemed it proper to make, are now in full operation. The sole question is, can a state regulate commerce with foreign nations and among the states, while Congress is regulating it?

The counsel for the respondent answer this question in the affirmative, and rely very much on the restrictions in the tenth section, as supporting their opinion. They say, very truly, that limitations of a power furnish a strong argument in favor of the existence of that power, and that the section which prohibits the states from laying duties on imports or exports proves that this power might have been exercised, had it not been expressly forbidden; and, consequently, that any other commercial regulation, not expressly forbidden, to which the original power of the state is competent, may still be made.

That this restriction shows the opinion of the convention, that a state might impose duties on exports and imports, if not expressly forbidden, will be conceded; but that it follows as a consequence, from this concession, that a state may regulate commerce, with foreign nations and among the states, cannot be admitted.

Powerful and ingenious minds, taking, as postulates, that the powers expressly granted to the government of the Union are to be contracted, by construction, into the narrowest possible compass, and that the original powers of the States are retained, if any possible construction will retain them, may, by a course of well digested, but refined and metaphysical reasoning, founded on these premises, explain away the constitution of our country, and leave it a magnificent structure indeed, to look at, but totally unfit for use. . . .

Questions

1.   Under this decision, may states ever regulate matters Congress has the power to regulate?

2.   Does it matter whether Congress has chosen to exercise its power in a matter the states might seek to regulate?

Court Limitation of the Commerce Clause

In spite of the Court's broad interpretation, Congress rarely used the commerce power until it passed the Interstate Commerce Act in 1887. Beginning with that act, Congress began to exert its power under the Commerce Clause. It enacted the Sherman Act in 1890, seeking to ensure the free flow of goods in interstate commerce (see Chapter 46); the Rivers and Harbors Act in 1899, seeking to prevent blockages of interstate waterways; and the Clayton Act of 1914, seeking to reinforce the intent of the Sherman Act (see Chapter 47). This expansion of Congress's use of the Commerce Clause power came to an abrupt halt in 1918, when the Supreme Court decided *Hammer v. Dagenhart*.

Congress had enacted a statute prohibiting the interstate transportation of goods manufactured with the use of child labor. The Court in *Hammer v. Dagenhart* held the statute unconstitutional, concluding that Congress was seeking to control

the elements of the manufacturing process, and manufacturing was a totally intrastate activity. This strict construction, and consequent limitation, of Congress's authority under the Commerce Clause continued until the New Deal years.

Court Expansion of Congressional Commerce Power

With the Great Depression, beginning in 1929, came increased recognition of the need for federal control over the business sector. During the first years of the New Deal, Congress enacted many statutes increasing federal control of business and the welfare of labor, including the Unemployment Compensation Act of 1933, the Social Security Act of 1935, and the Fair Labor Standards Act of 1938. During this period, Congress had attempted to control business and labor comprehensively by enacting the National Industrial Recovery Act of 1933. The Court held this act to be unconstitutional in *Schechter Poultry Corp. v. U.S.*, a 1935 landmark decision. Congress's enactment of the N.I.R.A. exceeded its limits under the Commerce Clause. In response to this defeat, however, Congress almost immediately enacted the Wagner Act (the beginning of the National Labor Relations Act). The consitutionality of this statute was upheld by the Court in another landmark decision, *N.L.R.B. v. Jones & Laughlin Steel Corp.* In this case, the Court ruled the Wagner Act constitutional. More important, however, the decision broadened Congress's authority under the Commerce Clause, holding that Congress has the power to regulate not only matters involved in interstate commerce but also those that have a close and substantial relationship to interstate commerce. As a result of this decision, the federal government acquired the power to control almost any matter it wishes under the notion of a rela-

tionship with commerce. Many activities that are not "involved in" interstate commerce may be found to have some substantial relationship to interstate commerce. This, the Court held, included the totally intrastate activity of manufacturing as long as raw materials used in the manufacturing process came from across state lines, or the finished product was shipped in interstate commerce. Suppose, however, the manufacturing process was totally intrastate, using only raw materials from within the state, and direct sales were only within state boundaries. What then?

The Present Status of Commerce Power

The final chapter was written by the Court in 1941 in the following case.

U.S. v. DARBY

312 U.S. 100, 61 S.Ct. 451, 85 L.Ed. 609 (1941)

Defendant Fred W. Darby was indicted for violation of Section 15(a) (1), (2), and (5) of the Fair Labor Standards Act of 1938. The alleged violation involved the shipment, in interstate commerce, of goods produced by employees whose wages did not comply with the requirements of the act.

Defendant's demurrer to the indictment was sustained by the district court for the Southern District of Georgia and the indictment was quashed. Appeal was taken directly to the Supreme Court. Reversed.

STONE, Justice.

The case comes here on assignments by the Government that the district court erred in so far as it held that Congress was without constitutional power to penalize the acts set forth in the indictment, and appellee seeks to sustain the decision below on the grounds that the prohibition by Congress of those Acts is unauthorized by the commerce clause and is prohibited by the Fifth Amendment. . . .

While manufacture is not of itself interstate commerce the shipment of manufactured goods interstate is such commerce and the prohibition of such shipment by Congress is indubitably a regulation of the commerce. The power to regulate commerce is the power "to prescribe the rule by which commerce is governed." Gibbons v. Ogden. . . . It extends not only to those regulations which aid, foster and protect the commerce, but embraces those which prohibit it. . . .

The power of Congress over interstate commerce "is complete in itself, may be exercised to its utmost extent, and acknowledges no limitations other than are prescribed in the Constitution." Gibbons v. Ogden, supra. . . . Congress, following its own conception of public policy concerning the restrictions which may appropriately be imposed on interstate commerce, is free to exclude from the commerce articles whose use in the states for which they are destined it may conceive to be injurious to the public health, morals or welfare, even though the state has not sought to regulate their use. . . .

In the more than a century which has elapsed since the decision of Gibbons v. Ogden, these principles of constitutional interpretation have been so long and repeatedly recognized by this Court as applicable to the Commerce Clause, that there would be little occasion for repeating them now were it not for the decision of this Court twenty-two years ago in Hammer v. Dagenhart. . . . In that case it was held by a bare majority of the Court over the powerful and now classic dissent of Mr. Justice Holmes setting forth the fundamental issues involved, that Congress was without power to exclude the products of child labor from interstate commerce. The reasoning and conclusion of the Court's opinion there cannot be reconciled with the conclusion which we have reached, that the power of Congress under the Commerce Clause is plenary [broad and complete] to exclude any article from interstate commerce subject only to the specific prohibitions of the Constitution.

Hammer v. Dagenhart has not been followed. The distinction on which the decision was rested that Congressional power to prohibit interstate commerce is limited to articles which in themselves have some harmful or deleterious property—a distinction which was novel when made and unsupported by any provision of the Constitution—has long since been abandoned. . . .

Congress, having by the present Act adopted the policy of excluding from interstate commerce all goods produced for the commerce which do not conform to specified labor standards, . . . may choose the means reasonably adapted to the attainment of the permitted end, even though they involve control of intrastate activities. Such legislation has often been sustained with respect to powers, other than the commerce power granted to the national government, when the means chosen, although not themselves within the granted power, were nevertheless deemed appropriate aids to the accomplishment of some purposes within an admitted power of the national government. . . .

Our conclusion is unaffected by the Tenth Amendment which provides: "The powers not delegated to the United States by the Constitution nor prohibited by it to the states are reserved to the states respectively or to the people." The amendment states but a truism that all is retained which has not been surrendered. There is nothing in the history of its adoption to suggest that it was more than declaratory of the relationship between the national and state governments as it had been established by the Constitution before the amendment or that its purpose was other than to allay fears that the new national government might seek to exercise powers not granted, and that the states might not be able to exercise fully their reserved powers. . . .

Since our decision in West Hotel Co. v. Parrish . . . it is no longer open to question that the fixing of a minimum wage is within the legislative power and that the bare fact of its exercise is not a denial of due process under the Fifth more than under the Fourteenth Amendment. Nor is it any longer open to question that it is within the legislative power to fix maximum hours. . . . Similarly the statute is not objectionable because applied alike to both men and women. . . .

The Act is sufficiently definite to meet constitutional demands. One who employs persons, without conforming to the prescribed wage and hour conditions, to work on goods which he ships or expects to ship across state lines, is warned that he may be subject to the criminal penalties of the Act. No more is required. . . .

Questions

1. How did the decision in this case differ from the decision in *Gibbons v. Ogden* concerning the limits of Congress's authority over interstate commerce?

2. After the decision in this case, what areas of commerce are left to the states to control?

Since the *Darby* decision, congressional authority under the Commerce Clause has gone largely unchallenged. The language of the Court makes it clear that almost any activity may be found, in some way, to affect interstate commerce. Under the Fair Labor Standards Act itself, even if a particular enterprise is not covered because of an insubstantial connection to interstate commerce, certain employees of that enterprise still may be covered if they regularly use interstate communications, such as the mail or the telephone, in conducting business.

THE FIRST AMENDMENT

The **First Amendment** consists of a cluster of rights that allow individual choice by each person; the freedoms of thought, belief, and expression. It states: "Congress shall make no law respecting an establishment of religion, or prohibiting the free exercise thereof; or abridging the freedom of speech, or of the press; or the right of the people peaceably to assemble, and to petition the Government for a redress of grievances." In its original form, as it passed the House of Representatives, this amendment contained language making its prohibitions applicable to the states as well as the federal government. The language, however,

was deleted by the Senate and never restored. But as will be discussed later in this chapter, the restrictions of the First Amendment and other key amendments now are made applicable to the states by virtue of the Fourteenth Amendment.

Freedom of Speech as a Relative Right

The right to express one's opinion, and even to persuade others to adopt a particular position, is inherent in a democratic system. It has been called "The Greatest Freedom." However, as is true of all other rights, freedom of expression is not absolute. The right to speak freely ends at the point at which it becomes an unreasonable infringement on the rights of others. Thus, defamatory statements (libel and slander) will result in liability to an injured party. The use of offensive and obscene language in public may be enjoined as an unreasonable invasion of the peace. Speech that presents a "clear and present danger" to the security of the nation also may be prohibited, such as statements made to obstruct military recruitment or to cause insubordination during times of war. As stated by Justice Holmes in *Schenck v. United States*, "The most stringent protection of free speech would not protect a man in falsely shouting fire in a theatre and causing panic." However, if the theater were empty or actually on fire, there would be no basis for prohibiting the utterance.

Protection of Commercial Speech

Although the First Amendment long has been held to protect free speech in a great variety of situations, including protest against governmental actions even in times of war, advertising has not always been so vigorously protected. As recently as 1942 the Supreme Court drew this distinction in *Valentine v. Chrestensen*. Chrestensen was charged with distribution of advertising leaflets on the streets, in violation of an ordinance. Later, he reprinted them with his advertisements on one side and a protest against the ordinance on the other. The Court, finding the ordinance valid and that Chrestensen's intent in printing the protest was to evade the ordinance, held against Chrestensen, stating that commercial speech was not entitled to First Amendment protection.

During the next thirty-three years, the Court's unanimous opinion in Chrestensen remained the law, with some erosion when the Court granted protection to paid political advertisements (*New York Times v. Sullivan*, 1964) and to abortion advertisements (*Bigelow v. Virginia*, 1975). Then, in the landmark case of *Virginia Pharmacy Board v. Virginia Citizens Commerce* (1976) the Court declared unconstitutional a Virginia statute that prohibited the advertising of prescription drug prices. In what may be characterized as a back-door approach, the Court held that the consuming public's "right to know competitive drug prices" outweighed the state's interest in prohibiting such advertising. Thus, the decision focused not on the right to publish advertisements, but on the right to receive the information. It was this case, then, that opened the door for a wide variety of previously prohibited professional advertising. The limits of that decision are examined in the following case.

OHRALIK v. OHIO STATE BAR ASSOCIATION
436 U.S. 447, 98 S.Ct. 1912, 56 L.Ed.2d 544 (1978)

The Ohio State Bar Association (Appellee) brought disciplinary proceedings against Albert Ohralik (Appellant) for personal solicitation of accident victims for the purpose of representing them on a contingent-fee basis. The Supreme Court of Ohio found Ohralik guilty of unethical conduct because of the alleged solicitation, and suspended him from practice indefinitely. Ohralik appealed, contending that his actions, involving commercial speech, were protected by the First and Fourteenth Amendments to the Constitution of the United States. Affirmed.

POWELL, Justice.

The solicitation of business by a lawyer through direct, in-person communication with the prospective client has long been viewed as inconsistent with the profession's ideal of the attorney-client relationship and as posing a significant potential for harm to the prospective client. It has been proscribed by the organized Bar for many years. Last Term the Court ruled that the justifications for prohibiting truthful, "restrained" advertising concerning "the availability and terms of routine legal services" are insufficient to override society's interest, safeguarded by the First and Fourteenth Amendments, in assuring the free flow of commercial information. Bates, 433 U.S., at 384,

97 S.Ct., at 2709; see Virginia Pharmacy Board v. Virginia Citizens Consumer Council, 425 U.S. 748, 96 S.Ct. 1817, 48 L.Ed.2d 346 (1976). The balance struck in Bates does not predetermine the outcome in this case. The entitlement of in-person solicitation of clients to the protection of the First Amendment differs from that of the kind of advertising approved in Bates, as does the strength of the State's countervailing interest in prohibition. . . .

Expression concerning purely commercial transactions has come within the ambit of the Amendment's protection only recently. In rejecting the notion that such speech "is wholly outside the protection of the First Amendment," Virginia Pharmacy, supra, . . . we were careful not to hold "that it is wholly undifferentiable from other forms" of speech. . . . We have not discarded the "common-sense" distinction between speech proposing a commercial transaction, which occurs in an area traditionally subject to government regulation, and other varieties of speech. . . . To require a parity of constitutional protection for commercial and noncommercial speech alike could invite dilution, simply by a leveling process, of the force of the Amendment's guarantee with respect to the latter kind of speech. Rather than subject the First Amendment to such a devitalization, we instead have afforded commercial speech a limited measure of protection, commensurate with its subordinate position in the scale of First Amendment values, while allowing modes of regulation that might be impermissible in the realm of noncommercial expression. . . .

It also is argued that in-person solicitation may provide the solicited individual with information about his or her legal rights and remedies. In this case, appellant gave Wanda Lou a "tip" about the prospect of recovery based on the uninsured-motorist clause in the McClintocks' insurance policy, and he explained that clause and Ohio's guest statute to Carol McClintock's parents. But neither of the Disciplinary Rules here at issue prohibited appellant from communicating information to these young women about their legal rights and the prospects of obtaining a monetary recovery, or from recommending that they obtain counsel. DR 2-104(A) merely prohibited him from using the information as bait with which to obtain an agreement to represent them for a fee. The Rule does not prohibit a lawyer from giving unsolicited legal advice; it proscribes the acceptance of employment resulting from such advice.

The state interests implicated in this case are particularly strong. In addition to its general interest in protecting consumers and regulating commercial transactions, the state bears a special responsibility for maintaining standards among members of the licensed professions. . . . ."The interest of the States in regulating lawyers is especially great since lawyers are essential to the primary governmental function of administering justice, and have historically been 'officers of the courts.'" Goldfarb v. Virginia State Bar. . . . While lawyers act in part as "self-employed businessmen," they also act "as trusted agents of their clients, and as assistants to the court in search of a just solution to disputes." Cohen v. Hurley. . . .

We need not discuss or evaluate each of these interests in detail as appellant has conceded that the State has a legitimate and indeed "compelling" interest in preventing those aspects of solicitation that involve fraud, undue influence, intimidation, overreaching, and other forms of "vexatious conduct." Brief for Appellant 25. We agree that protection of the public from these aspects of solicitation is a legitimate and important state interest.

Questions

1. If the advice the petitioner gave in this case really is of value to the public, is it realistic to assume that such information will flow freely if attorneys are *not* permitted to accept employment that might be prompted by that advice?

2. Is there really a public interest involved in prohibiting attorneys to solicit freely? Why is such solicitation considered unethical in the first place?

Free Speech Versus Private Property Rights

The Court, on numerous occasions, has dealt with other cases involving conflicts between the right of free speech and other constitutionally protected rights, including those in private property. To some extent, the Court has changed its stand both to suit the times and to suit situations.

In *Marsh v. Alabama* (1946), a case involving the distribution of religious material in a "company town," the Court held that the exercise of First Amendment liberties could not be prohibited in a place open to the public, even though it was privately owned. This line of reasoning was followed by the Court in *Amalgamated Food Employees Union Local 590 v. Logan Valley Plaza, Inc.* (1968), involving picketing, for organization purposes, of a store located in a shopping center. Then, in *Lloyd Corporation, Ltd. v. Tanner* (1972), the court reversed itself, holding that a shopping center does not become public by admitting the public for designated purposes. Thus prohibiting the distribution of antiwar literature by the owners of the shopping center did not constitute the kind of "state action" that would be a First Amendment violation. This holding was later approved in *Hudgens v. National Labor Relations Board* (1976), involving a labor dispute between a tenant of the shopping center and his employees. In this case, however, the Court left room for the possible need for accommodation between the conflicting rights. Most recently, in *Pruneyard Shopping Center v. Robins* (1980) the Court held that a state, by statute or constitutional provision, may restrict an owner of private property from prohibiting the exercise of First Amendment guarantees within reasonable limits. This case involved a California shopping center and the solicitation of signatures for a United Nations resolution. Thus, private property rights receive protection, even if the property is open for restricted public use. However, this protection may be removed by need or state law.

Other First Amendment Protections

In addition to providing for freedom of speech, the First Amendment protects other fundamental rights, including freedom of religion, freedom of the press, freedom of assembly, and the right to petition the government for redress of grievances. The last two rights ordinarily are not raised in a business context. Freedom of assembly sometimes becomes a question in cases involving picketing (the dissemination of information, often involving a labor or consumer dispute) and attendant patrolling (the physical presence of pickets). For example, courts are entitled to determine how many pickets may be present at a location. The question they must decide in each case is how many are needed to provide the necessary information without becoming a physical blockade or unreasonably intimidating. Although court-ordered limitations infringe on an absolute freedom of assembly, this freedom, as is true of all rights, is not absolute.

Freedom of religion has been involved in a substantial number of business-related cases, most frequently in those affecting rights of employees. For example, may the government require an employee to contribute to Social Security if his religion teaches that he should not accept Social

Security benefits? Should an employee be required, by Occupational Safety and Health Administration rules, to wear a hard hat if doing so would be against her religion? May an employer refuse to hire an applicant or discharge an employee on the basis of a rule that all employees must be clean-shaven, or because the person refuses to work on Saturday, when the requirements conflict with the tenets of the applicant's or employee's religion? With certain qualifications, the Supreme Court has answered *no* to the first two questions, and *yes* to the other two. In all such cases, courts have given great deference to freedom of religion, but have balanced the constitutionally mandated protection of that freedom against considerations of public policy and of the right of an employer to impose reasonable employee requirements.

DUE PROCESS

Due process of law may be defined as "fundamental fairness." The importance of due process is that any governmental action that involves taking private property for public use or depriving any other individual right is constitutional only if it is fair to do so (**substantive due process**), and if the means of taking ensures an opportunity for the rights of the individual to be fairly considered (**procedural due process**). The constitutional mandates of due process are found in the Fifth and Fourteenth Amendments. These amendments test the legitimacy of every action by the federal government (**Fifth Amendment**), and the governments of the states and their subdivisions (**Fourteenth Amendment**).

The Fourteenth Amendment

The first ten amendments to the Constitution of the United States, collectively, are referred to as the **Bill of Rights**. When adopted, their prohibitions applied only to actions of the federal government. With the enactment of the Fourteenth Amendment, in particular its due process provi-

sion, some parts of the Bill of Rights were interpreted as incorporated into the Fourteenth Amendment and thus act as limitations on the power of state and local governments. Thus, some of our most fundamental freedoms, such as speech, religion, and assembly, are protected against abuse by state and local officials. The precise extent to which this is true is not clear. Justice Hugo L. Black (1937–1971) represented one pole of the controversy. He stated that the Fourteenth Amendment was intended ". . . to extend to all the people of the nation the complete protection of the Bill of Rights. To hold that this court can determine what, if any, provisions of the Bill of Rights will be enforced, and if so to what degree, is to frustrate the great design of a written Constitution." Although certain other justices have agreed with Justice Black, this position never has been fully accepted. Most provisions of the Bill of Rights have now been incorporated on a case-by-case basis, and others undoubtedly will be in the future. Others may never be incorporated.

Public Taking of Private Property

Under the Fifth and Fourteenth Amendments, private property may not be taken by the government for public use without due process, including an opportunity for the property owner to have a full and fair hearing as to the necessity for the taking, and just compensation if the property is taken. Thus, the exercise of this right of **eminent domain** by the government may not be arbitrary or free of obligation to pay for what it takes.

Not all losses of private property for public purposes require compensation, however. The Supreme Court has interpreted the Fifth and Fourteenth Amendments to require compensation only if the loss constitutes a "taking for public use." For example, the right of the government to regulate the use of private property by prohibiting certain uses entirely (for example, gambling), or by selective regulation, as in zoning or environmental protection, does not constitute a compensable "taking." The economic loss to the owner is considered only incidental to the rightful exercise of the police power. Also, consider the circumstances of the following case. It illustrates that the courts also distinguish the "taking for public use" from the destruction of private property in the public interest.

U.S. v. CALTEX (PHILIPPINES), INC.
344 U.S. 149, 73 S.Ct. 200, 97 L.Ed. 157 (1952)

This was an action by Caltex (Philippines), Inc. and others (Plaintiff/Appellee) against the United States (Defendant/Petitioner) for compensation for the destruction of certain waterfront terminal facilities in Manila. These facilities were destroyed by the United States Army as it retreated from the island during World War II. The reason for destroying the facilities was to prevent them from falling into the hands of the enemy. Plaintiffs contended they were due compensation under the Fifth Amendment to the Constitution of the United States.
   Plaintiffs' claim was allowed by the United States Court of Claims. Reversed.

VINSON, Chief Justice.

As reflected in the findings of the Court of Claims, there were two rather distinct phases of Army operations in the Pandacan District in December 1941. While the military exercised considerable control over the business operations of respondents' terminals during the period between December 12 and December 26, there was not, according to the findings below, an assumption of actual physical or proprietary dominion over them during this period. Bound by these findings, respondents do not now question the holding of the Court of Claims that prior to December 27 there was no seizure for which just compensation must be paid.

Accordingly, it is the legal significance of the events that occurred between December 27 and December 31 which concerns us. Respondents concede that the Army had a right to destroy the installations. But they insist that the destruction created a right in themselves to exact fair compensation from the United States for what was destroyed.

The argument draws heavily from statements by this Court in Mitchell v. Harmony (US) 13 How 115, 14 L ed 75 (1855), and United States v. Russell (US) 13 Wall 623, 20 L ed 474 (1871). We agree that the opinions lend some support to respondents' view. But the language in those two cases is far broader than the holdings. Both cases involved equipment which had been impressed by the Army for subsequent use by the Army. In neither was the Army's purpose limited, as it was in this case, to the sole objective of destroying property of strategic value to prevent the enemy from using it to wage war the more successfully.

A close reading of the Mitchell and Russell Cases shows that they are not precedent to establish a compensable taking in this case. Nor do those cases exhaust all that has been said by this Court on the subject. In United States v. Pacific R. Co. 120 US 227, 30 L ed 634, 7 S Ct 490 (1887), Mr. Justice Field, speaking for a unanimous Court, discussed the question at length. That case involved bridges which had been destroyed during the war between the states by a retreating Northern Army to impede the advance of the Confederate Army. Though the point was not directly involved, the Court raised the question of whether this act constituted a compensable taking by the United States and answered it in the negative:

> The destruction or injury of private property in battle, or in the bombardment of cities and towns, and in many other ways in the war, had to be borne by the sufferers alone as one of its consequences. Whatever would embarrass or impede the advance of the enemy, as the breaking up of roads, or the burning of bridges, or would cripple and defeat him, as destroying his means of subsistence, were lawfully ordered by the commanding general. Indeed, it was his imperative duty to direct their destruction. The necessities of the war called for and justified this. The safety of the state in such cases overrides all considerations of private loss. . . .

The terse language of the Fifth Amendment is no comprehensive promise that the United States will make whole all who suffer from every ravage and burden of war. This Court has long recognized that in wartime many losses must be attributed solely to the fortunes of war, and not to the sovereign. No rigid rules can be laid down to distinguish compensable losses from noncompensable losses. Each case must be judged on its own facts. But the general principles laid down in the Pacific Railroad Case seem especially applicable here. Viewed realistically, then, the destruction of respondents' terminals by a trained team of engineers in the face of then impending seizure by the enemy was no different than the destruction of the bridges in the Pacific Railroad Case. Adhering to the principles of that case, we conclude that the court below erred in holding that respondents have a constitutional right to compensation on the claims presented to this Court.

Questions

1.   Did the fact that the action here in question was taken during wartime have any affect on the Court's decision?

2.   Should the right of a citizen to compensation really depend on whether his or her property was taken for public use or destroyed in the public interest?

Due Process in Administrative Proceedings

Although the question of due process is raised most frequently in connection with court proceedings, the elements of due process apply equally to other governmental actions including administrative proceedings. This is important because an increasing share of governmental regulation is being accomplished through the administrative process. As discussed more fully in Chapter 46, the legislature frequently establishes broad policy by statute, under the authority of which an administrative agency makes detailed rules and sees to the day-to-day policing function. In effect, administrative agencies are *quasi-legislative* (they make rules that have the same force and effect as statutes), *quasi-executive* (they police and investigate possible violations of these rules), and *quasi-judicial* (they hold triallike hearings to decide whether a rule has been violated and, if so, what should be done to remedy the violation).

The policing of regulated businesses is an essential element of the administrative process. This includes both the inspection of records that are required to be kept and on-sight investigations. As a result, questions arise concerning the Fourth Amendment's guarantee against unreasonable searches and seizures and the Fifth Amendment's privilege against self-incrimination.

The Supreme Court has ruled that records required by law to be kept are "public records" and, as such, are not protected by the Fifth Amendment guarantee. Howver, of course, an agency may demand to inspect records only at reasonable times and at a reasonable place, unless there is a court order to the contrary. More stringent restrictions have been placed on the right of agencies to conduct physical inspections of business premises, as the following case illustrates.

MARSHALL v. BARLOW'S, INC.
436 U.S. 307, 98 S.Ct. 1816 (1978)

This was an action by Barlow's, Inc. (Plaintiff/Appellee) against Ray Marshall, secretary of labor, and others (Defendants/Appellants) seeking to enjoin the enforcement of the inspection provisions of the Occupational Safety and Health Act of 1970. The provisions in question authorized inspectors to conduct unannounced inspections of the premises and the required records of covered employers without obtaining a warrant. On the morning of September 11, 1975, Ferrol G. Barlow, Plaintiff's president, had refused to allow an inspection without a warrant. When he was ordered to comply three months later, by a court order obtained by the secretary of labor, he again refused, contending that the provision for warrantless inspection was unconstitutional.

The district court held that the Fourth Amendment required a warrant for such inspections, and the defendants appealed. Affirmed.

WHITE, Justice.

The Warrant Clause of the Fourth Amendment protects commercial buildings as well as private homes. To hold otherwise would belie the origin of that Amendment, and the American colonial experience. . . . This Court has already held that warrantless searches are generally unreasonable, and that this rule applies to commercial premises as well as homes. In Camara v. Municipal Court, . . .we held:

> Except in certain carefully defined classes of cases, a search of private property without proper consent is 'unreasonable' unless it has been authorized by a valid search warrant.

On the same day, we also ruled:

> As we explained in Camara, a search of private houses is presumptively unreasonable if conducted without a warrant. The businessman, like the occupant of a residence, has a constitutional right to go about his business free from unreasonable official entries upon his private commercial property. The businessman, too, has that right placed in jeopardy if the decision to enter and inspect for violation of regulatory laws can be made and enforced by

the inspector in the field without official authority evidenced by a warrant. *See v. City of Seattle, supra, 387 U.S., at 543, 87 S.Ct., at 1739.*

These same cases also held that the Fourth Amendment prohibition against unreasonable searches protects against warrantless intrusions during civil as well as criminal investigations. . . .

The Secretary urges that an exception from the search warrant requirement has been recognized for "pervasively regulated business(es)," United States v. Biswell, . . . (1972), and for "closely regulated" industries "long subject to close supervision and inspection." Colonnade Catering Corp. v. United States, . . . (1970). These cases are indeed exceptions, but they represent responses to relatively unique circumstances. Certain industries have such a history of government oversight that no reasonable expectation of privacy . . . could exist for a proprietor over the stock of such an enterprise. Liquor (Colonnade) and firearms (Biswell) are industries of this type; when an entrepreneur embarks upon such a business, he has voluntarily chosen to subject himself to a full arsenal of governmental regulation. . . .

The Secretary submits that warrantless inspections are essential to the proper enforcement of OSHA because they afford the opportunity to inspect without prior notice and hence to preserve the advantages of surprise. While the dangerous conditions outlawed by the Act include structural defects that cannot be quickly hidden or remedied, the Act also regulates a myriad of safety details that may be amenable to speedy alteration or disguise. The risk is that during the interval between an inspector's initial request to search a plant and his procuring a warrant following the owner's refusal of permission, violations of this latter type could be corrected and thus escape the inspector's notice. To the suggestion that warrants may be issued ex parte and executed without delay and without prior notice, thereby preserving the element of surprise, the Secretary expresses concern for the administrative strain that would be experienced by the inspection system, and by the courts, should ex parte warrants issued in advance become standard practice.

We are unconvinced, however, that requiring warrants to inspect will impose serious burdens on the inspection system or the courts, will prevent inspections necessary to enforce the statute, or will make them less effective. In the first place, the great majority of businessmen can be expected in normal course to consent to inspection without warrant; the Secretary has not brought to this Court's attention any widespread pattern of refusal. . . .

Nor is it immediately apparent why the advantages of surprise would be lost if, after being refused entry, procedures were available for the Secretary to seek an ex parte warrant and to reappear at the premises without further notice to the establishment being inspected.

Whether the Secretary proceeds to secure a warrant or other process, with or without prior notice, his entitlement to inspect will not depend on his demonstrating probable cause to believe that conditions in violation of OSHA exist on the premises. Probable cause in the criminal law sense is not required. For purposes of an administrative search such as this, probable cause justifying the issuance of a warrant may be based not only on specific evidence of an existing violation but also on a showing that "reasonable legislative or administrative standards for conducting an . . . inspection are satisfied with respect to a particular [establishment]." . . .

Finally, the Secretary urges that requiring a warrant for OSHA inspectors will mean that, as a practical matter, warrantless-search provisions in other regulatory statutes are also constitutionally infirm. The reasonableness of a warrantless search, however, will depend upon the specific enforcement needs and privacy guarantees of each statute. Some of the statutes cited apply only to a single industry, where regulations might already be so pervasive that a Colonnade-Biswell exception to the warrant requirement could apply. Some statutes already envision resort to federal-court enforcement when entry is refused, employing specific language in some cases and general language in others. In short, we base today's opinion on the facts and law concerned with OSHA and do not retreat from a holding appropriate to that statute because of its real or imagined effect on other, different administrative schemes. . . .

We hold that Barlow's was entitled to a declaratory judgment that the Act is unconstitutional insofar as it purports to authorize inspections without warrant or its equivalent and to an injunction enjoining the Act's enforcement to that extent. The judgment of the District Court is therefore affirmed.

So ordered.

Questions

1. Can you think of any industries not mentioned by the court that might have such a history of governmental oversight as to be subject to administrative inspection without a warrant?

2. Can administrative agencies really do their jobs of inspecting in the face of this warrant requirement?

Equal Protection

Another important provision of the Fourteenth Amendment, although of secondary importance to due process in the business context, is equal protection. Perhaps more than with any other constitutional right, the precise limits of equal protection are vague and have been the subject of heated debate. Because the amendment was added to the Constitution after the Civil War, many legal scholars have argued that equal protection was intended to apply only to racial discrimination. Such a limited interpretation, however, is dubious. Just as rationally, it may be assumed that this mandate was intended to apply to unreasonable discrimination of any kind by a state or local government, in that citizens should not be subject to discriminatory treatment as they travel from state to state. Otherwise, the concept of the United States as a nation, and the public policy against impediments to interstate commerce, surely would suffer.

In one way or another, most laws are discriminatory since they usually promote some special interest. Therefore, other interests suffer, if only from inattention. However, when a question of equal protection is involved, discrimination against racial minorities and other classes within the coverage of civil rights legislation is particularly suspect. Interestingly, questions of equal protection also have been at the foundation of lawsuits involving reverse discrimination (the protection of minority interests at the expense of those of nonminorities).

Civil rights legislation, both federal and state, has been directed toward protecting classes that most frequently suffer from discrimination. These have included classifications based on race, creed, color, national origin, gender, age, and more recently others such as marital status and handicap. It is virtually certain that other classes will be added in the future as it becomes clear that they also need protection.

Equal protection cases concerning racial and color discrimination arising in the business context most often have involved either public accommodations (for example, restaurants and motels) or hiring and employment practices, while those concerning the other kinds of discrimination have been limited mostly to the latter. In all cases, the issues involved tend to be complex and perplexing to businesspeople. For example, does equal protection require only nondiscriminatory treatment, or does it demand affirmative action? In either case, does the law require an employer to set aside a certain number of positions to be filled only by minorities or other protected classes? What constitutes discrimination? For example, is it discriminatory to require that an applicant for employment reveal his or her arrest record or record of convictions, or be above a certain height, or below a certain weight? What if certain discriminatory characteristics are important to fulfilling a certain job? The answers to these and other such questions are not important here. In this chapter, we are seeking to understand the anatomy of the Constitution as it is important in business. However, such questions are addressed in Chapter 52.

TAXING POWER

Article I, Section 8 of the Constitution provides: "The Congress shall have the power to lay and collect taxes . . . and provide for the . . . general welfare of the United States. . . ." Compared to the Commerce Clause, relatively few congressional enactments have been grounded on this provision. However, those that have been so grounded significantly affect business on a broad scale. The Commerce Clause empowers Congress to legislate only concerning businesses that affect interstate commerce. There is no such limitation on Congress's power to tax.

Perhaps the best-known illustration of Congress's use of this power is the Social Security Act. It affects most employment situations—both employer-employee and self-employment. The benefits are distributed for a number of purposes that potentially can follow a person from cradle to grave. For example, a child born after the death of his or her father would be entitled to support under the act until age eighteen and, if handicapped and dependent, possibly until death.

Also of broad impact is the federal unemployment insurance plan. Enacted in 1935, the federal plan provided for a tax on employers of 3 percent of each employee's wages. It was provided, however, that if an employer made contributions to a federally approved state unemployment compensation program, a credit of 2.7 of the 3 percent would be granted. It took only two years for all of the states and most of the territories to enact legislation that qualified under the federal statute. Thus, Congress was able, under its taxing power, to "encourage" the states to adopt a program that could not be mandated federally.

INTERRELATIONSHIP BETWEEN THE FEDERAL GOVERNMENT AND THE STATES

With two levels of government, federal and state, what happens when their constitutions or laws conflict? Which set of rules must be followed?

Federal Supremacy

Article VI, Clause 2 of the Constitution provides: "This constitution, and the laws of the United States which shall be made in pursuance thereof, and all treaties made, or which shall be made, under the authority of the United States, shall be the supreme law of the land; and the judges in every state shall be bound thereby, anything in the constitution or laws of any state to the contrary notwithstanding." This provision, called the **Supremacy Clause**, makes two important points. First, federal treaties, statutes, administrative rules, and court decisions are valid only if they are within the limits of the powers granted to the federal government in the Constitution. Second, all state constitutional provisions, statutes, administrative rules, and court decisions that are contrary to any of the above are void. Thus, the

United States Constitution is supreme over all. Then come other valid laws of the United States, and then state law.

Since the laws of the United States are supreme, must every state law that contravenes a federal law be struck down? Of course not. This is the first point. The federal law will prevail only if it is valid under the Constitution. The federal government, remember, is a government of enumerated and limited powers. It possesses only those powers expressed or implied in the Constitution. All other powers expressly are reserved by the states. The following case illustrates this point.

A.L.A. SCHECHTER POULTRY CORPORATION v. UNITED STATES
295 U.S. 495, 55 S.Ct. 837, 79 L.Ed. 1570 (1935)

A.L.A. Schechter Poultry Corporation and others (Defendants/Petitioners) were charged with violations of the "Live Poultry Code," which was promulgated under Section 3 of the National Industrial Recovery Act of 1933. Defendants demurred to the indictment on the ground, among others, that Section 3 of the act was unconstitutional in that it attempted to regulate areas beyond Congress's authority, specifically intrastate transactions.

The demurrer was only partially successful and Defendants were tried and convicted in the district court, and the convictions were affirmed in part by the Circuit Court of Appeals. Defendants' petition for a writ of *certiorari* was granted by the Supreme Court, which reversed the conviction.

HUGHES, Chief Justice.

First. Two preliminary points are stressed by the government with respect to the appropriate approach to the important questions presented. We are told that the provision of the statute authorizing the adoption of codes must be viewed in the light of the grave national crisis with which Congress was confronted. Undoubtedly, the conditions to which power is addressed are always to be considered when the exercise of power is challenged. Extraordinary conditions may call for extraordinary remedies. But the argument necessarily stops short of an attempt to justify action which lies outside the sphere of constitutional authority, [*sic*] Extraordinary conditions do not create or enlarge constitutional power. The Constitution established a national government with powers deemed to be adequate, as they have proved to be both in war and peace, but these powers of the national government are limited by the constitutional grants. Those who act under these grants are not at liberty to transcend the imposed limits because they believe that more or different power is necessary. Such assertions of extra-constitutional authority were anticipated and precluded by the explicit terms of the Tenth Amendment, "The powers not delegated to the United States by the Constitution, nor prohibited by it to the States, are reserved to the States respectively, or to the people." . . .

The Government also makes the point that efforts to enact State legislation establishing high labor standards have been impeded by the belief that unless similar action is taken generally, commerce will be diverted from the States adopting such standards, and that this fear of diversion has led to demands for Federal legislation on the subject of wages and hours. The apparent implication is that the Federal authority under the commerce clause should be deemed to extend to the establishment of rules to govern wages and hours in intrastate trade and industry generally throughout the country, thus overriding the authority of the States to deal with domestic problems arising from labor conditions in their internal commerce.

It is not the province of the Court to consider the economic advantages or disadvantages of such a centralized system. It is sufficient to say that the Federal Constitution does not provide for it. Our growth and development have called for wide use of the commerce power of the Federal Government in its control over the expanded activities of interstate commerce and in protecting that commerce from burdens, interferences and conspiracies to restrain and monopolize it. But the authority of the Federal Government may not be pushed to such an extreme as to destroy the distinction, which the commerce clause itself establishes, between commerce "among the several States" and the internal concerns of a state.

Questions

1. Could this law have been enacted pursuant to Congress's taxing power so as to be constitutional?

2. Would this same decision have resulted if this case had been heard after *United States v. Darby* (1941), presented earlier in this chapter?

Exclusiveness of Federal Power

When the Constitution empowers the federal government to regulate on a particular subject, this does not mean that state laws on that subject are preempted in every case. Federal statutes sometimes expressly provide that the states may act. This is the case with the Federal Unemployment Tax Act and also the federal Occupational Safety and Health Act. Both statutes invited the states to enact comparable legislation, and if this was done, the federal acts would defer to those state laws. Some federal statutes set minimum standards, and the states are permitted to enact "tougher" regulations. Examples are the minimum-wage and maximum-hour provisions of the federal Fair Labor Standards Act. Many federal statutes assume jurisdiction in particular areas, and then create exempt classes that are subject to state control. This is done in the Fair Labor Standards Act by defining "covered enterprise" in terms of a certain volume of business. Under the National Labor Relations Act, the regulatory agency (National Labor Relations Board) imposes minimum size for employers covered under the act. In addition, the act allows individual states to determine the validity of certain union security clauses, such as "union shop" and "agency shop."

However, what if Congress is silent on the subject? Does that mean the states may legislate and regulate the area? The answer is "maybe." Some subjects are reserved *exclusively* for Congress, and others are open to the states, within limits, until Congress acts. Although the federal power to coin money and regulate bankruptcies is exclusive, its power to lay and collect taxes obviously is not. What about the power to regulate interstate commerce? In this area, the dividing line between exclusivity and the states' rights is not precise. It is clear that a state is entitled to regulate within the limits of its police power even if, in doing so, interstate commerce is affected, but not if the regulation unreasonably obstructs or burdens interstate commerce. The courts use a balancing test, weighing the states' interests against the need for uniformity of regulation and the burden on interstate commerce. The test is discussed in the following case.

PIKE v. BRUCE CHURCH, INC.
397 U.S. 137, 90 S.Ct. 844, 25 L.Ed.2d 174 (1970)

This was an action by Bruce Church, Inc. (Plaintiff/Appellee) against Loren J. Pike and others (Arizona state officials) to enjoin enforcement of a provision of the Arizona Fruit and Vegetable Standardization Act prohibiting Plaintiff's transportation of uncrated cantaloupes from its Arizona ranch in Parker to a nearby California city for sorting and distribution. Compliance with the provision would require an expenditure of approximately $200,000 to build a packing facility in Arizona. Plaintiff contended that the provision constituted an unlawful burden on interstate commerce.

The district court granted judgment for the Plaintiff, making its preliminary injunction permanent, and Defendants appealed. Affirmed.

STEWART, Justice.

Although the criteria for determining the validity of state statutes affecting interstate commerce have been variously stated, the general rule that emerges can be phrased as follows: Where the statute regulates even-handedly to effectuate a legitimate local public interest, and its effects on interstate commerce are only incidental, it will be upheld unless the burden imposed on such commerce is clearly excessive in relation to the putative local benefits. . . . If a legitimate local purpose is found, then the question becomes one of degree. And the extent of the burden that will be tolerated will of course depend on the nature of the local interest involved, and on whether it could be promoted as well with a lesser impact on interstate activities. . . .

At the core of the Arizona Fruit and Vegetable Standardization Act are the requirements that fruits and vegetables shipped from Arizona meet certain standards of wholesomeness and quality, and that they be packed in standard containers in such a way that the outer layer or exposed portion of the pack does not "materially misrepresent" the quality of the lot as a whole. The impetus for the Act was the fear that some growers were shipping inferior or deceptively packaged produce, with the result that the reputation of Arizona growers generally was being tarnished and their financial return concomitantly reduced. It was to prevent this that the Act was passed in 1929. The State has stipulated that its primary purpose is to promote and preserve the reputation of Arizona growers by prohibiting deceptive packaging.

We are not, then, dealing here with "state legislation in the field of safety where the propriety of local regulation has long been recognized," or with an Act designed to protect consumers in Arizona from contaminated or unfit goods. Its purpose and design are simply to protect and enhance the reputation of growers within the State. These are surely legitimate state interests. . . .

But application of the Act through the appellant's order to the appellee company has a far different impact, and quite a different purpose. The cantaloupes grown by the company at Parker are of exceptionally high quality. The company does not pack them in Arizona and cannot do so without making a capital expenditure of approximately $200,000. It transports them in bulk to nearby Blythe, California, where they are sorted, inspected, packed, and shipped in containers that do not identify them as Arizona cantaloupes, but bear the name of their California packer. The appellant's order would forbid the company to pack its cantaloupes outside Arizona, not for the purpose of keeping the reputation of its growers unsullied, but to enhance their reputation through the reflected good will of the company's superior produce. The appellant, in other words, is not complaining because the company is putting the good name of Arizona on an inferior or deceptively packaged product, but because it is not putting that name on a product that is superior and well packaged. As the appellant's brief puts the matter, "It is within Arizona's legitimate interest to require that interstate cantaloupe purchasers be informed that this high quality Parker fruit was grown in Arizona".

Although it is not easy to see why the other growers of Arizona are entitled to benefit at the company's expense from the fact that it produces superior crops, we may assume that the asserted state interest is a legitimate one. But the State's tenuous interest in having the company's cantaloupes identified as originating in Arizona cannot constitutionally justify the requirement that the company build and operate an unneeded $200,000 packing plant in the state. . . .

But in Toomer v. Witsell . . . the Court indicated that such a burden upon interstate commerce is unconstitutional even in the absence of such a purpose. In Toomer the Court held invalid a South Carolina statute requiring that owners of shrimp boats licensed by the State to fish in the maritime belt off South Carolina must unload and pack their catch in that State before "shipping or transporting it to another State." What we said there applies to this case as well:

> There was also uncontradicted evidence that appellants' costs would be materially increased by the necessity of having their shrimp unloaded and packed in South Carolina ports rather than at their home bases in Georgia where they maintain their own docking, warehousing, refrigeration and packing facilities. In addition, an inevitable concomitant of a statute requiring that work be done in South Carolina, is to divert to South Carolina, even though that be economically disadvantageous to the fishermen, employment and business which might otherwise go to Georgia; the necessary tendency of the statute is to impose an artificial rigidity on the economic pattern of the industry. . . .

While the order issued under the Arizona statute does not impose such rigidity on an entire industry, it does impose just such a straitjacket on the appellee company with respect to the allocation of its interstate resources. Such an incidental consequence of a regulatory scheme could perhaps be tolerated if a more compelling state interest were involved. But here the State's interest is minimal at best—certainly less substantial than a State's interest in securing employment for its people. If the Commerce Clause forbids a State to require work to be done within its jurisdiction to promote local employment, then surely it cannot permit a State to require a person to go into a local packing business solely for the sake of enhancing the reputation of other producers within its borders.

Questions

1. Would the Arizona statute be constitutional if its application had been restricted to cantaloupes identifying Arizona as the place they were grown?
2. Would the statute have been upheld if Arizona had alleged some heath-related reason for its enactment?

SUMMARY

All legal systems in the United States are based on written constitutions, one for the federal government and one for each state. The overall purposes of a constitution are to organize the government, to define its powers, and to protect the rights of the people from the unlimited, arbitrary exercise of power by the government. It should be clear at the outset that a constitution does not regulate the rights of one person vis-à-vis another person, but only the relationship between the individual and the government. Any action taken by the government, then, is valid only if it is within the limits of the powers granted to that government by the constitution.

The Constitution of the United States is unique. It provides for a federal form—a strong central government with residual, although important, powers retained by the states. It establishes a government that exists only by the consent of the governed. Its powers are divided among the three branches, with a system of checks and balances among the branches, and it is operated through elected representatives.

Questions arising under the Constitution are adjudicated by the courts, with ultimate authority resting with the United States Supreme Court. Whether the Court is empowered only to interpret the Constitution strictly as written, or to consider the changing needs of society, is a subject of ongoing controversy. During recent years, however, the Court has followed the latter course more frequently.

Among the more important provisions of the Constitution as they relate to the regulation of business are the Commerce Clause, the free-speech guarantees of the First Amendment, the Fifth and Fourteenth Amendment due-process provisions, and the taxing power. Of these, perhaps the single most important is the Commerce Clause, closely followed by the Fourteenth Amendment.

The Supremacy Clause of the Constitution provides a hierarchy of dominance for the laws in the United States. In rank order, they are the Constitution of the United States, laws of the United States validly promulgated under the Constitution, and finally state laws. Thus, any state law in conflict with a valid federal law or the United States Constitution is of no force or effect. The same is true of any federal law in conflict with the Constitution.

The powers granted to the federal government sometimes are exclusive, and sometimes are not. The Constitution provides several exclusive federal powers, such as the power to coin money, and several that clearly are nonexclusive, such as the taxing power. Federal legislation frequently expressly permits state action, as in the Occupational Safety and Health Act of 1970 and the wage and hour provisions of the Fair Labor Standards Act. Under the Commerce Clause, the power to regulate all matters affecting interstate commerce is recognized as nonexclusive, but the dividing line between federal and state powers is not precise when the federal government is silent on a matter. The relative state and federal rights are determined by weighing the state interests against the burden they impose on interstate commerce and the need for uniformity in regulation.

KEY TERMS AND CONCEPTS

constitution
sovereignty
separation of powers
checks and balances
federalism
enumerated powers
republic
Commerce Clause
First Amendment
substantive due process
procedural due process
Fifth Amendment
Fourteenth Amendment
Bill of Rights
eminent domain
Supremacy Clause

PROBLEMS

1. The city of New York Landmark Protection Commission designated Grand Central Station a historical landmark. Because of this designation, any alterations to the structure required approval of the commission. Penn Central Transportation, owner of Grand Central Station, wanted to con-struct a fifty-story office complex above the station, but the commission refused to grant permission, and offered to allow Penn Central to trade its property rights in the air space above the station for any other tract of city-owned land in the area on which its office complex could be constructed. Penn Central contended that the commission's action was an unconstitutional taking of its property without just compensation. Is Penn Central correct?

2. Emilee Harrison felt that she had been injured by the malpractice of a doctor and a hospital when she suffered complications following surgery. Edna Primus, an attorney for the American Civil Liberties Union, learned of this and contacted Ms. Harrison, advising her that the ACLU would represent her in a lawsuit against the doctor and the hospital. For doing so, Ms. Primus was charged with a violation of the state bar association canons of ethics, which prohibited soliciting employment. She challenged this action as unconstitutional. What was the probable result?

3. The owner of a restaurant sued to enjoin enforcement of Title II of the 1964 Civil Rights Act. It was his contention that application of the act to his business, thereby requiring that he not discriminate in serving customers, was contrary to his right to due process under the Fifth Amendment. This was grounded on the fact that his business was so small that it did not sufficiently affect interstate commerce. Should he prevail?

4. Section 524(c) of the federal Bankruptcy Act provides that one who is discharged in bankruptcy cannot be bound by a reaffirmation of discharged debts. That is, the discharge cannot be waived unless the waiver occurs before discharge, and then only with permission of the court in most cases. This section has been challenged as an unconstitutional impairment of contracts, and also on the ground that it takes away from the states their traditional right to determine the enforceability of contracts entered into within their respective boundaries. Is Section 524(c) unconstitutional?

5. A Massachusetts statute prohibited expenditures by corporations for the purpose of influencing or affecting a vote, other than one materially affecting its property or business. The statute further stated that expenditures to affect tax legislation particularly were prohibited. Is this statute in violation of the constitutional rights, if any, of corporations?

6. An Oklahoma statute allowed the sale of 3.2 percent beer to females at age 18 and males at age 21. This was challenged as an unconstitutional denial of equal protection under the Fourteenth Amendment. Should this challenge succeed?

7. Perez was involved in an automobile accident. As a result of the accident, she was sued for negligence, and a judgment was awarded against her. The judgment was not paid, and subsequently was discharged in bankruptcy. Nevertheless, the state of Missouri suspended Perez's operator's license pursuant to a statute providing for suspension in cases of unpaid judgments on personal injury claims. Perez challenged the constitutionality of the action on the ground that it was in violation of the Supremacy Clause. Was it?

8. Iowa enacted a statute prohibiting trucks to operate on its highways with trailers of a length of sixty-five feet or greater. This statute was challenged as an unconstitutional interference with interstate commerce. What was the result?

9. Following an accident, Schmerber was arrested for driving while intoxicated. He was taken to a hospital to attend to his injuries. While he was there, a sample of his blood was taken, without his permission, at the direction of the arresting officer. Schmerber challenged the use of the analysis of the blood sample to prove he was intoxicated, grounding his challenge on his Fifth Amendment right not to give evidence against himself in a criminal trial, and his Fourth Amendment right to be free from unreasonable searches and seizures. Should the challenge prevail?

10. A state statute permitted an abortion for an unmarried minor only (1) with the consent of both parents or, (2) if the parents would not consent, by court approval after notification of the parents. This statute was challenged as unconstitutional and contrary to the Supreme Court's ruling in *Roe v. Wade*, which upheld the right of a woman to have an abortion during the first trimester of pregnancy without fear of being prosecuted for a crime. There the court held that the woman's right to control her body exceeded any other constitutional considerations. What should the result be?

PART

II

The Common Law

Of Contracts

Of all of the areas of substantive law important in both the commercial and personal settings, contract law is perhaps the most important. Contract law addresses the question of which promises are enforceable by legal action. This concept of enforcement of certain kinds of promises transcends legal systems. It is not peculiar to the Anglo-American legal system, nor even to democratic societies. Contract law is more than substantive law; it is a social institution without which modern business could not operate in an efficient manner. Without contract law businesses could not depend on sources of products, supplies, and materials they might need in the future. Neither could they commit to sales of products to be manufactured in the future. Business could operate only on a "currently on hand" basis. A knowledge of contract law, then, enables each of us to plan our futures in reliance that promises made to us will be performed or that the law will provide redress if they are not.

Chapter | 6

Introduction to the Law of Contracts

INTRODUCTION

Any serious study of the substantive law in the commercial world must begin with the law of contracts. This body of legal principles impacts us directly or indirectly on a daily basis more than any other. During our lives we constantly will enter into contracts, discharge them, and depend on the performance of contracts entered into be-

tween others. The simple act of going to a grocery store and purchasing a loaf of bread involves the negotiation of a contract and the discharge of its obligations by the purchaser and the seller. The availability of gas, electricity, and water on a continuing basis depends on the proper performance of contracts by users and utility companies. The ability of a utility company to meet its contractual obligations to its customers depends on the performance of contracts between the utility company and others who supply it with fuel, labor, and other products and services. The ability of these suppliers to perform may depend, in turn, on other contracts being performed by those who furnish goods and services to them. The chain of contracts surrounding us in our daily affairs is endless. Thus, contract law is of prime importance in both our personal and business lives, and any-one who intends to alter his or her life by relying on a promise should make sure that the promise is enforceable under the law of contracts.

ELEMENTS OF A CONTRACT

The term *contract* has almost as many definitions as there are persons who wish to define it. William Blackstone, perhaps the best known of the early English legal scholars, wrote in his "Commentaries on the Law" that a contract might be defined as "an agreement, upon sufficient consideration, to do or not to do a particular thing." Although this definition is correct, it presumes a certain knowledge of contract law. For the purposes of our study, it probably would be better to define the term **contract** as *a promise or group of promises that the law, to some degree, regards as creating a legal obligation.*

Of greatest importance in this definition is the concept of "promise." This idea differentiates contract law from other areas of law such as tort law and criminal law. You may remember from Chapter 4 that duties in tort and criminal law arise by official imposition (operation of law); in contract law they arise only when a party voluntarily assumes them by making a promise. However, not all promises are contractual (governed by the law of contracts).

When the necessary elements of a contract are not present, the law will regard a promise as a mere "gift" promise. Although a **gift promise** may create a *moral* obligation, usually it will not be regarded as creating one that is legally enforceable. Generally the law will enforce only contractual promises, and the primary elements involved in the formation of a binding and enforceable contract are agreed to be: (1) offer, (2) acceptance, (3) consideration, (4) capacity of the parties, and (5) legal purpose.

The first two primary elements, *offer* and *acceptance*, deal with the necessity for an agreement (as does genuineness of consent) and are discussed more fully in Chapter 7. In that chapter we will concentrate on the making of promises and the parties' agreeing to their terms.

The concept of *consideration* is treated in Chapter 8 and focuses on what has been given by each party in return for the promises he or she has received. It is this exchange that makes a contract binding. This is the element that most pointedly differentiates "contractual" promises from "gift" promises.

Because every contract must involve a duty that is voluntarily and consensually assumed, the element of *capacity* is required—the parties must be mentally and otherwise capable of voluntary consent, as will be discussed in Chapter 9. Finally, the law will not recognize anything as an obligation that requires the performance of an illegal act (or a violation of public policy). The fifth element, *legal purpose*, will be discussed in Chapter 10.

These five elements form the major part of the structure of every contract, but they do not exhaust the list of concerns. Other matters of public policy must be considered. Also, some types of contracts are covered by special rules under special circumstances, such as those that are governed by the Uniform Commercial Code and those required to be in writing by virtue of the Statute of Frauds. Finally, there are procedural matters to be considered, such as general rules of evidence and specific rules like the parol evidence rule (discussed in Chapter 10).

CLASSIFICATION OF CONTRACTS

Contracts may be classified in a number of ways. It is important to understand each of these classifications in order to develop a vocabulary of commonly used terms, as well as to aid in understanding both the theory and rules of contract law. Throughout the discussions that follow, we will be referring to contracts as *simple, bilateral, executory, voidable,* and with various other terms. It will be important for you to understand both the reasons for these classifications and their effects on the rights and duties of the parties.

Valid, Void, Voidable, and Unenforceable

A contract is considered **valid** if it meets the first three of the five major elements for a contract described previously—offer, acceptance, and consideration. *Valid* is used as a "term of art" (a word or phrase that has a specific meaning in law). It simply means that these three elements were present in the agreement. It does not necessarily mean that all is well and there are no legal problems. In a **void contract**, one of these three elements is absent. A contract is classified as **voidable** if the circumstances entitle either of the parties to treat the contract as binding or to avoid performing his or her obligations thereunder. That is the case, for example, when one of the parties to the contract lacks full capacity (the fourth element). Finally, a contract is classified as **unenforceable** when there is a failure to meet the fifth element, that of legal purpose. Thus, a particular contract may be valid but also voidable and/or unenforceable. Technically, it would be incorrect to speak of a "void contract," although that term is used by many lawyers and judges. If an agreement is void, by definition it is not contractual.

It may occur to you that the terms *void* and *unenforceable* seem to be the same in effect—in neither situation will a court enforce the agreement. However, there is a subtle but important difference. In the case of a void agreement, the court will order that the parties be returned to the position they were in prior to entering into the agreement (status quo as of the time of the agreement), insofar as that is possible; in the case of an unenforceable agreement, the court generally will leave the parties in the position it finds them.

Suppose, for example, two persons agree to invest in an illegal poker game, each contributing $1000 on the understanding that one will do the playing and that they will split the profits 50-50. When the game is over, the player has won $10,000. In a lawsuit by the investor to enforce the promise to split the profits, the court will find that the agreement had an illegal purpose (gambling) and declare it unenforceable. Thus the investor will recover neither half of the profits nor the original $1000 stake. If the agreement were declared void rather than unenforceable, the court would order the return of the $1000.

Executory and Executed

A contract is classified as **executory** when one or both parties to it have not yet completely performed the obligations created by it. When both sides have completed their performance, the contract is classified as **executed**. Sometimes contracts are referred to as "partially executed," "partially executory," or "executed on one side and executory on the other." Just remember that *executed* means completed and *executory* means that some part of the obligation is yet to be completed.

Simple and Formal

A **simple contract** is one that requires offer, acceptance, and consideration in order to be valid. It is the type of agreement most generally thought of when the term *contract* is used, and is the kind of contract assumed in the above definitions of *valid* and *void*. The term **formal contract** is applied to another type of contract—one that must be in a prescribed *form* in order to be valid. Centuries ago, courts recognized only contracts "under seal." That is, a contract was valid only if it met the prescribed *form*—it had to be written and authenticated by affixing a proper seal. The seal requirement later was replaced by the requirement of consideration, and the concept of "simple" contracts emerged. Although most states no longer recognize the legal efficacy (legal effect) of the seal, there are other types of formal contracts that are very familiar to us today, the most common being the check. (Commercial paper, including checks, is discussed in Chapters 17–20.)

Concept outline: Contracts

Elements of a Contract

Offer—a proposal by an offeror to an offeree that will become legally binding upon acceptance

Acceptance—the agreement of the offeree to the proposal of the offeror

Consideration—a detriment to the promisee or benefit to the promisor that is bargained for

Capacity—the legal ability to perform an act

Legality—lawfulness

Types of Contracts

Valid—offer, acceptance, and consideration are present

Void—one of the three elements of a valid contract is missing

Voidable—may be legally annulled by one of the parties

Unenforceable—will not be enforced in a court of law

Simple—offer, acceptance, and consideration are required in order to be valid

Formal—A specific form is required in order to be valid

Unilateral—one party gives a promise, while the other party gives an act in return

Bilateral—one party makes a promise, and the other party gives a promise in return

Express—indicated by words, whether oral or written

Implied—conduct of parties and surrounding facts indicate the parties intended a contract

Executory—obligations created in the contract have not yet been completely performed

Executed—obligations in the contract have been completely performed by both parties

Noncontractual Remedies

Quasi contract—requires the payment of the reasonable value of a benefit received when no actual contract exists

Promissory estoppel—courts stop the offeror from revoking his or her promise in order to serve justice

Express and Implied

A contract may be classified as either express or implied depending on the manner in which it was created. If it came about by words, written or spoken, it is an **express contract**. If no words were used, but the conduct of the parties and the surrounding facts and circumstances indicate

that they intended a contract, it is an **implied contract**.

These terms have rather specific meanings and their definitions are mutually exclusive. However, their application is not. There are situations in which a purely implied contract may arise. For example, suppose Richie has a toothache; he is in pain, has a swollen jaw, and a towel wrapped around his face. He walks into the office of Bronski, a dentist. Richie says nothing, but Bronski, also saying nothing, sees Richie's circumstances, seats him in the operating chair, takes care of the tooth, pats Richie on the back, and sends him home. At the end of the month, Richie receives Bronski's bill for dental services. Even though nothing was said, either orally or in writing, a court probably would hold that a contract existed and that Richie owes Bronski for the services. It is clear from the facts and circumstances surrounding the event that both of them intended to enter into a contract (Bronski performed her usual professional services, and Richie willingly accepted them, with no circumstances to indicate that the services were performed as a gift).

Although we have just seen an example of a pure implied contract, as a practical matter there is no such thing as a purely express contract. If the parties in that example had entered into a long, wordy, written agreement prior to Bronski's performing the services, it really is impossible that the agreement would have left nothing to implication. For example, it might not mention that the payment would be in United States dollars, not Canadian dollars, or state precisely what law would govern the contract. However, any agreement that is entered into primarily by words may be called "express."

Bilateral and Unilateral

If you are somewhat conversant with Latin, you may note that now we will somehow classify contracts with reference to "two sides" and "one side." However, we are not referring to "one-sided contracts" as *unilateral* might be used in the vernacular. Instead, we are referring to the fact that some contracts are formed by promises on both sides, and others are formed by promises only on one side. That is, a **bilateral contract** is formed when one party makes a promise and the other party gives a promise in return. A **unilateral contract** is formed when one party gives a promise, and the other gives an act in return.

For example, suppose Taylor says to Baker, "If you *promise* to mow my lawn by Friday, I *promise* to pay you ten dollars." If Baker makes the required promise in return, a bilateral contract will be formed—Baker's promise to mow the lawn by Friday in return for Taylor's promise to pay the $10. Suppose instead that Taylor had said, "If you mow my lawn by Friday, I promise to pay you ten dollars." Now Taylor would be requesting an act (do it by Friday), not a promise, and any resulting contract would be *unilateral*—Baker's *act* of mowing the lawn by Friday in return for Taylor's promise to pay the $10.

The distinction between unilateral and bilateral is very important and must be understood in order to determine the precise moment at which the contract comes into being. In the bilateral situation, the contract exists at the moment Baker utters the requested promise. In the unilateral situation, the contract does not come into being until the requested act is performed. This difference can be critical, because neither party has any legal obligation until the contract is formed. Thus, if the above negotiations were being held on Tuesday and it was important either to Taylor that he have his lawn mowed by Friday, or to Baker that she is assured of the right to the $10 on Friday, the parties would be wise to enter into the transaction on a bilateral basis. If it is done on a unilateral basis, the lawn may not be mowed since Baker has not yet obligated herself to do the job, or Taylor may change his mind and revoke his offer, depriving Baker of the opportunity to earn the $10. As we will see in the next chapter, an offeror always has a right to revoke his or her offer at any time prior to acceptance, which would be

performance of the act in the unilateral situation.

The following section illustrates that failed attempts to accept unilateral offers can lead to problems for the parties and the courts. Because of this, accepted rules of interpretation prescribe that unless an offer is clearly unilateral, courts will interpret it as bilateral. Suppose, in the previous example, Taylor had said to Baker: "I will pay you ten dollars if you *will* mow my lawn by Friday." The word *will* is ambiguous—is Taylor requesting a promise or an act? Therefore, a court probably would hold that a promise was requested.

NONCONTRACTUAL REMEDIES

From the discussion of the evolution of our legal system in Chapter 2, you may remember that under early common law the courts were very strict. If the plaintiff did not have a cause of action that would fit neatly in one of the common-law-pleading "pigeonholes," no remedy would be available. This situation was relieved somewhat by the creation of courts of "equity" to supplement the remedies offered by the existing courts of "law." Today, in the United States, the once-separate systems of law and equity have been combined almost everywhere and, as a result, we boast that "for every wrong there is a remedy." That is, in some cases, justice may dictate that the plaintiff should recover even though applying the traditional rules of contracts (and torts) would not produce the desired result. Two theories used by the courts under these circumstances are *quasi contract* and *promissory estoppel*.

Quasi Contract

Quasi contract, based on equitable principles, found its way to the common law from the Civil (Roman) Law. **Quasi contract** is available only in cases in which no actual contract exists, and it is intended to prevent the *unjust enrichment of one party at the expense of another*. The remedy it affords is *the reasonable value of the benefits conferred*.

A quasi contract sometimes is more technically referred to as a "contract implied in law." Remember from the discussion of the classification of contracts that one of the classifications was "implied contract" (as opposed to "express contract"). More precisely, the contract referred to in that discussion is called a contract "implied *in fact*," because it is found not in the expressions of the parties, but from the surrounding *facts* and circumstances. A quasi contractual obligation to pay does not arise from the expressions of the parties, nor is it implied by the surrounding facts and circumstances. Rather, it is mandated by the desire of the courts to do justice or, to use the legal fiction, implied *in law*.

Consider our lawn-mowing case involving Taylor and Baker. Suppose they enter into the transaction on a unilateral basis—Taylor promising to Baker, "I will pay you ten dollars if you mow my lawn by Friday." Suppose further that on Friday Baker loads up her lawn mower, goes to Taylor's house, and begins mowing the lawn. When she is *almost* finished, Taylor comes out and says, "I've changed my mind—I don't want you to mow my lawn," and orders Baker to leave. At this point, there is no contract. The offer was unilateral and therefore could not be accepted until the re-quested act (mowing the lawn) was *performed completely*. Further, at this point, Baker cannot go ahead and accept the offer and form a contract because Taylor has revoked it. (Recall that, as a general rule, an offeror has a right to revoke his or her offer at any time prior to acceptance.) Although this is consistent with the common law contract rules, a question arises as to whether it would be fair or just, under the circumstances, to allow Taylor to retain the benefit of the lawn mowing without paying Baker something for her labors. If the answer is "no," a court could allow Baker to recover the reasonable value of the benefit to Taylor in an action based on quasi contract.

Note, however, that in quasi contract, as is the case with any extraordinary legal (or equitable) remedy, Baker has no *right* to a remedy as she would have had under the basic law of contracts, had a contract been formed. The courts grant extraordinary relief only when convinced that the dictates of justice demand it. Also, the amount awarded will be whatever the court deems to be the "reasonable" value of the benefit to Taylor, regardless of the amount of the loss to Baker or any amount established by the negotiations between the parties.

BLOOMGARDEN v. COYER, et al.
479 F. Supp. 201 (D.C. 1973)

This was an action by Henry S. Bloomgarden (Plaintiff/Appellant) against Charles B. Coyer and several other defendants including Coyer's business associate, Guy, to recover a finder's fee of $1,000,000 for bringing Defendants together with David Carley.

Carley was president of a corporation (PFA) that owned nearly half of another corporation that employed Plaintiff as president, Socio-Dynamics Industries, Inc. (SDI). He had requested that Plaintiff remain alert for any possible fruitful business investments in the Washington, D.C. area.

At the time, Coyer and Guy held contracts or options on several parcels of real estate on the Georgetown waterfront. Bloomgarden met Coyer in the summer of 1969 while arranging to lease office space in a building in which Coyer had an interest. At one of their meetings, Coyer revealed to Bloomgarden the details of a plan for the assembly and development of a sizable segment of the waterfront into a multipurpose business complex. Coyer explained that he and Guy lacked the financial resources needed to carry the project through, and Bloomgarden offered to put him in touch with Carley.

Bloomgarden promptly apprised Carley of Coyer's project and set up a meeting between them and others for January 26, 1970. Ideas were then exchanged but no suggestion was made by Bloomgarden to Carley or Coyer that he expected to be paid for bringing them together. By Bloomgarden's arrangement the group attended another meeting on February 19 in Chicago, with representatives of subsidiaries of Inland Steel Company.

An agreement in principle was reached between Coyer, Guy, and the Inland Steel group in early April 1970. This was formalized by a contract in June and a shareholders' agreement executed in August. Five corporations, among them Georgetown-Inland, were organized to handle the project. It was not until the end of March 1970 [*sic*; 1971], however, that Bloomgarden asserted any monetary claim on behalf of SDI for bringing about the initial contact, and it was not until May that he asked for compensation for himself. After each of these demands was rejected, Bloomgarden, on September 14, wrote to Coyer, again claiming a fee for sparking the business opportunity culminating in the Georgetown project. That likewise failing, Bloomgarden commenced his suit on October 1.

Bloomgarden sought a finder's fee on a twofold basis. He said that an agreement to pay such a fee, though not express, might be implied from the circumstances in which he brought the parties together, particularly in view of an alleged custom to reward those who discover advantageous business opportunities for others. Bloomgarden also said that in the context in which he introduced the parties, they came under a legal obligation—a quasi contract—to compensate him for his services whether or not the elements of an enforceable contract were present.

From a summary judgment granted in favor of Defendants, Plaintiff appealed. Affirmed.

ROBINSON, Circuit Judge.

[First we] examine the sufficiency of Bloomgarden's quasi-contract theory as a basis for recovery of the finder's fee which he sought. At the outset, we . . . call attention to the need for conceptual clarity. The quasi-contract, as we have said, is not really a contract, but a legal obligation closely akin to a duty to make restitution. There is, of course, no need to resort to it when the evidence sustains the existence of a true contract, either express or implied in fact. For the purpose of preventing unjust enrichment, however, a quasi-contract—an obligation to pay money to another—will be recognized in appropriate circumstances, even though no intention of the parties to bind themselves contractually can be discerned. Generally, in order to recover on a quasi-contractual claim, the plaintiff must show that the defendant was unjustly enriched at the plaintiff's expense, and that the circumstances were such that in good conscience the defendant should make restitution. Because quasi-contractual obligations rest upon equitable considerations, they do not arise when it would not be unfair for the recipient to keep the benefit without having to pay for it. Thus, to make out his case, it is not enough for the plaintiff to prove merely that he has conferred an advantage upon the defendant, but he must demonstrate that retention of the benefit without compensating the one who conferred it is unjustified. What must be resolved here is whether Bloomgarden made such a showing or evinced his capability of possibly doing so at trial.

By their very nature, the equitable principles of quasi-contracts are more difficult to apply where the court must determine whether services rendered by one person to another are to go unrewarded than where it must make that determination with respect to money or property unjustly retained. But since there is no general responsibility in quasi-contract law to pay for services *irrespective* of the circumstances in which they are carried out, a number of factual criteria have been utilized by courts to ascertain whether in a given case the defendant has undeservedly profited by the plaintiff's efforts. Thus, in situations involving personal services, it has been variously stated that a duty to pay will not be recognized where it is clear that the benefit was conferred gratuitously or officiously, or that the question of payment was left to the unfettered discretion of the recipient. Nor is compensation mandated where the services were rendered simply in order to gain a business advantage. And the courts have reached the same conclusion where the plaintiff did not contemplate a personal fee, or the defendant could not reasonably have supposed that he did. As one court has pointed out: . . . chagrin, disappointment, vexation, or supposed ingratitude cannot be used as a subsequent basis for a claim for compensation where none was originally intended or expected. Nor, we add, can an uncommunicated expectation of remuneration serve the plaintiff's purpose where the defendant had no cause to believe that such was the fact.

Thus we come full circle to the identical considerations which were dispositive of Bloomgarden's claim for recovery on an implied-in-fact contract. There simply was no basis on which a jury could rationally find that when he brought the parties together he entertained any thought of a finder's fee for himself, or that those with whom he dealt held the payment of such a fee in prospect. These circumstances defeat Bloomgarden's quasi-contract claim as well.

Questions

1. What factors do you think motivated the court to reach the result it did?

2. What would a businessperson like Bloomgarden have to do to make certain he or she receives a finder's fee?

Promissory Estoppel

This remedy was created by the equity courts and is founded on the principle that a person's words, acts, or omissions, under some circumstances, may *estop* him (close his mouth) from asserting certain rights. The elements of **promissory estoppel** are: (1) a promise was made; (2) at the time the promise was made the promisor knew, or should have known, that the promisee would change his position in reliance on the promise; (3) the promisee did change position; (4) the change was in justifiable reliance on the promise; and (5) there would be an unjust injury to the promisee if the promisor was not required to perform as promised. The remedy the courts grant in an action based on promissory estoppel, when there has been a unilateral offer, is that of *estopping* (stopping) the offeror from revoking his offer until the offeree has had a reasonable time to perform (and thus create a contract).

As in the case of quasi contract, promissory estoppel is founded on equitable principles and therefore the plaintiff has no *right* to the remedy. Unlike quasi contract, however, the remedy is not monetary relief, and it is not based on the *benefit* received by the promisor, but on the *detriment* suffered by the promisee. Also, note that although both quasi contract and promissory estoppel have been discussed as they may apply in situations of thwarted unilateral contracts, they also may apply in other kinds of situations, as when a benefit has been conferred by mistake or when a pure-gift promise has been made. In the following case, can you find each of the elements required for the application of the doctrine of promissory estoppel?

DRENNAN v. STAR PAVING COMPANY
51 Cal.2d 409, 33 P.2d 757 (1958)

This was an action by William A. Drennan (Plaintiff/Respondent) against Star Paving Company and others for damages for Defendant's refusal to honor its bid to do paving for Plaintiff.

On July 28, 1955, Plaintiff Drennan, a licensed general contractor, was engaged in bidding for a public-works construction job known as the "Monte Vista School Job" in the Lancaster school district. The bids of the general contractors for the complete construction job were required by the board of trustees of the school district to be submitted before 8:00 P.M. on July 28, 1955, in the office of the superintendent of the district. Drennan had advertised for bids to be submitted for various portions of the job that were to be subcontracted. On that day, Plaintiff received a bid from Defendant, Star Paving, which bid to do the paving work for $7131.60. Since the bid of Star Paving was the lowest bid received for the asphaltic-paving portion of the job, Drennan used it in making his final bid as general contractor and relied on the amount of the bid. Plaintiff's bid for the school job was accepted on the night of July 28, 1955. The general contract was awarded to him and thereafter he completed the job.

On the morning of July 29, 1955, Plaintiff, while on his way to Los Angeles, stopped at the office of Defendant company to talk to its representatives. The first person with whom he talked was Mr. Oppenheimer, a construction engineer employed by Defendant company. As soon as Plaintiff introduced himself, Mr. Oppenheimer told Plaintiff that there had been a mistake and that they could not do the work for the price bid. Plaintiff told Mr. Oppenheimer that he expected them to perform.

Defendant corporation refused to perform the asphaltic-paving work for any sum less than $15,000. Plaintiff then employed the L and H Paving Company to perform said work and was required to pay them the sum of $10,948.60.

From a judgment for Plaintiff in the amount of $3817 ($10,948.60 − 7131.60) and costs, Defendant appealed. Affirmed.

MUSSELL, Justice.

The trial court found, inter alia, that the Star Paving Company, through its agent K. R. Hoon, made a definite and specific offer or bid to perform the asphaltic paving portion of the Monte Vista job according to the official plans and specifications therefor for the sum of $7131.60; that in reliance upon defendant corporation's bid, plaintiff computed his final figures for said school job and submitted his bid in writing on the evening of July 28, 1955, specifically naming the defendant corporation as the subcontractor selected by him to perform said asphaltic paving work. These findings are supported by substantial evidence and cannot be here disturbed. . . .

In Wade v. Markwell & Co., 118 Cal. App.2d 410, 420, 258 P.2d 497, 502, 37 A.L.R.2d 1363, the court said, quoting from Carpy v. Dowdell, 115 Cal. 677, 687, 47 P 695: "'. . . he who, by his language or conduct, leads another to do what he would not otherwise have done, shall not subject such person to loss or injury by disappointing the expectations upon which he acted. Such change of position is sternly forbidden.'" And in Hunter v. Sparling, 87 Cal. App.2d 711, 725, 197 P.2d 807, 816, the doctrine of promissory estoppel is defined as "'A promise which the promisor should reasonably expect to induce action or forbearance of a definite and substantial character on the part of the promisee and which does induce such action or forbearance is binding if injustice can be avoided only by enforcement of the promise.'" This doctrine is applicable under the facts and circumstances shown by the record herein.

Questions

1. Would the result have been different if Star Paving had attempted to retract its bid on the afternoon of July 28, 1955?
2. Can you think of any way a businessperson, in Star's position, could avoid the risk of liability created by the doctrine of promissory estoppel?

THE UNIFORM COMMERCIAL CODE

The Uniform Commercial Code (UCC), first presented for adoption by the states in 1949, is the product of the combined efforts of the American Law Institute and the National Conference of Commissioners on Uniform State Laws. It has undergone a series of revisions since the first edition and has now been adopted in all states and the District of Columbia. Its purpose was, and is, to provide a uniform set of laws concerning commercial transactions for the entire United States. Its adoption by the states has done so with some exceptions. For example, Louisiana, whose legal system has its roots in the European Civil Law rather than the English Common Law, has not adopted Article 2 dealing with the sale of goods. Some sections of the UCC provide alternative wording, so different states may not have identical provisions in all cases (although these are few). Also, as the UCC undergoes periodic revision, some states, for a time, may retain the old version while others adopt the new.

Coverage

The UCC is composed of ten articles, each addressing a separate area of commercial transactions:

- Article 1—General Provisions, including "housekeeping" matters, general definitions, and rules of interpretation
- Article 2—Contracts involving the sale of goods
- Article 3—Commercial Paper
- Article 4—Bank Deposits and Collections
- Article 5—Letters of Credit
- Article 6—Bulk Transfers
- Article 7—Warehouse Receipts, Bills of Lading, and Other Documents of Title
- Article 8—Investment Securities
- Article 9—Secured Transactions
- Article 10—Effective Date and Repealer

Although each UCC article is distinct in its coverage, many cases involve the application of rules from more than one article.

Application

The common law rules are still in effect in all cases not covered by a conflicting UCC provision. Thus, the UCC does not apply to transactions involving only real estate or only the sale of services. In addition, even in situations covered by the UCC, there may be no UCC provisions that conflict with the common law. The UCC does not address all of the concerns that are dealt with by the common law, and also some UCC sections only restate the common law rules.

The UCC is written with equitable principles in mind, and many times the code alters the strict common-law rules to conform to common sense. Also, it imposes the obligation of "good faith" in every transaction covered by its provisions. The UCC imposes a higher legal duty on "merchants." For example, Section 2-205 provides that a merchant may be bound to his promise to hold an offer open for a period of time, even though he

has received no consideration for that promise. However, the UCC applies to nonmerchants as well, and in reading its provisions care must be taken to note which sections or parts of sections apply only to merchants (Section 2-205) or to transactions "between merchants" (Section 2-207(2)). Unless the particular section or subsection otherwise specifies, it applies equally to merchants and to nonmerchants. Finally, even in situations in which the code is not applicable, some courts have seen fit to apply its rules. This may occur either when the UCC simply has restated and perhaps clarified the common law, or when the court feels that the UCC rule is more just than existing legal precedents. Of course decisions of the latter type are constrained by the principle of *stare decisis*.

SUMMARY

The law of contracts touches the lives of most of us almost daily. Because of contract law we are able, within limits, to organize our affairs in reliance on things being done, or not being done, in the future. When a contractual promise is made and the promisor fails to perform it, the law will seek to vindicate the promisee's justifiable expectation of performance. Noncontractual or gift promises generally are not enforced by the courts.

Every contract involves one or more promises, and must comply with certain legal requirements. The required elements are *offer* and *acceptance* (mutual assent by the parties), *consideration* (something given to bind the promise of the other party), *capacity* of the parties, and *legal purpose*. In addition, some contracts are required to be in writing to be enforceable.

For the purpose of establishing common terminology for discussing contract law, contracts may be classified by type. The generally accepted classifications are: valid, void, voidable, and unenforceable; executory and executed; simple and formal;

express and implied (in fact); and bilateral and unilateral.

Although most obligations cannot be legally enforced if they are not contractual, the law does afford remedies in a few cases when justice—fairness—demands it. These cases most notably involve the doctrines of quasi contract (when there has been an unjust enrichment of one party at the expense of another) and promissory estoppel (when a party has suffered an unjust detriment in justifiable reliance on the promise of another). These are both noncontractual remedies governed by the principles of equity and, thus, are not granted freely, but only in the most deserving cases.

Most of the basic law of contracts is derived from the common law and has been developed by case decision. However, there are a number of important statutes in the area; the most notable is the Uniform Commercial Code, which establishes an almost completely uniform set of rules governing particular areas of contract law throughout the United States. To the extent that the UCC applies, it supersedes the common law. It especially is important in the context of commercial transactions, but its rules apply to laypersons as well as merchants except when the UCC specifies to the contrary.

KEY TERMS AND CONCEPTS

contract
gift promise
consideration
valid contract
void contract
voidable contract
unenforceable contract
executory contract
executed contract
simple contract
formal contract
express contract
implied contract
bilateral contract
unilateral contract
quasi contract
promissory estoppel

PROBLEMS

1. Schimmel Hotels was considering building an addition to an existing hotel. Clark & Enersen, an architectural engineering firm, asked to be allowed to submit a proposal for Schimmel's consideration. Schimmel's manager said the decision to go ahead with the project had not been made, but any proposals that were submitted would be considered. Clark & Enersen submitted blueprints and specifications, but construction never began. Later, Clark & Enersen filed suit for architectural and engineering services provided. Is Clark & Enersen entitled to recover?

2. Smith, a keno dealer at a hotel owned by Recrion Corp., presented the manager of the hotel with an idea for a recreational-vehicle park next to the hotel, and said he wanted to be paid if the idea was used. Two years later, the hotel built a park as suggested, but refused to pay Smith for the idea. Should Smith recover damages?

3. Compare and contrast the concepts of quasi contract and promissory estoppel, particularly in terms of the bases for applying each and the remedies provided.

4. A contract may be valid but a court still may not enforce it. Under what circumstances might this occur?

5. Ms. Richardson entered into a written contract with J. C. Flood Co. to repair a clog in a water pipe leading to her house. After excavating to remove the clog, it was discovered that one of the water pipes was defective and leaky. Although the contract did not provide for replacement of pipes, Flood replaced the defective section. Ms. Richardson knew this was being done and said nothing, but later she refused to pay for the pipe or the work involved in installing it. Should Flood recover?

6. Suppose Taylor says to Baker, "If you will mow my lawn, I will pay you fifteen dollars," and Baker says, "Okay." Is a contract formed? If so, is it unilateral or bilateral? In the case of a contract, why is it important to know whether it is unilateral or bilateral?

7. Miller leased a supper club to Overmeier. After operating for a short time, Overmeier contracted with Palmer to resurface the parking lot. When the work was completed, Overmeier failed to pay, and ultimately filed for bankruptcy. Palmer sued Miller for the value of the work done on his property. Is Palmer entitled to recover?

Mutual Assent

INTRODUCTION

As discussed in Chapter 6, every contract involves one or more promises and looks toward their performance in the future. This chapter explores the concept that contractual promises must be agreed to voluntarily by both parties. The very essence of contract law is that we have obligations that were voluntarily assumed (as opposed to ob-

ligations imposed by the legal system, as in tort law and criminal law). Therefore, for a contract to come into being, both parties must objectively manifest their willingness to enter into the contract (to be *legally* obligated to perform their respective promises) on a definite set of terms. This is accomplished by the process of offer and acceptance—one party (the **offeror**) stating the terms (the *offer*) and the other (the **offeree**) agreeing to those terms (the *acceptance*). In this way, the parties manifest their mutual assent.

INTENT TO CONTRACT

Since every contract involves a voluntary and consensual agreement, the court must be able to determine that the parties *intended* to agree to a common set of terms. Otherwise the courts will find no contract.

Intent—Subjective or Objective

Subjective **intent** may be defined as involving thoughts that were *actually* in the mind of a person at a given moment in time. It is this intent that the courts would like to ascertain. Unfortunately, this is impossible because there is no machine or other device that can be plugged into a person's mind to reveal its *actual* contents. Therefore, courts are forced to determine intent by the application of an *objective* standard—"what would a reasonable person, familiar with the surrounding facts and circumstances, believe the parties

intended?" It is accurate to say that what a person *actually* intended is unimportant legally (since it is not ascertainable). What *is* important is what that person *reasonably appeared* to have intended, which is judged by his or her words, conduct, and demeanor, given the surrounding facts and circumstances at the time and place of the alleged agreement. This rule will be applied uniformly unless the party to be bound can demonstrate that the other party knew his or her actual intention, which was different than his or her objective manifestation. Such a situation, however, is difficult to prove, as illustrated by the following case.

LUCY v. ZEHMER
196 Va. 493, 894 S.E.2d 516 (1954)

This was an action by W. O. Lucy and J. C. Lucy (Plaintiffs/Appellants) against A. H. J. Zehmer and Ida S. Zehmer, to compel specific performance of a contract to sell real estate.

On December 20, 1952, around 8:00 P.M., Plaintiff W. O. Lucy met with Defendants at a restaurant owned by them with the intention of purchasing their farm, although this intention was not then known to Defendants. After discussing the farm, Plaintiff said to A. H. Zehmer, "I bet you wouldn't take fifty thousand dollars for that place." Zehmer replied, "Yes I would too; you wouldn't give fifty." Lucy said he would and told Zehmer to write up an agreement to that effect. Zehmer took a restaurant check and wrote on the back, "I do hereby agree to sell to W. O. Lucy the Ferguson Farm for $50,000 complete." Lucy suggested the "I" should be changed to "We" because Mrs. Zehmer would have to sign too. Lucy tore up what he had written and wrote on another check as above, but with the change. He had Mrs. Zehmer sign it also and brought it back to Lucy, who offered him $5, which he refused saying, "You don't need to give me any money, you got the agreement here signed by both of us." Some discussion followed including some doubt about Lucy raising the $50,000. The next day, W. O. Lucy phoned J. C. Lucy and arranged for him to take a half interest. Thereafter Plaintiffs arranged for an attorney to examine the title to the farm and proceeded toward completion of the transaction. When Defendants refused to perform, on the ground that they were only joking (calling W. O. Lucy's bluff), this action ensued.

The trial court refused to grant specific performance and Plaintiffs appealed. Reversed and remanded.

BUCHANAN, Justice.

The appearance of the contract, the fact that it was under discussion for forty minutes or more before it was signed; Lucy's objection to the first draft because it was written in the singular, and he wanted Mrs. Zehmer to sign it also; the rewriting to meet that objection and the signing by Mrs. Zehmer; the discussion of what was to be included in the sale, the provision for the examination of the title, the completeness of the instrument that was executed, the taking possession of it by Lucy with no request or suggestion by either of the defendants that he give it back, are facts which furnish persuasive evidence that the execution of the contract was a serious business transaction rather than a casual, jesting matter as defendants now contend. . . .

Not only did Lucy actually believe, but the evidence shows he was warranted in believing, that the contract represented a serious business transaction and a good faith sale and purchase of the farm.

In the field of contracts, as generally elsewhere, "We must look to the outward expression of a person as manifesting his intention rather than to his secret and unexpressed intention. 'The law imputes to a person an intention corresponding to the reasonable meaning of his words and acts.'" . . .

The mental assent of the parties is not requisite for the formation of a contract. If the words or other acts of one of the parties have but one reasonable meaning, his undisclosed intention is immaterial except when an unreasonable meaning which he attaches to his manifestations is known to the other party. Restatement of the Law of Contracts, Vol. I., sec. 71, page 74. . . .

An agreement or mutual assent is of course essential to a valid contract but the law imputes to a person an intention corresponding to the reasonable meaning of his words and acts. If his words and acts, judged by a reasonable standard, manifest an intention to agree, it is immaterial what may be the real but unexpressed state of his mind. 17 C.J.S., Contracts, sec. 32, p. 361; 12 Am.Jur., Contracts, sec. 19, p. 515.

So a person cannot set up that he was merely jesting when his conduct and words would warrant a reasonable person in believing that he intended a real agreement.

Questions

1. Would the result have been the same if the parties had *not* written down the sale?
2. Which facts do you think were most critical to the court's finding mutual assent?

Definitions of Terms

A second intent factor is that the minds of the parties must "meet" on a common set of terms. That requires the offeror to state the offer in clear and definite terms. Even when it is certain that the parties have agreed, a court will not enforce an agreement if it cannot determine what that agreement was. Sometimes it is stated by the courts that if the parties have not made a clear contract, the court will not make one for them. Thus, vagueness of expression, or indefiniteness or uncertainty as to any term essential to the agreement, may prevent the formation of a contract even though the parties intended, in a general way, to be bound to an agreement of the type before the court.

In determining that terms are sufficiently definite and certain to form the basis for a contract, courts are faced with two basic tasks. First, they must decide what terms are necessary. Second, the court must decide whether the necessary terms are stated with reasonable certainty.

Obviously there is no practical limit as to what terms *might* be included in any particular contract. The question of what terms actually were included in an agreement will be determined by a court from the evidence brought before it. That process cannot begin until it is determined that at least the minimum terms were agreed upon.

Definite and *certain* are relative terms. The question, "just *how* definite and certain must the terms be?" inevitably arises. An examination of any dictionary reveals that most words have a variety of meanings. Nonverbal expressions may connote a variety of things depending on who observes them, and connotations may be varied further by the surrounding circumstances.

The often-stated rule is that there must be agreement as to *all* **material terms** (those that are so important that a court will not assume they are part of the contract, and will require that the parties actually agree to them) and that those terms must be stated with *reasonable certainty*. Of course, these statements give rise to further questions as to what terms are *material* and how certain *reasonable certainty* is. We then could define these terms using words that would be further defined, *ad infinitum*. However, perhaps the best statement to resolve this entire matter is given in Section 2-204(3) of the Uniform Commercial Code (UCC), which states: "Even though one or more terms may be left open a contract . . . does not fail for indefiniteness if the parties have intended to make a contract and there is a reasonable basis for giving an appropriate remedy." Although this section of the UCC applies mandatorily only to contracts for the sale of goods, it states the essence of the common-law notion of definiteness and surely would be approved by the courts in any contract case.

The idea underlying Section 2-204(3) is that a judge, in considering sufficiency of the terms, should ask: "Can I find a contract here and render a decision as to what was agreed upon, and then go home tonight and sleep well?" This does not mean that a judge should have no concerns, or that there must be absolute certainty, but only that there must be *reasonable* certainty.

Suppose, for example, Yvonne says to Bo, "I will sell my car to you for five hundred dollars."

Concept outline: Mutual assent

Intent to Contract

Subjective—thoughts that were actually in the mind of a person at a given time

Objective—what a person reasonably appeared to have intended

Definiteness of terms—parties must meet on a common set of terms

Writing anticipated—generally, contracts come into existence when the agreement is reached

Offer

Form—the way in which an offer is set up or proposed

Communication—occurs when the offeror's terms come to the attention of the intended offeree

Time offer remains open—stipulated by the offeror

Revocation—occurs when the offeror terminates the offer prior to acceptance

Termination—can be brought about by actions of either party or by operation of law

Acceptance

Unilateral—doing the requested act

Bilateral—making the requested promise

Silence as acceptance—silence alone generally will not be construed as acceptance

Communication—an acceptance is not effective until it has been communicated

Conditional acceptance—acceptance is contingent upon another condition put forth by the offeree

Rejection—occurs when the offeree rejects the terms of the offer

Bo replies, "I'll take it." Is there a reasonable basis on which a remedy might be granted should either Yvonne or Bo fail to perform and the question is brought before the court?

The material terms of a contract are those that must be supplied by the parties and will not be supplied by the courts. Material terms ordinarily include (1) the identity of the parties; (2) an adequate description of the contract's subject matter; (3) a statement of quantity; and (4) a statement of price. In the situation described above, assuming the parties were dealing face to face, there would be little doubt as to the identity of the parties. If Yvonne had shouted the statement into a crowd or had uttered it while looking at several people simultaneously, there would be a question as to the identity of the offeree. Since Yvonne stated "my car" (in the singular), a court reasonably would assume the quantity intended was "one." The statement of "five hundred dollars" is quite definite—the number of dollars is precise and a court reasonably could interpret "dollars" to be "United States dollars," assuming the contract was entered into and was to be executed in the United States. Is the subject matter adequately described?

If Yvonne owned only one car, presumably there would be no problem. Probably the statement "my car" would be sufficiently certain if Yvonne owned more than one car, but while speaking she and Bo were looking at and discussing one of them. Furthermore, if Yvonne owned two cars and one was worth around $500 and the other around $40,000, a court would feel reasonably certain which one the parties intended. If both were worth about the same, the statement "my car" probably would be too indefinite.

A court will supply some (nonmaterial) terms by construction. Such matters as method of payment, time of payment, time of delivery, and the car's condition upon delivery can be disposed of easily by accepted rules of interpretation. The method of payment, when credit is not mentioned, will be presumed to be cash and, as stated previously, payment will be in the currency of the place where the contract was made and executed. The times of payment and of delivery will be presumed to be concurrent—Bo pays the money when Yvonne delivers the car, and Yvonne delivers the car when Bo pays the money (sometimes called "conditions concurrent"), and it will be presumed that performance will be within a reasonable time. The condition of the car upon delivery should be substantially the same as when the agreement was made.

It is important to remember that the question of definiteness and certainty involves more than considering all material terms and the clarity with which they are stated. It also requires that these be evaluated against the backdrop of surrounding circumstances—the context in which the terms were agreed upon.

In cases involving merchants, and in dealings involving some special areas, custom and usage of a particular trade must be considered. For example, in purchasing bulk gold, the term "one ounce of gold" usually is intended to mean one *troy* ounce (31.1035 grams), not one ounce *avoirdupois* (28.3495 grams), and 99.9 percent pure, not 100 percent.

Also to be considered is the mood of the parties. For example, suppose Ike is walking down the street and sees Tina kicking the tire on a brand new car. When Ike asks what's wrong, Tina says, "I just paid $18,000 for this *@!* car and it quit running in the middle of the street during rush hour. If you want it, its yours for $5!" Ike's agreement to Tina's terms would not form a contract under the circumstances. In addition, the courts will consider any other circumstances that reasonably would aid in judging the intent of the parties.

Uniform Commercial Code Gap-Fillers

Courts generally are reluctant to hold agreements too indefinite to be enforced, but common law courts routinely did so when material terms were not stated by the parties or clearly implied. With the adoption of the Uniform Commercial Code, courts were permitted to apply more relaxed rules of interpretation. The most comprehensive of these is found in Section 2-204(3), as previously noted. This section provides that a contract for the sale of goods will not fail for indefiniteness if the parties have intended a contract and the court finds that it has a reasonably certain basis for granting an appropriate remedy. Perhaps the most striking gap-filler is found in Section 2-305, providing that the parties to a contract for the sale of goods may leave the price open, to be determined later. Others include Section 2-306, permitting flexible quantity terms based on the seller's output or the buyer's requirements; Sections 2-308 and 2-209, filling in delivery terms; Section 2-310, providing for time of payment; and Section 2-311, permitting the parties to leave particulars of performance to be specified by one of them. Overall, the UCC focuses on the intentions of the parties much more than does the common law, which has strict technical requirements.

When a Writing Is Anticipated

When parties enter into an agreement and it is contemplated that they will reduce their agreement to a signed writing, a question may arise as to exactly when they intend the agreement to become legally binding (contractual). As a general rule, courts hold that a contract comes into existence at the moment agreement is reached and that the writing is only a memorial of the contract already made. This usually is reasonable because agreement is of the essence of every contract—a contract is a meeting of the minds, not a piece of paper. However, circumstances may dictate to the contrary.

Courts tend to treat the fact that the parties contemplated a writing as some evidence, although not conclusive, that they intended *not* to be bound until the document was executed. Usage and custom also may be important, as in the case of collective bargaining agreements in the labor field.

The more complex the terms, the more likely it is that a court will find an oral agreement insufficient if contested by one of the parties. This especially is true when the terms have been negotiated item by item and the court feels uncertain that the parties reasonably could be expected to have in mind all of the provisions and their precise interrelationships without referring to a writing.

In cases involving contracts governed by the Statute of Frauds, which requires certain types of contracts to be in writing to be enforceable (discussed in Chapter 10), the courts frequently find that no contract exists until a sufficient writing is signed. An example would be contracts involving the sale and purchase of real estate. Finally, the conduct of the parties may answer the question for the courts. Thus, when both parties begin performance, or make preparations to perform or statements indicating an intent to be bound, without a writing, the courts may find the conduct strongly evidentiary. Of course, much of this problem can be precluded by including a specific term in the agreement providing that there is no obligation until a writing is signed.

THE OFFER

An **offer** may be defined as the initial proposal, by one of the parties, that begins the contract process. More importantly, it is the objective manifestation of the willingness of one of the parties (the offeror) to be bound to the other (the offeree) on a given set of terms. The offer may be made in any manner and any form sufficient to manifest objectively the intent of the offeror to enter into a contract with the offeree.

Form of the Offer

Every offer is composed of two parts—(1) what the offeror will do, and (2) what the offeror expects in return. Thus, the statement "I will sell my car to you for five hundred dollars" is interpreted to mean that the offeror *will* sell his or her car and, in return, *expects* $500 (or the promise of $500).

Preliminary Negotiations

In many cases, a transaction ending in a contract begins with a series of preliminary negotiations. The form and extent of these negotiations will vary with each situation. They may be initiated verbally, by conduct, in a letter, or by a newspaper or other advertisement, or may involve some combination of these. In its narrowest sense, the term **preliminary negotiations** refers to matters transpiring between the parties prior to the statement of any offer that could be accepted and form a contract. These may include general discussion of an indefinite character, the prodding by one of the parties in an attempt to determine the other's interest, sales talk concerning the desirability of a particular product—its qualities, price, and quantity, inquiries regarding terms, and requests for offers. Used in its broadest sense, the term can include all of these as well as offers, counteroffers, statements of conditions, and any other matters preceding the moment of final acceptance.

In evaluating preliminary negotiations, a court may be faced either with the question of whether a particular utterance constituted an offer or only a preliminary statement, or one of whether another utterance was an acceptance. In any case, preliminary negotiations are important in that they provide part of the backdrop (circumstances or context) that must be considered by the courts in interpreting the intent of the parties and in determining whether any contract has come into being. Among the commonly encountered situations in which special questions may arise are bids, auctions, advertisements, rewards, and those involving indirect methods of communication.

Bids and Auctions

Frequently preliminary negotiations include a request for the submission of offers. This is often the case in the construction industry. The person wishing to have the work done will request bids on the work, possibly by advertisement. Generally the request is not an offer, but the bid submitted in response frequently is. However, if the advertisement includes a formula for determining the winning bid, such as "job will go to the lowest bidder," the advertisement may be considered an offer. Generally this is not desirable; it may force

the advertiser into a contract with someone with whom he or she would rather not be involved.

Another common situation involving a request for offers is the auction. At an auction, the auctioneer generally is seen as requesting offers in the form of bids from the audience, any of which the auctioneer is free to reject or accept. This is true even though the advertisement for the auction may include a statement that "The goods being offered for sale include. . . ." Although an item almost always is sold to the highest bidder, there is no legal reason it *must* be. In addition, unless the advertisement for the auction states otherwise (as when it states "without reserve" or "all items will be sold"), an item placed on the auction block for sale may be removed and not sold even after bids have been solicited and received. Usually nothing is final until the auctioneer drops the hammer and says, "Sold to. . . ."

Advertisements

Advertisements to the general public usually are not considered to be offers, but are considered, again, as requests for offers—invitations to negotiate. In most advertisements, one of two common problems prevent them from being offers: (1) the terms are too indefinite to be enforceable and (2) an offer ordinarily must be made to an individual or a defined group of individuals. The reason for the latter rule involves, in part, the question of required intent.

If an advertisement to the general public constituted an offer, it could be accepted by everyone who heard or otherwise learned of it. The advertiser then theoretically could be liable on an unlimited number of contracts to supply a limited quantity of goods or services. Would a reasonable third party, familiar with the surrounding facts and circumstances, assume the advertiser intended that result? Arguably, of course, there is no danger of such a result. Only a limited number of people will desire to accept, and of them only a limited number will possess the means to do so.

However, one way to test a rule of law to determine whether it should be adopted is to take it to its logical possible (not probable) extreme. If it fails to hold up, it should be reconsidered.

The typical advertisement then, whether communicated locally or through some mass medium, generally is considered only an invitation to negotiate. For example, when a clothing store puts a sweater in the window prominently displaying a tag "SALE $65," it is inviting anyone who sees it to come in and make an offer to purchase it for $65. By the same token, when a grocery store advertises in the newspaper "Acme green beans, 3 one-pound cans for $1" and in response a customer comes into the store to purchase, the offer is extended by the customer bringing the goods to the cash register. This offer then is accepted by the clerk, typically by ringing up the purchase, taking the customer's money, giving back the change, bagging the purchase, and handing it to the customer. Thus, a contract is both entered into and immediately executed.

There are few exceptions to the rule that most advertisements are not offers. Two generally accepted ones involve the advertisement of rules for game prize contests and advertisements involving rewards. Consider, however, the following case.

LEFKOWITZ v. GREAT MINNEAPOLIS SURPLUS STORE
251 Minn. 188, 86 N.W.2d 689 (1957)

This was an action by Morris Lefkowitz (Plaintiff/Respondent) against Great Minneapolis Surplus Store arising out of his attempts, on two occasions, to accept the terms of Defendant's newspaper advertisements. Plaintiff claimed that each of these advertisements constituted offers.

On April 6, 1956, Defendant published the following advertisement in a Minneapolis newspaper: "Saturday 9 A.M. Sharp 3 Brand New Fur Coats Worth to $100.00 First Come First Served $1 Each." On April 13, the defendant again published an advertisement in the same newspaper as follows: "Saturday 9 A.M. 2 Brand New Pastel Mink 3-Skin Scarfs Selling for $89.50 Out they go Saturday. Each . . . $1.00; 1 Black Lapin Stole Beautiful, worth $139.50 . . . $1.00 First Come First Served." On each of the Saturdays following the publication of these advertisements, Plaintiff was the first to present himself at the appropriate counter in Defendant's store, and on each occasion demanded the merchandise advertised and indicated his willingness to pay the $1. On both occasions, Defendant refused to sell the merchandise to Plaintiff.

From a judgment for Plaintiff for the price of the lapin stole minus $1 ($138.50), Defendant appealed. Affirmed.

MURPHY, Justice.

The defendant relies principally on Craft v. Elder & Johnston Co. . . In that case, the court discussed the legal effect on an advertisement offering for sale, as a one-day special, an electric sewing machine at a named price. The view was expressed that the advertisement was . . . "not an offer made to any specific person but was made to the public generally. Thereby it would be properly designated as a unilateral offer and not being supported by consideration could be withdrawn at will and without notice." It is true that such an offer may be withdrawn before acceptance. . . . On the facts before us we are concerned with whether the advertisement constituted an offer, and, if so, whether the plaintiff's conduct constituted an acceptance. . . . The authorities . . . emphasize that, where the offer is clear, definite, and explicit, and leaves nothing open for negotiation, it constitutes an offer, acceptance of which will complete the contract. . . . Whether in any individual instance a newspaper advertisement is an offer rather than an invitation to make an offer depends on the legal intention of the parties and the surrounding circumstances. . . . We are of the view on the facts before us that the offer by the defendant of the sale of the Lapin fur was clear, definite, and explicit, and left nothing open for negotiation. The plaintiff having successfully managed to be the first one to appear at the seller's place of business to be served, as requested by the advertisement, and having offered the stated purchase price of the article, he was entitled to performance on the part of the deffendant.

Questions

1. What was the precise act of acceptance by the plaintiff in this case?

2. Another fact in this case, not discussed, is that when Lefkowitz responded to the first advertisement, he was told that the store had a "house policy" that the advertisements were for women only. Should the court have refused to grant judgment for Lefkowitz because of that fact, since he knew of the policy when he responded to the second advertisement?

Rewards

Advertisements of rewards form a common exception to the general rule that advertisements directed to the general public are not offers. This is because the courts feel that the general problem with advertisements—that they are subject to potential acceptance by everyone in the world—is not a problem with rewards because they typically are subject to only one acceptance—that is, by the person who "returns the lost article," "gives the requested information," or otherwise earns the reward.

Most jurisdictions consider advertisements of rewards as offers for unilateral contracts. A few consider them as offers for bounty, which is considered as owed to any person who does the requested act. To understand the importance of this distinction, and to judge the merits of the minority view, consider the following case.

GLOVER v. JEWISH WAR VETERANS OF UNITED STATES
68 A.2d 233 (D.C. 1949)

This was an action by Mary Glover (Plaintiff/Appellant) against Jewish War Veterans of United States, Post No. 50, to collect a reward of $500, having complied with the terms of the advertised offer of reward.

On June 5, 1946, Maurice L. Bernstein was murdered. On the following day, Defendant caused to be advertised in the newspapers an offer of a reward of $500 "to the person or persons furnishing information resulting in the apprehension and conviction of the persons guilty of the murder of Maurice L. Bernstein." Notice of the reward was published on June 7, 1947.

A day or so later, Plaintiff gave the information to the police that resulted in the apprehension and conviction of two persons guilty of the crime. Thereafter, on June 12, Plaintiff first learned of the offer above, and claimed right to it. Defendant refused to pay and this action ensued.

From a judgment for Defendant, Plaintiff appealed. Affirmed.

CLAGETT, Associate Judge.

The issue determinative of this appeal is whether a person giving information leading to the arrest of a murderer without any knowledge that a reward has been offered for such information by a non-governmental organization is entitled to collect the reward. The trial court decided the question in the negative and instructed the jury to return a verdict for defendant. . . .

We have concluded that the trial court correctly instructed the jury to return a verdict for defendant. While there is some conflict in the decided cases on the subject of rewards, most of such conflict has to do with rewards offered by governmental officers and agencies. So far as rewards offered by private individuals and organizations are concerned, there is little conflict in the rule that questions regarding such rewards are to be based upon the law of contracts.

Since it is clear that the question is one of contract law, it follows that, at least so far as private rewards are concerned, there can be no contract unless the claimant when giving the desired information knew of the offer of the reward and acted with the intention of accepting such offer; otherwise the claimant gives the information not in the expectation of receiving a reward but rather out of a sense of public duty or other motive unconnected with the reward. "In the nature of the case," according to Professor Williston, "it is impossible for an offeree actually to assent to an offer unless he knows of its existence." After stating that courts in some jurisdictions have decided to the contrary, Williston adds, "It is impossible, however, to find in such a case [that is, in a case holding to the contrary] the elements generally held in England and America necessary for the formation of a contract. If it is clear the offeror intended to pay for the service, it is equally certain that the person rendering the service performed it voluntarily and not in return for a promise to pay. If one person expects to buy, and the other to give, there can hardly be found mutual assent. These views are supported by the great weight of authority, and in most jurisdictions a plaintiff in the sort of case under discussion is denied recovery."

The American Law Institute in its "Restatement of the Law of Contracts"[11] follows the same rule, thus: "It is impossible that there should be an acceptance unless the offeree knows of the existence of the offer." . . .

We believe the rule adopted by Professor Williston and the Restatement and in the majority of the cases is the better reasoned rule and therefore, we adopt it.

Questions
1. Is the court's result, although technically correct, fair?
2. Would the plaintiff have won if she had sued on a quasi-contract theory?

Communication of Offers

In order to be effective and subject to acceptance, an offer must be communicated. Communication occurs when the offer's terms come to the attention of the intended offeree. A silent intention to make an offer is not sufficient. The offeror's intention must be manifested in order to be subject to objective measurement, and the mind of the offeree cannot meet with the offeror's mind if the offeree does not know the terms of the offer.

When the offeror's terms are communicated directly, as by parties speaking face to face, there is very little problem. The terms are considered communicated at the time and place they are uttered. Questions often arise, however, when the communication is by other means. For instance, an offer sent by letter may be lost in the mail. A situation that potentially is even more serious is when an offer consists of a number of separate terms, some of which are communicated while others are not. If the offeror does not realize that some of the terms were not communicated, he or she may enter into a contract that is not exactly what he or she subjectively intended.

For example, consider some very common situations—(1) a driver parks her car in a parking lot and receives a ticket indicating a license to park there and the time the car was parked, (2) a person enters a theater and receives a ticket evidencing the payment of an admission fee, and (3) a passenger checks his baggage and receives a claim check evidencing title to the property checked. In each of these cases the ticket or receipt may have printed on it terms that the issuer intends to communicate to the customer. Very frequently, these terms include some limitation of the issuer's liability arising from the transaction.

Suppose, for example, the theater patron enters the theater and is injured when the seat he is occupying collapses. When he demands payment for his injuries he is informed that there is a disclaimer on the reverse side of the admission ticket to the effect that the theater will not be responsible for injuries sustained by patrons while on theater premises. Is that statement a part of the contract between the patron and the theater? If the patron did not read or otherwise know of the disclaimer, has that term been communicated?

The law says that if the offeree either knew of the term, or should have known of it, then it has been communicated. The application of this rule may present significant questions of fact to courts, especially in cases in which the offeree actually did not know. *Should* she have known? This determination will rest on both subjective and objective analysis, and all lingering questions should be resolved against the offeror. It is the duty of the offeror to communicate the terms of the offer. If the question is raised, the burden of proving communication is on the offeror.

THE ACCEPTANCE

Just as the offer is the manifestation by the offeror of his or her willingness to be bound to the offeree on a given set of terms, the **acceptance** is the manifestation of the willingness of the offeree to be bound to those same terms. At this point we have "mutual assent," or what lawyers and judges are fond of calling a "meeting of the minds." From a technical standpoint, the acceptance comes in response to the second part of the offer. The offeree is giving what the offeror expects in return. In the bilateral situation, the acceptance is giving the requested promise. In the unilateral situation, it is doing the requested act (completion).

Acceptance by Bilateral or Unilateral Means

At common law the courts were very strict about the general form of an acceptance. A bilateral offer could be accepted only by bilateral means—the making of the requested promise—and a unilateral offer could be accepted only by unilateral means—the doing of the requested act. This rule has now been modified concerning contracts for the sale of goods. Uniform Commercial Code Section 2-206 states:

(1) Unless otherwise unambiguously indicated by the language or circumstances

  (a) an offer to make a contract shall be construed as inviting acceptance in any manner and by any medium reasonable in the circumstances.

  (b) an order or other offer to buy goods for prompt or current shipment shall be construed as inviting acceptance either by prompt promise to ship or by the prompt or current shipment. . . .

(2) Where the beginning of a requested performance is a reasonable mode of acceptance an offeror who is not notified of acceptance within a reasonable time may treat the offer as having lapsed before acceptance.

This latter rule, however, has not achieved general acceptance in cases not involving goods. The courts in these other cases have attempted to minimize questions of what means can be used in accepting by holding that unless the offer clearly and unambiguously requests an act in return, it will be construed as inviting a bilateral acceptance. Thus the problems sought to be alleviated by Section 2-206(2) are unlikely to occur.

Who May Accept an Offer

An offer may be accepted only by the one to whom the offeror intended to communicate it. Thus, if Johns says to James, "I will sell my car to you for five hundred dollars" and, before James can respond, Josephs, who overheard the offer, says "I'll take it," Josephs's utterance is not an acceptance. The offeror is the master of the terms of the offer and the master of the resulting contract. An offeree, as a general rule, cannot alter the terms of the offer unless he wishes to reject the offer and become the offeror. Nor can the offeror be forced to enter into a contract with anyone against his will.

Silence as Acceptance

As a general rule, silence alone will not be construed as an acceptance because, at best, mere silence is ambiguous. Suppose, for example, Johns writes to James, "I will sell my car to you for $500. If I don't hear from you within 10 days I will assume you accept." If James does not respond within ten days, is he bound to a contract? Probably not. Whether James failed to respond because he wanted to accept or because he had no duty to respond is unclear. The principal of requiring a manifestation of intent so that it can be measured by the objective standard seems to dictate that an offeree should do something in order to be bound to a contract, not to avoid one. The rule that silence will not be construed as acceptance, however, is subject to four exceptions: (1) prior arrangements, (2) past dealing, (3) acceptance of benefits, and (4) when the offeree intends silence as acceptance.

First, silence may constitute acceptance when there is a *prior arrangement*. Both of the parties must have agreed to this in advance. Examples of these arrangements are to be found in the contracts of various mail-in clubs involving everything from books, records, and tapes to fruit. The typical arrangement is that the club member will be notified each month, of the "special of the month." Unless she notifies the club by a certain date, she will be assumed to have ordered that special. Silence is considered appropriate and unambiguous since it was agreed to in advance.

A second exception may be found in the *past dealings* of two parties. The course of dealing between the parties simply is one of the circumstances that aid a court in determining intent. In this context, the intent of the parties in transacting business in the past may be used as a measure of their present intent to contract.

Third, one may accept an offer by silence by *accepting the benefits* of tendered performance. For example, when Graff is stuck in the street and

Garrison offers to push his car to the side of the street for $2, and Graff silently allows Garrison to do so, a court probably would find that Graff has accepted Garrison's offer. This, of course, simply is an example of a contract implied in fact, as discussed in Chapter 6.

Finally, silence may be considered an acceptance if *the offeree intends it* as such. For example, assume an offeror has made an offer and stated "If I don't hear from you within ten days, I will assume you accept." If the offeree remains silent for ten days and the offeror files suit to enforce an alleged contract, the offeror is not likely to be successful because of the general rule. But if suit is filed by the offeree to enforce the contract, the court probably would grant judgment in favor of the offeree. This is true because the offeror requested silence in return and the offeree complied with that request. Thus, in addition to being an exception to the rule that silence will not be construed as an acceptance, this situation also presents an exception to the general rule in contracts that unless both parties are bound, neither party is bound. The lesson is simple. An offeror never should invite acceptance by silence in the absence of a prior arrangement, especially if there have been no past dealings or acceptance of benefits. Otherwise, she may find herself bound under this fourth exception while the offeree is not.

Although the rules concerning silence as acceptance generally favor the offeree, the courts are aware that the offeree must not abuse the protections afforded. The following case illustrates a situation in which an offeree was prevented from taking advantage of the talents of a professional without payment.

STOUT v. SMITH
4 N.C.App. 81, 165 S.E.2d 789 (1969)

This was an action by Adrian P. Stout and Noell N. Coltrane Jr., dba Stout & Coltrane Architects (Plaintiffs/Appellants) against Joe F. Smith for payment of a professional fee. The complaint was based on alternative theories of agreement to build a home and *quantum meruit* (the value of the services provided).

Plaintiffs agreed to design a home for Defendant to his specifications, their fee to be based on a percentage of the cost of construction. When bids were submitted on the final plans, costs were much higher than reasonably expected by either party and the decision was made not to build the house. Later, Defendant built a house with many of the features suggested by Plaintiffs and on a site recommended by them.

The jury found for Plaintiffs in the amount of the reasonable value of their services ($3861.75). Defendant appealed. Reversed as to the measure of damages.

BRITT, Judge.

There is a difference between the measure of damages in a claim on express contract, one on implied contract, and one on *quantum meruit.* "A promise to pay for services is implied when they are rendered and received in such circumstances as authorize the party performing to entertain a reasonable expectation of payment for them by the party benefited. However, the law will not imply a promise to pay the value of services rendered and accepted, where there is proof of a special agreement to pay therefor a particular amount. . . ." 58 Am.Jur., Work and Labor, Sec. 6, pp. 514, 515. "If there is no special agreement as to the amount of compensation and the services are not intended to be gratuitous, the law implies a promise by the employer to pay what services reasonably are worth, which is determined largely by the nature of the work and the customary rate of pay for such work in the community and at the time the work was performed." Ibid, Sec. 10, p. 518. "The measure of recovery for services furnished or goods received under the doctrine of unjust enrichment, as distinguished from the doctrine of contracts implied in fact, is the value of the actual benefit realized and retained." Ibid, Sec. 32, p. 536.

It is permissible under our practice, in an action to recover for personal services, for the one rendering the services to abandon his allegations of special contract and proceed on the principle of *quantum meruit*. Lindsey v. Speight, 224 N.C. 453, 31 S.E.2d 371. But, the measure of such recovery, predicated on implied assumpsit [contract], is the reasonable value of the services rendered by plaintiff and accepted by defendant. . . .

In Thorner v. Lexington Mail Order Co. [241 N.C. 249, 85 S.E.2d 140], cited in defendant's brief, the action was instituted to recover for advertising material furnished by plaintiff. The Supreme Court held that if the material was not furnished in accordance with the contract, recovery on *quantum meruit* was limited to such materials and services as were accepted and appropriated by defendant, and an instruction permitting recovery for the value of all services and materials furnished by plaintiff, regardless of whether they were accepted or not, was reversible error. In an opinion by Bobbitt, J., and referring to the materials and services accepted and appropriated by defendant, the Court said: "As to these, and these alone, defendant must pay, on the basis of *quantum meruit*; and the basis of liability therefore is quasi contract, i.e., unjust enrichment."

The effect of the judge's charge in the instant case was that plaintiffs were entitled to recover the reasonable value of *all* services performed by them for or on account of the defendant. In view of the express contract pleaded by plaintiffs, it was error, prejudicial to the defendant, for the court to charge the jury that plaintiffs were entitled to recover for the reasonable value of their services, without limiting such recovery to the reasonable value of the services *accepted and appropriated* by defendant. Defendant's assignment of error is well taken.

Questions
1. How did the defendant "accept" the contract in this case?
2. Which principle of acceptance by silence is applicable to the *Stout* case?

In order to discourage the unsolicited sending of goods to unwary customers, several states and the federal government have enacted legislation making it illegal to send such goods. The federal statute covers only unsolicited goods sent by mail and allows the recipient to treat such goods as gifts; many state statutes apply to unsolicited goods sent by other means as well.

Communication of Acceptance

Just as an offer is not effective until it has been communicated, an acceptance is not effective until it has been communicated. It is especially important that the precise moments of communication be determined, because it is only then that the agreement becomes contractual, the offeror's right to revoke is cut off, and both parties are bound. Determining this precise moment of acceptance seldom is difficult when the parties are dealing directly, for example, face to face or by telephone. The acceptance is considered communicated at the time and place the words of acceptance are uttered. Problems may arise, however, when the acceptance is sent by a means that involves a delay between dispatch and arrival, such as the mail or telegram. Under these circumstances, the effective moment of communication must be determined by the application of a rather precise set of rules.

Delayed means of communication may be broken down into three basic categories: (1) stipulated, (2) expressly authorized, and (3) impliedly authorized. As long as one of these means is used, the acceptance is effective on dispatch—when it is placed into the hands of the "agency" of communication.

A means of communication is *stipulated* when the offeror states, in effect, "If you wish to accept you *must* respond by . . ." and names the method to be used. If the offeree uses the means stipulated, the acceptance is effective when dispatched. The use of any other means is not effective as an acceptance, although it may be considered an offer back that may be accepted or rejected by the other party. Thus, if the offer is made by mail and stipulates a response by mail, a telegram or even a telephone call would not be effective to create a contract. The reason is that a stipulation as to the means to be used in accepting is considered to be a term of the offer and, as a general rule, in tendering an acceptance the offeree must comply in all respects with the offeror's terms or no contract will result. Remember, the offeror is the

master of the terms of the ultimate contract.

When no means of acceptance is stipulated, one will be authorized. This authorization may be either express or implied. A means of communication is *expressly authorized* when the offeror states in words written or spoken, in effect, "If you wish to accept, you *may* respond by . . ." and names the method. Note that the use of the agency here is "permissive," but it is mandatory when the agency has been stipulated. If the offeree uses the authorized means, the acceptance is effective when dispatched. Use of any other means will result in a contract only when the acceptance actually arrives in the hands of the offeror, and then only if it arrives before the offer has terminated. Thus, the use of a nonconforming means of acceptance when another means has been stipulated will result in no contract, but its use when another means has been expressly authorized may be considered an acceptance, although the offeree assumes the risk of loss or late arrival.

If no means of acceptance is stipulated and none is expressly authorized, there always will be one or more *impliedly authorized* means. The effect of using or not using the impliedly authorized means is the same as for an expressly authorized means—if it is used, it is effective on dispatch and, if not used, the acceptance is effective only when and if it arrives. If it never arrives, or it arrives after the offer has terminated, no contract results. Remember, there is no impliedly authorized means if another means has been either stipulated or expressly authorized.

At common law, the *only* means that could be impliedly authorized was the same means as was used by the offeror to communicate the offer. Thus, an offer by mail, silent as to the means to be used in accepting, impliedly authorized only a reply by mail. Similarly, one sent by telegram impliedly authorized only telegraphic acceptance. This rule applies to all contracts except those for the sale of goods. In the latter case, UCC Sec. 2-206(1) states: "Unless otherwise unambiguously indicated by the language [as by stipulating or expressly authorizing another means] or circumstances . . . an offer to make a contract shall be construed as inviting acceptance . . . by any medium reasonable in the circumstances." Thus, although the common law provides only one impliedly authorized means, the Uniform Commercial Code, for *goods* contracts, may authorize several—any means "reasonable in the circumstances." Generally the courts resolve the question of what constitutes such a means by considering two factors: (1) relative speed, and (2) relative safety of the means used to communicate the offer and the means used by the offeree. Is the means used by the offeree as fast or faster and just as safe or safer? Consider the situation in which Shaw sends an offer to Vi by mail and mentions nothing about the means to be used in accepting. Vi responds by telegram. If the offer was for a car, a boat, a book, or some other item of "goods," Vi's response would be effective on dispatch. If it was one for the sale of real estate or services, Vi's response would be effective only when and if it arrived while the offer was still open. The common law disregards the fact that the means used by the offeree may be faster and safer than the means used by the offeror.

In summary, keep in mind that when an offeror *stipulates* a means, there is no means *authorized*, either expressly or impliedly; when no means is stipulated but one is *expressly* authorized, there is no means *impliedly* authorized; and when there is no stipulated or expressly authorized means there *always* will be one or more impliedly authorized means depending on whether the common law or the Uniform Commercial Code applies.

Communication of acceptance

WAS METHOD USED?

METHOD	Yes	No
Stipulated	Effective on Dispatch	Not Effective
Authorized	Effective on Dispatch	Effective on Arrival
Expressly Impliedly Common Law UCC	↓	↓

The table summarizes the effect of each on the communication of acceptance.

Given that an offer (and any revocation of an offer) are effective only upon arrival in the hands of the offeree, it can be very important to the offeree to use only stipulated and authorized means to communicate an acceptance. The violation of a stipulation results in no contract, while the use of a means not authorized places the risks of loss and late arrival on the offeree. The use of the stipulated or authorized means shifts those risks to the offeror. Of course, the offeror, as master of the terms of the offer, has the right to prevent this shifting of risks by stipulating that acceptance will be effective only upon arrival. The offeror can and always should, in addition, stipulate the means, the place, and the time for the acceptance to be effective. Doing so can do much to avoid unexpected acceptances such as the one in the following case.

MORELLO v. GROWERS GRAPE PRODUCTS ASSOCIATION et al.
82 Cal.App.2d 365, 186 P.2d 463 (1947)

This was an action by Euginio Morello (Plaintiff/Appellant) against Growers Grape Products Association (Defendant/Appellee) and others to recover $35,853 for breach of an alleged contract of November 1942.

On October 4, 1938, Plaintiff entered into an agreement with Defendant under which Defendant agreed to process a part of Plaintiff's grape crop. The agreement contained the following provision, among others: "The association shall not . . . sell at any price any quantity of commercial brandy processed for the association by the processor to any person, unless the association shall have first offered to sell the same to the processor at the same price and upon the same conditions, and unless the processor shall have failed or refused to accept said offer in writing or by telegraphic notification delivered within five (5) days from the date of the making of such offer."

Pursuant to that provision the association, on November 9, 1942, wrote to Plaintiff stating that the release had been ordered of the unsold brandy remaining in the pool, amounting to approximately four million gallons. The letter contained the following offer: "The unsold brandy of your distillation remaining in the pool, according to our records, amounts to approximately 23,902.46 original proof gallons. This amount, which is subject to our final verification, or any quantity thereof, is offered to you at $1.25 cash, per original proof gallon, f. o. b. the storage racks within the Internal Revenue Bonded Warehouse where it is now held, provided

"1. That you accept this offer in writing or by telegraphic notification delivered within five days from the date of this letter, in accordance with Paragraph 13 of the Brandy and High-Proof Processing Agreement.

"2. That you sign and return to the Growers Grape Products Association, four copies of the Brandy Purchase and Sales Agreement (copy of this is enclosed, and additional copies will be furnished upon request)."

Plaintiff telephoned his acceptance on November 13 and was told that he must put it in writing. On that same day, November 13, Plaintiff wrote a letter to Defendant and restated his acceptance as follows: "Confirming my telephone conversation with you this afternoon, I accept your offer of Nov. 9th and will purchase the 23,902.46 original proof gallons of commercial brandy at $1.25 cash per gal., all as set forth in said letter; so if you will send the contracts down to me I will immediately sign and return the same." November 14 was the fifth day, and it was a Saturday. Defendant refused to sell the brandy to Plaintiff contending that no contract came into being because its offer had not been properly accepted.

From a judgment for Defendants, Plaintiff appealed. Affirmed on grounds not relevant here.

GOODELL, Justice.

It is elementary that a contract is complete when the letter of acceptance is posted. . . The word "delivered" in the offer creates only an apparent, not a real difficulty, because under the law dealing with the formation of contract *delivery of an acceptance to the post-office operates as delivery to the person addressed*, except in unusual cases. . . .

There are many cases holding substantially that the deposit by one party in the mails of an instrument properly addressed to the other party, with postage thereon prepaid, constitutes a delivery to the other party, at the place where and the time when it is so deposited. . . .

The post-office was clearly the agent of the offeror, for the offer was itself sent by mail and it called for an acceptance in writing and thereby invited the use of the same medium as that chosen for the offer.

It is claimed by respondent and conceded by appellant that the acceptance of the 13th was not opened in the respondent's San Francisco office until Monday, November 16th. Appellant argues, however, that it might well have been mailed on the 13th, in which case it might have been received on the 14th had the respondent's office been open for business on that day, which was a Saturday. The case is susceptible of that inference, as there is no testimony as to whether the office was open or closed. Let it be conceded, however, that it was received on Monday, the 16th. If from that fact the inference could be drawn that it had been mailed in Fresno county on Saturday, the 14th—the fifth day—then a directed verdict, if based on the acceptance being too late, could not be sustained. [Plaintiff was successful in persuading the court on this point, but he lost the appeal on other grounds not important to our discussion of the effective moment of an acceptance sent by a delayed means of communication.]

Questions

1. In the case of the attempted acceptance by telephone, why was that not considered sufficient since it clearly manifested the plaintiff's intent to accept the offer?

2. What could the defendant have done to avoid this surprise acceptance?

TERMINATION OF THE POWER TO ACCEPT

Having considered how an offer comes into being, the nature of negotiations, the rules concerning acceptance, and the resulting formation of a contract, we must consider how long the offer will remain open, subject to acceptance. No offer remains open indefinitely, and termination may occur in various ways.

Lapse of Stated Time

Since the offeror is the master of the terms of the offer, he or she has a right to stipulate exactly how long the offer will remain open. Even if the time stated is unreasonably short or even impossible to comply with, any attempt to accept after the stated time will not be effective.

Lapse of a Reasonable Time

When no time is stated, an offer will remain open only for a reasonable time. What is reasonable will depend on the circumstances, which may include the nature of the subject matter, past dealings between the parties, conduct and other statements by the parties, and custom of the trade or business. For example, an offer to sell a parcel of real estate or a high-priced item of stable goods would remain open longer than an offer to sell securities listed on an organized exchange or a bushel of ripe peaches. It would be to the offeror's advantage to state a time of termination in every offer. Doing so eliminates the need for a court to determine just how long a "reasonable" time is.

Revocation

Since contract law requires *voluntary consent* on the part of both parties *at the time the contract comes into being*, an offeror may withdraw (**revoke**) his or her offer at any time prior to acceptance. This generally is true even though the offeror has promised to hold the offer open for a stated length of time. The reason is that the offeror's promise to hold the offer open for a stated period of time, like any other promise, generally is not enforceable in the absence of consideration. Thus, suppose on Wednesday Alice promises to sell her car to Mel for $500 and promises to allow Mel until Saturday to accept. Alice, without penalty, still can revoke her offer at any time prior to acceptance. To this general rule there are three generally recognized exceptions: (1) options, (2) firm offers, and (3) promissory estoppel.

An *option* is simply a separate *contract* to hold an offer open. In effect, the offeror sells to the offeree her (the offeror's) right to revoke. In the case of Alice's offer to sell her car, an option would have come into being if Alice had accepted money, or anything else of value, from Mel in return for her promise to hold the offer open. The option device is quite common in real estate transactions.

The *firm offer* is the creature of UCC Section 2-205. Although it has the same effect as an option, it differs in several important respects. (1) It

applies only when the offeror is a *merchant*; (2) it applies only to offers concerning *goods*; (3) it cannot be oral, but must be in a signed *writing*; and (4) its maximum duration is three *months*. In effect, under these circumstances a firm offer is like an option except that it is enforceable even though no consideration is given by the offeree. Note, also, that a firm-offer clause on a form supplied by the offeree must be separately signed by the offeror. This is an attempt by the UCC to ensure that, before taking away rights from the merchant-offeror, he was aware that he was extending a firm offer.

The concept of *promissory estoppel*, as used here, involves the same theory and the same five elements as discussed in Chapter 6. The courts may simply apply this doctrine in order to prevent an injustice. You should take a few minutes, at this point, to refresh your memory of promissory estoppel (see p. 133).

BUTLER v. WEHRLEY
5 Ariz.App. 233, 425 P.2d 130 (1967)

This was an action by Bob Wehrley dba Bob Wehrley Realty (Plaintiff/Appellee) against O. H. Butler for a real estate brokerage commission owing on an alleged listing contract Plaintiff contended Defendant breached.

Defendant was the owner of certain real estate located in Maricopa County, Arizona. On August 2, 1963, he signed an "agreement of exchange" on a form supplied by Plaintiff whereby he agreed to exchange his property for certain other property owned by one Perry. This agreement provided, in part:

This offer must be accepted by the second party on or before *August 5, 63*, and *1st* party agrees not to withdraw this offer prior to that date unless it is early rejected by second party. Each party covenants and agrees to and with the other that he has good right to sell and convey his respective property and that except as stated above he is the owner in fee simple [see Chapter 26] thereof and that the same is free of all encumbrances. And in consideration of the mutual promises herein contained it is further agreed that should either party hereto fail to perform and carry out his part of this agreement, such party, so failing, shall pay all the broker's commission below provided for, this promise being made directly for said broker's benefit.

Dated: *Aug 2, 1963*
signed: *O. H. Butler* (Seal)
signed: *J. C. Perry* (Seal)

The undersigned brokers agree to aid and assist in consummating the foregoing exchange.

signed: *A. W. Wehrley* (Seal) . . .

I hereby ratify and confirm the employment of *Bob Wehrley Realty*, Real Estate Broker, to procure a purchaser for my property above described in consideration of service performed by said broker in negotiating and bringing about the foregoing sale, and hereby agree to pay said broker forthwith a commission of *$5,000.00.*

signed: *O. H. Butler* (Seal)

After signing the above, Defendant began to have second thoughts and, after discussing the matter with his friend, Zona Wells (also a real estate salesman), asked Wells to phone Plaintiff and cancel the agreement. Wells did so on August 3.

Perry signed the agreement on August 5, and Defendant refused to sign the escrow instructions, contending he had revoked his offer.

From a judgment n.o.v. granted in favor of Plaintiff in the amount of $5000 commission agreed to by Defendant and $8500 Wehrley was alleged to be entitled to from Perry but for Defendant's breach, Defendant appealed. Affirmed as to the $5000 and reversed as to the $8500.

CAMERON, Chief Judge.

First we must discuss the exchange agreement between Wehrley and Perry. The evidence is clear that Wehrley signed the agreement which constituted an offer to Perry, if he (Perry) accepted by 5 August. The evidence indicated he did. Notwithstanding the fact that Butler promised to keep the offer open until then, he, Butler, could still withdraw the offer as to Perry at any time before Perry knew of the existence of the offer:

> As Professor Williston has said, there is nothing that can be regarded as an offer which is not communicated. Foster v. Udall, 10 Cir., 335 F.2d 828, 831 (1964).

And:

> An offer which is given without consideration to the offeror can be withdrawn at any time prior to the acceptance by the offeree. Patton v. Paradise Hills Shopping Center, Inc., 4 Ariz. App. 11, 417 P. 2d 382, 389 (1966).

Revocation of an offer, however, must be communicated to prevent an acceptance from changing it into a binding contract:

> The revocation of an offer, however, must ordinarily be communicated to prevent an acceptance from changing it into a binding contract, and it is not communicated to the offeree unless it is actually brought to his knowledge. . . . Formal notice is not always necessary, it being sufficient that the person making the offer does some act inconsistent with it, as, for example, selling the property, and that the person to whom the offer was made has knowledge of such act. . . .

We hold in the instant case that there was an offer when Butler signed the exchange agreement with the provisions contained therein and that there was no valid revocation of that offer communicated to Perry or Wehrley before the acceptance by Perry on 5 August. We do not feel that the telephone call by Zona Wells was sufficient notice of Butler's revocation of the written offer previously made and delivered.

The contract of exchange and the agreement for commission from Butler to Wehrley were shown to the extent that reasonable men could not have found to the contrary. There being a valid agreement for exchange of realty, Wehrley has earned his commission from Butler. The trial court was correct in granting a motion for judgment n.o.v. as to the $5,000 commission due Wehrley from Butler.

However, we must disagree with the court below as to the $8,500 for commission to be paid to Wehrley by Perry. The exchange agreement when signed by Butler contained the provision that Perry was to pay Wehrley a commission as "per separate agreement". The evidence is clear that this "separate agreement" was not in existence when Butler signed the agreement on 2 August 1963.

Questions
1. Do you agree with the court's holding that the communication here was insufficient to revoke?

2. What justification is there for the technicality in this area of law?

Like the offer and the acceptance, a revocation must be communicated in order to be effective. This may be done expressly, by the offeror's telling the offeree that the offer no longer is open. It also may be done by implication. An offer is considered revoked when the offeree learns of facts that would indicate to a reasonable person that the offeror no longer wishes to be bound to the offer. This may come by way of a statement from a reliable third person to that effect or by learning that the offeror no longer is able to perform, as in the case of the offeree of a car who learns that the offeror has since sold the car to someone else. It is the purpose of the law of contracts to vindicate the justifiable expectations of the parties. Thus an offer is revoked any time the offeree no longer can expect, justifiably, that performance will be rendered.

Rejection

Just as the offeror has a right to revoke the offer at any time prior to acceptance, the offeree has a right to reject it during the same time period. Rejection absolutely terminates the offer, and thereafter that offer never is subject to being accepted. Rejection occurs any time the offeree manifests his or her unwillingness to be bound by the terms of the offer. This may be express, as by the offeree's use of such words as "no" or "no, thanks," or it may be implied, as by the offeree's turning and walking away without saying anything when the offer was made face to face, or by the offeree's saying, "you're kidding" or "you must be crazy" and walking away.

An offer also may be rejected by the offeree's responding with a counteroffer or a conditional acceptance. A **counteroffer** is any response that indicates the offeree's unwillingness to comply with the terms of the original offer and offers back different terms. For example, Frank offers to sell his car to Margaret for $500, and Margaret responds, "I will give you $400."

A **conditional acceptance** is much the same as a counter-offer except that it includes a word or phrase that signals an express condition, such as *if*, *however*, *but*, or *as long as*. Thus, although Margaret's response in the previous example, "I'll give you $400," is a counteroffer, a response such as, "I will buy your car *if* you will take $400," or "*as long as* you will take $400," would be a conditional acceptance. At common law, this distinction is not particularly important. Either a counteroffer or a conditional acceptance operates as a rejection of the offer. However, UCC Section 2-207 makes a significant change in this rule concerning contracts for the sale of goods.

Under Section 2-207(1), a conditional acceptance still is regarded as a rejection, but some types of counteroffers—those that seem to be legitimate attempts to accept—are considered to be valid acceptances even though they may add new terms to those stated by the offeror, as long as they are "seasonable" (effective while the offer is still open). As noted, no change is made concerning conditional acceptances. Neither is the law changed concerning counteroffers that do not seem to be "definite" attempts to accept, such as the response "I'll give you $400" (those that *change* a term of the offer), those that delete a term of the offer, those that violate some stipulation of the offer, or those that do not become effective before the offer terminates. What UCC Section 2-207(1) does try to save are counteroffers such as, "Fine! I'll take it! *Bring it over on Friday*." Because Frank had stated nothing about delivery or a particular time for execution, this response could be treated as a rejection at common law even though it sounds like an excited attempt to accept.

Section 2-207(2) then deals with the next logical question. If the acceptance adds a term (such as "Bring it over on Friday"), is the offeror bound by that term? Subsection "(1)". says there is a contract on the terms stated by the offeror, and subsection "(2)" says that the additional term is to be construed as a *proposal* (by the offeree) for an addition of that term to the contract established by subsection "(1)."

As between merchants, the additional term *automatically* becomes part of the contract unless (a) the terms of the offer prohibit additions, (b) the additional term would change the obligation of the offeror materially, or (c) the offeror rejects the addition. As between *nonmerchants* or when one party is a nonmerchant and the other is a merchant, the additional term never becomes part of the contract unless the offeror actually agrees to it.

Note, again, that the UCC sometimes has a different rule for merchants than it does for nonmerchants. Subsection "(1)" and the first sentence of subsection "(2)" apply to everyone alike, and the remainder of subsection "(2)" applies only to transactions *between merchants*. Note, also, that this merchant provision applies only when both parties are merchants, while the merchant provision of Section 2-205, discussed earlier, required that the offeror be a merchant but said nothing about the offeree. Thus, under Section 2-205 the offeree might be either a merchant or a nonmerchant and the provision would apply. In any case, however, it is necessary to determine whether an acceptance that adds terms to the offer is conditional or unconditional. Consider the following case.

PODANY v. ERICKSON et al.
235 Minn. 36, 49 N.W.2d 193 (1954)

This was an action by Martin Podany (Plaintiff/Appellant) against Sadie U. Erickson and three of her children for specific performance of an alleged contract for the sale of certain real estate.

Plaintiff leased a building from Defendant Sadie U. Erickson for a term of five years beginning January 25, 1945. The lease contained a "continuing option" allowing Plaintiff the right to purchase the building at any time for $20,000. On March 19, 1949, Plaintiff, intending to exercise the option, sent a notice to Defendant, which read, in part as follows:

"Notice is hereby given that I have elected under the option provision on page 3 of said lease, to purchase the said property, for the sum of $20,000.00 within 30 days from the date of this notice and shall pay for the property with cash.

"Will you please furnish me with your abstract or registration certificate, brought down to date, so that I may have the title examined before completing the transaction and paying the money for it."

Defendant refused to accept, and offered to sell the building to Plaintiff for $38,000. Plaintiff did not accept, and Defendant sold the building to her children (the other defendants). Defendants contended that Plaintiff's notice constituted a conditional acceptance since nothing was mentioned in the offer about an abstract. Being a conditional acceptance, it was a rejection of the offer, not an acceptance.

The trial court agreed and gave a judgment for Defendants. Plaintiff appealed. Reversed and remanded for a new trial.

CHRISTIANSON, Justice.

It is a settled rule of law that, in order to form a contract, an acceptance must be coextensive with the offer and may not introduce additional terms or conditions. An acceptance which qualifies the terms of the offer amounts in legal contemplation to a rejection of the offer and is regarded as merely a counteroffer. However, it is equally well settled that requested or suggested modifications of the offer will not preclude the formation of a contract where it clearly appears that the offer is positively accepted, regardless of whether the requests are granted. Since no provision for an abstract was made in the lease and since defendant was under no legal duty to furnish an abstract, our only question is whether it appears that the furnishing of an abstract by defendant was intended as a condition precedent to plaintiff's acceptance of the offer.

The language of the controversial paragraph of plaintiff's letter is that of a request rather than a command. Nevertheless, where acceptance is expressly conditioned on acquiescence in the requested modification, or that is the necessary inference from the language employed, no contract is formed, even though precatory words of request [words asking, but not requiring] precede the condition. However, plaintiff's letter does not make the request an express condition, nor do we find the necessary inference of a condition. Instead, it appears clear to us that asking for an abstract was merely a request or suggestion on plaintiff's part looking toward per ance of the contract of sale, and not a qualification of the acceptance of the offer. Therefore, we hold as a matter of law that plaintiff's letter of intention to purchase was an unconditional acceptance.

Questions

1. Is the decision in this case fair and simply designed to avoid the application of a technical rule that would produce an unfair result? Does it destroy the predictability of result?

2. Should it make any difference that the property may have skyrocketed in value since the original offer?

Death

Death of either the offeror or the offeree will terminate an offer. The termination is automatic, by law, regardless of when the surviving party learns of the death. One basic reason for this is that every contract requires the existence of two parties. Also, especially in the case of the offeror's death, the court is concerned with the possibility that if the offeror had lived he or she might have revoked the offer prior to acceptance. For this reason, options, firm offers, and promissory estoppel (although the latter is difficult to apply against a dead promisor) are exceptions to the rule that death of the offeror will terminate an offer—in these situations, the ability to revoke is lost anyway.

Insanity and Incompetence

The distinction between *insanity* and *incompetence* must be understood because their effects in contract law are quite different. A person is considered *insane* if he or she is incapable of comprehending the nature of the business at hand at the time of the transaction in question. That is, **insanity** means the person simply lacks the mental capacity to be voluntary and consensual in entering into a contract. **Incompetence**, on the other hand, involves a judicial declaration, in a separate action (before a probate court in most states), that from that moment on, the person legally is incapable of entering into binding agreements until the court declares him competent again. Such a declaration is based on evidence demonstrating that the person, because of age or mental infirmity, has become a danger to himself or to others. Although insanity is judged as of a past or present moment in time, incompetence is judged as of the present and into the future.

Finally, although the acts of an insane person, like those of a minor, are declared to be *voidable*, those of an incompetent person are declared *void* by statute. Thus, although insanity of the offeror or the offeree usually will not terminate an offer, incompetence of either will. Also, this rule is subject to the same exceptions as were stated for death.

Generally, at common law, one who has been adjudicated incompetent is treated for most purposes as if he or she were dead, the theory being that an incompetent person "has no mind." The similarity between death and incompetency, for the purpose of determining contract liability, is considered in the following case.

UNION TRUST AND SAVINGS BANK v. STATE BANK
188 N.W.2d 300, 55 A.L.R.3d 336 (Iowa 1971)

This was an action by Union Trust and Savings Bank (Plaintiff/Appellant) against Union State Bank, in its capacity as conservator of the estate of Bonnie Semprini, to recover on a contract of guaranty on a note.

Semprini executed and delivered to Plaintiff a continuing guaranty (one that operates until it is revoked) to apply to any notes thereafter given to Plaintiff by her husband. Thereafter, on August 23, 1967, Defendant was appointed conservator of her estate. On November 4, 1969, James Semprini, Mrs. Semprini's husband, executed a note to Plaintiff in the amount of $85,000.

When the note was not paid, Plaintiff filed this suit on the instrument of guaranty. Defendant refused to pay contending that by its appointment as conservator, the guaranty was revoked. From a judgment for Defendant, Plaintiff appealed. Affirmed.

RAWLINGS, Justice.

August 23, 1967, defendant conservator was appointed. On October 3, 1969, plaintiff filed a claim in that conservatorship, on which the . . . prior action was premised. So it is apparent, plaintiff was aware of the conservatorship long before the subject note was taken.

The vital question now posed is whether appointment of a conservator for the guarantor served to effectively revoke this guaranty, then totally unaccepted by the obligee. Plaintiff concedes a continuing guaranty is usually terminated, in futuro, by death of the obligor. . . .

It is vigorously contended, however, the foregoing rule does not apply in event a conservatorship is established on behalf of a mentally competent guarantor.

In support thereof plaintiff inceptionally argues the revocation by death rule is founded upon the need to protect a deceased person's estate, which does not exist when a living competent party is placed under conservatorship since the conservator has power to revoke a continuing guaranty.

We perceive no such instantly persuasive distinction. An executor and a conservator have like powers in that regard. [The court then cited numerous authorities in support of its perception.]

It is to us apparent, (1) Bonnie Semprini executed and delivered to plaintiff, as sole obligee, a continuing accommodation guaranty limited only as to amount and nature of any debt to be thereby secured; (2) defendant was appointed conservator for said guarantor; (3) plaintiff had not then accepted the guaranty by any loan effected within the terms thereof; (4) plaintiff became aware of the aforesaid active conservatorship; and (5) subsequently attempted to effectuate a guaranty covered loan by a note renewal scheme never approved or ratified by the conservator or any court of competent jurisdiction. We are satisfied and now hold the appointment of a conservator for Bonnie Semprini, guarantor known to defendant bank, served to revoke the then unaccepted guaranty, making it thereafter and at all times here concerned of no legal force.

And it is of no consequence that the instrument here sued upon provides, in part, it shall "be a continuing guaranty . . . until revoked by me in writing and a copy of such revocation delivered to the bank."

Questions

1.   Who should be legally incompetent—infants, children, institutionalized people, resident aliens?

2.   Should courts be liberal or conservative in declaring people incompetent?

Intervening Illegality

Sometimes an offer is made and, prior to acceptance, performance of the terms of the offer becomes illegal. When this occurs, the offer is terminated automatically. Intervening illegality may arise as a result of a general change in the law, as would be the case if ABC Pharmaceutical offers to sell a quantity of a particular drug to WXY Wholesale Drugs and, prior to acceptance, the sale of the drug is banned by statute or Food and Drug Administration rule. It also may occur if a party to the negotiations loses a qualification necessary to perform the terms of the proposed contract legally, as would be the case if attorney A offered to represent party B in a lawsuit and, prior to B's acceptance, A was disbarred. In any case, the offer will terminate if the performance of the terms of the offer will *necessitate* illegal conduct.

Loss or Destruction of the Contract's Subject Matter

The loss or destruction of the subject matter of an offer will cause termination because any contract formed under the terms would be impossible to perform. This rule assumes that the loss or destruction was not the fault of either party, at least intentionally. Care must be taken, however, that the lost or destroyed property actually was the subject matter of the offer. For example, suppose Ashley finds she has more hay in her barn than she will need and states to Mark, "I will sell 200 bales of hay to you for $3.00 a bale." While Mark is considering the offer, Ashley's barn burns and the hay is destroyed. Thereafter Mark tenders his acceptance. Ashley probably is bound to a contract because the offer stated only "hay" and was not limited to the hay in Ashley's barn. Unless Mark actually understood that the offer was conditioned on the existence of that particular hay, Ashley probably would be required to purchase 200 bales of hay from another source and sell it to Mark for $3.00 a bale, or to pay damages for breach of contract.

SOME IMPORTANT UCC PROVISIONS

The Uniform Commercial Code varies somewhat in regard to the common law rules with respect to contracts for the sale of goods. Section 1-203 imposes an obligation of good faith in all transactions under the code, and "good faith" is defined in Section 1-201(19) as "honesty in fact." As

discussed previously, Section 2-204 sets the rule for certainty of terms; Section 2-206 allows variations on the strict rules of common law concerning the manner and means of acceptance; Section 2-205 makes certain promises to hold offers open irrevocable in spite of the fact that they are not supported by consideration; Section 2-207 allows an acceptance to be effective in spite of the fact that it alters the terms of the offer to some extent. In addition, two sections allow indefiniteness in the terms of a contract—Section 2-305 (open price term) and Section 2-306 (output, requirements, and exclusive dealing), although the latter, concerning output and requirements contracts, only codifies the common law. That is, it puts in statutory form the law as already set out in case decisions.

SUMMARY

Every contract requires that the parties mutually agree to a specific set of terms. These are dictated by the offeror. The mutual agreement must be based on a voluntary intention to enter into the contract. This is manifested by the offeror in communicating an offer, and by the offeree in communicating an acceptance. Generally, silent intent will be insufficient since contractual intent is measured by an objective standard that typically cannot be applied until there has been some communication.

An offer is the manifestation of the offeror's intent to be bound, and it generally can be made in any manner and by any means sufficient to communicate to the offeree the intent to be bound. In general, an offer is composed of two parts—(1) what the offeror will do, and (2) what the offeror expects in return. Special consideration must be given to some types of situations in order to judge when an offer has been made. Of particular importance are those involving auctions, advertisements, rewards, and those in which the offeror attempts to communicate through indirect means.

The acceptance is the manifestation of the offeree's willingness to be bound to the terms stated by the offeror. When this is done properly, the requirement of mutual assent is satisfied. Care must be taken to see that the tendered acceptance complies in all respects with the terms of the offer, although this requirement has been relaxed somewhat by the Uniform Commercial Code provisions concerning contracts for the sale of goods. Generally a unilateral offer must be accepted by unilateral means (performing an act) and a bilateral offer by bilateral means (making a promise). Also, an offer may be accepted only by the person to whom the offeror intended to communicate it. There are special rules governing the effective moment of acceptance when the acceptance is communicated by means involving a time lag between dispatch and receipt, but any acceptance sent by a means approved by the offeror is effective on dispatch.

Once communicated, an offer may terminate—and therefore no longer be subject to an acceptance—by the lapse of a time stated in the offer, by the lapse of a reasonable time when no other time was stated, by revocation by the offeror or rejection by the offeree, by the death or incompetency of either party, by intervening illegality, or by the loss or destruction of the subject matter of the proposed contract. It should be noted that there are significant exceptions to the general rules concerning death, incompetency, revocation, and rejection, and that the Uniform Commercial Code changes the common law rules in the contexts of revocation and rejection.

KEY TERMS AND CONCEPTS

offeror
offer
offeree
acceptance
mutual assent
intent
material terms
preliminary negotiations
revocation
counteroffer
conditional acceptance
insanity
incompetence

PROBLEMS

1. During Washington State Gambling Commission hearings, Treece, a vice-president of a punchboard manufacturing corporation, stated, "I'll offer a hundred thousand dollars to anyone to find a crooked board. If they find it, I'll pay it." The statement brought laughter from those who attended. Barnes heard the statement on TV and read it in the newspaper. He had two such boards in his possession, which he had purchased when he was a bartender, and presented them to Treece. He demanded the $100,000 but Treece refused, saying he was only joking. Is Barnes entitled to the reward?

2. As a general rule, an offeror may revoke the offer at any time prior to acceptance. Under what circumstances may this general rule *not* apply?

3. Since an offer may be held irrevocable under some circumstances, are there any circumstances under which an offeree may *not* be permitted to reject an offer?

4. Herndon and Armstrong entered into negotiations under which Herndon was to buy certain land belonging to Armstrong if she could arrange financing. Armstrong agreed to give her until January 15. Herndon diligently pursued financing and was able to secure it on January 17. Immediately, she tendered her acceptance to Armstrong, but was informed that Armstrong already had sold the land to someone else. Herndon sued Armstrong for breach of the agreement. Is she entitled to recover?

5. Peterson went to work for Pilgrim Village

at an agreed-upon salary. In addition to the salary, Pilgrim Village promised to pay him "a percentage of the profits." At the end of the first year, Pilgrim Village had paid Peterson the salary but refused to pay any more. Peterson sued and the trial court granted him judgment in an amount equal to what it considered a reasonable percentage of the profits. Pilgrim Village appealed. Should the decision of the trial court be affirmed?

6. Upon the expiration of her fire-insurance policy, Andrus told her insurance agent that she wanted coverage reduced from $40,000 to $24,000. The agent said the insurance company would insure only for 80 percent of the value of the insured premises which, in Andrus's case, was $48,000. Andrus then told the agent she would look elsewhere. The agent sent Andrus a policy for $48,000 together with a note stating, "Cancel if you don't want the policy." Andrus did not respond, and later the insurance company sued her for the premium on the policy. Is the insurance company entitled to recover?

7. Crouch was interested in purchasing an abandoned building owned by Purex Corporation, and wrote to Purex asking for its lowest price. Purex quoted $500 for the building and contents. Crouch wrote again, stating the price was too high, and offered to pay $300. Purex did not respond and, after awhile, Crouch sent another letter agreeing to the $500 price and enclosed a check in the full amount. In the meantime, Purex had sold the building to Marrs, but an officer of Purex endorsed Crouch's check and deposited it. Did the act of endorsing and depositing the check, under the circumstances, constitute the acceptance of the offer to sell the property to Crouch?

8. Morrison and Thoelke concluded negotiations concerning the purchase, by Thoelke, of certain land owned by Morrison. Morrison, in Florida, then signed a contract and mailed it to Thoelke for his signature. Thoelke, in New York, signed it and mailed it back to Morrison, retaining a copy for himself. Before the signed contract reached Morrison, Morrison called Thoelke and told him she had decided to revoke her offer to sell. Did a contract result?

9. Suppose, in the case of Morrison and Thoelke, the signed contract had been returned by mail but was lost and did not arrive for several weeks. Instead of calling to revoke, Morrison simply decided Thoelke did not wish to accept and sold the land to someone else. Would Thoelke be entitled to damages for breach of contract?

10. Dixon sent a letter to the Federal Mortgage Corp. offering to buy certain land owned by Federal, and specifying that he required an acceptance in writing. The offer was presented to the executive committee for its approval. Upon approval, a note was handwritten on the letter: "Approved by Executive Committee—Nov. 9, 1936—A. R. Murray." Some time later, the note was scratched out and another note was written under it: "Reconsidered and rejected—Miss A. R. Murray, Minute Clerk—Dated Nov. 17, 1936." Later, Dixon learned of all this and tendered the purchase price, demanding a deed to the property. Federal refused, contending no contract had been formed. Is Federal correct?

Chapter | 8

Consideration

INTRODUCTION

In the preceding chapter we focused on the necessity of mutual assent as expressed by the parties through the process of negotiations and, ultimately, offer and acceptance. This chapter focuses on the doctrine of *consideration*, the third of the three requirements for a valid contract. The doctrine provides that in order to bind the promisor contractually, the promisee must give something in return for the promise. For example, in a contract for the sale of a car for $500, the purchaser gives consideration for the seller's promise to sell the car by promising to pay the seller $500. Of the three contract requirements, consideration is the one most near the essence of contracts. This element distinguishes the contract from the gift.

Although records of the earliest common-law contract actions are too sketchy to be certain, the prevailing opinion among legal scholars is that, at early common law, the only contracts that were enforced were those "under seal." A contract's validity depended on its being put down in proper form—written and authenticated by each party's placing a personal seal on the document. In Chapter 6, contracts were classified as *formal* and *simple*. A contract under seal is an example of a *formal* contract—one that derives its validity from being put in proper form (the seal). In the interest of enforcing a broader class of promises, the law later replaced the seal requirement with that of consideration. A few jurisdictions still attach legal significance to the seal and give a sealed agreement validity even in the absence of consideration. However, all jurisdictions recognize the doctrine of consideration.

DEFINITION OF CONSIDERATION

Consideration may be defined as a legal benefit to the promisor *or* a legal detriment to the promisee, bargained for and given in exchange for a promise. Although this statement may seem relatively simple, it is highly technical and full of meaning. As is true of reading many statutes such as the Uniform Commercial Code, each word should be considered carefully.

Promise

Notice first that the entire definition focuses on *individual promises*—"legal benefit to the *promisor*," "legal detriment to the *promisee*," and "given in exchange for a *promise*." In Chapter 7 we were concerned with the offer and the acceptance, the offeror and offeree. In discussing consideration, we no longer are concerned with who gave the offer and who received it. We do not care if the promise in question was contained in the offer or the acceptance—a promise is a promise. We are concerned only with whether the particular promise sought to be enforced is supported by consideration.

Legal Benefit

Consideration may consist of a legal benefit to the promisor. **Legal benefit** may be defined as the acquisition of a right to which the person receiving it was not previously entitled. In other words, the person is receiving something new in return for his or her promise. Notice that when a benefit is used as the consideration, the benefit must flow to the promisor, not to the promisee. Notice further that the benefit must be a *legal* benefit, not necessarily an actual benefit. That is, it must be something the law recognizes as a benefit regardless of whether it actually appears to be beneficial or of value to the promisor. The requirement is satisfied if the promisor has received any right to which he or she was not previously entitled.

Legal Detriment

Notice that *either* a legal benefit *or* a legal detriment may be the basis for consideration. **Legal detriment** may be defined as giving up something a person was not previously obligated to give up. When a detriment is used as the consideration, it must be suffered by the promisee, not the promisor. Also, like the benefit, the detriment must be a *legal* detriment, not necessarily an actual detriment. This concept is illustrated in the following case.

The nature of consideration

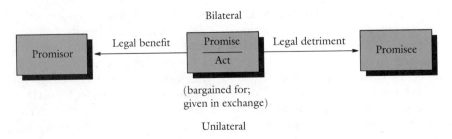

HAMER v. SIDWAY
124 N.Y. 538, 27 N.E. 256 (1891)

This was an action by Hamer (Plaintiff/Appellant), as assignee of William E. Story, II, against Sidway, the executor of the estate of William E. Story, Sr., to recover the sum of $5000 and interest claimed due on a contract entered into between William, Sr. and William, II.

On March 20, 1869, William, Sr., promised his nephew, William, II, that if he would refrain from drinking, using tobacco, swearing, and playing cards or billiards for money until his 21st birthday, he would pay him the sum of $5000. The nephew assented and fully performed. Thereafter, when he was 21 years of age, the nephew requested payment. The uncle told him, among other things, that the money was in the bank and that he would receive it when he (the uncle) felt that he (the nephew) was capable of taking care of it. The nephew consented to this arrangement. The uncle died in January 1887 without paying the money and Defendant refused to pay it on the ground that there was no contract because of lack of consideration—specifically, William, II, had suffered no detriment.

The trial court found in favor of Plaintiff. That decision was reversed on appeal to the Appellate Division of the Supreme Court of New York. The decision of the Appellate Division then was reversed here.

PARKER, J.

. . . The defendant contends that the contract was without consideration to support it, and therefore invalid. He asserts that the promisee, by refraining from the use of liquor and tobacco, was not harmed, but benefited; that which he did was best for him to do, independently of his uncle's promise,—and insists that it follows that, unless the promisor was benefited, the contract was without consideration—a contention which, if well founded, would seem to leave open for controversy in many cases whether that which the promisee did or omitted to do was in fact of such benefit to him as to leave no consideration to support the enforcement of the promisor's agreement. Such a rule could not be tolerated, and is without foundation in the law. The exchequer chamber in 1875 defined "consideration" as follows; "A valuable consideration, in the sense of the law, may consist either in some right, interest, profit, or benefit accruing to the one party, or some forbearance, detriment, loss, or responsibility given, suffered, or undertaken by the other." Courts "will not ask whether the thing which forms the consideration does in fact benefit the promisee or a third party, or is of any substantial value to any one. It is enough that something is promised, done, forborne, or suffered by the party to whom the promise is made as consideration for the promise made to him." *Anson*, Cont. 63. "In general a waiver of any legal right at the request of another party is a sufficient consideration for a promise." . . . "Any damage, or suspension, or forbearance of a right will be sufficient to sustain a promise." . . .

Now, applying this rule to the facts before us, the promisee used tobacco, occasionally drank liquor, and he had a legal right to do so. That right he abandoned for a period of years upon the strength of the promise of the testator that for such forbearance he would give him $5,000. We need not speculate on the effort which may have been required to give up the use of those stimulants. It is sufficient that he restricted his lawful freedom of action within certain prescribed limits upon the faith of his uncle's agreement, and now, having fully performed the conditions imposed, it is of no moment whether such performance actually proved a benefit to the promisor, and the court will not inquire into it.

Questions

1. Why did the court say a rule stating that anything not benefitting the promisor could not satisfy consideration "could not be tolerated"?

2. Does the Hamer case effectively destroy the doctrine of consideration?

Bargained For

Not every legal benefit to the promisor or legal detriment to the promisee will suffice as consideration—only those that are **bargained for**. That is, the legal benefit or detriment must be what the promisor intended to achieve by making the promise. Just as the requirement of consideration is the one that is most nearly the essence of contracts, the requirement of "bargained for" is the most critical element of consideration. In many **gift transactions** (those not supported by consideration) it is quite easy to find an offer and an acceptance with a legal benefit to the promisor or a legal detriment to the promisee, but the benefit or detriment never is bargained for in gift situations. This requirement will be discussed more fully toward the end of this chapter.

Consideration Applied

Having defined the term *consideration* and discussed each of its elements, let us completely analyze its application to a factual situation. Assume a case in which Sara has offered her car to Gary for $500, and Gary has agreed. Is consideration present?

Since the contract, if one exists, is bilateral—Gary having made a promise of $500 in return for Sara's promise of the car—consideration must be analyzed in terms of what consideration was given in return for each promise. Also, even though *either* a legal benefit to the promisor *or* a legal detriment to the promisee is sufficient, for the purpose of illustration we will see if we can find both for each promise. In most cases, when one is found, the other also is present.

For *Sara's promise* of the car, she (promisor) has acquired the right to Gary's $500 (legal benefit) and he (promisee) has given up the right to the $500 (legal detriment). Thus, Sara's promise is supported by consideration, assuming that by making the promise of the car, she was trying to acquire the right to the $500. For *Gary's promise* of the $500, he (promisor) has acquired the right to Sara's car (legal benefit) and she (promisee) has given up the right to the car (legal detriment). Thus Gary's promise also is supported by consideration, again assuming he bargained for the exchange. Therefore, a binding contract has come into being between Sara and Gary. Had only Sara's promise (or only Gary's promise) been supported by consideration, there would have been no contract because, as a general rule, unless both parties to a contract are bound, neither is bound. This is the notion of "mutuality of obligation."

How does this change in unilateral contract situations? Suppose Sara promises Gary, "If you come over and paint my garage by Friday, I will pay you $100." On Friday, Gary paints the garage (accepts the offer). Is there a contract entitling Gary to the $100? In other words, is Sara's promise to pay the $100 supported by consideration? Yes. Sara, in return for her promise to pay the $100, has received the legal benefit of having the garage painted, and Gary has suffered the legal detriment of doing the work (or giving up his right not to do the work).

What consideration then, has been paid to Gary? The answer is, "none." Payment of consideration to Gary is not necessary because he made no promise—he performed an act. Remember, consideration is "paid in return for a *promise*" (not an act). The purpose of consideration is to bind a person to a *promise* to do something in the *future*.

We have one final point concerning the application of the concept of consideration. Note that consideration in the bilateral case is found in the acquisition of *rights* by the promisor and the giving up of *rights* by the promisee. In the previous example, the car and the $500 are not the consideration. The consideration is the *right* to the car and the *right* to the $500. The car and the $500 are only the means of executing the contract. In effect, in most cases involving bilateral contracts, the promises that form the offer and acceptance, if mutually binding, also constitute the consideration. This important point is illustrated by the following case.

HOSPITAL AUTHORITY OF CHARLTON COUNTY v. BRYANT
157 Ga. App. 330, 277 S.E.2d 322 (1981)

This was an action by Bryant (Plaintiff/Appellee) against the Hospital Authority of Charlton County for damages for breach of an alleged contract of employment. Plaintiff requested compensatory damages in the amount of $1790 and punitive damages and attorney fees in the amount of $5000 each.

By written agreement to become effective February 1, 1978, Defendant agreed to employ Plaintiff, an independent service, to clean carpets and wax and buff tile floors at stated intervals at an agreed-upon price. The contract was to last one full year, but Defendant discharged Plaintiff on December 7, 1978 stating, among other things, that it could get the work done more cheaply. Defendant refused to pay Plaintiff thereafter on the theory that he was not entitled to pay since he did no further work.

From a judgment of the trial court awarding Plaintiff $4250 in damages, Defendant appealed. Reversed as to the damages only, the appeals court finding error in the instruction to the jury that punitive damages might be awarded.

QUILLIAN, Chief Judge.

There is no merit in appellant's anomalous contention that its motions for directed verdict and judgment notwithstanding the verdict should have been granted because there was no evidence establishing consideration for a promise by appellant to pay appellee for services he did not render in December 1978 and January 1979 after appellant prevented him from performing further.

The written contract was in evidence and its undisputed terms were that appellee promised to periodically perform floor maintenance service for specified fees for a period of one year and appellant promised to pay appellee for those services. The mutual promises of the parties provided the required consideration.

Questions

1.   If the plaintiff did no actual work, why should he be entitled to damages?
2.   Was the court correct in reversing the award of punitive damages in this case? Are punitive damages ever appropriate in a case of breach of contract?

SPECIAL PROBLEMS

Sometimes a promise is made that will not be sufficient as consideration, even though it might have been bargained for and given as requested. Although such promises may appear to be tendered in good faith, they create no legal detriment to the party making them nor any legal benefit to the other party.

Adequacy and Sufficiency of Consideration

As a general rule, courts do not question the "adequacy" of consideration—only its legal "sufficiency." That is, the court does not concern itself with **adequacy** (whether the thing given by one party in a transaction is equal in value to that given by the other party). Rather it concerns itself with **sufficiency** (whether that which was given in each case meets the legal definition of consideration stated before).

What a particular thing is worth is highly subjective; courts are unwilling to substitute their determinations of value for those of the parties. Amenity value (the value of the simple pleasure derived from having particular property) is a very important component of the entire question of value. For example, what is a pet worth? Most people who own a pet know that its value is immeasurable, and it is much more valuable to its owner than it is likely to be to anyone else.

Another factor affecting value is need. Which is worth more, ten gallons of water or a $150,000 Rolls Royce? Suppose your Rolls Royce broke down in the desert, ten days from water, and a passerby offered to trade his water for your car.

Would you trade? Probably. Would a court enforce such a contract? At common law a court would find that the passerby had suffered a legal detriment and you had acquired a legal benefit by his giving up his right to the water. Thus your promise to give up the Rolls Royce would be fully supported by consideration, and the court would give the passerby damages (probably $150,000) if you failed to turn over title to the car.

In two major situations the court may look at relative values. The first involves traditional equity law. Courts of equity may refuse equitable relief (specific performance) in cases of disparate relative values. Thus, an agreement by one party to pay another $100 for a $10,000 piece of real estate might be enforced by a court of law (by money damages) but not a court of equity (by ordering delivery of a deed to the property). The same would be true in the case of the Rolls Royce; although a court of law would give money damages, a court of equity would not grant specific performance. Courts of equity keep "hands off" in situations in which the exchange does not seem to produce fairness for both parties.

The second major situation involves Section 2-302 of the Uniform Commercial Code, Unconscionable Contract or Clause. This section provides that when a court finds a contract for the sale of goods, or any clause in the contract, to be **unconscionable** (grossly unfair), it is empowered to refuse to enforce it, or to eliminate or limit the unconscionable portion and enforce the rest. Unconscionability (which is not defined in the UCC) may come as a result of any number of circumstances including inadequate consideration. In general, it includes situations in which there is a great disparity in the values of the things given by the parties, and it appears that one party has extracted the contract from the other by exercising a position of superior power over him or her.

The effect of 2-302 is to give to courts of law powers that previously were held only by courts of equity—the power to remedy unfairness. As noted in the case of the Rolls Royce, without this power, courts of law were constrained to grant damage remedies even though it might seem that justice was not served. Probably, with its new power under Section 2-302, a court of law today would not grant money damages in that case.

Illusory Promises

An **illusory promise** is one that creates no binding obligation on the promisor. Although it may give the appearance of a binding promise, that appearance is false, an illusion. The most obvious type of illusory promise would be one such as, "I will do the job *if I want to*." Another common type is one based on a condition precedent and the promisor has the power to determine whether the condition ever occurs. For example, "I will purchase your car for $500 if I sell my boat by Friday." Although on the surface that promise seems to create an obligation, closer examination reveals that if the promisor wishes to avoid the obligation, he or she has the power to refuse to sell the boat until after Friday.

This is not to say that all promises based on conditions are illusory. For example, in the purchase of real estate, it is common for a purchaser to condition his or her promise on the availability of reasonable financing. In addition, many contractual promises are based on conditions over which the *promisee* (not promisor) has control, such as a promise to purchase a seller's entire production of certain goods during the coming year. These are not illusory.

Finally, illusory situations may arise as a result of apparent contracts, to be performed for indefinite periods, that either expressly or implicitly are terminable at the will of one or both of the parties. This is a common occurrence in employment "contracts," especially those entered into by young employees on their first jobs. When there is no commitment on the part of either the employer to employ, or the employee to work, for any particular time, the relationship is not contractual, at least not in the bilateral sense. When parties wish to have a contract that essentially is terminable at will, a provision for some notice of termination will prevent the promises from being illusory because the parties at least are bound for the notice period.

Special care should be exercised in cases of "contracts" that are long and detailed, because a single provision among the many may render the entire agreement illusory. It is not uncommon for a party to such an agreement to perform in good faith, as promised, for some extended period of time only to find, when he or she needs to enforce the "obligation" of the other party, that the "promise" of the other party is illusory; no contract ever existed, nor did any legal obligation. Of course, recovery may be had for the partial performance based on the performance of a continuing series of unilateral contracts or, at least, on a theory of quasi conract, but the expectation of future performance is lost. Consider the following case.

STREICH v. GENERAL MOTORS CORPORATION
5 Ill.App.2d 583, 126 N.E.2d 389 (1955)

This was an action by Frank Streich (Plaintiff/Appellant) against General Motors Corporation for damages for breach of an alleged contract for the purchase of machine parts.

Plaintiff entered into a long and complicated written agreement with Defendant under the terms of which Plaintiff was supposed to produce certain parts to Defendant's specifications and Defendant was to pay $13.50 per unit. Among the terms of the agreement appeared the following provisions:

> Deliveries are to be made both in quantities and at times specified in schedules furnished by Buyer. Buyer will have no liability for payment for material or items delivered to Buyer which are in excess of quantities specified in the delivery schedules. Buyer may from time to time change delivery schedules or direct temporary suspension of scheduled shipments.
>
> Buyer reserves the right to cancel all or any of the undelivered portion of this order if Seller does not make deliveries as specified in the schedules, or if Seller breaches any of the terms hereof including the warranties of Seller.

Defendant ordered no parts from Streich, who sued because he felt Defendant should have purchased something from him. From a judgment of the trial court dismissing the complaint for failure to state a cause of action, Plaintiff appealed. Affirmed.

McCORMICK, Presiding Judge.

This is an appeal from an order of the Circuit Court of Cook County sustaining a motion to dismiss the plaintiff's fifth amended complaint. The complaint was filed in an action for damages occasioned by the defendant's alleged wrongful cancellation of a contract. . . .

There is no question but that under the law a contract properly entered into whereby the buyer agrees to buy all its requirements of a commodity for a certain period, and the seller agrees to sell the same as ordered, is a valid and enforceable contract and is not void for uncertainty and want of mutuality. . . .

The contract in the instant case is not such a contract. Purchase Order No. 11925 states that it is issued to cover "shipments of this part, to be received by us from Sept. 1, 1948 to August 31, 1949 as released and scheduled on our series 48 'Purchase Order release and Shipping Schedule' No. 478412 attached and all subsequent Purchase Order releases." Construing the letter of April 1, 1948 as an integral part of the contract, the provisions therein contained are merely that it "now becomes necessary to issue our 48 series 'Open End' purchase order for our requirements from September 1, 1948, through August 31, 1949." Reading and construing the two documents together, notwithstanding the detailed provisions contained on the reverse side of the purchase order, the result is an agreement on the part of the seller to sell a certain identified valve at a certain fixed price in such quantities as the buyer may designate, when and if it issues a purchase order for the same. The word "release" as used throughout these documents is treated by both parties as equivalent to "order." . . .

Here, the buyer proffers purchase order 11925, with its twenty-five or more clauses, to the seller for acceptance. In the instrument it makes no promise to do anything. On the surface it appears to be an attempt to initiate a valid bilateral contract. The seller accepts, and as by a flash of legerdemain the positions of the buyer and seller shift. The buyer now becomes the promisee and the seller the promisor. The promise of the seller to furnish identified items at a stated price is merely an offer and cannot become a contract until the buyer issues a release or order for a designated number of items. Until this action is taken the buyer has made no promise to do anything, and either party may withdraw. The promise is illusory, and the chimerical contract vanishes. "An agreement to sell to another such of the seller's goods, wares, and merchandise as the other might from time to time desire to purchase is lacking in mutuality because it does not bind the buyer to purchase any of the goods of the seller, as such matter is left wholly at the option or pleasure of the buyer." . . .

Questions

1. Is there anything the seller could have done to avoid falling into the trap of the illusory promise?
2. Should the law do anything to protect people against illusory promises, or is the availability of quasi contract and other remedies sufficient?

Output, Requirements, and Exclusive Dealing Contracts

Not to be confused with illusory promises are output, requirements, and exclusive dealing contracts. A perfectly valid contractual commitment may be based on a promise to sell or purchase an indefinite quantity of goods or services when the quantity is to be established by the entire output of the seller (output contract) or the entire needs of the buyer (requirements contract). Contracts with these quantity terms received approval at common law, and subsequently under Section 2-306 of the UCC, because the law recognized that even though the quantity terms were indefinite, there existed some obligation and their use was demanded by practical commercial necessity. A promise to sell as much as I *produce* or to purchase as much as I *need* is wholly different than a promise to sell or purchase as much as I *want* to. The concept of reasonableness is imposed on these obligations. That is, the promisor is not allowed in an output contract to alter production drastically, or in a requirements contract to alter requirements in a way that goes beyond the reasonable expectations of the parties.

Exclusive dealing contracts are those giving one party the exclusive right to sell the goods (or other property) or services of another. The problem that arose when these contracts first became popular was that in many cases, the person receiving the right made no express commitment to the other party in return and the courts generally held such transactions to be noncontractual. This problem was remedied for contracts involving goods by UCC Section 2-206(2).

Forbearance to Sue

Fundamental to the legal system in the United States is the right to bring before a court any controversy concerning one's legal rights. Although asserting wholly bad-faith, spurious claims is prohibited, a person feeling wronged has a right to submit the dispute to the courts, regardless of the probability that he or she will be successful in pressing the claim. One person's giving up of such right is sufficient consideration to support a promise by another, as long as the claim could be brought in good faith. This frequently is referred to as an "out-of-court settlement."

Settlements may involve only the immediate two parties to a controversy, or may involve a promise by an interested third party. For example, Fred is involved in an automobile accident with Ginger. Fred promises to pay $5000 to Ginger if Ginger will agree not to sue. Ginger's agreement is sufficient consideration to bind Fred's promise as long as there is some basis to believe that Fred *might* have been found liable to Ginger had she brought suit. Also, the promise to pay the $5000 could have been made by another (for example, Fred's father) on Fred's behalf. The latter type of promise will be discussed in Chapter 11. The following case illustrates the legal effect of giving up the right to sue.

SCHIFFELBEIN v. SISTERS OF CHARITY OF LEAVENWORTH
190 Kan. 278, 374 P.2d 42 (1962)

This was an action by Celestine P. Schiffelbein (Plaintiff/Appellant) against the Sisters of Charity of Leavenworth dba St. Francis Hospital for breach of contract to employ Plaintiff for life. Plaintiff sought damages in the amount of $122,000.

It was alleged that on February 21, 1953, Plaintiff was severely and permanently injured while in the employ of Defendant. Two days later, Defendant orally promised Plaintiff that if Plaintiff would refrain from suing the defendant for his injuries, he could work for Defendant, doing what jobs he was capable of doing as long as he wished to remain at a rate of pay comparable to that paid to employees in similar institutions. It was further alleged that his employment was wrongfully terminated, contrary to this agreement, on January 12, 1960.

From an order of the trial court sustaining Defendant's demurrer to Plaintiff's second amended petition and rendering judgments for Defendant, Plaintiff appealed. Reversed.

JACKSON, Justice.

In the light of the facts aforementioned, this court has little difficulty finding the consideration for the contract, as alleged, to be sufficient, although the appellee would seem to assert the contrary.

There is no requirement that a legal obligation be pleaded and proved. The fact that the substance of a forbearance to sue need not be a legal claim is well established. . . .

Forbearance to sue can be good consideration for a promise, regardless of the actual validity of the claim, if the one who forbears has a reasonable and sincere belief in its validity.

"The view is taken that a reasonable and sincere belief in the validity of the claim is necessary and sufficient. It is sometimes stated that if an intending litigant bona fide forbears a right to litigate, he gives up something of value. The reality of the claim which is given up must be measured, not by the state of the law as it is ultimately discovered to be, but by the state of the knowledge of the person who at the time has to judge and make the concession." (12 Am.Jur.581, sec.87)

Construing the petition most favorably for the plaintiff, it can be said that some sincere right was forborne and that in reliance of such, the defendants acted accordingly.

Questions

1. How is a court supposed to determine whether a person has a "reasonable and sincere belief" in the validity of a claim?

2. Because of the uncertainty in determining "reasonable and sincere belief," may the courts be inviting fraud by granting recoveries in such cases?

Pre-Existing Obligations

Neither doing, nor a promise to do, that which one already is obligated to do will be sufficient consideration to support a promise on the other side. In these circumstances there is neither a legal benefit to the promisor (of the other promise) nor a legal detriment to the promisee. No new rights are created, nor new obligations assumed.

Pre-existing obligations may arise in any area of law—criminal, tort, contract, public, or private. For example, a promise to refrain from the commission of a crime or a tort is insufficient because the public and individuals are already the beneficiaries of laws prohibiting such conduct. Therefore, Fred's promise not to punch Barney in the nose in return for Barney's promise to pay $50 to Fred will be neither a legal benefit to Barney or the public, nor a legal detriment to Fred. The same may be said for a promise by the holder of a public office or one in a fiduciary relationship with another to do his or her legally prescribed duties. Thus, a sheriff in County A who, within the boundaries of County A, sees to the capture and conviction of a criminal for whom a reward is offered is *not* entitled to collect the reward. He or she is only fulfilling the duties of the office of sheriff. Generally, the same would *not* be true if the sheriff were to do the same thing in another county where he or she had no official jurisdiction.

Although these examples may seem obvious, situations arising under contract law may be less obvious. The potential for problems is increased because of the pervasive role of contract law in the personal and business lives of most people. Although the potential for problems is increased, the rule is the same—one who promises to do something he or she already is bound to do contractually cannot use that promise as consideration for a new promise. Again, the first party is not thereby giving up anything, nor is the other party acquiring anything to which he or she was not previously entitled. The fact that the promise is only a restatement of a pre-existing contractual obligation may be obvious, as where Carpenter and Phinney have a contract whereby Carpenter is bound to sell a house to Phinney for $50,000 and then promises to sell the same house, again to Phinney, for $55,000. Carpenter has paid no consideration for the promise of the extra $5000. Also, if Phinney were to promise to pay $45,000 instead of $50,000, this would not provide new consideration for any other new promise from Carpenter.

There are two major exceptions to the rule that a pre-existing obligation will prevent a promise from being sufficient consideration. The first involves unforeseen and unforeseeable difficulties, and the second is set out in UCC Section 2-209(1).

Sometimes, after performance of a contract has begun, it appears that performance is going to be more burdensome than expected because of difficulties that were **unforeseen and unforeseeable** at the time of contracting a promise. In this situation, a promise to pay an additional amount for completion of the work is enforceable. This is true even though the performance will be no more than already had been promised under the earlier contract. Notice, however, that the difficulties giving rise to this rule must be *both* unforeseen and unforeseeable. It is not sufficient that the promisor made a judgment error or was negligent in calculating the difficulties that might be encountered.

Even the fact that the difficulty might be an "act of God" is not always sufficient, as when the particular "act of God" was one that reasonably might be foreseen such as high winds, rain storms, lightning, or other natural conditions. Certainly a sudden sharp rise in performance costs is not unforeseeable.

Although the doctrine of unforeseen and unforeseeable difficulties generally is seen as an exception, in fact it finds a firm foundation in the law concerning mistakes. Cases in which the "exception" is applied, in reality may be cases involving mutual mistake of material fact, giving the person who would be burdened the right to rescind. That party may waive the right to rescind in consideration for the promise by the other party to pay an additional amount. Consider the reasoning of the court in the following case.

BRIAN CONSTRUCTION AND DEVELOPMENT CO., INC. v. BRIGHENTI
176 Conn. 162, 405 A.2d 72 (1978)

This was an action by Brian Construction (Plaintiff/Appellant) against John Brighenti for breach of a subcontract to remove rubble from an excavation site.

Plaintiff was the assignee of a contract to construct a post office building, including all necessary excavation work. This latter work was subcontracted to Defendant, who agreed to do the job for $104,326. When Defendant commenced work, he discovered considerable debris below the surface consisting of part of a foundation, slab floors, underground tanks, twisted metals, and various combustible materials. Prior to entering into the agreement, Plaintiff had done test borings on which Defendant relied, but the borings had shown no evidence of the debris and neither party was aware of its existence. Thereafter, following much negotiating and protesting, Plaintiff promised to pay Defendant the cost of the additional work plus ten percent. Defendant agreed and resumed work but did not complete the job. Plaintiff was forced to complete his own contract suffering considerable damage as a result of Defendant's abandonment. Defendant contended that the agreement to do the additional work was not binding because his promise was based on a pre-existing obligation.

From a judgment for Defendant, Plaintiff appealed. Reversed.

LOISELLE, Associate Justice.

It is an accepted principle of law in this state that when a party agrees to perform an obligation for another to whom that obligation is already owed, although for lesser remuneration, the second agreement [to perform the same obligation] does not constitute a valid, binding contract. . . . "The basis of the rule is generally made to rest upon the proposition that in such a situation he who promises the additional compensation receives nothing more than that to which he is already entitled and he to whom the promise is made gives nothing that he was not already under legal obligation to give. 1 Williston on Contracts, Sec. 130." Blakeslee v. Board of Water Commissioners, 106 Conn. 642, 652, 139 A. 106, 110. Where, however, the subsequent agreement imposes upon the one seeking greater compensation an additional obligation or burden not previously assumed, the agreement, supported by consideration, is valid and binding upon the parties. . . .

The unchallenged findings of the court reveal that the substantial rubble found beneath the surface of the site was not anticipated by either party, that its presence necessitated excavation beyond the depths required in the plans and specifications, that the cost of removing this rubble was not included in the contract price and that the parties entered into a separate oral agreement for the removal of the rubble. Under these circumstances, the subsequent oral agreement, that the defendant would remove this rubble in return for additional compensation, was binding as a new, distinct contract, supported by valid consideration.

Questions

1.   Why wasn't the rubble foreseeable? Does a decision such as this undermine the basic rule?

2.   Are there so many exceptions to the consideration rule that it is basically useless?

The second exception to the rule concerning pre-existing contractual duties, UCC Section 2-209(1) provides: "An agreement modifying a contract within this Article [Sale of Goods] needs no consideration." In theory, when two parties have entered into a contract for the sale of goods, they may agree mutually to change any of its terms including price, subject matter, or quantity.

Even though its application requires the existence of a traditional contract (offer, acceptance, and consideration) in the first place, beyond that Section 2-209(1) flies squarely in the face of the rule that every new promise (including a change in the terms of an existing promise) must be supported by new consideration. Courts have the power to apply Section 2-209(1) in all applicable cases; the tendency is to apply it sparingly—only in those cases in which its application is necessary to prevent a substantial injustice. In effect, it provides for the court's use of equitable discretion by a law court, as does UCC Section 2-302 (Unconscionable Contract or Clause), and thus should be used very sparingly.

Past Consideration

Like the terms *void contract* and *conditional acceptance*, the term *past consideration* is a misnomer. A void contract really is not a contract; a conditional acceptance really is not an acceptance; and past consideration really is not consideration. **Past consideration** is involved when a promise is made based on something the promisee has done in the past. For example, a child's parents are killed and the child's aunt takes him in, feeds, clothes, and educates him. Later the aunt falls on hard times and the nephew promises: "Since you helped me when I needed you, I will support you at the rate of $30,000 per year for the rest of your life." Does an enforceable contract exist? No. What the aunt did for the nephew was completed when the nephew's promise was made. This past consideration is not sufficient to support the promise. It constitutes neither a "legal benefit to the promisor" nor a "legal detriment to the promisee," nor is it "given in exchange for the promise."

Debt, Compromise, and Composition

Suppose Ron and Nancy enter into a contract under which Ron agrees to remove a dead tree for Nancy for $500 and Nancy agrees to pay the $500. Later, prior to paying, Nancy tells Ron that she is a bit short of money and asks Ron if he will take $400 in satisfaction of the $500 debt. Ron agrees to do so. Can Ron later change his mind and demand the other $100 from Nancy, or is the entire $500 debt discharged by the payment of the $400? The answer depends on whether the $500 debt was *liquidated* or *unliquidated*.

A **liquidated debt** arises when the parties agree (1) that a debt exists, and (2) on the exact amount of the debt. Consider the previous example. Presumably, the parties would agree that a debt existed and that its exact amount was $500. Thus the debt owed by Nancy to Ron would be considered "liquidated." The general rule concerning liquidated debts is that payment of the debt will come only by paying the face amount and no less. Therefore, in the above situation, Ron still has an enforceable right to the remaining $100 from Nancy. Why? When Ron agreed to take $400 in full satisfaction of the $500 liquidated debt, what he was saying, in effect, was "I will take $400 and I promise not to pursue you (Nancy) for the other $100." This promise is not enforceable because Nancy paid no consideration for it. Paying less than Nancy owed certainly constitutes neither a legal benefit to the promisor (Ron) nor a legal detriment to the promisee (Nancy). Suppose, however, that in addition to paying the $400, Nancy had done something else.

The payment of the $400 before the due date (early payment) would discharge the whole $500 debt—so would paying the $400 at a place other than where it was due, and so would the payment of $400 *plus* something else, such as a promise to paint Ron's house or a promise to fix Ron's car. Even the giving up of a 29-cent ballpoint pen in addition to the $400 would suffice. In all of these cases, Nancy would be doing something she was not previously obligated to do (legal detriment) and Ron would be acquiring something to which he had no previous right (legal benefit). Whether the court would feel that any of these additional things was worth $100 does not matter. Remember, generally a court looks only to see that the consideration is "legally sufficient," not whether it is "adequate."

Another possibility would be for Ron to make an *executed* gift of the $100 to Nancy. Although it is true that a *promise* to make a gift generally is not enforceable, a gift that is executed—handed over—passes title to the property, and cannot be taken back. In order to be executed, the thing given must be *delivered*. In order to make delivery of an intangible piece of property, such as a debt as in our example, a certificate of gift may be used. The donor simply may write down his or her intention to make the gift, and then hand over the writing to the donee. Once this is done, the gift is executed.

Any debt that is in dispute is classified as *unliquidated*. Recall that in order to be classified as liquidated, the parties must have agreed about (1) the debt's existence, and (2) its exact amount. The absence of either or both of these factors results in an **unliquidated debt**.

In the introductory chapter on contracts, an example was discussed involving a person who went to a dentist's office with a bad tooth. The dentist pulled the tooth and otherwise cared for the patient and, at the end of the month, sent a bill for $50. In spite of the fact that neither the dentist nor the patient had said a word, it was decided that a contract had been entered into by implication (implied in fact) requiring the patient to reimburse the dentist for the services. The question of importance in this chapter, however, is how much the patient owes. This is an example of an unliquidated debt. Although a debt exists, the parties have not agreed upon its exact amount.

The rule is that an unliquidated debt can be discharged by the payment of any amount agreed to by the parties. Thus, although the bill is for $50, the patient may offer to pay $20. The dentist may offer to take $35, the patient then offers to pay $25, the dentist offers to take $30, and the patient agrees and pays the $30. The debt is discharged by payment of the agreed amount. This is called a **compromise**, or an accord and satisfaction. The parties have negotiated the unliquidated debt, have reached an "accord" at $30, and the patient "satisfied" the debt by paying the $30.

Even though the example involves a situation in which there is agreement as to the debt's existence but not the amount, compromise works equally well when the debt's existence itself is in dispute. For example, following an accident, the parties involved may argue and finally agree to an out-of-court settlement, with one paying the other an agreed-upon sum to prevent a lawsuit. What all cases of compromise (or accord and satisfaction) involve is the taking of an unliquidated debt, liquidating it, and then paying off the liquidated amount.

In discussing the final method of satisfying debts, composition agreements, we return to the topic of liquidated debts. A **composition** is like a private, contractual form of bankruptcy. It is an agreement between a debtor and two or more of his creditors according to which the creditors agree to accept less than the face amounts in full discharge of their respective obligations. This type of contract has two major limitations. First, there must be agreement by all parties. Any creditor who does not agree cannot be bound. Second, two or more creditors must agree. A debtor cannot have a composition with only one creditor. If this were possible, the entire preceding discussion of discharging liquidated debts would have been unnecessary. Also, without at least two creditors, there would be no consideration, in that the consideration in every composition agreement is found in the cross promises of the creditors.

Since the debtor is doing less than he otherwise is obligated to do, he is suffering no legal detriment, nor is he conferring a legal benefit on the creditors. Suppose, for example, the debtor has $10,000 in assets and four creditors, to each of whom she owes $80,000. If they all enter into a composition agreement to take $10,000 apiece in full discharge of their respective $80,000 claims, each pays consideration to the others on behalf of the debtor. Thus, the consideration for Creditor A's promise to take ⅛ of face value in full payment of his claim is the promise of Creditors B, C, and D to do the same thing; the same may be said of each creditor. Each takes a loss to benefit all.

THE BARGAIN THEORY

Bargained For

The third part of the definition of "consideration" set out at the beginning of this chapter required that the legal benefit to the promisor or legal detriment to the promisee, given in exchange for the promise, had to be bargained for. The requirement of "bargained for" means that the legal benefit or legal detriment to be used to satisfy the element of consideration must have been what the promisor was trying to get by making the promise. It is intended specifically to differentiate between a contractual intent and a gift intent. Suppose, for example, that Hurd tells Blum, "If you come over to my house at 2:00 on Sunday afternoon, I will treat you to a steak dinner with all the trimmings." When Blum shows up as requested, Hurd explains that he has changed his mind and refuses to deliver the dinner. Is Hurd in breach of contract? Hurd made an offer. Blum did what Hurd requested and certainly suffered a legal detriment (gave up her right to be somewhere else). But was Blum's detriment bargained for? Did Hurd make his promise for the purpose of extracting this performance from Blum? Or, did Hurd make the promise with an apparent intent to make a gift? Probably the latter is the case and, therefore, Blum's detriment probably was not bargained for, and no contract resulted. If it could be shown that Hurd made the promise for the purpose of getting Blum to come over to his house at 2:00 Sunday, perhaps because he needed help with some work or for some other ulterior purpose, then a contract would result.

Nominal Consideration

The term *nominal* means "in name only." Thus **nominal consideration** means "consideration in name only." It is another of those legal terms, such as *void contract*, *conditional acceptance*, and *past consideration*, that may be misleading. Nominal consideration really is not consideration at all. It occurs when parties to a gift transaction place a statement in the agreement, such as "$1.00 given in consideration," in order to make it appear to be a contract. When the "$1.00" never was intended to be paid, and was not what the promisor was bargaining for in making the promise, the transaction is a gift.

The simple recital of nominal consideration does not change a gift intent into a contractual intent. A small minority of courts, however, hold that a recital in writing creates an obligation to pay and therefore is consideration, but that posture generally is recognized as unsound because it is contrary to the bargain theory.

PROMISES ENFORCEABLE WITHOUT CONSIDERATION

Although the general rule is that promises are enforceable only if supported by consideration, there are exceptions. Some are true exceptions; others are treated as such because they are complex and subject to disagreement as to theory, but not as to effect. Following are brief explanations of those exceptions thought most important.

Promissory Estoppel

This exception is discussed in Chapter 6. When the five elements of promissory estoppel are met, a court of equity may enforce the promise even though it was not supported by consideration. This is accomplished by "estopping" the promisor from exercising rights that otherwise would be hers, such as the right to revoke her offer or declare her promise to be only an unenforceable gift promise.

Charitable Pledges

Under appropriate circumstances, a pledge made to give a gift to a charitable institution may be enforceable even though it is intended as a gift and is not supported by consideration. Courts generally hold that the promise will be enforced when: (1) the promise was made, (2) the institution changed its position in (3) reliance on the promise, and (4) if the promise was not enforced, the institution would suffer an unjust injury. After all, the promisor (5) should have known that a change in position might occur. The reason for numbering the elements is to show that they are the same as those required for promissory estoppel. The only real difference is that when the promisee is a charitable institution, the courts more easily find that reliance was *justifiable* and that the resulting injury would be *unjust*. Thus, this exception is only a subset of the first.

Uniform Commercial Code

Under Section 2-205 of the UCC, a firm offer is "not revocable for lack of consideration during the time stated. . . ." Under Section 2-209(1), the parties to a contract for the sale of goods may agree mutually to cancel or modify the contract and no new consideration is required.

Debts Barred by a Statute of Limitations

When a debt is owed, the creditor must seek to enforce it within a certain length of time after it becomes due. Otherwise, the law will bar the creditor from enforcing it in court. Most obligations are controlled by a statute of limitations.

The time limit will depend on the type of obligation and the jurisdiction. Commonly the time
limit on an oral contractual debt is about five
years, and about ten years on a written one. However, if, after the applicable statute "has run," and
the party owing the debt promises to pay it even
though the creditor is barred from collecting it by
legal action, the courts generally will enforce the
new promise even though it is not supported by
new consideration. State laws often require that
such a promise be in writing.

Conditional Duties

Generally, the rule that a promise to perform a
conditional duty (a duty that arises only after
some special event occurs) is enforceable without
new consideration in spite of the fact that the
condition has not been met is viewed as an exception to the consideration requirement. Thus,
when Jeff promises to purchase Ginny's house for
$25,000 if sewer and water are extended by July 1
and, even though sewer and water are not extended by that date, Jeff promises to perform
anyway, Jeff's second promise is enforceable in
spite of the fact that Ginny has paid no new consideration. In reality, however, this "exception"
probably is nothing more than a case in which the
first contract lapsed because of non-occurrence of
the condition, and the parties then entered into a
second contract, consideration and all.

MORAL CONSIDERATION

Worthy of final note is some reference to the
concept of moral consideration. It represents a
view held by a small number of courts. It is not
settled as to whether this small following is evidence of an obscure minority opinion, or reflects
the fact that few cases have come forward to
which its principles might apply. It only is clear
that it eloquently bespeaks the fact that equity and
the courts may function to prevent a perceived
injustice. Consider the following case.

WEBB v. MCGOWIN et al.
27 Ala. 82, 168 So. 196 (1936)

This was an action by Joe Webb (Plaintiff/Appellant) against Joseph F. McGowin
and N. Floyd McGowin as executors of the estate of J. Greeley McGowin on an
agreement by the terms of which J. Greeley McGowin had promised to support
Plaintiff during Plaintiff's life.

On August 3, 1925, Plaintiff was working on the upper floor of a mill belonging to his employer. While he was in the act of dropping a 75-pound pine block
to the ground floor below, he saw J. Greeley McGowin directly below him.
Because he knew that if he dropped the block as planned, McGowin would likely
be seriously injured or killed, Plaintiff kept hold of the block and fell with it,
thereby diverting its course away from McGowin. Plaintiff was crippled for life
and unable to work thereafter.

On September 1, 1925, in consideration of Plaintiff saving him from death or
serious bodily harm, McGowin agreed to support Plaintiff at the rate of $15 every
two weeks for the rest of Plaintiff's life. McGowin paid regularly until his death
on January 1, 1934, and payments were discontinued after January 24, 1934.

Defendants' demurrers to Plaintiff's complaint on the grounds, among other
things, that it failed to show consideration for a contract, were sustained by the
trial court and Plaintiff appealed from the judgment of nonsuit. Reversed and
remanded. (Certiorari denied, 168 So. 199)

BRICKEN, Presiding Judge.

The averments of the complaint show that appellant saved McGowin from death or grievous bodily harm. This was a material benefit to him of infinitely more value than any financial aid he could have received. Receiving this benefit, McGowin became morally bound to compensate appellant for the services rendered. Recognizing his moral obligation, he expressly agreed to pay appellant as alleged in the complaint and complied with this agreement up to the time of his death; a period of more than 8 years.

Had McGowin been accidentally poisoned and a physician, without his knowledge or request, had administered an antidote, thus saving his life, a subsequent promise by McGowin to pay the physician would have been valid. Likewise, McGowin's agreement as disclosed by the complaint to compensate appellant for saving him from death or grievous bodily injury is valid and enforceable.

Where the promisee cares for, improves, and preserves the property of the promisor, though done without his request, it is sufficient consideration for the promisor's subsequent agreement to pay for the service, because of the material benefit received. . . .

Life and preservation of the body have material, pecuniary values, measurable in dollars and cents. Because of this, physicians practice their profession charging for services rendered in saving life and curing the body of its ills, and surgeons perform operations. The same is true as to the law of negligence, authorizing the assessment of damages in personal injury cases based upon the extent of the injuries, earnings, and life expectancies of those injured.

In the business of life insurance, the value of a man's life is measured in dollars and cents according to his expectancy, the soundness of his body, and his ability to pay premiums. The same is true as to health and accident insurance.

It follows that if, as alleged in the complaint, appellant saved J. Greeley McGowin from death or grievous bodily harm, and McGowin subsequently agreed to pay him for the service rendered, it became a valid and enforceable contract. . . .

Under the decisions above cited, McGowin's express promise to pay appellant for the services rendered was an affirmance or ratification of what appellant had done raising the presumption that the services had been rendered at McGowin's request.

Questions

1. Isn't the notion of "moral" consideration so obscure that it destroys the objective character of contractual arrangements?

2. Does the notion of "moral" consideration effectively allow courts to do what they please? Does it thereby destroy any ability to predict how courts will behave in the law of contracts?

SUMMARY

Consideration is the requirement that most clearly differentiates contract promises from gift promises. It represents what is "paid" by one party to bind the other to his or her promise. Either a legal benefit to the promisor or a legal detriment to the promisee is sufficient if it was bargained for by the promisor. It generally makes no difference whether that which was given by one party is of equal value to that which was given by the other. Exceptions may be found when an extreme injustice would result by enforcing the contract.

A legal benefit is anything that the promisor acquires to which he or she had no previous right. A legal detriment is anything done by the promisee that he or she had no prior duty to do. In the typical bilateral contract, the mutually binding promises of the parties form the consideration. In the typical unilateral case, consideration exists in the act of the offeree. Thus it may be said that the same things forming the offer and the acceptance also form the consideration.

In entering into contracts, some special problems must be considered. What appears to be a promise, but is based on a condition precedent over which the promisor has control, is an illusory promise because it carries no obligation, and thus does not constitute consideration. Although contracts usually must be based on specific terms, a quantity term based on the "needs" of the buyer or the "total output" of a supplier is sufficient. Also, a forbearance in bringing a legal action is sufficient to support a promise unless it would be based on a wholly bad-faith, spurious claim.

Neither a promise to do an act that a person already is obligated to do, nor something that already has been done at the time a promise is made, will constitute consideration for the promise. Neither situation provides a legal benefit to the promisor nor a legal detriment to the promisee.

Debts that are liquidated (agreed-to as to existence and exact amount) may be discharged only by paying the full amount. This is true even though the person to whom the debt is owed agrees to take *less*, unless some consideration is given for the promise to discharge the remainder, such as early payment, payments at a different place, or in a different medium of exchange, or if the creditor gives an *executed* gift of that portion. Execution of a gift generally requires some manual delivery of the thing given or of a certificate stating the donor's intent to make the gift. Debts that are unliquidated (do not meet the requirements of liquidated debts) may be discharged by the payment of any amount agreed to by the parties.

One other possibility for discharging a liquidated debt by payment of less than the full amount is by means of a composition agreement between the debtor and his or her creditors. This requires that they agree, and must involve at least two creditors. Any creditor who does not agree is not bound by the composition.

Some promises are considered enforceable in spite of the absence of consideration. Examples are those to which the principles of promissory estoppel apply, including pledges to charitable organizations, those evolving from offers under Section 2-205 of the UCC, and those involving modification of contracts for the sale of goods under Section 2-209 of the UCC. Some courts also recognize exceptions for promises to pay debts barred by the running of a statute of limitations and promises to perform a conditional duty even though the condition was not met.

A small number of courts recognize the concept of moral consideration. Judgments based on moral consideration generally are justified on the ground that a benefit was conferred in an emergency situation, and the person receiving the benefit would have agreed to pay if there had been an opportunity to negotiate. Generally, the theory is good, but its application is dangerous because of the lack of firm, objective limitations.

KEY TERMS AND CONCEPTS

consideration
legal benefit
legal detriment
bargained for
gift transactions
adequacy of consideration
sufficiency of consideration
unconscionable contract
illusory promise
pre-existing obligations
unforeseen and unforeseeable
past consideration
compromise
composition
liquidated debt
unliquidated debt
nominal consideration
moral consideration

PROBLEMS

1. Adams purchased a new computer and made a gift of his old one to his nephew, Bob. Bob thanked Adams and took the computer home. A few days later, Adams became dissatisfied with his new computer and asked Bob to return the old one. Bob refused. Adams sued Bob, contending he was entitled to the return of the computer because Bob had paid no consideration for it. Is Adams correct?

2. Wood and Gordon entered into a contract providing that Wood was to have the exclusive right to place Gordon's endorsements on clothing, and in return Wood was to receive one half of the profits. Although Wood performed as promised, Gordon decided to grant similar rights to another promoter. Wood sued to enjoin the granting of any rights contrary to the contract.

Gordon defended on the ground that Wood's promise was illusory because it obligated him to do nothing unless he wanted to, and therefore it was not sufficient consideration to support a contract. Is Gordon correct?

3. Carmichael purchased shoes for her store from International Shoe Company. Her account fell into arrears by a large sum, and International refused to extend further credit. International agreed, however, that it would ship more shoes if Carmichael would make an immediate part payment of $8000 and agree to pay the remainder at a rate of $50 per week. Carmichael agreed, paid the $8000, and made four weekly payments; International didn't ship the shoes, but sued Carmichael for the balance due ($5318.92). Is International entitled to a judgment in that amount?

4. In the case of International Shoe Company and Carmichael, would the decision be different if Carmichael had been insolvent and had agreed to pay the obligation as stated instead of filing for bankruptcy?

5. Rose owned a house with a fair market value of $25,000, in which she had equity of $3863. In order to get out of financial difficulty, Rose transferred the property to Lurvey, the son of Rose's sister. The deed recited consideration of $1.05. Thereafter, Lurvey paid the mortgage to date ($775) as well as back taxes. Then Rose, who continued to occupy the house, was served with an eviction notice. Rose sued to have the deed set aside on the ground of inadequate consideration. Is she entitled to the relief requested?

6. Brenner enrolled his daughter, Pam, in an exclusive private school, paying $2500 tuition at the time of registration and agreeing to pay an additional $500 each month during the first year. Prior to the first day of classes, Brenner changed his mind and requested the return of his $2500. The contract between Brenner and the school provided that the advance tuition was not refundable. In spite of this, the school promised to make the refund. When it failed to do so, Brenner sued, and the school defended on the ground that its promise to refund was not supported by consideration. Is the school correct?

7. Following the robbery of the Merchants Bank, the Kentucky Bankers Association offered a reward of $5000 for the capture and conviction of the robber. The offer provided that claims were to be filed with the Association. Thereafter, through the efforts of ten people, the capture and conviction were effected. The people involved were: (1) Denny, Buis, McCollum, and Snyder, all employees of the bank, who gave information and descriptions to the police; (2) Corbin, Julie, Alvie, and Gene Reynolds, who also gave information but did not file a claim with the Association; (3) Godby and Simms, who were the state police officers who captured the robber; and (4) Reppert, a Rockcastle County deputy sheriff who aided in the capture in Pulaski County. Which, if any of these claimants, is entitled to share in the reward?

8. The Robert Chuckrow Construction Co. was erecting a building for Gough. One night, a high wind blew down the trusses, a day before the roof was to be completed. The next morning, Gough instructed Chuckrow to disassemble, inspect, reassemble, and re-erect the trusses, promis-

ing to pay the cost of the additional work. Chuckrow complied. Thereafter, Gough refused to pay the charge for the extra work, contending Chuckrow paid no consideration for the promise. Is Gough correct?

9. During the probate of the estate of Frasier, the attorney for the estate, D. L. Carter, failed to file certain documents on time. As a result, Mrs. Frasier, one of the beneficiaries, became entitled to receive a smaller share of the estate than that to which she would have been entitled had the papers been filed properly. Carter admitted his error and promised to pay the difference to Mrs. Frasier personally. When he failed to do so, Mrs. Frasier sued. Carter defended on the ground that Mrs. Frasier had paid no consideration for the promise. Is Carter correct?

10. Moore borrowed $1466.67 from Lawrence. The obligation was evidenced by a promissory note, under which Moore agreed to repay the obligation within six days. He also orally promised to assign a certain life insurance policy as security. Moore died before the debt was repaid or the assignment was made. Mrs. Moore, the beneficiary of the policy, upon learning of these facts, promised to pay Mr. Moore's debt from the proceeds of the policy. When she failed to do so, Lawrence sued. Is Mrs. Moore obligated to pay?

Chapter | 9

Voidable Contracts

_____
_____
_____
_____

INTRODUCTION

Fundamental to the law of contracts is that every contract is based on the voluntary consent of all parties. This is the primary factor distinguishing contractual liability from tort and criminal liability, both of which involve duties imposed by society rather than duties voluntarily created by the parties. Because of the requirement of voluntary consent, the law recognizes that a binding contract will not come into being if one of the parties lacked the ability to be voluntary and consensual at the time an agreement was formed. The disqualifying disability may have been of a permanent or only a temporary nature, inherent in the individual or induced by the other party. In any case, contracts involving these problems are _voidable_. This means they may be canceled (declared void by a court) at the request of the disabled party.

CAPACITY

Full contractual capacity requires that the parties must be capable of voluntary consent in an arm's-length transaction. In some cases capacity is not present, either because of some inherent characteristic of one of the parties or because of wrong-doing or special circumstances.

Incapacity Inherent in the Individual

The law recognizes that certain persons, because of their individual characteristics, inherently are incapable of entering into an absolutely binding contract. Of primary concern are minors (infants), persons who are insane, and persons who are intoxicated. These people, because of their disabilities, are presumed to lack the requisite mental capacity to bind themselves contractually. The law feels that the estates of these persons should be preserved and protected against dissipation while they are incapable of dealing at arm's length (on a reasonably equal footing) to safeguard their own property. Of somewhat less concern, because of the infrequency with which problems arise, are other categories of incapacity, such as married women, aliens, and corporations acting in excess of their charter powers. These latter three types of incapacity rest solely on considerations of public policy rather than mental incapacity.

At common law it was said, metaphorically, that a husband and wife were one, and the husband was that one. In other words, when a woman was married, she lost her legal identity for many purposes. Her property vested in the husband and it was the husband who was the legal representative of the family. The woman lost her ability to contract individually. Although states have been revising their laws to remove this disability, married women still are not on an equal footing with their husbands in all respects. In addition, historically, some states discriminated against aliens concerning certain kinds of contracts. For example, aliens of Oriental descent, at one time, were prohibited from purchasing real estate in California. These laws are contrary to the equal protection clause of the Constitution and current civil rights legislation. Thus, for the most part, they have now been eliminated. Finally, the law always has questioned the extent to which a corporation and, derivatively, its shareholders should be bound by acts of the corporation's officers and other agents who were outside the powers granted to the corporation in its charter and bylaws. The once hard-line attitude of the courts has been liberalized over the years; today, there is a greater tendency to find liability for these *ultra vires* acts (acts that are beyond the authority granted) on equitable grounds.

Incapacity Induced by Wrongdoing or Mistake

Under certain circumstances, it may occur that the apparent consent of a party to a contract was not genuine because it was procured by means of wrongdoing by the other party or some mistake of material fact. This is the case when a contract has been induced by means of misrepresentation, fraud, duress, undue influence, or mistake. When any of these is a substantial factor in an agreement, the result is the same as if the party laboring under its effects was not mentally capable of true assent. In none of these situations was the party truly at arm's length or on an equal footing with the other, except in the case of mutual mistake, which has the effect of rendering both parties incapable.

Effect of Incapacity

Any time a contract is entered into by a person laboring under any of these disabilities, the contract is voidable at the option of that person. Note that the contract is not void. It is only subject to being rendered void (avoided) at the option of the party suffering the incapacity. The circumstances under which a contract may be avoided, and the rights and duties of the parties involved with such a contract, are the subjects of the remainder of this chapter.

MINORS

At common law, the age of majority (adulthood) for the purposes of contract law was 21. This was changed by some states and for a considerable period of time, state laws varied. Many retained the 21-year age limit; some lowered it to 18. Today, *most* states have adopted age 18, following the passage of the Twenty-Sixth Amendment to the Constitution of the United States, which lowered the age for voting in federal elections to 18.

This period of incapacity should not be confused with other age limits, such as those for the purposes of purchasing alcoholic beverages or for obtaining a marriage license. All of these may vary within a state and from state to state according to each state's perception of public policy issues surrounding the particular subject.

The question foremost in the minds of the legislature in adopting an appropriate age of majority is the age at which a person is old enough to possess sufficient mental capacity to protect himself or herself in dealing with others of that age or older. Some object to establishing a particular age for contractual capacity. They argue that some people are fully capable at, for example, 16, while others remain immature and gullible beyond 21. Undeniably this is true. However, the alternative would be to judge each person according to his or her characteristics. Although this might produce an extra measure of justice in some cases, this benefit would be far outweighed by the uncertainty it would inject into every contract involving a young person. Setting a particular age, even though somewhat arbitrary, at least provides a measure of calculability. Also, the age established has been determined, in a fairly precise way, as a judgment based on human experience. As a result, it is quite simple for anyone contemplating entering into a contract with a young person to determine age as opposed to subjective capacity.

Emancipation

Traditionally, parents have had an absolute right to the earnings and services of their unemancipated minor children. In a sense, unemancipated children are the property of the parents, who can require their services and, if an unemancipated child works for someone else, the parents—not the child—have a right to the wages earned. This right continues until the child's emancipation, which usually occurs upon the child's reaching the age of majority, but it may happen earlier. The parents can expressly emancipate a child by declaring it to be so. It can happen by implication when the parents allow the child to go forth into the world to support himself or herself. Marriage and entering military service traditionally have resulted in emancipation. However, except when modified by state law, an emancipated minor is no more bound to a contract than any other minor. Emancipation, alone, has no effect on contractual capacity.

Right to Disaffirm

As a result of the incapacity, a minor's contract is voidable at his or her option. That is, a minor has a right to continue the contract or to **disaffirm** (cancel) it. The choice is personal to the minor and may not be exercised by anyone else other than a guardian (including a parent) or someone acting on behalf of the minor as a "next friend." An adult who deals with a minor has no such option, but is subject to the will of the minor, who may rescind or enforce the contract. However, equity courts usually will not grant a minor specific performance of a contract because of the general rule in equity against awarding that remedy when a contract is not binding on both parties.

TIME OF DISAFFIRMANCE. As a general rule, the right to disaffirm may be exercised by a minor at any time during his or her minority and for a reasonable time after becoming of age. To this there is one generally recognized exception. If the contract involves title to real estate, most states require that the minor wait until he or she is of age to disaffirm. The reason lies in the law's reverence for real estate. Real estate frequently is treated differently from all other kinds of property. Some states, such as Michigan, provide that a minor must wait until majority to disaffirm *any* contract. This rule represents an attempt to prevent minors from using the defense of minority to defraud adults. The theory is that a minor is less likely to "go on a shopping trip" if he or she must wait to disaffirm. Also, upon reaching the age of majority the former minor may develop a greater sense of social responsibility.

CONTRACTS THAT CANNOT BE DISAF-FIRMED.   A few types of contracts are not subject to disaffirmance at all. These may vary from state to state. A contract to perform military service is one example. Some courts hold that a minor cannot disaffirm a partnership agreement if the effect is to work an injustice on partnership creditors. Under Michigan law, a minor 16 years or older can be bound as an adult to a life or disability insurance contract.

DUTIES ON DISAFFIRMANCE.   The minor's right to disaffirm a contract generally is considered absolute. To the extent possible, she has a right to receive back what she gave, and this right is not conditioned on her ability either to tender or to give back what she received. Thus, a minor who purchases a new car for $20,000, drives it for some time, and then totally destroys the car in an accident has a right to return to the seller and get his money back even though he is in no position to return the car (at least in acceptable condition). This rule has two important limitations. First, if the minor has given property that subsequently has been sold to a bona fide (good-faith) purchaser who had no notice that the seller's title was voidable, or if the property has been destroyed, the minor will have to settle for a judgment for its reasonable value. Second, although returning the adult party to status quo is not a condition precedent (a prerequisite) to disaffirmance, a court generally will order the minor to return any of the consideration still in his or her possession as a part of the judgment granting relief. However, as the following case illustrates, the latter may be an imperfect remedy for the adult.

ROTONDO v. KAY JEWELRY COMPANY
84 R.I. 292, 123 A.2d 404 (1956)

This was an action by Joseph Rotondo (Plaintiff/Appellant) against Kay Jewelry Company to recover money paid to Defendant as part of the price of an engagement ring purchased while Plaintiff was a minor.

Plaintiff purchased the ring from Defendant on August 8, 1953, when he was a minor of the age of 19 years, and made part payment of $93.39. On that same day, he gave the ring to his fiancee. On April 10, 1954, the engagement was terminated, and thereafter, while still a minor, Plaintiff notified Defendant of his intention to rescind the contract and demanded the return of his money. Defendant refused because, among other things, Plaintiff did not offer to return the ring.

The trial court entered a judgment in favor of Plaintiff in the amount of $93.39. Defendant appealed to the Superior Court, which found for Defendant. Reversed.

ROBERTS, Justice.

The plaintiff has elected to disaffirm his contract with defendant and sues to recover the consideration thereunder that moved from him. It is settled in this state that a minor, with regard to his contracts for non-necessaries, may disaffirm such contracts and recover the consideration that moved from him. It is also required that he return the goods or merchandise purchased under the contract if he is able to do so. . . .

The defendant contends, however, that as the law requires the infant to return the property purchased to the extent that he is able, the burden of proving that he is unable to return the property is on the infant. In other words, the defendant claims that an infant so disaffirming a contract must show by a preponderance of evidence that he is unable to return the goods which he received. Such rule in effect would impose a condition precedent upon an infant's right to recover the consideration that moved from him when he disaffirmed a contract for non-necessaries. . . .

We think it was error for the trial justice to require the plaintiff to prove by a preponderance of the evidence that he was unable to return the ring. Nothing in the nature of a condition precedent can be interposed to defeat the right of an infant to disaffirm his contracts for non-necessaries and to recover the consideration that moved from him.

Questions

1. What, if any, justification is there for the court's decision?
2. Why does the court limit its result to non-necessaries? What are necessaries?

Tort Versus Contract Liability

A minor may be liable for his own torts, even though liability cannot be predicated on his breach of a contract. The wrong committed must be more than the breach of a contract, and it must be separate and independent of the minor's contract obligations. By great weight of authority, the test is whether the liability can be established without taking notice of the fact that a contract was involved. Thus, when a minor rents a car and, as bailee, negligently causes damage to it, she cannot be held liable for that injury. The contrary would be true, however, if she rents the car and then fails to return it, converting it to her own use, selling it, or concealing it. Thus the courts will not allow the adult to "sneak through the back door" of tort law to enforce a contract against a minor. To hold otherwise would be to allow a contract to be enforced in an action *ex delicto* (in tort) that could not be enforced in an action *ex contractu* (in contract). Consider the following case.

CENTRAL BUCKS AERO, INC. v. SMITH
226 Pa.Super. 84, 310 A.2d 283 (1973)

This was an action in trespass by Central Bucks Aero, Inc. (Plaintiff/Appellant) against John Henry Smith, a/k/a John Henry Smith, Jr., a/k/a John Henry Smith, III for damages to an airplane leased to Defendant and also for damages to a landing field where Defendant crashed the airplane. Upon the filing of this lawsuit, Defendant, still a minor, disaffirmed the lease.

From a judgment for Defendant, Plaintiff appealed. Affirmed.

SPETH, Judge.

When a minor disaffirms a contract, unless the contract is for necessaries the other party cannot recover the value of any item that the minor has obtained pursuant to the contract. The only remedy the other party has is an action in replevin [an action to recover possession of property] to recover the item itself. If the minor no longer has the item, the other party is remediless. . . .

An action in trespass, which is the form of action selected by appellant, will not lie. As stated in *Penrose v. Curren*, 3 Rawle 351, 353 (1832): "The foundation of the action is contract, and disguise it as you may, it is an attempt to convert a suit, originally in contract, into a constructive tort so as to charge the infant." . . .

In Wilt v. Welsh, 6 Watts, 9, Gibson, J., said: "Indeed the privilege would be [of] little worth if it might be eluded by fashioning the action into a particular shape." The principle there maintained was, that whenever the substantive ground of an action against an infant is contract, as well where the contract is stated as incident to a supposed tort, as where it is not, the plaintiff cannot recover. In the course of his discussion of the cases in which infants may be sued in tort and those in which they cannot be, Judge Cooley says: "The distinction is this: If the wrong grows out of contract relations, and the real injury consists in the nonperformance of a contract into which the party wronged has entered with an infant, the law will not permit the former to enforce the contract indirectly by counting on the infant's neglect to perform it, or omission of duty under it as a tort. The reason is obvious: To permit this to be done would deprive the infant of that shield of protection which, in matters of contract, the law has wisely placed before him." 1 Cooley on Torts, 3d ed. 181. This principle is followed in most jurisdictions. See 42 Amer.Jur.2d Infants Sec. 145.

It may be granted that upon occasion the courts have decided to remove an immunity from legal responsibility by overruling the cases that created the immunity. Ayala v. Philadelphia Board of Education, . . . Flagiello v. Penna. Hospital. . . . In the present case, however, such a decision would be inappropriate.

In cases such as Ayala, and Flagiello, supra, the court was responding to an injustice; by removing the immunity in question the court extended protection to persons unable to protect themselves. No such situation is presented here. A businessman may protect himself from loss incident to a minor's disaffirmance of a contract by finding out whether the person with whom he is dealing is a minor. . . .

Inasmuch as appellant neglected such precautions, it has only itself to blame for its inability to recover for the damage to its airplane and landing field.

Apart from these considerations, to overrule the cases that permit disaffirmance would involve the court in a legislative function. Some age must be established as the age below which disaffirmance will be permitted; perhaps a twenty-year old person should not be protected, but surely an eight year old should be. If the age is to be changed, the legislature is better equipped than the court to decide whether the change should be to age 19, 18, 16, or some other age.

Questions

1. Can you really draw a line between contracts and torts in the manner this court did?

2. What should be the result if the minor lies about his or her age when renting a car or an airplane?

Misrepresentation of Age

If most torts of a minor committed in connection with a contract are not actionable, what of the situation in which a minor misrepresents his or her age, thereby fraudulently inducing an adult to enter into a voidable contract? Very simply, at common law, that made no difference. The general rules stated above still were applicable and the minor could assert his or her minority in an action to disaffirm the contract or as a defense to an attempt to enforce his or her obligation. Although authority is split, the great weight of it, as well as reason, dictates that the infant may be estopped in a court of equity. Equity maxims require that "one who asks equity must do equity" and "one who comes into equity must come with clean hands." To a considerable extent this equity theory has affected modern common law.

The majority of states now make some provision when a minor misrepresents his or her age. Some hold that the minor who has misrepresented his or her age still may disaffirm but is liable in an action for damages for deceit. Others conclude that the minor can disaffirm only by returning the adult party to his or her pre-contract position and accounting for any depreciation to the value of the property. Still others have general statutes disallowing disaffirmance of contracts induced by any misrepresentation of age. Michigan has a statute providing that a minor may be held liable on the contract, just as if he or she were an adult, if he or she misrepresents his or her age on a *separate* signed statement containing no more than a date, a statement of age, and the signature of the minor.

Those jurisdictions that still follow the common law rule seem to do so primarily because of a fear that, otherwise, the law's policy to protect the infant's property always will be undermined by its policy to enforce an infant's tort liability. This view, however, does not recognize the fact that liability in contract and liability in tort rest on different principles and involve different measures of recovery. Thus enforcement in an action in deceit would not, in fact, amount to enforcement of the contract.

Liability for Necessaries

Sometimes it is stated incorrectly that courts will enforce a minor's contracts for **necessaries**—that is, contracts involving things reasonably required for the continued health and well being of the minor. Although a minor generally is held liable in such transactions, that liability is not in contract, but is in quasi contract. A minor still will be allowed to disaffirm, but will be held liable for the reasonable value (not necessarily the contract price) of the necessaries furnished.

The items considered necessaries are determined by a subjective evaluation. A judgment must be made as to what things the particular minor needs for continued health and well being in light of surrounding circumstances and his or her station in life. Generally, reasonable items of food, clothing, shelter, basic education, medical attention, and tools of a trade have been held to be necessaries. The food category would not include a daily diet of steak and lobster, nor would it be limited to peanut butter and dog food. Clothing would depend, perhaps, on the minor's background and current situation. Although an infant sales representative might require a fair quantity of dress clothing, an infant farmer probably would not. Such a differentiation also might be made between the child of affluent parents and one from a poor family. Shelter probably would include a room, or possibly a modest apartment, but not an expensive house. Basic education almost certainly would include a high-school education and even trade school training. Anything beyond that point is questionable, but should seldom be a problem, especially since the age of majority in most states has been lowered to 18. Medical attention would include treatment for illnesses and probably a normal physical examination. It generally would not include plastic surgery or a hair transplant (unless, perhaps, it could be shown that without these, the minor's mental condition would deteriorate dangerously). Tools of a trade traditionally have been considered to be small equipment, such as hair clippers for a barber or wrenches for a mechanic, not large equipment such as an automobile, pickup truck, tractor, combine, or airplane. However, in today's world, wouldn't an automobile be a necessary? for a trav- eling salesperson? for one who was supporting a spouse and a child? How about adding a disabled, widowed mother? How far can this be taken? Would five Boeing 747s be necessaries for a minor who wants to open an airline? Is there a difference? Consider the following case involving an automobile.

BANCREDIT, INC. v. BETHEA
65 N.J.Super. 538, 168 A.2d 250 (1961)

This was an action by Bancredit, Inc. (Plaintiff/Respondent) against Lynn Bethea and his father, Tony Bethea, for payment of a promissory note given in partial consideration for the purchase of a car by Lynn Bethea. Among other grounds for complaint, Plaintiff argued that Defendant Lynn should be bound even though he was an infant at the time of the contract, because the automobile was a necessary.

From a decision of the trial court ignoring Defendant Lynn Bethea's defense of infancy and finding him liable on the note, Defendant appealed. Reversed and remanded concerning this issue for a decision by a jury.

FREUND, J. A. D.

We are in accord with the recognition, implicit in these holdings, that modern transportation habits and the definitional flexibility of "necessary," dependent as the term is upon the social position and situation in life of the minor, . . . may well combine to dictate that, under certain circumstances, an automobile is sufficiently indispensable to bind an infant who contracts for one. Whether, therefore, the automobile in the case at hand—allegedly used by young Bethea in driving to and from work—is a necessary should have been determined by the jury, taking into account such considerations as the defendant's station in life, his personal need of the vehicle, the type of work in which he is engaged, the travelling distance involved in going to and from his job, convenient alternative means of transportation, and the terms of his contract of employment. See 43 C.J.S. Infants Sec. 78 b, pp. 189-194. Also to be resolved by the jury is the question of whether, considering young Bethea's possession of another automobile (the one traded in) and the apparent willingness of his father to help him, the infant was in "actual need" of the car purchased. Finally, even if the automobile is found to be a necessary, the infant's liability must be limited to the reasonable value thereof; defendants have claimed all along that the worth of the vehicle is considerably less than the sales price.

We recognize that, in general, the burden of proving infancy is on the one who asserts it in defense. See 27 Am.Jur., Infants, Sec. 145, p. 862. However, once the defendant effectively demonstrates his infancy at the time of contracting the party seeking to recover for materials furnished has the burden of proving both that the articles supplied in fact constituted necessaries, and that the infant was in "actual need" of them. . . . It is also the duty of the creditor to establish the reasonable value of the alleged necessaries.

Questions

1. Why should there be a distinction between necessaries and non-necessaries?
2. If what are considered necessaries depends in part on the minor's station in life, does this unfairly discriminate between the rich and the poor? Which would suffer from the discrimination?

One final rule concerning necessaries merits mention. Nothing qualifies as a necessary if the minor's parents are ready, willing, and able to meet his or her reasonable needs. Thus, if a minor stops on the way home from school and purchases a hamburger, the hamburger ordinarily would not be a necessary in spite of the fact that it is a modest food item. On the other hand, for a minor at college, miles from home, it probably would be, and so would clothing and a room. Also, the field of possible necessaries is increased significantly by emancipation. Parents are not expected to provide support for emancipated minors.

Ratification

Although a contract entered into by an infant may be disaffirmed, it may be ratified instead. That is, the infant, after coming of age, may elect to bind himself to the same extent as he would have been bound if he had entered into the contract as an adult. This **ratification** will date back to the moment of the contract, and must be total or not at all—the law does not allow the ratification of the beneficial parts of the contract and disaffirmance of the rest. It is important to note that the contract will be binding only to the extent that it would have been binding if entered into by an adult. Any problems with the agreement other than the infancy are not eliminated.

Ratification can occur only after the infant reaches the age of majority. Since a minor does not bind herself at the time of contracting, she cannot bind herself by ratification during incapacity.

Ratification may be either express or implied. It occurs anytime the former infant objectively manifests his or her intent to be bound to the transaction. The person may tell the other party, "Though I was underage when the contract was made, you may be sure that I intend to honor it." Any words, even less formal ones, indicating a present intent to be bound will be sufficient to constitute an express ratification. But ratification also may occur by implication from the conduct of the party who has the right to disaffirm. Generally, retaining the consideration received for an unreasonable period of time after becoming of age is considered an act of ratification, although what constitutes an unreasonable time is a contextual matter, depending on the nature of the contract and other relevant circumstances. The better-reasoned cases hold that when a contract remains entirely executory, a failure to disaffirm is not ratification. Other conduct must be evaluated on a case-by-case basis, but such acts as continuing to make payments or selling or otherwise disposing of the consideration received after becoming of age, almost certainly will be considered as manifestations of an intent to ratify. Usually, the fact that the party is ignorant of his or her right to disaffirm will be unimportant in determining whether words or conduct amount to ratification. However, consider the following case.

LEE v. THOMPSON
124 Fla. 494, 168 So. 848 (1936)

This was an action by John E. Lee (Complainant/Appellant) against Elizabeth Celeste Thompson to foreclose a mortgage.

On June 1, 1928, Defendant, an unmarried minor of 18 years of age, executed a mortgage on the home in which she and her father resided. She signed at the request of her father with no knowledge of the nature of the writing she signed. Thereafter her father left town and, until early 1933, he sent checks to her regularly with instructions that she take them to the bank (Complainant's assignor) to pay the mortgage, which she did. Then between April 1933 and February 1934, there was correspondence between Defendant and representatives of the mortgagee with an eye toward renewal or refinancing of the mortgage. It was during this time that she first learned that she was not liable on the mortgage since she had executed it as an infant. She immediately took action to disaffirm. Complainant contended that her actions after becoming of age constituted ratification.

From a judgment in favor of Defendant, Complainant appealed. Affirmed.

TERRELL, Justice.

Since the contracts of an infant are voidable . . . that is to say, subject to the possibility of disaffirmance, it follows that when the infant attains his majority and ratifies a contract made in infancy its infirmity is removed and it will be treated as valid from inception and the optional right to disaffirm abandoned. Ratification does not now require a new consideration to make it binding. 14 R.C.L. 246.

Some of the early cases held that ratification required the same formality and proof as a new contract, but the later view is that ratification may be accomplished by exercising the option not to avoid the contract. The quondam [former] infant is required to do this in express terms, or he may do so by some act freely and voluntarily done. He may also ratify by conduct which shows a clear intent to do so or such as will work a fraud on the opposing party if not treated as a ratification. It has been held that if the quondam infant is aware of the existence of the contract, knowledge of his right to affirm or repudiate will be imputed to him. . . .

In the case of executed contracts, ratification is more often implied from the conduct of the quondam infant than from express declarations, but in the case of executory contracts ratification must be positive and explicit. It may be verbal if not required to be in writing. A mere acknowledgement is not sufficient. It must be a direct promise to pay or discharge the contract in question. This court has held that there must not only be an acknowledgement of liability, but an express confirmation or new promise voluntarily and deliberately made by the infant on coming of age, and with the knowledge that he is not legally liable, or bound by the original executory agreement. Summerall v. Thomas et ux., 3 Fla. 298, text 308. . . .

Acts and negotiations with reference to the payment of interest and taxes, some of which took place before and some after majority, were all done at the direction of the father and there is not a shred of evidence to show that appellee knew that she had made a contract or consciously intended to ratify one that she had made unwittingly. In fact the evidence shows conclusively that there was no intent whatever to ratify, and intent is one of the essentials of ratification. Intent must also be supported by some act amounting to ratification with full knowledge of its consequences. . . .

As to appellee, the contract in question was executory, and while the rule announced in Summerall v. Thomas, supra, is more rigid than that usually exacted in such cases, certainly appellee should not have been held to have ratified under the facts in this case before she was conscious of her status with reference to the mortgage and was advised as to the consequences of ratification. Up to the time she disaffirmed the contract there is no showing whatever that she was anything more than a conduit by which her father handled the charges on the mortgage.

Questions

1. Is there anything in the facts of this case that seems to compel its result?
2. Does this case violate the principle that ignorance of the law is no defense?

Minors' Tort Liability

As touched on briefly in the previous discussion of misrepresentation of age, a minor generally is fully liable for his or her own torts. Certain adjustments may be made for age, however. For instance, it is difficult to establish negligence by a child under the age of about 7. Between the ages of 7 and 14, children generally are judged not against the standard of a "reasonable person of ordinary prudence under the same or similar circumstances," but against that of "a child of like age and understanding." Intentional torts will proceed much as they do for adults.

The reason a minor may be liable for torts but not for contracts is that these two areas of law are founded on different principles. Contracts are the products of negotiation between the parties and adults presumably are fully capable of protecting their own interests. Torts, on the other hand, are visited on the victim without negotiation and frequently without his or her participation. Naturally, we have sympathy for a minor who injures another without really intending to do so, often acting without considering the possibility of an injury and perhaps even in complete good humor.

Although we would like to preserve his or her estate from dissipation caused by the payment of damages, another more important policy question is involved. That is, another person has been injured. The question, therefore, is who should suffer the consequences of that injury—the entirely innocent injured party or the child who, even though acting without malice and perhaps in the spirit of fun, caused the injury? The law says the latter.

Finally, although children ordinarily are liable for their own torts, their parents ordinarily are not liable for them. This has been changed by statute in some states and by municipal ordinances in some communities. These changes frequently apply to wanton and willful or intentional misconduct by unemancipated minors, and frequently are limited to destruction of public property, especially school property. Also, principles of agency law may impose vicarious liability on the parents when the minor commits a tort while on the business of the parents or the family, or while driving the family car. However, this liability is the exception, not the rule.

INSANE AND INTOXICATED PERSONS

Generally, the principles applicable to the liability of minors on contracts also are applicable to those who lack capacity because of insanity or intoxication. The only significant difference is found in the area of duties upon disaffirmance. Although a minor may disaffirm a contract without returning the other party to status quo, this is not true for insane persons and intoxicated persons.

Insanity (as distinguished from judicially declared incompetency, which causes all contracts entered into during the period of incompetency void) exists in the law of contracts when it is determined that, at the time of the contract, the complaining party was "incapable of comprehending the nature and consequences of the business at hand." In such a case, the complainant will be allowed to disaffirm. However, if he or she was dealt with fairly, benefited from the contract, and the other party dealt in good faith and without notice of the disability, disaffirmance will be conditioned on the ability of the insane party to return the other to status quo. The reason this requirement is imposed in the case of insanity, but not in the case of minority, is that although both insanity and minority presumably exist through no fault of the disabled party, the other party to the transaction usually is capable of determining age, but not necessarily sanity. Thus, in good faith transactions, some responsibility is shifted to the insane party.

Intoxication is another matter. The same rule used to determine insanity also is used to determine sufficient intoxication—was the complaining party capable of comprehending the nature and consequences of the business at hand? Indeed, intoxication is nothing more than a temporary, self-induced form of insanity. Intoxication may come as the result of being influenced by alcohol or any other mind-altering drug. The defense of intoxication is viewed more harshly by the law than the defense of insanity because it is

Mental incapacities that will void contracts

Type of Incapacity	Legal Rights
Minority	Contracts can be dissaffirmed at any time (real estate is usually an exception) during minority, with a full refund of what was paid, regardless of minor's ability to return the good received
Insanity	Contracts can be dissaffirmed, but the other party must be returned to status quo (earlier position) unless the insane party was taken advantage of
Intoxication	Contracts can be dissaffirmed if the intoxicated person was taken advantage of and the other party can be returned to status quo
Incompetence	Contracts are void

self-induced. In a case of "accidental intoxication," such as might occur if one person were to slip a drug in the complaining party's coffee without his or her knowledge, the complainant should be treated in the same manner as an insane person.

A party using the defense of intoxication is required to show, as a condition of disaffirmance, that he or she was dealt with in bad faith and taken advantage of because of his or her condition. In addition, he or she must be able to return the other party to status quo. By way of contract, only the latter was required of an insane person and then only if the other party acted in good faith. Neither generally is required of the infant.

MISREPRESENTATION

Like minority, insanity, and intoxication, misrepresentation can cause a party's consent to a contract to be involuntary. This is true even if the misrepresentation is innocent. Thus, the resulting contract is voidable.

Elements

A misrepresentation is actionable when there has been a (1) misrepresentation of material fact and (2) the other party justifiably relied on it in entering into a contract. Both elements are required.

In order to have a **misrepresentation**, there must be a statement that something exists when it does not exist, or that it does not exist when it does. The required misstatement may be made expressly, or may be created by conduct or even silence. Even statements that literally are true but misleading in effect may provide the foundation of a misrepresentation. Consider the following case.

OBDE v. SCHLEMEYER
56 Wash.2d 449, 353 P.2d 672 (1960)

This was an action by Fred Obde and his wife, Mary Obde (Plaintiffs/Appellees) against Robert L. and Cleone L. Schlemeyer, husband and wife, for damages for fraudulent concealment of termite infestation in an apartment house Plaintiffs purchased from them. Defendants knew, at the time of the sale, that the building had been invaded by termites, and that even though they had taken some steps to eradicate them, these steps were likely to be ineffective. However, at trial they contended that since the parties were dealing at arms length, they had no duty to tell Plaintiffs of the termite problem.

From a judgment for Plaintiffs in the amount of $3950, Defendants appealed. Affirmed.

FINLEY, Judge.

Without doubt, the parties in the instant case were dealing at arms length. Nevertheless, . . . we are convinced that the defendants had a duty to inform the plaintiffs of the termite condition. In Perkins v. Marsh, . . . a case involving parties dealing at arms length as landlord and tenant, we held that, "Where there are concealed defects in demised premises, dangerous to the property, health, or life of the tenant, which defects are known to the landlord when the lease is made, but unknown to the tenant, and which a careful examination on his part would not disclose, it is the landlord's duty to disclose them to the tenant before leasing, and his failure to do so amounts to a fraud."

We deem this rule to be equally applicable to the vendor-purchaser relationship. See 15 Tex.Law Review (December, 1936) 1, 14-16, Keeton: Fraud—Concealment and Non-Disclosure. In this article Professor Keeton also aptly summarized the modern judicial trend away from a strict application of caveat emptor by saying: "It is of course apparent that the content of the maxim 'caveat emptor,' used in its broader meaning of imposing risks on both parties to a transaction, has been greatly limited since its origin. When Lord Cairns stated in Peek v. Gurney that there was no duty to disclose facts, however morally censurable their nondisclosure may be, he was stating the law as shaped by an individualistic philosophy based upon freedom of contract. It was not concerned with morals. In the present stage of the law, the decisions show a drawing away from this idea, and there can be seen an attempt by many courts to reach a just result in so far as possible, but yet maintaining [*sic*] the degree of certainty which the law must have. The statement may often be found that if either party to a contract of sale conceals or suppresses a material fact which he is in good faith bound to disclose then his silence is fraudulent.

"The attitude of the courts toward non-disclosure is undergoing a change and contrary to Lord Cairns' famous remark it would seem that the object of the law in these cases should be to impose on parties to the transaction a duty to speak whenever justice, equity, and fair dealing demand it." . . .

A termite infestation of a frame building, such as that involved in the instant case, is manifestly a serious and dangerous condition. One of the Schlemeyers' own witnesses, Mr. Hoefer, who at the time was a building inspector for the city of Spokane, testified that ". . . if termites are not checked in their damage, they can cause a complete collapse of a building, . . . they would simply eat up the wood." Further, at the time of the sale of the premises, the condition was clearly latent—not readily observable upon reasonable inspection. As we have noted, all superficial or surface evidence of the condition had been removed by reason of the efforts of Senske, the pest control specialist. Under the circumstances, we are satisfied that "justice, equity, and fair dealing," to use Professor Keeton's language, demanded that the Schlemeyers speak— that they inform prospective purchasers, such as the Obdes, of the condition, regardless of the latter's failure to ask any questions relative to the possibility of termites.

Questions

1. Under what circumstances must a seller speak? Must a seller always speak, or only when the defect presents a danger to the other?

2. Would it have made this decision any easier if the purchaser had asked about termites and had been told there were none (the literal truth)?

In order to constitute a misrepresentation of fact, the misrepresentation generally must be of something past or present. A statement of opinion is not actionable unless it is *not* the speaker's opinion (a misrepresentation of his or her present state of mind). Neither is a statement concerning the future actionable unless, again, it constitutes a misrepresentation of the speaker's present state of mind (for example, that he will do something he has no intention of doing), or unless he holds himself out to be capable of accurately predicting the future or gives a warranty to that effect. It is in this latter case that professionals must be especially careful. The opinions of experts, even as to the future, may be considered statements of fact in some circumstances.

The misrepresentation also must be of material fact. A misrepresentation as to a fact that could have no important bearing on the parties' decision to contract is not actionable. Thus, a statement by the seller of a car that she is the second owner and that the car previously was owned by "John Smith" when, in fact, it previously was owned by John Smith's wife, is not material in the absence of any other factors. The same would be true of a statement that the car had been driven 30,000 miles when it had been driven for 30,010 miles.

There also must be justifiable reliance by the complaining party. When there has been a false statement, but the complaining party either knew or should have known it was false, then reliance is not justifiable and the misrepresentation is not actionable. For example, if the seller of a car has represented it as having been driven 30,000 miles when, in fact, it has been driven 130,000 miles, but it is in very bad repair, the interior is filthy with holes worn in the seat covers and the floorboard, and the brake and clutch pedals are worn off to the metal, reliance would not be reasonable. Even with less evidence than this, a purchaser hardly would be justified in relying on the statement. Although there has been much movement toward the elimination (or the minimizing) of the defense of caveat emptor, a buyer still is presumed to know what reasonable examination would reveal, assuming reasonable examination is possible.

Remedy

When an actionable misrepresentation is found, the contract is voidable and the innocent party is given the option to rescind it. She can return what she has received and get back what she has given. As a general rule, in the absence of fraud, if it is impossible for the victim to return the other party to status quo, he cannot rescind. However, he may pay only the reasonable value of what he received, rather than the contract price.

FRAUD

Elements

Fraud is basically an intentional misrepresentation. More specifically, **fraud** is (1) a misrepresentation of material fact, (2) knowingly made, (3) with intent to defraud, (4) upon which the other party justifiably has relied that (5) results in an injury to the party defrauded.

Fraud requires that the misrepresentation be made knowingly. Although an innocent misstatement may be sufficient for misrepresentation, it will not be sufficient to constitute fraud. Thus, a statement the speaker justifiably believes to be true is not fraudulent.

Fraud also requires the element of **scienter**—an evil mind. The misstatement must be made with intent to defraud. In the absence of such malice,

there is no fraud. For example, Weiss knowingly misrepresents to Schwartz the condition of Grey's car, having no reason to know that Schwartz has been considering buying the car. If Schwartz purchases the car in reliance on Weiss's statements, Schwartz has no action against Weiss for fraud. Because Weiss did not intend Schwartz to act (buy the car) as a result of the misrepresentation, there was no scienter attributable to Weiss. Nor does Schwartz have an action against Grey for either misrepresentation or fraud.

Finally, an injury must result. Without an injury there are no damages, and without damages, there is no purpose for bringing a fraud action.

Remedy

Since every contractual fraud involves the two elements of an actionable misrepresentation, the remedy of rescission is available. In addition, however, the victim has the right to sue for damages for the tort of deceit. An election of remedies is required—the injured party is not entitled to both. Thus, a party defrauded into a car purchase may seek to return the car and get his or her money back, or may sue to recover the difference between what the car is worth and what it would have been worth if it had been as represented.

In addition to these compensatory damages, the injured party may receive punitive (exemplary) damages if the court feels that the party who committed the fraud should be punished for his or her wrongdoing. Punitive damages are awarded to deter the offender, and others by example, from committing fraud in the future. They are possible in any case involving scienter, although they are not awarded frequently. Punitive damages involve an overlap between criminal theory and civil actions.

DURESS

Duress is unlawful pressure or coercion exercised over the will of another, forcing the other to do something he or she would not otherwise have done. Duress originated in the criminal law and was founded on actual imprisonment, physical violence, or the threat of either of these. Acts or threats directed toward one's family also were considered duress. This concept was brought over into civil law, and what constitutes civil duress has been expanded.

Today, what constitutes duress is determined by subjective evaluation—there is no precise rule. The court, in each case, seeks to determine whether the promisor was deprived of his or her free will by the acts or threats of the promisee (or someone acting in the promisee's behalf). It is the court's duty to see that every contractual obligation is assumed voluntarily. If not, the obligation is voidable. In reaching its decision, a court will consider the nature of the act or threat, the characteristics of the persons involved, and the surrounding circumstances. Every person is expected to resist duress to the extent expected of the *average* person of *normal* courage.

In addition to the types of duress recognized at common law, today threats to reputation or credit-worthiness, and sometimes even threats to destroy or injure property, *may* constitute duress. For some time, the threat to bring unfounded criminal prosecution has been considered a possible ground for duress; the threat to bring a civil suit generally has not. The difference is that the former carries with it the threat of facing the "unlimited" power of the state, but the latter does not. The former also involves an allegation of serious antisocial conduct, while the latter generally does not. However, if the threat to bring a civil suit could be expected to bend the will of the other party, as for instance if the person making the threat had reason to believe the other would fear that he or she would be unable to afford to defend the suit or would be driven into bankruptcy, duress might be found. In all cases, the question is whether, under the circumstances, the will of the party was, and should have been, controlled.

UNDUE INFLUENCE

As in cases of duress, undue influence involves an unlawful constraint on the will of a contracting party. However, in cases of **undue influence**, the constraint is not effected by injury or threats, but by the abuse of a position of superiority by one party over the other. This may occur because of a close, personal relationship or a relationship of trust or confidence. The point is that rules of contract law assume the existence of two parties in an adversarial transaction, dealing at arms length, from positions of relatively equal influence and power. When this assumption is incorrect, different rules must be applied.

Family relationships and relationships involving professionals and clients, trustees and their beneficiaries, and even people who love and admire each other may prevent the parties from regarding each other as objectively as they would in dealings with total strangers. When a contract or other transaction between such parties seems beneficial to one and unfair to the other, the implication of undue influence may arise and give the party taken advantage of the right to disaffirm. Undue influence also may underlie an action for fraud, as in the following case.

SYESTER v. BANTA et al.
257 Iowa 613, 133 N.W.2d 666 (1965)

This was an action by Agnes Syester (Plaintiff/Appellee) against James R. Banta, Mary L. Banta, George B. Theis, and Forest L. Theis, dba Arthur Murray Dance Studio, for damages for fraud.

Plaintiff, an elderly widow living alone, began going to Defendants' dance studio where she met a young, handsome dance instructor at that time employed by Defendants. From the fall of 1954 to May 2, 1955, Defendants sold Plaintiff 3222 hours of dancing lessons for which she paid $21,020.50. By March 2, 1960, she had purchased 4057 hours for $33,497.00. Included were three lifetime memberships. Plaintiff testified, "He promised me all the privileges of the studio and [that] I would be a professional dancer." More of the long and complicated facts revealed in this case are discussed in the court's opinion.

From a judgment for Plaintiff for $14,300 in actual damages and $40,000 in punitive damages, Defendants appealed. Affirmed.

SNELL, Justice.

Since the beginning of recorded history men and women have persisted in selling their birthrights for a mess of potage and courts cannot protect against the folly of bad judgment. We can, however, insist on honesty in selling. The old doctrine of caveat emptor is no longer the pole star for business. . . .

The members of defendants' staff were carefully schooled and supervised in the art of high-powered salesmanship. Mr. Carey, a witness for plaintiff, testified at length as to methods and as to his contact with plaintiff. There was evidence that Mr. Carey was a disgruntled former employee and instructor and had expressed hostility toward defendants, but his credibility was for the jury. . . .

Mr. Carey had received two months training including a course on sales technique taught by the manager. Plaintiff's Exhibit H is a revised edition of defendants' "Eight Good Rules For Interviewing." It is an exhaustive set of instructions, outlines and suggested conversations covering twenty-two pages. A few pertinent parts are:

"**1.** How to prevent a prospect from consulting his banker, lawyer, wife or friend.

"**2.** Avoid permitting your prospect to think the matter over.

"**3.** Tell the prospect that has never danced before that it is an advantage and tell the prospect that has danced before that it is an advantage.

"**4.** To dance with the prospect and then tell the prospect that their rhythm is very good, their animation or self confidence is good, that their natural ability is very good. That they will be an excellent ballroom dancer in much less time and that if they didn't have natural ability it would take twice as long.

"**5.** To summarize the prospects [sic] ability to learn as follows: 'Did you know that the three most important points on this D.A. are: Rhythm, natural ability and animation? You've been graded Excellent in all three.'

"**6.** In quoting the price for various courses, the instructor is supposed to say 'the trouble with most people is that they dance lifelessly, but as I told you on your analysis, you have animation—vitality in your dancing. No matter what course you decide on you're going to be a really smooth dancer (men would rather be a smooth dancer—women would rather be a beautiful, graceful dancer).'

"**7.** To use 'emotional selling' and the instructor is tutored as follows: 'This is the warm-up period and is a very important part of your interview. You have proved to him by now that he can learn to dance; now you must appeal to his emotions in such a way that he will want lessons regardless of the cost.'"

Theoretically, for advancing proficiency in dancing (the jury must have thought that $29,000 had something to do with it), plaintiff was awarded a Bronze Medal, then a Silver Medal and then a Gold Medal. These awards were given plaintiff all in the same year although defendants' manager testified that it takes approximately two to four years to qualify for a Bronze Medal, five to seven years for a Silver Medal and anytime after 1200 hours a student could qualify for the Gold Medal. Finally after considerable thought about new incentives for plaintiff to buy something more she was shown a film on Gold Star dancing. This is a difficult professional type of dancing. "The dancers on the film were brought in from Europe by Mr. Murray. The dancing is English quick step and is the type of dancing done by Ginger Rogers and Fred Astaire only about twice as difficult." This film had been studied 15 to 20 times to determine what parts to stress with plaintiff.

Plaintiff was easily sold a Gold Star course of 625 hours for $6250. A few days later she came into the ballroom, handed Mr. Carey an envelope and said "Well, it took some doing but here is the money." The money was delivered to the manager.

The Gold Star course was started although even the instructor was "faking it" and had no idea what he was doing.

Mr. Carey testified at length as to the attentions, inducements, promises and lies (he said they were) lavished on plaintiff. He became plaintiff's regular instructor. He was about twenty-five years old and apparently quite charming and fascinating to plaintiff. She gave him a diamond ring for his birthday in 1960. . . .

Mr. Carey was discharged by defendants in the fall of 1960. Plaintiff quit the studio shortly thereafter. She still had 1750 hours of unused time that she had purchased. She testified that she did so because she "was unhappy because things didn't go right and I was through with dancing, and that was the only reason I quit." Defendants' manager testified that plaintiff "became unhappy over the dismissal of Mr. Carey and left the studio." Another witness for defendants said plaintiff complained mostly about losing her instructor, Mr. Carey.

[The court then discussed the law regarding proof of fraud and the plaintiff's entitlement to punitive damages and had no difficulty in affirming the judgment of the trial court.]

Questions

1.   Has the court confused "gullibility" with "undue influence"?
2.   If undue influence can be based on the relationship between a dance instructor and a client, how about between a used car salesman and a customer?

MISTAKE

When an offer is stated in ambiguous terms, generally no contract results if the parties have attached different meanings to one of the ambiguous terms. There has been no "meeting of the

Actions that can result in voidable contracts

Action	Example
Misrepresentation	Mistaken statement that a car has been driven 50,000 miles when the actual mileage is 150,000
Fraud	Knowingly selling a zircon stone as a natural diamond in order to glean "excessive" profit
Duress	Entering into an unfavorable contract with someone who has threatened your spouse
Undue influence	Buying an overpriced automobile from an employer to keep your job
Mistake	Selling what you and the other party thought was a common collector's stamp only to find out that it was exceedingly rare

minds" (mutual assent to a common set of terms). This, however, presumes that the mistake was as to a material term, not one that was unimportant or collateral to the contract. Of course if both parties attached the same meaning to the term, a binding contract will result in spite of the fact that it was ambiguous.

When the terms of the offer are clear and unequivocal, only a non-negligent mistake by one party will excuse performance. If, however, the other party knows of the mistake and takes no steps to clear it up, even a negligent mistake may not be binding. The fact that the complaining party agreed to a contract not realizing that it was a contract generally is not sufficient to relieve him or her of responsibility. Remember, intent is measured objectively (by what has been manifested), not subjectively (by what the party "really" intended). Also, failure to read and understand the terms of a contract usually is not an excuse, even when the complaining party was unable to read and understand.

When an offer transmitted by an agent carries erroneous terms, performance is not excused as long as the offeree has accepted without notice or knowledge of the mistake. Normally a principal is responsible for errors committed by his or her agent. Thus a misstatement by a sales manager about the price or availability of a product is binding on the principal.

Bilateral Versus Unilateral Mistake

To be actionable, mistakes generally must be on the part of both parties. For instance, suppose Jan and Jim enter into a contract by which Jim agrees to purchase Jan's horse but, unknown to either, at the time of the contract the horse is dead. A **bilateral (mutual) mistake** existed. Both were dealing on the assumption of a live horse, not a dead one. However, mistakes as to the value of something usually are not actionable, even if bilateral. Remember, a court of law generally will not establish values. Of course, as always, equity has the power to intervene when necessary to avoid grossly inequitable results. The following case is a classic on the subject of whether a court should find a mistake when the effect of enforcing the contract would injure one of the parties far out of proportion to the effect on the other of not enforcing it.

SHERWOOD v. WALKER et al.
66 Mich. 568, 33 N.W. 919 (1887)

This was an action by T. C. Sherwood (Plaintiff/Appellee) against Hiram Walker & Sons and others employed by the Walker Farms for replevin of a cow. Plaintiff wished to buy some cattle and contacted Defendant, breeders and importers of angus cattle. After looking at Defendant's stock at one farm, Plaintiff found no cattle that suited him, and was told by one of Defendant's employees that he might look at some cattle they had at another farm. Plaintiff was told that the cattle there were probably barren and would not breed. Plaintiff looked at the cattle and selected one, "Rose II of Aberlone." Defendant agreed to sell the cow to Plaintiff at "five and one half cents per pound." She weighed 1420 pounds. When Plaintiff came to pick up "Rose," he found that Defendant, in the mean time, had found she was pregnant. She had been purchased by Defendant for $85 and, since not barren, was worth $750-$1000. Defendant, therefore, refused to deliver the cow.

From a judgment of the trial court for Plaintiff, Defendant appealed. Reversed and remanded with the costs of the appeal to Defendant.

MORSE, J.

The circuit judge ruled that [the fact that the cow was with calf] did not avoid the sale and it made no difference whether she was barren or not. I am of the opinion that the court erred in this holding. I know that this is a close question, and the dividing line between the adjudicated cases is not easily discerned. But it must be considered as well settled that a party who has given an apparent consent to a contract of sale may refuse to execute it, or he may avoid it after it has been completed, if the assent was founded, or the contract made, upon the mistake of a material fact,—such as the subject-matter of the sale, the price, or some collateral fact materially inducing the agreement; and this can be done when the mistake is mutual. . . .

If there is a difference or misapprehension as to the substance of the thing bargained for; if the thing actually delivered or received is different in substance from the thing bargained for, and intended to be sold,—then there is no contract; but if it be only a difference in some quality or accident, even though the mistake may have been the actuating motive to the purchaser or seller, or both of them, yet the contract remains binding. "The difficulty in every case is to determine whether the mistake or misapprehension is as to the substance of the whole contract, going, as it were, to the root of the matter, or only to some point, even though a material point, an error as to which does not affect the substance of the whole consideration." Kennedy v. Panama, etc., Mail Co., L.R. 2 Q.B.580, 587. It has been held, in accordance with the principles above stated, that where a horse is bought under the belief that he is sound, and both vendor and vendee honestly believe him to be sound, the purchaser must stand by his bargain, and pay the full price, unless there was a warranty.

It seems to me, however, in the case made by this record, that the mistake or misapprehension of the parties went to the whole substance of the agreement. If the cow was a breeder, she was worth at least $750; if barren, she was worth not over $80. The parties would not have made the contract of sale except upon the understanding and belief that she was incapable of breeding, and of no use as a cow. . . .

The mistake affected the substance of the whole consideration, and it must be considered that there was no contract to sell or sale of the cow as she actually was. The thing sold and bought had in fact no existence. She was sold as a beef creature would be sold; she is in fact a breeding cow, a valuable one.

Questions

1. What does the court mean when it says the mistake "went to the whole substance of the agreement?" Is that a reasonable test for determining which mistakes will permit rescission?

2. What if the cow's breeding potential became known after delivery? Could Walker have recovered her then? When does the possibility of mistake end?

Reformation

Although an actionable mistake generally allows rescission of the contract, when the mistake is not in the parties' understanding, but in the way their intent was expressed in a written document, equity will *reform* the writing to conform with the true agreement of the parties. The problem lies in convincing the court that a mutual mistake in the written expression actually occurred, rather than that one party simply maneuvered for advantage.

SUMMARY

Fundamental to the law of contracts is that every contract arises by the voluntary, consensual agreement of the parties. Sometimes, however, circumstances prevent voluntary consent by one party. This may involve the lack of mental capacity, as in the case of a minor or of a person who was insane or intoxicated at the time the contract came into being. The inability of the party to act voluntarily, however, also may result from a situation in which this ability was destroyed by the conduct of the other parties. Examples are misrepresentation, fraud, duress, and undue influence. Finally, the parties may have been mistaken concerning some material fact. When any of these situations occurs, the resulting contract is voidable at the option of the party suffering from the disability.

In cases involving mental incapacity, the incapacitated party must exercise his or her right to avoid the contract sometime during the period of his or her incapacity, or within a reasonable time after it is removed. One general exception to this rule is that courts generally do not permit a minor to disaffirm a contract involving the sale or purchase of real estate until he or she has become of age.

A minor usually has a right to disaffirm her contracts and receive back what she gave, regardless of her ability to return what she received. However, an insane person must give back what

---

Concept outline: Voidable contracts

Contracts are voidable at the OPTION of the plaintiff if one of the following exist:

Incapacity

    Inherent—individual characteristics make certain people inherently incapable

    Induced—primarily occurs because of wrongdoing by the other party

    Minors—are assumed incapacitated until they reach the age of majority (18 or 21)

    Insanity—exists when the party entering into the contract is incapable of comprehending the business at hand

    Intoxication—comprehension of business dealings is impaired by alcohol or other drugs

Misrepresentation

    Elements—misrepresentation of material fact on which the other party justifiably relied

Fraud

    Elements—misrepresentation of material fact, knowingly made, with intent to defraud, which the other party relied on and resulted in injury

    Duress—unlawful pressure or coercion exercised over the will of another

    Undue influence—abusing a position of superiority to unlawfully constrain the will of another

    Mistake—occurs when there is not a "meeting of minds" on a common set of terms, or when an assumption(s) of the contract is erroneous

he received, unless he can show that the other party took advantage of him because of his insanity. An intoxicated person must both show that she was taken advantage of and be able to return the other party to his earlier position. If the contract of any of these parties involved the purchase of "necessaries," upon disaffirming, he or she may be required to pay their reasonable value. Also, if a minor has misrepresented his age in entering into the contract, he may be required to do something, such as pay the reasonable value of what he has received or account for its depreciation and use. Some courts even allow the other party to bring a suit based on the tort of deceit.

Even though the party suffering the disability has a right to disaffirm, she also may elect to be bound by the transaction. This ratification may be accomplished only after the disability has been removed, and it may be done by words or conduct. Anything that objectively manifests her willingness to be bound will be considered a ratification, including retention of the consideration received for an unreasonable time after removal of the disability.

Although a party lacking capacity typically is not bound by his contracts, he generally is liable for his torts. In addition, with few exceptions, parents usually are not liable for the torts of their minor children.

Misrepresentation and fraud both involve a misstatement of material fact and justifiable reliance by the party seeking to avoid the contract. In addition, for fraud, the misrepresentation must be made knowingly with intent to defraud, and an injury must result. Fraud gives the injured party the right to elect either rescission or damages for the tort of deceit, but she cannot have both.

Duress and undue influence both involve one party constraining the free will of the other. In the case of duress, constraint occurs as a result of acts of imprisonment or violence, threat of such acts, or any other threat that would be calculated to overcome the will of the average person of ordinary courage, considering the personal characteristics of the parties and other relevant facts and circumstances surrounding the transaction. In the case of undue influence, the constraint occurs as a result of the abuse of one's position of dominance over the other. It can be created by the existence of a close personal relationship or one of trust and confidence between the parties. The theory of these cases is that the parties are not dealing at true arm's length.

Mistake justifying avoidance of a contract results either when the minds of the parties have not met on a common set of term, or when they enter into an agreement based on an assumption that is erroneous. Thus when two parties attach different meanings to an ambiguous term, or when they are mistaken as to the existence or nonexistence of a material fact, the resulting agreement is voidable. Generally, to be actionable, the mistake must be mutual (by both parties) and it cannot rest on a mistake concerning value or the fact that one did not read and understand the contract, although equity always has the power to intervene to prevent an unjust result. If the mistake of the parties is not in their understanding, but only in the way that understanding is expressed in a writing, a court of equity may reform the writing to make it reflect what the parties intended.

KEY TERMS AND CONCEPTS

minors (infants)
insane
intoxicated
voidable
emancipation
disaffirm
necessaries
ratification
misrepresentation
fraud
scienter
duress
undue influence
bilateral (mutual) mistake
reformation

PROBLEMS

1. Victor was a 50-year-old bachelor who lived with his mother. He married Jane, a 30-year-old divorcee who was the mother of two minor children. Victor was secure financially. Among other things, he owned his own home, some apartments, and stock of a value of $18,000 to $19,000. Within the first few months of marriage, trouble began. Jane expressed anxiety over her financial insecurity. To remedy this, Victor opened a joint savings account of $5000. Jane also complained about their home, and Victor purchased a house with a swimming pool for $107,000, taking title with Jane by the entireties (a type of joint ownership by husband and wife). Later, to soothe other complaints, he transferred title to the old house to Jane, along with a one-half interest in the stocks. He also sold $18,000 worth of stock to purchase a $17,000 boat for Jane, which she sold one year later for $16,000, investing the proceeds. Some four years after the marriage, Jane filed for divorce. Victor sought to set aside some of these transfers on the ground of undue influence. Should Victor succeed?

2. Taylor sold a certain motel to Beierle, telling him that it was "capable of producing $20,000 per year." After purchasing the motel and operating it for a substantial period, it produced nothing close to $20,000 per year, and Beierle sued Taylor for rescission on the ground of misrepresentation and fraud. Should Beierle succeed?

3. Sunderhaus purchased a diamond ring from Perel & Lowenstein Jewelers. The seller stated that the ring was worth $5000. Some time after the purchase, Sunderhaus became suspicious and took the ring to another jeweler for appraisal. She found it was worth not more than $1500. Sunderhaus sued Perel & Lowenstein for misrepresentation and fraud. Should Sunderhaus succeed?

4. Beachcomber Coins, Inc. purchased a coin for $500, believing it to be genuine. The seller, also believing it to be genuine, had purchased it along with two other cheap coins for $450. The coin turned out to be a fake. Is Beachcomber entitled to get its $500 back?

5. Laemmaru was an employee "at will" of the J. Walter Thompson Co. As such, he was entitled to purchase company stock under favorable terms. He did so for several years. Pending a merger with another corporation, the company's stock was predicted to rise sharply in value. The company, thereafter, gave Laemmaru the choice of selling his stock back to the company or being fired. Laemmaru sold the stock back. Later he sued to have the transfer set aside on the ground of duress. The company contended there was no duress because it threatened to do only what it had a legal right to do. In fact, it gave up its right to discharge Laemmaru in consideration for the transfer. Is Laemmaru entitled to rescind the transfer?

6. Roger was 19 years old, a high-school graduate, married and the father of an infant child. He was attending college in an effort to complete a technical education, and his wife worked. In an effort to secure a job to support himself and his family and to finance his education, Roger contracted with the Gastonia Personnel Corp. to secure a position for him, agreeing to pay a fee equivalent to the first month's wages. Gastonia secured a job for Roger, but thereafter Roger refused to pay the fee, and sought to rescind the contract on the ground that he was a minor (state law set the age of majority at 21). Is Gastonia entitled to recover anything from Roger?

7. Lee, a 20-year-old minor, purchased a car from Hadocy Pontiac. During the transaction, Lee misrepresented her age to be 21. Thereafter, she gave the car to a friend and refused to pay for it on the ground that she was, in fact, a minor at the time of the transaction. Is Lee entitled to rescind, assuming the car cannot be recovered?

8. Langstraat, a minor, purchased an automobile insurance policy from Midwest Mutual Insurance Co. In the application she waived "uninsured motorist" coverage, and paid a reduced premium. Thereafter, she was involved in an accident caused by the negligence of an uninsured motorist and sought to collect on her policy, contending her waiver of coverage was not binding because of her minority. Is Langstraat correct?

9. Fuld agreed to sell certain land to McPheters, executing a written contract. Prior to executing and delivering the deed, Fuld died. McPheters filed suit against the executor of Fuld's estate, demanding a deed to the land in question. During the trial, witnesses testified that at the time of the contract, Fuld had a mental disability and was very senile. He was confined to a nursing home and, according to witnesses, he appeared at times to be unaware that his wife had died and often confused the past with the present. A business associate testified that Fuld had become very confused as to business matters and at times sent the associate money that was not owed. He was unable to care for himself and, according to friends, had become so confused as to be unable to perform even basic tasks. All of this preceded both the signing of the contract and the execution of his will. In addition to a general denial that Fuld lacked contractual capacity, McPheters noted that the court had found Fuld competent to execute his will. Should the court conclude Fuld lacked the capacity to enter into the contract even though it found him competent to execute his will?

10. Matthews learned that Williamson wanted to sell her home. She had been threatened with foreclosure of a mortgage because payments had fallen in arrears, and she wanted to get enough equity to buy a mobile home. There was a dispute as to whether Williamson had quoted $1700 or $17,000 as the price, but on September 27, both parties went to an attorney and Williamson executed a contract to sell the property for $1800 (including $100 worth of furniture). On October 10, they went to close Matthews's loan at a savings and loan—enough to cover $1800 plus back payments on the mortgage. On October 11, Williamson filed for a court order to enjoin the transfer. The evidence disclosed the property was worth $16,500, and Williamson had $10,000 in equity (and a $6500 mortgage). The evidence also disclosed that Williamson had a long history of heavy drinking and had been drinking on the day the contract was signed. Is Williamson entitled to relief?

Unenforceable Contracts

INTRODUCTION

Certain contracts may be valid because they have met the requirements of offer, acceptance, and consideration, and may have been entered into entirely fairly and voluntarily by parties possessing full contractual capacity, but still may not be enforced by the courts because they violate public policy. These difficulties generally fall into two classifications—those involving contracts having improper subject matter, such as illegal or unconscionable clauses, and those involving contracts that do not satisfy the requirement that they be in writing.

Such contracts are classified as **unenforceable** and courts encountering them maintain a strict hands-off policy, leaving the parties where they found them. An unenforceable contract is different, in this respect, from an agreement that is void. When an agreement is declared to be void, the court generally will order that the parties be returned to their earlier positions. When a contract is decreed unenforceable, the court refuses to do anything further. It will not "stain its hands" by issuing any remedial orders. Our discussion will begin with illegal contracts.

CONTRACTS CONTRARY TO PUBLIC POLICY

Contracts may be illegal for either of two general reasons. They may be contrary to a positive law, or they may be illegal because they are contrary to general **public policy** (what is in the best interests of the public). For the most part, contracts contrary to general public policy involve those affecting public officers in the performance of their duties. An agreement to secure a public office for another in return for a promise by the office-seeker to exercise official discretion or political influence would fall in this category. So, too, would agreements: (1) to alter the pay of a public officer fixed by law (e.g., paying a reward for doing his or her public duty); (2) by the officer to exercise official or political influence for "lobbying purposes" or to procure government contracts; (3) by a quasi-public corporation to do favors (for example, if a railroad agreed to establish a station at a particular point or to build along a particular route); and (4) any other agreement to do something in conflict with public duty. Note that we are talking only about *agreements* to do any of these things in return for some consideration, not about whether they actually are done as a matter of *free* discretion. Only contracts that purport to compel such performance are illegal.

Agreements in Restraint of Trade

Although agreements in **restraint of trade** (those that interfere with free competition) frequently are declared illegal by statute, they also are against public policy and therefore are unenforceable even in the absence of a specific statute. For example, the seller of a business may agree, as part of the contract of sale, that he will not engage in a business that competes with the purchaser. An employee may agree, as part of an employment contract, that upon its termination she will not compete. Competitors may agree to fix the price or supply of a product, or otherwise do things

contrary to our economic model of free competition. All of these are subject to scrutiny as possible violations of public policy.

An agreement by the seller of a business not to compete with the purchaser may be perfectly legal as long as it is made in connection with the sale of "goodwill" along with the other business assets. Goodwill is simply the difference in value between a going, established business and a like business that is started from scratch. Since a purchaser presumably pays an extra amount in recognition of this "going business value," he or she has a right to protect this investment *to the extent reasonably necessary.* Any **covenant** (contractual promise) **not to compete** must be limited reasonably as to (1) duration and (2) geographical limits. Thus, an agreement by the seller of a neighborhood grocery not to open a competing business anywhere in the United States for the rest of his life patently would be illegal and, thus, unenforceable.

The same rules generally apply to covenants not to compete given by employees. However, courts tend to be more restrictive with these agreements concerning what time and geographical limits they will consider reasonable. There must be a balancing of conflicting interests both with regard to agreements involving the sale of a business and those involving employment. In the former, the interest in protecting the purchaser's investment in the asset goodwill conflicts with the interest of allowing free competition and the right to earn a living. In the latter, the interest in protecting the value of the cost of an employee's training and experience, and the trade secrets acquired, conflicts with the interest in preserving competition, as well as with the interests in the employee's mobility and right to earn a living, among others. These conflicts must be resolved in the public interest. The reason the two types of cases are treated differently is that the courts see a much greater potential for disproportionate impact when employees, rather than entrepreneurs, are involved. The following case illustrates how the courts balance the competing interests.

BAUER v. SAWYER
8 Ill.2d 351, 134 N.E.2d 329 (1956)

This was an action by August A. Bauer and four other partners of the Kankakee Clinic (Plaintiffs/Appellees) against P. W. Sawyer to enforce a covenant not to compete contained in the partnership's agreements. The other six partners in the clinic declined to participate in this suit as plaintiffs, so they were joined (sued) as defendants.

All of the parties to this suit were partners in a medical partnership known as the Kankakee Clinic until March 31, 1954, when Defendant withdrew from the partnership. In May 1954, he opened offices for the practice of medicine contrary to a clause in the partnership agreement providing that, upon withdrawal from the partnership, he would not practice medicine, surgery, or radiology within a radius of 25 miles from Kankakee for a period of five years. Defendant contended that the clause was unenforceable as an unreasonable restraint of trade and contrary to public policy.

The trial court granted judgment for Plaintiff. The Court of Appeals reversed and remanded. Affirmed.

SCHAEFER, Justice.

The principles governing cases of this kind were stated in Ryan v. Hamilton, 205 Ill. 191, 197, 68 N.E. 781, 783, in which a contract by a physician not to engage in practice in a specified community was enforced by injunction. That contracts in general restraint of trade are generally held to be illegal is beyond controversy. But the rule admits of well-defined exceptions, and among the exceptions are contracts of the kind and character presented in this case. Contracts of this class, where the limitation as to territory is reasonable, and there exists a legal consideration for the restraint, are valid and enforceable in equity, and in such cases relief by injunction is customary and proper. . . . In determining whether a restraint is reasonable it is necessary to consider whether enforcement will be injurious to the public or cause undue hardship to the promisor, and whether the restraint imposed is greater than is necessary to protect the promisee. . . .

In this case the interest of the public is in having adequate medical protection, and it is of course true, as suggested by Dr. Sawyer, that if the injunction is granted the number of doctors available in the Kankakee community will be reduced. A stipulation entered into by the parties, however, shows that there are now 70 doctors serving the area. We are unable to say that the reduction of this number by one will cause such injury to the public as to justify us in refusing to enforce this contract. In any case, there is no reason why Dr. Sawyer cannot serve the public interest equally well by practicing in another community. No special hardship to Dr. Sawyer appears which would justify the denial of relief in this case. He may resume practice in Kankakee after five years and in the meantime he may practice elsewhere. The territorial limitation to the city of Kankakee and the surrounding area is not, we think, unreasonable in the light of modern methods of transportation and communication.

Questions

1. Would the result have been the same if there were only twenty-five doctors in the community? seven? if the only doctors in the area all were partners in the Kankakee Clinic?

2. What if the nearest town in which the defendant could practice was 100 miles away?

Antitrust violations are in a special class. Although generally controlled by statute, as mentioned above, they also are subject to broad considerations of public policy. Basically, any agreement that is in restraint of free competition, at least to an unreasonable extent, is subject to being declared illegal. The restrictive agreements just discussed (those not to compete) would fall in this category if they had not been accorded special consideration.

It also should be noted that some restraints on free competition are considered necessary and beneficial, such as monopoly agreements concerning public utilities. It would make very little sense, and would raise costs unreasonably, if particular communities were serviced by competing electric or local telephone companies. In fact, this was the attitude concerning long-distance telephone service until technology made competition feasible. The belief still remains in many respects regarding the delivery of first-class mail. Since competition is not allowed in the public utilities areas, the effect of free competition is replaced by that imposed by a public regulatory agency such as a state public utilities commission, the Federal Aviation Agency (previously, also, the Civil Aeronautics Board), and others. The details of antitrust policy are covered more fully in Chapters 46 and 47, and regulatory agencies are discussed in Chapter 44.

Bribery

Bribery merits particular attention. It seems to go without saying that a contract involving **bribery** (payment in consideration for a breach of duty) is illegal and, therefore, unenforceable. The duties

mentioned in the beginning of this chapter mostly entail some form of bribery. Although the public policy forbidding bribery within the United States always has been firm, very little attention, historically, has been paid to bribery in foreign countries. To a considerable extent, in some countries the bribery of public officials was seen as a "normal method of doing business." The Watergate hearings in 1973 first brought the attention of the American public to the problem of domestic political contributions, especially by corporations. An investigation by the Securities and Exchange Commission uncovered a widespread practice of making questionable payments abroad. The Supreme Court held that a failure to disclose these payments was a violation of the Exchange Act of 1934. In many cases, bribes of foreign officials were treated, for income-tax purposes, as business expenses that were necessary to meet competition abroad.

Although the problem existed and could be addressed by various means, Congress decided there was a need for one comprehensive piece of legislation and, in 1977, passed the Foreign Corrupt Practices Act (see Appendix L). The act forbids the offering or authorizing of corrupt payments to foreign officials, foreign political parties or their officials, or a candidate for any foreign political office. Thus, the policy against bribery was extended legislatively to activities of American firms acting in foreign countries.

CONTRACTS TO INJURE THIRD PARTIES

Sometimes contracts are entered into for the purpose of injuring others. Because these contracts are intended to injure and are against public policy, courts will not enforce them.

Crime or Tort

Any contract requiring, as a necessary part of its performance, the commission of a crime or a tort is illegal and therefore unenforceable. Thus the principle applies when Wolf hires Katz to kill Fox. However, should Wolf hire Katz to deliver merchandise for Wolf's store, and in the course of making deliveries Katz runs over and kills Fox, the fact that a crime or a tort may have been committed does not render the employment contract illegal because it was incidental to the required performance.

Indemnity Against Tort Liability

A promise to indemnify someone against tort liability in order to induce the commission of a tort is illegal. Thus, when Wolf induces Katz to go with him and trespass on Fox's property by a promise to pay both his own and Katz's liability if they get caught, the promise is unenforceable. Insurance contracts, of course, are perfectly legal, at least insofar as they provide indemnity against liability for negligence. But public policy generally opposes allowing indemnity for liability for intentional torts, just as it opposes indemnity for the purpose of directly inducing a tort. The common component that renders these agreements illegal is the presence of an evil mind. Wrongdoing simply is not to be promoted or rewarded by the law.

In Fraud of Creditors

An agreement to aid a debtor in concealing his or her property from creditors is illegal. So, too, is an agreement to prefer one creditor to the detriment of the others. Thus, an agreement under which a debtor, for the purpose of inducing one of her creditors to enter into a composition agreement, secretly promises to give that debtor a proportionally greater part of her assets than similar creditors will receive is unenforceable. In addi-

tion, if one of the creditors who has agreed to the composition learns that this has occurred, he or she has the right to renounce the composition and recover on the original debt.

Breach of Trust

Any bargain that, either by design or otherwise, might tend to induce a **breach of trust** (breach of a close, confidential, trusting relationship), or that might raise a question in the mind of a reasonable person as to the propriety of a fiduciary's actions, is illegal. This may involve a trustee, executor, administrator, guardian, agent, partner, corporate officer or director, attorney, or any other person occupying a **fiduciary** position (a position of the highest trust and confidence) with respect to another. The agreement may be one that calls for the fiduciary to profit personally, to act in a transaction in which the fiduciary has a conflict of interests, or to act in a transaction that might create a reasonable inference of impropriety.

A contract by which an agent is to represent both parties in a transaction secretly, or is to receive extra compensation for doing his duty, or is to act in his own behalf contrary to the interests of his principal is unenforceable. So, too, would be a contract between two attorneys, representing opposing clients, to split their fees. Any agreement that might lead to a breach of trust, or even an apparent breach, is illegal and thus unenforceable.

Exempt from Negligence

When two parties are of equal bargaining power, an agreement that one is to be released from liability for the effects of his or her negligence is perfectly legal. The theory is the same as that allowing an insurance contract to indemnify someone against liability for negligence. However, if the party to be released is one whose business is permeated with the public interest—such as a public utility, a common carrier, a public warehouse, or a place of public accommodation—his or her ability to exempt himself or herself is limited. A total release is against public policy, although a contract to limit liability to some appropriate amount is not. Generally, an affected business is one that is regulated and required to have a license (this is discussed more fully below). It is subject to regulatory scrutiny and perhaps has its rates set by a regulatory commission, or is protected against competition to some degree. Of course, the business may insure itself against liability.

STATUTES AFFECTING THE LEGALITY OF CONTRACTS

The public policy against certain conduct may be so strong that it becomes enacted into a statute. Violations, then, are violations of positive law as well as public policy. Contracts that will involve such conduct, thus, are unenforceable.

Usury

Most states establish a maximum interest rate that may be charged on a loan. This legislation, called a **usury** statute, has its origin in the religious notion that charging a fee for the loaning of money was a sin—one in financial need should be helped out of the milk of human kindness. Today, a maximum rate is established for the public good. The precise rate often depends on the type of loan. The penalties for charging a usurious rate range from forfeiture of the excess amount to a forfeiture of the *entire* interest *and* principal. The regulated interest includes the actual stated interest and hidden interest, such as service fees and other amounts that must be paid by the borrower and might tend to understate the actual rate of interest being charged. The disclosure of true interest now is controlled closely by statutes and

rules on both the state and the federal levels, such as the Truth in Lending Act (Regulation Z).

Wagering

Almost all states have enacted statutes prohibiting wagering to some degree. **Wagering** generally is defined as the creation of a risk for the purpose of assuming it. Thus, although the purchase of corporate securities and commodities futures involves the assumption of a risk with the hope of profits, the difference is that in the case of these legal activities, the risk is not created for the purpose of the contract. These contracts merely involve the assumption of already existing business risks, spreading them much as insurance would. On the other hand, when a poker game is conducted, no risk exists until the game is begun.

Sunday Closing Laws

A number of states still have **Sunday closing statutes** providing that most business contracts entered into on Sunday are unenforceable. Although their provisions are by no means uniform, most prohibit performing certain labors and conducting certain business transactions on Sunday. Most exempt charitable pursuits and certain necessary services and sales. Although their basis may be found, directly or indirectly, in Christian religious observance, they have not yet fallen victim to either constitutional or civil rights challenges. Today, these ordinances generally are designed to equalize competition between those who observe a holy day and those who do not by making everyone take a day of rest. The following is the leading case on the subject of the constitutionality of Sunday closing laws.

McGOWAN v. STATE OF MARYLAND
366 U.S. 420, 81 S.Ct. 1101 (1961)

This was a criminal action by the State of Maryland (Plaintiff/Appellee) against Margaret M. McGowan and others (Defendants/Appellants) for violation of Maryland's Sunday Closing Law.

Defendants are seven employees of a large discount department store. They were indicted for selling a three-ring loose-leaf binder, a can of floor wax, a stapler and staples, and a toy submarine in violation of the Sunday closing law. The statute prohibited the sale on Sunday of all merchandise except certain items listed in the statute. The list did not include any of the above items. It also provided that any business employing not more than one employee in addition to the owner could operate on Sunday. The constitutionality of this provision and the rest of Maryland's entire "package" of Sunday closing laws was considered by the court.

From conviction in the trial court Defendants appealed. Affirmed.

WARREN, Mr. Chief Justice.

The standards under which this proposition is to be evaluated have been set forth many times by this Court. Although no precise formula has been developed, the Court has held that the Fourteenth Amendment permits the States a wide scope of discretion in enacting laws which affect some groups of citizens differently than others. The constitutional safeguard is offended only if the classification rests on grounds wholly irrelevant to the achievement of the State's objective. State legislatures are presumed to have acted within their constitutional power despite the fact that, in practice, their laws result in some inequality. A statutory discrimination will not be set aside if any state of facts reasonably may be conceived to justify it. . . .

Throughout this century and longer, both the federal and state governments have oriented their activities very largely toward improvement of the health, safety, recreation and general well-being of our citizens. Numerous laws affecting public health, safety factors in industry, laws affecting hours and conditions of labor of women and children, week-end diversion at parks and beaches, and cultural activities of various kinds, now point the way toward the good life for all. Sunday Closing Laws, like those before us, have become part and parcel of this great governmental concern wholly apart from their original purposes or connotations. The present purpose and effect of most of them is to provide a uniform day of rest for all citizens; the fact that this day is Sunday, a day of particular significance in the dominant Christian sects, does not bar the State from achieving its secular goals. To say that the States cannot prescribe Sunday as a day of rest for these purposes solely because centuries ago such laws had their genesis in religion would give a constitutional interpretation of hostility to the public welfare rather than one of mere separation of church and State. . . .

However, the State's purpose is not merely to provide a one-day-in-seven work stoppage. In addition to this, the State seeks to set one day apart from all others as a day of rest, repose, recreation and tranquility—a day which all members of the family and community have the opportunity to spend and enjoy together, a day on which there exists relative quiet and disassociation from the everyday intensity of commercial activities, a day on which people may visit friends and relatives who are not available during working days. . . .

Moreover, it is common knowledge that the first day of the week has come to have special significance as a rest day in this country. People of all religions and people with no religion regard Sunday as a time for family activity, for visiting friends and relatives, for late sleeping, for passive and active entertainments, for dining out, and the like. "Vast masses of our people, in fact, literally millions, go out into the countryside on fine Sunday afternoons in the Summer. . . ." 308 Parliamentary Debates, Commons 2159. Sunday is a day apart from all others. The cause is irrelevant; the fact exists. It would seem unrealistic for enforcement purposes and perhaps detrimental to the general welfare to require a State to choose a common day of rest other than that which most persons would select of their own accord. For these reasons, we hold that the Maryland statutes are not laws respecting an establishment of religion.

Questions

1. What about the freedom to work hard seven days a week?
2. Would a weekend closing ordinance be constitutional?

Regulation of Trade, Business, or Profession

All jurisdictions have legislation regulating certain trades, businesses, and professions. Regulation generally is accomplished by means of licensing requirements and some scrutiny by regulatory authorities. The degree of regulation typically is governed by the degree of perceived risk of injury to the public in the event of misfeasance by the licensee. Whether an agreement by an unlicensed business or professional is illegal or enforceable depends on the type of licensing statute violated. Basically, there are two types of statutes—those intended to regulate a certain trade, business, or profession and those enacted only for the purpose of providing revenue.

Regulatory statutes are not uniform, but the most common require that persons engaged in certain kinds of activities obtain a license in order to protect the public against dishonest and unskilled practitioners. Professionals such as lawyers, doctors, dentists, and certified public accountants must pass some type of examination of their knowledge before practicing their professions. In many states real estate agents, insurance agents, and securities dealers are subject to scrutiny concerning their moral character and also must pass a substantive examination. In addition, people who wish to operate some types of regulated businesses, such as those involving alcohol, tobacco, and pawnbroking, must first obtain a license. A contract to perform these activities is illegal, and therefore unenforceable, if entered into by a party lacking the required license.

The purpose of some licensing statutes is to raise revenue. Whether a particular statute is of this type or the regulatory type is a question of legislative intent. Generally, if the statute requires proof of skill, knowledge, or moral character it will be classified as regulatory. If it provides that a license will be issued to anyone who pays a fee, it will be classified as a **revenue-raising statute**. A good example is a city licensing fee that anyone operating a retail or a wholesale business pays to do business. Statutes providing for a possible fine or imprisonment for their violation generally are of the regulatory type; revenue-raising statutes usually provide for the payment of a larger fee or an interest (late) charge in case of violation. Failure to obtain a license required by a revenue-raising statute has no effect on the enforceability of contracts by unlicensed persons. As the following case illustrates, courts consider the legislature's intent to determine whether violations should render a contract unenforceable.

LEW BONN COMPANY v. HERMAN
217 Minn. 105, 135 N.W.2d 222 (1965)

This was an action by Lew Bonn Company (Plaintiff/Appellee) against Alen Herman and Tony L. Ferrara, dba Calhoun Terrace Company, to recover the price of work performed.

Plaintiff and Defendant entered into a contract under which Plaintiff was to do electrical work on a building belonging to Defendant. Although a building permit was obtained, Plaintiff failed to file separate plans for the electrical work as required by a city ordinance. Defendant contended that this failure rendered this contract illegal and therefore, unenforceable.

From a judgment for Plaintiff in the amount of $10,435.18 as requested, Defendant appealed. Affirmed.

MURPHY, Justice.

Although the general rule is that a contract entered into in violation of a statute which imposes a prohibition and a penalty for the doing of an act, such as the pursuit of a business, profession, or occupation without procuring a license or permit required by law for the protection of the public, is void, such rule is not to be applied without first examining the nature and circumstances of the contract in light of the applicable statute or ordinance. In construing such a statute or ordinance, courts will infer that the legislature did not intend that an instrument executed in violation of its terms should be void unless that be necessary to accomplish its purpose. 4 Dunnell, Dig. (3 ed.) Section 1873. The general rule has been applied in this state with varying results. In Ingersoll v. Randall, . . . and Leuthold v. Stickney, . . . contracts in violation of law were held to be unenforceable under circumstances where the violations offended important public policy with respect to health and safety of the public. However, in De Mers v. Daniels, . . . and in re Estate of Peterson, supra, the holdings indicate that the breach of a provision of law as it bears upon the performance of a contract will not necessarily render the agreement unenforceable where the legislative intent to be found in the act would not indicate that its sanction should apply where the violation is slight, not seriously injurious to the public order, and where no wrong has resulted from want of compliance.

The contentions of appellants come down to the proposition that they are entitled to a windfall of more than $10,000 because of the failure of their creditor to comply strictly with the provisions of a city ordinance. It could hardly be said that such a decision would be consonant with principles of justice where there is nothing in the record to indicate that when the contract was entered into there was any intention to violate the law, or to indicate bad motives or a design to deny the protection of law to one of a class for whose benefit the statute or ordinance was enacted. We do not think that the legislature intended that a slight violation relating to failure to comply with a collateral duty in the filing of plans and specifications should result in the forfeiture of a just debt.

Questions

1.   What led the court to the result it reached? Was the ordinance unimportant? Was the violation small? Would a contrary result have been inequitable? Were all three of these elements involved?

2.   Does the result in this case render the ordinance meaningless? Why should anyone obey it?

EFFECT OF ILLEGALITY

Courts usually refuse to enforce illegal contracts. As noted earlier, they will not grant a recovery for services or other transactions performed under the contract, and they will not grant damages for breach of the contract. Unlike situations in which agreements are declared void, when unenforceable contracts are involved the courts will refuse even to order the parties returned to their pre-contract positions. There are, however, some important exceptions to this rule.

Ignorance of Law or Fact

Generally, ignorance of the law is no excuse. Every person is assumed to know the law of his or her domicile, residence, the place where he or she finds himself or herself physically, and of any place where he or she conducts business, either for profit or gratuitously. However, ignorance of some special regulation involving a trade, business, or profession of the other party to a contract frequently is regarded as excusable. The same is true of good-faith ignorance of any noncompliance when such a regulation has not been followed. Under these circumstances, the innocent party may be granted an appropriate remedy—for example, return to status quo, payment for part performance, or, in some cases, recovery of damages—on a theory that the other party is in breach of an implied warranty concerning his or her qualification to do business.

Ignorance of a fact, as long as it was in good faith and excusable, generally will entitle the inno-cent party to some "make-whole" remedy if he or she ceases the activity promptly upon learning of the illegality. This especially is true when the other party knew of the illegality. For example, suppose Al steals Bjorn's horse and boards it in Carol's stable. Carol may recover from Al any boarding fee earned under these circumstances. Review the discussion of mistake in Chapter 9.

Knowledge of Illegal Use

When an article is sold or money is lent to be used for an illegal purpose, the enforceability of the underlying contract will depend on the knowledge of the illegality and perhaps on the seriousness of the crime. Suppose Clyde sells a car to Bonnie and, unknown to Clyde, Bonnie plans to use is as a getaway car during a bank robbery, and it is so used. Since Clyde had no knowledge of this planned use at the time of the contract, he can recover in a suit for the price of the car even though the crime is a serious one. The contrary would be true if Clyde had known of its intended use and had sold it to Bonnie because it was the "ideal getaway car." Both determining factors would be present. However, if Clyde had sold the car to Bonnie knowing that she was a bank robber and that the car probably would be used in a robbery, the contract would be enforceable because it was not entered into *for the purpose* of furthering the commission of a crime. Finally, if Clyde sold the car to Bonnie knowing that she would be leaving it illegally parked, even if Clyde participated by delivering it to the illegal parking space the contract would not be rendered unenforceable because the crime of illegal parking would not be considered sufficiently serious. Of course, it should be kept in mind that the lines dividing these situations can be very thin.

Parties Not in *Pari Delicto*

When the parties have entered into a contract involving an illegality, but they are not equally guilty—not in *pari delicto*—the courts generally will grant recovery to the relatively innocent, or less guilty, party as long as she acts in a timely fashion to disaffirm and the illegality did not involve a wrongful intent (moral turpitude) on her part. That would be the case in situations involving ignorance of a special regulation or fact, discussed previously, and those in which the more guilty party has induced the other to perform for the purpose of defrauding him. Many times "con games" fall into this classification.

Also included in this exception may be situations in which one party, although equally guilty in planning the wrongdoing, stopped short of the illegal performance and sought rescission of the contract. To grant recovery under these circumstances is thought to promote public policy by encouraging persons to back out before any harm is caused. Consider the following case.

DIAS v. HOUSTON
154 Cal.App.2d 279,315 P.2d 885 (1957)

This was an action by Edward Dias (Plaintiff/Respondent) against Hosle Houston, Jr., an unlicensed contractor, for breach of a contract to remodel Plaintiff's building.

The parties entered into a written contract by which Defendant was to remodel Plaintiff's building at an agreed-upon price of $4000. Later there was a supplemental agreement to do additional work for $1600. Plaintiff paid $1000 on the original contract and the full $1600 on the supplement. Shortly thereafter he discovered that Defendant was unlicensed and refused to allow him to continue working on the job.

The trial court entered a judgment for Plaintiff in the amount he had paid on his contract with Defendant. Defendant appealed. Affirmed.

PEEK, Justice.

Defendant's contention that the contract between the parties was illegal and void and for the reason, unenforceable, is without merit. The rule is well established in this state that ". . . when the Legislature enacts a statute forbidding certain conduct for the purpose of protecting one class of persons from the activities of another, a member of the protected class may maintain an action notwithstanding the fact that he has shared in the illegal transaction. The protective purpose of the legislation is realized by allowing the plaintiff to maintain his action against a defendant within the class primarily to be deterred. In this situation it is said that the plaintiff is not in pari delicto.

Defendant then goes one step further and contends that since the contract was void because of its illegality, it cannot be enforced by either party and hence the innocent party may recover only that for which he had received no value. Under the circumstances defendant's disagreement with the rule in the case of Ownes v. Haslett . . . is quite understandable. Nevertheless it is the rule that, "Where the illegality of a bargain is due to (a) facts of which one party is justifiably ignorant and the other party is not, or (b) statutory or executive regulations of a minor character relating to a particular business which are unknown to one party, who is justified in assuming special knowledge by the other party of the requirements of the law, the illegality does not preclude recovery by the ignorant party of compensation for any performance rendered while he is still justifiably ignorant, or for losses incurred or gains prevented by non-performance of the bargain." Restatement of Contracts, sec. 559.

If necessarily follows that under the facts and circumstances of the record before us, plaintiff comes within the exception to the general rule, and hence was properly allowed damages as in an action predicated upon an alleged wrongful breach of contract.

Questions

1. Is the court applying the rule correctly?
2. Is the result fair?

Divisible Agreements

When an agreement involves an illegality but is for the most part legal, courts will enforce the legal portion if it is able to separate it from the illegal portion. This generally requires that the consideration for the illegal part be separable and not inextricably mixed with that for the legal part. Thus, if Crisco hires Wesson to work as a bartender, agreeing to pay a bonus of $20 per day if Wesson will oversee the illegal poker game in the back room, a court probably would grant Wesson a recovery for his bartending wages but not for the bonus. However, if Crisco were to hire Wesson to make deliveries for a wage of $50 per day, some of the goods being legal and others, known to Wesson, being illegal, no recovery would be granted of any part of the wages. The entire contract would fall because of the illegal portion. Perhaps if Wesson were to be paid a set fee for each stop, the illegal stops might be separable from the legal ones, permitting Wesson to recover for the latter.

UNCONSCIONABLE CONTRACTS

At common law, courts sometimes encountered situations in which they were required to enforce contracts they felt were unfair. Although courts of equity could refuse to enforce such agreements specifically, law courts were without similar power when the remedy sought was damages, unless the unfairness was the result of actual fraud, duress, undue influence, or the like. The courts tried to be creative in dispensing justice regarding these contracts, and finally were given an express grant to do so concerning contracts for the sale of goods by Section 2-302 of the Uniform Commercial Code, which provides:

> *If the court as a matter of law finds the contract or any clause of the contract to have been unconscionable at the time it was made, the court may refuse to enforce the contract, or it may enforce the remainder of the contract without the unconscionable clause, or it may so limit the application of an unconscionable clause as to avoid any unconscionable result.*

What causes a contract or clause to be **unconscionable** (such as to shock the ordinary person's sense of fairness) is a matter of judicial judgment. (It is not defined in the Code.) The fact that a contract is "lopsided" usually is not sufficient, since a law court generally tries to avoid substituting its sense of value for those of the parties—a court normally will examine only the sufficiency of consideration, not its adequacy. However, when inequity is coupled with some other factor, such as gross inequality of bargaining position or a devastating effect on one party without a corresponding risk of a similar effect on the part of the other, unconscionability may be considered. The following case is a classic on the subject of unconscionable contracts.

WILLIAMS v. WALKER-THOMAS FURNITURE COMPANY
350 F.2d 445 (D.C. Cir. 1965)

This was an action by Walker-Thomas Furniture Company (Plaintiff/Appellee) against Ora Lee Williams for replevin (recovery) of furniture sold to Defendant on an "open-end" credit plan.

Plaintiff operated a furniture store and sold furniture on an open-end credit plan by which title to the goods remained with the seller until payment was made in full, at which time title would transfer to the purchaser. The written contract further provided that "the amount of each periodical installment payment to be made by [purchaser] to the Company under this present lease shall be inclusive of and not in addition to the amount of each installment payment to be made by [purchaser] under such prior leases, bills or accounts; *and all payments now and hereafter made by [purchaser] shall be credited pro rata on all outstanding leases, bills and accounts* due the Company by [purchaser] at the time each such payment is made." (Emphasis added.) The effect of this rather obscure provision was to keep a balance due on every item purchased until the balance due on all items, whenever purchased, was liquidated.

Defendant engaged in several transactions with Plaintiff and always had a running balance in her account. On April 17, 1962 she bought a stereo from Plaintiff for $514.95 and, shortly thereafter, defaulted. Plaintiff sought to replevy all items purchased since December 1957.

The trial court found for Plaintiff. Defendant appealed to the District of Columbia Court of Appeals, which expressed concern about Plaintiff's "sharp" practices but felt they were a matter to be addressed by the legislature, and affirmed (198 A.2d 914). The case then was reheard in the trial court, which again found for Plaintiff. On appeal of the second trial court decision, the United States Court of Appeals for the District of Columbia reversed and remanded.

J. SKELLY WRIGHT, Circuit Judge.

Congress has recently enacted the Uniform Commercial Code [for the District of Columbia], which specifically provides that the court may refuse to enforce a contract which it finds to be unconscionable at the time it was made. 28 D.C.CODE sec. 2-302 (supp. IV 1965). The enactment of this section, which occurred subsequent to the contracts here in suit, does not mean that the common law of the District of

Columbia was otherwise at the time of enactment, nor does it preclude the court from adopting a similar rule in the exercise of its powers to develop the common law for the District of Columbia. In fact, in view of the absence of prior authority on that point, we consider the congressional adoption of Sec. 2-302 persuasive authority for following the rationale of the cases from which the section is explicitly derived. Accordingly, we hold that where the element of unconscionability is present at the time a contract is made, the contract should not be enforced.

Unconscionability has generally been recognized to include an absence of meaningful choice on the part of one of the parties together with contract terms which are unreasonably favorable to the other party. Whether a meaningful choice is present in a particular case can only be determined by consideration of all the circumstances surrounding the transaction. In many cases the meaningfulness of the choice is negated by a gross inequality of bargaining power. The manner in which the contract was entered is also relevant to this consideration. Did each party to the contract, considering his obvious education or lack of it, have a reasonable opportunity to understand the terms of the contract, or were the important terms hidden in a maze of fine print and minimized by deceptive sales practices? Ordinarily, one who signs an agreement without full knowledge of its terms might be held to assume the risk that he has entered a one-sided bargain. But when a party of little bargaining power, and hence little real choice, signs a commercially unreasonable contract with little or no knowledge of its terms, it is hardly likely that his consent, or even an objective manifestation of his consent, was ever given to all the terms. In such a case the usual rule that the terms of the agreement are not to be questioned should be abandoned and the court should consider whether the terms of the contract are so unfair that enforcement should be withheld.

In determining reasonableness or fairness, the primary concern must be with the terms of the contract considered in light of the circumstances existing when the contract was made. The test is not simple, nor can it be mechanically applied. The terms are to be considered "in light of the general commercial background and the commercial needs of the particular trade or case." Corbin suggests the test as being whether the terms are "so extreme as to appear unconscionable according to the mores and business practices of the time and place." . . . We think this formulation correctly states the test to be applied in those cases where no meaningful choice was exercised upon entering the contract.

Because the trial court and the appellate court did not feel that enforcement could be refused, no findings were made on the possible unconscionability of the contracts in these cases. Since the record is not sufficient for our deciding the issue as a matter of law, the cases must be remanded to the trial court for further proceedings.

So ordered.

Questions

1. Shouldn't an unenforceable contract be unenforceable by either party?
2. How does this contract differ from a voidable contract?

STATUTE OF FRAUDS

Basically, a **Statute of Frauds** is a statute requiring that certain types of contracts be in writing in order to be enforceable. Each state has enacted its own, and the types of contracts included vary from state to state. However, the vast majority agree concerning certain types of contracts, and those will be the focus of this section.

One of the first things to understand about the Statute of Frauds is that it has nothing to do, directly, with fraud. It takes its name from the early statute after which it is patterned, enacted by the Parliament in England in 1677, entitled "An Act for the Prevention of Frauds and Perjuries."

The reason for this name is found in the rules of procedure in force in the English courts at the time. They provided that when two persons entered into a contract, the parties to it were disqualified from testifying in any litigation involving the existence or provisions of the contract because the courts felt that the parties, having an interest in the outcome of the controversy, would be unduly tempted to perjure themselves. This rule gave rise to a widespread practice of hiring "witnesses" who most certainly perjured themselves. In order to avoid some of the risk of perjured testimony in cases, Parliament simply required that certain contracts, which they felt would be sufficiently important, be evidenced by a signed writing in order to be enforceable.

Scope

The contracts listed in the 1677 act were (1) promises by an executor or administrator to answer out of his own pocket for the debts of the deceased, (2) promises to answer for the debt, default, or miscarriage of another, (3) promises on consideration of marriage or a promise to marry, (4) contracts not to be performed within one year, (5) contracts involving the sale of an interest in land, and (6) contracts involving the sale of goods above a certain value. These provisions, with some modifications and additions, continue to be found in contemporary statutes of frauds. The statutes generally do not apply to contractual obligations created by law, to those that are unilateral, or to those that have been executed fully by the parties.

When a contract is within the provisions of the Statute of Frauds but the requirements of the statute have not been met, the contract is unenforceable. The effect is the same as in the case of an illegal contract, but no wrongdoing is involved. The public policy involved is that of protecting against enforcement of apparent contractual obligations established by perjured testimony.

Complying with the Statute of Frauds usually requires that the existence of the contract be evidenced by a sufficient writing, although other evidence may be used to avoid unenforceability, as we will see in the discussion of the methods of satisfying the Statute of Frauds.

Collateral Promises

The first two types of promises covered by the original statute can be considered together under the term **collateral promises** in that both involve the same basis—one party promises to pay the debt of another if that person does not pay it. These are sometimes called "suretyship promises" or "promises of guarantee."

For a promise to be collateral, two elements are required: (1) there must be a promise in collateral form ("I will pay X's debt if X fails to pay") and (2) there must be a valid underlying debt. Suppose, for example, Chet owes $500 to David for the purchase of a boat. David threatens to take back the boat when Chet fails to pay on time. Diane, a friend of Chet's, tells David, "Don't worry about it. If Chet doesn't pay the $500 by the end of the month, I will pay it." This is a classic collateral promise and must be in writing to be enforceable. Suppose, however, Diane had induced David to sell the boat to Chet saying, "Give it to him. I will pay the $500." This promise is not collateral in that it is neither in collateral form nor based on a valid underlying debt owed by Chet to David. Suppose Diane "cosigns" Chet's obligation to David to pay for the boat. Her promise, again, is not collateral. Even though there is a valid underlying debt owed by Chet to David, a cosigner is not saying "I will pay if X doesn't." She is saying, "I will pay." This is a primary obligation; that of a collateral promisor is secondary. Suppose, finally, that Diane knows Chet wants the boat and tells David, "Send the boat over to Chet. If he doesn't pay for it, I will." Again, Diane's promise is original, not collateral. It is collateral in form but there is, at the time of the promise, no valid underlying debt since Chet has never agreed to pay for the boat.

Contracts in Consideration of Marriage or a Promise to Marry

Of primary interest under this provision are **prenuptial (antenuptial) contracts**. These are agreements by which persons about to be married may settle property rights in the event of divorce or death. In the absence of such an agreement, the law will dictate what rights each has in property belonging to the other and in property acquired during the marriage. Although state statutes differ significantly in the details, a split of 50-50 of the marital property is quite common, on the theory that during the course of the "normal" marriage each partner will contribute about half to the total accumulation of wealth. In the event that the parties feel this presumption may not be realistic in their particular case—as when there is a considerable difference in age, one of the couple has far more wealth than the other, or one has children by a former marriage—the parties may choose to enter into such an agreement by which the younger, less wealthy, or childless party agrees to give up some portion of the property rights to which he or she otherwise would be entitled in return for the agreement of the other to marry. When these agreements are used, they frequently involve substantial property rights.

It should be noted that this provision does not cover simple mutual promises to marry. Engage-

ment agreements really are not considered to be contractual. Jurisdictions that recognized "breach of promise suits" did so not on contract grounds, but on the ground of the public interest in maintaining a climate of moral behavior, it being felt that men too often became engaged to young ladies in order to induce them to engage in sexual activities outside of marriage.

Contracts Not to Be Performed Within One Year

The theory behind including these contracts in the Statute of Frauds is much the same as that behind statutes of limitations. When duties are to remain executory over a long period of time, the parties' memories may become less accurate, evidence may be misplaced, and witnesses may forget or become unavailable. Thus it is felt that when performance is to extend over a period longer than one year, the agreement should be evidenced by a writing. It should be noted that this provision applies to bilateral contracts only. Thus, if Robert promises Judy one thousand dollars if she walks across the George Washington Bridge three years from today, the Statute of Frauds does not govern Robert's promise.

In determining whether to apply this provision, courts have applied a strict negative standard. That is, in order for a contract to be covered, the language of the contract must make it impossible for full performance to occur within one year. A contract under which Turner promises to work for Cooper for two years would be such a contract. However, a promise by Turner to work for Cooper for life would not. Regardless of the probability that performance will extend beyond one year, and even regardless of the fact that it actually does, at the time the contract was entered into its provisions did not expressly prevent performance within one year.

This theory may be taken to extremes, such as exempting a contract involving a promise to walk back and forth across the United States four thousand times. Although performance within one year appears to be impossible according to known laws of physical science, nothing in the terms of the contract prohibit it from happening. Even more creatively, in a case involving a promise to provide support to another for 20 years, courts have reasoned that the promise was not covered because what the promisor actually meant was a promise of support for "20 years or the rest of the promisee's life, whichever occurred first." This conclusion is grounded on the premise that if the promisee dies within a year he or she will have no further need of support, and thus the promise will have been performed as fully as it ever could be performed. The same theory would not apply to the contract to work for two years. In that context, if the promisor died earlier, the work for the remainder of the two years would not be completed and would have to be performed by someone else.

In counting time, keep in mind that the one year begins on the date the contract is entered into, not on the date performance is to begin. Thus a promise to work for one year, with work to begin that same day or the following day, can be performed within one year. A promise on Saturday to work for one year beginning Monday cannot be performed within one year, and falls within the Statute of Frauds. Note also that for the purpose of counting time, one day is treated just like another. Weekends and holidays are of no particular significance. In the case of the promise on Saturday to begin work on Monday, the argument that "we don't work weekends" so the job would be finished on Friday, one year later would not prevail either. The obligation would be seen as extending to *Sunday* one year later, regardless of the expected work schedule.

Extensions of existing contracts present another problem. When the time of an existing contract is extended, time is calculated as of the date of the promise, not the beginning of the extension. Thus if Abner agrees to work for Russell for one year, beginning on January 1 and ending on December 31, and on April 1 agrees to extend the contract for 6 months, the promise to extend must be in writing. That is because the new agreement is not to be completely performed for 15 months (April 1 of that year through June 30 of the following year).

Some contracts overlap Statute of Frauds categories. For example, in applying the one-year provision, the question of whether a particular contract is one for the sale of services or some other kind of contract will be important in determining the rights of the parties, and is not always an easy question to answer. Consider the following case involving a mixed services and goods contract.

BUTTORFF v. UNITED ELECTRONIC LABORATORIES, INC.
459 S.W. 2d 581 (Ky., 1970)

This was an action by Gordon Stephen Buttorff (Plaintiff/Appellant) against United Electronic Laboratories, Inc. to recover commissions allegedly due under an oral contract whereby Plaintiff was to market Defendant's camera equipment.

According to Plaintiff, he and Defendant entered into an oral agreement in February 1961 whereby Plaintiff was to market Defendant's security cameras, purchasing them for $440 each and selling them for $985 plus installation. Orders were sent to Defendant, who billed the customers and then remitted Plaintiff's "commission" to him. Their relationship was then terminated by Defendant. When sued, Defendant's defense was that any such agreement would violate the Statute of Frauds.

In the trial court, there was a jury verdict for Plaintiff in the amount of $14,197.50. This was set aside by the judge, granting Defendant's motion for judgment n.o.v., and Plaintiff's complaint was dismissed. Plaintiff appealed. Reversed and remanded.

REED, Judge.

The next argument advanced by the defendant and one on which it appears to place great reliance is that the agreement was unenforceable because of the "sale of goods for the price of $500 or more" section of the statute of frauds which is now incorporated into the Uniform Commercial Code and is embodied as statutory law in Kentucky at KRS 355.2-201. Defendant argues that by the plaintiff's own pleadings the agreement between them was a sale of goods for a price of $500 or more. We are not so persuaded.

Anderson's Uniform Commercial Code, Vol. 1, Section 2-201:2, p. 93, points out that the pattern of the former Uniform Sales Act is continued in this new section except that the content of the writing is simplified, the exception of non-resellable goods is made more strict and the exception of giving something in earnest is deleted. Thus, we perceive no change in the basic law concerning whether a particular agreement is one for the sale of personal services or for the sale of goods.

Stone v. Krylon, Inc., 141 F.Supp. 785 (D.C.E.D.Pa. 1956), held that where the agreement was for performance of certain personal services for the defendant corporation and the defendant corporation promised to grant the plaintiff an exclusive agency to sell certain goods, the contract was one for employment and the consideration for the services was not wages or salary but a valuable franchise. There the court refused to declare the agreement unenforceable by reason of U.C.C. 2-201.

In his consideration of the Uniform Sales Act which preceded the U.C.C. as the law in Kentucky, Williston said: "A contract creating an agency to sell goods is not a contract for the sale of goods and is not within the statute." Williston on Sales Revised Edition (1948), Section 58, p. 153. A contract under which a distributor undertook to secure new customers' accounts, take orders for specific territory, sell only the goods of the seller, and he, at the same time ordered from the seller a one-half year's supply of goods, was held an agency contract and not within the statute of frauds in Fargo Glass and Paint Company v. Globe American Corporation, 161 F.2d 811 (7th Cir.1947).

In City of Owensboro v. Dark Tobacco Growers' Ass'n., 222 Ky. 164, 300 S.W. 350, we pointed out that in determining whether an agreement between parties is a sale or is a mere contract of agency, isolated expressions in the instrument indicating whether it is one or the other are not necessarily controlling; on the contrary, the courts will ignore apparently inconsistent language used, and look to the real nature of the agreement between the parties, what its real purpose was, and what, from the nature of the transaction, must have been in the minds of the parties. We have no hesitation, in view of the proof and considering the pleadings in their entirety, in concluding that this agreement is not a sale of goods as such but is a contract for personal services and, therefore, KRS 355.2-201 does not preclude its enforcement.

The plaintiff argues that the general rule pertaining to contracts of employment should be applicable. The general rule is that contracts for employment or other performance that is to begin within a year and is to continue for an indefinite, unspecified period are terminable by either party at any time and held not to be within the one-year clause of the statute. Salyers v. Kenmont Coal Co., 226 Ky. 655, 11 S.W.2d 705 (1928), is an example of the application of that principle.

Defendant argues that where, from the nature of the contract, it cannot be performed in a year and the parties so contemplated in making it, the statute applies and the contract is unenforceable. . . .

The enforceability of a contract under the one-year provision of the statute does not turn on the actual course of subsequent events, nor on the expectations of the parties as to the probabilities. Contracts of uncertain duration are excluded; historically, the statute has been consistently applied only to those contracts where performance cannot possibly be completed within a year. Therefore, although the criticism by Williston and Corbin of the cases cited by defendant may be valid when viewed in the light of the doctrine that expectations of the parties as to probabilities will not place a contract within the statute; nevertheless, if the testimony of the party seeking to enforce the contract is that it was factually impossible to perform his agreement within a year, then such contract must fall squarely within the statute.

Questions

1. Is there any real utility to the one-year provision given the judicial construction of it?

2. Does the Statute of Frauds have any continued utility in modern times?

Contracts for the Sale of an Interest in Land

The first thing to be understood concerning this provision is that the courts uniformly interpret the term *land* to mean "real estate." Although **land** generally is defined as "the earth's crust," **real estate** is defined as "the earth's crust and all things permanently attached thereto or used peculiarly therewith." Thus, real estate includes not only land, it also includes buildings, fixtures, trees, mineral rights, and air rights—anything that is naturally attached to or part of the land, or is later attached to it with the apparent intent that it remain there.

The Uniform Commercial Code, in Sections 2-105(1) and 2-107 does treat as *goods* some things that otherwise would be classified as real estate. Section 2-105(1) states that the term **goods** includes "growing crops and other identified things attached to the realty as described in . . . Section 2-107." Section 2-107 then includes, as goods, "minerals or the like (including oil and gas) or a structure or its materials to be removed from the realty . . . *if they are to be severed by the seller* . . . [and] growing crops or other things attached to the realty and capable of severance without material harm thereto . . . [or for timber to be cut] . . . *whether the subject matter is to be severed by the buyer or by the seller.* . . ." [Emphasis added.]

The second point to be understood is that this provision of the Statute of Frauds applies to *any* interest in land, not just the fee-simple title (complete ownership). Thus, also covered are *contracts to transfer* such interests as mortgages, easements, liens, and the like. Leases also are covered, although most states make special provisions with respect to them. Under Michigan law, leases for one year or less can be oral. Indiana has permitted oral leases of up to three years. State law must be examined to determine what rule applies in any particular situation.

Finally, this provision covers only *contracts* to transfer, not the *instruments* of transfer. That is, it does not cover deeds or wills, only contracts to make deeds or wills. The actual instruments of transfer typically are covered by other statutes.

Contracts for the Sale of Goods

This provision of the Statute of Frauds is found in Section 2-201 of the UCC, and thus is in force throughout the nation (except in Louisiana, which has not adopted Article 2). It covers all contracts for the sale of *goods* of a *price* of *$500 or more*. It is necessary to consider each word of this short provision in detail.

The types of property that constitute *goods* has been briefly noted. The term is defined in detail in Sections 2-105(1) and 2-107 of the UCC. Basically, 2-105(1) defines *goods* as all tangible personal property (thus excluding real estate and intangible personal property such as copyrights and patent rights), except (1) purchase-price money, (2) investment securities, and (3) things (choses) in action.

The reason for excluding purchase-price money is that the money to be paid is regarded as a medium of exchange, not something that is bought and sold. Of course, rare coins would be classified as goods since they are not purchase-price money. The reason for excluding investment securities is that they are given special, individual treatment under Article 8 of the UCC. Choses in action are obligations owed, such as accounts receivable. More technically, a **chose in action** is any property that is not usable in its existing form, but must be converted into something else to be used. Choses in action are excluded because even

though they may be bought and sold, they are unlike goods in that they are for investment, not for consumption or other immediate use.

Notice that goods contracts are covered only if the *price* is $500 or more. Under the Uniform Sales Act, which preceded Article 2 of the UCC, the provision was based on "value." This was changed because of the difficulty of determining what something is worth as opposed to its selling price. It should be noted, also, that the term *price* does not include "add-on" items such as sales tax and finance charges.

Finally, remember that this provision becomes applicable at the exact figure of $500 (not more than $500). A price of $499.99 is not included. Thus, when Abner agrees to sell a car to Russell for $500, the Statute of Frauds requires a writing for that contract to be enforceable.

METHODS OF SATISFYING THE STATUTE OF FRAUDS

This discussion has proceeded on the assumption that if a contract is covered by the Statute of Frauds it must be in writing in order to be enforceable. Unquestionably a writing is the best, most certain, and most universally applicable method of satisfying the requirements of the statute, but it is not the only way. In this section, writings will be discussed first, then other, secondary possibilities will be presented.

Writing

The Statute of Frauds usually requires that a contract within its provisions be "evidenced by a note or memorandum in writing." This statement raises three questions. (1) What is meant by "writing"? (2) What is meant by "note or memorandum"? (3) At what point in time must the note or memorandum be written?

In answer to the first question, the term **writing** may be defined as "the reduction of thought to tangible form." Thus, the statute does not require a formal, "whereas, heretofore, blue-backed, typewritten" contract. An adequate writing may be scratched out on a piece of notebook paper, or on a dinner napkin with a crayon—not that these methods are suggested, but they meet the requirement.

What must be contained within the note or memorandum? This depends on the type of contract involved. For the sale of goods, UCC Section 2-201 states that a sufficient writing must: (1) evidence a contract for the sale of goods, (2) specify quantity, and (3) be signed by the party to be charged (the party defending on the ground of the Statute of Frauds). If the quantity specified is inaccurate, the court will not refuse to enforce the contract, but will not enforce it beyond the quantity stated.

Concerning contracts for the sale of investment securities, Code Section 8-319 states that the writing must: (1) evidence a contract for the sale of securities, (2) identify the parties, (3) state the quantity, (4) state the price, (5) describe the securities, and (6) be signed by the party to be charged. Thus, a sufficient writing for the sale of securities requires more elements than are necessary for the sale of goods.

Other contracts are governed by the principles of common law, which requires that the writing contain all *material* terms, specifically including:

(1) identification of the parties, (2) description of the subject matter, including price, (3) any special terms (such as credit terms) and conditions, and (4) the signature of the party to be charged. Note that the signature requirements are the same for all Statute of Frauds contracts. Both parties need not sign; only the party invoking the statute as a defense must have signed. This means that it is *your* responsibility to see that the *other* party signs and it is *his* responsibility to see that *you* sign. If Abe has Ben sign but Ben does not see that Abe does, in a suit by Abe, Ben could not use the statute as a defense, but in a suit by Ben, Abe could. This obviously is not a desirable position in which to find oneself.

Finally, the rule provides that the writing may be created any time before the question of compliance with the statute is raised in court. The writing may be completed at the time of agreement or some time afterwards, but must be completed before it must be produced in court. It may be a writing that was drafted for the purpose of satisfying the statute, or it may consist of correspondence between the parties that meets the requirements stated above. As the following case illustrates, the court may well find *any* writing sufficient if it contains enough information about the transaction.

BARDO SALES, INC. v. MILLER-WOHL COMPANY, INC.
440 F.2d 962 (2nd Cir. 1971)

This was an action by Bardo Sales, Inc. (Plaintiff/Appellee) against Miller-Wohl Company, Inc. for a declaratory judgment to determine Plaintiff's rights in a lease contract entered into with Defendant.

For some time Plaintiff had done business on a lease arrangement in parts of Defendant's stores, paying rent calculated on a percentage of sales. In 1968 the parties entered into negotiations for the renewal of existing leases and the addition of a lease for a new store being opened by Defendant. The new leases were to be for six-year periods. On February 12, 1969, Victor Fortgang, Defendant's vice-president, sent an unsigned internal memorandum to one of his assistants concerning the leases. Thereafter, in March or April, Defendant sent Plaintiff ten new leases dated February 28, 1969. On April 7, 1969, Defendant sent a letter to Plaintiff mentioning, among other things, the lease agreements.

Plaintiff signed and returned them, but Defendant did not sign them and refused to honor the alleged agreement of the parties. When sued, Defendant defended on the grounds of the Statute of Frauds.

From a summary judgment for Plaintiff, Defendant appealed. Reversed and remanded for special findings, but not as to the substance of the lower court's decision.

J. JOSEPH SMITH, Circuit Judge.

[The court first found that the alleged agreement of the parties would be within the Statute of Frauds as a contract not to be performed within one year. Then the court discussed the question of an adequate writing.]

The appellee and the court below relied on the New York Court of Appeals decision in *Crabtree v. Elizabeth Arden Sales Corp.*, 305 N.Y. 48, 110 N.E.2d 551 (1953) which stated: "The statute of frauds does not require the "memorandum . . . to be in one document. It may be pieced together out of separate writings, connected with one another either expressly or by the internal evidence of subject matter and occasion." . . .

None of the terms of the contract are supplied by parol [orally]. All of them must be set out in the various writings presented to the court, and at least one writing, the one establishing a contractual relationship between the parties, must bear the signature of the party to be charged, while the unsigned document must on its face refer to the same transaction as that set forth in the one that was signed. Parol evidence—to portray the circumstances surrounding the making of the memorandum—serves only to connect the separate documents and to show that there was assent, by the party to be charged, to the contents of the one unsigned. . . . The district court correctly found that the signed letter of appellant's assistant comptroller dated April 7, 1969 which included the reference to "our agreement . . . to initiate the new leases" was sufficient to come within the Crabtree requirement that the signed document "establish a contractual relationship between the parties" and that the unsigned documents of February 12th and the agreements dated February 28, 1969 set forth all the material terms of the contract. . . .

Finally, appellant contends that even if the statute of frauds is satisfied as to the eleven stores where the previously existing leases were renewed, there is insufficient written memoranda to meet the Statute's requirements as to the new agreement regarding the Springfield store. The documents which set forth all the material terms of the agreements as required under Crabtree were the contract letters dated February 28, 1969. No such letter as to the Springfield store was ever sent to appellee. The only specific reference in the various writings to the Springfield store is in the Fortgang memo of February 12th. However, the basic terms covering the operations (except the percentage and fixed monthly rentals dealt with in the 1969 negotiations) were and had been standard in all the agreements since 1966. The Fortgang memo clearly included the Springfield store number 812. Therefore, while the statute of frauds issue is a closer question with respect to the Springfield store, we are of the view that the district court was correct in finding sufficient memoranda to include it within the Crabtree formula given the factual circumstances of the concurrent relations between the parties. See, Stulsaft v. Mercer Tube & Mfg. Co., 288 N.Y. 255, 43 N.E. 2d 31 (1942).

The judgment of the district court is therefore reversed and the case remanded for trial on the issue of contractual intent.

Questions

1. Is the law's attitude toward the writing requirement too permissive?
2. If you were the judge in this case, would you have included the Springfield store within the scope of the writing?

Although a writing is the safest and most certain method of satisfying the statute, there are other ways of doing so, most of which apply only to specific types of contracts. They should not be regarded as true alternatives, but only as possibilities when a party has failed to secure the required writing.

Admission

If a party admits, *on the court record*, either as a part of his pleadings or in his testimony, that the contract in question was entered into, he loses his right to use the statute as a defense. The purpose of requiring a writing is that the court needs to have some evidence of the contract in addition to the testimony of the plaintiff and his or her witnesses. This evidence requirement is for the protection of the defendant. If the defendant admits that there was in fact a contract, as the plaintiff has alleged, this eliminates any controversy as to the existence of the contract and any need to protect the defendant further. The only thing remaining to be considered is its terms. This exception applies to all contracts that do not otherwise satisfy the Statute of Frauds.

Part Performance

Part performance of some types of contracts will satisfy the Statute of Frauds. Remember that the statute generally applies only to *executory bilateral* contracts. The nature of the required part performance differs depending on the type of contract involved.

Concerning *contracts not to be performed within one year*, the statute is satisfied if the contract has been executed *fully* on one side. If neither side has been performed fully but *some* performance has been rendered, the contract is not enforceable, but there may be a recovery in quasi contract for what has been done if the circumstances are appropriate.

Concerning contracts for the *transfer of an interest in land*, the statute is satisfied if there has been *significant* part performance. In determining whether the part performance has been significant the courts generally look for some act done that would not likely have been done had a transfer of the interest not taken place. Generally, neither the payment of money nor possession of the property, alone or together, will be seen as "significant." Thus, when Rhom orally has transferred her house to Chee for $80,000, with Chee to pay the purchase price in installments of $600 per month, even if Rhom allows Chee to move in and Chee makes several of the monthly payments, the Statute of Frauds probably will not be satisfied. Chee's possession and payments are as consistent with rent as they are with purchase. However, if Chee pays the taxes or builds a permanent addition, paying for it out of her own pocket, these may be seen as significant. The same might be true if the amount of the payments was grossly disproportionate to (higher than) reasonable rent. Remember, however, that part performance as is true of part performance concerning the other types of contracts, only gets the plaintiff around the Statute of Frauds. It does not prove the contract. That burden remains unaltered.

Concerning contracts for the *sale of goods*, part performance satisfies the statute to the extent that there has been either partial delivery and acceptance, or there has been partial payment. In these situations, the contract will be enforceable up to the amount delivered or the amount paid. Thus, assume Huber and Lark enter into an oral contract under which Huber agrees to sell Lark 400 bushels of corn for $4.00 per bushel. If Huber delivers and Lark accepts 100 of the bushels, or Lark pays Huber $400, the contract is provable up to 100 bushels or $400, but not as to the remainder of the contract.

Part performance of contracts for the sale of *investment securities* (UCC Article 8) will satisfy the statute to the same extent as for the sale of goods.

Written Confirmation

Section 2-201(2) of the UCC provides a special rule concerning transactions *between merchants* involving *goods*. If one merchant sends to the other a written confirmation that is a sufficient memorandum to bind the sender under the statute, it also will bind the merchant who receives it, just as if she too had signed it, unless she sends an objection to its contents within ten days after receiving it. It is important for a merchant to watch her mailbox. If she receives a written confirmation of a contract she did not enter into, it is important that she object to it within ten days after receipt. Failure to do so may invite a lawsuit.

Special Manufacture

Section 2-201(3)(a) of the Uniform Commercial Code provides that the requirements of the statute may be satisfied if a manufacturer has produced goods that are not salable in the ordinary course of business and are of such a nature as to indicate that they were manufactured for a particular buyer. For example, Felix Fitzwilly is sued by Acme Glass Mfg. Co. for failing to follow through on an order for 100 beer glasses with his name etched in the side of each. The fact that

Acme has manufactured the glasses is sufficient to satisfy the Statue of Frauds so Acme can enter evidence concerning the alleged contract. The special glasses make the court comfortable enough to hear more evidence from the parties, just as a sufficient writing would have.

The Main Purpose Doctrine (Leading Object Rule)

This final exception concerns the making of a collateral promise for a selfish motive. When this occurs, the statute is satisfied for any collateral promise. One of the reasons collateral promises are within the Statute of Frauds is that they are unusual transactions. Why would one person promise to pay the debt of another? However, if the court can see that *if* the promise was made, it wasn't made out of "the milk of human kindness," but for personal gain of the promisor, the evidence will be heard. For example, Yard, a real estate broker, is negotiating the sale of Burns's home to Allen when he learns that Street has a lien on the property for $9000 of work and materials. Afraid that if the deal is delayed any longer he will lose the opportunity to earn a commission, Yard asks Street to release the lien, promising to pay the $9000 if Burns does not. Because of the Main Purpose Doctrine, Allen, if necessary, could enforce Yard's collateral promise even in the absence of a writing.

THE PAROL EVIDENCE RULE

The Parol Evidence Rule relates to the Statute of Frauds only in that they both deal with writings. Otherwise, they are two completely different concepts. The Statute of Frauds listed certain types of contracts that are required to be in writing to be enforceable; the Parol Evidence Rule comes into play any time *any* contract has been reduced to writing. It makes no difference whether the contract was written because the Statute of Frauds required it, or just because the parties wanted it that way. The rule applies to *all* written contracts.

The **Parol Evidence Rule** is an exclusionary

rule of evidence. Simply stated, it provides that if the parties' agreement has been reduced to writing and signed by both, the writing will be taken as the best evidence of that contract. No parol evidence will be allowed from outside the "four corners of the writing" that in any way would add to, delete from, modify, or alter the writing in any respect. The integrity of the writing is to be protected against all such assaults. Evidence is *parol* if it is not contained in or referred to within the four corners of the contract, regardless of whether it is written or oral (although most commonly it is oral).

Suppose April agrees to sell her car to Biff for $450 and, as part of the agreement, she promises to replace the clutch before delivery. April and Biff reduce their agreement to writing. The writing contains all material terms except that it does not mention the clutch. When Biff notices the omission, April says, "Don't worry about it. You know I'll take care of it." In reliance, Biff signs the writing. When the car is delivered, the clutch has not been replaced. In a suit for rescission or damages, Biff would not be allowed to testify concerning April's oral promise. The integrity of the writing would be protected.

Admissible Parol

Although parol evidence generally is not admissible to change the terms as they appear in the writing, it is admissible to prove circumstances under which the contract was entered into, such as to prove the contract is voidable because of misrepresentation, fraud, duress, undue influence, or lack of capacity of one of the parties. Parol evidence also is admissible to show that the terms of the contract are illegal. All of these may be allowed even if contrary to a declaration in the writing. Parol evidence may be admitted to fill in obvious gaps in the terms of the writing. This would include the omission of a term, such as price, that the court knows must have been agreed on in any contract of the type in question—a material term.

Parol evidence is admissible to clear up ambiguities in the writing, words or phrases that are susceptible to two or more interpretations. In the previous example concerning the promise to put in the new clutch, if Biff simply had handwritten on the agreement the word *clutch* the court would have allowed evidence to show what was meant by "clutch" and Biff would have been allowed to testify concerning April's promise.

Finally, parol evidence generally is admissible to show that a written contract was entered into on an oral condition precedent. A written agreement to purchase land may be conditioned orally on the availability of reasonable financing, or a stock subscription contract on the sale of a minimum number of shares to other investors. This type of condition precedent is different from just another term of a contract. It is something that must occur before the written agreement ever becomes contractual (binding). The distinction between "just another term" and "a condition precedent" sometimes is difficult to make. The rule has been criticized as illogical and, as illustrated by the following case, it is not accepted in all jurisdictions.

DECK HOUSE, INC. v. SCARBOROUGH, SHEFFIELD & GASTON, INC.
139 Ga.App. 173, 228 S.E.2d 142 (1976)

This was an action by Scarborough, Sheffield & Gaston, Inc. (Plaintiff/Appellee) against Deck House, Inc. (Defendant/Appellant) to recover money paid to Defendant under a contract for building materials. It was Plaintiff's contention that the written contract was formed on an oral condition precedent that did not occur, and that it therefore was entitled to the return of sums paid in part performance of the failed contract.

The trial court denied Defendant's motion for summary judgment on the complaint and granted Defendant leave to file appeal challenging that denial. Reversed with direction.

MARSHALL, Judge.

The "package contract" signed by plaintiff's vice-president as purchaser called for the plaintiff to purchase a "basic package" of building materials. . . . Plaintiff submitted with the order a check for $4,821 as what the contract specified was a "non-returnable deposit." There is no provision in the contract to the effect that the contract was contingent upon [an oral condition precedent]. . . . The contract does contain a clause which provides: "ORAL MODIFICATIONS: The terms and conditions within this contract constitute the entire contract and no other terms or conditions, verbal or written, which are not contained herein, shall be applicable to this contract." Plaintiff's vice-president states that he informed Deck House that he would not order any building materials from Deck House unless real property was purchased so that it would own land upon which to erect the townhouse. Plaintiff seeks by such evidence to prove by parol evidence a condition precedent to the formation of a contract. While the rule in many jurisdictions would permit parol evidence to show conditions precedent to the contract, Georgia's rule is to the contrary. . . . In the absence of such contingency in the written instrument and of allegations of fraud, accident or mistake in plaintiff's complaint, the contract is not invalid or unenforceable for that reason.

The trial court erred in denying the motion for summary judgment.

[NOTE: This case also is discussed in Chapter 15 concerning a different point of law.]

Questions

1. Would this court have entertained evidence of the oral agreement if the written agreement had not contained the integration clause ("ORAL MODIFICATIONS . . .")?

2. Should the courts ever accept evidence of oral conditions precedent to a written agreement? Would the failure to do so help perpetrate fraud?

Subsequent Modifications

The parties to a written agreement may later modify it. Generally, if the modification does not require a return of contractual subject matter covered by the Statute of Frauds, the modification may be oral. These oral modifications are not covered by the Parol Evidence Rule because they are *subsequent* to the writing. The Parol Evidence Rule covers only matters arising between the beginning of negotiations and the moment of the writing. The law does not presume that subsequent agreements were incorporated into the writing for the obvious reason that they occurred after the writing. Of course, whether these subsequent agreements can be enforced is a matter of substantive contract law—they must stand, independently, as enforceable agreements.

SUMMARY

Contracts may be partially or wholly unenforceable for a number of reasons. They may be illegal because they require, for full and complete performance, some act or omission in violation of law (such as the commission of a crime, a tort, or a breach of contract), or because they are in violation of public policy. When that is the case, courts generally will refuse to enforce the contract and even will refuse to order that the parties be returned to the positions they were in prior to beginning performance. The courts simply maintain a hand-off posture.

When a contract is partly appropriate for enforcement and partly not, if the inappropriate part can be severed, leaving the elements of a valid contractual obligation, the remaining part may be enforced. Section 2-209 of the UCC specifically empowers the court, when a contract is so one-sided as to be unconscionable and thus contrary to public policy, to refuse to enforce its terms or to reform it as the court deems necessary to avoid any unconscionable results. This is, in effect, a grant of equity powers to courts of law when dealing with contracts for the sale of goods. Courts also may permit some recovery to a party to an illegal contract if it finds that he or she is not as guilty as the other party in attempting to create or to continue the illegality.

Contracts, and parts of contracts, also may be unenforceable when they are entered into without meeting certain required formalities, such as being in writing. Whether a particular contract must be in writing is governed by statute in each state—a Statute of Frauds. The most typical contracts covered by such statutes are collateral contracts, contracts that cannot be performed within one year, those involving the transfer of an interest in real estate, and those involving the sale of goods of a price of $500 or more. Beyond these, the statutes differ from state to state.

Also of importance is the Parol Evidence Rule, which is an exclusionary rule of evidence. It is grounded on the assumption that when two parties have negotiated a contract and have reduced the fruits of their labors to writing, the writing should be the best evidence of what the parties had agreed to up to the moment it is signed. Therefore, with very few exceptions, the courts will not hear any evidence of matters not set down, or at least referred to, in the writing that in any way would add to, subtract from, alter, or modify the provisions of the writing. The most important exceptions are when the evidence is offered (1) to explain the circumstances surrounding the agreement, (2) to show that the agreement should not be enforced because its terms are illegal, (3) to fill in obvious gaps in the terms or to aid in the interpretation of ambiguous language, or (4) to show that the parties did not intend that the agreement be binding until a condition precedent was fulfilled. Thus the integrity of such writings is protected.

KEY TERMS AND CONCEPTS

unenforceable

public policy

restraint of trade

covenant not to compete

bribery

breach of trust

fiduciary

usury

wagering

Sunday closing statutes

revenue-raising statute

pari delicto

unconscionable

Statute of Frauds

collateral promise

prenuptial (antenuptial) contract

land

real estate

goods

chose in action

writing

part performance

Main Purpose Doctrine

Parol Evidence Rule

PROBLEMS

1. After dating for a substantial time, Lee and Michelle decided to be POSSLQs (Persons of Opposite Sex Sharing Living Quarters). They set up housekeeping and, although they never were married, they lived together as if they were husband and wife for four years. During that time, Lee earned the living and Michelle took care of the home. Upon parting company, Michelle sued for *palimony*. She contended that at the time they agreed to live together, they also orally agreed that in case they terminated their relationship she would receive certain property. Lee, in part, defended on the ground that such a contract would not be enforceable since it involved illegal sexual relations and enforcement therefore would be contrary to public policy. Is Lee correct?

2. Baker rented a golf cart from the city of Seattle while playing golf on a course owned and operated by the city. While operating the cart, a wheel came off and Baker was injured. The city refused to pay for his injuries, pointing out a clause in the middle of the contract disclaiming liability for injuries caused by mechanical failures. Baker filed suit contending the disclaimer should not be enforced. Is Baker correct?

3. Adams, a beer distributor, sold beer to Baker, a tavern owner. The transaction was wholesale and on credit, in violation of state law, which provided a fine of $500 and/or one year in prison for the offense. When Baker refused to pay for the beer, Adams filed suit. Baker defended on

the ground that the contract was illegal. Adams contended the statute was only for the purpose of imposing a tax and its violation would not render the contract unenforceable. Is Adams entitled to recover the purchase price?

4. Carson and Drew jointly purchased an Irish Sweepstakes ticket in Carson's name, agreeing to share the proceeds equally if the ticket was a winner. It was, but Carson refused to give Drew the agreed-upon share. When Drew sued, Carson defended on the ground the agreement was unenforceable since gambling on the Irish Sweepstakes was prohibited by state statute. Is Drew entitled to share in the winnings according to the agreement?

5. Elliot leased certain land to Fitzgerald. The parties also orally agreed that any payments on the lease would be credited toward the purchase of the property for a stated price. At the time of the agreement, Fitzgerald gave earnest money of $1000. She then took possession of the property and made substantial improvements, paying for them out of her own pocket. Thereafter, Elliot denied the existence of the agreement to sell the land. When Fitzgerald sued, Elliot objected to evidence of the oral agreement on Statute of Frauds grounds. Is Elliot correct?

6. Phillips engaged Quisling, a construction contractor, to build a house for him. Quisling subcontracted the masonry work to Richards, a masonry contractor. Just before work was to begin, Richards learned that Quisling had a reputation for not paying and for giving bad checks. He threatened to pull off the job, and Phillips orally promised that if he would go ahead and do the work, he (Phillips) would pay for the work if Quisling did not pay. When sued on his promise, Phillips invoked the Statute of Frauds defense. Is Richards entitled to a judgment against Phillips?

7. On July 6, Co-op Dairy agreed to employ Deana for "a minimum period of one year." The job required her to move to a town 120 miles away. Deana finished up some business, packed her possessions, and found a place to live. She reported to work on July 13. After working for Co-op for nine weeks, Deana was discharged. When she sued Co-op for breach of contract, Co-op defended on the grounds that the alleged contract was one that could not be performed within one year and, therefore, was in violation of the Statute of Frauds. Is Co-op correct?

8.   On December 5, 1965, Short orally agreed to work for Trimmer during the full year of 1966. It was agreed that he would receive a specified salary plus a stated share of the profits at the end of the year. Short completed the year, and although Trimmer paid the salary, he refused to pay a share of the profits. When sued, Trimmer defended on the grounds that the contract violated the Statute of Frauds because it could not be performed within one year. Should Short be allowed to enter evidence of the agreement?

9.   Orvis agreed to purchase a certain building from Perry. Orvis contends that during negotiations, she had stated that the building was to be used for the storage of crates of hardware and, therefore, the floors would have to be capable of bearing very heavy loads, and that Perry stated that the floors "would suit her needs." After Orvis took up occupancy and began stacking the crates in the building, the floor collapsed. When sued for rescission of the contract and sale, Perry contended that evidence of the statement guaranteeing the floor could not be entered into evidence because of the Parol Evidence Rule. The parties' agreement was in writing, and appeared complete on its face. It made no mention of the guarantee, and also contained an integration clause declaring that the writing contained the entire agreement of the parties. Should the court allow Orvis to testify as to the existence of the oral guarantee?

10.   Dallas and Rebecca Masterson sold their ranch to Medora and Lu Sine (Medora was Dallas's sister). The ranch had belonged to Dallas and Medora's parents, and both had grown up there. Dallas had purchased the property from the estate when his parents died. After the sale, Medora and Lu were declared bankrupt and the ranch was taken by the trustee. Dallas and Rebecca petitioned the court to allow them to exercise an oral option to repurchase, given because the parties intended that the ranch should stay in the family. The trustee objected to the evidence on the ground of the Parol Evidence Rule. Should the trustee succeed?

Chapter | 11

Third-Party Contracts

INTRODUCTION

Throughout the preceding discussion of the law of contracts, the focus has been on the rights and duties of the two parties directly involved. First we viewed them in terms of being the "offeror" and "offeree," then in terms of being the "promisor" and "promisee." Understandably, either "party" could have consisted of more than one person. That is, a promisor might make a single promise to more than one person—for example, to two or more persons jointly or to "the first three persons who apply"—or two or more persons might make a joint promise. In all cases, however, we have focused on the rights and duties of parties in a direct relationship. This chapter covers situations involving third parties who are indirectly related to a transaction but still may have rights under the contract, either by assignment or because it was the intent of the direct parties to the agreement to benefit the third party.

ASSIGNMENT

At early common law, all contractual relations were considered personal; therefore no contract was assignable. That is, the rights under a contract could not be transferred by either of the parties to

241

a third party. With the passage of time, the courts began to focus more on the property view of contracts and less on personal considerations. That is, courts placed more emphasis on the idea that a contract right was a piece of property (although intangible) and should be treated in the same fashion as other property such as a house or a book.

Courts of law then began enforcing the rights of *assignees* under the legal fiction that the assignee was an agent (attorney in fact) for the assignor and, as such, could collect on the obligation on behalf of the assignor. In courts of equity, an assignee for value was recognized as the actual owner of the right assigned.

Finally, courts of law came to recognize the assignee's "equity," holding the assignee to be the owner of the claim. This process of evolution was completed by the enactment of procedural statutes allowing an assignee to sue in his or her own name.

Today, the rights of assignees are fully recognized. Although not all contracts are assignable, the concept of assignment is supported on the ground that property rights should be freely transferable unless there is some overriding policy reason to the contrary.

Every contract is composed of a set of rights and corresponding duties. The transfer of some portion of these rights and their corresponding duties is called an **assignment**. To be more accurate, however, the transfer of the *rights* is called *assignment* and the transfer of the corresponding *duties* is called **delegation**. Therefore, care must be taken to consider the context when the term *assignment* is used.

What Constitutes an Assignment

Any manifestation by an owner of a contract right (meaning a debt is owed to him) of his intent to make a present transfer of that right to another person will constitute an assignment. This manifestation usually is made to the assignee, but may be made to a third party. Generally, no particular words or formalities are required. An oral assignment is just as valid as a written assignment except in states having a Statute of Frauds provision to the contrary. Also, an assignment may be made for consideration or entirely as a gift. No consideration is required because an assignment is not a contract (a promise to do something in the future). It is a present transfer of a property right.

Once a right is assigned, the assignor's claim against the debtor is extinguished and it becomes vested in the assignee. In order to perfect this claim (to protect herself against any subsequent devaluation of the claim by the conduct of others), the assignee must give notice to the debtor. If the debtor has no notice of the assignment and pays the debt to the assignor, the claim of the assignee is extinguished and her rights are against the assignor only. In the event that an assignor makes successive assignments of the same right to two or more assignees, notice also may be necessary for one assignee to perfect his or her right as against the other assignees. Although the majority of states still hold that in such cases the first assignee in time has the right, a significant minority takes the position that the first to give notice to the debtor has the better right. Consider the following case.

BOULEVARD NATIONAL BANK OF MIAMI v. AIR METALS INDUSTRIES INC.
176 So.2d 94 (Fla., 1965)

This was an action by Boulevard National Bank of Miami (Petitioner/Appellant) against Air Metals Industries, Inc. and others (Respondents/Appellees) to collect the amount due on an account receivable of which Petitioner was an assignee.

Respondent assigned the accounts receivable in question to American Fire and Casualty Ins. Co. on January 3, 1962. On November 26, 1962, Respondents executed an assignment of the same accounts receivable to Petitioner to secure a loan. In June 1963, Respondent defaulted on its contracts with American Fire and Casualty, and the latter gave formal notice of the assignment to the debtor, Tompkins-Beckwith, who agreed to pay the account to American. Thereafter, Petitioner also served notice on Tompkins-Beckwith, who refused to recognize Petitioner's claim.

The trial court found that American Fire and Casualty had a claim better than that of Petitioner, and granted summary judgment. Its decision was affirmed on appeal to the District Court of Appeal. Petitioner appealed the grant of summary judgment (wishing to argue the order in which the assignments became effective) by certiorari to the Supreme Court of Florida. The summary judgment in favor of American Fire and Casualty was affirmed.

WILLIS, Circuit Judge.

The American rule for which petitioner contends is based upon the reasoning that an account or other chose in action may be assigned at will by the owner; and that when such assignment is made the property rights become vested in the assignee so that the assignor no longer has any interest in the account or chose which he may subsequently assign to another. . . .

The English rule [the original case was an English case] has its origin in pronouncements made in Dearle v. Hall (1843). . . . Subsequent cases in England considered the question and it seems to have become the settled rule in England. . . . [Justice Butler, in his opinion in Salem Trust Co. v. Manufacturer's Finance Co., held] that in the case of a chose in action an assignee must do everything toward having possession which the subject admits and must do that which is tantamount to obtaining possession by placing every person who has an equitable or legal interest in the matter under an obligation to treat it as the assignee's property. It was stated:

> For this purpose you must give notice to the legal holder of the fund; in the case of a debt, for instance, notice is tantamount to possession. If you omit . . . to give that notice you are guilty of the same degree and species of neglect as he who leaves a personal chattel, to which he has acquired a title, in the actual possession, and, under the absolute control, of another person. . . .

It seems to be generally agreed that notice to a debtor of an assignment is necessary to impose on the debtor the duty of payment to the assignee, and that if before receiving such notice he pays the debt to the assignor, or to a subsequent assignee, he will be discharged from the debt. . . . To regard the debtor as a total non-participant in the assignment by the creditor of his interests to another is to deny the obvious. . . .

We do not hold that notice to the debtor is the only method of effecting a delivery of possession of the account so as to put subsequent interests on notice of a prior assignment. The English rule itself does not apply to those who have notice of an earlier assignment. The American rule is not in harmony with the concepts expressed. It seems to be based largely upon the doctrine of caveat emptor which has a proper field of operation, but has many exceptions based on equitable considerations. It also seems to regard the commercial transfers of accounts as being the exclusive concern of the owner and assignee and that the assignee has no responsibility for the acts of the assignor with whom he leaves all of the indicia of ownership of the account. This view does not find support in the statute or decisional law of this State. . . .

We thus find that the so-called English rule which the trial and appellate court approved and applied is harmonious with our jurisprudence, whereas the so-called American rule is not.

Questions

1.   Isn't the English rule inconsistent with general rules governing personal property, in that once an owner has made a valid transfer he or she has nothing further to give to the second transferee?

2.   How does the notice requirement enhance public policy, since notice to the debtor would not, in itself, provide notice to a subsequent, good-faith assignee?

Finally, the rights under a contract may be assigned without delegating the duties, or the duties may be delegated without assigning the rights. In fact, an assignment may be partial, transferring only some of the rights, and the same is true of a delegation. However, an assignment of "the contract" is presumed to be a transfer of all rights and a delegation of all duties under the agreement unless the circumstances or the nature of the rights or the duties dictate to the contrary.

Rights Acquired by the Assignee

Generally, an assignee can have no better rights than the assignor had at the time of the transfer. Therefore, if Howard defrauds Lee into purchasing his worthless car for $500 and assigns his right to the $500 to Grimm, upon discovery of the fraud Lee can refuse to pay Grimm just as she could have refused to pay Howard if he had tried to collect.

Any defenses, set-offs, or counterclaims good against the assignor before the debtor receives notice of the assignment also are good against the assignee. In the example above, suppose the sale of the car to Lee was proper and without fraud, but thereafter, following the assignment but prior

to notice, Howard ran into Lee's car and became indebted to her for $200 in damages. Grimm then would be entitled to collect only $300 from Lee. If notice of the assignment had been given prior to the accident, the entire $500 would have been due to Grimm.

Assignability of Rights

Whether a right is assignable depends on whether an assignment by the promisee would alter the promisor's obligation materially. If it would, the right is not assignable. The most common example of a right that *is* assignable is one to collect money owed. It should make no difference to the promisor whether he or she pays the money to the original promisee or to the assignee. The same is true of the promise to transfer most other types of property, whether the obligation is owed or is to become due in the future, whether it arises out of a bilateral contract or a unilateral contract, and whether the obligation is conditional or unconditional. Therefore, the right to receive an agreed-upon price for constructing a building may be assigned, although the right of the assignee to collect will depend on the degree to which the assignor performs his or her obligation.

The assignment of rights

When debtor is notified by assignee

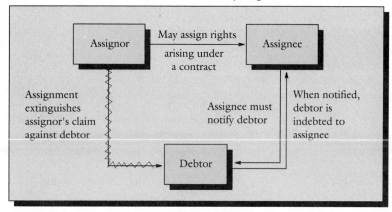

When debtor is not notified by assignee

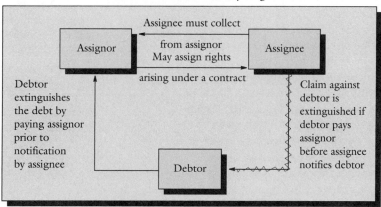

The delegation of duties

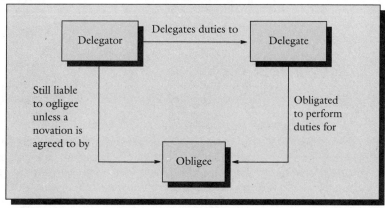

Rights are not assignable if they are of a personal nature. For example, the right to coverage under a fire insurance policy cannot be assigned. However, if a fire occurred and the insurance company became indebted to the insured for the amount of the damages, the right to collect for the damages could be assigned. The right to share a room with a roommate may not be assignable, although the right to the premises, when no such personal relationship is involved, usually would be. The right to receive goods based on the purchaser's requirements would not be assignable because the needs of the assignee presumably are not the same as those of the assignor.

Wage Assignments

The assignability of wages to be earned in the future has long been debated. At early Common Law, courts of law regarded these assignments as void because the assignor had not yet acquired any right. Courts of equity did recognize such assignments. The law gradually changed, first recognizing assignments of future wages under a contract of employment, but not when the assignor was working "at will." Today, such assignments generally are recognized so long as the assignor is regularly employed. For reasons of public policy, however, many states have limited the percentage of future wages that may be assigned (for example, 60 percent if single, 40 percent if married).

Prohibitions Against Assignment

Since contract rights are regarded as property, it generally is felt that they should be transferable (assignable) in the same way as is other property unless an assignment would have an unreasonably negative impact on the promisor. Public policy in our legal system favors the free transferability of property. The question, then, arises as to the extent to which courts should enforce a contract clause that seeks to prohibit assignment.

When a clause in a contract clearly prohibits the assignment of rights under the agreement, the provision generally will be enforced. However, a clause that simply prohibits the assignment of "the contract'" usually is interpreted as affecting only the delegation of duties, not the assignment of rights. If the clause requires permission of the promisor before an assignment of rights can be effective, courts generally require that any withholding of permission be in good faith, for some reasonable cause. Also, statutes may affect the enforceability of such provisions, as does UCC Section 2-210(2), discussed at the end of this section.

If a clause prohibiting assignment is desirable, care must be taken that its language accurately expresses the intentions of the parties. Otherwise, unanticipated interpretation may produce an unintended result. Consider the following case.

MUNCHAK CORPORATION v. CUNNINGHAM
457 F.2d 721 (4th Cir. 1972)

This was an action by Munchak Corporation and RDG Corporation, a joint venture dba The Carolina Cougars (Plaintiffs/Appellants) against William John Cunningham (Defendant/Appellee) to enjoin Defendant from performing services as a player for any other basketball club.

Defendant had entered into a contract to play basketball for the Carolina Cougars at a time the team was owned by Southern Sports Corporation. His contract prohibited assignment to "another club" without his consent. Thereafter, Southern Sports sold the Carolina Cougars to Plaintiffs, who thereby became assignees of Defendant's contract. Defendant then signed a contract with the Philadelphia 76ers, contending the contract with the Carolina Cougars and its assignment to Plaintiffs were void.

The trial court found for Defendant and Plaintiffs appealed. Reversed and remanded.

WINTER, Circuit Judge.

We recognize that under North Carolina law the right to performance of a personal service contract requiring special skills and based upon the personal relationship between the parties cannot be assigned without the consent of the party rendering those services. . . . [But] some such contracts may be assigned when the character of the performance and the obligation will not be changed. To us it is inconceivable that the rendition of services to a professional basketball club could be affected by the personalities of successive corporate owners. . . . Indeed, Cunningham had met only Gardner of Southern Sports Club, and had not met, nor did he know, the other stockholders. If Gardner had sold all or part of his stock to another person, Cunningham could not seriously contend that his consent would be required.

The policy against assignability of certain personal service contracts is to prohibit an assignment of a contract in which the obligor undertakes to serve only the original obligee. . . . This contract is not of that type, since Cunningham was not obligated to perform differently for plaintiffs than he was obligated to perform for Southern Sports Club. We, therefore, see no reason to hold that the contract was not assignable under the facts here.

Questions

1. Doesn't this decision amount to legalizing a form of slavery?
2. Is there room for the court to interpret the intent of the parties when the contract clearly prohibited assignment without the defendant's permission?

Generally, clauses concerning assignment do not prohibit assignment absolutely, but only establish some procedures that must be followed before an assignment can be effective. In these cases, courts usually will enforce strict compliance with the procedures as long as they are reasonable. An assignee always should insist on following the agreed-upon procedures; otherwise, a perfectly proper assignment may fail. Consider the following case.

NATIONAL LUMBER COMPANY v. GOODMAN
371 Mich. 54, 123 N.W.2d 147 (1963)

This was an action by National Lumber Company (Plaintiff/Appellant) against Albert J. Goodman and Jerome Goodman, Trustee in Bankruptcy of Elliott-Jared Investment Company, and others (Defendants/Appellees) to enjoin land-contract foreclosure proceedings.

Under a land contract dated January 12, 1956, Defendant Albert J. Goodman agreed to sell certain lots to Elliott-Jared Investment Company. The contract included the following clause:

> No assignment or conveyance by the purchaser shall create any liability whatsoever against the seller until a duplicate thereof, duly witnessed and acknowledged, together with the residence address of such assignee, shall be delivered to and accepted by the seller, and receipt thereof indorsed thereon.

Thereafter, Defendant executed to Plaintiff a note and mortgage on some of the lots to secure certain indebtedness. This was done without the permission of the seller (Albert J. Goodman). Upon default by the buyer, Plaintiff sought to pay the indebtedness on the lots that were the subject of the mortgage held by Plaintiff. Defendant Goodman refused to accept the tender and instituted foreclosure proceedings on the entire tract. Plaintiff contended that it was substituted for Elliott-Jared Investment Company and, as such, was entitled to require a transfer of the lots covered by its mortgage upon payment of the indebtedness.

The trial court found for Defendants and Plaintiff appealed. Affirmed.

KAVANAGH, Justice.

A similar provision to the one present in this land contract restricting alienation has been held by this Court not to be invalid because of being in restraint of alienation, since it does not bar assignment of the contract but merely is an agreement between the contracting parties as to the method in which an assignment or conveyance must be made to affect the rights of the vendor. . . .

Equally well settled is the rule that the term "conveyance" embraces a mortgage of lands. . . .

It is not disputed that at the time the negotiations took place between plaintiffs and defendant Goodman, the vendee, Elliott-Jared Investment Company, had the right to a release of any or all of the remaining lots upon payment of the same amounts offered by the plaintiffs. Defendant Goodman testified he had a legal obligation to convey upon payment by Elliott-Jared Investment Company of such sums.

Plaintiff contended that as mortgagees of a vendee's interest under a land contract, they have the right to step into the shoes of their mortgagor and exercise the right to obtain a release of the 8 lots in order to protect their interest. Accepting, *arguendo*, this basic contention, plaintiffs face a second hurdle, namely, whether their offer of payment is a sufficient basis for granting equitable relief, even though they breached the contract provisions requiring presentation and indorsement of the conveyance. Authority exists for such a rule . . . where the assignee of the vendee has acquired the full interest of the vendee and tenders full payment of the contract price.

The record in the instant case discloses there were several extensions and modifications of the contract, which were obviously concessions to the vendee to enable it to perform. This, together with the provisions relating to presentation and indorsement of an assignment or conveyance indicates the contract was of a personal nature.

The law recognizes the right of a person to choose those with whom he would contract. It would appear for reasons best known to himself, perhaps because of the promotional ability of Elliott Schubiner, that defendant Goodman was willing to grant personal extensions and release lots to him, fully confident that he would be able to perform the remainder of the contract.

We conclude that this personal element, which in no way affected the assignability of the contract, prevented any equities arising that would interfere with the vendor's right to insist upon strict compliance with the contract terms.

Questions

1. Would the court have decided this case differently if the so-called personal element had not existed in the vendor-vendee contract?

2. What harm would result from requiring strict compliance with the clause in question in any case, personal or not?

Delegation of Duties

Just as the rights under a contract may be assigned, the duties thereunder may be delegated, although not quite so freely. Duties that (1) are personal in nature, or (2) require the exercise of a particular skill or judgment for their performance or the promisee is relying on the character of the promisor, or (3) are of such a nature that delegation otherwise would alter materially the benefits to flow to the promisee are not delegable. Therefore, the duty of a person to be a live-in companion for another, and the duty of an agent to collect funds due his or her principal, are among duties that are nondelegable.

In terms of agency law, the duties of "servants" and "controlled agents" for which the employer or principal may be held liable in respondent superior (liable for the servant's or controlled agent's torts) are not delegable, but the duties of independent contractors and independent (professional) agents frequently are, because their torts would not create liability on their employers or principals. Suppose Arnold agrees with Ben to teach Ben to play the piano in his (Arnold's) own particular jazz style, and to provide Ben with a piano at Ben's home for the purpose of practicing between lessons. Although the duty to teach probably is not delegable, the duty to provide the piano probably is. Ben's duty to pay for the lessons quite clearly is delegable.

Whether a duty involves a relationship so personal that it should not be delegable is a question for the courts. As the following case illustrates, the fact that one of the parties to a contract has chosen the other because of certain personal characteristics does not always mean the latter's duties are nondelegable.

MACKE COMPANY v. PIZZA OF GAITHERSBURG, INC. et al.
259 Md. 479, 270 A.2d 645 (1970)

This was an action by the Macke Company (Plaintiff/Appellant) against Pizza of Gaithersburg, Inc. and others (Defendants/Appellees) for breach of contract.

Defendants entered into contracts with Virginia Coffee Service, Inc. for the placement of cold-drink vending machines in six of their locations. The contracts were all for one year, automatically renewable in the absence of a 30-day notice.

Plaintiff purchased Virginia's assets, becoming assignee of the contracts. Defendant sought to terminate early because of the assignments.

The trial court found for Defendants on the ground that in entering into the contracts they relied on the skill, judgment, and reputation of Virginia, thus making Virginia's duties under them nondelegable. Plaintiff appealed. Reversed as to liability and remanded for a new trial on the issue of damages.

SINGLEY, Judge.

In the absence of a contrary provision—and there was none here—rights and duties under an executory bilateral contract may be assigned and delegated, subject to the exception that duties under a contract to provide personal services may never be delegated, nor rights be assigned under a contract where *delectus personae* was an ingredient of the bargain. . . . Crane Ice Cream Co. v. Terminal Freezing & Heating Co. . . . held that the right of an individual to purchase ice under a contract which by its terms reflected a knowledge of the individual's needs and reliance on his credit and responsibility could not be assigned to the corporation which purchased the business. In Eastern Advertising Co. v. McGraw & Co. . . . our predecessors held that an advertising agency could not delegate its duties under a contract which had been entered into by an advertiser who had relied on the agency's skill, judgment and taste.

The six machines were placed on the appellees' premises under a printed "Agreement-Contract" which identified the "customer," gave its place of business, described the vending machine, and then provided [for installation of the machines, their location, that the customer would supply electricity and protect the equipment, that the company would be liable for licenses and taxes, the term of the contract, and the fee to be paid to the company]. . . .

We cannot regard the agreements as contracts for personal services. They were either a license or concession granted Virginia by the appellees, or a lease of a portion of the appellees' premises, with Virginia agreeing to pay a percentage of gross sales as a license or concession fee or as rent . . . and were assignable by Virginia unless they imposed on Virginia duties of a personal or unique character which could not be delegated. . . .

The appellees earnestly argue that they had dealt with Macke before and had chosen Virginia because they preferred the way it conducted its business. Specifically, they say that service was more personalized, since the president of Virginia kept the machines in working order, that commissions were paid in cash, and that Virginia permitted them to keep keys to the machines so that minor adjustments could be made when needed. Even if we assume all this to be true, the agreements with Virginia were silent as to the details of the working arrangements and contained only a provision requiring Virginia to "install . . . the above listed equipment . . . maintain the equipment in good operating order and stocked with merchandise." We think the Supreme Court of California put the problem of personal service in proper focus a century ago when it upheld the assignment of a contract to grade a San Francisco street:

> All painters do not paint portraits like Sir Joshua Reynolds, nor landscape like Claude Lorraine, nor do all writers write dramas like Shakespeare or fiction like Dickens. Rare

genius and extraordinary skill are not transferable, and contracts for their employment are therefore personal, and cannot be assigned. But rare genius and extraordinary skill are not indispensable to the workmanlike digging down of a sand hill or the filling up of a depression to a given level, or the construction of brick sewers with manholes and covers, and contracts for such work are not personal, and may be assigned.

. . . Moreover, the difference between the service the Pizza Shops happened to be getting from Virginia and what they expected to get from Macke did not mount up to such a material change in the performance of obligations under the agreements as would justify the appellees' refusal to recognize the assignment. . . .

Questions

1. Is it inconsistent with the principles of contract law that a party may be forced into a contractual relationship with another, even over his or her objection?
2. Why doesn't the service to be rendered by Virginia (now Macke) in keeping the machines in proper operating order qualify this contract as personal?

Delegation differs from assignment in another very important respect. When a right is assigned, the claim of the assignor against the promisor is extinguished entirely. However, when a duty is delegated, the obligation of the delegating party is not extinguished. He or she continues to be fully liable if the delegate fails to perform, or performs only partially or improperly. This liability can be extinguished only by the agreement of the party to whom the duty is owed.

Suppose, for example, Abel promises to mow Bess's lawn for $10 and wishes to delegate his duty of performance to Sue. Abel will remain liable unless Bess agrees to look only to Sue for performance. If this is done, the resulting agreement is called a **novation**. Novations occur with some frequency in real estate transactions. If Abel purchases property and mortgages it to Bess to pay the purchase price, then later wishes to sell it to Sue, a novation may be quite practical. Of course, Sue might pay cash, in which case she either could trust Abel to pay the mortgage from the proceeds (not a good idea) or could pay the mortgage and give Abel the remainder for his equity. When a cash transaction is not possible, Abel could transfer title to Sue and trust Sue to pay the mortgage (also not a good idea). The best resolution, when cash payment is not possible,

probably is a novation. Abel would transfer the property to Sue upon Sue's agreement to pay the mortgage and Bess's agreement to discharge Abel and look only to Sue for payment—the novation. Of course, Bess must agree to this, and when she does Sue's assumption of the obligation provides the consideration to support her agreement.

Delegate's Liability for Performance

When duties under a contract have been delegated, the delegate becomes liable to perform. This liability runs to the delegator (the person who delegated the duty) and, in many cases, also may extend to the person who was entitled to receive the performance. A delegate makes a promise, express or implied, to perform the duty properly. Therefore, he or she is liable to the delegator for any damages the delegator suffers. If, in addition, the delegate made his or her promise for the benefit of the person entitled to the performance, the delegate also will be liable to that person. Whether a promise is of the latter character is largely a matter of intent.

As a rule of thumb, if the delegate undertakes to perform only part of the delegator's duties, only the obligor may sue her for nonperformance. If, however, she undertakes to perform the delegator's entire obligation, she may be liable to both the delegator and the party entitled to performance. Suppose White promises to build an office building for Black. If White delegates to Green the duty to do the paving of the parking lot, only White can sue for nonperformance. If, instead, Green had agreed to perform the entire contract, substituting himself fully for White, then both White and Black could sue. If Green promised to do the essential portion of the contract—build the building—while the details of paving, painting, and other comparatively minor tasks were to be completed by White and/or other subcontractors, liability again probably would run to both White and Black.

Assignor's Liability to the Assignee

If an assignment is made for consideration, the assignor impliedly warrants that (1) he or she has title to the assigned claim, (2) he or she has the right to assign it (for example, he is not holding title in trust for someone else), (3) the claim is valid (for example, it has not been secured under circumstances that would render it voidable or unenforceable, and has not been discharged), (4) any documents evidencing the claim are genuine and have not been altered, and (5) the assignor will do nothing after assignment to defeat any part of the claim (for example, she will not take payment of it for herself or become indebted to the obligor in such a way as to establish a set-off or counterclaim). If the assignment is made as a gift, these warranties are not made (since there would be no consideration to support them). However, even in the case of a gratuitous assignment, conduct that would violate the fifth warranty might be actionable in tort as a trespass to the property right belonging to the assignee.

Assignments Under the UCC

If the rights assigned or the duties delegated arise under a contract for the sale of goods, UCC Section 2-210 is controlling. This section provides that, unless otherwise agreed, (1) a party can per-

form through a delegate unless the other party has a substantial interest in having the original promisor perform, and (2) all rights are assignable unless there is some substantial reason that they should not be, but rights arising as a result of a breach of the contract always can be assigned, even if the contract prohibits assignment. Subsection (3) provides that an assignment of "the contract" or "all my rights under the contract," will be construed as including, also, a delegation of the assignor's duties, unless circumstances indicate to the contrary. Also, the delegate's obligation to perform may be enforced by either the assignor or the other party to the original contract. Subsection (4) of the section provides that the other party to the original contract may treat a delegation of duties as grounds for insecurity and may demand further assurances under Section 2-609.

THIRD-PARTY BENEFICIARY CONTRACTS

Classifications

Sometimes two parties enter into a contract that will benefit a third person either directly or indirectly. These are called **third-party beneficiary contracts**. If the third person is intended to benefit, he or she is treated as any other party, and has the right to enforce the contract.

Third-party beneficiaries may fall into any of three classifications: donee, creditor, or incidental. A **donee beneficiary** is someone the parties to the contract intend to benefit for the purpose of conferring a *gift*. A **creditor beneficiary** is a person the parties intend to benefit for the purpose of *discharging an obligation* one of the parties owes to that beneficiary. The beneficiary of a life insurance policy is typically a donee beneficiary. The purpose of designating him as beneficiary is that the insured wishes to make a gift of the insurance proceeds on death. However, suppose the insured has purchased a house, paying for it with borrowed money, the repayment of which is secured by a mortgage. She purchased the life insurance policy and named the mortgage holder as benefi-

Third-party beneficiaries

Types of Beneficiaries	Definition	When Rights Take Effect	Example
Donee	Someone the parties to a contract intend to benefit for the purpose of conferring a gift.	Rights vest the moment the contract is entered into.	Life insurance policy naming your spouse as beneficiary.
Creditor	Someone the parties intend to benefit for the purpose of discharging debt.	The rights vest only when the creditor learns of the contract.	Life insurance policy naming a mortgage holder as beneficiary.
Incidental	A third person who will benefit from performance of a contract by the parties, although this benefit was not intended by the parties.	No rights are conferred to the incidental beneficiary.	Life insurance policy stipulating partial use of funds to erect a mausoleum. Builders of mausoleum benefit.

ciary for the purpose of paying off the mortgage indebtedness upon her death. In this case, the mortgage holder would be a creditor beneficiary.

An **incidental beneficiary** is a third party who will benefit from performance of a contract by the parties, although it was not the intent of the parties or the purpose of the contract to benefit him or her. For example, suppose Ann agrees to build a house for Steve. Performance of the contract may benefit the local bank because Steve must borrow money to finance the house, and it also may benefit the local building-supplies company in that building materials will be purchased there, but the intent of the parties and the purpose of the contract is to build the house, benefiting Ann and Steve, not to benefit either the bank or the building-supplies company. Thus, the bank and the building supplies company are incidental beneficiaries. Contracts of governmental units to benefit the general public result in members of the public becoming incidental beneficiaries, but the same is not true of government contracts entered into specifically for the protection of certain individuals.

Rights of Third-Party Beneficiaries

Both donee beneficiaries and creditor beneficiaries are considered parties to a contract made for their benefit. They differ, however, in when their rights become **vested** (cannot be taken away by the other two parties without the beneficiary's consent). The rights of a donee beneficiary vest at the moment the contract is entered into. The other parties have no right to modify or cancel the contract thereafter without the permission of the donee beneficiary, unless the right to do so specifically was reserved as a term of the contract. For example, if Win orders flowers from Jobst to be sent to Loos, from the moment of the contract Loos has a vested right to the flowers or to damages for nonperformance, which cannot be modified or taken away by Win and Jobst. The same would be true if Win purchased a life insurance policy from Haight Insurance Company and named Loos as (donee) beneficiary of the policy. However, in the case of life insurance, the policy generally provides that the insured retains the right to do with the policy as he or she sees fit, including the right to change the beneficiary or cancel the policy.

The rights of a creditor beneficiary vest at the moment he or she learns that the contract has been entered into for his or her benefit, and thereafter he or she has the same rights as the donee beneficiary. Until that time, the other two parties may do as they wish with the contract, including cancel it. At first thought, it may seem that the rules are backward. Why should a donee beneficiary have greater rights than a creditor beneficiary? The former received his or her rights as a gift. The reason is that if the parties are allowed to cancel the donee beneficiary contract, the donee beneficiary loses everything, but the cancellation of the creditor beneficiary contract results in no loss of expectation so long as the creditor beneficiary does not know of the contract. He or she still has the same rights against the debtor he or she had before the third-party beneficiary contract was entered into.

Incidental third-party beneficiaries have no rights under the contract. They derive any benefits only incidentally, not because it was within the enforceable intent of the parties. They cannot sue to enforce the contract or recover damages for its breach. Consider the following case.

MARTINEZ v. SOCOMA COMPANIES, INC.
11 Cal.3d 394, 521 P.2d 841 (1974)

This was a class action suit by Ignacio Martinez and others (Plaintiffs/Appellants) against Socoma Companies and others (Defendants/Appellees) to enforce certain contracts entered into between Defendants and the federal government. The trial court found for Defendants, and Plaintiffs appealed. Affirmed.

WRIGHT, Chief Justice.

Plaintiffs brought this class action on behalf of themselves and other disadvantaged unemployed persons, alleging that defendants failed to perform contracts with the United States government under which defendants agreed to provide job training and at least one year of employment to certain numbers of such persons. Plaintiffs claim that they and the other such persons are third party beneficiaries of the contracts and as such are entitled to damages for defendants' nonperformance. General demurrers to the complaint were sustained without leave apparently on the ground that plaintiffs lacked standing to sue as third party beneficiaries. Dismissals were entered as to the demurring defendants, and plaintiffs appeal.

We affirm the judgments of dismissal. As will appear, the contracts nowhere state that either the government or defendants are to be liable to persons such as plaintiffs for damages resulting from the defendants' nonperformance. The benefits to be derived from defendants' performance were clearly intended not as gifts from the government to such persons but as a means of executing the public purposes stated in the contracts and in the underlying legislation. Accordingly, plaintiffs were only incidental beneficiaries and as such have no right of recovery. . . .

A person cannot be a creditor beneficiary unless the promisor's performance of the contract will discharge some form of legal duty owed to the beneficiary by the promisee. . . . Clearly the Government (the promisee) at no time bore any legal duty toward plaintiffs to provide the benefits set forth in the contracts and plaintiffs do not claim to be creditor beneficiaries.

A person is a donee beneficiary only if the promisee's contractual intent is either to make a gift to him or to confer on him a right against the promisor. . . . If the promisee intends to make a gift, the donee beneficiary can recover if such donative intent must have been understood by the promisor from the nature of the contract and the circumstances accompanying its execution. . . . This rule does not aid plaintiffs, however, because, as will be seen, no intention to make a gift can be imputed to the government as promisee.

Unquestionably plaintiffs were among those whom the Government intended to benefit through defendants' performance of the contracts which recite that they are executed pursuant to a statute and a presidential directive calling for programs to furnish disadvantaged persons with training and employment opportunities. However, the fact that a Government program for social betterment confers benefits upon individuals who are not required to render contractual consideration in return does not necessarily imply that the benefits are intended as gifts. . . . The benefits of such programs are provided not simply as gifts to recipients but as a means of accomplishing a larger public purpose. The furtherance of the public purpose is in the nature of consideration to the Government, displacing any governmental intent to furnish the benefits as gifts. . . .

Even though a person is not the intended recipient of a gift, he may nevertheless be "a donee beneficiary if it appears from the terms of the promise in view of the accompanying circumstances that the purpose of the promisee in obtaining the promise . . . [is] to *confer upon him a right against the promisor* to some performance neither due nor supposed or asserted to be due from the promisee to the beneficiary." . . . The Government may, of course, deliberately implement a public purpose by including provisions in its contracts which expressly confer on a specified class of third persons a direct right to benefits, or damages in lieu of benefits, against the private contractor. But a government intent to confer such a direct right cannot be inferred simply from the fact that the third persons were intended to enjoy the benefits. . . .

The present contracts manifest no intent that the defendants pay damages to compensate plaintiffs or other members of the public for their nonperformance. To the contrary, the contracts' provisions for retaining the Government's control over determination of contractual disputes and for limiting defendants' financial risks indicate a governmental purpose to exclude the direct rights against defendants claimed here.

Questions

1. Why should members of the public, as incidental beneficiaries, not be permitted to sue to enforce such contracts?

2. Under what circumstances might the plaintiffs here have been entitled to sue for enforcement of the contract in question?

SUMMARY

Although most contracts involve two parties who are directly involved in their negotiation, third parties, under certain circumstances, may acquire rights in contracts negotiated by others. The third party may acquire rights by assignment of a contract already in existence, or may be made the beneficiary of a contract at the time it was entered into.

When rights in a contract are transferred to a third party, the transfer is called a *assignment*. When the duties are transferred, it is called a *delegation*. When it is said that "a contract is assigned," it usually is presumed to mean that both the rights and the duties under the contract have been transferred.

As a general rule, most rights under a contract may be assigned and most duties may be delegated. However, if the assignment or the delegation would alter materially the rights or duties of the other party to his or her disadvantage, the transfer will not be valid. Therefore, rights or duties that are personal in nature and duties that require the exercise of skill or judgment in their performance are not transferable.

When rights under a contract are assigned effectively, the claim of the assignor is extinguished and becomes vested in the assignee. The assignee has the same rights the assignor had at the time of the assignment, even though he immediately should give notice to the person who owes the obligation in order to perfect his right against payment to the assignor and, in some states, against possible assignees of the same right by the same assignor. Along with every assignment, the assignor who receives consideration impliedly warrants to the assignee that (1) she has valid title to the claim, (2) she has the right to transfer it, (3) the claim is valid, (4) any supporting documentation is genuine and unaltered, and (5) the assignor will do nothing to impair the value of the assignment. The UCC has special provisions regarding assignments of contracts for the sale of goods in Section 2-210.

When a contract is entered into between two parties but will benefit a third party, the extent of the rights of the third party will depend on whether he or she is a donee beneficiary, a creditor beneficiary, or an incidental beneficiary. A donee beneficiary is one whom the parties to the contract intend to benefit in order to give the beneficiary a gift. The rights of the donee benefi-

ciary vest at the moment the contract is entered into, and cannot be altered or cancelled without his or her consent. A creditor beneficiary is one the parties intend to benefit as a means of paying a debt owed to the beneficiary. The rights of this type of beneficiary vest only when he or she learns of the contract. Until that time, the other two parties may alter or cancel the contract without his consent. An incidental beneficiary is one who will benefit by performance of the contract, but it was not the intent of the parties nor the purpose of the contract to benefit him or her. He or she has no right to enforce the contract or to sue for its breach or cancellation.

KEY TERMS AND CONCEPTS

assignment

delegation

novation

third-party beneficiaries

donee beneficiary

creditor beneficiary

incidental beneficiary

vested rights

PROBLEMS

1. Berry purchased certain land from Wiscombe on a land contract. Thereafter Berry assigned the contract to Lockhart, who paid him $20,000, with Berry agreeing to continue making payments to Wiscombe. Lockhart did not notify Wiscombe of the assignment and, when Berry fell behind in making payments, Wiscombe notified Berry of his intent to foreclose. Berry made no further payments and the property was sold at an auction. When Lockhart learned of the sale, he brought suit to set aside the deed on the ground that his rights cannot be taken away without notice. Is Lockhart correct?

2. Charlotte borrowed money from Bigg Bank and gave Bigg Bank possession of a certificate of deposit as security. Thereafter, she assigned the certificate to Small Bank. Small Bank gave notice of the assignment to Bigg Bank. However, just prior to the notice, Charlotte defaulted on her loan with Bigg Bank. Who is entitled to the certificate?

3. Hastings Motor Truck Co. sold its business and, as part of the transaction, the buyer agreed to assume responsibility for a Small Business Administration loan. The SBA drew up an assumption of liability agreement, which the buyer signed and returned to the SBA. When the buyer defaulted on loan payments, the SBA sought to hold Hastings Motor Truck Co. liable, contending that the delegation of duty of payment did not relieve Hastings of liability when the delegate failed to perform. Is the SBA correct?

4. Nolan was the author of a popular song, "Tumbling Tumbleweeds." He assigned his rights in the song to "Fox Productions and its assigns." Fox was to promote the song and Nolan was to receive a percentage of the profits. Thereafter, Fox assigned the rights to Williamson Music, Inc. Nolan sought to set aside the assignment on the ground that the rights were too personal. Should Nolan succeed?

5. Chimney Hill Corp. was the owner of Chimney Hill, a recreational second-home development. Part of its agreement with purchasers was that all lots would be subject to an annual assessment for maintenance and upkeep. The corporation sold eleven lots to Eastern Woodworking Co. The agreement with Eastern provided that Chimney Hill Corp. would not charge the assessment on the eleven lots as long as they remained undeveloped. Later, Chimney Hill Corp. transferred its interest in the development to Chimney Hill Owners' Association, Inc. The latter then sought to collect assessments on undeveloped lots owned by Eastern. Is Eastern obligated to pay?

6. Contemporary Mission, Inc. was the owner of several songs. It entered into an agreement with Famous Music Corp. to promote and market its songs. Later, Famous Music Corp. assigned the contract to ABC Records, Inc. ABC then refused to market Contemporary's songs and Contemporary sued Famous Music Corp. for breach of contract. Is Famous liable?

7. Rogers entered into a contract to sell certain parts to Parton. Rogers also contracted with Nelson to supply those parts. Nelson defaulted on his obligation and Parton sued Nelson for non-performance. Is Parton entitled to recover as a third-party beneficiary of the contract between Rogers and Nelson?

8. Sprenger was an employee of Powder Power Tool Corp. After Sprenger terminated his employment in December 1983, the union representing employees of the corporation negotiated a contract with the corporation. Among the terms of the agreement was a clause granting retroactive pay increases to employees who were employed during 1983. When Sprenger did not get paid, he sued the corporation contending he was a proper party to sue in that he was a third-party beneficiary of the contract. Is Sprenger correct?

9. The Rensselaer Water Co. was a private company obligated by contract with the city of Rensselaer to provide water for the city water system. Moch Co. experienced a fire and was unable to get water from a nearby hydrant. As a result, its building burned to the ground. Moch sued the Rensselaer Water Co. for failure to supply water according to its contract with the city. Is Moch entitled to a judgment?

10. American Eastern Development Corp. kept its boat docked at a marina owned by Everglades Marina, Inc. The owner of Everglades intentionally set the marina on fire in order to collect insurance. In the fire, American's boat was destroyed. American submitted a claim with Everglades's insurance company but the company refused to pay on the ground that the fire had been set intentionally. Is American entitled to recover on the policy?

Chapter | 12

Discharge and Remedies

CONDITIONS

The previous chapters have focused on the nature and composition of contracts. This chapter will be concerned with what happens after a contract comes into being—its discharge by performance or otherwise, and the remedies available to ensure that the expectations of the parties are protected. In judging whether performance was proper, it is necessary to determine when performance was to begin, what it was intended to accomplish, and what was to constitute completion of performance. Therefore, we must examine the conditions for its complete performance.

A **condition** is any fact or event, other than the passage of time, that qualifies (limits) the promisor's present duty of performance. Conditions may give rise to a duty to perform; they may alter the method of performance; or they may cause an existing duty of performance to cease, temporarily or permanently.

Types of Conditions

Conditions may be classified as precedent, concurrent, and subsequent. A **condition precedent** is a condition that must occur before the duty to perform will arise. It precedes the duty. A **condition subsequent** is one that will terminate the

258

duty of performance when it occurs. **Conditions concurrent** are two conditions that must occur simultaneously, and they give rise to reciprocal duties of simultaneous performance.

For example, suppose Jack promises Jim, "I will come to work for you if I am laid off from my present job, and I will continue to work for you until my present employer calls me back to work." Jack's promise is based on both a condition precedent (being laid off) and a condition subsequent (being called back to work). Jack's duty to work for Jim arises when he is laid off. He will then work for Jim, but his duty to do so is terminated when he is called back to work.

For another illustration, suppose Louise promises to sell her car to Ann for $400 and Ann agrees. When does Louise have to deliver the car to Ann? When Ann pays her the $400. When does Ann have to pay the $400? When Louise delivers the car. Payment and delivery are conditions concurrent. These conditions frequently are implied by law (constructive conditions), but they may be expressed by the parties if they choose.

Creation of Conditions

Conditions may be either express or implied. When express, they are signaled by the use of such words as "if," "however," "but," or "as long as." Of course, all contracts, even those we call "express," are subject to some implied conditions, as with the conditions concurrent. Also, in employment contracts there is usually an implied condition that the employee lives to perform. As a general rule, conditions have no effect on the validity or the enforceability of a contract, but this rule is subject to two important exceptions.

If an acceptance of an offer is tendered on express conditions, it is considered to operate as a rejection of the offer both at common law and under Section 2–207(1) of the Uniform Commercial Code. This is the conditional acceptance discussed in Chapter 7. Second, if a condition is attached to the promise in either the offer or the acceptance, and is such that the promisor has

control over whether the condition occurs, the promise will not be sufficient consideration to support a contract. This is the illusory promise that was discussed in Chapter 7.

Independent Aleatory Promises

An **aleatory promise** is a promise conditioned on a fact or event other than performance by the other party. It operates independently and is not conditioned on performance or tender by the promisee. For example, ABC Insurance Company promises to pay Langton $40,000 if his house is destroyed by fire, and Langton promises to pay ABC a premium of $125. Langton's duty to perform is not conditioned on ABC's performance or offer of performance. It is aleatory. The same is true of a collateral promise. If Art promises to pay Tom $100 as the purchase price of goods, and Nancy promises that if Art does not pay, she will pay, Nancy's promise is not dependent on Tom's performance, but upon Art's refusal to pay.

In these examples, there is an aleatory promise on one side of the contract. Promises may be aleatory on both sides of a contract, as in the case of *reciprocal* collateral promises. For example, Sam promises to sell his house to Rebecca if he is relocated to another state by his employer, and Rebecca promises to purchase Sam's house if reasonable financing is available. When an aleatory promise is involved, nonperformance is not a breach or an excuse for nonperformance of the other promise, but if the aleatory promise actually is breached, the other party is discharged to the same extent as with nonaleatory promises.

PERFORMANCE AND BREACH

The Obligation to Perform

The performance of obligations is fundamental to all contracts. Exactly what constitutes performance may vary according to the nature of each obligation. However, when performance falls below some legally acceptable standard, a breach of the contract occurs.

Most contracts are discharged by performance. When a promise is performed, the promisor's duties under the contract end, leaving only his or her rights to receive complete performance from the other party. His or her performance caused these rights to arise. **Tender of performance** also will create these rights to performance by the other party. A *tender* is an offer to perform by someone who is ready, willing, and able to do so. If after tender by one party the other party fails to perform, the obligation of the first party is considered to have been met. Also, any surety (a person who has guaranteed performance) on the duty tendered is discharged. When performance actually is rendered, the question becomes, "What degree of performance is considered sufficient to meet the promisor's obligation?"

Complete and Satisfactory Performance

The degree and quality of peformance required to satisfy an obligation will depend on the nature of the contract and sometimes on its wording. Some obligations must be performed to perfection for the promisor to be fully discharged. These are obligations capable of perfect performance, such as an obligation to pay $500 as the purchase price for an automobile. Performance of other obligations must be measured by what the parties reasonably expected. Concerning the purchase of the car, although the obligation of the purchaser to pay must be performed to perfection, the obligation of the seller cannot. The obligation to deliver the car in the condition it was in when purchased must be considered satisfactorily performed if the car is delivered in such condition as would meet the reasonable expectation of the purchaser. In this context, perfection is impossible.

Performance to Personal Satisfaction

In some cases, performance is promised to the personal satisfaction of the promisee. For exam-

ple, suppose an artist is commissioned to paint a portrait. If the condition of personal satisfaction is expressed, or can be implied reasonably, and the promisee is not satisfied with the performance, the promisor's obligation is not discharged. A court will not apply a standard of merchantability or of reasonableness, or seek to substitute its judgment for that of the promisee, as long as the promisee's dissatisfaction is bona fide.

Substantial Performance

When performance has been rendered that is less than complete or satisfactory, but not so defective as to constitute a material breach, the other party's obligation is not discharged. However, his or her obligation may be diminished. For example, suppose Enslin promised to build a house for Wang, to Wang's specifications, for $50,000. Upon completion, Wang discovers that instead of using Acme water pipes in doing the plumbing as called for in the plans, Enslin used Becker pipes, and one of the bedrooms measures 12′ by 14½′ rather than 12′ by 15′. Although these differences constitute a breach and would entitle Wang to damages for any injury that resulted (such as the house being worth less than if it had been constructed to specification), the breach probably is not material. Justice would not be done by declaring Wang completely discharged from his obligation to pay. However, if the brand of plumbing pipes or the size of the room was an express condition for performance, most courts would not find substantial performance. Generally, express conditions, as distinguished from ordinary terms, must be performed at least satisfactorily (if perfection is not possible). Also, courts tend to be less sympathetic when the deviation was intentional rather than an oversight.

Even when there has been substantial performance, the party responsible for performance will be liable for damages to the extent the imperfections injure the party to whom performance was due. The following case first discusses the question of substantial performance and then the measure of damages.

PLANTE v. JACOBS
10 Wis.2d 567, 103 N.W.2d 296 (1960)

This was an action by Eugene C. Plante (Plaintiff/Respondent) against Frank M. and Carol H. Jacobs (Defendants/Appellants) to establish a lien and to recover the contract price, plus extras, for building a house. Defendants counterclaimed for faulty workmanship.

The contract price of the house was $26,765 plus $960 for an agreed-upon modification. On completion, Defendants claimed the contract had been breached. They alleged some 20 defects requiring repairs amounting to 25 to 30 percent of the contract price. Of particular concern was a misplaced wall between the living room and the kitchen that shortened the living room by one foot. Plaintiff contended that there had been substantial performance and that he was entitled to the agree-upon price less some adjustment for defects.

The trial court found for Plaintiff and Defendants appealed. Affirmed.

HALLOWS, Justice.

The question here is whether there has been substantial performance. The test of what amounts to substantial performance seems to be whether the performance meets the essential purpose of the contract. In [Manitowoc Steam Boiler Works v. Manitowoc Glue Co.] the contract called for a boiler having a capacity of 150 per cent of the existing boiler. The court held there was no substantial performance because the boiler furnished had a capacity of only 82 percent. . . . In Houlahan v. Clark . . . the contract provided the plaintiff was to drive pilings in the lake and place a boat house thereon parallel and in line with a neighbor's dock. This was not done and the contractor so positioned the boat house that it was practically useless to the owner. Manthey v. Stock . . . involved a contract to paint a house and to do a good job, including removal of the old paint where necessary. The plaintiff did not remove the old paint, and blistering and roughness of the new paint resulted. The court held that the plaintiff failed to show substantial performance. . . .

Substantial performance as applied to construction of a house does not mean that every detail must be in strict compliance with the specifications and the plans. Something less than perfection is the test of substantial performance unless all details are made the essence of the contract. In this case the plan was a stock floor plan. There were no blueprints. The specifications were standard printed forms with some modifications and additions written in by the parties. Many of the problems that arose during construction had to be solved on the basis of practical experience. No mathematical rule relating to the percentage of the price, of cost of completion or of completeness can be laid down to determine substantial performance of a building contract. Although the defendants received a house with which they are dissatisfied in many respects, the trial court was not in error in finding the contract was substantially performed.

The next question is what is the amount of recovery when the plaintiff has substantially, but incompletely, performed. For substantial performance, the plaintiff should recover the contract price less the damages caused the defendant by the incomplete performance. Both parties agree. Venzke v. Magdanz . . . states the correct rule for damages due to faulty construction amounting to such incomplete performance, which is the difference between the value of the house as it stands with faulty and incomplete construction and the value of the house if it had been constructed in strict accordance with the plans and specifications. This is the diminished-value rule. The cost of replacement or repair is not the measure of such damage, but is an element to take into consideration in arriving at value under some circumstances. The cost of replacement or the cost to make whole the omissions may equal or be less than the difference in value in some cases and, likewise, the cost to rectify a defect may greatly exceed the added value to the structure as corrected. The defendants argue that under the Venzke rule their damages are $10,000. The plaintiff on review argues the defendants' damages are only $650. Both parties agree the trial court applied the wrong rule to the facts.

The trial court applied the cost-of-repair or replacement rule as to several items, relying on Stern v. Schlafer . . . wherein it was stated that when there are a number of small items of defect or omission which can be remedied without the reconstruction of a substantial part of the building or a great sacrifice of work or material already wrought in the building, the reasonable cost of correcting the defect should be allowed. However, in Mohs v. Quarton . . . the court held when the separation of defects would lead to confusion, the rule of diminished value could apply to all defects. . . .

The item of misplacing the living room wall under the facts of this case was clearly under the diminished-value rule. There is no evidence that defendants requested or demanded the replacement of the wall in the place called for by the specifications during the course of construction. To tear down the wall now and rebuild it in its proper place would involve a substantial destruction of the work, if not all of it, which was put into the wall and would cause additional damages to other parts of the house and require replastering and redecorating the walls and ceilings of at least two rooms. Such economic waste is unreasonable and unjustified. The rule of diminished value contemplates the wall is not going to be moved. Expert witnesses for both parties, testifying as to the value of the house, agreed that the misplacement of the wall had no effect on the market price. The trial court properly found that the defendants suffered no legal damage, although the defendants' particular desire for specified room size was not satisfied.

Questions

1. Isn't it contrary to general concepts of contract law that a party may be required to accept some performance other than that called for in the contract?

2. How does a court know whether to apply the "cost-of-repair-or-replacement" test or the "diminished-value" test?

It should be noted that under the Uniform Commercial Code, Section 2–601, a buyer of goods is entitled to require that the goods tendered by the seller conform in all respects to the contract. Otherwise, the buyer has the right to accept the goods, reject the entire shipment, or accept part and reject part. This is called the "Perfect Tender Rule." It preserves the common law right of the buyer to demand perfect performance when perfection is possible.

Material Breach

When performance falls below the standard of substantial performance, there is a **material breach.** This may occur because the performance is so defective as to impair the value of the contract and make it substantially worthless. In the last example, if Enslin had constructed the house with materials that were so inferior that there was a risk that the house might collapse at any time, he would have been guilty of material breach and

Wang would have been discharged. Wang then would be entitled to rescind the contract or to keep the house and sue for damages.

Material breach also may occur if the party obligated notifies the other party, in advance of performance, that he or she does not intend to perform, or, after part performance, that he or she does not intend to complete the job. These circumstances constitute what is called an **anticipatory breach,** and entitle the other party to the same rights as those to which he or she would be entitled in the event of an actual breach. The following case is perhaps the classic on the question of anticipatory breach, firmly establishing the principle in English law. Substantially all American courts have adopted its rule and reasoning.

HOCHSTER v. DE LA TOUR
2 E. & B. 678 (Q.B. 1853)

This was an action in *assumpsit* (for breach of contract) by a performer (Plaintiff) who had agreed to perform for Defendant, accompanying him on tour for three months, to begin June 1, 1852. On May 11, 1852, Defendant wrote to Plaintiff that he had changed his mind. Plaintiff filed suit on May 22 and, prior to June 1, he obtained another engagement, on equally good terms, that would not commence until July 4, 1852. Defendant contended that there could be no breach until June 1, but the trial court refused to dismiss the complaint and the jury found for Plaintiff.

LORD CAMPBELL, C.J.

On this motion in arrest of judgment, the question arises whether if there be an engagement between A. and B. whereby B. engages to employ A. on and from a future day for a given period of time, . . . B. may, before the day, refuse to perform the agreement and break and renounce it, so as to entitle A. before the day to commence an action against B. to recover damages for breach of the agreement, A. having been ready and willing to perform it, till it was broken and renounced by B. The defendant's counsel very powerfully contended that, if the plaintiff was not contented to dissolve the contract, and to abandon all remedy upon it, he was bound to remain ready and willing to perform it until the day when the actual employment . . . was to begin; and that there could be no breach of the agreement, before that day, to give a right of action. But it cannot be laid sown as a universal rule that, where by agreement an act is to be done on a future day, no action can be brought for a breach of the agreement till the day for doing the act has arrived. If a man promises to marry a woman on a future day, and before that day marries another woman, he is instantly liable to an action for breach of promise of marriage. . . . If a man contracts to execute a lease on and from a future day for a certain term, and, before that day, executes a lease to another for the same term, he may be immediately sued for breaking the contract. . . . So if a man contracts to sell and deliver specific goods on a future day, and before the day he sells and delivers them to another, he is immediately liable to an action at the suit of the person with whom he first contracted to sell and deliver them. . . . One reason alleged in support of such an action is, that the defendant has, before the day, rendered it impossible for him to perform the contract at the day; but this does not necessarily follow; for, prior to the day fixed for doing the act, the first wife may have died, a surrender of the lease executed might be obtained, and the defendant might have repurchased the goods so as to be in a situation to sell and deliver them to the plaintiff. . . . The declaration in the present case, in alleging a breach, states a great deal more than a passing intention on the part of the defendant which he may repent of, and could only be proved by evidence that he had utterly renounced the contract, or done some act which rendered it impossible for him to perform it. If the plaintiff has no remedy for breach of the contract unless he treats the contract as in force, and acts upon it down to the 1st of June, 1852, it follows that, till then, he must enter into no employment which will interfere with his promise "to start with the defendant on such travels on the day and year," and that he must then be equipped in all respects as a courier for a three months' tour on the continent of Europe. But it is surely much more rational, and more for the benefit of both parties, that, after the renunciation of the agreement by the defendant, the plaintiff should be at liberty to consider himself absolved from any future performance of it, retaining his right to sue for any damage he has suffered from the breach of it. Thus, instead of remaining idle and laying out money in preparations which must be useless, he is at liberty to seek service under another employer, which would go in mitigation of the damages to which he would otherwise be entitled for a breach of the contract. It seems strange that the defendant, after renouncing the contract, and absolutely declaring that he will never act under it, should be permitted to object that faith is given to his assertion, and that an opportunity is not left to him of changing his mind. If the plaintiff is barred of any remedy by entering into an engagement inconsistent with starting as a courier with the defendant on the 1st of June, he is prejudiced by putting faith in the defendant's assertion; and it would be more consistent with principle if the defendant were precluded from saying that he had not broken the contract when he declared that he entirely renounced it. . . . The man who wrongfully renounces a contract into which he has deliberately entered cannot justly complain if he is immediately sued for a compensation in damages by the man whom he has injured; and it seems reasonable to allow an option to the injured party, either to sue immediately, or to wait till the time when the act was to be done, still holding it as prospectively binding for the exercise of this option, which may be advantageous to the innocent party, and cannot be prejudicial to the wrongdoer. An argument against the action before the 1st of June is urged from the difficulty of calculating the damages; but this argument is equally strong against an action before the 1st of September, when the three months would expire. In either case, the jury in assessing the damages would be justified in looking to all that happened, or was likely to happen, to increase or mitigate the loss of the plaintiff down to the day of trial. We do not find any decision contrary to the view we are taking of this case. . . .

If it should be held that, upon a contract to do an act on a future day, a renunciation of the contract by one party dispenses with a condition to be performed in the meantime by the other, there seems no reason for requiring the other to wait till the day arrives before seeking his remedy by action; and the only ground on which the condition can be dispensed with seems to be, that the renunciation may be treated as a breach of contract.

Upon the whole, we think that the declaration in this case is sufficient. It gives us great satisfaction to reflect that, the question being on the record, our opinion may be reviewed in a Court of Error. In the meantime, we must give judgment for the plaintiff.

Questions

1. Doesn't the rule in this case take away the opportunity for the "breaching" party to change his mind and do what is right?
2. How do we distinguish a "passing intention" of which a party may repent from an actionable repudiation?

Time of Performance as a Condition

The parties to a contract may specify the time for performance or a time by which performance must be completed. If no time is stated, the courts presume a reasonable time was intended. What constitutes a reasonable time must be determined from the nature of the contract and the surrounding facts and circumstances.

If the parties have stated a time for performance, or one can be implied, and the promisor fails to perform within that time, the court may or may not find a breach. Its decision will depend on whether "time is of the essence" of the contract. Courts generally hold that **time is of the essence** if the parties have set a particular time and the terms of the contract expressly state that time is of the essence. Also, time is of the essence if later performance would deprive the promisee of a substantial portion of the value of performance. Of course, late performance is always a breach, and entitles the promisee to damages for any injury that results. If time is of the essence, however, any

late performance will be considered a material breach and the promisee will be discharged.

Prevention of Performance

When two parties enter into a contract, each assumes an implied duty to refrain from interfering unreasonably with the other's performance. If performance is prevented unreasonably, the interfering party is considered in material breach of the contract because of the failure to comply with this constructive obligation. If the interference does not prevent performance but makes it significantly more cumbersome, it is a partial breach and the promisor, although not discharged, is entitled to damages for the additional burden. For example, suppose Davis contracts with Egan Construction to build a house for her. If Davis then prevented Egan from coming on the proposed building site, her actions would constitute a material breach. If, however, she decided that she didn't like the way Egan had laid a tile floor and tore up the tile after Egan left one evening, Egan could be entitled to damages only—the cost of laying the floor again.

IMPOSSIBILITY

Ordinarily the parties to a contract are expected to perform their obligations, even though their performance proves to be more burdensome than expected. However, the sources of the burdens and the degree to which they alter the parties' justifiable expectations must be examined to determine when performance will be insisted upon. When performance becomes objectively impossible ("it cannot be done" rather than subjectively impossible, "I cannot do it") or highly impracticable, performance may be excused.

Nature of the Doctrine

The performance of a contract may become impossible because of circumstances not attributable to any wrongdoing or negligence on the part of the parties involved. If this occurs, both parties are discharged. If it occurs after performance has begun, the parties are entitled to be returned to status quo insofar as that is possible. If a complete return to status quo cannot be accomplished, and one of the parties has received a benefit that justice demands he or she should not be allowed to retain without paying for it, the other party may be entitled to recover in an action in quasi contract for the reasonable value of that benefit. Any additional detriment suffered by either party must be borne by that party alone.

Grounds of Impossibility

ILLNESS OR DEATH.   Death of the promisor will excuse performance of any contract that requires his or her existence for proper performance. Therefore, performance of a contract under which Brink had agreed to work for Jonas for a stated time would be excused by Brink's death, but the same would not be true if Brink had agreed to sell a car to Jonas for $500. The latter contract could be fully performed by Brink's executor or administrator. Illness of the promisor may excuse performance entirely or may operate only to postpone it, depending on the nature of the illness and the nature of the contract. A short illness, or even a lengthy one for a period that was not critical, would fall under the latter rule.

Death or illness of the promisee is less likely to excuse or delay performance, but will do so in circumstances in which performance was personal to the promisee or the value of the contract would be impaired substantially by the promisee's circumstances. For example, a contract to provide medical attention to the promisee would be excused by his or her death. A promise to provide the promisee with racquetball instruction would be excused by his or her death but only delayed by his or her illness in most circumstances. A contract to sell a car to the promisee probably would not be excused or delayed by either. Note that in any of these situations, the obligation has not been *performed*. Its performance only has been, at the most, excused or delayed. Note also that in all cases, we are presuming no wrongdoing on the part of either party. That would change the case to the category discussed at the end of the last section—prevention of performance.

PERFORMANCE DECLARED ILLEGAL.   If by virtue of some intervening circumstances performance of a contract became illegal, both parties would be discharged. The illegality would render the contract unenforceable and the courts, therefore, would refuse to interfere. However, if the obligations of the parties are severable—and if the illegality affects only a portion of the obligation and that portion can be severed from the rest, leaving complete matching obligations on both sides—then the illegality does not completely discharge either party. For example, suppose Dalloway promises to sell to Woolf 100 wild rabbits, 100 chickens, and 50 ducks at $2 per animal. Prior to performance, the sale of wild rabbits is made illegal by statute. Only the part of the contract relating to the rabbits is discharged; the remainder will be enforced.

DESTRUCTION OF THE SUBJECT MATTER. When the contract's subject matter is destroyed through no fault of either party, the obligations of the parties are discharged. If any performance has been rendered at the time of the destruction, the party receiving any severable performance of value will (1) be required to pay for the part received according to the contract, (2) if the value of the part is diminished by less-than-full performance, he or she may be required to pay the reasonable value of the part performed, or (3) the parties may be returned to status quo, whichever seems appropriate. Of course, if the destruction resulted from the wrongdoing of one of the parties, that party will be liable for any damages suffered by the other party.

As we discussed in Chapter 7 relating to termination of an offer by destruction of the subject matter, care must be taken that what was destroyed actually was the subject matter. For example, if Dalloway agrees to sell 500 bales of hay to Woolf at $4 per bale and, prior to delivery, fire destroys all of Dalloway's hay, the "subject matter" has been destroyed only if the terms of the contract specified that the hay was to come from the particular lot of hay owned by Dalloway, not just hay in general. Finally, care must be taken concerning when title passes from the seller to the buyer. Once title has passed to the buyer, the obligation to pay will not be discharged by destruction. Generally this occurs on delivery if the contract calls for delivery by the seller, or after the passage of a reasonable time if the buyer is supposed to pick up the property. Regarding contracts for the sale of goods, the rules allocating the risk of loss are set out in detail in Sections 2–509 and 2–510 of the UCC, and Section 2–501 specifies when a buyer obtains an insurable interest in goods.

Commercial Frustration

At common law, a party was not excused from performing a contractual obligation by the mere fact that circumstances had rendered performance more burdensome than expected, unless the circumstances amounted to an unforeseen and unforeseeable difficulty or mutual mistake of material fact. Today there is a tendency to relax the rules in cases in which their strict application appears to work an injustice. The circumstances warranting special treatment have been termed **commercial frustration.** The application of this equity principle by law courts is, at least in part, an outgrowth of the Uniform Commerical Code.

Section 2–615(a) of the Code provides that performance may be excused if made impracticable by good-faith compliance with any applicable foreign or domestic government regulation or order. Subsection (b) then provides that when only part of the seller's capacity to perform is affected, he or she must allocate remaining production and delivery among customers in a manner that is fair and reasonable. However, as the following case illustrates, the term *impracticable* is not as broad as it may seem.

WOOD v. BARTOLINO et al.
48 N.M. 175, 146 P.2d 883 (1944)

This was an action by Lena Rohr Wood (Plaintiff/Appellant) against Andrew Bartolino and Mary Bartolino (Defendants/Appellees) to enforce payment of rent under a lease.

Plaintiff leased property to Defendants to be used "solely as a filling station." The lease was for five years, commencing June 1, 1939. The property was used as a filling station until July 1, 1942, when Defendants ceased operation and sought termination of the lease because of "commercial frustration." Defendants' position was that government wartime regulations freezing the sale of automobiles, tires and tubes, and rationing the sale of gasoline made continuance of the lease "impossible and impracticable."

From a judgment for Defendants, Plaintiff appealed. Reversed and remanded, with directions.

BRICE, Justice.

The doctrine of "commercial frustration," or, as more often called by the courts of this country, the doctrine of "implied condition," has been developed by a process of evolution from the rules: (1) A party to a contract is excused from performance if it depends upon the existence of a given person or thing, if that person or thing perishes. . . . (2) A party to a contract is excused from performance if it is rendered impossible by act of God, the law, or the other party. . . . The rules are otherwise stated, as follows:

(1) Impossibility due to domestic law;

(2) Impossibility due to the death or illness of one who by the terms of the contract was to do an act requiring his personal performance.

(3) Impossibility due to fortuitous destruction or change in character of something to which the contract related, or which by the terms of the contract was made a necessary means of performance. 6 Williston on Contracts, Sec. 1935.

Regarding a fourth and fifth class, Williston States:

The fourth class of cases, to which allusion was made above as standing on more debatable ground, comprises cases where impossibility is due to the failure of some means of performance, contemplated but not contracted for.

The fifth class does not strictly fall within the boundaries of impossibility. Performance remains entirely possible, but the whole value of the performance to one of the parties is at least, and the basic reason recognized as such by both parties, for entering into the contract has been destroyed by a supervening and unforeseeable event. This does not operate primarily as an excuse for the promisor, the performance of whose promise has lost its value, but as a failure of consideration for the promise of the other party, not in a literal sense it is true, since the performance bargained for can be given, but in substance, because the performance has lost its value. The name "frustration" has been given to this situation. Until recently, it has received little clear recognition, but its adoption seems involved in some decisions, and their justice is plain.

Id. Sec. 1935.

Regarding the meaning of "impossibility" as used in the rules that excuse the non-performance of contacts, it is stated:

As pointed out in the Restatement of Contracts, the essence of the modern defense of impossibility is that the promised performance was at the making of the contract, or thereafter became, impracticable owing to some extreme or unreasonable difficulty, expense, injury, or loss involved, rather than that it is scientifically or actually impossible. . . . The important question is whether an unanticipated circumstance has made performance of the promise vitally different from what should reasonably have been within the contemplation of both parties when they entered into the contract. If so, the risk should not fairly be thrown upon the promisor.

Id. Sec. 1931.

We need not determine whether the doctrine of "commerical frustration" can, under the circumstances, apply to a worthless business, as we have concluded that ordinarily it does not apply to demises of real estate, and if at all, then only as limited hereinafter.

The courts of this country, Federal and State, have cited with approval, and generally followed, the decisions of the English courts that the doctrine has no application to an ordinary lease of real property. . . .

First, it is the rule that in the absence of an eviction, actual or constructive, or complete destruction of the leasehold, a tenant is bound to discharge his covenant to pay rent, unless he is relieved therefrom by the happening of some event which by the convenants of the lease terminates it. . . .

It was the rule at common law and is now the rule generally in this country, that a lessee of premises destroyed during the term of the lease by unavoidable accident, is not relieved from an express and unconditional promise to pay rent, unless the destruction of the premises is of the entire subject matter of the lease so that nothing remains capable of being held or enjoyed. . . .

Under this rule the mere frustration of the business permitted to be conducted upon the premises did not relieve the tenant from his obligation to pay rent. It is the basis of the decisions of a number of courts holding that the adoption of the 18th amendment to the Federal Constitution, prohibiting the sale of intoxicating liquors, did not absolve the tenant from paying rental on premises leased to be used exclusively for the conduct of the liquor business, in the absence of a convenant in the lease relieving the tenant from the payment of rent upon the happening of such contingency. . . .

There are no Federal regulations prohibiting the sale of gasoline, oil, tires, tubes and other merchandise ordinarily sold at filling stations, though the enforcement of such regulations [*sic;* probably, regulations limiting these sales] has drastically reduced appellees' income, which before was less than operating expenses; nor has Federal law, rule or regulation deprived appellees of the use of the premises as a filling station. It follows that the trial court erred in denying recovery of rent by appellant.

Questions

1. Doesn't the rule in this case fail to give due regard to the obvious intentions of the parties?

2. Why does the court refuse to apply the doctrine of commercial frustration to cases involving real estate to the same extent as those involving other kinds of contracts?

DISCHARGE

A contract is **discharged** when the parties no longer have any obligation of performance. This generally occurs as a result of complete performance. However, it also may occur by agreement of the parties or by operation of law.

Discharge by Agreement

Discharge by agreement may come about under a variety of circumstances. First, because a contract is entered into by mutual agreement, it may be cancelled by mutual agreement. This mutual cancellation may be written or oral, and evidence of an oral cancellation of a written agreement is admissable under the Parol Evidence Rule as a subsequent oral contract. However, most courts require the cancellation to be written if it will involve the re-transfer of any subject matter governed by the Statute of Frauds.

Second, a party to whom performance is due may waive his or her right either expressly or by implication. For example, if a purchaser accepts defective performance without objection, knowing that the other party does not intend to cure the defect, he or she will be held to have waived his or her right to complete performance.

Finally, the parties may discharge a liquidated obligation by composition or an executed gift, or an unliquidated debt by accord and satisfaction. These methods were discussed in Chapter 8.

Discharge Under the UCC

Three sections of the Code are relevant to discharge by agreement of contracts for the sale of goods. Section 1–107 provides that any claim or right arising out of an alleged breach can be waived without consideration by a signed writing delivered to the obligor. Section 2–209 allows a waiver without consideration of any executory portion of a contract, but subsection (5) provides that the waiver may be retracted unless that would produce an injustice. Section 2–725 provides a four-year statute of limitations for any action for breach of a contract for the sale of goods.

Discharge by Alteration

Forgery of a writing creates no obligation on a party if the forgery is of his or her signature. Material alteration is another kind of forgery, and it will discharge the obligation of the party whose rights or duties were changed thereby if the alteration is (1) material, (2) by a party to the contract or by his or her agent, (3) intentional, and (4) without consent. The resulting discharge is complete as to the party who did the altering personally or through an agent, and as to any assignee thereafter.

Discharge by Statute of Limitations

The right to bring suit on a contract may be barred if the party having the right to sue waits too long. The exact time depends on the nature of the claim and the state in whose courts the suit is being brought. As noted above, the UCC provides a four-year statute of limitations on claims arising out of contracts for the sale of goods. Other contracts are controlled by other limitations provisions that vary state by state. The time generally begins running at the moment the right to sue arises, but in the case of fraud and misrepresentation it typically does not begin until the party discovers, or reasonably should have discovered, the fraud or misrepresentation. Once begun, the running of the statutory period may be "tolled" (temporarily stopped) under certain circumstances, such as flight of the wrongdoer to avoid being served with process, or incompetence of the claimant. The period may be stopped and started all over again if the other party reaffirms his or her obligation either expressly or by implication (for example, by part performance). It always is stopped when a lawsuit on the claim is filed. If the lawsuit is one in equity, such as for specific performance, generally there is no statute of limitations. In its place, the doctrine of **laches** is applied, which provides for a "reasonable" time instead of a prescribed period. Although the defense of the statute of limitations or laches may be waived by the claimant, many states require a waiver to be in a signed writing.

Discharge by Bankruptcy

Title 11 of the United States Code provides that the debts of an individual may be discharged by a bankruptcy proceeding. Bankruptcy is, therefore, another form of statutory (or "operation-of-law") discharge. Bankruptcy is discussed more fully in Chapter 24.

THE NATURE OF REMEDIES

Purpose

The objective in granting remedies is to make the injured party whole to the extent possible. When this can be done by returning the parties to the positions they were in prior to entering into contractual negotiations, the court usually is willing to do so. Sometimes this is not possible, and even when it is, the remedy may not be completely satisfactory. Even if the court orders the return to each of all the money or other property he or she gave, the process of negotiation and settlement causes a loss of time and energy, and some of the parties' expectations have been lost. Therefore, the court can do only whatever seems to produce the most effective justice under the circumstances.

Remedies may be "at law" or "in equity." As discussed in Chapter 2, the distinction is less important today than it once was, but it is still significant procedurally. Generally speaking, the remedy at law is money damages. At early common law, money damages was the only common remedy known to the law courts. Over the course of time, other "extraordinary" remedies at law were developed, but money damages remains by far the most frequent.

Sometimes the remedy of money damages is inadequate. For example, suppose Sawyer agrees to sell to Thatcher, for $800, a Rembrandt painting. If Sawyer fails to perform, no amount of money damages will place Thatcher in the position she would have been in if Sawyer had performed. Presumably the painting is a "one-of-a-kind" item. If the contract had been one for a car with no unique qualities, damages probably would be adequate. Thatcher could take the $800 she was prepared to pay plus the damages and purchase a similar car. In cases in which money damages are not adequate, the courts may grant an equitable remedy, the most common for breach of contract being an order directing the party to perform the contract as he originally promised. This remedy is called **specific performance** and is discussed later

in the chapter. Justice probably would require specific performance in the case of an heirloom (see Chapter 2) but not in the case of the car. Just as courts of law have some "extraordinary" legal remedies, courts of equity, when justice requires it, *may* give money damages incidental to equitable relief.

Enforcement

When a plaintiff has been successful in court and has been granted a remedy, two major risks remain. First is the risk that the party against whom judgment was granted may not be able to satisfy the judgment. In addition to the risk of ability to pay, a second risk lies in the defendant's willingness to pay. In order to alleviate these problems, three principal procedures are available—attachment, execution, and garnishment.

Attachment is a process by which a claimant may have the property of the other party seized at the beginning of the lawsuit in order to assure that it will be available for payment of a judgment if he or she is successful in pursuing his or her claim. **Execution** is a process by which a judgment debtor's property is seized, after judgment, to satisfy the claim. In the case of specific performance, the property will be turned over to the claimant. In the case of a money-damage judgment, the property may be sold to pay the judgment or it may be redeemed by its owner upon payment of the judgment. If the property is sold but the money generated is insufficient to satisfy the judgment, the court will grant a "deficiency judgment." If the money generated is more than the judgment, the owner is entitled to the excess. **Garnishment** is similar to execution except that it is used to seize the judgment debtor's property in the hands of a third party. The most common objects of garnishment are bank accounts and wages.

The rules governing attachment, execution, and garnishment are quite detailed and vary greatly from state to state. Most states have property exemption statutes providing that certain kinds of

Concept outline: Contract discharge

Performance

Complete—performing all obligations required satisfactorily

Personal satisfaction—obligation is not discharged until the other party is personally satisfied

Substantial performance—performance has been rendered but is less than complete or satisfactory

Impossibility

Death—will excuse performance of a contract

Illness—may excuse performance entirely or merely postpone it

Illegal—both parties will be discharged if performance becomes illegal

Destruction of subject matter—both parties are discharged if subject matter is destroyed through no fault of either party

Commerical frustration—performance may be excused if rendering performance becomes unduly burdensome

Discharge

By agreement—mutual cancellation will result in a discharge

Under the UCC—discharge may be mandated by sections of the UCC

By alteration—material alteration of a writing will discharge the party whose rights were changed by the alteration

By statute of limitations—discharge may result because a sufficient amount of time has passed

Discharge, continued

Bankruptcy—Title 11 provides the discharge of debts under bankruptcy proceedings

Damages

Compensatory—awarded to compensate for loss suffered

Consequential—awarded to compensate for loss due to a particular situation

Punitive—awarded to punish the wrongdoer

Liquidated—amount of damages is agreed to in advance by the parties if there is a breach of contract

Equitable Remedies

Specific performance—breaching party is made to perform as promised

Rescission—contract is terminated by the courts

Restitution—returning goods received or making payment for the goods received

Reformation—used to remedy an understanding by the parties that was not accurately reflected by the written contract

Non-Contract Remedies

Promissory estoppel—courts, in order to serve justice, enforce a promise made even though no contract existed

Quasi contract—payment of the reasonable value of benefits received when a contract did not exist

---

property (such as a homestead, furniture, and working tools) or only property in excess of a certain minimum value can be taken by these processes. Wages may be subject to special rules, such as limiting the amount that may be reached to 60 percent of wages (or 40 percent if the judgment debtor is married) to enable the debtor to have enough money for daily living.

Remedies Under the UCC

Section 1–107 of the Uniform Commercial Code provides that remedies under its provisions are to be liberally administered to the end that the aggrieved party may be placed as nearly as possible in the same position he or she would have been in had the contract been fully performed. Also, this

section makes it clear that only compensatory damages that reimburse the plaintiff for losses normally are authorized. The grant of other damages, such as punitive damages that punish the defendant, must be provided for specifically in the Code.

DAMAGES

Money damages in a case may be (1) compensatory, (2) consequential or special, or (3) punitive or exemplary. These may be awarded individually or in some combination as justice dictates.

Compensatory damages are the most common. They are awarded in an amount determined sufficient to compensate the aggrieved party for the loss he or she suffered as a normal consequence of the breach. For example, suppose Carol promised to sell her car to Mike for $500 and then refused to deliver. If the court determined that it would cost Mike $800 to buy a comparable car on the open market, compensatory damages of $300 would be in order. If a comparable car would cost $500 or less, there would be no basis for compensatory damages.

Consequential (special) damages are awarded to compensate for losses that do not flow as a normal result of a breach of the type being considered, but have been suffered by the plaintiff in the particular situation. Therefore, in the preceding example, if because of the nondelivery of the car Mike had missed meeting with a customer and could establish that the missed appointment resulted in the loss of a $400 sales commission, this amount might be added to the $300 compensatory damages. Consequential damages may be granted only to the extent that they reasonably were foreseeable as a consequence of the particular breach. In the example, if Carol knew Mike's business and knew or should know that he used

his car to conduct his business, this requirement probably would be satisfied.

Punitive (exemplary) damages are awarded to punish the wrongdoer and to deter the wrongdoer, and others by example, from engaging in similar conduct in the future. In granting this remedy, the purpose of civil law overlaps that of criminal law. Malice is the element that raises the possibility of punitive damages.

The amount of punitive damages sometimes is set by statute, but is more frequently set by the courts in an amount the court—or the jury—feels necessary to provide a deterrent. In the case of an individual, this may be a few hundred or a few thousand dollars. In a case against Ford Motor Company concerning deaths resulting from an alleged design defect in its Pinto, the original award by a California court was in excess of $121 million.

Punitive damages are granted less frequently in contract cases than in tort cases, and are not permitted in cases brought under Article 2 of the UCC. As the following opinion illustrates, however, they may be appropriate in some unusual contract cases.

WRIGHT v. PUBLIC SAVINGS LIFE INSURANCE COMPANY
262 S.C. 285, 204 S.E.2d 57 (1974)

This was an action by Mamie L. Wright (Plaintiff/ Respondent) against Public Savings Life Insurance Company (Defendant/Appellant) for compensatory and punitive damages for fraudulent cancellation of life and health-and-accident insurance policies.

In May 1963, Plaintiff purchased a life and a health-and-accident policy from Defendant. The premiums were 99 cents per week and 60 cents per week respectively. She made two claims for illness thereafter. In May 1971, she was informed that her policies had lapsed for nonpayment of the premiums. The evidence was undisputed that the required premiums, in fact, had been fully paid. When Plaintiff protested, the response of Defendant's Lancaster office manager was "you are getting too old anyhow." The manager then tendered a return of $6.36 of prepaid premiums and requested that Plaintiff sign a receipt, which she declined. In the meantime, a Multiple Revival Application was submitted to Defendant, without Plaintiff's knowledge and bearing a forgery of her signature. It acknowledged termination of the policies in question and requested reinstatement. Plaintiff contended all of this demonstrated a plan by Defendant to cancel her policies because of her age and ill health.

The jury returned a verdict for Plaintiff in the amount of $600 actual damages and $1700 punitive damages, and Defendant appealed. Affirmed.

PER CURIUM.

This Court has consistently adhered to the rule that the breach of a contract, committed with fraudulent intent, and accompanied by a fraudulent act, or acts, will entail liability for punitive as well as actual damages. . . .

In the case of Sullivan v. Calhoun . . . this Court quoted with approval from 12 R.C.L. 229, the following language: "Fraud assumes so many hues and forms, that courts are compelled to content themselves with comparatively few general rules for its discovery and defeat, and allow the facts and circumstances peculiar to each case to bear heavily upon the conscience and judgment of the court or jury in determining its presence or absence. While it has often been said that fraud cannot be precisely defined, the books contain many definitions, such as unfair dealing; the unlawful appropriation of another's property by design." We think that the evidence hereinabove recited was quite sufficient, under settled principles of law, to warrant a finding that there was a breach of contract, with fraudulent intent, accompanied by a fraudulent act or acts on the part of the insurer and accordingly sufficient to support a verdict for punitive damages.

Questions

1. What other conduct in connection with a contract should give rise to punitive damages?

2. How should a court compute punitive damages? What factors should be taken into account?

Sale of Goods

Under Section 2-708 of the UCC, if a buyer refuses to accept delivery or repudiates, the seller is entitled to direct compensatory damages (Sec. 2-110). If these are inadequate, the seller is entitled to lost profits, including reasonable overhead, and **incidental damages** (additional compensatory damages). Section 2-713 provides for damages to the buyer in the event of seller's nondelivery or repudiation (refusal to perform). The measure is the difference between the market price when the buyer learns of the breach and the contract price, together with any incidental and consequential damage suffered.

Mitigation of Damages

Mitigation of damages means that if one of the parties breaches the contract, the other is under a duty to exercise reasonable effort to minimize the effect of the breach. Although this principle is applicable to all contracts, it is most apt to be seen in connection with contracts requiring continued performance over an extended period of time, such as leases and employment contracts. In the event of breach of a lease by a lessee, the lessor is under a duty to make a reasonable effort to find a new tenant. Failure to do so will result in a reduction of damages received by the lessor by the amount of the rent he or she could have received by finding a new tenant. An employee, discharged wrongfully is under a duty to seek comparable employment. However, Section 2–712 of the UCC expressly exempts the buyer, under contract for the sale of goods, from any duty of mitigation if the seller breaches the obligation.

When there is a duty to mitigate damages, particularly in cases of breach of employment contracts, the question of what substitute performance may be considered reasonably comparable can be difficult. Consider the following case.

PARKER v. TWENTIETH CENTURY–FOX FILM CORPORATION
3 Cal.3rd 176, 474 P.2d 689 (1970)

This was an action by Shirley MacLaine Parker (Plaintiff/Respondent) against Twentieth Century-Fox Film Corporation (Defendant/Appellant) to recover agreed compensation under a contract for her services as an actress in a motion picture.

Under a contract dated August 6, 1965, Plaintiff agreed to play the female lead in a motion picture entitled "Bloomer Girl" at a guaranteed compensation of $750,000. Defendant later notified Plaintiff of its decision not to produce the film, and offered her a leading role in another picture, "Big Country, Big Man" at the same compensation. "Bloomer Girl" was a musical to be filmed in California, and "Big Country, Big Man" was a western to be filmed in Australia. Plaintiff refused the substitution and filed suit. Defendant pleaded, as an affirmative defense, Plaintiff's failure to mitigate damages by accepting the substitute role.

From a summary judgment for Plaintiff, Defendant appealed. Affirmed.

BURKE, Justice.

The general rule is that the measure of recovery by a wongfully discharged employee is the amount of salary agreed upon for the period of service, less the amount which the employer affirmatively proves the employee has earned or with reasonable effort might have earned from other employment. . . . However, before projected earnings from other employment opportunities not sought or accepted by the discharged employee can be applied in mitigation, the employer must show that the other employment was comparable, or substantially similar, to that of which the employee has been deprived; the employee's rejection of or failure to seek other available employment of a different or inferior kind may not be resorted to in order to mitigate damages. . . .

In the present case defendant has raised no issue of *reasonableness of efforts* by plaintiff to obtain other employment; the sole issue is whether plaintiff's refusal of defendant's substitute offer of "Big Country" may be used in mitigation. . . .

Applying the foregoing rules to the present case, with all intendments in favor of the party opposing the summary judgment motion . . . it is clear that the trial court correctly ruled that plaintiff's failure to accept defendant's tendered substitute employment could not be applied in mitigation of damages because to offer of the "Big

Country" lead was of employment both different and inferior, and that no factual dispute was presented on that issue. The mere circumstance that "Bloomer Girl" was to be a musical review calling upon plaintiff's talents as a dancer as well as an actress, and was to be produced in the City of Los Angeles, whereas "Big Country" was a straight dramatic role in a "Western Type" story taking place in an opal mine in Australia, demonstrates the difference in kind between the two employments. . . .

Additionally, the substitute "Big Country" offer proposed to eliminate or impair the director and screenplay approvals accorded to plaintiff in the original "Bloomer Girl" contract . . . and thus constituted an offer of inferior employment.

Questions

1. What if Ms. Parker had been offered the lead in a musical western filmed in a small cow town on the American plains?

2. Can you formulate a test for what is comparable employment?

Liquidated Damages

When the parties agree in advance as to the amount of damages to be recovered in the event of a breach, called **liquidated damages,** a court generally will enforce the agreement rather than determining the amount itself. This approach is favored under appropriate circumstances since it carries out the will of the parties. However, for a liquidation agreement to be enforced it must appear to the court that (1) the actual damages are uncertain in amount or difficult to prove and (2) the agreed-upon (liquidated) damages bear some reasonable relationship to the actual damages and, therefore, would not constitute a penalty. Of the two requirements, the courts apply the second more strictly, the purpose of a civil remedy ordinarily being compensation, not punishment (punitive damage cases excepted).

Nominal Damages

Nominal damages are damages "in name only." They are awarded in cases in which the court finds that a breach has occurred, but the complaining party has suffered no real economic loss. Nominal damages are granted only to vindicate the claimant's right. The amount is typically $1 or some other insignificant sum.

Costs and Attorney Fees

Costs of the proceedings, including filing fees and fees for any witnesses and jurors, may be awarded if the court feels it is in keeping with justice. Although they normally are awarded to the successful party, either plaintiff or defendant, they may be awarded to the loser in cases in which the court feels it was required by law to find for one party though its sympathies were with the other. They also may be divided evenly between the parties when it is felt that the equities lie with neither.

Attorney fees normally are not awarded, which means that the costs awarded are but a small fraction of the actual costs of litigation. Each party must pay his or her own attorney. However, attorney fees may be granted in the court's discretion in a limited number of cases, and may be provided for by statute or by agreement of the parties. Clauses calling for reasonable attorney fees and costs of collection on default are common in commercial promissory notes.

EQUITABLE REMEDIES

Although the usual common-law remedy of money damages is adequate to satisfy most problems arising out of contract performance, this is

not true in all situations. Sometimes fairness requires that courts provide other, less common remedies. Collectively, these fall into a category called equitable remedies.

Specific Performance

The most common of the equitable remedies in contract law is specific performance, which requires that the breaching party perform as promised. This seems to be a highly desirable remedy since it most effectively conforms to the expectations of the parties, but it is granted relatively infrequently because it is considered extraordinary in nature. That is, it is to be granted only when the remedy at law (money damages) is inadequate and it is necessary in order to avoid an injustice.

Contracts for the sale of goods rarely merit specific performance because goods comparable to those promised are usually available on the open market and/or the purchaser normally is not in urgent need of the goods. This rule would not pertain, however, in cases involving heirlooms, works of art, and other one-of-a-kind goods.

Contracts for the sale of land almost always are considered to justify specific performance. This is probably due mostly to tradition because of the unique value of land and its meaning as a symbol of wealth and power during feudal times in England. Also, it is felt that each parcel of land is unique (one of a kind), and amenity values may vary widely among parcels in the eyes of a particular purchaser.

Usually, employment contracts will not be specifically enforced. To order specific performance would smack of slavery. Also, there is considerable question as to how satisfactorily an employee would perform if forced to work for another. The relationship of employment generally is considered highly personal. Finally, courts usually are unwilling to order specific performance in situations that would require a constant monitoring to ensure continued compliance. However, the courts normally are quite willing to enforce clauses prohibiting an employee from working for a competitor within a reasonable time and within reasonable geographic limits. Also, more and more courts are finding circumstances that justify ordering an employer to hire a person wrongfully denied employment, or to rehire a person wrongfully discharged. Both especially have been common when it has been necessary to remedy a civil rights violation. The following case illustrates the general problems concerning specific enforcement of employment contracts.

FELCH v. FINDLAY COLLEGE
119 Ohio App. 357, 200 N.E.2d 353 (1964)

This was an action by William E. Felch (Plaintiff/Appellant) against Findlay College (Defendant/Appellee) for specific performance of a contract of employment. Plaintiff contended that he was a faculty member on "continuing" appointment, and was discharged in violation of required procedures for dismissal. The trial court found for Defendant and Plaintiff appealed. Affirmed.

GURNSEY, Judge.

In 81 C.J.S. Specific Performance Section 82, p. 591, the rule is stated as follows:

> In general, specific performance does not lie to enforce a provision in a contract for the performance of personal services requiring special knowledge, ability, experience, or the exercise of judgment, skill, taste, discretion, labor, tact, energy, or *particularly where the performance of such services would be continuous over a long period of time*. This rule is based

on the fact that mischief likely to result from an enforced continuance of the relationship incident to the service after it has become personally obnoxious to one of the parties is so great that the interests of society require that the remedy be denied, and on the fact that the enforcement of a decree requiring the performance of such a contract would impose too great a burden on the courts. . . .

On the other hand, where services have an unique and peculiar value, specific performance has been awarded under some circumstances. . . . (Emphasis added.)

Assuming plaintiff's claim of continuing contract status, the services to be performed would "be continuous over a long period of time" and although his services might once have had a unique and peculiar value they no longer have any value as far as the defendant is concerned. Moreover, the rule of uniqueness is applicable to an action to require specific performance of a contract by an employee who refuses to perform personal services and not applicable to an action to require specific performance by the employer.

Questions

1. Does this decision mean that the plaintiff has no remedy?

2. Does the rule against specific performance in employment cases make any sense when the employer is a giant company?

Rescission and Restitution

When a contract is breached, an innocent aggrieved party usually is entitled to rescission. This is particularly true when the claimant has entered into a contract because of misrepresentation, fraud, duress, or undue influence, or when the claimant lacked the required contractual capacity. **Rescission** simply is cancellation of the contract.

Whenever rescission is granted, the parties become obligated to make **restitution** to each other. Each must return what he or she has received. If restitution *in specie* (the goods themselves) is not possible, as when goods have been consumed or sold to a good-faith purchaser, restitution must be made by payment of the reasonable value of the goods.

Reformation

Reformation is a remedy available in cases in which the understanding of the parties is not reflected accurately by the writing they have drafted to memorialize, or to embody, their agreement. Clerical errors are the most frequent subjects of reformation. For example, suppose Bach agrees to purchase Bartok's home and, in the writing, the parcel is described as "Lot *36* in the Miller Addition to the City of Springfield, Maine" but Bartok's home is located on Lot *35* in that addition. The court, on the application of either party, would reform the writing to reflect the correct lot number.

Because of the restrictions of the Parol Evidence Rule, a writing may be reformed only to correct a *patent* (very obvious) error or to supply a *patent* omission, unless both parties agree. Also, under Section 2–302 of the UCC, the power to reform is implicit in the power of a court to enforce an unconscionable contract for the sale of goods in a way that avoids an unconscionable result.

NON-CONTRACT REMEDIES

In the interest of fairness, courts sometimes enforce promises that are not truly contractual. They

also may create obligations not founded on traditional contract or tort theory. In doing so they reinforce the notion that for every wrong there should be a remedy.

Promissory Estoppel

In situations in which no contract exists, but the court feels that one who has made a promise should be bound to perform anyway, equity can enforce the promise. This is an intermediate step leading to a remedy, which may be either specific performance or damages. In order to establish this cause of action the circumstances must meet certain requirements. Promissory estoppel is discussed more fully in Chapter 6.

Quasi Contract

Although not technically an equitable remedy, quasi contract is a cause of action brought to the common law from the civil law and proceeds according to equity principles. It allows recovery of the reasonable value of benefits conferred in situations in which no contract exists, but justice requires that the person receiving the benefits should be required to pay for them. Quasi contract also is discussed more fully in Chapter 6.

SUMMARY

A condition is any fact or event, other than the passage of time, that qualifies (limits) a promisor's present duty of performance. Conditions precedent give rise to a duty and conditions subsequent terminate a duty. Conditions may be created expressly or impliedly, or may be construed into a contract by law. Conditions of all kinds may be part of a valid contract, but if a promisor's duty is dependent on a condition that he or she can control, his or her obligation to that extent is illusory.

Performance of an obligation is the object of every contract. It serves to discharge the promisor and to give rise to a duty of performance by the other party if it is complete or satisfactory. Performance to a lesser degree constitutes a breach.

The effect of the breach depends on its seriousness. If it is not substantial, the other party may reduce his or her promised performance by the amount by which the less-than-complete, but substantial, performance reduced the value below that of complete performance. Performance that is so defective as to be rendered substantially worthless constitutes a material breach and discharges the other party of his or her entire obligation, although he or she still may have an obligation of restitution, or be liable in quasi contract for any benefits he or she has received. If time is of the essence in the performance of a particular contract, failure to perform on time may constitute a material breach. But if a promisor is prevented from performing by the wrongful act of the promisee, the promisor is discharged.

If performance of a promise becomes impossible through no fault of either party, both are discharged, although some obligation of restitution or quasi contract still may exist. Impossibility may result from the illness, death, or incompetence of one of the parties, or from intervening illegality or destruction of the subject matter. A growing number of courts hold that if unforseen circumstances render performance substantially more burdensome than anticipated by the parties, this "commercial frustration" may result in discharge.

Discharge may be total or partial. It may occur by agreement, by wrongdoing of one of the parties, or by operation of law as in the case of a claim that is barred by the running of a statute of limitations, or by bankruptcy proceedings. These, of course, are in addition to discharge by performance or by breach.

Remedies available to an aggrieved party may be at law for money damages, or may be in equity for specific performance or some other nonmonetary relief such as rescission, restitution, or reformation. In addition, some noncontractual remedies may be available by a cause of action in promissory estoppel or quasi contract. Equitable remedies are granted only when money damages would be inadequate, and then only if necessary to prevent a substantial injustice.

KEY TERMS AND CONCEPTS

condition
condition precedent
condition subsequent
conditions concurrent
aleatory promise
tender of performance
complete and satisfactory performance
substantial performance
material breach
anticipatory breach
time is of the essence
commercial frustration
discharge
laches
specific performance
attachment
execution
garnishment
compensatory damages
consequential (special) damages
punitive (exemplary) damages
incidental damages
mitigation of damages
liquidated damages
nominal damages
rescission
restitution
reformation

PROBLEMS

1. CMS&P operated a railroad. Under its certificate, the federal government required it to service certain railroad lines. In order to do so, it rented terminal facilities from Chicago & Northwestern Transportation Co. After operating for some time, CMS&P joined the Amtrack system. As a result, it no longer was required to service the additional lines. Therefore, CMS&P sought to terminate its lease with Chicago & Northwestern on the ground of commerical frustration. Is CMS&P's position correct?

2. Friedman contracted to move certain large stones from the east bank of the White River across to the west bank. It was agreed that the work was to be done during the months of December and January so the stones could be taken across the river on ice skids. The work was to be completed by January 31. Because of a mild winter, the ice on the river never did become sufficiently thick to allow the work to be done. Friedman was sued for breach of contract. Should the plaintiff succeed?

3. Carnera, a professional prize fighter, agreed to participate in a prize-fighting tournament promoted by Madison Square Garden Corp. He was to fight the winner of a particular elimination contest. As part of the contract, he also agreed not to fight any of the other tournament participants before this fight. Thereafter, he signed an agreement to fight one of the other contenders. Madison Square Garden sought an injunction to enforce its contract with Carnera, who defended on the ground that an injunction would not be proper because his was a contract for personal services. Is Carnera correct?

4. Milstead agreed to do certain earth moving and grading on a site to be used in the construction of a new drive-in theater. Problems developed, and construction was delayed through the fault of Milstead. Evergreen Amusement Corp., for whom the grading was to be done, sued Milstead for damages caused by the delay. Evergreen contended that the proper measure of damages was the lost profits during the delay, which it calculated at $12,500. Milstead contended the proper measure was the reasonable rental value of the property during the period, which was $4500. Which is correct?

5. Jean Vincent, Inc., a real-estate broker, sued Chef Joe's, Inc. for an agreed-upon commission under a real-estate listing contract. The contract provided that if the property was sold during the listing period, the commission was to be paid regardless of who made the sale. The defendant sold the property himself, and contended the provision should not be enforced because it constituted a penalty. Is the defendant correct?

6. Lawrence borrowed $24,000 from Madison, executing a promissory note calling for repayment at the rate of $500 plus 6 percent interest per month for 48 months. Lawrence made regular payments for 14 months, and then made no payments during the next two months. Madison sued for the unpaid balance ($17,000). Is Madison entitled to a judgment?

7. The Terrys owned and operated an Arco service station under contract with Atlantic Richfield Co. Under the terms of the contract, Atlantic Richfield was obligated to supply their needs for gasoline, oil, and other petroleum products. During the "Arab oil embargo," Atlantic Richfield was unable to secure enough oil to meet all of its obligations. Therefore, it determined to allocate available supplies to its customers on a ration based on the previous year's sales. The Terrys objected on the ground that their station had been closed during part of the previous year due to a leak in its tanks and other maintenance problems. Should the Terrys prevail?

8. Johnson was hired as a bus driver by the Wallowa County School District. The contract provided that her contract would continue as long as she rendered "satisfactory service." Although she performed her job reasonably, she was discharged. Johnson sued and the school district defended on the ground that it was not personally satisfied with Johnson's service. Is Johnson entitled to a judgment?

9. Cartozian contracted with Ostruske to supply carpeting for an apartment house Ostruske was constucting. Cartozian was to supply the carpeting by July 1. On July 1, Ostruske called and cancelled the contract for nonperformance. Thereafter, Ostruske was able to contract for other carpeting to be delivered no sooner than September 1. Cartozian sued for breach of the agreement. Is Cartozian entitled to a judgment?

10. Marshall and Nolan entered into a contract under which Marshall was to purchase a factory building and its equipment, operated as a bottling business, along with a Coca-Cola franchise. It also was agreed that Marshall would employ Nolan or one of his sons as a consultant for six years. Nolan later refused to perform, and Marshall sued asking for specific performance of the contract. Is this a proper case for the granting of specific performance?

PART III

Sales and the Uniform Commercial Code

The preceding seven chapters discussed contracts under the common law, and some reference was made to sales contracts under the Uniform Commercial Code. The following four chapters address sales contracts under Article 2 of the Code, building on the common law principles. Chapter 13 provides an overall introduction to the relationship of the Code to contracts. Chapter 14 discusses the formation of sales contracts and the relative positions of the parties with respect to the passing of title and risk of loss. Chapter 15 then addresses the questions of performance, including what constitutes breach of obligation, and the remedies the Code provides for breach. Finally, Chapter 16 is devoted to sales warranties and the broader question of liability of a seller for faulty products.

Introduction to Sales

CONTRACT LAW AND THE UNIFORM COMMERCIAL CODE

The most common type of contract today is a contract for the purchase and sale of goods. In addition to its effect in commercial transactions, the law governing sales transactions touches our personal lives daily—or almost daily—and comes into play whenever we purchase groceries, clothing, and a myriad of other basic consumer items or larger goods such as furniture, appliances, and automobiles. In addition, the law of sales can be important long after an actual sales transaction because it controls, to a large extent, the rights and liabilities of the purchaser and the seller during the useful life of the goods.

Early English contract law was designed to meet the needs of an agricultural economy, and accordingly paid particular attention to transactions affecting land but very little to other types of sales. Later, as a new mercantile economy arose, traditional land-based contract law became increasingly inadequate to meet society's needs. As a result, merchants developed an entirely separate body of commercial law, including contract law. This body of law, called the "Law Merchant," was administered by a separate court system, established by merchants who voluntarily submitted to the jurisdiction of merchants' courts to settle disputes among themselves.

As commerce became more established, the Law Merchant was tried and tested in the merchants' courts. Eventually it became apparent that its principles should be applied by the general courts of England as well, and the Law Merchant was adopted by the common law, and the merchants' court system disappeared.

In 1853, the common law of sales in this country was codified as the Sales of Goods Act. This act served as the basis for the Uniform Sales Act, drafted by the National Conference of Commissioners on Uniform State Laws in the early 1900s, which eventually was adopted in more than thirty states. In 1932, the Commissioners modernized the Uniform Sales Act and incorporated it into the first draft of the Uniform Commercial Code, in which—as Article 2—it has remained to the present day. The Uniform Commercial Code has been revised periodically, most notably in 1964 and 1978. To date, the UCC has been adopted in every state except Louisiana, which has adopted only parts of the Code and has not adopted Article 2.

In studying contracts for the sale of goods, remember that the general common law of contracts governs an issue unless UCC Article 2 speaks to the point under consideration. Therefore, you should familiarize yourself with the material contained in Chapters 6 through 12 before proceeding with the chapters in this part of the book. In analyzing any given case, you should first ask whether the common law of contracts or the UCC governs, and next ask how the substantive issues should be resolved under the applicable law. In accomplishing this you may find it convenient to look first at the common law, and then treat any applicable sections of the UCC as exceptions to the common law.

Reading and understanding the UCC can be difficult. Code sections tend to be written very concisely, and the meaning of a section may be missed entirely unless each word is examined closely. Therefore, you should read through the applicable section or part of a section first in order to obtain a general idea of what the provision says. It may be necessary to read it a second time to get the sense of it if the section is particularly complicated. The next reading should be word-by-word, and you should stop to look up the definition of any words that might be "terms of art," that is, words that have special legal meanings. Definitions of UCC terms can be found either in Article 1, if the term is used throughout the Code, or in the first part of Article 2 (sections numbered 2–1 . . . , such as 2–103 and 2–104) if the term is peculiar to the law of sales. If not defined in the UCC, then that term should be given its "plain meaning" according either to legal or common usage, depending on its context. Finally, it often is necessary to read the material one last time to bring everything together.

SCOPE OF ARTICLE 2

The provisions of Article 2 of the UCC are intended to apply only to contracts for the sale of goods. Some sections, or parts of sections, apply only to merchants, and so state. Otherwise, Article 2 applies to merchants and nonmerchants alike.

"Goods" Defined

Article 2 of the UCC governs only contracts for the sale of "goods." In common usage, the term *goods* is equivalent to "personal property." However, Section 2–105 defines **goods** more precisely as including all personal property *except* (1) money (other than money that actually is purchased because it has some special value beyond its value as a medium of exchange); (2) investment securities (these are treated specially under Article 8); and (3) choses in action, which are intangible obligations, such as accounts receivable. Section 2–107 then adds some real property (as opposed to personal property)—such as growing crops and timber—to the definition of *goods* if those things are to be severed by the seller and sold separate from the land.

Section 2–105. Definitions: Transferability; "Goods"; "Future" Goods; "Lot"; "Commercial Unit."

(1) "Goods" means all things (including specially manufactured goods) which are movable at the time of identification to the contract for sale other than the money in which the price is to be paid, investment securities (Article 8) and things in action. "Goods" also includes the unborn young of animals and growing crops and other identified things attached to realty as described in the section on goods to be severed from realty (Section 2–107).

Section 2–107. Goods to be Severed from Realty; Recording.

(1) A contract for the sale of minerals or the like (including oil and gas) or a structure or its materials to be removed from realty is a contract for the sale of goods within this Article if they are to be severed by the seller but until severance a purported present sale thereof which is not effective as a transfer of an interest in land is effective only as a contract to sell.

(2) A contract for the sale apart from the land of growing crops or other things attached to realty and capable of severance without material harm thereto but not described in subsection (1) or of timber to be cut is a contract for the sale of goods within this Article whether the subject matter is to be severed by the buyer or by the seller even though it forms part of the realty at the time of contracting, and the parties can by identification effect a present sale before severance.

Thus, Article 2 of the Code governs most kinds of personal-property contracts, but does not affect contracts for the sale of services or most sales of

Applications of Article 2 of the Uniform Commercial Code

The Uniform Commercial Code normally governs contracts when:

tangible and portable goods (not services or paper securities alone) are bought and sold
the seller is a merchant, or a merchant is used as a "middleman"

The Uniform Commercial Code may not apply to a contract if:

neither the buyer nor the seller is a merchant

The Uniform Commercial Code seldom applies to any contract if:

services or securities alone are bought and sold
real estate is transferred
transactions primarily involve gifts, choses in action (e.g., accounts receivable), or bailments

real estate. However, sometimes it is difficult to be certain whether a particular contract is to be covered under Article 2 as one for the sale of goods. For example, in cases involving the purchase of services, goods sometimes are involved as a part of rendering the service. Does that make the total contract one for the sale of goods? Consider the following case.

ELLIBEE v. DYE
15 UCC Rep. 361 (Pa. Ct. of Common Pleas, 1973)

This was an action by Plaintiff Ellibee for injuries suffered as a result of a "French Perm" applied by an employee of Defendant's beauty parlor. Shortly after the treatment Plaintiff's hair began to fall out as it was being washed by Defendant's employee. Plaintiff alleged that the perm solution was defective, and her complaint contained five counts. Pertinent here is the fourth count—Plaintiff's claim based on Defendant's breach of an implied warranty of fitness for the particular purpose for which the product was intended. Defendant contended that the theory of implied warranty should not apply because the case involved the sale of a service rather than the sale of goods within the meaning of Article 2. Defendant, therefore, demurred (moved to dismiss for failure to state a cause of action) to the complaint. The court denied the demurrer in its entirety.

ACKER, J.

The starting point is Hoffman v. Misericordia Hospital of Philadelphia, . . . (1970). Indeed, Hoffman could be dispositive of this case. There, also, a demurrer was filed to a complaint in an assumpsit [contract] action claiming breach of implied warranty of merchantability and/or fitness for a particular purpose. The action was for death caused by a transfusion of blood containing hepatitis virus. The claim was that there was no sale. The lower court sustained the demurrer. This was reversed on appeal and remanded with appropriate language applicable to the case at bar, at page 507:

> We therefore do not feel obligated to hinge any resolution of the very important issue here raised on the technical existence of a sale. In this respect, we agree with the following statement made by a court of a sister state: 'It seems to us a distortion to take what is, at least arguably, a sale, twist it into the shape of a service, and then employ this transformed material in erecting the framework of a major policy decision.': Russel v. Community Blood Bank, Inc., 185 So.2d 749, 752 (Fla Ct App 1966). In view of our case law implying warranties in non-sales transactions, it cannot be said with certainty that no recovery is permissible with the claim here made, even if it should ultimately be determined that the transfer of blood from hospital for transfusion into a patient is a service.

By footnote 11, page 507, the court quotes Comment 2 to Section 2–313 of the Uniform Commerical Code to the effect that the warranty section was not designed in any way to disturb that line of case law growth which has recognized that warranties need not be confined either to sale or contract or to the direct parties to such contract. . . .

California has recognized that an implied warranty may be found even though the contract is for labor and materials rather than a sale: Aced v. Hobbs-Sesack Plumbing Co. . . . There, the court concluded that the contract was one for labor and materials but that, nevertheless, there may be an implied warranty.

Although there is a conflict in jurisdictions as to whether the furnishing of materials by a beautician constitutes a sale, a well-reasoned opinion holding a sale is Newmark v. Gimbel's, Inc. . . .

There, plaintiff, at defendant's establishment, secured a permanent wave, the type being at the suggestion of defendant's representative. Certain injuries were alleged to have resulted. The lower court had concluded that it was merely a transaction between parties amounting to a rendition of services rather than the sale of a product. The appellate court reversed concluding that there was no good reason for restricting warranties to sales. Where one person supplies a product to another, whether or not the transaction be technically considered a sale, warranties should be applicable. The court stated, *Newmark v. Gimbel's, Inc.,* supra, at page 15:

> Weighing the foregoing policy considerations, we are satisfied and hold that, stripped of its nonessentials, the transaction here in question, consisting of the supplying of a product for use in the administration of a permanent wave to plaintiff, carried with it an implied warranty that the product used was reasonably fit for the purpose for which it was to be used.

The policy reasons were that the risk from use of the lotion was incident to the operation of defendant's business. A business which yielded it a profit and placed it in a position to promote safety through pressure on suppliers. [*sic*] Defendant was in a position to protect itself by making inquiry or to test to determine the susceptibility of customers to the use of the product by using another lotion which did not present the possibilities of an adverse effect. The fact that there was no separate charge for the product did not preclude it being considered as having been supplied to the customer in a sense justifying the imposition of the implied warranty against injurious defects. Perlmutter v. Beth David Hospital case, supra, used by defendant in the case at bar, was likewise cited and distinguished on policy reasons in favor of hospitals.

The trend in Pennsylvania law has been to extend warranties in new directions and for situations previously denied. . . .

This court is of the opinion that accepting the facts of plaintiff as true, as it is required to do at this posture of the case, the supplying of the product was a vital part of the performance of the service. Without the product, the service could not have been successfully accomplished. This was contemplated by all parties. The cost of the service must necessarily have included the cost of the product. If a supplier of a product over the counter would be liable to plaintiff under either a Restatement or warranty theory, certainly in logic and reason a beauty shop operator, who has the opportunity to examine the product as it is being applied and to be assured that it is properly applied, should be held responsible if the product is defective. Plaintiffs in the case at bar must be given the opportunity to prove their case. They may do so under a theory of absolute liability, breach of warranty or negligence or all three or a combination thereof at the trial.

Wherefore, the demurrer of defendant is denied.

Questions

1. Does the result in this case indicate that the use of any product in connection with providing a service means that there has been a sale of goods contract? Is very much left of the distinction between contracts involving goods and those involving services if this is true?

2. Do you think the time has come for the UCC to be extended to service contracts as well as to those involving sales of goods?

Types of Transactions Under Article 2

Section 2–102 provides that Article 2 applies to all "transactions in goods" with some stated exceptions. However, the term *transaction* is not defined in the UCC, either in Article 1 or Part 1 of Article 2. The courts, therefore, have some latitude to interpret Article 2 as applying to some types of transactions other than mere sales. The courts generally have refrained from exercising this apparent power broadly. However, they have concluded that Article 2 warranties may run in favor of persons injured by goods even if they did not purchase the goods themselves, and that Article 2 applies equally to a **present sale** (present transfer of title) of goods and to a contract to sell goods in the future. In contrast to its ambiguity concerning the meaning of *transaction,* the UCC defines the term *sale* clearly: a sale is a transaction by which the title to specified goods passes from a seller to a buyer. The rules concerning the point at which title actually passes are discussed in considerable detail in the next chapter.

Article 2 specifically excluded from coverage "any transaction which . . . is intended to operate only as a security transaction." Thus, Article 2 excludes pledges and "chattel mortgages," which means all mortgages on personal property. The Code does not exclude conditional sales contracts, however, if title passes to the buyer, even though the seller retains a security interest in the goods. Section 2–102 also specifies that Article 2 does not supersede any other state statute regulating sales of goods to special classes of buyers such as consumers or farmers. Additional transactions excluded from coverage under Article 2 are those involving gifts, leases, and bailments, because those transactions do not involve the transfer of title to goods in return for consideration.

Whether Article 2 applies to transactions involving a sale of a mixture of goods and non-goods is a matter for the courts to decide case by case. This does not mean that courts are inconsistent in their holdings, but rather that the unique features of each transaction must be considered.

POLICY ELEMENTS OF ARTICLE 2

Article 2 of the UCC implements a new policy concerning contracts for the sale of goods. In many situations, it departs from the strict application of common law rules. Also, it directs judicial decisions toward a goal of fairness much more than did the common law, and expands the power of the courts to deal with unfairness.

Equity

In drafting Article 2, the Commissioners on Uniform State Laws were concerned about the harsh inequity of some of the strict common law rules relating to sales. The Commissioners therefore adopted a number of modifications of the common law that previously had been applied, for the most part, only in courts of equity. The Code's common-sense treatment of counteroffers under Section 2–207(1), and its enforcement under Sections 2–205 and 2–209(1) of promises not supported by consideration (discussed in Chapter 14), are important instances. Moreover, the Commissioners' concern for fairness is illustrated dramatically by the fact that the terms *reasonable* and *unreasonable,* and variations of these terms, appear in Article 2 some 96 times.

Merchants

Students often are confused about whether the rules in Article 2 apply only to merchants or to nonmerchants as well. The answer is that Article 2 applies to everyone, not just to merchants, unless the particular section under consideration states to the contrary. For example, Section 2–207(1) begins by stating that "[a] definite and seasonable expression of acceptance . . . will operate as an acceptance . . . and therefore applies to laypersons and merchants alike." Section 2–205, however, refers specifically to "[a]n offer by a merchant" and therefore applies more restrictively. Moreover, some Code sections apply only when both parties to the transaction are merchants. Although Section 2–205 as just quoted requires that the offeror be a merchant, Section 2–207(2), beginning with the second sentence, applies only "between merchants." Thus, Article 2 applies to merchant and nonmerchant alike except when, as often happens, the Code section explicitly limits its scope.

The purpose of making a section of Article 2 applicable only to merchants usually is to place a higher duty on merchants than on ordinary individuals. In part this is because the roots of Article 2 are in the Law Merchant which, from its very beginning, concerned dealings among merchants. More important, perhaps, is the fact that the law considers merchants to be, to some extent, experts in their own fields. Therefore, merchants probably need the special protections of the Code less than lay consumers, especially when fairness and utility can be achieved best by a relaxation of some of the common law's harsh rules.

Section 2–104(1) defines **merchant** as:

a person who deals in goods of the kind or otherwise by his occupation holds himself out as having knowledge or skill peculiar to the practices or goods involved in the transaction or to whom such knowledge or skill may be attributed by his employment of an agent or broker or other

intermediary who by his occupation holds himself out as having such knowledge or skill.

Thus, one may be a merchant because his or her business involves dealing in goods, but also may be considered a merchant because he or she has regular dealings with goods as an avocation or hobby, such as a stamp or coin collector. In addition, one who sells goods through a merchant, such as a new-car buyer who sells an old car through a used-car lot, also is classified as a merchant.

Whether a person is a merchant can be important in the application of many sections of Article 2. As the following case illustrates, however, determining whether someone is a merchant can be difficult.

LOEB AND COMPANY, INC. v. SCHREINER
294 Ala. 722, 321 So. 199 (1975)

Loeb and Company, Inc. (Plaintiff/Appellant) engaged in the marketing of raw cotton. Plaintiff alleged that it and Charles Schreiner (Defendant/Appellee) entered into an oral contract under the terms of which Defendant, a farmer who had grown cotton and other crops during the previous ten years, agreed to sell cotton to Plaintiff for a price in excess of $500. Plaintiff sent a written confirmation to Defendant; Defendant did not reply. In the meantime, the market price of cotton rose from approximately $0.37 to approximately $0.85, and Defendant refused to perform. At trial, Defendant asserted the Statute of Frauds in the UCC as a defense.

The trial court found for Defendant, and Plaintiff appealed. Affirmed.

ALMON, Justice.

Tit. 7A, Section 2–201 . . . sets out the statute of frauds for Article 2 of the Uniform Commercial Code. It governs all contracts for the sale of "goods." Cotton is included within the definition of "goods" as defined by the Code. . . . Section 2–201 provides in pertinent part as follows:

Except as otherwise provided in this section a contract for the sale of goods for the price of $500 or more is not enforceable by way of action or defense unless there is some writing sufficient to indicate that a contract for sale has been made between the parties and signed by the party against whom enforcement is sought or by his authorized agent or broker. A writing is not insufficient because it omits or incorrectly states a term agreed upon but the contract is not enforceable under this paragraph beyond the quantity of goods shown in such writing.

(2) *Between merchants* if within a reasonable time a writing in confirmation of the contract and sufficient against the sender is received and the party receiving it has reason to know its contents, it satisfies the requirements of subsection (1) against such party unless written notice of objection to its contents is given within ten days after it is received. (Emphasis added.)

Appellant contends that the trial court erred in finding that the appellee cotton farmer was not a merchant and that Section 2–201 would act as a bar to the enforcement of the contract in question. However, if appellee is a "merchant," he would be liable on the contract because he did not within ten days give notice of objection to appellant's confirming statement. Tit. 7A, Section 2–104(1) defines "merchant" as follows:

(1) 'Merchant' means a person who deals in goods of the kind or otherwise by the occupation holds himself out as having knowledge or skill peculiar to the practices or goods involved in the transaction or to whom such knowledge or skill may be attributed by his employment of an agent or broker or other intermediary who by his occupation holds himself out as having such knowledge or skill.

Only a few courts have considered the question of whether a farmer is a "merchant." In Cook Grains v. Fallis . . . the Arkansas Supreme Court held that a soybean farmer was not a merchant when he was merely trying to sell the commodities he had raised. . . .

In Oloffson v. Coomer, . . . the Third Division of the Appellate Court of Illinois stated in dictum that a farmer in the business of growing grain was not a "merchant" with respect to the merchandising of grain. However, in Campbell v. Yokel, . . . the Fifth District of the Appellate Court of Illinois dealt with a case that involved an action against some soybean farmers on an alleged breach of an oral contract for the sale of soybeans. The court held that the soybean farmers, who had grown and sold soybeans for several years were "merchants" when selling crops and were therefore barred by Section 2–201(2) from asserting the statute of frauds as a defense.

One court has suggested that whether or not a farmer is a "merchant" within the meaning of Section 2–104 should turn upon whether or not he has engaged in a particular type of sale in the past. In Fear Ranches, Inc. v. Berry, . . . a breach of warranty case, the court held that where the defendant cattle farmers made a sale to a non-meatpacker for resale when they had previously sold all of their cattle to meat-packers, they were not "merchants" with respect to the sale to the non-meatpacker. The court felt that the sale of cattle for resale was a sale of a different type of goods and made up a different type of business than the sale of cattle to meat-packers.

We hold that in the instant case the appellee was not a "merchant" within the meaning of Section 2–104. We do not think the framers of the Uniform Commercial Code contemplated that a farmer should be included among those considered to be "merchants."

In order for a farmer to be included within the Section 2–104 definition of "merchants," he must do one of the following:

1. deal in goods of the kind;
2. by his occupation hold himself out as having knowledge or skill peculiar to the practices or goods involved in the transaction; or

3. employ an agent or broker or other intermediary who by his occupation holds himself out as having such knowledge or skill.

Since the farmer in the instant case did not qualify as a merchant under 3 above, he would have to qualify under 1 or 2. It is not sufficient under 2 that one hold himself out as having knowledge or skill peculiar to the practices or goods involved, he must by his occupation so hold himself out. Accordingly, a person cannot be considered a "merchant" simply because he is a braggart or has a high opinion of his knowledge in a particular area. We conclude that a farmer does not solely by his occupation hold himself out as being a professional cotton merchant.

The remaining thing which a farmer might do to be considered a merchant is to become a dealer in goods. Although there was evidence which indicated that the appellee here had a good deal of knowledge, this is not the test. There is not one shred of evidence that appellee ever sold anyone's cotton but his own. He was nothing more than an astute farmer selling his own product. We do not think this was sufficient to make him a dealer in goods.

Questions

1. Do you agree with the court's result? Why or why not?

2. Is it fair to let the defendant out of his obligation to perform the contract just because he is not a "dealer" in the goods? Do you think this decision merely reflects the court's desire to protect farmers?

Good Faith

Section 1-201(19) defines **good faith** as "honesty in fact in the conduct or transaction involved." Section 1-203 then imposes an overriding obligation of good faith on "every duty" arising under the Uniform Commercial Code, including Article 2. Although the Code's definition of good faith does not set forth precise limits on conduct, its intent is clear. It allows the courts to look at all of the facts involved in a given transaction and to determine, in their discretion, whether the parties' conduct was fair and appropriate. It also requires the parties to act fairly when the general circumstances would lead a reasonably prudent and honest person to question the propriety of a transaction. In addition to the obligation of good faith, Section 2-103(b) imposes the requirement that merchants observe "reasonable standards of fair dealing in the trade."

Unconscionable Contracts

Section 2-302 empowers courts to deal almost as they see fit with contracts containing provisions they consider unconscionable. This section is one of the most controversial in the entire UCC, although criticism of its provisions seems to have decreased steadily since the Code first was adopted. There is no doubt that Section 2-302 creates an important exception to the basic principle of freedom of contract, but the extent of this limitation is not clear. In part this is because the term *unconscionable* is not defined in the Code.

Decisions of law courts prior to the UCC provide no clear guidance in determining the extent of the courts' power under Section 2-302. The common law had no well-defined rules to police the imposition of outrageous provisions in a contract. These terms ordinarily came about as a result of some disparity in bargaining power between the contracting parties. They were up-held because the common law typically regarded power as a legitimate property right to be exercised by its possessor for his or her own benefit. Further, the courts resisted substituting their own values for those of the parties to the contract except under compelling considerations of public policy.

The equity courts, however, traditionally adopted a different approach. They focused on ensuring that transactions were "fair," and accordingly their decisions can provide some guidance as to the meaning of Section 2–302. Consider, for example, the following equity case, and compare it with the decision in *Williams v. Walker-Thomas Furniture Co.*, which appears in Chapter 10.

CAMPBELL SOUP CO. v. WENTZ et al.
172 F.2d 80 (3d Cir. 1949)

This was an action by Campbell Soup Co. (Plaintiff/Appellant) against George B. Wentz and another (Defendants/Appellees) for specific performance of a contract to sell carrots. Wentz sold 62 tons of carrots to Walter M. Lojeski in violation of his contract with Plaintiff. Other pertinent facts are set forth in the opinion.

The trial court found for Defendants, denying equitable relief on the ground that the contract did not concern a unique subject matter and that, therefore, Plaintiff's remedy at law for damages was adequate. The Court of Appeals for the Third Circuit affirmed, but for different reasons.

GOODRICH, Circuit Judge.

[The court first discussed the uniqueness of the contract's subject matter and determined, contrary to the trial court, that it might justify an award of specific performance.] The reason that we shall affirm instead of reversing with an order for specific performance is found in the contract itself. We think it is too hard a bargain and too one-sided an agreement to entitle the plaintiff to relief in a court of conscience. For each individual grower the agreement is made by filling in names and quantity and price on a printed form furnished by the buyer. This form has quite obviously been drawn by skillful draftsmen with the buyer's interests in mind.

Paragraph 2 provides for the manner of delivery. Carrots are to have their stalks cut off and be in clean sanitary bags or other containers approved by Campbell. This paragraph concludes with a statement that Campbell's determination of conformance with specifications shall be conclusive.

The defendants attack this provision as unconscionable. We do not think that it is, standing by itself. We think that the provision is comparable to the promise to perform to the satisfaction of another and that Campbell would be held liable if it refused carrots which did in fact conform to the specifications.

The next paragraph allows Campbell to refuse carrots in excess of twelve tons to the acre. The next contains a covenant by the grower that he will not sell carrots to anyone else except the carrots rejected by Campbell nor will he permit anyone else to grow carrots on his land. Paragraph 10 provides liquidated damages to the extent of $50 per acre for any breach by the grower. There is no provision for liquidated or any other damages for breach of the contract by Campbell.

The provision of the contract which we think is the hardest is paragraph 9, set out in the margin. ["Grower shall not be obligated to deliver any Carrots which he is unable to harvest or deliver, nor shall Campbell be obligated to receive or pay for any Carrots which it is unable to inspect, grade, receive, handle, use or pack at or ship in processed form from its plants in Camden (1) because of any circumstance beyond the control of Grower or Campbell, as the case may be, or (2) because of any labor disturbance, work stoppage, slow-down, or strike involving any of Campbell's employees. Campbell shall not be liable for any delay in receiving Carrots due to any of the above contingencies. During period when Campbell is unable to receive Grower's Carrots, Grower may with Campbell's written consent, dispose of his Carrots elsewhere. Grower may not, however, sell or otherwise dispose of any Carrots which he is unable to deliver to Campbell."] It will be noted that Campbell is excused from accepting carrots under certain circumstances. But even under such circumstances the grower, while he cannot say Campbell is liable for failure to take the carrots, is not permitted to sell them elsewhere unless Campbell agrees. This is the kind of provision which the late Francis H. Bohlen would call "carrying a good joke too far." What the grower may do with his product under the circumstances set out is not clear. He has covenanted not to store it anywhere except on his own farm and also not sell to anybody else.

We are not suggesting that the contract is illegal. Nor are we suggesting any excuse for the grower in this case who has deliberately broken an agreement entered into with Campbell. We do think, however, that a party who has offered and succeeded in getting an agreement as tough as this one is, should not come to a chancellor and ask court help in the enforcement of its terms. That equity does not enforce unconscionable bargains is too well established to require elaborate citation.

The plaintiff argues that the provisions of the contract are separable. We agree that they are, but do not think that decisions separating out certain provisions from illegal contracts are in point here. As already said, we do not suggest that this contract is illegal. All we say is that the sum total of its provisions drives too hard a bargain for a court of conscience to assist.

Questions

1. Does this decision and UCC Section 2–302 really permit a court to "do what it wants" and simply disregard a contract's terms?

2. What is the impact of cases like this one, and of UCC Section 2–302, on the stability of contracts?

3. Can you articulate any standards a court might use in determining whether a contract is unconscionable?

Assignments

Generally, both the assignment of rights and the delegation of duties under sales contracts are allowed under Section 2–210 of the Code. These are considered normal incidents of contracts for the sale of goods. However, as under the common law, the UCC imposes some important limitations on assignment and delegation.

The right to assign or to delegate may be limited by the parties in their agreements. In particular, the delegation of duties may be prohibited if the promisee has a substantial interest in having the original promisor perform or control the acts required by the contract. Further, rights are not assignable if: (1) the assignment would affect the duty of the other party materially as it typically would, for example, under a "requirements" contract; (2) the assignment would increase the burden or risk imposed on the other party significantly, as it would if a contract providing for the free shipment of goods by truck to the promisee's warehouse was assigned to an assignee whose warehouse was located much farther from the point of shipment than the promisee's; or (3) the assignment would impair materially the other party's chance of obtaining return performance, as might happen if a sales contract providing credit terms to the buyer was assigned to a poor credit risk. In addition, as noted above, the parties may agree that rights cannot be assigned. However, a right to damages for the breach of the contract as a whole rather than a portion of it, and any right the assignor obtains by due performance of his or her entire obligation, may be assigned even contrary to such an agreement.

Interpretation of Contracts

In addition to the ordinary rules of construction, the Uniform Commercial Code explicitly recognizes "course of dealing" and "usage of trade" as tools for interpreting the intent of the parties to any contract for the sale of goods. **Course of dealing** refers to the conduct of the parties in previous transactions between them, and courts may interpret a contract in light of prior conduct when it appears to have formed the basis for an understanding between the parties. By way of contrast, **usage of trade** is any practice commonly observed in a place, vocation, or trade. Unless it appears that the parties were unaware of the practice in question, it may be employed in interpreting their contract. Although courts can use these tools in construing any contract under the Code, it is interesting that interpretation in light of trade

usage appears to be mandatory rather than permissive. This is because Section 1-205(5) provides: "An applicable usage of trade in the place where any part of performance is to occur *shall* be used in interpreting the agreement as to that part of performance." [Emphasis added.]

Technical Provisions

As described in *Loeb & Company, Inc. v. Schreiner,* earlier in this chapter, the Statute of Frauds provision of Article 2, Section 2-201, applies to contracts for the sale of goods of a price of $500 or more. This Code provision differs from the comparable provision of the Uniform Sales Act, which used "value" rather than price as its measure. In addition, subsections (2) and (3) of Section 2-201 provide four means for satisfying the statute in the absence of a signed writing. Three of these—specially manufactured goods, admission on a court record, and part payment or part delivery—apply to all Article 2 contracts. The fourth, however, provides that if the contract is *between merchants,* a written confirmation of an oral contract that is sufficient against the sender also will bind the other party unless the latter objects to the confirmation within ten days after receiving it.

Section 2-202, the Code's parol evidence provision, prohibits the introduction of evidence of prior or contemporaneous agreements offered to alter the interpretation of a final contract's terms. In other words, courts do not want to go outside the four corners of the writing under consideration. However, it is permissible to supplement the writing with evidence that explains it rather than changes it, as by introducing proof of any applicable course of dealing or usage of trade. Of course, if the court determines that the writing was not intended to be the final and complete agreement of the parties, the parol evidence rule does not apply. (The Statute of Frauds and the Parol Evidence Rule are discussed more fully in Chapter 10.)

An action for breach of an Article 2 contract must be commenced within four years from the time the breach occurred or it will be barred, even if the aggrieved party did not know of the breach. The parties may reduce this time limit to no less than one year, but they may not extend it. In the usual case in which an action is filed within the proper time and is terminated in a way that permits another action for the same breach, the normal four-year limitation period is extended by six months to enable the plaintiff to organize the bringing of a new lawsuit.

SUMMARY

The most common type of contract today is one involving "goods." Because of this, a thorough understanding of the provisions of Article 2 of the Uniform Commercial Code (UCC) is of special importance to everyone, because it affects both our business and our personal lives.

Article 2 deals only with "goods" as defined in UCC Sections 2–205 and 2–207. Most personal property and even some elements of real estate are goods. And Article 2 does not deal with most real estate contracts, nor does it touch on contracts for the sale of services. Classification of contracts can be difficult when more than one of these is involved, such as a contract for the sale of goods along with service.

Most of the provisions of the Code apply to everyone, but some are applicable only to merchants or to transactions between merchants. Basically, a merchant is someone who deals in the type of goods involved on regular basis, either in business or personal life, or who sells goods through an intermediary who is a merchant.

Some provisions of the Code merely restate common law principles. Others change the common law rules for sale of goods contracts. Still others grant new powers to law courts in enforcing contracts of the sale of goods. When the Code is silent on a question, the common law continues to govern the transaction.

In every transaction involving a contract for the sale of goods, the Code imposes on the parties an obligation to act in good faith, which the Code defines as "honesty in fact." In keeping with its policy of fairness, the Code permits courts to refuse to enforce unconscionable contracts and clauses or to rewrite such contracts so the parties are treated fairly. Courts have broad latitude in determining unconscionability, although most decisions involving this question focus on gross disparity of benefits gained by the parties under the contract and great inequality of bargaining power between them as the two factors to be considered in finding a contract unconscionable.

Generally, contracts under Article 2 of the Code are assignable, and general principles of contract law are followed. Thus, rights may be assigned and duties may be delegated unless they are so personal, or the other party's obligations are altered to such an extent, that the court is uncertain that the other party would not object to the assignment or delegation.

Technical provisions of the Code include a Statute of Frauds provision requiring that contracts for the sale of goods be in writing when they involve a price of $500 or more, with some exceptions. Also included is a parol evidence provision requiring that, in most cases, a court must regard a written contract as the best evidence of what the parties agreed to, and must not permit oral evidence offered to prove that the writing was incomplete or in error.

KEY TERMS AND CONCEPTS

Uniform Commercial Code
goods
transaction
present sale
merchant
good faith
unconscionable contract
course of dealing
usage of trade

PROBLEMS

1. Osterholt entered into a contract with St. Charles Drilling Co. to have a water system installed. When work was completed, Osterholt was dissatisfied with the flow of the water and sued St. Charles for breach of an implied warranty of fitness for the intended purpose under the Uniform Commercial Code. St. Charles contended that the contract was not one for the sale of goods and thus was not covered by the Code. Is St. Charles correct?

2. Jones, who was receiving welfare payments at the time, agreed to purchase a home freezer from a seller of home freezer plans for $900. However, after time-credit charges, credit life insurance, credit property insurance, and sales tax were added the total charge came to $1439.69. The retail value of the freezer was only $300. The contract was assigned to Star Credit Corp. to whom Jones made payments totaling $600. When he discontinued paying, Star Credit sued. Jones contended that the contract was not fair, but Star Credit maintained that it should be enforced because it was entered into voluntarily and was supported by legally sufficient consideration. Should this contract be enforced? If not, what legal concept would allow Jones to undo the initial transaction?

3. Baker Container Corp. entered into a contract with Carson, Inc., agreeing to produce 1000 special containers at $125 per container to Carson's detailed specification. The containers were to be used to ship vehicles to Southeast Asia. All negotiations were oral. After Baker completed the first installment of 100 containers, Carson refused to accept delivery. When sued, Carson objected to evidence of the agreement on the ground of the Statute of Frauds. Should the evidence be admitted? Would your answer change if Carson were not a merchant?

4. The Campbell Grain & Seed Co. orally contracted with Yokel, a farmer, to purchase between 6800 and 7200 bushels of yellow soybeans grown by Yokel. The price was to be $5.30 per bushel. Campbell sent a written confirmation of the agreement to be signed by Yokel and returned. Yokel neither signed nor returned the confirmation. After 30 days, Campbell inquired about delivery, and Yokel informed Campbell that he did not intend to perform because he had sold the soybeans to someone else. When sued, Yokel asserted the Statute of Frauds as a defense, and Campbell contended that the Statute was satisfied by the written confirmation. Yokel claimed that the confirmation was ineffective because he was not a merchant. Campbell disagreed because Yokel had earned his living growing soybeans and selling them on the market for several years. Who is correct, and why?

5. Adams and Bates made a contract under which Adams would pick up, advertise, and sell goods for Bates in exchange for a fee based on a percentage of the selling price. Was this a contract for the sale of goods?

6. Weaver's Kiddy Shoppe, Inc. entered into a contract to purchase a quantity of children't clothing from Seller, Inc. The contract provided for delivery "June-August." Seller shipped for the first time in late August, and Weaver's refused delivery on the ground that Seller had breached the contract by not delivering in installments beginning in June as was the industry practice. Seller contended that the contract called for delivery any time during the specified period, and that what other buyers and sellers did was irrelevant parol evidence. Is Seller correct?

7. On September 15, Builders Supply contracted to furnish building materials to Ludwig for a construction project. Builders provided a price sheet that stated that the prices listed were good "for the year," but on January 1 Builders gave notice of a 6-percent price increase to begin March 1. Builders continued to supply materials to Ludwig and on June 1, when the job was completed, Ludwig objected to the increased prices for materials supplied after March 1. Was Ludwig within his rights to withhold payment to the extent of the increases? Why or why not?

8. Thompson and B. F. Goodrich entered into an oral agreement under which Thompson was to purchase $9000 worth of used printing presses from Goodrich. Thompson sent a written confirmation of the agreement, but because of a mixup in the mailroom at Goodrich the confirmation never came to the attention of the equipment manager. Subsequently the machines were sold to another purchaser. Goodrich contended that the confirmation was not binding because the proper person did not learn of it, and nothing on the envelope indicated its contents. Should Goodrich be bound?

9. Notaras purchased a used car from Leveridge Motors on January 15, 1964. The written contract provided that the car was sold with "no warranties." However, in the margin was the handwritten notation "30-day warranty—Repair clutch as needed—not to exceed $100—date no later than Sat.—Feb. 24, 1964." If Notaras had difficulty with the clutch within 30 days, was Leveridge obligated to repair it under warranty?

10. Phillips entered into an oral contract with Quarry under which Phillips was to tear down a building belonging to Quarry and remove the materials. Phillips was to pay Quarry $450. Thereafter, Quarry refused to perform. When sued, Quarry defended on the ground of the Statute of Frauds. Phillips contended that the statute did not apply because the contract was for the sale of goods of a price under $500. Who is correct, and why?

Chapter | 14

Sales: Formation, Title, and Risk

FORMATION

Contracts for the sale of goods under Article 2 are formed in substantially the same way as other contracts. The law requires a voluntary manifestation of the mutual assent of the parties to enter into a contract—in other words, an offer and an accep-tance—and valid consideration. However, some aspects of contract formation under Article 2 de-part from the general common law of contracts.

Under common law principles, an offer usually is revocable at any time unless the offeree has paid the offeror to grant him an option. However, under Section 2–205, if a merchant, in a signed writing, promises to keep her offer open she must do so even if she received no consideration in return for her promise. The offer must be kept open for the time stated or, if no time is stated, for a reasonable time, but in no case for longer than three months. This is known as a merchant's "**firm offer,**" and in effect amounts to a statutory ap-plication of the common law doctrine of estoppel. Since the firm-offer rule deprives offeror-mer-chants of rights that nonmerchant offerors have, if a promise to keep an offer open is included on a form supplied by the offeree the promise must be signed separately by the offeror. This protects merchants from being trapped into extending a firm offer unwittingly.

The common law of contracts also differs from the UCC because it treats both counteroffers and conditional acceptances as rejections of the offers to which they respond. The common law of contracts requires an acceptance to manifest the offeree's willingness to be bound to the terms stated in the offer, without any "ifs," "ands," or "buts"; in other words, an acceptance must be a "mirror image" of the offer. Under Section 2-207, by way of contrast, although a conditional acceptance still is treated as a rejection, counteroffers are considered acceptances if they seem to be genuine attempts to accept. For example, suppose Ed offers to sell his car to Jane for $500. If Jane responds, "I'll give you $400," the UCC considers the counteroffer ($400 instead of $500) a rejection because it does not indicate a definite attempt to accept. However, if Jane responds, "I'll take it. Bring it over on Friday," this counteroffer (addition of "bring it over on Friday") would be considered an acceptance of the car for $500, coupled with a proposal to add the term "bring it over on Friday" to the contract.

Section 2-207(2) provides that if Ed and Jane *both* were merchants, the new term would become part of the contract automatically unless the offer prohibited additions, the added term materially altered the terms stated in the offer, or the offeror objected to it within a reasonable time. If either Ed or Jane, or both, were nonmerchants, the proposed term would have to be agreed upon explicitly in order to become part of the contract.

Although all Article 2 contracts must be supported by valid consideration, the parties are free to make subsequent modifications without further consideration. This, of course, is contrary to the common law rule. Section 2-209 provides, however, that if the agreement of the parties or the Statute of Frauds requires modifications to be in writing, they must be written in order to be irrevocable. Nevertheless, even when modifications must be in writing, an oral modification may operate as a waiver of the rights modified, although the waiver may be revoked at any time before the other party has materially changed position in reliance on it.

Completeness of Terms

The extent to which the terms of an offer must be complete is stated in Section 2-204(3), which provides: "Even though one or more terms may be left open, a contract for sale [of goods] does not fail for indefiniteness if the parties have intended to make a contract and there is a reasonably certain basis for giving an appropriate remedy." This section is in accord with the common law rule, except that other sections of Article 2 allow the parties to postpone agreement on some terms that the common law considers too material to be left indefinite.

Price

The material terms in every contract include (1) the identification of the parties, (2) an adequate description of the subject matter of the agreement, and (3) the price to be paid by the purchaser. However, under Section 2-204(3), the parties to a contract for the sale of goods may have a valid contract even though they leave the price to be agreed upon later. The parties may provide a formula by which the price will be determined, or merely may "agree to agree" on a price. Of course, they are bound by the requirement of good faith, and if they fail to agree on a price a court may supply a reasonable one. A court would not do this under the common law contract rules. Even under Section 2-204(3), however, if the parties omit a price and make it clear that they do not intend a contract to bind them unless and until they agree on one, no contract arises until an agreement on price is reached.

Quantity

Article 2 treats quantity as a material term but, like price, quantity need not be stated with precision. For example, Section 2–306(1) provides that quantity may be described as the output of the seller or the requirements of the buyer. The contract must be executed in good faith, and no quantity unreasonably disproportionate to any estimate may be tendered or required. In the absence of an estimate, reasonableness is measured by reference to prior comparable output and requirements. The Code treats quantity as more important than price in one respect, however: the Statute of Frauds provision in Section 2–201 provides that although "a writing is not insufficient because it omits or incorrectly states a term agreed upon" a contract "is not enforceable under this paragraph beyond the quantity of goods shown in such writing."

Delivery

A contract under Article 2 may be formed even though no provision has been made concerning the place, time or method of delivery. Section 2–308 provides that, in the absence of an agreement to the contrary, the ordinary place of delivery is the *seller's* place of business, or her residence if she has no other place of business. However, if the contract is for the sale of specific, identified goods that to the knowledge of the parties at the time of the contract are located somewhere else, that place is the place of delivery.

If no time of delivery is stated in a contract, Section 2–309 provides that delivery shall be made within a reasonable time. Of course, what constitutes a reasonable time depends on the circumstances of each case. In addition, if performance is to be in successive installments and no duration is stated, the contract is valid for a reasonable time but may be terminated at any time by either party, unless they agree to the contrary. Termination at the will of one of the parties is effective only after reasonable notice, however,

and the notice requirements cannot be waived by agreement.

Performance

The policy of Article 2 clearly is to preserve contracts if the parties intended to be bound by one. In addition to the idefiniteness permitted by the provisions discussed above, Section 2–311(1) provides that agreements that otherwise are sufficiently definite are not made invalid simply because they leave specification of the particulars of performance to one of the parties. Of course, the requirement of good faith is imposed on that party, as is the requirement of commercial reasonableness.

METHODS OF ACCEPTANCE

Article 2 departs from the common law of contracts concerning methods of acceptance in a number of ways. Of particular importance is Section 2–206(1), which provides: "Unless otherwise unambiguously indicated . . . an offer to make a contract shall be construed as inviting acceptance in any manner and by any medium reasonable in the circumstances. . . ." An important effect of this provision relates to "impliedly authorized means of acceptance," which, if used, ordinarily make an acceptance effective upon dispatch rather than upon arrival. Under the common law, an offeree could bind the offeror immediately upon sending his acceptance only if he transmitted his acceptance by a means expressly authorized by the offeror or, if the offeror was silent as to the means to be used, by using the same means employed by the offeror to communicate the offer. Under this UCC section, therefore, an acceptance by telegram of an offer sent by mail would bind upon dispatch even though it would not under the common law. Also Section 2–206(1) authorizes acceptance of a bilateral offer by performance, which is not allowed under the common law.

Acceptance by Shipment

Section 2-206(1) (b) effectively eliminates the common law's technical distinction between unilateral and bilateral contracts to a limited extent by providing that "an order or other offer to buy goods for prompt or current shipment shall be construed as inviting acceptance either by a prompt promise to ship or by the prompt or current shipment of . . . goods." If acceptance is unilateral (by performance), the acceptance is effective upon dispatch of the goods regardless of when title passes to the buyer. However, under Section 2-206(2), if acceptance is by performance (shipment), the seller must notify the buyer of shipment within a reasonable time. Otherwise, the buyer may treat the offer as lapsed, although she may not do so until the reasonable time has passed. Generally, it is the trust of Section 2-206 that shipment is a sufficient manifestation of the intent of the shipper to enter into a contract, as the following case illustrates.

NATIONS ENTERPRISES, INC. v. PROCESS EQUIPMENT CO.
40 Colo.App. 390, 579 P.2d 655 (1978)

This was an action by Nations Enterprises, Inc. (Plaintiff/ Appellee) against Process Equipment Co. (Defendant/Appellant) for breach of a contract to supply pumps to Plaintiff. Defendant denied that a contract existed, but also counterclaimed for the price of pumps delivered to Plaintiff during the period of negotiations.

In response to a request from Plaintiff, Defendant sent two written proposals to supply pumps in February and June 1972. Two months later the parties met and discussed requirements, including specifications for the pumps. Following that meeting, Plaintiff sent a purchase order with the notation: "NOTE: THIS ORDER IS NOT VALID UNTIL ACCEPTANCE COPY SHOWING SHIPPING DATE IS RECEIVED BY THIS OFFICE." Process Equipment did not execute and return the acceptance copy but, approximately one year later, shipped a number of pumps, some of which met the requirements discussed a year earlier.

The trial court found that Plaintiff's purchase order constituted a contract that was breached by Defendant, but found for Defendant on the counterclaim, holding that Defendant was entitled to the purchase price of the pumps that had been delivered and met the Plaintiff's requirements. Defendant appealed. The court affirmed the finding on the counterclaim, but reversed the finding that Plaintiff's purchase order constituted a contract.

KELLY, Judge.

Process admits that it entered into a contract with Nations. However, it argues that it fulfilled its contractual obligations and that the trial court's finding of breach resulted from its erroneous determination that Nation's purchase order constituted the terms of the contract. We agree. . . .

Ordinarily, an offer to make a contract invites acceptance in any manner reasonable in the circumstances. Section 4-2-206, C.R.S. 1973. However, here, Nations' purchase order provided for an acceptance in writing, and the acceptance copy pointed out that the order was not valid until the acceptance copy was received by it. Nations' purchase order did not invite acceptance by partial performance, and the trial court erred in finding that Process' conduct in shipping some of the pumps more than a year after the date of the purchase order amounted to acceptance. Section 4-2-206, C.R.S. 1973. . . .

Alternatively, Nations argues that, if its purchase order was not accepted by Process' partial performance, then, under the circumstances, its purchase order was an acceptance of an offer made by Process to supply pumps. We do not agree. Process' April letter, which contained a proposal to supply pumps, recognized that further negotiations were necessary between the parties. . . . Fairly read, the letters sent by Process to Nations were preliminary negotiations soliciting an offer from Nations. . . .

However, it is undisputed, and the trial court found, that nine pumps were shipped to Nations. From this finding, the trial court correctly ruled that Process was entitled to the purchase price for the pumps delivered, and thus judgment on the counterclaim was properly entered.

The continuing negotiations between the parties, the pump supplier, and the Corps of Engineers regarding the shock specifications and the efforts to have them reduced, which culminated in the shipment of the acceptable pumps, is conduct which shows that the parties intended to enter into a contract for the sale of pumps which were acceptable to the Corps of Engineers. . . . Thus, since the pumps which were acceptable were shipped to Nations and accepted by it, the contract for their sale, although not in writing, is enforceable, and Process is entitled to the purchase price. . . .

Questions

1. Is the result in this case based more on an accurate reading of the agreement or on a desire to be equitable?

2. Isn't it inconsistent for the defendant to say, "There was no contract but pay me for what I delivered under the arrangement"?

3. Can you identify the offer and the acceptance that formed the contract for the nine pumps that were delivered?

Section 2-206 further provides that if acceptance is by the shipment of goods, the goods may be either "conforming" or **nonconforming goods** (goods that differ in some material respect from those ordered by the buyer). Shipment of either is taken to signify the intent of the seller/offeree to accept, unless he or she "seasonably [within an appropriate time] notifies the buyer that the shipment is offered only as an accommodation to the buyer." This "accommodation" provision is intended to foreclose what had come to be known as "the unilateral contract trick." Prior to the adoption of the Code, a seller could ship nonconforming goods and then contend, if sued for breach, that the nonconforming character of the goods changed shipping them from an acceptance into an offer that the buyer accepted by taking possession of the goods. Therefore, no breach of contract occurred. Now, however, the Code treats shipment of nonconforming goods as simultaneously an acceptance and a breach of contract.

Utility of Shipping Nonconforming Goods

Allowing the seller to ship nonconforming goods as an "accommodation" permits a seller who has run out of the particular goods ordered but *does* have goods that may be a reasonable substitute to ship them for the buyer's approval. If the buyer needs the goods promptly and agrees to the substitution, both the buyer and the seller will be happy. If not, the buyer may reject the goods. Prior to the Code, the seller who attempted to help a customer in this way risked a breach of contract suit each time he or she did so.

TRANSFER OF TITLE

The term **title** refers to a person's rights of ownership of property. Ordinarily, someone owns property when title passes and, at that time, assumes the risk of loss if the property is lost or destroyed; he or she is able to insure the property and otherwise is responsible for it. However, the UCC contains some very important rules governing these matters.

Importance of the Rules

One of the most widely criticized sections of Article 2 is Section 2-401, which deals with the passage of title. The introduction to this section makes it clear that, except when a Code provision specifically refers to title, the parties' rights do not depend on who actually has it. Although practical consequences of Section 2-401 probably do not differ markedly from those under prior law such as the Uniform Sales Act, the Code provision sets out a new, direct approach to problem solving that probably is an improvement. Some specific UCC provisions that traditionally would be thought to depend on passage of title include: Section 2-501 (when the buyer obtains an insurable interest); Section 2-509 (who bears the risk of loss in the absence of a breach); Section 2-510 (who bears the risk of loss in the event of a breach); and Section 2-709 (the seller's right to obtain the purchase price).

General Rules

Section 2-401(1) provides that title to goods cannot pass until the goods have been **identified to the contract** (see Section 2-501(c)). Identification may take place either at a time and in a manner explicitly agreed upon by the parties, or according to rules established by Section 2-501. Once goods have been identified, the buyer acquires a special property right in them, and the seller has retained no more than a security interest (if he or she purportedly has reserved title). Of course, this rule can be modified by explicit agreement.

In the absence of agreement on this point, the question of when title passes is answered by the Code. Most cases involving questions of title fall into one of four categories: (1) shipment of the goods, (2) delivery of the goods, (3) delivery of documents of title only, (4) delivery of the goods without moving them or delivering documents of title. The primary question for the courts is, "at what point has the seller manifested an intent to make the transfer?"

TRANSFER BY SHIPMENT. A buyer often orders goods without stipulating a method of delivery. In these cases, Section 2-401(2)(a) provides that title passes upon shipment by the seller.

TRANSFER BY DELIVERY. If the goods are to be moved from their location at the time of contract and the contract specifies either the time or place of delivery, or even that delivery must be made by the seller, then title will pass at the time and place of delivery.

TRANSFER BY DELIVERY OF DOCUMENTS OF TITLE. The term **documents of title** is defined more fully in Section 1-201(15) of the UCC. However, in simplistic terms, a document of title is a written instrument that evidences title to goods that are in the possession of some third party, such as a warehouse or a common carrier, who is holding them for delivery to the person who has the document. In some cases the parties provide neither for shipment nor delivery of the goods in their agreement, they mention only delivery of documents of title. The parties may intend that the buyer will pick up the goods, or that the goods will be used at or resold from their location at the time of the contract. In these cases, Section 2–401(3)(a) provides that title passes at the time and place of delivery of the documents.

TRANSFER WITHOUT DELIVERY OF THE GOODS OR DOCUMENTS OF TITLE.   Finally, if goods are not to be moved and documents of title are not to be delivered, Section 2–401(3)(b) provides that title passes at the time and place the contract is entered into. If the parties are in different locations at the time, the place of contracting generally is considered to be the location of the acceptance.

RISK OF LOSS AND INSURABLE INTEREST

Sometimes goods are destroyed before the buyer has received them or the transaction has been completed. In these cases the parties' rights depend on when the risk of loss is transferred from the seller to the buyer. Usually, because the goods will have been moved, the risk will have followed title. In shipment contracts risk passes at the time of shipment, and in destination contracts it passes at the time delivery is tendered (offered by one who is ready, able, and willing to perform). If the goods are not to be moved, Section 2–509(2) prescribes rules that assign the risk: (1) when the buyer receives a *negotiable* document of title; (2) when the bailee (a third person who holds the goods for the owner) acknowledges the buyer's right to take possession of the goods if no negotiable documents have been delivered; or (3) when the seller gives the buyer a non-negotiable document of title or a written direction to a bailee to deliver the goods to the buyer and the buyer has had a reasonable time to present the document or direction. In cases not covered by any of the described rules, Section 2–509(3) provides that if the seller is a merchant, risk passes to the buyer upon receipt of the goods, and if he or she is not, it passes when the seller tenders delivery. Of course, any of these provisions for the passing of risk can be modified in an agreement between the parties. Consider the following case.

CAUDLE v. SHERRARD MOTOR COMPANY
525 S.W.2d 238 (Tex.Ct.Civ.App., 1975)

This was an action by Sherrard Motor Company (Plaintiff/Appellee) against John B. Caudle (Defendant/Appellant) to recover the purchase price of a trailer. Defendant agreed to purchase the trailer on February 10, 1972 and paid a deposit. When he returned to take delivery, he was told that the trailer was not ready and, accordingly, he agreed to return later. Before he returned, however, and after only a few days, the trailer was stolen. Defendant stopped payment on the check he had given as a deposit. Plaintiff demanded full payment, contending that the risk of loss had passed to Defendant before the theft.

The trial court denied Defendant's motion for an instructed (directed) verdict because it found that the risk of loss had passed, and Defendant appealed. Reversed, and judgment rendered for Defendant.

AKIN, Justice.

Plaintiff contends . . . that if Section 2.509(b) is inapplicable then the risk of loss passed to the defendant pursuant to Section 2.509(d). This section provides that a buyer and seller may specifically enter into a contract contrary to the other provisions of Section 2–509. Plaintiff argues that such a contrary agreement was made because the terms of the contract for the sale of the trailer provided that the risk of loss passed to the defendant when the contract was signed by the parties.

The pertinent clause of the sales contract states:

> No transfer, renewal, extension or assignment of this agreement or any interest hereunder, and no loss, damage or destruction of said motor vehicle shall release buyer from his obligation hereunder.

We hold that this language is insufficient to constitute a "contrary agreement" between the parties pursuant to Section 2.509(d). A contract which shifts the risk of loss to the buyer before he receives the merchandise is so unusual that a seller who desires to achieve this result must clearly communicate his intent to the buyer. . . . This clause was apparently intended to fix responsibility for loss after the defendant had taken possession of the trailer. This interpretation is consistent with other provisions of the contract. For example, the contract provides that the "buyer shall keep said motor vehicle in good order and repair. . . ." It would indeed be difficult for the buyer to honor this responsibility without having acquired actual possession of the trailer. It is also apparent that the provisions of the contract were drafted for the benefit of a third party—the bank or other lending institution to which the contract would be sold. The contract was assigned to the Citizens National Bank of Denison, Texas with recourse on Sherrard. Furthermore, since risk of loss is not specifically mentioned in the contract, we cannot say that an agreement to the contrary may be inferred from reading the document as a whole. We, therefore, conclude that it was not the intention of the parties to transfer risk of loss of the trailer *prior to delivery of possession to the buyer*. To hold otherwise would be to set a trap for the unwary. If parties intend to shift the burden of the risk of loss from the seller to the buyer before delivery of the goods, then such must be done in clear and unequivocal language.

It is defendant's contention that pursuant to Section 2.509(c) the risk of loss remained with the plaintiff because he had not taken actual physical possession of the trailer. We agree. That section provides,

> In any case not within Subsection (a) or (b), the risk of loss passes to the buyer on his receipt of the goods if the seller is a merchant; otherwise the risk of loss passes to the buyer on tender of delivery.

To determine if this section applies, the following questions must be resolved: (1) was the plaintiff a merchant? and (2) did the defendant receive the trailer? The plaintiff is a merchant under Article 2 of the Code as it "deals in goods of the kind . . . involved in the transaction. . . ." Section 2.104(a). The language "receipt of goods" is defined in the code as "taking physical possession of them." Section 2–103(a)(3). It is undisputed that the defendant never took physical possession of the trailer; therefore, he had not received the goods. Accordingly, we hold that the risk of loss did not pass to the buyer before the trailer was stolen. It follows, therefore, that no breach of contract occurred.

Our holding is in accordance with the underlying principles of Section 2.509 dealing with risk of loss. Under the Uniform Commercial Code, the risk of loss is no longer determined arbitrarily by which party had title to the goods at the time of the loss. Instead, as the drafters of the Code state: "The underlying theory of these sections on risk of loss is the adoption of the contractual approach. . . ." Uniform Commercial Code, Section 2-509, Comment 1. For example, under Tex.Bus. & Comm.Code Ann. Section 2.509(a)(1) and (2) (Tex.UCC 1968), the risk of loss depends on whether the goods are shipped by a carrier pursuant to a "destination" or "shipment" contract. In addition, Section 2.509(d) provides that the buyer and seller are free to adjust by contract their rights and risks contrary to the other provisions of Section 2.509. Subject to the placement of a contractual approach at the analytic center of risk of loss problems is the policy that a party who had control over the handling of goods should bear their loss. For example, under Section 2.509(a)(1) and (2), the seller must bear the risk of loss until the goods reach the control of the carrier, if it is not a "destination" contract. Strong policy reasons support this approach. The party in control is in the best position to handle properly the goods, to contract for shipment with a reliable carrier, and to insure the goods. This theory is particularly applicable when the buyer is not a merchant and is unfamiliar with the problems of handling the goods.

Questions

1. Although the result is "fair" to an innocent buyer, is the court's opinion consistent with UCC Section 2-509? Why or why not?

2. What would the contract have had to say in this case for the court to declare it a "contrary agreement" under Section 2-509?

Risk of Loss upon Breach

The general rules of Section 2-509 assume that the parties have conducted themselves properly. If either breaches the agreement, the rules change. Section 2-510 provides for the allocation of risk upon a breach by one of the parties. If the seller breaches by a tender or delivery of goods so defective as to give the buyer the right of rejection, the risk of loss remains with the seller until the defect is cured or there is a subsequent acceptance. If the goods have been accepted, but the buyer rightfully revokes the acceptance, the risk of loss he assumed by his acceptance remains with him, but only to the extent that he has insurance to cover it. If the buyer breaches after the risk of loss has passed to him, the risk remains his; if before, he assumes any portion of the risk that exceeds the seller's insurance coverage.

Suppose, for example, that Dave contracted to sell 1000 wooden beams to Lisa at $100 per beam, and the beams were identified to the contract. Prior to shipment, Dave's warehouse burned down and the beams were destroyed. Who bears the loss, Dave or Lisa? Consider two variations on these facts: (1) Dave was in breach because he had failed to ship in a timely manner; and (2) Lisa was in breach because she had not picked the beams up within the time specified or a reasonable time. In the first case, the loss would fall on Dave, and in the second, on Lisa. If Lisa had given Dave notice of her desire to breach before the fire occurred, the risk would be on Dave to the extent of his insurance coverage, and the remainder would be on Lisa. However, if Lisa had accepted delivery with the right to return any unused portion, and had given notice that she was exercising that right, she would bear the loss to the extent of her insurance coverage and the remainder would be on Dave. Of course, as already indicated, the parties are free to allocate the risk in a different way by saying so in their contract.

Insurable Interest

An **insurable interest** gives its holder legal permission to obtain insurance to cover a risk of loss. Without a stake in goods sufficient to qualify as an insurable interest, allowing someone to insure them would constitute gambling rather than insurance. The Code, in Section 2–501, specifies what constitutes an insurable interest. This requirement cannot be altered by contract, although Subsection (3) states that the provisions of the section are intended only to add to the other provisions of state law regarding what is an insurable interest rather than to replace or impair them.

Under Section 2–501, the seller always has an insurable interest in goods to the extent that he retains title to them or a security interest in them. The buyer acquires an insurable interest as follows: (1) if the goods exist and are identified to the contract when the contract is made, her interest is acquired at the time of the contract; (2) if the contract is for goods not yet in existence, her interest is acquired when the goods come into existence and are identified to the contract, whether by marking the goods and setting them aside or by shipping them; (3) if the goods are growing crops, the buyer's interest is acquired when they are planted, and if they are unborn animals, at the moment of conception. Growing crops, for the purposes of this provision, are limited to those intended to be harvested either within twelve months or at the next regular harvest, whichever is later. Therefore, the term would not include growing timber or other plants unless they were planted for the purpose of regular harvest, as in the case of Christmas trees. Similarly, for purposes of Section 2–501, "unborn young of animals" is limited to those to be born within the twelve months.

It should be noted that an insurable interest does not necessarily follow title. For example, suppose Hillary and Blake agreed that Blake would purchase a particular car belonging to Hillary for $500. Because the car is in existence and has been identified to the contract, Blake has acquired an insurable interest even though he does not yet have title. Also, if Hillary turned title over to Blake and Blake both paid $100 and promised to pay the remaining $400 within 30 days, Hillary would retain an insurable interest because of her security interest in the car even though Blake would have gained the title. It also should be noted that, in contrast to title and risk of loss, more than one person can have an insurable interest in an item of property at the same time. This is true, for example, in the case just discussed in which Hillary and Blake have insurable interests, but only Blake has title and has assumed the risk of loss. Why should Hillary have an insurable interest even though she does not bear the risk of loss? Because if Blake defaults after taking title so that Hillary is not paid, and the property is destroyed, Hillary stands to lose $400. That possibility is sufficient to give her an insurable interest.

SHIPPING TERMS

In the discussion of transfer of title and the risk of loss, it was noted that the Code allows the parties to modify the usual rules. This is done most frequently by agreeing to shipping terms such as F.O.B., C.I.F., or the like.

F.O.B. stands for "Free On Board." This term is meaningless unless it specifies a location, which is generally the place of shipment or destination, although the location could be some intermediate stop during shipment, or, indeed, anywhere else. **Shipment F.O.B.** to a particular location means that the seller bears the expense and the risk of loss until delivery to the specified location; thereafter, expense and risk shift to the buyer. Therefore, a contract providing for shipment "F.O.B. San Francisco" means that the seller bears the expense of shipping the goods to San Francisco as well as the risk of loss until they reach that point. Consider the following case.

NATIONAL HEATER COMPANY, INC. v. CORRIGAN COMPANY MECHANICAL CONTRACTORS, INC.
482 F.2d 87 (8th Cir. 1973)

This was a diversity-of-citizenship action in federal court brought by National Heater Company, Inc. (Plaintiff/Appellant) for the balance due on a contract for heaters sold to Corrigan Company Mechanical Contractors, Inc. (Defendant/Appellee). Defendant counterclaimed for damages to the heaters in transit, late delivery, and work to conform the heaters to the contract. The heaters were damaged in transit, and the parties disagreed as to when the risk of loss passed from seller to buyer under the terms of the contract. The pertinent facts are set out in the court's decision.

The trial court rendered judgment for Defendant on both the complaint and the counterclaim. Plaintiff appealed. Affirmed.

STEPHENSON, Circuit Judge.

On March 1, 1969 National Heater made a proposal "to the trade" concerning the price of certain heating units to be used in construction at the Chrysler automobile plant in Fenton, Missouri. The proposal priced the merchandise F.O.B. St. Paul, Minnesota "with freight allowed." Based in part upon National Heater's proposal, Corrigan made its bid on the construction job and was awarded the contract. Thereafter, appellant received appellee's purchase order listing "Price $275,640.00 Total Delivered to Rail Siding." Expressly made a part of this acknowledgment was the condition that "delivery of equipment hereunder shall be made f.o.b. point of shipment unless otherwise stated." The trial court determined that the parties had by these writings contracted for appellant to deliver the goods to the construction site and that the attendant risk of loss in transit therefore was appellant's burden. The court states:

> [t]he statement on the face of the acknowledgment which obligated plaintiff to deliver the merchandise 'to rail siding' comes clearly within the 'otherwise stated' provision of the condition. The manifest intention of the parties, in view of their entire course of conduct, was that delivery was to be made not F.O.B. point of shipment but to the rail siding on the job.

We agree. To hold otherwise would contradict the writing. We must give effect to the intention of the parties as expressed in the unequivocal language employed. . . .

Several circumstances surrounding this contract further convince us that the trial court was correct. Both litigants agree that the Uniform Commercial Code having been adopted in Minnesota and Missouri prior to the formation of this contract, should apply to this lawsuit. The Code provides that evidence relating to course of performance between the parties is relevant in determining the meaning of the agreement. Uniform Commercial Code Section 2-208.

Appellant argues that the term "delivered" in appellee's purchase order and the term "delivered to rail siding" in the acknowledgment referred only to price. As heretofore mentioned the original proposal to the trade made by appellant had previously established that freight would be allowed. Yet both parties typed in the provisions concerning delivery on their forms. In addition appellant made no protest about the "delivered" term in a letter he sent to appellee accompanying the acknowledgment. He did take exception to another provision of the purchase order concerning a ten percent retainage by the buyer pending acceptance. It seems to us as it did to the trial court that the parties were contemplating where delivery would take place rather than price.

When a contract is partly written or typewritten and partly printed any conflict between the printed portion and the written or typewritten portion will be resolved in favor of the latter. . . . It is also true that any ambiguity in the acknowledgment must be construed against appellant since it drafted the document. . . . We conclude that the parties by their written documents agreed that appellant was to deliver the goods to the job site. . . .

In reaching our result we are not unmindful that the F.O.B. term usually indicates the point at which delivery is to be made and will normally determine risk of loss. . . . We also note that the "destination" type contract which we envision this to be is the variant rather than the norm. . . . The provisions of the Uniform Commercial Code may nevertheless be varied by agreement. Uniform Commercial Code Section 1-102 and Comment 3. The written documents persuade us that National Heater specifically agreed to deliver the goods to their destination.

Questions

1. Are you persuaded that the court has interpreted the parties' intentions correctly? Why or why not?

2. If you believe that the agreement is inherently ambiguous and that the parties never really agreed on the question of risk of loss, who should bear it?

F.A.S. and Ex Ship

F.A.S. stands for "Free alongside ship." **Shipment F.A.S.** is the maritime equivalent of F.O.B. and means that the seller bears the expense and risk of loss until the goods are delivered to the place of the carrier. F.A.S. differs from F.O.B., however, in that both expense and risk shift from seller to buyer when the goods are available to the carrier rather than when the carrier takes possession. **Ex ship** stands for "from the ship or carrier." Expense and risk do not pass to the buyer under this term until the goods have been unloaded at their destination. This term is similar to "F.O.B.

destination," except that there the expense and risk shift to the buyer upon arrival, prior to unloading.

C.I.F. and C. & F.

The "C" stands for "cost," the "I" for "insurance," and the "F" for "freight." These initials indicate what the purchase price of the goods covers. Thus, a price quoted as "$500 C.I.F. San Francisco" means that the $500 price includes all expenses of shipment to San Francisco plus insurance to cover any loss prior to that point. More specifically, Section 2–320 provides that unless otherwise agreed, the term **C.I.F. destination** requires the seller, at his or her own expense, to: (1) place the goods in the possession of the carrier and obtain a negotiable bill of lading to the destination; (2) load the goods and obtain a receipt showing that freight costs have been paid or provided for; (3) obtain an insurance policy covering the goods that meets the requirements set out in Section 2–320 (2)(c); (4) prepare an invoice and procure any other documents required for shipping the goods to their destination (such as customs clearance); and (5) tender all necessary documents, together with any necessary endorsements, to the buyer. The term **C. & F. destination** requires the same except that it does not include insurance.

No Arrival, No Sale

This term differs from "F.O.B. Destination" in that the seller promises to ship conforming goods but does not guarantee their delivery to the destination. Therefore, although the seller pays the expense of shipping, the buyer assumes the risk of loss, destruction, and deterioration unless the seller is at fault. If the goods are lost or destroyed, or have deteriorated so completely that their entire value is compromised, there is no further obligation on the part of either party—the transaction is off. If the deterioration is only partial so that the goods still have value but do not conform to the agreement, the buyer has the right to inspect them and either to treat the loss as total or to take the goods at a reasonably adjusted price. This term is useful particularly during times of civil unrest or when the transaction involves goods

---

Shipping terms

Term	Meaning/Definition	Legal aspects
F.O.B. (Free on board)	Takes on meaning only when a location suceeds the term.	Seller bears expense and risk to the location.
F.A.S. (Free alongside ship)	The maritime equivalent of F.O.B.	Expense and risk borne by seller until goods are delivered to the carrier, then the buyer assumes the risk.
Ex Ship (From the ship or carrier)	Similiar to F.O.B.	Expense and risk shift to the buyer upon unloading.
C.I.F. (Cost, insurance, and freight)	The initials indicate what the purchase price covers.	Expense on seller as indicated by initials, and risk on seller to specified location.
No Arrival, No Sale	Seller promises to ship conforming goods but does not guarantee their delivery to destination	Seller pays for shipping, buyer assumes risk (unless seller at fault) but is not obligated if goods are lost, destroyed, or compromised.
Sale on Approval	Buyer is not obligated to keep goods unless he or she is satisfied.	Title and risk remain with the seller until the buyer accepts the goods.
Sale or Return	Buyer is not obligated to keep goods unless he or she is satisfied.	Title and risk pass according to the rules of a normal sale.

such as fresh fruit or nitroglycerin, which are highly susceptible to deterioration.

Sale on Approval and Sale or Return

These terms both describe sales that do not obligate the buyer to keep the goods unless he or she is satisfied. The two are similar except that **sale on approval** is used in connection with goods primarily intended to be consumed by the buyer, and **sale or return** with goods intended primarily for resale. However, in a sale on approval, both title and risk of loss remain with the seller until the buyer accepts the goods; by way of contrast, in a sale or return, title and risk pass according to the rules for a normal sale. If the buyer elects to return the goods, the return is then treated as a separate contract of sale, and title and risk again shift as under a regular sale contract. Sale or return contracts frequently are used when goods are transferred to a buyer on consignment. The remaining special features of approval and sale or return contracts are important only in regard to the rights of creditors, and are discussed in this book under secured transactions.

PURCHASE OF DEFECTIVE TITLE

A fundamental rule in personal property law is that title to property cannot be transferred by someone who does not have it. That is, someone who has nothing has nothing to sell. Like most rules of law, however, this one is not without exception. One broad exception recognized by the common law is estoppel. Other exceptions are addressed specifically by the code.

Estoppel

Applying this doctrine in extraordinary cases when fairness demands, courts will estop (stop) an owner from asserting his or her title to property against a good-faith purchaser who acquired it from someone who did not own it. These cases occur when the owner has been culpable in allow-

ing the purchaser to be misled. Analysis of whether estoppel applies in a particular case must proceed in five steps. To be applicable, there must have been: (1) an action or inaction by the true owner (2) at a time when the owner knew or had reason to know that someone might be misled by his or her action or inaction (3) causing the innocent party to change his or her position in reliance on the owner's behavior (4) in a situation in which the innocent party's reliance was justifiable so that (5) estopping the owner from asserting a title to reclaim the property from the innocent party is necessary to prevent injustice to the innocent party. The two elements most difficult to prove are the last two—that the purchaser's reliance was *justifiable* and that forcing the innocent party to return the property would be *unjust*.

Estoppel is not discussed specifically in the Code as are the legal concepts of "voidable title" and "entrustment." However, estoppel is the basis underlying both, and may be used independently in situations that do not fit neatly within either specific exception.

Voidable Title

Restating the fundamental rule of property law mentioned above, UCC Section 2–403(1) states: "A purchaser of goods acquires all title which the seller had. . . ." It adds, however, "or had a power to transfer." This should alert the reader to the fact that the Code intends to establish rules by which a seller may transfer greater title than he or she owns—and so it does.

Section 2–403 continues: "A person with voidable title has power to transfer good title to a good faith purchaser for value." Note first that this provision relates only to *voidable*, not void, title. The reasons that make a title voidable, such as fraud, duress, undue influence, and lack of capacity, are discussed in Chapters 6 and 10. The term *purchaser* is defined by Section 1–201(32) and (33) to include the recipient of a sale, pledge, or gift, or *any* other voluntary transfer. *Good faith* is defined, in subsection (19) of that same section, to mean "honesty in fact." Of course, the obligation of good faith is imposed by Section 1–203 on all parties to every transaction under the Code. **Value** is defined in subsection (44) of Section 1–201 to refer to anything that would be valid consideration for a contract as well as security interests or the satisfaction of all or part of a preexisting obligation.

According to Section 2–403(1), the rules stated above apply even though: (1) the transferor (true owner) was deceived as to the identity of the purchaser; (2) the delivery was in exchange for a check that later was dishonored; (3) it was agreed that the transaction was to be a "cash sale" but the cash never was paid; or (4) the delivery was procured through fraud that would be punishable as larceny under criminal law.

Suppose, for example, that a minor trades his car for another at a car dealership. The dealership then sells the trade-in to a good-faith purchaser for value, which as a practical matter would include almost any ordinary purchaser. The minor has a right to avoid his contract with the dealership and get back all he gave. However, the dealership will have to pay the reasonable market price of the trade-in rather than produce the car, because neither the minor nor the dealership can reclaim the car from the good-faith purchaser for value. Title passed to the good-fath purchaser of the car under Section 2–403(1).

Entrusting

Section 2–403(2) of the Code provides: "Any entrusting of goods to a merchant who deals in goods of that kind gives the merchant the power to transfer all rights of the entruster to a buyer in ordinary course of business." **Entrusting** includes any delivery into, or acquiescence in, the merchant's possession of the entrusted goods by the owner. For example, if Patty takes her watch to a jewelry store to have it repaired and the jeweler sells it to a good-faith purchaser in the ordinary course of business, Patty will lose title to the watch, and her only recourse is against the jeweler for damages from the loss of the watch.

The substance of Section 2–403(2) is basically the same as that of the common law doctrine of "Market Overt." Like Section 2–403(1), Market Overt is embraced under the general theory of estoppel. All three concepts are based on the idea that at some point the rights of a good-faith purchaser outweigh those of the real owner of the goods. Of course, it is the purpose of both subsections of Section 2–403 not only to promote fairness but also to encourage confidence in commercial transactions by protecting the good-faith purchaser and, thus, by stabilizing ordinary buy-and-sell agreements. Consider the following case.

TOYOMENKA, INC. v. MOUNT HOPE FINISHING COMPANY
432 F.2d 722 (4th Cir. 1970)

This was an action by Toyomenka, Inc. (Plaintiff/Appellee) against Mount Hope Finishing Company (Co-Defendant/Appellant). Toyomenka shipped certain textile goods via Wilmington Shipping Company to Harold A. Jason, Inc., but in order to secure payment from Jason, Toyomenka instructed Wilmington to deliver the goods to Mount Hope's plant, to be held in Toyomenka's name until Jason paid its bill. Wilmington negligently delivered the textiles to Mount Hope in Jason's name instead of Toyomenka's. Relying on authority from Jason, Mount Hope delivered the goods, after finishing, to Hampton Shirt Company. The evidence was conflicting as to whether this was done by Mount Hope before or after it was notified of Toyomenka's interest. The question of primary importance was whether Wilmington's negligent shipment of the goods to Mount

Hope in the name of Jason instead of Toyomenka constituted an "entrusting" of the goods by Toyomenka to Jason. The trial court found in favor of Toyomenka and Mount Hope appealed. Affirmed.

DONALD RUSSELL, District Judge.

The primary thrust of Mount Hope's motion both for a directed verdict and for judgment n.o.v. rests on Section 25-2-403, subsection (2), General Statutes of North Carolina, which is a part of the Uniform Commercial Code. This subsection provides:

> (2) any entrusting of possession of goods to a merchant who deals in goods of that kind gives him power to transfer all rights of the entruster to a buyer in ordinary course of business.

It is clear that, for this subsection to be applicable, there must be three essential steps: (1) An entrustment of goods to (2) a merchant who deals in goods of that kind followed by a sale by such merchant to (3) a buyer in ordinary course of business. And the phrase "deals in goods" is to be construed as one who is engaged regularly in selling goods of the kind. . . . It is unquestionably true that Toyomenka entrusted its goods to another but that bailee was not Jason, as Mount Hope argues, but Wilmington. And Wilmington was not a merchant regularly engaged in selling textile goods, as the statute requires; its business was strictly that of a customs broker. Mount Hope seeks to escape this dilemma by urging that Wilmington, in negligently billing the goods in the name of Jason, was acting as the agent of Toyomenka and that its act, which amounted to an entrustment to Jason, is imputed on familiar principles of agency to Toyomenka. The difficulty with this argument is that the law of North Carolina, which all parties assume to be controlling, is clear that the unauthorized act of Wilmington, the bailee, may not be imputed to Toyomenka. . . . In short, Toyomenka at no time entrusted its goods to a merchant engaged in dealing in such goods or authorized any such entrustment. Its express instructions were to the contrary. Nor for that matter was Mount Hope a "buyer in ordinary course of business", a purchaser who "bought goods in the open market". See Independent News Co. v. Williams, *supra*. It did not acquire possession of the goods as a purchaser in the ordinary course of business but received those goods in its capacity of a textile finisher, for the specific purpose of processing them on behalf of the owner. Mount Hope, also refers in its brief to that portion of Section 2-403 as provides that one with voidable title has "power to transfer a good title to a good faith purchaser for value". Such provision is clearly irrelevant to this controversy. The basic predicate for the operation of this subsection is title, either actual or voidable, in the transferee (in this case, Wilmington). Wilmington neither had nor claimed any such title. Even less can it be said that Jason acquired any such title. Jason could only acquire title if there had been a valid delivery to it. Toyomenka, the owner, never made or authorized such delivery, and, if it be asserted the negligent act of billing by Wilmington may be deemed to constitute delivery, it is sufficient answer that an unauthorized act by the bailee cannot bind Toyomenka or operate to forfeit its property rights. The cases cited by Mount Hope in suppport of this phase of its arguments involved instances in which undisputed delivery had been made to the buyer. In those situations, where there has been "delivery to the buyer", a reservation of title by the seller, by express provision of the Code, is "limited in effect to a reservation of a security interest". Section 2-401(1). . . . This is not such a case. It is manifest, therefore, that the provisions of the Uniform Commercial Code, relied on by Mount Hope, were inapplicable. . . .

Questions

1. Is the result in this case "fair" to Mount Hope? What policies does it promote?
2. Is there any way Mount Hope realistically can protect itself from having this happen again?

SPECIAL TRANSACTIONS

Article 2 applies to all transactions involving goods. Broadly, it covers ordinary sales, and it also addresses certain special transactions such as auctions.

Auctions

A sale by auction presents many of the same considerations as other transactions in goods, but also involves some that are peculiar to auctions. As discussed in Chapter 7, all bids at auctions are offers to buy by those who attend, and the auctioneer is the offeree or, in many cases, the agent of the offeree. The auctioneer generally is free to accept or reject any and all offers.

Section 2-328 of the UCC provides that, at auction, an offer is accepted and a sale is completed "by the fall of the hammer or in other customary manner." The key, of course, is a manifestation of the willingness of the auctioneer/ offeree to accept, thus forming a contract with the high bidder. If a new bid is made while the hammer is falling, however, the auctioneer is entitled to reopen the bidding if he or she wishes. Because the auctioneer is the offeree and has the power either to accept or reject each bid, ordinarily he or she also is under no duty to sell any item, even if it has been placed on the auction block and the bidding has begun. The auctioneer may withdraw an item any time, and of course a bidder may retract a bid at any time prior to acceptance. If, however, the auction advertisement or the auctioneer states explicitly that the auction is to be "without reserve," once an item has been placed on the block and at least one bid has been received the item must be sold. An item can be removed from the block only if no bid is received after a reasonable time, which means that it cannot be placed on the block and immediately removed in order to defeat the purpose of the without-reserve provision.

Bidding at an auction by, on behalf of, or at the procurement (request) of the seller is forbidden unless the seller gives notice that he or she has reserved these rights. If the autioneer knowingly receives a bid in violation of this rule, the buyer of any item has the option to avoid the sale or to take the goods at the last good-faith bid before the seller began bidding. This is intended to prevent a seller from inflating bids artificially or from circumventing the rule concerning auctions without reserve. This limitation does not apply to forced (court-ordered) sales, however, such as a foreclosure sale.

Bulk Transfers

A bulk transfer is a special kind of sale that is covered by Article 6 rather than by Article 2 of the UCC. A **bulk transfer** is defined in Section 6-102 as "any transfer in bulk and not in the ordinary course of the transferor's business of a major part of [the business's] materials, supplies, merchandise or other inventory." Although what constitutes "a major part" cannot be defined precisely, courts have held bulk transfers to range from 10 percent all the way to 70 or 75 percent of a business's assets.

The basic purpose of Article 6 is to prevent fraud on creditors. Therefore, it requires that prior to any bulk sale: (1) the transferor and buyer must prepare a list of the property to be transferred; (2) the buyer must obtain a list of the transferor's creditors; (3) the transferor must sign and swear to the list; (4) the buyer must notify all creditors on the list at least ten days before taking possession of the goods; and (5) the list of cred-

itors must be preserved for at least six months following the transfer and must be available to all creditors during that period. If the buyer fails to ensure that these requirements are met, the rights of affected creditors are not cut off; instead, they can be exercised against the buyer any time if the transfer was concealed, and if it was not, they can be exercised for six months after the date of the transfer. However, these rights are restricted by a subsequent sale to a good-faith purchaser. To what extent may a buyer in bulk depend on the affidavit of the seller indicating the property to be transferred and the seller's creditors? Must the buyer conduct an independent investigation into the facts? Consider the following case.

ADRIAN TABIN CORPORATION v. CLIMAX BOUTIQUE, INC.
34 N.Y.2d 210, 313 N.E.2d 66 (1974)

This was an action by the Adrian Tabin Corporation (Plaintiff/Appellant) against Climax Boutique, Inc. (Defendant/Appellee) to set aside a bulk sale of property to Defendant by Plaintiff's debtor. The evidence showed that Plaintiff was a creditor of Paul Warman, who sold the goods in bulk to Defendant. Warman gave Defendant an affidavit swearing that he had no creditors. Defendant also had investigated lien records, but they revealed no creditors, and had checked with Warman's attorney, who stated that Warman had no creditors. Plaintiff's suit was grounded on Defendant's failure to notify it, as a creditor, of the bulk sale as required by law.

Defendant appealed from a judgment of the trial court (the Supreme Court, Special Term, of Queen's County) that the sale was void as against Plaintiff. The intermediate appellate court (the Supreme Court, Appellate Division) reversed, and Plaintiff appealed. The decision of the Appellate Division that Plaintiff had no rights in the goods was affirmed by New York's highest court, the Court of Appeals.

JASEN, Judge.

The language of section 6–104 is simple and unambiguous. In pertinent part, subdivision (1) provides that a bulk transfer is ineffective as against creditors of the transferor unless the transferee requires the transferor to furnish a list of creditors and the transferee preserves the list for six months and allows reasonable inspection thereof. Subdivision (3) places upon the transferor the responsibility for the accuracy and completeness of the list and provides that the transfer is not ineffective because of errors or omissions in the list unless the transferee had knowledge. "Knowledge", as carefully defined by the code draftsmen, means actual knowledge (Uniform Commercial Code, Section 1–201, subd. [25]), not constructive knowledge. And as the official comment to subdivision (3) above makes clear, the sanction for the accuracy of the list of creditors is the false swearing statute of the State.

Concededly, cases interpreting the pre-Uniform Commercial Code New York Bulk Sales Act (former Personal Property Law, Section 44) stand for the proposition that before a transferee may rely on an affidavit of no creditors, he must make careful inquiry and otherwise have no knowledge of such creditors of the transferor. . . . But on the face of section 6–104 of the Uniform Commercial Code, there is no requirement of careful inquiry. Notwithstanding the commentary accompanying subdivision (3) of section 6–104 that it is declarative of precode New York law, in our view, the judicial gloss on the former law has not been carried over. As the report of the New York Law Revision Commission more accurately states, subdivision (3) of section 6–104 is merely in "general accord" with precode law. . . . Although at first reading this provision may seem harsh on the transferor's creditors, a requirement of careful inquiry might, on the other hand, tend to restrain the free alienation of property. Hence, it is in this situation that the code protects the innocent transferee because "the desirability of allowing transfers to go forward outweighs the value of protecting the omitted creditor." . . .

This is not to say, however, that the omitted creditor is entirely without remedy. The Uniform Fraudulent Conveyance Act (Debtor and Creditor Law, Section 270 et seq., Consol.Laws, c. 12) was not repealed by the enactment of the Uniform Commercial Code. Under section 276 of that law, if a transferee knowingly participates in a conveyance made with actual intent to "hinder, delay, or defraud . . . present and future creditors" of the transferor, the goods may be recovered from the transferee by the transferor's creditors notwithstanding literal compliance with the bulk transfer provisions of the Uniform Commercial Code. . . . Also, section 60 of the Bankruptcy Act (U.S. Code, tit. 11, Section 96) proscribing preferential transfers may apply in a given context. Conceivably . . . [u]pon adjudication of the transferor as a bankrupt, the transferee could be required to turn the property over to the trustee if, at the time of the conveyance, the transferee had reasonable cause to believe the transferor was insolvent. . . .

We recognize, as is so ably stated in the dissenting opinion, that strong reasons grounded in public policy and in the equities of the situation can be raised as a basis for imposing a duty of careful inquiry upon the transferee of a bulk sale. Nevertheless, it is our view that the simple and unambiguous language of section 6–104 and the precise and careful definition of knowledge as used in the code (Section 10291, subd. [25]) preclude such a construction.

Questions

1. How can creditors protect themselves from bulk transfers, like the one in this case, that do not take account of their rights?

2. How meaningful are the two protections for creditors mentioned toward the close of the court's opinion?

3. Should bulk purchasers be required to do more than the defendant did in this case? Why or why not?

SUMMARY

The law governing contracts for the sale of goods is founded on the general law of contracts, with some important modifications found in Article 2 of the Uniform Commercial Code. In some respects, Article 2 merely restates, or codifies, common law principles. In other respects, it applies equity principles to provide flexibility in resolving special contractual problems. Also, Article 2 provides several entirely new rights and duties in order to ensure that commerce operates smoothly. For example, Section 2–205 requires a merchant who promises in writing not to revoke an offer for a time to keep that promise even though he or she has not been given consideration to do so. Section 2–207 provides that some counteroffers, if they seem to be attempts to accept, can operate as acceptances. And Section 2–209 allows modifications of contracts without new consideration.

In addition, the Code considerably relaxes the common law requirements for definiteness of contract terms. Article 2 allows the price for the goods to be left open, to be agreed upon after the contract is formed. It also allows for the absence of a specific quantity term, and for a quantity based on either the seller's total output or the buyer's needs. Article 2 further provides rules for determining the time and place of delivery if these are not specified by the parties, and does away with the strict common law rule requiring a bilateral acceptance of a bilateral offer and a unilateral acceptance of a unilateral offer.

Also, the moment of shipment becomes important for many purposes, especially determing title, risk of loss, and insurable interest. The Code has provided rather elaborate rules for these problems.

When goods are to be shipped, the price frequently is quoted with terms indicating who will be responsible for shipping costs and insurance, and at what point the risk of loss shifts from the seller to the buyer. For example, "F.O.B. destination" means that the costs of shipping must be paid to the destination, and "C.I.F. San Francisco" means that the price includes cost, insurance, and freight as far as San Francisco.

An important contribution of Article 2 is its protection of good-faith purchasers. In many circumstances, when goods are sold in the ordinary course of business to a good-faith purchaser, title can pass even though the title held by the seller was defective. Three general categories of transactions in which this protection is afforded are those giving rise to promissory estoppel, those involving voidable title, and those concerning entrusting under Section 2–403.

In addition to the basic provisions in Article 2 relating to the sale of goods, two somewhat more unique types of sale transactions are given special treatment by the Code. These are auctions and bulk transactions under Article 6.

KEY TERMS AND CONCEPTS

firm offer
estoppel
non-conforming goods
title
goods identified to a contract
documents of title
insurable interest
shipment F.O.B.
shipment F.A.S.
Ex ship
C.I.F. destination
C. & F. destination
no arrival, no sale
sale on approval
sale or return
value
entrusting
bulk transfer

PROBLEMS

1. Moore entered into a contract with Lisko Motors, agreeing to purchase the first Corvette to come to Lisko from the factory. The price was to be the "sticker price," estimated at $14,000 to $18,000, and Moore paid $100 down. When the

car arrived it had a sticker price of $14,688.21, but the demand for Corvettes had far exceeded the supply and Lisko demanded $22,000. Lisko contended that the arrangement with Moore was too indefinite to be a contract. Is Lisko correct? If Moore and Lisko have a contract, at what price must Lisko provide the car?

2. The Massachusetts Gas & Electric Supply Co. agreed to furnish to V. M. Corporation sufficient gas to meet all of V. M.'s requirements during the following year at an agreed-upon price. The contract provided that either party could cancel upon giving 30 days notice. When gas prices rose sharply and V. M. learned that Massachusetts Gas was going to cancel, it ordered 892 units on June 28. Massachusetts Gas objected because V. M.'s normal usage had been around 100 units per month. Must Massachusetts Gas supply V. M. the quantity ordered?

3. In an action by a carpet dealer against a manufacturer for fraud, the manufacturer challenged the jurisdiction of the court to hear the merits of the case. On the back of the manufacturer's form, sent in response to the dealer's order, was a clause providing that the parties agreed to arbitrate any disputes that arose out of the order. The trial court held that the clause was binding and granted summary judgment on the issue for the manufacturer. When the carpet dealer appeals, should the decisions be affirmed?

4. Royal Store Fixture offered to pay "a competitive price" for "store fixtures and refrigeration equipment." The offer was made to Bucci, who was quitting the business. Did Royal's statement constitute a valid offer?

5. Ramos purchased a motorcycle from the Wheel Sports Center. He paid for it, but before he could return to pick it up it was stolen. Who must bear the loss? Would your answer be the same if Wheel Sports had agreed to keep an eye on the motorcycle for Ramos?

6. ABC Motors sold a car to Mann, who paid for it and was to return the following day to pick it up. ABC assured her than the title would be sent to the state for registration. Later the same day, ABC gave the title to the National Exchange Bank to secure a loan. When ABC defaulted on the loan, the bank sought possession of the car. Must Mann give the car up?

7. Archer purchased clothing for his store. It was to be shipped "FOB Los Angeles" by truck. When the clothing arrived, Archer asked the driver to unload it, but the driver refused, saying he was not obligated to do so. Archer disagreed and refused to unload the truck. The driver then left with the shipment, and despite careful precautions, the clothes were stolen from the truck later that evening. Who must bear the loss, Archer or the seller?

8. Suppose a debtor who owes money to a number of unsecured creditors (who have no recourse in property interests) goes out of business, sells her assets in bulk without notice to her creditors, then distributes the proceeds to only one of the creditors. What remedy, if any, is available to the other creditors under the Uniform Commercial Code?

9. Alpha Wines agreed to purchase grapes from a German grower, Gellerhaus, under a "shipment" contract. When the grapes were ready Gellerhaus shipped them to Alpha, but they were lost at sea. Gellerhaus contended the risk of loss passed to Alpha when the grapes were shipped, and Alpha contended the risk remained with Gellerhaus because it had not been notified of shipment. Who is corrrect?

10. Masters was having trouble with his computer and mentioned it to his friend, Parr, who offered to take a look at it. Masters took the computer to Parr at her home, and left it. Before Masters could return to pick it up, Parr sold the computer to a good-faith purchaser. As it turned out, Parr was in the business of repairing and selling used computers, although Masters did not know this. When Masters learned of the sale, he contacted the purchaser and demanded the return of his computer. The purchaser refused on the ground that the computer was a consumer good he had purchased, in good faith, from a dealer. Is Masters entitled to recover the computer?

Chapter 15

Sales: Performance, Breach, and Remedies

OUTLINE

INTRODUCTION

The performance of contracts for the sale of goods involves substantially the same concepts as performance of other kinds of contracts. The problems of performance, breach, and remedies under the common law are discussed in Chapter 12.

Many of the common law rules have been codified in Article 2 of the Uniform Commercial Code, but some have been changed in material respects. It is one of the purposes of Article 2 to establish rules to promote fairness in circumstances in which the common law rules are too rigid. The changes under Article 2 are too numerous to be listed in this introduction, but discussion can begin with a reminder of the good-faith requirement and a few remarks about commercial reasonableness.

Good Faith and Commercial Reasonableness

The obligations of good faith and **commercial reasonableness** (the obligation to act reasonably in light of the specific needs of the parties in a commercial, rather than a personal, setting) are imposed on the parties to every contract for a sale of goods. Good faith is defined in Section 1-201(19) as "honesty in fact," and is required in all sales transactions by Section 2-103. Section 2-103(1)(b) also imposes upon every merchant an obligation of "observance of reasonable commercial standards" of fair dealing in the trade. As mentioned in Chapter 14, merchants sometimes are held to higher standards than laypersons. Although the good-faith requirement of Section 2-103 applies to both, the requirement of commercial reasonableness applies only to *merchants* as defined in Section 2-104(1). Further, note that merchants are held to higher standards by Sections such as 2-205 and 2-207.

Judicial Construction of the UCC

Generally, courts construe statutes strictly if they are in derogation of (contrary to) the common law. What this means is that judges are reluctant to construe the language of those statutes broadly or to cover a wide range of situations, and instead confine them as narrowly as their words will permit. However, this rule is not applied in construing provisions of the Uniform Commercial Code. Section 1-102(1) provides that the UCC "shall be liberally construed and applied to promote its underlying purposes and policies [stated in subsection (2)]." Further, Section 1-103 provides: "Unless displaced by particular provisions . . . the principles of law and equity, including . . . estoppel . . . or other validating or invalidating cause shall supplement its provisions." Therefore, in addition to sections applying canons of commercial reasonableness such as Sections 2-305 through 2-311 concerning indefiniteness in contract terms, courts are permitted to seek justice based on the individual circumstances of each case when they interpret the UCC.

DELIVERY

Chapter 14 emphasized the obligations of the seller concerning the shipment of goods. In order to complete performance, the seller must deliver the goods. This may be accomplished in a variety of ways.

Time

The time for shipment or delivery of all or any part of an order for goods may be specified by the parties as they see fit. There is no requirement that the parties must be reasonable. However, if no time for delivery is agreed upon, Section 2-309 provides that the time shall be a "reasonable time." What constitutes as reasonable time, of course, depends on the nature of the contract and the circumstances surrounding it. For example, the reasonable time period for shipment or delivery of specially manufactured goods is likely to be longer than that for items from stock. Also, if the seller has notice—either expressed by the buyer or indicated by the circumstances—that the goods are expected or needed quickly or by a certain date, delivery must be made accordingly. Therefore, it always is to the buyer's advantage to specify a time for delivery, and if time is important, to state in the contract that "time is of the essence." This avoids the uncertainty that results from relying on a court to determine a reasonable time.

Manner

In order to meet the obligation to deliver, the seller must make an appropriate "tender" of the goods. This requires the seller to put conforming goods at the buyer's disposal and notify the buyer in a manner that enables the buyer to take delivery. The tender must be made at a reasonable time, and if the goods are to be held by the seller or a third party they must be kept available for the period reasonably necessary for the buyer to take possession. Under some circumstances, the tender requirement may include the tender of documents of title or written directions to a bailee who is temporarily in possession of the goods. Consider the following case concerning whether a proper tender or delivery has been made.

CONSOLIDATED BOTTLING CO. v. JACO EQUIPMENT CORP.
442 F.2d 660 (2d Cir. 1971)

This was an action by Consolidated Bottling Co. (Plaintiff/Appellant) against Jaco Equipment Corp. (Defendant/Appellee) to recover the purchase price of certain used can-filling equipment sold to Defendant. The shipping terms in the contract were "F.O.B. purchaser's truck." Plaintiff notified Defendant that the equipment was ready to be delivered, but before it was placed in Defendant's hands vandals broke into Plaintiff's warehouse and removed essential parts from the equipment, rendering it valueless to Defendant. The question before the court was whether delivery or proper tender had taken place, passing the risk of loss to Defendant, prior to the vandalism.

The trial court determined that there had been no delivery or tender and found for Defendant. Plaintiff appealed. Affirmed.

MOORE, Circuit Judge.

Consolidated's theory of the case is that it "put and held the can filler at the disposition of Jaco within the meaning of Section 2–503(1) of the Uniform Commercial Code." Accepting this allegation that Consolidated did all that it could do to put the can filler in a "deliverable state," and further assuming *arguendo* [for the purpose of argument, without treating it as a fact in deciding the case] that Consolidated gave Jaco the required notification "reasonably necessary to enable [the buyer] to take delivery," under the same section, we still find Consolidated's position untenable because it ignors an integral part of the parties' agreement—i.e., the term "f.o.b. purchaser's truck." . . .

Employment of the f.o.b. term in the contract (i.e., in both the purchase order and the acknowledgement invoice) obviates the necessity of deciding whether there was "tender of delivery" within the meaning of Section 2–509(3), because Section 2–509(4) provides that "[t]he provisions of this section are subject to contrary agreement of the parties. . . ." N.Y.U.C.C. Section 2–509(4), at 440 (McKinney 1964). We hold that the term "f.o.b. purchaser's truck" is such a "contrary agreement" under Section 2–509(4), bringing into force application of N.Y.U.C.C. Section 2–319(1)(c) (McKinney 1964). . . .

Section 2–319(1)(c) of the Code provides that under a contract containing a term such as the one at bar, "the seller must . . . at his own expense and risk load the goods on board." N.Y.U.C.C. Section 2–319(1) (c), at 327 (McKinney 1964). The New York Annotations to this section note that "[a]ny question as to when the risk passes to the buyer can be avoided by the use of the appropriate F.O.B. term." N.Y.U.C.C. Section 2–319, at 328,329 (McKinney 1964). This was clearly done here, and the judgment must, therefore, be affirmed.

Questions

1. Is the court's result fair or "hypertechnical"?

2. How long would the seller have to wait for the buyer's truck before the risk of loss would pass to the buyer?

TENDER

To complete performance of a contract for sale, the seller must deliver the goods as agreed. Or, the seller must *tender* them at the time and place agreed-upon for delivery.

Place

As discussed in Chapter 14, the place of delivery frequently is specified by the parties, either specially or by the use of shipping terms. If it is not, Section 2-308 establishes three applicable rules: (1) the place of delivery will be the buyer's place of business or place of residence if the buyer has no place of business; (2) if at the time of the contract both parties know that the goods are located at some other place, that is the place of delivery; and (3) documents of title may be delivered through customary banking channels. For example, suppose the contract is for a defined lot of goods, and is between a seller in Los Angeles and a buyer in New York. Suppose further that both parties know that the goods were shipped from Dallas and are being held in a trucking company's warehouse in Philadelphia. Unless otherwise agreed, proper tender could be made by the seller's sending a negotiable warehouse receipt or bill of lading, which is a receipt for goods that are shipped aboard a common carrier, (depending on the shipper's arrangements with the trucking company) to the buyer through banking channels. The buyer would be expected to pick up the document at his or her bank and either take it to Philadelphia to pick up the goods or arrange with the trucking company for delivery.

Perfect Tender Rule

The rules concerning tender assume that the seller has tendered or delivered conforming goods and has fulfilled the terms of the contract to the letter. The rights of the buyer and seller concerning nonconforming goods are governed by the perfect tender rule stated in Section 2-601, which provides: "if the goods or the tender of delivery fail in any respect to conform to the contract, the buyer may (a) reject the whole; or (b) accept the whole; or (c) accept any commercial unit or units and reject the rest." This seemingly demanding and inflexible rule, although derived from the common law tradition, is not consistent with the purpose of the UCC stated in Section 1-201 (2)(a), "to simplify . . . and modernize the law governing commercial transactions." Therefore, Section 2-601 provides three exceptions to the perfect tender rule.

First, the parties may agree to a different rule. For example, if the goods are perishable or otherwise subject to damage or deterioration, they may agree to a reasonable reduction in purchase price according to the condition of the goods on arrival, or they may agree that the seller will repair any damaged items. This term would help prevent economic waste, and the courts therefore might prefer it to the "all-or-nothing" standard of the perfect tender rule.

Second, Section 2-508 provides that if the buyer rejects nonconforming goods, the seller must be allowed to "cure" the problem. The seller may do so as long as he or she notifies the buyer of his or her intention and can tender conforming goods prior to the expiration of the time for performance called for by the original contract. Also, if the seller had reasonable grounds to believe that the goods would be accepted by the buyer whether or not they were conforming, the seller may notify the buyer of this and employ a further reasonable time to tender conforming goods.

Third, if the parties have agreed to delivery in installments and one installment is so defective as to impair its value, Section 2–612 provides that (1) the buyer may reject the installment, but (2) if the defect in the installment does not impair the value of the contract as a whole and the seller gives adequate assurance of its intent to cure, the

buyer must accept the defective installment, and (3) if the buyer accepts the installment without reasonably notifying the other party of his or her desire to cancel, or brings a cause of action with respect only to past installments or demands performance of future installments, the aggrieved party waives his or her rights concerning any nonconforming installment and the contract as a whole. The following case illustrates a situation in which a nonconforming installment has dire consequences.

GRAULICH CATERER, INC. v. HANS HOLTERBOSCH, INC.

101 N.J.Super. 77, 243 A.2d 253 (1968)

This was an action by Graulich Caterer, Inc. (Plaintiff/Appellant) against Hans Holterbosch, Inc. (Defendant/Appellee) to recover expenses and lost profits from Defendant's cancellation of a contract to purchase food. Defendant had entered into the contract on the basis of samples. The food was to be sold in Defendant's Lowenbrau Pavillion at the World's Fair.

When Plaintiff delivered the first installment of food on April 23, 1964, it was determined that it did not conform to the sample; it was "tasteless" and of low quality. Defendant rejected the installment and Plaintiff promised to cure. A second installment was delivered on April 25, and it is agreed that it was no better than the first. Defendant then gave notice of cancellation and changed its operation to prepare its own food.

The trial court found the cancellation proper and rendered judgment for Defendant. Plaintiff appealed. Affirmed.

FOLEY, J.A.D.

Giving due regard to the original trier's opportunity to observe the demeanor and to judge the credibility of the witnesses, we find as a matter of fact that the deliveries of April 23 and 25, 1964 did not conform to the samples originally presented and approved. Since warranties of sample and description are characterized as "express warranties," the "whole of the goods shall conform to the sample or model." N.J.S. 12A:2–313(1) (C), N.J.S.A. The "goods" to "conform" to the sample or model must be "in accordance with the obligations under the contract" N.J.S. 12A:2–106(2), N.J.S.A.; here, to comply with the standards established by the March 17 taste-test of the samples. Any distinguishing language would be controlled by the sample as presented on March 17. Additionally, the implied warranty of fitness for purpose attaches to contracts of this type, where, as here, they are not specifically excluded. A breach of these warranties triggers a buyer's rights following seller's breach as catalogued in N.J.S. 12A:2–711(1), 2–106(4), N.J.S.A. "if the breach goes to the whole of the contract." N.J.S. 12A:2–612(3), N.J.S.A. . . .

Here, Holterbosch had the right to reject any installment that was non-conforming, provided that the nonconformity substantially impaired the value of that installment and could not be cured. N.J.S. 12A:2–612(2), N.J.S.A. "Cure," novel to New Jersey's jurisprudence, permits the seller to cure a defective tender through repair, replacement or price allowance if he reasonably notifies the buyer of his curative intention and, in effecting the cure, makes a timely conforming delivery. N.J.S. 12A:2–508(1), N.J.S.A.

The effect of the installment contract section N.J.S. 12A:2–612(2), N.J.S.A., is to extend the time for cure past the contract delivery date for that non-conforming installment, provided the nonconformity does not "substantially [impair] the value of that installment" and can be cured. We find that Holterbosch was justified in rejecting Graulich's tender of the April 23 initial installment since the nonconformity of the tendered goods with the accepted sample was incurable, and thus substantially impaired the value of that installment.

. . . To allow an aggrieved party to cancel an installment contract, N.J.S. 12A:2–612(3), N.J.S.A. requires (1) the breach be of the whole contract which occurs when the nonconformity of "one or more installments substantially impairs the value of the whole contract;" and (2) that seasonable notification of cancellation has been given if the buyer has accepted a non-conforming installment.

What amounts to substantial impairment presents a question of fact. Analyzing this factual question, the New Jersey commentators counsel that the test as to whether the nonconformity in any given installment justifies cancelling the entire contract depends on whether the nonconformity substantially impairs the value of the whole contract, and not on whether it indicates an intent or likelihood that the future deliveries also will be defective. Continuing, the Comment relates the intent underlying a breach to insecurity and those sections of the Code providing buyer with adequate assurance of performance, Section 2–609, and anticipatory repudiation, Section 2–610. More practical in its treatment of "substantial impairment," the official Comment states that "substantial impairment of the value of an installment can turn not only on the quality of the goods but also on such factors as time, quantity, assortment and the like. It must be judged in terms of the normal or specifically known purposes of the contract." Comment to Section 2–612, par. 4. . . .

At the Lowenbrau Pavilion on April 23, 1964 plaintiff Graulich, timely notified of the non-conforming initial tender, gave assurance that future tenders would be cured to match the original samples. Unequivocally committed to the microwave kitchen method, defendant lent plaintiff three members from its staff in aid of this adjustment. Since plaintiff was given the opportunity to cure, there is no need to touch upon the substantiality of the initial non-conforming installment.

The second installment tender was as unsatisfactory as the first. The meat was dry, the gravy "gooey" and the complaints abundant. After the non-conforming second delivery it became apparent that eleventh-hour efforts attempting to rework and adjust the platters failed. Translating this into legal parlance, there was a non-conforming tender of the initial installment on a contract for the sale of goods; upon tender the buyer Holterbosch notified the seller Graulich of the nonconformity and unacceptable nature of the platters tendered; the failure of the cure assured by plaintiff, seller, was evidenced by a subsequently defective non-conforming delivery. The second unacceptable delivery and the failure of plaintiff's additional curative efforts left defendant in a position for one week without food. Time was critical. Plaintiff knew that platters of maximum quality were required on a daily installment basis. Because of defendant's immediate need for quality food and plaintiff's failure to cure, we find that the nonconformity of the second delivery, projected upon the circumstances of this case, "substantially impair[ed] the value of the whole contract [and resulted in] a breach of the whole." N.J.S. 12A:2–612(3), N.J.S.A. If the breach goes to the whole contract the buyer may cancel the whole contract. N.J.S.A. 12A:2–711(1), N.J.S.A. Accordingly, we find that Holterbosch was justified in cancelling the installment agreement signed on April 1, 1964.

Questions

1. What else might the court have done to salvage the situation?
2. Can you articulate the reasons why the court concludes that the nonconformity impairs the value of the entire contract? Can you state a general test for determining when the defect justifies ending the entire contract?

Although defective tender ordinarily involves the seller's performance, it may result from the buyer's failure to tender payment on time. For example, suppose that goods are to be delivered in ten installments, that payment is due within ten days after delivery, and that the buyer fails to pay on time after the fourth delivery. Does this allow the seller to declare a breach of the entire contract and refuse to make punctual delivery of the remaining installments? The answer will depend on the materiality of the breach, the buyer's ability to give reasonable assurance of a timely cure, and whether the breach happens a second time. Remember, good faith and commercial reasonableness apply in all cases of technical breach.

BUYER'S PERFORMANCE

When the seller's performance has been completed, the buyer must perform or complete his performance. Ordinarily, that means the buyer is obligated to pay for the goods. However, the buyer has certain rights with respect to performance.

Obligation of Payment

The basic obligation of the buyer is to tender payment; meeting this obligation gives rise to the seller's obligation to tender the goods. In fact, tender of payment and tender of the goods are concurrent conditions; that is, each obligation is a condition of the other, and both are intended to occur at the same time.

Unless the parties agree to the contrary, cash on delivery at the place of delivery is assumed, and a seller is not required to extend credit or to accept a check. However, if payment by check usually is acceptable in the ordinary course of the business involved in the transaction, tender of a check will meet the buyer's obligation, and if the seller demands cash, the seller also must extend the time of payment as long as is reasonably necessary for the buyer to procure cash. If the seller accepts the buyer's check and the check is dishonored on due presentment (when it properly is presented to the bank for payment), payment is defeated.

Right of Inspection

Section 2-513 gives buyers the right to inspect goods prior to payment. Generally, a seller's right to tender of the purchase price is conditioned on this right. The buyer, however, may give up this right by agreement; he or she may contract for delivery "C.O.D." or on similar terms, or may agree to pay upon receipt of documents of title without the right to inspect.

A buyer's right to inspect may be exercised at any reasonable time and place, and in any reasonable manner, unless the contract specifies to the contrary. If the goods are to be delivered to the buyer, inspection may occur after arrival, and receipt of the goods does not constitute acceptance or give rise to a duty to pay until the buyer has had a reasonable opportunity to inspect. Failure to exercise this right within a reasonable time may constitute waiver of the buyer's right to reject or to revoke acceptance of the contract.

All expenses of inspection are borne by the buyer unless the buyer rejects the goods as nonconforming. Remember, however, that in the case of nonconforming goods Section 2-601 provides that the buyer may reject the whole, accept the whole, or accept any commercial unit or units and reject the rest. In the case of a partial rejection, inspection costs may be divided between the parties proportionately.

Rejection

Sections 2-602 to 2-604 govern a buyer's rights and obligations concerning rejection of goods. If a buyer exercises his or her right to reject nonconforming goods, this right must be exercised prior to acceptance and within a reasonable time after tender or delivery. It also must be accompanied by reasonable notice to the seller. If rejection is wrongful, the buyer is liable for all foreseeable damages that the seller suffers as a result. Generally, the exercise of ownership by the buyer after rejection is considered just as wrongful as the rejection of conforming goods.

Upon rejecting goods in his or her possession, the buyer becomes an involuntary bailee of the goods and is obligated to hold them with reasonable care for a time sufficient to permit the seller to remove them. Unless the buyer is a merchant or the seller has no agent or place of business at the place of rejection, the buyer has no further obligation.

If the buyer *is* a merchant *and* the seller has no agent or place of business at the place of rejection, the buyer is obligated to aid the seller by mitigating the seller's damages, even if the buyer's rejection was rightful. The buyer must follow any reasonable instructions from the seller, who even may require the buyer to sell the goods on the seller's account. If the seller gives no instructions and the goods are either perishable or otherwise likely to decline in value rapidly, the buyer must make a reasonable effort to sell them for the seller. If the buyer succeeds in selling the goods, the buyer then is entitled to reimbursement of all expenses reasonably incurred plus a commission on the sale. The amount of the commission may be what is usual in the trade or, if there is no customary usage, it may be a reasonable commission; in either case, the commission cannot exceed ten percent of the gross proceeds.

Acceptance

Generally, an acceptance is a manifestation by the buyer of his intent to be bound to discharge his obligations under the contract. Specifically, Section 2-606 provides that an acceptance occurs when the buyer: (1) after a reasonable opportunity to inspect, signifies to the seller that the goods are conforming *or* that he is willing to accept them in spite of their nonconformity; or (2) after a reasonable opportunity to inspect, fails to make an effective rejection; or (3) acts inconsistently with the seller's ownership by, for example, selling the goods to a third party. Under Section 2–607(2), acceptance in any of these ways precludes rejection or revocation of acceptance unless, as described below, the goods were nonconforming.

Revocation of Acceptance

Under Section 2–608, a buyer who has accepted may revoke her acceptance as to a lot or a commercial unit that is so nonconforming that its value is impaired substantially. Revocation is possible if she accepted it (1) under a reasonable belief that the seller would cure any defect seasonably, as provided in Section 2–607(2), or (2) without discovery of the nonconformity if her acceptance was induced either by the difficulty of reasonable discovery prior to acceptance or by the seller's assurances that the goods were conform-

ing. In order to revoke, the buyer must notify the seller within a reasonable time after she discovers or should have discovered the nonconformity, and prior to any substantial change in the goods caused by something other than the defect. If the buyer properly revokes, she has the same rights she would have had if she had rejected. Suppose, for example, Acme Appliances receives a lot of twenty toasters from Toastkin, Inc., each toaster packaged in a separate sealed box. Acme probably would be on notice of a possible problem if the shipping carton arrived with substantial physical damage. Otherwise, Acme normally would not be expected to open, inspect, and test each toaster. Therefore, a substantial period of time might pass before enough sales were made and toasters were returned or complaints were received to cause Acme to open the remainder of the lot and to check it. As this illustration suggests, what constitutes a reasonable time always depends on the circumstances. Consider the following case.

BOWEN v. YOUNG
507 S.W.2d 600 (Tex. Civ.App. 1974)

This was an action by Orris W. Bowen, dba Bowen Mobile Homes (Plaintiff/Appellant), against Jack Young (Defendant/Appellee) for the unpaid balance of the purchase price of a mobile home Defendant purchased. After delivery, Defendant found may substantial defects in the home. Plaintiff failed to make repairs within a reasonable time, so Defendant gave notice of cancellation. Then, because Plaintiff made no effort to return his deposit, Defendant moved in and lived in the mobile home for a little more than a year before moving to South Carolina. While in South Carolina he spent $581 making repairs and converting the heating system to gas.

   The trial court found that Defendant had rejected the mobile home rightfully and granted him judgment. Plaintiff appealed. Reversed and remanded.

OSBORN, Justice.

Although Section 2.711(c) gives a buyer a security interest in goods in his possession, and even a right to resell them, it does not give a right to continued use of the goods until the security interest is satisfied. The Appellee testified that after discovering the defects in the mobile home, he telephoned both the seller and manufacturer to obtain some satisfaction toward the repairs and change of the defects. When he sent his

telegram on January 21st to the seller, he said therein "Unable to secure commitment from factory." A week earlier he had wired the seller and General Electric Credit Corporation, who was to originally finance the mobile home, that the unit was damaged and that he would not pay until it was completely repaired.

Failing to get satisfactory assurance from either the seller or manufacturer concerning the damaged and non-conforming mobile home, Appellee did not seek to foreclose his security interest for the down-payment, transportation and storage expense. Nor did he act in accordance with Section 2.604, which provides: ". . . if the seller gives no instructions within a reasonable time after notification of rejection the buyer may store the rejected goods for the seller's account or reship them to him or resell them for the seller's account with reimbursement as provided in the preceding section. Such action is not acceptance or conversion." Instead, he decided sometime in February to move into the mobile home and spent nearly $600.00 to repair the heating unit and change from an electric to a gas heater. By doing so he accepted the goods under Section 2.606, and under Section 2.607 became obligated to pay at the contract price for the goods accepted, retaining such rights, if any, as existed for damages under Section 2.714 and Section 2.715. Melody Home Manufacturing Company v. Morrison, 502 S.W.2d 196 (Tex. Civ.App.—Houston (1st Dist.) 1973, writ filed).

On numerous occasions Courts have held that one who exercises dominion over or alters goods in his possession thereby accepts the goods as delivered. . . .

The action which the buyer may take once he has rejected the goods is summarized in Bender's UCC Service, Vol. 3, Section 14.02(1)(c)(i), as follows:

> If the seller does not give reasonable instructions, or does not give any instructions at all, or if the buyer makes such a demand but the seller does not provide indemnity for expenses, then the buyer is entitled to attempt reasonably to sell the goods. In any resale of the goods, it would be for the seller's account. . . . However, looking at the terms in Section 2-604, the buyer (merchant or nonmerchant) is given an option to resell goods for the seller's account even if they are not perishable or do not threaten to decline in value speedily. Under Section 2-604, if the buyer notifies the seller of his rejection within the time required, and if the seller does not remit instructions to the buyer within a reasonable time, then the buyer may either store, reship, or resell the goods. These are optional alternatives but, obviously, the buyer is going to have to do one of these three things.

In this case, Mr. Young did not exercise any of these three options permitted by the Code, but instead took a course of conduct clearly inconsistent with the seller's continued ownership of the mobile home.

Questions

1. Would the result have been different if the mobile-home buyer had no other place to live? What if it could be shown that, if he had sold the home, it would not have yielded enough money to rent an apartment for any appreciable period?

2. Would the result have been different if the buyer had merely lived in the home and had not converted the heating system?

Sales performance

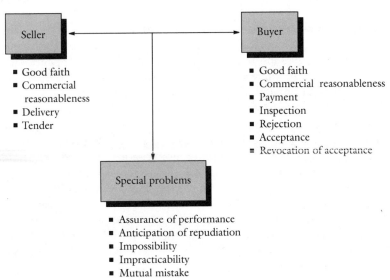

SPECIAL PROBLEMS

Although most sales transactions are completed routinely, a small percentage are not. Unusual circumstances may give rise to special problems. When this occurs, the rights and duties of the parties may be altered.

Assurance of Performance and Anticipation of Repudiation

When one party is unwilling or unable to perform, the party to whom performance is due or will be due should have a more convenient remedy than the ultimate and cumbersome weapon of a lawsuit. For this reason, under Section 2–609, if either party has reasonable grounds for doubting that the other will perform as promised, he or she may demand (in writing) an adequate assurance of proper future performance. Then the other party, within a reasonable time not exceeding 30 days, must give the requested assurance. During the period following notice, if it is commercially reasonable to do so, the party giving notice may

suspend any performance for which he or she has not already received the agreed-upon return and, if adequate assurance is not provided, may treat the failure as a **repudiation** (disavowal) of the transaction. He then is entitled to await performance from the repudiating party, to resort to any remedy for breach even if he has notified the repudiating party that he would await performance, or to claim identified goods or salvage unfinished goods (put the goods to some reasonable use so as to avoid loss) under Section 2–704.

Until the repudiating party's next performance is due, she may retract her repudiation unless the aggrieved party has cancelled, materially changed his position, or otherwise indicated that he considers the repudiation final. The retraction may be accomplished by any method that indicates to the other party that she intends to perform, accompanied by any assurance justifiably demanded. This reinstates the contract with any allowances due to the aggrieved party because of the repudiation. Consider the following case.

AMF, INCORPORATED v. McDONALD'S CORPORATION
536 F.2d 1167 (7th Cir. 1976)

This was an action by AMF, Incorporated (Plaintiff/Appellant) against McDonald's Corporation (Defendant/Appellee) for damages for Defendant's wrongful cancellation and repudiation of a contract to purchase 23 computerized cash registers. A prototype unit was installed in Defendant's Elk Grove, Illinois, restaurant in April 1968. Between August and December 1968, Defendant ordered 16 machines, and 7 more were ordered by Defendant's franchisees. AMF proposed to deliver the first unit in February 1969, and the remainder during the first half of 1969. However, Plaintiff revised its schedule in February 1969 to begin deliveries by the end of July 1969, assuming that the first test unit being built at Plaintiff's Vandalia, Ohio, plant was completed and satisfactorily tested by the end of July 1969. This never was accomplished. The prototype unit installed in Elk Grove performed unsatisfactorily, and required frequent service calls until it finally was removed by Defendant in April 1969. Plaintiff and Defendant met in March and May 1969, and at the May meeting it became clear that Plaintiff could not produce a satisfactory unit within a reasonable time because its Vandalia plant personnel were too inexperienced. Because of the poor performance of the prototype machine and the lack of assurance that a workable machine would be available within a reasonable time, Plaintiff subsequently concluded that Defendant had decided to cancel and repudiate its order, and this was confirmed at a July 29, 1969 meeting.

The trial court found that Defendant had canceled and repudiated its contract justifiably, because Plaintiff already had repudiated it by failing to provide adequate assurance of performance, and granted judgment accordingly. Plaintiff appealed. Affirmed.

CUMMINGS, Circuit Judge.

Whether in a specific case a buyer has reasonable grounds for insecurity is a question of fact. . . . On the record, McDonald's clearly had "reasonable grounds for insecurity" with respect to AMF's performance. At the time of the March 18, 1969, meeting, the prototype unit had performed unsatisfactorily ever since its April 1968 installation. Although AMF had projected delivery of all twenty-three units by the first half of 1969, AMF later scheduled delivery from the end of July 1969 until January 1970. When McDonald's personnel visited AMF's Vandalia, Ohio, plant on March 4, 1969, they saw that none of the 72C systems was being assembled and learned that a pilot unit would not be ready until the end of July of that year. They were informed that the engineer assigned to the project was not to commence work until March 17th. AMF's own personnel were also troubled about the design of the 72C, causing them to attempt to reduce McDonald's order to five units. Therefore, under Section 2–609 McDonald's was entitled to demand adequate assurance of performance by AMF.

However, AMF urges that Section 2–609 of the UCC . . . is inapplicable because McDonald's did not make a written demand of adequate assurance of due performance. In Pittsburgh-Des Moines Steel Co. v. Brookhaven Manor Water Co., . . . we noted that the Code should be liberally construed and therefore rejected such "a formalistic approach" to Section 2–609. McDonald's failure to make a written demand was excusable because AMF's Mr. Dubosque's testimony and his April 2 and 18, 1969, memoranda about the March 18th meeting showed AMF's clear understanding that McDonald's had suspended performance until it should receive adequate assurance of due performance from AMF. . . .

After the March 18th demand, AMF never repaired the Elk Grove unit satisfactorily nor replaced it. Similarly, it was unable to satisfy McDonald's that the twenty-three machines on order would work. At the May 1st meeting, AMF offered unsatisfactory assurances for only five units instead of twenty-three. The performance standards AMF tendered to McDonald's were unacceptable because they would have permitted the 72C's not to function properly for 90 hours per year, permitting as much as one failure in every fifteen days in a busy McDonald's restaurant. Also, as the district court found, AMF's Vandalia, Ohio, personnel were too inexperienced to produce a proper machine. Since AMF did not provide adequate assurance of performance after McDonald's March 18th demand, UCC Section 2–609(1) permitted McDonald's to suspend performance. When AMF did not furnish adequate assurance of due performance at the May 1st meeting, it thereby repudiated the contract under Section 2–609(4). At that point, Section 2–610(b) . . . permitted McDonald's to cancel the orders pursuant to Section 2–711 . . . as it finally did on July 29, 1969.

Questions

1. Since the Code calls for a written demand for assurance of performance, was it right for the court to call the plaintiff's insistence on compliance a "formalistic approach"?

2. What should happen if a buyer gives notice of insecurity (a lack of confidence that the seller will perform) prematurely? How should the seller be protected?

These provisions concerning *anticipatory repudiation* (justifiable belief that the other party will fail to perform in the future) serve the important Article 2 purpose of encouraging performance of sales transactions. They provide security to the party to whom performance is due, yet keep mistakes from being terminal in many circumstances. By doing so, they encourage continuity in commerical relationships.

Impossibility of Performance

The parties to a contract may find that they are unable to perform because of circumstances that intervene between the time they contract and the time performance is due. If these circumstances are beyond the reasonable control of the parties, full performance usually is excused. One such circumstance may be some irrecoverable damage to the goods.

Section 2–613 provides that if goods are lost or destroyed, or if they are partially lost or suffer deterioration to the extent that they no longer conform to the contract, the buyer may be excused from all or part of his or her performance. If the loss is total, the contract is avoided. Otherwise, the buyer either may treat the contract as avoided or may accept the goods with allowance from the contract price for the deficiency. In making this decision, and in determining how much allowance is due, the buyer must observe the limitations of good faith and commerical reasonableness required by the Code.

It should be noted that these rules do not apply until the goods have been *identified* to the contract. That is, the goods suffering the casualty must have been specifically referred to in the terms of the contract, or must have been shipped to or marked for the buyer. Suppose Dan harvests his crop of hay and puts it in his barn. He determines that he has 250 bales more than he needs and says to Roseanne, "I will sell you 250 bales of hay at $4 per bale." Roseanne accepts this offer, but prior to delivery, Dan's barn burns down and the hay is destroyed. The contract in this case is not avoided. Because the hay in the barn was neither specified nor otherwise identified to the contract, Section 2–613 does not apply. Dan would be obligated to purchase hay on the open market to deliver to Roseanne. The reason for this outcome is simple: Dan offered to sell 250 bales of hay, not any particular 250 bales of the hay he had in his barn. Clearly, if any conditions (such as the source of particular goods) are important to an offeror, he must be sure to include them in his offer. The objective meaning of an offer, not the offeror's secret subjective intent, will determine his rights if a dispute arises.

Impracticability of Performance

Although the parties are ready and willing to perform fully and the goods have remained unchanged after having been identified to the contract, circumstances still may intervene to prevent the planned performance. This might happen if the agreed-upon method of shipment becomes unavailable. For example, the contract might call for shipment by truck, and a strike of truck drivers or warehouse employees could make shipment by truck either impossible, unacceptably costly, or subject to delay. Section 2–614 provides that under these circumstances—if delivery in the agreed-

upon manner becomes either impossible or **commerically impracticable** and a commerically reasonable substitute is available—delivery by the substitute means must be tendered and accepted. By this provision, the UCC again places the goals of continuity of commerical obligations and the completion of performance above technical requirements, even when those requirements are stated in the agreement between the parties.

Mutual Mistake

Prior to performance of a contract, the parties may find out they both were mistaken about a basic fact or may learn of intervening circumstances that were not contemplated when they entered into the contract. If the subject of the mistake or nonexistence of these factors was a basic assumption on which the contract was made, delay in delivery or nondelivery in whole or in part may be excused. If the circumstances affect only part of the seller's capacity to perform, she must allocate production and delivery among her customers in any manner that is fair and reasonable. In establishing this allocation she may consider her future capacity for production, and, if she wishes, may take account of regular customers not then under contract. Customers affected are entitled to notice and an estimate of the quota available to them. Circumstances to which these rules apply include an unavailability of raw materials, labor problems, loss of production facilities, and some problems concerning warehousing or shipping.

It should be noted that the doctrine of mutual mistake comes into play when important conditions of performance fail to occur without the fault of either party. The conditions are assumed and could be, but often are not, stated in the contract. All contracts of every kind are based on some fundamental, and often unstated, assumptions. For example, in entering into a contract for the sale of a horse, it normally would be assumed that the horse was alive, unless circumstances or the stated terms dictate to the contrary. The doctrine of mutual mistake not only ensures just outcomes by preventing unfair surprises, it also saves contracting parties from having to specify the infinite number of conditions that must occur for their performance to be possible.

SELLER'S REMEDIES

At any point after agreement is reached, a buyer may fail in his obligations to the seller. The buyer might wrongfully reject the goods or revoke his acceptance by failing to pay the purchase price or by repudiation. In any of these events, the seller's justifiable expectations of performance are impaired, and the seller is entitled to relief. The possible remedies, depending upon the type of breach, the circumstances, and sometimes the desire of the seller, are to:

1. withhold delivery of the goods (Section 2-703);
2. stop delivery by any bailee (Section 2-705);
3. proceed to identify the goods to the contract or to salvage (Section 2-704);
4. resell the goods and recover damages (Section 2-706);
5. recover damages for nonacceptance (Section 2-708);
6. recover the price (Section 2-709);
7. cancel.

When appropriate, these remedies may be used in combination.

To Withhold Goods or Stop Delivery

Upon the buyer's breach, the seller may withhold any goods still in her possession. If the goods have been placed for shipment or otherwise put into the possession of a bailee with instructions to deliver them to the buyer, the seller may retract her instructions and stop delivery only until: (1) delivery of the goods to the buyer; (2) acknowledgment to the buyer, by any bailee except a carrier (for example, a warehouse), that the goods are being held for the buyer; (3) such acknowledgment by a carrier through shipment by the carrier (not the seller) to the buyer or by the carrier as warehouseman; or (4) negotiation to the buyer of any *negotiable* document of title, unless the seller has recovered the document of title and returned it to the bailee. (A document of title is negotiable if the party holding the goods is obligated to deliver them only to the person who has possession of the document, rather than to a person named on the face of the document. The latter is called the *nonnegotiable* document of title.) No bailee is obligated, however, unless notified either by the seller or by someone on the seller's behalf and the notice comes while the bailee reasonably can honor the order. Also, if the bailee has delivered to the buyer a *nonnegotiable* document of title, he is not obligated to honor notice given by anyone except the consignor (*usually* the seller). Therefore, notice is effective to stop delivery only if given in time for the bailee to act and before the bailee has made either delivery or an irrevocable commitment to the buyer.

To Identify or to Salvage Goods

Upon the buyer's breach, the seller, if he wishes, may identify to the contract any conforming goods still within his possession or control, or may treat the goods as independent of the contract and sell them to other buyers in the course of business. In addition, any unfinished goods that are in the process of manufacturing or completion, and clearly are intended to fill the contract with the breaching buyer, may be salvaged by the seller. In good faith, and as commercially reasonable, the seller may elect either to complete the goods and hold them for resale or to sell them in their unfinished form for scrap or otherwise (perhaps "kit" form). These rights, in effect, promote reasonable mitigation of damages by the seller.

To Resell Goods and Recover Damages

Upon breach by the buyer, the seller may elect to resell any undelivered goods that were the subject of the contract. This includes all goods identified to the contract, any unfinished goods, and even future goods (not yet in existence) if there is a recognized market for them. The sale may be either public or private and by any method or in any manner, at any time and place, and on any commerically reasonable terms. The resale must identify the goods as belonging to the broken contract.

If the resale is a private sale, the seller must give the buyer reasonable notification of her intention to sell. If at public sale, the buyer is entitled to reasonable notification of the time and place, ex-cept if the goods are perishable or are subject to rapid decline in value. A public sale must be held at a usual place or market for public sale if one is available, and the seller is entitled to buy. A pur-chaser who buys goods at resale takes them free and clear of all rights of the buyer, as long as the transaction was in good faith. This is true even if the seller has violated one or more of the UCC requirements regarding the sale. Finally, the seller is not accountable to the buyer for any profits above the price of the broken contract. Consider the following case.

WOLPERT v. FOSTER
312 Minn. 526, 2554 N.W.2d 348 (1977)

This was an action by Herschel Wolpert, individually and dba Sales Enterprises (Plaintiff/Respondent) against Charles R. Foster and others (Defendants/Ap-pellants) to recover (1) principal and interest on an open account and (2) the contract price of goods held for Defendant Foster. The parties entered into an agreement under the terms of which Plaintiff would purchase fishing equipment for Foster, reselling it at cost plus ten percent. Many of these sales were on open account. When the parties terminated the contract, Plaintiff held goods pur-chased for Foster at a cost of $19,055.08, and the open account for goods previously received by Foster had a balance of $21,817.50. By means of various kinds of sales, Plaintiff sold off much of the $19,055.08 of goods after Foster failed to take and pay for them. At the time of suit, Plaintiff remained in possession of goods of a cost of $4703.43 (the contract price to Foster was $5515.56).

The trial court found for Plaintiff and Defendants appealed. Affirmed as to all matters material here.

KELLY, Justice.

Plaintiff brought this action for the price of the remaining inventory under Minn.St. 336.2–709. That section provides in part:

(1) When the buyer fails to pay the price as it becomes due the seller may recover, together with any incidental damages under the next section, the price . . .
(b) of goods identified to the contract if the seller is unable after reasonable effort to resell them at a reasonable price or the circumstances reasonably indicated that such effort will be unavailing.
(2) Where the seller sues for the price he must hold for the buyer any goods which have been identifed to the contract and are still in his control except that if resale becomes possible he may resell them at any time prior to the collection of the judgment. The net proceeds of any

such resale must be credited to the buyer and payment of the judgment entitles him to any goods not resold.

Plaintiff held the remaining goods for delivery to defendant upon payment of the contract price. Defendant concedes the goods have been identified to the contract and does not challenge the reasonableness of plaintiff's efforts to resell the remaining inventory. Instead, defendant contends that plaintiff has failed to adequately credit under Section 336.2-709(2) the part of the inventory that plaintiff was able to resell, because those resales did not comport with Minn.St. 336.2-706. It should be noted that plaintiff is not seeking damages with respect to that part of the inventory which has been resold. The trial court found that plaintiff "neither made nor lost any substantial amount of money" on the resales. Our perception of the evidence similarly reveals that the net proceeds from the resales were less than the contract price for those goods.

We find that Section 336.2-709 does not incorporate the resale requirements of Section 336.2-706. The Uniform Commerical Code makes it clear that a seller's remedies are cumulative. . . . A resale of goods conforming to the requirements of Section 336.2-706 entitles a seller to damages measured by the resale price. Minn.St. 336.2-706(1). A resale failing to conform to these requirements may relegate the seller to measurement of his damages based on the market price at the time and place of tender. . . . An action for the price arises in this situation only when reasonable resale efforts do not dispose of the goods. It is a remedy distinct from an action for damages under Section 336.2-706 or Section 336.2-708, and thus we would hesitate to incorporate the requirements of Section 336.2-706 with respect ot the goods that have been sold as a prerequisite for maintaining an action under Section 336.2-709 for the price of the remaining goods. Minn.St. 336.2-709 confirms our conclusion. It mandates crediting resale proceeds only of goods still held for the buyer at the time of suit and not of goods amenable to sale by reasonable efforts and for which no action for the price would lie. Minn.St. 336.2-709(2): ". . . The net proceeds of any such resale. . . ." Because the trial court found that plaintiff handled the resold goods in a commerically reasonable manner and because plaintiff's net proceeds from the resale were less than the contract price for the items, no factor appears in the instant case to alter our conclusion.

In sum, plaintiff resold some of the goods identified to the contract but decided not to seek damages with respect to those goods. Instead, he sought to recover the contract price for the goods he could not resell. He has satisfied the requirements of Section 336.2-709 and is entitled to the contract price, even though he failed to comply with the requirements that Section 336.2-706 imposes on an action to recover damages measured by the resale price. Thus, the trial court's judgment in this respect is affirmed, and defendant is entitled to the goods in plaintiff's possession upon payment of the contract price.

Questions

1. What does the court mean when it says that a seller's remedies under the UCC are *cumulative?*

2. Might a seller's decision to hold goods and sue for the contract price be considered a failure of his or her duty to mitigate damages? Why or why not?

To Recover Damages for Nonacceptance or Repudiation

In the event of nonacceptance or repudiation by the buyer, the seller is entitled to damages for breach of contract. Ordinarily, the measure of damages is the market price of the goods at the time and place of tender and the unpaid contract price, together with any incidental damages, but less any expenses saved as a consequence of the breach. If the seller's action for damages is brought on the ground of anticipatory repudiation (prior to the time of tender), then the measure of damages begins with the market price at the time the seller learned of the repudiation rather than the market price at the time of tender. Therefore, the timing of an action for breach may be subject to the seller's assessment of the future market for goods such as those involved in the repudiated contract. If the seller elects to hold the goods during a period of rising market price, it may affect mitigation of the damages to be paid by the buyer. If the seller holds the goods during a declining market, the damages, of course, may be increased. However, the seller is permitted to make the choice, but it must be exercised in good faith and according to standards of commerical reasonableness if the seller is a merchant—the choice may not be made for the purpose of increasing the amount of damages due from the buyer.

If the general measure of damages just discussed is inadequate to put the seller in as good a position as he would have been in had the contract been performed, Section 2–708(2) provides an alternative. Under these circumstances the measure of damages is the profit (including reasonable overhead) that the seller would have made from the buyer, together with incidental damages and an allowance for costs reasonably incurred, reduced by any payments by the buyer and any proceeds of resale. This section applies technically to the "lost-volume seller," a seller of goods whose price does not change and who, therefore, would gain nothing by damages computed by subtracting the market price from the identical price in the contract. The Code recognizes that the lost-volume seller in fact has lost profit even though he can resell the goods for the contract price, and therefore provides him with a lost-profits remedy.

Incidental Damages

The discussion above has mentioned incidental damages. Under Section 2–710, these include any commerically reasonable charges, expenses, or commissions incurred (1) in stopping delivery, (2) in the transportation, care, or custody of goods after the buyer's breach, (3) in connection with the return or resale of the goods, or (4) otherwise as a result of the breach. Incidental damages generally are limited, however, to damages that reasonably are foreseeable as a consequence of the type of breach involved.

To Recover the Purchase Price

Instead of reselling the goods that were the subject of a contract and bringing a lawsuit for damages, the seller may sue the buyer for the purchase price of the goods the buyer accepted, goods lost or damaged within a commerically reasonable time after the risk of loss passed from the seller to the buyer, and any other goods identified to the contract, together with incidental damages. This excludes goods in process that are incomplete and other future goods. However, before the seller in effect can force the buyer to buy the goods, she first must make a reasonable effort to resell them in the marketplace.

When the seller brings an action for the price, she must hold the goods at the buyer's disposal unless she is able to sell them before collection of the judgment. The net proceeds of any such sale then must be credited to the buyer. Of course, any seller who does not meet the criteria necessary to allow a suit for the purchase price still may maintain an action for damages as described above. For example, a seller who is not in possession or control of identified goods may sue for the difference between the contract price and the market price, or for lost profit.

Action upon Buyer's Insolvency

Section 2–702 provides for sellers' remedies in the event that the buyer is insolvent. A buyer's insolvency may be proved by an order for relief in a bankruptcy action, by his involvement in a composition agreement, or by other relevant facts. An insolvent buyer is one whose liabilities exceed his assets or, according to the current Bankruptcy Code, one who is unable to pay his debts as they come due. A buyer's insolvency, of course, gives the seller ample cause to doubt the buyer's present and future ability to perform.

If the buyer is insolvent, the seller may elect to withhold delivery until the buyer has paid fully for past deliveries even if, according to the contract's terms, payment is not yet due. The seller then may condition all further deliveries on the payment of cash, and may reclaim any goods delivered while the buyer was insolvent.

A seller's right to reclaim goods sold on credit to an insolvent buyer is conditional upon the seller's having made a demand for payment within ten days after the goods were received. However, if the buyer has misrepresented her solvency to the seller in writing within three months before delivery, the ten-day limitation does not apply. The seller's right to reclaim is allowed only by complying with these rules. It should be noted that the seller's right to reclaim is subject to the rights of a buyer in the ordinary course of business, or a good-faith purchaser under Section 2–403, and that successful reclamation of goods excludes all other remedies available to the seller. Creditors' rights in bankruptcy actions are discussed more fully in Chapter 24.

BUYER'S REMEDIES

Just as a buyer may fail in his obligations to the seller, so may the seller breach the contract. This may occur as a result of a failure to make delivery or a repudiation, or because of the seller's shipment of nonconforming goods. Upon the seller's breach, the buyer is entitled to cancel with respect to some of the goods, or with respect to all of them if the breach goes to the entire contract. In addition, whether or not he cancels, the buyer may recover as much of the price as he has paid *and* (1) "cover" and have damages, *or* (2) recover damages for nondelivery. If the seller fails to deliver or repudiates, the buyer also may (1) recover any goods that have been identified to the contract *or* (2) obtain specific performance or replace the goods in appropriate cases.

Upon rightful rejection or revocation of acceptance, the buyer has a security interest in any of the seller's goods that are in her possession or control. This interest secures all payments made and any expenses reasonably incurred in the inspection, receipt, transportation, or care and custody of the goods. The buyer also may resell the goods in the same manner as an aggrieved seller.

Cover

The buyer's right to *cover* under Section 2–712 is similar to the seller's right to resell under Section 2–706. It is the buyer's method of mitigating damages. **Cover** is the purchase of sustitute goods to replace those the seller failed to tender. If the buyer elects to cover, he is entitled to recover from the seller the difference between the cover price and the contract price together with any incidental and consequential damages, but less any expenses saved as a consequence of the seller's breach. A buyer is not required to cover, however, and failure to do so does not affect his right to any other available remedies. Consider the following case.

BIGELOW-SANFORD, INC. v. GUNNY CORPORATION
649 F.2d 1060 (5th Cir. 1981)

This was an action by Bigelow-Sanford, Inc. (Plaintiff/Appellee) against Gunny Corporation (Defendant/Appellant) for the cost of cover to replace a promised shipment of jute. Defendant had contracted to sell to Plaintiff, a carpet manufacturer, 100,000 linear yards of jute at 64 cents per yard. Defendant failed to deliver 72,265 yards and Plaintiff purchased jute elsewhere to cover. The average price paid was $1.21 per yard. It appeared that Defendant owned enough jute to meet its obligation, but held the jute in its warehouse to sell at a higher price.

The trial court awarded damages to Plaintiff in the amount of $41,683.11. In addition, the jury found that Defendant had been "stubbornly litigious," and awarded Plaintiff $7500 in attorney fees. Defendant appealed. Affirmed.

KRAVITCH, Circuit Judge.

. . . Gunny contends that appellee's alleged cover purchases should not have been used to measure damages in that they were not made in substitution for the contract purchases, were not made seasonably or in good faith, and were not shown to be due to Gunny's breach. . . . [W]e disagree. . . . Ga.Code Ann. Section 109A-2-711 (UCC Section 2-711) provid[es] in part for cover damages where the seller fails to make delivery or repudiates the contract. . . .

. . . The district court thus acted properly in submitting the question of cover damages to the jury, which found that Gunny had breached, appellee had covered, and had done so in good faith without unreasonable delay by making reasonable purchases, and was therefore entitled to damages under Section 2-712. Gunny argues Bigelow is not entitled to such damages on the ground that it failed to make cover purchases without undue delay and that the jury should not have been permitted to average the cost of Bigelow's spot market purchases totalling 164,503 linear yards Gunny failed to deliver. Both arguments fail. Gunny notified Bigelow in February that no more jute would be forthcoming. Bigelow made its first spot market purchases in mid-March. Given that it is within the jury's province to decide the reasonableness of the manner in which cover purchases were made, we believe the jury could reasonably decide such purchases, made one month after the date the jury assigned to Gunny's breach, were made without undue delay. The same is true with respect to Gunny's second argument: Bigelow's spot market purchases were made to replace several vendors' shipments. Bigelow did not specifically allocate the spot market replacements to individual vendors' accounts, however, nor was there a requirement that they do so. The jury's method of averaging such costs and assigning them to

Gunny in proportion to the amount of jute it failed to deliver would, therefore, seem not only fair but well within the jury's permissible bounds.

Questions

1. Does the court leave the buyer too much discretion in timing the cover? Can abuse be prevented?
2. Does it make sense to ask juries to decide commerical matters such as the one in this case?

Damages for Nondelivery or Repudiation

If the seller repudiates or fails to deliver, the buyer is entitled to damages for breach comparable to a seller's right to damages for nonacceptance or repudiation. The ordinary measure of damages is the difference between the market price at the time the buyer learned of the breach and the contract price, together with incidental and consequential damages, but less expenses saved as a consequence of the seller's breach. The market price is determined as of the place of tender, or as of the place of arrival in the case of rejection of the goods or revocation of acceptance after arrival. If the buyer has received any goods under the contract for which payment has not been made, upon notifying the seller of an intention to do so the buyer is entitled to deduct the amount of the damages from any payment due under the contract.

Damages for Breach after Goods have been Accepted

If the buyer has accepted the seller's goods and has given notice to the seller as required under Section 2-607(3), she may recover damages for any reasonable loss resulting in the ordinary course of events from the seller's breach. The damage include only those injuries that reasonably might have been expected to flow as a normal, foreseeable consequence of the breach. The measure of damages is the difference between the value of the goods and their value if they had been as warranted, judged as of the time and place of acceptance, together with incidental and consequential damages. The subject of damages for breach of warranty is discussed more fully in the next chapter.

Buyer's Incidental and Consequential Damages

Incidental damages from a seller's breach may include expenses reasonably incurred in inspection, receipt, transportation, and care and custody of goods rightfully rejected, as well as any commercially reasonable charges, expenses, or commissions incurred in connection with effecting cover, and any other expenses resulting from the breach.

Consequential damages include any loss resulting from the buyer's requirements or needs that the seller had reason to know of at the time of contracting and that could not reasonably have been avoided by cover or otherwise. Also included are damages for any injury to persons or property proximately resulting from the seller's breach of warranty.

The elements of consequential damages are set out in Section 2-715(2). The portion dealing with cover, which describes consequential damages, in part, as those "which reasonably could not have been prevented by cover," appears

Summary of remedies

Seller	Buyer
▪ Withhold goods ▪ Resell goods ▪ Recover damages after goods resold for nonacceptance for repudiation incidental damages recover purchase price replevin	▪ Cover (purchase of substitute goods) ▪ Recover damages nondelivery repudiation breach of contract incidental damages consequential damages ▪ Specific performance ▪ Replevin

to conflict with Section 2–712(3), which provides: "Failure of the buyer to effect cover within this section does not bar him from any other remedy." However, it should be understood that although the buyer's failure to cover when substituted goods reasonably are available will not bar the recovery of consequential damages, it may be considered in assessing their amount. It is the purpose of Section 2–712(3) to insulate courts from being forced to substitute their opinions as to the reasonableness of effecting cover for those of buyers in determining whether damages should be awarded.

Specific Performance and Replevin

Section 2–716(1) restates the common law's general rule concerning the remedy of specific performance. Although this remedy is described as a right, in fact it still is regarded as a privilege, to be granted at the discretion of the court, not according to any fixed formula, but only when "the goods are *unique* or in other *proper* circumstances." [Emphasis added.]

To assert the right to **replevin** (to take goods that are rightfully his), the buyer first must make a reasonable effort to go into the marketplace and cover or to demonstrate that a reasonable effort would be unavailing. He then is entitled to re-plevin of goods identified to the contract. He also is entitled to replevin of goods shipped under reservation of title after he has made tendered satisfaction of the seller's security interest in them. The major difference between the remedies of specific performance and replevin is that specific performance is a privilege to receive the title to specified goods as the seller promised, whereas replevin is a right to take possession of goods to which the buyer already has title. Moreover, historically, the former is an action in equity and the latter is an action at law.

CONTRACTUAL PROVISIONS AFFECTING REMEDIES

To some extent the agreement of the parties can alter the buyer's and seller's rights to remedies. This is consistent with the notion that the law favors the resolution of legal problems concerning the available remedies and measures of damages by the parties themselves. However, the law also recognizes that parties sometimes have grossly unequal bargaining power. It therefore places some limitations on agreements between them. Contractual provisions affecting remedies may be of two general types: (1) liquidation or limitation of damages and (2) modification or limitation of remedies.

Liquidation or Limitation of Damages

In order to ensure that their commercial relations will be predictable, the parties to a contract may agree on an amount to be paid to the aggrieved party in the event of breach. A provision for liquidated damages must be reasonable in light of (1) the anticipated or actual harm caused by the breach, (2) the difficulties of proof of loss, and (3) the inconvenience or infeasability of otherwise obtaining an adequate remedy. If a liquidated-damages provision is unreasonable in any of these respects, Section 2–718 provides that it is a penalty rather than a true measure of damages, and is therefore void. Most cases involving liquidated-damages clauses that have been challenged as unreasonable involved allegations that the agreed-upon damages are too large. However, a provision for liquidated damages also can be a penalty if it is unreasonably small. An unreasonable liquidated-damages provision, whether the liquidated amount is too large or too small, also is subject to challenge under Section 2–302 as unconscionable.

In the absence of a clause providiing for liquidated damages, Section 2–718 places another important limitation on damages. Subsection (2) provides that if the seller justifiably withholds delivery because of the buyer's breach, the buyer is entitled to restitution of any down payment that has been made to the extent that it exceeds 20 percent of the value of total performance or $500, whichever is smaller.

Contractual Modification or Limitation of Remedy

Within certain limits, the parties are free to shape remedies to suit their needs. Their agreement may provide for remedies in addition to or in substitution for those provided in Article 2 of the UCC. For example, the parties may limit the buyer's remedies to the return of the goods and repayment of the purchase price, or to the repair and replacement of nonconforming goods and parts.

Whether substituted remedies are exclusive depends on the language of the agreement and, unless it *expressly* provides that the substituted remedies are exclusive, the aggrieved party may choose between the contractual remedies and the remedies provided by Article 2 as he or she wishes.

If the remedies provided by the parties are intended to be exclusive, but fail in their essential purpose to make the aggrieved party whole or are unconscionable in their application to the facts of the case, their application may be limited or excluded. Section 2–719(3) specifically provides that limiting consequential damages for injury to persons in the case of consumer goods is *prima facie* unconscionable. When the contract limits damages, the breaching party must establish by a preponderance of the evidence that the limitation is reasonable. In judging reasonableness, a court will consider, among other things, factors it would think relevant under Section 2–718(1) in determining the reasonableness of a liquidated-damages clause.

STATUTE OF LIMITATIONS

The purpose of a statute of limitations is to provide peace of mind to potential defendants by requiring plaintiffs to bring their lawsuits within a limited period of time after their causes of action accrue. The statute lessens the chance that evidence will be lost, or that the memories of the parties and witnesses will become "foggy" concerning the crucial details of a transaction, so that the truth will be lost or the defendant will be unable to defend.

Under Section 2–725, an aggrieved party must bring suit within four years on a sales transaction covered by the Code, although the parties may agree to a shorter period of no less than one year. A cause of action accrues when the breach of contract occurs, even if the aggrieved party does not know of the breach. A breach of warranty (a promise concerning the nature or quality of the goods) accrues when delivery is tendered, except when the warranty explicitly extends to future performance and discovery of the breach must await the time of performance. In that situation, the cause of action accrues when the breach is or should have been discovered, whichever occurs first. For example, suppose an automobile manufacturer sells its products with a five-year extended warranty on parts and workmanship. Four and a half years after purchase the brakes fail on one of the cars, causing an injury to the owner. Since the manufacturer explicitly warranted future performance, and discovery of the breach reasonably could not have occurred earlier, the statute of limitations would begin to run at the time of the failure, unless the brake problem should have been discovered earlier.

Section 2-725 has been questioned because it sets accrual at the time of the breach rather than when the breach was or should have been discovered, which is thought by some to be fairer to the buyer. However, those who drafted Article 2 concluded that the advantages of having a fixed time for accrual exceeded those of a more flexible approach. Also, it should be remembered that, in cases in which a fraud prevents a buyer from discovering the breach or in cases in which the limitation period rightfully should be "tolled" (stopped temporarily), a court under Section 2-725(4), is free to fiind that the buyer's cause of action accrued at a later time.

SUMMARY

The law related to performance of contracts for the sale of goods under Article 2 does not differ significantly from the law related to the performance of other contracts. However, many contractual requirements and remedies have been changed by the Uniform Commerical Code to suit the commerical context, and merchants frequently are held to higher standards than are laypersons.

A seller's primary obligation to perform a sales contract is satisfied by a tender of conforming goods. Unless the agreement or the circumstances indicate to the contrary, tender must be provided at a reasonable time and by any reasonable method. The place of tender ordinarily is dictated either by the circumstances or by the shipping terms.

A buyer's primary obligation is satisfied by acceptance and payment if the goods are conforming. If only some of the goods conform, the buyer's obligation is satisfied by acceptance of and payment for units that do conform, coupled with notice to the seller of any problems with the remainder. These obligations are conditioned on the buyer's right to inspect the goods and the seller's right to cure nonconforming tender.

Prior to completion of performance, if either party has just cause to doubt the other's ability or willingness to perform, he or she is entitled to demand adequate assurance of due prformance in any manner and by any means reasonable under the circumstances. If assurance is not forthcoming, the aggrieved party is entitled to suspend performance and eventually declare a breach.

If, without the fault of either party, performance becomes impossible, further performance is excused, and if the impossibility materially impairs the value of the entire contract, the contract is avoided. If performance as promised becomes impracticable because of intervening circumstances, the contract continues if substitute performance is reasonable. Otherwise it is avoided. If the parties have entered into a contract, and were mutually mistaken concerning some basic assumption on which the contract was entered into, performance is partially or wholly excused as is appropriate under the circumstances.

Sellers' and buyers' remedies are roughly counterparts of each other under Article 2. They include the right to suspend performance, the right to recover damages that are either incidental or consequential results of the breach, the seller's rights to sue for the purchase price, and the buyer's right to seek possession of the goods. In exercising these rights, however, both parties must mitigate the damages flowing from the breach to the extent reasonably possible. In addition, the parties are entitled to tailor the available remedies to suit their particular needs within the limits of reasonableness and conscionability.

The general statute of limitations in Section 2–725 is four years. This may be reduced to no less than one year by agreement, but cannot be extended. In most cases, the period of limitations begins running at the time of the breach, which is ordinarily the time of tender of delivery. This is true regardless of the aggrieved party's lack of knowledge of the breach. However, in appropriate situations, a court may declare the time of accrual to be a later time.

KEY TERMS AND CONCEPTS

commercial reasonableness
repudiation
commercially impracticable
cover
replevin

PROBLEMS

1. Simmons ordered cable from Terrell to be used in extending buried electric lines among buildings on a construction project. When the order arrived, two of the three spools were of the above-ground type and were not usable. Simmons notified Terrell and Terrell asked that they be sent back and Simmons's account would be credited. Simmons tried to arrange for shipment but was unable to do so because of a trucking strike. In the meantime, the cable was stored in a building next to Simmons's property. Four months later, the storage building was burglarized and the cable was stolen. Who must bear the loss, Simmons or Terrell?

2. Undermeire agreed to sell certain goods on credit to Wood, with whom he had not dealt before. Prior to delivery, Undermeire became un-comfortable about the transaction and tried to contact Wood. He was unable to do so. In pursuing his investigation, Undermeire learned that the telephone number Wood had given him was that of a telephone booth, that Wood did not have a factory at the address he had given, and that Wood had a bad reputation among those with whom he had dealt. What recourse may Undermeire have in order to lessen the possibility of injury?

3. Consolidated Edison Co. entered into a contract to purchase oil, then at sea, from T. W. Oil, Inc. T. W. had been informed that the sulfur content of the oil was 0.52 percent. The contract with Consolidated Edison provided that the sulfur content of the oil should not exceed 0.50 percent rounded off, as was industry practice. When the oil arrived, it contained 0.92 percent sulfur, and Consolidated Edison rejected it even though, as T. W. learned, Consolidated Edison was permitted to use oil with a sulfur content as high as 1.00 percent and sometimes mixed oils to maintain a legally acceptable percentage. The next day, T. W. offered to cure, but the offer was rejected. It turned out that between the time the oil was ordered and its arrival, an oil embargo that had been in force by certain countries had been removed, and oil prices had dropped sharply. T. W. was forced to sell the oil on the open market and sued Consolidated Edison for $1,385,512.83, the difference between the contract price and the selling price. Is T. W. entitled to a judgment? If so, for what amount?

4. Under a contract with B.A.S.F. Systems, Inc., Holiday Mfg. Co. was to supply cases for cassette tapes, manufactured to specifications supplied by B.A.S.F. When the first installment was shipped the cases were not suitable for use, and B.A.S.F notified Holiday. Holiday fixed the problem. Thereafter, from time to time, other problems developed, although none of them were of a serious nature. B.A.S.F. then notified Holiday that it considered the contract terminated. Was B.A.S.F. entitled to take this action?

5. Maple Farms, Inc. contracted to sell milk to the City School District at an established price. During the contract period, because of sales of huge amounts of milk to Russia, prices increased some 23 percent. In the previous years, prices had fluctuated within a range of 1 percent to 4.5 percent. Because of the circumstances, Maple Farms sought to be relieved of its obligation under the contract on the ground of commerical frustration. Is Maple Farms entitled to the relief?

6. On December 1, 1967, Anderson ordered a tractor and loader from ABC Equipment to be delivered during September of the following year. The seller failed to deliver the equipment, and in December 1968 Anderson purchased a similar tractor and loader from another dealer at a cost of $1000 more than she was to have paid ABC. Anderson contends that she is entitled to recover the $1000 from ABC because of it's breach. ABC contends that since Anderson bought equipment different from what was called for in the contract, it does not have to pay the difference in price. Who is correct?

7. Lewis entered into a contract, agreeing to purchase from Meadows a certain laundry and dry cleaning business. When Meadows attempted to cash the check he had received in payment, it was dishonored because of insufficient funds. Lewis failed to make the check good and Meadows sold the business to another purchaser. Meadows then demanded from Lewis the difference between the contract price and the price paid by the substitute purchaser. Lewis refused on the ground that he was not notified of the sale. Is Meadows entitled to the amount demanded?

8. Irwin purchased a tractor for her trucking business from Keystone Diesel Engine Co. The engine was defective and could not be repaired for almost a month. When the repair was completed, Irwin refused to pay for the parts as she had agreed. When sued for the price of the parts, Irwin counterclaimed for damages for lost profits for 27 days. Keystone contended that such damages should not be awarded because Irwin never notified them that she was losing profits during the period. Is Irwin entitled to recover?

9. Davis purchased hogs from Edgewater Livestock Co. After he had them for a few days, it became apparent that many were sick. During the next 30 days he was able to restore the herd to health, but in the meantime more than half of the hogs died. To what damages is Davis entitled?

10. Wilson Sweater Co. purchased yarn from Paulson Mills. The contract between the parties contained a clause limiting the time to reject any yarn purchased. The clause provided that no adjustments would be made for yarn after it had been processed. No defects in the yarn were apparent when Wilson took delivery. However, after it had been woven into sweaters and washed, the color "shaded." Paulson refused to make an adjustment because of the clause. Wilson claimed that the clause was not enforceable because the defect was not discovered until after processing. Is Wilson correct?

Warranties and Product Liability

INTRODUCTION

Historically, the relationship between the parties to a contract for the sale of goods has been characterized by the doctrine of *caveat emptor,* or "let the buyer beware." In the absence of fraud or misrepresentation concerning specific, present, and material aspects of the goods involved, the parties had no duty to reveal hidden defects in their wares. Instead, they were considered to be almost total adversaries. In some transactions, such as "horse-trading," the parties even were expected to make substantial false representations as part of the negotiations.

The law has changed over time. The first signs of this came with the erosion of the doctrine of *caveat emptor,* first in fraud and then in misrepresentation cases. By the middle of the nineteeth century the law of negligence was developed. In the early part of the twentieth century there came a breaking down of the restriction placed on a manufacturer's liability by the doctrine of **privity**

of contract (the requirement that a direct or formal contractual relationship exist between the plaintiff and the defendant in a product-liability lawsuit). This was followed by the courts' increased acceptance of the theory of strict liability for personal injuries caused by product defects (strict liability is discussed in depth in Chapter 4). The Uniform Commerical Code also has made great inroads on *caveat emptor* by imposing certain warranty protections in transactions involving goods, and by limiting the right of sellers to modify or seek waiver of these warranties. Finally, the Federal Consumer Product Safety Commission and the Magnuson-Moss Warranty Act have extended the liability of sellers in transactions involving consumer goods yet further. This chapter will discuss these changes and the current state of warranty and product liability law. Consider the following case. It is, perhaps, the classic case demonstrating the erosion of the privity requirement.

MacPHERSON v. BUICK MOTOR CO.
217 N.Y. 382, 111 N.E. 1050 (1916)

This was an action by Donald C. MacPherson (Plaintiff/Appellee) against the Buick Motor Co. (Defendant/Appellant) for injuries sustained in an automobile mishap. Plaintiff was driving an automobile manufactured by Defendant, which sold it to an automobile dealer who resold it to Plaintiff. While the automobile was in motion, the spokes of one of its wooden wheels crumbled, causing the automobile to collapse. Plaintiff was thrown out and injured. Defendant based its defense on two main points—(1) there was no privity of contract between Plaintiff and itself and (2) Defendant was not negligent because the defective wheel was manufactured by a reputable supplier, not by itself.

The trial court found for Plaintiff and Defendant appealed. Affirmed.

CARDOZO, J.

We hold, then, that the principle of Thomas v. Winchester [the case in which New York's highest court first recognized the legal theory of negligence but seemed to limit it to "inherently dangerous" products] is not limited to poisons, explosives, and things of like nature, to things which in their normal operation are implements of destruction. If the nature of a thing is such that it is reasonably certain to place life and limb in peril when negligently made, it is then a thing of danger. Its nature gives warning of the consequences to be expected. If to the element of danger there is added knowledge that the thing will be used by persons other than the purchaser, and used without new tests, then, irrespective of contract, the manufacturer of this thing of danger is under a duty to make it carefully. That is as far as we are required to go for the decision of this case. There must be knowledge of a danger, not merely possible, but probable. It is possible to use almost anything in a way that will make it dangerous if defective. That is not enough to charge the manufacturer with a duty independent of his contract. . . . There must also be knowledge that in the usual course of events the danger will be shared by others than the buyer. Such knowledge may often be inferred from the nature of the transaction. But is is possible that even knowledge of the danger and of the use will not always be enough. The proximity or remoteness of the relation is a factor to be considered. We are dealing now with the liability of the manufacturer of the finished product, who puts it on the market to be used without inspection by his customers. If he is negligent, where danger is to be foreseen, a liability will follow.

We are not required, at this time, to say that it is legitimate to go back of the manufacturer of the finished product and hold the manufacturers of the component parts. To make their negligence a cause of imminent danger, an independent cause must often intervene; the manufacturer of the finished product must also fail in his duty of inspection. . . . We have put aside the notion that the duty to safeguard life and limb, when the consequences of negligence may be foreseen, grows out of contract and nothing else. We have put the source of the obligation where it ought to be. We have put its source in the law [tort law].

From this survey of the decisions, there thus emerges a definition of the duty of a manufacturer which enables us to measure this defendant's liability. Beyond all question, the nature of an automobile gives warning of probable danger if its construction is defective. This automobile was designed to go 50 miles an hour. Unless its wheels were sound and strong, injury was almost certain. It was as much a thing of danger as a defective engine for a railroad. The defendant knew the danger. It knew also that the car would be used by persons other than the buyer. This was apparent from its size; there were seats for three persons. It was apparent also from the fact that the buyer was a dealer in cars, who bought to resell. . . .

We think the defendant was not absolved from a duty of inspection because it bought the wheels from a reputable manufacturer. It was not merely a dealer in automobiles. It was a manufacturer of automobiles. It was responsible for the finished product on the market without subjecting the component parts to ordinary and simple tests.

Questions

1. Is Judge Cardozo suggesting that a manufacturer should be liable for all foreseeable injuries caused by a product, or only for injuries caused by very dangerous products?

2. Why wasn't the fact that MacPherson could have inspected the wheels enough to relieve Buick of liability? Does your answer suggest that an intermediary, such as the auto dealer, also should be relieved of liability?

3. If Buick ultimately was found liable to MacPherson, but the negligence of a supplier, such as the wheel maker "back of the manufacturer," clearly caused MacPherson's injury, wouldn't it be unfair to make Buick pay? If so, how do you think the law should solve this problem?

Bases of Liability

Generally, the liability of sellers in transactions involving the sale of goods arises from two sources, warranties in the law of contracts and various theories of the law of torts. More specifically, one or more of the following theories may be the basis of liability: (1) misrepresentation, (2) fraud, (3) negligence, (4) strict liability under statute or common law, and (5) breach of warranty. The first topic for discussion will be warranty law.

Sources of Warranties

The term **warranty** may be defined as "a contractual promise." In the context of this chapter, we are concerned particularly with these promises as they relate to the state of the title to goods, their nature, and their quality. These warranties may arise expressly if a seller, in words written or spoken, makes specific guarantees concerning the goods. They also may arise by implication from a fair examination of the facts and circumstances surrounding each transaction. Most important, however, are the warranties imposed by Article 2 of the Uniform Commercial Code and the rules governing them.

WARRANTY OF TITLE

Under early English Law, a sale of goods did not include any implied promises. In fact, the contract itself would not be found to promise anything unless it was stated very clearly. As previously noted, transactions were characterized by *caveat emptor*. This theory was based on the idea that the parties had relatively equal bargaining power, and each was allowed to negotiate in any manner, short of actual fraud, that would promote his personal interests. Entering into a contract was an arms-length transaction; there was not even an implied promise that the seller owned the goods he sought to sell. This no longer is true.

Under Section 2–312 of the UCC, unless excluded or modified by specific language or by circumstances that give the buyer reason to know that the seller does not claim title for herself, or alternatively, that she is purporting to sell only such title as she or a third party may have, every seller makes a **warranty of title.** This warranty includes three separate guarantees: (1) that the title conveyed is good; (2) that the seller has a right to convey that title; and (3) that the goods are free from any security interest or other lien or encumbrance the buyer has no actual knowledge of at the time of contracting. If the seller is a merchant, her warranty of title carries an additional guarantee: (4) that the goods will be delivered free of the rightful claim of any third person by way of infringement of a patent or trademark or the like, except when the buyer furnishes specifications to the seller. In the latter case, the seller is relieved from the fourth guarantee if she simply follows the specifications.

The warranty of title is a special warranty under Article 2. It is not created by words, so it is not an express warranty. Neither is it an "implied warranty" under Section 2–314. It is treated separately by the Code so that the disclaimer rules that apply to warranties will not also apply to it.

EXPRESS WARRANTIES

An **express warranty** is one created by words, whether written, spoken, or a combination of the two, or by a sample or a description. The seller need not use the words *warrant* or *promise,* and need not even have a specific intention to create a warranty. An express warranty may arise from any statement of fact concerning the goods to be sold. This may be a direct statement or it may be an affirmation, a promise, a description, or even a sample.

The idea of express warranty is similar to that of misrepresentation under the common law. It is not necessary that the statement be made with knowledge of its falsity, or with an intent to defraud, for there to be a breach of warranty. Any statement that becomes part of the basis for the bargain may constitute an express warranty. However, it must be more than a statement of the value of the goods, the seller's opinion, or a mere commendation of the goods; ordinarily, it must be a statement of past or present fact. A speculation as to the future usually will not suffice, although if the statement is made by one who holds himself out as having the ability to make predictions accurately, it may be considered a statement of fact. This rule has been explained on the ground that someone who claims an ability to predict the future misrepresents his present ability, and that is a statement of fact. Similarly, a seller who holds himself out as an expert concerning matters relating to the goods, or misrepresents his actual opinion, may be held for breach of an express warranty. For example, a mechanic may state that, in his opinion, a car he is selling is in "top mechanical condition." If he is mistaken, or if his statement is untruthful because he knows the car has mechanical problems, liability for breach of warranty may result.

Finally, express warranties must be distinguished from mere **sales talk** or **puffing.** These are general statements that one reasonably might expect a seller to make in bragging about her wares. For example, she might say, "This is the best product on the market," or "you won't find one nicer," or "you will be proud to own it." These statements are not regarded as warranties. Consider the following case.

BIGELOW v. AGWAY, INC.
506 F.2d 551 (2d Cir. 1974)

This was an action by Harold and Virginia Bigelow (Plaintiffs/Appellants) against Agway, Inc. (Defendant/Appellee) for losses suffered when Plaintiffs' barn caught fire and burned. Hay sprayed with a chemical produced by Defendant had been stored in the barn. The hay was stored "green," and that caused the fire. The chemical, "Hay Savor," was advertised as retarding mold, thus allowing hay to be stored with a higher moisture content (good farming practice requires hay to be dried until its moisture level is 20 to 25 percent before it can be considered safe for storage). Plaintiffs baled the hay and stored it, in spite of Harold Bigelow's opinion that it was yet too green to be safe, because of the insistence of an authorized representative of Defendant who assured Plaintiffs that it would be safe if sprayed with "Hay Savor."

The trial court directed a verdict for Defendant and Plaintiffs appealed. Reversed and remanded.

MANSFIELD, Circuit Judge.

In determining whether a motion for a directed verdict should be granted, the evidence must be viewed most favorably to the party against whom the motion is made. . . . The non-moving party is given the benefit of all reasonable inferences from the evidence, and evidence unfavorable to it may be considered only if that evidence stands uncontradicted and unimpeached. . . . Applying this standard, we find that, despite the proof supporting defendants' position, there was evidence upon which a jury could reasonably find for the plaintiffs. . . .

Plaintiffs' complaint alleged that products manufactured by Kemin Industries and sold by Agway to them were "defective and unfit for the purpose of which they were sold." In support of this general claim of breach of warranty plaintiffs' principal contention was that Hay Savor was defective in that it did not in fact allow farmers to put up high moisture hay, as was represented. We agree with Chief Judge Holden that there is no evidence that Hay Savor was defective or that it would not be effective if properly used. Moreover, proper usage, as specified in Hay Savor literature, required that moisture levels in hay be 25% or less before bailing. Plaintiffs cannot recover on the ground that Hay Savor did not live up to its advertising claims since there is no evidence that plaintiffs complied with this instruction in using the product. . . .

Plaintiffs, however, contend that their broad warranty claim could be established by proof that on the June 15th visit Mr. Nelson represented that Hay Savor enabled 32% moisture hay to be safely bailed, and that in fact the product failed to prevent a fire at this moisture level. Although plaintiffs may have placed most of their emphasis at trial on the properly rejected theory that the product was inherently defective, their claim was expressed in sufficiently general terms to embrace Nelson's representations, see 9A Vermont Statutes Annotated Section 2-313, 2-315, and at trial plaintiffs' counsel asserted the latter theory. Since the elements of this claim are essentially the same as those of the negligence claim, we believe there was adequate evidence to go to the jury on the breach of warranty claim as well.

Questions

1. If Mr. Nelson had not been a Hay Savor salesman, but only an interfering neighbor, could Agway still be held liable? Could Mr. Nelson?
2. If the Bigelows win their suit, what will their damages be? If unusually strong winds caused the fire to spread to their house and also to an oil slick a neighbor's leaky oil tank had caused on their creek, and thence to the Jones's barn three miles away, would Agway or Nelson be liable for all of the damage?

Classifications of warranties

1) **Warranty of Title**	title is clear and free when conveyed created orally, in writing, or by a sample imposed by law
2) **Express Warranties**	
3) **Implied Warranties**	
a) Warranties of merchantibility	goods sold must be of merchantable quality
b) Warranties of fitness	goods purchased on seller's advice must be "fit" for the purpose they were intended
c) Warranties arising from course of dealing or usage of trade	arises due to past dealings between parties because certain expectations are set or trade custom
d) Implied warranties regarding food and drink	applies to food and drink purchased, but is frequently dealt with by state laws

IMPLIED WARRANTIES

In every contract for the sale of goods the seller makes certain implied warranties unless the agreement explicitly states to the contrary. Implied warranties arise not as a result of some statement by the seller as do express warranties, nor do they concern the quality of the seller's title to the goods as does a warranty of title. Instead, **implied warranties** are imposed by law, and guarantee the quality of the goods themselves.

Three general types of implied warranties are recognized by the UCC: (1) warranties of merchantability, (2) warranties of fitness, and (3) warranties arising from the parties' course of dealing or usage of trade. Which of these warranties arises in a transaction depends on a number of factors, including the type of goods, the relationship of the parties, whether the seller is a merchant, and the application of other state and federal laws.

Warranty of Merchantability

Unless warranties are excluded or modified by contract, a seller who is a merchant with respect to the goods sold impliedly warrants that they are of merchantable quality. That is, he warrants that they are reasonably adequate for the *general purpose* for which they are intended. The question of what quality of performance is required for the goods to be reasonably adequate may depend on the nature of the goods. For example, a cheap tape player would be required to produce only passable sound quality, whereas an expensive tape player or a compact disc player would be expected to produce far superior sound. An electronic calculator, moreover, would be required to perform to perfection because only perfect calculation, not just approximate accuracy, is reasonable for that type of goods.

In defining **merchantability** Section 2–314 of the Code establishes some specific qualities to be considered. Subsection (2) provides: Goods to be merchantable must be at least such as

(a)   pass without objection in the trade under the contract description; and

(b)   in the case of fungible goods [one unit is like another, such as 12-ounce cans of cola], are of

fair average quality within the description; and

(c)   are fit for the ordinary purposes for which such goods are used; and

(d)   run, within the variations permitted by the agreement, of even kind, quality and quantity within each unit and among all units involved; and

(e)   are adequately contained, packaged and labeled as the agreement may require; and

(f)   conform to the promises or affirmations of fact made on the container or label if any.

Items (a) and (c) set out the general provisions; (b) and (d) basically concern fungible goods and units; and (e) and (f) address packaging and labeling. Note that this list is not intended to be exhaustive. It only sets a minimum threshold for meeting the merchantability requirement. Goods are not merchantable if they fail in any of these respects. Note also that this warranty applies only if the seller is a merchant. The following case concerns a rather pronounced breach of the implied warranty of merchantability.

TWIN LAKES MANUFACTURING COMPANY v. COFFEY
222 Va. 467, 281 S.E.2d 864 (1981)

This was an action by Davis F. and Evada J. Coffey (Plaintiffs/Appellees) against Twin Lakes Manufacturing Co. (Defendant/Appellant) for breach of an implied warranty of the merchantability of a mobile home manufactured by Defendant and purchased by Plaintiffs. Although Plaintiffs inspected the home at the dealership, it was not until it was taken to its destination and its two sections were assembled that substantial defects became discoverable. The assembler listed 72 defects, among them bulges, creases, and buckles in the interior and exterior walls. There also were gaps between the walls and ceiling and the floors had become very uneven. Plaintiffs occupied the home for a while at the insistence of the dealer, who promised that the problems would be taken care of.

From a judgment for Plaintiffs, Defendant appealed. Affirmed.

POFF, Justice.

In the first of two assignments of error, Twin Lakes asserts that "the plaintiffs failed to establish . . . that the implied warranty of merchantability . . . was breached by the defendant" and that the trial court erred in overruling the motion to strike the plaintiffs' evidence. Preliminarily, the defendant argues that "the implied warranty of merchantability [was] waived by the plaintiffs when they inspected the mobile home." We reject this argument. "[W]hen the buyer before entering into the contract has examined the goods . . . there is no implied warranty with regard to defects which an examination ought in the circumstances to have revealed to him". Code Section 8.2-316(3)(b). The superficial defects the Coffeys observed when they examined the separated sections of the mobile home had only a marginal effect on the merchantability of the goods. The skewed frame and the resulting distortion in construction of the superstructure were the essence of the breach of warranty. The defects in manufacture did not become apparent, even to experienced workmen, until pressure was applied to join the two sections and level the unit on its foundation. Such latent defects are not those contemplated by Section 8.2-316(3)(b).

Addressing the gravamen [the most important allegation] of its first complaint, Twin Lakes maintains that the evidence was not sufficient to prove a breach of the implied warranty of merchantability. "Goods to be merchantable must be at least such as . . . are fit for the ordinary purposes for which such goods are used". Code Section 8.2-314(2)(c). Alluding to this language, the defendant insists that "the home was obviously reasonably fit for the ordinary purpose for which it was intended . . . in that it was habitable." In support of that argument, Twin Lakes relies on the fact that the defects were not serious enough to prevent the Coffeys from living in the home, and upon the building official's testimony that the home complied with state safety and sanitary regulations.

The flaw in this argument is that it equates "merchantability" with "habitability". Certainly, the latter is an element of the former, but the fact that people may be able to live safely in a mobile home does not mean that it satisfies the warranty of merchantability. . . . While the repairs reported by the building official made the home safe and sanitary for purposes of human habitation, they did not render the home merchantable for purposes of the warranty. Indeed, Gleaton, Twin Lakes' own agent, testified that he would not have it as a gift. All the witnesses agreed that the defects were extensive and substantial. Not unexpectedly, the experts disagreed whether they could be satisfactorily repaired. But the trial judge resolved all conflicts in the testimony, and we hold that the evidence was sufficient to support his decision that Twin Lakes breached its implied warranty of merchantability.

Questions

1. By what conduct could the plaintiffs actually have waived their home's warranty of merchantability? Would a deliberate refusal to inspect the home have sufficed?

2. If the doctrine of *caveat emptor* were still in force, how would this case have been decided?

3. If the flaws in the home had developed two months after the house was assembled, would the result have been the same? Would your answer change if the defects developed only after completion of remodeling work that the plaintiffs asked Twin Lakes to undertake to improve the home's otherwise unacceptable appearance?

Warranty of Fitness for a Particular Purpose

Unless excluded or modified, if the seller, at the time of contracting, either knows or should know that the buyer intends to use the goods for a particular purpose, and that she is relying on the seller's skill and judgment to furnish suitable goods, a **warranty of fitness** arises. If the goods furnished are not reasonably fit for the buyer's particular purpose, this warranty is breached.

This warranty should not be confused with the warranty of merchantability. Goods may be merchantable yet unfit for a particular purpose. For example, suppose Ruiz goes to Holm's store and purchases shoes for work. Ruiz is an employee of a grinding and fabricating plant, and during most of his work day he walks on floors covered with oil and various caustic chemicals. Ruiz's new shoes fall apart within two weeks, victims of the oil and chemicals. Although the shoes may have been suitable for ordinary wear and therefore merchantable, they clearly were not fit for the particular purpose for which Ruiz intended them. If at the time of the sale Holm knew or should have known of these special circumstances, Holm would be in breach of an implied warranty that the shoes would be fit for Ruiz's particular purpose.

In judging a breach of this warranty the court must determine the degree to which the seller possessed particular skill and judgment, or the degree to which she held herself out as possessing them. It also must determine the extent to which the buyer relied on these characteristics of the seller, the reasonableness of his reliance, and whether the buyer acted properly to protect his own interests. Therefore, each case must be judged in light of its particular circumstances. Consider the following case.

CATANIA v. BROWN
4 Conn.Cir. 344, 231 A.2d 668 (1967)

This was an action by Michael Catania and others (Plaintiffs/Appellees) against Charles J. Brown (Defendant/Appellant) for breach of warranty of fitness. Plaintiff Catania asked Defendant, who operated a paint store, to recommend a paint to be used on the stucco walls of his house. The parties discussed the condition of the surface and Defendant recommended, and sold to Catania, Pierce's shingle and shake paint. Catania followed Defendant's instructions, but within five months the paint began to blister and peel. This necessitated thoroughly brushing, sandblasting, and repainting.

From a judgment for Plaintiffs, Defendant appealed. Affirmed.

JACOBS, Judge.

. . . Under the statute governing implied warranty of fitness for a particular purpose (Section 42a-2-315), two requirements must be met: (a) the buyer relies on the seller's skill or judgment to select or furnish suitable goods; and (b) the seller at the time of contracting has reason to know the buyer's purpose and that the buyer is relying on the seller's skill or judgment. "It is a question of fact in the ordinary case whether these conditions have been met and the warranty arises." . . .

The implied warranty of fitness is not founded on negligence; . . . nor is it founded on fraud or lack of good faith. . . .

The raising of an implied warranty of fitness depends upon whether the buyer informed the seller of the circumstances and conditions which necessitated his purchase of a certain character of article or material and left it to the seller to select the particular kind and quality of article suitable for the buyer's use. . . . So when the buyer orders goods to be supplied and trusts to the judgment or skill of the seller to select goods or material for which they are ordered, there is an implied warranty that they shall be reasonably fit for that purpose. . . . Reliance can, of course, be more readily found where the retailer selects the product or recommends it.

Questions

1. If the plaintiffs told the defendant the purpose for which the product was being purchased, and the defendant told them it was suitable and gave instructions for its use, why was this not an express warranty? Or was it?

2. If an express warranty was made and breached in this case, which might be more advantageous to the plaintiffs—to sue on the theory of express warranty or implied warranty? Why?

Warranties Arising from Course of Dealing or Usage of Trade

Section 2-314(3) provides for special implied warranties that may arise as a result of past dealings between the parties, and the substance of these warranties may be entirely peculiar to the parties involved. For example, suppose Delta regularly purchased registered beagles from Gerald and Gerald always had taken care of the procedures for the registration of the animals in Delta's name as purchaser. Delta may have been the only customer for whom Gerald routinely had performed this additional service. However, Gerald is required to continue this practice until he notifies Delta to the contrary prior to a sale because of their **course of dealing.** The purpose of this warranty is to protect the buyer who has built up legitimate expectations in the seller over the course of the seller's performance.

The same general reasoning may apply to all those who buy certain kinds of goods, not just to particular buyers, if it is commonly understood in a particular trade that transactions are handled in a certain way **(usage of trade).** For example, someone who purchases a pedigreed dog is entitled to expect that the seller, as a part of the transaction, will provide sufficient documentation of breeding

to have the dog registered with an appropriate kennel club. This warranty is implied in favor of all such buyers, not just those with whom the seller may have dealt frequently in the past.

Implied Warranties Regarding Food and Drink

Section 2-314(1) of the UCC provides that serving food or drink to be consumed on the premises or elsewhere is a sale within the meaning of Article 2. However, state laws frequently have special provisions concerning these goods because unhealthy food and drink products present unusual hazards to the public.

By way of illustration, suppose Dean purchases a martini in Lewis's restaurant. In attempting to eat the olive that accompanied the drink, Dean bites down and breaks a tooth on the olive pit. Is Dean entitled to damages from Lewis for breach of warranty? The answer will depend, in part, on the law of the particular state. A minority of states would not treat the presence of the pit in the olive as a breach of warranty because it is an object that is *natural to the product.* A majority of states, however, would examine the facts to determine the *reasonable expectations of the buyer*. Should a person reasonably expect to find a pit in an olive served as a garnish in a martini? Liability would be universal, however, if a buyer is injured by a tack in an olive.

EXLUSION AND MODIFICATION OF WARRANTIES

The exclusion and modification of warranties in the contract is permitted under Article 2, but neither exclusion nor modification is favored. This is because there is a tension between protecting the law's goals of ensuring that parties can bargain freely on any legal terms they wish, on the one hand, and protecting buyers, especially consumers, by extensive warranties on the other. In Comment 4 to Section 2-313, the UCC drafters state that the purpose of warranty law is to determine what, in essence, the seller has agreed to sell. Therefore, a material reduction in the seller's obligations should be allowed only in unusual cases. The drafters' comments also suggest that exclusions and modifications of warranties should be allowed only in cases in which the parties clearly, not just arguably, intended for the modifications to exist. Any ambiguities must be resolved in favor of the buyer.

Warranty of Title

A warranty of title may be excluded or modified only by specific language or the circumstances of the transaction. The three elements of the warranty must be excluded specifically. The following would be sufficient: "It is understood by the parties that the seller does not warrant, promise or guarantee that (1) the title to the goods is transferred to the buyer, (2) the transfer is rightful, or (3) the goods are free of security interests or other encumbrances." Otherwise, a court is likely to construe any exclusion or modification so as to have the least possible impact on the buyer.

Exclusion or modification of this warranty also may arise because of circumstances that should lead a reasonable buyer to understand that the seller does not claim perfect title. Examples would be sales by a sheriff, a trustee, an executor or administrator, or a lienholder. In these circumstances, the seller will be understood to convey only the title he holds or the title the prior owner held. In addition, in some cases a sale of goods may be subject to a statutory "right of redemption."

Express Warranties

As previously discussed, express warranties may be created by any statement or affirmation of fact, promise, description, or sample. They may be excluded or modified by appropriate words or by the conduct of the parties. However, Section 2-316 provides that any conflict between an express warranty and a disclaimer must be resolved in favor of the warranty. For example, suppose the literature accompanying a battery states that it will provide "1000 hours of service," but several paragraphs later the literature states that the seller makes "no warranties express or implied." In this situation, the disclaimer fails to undermine the express warranty. Section 2-316 provides that all warranties and disclosures, whenever reasonable, will be construed as consistent with each other. However, when that is not possible, the disclaimer will be inoperative.

Difficulties may arise in cases involving oral warranties and written disclaimers. Proof of oral warranties may be excluded by the Parol Evidence Rule embodied in Section 2-202. In the example above, if the statement concerning 1000 hours of battery service had been made orally by the seller instead of appearing in the literature, it probably could not be entered as evidence. Remember, the Parol Evidence Rule excludes evidence of any prior or contemporaneous oral agreement that conflicts with any writing that purports to be the final expression of the parties' agreement.

Implied Warranties

In order to exclude the implied warranty of merchantability, Section 2–316(2) provides that the disclaimer must mention merchantability and, if the disclaimer is in writing, it must be "conspicuous." Therefore, a statement such as "Buyer understands that these goods are provided with no implied warranty of merchantability" is sufficient. If in writing, it may be made "conspicuous" by the use of larger type or a typeface different from that in the body of the contract. It probably would be even better to set out the disclaimer in a separate paragraph to be separately signed or initialed by the buyer.

Subsection (3) states that notwithstanding subsection (2), further rules are to be applied to all implied warranties, including the warranty of merchantability. The subsection provides that all implied warranties may be excluded by expressions such as "as is," "with all faults," or other language that in common understanding calls the buyer's attention to the exclusion of warranties and makes it plain to the buyer that she is not receiving any implied warranty. Also, if the buyer has examined the goods, a sample, or a model prior to entering into the contract, or has refused to exercise her right to examine, there is no implied warranty concerning any defect that an examination should have revealed. In addition, an implied warranty may be excluded by a course of performance or usage of trade. Consider the following case.

HENNINGSEN v. BLOOMFIELD MOTORS, INC.
32 N.J. 358, 161 A.2d 69 (1960)

[NOTE: This very famous case was decided under the Uniform Sales Act, which preceded Article 2 of the Uniform Commerical Code. The decision reveals the character of the law at that time concerning disclaimers of warranties accompanying sales of goods, but many of the principles the court employs still are good law today.]

This was an action by Claus H. and Helen Henningsen (Plaintiffs/Respondents) against Bloomfield Motors, Inc. and Chrysler Corporation (Defendants/Petitioners) for injuries to Mrs. Henningsen caused when she crashed while driving an automobile manufactured by Chrysler Corporation and purchased by Mr. Henningsen from Bloomfield Motors, Inc. The cause of the accident was defective workmanship on assembly of the steering mechanism. Among the questions before the court was whether Defendants were liable on an implied warranty of merchantability. Defendants contended that there was no warranty in effect because it had been disclaimed by agreement of the parties.

The trial court found for Plaintiffs. Affirmed.

FRANCIS, J.

In the ordinary case of sale of goods by description an implied warranty of merchantability is an integral part of the transaction. R.S. 46:30–20, N.J.S.A.

If the buyer, expressly or by implication, makes known to the seller the particular purpose for which the article is required and it appears that he has relied on the seller's skill or judgment, an implied warranty arises of reasonable fitness for that purpose. R.S. 46:30–21(1), N.J.S.A. The former type of warranty simply means that the thing sold is reasonably fit for the general purpose for which it is manufactured and sold. . . . As Judge (later Justice) Cardozo remarked in [Ryan v. Progressive Grocery Stores] . . . the distinction between a warranty of fitness for a particular purpose and of merchantability in many instances is practically meaningless. In the particular case he was concerned with food for human consumption in a sealed container. Perhaps no more apt illustration of the notion can be thought of than the instance of the ordinary purchaser who informs the automobile dealer that he desires a car for the purpose of business and pleasure driving on the public highway. . . .

The general observations that have been made are important largely for purposes of perspective. They are helpful in achieving a point from which to evaluate the situation now presented for solution. Primarily, they reveal a trend and a design in legislative and judicial thinking toward providing protection for the buyer. It must be noted, however, that the sections of the Sales Act, to which reference has been made, do not impose warranties in terms of unalterable absolutes. R.S. 46:30–3, N.J.S.A., provides in general terms that an applicable warranty may be negatived or varied by express agreement. As to disclaimers or limitations of the obligations that normally attend a sale, it seems sufficient at this juncture to say they are not favored, and that they are strictly construed against the seller. . . .

Moreover, it must be remembered that the actual contract was between Bloomfield Motors, Inc., and Claus Henningsen, and that the description of the car sold was included in the purchase order. Therefore, R.S. 46:30–21(2), N.J.S.A., annexed an implied warranty of merchantability to the agreement. . . . It remains operative unless the disclaimer and liability limitation clauses were competent to exclude it and the ordinary remedy for its breach. It has been said that this doctrine is harsh on retailers who generally have only a limited opportunity for inspection of the car. But, as Chief Judge Cardozo said in Ryan, supra:

> The burden may be heavy. It is one of the hazards of the business. . . . In such circumstances, the law casts the burden on the seller, who may vouch in the manufacturer, if the latter was to blame. The loss in its final incidence will be borne where it is placed by the initial wrong. 175 N.E. at pages 106 and 107.

Re-examination of the purchase contract discloses an ambiguous situation with respect to the warranty position of the dealer. Section 7, on the reverse side thereof, says no warranties, express or implied, are made by the dealer or manufacturer except the express warranty of the manufacturer discussed above. However, the last paragraph of the section says that: "The dealer also agrees to promptly perform and fulfill all terms and conditions of the owner service policy." That policy, as noted above, sets forth the same manufacturer's warranty and then adds a stipulation substituting "dealer" in the context wherever "manufacturer" appears. Presumably the intention was to incorporate the policy into the sales contract by reference. Accepting that to be the dealer's intention, the binding character of the limitation on its liability to the buyer under the warranty is even less apparent than in the case of Chrysler. The uncontradicted proof shows that the policy was not shown or given to Henningsen prior to or at the time of execution of the sales agreement; it was delivered with the car. No one suggests that the clause limiting the dealer's liability to replacement of defective parts and excluding implied warranties as well as responsibility for personal injury claims was specifically brought to Henningsen's attention, or that any attempt was made to make him understand that he was yielding his right, and that of any third person claiming in his right, to recover for such injuries.

For the reasons set forth [previously] . . . we conclude that the disclaimer of an implied warranty of merchantability by the dealer, as well as the attempted elimination of all obligations other than replacement of defective parts, are violative of public policy and void.

Questions

1. How would *Henningsen* be decided under today's UCC?

2. Does *Henningsen* show that the trend "toward providing protection for the buyer" has gone too far? If not, what principles should limit the protections the law affords to consumers?

3. Does *Henningsen* imply that a warranty never can be disclaimed effectively against someone who does not notice the disclaimer even if it was reasonably conspicuous? Does the case imply that warranties never can be disclaimed in transactions with minors, the mentally handicapped, or the mentally ill?

4. Would *Henningsen* have been decided the same way if the car had been defective but no one had been injured? What if Mr. Henningsen had lent the car to his neighbor, and the neighbor had been injured?

The exclusion of warranties by the course of performance or usage of trade particularly may be important because these exclusions may be less obvious to the casual buyer. **Course of performance** means the manner in which the current contract is being performed, as opposed to "course of dealing," which refers to "the manner of performance of past contracts between the parties." Exclusion by course of performance, for example, will arise in the event that a contract is performed in installments and the buyer receives defective goods during performance of one or more of the installments, but fails to give proper notice to the seller.

Concerning exclusion of warranties by usage of trade, suppose a clothing manufacturer sent 100 three-piece suits to a clothing store and a store employee replaced the manufacturer's label with the store's own. The store manager then discovered that the manufacturer had shipped the wrong order to the store; the store actually had ordered 100 two-piece suits. In these circumstances, if a usage of trade precluded returns after relabeling, the store might be unable to recover for breach of warranty just as if the statute of limitations had run.

Exclusion of Warranty of Fitness for a Particular Purpose

A warranty of fitness may be excluded if it is disclaimed in writing with conspicuous words. This warranty also may be excluded by such language as: "There are no warranties beyond the description on the face hereof." In addition, this warranty may be excluded as provided in Section 2–316(3), described above. Consider the following case.

O'NEIL v. INTERNATIONAL HARVESTER CO.
40 Colo.App. 349, 575 P.2d 862 (1978)

This was an action by Albert M. O'Neil (Plaintiff/Appellant) against International Harvester Co. (Defendant/Appellee) for breach of an implied warranty of fitness for a particular purpose. Plaintiff purchased a used diesel tractor and trailer. The contract between the parties provided: "Each USED motor vehicle covered by this contract is sold AS IS WITHOUT WARRANTY OF ANY CHARACTER, expressed or implied, unless purchaser has received from seller a separate written warranty executed by seller." No written warranties were received by O'Neil, and Defendant contended that this exclusion was effective to disclaim an oral warranty of fitness.

The trial court found for Defendant the Plaintiff appealed. Affirmed insofar as it is relevant here.

RULAND, Judge.

Pursuant to the Uniform Commerical Code, one way an implied warranty of fitness for a particular purpose can be excluded is by a conspicuous writing which states generally that there are no warranties extending beyond the description in the contract. Section 4-2-316(2) C.R.S. 1973. O'Neil admits reading the warranty disclaimer provision. Thus, we need not decide whether as a matter of law it was "conspicuous." See Section 4-1-201(10),C.R.S.1973. And, we hold that the language "AS IS WITHOUT WARRANTY OF ANY CHARACTER expressed or implied" was sufficient to inform O'Neil that there was no implied warranty in effect for the truck. See Section 4-2-316(2), C.R.S. 1973.

Questions

1. If O'Neil had sought to appeal this case to the Colorado Supreme Court, what would his strongest argument have been?

2. If O'Neil never read the exclusionary clause, would the result have been the same? Would the result have been the same if he had read it only after he had driven the tractor and trailer to his home? What if he had read it after signing the contract but before the tractor and trailer arrived?

Conflicts of Warranties

Sometimes, when more than one warranty is extended by a seller, their provisions may conflict. Section 2-317 provides that warranties, express and implied, are to be construed as consistent and as cumulative. If that is unreasonable, the intent of the parties must be determined according to which warranty is dominant, applying the following rules:

(a) Exact or technical specifications displace an inconsistent sample or model or general language of description.

(b) A sample from an existing bulk displaces inconsistent language of description.

(c) Express warranties displace inconsistent implied warranties other than an implied warranty of fitness for a particular purpose.

If a conflict cannot be resolved by the application of these rules—for example, if two express warranties are inconsistent—an ambiguity is created that may be resolved by other evidence, either written or oral. Failing that, both warranties may be considered inoperative.

Unconscionability

There has been considerable debate about whether the provisions of Section 2–302 concerning unconscionable contracts and clauses should be applied to attempts to exclude or modify implied warranties under Article 2. One view is that since Section 2–316 specifically addresses the subject and sets out clear procedures, Section 2–302 should not apply. On the other hand, one of the paramount purposes of Article 2 is to promote fairness, and the courts will not enforce contractual provisions they find so unfair as to be truly unconscionable. Therefore some courts can be expected to apply Section 2–302 to warranties, although it should be remembered that the application of Section 2–302 is permissive, not mandatory.

LIMITATION OF REMEDIES FOR BREACH OF WARRANTY

Remedies for breach of warranty may be limited in the same manner as remedies for any other breach under Article 2. Section 2–316(4) provides that the rules concerning liquidation or limitation of damages in Section 2–718 and those concerning contractual modification of remedies in Section 2–719 are applicable. These sections were discussed in the preceding chapter. Interestingly, these sections specifically provide that limitations must be reasonable, and Section 2–719(3) provides that any attempt to limit consequential damages for personal injury is *prima facie* unconscionable.

DEFENSES IN WARRANTY ACTIONS

Proof problems in actions for breach of warranty begin with establishing the existence of a warranty and that it was broken. These have been discussed previously. Next, the defenses the seller may have must be considered.

Causation

In every warranty action, it is necessary to establish that a loss was suffered and, more importantly, that the breach of warranty caused that loss. This requires the same proof as that required in any negligence action; causation is simply an unbroken chain of events leading from the breach to the injury. Also, as in a negligence case, this chain may be broken if the buyer acts unreasonably in the face of the risk occasioned by the breach. For example, suppose Mary purchases a new car from Grimes Motors. While driving it home, she notices that she is having a very difficult time steering because of slack in the steering wheel. Nevertheless, Mary continues to drive the car, and a few minutes later loses control and hits a tree. The cause of the accident was a loose gear in the steering box. Mary's cause of action against Grimes nevertheless may be defeated by a finding that Mary's conduct—failing to stop driving the car when she experienced difficulty—constituted "contributory negligence" or "assumption of risk." These simply mean that the line of causation from Grimes's breach to Mary's injury was broken by Mary's own negligence in continuing to drive the car when it obviously was impaired.

Statute of Limitations

Section 2–725 provides that a plaintiff must sue for the breach of a contract for the sale of goods within four years after the cause accrued. Generally, this means that the plaintiff must sue within four years after the goods were delivered to the buyer. If a warranty explicitly extends to future performance of the goods, and thus discovery of the breach must await such performance, the cause of action accrues when the breach should have been discovered. For example, if a toaster is warranted to be free of defects for one year from the date of purchase, the cause of action may accrue at any time within one year after purchase. The buyer need not know that the toaster has failed for her cause of action to accrue, however. If the toaster broke due to a defect covered by warranty while the buyer's son was using it, and the embarrassed son then hid the toaster for a year and a day, the buyer would have lost both her toaster and her right to sue. After a contract for the sale of goods has been made, the parties may agree to reduce the warranty period to no less than one year, but the Code prohibits them from extending it. Of course, if the seller wishes, he simply may give a longer warranty before the sale is made.

Some state legislatures have been concerned that product liability law has been slanted too much in favor of purchasers, and have enacted legislation designed to help sellers. Two examples of such legislation are "consolidated product liability statutes" and "statutes of repose." The former require that all product-liability actions are subject to a single statute-of-limitations time period, regardless of whether they are brought under a tort theory, such as negligence or strict liability, or under a contract theory for breach of warranty. The latter provide that a buyer's cause of action accrues at the time of the sale of the defective goods, rather than at the time of injury or discovery of the defect. Thus, both are aimed at enabling sellers to predict the magnitude of potential future liability more accurately.

Parol Evidence Rule

As previously discussed, the Parol Evidence Rule, Section 2–202, may bar a buyer from introducing evidence about an oral express warranty if the parties' agreement is in writing, appears complete on its face, and does not mention the warranty. Although this rule may seem to facilitate fraud by the seller, it actually serves mainly to make the buyer responsible for mentioning in the writing anything in the transaction that is important to him. Of course, the seller has a corresponding interest in protecting herself.

Notice of Breach

When a breach occurs, the buyer must give timely notice to the seller or he will be barred from any remedy. Section 2–607(3) provides that notice must be given within a reasonable time after the breach was or should have been discovered. If the claim is that, due to the seller's fault, the buyer has been sued for patent infringement or a similar violation of another's rights, the buyer must give notice to the seller within a reasonable time after he has received notice of the litigation.

Generally, the notification need not precisely specify the details of the breach, but only the fact that a breach has occurred in the specified transaction. In addition, timeliness of notification may vary widely from case to case, and the time period ordinarily is longer if the transaction involved consumer goods rather than commerical or industrial goods. Beyond this, generalization is impossible.

The purpose of the notice requirement is twofold. First, timely notice gives the seller an early opportunity to cure the defect and save the transaction, or to take other action to minimize any loss to the buyer that may result from the breach.

Also, the requirement makes it harder for a bad-faith buyer to make groundless claims, for example, simply as an offset to a seller's action for the price.

PRODUCT LIABILITY AND CONSUMER PROTECTION

Product liability actions primarily involve injuries caused by defects in consumer goods such as appliances, automobiles, and food products. Although industrial goods sometimes are involved, this happens less frequently and involves the application of some different standards.

The defects at issue in product liability actions may involve product design, construction, or labeling. Design defects affect every one of a particular good equally. For example, according to several plaintiffs' allegations, the Ford Motor Company designed its Pinto automobile defectively because it placed the gas tank too far toward the front of the car and immediately behind a large, protruding bolt. The plaintiffs claimed that this made the Pinto unreasonably vulnerable to explosion and fire in rear-end collisions.

Construction defects are those that arise during production, and generally involve a failure to comply with design specifications or faulty workmanship. For example, a worker's intoxication may cause her to forget to insert a special washer in a pressure cooker's pressure release valve, and the result may be an explosion in a consumer's home. A labeling defect simply is either incorrect or inadequate labeling. For example, a food-product label may fail to disclose the presence of a chemical that commonly causes an allergic reaction; a lawn mower may fail to have a conspicuous label warning of hazards connected with normal use; or a chemical container, such as a canister of gas used in recharging air conditioners, may fail to have labels warning of the possibility of explosion if stored at temperatures above a certain maximum.

A product liability case may be based on various legal theories: negligence or strict liability, breach of warranty under the UCC or other applicable state law, or a violation of federal legislative or administrative rules. An injured buyer therefore may be able to choose among these legal grounds, although under modern rules of procedure, he usually will advance multiple theories in a single complaint.

Negligence

Negligence is one of the oldest theories allowing recovery for personal injuries based on negligence rather than wrongful intent. As discussed in Chapter 4, all tort law concerns breaches of duties to an individual that arise from sources other than contract. A cause of action for negligence requires the proof of three elements—a negligent act, proximate cause, and injury. The absence of any of these will deny the plaintiff a cause of action.

The law imposes a duty of reasonable care on all human conduct. *Negligence* simply is a failure to live up to this duty, and typically is defined as a failure to behave as would a "reasonable person of ordinary prudence under the same or similar circumstances." This standard may be raised or lowered in some situations, however. If an actor possesses or holds himself out as possessing certain skills, he may be judged according to the standard of "a reasonable person in possession of like skills and understanding." A doctor, for example, cannot show that she was not negligent by showing that she was as careful as an ordinary person—she must show that she was as careful as an ordinary *doctor* of like skill and training. By the same token, a manufacturer of electrical products will be judged according to a standard appropriate for an electrical engineer. Two questions must be asked to determine the proper standard of care—what skills did the defendant possess, and what skills could the plaintiff reasonably have assumed that the defendant possessed?

To establish proximate cause, a plaintiff must show an unbroken chain of events leading from the defendant's negligent act to the injury complained of. This was discussed earlier in this chapter as it related to a breach of warranty action under the heading of "causation." In a tort action, proximate cause must be proved in two steps. First, the plaintiff must show "cause in fact," that is, that the injuries would not have occurred but for the defendant's action or failure to act. Then, the plaintiff must show that his injuries were foreseeable by the defendant as a consequence of his conduct. For example, although the want of a nail may cause the loss of a shoe, which may cause the loss of a horse, which may cause the empire to fall, it is most unlikely that a court would hold the blacksmith liable to the emperor.

In some negligence cases, courts allow the plaintiff to make use of the doctrine of *res ipsa loquitur,* which is Latin for "the thing speaks for itself." This doctrine raises a rebuttable presumption of negligence, allowing the plaintiff to recover on proof of only the other two elements—proximate cause and injury. For example, a plaintiff who found a dead mouse in his chewing tobacco did not need to prove that the mouse got there because of the defendant's negligence—the mouse's unexpected presence spoke for itself. *Res ipsa loquitur* typically applies when: (1) the injury is of a type that usually does not occur absent the defendant's negligence and (2) the cause of the injury and the evidence that would prove or disprove negligence are within the defendant's control. The theory underlying *res ipsa loquitur* is that when these two criteria are met, the defendant is in a better position to prove that she was not negligent than the plaintiff is in to prove negligence affirmatively.

Also, in appropriate cases, many jurisdictions allow the plaintiff in a negligence action to use the doctrine of "negligence *per se.*" This term, which means "negligence as such," provides that the defendant's violation of a statue or regulation imposed for the public's safety is sufficient proof of negligence. For example, if the plaintiff were injured because the defendant was driving on the left-hand side of the road, the plaintiff need not show that driving on the left side was negligent—it was illegal, and that is enough. In order to make use of this doctrine, the plaintiff must show that: (1) he is a member of the class of persons sought to be protected by the statute or regulation, and (2) his injury is of the type it sought to prevent. Suppose, for example, that a health-department regulation requires all restaurants to have smooth floors in order to facilitate cleaning. A restaurant disregards the regulation and installs "tongue and groove" flooring, and a customer is made ill by contamination that was bred in the grooves of the floor. The doctrine of negligence *per se* would allow the customer to recover upon proof of proximate cause and injury, without any other proof. However, suppose the customer had slipped and fallen on the floor. Negligence *per se* would not apply because the plaintiff's injury was not of the type the regulation was intended to prevent.

The most common affirmative defenses in a lawsuit based on negligence are "assumption of risk" and "contributory negligence." **Assumption of risk** applies when an injured plaintiff, knowing of a given danger, ignores it and is injured as a result. **Contributory negligence** applies in the slightly different circumstances in which the plaintiff is injured by the defendant's negligence, but also, in part, due to her own negligence. A plaintiff may both assume the risk and be contributorily negligent. For example, a plaintiff, knowing that her new lawn mower had not yet been completely assembled and checked by the seller, might not only take it after having been warned, but also may decide not to inspect it carefully before using it. If she then is injured when a blade that had not been tightened properly flies off, both defenses would apply. Moreover, either assumption of the risk or contributory negligence will defeat the plaintiff's cause of action for negligence completely.

A number of jurisdictions now have substituted

"comparative negligence" in place of contributory negligence. This has been done because it seems unfair to defeat a plaintiff's cause of action completely when his contributory negligence was only slight. **Comparative negligence** provides that each party should pay for the costs of an injury in proportion to the degree to which his or her negligence contributed to that injury. Thus, in a pure comparative negligence jurisdiction, if the defendant's negligence was 70 percent of the cause of an injury and the plaintiff's was 30 percent, the plaintiff would recover only 70 percent of the damages resulting for his injury.

"Strict" or "Absolute" Liability

Although strict liability has existed in tort law for a long time, its application to product liability is relatively recent. In fact, strict liability did not come into real prominence until the 1963 California Supreme Court decision in *Greenman v. Yuba Power Products, Inc*. In that case, the court held that a manufacturer should be liable in tort whenever he markets a product so defective as to cause personal injury, and knows that it will be used without inspection for defects. On this ground, liability was imposed on the manufacturer even though he was not shown to have been negligent. The *Greenman* rule is substantially that adopted by the Second Restatement of the Law of Torts, Section 402A(1), which states:

> One who sells any product in a defective condition unreasonably dangerous to the user or consumer or to his property is subject to liability for physical harm thereby caused to the ultimate user or consumer, or to his property if:
> a. the seller is engaged in the business of selling such a product, and
> b. it is expected to and does reach the user or consumer without substantial change in the condition in which it was sold.

Although not officially "the law" in any jurisdiction, courts frequently rely on the Restatement's provisions as persuasive authority, especially in cases of "first impression." Therefore, it properly may be regarded as a true, although not a binding, source of law.

There can be no finite list of the products that may invite the application of strict liability, but some generalizations are possible. Food, drugs, cosmetics, automobiles, power tools, explosives, and some electric products all have been treated as proper subjects. On the other hand, ballpoint pens, clothing, light bulbs, and books ordinarily would present no real danger from defects. Neither would a transistor radio, although a transistor television might because of the greater danger of an explosion or serious electrical shock.

The definition of *seller* for strict liability purposes has been expanded over the years. Although casual sellers are not included, teachers "selling" lessons have been, and persons furnishing goods incidental to the sale of services, such as beauty parlor operators, have been found to be "sellers" as well.

The requirement that the goods must have been actionably defective when they passed from the hands of the defendant may make recovery difficult. For example, a buyer who is injured by a foreign object in a package of cheese may have a cause of action against the manufacturer, the wholesaler, the retail seller from whom the cheese was purchased, and anyone else in the chain of distribution, including perhaps the dairy that produced the milk used in making the cheese. However, the buyer can recover only from those in whose hands the product contained the adulteration, and she may find that difficult to trace beyond the person who sold the cheese to her.

The concept of strict liability is founded on two principles. First, some products are so dangerous that, even with the exercise of reasonable care by the manufacturer and the seller, the safety of the public is not adequately assured and, therefore, manufacturers and sellers of such products must be encouraged to exercise extraordinary or ultimate care. Second, manufacturers and sellers should be required to bear the loss of the injuries that result from the use of these products, so that the risk of costly injuries may be spread among all of the wide group of users of the product in the form of higher prices. The latter principle certainly is practical, if it seems a bit socialistic.

Ordinarily the only defense to a strict liability claim is misuse of the product. For example, someone who removes the blade guard from a power saw, or disables a safety switch, will defeat his cause of action. This particularly is true when warning labels have been ignored. Ordinary contributory negligence, however, will not bar recovery. Primarily, this is to promote both of the two principles stated above, especially that of "risk spreading."

Shared Responsibility

In recent years the law has moved in away from the traditional notion of individual liability toward a concept of **shared responsibility.** Sometimes injuries occur, not because of the fault of any one individual, but because of the combined effect of acts of wrongdoing by a number of individuals. For example, five companies may discharge identical pollutants into a river and thereby cause the produce of the river to be unfit for human consumption. It could be that the amount discharged by any single individual would be harmless, but when the pollutants combine, they reach a critical concentration and become harmful. Traditionally, the courts have refused to grant recovery in such cases unless the plaintiff could show that the defendants acted in concert in some way, shared a common ownership, or agreed to enter jointly into the offending activity. This result follows from the principle that one should be liable only if his or her own conduct has caused the harm without any intervening cause. However, it can seem grossly unfair to deprive a victim of a remedy simply because his or her losses were due to the acts of multiple tortfeasors. Consider the following case.

SINDELL v. ABBOTT LABORATORIES, et al.
163 Cal.Rptr. 132, 607 P.2d 924 (1980)

This was a class action suit brought by Judith Sindell on her own behalf and on behalf of others similarly situated (Plaintiffs/Appellants) against Abbott Laboratories and four other drug manufacturers (Defendants/Appellees) for injuries sustained as a result of the administration of a drug called DES to their mothers while pregnant with Plaintiffs. Defendants were major manufacturers of this drug between the years 1941 and 1971. It was advertised as a miscarriage preventative. In 1971, the Food and Drug Administration banned DES after it was found to cause cancer in children whose mothers had taken it during pregnancy. Plaintiffs were unable to establish precisely which drug manufacturers produced the DES used by their mothers.

The trial court found for Defendants, and Plaintiffs appealed. Reversed.

MOSK, Justice.

[The court first discussed the traditional theories of liability. In particular, it discussed those in *Summers v. Tice* and *Hall v. E.I. DuPont de Nemours & Co., Inc.* The court determined, however, that none of the theories was applicable because all required the plaintiffs to establish which defendant manufactured the drugs in each case.]

If we were confined to the theories of *Summers* and *Hall*, we would be constrained to hold that the judgment must be sustained. Should we require that plaintiff identify the manufacturer which supplied the DES used by her mother or that all DES manufacturers be joined in the action, she would effectively be precluded from any recovery. As defendants candidly admit, there is little likelihood that all the manufacturers who made DES at the time in question are still in business or that they are subject to the jurisdiction of the California courts. There are, however, forceful arguments in favor of holding that plaintiff has a cause of action.

In our contemporary complex industrialized society, advances in science and technology create fungible goods which may harm consumers and which cannot be traced to any specific producer. The response of the courts can be either to adhere rigidly to prior doctrine, denying recovery to those injured by such products, or to fashion remedies to meet these changing needs. Just as Justice Traynor in his landmark concurring opinion in *Escola v. Coca Cola Bottling Company* . . . recognized that in an era of mass production and complex marketing methods the traditional standard of negligence was insufficient to govern the obligations of manufacturer to consumer, so should we acknowledge that some adaptation of the rules of causation and liability may be appropriate in these recurring circumstances. The Restatement comments that modification of the *Summers* rule may be necessary in a situation like that before us. . . .

The most persuasive reason for finding plaintiff states a cause of action is that advanced in *Summers:* as between an innocent plaintiff and negligent defendants, the latter should bear the cost of the injury. However, as in *Summers,* plaintiff is not at fault in failing to provide evidence of causation, and although the absence of such evidence is not attributable to the defendants either, their conduct in marketing a drug the effects of which are delayed for many years played a significant role in creating the unavailability of proof.

From a broader policy standpoint, defendants are better able to bear the cost of injury resulting from the manufacture of a defective product. As was said by Justice Traynor in *Escola,* "[t]he cost of an injury and the loss of time or health may be an overwhelming misfortune to the person injured, and a needless one, for the risk of injury can be insured by the manufacturer and distributed among the public as a cost of doing business. . . . The manufacturer is in the best position to discover and guard against defects in its products and to warn of harmful effects; thus, holding it liable for defects and failure to warn of harmful effects will provide an incentive to product safety. . . ." These considerations are particularly significant where medication is involved, for the consumer is virtually helpless to protect himself from serious, sometimes permanent, sometimes fatal, injuries caused by deleterious drugs.

Where, as here, all defendants produced a drug from an identical formula and the manufacturer of the DES which caused the plaintiff's injuries cannot be identified through no fault of plaintiff, a modification of the rule of *Summers* is warranted. As we have seen, an undiluted *Summers* rationale is inappropriate to shift the burden of proof of causation to defendants because if we measure the chance that any particular manufacturer supplied the injury-causing product by the number of producers of DES, there is a possibility that none of the five defendants in this case produced the offending substance and that the responsible manufacturer, not named in the action, will escape liability.

But we approach the issue of causation from a different perspective: we hold it to be reasonable in the present context to measure the likelihood that any of the defendants supplied the product which allegedly injured plaintiff by the percentage which the DES sold by each of them for the purpose of preventing miscarriage bears to the entire production of the drug sold by all for that purpose. Plaintiff asserts in her briefs that Eli Lilly and Company and 5 or 6 other companies produced 90 percent of the DES marketed. If at trial this is established to be a fact, then there is a corresponding likelihood that this comparative handful of producers manufactured the DES which caused plaintiff's injuries, and only a 10 percent likelihood that the offending producer would escape liability.

If plaintiff joins in the action the manufacturers of a substantial share of the DES which her mother might have taken, the injustice of shifting the burden of proof to defendants to demonstrate that they could not have made the substance which injured plaintiff is significantly diminished. While 75 to 80 percent of the market [has been] suggested as the requirements by [one commentator], we hold only that a substantial percentage is required.

The presence in the action of a substantial share of the appropriate market also provides a ready means to apportion damages among the defendants. Each defendant will be held liable for the proportion of the judgment represented by its share of that market unless it demonstrates that it could not have made the product which caused plaintiff's injuries. In the present case, as we have seen, one DES manufacturer was dismissed from the action upon filing a declaration that it had not manufactured DES until after plaintiff was born. Once plaintiff has met her burden of joining the required defendants, they in turn may cross-complaint against other DES manufacturers, not joined in the action, which they can allege might have supplied the injury-causing product.

Questions

1. Is it fair to find liability on a defendant regardless of the fact that it may not have been involved at all in the plaintiff's injuries? How broadly should this principle apply?

2. Is the idea of spreading the risk of this kind of activity among users of drug products a sound idea? Doesn't it make just as much sense to hold manufacturers of *all* products liable so the users of *all* products will bear the risks for individual users?

3. Why shouldn't the court in this case require Sindell to sue her mother's doctor or druggist who, in turn, might check his or her records to determine who manufactured the DES sold to her mother? Doesn't that seem more fair and efficient?

Breach of Warranty and Tort Liability

Until early in the twentieth century, the primary distinction between contract actions for breach of warranty and tort litigation was substantial. A contract action required proof of privity—a direct contractual relationship between the seller and the injured party. In many cases, the privity requirement prevented recovery by third parties who were injured by defective products. On the other hand, when the injured party had bought directly from the defendant, or otherwise was in privity with him, he could sue for breach of warranty, which did not require proof of negligence. The buyer had to prove that the warranty was breached, but not that the seller's conduct was unreasonable or that he was in any way at fault in making the defective product.

In the *MacPherson v. Buick Motor Co.* case, the court held that privity no longer should be required in some product liability cases. The court's reasoning in *MacPherson* soon began to convince other courts as well, and gradually they began to drop the privity requirement. Finally, as the theory of strict liability became accepted, the warranty and strict liability theories began to converge in product liability cases.

Today, the differences between an action under UCC Section 2–314 for breach of warranty and one for strict liability in tort, assuming state law conforms to Section 402A of the Restatement, are slight. Four points of difference may be material, however. (1) A warranty action requires only that the goods be nonmerchantable, that is, not fit for ordinary use, while strict liability requires that the goods' defects cause them to be unreasonably dangerous, and this usually requires proof by expert testimony. (2) The buyer must give reasonable notice of breach of warranty, whereas there is no such requirement in an action for strict liability. (3) Warranties run in favor not only of the ultimate user or consumer, but also of all persons who reasonably might be expected to be affected by the goods, whereas only the ultimate user or consumer is protected under Section 402A. (4) The statute of limitations for warranty actions is four years, and begins to run at the date of the transaction unless modified by the parties, but the statute of limitations for strict liability actions varies from state to state, frequently is shorter than four years, and does not begin to run until the plaintiff is injured. Beyond these differences, the pleadings and proof in the two actions are

substantially the same, which gives the injured party an effective battery of remedies to chose from. Indeed, many people believe that the pendulum has swung too far in favor of consumers, and that the cost of litigation and liability is damaging American business and making it less competitive in the world market.

FEDERAL LAW AFFECTING PRODUCT LIABILITY

The expansion of liability under state law due to both the UCC and the development of strict liability has provided consumers and the general public with increased protection from defective products. One weakness in these remedies, however, is that they apply only after an injury has occurred. For this reason, the federal government, like some states, has passed legislation in an attempt to prevent injuries, both by setting minimum standards for warranties and by regulating consumer products to ensure their safety. The Magnuson-Moss Warranty Act and the Consumer Product Safety Act are of particular importance.

The Magnuson-Moss Warranty Act

Passed as an amendment to the Federal Trade Commission Act, the **Magnuson-Moss Warranty Act** seeks to improve the quality of warranties given by manufacturers. The act's stated purpose is "to improve competition in the marketing of goods," and it has three main provisions: the act (1) requires certain disclosures concerning written warranties, (2) places limitations on disclaimers concerning written warranties, and (3) places limitations on disclaimers of implied warranties. The act's primary focus is on protecting the consumer, however, and it applies only to goods normally sold for personal, family, or household use. Also, the act affects only warranties on products costing $15.00 or more.

One specific target of the act is vagueness as to the coverage of warranties. Accordingly, it requires that warranties on products costing more than $15.00 must "fully and conspicuously disclose in simple and readily understandable language the terms and conditions of the warranty." The Federal Trade Commission has promulgated further restrictions and standards under the act. For example, the Commission has issued a regulation requiring that any warranty seeking to limit or exclude consequential damages flowing from its breach (for example, limiting the warrantor's liability to repair or replacement) must be accompanied by a disclosure: "Some states do not allow the exclusion or limitation of . . . damages, so the above limitation or exclusion may not apply to you."

The act requires a written warranty accompanying any product costing more than $10.00 to be designated clearly and conspicuously as "FULL" or "LIMITED." In order to be designated as "FULL," the warranty must meet four standards:

1. In the case of a defect, malfunction, or failure to conform to the warranty, the warrantor must agree to fix the product within a reasonable time, without charge.
2. The warrantor must not limit the duration of any implied warranty.
3. The warrantor must not exclude or limit damages for breach of the warranty *unless the exclusion or limitation appears conspicuously on the face of the warranty.*
4. The buyer must be entitled to elect a refund or replacement if a defect cannot be remedied after a reasonable number of attempts.

A failure to meet any of these standards means that the warranty must be designated as "LIMITED."

The first and fourth standards above are self-explanatory. They really do little more than codify what probably were a consumer's reasonable expectations anyway. However, it is important that the act turned these expectations into legal reality. One of the major problems with warranties has been the necessity for the buyer simply to make reasonable assumptions and hope that a court would agree; now warranty law has become both more predictable and fair.

The second standard imposes definite limitations, but is not as comprehensive as it may appear at first reading. Note that it only prevents warrantors from limiting the durations of *implied* warranties and only when they are *written* warranties. Therefore, a sale "as is" with no written warranty still can exclude all liability for breach of implied warranties. In addition, a seller may limit the duration of implied warranties to the duration of the written warranty as long as the limitation is not unconscionable and the warranty is designated conspicuously as "LIMITED." For example, a seller may give a one-year limited warranty, and limit the implied warranties to one year as well.

The third standard seems to permit the exclusion or limitation of consequential damages for personal injury. However, it should be read in conjunction with Section 2–719(3) of the UCC, which provides that it is *"prima facie* unconscionable" to limit consequential damages stemming from injuries to persons caused by the use of consumer goods. Therefore, although limitations on consequential damages are permitted under Magnuson-Moss, they nevertheless are *prohibited* in most cases under the UCC. Accordingly, a limitation generally would be enforceable only in cases involving nonconsumer goods, and perhaps in Louisiana.

A breach of warranty that involves a violation of the Magnuson-Moss Act entitles the buyer to any remedies provided by state law. In addition, if he wins his suit under the act, he also is entitled to reimbursement for the costs of the lawsuit, including reasonable attorney fees. This, of course, is designed to encourage private enforcement of the act in addition to enforcement by the Federal Trade Commission.

The Consumer Product Safety Act

The **Consumer Product Safety Act** established the Consumer Product Safety Commission to oversee the safety of consumer products. The commission also took over responsibility for enforcing some existing statutes and was empowered to pass and enforce new regulations to ensure the safety of consumer goods.

For the purposes of the act, a **consumer product** is one that was produced or distributed for use by consumers in the home, at school, or for recreation. The fact that the product also may be used for commerical or industrial purposes is of no consequence. However, the mere fact that a few consumers use the product will not make it a consumer product if it was neither produced nor distributed for consumer use.

The act requires producers to comply with regulations concerning product safety, to keep and maintain records, and to supply the Consumer Products Safety Commission with information concerning their products, including advance notice of new consumer products if the Commission so requires.

The **Consumer Products Safety Commission** imposes two general types of standards—performance standards and labeling standards. The former set out minimum safety requirements. For example, one standard requires that automobiles must be equipped with shatter-proof glass that will withstand pressures of up to a certain number of pounds. Another performance standard prohibits manufacturers from giving teddy bears detachable glass eyes. Labeling standards, in contrast, simply require warnings of permissible hazards. For example, some products may be permitted to contain materials that are particularly flammable, but only when sold with a label warning of every conceivable hazard. Cigarette warning labels are another well-known requirement, although there is considerable debate over whether these have any substantial beneficial effect. Finally, the Commission can seek to ban products that are unreasonably dangerous.

SUMMARY

The doctrine of *caveat emptor* for the most part has been replaced by a large number of new manufacturer and seller duties, which have caused a corresponding increase in liability. These duties are imposed both by the law of contracts and by the law of torts, and particularly by Article 2 of the Uniform Commerical Code.

There are three main types of warranties under the UCC—warranties of title, express warranties, and implied warranties. Warranties of title guarantee the lawful transfer of clear title to goods. They are special warranties that accompany every sale of goods unless negated or limited by the parties or the five circumstances of the transaction. Express warranties are self-explanatory, and the most important implied warranties are those of merchantability and fitness for a particular purpose.

Generally, all of these warranties may be modified or even entirely excluded by the sales contract, but only if certain rules are observed. The warranty of title may be excluded, but only by clear and specific language. Once made, express warranties are almost impossible to exclude. The warranty of merchantability may be excluded, but only in very special circumstances and by unambiguously notifying the buyer of its exclusion. The warranty of fitness for a particular purpose, in contrast, may be excluded even by very general language. Remedies for breach of warranty may be modified to the same extent as the warranties themselves, except that any attempt to limit consequential damages for injuries to a person are *prima facie* unconscionable, and therefore normally unenforceable.

There are three general defenses in warranty actions. First, a seller may prove that the breach was not the legal cause of the buyer's injuries, perhaps because the buyer was guilty of negligence contributing to her injuries, or because she assumed the risk. Second, the statute of limitations requires that every warranty action be brought within four years from the time it accrued, although the parties, by agreement, may reduce this to not less than one year. Failure to sue within the limitation period will bar recovery completely. Third, unless the buyer gives the seller notice of the breach within a reasonable time after it occurred, or within a reasonable time after she should have discovered a breach of an extended warranty, her action will be barred.

Historically, the most common basis for actions concerning personal injuries almost certainly has been negligence. Negligence requires proof of a negligent act by the seller that proximately caused the injuries of the complaining party. In some areas of the law, however, although negligence suits are still an available option, negligence has been replaced to a great extent by strict liability and the Article 2 warranties discussed above. Today, most actions for injuries caused by defective products probably are brought under one of these two theories. The strict liability and warranty theories overlap substantially in the area of product liability, although they differ in four important ways—the condition of the goods necessary to support an action, the requirement of notice of a breach of warranty, the persons protected, and the statutes of limitations.

Federal law also has developed to protect consumers from defective products and attempts by sellers to escape their responsibilities. The Magnuson-Moss Warranty Act sets standards for warranties, requiring that they be expressed in clear and understandable language. It also specifies requirements that must be met before labeling a warranty as "FULL" or "LIMITED." The federal Consumer Product Safety Act established the Consumer Product Safety Commission to oversee product safety in the area of consumer goods. The Commission has promulgated regulations concerning product performance and labeling, has established record-keeping and reporting requirements with which manufacturers must comply, and has monitored new consumer products as they have come onto the market.

KEY TERMS AND CONCEPTS

privity of contract
warranty
warranty of title
express warranty
sales talk or puffing
merchantability
implied warranty
warranty of fitness
course of dealing
usage of trade
course of performance
res ipsa loquitur
assumption of risk
contributory negligence
comparative negligence
shared responsibility
Magnuson-Moss Warranty Act
Consumer Product Safety Act
Consumer Product Safety Commission
consumer product

PROBLEMS

1. While eating fish chowder at the Blue Ship Tea Room in Boston, a fish bone became lodged in Webster's throat. Although his injuries were not great, he sued Blue Ship for breach of warranty of merchantability. Is Blue Ship liable?

2. Branch Moving and Storage Co. leased a truck from Robinson. Although Robinson repeatedly advised Branch to inspect the truck before taking it, Branch did not do so. Thereafter, over the course of a three-month period, defects caused the truck to break down a number of times. Some of the defects probably would not have been discovered even if Branch had performed a reasonable inspection. Branch sued Robinson for breach of warranty, claiming $5000 in lost wages. Is Branch entitled to recover?

3. While working in an underground tunnel, Anderson's oxygen mask failed and she was overcome by gas. In an attempt to rescue Anderson, four of her co-workers entered the tunnel without oxygen masks. Although Anderson was rescued, her rescuers were injured by the gas. When the rescuers sued Mine Safety Appliance Co., the supplier of Anderson's mask, Mine Safety defended on the ground that the rescuers had assumed the risk of injury by entering the tunnel without masks. Is Mine Safety Appliance Co. correct? Why or why not?

4. Mobly purchased a car from Century Dodge, Inc. The sale contract described the car as "new," and also contained a clause disclaiming all warranties, express or implied, other than those made by the manufacturer, Chrysler Corp. After driving the car for a while, Mobly discovered that it had been wrecked and repaired before it was sold to him. When sued, Century Dodge defended on the ground that the disclaimer relieved it of all liability. Is Century Dodge correct? If not, how would Mobly's damages be measured?

5. Associated Grocers, Inc. delivered a pallet of produce to Anderson's grocery store. It had a box of bananas on top, then a piece of wet burlap, then a box of radishes, then various other types of produce. After Anderson began to unload the pallet and had removed the box of bananas, a "banana spider" jumped on him from the wet burlap and bit him. After a lingering illness caused by the bite, Anderson died and his widow sued Associated for wrongful death. Should Associated be held liable? Should the spider?

6. Bashada contracted asbestosis after working for years with asbestos produced and distributed by Johns-Manville Products Corp. Bashada sued Johns-Manville for damages on the theory of strict liability. Johns-Manville defended on the ground that at the time it produced and distributed the asbestos for the use to which Bashada was exposed, it did not know of asbestos's potentially harmful effects. Should Bashada recover?

7. The Consumer Products Safety Commission sued Kaiser Aluminum and Chemical Co. alleging that Kaiser's aluminum branch-wiring circuits were unsafe. Kaiser said the circuits were produced and sold only to wholesalers who later resold them to electrical contractors, who installed them in homes and other buildings. Kaiser challenged the jurisdiction of the Consumer Products Safety Commission on the ground that the circuits were not consumer products. Is Kaiser correct?

8. Fairchild Industries sold a helicopter to Maritime Air Services, Ltd. The contract provided that the helicopter was sold "as is," and that the seller made no warranties either express or implied. This disclaimer appeared in the middle of the contract and was not distinguished by large type or in any other way. The helicopter crashed because of defects. Maritime sued Fairchild for breach of its implied warranty of fitness. Is Fairchild entitled to rely on its disclaimer?

9. Abernathy purchased a car from ABC Motors. The contract contained a disclaimer of warranties. Soon after the purchase, Abernathy became involved in an accident because the right front wheel collapsed. Barnes, a passenger in the car, sued ABC for breach of the warranty of merchantability. Should Barnes recover?

10. Gates decided to purchase a dress for his wife. He did not know her size, so he went to the Pretty Ms. Shoppe, where Mrs. Gates regularly purchased dresses. He told the owner his problem, and the owner selected three dresses, claiming that they would suit Gates's needs. On Christmas day, when the package was opened, Mrs. Gates discovered that the dresses were not her size. Mr. Gates then made several attempts to exchange the dresses but could find none that were suitable in Mrs. Gates's size. Gates then sued Pretty Ms. Shoppe for breach of warranty of fitness for the particular purpose. Is Gates entitled to recovery?

PART IV

Commercial Paper

The law of commercial paper involves such common written instruments as checks and promissory notes. More generally, it involves written instruments calling for the payment of money. Although the promises contained in these instruments bear similarity to promises under the law of contracts, as discussed in Parts II and III of this book, it is the dissimilarity between the two that is important. Commercial paper promises may be legally enforceable in a variety of situations in which the law of ordinary contracts provides no protection to the promisee or others who may have been assigned the rights of the promisee. Because of this, most businesses will accept commercial paper as a temporary substitute for cash payment and as a basis for extending credit to a purchaser of goods or services although they might not extend ordinary contract credit to the same purchaser. As a result, the ease, speed, and convenience of ordinary commercial transactions are greatly enhanced by the law of commercial paper.

Chapter 17

Commercial Paper: Introduction and Negotiability

OUTLINE

INTRODUCTION

Every piece of **commercial paper** is basically a contract for the payment of money. Rather than being a simple contract (requiring offer, acceptance, and consideration to be valid), commercial paper involves a type of formal contract; its validity stems from being set down in a prescribed form. The particular formal requirements are discussed in detail below.

The precise origin of commercial paper is not known, although it is known that written contracts for the payment of money have been in existence for more than 4000 years. Instruments somewhat akin to modern commercial paper came into common use among merchants with the rise of the mercantile era, beginning in the thirteenth century. At the time, merchants trading in goods were primarily itinerant, traveling through Europe selling goods often purchased in Asia or in other cities in Europe. Of course, it was dangerous to carry gold and money. In order to meet the need for a safe medium of exchange, these merchants developed the concept of commercial paper and devised their own rules to govern its use. These rules originally were enforced in merchants' courts that adjudicated the Law Merchant—the special body of law by which merchants agreed to abide.

By the end of the nineteeth century, the concept was adopted in England by Parliament's passage of the Bills of Exchange Act of 1882. It then was adopted in the United States, embodied in the Uniform Negotiable Instruments Act, and later in Article 3 of the Uniform Commercial Code (UCC).

NEGOTIABLE INSTRUMENTS DISTINGUISHED

The term *negotiable* is defined in various ways depending on the context, but generally it has some reference to transferability. For example, the term sometimes is used in connection with bonds to distinguish those that can be transferred without formality (also known as "bearer" or "coupon" bonds) from those that require every transfer to be registered with the issuing corporation. The same concept of negotiability also is applied to such instruments as warehouse receipts and bills of lading. These documents, however, are not commercial paper.

Requirements for Commercial Paper

In order to be classified as commercial paper, The Uniform Commercial Code requires that an instrument (1) be payable in money (Section 3-104(1)(b) since it is intended to be used as a substitute for money, and (2) does not include investments securities (Section 3-103(1) because they are not used currently in trade. The latter

simply means that they are not instruments of the type one might expect to find evidencing an obligation in a transaction involving the purchase and sale of goods or other property or services.

Other Negotiable Instruments

A share of corporate stock may be termed "negotiable" but it is not payable in money. It is intended to evidence ownership of a share of the issuing corporation. A corporate bond is payable in money, and certainly is of value, but it is not used currently in trade. Warehouse receipts and bills of lading are not used currently in trade, and are not payable in money but are payable in goods. Therefore, in classifying **negotiable instruments** as commercial paper, Article 3 of the UCC concerns itself with only those instruments that are accepted as substitutes for money in the conduct of daily business affairs.

TYPES OF COMMERCIAL PAPER

Instruments covered by Article 3 may be divided broadly into two classifications, *notes* and *bills of exchange*. It is for this reason that the governing law prior to the Uniform Negotiable Instruments Act was referred to as the "Law of Bills and Notes."

Notes

A **note** is a two-party instrument by which one party, called the **maker,** promises to pay money to a second party, called the **payee.** It is the simplest form of negotiable instrument. For example, "I promise to pay to the order of A. Adams $500. (signed) B. Baker" would comply with the requirements for a negotiable note.

If a note is generated by a deposit of money with a bank (or, under more recent law, any financial institution), it is referred to as a **certificate of deposit** (or C.D.). All other notes simply are called "notes" or "promissory notes."

Commercial paper

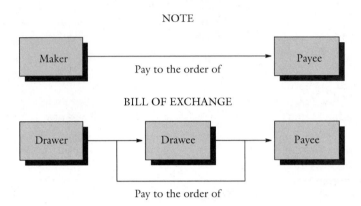

Bills of Exchange

A **bill of exchange** is a three-party instrument by which one party, called the **drawer,** orders a second party, called the **drawee,** to pay money to a third party, called the **payee.** This is the form of commercial paper with which most people are familiar. It includes the check. A **check** is simply a bill of exchange drawn on a bank and payable on demand. All other bills of exchange are called *drafts.*

The concept of a bill of exchange is that one party is holding money belonging to another and agrees, expressly or impliedly, to pay out those funds, or any part of them, to the creditor or to anyone the creditor designates. If money is paid to a third party because the creditor has ordered it, the debtor acts as an agent for the creditor to dispense the creditor's funds according to his lawful orders. The order—the debtor's authority to do so—is considered inherent in the check or other draft issued by the creditor. Failure to comply with a lawful order may render the debtor liable to both the creditor and the third party entitled to payment.

The use of checks is quite familiar to us, but the use of **drafts** may not be. One example of a use of drafts, which is steadily becoming more popular,

is in withdrawing funds from a draft account at a credit union or savings and loan institution. These drafts seem identical to checks in their form and in the information contained on them; and because drafts are used to pay obligations and the persons who receive them submit them to the drawee institution for payment. However, they are drafts, not checks, because the drawee is not a bank, but some other type of financial institution. A check must be drawn on a *bank.* Also a check could be converted to a draft by changing it so that it was payable after some time period following demand. A notation on the check *"10 Days After Demand,* pay to the order of" would render it a draft. A check must be payable on demand.

Another common use of the draft in commercial transactions is to secure payment for goods that must be shipped some distance to the purchaser. A seller may ship the goods with a negotiable bill of lading. When the seller gives the goods to a trucking company she may get the bill of lading, which evidences title to the goods being shipped. She then fills out a draft, naming herself as drawer and as payee and naming the purchaser as drawee. The bill of lading and the draft are then sent to the purchaser's bank (usually by the seller's bank). In order to get possession of the goods the purchaser must have the bill of lading. In order to get the bill of lading, the purchaser must accept the draft. After he does, his bank will take the money from his account and send it to the seller at her bank. In the case of a demand draft, the money will be sent immediately. If the draft is a time draft, used to extend credit to the purchaser, the money will be sent at the stated time. In transactions of this type, the draft frequently is called a **trade acceptance** because it is used to pay for goods. The banks charge a fee, called *exchange,* for their services. A trade acceptance normally is designated on its face as such, because trade acceptances typically receive a more favorable exchange rate than do other drafts.

BENEFITS OF NEGOTIABILITY

The main objective of Article 3 and the law of commercial paper is to create an instrument that will be accepted in place of money in ordinary commercial transactions. In order to meet this objective, the law reduces the number of defenses to payment that are available to the issuing party. In Chapter 19, defenses to the payment of a simple contract will be classified into twelve general categories. Five of these, including fraud and lack of consideration, are eliminated if the requirements of Article 3 are met. The elimination of these five very important defenses is the crux of the difference between the effect of the assignment of a simple contract and the negotiation of an item of commercial paper. The assignee of a simple contract ordinarily is subject to all defenses that would be available against the assignor (all twelve defenses).

The law of simple contracts still may be of importance in cases involving commercial paper. For one thing, if in attempting to comply with Article 3 of the UCC there is a failure to meet its requirements (no matter how small the failure), liability on the instrument will not be determined under Article 3. But, if the instrument meets the requirements of simple contract law, there may be liability on it. Also, although the requirements of Article 3 have been met, it still may be advantageous for the holder of the instrument to file a simple contract action instead of one under Article 3. For example, it may be necessary to hold liable an undisclosed or partially disclosed principal whose agent has signed a negotiable instrument on her behalf. Since the principal is not identified on the instrument she would not be liable under Article 3.

RISKS NOT ELIMINATED

Although the law of commercial paper seeks to create instruments that will be accepted in place of money, the acceptance of commercial paper is never as safe or as certain as payment in money. Even a demand instrument (such as a check) is subject to some risks that are not eliminated by the law. The most obvious of these are the risks of willingness and ability to pay. A $1000 check drawn by someone who never will have $1000 is worthless, or its worth is limited. The value of a check or note also may be limited by the fact that the maker or drawer will refuse to pay or will make collection difficult. In addition, the law does not eliminate defenses that arise from some circumstances involving the creation of the instrument itself, such as forgery or fraud in the execution of the instrument. Nor does it eliminate the defenses of lack of capacity or conflict with applicable law. Thus, a negotiable instrument that is void, voidable, or unenforceable in its inception may be no better than a simple contract with the same disabilities.

FORM OF COMMERCIAL PAPER

The importance of form in the law of commercial paper cannot be overstated. The formal requirements of Article 3 constitute the first of three major steps in using the protections of that article. If the formal requirements are met, the instrument is classified as negotiable. An instrument meeting these requirements may be void, voidable, or unenforceable, but still *negotiable.*

Formal Requirements

UCC Section 3-104 sets out seven formal requirements for commercial paper to be negotiable. The instrument must (1) be in *writing,* (2) be *signed* by the maker (note) or drawer (bill of exchange), (3) contain an *unconditional promise* (note) or *order* (bill of exchange), (4) to pay a *sum certain,* (5) in *money,* (6) on *demand* or at a *definite future time,* and (7) be payable to *order* or to *bearer.* The failure to meet any of these seven requirements will prevent the operation of Article 3.

Writing

The term **writing** may be defined as "the reduction of thought to tangible form." This requirement may be met in any number of ways. A proper negotiable instrument may be written in pencil on a piece of notebook paper, on a paper napkin, or on a tablecloth. One drawer carved his check into the side of a pumpkin and gave it as his donation to a pumpkin festival. Other examples of odd checks include one written on a woman's stomach. Of course these are exaggerated forms of writings, but they serve to illustrate that the requirements may be met by *any* reduction of thought to tangible form, and that the "normal" form in which we ordinarily find checks is not sacred.

Check forms came into common use so the average person could fill in the blanks and meet the seven requirements for negotiability without knowing the specifics of the law. Today, check forms also are personalized and coded to allow electronic processing. Under current federal law, although a drawer still may make out a perfectly valid negotiable check in any of the unusual ways noted above, she may find that doing so will result in the assessment of a special processing fee.

Signed

UCC Section 3-401(2) provides: "A signature is made by use of any name, including any trade or assumed name, upon an instrument, or by any word or mark used in lieu of a written signature." Therefore, in essence, any mark someone places on an instrument for the purpose of authentication (any mark someone intends as a signature) is sufficient to meet the requirements of a signature. Although a signature generally is thought of as being a script version of one's name, it may be printed, initials or a rubber stamp may be used, or someone else's name may be used. Early in the history of European civilization, a seal often was pressed into sealing wax to make a signature because even the wealthy were unable to write. In more modern times, people sometimes have used an "X" as a signature. Any of these is sufficient to meet the requirement. Under Section 3-403(1), a proper signature may be executed even by an agent.

It also should be noted that Article 3 does not limit the placement of the required signature. Although it normally is located below the text, it properly may appear anywhere on the instrument. The law simply says **signed,** not "subscribed." However, rules of interpretation provide that a signature on the face of an instrument will be presumed to be that of a maker, drawer, or acceptor, and one on the back will be presumed to be an indorsement. In case of doubt, Section 3-402 provides: "Unless the instrument clearly indicates that a signature is made in some other capacity it is an indorsement." The following case illustrates the force of presumptions. (*Note:* the UCC uses the term *indorse,* and most legal texts follow that practice. It means the same thing as the more familiar term *endorse.*)

CHRISMER v. CHRISMER
103 Ohio App. 23, 144 N.E.2d 494 (1956)

[Note: This case was tried under the Ohio negotiable instruments law prior to the enactment of the Uniform Commercial Code. However, the same principles would be applied today under Article 3.]

This was an action by Vern Chrismer and Marie Chrismer (Plaintiffs/Appellants) against the estate of Francis M. Chrismer, deceased, to collect the face amount of an alleged promissory note.

Upon Francis M. Chrismer's death, Plaintiffs submitted to the estate a carbon copy of a promissory note in the amount of $6000. The executor of the estate refused to allow it as a claim, and Plaintiffs filed suit.

From a judgment for Defendant estate, Plaintiffs appealed. Affirmed.

WISEMAN, J.

First, is the instrument a negotiable instrument within the meaning of the negotiable Instruments Act? We think it is not. Without question, the instrument is but a carbon copy of an original. The signature is made by imprint of the carbon paper. In our opinion the signature of the maker must be an original signature to be genuine and legal within the meaning of the Act. Section 8106, General Code, sets forth the requirements of a negotiable instrument, the first being that "it must be in writing and signed by the maker or drawer." Section 8123, General Code, provides that no person shall be liable on an instrument whose "signature does not appear thereon." Section 8289, General Code defines a negotiable promissory note, and one of the requirements is that it be "signed by the maker." In our opinion, a carbon copy of an instrument, which bears a carbon copy of what purports to be the signature of the maker, does not meet the requirements of the statute.

Finding no reported opinions on this proposition, it becomes a matter of first impression. In our opinion, the execution of a duplicate original negotiable promissory note is not contemplated by the Act, and, further, to do so would not be a sound trade practice or usage. We are cognizant of the fact that in modern trade practice carbon copies of negotiable promissory notes are made and retained for limited record purposes. However, in no sense can a carbon copy meet the statutory requirements of negotiability.

Questions

1. Does the judge really mean that a carbon rendition of the script version of someone's name *cannot* be a signature, or only that, in this case, the plaintiff's evidence was insufficient to overcome the presumption that it was not?

2. Is there any other way the plaintiff can seek payment at this point?

Unconditional Promise or Order

Every negotiable instrument involves either a promise to pay money in the future (a note), or an order from the drawer that a drawee pay money for the drawer's behalf (a bill of exchange). A **promise** is simply a binding obligation to do something in the future. It must arise from the language of the instrument, but the word *promise* need not be used. Such language as "I will pay" or "you are hereby assured of receiving payment from me" is sufficient. In most cases, however, the word *promise* is used. Section 3-102(c) states: "A 'promise' is an undertaking to pay and must be more than an acknowledgement of an obligation."

The term **order** is defined by Section 3-102(b) as: ". . . a direction to pay and must be more than an authorization or request. It must identify the person to pay with reasonable certainty. It may be addressed to one or more such persons jointly or in the alternative but not in succession." Therefore, an order is a mandate. The word *order* need not be used, and frequently is not. "Pay to the bearer" is an order. An order may be in polite terms such as "please pay to bearer," but language such as "you would do me the greatest favor if you would pay the bearer" has been held to be nothing more than a request or authorization, and is not an order. An "I.O.U." is not negotiable because it states only that a debt is owed, not a promise or order to pay the debt.

The required promise or order must be **unconditional.** That means it must be absolutely determinable from the language of the instrument that the obligation is payable in all events. Section 3-105 discusses in great detail the circumstances under which a promise or order is, and is not, considered conditional. The fact that an instrument is subject to implied or constructive conditions does not violate this requirement. In the first place, the law takes notice only of matters that appear on the instrument itself. Also, no written contract ever can be so complete that it leaves nothing to implication or to be construed by the court (such as "dollars" means "United States Dollars," which states of law will apply, and what is a "ton.") The fact that the instrument states that consideration existed or what that consideration was, that the instrument was given as required by another agreement, that it was given under a letter of credit or otherwise is secured does not make it conditional. These are all circumstances surrounding the creation of the instrument, not events whose occurrence will alter the obligation to pay. The fact that an instrument designates a particular account to be debited (as does every check) does not make it conditional. Such a designation does not limit payment only if funds are available in that account. Instead, it is construed as an "accounting advice."

A promise or order stating that it is "subject to" or "governed by" an outside instrument does not meet the requirement, even if the other instrument states no conditions. The mere fact that the holder was required to go outside the instrument to make that determination makes the instrument conditional. Finally, if the instrument states that it is payable *only* out of a particular account or fund, not just an accounting advice, it is conditional unless the maker or drawer is a government or a governmental agency or unit.

The "bottom line" of the requirement that the promise or order must be unconditional is that the extent and the nature of the obligation must be determinable from what appears on the instrument, because the instrument is intended to be transferable from hand to hand and may end up many miles from its origin. Parties at any distance certainly would be less willing to accept commercial paper in lieu of money if this requirement were not imposed. Consider the following case.

FIRST STATE BANK OF GALLUP v. CLARK et al.
91 N.M. 117, 570 P.2d 1144 (1977)

This was an action by the First State Bank of Gallup (Plaintiff/Appellee) against M. S. Horne (Defendant/Appellant) and other defendants, including R. C. Clark, to collect the amount due on a promissory note.

Horne had executed a promissory note in the amount of $100,000 payable to R. C. Clark. The note contained a provision, on the back, prohibiting transfer of the note without the written consent of Horne. As a part of the transaction, Horne gave Clark a letter of consent allowing Clark to pledge the note as collateral for an anticipated loan at the First State Bank of Gallup. Clark obtained the loan and pledged the note. When First State Bank attempted to collect on the note, Horne refused, stating that Clark had given him an offsetting note in case he defaulted on the loan. The bank contended that it was entitled to payment as a holder in due course of the note.

The district court granted summary judgment for Plaintiff and Defendant appealed. Affirmed (in result).

EASLEY, Justice.

The note in question here failed to meet the requirements of Section 3-104, since the promise to pay contained in the note was not unconditional. Moreover, the note was expressly drafted to be non-negotiable since it stated:

> This note may not be transferred, pledged, or otherwise assigned without the written consent of M. S. Horne.

These words, even though they appeared on the back of the note, effectively cancelled any implication of negotiability provided by the words "Pay to the order of" on the face of the note. Notations and terms on the back of a note, made contemporaneously with the execution of the note and intended to be part of the note's contract of payment, constitute as much a part of the note as if they were incorporated on its face. Williams v. Wisowaty, 2 Ill.App. 3d 400, 276 N.E.2d 424 (1971).

Counsel argue that Section 3–119 applies and allows incorporating other documents to remove the defects on the face of the instrument. They argue that Horne's separate letter to Clark authorizing the pledging of the note to First State removed the conditions in the note and the express prohibition therein against its negotiability and rendered the note negotiable for Article 3 purposes. This is incorrect. An instrument which in and of itself does not meet the requirements of Section 3-104 cannot be made negotiable for Article 3 purposes by reference to another document which purports to cure the defects in the note's negotiability. . . .

The whole purpose of the concept of a negotiable instrument under Article 3 is to declare that transferees in the ordinary course of business are only to be held liable for information appearing in the instrument itself and will not be expected to know of any limitations on negotiability or changes in terms, etc., contained in any separate documents. The whole idea of the facilitation of easy transfer of notes and instruments requires that a transferee be able to trust what the instrument says, and be able to determine the validity of the note and its negotiability from the language of the note itself. . . .

Even though a note or instrument is not a "negotiable instrument" for Article 3 purposes, it may nevertheless be negotiable between the parties involved under ordinary contract law. . . . As between Clark and Horne, Clark had a contract right to pledge Horne's note to First State as security. Clark had a contract right to negotiate the note. Thus the note was negotiable for Clark's limited purposes even though it was not an Article 3 negotiable instrument. Before accepting Clark's pledge, First State verified by direct conversation with Horne that Clark had Horne's authority to pledge the note as the letter permitted. Horne in no way suggested that he had any offsetting defense to the validity of the note. Horne failed to notify First State that Clark had given him an offsetting note which was intended to nullify the effect of Horne's note to Clark should Clark default on his loan obligation secured by that note. [The court estopped Horne from asserting his setoff as a defense.]

Questions

1. Is the result in this case fair to the defendants?
2. Hasn't the court misused the terms "negotiable" and "negotiate" in the last paragraph of its opinion? Is that wise?

Money

The term **money** is defined in Section 1-201(24) as "a medium of exchange adopted by a domestic or foreign government as a part of its currency." This would include United States dollars, Canadian dollars, Italian lira, and German marks. On the island of Yap, certain designated stones are currency, having been authorized as such by the government. Gold, silver, and diamonds are not money, even though some may consider them more valuable. Also, for our purposes, currency issued by the Confederate States of America was not money because that government was not recognized by the United States of America, although it was money under Confederacy "law."

Checks and notes are not money; they are payable in money. However, a Federal Reserve Note (for example, a one-dollar bill or a five-dollar bill) is money because it is part of the currency of the United States government. Section 3-107 discusses some details concerning this requirement.

An instrument payable in either money or non-money (such as goods) still may be negotiable if the holder of the instrument has the option to accept either, but not if it is the option of the maker or drawer to pay either. For example, a note in which Jeff promises to give Wendi $5000 or a diamond ring, whichever Wendi chooses, can be negotiable. Wendi's right to the money is protected, and protection of the holder of the instrument is the underlying motive for most of the rules in Article 3.

Sum Certain

The requirement that the money be stated as a **sum certain** simply means that the instrument must state a fixed or absolute sum. The person holding the instrument must be able to determine from the face just how much is due to him at any point in time. An obligation to pay "$500," of course, would be a sum certain; so would "$500 together with 6 percent interest." In the latter case, the exact amount is not stated, but a means of precise calculation appears on the instrument. Ordinary rules of construction apply to construe "6 percent" to mean "6 percent per annum on the face of the obligation until it is paid." Section 3-106 provides that a stated sum is sufficiently certain even though it is to be paid with stated interest or in installments, with stated different rates of interest or discounts or additions payable at different stated times, "with exchange" or "less exchange," or with attorney fees and costs of collection if not paid by the due date. In all of these circumstances except the last two, the precise amounts of additions or discounts are stated in, or calculable from, the language of the instruments.

In the case of exchange, it may be at the "current rate." This exception is a matter of commercial necessity. The precise amount of exchange to be charged will depend on which banks handle collection of an instrument, but it is expected that the rate will not vary to any material degree. The same is true in the case of attorney fees and costs of collection. Also, since these latter additions are generated only by default, and Article 3 concerns itself with matters only up to default, they should not render the instrument nonnegotiable.

If an instrument calls for the payment of interest but no rate is stated, the rate is construed to be the statutory rate of interest that runs on unpaid judgments in the jurisdiction in which the instrument is payable. (In Michigan, that rate is 12 percent.)

Demand or Definite Future Time

Every instrument must be payable either on demand or at some definite future time. The holder of the instrument must be assured that he has a right to the money either whenever he wants it or no later than a particular point in time in the future.

An instrument payable on **demand** is one that, by its terms, is payable at any time the holder of the instrument properly requests payment from the maker or the drawee. The word *demand* need not be used, but the language of the instrument clearly must imply demand. Section 3-108 specifically authorizes the use of "sight" and "presentation" to mean demand. Under the same section, the Code provides that if an instrument states no time of payment, it is payable on demand. A familiar example of this is the ordinary check, which states the date of execution but makes no reference to any particular time for payment. Also, consider the following case involving a note.

MASTER HOMECRAFT COMPANY v. ZIMMERMAN
208 Pa.Super. 401, 22 A.2d 440 (1966)

This was an action by Master Homecraft Company (Plaintiff/Appellant) against Edward T. Zimmerman and Alice Zimmerman (Defendants/Appellees) and First National Bank of Export (Garnishee). Plaintiff procured a levy of execution (a court order to collect the judgment) by garnishment on a judgment Plaintiff held against Defendants. Defendants moved to vacate the judgment on the ground that it was based on an invalid promissory note. The note in question read, in part, as follows:

$9747.00   No _____
(Total Amount of Note)

Pittsburgh, Pa. 8/4/64

For value received, I/we or either of us promise to pay to the order of MASTER HOMECRAFT COMPANY, the sum of Nine Thousand Seven Hundred Forty-seven Dollars in _____ monthly installments of $ _____ each, beginning on the day of _____, 19 ____, and continuing on the same day of each and every month thereafter until the full amount thereof is paid. . . .

The Defendants contended that the instrument is not written in the form of a demand note, and also specifies no date for payment. As such, it does not constitute a valid obligation.

From a judgment for Defendants, Plaintiff appealed. Reversed and remanded with instructions to allow Defendants to file a motion to open the judgment (to have the court hear more evidence about the legitimacy and correctness of the judgment).

SPAULDING, Judge.

The law is clear that a motion to strike a judgment operates as a demurrer to the record and will be granted only when there are defects apparent on the face of the record. . . . In the instant case there were no such defects because both the time of default and the amount due were ascertainable from the face of the instrument.

The Uniform Commercial Code provides: "Instruments payable on demand include those payable at sight or on presentation and those in which no time for payment is stated." April 6, 1953, P.L. 3 12A P.S. Section 3-108. . . . Under this section, the note in question is a demand note, due and payable immediately. This presumption as to payment on demand existed long before the Code, Horner v. Horner, 145 Pa. 258, 23 A. 441 (1892); Hall v. Toby, 110 Pa. 318, 1 A. 369 (1885), and applies whether or not the note is negotiable. . . .

The note is not rendered defective because the blanks for alleged installment payments appear unused. On its face the note designates a principal sum of $9747. The failure to fill in the monthly installment blanks does not indicate that no principal sum was intended.

On this issue the court below stated: "This Court does not know the reason for the failure to complete the note. The parties to this note either inadvertently or unintentionally failed to complete the blanks." This conclusion is without support in the record. . . .

In Hinkson v. Southard . . . , which involved a judgment note with unused installment blanks, the court granted a petition to strike. This case, decided before the Code, is not controlling since under the Code the absence of a specific maturity date is not a fatal defect.

If the appellees wish to raise a defense, the proper remedy would be a petition to open the judgment which would permit additional evidence.

Questions

1. Does this case further the policies underlying negotiability?

2. Given the technicality and insistence on form that characterized some of the earlier cases in this chapter, how do you explain the permissiveness of the court in this case?

An instrument is payable at a **definite future time** if it fixes a stated time by which the instrument must be paid if the holder wishes, and that stated time is certain of occurrence and can be calculated at any moment in time. The essence of definite time would be, for example, "12:00 Noon, December 25, 1991." However, "December 25, 1991" is sufficiently definite, as is "Christmas Day, 1991," or "One year after Christmas Day 1990." On the anniversary day of the birth of the seventh president of the United States" is sufficient, since the seventh president of the United States was dead at the time the instrument was issued. All of these are definite times that may be calculated, although the last may require some research. "Ten days after my death" is not sufficient because it is not calculable at any moment in time. It may be calculated only after the maker or drawer's death, and even that supposes that the death will occur. The calculation may not depend on an event that is uncertain as to time of occurrence at the moment the instrument is executed. Failure to meet this requirement is not cured even if the uncertain event, in fact, does occur (Section 3-109(2)).

Section 3-109(1) provides that an instrument is payable at a definite time if it is payable (a) on or before a stated date or at a fixed period after a stated date, or (b) at a fixed period after sight (that is, demand). These certainly are calculable. Subsection 3-109(1)(c) states that the requirement is met even if the instrument is subject to "acceleration" of the definite time. That is, the holder may elect to demand earlier payment, a party obligated may elect to pay early, or the date of payment may be accelerated automatically by the occurrence of an uncertain future event. In all of these cases, the holder is assured of the right to be paid no later than the stated final date. Subsection 3-109(1)(d) then provides that the definite time also may be subject to extension to a later time. This extension may occur freely at the option of the holder. That is, the holder may be entitled to receive payment on the stated date or whenever, thereafter, he or she wishes. However, if the extension is to occur at the option of the party obligated, or upon the occurrence of some uncertain future event, the extension must be to a further definite time. If there were no such limitation on these two situations, the holder would not be assured that he or she would be paid at all.

Order or Bearer

The requirement that commercial paper is valid only if it is made payable to order or to bearer is unique. Unlike the other six, its purpose is only to act as a "stumbling block." It is the one requirement that a promisor would not be likely to meet by accident if he or she intended to write up a simple contract rather than commercial paper. It serves to help assure the court that the maker or drawer intended that the instrument be governed by Article 3, and therefore intended to give up certain defenses to paying it. Actually this requirement could be replaced by a requirement that the maker or drawer print "garbage can" across the face of the instrument, since it is intended only as a signal.

Section 3-111 provides that an instrument is **payable to bearer** if it is payable to (1) "bearer," (2) "the order of bearer," (3) "[a specified person] or bearer," (4) "cash," (5) "the order of cash," or (6) any other indication that does not purport to designate a specific payee. In other words, a bearer instrument is one that does not purport to name a specific payee who is capable of indorsing it either personally or through an authorized agent. Therefore, an instrument made payable to "the old oak tree at the corner of Fifth and Main" presumably would be considered a bearer instrument. In a real sense, then, an instrument is considered to be payable to bearer when it is made payable to no one in particular.

Section 3-110 then discusses instruments **payable to order.** Subsection (1) begins with an implied warning. If an instrument purports to name a payee (one capable of indorsing it), then the "order" form must be used. The use of the specific word *order* is ideal, but is not required. The word *assigns* specifically is authorized to mean "order." The requirement also is met if "Exchange" is written conspicuously on the face of the instrument.

The payee may be anyone, including the maker, the drawer, the drawee, or two or more persons either together or in the alternative ("A and B" or "A or B"). The payee also may be a partnership, corporation, estate, trust fund, or an office (for example, San Diego City Treasurer), among others.

In the event that an instrument is made payable both to order and to bearer, rules of construction (Section 3-118) will apply. Handwriting takes precedence over typewriting, and typewriting takes precedence over printing (as in a printed form). If both the order and the bearer designations are handwritten, or they are both printed, then under subsection (3), the instrument is considered payable to order. As the following case illustrates, confusion generated by the form of an instrument may cause the instrument to be considered nonnegotiable.

BROADWAY MANAGEMENT CORPORATION
v. BRIGGS
30 Ill.App. 488, 332 N.E.2d 131 (1975)

This was an action by Broadway Management Corporation (Plaintiff/Appellee) against Conan Briggs (Defendant/Appellant) to obtain a garnishment of certain property that was in the hands of another and belonged to Plaintiff's judgment debtor, Briggs.

Plaintiff had obtained a judgment against Briggs on a promissory note, under a power purportedly granted in a confession of judgment *(cognovit)* clause contained in the note. Defendant challenged the validity of the judgment because of the form of the note, which read, in part: "<u>Ninety Days</u> after date, I, we, or either of us, promise to pay to the order of <u>Three Thousand Four Hundred Ninety Eight and ⁴⁵/₁₀₀-----------------</u>Dollars." (The underlined words and symbols were typed in. The remainder was part of a printed form.)

The trial court denied Briggs's motion to vacate the judgment and Briggs appealed. Reversed.

CRAVEN, Justice.

Thus the critical question of whether this is order or bearer paper is to be determined by section 3 of the Uniform Commercial Code, which governs negotiable instruments. If this is bearer paper, the plaintiff's possession was sufficient to make it a holder (Uniform Commercial Code, section 1-201(20) (Ill.Rev.Stat.1971, ch. 26,

Section 1-201(20)), and this note on its face authorizes the holder to confess judgment against the maker.

On the other hand, if the instrument is order paper, it becomes apparent that the payee cannot be determined upon the face of the instrument. The power to confess judgment must be clearly given and strictly pursued. . . . The warrant of authority in this case cannot be read to extend to "bearer," then it may not be exercised, since the strict construction mandated by Illinois decisions will not allow a court to guess in whose name such a power may be exercised.

Under the Code, an instrument is payable to bearer only when by its term it is payable to:

(a) bearer or the order of bearer; or
(b) a specified person or bearer; or
(c) 'cash' or the order of 'cash', or any other indication which does not purport to designate a specific payee. (UCC, Section 3-111) . . .

The official comments to the section note that an instrument made payable "to the order of _____" is not bearer paper, but an incomplete order instrument unenforceable until completed in accordance with authority. (UCC, Section 3-115). . . .

The instrument here is not bearer paper. We cannot say that it "does not purport to designate a specific payee." Rather, we believe the wording of the instrument is clear in its implication that the payee's name is to be inserted between the promise and the amount, so that the literal absence of blanks is legally insignificant.

Since the holder could not be determined from the face of the instrument, the trial court was in error in allowing plaintiff Broadway Management Corporation to exercise the warrant of attorney granted by this instrument to its holder. The judgment by confession therefore must be vacated.

Questions

1. Is the result in this case fair to the plaintiff? What can the plaintiff do now?
2. Does this case promote the policies underlying negotiability?

INCOMPLETE INSTRUMENTS

An instrument must be complete in meeting the requirements of negotiability. However, if the instrument is incomplete at the time it is signed, although it is not negotiable at that time it may become negotiable later if it is completed properly. Under Section 3-115, as long as the maker or drawer intended that the instrument be negotiable at the time of signing, it may be completed later by anyone acting in good faith, and it will be negotiable. For example, a note may promise payment "60 days after date," but no date is placed on the instrument by the time it is signed. Any holder of the instrument later may supply the necessary date and the instrument will become negotiable. The maker will be presumed to have authorized the completion on her behalf unless the instrument is completed in such a way as to increase her obligation or to harm her in any fashion. If the contract is altered in a way that harms her, the maker will have either a partial or complete defense to payment of the instrument under Section 3-407.

SUMMARY

The law of commercial paper in Article 3 of the Uniform Commercial Code involves the creation of a special kind of contract. Commercial paper involves formal contracts for the payment of money, which are intended to be accepted in commercial transactions as temporary substitutes for money. This is achieved by eliminating the use of five of twelve common defenses that could be used against paying a simple contract obligation.

There are two general classifications of commercial paper, bills of exchange and notes. Bills of exchange are three-party instruments by which a drawer orders a drawee to pay money to a payee. An example is a check, which is any bill of exchange that has a bank as drawee and is payable on demand. A note is a two-party instrument by which a maker promises to pay money to a payee. An example is a certificate of deposit, which is a note generated by a deposit of money with a financial institution.

In order to qualify as commercial paper, an instrument must meet seven requirements of negotiability. It must (1) be in writing, (2) signed by the maker or drawer, (3) contain a promise or order, (4) to pay a sum certain, (5) in money, (6) on demand or at some future time, and (7) it must be payable to order or to bearer. If all of these requirements are met, the instrument is considered negotiable, and the first of three general steps necessary to use the protections of Article 3 has been met.

KEY TERMS AND CONCEPTS

commercial paper
negotiable instrument
note
maker
payee
certificate of deposit
bill of exchange
drawer
drawee
check
draft
trade acceptance
writing
signed
promise
order
sum certain
money
demand
definite future time
payable to bearer
payable to order

PROBLEMS

1. A promissory note, otherwise negotiable in form, provided that it was due and payable one year from the date of the instrument. It also contained a clause entitling the holder to confess judgment against the maker any time during the term of the note. Is the note negotiable?

2. The holder of a negotiable note dated May 25, 1963 that provided for payment "within ten years after date" brought an action against the maker seeking to collect the instrument in 1965. She wanted to introduce testimony that the parties had orally agreed that the maker would pay the note earlier if the holder wished. Should the testimony be permitted?

3. An instrument is completed in all respects except that the space for filling in the name of the payee is left blank. Can this instrument be negotiable?

4. Smith agreed to lend $20,000 to Tucker and Tucker executed and delivered to Smith a mortgage note made payable "Pay to S. Smith" on its face. Smith took the note and endorsed it "Pay to the order of B. Burnes—/x/ S. Smith" and gave it to Burnes. Was this note negotiable?

5. Assuming all are valid items of commercial paper, which of the following is more desirable to you as a holder: (1) a check, (2) a draft drawn on a credit union, (3) a promissory note payable on demand, or (4) a certificate of deposit that is due and payable?

6. Assume a note is given and payment is secured by a mortgage. The note provides ". . . the terms of the mortgage are by this reference made part hereof." Can the note be negotiable?

7. Locke gave Phillips a note payable "Pay to P. Phillips" to secure payment for services rendered. Phillips sold the note to Aetna Acceptance Corp. and, when Aetna sought to collect on it, Locke contended that since it was not made payable to order or to bearer it was void except as between the original parties and Aetna was not entitled to collect on it. Is Locke correct?

8. A note, otherwise negotiable in form, contained a provision "In case of death of the maker all payments not due at date of death are cancelled." Is this note negotiable?

9. Suppose Carr owes Able $1000, and Able owes Brown $200. Able gives the following letter to Brown to take to Carr: "To: C. Carr, 102 E. 2nd St., Carroll, Colo.—Please give the bearer of this letter $200 of the $1000 you owe me.—/x/ A. Able." Is the instrument a check, a draft, a promissory note, or none of these? Is it negotiable?

10. The Feldman Construction Company issued a check to pay its obligations to a subcontractor who owed a material supplier for materials furnished on a contruction project. The check was made payable "Pay to the order of Interstate Steel Corp., General Pipe & Supply." Who must indorse the check in order to negotiate it?

Negotiation and Holder in Due Course

INTRODUCTION

Once the seven requirements for negotiability discussed in Chapter 17 have been met, the resulting instrument is classified as negotiable. This satisfies the first of three general prerequisites for using the protections of Article 3 of the Uniform Commercial Code. Failure to meet any one of the seven requirements means that the instrument is not commercial paper and Article 3 does not apply, but it still may qualify as a simple contract if the elements of offer, acceptance, and consideration are present.

A purpose of Article 3 is to create an instrument that can be transferred freely from hand to hand. When dealing with simple contracts, the process of transfer was called *assignment*. Although commerical paper also can be assigned rather than negotiated, if it is assigned Article 3 does not come into play and the law of contracts will govern. The value of having commerical paper is to enable the parties to negotiate it so the advantages of Article 3 can be used.

NEGOTIATION AND ASSIGNMENT

The process of negotiation is very similar to that of assignment. In both cases, a contract is transferred to a third person. The difference is that assignment is governed by the law of contracts and, if the assignment is completely successful, the assignee still can have no better rights than were possessed by the assignor at the time of assignment. She will be subject to twelve possible defenses. By way of contrast, negotiation is governed by the law of commercial paper (Article 3) and, if negotiation is completely successful, it is possible for the recipient to have greater rights than were possessed by the person who negotiated the instrument to him. Rather than being subject to the twelve defenses, he will be subject to only seven. Exactly which defenses these are will be discussed in detail later.

If the instrument to be transferred is not negotiable (see Chapter 17), it may be assigned, but it cannot be negotiated. If it is negotiable, but is transferred in a way that fails to meet the requirements for negotiation, the transfer may qualify as an assignment. Keep in mind that whenever there is a failure to meet the requirements of Article 3,

the transaction still may be governed by contract law. If contract law cannot be satisfied, the transaction will be considered in the nature of a gift and any executory promises probably will not be enforceable.

In a general way, the term **negotiation** may be defined as the transfer of a negotiable instrument in a manner that makes the transferee a holder. The term **holder** is then defined in Section 1-201(20) of the Uniform Commercial Code (UCC) as "a person who is in possession of an instrument . . . drawn, issued or indorsed to him or to his order or to bearer or in blank." Otherwise stated, a *holder* is anyone who is in possession of an instrument that was negotiated to him or her. If it is an "order" instrument, it must be both indorsed and delivered to be negotiated. If it is a "bearer" instrument, delivery alone is sufficient. (A bearer instrument may be indorsed also, but indorsement is not required for negotiation.) However, if an order instrument is transferred without indorsement, the transfer is only an assignment and Article 3 will not apply to that transferee or anyone who takes the instrument thereafter. All subsequent transferees will be assignees.

FIRST NATIONAL BANK OF GWINNETT v. BARRETT
141 Ga.App. 161, 233 S.E.2d 24 (1977)

The Barretts, husband and wife, (Plaintiffs/Appellees) brought an action against the First National Bank of Gwinnett (Defendant/Appellant) to recover for an alleged unauthorized payment from their checking account.

On July 19, 1975 Mr. Barrett issued a check for $1500 drawn on Plaintiffs' joint account in Defendant Bank, payable to the order of Acquatic Industries. Acquatic deposited the check in the Roswell Bank but failed to indorse it. The Roswell Bank indorsed the check and forwarded it to Defendant Bank, and Defendant Bank debited Plaintiffs' account for $1500.

The trial court found for Plaintiffs on their motion for summary judgment and Defendant appealed. Reversed.

Rights and defenses when value is transferred

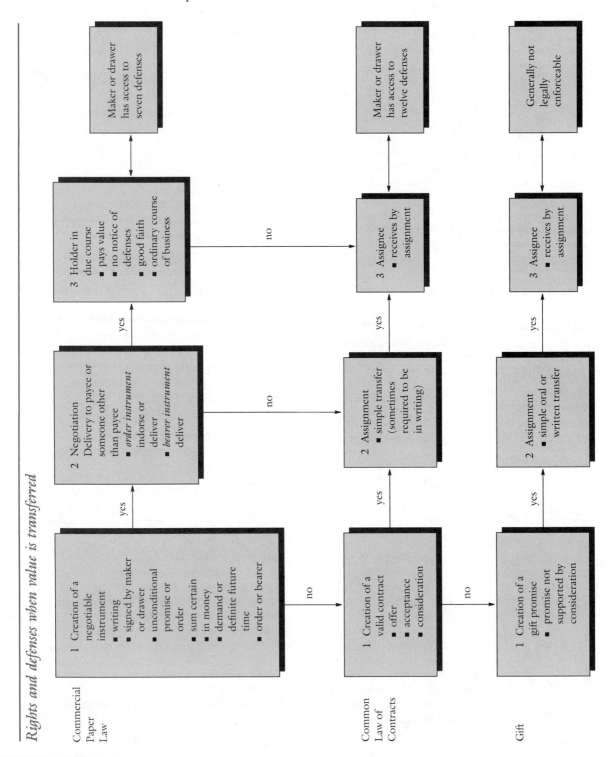

BELL, Chief Judge.

. . . The absence of the payee's indorsement . . . did not affect the payor bank's right to pay this check and to debit the plaintiffs' account. In absence of the indorsement of the payee the instrument was not transferred by negotiation and any subsequent transferee of the instrument could not acquire the status of holder in due course. UCC § 3-202(1) . . . Although the check was not negotiated, it was transferred [assigned] from the payee to the Roswell Bank and by Roswell to the defendant bank. . . . The Uniform Commercial Code does not prevent transfers of negotiable order paper without indorsement. See UCC § 3-201(1) . . . Indeed, where the holder of an instrument payable to order transfers it for value without indorsing it, the transfer vests in the transferee all the title that the transferor had in the paper. . . .

Questions

1. Does the distinction between assignment and negotiation make any sense?
2. Would there be any advantage to eliminating the notion of assignment in connection with commercial paper and insisting on negotiation or nothing? Would there be any disadvantages?

INDORSEMENTS

An **indorsement** is simply a signature on the instrument or on a separate piece of paper firmly attached to the instrument (called an **allonge**), and it must be made by or on behalf of the indorser (Sec. 3-202(2)). An indorsement normally appears on the back of the instrument, but it may appear anywhere. The following case considers the requirements for attaching an allonge to an instrument.

LAMSON v. COMMERCIAL CREDIT CORPORATION
531 P.2d 966 (Colo. 1975)

This was an action by Robert S. Lamson (Plaintiff/Petitioner) against Commercial Credit Corporation (Defendant/Respondent) to recover the face value of two checks plus interest.

Defendant drew and issued two checks payable to Ranch Motor Company. Ranch indorsed them and deposited them to its account at University National Bank. University National, to settle a dispute with Plaintiff, transferred the two checks to him, attaching a special two-page indorsement to the checks with a staple. Commercial Credit refused to pay the checks, defending in the trial court on grounds not material here. The trial court granted judgment to the Plaintiff. This judgment was overruled by the Court of Appeals on the ground that Plaintiff was not a holder of the checks because University National Bank's indorsement to him was not in compliance with the requirements of the Uniform Commercial Code. Reversed.

DAY, Judge.

We agree with the Court of Appeals' statement that a separate paper pinned or paper-clipped to an instrument is not sufficient for negotiation. Section 4-3-202(2), comment 3. However, we hold, contra to its decision, that the section does permit stapling as an adequate method of firmly affixing the indorsement. Stapling is the modern equivalent of gluing or pasting. Certainly as a physical matter it is just as easy to cut by scissors a document pasted or glued to another as it is to detach the two by unstapling. Therefore we hold that under the circumstances described, stapling an indorsement to a negotiable instrument is a permanent attachment to the checks so that it becomes a part thereof."

Section 4-1-201(20) defines a holder as "a person who is in possession of . . . an instrument . . . indorsed to him. . . ." The Bank's special indorsement, stapled to the two checks, effectively made Lamson a holder, although not a holder in due course.

Once signatures are proven, Lamson, as a holder was entitled to payment by mere production of the instrument unless the corporation established a defense.

Questions

1. Should the sufficiency of an indorsement turn on whether it is pinned or stapled to an instrument?

2. How can an indorsement requirement be taken seriously if a mere mark suffices? What is the justification for this?

There are two basic reasons for indorsements. The first is that if the instrument is an order instrument, an indorsement is necessary to permit negotiation. Second, an indorsement adds, or increases, the liability of the indorser to those who take the instrument thereafter. The nature and extent of an indorser's liability is discussed fully in this chapter under qualified and unqualified indorsements.

In order to be effective for negotiation, an indorsement must carry title to the entire instrument or any remaining unpaid portion. If it purports to convey any less, it is considered only a partial assignment.

If an instrument is made payable to a person under a wrong or a misspelled name, he may indorse and negotiate the instrument by signing in the wrong or misspelled name, or in his own name. Anyone taking the instrument from him and paying value for it has a right to require that he indorse in both names. The latter only minimizes problems in further negotiation by the holder. Subsection 3–401 (2) authorizes the use of any mark, not just a name, as an indorsement sufficient for negotiation.

TYPES OF INDORSEMENTS

Every indorsement may be classified in terms of three characteristics. An indorsement will be either (1) special or in blank, (2) restrictive or nonrestrictive, and (3) qualified or unqualified, taking one characteristic from each category.

Special or In Blank

An indorsement is special if it identifies the indorsee. Every other indorsement is in blank. Thus, assume an instrument is made payable to A. Adams, and Adams turns it over and indorses it "pay to B. Baker, (signed) A. Adams." This is an example of a **special indorsement.** If Adams simply had written "(signed) A. Adams," it would be **indorsement in blank,** since it did not name the indorsee. This, of course, is the most common type of indorsement.

The effects of these types of indorsements are important in that they dictate what must be done to negotiate the instrument further. Specifically, if the last indorsement on an instrument is special, the instrument is an order instrument and it must be both indorsed and delivered to be further negotiated. If the last indorsement is in blank, it is a bearer instrument and may be negotiated by delivery alone. Suppose, for example, an instrument is drawn "Pay to the order of A. Adams" and Adams indorses it with a blank indorsement and transfers it to Baker, who indorses it "Pay to C. Carson" and transfers it to Carson, who indorses it in blank and transfers it to Drew. The instrument was drawn as an order instrument; it became a bearer instrument by Adams's blank indorsement; it was converted back to an order instrument by Baker's special indorsement, and back to a bearer instrument again by Carson's blank indorsement. With each indorsement, the requirements for further negotiation changed back and forth.

As noted, the more common type of indorsement is the indorsement in blank. One who takes an instrument indorsed in blank must be very careful. It is much like carrying cash in that if the instrument is lost, it can be negotiated by anyone who finds it. This is because it is a bearer instrument and, therefore, no further indorsement is necessary. For this reason, Subsection 3–204(3) authorizes the holder of such an instrument to go in above the blank indorsement and convert it to a special indorsement. Therefore, if Adams has indorsed with a blank indorsement and transferred an instrument to Baker, Baker is authorized to add his name as special indorsee, so the indorsement will appear "Pay to B. Baker, (signed) A. Adams."

One final point. Notice that the special indorsements in the examples state "Pay to . . . ," rather than "Pay to *the order of.* . . ." The requirement that an instrument must be payable to order or to bearer must be met initially on the face of the instrument, but does not apply thereafter to indorsements. Once an instrument meets the seven requirements, and therefore is negotiable on its face, it will remain negotiable regardless of what language is used in later indorsements. Notice that the restrictive indorsements discussed next also contain language that, if found on the face of the instrument, would render it nonnegotiable.

Restrictive or Nonrestrictive

Just as every indorsement is either special or in blank, it also will be either restrictive or nonrestrictive. A **restrictive indorsement** is one that either (1) places a condition on the transfer of the instrument or (2) *purports* to prohibit further negotiation. Every other indorsement is a **nonrestrictive indorsement.**

Just as the characteristic of special or in blank determined whether the instrument had to be indorsed to be further negotiated, the characteristic of restrictive or nonrestrictive determines whether there are any limitations on payment of the instrument to the indorsee. The next transferee following a holder who received an instrument under a restrictive indorsement must see that any value she pays to that holder is paid consistent with the restriction, or without notice that the money will be use for improper purposes.

The most common restrictive indorsement contains the words "for deposit only." Therefore, if an instrument issued or indorsed to A. Adams is indorsed "for deposit only (signed) A. Adams" and is given to Baker, the person who takes it from Baker must pay the proceeds of the instru-

Requirements for negotiability of commercial paper

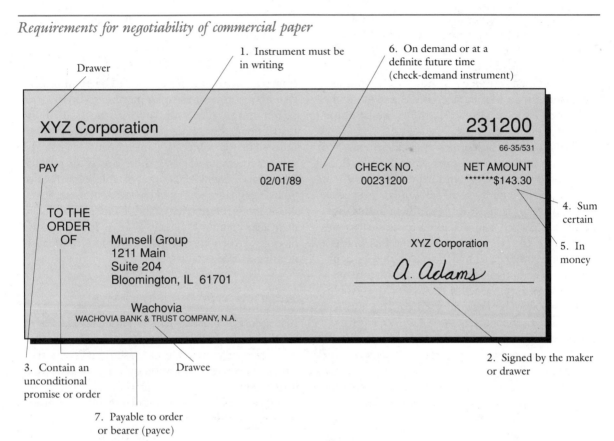

1. Instrument must be in writing

6. On demand or at a definite future time (check-demand instrument)

Drawer

XYZ Corporation   231200

66-35/531

PAY   DATE   CHECK NO.   NET AMOUNT
                                 02/01/89   00231200   *******$143.30

4. Sum certain

5. In money

TO THE
ORDER
OF   Munsell Group
        1211 Main
        Suite 204
        Bloomington, IL 61701

        Wachovia
        WACHOVIA BANK & TRUST COMPANY, N.A.

XYZ Corporation

a. adams

2. Signed by the maker or drawer

3. Contain an unconditional promise or order

Drawee

7. Payable to order or bearer (payee)

ment into an account for Adams. The money must not be paid to Baker or applied to Baker's use. Words such as "for collection," "pay any bank," or the like also are effective to restrict an indorsement. They purport to prohibit further negotiation of the instrument, although further negotiation never can be prohibited, regardless of what type of indorsement is used. If, in the above example, Adams had indorsed "Pay to B. Baker in trust for C. Carson (signed) A. Adams," again this would be a restrictive indorsement. A condition is placed on payment of the instrument, requiring that the proceeds be used for the benefit of C. Carson. If the next transferee were to allow Baker to use the instrument to pay his own bills or to purchase items that obviously were for his own

use, the restriction would be violated. But, simply paying the money to Baker would not be a violation, unless some other factor gave the transferee knowledge that Baker was in the process of violating his fiduciary duty to Carson. See Section 3-206 of the UCC for a more detailed discussion of the effect of restrictive indorsements.

Consider, again, the previous illustrative indorsements. The first, "for deposit only (signed) A. Adams," is an example of a blank restrictive indorsement. The second, "pay to B. Baker in trust for C. Carson," is an example of a special restrictive indorsement. Had Adams indorsed, simply, "(signed) A. Adams," the indorsement would have been classified as blank and nonrestrictive.

Examples of indorsements

	Special	Blank
Restrictive	Pay to B. Baker in trust for C. Carson A. Adams	For Deposit Only A. Adams
Non-Restrictive	Pay to B. Baker A. Adams	A. Adams

Add "without recourse" to any of these and it becomes qualified.

SALSMAN v. NATIONAL COMMUNITY BANK OF RUTHFORD
102 N.J. SUPER. 482, 246 A.2d 162 (1968)

This was an action by Elizabeth A. Salsman (Plaintiff) against National Community Bank of Rutherford (Defendant) to recover the amount of a check paid by Defendant on an improper indorsement. Plaintiff sued in her individual capacity and in her capacity as administratrix of the estate of her deceased husband.

Plaintiff received a check, made payable to her order, in the amount of $159,770.02. The check was in payment of benefits from her husband's employer upon her husband's death. Breslow, whom Plaintiff had employed as attorney for the estate, informed her that the check was not hers, but belonged to the estate. Plaintiff indorsed the check "Pay to the order of the Estate of Arthur J. Odgers" together with her signature. (Plaintiff's married name was Odgers.) Under this indorsement, when no longer in Plaintiff's presence, Breslow wrote, "Estate of Arthur J. Odgers—for deposit Harold Breslow, Trustee." Under this purported indorsement Breslow's secretary then wrote, "For deposit Harold Breslow, Trustee." The check was then collected and deposited in Breslow's general trustee account. When Plaintiff learned that Breslow had appropriated the funds for his own use, she commenced this action. The court granted judgment for Plaintiff for $117,437.43 plus interest and costs.

BOTTER, J.S.C.

In the absence of defenses such as negligence, estoppel or ratification, the payee of a check is entitled to recover against a bank making collection from the drawee based upon a forged or unauthorized indorsement of a check. . . . This has been the established law throughout the country and continues to be the rule in states which have adopted the Uniform Commercial Code. . . .

The check in question was indorsed by the payee, Mrs. Odgers, to the order of the Estate of Arthur J. Odgers. There was no valid indorsement thereafter by the estate of Arthur J. Odgers. N.J.S. 12A;3-110(1) (e), N.J.S.A. provides that an instrument may be payable to the order of "an estate, trust or fund, in which case it is payable to the order of the representative of such estate, trust or fund. . . ." The check was not indorsed by the administratrix of the estate, the only person who had authority in law to indorse the check. Breslow was not a trustee of the estate, and the purported indorsement for the estate by "Harold Breslow, Trustee" was unauthorized and ineffective. Breslow testified that he never told plaintiff that he would act as her agent. His purported indorsement was not authorized as the agent for the administratrix nor as a representative of the estate. . . .

Receiving the funds without a proper indorsement and crediting the funds to one not entitled thereto constitutes a conversion of the funds.

Questions

1.   How can banks protect themselves against forgeries as in this case?
2.   Why shouldn't the estate, rather than the bank, be required to seek recovery against the forger?

Qualified or Unqualified

The UCC provides that the use of the words "without recourse," or words of similar import, makes an indorsement qualified. All other indorsements are unqualified. Whether an indorsement is qualified or unqualified determines the extent to which an indorser is liable on the instrument.

One who indorses with an **unqualified indorsement** will be liable under Section 3-414, called the contract liability, and also under Section 3-417(2), warranties. Under Section 3-414, an unqualified indorser makes an absolute promise to pay the instrument, according to its tenor at the time of her indorsement, to any subsequent indorser *no matter why* it was not paid by the maker or drawer. In other words, the unqualified indorser makes an absolute guarantee of payment. Under Section 3-417(2), the unqualified indorser also automatically makes five specific warranties. She warrants (contractually promises) that (1) she has title to the instrument, or is authorized to obtain payment, and has the right to convey it;

(2) none of the signatures have been forged; (3) the instrument has not been altered materially; (4) no party to the instrument has a good defense against her; and (5) that she has no knowledge of any insolvency proceedings instituted against the maker or acceptor or the drawer of an unaccepted draft.

One who uses a **qualified indorsement** does not make the Section 3-414 contract guarantee, but does make the Section 3-417(2) automatic warranties, except that the fourth warranty is altered to *no knowledge* of defenses (UCC 3-417(3)).

One who transfers an instrument *without indorsing* it also does not make the Section 3-414 contract guarantee, but does make the same five Section 3-417(2) automatic warranties as the unqualified indorser. However, the warranties extend only to his immediate transferee, unlike those of the indorsers, which extend to everyone who takes the instrument thereafter in good faith. Also, note that since warranties are contractual promises, they are made only if the indorser, or the transferor without indorsement, has received consideration for the transfer.

Returning to classifications of indorsements, suppose an instrument is made payable to A. Adams, and she indorses it "(signed) A. Adams" and transfers it to Baker, who indorses it "without recourse, pay to C. Carson in trust for D. Drew." Adams's indorsement is in blank, nonrestrictive, and unqualified. Therefore, Baker could have negotiated it without further indorsement; the proceeds could have been paid to Baker with no restrictions on how they were to be used, and Adams rendered herself fully liable on the instrument under Sections 3-414 and 3-417(2). Baker's indorsement was special, restrictive, and qualified. Therefore, Carson would have to indorse the instrument to further negotiate it, the proceeds should be paid to Carson only to be used for the benefit of Drew, and Baker's liability on the instrument would be governed only by Section 3-417(2) and (3).

HOLDER IN DUE COURSE

The third and final step that must be met in order to use the protections of Article 3 is that the negotiable instrument must be negotiated to a holder in due course. A **holder in due course** is (1) a holder, who takes the instrument (2) for value, (3) with no notice of defenses, (4) in good faith, and (5) in the ordinary course of business. It even is possible for the payee to be a holder in due course. If the person who takes the instrument falls short of any of these five requirements, again, he is an assignee and the law of contracts will govern his rights. A *holder* simply is one who has received a negotiable instrument by negotiation. In other words, the first two steps in the three-step process have been met.

Taking for Value

The term *value* as used in Article 3 is very similar to the concept of consideration in contract law. Section 3-303 provides that a holder takes for **value** "(a) to the extent that the agreed consideration has been performed . . . ." So, although an executory promise may constitute consideration for a contract, it must be executed before it can constitute value. A holder also takes for value to the extent that ". . . he acquires a security interest in or a lien on the instrument otherwise than by legal process; or (b) when he takes the instrument in payment of or as security for an antecedent claim . . . or (c) when he gives a negotiable instrument for it or makes an irrevocable commitment to a third person." Concerning provision (b), although an antecedent debt will not constitute consideration for a simple contract, it will constitute value under Article 3.

It should be noted that a holder who pays only partial value may be a holder in due course of only part of an instrument. For example, suppose Arthur brings a $500 check to First Bank, takes $200 in cash and has the remaining $300 deposited in his checking account. The bank can be a holder in due course as to the $200 instrument.

As funds created by the deposit are withdrawn later, the extent of the bank's holder-in-due course protection will increase proportionally. The requirement that value actually must be *given*, and not merely *promised*, is illustrated by the following case.

KORZENIK v. SUPREME RADIO, INC.
347 Mass. 309, 197 N.E.2d 702 (1964)

This was an action by Arnold A. Korzenik and his partner in the practice of law (Plaintiffs/Appellants) against Supreme Radio, Inc. (Defendant/Appellee) on two promissory notes of which Plaintiffs were indorsees.

The notes in question were given by Defendant to Southern New England Distributing Corporation as trade acceptances. They were in the face amount of $15,000. Southern then indorsed the notes to Plaintiffs "as retainer for services to be performed" by Korzenik. When Defendant discovered it had been defrauded in the transaction giving rise to the notes, it refused to pay them. Between the date of receiving the notes and the refusal to pay, Plaintiffs had done "some" work for Southern, but there was no evidence as to how much.

From a judgment of the district court in favor of Defendant, and the affirming of that judgment by the Appellate Division, Plaintiffs appealed. Affirmed.

WHITTEMORE, Justice.

Decisive of the case, as the Appellate Division held, is the correct ruling that the plaintiffs are not holders in due course under G.L. c. 106, section 3-302; they have not known to what extent they took for value under Section 3-303. That section provides: "A holder takes the instrument for value (a) to the extent that the agreed consideration has been performed or that he acquires a security interest in or a lien on the instrument otherwise than by legal process; or (b) when he takes the instrument in payment of or as security for an antecedent claim against any person whether or not the claim is due; or (c) when he gives a negotiable instrument for it or makes an irrevocable commitment to a third person."

Under clause (a) of Section 3-303 the "agreed consideration" was the performance of legal services. It is often said that a lawyer is "retained" when he is engaged to perform services, and we hold that the judge spoke of "retainer" in this sense. The phrase that the judge used, "retainer *for services*" (emphasis supplied), shows his meaning as does the finding as to services already performed by Korzenik at the time of the assignments. Even if the retainer had been only a fee to insure the attorney's availability to perform future services, . . . there is no basis in the record for determining the value of this commitment for one week.

The Uniform Laws Comment to Section 3-303 points out that in this article "value is divorced from consideration" and that except as provided in paragraph (c) "[a]n executory promise to give value is not . . . value. . . . The underlying reason for policy is that when the purchaser learns of a defense . . . he is not required to enforce the instrument, but is free to rescind the transaction for breach of the transferor's warranty." . . .

The only other possible issue under Section 3-303 is whether, because of or in connection with taking the assignments, Korzenik made "an irrevocable commitment to a third person." There is no evidence of such a commitment. The finding as to a payment to cocounsel shows only that some of the proceeds of other assigned items have been expended by Korzenik.

Questions

1. Why isn't the lawyer's availability to the client sufficient value for the purposes of Article 3?

2. Why shouldn't a promise be sufficient value for Article 3?

Taking without Notice

In order to be free of **notice of defenses** a holder not only must have no knowledge of defenses, but also must not take the instrument under circumstances that would lead a reasonable person to *suspect* that a particular defense *might* exist. Many specific circumstances constituting notice are set out in Section 3-304.

A purchaser has notice of a claim or defense if the instrument is so incomplete, bears such visible evidence of forgery or alteration, or is otherwise so irregular as to call into question its validity, terms of ownership or to create an ambiguity as to who to pay, or if the purchaser has notice that the obligation of any party is voidable in whole or in part, or that all parties have been discharged (UCC 3-304(1)).

A purchaser also has notice of a claim if she has *knowledge* that a fiduciary has negotiated the instrument for her own benefit and contrary to her duty. Therefore, if an instrument is indorsed "pay to B. Baker in trust for C. Carson," and Baker negotiates it in payment of, or security for, her own debt, or to purchase items for herself and patently not for C. Carson, the transferee will be on notice of Carson's claim. If, however, the transferee pays the amount of the instrument to Baker without knowledge that Baker will misapply the money, the transferee will not have notice.

A purchaser has notice of a claim or defense if he takes an instrument that is overdue, because he must wonder why it was not paid when due. Therefore, if he knows that part of the principal (but not the interest) is overdue, or if a series of instruments was created by the same transaction and any instrument in that series is overdue, he is on notice. If the instrument is a time instrument, it becomes overdue after the due date. If it contains an acceleration clause and the purchaser knows it was accelerated but not paid as required, he is on notice. If the instrument is a demand instrument and the purchaser knows there was a demand but it was not paid, or if more than a reasonable time has elapsed since the time of issue, the purchaser is on notice. What constitutes a reasonable time depends on the nature and character of the instrument and the circumstances under which it was issued. For example, a note given to secure the purchase price of seed in a farming community normally is not expected to be paid until the crops have been harvested and sold, perhaps six months to a year after the purchase. Section 3-304(3)(c) provides that a reasonable time for a domestic check is presumed to be thirty days.

Section 3-304(4) provides a list of matters that do not, of themselves, give notice of a claim or defense. The list includes knowledge or notice: (a) that the instrument was antedated or postdated; (b) that it was given in return for an executory promise or was accompanied by a separate instrument; (c) that any party has signed for accommodation (to add her liability to an instrument in which she has no other interest); (d) that incomplete paper has been completed, unless she has actual notice of improper completion; (e) that any person negotiating the instrument was a fiduciary, or that there has been a default in paying interest, or even principal if the default was not on the instrument itself or another instrument in the same series. Finally, the filing or recording of a document does not give notice to a person who otherwise would be a holder in due course.

Taking in Good Faith

The term *good faith* is defined in Section 1-201(19) as "honesty in fact." This requirement substantially overlaps the requirement of "no notice of defenses," but it is intended to be an entirely subjective question of fact. It is meant to cover situations in which the purchaser has participated in a questionable transfer, but the circumstances would not necessarily alert him to the possible existence of a *particular* defense. One example of bad faith would be paying $100 for a $1000 demand instrument purporting to be an obligation of a readily accessible maker. The circumstances do not indicate exactly what might be wrong, but the transaction "smells fishy." In other words, the protections of Article 3 should be

extended only to the most deserving holders who, in equity, merit protection.

The final requirement, that the transferee take the instrument in the **ordinary course of business** is designed to allow Article 3 to be used only in ordinary commercial transactions—those involving the purchase and sale of property and services. The drafters of the original law of negotiable instruments intended that the use of commercial paper in such transactions be promoted. In keeping with this intent, Section 3-302(3) provides that a holder does *not* become a holder in due course of an instrument by (a) purchase of it at judicial sale or taking it under legal process; (b) acquiring it in taking over an estate; or (c) purchasing it as a part of a bulk transaction not in the regular course of the transferor's business. As the following case illustrates, courts are not unmindful of differences in customary and ordinary practices from one type of business to another.

Summary: Requirements for holder in due course

Takes the instrument by negotiation
For value (consideration)
No notice of defenses
Good faith
Ordinary course of business

NIDA v. MICHAEL
34 Mich.App. 290, 191 N.W.2d 151 (1971)

This was an action by Edmund A. Nida (Plaintiff/Appellant) against William R. Michael, City National Bank, and Manufacturers National Bank (Defendants/Appellees) to recover on an alleged breach of statutory warranties arising out of the transfer and presentment of a check.

On November 7, 1968, Plaintiff issued a check to the order of Michael based on certain fraudulent misrepresentations by Michael. On the same day, Michael delivered the check to City National Bank, which paid $5000 to Defendant and deposited the remaining $16,000 in his account. Michael did not indorse the check, but City National stamped it ". . . prior indorsements guaranteed" and sent it to the drawee, Manufacturers National Bank, for payment. Manufacturers

National paid the $21,000 to City National and deducted the same from Plain-
tiff's account.

Four months later, Plaintiff discovered the fraud and notified both banks. In
the meantime, Michael had departed for parts unknown.

Plaintiff claimed City National was not a holder in due course, and therefore
was subject to the personal defense of fraud in indorsement, because it did not
receive the order instrument by indorsement. From a summary judgment in favor
of both banks, Plaintiff appealed. The judgment was affirmed by the Court of
Appeals. Affirmed.

V.J. BRENNAN, Judge.

Section 3-302 of the Code defines a holder in due course as a holder who takes an
instrument for value in good faith and without notice that it is overdue or has been
dishonored or of any defense against or claim to it on the part of any person. It is not
claimed here that City Bank acted in bad faith or that it did not pay value. Nor is it
claimed that the bank had notice of the plaintiff's potential defense. The sole obstacle
interposed is that City Bank was not a holder because the check was not indorsed to it.

Negotiation is the transfer of an instrument in such form that the transferee
becomes a holder. Section 3-202. Plaintiff contends that since instruments payable to
order cannot be negotiated except by indorsement and delivery, City Bank was not a
holder and therefore not a holder in due course. As a general proposition, plaintiff is
totally correct. However, when we are dealing with a depository bank which accepts a
check from a customer as agent for collection it has been held that it need not take by
negotiation in order to be a holder in due course. In [Bowling Green, Inc. v. State
Street Bank & Trust Co.] it was said:

> We doubt, moreover, whether the concept of 'holder' as defined in Section 1-201(20)
> applies with full force to Article 4. Article 4 establishes a comprehensive scheme for
> simplifying and expediting bank collections. Its provisions govern the more general rules of
> Article 3 wherever inconsistent. Mass.Gen.Laws Ann. c. 106 Section 4-102(1). As part of
> this expediting process, Article 4 recognizes the common bank practice of accepting unin-
> dorsed checks for deposit. See Funk, Banks and the UCC 133 (1964). Section 4-201(1)
> provides that the lack of an indorsement shall not affect the bank's status as agent for
> collection, and Section 4-205(1) authorizes the collecting bank to supply the missing
> indorsements as a matter of course. In practice, banks comply with Section 4-205 by
> stamping the item 'deposited to the account of the named payee' or some similar formula.
> Funk, supra at 133. We doubt whether the bank's status should turn on proof of whether a
> clerk employed the appropriate stamp, and we hesitate to penalize a bank which accepted
> unindorsed checks for deposit in reliance on the Code, at least when, as here, the customer
> himself clearly satisfies the definition of 'holder'. Section 4-209 does provide that a bank
> must comply 'with the requirements of section 3-302 on what constitutes a holder in due
> course,' but we think this language refers to the enumerated requirements of good faith and
> lack of notice rather than to the status of holder, a status which Section 3-302 assumes rather
> than requires. We therefore hold that a bank which takes an item for collection from a
> customer who was himself a holder need not establish that it took the item by negotiation in
> order to satisfy Section 4-209.

Since it is clear that Michael, as payee, was himself a holder, we conclude that City Bank was holder in due course and unaffected by the plaintiff's merely personal defense of fraud in the inducement. In other words, we will not compel a bank to disgorge funds received from the drawer in collecting an item on which the bank could have successfully sued had the positions of the parties been reversed. The grant of summary judgment in favor of City Bank was proper.

We also feel that summary judgment was proper in the case of defendant Manufacturers. Manufacturers paid according to the genuine order of the drawer. As such it had the right to charge the item to his account. See Section 4-401. No stop order was made prior to payment of the check, nor was Manufacturers put on notice of any defense prior to payment. Furthermore, the warranties arising on presentment or transfer of a negotiable instrument upon whose breach plaintiff bases his case do not run in favor of a drawer of a check. Plaintiff has failed to state a claim upon which relief can be granted.

Questions

1. What justifies the special rule for banks?
2. Is there anything the plaintiff can do at this point?

DECLINE OF THE DOCTRINE OF HOLDER IN DUE COURSE

With the sudden, sharp rise in consumer protection during the late 1960s and early 1970s came an increase in the assault on the doctrine of holder in due course. Many advocated a complete repeal of the doctrine on the ground that it unjustly deprived consumers of their most important defenses, especially those of lack (failure) of consideration and fraud in the inducement. On the other hand, those who advocated retaining the doctrine did so on the ground that its repeal would defeat the whole purpose of commerical paper—to have an instrument that can be used freely as a temporary substitute for money in commerical (and other) transactions. To date, the doctrine has suffered some selective erosion, but remains strong.

State Laws and the Uniform Consumer Credit Code

Some states have limited the application of the holder-in-due-course doctrine by statute, others by court decision. These laws are far from uniform, and range from restricting the doctrine's application to specific kinds of transactions to an almost complete ban on its use. One attempt to limit it was drafted by the National Conference of Commissioners on Uniform State Laws in 1968. It was entitled the **Uniform Consumer Credit Code (UCCC),** and it virtually eliminated commerical paper in the area of consumer transactions by prohibiting a seller from taking a UCC Article 3 instrument, other than a check, as evidence of the purchaser's indebtedness. It obviously was intended to have a profound effect on the use of promissory notes. The Uniform Consumer Credit Code, however, was adopted by very few states. The trend in the state law today is away from further limits on the doctrine, but it is unlikely ever to return, completely, to its previous status.

Federal Trade Commission Rules

The Federal Trade Commission has promulgated a rule directed toward consumer transactions and the use of notes. It makes it an unfair trade practice for a seller to use any procedure that would make the purchaser's obligation to pay independent of the seller's obligation to perform. Any defenses the purchaser might have against the seller arising out of the transaction must continue to be good against any subsequent transferee of the purchaser's obligation. Even transactions in which the seller arranges financing for the purchaser through a third party are covered by the rule. Finally, the rule requires that a printed statement, in boldface type on the face of the instrument, give notice to potential transferees that personal defenses are retained. If the required statement is omitted from the instrument, any transferee could be a holder in due course, free of those defenses, but the seller would be subject to a possible penalty of up to $10,000. The following case illustrates the effect of the FTC rule.

JEFFERSON BANK AND TRUST COMPANY v. STAMATIOU
384 So.2d 388 (La. 1980)

This was an action by Jefferson Bank and Trust Company (Plaintiff/Appellee), as assignee of a promissory note, against Christos G. Stamatiou (Defendant/Appellant), maker of the note, for payment.

Defendant purchased a truck from Key Dodge, Inc. At the time of the purchase he signed an instrument that included a contract of sale, a chattel mortgage, and the promissory note in question. Among the numerous provisions of the contract and mortgage sections of the instrument, the following notice appeared in bold type:

> NOTICE: ANY HOLDER OF THIS CONSUMER CREDIT CONTRACT IS SUBJECT TO ALL CLAIMS AND DEFENSES WHICH THE DEBTOR COULD ASSERT AGAINST THE SELLER OF GOODS OR SERVICES OBTAINED PURSUANT HERETO OR WITH THE PROCEEDS HEREOF. RECOVERY HEREUNDER SHALL NOT EXCEED AMOUNTS PAID BY THE DEBTOR HEREUNDER.

The instrument was then assigned to Plaintiff.

Defendant refused to pay the note when the truck became inoperable and unusable a short time after the purchase. Plaintiff contended that it was entitled to payment because it was a holder in due course. Plaintiff further contended that the notice was inoperative because the truck was purchased for commerical use, and was not therefore part of a "consumer credit transaction."

The trial court found for Plaintiff, and the decision was affirmed on appeal to the Court of Appeals. Reversed and remanded by the Louisiana Supreme Court to the district court.

CALOGERO, Justice.

Plaintiff makes the following argument: that the preservation of defenses language is included in all credit contracts to insure compliance with federal regulations but is only intended to apply to the appropriate transactions even though there is no notation to the effect that the clause is possibly inapplicable; absent inclusion in all credit contracts, the vendor and/or finance company would be required to have two different forms and to hire a staff attorney to instruct them each time which to use; and that the sale of the truck to defendant for use in his tow truck business takes the transaction out of the consumer credit contract category as defined by the FTC, and thus the provision, although there in the contract, was not applicable to this transaction and should be ignored.

Defendant on the other hand claims that the preservation of defenses language (whether federally required in this contract or not) was included in the contract and as such become a part of that contract. Defendant relies on La.Civ.Code art. 1901 and La.Civ.Code art.1945 in support of his argument.

We conclude that defendant's argument is the more persuasive and is more supported by the law. Under the provisions of the Civil Code, parties are free to govern their relationships through their contracts, and the contractual provisions have the effect of law on the parties. The contract between Stamatiou and Key Dodge, as assigned to plaintiff, provided "Any holder of this . . . contract is subject to all claims and defenses which the debtor could assert against the seller." That the parties to the contract mistakenly asserted that it was a consumer credit contract ("any holder of this consumer credit contract") is of little consequence. In looking at the contract, there was nothing on the face of the instrument to indicate that this was not a "consumer credit contract." The assignee/holder was put on notice that all defenses were available to the buyer against him at the time he acquired the instrument. In looking at the face of the instrument, plaintiff could not have expected to be a holder in due course, and is not now entitled to be so treated. At best the contract is ambiguous and is surely not to be construed against the purchaser who did not confect it.

Questions

1. What are the policy arguments that support the court's decision that the contract be enforced according to its terms despite the fact that those terms were inappropriate to the transaction? What are the arguments against the result?

2. Can you define "consumer transaction"? Is it a proper category of cases for special treatment?

SUMMARY

The objective of the law of commerical paper is the creation and management of certain contracts for the payment of money in such a manner as to make them comparatively freely accepted in commerical transactions as temporary substitutes for money. In order to accomplish this objective, three general steps are required: the instrument must be negotiable in form, as discussed in the preceding chapter; the instrument must be negotiated; and the person receiving it must qualify as a holder in due course. When all three steps have been complied with, the defenses available to avoid paying the obligation are reduced from twelve to seven. Failure to meet any of these prerequisites places the transaction under the law of contracts.

The second step requires that the negotiable instrument be negotiated, which is accomplished by delivery of a bearer instrument or indorsement and delivery of an order instrument. One to whom a negotiable instrument has been negotiated is called a *holder*.

Every indorsement has three characteristics. It is either special or in blank; it either is restrictive or nonrestrictive; and it either is qualified or un-qualified. Whether it is special or in blank determines whether it must be indorsed in order to be further negotiated. Whether it is restrictive or nonrestrictive detemines whether there are limitations placed on payment of the proceeds of the instrument at the time it is further negotiated. Whether it is qualified or unqualified determines the extent to which the indorser is liable on the instrument under Section 3-414 and Section 3-417(2). For example, the simplest form of indorsement, in which the indorser simply signs his or her name, is classified as in blank, nonrestrictive, and unqualified. This means that the instrument is a bearer instrument, so it can be negotiated further by delivery alone, the proceeds can be paid to the holder without any restrictions, and the indorser is fully liable under Sections 3-414 and 3-417.

If a negotiable instrument has been negotiated properly and the holder meets four qualifications, Article 3 will apply to the transaction. The holder must take the instrument for value, without notice of any defenses to payment of the instrument, in good faith, and in the ordinary course of business. This simply means that the transferee must be a holder who has paid over something for the instrument, has taken it with no reason to believe that it should not be paid, and received it in the course of an ordinary commerical transaction involving the purchase and sale of property or services. The law of commerical paper does not govern instruments acquired as part of bulk purchase, in connection with an estate, or by legal process.

KEY TERMS AND CONCEPTS

negotiation
holder
indorsement
allonge
special indorsement
indorsement in blank
restrictive indorsement
nonrestrictive indorsement
qualified indorsement
unqualified indorsement
holder in due course
value
notice of defenses
ordinary course of business
Uniform Consumer Credit Code (UCCC)

PROBLEMS

1.   Barrett drew a check payable to the order of Phillips, who took it to the Bank of Gannett, the drawee bank, and cashed it. The Bank of Gannett failed to get Phillips's indorsement. A later check created an overdraft in Barrett's account and Barrett claimed the overdraft was the fault of the bank because, in paying the Phillips check without Phillips's indorsement, it made an improper payment. Is Barrett correct? Why or why not?

2.   Bates drew a check payable to the order of Fredson, naming him as a fiduciary. Fredson's bank allowed him to deposit the check in his personal account. Did this prevent the bank from taking the check as a holder in due course?

3.   Patsy and Jerry were divorced and, as part of the property settlement, Jerry executed a note to the order of Jim Stall, Patsy's father. The note stated no time for payment, but Patsy and Jerry agreed the note would be transferred to Patsy and paid in installments, and not on demand. Stall transferred the note to Patsy, but did not indorse it. Patsy immediately sued Jerry on the note, and Jerry wanted to offer testimony of the oral agreement to pay in installments. Should the evidence be permitted?

4.   A bank was presented with two checks, drawn on another bank, one for $3000 and the other for $3500. In return for the $3000 check it gave a draft for $3000; in return for the $3500 check, the bank gave a draft for $2900 and $600 in cash. The drawer of the two checks sought to assert personal defenses to their payment, and the bank claimed to be a holder in due course to the full extent of both of them. The drawer denied this, contending the bank was a holder in due course only to the extent of the $600 cash paid. Is the drawer correct?

5. Starr purchased an automobile from Moon, giving Moon a check for $1400. Moon took the check to the Falls Church Bank and deposited it. Later that day, Moon withdrew $400. When the check was dishonored, the bank sued Starr, who defended on the ground that he had been defrauded in the transaction. The bank claimed it was a holder in due course. Is the bank correct? Why or why not?

6. Westerly Hospital sold a note at its bank, indorsing the note in blank. When the maker defaulted, the hospital paid the amount due and the bank returned the note without indorsement. When the hospital sued the maker, the maker defended on the ground that the bank, not the hospital, was the proper party to sue on the note. Is the maker correct?

7. Saka employed Bates as a sales representative. When Bates left on a trip, Saka gave her a check made payable to the Sahara-Nevada Hotel, completed except that the amount was left blank. Bates was authorized to complete the check for the amount of the hotel bill. Upon leaving the hotel, Bates filled in the amount for the hotel bill plus $400, which she took in cash. Saka refused to pay the check, contending that since Bates completed it beyond her authority, and the hotel, as payee, could not qualify as a holder in due course, so he was not liable. Was Saka correct?

8. Mrs. Kilroy signed two blank checks and gave them to her husband. Later they were stolen by William Kilroy, who cashed one of them at a bank. The check was returned marked "NSF" (Not Sufficient Funds). Thereafter, he cashed the second one at the same bank. Mrs. Kilroy paid the first check, but refused to pay the second, contending the bank, having had the first one returned "NSF" was not a holder in due course of the second. Is she correct?

9. Greenlaw & Sons Roofing & Siding Co. completed a job for Spanks, and was paid by a check made payable to "Greenlaw & Sons Roofing & Siding Co." Greenlaw then cashed the check at Watertown Federal Savings & Loan, indorsing it "Greenlaw & Sons." Spanks refused to pay the check, claiming the work done by Greenlaw was defective, and that Watertown was not a holder in due since the check was not indorsed in the name of the payee. Is Spanks correct about the indorsement?

10. The Silver Slipper, Inc. issued a payroll check to Bluiett in the amount of $185.59. Bluiett indorsed it in blank and left it on her dresser at home. The check was stolen by Watkins, who used it to purchase two tires at the Western Auto store, receiving the tires and $73.21 change. Is Western Auto a holder in due course? Is it subject to the defense of theft of the check?

Chapter | 19

Liability of the Parties
and Discharge

INTRODUCTION

In the two preceding chapters we focused first on the technical requirements for creating commercial paper and then on the rules governing its transfer and the holder's acquiring the status of a holder in due course. In doing so, we completed the steps required to have an instrument that would be governed by Article 3 of the Uniform Commercial Code. This chapter will address the liabilities created, the requirements for obtaining payment, and ultimately the question of when the liabilities of the parties are discharged. It should be kept in mind that we are dealing with a special kind of contract, governed by a complex body of law that requires compliance with a great number of details. A basic tenet of commercial-paper law is that the liabilities of a party to commercial paper arise only when that person signs the instrument, as drawer or acceptor of a check or draft, as maker of a note, or as an indorser.

SIGNATURES

"No person is liable on an instrument unless his signature appears thereon" (Uniform Commerical Code Section 3-401(1)). This is true of the maker of a note, of the drawer and the acceptor of a bill of exchange, and of a transferor of the instrument. For this reason, an undisclosed or partially disclosed principal is not liable under Article 3 of the Uniform Commerical Code (UCC) when his agent, even with authority, signs a negotiable instrument on his behalf. Neither is the transferor who conveys an instrument without indorsing it. However, both may be liable to the other party for the transaction under contract law.

As explained earlier, a signature is any mark placed on an instrument for the purpose of authentication, including any name, any trade or assumed name, or any word or other mark (Section 3-401(2)). A signature may be made personally or placed on the instrument mechanically or by an authorized agent. Therefore, any mark placed on an instrument by or at the direction of a party intending that it be her signature *is* her signature.

Signature by an Agent

Section 3-403 states that an agent may bind his or her principal on a negotiable instrument as long as he or she is authorized by the principal. No particular formality is required to create that authority. In order to avoid personal liability on the instrument, the agent must (1) clearly identify the principal and (2) clearly indicate that he or she is signing the instrument in a representative capacity only. For example, assuming authority, A. Adams, president of ABC Corporation, should sign:

> ABC Corporation
> by A. Adams, President.

In addition to these two requirements, it is good practice for an agent to indent his name relative to that of the principal, and to use a signaling word such as "by" or "per," as in the illustration. This is considered further evidence that the signature was representative only. A signature such as the following would meet the disclosure requirement, but is more likely to generate a lawsuit:

> ABC Corporation
> A. Adams, President.

A signature in the following manner would cause Adams to be liable jointly with the corporation because of failure to disclose his representative capacity:

> ABC Corporation
> A. Adams.

Signing in the following manner would render Adams solely liable, since his principal's name does not appear on the instrument, even though Adams has disclosed his agency capacity:

> A. Adams, President.

If an agent meets neither of the first two requirements, as would be the case if Adams signed the instrument simply "A. Adams," then the agent is personally liable on the instrument. If he meets either one of the requirements but not the other, he again, is personally liable unless *as between the immediate parties* (only) to the transaction, parol evidence is admissible to show that the parties intended that the signature be representative only.

Unauthorized Signature

If a person's name is signed to an instrument without that person's consent or knowledge (that is, without her authorization), she is not liable on the instrument. For example, Davis signs Carson's name without authority. Carson is not bound, assuming he was not chargeable with negligence in inviting the forgery. It will operate as *Davis's* signature in favor of any person who pays the instrument in good faith or takes it for value (Section 3- 404).

Accommodation Signature

An **accommodation signer** is any person, not otherwise a party to the transaction, who signs an instrument for the purpose of lending his or her liability to the instrument. An accommodation signer is liable on an instrument to the same extent as any other person who signs in the same capacity (maker, drawer, or indorser). A person taking the instrument, even with knowledge that one of the parties has signed for accommodation, has full rights and can be a holder in due course if he or she otherwise qualifies. Rights against the accommodation signer do not extend to the party accommodated, however, and if the signer has to pay the instrument, he is entitled to reimburse-

ment from the party accommodated. Suppose, for example, Adams is willing to sell her car to Baker, and to take a $1000 promissory note to secure payment as long as Baker's father will sign the note along with Baker. Baker's father will be liable to the same extent as Baker, who has the principal obligation on the transaction, to Adams or any subsequent transferee of the note. He will not be liable to Baker, however, and if the father pays the note, either because of Baker's default or because the party entitled to payment otherwise elected to seek payment from him rather than Baker, he is entitled to be reimbursed by Baker (Section 3-415). Consider the following case concerning the liability of accommodation indorsers.

DAIGLE v. CHAISSON
369 So.2d 573 (La.App. 1981)

This was an action by Alvin Daigle (Plaintiff/Appellant) against David Chaisson and Marlene Daigle (Defendants/Appellees) for contribution of their shares of liability as co-indorsers.

On March 22, 1979, Jerry Iguess made a promissory note payable to the Calcasieu Marine National Bank in the amount of $7000 plus 10 percent interest and attorney fees. On the reverse side appeared the signatures of Arvin Daigle, David Chaisson, and Marlene Daigle. Under each signature was the word *indorser*. The note was not paid when due, and in the meantime Iguess had filed a petition in bankruptcy. The bank therefore demanded payment of Plaintiff and Chaisson. Chaisson refused, and Plaintiff paid the entire amount to avoid damaging his credit. Defendants refused to contribute on the theory that they were not co-indorsers, but only individual indorsers.

After Plaintiff dismissed Iguess as a party, the trial court found for Defendants, holding that, even as co-indorsers, they could not be liable without Plaintiff first pursuing recourse against the maker.

CULPEPPER, Judge.

Under the Commercial Laws, La.R.S. 10:1-101, et seq. adopted in 1975 and repealing the former Negotiable Instruments Law, an accommodation party is "one who signs the instrument in any capacity for the purpose of lending his name to another party to it." La.R.S. 10:3-415(1). From the note itself, it is apparent that Daigle, his wife and Chaisson signed the note as indorsers. The accommodation character of the three indorsements is also clear since they do not appear in the chain of title to the note. La.R.S. 10:3-415(4). This finding is also supported by the testimony which reflects that the names of the three indorsers were added to the instrument as additional security for the bank.

Directly above the three indorsements on the note is found the following language: ". . . the undersigned hereby jointly and severally guarantee to the Calcasieu Marine National Bank of Lake Charles, its successors, indorsers or assigns, the punctual payment at maturity of said loan;". [*sic*] The three indorsements on the reverse side of the note appear in a horizontal line rather than vertical. Plaintiff's indorsement is farthest to the left followed by that of Chaisson and then plaintiff's wife.

Initially, we interpret the phrase "jointly and severally" to mean that the three indorsers bound themselves in solido with the principal obligor. The common law term "joint and several" has been held synonymous with our Civil Law term "in solido". Johnson v. Jones-Journet, 320 So.2d 533 (La.1975), Ford Motor Credit Company v. Soileau, 323 So.2d 221 (La.App. 3rd Cir. 1975). Moreover, as these parties "guaranteed" the punctual payment of the loan, the bank could proceed directly against each indorser for the whole amount without first making demand upon the maker. La.R.S. 10:3-416(1). The Official Comment to Uniform Commercial Code, Section 3-416 states:

> An indorser who guarantees payment waives not only presentment, notice of dishonor and protest, but also all demand upon the maker or drawee. Words of guarantee do not affect the character of the indorsement as an indorsement [Section 3-202(4)]; but the liability of the indorser becomes indistinguishable from that of the co-maker.

The order of liability of indorsers is provided in La.R.S. 10:3-414(2) as follows:

> Unless they otherwise agree, indorsers are liable to one another in the order in which they indorse, which is presumed to be the order in which their signatures appear on the instrument.

It could be argued under Section 3-414(2) that since plaintiff signed farthest to the left, followed by Chaisson, on the horizontal line on which all three indorsers signed, that plaintiff indorsed first and is precluded by this section from any recourse against Chaisson. However, the presumption of Section 3-414(2) may be rebutted by evidence which shows a different order or division of liability was intended or agreed to by the parties. See La.R.S. 10:3-415(3). . . .

In the instant case, the testimony shows that Jerry Iguess and David Chaisson were business partners engaged in a welding business. The present debt was incurred to purchase land and equipment for their welding shop. Plaintiff testified that his and his wife's names were supplied to the instrument only to accommodate Iguess. Daigle testified that he had no financial interest in defendants' business, nor did he receive any of the funds borrowed. The record also shows that all three indorsements were affixed to the instrument simultaneously.

We think the circumstances surrounding the signing of the note, as well as the other factors mentioned, negate any intent on the part of the indorsers to be bound in the order in which they signed. All of the evidence in the record shows no indorser was to share a greater portion of the liablity than the other co-indorser. Chaisson makes no contention to the contrary.

Questions

1.   Did the court play fast and loose with the technicalities simply to achieve a just result? If so, how?

2.   Is it desirable for judges to scrutinize the circumstances of indorsement in such detail? Should they do it in every case?

CONTRACT LIABILITY

Anyone who signs a negotiable instrument becomes liable on the instrument. The nature and extent of that liability will depend on the capacity in which he or she signs the instrument—as maker, drawer, acceptor, or indorser. The contract liability of the party is dictated by Article 3 of the Uniform Commercial Code.

Primary and Secondary Liability

A person signing a negotiable instrument either may be primarily or secondarily liable. A party **primarily liable** is one who has agreed to pay the instrument in all events. A party **secondarily liable** is one who has agreed to pay the instrument only if the party primarily liable does not. His promise is collateral, and his obligation is contingent upon the obligee's going first to the party primarily liable and getting a refusal to pay (dishonor).

CONTRACT OF A MAKER.   The maker of a note is primarily liable on that note. Her obligation is absolute, and she promises to pay the note according to its tenor at the time of her signing, or according to its terms when completed if she signs it while it is still incomplete in some material respect (UCC Section 3-413(1)).

CONTRACT OF A DRAWER.   The party who draws a bill of exchange (draft or check) is secondarily liable. He pays the instrument only if the drawee fails to pay it. However, he can avoid *all* liability by drawing without recourse (UCC Section 3-413(2)). As the following case illustrates, the drawer's liability is conditioned on the duty to present it for payment properly.

ENGELCKE v. STOEHSLER
273 Or. 937, 544 P.2d 582 (1975)

This was an action by Gene M. Engelcke (Plaintiff/Respondent) against Leland J. Stoehsler and Juanita Stoehsler (Defendants/Appellants) for payment of a check dishonored because of insufficient funds. Defendants contended that the action should be dismissed because Plaintiff had agreed orally that he would not present the check for payment until Defendants had received certain insurance proceeds, which had not been received at the time of presentment.

During the trial, over Plaintiff's objections, the judge admitted evidence of the oral agreement although it had not been pleaded prior to the trial. At the close of Defendants' evidence, the court sustained Plaintiff's demurrer to Defendants' counterclaim, refusing to allow Defendants to amend to conform with the proofs during trial, and directed a verdict for Plaintiff. Defendants appealed. Reversed (on points material here).

HOLMAN, Justice.

Defendants . . . contend the trial court erred in granting a directed verdict upon the check because of defendants' testimony to the effect that the parties orally agreed that the check was not to be effective and should not be presented for payment until defendants received the insurance money from the destruction of the hay crops by fire. Parol evidence is admissible to show that the check was not to be operative as a binding obligations until the occurrence of some condition precedent. . . . The issue should have been submitted to the jury and the trial court was in error in directing a verdict upon the check.

Plaintiff contends that the insurance proceeds had been received by the time of trial and, therefore, the check was payable at that time and the judgment should be sustained. This is an action on the check, not on the underlying debt. The drawer is liable upon the check only if the bank on proper presentment refuses to honor it and the holder thereafter gives the necessary notice of dishonor and protest. ORS 73.1020(1)(d), 73.4130(2); White and Summers, Uniform Commercial Code 411, Section 13-9 (1972). Proper presentment to the bank was a condition precedent to defendants' liability. If there was a condition precedent to the effectiveness of the check, as defendants contend, the presentment prior to the time it was a binding obligation was a nullity because it was not intended to be a valid check at that time. There was no evidence of any presentment subsequent to the receipt by defendants of the proceeds of the insurance.

Questions

1. Is this just another hypertechnical decision, or is there some policy for the court's treatment of the case?

2. Once again, hasn't the court undermined principles of efficiency and predictability by engaging in a detailed analysis of the intentions of the parties?

CONTRACT OF AN ACCEPTOR. Although the drawer is secondarily liable when a bill of exchange is drawn, the drawee has no liability until the instrument is accepted. At the moment of acceptance, the drawee becomes the acceptor and is primarily liable to pay it. The acceptor agrees to pay it just as the maker of a note does (UCC Section 3-413(1)).

CONTRACT OF AN INDORSER. The contract liability of an indorser was discussed in Chapter 18 in the section concerning qualified and unqualified indorsements. The liability of indorsers is secondary, and the liability of each one extends to all transferees who take the instrument after his indorsement.

By using a qualified indorsement ("without recourse" or words of similar import), an indorser has no contract liability. An unqualified indorser promises to pay the instrument if, *for any reason*, it is not paid by the party primarily liable.

PRESENTMENT, ACCEPTANCE, AND DISHONOR

In order to activate the liabilities of the parties on a negotiable instrument, certain procedures generally must be followed. The liability of the maker of a note or the drawee of a draft is activated by presenting the note for payment or simply presenting the draft for acceptance. The liability of the drawer of a draft and all indorsers is activated by presentment and dishonor, and proper notice or protest of that dishonor.

Presentment

Presentment may be made for either acceptance or payment. Acceptance is simply the act by which a drawee of a draft agrees to be liable on the instrument. This usually is done by signing the instrument across its face.

Section 3-305(1) states that **presentment for acceptance** is necessary to charge the drawer and the indorsers of a draft if (1) the draft so provides, (2) it is payable other than at the residence or place of business of the drawee, or (3) its date of payment depends on presentation (for example, a draft made payable "30 days after sight"). **Presentment for payment** is necessary to charge any indorser, and it also is necessary to charge a drawer, the acceptor of a draft payable at a bank, or the maker of a note payable at a bank. However, failure to make presentment will discharge such a drawer, acceptor, or maker, only if he is deprived of funds held at the bank for payment of the instrument because of the bank's insolvency during the delay, and he makes a written assignment to the holder of the instrument of his rights against the bank (UCC Section 3-502(1)(b)).

TIME OF PRESENTMENT. Presentment for acceptance, when necessary (UCC Section 3-305(1), is due on the due date of a time instrument (one having a fixed due date). For a demand instrument, presentment is due within a reasonable time after the later of its date (if dated) or date of issue. Presentment for payment is due on the due date of a time instrument or within a reasonable time after acceleration if an instrument has been accelerated. Concerning parties secondarily liable, demand instruments must be presented within a reasonable time after they became liable on the instrument. A reasonable time for presentment of a domestic check (one drawn and payable in the United States) is presumed to be thirty days after the later of the date of the instrument or the date of its issue for liability of the

drawer. Otherwise, the check is considered "stale" (in effect, overdue). For determining the liability of an indorser, the rule is seven days after his or her indorsement.

Suppose, for example, Alverez issued a check on June 3, payable to Berghorst. On June 12, Berghorst indorsed the check to Chen, who presented it to the drawee bank for payment on July 5. Because presentment was made more than seven days after Berghorst indorsed the check, unless the delay can be excused or the seven-day presumption is invalid for some reason, Berghorst will not be liable on the check if the bank refuses to pay. Alverez, however, will be discharged only to the extent that she can prove she was harmed by the delay.

RIGHTS OF THE PARTY TO WHOM PRESENTMENT IS MADE. The party to whom presentment is made may require, without dishonoring, that the presenting party exhibit the instrument, show reasonable identification, and, if he is acting as agent for someone who is entitled to payment, show reasonable evidence of his authority to make presentment. (This is because paying an instrument before the due date without taking possession of the instrument or seeing to its physical cancellation can render the party paying it liable to pay it again if it later falls into the hands of a holder in due course. The same is true if she pays an imposter.) The payor may require presentment at the place specified in the instrument or, if no place is specified, at any place reasonable under the circumstances. Failure to comply with any of these payor requirements will invalidate the presentment (UCC Section 3-505).

Acceptance

Acceptance is defined as the "drawee's signed engagement to honor the draft as presented," which is written on the draft (UCC Section 3-410(1)). Once the drawee has accepted, he is absolutely liable to pay the instrument according to its tenor at the time of acceptance, and has no defenses to payment of the instrument even if it was forged, was materially altered, was given by a drawer who lacked capacity, lacked the signature of the drawer, was incomplete in one or more material respects at the time of acceptance, or contained any other irregularity. Acceptance normally is expected at the time of presentment, but it can be delayed until the close of the next business day (UCC Section 3-506).

Dishonor

An instrument is **dishonored** if it is not accepted or paid as required. Payment normally is expected at the time of presentment, but it may be delayed if it is necessary for the party paying on the instrument to determine that it is properly payable. In any event, however, payment must be made before the close of business on the day presentment is made. Subject to any necessary notice of dishonor, dishonor of an instrument gives the party presenting it an immediate right of recourse against parties secondarily liable (the drawee and indorsers).

NOTICE OF DISHONOR.   Notice of dishonor of an instrument is necessary to charge any party secondarily liable. Unless notice is excused, failure to give notice will discharge all indorsers and may discharge the drawer. The discharge of the drawer is limited to the same extent as failure to present properly (UCC Section 3-502(1)(b)).

Notice may be given by the holder, her agent, or any other person, including a bank, in whose hands the instrument was dishonored. The party receiving notice then may give notice to other parties secondarily liable. Notice may be given in any manner, oral or written, that identifies the instrument and communicates the fact that it has been dishonored, and a *written* notice is effective *when sent* even if it is not received.

Any notice must be given by midnight of the third business day after dishonor or, by a party receiving notice, by midnight of the third business day after notice was received (UCC Section 3-508). Consider the following cases concerning the necessity for giving notice, and then the manner of giving notice and the midnight deadline.

LUSTBADER v. LUSTBADER
48 Misc.2d 133, 264 N.Y.S.2d 307 (1965)

This was an action by Morris S. Lustbader (Plaintiff) against Sol Lustbader (Defendant) to recover on a promissory note made and issued by a corporation of which Defendant was an officer. Defendant had used an accommodation indorsement on the note, which was payable on demand. He left employment of the corporation while it was insolvent. The corporation then ceased doing business and Plaintiff demanded payment by Defendant, who refused.

This action was in the Supreme Court, Special and Trial Term, New York County. The court dismissed the complaint for failure to make presentment to the maker and then notice of the dishonor.

ABRAHAM N. GELLER, Justice.

[The court first discussed Plaintiff's pleadings. It the noted that Plaintiff's case was grounded on a theory that the necessity for presentment to the maker and notice of dishonor should be waived.] Plaintiff's main reliance as to waiver is that it should be implied from the fact that defendant as an officer of the corporate maker knew that it was insolvent and out of business and, therefore, knew that it would have been useless to make presentment to the corporation.

Here, of course, the evidence is that defendant left the corporation while it was still functioning, albeit in greatly reduced circumstances, so that such knowledge on his part cannot be conclusively presumed. Moreover, it has been definitely settled that the facts upon which plaintiff relies do not constitute a waiver of the statutory requirements (Goldstein v. Brastone Corporation . . .).

The mere insolvency of the maker of an instrument and the knowledge thereof by the indorser furnishes no excuse for failure to present it and give notice of dishonor to the indorser. It was formerly held that, where the indorser, an officer of the corporate maker, by his affirmative act and signed assent caused it to be adjudged a bankrupt prior to maturity of the note, presentment and notice of dishonor were excused (O'Bannon Co. v. Curran . . .). It should be noted in this connection that . . . Uniform Commercial Code, Section 3-511(3) provides that presentment is excused when the maker is in insolvency proceedings instituted after the issue of the instrument. Here there is merely a claim of insolvency and alleged knowledge thereof by defendant as an officer of the corporate maker.

In Goldstein v. Brastone Corporation, supra, the court said . . . "The law treats him as it would a stranger." Pointing out the need in commercial transactions for uniformity of prescribed rules of liability, the court concluded . . . "It may seem a drastic rule to require notice of dishonor under such circumstances; but by long custom and by statute the rules of liability and nonliability have been determined. If exceptions are made to fit particular circumstances, then the purposeful rigidity of the law is frittered away."

The complaint must accordingly be dismissed. However, the dismissal is without prejudice, in order to permit plaintiff, if so advised, to make due presentment of this demand note, give notice of dishonor and sue thereon within the applicable period of limitation, with all defenses available to defendant, including the defense that presentment was not made within a reasonable time (UCC, Section 3-503 (1)(e)), a question to be determined by the nature of the instrument, any usage of business and the facts of the particular case.

Questions

1. Would anyone really be harmed or legally prejudiced if presentment had been waived in this case?

2. Should the result be the same if the defendant is a partner and the maker is a partnership?

LEADERBRAND v. CENTRAL STATE BANK OF WICHITA
202 Kan. 450, 450 P.2d 1 (1969)

This was an action by Charles L. Leaderbrand (Plaintiff/Appellant) against the Central State Bank of Wichita (Defendant/Appellee) to recover the face amount of a check. Defendant had received the check as drawee bank; the check was dishonored because of insufficient funds in the drawer's account; and Defendant failed to give notice of dishonor before the "midnight deadline."

Plaintiff presented a check to Defendant on two occasions and was, each time, notified that the drawer's account was insufficient to cover the amount of the check. Thereafter, Plaintiff deposited the check in his account at another bank, and it was sent to Defendant for collection by mail. Defendant failed to give either Plaintiff or his bank notice of the drawer's default by midnight of the day following the day it received the check. Defendant contended that its failure to give the required notice should be excused because Plaintiff already had been notified of drawer's default on two previous occasions when he attempted to cash it.

From a summary judgment entered for Defendant in the trial court, Plaintiff appealed. Affirmed.

SCHROEDER, Justice.

Under 84-4-302, the payor bank is required to handle a demand item promptly, and upon failure to do so is made accountable for the amount of the item to the person presenting it.

Under the previous section of the Uniform Commercial Code (K.S.A. 84-4-301) a demand item received by the payor bank for credit on its books may be returned or notice of dishonor sent if it acts before its midnight deadline. Subparagraph (3) of this section reads:

> (3) *Unless previous notice of dishonor has been sent* an item is dishonored at the time when for purposes of dishonor it is returned or notice sent in accordance with this section. (Emphasis added.)

"Midnight deadline" is defined in K.S.A. 84-4-104(1) (h) as follows:

> 'Midnight deadline' with respect to a bank is midnight on its next banking day following the banking day on which it receives the relevant item or notice or from which the time for taking action commences to run, whichever is later;

Under the provisions of K.S.A. 84-3-508(3) notice of dishonor may be given in any reasonable manner. It may be oral or written and in any terms which identify the instrument and state that it has been dishonored.

Under the admitted facts and circumstances of the instant case, the check in question came to the Central State Bank of Wichita, the payor bank, for collection, after having been twice orally dishonored by the payor when the appellant presented the check over the counter at such bank for payment.

K.S.A. 84-3-511(4) reads:

> Where a draft has been dishonored by nonacceptance a later presentment for payment and any notice of dishonor and protest for nonpayment are excused unless in the meantime the instrument has been accepted. . . .

A study of the various sections of the Uniform Commercial Code adopted by Kansas as they relate to the facts in this case, and in particular sections 84-4-301(3), 84-3-511(4) and 84-1-203, supra, discloses a statutory scheme designed to impose a duty upon the payor bank, where a check is presented for payment and the drawer has insufficient funds on deposit to cover the item, to give timely notice of dishonor to the party presenting the check for payment just once. Such notice of dishonor *fixes the time at which the item is dishonored by the payor bank* as to the party presenting such item, and subsequent presentment of the item for collection, where the drawer still has insufficient funds on deposit to cover the item, does not require an additional notice of dishonor by the payor bank to such party. Under these circumstances any further notice of dishonor is excused.

Questions

1. Is this case inconsistent with the one immediately preceding it (*Lustbader*), or at least very different in attitude?

2. Is anyone disadvantaged by waiving further notice of dishonor?

EVIDENCE OF DISHONOR. Section 3-510 provides that three things are admissable as evidence of dishonor and of any notice of dishonor written on them. They are (1) a protest, (2) a bank stamp or other written memorandum, and (3) any book or record of a bank.

A **protest** is a formal, written notice witnessed by a notary public, a consul or a vice-consul, or any other public official authorized to certify dishonors. It is used frequently in connection with international transactions, although it may be used in any other situation of dishonor. It is a formal notice.

A *stamp* purporting to be that of the drawee, payor, or presenting bank, or a written memorandum of such bank, frequently is used. The most common are probably stamps across the instrument such as "Payment Stopped" or "Insufficient Funds." A memo written on the instrument, or accompanying it, also is sufficient.

As a third possibility, any *book or record* of the drawee, payor bank, or any collecting bank that is kept in the usual course of business may be used even though there is no evidence of who made a particular entry. Such entries are considered credi-ble because they are kept in the ordinary course of the bank's business, not made up for the sole purpose of providing evidence of a dishonor.

Excuses for Delay or Omission of Presentment, Notice, or Protest

Delay in presentment, notice, or protest may be excused for a period during which the party does not know that payment is due, or may be excused by circumstances beyond his control. The party must use reasonable diligence in correcting the situation once the cause of the delay is removed.

Presentment, notice, or protest are excused entirely as to a party who has (1) expressly waived them, or (2) himself dishonored them or otherwise knows of facts that do not entitle him to presume the instrument will be accepted or paid. Also, they are excused when (3) by reasonable diligence presentment or protest cannot be made or notice given, or (4) the maker, acceptor, or drawee is dead, incompetent, or the subject of insolvency proceedings instituted after the instrument was issued. They also are excused if (5) acceptance or payment has been refused for reasons other than lack of proper presentment. An example of the latter would be nonpayment of an instrument because of the lack of a proper indorsement.

WARRANTIES OF THE PARTIES

Every party who presents an instrument for acceptance or payment, or transfers the instrument for consideration, makes certain warranties. These warranties are provided by Section 3-417 of the Code and are implied into the foregoing situations. They need not be written on the instrument.

Presentment Warranties

Whenever an instrument is presented to the maker or the drawee for acceptance or payment, the party presenting makes three presentment warranties. These are: (1) she is the owner of the instrument, or is authorized by the owner to obtain acceptance or payment; (2) she has *no knowledge* that the signature of the maker or drawer is not authorized (forged); and (3) the instrument has not been altered materially. However, the latter two warranties are not made by a holder in due course, acting in good faith, and neither is made to a maker or drawer with respect to her own signature, regardless of whether or not the drawer is also the drawee—the drawer and the maker are expected to know their own signatures. The second warranty is not made to an acceptor of a draft if the holder in due course took the instrument after acceptance or obtained the acceptance without knowledge of the forgery—a drawee, in accepting an instrument, is expected to know the signature of his own drawer, and by accepting is guaranteeing payment of the instrument as it appeared at the time of acceptance, regardless of forgeries or anything else. For the same reasons, the third warranty is not made to an acceptor if the alteration was made prior to acceptance and the holder in due course took it after acceptance, or if the alteration is made after acceptance.

Finality of Payment

Generally, payment or acceptance of any instrument is final, and cannot be recovered by the maker or the drawee, when made to a holder in due course or to a person who, in good faith, has changed her position in reliance on the payment. However, the drawee may recover from the presenter if there has been a breach of one of the presentment warranties. Certain exceptions also are provided in Article 4 of the UCC, Bank Deposits and Collections.

Transfer Warranties

Every person who transfers an instrument and receives consideration makes five warranties. The reason consideration is required is, again, that these warranties are contractual promises and consideration is necessary to make a contract valid.

The first three of these warranties are the same as the three warranties made by a presenter—(1) title, (2) against forgeries, and (3) against material alterations. Then, the transferor also warrants that (4) no party has an effective defense against him, and (5) he has no knowledge of any insolvency proceedings (for example, bankruptcy) instituted against the maker, the acceptor, or the drawer of an unaccepted instrument.

If the transfer is by a qualified indorsement ("without recourse"), the fourth warranty above is altered to a warranty of no *knowledge of* such defenses rather than knowledge that they do not exist. If the transfer is without indorsement, the transferor makes the same five warranties as an unqualified indorser, but they run in favor of that transferor's immediate transferee only.

Suppose a check is drawn payable to "A. Adams," and Adams indorses it with an unqualified indorsement and transfers it to Baker. Baker then indorses it with a blank, qualified indorsement ("Without Recourse. (signed) B. Baker") and transfers it to Carson. Since the instrument is now a bearer instrument, Carson can negotiate it to Davis without indorsement, and he does so. Davis then transfers the instrument (with or without indorsement) to Egan. Suppose further that, unknown to any of the other parties, including Adams, the drawer was a minor and thus has a defense to payment of the check. Adams is liable to Baker, Carson, Davis, and Egan on the fourth warranty because of the defense. Baker is liable to no one because he had no knowledge of this defense. Carson is liable only to Davis (her immediate transferee) on the fourth warranty.

DEFENSES

The matter of what defenses against paying an instrument are available to a maker or drawer is the major, and almost the entire, focus of Article 3. Taking away some of these defenses in favor of a holder in due course is the means by which Article 3 makes commercial paper more freely accepted in commerce than ordinary contract promises as a temporary substitute for money.

Defenses to the payment of contract obligations may be classified into twelve basic categories: (1) fraud in the inducement, (2) lack (or failure, or want) of consideration, (3) payment before maturity, (4) nondelivery of a completed instrument, (5) undue influence, (6) forgery, (7) material alteration, (8) fraud in the execution, (9) incapacity of the obligor, (10) discharge in insolvency proceedings, (11) duress, and (12) illegality. The first five are known as **personal defenses;** the next five are known as **real (absolute) defenses;** and the last two may be either personal or real, depending on the circumstances. All twelve are valid against payment of a simple contract obligation. However, when a negotiable instrument is negotiated to a holder in due course (so Article 3 governs the instrument), the personal defenses are cut off. At that point, they are lost forever.

Suppose, for example, Adams agreed to purchase a car from Baker for $500 and gave him a check for the purchase price, but Baker did not deliver the car and vanished. Baker then gave the check to Carson as a birthday gift and Carson negotiated the check to Davis, who paid her $500 for it and otherwise met the qualifications of a holder in due course. Davis then negotiated the check to Egan who, at the time he received it, knew that Baker had procured it by fraud (or lack of consideration). Therefore, Egan was not a holder in due course.

Is Egan entitled to collect the $500 from Adams or the drawee bank? The answer is *yes*. Had Baker demanded payment, the personal defense would have been good against him. He created the defense and, therefore, was not a holder in due course. Had Carson demanded payment, she could not have collected either. Since she was not a holder in due course, she was in the position of an assignee, and an assignee has no greater rights than her assignor (Baker) had. Since Baker could not have collected, neither can Carson. Davis would be entitled to payment. He was a holder in due course, and therefore cut off Adams's personal defense. Egan also would be entitled to payment. When the instrument came into the hands of Davis, the holder in due course, the defense was lost forever. Since Egan was not a holder in due course, he was in the position of an assignee with the same rights as his assignor (Davis), who had the rights of a holder in due course. If Egan had transferred the instrument to Fisher, and Fisher was not a holder in due course, the same would result. Fisher would have the rights of Egan, who had the rights of Davis, the holder in due course. This is called the **Shelter Rule**—a holder in due course cuts off all personal defenses and shelters all transferees after him (UCC Section 3-201(1)).

An exception to the Shelter Rule is found in Section 3-201(1). It provides that a person who has been a party to any fraud or illegality affecting the instrument, or who as a prior holder had notice of a defense or claim against it, cannot *improve* his or her position by transferring the instrument and later reacquiring it after it has "been laundered" through the hands of a holder in due course. Consider the following case.

COPLAN PIPE AND SUPPLY COMPANY v. BEN-FRIEDA CORPORATION
256 So.2d 218 (D.Ct. of App. of Fla. 1972)

This was an action by Coplan Pipe and Supply Company (Plaintiff/Appellant) against Ben-Frieda Corporation (Defendant/Appellee) on certain promissory notes indorsed by Defendant.

On March 31, 1969, Dade Plumbing (not a party here) made and issued a series of promissory notes, payable to Plaintiff, in the amount of $50,000. The notes were indorsed by Plaintiff and then by Defendant (in that order) and transferred to Jafee (not a party in this action) in return for $50,000, which was deposited in Plaintiff's bank account. In September 1969, Dade Plumbing went into bankruptcy and paid only part of the $50,000. Plaintiff paid the remainder of the amount due on the notes and received an assignment of them from Jafee. Thereafter, Plaintiff demanded payment from Defendant, and Defendant refused.

From a judgment of the trial court denying Plaintiff's motion for summary judgment and finding for Defendant, and an affirmance of this judgment by the court of appeals, Plaintiff appealed. Affirmed.

HENDRY, Judge.

Appellant . . . argues that it sued as an assignee for value of a holder in due course, citing Section 68.06, Fla.Stat., F.S.A. Thus, in broad terms, appellant asserts that it is a successor, under Section 673.201(1), Fla.Stat., F.S.A., to the rights of a party who is a holder in due course without notice that an instrument is overdue, dishonored or subject to a defense. Thus, appellant concludes that only real and not personal defenses may be asserted against it. Appellee, however, argues that it was discharged as a party to the note under Section 673.208, Fla.Stat., F.S.A., and that this defense of discharge of a party may be asserted against appellant, as a prior indorser, under Section 673.602, Fla.Stat., F.S.A.; see also Section 673.304(1)(b), Fla.Stat., F.S.A. Ben-Frieda, the appellee, also contends that Coplan lacks the status of a holder in due course or successor to such a holder. . . .

We agree in general with the appellee, and affirm, but not for precisely the reasons assigned. We reason as follows: First, if one assumes Coplan had holder in due course status (as a successor to a holder in due course), by reacquiring the notes after participating fully in the underlying transactions, it had actual notice of the personal defense of discharge, so that the defense could be asserted; second, Coplan did not have holder in due course status because it had full knowledge of the transactions.

To begin with, assuming Coplan had holder in due course status, under Section 673.201(1); Fla.Stat., F.S.A.:

> Transfer of an instrument vests in the transferee such rights as the transferor has therein, except that a transferee . . . who as a prior holder had notice of a defense or claim against it cannot improve his position by taking from a later holder in due course.

Official Comment 3 to this section explains:

. . . The provision is not intended and should not be used to permit any holder . . . who has received notice of any defense or claim against it [the instrument], to wash the paper clean by passing it into the hands of a holder in due course and then repurchases it. . . .

We have concluded that the trial court's rulings and the judgment appealed are amply supported in law and fact; therefore we must affirm.

Questions

1. Is there any argument against the result in this case or against the rule on which it was based?

2. Should the exception to the Shelter Rule apply to all of the defenses equally?

Personal Defenses

Although, numerically, only about half of the available defenses, called *personal defenses*, are lost when an instrument falls into the hands of a holder in due course, the impact is much greater than half. This is because the first two personal defenses to be cut off are the two used most frequently in defending against a contract obligation. They are, (1) **fraud in the inducement** occurs when, by fraudulent misrepresentation, one is induced to sign an instrument to secure payment of an obligation. In defenses, (2) *lack of consideration* means you did not receive the agreed-upon performance from the other party to the transaction. Suppose, for example, Adams sells a car to Baker for $500 and Baker gives Adams a check in payment. After driving the car for a short time Baker finds that the car is not as promised; furthermore, it is worthless if Baker's check has been transferred to a holder in due course. Baker will have to pay on the check, and his only recourse will be against Adams. (3) *Payment before maturity* contemplates a situation in which a person pays an instrument before its final due date, but fails to take possession of it, to have it marked "paid," or to have it destroyed. If the instrument then is transferred to a holder in due course, the maker or drawer will be obligated to pay it again. The reason we are worried about situations of payment *before maturity*, not after, is that someone who takes the instrument after ma-

turity could not be a holder in due course, and would be subject to the defense that the obligator had been paid.

The defense of (4) *nondelivery of a completed instrument* involves the situation in which a maker or drawer completes the face of an instrument but does not deliver it to the payee, yet the payee finds it and takes it without permission. The maker or drawer would not have to pay it while it is in the hands of the payee, but will have to pay it if it gets into the hands of a holder in due course.

(5) **Undue influence** as a defense was discussed earlier in Chapter 9 on voidable contracts. It involves a situation in which a person is persuaded to part with property (a negotiable instrument) by someone in a relationship of trust, authority, or control. For example, a granddaughter cares for her sickly grandfather, lavishing him with attention and affection, and induces him to part with a check for $15,000 so that she can purchase the car she has "always wanted and thought she never would have." The defense of undue influence will be lost if the check is negotiated to a holder in due course.

Real (Absolute) Defenses

Real defenses remain with the instrument and are not cut off by a holder in due course. They differ in quality from personal defenses in that they either involve conduct of a more serious nature or involve problems in the creation of the instrument itself, rather than problems arising personally from the negotiations between the original two parties.

They are: (1) Forgery and (2) **material alteration** both occur, presumably, without participation by the supposed maker or drawer. They both involve the attempt to alter the obligation of another party on an instrument of legal efficacy, and in fact they are both types of forgery, but are treated separately because their effects are different. Forgery, in the sense of signing someone else's name to an instrument without authority, is a complete defense to payment of an instrument. Material alteration most frequently is a defense only to the extent of the increase in the obligation of the maker or drawer. The instrument still is payable according to its original tenor except in the hands of the person who altered it and anyone who takes it thereafter until it gets into the hands of a good-faith transferee. For example, suppose Adams draws a check payable to Baker for $100, then Baker alters it to read $150 and negotiates it to Carson, who knows of the alteration. Carson then negotiates it to Davis who takes it in good faith. This alteration completely discharges Adams's obligation as to Baker and Carson, but Adams still is liable on the instrument for $100 (the original tenor) to Davis. Had Baker forged Adams's signature to an instrument, Adams would not have been liable on the instrument to anyone.

Negligence is an exception to the rule that forgery and material alteration are absolute defenses. If the maker or drawer is negligent and thereby invites a forgery or material alteration, these defenses become personal only. For example, if someone leaves her check blanks and checkwriter unlocked on her desk when she leaves work one evening, and the custodian prints up a few checks payable to himself—or signs a blank check and carries it around in his pocket and loses it and someone finds it and completes it payable to himself—or he fills in the blanks of a check in such a way that it is easy to alter, by not completing the "Dollars" blank or the payee blank, the forged or altered instrument would not obligate the negligent person until the instrument came into the hands of a holder in due course. At that point, the negligent person would become fully liable.

A second exception to the rule concerning forgeries is the *imposter rule* (UCC Section 3-405). Under the **imposter rule,** a maker or drawer who places commercial paper into the hands of anyone other than the payee risks his defense to payment on a forged indorsement. The Code provides that anyone can indorse the instrument in the name of the named payee and negotiate it. The defense of forgery does not apply to anyone who takes the instrument in good faith or to those who come thereafter. Note that the "imposter" may be someone entirely foreign to the parties to the instrument, or may be an agent or employee of the drawer or maker. The potential for the application of this rule is especially obvious when a person either authorizes an agent to sign his name to negotiate instruments or signs negotiable instruments prepared by an employee and returns them to that employee for distribution. The following case illustrates the effect of the imposter rule.

BRIGHTON, INC. et al. v. COLONIAL FIRST NATIONAL BANK et al.
176 N.J.Super. 101, 422 A.2d 433 (1980)

[This decision was affirmed by the Supreme Court of New Jersey in a brief opinion for the reasons stated here. 86 N.J. 259, 430 A.2s 902 (1980).]

This was an action brought by a group of real estate management firms including Brighton, Inc. (Plaintiffs/Appellants) against Colonial First National

Bank and others (Defendants/Appellees) seeking to determine the liabilities of the defendants for checks drawn and checks indorsed by an unfaithful employee.

Between 1973 and 1978, Norman Hirschfield, an employee of Plaintiffs, embezzled well over $300,000 from Plaintiffs. He was authorized to draw checks on his employers' accounts. He drew checks payable to payees who did business with the Plaintiffs but to whom no money was owing, indorsed the checks in the names of the payees, then in his own name, and deposited them to his own account. The checks were then paid in the normal course of the banks' affairs. Some of these checks he signed using his own name, as he was authorized to do. Others were signed by forging the names of his employers. Notice of forged indorsements on checks of the first type was first given by Plaintiffs and Defendants on June 21, 1978. Notice of checks bearing the forged signatures of the drawers (the checks of the second type) was first given on July 17, 1979.

From a judgment determining that Defendant banks were not liable for honoring the checks, Plaintiffs appealed. Affirmed.

MORGAN, J.A.D.

[This abstract of the court's opinion addresses only the question of the liability of the parties on those checks properly signed by Hirschfield, using his own name. The parties' liability on the other checks is treated in a continuation of the opinion set out in the next chapter.]

With respect to checks bearing forged indorsements the amounts of which were debited to a plaintiff's account more than three years prior to return of the forged item, no claim against a drawee may be pressed for reasons given in the first point. Section 4-406(4). With respect to the many items not so barred as untimely, summary judgment was entered in the drawees' favor on the basis of Section 3-405, the so-called fictitious payee rule.

Section 3-405(1)(b) provides: "[a]n indorsement by any person in the name of a named payee is effective if . . . a person signing as or on behalf of a maker or drawer intends the payee to have no interest in the instrument. . . ."

This statute was designed to place the loss from the activities of a typical "faithless employee" upon the employer rather than upon the bank. As stated in Official Comment 4:

> . . . The principle followed is that the loss should fall upon the employer as a risk of his business enterprise rather than upon the subsequent holder or drawee. The reasons are that the employer is normally in a better position to prevent such forgeries by reasonable care in the selection or supervision of his employees, or, if he is not, is at least in a better position to cover the loss by fidelity insurance; and that the cost of such insurance is properly an expense of his business rather than of the business of the holder or drawee.

The loss is shifted by making the indorsement effective rather than by explicitly imposing it upon the drawer. By declaring a forged indorsement "effective," a collecting bank's liability on a Section 4-207 warranty and a drawee bank's liability to its customer under Section 4-401 are precluded, with the result that loss is borne by the drawer. . . .

A typical situation to which Section 3-405 applies is given as an example in Official Comment 3 to Section 3-405:

> The drawer makes the check payable to P, an existing person whom he knows, intending to receive the money himself and that P shall have no interest in the check.

Plaintiffs' complaint pleads facts directly congruent to the given example. Hirschfield drew checks to the order of payees he intended to have no interest therein. In such circumstances Section 3-405 mandates that anyone's indorsement for the payee, even Hirschfield's, is "effective," thus passing title and making the item properly payable under Section 4-401. A drawee receiving that item, as did the three drawee banks in this matter, is authorized to debit the customer's account in the amount of such a check. Any loss thereon is borne by the customer as the Code clearly intended.

Questions

1. Is there any way to protect against the problem of an imposter?
2. Although the propriety of the imposter exception seems sound in the principal case, should it apply to people who do not have some relationship to the parties?

Fraud in the execution differs from the personal defense of fraud in the inducement in that, in fraud in the inducement, the party defrauded realizes that she is signing a negotiable instrument, but her willingness to do so has been induced by fraud. In cases of **fraud in the execution,** the party, through no fault of her own, is justifiably unaware that she is signing a negotiable instrument. For example, suppose Baker induces Adams to sign what appears to be a simple installment contract. In fact, the document has a negotiable promissory note laminated to the back with the lower edge exposed so that Adams's signature actually is affixed to the note instead of the contract. Adams would have the defense of fraud in the execution. Of course, the fact that a person signs an instrument without reading or understanding it will not by itself constitute fraud in the execution. It must be shown that the person reasonably could not have been expected to know its contents. Also, evidence of such fraud can be a problem. It is partially for this reason that people who sign autographs seldom, if ever, will sign only their names. They will usually include such notations as "Best Wishes," and frequently will sign at an angle to the bottom of the paper instead of straight across the bottom (as one normally would sign a document).

(4) *Contractual incapacity* of a party is also a real defense. For the reasons discussed in Chapter 9, the law—to a greater or lesser extent depending on the type of incapacity—seeks to preserve the estates of individuals while they are incapacitated. Therefore, they are liable on negotiable instruments only to the extent that they are liable on any other contract.

(5) *Discharge in insolvency proceedings*, such as bankruptcy, will relieve a party of all obligations that are dischargeable, regardless of whether they are evidenced by negotiable instruments, simple contracts, or otherwise. Commercial paper takes no priority over any other debt.

Defenses that May Be either Personal or Real

The remaining two defenses of the twelve listed may be either personal or real, depending on the circumstances. (1) *Ordinary duress* is a personal defense, but it becomes a real defense if it is *extreme.* There is no precise dividing line but, as a rule of thumb, if the duress is so extreme that a person of ordinary courage would not be expected to consider seriously whether or not to comply, it will create a real defense. For example, a threat to be punched in the nose might not be very threatening in many circumstances, but one who has a loaded gun pointed at his head is not expected to think long before signing.

The fact that (2) the transaction underlying a negotiable instrument was *illegal* will create a personal defense, just as it does under contract law. However, if the state also has a statute declaring that instruments arising out of such transactions are *void*, then the defense is real. Taking illegal gambling as an example, the difference will be whether applicable state statutes simply provide that the gambling activity is illegal or that, *in*

Summary of defenses

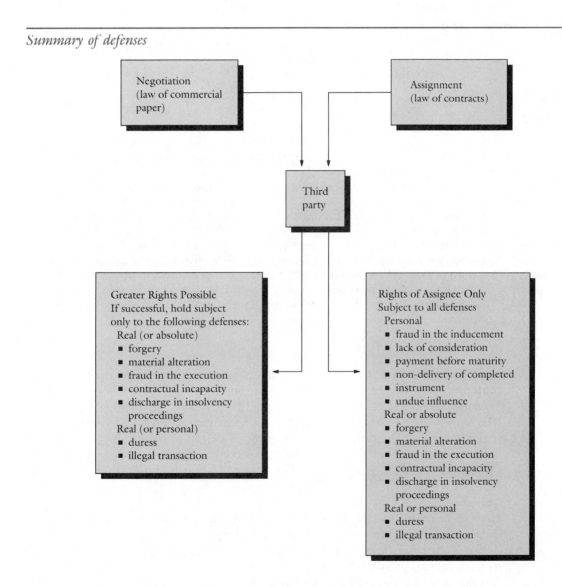

addition, instruments given in payment of gambling debts are void.

Conversion

Section 3-419 of the Code provides certain rules concerning conversion of an instrument. **Conversion** basically is defined as the unauthorized assumption of control over the property of another. It is the civil equivalent of the crime of "theft." An instrument is considered converted when it is presented properly and the person to whom it was presented refuses to accept, pay, or return it on demand. Conversion also occurs if a drawee pays a forged instrument because he has dispensed the funds of the drawer without a lawful order (authority) to do so. Upon conversion, the party who converted generally is liable for the loss suffered by the true owner, up to the face amount of the instrument. Consider the following case involving conversion.

SMITH v. GENERAL CASUALTY COMPANY OF WISCONSIN
75 Ill.App.3d 971, 31 Ill.Dec.602, 394 N.E.2d 804 (1979)

This was an action by William Smith (Plaintiff/Appellee) against General Casualty Company of Wisconsin (Defendant/Appellant) for conversion of a draft paid on an alleged forged indorsement.

In settlement of a previous lawsuit against Defendant's insured, Defendant issued a draft in the amount of $7000, payable to the order of Plaintiff and his attorney, Donald S. Frey. This draft was "payable through" First Wisconsin Bank of Madison. Attorney Frey indorsed the draft, and also penned, or caused to be penned, what purported to be Plaintiff's signature. The draft was paid by Defendant through the bank. Defendant contended that the purported signature of Plaintiff was not a forgery because of the attorney-client relationship.

From a judgment of the trial court denying Defendant's motion for summary judgment and finding for Plaintiff in the amount of $7000, Defendant appealed. Affirmed.

SCOTT, Justice.

[After discussing that Defendant was both drawer and drawee of the draft, the court continued.] The rule of decision followed in Illinois is set out in Crahe v. Mercantile Trust & Savings Bank (1920), 195 Ill. 375, 129 N.E. 120. That case holds that one who stands in the position of attorney or agent may well have, by virtue of his position, the authority to collect the proceeds of a claim or judgment. That case also holds as a matter of law that such person does not have, by virtue of his position, the authority to indorse an instrument of settlement on behalf of his client. Indeed, the Crahe court expressly labels as a forgery any such unauthorized indorsement. It is clear that under Crahe the action for a conversion, which under section 3-419(c) arises in the presence of a forgery, is not cut short merely because the converter's stylus is directed by the hand of an unscrupulous attorney or agent.

The policy of casting losses on the party best able to prevent same permeates the nine articles of the Commercial Code. We believe that the bank to which the draft was first presented for payment and the bank with the only opportunity to ascertain the identity of the indorser was, under these facts, the bank best able to have prevented Smith's $7,000 loss from occurring. In his treatise, Professor Hawkland suggests that where the drawee is found liable to the payee for conversion, the same drawee can pass the loss back to its transferor until the loss is ultimately cast upon the bank or institution to which the draft was first presented for payment. Hawkland, Commercial Paper, pages 66-67; see also warranties of collecting banks, Illinois Revised Statutes 1973, ch. 26, sec. 4-207. We believe Professor Hawkland has correctly explained the functioning of the Article Four warranties as envisioned by the Code authors. Only if the plaintiff in the case at bar is allowed his cause of action against the drawee for conversion can the loss shifting mechanism of the Commercial Code operate in accordance with the design of the drafters. And only if we adopt the conclusion, as did the trial court below and our supreme court in Crahe, that William Smith's purported signature is, under the terms of section 3-419, a forgery, can plaintiff's cause of action be sustained. Because we believe a comprehensive reading of the Commercial Code compels this result, we conclude that the plaintiff's purported signature is a forgery within the meaning of the Code.

Questions

1.   Doesn't this decision prevent the bank from relying on anyone other than the payee? Is it sound?

2.   To protect itself against the type of liability imposed on banks by cases like Smith, doesn't a bank have to insist on in-person presentation with strong identification? Is this commercially desirable?

DISCHARGE

At some point, every negotiable instrument will have served its intended purpose. This will occur when all parties to the instrument finally have been discharged of further liability. Every party has some liability, either primary or secondary, and each will be discharged, in whole or in part, either individually or because of some circumstances that discharges all parties at one time.

Discharge under Contract Law

Section 3-601(2) of the UCC provides that any act of agreement that would discharge a party of liability under simple contract law will discharge her of liability on a negotiable instrument. This would include discharge by accord and satisfaction (compromise), composition, a novation, rescission, mutual agreement, substitution of a new

contract, and provisions of the agreement (see Chapter 12).

Operation of Law

The liability of parties also may be discharged by operation of law. Bankruptcy discharges obligations evidenced by commercial paper to the same extent that it discharges obligations under simple contracts. That also is true of the running of an applicable statute of limitations. Liability on a negotiable instrument also may be discharged by merger of the obligation into a judgment in favor of a holder when an action has been brought on an instrument.

Payment

Payment of an instrument to the holder is the most common way of achieving discharge, and the discharge may occur by the payment of something other than money, with the agreement of the holder. Either type of payment will result in a discharge even if it is made with knowledge that another person has a claim on the instrument, unless that other person supplies indemnity or obtains an injunction. Neither will result in a discharge, however, if made in bad faith; if made to a thief or his successor prior to a holder in due course; if early payment is made but not indorsed on the instrument, and the instrument then falls into the hands of a holder in due course; or if paid to a holder in violation of a restrictive indorsement. Consider the following case.

RUSSELL v. MAXON SALES COMPANY
591 P.2d 703 (Okl. 1979)

This was an action by Leon Russell and Truman Coffey, dba McDonald County Livestock Market (Plaintiffs/Appellees) against Maxon Sales Company (Defendant/Appellant) to collect the face amount of a check. Defendant contended that it had been discharged of liability by payment to the McDonald County Bank.

As part of a livestock transaction, Defendant drew a check to Paul Durbin in the amount of $29,290.86. On the same day, Durbin repurchased part of the livestock, drawing a check to Defendant in the amount of $16,002.34. Durbin then indorsed the $29,290.86 check and another (total of $38,533.29), took them to the McDonald County Bank, and instructed the bank to deposit $38,145.06 of the total in the account of Plaintiffs. When Defendant attempted to cash Durbin's $16,002.34 check at the bank, it was dishonored for insufficient funds. Defendant then stopped payment on its $29,290.86 check. When the McDonald County Bank discovered that payment had been stopped, it called Defendant, and agreed to accept $13,288.52 in satisfaction of its $29,290.86 check (the difference between Defendant's check and Durbin's check). The bank then charged back this difference (the amount of Durbin's check) to the account of Plaintiffs. Plaintiffs contended that they, not the bank, were holders of Defendant's check by virtue of Durbin's instructions at the time of his deposit, and thus only they could discharge Defendant.

From a judgment for Plaintiffs, Defendant appealed. Reversed and remanded.

BARNES, Justice.

Under the provisions of 12A O.S. 1971, Section 3-301, a holder of an instrument, whether or not he or she is the owner, may on payment or satisfaction discharge the instrument.

The Uniform Comment to that Section indicates that every holder has such rights. A holder is defined at 12A O.S.1971, Section 1-201(20), which provides:

'Holder' means a person who is in possession of a document of title or an instrument or an investment security drawn, issued or indorsed to him or to his order or to bearer or in blank. . . .

Despite the fact that Livestock may have rights to the proceeds of the check, it is clear that Livestock was at no time the holder of the check, for at no time did

Livestock have possession of that check, either by virtue of personal possession or possession by an agent.

Despite the fact that Livestock did not have possession of the instrument, Livestock urges this Court to hold that they were nonetheless holders of the check. If we were to rule that one not in possession of an instrument were the holder, an inordinate burden would be put upon drawers, makers and acceptors of negotiable instruments, for they would be required to ascertain who the holder of a particular instrument was prior to payment or satisfaction. Otherwise, these makers, drawers or acceptors would run the risk of paying a party in possession of the instrument who presented it for payment, but who, in fact, was not the holder, and therefore would not have the power to discharge the instrument.

To avoid such difficulty, the drafters of the Code provided that in order to be a holder one must have possession of an instrument. One of the underlying purposes and policies of the Uniform Commercial Code, as set forth at 12A O.S. 1971, Section 1-201, is to simplify, clarify and modernize the laws governing commercial transactions. That Section also provides that the Code shall be liberally construed and applied to promote its underlying purposes and policies. To hold that one not in possession of an instrument were its holder would clearly not simplify commercial transactions, but would, as shown above, create virtual chaos in the commercial world. This being so, we cannot accept Livestock's argument that they were the holder of the instrument, although they never had possession of the same. Rather, the depository bank, who had physical possession of the instrument, which was a bearer instrument, was the holder, whose discharge of Maxson's obligations on the check relieved Maxson of its obligations on the check, as the bank, being the holder, had the power to discharge the instrument, pursuant to the provisions of 12A O.S. 1971, Section 3-301 and 3-603.

Questions

1. Do you think the court is right, or is it putting too much emphasis on technical possession?

2. On the basis of what you have read thus far, do you think the UCC has achieved the purposes described in *Russell*?

Tender

If tender of payment is refused, the party making tender is discharged of liability for any subsequent interest, costs, or attorney fees. Also, anyone who has a right of recourse against the party making tender is discharged.

Suppose Arthur gave Busch a $10,000, six-percent, 60-day note to secure the purchase price of an automobile he bought from Busch. When the note came due, it was discovered that Arthur had left town but provided no forwarding address. In the meantime, Busch had indorsed the note to Crane, who had indorsed it to Diaz. Busch tendered payment of the note ($10,000) to Diaz, but Diaz refused, vowing to find Arthur and make him pay. When Diaz was unsuccessful in his search, he requested that either Busch or Crane pay the note. Who is liable for what to Diaz and for how much? Because of Diaz's refusal to accept Busch's earlier tender of payment, Crane (who, if he was required to pay, would have recourse against Busch) would not be liable. Busch would be liable, but only for the $10,000—not for interest or other costs arising after his tender.

Cancellation or Renunciation

The holder of an instrument may discharge all parties to an instrument by cancelling it. This may be done in any manner that makes it apparent on the face of the instrument, such as marking it "paid" or "cancelled," destroying it, or mutilating it. The holder also may cancel the obligation of any indorser by striking out that person's indorsement. The latter does not affect the title to the instrument even if the cancelled indorsement otherwise is necessary to the chain of title. The holder also may renounce her rights against any party by either delivering a signed writing, or the instrument itself, to the party to be discharged.

Impairment of Recourse

If a party secondarily liable on an instrument is required to pay it, he may have a right of recourse against the party primarily liable and against other parties prior to him in the instrument's chain of title. If a holder of the instrument impairs that right of recourse, the party whose right is impaired is discharged. (**Impairment of recourse** may occur by the holder's release of the other party, his promise not to sue him, his extension of the time for payment, or any other discharge. It also may occur by a surrender or other impairment of collateral.) However, if the holder expressly reserves rights against the party with the right of recourse, that party is not discharged, but her right of recourse remains unimpaired as to the party against whom she had the right.

Material Alteration

An alteration of an instrument by the holder, which is both material and for fraudulent pur-

poses, will discharge any party whose obligation is changed. However, a subsequent holder in due course has a right to enforce the instrument according to its original tenor. This is an example of one of the extraordinary situations in which the civil law imposes a penalty on a wrongdoer.

Certification of a Check

The **certification of a check** is acceptance by the drawee bank. By acceptance, the bank obligates itself to pay the check according to its tenor at the time of presentation. If the certification is procured by a holder of the instrument, the drawer and all prior indorsers are discharged. However, unless otherwise agreed, a bank has no obligation to certify a check.

SUMMARY

In order to be liable on a negotiable instrument, a party must sign the instrument either personally or by an authorized agent. In signing on behalf of a principal, an agent must both identify his principal and indicate his representative capacity. If he fails to meet either requirement, the principal is not liable but the agent is, except that between the immediate parties parol evidence is admissable to bind the principal and relieve the agent of liability. Even a person who has no interest in the transaction may sign "for accommodation." She then will be liable as would any other signer, but she is entitled to reimbursement from the party accommodated.

Contract liability on an instrument may be either primary or secondary, depending on whether the party's promise is to pay in all events or only after the default of another party. A maker is primarily liable on a note. No one is primarily liable on a draft until it is accepted by the drawee, then the drawee (acceptor) becomes primarily liable. The drawer of a draft, and the indorser of either a draft or a note, are secondarily liable.

In order to activate the liability of parties primarily liable, the instrument must be presented

Summary: Discharge

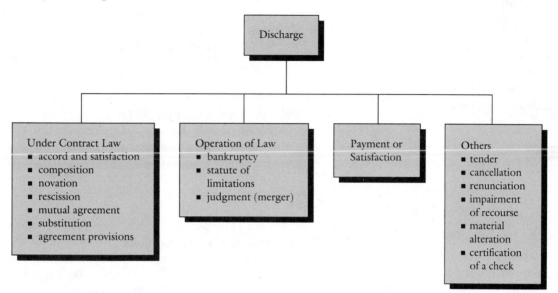

for acceptance or payment. Then, dishonor, and sometimes notice or protest, is required for parties with secondary liability.

In addition to contract liability, the party presenting the instrument, and all transferors, make certain warranties. These obligations are implied by the code, and the warranties of indorsers run in favor of all parties taking the instrument thereafter, while those of a transferor without indorsement run in favor of only the immediate transferee.

The liability of the maker and the drawer are subject to certain defenses. These defenses may be either personal or real. Personal defenses are cut off when the instrument comes into the hands of a holder in due course, but real defenses generally remain with the instrument forever. Examples of personal defenses are fraud in the inducement and lack of consideration. Examples of real defenses are forgery, material alteration, and incapacity.

The obligations of parties liable may be discharged in any number of ways. The most obvious way to achieve discharge is by payment.

However, other circumstances also will create discharge, either of individuals or of all parties to the instrument. Among them are tender, cancellation or renunciation, impairment of recourse (including collateral), material alteration by a holder, and certification of a check.

KEY TERMS AND CONCEPTS

accommodation signer
secondary liability
primary liability
acceptance
presentment for acceptance
notice
presentment for payment
dishonor
protest
Shelter Rule
personal defenses
real (absolute) defenses

fraud in the inducement
undue influence
material alteration
fraud in the execution
imposter rule
conversion
impairment of recourse
certification of a check

PROBLEMS

1. Morris stole a car belonging to Nolan and sold it to A&D Motor Sales, representing himself as Nolan. A&D gave Morris a check made payable to Nolan. Morris then took the check to Greenberg, who cashed it after first calling A&D. When A&D discovered the fraud, it sought to stop payment on the check and refused to pay it, contending that Greenberg did not have title because the check was drawn payable to Nolan but cashed by Morris. Is Greenberg entitled to payment?

2. The drawer of a check drew it in 1955; the instrument was complete except that the date was left blank. In 1964, the holder filled in the date and cashed the check at the drawee bank. The drawer objected when she learned of the transaction, contending that forgery of the date gave rise to a real defense to payment, and also that the bank was not a holder in due course. Is the drawer correct?

3. Terry, an employee of the drawer, was responsible for preparing checks for the drawer's signature. After they were signed, he mailed them to the proper persons. On one occasion, among the checks was one made payable to Fred Willard, whom Terry intended to have no interest. When the checks were signed, Terry took the one payable to Willard and cashed it at the drawee bank. Is the drawer entitled to recover the amount of the check from the bank?

4. Masters received a check from Simpson and deposited it in her bank account. The check was returned by the drawee bank because of a stop-payment order. Masters received notice of the dishonor and the check was returned to her by her bank. Masters filed suit on the check but, by the time of trial, the check had been lost or stolen. Masters offered in evidence a photocopy of the check, taken by the drawee bank at the time it returned the check to Masters's bank. Should the copy be admitted into evidence?

5. An aluminum siding company sold siding to Matthews, who signed a contract and an installment note to secure payment. Matthews was partially blind and could see only the largest print on the instruments. The contract price of the siding was $3250. The note called for 84 equal monthly payments at the rate of $61.04—a total of $5127.36. Thereafter, the contract and note were transferred to Aluminum Acceptance Corp. When it was determined that the note was contrary to the state usury statute, Matthews sought to avoid his obligation. Aluminum Acceptance Corp. contended that it was not subject to the defense since it was a holder in due course. Was Aluminum Acceptance Corp. a holder in due course?

6. Berenyi purchased carpeting from ABC Carpets, signing a contract and giving a promissory note to secure payment. At the time, ABC was not supposed to be doing business in the state because of an injunction granted against it for fraudulent business practices. ABC sold the note at New Jersey Mortgage and Investment Corp.; New Jersey Mortgage took the note as a holder in due course. Berenyi later refused to pay the note on the ground that the carpeting never had been installed as promised and also because the transaction was illegal since it was in violation of a valid injunction. Is New Jersey Mortgage entitled to payment?

7. Lacey purchased a tractor and a dump truck from Anderson Equipment Co., and gave a promissory note to secure payment. The note was sold at the Capital Bank and Trust Co. The tractor and dump truck proved defective and Lacey refused to pay the note. Capital repossessed the equipment, sold it at public sale, and sued Lacey for the deficiency. Lacey defended on the ground that the note was for the purchase of consumer goods and, therefore, the bank was subject to the same defenses as the seller. The bank agreed that the contract might have been for consumer goods, but contended it was not subject to the seller's defenses because the contract did not contain the notice required by federal regulation (16 C.F.R. 443). Is the bank correct?

8.   Suppose a drawee bank refuses to honor a check for the payee even though the payee has proper identification and the bank admits the check is "good." Is the payee entitled to sue the bank for damages caused by the dishonor?

9.   Hiram executed a promissory note in the amount of $25,000, payable to Rubin, who indorsed it and sold it to the First Bank and Trust.

When the note was dishonored, First Bank promptly mailed a notice of dishonor to Rubin, but the notice did not arrive. Later, when the bank sued Rubin to recover under her indorsement, Rubin defended on the ground that the bank had not given her notice as required by UCC Section 3-508. Is Rubin correct?

10.   Suppose Schmidt defrauds Humbrock into giving him a check for $500. Schmidt then negotiates the check to Czarnecki who, at the time of negotiation, is aware of the fraud by Schmidt. Czarnecki then negotiates the check to Drew, who takes it as a holder in due course. Drew then gives it to his son, Ed, as a birthday gift, and Ed negotiates it back to Czarnecki. If Ed still had the check, would he be entitled to payment from Humbrock? Is Czarnecki entitled to payment?

Chapter 20

The Relationship between a Bank and Its Customer

INTRODUCTION

This chapter is devoted to the law concerning the use of checking accounts. The preceding chapters discussed checks, as one type of commercial paper, and the basic law was found in Article 3 of the Uniform Commercial Code (UCC). The relationship between the drawee bank and the drawer of a check is governed, for the most part, by Article 4. It should be recognized at the outset, however, that the rules stated in Article 4, within

The dual relationship between a bank and its customer(s)

Customer's Role	Bank's Role	Obligation
Creditor	Debtor	Bank is obligated to return creditor's deposit on request.
Principal	Agent	Bank is obligated to dispense money according to principal's lawful orders (checks).

stated limits, may be modified by agreement between the bank and its customer, except that a bank may not disclaim its responsibility to act in good faith or to exercise ordinary care. Nor can it limit the measure of damages for its failure to meet these responsibilities (UCC Section 4-103).

TYPES OF CHECKS

The term *check* was defined in Chapter 17 as a "bill of exchange drawn on a bank and payable on demand." Sometimes checks are referred to as drafts or bank drafts, although such terminology technically is incorrect. However, it is in order to describe some other common terms at this point.

Certified Check

A certified check is a check that has been accepted for payment by the drawee bank, but has not been paid. The bank's acceptance, or certification, is written (stamped) on the check, which then is returned to the person (drawer or holder) who presented it for certification. Upon certification, the bank becomes primarily liable to pay the check as it appeared at the time of certification, even if the check was forged, materially altered, or subject to any other defense. Of course, the bank's liability runs in favor of holders in due course who hold the check after certification. When a check is certified, the bank takes the amount of the check out of the drawer's account and places it in a special trust account for certified checks.

Cashier's Check

A cashier's check is like any other check except that a bank is both drawer and drawee. This type of check is similar to a teller's check, except that a teller's check is drawn by the bank on its own funds deposited in another bank. Only the bank has a right to stop payment on either of these types of checks, since it is the drawer in both cases.

Traveler's Check

A traveler's check ordinarily is only a type of cashier's check, distinguished by the fact that it is sold, in varying face amounts and quantities, to travelers. When drawn on an institution other than a bank, it frequently is designated a "traveler's *checque*," as is true of American Express, which draws its traveler's checks on itself. However, the rights and obligations of the parties are the same as for any cashier's check.

GOVERNING PRINCIPLES

When a customer opens a checking account with a bank, two relationships are established. First is the relationship of debtor and creditor. The customer (creditor) has deposited money in the bank, and the bank (debtor) is obligated to return it upon request. Second, and of greater potential importance, is the relationship of principal and agent. By the terms of their agreement, the bank (agent) undertakes the obligation to dispense the money deposited by the customer (principal) according to his or her lawful orders. Authority to do so is granted to the bank, transaction by transaction, by the customer's drawing of a check. The check, therefore, is a written grant of agency authority.

Bank's Right to Charge the Account

The bank may charge the drawer's account with the amount of any instrument properly chargeable against the account. However, it has no right to charge other obligations the customer may owe without express authority to do so. Also, the bank has a right to charge the account even if, by doing so, an overdraft is created. If in paying a check the bank meets the requirements, the bank will be in the position of a holder in due course. Therefore, if the check has been altered, the bank may charge the account according to its original tenor. Also, the bank is protected in all cases of forgery by the rules concerning its customer's negligence and the imposter rule. The following case concerns the bank's right to charge a customer's account for amounts due the bank.

MERCANTILE SAFE DEPOSIT AND TRUST COMPANY v. DELP & CHAPEL CONCRETE AND CONSTRUCTION COMPANY et al.
44 Md.App. 34, 408 A.2d 1043 (1980)

This was an action by Delp & Chapel Concrete Construction Company and others (D & C) (Plaintiffs/Appellees) against Mercantile Safe Deposit and Trust Company (Defendant/Appellant) for, among other things, damages for wrongful dishonor of twelve checks.

D & C desired to obtain certain commercial loans from Defendant, which Defendant granted. As part of the transaction, D & C established a checking account with Defendant. At first, the loans were paid on time, but D & C later became progressively slower in paying until, at one point, three loans totalling $8913.62 were substantially overdue. Defendant then charged D & C's account with the balance due. This resulted in the dishonor of twelve outstanding checks. The court examined the right of Defendant to set off the loans against D & C's account.

From a judgment of the trial court awarding Plaintiff compensatory damages of $9343.60 and punitive damages of $25,000, Defendant appealed. Reversed.

COUCH, Judge.

Count One, which alleges Mercantile's wrongful dishonor of checks drawn on D & C's checking account, is premised upon the theory that the set off against the corporate checking account was improper. This, we have decided, was not the case. In reviewing the propriety of the denial of Mercantile's motion for directed verdict we must, of course, consider all evidence and inferences rationally drawn therefrom in the light most favorable to the party against whom the motion is made. If there is in the record any legally relevant and competent evidence to prove the appellees' case then we must uphold the trial court's denial of the motion. . . . We find no such evidence here.

The Commercial Law Article of the Annotated Code of Maryland, (1975), Section 4-402, (hereinafter U.C.C.) sets forth the cause of action known as wrongful dishonor:

> Section 4-402. Bank's liability to customer for wrongful dishonor.
>
> A payor bank is liable to its customer for damages proximately caused by the wrongful dishonor of an item. When the dishonor occurs through mistake liability is limited to actual damages proved. If so proximately caused and proved damages may include damages for an arrest or prosecution of the customer or other consequential damages. Whether any consequential damages are proximately caused by the wrongful dishonor is a question of fact to be determined in each case. . . .

A payor bank, in this instance Mercantile, generally has a duty to its customer to pay items "properly payable" and drawn against the customer's account. U.C.C. Section 4-401; 4-104(1)(i). If this duty is breached, then the bank is liable to its customer for wrongful dishonor under Section 4-402. Comment 2 of that section states, "'Wrongful dishonor' excludes any permitted or justified dishonor . . ." The actions taken by Mercantile amount to a permitted, rather than wrongful, dishonor. . . .

There were a total of twelve D & C checks which were allegedly dishonored by Mercantile. Of those twelve checks, nine were charged to D & C's account on November 4 and returned to the payees for non-sufficient funds on November 5. While the posting of an item (in this instance the entering of a debit to the customer's account), Section 4-109(d), is a measuring point in the process of determining when an item may be finally paid, it does not mean that Mercantile's set off was too late to include those funds. See Section 4-109 Comment. Mercantile's return of the nine checks is perfectly acceptable under Section 4-301 which provides:

> (1) Where an authorized settlement for a demand item. . . received by a payor bank otherwise than for immediate payment over the counter has been made before midnight of the banking day of receipt the payor bank may revoke the settlement and recover any payment if before it has made final payment . . . and before its midnight deadline it
> (a) Returns the item . . .

Mercantile's charges against the account on November 4 used all available funds, thus the bank's return of the checks for what Mercantile termed "non-sufficient funds" amounted to a rightful dishonor since the set off was exercised prior to midnight of the banking day (November 5) following receipt of the checks on November 4.

Questions

1. Should the bank have been permitted to make the set-off without notifying D & C? If so, how is a depositor ever certain how much money is in his or her bank account?

2. What if D & C had a good defense to the bank's claim? Would the dishonor have been wrongful?

Bank's Duty to Pay

By virtue of the agreement between the bank and its customer, the bank is obligated, just as is any agent, to obey its principal's instructions. Therefore, it is obligated to pay all checks properly presented. Failure to do so will subject the bank to liability for any damages proximately caused by the failure. These may include damages arising from the arrest or prosecution of its customer. However, the bank's obligation to pay ceases if the check is not presented within six months after its date, although it *may* pay the check thereafter if it does so in good faith.

Stop-Payment Orders

A customer has a right to stop payment on any check he has drawn. It is important to understand that a stop-payment order does not change the drawer's obligation on the instrument or on the underlying transaction. It simply gives him temporary control over his cash. A **stop-payment order** is only a revocation of the authority granted to the bank. It is effective only if received by the bank in such time as to afford the bank a reasonable opportunity to act on it. An oral stop-payment order is effective for fourteen days, and a written stop-payment order is effective for six months. Either can be renewed. If the bank pays a check contrary to an effective stop-payment order, it is not a holder in due course in its own right (since it has notice of a defense), but has only the rights of the person who transferred the check to it. Consider the following cases.

BRUNO v. COLLECTIVE FEDERAL SAVINGS AND LOAN ASSOCIATION
147 N.J.Super. 115, 370 A.2d 874 (1977)

This is an action by Madison Bruno (Plaintiff/Appellant) against Collective Federal Savings and Loan Association (Defendant/Appellee) to recover the amount she had deposited in the savings and loan.

Plaintiff had deposited some $12,000 in Defendant savings and loan. She sought to withdraw $5000, and Defendant issued its check for that amount, drawn on its account at Federal Home Loan Bank and made payable, at Plaintiff's request, to her uncle, Samuel Clerico. Plaintiff took the check and gave it to the payee's son, who indorsed Samuel Clerico's name and left with it. Fearing that the indorsement was not authorized, Plaintiff asked Defendant to stop payment on the check. Defendant did so, notifying Federal Home Loan Bank and returning the $5000 to Plaintiff's account. It was then learned that the stop-payment order was too late to be effective—the check already had been cashed by the bank, so Defendant re-debited Plaintiff's account, again withdrawing the $5000. Plaintiff contended the re-debit was improper because she had requested the stop-payment order before the check was cashed.

From a judgment for Defendant, Plaintiff appealed. Affirmed.

PER CURIAM.

Although we agree with plaintiff that the provisions of the Uniform Commercial Code relied upon by the trial judge have no application to this case, we nonetheless conclude that the result reached was a partially correct one although for different reasons. It is essential to an understanding of this case to emphasize that plaintiff was not a party to the check in question; defendant bank was the drawer, the Federal Home Loan Bank of New York was the drawee, and Samuel Clerico was the payee. Clerico, who admitted during the trial that the indorsement of his name was not authorized, appeared as an indorser as well as did Martin Simon. Clearly, since plaintiff is not a party to the check in question, her rights with respect to it are not governed by that section of the Uniform Commercial Code defining rights and liabilities with respect to parties to negotiable instruments. Hence, contrary to the ruling of the trial court, N.J.S.A. 12A:4-303 does not control disposition of this case. The same is true with respect to N.J.S.A. 12A:4-403 and N.J.S.A. 12A:4-407.

Rather, the rights of plaintiff against defendant bank, if any, in the given circumstances are governed by the contract of deposit between plaintiff and bank, the specific contents of which were never disclosed by the record. Nonetheless, certain aspects of the relationship are inferable from what occurred in this case. Traditionally, the relationship between a depositor and bank is viewed as that of creditor and debtor. . . . When plaintiff withdrew $5,000 defendant bank ceased to be her debtor in that amount. Had the withdrawal been made in cash, and had she lost the cash or had it been stolen from her, she would have had no recourse against the bank. We can, nonetheless, infer from this record that the fact that the withdrawal was made by check still left plaintiff with certain rights against the bank for the amount of the check, at least until it was cashed, that is, until it assumed the form of cash. We draw this inference from the bank's actions in attempting, unsuccessfully in this case, to stop payment thereon at the request of its depositor.

Once it undertook this course of action, it was under an obligation to exercise due care in connection with this attempt. . . .

The fact that defendant bank recredited plaintiff's account in the amount of the check on the mistaken assumption that the check had not been cashed does not alter the result. The funds had been withdrawn by the date the bank corrected its error. All the bank was doing was correcting the statement of the amount of its debt owing to plaintiff on the basis of its later discovery of the truth—that the check covered by the debit of plaintiff's account had been cashed and the withdrawal therefore completed. . . .

Hence, the trial judge correctly held that the bank was not liable to plaintiff in the amount of $5,000. . . .

Questions

1. Is there anything wrong with the court's analysis?
2. Is there any rational way of reaching the opposite result in this case?

FEDERAL DEPOSIT INSURANCE CORPORATION
v. WEST
544 Ga. 396, 260 S.E.2d 89 (1979)

This was an action by the Federal Deposit Insurance Corporation (Plaintiff/Appellant) as assignee of the Hamilton Bank & Trust Company, a defunct bank, against A. Davidson West (Defendant/Appellee) to collect on certain checks that had created an overdraft at the assignor bank.

An account was opened with Hamilton Bank & Trust in the name of Davidson-Sarasota. The checks were imprinted with the corporate name, and according to the signature card required the countersignature "A. Davidson West as Pres." At the time Hamilton Bank & Trust was taken over by Plaintiff, overdrafts to the account amounted to $36,715.15. A number of the checks, imprinted with the corporate name and account number, had been signed "A. Davidson West" (not indicating his agency capacity).

The trial court granted summary judgment for Plaintiff. This decision was reversed on appeal by the Court of Appeals, and Plaintiff appealed. Affirmed.

BOWLES, Justice.

[The court agreed with the decision of the Court of Appeals, but disagreed with some statements made in its decision. Therefore, the decision of the Georgia Supreme Court presents the grounds for affirmance, and also some very important dicta concerning the right of a drawee bank to assume the position of a holder in due course of a check drawn on it.]

We have carefully studied all sections of Articles 3 and 4 of the U.C.C. along with their official comments to try and determine what the drafters' intent might have been. We find no direct answer but rather discover that some sections and comments seem to indicate one answer while others indicate another. We conclude that there is no compelling reason that a bank cannot be a holder in due course of an instrument drawn on it if it meets all the qualifications of the status. One simple way for a drawee bank to gain holder in due course status would be to take the instrument from a transferor who is a holder in due course. Code Ann. Section 109A-3-201. One of the most useful occasions to assert holder in due course status would be in a case *similar* to the case at bar. If a drawee bank turns money over to a collecting bank who is a holder in due course on an instrument which would overdraw the drawee bank's customer's account, it has turned over its own money on the instrument. While the drawee bank has a remedy against its customer under Code Ann. Section 109A-4-401, we conclude that it also has a remedy on the instrument *against the drawer* provided the drawee does not give up possession of the instrument. A drawee bank cannot sue on an instrument as a holder in due course if it does not continue to be a holder.

While the record is not clear in the case at bar, it seems likely that the checks in issue here were returned to the bank's customer in its bank statement. If the bank has given up possession of the instruments, it is no longer a holder of them. Since this case is being reversed for further proceedings, that issue may still be developed.

For now we will assume that the instruments causing the overdrafts were returned to the bank's customer. The drawee bank, having elected to pursue its remedy of charging its depositor's account under code Ann. Section 109A-4-401, must look to its depositor for repayment. The deposit agreement, if any, the signature card and the checks drawn against the account are the contract documents between the bank and the customer. The identity of the depositor, Davidson-Sarasota, as amplified by the signature card, and the checks drawn on that account number, in this case is ambiguous and so parol evidence is necessary to determine the correct identity. Code Ann. Section 109A-3-403 is not involved as this is not a suit on the instrument itself but rather on the underlying debt caused by the overdrafts.

Questions

1. What issues will be litigated when this case returns to the trial court?

2. Should cases like this one be handled outside the UCC in light of their close relationship to commercial instruments?

Death or Incompetency of the Customer

Ordinarily, the relationship of principal and agent is terminated upon either the death or the incompetency of the principal (see Chapter 34). However, under Section 4-405(1) of the UCC, the authority of the bank, granted by the drawing of a check, is not terminated until the bank knows of the death or the adjudication of incompetence and has a reasonable time to act on it. Under Section 4-405(2), even with knowledge, the bank may continue to pay or certify checks for a period of ten days after the customer's death (but not incompetence) unless ordered to stop payment by a person claiming an interest in the account.

Customer's Duty to Report Forgeries

The forgery of a check may occur by an unauthorized signing of the drawer's name, by an alteration of the terms of the check in some material respect, or by the forgery of a necessary indorsement. A forgery creates a real (absolute) defense to the payment of the check, and the drawer, or purported drawer, is not liable on it (or, perhaps, not liable for the amount of the alteration), even to a holder in due course. Therefore, if the bank charges the customer's account with the amount of such an instrument, it is obligated to reimburse the account when ordered to do so by the customer. However, this right of the customer may be lost if he or she does not act reasonably to discover the forgery and to report it to the bank.

In the event that there is a forgery, including a material alteration, on the face of the instrument, the customer must notify the bank within one year of the time the instrument was first made available to him. This ordinarily would be from the time it arrived in his mailbox. For a forged indorsement, the period is three years.

The foregoing rules apply only to "one-time" forgeries, however. In the case of a **series of forgeries,** a different rule applies. A series consists of two or more forgeries, including material alterations, by the same wrongdoer or by two or more wrongdoers working in concert. In this circumstance, the customer must report the forgery within a reasonable time, not to exceed *fourteen days* from the time the *first* forgery in the series was made available to her. This presents an obvious problem for the customer. When she first discovers a forged check among the cancelled checks returned to her, she probably will have no way of knowing if it is a "single" or the first in a series. Therefore, wisdom dictates that she should assume the worst.

For the purpose of illustration, suppose the customer receives her cancelled checks from the bank on August 31. Among them is one forged check. Thereafter, forged checks *in the same series* are cashed by the bank on September 8, 13, 16, 23, and 30. Meanwhile, the customer, having noticed the first forgery, gives the bank notice on September 26. Who is liable on each of these checks? As to those cashed on September 8 and 13 (within fourteen days of August 31), the bank will be liable if the customer reports them within one year from the time they are made available to her (probably September 30). Those cashed on September 16 and 23 (after September 14 and prior to September 26) are the sole responsibility of the customer. The bank is not liable even if notified. The bank will be liable for the check cashed on September 30 if the customer gives the bank notice within one year after it is made available to her (probably October 31). Consider the following case concerning the duty of the customer to report forgeries.

BRIGHTON, INC. et al. v. COLONIAL FIRST NATIONAL BANK et al.
176 N.J.Super. 101, 422 A.2d 433 (1980)

[For a discussion of the facts, see this case in Chapter 19, p. 426–27.]

MORGAN, J.A.D.

[Presented here is the court's discussion concerning the liability of the parties on checks bearing forgeries of the drawer's signatures and forgeries of necessary indorsements.]

N.J.S.A. 12A:4-406(4) provides as follows:

> *Without regard to care or lack of care* of either the customer or the bank *a customer who does not within one year from the time the statement and items are made available to the customer* (subsection (1)) *discover and report his unauthorized signature* or any alteration on the face or back of the item or does not within three years from that time discover and report any unauthorized indorsement *is precluded from asserting against the bank such unauthorized signature or indorsement or such alteration.* [Emphasis supplied]

The one-year period limitation in Section 4-406(4) is not merely a statute of limitations, but a rule of substantive law barring absolutely a customer's untimely asserted right to make such a claim against the bank.

The purpose of the statute is to have one uniform rule throughout the country in place of the various time periods that existed prior to the U.C.C. As stated in Official Comment 7 thereto, the statute sets forth

> . . . a public policy in favor of imposing on customers the duty of prompt examination of their bank statements and the notification of banks of forgeries and alterations and in favor of reasonable time limitations on the responsibility of banks for payment of forged or altered items . . .

The statute is clearly applicable to the facts of this case. By plaintiffs' own admission in their complaint, they did not give the drawee banks' notice of any impropriety with respect to the subject checks until June 21, 1978. That notice dealt only with a claim of forged indorsements which we will hereinafter be discussing. No notice was given to drawees of any alleged unauthorized signatures until plaintiff filed and served its amendment in this action on July 17, 1979. That notice was well beyond the one-year time limit—and summary judgment dismissing the seventh, eighth and ninth counts was clearly warranted. . . .

We start with the general proposition that a drawee bank may not properly debit the account of a customer whose check bears the forged indorsement of a payee. (Section 3-404). Where it does so and where the drawee is so notified within three years from the date the statement and the challenged item is made available to the customer that such is the case, Section 4-406(4), it will be required to recredit the customer's account by the amount of the check bearing the forged indorsement. Section 4-401. A forged indorsement is normally ineffective to pass title to the instrument on which it appears.

With respect to checks bearing forged indorsements the amounts of which were debited to a plaintiff's account more than three years prior to return of the forged item, no claim against a drawee may be pressed for the reasons given [concerning the one year limitation on items bearing a forged signature of the drawer].

Questions

1. Why shouldn't a bank be required to reimburse depositors' accounts for all forgeries with no time limit?

2. Are the rules regarding reporting forgeries too complicated for ordinary depositors? Can they be simplified?

ELECTRONIC FUNDS TRANSFERS

With the arrival of the computer age has come a new system of handling financial transactions, the electronic fund transfer. This system already has replaced the traditional paper check to a considerable extent, and its effect is expected to increase, possibly to the extent of almost entirely replacing money. This revolution created a need for new legislation. Federal law, state statutes, and the UCC all were inadequate to deal with the new technology. Today states have made some progress in passing new legislation, and a revision of the Code is in the offing. However, the most significant regulation is found on the federal level.

A special subchapter (VI) was included in the 1978 Financial Institutions Regulatory and Interest Rate Control Act (15 U.S.C. 1693 et. seq.). This subchapter is known as the **Electronic Fund Transfers Act,** and its purpose is "to provide a basic framework establishing the rights, liabilities, and responsibilities of participants in electronic fund transfer systems." The primary objective of the act, however, is stated to be the protection of individual consumer rights, and it allows the states to pass more stringent rules to achieve this.

The act regulates any means of transfer of funds by the use of an electronic terminal, telephone, computer, or magnetic tape. These means include point-of-sale transfers, automated teller machine transactions, direct deposits or withdrawals of funds, and transfers initiated by telephone.

Point-of-sale (POS) transfers involve automated transfers from terminals located in business places. In purchasing goods, the customer, electronically, by the use of a "debit card," will authorize the transfer of funds from his account directly to an account of the seller. This method eliminates risks and delays that attend the use of checks, although certain other risks may be created, such as risks to the customer's privacy.

Automated teller machines (ATMs) are more common than POS transfers. They go by many names, such as "24-Hour Teller," "Cash Station," and "Ready Teller." A bank typically places terminals at several locations around its banking area. Access to these terminals generally is by use of a magnetic card and a secret personal identification number. Services offered range from withdrawals of cash from checking accounts to a full range of deposit, withdrawal, and transfer services.

Direct deposit and withdrawal arrangements are common. Frequently an employee will authorize her employer to send her net pay to a bank via electronic transfer. A borrower may authorize a lender to withdraw payments from his checking account. This particularly is common in the payment of a home mortgage indebtedness. Automatic withdrawal authorizations also are used with some frequency to pay insurance premiums.

Banking by telephone is in the early stages today. Monthly bills for utilities, department stores, and other business may be paid by using a touch-tone telephone system whenever a bank offers this service. By "punching in" the appropriate numbers after being connected to the bank's system, the transfers may be made from the home or office.

Terms and Conditions of Transfer

The first substantive section of the Electric Fund Transfers Act provides for a disclosure of the terms and conditions that apply to electronic fund transfers. The disclosure is to be in readily understandable language and must include, to the extent applicable:

1. the consumer's liability for unauthorized transfers;
2. the telephone number and address of the person or office to be notified concerning unauthorized transfers;
3. the type and nature of transfers that the consumer can initiate, and any applicable limitations;
4. charges for the service;
5. the consumer's right to stop payment on preauthorized transfers and the procedure for doing so;
6. the consumer's right to receive documentation of transfers;
7. a summary of error-resolution procedures;
8. the financial institution's liability to the consumer; and
9. the circumstances under which the financial institution will disclose information about the consumer's account to third persons.

Documentation of Transfers

For each transfer initiated from a terminal, the financial institution must make available to the consumer documentation setting forth:

1. the amount and date of the transfer;
2. the type of transfer;
3. the identity of the consumer's account;
4. the identity of the third party to whom or from whom the transfer was made; and
5. the location or identity of the terminal involved.

This information is a substitute for the return of cancelled checks. It is important not only for the protection of the consumer, but also as a basis for activating the consumer's duty to report unauthorized transfers.

Preauthorized Transfers

These transfers may be authorized by a consumer only in writing. A stop payment on such transfers may be either written or oral and may be given at any time up to three business days prior to the scheduled date of the transfer, but the financial institution may require a written confirmation of an oral order within fourteen days after it is made. This provision is quite different than the Article 4 provision relating to checks. The time period required to allow the financial institution to act is stated, rather than resting on a determination of what constitutes a reasonable time.

Error Resolution

In order to activate the liability of the financial institution for unauthorized transfers, the consumer must report the error to the institution within sixty days of receiving notification of the transfer. This report may be either written or oral, and it must: inform the institution of the consumer's account number, or enable the institution to determine it; indicate the consumer's belief that an error has occurred; and set forth the reasons for this belief. Following this report, the financial institution is under a duty to investigate and report the results of its investigation to the consumer within ten days. If the institution determines that an error has been made, it must correct the error within one business day of that determination. In lieu of these time limits, the institution, within ten days, may recredit the consumer's account and investigate. As long as the consumer has use of the money recredited, the institution may extend its investigation up to forty-five days after receipt of the notice of error. If the institution determines that no error was made, it must notify the consumer within three business days of the determination, and provide copies of any documentation it relied on in reaching its conclusion. Any violation of the provisions of the act subject the financial institution to treble damages.

Consumer Liability

In order for a consumer to be liable on an unauthorized transfer, it must have been effected by the use of an accepted card or other means of access (that is, not by a mechanical or an electrical problem or by tampering) and the financial institution must have provided a means of identifying the intended user of the card (for example, a photograph or a secret identification number). The consumer's liability is limited to the lesser of $50 or the amount of money or value of property or services obtained by the transaction.

In order to preserve the limitation on the dollar amount of liability, the consumer is under a duty to report any errors to the institution as required above (the sixty-day requirement) and to report the loss or theft of his or her card within two business days of discovering the loss or theft. Failure to comply discharges the financial institution's liability to reimburse to the extent of the loss it suffers because of the failure, but the discharge is limited to the lesser of $50 or the amount of the loss. The burden of proving that a transfer was authorized, and that the consumer is not entitled to the ordinary limitations on his or her liability, rests with the financial institution.

Other Liability of Financial Institutions

The financial institution is liable to the consumer for all damages proximately caused by the institu-

tion's improper handling of transfers. The improper acts are specified as unexcused failure to make a transfer in the correct amount in a timely fashion, failure to make a transfer because of insufficient funds if the shortfall was caused by the institution's failure to credit properly a deposit to the consumer's account, and the institution's failure to stop payment as instructed by the consumer. Specifically excluded as bases of liability are acts of God and technical malfunctions known to the consumer at the time he attempted a transfer or at the time a preauthorized transfer was scheduled to occur.

Issuance of Means of Access

The Electronic Fund Transfers Act forbids a financial institution from issuing cards or other means of access to permit electronic fund transfers except on request (not unsolicited) or as a renewal. A general exception is provided for cards and other means of access that are sent unsolicited, but are not validated for use until validation is requested.

Compulsory Use

The act forbids placing a condition on the extension of credit such that repayment must be by means of electronic fund transfers. It also forbids the conditioning of employment or the receipt of a government benefit on the consumer's establishing an account with a particular financial institution for the receipt of transfers.

Liability for Failure to Comply

Failure to comply with the provisions of the act subjects the non-complying party to both civil and criminal liability. The civil liability includes provision for costs of the action and a reasonable attorney's fee.

OGNIBENE v. CITIBANK, N.A.
112 Misc.2d 219, 446 N.Y.S.2d 845 (1981)

This was an action by Frederick P. Ognibene (Plaintiff) against Citibank, N.A. (Defendant) in the Small Claims Part of the Civil Court of New York City (a trial court). Plaintiff sought to recover $400 withdrawn from his account by an alleged unauthorized person by use of an electronic teller machine. The method by which the withdrawal was effected is set out in the opinion of the court.

The court granted judgment for Plaintiff in the amount of $400, as requested.

THORPE, Mara T., Judge.

Plaintiff seeks to recover $400.00 withdrawn from his account at the defendant bank by an unauthorized person using an automated teller machine. The court has concluded that plaintiff was the victim of a scam which defendant has been aware for some time.

Defendant's witness, an assistant manager of one of its branches, described how the scam works: A customer enters the automated teller machine (ATM) area for the purpose of using a machine for the transaction of business with the bank. At the time that he enters, a person is using the customer service telephone located between the two automated teller machines and appears to be telling customer service that one of the machines is malfunctioning. This person is the perpetrator of the scam and his conversation with customer service is only simulated. He observes the customer press his personal identification code into one of the two machines. Having learned the code, the perpetrator then tells the customer that customer service has advised him to ask the customer to insert his Citicard into the allegedly malfunctioning machine to check whether it will work with a card other than the perpetrator's. When a good samaritan customer accedes to the request, the other machine is activated. The perpetrator then presses a code into the machine, which the customer does not realize is his own code which the perpetrator has just observed. After continuing the simulated conversation on the telephone, the perpetrator advises the customer that customer service has asked if he would try his Citicard in the allegedly malfunctioning machine once more. A second insertion of the cards permits cash to be released by the machine, and if the customer does as requested, the thief has effectuated a cash withdrawal from the unwary customer's account. . . .

The EFT Act places various limits on a consumer's liability for electronic fund transfers from his account if they are "unauthorized." Insofar as is relevant here, a transfer is "unauthorized" if 1) it is initiated by a person other than the consumer and without actual authority to initiate such transfer, 2) the consumer receives no benefit from it, and 3) the consumer did not furnish such person "with the card, code or other means of access" to his account. 15 U.S.C.A. 1963a(11).

In an action involving a consumer's liability for an electronic fund transfer, such as the one at bar, the burden of going forward to show an "unauthorized" transfer from his account is on the consumer. The EFT Act places upon the bank, however, the burden of proof of any consumer liability for the transfer. 15 U.S.C.A. 1963g(b). To establish full liability on the part of the consumer, the bank must prove that the transfer was authorized. To be entitled to even the limited liability imposed by the statute on the consumer, the bank must prove that certain conditions of consumer liability, set forth in 15 U.S.C.A. 1963g(a) have been met and that certain disclosures mandated by 15 U.S.C.A. 1963c(a)(1) and (2) have been made. Id.

Plaintiff herein met his burden of going forward. He did not initiate the withdrawals in question, did not authorize the person in the ATM area to make them, and did not benefit from them.

However, defendant's position is, in essence, that although plaintiff was duped, the bank's burden of proof on the issue of authorization has been met by plaintiff's testimony that he permitted his card to be used in the adjoining machine by the other person. The court does not agree.

The EFT Act requires that the consumer have furnished to a person initiating the transfer the "card, code, or other means of access" to his account to be ineligible for the limitations on liability afforded by the Act when transfers are "unauthorized." The evidence establishes that in order to obtain access to an account via an automated teller machine, both the card and the personal identification code must be used. Thus, by merely giving his card to the person initiating the transfer, a consumer does not furnish the "means of access" to his account. To do so, he would have to furnish the personal identification code as well. See 12 C.F.R. 205.2(a)(1), the regulation promulgated under the EFT Act which defines "access device" as "a card, code or other means of access to [an] . . . account *or any combination thereof.* (emphasis added).

The court finds that plaintiff did not furnish his personal identification code to the person intiating the $400.00 transfer within the meaning of the EFT act. There is no evidence that he deliberately or even negligently did so. On the contrary, the unauthorized person was able to obtain the code because of defendant's own negligence. Since the bank had knowledge of the scam and its operational details (including the central role of the customer service telephone), it was negligent in failing to provide plaintiff-customer with information sufficient to alert him to the danger when he found himself in the position of a potential victim. . . .

Since the bank established the electronic fund transfer service and has the ability to tighten its security characteristics, the responsibility for the fact that plaintiff's code, one of the two necessary components of the "access device" or "means of access" to his account, was observed and utilized as it was must rest with the bank.

Questions

1. After all is said and done and the court has concluded its legal analysis, doesn't common sense tell us that the banks want customers to use these machines and, therefore, should bear the basic risks that they will be misused?

2. Having said that, however, aren't there circumstances in which the customer should bear the risk of loss through the machine? What are they and what standard of care should be imposed on the customer?

SUMMARY

When a depositor opens a checking account with a bank, two relationships are formed—debtor/creditor and principal/agent. The bank, as agent of the depositor, is obligated to honor all lawful orders (checks) sent to it by the depositor as long as they are presented within six months of the date of issue. Thereafter, the bank *may* honor them if it wishes, and if it does so in good faith.

The bank also is obligated to honor all stop-payment orders issued by its depositor. Failure to do so will result in the bank's taking only such rights as were possessed by the person from whom it took the check, and the bank will be liable to the depositor for any damages caused by cashing the check. Stop-payment orders are effective for fourteen days if oral and six months if written.

A bank is liable for cashing forged checks if the depositor gives proper notice. After the forgery first is made available to the depositor, the notice must be given within one year for a forgery on the face of the check and within three years for a forged indorsement. If notice is not given within the required time, the bank's liability ceases. Additionally, there is a fourteen-day rule governing series forgeries.

In recent years banks have added a new service—automated teller machines (ATMs). The rights and duties of the bank and the depositor concerning the use of ATMs are governed principally by federal law—the Electronic Fund Transfers Act.

KEY TERMS AND CONCEPTS

stop-payment order
series of forgeries
Electronic Fund Transfers Act

PROBLEMS

1. Within what period of time after a stop-payment order is given to a bank should the bank be prepared to honor it?

2. Granit Equipment company issued a written stop-payment order on one of its checks in October 1968, and it was effective for six months. Granit did not renew the order, and in November 1969 the bank cashed the check. Is Granit entitled to have the funds returned to its account because of the age of the check and the bank's knowledge of the stop-payment order?

3. Skov issued a check to Nielson. Although Skov's account was sufficient to cover the check, the check was dishonored by the bank due to a mixup in account numbers. As a result of the dishonor, Nielson refused to do any more business with Skov. Skov sued the bank for damages for wrongful dishonor. Is the bank liable?

4. Franklin National Bank certified a check in the amount of $2000, at the request of the drawer. Thereafter, it was altered to read $2900. To what extent is the bank liable to a holder in due course of the altered instrument?

5. Reinhard purchased a cashier's check from the Marine Midland Bank and indorsed it to Moon Over The Mountain, Ltd. in payment for goods. Moon Over The Mountain deposited the check in it's account, but it was returned stamped "Payment Stopped." The payment had been stopped by Marine Midland at the request of Reinhard. Is Moon Over The Mountain entitled to payment of the check?

6. Over a period of seven years, a secretary for Kidwell Construction Co. forged checks on the company account. When this finally was discovered by Kidwell's treasurer, Kidwell demanded that the bank return to its account the total amount of the forgeries. The bank contended it was not liable because Kidwell should have discovered the forgeries earlier. What should be the result?

7. Thomas purchased four area rugs from Imports Unlimited at $500 each. When the rugs were delivered, Thomas gave Imports a check for $2000. Upon unpacking the box, Thomas found that one of the rugs was missing and called Imports. The manager of Imports claimed four rugs had been shipped and refused to aid Thomas fur-

ther. Thomas then stopped payment on the check, but a day and a half later the bank cashed it anyway. What are the rights of Thomas and the bank?

8.   During a period of eleven months, an employee of Zenith Syndicate forged on its account eighteen checks totalling $22,000. When Zenith discovered the forgeries, it notified the bank and demanded the bank return the $22,000 to it's account. To what extent is the bank liable?

9.   Ulibarri sold goods to Jacobson in the amount of $1783. When Jacobson tendered his check for that amount, Ulibarri called the drawee bank to inquire, and an officer of the bank said the check was "OK." Ulibarri deposited the check, and in a few days it was returned stamped "No Account." Ulibarri contends the bank should be liable to her for the amount of the check. Is Ulibarri correct?

10.   Rock Island Auction Sales, Inc. sold cattle to the Empire Packing Co, Inc. and received Empire's check in the amount of $14,706.90, dated September 24, 1962. The check was deposited the same day. The check reached the payor bank on September 27. At that time, Empire did not have sufficient funds to cover it. The bank held the check until October 2 in reliance on Empire's promise to make it good. The bank then returned the check, marked "NSF" (Not Sufficient Funds), and it was received by Rock Island on October 4. From October 4 through November 7, the bank requested that Rock Island send the check through again, which Rock Island refused to do. The bank was negotiating with Empire to deposit enough to cover the check. Finally, on November 7, Empire was adjudicated bankrupt. Is the bank liable to Rock Island for the amount of the check?

PART V

Credit and

Secured

Transactions

The importance of credit in modern business transactions can hardly be overstated. Literally billions of dollars of credit are extended each year by sellers and third-party lenders. Without credit, a great percentage of all real estate transactions might never have been negotiated, and sales of even ordinary consumer goods would be greatly hampered. It is the purpose of this part of the book to discuss various methods of securing creditors' rights to payment of credit obligations. Chapter 21 addresses security devices as they relate to personal property, and Chapter 22 discusses security interests in real property. Chapter 23 presents an alternative to security interests in property—suretyship contracts, or guarantees of payment made by third persons who are not otherwise parties to the transaction between the creditor and the debtor. Finally, the law of bankruptcy is considered in Chapter 24.

Chapter | 21

Security Interests in Personal Property

OUTLINE

INTRODUCTION

Whenever credit is extended, certain rights arise. These rights may be protected by a creditor's obtaining a specific **security interest,** which is a creditor's interest in property belonging to the debtor, taken by the creditor to secure performance of the debtor's obligation. It also commonly is referred to as a **lien.** That security interest may be further strengthened by perfecting it. (A security interest is perfected when the creditor has followed legal procedures required to obtain a right in a debtor's property that is protected against the claims of other creditors.) As will become obvious, an unperfected security interest is of little value in the event of the debtor's dishonesty or insolvency. Therefore, knowledge of the manner of creating and perfecting security interests may be as important to a businessperson as knowledge of the product or the ability to make a sale.

THE SCOPE OF UNIFORM COMMERCIAL CODE ARTICLE 9

The law governing security interests in personal property is found primarily in Article 9 of the Uniform Commercial Code. Generally, Article 9 applies to every transaction intended to create a security interest in personal property or fixtures, and also to any sale of accounts or chattel paper. Prior to the adoption of Article 9, the law was fragmented somewhat, treating separately **pledges** (if the creditor has possession of the debtor's property as security for the debt), assignments, **chattel** (personal property) **mortgages,** chattel trusts, trust deeds, factors' liens, equipment trusts, **conditional sales contracts** (title to the property transfers to the buyer when he fully performs his obligation), trust receipts, other liens and title-retention contracts, and leases and consignments intended as security. All of these now are treated as "security transactions" under Article 9. The UCC, therefore, takes what may be called a "unitary approach" to security transactions.

Transactions Excluded

Article 9 is intended to cover only private, consensual security interests in personal property and fixtures that are given in the ordinary course of business. Therefore, several types of transactions are excluded from coverage by Section 9-104, including:

1. Security interests governed by any *statute of the United States* to the extent that the statute covers the rights and obligations in question. This is in recognition of the supremacy of federal law over state law in this area (UCC Section 9-104(a)).
2. *Nonconsensual liens,* such as a landlord's lien, a mechanic's or materialman's lien for services or materials, or any other statutory lien. Article 9 is intended to cover only consensual liens (UCC Section 9-104 (b), (c)).

3. Transactions *not concerning financing in the ordinary course of business,* for example: assignments of wage claims; assignments in connection with the sale of a business, or for collection, or as an assignment of the whole contract, or in satisfaction of a preexisting debt; assignments of judgment claims; assignments of rights of set-off; or assignments of rights under a tort claim. These are excluded as not being *ordinary* transactions in commercial financing (UCC Section 9-104 (d),(f),(h),(i),(k)).
4. Certain commercial financing *transactions that are covered adequately by other law,* such as assignments of insurance claims (not proceeds) and the transfer of rights in any deposit account (UCC Section 9-104 (g),(i)).
5. Transfers *by a government,* or governmental agency or subdivision. Article 9 is intended to cover only *private* transfers (UCC Section 9-104(e)).
6. Transfers of liens or security interests in *real estate* (except fixtures), including leases and rents. Article 9 is intended to cover only transactions involving personal property and fixtures (UCC Section 9-104(j)).

Some of these excluded categories are modified by UCC Sections 9-306 (proceeds), 9-310 (priority of certain liens), and 9-312 (priority of conflicting liens). In addition, the coverage of Article 9 may be subject to modification by local or state law. Section 9-203(4) allows each state to provide that, in the case of a conflict between Article 9 and certain prescribed local or state laws—such as local statutes regulating small loans, retail installment contracts, *"and the like"* (for example, the Uniform Consumer Credit Code)—the latter will govern.

"Purchase Money" Security Interests

Perhaps the most common type of security transaction under Article 9 is the **purchase money security interest.** This is the security interest a seller retains, or a right held by a lender who has lent money used to purchase goods, in goods sold. Upon the purchaser's default, the seller or lender is entitled to take the goods. This security interest is similar in effect to the purchase of real estate on a land contract or with a mortgage. It differs, however, from transactions involving **collateral** (a security interest in property other than the goods sold). Purchase money security interests are given special priority relative to other security interests, a subject discussed later in this chapter.

Leases

There is considerable confusion concerning whether leases are included under Article 9. They are if intended as security, but not if they simply are general leases. Section 1-201(37) provides that each lease must be considered according to its own circumstances. The inclusion of an option to purchase does not of itself make a lease one that is intended as security, but if at the end of a lease the lessee is entitled to become the owner of the property for no additional consideration, or for only nominal consideration, the lease is one for security.

Consignments

Article 9 applies to **consignments** intended as security, but not to "true" consignments. The two are distinguished by examining the obligations of the consignee. In a "true" consignment, the consignee receives the goods to hold for sale, and any unsold goods are returned to the consignor. Consignments are common in the greeting-card industry. A gift shop may have a large display of cards. The shop has not purchased the cards from the manufacturer. Rather, it pays for those sold, retaining part of the price, and returns any unsold cards to the manufacturer. If the consignee is required to purchase goods not sold, the consignment is one for security. Section 1-201(37) provides that this determination is not affected by the

fact that the consignor retains title to the goods during the consignment period.

Security Interests under Article 2

In addition to security interests under Article 9, the UCC grants security interests under Article 2. Those security interests include, among others: the right of a shipper, shipping "under reservation of title," to exercise control over goods while in transit (UCC Section 2-505); the rights of a shipper to stop goods in transit and to withhold delivery (UCC Section 2-703 and 2-705); the rights of a financing agency or "person in the position of a seller" to exercise the rights of the seller to go against the goods (UCC Section 2-506 and 2-707); and the rights of a buyer, in goods in his possession or control, to secure repayment of expenses attendant to his rightful rejection of goods or revocation of his acceptance (UCC Section 2-711(3)).

PROPERTY THAT MAY BE THE SUBJECT OF A SECURITY INTEREST

A security interest may be taken in specific tangible or intangible property. In addition to the specific security interest, a creditor also may extend the security interest to property the debtor may acquire in the future, and to proceeds from the sale of any property that is subject to the security interest. The interest also may secure any future credit extended by the creditor to the debtor.

Tangible Property

This category includes *goods*, defined in Section 2-105 as including all things movable at the time of identification to the contract, except purchase price money, investment securities, and **things in action** (money due a person, such as accounts receivable), plus some items specifically designated as goods in Section 2-107. The broad term *goods* then may be subdivided into five recognized subcategories: (1) **consumer goods,** those purchased or used primarily for personal, household, or family purposes; (2) **equipment,** goods held primarily for business purposes; (3) **inventory,** goods held for sale or lease or to be furnished in performing business services; (4) **fixtures,** goods attached to real estate that become part of it, which may be treated as either real or personal property depending on circumstances; and (5) **farm products,** including goods such as crops, livestock, and personal property used or produced in farming operations.

Intangible Property

This category includes personal property having no physical existence. These are naked rights. The six subcategories of **intangible property** recognized by Article 9 are: (1) *debt instruments*, which are those generally involved under Article 3—bills of exchange (checks and drafts) and notes (certificates of deposit and other promissory notes); (2) *investment securities*, specifically covered under Article 8, including stocks and bonds; (3) *documents of title* such as warehouse receipts, bills of lading, dock warrants, and dock receipts; (4) *accounts receivable* (a type of "thing in action"), which represent a right to receive payment for goods or services not evidenced by chattel paper or debt instruments—often referred to as "open account"; (5) *chattel paper*, which includes instruments evidencing both an obligation to pay money and security in specific goods, such as a conditional sales contract; and (6) *general intangibles* as defined in Section 9-106, including other intangible property such as patents, copyrights, and franchises.

The Floating Lien

The **floating lien** is so called because it does not simply remain attached to a single piece of property at a fixed location, but adjusts to accommodate any of three common changes—**after-acquired property** (property the debtor purchases after giving the security interest), **future advances** (additional credit given to the debtor by the creditor after the security interest was taken), and the conversion of the secured property to proceeds (for example, the sale of an automobile for cash).

In their security agreement, the parties may provide that the subject property will secure not only the original obligation, but any future obligations that become owed by the debtor to the secured party while the security agreement is in effect. This clause is particularly common in contracts that involve lending in a series of installments and in amounts to be determined in the future. Also, the parties may provide that in addition to the subject property, any other property acquired by the debtor in the future also will be subject to the security interest created by the agreement. For example, ABC Bank lends Adams $100,000 to purchase inventory. The loan will be secured not only by the first inventory purchased, or even by the first $100,000 of inventory, but by all inventory held by Adams until the loan is repaid in full. These are examples of the first two types of changes, previously noted, that are affected by floating liens, and they arise only if agreed to by the parties. Consider the following case involving a security agreement with a broad, general, after-acquired property clause.

NATIONAL CASH REGISTER COMPANY v. FIRESTONE & CO.
346 Mass. 255, 191 N.E.2d 471 (1968)

This was an action by National Cash Register Company (Plaintiff/Appellee) against Firestone & Co. (Defendant/Appellant) for conversion (theft) of a cash register.

Plaintiff sold a cash register to Carroll on a conditional sales contract. Thereafter, and prior to delivery of the cash register, Defendant made a loan to Carroll who conveyed certain property to Defendant as collateral under a security agreement. Defendant filed a financing statement with the town clerk on November 18, 1960, and with the secretary of state on November 22, 1960. Plaintiff delivered the cash register between November 19 and November 23. A new conditional contract superceding the previous one, covering the cash register, was entered into between Plaintiff and Carroll on November 25, and a financing statement was filed with the town clerk on December 20 and with the secretary of state on December 21 by Plaintiff. Carroll defaulted on the loan extended by Defendant, and Defendant took possession of the cash register in December. He sold it at auction in January with notice of Plaintiff's claim.

Defendant's security agreement provided that it covered equipment acquired by Carroll after the date of the agreement, but made no specific mention of the cash register among the items specified. Plaintiff's financing statement gave the same detailed description of the items but also did not mention the cash register, and made no mention of property to be acquired later.

The trial court found for Plaintiff and the appellate division agreed. Defendant appealed to the Supreme Judicial Court. Reversed.

WILKINS, Chief Justice.

Under the Uniform Commercial Code, . . . after-acquired property, such as this cash register, might become subject to the defendant's security agreement when delivered, Section 9-204(3); and likewise its delivery under a conditional sale agreement with retention of title in the plaintiff would not, in and of itself, affect the rights of the defendant. . . . Section 9-202. Although the plaintiff could have completely protected itself by perfecting its interest before or within ten days after delivery of the cash register to Carroll, it did not try to do so until more than ten days after delivery. Thus the principal issue is whether the defendant's earlier security interest effectively covers the cash register. . . .

In Section 9-110, it is provided: "For the purposes of this Article any description of personal property or real estate is sufficient whether or not it is specific if it reasonably identifies what is described." In Section 9-203 it is provided: (1) ". . . a security interest is not enforceable against the debtor or third parties unless . . . (b) the debtor has signed a security agreement which contains a description of the collateral. . . ."

Contrary to the plaintiff's contention, we are of opinion that the security agreement is broad enough to include the cash register, which concededly did not have to be specifically described. The agreement covers "All contents of luncheonette including equipment such as," which we think covers all those contents and does not mean "equipment, to wit." There is a reference to "all property and articles now, and which may hereafter be, used . . . with, [or] added . . . to . . . any of the foregoing described property." We infer that the cash register was used with some of the other equipment even though the case stated does not expressly state that the luncheonette was operated. . . .

We now come to the question whether the defendant's financing statement should have mentioned property to be acquired thereafter before a security interest in the cash register could attach. . . . Section 9-402(1), reads in part: "A financing statement is sufficient if it is signed by the debtor and the secured party, gives an address of the secured party from which information concerning the security interest may be obtained, gives a mailing address of the debtor and contains a statement indicating the types, or describing the items, of collateral."

In the official comment to this section appears the following: "2. This Section adopts the system of 'notice filing' which has proved successful under the Uniform Trust Receipts Act. What is required to be filed is not, as under chattel mortgage and conditional sales acts, the security agreement itself, but only a simple notice which may be filed before the security interest attaches or thereafter. The notice itself indicates merely that the secured party who has filed may have a security interest in the collateral described. Further inquiry from the parties concerned will be necessary to disclose the complete state of affairs. . . .

The framers of the Uniform Commercial Code, by adopting the "notice filing" system, had the purpose to recommend a method of protecting security interests which at the same time would give subsequent potential creditors and other interested persons information and procedures adequate to enable the ascertainment of the facts they needed to know. In this respect the completed Code reflects a decision of policy reached after several years' study and discussion by experts. We conceive our duty to be the making of an interpretation which will carry out the intention of the framers of uniform legislation which already has been enacted in twenty-five States. That the result of their policy decision may be asserted to favor certain types of creditors as against others or that a different policy could have been decided upon is quite beside the point.

Questions

1.   What are the competing arguments for requiring or not requiring the notice to specify after-acquired property?

2.   How could the plaintiff have protected itself?

The third type of change affecting floating liens arises automatically under Section 9-203(3), unless the parties agree to the contrary. Upon the sale of property that is the subject of a security agreement, or upon the collection of insurance because of its injury or loss, the secured party automatically has a substituted security interest in the proceeds. This is not a general security interest in the money of the debtor, but only in the portion directly traceable to the subject property. If the proceeds are mixed with other money of the debtor, the courts usually consider it traceable under a "FIFO" (first in, first out) method. For example, if $2000 of proceeds were mixed in an account having a balance of $10,000 immediately before the deposits, and then $11,000 was expended from the account, the courts would consider the remaining $1000 balance to be proceeds. Of course, the parties may agree to the contrary.

CREATION OF SECURITY INTERESTS

The purpose of a security interest is to create an interest in property that is enforceable by a creditor against the debtor, other creditors of the debtor, and third parties who may purchase the property subject to the security interest. The extent to which this purpose is achieved depends on both the circumstances and the degree of compliance with the requirements of Article 9. Such an interest typically is created in two steps, attachment and perfection.

Attachment

When a valid security interest is created, as between a creditor and a debtor, the security interest is said to attach to the subject property, which is called the *collateral*. Under Section 9-203, **attachment** occurs (1) when either the creditor takes possession of the collateral pursuant to an oral or written agreement or the parties have executed a sufficient writing; (2) value thereby has been paid to the debtor; and (3) the debtor thus has rights in the collateral.

The term *possession* means that the property is in either the actual or constructive possession of the secured party, and out of the debtor's possession or control. If attachment depends on a written security agreement, the writing must contain a description of the collateral and be signed by the debtor. In addition, if the collateral is crops (either growing or to be grown) or timber to be cut, the writing also must contain a description of the land involved. The following case illustrates these two prerequisites.

M. RUTKIN ELECTRIC SUPPLY CO., INC. v. BURDETTE ELECTRIC, INC.
98 N.J.Super. 378, 237 A.2d 500 (1967)

This opinion involves a hearing on a motion to declare an assignment void. The motion was made by a receiver in bankruptcy for Burdette Electric, Inc. (Defendant) in an action brought by M. Rutkin Electric Supply Co., Inc. (Plaintiff).

Defendant held an account receivable owed by B. J. Builders, Inc. This account was allegedly assigned by Defendant to Milton Rabin as security for a loan Rabin made to Defendant. A financing statement signed by Rabin and Defendant was filed properly, but Rabin could not produce a written security agreement.

The court ordered that the alleged assignment was void.

MINTZ, J.S.C.

N.J.S.A. 12A:9-204(1) provides in part:

> (1) A security interest cannot attach until there is agreement . . . that it attach and value is given and the debtor has rights in the collateral. . . .

The debtor, Burdette Electric, had rights in the collateral, and Rabin, the alleged secured party advanced value. But as noted earlier, Rabin has failed to produce a written security agreement to document his acquisition of a security interest in the B. J. Builders account receivable. Thus Rabin's claim falls unless he can prove the existence of some form of enforceable "agreement" which provides that his security interest in the account receivable be created.

N.J.S.A. 12A:1-201(3) defines "agreement" as:

> . . . the bargain of the parties in fact. . . . Whether an agreement has legal consequences is determined by the provisions of this Act, if applicable. . . .

New Jersey Study Comment, Note 2, to N.J.S.A. 12A:9-204 indicates that in order to ascertain whether an "agreement" to attach a security interest has legal sufficiency, N.J.S.A. 12A:9-203(1), chapter 9's statute of frauds must also be considered. The Study Comment reads:

> This requirement that there must be an agreement must be read not only in connection with Section 1-201(3), but also in connection with Section 9-203 which requires that the security agreement be written (see, Comments, Section 9-203) unless the collateral is in the possession of the secured party. So much of Section 9-204(1) as requires an 'agreement' expressing an intent that a secured interest be created makes no change in New Jersey law. . . . (at p. 383)

Accordingly, in order for an "agreement" to arise, signifying the creation of an enforceable security interest, either the collateral must be in the possession of the secured party or the debtor has signed a security agreement which contains a description of the collateral. N.J.S.A. 12A:9-203(1). An account receivable is an intangible and as such cannot be "possessed" within the meaning of the Code. . . .

Hence, "possession" is unavailable to Rabin as a means of signifying an agreement with the insolvent that the security interest attach. [Under New Jersey Statute of Frauds, a] security interest in an account receivable must be evidenced by a security agreement signed by the debtor and containing a description of the collateral. . . . In the instant situation, since Rabin can proffer no writing signed by the debtor giving, even sketchily, the terms of the security agreement, it is unenforceable. The financing statement signed by the parties and duly filed with the Secretary of State is no substitute for a security agreement. It alone did not create a security interest. It was but notice that one was claimed.

Questions

1. What are the policy reasons for the requirement of either possession or a writing?
2. What happens to a creditor when no attachment occurs?

Value is defined in Section 1-201(44), and is similar to the concept of "consideration" under the law of contracts. In addition, however, value may be constituted by (1) a binding commitment to extend credit, or its extension; (2) receipt of the instrument as security for, or in partial or complete discharge of, a pre-existing obligation; or (3) accepting delivery pursuant to a pre-existing contract for purchase.

The third requirement—"the debtor has rights in the collateral"—serves only to remind the secured party that a creditor cannot legally convey what he does not own. The debtor's "rights" need not be full title, however; *any* right is sufficient.

Agreement not to Assert Defenses

Section 9-206 allows a purchaser to agree in a security agreement that he will not assert against an assignee any defenses he may have against the seller (or a lessee may agree as to defenses against the lessor). The purpose is to make it easier for a seller to assign an installment-sale contract. This type of agreement encourages a financial institution to purchase such a contract, and the institution probably will pay a higher percentage of its face value to the seller (apply a lower discount rate). The waiver of defenses, of course, is to the buyer's disadvantage, and is not permitted without some limitations.

First, if the contract involves consumer goods, the clause is permitted only in the absence of any statute or court decision to the contrary. During the late 1960s and 1970s many states enacted statutes protecting consumers' rights. For example, the Commissioners on Uniform State Laws offered the Uniform Consumer Credit Code (UCCC) to the states for adoption, although it was adopted by only a few. Among other things, the UCCC sought to eliminate waivers of defenses, even to the extent of altering the "holder in due course" doctrine applied to commercial paper (Article 3 of the UCC). The Federal Trade Commission (FTC) promulgated a rule requiring that a seller, on every installment-sale contract involving consumer goods, include a bold-type notice that any assignee of the contract was subject to all defenses of the buyer against the seller. This, of course, would negate any "waiver of defenses" clause in the contract. The seller's failure to comply, however, would not help the buyer who had signed a waiver, but the seller would be subject to a fine of up to $10,000 for an unfair trade practice.

Second, the defenses waived are only those not available against a holder in due course under Article 3; the most important of these are fraud in the inducement, failure of consideration, and breach of warranty. Note that these are the defenses used most frequently by purchasers of defective or inadequate goods and in circumstances of nondelivery.

Finally, in any contract involving goods, when the seller retains a purchase money interest in the goods, the provisions of Article 2 apply—specifically those governing disclaimer, limitation, and modification of warranties. These provisions are discussed more fully in Chapter 16.

The following case considers the affect of a general waiver clause.

ROOT v. JOHN DEERE COMPANY OF INDIANAPOLIS, INC.
413 S.W.2d 901 (Ky. 1967)

This was an action by John Deere Company of Indianapolis, Inc. (Plaintiff/Appellee) against Lester C. Root (Defendant/Appellant) to collect the balance due on a note.

Defendant purchased a tractor from Anderson Sales and Service and gave a note to secure payment of approximately $10,000. The note included a clause providing that Buyer (Defendant Root) would settle any defenses with Seller (Anderson) and would not assert any in defense to payment of the note. Anderson assigned the note to Plaintiff. Defendant defaulted on payment and Plaintiff repossessed the tractor, sold it, and sued for a deficiency. Defendant wished to assert two defenses to payment of the note.

Plaintiff moved for, and was granted, summary judgment and Defendant appealed. Affirmed.

STEINFELD, Judge.

Root interposed two defenses. He claimed that Anderson Sales and Service was an indispensable party pursuant to CR 19.01 and that the failure to join Anderson was fatal. The trial court overruled a motion to dismiss. This ruling was correct. CR 19.01 does not apply. Deere, the assignee was the real party in interest; therefore, it could sue in its own name. CR 17.0. Joining the assignor was unnecessary. 6 Kentucky Practice, Clay, page 293.

Secondly, Root argues that the following statement in the agreement is significant:

I (We) acknowledge receipt of the items sold hereunder and consent to the warranty agreement on the reverse side hereof, which is expressly made a part hereof.

He claims that Deere became obligated to fulfill the provisions of the warranty and that the tractor was defective. The trial court was not in error in entering the summary judgment for there is no merit in this defense. The latter quotation obviously is an agreement by Root and not Deere. Furthermore, Root agreed to seek redress from the SELLER for any breach of warranty and if the note was assigned not to "use any such claim as a defense against any effort by the holder to enforce this instrument."

Such an agreement is authorized by KRS 355.9-206(1), a provision of the Uniform Commercial Code. Similar provisions have been approved in Hieb Sand and Gravel, Inc. v. Universal C.I.T. Credit Corp. . . . and Morgan v. John Deere Company of Indianapolis, Inc. . . .

The statement that Root would NOT use such claim against the holder is a form of negative covenant and is valid.

Questions

1. Why should a buyer like Root agree not to assert any defense to payment of the note?

2. What are the arguments for and against the court's enforcing such an agreement?

Security interests are typically created in two steps

ATTACHMENT

The security interest is attached to the subject property (the collateral) when a valid security is created.

Attachment occurs when:
1. the creditor takes possession of the collateral or with the execution of sufficient writing,
2. value has been paid to the debtor, and
3. the debtor has rights in the collateral.

and

PERFECTION

Perfection extends the creditor's rights with regard to other creditors of the debtor and purchasers of the collateral.

Three methods of perfection are:
1. filing of a notice on public record,
2. possession of the collateral by the creditor, and
3. automatic perfection.

PERFECTION OF SECURITY INTERESTS

Although attachment of a security interest gives the secured party enforceable rights as between herself and the debtor, **perfection** is necessary to extend her rights as to other creditors of the debtor and to purchasers of the collateral. The method of perfection used may depend on the nature of the subject goods and the circumstances. Generally, there are three methods: *filing* of a notice on public record, *possession* of the collateral by the secured party or someone on her behalf, and *automatic perfection*.

Filing

The most common method of perfecting a security interest is by filing a **financing statement.** However, this requires compliance with the statutory procedures provided for in Part 4 of Article 9. Any failure in meeting these requirements may result in a failure to perfect as against other creditors of the debtor or good-faith purchasers of the collateral.

The first step toward proper filing is to obtain a financing statement, although any writing, including the contract of sale or a copy of the security agreement, is sufficient. All that is required is that the writing contain certain elements specified by Section 9-402. The writing must: (1) give the names of the parties; (2) provide the address of the secured party, from which information concerning the security interest may be obtained; (3) give the mailing address of the debtor; (4) indicate the types of collateral or describe the items; and (5) be signed by the debtor. In addition, if it covers crops growing or to be grown, the statement must contain (6) a description of the real estate concerned. Finally, a financing statement covering (a) timber to be cut, or minerals, or the like (including gas and oil), or (b) accounts subject to Section 9-103(S), or (c) a financing statement filed as a fixture filing (filed in the real estate

records in the county where the fixture is located) must show that it covers collateral of this type, recite that it is filed in the real estate records, and contain a sufficient description of the real estate concerned.

A financing statement is effective even if it contains minor errors. The critical question is whether the statement gives adequate notice of the security interest. For example, the name of the debtor may be misspelled as long as the debtor is reasonably identifiable. However, if the debtor changes her name (for example, into a corporation), or the identity of the debtor otherwise is changed so that it becomes seriously misleading, the statement will not perfect a security interest in collateral acquired more than four months after the change. In any event, a financing statement may be amended as necessary. Doing so, however, does not change the period during which the financing statement will be effective.

Financing statements remain in force for five years from the date of filing, except in the case of a mortgage that is effective as a fixture filing. These are operative until released and terminated of record. The effectiveness of an ordinary financing statement may be continued by filing a **continuation statement** within six months prior to the expiration of the previous financing or continuation statement. If a statement is allowed to lapse, it becomes ineffective both as against a purchaser or lien creditor who became so before the lapse, and as against those who became so during the lapse period.

When the obligations of the debtor have been performed, it is expected that the secured party will file a **termination statement;** in the case of a security interest in fixtures perfected by the filing of a mortgage, this can be done by filing a proper release. In the case of consumer goods, this must be done either within one month after termination or within ten days following a written demand by the debtor, whichever is earlier. In all other cases, there is no duty to file a termination statement or release, but one must be sent to the debtor within ten days following termination after the necessary written demand by the debtor. Failure to do so renders the secured party liable to the debtor for $100 plus any loss caused to the debtor by the failure to comply.

The proper place of filing varies from state to state and also according to the collateral involved and the use for which the debtor holds it. Generally speaking, financing statements involving consumer goods, equipment, and inventory must be filed in the office of the secretary of state. Those involving fixtures, crops, timber to be cut, material, and the like—because they relate in some way to real estate—ordinarily must be filed in the county in which the real estate is located. The precise county office varies from state to state, but is the office that maintains real estate records. Also, some states require additional local filing for other financing statements. In any case, individual state statutes should be consulted, particularly the portion embodying UCC Section 9-401.

Possession of Collateral

Prior to the adoption of rules allowing perfection by filing, perfection ordinarily was achieved, if at all, by possession of the collateral by the secured party or someone holding it on his behalf. Possession remains an important, and sometimes necessary, method of perfecting and may be used as an alternative to filing. However, secured interests in accounts and other intangibles *must* be perfected by filing. A security interest in money or instruments can be perfected *only* by possession.

If the secured party perfects by possession of the collateral, she is under an obligation to use reasonable care to protect and preserve it. However, during possession by the secured party, the risk of loss to the collateral remains with the debtor to the extent that insurance coverage is inadequate. The secured party is under a duty to keep the collateral separate or otherwise identifiable from her own, except in the case of fungible goods. All reasonable costs of custody and preservation of the collateral must be borne by the debtor.

Automatic Perfection

Remember that attachment of a security interest generally vests a security interest in the secured party that is good against the debtor, but not against other existing creditors of the debtor or a subsequent good-faith purchaser of the collateral. Under Article 9, attachment may perfect the attached security interest automatically as against other creditors. **Automatic perfection** may occur in three important situations: (1) temporary perfection in certain instruments and in documents of title under Section 9-304(4); (2) temporary perfection in proceeds from collateral under Section 9-305(3); and (3) perfection of purchase money security interests in consumer goods.

A security interest in "bearer" (noncertificated) securities, and negotiable documents of title, to the extent that it arises for new value under a written security agreement, is automatically perfected for twenty-one days from the time it attaches. Thereafter, perfection may continue only by filing in the case of securities, or by possession in the case of documents. However, the security interest remains perfected during the twenty-one day period even if the secured party makes the securities or documents available to the debtor to deal with them in some manner preliminary to their sale or exchange or, in the case of instruments, for the purpose of sale or exchange or of presentation, collection, renewal, or registration of transfer. This underscores the rule that possession by the secured party during that period is not necessary to perfection, and also that the collateral may be dealt with normally during the twenty-one days.

Under Section 9-306, the term **proceeds** includes whatever is received upon the sale, exchange, collection, or other disposition of collateral, or the proceeds of prior collateral. It also includes insurance payable by reason of the loss of collateral, except to the extent that the insurance is payable to a third party. A party having a perfected security interest in the original collateral also has an automatically perfected security interest in the proceeds of that collateral for a period of ten days from the time the proceeds are paid to the debtor. At the expiration of that period, the interest no longer is perfected, unless it was included properly in the original security agreement. Then that agreement must have been filed in the office or offices appropriate for filing a security interest concerning such proceeds, or the proceeds must be identifiable (traceable) cash proceeds, or a proper financing statement covering the proceeds must have been filed before the expiration of the ten days.

The most widespread application of the rules of automatic perfection involves purchase money security interests. These include any security interest in favor of a seller of consumer goods, or in favor of a lender who provides money used to purchase consumer goods, if the security interest is taken to protect the purchase price of the goods. This rule does not apply, however, if the goods are either a motor vehicle required to be registered under state law or a fixture. In these cases, filing is required. Most states have statutes permitting security interests in motor vehicles to be perfected by indorsing notice of the interest on the motor vehicle title which, then, is filed with the secretary of state.

In drafting Article 9, the Commissioners on Uniform State Laws have treated purchase money security interests differently than other security interests. Why are they perfected by attachment alone, although the others may be perfected only by filing or possession? Perhaps one reason is that the UCC primarily is interested in commercial transactions rather than sales of consumer goods. However, the more important reason is that consumer sales on credit are so frequent that a filing requirement would be cumbersome, probably would lead to too much restriction on the availability of credit, and would clutter the system of records far out of proportion to the benefits realized. The following case illustrates the effect of a purchase money security interest.

IN RE NICOLOSI
4 U.C.C. Rptr. 111 (S.D. Ohio, 1966)

This action came before the bankruptcy court on a petition by the trustee in bankruptcy in the matter of the estate of Nicolosi. A hearing was conducted to determine the priority between a lien holder and the trustee concerning an engagement ring.

On July 7, 1964, Nicolosi purchased the ring and signed a purchase money security interest in favor of the vendor, which the vendor did not file. Nicolosi gave the ring to his fiancee, and upon termination of their relationship she delivered the ring to the trustee.

The court determined that the purchase money security interest prevailed.

ANDERSON, Charles A., Referee in Bankruptcy.

If the diamond ring, purchased as an engagement ring by the bankrupt, cannot be categorized as consumer goods, and therefore exempted from the notice filing requirements of the Uniform Commercial Code as adopted in Ohio, a perfected security interest does not exist. . . . (UCC Section 9-302).

No judicial precedents have been cited in the briefs.

Under the commercial code, collateral is divided into tangible, and documentary categories. Certainly, a diamond ring falls into the tangible category. The classes of tangible goods are distinguished by the primary use intended. . . . (UCC Section 9-109) . . . [T]he four classes are "consumer goods," "equipment," "farm products" and "inventory."

The difficulty is that the code provisions use terms arising in commercial circles which have different semantical values from legal precedents. Does the fact that the purchaser bought the goods as a special gift to another person signify that it was not for his own "personal, family or household purposes?" The trustee urges that these special facts control under the express provisions of the commercial code.

By a process of exclusion, a diamond engagement ring purchased for one's fiancee is not "equipment" bought or used in business, "farm products" used in farming operations, or "inventory" held for sale, lease or service contracts. When the bankrupt purchased the ring, therefore, it could only have been "consumer goods" bought for use "primarily for personal use." There could be no judicial purpose to create a special class of property in derogation of the statutory principles.

By the foregoing summary analysis, it is apparent that the diamond ring, when the interest of the bankrupt attached, was consumer goods since it could have been no other class of goods. Unless the fiancee had a special status under the code provision protecting a bona fide buyer, without knowledge, for value, of consumer goods, the failure to file a financing statement is not crucial. . . .

Is a promise, as valid contractual consideration, included under the term "value"? In other words, was the ring given to his betrothed in consideration of marriage (promise for a promise)? If so, and "value" has been given, the transferee is a "buyer" under traditional concepts. . . .

The Uniform Commercial Code definition of "value" (because of the code purpose of being so broad as to not derogate from the ideal ubiquitous secured creditor), very definitely covers a promise for a promise. The definition reads that "a person gives 'value' for rights if he acquires them . . . (4) generally, in return for any consideration sufficient to support a simple contract."

It would seem unrealistic, nevertheless, to apply contract law concepts historically developed into the law of marriage relations in the context of new concepts developed for uniform commercial practices. They are not, in reality, the same juristic manifold. The purpose of uniformity of the code should not be defeated by the obsessions of the code drafters to be all inclusive for secured creditors.

Even if the trustee, in behalf of the unsecured creditors, would feel inclined to insert love, romance and morals into commercial law, he is appearing in the wrong era, and possibly the wrong court.

Questions

1. Are there any flaws in the court's legal reasoning?

2. Would there have been any serious impairment of the policies underlying the UCC if the court had decided to remove transactions like the one in this case from the Code?

PROTECTION OF THIRD PARTIES

Perfection of a security interest may not give complete protection to its holder. Under some circumstances, subsequent third parties may obtain rights as a matter of public policy in spite of perfection.

Protection of Buyers of Goods

Section 9-307 provides that a **buyer in the ordinary course of business** (Section 1-201(9)) takes the item free of any security interest created by the seller *even though the security interest is perfected and even though the buyer knows of its existence.* This rule, however, does not apply to a buyer of farm products from a person engaged in farming operations (according to a 1972 amendment).

The rule covers transactions in which the seller is a merchant who ordinarily sells goods of the type involved. However, in all cases involving the purchase of consumer goods, if the buyer purchases for personal, family, or household purposes, he takes the goods free of even perfected security interests he does not know of other than those perfected by filing. Thus, someone who purchases consumer goods other than from a merchant in the ordinary course of business assumes the risk of a filed financing statement. However, regardless of whether the goods are consumer goods, such a buyer still takes the goods free of a security interest to the extent that it secures future advances made after the time the secured party acquired knowledge of the purchase, or more than forty-five days after the purchase, whichever occurs first. Future advances involve situations in which a security agreement provides it is to secure not just the loan that led to its creation, but to future loans as well.

Therefore, even filing does not completely perfect a security interest, even as against a buyer not in the ordinary course of business. Perhaps the lesson to be learned is that a seller, even one who is to be secured, still should consider the personal and business characteristics of the buyer if credit is to be extended. Consider the following case, which presents an important exception to the policy of protecting buyers in the ordinary course of business.

EXCHANGE BANK OF OSCEOLA v. JARRETT
180 Mont. 33, 588 P.2d 1006 (1979)

This was an action by Exchange Bank of Osceola (Plaintiff/Appellant) against Spencer Jarrett, dba Jarrett Construction Co. (Defendant/Appellee) to foreclose a lien on a tractor.

The tractor was purchased through Plaintiff on September 8, 1976 in Florida, and Plaintiff perfected a security interest under Florida law. On February 1, 1977, Holland (the purchaser) sold the tractor to C. B. and O. Equipment in Council Bluffs, Iowa, without Plaintiff's permission and in violation of the security agreement. The tractor was taken to Iowa, and on February 21, 1977 it was sold to Defendant, who took it to Montana. On April 4, 1977 (within four months of the time the tractor arrived in Iowa), Plaintiff filed a financing statement in Iowa, pursuant to Iowa law. Holland defaulted on payment and Plaintiff brought this action.

The trial court sustained Defendant's motion to dismiss the complaint for failure to state a cause of action (demurrer) and Plaintiff appeared. Reversed.

SHEEHY, Justice.

The sole issue for our determination is whether Spencer Jarrett purchased the tractor-scraper "free of" or "subject to" the bank's security interest. It is agreed that the bank perfected its security interest in the tractor-scraper by filing the financing statement required by Fla.Stat. Section 679.302. The Uniform Commercial Code contemplates the continued perfection of a security interest if there has been no intervening period when it was unperfected. Fla.Stat. Section 679.303. A perfected security interest is generally not destroyed by the sale, exchange or other disposition of the collateral:

> (2) Except where this chapter otherwise provides, a security interest continues in collateral notwithstanding sale, exchange or other disposition thereof by the debtor unless his action was authorized by the secured party in the security agreement or otherwise, and also continues in any identifiable proceeds including collections received by the debtor. Fla.Stat. Section 679.306(2).

Since Daniel Holland sold the tractor without plaintiff's permission and in violation of the security agreement, it is clear the C. B. and O. purchased the tractor-scraper "subject to" the bank's security interest.

When C. B. and O. transported the tractor from Florida to Iowa, the continued existence of the bank's security interest was contingent on the provisions of Iowa's Commercial Code. Iowa Code Section 554.9103, provides:

> When collateral is brought into and kept in this state while subject to a security interest perfected under the law of the jurisdiction from which the collateral was removed, the security interest remains perfected, but if action is required by Part 3 of this Article to perfect the security interest,
> i. if the action is not taken before the expiration of the period of perfection in the other jurisdiction or the end of four months after the collateral is brought into this state, whichever period first expires, the security interest becomes unperfected at the end of that period and is thereafter deemed to have been unperfected as against a person who became a purchaser after removal;
> ii. *if the action is taken before the expiration of the period specified in subparagraph (i), the security interest continues perfected thereafter:* (Emphasis supplied.)

The courts uniformly hold that section 554.9103 gives a secured party a four-month grace period during which his security interest is protected without any further action on his part. . . .

Applying the provisions of Iowa Code Section 554.9103 to our fact pattern, it is obvious that the bank's security interest was viable at the time defendant purchased the tractor-scraper from C. B. and O. Equipment Company. The bank fully complied with section 554.9103 by filing its financial statement in Iowa on April 4, 1977, well within the four-month period. Therefore, plaintiff's security interest continued unless Article 9 provides otherwise.

Defendant contends that Iowa Code Section 554.9307 allowed him to purchase the tractor-scraper "free of" plaintiff's security interest. Section 554.9307 provides:

> Protection of buyers of goods. 1. A buyer in ordinary course of business (subsection 9 of section 554.1201) other than a person buying farm products from a person engaged in

farming operations takes free of a security interest created by his seller even though the security interest is perfected and even though the buyer knows of its existence.

In the present case, defendant Jarrett purchased in good faith and without knowledge that the sale to him was in violation of the bank's security interest. Defendant also purchased the tractor in the ordinary course from a person in the business of selling tractors, therefore, he was a "buyer in the ordinary course of business". Iowa Code Section 554.01(9).

However, section 554.9307 contains the further limitation that the security interest must be "created by his [defendant's] seller". This Court has never interpreted the "created by his seller" limitation. . . .

As an alternate theory, defendant claims Iowa Code Section 554.2403 allows him to take the tractor-scraper "free of" plaintiff's security interest. Section 554.2403 provides:

> Any entrusting of possession of goods to a merchant who deals in goods of that kind *gives him power to transfer all rights of the entruster* to a buyer in ordinary course. (Emphasis added.)

The emphasized language of section 554.2403 disposes of defendant's alternative claim. The "entruster" in this case would be Daniel Holland, however, his title was encumbered by plaintiff's security interest. Therefore, C. B. and O. could transfer all rights of Daniel Holland, but such transfer would still be "subject to" the bank's security interest.

This Court recognizes that this is a harsh result, since the purchaser, on the date of purchase in Iowa, had no means to learn in Iowa that the property he purchased was subject to a security interest. It may be that legislative action is necessary to prevent such results in the future. Since we are bound by the enacted laws, and must give full faith and credit to the laws of our sister states, no other course is open to us here.

Questions

1. Is there any way for the buyer to protect itself against the possibility of there being an unfiled security interest that was within the four-month grace period?

2. What is the purpose of the four-month grace period?

Purchase of Chattel Paper and Instruments

A purchaser of chattel paper or an instrument receives certain protections if he gives new value and the purchase is in the ordinary course of business. If he acts without knowledge that the specific chattel paper or instrument is subject to a security interest, he takes it free of a security interest perfected under Section 9-304 (permissive filing and automatic perfection) or under Section 9-306 (perfection as to proceeds). In addition, he takes free of a security interest that is claimed merely as proceeds of inventory subject to a security interest (Section 9-306) even though he knows that the specific paper or instrument is subject to the security interest. A rule to the contrary, of course, would complicate unduly the process of converting noncash proceeds to cash. Also, remember that the secured party still has a security interest in traceable cash proceeds resulting from the sale of the chattel paper and interests.

Protection of Purchasers of Instruments, Documents, and Securities

Section 9-309 provides that the rules under Article 9 make no change in the rights of purchasers and holders granted in Articles 3, 7, and 8 concerning commercial paper (Article 3), negotiable documents of title that have been negotiated (Article 7), and securities sold to a bona fide purchaser (Article 8). They continue to take priority over earlier Article 9 security interests, even though perfected. Also, filing under Article 9 does not give notice to prevent a purchaser or holder from being in good faith and without notice of interests or defenses. Therefore, the rights created under these other articles remain intact unless other notice of the existence of a security interest is involved.

PRIORITIES

In considering priorities among security interests (who prevails in cases of conflicts among the interests of concerned parties), in addition to the rights of good faith buyers in the ordinary course of business as previously discussed, a number of principles should be kept in mind. These are: (1) the rules set out in Article 9 are concerned primarily with the limits of a secured party's protection against (a) purchasers from the debtor and (b) other creditors of the debtor; (2) in general, the secured party is protected against transferees and other creditors of the debtor after perfection, and in particular against creditors who may claim their interests in bankruptcy proceedings in-

stituted by or against the debtor; and (3) even unperfected security interests may afford the secured party some protection, particularly against the debtor and some third parties.

Specific types of third parties with whom Article 9 is concerned are purchasers from the debtor and other creditors of the debtor. The latter may be further subdivided into: (1) general (unsecured) creditors; (2) creditors secured under Article 2, 4, or 9; (3) lien creditors (by attachment, levy, or the like); (4) lienors by operation of law (for example, a mechanic's lien by possession); (5) governmental liens (for example, tax liens); (6) a trustee in bankruptcy.

The general rule concerning priority of conflicting interests in the same collateral is "first in time, first in right." That is, the first interest will prevail over subsequent interests of the same type. In judging who is "first," the decision is governed by the earlier of two events—filing of a proper financing statement or perfection by other means. If neither party has perfected his or her security interest, the first to attach will prevail. Again, these rules govern only cases involving security interests of the same type.

Purchase Money Security Interests

As previously noted, purchase money security interests are treated specially in Article 9. Under Section 9-312(4), purchase money security interests in collateral other than inventory take priority over all conflicting security interests in the same collateral or its proceeds, as long as the purchase money security interest is perfected at the time the debtor takes possession of the collateral or within ten days thereafter.

The rule is more complex concerning priority of conflicting security interests in inventory. The purchase money security interest still is given priority concerning inventory, and also concerning identifiable cash proceeds received by the debtor on or before delivery of the inventory to the buyer, but only if certain other requirements are met. They are: (1) the purchase money security interest was perfected at the time the debtor received possession of the inventory; (2) the purchase money secured party gives notice to the holder of the conflicting security interest as required by Section 9-312(3)(b); (3) the holder of the conflicting security interest receives the notification within five years before the debtor receives possession of the inventory; and (4) the notification states that the purchase money secured party has or expects to acquire a purchase money security interest in inventory of the debtor, describing the inventory by item or type.

In summary, it is the intent of Section 9-312(3) to allow a purchase money security interest to prevail over a security interest created by an after-acquired property clause in a previous security interest. Although at least three major rationales have been advanced for the preference of purchase money security interests, the best reasoned is that in the case of a seller on credit, she had an interest in the property that never left her at the time of sale and, therefore, was created prior to any other competing interest. Much the same theory may be applied to a purchase money security interest in favor of a third-party lender. In extending the loan he has relied on getting a security interest in the specific property, and without the loan the debtor never would have had an interest in the first place.

Fixtures

Fixtures generally may be defined as goods so attached to real estate as to become part of it. Article 9 recognizes three types of fixtures: those that retain their character as goods (for example, trade fixtures); those that become real estate; and building materials. The latter are not covered by Article 9.

As for the first two types of fixtures, the interest of a purchase money secured party prevails over an interest of encumbrancers (for example, mort-gage holders) or the owner of the real estate if it was perfected before the collateral became a fixture or within ten days thereafter, the conflicting interest was created before the collateral became a fixture, and the debtor has a recorded interest in the real estate. A nonpurchase money security interest in fixtures is given priority over the interests of encumbrancers and the owner if it was perfected by fixture filing before the other interest is of record, it has priority over any conflicting security interest of a predecessor of the encumbrancer or owner, and the debtor has an interest in the real estate.

A security interest in fixtures that is perfected before they became fixtures also will prevail over the interests of encumbrancers and the owner if the fixtures are readily removable factory or office machines or readily removable replacements of domestic appliances that are consumer goods. In this context, Section 9-313 has accorded special treatment to trade and domestic consumer fixtures that frequently are moved upon vacating the real estate to which they are attached. The key is the frequency of removal.

Finally, a security interest in fixtures is given priority over liens obtained by judicial process as long as it was perfected by any method under Article 9. Liens acquired by judicial process should grant to the lienholder no greater interest than was possessed by the debtor other than as against unperfected interests. In summary, assuming interests are perfected properly, Article 9 prefers, in descending rank of priority: (1) purchase money security interests, (2) other security interests in fixtures, (3) interests of the owner or encumbrancers of the whole property, and (4) interests of holders of judicial liens.

Any creditor intending to take a security interest in a fixture should be aware that the real estate records may not reveal all outstanding interests, even though the fixture has acquired the status of real property. This point is illustrated by the following case.

BARNETT BANK OF CLEARWATER, N.A. v. ROMPON

377 So.2d 981 (Ct.App.Fla. 1979)

This was an action by Barnett Bank of Clearwater, N.A. (Plaintiff/Appellant) against Nickolas J. and June P. Rompon, J. Maurice Langelier, and Jacques A. Corbeil (Defendants/Appellees) to foreclose a lien on a mobile home. The Rompons purchased a mobile home and financed it with Plaintiff, which perfected its lien by notation on the title filed with the Department of Highway Safety and Motor Vehicles. The mobile home was then moved to a lot and permanently affixed to a foundation, making it real estate, and thereafter it was taxed as such. Later, Langelier and Corbeil purchased it at a sheriff's auction after having searched the real estate records to make sure title was clear.

The trial court found for Defendants and Plaintiff appealed. Reversed.

OTT, Judge.

It may well be that the mobile home was so affixed to the land as to become a fixture, but that is not the determinative factor here. If a mobile home must be registered and titled as a motor vehicle under Florida law, then the provisions of Chapter 679 do not even apply. Section 679.9-302(3)(b).

There can be no doubt that a mobile home is classified as a motor vehicle under Florida law and must be registered with and titled by the Department. . . . At the time appellant financed Rompon's purchase of the mobile home it was registered and titled by the Department. Appellant could only perfect its lien on it by filing notice thereof with the Department and having it noted on the certificate of title. . . . Even when a mobile home is permanently affixed to land and taxed as real property, it still must have an RP license plate issued by the Department and attached to the rear of the mobile home in a conspicuous place. . . .

At the time of financing the Rompon purchase of the mobile home, the appellant perfected its security interest according to law. There is no requirement that appellant reperfect its security interest pursuant to Chapter 679 in the event the mobile home subsequently becomes a fixture to real property. Under the provisions of Chapters 319 and 320, Florida Statutes, appellees' interest in the mobile home is subject to appellant's perfected security interest. A check of the records of the Department is required even though a mobile home has actually become a fixture to real property.

Questions

1. Why shouldn't the law have required the security to be reperfected when the mobile home was affixed to the land?

2. Can you think of other types of property that have "dual" characteristics? How should they be treated?

Accessions

Sometimes goods are attached to other goods so as to combine with them to make a whole. This is called **accession.** For example, an engine is attached to a body and other components that combine to make up a car. As a general rule, a security interest attached (not necessarily perfected) before the collateral is affixed to the other goods will prevail over the interest of a person claiming an interest in the whole.

A security interest that attaches to collateral *after* it is affixed prevails over any interest subsequently acquired in the whole. However, it is subordinate to any interest that existed at the time of attachment, unless the holder of that interest consents in writing to the security interest or disclaims any interest in the goods as part of the whole.

The treatment of conflicting interests in accessions may be compared to that of conflicting interests in fixtures. Again, to the extent reasonably possible, the holder of the specific security interest is preferred over the holder of an interest in the whole. However, neither of these interests will prevail over: (1) a subsequent purchaser for value, including a purchaser at a foreclosure sale; (2) a holder of a judgment lien; or (3) a creditor with a prior perfected security interest in the whole. However, in order to prevail, the purchase must have been made, or the interest obtained, without knowledge of the security interest and before it was perfected.

When Goods are Commingled or Processed

Sometimes goods are commingled with others, as in a case of fungible goods belonging to two or more owners (for example, corn belonging to several farmers may be stored in a grain elevator), or are processed with other types of goods, as in the case of flour processed into loaves of bread. In these cases, a perfected security interest in the goods continues if they are so commingled or processed as to lose their individual identity, or if a financing statement covering them also covers the mass or end product. In the case of a conflict between or among security interests in the mass or end product, they will rank according to the ratio each of the attached goods bears to the total cost of the mass or end product. This seems the only fair solution even though a holder of such an interest may find that the value of the mass or end product is less than the sum of the values of the goods that were commingled or processed. For example, if 50,000 bushels of top-grade wheat are mixed with 50,000 bushels of low-grade wheat, the value of the mass is unlikely to approximate an average of the values of the two.

Possessory Liens of Bailees

Someone who furnishes services or materials with respect to goods ordinarily is granted a lien to secure payment for them. This may be prescribed by statute or judicial decision. These liens are perfected by the lienholder's retaining possession of the goods improved by the services or materials. For example, a mechanic who repairs a customer's automobile is entitled to retain possession of the automobile until the charges for repairs are paid. The lien takes priority over all other security interests in the goods, unless it is created by statute and the statute provides to the contrary. The rationale for this rule is that the value of the goods has been increased by the value of the services and materials. Therefore, the interests of prior secured parties is not really diminished if the artisan's lien is given priority.

RIGHTS OF CREDITORS ON DEFAULT

The term *default* is not defined in the UCC. However, **default** normally is considered to mean that a debtor has failed to comply with some term of the security agreement. This may result from nonpayment of principal or interest due, failure to insure the collateral, a decline in the value of the collateral without additional security called for in the agreement, or insolvency proceedings being instituted by or against the debtor. In any case, the secured party may take action under Part 5 of Article 9 of the Code. In addition, he or she may proceed according to any rights provided by the security agreement, within limits specified in Section 9-501(3).

In addition to the common law right to self-help repossession, as long as it can be accomplished peacefully, the rights of a creditor on default typically include taking judgment against the debtor or foreclosing against the collateral. If the collateral is documents, the creditor is entitled to proceed against either the documents themselves or the goods underlying them. If the secured party elects to take judgment against the debtor, the levy based on any execution of the judgment will date back to the date of the security interest in the collateral.

Sale

Foreclosure ordinarily is accompanied by a sale of the collateral, and a sale caused by a levy of execution of a judgment against the debtor is considered a foreclosure. Section 9-504 sets out rules and procedures concerning foreclosure sales. The sale may be public or private, must be conducted in a commercially reasonable manner, and the secured party is allowed to bid.

Proceeds of a sale under this section are applied first to pay the costs of retaking, holding, and preparing the property for sale and, if allowed by the security agreement, reasonable attorney fees and other legal costs of the sale. Second, the proceeds are applied to satisfy the debt itself. Finally, any remaining proceeds are paid to subordinate interest holders. Generally, the secured creditor must account to the debtor for any excess proceeds, and the debtor is liable for any deficiency. However, if the underlying transaction was a sale of accounts or chattel paper, the debtor is entitled to the excess proceeds and is liable for any deficiency only if this is called for in the security agreement.

Strict Foreclosure

Instead of being put to the complexities and expense of a sale, a secured party, upon default, may elect to take the collateral in full satisfaction of the debt. This is called **strict foreclosure** and is provided for under Section 9-505 of the Code. The debtor must be notified of the decision to elect strict foreclosure. In cases involving consumer goods, this is the only notice required. In all other cases, the secured party also must notify other creditors of the debtor who have notified the secured party of their claims. All notices must be written. However, the requirement of notice may be waived by a debtor, either expressly or by conduct. Consider the following case.

GRANT COUNTY TRACTOR CO. v. NUSS
6 Wash.App. 866, 496 P.2d 966 (1972)

This was an action by Grant County Tractor Co. (Plaintiff/Appellant) against Vernon E. and Jane Doe Nuss (Defendants/also Appellants) for a deficiency judgment on a contract and security agreement.

On July 1, 1969, Defendants purchased a tractor and equipment from Plaintiff and executed a security agreement to secure the purchase price. Defendants defaulted and, without request, delivered the tractor and equipment to Plaintiff's sales yard on January 8, 1970. On January 13 they gave notice of their election to rescind the contract. (The rescission was not effective, however, because there were no legal grounds for rescission.) In April, Plaintiff sold the tractor without notice to Defendants. A balance of $3507 remained.

To Plaintiff's complaint seeking to recover the deficiency, Defendants answered and counterclaimed for rescission. The trial court denied relief to both parties and both appealed. Reversed and remanded, the appellate court finding Plaintiff did not forfeit its right to a deficiency judgment by selling the tractor without notice to Defendant.

GREEN, Judge.

This issue is one of first impression in this state. Other jurisdictions have reached opposite results under similar provisions of the Uniform Commercial Code. One line of authority holds that failure to comply with the notice requirements of RCW 62 A.9-504(3) results in a forfeiture of the right to a deficiency. . . . The other line of authority holds that the failure to give notice does not prevent a deficiency. . . . We adopt the reasoning of the second line of cases.

RCW 62 A.9-504(2), . . . provides that the debtor is liable for a deficiency, if there is no agreement to the contrary. RCW 62 A.9-507(1) provides:

> (1) If it is established that the secured party is not proceeding in accordance with the provisions of this Part disposition may be ordered or restrained on appropriate terms and conditions. If the disposition has occurred the debtor or any person entitled to notification or whose security interest has been made known to the secured party prior to the disposition has a right to recover from the secured party any loss caused by a failure to comply with the provisions of this Part.

Under this provision if the creditor fails to give notice to the debtor as required by RCW 62 A.9-504(3), the debtor has a right to recover from the creditor any loss caused by the failure to give that notice. Thus, in the instant case if the sale of the tractor without notice had resulted in a loss to the defendants, the defendants would have a right in the instant proceeding to claim that loss against the deficiency sought by the plaintiff. In view of this remedy, we are of the opinion the writers of the Uniform Commercial Code did not intend that the creditor's failure to give notice would result in a forfeiture of the creditor's right to a deficiency. See Hogan, Pitfalls in Default Procedure, 2 UCC L.J. 244,257 (1969).

Further, it should be noted that defendants unilaterally and voluntarily delivered to plaintiff complete control of the security and gave written notice of their election to rescind the transaction. It has been held that such conduct constitutes a waiver of the debtor's right to reasonable notice of an impending sale or estops the debtor from claiming a violation of the statute.

Questions

1.   What are the arguments for requiring notice in order to preserve the right to seek a deficiency?

2. Do you think the result in the case would have been the same had the defendants not delivered the tractor, or is the court just throwing that in as a make-weight to bolster its conclusion?

Either of two circumstances may prevent strict foreclosure, requiring the collateral to be sold under Section 9-504. First, any other creditor of the debtor may object to strict foreclosure by sending a written notice to the secured party, which must be received by the secured party within twenty-one days after his notice was sent. Also, if the collateral was consumer goods, and the debtor has paid 60 percent of the price in the case of a purchase money security interest or 60 percent of the loan in the case of any other security interest, the debtor may require a sale.

Right of Redemption

At any time before the secured party has disposed of the collateral or entered into a contract for its disposition as a result of a sale under Section 9-504, or before the obligation has been discharged by strict foreclosure under Section 9-505(2), either the debtor or a creditor of the debtor may redeem the collateral. The **right of redemption** may be exercised by notifying the secured party of this intention, and then tendering to the secured party the amount of the obligation, the expenses of retaking, holding, and preparing the collateral for sale, the expenses of arranging for the sale, and, if provided in the contract, reasonable attorney fees and other legal expenses incurred by the secured party. This provides the debtor and other creditors with a hedge against the possibility of a low sale price at a foreclosure sale.

SUMMARY

The main purpose of the law governing security interests is the allocation of rights among a secured party, the debtor, other creditors of the debtor, and purchasers of the collateral from the debtor. The rules of law are found in Article 9 of the UCC. Article 9 covers every transaction intended to create a security interest (regardless of type) in personal property or fixtures, and every sale of accounts or chattel paper. A number of transactions are excluded from Article 9 by Section 9-104. They are generally those that fall outside of the ambit of Article 9—private, consensual security interests in personal property or fixtures given in the ordinary course of business. These include purchase money security interests, leases intended as security, consignments intended as security, security interests created under Article 2, and various other transactions.

Specific property that may be subject to an Article 9 security interest may be tangible property, including consumer goods, equipment, inventory, fixtures, and farm products. It also may be intangible, including debt instruments, investment securities, documents of title, accounts receivable, chattel paper, and general intangibles. In addition, a security interest may arise in proceeds from the disposal of collateral, insurance proceeds generated by loss of or injury to collateral, property acquired after the security interest was given, and property already the subject of a security interest for later credit extended by the secured party to the debtor.

When a security interest is created, it is said to *attach* to the *collateral*. This occurs when the creditor takes possession of the collateral or when a sufficient writing is executed, value is paid to the debtor, and the debtor has an interest in the property. Attachment gives the secured party rights only as against the debtor. In order to have rights as against other creditors of the debtor and purchasers of the collateral from the debtor as well, it is necessary that the attached security interest be perfected.

A security interest usually may be perfected by filing a financing statement or other sufficient notice, by possession of the collateral by the secured party, or in some cases automatically by attachment under Sections 9-304 and 9-305. Some security interests may be perfected by any of these methods, and some require a particular method (for example, possession is required for negotiable documents and instruments).

Rights of certain third parties are protected under Article 9, including subsequent purchasers of goods, purchasers of chattel paper and instruments, and purchasers of documents and securities. Third parties generally are protected if they purchase for value, without notice of the security interest and in the ordinary course of business. A purchaser of goods ordinarily is protected even if he or she knows of the security interest, as long as he or she purchases in good faith.

In the event of a conflict among security interests in the same collateral, rights of the parties are governed by an elaborate set of rules setting priorities. However, the general rule is "first in time, first in right." Among unperfected interests, the first to attach will prevail. Among perfected interests, the earlier filing of a proper financing statement or perfection by other means will prevail. However, major exceptions to these rules are found with respect to purchase money security interests and fixtures. The "first in time" rule tends to favor purchase money secured parties, and the "first to file" rule tends to favor holders of security interests in a specific fixture as opposed to the holder of an interest in the entire property to which the fixture was affixed. Special rules also are provided concerning accessions, commingled goods, and goods processed into an end product. As was the case with regard to fixtures, these rules generally tend to protect the interests in specific collateral as opposed to interests in the whole.

In case of default by the debtor on his obligations under a security agreement, the secured party normally has two principle courses of action. She may take judgment against the creditor personally, or she may proceed against the collateral. The latter course is called *foreclosure*. Upon foreclosure, the collateral may be disposed of by sale, or the creditor may take the collateral in full discharge of the obligation it secured (called *strict foreclosure*). If the secured party elects strict foreclosure, the debtor must be notified of this decision in writing, and if the collateral is other than consumer goods, other creditors also must be notified in writing if they have given the secured party written notice of their claims. Strict foreclosure may be prevented by objection of any creditor notified, or by the debtor if he has paid 60 percent or more of the obligation secured by the collateral and the collateral is consumer goods.

KEY TERMS AND CONCEPTS

security interest
pledge
lien
chattel mortgage
conditional sales contract
purchase money security interest
collateral
consignment
things in action
consumer goods
equipment
inventory
fixtures
farm products
intangible property
floating lien
after-acquired property
future advances
attachment
value
perfection
financing statement
continuation statement
termination statement

automatic perfection

proceeds

buyer in the ordinary course of business

accession

default

foreclosure

strict foreclosure

right of redemption

PROBLEMS

1. Kimbrell's Furniture Co. sold a tape recorder and a television to Casey on a conditional sales contract, but did not record it. Later, Casey pawned the items with Friedman, a pawn broker. When Casey failed to make payments, Kimbrell's Furniture sought to recover the tape recorder and television from Friedman. Friedman objected, contending his lien was superior to the unrecorded conditional sale contract. Is Friedman correct?

2. Arthur sold certain furniture and appliances to Bates and took a security interest to secure payment. The security agreement listed all of the furniture items, and the financing statement listed the same plus the appliance items. The financing statement was filed properly. Later, Carter Bank & Trust gave Bates a loan and took a security interest in the same items of furniture and appliances. Bates defaulted on the loan, and when Carter Bank sought to foreclose on the security Arthur contended his security interest was superior to that of Carter Bank. Carter Bank contended its security interest was superior as to the appliances not covered in Arthur's security agreement. Who is correct?

3. On March 7, Ultra Precision Industries borrowed money from National Acceptance Co., in the amount of $692,000, secured by its equipment. The security agreement had an "after-acquired property" clause. The following year, machinery was delivered by the seller, Wolf, on April 30 and June 20, under an agreement that

Ultra could test the machinery and, if it was satisfactory, Ultra would purchase it. On July 31, after testing, Ultra executed a purchase money security interest to Wolf, who assigned it to a bank under a prearranged condition of the sale. The bank filed the security interest on August 5. National Acceptance sought to foreclose on the machinery by virtue of its after-acquired clause, contending that its interest was superior to that of the bank because the bank did not file its security interest within ten days after Ultra came into possession of the machinery. Is National Acceptance correct?

4. Phillips purchased a new car with the proceeds of a loan from National Bank, giving the bank a security interest in the car, and the security interest was properly filed. Later, Phillips took the car to Bergeron Cadillac for repair. When repairs were finished, Bergeron refused to release the car until the repair bill was paid. In the meantime, Phillips defaulted on the loan and the bank sought to foreclose on the car. Is the security interest of the bank superior to that of Bergeron?

5. Upon the default of the buyer, a seller of a truck on a conditional sales contract sought to repossess. This was effected when an agent of the seller found the truck parked, unscrewed a small vent on the door, got into the truck, and drove it to the seller's place of business. When the buyer learned of this, she sought to recover the truck, contending the seller was not entitled to trespass and burglarize the truck to recover possession. Is the buyer correct?

6. Davis regularly purchased cattle, ranching equipment, and supplies from the Filmore Auction Co. on credit. All purchases were secured by an agreement that provided, in part, that Davis would not "sell, assign, or transfer any cattle, equipment, or supplies" purchased under the agreement without the written consent of Filmore. In spite of this, Davis regularly sold cattle without Filmore's written consent but with his knowledge, and had done so for several years. Davis sold some 2500 head of prime beef cattle to Myers, and when he defaulted on his obligation to Filmore, Filmore sought to recover those cattle. Myers contended that under the facts, Filmore had waived its right to enforce the requirement of written consent. Is Myers correct?

7. Myrick ordered building materials from National Steel Products. When the materials arrived, Myrick gave a check for the purchase price. The check was dishonored and National Steel Products sought to recover the materials. Myrick contended National Steel had no right to do so because it had failed to get a security agreement covering the sale. Is Myrick correct?

8. Manger gave Davis a diamond ring to sell for her. Davis took the ring and pledged it to CD&M Co. as security for a loan. When Manger learned of this, she demanded the return of the ring. CD&M refused, contending it had a security interest and would not return the ring until the loan was repaid. Is Manger entitled to the return of her ring?

9. Walters purchased a car with the proceeds of a loan from National Shawmit Bank and gave the bank a security interest in the car, which was filed properly by the bank. Walters then sold the car to a car dealer who sold it to Jones. When the bank sought to foreclose on the car, Jones defended that, as a bona fide purchaser of consumer goods, his purchase cut off the security interest held by the bank. Is Jones correct?

10. Thompson bought a barn cleaner and gave the seller a security interest, which the seller filed properly. Thereafter, the barn cleaner was affixed to the barn in such a manner as to become a fixture. Thompson then sold the farm to Kibbe, who purchased it after a complete search of the real estate records. Did Kibbe buy the farm free and clear of the security interest?

Chapter | 22

Security Interests in Real Property

INTRODUCTION

The preceding chapter focused on security interests in personal property. Real property was not involved except with regard to fixtures, and the governing law was found primarily in Article 9 of the Uniform Commercial Code. This chapter continues the discussion by examining security interests in real property. The governing law is found almost entirely in the common law and statutes outside of the UCC.

Security interests in real property may take the form of mortgages, land contracts, trust deeds, or one of a variety of possible lesser liens. Each is important. All attach themselves to the title to real property, and if handled properly they remain with the title until they are discharged. For this reason, and because the subject property always remains in one location, a security interest in real property is considered particularly desirable by lenders and sellers on credit.

MORTGAGES

In its earliest common law form, a **mortgage** involved a transfer of the title to real property by the debtor (called the *mortgagor*) to the lender (called the *mortgagee*) with an agreement that it would be returned upon payment of the indebtedness. This could be accomplished by means of a deed executed by the mortgagor and handed over to the mortgagee, and generally an instrument of defeasance (an instrument promising to return the property upon payment of the debt) executed by the mortgagee and handed over to the mortgagor. In more recent times, a mortgage normally is accomplished by the use of a special mortgage instrument. However, consider the following case.

SPATARO, et al. v. DOMENICO, et al.
96 Cal.App.2d 411, 216 P.2d 32 (1950)

This was an action by Vito and Antonia Spataro and others (Plaintiffs/Appellants) against Domenico and others (Defendants/Appellees) to have a deed declared a mortgage.

The Spataros found themselves in debt beyond their abilities to pay. One creditor was the Domenicos, to whom they owed $1300. On March 14, 1938, they went to the bank that held a mortgage on the property in question. The Domenicos agreed to assume liability on the mortgage and paid $500 to the bank as part of the mortgage indebtedness. The Spataros then executed a deed to the Domenicos, and it was recorded the same day. The deed was absolute on its face. Other relevant facts are discussed by the court in its opinion.

The trial court found that the evidence was insufficient to prove the deed was intended as a mortgage, and Plaintiffs appealed. Affirmed.

VALLEE, Justice.

In determining whether a deed, absolute on its face, is a mortgage, the intention of the parties is controlling, and in the absence of any writing this intention is manifested by, and inferred from, all of the facts and circumstances of the transaction under which the deed was executed, taken in connection with the conduct of the parties after its execution. . . . Whether a deed absolute is in fact a mortgage is a mixed question of law and fact. . . . The test by which to determine whether the instrument is a mortgage is—was there a subsisting, continuing debt and a continuation of the relation of debtor and creditor? The fact is not only a circumstance tending to show that the conveyance is a mortgage, but is indispensable to the existence of a mortgage; if there is no indebtedness for which the conveyance is security, there can be no mortgage. . . . Ordinarily, there must be an agreement, express or implied, on the part of a mortgagor to pay the mortgagee a sum of money. Where there is no promise to pay, the deed will not be construed to be a mortgage. . . .

The presumption is that a deed is what it purports to be and one who seeks to overcome such presumption has the burden of producing clear and convincing proof. . . . Such evidence must be " 'clear, convincing, and conclusive—something more than that modicum of evidence which appellate courts sometimes hold sufficient to warrant a finding where the matter is not so serious as the overthrow of a clearly express deed, solemnly executed and delivered.'" . . . Whether the evidence offered to change the ostensible character of an instrument is clear and convincing is a question for the trial court and its determination in favor of either party upon conflicting or contradictory evidence is not open to review on appeal. . . .

After execution of the deed, plaintiffs did not exercise any of the prerogatives usually exercised by owners, with the possible exception of small expenditures for materials used in minor repairs. The Domenicos, on the other hand, did so. They paid all taxes on the premises from 1938 on, and spent $3700 repairing the premises. They rented the premises, collected all rentals from the tenants, with the exception of plaintiffs, and paid all utilities. There is testimony that plaintiffs paid the water bills on the residence they were occupying until 1947, when the bills were changed into Mrs. Domenico's name, but this is directly contradicted by testimony that Marie Principi, on behalf of her mother, gave plaintiffs the money with which to pay these bills. No debtor-creditor relationship was shown to have existed between the parties after the execution of the deed.

Vito testified that the property was worth $22,000 in 1938. Mrs. Domenico placed the value at $3500. The bank appraisals of the two parcels as of January 10, 1938, totaled $3750. The 1938 tax bills on both parcels reflect a total of $2000.

It is obvious that appellants' contention that the evidence is insufficient to support the findings that (a) a good and sufficient consideration was paid by the grantees, (b) the deed was intended as an absolute conveyance, and (c) appellants were guilty of laches, cannot be upheld. The consideration for the transaction was the extinguishment of the grantors' debt to the grantees and the assumption by the latter of the encumbrance and the delinquent taxes. That the relationship of debtor and creditor no longer existed between the parties subsequent to the execution of the deed is amply supported by the record. The total consideration paid by the grantees was $5,887.51, which included the preexisting $1300 indebtedness extinguished by them, the $4,465.24 mortgage assumed by them, and $122.27 paid by them in redeeming the property from delinquent taxes. Disregarding the valuation placed upon the premises by appellants, in view of the conflict in the evidence, it is evident, contrary to appellants' claim, that there was no great disparity between the value of the property and the consideration paid. The fact that the grantors received no money at the time of the execution of the deed is not, of itself, controlling. . . .

Since the evidence fully justifies the conclusion that the deed was not a mortgage, no purpose would be served in discussing the several other contentions made by appellants. They are inconsequential and a ruling one way or another would in no wise affect the judgment on its merits.

Questions

1.   What policies motivated the court to put a heavy burden of proof on the plaintiffs to show that the deed was a mortgage?

2.   Are you as confident as the court seemed to be that the result reached in this case is right?

In early practice, if the mortgagor defaulted, the condition necessary to cause defeasance was broken and title vested in the mortgagee permanently. Also, the mortgagee, in addition to keeping the property, could sue the mortgagor on the indebtedness. This, of course, imposed a penalty on the mortgagor, and the law soon began to move to the position that the mortgagee was required to elect between these remedies. Today, the law even goes one step further to protect the debtor, giving to the mortgagor the right to redeem the property after default.

Creation

The precise form for a mortgage is controlled primarily by common law. However, many matters concerning the mortgage transaction are statutory. Among the more important federal statutes are the Truth in Lending Act, the Equal Credit Opportunity Act, the Real Estate Settlement Procedures Act, the Home Mortgage Disclosure Act, and the Community Reinvestment Act. In addition, several states have enacted legislation aimed at preventing the practice of "redlining" (a practice of lenders refusing to make loans on real estate in certain, usually low-income, areas). Although important, a discussion of these statutes is beyond the scope of this chapter.

As noted earlier, a mortgage at early common law consisted of a deed from the mortgagor to the mortgagee and an agreement providing for defeasance upon payment of the loan. In many states a mortgage still may be created in this manner, and in most of these the defeasance agreement may be oral. Parol evidence is permitted to prove that a deed was intended only as a mortgage. Of course, this practice is not recommended, especially because of the difficulties of proof and because the mortgagor easily could lose the property if the mortgagee conveys it to a good-faith purchaser. The latter problem is discussed later in connection with recording.

Today, most mortgages involve use of a special mortgage form. The language of the instrument usually is similar to that found in a deed, except that it does not use words of conveyance, but language such as "mortgage and warrant" instead. The form also contains a defeasance clause. In addition, the mortgagor executes a promissory note setting out the details of the loan and provisions concerning its repayment.

Because the mortgage involves a conveyance of an interest in real estate, it must be executed in a manner meeting the same requirements as for a deed. Each state specifies, for example, how many witnesses are required. The statutes generally do not require a mortgage to be executed before a notary public to be valid. However, this usually is required in order to have a mortgage recorded. Therefore, in essence, a mortgage must be certified by a notary.

In addition, when title to the real estate is owned by two or more owners (see concurrent ownership, Chapter 26), all of the owners must sign the mortgage. Otherwise the mortgage will be binding only as to the individual interest of those who do sign. In the case that the owners are husband and wife, and hold the title as tenants by the entireties, it may not be binding at all.

In order to perfect a mortgage security interest, it normally is necessary for the mortgagee to record it. Anyone taking an interest in real estate does so subject to rights evidenced on the record and those apparent on the land. Since the mortgagor usually remains in possession of the property, recording probably will be required.

Recording statutes vary from state to state. One thing they have in common, however, is a requirement that all matters concerning real estate be recorded in an appropriate office in the county in which the affected real estate is located. The particular office varies; such titles as "Recorder" and "Register of Deeds" are common. When properly recorded, any document provides notice to anyone dealing with the named real estate.

In case of a conflict between interests, the one that prevails depends on the type of recording statute. The common types are *race, notice, race-notice,* and *torrens.* A **race recording statute** gives priority to the first to record. A **notice recording statute** provides that in order to provide notice, an interest must be recorded, and a subsequent good-faith purchaser of an interest will prevail over a previous interest if it was not recorded prior to the second transaction. A **race-notice recording statute,** then, is a mixture of the two; it gives priority to the first good-faith purchaser who records. For example, suppose Hopkins sells a certain parcel of real estate to Dawkins on January 10, and later purports to mortgage the same property to Cornett on February 10. On February 15, Cornett records the mortgage and Dawkins records the deed on February 20. Who will prevail?

At *common law* the first instrument in time would prevail. That would be Dawkins. Under a *race* statute, Cornett would prevail since he was the first to record, regardless of whether he knew of Dawkins's interest at the time he took the mortgage. Under a *notice* statute, Cornett should prevail if he took the mortgage in good faith, for value, and with no notice of Dawkins's claim. If Cornett knew of Dawkins's claim, recorded or not, then Dawkins would prevail. Under a race-notice statute, the result would be the same as under the notice statute. However, if Dawkins had recorded first, and then Cornett, the two would yield different results. Then, if both parties recorded without notice of the interest of the other, Cornett would prevail under a notice statute since he had no notice at the time he took the mortgage, but under a race-notice statute Dawkins would prevail, being the first good-faith party to record.

A **torrens recording statute** is unlike any of the other three. The torrens system provides for interests to be recorded on a certificate called a *torrens certificate* rather than on another public record. Generally, interests are valid only if recorded on the certificate, and conflicting interests have priority in the order in which they are recorded. A few torrens statutes permit certain interests, such as tax liens, public easements, and short-term leases to prevail even if not recorded. Torrens statutes, although attractive in theory, never have achieved much popularity in practice.

Rights and Liabilities of the Mortgagor

In a mortgage transaction, the mortgagor usually remains in possession of the mortgaged property and retains the same rights in it as any other owner. She may lease the property to a tenant and is entitled to collect the rent. She may further encumber the property, as by giving a second mortgage, granting an easement, or allowing the creation of lesser liens. She may transfer her ownership rights in the property and, upon her death, title will pass according to her will or to her heirs. If the mortgagor marries during the mortgage period, her spouse may be entitled to a spousal interest in property, if provided by state law. In all cases, however, the interest granted is taken subject to the mortgagee's interest if the mortgage is recorded properly. Of course the mortgagor's principal obligation is to repay the accompanying loan according to the terms of the mortgage agreement. In addition, the agreement often provides for other duties, such as the payment of taxes, the maintenance of adequate insurance, and the general upkeep of the property. If the mortgagor transfers the property to a purchaser who assumes the mortgage, even if she also delegates her duty to pay the mortgage loan, she remains liable in the event of default by the purchaser. Also, if the mortgagee properly forecloses on the property for breach of the mortgage agreement, the mortgagor remains liable for any deficiency. The mortgagor may be relieved of this obligation only if the mortgagee agrees to the delegation of the duty to the purchaser and agrees to look only to the purchaser for performance. Such an agreement among a mortgagor, a mortgagee, and a purchaser is termed a *novation*.

It should be noted that some mortgages include due-on-sale clauses. These clauses provide that the entire mortgage indebtedness becomes due if the property is sold. The validity of such clauses may be subject to state law.

Mortgagee's Assignment of the Mortgage

Generally, the rights of a mortgage are assignable. However, remember that the mortgagee's interest involves both a note evidencing the mortgagor's indebtedness and a security interest in the mortgaged property. Ordinarily both are transferred, but they may be separated. Of course, the security interest is of little value without the note, except to secure any liability the mortgagee may have to an assignee if the note is not paid. Also, the note is less valuable without the security interest. Most states assume that every transfer of a mortgage note automatically includes the rights to the security unless these are specifically excluded. Nevertheless, a prudent assignee should take care to see that he receives both from the mortgagee. If the note is negotiable (commercial paper under

Article 3 of the UCC), it should be negotiated rather than simply assigned.

Foreclosure

If the mortgagor defaults on performing her obligations under the mortgage, notably by not making the required payments, the mortgagee may seek *foreclosure*. Statutes vary concerning the precise procedure, but most require some notice, by the mortgagee to the mortgagor, of intent to foreclose, a petition to the appropriate court, and a hearing on the merits of the petition. Courts ordinarily do not grant this ultimate remedy in cases of minor defaults, such as a late payment or the commission of technical waste (unreasonable use that would impair the mortgagee's security interest, such as allowing the property to fall into disrepair or cutting down all the trees) by the mortgagor. In addition, the mortgagor may cure any default any time before the court finally decrees foreclosure. When foreclosure is granted, the court will place the property in the hands of the county sheriff or some other court officer, to be sold at public auction. Most states no longer allow "strict foreclosure" as is permitted in foreclosures of security interests in personal property. After the sale is completed, the purchaser will receive a special deed, sometimes a *sheriff's deed*. A

Typical foreclosure procedures

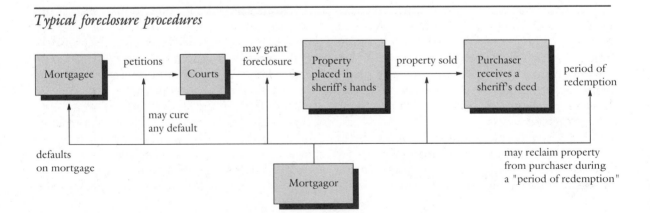

sheriff's deed transfers title to the purchaser subject to a *right of redemption* on the part of the mortgagor. The right of redemption allows the mortgagor to reclaim the property from the purchaser upon payment to the latter of the sale price. The right also may be exercised any time during the **period of redemption,** which is set by statute (for example, six months from the date of the sale). A mortgagor who wishes to redeem her property after foreclosure must act during the period specified in the statute. If the mortgagor dies during the period of redemption, her right will pass to, and may be exercised by, her executor, administrator, or a person specified by will.

GUIDARELLI v. LAZARETTI
305 Minn. 551, 233 N.W.2d 890 (1975)

This was an action by Elio Guidarelli (Plaintiff/Appellant) against Raymond Lazaretti (Defendant/Appellee) to set aside a mortgage foreclosure solely on the ground that Defendant, who was the mortgagee and also the purchaser at the sale, was enriched unjustly. It is alleged that the foreclosed property was worth $100,000 at the time of the sale but Defendant purchased it for $37,782.02. There was no allegation of any other irregularity concerning the sale. Plaintiff took no action during the one year redemption period after the sale, but instituted this action some four years later.

The trial court dismissed Plaintiff's complaint and Plaintiff appealed. Affirmed.

PER CURIAM.

The sole issue raised by plaintiff is whether he as a defaulting mortgagor can maintain an action for unjust enrichment against the purchaser at a foreclosure sale when the action is commenced following expiration of the redemption period, in the absence of any fraud or irregularity in the proceedings.

Plaintiff alleges that he should be allowed to show unjust enrichment, conceding that there was no fraud or other irregularity involved in this foreclosure sale. This claim has been raised in this court several times, and has been rejected each time. In Kantack v. Kreuer . . . , relied on by the lower court, we most recently restated the general rule:

> With respect to the claim that the foreclosure sale should be invalidated because the bid was grossly inadequate, about all that needs be said is that the general rule is that a foreclosure sale free from fraud or irregularity will not be held invalid for inadequacy of the price.

The reason or basis for this rule was set forth in Stearns v. Carlson, . . . (1925), a case in which the mortgagee purchased the realty at the foreclosure sale and then brought an action against the mortgagor for the deficiency on the note. This court held that a claim of inadequate price received at the sheriff's sale could not be asserted as a defense. . . .

Under the circumstances of the present case, where plaintiff did not even allege any fraud or irregularity surrounding the foreclosure sale and where none appears from our examination of the record, we hold that the lower court was correct in ruling that plaintiff could not maintain a cause of action for unjust enrichment. Plaintiff's remedy was to redeem within the year granted by Minn.St. 580.23. Having failed to do so, he cannot complain unless he can show fraud or irregularity to support his claim of unjust enrichment.

Questions

1.   Are there reasons for requiring that the redemption right be exercised within the period provided by statute, or is the Minnesota court just being very technical?

2.   Should the mortgagor be protected against the property's being sold at an inadequate price at public auction?

TITLE-RETAINING SECURITY INTERESTS

In many cases a purchaser of land may receive title at the time of sale, subject to a security interest, such as a mortgage. In other cases the seller may retain title until the purchase price is paid. Examples of the latter include land contracts and trust deeds.

Land Contracts

A seller of real estate may take a security interest in the real estate to secure the sale price by *retaining* title until the debt is paid. The effect is much the same as transferring the title and *taking back* a mortgage at the time of the sale. The difference is that with a **land contract,** the title is encumbered by the purchaser's interest, rather than by the seller's interest as in the case of a mortgage. (When deeds first came into use, they actually were *contracts* for the sale of real estate. They differed from other contracts, however, in that courts of equity always would grant specific performance upon the purchaser's petition. Therefore, they soon were seen as self-executing contracts and, in later years, as instruments of transfer rather than contracts. One requirement for a deed that betrays its contract origin is the necessity of reciting consideration.)

In order to be valid, a land contract must comply with the general requirements for all valid contracts—offer, acceptance, and consideration. In addition, it must be in writing to be enforceable under the Statute of Frauds. If entered into by a person who, at the time of the contract, was a minor, insane, intoxicated, or otherwise lacked contractual capacity, the contract will be voidable at his option.

Land contracts, like mortgages, should be recorded in order to assure perfection of the security interest. As an alternative, most states allow the recording of a "Notice of Land Contract" rather than the contract itself. The effect is the same. These are recorded in the same office as that designated for recording mortgages, and the procedure is the same. In the case of a land contract, however, it is the buyer's interest that must be protected instead of the seller's, so it is the buyer who would see to the recording.

Most states provide specific statutory procedures to be followed by a seller upon default of land contract obligations by the purchaser. If not, the seller simply is entitled to reclaim possession of the property or to sue for breach of the contract, or both in unusual cases. Those states having statutory provisions require that if the seller elects to reclaim possession, foreclosure procedures, similar to those required for foreclosure of a mortgage, must be observed. Florida has such a requirement, as the following case illustrates.

MID-STATE INVESTMENT CORPORATION v. O'STEEN
133 So.2d 455 (Fla. 1961)

This was an action by C. B. and Nell O'Steen (Plaintiff/Appellees) against Mid-State Investment Corporation (Defendant/Appellant) for trespass to real property and conversion of personal property.

Plaintiffs purchased a house and assigned the deed to Defendant as security for a loan, receiving a contract in return. The contract contained a provision:

> And in case of failure of the said parties of the second part to make either of the payments or any part thereof, or to perform any of the covenants on their part hereby made and entered into, this contract shall, at the option of the party of the first part, be forfeited and terminated, and the party of the second part shall forfeit all payments made by them on this contract; and such payments shall be retained by the said party of the first part in full satisfaction and liquidation of all damages by them sustained, and said party of the first part shall have the right to re-enter and take possession of the premises aforesaid without being liable to any action therefor.

Upon Plaintiffs' default, while they were absent, Defendant took possession of the house and contents and almost immediately sold the house to the half-brother of a neighbor.

The trial court found for Plaintiffs. The District Court of Appeal agreed that Defendant was not entitled to repossess the house summarily, but it reversed because of an error in an instruction to the jury.

CARROLL, Donald K., Chief Judge.

We think, and we hold, that the contract involved in this appeal falls within the ken of the provisions of Section 697.01, Florida Statutes, F.S.A., which reads in pertinent part:

> 697.01 Instruments deemed mortgages
> All conveyances, obligations conditioned or defeasible, bills of sale or other instruments of writing conveying or selling property, either real or personal, for the purpose or with the intention of securing the payment of money, whether such instrument be from the debtor to the creditor or from the debtor to some third person in trust for the creditor, shall be deemed and held mortgages, and shall be subject to the same rules of foreclosure and to the same regulations, restraints and forms as are prescribed in relation to mortgages.

In our opinion the contract before us was clearly intended to secure the payment of money and must be deemed and held to be a mortgage, subject to the same rules of foreclosure and to the same regulations, restraints, and forms as are prescribed in relation to mortgages, to use the words of the statute. This being so, the defendant had only a naked legal title as security for the indebtedness, had no legal right to repossess the real or personal property, and had no such right to trespass upon the real property or exercise dominion over the personal property. The courts of this state have many times applied the principle of the quoted statute to instruments of writing in circumstances analogous to those on this appeal. . . .

In this state of the evidence at the close of the trial, which evidence we think permitted no reasonable inference other than that the defendant was liable in trespass and conversion as charged, the trial court correctly directed the verdict against the defendant on the issue of liability and properly submitted the question of damages to the jury.

Questions

1. What are the policy reasons for requiring formal foreclosure proceedings when creditors exercise their security interests in real estate?

2. Should a debtor be permitted to waive formal foreclosure proceedings at the time the security interest is given? at the time foreclosure is to occur?

Trust Deeds

Trust deeds are not as common a security device as mortgages or land contracts. They are recognized in about half the states, and are a popular device in those places. Although similar to a mortgage, a trust deed has some very significant advantages.

The procedure for creating a **trust deed** involves three parties—the debtor, who may be called the settlor or trustor, the creditor, who will be the beneficiary of the trust, and a trustee. The debtor will transfer title to the trustee, who will hold legal title in trust to secure fulfillment of the debtor's obligations to the creditor. In the event of default, the trustee will be empowered to sell the property and apply the proceeds to the obligation owed to the beneficiary. Unless required by state law, the trustee need not follow the procedures required for foreclosure. The sale may be

Creating a trust deed

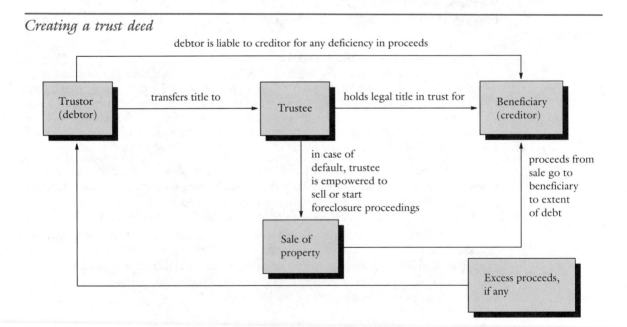

either public or private, with or without notice, as specified by the trust agreement. Generally, the parties may agree to any terms and conditions they see fit.

The reason the trust deed device is not accepted by so many states is that it favors the creditor at the expense of the debtor. First, the trustee is empowered to sell the property without resort to court proceedings. This avoids a great deal of potential expense and delay, but deprives the settlor of the protection afforded a mortgagor. Second, the power to sell the property and to apply the proceeds to payment of the debt is still effective in spite of the fact that the Statute of Limitations may have run on the underlying debt. Finally, there is no right of redemption after a sale under a trust deed. In order to mitigate these effects, a number of states that allow the use of trust deeds simply have required that trust deed security interests be foreclosed in the same manner as mortgages.

MECHANIC'S LIENS

A **mechanic's lien** is a statutory interest in real estate, granted to secure the price of services or materials furnished in the construction, repair, or improvement of real estate. The lien is purely a creature of statute; no lien on real estate was recognized at common law. All states have such statutes, but they vary considerably.

Persons Entitled to Lien

Typically, every person who supplies materials or renders services directly for the construction, repair, or improvement of real estate is entitled to a lien. Whether subcontractors supplying either services or materials also are entitled varies from state to state. For example, suppose landowner Bell contracts with contractor Arntz to build a house. Arntz subcontracts the plumbing and electrical work to Dee. In addition, he orders lumber from Carver. In order to fill the order, Carver purchases the necessary rough boards from a sawmill. Of these, who is entitled to a lien against Bell's property for services and materials?

Arntz will be entitled to a lien in all states. However, the states are split as to the approach taken for Dee's rights. Although Dee is entitled to a lien, under the "Pennsylvania Rule" he has a direct right, and under the "New York Rule" his rights are only derivative of Artnz's rights. Under the former, his right is independent of performance by Arntz. Under the latter, his lien is limited to the amount owed to Arntz, and any breach by Arntz may reduce or eliminate his lien.

Materialman Carver will be entitled to a lien in all states. The sawmill will be entitled to a lien only if *sub*materialmen are expressly protected by the governing statute. In addition, in order to be entitled to a lien, many courts require that a material supplier prove that the materials actually were used on the property that is to be the subject of the lien. It is not sufficient simply to prove that they were ordered for the particular job. This, of course, presents problems of tracking materials, and makes it important to the supplier to establish some means of hedging against the possibility that the contractor may direct materials from one job to another. The importance of adopting such a procedure is illustrated by the following case.

BOWEN v. COLLINS
135 Ga. 221, 217 S.E.2d 193 (1975)

This was an action by G. W. Bowen and one Rogers, his partner (Plaintiffs/ Appellants) against Ronald A. and Carol C. Collins (Defendants/Appellees) for a judgment *in rem* (for a lien) against Defendants' property. Plaintiffs allege material for Defendants' house were charged to their account at Plaintiffs' place of business by a contractor and were not paid for. Defendants contended that the material charged to the account did not go into their home.

The trial court found for Defendants on the ground that Plaintiffs had failed to prove the material was used to construct Defendants' house, and Plaintiffs appealed. Affirmed.

EVANS, Judge.

Laws as to liens of mechanics and materialmen who supply labor or materials for the improvement of realty are in derogation of the common law and must be strictly construed; and one who claims such a lien must bring himself clearly within the law. . . .

The burden was on the plaintiffs to prove that the materials furnished actually went into construction of defendants' building, under a contract and the value of same. . . .

Since there was evidence here from which the jury could infer that much of the material charged against the defendant's job did not go into the construction of defendants' dwelling, the court did not err in charging the jury that to obtain a lien, the supplies must be furnished for the purpose of improving the owner's property and that they were in fact used in such improvements. In Schofield v. Stout . . . it was held that such improvements must be attached to and become incorporated in the reality.

Where a materialman furnishes and delivers material to the owner's premises in reliance on the owner's representation that the material is intended to be used for the improvement of the property, the owner is estopped as between the parties to contend that the material was not in fact so used. . . . But there was no estoppel of the owner under the facts here, and the above statement of law does not apply.

Plaintiff proved the material was charged to the contractor but did not prove that all of same was delivered to defendant's job. Materials were supplied to several other houses in the immediate area, and some of the materials were supposedly delivered to the job by the contractor's employees. Accordingly, the general grounds of the motion for new trial are not meritorious, and the evidence does not demand a finding that the material was delivered to defendant's home construction site and used to improve his dwelling.

Questions

1. How can a home builder protect himself against a mechanic's lien being put on his property for material or work not connected to it?
2. Why should mechanic's lien laws be strictly construed?
3. What can the plaintiffs do now?

Obtaining a Lien

Because the requirements for obtaining a lien are statutory, they must be complied with strictly. Generally, statutes require the lienholder to file a notice of lien in an appropriate county office, such as Register of Deeds, Recorder, or County Clerk. Some also require that notice be given to the landowner, perhaps by service. The filing ordinarily must be accompanied by the claimant's affidavit (sworn statement).

There is considerable variation from state to state concerning the time of filing, such as thirty, sixty, or ninety days after the last work was done or materials were furnished. Frequently, statutes distinguish between those who supply labor and those who supply materials, often allowing a longer filing period for the former.

Foreclosure and Priorities

The procedure for foreclosing a mechanic's lien is substantially the same as that for foreclosing a real estate mortgage. Some statutes, however, provide that a mechanic's lien may attach to only part of the subject real estate rather than to all, as is true of a mortgage. For example, a contractor who

digs a 20-acre pond on a 1500-acre tract of land may be entitled to a lien only on the 20 acres, together with some specified surrounding land.

Mechanic's liens usually take priority over other liens and interests acquired after it was recorded. Some states provide, however, that these liens attach from the time work begins or the first material is furnished, and may be effective even though they are "secret" prior to filing. One notable exception to subordination of other liens is tax liens. Frequently they are given priority regardless of the date on which mechanic's liens are filed.

Mechanic's liens may be waived, or subordinated to other liens, by agreement of the lienholder. Because such an agreement constitutes a contract to transfer an interest in real estate, the Statute of Frauds requires it to be in writing to be enforceable. In addition, some states require that it be recorded. Consider the following case.

KEMP v. THURMOND
521 S.W.2d 806 (Tenn. 1975)

This was an action by Builders Supply Company, Inc. and K-T Distributors, Inc. (Petitioners/Appellants) against E. C. Thurmond III and his wife Doris (Defendants/Appellees) to enforce a materialmen's lien on Defendants' house. Defendants had a home built with materials purchased on credit from Petitioners. [Kemp was probably a representative of one of the petitioners.] The cost was borrowed by Defendants from the Martin Bank, and the bank took and recorded a trust deed to secure repayment of the loan. At the time, the bank gave Petitioners $2500, and the trust deed secured that amount and future advances up to a total of $25,000. The entire amount eventually was lent. After the trust deed was recorded Petitioners began furnishing materials and construction began. The question before the court was whether the trust deed or the materialmen's lien took priority.

The trial court held that the trust deed prevailed and Petitioners appealed. Affirmed.

COOPER, Justice.

In determining whether advances made after the giving of a mortgage shall receive priority over intervening mechanics' liens, courts generally look to whether the mortgagee is under an obligation, pursuant to the terms of his agreement with the mortgagor, to advance the sum or sums called for by the instrument. Many courts, including this Court, "have recognized that where the making of the advances is obligatory upon the mortgagee or beneficiary, the lien of a mortgage or trust deed that has been recorded before the mechanic's lien attaches, despite the fact that advances are actually given subsequently to this time." . . .

Petitioners do not take issue with the above statement of applicable law, but insist that the Court of Appeals erred in finding that "it was an obligation on the part of The Martin Bank to make additional loans." The Martin Bank, in turn, insists that this Court is faced with a concurrent finding of fact by the chancellor and the Court of Appeals on the issue, and that the only question is whether there is any material evidence in the record to support the finding that The Martin Bank was under legal obligation to make additional loans up to $25,000.00.

While a finding of an obligation on the part of The Martin Bank to make additional loans to the Thurmonds may be implicit in the chancellor's holding that The Martin Bank's lien under the deed of trust included the advancements up to $25,000.00, the chancellor made no such specific finding. Absent this, we do not feel bound by the "concurrent finding of fact" rule, but have reviewed the record with a view of determining where the preponderance of evidence lies on the issue. On doing so, we find ourselves in agreement with the finding of the Court of Appeals that "The Martin Bank was under a legal obligation to make its advances, pursuant to its agreement with Thurmond to make those advances, so long as the work progressed. . . . Therefore, the lien (of The Martin Bank) is for the full amount of the recited amount to be advanced. The lien thereof relates back to the filing of the Trust Deed and it is superior to the appellant's lien."

Questions

1. Why should the law have preferred the bank over the material supplier in this case?

2. What is the importance of the recording requirement? Would the result have been different if it had not been met?

OTHER NONCONSENSUAL LIENS

Other liens may be obtained on property without the consent of the property owner. These include liens arising out of judicial proceedings and liens securing obligations owed to the government.

Judicial Liens

Upon filing an action against a debtor, the creditor may seek a court order granting an *attachment* of certain property of the debtor in order to secure payment of any judgment that may be granted in the action. **Attachment liens,** like other interests in real estate, must be recorded properly on the appropriate county records. In order to obtain an attachment lien, the creditor ordinarily must show some overpowering necessity, such as reason to believe the debtor may transfer her property prior to judgment for the purpose of avoiding collection of a judgment. In addition, the creditor must post a bond to secure the payment of any costs and any damages to the debtor that might arise if it later is determined that the creditor's action was brought in bad faith.

When *judgment* is granted to a plaintiff in a civil lawsuit, it becomes a **judgment lien** on any of the defendant's real estate in the county in which the judgment was granted. Anyone purchasing or taking an interest thereafter takes it subject to the rights of the judgment creditor (plaintiff) until the judgment is paid and discharged. Suppose a debtor owned two parcels of real estate in the county, and attachment was granted as to one of them prior to trial. If judgment is granted against him in the later civil suit, the automatic judgment lien still would attach, and both parcels would be encumbered in favor of the judgment creditor. In addition, a copy of the judgment may be certified and recorded in any other county in the state, and it will become a lien against real estate owned by the judgment debtor in each county where it is recorded.

In addition to the judgment lien, a successful plaintiff may request *execution* against any specific real estate owned by the judgment debtor. The result is the same as with a judgment lien except that a recorded execution lien will encumber only a specific parcel, rather than all real estate owned by the judgment debtor in the county.

Tax Liens

A **tax lien** is a very special type of nonconsensual lien. It is taken by a government or governmental agency to secure the payment of various kinds of taxes. The lien to secure the payment of real estate taxes is especially important. Real estate taxes are assessed against most real estate in the United States, usually by the state and its subdivisions. Also, it is important because it attaches to the property automatically, without special filing. The reason for this is that the current status of real estate taxes on each parcel of real estate in a county is already on record. In examining the title to real estate, tax records are among the kinds of records that must be checked as a normal part of a search.

Other tax liens, such as to secure the payment of estate, inheritance, income, or unemployment taxes, also may be recorded, but they are not automatic. They require the filing of a notice of tax due or of delinquency. By law, tax liens frequently are given priority over all other liens. Also, foreclosure of tax liens often provides for a period of redemption, such as six months from the date of the foreclosure sale.

SUMMARY

Security interests in real property may be consensual, such as a mortgage, a land contract, or a trust deed, or they may be nonconsensual, such as a mechanic's, a judicial, or a tax lien. All are perfected by recording in the real estate records in the county in which the subject property is located, except real estate tax liens. They are already on record, without special filing.

A mortgage may be created either by the giving of a deed by the mortgagor to the mortgagee and the taking back by the mortgagor of a right of defeasance, or by the use of a special mortgage instrument. The latter is the most common today. A mortgage transaction usually also includes the mortgagor's signing of a promissory note evidencing the underlying debt and the terms of its repayment.

Recording statutes may be of four types: (1) *race* statutes, giving priority to the first to record; (2) *notice* statutes, which provide that an interest is of no effect until recorded; (3) *race-notice* statutes, giving priority to the first interest acquired in good faith and recorded, and (4) *torrens-system* statutes, giving priority to interests in the order they are recorded on the torrens certificate covering the property.

The interests of the mortgagor and the mortgagee generally may be freely assigned, and the duty of the mortgagor to pay the mortgagee may be delegated. However, if the delegate fails to perform, the mortgagor remains fully liable on the mortgage unless there has been a novation.

Upon default of the mortgagor's obligation, the mortgagee is entitled to give notice of default and to secure a foreclosure order from a court.

The property then can be sold to pay the mortgage. Any excess proceeds are returned to the mortgagor; conversely, the mortgagor is liable for any deficiency. In most states, a mortgagor is entitled to "cure" any defect in performance prior to the sale and thereby stop the sale, or to "redeem" during a statutory period after the sale and reclaim the property. Most states no longer permit strict foreclosure, which allows the mortgagee simply to take the property on default without following foreclosure procedures.

Two other methods of taking voluntary security interests in real estate are the use of a land contract or a trust deed. The former is simply a type of conditional sales contract, and the latter involves the mortgagor's deeding the property to a trustee who holds title for the benefit of the creditor until the underlying debt is repaid. Although the latter originally were used to escape the necessity for meeting foreclosure procedures, most states now require that foreclosure procedures by used.

A mechanic's lien is a type of nonconsensual security interest in real property. It is created by statute to secure the price of services or materials used in the construction, repair, or improvement of real property. Who is entitled to a mechanic's lien, rules concerning priorities, and other matters related to mechanic's liens vary considerably from state to state. Each state's statutes should be consulted for particulars.

Other nonconsensual liens include judicial liens, which include attachment liens, judgment liens, and execution liens. These are granted in connection with a lawsuit in order to secure the payment of any judgment that may be awarded. Attachment liens may be granted prior to trial, and are permitted only when necessary. Judgment liens are automatic with the entry of a judgment, and execution liens are available when a judgment is not paid as required by the court.

Tax liens are a special category of liens. They are granted to secure the payment of various taxes to the federal government, the state government or subdivision, or some governmental agency. They are recorded in a manner similar to other liens and real estate tax liens automatically are part of the real estate records. Tax liens frequently are given priority over all other liens and other interests.

KEY TERMS AND CONCEPTS

mortgage
race recording statute
notice recording statute
race-notice recording statute
torrens recording statute
sheriff's deed
period of redemption
land contract
trust deed
mechanic's lien
attachment lien
judgment lien
tax lien

PROBLEMS

1. Jerry and Barb were married and held their home in their joint names. When they were separated, Jerry agreed to have certain work done on the home. After the work was completed, Jerry failed to pay one subcontractor, Jeffers, for his work. Jeffers served a notice of mechanic's lien on Jerry but not Barb. Later, Jerry and Barb executed a morgage to the bank. What are the relative rights of Jeffers and the bank?

2. Pilson gave a deed instrument to Talbot, directing that in the event of his default on a loan from Landers Bank, Talbot should deliver the deed to the bank. When Pilson defaulted, Talbot did as he was instructed. Five years later, when an oil company showed an interest in the property, Pilson sought to recover it. The bank contended that when Talbot delivered the deed as instructed by Pilson, Pilson lost all of his interest in the property absolutely, with no right of redemption. Is the bank correct?

3.   Land belonging to Gwinn was sold at a mortgage foreclosure sale on February 16, 1942. He sought to exercise his right of redemption on June 20, 1944. The evidence established that he left for military service in December 1941 and was discharged on June 20, 1944. The statutory period of redemption is one year. Might Gwinn be entitled to redeem?

4.   Kelly sold certain land to Lambert. Prior to closing, Lambert searched the records in the county in which the land was located. Among other things, the records showed all taxes were paid to date. After Lambert purchased the land, the county treasurer notified her that the records were in error and taxes for the last three years were still outstanding. When Lambert refused to pay, the treasurer sought to foreclose the tax lien. What might be the result?

5.   McDonald borrowed money from the National Bank of Washington to finance a construction project, giving the bank a security interest in the form of a trust deed. The security agreement covered future advances. Later, McDonald sold the land to Security Investors. In order to help Security Investors obtain a loan from the same bank to continue construction, McDonald subordinated his interest in the trust deed to that of the bank concerning all future advances. Thereafter, Columbia supplied materials for the project and, when Security Investors did not pay, Columbia sought to enforce a mechanic's lien. The bank had given proceeds of the loan to Security Investors, and claimed its interest under the future-advances clause was superior to that of Columbia. Is the bank correct?

6.   McKeighan obtained a loan from Citizens Bank, giving the bank a deed to be held as a mortage. McKeighan retained possession of the land and lived there. When she defaulted on the loan, the bank sold the property to Stockton, who demanded possession. Did the sale foreclose McKeighan's rights?

7.   During the term of a mortgage, the mortgagor was in possession of the property. While there, he involved himself in distilling illegal "moonshine" on the property, which gave rise to a petition by the Solicitor General to have the property padlocked. Also, the mortgagor was not repairing or maintaining the property so it was deteriorating seriously. Does the mortgagee have the right to intervene and either dispossess the mortgagor or repair the property and charge the mortgagor with the cost?

8.   David operated a restaurant on property covered by a mortgage. She purchased certain kitchen equipment from Intermountain Food Equipment Company on a conditional sales contract. The contract was recorded properly. Thereafter, the mortgage holder foreclosed the mortgage. Who has the superior right to the security in the kitchen equipment that was attached as a fixture?

9.   There has been much resistance to "due-on-sale" clauses (clauses providing that the entire amount of the debt becomes due upon sale of the property securing the debt), but those contained in mortgage agreements generally have been held valid. Are they also applicable if the mortgagor then sells the property on a land contract? Why?

10.   Suppose a property owner pays a contractor the full price of the job upon the contractor's showing releases of all subcontractor liens. If the releases of the subcontractors had been obtained by the contractor's fraud, would the releases be binding as to the property owner?

Chapter | 23

Suretyship

INTRODUCTION

Terminology is a problem when beginning a study of suretyship. As discussed below, the term *suretyship* may be interpreted in two ways. Also, the parties involved may be referred to by a variety of names. In this chapter, the parties will be designated as *surety* (one who agrees to be responsible for the debt of another), *principal* (the one who owed the debt), and *creditor* (the person to whom the principal owes the debt).

Suretyship and Guaranty

In modern legal terms, *suretyship* generally is considered to encompass both the contract of suretyship and the contract of guaranty. The term covers all situations in which one party agrees to be answerable for the debt, default, or miscarriage of another and has a right to reimbursement from the other in the event that she actually must pay the obligation. Historically, contracts of suretyship and those of guaranty were treated separately by the law. Technically, **suretyship** involves a situation in which the surety becomes a party to a contract with the principal, rendering herself *primarily* liable thereon. A **contract of guaranty,** on the other hand, involves a situation in which the guarantor renders herself *secondarily* liable, under a separate contract of guaranty and upon separate consideration. The surety's primary liability

Creation of a suretyship

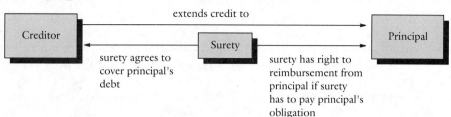

allows the third party to go either to him, his principal, or both to collect the debt. The guarantor's secondary liability requires that the third party must go first to the primary obligor and be turned down before going to the guarantor. The surety is obligated to pay in all events, but the

guarantor is obligated to pay only if the other party does not. The promise of the guarantor sometimes is referred to as a collateral promise. In the following case, the court dealt at some length with the nature and formation of suretyship contracts.

UNITED STATES v. TILLERAAS
709 F.2d 1088 (6th Cir. 1983)

This was an action by the United States (Plaintiff/Appellee) against Elizabeth A. Tilleraas (Defendant/Appellant) to recover principle plus interest on defaulted student loans guaranteed by Plaintiff under the Higher Education Act of 1965. The loans had been made by Dakota National Bank & Trust Co., Fargo, North Dakota on September 4, 1969, June 18, 1970, and October 5, 1970. The bank assigned Defendant's notes to Plaintiff on May 10, 1974, and the bank's claims were paid fully by Plaintiff on July 5, 1974. Plaintiff filed this suit on July 4, 1980.

Defendant moved for summary judgment on the ground that Plaintiff's cause of action was barred by a six-year federal statute of limitations applicable to actions for money damages brought by the United States upon "any contract express or implied." The motion was overruled and Defendant appealed. Affirmed.

WELLFORD, Circuit Judge.

It is clear that we must apply federal law, not state law in determining the validity of appellee's statute of limitations defense. . . . This rule of law applies because of the federal interest in the protection of its funds. It is crucial, then, to determine under that federal law when the government's cause of action "accrued." Appellant asserts that it accrued when she first defaulted, July 27, 1972. The government responds that the limitation period . . . was tolled because of appellant's failure to notify the creditor Bank (or the United States) of her change of address, preventing by this omission the commencement of suit against her. The government further contends that its cause of action accrued when it paid the insurance claim filed by the lender Bank.

The government admits that under [the Higher Education Act of 1965], which provides that upon payment of the lender's claims the government becomes subrogated to all of the lender's rights and is entitled to assignment of the note, and that its rights as assignee are co-extensive with those of the lender. . . . [T]he government argues, however, that it is not limited to assignee status, since it may also rely on its common law right as a surety to bring an action against the principal for reimbursement. Since a surety's or guarantor's cause of action for indemnity does not accrue until payment of the principal's liability, . . . the government claims that it also has a cause of action which accrued on the date it paid the lender, July 6, 1974, a cause which was timely when this action was filed.

It is uncontroverted that Tilleraas did not inform the lender Bank, nor the United States, of her change of address from North Dakota to Cleveland upon her marriage and move to Ohio. The government claims that it was not until 1979 that it finally obtained a current address on appellant prior to institution of suit in 1980. Thus, the government would exclude this approximate five year period from the running of the six year statute here involved.

We agree with the district court . . . that it is unnecessary to decide this contention of the United States, because we affirm the judgment of District Judge William K. Thomas that the government's right of action did not accrue, for the purposes of this statute, until July of 1974.

The use of the word "insurance" in the statute is not determinative in light of the realities existing between the relevant parties. The nature of the substantive rights and duties among the parties clearly reflects a surety-principal-lender relationship. Insurance is a contract where one undertakes to indemnify another against loss, damage or liability caused by an unknown or contingent event. Since the insured pays the insurer for the promise of indemnity, the insurer benefits to the extent that a contingency never occurs. Where a contingency does occur, the insurer can still be made whole, by virtue of subrogation, to the extent that the insured would be able to recover damages from a third party. Despite the presence of this right of subrogation it is clear that *when the contract is formed* all legal rights and obligations flow between the insurer and the insured. At this initial stage, there is no legal obligation owing from the third party to the insurer. In fact, it is unknown at that stage whether such a third party obligation will ever arise and, if so, who that third party will be.

A surety, on the other hand, promises to assume the responsibility for the payment of a debt incurred by another should he or she fail to repay the creditor. The arrangement is made to induce the creditor to deal with the borrower where there might otherwise be reluctance to do so. Under this arrangement, the nature, size, and source of the possible loss to the creditor is known from the start. In addition, there is no payment from the creditor to the surety or guarantor for this "insured" payment. Rather, a kind of tripartite relationship is formed. The consideration running from the creditor to the debtor is deemed sufficient to support the surety's promise to make the debt good. In turn, the benefit flowing to the debtor by virtue of the surety's promise places that debtor under an implied legal obligation to make good any loss incurred by any payment the surety must ultimately make to the creditor. . . . It is clear than that the two contracts are materially distinguishable, as are the rights and duties of the parties involved. . . .

Under the FISLP [Federally Insured Student Loan Program] the student contracts to borrow money with no collateral and upon favorable interest and repayment terms. The lender, in turn, contracts with the Department of Education to insure repayment should the student default. This has consistently been interpreted as creating a third-party surety contract, despite its nomenclature. . . .

We conclude, therefore, that the United States in this instance stands in the position of a surety-guarantor, and therefore it may pursue its rights as a surety under FISLP. As pointed out, it was not until July of 1974 that the government paid the Bank's claim and obtained its right to sue the defaulting appellant on the underlying loan. Under the realities of the FISLP, the government is a surety of the borrower and is entitled to its rights as such. This is the position supported by the other Courts of Appeals that have considered the same issue under this law.

Questions

1. What would be the consequences of a contrary result in this case—namely, that the surety's right to collect accrued when the debtor defaulted?

2. Is the result in this case fair to the debtor—the student?

Circumstances of Suretyship

Suretyship contracts are found in three major circumstances. The first is *credit extension*. When a seller is uncertain about the credit-worthiness of the buyer, the seller may require that a third party act as surety. This may be done by **co-signing** (true suretyship) or by collateral obligation. The surety may be an agent of the primary obligor (a *del credere* agent) or may be some other person in whom the seller has confidence. The use of a surety for this purpose may be particularly important when the principal obligor is a minor or when there is no other security for an obligation.

A second common circumstance under which suretyship contracts arise is in **bonding.** This is an important aspect of the business of many insurance companies. A bail bond or appearance bond may be issued guaranteeing a defendant's appearance in court to face criminal charges. To obtain the bond, a defendant will pay a premium calculated as a percentage of the face amount of the bond—perhaps ten percent. If the defendant

then fails to appear, the bond is forfeited. Bail actually is the obligation of the defendant, but it is paid on her behalf by the insurer and is recoverable by the insurer from the defendant in the case of default. Other situations that may require the posting of a bond are handling of public funds by a public official, obtaining a notary public certificate, becoming a fiduciary such as an executor or administrator of an estate or a guardian of an incompetent person, guaranteeing the honesty of certain employees or the proper performance of a contract by an independent contractor, and securing some requested relief in judicial proceedings, such as an appeal or an attachment of property. A bond may be appropriate whenever a person might create liability by her conduct. For example, an employee who handles cash or valuable property for an employer might be bonded to secure any loss to the employer in the event of theft by the employee.

Finally, *third-party creditor beneficiary contracts*

involve suretyship. This situation differs from the previous two in that in these contracts, the third party is not the surety. By virtue of the creditor beneficiary contract, the third party becomes principal debtor and the promisee-debtor becomes a surety by operation of law. As discussed below, the promisee-debtor has the same rights and defenses as any other surety, including the right to be reimbursed by the principal debtor if he has to pay the creditor.

THE SURETYSHIP CONTRACT

Since a suretyship obligation is contractual, the general rules of contract apply. In order to be valid, there must be offer, acceptance, and consideration. In the true suretyship situation, in which primary liability is assumed by the surety, the consideration for the surety's promise will be the same as the consideration for the principal debtor's promise. In the guarantee situation, since the guarantor is assuming secondary liability under a separate contract, independent consideration is required.

As already noted, in modern terms, suretyship may involve the assumption of either primary or secondary liability. When the liability is primary, the surety's contract may be either oral or written unless the consideration paid for her promise involves subject matter within the Statute of Frauds. When the liability is secondary, her promise *always* must be in writing unless her motivation invites application of the "Main Purpose Doctrine," which provides that collateral promises made for the direct benefit of the promisor need not be in writing. Collateral promises and the requirements of the Statute of Frauds are discussed in more detail in Chapter 10.

DEFENSES OF A SURETY

Certain defenses may be available to a surety who is sued on the underlying obligation. These in-clude payment by the principal, acts of the creditor that might harm the surety, and certain personal defenses. These defenses may be complete or only partial.

Payment of a Debt by the Principal

The surety is discharged to the extent that the principal pays the debt. The surety then owes no further obligation to either the principal or the creditor.

Rejection of Tender

When payment of a debt is tendered and that tender is rejected by the creditor, the principal and the surety are both discharged of the *obligation of immediate performance*. Also, the refusal of valid tender has the effect of stopping the accumulation of interest. The debt itself is not discharged, but the obligation of the surety is discharged. It would not be fair for the creditor to increase the surety's risk by refusing immediate payment. The principal is obligated only to make payment available to the creditor in a reasonable manner.

Alteration of the Original Contract

Any change in the terms of the original contract between the creditor and the primary debtor, without the consent of the surety, will discharge the surety either completely or at least to the extent that he is adversely affected. Since the suretyship agreement has made the surety a party to the original contract, either primarily or collaterally, changes that adversely affect him would be invalid because they would be unilateral. As with any contract, the unilateral imposition of different or additional terms is not allowed. Consider the following case.

GILBERT v. COBB EXCHANGE BANK
140 Ga.App. 514, 231 S.E.2d 508 (1976)

This was an action by Cobb Exchange Bank (Plaintiff/Appellee) against L. A. Gilbert (Defendant/Appellant) to recover the amount due on a defaulted note pursuant to a contract of guaranty. Defendant contended that he was discharged by certain events described in the court's opinion.

From a judgment granting Plaintiff's motion for a directed verdict, Defendant appealed. Reversed with direction.

BELL, Chief Judge.

Plaintiff's evidence established that Defendant's son on July 31, 1970 executed a promissory note to plaintiff in the amount of $3100. The defendant executed an unconditional guaranty of payment of the note and of all extensions or renewals. On October 10, 1971 the note was renewed for an additional $600 cash and added to the principal amount of the original. The defendant argued at trial and here that the addition of the $600 constituted a novation and was accomplished without his consent which operated to discharge him. A novation without the consent of the surety will discharge the surety under Code Section 103-202. This statute has been held to apply to a contract of guaranty. . . . Plaintiff contends that since the guaranty covered all renewals of the note, there was no discharge. While the guaranty did cover extensions or renewals, it could only apply to a renewal of the same obligation and not a new one. The guaranty very clearly guaranteed payment of "that certain note dated July 31, 1970 in the amount of $3,100.00 . . . and all extensions or renewals thereof, . . ." and nothing else. The addition of the $600 to principal constituted a material change in the terms of the note. A novation resulted which discharged defendant. [A *novation* is an agreement by a creditor to discharge the debtor and to look only to a specified third party for payment of the debt.]

Questions

1. What should the bank have done to avoid discharging the surety when it renewed the note and increased it by $600?
2. Why is the court being so protective of the surety?

Discharge of the Principal

Discharge by the creditor of the principal debtor, or any principal debtor when there is more than one, will operate to discharge the surety unless the surety has consented to the discharge or the third party *specifically* has reserved rights against the surety. Although such a discharge has no effect on the surety's right to reimbursement from the principal, it does constitute a change in her expectation that it is the principal who will pay. Therefore, the law will dictate that discharge of the principal presumably is intended to discharge the surety also, unless the creditor makes his intent to the contrary clear prior to the discharge.

Principal's Defenses

The surety has available many of the same defenses that would be available to the principal if the principal were sued. These are defenses arising out of the transaction, such as misrepresentation, fraud, duress, undue influence, and illegality. Defenses entirely personal to the principal, however, such as minority, insanity, and bankruptcy, cannot be used by the surety. One factor frequently giving rise to the need for a surety is a concern about some personal characteristic of the principal such as age, sanity, or credit-worthiness. For ex-

ample, it is common for a merchant to require that a parent or some other adult co-sign an obligation with a minor.

Personal Defenses

Personal defenses not arising out of the transaction are available to the surety if they are personal to her and not to the principal. Thus, if the surety is a minor, insane, or intoxicated at the time the suretyship contract is entered into, that agreement is voidable the same as any other agreement, as discussed in Chapter 9. In addition, the surety may defend on the ground of the running of the applicable statute of limitations and, if the suretyship promise is collateral, the Statute of Frauds as well. The death of the surety may or may not provide a defense, as illustrated by the following case.

AMERICAN CHAIN CO., INC. v. ARROW GRIP MFG. CO., INC. et al.
134 Misc. 321, 235 N.Y.S. 228 (1929)

This was an action by American Chain Co., Inc. (Plaintiff) against a number of defendants, including the executors of the estates of three deceased guarantors of a contract under which Plaintiff and Arrow Grip Mfg. Co., Inc. (one of the defendants) were principal parties.

The contract in question was executed on May 21, 1923. Although not named in the contract, George F. Underwood, Louis W. Emerson, and William H. Gelshenan (stockholders in Arrow Grip) signed as guarantors, apparently to secure favorable credit terms for their corporation. The contract provided that the guaranty would be a continuing one, applying not only to purchases at the time of the contract but to future purchases by Arrow Grip from Plaintiff as well. It further provided: "This agreement shall be enforceable by and against the respective administrators, executors, successors and assigns of the parties hereto, and the death of the guarantors shall not terminate the liability of such guarantors under this agreement, except by the giving of notice of termination of this agreement by the representatives of the since-deceased in the manner hereinbefore provided with respect to termination of this agreement."

Underwood died in 1923, and Gelshenan and Emerson died in 1924. Their estates were properly probated and closed. The purchases giving rise to this suit were made after the guarantors' deaths, and the representatives of the estates had no knowledge of Plaintiff's claim until after January 1927. Plaintiff's claims had never been filed with the estates.

The trial court rejected the claim of guaranty. The decision was not appealed.

HEFFERNAN, J.

It seems to me that the failure to name all the guarantors in the body of the instrument is of no importance. It is not disputed that the guarantors affixed their names to the contract with the intent to sign the same. That being so, they thereby became parties to it and are bound by its provisions although not named in the body of the writing. . . .

The important question to be decided in this case is whether the contract, so far as the liability of the decedents is concerned, was revoked by death. There is no parallel case in this state, nor is the language contained in the instrument under consideration substantially identical with that used in any of the cases arising in other jurisdictions. It is distinguishable in that it provides that it shall be enforceable by and against the respective administrators, executors, successors, and assigns of the parties thereto and that death of the guarantors shall not terminate their liability. The mere fact, however, that it purports to bind the representatives of the guarantors does not impose any greater obligation. The presumption is, in the absence of express words to the contrary, that every person who makes a contract intends to bind his executors and administrators. . . .

The confusion in the cases dealing with the subject of guaranty can be clarified by determining first whether the contract was revocable during life though continuing until notice given by the guarantor, or whether the obligation be considered as one which is entire and indivisible. If the latter be the proper construction of the guaranty, the responsibility for advances made after death continues until the completion of all the acts contemplated. If, however, the consideration passes at each time a separate sale is made, and the contract is therefore severable, death ends the liability as to transactions occurring thereafter. . . . The decease of a guarantor in a divisible contract of indemnity revokes the obligation as to advances thereafter made. In case of a continuing guaranty, each advance made by the guarantor [*sic*] constitutes a fresh consideration and, when made, an irrevocable promise on the part of the living guarantor. Guaranties have, therefore, been divided into two classes. The first is where the entire consideration passes wholly at one time; the other where it passes at different times and is separable or divisible. The former are not revocable by the guarantor and are not affected by his death. The latter, on the contrary, may be revoked as to subsequent transactions by the guarantor upon notice to that effect and are determined by his death. The guaranty in the case at bar is in the latter class. . . . Where the consideration for the guaranty is given once for all, such as in the case of a surety upon a lease or when the liability is upon a bond given to secure the faithful performance of his duties by a person occupying a position of trust and confidence, the estate of the surety is liable after death. In case of a contract for the payment of money or the sale or purchase of property or of covenant of warranty, it would be an unreasonable supposition that the parties intended that the obligation should not survive against their representatives although not specifically named. . . .

Whether the fact of death must be made known to the one advancing credit before liability ends has caused a divergence of opinion. In some states, it has been held that actual or constructive notice must be shown to relieve from liability, and until that is received responsibility continues, but not beyond. . . . In other jurisdictions, it is decided that death ipso facto ends the relationship as of the date thereof. . . . Testing the rules of law laid down in the conflicting authorities referred to and having in mind the practical results that are likely to flow from them, reason, it seems to me, dictates that the latter doctrine is preferred. If death ends liability on an instrument of this character, then, as I view it, it is wholly irrelevant whether or not the guarantor [*sic*] acquires notice thereof.

Questions

1. What policy reasons support the court's ruling about the guaranty in this case not surviving death?
2. Is the distinction drawn by the court between single transactions and continuing guarantees sound?

Fraud in Inducing the Suretyship

Fraud by the creditor in inducing someone to become surety on an obligation will render the suretyship contract voidable. Fraud by the principal will not have that effect on the creditor, who should be liable only for his own wrongdoing. Such wrongdoing may occur by silence. Most jurisdictions impose upon a creditor the duty to inform the prospective surety of all risks that are known to the creditor and which the creditor has no reason to believe are known to the prospective surety.

Impairment of Security

If there is security for the debt in addition to the promise of the surety, the creditor is not allowed to surrender the security or unreasonably to allow its value to be diminished without the consent of the surety. If the creditor does so, the surety will be discharged to the extent that the surrender or **impairment of security** has injured her. The security may be collateral that she returns to the principal or allows to fall into disrepair, or it may be the release of another surety on the same obligation. In either situation, this rule applies only to security existing at the time the suretyship contract was made and on which the surety relied in entering into the obligation. In the following case, the court deals with questions concerning whether impairment of collateral should discharge the surety, and to what extent.

LANGEVELD v. L.R.Z.H. CORPORATION
74 N.J. 45, 376 A.2d 931 (1977)

This was an action by John P. Langeveld (Plaintiff/Respondent) against L.R.Z.H. Corporation and others (Defendants) and Joseph A. Higgins, Sr. (Defendant/Appellant) to recover on a contract of guaranty.

On March 10, 1972, L.R.Z.H. Corporation made and delivered to Plaintiff a promissory note for $57,500, secured by a third-priority mortgage on certain real estate. Defendant Higgins, among others, also signed the note as guarantors. The note matured on February 15, 1973, and was not paid. It was then discovered that Plaintiff's mortgage had never been recorded, and Plaintiff recorded it on March 1, 1973. However, in the meantime, since March 10, 1972, (1) another mortgage by L.R.Z.H. Corporation, in the amount of $100,000, (2) a Mechanic's Notice of Intention in the amount of $111,825.48, and (3) a Mechanic's Notice of Intention in the amount of $12,804.56 had been recorded. Defendant contended that, in view of these facts, Plaintiff had allowed the collateral to become so impaired that he, as guarantor, should be discharged of liability.

The trial court found for Plaintiff, and its decision was affirmed on appeal to the Superior Court, Appellate Division. Reversed and remanded by the New Jersey Supreme Court.

MOUNTAIN, J.

[The court first noted that the parties had drawn particular attention to Section 3-606 of the Uniform Commercial Code] . . . which in pertinent part reads,

Impairment of Recourse or Collateral.

(1) The holder discharges any party to the instrument to the extent that without such party's consent the holder

•   •   •   •   •

    (b) unjustifiably impairs any collateral for the instrument given by or on behalf of the party or any person against whom he has a right of recourse. . . .

It is a well-recognized principle of the law of suretyship that a release of collateral held by a creditor, or its impairment by improper action or inaction on his part, will extinguish the obligation of the surety, at least to the extent of the value of the security released or impaired. This rule has come to be accepted as the law of our state. . . . The section of the Uniform Commercial Code we are considering is essentially a restatement of this rule, as the courts that have examined it have consistently held. . . .

The doctrine is an equitable one, designed to protect the surety's right of subrogation. Upon paying the debt, the surety is, as a matter of law, subrogated to all the creditor's rights against the principal debtor and is entitled to all benefits deriveable from any security of the principal debtor that may be in the creditor's hands. The rule forbidding impairment of collateral has as its chief aim the protection of these potential benefits made available through subrogation.

Defendant has made out a prima facie case to support his contention that he comes within the favor of this rule. Relating his contentions to the language of the act clearly demonstrates that this is so. Thus we see that plaintiff is the "holder" of collateral, as the word is used in the statute. Defendant is a "party to the instrument" in his capacity as guarantor. A failure to record a mortgage held as collateral security—absent waiver, estoppel or the like—seems clearly to be an instance of unjustifiable impairment. Common law authorities so held, almost without exception. . . .

Plaintiff essentially disputes defendant's position on two grounds. He urges, first, that the guaranty is unconditional in form and that this being so, the alleged impairment of collateral in no way affects the obligation to which the guaranty gives rise. In the second place he contends that there has in fact been no impairment of collateral, or at least none that has caused defendant to suffer loss. . . .

The point to be made and emphasized is that absent express agreement, waiver or renunciation, a surety's right of subrogation to *unimpaired* collateral will be protected. We do not find this right to have been waived or relinquished by anything contained in this guaranty.

Plaintiff's second contention is that the collateral has not as a matter of fact been impaired, or at least not to an extent that it has caused defendant any loss. [The Court did not agree with this contention.] . . .

The parties express sharply differing views as to the extent to which an impairment of collateral should be held to discharge one secondarily liable. Defendant suggests that the Code has adopted the rule, sometimes referred to as that of *strictissimi juris*, that a surety is completely discharged by any impairment of collateral, whether or not he has sustained loss or prejudice. Plaintiff, on the other hand, contends that the surety should only be released from liability to the extent that actual, calculable monetary loss can be shown to have occurred.

We think the statute should be read as adopting a rule somewhere between these extremes. If the impairment of collateral can be measured in monetary terms, then the calculated amount of the impairment will ordinarily measure the extent of the surety's discharge. But there are factual situations—this may or may not be one of them—where a surety may be able to establish that he has sustained prejudice, but be unable to measure the extent of the prejudice in terms of monetary loss. Where such a situation is presented the surety will normally be completely discharged.

Questions

1. Would it have made more sense for the court to adopt the strict rule on the theory that its application would be simpler?

2. Is the result in this case fair or unfair? to whom?

RIGHTS OF THE SURETY

When a surety is called upon to pay the guaranteed obligation, he or she may have certain rights. These include demanding payment by the principal, assuming the principal's rights against others, and requiring some contribution by cosureties.

Exoneration

It is not expected that the surety ultimately will be liable for the obligations; it is the principal who should pay. Therefore, in all cases, if the creditor demands payment from the surety, the surety is entitled to demand of the principal that he pay instead. In a lawsuit for payment of the obligation brought by the creditor against the surety, the latter even may join the principal as a party to the suit, thus establishing the primary obligation of the principal at the same time as the surety's obligation is adjudicated.

Subrogation

A surety who pays the principal's obligation to the creditor is automatically the owner of the creditor's rights against the principal. This is called **subrogation.** Of course, subrogation does not ensure that the surety will have a right to recover against the principal. If the principal was a minor, insane, or otherwise incapacitated at the time of her contract, or if there were other defenses available to the principal that were not available to the surety, then the surety, by subrogation, will obtain only a voidable right or less.

Reimbursement

Again, because the obligation is supposed to be paid by the principal, payment by the surety entitles the surety to reimbursement from the principal. This is much the same as acquiring rights by subrogation but it is an independent right and is not dependent on the validity of the creditor's rights. For example, although the obligation of a principal to the creditor may be discharged by composition or other insolvency proceedings, the surety might not join or might not be joined, and the creditor expressly may reserve rights against the surety. In such a case, although the principal will be discharged as to the creditor on the original obligation and thus any subrogation, the obligation to reimburse the surety will not be discharged. In the case of bankruptcy, a surety, by right of reimbursement, also may occupy a position superior to that of the creditor, which he would get by subrogation, as when a surety's claim is secured but the creditor's is not.

Contribution

Sometimes more than one person is surety on a principal's obligation. These may be joint or independent sureties. When one surety is required to pay the obligation, she is entitled to **contribution** from the others of their proportional shares. In the case of joint sureties, the contribution obligation will be shared *pro rata*. In the case of independent sureties, the percentage each will bear is subject to agreement between each surety and the creditor or the other sureties. In the absence of an agreement to the contrary, the liability is presumed to be in the same proportion as the relative consideration received by each. Therefore, if the sureties are members of a partnership, and the consideration was taken as a partnership asset, each will be liable for contribution in a percentage equal to his percentage share of partnership debts.

SUMMARY

Suretyship is created when one person called the *surety* agrees to be responsible to pay the obligation of a second person, called the *principal*, to a third party, called the *creditor*. The surety's obligation may be primary (true suretyship), or it may be secondary (collateral, or technical guaranty). If it is of the latter type, it must be in writing to be enforceable under the statute of frauds. As with any other contract, any suretyship agreement must comply with the requirements of the law of contracts.

A surety may defend against payment of an obligation under certain circumstances. These include when (1) the principal and the creditor materially alter the principal's obligation; (2) there has been a discharge of the principal by the creditor; (3) the principal has paid the obligation or the creditor has refused valid tender of payment; (4) there have been defenses created by the transaction, such as fraud, duress, or undue influence; (5) the surety has personal defenses such as his own incapacity or bankruptcy; (6) the surety was induced fraudulently, by the creditor, to enter into the suretyship agreement; or (7) collateral or other security has been surrendered, or unreasonably impaired, by the creditor.

Every demand for, or payment of, the principal's obligation is accompanied by certain rights in the surety. They are exoneration by the principal (the right to require the principal to pay instead of the surety), subrogation to the rights of the creditor, reimbursement by the principal, and contribution by other co-sureties of their proportionate shares.

KEY TERMS AND CONCEPTS

suretyship
contract of guaranty
co-signing
bonding
impairment of security
subrogation
contribution

PROBLEMS

1. Carter owed the Bank of Waynesboro $10,000 on a promissory note due May 13. Carter then experienced business difficulties and was unable to pay the note when due. The bank extended the time of payment for six months. However, during that period Carter was declared bankrupt, and the bank sought to collect the amount due from Ghosh, who had signed the note as surety for Carter. Ghosh contended he was not liable on the instrument because the due date had been extended without his permission. Is Ghosh correct?

2. Vaccaro and Anderson were stockholders and directors of a corporation. When the corporation experienced financial difficulties, Vaccaro

lent $2000 to the corporation, which it carried on it's books as a liability. Thereafter, Anderson guaranteed payment of the note to Vaccaro. When the corporation was unable to pay, Anderson paid $581 of the obligation and then refused to pay more, contending she was not liable because she had been paid no consideration for the guaranty. Is Anderson correct?

3. Burns operated an appliance store, primarily selling Sylvania appliances. In order to aid Burns in securing financing for inventory, Burns's brother, Philip, signed a form entitled "Guarantee of Past and Future Indebtedness" with "Sylvania Electric Products and/or John P. Maguire" as addressees. Thereafter, Burns secured inventory on credit from Sylvania and other financing from Maguire. Maguire subsequently assigned Burns's account to Financeamerica. When Burns defaulted, Financeamerica sought to enforce the guarantee signed by Philip, and Philip defended on the ground that the guarantee was for the benefit of Sylvania and Maguire only, and was not assignable. Is Philip correct?

4. Arnold, Ben, and Carl were joint sureties on an 8-3/4 percent promissory note. When the note was defaulted, Arnold paid the entire amount of $12,465.23. Arnold then sued Ben and Carl for contribution. The court granted judgment in favor of Arnold and against Ben and Carl, each for one-third of the amount paid by Arnold, together with 8-3/4 percent interest on the amounts prior to judgment—interest at the legal rate after judgment—and attorney fees. Was this judgment proper?

5. On January 15, Black sent a letter to the Electric Storage Battery Co. guaranteeing credit extended to his son on his purchase of batteries. Electric Storage then sold some $2500 worth of batteries to Black's son, although nothing was said to Black. Sixteen months later, when Black's son defaulted on the obligation, Electric Storage sued Black on his guarantee. Black defended on the ground that he never had been notified that credit had been extended in reliance on his guarantee. Is Black correct?

6. Davis lent $15,000 to Edwards on an oral promise by Edwards to pay on demand. The loan was granted on the condition that Finley would guarantee payment. Finley did so, executing a written contract of guarantee. The obligation remained unpaid for eight years. When her demand for payment was refused, Davis sued both Edwards and Finley. In the jurisdiction, the statute of limitation on oral obligations was five years, and ten years on written obligations. The court, therefore, dismissed the suit as to Edwards, but not as to Finley. Finley appealed on the ground that since the debtor was discharged, so was the surety. Is Finley correct?

7. Sanders became obligated to the Kitsap County Credit Bureau on a $5000 note executed to secure the purchase price of an automobile. Richards also signed the note, guaranteeing payment by Sanders. Thereafter, a dispute arose, and in settlement the Credit Bureau agreed to accept $3500 from Sanders in full payment of the obligation. The Credit Bureau then sued Richards for the other $1500. Is Richards liable?

8. Collins lent Darby $25,000, and Darby executed a promissory note due in six months. The face of the note called for payment of $30,000. Payment of the note was guaranteed by the Evans Bonding Co. When the note was not paid, Collins sued both Darby and Evans. The note and its underlying obligation were determined to be illegal and void, under the usury laws of the jurisdiction. The court therefore dismissed the suit against both Darby and Evans. Collins contended that although the illegality relieved Darby of liability, it did not discharge the surety. Is Collins correct?

9. Arvin contracted with the City of Buckner, Missouri, to install sewer lines in certain areas of the city. The contract provided that work would begin as soon as the city could obtain funding. Arvin's performance was secured by a bond issued by Phoenix Assurance Co. After a delay of eleven months, Arvin gave notice to the city that he was quitting because the city did not have the funds to pay the contract and it had delayed too long in getting the contract started. The city sued Phoenix, and Phoenix contended that it was not liable for the reasons stated by Arvin. Is Phoenix liable?

10. Watkins and Lankford signed a promissory note as joint obligors. When the note was not paid, Watkins paid the entire amount due and then sued Lankford, offering evidence that, in signing the note, she was acting only as surety for Lankford. Lankford objected to the evidence on the ground that nowhere on the note did it disclose Watkins as a surety only. Should the evidence be admitted?

Chapter | 24

Bankruptcy

INTRODUCTION

The Constitution of the United States, Article 1, Section 8, clause 4 provides, "The Congress of the United States shall have the power . . . to establish . . . uniform laws on the subject of bankruptcy throughout the United States." Bankruptcy is entirely federal; states are prohibited from enacting bankruptcy laws, although the federal Bankruptcy Act incorporates state law under certain circumstances. In addition, state law may provide for similar proceedings.

The purpose of bankruptcy law as it originated in England was to protect creditors. Bankruptcies were set in motion at the insistance of creditors, and operated against the debtor contrary to his or her wishes. Bankruptcy law was intended to ensure a fair distribution of the debtor's assets to the creditors, although the debtor also benefited by being discharged from his or her obligations. In the United States, especially in the past fifty years, bankruptcy policy has been justified on humanitarian grounds of granting relief to debtors from a lifetime of hopeless debt with no opportunity to recover.

Today's use of **voluntary bankruptcy** (initiated by the debtor) sometimes is thought of as immoral; some people believe it allows a debtor to cheat creditors out of money honestly owed. However, the truth is that both the debtor and his creditors usually play some part in creating the circumstances leading to a bankruptcy. An average bankruptcy estate may involve debts to assets in a ratio of 20 or so to 1, and the debtor's insolvency usually has evolved over a substantial period of time. Frequently, the debtor has continued to borrow during this period in the hope of "bailing himself out," and creditors have continued to lend. Therefore, most often, both debtors and creditors must share the blame.

Since the Bankruptcy Reform Act of 1978, some corporations have used bankruptcy law for two other purposes. First, faced with the threat of a multitude of lawsuits after a catastrophe, corporations sometimes have filed for reorganization under Chapter 11 of the act in order to delay the immediate effects of the lawsuits. Second, corporations have filed as an attempt to force the adjudication of all future claims arising out of a single cause (for example, injuries from exposure to asbestos), again by filing under Chapter 11. One airline even was accused of filing a Chapter 11 proceeding for the purpose of "breaking" the union representing its pilots. However, for purposes of our discussion, these possible uses must be considered incidental to the main purposes of bankruptcy.

HISTORY

Bankruptcy law is a direct descendant of the English law, although its focus in this country has been somewhat different. The first reasonably comprehensive bankruptcy law in the United States was enacted by Congress in 1898. Prior to that time there had been only faltering attempts to maintain an act. The 1898 statute was only a beginning, however. Except for provisions concerning railroad adjustments, it provided only for

individual bankruptcies, and the only remedy was liquidation. in 1938, Congress passed the Chandler Act, amending the original act to include provisions for corporate reorganization and for wage-earner plans. Prior to 1978, the Chandler Act was the only major revision of bankruptcy law in the United States.

In 1978 Congress enacted a major revision of the Bankruptcy Act. The 1978 Act, then, was amended in a number of substantial ways in 1984 and 1986. The changes were both broad and far-reaching, and spurred a wave of concern throughout the business community. However, in spite of the amendment of the act since that time, most of the 1978 changes remain law today. The most important provisions will be discussed in turn in this chapter.

TYPES OF BANKRUPTCY PROCEEDINGS

Proceedings under the Bankruptcy Act may be pursued under any of five chapters: (1) Chapter 7, Liquidation; (2) Chapter 9, Adjustment of Debts of a Municipality; (3) Chapter 11, Reorganization; (4) Chapter 12, Adjustment of Debts of Family Farmers; and (5) Chapter 13, Adjustment of Debts of an Individual with Regular Income. Only the first is *bankruptcy* as the term commonly is used. The other four involve proceedings aimed at the bankrupt's possibly paying the full amounts of his or her debts. Of the five, Chapters 7, 11, and 13 are of the most interest to businesspersons.

Liquidation

Liquidation under Chapter 7 is what is most commonly thought of when the term *bankruptcy* is used. The bankrupt's nonexempt assets are taken by the court and divided among the creditors on a priority and *pro rata* basis. At the conclusion of these proceedings, the full amounts of the debts are discharged even though the creditors may have received only a few cents on the dollar, or nothing at all.

Reorganization

This option, under Chapter 11, is available basically to businesses. **Corporate reorganization** involves the filing of a repayment plan for all or some portion of a corporation's debts. If the plan is approved, the corporation will continue operation under the direction of the bankruptcy court. Debts of corporate creditors will be paid according to the terms set out in the plan and, if all goes well, the corporation will be discharged of its debts and will resume functioning independently.

Adjustment of Debts of an Individual with Regular Income

Chapter 13 is an underutilized provision of the Bankruptcy Act. It allows proceedings comparable to those under Chapter 11 for individuals (rather than businesses). The equivalent provision under the 1938 act was referred to as **"wage-earner" bankruptcy**—a term often still used in referring to present Chapter 13 proceedings, although it is technically incorrect. The previous Chapter 13 required that the bankrupt have wages from employment as his or her principal source of income. The present Chapter 13, however, allows earnings from any source, as long as they are regular. We will discuss more about this, and corporate reorganization, later in this chapter. Chapter 12 bankruptcy provides similar treatment of family farmers.

COMMENCEMENT OF BANKRUPTCY PROCEEDINGS

The model for this discussion will be Chapter 7 liquidation. Much of the substance also is applicable to other proceedings under the 1978 act. Appropriate modifications will be made for the other chapters as they are discussed in more detail.

All bankruptcy proceedings begin with the filing of a petition with the court. Filed by the debtor, the proceedings are termed *voluntary*. Filing also may be initiated by one or more creditors, in which case it is termed **involuntary.** As noted previously, true bankruptcy historically was instigated by the creditors (today's "involuntary" proceeding), and voluntary proceedings were not "bankruptcy" proceedings. Instead, they were called "insolvency" proceedings and were governed by a different statute and different rules. Today, both are treated as bankruptcy and are governed by the same rules.

Who May Be Bankrupt

Since the 1978 act, the subject of bankruptcy proceedings no longer is referred to as the *bankrupt*, but is called the *debtor*. Section 101(12) of the act defines *debtor* to mean any "person or municipality," and subsection (30) defines *person* to include "individual, partnership, and corporation," but not "government agency." Therefore, the only general exclusion is for governmental agencies other than municipalities. The "debtor" must reside in the United States, or have a domicile, a place of business, or property in the United States, or be a municipality (Bankruptcy Act Section 109(a)). However, the act has additional specific exclusions concerning certain types of proceedings.

Bankruptcy Act Section 109(b) provides that railroads, insurance companies, and most financial institutions such as banks, savings and loan institutions, and credit unions cannot be debtors under Chapter 7. Further, Section 303(a) provides that involuntary proceedings under Chapters 7 or 11 may not be brought against a municipality, a farmer, or a corporation that is not a "moneyed, business or commercial corporation" (for example, a charity). Section 109(d) also provides that Chapter 11 reorganization is available only to debtors qualified under Chapter 7, except stockbrokers and commodities brokers. Finally, only voluntary proceedings are allowed under Chapter 13; the debtor must be an individual (not a corporation, partnership, or a municipality), and may not be a stockbroker or a commodities broker.

Involuntary Proceedings

Involuntary proceedings may be brought only under Chapters 7 or 11. This generally may be done by: (1) three or more entities, each of which is a holder of a claim against the debtor, if their claims aggregate to at least $5000 more than the value of any lien on any property securing these claims; (2) if there are fewer than twelve claimholders, with certain exclusions, by one or more holders of a claim or claims aggregating to at least $5000; or (3) if the debtor is a partnership, by any of the general partners (but not all, as that would make the petition voluntary), or by the holder of any claim against the partnership. These requirements are designed to ensure that the petitioner in an involuntary proceeding has a substantial interest.

Because of the potential negative effect on the debtor of a petition in bankruptcy, there are penalties for false filing of an involuntary petition, and filing creditors may be required to post a bond to guarantee payment of any damages. If the court dismisses the petition, the debtor is entitled to (1) any damages caused by the taking of possession of the debtor's property by the trustee appointed by the court; (2) costs; and (3) reasonable attorney's fees. If, in addition, the filing was in bad faith, the debtor also is entitled to any other damages caused by the filing and to punitive damages in an amount determined by the court.

Grounds for Relief

Upon approval of the petition, the court will grant an **order for relief.** Under the 1938 Act, the debtor had to be "insolvent" according to a "balance-sheet test." This meant that she had to have liabilities in excess of her assets. In addition, if the case was involuntary, the petitioning creditor or creditors were required to prove that the debtor had committed an "act of bankruptcy," such as a transfer of property apparently for the purpose of defrauding creditors during the debtor's insolvency. Under the 1978 Act, a new test was imposed—the **cash-flow test.** This requires only that the debtor generally is not paying her debts as they become due. In addition, in involuntary cases, the requirement of proving the debtor committed an act of bankruptcy was eliminated (Bankruptcy Act Section 303(h)). The only reasons a court usually may refuse a petition are: (1) failure of the debtor to meet the "cash flow test"; (2) if the interests of the debtor and creditors would be better served by a dismissal of the petition; or (3) failure to pay the required filing fee. Consider the following case.

IN RE R.V. SEATING, INC.
8 B.R. 663 (1981)

This matter arose from an involuntary petition under Chapter 7, filed by Tri B Manufacturing, Inc. against R. V. Seating, Inc. The question before the court was whether granting an order for relief would be in the best interests of the parties. Petition dismissed.

WEAVER, Sidney M., Bankruptcy Judge.

The petitioning creditor is the only creditor of the alleged debtor. It is undisputed that the petitioning creditor has not been paid in full, that the judgment in its favor was entered more than two years prior to the trial of the involuntary petition, and that the other creditors of the alleged debtor were paid in August of 1977. . . .

In the situation before the Court, the petitioning creditor has failed to show any special circumstances or that it would not be able to obtain as much relief as the Bankruptcy Code provides by proceedings supplementary to its judgment in the state courts. (In fact, considering the expenses involved in the administration of a bankruptcy case, the petitioning creditor might well receive more by proceeding in state court to enforce its judgment than by the results achieved by bankruptcy.) And there is evidence that there are assets, in the form of claims or accounts receivable, which apparently could be garnished by the petitioning creditor. Thus, under the authority of 7H Land & Cattle Co. and Sol Arker cases, the involuntary petition should be dismissed. The legal test set forth in the 7H Land & Cattle Co. and the Sol Arker cases perhaps can be better understood as an application of the abstention doctrine:

> The adoption of the doctrine of abstention by Section 305 of the Bankruptcy Code is nothing more than a recognition of the well-recognized fact that there are instances where it appears to be proper for the Court to decline jurisdiction. However, it is clear that abstention is improper unless the interest of the debtor and all creditors would be better served by dismissal or suspension of all proceedings. . . .

One factor to be considered in determining whether the interests of creditors and the debtor would be better served by dismissal is the economy of bankruptcy administration. . . . To allow the recovery of the alleged debtor's claims or accounts receivable to be eaten up by the expenses of bankruptcy administration would serve the interests of neither the petitioning creditor nor the alleged debtor. This factor and the adequacy of the remedies available to the petitioning creditor under Florida law lead the Court to conclude that the interests of the petitioning creditor and the alleged debtor would be better served by the dismissal of this case. (Of course, in other situations, other factors might be paramount. . . .) Accordingly, this Court will exercise its discretion to dismiss this case.

Questions

1. Can you think of any other circumstances in which the Bankruptcy Court should "abstain" from taking jurisdiction?

2. Should the court have gone forward if the debtor did not object? Suppose the debtor affirmatively wanted the petition to be granted?

POST-PETITION PROCEDURE

Order for Relief

An order for relief is, in effect, a decision of the bankruptcy court to assume jurisdiction of a case brought before it. In a voluntary case, the filing of the petition itself constitutes an order for relief under Section 301. In an involuntary case, an order for relief is granted only after the debtor has

Typical bankruptcy procedures under Chapter 7

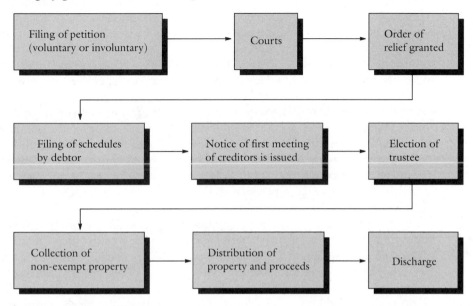

```
Filing of petition          →    Courts    →    Order of
(voluntary or involuntary)                       relief granted

Filing of schedules         →    Notice of first meeting    →    Election of
by debtor                        of creditors is issued          trustee

Collection of               →    Distribution of            →    Discharge
non-exempt property              property and proceeds
```

an opportunity to be heard on the merits of the petition. During the hearing, the debtor may wish to prove such matters as that he is able to pay his debts as they come due or that the best interests of the parties requires that the court abstain and deny the petition. However, if he waives his rights, an order for relief will be granted. Consider the following case involving a hearing on an involuntary petition.

IN RE REED
11 B.R. 755 (1981)

Creditors filed an involuntary bankruptcy petition under Chapter 7 against Del H. Reed, Jr. The question before the court was whether Reed was or was not generally paying his debts as they came due. The court found for the creditors.

FLOWERS, Edwin F., Bankruptcy Judge.

A debtor must neglect more than one debt for the nonpayment to be general, unless there are exceptional circumstances. . . . Ordinarily, for the number of debts to have any significance in the determination, the number not paid each month must be compared to the number which were paid. The ratio of unpaid to accruing debts is more revealing than a simple count of unsatisfied creditors.

Without ascertaining dollar amounts, however, the ratio of unpaid to accruing debts does not supply very useful data. The size of the debts, separately and in the aggregate, must be examined to determine whether a seemingly high number of unsatisfied claims are *de minimis* [too insignificant to worry about] in amount. Moreover, total past due indebtedness can be weighed more accurately when the debtor's liquid assets are known and when the past due amount is compared to the amount of new indebtedness accruing monthly. Accordingly, the initial factors of the number and amount of debts and their relationship to aggregate indebtedness and monthly accruals should be viewed in the context of the debtor's liquidity. . . .

Apart from the number of debts and their amount, the court must consider the materiality of the nonpayment of debts. A default of short duration should be viewed differently than one which is longer. Obviously, even a substantial amount of indebtedness which is only thiry-one days past due should be viewed differently from the same group of debts which are ninety days old. . . . Further, the debts should be examined to determine whether there is any reasonable basis for nonpayment. Either a bona fide dispute or commercial practice might not only explain, but in fact fully justify the debtor's failure to pay. . . .

Finally, the factors of number, amount and materiality of non-payment must be viewed in the context of the debtor's overall handling of his financial affairs. If the debtor is winding up his business or personal affairs, selling assets in a liquidating fashion, paying only nondischargeable or co-obliger debts, kiting checks, or otherwise is conducting his financial affairs in a manner not consistent with one operating in good faith and in the regular course of business, then the interpretation of nonpayment could be quite different.

Applying these standards to Reed's situation leaves little doubt that he is generally not paying his debts as they become due. Reed owes fourteen creditors and is delinquent on each debt. He is paying only modest household expenses of $700.00 to $800.00 per month. Total past due debts amount to $117,753.04, while his liquid assets are admittedly insufficient to pay any amount now to these creditors. His current income of $400.00 to $500.00 per month is not likely to produce the estimated $18,000.00 he earned last year. Even if his previous year's income was matched by his current earnings, the delinquent portion of his indebtedness is more than six times those earnings. He has no personal financial net worth. His hope for financial relief lies only in a substantial recovery from two law suits filed by a corporation, fifty percent of which he owns, and in a $300,000.00 line of credit, which has been rejected by his bank, one of the Petitioners here. His debts range in size from two of less than $100.00 to one over $84,000.00. Of the fourteen debts, none were current at the time of the petition. As of the filing date, the debts were from four to thirty-two months delinquent. , . . The only debt for which any credible explanation of default was given was the first mortgage delinquency to Charleston Federal Savings & Loan. Reed had forestalled foreclosure against the collateral once before and foreclosure was halted voluntarily on the most recent occasion upon the filing of this petition. The Debtor explains that, since his former wife owns an undivided one-half interest in the mortgaged property and this interest has been the object of both negotiation and litigation between them, he would not make further payments to improve her equity in the property. However, his defense for nonpayment of some of the debts because they were also debts of certain of his corporations is inadequate. These debts are also his personal debts by recordation of judgments, though he might have hoped to satisfy them otherwise. Moreover, while his debts were accumulating, the Debtor made an undisclosed transfer of unencumbered real estate to his present wife. . . . Finally, the Debtor has defaulted on four agreements to purchase his former wife's interest in his residence. This related conduct of the Debtor certainly does not put his creditors at ease.

The Debtor rather vehemently insists that his financial distress is the result of the malicious actions of the Petitioners, who are accused of filing this petition in bad faith and for purposes "inconsistent with the intent and spirit of the bankruptcy laws." . . .

Conceivably, a debtor who is the victim of a malicious conspiracy by his creditors might be spared the consequences of their improper acts. General equitable principles applicable to bankruptcy matters would bar relief to those who come to court with unclean hands. However, inequitable conduct by the Petitioners is not established by the evidence in this case. . . . Accordingly, it is found that the Debtor, Del H. Reed, Jr., is not paying a significant number and amount of his debts, either in the regular course of his business or in his personal affairs. Considering the materiality of the nonpayment and the contemporaneous conduct of his affairs, an involuntary order for relief should be entered against him.

Questions

1. Given Mr. Reed's finances, why do you suppose he was contesting the bankruptcy?

2. What should a court do when the debtor clearly is not viable economically, but the bankruptcy is being sought by malicious creditors?

The effect of an order for relief, in addition to the assumption of bankruptcy jurisdiction by the court, is that it operates as a stay of further attempts by creditors to collect debts to be adjudicated in the bankruptcy proceeding, and of most other actions against the debtor or her property. This **automatic stay** under Section 362 is one of the fundamental protections afforded the debtor in a bankruptcy action. It gives the debtor a "breathing spell" from creditors and provides an opportunity to begin to arrange her affairs without the financial pressures that necessitated the bankruptcy in the first place. However as the following case illustrates, not every action by a creditor will be viewed as a violation of an order for relief.

IN RE ROACH
660 F.2d 1315 (9th Cir. 1981)

This matter came before the court on appeal of an order of the Bankruptcy Court granting relief from an automatic stay on petition of First National Bank of Anchorage and Alaska Title Guarantee Company (Plaintiffs/Appellees) in the matter of the bankruptcy petition of Hilliard T. Roach. Roach had borrowed money from the bank to finance a residential subdivision. When he stopped making payments the bank elected to foreclose nonjudicially. Sale of the property was scheduled for February 4, 1980. On that day, Roach filed a petition under Chapter 11. The sale was postponed and the bank advertised a new, later date for the sale. Roach contended this action violated the automatic stay granted when he filed for relief under bankruptcy law.

The Bankruptcy Court granted the petition for relief and Roach appealed. Affirmed.

FARRIS, Circuit Judge.

. . . [T]he bankruptcy court's conclusion that Roach did not have an equity interest in the subject property was not clearly erroneous. The property was encumbered by liens totalling approximately $625,000, and though the bankruptcy court heard conflicting testimony regarding the value of the property, one appraiser testified the value was not greater than $480,000. In addition, the bankruptcy court also concluded that the Bank lacked adequate protection of its interests in the property, and Roach has not challenged this independent basis for the judgment. . . .

Postponement notices which specify a new sale date do not violate [Section 362].

The purpose of the automatic stay is to give the debtor a breathing spell from his creditors, to stop all collection efforts, harassment and foreclosure actions. . . . The automatic stay also prevents piecemeal diminution of the debtor's estate. . . . The automatic stay does not necessarily prevent all activity outside the bankruptcy forum. See David v. Hooker, Ltd. . . . (automatic stay under old bankruptcy act did not prevent trial judge in a separate case from requiring the debtor to comply with a discovery order issued prior to the filing of the insolvency petition).

Here, the Bank merely maintained the status quo, and did not harass, interfere or gain any advantage. This is consistent with the purpose of the automatic stay provision.

Questions

1. Did the bank merely maintain the status quo by advertising?
2. What other activities might a creditor engage in without violating the stay?

Duties of the Debtor

Among the first duties of the debtor, once proceedings have begun, is to submit to the court a list of creditors and the amounts owed to each. This is important to enable the court to notify creditors so they may have an opportunity to participate in the proceedings. Unless the court orders otherwise, the debtor also is required to submit a schedule of assets and liabilities, and a statement of the debtor's financial affairs. If a trustee is serving in the case, the debtor must surrender to the trustee all property of the estate and any recorded information, including books, documents, records, and papers relating to the estate's property. Other duties are listed throughout the act, such as the debtor's duty to cooperate with the trustee in the performance of his duties, to submit to examination, and to attend any hearing on discharge.

First Meeting of Creditors

Within a reasonable time after the order for relief has been granted, notice of the first **meeting of the creditors** is issued. The court also may order a meeting of any equity security holders (for example, stockholders if the debtor is a corporation). The court may not preside at or even attend this meeting. The meeting typically will be called to order by the trustee in bankruptcy, if one has been appointed by the court under Section 303(g). Otherwise, the creditors will do so, first by electing a presiding member. Creditors are not required to attend this meeting, but the debtor is, and is required to submit to examination under oath.

Duties of the Trustee

The **trustee,** coming out of the national trustee system established by the 1986 amendments, is the representative of the bankruptcy estate and is responsible to the court for its proper administration. The trustee is not an agent either of the debtor or the creditors, but is a special fiduciary. His or her duties are established by Section 704, which provides:

> The trustee shall—(1) collect and reduce to money the property of the estate for which such trustee serves, and close such estate as expeditiously as is compatible with the best interests of parties in interest; (2) be accountable for all property received; (3) ensure that the debtor shall perform his intention as specified in section 521(2)(B) of this title; (4) investigate the financial affairs of the debtor; (5) if a purpose would be served, examine proofs of claims and object to the allowance of any claim that is improper; (6) if advisable, oppose the discharge of the debtor, (7) unless the court orders otherwise, furnish such information concerning the estate and the estate's administration as is requested by a party in interest; (8) if the business of the debtor is authorized to be operated, file with the court and with any governmental unit charged with responsibility for collection or determination of any tax arising out of such operation, periodic reports and summaries of the operation of such business, including a statement of receipts and disbursements, and such other information as the court requires; and (9) make a final report and file a final account of the administration of the estate with the court.

Obviously, these duties involve most of the day-to-day activities to be handled during the bankruptcy proceeding. Although the trustee actually does not approve the validity of claims (this is done by the court), he does challenge those he believes to be invalid, or for which he believes sufficient proof has not been made. Therefore, initially the allowance of claims effectively is decided by the trustee.

Property of the Estate

Broadly speaking, all property owned by the debtor at the time the bankruptcy proceedings are commenced will be taken by the trustee for possible inclusion in the **bankruptcy estate.** From that, then, certain exempt property will be returned to the debtor. Some property acquired after the commencement of proceedings will be added, and certain property that was the subject of a preferential transfer or a fraudulent conveyance, prior to commencement of proceedings or conveyed thereafter, will be reclaimed by the trustee.

"All property of the debtor" includes both legal and equitable interests in both tangible or intangible property. The most easily understood elements are interests in tangible real or personal property. However, also included are such rights as an interest in a lease, a tax benefit (such as a refund, or a carryover of an investment credit or a loss), an expectancy, or a contract claim. Remember that the term *property* may be defined simply as "anything of value that can be owned."

Preferential transfers, those that favor one creditor over others, may be voided by the trustee under certain conditions. If the transfer was (1) to or for the benefit of a creditor, (2) for or on account of a debt incurred before the transfer was made (an antecedent debt), (3) made while the debtor was insolvent, (4) within ninety days before filing of the petition or within one year if the creditor was an insider and had reasonable cause to believe the debtor was insolvent at the time of the transfer, and (5) enabled that creditor to receive more than he or she otherwise would have received under Chapter 7, the trustee may rescind the transfer and reclaim the property. The primary reasons for this provision are to assure equal treatment of all creditors and to avoid a race to the courthouse by creditors attempting to dismember the debtor when he or she becomes insolvent.

Generally, contemporaneous exchanges of property for new value and the payment of ordinary obligations within forty-five days from the time they were incurred are not treated as preferential. However, the 1984 amendments provide that a consumer-debtor may transfer any property of a value up to $600 without the transfer constituting an illegal preference. In the following case the court must determine whether a transfer constituted an illegal preference.

IN RE FULGHUM CONSTRUCTION COMPANY
7 B.R. 629 (1980)

This was an action by Robert H. Waldschmidt, as trustee of the bankruptcy estate of Fulghum Construction Company (Plaintiff) against Ranier & Associates and others (Defendants) to set aside certain payments by the debtor to Defendants as preferences.

Ranier, a partnership, was the sole shareholder of the debtor. Ranier made certain advances to the debtor to help debtor make its payroll. While insolvent, debtor repaid some of these advances to Ranier. The question before the court was whether these payments constituted preferences. The court held that under the "net-result" test they were not.

HIPPE, Russell H. Jr., Bankruptcy Judge.

. . . The party seeking to void a preference thus must establish the fair valuation of all of the debtor's assets at the time of the transfer. . . . The cases under the prior Act established that "fair valuation" signified the reasonable estimate of what could be realized from the assets by converting them into, or reducing them to, cash under carefully guarded, if not ideal, conditions. . . . Fair valuation was held by the courts not to be synonymous with a distressed or forced sale price. . . .

The fair value of the debtor's property may be established from balance sheets, financial statements, appraisals, expert testimony, and other affirmative evidence. . . . Reduction in the face value of the debtor's assets may be appropriate if those assets are not susceptible to liquidation and thus cannot be made available for the payment of debts within a reasonable time. . . .

Section 547(b)(4)(B) provides that the trustee may avoid any transfer of the debtor's property made between 90 days and one year before the filing date if the creditor-transferee was an insider and had reasonable cause to believe the debtor was insolvent at the time of such transfer. Under Section 101(25), an "insider" includes, if the debtor is a corporation, a director of the debtor, an officer of the debtor, and a person in control of the debtor. Both of the general partners were officers and directors of the debtor. The shareholder and its general partners were insiders for the purpose of Section 547(b)(4)(B). . . .

The court has little difficulty in concluding that the shareholder and its two general partners had reasonable cause to believe that the debtor was insolvent at all times subsequent to June 5, 1980. . . .

Section 547(b)(5) requires a comparison between what the creditor actually received and what the creditor would have received in a chapter 7 liquidation but for the transfer. 4 Collier, Bankruptcy Section 547-35 (15th ed. 1980). The court must focus upon the relative distribution between classes as well as the amount that will be received by the members of the class of which the transferee is a member. . . . The test under Section 547(b)(5) is whether the creditor obtained from the debtor's property a greater percentage of his debt than some other creditor would have received under the distributive provisions of the Code had the transfer not occurred. . . . Whether a creditor had received a preference under the prior Act was determined not by what the situation would have been if the debtor's assets had been liquidated and distributed among his creditors at the time the alleged preferential payment was made, but by the *actual effect* of the payment as determined when bankruptcy results. . . .

This shareholder is an unsecured creditor. The trustee demonstrated at trial that, after adding the total amount of the transfers herein at issue to the debtor's total assets, subtracting the total of all priority claims, and dividing the total assets by the total unsecured debt (including that owed to shareholder), unsecured creditors would receive .775054 percent of their indebtedness. The trustee then attempted to show that, because of the transfers, the shareholder actually received .885750 percent of its indebtedness.

Although not challenging the accuracy of the trustee's computations, the shareholder asserts that Section 547(b)(5) requires a determination that the net effect of all of the transactions between itself and the debtor was to deplete the debtor's estate and thus to interfere with the otherwise equal distribution of the debtor's assets among the debtor's creditors. The shareholder asserts that when otherwise preferential transfers are followed by extensions of credit that result in a net increase in the debtor's estate to the benefit of all of the debtor's creditors, such transfers are not voidable preferential transfers as defined by Section 547(b)(5). The defendants, in short, urge the court in its interpretation of Section 547(b)(5) to adopt the "net result" rule that was applicable under Section 60(a) of the prior Act. . . .

The legislative history of Section 547(c)(1) indicates that this exception was intended to codify "the net result rule in section 60c of current law." . . . There is no indication that the Congress intended to effect any change in the separate "net result" rule that the courts had developed under the definitional provisions of Section 60(a) of the prior Act. The latter "net result" rule, therefore, will continue to apply under Section 547(b)(5). Although Section 547(b)(5) modifies the old greater percentage test under Section 60(a) of the prior Act. The latter "net result" rule, therefore, will continue to apply under Section 547(b)(5). . . . Accepting the debtor's assets at face value, the trustee's computations might very well accurately reflect that the defendants would have received a lesser percentage of their debt than would have been the case had the assets represented by the payments remained a part of the debtor's estate. This analysis neglects to consider, however, that the debtor's estate was increased to the extent that the extensions of credit by the shareholder exceeded the payments made by the debtor and that to this extent all of the debtor's creditors benefited from the transactions' having occurred.

It is the court's opinion, therefore, that the transfers herein at issue do no constitute preferential transfers.

Questions

1. Is there anything objectionable about the court's analysis or result?
2. Is the "net result" test fairer than the "actual effect" test?

Fraudulent conveyances also may be avoided by the trustee. These are transfers or obligations made with actual intent to hinder, delay, or defraud a creditor. For example, a debtor planning to file a voluntary petition, or fearing creditors may file an involuntary petition, transfers some or all of his property to a friend. Transfers made for less than reasonably equivalent consideration also may be avoided if the debtor was, or as a result became, insolvent, was engaged in business with an unreasonably small amount of capital, or intended to incur debts beyond his or her ability to pay. All of these may be avoided if made within one year prior to filing the petition.

Most transfers of substantial property by the debtor after the filing of the petition also are avoidable by the trustee. However, in involuntary cases this does not include transfers between the time of filing of the petition and the granting of an order for relief, notwithstanding any notice or knowledge of the transferee. Neither does it include most transfers to good-faith purchasers who have no knowledge of commencement of proceedings and who also pay fair present consideration. Special exceptions also are made for certain transfers of real estate to good-faith purchasers. Any action by the trustee to avoid post-petition transfers must be commenced within the earlier of (1) two years after the date of the transfer or (2) the time the bankruptcy action is terminated.

Finally, after notice and a hearing, a trustee may abandon any property of the estate that is burden-some to the estate or that is of inconsequential value (more trouble than it is worth). Also, the court may order the trustee to abandon such property, and property that is scheduled but is not administered prior to the close of the case is considered abandoned. The reason is that property of the estate should include only what is beneficial to the parties or to the administration of the case, and not items that are detrimental. For example, suppose the debtor had rights, under an executory contract, to receive certain inventory for her business, but her business was to be liquidated in the bankruptcy proceedings. Absent unusual circumstances, it probably would be advantageous if these rights were abandoned.

Debt not Dischargeable under Chapter 7

Not all debts may be discharged under Chapter 7. That is, a debtor may not avoid them by filing for liquidation. A careful study of Section 523 is required to understand fully the details of these exemptions. However, they may be summarized as follows:

1. certain taxes and customs duties, notably those with respect to which no return was filed or was filed late and within two years of filing the bankruptcy petition, and those the debtor fraudulently or willfully tried to evade;

2. claims for money, property, services, or credit secured by fraud, false pretenses, or false representation;
3. debts not properly listed in the debtor's bankruptcy schedules;
4. claims for fraud or wrongdoing while acting in a fiduciary capacity, embezzlement, or larceny;
5. with limited exception, obligations for alimony, separate maintenance, or spouse or child support arising under a court decree;
6. claims for willful or malicious injury to the person or property of another;
7. most fines, penalties, and forfeitures to a governmental unit;
8. most debts owed to a governmental unit or nonprofit institution of higher education on account of student loans;
9. debts that were or could have been scheduled in a previous bankruptcy in which discharge was waived or denied; and

10. liability on a judgment based on operating a motor vehicle while intoxicated.

It might be said more generally that **nondischargeable debts** fall into classifications of those owed to a government, those arising from intentional torts, and those involving alimony, separate maintenance, and support. Presumably these are exempt because they are either debts owed to the public rather than a person who may be represented adequately in the proceedings, or those for which discharge would be inconsistent with public policy. In addition, the 1984 amendments provide that consumer debts for luxury good or services of more than $500 that were incurred within forty days of an order for relief, and cash advances over $1000 within twenty days before, are presumed nondischargeable. The purpose of these additions is to prevent debtor fraud. Consider the following case.

IN RE RAHM
641 F.2d 755 (9th Cir. 1981)

This was an action by Ronald E. Gregg (Plaintiff/Appellant) seeking to establish an exemption from the rules of dischargeability of debts in the matter of the bankruptcy of Charles Barry Rahm. Plaintiff contended that his judgment against the debtor for illegally tape recording a telephone conversation was a nondischargeable debt.

The bankruptcy court refused to grant the relief requested, holding the debt dischargeable and Plaintiff appealed. Affirmed.

FERGUSON, Circuit Judge.

Under 11 U.S.C. Section 35(a)(8), a liability stemming from the "willful and malicious" conduct of the debtor is not dischargeable in bankruptcy. The creditor has the burden of proving both willfulness and malice. . . . This burden is weighty in light of the rule that exceptions to dischargeability are to be strictly construed so as to effectuate the Congressional policy of permitting bankrupts a fresh start. . . .

Gregg appears to argue that the default judgment required the bankruptcy court to find willfulness and malice. This argument is without merit. First, in this circuit a prior state court judgment has no collateral estoppel force on a bankruptcy court considering dischargeability unless both parties agree to rest their cases on that judgment. . . . At most, a prior judgment establishes a prima facie case of non-dischargeability which the bankrupt is entitled to refute on the basis of all relevant evidence. . . .

Second, on the record under consideration it is doubtful that even a prima facie case was established. Gregg has not cited any authority for the proposition that a judgment under Section 632 and 637.2 implies malice; further, the statute on its face requires no mental element beyond the intention to record. . . . This intent requirement is consistent with the meaning of willfulness under Section 35(a)(8), see Kasler, supra, at 310 but has no bearing on the question of malice.

In Tinker v. Colwell, . . . the Supreme Court defined "malice" under Section 17(2) of the Bankruptcy Act of 1898. That section contained language identical to 11 U.S.C. Section 35(a)(8). Tinker held that an act which is against good morals and wrongful in and of itself, and which necessarily causes injury and is done intentionally." . . . Matter of Kearney Chemicals, . . . (under Section 35(a)(8), an act is malicious if "wrongful and without just cause or excuse . . .").

The default judgment provides no basis for concluding that Rahm's conduct in recording the phone call was "against good morals and wrongful in and of itself." Since Gregg has offered no evidence beyond that judgment, he has failed to meet his burden of proof as to malice. This lack of proof is fatal to his appeal.

Questions

1. Would the result in this case have been different if a state statute made it a crime to record someone's telephone conversation?

2. Would a damage claim for assault and battery be exempt from discharge? for sex discrimination?

Exempt Property

Not all property owned by the debtor who is a natural person may be taken to pay his or her debts. Prior to the 1978 revision, the Bankruptcy Act referred to state law to establish what property was exempt in each case. However, state provisions were far from uniform, and many states had done little to keep their exemption statutes up to date. For example, Michigan law still provided exemption for such items as "10 sheep, 2 cows, 5 swine, 100 hens, 5 roosters and a sufficient quantity of hay and grain . . . for properly keeping such animals and poultry for 6 months." In general, property exempted included mostly necessities and highly personal items.

In Section 522 the 1978 Act, Congress provided a list of **exempt property** that could be used by a debtor unless the law of the state of the debtor's residence required the use of the state list. To date, some forty states have passed legislation so requiring. However, while doing so, most also took the opportunity to update their lists. Some, such as Ohio, virtually have duplicated the federal provisions. Under federal law, the following property is exempt:

(1) *The debtor's aggregate interest, not to exceed $7,500 in value, in real property or personal property that the debtor or a dependent of the debtor uses as a residence, in a cooperative that owns property that the debtor or a dependent of the debtor uses as a residence, or in a burial plot for the debtor or a dependent of the debtor.*

(2) *The debtor's interest, not to exceed $1,200 in value, in one motor vehicle.*

(3) *The debtor's interest, not to exceed $200 in value*

in any particular item or $4,000 in aggregate value, in household furnishings, household goods, wearing apparel, appliances, books, animals, crops, or musical instruments, that are held primarily for the personal, family, or household use of the debtor or a dependent of the debtor.

(4) The debtor's aggregate interest, not to exceed $500 in value, in jewelry held primarily for the personal, family, or household use of the debtor or a dependent of the debtor.

(5) The debtor's aggregate interest in any property, not to exceed in value $400 plus up to $3,750 of any unused amount of the exemption provided under paragraph (1) of this subsection.

(6) The debtor's aggregate interest, not to exceed $750 in value, in any implements, professional books, or tools of the trade of the debtor or the trade of a dependent of the debtor.

(7) Any unmatured life insurance contract owned by the debtor, other than a credit life insurance contract.

(8) The debtor's aggregate interest, not to exceed in value $4,000 less any amount of property of the estate transferred in the manner specified in section 542(d) of this title, in any accrued dividend or interest under, or loan value of, any unmatured life insurance contract owned by the debtor under which the insured is the debtor or an individual of whom the debtor is a dependent.

(9) Professionally prescribed health aids for the debtor or a dependent of the debtor.

(10) The debtor's right to receive—

    (A) a social security benefit, unemployment compensation, or a local public assistance benefit;

    (B) a veterans' benefit;

    (C) a disability, illness, or unemployment benefit;

    (D) alimony, support, or separate maintenance, to the extent reasonably necessary for the support of the debtor and any dependent of the debtor;

    (E) a payment under a stock bonus, pension, profitsharing, annuity, or similar plan or contract on account of illness, disability, death, age, or length of service, to the extent reasonably necessary for the support of the debtor and any dependent of the debtor, unless—

    (i) such plan or contract was established by or under the auspices of an insider that employed the debtor at the time the debtor's rights under such plan or contract arose;

    (ii) such payment is on account of age or length of service; and

    (iii) such plan or contract does not qualify under section 401(a), 403(b), 408, or 409 of the Internal Revenue Code of 1954 (26 U.S.C. 401(a), 403(b), 408, or 409).

(11) The debtor's right to receive, or property that is traceable to—

    (A) an award under a crime victim's reparation law;

    (B) a payment on account of the wrongful death of an individual of whom the debtor was a dependent, to the extent reasonably necessary for the support of the debtor and any dependent of the debtor;

    (C) a payment under a life insurance contract that insured the life of an individual of whom the debtor was a dependent on the date of such individual's death, to the extent reasonably necessary for the support of the debtor and any dependent of the debtor;

    (D) a payment, not to exceed $7,500, on account of personal bodily injury, not including pain and suffering or compensation for actual pecuniary loss, of the debtor or an individual of whom the debtor is a dependent; or

    (E) a payment in compensation of loss of future earnings of the debtor or an individual of whom the debtor is or was a dependent, to the extent reasonably necessary for the support of the debtor and any dependent of the debtor.

The inclusion of this exemption list gave rise to much concern in the business community. Two particularly troublesome problems were created. First, in cases involving the joint bankruptcy of a husband and wife, one was permitted to take the state exemptions and the other the federal, thus enjoying the best of both. This was corrected by the 1984 amendments, which require them to select the same—federal or state—option. The second problem involves the third exemption. Initially, no aggregate limit was placed on the value of the "debtor's interest, not to exceed $200 in value in any particular item . . . ." Therefore, prior to the addition of the aggregate limit of $4000, it would have been in a debtor's interest before bankruptcy to convert his property to such items to the extent possible. For example, it would have been possible to purchase and exempt a set of sterling silverware as long as no individual knife, fork, or spoon had a value of more than $200.

IN RE CANNADY
653 F.2d 210 (5th Cir. 1981)

The Cannadys, husband and wife, filed a joint bankruptcy petition. Mr. Cannady elected to take exempt property under state law (Texas) in order to take advantage of a "homestead" exemption. Mrs. Cannady elected exemptions permitted under federal law. The question before the court, upon petition by the trustee, was whether debtors under a joint petition were required to choose exceptions under the same law. The bankruptcy court held that one could not choose state, and the other, federal exemptions. The federal court of appeals reversed and remanded.

RANDALL, Circuit Judge.

In the context of this legislative history we decline to read section 522(m) as did the bankruptcy court, i. e., to deny one spouse the right to choose federal exemptions when the other spouse claims a family exemption under state law. Although in some cases the debtors in a joint bankruptcy case may thereby achieve "instant affluence" rather than just "a fresh start," we think it clear that the Congress contemplated that possibility. The Congress did nothing to prevent such a result, but instead delegated to the states the authority to prevent it by appropriate state legislation. In short, the legislative history behind section 522 demonstrates that the Congress intended to allow each debtor in a joint case to choose the federal exemptions regardless of his or her spouse's choice of a family exemption under state law—unless and until the applicable state law precludes such a result. . . . Since Texas has not yet enacted legislation to restrict a debtor's right to choose federal exemptions in such circumstances, we conclude that Mrs. Cannady may claim federal exemptions under section 522(d) of the Bankruptcy Code despite Mr. Cannady's choice of state exemptions under . . . [Texas Law].

Our conclusion might be different had the applicable state law required Mrs. Cannady to join her husband in choosing to assert a family exemption, for in that event Mrs. Cannady would herself have chosen to claim both state and federal exemptions. This situation arose under Arizona law in In Re Ageton. . . . Under Arizona law both spouses must join in making any homestead claim as to community or joint property, and this fact led the bankruptcy court to deny a separate federal exemption claimed by the wife:

Upon her joining in the homestead exemptions under the State statute, [the wife] may not then claim a separate federal exemption. Section 522(m) does not state that one spouse is entitled to claim both a state and federal exemption.

5 B.R. at 325. We agree that section 522(m) does not contemplate the selection by one spouse of both state and federal exemptions. However, Texas law does not require both spouses to join in the designation of property sought to be exempted.

Questions

1. Didn't this construction of the statute give the joint bankruptcy couple "the best of two possible worlds"?
2. Why should state law govern this right? Shouldn't the rule be uniform?

Priority of Distribution

Following the collection and any necessary liquidation of the debtor's nonexempt property, the property and proceeds are distributed according to an order established by Section 726.

First, secured creditors are paid. This may be by receiving the specific property subject to the security interest or the proceeds of its sale. Any amount by which the secured creditor's claim exceeds the value of the property or its proceeds is treated as an unsecured claim and is added to the claims of other general unsecured creditors. Any amount by which the value or proceeds exceed the claim is placed into the general assets of the estate.

Second, the remaining, non-exempt property is distributed according to priorities set out in Section 507 as follows:

1. costs of administration and necessary fees of other professionals such as attorneys and accountants;
2. in involuntary cases, unsecured claims arising in the ordinary course of the debtor's business after the filing of the petition, but before the granting of an order for relief or the appointment of a trustee;
3. claims of employees for wages earned within 90 days before filing of the petition, up to $2000;
4. unsecured claims for contributions to employee benefit plans resulting from services rendered within 180 days before the filing of the petition, limited to $2000 times the number of employees covered by the plan;
5. unsecured claims up to $900 based on money given to the bankrupt (prior to the bankruptcy) in payment for property or services not delivered or rendered; and
6. certain taxes owed for a period of three years prior to the filing of the petition.

Third, any property still remaining is paid in satisfaction of general unsecured claims. This is done on a *pro rata* basis. If unsecured creditors receive any payments at all, it is a virtual certainty that all property of the bankruptcy estate will be exhausted at this point. If not, the act sets out four further steps of distribution, the last of which is the return of remaining property to the debtor.

Discharge

The final step in the administration of a bankruptcy case is discharge. Section 725 provides that the court *shall* grant discharge unless one or more of a long list or circumstances has occurred. Generally, these involve either wrongdoing in connection with the bankruptcy proceeding or having received a discharge under any chapter of the act within the previous six years. Note that the discharge need not have been granted under the same chapter as the present proceedings. Also, subsections (d) and (e) of Section 725 provide for revocation of a discharge within one year, at the request of either the trustee or a creditor, for certain wrongdoing by the debtor.

Revival of Claims (Reaffirmation)

When discharge has been granted, it operates to enjoin the legal pursuit by creditors of any claim that was discharged. Although a debtor may pay such claims voluntarily, she cannot legally bind herself to do so. Prior to the 1978 act, a discharged claim could be revived by a new promise to pay it. Most states, however, required that the promise be in writing to be enforceable. Under present law, claims can be revived only by agreement of the parties and approval of the court *prior to discharge*. It may be argued that this provision of Section 725(c) and (d) deprives the states of their traditional right to determine the validity of contracts entered into within their respective borders, and so it does. Congress, however, determined that the incident of debtors reviving particular claims worked an unreasonable mischief on the underlying purpose of bankruptcy law, and no longer could be tolerated. This is the supreme law of the land.

REORGANIZATION

Unlike a liquidation case, the purpose of reorganization under Chapter 11 of the Bankruptcy Act is to help a corporation out of temporary financial distress and aid it in continuing business. This is done by implementing a plan for repayment of debts, the amounts and timing of payments being structured to the needs of the debtor. If the plan is successful, the corporation will emerge as a fresh new business.

Under prior law, reorganization was divided among three chapters of the act—Chapter 10 for general reorganization of a public company, Chapter 11 for a small nonpublic company, and Chapter 12 for a real estate arrangement by a noncorporate debtor. Proceedings under Chapters 10 or 12 could be voluntary or involuntary, and those under Chapter 11 were voluntary only. Since the 1978 act, reorganization proceedings primarily have been consolidated under Chapter 11. Most persons, including individuals, partnerships, and corporations, may be debtors under Chapter 11. The act, however, excludes municipalities (Chapter 9), insurance companies, stockbrokers, commodities brokers, and certain banking institutions. Proceedings under Chapter 11 may be either voluntary or involuntary, except that involuntary proceedings may not be brought against a farmer or a business that is not a "moneyed business or commercial corporation."

Upon the filing of a petition, the court, if requested to do so by a creditor, may appoint a trustee (receiver) to operate the business. If not, the debtor may continue. Trustees ordinarily are not appointed in Chapter 11 proceedings. Thereafter, initial procedures are very much the same as under Chapter 7—the filing of schedules by the debtor, notice to the creditors, and a first meeting of creditors. The court will then appoint a committee of unsecured creditors, and also may appoint a committee of secured creditors and one of equity shareholders, to assure representation by each of these distinct groups. The powers and duties of creditors' committees, as set out in Section 1103, are:

1. with the approval of the court, to select and authorize the employment by the committee of one or more attorneys, accountants, or other agents to represent and perform services for the committee;
2. to consult with the trustee or debtor in possession concerning administration of the case;
3. to investigate and monitor all aspects of the business and the desirability of its continuance, and any other matters relevant to the case or the formation of a plan;

4. to participate in the formation of a plan and collect and file with the court acceptances of the plan;

5. to request the appointment of a trustee or examiner if the need arises; and

6. to perform any other services that are in the interest of those represented.

The next step is the filing of a plan by the debtor. If this is not done within 120 days after the granting of the order for relief, under specified conditions a plan may be filed by any other party in interest. The plan must: specify classes of claims or interest, those not impaired under the plan, and the treatment of any that are impaired; provide for equal treatment of claims within a class unless the holder agrees to less favorable treatment; and provide adequate means for the plan's execution. If the debtor is a corporation, the plan also must provide for certain amendments to its charter.

A plan must be accepted by vote of the holders of *two-thirds* of the dollar amount of claims voting and *one-half* of the number of claims voting. For example, suppose claims totaled $800,000, held by 100 creditors, and that 70 creditors with claims totaling $600,000 actually voted. Acceptance would require an affirmative vote by at least 35 creditors (one-half of the claims) holding at least $400,000 (two-thirds) of the claims. A plan that has been accepted may be modified later if needs or other circumstances require.

If the proposed plan is "fair and equitable," and is accepted by all classes whose claims will be impaired by it, it may be confirmed by the court after hearing. Thereafter the plan must be executed. Under appropriate circumstances and conditions set out in Section 1112, a plan under Chapter 11 may be converted to liquidation under Chapter 7. This may be done by the debtor, or by any other party in interest after a hearing and court approval. On the other hand, if the plan is executed successfully, the debtor will be discharged from liability for all claims administered under the plan, but not those that are not dischargeable under the act.

"WAGE-EARNER" BANKRUPTCY

On the heels of the Great Depression, Congress added Chapter 13 proceedings to the Bankruptcy Act in 1938. They are intended to provide debt adjustment for individuals as an alternative to Chapter 7 liquidation. However, until the act was amended in 1978, this provision was used infrequently. It provided no real advantage to most debtors over liquidation. Since that time, Congress has attempted to make Chapter 13 more attractive to individuals, first by eliminating the requirement that a debtor under Chapter 13 must have wages as his or her principal source of income.

Proceedings under this chapter may be initiated by *voluntary* petition only. The debtor must be an *individual* with regular income, regardless of principal source, and must owe unsecured debts of less than $100,000 and secured debts of less than $350,000. Upon the filing of the required petition, the court appoints a trustee, and a plan for payment must be proposed, confirmed, and executed. Upon successful completion of all obligations under the plan, the debtor will be discharged of all debts covered by the plan.

As under Chapter 11 proceedings, a plan for repayment of debts must be proposed, and the plan may be modified at any time before confirmation. The plan must meet three requirements set forth in Section 1322. It must: (1) provide for the submission of all or such portion of future earnings or other future income of the debtor to the supervision and control of the trustee as is necessary to execute the plan; (2) provide for full payment of all claims entitled to priority under Section 507 (discussed above as the second step in distribution under Chapter 7), unless the holder of such a claim agrees to different treatment; and (3) if the plan classifies claims, provide the same treatment for each claim in the same class. The plan may not provide for payments over a period longer than three years, except the court may approve a period no longer than five years.

Unlike a debt adjustment plan under Chapter 11, a Chapter 13 plan need not be approved by the unsecured creditors. It only must be confirmed by the court. However, confirmation may be granted only after notice and a hearing. At the hearing, creditors or any other party in interest may object to the plan.

Section 1325 provides that the court *shall* confirm the plan if certain further requirements are met. In addition to meeting other requirements of the act and the payment of fees: (1) the plan must be proposed in good faith; (2) the value of property to be paid under the plan on each unsecured claim must not be less than the amount that would be paid on that claim under a Chapter 7 liquidation; (3) the plan must be accepted by each holder of a secured claim, and must provide that the holder of each secured claim retains the lien securing it, that the value of the property on the effective date of the plan is not less than the allowed amount of the claim, and that the debtor must be able to surrender possession of the property to the holder; and (4) it must appear that the debtor will be able to make all payments under the plan and otherwise comply with its terms. Once confirmed, the plan binds the debtor and all creditors included in its terms. Unless otherwise specified in the plan, confirmation vests in the debtor title to all property included in the estate free and clear of claims of all creditors provided for in the plan.

After confirmation, the debtor may modify the plan unless the changes are disapproved by the court. Also, the debtor, if not successful in executing the plan, may convert the case into liquidation under Chapter 7. Finally, if the plan is executed fully by the debtor, he may seek discharge.

Discharge under Chapter 13 has the same effect as discharge under Chapters 7 and 11. However, the only nondischargeable debt not extinguished under Chapter 13 is one for alimony, maintenance, or support. Notably, unpaid student loans, and debts arising from unintentional torts and even criminal wrongdoings are subject to discharge under Chapter 13. This is one of the advantages to using Chapter 13 rather than Chapter 7. Another is that a debtor who has been granted a discharge under Chapter 7 within the previous six years cannot petition again under Chapter 7, but can obtain an order for relief under Chapter 13 and then convert the plan to a proceeding under Chapter 7 upon the expiration of the six years. Further, a debtor under Chapter 13 may retain title to and the use of her property during the proceedings, and it is free of the claims of most creditors. Finally, if the debtor has suffered foreclosure of her property pursuant to a security agreement, a Chapter 13 proceeding may be used to extend the debtor's period of redemption allowed under the law. Because of these advantages, Chapter 13 adjustment has become a more attractive alternative in recent years.

BANKRUPTCY COURTS

The 1978 act provided for the creation of special bankruptcy courts in every United States court district. These courts were to be presided over by special bankruptcy judges. However, this provision was held unconstitutional by the Supreme Court. The reason was that Article 3 of the Constitution provides that federal judges are to be appointed for life, and that their salaries could not be reduced. The bankruptcy judges were given fourteen-year terms, and their salaries were subject to annual adjustment (including reduction). The 1984 amendments cured these problems, making the bankruptcy courts adjunct to the district courts, rather than separately existing courts.

SUMMARY

Bankruptcy law is a creature of federal statute, and laws pertaining to bankruptcy are within the exclusive dominion of Congress, although the Bankruptcy Act refers to state law to determine some matters, such as the validity of most contracts and the disposition of property within state boundaries. Originally conceived as a creditor's remedy, modern bankruptcy law is more often thought of as protection for debtors. In fact, it seeks to protect the rights of both. The two principal policies underlying bankruptcy law are to enable an insolvent debtor to get a fresh start and to see that an insolvent debtor's assets are distributed fairly among his or her creditors.

The three principal types of bankruptcy are liquidation, corporate reorganization, and "wage-earner" bankruptcy. Of the three, the type most familiar to people is liquidation. Liquidation involves taking a debtor's nonexempt assets and distributing them to creditors according to priorities established under the Bankruptcy Act. Corporate reorganization and "wage-earner" bankruptcy involve establishing a court-approved plan of gradual repayment of all or some portions of the bankrupt's obligations.

At the conclusion of bankruptcy proceedings, most of the bankrupt's debts will be discharged. Bankruptcy law, however, provides that some kinds of debts cannot be discharged, and they remain as obligations.

KEY TERMS AND CONCEPTS

voluntary bankruptcy
liquidation
"wage-earner" bankruptcy
involuntary bankruptcy
corporate reorganization
order for relief
cash-flow test
automatic stay
meeting of the creditors
trustee
bankruptcy estate
preferential treatment
fraudulent conveyances
nondischargable debt
exempt property

PROBLEMS

1. On February 10, Dickey, while he was insolvent, paid his telephone bill ($1753.34) for the previous December, January, and February. He was declared bankrupt on February 14. Dickey's trustee sought to recover the payment to the telephone company. Should she be allowed to do so?

2. When Rosow, Inc. was declared bankrupt, one of its creditors discovered that it had been double-billed on recent transactions in the amount of $7420. The creditor petitioned the bankruptcy court to put its claim above those of other unsecured creditors under a theory of "equitable subordination," as provided in Section 510(c) of the Bankruptcy Act. Should the petition be granted?

3. Johnson owed some $14,000 on a federally insured student loan. The full amount was paid to the bank by the government, which then demanded payment from Johnson. Johnson filed for bankruptcy under Chapter 13 and submitted a plan to pay off the loan in the amount of 39 percent. This was Johnson's only debt. Should his plan be approved?

4. Acker was insolvent. She had no assets, and had only one creditor, to whom she owed approximately $17,000. The creditor petitioned the bankruptcy court for involuntary bankruptcy against Acker. Should the court grant relief?

5. Harris, who made his business of purchasing property at foreclosure sales, purchased certain land belonging to Madrid at a nonjudicial foreclosure sale for $256,000. The property had a fair market value of $380,000 to $400,000. Soon thereafter, Madrid was adjudicated bankrupt. The trustee in bankruptcy sought to set aside the sale as a fraudulent transfer. Should the court grant the relief?

6. While insolvent, the president of SLF News Distributors, Inc. used the corporation's funds to pay the debts of a related company. When SLF was adjudicated bankrupt shortly thereafter, the

trustee sought to set aside the transfer as fraudulent. Should the relief be granted, assuming the creditor who received the payment was in good faith and did not know the source of the funds?

7. Under Section 522(f)(2), a debtor is permitted to avoid liens on certain items of property specifically exempt under Section 522(d). Should this right also pertain to property exempt under the "wild-card" provisions of Section 522(d)(5)?

8. Manglove filed for Chapter 13 bankruptcy. A notice of the pending bankruptcy was filed with the county but was docketed improperly by the clerk and misfiled. Thereafter, the county court, not knowing of the action, sold certain real estate owned by Manglove at a foreclosure sale, and the clerk gave the purchaser a deed to the property. Should the bankruptcy court set aside the transfer?

9. Mansfield Tire and Rubber Co. filed a petition for Chapter 11 bankruptcy. Thereafter, the state Workers Compensation Commission commenced hearings on workers' compensation claims filed against Mansfield. The trustee sought to enjoin the hearings as a violation of the automatic stay. Should the relief be granted?

10. As part of a divorce settlement, Ms. Geiger agreed to pay her husband $10,233 for his interest in certain real estate. In return, Mr. Geiger transferred to her the title to the property and retained a lien to secure payment. Almost immediately, Ms. Geiger petitioned the bankruptcy court and was adjudicated bankrupt. Mr. Geiger received nothing in the proceeding, but the debt probably was discharged (although there was disagreement, and neither the debt nor the lien were mentioned in the discharge). Thereafter, Mr. Geiger sought to enforce the lien. Ms. Geiger contends that the lien is not enforceable if the underlying debt was discharged. Is she correct?

PART VI

Property

Perhaps the most important social institution established by American law is that of property ownership. Property ownership is jealously guarded under our legal system. Private property rights can be taken away only by due process of law. Unlike most areas of civil law, property law (especially as it concerns real property) is significantly based on statutes, and many aspects of ownership and sale of personal property are found in the Uniform Commercial Code. In this part of the book, Chapter 25 addresses the nature of personal property and bailments, and Chapters 26 and 27 involve real property, including its nature and ownership, and transfer and encumbrance. Chapter 28 covers special kinds of personal property—intellectual property and computer law. Finally, Chapters 29 and 30 discuss special types of real and personal property transfers—the creation of trusts and transfer upon the death of the owner.

Personal Property and Bailments

INTRODUCTION TO PERSONAL PROPERTY

Chapter 21 addressed personal property in the context of security interests. In this chapter, we will discuss the nature of personal property, its acquisition, and its transfer.

Nature of Property

For legal purposes, the term **property** may be defined as a bundle of rights—the rights to use, possess, enjoy, and dispose of things of value.

Although it is common to think of an object as being property, that is not the way a lawyer would think. When property is transferred, it is actually the rights in the object that are conveyed. In fact, the "property" (rights) in an object may be divided among a number of recipients. For example, one person may receive the right to use the property for a period of time, another the right to collect rent from the first during that period, and another all rights after the period ends. Each has received property.

The ownership of property is an incident of organized society. Without the force of society (the law), property rights cannot exist. The idea of ownership would be more akin to possession than to rights as we know them. That is, a person would have property only as long as he had the might to ward off those who would take it away from him. In the United States, property is not only protected by common law and statutory principles, but its protection specifically is provided for in the Fifth and Fourteenth Amendments to the Constitution, providing that no person shall be deprived of life, liberty, or property without due process of law.

However, property rights are not absolute. Although they may not be taken away without due process of law, they may be limited, or even taken away entirely, under appropriate circumstances and within the limits of due process. Moreover, a citizen's use of her property may be regulated so that it does not infringe on the rights of another. Zoning ordinances and nuisance law serve this end. Also, the government may take private property for public use through its right of eminent domain, or may destroy it for the public good by virtue of its power of condemnation. Thus, in addition to being widely varied in character, property rights are relative with regard to the ability to exercise them.

Possession

As noted above, the right to possession is one of the key elements of property, and in the absence of law possession itself would be the only right. The importance of possession is indicated by the saying, "possession is nine-tenths of the law." The law even regards the fact of possession as some evidence of ownership. For example, someone who buys property is considered on notice of the rights of anyone in possession. Because property rights are not always evidenced by written documents or public records, as they typically are for land and motor vehicles, possession is often the best evidence of ownership.

Depending on the context, the term **possession** has at least two distinct meanings. A person is said to have "actual" possession when he has immediate physical control over property. However, he is considered to have **constructive possession** of property to which he holds legal title, even in the absence of immediate physical control. The term *legal possession,* then, is used to mean either rightful, actual possession or constructive possession or both. Therefore, anyone who occupies the house he or she owns has legal possession, and is in both actual and constructive possession of it. When the owner leaves the house temporarily, perhaps to go to the grocery store or on vacation, he or she still has legal possession, and is in constructive possession until he or she returns. If a trespasser enters the house while the owner is gone, the trespasser will be in actual, but not constructive, possession, and will not have legal possession. If the owner rents the house to someone else who occupies it for a period of time, the tenant will have actual possession, the owner will have constructive possession, and both will have legal possession. To complicate matters even further, if an owner places the property in the hands of an employee, the owner will be in constructive possession and the employee will be in actual possession, and the owner will have legal possession but the employee will not. Instead, the employee is said to have only "custody," since his rights in the property are not for himself, but for the benefit of the owner. The importance of these distinctions will become more clear as your study of property law continues. The distinction between possession and custody may be important because one who is in legal possession of property, such as a tenant, is entitled to maintain an action in trespass against anyone who wrongfully interferes with her possession.

CLASSIFICATION OF PROPERTY

All property is either real or personal. Personal property must be further classified into a number of subclasses, the most useful of which are tangible and intangible, fixtures, and public and private.

Tangible and Intangible

Tangible property is any property in an object having physical existence. Obvious examples are an automobile or a book. **Intangible property** is all other property not having any physical manifestation, such as a patent, a copyright, or an account receivable. Even the property in a check is intangible. Although the piece of paper we refer to as a check has a physical existence, the check itself is not the property we are primarily concerned with or that has the true value. The piece of paper, although it is certainly tangible property, is more importantly evidence of title to an obligation. That obligation is intangible.

Understanding property as either tangible or intangible is important for two reasons. First, it reinforces the concept that property is a bundle of rights rather than merely an object. Further, it becomes important when considering matters such as the execution of contracts. For example, when payment for an automobile purchase is made by check, is the purchaser's obligation fully performed? Ordinarily it is not, because by presenting the check the purchaser has not yet turned over the property he or she has agreed to pay (the money). Second, the distinction is important in tax law. Some state and local governments assess an annual tax on tangible personal property; others tax intangible personal property; others tax both. Also, in the automobile transaction, suppose the purchaser gave the seller the check on December 15 of one year, but the check was not cashed until January 10 of the following year. In which year is the income from the sale taxed, assuming the seller pays income tax on a cash basis?

Real property is defined as the earth's crust and all things permanently attached thereto or used peculiarly therewith, along with the space above and all things below. Beginning with the crust of the earth, these rights extend in a pie-shaped wedge up to "the heavens," to the extent usable, and down to the center of the earth. This includes rights in the air, light, and space above the land, and such things as the soil, rocks, minerals, oil, and water below. In addition, it includes such things as trees, grass, buildings, and fences attached to the land, either rising out of it or attached to it with an apparent intent that it remain there permanently. All other property may be classified as **personal property.**

Personal property may become real property by "attachment," and real estate may become personal property by "severance." For example, an acorn in your hand is personal property until it is planted. The resulting tree is real property until it is cut down. If the tree was sawed into boards, the boards would be personal property until they were used in constructing a building, which would be part of the real property to which they were attached. If the building was later torn down, the boards would become personal property again.

The Uniform Commercial Code, in Sections 2-105 and 2-107, has led to some confusion concerning timber to be severed by the seller, minerals, and growing crops. These are defined as *goods,* even though that term ordinarily is considered to include only personal property (movable things). It is important to understand that even though these things are considered goods under the UCC, they are still real estate, and real estate law applies to them fully.

Fixtures

A **fixture** is an item of personal property that is affixed to real estate and has become real property. For example, a television set that is built into the wall of a building is a fixture if its removal would cause unreasonable damage to the building. More familiar to most people, however, would be plumbing and electrical fixtures.

In determining whether fixtures must remain with the real estate when it is sold or vacated, courts distinguish between "ordinary"—personal—fixtures and "trade fixtures." **Trade fixtures** are those that are attached for the purpose of conducting a trade or business, and ordinarily are attached by a tenant rather than an owner of the premises. Typically, trade fixtures remain the personal property of their owner as long as they can be removed without structural damage to the premises. For example, a dentist might rent office space in a building and attach her dental chair and other equipment. In doing so, the dentist may even drill holes in the floor and walls, significantly altering the structure of the building. Nevertheless, the chair and equipment probably will remain her personal property. The contrary probably would be true if they were not trade fixtures. This topic is discussed more thoroughly in Chapter 26.

Public and Private

Property may be either "public" or "private," depending on who owns it. Public property is that owned by the United States, a state, or some political subdivision such as a town or county. All other property, such as that owned by a person, a group of people, or a corporation is private property. The classification of public or private relates only to ownership, not use. Private property such as a hotel or a restaurant may be open to public use, and the public may be restricted from using certain public property, for example a military base.

OWNERSHIP OF PROPERTY

The term *ownership* is subject to a variety of definitions. Generally, it is considered to refer to the possession of the entire "bundle of rights" in something, or what often is called the title. In essence, it is the permanent right of dominion and control over property. Ownership may be acquired in a number of ways.

Creation

One who creates something of value ordinarily is entitled to the fruits of his or her labors, draftsmanship, and genius. Sometimes the property produced comes about by the combination of other properties, like planning and constructing a house; sometimes it comes about by an alteration of other property, as would be true of constructing a road; and sometimes the property is originated, as in the case of a musical score or a computer program. In any case, the value added or created is the property of the person who brought it about.

Purchase

The most common method of acquiring ownership is by purchase. The rights of the creator of the property are transferred, for consideration, to another. The purchaser may transfer the rights again, and so on. The law concerning the sale and purchase of property is treated more fully in the next chapter, and in Chapters 13–16.

Gifts

A *gift* is a transfer of property without receiving something in exchange. The transfer of property by gift is just as binding as a transfer by purchase, although, as discussed in Chapters 6–12, a *promise* to make a gift generally is not enforceable.

In order to transfer property by gift validly, five

basic requirements must be met: (1) the person making the gift (the donor) must be voluntary; (2) the donor or his or her agent, must make a present delivery of the property to the donee, or to someone to hold for the donee; (3) the transfer must appear to be unconditional; (4) the donor must intend to divest himself or herself of the property and to vest title in the donee; and (5) the donee must accept the gift.

Of the five requirements, second only to the questions of voluntariness and intent, the most often litigated is the question of delivery. Although contractual promises generally are enforceable, a gift promise is not enforceable until delivery has taken place. What is required for delivery will depend a great deal on the circumstances of each case. In general, however, what is necessary is some sufficient *manifestation* of intent to make a present transfer. This may involve the manual delivery of an object, such as placing a book into the hands of the donee. If physical delivery is not possible or practical, symbolic delivery generally is sufficient. For example, it is not practical to make a gift of a car or a yacht by handing over the object itself. Sufficient delivery could be made, however, by handing over a signed, sworn document of title or (in some jurisdictions) by handing over the keys while uttering words of gift. If the donee is already in possession of the property, a clear and unmistakable declaration, by the donor, of his intent to make a present transfer is sufficient. The key, then, is actual or symbolic possession by the donee concurring with the required intent of the donor. The following case illustrates the importance of delivery in making a gift.

MOLL v. MOLL
109 Ohio.App. 393, 166 N.E.2d 531 (1959)

This was an action by Everett E. Moll, as executor of the Estate of Ira J. Moll (Plaintiff/Appellee), against Louis S. Moll (Defendant/Appellant) to have money in the sum of $14,500 declared the property of the estate. The evidence disclosed that on July 23, 1954, Ira gave Louis a duplicate key to a safe deposit box rented in Ira's name, stating to Defendant, "There is something in there which belongs to you. It is money." Defendant did not enter the box, but after Ira's death the box was opened and was found to contain, among other things, an envelope containing the money in question. On the envelope was written: "To whom this may concern: Contents are the property of Louis S. Moll."

Defendant asserted his ownership of the money on the alternative theories of trust and gift *inter vivos* (an ordinary gift during the donor's lifetime). The trial court found for Plaintiff on both theories and Defendant appealed. Affirmed.

CRAWFORD, Judge.

[The court disposed of the theory of trust, finding none. It then continued to consider the theory of gift.]

The most likely theory upon which Louis S. Moll could rest his claim is that of a gift of inter vivos. The Probate Court found the necessary donative intent in the mind of the decedent as expressed by the donative words "There is something in there which belongs to you. It is money." But that court found that there was not an effective delivery.

We concur in this finding. Decedent never parted with control of the box nor did appellant Louis S. Moll ever take possession. While we do not know whether the amounts or identities of the items were changed after the purported gift, it is clear that decedent continued to enter the box from time to time and apparently opened and then sealed at least one of the envelopes. If the gift had been completed, title would thereupon have passed, and he would thereafter have been without authority or right to do anything affecting the money. On the other hand Louis S. Moll, if a donee, was a very indifferent one; he did nothing whatever regarding the money, never even entering the box to discover the form or extent of the purported gift.

The Supreme Court has made it clear that in situations similar to the one now before us an intended gift inter vivos must fail for want of effective delivery.

Questions

1. Why weren't the giving of the duplicate key and the note in the box enough to satisfy the court?
2. What is the reason for the law's insistence on strict compliance with the formalities of gift giving?

There are two types of gifts generally recognized by the law—gifts *inter vivos* and gifts *causa mortis*. A **gift *inter vivos*** is an ordinary gift during life; a **gift *causa mortis*** is a gift in contemplation of death. The former is regarded as absolute, but the latter is not. Unlike an *inter vivos* gift, a gift *causa mortis* does not become absolute until the death of the donor in the manner anticipated, and then only if the gift has not been revoked and the donee survives the donor. Otherwise, the gift will be valid only if the requirements for an *inter vivos* gift have been met.

Gifts *causa mortis* should be distinguished from testamentary dispositions (wills), since the requirements for testamentary dispositions are different. The distinction is that a gift *causa mortis* is a transfer during life, to become perfected upon the death of the transferor, while a testamentary disposition involves a pre-arranged transfer, by law, that is to take place at the moment of death but not before. The latter are discussed more fully in Chapter 49.

Lost and Mislaid Property

Although technically not the owner, a finder of **lost property** acquires rights in it that are good against everyone but the true owner. For example,

suppose Adams lost her ring and it was found by Baker, and then Carson stole it from Baker. Baker could maintain an action to recover the ring or its value from Carson, and Carson's act would constitute the crime of theft. Adams's rights, however, would be superior to Baker's.

If the finder of lost property knows the identity of its true owner, or he could determine the owner's identity by the exercise of reasonable effort, he is bound to do what is reasonable to see to its return. Failure to do so will constitute conversion and theft. In many states, **estray statutes** provide procedures to be followed by the finder. These statutes commonly include a requirement that the property be advertised, and provide a period of time that must pass before title can be perfected in the finder.

Most courts, when possible, will distinguish between lost property and **mislaid property.** Property is considered mislaid when the owner places it somewhere and then goes off and leaves it. Property is considered *lost* when it is separated from its owner under circumstances indicating that the separation took place without conscious effort on the part of the owner. Stated in simplistic terms, an owner departs from mislaid property; by way of contrast, lost property departs from its owner.

If property has been mislaid, the owner of the premises on which it is found has rights superior to those of the finder. For example, suppose Field comes into Olson's restaurant and finds a watch on the table. The watch probably was mislaid by its owner, and Olson would have the right to retain it. However, if it was found on the floor, perhaps with a broken band, Field would have the superior right because the watch probably is lost rather than mislaid. The reason for this distinction is based on the likelihood that the owner will know where to come to look for his or her property when it is mislaid. Of course, the true owner still has the best right of all. Consider the following case.

DOLITSKY v. DOLLAR SAVINGS BANK
203 Misc. 262, 118 N.Y.S.2d 65 (1952)

This was an action by Betty Dolitsky (Plaintiff) against the Dollar Savings Bank (Defendant) to recover the sum of $100 found by Plaintiff on premises owned and controlled by Defendant. Specifically, the Plaintiff entered the safe-deposit room of Defendant bank, took a brochure from a rack in that room, and found the $100 inside. The safe-deposit room was a restricted area, not open to the public. Admission was gained only by owners and authorized users of safe-deposit boxes, upon showing proper identification. The question before the court was whether the $100 was "lost" or "mislaid." Judgment for Defendant, Dollar Savings Bank.

TRIMARCO, Justice.

At common law property was lost when possession had been casually and involuntarily parted with, so that the mind had no impress of and could have no knowledge of the parting. Mislaid property was that which the owner had voluntarily and intentionally placed and then forgotten. . . . The New York cases have consistently recognized this classification. . . .

Property in someone's possession cannot *be found in the sense of common law lost property*. If the article is in the custody of the owner of the place when it is discovered it is not lost in the legal sense; instead it is mislaid. Thus if a chattel is discovered anywhere in a private place where only a limited class of people have a right to be and they are customers of the owner of the premises, who has the duty of preserving the property of his customers, it is in the possession of the owner of the premises. . . .

In the case of mislaid property discovered on the premises of another, the common law rule is that the proprietor of the premises is held to have the better right to hold the same for the owner, Loucks v. Gallogly . . . or the proprietor has custody for the benefit of the owner, Silcott v. Louisville Trust Co. . . . or the proprietor is the gratuitous bailee of the owner, Foulke v. New York Consolidated R. Co. . . . The effect of the above cases, despite their different description of the relationship, is that the proprietor is the bailee of the owner. Thus the discoverer of mislaid property has the duty to leave it with the proprietor of the premises, and the latter has the duty to hold it for the owner. New York statutory requirements do not change this rule.

The bank is a gratuitous bailee of mislaid property once it has knowledge of the property. . . . As such the bank has the duty to exercise ordinary care in the custody of the articles with a duty to redeliver to the owner. . . .

No authority has been discovered as to how long a gratuitous bailee in the bank's position is expected to hold mislaid property for the owner. The broad statement of the cases that the holder of mislaid property is a gratuitous bailee for the owner seems to indicate that the Bank would have to hold the property indefinitely.

The recent case of Manufacturers Savings Deposit Co. v. Cohen . . . which held that property found on the floor of a booth located in an outer room used by a safe deposit company in conjunction with a Bank access thereto not being limited to box holders or officials of the safe deposit company was lost property and as such should have been turned over to the property clerk of the Police Department, can be distinguished from the present case. In the Cohen case the court found that the booth on the floor of which the money was found was not located within a safe deposit vault but rather in an outer room adjoining said vault and in a part of the bank which was accessible to the ordinary customer of the bank for the purchase of bonds and the opening of new accounts; as such the court considers the room in which the booth was located a public place not restricted to safe deposit officials and persons having safe deposit boxes in the vault. The case is further distinguished from the present case since its facts disclose that the money was found on the floor of the booth which indicated to the court that the money was not mislaid. The court points out that the testimony shows the money to have been found on the floor of the booth and not on any table or other normal resting place.

Questions

1. Are you persuaded by the court's distinguishing of the Cohen case? After all, the booth was still inside the bank's property.
2. How long should the proprietor be required to hold mislaid property in the hope that the owner will return?
3. Who should have the right to unclaimed mislaid property—the finder, the store owner, or someone else?

Confusion

When the property of the two persons becomes so commingled that it is impossible to separate the parts belonging to each, the situation is called **confusion.** Questions then arise as to who is entitled to the resulting mix, if the confusion causes a loss in value of the property of one of the parties, and who will bear the loss if the resulting property is diminished by loss or theft.

If the confusion is rightful or innocent, as by agreement, innocent mistake, or the act of some disassociated third party, each owner will share in the resulting property, or any losses, either according to their agreement or in proportion to their relative contributions to the whole. Confusion by agreement ordinarily occurs only when *fungible* goods are involved—goods that are of a nature that one unit is essentially the same as any other. An example would be corn of a particular type and grade. For all practical purposes, one bushel is indistinguishable from another. In these circumstances, it is common for many owners to store their corn in a mass storage unit. When their corn is returned, they do not get the same kernels they put in, but that is unimportant.

If the confusion is the result of one of the owners' negligence, then the innocent owner is entitled to the return of his or her property insofar as is possible, and the negligent party must suffer any loss and will be liable in damages for any injury to the innocent owner. For example, suppose the tangible goods of Zaid and Malik are mixed by the negligence of Malik, and half of the resulting property is stolen by a third person. Zaid will be entitled to the return of the amount that was his, up to the entire remaining amount. If his right exceeds the remaining amount, Malik will be liable to him in damages for the remainder. Suppose, however, that instead of identical or fungible goods the property mixed was 500 bushels of number-1-grade spring wheat, belonging to Zaid and worth $8.00 per bushel, and 400 bushels of number-3-grade winter wheat worth $3.00 per bushel. Assume the resulting mix is worth $5.00 per bushel. Zaid would be entitled to 800 of the 900 mixed bushels, and could collect from Malik any consequential damages that might result (for example, Zaid might have to pay damages to a purchaser to whom he had contracted to sell his 500 bushels of number-1 wheat).

Finally, if the confusion was the result of the intentional wrongdoing of one of the parties, and the property of the innocent party cannot be separated, ordinarily the entire resulting property belongs to the innocent party. Suppose, for example, Blunt steals Sharp's car, overhauls it and otherwise fixes it up, including giving it a new paint job and interior. This particular type of confusion often is called **accession** (or **accretion**); it means that property of a totally dissimilar kind is added to the property of another. Although the resulting car has been increased in value greatly by Blunt, Sharp is entitled to its return without paying Blunt even for her expenditures, since Blunt's efforts have been imposed on Sharp wrongfully.

Possession of Unowned or Abandoned Property

A person may become the owner of some kinds of property merely by taking possession. This is true of **unowned property,** such as a wild animal. It also is true of property that has been abandoned by its owner.

Wild animals are considered to belong to no one, although some are protected by statute or regulation. They usually are distinguished from domestic animals by the absence of a quality called *animus revertendi* (a mind to return). Domestic animals have owners, and when gone from their homes, if left to their own devices, are expected to return to their owners. When captured, a wild animal belongs to its captor. This generally is held to include animals caught in a trap. If the animal escapes, however, it belongs to the next person who takes possession. An animal that is wounded presents a dichotomy. If it is *mortally* wounded and is being actively pursued by the person who inflicted the wound, it belongs to the pursuer; otherwise it belongs to anyone who captures it.

Suppose a commercial fisherman has fish in his net and a competitor cuts the net and takes the fish. Has the competitor trespassed (violated property rights) against the first fisherman? The answer is yes, and the first fisherman would be entitled to sue the second for the value of the fish lost. By the same token, if a fur trader has trapped an animal and it is released from the trap by someone who happens along, that person has violated the trapper's property rights in the animal, and is subject to paying damages for the loss.

Property is considered **abandoned** when its owner either has discarded it or has lost or mislaid it and given up all intention of trying to find it. Cases involving the latter type of abandonment often present difficult fact situations. One need not pursue his property during every waking moment to still have a hope and a desire to find it.

Various ways of acquiring ownership of property

Way	Example
Creation	painting a landscape on canvas
Purchase	buying an antique at an auction
Gifts	
inter vivos	receiving a bicycle from your uncle
causa mortis	receiving a stereo from your aunt while she is on her deathbed
Lost property	finding a diamond ring buried in the sand
Mislaid property	finding a pair of sunglasses on the dash of a rented car
Taking possession of unknown property	catching a rainbow trout in a public stream

For this reason, some states have passed statutes concerning a finder's right to title to found property stating, for example, that the finder holds clear title after six months. Although it may seem that it is likely to be more obvious when property has been discarded, and that ordinarily is true, interesting cases sometimes arise. Keep this in mind as you consider *H. S. Crocker Co., Inc. v. McFaddin,* which appears later in this chapter.

EVIDENCE OF TITLE

Proving title to the vast majority of personal property can be difficult, because there is nothing to evidence title other than possession. This is understandable because of the numbers of items owned, and the frequency with which they are purchased makes it impossible to have an acceptable system of registration and title. Therefore, individual owners are wise to keep their own records—such as descriptions and serial numbers, or perhaps even photographs—of their more important items. This, of course, also is handy for tax and insurance purposes.

Statutes provide for systems of registration and certification of title for real estate and for certain kinds of personal property, including motor vehicles, bicycles, and firearms. These statutes may serve three important purposes—a means of searching title by official records, provision for written means of conveyance, and, of course, a system for collecting taxes.

The use of *documents of title* in connection with goods provides an excellent means of both proving title and facilitating the conveyance of goods, especially in commercial transactions. Two important kinds of documents are warehouse receipts and bills of lading. A *warehouse receipt,* as the name implies, is simply a written receipt evidencing title to goods stored in a warehouse. A *bill of lading* is similar, except that it evidences title to goods that have been placed in the hands of a carrier for shipment. Their utility as evidence of title is obvious. If evidence of title is all that is desired, it is sufficient to use a simple *non-negotiable* document. However, for convenience in commercial transactions, a *negotiable* document (especially a negotiable bill of lading) often is desirable. Although a non-negotiable document provides strong evidence of the right to possession of the goods described, a negotiable document is almost conclusive. In addition, it provides an easy means for the transfer of that right by vesting it in the person who has possession of the document, with any necessary indorsements. For example, suppose Archie, in California, wishes to send to Veronica, in New York, certain goods to be shipped via ABC Trucking Co. Archie could place the goods in the hands of ABC Trucking and obtain a negotiable bill of lading, which he would endorse, naming Veronica as endorsee, and send it to her. When the goods arrive, Veronica could take possession of them, evidencing her right by the properly endorsed bill of lading. In fact, if Veronica were to pay for the goods upon arrival, Archie could ensure that he would get the money before Veronica could get the goods by sending the document to an escrow agent in New York (perhaps a bank). The escrow then would collect the amount due, to be sent to Archie, before turning the necessary document over to Veronica. Documents of title and their uses in commercial transactions are discussed in more detail in Chapters 21–23.

BAILMENTS

NATURE AND CREATION OF A BAILMENT

The term *bailment* is strange, and unknown to most people before they study the law. In fact, however, most people encounter bailments frequently, both in their personal lives and in conducting business affairs. Each time that happens, they are subject to a unique set of rights and liabilities imposed by the law. For the most part, these rights and liabilities may be altered by agreement between the parties. Many times it is desirable that this be done. In order to do so, however, it is necessary to understand the basic principles of bailment law.

Nature

A **bailment** occurs whenever one person (called the bailor) turns over possession of his property to another (called the bailee) to return it, or otherwise to dispose of it, according to his instructions. For example, you check your coat and hat at a checkstand in a restaurant or theater, or you leave your television with a repair shop to be repaired,

or you lend your book to a friend. Each of these transactions involves a bailment relationship.

It should be noted that bailment involves only the turning over of possession, not title. In this respect bailment differs from a "trust" relationship as discussed in Chapter 50. The latter entails a transfer of legal title to a trustee with the vesting of beneficial (equitable) title in a beneficiary. Also, bailment should be differentiated from lease or license arrangements. For example, as noted above, if someone checks her personal possessions at a checkstand, turning over possession to its operator, a bailment is created. However, if she merely places those possessions on a shelf or a hook provided for such purposes, there is no bailment, but only a license to use. The same distinction exists when you park your car in a parking lot. If you simply take a ticket and park the car, the relationship is one of lease of a parking space, but if you turn your car over to an attendant to be parked and cared for, a bailment is created. The key is whether actual possession is transferred.

Creation

The essential elements of every bailment are: (1) two parties, called the *bailor* and the *bailee;* (2)

Creation of a bailment

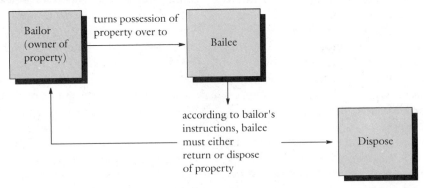

intent to create a bailment; (3) subject matter that is personal property, not real property; (4) the separation of ownership and actual possession; and (5) an absolute obligation on the part of the bailee to return, or to dispose of, the property according to the directions of the bailor. Of these elements, the last two are most frequently involved in litigation. Consider the following case.

H. S. CROCKER CO. v. Mc FADDIN
148 Cal.App.2d 307, 307 P.2d 419 (1957)

This was an action by H. S. Crocker Co. (Plaintiff/Appellant) against Mrs. Claude L. McFaddin (Defendant/Appellee) to recover 220,970 greeting cards claimed by Defendant.

Plaintiff distributed greeting cards. Any not sold the first year were placed on the market a second year at a reduced price. The third year, some were distributed again and others were hauled to a dump to be destroyed. The cards in question were hauled to a dump maintained by City Dump & Salvage. Although Plaintiff had instructed its employees to see that the cards were destroyed, they only hauled and dumped them and did not request that they be destroyed, nor did they pay the fee required to have them destroyed. The cards were salvaged by City Dump and sold to another party, who resold them to Defendant.

Defendant claimed that Plaintiff abandoned the cards, that title then vested in City Dump by right of salvage, and that title passed to her by sale. Plaintiff contended that City Dump was a bailee, and therefore had no title to pass. The trial court found for Defendant and Plaintiff appealed. Affirmed.

VALLEE, Justice.

Plaintiff says the finding that defendant is the owner of the cards is contrary to the evidence. It argues the evidence is insufficient as a matter of law to establish a divestiture of plaintiff's title. Plaintiff characterizes the transaction as a bailment for destruction. Defendant asserts the finding was supported by the evidence; there was a sale of the cards to City Dump & Salvage; alternately, plaintiff divested itself of all rights in the property by abandonment; alternately, if not an abandonment to all the world, there was a gift of the cards to City Dump & Salvage. It appears to be agreed that if one delivers property to another as a mere bailee, a purchaser from the bailee, however innocent he may be, acquires no title as against the bailor. . . .

In a broad sense a bailment is the delivery of a thing to another for some special object or purpose, on a contract, express or implied, to conform to the objects or purposes of the delivery which may be as various as the transactions of men. . . . Ordinarily the identical thing bailed or the product of, or substitute for, that thing, together with all increments and gains, is to be returned or accounted for by the bailee when the use to which it is to be devoted is completed or performed or the bailment has otherwise expired. If there is a transfer of ownership the transaction is a sale. . . . The general rule that the assent of both parties is necessary before a contract, either express or implied in fact, can come into existence, is applicable to the ordinary case of a contract of bailment. . . .

No bailment can be implied where it appears it was the intention of the parties, as derived from their relationship to each other and from the circumstances of the case, that the property was to be held by the party in possession in some capacity other than as bailee. . . .

While the word "sale" is commonly understood to mean a transaction by which the property of one of the parties thereto is exchanged for the money of the other, the legal meaning of the word is not so limited. The consideration need not be money; it may be money or its equivalent; it may be any valuable consideration. . . .

Applying these principles to the facts, we have concluded the transaction between City Dump & Salvage and plaintiff was not a bailment: it was a sale. City Dump & Salvage conducted both a dump and a salvage operation. It offered an opportunity for choice between two things to those who brought material to its dump. For a small charge such persons were accorded the privilege of dumping their material into a pit on the property of City Dump & Salvage, and a salvage operation followed. This was the normal course unless a special contract of a different character was made. If the person bringing the material requested that it be destroyed he was charged a greater sum; he was directed to dump the material in a hole dug by City Dump & Salvage—a different place from that in which he would have dumped it if the request had not been made—and the latter destroyed it without salvaging. Plaintiff concedes there was "a delivery, for a consideration, to a particular person." The early case of Stephens v. Mansfield, 11 Cal. 363, held that the relinquishment of property for a consideration is a sale or barter.

Plaintiff took the cards to City Dump & Salvage. It paid the fee for the privilege of dumping the cards only. It received a receipt with the name "City Dump & Salvage, Inc." on it, which in effect told it that if the cards were merely dumped into a pit they might be salvaged. It did not manifest in any way any intention or desire that the cards be handled so as not to be subject to salvage or that it wanted them destroyed. Plaintiff had no further use for the cards. In consideration for the privilege of dumping the cards on the property of City Dump & Salvage and thereby relinquishing them, plaintiff paid the latter $2.50 a load and dumped them. Plaintiff thereby sold the cards to City Dump & Salvage, and title to them passed to it.

Questions

1. What is the legal status of old appliances that you put outside as part of your weekly garbage?
2. What is the legal status of clothes left at a dry cleaner for several months when there is a sign posted that says "items left must be claimed within 30 days"?

Two Parties

It seems to be fairly obvious that one person cannot be both bailor and bailee of a single piece of property. However, if two people jointly own an object, for example a car, possession by one would create a bailment concerning the interest of the other. But, the transfer of corporate property from one division to another would not. Neither would the possession of lost property by a finder if abandonment could be proven.

Intent

The required intent to create a bailment may be expressed by the parties or implied from the circumstances; most frequently the latter is the case. That is, when litigated, the intent of the parties usually must be determined by the court from what ordinarily would be intended by the parties in each given situation. As previously noted, the element of intent, although strictly required, is not litigated frequently. However, as the following case illustrates, it may be the key factor in determining the rights of the parties.

BERGLUND v. ROOSEVELT UNIVERSITY
18 Ill.App. 842, 310 N.E.2d 773 (1974)

This was an action by Richard C. Berglund (Plaintiff/Appellee) against Roosevelt University (Defendant/Appellant) for the value of property allegedly held by Defendant as bailee and lost.

Plaintiff, a student at Roosevelt University, worked on the school newspaper and used offices of the newspaper located in a building owned and controlled by the university. The property in question was his own property intended for his personal use, which he had stored in one of the offices. The university did not know the property was stored there. It was stolen during a weekend by a party or parties unknown. The primary question before the court was whether the university was a bailee.

The trial court found for Plaintiff and Defendant appealed. Reversed.

McNAMARA, Presiding Judge.

Bailment is defined as the rightful possession of goods by one who is not an owner. The characteristics common to every bailment are the intent to create a bailment, delivery of possession of the bailed items, and the acceptance of the items by the bailee. . . . A bailment can be established by express contract or by implication, with the latter designated as implied-in-fact or implied-in-law. . . . In determining the existence of an implied-in-fact bailment, one must analyze the facts surrounding the transaction, such as the benefits to be received by the parties, their intentions, the kind of property involved, and the opportunity of each to exercise control over the property. . . .

In the present case, plaintiff attempted to show that an implied-in-fact bailment had arisen between the parties. It is clear, however, that the failure of the plaintiff to prove any knowledge on the part of the defendant of the storage of the items doomed this attempt.

Knowledge on the part of the bailee is essential to prove proper delivery and acceptance. Physical control over the property allegedly bailed and an intention to exercise that control are needed to show that one is in possession of the bailed item. . . . And before acceptance can be inferred on the part of the alleged bailee of the goods purportedly bailed, there must be evidence to show notice or knowledge on the part of the bailee that the goods are in fact in his possession. . . . We conclude that plaintiff's failure to prove knowledge on the part of defendant of the goods stored resulted in his inability to prove a valid delivery of the camera equipment and a true acceptance of the goods by defendant. The trial court erred in holding to the contrary.

Questions

1.   Is the knowledge requirement met in the case of the contents of a bank safe-deposit box?
2.   What difference does it make whether the relationship between the plaintiff and defendant in this case is categorized as a bailment?

Personal Property

Only personal property can be the subject matter of a bailment. Further, it may be argued that only tangible personal property may be involved because it is necessary to hand over possession, which cannot be done with intangible property. This point is largely academic, however, in that it is quite clear that documents evidencing title to intangible property such as stock certificates, bonds, and promissory notes can be the subject of bailments. As to real property, there is perhaps no logical reason why a bailment cannot be created, other than the fact that similar relationships involving real estate are covered by a separate body of law, which is discussed in the next two chapters.

Possession

The delivery of *actual* possession from the bailor to the bailee is crucial to the establishment of a bailment. As noted in the introduction to this material, the delivery of actual possession distinguishes bailment situations from mere leases or licenses to use. In addition, it is necessary that only possession, and not title, be transferred. Otherwise, the transaction probably will constitute the formation of a trust. Each of these similar arrangements is governed by a separate body of law distinct from the law of bailment.

Delivery of possession must be actual (not symbolic), but need not be voluntary on the part of the bailor. However, acceptance must be voluntary on the part of the bailee. Although the intent of the bailor is ordinarily either express or implied in fact, it also may be implied in law. For example, suppose during a storm a lawn chair belonging to Montague is picked up by the wind, carried into Capulet's back yard, and Capulet picks it up to carry it inside. At that moment, a bailment is created. Montague's delivery to Capulet was involuntary and his intent to create a bailment is implied by law. Capulet's taking possession is actual and her intent to create a bailment is implied by the fact that she took possession of the chair. She thereby undertook certain duties to Montague, discussed more fully in the next section. Had she simply left the chair where it was, no bailment would have been created and no duty to Montague would have arisen, absent some other prior duty. The bailee's willingness to accept responsibility must be demonstrated clearly.

Termination of Bailment

Ordinarily a bailment relationship is terminated by the return of the property to the bailor or its disposal according to the bailor's instructions. The obligation to do one of these must be absolute. If title passes to the recipient, the title is supposed to transfer to him in the future, or the duty to return or dispose of the property is conditional, the transaction is not a bailment. If title passes absolutely, the transaction will be considered a *sale* if consideration is to be returned, or a *gift* if the transfer is without consideration. If title is to transfer in the future, upon payment, the transaction is a *conditional sale;* it is a *consignment* if the property is to pass to a third party purchaser or is to be returned if not sold. A *sale on approval* occurs if title passes conditionally with a right of return. Finally, if the owner has abandoned the property, the person in possession has no duty to return it, so of course there is no bailment. Other ways in which a bailment can terminate are by agreement of the parties or destruction of the subject matter.

Custody of Agent or Servant

In carrying on business, it is common for an owner of property to place it in the hands of his agent or servant, to be used in connection with the business or disposed of for the benefit of the owner. Although similar, such a transfer does not create a bailment because only **custody** is transferred, with possession remaining with the owner. This distinction is subtle, but important, and is discussed more fully in the chapters on agency law.

BAILEE'S DUTY OF CARE

In every bailment relationship, the bailee owes a duty of care to protect the property in his or her possession from loss or harm. The degree to which the duty is owed will depend on the type of bailment. Bailments generally may be classified as: (1) for the benefit of the bailee; (2) for the mutual benefit of both parties; (3) for the benefit of the bailor; and (4) involuntary.

Bailment for the Benefit of the Bailee

A loan of property for the exclusive benefit of the bailee is an example of this type of bailment. Under these circumstances, the bailee owes the highest duty of care, and basically becomes a guarantor of the safety of the property. If it is lost or harmed, other than by an "act of God," the bailee

may be liable. For example, suppose Fred lends his car to his roommate Ricky, and while in Ricky's possession it is damaged while parked in a parking lot. Ricky probably will be liable even if he is not at fault in causing the damage. In a bailment for the benefit of the bailee, sometimes called "gratuitous bailment," the duty to return the property in substantially the same condition as when it was received is almost unqualified.

Mutual-Benefit Bailment

When the purpose of a bailment is to benefit both the bailor and the bailee, it is called a **mutual-benefit bailment.** For example, the bailor leaves her watch at a repair shop to be repaired. In this situation, the duty of care required of the bailee, although substantial, is somewhat less than in the gratuitous bailment. He would be liable to the bailor only if he is at fault in reducing the value of the watch, including loss or injury caused by his ordinary negligence. However, assuming he exercised due care, if his shop was burglarized and the watch was stolen, he would not be liable.

Bailment for the Benefit of the Bailor

If the bailee does not benefit in any way from the bailment, but takes possession of the property solely as an accommodation to the bailor, the duty of the bailee is further decreased. Suppose for example, Marsha agrees to take care of Greg's dog without compensation while Greg is on vacation. If the dog is injured or lost, Marsha probably will not be liable unless it can be shown that the loss or injury was due to her gross negligence, or intentional misconduct. Therefore, if she allowed the dog to run free against the expressed wishes of Greg, she probably would be liable, but not if the dog escaped or was stolen while on a chain in her backyard, absent some additional wrongdoing.

Involuntary Bailment

Someone who is the involuntary bailee of the property of another owes the owner only a slight duty of care. That is, an involuntary bailee probably will not be liable unless he is intentionally wrongful. An **involuntary bailment** may arise by taking possession of property that has been lost by its owner or by taking delivery of property sent by mistake, if the mistake is known to the person who receives the property. For example, after terminating his membership in the Record-By-Mail Club, Anton continues to receive the record of the month in the mail. Anton's obligation as bailee is not to use the records and to refrain from intentionally damaging them or causing their loss. It might be said that if his apartment were to catch fire, the records are the last things he should worry about removing.

ALTERATION OF BAILEE'S LIABILITY

Most bailments are voluntary. Therefore, the parties are free to alter the rights and duties between themselves as they see fit. The most frequent alteration of the bailee's liability involves placing a dollar limit on losses for which the bailee will be liable. This agreed-upon limitation generally is accompanied by a provision for the bailor's obtaining insurance to cover any loss above the established limit. Attempts by bailees to eliminate all liability, including liability for an intentional breach of the bailment contract, generally are held unenforceable.

Common carriers and *innkeepers* ordinarily are subject to special rules concerning responsibility for property belonging to their customers and guests. A common carrier is a business that is open for hire by the general public to transport property from place to place. An innkeeper is someone who opens his or her property for public accommodation, to feed and house transients—for example, a hotel.

At common law, both common carriers and innkeepers were considered insurers of the safety of the property belonging to their customers and guests. The rule of strict liability was applied to these businesses because of a perceived need to protect the public from dishonest practices. In the case of common carriers, it was feared that if they were left with only ordinary legal restraints, there was a substantial danger they would collude with highwaymen. In the case of innkeepers, it was felt that the liability should be increased because the guests, being largely transient, otherwise would have little incentive to pursue legitimate claims. Today, the rule of strict liability remains, and both common carriers and innkeepers generally are relieved of liability only for "acts of God."

Two points should be noted. First, the liability described above applies only to a common carrier or an innkeeper as a bailee. Although the surrender of property to a common carrier certainly will constitute a bailment, an innkeeper is not the bailee of all the property brought by his or her guests. A bailment is created only with respect to property the guest actually turns over to the innkeeper for safekeeping—for example, property handed over to be placed in the hotel safe. However, if no place of safekeeping is provided, an innkeeper may be strictly liable even for property that a guest must leave in a room. Second, the liabilities of these businesses is controlled heavily by state statute. These statutes generally restate the principles just described and place a maximum dollar amount on liability for loss or damage.

BAILEE'S RIGHT TO COMPENSATION

Most bailments are entered into based on a contract, either express or implied in fact. When an express contract is involved, the bailee's compensation ordinarily is handled by an express provision. Otherwise (or when the relationship is created by an implied contract), the bailee is entitled to the reasonable value of the services performed, with two important exceptions. If the bailment is for the sole benefit of the bailee, no right to compensation is implied because of the nature of the bailment. Second, circumstances such as the relationship of the parties may negate any presumption that compensation is due. For example, a person takes care of his sister's dog for a weekend while she is out of town to visit the family. There would be a very strong implication against the bailee's right to be compensated.

Involuntary bailments give rise to a slightly different rule. Suppose, for example, that Jean's dog ran away and Kevin took it in as a stray, keeping it for two days until its owner could be located. Kevin would be entitled to some compensation for his services. Although a recovery of the reasonable value of those services under the theory of a contract implied in fact is a possibility, the better-reasoned rule would allow him a recovery for the reasonable value of the benefit conferred on Jean, under the theory of quasi contract. Either way, it is clear that Kevin would be entitled to just compensation. The same rule would apply to the previous "Records-By-Mail Club" example.

A final consideration regarding a bailee's right to compensation is the matter of enforcing the right. The law provides, generally, that when services are performed involving the creation, maintenance, or preservation of property, the party performing the services, if entitled to compensation, also is entitled to a lien to secure payment. A lien is a security interest in property. It may be quite formal, as is usually the case with a mortgage on real estate. However, it also may be much less formal. Chapter 21 discusses the intricacies of security interests involving personal property. Here, it simply should be noted that liens against personal property may be perfected by meeting certain filing requirements, but also may be perfected by the bailee's retaining possession of the property involved until the bailor pays.

BAILOR'S LIABILITY

Although questions of liability in bailment situations ordinarily focus mostly on the bailee's liability, it is important to note that a bailment can impose liablity on the bailor in addition to his or her liablity for compensation. The bailor is obligated to exercise reasonable care to prevent injury to the bailee resulting from the bailee's taking possession of the property bailed.

The degree of care required of the bailor depends on the type of bailment and the circumstances. If the bailment is for the sole benefit of the bailor, the bailor usually is liable for any injuries resulting to the bailee caused by a defect or hazard connected with the property bailed. Of course, this presumes that the bailee exercises reasonable care. If the bailment is for the sole benefit of the bailee, on the other hand, the bailor is expected to exercise reasonable care with respect to hazards known to him and of which he has no reason to believe the bailee is aware. Therefore, if Shawn lends his car to Julie, and Julie is injured because of a mechanical failure, the purpose for which the car was being used may well be determinative of Shawn's liability. Was the car being used for the benefit of Shawn, or Julie, or for the benefit of both?

Mutual-benefit bailments, by far the most common in the commercial context, give rise to a duty on the bailor that is in between the two extremes. The bailor assumes liability for injuries caused to the bailee as a result of hazards or defects either known by the bailor or that she could have discovered by the exercise of reasonable care. Again, this assumes the bailee justifiably is unaware of the problem. Consider the following case.

MOORE v. ELLIS
385 S.W.2d 261 (Tex.Ct.Civ.App. 1964)

This was an action by Harold Ellis, a minor, by his next friend A. G. Ellis (Plaintiff/Appellee) against John I. Moore and H. R. Wardlaw, dba Red Town Farm (Defendants/Appellants) to recover damages for injuries sustatined while operating farm machinery supplied by Defendants. The machinery was defective and the defect was known by Plaintiff prior to sustaining the injuries in question, which resulted because of the defect. The question before the court was whether Defendants had failed in their duty as bailors to supply machinery in safe condition.

The trial court found for Plaintiff in the amount of $126,500 and Defendants appealed. Reversed with judgment ordered for Defendants.

DUNAGAN, Chief Justice.

The record establishes without dispute that the relationship of the parties herein is that of bailor-bailee, although there is no jury finding to this effect.

. . . As we view the situation before us, the question which is here presented is whether the defendants breached a duty owed by a bailor to a bailee, or one standing in the place of the bailee, or whether, as a matter of law from the undisputed evidence, all duties owed by the defendants were performed, thereby absolving them from any liability in this matter. . . .

The law of Texas and the other jurisdictions of the United States makes a distinction in the duty owed by different types of bailors to their bailees. Irrespective of whether it be a gratuitous bailor, a bailor for mutual benefit, or bailor for hire, there is no duty to act if the bailee knows of the defect. If the bailee does not know of the defect, there is no duty other than informing him of such defect. . . .

In the case of Nesmith v. Magnolia Petroleum Co, . . . the court said:

'One who supplies directly or through a third person a chattel for another to use, is subject to liability to those whom the supplier should expect to use the chattel with the consent of the other or to be in the vicinity of its probable use, for bodily harm caused by the use of the chattel in the manner for which and by a person for whose use it is supplied, if the supplier (a) knows, or from facts known to him should realize, that the chattel is or is likely to be dangerous for the use for which it is supplied; (b) and has no reason to believe that those for whose use the chattel is supplied will realize its dangerous condition; and (c) fails to exercise reasonable care to inform them of its dangerous condition or of the facts which make it likely to be so.' These general principles apply alike to donors, lenders, and lessors of chattels. . . .

Therefore, all three of the above elements must exist concurrently before liability can be assessed against the defendants.

In the case at bar it is undisputed that Harold Ellis knew of the inoperable cylinder lift, and it is further undisputed that McCrary told Harold Ellis about the inoperable cylinder lift. Furthermore, the jury found that at the time and on the occasion in question, Harold Ellis knew that the cylinder lift was not in operating condition. Therefore, elements (b) and (c) did not exist, but rather, the evidence showed that the duty imposed was fulfilled and not breached.

The rule appears to be general and firmly established that where a bailee-plaintiff voluntarily continues to use a defective machine after knowledge of the defect, he cannot recover for injuries resulting from such defect. . . .

Questions

1. Why doesn't the law impose a greater duty on the bailor, especially when the subject of the bailment is something that is potentially dangerous, such as machinery?
2. Should the fact that the plaintiff was a minor make a difference to the court in this case?

SUMMARY

The term *property* is defined as a bundle of rights to use, possess, enjoy, and dispose of something of value. These rights may be owned entirely by one person, or divided among two or more. The ownership of property is considered so important in the United States that it is protected by two amendments to the Constitution—the Fifth and the Fourteenth.

Property may be classified as tangible or intangible, real estate or personal, as a fixture, or as public or private. A working knowledge of property law requires an understanding of each of these terms.

The ownership of property may be acquired by creation, purchase, executed gift (*inter vivos* or *causa mortis*), finding lost or mislaid property that has been abandoned by its owner, or by taking possession of unowned property such as a wild animal. Ownership of personal property ordinarily is not evidenced by a formal certificate of title, and possession alone may be the best evidence. However, negotiable or non-negotiable warehouse receipts and bills of lading are used commonly to show title to such property when it is placed in the hands of a warehouse employee for storage or a carrier for transportation to another location. In addition, special statutes provide for the registration of some kinds of personal property, such as motor vehicles and firearms.

A bailment is a special relationship created when the owner of property (bailor) transfers possession of that property to another (bailee) to be returned or disposed of according to his instructions. The creation of a bailment requires:

(1) two parties; (2) intent; (3) the property must be personal property; (4) a separation of title and possession; and (5) an obligation to return, or dispose of, the property according to the bailor's instructions. Perhaps the most distinguishing feature of a bailment is that possession is transferred, not title or mere custody.

Bailments may be classified generally into four types: (1) those for the benefit of the bailee; (2) mutual-benefit bailments; (3) those for the benefit of the bailor; and (4) involuntary bailments. With each, the bailee owes a descending obligation of care, from ensuring the safety of property bailed for her benefit, to a very slight degree concerning property of which she is an involuntary bailee. The bailor's duty to see that the property is safe for the bailee increases from a duty only to either cure or warn of known defects in a bailment for the benefit of the bailee, to strict liability in the case of a bailment for his own benefit. The liability of the parties, however, may be altered by contract, and in the case of some special bailments, such as those involving common carriers and innkeepers, liability is altered significantly by special statute.

KEY TERMS AND CONCEPTS

property
possession
constructive possession
tangible property
intangible property

personal property
real property
fixture
trade fixture
gifts *inter vivos*
gifts *causa mortis*
lost property
estray statutes
mislaid property
confusion
accession (or accretion)
unowned property
abandonment
bailment
mutual-benefit bailment
involuntary bailment

PROBLEMS

1. Arthur Adams owned an old manuscript that he wished to donate to Tamberton University. He gave it to his sister, Martha, with instructions that it was to be delivered to the university upon his death. Two years later, while Martha was still in possession of the manuscript, Arthur was adjudicated incompetent and confined to a state mental hospital. Six months later he died. Martha delivered the manuscript to the university as she was instructed, but the executor of Arthur's estate demanded that it be returned as property of the estate. Who is entitled to the manuscript?

2. Sears sold drapes and matching bedspreads to Seven Palms Motel, which used them in furnishing 120 rooms at the motel. When Seven Palms failed to pay for the merchandise, Sears sought a mechanic's lien as security. Is Sears entitled to its lien?

3. Ochoa's truck was stolen. Eventually it ended up in a junkyard, in pieces. Rogers saw the pieces and purchased them. She spent many hours reassembling the truck and restoring it. Some time after the job was finished, Ochoa saw the truck and demanded it. When Rogers refused, Ochoa filed suit contending that, since the truck was stolen property, Rogers had no title. Is Ochoa correct?

4. Van Dyke sent several rolls of movie film to Kodak for processing. During development, a substantial portion of the film was damaged due to the negligence of Kodak. Van Dyke incurred a $1500 expense in reshooting the pictures. Kodak denied liability on the ground that a disclaimer on the film box limited the liability of Kodak to replacement of the film, and disclaimed any other liability in connection with the sale *or subsequent handling* of the film. Should Kodak prevail?

5. While in Germany during World War II, Lieber came into possession of certain Adolf Hitler relics and brought them home with him when he was discharged from military service. They remained in his home for some 20 years, at which time they were stolen in a burglary. Sometime later, Lieber located the articles, which in the meantime had been sold to a dealer who had resold them to a good-faith purchaser. Is Lieber entitled to the return of the articles?

6. Capezzaro was robbed and a suspect was arrested in possession of the stolen property, which Capezzaro identified at the police station. Because of a technical mistake in making the arrest, the suspect was not indicted. When she was released, the property was returned to her by the police department's property officer. Capezzaro sued the department contending the officer should not have released the property to the suspect. Is Capezzaro correct?

7. Central Chrysler Plymouth rented a building from Holtz from which it operated its automobile agency. While there, it installed two hydraulic lifts in the garage area. Upon termination of the lease, Central negotiated with its successor, American Central Automotive, Inc., to sell the lifts to American. Thereafter, when Holtz and American executed the lease, the lease provided that the lifts went with the property, and American refused to negotiate further with Central. Central sued Holtz for conversion of the lifts, and

Holtz defended on the ground that Central had abandoned them. Who is correct?

8. Ikeda, an employee of United Construction Co., was injured when a bucket of a crane came loose from the cable and fell on him. Ikeda sued Okada Trucking, the lessor of the crane, contending it was liable for leasing the crane to his employer in an unsafe condition. If it is proven that the bucket was not properly attached when the crane was leased, is Okada liable?

9. Hines leased a donkey engine to Purvine to be used in powering saws Purvine used in her logging operation. While the engine was in Purvine's possession, it was destroyed by a fire of unknown origin. Hines demanded payment for the engine. Is he entitled?

10. During the county fair, Dundas leased space in a stable at the fairground for the purpose of housing her horse for the week. Fire broke out in the stable and Dundas's horse died. Dundas sued Lincoln County, owner of the fairground and lessor of the stable space, contending it was liable for failing to keep the horse safe and, among other things, failing to equip the stable with fire extinguishers properly. Is the county liable?

Chapter | 26

Interests in Real Property

_____

_____

_____

_____

INTRODUCTION

In the previous chapter, the term *real property* was defined for the purpose of contrasting it to personal property. It is important to consider the term again, and to expand on the definition.

Definition

Real property is basically property that has a relatively fixed, or permanent, location, and includes the earth's crust and all things permanently attached thereto or used peculiarly therewith. "Permanently attached" does not mean absolutely immovable, since any particular item of tangible property probably can be moved with some degree of effort. Rather, whether something is attached permanently is to be determined from the apparent intent of the person who attached it. Does it appear that he would have intended to pick it up and take it away if he moved to another location?

According to the common law, someone who owns a portion of the earth's crust also owns the airspace above and all things below, in a pie-shaped wedge out to "the heavens" and down to the center of the earth. This includes the right to such things as oil, minerals, and water located below, and the "natural lights and breezes" above. This remains the basic rule today, although it is subject to some limitations such as the right to reasonable flight by aircraft, the loss of natural light and breeze because of the erection of tall buildings on adjoining land (when permitted by local law), the extent to which air space can be utilized, and some alteration of rights in oil and water in some jurisdictions. Consider the following case.

SOUTHWEST WEATHER RESEARCH, INC.
v. DUNCAN
319 S.W.2d 940 (Tex.Ct.Civ.App. 1959)

This was an action by Jim Duncan and others (Petitioners/Appellees) against Southwest Weather Research, Inc. (Respondent/Appellant) for an injunction to stop Respondent from seeding clouds over land belonging to Petitioners. The seeding was being conducted under contract with other area farmers for the purpose of preventing hail that could damage crops. Respondent contended that Petitioners had no right to an injunction because the seeding operation was not harmful to them, and they would continue to receive any rain the clouds otherwise would provide. Petitioners contested this conclusion.

The trial court found for Petitioners and granted a temporary injunction. Respondent appealed. Judgment modified and affirmed.

PER CURIAM.

First of all, it must be noted that here we do not have any governmental agency, State or Federal, and find no legislative regulation. This is exclusively a dispute between private interests. It has been said there is no precedent and no legal justification for the trial court's action. It has long been understood that equity was created for the man who had a right without a remedy, and, as later modified, without an adequate remedy. Appellees urge here that the owner of land also owns in connection therewith certain so-called natural rights, and cites us the following quotations from Spann v. City of Dallas, . . . in which Chief Justice Nelson Phillips states:

> Property in a thing consists not merely in its ownership and possession, but in the unrestricted right of use, enjoyment and disposal. Anything which destroys any of these elements of property, to that extent destroys the property itself. The substantial value of property lies in its use. If the right of use can be denied, the value of the property is annihilated and ownership is rendered a barren right. . . .
> . . . The very essence of American constitutions is that the material rights of no man shall be subject to the mere will of another. Yick Wo. v. Hopkins, 118 U.S. 356, 6 S.Ct. 1064, 30 L.Ed. 220.

In Volume 34, Marquette Law Review, at Page 275, this is said:

> Considering the property right of every man to the use and enjoyment of his land, and considering the profound effect which natural rainfall has upon the realization of this right, it would appear that the benefits of natural rainfall should come within the scope of judicial protection, and a duty should be imposed on adjoining landowners not to interfere therewith.

In the Stanford Law Review, November 1948, Volume 1, in an article entitled, "Who Owns the Clouds?", the following statements occur:

> The landowner does have rights in the water in clouds, however. The basis for these rights is the common-law doctrine of natural rights. Literally, the term 'natural rights' is well chosen; these rights protect the landowner's use of his land in its natural condition. . . .
>
> All forms of natural precipitation should be elements of the natural condition of the land. Precipitation, like air, oxygen, sunlight, and the soil itself, is an essential to many reasonable uses of the land. The plant and animal life on the land are both ultimately dependent upon rainfall. To the extent that rain is important to the use of land, the landowner should be entitled to the natural rainfall.

In California Law Review, December 1957, Volume 45 No. 5, in an article, "Weather Modification," are found the following statements:

> What are the rights of the landowner or public body to natural rainfall? It has been suggested that the right to receive rainfall is one of those 'natural rights' which is inherent in the full use of land from the fact of its natural contact with moisture in the air. . . .
>
> Any use of such air or space by others which is injurious to his land, or which constitutes an actual interference with his possession or his beneficial use thereof, would be a trespass for which he would have remedy. . . .

We believe that under our system of government the landowner is entitled to such precipitation as Nature deigns to bestow. We believe that the landowner is entitled, therefore and thereby, to such rainfall as may come from clouds over his own property that Nature, in her caprice, may provide. It follows, therefore, that this enjoyment of or entitlement to the benefits of Nature should be protected by the courts if interfered with improperly and unlawfully. It must be noted that defendant's planes were based at Fort Stockton, in Pecos County, and had to fly many miles to seed clouds over defendants' lands in Jeff Davis County. We do not mean to say or imply at this time or under the conditions present in this particular case that the landowner has a right to prevent or control weather modification over land not his own. We do not pass upon that point here, and we do not intend any implication to that effect.

There is ample evidence here to sustain the fact findings of the trial court that clouds were destroyed over property of appellees by operations of the appellants. The trial court chose to believe the evidence to that effect, and we hold there was ample evidence to support him [*sic*] in so holding and finding. We further hold that the trial court was justified in restraining appellants from modifying or attempting to modify any clouds or weather over or in the air space over lands of the appellees.

Questions

1. Should a landowner be allowed to stop cloud seeding when there is a drought in the general area?

2. Does this case permit a landowner to prevent kites, gliders, hot-air balloons, airplanes, and space vehicles from passing over his or her property?

Types of Interests

Remembering the definition of property as a bundle of rights, and that these rights may be possessed by one person or divided among two or more persons, it should be clear that the interests of the various owners may differ quite widely in nature and quality. For convenience, however, these interests may be classified into four general categories, each with a number of subcategories— (1) freehold estates, (2) leasehold estates, (3) nonpossessory interests, and (4) future interests.

FREEHOLD ESTATES

Broadly speaking, the term *estate* applies to *any* interest in either real or personal property. As used here, however, **estate** means only those interests that include the exclusive right to present possession. All other interests are "less than estates," or simply "interests." Estates, then, are of two types—freehold and leasehold. A **freehold estate** is one that continues for an indefinite period and, theoretically, may continue without end. The common law recognized four types of freehold interests. They were (1) fee simple, (2) fee simple determinable, (3) life estate, and (4) fee tail. The **fee tail** estate was an estate that passed automatically from a person to the "heirs of his body" (ordinarily the eldest son). Its use has been abolished in the United States in all except a few states. Therefore, it will not be discussed in further detail.

Fee Simple

When a person says he or she owns real property, that ordinarily means the speaker owns a *fee simple* interest in the property. The **fee simple** interest is

the most comprehensive form of property interest. It embraces the ownership of every interest concerning the property, absolutely and in perpetuity. As a practical matter, however, someone who owns in fee simple today is unlikely to own every interest. For example, as noted above, every parcel of real property in the United States is subject to the ability of others to make reasonable flights over it. Most property also is subject to other public rights for roads, utilities, and the like. Therefore, a complete fee simple title exists today only in theory.

A fee simple title is conveyed by the use of such words as "To A in fee simple," or "To A and her heirs." In the United States, a transfer of a fee simple title is assumed unless it is specifically negated in the language of the conveyance. Characteristics of the fee simple title are that it is absolute, freely transferable, and it is an estate of inheritance.

Fee Simple Determinable

A **fee simple determinable** interest differs from a fee simple in that it is not absolute, but is conditional. It may exist forever, but only if the condition upon which it is based is not broken. This interest also sometimes is called a *base fee, qualified fee, fee simple conditional,* or *fee simple defeasible*. The fee simple determinable is created by the use of such words as "To the City of Kalamazoo as long as the property is used as a public park." The use of the words "as long as" signals an express condition, and when taken in connection with the words that follow negate the presumption of a fee simple absolute. Characteristics of the fee simple determinable thus are that it is conditional rather than absolute, it is in perpetuity as long as the condition is not violated, it is transferable, but only for the purpose stated, and it is an estate of inheritance.

Life Estate

A **life estate,** as the name implies, is an estate granted for the lifetime of one or more persons—

for example, "To Fred for his life," "To Fred and Wilma for their lifetimes, and the lifetime of the survivor of them," or "To Fred for the lifetime of Wilma." All of these convey individual and concurrent life estates. The use of the terms *life* and *lifetime* negates the legal presumption of a fee simple. Consider the following case, in which the court must determine whether a fee simple or a life estate was granted.

ROOT, et al. v. MACKEY, et al.
486 S.W.2d 449 (Mo. 1972)

This was an action by Fannie Snow Root and others (Plaintiffs/Respondents) against Mildred Mackey and others (Defendants/Appellants) to determine title to land. Plaintiffs are the brothers and sisters of Sam H. Snow and J. Edgar Snow. Defendants are the children of the same.

A deed was executed by H. P. Snow granting certain land to his sons, Sam H. Snow and J. Edgar Snow. The deed provided that the grantor did "Grant, Bargain and Sell, Convey and Confirm, unto the said parties of the second part, their heirs and assigns [certain described land]." It also provided, at the end of the deed, that "in case of the death of either or both of the grantees, the share of such deceased shall revert to the living brothers and sisters." Plaintiffs are living brothers and sisters of the deceased Sam H. and J. Edgar Snow. The deed was prepared by the grantor and his two sons, all of whom were laymen in the law.

The question before the court was whether the deed granted a fee simple or only a life estate in Sam H. and J. Edgar Snow. The court held that it granted only a life estate, and thus Plaintiffs held fee simple title as "remaindermen." Defendants appealed. Affirmed.

HYDE, Lawrence M., Special Commissioner.

Obviously this deed was not prepared by a lawyer. Such "do it yourself drafting" frequently makes judicial interpretation necessary and difficult. Defendants cite Knox College v. Jones Store Co. . . . for the rule of construction: ". . . the rule to be observed in the construction of deeds as well as wills is to ascertain the intention of the grantor from the whole of the instrument in question, allowing them to be effective 'in line with the intent of their faces as gathered from the everyday, good sense of their language.'" Although the deed uses words such as "Grant, Bargain and Sell," etc., courts "to give effect to the grantor's intention, . . . make it the paramount rule to read the whole instrument, and, if possible, give effect and meaning to all its language." . . .

Plaintiffs claim Sam H. Snow and J. Edgar Snow had only life estates and that defendants, children of J. Edgar Snow, have no interest. . . .

"No particular words are required or are necessary to create a life estate. The use of the term 'life estate' is not necessary, but the intention to create a life estate may be expressed in any equivalent and appropriate language." . . . Cross v. Hoch. . . . In Cross, a will gave certain described land to the testator's daughter Sarah Cross and her heirs but provided: "the property here devised to Sarah Cross be subject to the trust, care, and control of my son Turner Maddox, for her use, and, should the said Sarah Cross die without children, then said property shall be divided among my other daughters." The court held this "a life estate for his daughter Sarah Cross, by necessary implication from the terms of the grant." . . . It was considered that the testator was not a lawyer; that he "evidently used the term 'her heirs' as meaning her 'children.'" The court said it was not the law "that a life estate could only be created by the use of the express term 'life estate,'" but instead "[t]he same intention, may be expressed in any appropriate equivalent words." . . .

The provision in the grantor's deed that the land shall not be sold or mortgaged for a period of ten years is relied on by defendants as showing a fee simple grant to J. Edgar Snow and Sam H. Snow was intended. However, a life estate is a freehold estate and can be sold or mortgaged. . . . Thus this restriction is not determinative of the estate conveyed. What is determinative is the restriction on the grantees' right to determine to whom the title goes on the deaths of the grantees, by specifically providing that upon the death of either grantee his living brothers and sisters take his share. This is similar to the provision construed in Cross v. Hoch, supra.

Questions

1. Are you convinced that this case is "similar" to the Cross case? Why or why not?
2. Can you think of any policy reason why there should be a judicial preference for a transfer of a fee simple or a life estate?

In addition to the above, which are consensual life estates, life estates also are created by law. For example, at common law, a wife who survived her husband was entitled to a life estate in one-third of all of the real property owned by her husband during their marriage. This right was called **dower.** Most states, other than "community property" states, still recognize the concept of dower, either expressly or in spirit. However, by statute in a number of states, the right has been expanded to a one-third or one-half interest in fee simple rather than in a life estate. In addition, many states today permit a surviving spouse to elect a life estate in the entire property in lieu of a fee simple in one-third or one-half.

During the marriage, while the husband survives, the dower right is not absolute, but is contingent on the survival of the wife, and therefore is referred to as *inchoate.* After the death of the husband, it is referred to as *consummate.* Any transfer of the property by the husband, as long as the wife survives, will carry with it the continuation of her dower interest unless she also signs the conveyance. For this reason it is common for deeds to state the marital status of the conveyor, and to have the signature of the wife if she is alive. Death of the wife, or divorce prior to the death of the husband, automatically terminates dower rights, even in property already conveyed.

At common law, the husband's **curtesy** right was comparable to the wife's dower right. It also was a life estate, and operated in a manner similar to the dower right. A number of states, although they adopted dower, did not adopt curtesy. The theory was that a surviving husband, unlike a surviving wife, had no real need for protection. Today, as part of the process of "degenderizing" statutes, many states no longer provide for either dower or curtesy specifically, but instead simply grant a "spousal right" to both. This subject is discussed more fully in Chapter 49.

LEASEHOLD ESTATES

It is important to note that the **leasehold estate** is an estate in real property because it includes the right of exclusive possession. However, it differs from the freehold estates discussed above in that it is for a definite period rather than for an indefinite time. It is created by a contract between the landowner and the tenant called a *lease*. The relationship of the parties to a lease is controlled by a distinct subcategory of the law of real property called the *law of landlord and tenant*. In many ways, the leasehold estate resembles two interests already discussed—bailments and life estates. It differs from these two, however, in that real property cannot be the subject of a bailment, and a life estate is for an indefinite number of years. Beyond these, the rights and obligations are very similar.

The duration of a leasehold estate may be any limited period of time. Frequently it is one *for years*. This means that the leasehold interest is granted to the tenant for a stated period, such as one year, ten years, or ninety-nine years. The other common type of leasehold is one *from period to period*. Under this arrangement, the lease continues for a stated period, such as one month, and is renewed automatically until one of the parties gives notice of termination. When the lease is from month-to-month, state laws usually establish when notice must be given, unless the parties have agreed to the contrary. The usual statutory provision is that notice must be given at least 30 days, and no later than the beginning of the last rent-paying period, prior to termination. So, assuming a lease from calendar month to calendar month, if one of the parties wishes to terminate the lease at the end of July (a 31-day month) she would be required to give notice no later than July 1. If she

wishes to terminate at the end of February (a 28-day month) she would have to give notice no later than January 30 to comply with the 30-day requirement.

Less commonly, a lease may be *at will*. This means that it is without an established time limit, and continues until one of the parties gives notice, at which time the lease will terminate immediately. In the absence of a statute to the contrary, the tenant must leave the property at the time notice is given, and has no grace period. Such an arrangement may be appropriate in cases in which the tenant can comply without great preparation, as giving up a parking space for a motor vehicle. In most cases involving leases of living quarters, however, it probably would not be appropriate.

If a tenant holds over after the termination of a lease, his tenancy becomes one *at sufferance*. He has a leasehold interest in spite of the fact that, technically, he is a trespasser. State laws generally establish the rights of parties in this circumstance. Commonly, the landlord is entitled to choose either to consider the tenancy one at will, or treat it as a renewal of the terminated lease, for a like period, but up to some maximum period such as one year. In this case, the provisions of the terminated lease continue to apply.

The Lease

In some respects a lease is contractual, and in others it evidences title to a leasehold estate. Therefore, a lease really is a mixture of personal and real property rights. Frequently, in writing such documents as wills attorneys will include in the words of transfer "all property, real, personal, and mixed." "Mixed" refers to the property rights in a lease.

In judging the validity of a lease, courts have applied contract law. There must be mutual agreement of the parties (offer and acceptance); there must be consideration; the parties must have capacity; and the lease must be for a legal purpose. The parties then set forth the agreed-upon terms and conditions. On matters to which the parties are silent, state law will govern (normally the law of the state in which the land is located). As to the question of legal purpose, the courts usually hold that even the landlord's knowledge of the tenant's illegal use does not void the lease unless it is determined that, in some way, the landlord consented to the illegality. Silence alone normally is not sufficient to prove consent. Also, although prohibitions contained in the lease are some evidence of the landlord's good faith, they are not conclusive.

As a general rule, leases must be in writing under the Statute of Frauds. The reason is that every lease is, in part, a contract to transfer an interest in land. However, the Statute of Frauds of many states contains special provisions concerning leases. For example, under Michigan law, leases up to one year may be oral, and Indiana law allows oral leases for up to three years. In the absence of these statutory provisions, all leases would have to be in writing. Failure to comply with the requirements of the Statute of Frauds renders the lease unenforceable, and any occupancy by the tenant generally is considered to be at will. Such a lease can be terminated by either party at any time, although it is common for statutes to require some notice period, such as one month.

Ordinarily, a lease must be signed by both parties. At the very least, the landlord must sign it in order to comply with the Statute of Frauds. However, if the lease is for a period exceeding one year and the tenant does not sign it, his obligations under the lease may not be enforceable because of another provision of the Statute of Frauds requiring that every contract "not to be performed within one year" be in writing and signed by the party to be obligated.

Care also should be taken to describe accurately the property to be covered by the lease. If the leased property is an apartment, a description by street address and apartment number probably is adequate. If the property is a house located on a city lot, to be used for residential purposes, the courts probably would construe the lease as including the use of the entire lot, since the entire lot normally is associated with the building. How-ever, suppose the lease is for a commercial building located in an industrial park. Greater questions may arise as to exactly what property is comprehended by the lease. For example, does the leased property include the grounds around the building, or is that held in common by tenants of the park? Therefore, an accurate description of the property is essential.

Rights and Duties of the Tenant

In most states, the tenant is entitled to immediate possession of the property. If it is occupied, for example by a holdover tenant, the landlord is obligated to do whatever is necessary to recover possession. Some courts hold that a lease conveys only the *right* to possession, and actual possession must be obtained by the tenant. In any case, the tenant should insist on a lease provision covering this point.

A lease normally includes an obligation to pay rent, but the payment of rent is not essential to the lease's validity. A lease may be entirely gratuitous. However, if there is no express provision for rent, most courts, consistent with the common law view, find an implied obligation unless the circumstances dictate the tenant reasonably could believe the conveyance was intended as a gift. Also, unless the lease contains provisions to the contrary, any agreed-upon rent is presumed to be payable in one lump sum, in cash, at the time of the conveyance.

At common law, a lease was held to convey the right to possession and use of the described premises. Although it was required that the premises be habitable at the time the lease was to begin, there was no implication that the landlord guaranteed the condition of the premises in the future. If the tenant rented a house for the purpose of occupying it as a residence and the house was destroyed, the obligation to pay the full rent continued, unless the destruction was the landlord's fault. This has now been changed by statute or court decision in many states under the theory that such circumstances have thwarted the parties' intentions. Of course, if the destruction is caused by the wrongful act or omission of the tenant, his or her obligations will continue. It always is best to include some provision in the lease for such contingencies, and for the obligations of the parties concerning insurance. Unquestionably, a tenant has an insurable interest in the property, and most insurance companies offering homeowner policies also offer low-cost renter policies.

A tenant ordinarily is entitled to the exclusive possession of the property and has the right to use it for any legal purpose. Anyone, including the landlord, who wrongfully interferes with the tenant in his or her enjoyment of the property is considered a trespasser, and an action for trespass may be brought by the tenant. Understand that a tenant's estate is a property right just the same as the landlord's estate.

Because a tenant has a property right in the leased premises, she generally may assign, sublet, or mortgage her interest, absent statutory or lease restrictions to the contrary. The law favors the free alienation of property, so any lease provision purporting to prohibit absolutely the transfer or encumbrance of the tenant's interest usually will be void as against public policy. A landlord, however, may place reasonable restrictions on the exercise of these rights. The most common restriction concerning assignment and subletting is one requiring the prior written consent of the landlord. The courts generally hold that the landlord must exercise this right in good faith only, and cannot withhold consent without valid reason. In addition, some leases involve rights so personal that assignment or subletting may be prohibited by general principles of property law. For example, the right to share a single room, or perhaps a lease involving the sharing of a common bath, kitchen, and other facilities, may not be transferable by the tenant without the consent of the other tenants, even in the absence of a specific lease provision.

A tenant who assigns, sublets, or mortgages his interest can transfer or encumber no more than he owns. In addition, he remains liable to the landlord for any nonperformance or injury to the property caused by the assignee or sublessee. This can be changed only by a novation, which requires that the landlord consent and agree to look only to the new tenant for performance. The difference between an assignment and a sublease is that an **assignment** transfers all of the tenant's rights to the assignee, creating a relationship of landlord and tenant between the landlord and the assignee. A **sublease,** on the other hand, creates a relationship of landlord and tenant between the tenant and the sublessee.

Because the tenant's use and occupancy of the leased premises is only temporary, the tenant is under an obligation, by law, to do nothing that would diminish the value of the property for the landlord unreasonably. A breach of this obligation is the basis of the common law cause of action for "waste." When most leases were for agricultural purposes, it ordinarily was assumed that the tenant had the duty to do repairs and to maintain the leased property. Generally, this no longer is true since most leases today are for residential purposes. However, when the tenant has the duty to maintain and repair, his or her failure to do so reasonably would constitute waste. Also, to cut trees for the purpose of making lumber to do ordinary repairs would be permitted. However, to cut trees for sale would not, unless that right specifically was granted by the landlord.

Because the rights of a tenant in the property are possessory, he may be liable for injuries to others while they are on the property. If the other person is a **business invitee** (one who is on the property for the mutual benefit of herself and the tenant), the tenant is liable for any injuries caused by defects on the property of which he knew, or which he reasonably should have discovered. If she is a **licensee** (someone on the property for only her own benefit), the tenant is liable for injuries only if caused by defects of which he had knowledge. If the other is a **trespasser** (someone on the property without permission or privilege), the tenant is obligated only to avoid doing anything to injure the trespasser once her presence is known. It should be noted at this point that some states have altered these liabilities by statute. In addition, the **attractive nuisance doctrine** may impose liability on the tenant if he maintains a condition on the property that is likely to attract children of "tender age," and to cause injury. This doctrine usually applies to children under fourteen years of age. Many cases have involved farm ponds close to a road and unprotected swimming pools. Of course, the landlord also may be liable in all of these circumstances since she is in constructive possession of the leased property by virtue of her title, and either she or the tenant may sue in trespass for the violation of their possessory rights.

Rights and Duties of the Landlord

As discussed previously, the obligation of the landlord concerning turning over possession of the leased property to the tenant has undergone a change from the common law rule. Most states today require that the landlord do so. This change has come about as a result of the transition from primarily agricultural leases to residential leases. The obligation to give the tenant possession applies unless the tenant has agreed, or is otherwise on notice, to the contrary. In return, the landlord has two primary rights—the right to the agreed-upon rent (or, if there has been no agreement but the circumstances are appropriate, rent in the amount of the reasonable value of the benefit of the lease to the tenant) and the right to protection against waste of the property by the tenant.

Although the tenant is entitled to exclusive possession of the premises, the landlord has the right to enter at reasonable times for reasonable purposes. This is to allow the landlord to make sure that waste is not being committed. Also, it is needed to afford the landlord the opportunity to make necessary or agreed-upon repairs. In the absence of an agreement to the contrary, it is ordinarily the landlord's obligation to make necessary repairs. In addition, the landlord has an obligation to maintain and repair common ways when more than one tenant occupies the premises, each having a separate unit—for example, stairs, hallways, and walkways in an apartment or office building.

Upon the tenant's default on any obligation under the lease, particularly the payment of rent, the landlord is entitled to re-enter the premises. The landlord also is entitled to take possession of the tenant's personal property located on the premises, and to retain possession as security for unpaid rent. This is called *landlord's distress for rent*. Today, some states control these rights by statute. In all cases, however, the lease should contain a provision dealing with default and re-entry. For the tenant's protection, there should be a provision to the effect that the landlord's rights can be exercised only after serving notice of default and allowing for a reasonable time to cure. For the protection of the landlord, the lease should provide that upon default and re-entry by the landlord, the lease will *not* terminate and the tenant will remain liable for all damages from his or her default. It also should state that when the landlord re-enters and takes possession he does so as agent for the tenant, has a right to relet the premises as agent of the tenant, and the tenant remains liable for the agreed-upon rent less any rent received from reletting. Consider the following case.

DAHL v. COMBER
444 A.2d 392 (Me. 1982)

This was an action by Bernhoff A. Dahl (Plaintiff/Appellee) against Edward Comber (Defendant/Appellant) for rent and damages for breach of a lease. Defendant entered into a lease for a building with Plaintiff, agreeing to pay a stated rent of $1852 per month. Defendant failed to pay the rent for the months April, May, and June 1979, but did pay rent for July. On August 16, 1979, Plaintiff obtained a writ of possession and retook the premises. Plaintiff then leased the premises to a third party who paid rent through April 1980. Plaintiff was unable to rent the entire building again, but did rent parts of it.

Defendant contended that his obligations under the lease were terminated by Plaintiff's acceptance of a "substitute tenant." The trial court entered a judgment for Plaintiff for $27,110 and Defendant appealed. Affirmed.

McKUSICK, Chief Justice.

On appeal, Comber argues that Dahl's consent to a "substitute" tenant (Bushmaster Firearms, guaranteed by Dyke) constituted acceptance of Comber's surrender of the lease, thereby discharging him from further liability for rent. The existence of surrender and acceptance depends on the intent of the parties and is a question of fact. Moreover, the tenant bears the burden of proof that his attempted surrender was accepted by the landlord. . . . In this case, the evidence against termination by surrender included 1) Dahl's testimony as to his subjective intent; 2) the equivocal nature of the manifestations of Dahl's intent testified to and relied upon by Comber; and 3) paragraph 10 of the lease forbidding cancellation or surrender of the lease except by a writing signed by the landlord. There being competent evidence in the record to support the conclusion that Comber failed to carry his burden of proof, we cannot say that the justice below clearly erred in her finding that there was no surrender and acceptance. . . .

Alternatively, the tenant, Comber, argues that in subsequently reletting parts of the building to other tenants after Bushmaster's demise but during the term of the unexpired lease, Dahl (who claims only to have been acting for Comber's account to mitigate damages) effectively accepted surrender of the leasehold. This alternative argument of Comber is in part founded on paragraph 9 of the lease agreement, which provides that "[i]n case of default by the Tenant in the payment of rent, . . . the Landlord may at any time thereafter resume possession [of the building] by any lawful means . . . and hold the premises as if this lease had not been made." Thus, Comber urges a construction of this clause that would have resulted in rescission of the lease agreement upon Dahl's taking possession. When read in context, however, the ambiguous language of paragraph 9 is equally amenable to interpretation as assuring the landlord the right, in order to mitigate damages, to reenter and relet the premises after the tenant's default. The paragraph 9 language relied on by Comber must be read along with the other provision of that paragraph stating that after his surrender of the premises, "the Tenant shall remain liable as hereinafter provided" has meaning only if it refers to paragraph 18 of the lease entitled "Payment of Rent" and prescribing the obligation of the tenant to pay rent to the landlord "when due," by hand delivery or mail. Since the parties offered no parol evidence to clarify their intent in drafting paragraph 9, construction of the ambiguous language constituted a question of law. . . . The justice below necessarily rejected Comber's interpretation and held that Dahl could, consistent with the terms of the agreement, relet the building after default without forfeiting his right to future rent from the original tenants. . . .

Since the record supports the view that upon Comber's default in his obligation to pay rent Dahl merely attempted in good faith to mitigate the damages, the finding below that there was no effective surrender and acceptance is unassailable on appeal.

Questions

1. How can a tenant protect himself against a landlord who accepts someone as a substitute tenant for rent that is far below the marketplace value of the premises?
2. How can a landlord protect herself against a default and disappearance by the tenant and an inability to find a substitute tenant?

Eviction is the ultimate weapon for a landlord if the tenant defaults. In most states, eviction has become a statutory process, complicated and attended by considerable delay. Easily a delay of six or more months may be anticipated if notice and a hearing are involved. In many cases, eviction is an inadequate remedy from a practical perspective. It should be noted however, that eviction does not always result from a tenant's default; sometimes it occurs because of some wrongdoing by the landlord. **Eviction** is any depriving of the tenant of the beneficial use or enjoyment of all or any part of the leased premises by the intentional act or inaction of the landlord or caused by him. Therefore, the landlord's refusal to meet his obligation to repair or to provide heat may constitute a constructive eviction if the tenant's use or enjoyment are materially impaired. In the case of this type of eviction, the tenant may have a right to declare the lease terminated and pursue a damage remedy.

If a tenant remains in possession of the leased premises beyond the term of the lease, she is called a **holdover tenant.** At common law, the landlord then was given the option of proceeding with eviction or considering the tenant's act a renewal of the expired lease for the same term, and under the same terms and conditions. Today, this circumstance generally is controlled by statute. Some provide that the lease may be considered renewed, but for not longer than a specified period—for example, one year. Most, however, provide that the tenant becomes a **tenant at sufferance** from

month to month. These statutes also ordinarily provide for some notice of termination, such as one month from the beginning of any rent-paying period. However, this again is a matter that should be provided for in the lease.

CONCURRENT OWNERSHIP

It should be clear, by this point, that a parcel of real estate may be owned by more than one person simultaneously. The nature of concurrently owned estates, and the rights and obligations of the owners, depend on the type of concurrent ownership. The two major types of concurrent ownership are *tenancy in common* and *joint tenancy*. Although they differ in many important respects, they share many common characteristics: (1) the co-tenants each own an individual interest in the entire property, (2) they have equal rights to possession, and (3) their individual interests may be transferred or encumbered. Other types of concurrent ownership that will be discussed in this section are tenancy by the entireties, tenancy in partnership, community property, cooperatives, and condominiums.

Tenancy in Common

Tenancy in common is the most basic type of concurrent ownership in real property. It requires only that two or more persons hold the property as co-tenants, each having an equal right to possession. A tenancy in common may be created by providing in the instrument of transfer something like: "To A and B as tenants in common," or "To A and B," or even "To A and B jointly." As will be noted in the discussion that follows, there is a strong presumption in the law that co-tenants take as tenants in common unless the language of the transfer is sufficiently clear to overcome this presumption.

Joint Tenancy

A **joint tenancy,** like a tenancy in common, involves two or more co-tenants, each taking an undivided interest in the entire property and each having an equal right to possession. However, that is the extent of the similarity. Unlike the tenancy in common, the joint tenancy is not inheritable; it is not transferable as such; and the "four unities" must exist.

The most significant characteristic of the joint tenancy is that it is accompanied by a **right of survivorship.** This means that upon the death of any joint tenant, his interest does not become a part of his estate, but is transferred automatically to the surviving tenants. For example, if Rob and Laura own property as joint tenants and Laura dies, Rob becomes the sole owner of the prop-erty. Laura's heirs take no interest, and if Laura had included her interest in her will, that portion of the will would be invalid, since at the moment of her death she no longer had an interest to transfer.

Although a joint tenant is entitled to transfer his interest during his lifetime, the interest is not transferable as a joint tenancy. For the transfer to take place, the joint tenancy first must be *severed.* Following the **severance,** the co-tenancy becomes a tenancy in common; then the transferring tenant's interest in common may be transferred. At common law, this procedure required the filing of an action in an equity court (Petition for Severance), and a later transfer after the judgment granting the petition. This is still the procedure in some states, although a number now deal with the severance as a legal fiction whenever a joint tenant executes a transfer of his interest.

In order to create a valid joint tenancy, the requirement of the **four unities** must be met. They are (1) time, (2) title, (3) interest, and (4) possession. The failure to comply with any of them will result in a tenancy in common.

The unity of *time* requires that the co-tenants receive their interests at the same time. If the interest of one of the co-tenants is to vest either before or after the interest of the others, this unity

---

The "Four Unities"

TIME	TITLE
Co-tenants must receive their interest at the same time.	Co-tenants must receive their interest by the same instrument.
INTEREST	POSSESSION
Each co-tenant must receive an interest equal to those of the other tenants.	Co-tenants must have equal rights to possess the property.

is violated. The unity of *title* requires that the co-tenants must receive their interests by the same instrument (deed or will). The unity of *interest* means that each tenant must receive an interest equal to those of the other tenants. If there are two tenants, each must receive a one-half interest of the same scope as the other. If there are four tenants, each must receive a one-fourth interest.

The unity of *possession* requires that all tenants have equal rights to possess the property. Of course, once the four unities have been complied with and the joint tenancy has been created, the tenants are then free to make any arrangements they wish concerning possession and use of the property. The following case considers the four unities.

DESLAURIERS v. SENESAC, et al.
331 Ill. 437, 163 N.E. 327 (1928)

This was an action by Eustache Deslauriers, executor of the estate of Homer Deslauriers (Plaintiff/Appellee) against Belle Senesac and others (Defendants/Appellants) for construction of a deed.

Ida Boudreau acquired title to certain property by deed on July 20, 1903. Thereafter she married Homer Deslauriers, and on April 22, 1911, she and her husband executed a deed purporting to grant the property to themselves as joint tenants. The language of the grant stated: "Said grantors intend and declare that their title shall and does hereby pass to grantees not in tenancy in common but in joint tenancy." After Ida's death, leaving no children, but leaving brothers and sisters, Homer entered into a contract to sell the property to Martin Drendel and Edward West. Homer died prior to delivering a deed. When title to the property was examined, attorneys for Drendel and West doubted that the deed of April 22, 1911, created joint title. If it did not, the interest of Ida Deslauriers vested in Defendants, her brothers and sisters, upon her death.

The trial court found that the deed had created a valid joint tenancy, and Defendants appealed. Reversed and remanded.

DE YOUNG, C. J.

A transaction involving the transfer of title to real estate presupposes the participation of two or more parties. For every alienation there must be an alienor and an alienee, for every grant a grantor and a grantee, and for every gift, a donor and a donee. The words "convey," "transfer," and similar words employed in conveyancing, signify the passing of title from one person to another. To make a deed effective, the grantor is divested of, and the grantee is vested with, the title. The requisites of a deed purporting to grant an immediate estate in possession are that there be a grantor, a grantee, and a thing granted. . . . A person cannot convey or deliver to himself that which he already possesses. . . .

An estate in joint tenancy can only be created by grant or purchase—that is, by the act of the parties. It cannot arise by descent or act of law. The properties of a joint estate are derived from its unity, which is fourfold, the unity of interest, the unity of title, the unity of time, and the unity of possession; or, in other words, joint tenants have one and the same interest, accruing by one and the same conveyance, commencing at one and the same time, and held by one and the same undivided possession. . . .

Ida Deslauriers was the sole owner of the half lot prior to the execution of the deed from herself and husband to themselves. She could not by that deed convey an interest in the property to herself. It is manifest from the deed that she did not intend to convey the whole and entire interest to her husband, for she retained an equal share or interest. Hence the interests of Ida Deslauriers and her husband were neither acquired by one and the same conveyance, nor did they vest at one and the same time. Two of the essential properties of a joint estate—the unity of title and the unity of time—were therefore lacking. Where two or more persons acquire individual interests in a parcel of property by different conveyances and at different times, there is neither unity of time, and in such a situation a tenancy in common, and not a joint tenancy, is created.

Questions

1. Can you think of reasons for each of the four unities?
2. Why should a joint tenancy be more difficult to achieve than a tenancy in common?

Today, title standards in many states soften the strictness of the common law standards. For example, many dispense with the requirements of unity of time and unity of title. That is, an owner of the whole title may convey title to herself and a co-owner as joint tenants. Some also permit a joint tenant to re-convey to himself as a tenant in common.

In order to create a joint tenancy, the legal presumption in favor of a tenancy in common must be overcome clearly. The recommended language to use, in order to be safe, is "To A and B as Joint Tenants, with rights of survivorship, and not as Tenants in Common." This specifically designates the parties as joint tenants, provides for the right of survivorship (which is inconsistent with a tenancy in common), and specifically states that the tenancy is not to be considered one in common. Most courts are now more liberal in construing language of transfer to create a joint tenancy, but using the recommended language takes very little extra effort, and always is safe.

Tenancy by the Entireties

A **tenancy by the entireties** is simply a joint tenancy between a husband and wife. It must meet all the requirements for establishing a joint tenancy. However, it differs from a joint tenancy in two material respects. It cannot be encumbered or taken for the payment of any debt, except a joint debt of the husband and wife. Also, it is severed automatically, and becomes a tenancy in common, in the event of divorce.

The four unities must exist to create a tenancy by the entireties. Also, it is recommended that the same considerations be given concerning drafting to avoid an interpretation of tenancy in common as were recommended for a joint tenancy. In addition, the parties should be designated as husband and wife. Therefore, the appropriate language would be "To Fred and Wilma, Husband and Wife, as Tenants by the Entireties, with rights of survivorship, and not as Tenants in Common." Note that it is necessary specifically to negate only the legal presumption in favor of a tenancy in common. There is no comparable presumption favoring joint tenancy over tenancy by the entireties. However, if the grant is intended to create a true joint tenancy rather than a tenancy by the entireties between a husband and wife, some caution should be exercised in wording the grant.

Tenancy in Partnership

When a valid partnership is formed, each partner becomes the owner of specific partnership property as a tenant in partnership. This is automatic regarding any property originally contributed by the partners, and any property thereafter acquired in the partnership name. Section 25 of the Uniform Partnership Act sets out the incidents of the **tenancy in partnership** as follows:

1. Each partner has an equal right to possess specific partnership property, but only for partnership purposes;
2. A partner's interest in partnership property cannot be individually assigned;
3. Partnership property cannot be attached, or otherwise taken, for individual debts of any partner—only partnership debts;
4. Death of a partner vests his or her rights in the surviving partners, and
5. A partner's interest is not subject to curtesy, dower, or any other allowance to spouse, heirs, or next of kin.

Therefore, a tenancy in partnership closely resembles a joint tenancy, except with additional limitations. Like a joint tenancy, it may be severed to become a tenancy in common.

Community Property

The concept of **community property** is based on a theory similar to that supporting the concepts of curtesy and dower. However, it has its roots in the Civil Law tradition rather than the Common Law. It is recognized in only eight states (Arizona, California, Idaho, Louisiana, Nebraska, New Mexico, Texas, and Washington). Interestingly, it is the recognition of community property by these states that caused the addition of the rules for filing joint federal income tax returns to the Internal Revenue Code. It also has transformed divorce law in many states, causing them to move toward "equitable distribution" of marital property, which is community-property-like. In divorce situations, equitable distribution may be given in lieu of traditional alimony, which involves a continuing obligation to support instead of a division of marital property.

In community property states, all property *acquired during the marriage* by the *efforts* of either party belongs one-half to each spouse. It does not apply to property brought into the marriage by either party. It also does not apply to property acquired during the marriage by gift, inheritance, or under a will. In this respect, it differs from curtesy and dower. Upon the death of one spouse, that spouse's one-half interest ordinarily will go to his or her heirs, or may be disposed of by will.

Cooperatives

The cooperative ownership of apartments was common in England and the Scandinavian countries prior to gaining attention in the United States in the 1920s. A **cooperative** may take the form of a trust or corporation that purchases the land and constructs the building that is then divided into apartment units. The corporation holds title, and then lets apartments to the owners by long-term proprietary leases. In the trust form, which is less common than the corporate form, the tenants acquire their rights to occupancy by the trust's issuance of certificates of beneficial interest. Decisions concerning the operation of the cooperative are made by officers, or a board, elected by the tenants. Cooperatives in the corporate form, which create apartments in the individual rather than the cooperative form, provide the framework for condominium apartments.

Condominiums

The condominium concept, of more recent general interest in the United States, is of ancient origin, dating back to the Romans. The **condominium** differs from the cooperative apartment in that the owners hold fee simple title in their separate units, with common parts such as hallways, stairs, any lounge area or club facilities, and surrounding land being held in common. Condominium owners then pay a maintenance fee for the upkeep of these common areas. Decisions concerning the operation of the project are made by a committee elected by the owners. Although condominiums ordinarily take the form of residential apartments in multi-unit buildings, they may be in the form of separate units and, with increasing frequency, are occupied as offices and shops—for example, a condominium shopping center.

NONPOSSESSORY INTERESTS

The interests discussed in this section are not estates like the interests discussed previously. **Nonpossessory interests** involve only limited rights to use real property, rather than the right to possession.

Easements

An **easement** is a nonpossessory interest in real estate belonging to another. It is irrevocable once granted, and constitutes a burden on the title to the property to which it attaches. Since it represents the transfer of an interest in land, an easement is required by the Statute of Frauds to be in writing. In addition, easements should be recorded as is required for any other instrument evidencing an interest in real property. Easements are intangible, and may be either appurtenant or in gross, and affirmative or negative.

An **easement appurtenant** is any easement granted for the benefit of another tract of real estate. For example, suppose Hatfield owns land between McCoy's land and a major highway. McCoy may purchase from Hatfield an easement to construct a road between his land and the highway. That easement, over Hatfield's land to allow better access to McCoy's land, would be appurtenant, and Hatfield's land would be called the **servient tenement,** and McCoy's, the **dominent tenement.** McCoy's easement would be irrevocable during the period for which it was granted, or forever if no time limit was placed on the grant. Upon sale of either tract by Hatfield or McCoy, the easement would continue. It would burden the new owner of Hatfield's tract, and continue to benefit the new owner of McCoy's.

An **easement in gross** is an easement for the benefit of a particular individual. It is not intended for the benefit of any other tract of land. For example, in the previous illustration McCoy also might purchase from another neighbor, Crockett, the right to cross her property for the purpose of going to a river to fish. That easement would be a personal right belonging to McCoy. If Crockett sold her land, the easement in favor of McCoy would continue to burden the title. Moreover, if McCoy sold his land, the easement would remain his and would not be transferred with his land. Whether an easement in gross may be assigned depends upon its nature—how personal it is. Generally, the assignability of easements in gross is determined by the same rules as are used in determining the assignability of contracts. Assignments are discussed in Chapter 11.

An **affirmative easement** involves the right to make use of the real estate of another. The examples discussed above are both illustrations of affirmative easements. A **negative easement,** then, is a right of a real estate owner to have another refrain from some lawful use of his land. For example, suppose George owns a vacant lot between Dan's home and a lake. Dan may purchase from George an easement preventing George from constructing a building or otherwise interfering with Dan's view of the lake. This would be a negative easement appurtenant. Of course Dan also might wish to purchase an affirmative easement, either in gross or appurtenant, to cross George's lot to make use of the lake.

An easement may be granted either for general or for limited purposes. In the preceding example, Dan's easement to cross George's lot on his way to the lake may be restricted to foot travel only, for the purpose of putting in and taking out his boat, both of these, or possibly any nonpossessory purpose Dan wished. It should be clear at this point that an easement may be only a very slight burden on the title to land, or it may be so great that it constitutes most of the value of the title.

Although easements come in a variety of types and are for a variety of purposes, like other property they must be granted by the owner of the servient property or by law; they may not simply be assumed. Consider the following case.

HELMS v. TULLIS
398 So.2d 253 (Ala. 1981)

This was an action by Oscar and Martha Helms (Plaintiffs/Appellants) against Ida and Elizabeth Tullis (Defendants/Appellees) seeking an order enjoining the defendants from interfering with the installation of a power line across property owned by Defendants.

Plaintiffs purchased a 40-acre tract of land from Defendants, and moved into a house trailer located on the property. They sought to have a power line installed over an adjoining one-acre tract belonging to Defendants. When Defendants became aware that trees were being cut on their property to install the line, they ordered the power company to cease work, and Plaintiffs sought this injunction.

The trial court denied the injunction and Plaintiffs appealed. Affirmed.

TOBERT, Chief Justice.

There are several ways by which an easement may be acquired. These are: (1) by express conveyance, (2) by reservation or exception, (3) by implication, (4) by necessity, (5) by prescription, (6) by contract, and (7) by reference to boundaries or maps. . . . An examination of the facts in the case before us fails to show that an easement was created under any theory.

The Helmses do not claim, nor did they seek to prove at trial, that an easement was created across the one-acre tract owned by the Tullises by conveyance, by reservation, by contract or by reference to boundaries or maps. We will therefore not consider these methods of creating easements in our discussion.

The only remaining possible ways an easement could have been created in the case before us are by necessity and by implication. Creation by necessity is actually a form of creation by implication, but is treated separately by some authors. . . .

The rationale for allowing an easement by necessity is that public policy demands that land not be rendered unusable. . . . Under Alabama law, however, there must be a genuine necessity; mere convenience is not enough. . . . The burden is on the one seeking to establish the easement to prove the easement is "reasonably necessary for the enjoyment" of the land. . . . Original unity of ownership of the dominant and servient tenements is always required for an easement by necessity. . . .

Easements created by implication cover a variety of types of easements. Creation by this method requires not only original unity of ownership, . . . but also that the use be open, visible, continuous, and reasonably necessary to the estate granted. . . . The implication is that the parties implied such an easement because the grantee, having seen the use the grantor made of the property, can reasonably expect a continuance of the former manner of use. . . .

In the present case there is no easement created by either necessity or implication. The Helmses failed to show that there was no other route by which a power line could be brought to their property. Thus, there was no necessity. Furthermore, electrical service was not shown to be necessary to the reasonable enjoyment of the property, although it was shown to be necessary to one use of the property, i.e., as a site for a residence. There was no easement created by implication, since there had never been a power line run over that strip of land; thus there was no open, visible and continuous use.

Questions

1. Would the case have come out differently if the plaintiffs were building a residence on the property? What else would the plaintiffs have to establish, if you don't think the residential use would be sufficient?

2. Would a pathway to the property be a necessity? a water line? a mailbox? anything else?

Licenses

A **license** is a right to use land belonging to another, but unlike an easement it is revocable at the will of the grantor, and is considered a personal interest rather than an interest in real estate. Because it is an irrevocable right, a license is not required to be in writing under the Statute of Frauds. In fact, an intended easement that fails to comply with the Statute of Frauds is considered a license. Also, a license that, for any reason, is held by a court to be irrevocable is considered an easement.

Continuing the examples, suppose Dan was on vacation and asked Ed for permission to cross Ed's land to take his boat to the lake to fish for the day. Ed's permission, if granted, would be a license. The parties would be intending that Dan use Ed's land for a short-term, single purpose rather than a continuing relationship. Another common example of a license is shopping in a store. The merchant grants a license to each cus-tomer to enter her premises for the purpose of looking over, and perhaps purchasing, her merchandise. Because it is revocable at the will of the grantor and does not constitute an actual interest in the real property to which it attaches, a license is not a burden on title, as is an easement.

Profits à Prendre

A **profit à prendre** is a right to remove the produce of the property of another, such as timber, minerals, or crops. It is an interest in real property, like an easement, and by implication carries with it a license to enter the property if removal is to be by the holder. Under some circumstances, the produce to be removed is treated as "goods" by the Uniform Commercial Code. Section 2-105(1) provides that the term "goods" includes ". . . growing crops and other identified things attached to the realty as described in the section on goods to be severed from realty (Section 2-107)." The first two subsections of Section 2-107 then state which things are to be considered goods and which are not. Depending on its nature, a profit à prendre may be a very important interest, as would be true, for example, of a right to take oil or gold.

Lateral Support

At common law, each parcel of real estate was entitled to lateral support by all adjoining parcels. This right continues today, basically unchanged. For example, suppose George decided to build a pond on his property. He would not be entitled to dig it so close to his property line as to cause Ed's property to cave in. Ed's right to support is an interest in George's property, granted by law, and is in the nature of a negative easement. At common law, this right extended to only unimproved property. That is, if George dug the pond and Ed's property caved in, but it could be shown that it would not have caved in but for the presence of Ed's house, Ed's right to lateral support would not have been violated. Most courts no longer take that position in circumstances in which the nature and extent of the improvements are sufficiently obvious to place the neighboring property owner on notice.

Riparian Rights

Riparian rights are rights belonging to the owner of the property along a waterway. At common law these included rights to use the water for ordinary purposes, such as drinking or bathing, and for other purposes such as building a wharf or floating a boat out to navigable waters. Of particular importance today, however, is the right to have the flow of water continue. In most states, riparian rights encompass the right to a flow of water not diminished unreasonably in either quantity or quality. These rights could be violated, therefore, if another person erected a dam upstream, diverted the stream away from its

course, used an unreasonable amount of water as it passed by, or polluted it so that it was unfit for normal use. In some states in which water is in short supply, the courts apply the **rule of prior acquisition.** This allows the owners upstream to use as much water as necessary to meet their reasonable needs, even if the supply is entirely depleted. Although this allocates scarce water to fewer people, it is supported on the idea that the ordinary riparian rule would result in insufficient water for everyone.

FUTURE INTERESTS

All of the estates and other interests discussed thus far in this chapter may be described as "present" interests. They all have had in common present rights to possess, use, or remove property. **Future interests,** however, include only rights to *future* possession. Future interests generally arise because the grantors intentionally created them. Sometimes, however, a future interest may be implied by law because a grantor has transferred less than the complete title to his or her real property. In general, future interests are divided into three types—reversions, remainders, and rights of entry.

Reversions

A **reversion** is a right of the grantor to a return of the property upon the termination of the present estate. For example, if Nils owns a fee simple and grants a life estate to Hedda and makes no provision as to what is to be done with the property upon Hedda's death, title automatically will revert to Nils. This type of reversion is implied by law and is contingent on nothing except the death of Hedda.

A different type of reversion is one that is contingent on something in addition to the life tenant's death. This type of reversion is called a **possibility of reverter** and accompanies the grant of every fee simple determinable. For example, if Hedda grants property to the City of Kalamazoo "as long as the property is used for a public park," and makes no further disposition, then Hedda will have a possibility of reverter. Both the common reversion and the possibility of reverter are considered rights in real property, even though they are not to be possessory until sometime in the future, and in the case of the possibility of reverter, perhaps never. However, they are of value and may be transferred by the holder, and upon the death of the holder they are transferred to her heirs or according to her will.

Remainders

A **remainder** is a future interest similar to a reversion except that it is held by someone other than the grantor or the owner of the present estate. In the first example, when Nils conveyed the life estate to Hedda, instead of making no further disposition and thus retaining the reversion, he might have granted the remaining interest to Chris. In that case, Chris would have become the holder of a remainder.

It is important to note that a remainder must be created by the same instrument that created the present estate. That is, if Nils had granted the life estate to Hedda and retained the reversion, and later had transferred his reversion to Chris, its character as a reversion would remain unchanged. Rather than becoming a remainder, it simply would be a reversion held by Chris as a transferee.

Just as a reversion may be a common reversion or a possibility of reverter, a remainder may be either vested or contingent. In the case in which Nils granted the life estate to Hedda with a remainder in Chris, the remainder held by Hedda would be classified as vested. It will become possessory upon the occurrence of no other contingency than the death of Hedda. However, in the case in which Hedda granted the property to the City of Kalamazoo as long as it was used for a public park, if she had provided that upon the breach of the condition the property would go to Chris, then Chris would have held a contingent remainder. Her interest would have been contingent upon the happening of some uncertain future event. Therefore, the vested remainder is similar to the common reversion and the contingent remainder is similar to the possibility of reverter.

Right of Entry

The **right of entry** sometimes is called a "right of entry on condition broken." It resembles a possibility of reverter in that it is held by the grantor, and upon the occurrence of an uncertain future event the property reverts. The distinction is that in the case of the possibility of reverter, the transfer of the title back to the grantor is automatic (self-executing), but in the case of a right of entry, the grantor must take action to reclaim title. For example, in a grant from Hedda to the City of Kalamazoo, instead of stating "as long as it is used as a public park," Hedda stated "to be used as a public park only." The absence of the words "as long as," allowing self-execution, would create a right of entry, rather than a possibility of reverter, in Hedda. In the following case the court must deal with the difference between these two closely related interests.

OLDFIELD v. STOECO HOMES, INC. et al.
26 N.J. 246, 139 A.2d 291 (1958)

This was an action by taxpayers of the City of Ocean City (Plaintiffs/Appellants) against Stoeco Homes, Inc. and others (Defendants/Appellees) to have certain resolutions of the city set aside. These resolutions sought to extend the time for performance of certain conditions in a deed granting property to Defendant.

The deed in question granted title to Defendant on certain conditions, and provided: "A failure to comply with the covenants and conditions of paragraphs (a), (b) and (c) hereof will automatically cause the title to revert to the City as to any particular land, lot or lots involved in any violation." The question before the court of interest here was whether the deed created a "possibility of reverter" or a "right of entry" in the city. The court held the latter and Plaintiffs appealed. Affirmed.

BURLING, J.

First, we consider the issue relating to the nature of the estate created. It is said that a fee simple determinable differs from a fee simple subject to a condition subsequent in that, in the former, upon the happening of the stated event the estate "ipso facto" or "automatically" reverts to the grantor or his heirs, while in the latter the grantor must take some affirmative action to divest the grantee of his estate. . . . The interest remaining in the grantee in a fee simple determinable has been denominated a possibility of reverter, . . . while the interest remaining in the grantee of a fee simple subject to a condition subsequent, i.e., the right to re-enter upon the happening of prescribed contingency, has been denominated a power of termination. . . .

It is further alleged that a fee simple determinable estate is more onerous than an estate in fee simple subject to condition subsequent in that in the defenses of waiver and estoppel which are applicable to the latter are unavailing in the former. But cf. Dunham, "Possibility of Reverter and Powers of Termination—Fraternal or Identical Twins?" . . . We can assume, without deciding the point, that such a distinction exists between the two estates, for the reason that, as will be hereafter developed, the estate created in the instant case was one subject to a condition subsequent. . . .

If the four corners of the deed provide a coherent expression of the parties' intent, we need search no further, but if an ambiguity or a reasonable doubt appears from a perusal of the particular symbols of expression our horizons must be broadened to encompass the circumstances surrounding the transaction. . . . To the foregoing must be added certain constructional biases developed in a hierarchical fashion and predicated upon the proposition that the law abhors a forfeiture. Thus, if the choice is between a condition subsequent and a restrictive covenant, the former is preferred. . . . And where the choice is between an estate in fee simple determinable and an estate on condition subsequent, the latter is preferred. . . .

To focus attention solely on the words "automatically cause title to revert" is to ignore and refuse effect to the following provisions:

This conveyance is also subject to the following *conditions,* requirements, reservations, covenants and restrictions:" (Emphasis supplied.) and

A failure to comply with the covenants and *conditions of paragraphs (a), (b) and (c) hereof.* . . . (Emphasis supplied.)

Moreover, the deed contained the following clause:

The City of Ocean City reserves the right to change or modify any restriction, condition or other requirements hereby imposed in a manner agreeable to or as permitted by law.

The repeated use of the word "condition" and the provision reserving the right to alter the arrangement in the clauses are sufficient to cast a reasonable doubt upon what was intended. Accordingly, we shall consider the surrounding circumstances in order to ascertain the intention of the parties in creating the estate. . . .

To hold that the condition as to time was so essential to the scheme of the parties that to violate it by a day would result in an immediate and automatic forfeiture of the estate is to distort beyond recognition what the parties intended. There is no indication that time was of the essence of the agreement. . . .

It is our conclusion that the parties contemplated that the estate created was not to expire automatically at the end of a year and that therefore it is one subject to a condition subsequent.

Questions

1.   Do you agree with the court that the agreement was ambiguous and required interpretation?

2.   What is the effect of the court's ruling?

Rule Against Perpetuities

In the discussion of remainders, a distinction was drawn between vested and contingent interests. The distinction is important because the **Rule Against Perpetuities** requires that all contingent future interests must vest, if at all, within a period established as "a life in being plus twenty-one years" from the time they were created. For example, suppose Carol willed her estate "to my daughter, Pamala, for her lifetime, and then to the first of her children who shall attain the age of 25 years." The life estate in Pamala would be valid, but the contingent remainder in her child would be void unless Pamala had at least one child who was of the age of four years or older at the time of her mother's death. Pamala would be the life in being for purposes of the Rule. It should be noted that probabilities play no part in the application of this rule. If a contingent interest is 99-percent certain to vest, if at all, within the period, the one-percent possibility that it will not makes it void. The purpose of the rule is to prevent the clouding of title to real property by the inclusion of contingent interests that may vest only after a long period of time. The effect of the rule is to reduce

Classification of real property interests

Freehold Estates	Co-ownership of Real Property	Leasehold Estates	Nonpossessory Interests	Future Interests
fee simple	tenancy in common	term of years	easements	reversions
fee simple determinable	joint tenancy	period-to-period	licenses	remainders
life estate	tenancy by the entireties	at will	profits á prendre	rights of entry
fee tail	tenancy in partnership		lateral support riparian rights	

the ability of a landowner to control the alienation of the property for any extended period after his or her death. The failure of an interest because of the Rule Against Perpetuities ordinarily will leave a gap in the title that will be filled, by law, with a reversion in the grantor and his or her heirs.

SUMMARY

Possible interests in real property are many and varied. Some give the right of possession and are called estates. Others carry with them only the right to use the property for general or limited purposes. Some are present interests, and some provide for possession at a future time.

The estates in real property are fee simple, life estates, and leasehold estates. Fee simple connotes ownership of the entire freehold title (the title to property for an indefinite time), although it may terminate on the occurrence of some uncertain future event, in which case it is called a fee simple determinable. A life estate is for the period of the life of one or more named persons. A leasehold estate is an estate for a definite period, and is created by a contract called a lease.

The title to any of these interests may be held by two or more persons concurrently. This may be by tenancy in common; it may be by joint tenancy, which includes the right of survivorship; or it may be as tenants by the entireties, which is a joint tenancy between a husband and wife. Other possible types of concurrent ownership include tenancy in partnership, community property, and ownership of part of a cooperative or condominium project.

Nonpossessory interests in real property include easements, profits à prendre, the right to lateral support, and riparian rights. In addition, a license is a right much like an easement, but it is revocable at the option of the grantor, and therefore is considered a personal interest rather than an interest in real property. These interests differ from estates because they involve only the right to use real property, not the right to possess it.

Interests involving a future, rather than a present, right to possession are called future interests. They entitle their holders to possession upon the termination of limited present estates such as the fee simple determinable, the life estate, and the leasehold estate. If the future interest is in the grantor of the present estate, it is known as a reversion, a possibility of reverter, or a right of entry, depending on its nature. If it is held by someone other than the grantor or his heirs or assigns, it is called a remainder. These interests are vested if they come into effect upon the death of the owner of the present estate, and are contingent if they depend, for vesting, upon some other condition. In order to be valid under the rule against perpetuities, every contingent future interest must vest within a life in being plus 21 years from the time of the grant.

KEY TERMS AND CONCEPTS

real property
estate
freehold estate
fee simple
fee simple determinable
life estate
dower
curtesy
leasehold estate
assignment of a lease
sublease
business invitee
licensee
trespasser
attractive nuisance doctrine
eviction
holdover tenant
tenant at sufferance
tenancy in common
joint tenancy
right of survivorship

severance
four unities
tenancy by the entireties
tenancy in partnership
community property
cooperative
condominium
nonpossessory interest
easement
easement appurtenant
servient tenement
dominent tenement
easement in gross
affirmative easement
negative easement
license
profit à prendre
riparian rights
rule of prior acquisition
future interest
reversion
possibility of reverter
remainder
right of entry
Rule Against Perpetuities

PROBLEMS

1. Bradshaw inherited certain property from his father. When he came to see it, he found Ashley living there, and she had for some five years. Both contended they owned the property. However, Bradshaw took possession when Ashley left for a period and refused to allow Ashley back on when she returned. Ashley brought an action in ejectment. At the trial, the court determined that neither had title under the deeds they were relying on. Who is entitled to the property?

2. In his will, Simpson left certain land to his wife, Georgia, by the following grant: "To my wife as long as she remains my widow. In the event of remarriage, to my sons and their heirs."

When Georgia Simpson died, she left the property to Alexandria Hospital in her will. Simpson's sons contend that their mother had only a life estate under their father's will, and now that she is dead, the property is theirs. Are they correct?

3. Upon the owner's death, a tract of land was divided into two parcels, the front parcel abutting a highway and the back parcel accessed by means of a road over the other. Although the road had been used for years, Helton, who owned the front parcel, put a gate across it and prohibited Jones, the owner of the other, from reaching her parcel. When Jones tried to use the road, she was arrested for trespass. In return for a dismissal of the charge, she granted to Helton all of her interest in the road. She then brought an action to determine her right to an easement. Is she entitled to relief?

4. Lemle rented a house from Breeden, to be used as a home for his family. Shortly after moving in, he found the house to be rat infested, and the family slept in the middle of the living room floor the first three nights, fearing rat bites. Lemle demanded the return of his deposit and first month's rent. Breeden refused on the ground that, according to the lease, they were not refundable, and nothing in the lease warranted the condition of the premises. Is Lemle entitled to relief?

5. Offut, an apartment-building owner, sold an adjoining house to Maris. The contract of sale included a right of Maris and her family to use the apartment swimming pool, but nothing was stated in the deed. When Maris sold the house to Bunn, she told Bunn he would have the use of the pool. When Offut refused to allow Bunn to use the pool, Bunn sued, contending he was an assignee of the easement to the pool. Is Bunn correct?

6. By his will, Neil Duffy conveyed certain property to his sisters, Nellie Duffy, Anna Duffy, and Katherine O'Connel, as joint tenants. Thereafter, Nellie conveyed her interest to Anna. When Annie died, her heirs sued to partition the property. They contended that the conveyance by Nellie to Anna severed the joint tenancy and, therefore, they were entitled to two-thirds of the property as her heirs. Are they correct?

7. Certain land was granted to Sauls for life, with a remainder interest in Crosby. While Sauls was on the land, he began cutting timber and selling it as a means of earning a living. Crosby sued to stop this on the ground that Sauls's life estate did not carry with it the right to cut timber commercially. Is Crosby correct?

8. Ritchy purchased a condominium in Villa Nueva. Her deed included restrictions provided in the rules of the Villa Nueva Condominium Association, one of which was that children under the age of 18 were prohibited from living in the complex. When Ritchy decided to sell her condominium, she found a buyer who was ready and able to purchase, but he had children under 18. Ritchy sued the association, contending the rule was discriminatory and, therefore, unenforceable. What should be the result?

9. Burnham owned a home near an airport. Regularly, Beverly Airways, Inc. flew its airplanes less than 500 feet above his land. He brought an action in trespass, seeking to enjoin the flights. Is he entitled to relief?

Chapter | 27

Transfer and Encumbrance of Real Property

_____

_____

_____

_____

OUTLINE

INTRODUCTION

As briefly noted in the preceding chapters, real property historically has occupied a unique place in the law. This undoubtedly is due in part to the fact that the available quantity of real property is finite, and that for centuries land was considered the source of all wealth and power. We now have as much real property as we can anticipate having in the foreseeable future. In addition, the modern law of real property, as it concerns private ownership, has developed largely since the feudal period in England. It was during that period that one who "owned" real property (actually, as a tenant of the king) effectively was a quasi-government—handing down laws governing his "realm," being master of those who worked on the land, and even levying and collecting taxes from tenants who held their land at his pleasure.

As a general proposition, the rules governing the transfer and encumbrance of real property rights include the same rules that apply to personal property transactions with the addition of certain formalities. We will pay special attention to these formalities in this chapter.

The term *transfer*, as it is used in this chapter, is limited to the conveyance of the basic title to real property. **Encumbrance** refers to various restrictions placed on that basic title. These may be created by either private or public action.

There are five common methods of transferring real property. First, during the lifetime of the owner, transfer may be by land contract or by deed. Second, upon death, the deceased's title may be transferred by will or by intestate succession. Third, the title to property may be taken by adverse possession. Fourth, the title may provide for automatic transfer as in cases of determinable fees, life estates, and joint tenancies. Finally, encumbrances may be placed on the property, including mortgages, private covenants, and governmental restrictions. Transfers upon death will be discussed in detail in Chapter 49. Mortgages were discussed in Chapter 23, involving security interests, and the remainder will be treated in detail in the pages that follow.

MARKETABLE TITLE

Prior to discussing transfer and encumbrance, it is desirable to examine briefly the concept of marketable title. When a transfer is made, it normally is expected that the transferee will receive marketable title. Further, encumbrances of the type touched on and discussed in this chapter are, typically, the most important in terms of placing a cloud on title and preventing complete marketability.

A **marketable title** is one that is free of defects that would make the property unsalable in the ordinary course of business to a person of reasonable prudence who was familiar with the facts relating to the title. Someone who has marketable title, then, reasonably is assured that she will have quiet and peaceful enjoyment of the property. This does not mean that there are no outstanding restrictions and possible questions as to the title, only that there should be no reasonable objection to those that do exist. Of course, the exact nature of the title to be conveyed may be stipulated by the parties to the transfer, and they may agree to less than marketable title. In the absence of such a provision, however, the law assumes that marketable title was intended, and what is necessary for marketable title often is established by statute and court decision.

Marketable Title Acts

A number of states have enacted statutes that provide for the clearing of some of the more common title defects, in particular those concerning the possible existence of rights in the heirs of previous owners, and sometimes those relating to dower and curtesy rights. For example, under Michigan's act, the defects to which it relates are cleared after 45 years. Other states have similar time limits. The following case considers one such statute.

TISDELL v. HANES, et al.
248 Iowa 742, 82 N.W.2d 119 (1957)

This was an action by E. S. Tisdell, Jr. (Plaintiff/Appellee) against Lawrence D. and Carol M. Hanes and Iowa Savings and Loan Association (Defendants/Appellants) for a declaratory judgment that his title to certain real estate is "good and merchantable."

Under Iowa's statute, claims to real estate arising or existing prior to January 1,

1940, were declared invalid as against a holder of record title in possession, unless a written claim was recorded prior to July 4, 1951. The purpose of this statute, referred to as a "Marketable Title Act," was to clear real estate titles of old claims that probably would not be asserted anyway, but which created technical defects. Defendants challenged the act and the sufficiency of an affidavit of Plaintiff's occupancy to clear the defects complained of and make Plaintiff's title "merchantable" (marketable).

The trial court found the title "good and merchantable," and Defendants appealed. Affirmed.

WENNERSTRUM, Justice.

A merchantable or marketable title has been defined as one that later can be sold to a reasonable purchaser, ". . . a title that a man of reasonable prudence, familiar with the facts and apprised of the questions of law involved, would in the ordinary course of business accept." . . .

Iowa was the first of several states to pass a statute which bars all claims to real property arising prior to a stated date without regard to the nature of any legal condition on the part of a possible claimant. This initial legislation was enacted in 1919. . . .

In order to comply with the statute and to make possible a reliance upon it the required affidavit must be filed by the owner in possession. In Lytle v. Guilliams . . . in discussing the statute in question, we stated: ". . . Only those who possess a title which complies with the conditions of the statute are qualified to invoke its aid. . . ." As provided in the statute no action may be brought against the holder of the record title who has been in possession on any claim arising or existing prior to January 1, 1940. However, the declaration, as set out in the statute, is subject to two exceptions. (1) The holder of the record title and his predecessors must be shown to have held a record chain of title since January 1, 1940, and (2) an action is barred only if the claimant failed to preserve his claim by filing a duly acknowledged description of it within one year from July 4, 1951. Drake Law Review, Vol. 2, No. 2, pp. 76, 78. And in the foregoing article it is stated: ". . . The statute thus operates both as a statute of limitation and as a method of forcing claims to be recorded. The statute applies irrespective of any disability of the claimant; it defines what transfers are included in determining the record chain of title; and it authorizes affidavits to prove the possession of the record title."

We hold the title holder at the time of the submission of the abstract of title and prior to the giving of the deed to the purchaser complied with the statute in that an affidavit of possession was filed by him as one of the owners in possession and therein stated no claimant had sought to maintain a claim to the property prior to July 4, 1951. In filing such an affidavit a good and merchantable title was effected as provided by the purchase agreement. It has been suggested the section in question is a bar to all claims affecting title to real property except claims of a state or the United States. As to these possible claimants we are not required to comment in this appeal.

Questions

1. What are the arguments for and against the Iowa statute?
2. Is there anything someone with a claim to real property can do to protect that claim from being cut off?

Quiet Title Action

When questions exist concerning the marketability of title, or the possibility of any other claim to a particular parcel of real property, anyone having an interest in the property may bring an action in equity to "quiet" the title to that property. The rules of procedure require that any identifiable person suspected of having an interest must be served with process personally. Others whose identities are not known may be notified "by publication." This ordinarily requires the publication of notice of the suit in a newspaper of general circulation in the county in which the property is located. The publication period usually is quite long, from 13 to 26 weeks. The court's jurisdiction to quiet title is based on the fact that the property is located in its bailiwick. The action is one *in rem* (concerning the property itself) rather than one *in personam* (concerning the person apart from the property). When judgment is rendered properly, it clears the title of most, but not all, outstanding clouds. For example, a **quiet title action** usually will not be effective against the rights of an insane person or those of someone who was in military service at the time of publication of the notice.

LAND CONTRACTS

For many years, the use of land contracts has been one of the most popular methods of financing real estate transactions. Because a **land contract** is an agreement directly between the buyer and seller, the buyer may be able to finance the purchase at a rate less than the prevailing commercial mortgage rate. The seller who is willing to sell on a land

contract may find the available pool of potential purchasers significantly increased. The possible disadvantage to the seller is that, unlike mortgage financing, the purchase price is not received at the time of sale. Instead, the purchase price is paid over the course of 10, 20, or even 30 years. Delivery of the deed, then, comes at the time of final payment. During the payment period, the purchaser ordinarily undertakes ownership obligations such as maintenance and repair and the payment of insurance against the risks of fire or other loss, taxes, and assessments.

Form of a Land Contract

A land contract is an ordinary, simple contract. It must satisfy the same formalities as other simple contracts (offer, acceptance, consideration, capacity of the parties, and legal purpose). Of course, because it involves a promise, by the seller, to transfer an interest in land, it is required to be in writing under the Statute of Frauds.

The importance of two points regarding land contracts cannot be overstated. First, as with any transaction involving real estate, it is necessary to incorporate a precise, accurate description of the property in the agreement. Any vagueness or other irregularity in the description may render the contract void. In this respect, courts are less permissive in interpreting the parties' intent than with any other kind of contract. Second, for the purchaser's protection, every land contract, or notice of it, should be recorded in the county in which the property is located. This ordinarily is done in the office of the same county official responsible for other real estate records. This is necessary in order to give notice to anyone who subsequently may seek to become the owner or the holder of a security, or any other interest in the property. Property descriptions and the effects of recording are discussed in more detail in later sections of this chapter.

Rights under a Land Contract

The buyer under a land contract has a property interest (equitable title) in the real estate that is covered by the contract. This interest, and the rights under the contract, ordinarily may be as-signed to a third party. Upon assignment, the assignee receives the rights, and undertakes the obligations, of the assignor (buyer). However, the assignment does not free the buyer of his obligations to the seller unless the seller agrees to look only to the assignee for performance (agrees to a novation). If the land contract contains a provision prohibiting assignment without the seller's consent, any assignment in violation thereof would entitle the seller to declare a for-feiture. The forfeiture then could be avoided only by the tender of full performance by either the buyer or the assignee. The following case presents an interesting land contract situation.

DAVIS v. DEAN VINCENT, INC.
255 Or. 233, 465 P.2d 702 (1970)

This was an action by Leonard S. and Margaret M. Davis (Plaintiffs/Respondents) against Dean Vincent, Inc. and Howard Angell (Defendants/Appellants) for rescis-sion of a contract for land on the ground of misrepresentation.

Plaintiffs saw certain real estate owned by Howard Angell and his wife and listed for sale by Dean Vincent, Inc., a real estate broker. They negotiated and entered into a contract to purchase the property. During negotiations, Howard Angell represented himself to be the sole owner, and only he signed the contract as vendor. When it was discovered that the title, in fact, was held in entireties, Plaintiffs gave notice of their desire to rescind the contract. Defendants refused because Mrs. Angell was willing to sign the deed and the contract provided for a period of 30 days in which Plaintiffs could clear any defects.

The trial court entered judgment in favor of Plaintiffs, granting rescission for misrepresentation of ownership, and Defendants appealed. Reversed.

TONGUE, Justice.

The contract between the parties provided that each party should have a period of 30 days "after written notice of defects to correct defects in his title." We do not consider the preliminary title report, a copy of which was appparently mailed by the title company to Angell, as satisfying the requirement of "written notice of defects", as that term was used by the parties in their contract. At no time prior to the filing of their complaint did Davis ever complain that Angell had either misrepresented his title or that his title was defective. Much less did Davis give written or any notice to Angell complaining of any defect in title, as clearly intended by the terms of the contract to be a condition precedent to any suit for rescission based upon any such defect.

But even if the preliminary title report be considered [*sic*] as satisfying the require-ment of written notice of defective title, requiring correction in 30 days, it does not follow that plaintiffs were entitled to relief.

Even before the expiration of the 30 day period Dr. Davis demanded the return of the earnest money and refused to proceed further. In addition, there is ample authority to support the proposition that the purchaser has no right to rescind a contract for the sale of land because of a defect in the vendor's [defendants'] title prior to the time for performance of the contract. . . .

As we view it, a defect arising from the failure to have the vendor's wife (with whom title is held in an estate by the entirety) sign the preliminary earnest money contract or one arising from the fact that such a contract incorrectly describes the husband as the sole owner of the property, as in this case, is a defect that can be removed, as a practical matter, within the meaning of the foregoing rule, where, as in this case, testimony was offered that the wife had authorized a listing of the property for sale and was willing to join in the conveyance. Indeed, in view of such testimony she probably could not have later disaffirmed it, in any event, under the facts of this case. . . .

Although there are no previous Oregon cases involving such a defect in title, and thus none directly in point, this result is entirely consistent with the previous decisions by this court. Thus, in Wade v. James . . . it was held (although under somewhat different facts), that:

> There can be no rescission and recovery of purchase price by the purchaser where the vendor is able and willing to perform within the time limited by the contract of sale. 39 Cyc. 2006. If the vendor fails to furnish good title at the time fixed for performance, the purchaser may maintain an action to recover the price paid. . . .

If the case is considered as one based upon a misrepresentation of ownership, the same result follows, in view of the rule that a contract may not be rescinded because of a misrepresentation in the absence of a showing that some damage has or will result. Thus, as the rule is stated in 8A Thompson on Real Property 417-418 Section 4473:

> Misrepresentation of title is fraud if it results in injury to the purchaser, but no fraud justifying rescission exists where the purchaser sustained no injury and the vendor entered into the contract in good faith, and is able to furnish a good title upon demand. Thus, representations by a vendor as to the title he holds at the time of the sale, which he believes to be true, but which are in fact untrue, will not authorize a rescission of the contract. See also 55 Am.Jur. 542-543, Vendor and Purchaser, Section 70.

Thus, in this case, since there was testimony that Angell's wife had authorized a listing of the property for sale and since testimony was offered that she would have joined in a deed for conveyance of the property, it follows that Davis had not and would not have suffered damage as a result of the alleged misrepresentation of title.

Questions

1. Why is the court so willing to forgive a clear misrepresentation of title?

2. Since Davis apparently will not be damaged by the misrepresentation, why do you suppose he is seeking rescission? Is his motivation relevant to what the court should do?

The seller under a land contract has rights both as promisee of performance by the buyer and as the holder of legal title to the real estate that is the subject of the contract. She may assign her rights to the purchase price freely, although the assignee takes them subject to the seller's obligations to the buyer. In addition, she may convey her legal title. Again, however, the purchaser takes equitable title subject to the rights of the buyer under the land contract, but only if he has notice of those rights. For this reason, it is important that the buyer under a land contract records the contract. The recording provides notice of the buyer's rights.

The rights of the seller upon default by the buyer vary widely depending on state law, provisions of the contract, and the circumstances of the default. Most states have some requirement for service of the notice of default by the seller on the buyer, and also provide that the buyer may cure the default. A proper cure may require the buyer's full performance or only performance to date and costs, with assurances of future performance. In addition, for the seller to retake possession upon default, many states require that the formal foreclosure procedure be followed. Contracts may contain such provisions as buyer's waiver of notice of default, waiver of the necessity of foreclosure, and the right of the seller to retain all payments to date in addition to repossessing the real estate. The extent to which these provisions are enforceable, however, depends upon state law. Generally, state statutes and the courts do not uphold contractual provisions allowing the seller to retake possession without first giving the buyer notice and an opportunity to be heard. Also not favored are forfeitures of payments that have been made by the buyer when the amount of the forfeiture would constitute a penalty because it does not bear any reasonable relationship to the injuries suffered by the seller. In states in which foreclosure proceedings are required, because such proceedings are in equity, the courts will not grant foreclosure if the amount due on the contract is small in relation to the value of the property. Under these circumstances, the seller is allowed only an action at law for breach of contract.

In the vast majority of cases, when a breach of a land contract occurs, it is the buyer who defaults. This is true because it is the buyer who has almost all of the continuing obligations that are performed during the contract period. However, when the buyer has executed his obligations fully, the seller sometimes refuses to execute and deliver a deed to the property. When this occurs, the buyer, at his election, may rescind the contract, or he may sue for damages suffered and specific performance. If the buyer elects to rescind, he may recover all payments made and any reasonable costs arising out of the breach. In addition, he may recover the value of any improvements he made to the property in good faith. If the buyer elects to sue for specific performance, the courts ordinarily will grant the remedy. If the seller still refuses to convey the title, the courts will execute the deed in the seller's name.

DEEDS

Early in the history of the Common Law system, when reading and writing were virtually unknown, land was transferred routinely by **enfeoffment.** The seller simply took the buyer to the property, picked up a handful of soil and placed it in the buyer's hand while uttering words of conveyance. This practice, for a number of reasons, is not recognized in the United States. It has given way to the more formal method of transferring real estate by means of a written instrument of conveyance called a deed. This provides clearer evidence of title and facilitates the recording of such transfers.

In essence, in its first use, a **deed** was nothing more than a contract under the terms of which a seller acknowledged the receipt of certain consideration in return for which the seller was obligated to transfer title immediately to certain described real estate. Because courts of equity always would grant specific performance of written contracts to convey an interest in real estate, these contracts were seen as essentially self-executing. Today, although deeds still carry the earmarks of contracts, they usually are viewed as instruments of conveyance rather than contracts.

Types of Deeds

The most basic form of deed is the **quitclaim** deed. It purports to do no more than convey to the transferee such rights as the transferor has in the subject property. It does not purport to convey title, nor does it make any guarantees concerning the quality of any interest being conveyed. Therefore, anyone may be the grantor under a quitclaim deed since, in essence, it states: "Whatever interest I may own in the property, if any, is yours." Quitclaim deeds are used quite commonly as a means of clearing possible defects in the title to real property. If a question arises as to a possible outstanding interest held by someone, a quitclaim deed executed and delivered by that person, and properly recorded, will clear the title of that defect, and the grantor makes no guarantee that he has any interest to transfer.

The other basic type of deed is the **warranty deed.** In effect, a warranty deed is like a quitclaim deed with the addition of certain contractual guarantees called warranties. Unless the deed specifies to the contrary, every warranty deed carries with it five guarantees:

1. that the grantor has title to the real estate being conveyed;
2. that the title is good against all other persons (no one else has an interest in the property);
3. that there are no encumbrances against the property (such as mortgages, other liens, and easements);
4. that the grantee will not be disturbed in the quiet and peaceful enjoyment of the property; and
5. that in the event that any other person claims an interest in the property, the grantor will aid the grantee in defense of the title.

These five warranties are made even if they are not spelled out in the warranty deed.

There are two subcategories of warranty deeds. The most common, known as a **general warranty deed,** makes the listed warranties with respect to the title for the period beginning when the property first came under private ownership. Less common is the **special warranty deed,** which makes the same five warranties, but only as to defects arising since the grantor took title. This is the type of deed that generally is given by a trustee or any other person holding title for the benefit of someone else, such as an executor, an administrator, or a guardian.

Formal Requirements

State laws are not completely uniform as to the requirements for a valid deed. However, the following fundamental elements typically are necessary for all deeds: (1) legal capacity of the grantor; (2) a grantee identified with reasonable certainty; (3) a recital of consideration; (4) words of conveyance; (5) a description of the real estate; (6) execution of the deed by the grantor; (7) delivery to the grantee; and (8) acceptance by the grantee. Beyond these requirements, state law may require other formalities, such as identification of the preparer of the deed. In addition, the deed may contain other matters, details, or restrictions, depending on the circumstances of each transaction.

The *capacity of the grantor* necessary for the execution of a valid deed is governed by state law. To begin with, the grantor must be either a natural person or an artificial person recognized by the law. The latter includes corporations, duly appointed trustees, and other fiduciaries approved by a court such as executors, administrators, and guardians. Also included are public officials acting within the limits of their statutory authority. In addition, many states recognize some noncorporate associations, such as partnerships or limited partnerships, as legal persons. Of course, it must be noted that the procedures required for corporate and noncorporate entities to transfer real estate are governed by state laws regulating business organizations, and sometimes by the provisions of their charters and bylaws.

Natural persons must be of legal age and sound mind. At common law, the age of capacity was 21. Many states now have changed the age to 18 by statute. Sound mind requires that the grantor be capable of comprehending the nature and consequences of her act, and not have been officially adjudicated incompetent. Deeds executed by infants and insane persons are voidable, and those executed by incompetent persons generally are declared void by statute. In these respects, the rules for grantor's capacity are the same as those for contractual capacity, which is discussed in Chapter 9.

Since it is clear that the title to all property in the United States must vest in someone, a deed purporting to transfer title is effective as a transfer only if it *names the grantee* with reasonable certainty. If the space for the grantee's name is left blank, the deed is not valid until it is filled in by the grantor or with his authority. A misspelled or an assumed name will not invalidate a deed, as long as it identifies the grantee with reasonable precision. For example, a grant to John Albert Adams in the name "Jack Adams" may be held sufficient, although identification may require outside testimony and other proof. Of course, such carelessness should not be encouraged. Also, any subsequent grant should be in the name as title was received, in order to prevent further clouding of the title. Remember also that any grant to someone who is not a natural person must comply with state laws governing business organizations. For example, a deed naming an

unincorporated association as grantee is not valid unless the association is recognized as an entity capable of holding title. However, the fact that such an association, or a corporation, is prohibited by its articles or its bylaws from owning the property normally will not invalidate the grant, although the organization may be required to divest itself of the property immediately.

As noted in the introductory discussion of deeds, in its original form a deed was a contract. Therefore, *consideration* was necessary for the validity of a deed (perhaps even fair and adequate consideration). In most jurisdictions today, a recital of consideration generally is included (commonly, "$1.00 and other valuable consideration") but is unnecessary for the validity of a deed. Therefore, the title to real estate ordinarily now may be conveyed, by deed, as a gift. The only universal exception to this rule is the deed of "bargain and sale" (the first kind of deed used), which by definition recites consideration to support it as a contract. This deed may be in the form of a quitclaim, or may be a general or special warranty deed. It purports to do nothing other than those things stated in the deed, except that there is an implication that the grantor purports to transfer legal title unless the deed states to the contrary. However, no warranties are implied as in the standard form of warranty deed. Of course, if warranties are to be enforced, even under the standard form of warranty deed, there must be consideration.

Although title would pass without consideration, any warranties would be void. Also, consider the following case in which the agreed-upon consideration for a deed was not fully paid.

WORRELL v. WEST
129 Kan. 467, 296 P.2d 1092 (1956)

This was an action by Nellie Mae Worrell (Petitioner/Appellant) against Thomas C. and Grace S. West (Respondents/Appellees) to cancel a deed for failure of Respondents to pay the stated consideration.

Plaintiff, by deed, granted her home to Respondents who agreed, in return, to allow her to live in the home. Her petition alleged that Respondents made life miserable for her in a number of stated respects, and as a result she was forced to leave her home.

Respondents demurrered to the petition and the trial court granted the demurrer. Petitioner appealed. Reversed.

WERTZ, Justice.

At the outset it may be stated that we are called upon to review the sufficiency of plaintiff's evidence as against defendants' demurrer, and not to weigh the evidence for the purpose of rendering a decision on the merits of the action, and this same duty was incumbent upon the trial court. . . .

In considering and deciding a demurrer to plaintiff's evidence in a case tried to the court, the same rule obtains as in cases tried by a jury. . . . Considering plaintiff's evidence in its most favorable aspects in accordance with the rules enumerated, we are of the opinion that there was ample evidence to support plaintiff's cause of action as set forth in her petition, and the court erred in sustaining the demurrer.

In this and other jurisdictions, a grantor who conveys land in consideration of an agreement by the grantee to support, maintain, and care for the grantor during his lifetime, may, upon the neglect or refusal of the grantee to comply with the contract, have a decree setting aside the deed and reinvesting him with the title to the real estate. The intervention of equity in such cases is sanctioned on the theory that the neglect or refusal of the grantee to comply with his contract raises a presumption that he did not intend to comply with it in the first instance, and that the contract was fraudulent in its inception, wherefore a court of equity will not permit him to enjoy the conveyance so obtained. Rescission of such a conveyance has been granted upon the theory that the conveyance is one upon a condition subsequent, which is broken by the failure to provide support. . . .

We have held, in contracts of the character of the one under consideration, that nonperformance by the grantee of his covenant to furnish support and maintenance to the grantor constitutes sufficient ground for the rescission and cancellation of the conveyance.

Questions

1. The court makes it clear that it is not deciding the case on the merits of this appeal. Why not? What happens next?

2. In the *Davis* case the court was unwilling to grant rescission of a land contract despite a clear misrepresentation, yet the court in this case has not found such a misrepresentation. What is the difference between the two cases, or are they just inconsistent?

The requirement that all deeds must contain *words of conveyance* may be satisfied by using any language that signifies the grantor's intention to make a present transfer. Very commonly used are words such as "convey and quitclaim," "convey and warrant," and "grant," "bargain and sell," "set over," and "assign." Words indicating an intent to convey in the future must be avoided.

The *description* of the property to be conveyed *must* be clear and accurate. Historically it was common for property to be described according to natural monuments. For example, "Beginning at the big oak tree on the southwest corner of the Jones farm, east along the creek bank 550 yards to the edge of the Phillips ford, then northeast. . . ." Although arguably adequate, such descriptions lack permanence. With the passage of time people will forget the location of the Jones farm; the big oak tree will die and rot away; the creek will change course (which raises an interesting problem, itself); and the Phillips ford will be no more. Today, most property is described by the use of metes and bounds and the rectangular survey system, or by lot numbers corresponding to a recorded plat. For example, a residential property may be described as "Lot Number Seventeen (17) in the Morrison Addition to the town of Iowa City, Iowa." In turn, when the Morrison Addition was platted, and the plat map was recorded, it may have been described as "The southwest quarter of the northeast quarter of Township 14 North, Range 6 East, near the town of Iowa City, Iowa." Metes and bounds might then have been necessary if the boundaries of the Morrison Addition were irregular. Beyond being clear, the description should be accurate. Otherwise, questions will arise concerning the need for a court action to reform the description or to quiet title. Also, the grantee may receive less property than he bargained for, or the grantor may be subject to a suit for breach of warranty. To say the least, the courts are not particularly flexible about real property descriptions, except that it is conventional to see the statement of acreage that accompanies the description qualified by the declaration "more or less." The reason for this is that surveys cannot be perfectly accurate, and acreage measurements usually will be rounded slightly.

Execution of the deed by the grantor, of course, is necessary to the validity of any deed. This requires that the deed be signed by the grantor or her authorized agent. Obviously, execution by an agent is necessary in the case of a grantor who is not a natural person. Although it is customary to date a deed when it is executed, a date is not necessary for its validity. With the exception of a few states, primarily in the East, if the grantor is a natural person, a seal no longer is required. When the grantor is not a natural person, however, the seal requirement is much more common. In most jurisdictions, deeds must be acknowledged, which means they must be signed before an official authorized to take oaths, such as a notary public. The acknowledgement, however, is not necessary for the validity of a deed, but only to qualify it to be recorded on a public record.

Although the preceding paragraph sets out the basic requirements for execution of a deed, some other matters must be considered. If the grantor is the sole owner of the property conveyed, but is married at the time the deed is executed, the signature of the grantor's spouse also will be necessary to release any of the spouse's rights, such as dower. If not released, these rights will continue. If the grantor is not married, it is customary to state that fact along with the signature. Otherwise, the question of the grantor's marital status will be a cloud on the title. Also, if the property is held by a husband and wife as tenants by the entireties, execution by both is necessary to convey any interest in it. This is not, however, true of property held as tenants in common or as joint tenants. Under these circumstances, the interests of the individual tenants may be transferred freely. Any transfer executed by a trustee, guardian, or other fiduciary should indicate the capacity in which the deed was executed clearly, and the record should show the source of authority to do so, such as a trust agreement or a court order.

Delivery of the deed to the grantor is necessary for the conveyance to become operative. There are no absolute rules as to what constitutes delivery, and each case must be reviewed on its individual merits. Delivery does not mean simply the manual handing over of possession of the deed. More accurately, it means the objective manifestation of the grantor to make a present transfer of the property. Of course, this frequently is accomplished by surrendering possession of the deed. However, a deed may be delivered to the grantee for other purposes, such as reading it or checking the description. Delivery of a deed even may be for the purpose of transferring a mortgage interest rather than the absolute title, as discussed below. It even is possible to deliver a deed without turning over actual possession of the document. For example, the grantor may execute the deed and have it recorded in the name of the grantee. Again, what is necessary is a clear and objective manifestation of the grantor's intent to convey

presently. Therefore, it should be clear that delivery of a deed is effective only if it takes place during the grantor's lifetime. If the grantor retains possession of the deed, with instructions that it be delivered after his death, delivery would not be effective to transfer title. However, an *inter vivos* delivery by the grantor to a third person, with instructions to deliver to the grantee after the grantor's death, would be effective if the transfer to the third person was irrevocable—for example, a delivery in trust. Consider the following case.

BURY v. YOUNG
98 Cal. 446, 33 P. 338 (1893)

This was an action by Bury (Plaintiff/Appellee) against Young (Defendant/Appellant) to have a declaration of the validity of a deed and conveyance of real estate.

The parties are both daughters of M. A. Hinkson. While recovering from an illness, Hinkson called his attorney to his bedside, executed a deed to certain real estate naming Plaintiff as grantee, and gave it to the attorney instructing him to give it to Plaintiff upon his death. Hinkson did not expressly reserve a power to revoke. Hinkson recovered from the illness and demanded return of the deed from the attorney, but the demand was refused. Then he executed a will leaving the subject real estate to Defendant. Thereafter, Hinkson died.

The trial court found that the delivery of the deed to the attorney without reserving the power to revoke constituted a binding delivery of the deed into escrow, and thus satisfied the requirement that a deed be delivered. Judgment for Plaintiff was appealed by Defendant. Affirmed.

GAROUTTE, J.

It may be conceded that the roads traveled by courts in arriving at this conclusion have not always been the same, but, whatever may have been the various lines of reasoning pursued, the same result had always been reached, and a valid delivery declared. We shall not enter into a discussion of the elementary principles of law supporting the proposition here involved, but content ourselves with a reference to the views of various courts as to the law applicable to the state of facts here presented. In the well-considered case of Cook v. Brown, . . . the decision of the court upon this question concludes as follows: "If the owner of land desires to convey the same, but not to have his deed take effect until his decease, he can make a reservation of a life estate in the deed, or it may be done by the absolute delivery of the deed to a third person, to be passed to the grantee upon the decease of the grantor, the holder in such case being a trustee for the grantee." In Prutsman v. Baker, . . . Chief Justice Dixon, speaking for the court, approved the doctrine cited from Cook v. Brown, supra, and declared the same rule in the following language: "As to the grantor, delivery is absolute and final, and so is his conveyance of the land, the title to which passes at once to the grantee, qualified only by the right of the grantor to use and occupy, or take and receive the rents and profits during his life, or until the event shall have happened upon which second delivery be made. The grantor in such case converts his estate into a life tenancy, and makes himself the tenant of the grantee. These conclusions result unavoidably from the certainty of the event upon which the second delivery is made to depend, and from the impossibility, under the circumstances, that the grantor will ever be able to recall or repossess himself of the deed. He delivers the writing, therefore, as his deed, always so to remain, and never to return to him, and it becomes presently operative, and the title vests immediately in the grantee." [Other authority also was quoted.]

Upon a careful examination of the authorities cited by appellant, and other cases, bearing upon this question, not cited, we have failed to find a case supporting a contrary doctrine to that announced in the foregoing citations. In every case where the deed has been declared invalid by reason of failure of delivery it will be found that the grantor reserved some rights over the instrument; the he failed to part with all control and dominion over it; that, upon the happening of some event or contingency or condition, he had the right, if so disposed, to reach out, and take it from the possession of the depositary. Such is not the case under consideration, for here the court finds as a fact that "the grantor parted with all dominion over said deed." There are well-considered cases holding that, even though the grantor delivers the deed to the depositary, reserving the right to recall it, yet if he dies without recalling it, and the deed is then delivered, such delivery is complete and entire, and carries title. We are not disposed to indorse that doctrine, and think the principle recognized in this case goes far enough for all proper purposes. The essential requisite to the validity of a deed transferred under circumstances as indicated in this case is that, when it is placed in the hands of a third party, it has passed beyond the control of the grantor for all time. That question is determined by the grantor's intention in the matter, and his intention in making the delivery is a question of fact, to be solved by the light of all the circumstances surrounding the transaction. . . .

Appellant offered in evidence a deed from M. A. Hinkson to A. C. Hinkson, and a deed back to M. A., of the realty here involved. These deeds were made subsequent to the deed which we have had under consideration, and were offered as tending to show the grantor's intentions at the time he made the original deed. The proposed evidence was rejected, and rightly so. The consideration in both deeds was nominal. They were executed about the same time, and were recorded upon the same day. It was a very poor attempt upon the part of the grantor to create evidence in his own favor. Neither was the grantor's order upon the depositary to redeliver the deed to him proper evidence. If offered as tending to show a revocation was not involved in the case. [*sic*] The question involved was the power of the grantor to revoke or recall the deed.

Questions

1. How could the giving of a deed to one's own lawyer be an irrevocable act, given the fact that an attorney is supposed to act for the client?
2. Does the court indicate whether the power to revoke would have to be in writing and, if so, would it have to comply with the formalities of a deed?

The last requirement is *acceptance* by the grantee. Although mandatory, this requirement seldom presents a problem. Ordinarily, the courts will assume acceptance as long as the grant is beneficial. Otherwise, of course, proof of acceptance is necessary.

Finally, it should be noted that most states tax real estate transfers, and require that tax stamps be affixed to every deed prior to recording. The amount of the tax usually depends on the selling price; for example, 55 cents per 1000 dollars. In an effort to conceal the selling price on the public record, it is a common practice to purchase significantly more tax stamps than are necessary, and not reveal the true consideration on the deed. For example, the consideration may be recited as "$1.00 and other valuable consideration" or "$1.00 O.V.C." However, concealment is not always possible. Some states reassess property values each year, based in part on the selling prices of properties during the year. In these states, if the correct consideration is not recited in the deed, it is necessary to reveal it in a separate affidavit that is filed along with the deed, making it impossible to conceal the selling price completely.

Although it is important to record all documents relating to rights in real property, it is just as important that the buyer physically inspect the property before purchasing it. Consider the following case.

HENDERSON v. LAWRENCE
369 S.W.2d 553 (Tenn. 1963)

This was an action by Eurydice Henderson (Complainant/Appellant) against Robert H. Lawrence and George G. Nowlin (Defendants/Appellees) to have the court declare her title to certain real estate.

In substance, so far as important here, Complainant became the sole owner of certain real estate in 1934, as sole surviving heir of her mother and father. She had occupied the property as a home, and briefly rented it and collected rent, continuously from 1930 until the present lawsuit. On February 5, 1953, she executed a deed to the property to Vernon and Lila Lloyd. She alleges that the consideration for the deed was the promise of the Lloyds to improve and maintain the property, and to allow her to live there for the rest of her life. She alleges that this was not done and the deed to the Lloyds was procured by fraud, and therefore was voidable. In the meantime, through a series of conveyances and legal procedures, Defendants became the owners of the property, their title being proximately derived from the title of the Lloyds. The question before the court was whether Defendants were good-faith (bona fide) purchasers.

The trial court dismissed Complainant's complaint on demurrer and Complainant appealed. Reversed.

WHITE, Justice.

It is a general rule of procedure that the courts engage in every reasonable presumption in favor of the bill when assailed by a demurrer. . . .

The defendant Lawrence claims that he is an innocent purchaser for value, but at the same time, by filing a demurrer he admits the averments in the original bill and the bill as amended.

A bona fide purchaser is one who buys for a valuable consideration without knowledge or notice of facts material to the title. . . .

It is well established in this State that there can be no innocent purchase of land from a vendor who was out of possession at the date of the conveyance. . . .

The appellant, Eurydice Henderson, was in actual possession of the property in question and this alone is sufficient notice to the purchaser to put him on inquiry as to her rights in and to the possession of the property in question. . . .

In the case of Nikas v. United Construction Company, . . . it was held that the purchaser of a lot which had a wall encroaching eleven inches over the boundary line at the time of purchase was not an innocent purchaser.

In the case of Macon v. Sheppard, . . . one acre of land was regularly occupied by a church. The congregation had been promised a deed but same had never been executed and the vendee of the entire tract of which this was a part claimed he had no notice. The Court said:

> And it is settled that if a person purchase an estate from the owner, knowing it to be in possession of tenants, he is bound to inquire into their estates, and is affected with notice of all the facts in relation thereto.

And in the case of Walgreen Company v. Walton . . . the Court said:

> Where the lessee is in possession, the purchaser takes subject to the lease.

In the instant case, the averments in the original and amended bills are that the appellant, original complainant, was in actual possession of the property in question and that the defendant Lawrence knew of this possession, and knew also that the appellant claimed that the defendants, Lila Lloyd and her husband, had obtained title to the property through fraudulent means. Therefore, it cannot be said that Lawrence was an innocent purchaser. That is, that he was innocent of the claims made by Eurydice Henderson.

Questions

1. Does the rule in this case apply to problems other than a tenant in possession? What would they be?

2. What should a buyer who cannot visit the land or who feels ill-equipped to identify problems do to protect herself against the charge that she is not an innocent purchaser?

MORTGAGES

In the simplest of terms, a **mortgage** is a security interest in property that is not in the possession of the mortgage holder. The property may be either personal or real, and if it is personal property, the mortgage is referred to as a *chattel mortgage*. In this section, however, we will deal only with real property mortgages.

In its original common law form, a mortgage involved lending money, the obligation to repay being evidenced by a promissory note and secured by the transfer of title to the real estate by the borrower/mortgagor to the lender/mortgagee, who in turn signed and gave back a separate instrument of defeasance. What all of this means is that the typical mortgage transaction involved three separate documents: (1) a promissory note containing the agreement of the parties concerning the debt and the terms of repayment; (2) a deed transferring the borrower's title in certain real estate to the lender; and (3) an instrument that required the lender to transfer the title back to the borrower upon repayment of the loan. The functions of these three separate instruments are all combined in the modern mortgage instrument. In fact, the majority of states now view a mortgage as creating only a security interest in the property, rather than involving an actual transfer of title from the mortgagor to the mortgagee. However, most states also recognize the more cumbersome procedure of transferring title, and even allow oral evidence to establish that a deed, in fact, was intended as a mortgage. The creation of a mortgage in this matter, with an oral obligation to retransfer title upon repayment of the debt, of course is risky and the practice is not recommended.

Formal Requirements

Very little need be said concerning a mortgage's formal requirements. Basically they are the same as those required for a valid deed. This should be clear because of the nature of a mortgage as described above. One difference, in modern practice, is that even though a mortgage ordinarily is not treated as a transfer of title, it should be recorded in the same manner as a deed.

Transfer of Interests

As a general rule, the rights of both the mortgagor and the mortgagee may be assigned, and the mortgagor's obligation to pay the underlying debt may be delegated. Of course, as is true of other assignments, neither assignment nor delegation eliminates the mortgagor's duty of performance unless the mortgagee also agrees to a novation. However, prior to the mid-1970s, it was fairly common for mortgage agreements to be "assumable," with the mortgagee agreeing in advance that the mortgagor could delegate his obligation under the mortgage, along with the assignment of his rights, in the event that he sold the property. The mortgagee could object only upon a showing of reasonable cause for insecurity. However, when interest rates rose suddenly during the recession of the 1970s—with the prime rate peaking at 22–23 percent—the financial community suddenly became aware of the need to protect itself in the future. Mortgage lenders almost eliminated the use of standard assumable mortgages. Along with other devices such as "balloon" and "variable-rate" mortgages, the use of "due on sale" clauses became common. Not only was the mortgage not assumable, but upon the sale of the property by the mortgagor, the entire balance of the mortgage indebtedness becomes due and payable. Therefore, the assignment of mortgages by the mortgagor became the exception rather than the rule, other than for older mortgages.

Foreclosure

In technical terms, **foreclosure** is a process by which the mortgagor's right of redemption is cut off (foreclosed), and title to the mortgaged property is perfected in the mortgagee. Under modern state law, foreclosure proceedings can be laborious and complicated, and usually involve the sale of the mortgaged property rather than the automatic assumption of continuing title by the mortgagee. When the property is sold, the proceeds are first applied to the costs of foreclosure and then to the mortgage indebtedness. Any excess over the amount necessary to pay these obligations is given to the mortgagor. Any deficiency becomes a general, unsecured debt to the mortgagee. Statutes generally provide that for some period after the sale, typically one year, the mortgagor may reacquire the property from the purchaser upon payment of the purchase price, together with interest and costs. This is called the **right of redemption,** and is discussed more fully in Chapter 22.

Although the details of foreclosure differ from state to state, there is a general pattern. Most states require notice of the mortagee's intent to foreclose, a hearing on the merits of foreclosure if the mortgagor desires, notice of sale, and a public auction. In states in which a public sale is not required, it usually is more expedient to include a clause in the mortgage agreement allowing foreclosure without it. This may avoid costs and delays attendant to judicial proceedings. Moreover, proceeds from foreclosure sales often do not equal the fair value of the property. For this reason, it is common that the mortgagee, and even the mortgagor, may bid at the sale. Sometimes the property is purchased by a sympathetic friend who holds it for the mortgagor. In any case, foreclosure seldom is desirable from the standpoint of either the mortgagor or the mortgagee. Unfortunately, it is often the only viable option for the parties.

ADVERSE POSSESSION

Title to real property may be acquired by possessing it for some statutorily prescribed period of time and meeting certain legal requirements. This is the concept of **adverse possession**—sometimes referred to as "squatter's rights." Once title is acquired by this means, it usually is perfected on record by a court judgment, frequently as a result of a suit to quiet title.

Although it is possible that a possessor might acquire title to the property of another by conscious design, these situations are rare, and are not consistent with the intent of adverse-possession law. Instead, that law is designed to serve the dual purposes of encouraging the productive use of land and clearing clouds on the title. Productive use of land is encouraged by threatening the possible loss of title if the owner does not pay at least some minimum attention to the property during the statutory adverse-possession period. As to the second purpose, it should be understood that many clouds on the title to real property are of a technical nature, and occurred so long before they became problems that evidence is lost and witnesses who could have testified to the facts have long since died or disappeared. Therefore, the means of presenting proof and setting the record straight frequently are unavailable.

Requirements

In order to result in adverse possession, the possession must meet certain requirements. Generally, it must have been (1) actual, (2) open and notorious, (3) hostile, and (4) continuous (5) for a statutory period of time. In addition, some states also require that, during the entire period of possession, the possessor must have paid the taxes on the property.

The requirement of *actual* possession simply means that the possessor must be physcially present on the land. An adverse-possession claim cannot be supported by a showing of only constructive possession, because the possessor should be present to be discoverable by the true owner should she choose to check her land.

The requirement that possession be *open and notorious* means that it cannot be hidden from reasonable view, and it must continue with an open claim of title or, at least, the appearance of a claim of title without the possessor denying it. Although this element is seldom a problem in cases involving adverse possession, the following case illustrates the reason for requiring it and its application in a most unusual setting.

MARENGO CAVE CO. v. ROSS
212 Ind. 624, 10 N.W.2d 917 (1937)

This was an action by John E. Ross (Plaintiff/Appellee) against Marengo Cave Co. (Defendant/Appellant) to quiet title to certain real estate.

Plaintiff and Defendant were owners of adjoining land in Crawford County, Indiana. On Defendant's land was the opening to a cave that Defendant developed and opened for commercial tours. Plaintiff purchased his land in 1908. The commercial tours through Defendant's cave had begun some 25 years before that time and continued more than 21 years afterward. During that time, possession of the cave had been held exclusively by Defendant and his remote and immediate grantors. Part of the cave extended under Plaintiff's land, a fact he did not ascertain until 1932. Defendant contended that he had acquired the portion of the cave under Plaintiff's land by adverse possession. The trial court found for Plaintiff and Defendant appealed. Affirmed.

ROLL, Judge.

It will be noted that neither appellee nor his predecessors in title had ever affected a severance of the cave from the surface estate. Therefore the title of the appellee extends from the surface to the center but actual possession is confined to the surface. Appellee and his immediate and remote grantors have been in posseion of the land and estate here in question at all times, unless it can be said that the possession of the cave by appellant as shown by the evidence above set out has met all the requirements of the law relating to the acquisition of land by adverse possession. A record title may be defeated by adverse possession. All the authorities agree that, before the owner of legal title can be deprived of his land by another's possession, through the operation of the statute of limitation, the possession must have been actual, visible, notorious, exclusive, under claim of ownership and hostile to the owner of the legal title and to the world at large (except only the government), and continuous for the full period prescribed by the statute. The rule is not always stated in exactly the same words in the many cases dealing with the subject of adverse possession, yet the rule is so thoroughly settled that there is no doubt as to what elements are essential to establish a title by adverse possession. . . .

(1) The possession must be actual. It must be conceded that appellant in the operation of the "Marengo Cave" used not only the cavern under its own land but also that part of the cavern that underlaid appellee's land, and assumed dominion over all of it. . . .

(2) The possession must be visible. The owner of land who, having notice of the fact that it is occupied by another who is claiming dominion over it, nevertheless

stands by during the entire statutory period and makes no effort to eject the claimant or otherwise protect his title, ought not to be permitted, for reasons of public policy, thereafter to maintain an action for the recovery of his land. But, the authorities assert, in order that the possession of the occupying claimant may constitute notice in law, it must be visible and open to the common observer so that the owner or his agent on visiting the premises might readily see that the owner's rights are being invaded. . . . What constitutes open and visible possession has been stated in general terms, thus; it is necessary and sufficient if its nature and character is such as is calculated to apprise the world that the land is occupied and who the occupant is; . . . and such an appropriation of the land by claimant as to apprise, or convey visible notice to the community or neighborhood in which it is situated that it is in his exclusive use and enjoyment. . . . It has been declared that the disseisor [the person who wrongfully puts the owner out of possession] "must unfurl his flag" on the land, and "keep it flying," so that the owner may see, if he will, that an enemy has invaded his domains, and planted the standard of conquest. . . .

(3) The possession must be open and notorious. The mere possession of the land is not enough. It is knowledge, either actual or imputed, of the possession of his lands by another, claiming to own them bona fide and openly, that affects the legal owner thereof. Where there has been no actual notice, it is necessary to show that the possession of the disseisor was so open, notorious, and visible as to warrant the inference that the owner must or should have known of it. . . .

(4) The possession must be exclusive. It is evident that two or more persons cannot hold one tract of land adversely to each other at the same time. "It is essential that the possession of one who claims adversely must be of such an exclusive character that it will operate as an ouster of the owner of the legal title; because, in the absence of ouster the legal title draws to itself the constructive possession of the land. A possession which does not amount to an ouster or disseisin is not sufficient." . . .

Here the possession of appellant was not visible. No one could see below the earth's surface and determine that appellant was trespassing upon appellee's lands. This fact could not be determined by going into the cave. Only by a survey could this fact be made known. The same undisputed facts clearly show that appellant's possession was not notorious. Not even appellant itself nor any of its remote grantors knew that any part of the "Marengo Cave" extended beyond its own boundaries, and they at no time even down to the time appellee instituted this action made any claim to appellee's lands. . . .

Even though it could be said that appellant's possession has been actual, exclusive, and continuous all these years, we would still be of the opinion that appellee has not lost his land. It has been the uniform rule in equity that the statute of limitation does not begin to run until the injured party discovers, or with reasonable diligence might have discovered, the facts constituting the injury and cause of action. Until then the owner cannot know that his possession has been invaded. Until he has knowledge, or ought to have such knowledge, he is not called upon to act, for he does not know that action in the premises is necessary and the law does not require abjured or impossible things of any one. . . .

So in the case at bar, appellant pretended to use the "Marengo Cave" as his property and all the time he was committing a trespass upon appellee's land. After 20 years of secret user, he now urges the statute of limitation, section 2-602, Burns' St. 1933, section 61, Baldwin's Ind.St. 1934, as a bar to appellee's action. Appellee did not know of the trespass of appellant, and had no reasonable means of discovering the fact. It is true that appellant took no active measures to prevent the discovery, except to deny appellee the right to enter the cave for the purpose of making a survey, and disclaiming any use of appellee's lands, but nature furnished the concealment. . . .

Questions

1. Does the result of this case permit the plaintiff to require the defendant to stop bringing tours into the portion of the cave under the plaintiff's land?

2. If the defendant had discovered the true facts, what could he have done to start the adverse-possession clock running?

In order for possession to be *hostile*, it is not necessary that the adverse possessor and the owner get into a fist-fight or some other unpleasantry. It only is necessary that the possession conflict (be hostile to) the owner's title. That is, the adverse possessor must be a trespasser, possessing the property without permission from the owner or any privilege granted by law.

The possession must be *continuous*, although this does not mean that the adverse possessor must be on the property 100 percent of the time. It means only that he must occupy the property as a true owner reasonably might do. What is required to meet this test may depend on the nature of the property. A full-time residence should be occupied as such; a vacation cabin in the "great north woods" would require, perhaps, occupancy only a few weeks out of the year; and commercial property would require something quite different.

Most states allow the requirement of continuity of possession to be met by more than one possessor, as long as continuity is not broken and each successive possessor occupies the property under claim of right from the previous possessor, such as by a purported grant of title. This is called **tacking.** Thus, tacking would not apply if pos-

sessor A occupied the property for half the period and then left, and B immediately took possession, not knowing about A's prior possession.

The *period of time* during which possession must continue varies from state to state, and is generally between 5 and 20 years (20 years was the requirement at common law). The period is set out in the Statute of Limitations for bringing an action for trespass to land. One theory supporting the right of an adverse possessor to title is that the true owner, by the running of the applicable statute of limitations, has lost the right to sue for trespass. Therefore, the courts hold, the "trespasser" has acquired an enforceable interest in the property.

Scope of Rights Acquired

Upon meeting the requirements for adverse possession, the adverse possessor is entitled to the entire present estate held by the "owner" during the period of possession. She takes her title subject to any perfected (ordinarily, recorded) interests, such as future interests and easements. That is, she acquires the same rights owned by anyone entitled to possession. This, of course, is ordinarily a fee simple title.

Under the general rules of adverse possession, the adverse possessor is entitled to all property he actually occupied and used. However, most states also recognize adverse possession under **color of title.** This means that if the adverse possessor took possession under an apparent grant of title, such as by a deed, his rights would extend to all property covered by that grant. Suppose, for example, he took possession of a farm, but made no actual use of one ten-acre field included in his deed. The adverse possessor would acquire title to that ten acres without actual occupancy, as long as it adjoined the property he did occupy.

Prescriptive Rights

Akin to the legal concept of adverse possession is the concept of prescriptive rights. The difference is simply that adverse possession gives the possessor actual title; **prescriptive rights** involve only a right to *use* property belonging to another. Therefore, if the requirements for adverse possession are met, but only use rather than possession was involved, the adverse user will acquire a right to continue the use and, therefore, will have a **prescriptive easement.** This use may be in the form of a road, or a path, or perhaps a right to discharge wastes onto the servient property. The time period necessary to acquire a prescriptive right is the same as for adverse possession, as long as the owner of the property is bringing an action at law (for damages) against the user. However, if the action is one in equity (to enjoin the continuation of the user's nuisance), the rule of *laches* applies, since statutes of limitations apply only to actions at law. Rather than a set number of years, **laches** involves the running of a reasonable period of time. The period of laches generally is shorter than the statutory period for trespass.

RESTRICTIONS ON USE AND POSSESSION

Today, when property is conveyed, title almost always is taken subject to some restrictions. As previously discussed, these frequently include such things as future interests, easements, and public rights. Broadly speaking, these limitations may be of two general types—private and public. In most modern cases, the latter are the most important. However, this was not always so. Private restrictions antedate public restrictions by a considerable length of time and were quite important. Prior to the advent of public restrictions, unless some private control was exercised, the value of a particular parcel of land could be freely, and severely, affected by the use of neighboring land. For example, someone could buy property and build a beautiful home and then a neighbor could decide to erect a pig farm or a slaughter house next door.

Restrictive Covenants

A covenant is a contractual promise. **Restrictive covenants,** then, are contractual limitations placed on the title by the parties at the time of transfer. Within the limits of public policy, they may be as broad or limited as the parties agree.

Restrictive covenants may be classified into three broad categories. First, they may be arbitrary, capricious limitations that suit the seller's fancy—for example, a provision that no person may consume alcoholic beverages on the premises or plant sycamore trees. Of the three categories, covenants of this type run the highest risk of conflicting with public policy. Second, covenants also may be for the benefit of land sold or land retained. For example, an owner of two adjoining lots may sell one and impose a restriction on either lot concerning the height or location of any buildings. This sometimes is done to protect such amenities as an unobstructed view or a breeze. Third, restrictions frequently are imposed by a subdivider or a developer of a tract of land to ensure not only conformity of use, but also to assure safety or beautification.

Zoning

Public restrictions on land most frequently are imposed by local units, such as a city, a township, or a county government in the form of **zoning** ordinances. These generally restrict structural and architectural designs, and also the uses to which the property may be subject. The affected city, township, or county is divided into districts (zones), each controlled by a different set of restrictions. In order to be upheld, zoning ordinances must be legislated in conformity with the government's police power to protect the public health, safety, morals, or welfare.

When a new zoning ordinance is enacted, there may be property within a particular district that by structure, architecture, or use does not meet the requirements of the ordinance. Such property is called a **nonconforming use.** For example, there may be a commercial property, such as a grocery store or a neighborhood tavern, in a district zoned for single-family dwellings. Such uses usually are permitted to continue. To order them removed might be illegal as retroactive legislation or a taking of property without just compensation. However, expansion of a nonconforming use will not be permitted. Sometimes ordinances even prohibit repairs to buildings in order to phase out the use. It ordinarily is possible for the owner to change the use to one that is still nonconforming, but less "offensive." Also, such property will lose its exemption whenever it is abandoned or sold. Once a property is held in conformance with the ordinance, any subsequent change to a nonconforming use may be permitted only by application for a **variance** to the appropriate governmental authority.

Eminent Domain

Eminent domain is the power of the government to take private property for public use. It is of ancient origin, beginning with the absolute power over and ownership of all property in the realm by the sovereign. Today, the power is limited by statute in most states. For example, before the power can be exercised, the government may be required to show the necessity for the taking and, in some states, even may be required to show the necessity for taking the *particular* property involved to meet the public need. An important limitation also is imposed by the Fifth and Fourteenth Amendments to the Constitution, which prohibit the taking of property without due process of law and just compensation. Therefore, the government exercising its eminent domain power must pay the owner the fair market value of the property taken. This is not true, however, of property that is not taken for public *use* but is **condemned** (destroyed in the public interest, although the term sometimes is used interchangeably with eminent domain). This is illustrated by the case of *U.S. v. Caltex (Philippines), Inc.*, which appears in Chapter 5, involving the destruction of the plaintiff's oil storage tanks to prevent the oil from falling into enemy hands during World War II. Also, as the following case illustrates, in addition to zoning, a government properly may impose burdens on property, in the public interest, without any compensation.

POLETOWN NEIGHBORHOOD COUNCIL v. CITY OF DETROIT
410 Mich. 616, 304 N.W. 455 (1981)

This was an action by Poletown Neighborhood Council and individual residents of an affected area (Plaintiffs/Appellants) against the City of Detroit, Michigan, and others (Defendants/Appellees) challenging condemnation of their area by the city's economic development corporation. The purpose of the condemnation was to turn the property over to General Motors Corporation for the construction of an assembly plant. Plaintiffs alleged that (1) the purpose of the condemnation was not a "public" one as is required for the city to exercise its power of eminent domain, and (2) the action would be in violation of the Michigan Environmental Protection Act.

The trial court found for Defendant. Plaintiffs appealed to the State Supreme Court by leave without awaiting a decision of the Court of Appeals. Affirmed.

PER CURIAM.

The Economic Development Corporations Act is a part of the comprehensive legislation dealing with planning, housing and zoning whereby the State of Michigan is attempting to provide for the general health, safety, and welfare through alleviating unemployment, providing economic assistance to industry, assisting the rehabilitation of blighted area, and fostering urban redevelopment. . . .

To further the objectives of this act, the legislature has authorized municipalities to acquire property by condemnation in order to provide industrial and commercial sites and the means of transfer from the municipality to private users. . . .

Plaintiffs-appellants do not challenge the declaration of the legislature that programs to alleviate and prevent conditions of unemployment and to preserve and develop industry and commerce are essential public purposes. Nor do they challenge the proposition that legislation to accomplish this purpose falls within the Constitutional grant of general legislative power to the legislature in Const. 1963, Art. 4, Section 51, which reads as follows:

> The public health and general welfare of the people of the state are hereby declared to be matters of primary public concern. The legislature shall pass suitable laws for the protection and promotion of the public health.

What plaintiffs-appellants do challenge is the constitutionality of using the power of eminent domain to condemn one person's property to convey it to another private person in order to bolster the economy. They argue that whatever incidental benefit may accrue to the public, assembling land to General Motors' specifications for conveyance to General Motors for its uncontrolled use in profit making is really a taking for private use and not a public use because General Motors is the primary beneficiary of the condemnation. . . .

There is no dispute about the law. All agree that condemnation for a public use or purpose is permitted. All agree that condemnation for a private use or purpose is forbidden. Similarly, condemnation for a private use cannot be authorized whatever its incidental public benefit and condemnation for a public purpose cannot be forbidden whatever the incidental private gain. The heart of this dispute is whether the proposed condemnation is for the primary benefit of the public or the private user.

The Legislature has determined that governmental action of the type contemplated here meets a public need and serves an essential public purpose. The Court's role after such a determination is made is limited. . . .

The United States Supreme Court has held that when a legislature speaks, the public interest has been declared in terms "well-nigh conclusive.". . .

In the court below, the plaintiffs-appellants challenged the necessity for the taking of the land for the proposed project. In this regard the city presented substantial evidence of the severe economic conditions facing the residents of the city and state, the need for new industrial development to revitalize local industries, the economic boost the proposed project would provide, and the lack of other adequate available sites to implement the project. . . .

In the instant case the benefit to be received by the municipality invoking the power of eminent domain is a clear and significant one and is sufficient to satisfy this Court that such a project was an intended and a legitimate object of the Legislature when it allowed municipalities to exercise condemnation powers even though a private party will also, ultimately, receive a benefit as an incident thereto.

The power of eminent domain is to be used in this instance primarily to accomplish the essential public purposes of alleviating unemployment and revitalizing the economic base of the community. The benefit to a private interest is merely incidental.

Our determination that this project falls within the public purpose, as stated by the Legislature, does not mean that every condemnation proposed by an economic development corporation will meet with similar acceptance simply because it may provide some jobs or add to the industrial or commercial base. If the public benefit was not so clear and significant, we would hesitate to sanction approval of such a project. The power of eminent domain is restricted to furthering public uses and purposes and is not to be exercised without substantial proof that the public is primarily to be benefited. Where, as here, the condemnation power is exercised in a way that benefits specific and identifiable private interests, a court inspects with heightened scrutiny the claim that the public interest is the predominant interest being advanced. Such public benefit cannot be speculative or marginal but must be clear and significant if it is to be within the legitimate purpose as stated by the Legislature. We hold this project is warranted on the basis that its significance for the people of Detroit and the state has been demonstrated.

Plaintiff's complaint also alleged that the proposed project violates the Michigan Environmental Protection Act (MEPA), M.C.L. Section 691.1201 et seq; M.S.A. Section 14.528(201) et seq, because it "will have a major adverse impact on the adjoining social and cultural environment which is referred to as Poletown". The trial court dismissed this claim, stating that " 'social and cultural environments' are matters not within the purview of the MEPA and outside its legislative intent". We agree.

Questions

1. If the government changes the character of an area, as is alleged in *Poletown*, are people whose property is not taken, but who are affected by the changes, entitled to compensation?

2. Isn't the language in *Poletown* so broad that it enables the government to take any property and give it to someone else as long as there would be a marginal benefit to the community? Can you think of any takings to which it would not apply?

SUMMARY

Generally, the transfer of an interest in real property may occur (1) by contract or deed during the lifetime of the owner, (2) upon death, by will or intestate succession, (3) by adverse possession, (4) by provisions of the title, as in the case of a life estate or a determinable fee, or (5) by encumbrance, such as by mortgage or even by governmental action. When it is by contract or deed, it is presumed that the seller will convey *marketable title* unless it is agreed to the contrary. A marketable title is one that would be acceptable to a reasonably prudent buyer familiar with the surrounding facts and circumstances.

A land contract is similar to other contracts except that it involves the title to land. The general requirements for all simple contracts must be met, although unlike most other contracts, a land contract generally is subject to specific performance in the event that the seller seeks to breach the agreement.

A deed is an instrument by which the title to real property ordinarily is transferred. It may be a bare transfer of whatever rights are possessed by the grantor, with no promise that she had anything to transfer. Such a deed is called a *quitclaim* deed. It also may carry warranties (contractual promises) to any extent agreeable to the parties. These deeds are called warranty deeds and may be *general* (relating to the title absolutely) or *special* (concerning only matters that have occurred since the grantor took title). Every deed must conform to certain statutory requirements, specified in the statutes of each state, in order to be valid.

A mortgage is an instrument by which the title to property is encumbered by a security interest, usually to secure the repayment of a loan. It generally is made up of a promissory note, an instrument of transfer of title, and a provision for the retransfer of title upon payment of the obligation. As is the case with land contracts and deeds, it is wise to record mortgages on a public record in the county in which the subject property is located. By doing so, the public is put on notice of the interest so that it ordinarily cannot be defeated by a subsequent transfer of the property.

Adverse possession is a means of acquiring title to real estate. The law provides that if a stranger to the title takes possession of property, and that possession is actual, open and notorious, hostile to the owner's title, and continuous for a specified statutory period, the possessor will acquire the owner's title. A comparable rule of prescriptive rights can give someone the right to use, as opposed to possess, the property of another under similar circumstances.

In addition to these various transfers, the use of property may be restricted, or title even may be taken, by other private or public means. These include restrictive covenants, zoning laws, and eminent domain.

KEY TERMS AND CONCEPTS

encumbrance
marketable title
quiet title action
land contract
enfeoffment
deed
quitclaim
warranty deed
general warranty deed
special warranty deed
mortgage
foreclosure
right of redemption
adverse possession
tacking
color of title
prescriptive easement
laches
restrictive covenant
zoning
nonconforming use
variance
eminent domain
condemnation

PROBLEMS

1. Allen lived in a subdivision in which a plat restriction, referenced in all deeds, prohibited

"commercial establishments." Allen sued to enjoin Forbes, a neighbor, from operating his worm farm at his home. The "farm" was constructed using several layers of wooden trays, which Forbes kept behind his house. They were visible from the street and, particularly, from Allen's back windows. Forbes contended the property owners had waived the restriction by allowing five other commercial establishments, such as a gun shop, to operate in the area. Is Forbes entitled to continue his use?

2.   Goldthorp sold land to Morris. The contract did not specify the type of deed that would be used, but when Goldthorp tendered a quitclaim, Morris objected, contending it was "normal" that a warranty deed be used. Is Goldthorp required to deliver a warranty deed?

3.   Dundas purchased land from Foster on a land contract. She fell behind in payments. In order to get out of financial difficulty, she accepted a lease from Foster. Later, when an oil company became interested in the land, Dundas sued Foster to require him to give back the land contract. Dundas contended that the parties had agreed orally that the lease was "only temporary." Is Dundas entitled to relief?

4.   Moroz tried to record a deed in New York, but the clerk of the court refused to accept it for recording because material portions were written in Polish. Did the clerk err?

5.   Beginning in 1957, the Gerwitzes owned and resided on lot #24 of the Belleville Tract. Shortly thereafter, they began to use the adjacent vacant lot #25. At various times they planted grass seed, flowers, and shrubs on the land and used it for picnics and cookouts. They knew the lot did not belong to them, and they did not pay taxes on it. When the lot was purchased by Gelsomin in 1978, and he constructed a foundation on it for the purpose of moving a house there, Gerwitz sued to quiet title, claiming title by adverse possession. Is Gerwitz entitled to the relief?

6.   Ethel Nivens purchased a home for her sister, Carrie Johnson, because Carrie was pregnant and could not afford a home for herself. The arrangement was that Ethel was to advance the money for the home as a loan. Carrie took title, and immediately executed and delivered a deed back to Ethel, but the deed was never recorded. When Carrie died, her daughter Karen Johnson claimed title to the property as Carrie's only heir. In view of the unrecorded deed, to whom does the property now belong?

7.   Barrows purchased a home near a lake. It was located on a dirt road leading back from a highway. At the time of transfer, he purchased a title insurance policy insuring against, among other things, "lack of right of access." When spring came, he found the road flooded. Upon inquiring, he learned that it was flooded each spring and fall by high water, and access to his house would be cut off for a period of two to three months each year. Barrows sought to recover from the insurance company. Is he entitled to payment?

8.   John and Lottie Wondering executed a deed to their home, naming two of their grandchildren, Lois Haasjes and Dorothy Miles, as grantees. The deed was never delivered, but was kept by the Wonderings, who continued to live in the house, pay the taxes, and otherwise acted as owners. Lottie died first, and when John died, he left the property to his son, John, in his will. Haasjes and Miles sued to quiet title. Are they entitled to relief?

9.   Nash sold certain land to Mills. The deed contained the standard warranties and provided that it was "subject to deed restrictions and easements of record." After taking possession, Nash determined that a ditch across the property, used by a neighbor for the discharge of waste water from a manufacturing process, could not be filled in because the neighbor had acquired a prescriptive easement by continued use. Mills sought to recover from Nash for breach of his warranty

against encumbrances. Nash defended on the ground that since the ditch was apparent on the property at the time of transfer, the warranty was not breached. Is Nash correct?

10. Mowris sold a portion of her farm to Gravin, reserving in the deed a right to use a dirt road across the parcel for the purpose of ingress and egress to and from an adjoining river. She used the road very seldom—only when she went to the river to fish. Graven then sold the land to Piper, the deed making no mention of the use reserved by Mowris. Piper plowed up the road to plant crops. When Mowris learned of this, she objected, and Piper sued to prevent further use of the former road by Mowris, contending he had no knowledge of the use. Is Piper entitled to relief?

Intellectual Property
and Computers

INTRODUCTION

Intellectual property is a catch-all phrase that encompasses the four legal areas of patents, trademarks, copyrights, and trade secrets. These sub-jects all involve a highly abstract concept of property. The "property" of intellectual property is not in a concrete and tangible form that charac-terizes real property, for instance. It has been said, with respect to tort law and the ease with which students grasp its basics, that anyone can recog-nize a punch in the nose. Unlike a punch in the nose, though, the basic concepts of intellectual property are more like the invisible beams of Buck Rogers's ray gun. This abstract quality has led some to describe intellectual property as part of "the metaphysics of the law."

Despite its abstract quality, however, intellec-tual property is familiar to all of us. The trade-mark, for instance, is even more commonplace, it is hoped, than a punch in the nose. We all have seen *Xerox* machines, *Kodak* cameras, and *Rolls Royce* cars, as well as the ads that manufacturers place periodically to reinforce the strength of their marks. We have used aspirin, which once was a trademark but is no longer. Likewise, even though most people have not seen a patent document, we all have seen, used, and benefited from patented items, processes, combinations, and the like. We have seen and used copyrighted materials such as music, motion pictures, and books (including this one) and have enjoyed many of them. Without patented and copyrighted items, our lives would be quite different. The richness they bring to us is one of the justifications for the protection the law gives them (although one always should remember that copyright protection was not necessary to inspire Shakespeare to write, nor was the patent system necessary to encourage the inventor of the wheel).

This chapter explains the basic framework of each of the four areas of intellectual property and the differences among them. It then discusses the special problems that computer programs and data bases pose for traditional legal concepts. Finally, it touches briefly on some other contexts in which the computer revolution has raised new and important legal questions.

PATENTS

A **patent** is a monopoly granted by the federal government. During the life of the patent, the owner has the exclusive right to determine who, if anyone, will be permitted to use, make, or sell the patented item. The authority for the government to grant this unusual privilege stems from the Constitution, which gives Congress the power "To promote the Progress of . . . the useful Arts by securing for limited Times to . . . Inventors the exclusive Right to their . . . Discoveries." In theory, then, a patent is a simple reward or inducement to inventors for the benefit of society.

But the theory behind the constitutional provision, as well as the federal Patent Act, has a tension between its two halves. Normally, we associate the "Progress of the useful Arts" (science, technology, and knowledge in general) with the free flow of ideas and competition in the marketplace. Patent law, however, promotes this progress by granting to inventors "exclusive rights" or monopolies that often prevent the free use of ideas and inhibit competition. Some critics of the patent system point out that many of history's greatest inventions were created without patent protection at all—the printing press, early explosives, and the wheel, to name a few. Many patents are produced under government contracts with no absolute assurance of eventual exclusive rights. The atomic bomb and Einstein's work were produced without patent incentives, and Benjamin Franklin donated all of his inventive works to the public without ever attempting to patent them.

On the other hand, commentators have amassed data seeming to support the proposition that the American patent system has been extremely successful in furnishing the incentive to invent. Countries having less-developed and less-sophisticated patent systems do not appear as successful in producing the number of patentable inventions as the United States. Patents as a system of rewards for inventiveness also seem to be supported by common sense and the theory of the free-enterprise system.

These opposing impulses, which will reappear throughout this chapter's consideration of intellectual property, never can be reconciled completely. As a result, the Patent Act strikes several compromises. It grants a powerful monopoly to the owner of a patent, but strictly limits the items that may be patented. In addition, it compels the owner, as a condition for receiving the patent, to make public certain information about the invention. Finally, the life of the patent is kept comparatively short—it is currently seventeen years.

THE PATENT ACT

The Patent Act limits what inventions are entitled to patent protection. Certain important requirements must be met to obtain a patent.

The Subject Matter of Patents

According to the United States Patent Act, to be patentable an invention must be a new and useful "(1) process, (2) machine, (3) manufacture, or (4) composition of matter, or any new and useful improvement thereof." Those four categories exhaust the possible things for which a patent may be obtained.

A **process** may be defined as a means to an end. The remaining three categories (machine, manufacture, or composition of matter) may be defined as ends in themselves—"products." Thus, there are essentially only two categories of patentable subject matter: processes and products. Products are physical entities—**machines,** perhaps, are the most obvious of the three. **Manufactures** are any fabricated products that otherwise satisfy the requirements of patentability. Finally, a **composition of matter** describes what most people imagine to be the goal of the typical laboratory inventor, since it usually is a new chemical formulation, although it can be any composition of materials, not limited solely to chemicals.

Processes are more intangible and difficult to define than products. In a sense, they are a way of getting somewhere else from where one starts, and they may be either a way of getting to something inventive or they may be an inventive way of getting to something already known. A typical process it the chemical one, which produces a compound through a series of steps that may be embodied in a particular machine, in which case both the process and the machine may be patentable, although that is not always true.

In addition to the four categories of patentable subject matter, the statute also permits a patent to issue on "any new and useful improvement" on a process, machine, manufacture, or composition—a better light bulb or chemical composition, for example. Obviously, though, an improvement still must fit in one of the four categories before it can be a new and useful improvement thereof.

To be patentable, an invention fitting one of the four categories also must meet three explicit conditions: It must be "novel," "useful," and "non-obvious" to people skilled in the field of knowledge or technology in which it is applied. The first two of these conditions are relatively straightforward. **Novelty** means that the invention must be something new. An invention that already has been patented, that already is in public use, or that has been described in detail in publications is not "novel" and cannot be patented. **Usefulness** requires that the invention have some specific, beneficial utility. That use may be trivial, but it must be real, not speculative. The requirement of usefulness serves two purposes. First, it prevents open-ended patent claims from monopolizing entire fields of knowledge and, second, it furthers the basic incentive goal of patent law by rewarding only those inventions that actually increase the fund of practical knowledge.

The third consideration, **non-obviousness,** is a more slippery concept than novelty or utility. In a sense, it is related to novelty, but it is distinctively different. An invention may not have been developed before a certain date. It is, at that point in time, new; it has novelty. However, just because it never *actually* was invented before does not mean it could not have been done. It is possible that someone skilled in the relevant field of technology and familiar with its subject matter could have invented it with comparative ease had he or she tried; such an "invention" would be novel but obvious to that person, and therefore not patentable.

The reason for requiring non-obviousness is to distinguish between pedestrian advances that would be disclosed naturally without patent protection because they are easily accessible to the ordinary mechanic, and true inventions that would be disclosed only in return for patent protection. The distinction is somewhat metaphysical, but is an important part of the compromise between free competition and the monopoly power of patents. In order to protect free competition as much as possible, the person applying for a patent has a heavy burden to prove non-obviousness. As the Supreme Court has said: "He who would build a better mousetrap today has a long path to tread before reaching the Patent Office."

It is necessary to go beyond saying that a product or process may qualify for patent protection, however, because there is a negative and prohibitive aspect to the definition of patentability—ideas are not patentable. If a claimed invention too closely resembles the broad prohibited category of an abstract idea, rather than what accurately could be described as a product or process, it is not patentable.

Although mere ideas are ineligible subject matter, the application of an idea is not. In fact, it is the distinction between the idea and its application that defines the area of patentability. Mere novelty, utility, and non-obviousness is not enough to gain protection for an idea. All of the specified patentable categories are at lease one step beyond the mere idea stage. For instance, Einstein's formula $E = MC^2$ is a mere idea. It is not a particular concrete application of the principle of atomic energy, but the very idea itself. A particular atomic power plant, a method of measuring atomic energy, or countless other applications based on this idea might well be patentable, but the bare idea lies outside the scope of patentable subject matter. In other words, to be patentable, an inventive idea must be reduced to an applied form.

Obtaining a Patent

To obtain a patent someone must demonstrate that he or she has developed a new, useful, and non-obvious product or process. This demonstration is made through the patent application, which contains a "specification" describing how the invention works. A second part of the patent application consists of "claims," under the preceding specification. They are the actual patentable features of the invention. The claims are the asserted new, useful, non-obvious advances beyond the prior state of the art that are embodied in the invention. The relation between the specification and the claims is that the claims point out what it is that is patentable about the specification.

Patent applications are public documents, thereby disclosing to everyone information about new inventions. The goal of disclosure is served by the requirement that the specification contain a complete description of the new invention, revealing how it works and how to reproduce it. This effectively discloses all advances in an art to those who practice it.

The patent application is submitted to the Patent Office. No monopoly right in an invention exists until a patent actually is issued by the Patent Office. (There may be other rights created by state common law protecting an invention prior to the grant of a patent application, however, such as the law of trade secrets or unfair competition.) The Patent Office examines the application and conducts a search of past patents and of relevant technical literature to ascertain whether the claims actually are new, useful, and non-obvious. The Patent Office examiner frequently denies patentability to some, or perhaps all, of the claims, and the application then may be revised to meet the examiner's objections. Sometimes, the application is resubmitted with an explanation of why the examiner was mistaken.

Frequently, this process goes back and forth several times until the patentee and the examiner are in agreement. The file of the patent application can become extraordinarily voluminous, and much time and money may be expended.

During the life of a patent, the owner has the complete right to determine who, if anyone, will have the right to use, make, or sell the patented item and, to a more limited extent, how or where it will be exploited initially. It is important to understand that American law does not require

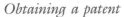

Obtaining a patent

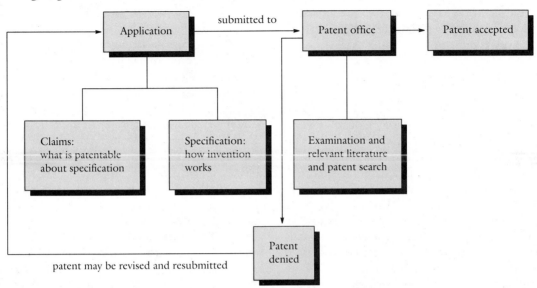

the patentee to put the patent into use or to allow others to do so. The first requirement, of putting the device to use, is called "working" the patent, a requirement with some historical meaning and of considerable foreign patent law significance. The second requirement, of allowing others to use the patent, is called "compulsory licensing." Like working an invention, there is no absolute American requirement of compulsory licensing, but other aspects of the law, especially antitrust, may have the effect of obliging a patent owner to license others to use the patent.

Although the patent owner is not required either to work the patent or allow others to do so, he or she normally will find it counterproductive not to put the patent to use. Moreover, from a societal point of view, the exclusive right is supposed to be the incentive that the patent system offers the new patent owner to exploit the invention and make its benefits available to the public.

The patentee has different ways of using the patent, either himself or by allowing others to do so. The patentee can sell the patent outright by

assigning all the rights to it, or may license others to use it, either exclusively, by allowing only one other person to use the item and promising not to let others do so, or nonexclusively, by granting patent rights to a variety of persons. The patentee also has the right under the Patent Act to grant the patent privilege, through licensing or otherwise, on a geographic basis. But there are antitrust implications in geographically limited licenses, and in order to avoid committing an antitrust violation a patentee must not exceed the rights granted by the Patent Act.

A patent owner may sue anyone she believes has been using part or all of the patent without authorization. If successful, she can recover damages and secure an injunction against further infringement. It is a valid defense to a charge of infringement to show that the grant of a patent somehow was unwarranted. The defendant must prove that the Patent Office was mistaken by establishing that the owner's patent does not possess the required amount of novelty, utility, and non-obviousness. A challenge alternatively can be based on some inequitable conduct by the patentee before or after the patent grant, such as the use of the invention in a way that violates antitrust laws. Alleged infringers have been quite successful in attacking patents, and some federal courts have found more patents invalid than valid.

COPYRIGHTS

Copyrights, like patents, involve a form of limited monopoly granted by the federal government. In fact, both stem from the same provision of the Constitution, which, in addition to authorizing Congress to establish a patent system, authorizes Congress "to promote the Progress of" authors by giving them "the exclusive Right to their Writings" for "limited times." Because of this common origin, copyrights are subject to the same theoretical criticisms and defenses discussed earlier in connection with patents.

Despite this common origin, however, copyright law differs from patent law in four significant respects. First, copyright protects only "writings," not products or processes. Second, copyrights are far easier to obtain than patents. Third, copyright protection is less comprehensive than the patent monopoly, and fourth, a copyright lasts much longer than a patent.

Writings

The "writings" protectable under copyright law include many things. The Copyright Act defines **writings** as all "original works of authorship fixed in any tangible medium of expression, now known or later developed, from which they can be perceived, reproduced, or otherwise communicated, either directly or with the aid of a machine or device." The act then lists seven categories of copyrightable materials including: (1) literary works; (2) musical works; (3) dramatic works; (4) pantomimes and choreographic works; (5) pictorial, graphic, and sculptural works; (6) motion pictures and other audiovisual works; and (7) sound recordings. Although useful as a guide, this list does not exhaust the universe of copyrightable

material. Instead, the boundaries of copyright are defined by the double-barrelled concept of "original works of authorship fixed in any tangible medium of expression."

The requirement of fixation in a "tangible medium of expression" is not hard to meet. Nevertheless, it does mean that a speech, a casual conversation, or an improvised jazz performance is not copyrightable unless it either is written down or recorded on tape or film. If it is not somehow "fixed" in some tangible medium of expression, it evaporates into the air and is ineligible for copyright.

"Originality" is a more subtle concept. It is the essence of copyright, and requires that the copyright owner or claimant "originated" the work. By contrast to a patent, however, a copyrightable **original work** need not be novel. An author can claim copyright in a work as long as he created it himself, even if a thousand people created it before him. Originality does not imply novelty; it only implies that the copyright claimant did not take it from someone else. From that definition of originality comes the common but true example that an author could gain a copyright on his text of the *Romeo and Juliet* story as long as he made it up himself and did not copy it from Shakespeare. That copyright would prevent anyone else from copying the work of the copyright owner (but it would not prevent others from copying Shakespeare's creation, since that is in the public domain).

Two other concepts form the remaining boundaries of copyright law—utilitarian objects and ideas are non-copyrightable. With respect to utilitarian objects, an exception is made for those portions of the work that are nonutilitarian and *separable* from the utilitarian object. This exception, however, is rather narrow and at time bewildering. For example, a floral relief pattern on silver flatware can be copyrighted, but the graceful shaping of the flatware itself cannot. Similarly, a statuette of a dancer can by copyrighted, but a lamp in which it serves as a base cannot.

One reason the courts are unwilling to grant

copyright protection to purely utilitarian works is that patent protection is reserved to works of utility. Because copyright protection lasts longer than patent protection, and also because copyright protection is granted upon fixation and is subject only to a very minimal showing of originality as opposed to the rigorous demonstration of novelty, non-obviousness, and utility required for patent protection, courts attempt to keep the borders between copyright and patent well defined and clear. Thus, to allow copyright protection for a utilitarian object would allow monopoly control over something that more appropriately might be subject to the very different protection of patent law.

A similar argument is posed by the question of whether forms, systems, contest blanks, tests, and similar items are copyrightable. Once again, a basic copyright concept is at work. The federal courts and the current Copyright Act have made it clear that copyright is reserved for the *expression* of an idea; it does not extend to the *idea* itself. For instance, in 1879, the copyrightability of an accounting system was at issue. The Supreme Court held, in *Baker v. Selden,* that since the defendant's account books were arranged differently than those of the original author, it was not an infringement to use the principles or ideas of double-entry bookkeeping expounded by the original author in his book. The Court emphasized the difference between the "art," or subject matter of the book, and the "description" of the art, or its

Copyright registration (1986)

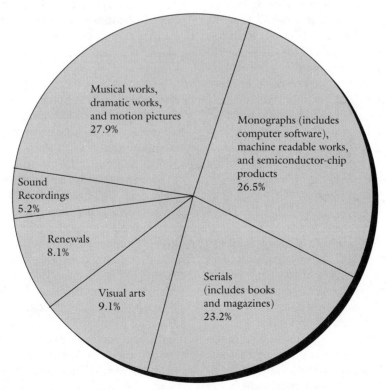

Musical works, dramatic works, and motion pictures
27.9%

Monographs (includes computer software), machine readable works, and semiconductor-chip products
26.5%

Sound Recordings
5.2%

Renewals
8.1%

Visual arts
9.1%

Serials (includes books and magazines)
23.2%

Source: Statistical Abstract of the United States (1988), Table 895.

expression. The idea underlying the system of accounting was not copyrightable, although the expression was. Thus, if there had been literal copying of the original author's forms of account, it would have been infringement. Since the defendant had arranged his account books differently, all that had been taken from the author was the idea, or the "art," which is not protectable under copyright.

Naturally, the more basic issue involved in this venerable case is the copyrightability of ideas. Since everyone is free to borrow an idea, there is very little protection available to the original author of an accounting system or business method or commercial plan, except the copyright law's prohibition against copying the original explanation of the system. As a result, numerous valuable works have very little protection other than against literal copying of the expression itself. In 1958, a court held that insurance forms and instruments are copyrightable, but found that the scope of protection of forms varies according to the degree of variation inherently available to potential competitors. In other words, to the extent that the ideas in a form can be expressed in many different ways, an original author will be protected against copying. However, as the form becomes more simple and the possibilities of expressing the underlying idea in different ways become fewer, only a strictly literal reproduction would constitute infringement, if at all.

Obtaining a Copyright

Coypright protection is automatic. It attaches to any original work of authorship at the moment the work is fixed in a tangible form of expression. Thus, as an author's pen moves across the page, or the painter's brush touches the canvas, or the student writes her paper, their works are protected instantly. Unlike patents, no official examination and certification takes place. With some minor exception, however, protection will not be complete unless the originator marks the work with the universal symbol ©(℗ in the case of sound recordings), his or her name, and the date of first publication (dissemination) of the copyrighted material. This is required so that others who see, read, or hear the work will know that it is protected by copyright and is not in the public domain. Once the work is published, each copy must bear the copyright notice; otherwise, the owner may lose his or her protection.

A procedure exists for registering copyrights with the U.S. Copyright Office in Washingtion, D.C. The person seeking registration fills out a simple application, sends a copy of the work, and pays a small fee, currently ten dollars. Strictly speaking, this procedure is not necessary for obtaining copyright protection. However, certain benefits are available to people who deposit their work and register. Primarily, registration is a prerequisite for an owner to sue someone else under the act for infringing a copyright. Also a successful plaintiff who has complied with the formalities is entitled to reasonable attorney fees.

What Copyright Protects

The federal copyright statute grants the owner of a copyright five exclusive rights: (1) to reproduce the work; (2) to make derivative works; (3) to distribute the work; (4) to perform the work in public; and (5) to display the work publicly.

The reproduction right, or the right to produce copies, is the most basic. The right protects against verbatim copying and against paraphrasing, but it prohibits only actual use of the copyright owner's work as a model, either directly or indirectly; it does not cover coincidental similarities in a work created independently and without reference to the first. High degrees of noninfringing similarity occur most commonly in works of nonfiction as opposed to more creative writing or poetry. Thus, for example, if two historians research the same event and describe it the same way, yet do not consult each other's works, neither infringes the other, regardless of how similar their final products are. Neither can monopolize historial events or facts. But if we were discussing patents, the result would be opposite. A patent owner is protected absolutely against a competitor putting a similar product or process on the market, even if the second person did not copy from the original patent.

Although our two historians may not copy each other's expression or particular manner of presenting the facts or ideas, they are free to borrow facts and ideas from each other's works only as long as they set out these facts and ideas in their own words. This is because of the idea/expression dichotomy noted earlier, which prohibits copyrighting of ideas. In addition, our historians are protected only against "substantial and material" copying. However, no set rule or formula can determine how much copying is substantial and material. Even an important small extract from a larger work may be substantial and material, depending on the nature of the copyrighted work and of the portion copied.

The right to make derivative works safeguards a copyright owner from what otherwise might be an unduly narrow interpretation of the reproduction right, which then could permit another to vary elements of the work sufficiently to assert that it is not actually a copy. The right thus protects the owner against others creating works based on her own. The statutory definition of a "derivative work" includes such things as translations, arrangements, dramatizations, fictionalizations, film, recordings, abridgments, condensations, "or any other form in which a work may be recast, transformed, or adapted." Thus, only the copyright owner of a book has the right to prepare or to license the preparation of a motion picture, play, musical, television show, or any work based on the book.

The right of distribution assures the copyright owner that, until she parts with ownership, she has the right to prohibit all others from distributing the work. On the other hand, once a sale of a copyrighted work has occurred, the new owner is allowed to treat the object as his own. Thus, when a copyright owner sells a copy of his protected book, it is not a violation of copyright for the buyer to resell the book to another, even if the copyright owner had conditioned the sale upon a promise of no resales. The buyer, of course, may not reproduce the work or convey the right to do so because he doesn't have it. The distribution right only secures to the copyright owner the right to control the first transfer of a copy of the work.

The rights of public performance and display are of great importance to dramatic, musical, and audiovisual works. This last category includes both conventional works such as motion pictures and works in new media such as computer-generated video games. The display right also covers pictorial, graphic, and sculptural works, although the copyright proprietor may not prevent the owner of a particular copy (including the original) from displaying it in a museum, art gallery, or other public place. The copyright proprietor, however, may prevent the owner of a particular copy from making further copies and displaying these. The statute defines a public performance or display as one presented at a place open to the public or where a substantial number of persons outside of a normal circle of a family or its social acquaintances is gathered, or as one presented by a transmission, such as a radio or television broadcast.

Duration

Copyright protection lasts for the life of the author plus 50 years. However, if the work was made "for hire" so that the copyright is owned by an employer instead of the author, the copyright expires after a fixed number of years—75 years after publication or 100 years after creation, whichever occurs first. In the case of anonymous or pseudonymous works, the same 75/100-year scheme applies. As you can see, the duration of copyright protection is substantially longer than patent protection.

HARPER & ROW, PUBLISHERS, INC. v. NATION ENTERPRISES
471 U.S. 539, 105 S.Ct. 2218, 85 L.Ed.2d 588 (1985)

In February 1977, shortly after leaving the White House, former President Gerald R. Ford contracted with Harper & Row and The Reader's Digest (Petitioners) to publish his as yet unwritten memoirs. The memoirs were to contain "significant hitherto unpublished material" concerning the Watergate crisis, Mr. Ford's pardon of former President Nixon, and "Mr. Ford's reflections on this period of history, and the morality and personalities involved." The agreement gave Petitioners the exclusive right to license prepublication excerpts, known in the trade as "first serial rights." Two years later, as the memoirs—*A Time to Heal: The Autobiography of Gerald R. Ford*—were nearing completion, Petitioners negotiated a prepublication licensing agreement with *Time*, a weekly news magazine. *Time* agreed to pay $25,000, $12,500 in advance and an additional $12,500 at publication, in exchange for the right to excerpt 7500 words from Mr. Ford's account of the Nixon pardon. The issue featuring the excerpts was timed to appear approximately one week before shipment of the full-length book version to bookstores. Exclusivity was an important consideration; Harper & Row instituted procedures designed to maintain the confidentiality of the manuscript, and *Time* retained the right to renegotiate the second payment should the material appear in print prior to its release of the excerpts.

Two to three weeks before the *Time* article's scheduled release, an unidentified person secretly brought a copy of the Ford manuscript to Victor Navasky, editor of *The Nation*, a political commentary magazine (Respondent). Mr. Navasky knew that his possession of the manuscript was not authorized. He hastily put together what he believed was "a real hot news story" composed of quotes, paraphrases, and facts drawn exclusively from the manuscript. Mr. Navasky attempted no independent commentary, research, or criticism, in part because of the need for speed if he was to "make news" by publishing in advance of publication of the Ford book. The 2250 word article, entitled "The Ford Memoirs—Behind the Nixon Pardon," appeared on April 3, 1979. As a result of *The Nation's* article, *Time* canceled its piece and refused to pay the remaining $12,500.

Petitioners brought a successful copyright action against *The Nation*. On appeal, the Second Circuit reversed the lower court's finding of infringement, holding that *The Nation's* act was sanctioned as a "fair use" of the copyrighted material. Harper and Row appealed to the United States Supreme Court. Reversed and remanded.

O'CONNOR, Justice.

We agree with the Court of Appeals that copyright is intended to increase and not to impede the harvest of knowledge. But we believe the Second Circuit gave insufficient deference to the scheme established by the Copyright Act for fostering the original works that provide the seed and substance of this harvest. The rights conferred by copyright are designed to assure contributors to the store of knowledge a fair return for their labors. . . .

. . . The book at issue here, for example, was two years in the making, and began with a contract giving the author's copyright to the publishers in exchange for their services in producing and marketing the work. In preparing the book Mr. Ford drafted essays and word portraits of public figures and participated in hundreds of tapes interviews that were later distilled to chronicle his personal viewpoint. It is evident that the monopoly granted by copyright actively served its intended purpose of inducing the creation of new material of potential historical value.

Section 106 of the Copyright Act confers a bundle of exclusive rights to the owner of the copyright. Under the Copyright Act, these rights—to publish, copy, and distribute the author's work—vest in the author of an original work from the time of its creation. In practice, the author commonly sells his rights to publishers who offer royalties in exchange for their services in producing and marketing the author's work. The copyright owner's rights, however, are subject to certain statutory exceptions. Among these is § 107 which codifies the traditional privilege of others to make "fair use" of an earlier writer's work. In addition, no author may copyright facts or ideas. The copyright is limited to those aspects of the work—termed "expression"—that display the stamp of the author's originality.

. . . [T]here is no dispute that the unpublished manuscript of "A Time to Heal," as a whole, was protected by § 106 from unauthorized reproduction. Nor do respondents dispute that verbatim copying of excerpts of the manuscript's original form of expression would constitute infringement unless excused as fair use. . . . Yet copyright does not prevent subsequent users from copying from a prior author's work those constituent elements that are not original—for example, quotations borrowed under the rubric of fair use from other copyrighted works, facts, or materials in the public domain—as long as such use does not unfairly appropriate the author's original contributions. . . .

. . . The Nation has admitted to lifting verbatim quotes of the author's original language totalling between 300 and 400 words and constituting some 13% of The Nation article. In using generous verbatim excerpts of Mr. Ford's unpublished manuscript to lend authenticity to its account of the forthcoming memoirs, The Nation effectively arrogated to itself the right of first publication, an important marketable subsidiary right. For the reasons set forth below, we find that this use of the copyrighted manuscript, even stripped to the verbatim quotes conceded by The Nation to be copyrightable expression, was not a fair use within the meaning of the Copyright Act.

Though the right of first publication, like the other rights enumerated in § 106 is expressly made subject to the fair use provision of § 107, fair use analysis must always be tailored to the individual case. . . . The nature of the interest at stake is highly relevant to whether a given use is fair. . . . The right of first publication implicates a threshold decision by the author whether and in what form to release his work. First publication is inherently different from other § 106 rights in that only one person can be the first publisher; as the contract with Time illustrates, the commercial value of the right lies primarily in exclusivity. Because the potential damage to the author from judicially enforced "sharing" of the first publication right with unauthorized users of his manuscript is substantial, the balance of equities in evaluating such a claim of fair use inevitably shifts.

. . . The obvious benefit to author and public alike of assuring authors the leisure to develop their ideas free from fear of expropriation outweighs any short term "news value" to be gained from premature publication of the author's expression. . . . The author's control of first public distribution implicates not only his personal interest in creative control but his property interest in exploitation of prepublication rights, which are valuable in themselves and serve as a valuable adjunct to publicity and marketing. . . . Under ordinary circumstances, the author's right to control the first public appearance of his undisseminated expression will outweigh a claim of fair use.

Respondents, however, contend that First Amendment values require a different rule under the circumstances of this case. The thrust of the decision below is that "[t]he scope of [fair use] is undoubtedly wider when the information conveyed relates to matters of high public concern." . . . Respondents advance the substantial public import of the subject matter of the Ford memoirs as grounds for excusing a use that would ordinarily not pass muster as a fair use—the piracy of verbatim quotations for the purpose of "scooping" the authorized first serialization. Respondents explain their copying of Mr. Ford's expression as essential to reporting the news story it claims the book itself represents. . . . Respondents argue that the public's interest in learning this news as fast as possible outweighs the right of the author to control its first publication.

The Second Circuit noted, correctly, that copyright's idea/expression dichotomy "strike[s] a definitional balance between the First Amendment and the Copyright Act by permitting free communication of facts while still protecting an author's expression." No author may copyright his ideas or the facts he narrates. . . . As this Court long ago observed: "[T]he news element—the information respecting current events contained in the literary production—is not the creation of the writer, but is a report of matters that ordinarily are *publici juris;* it is the history of the day." International News Service v. Associated Press, 248 U.S. 215, 234, 39 S.Ct. 68, 70, 63 L.Ed. 211 (1918). But copyright assures those who write and publish factual narratives such as "A Time to Heal" that they may at least enjoy the right to market the original expression contained therein as just compensation for their investment. . . .

Respondents' theory, however, would expand fair use to effectively destroy any expectation of copyright protection in the work of a public figure. Absent such protection, there would be little incentive to create or profit in financing such memoirs and the public would be denied an important source of significant historical information. The promise of copyright would be an empty one if it could be avoided merely by dubbing the infringement a fair use "news report" of the book. . . .

Nor do respondents assert any actual necessity for circumventing the copyright scheme with respect to the types of works and users at issue here. Where an author and publisher have invested extensive resources in creating an original work and are poised to release it to the public, no legitimate aim is served by preempting the right of first publication. The fact that the words the author has chosen to clothe his narrative may of themselves be "newsworthy" is not an independent justification for unauthorized copying of the author's expression prior to publication. . . .

In our haste to disseminate news, it should not be forgotten that the Framers intended copyright itself to be the engine of free expression. By establishing a marketable right to the use of one's expression, copyright supplies the economic incentive to create and disseminate ideas. . . .

It is fundamentally at odds with the scheme of copyright to accord lesser rights in those works that are of greatest importance to the public. Such a notion ignores the major premise of copyright and injures author and public alike. . . .

In view of the First Amendment protections already embodied in the Copyright Act's distinction between copyrightable expression and uncopyrightable facts and ideas, and the latitude for scholarship and comment traditionally afforded by fair use, we see no warrant for expanding the doctrine of fair use to create what amounts to a public figure exception to copyright. Whether verbatim copying from a public figure's manuscript in a given case is or is not fair must be judged according to the traditional equities of fair use. . . .

Questions

1. Since the language taken from President Ford's book only amounted to between 300 and 400 words, what factor led everyone to assume that there had been an infringement if the defense of fair use did not apply?

2. What types of uses of a copyrighted work would fall within the "fair use" doctrine?

TRADEMARKS

Trademarks are symbols used to perform an identification function. Thus a word, name, logo, or design may signify to the public some kind of association between a product or service and a particular source. When most people see the designation "Coke," a product and its source spring to mind.

The law of trademarks serves twin objectives—to protect both producers and consumers in the marketplace. It protects producers by allowing them to prevent competitors from "palming off" their goods as those of the trademark owner. In this sense trademark law is part of the law of unfair competition; it protects trademark owners from losing their markets. Similarly, by preventing palming off, trademark law protects the public

from being confused; it allows consumers to purchase goods without fear of unwittingly buying imitations or knock-offs that may not have the same market value or may be of inferior quality.

Trademarks cannot be claimed simply because someone thinks them up and registers them. A trademark is something that exists only with respect to some other commercial activity. It must identify a businessperson's goods or services, and a businessperson can acquire federal protection for a mark only by first actually using it in the market. A mark meant to identify the origin of goods that identifies neither origin nor goods simply is not a trademark.

Like patents and copyrights, trademarks are governed by a federal statute, known as the Lanham Act, which is essentially a nationwide registration system. The act demands that the applicant demonstrate that the mark is used "in commerce" and "in connection with" products specified in the application; the applicant must specify the date of "first use." The meaning of "first use" is critical, as well, because it assures that actual use preceded registration, and it determines priority so that the first user (as is normally the case) obtains registration.

No specified amount of use in commerce is needed before a trademark may be registered. Indeed, a single sale appears adequate. But more is required to establish a lasting claim to ownership. As an example, a perfume manufacturer owned the registration to the mark SNOB for a perfume that it never made a serious effort to merchandise and sold in only minimal quantities. When a competitor later challenged the trademark, it was found to be invalid because the real purpose of the registration was to reserve the name for future use as part of a "trademark maintenance program."

In addition to being used in commerce, a mark must be "distinctive" in order to qualify for trademark protection. The requirement of distinctiveness is roughly analogous to the requirement of novelty for patent rights and to the requirement of originality for copyright. Without distinctiveness, either based on the inherent nature of the mark or developed by the owner through marketing, trademark rights fail.

Naturally, a trademark must be distinctive if it is to serve the function of identifying the origin of goods and thereby avoid confusion, deception, and mistake. If a trademark is to protect purchasers from confusion over what they are purchasing, the trademark somehow must be recognizable, identifiable, and different from other marks.

A merely generic or descriptive mark is not distinctive. As an obvious example, "apple" would be a descriptive name for that fruit, and as a mark would serve only to confuse the consumer, for it would tell nothing about the different origins of a selection of apples produced by different producers. Moreover, to allow an owner to preempt the term "apple" would afford the owner a monopoly of something that is necessary to describe the goods for sale.

Of course, it is possible that a descriptive term could indicate the origin of goods. For instance, the mark "red" would be descriptive of apples and thus ineligible for trademark appropriation. However, if a producer effectively markets his apples with the term "Red" so that after a while consumers immediately associate the mark "Red" with only one producer of apples, that consumer identification is a sign of secondary meaning. A "Red" apple, under the example, connotes a certain producer, and not color at all. In a sense, this says that a descriptive word may be appropriated as a trademark once it becomes nondescriptive and acquires what the law calls a "secondary meaning" that identifies the source of the goods. That is what has happened to "Sunkist," which identifies a particular cooperative of orange growers.

As trademarks become less descriptive and more fanciful, they become "stronger" and more easily protected. Names like Kodak and 7-Up are good examples. But because the marketplace is the final judge of whether a mark truly is distinctive, even a strong mark may lose its status by becoming descriptive or even generic. History is full of examples. The term *aspirin* was originally a trademark for the Bayer Company's product, but by 1921 it became a generic term for describing a certain class of pain relievers. Similarly, *cellophane* ceased to be a protected trademark in 1936 when it was found that the public had come to identify all plastic wrapping material by that name.

The centrality of the marketplace in determining whether a term truly is distinctive is best illustrated by the phenomenon of "recapture." In 1896 the Supreme Court decided that the symbol "Singer" had lost its distinctiveness as the public came to identify all sewing machines as Singers. However, the company continued to use its name on all its products and, after more than a half century, it succeeded in regaining exclusive rights to the term.

Unlike patents and copyrights, trademarks do not expire after a set number of years. Instead, they continue for as long as their owners use them. As you would guess, then, a trademark can be lost through abandonment or non-use. A trademark generally will be considered abandoned after a period of two years of non-use unless the owner can prove otherwise. The owner of a valid, distinctive trademark can prevent others from using an identical mark in commerce. The owner also can prevent the use of different marks as long as there is a "likelihood" of confusion caused by the different marks. Basically, confusion will stem either from similarity of the marks or similarity of the goods.

A famous example is the "Dramamine" case in which the identical goods—motion-sickness medicine—were marketed under somewhat similar marks, "Dramamine," and "Bonamine." It is possible that the use of the identical mark "Dramamine" on a completely dissimilar and nonrelated product would not give rise to infringement. This certainly is true in the case of nonfanciful names that, unlike an arbitrary mark like "Dramamine," have considerably less strength. Thus, if the motion-sickness pills were named "Steady" pills, it is unlikely that the manufacturer of "Steady" typewriters would be liable for infringement of trademark. There is no likelihood of confusion even with identical marks in completely unrelated markets for unrelated goods or services.

Similarity of goods or services is determined by inquiring whether the products or services are similar in the eyes of the average consumer. From the standpoint of the consumer, goods are similar when they serve the same purposes, relate to the same activities, or fulfill the same needs. For instance, although dog food and dog vitamins are dissimilar in form, appearance, and many other ways, they serve the same purpose of nourishing domestic pets, relate to the activity of caring for

animals, and fulfull the need of maintaining the health of those creatures. When a dog-food manufacturer marketing its product under the mark "Doggie Dinner" opposed the registration of "Dog-E-Diet" as the mark for dog vitamins, it was successful despite the substantial dissimilarity of the marks because of the close similarity of the products.

Whether the average consumer is likely to be confused by similar marks applied to similar products may depend on many other factors. When dealing with impulse buying in a supermarket, for instance, where goods are stocked closely together and the consumer may be relatively inattentive, confusion may be a common phenomenon. When considering purchases of expensive automobiles or highly technical equipment in which the consumers exercise sophisticated judgments, confusion may be almost nonexistent. Quite appropriately, therefore, similarity of goods and similarity of marks are weighed on a scale that is adjusted by considering the character of the market; the scale is recalibrated as the sophistication of the market changes. The "discriminating purchaser" theory frequently is decisive. For instance, in a controversy between a registrant of the mark "Climatrol" for air conditioning equipment and an applicant for the mark "Clime-matic" for identical equipment, the court held that the marks were not confusingly similar, considering the expensive nature of the products and the probable care that purchasers would use in making purchases. Distinctions such as these illustrate the metaphysical quality of intellectual property mentioned at the beginning of the chapter.

TRADE SECRETS

Trade secrecy is a creature of state statute or common law. It differs somewhat from state to state, but is known everywhere. The premise on which **trade secrecy** is based is this: if a business maintains confidentiality concerning either the way in which it does something or some information that it has, courts should protect the business against the misappropriation of that secret. Because secrecy is paramount, it is inappropriate for protecting works that contain the secret and are designed to be distributed widely. Protection is lost when the secret is disclosed, no matter what the circumstances of the disclosure. Because the secret may never be disclosed, the protection theoretically is perpetual. Thus, trade secrecy fundamentally is inconsistent with patents and copyrights, both of which require disclosure of information in return for a limited monopoly. The lack of uniform national law in this area also reduces the utility of this method of protection.

COMPUTERS

Computer technology has revolutionized our lives during the recent past, and undoubtedly will continue to do so. Not surprisingly, it has had a profound effect on our business lives as well. During the last ten to fifteen years, there has been a growing recognition that this new technology will generate many legal problems as the law struggles to keep pace with it. Space permits only the exploration of a few of them.

Computers and Intellectual Property

Computer programs and data bases do not always fit neatly into the traditional categories of intellectual property. For example, for many years there were serious doubts as to the copyrightability of computer programs based on a number of objections, one of them being that a computer program was not a writing as required by the constitution. After all, by itself the program does not communicate anything the way a book, a work of art, or music does. A program's significance is in its operation in conjunction with a machine and, therefore, the argument went, it was part of a utilitarian device and not a writing. Nevertheless, the Copyright Act fully accepts computer programs as copyrightable. The protection is virtually identical to that given other works of authorship, and the scope of protection is governed by the idea/expression dichotomy discussed earlier. One exception, however, is that the purchaser of a program legally may copy the program if it is necessary to do so to operate the program properly or to protect it from accidentally being erased.

COPYRIGHTS. The decision to use copyright as the primary form of protection for programs stemmed from Congress's acceptance of the report of the National Commission on New Technological Uses of Copyrighted Works (CONTU). The commission recognized that the cost of developing computer programs is far greater than the cost of their duplication. Consequently, computer programs are likely to be disseminated only if the creator may spread costs over multiple copies of the work with some form of protection against unauthorized duplication of the work. Since this is a classic objective of copyright law, that mode of protection was chosen by CONTU.

CONTU also recognized that the automated data base represents a new technological form of a type of work long recognized as eligible for copyright. Dictionaries, encyclopedias, and tables of numeric information are all forms of data bases that long antedate the computer and for which copyright protection has been available under federal statute. Adequate legal protection for proprietary rights in extracts from data bases exists under traditional copyright principles, supplemented by relief under common-law principles of unfair competition. The unauthorized taking of substantial segments of a copyrighted data base will be considered an infringement. In addition, some common-law tort principles of misappropriation are available to enforce proprietary rights in these works.

WHELAN ASSOCIATES, INC. v. JASLOW DENTAL LABORATORY, INC.

797 F.2d 1222 (3d Cir. 1986)

Whelan Associates, Inc., a developer of a custom computer program for dental-laboratory record keeping (Plaintiff/Appellee), brought a copyright infringement action against Jaslow Dental Laboratory, Inc., a dental laboratory, for whose benefit the program had been developed, and related parties (Defendants/Appellants), as a result of the development by Jaslow of another program with similar purpose in another computer language and the distribution of both programs. The District Court entered judgment in favor of Whelan, awarding damages for copyright infringement and enjoining the dental laboratory from selling any more copies of the programs. Defendants appealed. Affirmed.

BECKER, Judge.

It is well, though recently, established that copyright protection extends to a program's source and object codes. . . . In this case, however, the district court did not find any copying of the source or object codes, nor did the plaintiff allege such copying. Rather, the district court held that the Dentalab copyright was infringed because the *overall structure* of Dentcom was substantially similar to the overall structure of Dentalab. . . . The question therefore arises whether mere similarity in the overall structure of programs can be the basis for a copyright infringement, or, put differently, whether a program's copyright protection covers the structure of the program or only the program's literal elements, *i.e.,* its source and object codes.

Title 17 U.S.C. § 102(a)(1) extends copyright protection to "literary works," and computer programs are classified as literary works for the purposes of copyright. . . . The copyrights of other literary works can be infringed even when there is no substantial similarity between the works' literal elements. One can violate the copyright of a play or book by copying its plot or plot devices. . . . By analogy to other literary works, it would thus appear that the copyrights of computer programs can be infringed even absent copying of the literal elements of the program. Defendants contend, however, that what is true of other literary works is not true of computer programs. They assert two principal reasons, which we consider in turn.

. . . It is axiomatic that copyright does not protect ideas, but only expressions of ideas. This rule, first enunciated in *Baker v. Selden*, 101 U.S. (11 Otto) 99, 25 L.Ed. 841 (1879), has been repeated in numerous cases. . . . The rule has also been embodied in [the copyright] statute. . . .

Defendants argue that the structure of a computer program is, by definition, the idea and not the expression of the idea, and therefore that the structure cannot be protected by the program copyright. Under the defendants' approach, any other decision would be contrary to § 102(b). . . .

[The court rejected the defendants' argument and established the rule that "the purpose or function of a utilitarian work (like a computer program) would be the work's idea, and everything that is not necessary to that purpose or function would be part of the expression of the idea."]

. . . [A]mong the more significant costs in computer programming are those attributable to developing the structure and logic of the program. The rule proposed here, which allows copyright protection beyond the literal computer code, would provide the proper incentive for programmers by protecting their most valuable efforts, while not giving them a stranglehold over the development of new computer devices that accomplish the same end.

The principal economic argument used against this position—used, that is, in support of the position that programs' literal elements are the only parts of the programs protected by the copyright law—is that computer programs are so intricate, each step so dependent on all of the other steps, that they are almost impossible to copy except literally, and that anyone who attempts to copy the structure of a program without copying its literal elements must expend a tremendous amount of effort and creativity. . . . According to this argument, such work should not be discouraged or penalized. A further argument against our position is not economic but jurisprudential; . . . the concept of structure in computer programs is too vague to be useful in copyright cases. . . .

Neither of the two arguments just described is persuasive. The first argument fails for two reasons. In the first place, it is simply not true that "approximation" of a program short of perfect reproduction is valueless. To the contrary, one can approximate a program and thereby gain a significant advantage over competitors even though additional work is needed to complete the program. Second, the fact that it will take a great deal of effort to copy a copyrighted work does not mean that the copier is not a copyright infringer. The issue in a copyrighted case is simply whether the copyright holder's expression has been copied, not how difficult it was to do the copying. Whether an alleged infringer spent significant time and effort to copy an original work is therefore irrelevant to whether he has pirated the expression of an original work.

As to the second argument, it is surely true that limiting copyright protection to computers' literal codes would be simpler and would yield more definite answers than does our answer here. Ease of application is not, however, a sufficient counterweight to the considerations we have adduced on behalf of our position. . . .

We are not convinced that progress in computer technology or technique is qualitatively different from progress in other areas of science or the arts. In balancing protection and dissemination . . . the copyright law has always recognized and tried to accommodate the fact that all intellectual pioneers build on the work of their predecessors. Thus, copyright principles derived from other areas are applicable in the field of computer programs. . . .

We hold that (1) copyright protection of computer programs may extend beyond the programs' literal code to their structure, sequence, and organization, and (2) the district court's finding of substantial similarity between the Dentalab and Dentcom programs was not clearly erroneous. . . .

Questions

1. Do you think the court's result underprotects or overprotects computer programs?

2. Define a computer program's "structure," "sequence," and "organization."

3. Given the fact that a copyright in a computer program may extend beyond the literal instructions, if your company purchased or produced computer programs, what instructions would you give to the appropriate managers to avoid any possibility that your organization could be charged with copyright infringement?

PATENTS. In certain circumstances, computer program proprietors may find patent protection more attractive than copyright, since it gives them the right not only to license and control the use of their patented devices or processes, but also to prevent the use of such devices or processes when they are developed independently by third parties. The acquisition of a patent, however, is time consuming and expensive. In addition, a program can be protected by a patent only insofar as it is part of a patentable product or process. Otherwise the program would be disqualified as a mathematical formula or idea.

To date, the Patent Office and the courts have rejected most attempts to patent programs, typically because they do not meet the novelty and non-obvious criteria. However, the Supreme Court has approved a patent for a program as part of a process for curing rubber. Prior to this invention the industry was unable to obtain a consistently accurate cure; overcuring and undercuring were typical, caused by the lack of control over the internal temperature of the rubber mold. The inventors developed a method through which the mold temperature could be measured constantly. These measurements then were input into a computer that repeatedly recalculated the cure time. When the recalculated time equaled the actual elapsed time, the computer signaled the mold, which was sealed, to open.

The decision to allow this process to be patented is important because many advances in old technologies will be made possible through the use of computers and algorithms. Although an isolated computer program that is not entwined in a specific process will be labeled a mere method of calculation and, therefore, will not be patentable, an inventor no longer need avoid using a computer in a process for fear that its presence will jeopardize the claim's status as patentable subject matter. The program that stands alone, though not patentable, will remain copyrightable.

TRADEMARKS. Trademark, which protects the name given to a computer program (and sometimes the name of a company, such as Exxon and Xerox when applied to their products) is of course available. It is used widely in the computer software field to prevent misuse of the product name and counterfeiting, particularly for programs that are mass marketed. It also is available to identify the source of particular data bases, as is true of the two national data bases of legal materials that now exist—Westlaw and Lexis. So far, there has been comparatively little litigation in this area.

TRADE SECRETS. Proprietors face several problems in using trade secrecy for protecting computer software. Trade secrecy does not protect against independent discovery or against reverse engineering (buying a washing machine, taking it apart to see how it works, and then building a new and perhaps better one). Because secrecy is paramount, the law of trade secrets is inappropriate for protecting programs or data bases sold in multiple copies over the counter to small businesses, schools, consumers, and hobbyists. On the other hand, trade secrecy may be useful in the case of unique programs and data bases prepared for large commercial customers or made accessible from remote locations on a use or service basis. Such material normally will be leased to the customer, and the lease contract will contain a provision obligating the customer to keep the program and data base secret.

WHO OWNS THE SOFTWARE? Thus far we have not asked the question "Who owns the intellectual property rights in a computer program?" In many situations the answer will be obvious. However, in several others—especially when trade secrecy is the only form of protection—several possibilities exist.

One easy case occurs when a computer user, either an individual or a corporation, writes its own programs. The creator then also owns the programs. Equally simple is the case in which the user buys or leases ready-made programs. These invariably have been copyrighted by the author or producer of the program, who is protected just like an author who sells books in a bookstore. Indeed, if the program is encoded on a Read-Only Memory chip, the copyright owner is further protected by the fact that the program cannot be copied readily from this format.

A tougher case arises when the owner of the computer contracts out for a custom-made program. Whether the purchaser or the producer owns the rights should be negotiated between the parties. If they fail to negotiate, in all probability the producer will own the copyright. Through a contract with the producer, however, the purchaser can acquire the rights either for resale or to prevent immediate competitors from getting access to the same program. If the purchaser negotiates to acquire these rights before the program has been created, the program may be considered a "work for hire" and the copyright will last 75 years from publication or 100 years from creation, whichever comes first. If, on the other hand, the

purchaser acquires the rights to a program already written, the copyright will last for the life of the program's author plus 50 years.

But to say that the producer in some cases owns a program leads to a new question. When the producer is a company rather than an individual, who is the real owner? Is it the company or the individual who authored the program? The rules relating to patents and copyrights, when applicable, answer most disputes of this kind. The employment contract generally will specify whether works produced during work hours are considered to belong to the employer.

Trade secret law, however, is much less clear because the question becomes "what information is an employee free to take when he or she goes to a new company?" Although this question arises in many business contexts, it is particularly acute in the computer industry, which is young, idea-intensive, changing rapidly, and marked by a high degree of employee mobility.

No precise formula determines what information an employee may or may not take to a new job. However, a few generalizations help guide decisions in particular cases. One involves the degree of specificity of the information. Broadly speaking, the more basic and general the information, the greater the employee's freedom to take it when she leaves. This furthers the general policies of preserving incentives for individuals to innovate, promotes competition through the free flow of information and ideas, and protects the freedom of employees to change jobs. In contrast, highly specific information about a particular piece of software must be left behind. It would be unfair for a company to invest heavily in research and development, and to pay an employee to develop a special device or program, only to have the employee leave and give the technology to a competitor.

Another factor is the rank and special knowledge of the employee. A high-ranking employee who is privy to all of the company's closely held secrets may be held to a more stringent trust relationship with his former employer than a lower-level employee. Correspondingly, a court will be concerned with the new company's motive in hiring away a competitor's employees. The court will ask whether the new company is hiring someone with general expertise or "stealing" a possessor of specific secrets. These disputes often are quite bitter and will continue to be a large factor in the computer industry as long as there is hot competition to attract software specialists to new companies.

Other Areas of the Law

Computer technology has led to the development of a new body of law relating to many subjects of great interest. Space permits touching on only a few of them.

CONTRACTS.   Contracts for computer services sometimes raise interesting legal questions. For instance, when a company engages a computer service bureau to do its data processing, information storage, payroll, or other services, or has an outside service devise a specialized program for an in-house computer, has the company contracted for "goods" or for "services"? This seemingly trivial distinction can have tremendous implications for tax purposes, and in determining what law applies to the transaction, because Article 2 of the Uniform Commercial Code applies only to sales of goods. Similarly, suppose the company consistently fails to pay its bills to a service bureau that stores its data. Would the bureau be justified in withholding the data as a lien for monies due? No law speaks directly to this issue, and its resolution will be controversial when it finally is faced. The moral of this story is that contract law has not kept pace with the computer revolution, and that there are no standard terms for a court to infer into an agreement when conflicts arise. Parties contracting for computer services, therefore, are well advised to negotiate explicitly over many issues that in other contexts they safely assume are covered by generations of accumulated experience in the courts.

TORTS AND CRIMES.   In the field of torts and criminal law, computers have not so much changed the law as merely provided individuals with new means to run afoul of it. Perhaps the only important question to surface has been whether taking a program or information from a data base by receiving it over a transmission or breaching the computer's security system—as many computer hackers like to do—could constitute theft or conversion, since nothing tangible had been taken. For the most part, this controversy has now been eliminated either by the enacting of new statutes or by judicial interpretation of existing ones. Thus talk of "computer crime" suggests little more novel than a crime committed with a computer rather than with a gun. Likewise, the laws of negligence and product liability do not change when computers are used. All that is involved is a new technology and new contexts. Thus no special discussion of these topics really is necessary.

THE LAW OF EVIDENCE.   One final area in which computers have raised special legal problems is the field of business records. As more and more businesses place their records in computers, and as more and more complex litigation requires sophisticated inquiries concerning information, courts have had to accept computerized data as a valid form of evidence at trial. Prior to trial, when the opposing parties in a lawsuit seek information (through discovery) from one another upon which to build their cases, many issues of access to computerized data may arise. A party may be required not only to furnish pre-existing hard copies of computerized data but also to provide new printouts of pertinent items or of data bases. Sometimes a party may be required to provide this information in machine-readable form, so that the data may be stored by the discovering parties for later analysis on their own computers without the time, expense, and potential for errors that would result if data from a printout had to be reentered manually.

Parties sometimes request production in a form that can be created only at substantial expense for additional programming; if so, payment of those costs by the requesting party often is made a condition of production. Because trade secrets, privileged information, and trial-preparation materials may require protection, and indeed the methodology of a company's computer system itself may be a valuable asset that should not be handed over to others without good reason, the court sometimes will enter protective orders to prevent abuse or misuse.

A party who wants to use computerized evidence has the burden of establishing its accuracy. Notwithstanding the capacity of computers to make tabulations and calculations involving enormous quantities of information—and to do so far more quickly and reliably than if done manually—several sources of potential errors of great magnitude exist. The more common include incorrect or incomplete entry of data, mistakes in output instructions, programming errors, damage and contamination of storage media, power outages, and equipment malfunction. Exploring matters relating to the reliability of this data for the first time at trial, however, may waste time, and either be unfair to the parties against whom they are offered, or result in the elimination of evidence that, had problems been identified and corrected earlier, would have helped to expedite trial and understand the issues. Therefore, the trustworthiness of computerized evidence will be tested well in advance of trial. This usually will include inquiry into the accuracy of the underlying source materials, the procedures for storage and processing, and some testing of the reliability of the results obtained.

The goal of these procedures is to eliminate, to the extent practicable, any disputes about the accuracy of the information. Obviously, complete accuracy cannot be assured. Nevertheless, the potential benefits that may be derived from using computerized data often outweigh the problems it may create, and courts have recognized this fact.

SUMMARY

"Intellectual property" is a name given collectively to the four legal areas of patents, copyrights, trademarks, and trade secrets. Patents are powerful monopolies, granted by the federal government, that give to inventors the complete right to determine who, if anyone, will be able to use their patented inventions. Independent invention is not a defense to an infringement action. Patents last for seventeen years. Patentable inventions include products, processes, and "any new and useful improvement" on a product or process. Ideas, however, are ineligible for protection. The acquisition of a patent is time-consuming and expensive. An applicant must prove to the Patent Office that the invention is useful, novel, and non-obvious to those familiar with the state of the art in which the patent is sought.

Copyrights also are monopolies granted by the federal government. Copyrights, however, protect "writings," not products or processes. In fact, if an item is found to be utilitarian—a prerequisite to patentability—its utilitarian aspects are ineligible for copyright. *Writings* are defined broadly as "original works of authorship." Common examples include literary works, musical works, pictorial or sculptural works, and sound recordings. As with patents, abstract ideas are ineligible; only a particular, original expression of an idea can by copyrighted, not the idea itself. Copyrights last much longer than patents—the life of the author plus 50 years—but provide less monopoly power to the owner.

Trademarks, like patents and copyrights, are governed by a federal statute. Unlike those other forms of intellectual property, however, trademarks cannot be claimed simply because someone thinks them up and registers them. A trademark is something that exists only with respect to some other commercial activity. It must identify a particular business, goods, or services, and a business can acquire federal protection for a trademark only be first actually using it in the market. Theoretically, the trademark can last forever, as long as it is used and does not become generic.

Trade secrecy is very different from the other forms of intellectual property. It is not governed by a federal statute. Instead, it is a creature of state statute or common law, and therefore varies from state to state. All trade secrecy law, however, is founded on the basic premise that if a business maintains confidentiality concerning information, the courts should protect that business against misappropriation of the secret. Protection is lost when the secret is disclosed by any means other than theft.

Computer programs and data bases do not always fit neatly into the traditional legal categories of intellectual property. At times they resemble "writings," and at other times "inventions." Moreover, because the computer industry is young and marked by mobility of employees from one company to another, questions of trade secrecy are common. Nevertheless, copyright has emerged as the most logical, as well as the dominant, form of legal protection for computer software and data bases.

The computer revolution has had an impact on virtually all areas of the law. Interestingly, in most contexts, computers have not so much changed the law as provided individuals new tools with which to violate it and new contexts in which legal problems can arise. In the areas of contracts, torts, and evidence, however, computers have raised new and important legal questions about how to handle new forms of commercial values and records.

KEY TERMS AND CONCEPTS

intellectual property
patent
process

machine
manufacture
composition of matter
novelty
usefulness
non-obviousness
copyright
writings
original work
trademark
trade secrecy

PROBLEMS

1. The Miller Brewing Company began marketing a new, lower-calorie light beer under the name "Lite." Thereafter, the G. Heilman Brewing Company began marketing a similar product, designating it as "Light" on the label. Miller sued Heilman to enjoin its use of the word "Light," contending it was a violation of Miller's trademark. Should Miller prevail? Why or why not?

2. Rosenthal Jewelry Corp. produced and coyprighted a jewel-encrusted gold pin in the shape of a bee. It was a considerable commercial success, and thereafter, Kalpakian, a competitor, produced and marketed a similar pin. Rosenthal sued claiming infringement of its copyright. What should be the result?

3. Dr. Chakrabarty was successful in producing a new strain of living microorganism in a laboratory. He sought to patent it. Is such a creation patentable?

4. On one particular college campus, it became a profitable business to sell outlines of lectures for particular courses. In pursuance of such a business, Weisser employed a young person to enroll in a class taught by Professor Williams, take detailed notes of the lectures, and type them up. Later, Weisser sold the notes, identifying them as lecture notes from Professor Williams's class.

Williams sued, claiming a common-law copyright in his lectures and lecture notes. Is Professor Williams entitled to a judgment?

5. With the production of the Apple II computer, computers became popular consumer items, and Apple met with much success. Soon after companies began producing similar, lower-priced computers, some advertised as "Apple compatible." One such company, Franklin, produced a compatible computer and copied Apple's operating system program to run its product. When Apple sued for copyright infringement, Franklin contended that the program was not copyrightable, but was a "process system" or "method of operation," which, if it was to be protected, should have been patented; it also argued that the program was "utilitarian" and, therefore, not subject to copyright protection. Is Franklin correct?

6. Arthur Young & Co. operated an executive search service in the area of Birmingham, Alabama. It had operated in the area since 1960, and had its name registered under the Lanham Act. In 1981, another company, Arthur Young, Inc., began operating an executive search company in the same area. Both companies had been named for their founders. After receiving a number of calls from persons seeking Arthur Young, Inc., Arthur Young & Co. claimed infringement of its trade name and asked for an injunction. Should the court grant the relief?

7. Ag Pro developed, and successfully marketed, a system for cleaning the floors of dairy barns by flushing them with water under high pressure. The refuse then flowed into a holding tank. It received a patent on the system. There-after, Sakraida began marketing substantially the same system under its own name. When sued for patent infringement, Sakraida defended on the ground that Ag Pro's patent was invalid because the system was not patentable. What might result?

8. Kewanee Oil Co. manufactured a synthetic crystal useful in the detection of ionizing radium. Some of its employees left and formed a new, competing company, also manufacturing such a crystal. Kewanee sued for a violation of its rights in trade secrets concerning the crystal. The new company defended on the ground that the process for producing the crystal, in which Kewanee claimed trade-secret rights, was patentable but had not been patented. Therefore, any rights in the invention were not protected. Is the defendant correct?

9. Jenkins had a conversation with the editor of a newspaper, describing in detail a story she intended to write. She later decided not to write it, and the newspaper published the interview with her, telling her story. Jenkins sued for infringement of her common-law copyright. The newspaper defended on the ground that its story was "news" only, and thus not a violation of any copyright. Is the newspaper correct?

10. During negotiations toward the manufacture of his patented invention, an electric steam iron, Schreyer revealed blueprints and specific details to an agent of Casco Products Corp. The negotiations were unsuccessful. Later, Casco used the information from the plans and produced its own iron. When Schreyer sued for patent infringement, Casco defended on the ground that it had not taken anything patentable from Schreyer. Is Schreyer entitled to a judgment?

Chapter | 29

Trusts

INTRODUCTION

A **trust** is a property arrangement involving at least three parties. A person called a **settlor** or **trustor** creates a trust by transferring property, called the *res* or *corpus,* to a **trustee** to hold and administer the property for the benefit of a **beneficiary.** In legal terms, the trustee holds **legal title** and the beneficiary holds **equitable title.** It is this split in the title to the property that is the essence of a trust.

Classification of Trusts

Trusts may be either *express* or *implied*. That is, they may arise either at the verbal or written direction of the settlor or by operation of law. In the latter case, a trust may be imposed upon the title to certain property in order to reflect a transferor's true intent, or to prevent some injustice. The law will require that the property be administered or disposed of for the benefit of some person to protect against an inequitable result. Express trusts may be established to be effective during the lifetime of the settlor, or to become effective upon the settlor's death. The former are called **inter vivos** or "living" trusts, and the latter are called **testamentary trusts.** Trusts also may be either *private* or *charitable,* depending on the purpose for which they are established. Finally, a trust may be **revocable** (subject to cancellation) or **irrevocable** by the settlor.

Purpose of Trusts

Generally, trusts are created for any of three basic purposes—to preserve property, to provide for maintenance and support, or to achieve tax advantages. A single trust may be created for one, two, or all three of these purposes.

A trust created for the purpose of preserving property may accomplish any number of specific objectives. For example, it might be created for the purpose of keeping certain property in the family for as long as possible. With legal title in the trustee, the settlor may be assured that the property will not be sold unless necessary. In the alternative, a trust might be created to allow full management and control of property by the trustee. This arrangement would relieve the settlor of the task of maximizing the utility of the property, having this done by a professional property manager. This kind of arrangement may be attractive when the trust involves a large amount of property, property that requires expert administration such as securities or a going business, or when the settlor wishes to be a beneficiary of the trust.

A trust created for maintenance and support may name an individual or a charity as beneficiary. When an individual is named, the objective simply may be to provide for management of the prop-erty so the beneficiary will be relieved of the responsibility. This technique is common when the beneficiary is incompetent or someone who is not able to manage property effectively. However, the objective also may be to see that the person is supported and has no power to dispose of the *res* (property), thus preventing the property from being squandered. A trust for the latter purpose sometimes is called a *spendthrift trust*. If the beneficiary is a charity, the objective often simply is to see that the charity is supported and thereby perpetuated.

Concerning taxation, the trust often is used in connection with estate planning to reduce taxes. Property may be placed in trust, the income being used to support people such as retired parents or minor children. The income from the trust then is taxed to the beneficiaries or the trust (which is an entity for tax purposes) at a lower rate than the settlor would pay if the income went to him before it was given to the beneficiary. Of course, the creation of a trust may shift taxation from an estate tax to a lower-rate gift tax in the case of a living trust. Also, property placed in a charitable trust may provide the settlor with an attractive tax deduction.

Care should be taken in the creation of any trust. A trustee who is a poor manager may cause more loss than benefit to the trust assets, and a settlor who creates a trust with too many strings attached may lose some or all of the anticipated tax advantages.

Creation of a trust

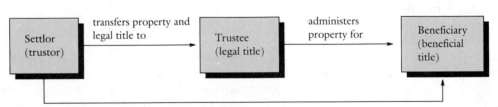

transfers equitable (beneficial) title

EXPRESS TRUSTS

Creation

As previously noted, an **express trust** is one created by the articulated intent of the settlor. Although it may be created orally, some states require that a trust be written or later evidenced in writing, although a formal trust document is not required. However, in every state five basic elements generally are required for the creation of an express trust. They are: (1) the settlor must have legal capacity; (2) the settlor must intend to establish a *present* trust; (3) the *corpus* must be specific property; (4) the beneficiary must be identifiable with reasonable certainty; and (5) the purpose of the trust must be consistent with public policy.

The first requirement means that the settlor must have legal capacity to convey property. In most states, this means that the settlor must be of legal age, of sound mind, sober, and not under an adjudication of incompetency at the time the trust is created. If he thereafter becomes insane or is adjudicated incompetent, the condition has no effect on the trust, unless the trust agreement provides to the contrary. Remember, a trust is not a contract, but involves an executed conveyance.

The settlor's intent must be to create a *present* trust, not a trust in the future. That is, it must involve a conveyance, not a contract for a future conveyance. This intent is measured by the same objective standard as is used to determine a party's intent to contract—what would it appear to a reasonable person, familiar with the surrounding facts and circumstances, that the settlor intended? In addition, this intent sometimes must be manifested by some required formality. For example, if the *corpus* of the trust involves real estate, a writing ordinarily is required to satisfy the Statute of Frauds. If the trust is created by a will, there must be compliance with the requirements for a valid will. Consider the following case, in which the court is faced with the question of whether the language of a will was sufficient to demonstrate the testator's intent to impose a trust on his property.

COMFORD v. CANTRELL
177 Tenn. 553, 151 S.W.2d 1076 (1941)

This was an action by William Harrison Comford, executor of the estate of Clara Augusta Cantrell, and others (Complainants/Appellees) against Lee Cantrell and others (Defendants/Appellants) for the construction of two wills.

James G. Cantrell died leaving the bulk of his estate to his wife according to the following provisions of his will:

> *Third: I give, devise and bequeath all the rest, residue and remainder of my estate and property of whatsoever kind and nature, wherever situated, both real and personal, to which I am entitled, or which I may have the power to dispose of at my death, to my wife, Clara Augusta Cantrell, to be her absolute estate forever; but if said Clara Augusta Cantrell dies in my lifetime, I then bequeath the property described in the next succeeding paragraph to the persons and in accordance with the request therein contained.*
>
> *Fourth: It is my request that upon her death my said wife, Clara Augusta Cantrell, shall give devise and bequeath my interest in the following described property in Nashville, Tennessee, to wit: (Description follows) . . .*

> *One quarter interest in my interest of the property described in the fourth section of this will to each of my brothers, Harvey W. Cantrell, Lee Cantrell and Julian Cantrell, or their heirs, and one quarter interest in my interest in said property to Charles E. Boisseau, Jr., and his sister Marguerite Boisseau, to be held by them jointly during the life of said Marguerite Boisseau, and at her death, the interest of said Marguerite Boisseau to revert to said Charles E. Boisseau or his heirs.*

Defendants contended the above language gave Clara Augusta Cantrell only a life estate and impressed a trust on the property by which she was required to pass it to Defendants by her will.

The trial court found for Complainants, that Clara Augusta Cantrell held the property in fee simple with no trust, and Defendants appealed. Affirmed.

GREEN, Chief Justice.

As observed by the chancellor, the testator used strong language in describing the character of the estate conferred upon his wife under his will. He said it was "to be her absolute estate forever." Absolute means without limitation or restriction. The word forever is almost invariably used in an instrument which creates an estate in fee simple. Forever is said to be an adjunct of a fee-simple estate. This will was obviously prepared by a lawyer and it is hard to conceive of words more clearly designed to pass a fee-simple estate than those quoted above.

Such being the will before us, we think the case falls under the authority of Smith v. Reynolds. . . . In that case the court reviewed earlier decisions and re-affirmed the rule that a clear and certain devise of a fee, about which the testamentary intention was obvious, would not be cut down or lessened by subsequent words which are ambiguous or of doubtful meaning. Although the will said that the estate devised to his wife "is by my wish returned to my nearest blood kin" at her death, the court held that the wife took the fee, it having been clearly and without ambiguity given to her previously in the instrument. The court said that the testator did not use the word wish as a command. And further that a trust would not be declared on the basis of precatory words where the will showed an intention to leave property absolutely.

In Smith v. Reynolds the court noted the change in the trend of authority as to the force of precatory words. This change has been very clearly discussed by two eminent authorities—Professor Scott of Harvard Law School and Professor Bogert of the University of Chicago Law School.

In Scott on Trusts, Section 25.2, it is said:

> Under the older view the question was whether the testator desired that the legatee should make a particular disposition of the property. If he did and if that disposition was one which could be enforced, the courts held that a trust was created. Under the modern cases the question is: Did the testator not only desire that the legatee should make a particular disposition of the property, but did he intend to impose a legal obligation upon him to make the disposition? Under the earlier rule it was easier to determine whether or not a trust was created than it is under the modern view, which makes the question one of interpretation of each particular will.

In 1 Bogert on Trusts and Trustees, Section 48, it is said:

> The words 'request,' 'desire,' and the like, do not naturally import a legal obligation. But the early view in England was that such words, when used in a will, were to be given an unnatural meaning, and were to be held to be courteous and softened means of creating duties enforceable by the courts. According to that opinion words of request prima facie created a trust. But since the beginning of the nineteenth century the English courts have changed their stand upon this question, and now hold that the natural significance of precatory words is not a trust, but that such an obligation may be shown by other portions of the instrument or by extrinsic circumstances. The American courts have adopted this natural construction of precatory expressions. . . .

Counsel for defendants rely on Daly v. Daly, . . . in which precatory words were treated as imperative. There, however, the court analyzed the whole will and showed that throughout the testator used such words as expressing a command rather than a mere desire. In Daly v. Daly our earlier cases were all set out and need not here be considered. In none of these cases was a trust held to exist where the recipient of the gift was to take it as an "absolute estate forever." These words are just incompatible with any other interest in the estate.

Questions

1. Are you convinced that the court reached a correct conclusion?

2. Should a document drafted by a lawyer be interpreted differently than one drafted by a non-lawyer? If so, what are those differences?

3. If the court had reached the opposite conclusion, what type of trust would have been created—an express or an implied trust? Why?

Because a trust involves a conveyance of property, the third requirement is that the property must be identified with reasonable certainty. Otherwise, no conveyance can occur. Of course, the settlor also must have had the right to convey the property. This does not mean that the property may be in no way encumbered; all it means is that the settlor owned or had the right to convey a transferable property right. For example, real estate owned by the settlor but subject to a mortgage and various easements properly may be the *corpus* of a trust.

A failure to identify the beneficiary with reasonable certainty has no effect on the validity of the conveyance to the trustee, as do the first three requirements, but will cause the trust to fail for indefiniteness. The result is that the trustee would

be required to reconvey the property to the settlor and no trust would be created. In effect, until the reconveyance, the trustee will hold the property for the benefit of (in trust for) the settlor.

The stated beneficiaries may be a person, two or more persons, or an identified group, such as all blind persons residing in a particular county. As already indicated, it also may be an entity, such as a university, church, or a charitable organization. The beneficiaries need not be specified, but must be reasonably identifiable.

The last requirement is that the purpose of the trust must be legal. A failure to satisfy this obligation causes the trust to fail. Illegal purpose does not mean that there might be some incidental illegal activities by one trustee or that execution of the trust incidentally might further some illegality. It means that an illegality is *required* if the trust is executed as stated. For example, the fact that the trustee might use the funds for an illegal investment would not void the trust, but *if the trust agreement provided* that the funds be illegally invested, for gambling or the overthrow of the government, it would fail for lack of illegal purpose. There is some controversy as to whether, in the case of an improper purpose, a court of equity would require that the trustee hold the *corpus* for the benefit of the settlor, or require that it be retransferred to the settlor. It is doubtful that an equity court would intervene at all since both parties conspired to commit an illegal act.

Charitable Trusts

A **charitable trust** is one created to benefit the public or some defined segment of the public. Its purpose may be to further purely public ends or those of religion, education, science, research, health, helping the needy, or any other of a host of charitable works. Charitable trusts are characterized by a definite charitable intent and indefiniteness of the specific persons who actually will benefit. Typically, a charitable trust is administered by a board rather than one person as trustee, but this is not an essential element.

Once a charitable trust is created, courts will do what they reasonably can to prevent it from failing for want of a beneficiary. If the class of beneficiaries stated in the trust document ceases to exist, if the application of the *corpus* as stated would be illegal, or if the language is so vague or uncertain that the settlor's intent must be ascertained by construction, the courts will seek to apply the trust as nearly as possible to what it determines the settlor's intent to have been. In doing so, the court applies the **cy pres** (pronounced "see pray") **doctrine,** which means "as near as possible." For example, upon the death of a sufficient number of qualified beneficiaries, a charitable trust to provide for needy veterans of World War I might be construed to be open to benefit veterans of World War II. Years later, the beneficiaries might become needy veterans of the Korean War, and so on. The questions would be whether (1) failure to reconstrue would cause the trust to fail; (2) the settlor intended to benefit only World War I veterans, veterans of a world war or any war, veterans of declared wars only, or veterans in general; (3) the trust should remain as is until the passing of the last World War I veteran; and (4) what would be best for the public interest. Obviously the final decision would not be an easy one for the court. Consider the following case illustrating the application of the *cy pres* doctrine.

WESLEY UNITED METHODIST CHURCH v. HARVARD COLLEGE
366 Mass. 247, 316 N.E. 2d 620 (1974)

This was an action by Wesley United Methodist Church as trustee of a charitable trust created by the will of Harold E. Colson (Petitioner/Appellee) against Harvard College and certain heirs of Harold E. Colson (Respondents/Appellants) seeking modification of the terms of the trust under the doctrine of *cy pres*.

Harold E. Colson's will gave the trust in question the "rest, residue, and remainder" of his estate. The petitioner, as trustee, was charged to provide a $500 scholarship for a student to Harvard College, and as the income from the trust exceeded $500, to provide another, and so on as the trust income accumulated. At the time the will was executed the amount involved was modest. By the time of Colson's death, the amount exceeded $55,000, producing annual income of approximately $3200. The scholarships were to be provided to male members or communicants of the Wesley United Methodist Church, and at the time of trial the church had received no scholarship applications. The heirs contended the doctrine of *cy pres* was inapplicable, and a resulting trust should be declared in their favor.

The probate court granted the petition and the heirs appealed. Affirmed.

TAURO, Chief Justice.

The Probate Court found that "the express terms of the trust . . . are literally impracticable of operation in limiting the beneficiaries to male members or communicants of Wesley Methodist Church," and that "the testator's intention to provide scholarships for students attending Harvard College as a memorial for his mother may be fulfilled to promote and accomplish the general charitable intent of the testator under the application of cy pres." It was ordered that "the Board of Trustees of the Petitioner apply income and accumulations of the trust fund in the awarding of annual scholarships, in their discretion, unlimited in amount, to worthy male or female applicants, not restricted to members or communicants of the petitioner if there are no such applicants, for undergraduate or graduate education in Harvard University."

The defendant heirs at law argue that both the findings as to impracticability and general charitable intent are erroneous. Each is a necessary element for the application of the cy pres doctrine: "Where property is given in trust for a particular charitable purpose, and it is impossible or impracticable to carry out that purpose, the trust does not fail if the testator has a more general intention to devote the property to charitable purposes. In such a case the property will be applied under the direction of the court to some charitable purpose falling within the general intention of the testator." . . . Cy pres will not apply, however, if the trust remains capable of meaningful application, or if, despite impracticability, there is a lack of general charitable intent on the testator's part. In the latter situation, ". . . in the absence of any limitation over or other provision, the legacy lapses." . . .

We hold that the Probate Court's findings were warranted and the decree was not erroneous. It is true, as the respondent heirs argue, that the Colson trust is theoretically capable of application, in that (1) a male undergraduate student at Harvard might at some point in the future join the Wesley United Methodist Church; (2) an adult male member of the church might himself enroll at the college, or (3) eligible male children might be born to the present predominantly adult membership. Nevertheless, it is clear that literal compliance with the terms of the trust is now preventing, and will most likely continue to prevent, any use of the funds. Of the 236 members, only a portion are males, and most of them are adult, past college age. It is obvious that the Wesley United Methodist Church, in bringing this suit, sees very few or even no present or prospective scholarship applicants among that slim percentage of its congregation that is even eligible under the terms of the trust. This and other courts have found impracticability where a present and probably continuing lack of specified beneficiaries serves effectively to freeze disbursement of charitable funds. . . . This rule is a sound one, as no purpose, least of all the settlor's, is served by tying up funds intended for charitable use with the thin thread of a theoretically possible (but unlikely) change in circumstances. . . . We believe that in the instant case, in view of the size and character of the Wesley United Methodist Church membership, the Probate Court was correct in its finding that the Frances L. Colson trust is impracticable.

Moreover, we believe that the settlor displayed a general charitable intent, as distinguished from an intent "limited to . . . a specific charitable purpose." . . . Ultimately, the question is whether the settlor would have preferred that his bequest be applied to a like charitable purpose in the event that his original scheme did not work out, or would have instead desired that the unused funds be diverted to private use. This analysis is often difficult since more often than not the settlor, fully expecting his scheme to be effective, never contemplates alternative dispositions, or at least fails to include them in his testamentary design. This appears to be the case here, as the settlor's will contains neither an express statement of general charitable intent, nor specific instructions for the disposition of the trust funds in the event of a failure or impracticability. Thus, the general charitable intent, or lack of it, must be inferred from the language of the trust provisions contained in the will, and from the language of the will as a whole. . . .

We are satisfied that the settlor would have wished that the funds be applied to a like charitable purpose rather than be removed from charitable use entirely. The applicable provision established a $500 scholarship in his mother's name to assist "one worthy male member of the congregation or communicant of . . . [the Wesley United Methodist] church, to be selected each year at the discretion of . . . [the] Board of Trustees, to attend Harvard College . . . for undergraduate education." While "[t]he class whom . . [the testator] sought to benefit is narrowly circumscribed," . . . that fact alone does not preclude a finding that the testator was motivated by broader, overriding charitable considerations. . . . Relevant in this regard, and indicative of a general charitable intent, is the absence of a gift over [an alternate person to receive the proceeds if the trust fails] in the event that the trust should fail. . . . The decedent's will contains no gift over clause. Nor does the language of the controlling trust provision indicate a purposeful and permanent exclusion of all others from his beneficence. Another factor pointing to a general charitable intent is the disposition of gifts to other charities. . . .

In view of the foregoing, we conclude that the case was a proper one for the application of the cy pres doctrine. No question is raised as to the manner in which the doctrine was applied.

Questions

1. Doesn't the *cy pres* doctrine give the court too much authority to do whatever it wants with the trust?

2. Are you satisfied that the probate court changed the trust properly? Was it necessary to change as many conditions as it did?

3. What should happen if there still aren't enough applicants?

Private Trusts

A **private trust,** as opposed to a charitable trust, is one established for the benefit of a certain specified individual or individuals, or a known and clearly identifiable class of persons. Its distinguishing characteristics are private, rather than charitable, intent and definiteness of the person or persons to benefit.

Unlike a charitable trust, a private trust may not have perpetual existence. It may be for the benefit only of persons known and identifiable as existing within a time limit allowed by the **rule against perpetuities.** That is, the beneficiary must exist and be identifiable, if at all, not later than 21 years, plus the period of gestation, after some life or lives in being at the time the trust first became effective. The rule is intended to prevent a property owner from controlling the disposition of his or her property forever "from the grave." Its application has been modified by statute in some states, but its purpose has been preserved. (The rule is discussed further in Chapter 26.)

When the last permissible beneficiary of a private trust dies or becomes permanently disqualified from receiving benefits, the trust terminates. The *cy pres* doctrine has no application. Any property remaining will be disposed of as directed when the trust was established. If no directions were made, trust assets will revert, to be distributed to the heirs of the settlor.

Totten Trust

Although most trusts involve three separate parties who act as settlor, trustee, and beneficiary, an exception to this rule is the so-called **totten trust.** This is a trust created by the deposit by one person of his own property in his own name as trustee for another. For example, a surviving parent dies leaving two children—a daughter and a mentally handicapped son. All of the deceased's property is willed to the daughter with the request that the son be cared for out of the income. The daughter may set aside one-half, or some other appropriate portion, of the parent's estate and put it in trust (perhaps in a bank or securities account) for the brother. Care should be exercised in creating these trusts, especially if they involve real property. Some states do not recognize a transfer to oneself. Instead, the property must first be transferred to a "straw man," who will then retransfer in trust. Obviously this procedure does not involve any real substantive difference.

Generally, a totten trust is considered a tentative trust revocable until the settlor/trustee dies or completes the gift during her lifetime. This requires some unequivocal act, such as the delivery of a passbook to a bank account, or some equivalent act. If the settlor/trustee dies without revocation or some decisive act or declaration of disaffirmance, a presumption arises that an absolute trust was created as to the balance on hand at the time of death. A new trustee will be appointed to serve until the death of the beneficiary. In this regard, consider the following case.

WRIGHT'S ESTATE
17 Ill. App.3rd 894, 308 N.E.2d 319 (1974)

The decedent, Charles R. Wright, opened a savings account at Farmers State Bank of Ferris in the name "Charles Wright, Pay on Death to Mary Lowe." Subsequently deposits were made during the decedent's lifetime, as was one withdrawal of $500. The decedent's will made no mention of the account. This action was brought by his sons (Petitioners/Appellees) against Mary Lowe (Respondent/Appellant) to have the account declared part of the estate.

The Probate Court found for Petitioners and Respondent appealed. The Court of Appeals, noting that it was not deciding any rights that might be held by a surviving spouse since there was none, reversed and remanded to the lower court.

ALLOY, Justice.

It is principally maintained by appellant that decedent, in opening and maintaining the account in question, established a so-called "Totten" or tentative trust, which device was recognized as valid in Illinois by our Supreme Court in the case of In re Petralia, . . . by the following language . . .

> We accept the position adopted by the American Law Institute in Section 58 of the Restatement (second) of Trusts: 'Where a person makes a deposit in a savings account in a bank or other savings organization in his own name as trustee for another person intending to reserve a power to withdraw the whole or any part of the deposit at any time during his lifetime and to use as his own whatever he may withdraw, or otherwise revoke the trust, the intended trust is enforceable by the beneficiary upon the death of the depositor as to any part remaining on deposit on his death if he has not revoked the trust . . .

In support of the proposition that a recognized "Totten" or tentative trust was here created, appellant refers us to, inter alia, the following circumstances: at the time the account in question was opened the decedent apparently withdrew $2000 from his regular savings account (held in his name alone) and immediately used such money to fund the new account. Further, decedent continued to make significant deposits to the account in question throughout the rest of his life, while making only one withdrawal of $500, which withdrawal was "made up" with a deposit in the amount of $500 only 9 days later. Decedent and appellant were affectionate friends; their plans for marriage being thwarted, however, by the condition of decedent's health.

Appellant points out that the primary object of all rules of construction in interpretation is to arrive at and give effect to the mutual intentions of the parties as expressed in the whole agreement and the circumstances surrounding the transaction.

> In the interpretation of any particular trust agreement, the Court is required to examine the entire agreement and it may also consider the relation of the parties, their connection with the subject matter of the agreement, the circumstances under which it was made, and the purpose for which it was made. . . .

In addition, we are reminded by appellant of the admonitions contained in Goldstein v. Handley, . . . that "[n]o particular form of words or language is necessary in a gift of property to create a trust," and in Pap v. Pap . . . where it is said that "it is not necessary that the word "trust" or "trustee" be used in order to create a trust . . . ." Moreover, argues appellant, it is clear that wholly parol trusts in personal property are recognized in Illinois . . . and since a trust has been here established, there is no compelling reason for this court to thwart the settlor's intent.

Under the circumstances, we do not believe it may properly be said, as maintained by appellee, that appellant had no "present interest" in the account during the lifetime of decedent. On the contrary, she was a beneficiary named in the account and in our judgment thus held a present, although wholly defeasible, interest therein contemporaneous with decedent's superior rights. The latter's death, however, terminated his rights, and rendered appellant's indefeasible.

That we find, in accordance with the foregoing, that a tentative trust has been here established would seem to end our inquiry. However, a further argument advanced by appellant in our view serves as a basis for an alternate holding which we deem to be valid whether or not decedent established a trust in creating the account in question. We accordingly deem it wise to consider appellant's alternate theory, which maintains that the decedent in this case entered into a perfectly valid contract with the bank naming her as a third party beneficiary thereto. As such, she is entitled to whatever funds were contained in the account at decedent's death, pursuant to the explicit terms of the contract. In support of this proposition, we are referred , *inter alia*, to 4 Corbin on Contracts, Sec. 783, at pages 89–90 (1951), where it is said as follows: ". . . Rarely has the third party been regarded as the beneficiary of a contract between A [the depositor] and the bank. This is due either to insufficient analysis or to the uncertainty and conflict that until recently existed in third party beneficiary law. In all cases, so long as there is no fraud on A's creditors, C [the named beneficiary] should get the money that A has not drawn out . . . as . . . beneficiary of the banking debtor's promise to the creditor [depositor]." . . .

We find appellant's third-party beneficiary contract theory quite compelling and entirely consistent with sound principles of jurisprudence. . . . It is absolutely clear that decedent named appellant as the death beneficiary of the account in question, and it is equally clear that he entered into a binding contractual arrangement with the bank in connection therewith. There being no rights of creditors or a surviving spouse here in question, we see no legally cogent reason for thwarting the decedent's clear dispositive intent concerning the sums held in the account at decedent's death.

In accordance with the foregoing, we find that decedent either established a valid "Totten" trust with respect to the account in question, or entered into a valid third-party beneficiary contract naming appellant as the beneficiary thereof. In either case, appellant is entitled to all sums in the account at the time of decedent's death.

Questions

1. Should the court have preferred the "fiancée" over the sons?
2. What difference would it make if the deceased was survived by a wife and the bank account was in the name of a friend?

Spendthrift Trusts

A "spendthrift" may be defined as a person who spends money lavishly and improvidently, perhaps because of habitual intoxication, gambling, idleness, or simply the exercise of poor judgment. Some states, by statute, provide that the estate of a spendthrift may be placed in guardianship for the protection of the spendthrift, his or her family, and the public, upon whom the ultimate burden of support might fall. Similarly, money or other property intended for such a person may be put into a **spendthrift trust,** instead of given absolutely.

To create a valid spendthrift trust the same requirements must be met as for any other private trust. However, the gift must be only of the income. The beneficiary must take no estate in the property, or have any right of alienation or possession. The beneficiary must have no beneficial interest in the property except a qualified right to support and an equitable interest in the income. The trust must be an active one. That is, the trustee must have ongoing duties of trust management and distribution of the income. Spendthrift trusts most commonly are created by wills, and the concept is illustrated by the following case.

AMERICAN SECURITY AND TRUST COMPANY v. UTLEY
382 F.2d 451 (D.C.Cir. 1967)

This was an action by Freda Utley (Plaintiff/Appellee) against American Security and Trust Company (Defendant/Appellant) to secure a writ of attachment garnishing the accrued income of a "spendthrift" trust, held by Defendant, to secure payment of a promissory note, in the amount of $4500, executed by Sidney R. Graves, beneficiary of the trust. The trust had been created by the will of Mr. Graves's wife.

The trial court granted the writ and Defendant appealed. Reversed and remanded.

BURGER, Chief Judge.

On this premise the District Court then applied the well-known rule that where the settlor-creator of the trust is also the beneficiary, the interest in the trust can be invaded. . . . We have no quarrel with the rule that one may not create a trust for his own benefit and place the income beyond reach of his creditors. However, the view adopted by the District Court is contrary to the settled weight of authority and we think not warranted as a matter of sound policy. . . .

Professor Scott, while recognizing the criticism of complete immunity for trust income concludes:

> On the whole the better view would seem to be that where a husband creates a trust for his wife by will, the mere fact that she surrenders her right to dower or to a distributive share of his estate does not make her the creator of the trust, even to the extent of the value of the interest which she surrendered. If spendthrift trusts are to be permitted at all, it would seem that a husband should be allowed to create such a trust for his widow, even though she may have power to refuse to accept the provisions of his will and take her dower or distributive share in lieu thereof.

2 SCOTT, TRUSTS Section 156.3, at 1105-1106 (2d Ed. 1956).

We have long recognized the validity of the so-called spendthrift trust, but not without limitation. The historical purpose of a settlor or testator in creating a trust, the income of which was protected from invasion, was to protect the interests of the beneficiary. This purpose has been held to render the income totally immune from claims, including claims for debts incurred by the beneficiary for the necessaries of life. . . . We see no reason for an absolutist "all or nothing" approach. . . . Traditionally, in the absence of a statute, several distinct classes of claimants have been permitted to invade the beneficiary's interest. . . . This court has permitted the interest of a father in a spendthrift trust to be subjected to claims for the support of his minor children, Seidenberg v. Seidenberg. . . . Our holding in *Seidenberg* indicates that it does not necessarily follow from the general validity of spendthrift trusts that trust income is protected from all obligations. We view the primary purpose of such a trust to assure that the beneficiary will be provided for, independent of his own improvidence. To accomplish this the income need not be made immune from debts incurred for the necessities of life; indeed to allow such claims is entirely compatible with the purpose of the trust. . . .

The District Court had no occasion to inquire into the circumstances which gave rise to the indebtedness, and we therefore remand for a determination of the basis of the debt incurred and the purposes to which the proceeds of the loan were devoted. If the District Court finds the debt to have been incurred for necessaries such as those for which an infant would be held liable in contract in otherwise comparable circumstances, the claim may be allowed against the income of the trust; if not, judgment must be for the Appellant.

Questions

1. Why does the court recognize an exception for necessaries to the protections for spendthrift trust beneficiaries?

2. How can a court guard against the possibility that a spendthrift trust is being used to avoid creditors?

3. Should a court limit the ability to create a spendthrift trust to those situations in which the beneficiary really is a spendthrift? Why or why not?

Modification and Revocation of Trusts

As a general rule, a settlor may modify or revoke a trust only if the power to do so was retained validly at the time the trust was created. Ordinarily this would be by express reservation in the trust agreement. Of course, a trust created by a will does not become effective until the death of the testator, and may be modified or revoked until that time.

If the terms of a trust do not provide for modification or revocation, the settlor may attempt to prove to a court that it was intended that these rights be reserved. If convinced, a court may allow modification or revocation. Also, as discussed previously, the reservation of these powers is presumed when a totten trust is created. However, if a settlor received consideration in return for the creation of a trust, the law of contracts ordinarily will prevent modification or revocation when not provided for expressly, unless the mistake was patent and bilateral.

Of course, if a settlor is induced to create a trust by misrepresentation, fraud, duress, or undue influence, the trust may be modified or revoked. Also, these powers may be exercised with the consent of the beneficiaries. Finally, since the courts have continuing jurisdiction over all trusts, a court may allow a deviation from the terms of a trust when the settlor is dead and unanticipated changes in circumstances threaten the settlor's dominant purpose in creating the trust.

Termination

Most trusts terminate when a period stated in the instrument creating the trust—if there is such a term—has elapsed, when its stated purpose has been accomplished, or when it has been revoked by the settlor. In addition, if the purpose of a trust becomes illegal, it will terminate, except in the case of a charitable trust to which the *cy pres* doctrine may apply. In all cases a trust will terminate if its promise becomes impossible to accomplish.

Destruction of the subject matter of a trust may cause termination. However, if the subject matter was insured against loss, or the destruction was by wrongful act of the trustee or a third person against whom a claim may be collected, the trust will not terminate, but will continue to operate on the proceeds. Of course, any trust may be terminated by consent of the settlor and all of the beneficiaries or when termination by the settlor is provided for in the agreement. The death, incapacity, or unwillingness of the trustee to continue to serve will not terminate a trust, unless the agreement provided that the trust was to continue only as long as the named trustee functioned. Ordinarily, another trustee will be appointed.

TRUSTEES

Who may be a trustee is defined by state statute. The position may be held by an individual or a corporation, or in many states by a partnership or other unincorporated association. If the trustee is an individual, the person ordinarily must be of legal age to hold title to property—commonly 18 or older. The trustee cannot be the beneficiary. Otherwise the merger of both legal and equitable title in one person would cause a transfer of the *corpus* to be absolute rather than one into trust.

The qualities to be sought in a trustee, of course, are honesty, diligence, and skill in dealing with the type of property making up the particular trust. For example, portfolios of securities, real estate, or cash each require a different kind of expertise. If the beneficiary has special needs, such as a handicapped child, the trustee should have some understanding of those needs and how they are to be met.

Whether the trustee is an individual or a corporate trustee is a personal decision. Each has advantages and disadvantages. Many times a corporate trustee, such as the trust department of a bank, is chosen because of continuity. A corporate trustee does not die or become incapacitated, in the normal sense. In addition, the trust department of a bank is likely to be staffed by individuals who have some background and skill in dealing with different kinds of property and investments. Of course, there is likely to be some turnover of personnel. Because of that, and because of the general impersonal nature of corporations, there is less likelihood of maintaining a close, personal relationship among the settlor, the trustee, and the beneficiary than in the case of an individual trustee. Also, a corporate trustee almost always will require a fee, frequently in an amount established "across the board" by the corporation. An individual—particularly a friend or family member—may serve without a fee, or at least be flexible as to the amount.

Duties of the Trustee

Every trustee is a **fiduciary.** This means that every trustee owes a duty of loyalty exceeding that owed by parties in ordinary relationships. In essence, owing a fiduciary duty means that the relationships between the trustee and the settlor, and the trustee and the beneficiary, are not considered "arm's length." Instead, the trustee owes the highest duty of trust and confidence. This includes not only acting with complete honesty and good faith, but doing nothing that might lead a reasonable person to question the propriety of his actions concerning the interests of the settlor or the beneficiaries. Examples of actions in breach of the fiduciary duty are self-dealing, favoring the interests of one beneficiary over others, and acting for the benefit of any third party against the interest of any beneficiary.

In conducting the affairs of the trust, a trustee is expected to exercise reasonable care and skill to preserve the *corpus* and to make it productive. In addition, if the trustee holds herself out as having special skill or knowledge relative to the affairs of the trust, she is held to a standard commensurate with that degree of skill or knowledge. For example, a trust department of a bank, or a securities broker, may be held to a higher standard in financial matters than would a lay trustee. Consider the following case involving an obvious breach of duty by the trustee.

WIEMER v. HAVANA NATIONAL BANK
96 Ill. App.3rd 549, 52 Ill.Dec. 139, 421 N.E.2d 1002 (1981)

Northwestern Mutual Life Insurance Company brought an action to foreclose a mortgage held in trust for Amelia E. Wiemer by Havana National Bank as trustee. Amelia E. Wiemer (third-party Plaintiff/Appellant) then filed a complaint in that action against Havana National Bank (Defendant/Appellee), seeking indemnification for breach of trust.

On March 28, 1968, Mr. and Mrs. Wiemer (Mr. Wiemer was deceased at the time of the trial) executed a trust naming Havana National Bank as trustee. To fund the trust in part, Havana Bank lent $35,000 to the trust, secured by a mortgage to Havana Bank. On June 24, 1968, Havana Bank (as trustee) and the Wiemers (as beneficiaries) executed a mortgage note to Northwestern Mutual Life Insurance Company. Havana subordinated its lien to that of Northwestern Mutual.

As trustee, Havana had the duty to manage the trust property, a farm, and to apply its income to pay existing debts. On January 21, 1976, Mrs. Wiemer's attorney sent a letter to Havana Bank requesting termination of the trust. Havana Bank replied that Mrs. Wiemer did not have the authority to end the trust in such a manner. On February 4, 1976, approximately $8000 was in the trust's account. A mortgage payment of $4035.50 was due to Northwestern Mutual on April 1, 1976. Havana applied the entire $8000 to partial satisfaction of its own mortgage and the Northwestern Mutual was defaulted, giving rise to its foreclosure action.

The trial court denied Mrs. Wiemer's motion for summary judgment and Mrs. Wiemer appealed. Reversed and remanded.

HEIPLE, Justice.

Emerging from this factual backdrop is a single issue. Was the trial judge correct in finding the trustee did not breach the trust and ordering summary judgment for Havana Bank? Responding in the negative, we reverse.

A trust relationship existed between Havana Bank and Mrs. Wiemer by virtue of the trust agreement. . . . Ascertaining whether the trust was breached requires scrutiny of the trustee's conduct as well as the written trust agreement creating the trustee's duties. What does the trust say? . . .

When a trustee fails to administer a trust according to its terms, a breach of trust results. White v. Macqueen (1935), 360 Ill. 236, 248, 195 N.E. 832. Havana Bank, as trustee, has a duty to pay the semi-annual payments on the Northwestern mortgage. The trustee knew that mortgage had priority since it not only prepared the trust agreement, but expressly subordinated its lien to that of Northwestern. Nonetheless, it breached the trust by applying the $8,000 to partially discharge its own second mortgage.

Havana Bank argues Mrs. Wiemer's letter of January 21, 1976, and her subsequent repossession of the farm repudiated the trust relationship. This contention is unpersuasive. The purpose of the trust was consolidation of the Wiemer's debt so they could buy a farm and work it. The trust was valid for twenty years. A beneficiary cannot terminate a trust where its object has not been accomplished in the absence of a provision allowing her to do so. . . . The trust did not give Mrs. Wiemer any such right nor had its purpose been accomplished. The liability of the trustee, Havana Bank, for breach of trust is abundantly clear. If the trustee had paid Northwestern instead of Havana Bank, the first mortgage would not have been foreclosed. The burden and expense of this latter litigation would have been avoided. Since the trial court incorrectly denied Mrs. Wiemer's motion for summary judgment, we do not know what the evidence, if any, might show as to the extent of her damages due to the trustee's breach. Therefore, a remand for a trial to ascertain those damages is required.

Questions

1. Would the trustee have been permitted to pay itself its fees and expenses before paying Northwestern Mutual, or would that have been a breach of trust?

2. Would it have been a breach of trust if the trustee had paid unsecured creditors before paying Northwestern Mutual?

A trustee is liable for any loss occasioned to the trust by any breach of his duties. In addition, a trustee also is personally liable on every transaction entered into for the trust, although he is entitled to indemnity and reimbursement from the trust, as long as transactions are conducted properly.

It should be noted that two factors may bear significantly on the trustee's duties. First, the trust document may establish obligations more precisely, or new obligations, or even waive some that would be imposed on the trustee by the general law in the absence of specific language. Also, state statutes frequently place obligations,

often extensive ones, on trustees. For example, statutes often dictate the permissible investments into which trust funds may be placed. In every case, the trustee must consult the language of the trust documents and applicable state statutes.

Powers of the Trustee

Although a trustee is not an agent, but a special type of fiduciary, the duties, and especially the powers, of a trustee are very similar to those of an agent. The powers of a trustee primarily are express, implied, or arise by operation of law. Generally, the trust document will grant certain specific powers, and may refer to others in general terms. In addition, however, a trustee ordinarily also will have all powers reasonably necessary to carry out the purposes of the trust, to preserve the trust property (*corpus*), and to make it productive. This may include the power, and even the duty, to act contrary to express provisions of the trust document in emergency situations, as long as doing so appears reasonably necessary to meet her general obligations as trustee. For example, the trust document may require that ten percent of the trust funds be invested in stock of a particular company. However, due to circumstances unforeseeable to the settlor, it becomes apparent that the company is about to fail, and its stock should be sold immediately in order to avoid substantial loss to the trust. If the trustee must act quickly, there being no time or ability to get specific instructions from the settlor or an appropriate court, she probably will be empowered to take the necessary action as long as she does so in good faith, acts reasonably, and there are no extenuating circumstances.

IMPLIED TRUSTS

The discussion thus far has focused on express trusts—those created by the voluntary and intentional act of the settlor. However, trusts also may be implied. Rather than depending on the voluntary intent of a settlor, **implied trusts** are created by operation of law. Many of the rules applicable to express trusts also apply to implied trusts, when the context permits. The remainder are created by courts in order to achieve equitable results in particular circumstances. Implied trusts may be of two general types—resulting trusts and constructive trusts.

Resulting Trusts

When the owner of property has transferred legal title to another, but it appears from the conduct of the parties, or other facts and circumstances surrounding the transfer, that the transferor did not intend to transfer the equitable title (beneficial interest) or has done so imperfectly, a trust will "result" in favor of the transferor. The intent to create such a trust arises by implication of law, or by operation and construction of equity. In other words, it is presumed or inferred that the transferor intended that the beneficial interest vest in himself and his heirs in the given situation.

A great variety of specific circumstances may cause a court to impose a **resulting trust** on property. It may result from an imperfect attempt to create an express trust. For example, the proposed settlor may fail to identify the beneficiaries sufficiently, the purpose of the trust may be illegal, impossible, or impractical to accomplish, or a trust may terminate because it has accomplished its purpose or because of unanticipated circumstances, but the settlor failed to provide for disposition of the remaining *corpus*.

If one person purchases real property with his or her own money and directs the seller to transfer title to a third person, the laws of most states provide that these circumstances raise a presumption of a resulting trust in favor of the purchaser. This presumption may be overridden, however, by proof that the transfer was intended as a loan, to pay an obligation, as a resale of the property, or as a gift. If not overridden by evidence offered by or on behalf of the transferee, the presumption of a resulting trust will be conclusive. Most courts find it easier to accept the theory that a gift was intended when the purchaser and the transferee are closely related—for example, when the transferee is the child or spouse of the purchaser.

When a resulting trust is imposed by law, it becomes the duty of the trustee to preserve the property for the beneficiary. However, generally no fiduciary duty arises, at least if the trustee is holding the property as an involuntary bailee. Also, the trustee normally owes no duty to see that the property is productive. A duty does arise, however, that the beneficiary act with reasonable promptness to recover legal title and possession or establish an express trust.

Constructive Trusts

Although, like a resulting trust, a **constructive trust** arises by operation of law, it is unlike a resulting trust in that its creation is not based on an assumption of some intent on the part of the transferor. Instead, it is imposed to redress a wrong or to prevent an unjust enrichment—it is a device created by the law to make sure that equity is done. Circumstances compelling a constructive trust are those in which the person who received legal title to property, in fairness, is not entitled to enjoy the fruits of equitable title. At the foundation of every constructive trust is fraud or wrongdoing by the transferee, either actual or constructive. A constructive trust also may be referred to as a trust *ex maleficio* or *ex delicto*.

Constructive trusts may be imposed in a great variety of situations. For example, suppose an insurance company, intending to send a claim check to a policy holder, Ronald Stevens, mistakenly sends it to a different Ronald Stevens at a wrong address. A court would impose a constructive trust on the check, in the hands of the wrong Stevens, in favor of the insurance company, especially when it is clear that the recipient knew that he was not entitled to the check. The same result would be obtained concerning property in the hands of a thief or in the hands of someone who obtained it by misrepresentation, duress, or undue influence. Finally, an agent who obtained secret profits by self-dealing in breach of her fiduciary duty to her principal would find them subject to a constructive trust in favor of the principal. Generally, constructive trusts are said to arise through the application of the doctrine of equitable estoppel, or under the broad doctrine that equity regards and treats as done what in good conscience ought to be done. The following case provides an example of circumstances that may justify the imposition of a constructive trust.

SHARP v. KOSMALSKI
40 N.Y.2d 119, 351 N.E.2d 721 (1976)

This was an action by J. Rodney Sharp (Plaintiff/Appellant) against Jean C. Kosmalski (Defendant/Appellee) to impose a constructive trust on property. Upon the death of his wife of thirty-two years, Plaintiff developed a close relationship with Defendant, a school teacher sixteen years his junior. Defendant performed many domestic services for Plaintiff, such as keeping house and ironing his shirts. They were frequent companions and Plaintiff showered her with many gifts, hoping she would agree to marry him. Plaintiff made Defendant joint owner of his bank account, from which she withdrew substantial sums, made her sole beneficiary under his will, and made her joint owner of his farm. Later he deeded his interest to her as well, and instructed his insurance agent to list Defendant and her children as additional insureds under his farm liability policy, and to change the policy to read, "J. Rodney Sharp, life tenant. Jean C. Kosmalski, owner." Thereafter, Defendant ordered Plaintiff off the farm.

From a judgment dismissing the complaint, Plaintiff appealed. Reversed and remanded.

GABRIELLI, Judge.

Generally, a constructive trust may be imposed "[w]hen property has been acquired in such circumstances that the holder of the legal title may not in good conscience retain the beneficial interest." . . . In the development of the doctrine of constructive trust as a remedy available to courts of equity, the following four requirements were posited: (1) a confidential or fiduciary relation, (2) a promise, (3) a transfer in reliance thereon and (4) unjust enrichment. . . .

Most frequently, it is the existence of a confidential relationship which triggers the equitable considerations leading to the imposition of a constructive trust. . . . Although no marital or other family relationship is present in this case, such is not essential for the existence of a confidential relation. . . . The record in this case clearly indicates that a relationship of trust and confidence did exist between the parties and, hence, the defendant must be charged with an obligation not to abuse the trust and confidence placed in her by the plaintiff. The disparity in education between the plaintiff and defendant highlights the degree of dependence of the plaintiff upon the trust and honor of the defendant. . . .

Unquestionably, there is a transfer of property here, but the Trial Judge found that the transfer was made "without a promise or understanding of any kind." Even without an express promise, however, courts of equity have imposed a constructive trust upon property transferred in reliance upon a confidential relationship. In such a situation, a promise may be implied [*sic*] or inferred from the very transaction itself. As Judge Cardozo so eloquently observed: "Though a promise in words was lacking, the whole transaction, it might be found, was 'instinct with an obligation' imperfectly expressed. . . ." In deciding that a formal writing or express promise was not essential to the application of the doctrine of constructive trust, Judge Cardozo further observed in language that is most fitting in the instant case:

"Here was a man transferring to his sister the only property he had in the world . . . He was doing this, as she admits, in reliance upon her honor. Even if we were to accept her statement that there was no distinct promise to hold for his benefit, the exaction of such a promise, in view of the relation, might well have seemed to be superfluous". . . .

The salutary purpose of the constructive trust remedy is to prevent unjust enrichment and it is to this requirement that I now turn. The Trial Judge in his findings of fact, concluded that the transfer did not constitute unjust enrichment. In this instance also, a legal conclusion was mistakenly labeled a finding of fact. A person may be deemed to be unjustly enriched if he (or she) has received a benefit, the retention of which would be unjust (Restatement, Restitution, Section 1, Comment a). A conclusion that one has been unjustly enriched is essentially a legal inference drawn from the circumstances surrounding the transfer of property and the relationship of the parties. It is a conclusion reached through the application of principles of equity. Having determined that the relationship between plaintiff and defendant in this case is of such a nature as to invoke consideration of the equitable remedy of constructive trust, it remains to be determined whether defendant's conduct following the transfer of plaintiff's farm was in violation of that relationship and, consequently, resulted in the unjust enrichment of the defendant. This must be determined from the circumstances of the transfer since there is no express promise concerning plaintiff's continued use of the land. . . .

Accordingly, the order of the Appellate Division should be reversed and the case remitted to that court for a review of the facts, or, if it be so advised, in its discretion, to order a new trial in the interests of justice.

Questions

1. What made the relationship one of trust and confidence in this case? After all, weren't there mutual benefits from the arrangement?
2. What remedies might the plaintiff recover? possession of the property? title to the property? damages?
3. Can the defendant bring a separate lawsuit for the value of the services she rendered?

SUMMARY

A trust involves the transfer of legal title to property by a settlor to a trustee, with equitable title going to a beneficiary. It may be created expressly, or by implication, the former involving a manifestation of direct intent by the settlor, and the latter either implied intent or an attempt by the law to prevent an injustice. Trusts may be created for a variety of reasons, among the most important being the preservation of property or title, the maintenance and support of a beneficiary, and tax advantages.

The creation of an express trust involves five basic elements: (1) the settlor must have legal capacity; (2) the settlor must intend presently to establish a trust; (3) the *corpus* must be specific property; (4) the beneficiary must be identifiable with reasonable certainty; and (5) the purpose must be consistent with public policy.

An express trust may be private or charitable. The latter is characterized by a definite charitable intent and indefiniteness of the specific beneficiaries. When properly created, a court will seek to prevent the failure of a charitable trust for want of a proper beneficiary. This may be done by the application of the *cy pres* doctrine, under which a court will seek to apply the trust as nearly as possible to the settlor's purpose, consistent with public policy. This doctrine is not applied to private trusts. Upon the failure or other termination of a private trust, the remaining *corpus* is returned to the settlor, or distributed to his heirs or according to directions in the trust document.

Classification of trusts

Express Trusts	arise by express direction of the settlor
Totten trusts	settlor and trustee are the same person
Spendthrift trusts	created to support beneficiary who might squander the money
Implied Trusts	arise by operation of law
Resulting trusts	arise when a transfer of property was meant to transfer legal title alone
Constructive trusts	created by courts to redress a wrong or injustice
***Inter Vivos* Trusts**	become effective during the lifetime of the settlor
Testamentary trusts	become effective upon settlor's death
Private Trusts	established for private individuals
Charitable trusts	established to benefit the public or some subset of the public
Revocable Trusts	can be revoked or modified by settlor
Irrevocable trusts	cannot be revoked or modified by settlor

Two special types of express trusts worthy of note are the totten trust and the spendthrift trust. The rules governing these are the same as for other express trusts, but they present interesting situations. A totten trust is a trust created when the settlor places his own property in his own name as trustee for another person. The settlor and the trustee are the same person.

A spendthrift trust is one created for the maintenance and support of a person who otherwise would be likely to dispose of property foolishly. The beneficiary of this kind of trust ordinarily is entitled only to income from the trust, without any right to the *corpus*.

Generally, a settlor may modify or revoke a trust only if the power to do so was reserved specifically in the trust document. Otherwise the settlor may do so only in cases of a totten trust, or if the settlor can convince a court that it was intended that these powers be reserved, or when equity would allow it, as in the case of fraud, duress, or undue influence in the creation of a trust.

A trustee must be a "person," whether an individual, a corporation, or an unincorporated association (if permitted under state law). If an individual, the trustee must be of legal age. When acting as such, a trustee is a fiduciary, owing the settlor and the beneficiaries the highest duty of trust and confidence. This requires that the trustee be honest and appear honest in the transaction of all trust business. She is expected to exercise ordinary care and skill in preserving the trust and making it productive. In addition, if she holds herself out as having special knowledge or skills, like a bank or a professional trustee, she must exercise them. Failure to perform faithfully will render the trustee liable for all losses to the trust occasioned to the trust by that failure. The trustee is liable personally on all trust transactions, but is entitled to reimbursement from the trust when acting in the proper discharge of her duties. The trustee is the representative of the estate. She has all powers granted in the trust document, and powers that reasonably are necessary to effect the express purpose of the trust.

Implied trusts differ from express trusts in that they arise, not from an expressed intent by the settlor, but by operation of law. Two types of implied trusts are resulting trusts and constructive trusts. The first involves a transfer of property by the owner under circumstances indicating that the transferee was intended to receive only legal title, with equitable title remaining with the transferor. This intent of the transferor is presumed or inferred from the circumstances. A constructive trust arises in an effort by a court to prevent an injustice; specifically, it seeks to redress a wrong or prevent an unjust enrichment of the person holding property. Constructive trusts are founded on the application of the doctrine of equitable estoppel, and permit the court to do what seems fair under the circumstances.

KEY TERMS AND CONCEPTS

trust
trustee
beneficiary
legal title
equitable title
inter vivos trust
testamentary trust
revocable trust
irrevocable trust
settlor or trustor
express trust
charitable trust
cy pres doctrine
private trust
Rule Against Perpetuities
totten trust
spendthrift trust
fiduciary
implied trust
resulting trust
constructive trust

PROBLEMS

1. Auffaker conveyed certain land into trust, with Continental Bank as trustee. The property was subject to a lease, with an option to purchase, in favor of Country Club Mobile Home Estates. Twice, after the expiration of the option term, and after establishing the trust, Auffaker purported to extend the option term for additional five-year periods. Were the extensions binding on the trust?

2. After DeVries's death and the death of his second wife, the children of his first marriage sued the children of his second marriage to establish a constructive trust in his second wife's estate. De-Vries's will left all of his property to his second wife, and included a provision: "I give, devise and bequeath to my beloved wife, Amanda DeVries, all the balance, residue and remainder of my property . . . with the knowledge that she will be fair and equitable to all of my children, the issue of myself and my former wife, as well as the issue of herself and myself." Are the petitioners entitled to share by virtue of this provision?

3. By will, the testator empowered the executor of her estate as a "trustee" to distribute to her "friends" such of her property as they considered suitable mementos. The determination of who would share and what property would be distributed was left to the friends' discretion. Was a valid trust created?

4. Sidney Graves owed Utley $4500 on a note dated April 30, 1963. Graves's wife had died on April 11, 1962, leaving Graves only a spendthrift trust for necessaries. Graves had elected to take under the will creating the trust rather than to take a spouse's share under statute. Utley sued Graves on the unpaid note and contended that doing so caused Graves to become both settlor and beneficiary, thus causing the trust to dissolve. As a result, the *corpus* of the failed trust should be subject to his (Utley's) claim. The trial court agreed. Should this judgment be reversed?

5. A testamentary trust was created naming "Carthage College, Carthage, Illinois" as beneficiary. The trust funds were to be used to provide scholarships to needy, deserving, Carthage College students. When Carthage College moved to Wisconsin, Bell petitioned a court to declare the trust beneficiary no longer existed, and to designate another Carthage, Illinois, institution beneficiary by applying the *cy pres* doctrine. Should the court grant the petition? Articulate your reasons.

6. Earl Payne sued to set aside a land trust established by his wife, Emily, prior to their marriage. His contention was that the land should be included in Emily's estate because she had reserved the power to amend and revoke. Should the trust be set aside for this reason?

7. A & M produced and manufactured tapes and records of musical performances. Heilman admitted copying and distributing several selections from these tapes and records. A & M sued to have a constructive trust declared on Heilman's assets in an amount sufficient to reimburse A & M for lost profits. Is this an appropriate remedy for A & M?

8. Barnette signed a document entitled "Declaration of Trust," which stated that he was holding certain shares of stock he then owned in trust for his wife. The share certificates never were indorsed, and the corporation never was notified. After his death, the question arose of whether a valid trust had been created since there had been no transfer of the property. Was a valid trust created?

9. Nussbaum, by will, left $1950 in a checking account, $5000 in certificates of deposit, and a house valued at $6000 to his granddaughter, Whitmer, who was nine years old at the time of Nussbaum's death. The property was willed in trust, with Whitmer's aunt, Blair, as trustee, to be held for Whitmer's education. The house was sold, netting $4467. The entire amount, except for the certificates, was held in a non-interest-bearing checking account. When Whitmer was ready for college, at age twenty-three, she sued Blair for improper administration of the trust on the ground that the funds should not have been held in a checking account. Is she entitled to a judgment?

10. The Industrial Valley Bank was named trustee of a continuing trust under Hammil's will. Over the objections of current-income beneficiaries, the entire *corpus* was invested in treasury bills. The beneficiary then filed suit to compel the trustee to reinvest the money in other investments that would earn a higher rate of return. Is the beneficiary entitled to relief?

Decedents' Estates

OUTLINE

INTRODUCTION

Most of us will accumulate property during the course of our lifetimes. Few of us are likely to accumulate vast sums, but fortunately few of us will die penniless. Thus, it is important to give some consideration to what happens to our property upon death, and to think about the possible need for estate planning.

Disposition of Property upon the Owner's Death

After death, property belonging to the decedent must be distributed either to heirs, according to the laws of intestate succession, or according to a will, if the decedent executed a valid one during his or her lifetime. Formal distribution by a court is called **probate,** and is administered by a personal representative of the estate, sometimes called an *executor* or *administrator*. Administration of a decedent's estate is accomplished by a continuing proceeding through a special court, often called a *probate, surrogate,* or *family court.*

Probate proceedings are conducted according to state law. There is no national statute concerning descent and distribution. Generally, it is recognized that each state has a fundamental right to regulate the disposition of property of those who die within its borders. Although the various states' laws are not uniform, they are quite similar in theory and in their basic provisions. However, differences become particularly important when more than one state is involved in the probate process. For example, a resident of Michigan might die in his winter home in Florida, owning real estate in Arizona and an interest in a partnership in Massachusetts. As more states become involved, the potential for conflicts of laws is increased, including questions concerning which state or states may tax the decedent's estate.

The question of taxation is important in the probate of many estates. In this context, federal laws concerning both estate and gift taxation may be a factor in probate, as may state inheritance tax laws. To a substantial degree, therefore, a desire to avoid tax problems stimulates a need for estate planning.

Federal estate tax is assessed on all property belonging to a person at the date of death. However, beginning in 1986, the tax law made the first $600,000 exempt. Thus, many estates pay no federal tax. Still, state inheritance taxes may apply. In most cases, state inheritance taxes are assessed only on property located in the state. Thus, a single estate may be subject to taxes in two or more states.

Sometimes people whose estates are subject to estate and inheritance taxes can minimize their impact by making gifts of money and property during their lifetimes. Although this tactic is effective, gifts of more than $10,000 per year are subject to gift taxes. Also, if gifts are made in contemplation of death, and are intended to circumvent estate taxation, the amounts of the gifts may be included in the donor's estate for estate-tax purposes.

Estate Planning

Estate planning is a process of planning for the accumulation and the distribution of a person's property. Accumulation refers to the sources of additions to a person's estate, as well as to its productive use during the person's lifetime. Distribution involves both transfers of property during lifetime and after death. Depending upon an individual's circumstances, estate planning can have a number of objectives: minimizing the impact of death taxes, avoiding the forced sale of assets at the time of death, assuring that certain property passes to those the deceased wishes to receive it, and providing for the care and support of dependents.

Death taxes may be minimized by the use of such techniques as gifts during the person's lifetime and the creation of trusts. In addition, the use of readily available after-death dispositions such as life insurance, passing appreciated property instead of cash, and providing for the creation of life estates instead of fee simple estates in appropriate circumstances may do much to minimize taxes. Forced sales may be avoided by providing sufficient cash to pay off the estate's obligations, and by providing for the transfer of particular undivided property to specific beneficiaries, or by transferring joint interests in divisible property so that the property does not have to be partitioned. Special assets, such as grandmother's ring or an antique car, may be given to particular people by an express provision in a will. Finally, trusts may be used to see to the care and support of dependents. Taxes are discussed in more detail at the end of this chapter, and trusts were discussed in the preceding chapter.

INTESTATE SUCCESSION

When a person dies without leaving a will, his estate will be distributed to his spouse and heirs according to a statutory formula. If he has no spouse or heirs, the property will go to the state. Receiving property under such a statute is called **intestate succession.** Often this statutory method is not a good idea for a variety of reasons.

Generally

Most of us do not like to think about death, let alone plan for it. As a result, it is not uncommon that a person dies without leaving a will. Another reason for not making a will is that some people believe it is the way to avoid probate, with its attendant costs and delays. For the most part, that simply is not true. As one philosopher stated, the best way to avoid probate is to eat only healthy foods, get plenty of rest, and look both ways before crossing the street. Although this may be a bit tongue-in-cheek, it is essentially true. The distribution of most estates will involve some kind of probate proceeding, and if an estate is substantial, the costs, especially in terms of taxes, easily may be greater if there is no will. The only thing really accomplished by not making a will is that the property of the deceased will be distributed according to the rules provided in the state's intestacy statute. Although these rules may be appropriate in many cases, very often they do not suit the needs of most persons, and having a well-written will may avoid the almost inevitable fighting among heirs as they descend on the estate.

Rules of Distribution

Although not uniform, the rules for intestate distribution in the statutes of the various states follow a common pattern. The distribution of personal property will be governed by the laws of the state of the decedent's *domicile;* real property is distributed according to the laws of the state in which it is located.

In order to inherit property under the laws of intestate succession, one generally must be an **heir**—a *blood* relative of the deceased, although the intestacy statutes of many states, and the **Uniform Probate Code (UPC),** which is a uniform distribution statute adopted by many states, define the term *heir* as including a spouse. Heirs then may be *ascendents* (such as parents or grandparents), *descendants* (such as children and grandchildren), or *collateral* (such as brothers and sisters). Other than a spouse, non-blood relatives *ordinarily* take no interest under intestacy laws. Neither do non-relatives such as friends, acquaintances, and live-in mates.

Under most laws of intestate succession, the first to be provided for are the surviving spouse, issue (lineal descendants, such as children, grandchildren, and great grandchildren), and parents in some cases. Under Section 2-102 of the Uniform Probate Code, if there is a surviving spouse, the estate is distributed as follows:

1. if there is no surviving issue or parent of the decedent, the entire estate passes to the spouse;
2. if there is no surviving issue, but the decedent is survived by a parent or parents, the spouse receives the first $50,000 plus one-half of the balance of the estate, and the remainder goes to the parent or parents;
3. if there are surviving issue, all of whom are also issue of the surviving spouse, the spouse, again, receives the first $50,000 plus one-half of the balance of the estate, and the remainder is divided among the issue (surviving parents of the deceased receive no interest); and
4. if there are surviving issue, one or more of whom are not issue of the surviving spouse, the spouse receives one-half (only) of the entire estate, and the remainder is divided among the issue.

These rules probably will satisfy the needs of the majority of intestate estates in most jurisdictions. The $50,000 figures is only recommended by the UPC and states adopting the code may substitute another amount. Also, an alternative, Section 2-102A, is provided for community property states. In those states, a surviving spouse generally is given a one-half interest in property accumulated during the marriage with some exceptions (such as property received by either spouse as a gift or by inheritance), and the remainder of the decedent's property is distributed as above.

Section 2-103 of the UPC then governs the

distribution to heirs other than the surviving spouse. The portion of the estate not passing to the spouse, or the entire estate if there is no surviving spouse, passes as follows.

1. If there is issue of the decedent, they share equally according to degree of kinship, the closest taking equal shares *(per capita),* and the more remote taking by representation *(per stirpes).* For example, suppose the deceased had three children; Al, Beth, and Cy. Suppose also that Cy predeceased his father, leaving two children, Quincy and Rose, and that Rose also was dead, leaving two children, Zeke and Zach. The portion to be distributed under Section 2-103 would pass one-third to Al, one-third to Beth, one-sixth to Quincy (half of Cy's third), and one-twelfth each to Zeke and Zach (one-half each of Rose's sixth). Note that Cy's spouse and Rose's spouse take nothing. They are not *heirs* of the deceased.

2. If there are no issue of the deceased, the parents of the deceased share equally.

3. If there are no issue or parents, the brothers and sisters of the deceased will share equally. The issue of any deceased brother or sister will take equally according to degree of kinship, the more remote taking by representation, as in the first example.

4. If there are none of the above, then grandparents and their issue take, again equally according to degree of kinship, the more remote kin taking by representation. One-half is distributed on the paternal side and the other half on the maternal, if representatives of both survive. Otherwise, all descends to one side.

States may provide for distributions to even more remote kin if there are no representatives of any of the above classes. However, beyond grandparents and their issue, distributions may become very complicated, with relatives becoming difficult to locate and shares becoming fractionally very small. In any case, if no eligible heirs can be located, a decedent's undistributed estate will *escheat* to the state. Escheat, however, is rare. But, even someone with no relatives should have a will to make sure that her property goes to a favorite charity, educational institution, religious organization, friend, or even a pet rather than to the state's treasury.

The following case illustrates some of the problems encountered by probate courts when a substantial estate is involved and no close heirs can be located. Involved are what are sometimes referred to as "laughing heirs" (those of remote kinship) and the inevitable emergence of parasites advancing fraudulent claims.

IN RE WENDEL'S ESTATE
159 Misc. 443, 287 N.Y.S. 893 (1936)

In this case, the court denied the claims of Petitioners and admonished their attorneys to consider the Canons of Ethics of the American Bar Association before representing such clients again.

FOLEY, Surrogate.

This proceeding involves the latest, and it is hoped the last, attempt to impose a fraudulent claim of relationship upon the members of the family of Ella V. von E. Wendel. Meta Wendel Strauch, the petitioner, claiming to be the illegitimate daughter of decedent, Georgiana G. R. Wendel, sought to have established her status as sole next of kin, and applied to have opened the final decree made by this court on December 29, 1933, settling the accounts of the administrators of the estate. Under that decree, distribution was made to her two sisters, Rebecca A. D. Wendel Swope, and Ella V. von E. Wendel, as her sole next of kin. Georgiana died on January 19, 1919, Rebecca died on July 20, 1930, and Ella died on March 13, 1931. Georgiana left an estate approximating $5,000,000. Most of her property found its way into Ella Wendel's estate.

The first formal claim that the petitioner, Meta Wendel Strauch, was an illegitimate daughter of the decedent was made upon the filing of the petition in the present proceeding on May 1, 1935. In it Meta Wendel Strauch asserts that she was born the daughter of the decedent on July 3, 1879, in the city of Bremen, Germany. The evidence submitted upon the hearing before the Surrogate completely destroys the contentions of the petitioner and brands her claim as a crude fraud. In the process of exposure, however, it has been necessary for the representatives and the beneficiaries of this estate and of the estate of the decedent's sister to conduct an expensive investigation into the allegations of the petition, to examine 24 witnesses in Germany upon commissions issued out of this court, to take the testimony of other witnesses in Massachusetts and New Jersey, and to produce witnesses upon the formal hearing before the Surrogate.

This proceeding is of special interest because of similar attempts by fortune seekers to assert claims of relationship to Ella Wendel, the decedent's sister. In the estate of Ella, 2,303 persons filed claims to varying degrees of relationship. Nine finally established their status as the lawful next of kin as relations of the fifth degree of kinship. The claims of 2,294 persons were dismissed. Of this number the greater majority pretended to be related in more distant degrees beyond the fifth degree of kinship. The establishment of kinship of persons within that degree necessarily led to a dismissal of those asserting a relationship beyond it. There were other claimants who asserted that they were within the third, fourth, and fifth degrees. The trials of the status of these claimants revealed the falsity of their pretensions and exposed the spurious, forged, and fraudulent evidence upon which they were based.

Thomas Patrick Morris claimed to be the nephew of Ella Wendel and the son of her brother, John G. Wendel. The nature of the evidence in his case was considered by me and his claim dismissed in Matter of Wendel's Estate, 146 Misc. 260, 262 N.Y.S. 41. It was shown that he had attempted to perpetrate a fraudulent marriage certificate of his alleged mother and father, a spurious will of his alleged father and other fabricated documents in order to substantiate his claim. The record in the case was directed by the Surrogate to be transmitted to the district attorney of New York county for appropriate action. Morris was indicted and convicted of conspiracy and sentenced to a term of three years. He subsequently sought to set aside his conviction with his claim that he was the son of John G. Wendel and one Mary Ellen Devine. In the same application, and by way of contradiction, he presented an additional claim that he was the illegitimate child of John G. Wendel and his sister, Mary Wendel, by an incestuous relationship. The motion for a new trial was denied by Judge Morris Koenig of the

Court of General Sessions of New York County in a very comprehensive opinion. New York Law Journal, October 20, 1934, p. 1353.

A second group of claimants, the so-called Dew claimants of Tennessee, in three successive applications, sought to establish their relationship as of the fifth degree. Their claims were based upon an attempt to identify one of their ancestors as an ancestor of Ella Wendel. These claims were dismissed upon the ground that no relationship whatsoever existed between them and Miss Wendel. Again forged documentary evidence was attempted to be foisted upon the court. The judicial records of the courts of Tennessee were shown to have been deliberately altered. The spurious nature of these documents and the willful alterations made in them were revealed upon the trials and discussed in my decisions. Matter of Wendel's Estate, 148 Misc. 884, 267 N.Y.S. 33; Id., 146 Misc. 260, 262 N.Y.S. 41, and N.Y. Law Journal, April 8, 1933, p. 2101.

A third group of claimants, residing in Illinois, likewise attempted to prove relationship by spurious documentary evidence consisting of letters claimed to have been written by the relations of Ella Wendel. Two of these letters were dated 1836 and 1841. Investigation revealed that they were written upon paper purchased from the F.W. Woolworth Five and Ten Cent Stores. The paper was manufactured not earlier than 1930, although the writings were dated almost a century before. Their claims were dismissed. New York Law Journal, November 18, 1932, p. 2218.

It is significant as bearing upon the motives of conspirators in the present application in the estate of Georgiana Wendel that they were associated with a group of persons who sought to establish that they were related to Ella Wendel in the proceedings in her estate. Their contention was that they were distant cousins of Ella Wendel through an alleged common ancestor, one Johann Christian Heinrich Wendel. They found an association in Bremen, Germany, and raised funds to prosecute their claims. Meta Strauch, the petitioner here, was not included in the group for some unexplained reason, although 23 of her close relations filed formal claims in this court. The testimony in this proceeding however shows that she contributed 500 marks to the expenses of Emil Wendel, one of the agents of the group. Since all of their contentions involved a pretense to relationship beyond the fifth degree of kinship, it became unnecessary to take testimony to determine their status. Sufficient evidence has been adduced in this proceeding to show that they were not in the slightest degree related to Ella Wendel.

Questions

1. What methods should be used by the legal system to deter fraudulent claims against an estate?

2. Does a will prevent the problems presented in this case? Does a will create other problems?

3. How much proof is needed to convince a judge who constantly faces fraudulent claims that a particular claim is genuine?

SPECIAL RULES GOVERNING DISTRIBUTION

Some situations are subject to special rules governing distribution. These affect who is entitled to inherit or receive property under a will, and what taxes may apply to the estate.

Heirs

As previously discussed, only a spouse and heirs are entitled to take by intestate succession. This includes all children of the deceased, both legitimate and *illegitimate*. Children of a decedent born after his death inherit as any other child. Also, children legally *adopted* by the deceased are allowed to inherit by specific statutory provision. In addition, most states also provide that *half-blood* brothers and sisters inherit the same as full-blood. *Stepchildren* however, do not inherit unless legally adopted.

Homicide Disqualification

Most states specifically provide that someone who is convicted of the homicide (murder, and usually manslaughter also) of a person may not inherit from, or take under the will of, that person. The same generally is true concerning proceeds of a life insurance policy or any other interest arising as a result of the death of the victim, including a right of survivorship in jointly held property. If not excluded specifically by state law, the passage of property interests under these circumstances is subject to attack in the courts as being contrary to public policy. Judges typically refuse to reward criminal activity by allowing fruits of the crime to pass to the guilty party.

Simultaneous Death

Suppose two persons, for example a husband and wife, die as a result of the same catastrophe, such as a fire, an airplane crash, or an automobile accident. Whether one will inherit from the other normally depends on who died first. If it could be proven that one survived the other by as little as one second, the surviving spouse would inherit. The surviving spouse's inheritance would become part of that spouse's estate and would be distributed accordingly. This multiple-death situation creates two problems. First, under these circumstances, it often is difficult, if not impossible, to determine who survived. Second, the rule may lead to double taxation since the property must be probated through two estates. In order to avoid these problems, most states have adopted specific provisions concerning simultaneous death.

Section 2-104 of the Uniform Probate Code provides that an heir must survive the decedent by 120 hours or that heir will be deemed to have predeceased the decedent. Of course, the heirs of that heir may take some share of the estate of the deceased by representation in appropriate circumstances. This provision is of general application to all heirs and primarily is aimed at avoiding the multiple administration of estates. However, it is applicable only to cases of intestacy, and does not apply if its operation would result in property escheating to the state (when the heir concerned would be the last heir of the decedent). The UPC does have a comparable provision involving wills, in Section 2-601, and of course a will itself may contain a provision for avoiding the problem of simultaneous death.

Another "uniform" statute, the Uniform Simultaneous Death Act, also offers some solution to this problem, but is in some respects less comprehensive than the UPC. It offers only partial assistance because it applies only if there is no proof that the parties died otherwise than simultaneously. When applicable, the USDA provides that the property of each party will be distributed *as though he or she survived*. This means that the property of each will be distributed to his or her heirs. Of course, again, any part of the estate of one that would be distributed to the heirs of the other by representation will be distributed in the same manner under the USDA.

Gifts Prior to Death

Gifts of money and other property may be made during the lifetime of the donor, and this is done commonly to avoid death taxes when there has been estate planning. These may be absolute gifts, advancements of property to be received by the recipient upon the death of the giver, gifts *causa mortis,* or gifts in contemplation of death intended to evade federal estate tax. If the gift exceeds deductible amounts set out in the statute, all of these are subject to gift taxation. In order to prevent double taxation of transfers, federal laws concerning gift and estate taxation are intended to be complementary. Those transfers taxed as gifts will not be taxed as part of the estate, and vice versa. One method used in proper estate planning is to find the optimum mix of these taxes and distribute a person's property during life and at death accordingly.

In order to avoid being taxed as part of the donor's estate, absolute gifts during lifetime must be just that—absolute. They must be made unconditionally and irrevocably. However, they may be made either directly or in an irrevocable trust. Any rights retained by the donor are subject to estate taxation. Absolute gifts, however, may be taxable under federal gift tax laws beyond the one-time and annual deductible amounts set out in the statute.

Advancements are gifts during a lifetime intended by the giver as a prepayment of some portion of the recipient's share of the giver's estate upon death, such as giving a son a home to live in with his new wife, the property being part of the parent's estate that was intended to go to the son upon death. Advancements are considered part of the giver's estate for estate-tax purposes, and are deducted from the recipient's share upon distribution of the estate. In order to avoid adverse tax effect, any property given as an advancement should be deleted from the giver's will.

Gifts *causa mortis* are contingent gifts during the lifetime of the donor, intended to become effective upon the donor's death. "Because I am about to die of cancer, I want you to have my antique watch when I pass." In order to be effective, the donor must die of the peril that motivated the giving of the gift. Otherwise the subject of the gift remains the property of the donor. Since gifts *causa mortis* become effective upon the owner's death, the donor has full rights in the subject property at the moment of death. Therefore, the subject property is taxed as a part of her estate.

Sometimes the giving of property is motivated by the fear of impending death, but the donative intent arises from a desire to avoid estate taxation by making the transfer during life and thus taking advantage of favorable gift-tax exemptions. When it is determined that this is the donor's motivation, the subject property will be taxed as part of the estate even though it was transferred as an absolute gift during the donor's lifetime. Any gifts made within a prescribed period prior to the donor's death are subject to the presumption that they were given for the purpose of evading estate taxation. It is important to understand that these gifts differ from gifts *causa mortis* in that they are given absolutely, rather than being contingent on death, and their purpose is to avoid estate taxation.

WILLS

A **will** is an instrument of conveyance by which title to property is transferred at the time of death. It should be noted that a will is not a contract. It gives no assurance that the property ever will be transferred, and it may be revoked at any time prior to death. Unlike a deed, it grants no immediate rights in property even when a valid will is executed during the testator's lifetime. Its effectiveness awaits the death of the person making the will—the **testator** or **testatrix.** At the moment of death, the interests it provides for are transferred immediately, subject, of course, to probate proceedings.

The requirements for wills are not completely uniform among the states, although there is much similarity in the basic statutory provisions. Also, the courts of most states will recognize a will that is defective under local law if it is valid under the laws of the state in which it was executed. In the discussion that follows, the Uniform Probate Code will be used as a model for examining the basic requirements for a valid will.

Requirements for a Formal Will

A formal will is a will that meets all of the state requirements for a valid will, without resort to special rules for will forms such as the *holographic* (handwritten) *will* or the *nuncupative* (oral) *will*. Statutes typically require that the testator or testatrix be of legal age. Under the UPC and the laws of most states, the legal age is 18. At common law, an infant (minor) technically could not hold legal title to property, but could hold only equitable title, which is voidable title under contract law, or beneficial title as the beneficiary of a trust. Therefore, an infant ordinarily would have no property to dispose of under a will. Of course, this may be changed by statute, but it still is true in the vast majority of states.

Beyond the legal age requirement, a formal will must be in writing, signed by the testator or by an authorized agent in the presence of the testator, and must be witnessed. The UPC and the statutes of most states require a minimum of two witnesses, although a few require three. The testator normally must sign in the presence of the witnesses, and they must sign in the presence of the testator. Indiana law, however, requires that the testator sign in *the sight and the presence* of the witnesses, and that they sign in the sight and the presence of the testator and in the sight and the presence *of each other*. Such technical requirements are of great importance in the law concerning wills. The failure to meet all of them to the letter may well result in the will's being declared void, and the decedent's property being distributed as an intestate estate. Unfortunately, that fact probably will come to light only after the death of the testator, when it is too late to remedy the defect.

In addition to these prerequisites, most states insist that wills be **acknowledged and published.** That is, the testator must state that he is acting freely and voluntarily, and declare the document to be his "last will and testament." The witnesses then attest the fact that the testator did so. Part of the reason for the witness requirement is to have two or more persons to whom the testator may make this declaration, in addition to having witnesses who can testify that the testator signed the document.

Ordinarily it is not necessary that a will be notarized (sworn and signed before a notary public). However, Section 2-504 of the UPC, and the statutes of a number of states, provide that if a will is executed, or later acknowledged, by the testator, and affidavits are executed by witnesses before a notary public or other officer authorized by the state to administer oaths (for example, a judge), then the will is **self-proved.** This means that it may be admitted to probate without the testimony of any witnesses. Thereafter, however, it is treated as is any other will, and may be challenged for any reason other than the validity of the testator's signature.

Contents of a Will

A will generally begins with a clause naming the testator, stating that he or she is of full age, sound mind, and disposing memory, and declaring the document to be his or her last will and testament. Thereafter, provision is made for the disposition of the testator's estate. Usually the first disposition clause directs payment of all valid debts, often including charitable pledges, and the costs of administering the estate. If the testator owns property subject to the probate law of other states, provision generally is made for payment of the costs of ancillary probate proceedings from the *corpus* of the main estate. The next clause or clauses typically set out bequests of particular property to specified persons, and a final disposition clause provides that all of the "rest, residue, and remainder" of the estate will be distributed in a certain manner. (This is called a *residual* or *residuary clause*.) Provision then is made for an executor (or executrix) or the appointment of an administrator (or administratrix), any request concerning the bonding of the executor or administrator, and any request concerning his or her compensation. Under the laws of some states, the testator even may request that, within limits stated or provided by statute, the executor or administrator be allowed to exercise independent judgment in some matters without being required to seek prior court approval. Finally, there is an execution clause and an attestation clause. In addition to these standard clauses, provision may be made for the creation and administration of one or more trusts, and the testator may make nonbinding requests of the court or particular parties. These requests sometimes are called *precatory* provisions.

Holographic Wills

A **holographic will** is one written and signed in the handwriting of the testator. A valid holographic will needs no witnesses. The fact that its provisions are set down in the handwriting of the testator is considered sufficient to prove the intent of the testator.

Many states that recognize the validity of holographic wills require that the entire document be in the handwriting of the testator. This strict approach is rejected by the UPC. Section 2-503 of that Code requires only that, in addition to the signature, *material* provisions must be in the hand of the testator. This was done to avoid invalidating a holographic will because of the printing or stamping of immaterial parts such as a date or introductory wording. In addition, it permits the use of printed forms, as long as the material provisions are handwritten. This seems adequate to serve the purpose of allowing persons unable to secure legal assistance to make valid wills. Although a holographic will is sufficient and sometimes necessary, a formal will still is preferable. In spite of the simplification of requirements regarding handwritten wills, care must be exercised that the minimum formal requirements are met, as the following case illustrates.

IN RE ESTATE OF HALL
238 F.Supp. 1305 (A.C. D.C. 1971)

This was an action by the Navy Relief Society to have a holographic writing of decedent, Francesca Ross Hall, admitted to probate as her last will and testatment.

In the course of the administration of the decedent's estate, a one-page handwritten document was found in a safe deposit box. The document was written in 1932, and purported to give approximately 70 percent of her estate to "whatever organization cares for the disabled sailors and seamen of the United States Navy and their families." The page was written on both sides, and on the back side it ended with an incomplete line, "All personal effects to be left to . . ." The writing was not signed, but the decedent's name appeared in her own handwriting at the top of the first side of the page. The signatures of two witnesses also appeared at the top of the front. Testimony was given that the entire document, at the time it was made out, consisted of three pages. Neither witness was present or saw the other sign, and one was not present when the first page was written.

PRATT, John H., District Judge.

Of course the burden of proving formal execution of a will rests on the party wishing to have the document admitted to probate, in this case the plaintiff Navy Relief Society. . . . *Where a will appears regular* on its face, the normal presumption of regularity would lighten the burden on the moving party. . . . The document before the Court, however, is not regular on its face. The last two pages of the original document, including the page with Francesca's signature, and that of the witness Cousins, are missing under unknown circumstances. It is uncertain whether the second witness, Mrs. Lockner, ever attested the original complete document on the last page. It is certain that Mrs. Lockner did not see decedent sign her name or write any part of the paper. The writing does not effect a complete disposition of decedent's assets. These facts, coupled with Miss Hall's admitted mental problems, place a heavy burden on plaintiff in its effort to show due execution. . . .

The purported will was not validly attested by Lockner. There is no evidence at all, nor could any be presented if there was a trial, on attestation of the complete original document by Lockner. We know that she signed on the first page, although we do not know when. But the testimony of Cousins in his deposition is clear that Francesca finished the entire document in one sitting, signed it, and then went upstairs to bed. Since the last pages are missing, we just do not know if Lockner ever signed at the end. Even if Lockner signed, there is no evidence that the signing by Francesca and attesting of the paper by Lockner was a substantially contemporaneous transaction. As discussed above, District [of Columbia] law requires that even holographic wills be attested and subscribed in the presence of the testator by two witnesses, although they need not sign in each other's presence or physically observe the other's signature. . . . Plaintiff urges that the normal presumption of regularity should apply since we have admittedly authentic signatures of the testator and the two witnesses on the present document. It is the Court's view, however, that for all of the reasons discussed above, this document cannot be viewed as being regular on its face, and that therefore due execution cannot be presumed. Plaintiff has not and cannot meet its burden of showing that we have a portion of a longer, duly executed document, which should be given present effect.

Questions

1. Since the will clearly is in the deceased's handwriting and there is some testimony by witnesses, what is the court worried about?
2. Isn't it better to follow the handwritten desires of the deceased than to give the property to the state?
3. Does this case mean that each and every formality must be met before a holographic document will be accepted?

Nuncupative Wills

A **nuncupative will** is an oral will. Where recognized, a nuncupative will normally is effective only if it is made in the reasonable fear of impending death, disposes of only personal property (frequently only up to a maximum value and only if the property is then in the possession of the testator), and is proven by disinterested witnesses. One important circumstance that often is held to justify a nuncupative will is its use in time of war under battlefield conditions. Nuncupative wills are not recognized under the UPC.

Modification

Once executed, a will may be modified freely or revoked by the testator. Although it is possible to modify terms by erasing, marking out, or inserting new provisions, this procedure certainly is not recommended. Alterations to the document raise questions of forgery. In addition, the law requires changes to be made and attested to with the same formalities necessary to execute a valid will. These present enormous problems of both logistics and proof.

Two methods of modification are recommended. The entire will may be rewritten and the old one physically destroyed, or the testator may execute a *codicil*. The first method, although always appropriate, generally is unnecessary unless the modifications involve a major revision of the existing will, such as taking account of a new child or creating a trust to take care of a spouse who has become incompetent. A **codicil** is simply a written statement of the changes to the existing will, perhaps adding a specific bequest of some recently acquired asset. It must be executed with the same formalities required for a will, including publishing, executing, and attesting by witnesses. When the proper procedure is followed, the codocil has the effect of republishing the will as modified by the codicil. The codicil then should be attached to the front of the will and the entire document should be put in a safe and obvious place.

Revocation

As noted above, in addition to the right to modify, the testator has a right to revoke any will prior to her death. Modification, of course, acts as a revocation of the specific provisions changed. However, the testator may choose to revoke the will in its entirety.

A will may be revoked by act of the testator. This includes the execution of a valid subsequent will. A will also may be revoked by being burned, torn, canceled, obliterated, or destroyed, with the intent and for the purpose of revoking it, by the testator or by another person in the testator's presence and at his direction (UPC, Section 2-506). As long as the court can determine that at the time of his death the testator no longer intended that the will be effective, it will be considered revoked. The safest procedure is to both execute a statement revoking the previous will and destroy it.

If the revoked will is not replaced by a new one, the testator will be considered to have died intestate. Also, although copies of a will generally are not effective, they also should be destroyed. Consider the following case dealing with the question of probating a will that was lost or accidentally destroyed.

BARKSDALE v. PENDERGRASS
294 Ala. 526, 319 So.2d 267 (1975)

This was an action by Rita Jan Pendergrass (Petitioner/Appellee) to have a copy of a will admitted to probate as the last will and testament of Mamie C. Henry, a widow. The writing purported to leave the entire estate to Petitioner. The petition was contested by Joe Barksdale, administrator of the estate, and Olen Barksdale (Respondents/Appellants). They contended that the purported will never was executed or, if executed, was destroyed by the decedent. No other will was found.

The court found for Petitioner and admitted the will to probate, and Respondents appealed. Affirmed.

MERRILL, Justice.

In a proceeding to probate an alleged lost or destroyed will, the burden is on the proponent to establish, to the reasonable satisfaction of the judge or jury trying the facts:

(1) The existence of a will—an instrument in writing, signed by the testator or some person in his presesnce, and by his direction, and attested by at least two witnesses, who must subscribe their names thereto in the presence of the testator. . . .

(2) The loss or destruction of the instrument. . . .

(3) The nonrevocation of the instrument by the testator. . . .

(4) The contents of the will in substance and effect. . . .

The evidence produced at trial showed that Charles M. Scott, a Ft. Payne attorney, prepared a will for Mrs. Henry in November of 1963. She did not execute the will in Scott's office because she wanted to "get her own witnesses" in Collinsville where she lived. Scott subsequently made several minor changes in the will and mailed her a final version in January of 1964. Rita Jan Gray was named as beneficiary in every version of the will. . . .

The second thing which the proponent must prove is the loss or destruction of the instrument. Billy McDowell, who rented an apartment from Mrs. Henry between 1967 and 1969, testified that Mrs. Henry showed him a will; that she said Charles M. Scott prepared it; that Cecil Sharp's name was on the will as a witness, and that Rita Jan Gray was the sole beneficiary. He also said that Mrs. Henry kept the will in a purse under a mattress in a spare room. Floyd Gray, the father of the beneficiary, testified that he saw one of Mrs. Henry's nephews at her house shortly after her death. Willard Reaves, an employee of the funeral home, testified that several of Mrs. Henry's relatives visited her house that day after she died. There was also an abundance of testimony that the will might have been lost or destroyed by accident. Finally, attorney Scott testified that several weeks after Mrs. Henry's death he searched the house himself. Proponent Rita Jan Gray Pendergrass subsequently filed an application to compel production of the will. Appellants Barksdale responded "That the said purported will, if executed, has been destroyed prior to the death of the Testatrix, and was not found in her possession nor among his [*sic*] effects at the time of her death, and is presumed, if ever executed, to have been destroyed in accordance with law."

The third element of proof involved the presumption of revocation. When the will is shown to have been in the possession of the testator, and is not found at his death, the presumption arises that he destroyed it for the purpose of revocation; but the presumption may be rebutted, and the burden of rebutting it is on the proponent. . . .

Billy McDowell, attorney Scott, and Mildred Johnson, a former neighbor of Mrs. Henry, testified that Mrs. Henry said that she did not want her nieces and nephews to have anything she had; that she had always made it abundantly clear that she wanted to select somebody other than her nieces and nephews; that she was afraid they were going to get her property; that she knew that her nieces and nephews would get her property if she died intestate; that she wanted Rita to have it, and that this was her fixed opinion.

Finally, proponent offered the copy of the will in evidence as proof of its contents.

A jury question was adequately presented under the authorities cited supra, and the jury found for the proponent. . . .

While the usual method of authenticating a copy is by the testimony of someone who has compared the copy with the original and found the copy to be correct, other evidence may suffice. . . .

In the instant case, Billy McDowell testified that Mrs. Henry showed him her will; that he remembered seeing Cecil Sharp's signature; and that Mrs. Henry told him that her attorney Scott had written the will, and that Rita Jan Gray was her sole beneficiary. It would appear that there was sufficient evidence from which too identify the copy.

Questions

1. Is it inconsistent to insist that the formalities for a valid will be complied with and then accept a copy rather than the original? Why or why not?

2. What is wrong with using a copy of a will?

3. Are you persuaded by the proof in this case?

Under the laws of most states, and under Section 2-508 of the UPC, termination of a marriage, as by divorce or annulment, will revoke any existing testamentary disposition to the former spouse. Note, however, that this does not revoke the entire will. Also, other changes, such as separation, even by court decree, ordinarily do not revoke the will. Normally, a provision in a well-drafted divorce or annulment decree explicitly will revoke other dispositions to the spouse. However, again, the safe procedure is to revoke these other grants expressly, either in a new will or by codicil.

ADMINISTRATION OF ESTATES

Some kind of probate proceeding is likely to be necessary upon the death of any person unless she dies without any property to be distributed. This is true whether the person has a will or dies intestate. Probate proceedings generally are necessary to transfer any property interests owned by the deceased at the time of death. Some interests pass automatically without the necessity of probate, such as those to beneficiaries under life insurance policies and to surviving joint or entireties tenants. However, even these may have estate and inheritance tax implications, both for the decedent's estate and the recipient.

The Representative of the Estate

Someone must be empowered to administer the details of the probate of an estate. This person may be referred to as executor, executrix, administrator, or administratrix. The term **executor** is used when the person was named by the testator in the will, and **administrator** is used when appointed by the court. The suffix *rix* indicates that the person is female. Many states have now "degendered" their probate statutes, and the term **personal representative** often is used, regardless of how the person was empowered and regardless of sex.

The personal representative may be any "person," including an individual, a partnership, or a corporation. Normally, the only specific requirement is that the person must be a resident of the state in which the probate proceedings are to take place, although a few states do not require residency. This is for the purpose of giving the court jurisdiction over that person. In cases of ancillary proceedings in another state, it usually is sufficient if the personal representative complies with this requirement in the state having primary jurisdiction and agrees to submit to jurisdiction in the other states. When the estate is to be administered by co-representatives, only one is required to be a resident. The fact that the personal representative has an interest in the estate is not a disqualification.

The job of the personal representative is to see that probate proceedings are commenced, to accumulate the property of the decedent, to pay debts and the expenses of the last illness and funeral, to pay the expenses of probate, to see that all taxes are paid, and to make reports to the court as necessary. The representative is entitled to compensation for all reasonably necessary services rendered to the estate, unless waived or otherwise provided by the will. The personal representative is not an agent either of the deceased or the beneficiaries of the estate. Instead, he or she is a fiduciary owing a duty to the court. The nature and limits of the representative's duties are prescribed by statute and administered under scrutiny by the court from which he receives his power and authority.

The degree to which a personal representative's actions must be approved by the court at the time they are undertaken depends on the type of probate proceedings involved and the provisions of the will, if one exists. In cases involving full, formal proceedings, most actions taken by a personal representative must be approved individually. However, many states allow a testator to provide that the personal representative may act according to her best judgment without prior approval of or intervention by the court. Within limits, then, the personal representative will be relatively unfettered. This generally speeds up the probate process.

A personal representative normally is liable for any injury or loss to the estate occasioned by even common negligence. In order to assure payment for such damages, a personal representative must be bonded. However, the testator may provide in the will that the representative will be liable only for reckless or intentional loss, and also may *request* (but not require) that only minimal, or nominal, bond be required. The expense of bonding the personal representative is an ordinary expense chargeable against the estate. The representative is entitled to compensation, the amount of which is prescribed by statute in many states. The fee often is waived in the case of a representative who is a relative or a family friend.

Steps in Administration

The first step in the probate process is placing the estate before the appropriate court. This may be a special court, called the probate court or some other special name, or it may be a division of a county court, especially in less-populated areas. This varies from state to state and occasionally from county to county. The estate comes before the court by the filing of a will or, in the case of an intestate estate, by petition of someone interested in the estate.

The next step is selecting a personal representative for the estate. This may be a person named in the will, or someone appointed by the court if no one is named or the person named is unable or unwilling to serve. If appointed, the person is frequently the spouse, another family member, or

Typical steps in the administration of an estate

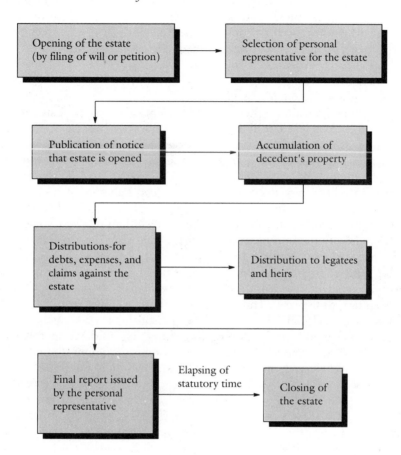

a friend. The personal representative's authority then comes from the court's granting of **letters testamentary.**

The first work of the personal representative ordinarily is seeing to the publication of a notice that an estate has been opened for the deceased. This notice is published in a newspaper of general circulation in the county in which probate is to proceed for a minimum time established by statute. Its purpose is to inform anyone who might be interested in the estate, whether debtor, creditor, or potential beneficiary, of the basic facts and how to communicate with the representative of the estate.

Subsequent steps involve the accumulation of the decedent's property, including the collection of debts owed to him. If the decedent had a safe deposit box, it will have been sealed by the bank upon notice of the death and may be opened only in the presence of a county tax official, often called the County Assessor. The assessor then may take an inventory and will release the contents of the box only if otherwise assured that all taxes will be paid by the estate. Other property must be appraised both for the purpose of determining whether any tax is owed, and to determine the value of any distributions "in kind" (property other than cash) to beneficiaries of the estate.

Thereafter, distributions may be made with approval of the court. These sometimes are made at one time, and sometimes in stages called "partial distributions." Much depends on whether property has to be sold to generate cash to pay the decedent's debts and the estate's expenses. If so, distributions may be made over a longer period. Throughout this process, the representative will receive claims against the estate, including preexisting debts, expenses of the decedent's last illness and funeral, and expenses generated by the probate of the estate. These may be paid or may be challenged by the representative, in which case court hearings may be held to determine the validity of claims. Sometimes claims are made based on oral contracts. These may be the most difficult for the estate to handle because of proof problems.

When all debts have been paid, including death, income, and other taxes, and all property has been distributed, the personal representative will issue a final report and accounting to the court and, if all is in order, the estate will be closed. This may not occur for a statutory period after notice during which claims may be filed—commonly six months.

Challenges to the Will

In most cases the administration of the estate will proceed smoothly and it will be closed in due course. However, the law books are filled with cases involving "will challenges," typically brought by disgruntled or vindictive family members who are dissatisfied with their shares of the estate or are angry at what others have been given. The challenges may be based on a variety of grounds, most notably noncompliance with the statutory prerequisites or the contention that the testator was not of sound mind when the will was executed, the will offered for probate was revoked, or even that it is a forgery. The larger the estate, the greater the potential for conflict, and situations like that in Wendel's estate, studied in the context of intestacy, are not unusual. For example, following the death of the eccentric billionaire Howard Hughes, dozens of people came rushing forward with documents purporting to be his will naming them the primary beneficiaries. One claimant's story was so engaging that it was made into a motion picture.

Mini Probate

As previously noted, probate proceedings may be more or less elaborate. Some states require no proceedings at all if estates are sufficiently small and simple. Many also provide for a **mini probate** under appropriate circumstances. This simply involves less elaborate proceedings than are involved in a full, formal administration. Part 12 of Article 3 of the UPC is devoted to such proceedings, and is entitled "Informal Probate and Appointment Proceedings." Section 3-1201 provides that a person claiming to be the successor of the decedent leaving an intestate estate may collect obligations owed to the decedent, and tangible personal property belonging to him, by presenting an affidavit to the party owing the obligation or holding the decedent's property. The affidavid must state that: (1) the net value of the entire estate does not exceed $5000; (2) 30 days have elapsed since the decedent's death; (3) no application or petition for appointment of a personal representative is pending or has been granted in any jurisdiction; and (4) the claiming successor is entitled to payment or delivery. Existing statutes in most states generally provide that a surviving spouse or children of the decedent may collect wages and other small amounts of liquid funds. This section of the UPC only takes this principle a step further. Real estate is not handled under these proceedings, since the appointment of a personal representative ordinarily may be obtained easily.

Someone who pays an obligation or delivers evidence of indebtedness or property pursuant to an affidavit is discharged as if she had made payment or delivery to the decedent. Any problem that arises, such as untruthfulness of the affidavit or that the estate is not qualified for such proceedings, has no effect other than to permit petition to the court for more formal proceedings.

Small estates may be distributed and closed by summary administrative procedure. No notice to creditors is required prior to distributions of property to those entitled to it. The estate then may be closed by the filing of a verified statement by the personal representative. If no actions or proceedings involving the personal representative

are pending in the court one year after the closing statement is filed, the appointment of the personal representative terminates.

In some cases, family agreements among the heirs also may simplify distribution. However, such an agreement must meet certain requirements, and should be used to supplement, not to replace, probate proceedings. Consider the following case.

IN RE ESTATE OF McCREA
475 Pa. 383, 380 A.2d 773 (1977)

Katherine Jane Wiest McCrea, a widow, died testate. Her will divided her property among her six children, and named her children John, William, and Sarah (all law school graduates) as executors of her estate. These executors sought no distribution of the estate until twelve years after decedent's death. In the meantime, John and William used the property. When the executors submitted their first and final accounting, the Orphan's Court Division of the Court of Common Pleas, Cumberland County, refused to allow them to charge certain expenses and claims against the estate, ordered that they pay a surcharge of 3.5 percent per year on the value of the estate (some $60,000) for failure to seek a timely distribution, and revoked their letters testamentary, appointing a bank as administrator. They appealed contending (1) the surcharge was improper because the value of the estate had increased during those years and, thus, there was no loss to the estate; and (2) there was a family agreement among the heirs to accept cash from the estate instead of the property. The order of the Orphan's Court was affirmed.

ROBERTS, Justice.

Although family settlement agreements are favored because they avoid potentially divisive litigation, . . . the existence of such an agreement must be clear and unambiguous, . . . and the agreement must be binding on all parties. . . .The orphans' court concluded that clear and unambiguous evidence of an agreement binding on all parties did not exist. This conclusion is supported by the testimony of the children of Mrs. McCrea. Sarah and Katherine testified that they had no recollection of an agreement among the devisees; appellant William's testimony, intended to demonstrate the existence of an agreement, in fact supported the conclusion of the orphans' court. According to William, Sarah and Katherine never agreed to the terms of the purported settlement. . . .

Appellants also argue that the orphans' court improperly imposed a surcharge upon the former executors. We do not agree.

An executor is required to exercise the same degree of judgment that a reasonable person would exercise in the management of his own estate. . . . This duty includes the responsibility to distribute the estate promptly. . . . If the executor breaches this duty, he may properly be surcharged for interest on the assets not expeditiously distributed. . . .

[T]he evidence supports the imposition of a surcharge. The former executors, through their positions of trust, took control of the farm operations and all the accompanying realty. They made no effort to distribute the estate promptly. They never petitioned the orphans' court to allow continued operation of the farming business. . . . Instead, the former executors delayed the final settlement of this estate for twelve years, and allowed the property to remain unproductive.

The former executors' failure to distribute the property over twelve years is inexcusable, particularly in view of the executors' legal training. . . . This breach of duty has deprived one devisee, Margaret, who died before these proceedings began, of all benefits; it has deprived the others of their benefits until now.

Appellants assert that because the real estate in this case has appreciated in value since Mrs. McCrea's death—from an estimated $39,000 to an estimated $218,000—there has been no loss to the estate and its beneficiaries. We find this argument unpersuasive. It is hardly surprising that the value of the real estate has increased over the twelve years that the appellants wrongfully withheld it from the beneficiaries. The beneficiaries have nonetheless been denied its beneficial enjoyment by the former executors' unwarranted delay.

Questions

1. Since the beneficiaries were all children of the deceased, what business did the court have interfering with a family matter?

2. Is the court being particularly tough because three of the children are lawyers? Is that proper?

SUMMARY

Upon death, property owned by the decedent will be distributed to his heirs or to persons named in a will, if he has executed one. This process, called *probate,* is administered by a personal representative under authority of a probate court. These proceedings are conducted according to state law since there is no national probate law. National law does touch probate, however, in the area of taxation. One of the important purposes of estate planning, then, becomes reducing death taxes. Creative planning can do much to maximize the utility of property during a person's lifetime, arrange for its distribution on death, and minimize the impact of taxes of all kinds.

It should be clear that if someone dies without having executed a valid will, this does not eliminate the necessity of probate. It even may increase the costs and delays otherwise attendant to distributing an estate. In addition, the distribution will be according to state statutes governing intestate succession. Although not uniform in their provisions, the laws of most states are similar. The first to be cared for ordinarily are the decedent's spouse and any children.

If the decedent is not married and has had no children, the estate will be distributed to other heirs, first to those closest in relationship to the decedent, and if there are none, then to those more remote. An *heir* is anyone related by blood to the decedent, including ascendents, descendants, and collateral kin. If none can be found, the state will take the property by *escheat*. Many special rules govern distributions to heirs, and state laws should be examined closely.

A will is a written document executed by a person directing the disposition of her property upon death. It is an instrument of conveyance that becomes effective only on death. During lifetime, the testator may modify or revoke it freely.

In order to be valid, state laws generally require that a will be in writing, published and executed by a testator of legal age and sound mind, and attested to by a specified number of witnesses. A number of states, however, recognize holographic wills—those written in the hand of the testator. A valid holographic will requires no witnesses. Some states also recognize nuncupative wills for the distribution of limited personal property in possession of the testator. This is an oral will, and ordinarily is allowed only in cases of fear of impending death, such as in military combat.

Administration of an estate is accomplished in proceedings in a probate court. After an estate is opened by petition of an interested person or by the filing of a will, the court will authorize a personal representative to handle the details of administration. This may be a person named in the will or one appointed by the court. Ordinarily the person acting as personal representative must be a resident of the state in which the proceedings are held.

Following the determination of who will serve as personal representative, letters testamentary are issued by the court and the representative will proceed first to publish notice that the estate has been opened so creditors may submit claims, then to pay all obligations of the decedent, taxes, and costs of administering the estate, and finally to see to the distribution of the remaining property either according to the will or under the laws of intestate succession. Upon completion of these duties, the representative will make a final report to the court. If the statutory time for submission of claims has passed, the estate will be closed and the personal representative will be discharged.

Many states provide for a shorter form of probate for small estates. Obligations owed to the deceased may be collected by the successor to the estate by presenting debtors with an affidavit of claim. Tangible personal property belonging to the deceased but in the hands of a third party may be reclaimed by the same method. Only the distribution of real estate requires the appointment of a personal representative. However, the laws of most states have simplified the obtaining of such an appointment. The probate court still governs these mini probate proceedings, and must approve the distribution and closing of the estate.

KEY TERMS AND CONCEPTS

probate
estate planning
intestate succession
heir
Uniform Probate Code (UPC)
gifts *causa mortis*
will
testator(rix)
formal will
acknowledge and publish a will
self-proved will
holographic will
nuncupative will
codicil
executor(rix)
administrator(rix)
personal representative
letters testamentary
mini probate

PROBLEMS

1. An eleven-page document, purported to be the will of one Anna Miller, was offered for probate. It was written in the hand of Anna Miller and met all requirements, except that none of the pages were signed. Instead, the pages were placed in an envelope which was sealed, and the envelope was signed by Anna. Should the "will" be admitted to probate?

2. A testator's second marriage had been an unhappy one, and his will provided that any children raised by his second wife were to receive nothing. His two children by his second wife, raised by her but 30 years old at the time of the testator's death, claimed the provision was void as contrary to public policy. The trial court agreed. Should this judgment be reversed?

3. A residuary clause in a will gave one-fourth of the remainder to one beneficiary and one-half to another. Upon petition by the testator's daughter seeking to have the residuary clause invalidated so she would receive the residual estate, the probate court ruled that the clause meant one-third and two-thirds. The daughter, being the testator's only heir, appealed. Should the court's decision be reversed?

4. Smith's will contained a provision: "I devise my money and coin collection to Todd Fehlhaber and Sue Fehlhaber in equal shares, or to the survivor thereof." Upon Smith's death, an inventory of the estate disclosed, under "money and coin collection," thirty-six coins and six $2 bills, having a total value of $49. Bank accounts, including checking and savings, totaled $75,336.71, and other property had a value of $31,414.88. A question was raised whether the bank accounts should be included in "money and coin collection." Smith's attorney testified that when she spoke of the money, she spoke of the $2 bills, and possibly other denominations, in her safe deposit box. The Fehlhabers appealed, contending the court should not have permitted oral testimony in evidence in interpreting a written will. Is this contention correct?

5. Wolfe left his car to Evans in his will. Wolfe died in an accident while driving the car. Evans contended he was entitled to the proceeds of Wolfe's automobile insurance policy, and Wolfe's personal representative argued that Evans was entitled to nothing. Who is correct?

6. When Peterson's will was admitted for probate, heirs challenged its validity on the ground of undue influence. Peterson was a 78-year-old spinster at the time of her death. During the years prior to her death, she had developed a close relationship to her attorney. He had lavished her with constant attention, flowers, and flattery. He drew seven wills for her, each one giving successively more to his children, who were brought by to visit with her frequently. The attorney contended the will should not be voided because, if there had been inadvertent undue influence, the beneficiaries were innocent of it. What should be the decision?

7. When the will of J. T. Payne was presented for probate, his son and two daughters objected, claiming the will had been revoked. Evidence showed that the testator had thrown it into a fireplace, stating: "I'm going to get rid of that damned thing," but it was pulled from the fire by the testator's wife, only slightly discolored on the edge. Did the testator's act constitute a revocation?

8. Upon the death of E. A. Mumaw, his son produced a letter from the decedent stating that he had left a farm to the son in a will in his safe deposit box, and that the will revoked his prior will. No will was found in the safe deposit box, but the son contended the letter, signed by the decedent and in his own handwriting, was sufficient to show a revocation of the prior will and a devise of the farm to him. Is the son correct?

9. The sons of testator, Miller, sued the executor of Miller's estate, challenging the right of the executor to pay the debts of Miller's business out of the general assets of the estate. The will provided only that the executor was empowered to continue the business. Should the challenge be upheld?

10. For most of the latter years of her life, Podgursky suffered from continued schizophrenia. She had been adjudicated incompetent, with a guardian appointed, and was confined to a foster home. She was kept on drugs and required constant care. When she died, her heirs challenged her will, which has been executed during this period. Upon proof of these facts, they moved for summary judgment that the will was invalid because of lack of testamentary capacity. Should the motion be granted?

P A R T
VII

Agency

Agency law might better be termed "the relationship of employment," because it involves the rights, duties, and liabilities that exist between principals and their agents and between employers and their employees, and the liabilities of each to third parties. In this part of the book, Chapter 31, addresses the formation and nature of agency relationships. In this chapter the student should be especially careful to study and understand the relevant terminology. Chapters 32 and 33 discuss the liabilities of the parties (principal or employer, agent or employee, and third party) under contract, tort, and criminal law. Chapter 34 then looks at the duties between the principal and agent, and the employer and employee, and the manner of termination of these relationships.

Chapter 31

Formation and Nature of the Agency Relationship

INTRODUCTION

The law of agency today encompasses all of those varied relationships created any time one person either requests or permits another to perform services for him. The employing person is called either a **principal** or an **employer,** and the one employed is called either an **agent** or **employee.** Although the term *employ* normally connotes hiring for compensation, we will find that compensation is not necessary for the creation of an agency relationship. What is necessary is that both parties have consented to the relationship, either expressly or impliedly, or have entered into, or remained in, a situation in which the agency relationship is imposed by some rule of law.

Once the relationship is established, the law of agency in effect considers the principal or employer as having duplicated herself (become more than one person), and the agent or employee as having become, to the extent consented to by the parties, the "alter ego" of the principal or employer.

Business organizations may be classified into three categories: proprietorships, partnerships, and corporations. A person can operate a sole proprietorship and have only minimal involvement with agency relationships, but the proprietor would find doing business cumbersome and inconvenient, and the business would remain very small. Minimizing agency relationships would require that he perform all phases of the business operation himself—serve as store clerk and cashier, stock the shelves, clean the store, and keep the records. To avoid indirect agency relationships, he would not deal with suppliers or customers who operate through their own agents, and would not even have a checking account. Of course, in his relationships with the government—procuring its services and meeting its requirements—some connection with agency law is unavoidable.

The operation of a partnership would be impossible without agency law. The very nature of this business form is that each partner is both the principal and the agent of the other. *Partnership* is, in reality, a collective term referring to the association of individuals we call partners. A partnership has no legal existence apart from the collective identities of its partners. Upon the death or withdrawal of any partner, or upon the addition of a new partner, the old partnership technically ceases to exist; to continue to function, a new one has to come into being. When any partner transacts authorized business for the partnership, in reality she is acting directly on her own behalf and on behalf of each of the other partners as their agent.

A corporation also could not exist in the absence of agency. This business form is a fictitious legal entity created by the state; although it is a legal person, it has no physical existence. A corporation exists only on paper, on the records of the Secretary of State of the state in which it is incorporated or registered. As a result, it can function only through its directors, officers, and those employed by it to perform the day-to-day details of its operations—in other words, its agents and employees.

CREATING AGENCY RELATIONSHIPS

Agency relationships may be created either formally or informally. This may happen by contract, which may be written or oral, or without a contract; they may come into existence by virtue of some act or omission on the part of the prospective principal or employer, or by virtue of some rule of law. The agency may involve compensation or be entirely gratuitous. Although agency law is quite specific concerning the rules for the creation of these relationships, compared to other areas of law it also is quite liberal in terms of providing circumstances under which they may come into existence. The reason for this is that even though agency law strives to facilitate the ability to carry on business according to the needs of today's commercial world, it also recognizes the need to protect the rights of third parties who deal with agents or employees. Thus, although the businessperson may use agency law to enhance his own ability to carry on a large enterprise, he is required by the same law to assume certain responsibility for the increased risk to third parties inherent in its operation.

A **power of attorney** is a formal, written grant of agency authority. The term *attorney* simply means "agent," and one who has authority to act by virtue of a power of attorney often is called an **attorney in fact** (as opposed to an *attorney at law*, who is an agent authorized to handle legal affairs for the principal). More frequently, agency relationships are created less formally and, many times, more subtly. Consider the case of a truck driver who is parked on the street and is carrying boxes into a building from the back of the truck, all of which is being observed with great adoration by a ten-year-old bystander. Pretty soon the child takes a box from the back of the truck and carries it into the building, probably fantasizing that he, too, is a truck driver. This process continues, much to the amusement of the driver, but neither she nor her volunteer helper says anything about their relationship. At some point the child, while carrying a box, carelessly injures a passer-by, perhaps poking him in the eye with a corner of the box he is carrying. If the injured passer-by sues the truck driver for the injury, the court probably will find that the child is the employee of the truck driver. An agency relationship was established even though nothing had been said by either the driver or the child, and quite possibly the child was helping only to be friendly and to enjoy his fantasy—not expecting to be paid. Nonetheless, an agency relationship is created any time one person either requests or permits another to perform services for her. Thus, along with the benefits of the agency relationship, the principal or employer must assume certain duties and increased potential liability.

TYPES OF AGENCY RELATIONSHIPS

One difficulty in any discussion of agency law is that there seems to be only general agreement as to the meanings of certain terms. In addition, courts and authors sometimes use terms too broadly. Thus, care should be taken to consider the meaning of such words as *agent, employee,* and *servant,* especially as they are used in cases. Context is important, and so is a recognition of individual differences among writers. In order to avoid unnecessary confusion, we will begin by defining some of the important terms and establishing some basic concepts.

The relationships contemplated by the term *agency law,* may be visualized as illustrated in the figure. Note that the diagram is divided, top to bottom, into two sections—Principal-Agent and Employer-Employee. It is divided, left to right, into two sections, the lower left quadrant being labeled "Master-Servant," and the lower right quadrant "Employer-Independent Contractor," with the upper half of the diagram also divided into two quadrants by a dotted line, but not individually labeled. Thus, half of the possible agency relationships (conceptually, not numerically) fall into the category of principal-agent, and the other half employer-employee. Of those falling into the employer-employee category, one half (conceptually) are more specifically referred to as master-servant, and the other half employer-independent contractor. The reason for the broken line through

Agency law

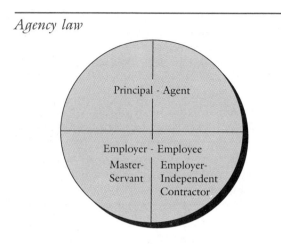

the principal-agent category is to alert you to the fact that there are some agents who are much like servants, and some who are more akin to independent contractors. The latter frequently are called *independent* (or *professional*) *agents,* but there is no generally accepted term for the former. (We might refer to them as *controlled agents.*) The significance of these divisions will become clear as we discuss the different characteristics of the possible relationships.

Principal-Agent

An agent's actions can alter the legal contractual relationships between the principal and third persons. Thus, it is the primary job of an agent to represent (be the alter ego of) the principal concerning contractual relations with others. When the agent's authority to act on behalf of the principal relates to a wide range of contractual affairs, the agent is sometimes called a **general agent,** as opposed to a **special agent,** whose authority is limited to only one or a few types of contracts. For example, a store clerk typically is a special agent. Each time a customer purchases an item, the clerk acts on behalf of the store owner in entering into a contract to sell the item to the customer, transferring title to the principal's goods and receiving payment, and thus discharging a debt owed by the customer to the principal as a result of the transaction. Although the clerk usually is authorized to act on behalf of the principal in transactions of that type, he typically is not authorized to purchase stock in trade to be sold in the store, to pay the principal's general obligations, or to hire and fire other employees. The latter powers might be possessed by the store manager, however, who very well might be classified as a general agent, depending on the overall extent of her authority.

Agents sometimes also are classified into other categories describing particular characteristics of their agency relationships. An **independent agent** is one who is in business for himself, generally operating a separate business, working for more than one principal simultaneously, and operating according to his own judgment rather than under the close direction and control of his principal. An example would be an attorney. A *del credere* **agent** is one who guarantees the credit of the principal's customers. In the event that one of the customers fails to pay, the *del credere* agent is liable to the principal for the amount of the unpaid obligation. A **broker** is a special agent whose job is to procure the purchase, sale, or exchange of property or services. A broker works as a middleman or negotiator. An example would be a real estate broker. A **factor** is an agent entrusted with possession and control of the principal's property consigned to him for sale. He is compensated by commission (called *factorage*) and differs from a broker in that he has possession, management, and control of the principal's property and usually sells in his own name, not the name of the principal. These relationships are common in the greeting-card industry because manufacturers frequently consign cards to various merchants who sell them, paying for those sold and returning the rest.

In addition to these common categories of agents, we find some people who occupy positions similar to those of agents, but who really are not agents. For example, even though the ex-

ecutor or administrator of the estate of a deceased person and a guardian of an incompetent person owe duties arising from their positions, they really are not agents of those other persons. They are special fiduciaries of the courts that approve their appointments, and their duties are owed to the courts. The trustee of a trust is in a similar position and is not an agent of the beneficiary, but of the trust itself. Although the relationship of a factor to a principal sounds similar to that of a franchisee and a franchisor, a franchise also is not an agency relationship. Even though a General Motors dealer's business may be referred to as a "Chevrolet Agency" in the vernacular, the franchisee generally is not regarded as an agent, but as an independent businessperson who has been licensed by the franchisor to use the latter's trade name, trademark, service mark, and the like in selling products or services. The franchise relationship is unique in providing the franchisor with a great deal of control over sales by the franchisee without necessarily assuming the normally attendant liability for the latter's acts.

Employer-Employee

An employee is someone who is employed to do a job of physical or mental work. (The term *employee* sometimes is used inaccurately to mean "servant," and may be so defined when used in statutes, such as the Fair Labor Standards Act. Here, it is used in a broader sense.) Examples of employees are teachers, accountants, drill-press operators, and custodians. These persons generally are not authorized to alter their employers' legal relations with third parties. However, it should be understood that being an employee is not a position of *lesser* dignity than that of an agent. It simply is *different*. Also, it should be understood that one person may act in both capacities for another, sometimes as an agent and sometimes as an employee. For instance, although we classified the store clerk in our example as an agent, the same clerk also performs some duties as an employee—stocking the shelves and keeping them straight, calculating price, discounts, and sales tax on individual transactions, making delivery of purchased items to the customers, and taking money, ringing it up, and placing it into the cash register. Thus, the clerk, during a single working day, typically will act alternately as an agent and as employee, depending on the nature of the particular task he or she is performing at a particular time.

Differentiating between the employee called a servant and the independent contractor depends on the degree to which the employer maintains the right to exercise control over the details of the employee's job. When the employer has the right to close, detailed control, the employee is considered a **servant.** When that right to control is not contemplated, rather the employer simply tells the employee what the end product is to be and leaves it to her judgment as to how best to achieve the objective, the employee is considered an **independent contractor.** There also are other characteristics distinguishing the two. Generally, the servant works for only one employer and, in a sense, all of her services are "bought" by the employer for certain hours during the day, for a given number of days each week, and for a certain number of weeks each year. It might be helpful to keep in mind that the concept of master-servant comes to us from ancient times (particularly feudal England) when a servant was truly a person dependent on her master, having no independent means, and frequently occupying the position of slave. The teacher, the drill-press operator, and

the custodian would be modern examples of employees who are likely to be classified as servants. The independent contractor, on the other hand, typically works for more than one employer at a time and operates her own business, "renting" herself to various employers by the job, and usually working for the employer for a fee instead of a wage or salary. Examples would be a building contractor, a plumber, and a TV repairperson. The counterpart of an independent contractor in the principal-agent relationship is the independent agent.

In most cases an employee can be classified rather easily as either a servant or an independent contractor. Some cases, however, involve considerable analysis of the particular relationship with the employer before a decision can be made. Of the factors the courts consider in arriving at a decision, the right to control the details of the employee's performance is undoubtedly the most important. But note that courts are looking at the *right* to control, not at whether it actually is exercised. Obviously, if the employer chose to exercise that right at all times, much of the benefit of the employer-employee relationship would be lost. In many cases, it would be better for the employer to avoid the cost of an employee and do the job himself. Of course, the fact that an employer *does* exercise a high degree of control is substantial evidence that *the right* to do so exists, but it is not conclusive. Other factors considered by the courts are summarized in the following case.

FLICK v. CROUCH
434 P.2d 256 (Sup.Ct.Okla., 1967)

This was an action by Melba Jean Flick, wife and administratrix of the estate of Ray Louis Flick (Plaintiff/Plaintiff In Error) against Elmer Crouch, dba Crouch Welding Service (Defendant/Defendant In Error), for damages for the wrongful death of her husband.

Plaintiff's husband was killed while working for his employer, Parker Drilling Company (Parker), when a drilling tower collapsed. Plaintiff attributed the collapse to faulty welding at the base of the tower; this welding was done under the direction of Defendant. Defendant claims that, at the time in question, he was working as a servant of Parker and therefore, under applicable workers' compensation law, was not subject to suit for the death. Plaintiff denies this, asserting that Defendant was an independent contractor. Evidence adduced during the trial disclosed the following facts:

Crouch was employed by Parker to see to the welding in question; he engaged other welders of his own choice, and in numbers as he saw fit, to do various parts of the job; he signed invoices submitted by the other welders. Crouch did business with Parker under the name "Crouch Welding Company." He owned his own truck and welding equipment and supplied his own welding rods. By his own testimony, he had the right to take other jobs but he worked only for Parker because Parker kept him busy. Crouch maintained his own insurance; he was not required to work any particular hours; he billed Parker monthly for his services at $7.00 per hour. He was told neither how to use his equipment nor what equipment to use. According to the testimony of Parker's drilling superintendent and his assistant, Crouch was instructed only as to what was "ultimately" sought to be accomplished, and Parker was interested neither in the details of the welding activities nor in how many welders were engaged to do the job.

From a decision of the District Court, Oklahoma County, sustaining Defendant's plea that he was only a servant of the Parker Drilling Company, and the Plaintiff's action was therefore abrogated by the Workmen's Compensation Law, Plaintiff appealed. Reversed.

McINERNEY, Justice.

As a general rule the line of demarcation between an independent contractor and a servant is not clearly drawn. The question of such relationship must be determined from the facts peculiar to each case. The various elements to be considered, as set forth in Page v. Hardy, Okl., 334 P.2d 782, 784, are: "(a) the nature of the contract between the parties, whether written or oral; (b) the degree of control which, by the agreement, the employer may exercise on the details of the work or the independence enjoyed by the contractor or agent; (c) whether or not the one employed is engaged in a distinct occupation or business and whether he carries on such occupation or business with others; (d) the kind of occupation with reference to whether in the locality, the work is usually done under the direction of the employer or by a specialist without supervision; (e) the skill required in the particular occupation; (f) whether the employer or the workman supplies the instrumentalities, tools and the place of work for the person doing the work; (g) the length of time for which the person is employed; (h) the method of payment, whether by the time or by the job; (i) whether or not the work is a part of the regular business of the employer; (j) whether or not the parties believe they are creating the relationship of master and servant; and (k) the right of either to terminate the relationship without liability."

An independent contractor is one who engages to perform a certain service for another, according to his own method and manner, free from control and direction of his employer in all matters connected with the performance of the service, except the result thereof. Those who render service but retain control over the manner of doing it are not servants. Where the defendant's status forms a material issue in the case and the facts bearing on that issue are disputed, or where there is room for reasonable difference of opinion as to the proper inference to be drawn from the known facts, the issue is for the jury under proper instructions by the court. . . .

Judgment dismissing cause for want of jurisdiction of the subject matter is accordingly reversed.

Questions

1. What important elements of the relationship between Crouch and Parker led the court to conclude as it did?

2. Would the result have been different if Parker had inspected Crouch's work every day or every week?

The Reason for Classifying Types of Agency Relationships

Considering again the diagram presented earlier in the chapter, our reason for distinguishing among the different relationships is to enable us to determine the potential liability of the principal or employer for the acts of agents or employees. Specifically, these liabilities will fall in the two legal areas of contracts and torts.

Vicarious contract liability is imposed on the principal only for the acts of his agents (the upper half of the circle). An employee does not render her employer contractually liable. Concerning tort liability, we look at the left side of the circle. The employer we call a "master" can be vicariously liable for torts committed by his servants, as can a principal for the conduct of those agents over whom he maintains a detailed right of control. However, the relationships of employer-independent contractor and principal-professional agent (the right half of the circle) do not generate this type of liability, with certain limited exceptions discussed in Chapter 33. The legal doctrine that makes a principal or employer liable for the torts committed by his agent or employee is termed *respondeat superior*. Vicarious contract and tort liability, and the liability of agents and employees in

these two areas, will be the subject of the next two chapters.

CAPACITY TO BE A PRINCIPAL OR AN AGENT

A person may be a principal even though he lacks contractual capacity. The same is true of being an agent. However, a principal's lack of capacity will affect any contracts underlying the agency relationship as well as those negotiated with third parties.

Capacity of the Principal

A principal can act through an agent to the same extent she can act for herself. Although there are no fixed rules as to the limits on the capacity one must possess in order to be called a principal, it is the rule that a principal's contractual capacity is neither enlarged nor diminished by the capacity of an agent. That is, whether or not an agent can bind the principal in any particular transaction can be determined by asking whether or not the principal could have bound herself. This is consistent with the concept that the agent is the "alter ego" of the principal. Thus, if an adult agent deals on behalf of a minor principal, the resulting contract is voidable by the principal just as if he had entered into it on his own behalf. Conversely, if a minor agent enters into a contract on behalf of an adult principal, the contract is binding on the principal and the agent's minority has no effect on it. In both situations, only the principal's capacity is important.

SIEGELSTEIN v. FENNER & BEANE
66 Ga.App. 345, 17 SE.2d 907 (1941)

This was a suit brought by M. J. Siegelstein (Plaintiff/Plaintiff In Error) against Fenner & Beane (Defendant/Defendant In Error), stockbrokers, to recover money following Plaintiff's rescission of a contract on the ground of minority.

The evidence, and reasonable deductions therefrom, showed that when Plaintiff was 19 years old he was given $1600 by his grandmother, presumably to be used for his education at the Georgia School of Technology. Sometime prior to his leaving home for Atlanta, he had a transaction with Fenner & Beane in which he purchased stock through Defendant that he later sold at a profit. On that occasion, he had represented himself to be 21 years old. After coming to Atlanta, he opened an account with Defendant, depositing the entire $1600, but made no further statements concerning his age until, after the account had been running for some time, he applied for employment with Defendant, representing himself to be over 21 years of age. After several months of unsuccessful trading, Plaintiff closed his account, which at that time had a balance of $96. He then gave Defendant notice that he rescinded his agreement and demanded the return of the entire $1600 deposited. From a judgment for Defendant, Plaintiff appealed. Reversed.

STEPHENS, Presiding Judge.

The court instructed the jury that if the defendants acted only as brokers or agents for the plaintiff, he could not recover any sums which were paid by the defendants to third persons in accordance with his instructions. This instruction is excepted to. At common law powers of attorney and agencies of all sorts were among those contracts of an infant which were absolutely void [*sic,* voidable], the reason being that the infant could not impart a power which he did not himself possess, that is, of doing valid acts. . . . In this case the minor, after coming of age, disaffirmed all transactions he had had with the brokerage firm. No authority has been cited to show that a contract of agency or the acts of an agent are any more binding on the minor than other contracts. The charge complained of was erroneous. . . .

It has been several times decided by this court that a minor may under certain circumstances be estopped from avoiding a contract which was induced by false representation as to his age. . . . The case of Woodall v. Grant & Co., 62 Ga.App. 581, 9 S.E.2d 95, is in some respects different from the case at bar. It was there held that the minor could avoid because of minority a contract to purchase an option from a brokerage concern, although he had signed, without reading, a statement that he was of age. In [some earlier] decisions it is pointed out that the doctrine of estoppel has no application to infants, but in this state "the doctrine of estoppel is not altogether inapplicable to infants; but that it may in a proper case be given effect against them." [The possible application of this doctrine to the case at bar may be considered by the trial court on retrial.]

Questions

1. Why shouldn't the plaintiff's right to disaffirm be limited to the third parties who sold the stock to him through the defendant, freeing the defendant from liability?
2. Should the right to disaffirm be permitted in business cases such as this to the same extent as it is in cases involving personal transactions?

Associations as Principals

It is clear that a corporation can act as a principal (or an agent) since a corporation is recognized by law as a legal "person." The limits of its ability to so act are found in its articles of incorporation and its by-laws. Unincorporated associations such as partnerships and trade associations, however, are not recognized as persons under the common law. As a result, traditionally, they could not sue or be sued, enter into contracts, or hold property in their own names. Thus, they acted neither as principals nor agents, even though their members can, individually and collectively. This disability of unincorporated associations generally has been removed by special statutes.

Capacity of Agents

Since the validity of agency authority and the degree to which contracts entered into through an agent are binding depend on the capacity of the principal and not the agent, there is no particular capacity required for a person to act as an agent. As a practical matter, it is sufficient if the agent has the ability to follow instructions and carry them out, as the following case makes clear.

CHASTAIN v. BOWMAN
1 Hill 270 (S.C. 1833)

This was an action by Richard Chastain (Plaintiff) against Zach and W. W. Bowman (Defendants) for the value of his cotton, which was burned in a fire aboard Defendants' boat. The evidence showed that when the boat, passing down the Savannah River, came to a landing, Plaintiff asked if it could carry his cotton. A slave belonging to a Defendant replied that it could. It was received on board and was burned aboard the boat before it reached its destination.

It was proved that Defendants had given general instructions to their slaves to take in freight whenever it could be had, and that in one instance, one Defendant had received pay for freight engaged by his slave. There was also some evidence to show the general custom of the river. Some witnesses proved that it is the custom to allow slaves to take in freight generally, and others stated that they are only allowed to receive freight when a boat is not fully laden.

The presiding judge charged the jury that Defendants were not liable unless the . . . [slave] was his master's agent and authorized to take in freight. From a judgment in favor of Plaintiff, Defendants appealed, contending, among other things, that the slave, being not a freeman, lacked the capacity to act as an agent. Affirmed.

JOHNSON, Judge.

From the instructions given to the jury, it is more than probable that they found the verdict on the ground that the defendants had constituted their patroon, the slave Jack, their agent to contract with the plaintiff for carrying his cotton, and on that ground it can be well sustained.

It is not questioned, that a master may constitute his slave his agent, and I cannot conceive of any distinction between the circumstances which constitute a slave and a freeman an agent—they are both the creatures of the principal, and act upon his authority. There is no condition, however degraded, which deprives one of the right to act as a private agent—the master is liable even for the act of his dog, done in pursuance of his command.

Questions

1. Is the proposition of law, enunciated by the court in extreme form in this case, sound?
2. Should the courts require particular skills of an agent? What skills?

CREATION OF AGENCY AUTHORITY

All agency is derived from the will of the principal and, in general, continues only as long as the principal consents to its existence. The principal's will may be manifested by words, either written or spoken, or by conduct, either action or inaction. An agent cannot confer authority on herself and neither, as a general rule, can an agency relationship be imposed on a principal, against his will, by a third party.

Sources of Authority

Sources of agency authority may be classified as (1) express, (2) implied, (3) apparent (ostensible), (4) by estoppel, (5) by ratification, and (6) by operation of law. The first two, express and implied, sometimes are lumped together under the heading "actual" authority. This does not mean, however, that these sources are more real or legally binding than the others. A principal can be bound by any of these forms of authority. The term *actual authority* refers, instead, to the fact that express and implied authority, unlike the other sources, always arise as a result of a direct communication from the principal to the agent.

EXPRESS.   **Express authority** is created by an expression, from the principal to the agent, in words, either written or spoken. For example, Peterson tells Claven, either orally or in writing, "I want you to go downtown to ABC Office Supplies, get a case of the duplicator fluid we use, charge it to the company account, and bring it back." The agent is said to have express authority to do any acts specifically mentioned by the principal. That is, Claven now has express authority to charge the company account for the purchase price of the fluid.

IMPLIED. Unless the principal clearly prescribes every last detail of what the agent is authorized to do (which, for all practical purposes, is impossible), the agent also will have some **implied authority** to do all things reasonably necessary to accomplish the purpose of the express authority. In the example, if Claven is to accomplish the task assigned, she must have some means of transportation down to the store and back. She therefore might be impliedly authorized to take a car from the company's carpool or be reimbursed for bus or cab fare, assuming walking was not an option. Hiring a chauffeur-driven limousine probably would be beyond the bounds of what is "reasonably necessary." As the limits of an agent's express authority are expanded, so too will be the probable scope of her implied authority. This type of implied authority is called "incidental." It should not be surprising that a general agent typically will have greater implied authority than a special agent.

COBLENTZ v. RISKIN
74 Nev. 53, 322 P.2d 905 (1958)

This was an action brought by Akim Riskin (Plaintiff/Respondent) against Alexander Coblentz and Jerry Fox, dba Thunderbird Jewel Shop, and others (Defendants/Appellants) to recover the value of jewelry consigned to them. From a judgment in favor of Riskin in the amount of $16,300, Defendants appealed, contending that there was no real evidence from which the trial court could have found that the essentials of either actual or apparent authority existed. Affirmed.

MERRILL, Justice.

Appellants are owners of the Thunderbird Jewel Shop in Clark County, Nevada. Respondent Riskin is a diamond broker and wholesale jeweler of Los Angeles, California. In August, 1955, appellants employed Hyman Davidson for services in connection with their store. In January, 1956, Davidson entered into a consignment agreement with Riskin pursuant to which he received, for purposes of retail sale, two expensive items of jewelry. In his dealings with Riskin, Davidson represented himself as manager of the jewel shop with full authority to receive merchandise on consignment. Riskin did not check these representations with appellants but did check with others in the jewelry trade and satisfied himself as to Davidson's authority. The jewelry pieces were reconsigned by Davidson without Riskin's approval or consent. The person to whom they were reconsigned has disappeared. Riskin demanded of appellants the return of the jewelry or its agreed value pursuant to the terms of the agreement. Upon failure of appellants to comply with his demand this action was brought.

Riskin testified that it was the custom in the jewelry trade to take expensive pieces of jewelry on consignment rather than by purchase at wholesale. This testimony is compellingly supported by reason when the nature of consignment transactions and the benefit to retail merchants of this commercial practice are considered. By consignment retail merchants are not financially committed to the purchase of expensive items until they have themselves resold the items. Until resale their only financial commitment is that of safekeeping. . . . It can hardly be questioned that the engaging in consignment transactions would be regarded by those in the jewelry trade as a customary, proper and necessary function of store management.

Davidson testified positively that he had been employed as manager of the store with instructions to run the store as he saw fit; that he had discussed with appellants the matter of taking merchandise on consignment and that appellants had approved; that he had received merchandise on consignment from five firms other than Riskin; that in at least three of these cases appellants knew of the transactions and that they were consignments and had made no protest; that in some cases the pieces were returned unsold while in others, they had been sold by the store; that when sold, appellants had shared the profits of sale and had signed the checks to the consignor for the agreed value; that most consignment pieces were placed on display at the store and were seen by appellants; that of the pieces here involved, at least one (an obviously expensive piece) had been seen on display by appellants; that another piece received from Riskin (an expensive emerald ring subsequently returned unsold) had been seen by appellants on display; that appellants had indicated approval of Davidson's success in securing such quality pieces and had never said anything about restrictions upon his authority to deal on consignment.

Actual authority includes . . . implied authority. . . . Implied authority is that which the agent reasonably believes himself to possess as a result of representations by the principal or of acts of the agent permitted by the principal over a course of time in which the principal has acquiesced, . . . [and] that which is reasonably necessary, proper and usual to carry into effect the main authority granted. . . .

The trial court has found that Davidson was employed to serve as manager and that he did so serve. The evidence we have recited presents a clear case of . . . implied. . . . We conclude that the trial court's determination of actual authority is supported by the record and that appellants are bound by Davidson's actions in their behalf in committing them to the consignment agreement with Riskin.

Questions

1. How can a merchant effectively restrict the implied authority of agents like Davidson?
2. Do you think it is fair to put the risk of loss on the jewelry store rather than Riskin? Why or why not?

The other type of implied authority agents possess is called implied authority "by necessity." This type is found only in emergency situations in which the agent must decide how, or whether or not, to act, and is unable to get instructions from the principal. It arises out of an agent's affirmative duty to act in the principal's best interests, a concept that will be developed more fully when we discuss the agent's "fiduciary" duty in Chapter 34. For example, imagine a train wreck in which the firefighter is injured; among other things, his arm is almost severed. In response, the conductor of the train contracts medical attention for him on behalf of the railroad. Although the conductor is not expressly authorized to do so, the principal (the railroad) probably will be bound to the contract under the theory of implied authority "by necessity," in that this type of authority covers unusual emergency situations not commonly "incidental" to the duties assigned to the agent.

PRISUDA v. GENERAL CASUALTY CO. OF AMERICA
272 Wis. 41, 74 N.W.2d 777 (1956)

This was a personal injury action brought by Audrey Prisuda and two other minors (Plaintiffs/Appellees) against General Casualty Insurance Co. of America (Defendant/Appellant), the insurer of the automobile in which they were riding when a collision occurred.

The automobile in question was owned by Mrs. Lucille Minnihan Allen, and she was the named insured. On the evening prior to the accident, William Allen had obtained permission from his mother to use the car. At that time, Mrs. Allen told William that no one but he was to drive the car on the trip.

Early that evening, while driving Plaintiffs and another passenger to a party, William momentarily lost control of the car and narrowly escaped rolling into a deep roadside ditch. Though shaken, William continued to the party. Some five hours later, when they left the party, William requested that his friend George Rogers drive on the way home, stating that he was too tired and nervous to drive. Rogers did so and was driving at the time of the accident.

The insurance policy covering the car, issued by Defendant, stated, in part: "Definition of 'Insured.' With respect to the insurance for bodily injury liability and for property damage liability the unqualified word 'insured' includes the named insured and also includes any person while using the automobile and any person or organization legally responsible for the use thereof, provided the actual use of the automobile is by the named insured or with his permission. The insurance with respect to any person or organization other than the named insured does not apply. . . ."

From a judgment for Plaintiff, Defendant appealed. Reversed and remanded.

STEINLE, Justice.

Respondents contend that an emergency situation was created when William found himself tired and nervous and requested Rogers to drive before the party left Pewaukee, and that hence the consent of Mrs. Allen to permit George Rogers to drive, was implied from the circumstances. The court determined that William Allen had requested George Rogers to drive because he was too tired. That finding was based upon credible evidence. Respondents urge that the situation, while not one of principal and agent, nevertheless is analogous in principle to such relationship, and that the rules applicable to agency by emergency or necessity ought to control here. They submit that the unforseen emergency reasonably enlarged the existing authority conferred by Mrs. Allen upon her son. However, it must be borne in mind, that under the law of agency, it is the principal's purpose and plans that are to be subserved, and he is the one to decide, where possible, how the emergency is to be met. If it is possible to communicate with the principal when emergency arises, it is the duty of the agent to do so in order that the principal's advice or direction can be obtained. . . . In the present circumstances were it to be considered that an emergency had been created, Mrs. Allen would have been entitled to have been notified of it in order that her direction could be obtained. It does not appear that any effort was made to communicate with her or that it was impossible to do so. The proof falls short of establishing implied consent because of emergency.

The driving of the car by Rogers was without the express or implied consent of the named insured, and hence was not within the protection of the policy.

Questions

1. Do you think the court was too demanding in defining *emergency*? Why do you think the court reached the decision it did?

2. What should Allen and Rogers have done to make certain the insurance policy was in effect?

APPARENT (OSTENSIBLE). **Apparent (or ostensible) authority** arises in situations in which the principal has led a third party to believe that the agent has authority and the third party acted on the reasonable belief it did exist. Suppose, in our example, that Claven picks up the duplicator fluid and informs the clerk at ABC that it is to be charged to the account of Peterson, her principal. The clerk, not being acquainted with Claven, calls Peterson, who says, "Yes, I told Claven to do that." Claven now is vested with apparent authority in addition to express and implied authority. These situations normally do not present problems. However, care must be taken to avoid circumstances that might lead third parties to believe erroneously that an agent is authorized to conduct certain types of business. For instance, suppose an agent, while selling sporting goods for his principal, sells to some customers his own hand-loaded ammunition. The principal knows of this and does not object. If someone is injured by a defect in the hand-loaded ammunition, the principal may find herself liable, having allowed the purchaser to assume reasonably that the agent was acting for her in making the sale. Note two things

at this point. First, apparent authority is just as real and binding as express and implied authority. Second, as mentioned above, while express and implied authority originate from a communication from the principal directly to the agent, apparent authority originates from some communication from the principal to the third party with whom the agent deals. As the preceding two examples show, this communication may be by words or by conduct.

ESTOPPEL. Authority by estoppel is very similar to apparent authority. Both arise from communication from the principal to a third party. The difference is subtle but important. **Authority by estoppel** involves the same theory and elements as were discussed concerning promissory estoppel in Chapter 6. Authority by estoppel is a "legal fiction" engaged in by courts to prevent a perceived injustice. For example, suppose Able steals Parker's horse, takes it to Terry, and offers it for sale, claiming it to be his own. Terry, thinking the horse looks like Parker's, calls Parker and inquires. Parker, who had seen the horse in the barn only shortly before, says, "It's not my horse. I just

Sources of agency authority

Type of Authority	How Created	Example
Express	created by written or spoken expression to agent	instructing an employee to purchase office supplies
Implied	derived from agent's position or responsibilities	an employee purchasing needed goods during her employer's vacation
Apparent (Ostensible)	arises when a principal leads a third party to believe that the agent has authority	an employer writes to a business contact telling her that an employee will conduct business for him
Estoppel	arises when used by courts to prevent a perceived injustice (similar to apparent)	leaving a watch to be repaired at a place of business that repairs watches and also sells used watches, and the repairperson sells the watch to a good-faith purchaser
Ratification	created when a principal assumes liability for an unauthorized act (after the fact) by an agent of the principal	an employee purchases securities with the company's funds without authorization, but a sudden surge in the securities' value leads the owner to approve the purchase
Operation of Law	imposed for reasons of public policy	union bargains for all employees in the bargaining unit established by the NLRB

put mine in the barn." Acting on this, Terry buys the horse. When Parker finds his horse gone, he goes to Terry, examines the animal, and claims it. The courts probably will hold that Parker lost title to the horse because (1) he disclaimed titled when Terry inquired, (2) he knew or had notice that Terry might change position by buying the animal, believing Parker's disclaimer, (3) Terry did buy the horse, (4) the purchase was in justifiable reliance on Parker's disclaimer, and (5) Terry would suffer an unjust injury if Parker was allowed to reclaim the horse. (Able probably is unavailable or insolvent by this time.) Thus, the court would use the legal fiction of agency by estoppel in order to allow a thief to pass title to the stolen goods when justice demands that result. Although the concept is very similar to apparent authority, note that the communication from the principal was not that Able was his authorized agent, but something else—a denial of title to goods.

RATIFICATION.   **Authority by ratification** is the one type of authority among the six that is conferred by the principal after the fact. It is created when a principal manifests a willingness to assume liability for an act that, although done by someone purporting to be her agent, was not authorized. The principal's willingness may be made clear by either word or conduct, and may be communicated either to the agent or to the third party involved in the transaction. Once the principal has ratified, the authority dates back to the moment of the transaction and, with respect to the rights of third parties, makes the agent's act just as binding as if it had been authorized properly when it was done.

Courts generally agree that to ratify an act: (1) the act must have been one that the principal could have done personally or authorized at the time the act was done; (2) it must have appeared at the time of the transaction that the act was being performed on behalf of that specific principal; (3) the principal must have known all material facts concerning the transaction at the time of ratification; (4) the third party must not have attempted cancellation of the transaction prior to the time of ratification; and (5) it must not appear to the court that the rights of any third party would be unjustly impaired by the ratification. In addition, (6) the ratification must cover the entire transaction. A principal is not allowed to pick and choose and ratify only the parts she finds advantageous.

DAVID v. SERGES
373 Mich. 442, 129 N.W.2d 882 (1964)

This was an action by T. G. David (Plaintiff/Appellant) against Steve Serges, (Defendant/Appellee), dba Gracelawn Meat Outlet, to recover the amount of a loan made by Plaintiff to Defendant's agent. Defendant claimed that his agent had no authority to procure the loan and there was apparently some evidence that the proceeds of the loan were not used for the benefit of Defendant/ principal.

In this case the only testimony taken was Plaintiff's; David testified that Defendant's managing agent had borrowed $3500 from him on Defendant's behalf for use in Defendant's business, a retail meat market. Plaintiff further testified that Defendant subsequently had paid $200 to him on the alleged loan and upon several occasions had stated to him that the full sum eventually would be paid. At the conclusion of this evidence, Defendant moved for a judgment of no cause of action on the ground that Plaintiff had failed to prove a *prima facie* case. From a decision of the trial court granting Defendant's motion, Plaintiff appealed. Reversed and remanded, costs to Plaintiff.

SOURTS, Justice.

When an agent purporting to act for his principal exceeds his actual or apparent authority, the act of the agent still may bind the principal if he ratifies it. The Restatement of Agency 2d, Sec.82, defines ratification thusly: "Ratification is the affirmance by a person of a prior act which did not bind him but which was done or professedly done on his account, whereby the act, as to some or all persons, is given effect as if originally authorized by him."

"Affirmance" is defined in Sec. 83 of the Restatement: "Affirmance is either (a) a manifestation of an election by one on whose account an unauthorized act has been done to treat the act as authorized, or (b) conduct by him justifiable only if there were such an election."

Although Michigan cases in which ratification has been discussed usually involve receipt of direct benefits by the ratifying principal, evidence of receipt of benefits, while it lends plausibility to an allegation of ratification and, indeed, may in itself constitute ratification, is not a *sine qua non* of ratification. . . .

Even if borrowing money were not within the agent's actual or apparent authority, plaintiff's evidence, viewed favorably, was legally sufficient to establish defendant's liability for the alleged loan upon a theory of ratification. Thus, plaintiff's evidence was sufficient to require defendant to be put on his proofs.

Questions

1. Once the defendant stated that the money would be repaid, should there have been any question about the propriety of finding ratification?

2. Are there any types of transactions that should *not* be subject to ratification?

We have one note of caution concerning ratification. Although it is true that ratification relates only to the single transaction ratified and does not bind the principal to other transactions before or after it, there is a danger that a series of ratifications may result in giving an agent apparent authority. Consider the case of the store clerk who has been told that he has no authority to buy stock in trade for the store. One day, when the principal is gone for lunch, a sales representative talks the clerk into buying a gross of "widgets" for the store. On her return, the principal explains to the clerk the error of his ways, but says, she will take care of it and sends the company a check for the widgets. Next month, again when the principal is gone, the same representative appears and the clerk buys more widgets. Again the principal ratifies. After the same thing occurs during the next three months, the principal finally fires the clerk and refuses to pay for the last batch of widgets. The principal probably will find that by the fifth month, her continued ratifications have clothed the clerk with apparent authority to deal with the widget representative. By that time, the principal probably has led the representative and the company to believe reasonably that the clerk was authorized to make these purchases. At exactly what point apparent authority was created may not be known—that is a judicial judgment call.

OPERATION OF LAW.   Under certain circumstances, an agency relationship may be imposed on parties for reason of public policy (**authority by operation of law**). An example is a "non-resident motorist statute." Most states have these statutes, which provide that if a non-resident of the state operates a motor vehicle on its roads and becomes involved in an accident during the visit, some official (usually the secretary of state) becomes the agent of that non-resident for the purpose of receiving service of process in any civil case arising out of the accident. The purpose of these statutes is to allow a lawsuit to be brought, in the state where the accident occurred, against a

non-resident who is not physically located in the state when it is commenced. Other examples are found in the National Labor Relations Act and the labor laws of the states. According to these acts, once a union has been voted in and certified as the collective bargaining agent for the workers in a particular unit, it acts as agent for all workers in that unit, regardless of whether they voted for the union or not. The individual workers no longer are allowed to discuss wages, hours, or other terms or conditions of employment with their employers except through their agent, the union.

These are only two examples of agency created by operation of law, and they may seem contrary to the first statement in this section that "All agency authority is derived from the will of the principal. . . ." Remember, however, that when the "principal" drives into another state or continues to work in that organized unit, he or she willingly submits to the respective agency relationships.

Other Special Considerations

DELEGATION OF AUTHORITY.   It often is said that, as a general rule, delegated authority is not delegable. That is, the authority the principal has delegated to the agent cannot be further delegated by the agent to anyone else (a subagent). This is, however, a general rule, and does not apply in situations in which authority exists for the delegation. Even though any of the six types of authority would be sufficient for the delegation, of greatest importance would be express and implied authority, which are the most subject to controversy. In the final analysis, a principal is liable for the contracts of a subagent only if the delegation of authority from the agent to the subagent was authorized. Subagents are discussed more fully in Chapter 32.

KNOWLEDGE AND NOTICE.   An agent's knowledge or notice of facts related to the duties entrusted to him by his principal are imputed to the principal, unless circumstances dictate that the third party relying on this rule had reason to know that the facts would not be communicated to the principal or, if they were, that the principal would not have had a reasonable time to act on them. Therefore, in most circumstances, when the agent knows or has notice of facts pertaining to the general area of duties assigned to him by his principal, it is presumed that the principal knows them also. For example, when an agent purchases a piece of property for his principal, knowing of a defect in the title, the principal generally has no right against the seller when he actually discovers the defect. This rule would not apply, of course, if the agent and the third party had colluded to prevent the principal from learning of the fact.

REPRESENTATIONS AND WARRANTIES OF THE AGENT.

Agents are likely to make statements to third parties in the course of normal business affairs that may constitute representations or warranties concerning the principal's property or services. The extent to which the principal will be bound by them is determined, again, by the limits of the agent's authority. Although the extent of express authority may be quite clear, the extent to which implied and apparent authority may exist can be the subject of considerable debate. In general, a principal will be liable for representations and warranties by her agents, related to the area of the agent's assigned duties, that may be considered ordinary or customary in the trade or business. In order to avoid some of the undesirable possibilities of this rule's application, principals sometimes include **exculpatory clauses** in contracts that were negotiated by their agents. These clauses in essence say: "If my agent has made any statement that does not appear somewhere in this writing, you must tell me or I will not be liable for it." The effect of these clauses is that if a customer brings an action based on an agent's representation that was not disclosed to the principal, the principal can be held liable to the extent of allowing rescission of the contract, but cannot be held liable for damages for fraud.

The theory of the law is that a principal who did not directly commit or authorize the fraud and who, by using the exculpatory clause, has done what she reasonably could do to prevent fraud by the agent should, however, be required to pay damages; nor should she be permitted to profit from the misrepresentation.

PAYMENTS TO AN AGENT.

Payments made to an agent by a third party to be given to the agent's principal will discharge the debt to the principal only if the agent has authority to receive the money. Once again, we are involved with implied and apparent authority and, again, an agent normally is considered to have authority in situations in which payments to the agent could be considered ordinary or customary in the trade or business. Courts generally hold that when an agent actually delivers the goods or services, he ordinarily will have authority to receive payment unless the customer has notice to the contrary. This rule does *not* apply to situations in which the agent merely is soliciting orders for future delivery. Courts generally discourage payments to agents significantly before the due date, or under other circumstances that might tempt the agent to breach his duty to the principal unreasonably. For example, although the manager of an apartment building ordinarily may be assumed to have authority to receive payments of rent due, the same is not true of payments of several months' rent in advance or payment of personal debts owed to the principal that are not connected with the apartments.

NEGOTIABLE INSTRUMENTS.

In addition to liability under the law of contracts and torts, agency relationships can create liability on negotiable instruments such as checks and promissory notes. This is governed by a very special—and sometimes quite different and strict—area of law, that of commerical paper. When an agent signs a negotiable instrument on behalf of the principal, the agent's authority to do so is construed strictly by the court. Also, if an agent signs her own name to such an instrument, she must be careful both to identify the principal and to disclose clearly that she is signing her own name only in a representative capacity. If the agent fails to do either of these she will be liable, and if she fails to identify the principal, *only* the agent will be liable on the instrument if suit is brought under commerical-paper law. Both of these must be done on the document itself. Under commerical-paper law, only someone identified on an instrument can be liable on it. The law of commerical paper is discussed more fully in Chapters 17–20.

As for payments made to agents in discharge of obligations owed to the principal, when those obligations are evidenced by negotiable instruments, the rule is generally the same as that for other payments to an agent, discussed earlier. However, the courts are somewhat more liberal in finding authority when amounts due are paid to an agent who, in the original transaction, received the negotiable instrument from the third party on behalf of the principal for whose benefit the payments are being made.

SUMMARY

The scope of modern agency law includes all of the relationships that can come into being when one person requests or permits another to perform services for him. These relationships may be created either formally or informally and may exist even in situations in which the services are extended as a gift rather than for pay. The various possible relationships include those commonly referred to as principal-agent and employer-employee, including independent contractors and professional agents. The effect of these relationships is to place a risk of liability on the recipient of the services—the principal or employer—for the acts of the other. These liabilities may be on contracts, when an agent is authorized by some words or conduct by the principal to negotiate them, or for torts, when the principal or employer maintains a close right to control the

details of the performance of the duties of the agent or employee.

Possession of full capacity to contract is not necessary in order to be either a principal or an agent. However, it is fundamental that a principal neither can enlarge nor diminish her own capacity by having an agent with more or less capacity.

The authority of an agent to bind the principal can come into existence only with the principal's consent, and generally it will continue only as long as the principal wills that it continue. This authority may arise by words or conduct of the principal, either expressly or by implication. It may be granted by ratification after the fact, within certain guidelines. Sometimes it is imposed by law in order to prevent an injustice or in order to further public policy.

Special situations may arise in the course of the relationship of principal-agent, such as the principal's liability for having notice of certain facts known by the agent, misrepresentations and warranties made by the agent in the course of business, payments made by third parties to the agent for the benefit of the principal, and the handling of negotiable instruments by an agent. These situations merit specific, close consideration, and should be studied in light of the general rules governing the law of agency.

KEY TERMS AND CONCEPTS

principal
employer
agent
employee
power of attorney
attorney in fact
general agent
special agent
independent agent
del credere agent
broker

factor
servant
independent contractor
express authority
implied authority
apparent authority
authority by estoppel
authority by ratification
authority by operation of law
exculpatory clause

PROBLEMS

1. Massey sued Tube Art Display for damages to his apartment that resulted when a back-hoe operator employed by Tube Art negligently dug into a gas line, causing an explosion. The operator worked about 90 percent of his hours for Tube Art and 10 percent for other employers. However he was not registered as a contractor or sub-contractor, he had no employees, he was not bonded, he did not obtain any of the licenses or permits for work he did, and he dug holes in locations and dimensions as instructed by Tube Art. Should Tube Art be liable for the operator's negligence?

2. While a guest at a Holiday Inn franchised motel, Murphy was injured in a slip-and-fall accident. The motel was operated independently by the franchisee, with no participation by Holiday Inns other than allowing the use of its trade name and dictating the architecture and paint color for the building. However, Murphy sued Holiday Inns, contending the company should be liable for her injuries since its name was being used in connection with the motel. Is Murphy correct?

3. Kyle Furniture sold furniture to Russell Dry Goods. The furniture was ordered by the general manager of Russell, apparently to be used as the store's stock in trade. In fact, most of the items were diverted to the manager's private use. When the owner learned of the purchases and their di-

version, he refused to pay for them, contending the general manager was not authorized to make the purchases. Is Kyle entitled to payment?

4. In August 1971, Melancon had her house treated for termites by A & M Pest Control, receiving the service and a one-year warranty against reinfestation. The warranty provided that it was "non-assignable." In spite of this, when Melancon sold the house to Ruiz she purported to assign the warranty. Thereafter, in November 1971 and January 1972 Ruiz called A & M and complained of insects. A & M diagnosed them as flying ants and treated them accordingly. In February 1972, Ruiz again called A & M, set up an appointment for an inspection, and paid a renewal fee. In late April, termites were discovered along with considerable damage. A & M refused to do repairs, contending that the warranty given to Melancon was not assignable. Is A & M liable?

5. Taylor traded stock from time to time and maintained a trading account with Merrill Lynch. Without Taylor's knowledge or consent, his wife went to Merrill Lynch and drew a draft on the account. The draft was honored. When the Taylors separated and Mr. Taylor learned of the transaction, he demanded that Merrill Lynch return the money to his account. Merrill Lynch contended that Mrs. Taylor, as wife of the depositor, had apparent authority to draw the draft. Is Mr. Taylor entitled to the return of the money?

6. Miotk was involved in an automobile accident and sustained personal injuries. She hired Phelps, an attorney, who filed a complaint on her behalf. Thereafter, without Miotk's knowledge or consent, Phelps signed a settlement agreement with the defendant on Miotk's behalf. Is the settlement binding on Miotk?

7. Johnson was injured by a defective coffeemaker purchased at the Ginny Mae Stamp Store. The coffeemaker had been manufactured by National Appliance and sold to an appliance wholesaler in Wisconson, who resold it to Ginny Mae in Iowa, where it was purchased by Johnson.

When sued by Johnson in Iowa, National Appliance moved to dismiss the complaint on the ground that it had not been served with process in Iowa, service having been made on the Iowa Secretary of State pursuant to a statute providing for such service in suits against nonregistered corporations doing business in Iowa. Was the service proper, so that the action may proceed in Iowa?

8. Davis went to Acme Hardware to purchase a chain to be used with a hoist in loading glass panes. Davis explained the use to the salesman and the weights involved, and the salesman assured him "this is the one you want." Davis purchased the chain; after a few uses it broke, causing the loss of $1200 worth of glass panels. Davis sued Acme for the loss, and Acme defended on the ground that the chain was not intended to hold such weights and its salesman had been so instructed. Should Acme be liable?

9. Sanders lived in an apartment building owned by Gregory. During her tenancy, she invested some $20,000 in savings certificates being sold by the building manager, Bilkos. The certificates were issued in the name of Gregory Apts. and were signed by Bilkos as manager. Bilkos then left town with the money collected from Sanders and other residents. When Sanders demanded payment from Gregory, Gregory said he knew nothing about the transactions and that Bilkos never had been authorized to sell such certificates. Assuming Gregory was truthful, should he be liable to Sanders?

10. Joe Jezisek was a minor with a poor driving record. As a result, he was uninsurable. In order to obtain insurance, his brother, George, purchased a policy from Southern Farm Bureau Insurance, falsely stating that Joe's car was his and for his use. This was done at the suggestion of the insurance agent. When Joe was involved in an accident and Southern Farm Bureau learned of the fraud, it brought an action for a judgment declaring the policy void. The Jeziseks contended the policy was payable because Southern Farm Bureau's agent knew the circumstances. Should the policy be declared void?

Chapter | 32

Contract Liability

_____

_____

_____

_____

OUTLINE

INTRODUCTION

Normally we assume that when an agent enters into a contract on behalf of a principal, it is the principal who will be bound to the third party, not the agent. As a general rule, this assumption is correct, but it presumes that (1) the agent is acting with authority, (2) the agent is acting only as authorized, (3) the identity of the principal is known to the third party, (4) the third party understands that the agent is acting only in a representative capacity (not also for herself), (5) the principal is capable of granting authority to the agent, and (6) the authority granted has not terminated in some way by the time the agent acts. Thus, in this chapter, we will examine the circumstances under which the principal can be liable, the agent can be liable, and both can be liable in situations involving contracts with third parties.

LIABILITY OF THE PRINCIPAL

The Rule

The principal will be liable on contracts entered into by an agent on the principal's behalf whenever the agent has acted with authority. The rule is as simple as that. Thus, when the agent is authorized, acts within the limits of that authority, and the authority is still in effect at the time of the act, the principal is liable. This is an absolute rule with no exceptions, and it operates independently of whether the agent *also* may be liable on the contract.

The Burden of Proving Authority

When an agent has acted and entered into a contract purportedly on behalf of a principal, and the third party wishes to hold the principal liable, the burden of proving the requisite authority is on the third party. That is, the third party must prove that the agent was authorized; the principal need not prove that the agent was *not*. This is consistent with the general rule of evidence requiring that the party alleging a fact carry the burden of proving it in court. The rule is based, in part, on the *a priori* concept that it usually is more difficult to prove a negative (authority *did not* exist) than a positive (authority *did* exist). Thus, the third party assumes the risk of lack of authority anytime he deals with an agent; he should understand that this risk is assumed and always exercise caution to satisfy himself that the agent is authorized.

ZEESE v. ESTATE OF SIEGEL
524 P.2d 85 (Utah, 1975)

This was an action brought by George Zeese and his wife Emily Zeese (Plaintiffs/Appellants) against the estate of Max Siegel, and others (Defendants/Respondents), to recover possession of approximately one acre of land then being used by one Defendant, Trailer Mart, Inc., dba Patton's Travelers, as a sales lot.

Plaintiffs had leased the land to Saturn Oil Company for a period of ten years commencing December 18, 1959. After a series of intermediate conveyances, the lease was assigned to Max Siegel on May 1, 1969. Max died on June 3, 1969, and in a letter dated June 16, 1969, his widow, as executrix, notified Plaintiffs of the exercise of an option to renew the lease for a period of an additional ten years, as provided by the lease. In June 1973, after a breakdown in negotiations between Plaintiffs and Defendant Trailer Mart, Inc., Plaintiffs served a notice-to-quit (a notice from a landlord to a tenant that the landlord wishes to repossess the property).

Plaintiffs contend that when Max Siegel took the assignment of the lease, and when the notice of exercise of the option to renew was given by Eva Siegel, they were acting in their individual capacities and not as agents of Defendant Trailer Mart, Inc., because at neither time were Plaintiffs notified that they were acting as agents for Trailer Mart, Inc. From a judgment in favor of Defendants, Plaintiffs appealed. Affirmed.

MAUGHAN, Justice.

The contract of an agent is the contract of the principal, and the principal, although not named therein, may sue or be sued thereon. Although an agreement reduced to writing may not be contradicted or varied by parol evidence, the principal may introduce evidence to show that the agent, who made the contract in his own name, was acting for him. This proof does not contradict the writing but merely explains the transaction.

Plaintiffs further contend that Max Siegel was not authorized in writing by defendant [Trailer Mart, Inc.] to act as its agent and, therefore, the assignment was void under . . . the Statute of Frauds.

Defendant was an assignee and lessee under the assignment of the lease agreement. [The statute requires] . . . that an agent of the lessor, or the assignor, granting an interest in land for a term exceeding one year, must be authorized in writing. There is no requirement within the [Statute of Frauds] that an agent of an assignee or lessee must be authorized in writing. . . .

Plaintiffs claim that the trial court erred in its determination that Eva Siegel was the agent of defendant and acting in its behalf when she exercised the option to renew the lease. In the written notice sent to plaintiffs, Eva Siegel stated that on behalf of the estate of Max Siegel, she was advising and notifying the Zeeses of the exercise of the option to renew the lease assigned by Husky Oil Company to Max Siegel. Eva identified herself as the executrix named in the last will and testament of her husband, Max Siegel. Plaintiffs urge that this letter was sent on behalf of the estate of Max Siegel and not on behalf of the defendant; and, therefore, it constituted neither notice nor an exercise of the option to renew.

This letter was sent fifteen days after the death of Max Siegel. The defendant was wholly owned by the Siegel family, who intended to continue the family business. . . .

If there was confusion as to the authority of Eva Siegel to act in behalf of the defendant, her exercise of the option was ratified, by the acts and conduct of the defendant, the principal. Even if Eva's act were deemed unauthorized, plaintiffs right to withdraw from the transaction was only prior to the time that it was ratified by the principal, thereafter, they were bound. Ratification relates back to the time when the unauthorized act was done; and although the act may have done without any precedent authority, ratification creates the relation of principal and agent. Eva exercised the option in June, 1969; plaintiffs did not challenge the validity of her act until June 1973; during the interim, the acts and the conduct of plaintiffs indicated an acceptance of the notice as an effective exercise of this contract right. For a period of four years plaintiffs dealt with defendant as the lessee, [*sic*] they are estopped by this conduct to take the inconsistent position that defendant did not have a leasehold interest.

Questions

1. Review Chapter 31. Which of the principles discussed there were applied by the court in *Zeese?*

2. Who had the burden of proof on the agency in question in this case? Why?

LIABILITY OF THE AGENT

Usually, when an agent enters into a contract on behalf of her principal, only the principal and the third party are bound by that contract. However, many situations that occur from time to time involve exceptions to that rule.

Disclosure of the Relationship

Every possible principal-agent relationship may be classified into one of three categories—disclosed, partially disclosed, or undisclosed. The **disclosed principal** (sometimes termed fully disclosed principal) exists when the third party dealing with the agent knows *both* that the agent is acting in a representative (agency) capacity and the exact identity of the principal. For example, a salesperson introduces herself to a potential customer saying, "Hello. My name is Phillis Archer and I represent ABC Auto Supply." Since this is a disclosed agency, Archer is not a party to any contract that might arise, and under normal circumstances she will not be liable if ABC fails to perform properly. This is in keeping with the concept that the law of contracts seeks to vindicate the justifiable expectations of the parties and, at the time the contract was entered into, the customer had no expectation that Archer would be performing it.

When an agent negotiates a contract on behalf of a principal and, even though the third party knows he is acting as an agent, he does not know the principal's identity, the agent is said to be dealing for a **partially disclosed principal.** If the third party knows neither the principal's identity nor that the agent is acting as an agent, but rather assumes that the agent is acting on his own behalf, then the principal is referred to as an **undisclosed principal.** If, in the example, Archer had introduced herself to the potential customer by saying, "Hi. My name is Phillis Archer and I am acting as agent for a principal whose identity I am not at liberty to disclose," Archer's principal would be partially disclosed. If she had said, "Hi. My name is Phillis Archer," the relationship would be undisclosed.

These latter relationships are far less common than the disclosed ones. They are essentially neither illegal nor immoral; they may be quite useful and, at times, even necessary. For example, suppose a major corporation wants to purchase several adjacent parcels of real estate for the purpose of building a new manufacturing plant. It is a fair guess that if potential sellers know the purchaser is a "wealthy" corporation, the price of the property will go up. This especially is true as each seller senses that the corporation's needs have increased. In such a case, it is only good business—and in the best interests of its stockholders—for the corporation to have its purchasing agent act in a partially disclosed or an undisclosed capacity.

When an agent acts on behalf of either a partially disclosed or an undisclosed principal, the agent always initially is liable on every contract entered into. The theory is that in both cases the third party does not know the identity of the principal, and therefore must be contracting in reliance on the credit of the agent alone. This, however, does not relieve the principal of liability. Remember, the principal always is liable in every case in which the agent has acted as authorized, and the third party is entitled to take advantage of this rule. The partially disclosed and undisclosed situations only add the liability of the agent to that of the principal.

Nature of the Agent's Liability

When the agent has acted as authorized, but in a partially disclosed or an undisclosed situation, the liability of the principal and the agent is said to be **several liability**—that is, separate. Although in the event of breach the third party can file suit against both the principal and the agent, can present evidence against both, and even can get a jury verdict against both, the court will require that the third party make an election when it comes time to enter the judgment. The third party either can recognize the existence of the agency relationship and hold the principal, or can ignore it and hold the agent. He cannot hold both. Of course, if the third party chooses the agent and the agent has acted only as authorized by the principal, the agent, as was discussed in Chapter 34, is entitled to reimbursement from the principal.

BERTRAM YACHT SALES, INC. v. WEST
209 So.2d 677 (Fla. App. 1968)

This was an action by William R. B. West (Plaintiff/Appellee) against the University of Miami and Bertram Yacht Sales, Inc. (Bertram) (Defendants/Appellants) for breach of a contract to sell a particular boat to Plaintiff.

Bertram, acting as authorized agent for the University of Miami, the owner of the boat in question, entered into a contract to sell the boat to Plaintiff. In doing so, Bertram signed the contract, naming itself as owner of the boat and not disclosing that it was acting as an agent for the university. However, thereafter the boat was sold to another purchaser, and Plaintiff brought this action.

The trial of the case before a jury resulted in a verdict in favor of Plaintiff against both Bertram and the university in the amount of $5000. Both Defendants appealed. Affirmed in part and reversed in part and remanded.

CHARLES CARROL, Chief Judge.

The appellant University of Miami argues that the court committed error by granting judgment against both defendants and by failing to require the plaintiff, after verdict, to elect to take judgment against only one or the other. With that contention we agree. . . . The effect of the verdict was to find the University was the owner of the boat and that Bertram was acting as agent for the University as its undisclosed principal [*sic*]. In those circumstances, as this court stated in Hohouser v. Schor . . ., ". . . when the issue of the agency relationship should be submitted to the jury for determination, then the plaintiff should be required to elect *after* verdict against which defendant he wishes to take judgment. . . ."

The appellee, while conceding the correctness of the contention, as held in Hohauser v. Schor . . . argues it should be rejected here because the contention was not also asserted by Bertram. We can not agree. The fact that Bertram has not raised the point does not destroy its validity when duly preserved and asserted on appeal by the University.

Accordingly, the judgment is affirmed in part, but the cause is remanded to the circuit court with direction to require the plaintiff to elect (after verdict) to take judgment against either the agent Bertram Yacht Sales, Inc. or against the undisclosed principal, the University of Miami, and thereupon the trial court shall vacate the judgment as to the one against which the plaintiff elects not to take judgment.

Questions

1. Why should the plaintiff have rights against the university, since it did not know of, and did not rely on, its ownership of the boat?
2. Why shouldn't the plaintiff be entitled to a joint judgment against both the university and Bertram, if both are liable?

Agent as a Partner

As discussed in the previous chapter, the essence of a common law partnership is that each partner is both the principal and the agent of the other partners. Thus, when one of the partners acts, as authorized, on behalf of the partnership, that act binds both that partner (as principal) and the other partners by virtue of the agency relationship. The fact that the agent binds herself as well as her partners is not a rule derived from the law of agency. It is a matter of simple contract law combined with the recognition that under these circumstances the individual is acting simultaneously in two capacities.

Agent as a Guarantor

Some agents, in carrying out their duties for their principals, not only enter into relations with third parties directly on behalf of their principals, but also bind themselves to contracts of guarantee in order to induce third parties to deal with their principals. In the event that the principal fails to perform properly, the agent is liable to the third party for the breach. The personal commitment by an agent is, of course, a separate contract, related only collaterally to the main contract between the principal and the third party. It is an example of the type of contract discussed in Chapter 23 on suretyship.

Agent for a Nonexistent Principal

It is fundamental that two persons are required in order to have an agency relationship—a principal and an agent. Therefore, when no principal exists, the agent is acting alone and his actions will bind only himself. This conclusion is founded, in part, on the concept that when one purports to act as an agent, he impliedly represents and warrants that he is acting with authority from a principal presently capable of granting that authority. Since, that representation is false in the case of a nonexistent principal, the third party may have an action against the agent under the contract theory of breach of warranty or the tort theory of deceit.

There are three general circumstances under which a purported principal may be nonexistent. First, the principal may be fictitious. An example would be when an agent states that he has been authorized by "John Smith," but there either is no such person or the John Smith who is alleged to be the principal never has granted the necessary authority as represented by the agent. For a more subtle example of the nonexistent principal, consider the following case.

DIXIE DRIVE IT YOURSELF SYSTEM v. LEWIS
78 Ga. App. 236, 59 S.E.2d 843 (1948)

This was an action by Dixie Drive It Yourself System (Plaintiff/Plaintiff In Error) against J. G. Lewis (Defendant/Defendant In Error) for breach of a contract for the rental of two automobiles rented by Defendant, the principal of Hapeville

High School, for the purpose of transporting students in connection with athletic activities. One of the terms of the contract signed by Defendant "Hapeville High School, John G. Lewis, Principal" provided that the customer would be liable for any damage to the vehicle while it was rented to the customer. The vehicle in question was obtained on a delivery ticket made out in the name of "Hapeville High School" and, during the rental, was involved in an accident to the alleged extent of $400. Defendant refused to pay for the damage, contending that he had acted only as an authorized agent for Hapeville High School.

From a judgment of the Civil Court of Fulton County, sitting without a jury, rendered for Defendant, Plaintiff appealed. Reversed.

GARDNER, Judge.

The only question presented here for decision is whether the contract in question is the individual undertaking of the defendant. It is clear that both parties to the contract knew that the Hapeville High School had no legal entity. It could not sue or be sued. So neither the plaintiff nor the defendant were [*sic*] misled. They were both bound by this knowledge. This is true even though the Hapeville High School is a unit of the Fulton County School System. Therefore, as a legal entity the Hapeville High School was nonexistent. The question before us was discussed at length in Hagan v. Asa G. Candler, Inc. . . . The court in that case said: "One who professes to contract as agent for another, when his purported principal is actually nonexistent, may be held personally liable on the contract, unless the other contracting party agrees to look to some other person for performance." In a similar case, Wells v. J.A. Fay and Egan Company, . . . the [Georgia] Supreme Court said: "If one contracts as agent, when in fact he has no principal, he will be personally liable."

In view of the authorities cited and the record in the instant case, the contract was the individual undertaking of the defendant.

The court erred in overruling the motion for new trial.

Questions

1. What should Mr. Lewis have done in order to protect himself against personal liability?

2. Is there any way a merchant can protect himself against nonexistent principals, since not all agents are financially able to pay damages?

A second circumstance under which a principal may be nonexistent is when the principal has authorized an agent to conduct certain business, but at the time the agent actually enters into a contract with a third party, unknown to the agent, the principal is dead. The agent will be liable on the contract, although when the agent has acted in good faith without notice of the death, courts tend to do everything reasonably possible to insulate the agent from being injured. But if there is no reasonable alternative, the rights of the third party will be protected over those of the agent.

The same notion underlies the third circumstance—an agent acting on behalf of an **incompetent principal.** It should be understood at this point that the term *incompetent* is not interchangeable with the term *insane.* As was discussed in Chapter 9 on voidable contracts, someone may be insane in fact, but is not incompetent until she is taken before a court (probate court in most jurisdictions) and, in a separate hearing, adjudicated incompetent. Normally, at this point, the person's affairs are turned over to a guardian and she is placed into some type of custodial care. By statute in most states, the acts of an incompetent person are void. The common law considered such a person as having no mind and thus, for most purposes, as being the same as if she were dead.

CHEDA v. GRANDI
95 Cal.App.2d 513, 218 P.2d 97 (1950)

This was an action by Adolf R. Cheda (Plaintiff/Respondent) against F. Lloyd Grandi (Defendant/Petitioner) for money damages for breach of an implied warranty of authority to act as an agent for his brother, Henry E. Grandi. (This action also was against other defendants for other reasons not material here.)

In August of 1941, Henry E. Grandi suffered a mental deterioration caused by high blood pressure and was confined to hospitals and sanitariums thereafter. He was declared incompetent in February 1943, and died in April of 1943. After August of 1941, Defendant assumed to act for Henry in matters relating to a garage owned by Henry, which had been rented to Plaintiff, month-to-month, since 1934.

In February 1942, Plaintiff talked with Defendant about securing a lease to the garage. Under the date of March 11, 1942, Defendant wrote Plaintiff a letter offering a five-year lease with an option to renew for an additional five years, stating in part, "I have analyzed the matter of your leasing Henry's garage . . . and I have attempted to arrive at a solution which would be fair to you and also to him. I have decided as follows: . . . [the letter then stated the terms]." Shortly thereafter Plaintiff executed three copies of the resulting lease and returned them to Defendant. In February 1943, Plaintiff requested a reduction in rent, and under the date of February 12, 1943, Defendant wrote to Plaintiff, "Regarding your request to eliminate the $15.00 payment on the equipment for 1943, I am willing to accept only the $40.00 garage rent until such time as in my opinion conditions are such that the payments on the equipment should be renewed."

Throughout the entire period, Plaintiff paid the agreed-upon rent to Defendant, who deposited it in a trustee account with records indicating that the money was Henry's. About July of 1946, parties named McFadden began negotiating to purchase the garage. Though they knew of Plaintiff's lease with the option to renew, they were told by Defendant that Plaintiff did not have a proper lease and, seeing that the lease was signed only by Defendant (not Henry), they believed it to be invalid. Immediately upon paying the purchase price, the McFaddens sought to raise the rent, and the present action ensued.

From a judgment in favor of Plaintiff in the amount of $2572.50, Defendant appealed. Affirmed.

PETERS, Presiding Judge.

[The court resolved the question of whether Plaintiff knew that Henry was incompetent, concluding that he did not. Had the court found to the contrary, Plaintiff would not have been entitled to the judgment granted.]

We think the evidence shows that Lloyd held himself out to be more than an ordinary agent with power simply to negotiate. Lloyd's letter of March 11, 1942, states that "*I have analyzed the matter,*" and "*I have attempted to arrive at a solution,*" and "*I have decided.*" The transaction outlined in the letter was an integrated transaction. Reasonably construed it impliedly represented that Lloyd had power to execute the lease. The subsequent actions of Lloyd strengthens [*sic*] this construction. It was Lloyd who collected all payments, and they were the very payments called for in the lease. It was Lloyd who granted Cheda permission to make alterations in the premises, the lease providing that such permission had to be secured from the lessor. It was Lloyd who, by letter dated February 12, 1943, allowed Cheda to discontinue the $15 monthly payments on the equipment, and in that letter states: "*I am willing to accept only the $40.00 garage rent until such time as in* my *opinion*" etc. Lloyd admitted that he often acted as Henry's agent in real estate and other business transactions. All of this evidence demonstrates that Lloyd represented by his actions that he had authority to execute the lease for Henry. There was, therefore, a breach of the warranty [of authority]. . . .

While the rule is that an agent does not normally warrant the capacity of his principal to contract (Restatement of Agency, Sec. 332), that is not an absolute rule. As stated in "Comment a" to section 332, "if the principal is completely incompetent so that he cannot be a party to a contract, the agent may be liable on a warranty." . . . Lloyd's statements to Cheda that he would submit the contract to Henry, if he then knew that Henry was totally incompetent, would be a sufficiently material misrepresentation to impose liability upon Henry upon the warranty [Henry's implied warranty, or promise, that he was authorized].

The portion of the judgment appealed from by F. Lloyd Grandi is affirmed.

Questions

1. Is the rule holding the agent of a dead or incompetent principal liable to a third party fair?

2. What other disabilities of a principal might activate the rule applied in the *Cheda* case?

There is one important exception to the rule that someone cannot be the agent of a dead or incompetent principal, which is found in Section 4-405 of the Uniform Commercial Code, dealing with banks and checking account customers. This section provides that a bank can continue to act as agent for the customer, paying out the customer's money on checks properly drawn prior to the death or incompetency, until the bank knows of the death or adjudication and has had time to act on it. Subsection 2 of the section further allows the bank, with such knowledge, to continue to pay and certify checks for a period of ten days after the customer's death (but not after the adjudication of incompetency) unless ordered to stop by a person claiming an interest in the account.

Agent for a Principal Lacking Contractual Capacity

When an agent acts on behalf of a principal who lacks full contractual capacity (short of incompetency), the resulting contract is voidable at the principal's option. If that happens, the third party may want to look to the agent for performance. The courts, however, hold that an agent will not be liable under this circumstance (see the *Cheda* case) unless it can be shown that he acted in bad faith, misrepresenting or concealing the inca-pacity. Although the law places the risk of the principal's existence and competency on the agent, it places the risk of the principal's other contractual capacity on the third party if there is no deception by the agent.

GOLDFINGER v. DOHERTY
276 N.Y.S. 289, 153 Misc. 826 (1934)

Originally this was an action by Ruth Goldfinger (Plaintiff) against Henry L. Doherty (Defendant/Appellant) to disaffirm certain purchases of stock, made on her behalf by her duly authorized agent, on the ground that she was an infant at the time of the transactions. Defendant then served a supplemental complaint and summons on the agent, Samuel Goldfinger (Supplemental Defendant/Respondent), joining him in the case and alleging that if Plaintiff is allowed to disaffirm the purchases, Samuel Goldfinger should be liable for Defendant's damages on the ground of breach of an implied warranty that he was authorized to bind Plaintiff to contracts. [The relationship, if any, between Samuel and Ruth Goldfinger was not disclosed in the pleadings.]

From a judgment dismissing the supplemental complaint, Defendant appealed. Affirmed.

SHIENTAG, Justice.

. . . "An agent does not warrant that his principal has full contractual capacity, any more than he warrants that his principal is solvent. Thus an agent for one not of legal age is not necessarily liable if the infant avoids the obligation of the contract made on his account." Comment (a) on section 332, Restatement of the Law of Agency. An agent who misrepresents the capacity of his principal to contract is liable as for any other misrepresentation, and this [is true] whether he misrepresents tortiously or innocently.

In the absence of misrepresentation, under what circumstances, if any, is an agent acting for an infant, who subsequently disaffirms, not the agency, but the transaction of the agent, liable to the other contracting party? It must appear that the agent knew or had reason to know of his principal's lack of full contractual capacity, and it must further appear that the other contracting party was in ignorance thereof. The theory of breach of warranty of authority is that one dealing with an agent has been misled by him. This could hardly be deemed to have occurred, if all the facts were known. "It is material, in these cases, that the party claiming a want of authority in the agent should be ignorant of the truth touching the agency." . . . If the agent "acts within his instructions, and in good faith, especially when the facts are equally known to both parties, he is not personally responsible, although it may happen that the authority itself is void." . . .

Assuming that the agent knows or has reason to know of the principal's lack of full capacity, and of the other party's ignorance thereof, what, if any, is the agent's liability? . . .

Clear authority on this point is lacking. Ordinarily, the duty to speak has been limited to a situation where there is either a pre-existing fiduciary relationship, or one expressly created by a repose of confidence, or where the contract itself calls for disclosure.

In a case as here presented, however, the duty imposed, if any, must rest on a broader basis. Concealment involves a suppression of truth, and, when accompanied by a statement in itself true, they together may create such a misleading impression as to cause the statement made to be in effect false and actionable. "Half the truth may be a lie in effect." . . .

The basis of the liability of an agent, in a situation such as we are here considering, is that he has produced "a false impression upon the mind of the other party; and, if this result is accomplished, it is unimportant whether the means of accomplishing it are words or acts of the defendant [Samuel Goldfinger], or his concealment or suppression of material facts not equally within the knowledge or reach of the plaintiff [Henry Doherty].

If, therefore, the liability of the agent is to be based on his failure to disclose facts in connection with his principal's lack of full capacity to the other contracting party, it must appear (1) that the agent knew or had reason to know the facts indicating his principal's lack of full capacity; (2) that the other contracting party was in ignorance thereof and the agent had reason so to believe; (3) that the transaction is one in which lack of full capacity was a material fact.

Drawing the most favorable inferences from the pleading under consideration, we find that it fails to set forth enough facts to constitute a cause of action. We feel, however, that the defendant Doherty should have an opportunity to amend, if he be so advised, so as to conform his pleading to the requirements herein set forth.

The order dismissing the supplemental complaint is affirmed, with $10 costs and disbursements, with leave to the defendant to serve an amended supplemental complaint within six days after service of order entered hereon upon payment of said costs.

Questions

1. What other contractual incapacities should be covered by the principle of the *Goldfinger* case?
2. What kinds of facts might Doherty include in his amended supplemental complaint against the agent to meet the court's standard?

LIABILITY UPON RATIFICATION BY THE PRINCIPAL

Just as a principal can bind herself by authorizing the conduct of an agent before the fact, she can bind herself by ratification after the fact. As a general rule, however, ratification only adds the liability of the principal to that of the agent; it does not eliminate the liability of the agent to the third party.

When the agent has acted as a partner or a

guarantor, there is nothing to ratify, because in both cases the agent has sought to act on behalf of both himself and the principal. A dead principal cannot ratify, and a principal who was incompetent at the time the agent acted cannot ratify because she could not have entered into the contract on her own behalf at the time it came into existence—remember, the acts of an incompetent generally are declared void (not voidable) by statute. Nor is there anything to ratify in the case of an undisclosed or partially disclosed principal. The authority already was there, but the law has given the third party the option to hold either the agent or the principal liable (once the identity of the principal is discovered) in order to give the third party someone absolutely identifiable against whom he can take action in the event of breach. This right is not altered either by discovery of the principal's identity or by the principal's ratification.

The exceptions to this general rule occur when the agent purportedly has acted on behalf of a principal who was fictitious (the agent was not authorized in the first place), has exceeded his existing authority, or has acted on behalf of a principal lacking full contractual capacity (one who is insane or a minor). In the last circumstance, ratification by the principal will terminate the agent's liability. In the other situations this exemption does not pertain.

SUBAGENTS

In many cases, an agent acting on behalf of a principal may find it convenient or necessary to employ the services of another person to help. This additional person, employed by an agent, is known as a **subagent.** Whether or not the principal is liable for contracts entered into or discharged by a subagent, as with the agent, is resolved by looking at the presence or absence of authority. Briefly, if the agent's hiring of the subagent was authorized by the principal and the subagent acted within the limits of that authority, the principal is bound. Otherwise she is not. Authority to hire subagents may arise in the same circumstances as described in Chapter 31 for agents. It may be express, implied, or apparent. The liability of a subagent on contracts entered into on behalf of the principal then will arise under the same circumstances as for any agent. The relationship established, for the purpose of contractual liability, is considered to be only between the principal and the subagent. The agent is not involved except as a conduit of the necessary authority.

TRANE COMPANY v. GILBERT
73 Cal.Rptr. 279 (1968)

This action is the result of the consolidation of two separate cases brought against Arthur Gilbert, Edward Rothschild, and others (Defendants/Appellants) by the Trane Company, English & Lauer, and others (Plaintiffs/Respondents). Trane sought to recover $8405.13 as the purchase price of a replacement motor that was sold to Defendants in April 1962, to be installed in their building; English & Lauer sought $5659.37 for labor and materials furnished in the installation of the motor.

In 1959, Defendants employed Sidney Eisenshtat, an architect, to prepare plans for their building. Eisenshtat employed Samuel L. Kaye, a mechanical engineer, to plan and draw specifications for the heating, ventilation, and air-conditioning system. After extended negotiations—on the basis of the statements in a brochure that the system was "foolproof," "failsafe," and "automatically protected against damage"—Defendant Rothschild approved the purchase of the Trane air-conditioning system.

The statements in the brochure were not qualified by any time limitation. Undisputed evidence, however, showed that at the time of the purchase Kaye had actual knowledge that relevant warranties on the system were limited to one year.

In April 1962, the motor in the system that was installed in 1959 burned out. It was replaced by Plaintiff Trane and installed by Plaintiff English & Lauer. Defendants refused to pay either for the motor or for the installation, contending that since they had no notice of the one-year limitation, the motor was still under warranty. Plaintiffs contended that Kaye was an authorized subagent of Defendant and that his knowledge of the warranty limitation was imputed to Defendant. Though it was uncontradicted that Defendant knew of the employment of Kaye, Defendant urged that there was no evidence to support a finding that Kaye was Defendant's agent.

From a finding for Plaintiffs on the issue, Defendant appealed. Affirmed.

STEPHENS, Associate Justice.

Defendant Rothschild testified that he had a "turn key contract" in which architect Eisenshtat was responsible in his supervisory capacity for handling all negotiations with third persons concerning the construction of the building. As a general rule, an architect, as far as the preparation of plans and specifications is concerned, acts as an independent contractor; but so far as the performance of his supervisory functions with respect to a building under construction is concerned, he ordinarily acts as an agent and representative of the person for whom the work is being done. (5 Am.Jur.2d, Architects, Sec. 6, p. 668; . . .) Whether in fact an agency has been created is to be determined by the relation of the parties as they exist under their agreement or acts. . . . By defendant Rothschild's own admission and from other evidence adduced at trial as to the nature of his employment, it is clear that architect Eisenshtat was a general supervising agent for defendants. The scope of the authority conferred may be determined by the conduct of the principal and agent in their business relationships. (Civil Code, Sec. 2315 . . .) The authority to appoint a subagent may be inferred from the employment of the agent in a position of general authority, which, in view of business custom and usage, or because of the nature and necessities of the business entrusted to the agent, ordinarily includes authority to appoint other agents. (Civil Code, Sec. 2349 . . .) In the present case, the evidence established that architect Eisenshtat employed Kaye in his capacity as mechanical engineer to plan and draw the specifications for the heating, ventilation, and air conditioning systems to be used in the building. Furthermore, defendant Rothschild was personally aware that Kaye was so employed. Under such circumstances, it is inferable that the agent Eisenshtat was authorized to employ Kaye as subagent. Even if unauthorized, it is evident that defendant Rothschild must be held to have acquiesced in or ratified Kaye's employment. Where an agent is authorized to employ a subagent, or his act in doing so is ratified by the principal, the latter is, as to third persons, bound by the acts of the subagent to the same extent as if they had been performed by the agent. That is, the relation of principal and agent exists between the principal and subagent. (Civil Code, Sec. 2351.) The evidence and reasonable inferences drawn therefrom are clearly sufficient to sustain the trial court's determination that Kaye was an agent of defendants. Consequently, and as in the case of an agent employed directly by the principal, notice to the subagent is imputable to, and is the equivalent of, notice to the principal. (Civil Code, Sec. 2332; . . . 3 Am.Jur.2d, Agency, Sec. 152, p. 543; Rest., Agency (2d ed.), Sec. 283.) Thus, it is a well established rule in California that the principal is chargeable with, and is bound by the knowledge of, or notice to, his agent, received while the agent is acting within the scope of his authority, and which is in reference to a matter over which his authority extends. . . . Kaye, as the mechanical engineer in charge of planning the air conditioning system, was certainly the proper person to receive literature concerning air conditioning equipment and terms of warranty. As stated in Granberg v. Turnham, 166 Cal.App.2d 390, 395, 33 P.2d 423, 426: "The fact that he may or may not have reported this information to his principal is immaterial, for he was acting in the course of his employment and the principal was charged with knowledge of information acquired by him in the transaction of her business. . . . An agent's knowledge of the content of a contract is imputed to his principal. This rule of law is not a rebuttable presumption. It is not a presumption at all. It is a rule which charges the principal with the knowledge possessed by [her or] his agent."

Questions

1. Is it realistic or fair to charge the principal with everything known to each of the subagents?

2. Does it make sense for a principal to insist that each subagent disclose everything it knows before contracting on behalf of the principal?

RIGHTS OF THE PRINCIPAL AND THE AGENT

In the typical situation in which the agent has entered into a contract on behalf of a fully disclosed principal and has acted only as authorized, the agent has no right of action against the third party for breach. This is based on the proposition that the resulting contract is between the principal and the third party, and the agent is not a party to it. This rule does not apply, however, when the agent is a party to the contract as a result of acting on behalf of a principal who is undisclosed, partially disclosed, nonexistent, or who lacked full contractual capacity, and the principal chooses to exercise his right to avoid the contract. Since the third party is able to hold the agent liable, the agent becomes a party to the contract with full rights against the third party. The rule also does not apply in suits by an agent in her own name, on behalf of her principal, against one wrongfully interfering with her rightful possession of the principal's property. Under these circumstances, the agent has a right of action just as would any other party.

When the agent has acted properly, with authority from the principal—or when the principal has ratified the agent's unauthorized act—it is the principal who has the first right of action. However, this right may be assigned to the agent if the principal and agent agree. Therefore, whoever is to be held liable on the contract has a right to secure the benefits of that contract.

In an action by a third party against the principal based on a contract entered into by the agent on the principal's behalf, the principal, as a general rule, will have available all defenses arising out of the contract itself (those available to the agent had he been sued as a party to the contract) as well as personal defenses. Thus, when an agent enters into a contract that does not satisfy the Statute of Frauds, a defense based on the Statute of Frauds is available to the principal, as would the defenses of misrepresentation, fraud, duress, undue influence, and the parol evidence rule. In addition, the principal also has available other defenses personal to herself, such as incompetence, minority, and the statute of limitations, and may assert her own claim by way of set-off, recoupment, and counterclaim. On the other hand, she cannot take advantage of defenses purely personal to the agent, such as the agent's incapacity, a statute of limitations applicable to the agent but not to her (for example, the rule that stops the statute from running while the agent is out of the jurisdiction), or a set-off personal to the agent.

Finally, when the agent is held liable personally on a contract negotiated in good faith and as authorized by the principal—as when the principal was undisclosed or partially disclosed—the agent has a right either to keep the benefits of the contract or to tender them to the principal and sue the principal for reimbursement. In a suit for reimbursement, the burden of proving the existence of authority is on the agent, and courts generally hold that this fact cannot be proven by the testimony of the agent alone. Corroborating evidence is required, just as it is in a suit by the third party against the principal.

SUMMARY

When an agent has acted as authorized by his principal, the principal generally is bound, not the agent. This is consistent with the concept that the agent is the alter ego of the principal, and thus when the agent acts it is, in contemplation of law, the principal acting on her own behalf. The application of this concept, however, does have specific limitations.

Whether the principal is bound by the acts of her agent depends on the presence or absence of authority. If authority was granted to the agent, the principal is bound. If not, she is not bound. In a suit to enforce the liability of the principal, the burden of proving the required authority is on the third party.

The agent may be liable in addition to the principal when the principal is undisclosed or partially disclosed, or instead of the principal when the principal is dead, incompetent, otherwise nonexistent, or lacks full contractual capacity. In the event that the agent also is acting as a partner of, or a surety for, the principal, the agent also renders himself liable by his personal undertaking. When ratification is possible, and the principal ratifies the unauthorized act of the agent, the agent is relieved of liability.

The principal is liable for the acts of subagents as long as the agent's hiring of the subagent was authorized and the subagent acted within the limits of his authority. A subagent can be liable on resulting transactions to the same extent as any other agent.

When both the principal and the agent are liable on a particular transaction, other than when the agent has acted as a co-partner or a guarantor, the liability is "several." This means the third party can secure judgment against either the principal or the agent, but not against both.

As to the rights of the principal and the agent, whoever is liable on the contract has a right to the benefits of the contract as well. Defenses available to the person liable on the contract include those arising out of the transaction and those personal to himself or herself. If the agent is liable on a contract when the liability, in fairness, should be assumed by the principal, the agent has a right to tender the benefits of the contract to the principal and seek reimbursement from the principal.

KEY TERMS AND CONCEPTS

disclosed principal
partially disclosed principal
undisclosed principal
several liability
incompetent principal
subagent

PROBLEMS

1. The Brotherhood of Missionary Churches, an unincorporated association, acting through its executive committee, asked Faush to have minutes of the annual meeting printed for distribution to its membership. Faush did so, signing the contract with the printer "Brotherhood of Missionary Churches—by F. Faush, Agent." When the Brotherhood failed to pay, the printer sued Faush personally. Is Faush liable?

2. In June 1976, Mary Losenski, vice-president of American Dry Cleaning Co., executed a lease with an option to purchase for the company's store, in favor of her son. The store constituted 90 percent of the company's assets. When the lessee sought to exercise his option to purchase, the board of directors, first learning of the transaction, refused to sell, contending Losenski was not authorized to give the option in the lease. Should American Dry Cleaning be bound?

3. Bruce Advertising sued Crane-Maier, a developer, and Sherrill, a trustee of a trust that owned land being developed, for payment for advertising services in connection with the development. The suit alleged that the defendants were

partners, when in fact Crane-Maier was acting as agent for the trust. As a result, judgment was granted against Crane-Maier only. Thereafter, Bruce filed a second suit seeking to hold Sherrill liable as principal. Sherrill contended that the judgment in the first suit discharged him. Is Sherrill correct?

4. Coats purchased certain goods from Harris Sales Corp., signing a contract that provided "It is hereby declared, agreed, and understood that there are no prior writings, verbal negotiations, understandings, representations, or agreements between the parties, not herein expressed." When Coats discovered he had been defrauded by a saleswoman for Harris, because of oral statements not contained in the writing, he sued Harris. Is Coats entitled to recover?

5. Romain employed various sales representatives to sell books door-to-door. They were paid on a commission based on their individual sales. Romain was sued by the attorney general of New Jersey for prohibited sales practices by the sales representatives; Romain defended on the ground that the representatives were independent contractors. Should Romain be liable?

6. Buford, acting as agent for Cooper, purchased land for Cooper without disclosing the agency to the seller, Epstein. When the sale was made, Epstein thought he was dealing with Buford only. The contract executed contained a clause prohibiting assignment. Is Cooper entitled to enforce the contract?

7. For years, Abell, a newspaper publisher, had published advertisements for Warren & Co., a corporation. On one occasion when an advertising bill of $3730.97 was not paid, Abell sued Skein on the contract signed "Warren & Co. (Firm Name)—Richard I. Skein (Partner of Firm or Officer Signing)." Abell contended Skein was liable because nothing indicated that Warren & Co. was a corporation or that he was *not* signing for himself, personally, as well as the company. Should Skein be held personally liable?

8. Frank Pierson contracted, as president of the Great River Steamboat Co., to purchase music services to be supplied by Wired Music, Inc. The contract contained a provision that stated, "The individual signing this agreement for the subscriber guarantees that all of the above provisions shall be complied with." The contract was signed "Great River Steamboat Co.—by Frank C. Pierson, Pres." When Great River failed to perform, Wired Music sought to hold Pierson personally liable on the guarantee. Should Pierson be liable?

9. Suit was brought by the Adam Miguez Funeral Home against First National Life Insurance Co. to collect benefits under a life-insurance policy on the life of Joe Trehan. When the policy was purchased, Trehan was in prison, and his father signed the application for him at the suggestion of the agent who sold the policy. The agent falsely certified that Joe had signed in his presence. Should First National be liable on the policy?

10. Ellenger agreed to work on a project; she thought she was working for Griffen. In fact, the project was owned by a corporation, of which Griffen was president. Ellenger was paid with a check signed by Griffen. The check was imprinted with a check protector, and the imprint contained the corporate name. The check was not honored, and Ellenger sued Griffen, who defended on the ground that he was acting only as agent for a fully disclosed principal. Should Griffen be liable?

Chapter | 33

Tort and Criminal Liability

OUTLINE

INTRODUCTION TO TORT LIABILITY

A principal or employer generally is liable for the torts committed by an agent or employee acting within the course and scope of employment *only* if the principal or employer maintains the right to control the details of that agent's or employee's performance. In terms of the diagram presented in Chapter 31, now we primarily are concerned only with relationships falling on the left side of the circle—the master-servant and the principal-controlled agent.

Rationale

The origins and reasons behind the concept of *vicarious liability* (liability without a direct breach of duty by the principal or employer personally, but based on a breach by an agent or servant) have been the subject of some debate by legal historians. It generally is agreed, however, that they are to be found in the feudal law of England. During the feudal period, servants and agents over whom close control was exercised were likely to be slaves who possessed no independent property that could be taken to pay judgments rendered against them. Thus, vicarious liability was a matter of necessity if the rights of third parties were to be protected. In addition, however, the rule seems to be fair, in that one who expands his ability to transact business or to perform labor by employing agents and servants should be liable for injuries to third parties occurring during periods of increased risk caused by this increased activity. This is especially true because the principal or employer has the right to control, and the activities are for his benefit.

The term applied to this type of liability is *respondeat superior* ("let the master answer"). It is applied only in cases involving tort liability, and then only in situations in which, at the time she committed the tort, the agent or employee was subject to detailed control by the principal or employer and was performing duties within the course and scope of employment. The student may wish, at this point, to refer back to Chapter 31 to recall what factors are considered of importance in distinguishing between a servant, an independent contractor, a controlled agent, and a professional agent.

The Loaned-Servant Doctrine

It has been said that a person cannot serve two masters. Although this may be true in a poetic context, it is not true of vicarious liability under the law of agency. For instance, one may act as the agent of a partnership, thus acting simultaneously as the agent for all the partners. So, too, a nurse who is negligent in administering care to a patient while under the direction and control of the attending physician may be found to be a servant of both the doctor and the hospital. As you can see, whether to one master or more, vicarious tort liability will extend to all those with a right to control.

Another application of this concept is found in the category of cases governed by the **loaned-servant doctrine.** These cases differ from the previous examples in that they involve situations in which the control of the services of a servant are transferred from one master to another temporarily. With this transfer of control goes the transfer of *respondeat superior* liability. Although the servant remains the servant of the first master for the purposes of any relevant statutes concerning such matters as Social Security, income-tax withholding, workers' compensation, and the like, in determining vicarious liability for tortious conduct he may be considered the servant of the second master. Once again, *respondeat superior* liability attaches to the right to control. Consider the following case involving the doctrine.

N.Y. CENTRAL R.R. CO. v. NORTHERN INDIANA PUBLIC SERVICE CO.

40 Ind.App. 79, 221 N.E.2d 442 (1966)

This was an action by the New York Central Railroad Company (NYC) (Plaintiff/Appellant) against Northern Indiana Public Service Company (Nipsco) (Defendant/Appellee) for reimbursement, pursuant to a contract of indemnity, of $30,000 in damages paid by Plaintiff to the widow of an employee killed while working for Plaintiff.

Plaintiff was the owner of some railroad tracks Defendant wished to cross with its power lines. Plaintiff granted permission by a written licensing agreement containing an indemnity provision that read as follows: "Sixth: Second Party (Nipsco) shall and will at all times hereafter indemnify and save harmless First Party (NYC) from and against any and all detriment, damages, losses, claims, demands, suits, costs, or expenses which First Party (NYC) may suffer, sustain, or be subject to, directly or indirectly, caused either wholly or in part by reason of the location, construction, maintenance, use or presence of said Work as permitted by this licence or resulting from the removal thereof, except *such as may be caused by the sole* negligence *of First Party (NYC), its* agents *or* employees." (Emphasis added.) The relevant facts were stated by the court: "After the power lines had been built over the tracks for some time, appellant undertook to replace the steel rails of the center set of tracks. To effectuate this replacement, appellant moved a gondola car loaded with steel rails to the section of the tracks just below the overhead wires. To unload the rails, appellant rented a twenty-five (25) ton truck crane with a forty (40) foot boom maintained by an operator and an oiler from another corporation engaged in the crane rental business. While the crane operator was unloading sections of track with the help and direction of appellant's employees, the end of the boom struck one of appellee's high tension wires. The current from the wire went down the cable attached to the boom into a gondola car grounding through one of appellant's laborers causing fatal injuries to him."

From a judgment for Defendant, Plaintiff appealed. Affirmed.

HUNTER, Judge.

Both the appellant and appellee seem to agree that the determining question placed before this court involves the borrowed servant doctrine which states that an employee while generally employed by one party, may be loaned to another in such a manner that the special employer may be responsible for the acts of the employee under the doctrine of *respondeat superior*. Indiana has recognized this doctrine. . . . If the operator were the borrowed servant of the appellant, then under the terms of the contract the "claim" was "caused by the sole negligence of" the appellant, "its agents or employees." Therefore, it would not be within the indemnity provision. . . .

. . . [T]he Indiana cases have broadly defined the methods of analysis. In Sargent Paint Co. v. Petrovitzky, supra, 71 Ind.App. p. 359, 124 N.E. p. 883, the court stated that in determining who the master is, it "becomes necessary to ascertain who was the master *at the very time of the* negligent *act*." (Our [the court's] emphasis.) The court also stated that in determining who is the master . . . "we must inquire whose work is being performed." This question is answered by ascertaining ". . . who has the power to direct and control the work being performed. . . ." In addition, it is not who actually controlled the actions of the servant ". . . but who had the right to control.". . .

These principles are deceivingly simple. The annotation noted above shows that while most of the jurisdictions purport to use the same methods of analysis, those being the "control" and "whose business" tests, with the recent development of the "scope of business" test, the results obtained by the various jurisdictions are conflicting as to one another and even within a single jurisdiction. . . .

[The court then discussed the merits of the three conflicting tests.]

In the facts at bar the general employer had the right to hire and fire the servant. It paid the servant's wages and was in charge of the care and maintenance of the machine. Additionally the general employer was in the business of renting similar machines and the operator was a semi-skilled employee. In some respects these uncontroverted facts would indicate that the general employer had a right to control the specific acts in question.

However, other facts indicate the contrary. The appellant in leasing the machine did not indicate what work was to be done. The testimony in the record indicates that the general employer was merely told to send a crane with an operator and oiler to report to the railroad who would have someone to direct them. When the operator and oiler arrived at the job, the foreman asked them if they were the crew that was to work for him. He explained the method of operation required as to where to lay the rails upon being unloaded from the gondola car. The yard foreman hooked a type of tongs onto the cable of the crane. He had previously directed the placement of the gondola below the high tension wires. The crane was working in close contact with the other employees of the railroad. The crane operator could not see into the gondola car where the men were working and attaching the tongs to the rails. In regard to the directions being given by the foreman in the way of hand signals to the operator, the evidence is in conflict. However, it is certain that the operator was looking for some signals from the foreman at the moment the boom hit the overhead wires. There had been some directions given by the foreman previously. In addition the general employer had no idea of the nature of the work. The lease was to continue for an indeterminate period at the option of the appellant. Also the nature of the work was well within the scope of business of the railroad, that of unloading a car of rails, and there is testimony in the record to the effect that the foreman was an experienced crane operator. From all of these facts the court could have concluded that the special employer (appellant) had the right to control the operator in the operation of the crane as to the act in question, and that the work being done was within the scope of the appellant's business.

We therefore hold that there is sufficient evidence of probative value and reasonable inferences to be drawn therefrom to support the lower court's special findings of fact and conclusions of law.

Questions

1. Would it make sense to hold both masters of a loaned servant liable to third parties?

2. Since the general master has the right to "loan" the servant, why doesn't that power determine the question of liability?

COURSE AND SCOPE OF EMPLOYMENT

To hold a principal or employer liable for the torts of an agent or employee, the court not only must find that the principal or employer reserved the right to control the details of the agent's or employee's work, it must conclude that the tort was committed while the agent or employee was in the **course and scope of employment.** A number of factors have to be considered in arriving at this determination. The single most important of these is whether the act was done by the servant with the intent, at least in part, to serve the master's interests. This must be determined by an objective evaluation of the servant's conduct in light of the surrounding facts and circumstances. Among the factors to be considered are the time and place of the act.

Time and Place

The basic notion of the time and place limitation is that the master normally is not liable for the torts of his servants 24 hours of the day, every day of the week. This liability occurs only while the servant is "on the job," which usually may be considered to begin when the servant "punches in" and to end when he "punches out," although this rule is subject to numerous exceptions.

Typically, a person is not in the course and scope of employment while traveling to or from the work place. This exclusion may not pertain, however, when the employer requests the employee to perform services of employment during those times, as when the employer requests one of his plumbers to do a job for a customer on her way home, or where the owner of a bakery requests his route driver to have the delivery truck serviced on the way home and bring it back the next morning. An employee who travels as a regular part of her job may be held to be in the course and scope of employment during the entire period if her expenses are paid from the time of leaving home until the time of returning.

When an employee is "on call" during normal off-duty hours, she is likely to be considered in the course and scope of employment if she is required to remain by a telephone awaiting a call. If the employee can use this time with relative freedom and generally for her own purposes, as when she is only required to call in at intervals or is equipped with an adequate "beeper," she is likely to be considered on her own time.

Lunch periods may be treated as working time if the employee cannot effectively use the time for his own purposes, as when the period alloted is too short or he is required to remain on the premises. Normal coffee breaks of 15 or 20 minutes universally are considered as working time, both because of the short length of time and because they really are as much for the benefit of the employer as for the benefit of the employee in terms of increased morale and productivity.

Motive

Implicit in every agency relationship is the notion that the agent or employee is hired to pursue the best interests of the principal or employer. Thus, there is very little question that the principal or employer will be liable when an agent or employee negligently commits a tort while pursuing assigned duties. On the other hand, if the tort is committed when the agent is acting in disregard of those duties and solely in his own personal interest, the principal or employer will not be liable. Between those two extremes lie the problems.

It usually is held that if pursuit of the employer's interests is a substantial part of the employee's motivation, the employer may be liable. Courts often have stated that it is unreasonable to expect employees to act completely without self-interest 100 percent of the time. Thus, relatively minor breaches of duty, such as "goofing off" and moderate "horseplay," will not take the employee out of the course and scope of employment. For instance, suppose a delivery truck driver is told to drive from point A to point B and back, making deliveries along the way. She also is told not to leave the route. One day, while on her route, she drives a few blocks away to get a cup of coffee or to see a friend. She is likely to be considered still in the course and scope of employment the entire time. Such a departure probably will be seen as a "deviation" that reasonably can be expected from time to time; this is in spite of the fact that it was contrary to the employer's express orders. On the other hand, were she to drive ten miles off the route to see her boyfriend, this probably will be considered a "frolic" because of the magnitude of the departure from the employer's business, both in terms of the detour's distance and purpose. She will be considered to have left the course of employment. It should be noted that there is a substantial split of opinion as to the precise point at which she will be considered back in the course of employment. Some courts say it will be at the time she starts back to her route, because at that moment she again begins to pursue the interests of her employer. Others say it is not fair to place liability on the employer until the employee is back at or near her route.

Assault

Cases of assault are particularly troublesome, as are those involving other intentional torts such as trespass, conversion, and defamation. Historically, the master was not held liable for the intentional torts of his servant unless he had authorized them. The concept of *respondeat superior* was reserved for cases of negligence only. Today the liability of masters has been expanded, and may include liability for intentional torts when it is found that the act had a substantial relationship to the job. If the act is motivated by the servant's own ill will and the only connection with the servant's employment is time and place, most courts conclude the master is not liable. In deciding these cases, the major considerations seem to be whether the job is likely to lead the servant to do an act similar to that which was done, and whether a desire to do the job was a part of the motive or, if not, whether it was a reaction that reasonably might be expected to be created by the job. Thus, although an assault on an unruly customer by a bouncer in a waterfront bar might well visit liability on the master, an assault by a clerk of a hardware store probably would not. In the following case, the court obviously was interested in avoiding the complexities and uncertainties of concentrating solely on motivation as the standard for imposing liability.

LANGE v. NATIONAL BISCUIT COMPANY
297 Minn. 399, 211 N.W.2d 783 (1973)

This was an action by Jerome Lange (Plaintiff/Appellant) against the National Biscuit Company (Defendant/Respondent) for damages for an assault and battery committed on him by one Ronnell Lynch, an employee of Defendant. Plaintiff was the manager of a small grocery store that did business with Defendant. Ronnell Lynch was a route driver employed by Defendant to service one of its delivery routes, including Plaintiff's store. Between the date of Lynch's employment with Defendant and the date of the assault, Defendant had received numerous complaints from grocers served by Lynch that he was overly aggressive and that he was taking the shelf space reserved for competing cookie companies.

On May 1, 1969, Lynch came to the store managed by Plaintiff to service his stock. An argument developed between Lynch and Plaintiff. Lynch began swearing and became uncontrollably angry, saying to Plaintiff, "I ought to break your neck." He then went behind the counter and dared Plaintiff to fight; when Plaintiff refused, Lynch assaulted him viciously, then left after throwing merchandise around the store.

The jury found that though Lynch had not been acting within the scope of his employment at the time of the assault, Defendant had been negligent in hiring and retaining him in its employ. The trial court then granted Defendant's motion for judgment notwithstanding the verdict on the issue of negligence and denied Plaintiff's motion for judgment notwithstanding the verdict on the issue of *respondeat superior*. Plaintiff appealed. Reversed.

TODD, Justice.

There is no dispute with the general principle that in order to impose liability on the employer under the doctrine of respondeat superior it is necessary to show that the employee was acting within the scope of his employment. Unfortunately there is a wide disparity in the case law in the application of the "scope of employment" test to those factual situations involving intentional torts. The majority rule as set out in Annotation 34 A.L.R.2d 372, 402, includes a twofold test: (a) Whether the assault was motivated by business or personal considerations; or (b) whether the assault was contemplated by the employer or incident to the employment. . . .

In developing a test for the application of respondeat superior when an employee assaults a third person, we believe that the focus should be on the basis of the assault rather than the motivation of the employee. . . .

Attempts in cases where altercations arise, to distinguish the doctrine of respondeat superior on the theory that at some point the argument becomes personal and not related to the scope of employment are unduly restrictive and attribute to the employee, enraged by reason of his employment, a rational decision, that he is crossing some imaginary line to pursue personal business. . . .

We hold that an employer is liable for an assault by his employee when the source of the attack is related to the duties of the employee and the assault occurs within work-related limits of time and place. The assault in this case obviously occurred within work-related limits of time and place, since it took place on authorized premises during working hours. The precipitating cause of the initial argument concerned the employee's conduct of his work. In addition, the employee originally was motivated to become argumentative in furtherance of his employer's business. Consequently, under the facts of this case we hold as a matter of law that the employee was acting within the scope of employment at the time of the aggression. . . .

Plaintiff may recover damages under either the theory of respondeat superior or negligence. . . . Having disposed of the matter on the former issue, we need not undertake the questions raised by defendant's asserted negligence in the hiring or retention of the employee.

Reversed and remanded with instructions to enter judgment for the plaintiff.

Questions

1. Would the result have been the same if the plaintiff was a customer who was beaten up by the driver because she was buying a competing brand of cookies?
2. What if the beating followed an argument between the store manager and the driver about politics or baseball? about whether cookies are good or bad for your health?

PROFESSIONAL AGENTS AND INDEPENDENT CONTRACTORS

Since the relationships of principal-professional agent and employer-independent contractor, by definition, do not embrace the right to control details of the duties by the principal or employer (see the right side of the diagram presented in Chapter 31), the principal or employer generally has no vicarious tort liability arising out of these relationships—the doctrine of *respondeat superior* does not apply.

As to professional agents in particular, the principal's liability is limited to deceit, as a practical matter. The principal certainly is liable if he intends an untrue statement to be made, whether he intended the particular harm or not. Also, a principal may be liable when he has created a situation enabling the agent to deceive others or when he, actually or apparently, has authorized the agent to make the statements. Thus, someone who employs a real estate broker to sell a house may well be liable if the broker deceives a potential buyer by forging the owner's name to an offer to sell that requires the purchaser to pay earnest money, and the broker diverts that money to her own use. The same would be true when the broker simply deceives the purchaser concerning the condition of the house.

As to independent contractors, the employer's general liability is limited to employment involving **non-delegable statutory duties** or **ultra-hazardous activities.** The reason for these exceptions is public policy. In these areas there is a special need to encourage maximum effort to protect the public from harm.

Non-Delegable Statutory Duties

This category of duties involves situations in which a legislative enactment, such as a statute or an ordinance, mandates the performance of a particular duty. Examples of such enactments are ordinances requiring that the owner of real estate keep the public sidewalks adjoining his property free of ice and snow during certain hours, and statutes requiring the owner of a motor vehicle operated on the public highways to keep it free from dangerous mechanical defects. These duties cannot be delegated; if the person on whom the duty is imposed employs an independent contractor to see that it is done, and the independent contractor fails to perform properly, the employer will be liable for any resulting injuries to third persons.

Ultrahazardous Activities

Exactly what constitutes an ultrahazardous activity is difficult to define. There is no finite list of such activities, although there is general agreement on the use of explosives, the demolition of buildings, the manufacture and sale of food, drug, and cosmetic products, and the keeping of wild animals. The question of what is ultrahazardous must be determined on a case-by-case basis. The courts basically are trying to determine whether a particular activity presents such a risk of harm that the public cannot be protected adequately by the exercise of ordinary care. To encourage greater care, the activity is classified as ultrahazardous, and the actor becomes liable under theory of strict (absolute) liability. The employer of an independent contractor entrusted to perform the activity also will be liable, under the same theory, for injuries to third parties caused by the activity. This is liability without fault. Both the actor and the employer become insurers of the safety of everyone affected by the activity.

LUTHRINGER v. MOORE et al.
31 Cal.2d 489, 190 P.2d 1 (1948)

This was an action by Albert L. Luthringer (Plaintiff/Respondent) against a number of defendants, including R. L. Moore individually and dba Orchard Supply Company, and Sacramento Medico-Dental Building Company, for damages for personal injuries that resulted when Plaintiff breathed hydrocyanic acid gas being used by Defendant Moore to fumigate the basement of a building adjoining the building in which Plaintiff was employed. The buildings were owned by Defendant Sacramento Medico-Dental Building Company, which had employed Moore to do the work. From a judgment in favor of Plaintiff, Defendant Moore appealed. Affirmed.

CARTER, Justice.

Defendant Moore was engaged to exterminate cockroaches and other vermin in the basement under the restaurant and that part under the dress shop. He made his preparations and released hydrocyanic acid gas in those rooms about midnight on November 16, 1943. Plaintiff, an employee of Flynn in the latter's pharmacy, in the course of his employment, arrived at the pharmacy about 8:45 a.m. on November 17, 1943, with the purpose of opening the store. . . . After entering the store he proceeded to a small mezzanine floor to put on his working clothes. Feeling ill he returned to the main floor and lost consciousness. He was discovered in that condition by Flynn's bookkeeper who arrived at the pharmacy between 9:15 and 9:30 a.m. Plaintiff was removed from the store, treated by the firemen of the city with a resuscitator and taken to the hospital where he received medical attention. He was found suffering from hydrocyanic acid gas poisoning and his injuries are from that source. . . .

It appears to be settled that the question of whether the case is a proper one for imposing absolute or strict liability is one of law for the court. . . .

Turning to the question of whether absolute or strict liability is appropriate in the instant case, we find that according to witness Bell (a man engaged in the pest control business), there are only three operators licensed to use lethal gas in pest control in Sacramento. And in regard to the nature of hydrocyanic acid gas he testified:

Q. Do you know whether hydrocyanic acid gas is a poisonous gas or a lethal gas?

A. It definitely is.

Q. By lethal, you mean it is deadly, or causes death?

A. That's right. . . .

Q. How about the quantities of it that are required to cause death to animals or human beings?

A. Minimum amount would be about 300 parts per million, would be a lethal dosage.

Q. The amount to 300 parts by volume.

A. Yes, sir.

Q. That amount would be lethal to human beings?

A. That is correct.

Q. Do you know how long a time would be required?

A.   It would take very little time with that amount.

Q.   Can you tell us what the physical characteristics of hydrocyanic acid gas are?

A.   It is a little lighter-than-air gas; a very highly penetrative gas; susceptible to moisture quite a bit, it will follow moisture; it is noninflammable; the flashpoint is very low so that it can be used without much hazard of fire. . . .

Q.   I think you said the gas was very penetrative?

A.   Definitely.

Q.   What do you mean by that?

A.   That is one of the advantages of the gas; why they use it in fumigation. It will penetrate behind baseboards, cracks and crevices that we couldn't get at with any type of liquid insecticide. It will go through mattresses, chesterfields, furniture, some types of porous walls. . . .

Q.   Is it difficult to keep that gas confined?

A.   Yes, because of the fact it will penetrate you have to be careful to keep it in a definite area. . . .

Q.   In the ordinary operation, if you go in and seal up so that you consider it is adequately sealed, you still have some leakage of gas, or not?

A.   You will have some, yes, sir, unless it is a very well built building. . . .

It has been said: "One who carries on an ultrahazardous activity is liable to another whose person, land or chattels the actor should recognize as likely to be harmed by the unpreventable miscarriage of the activity for harm resulting thereto from that which makes the activity ultrahazardous, although the utmost care is exercised to prevent the harm. . . . An activity is ultrahazardous if it (a) necessarily involves a risk of serious harm to the person, land or chattels of others which cannot be eliminated by the exercise of the utmost care, and (b) is not a matter of common usage." . . .

The above quoted evidence shows that the use of gas under the circumstances presented a hazardous activity; that it is perilous and likely to cause injury even though the utmost care is used; that defendant Moore knew or should have known that injury might result; and that the use of it under these circumstances is not a matter of "common usage" within the meaning of the term.

The judgment against the defendant Moore is affirmed.

Questions

1.   On the basis of this case, would you conclude that the operation of an airline is an ultrahazardous activity?

2.   What are the competing arguments for expanding and contracting the list of activities to be classified as ultrahazardous?

LIABILITY OF AGENTS AND SERVANTS

One who commits a tort is liable to anyone injured thereby. The fact that the tort was committed in the course and scope of his duties for his principal or employer, or even that it was committed at the direction and under the control of the principal or employer, will not relieve the agent or employee of liability. This conclusion is not changed by the doctrine of *respondeat superior*. That doctrine simply adds the liability of the principal or employer to that of the agent or employee.

Conversion

The tort of conversion is a possible exception to the otherwise absolute rule presented above. Conversion is defined as the exercise of unlawful dominion and control over the property of another. It is, roughly, the civil form of theft, *theft* being defined in criminal law as conversion with the intent to deprive the owner of the property permanently. In part because of the frequency with which agents and employees handle and deal with property apparently belonging to their principals and employers, the law provides that an agent or employee who acts in good faith and (1) takes the property from the possession of the principal or employer and (2) deals with it as directed, without notice of any conflicting rights of third parties, will *not* be liable for conversion. For example, Ann steals Abby's fur coat and wears it to dinner at a restaurant, where she gives it to Clark, the clerk at the restaurant checkstand, who returns it to Ann when she claims it following dinner. Under these circumstances Clark will not be liable to Abby for conversion, even though he has dealt with the coat contrary to Abby's title. If, however, while the coat was in Clark's possession, Abby had seen it and claimed it (thereby giving Clark notice of her possible conflicting rights), Clark would be liable for conversion if he had returned it to Ann. The exception is applicable only if both of the requirements are met.

What, then, should be done when an agent or servant is in possession of goods received from the principal or employer and is notified of a possible conflicting claim? In the second example Clark is obviously in a dilemma. If an agent or servant in such circumstances retains possession of the property no longer than reasonably necessary to ascertain the facts, the agent or servant will not, during that time, be liable for conversion. The trick, however, will be to get the property into the hands of the true owner. This may be done by filing for *interpleader,* which will bring the property and the two conflicting claimants before the court so that a judge can resolve the conflict and relieve Clark from potential liability.

GLASS v. ALLIED VAN LINES, INC.
450 S.W.2d 217 (1970)

This was an action by Lutricia Glass (Plaintiff/Respondent) against Allied Van Lines, Inc. (Defendant/Appellant) for damages for conversion of certain property owned by Plaintiff and given to Mary Baker by Defendant.

Plaintiff began living with James H. Baker without benefit of wedlock in May 1967. They lived first in Hollywood, Florida, and later moved to Winter Park, Florida. On about June 10, 1967, Plaintiff and Baker left on a trip to Washington, D.C. During their absence, Baker's wife, Mary Baker, then living in Orlando, Florida, called Defendant and arranged to have the household goods shipped from her home in Orlando to Hyattsville, Maryland. Later, James Baker called

Defendant and asked them to include in the shipment the household goods at the home he shared with Plaintiff in Winter Park, and to send the shipment to Baltimore, Maryland. Defendant did so.

When Plaintiff and Baker returned in August and she learned that Defendant "had picked the stuff up," she contacted Defendant asking to discuss the shipment with someone, though no discussion took place. A few days later, she called Defendant's office in Baltimore to inquire about the shipment and, after a few more days, went to the Baltimore office to pick up the goods. The agent refused to give them to her because of lack of identification. On November 1, 1967, Mary Baker went to the Baltimore office with a signed authorization from James H. Baker, paid the transportation and storage fees, and picked up all of the goods.

From a judgment for Plaintiff in the amount of $4500, Defendant appealed. Judgment reversed.

TITUS, Presiding Justice.

Bailment is a contract resulting from the delivery of goods by the bailor to the bailee on condition that they either be restored to the bailor or delivered to someone designated by the bailor, according to the bailor's directions, when the purpose for which the goods are bailed have been answered . . . and a bailee who makes delivery of the goods to a third person without the assent of the bailor, does so at his peril. . . . Possession of personal property is prima facie evidence of ownership . . . so if a bailee receives property in bailment from one in possession, although the possessor is not rightfully entitled thereto, the bailee is not guilty of conversion if he delivers the goods pursuant to the bailment contract, provided the delivery is accomplished before he has adequate notice of the rights of the real owner.

Proof of conversion may be made in either [*sic*] of three ways: (1) by a tortious taking, (2) by any use, or appropriation of the use of the person in possession, indicating a claim of right in opposition to the rights of the owner, or (3) by refusal to give up possession to the owner on demand. . . . In the first two instances, supra, the fact of conversion becomes self evident through proof of the overt acts of the converter. . . . On the other hand, if possession was not acquired by a tortious taking or the possessor does not appropriate or use the property in a fashion to indicate a claim thereto adverse to the owner, then no evidence of a conversion exists until there is proof, first, that a proper demand for possession was made by one who is entitled thereto and, second, that the possessor wrongfully refused delivery. Consequently, if a bailee's possession is innocent, as where he receives property from the bailor in good faith believing the bailor to be the owner, he is not liable in conversion to a third person who claims the property unless that person asserts a paramount right to immediate possession and makes sufficient demand for the property before the bailee delivers it to the bailor.

According to her proof, plaintiff never asserted to defendant's agents that she alone had the sole and exclusive right to the possession of the shipment, or any part thereof; she did not once deny the title of James Baker and Mary Baker in and to the property or tell the agents that James Baker and Mary Baker had no right to the possession of the shipment. Neither did the plaintiff ever undertake to specify what particular articles contained in the 1630 pound shipment she was personally claiming. . . .

The trial court should have sustained defendant's motion for a directed verdict in its favor. Accordingly, the judgment . . . for the plaintiff is reversed.

Questions

1. Is the result in this case fair? Does it make sense?
2. How does the plaintiff recover her property?

Breach of Duty Owed to Principal or Employer

Agents and employees, including professional agents and independent contractors, may be liable for injuries to third parties caused by breaches of duties owed to their principals or employers. This has long been true to some degree, but the trend today is toward increased liability, especially when the breach is one of **malfeasance** (doing poorly or improperly) as opposed to one of **nonfeasance** (not doing). To illustrate, suppose the owner of an apartment building directs an employee to repair the stairway in a common part of the building. A few days later, a guest is injured when a step on the stairway breaks. If the incident occurred because the employee had failed to do the repairs as directed (nonfeasance) the employee would not be liable to the guest. If, however, the step had broken because the employee had done the job but did it negligently (malfeasance), the employee would be liable. Of course, in either case, the employee is liable to the employer for the breach, and the third person may sue the employer.

Among the recent cases of greatest importance are those involving professionals such as accountants. Earlier cases involved information provided for the purpose of perpetrating fraud and information that was the product of gross negligence. More recently, courts have extended the rule to find liability for ordinary negligence in obtaining or communicating the information, such as might be involved in the preparation of financial statements. This liability generally is limited to losses sustained by persons to whom the accountant intended to supply the information or knew it would be supplied, who relied on it for the intended purpose. For more information on the subject of professional liability of accountants, see Chapter 54.

Liability in agency relationships

	Liability		
	Contracts	**Torts**	**Crimes**
Principal/Employer	when agent acted with authority	1. right to control 2. course and scope of authority (with exceptions)	usually none
Agent/Employee	not liable as a general rule (with exceptions)	always liable (with conversion exception)	always liable

Nature of the Liability of Agents and Servants

The liability of the agent or servant is **joint and several** with the principal or employer. That is, the injured third party may sue and recover a judgment against either individually, or against the two as a unit. There is no mandatory election as there was in the case of liability between the agent and his undisclosed or partially disclosed principal in contracts (in which the liability was only several). In the event of a joint judgment, each is liable for the entire amount (although the plaintiff can collect the judgment only once), and the question of which one pays initially may be resolved by the "deep-pocket" theory (whoever has the most money and other property pays the judgment).

MOSS v. JONES
93 N.J.Super. 179, 225 A.2d 369 (1966)

This was an action by Frank A. Moss (Plaintiff/Appellant) against Robert P. Jones (Defendant/Appellee) for damages for injuries sustained by Plaintiff when struck by an automobile driven by Samuel V. Jones, who at the time of the accident was alleged to have been the agent, servant, and employee of Defendant. At the time of this suit, Plaintiff previously had sued Samuel V. Jones, the driver, and had been awarded a judgment for $20,000 that remained in full force and effect, but was unpaid. Defendant Robert P. Jones contended that by virtue of that judgment, his liability as principal or employer was discharged because of, among other things, the doctrines of *res judicata* and collateral estoppel, which prevent someone from bringing more than one law suit on the same claim.

From a decision of the trial court granting Defendant's pretrial motion for dismissal, Plaintiff appealed. Reversed.

KILKENNY, J.A.D.

Coles v. McKenna and Tabloid Lithographers, Inc. v. Israel . . . are readily distinguished. They were contract cases, in which the remedy against the principal or agent was in the alternative. Under familiar principles of agency law, if an agent discloses his principal and acts within his authority, suit can be brought only against the principal. If the agent does not disclose his principal and purports to be acting for himself, the third person, upon ascertaining the principal-agent relationship has an alternative remedy, i.e., he may elect to hold the agent personally liable, *or* he may sue the principal. He is then bound by his choice of remedies. . . . Tort liability of a principal and agent, on the other hand, is both joint and several. This simply means, as expressed in Harris, Pleading and Practice in New Jersey (rev. ed. 1939), Sec. 229, p. 239: "Where an injury is caused by the negligence of a servant acting in the line of his employment, a joint action may be maintained against the servant and the master, or against either of them separately.". . .

We conclude that a person injured by the negligence of an agent or servant may sue the agent or servant and the principal or master in one suit, or may proceed against them in separate suits, and the recovery of a judgment, not satisfied, against the agent or servant does not bar a separate suit against the principal or master.

Accordingly, the judgment under review is reversed and the matter is remanded to the Law Division for trial.

Questions

1. Can you articulate the justification for giving the plaintiff "two bites of the apple"?

2. Wouldn't it be more efficient to make the plaintiff pick one defendant, or to require a single suit against both, than to permit two actions?

SUBAGENTS

The term *subagent,* as used here, includes both an agent who is hired by an agent and an employee who is hired by another employee. The liability of a subagent for her own torts is the same as that of any agent or employee—it is absolute, with a possible exception in the area of conversion. Although in the contract context we found that the principal is liable for the contracts of subagents as long as the hiring of the subagent was authorized, the rule is not so simple with regard to tort liability. Instead, whether the liability under *respondeat superior* will run to the principal/employer or the the agent/employee who hired the subagent depends on a determination of "for whose benefit the subagent was employed."

Suppose that ABC Insurance Company sends an agent to a particular place to set up a branch office, and that agent hires a sales representative to help sell policies there. In the alternative, suppose ABC elects to sell its policies through an independent insurance agent in the area and that agent hires a sales representative. In the event of a tort committed by the sales representative, in the first case ABC would be vicariously liable, but in the second case the independent insurance agent would be liable. This difference in result is best understood by following the rules we have established for *respondeat superior* liability. That is, in both cases, vicarious liability flows to the superior" who has the direct right of control. In the first case, the sales representative is under the control of ABC being exercised through the inter-

mediate agent. In the second, although the sales representative is a controlled agent of the independent insurance agency, he is a professional agent with respect to ABC.

CRIMINAL LIABILITY

An agent or employee always is liable for crimes he commits. This is true whether or not the agent is acting within the scope of employment and whether he was acting under the direction and control of the principal or employer or was motivated personally. The individual's duty to society is separate and apart from any agency relationship.

A principal or employer will be liable for crimes committed by the agent or employee with the authority or at the direction of the principal or employer. However, as a general rule, there is no true vicarious liability for crimes. This is because criminal law requires proof of an intent to commit the crime. As discussed in Chapter 4, the purpose of criminal law is to punish and deter the evil mind. For the most part, courts have resisted finding that the requisite evil mind existed vicariously. This resistance, however, has lessened to some extent in recent years, and there have been highly publicized homicide prosecutions for deaths caused by allegedly defective automobiles and the handling of toxic substances. Today, there are some state statutory exceptions, such as Indiana's statute rendering a corporation criminally liable if one of its agents or employees blocks a highway. In addition, in a variety of situations, a principal or employer may be held liable when an agent or employee violates government regulations such as the security antitrust laws. This type of liability is more likely to occur in closely regulated businesses such as those involving the sale of alcoholic beverages. All of these, however, remain as only exceptions to the firmly grounded general rule.

STATE v. SALONE
22 Conn.Sup. 482, 174 A.2d 803 (1961)

This was a criminal action by the State of Connecticut (Prosecution/Appellee) against Joseph Salone (Defendant/Appellant) for violation of a state statute that read, in part, as follows: "No person shall operate any commercial motor vehicle, nor shall the owner of any commercial vehicle allow such motor vehicle to be operated, on any public highway or bridge [while overloaded]. . . ." Defendant was the owner of a 1949 Mack dump truck, which on March 1, 1961, was being operated by an employee of Defendant. The gross weight of the truck, when stopped, was 35,200 pounds, an overload of 5100 pounds. Defendant had no actual knowledge of the overloading of the truck and never was present on the job during the overloadings; in fact, according to Defendant's testimony, on several previous occasions he had told the driver not to overload.

From a judgment of guilty, Defendant appealed. Affirmed.

CIANO, Judge.

. . . [T]he state may prove facts which will justify the trier in finding beyond a reasonable doubt that the motor vehicle was overloaded (1) either by the voluntary act of the owner or custodian, or (2) by the reason of his negligent failure to prevent overloading, as a reasonably prudent and careful truck operator or owner would have done under like circumstances.

In Guastamachio v. Brennan, 128 Conn. 356, 357, 23 A.2d 140, the court construed a regulation of the liquor control commission which provided that "[n]o permittee shall allow, permit or suffer" any immoral activities in or upon the permit premises. The responsibility for making effective this prohibition was placed upon the permittees.

Knowledge by the owner of the overloading is not an essential element of the crime; and to make the statute effective, the owner is held responsible, regardless of knowledge, by reason of his failure to take effective measures to prevent and prohibit conduct by those controlling the trucks under his authority. The rule of strict accountability is imposed by the statute on the owner. . . .

A claim urged by the defendant is that as a general rule a master is never criminally responsible for the acts of a servant done without the master's consent and against his expressed orders. The rule is restated in State v. Curtiss, 69 Conn. 86, 89, 36 A. 1014, 1015; "Criminal responsibility on the part of the principal for the act of his agent or servant in the course of his employment implies some degree of moral guilt or delinquency, manifested either by direct participation in or assent to the act, or by want of proper care and oversight or other negligence in reference to the business which he has thus entrusted to another." Ordinarily, a principal is not criminally liable for the acts of his agent in which he did not participate and of which he had no knowledge, if his directions were bona fide and the employee acted beyond the scope of his employment. The state produced prima facie evidence of the operation of an overloaded truck by an employee of the accused. The burden rested upon the defendant to rebut this presumption.

Questions

1. Is it fair to put this burden of proof on an employer?
2. How can an employer protect itself against such criminal liability?

SUMMARY

Generally, a principal or employer is liable for the torts committed by the agent or employee only when the agent or employee is subject to detailed control and commits the tort in the course and scope of employment. This includes "loaned servants." The vicarious tort liability of the principal or employer is termed *respondeat superior*. Vicarious liability for the torts of professional agents and independent contractors, as a rule, does not exist, except in some closely defined circumstances, including those involving certain statutory duties and those involving ultrahazardous activities.

The same rules that apply to agents and employees regarding tort liability apply equally to subagents (including subemployees), as long as the subagent's hiring was authorized and the subagent was hired on behalf of the principal or employer rather than on behalf of the agent or employee.

For the most part, principals and employers are not vicariously liable in the criminal area. Courts and other lawmakers largely have resisted finding the required criminal intent (evil mind) without some direct involvement in the commission of the crime. Significant exceptions are to be found, however, especially in cases involving violations of governmental regulations, and more often with regard to highly regulated businesses.

Agents and servants always are liable for their own torts and crimes, whether they were committed in the course and scope of employment, with

or without direction or control of the principal or employer. In the context of torts, there is a closely defined exception for conversion, when the agent or employee takes the property in question from the actual possession of the principal or employer and deals with it as directed, without notice of a conflict as to title or the right to possession.

KEY TERMS AND CONCEPTS

respondeat superior
loaned-servant doctrine
course and scope of employment
non-delegable statutory duties
ultrahazardous activities
malfeasance
nonfeasance
joint and several liability

PROBLEMS

1. Phillips listed her house for sale with Terrel & Garret, a real estate brokerage firm. She stated in the listing application that the house had 2400 square feet of floor space. Terrel & Garrett sold the house to Cameron, using Phillips's figures. When Cameron determined the house had only 2245 square feet, he sued Terrel & Gilbert for deceit. Should Terrel & Gilbert be liable?

2. Gatzke was employed by Walgreen. He was

sent out of town to oversee a project, and lived at the Edgewater Motel while away from home. One night he was working on reports to be sent back to Walgreen and having a few drinks. After he was finished, he left the room. However, he had disposed of a cigarette negligently, and a fire started. The motel sued Walgreen; Walgreen defended on the ground that in smoking and drinking "on the job," Gatzke had put himself out of the course and scope of his employment. Is the motel entitled to recover from Walgreen?

3. Gobea was told by her employer to pick up an air compressor on her way home and bring it with her the next morning. On her way to work the next morning Gobea was involved in an accident, negligently causing injuries to Anderson. Anderson sued Gobea's employer, who defended on the ground that in coming to work, Gobea was not yet in the course and scope of employment. Is this correct?

4. Hecht, a real estate broker, had an exclusive listing to sell Meller's house. He sold the house and took a signed contract to purchase, but before the closing date the house was destroyed by fire. Hecht claimed he was entitled to his commission and Meller disagreed. Who is correct?

5. The Maxwell Construction Company, a concrete contractor on a freeway job, employed Marsh, who was injured by the negligence of Wynglatz, a regular employee of one of the subcontractors, Tilley Steel Co. At the time of the injury, Wynglatz was operating a crane on the freeway job, apparently under the control of Maxwell. Marsh sued Tilley for the injury and Tilley disclaimed on the ground that Maxwell, not it, was controlling Wynglatz at the time of the injury. Is Marsh entitled to judgment against Tilley?

6. McCutcheon, a police officer employed by the city of Philadelphia, shot Fitzgerald during a disagreement in a tavern. At the time, McCutcheon was off duty but was carrying a revolver, as she was authorized by the city to do. Fitzgerald sued the city for his injuries. Is he entitled to recover?

7. Mittlestadt was involved in a collision on a highway in Arkansas. The accident was caused by the negligence of Ralls, a state highway employee. When sued by Mittlestadt, Ralls claimed he was not liable because at the time of the accident he was in the course and scope of his employment by the state. Is Ralls correct?

8. Brown, an employee of the Pines Hotel, was involved in an argumemt with a hotel guest. Sometime during the affray, she intentionally dropped a vacuum cleaner on the guest's foot, causing a painful injury. When sued by the guest, the hotel defended on the ground that in committing the intentional tort, Brown was not acting within the course and scope of her employment. Is the hotel correct?

9. Wayne Jack, an employee of the Rogers and Babler Construction Company, was assigned to work at a job site 25 miles from his home. Jack regularly drove to the site in the morning and back home in the evening. One evening, when returning home, Jack was involved in an automobile accident caused by his negligence. One of the injured parties sued Rogers and Babler. Finding as a matter of law that Jack was not in the course and scope of employment while commuting home after work, the court granted summary judgment for Rogers and Babler. Should the decision be upheld on appeal?

10. The Bank of New York employed Merola Bros. Construction Corp. to do certain renovation work on its building, and Merola Bros. subcontracted the terrazzo work to New Deal. During the work, New Deal piled bags of pebbles on the sidewalk. Although it had a permit to do so, the bags were piled negligently so as to be an obvious hazard to passersby. Merola Bros. came and inspected the project every day and saw the hazard, but it did nothing to correct it. Finally, one day, some of the bags fell on Schwartz, a pedestrian. When Schwartz sued Merola Bros. for his injuries, Merola Bros. defended on the ground that New Deal was an independent contractor. Should Merola Bros. be held liable?

Chapter | 34

Duties and Termination

INTRODUCTION

Although agency relationships may be based on express or implied contracts, it is important to understand that rights and duties may arise both under contract law and pure agency law. To the extent that a contract is involved, the general rules of contract interpretation are applicable. Even in the absence of a contract, however, agency duties are viewed under the same theory. In other words, the law treats the parties as if they were bound to a fictitious contract.

DUTIES COMMON TO THE PRINCIPAL AND THE AGENT

Some duties are owed only by a principal to an agent, and others only by an agent to the principal. Still others are reciprocal—owed by each to the other—such as those that follow.

Duty to Account

The principal and the agent each have a duty to the other to keep accurate accounts when it is appropriate to do so. The duty of the principal in this respect is general, in that in compensating the agent, amounts usually are deducted for tax and social security obligations owed to the government, and compensation paid to agents is reported as a business expense. Of course, when the agent is paid on a contingent basis, such as with a percentage of sales, the accounting duty is even more obvious. The agent is under a duty to account for all money and property received on behalf of the principal, and upon termination of the agency is required to render a full and *final* accounting.

Duty to Indemnify

When an agent, in the lawful performance of her authorized duties, suffers personal loss because of the performance, the principal is under a duty to indemnify and reimburse the agent for the loss.

This duty may arise as a result of authorized payments made by the agent out of her own pocket, the payment of necessary expenses by the agent, or by the agent's being held personally liable on a contract properly entered into on behalf of the principal. The latter situation, of course, may occur in any transaction in which the principal's identity is not known to the third party at the time the contract is made.

When the principal is held vicariously liable for the torts of an agent, the agent is under a duty to reimburse him for the loss. The theory of *respondeat superior* is recognized as a protection for the third party, not as a resolution of who ultimately is liable. The law is best served when the person actually responsible for the wrongdoing pays for its consequences.

MULDOWNEY v. MIDDLEMAN
176 Pa.Super. 75, 107 A.2d 173 (1954)

This action involved a lawsuit by Muldowney (Plaintiff) against Middleman (Defendant/Appellee) arising out of an automobile accident. Plaintiff was injured when struck by an automobile being driven in a negligent manner by Middleman. At the time of the accident Middleman was on the business of his employer, Cooper (Defendant/Appellant). After the trial, the judge entered a judgment on the jury's verdict for Plaintiff. The full amount of the judgment was paid by Cooper.

Approximately two months after the trial, Middleman petitioned the court to mark the judgment paid as against him as well as Cooper and to forward a copy of the discharge to the Secretary of Revenue of the Commonwealth. The court granted Defendant Middleman's petition over the objections of Defendant Cooper, holding that the judgment did not, itself, impose a duty on Middleman to indemnify Cooper. From this decision Cooper appealed. Reversed.

HIRT, Judge.

The suit was against the defendants as principal and agent and Cooper, as principal, was liable only in the application of the common law doctrine of respondeat superior. The defendants were not charged with independent acts of negligence which concurred in causing the injury. Cooper as Middleman's employer was liable only vicariously for the result of his employe's negligence; Middleman was primarily liable and Cooper's liability was secondary. Accordingly there can be no question as to the right to indemnity of the principal Cooper from his agent Middleman. "The right of *indemnity* rests upon a difference between the primary and secondary liability of two persons each of whom is made responsible by the law to an injured party. It is a right which enures . . . to a person who, without active fault on his own part, has been compelled, by reason of some legal obligation, to pay damages occasioned by the initial negligence of another, and for which he himself is only secondarily liable." . . . An agent is subject to liability for loss caused to the principal by any breach of duty except when arising from a contract with the principal. "Thus, a servant who, while acting within the scope of employment, negligently injures a third person, although personally liable to such person, is also subject to liability to the principal if the principal is thereby required to pay damages." Restatement, Agency, Sec. 401(c). . . .

[S]ince Middleman as a party defendant to the action appeared at the trial of the case with counsel and had the opportunity to participate in the defense, the judgment against him determined his liability not only to the plaintiff but his liability for indemnity to Cooper, as well. Restatement, Judgments, Sec 106(d).

Questions

1. Can you think of any circumstances in which the employer should not be able to recover reimbursement for damages paid for a tort committed by an employee?

2. Would the result have been different if Middleman (the employee) was not a party to the first suit? Why or why not?

Duty of Proper Conduct

Because of the nature of agency relationships, the identity of the principal and that of the agent often are closely linked in the minds of others. The ability of one to conduct business is very much affected by the reputation of the other. Thus, the principal and the agent are under corollary duties to conduct their affairs with propriety so that neither brings disrepute on the other. This duty is of particular significance for the agent. It may affect the manner in which he conducts his personal life as well as his actions and appearance while on the job. The breach of this duty is more likely to result in dismissal for cause than in a separate suit for damages.

PRINCIPAL'S DUTIES TO AGENT

In addition to the reciprocal duties common to an agent and principal, certain duties are owed only by the principal to an agent. The following are two such duties.

Duty to Refrain from Interfering

The principal does not guarantee the agent an opportunity to work by the mere creation of an agency relationship. A distinction must be drawn between the creation of the relationship itself (agency law) and affirmative obligations agreed to under that relationship (contract law). However, the duty to provide work certainly may be expressed, or even implied under certain circumstances. In addition, it is clear that when the opportunity to work is provided, the principal is under a duty not to interfere unduly with the agent's performance, especially when the agent's compensation is calculated according to the quantity and/or quality of her performance.

Duty to Compensate

Except under a specific agreement to the contrary, it is implied that a principal will pay an agent for all services he either requests or permits the agent to perform. This implication, of course, may be overridden by circumstances such as the existence of a family or some other close, personal relationship between the principal and the agent. When no amount is specified, a reasonable amount will be presumed. (The theory here would be in contract implied-in-fact for the reasonable fee for the services, not in contract implied-in-law—quasi contract—for the reasonable value of the benefits conferred.)

AGENT'S DUTIES TO PRINCIPAL

Agents owe several nonreciprocal duties to their principals. Most are quite specific. The fiduciary duty, however, is very broad.

Duty of Obedience

Every agent is bound to act only as authorized by the principal and according to the principal's instructions. This may be true even when the contract of employment does not provide for giving instructions of the kind, as long as the instructions given are reasonable. Any violation of this duty may lead to dismissal for cause, and even a gratuitous agent, before disobeying instructions, must give the principal reasonable notice of her intention to do so.

The duty of obedience must be considered in conjuction with the agent's general obligation to act only in best interests of the principal, and as she reasonably believes the principal would act on his own behalf. Unlike most contractual relations, the agent's duty may override express instructions in proper situations, such as a change in conditions or the encountering of unanticipated circumstances in performing the job. Thus, an agent may not only be allowed, but actually may be under an affirmative duty, to ignore the principal's express instructions. Authority to do so may be found specifically in the agent's implied authority—especially implied authority by necessity—which was discussed in Chapter 31.

Duty to Exercise Care and Skill

In the absence of an agreement to the contrary, every agent owes a duty to the principal to exercise reasonable care and skill in the performance of her job. This usually is considered to be the degree of care and skill that is standard in the locality of the particular job undertaken. However, the agent also will be expected to exercise any special skills she possesses. Thus, a professional accountant (not necessarily a CPA), in the execution of any duties involving accounting, will be held to a higher standard than would a layperson. However, unless she does so specifically, an agent normally does not warrant either the success of her performance or the principal's satisfaction. These risks normally are assumed by the principal.

SIMMERSON v. BLANKS
149 Ga.App. 478, 254 S.E.2d 716 (1979)

This was an action by Simmerson (Plaintiff/Appellant) against Blanks (Defendant/Appellee) for damages resulting from an alleged failure of Defendant to file a financing statement properly. Plaintiff contracted to sell certain real and personal property to Spillman. Plaintiff and Blanks, who was Spillman's attorney, first met on the day of the closing; this lawsuit was based in part upon the following conversation between the two, which occurred moments after the closing was completed: Defendant Blanks said, "I'll take care of the filing of the papers." This statement included the financing statement in question. Plaintiff said, "Fine." Less than a month after the closing, Defendant wrote a letter to Plaintiff informing him, "Financing statement executed by Emil V. Spillman in your favor [has been] recorded in Houston County. . . ."

The financing statement was filed in Houston County (the county where the personal property covered in the financing statement was located) but not in Cobb County (the county of the real property sold by Spillman). Defendant denied liability for the misfiling on the ground that he was acting only as a gratuitous agent (without pay) and, therefore, owed no duty to Plaintiff.

From a summary judgment entered for Defendant, Plaintiff appealed. Reversed.

SMITH, Judge.

As to appellant's claim that his postclosing conversation with appellee constituted the formation of an express attorney-client contract, which appellee breached, we find no error in the trial court's grant of summary judgment. From the evidence before the court it appeared conclusively that the alleged contract lacked consideration, the only bargained-for consideration having flowed from Spillman to appellee for the latter's services to the former. . . .

As to appellant's claim that appellee was a "voluntary agent, without hire or reward" and his misfiling constituted actionable "gross neglect" . . . we believe the trial court erred in sustaining appellee's motion for summary judgment. On the issue of asserted voluntary-agent status on the part of the appellee, appellee cannot prevail since the evidence did not conclusively disprove that he gratuitously undertook to perform a legal service on appellant's behalf and with his approval. "One who, by a gratuitous promise or other conduct which he should realize will cause another reasonably to rely upon the performance of definite acts of service by him as the other's agent, causes the other to refrain from having such acts done by other available means is subject to a duty to use care to perform such service or, while other means are available, to give notice that he will not perform." Restatement 2d Agency, Sec. 378 (1958). . . .

Furthermore, as to the question of whether the action of appellee was in compliance with the applicable standard of care, . . . it was for the jury to decide whether appellee's actions were grossly neglectful. Contrary to appellee's contention, appellant's supposed contributory negligence, his failure to remedy the alleged misfiling after receiving notice of it, cannot be a defense to liability. Appellant's "diligence, or want of it, does not in any way affect the liability of his attorney, unless stipulated for by special contract." . . .

There is no merit in appellee's proposition that, by bestowing "upon appellee the appellation of 'voluntary agent'" appellant "strip[ped]" appellee "of his status as an attorney . . . [and]concurrently strip[ped] him of the concomitant duties imposed upon him as a lawyer, such as the duty to know the law." As we have indicated, a gratuitous agent owes his principal the duty to exercise . . . diligence, and a proper appraisal of the agent's conduct encompasses the knowledge which he professes to possess. . . .

Questions

1. What policy reasons support the court's result?
2. Can you think of any other circumstances in which an agent should be held liable to the other party to the transaction?

Duty Not to Disclose Confidential Information

Confidential information includes information concerning matters personal to the principal such that, if it becomes known to third parties, the principal might be held up to contempt or ridicule, or might sustain some other personal loss. It includes trade secrets, which are defined by most courts as including ". . . any formula, pattern, device or compilation of information that is used in one's business, and that gives him an opportunity to obtain an advantage over competitors who do not know or use it. The secret may be a formula for a chemical compound, a process of manufacturing, treating or preserving materials, a pattern for a machine or other device, or a customer list." An agent always is under an affirmative duty not to disclose this information, even in the absence of a contract provision requiring confidentiality.

STANDARD BRANDS, INC. v. ZUMPE et al.
264 F.Supp. 254 (E.D. La. 1967)

This was an action brought by Standard Brands, Inc. (Plaintiff) against Walter T. Zumpe and William B. Reily & Company, Inc. (Defendants) seeking an injunction. The complaint asked that Defendant Zumpe be enjoined from (1) working for a competitor, Defendant William B. Reily & Company, Inc., and (2) disclosing trade secrets and confidential information to the competitor.

Through what was known as its Chase and Sandborn Product Division, Plaintiff developed, processed, and manufactured coffee and tea products. It operated a pilot plant in New Orleans, where it sought to improve its coffee and tea products, and a manufacturing plant in New Orleans, where it made all of the instant coffee it sold throughout the nation.

Defendant Zumpe began to work for Standard in 1946 as a shipping clerk. He was promoted successively; in 1954 he was transferred to New Orleans to become plant manager of Plaintiff's Chase and Sandborn Product Division. Because Zumpe's work afforded him access to information that Standard considered confidential, he signed two agreements. These agreements provided that, in consideration for his employment, Zumpe agreed: "2. That except as required in the performance of his duties to the Company, he will not disclose or use at any time during his employment any of the Company's manufacturing processes, techniques, types of machinery and equipment used together with improvements and modifications thereof, product formulae and ingredients, including raw materials used, discoveries, inventions, ideas, . . . projects or programs, customer lists or any information disclosed to him in confidence or any information held in secret by the Company, of which he became informed during the term of his employment with the Company; and 3. That he will not disclose or use at any time after the termination of his employment any of the foregoing information which may be trade secrets or confidential information of the Company unless he shall first request and obtain the written consent of the Company."

Defendant William B. Reily & Company, Inc. was a family firm engaged in the coffee and tea business and in the distribution of other food products. Reily needed a production manager and was particularly interested in finding someone who could work well with people. One of its executive officers had heard favorable reports about Zumpe, looked him up, and, after a series of conferences, engaged him as Reily's vice-president and general manager in charge of production. He was hired principally as an executive and to take charge of production processes, not to engage in improvement of coffee or tea products, research, or new product development.

The court held, *inter alia*, that an injunction should not be issued because there was no showing that Defendant Zumpe had violated his express agreement with Plaintiff not to reveal confidential information, and disclosure was not shown to be imminent or inevitable.

RUBIN, District Judge.

An employer who discloses valuable information to his employee in confidence is entitled to protection against the use of these secrets in competition with him. But the employee who possesses the employer's most valuable confidences is apt to be highly skilled. The public is interested in the reasonable mobility of such skilled persons from job to job in our fluid society, which is characterized by and requires the mobility of technically expert persons from place to place, from job to job and upward within the industrial structure. And the employee himself must be afforded a reasonable opportunity to change jobs without abandoning the ability to practice his skills. . . .

It is doubtless true that Zumpe may be tempted to use his confidential information to Reily's benefit, but, because of the nature of Reily's business, it does not follow that disclosure is inevitable. This conclusion is reached by considering each of the "confidential areas" separately and specifically. The evidence presented to the court indicates that the nature of Reily's business both with respect to pure coffee and coffee with chicory, instant and roasted, as well as with respect to tea, make it entirely possible for Zumpe to work for Reily for the two years estimated by Standard as the useful life of its confidential information without disclosing any of it. . . .

Even in the absence of a contract not to disclose confidential information, an agent has a duty not to use or communicate information given to him in confidence in competition with or to the injury of the principal unless the information is a matter of general knowledge. The agent has a duty after the termination of the agency "not to use or disclose to third persons, on his own account or on account of others, in competition with the principal or to his injury, trade secrets . . . or other similar confidential matters. . . ." The Restatement of the Law of Agency indicates that these rules apply "not only to those communications which are stated to be confidential, but also to information which the agent should know his principal would not care to have revealed to others or used in competition with him. It applies to unique business methods of the employer, trade secrets, lists of names and all other matters which are peculiarly known in the employer's business."

Trade secrets and confidential information are protected on the basis that their disclosure is a breach of trust. In the present case Zumpe would in addition violate his contract with Standard by disclosing any information imparted to him in confidence. Therefore it is unnecessary to determine which of the types of information listed above is technically a trade secret. All of it is confidential, all of it was imparted to Zumpe in the belief that it was confidential, and all of it should be held in confidence by him.

Questions

1. Was it unrealistic of the court to think Zumpe wouldn't disclose confidential information to his new employer?

2. Suppose Zumpe's contract with Standard Brands had stated that he would not work for a competitor. Should that provision be enforced by a court?

Duty to Inform

An agent owes the duty to disclose all information concerning matters of which he has either knowledge or notice, when they relate to the duties assigned to him and about which he should know the principal would *not* know. Failure to comply with this duty may expose the principal to unreasonable risks of loss, since the law imputes to the principal knowledge or notice of such matters. Thus, when an agent purchases real estate for his principal with knowledge or notice of facts indicating a defect in the title, the principal cannot rescind the transaction once he learns of the defect, although the agent may be liable for the loss if he should have known the facts were important to the principal.

Duty to Refrain from Acting as Agent after Termination of Authority

Once authority has been terminated and the agent is notified that he no longer is authorized, he is under a duty to refrain from further acting on behalf of the principal. This duty exists even though terminating the agent's authority may be in violation of a contract between the agent and the principal. (In this latter case, however, the agent will have an action for breach of contract.) If the authority has been terminated without notice to the agent, such as by the death of the principal or destruction of the agency's subject matter, the agent will not be liable for breach of duty until he has notice, but may be liable for all subsequent contracts, as discussed in Chapter 32 and as discussed later in this chapter.

Fiduciary Duties

Every agent owes her principal the duty of absolute loyalty. This **fiduciary duty** is defined as the highest duty of trust and confidence one can owe to another. It is the type of duty a lawyer owes to a client, a doctor to a patient, and a trustee to a trust beneficiary. It is the duty to act in the utmost good faith and only in the best interests of the principal. Consistent with this duty, the law allows the principal to assume the agent will not harm him, unless he has some reason to believe to the contrary. Thus, there is no presumption that a principal and his agent are dealing at arm's length, and the ordinary rules pertaining to adversary relationships do not apply.

The agent's fiduciary duty forbids her to act in her own self-interest in competition with the principal or to profit secretly in carrying out her assigned duties. The agent is required to be completely honest, open, and above-board, and to do nothing that would subject the principal to any unreasonable risk of loss. Thus, an agent who cheats her principal, or without telling him also represents the party on the other side of the transaction, or who has her own "deal on the side," violates her fiduciary duty. So does an agent who mixes a principal's money or other property with her own. In the latter case, even though the agent may not intend to harm the principal, the principal's property might be lost if the agent were to die or her personal assets were to be attached.

The agent's fiduciary duty goes even further than being honest, however. It also requires that the agent *appear* honest. Thus, even the suggestion that the agent *might* be acting contrary to the interests of the principal may be considered a breach of duty. A sales representative who collects money for his principal and, in the presence of the third party, places it with his own funds, has breached his fiduciary duty by the commingling *and* because it reasonably might raise a question in the mind of a third party.

It is possible for an agent to do anything that otherwise would constitute a breach of fiduciary duty if the principal consents after the agent fully and completely discloses all relevant known facts. However, this rule subjects the agent who relies on it to a significant risk. Dealings between a fiduciary and a beneficiary are scrutinized closely by the courts. For example, suppose an agent is out looking for real estate investment opportunities for a principal and finds a piece of property she would like to buy for herself as a home site. She tells the principal all about the property and says she would like to purchase it for herself if the principal does not want it. After considering the matter, the principal gives the agent permis-

sion to buy it for herself, and the agent does so. Within a short time, something unforeseen occurs, such as the erection of a new school and a shopping center nearby, or the discovery of oil on neighboring property, and the value of the property increases dramatically. Even though the agent has been completely honest, in a suit by the principal to force the agent to convey the property to him, the court will examine the situation carefully to determine whether the agent, in fact, fully and completely disclosed all facts known to her at the time she secured the principal's permission. If the court finds itself uncertain, it probably will decide against the agent because of the primacy of the fiduciary concept. This actually may constitute a shifting of the burden of proof from the plaintiff (principal) to the defendant (agent), contrary to accepted rules of procedure, and is a serious practical problem any agent potentially will face is she tries to benefit from opportunities acquired in the course of the agency.

SCIENCE ACCESSORIES CORPORATION v. SUMMAGRAPHICS CORPORATION
425 A.2d 957, 16 A.L.R.4th 170 (1980)

This was an action by Science Accessories Corporation (Plaintiff/Appellant) against Summagraphics Corporation and former employees Albert Whetstone, Edward Snyder, and Stanley Phillips (Defendants/Appellees) for damages and equitable relief. The equitable relief sought was to require an accounting for profits made, and the imposition of an equitable trust, on an invention called the "magnetostrictive digitizer."

Plaintiff (SAC) was engaged in the business of manufacturing and selling high-technology instruments, including a digitizer known as "grafpen." Defendants Whestone, Snyder, and Phillips were key employees of SAC. During their employment they learned of the invention by Brenner of the magnetostrictive digitizer (magwire digitizer). They helped Brenner convert his plans into a working model, and later terminated their employment with SAC and formed a competing high-tech corporation, with Brenner, to produce and market the magwire digitizer. It was conceded that this new product was in direct competition with SAC's grafpen and was superior to it in both cost of production and reliability. SAC contended that such action amounted to breach of the fiduciary duties of Defendants in three respects. First, Defendants breached a duty to disclose

Brenner's magwire digitizer concept to SAC even though it had been revealed to Whetstone in confidence and subject to an agreement not to disclose it to SAC. Specifically, SAC argued that Whetstone's agency duty to disclose overrode his agreement of confidentiality with Brenner. Second, they breached a duty not to compete with or act adversely to SAC's interest by diverting the digitizer concept from SAC to themselves through Summagraphics. Here, SAC particularly contested the trial court's conclusion that Brenner's concept would have been useless to SAC as erroneous, factually as well as legally. Third, they breached a duty not to engage in ''illegal, immoral and bad faith'' behavior while making preparations to leave SAC's employ.

From a judgment of the trial court dismissing Plaintiff's complaint, Plaintiff appealed. Affirmed.

HORSEY, Justice.

The thrust of SAC's fiduciary breach of duty argument is that the Trial Court's conceded finding—that Brenner's concept was not an opportunity available to SAC but one that defendants could take for themselves—is not determinative of SAC's right to equitable relief by reason of defendant's breach of so-called "independent" fiduciary duties owed to SAC. It is true, of course, that under elemental principles of agency law, an agent owes his principal a duty of good faith, loyalty and fair dealing. 3 CJS Agency Sec. 271; Restatement (Second) of Agency Sec. 387 (1957). Encompassed within such general duties of an agent is a duty to disclose information that is relevant to the affairs of the agency entrusted to him. . . .

Since Brenner's concept was found to be an "outside" opportunity not available to SAC, defendants' failure to disclose the concept to SAC and their taking it to themselves for purposes of competing with SAC cannot be found to be in breach of any agency fiduciary duty. Further, defendants cannot be said to have diverted anything from SAC once it was determined that SAC had no prior interest or expectancy in Brenner's concept. . . .

Defendants were not under employment contracts with SAC or convenants not to compete. Thus, they were free to make reasonable preparations to compete while still employed by SAC and after quitting SAC's employ, to compete with SAC. . . . Further, defendants' concealment from SAC of their plans to enter into competition with SAC was not, without more, a violation of their fiduciary duty of loyalty. To require employees to divulge such information to their employers ". . . would create an undesirable impediment to free competition in the commercial and industrial sectors of our economy." . . .

Questions

1. Isn't it clear that the defendant employees played it as close to the line as possible? Why does the court allow them to get away with it?

2. What kinds of activities would fall within the notion of "reasonable preparations to compete" that the court states is permissible?

Possible duties arising out of agency relationships

Duty	Principal	Agent
Duty to account	x	x
Duty to indemnify	x	x
Duty of proper conduct	x	x
Duty to provide work	x	
Duty to compensate	x	
Duty of obedience		x
Duty to exercise care and skill		x
Duty not to disclose confidential information		x
Duty to refrain from acting as agent after termination		x
Duty to act as fiduciary		x

TERMINATION

Having studied the natures of the various agency relationships and the numerous rights, duties, and liabilities surrounding these relationships, our final inquiry concerns their termination. Specifically, what circumstances will cause termination? Two considerations are important. *First,* as a general rule, an agency relationship must be terminated by substantially the same means used to create it. That is, some agencies are created by a communication from the principal to the agent. They may be terminated by another communication. Those that were created by a communication, express or implied, from the principal to a third party must be terminated by another communication of that character. The same is true of those created by operation of law. *Second,* when the attempt at termination is defective, an agent may retain the *power* to bind the principal, even though he no longer has the *right*. That is the case when an agent is "fired" by a communication from the principal to the agent. Although the agent's express authority is terminated properly, any apparent authority he might possess (for example, based on past dealings with customers) is not, and the agent may be able to bind the principal in subsequent transactions with those cus-

tomers who receive no notice that the agent has been fired.

Will of the Parties

Just as an agency relationship may arise by mutual agreement of the parties, it may terminate this way. Further, since all agency relationships are created by the voluntary, consensual granting of authority from the principal to the agent, as discussed in Chapter 31, as a general rule they also may be terminated by the principal's withdrawal of authority. Inherent in this power, however, are two possible problems. (1) Under circumstances in which an agency is based on an underlying contract of employment, the principal may withdraw the agency authority but still may be subject to suit for breach of contract. Thus, it must be recognized that the relationship between the agent and the principal actually may be composed of *two* relationships—contract and agency. (2) When the agency is **coupled with an interest,** the general rule does not apply. These agencies arise under circumstances in which an agent has more at stake in the continuation of the agency relationship than simply wanting to remain employed. For example, an agent may make certain advances out of his own pocket on behalf of the principal, with the understanding that as he makes collections, he will take out the amount of the advances first and remit the remainder to the principal. In this situation, the principal is not allowed to terminate the agency until the agent is first fully reimbursed. Another example would be a creditor's authority to sell collateral if a loan is not paid when due.

From a strict technical standpoint, agencies may not be terminated at the will of the agent alone. When authority is granted, an agent, in fact, is authorized whether she likes it or not. From a practical standpoint, however, the agent may choose not to exercise the authority so granted, and may give notice to the principal of this election. Thus, the agent would owe no duties to the principal except the duty not to act on the authority.

HILGENDORF v. HAGUE
293 N.W.2d 272 (Iowa 1980)

This was an action by Harvey C. Hilgendorf (Plaintiff/Appellee) against Mervin D. and A. Joan Hague, husband and wife, (Defendants/Appellants), for damages for breach of a real estate listing contract.

On March 29, 1976, Defendants listed two parcels of land with Plaintiff, a real estate broker. One parcel was 80 acres, the other 160 acres. The listings gave Hilgendorf the exclusive right to sell the two parcels for a period of twelve months. The 160-acre parcel was priced at $1400 per acre ($224,000). Hague agreed to pay Hilgendorf a commission of six percent of the price if, during the twelve months, Hilgendorf found a buyer ready, willing, and able to purchase on those terms or other agreed-upon terms. Both Defendants signed the listings. Thereafter, Defendants were notified by their principal creditor, Production Credit Association, that PCA would not renew their loan, which was then due. Defendants realized that this probably would cause them to have to liquidate, and they became impatient to sell the land. Defendants then sent Plaintiff a letter dated August 13, 1976, purporting to revoke the listing agreement. Plaintiff ignored the letter and, thereafter, on more than one occasion, produced offers to purchase the land at the listed price from purchasers ready, willing, and able to purchase on the terms stated in the listing agreement. These offers were ignored by Defendants.

From a judgment for Plaintiff in the amount of six percent of the offered price, Defendant appealed. Affirmed.

UHLENHOPP, Justice.

Right to terminate listing. Since agency is a consensual relationship, a principal has *power* to terminate an agency which is not coupled with an interest, although the contract is for a period which has not expired. Ordinarily the agent's authority thereupon ceases. Absent some legal ground, however, the principal does not have a *right* to terminate an unexpired agency contract, and may subject himself to damages by doing so. . . . Restatement (Second) of Agency Sec. 386 (1958).

The whole question regarding liability here turns on whether the Hagues had a legal ground for terminating Hilgendorf's agency before the expiration of the year. All agree that they had power to terminate, but they contend they also had a right to do so. They say PCA would not renew their loan, they had to sell the 80 acres in addition to their other land, and the best way to sell the 80 acres was with the 160 acres. Did these circumstances give them a "right" to terminate the listing contract they had signed on the 160 acres, and cast on Hilgendorf a "duty" to give up his listing contract as a matter of an agent's loyalty to his principal?

The Hagues appear to confuse the two roles an agent occupies. In performing agency functions for the principal an agent does indeed occupy a fiduciary position, and his duty of loyalty requires him to place the principal's interests first. . . . But in the contract of agency itself between the agent and the principal [a relationship of employer-employee, rather than principal-agent], neither of the parties is acting for the other; each is acting for himself.

This case involves the latter role. . . .

Several circumstances are given in the texts as grounds for terminating fixed-term agencies, but coming upon hard times is not among them.

Questions

1. Do you think the result in this case is too harsh? What arguments support it?

2. Is there a better measure for compensating the broker in these circumstances than giving him the full commission?

Contract Provisions

A contract that establishes the basis of an agency relationship also may provide a set time for its termination (for example, one year). Remember, however, in this context, as in the previous case and some that follow, this method of termination will end only express and implied authority, leaving apparent authority intact.

Accomplishment of Purpose

At this point we are concerned primarily with special (not general) agents. Very simply, when an agent is hired for a particular purpose, once that purpose is accomplished, the agency is terminated, there no longer being any reason for its existence.

Death of the Principal or Agent

It is fundamental that any relationship requires the existence of two persons. Thus, death of either the principal or the agent will terminate the agency relationship. Any existing third-party rights would be adjudicated through the estate of the deceased party. To this rule, however, there is one relatively minor exception. Under U.C.C. 4-405(a), the agency relationship between a depositor (principal) and a bank (agent) created when the depositor opens a checking account is not terminated until the bank knows of the customer's death. Further, under Subsection (b) of that section, even with such knowledge, the bank may continue to pay or certify checks drawn prior to the date of death for a period of ten days after the date of death.

Incompetency of the Principal

Although the continued mental capacity of the principal may affect an agency relationship, the same is not true for the agent. The principal's incompetency will terminate all agency relationships and the principal's insanity will render any authorized contracts made by his agent voidable. The capacity of the agent, however, as discussed in Chapter 31, generally is of no importance to the existence of the agency. Anyone may be an agent, regardless of mental capacity. Also, U.C.C. 4-405(a) (but not (b)), discussed immediately above, applies to incompetent principals.

Bankruptcy

The bankruptcy of the principal usually will terminate business agencies, although a principal *may* be allowed to continue business under the Bankruptcy Act (especially Chapter 11), in which case some business agencies will continue (those that are necessary). Personal agencies necessary to the continued health and well-being of the principal will continue, such as sending an agent to the store to purchase a loaf of bread. Unless the agent's credit is necessary to the agency, an agent's bankruptcy probably will have no effect.

Intervening Illegality

If the exercise of the agent's powers under an existing agency would *necessitate* the commission of an illegal act, then the agency is terminated. This may involve an illegality that nullifies the purpose of the agency, as in the case of an agent who is hired to sell wild rabbits and a new statute makes the sale of wild rabbits illegal. It also may involve a loss of qualification by either the principal or the agent, such as when an agent who is licensed as a real estate salesperson under a licensed broker (or the broker) loses the required license. In any of these situations, the law will not recognize the validity of a relationship since it is not the purpose of the law to promote illegal activities.

Impossibility of Performance

After agency authority has been granted, circumstances that formed a material part of the basis of the relationship may change in a way that renders performance of the agent's duties impossible. For example, during time of war, an agent might be drafted into military service, or supplies of a product no longer may be available. Perhaps a more common impossibility occurs when the subject matter of the agency is lost or destroyed. In these circumstances, the agency is considered terminated because it no longer has a purpose.

Change in Business Conditions

Finally, between the time the agency is created and the time the agent is to perform, the agent may have notice or knowledge that circumstances have changed in such a way that she reasonably should know the principal no longer would want her to act as previously authorized. For example, an agent is authorized to sell the principal's land for $20,000. Thereafter the agent learns that oil has been discovered on land next to the property she was authorized to sell. Since exercising the authority granted undoubtedly would involve a breach of the agent's fiduciary duty, the agency simply terminates. Note that in this situation, unlike the other methods, termination is not automatic upon the change, but occurs only when the agent has notice or knowledge of the change.

Duties on Termination

When agency authority is terminated by any of the means described above, the agent is under a duty, as discussed in the first part of this chapter, to refrain from further acting as an agent. In addition, when the agency authority was apparent, the principal is under a duty to see that third parties with whom the agent has dealt on his behalf are informed that the agent no longer is authorized. Otherwise, as noted, the agent still will have the power to bind the principal to these third parties though he no longer has the right to do so.

LAZOV et al. v. BLACK
88 Wash.2d 883, 567 P.2d 233 (1977)

This was an action by Spirdon Lazov (Plaintiff/Respondent) to recover real estate his wife had purchased from Defendants William C. and Betty A. Black under a power of attorney from Plaintiff, and subsequently had quitclaimed back to Defendants. Plaintiff contended that the transfer from his wife to Defendants was not effective as against him because, prior to the transfer, he had revoked the power of attorney.

On September 10, 1973, Plaintiff executed a power of attorney, recorded in Pierce County, naming his wife as his attorney in fact. Thereafter, he left the state and Mrs. Lazov purchased certain real estate from Defendants. Plaintiff returned to the state in September of 1974, instituted dissolution proceedings against his wife, gave her notice of his intent to revoke the power of attorney and, on November 8, 1974, filed the revocation instrument in Pierce County. On November 19, 1974, Mrs. Lazov conveyed her interest in the property purchased from Defendants, and purportedly also that of Plaintiff, back to Defendants. When the Plaintiff attempted to take possession, he was prevented from doing so by Defendants.

From a judgment for Plaintiff, Defendants appealed. Affirmed.

UTTER, Associate Justice.

Generally, termination by a principal of an agency relationship is not effective as to the agent and third parties who have previously dealt with the agent in that capacity until notice of the termination of the relationship is conveyed to them. . . .

The effect of recording a power of attorney is determined by statute in this state, however, and the general rule otherwise applicable in the absence of a statute is not controlling. RCW 65.08.130 provides: "A power of attorney or other instrument recorded pursuant to RCW 65.08.060 through 65.08.150 is not deemed revoked by any act of the party by whom it was executed unless the instrument of revocation is also recorded in the same office in which the instrument granting the power was recorded." The trial court found and the record substantiates the fact that this statute was complied with. While RCW 65.08.130 does not expressly provide that recording constitutes constructive notice to third parties of termination of the previously existing agency relationship, this is provided for in other statutes. A "conveyance" for purposes of the recording statute is defined as a "written instrument by which . . . title to any real estate may be affected, including an instrument in execution of a power, although the power be one of revocation only . . ." RCW 65.08.060(3). The effect of recording a conveyance is expressed in negative terms in RCW 65.08.070 but its meaning is nonetheless clear. The recording of a "conveyance" is notice to subsequent purchasers of the interest which it creates. . . .

We have previously held . . . that the legislative purpose in enacting RCW 65.08.070 was "to give stability to land titles, by authorizing prospective purchasers or encumbrancers to rely upon the title as disclosed by the record." We also noted . . . that "[t]he method to be followed in revoking a power of attorney is provided by the act, and affords one who has executed such a power an easy method by which the same may be rendered void from the date the instrument of revocation is recorded."

Questions

1. Would the result have been the same if the revocation had not been filed? Why or why not?

2. Is there any argument that the Blacks should have prevailed?

SUMMARY

Every agency relationship creates a unique set of rights and duties between the principal/employer and the agent/employee. The precise mix of these rights and duties will depend on the contract, if any, between the parties and on whether the relationship is one of principal-agent, master-servant, or employer-independent contractor. Primary among the duties of the principal/employer, however, is the duty to compensate the agent/employee for all services performed on his behalf, unless circumstances indicate that the parties intended the services to be rendered as a gift. Also, the principal/employer is under a duty to reimburse the agent/employee for any reasonable sums expended in the performance of her authorized duties. Primary among the duties of the agent/employee are to exercise proper skill and care in the performance of her duties, to act only as authorized or directed (including authority by necessity), to refrain from performing after termination of the agency/employment, and to reimburse the principal/employer when the principal/employer is held liable in *respondeat superior* and for other costs or expenses generated by a breach of duty by the agent/employee. An agent also owes to her principal the duty of utmost loyalty and faithfulness—the fiduciary duty.

An agency relationship may terminate in a variety of ways, including by the will of the parties, revocation of authority by the principal, the occurrence of some condition, or operation of law. As a general rule, agency authority must be terminated in substantially the same way as it was created. Failure to see that this is done may result in the principal being held liable for the agent's acts because the agent has retained the "power" to bind the principal, even though he no longer has the "right" to do so. At any rate, the practical obligation to see to proper termination rests primarily with the principal.

KEY TERMS AND CONCEPTS

fiduciary duty
agency coupled with an interest

PROBLEMS

1. O'Day employed Kirchberg, a food broker, to purchase lettuce for him. During their relationship of some 14 months, Kirchberg placed 55 orders with Arkelian, and O'Day paid Arkelian for them. O'Day then discharged Kirchberg; thereafter, Kirchberg placed another 20 orders with Arkelian, who did not know of the termination of Kirchberg's authority. Is O'Day liable to Arkelian on those 20 orders?

2. McDonald listed her house for sale with Dowd More Co. Realtors, giving the broker an exclusive right to sell her property during the next 90 days. Approximately one month later, McDonald notified Dowd More that its services no longer were needed, and then sold the house herself. Dowd More sued for its commission, and McDonald defended on the ground that the agency was terminable at her will. Is McDonald correct?

3. Desfosses employed Notis, on salary, to find real estate investments for him. Notis located an attractive parcel and told Desfosses the price was $32,400, when in fact the price was $16,474. Notis took the property in his own name and transferred it to Desfosses for $32,400. When Desfosses learned the truth he refused to pay Notis his salary and demanded the return of the secret profit Notis had pocketed. Notis contended Desfosses was entitled only to rescission of the contract. Is Notis correct?

4. Sierra Pacific Industries employed Carter, a licensed broker, to sell certain real estate. The asking price was $85,000, and Carter was to receive a $5000 commission. Carter sold the property for $85,000 to his daughter and son-in-law, but did not inform Sierra Pacific of the relationship. Is Carter entitled to the commission?

5. For years, Mr. Campagna, a contractor, had done renovation work for Mautner-Glick, a real estate developer. When he died, he had four projects in various states of completion. Mrs. Campagna undertook to complete them and Mautner-Glick, in order to help, began paying wages to Campagna's employees and sending the net amount remaining to Mrs. Campagna. After two years Mrs. Campagna was contacted by the Internal Revenue Service because when the wages had been paid, Mautner-Glick had not deducted and reported withholding taxes. In addition to back withholding, Mrs. Campagna was assessed interest and penalties, and incurred substantial legal costs. Mautner-Glick refused to reimburse her for these on the theory that it was only doing her a favor and was not compensated. Is this position sound?

6. Oramundo, chairman of the board of directors of Management Assistance, Inc., learned of a drop in earnings of the corporation and sold her stock before permitting publication of the figures. The price of the stock then dropped significantly, and she repurchased the same number of shares at the lower price. Diamond brought a shareholders' derivative action to recover the amount of the price difference. Should Diamond recover?

7. Upton owned certain land subject to a lease to Suckow, and wanted bulldozing done on it. He authorized Suckow to arrange for the work. Suckow obtained the services of Johnson and, during the bulldozing, Upton observed the progress. When Upton failed to pay the bill, Johnson sued Suckow. Is Suckow entitled to recover the attorney fees and costs of his defense from Upton?

8. Bowling gave National Convoy & Trucking an idea for a new business, in return for which National agreed to employ Bowling as manager. He was to continue until age 65, and was to be paid a salary plus a stated percentage of the profits. When Bowling reached 62, National sought to terminate him as manager and put him in another position with the same compensation. Is National free to terminate Bowling's agency at will?

9. Turley worked as a sales representative for Hollingsworth. When she left her position, she took with her certain papers concerning customers. She worked in an unrelated field for three months, and then went to work for a competitor of Hollingsworth, for whom she prepared a customer list, partially from the papers she had taken when she left Hollingsworth. Hollingsworth sued alleging a breach of duty, but the trial court granted a summary judgment for Turley. Was this decision correct?

10. Keolian, a security guard furnished by Chuck's Guard Service, while working in a store owned by Sears, Roebuck & Co., arrested a customer for shoplifting. In a suit by the customer against Sears for false arrest, it was revealed that there were no grounds for the arrest. Is Sears entitled to reimbursement from Keolian or Chuck's Guard Service for the damages paid out and the costs of its defense?

PART
VIII

Business

Organizations

Following on the heels of agency law, this part of the book addresses the law of business organizations. A knowledge of business organizations is particularly important to business students because all business is conducted through some form of organization, a sole proprietorship, a partnership, a corporation or, perhaps, one of the less-familiar forms, such as a syndicate or a business trust. In addition, many of these organizations operate as cooperatives or, of more recent and growing importance, as franchises. All students of business management, and particularly those who have some specialty in accounting and finance, possess the statistical tools necessary to viewing a business as a whole. An understanding of the law of business organizations is necessary to help managers understand the actual working potential of a business and, thus, plan for the future.

Chapter | 35

Business Organizations: Introduction

MAJOR FORMS OF BUSINESS ORGANIZATION

To start at the beginning, we must face the fact that the term *business organization* is impossible to define. Indeed, *Black's Law Dictionary* states that there is no precise or legal meaning of the term *business*. Normally we think of a **business organization** as an entity involved in commerical transactions for the purpose of earning a profit. However, the principles that apply to these organizations generally are applicable to not-for-profit organizations and to individuals as well. Moreover, in a sense, each of us is an individual organization (proprietorship) that exists for the purpose of conducting the business of life. In addition, people not otherwise directly involved in a commerical business organization doubtlessly will do business with others who are involved directly with such organizations. Thus, a general knowledge of the basic governing principles of business organizations is desirable for anyone.

Sole Proprietorship

The sole proprietorship is the simplest and most common type of business organization. The sole proprietor both owns and manages the business himself. Those who are employed as agents or employees of the business are agents and employees of the sole proprietor. Any debt of the business binds the sole proprietor individually. A **sole proprietorship** is typically a small business and takes many forms, including the business of a craftsperson (a carpenter, for example) a small retailer, a sole professional practitioner, such as a doctor or an attorney, or even a youngster who mows lawns during the summer.

One of the greatest advantages to the proprietorship form is that it is easy to organize. No formalities are required. No registration is required, except that some states insist that if the proprietorship is to be operated under a name other than that of the owner, the assumed name must be registered together with information identifying the owner. For example, if Alice Banks wished to operate a service garage under the name "Alice's Car Hospital," these states would require registration. This registration usually is on the county level.

Another advantage of the sole proprietorship is that management responsibilities are not shared. When a decision is to be made, there is no need for the proprietor to secure the approval of anyone else. Even though, there may be a corresponding disadvantage in that there is no one else to blame if problems arise or things go wrong. Of course, the sole proprietor can hire management talent to help in the decision-making process, but ultimate responsibility still rests with him.

Among the major disadvantages of this form of organization is that liability is unlimited and is borne by the proprietor personally. Generally, debts of the business are backed by the entire business and all the personal assets of the owner. Of course, insurance is available to spread most risks of this type, but the availability of insurance

is dependent on the proprietor's ability to pay the premiums. Also, liability may be limited by contract provisions, on a contract-by-contract basis. However, contracts that limit the proprietor's liability to the assets of the business are more difficult to negotiate. Moreover, there is a vast area of tort liability, and even criminal liability, that cannot be limited by contract.

Another disadvantage to the proprietorship form is the difficulty of raising operating capital. There are no other owners to provide additional capital, as there are in a partnership or a corporation. Also, since debts of the business are secured only by the assets and the credit-worthiness of the proprietor, the ability to borrow is limited, which can have a significant adverse impact in terms of business growth and in coping with emergency situations.

Taxation of a business organization may differ markedly depending on its form, and this may be advantageous or disadvantageous to the proprietorship. The income of a sole proprietorship is taxed as part of the personal earnings of the proprietor, and any losses are written off against other income. This also largely is true of partnership income. A corporation, however, is taxed as a separate entity on a different rate scale. Any distributed profits then are taxed to the individual owners of the corporation as part of their personal income. The point at which the sole proprietor will acquire a tax advantage by incorporating depends on the amount of business income and the amount of the proprietor's other (personal) income. As a rule of thumb, when an individual's other income exceeds about $15,000, there may be an advantage to the corporate form.

Finally, if continuity is important, the sole proprietorship may be undesirable. When the owner dies, the sole proprietorship terminates. On the positive side, there are no formalities to the winding up of this type of business as there are with partnerships and corporations. The business's assets become part of the estate of the proprietor, and the estate is chargeable with its debts.

Whether or not the business itself continues or starts up again is a matter to be decided by the beneficiaries of the estate. This, of course, makes the contractual commitments, including warranties, of a sole proprietor less stable than those of a corporation.

Partnership

A **partnership** is an association of two or more persons to carry on an ongoing business for profit. They also share responsibility for its management. A **general partnership** is very much like a combination of two or more proprietorships, with each partner sharing in the proprietorship venture of the other and sharing management responsibility as well. For the most part, the partners share the same liabilities as proprietors.

A general partnership may be formed either with or without a formal agreement. State law, such as the Uniform Partnership Act that has been adopted by most states, will govern the rights and duties of the parties when there is no agreement to the contrary. Each partner is both the principal and the agent of each of the other partners. Thus, the transaction of authorized partnership business by any one partner binds not only that partner but the other partners as well. The general partnership

usually is not considered a separate legal entity (although a few states are to the contrary, and the UPA treats partnerships as entities for a few purposes, such as holding property in its own name), and its existence depends on the continued existence of all the partners. Most general partnerships suffer from the same disabilities as a proprietorship in terms of unlimited liability and difficulties in securing new capital, although the ability to attract new capital is somewhat better than in the case of a proprietorship.

A special type of partnership is the **limited partnership.** It is formed by the association of at least one general partner and one or more limited partners. The rights, duties, and liabilities of the general partner are the same as in other partnerships. The most notable feature is that the general partner has unlimited personal liability for debts and obligations of the limited partnership. Limited partners, on the other hand, are treated as investors only. Their liability for partnership debts generally is restricted to the amount of their investment in the partnership, and they can have no voice in management, as the following case illustrates. The limited partnership is thus a hybrid between the general partnership and the corporation.

DELANEY v. FIDELITY LEASE LIMITED
526 S.W.2d 543 (Tex. 1975)

This was an action by Neil G. Delaney (Plaintiff/Petitioner) against the limited partnership of Fidelity Lease Limited, its limited partners, and its corporate general partner (Defendants/Respondents) for breach of a lease. The cause of action against the limited partners was severed to be decided separately in this case.

The sole business of the limited partnership in question involved a lease with Plaintiff by the limited partnership as tenant. The lease was breached by the limited partnership, and Plaintiff sought to hold the limited partners personally liable because they also acted as officers, directors, and shareholders of the corporate general partner, thus controlling the business of the limited partnership.

The trial court found for Defendant limited partners, and the Court of Appeals affirmed. Plaintiff appealed. Reversed as to the questions material to this chapter.

DANIEL, Justice.

It was alleged by plaintiffs, and there is summary judgment evidence, that the three limited partners controlled the business of the limited partnership, albeit through the corporate entity. The defendant limited partners argue that they acted only through the corporation and that the corporation actually controlled the business of the limited partnership. In response to this contention, we adopt the following statements in the dissenting opinion of Chieft Justice Preslar in the court of civil appeals:

> I find it difficult to separate their acts for they were at all times in the dual capacity of limited partners and officers of the corporation. Apparently the corporation had no function except to operate the limited partnership and Appellees were obligated to their other partners to so operate the corporation as to benefit the partnership. Each act was done then, not for the corporation, but for the partnership. Indirectly, if not directly, they were exercising control over the partnership. Truly 'the corporation fiction' was in this instance a fiction. . . .

Thus, we hold that the personal liability, which attaches to a limited partner when "he takes part in the control and management of the business," cannot be evaded merely by acting through a corporation. . . .

The defendant limited partners also contend that the "control" test enumerated in Section 8 of Article 6132a [of the Texas Uniform Limited Partnership Act] for the purpose of inflicting personal liability should be coupled with a determination of whether the plaintiffs relied upon the limited partners as holding themselves out as general partners. Thus, they argue that, before personal liability attaches to limited partners, two elements must coincide: (1) the limited partner must take part in the control of the business; and (2) the limited partner must have held himself out as being a general partner having personal liability to an extent that the third party, or plaintiff, relied upon the limited partners' personal liability. . . . They observe that there is no question in this case but that the plaintiffs were in no way misled into believing that these three limited partners were personally liable on the lease, because the lease provided that the plaintiffs were entering into the lease with "Fidelity Lease, Ltd., a limited partnership acting by and through Interlease Corporation, General Partner."

We disagree with this contention. Section 8 of Article 6132a simply provides that a limited partner who takes part in the control of the business subjects himself to personal liability as a general partner. The statute makes no mention of any requirement of reliance on the part of the party attempting to hold the limited partner personally liable.

Crombie, Kahn, and Sanders argue that, since their only control of Fidelity's business was as officers of the alleged corporate general partner, they are insulated from personal liability arising from their activities or those of the corporation. This is a general rule of corporate law, but one of several exceptions in which the courts will disregard the corporate fiction is where it is used to circumvent a statute. Pacific American Gasoline Co. of Texas v. Miller, 76 S.W.2d 833 (Tex.Civ.App. 1934, writ ref'd). See also Drye v. Eagle Rock Ranch, Inc., 364 S.W.2d 196, 202 (Tex.1962), and Pace Corporation v. Jackson, 155 Tex. 179, 284 S.W.2d 340 (1955). That is precisely the result here, for it is undisputed that the corporation was organized to manage and control the limited partnership. Strict compliance with the statute is required if a limited partner is to avoid liability as a general partner.

Questions

1. Why does the law insist that limited partners not be involved in the management of the partnership?

2. Why does the court reach the result it does if the plaintiffs were not misled into thinking the limited partners would be personally liable?

Corporation

A **corporation** is a completely separate legal entity, or legal person. It is formed by the grant of a charter, generally by the state. Its owners are only investors who will share in the profits and losses of the corporation, usually in proportion to the amounts of their investments. They may have management responsibilities to the extent that they do not delegate these responsibilities to oth-

Summary of legal forms of business organization

Form of Business	Advantages	Disadvantages
Sole proprietorship	1. easy to organize 2. simple to control 3. freedom of operation 4. not subject to much government regulation	1. difficult to acquire funds for expansion 2. firm lacks permanence 3. unlimited liability 4. owner must perform all management functions
Partnership	1. easy to organize 2. greater specialization of management is possible 3. securing financial resources easier than in sole proprietorship 4. subject to limited regulation	1. division of ownership may lead to disagreements 2. death or withdrawal of one partner automatically ends the organization 3. subject to unlimited liability 4. financial resources are typically quite limited
Corporation	1. capability of raising large amounts of capital through sale of stocks and bonds 2. limited liability of stockholders 3. stability and permanence 4. employment of specialized management personnel	1. subject to considerable government regulation 2. taxes and organizing costs for corporations are heavy burdens 3. double taxation of corporate income and dividends 4. separation of ownership and control

Source: *Economics* 4th ed. by Ralph T. Byrns and Gerald W. Stone. Copyright © 1989, 1987, 1984, 1981 Scott, Foresman and Company.

ers. Although every corporation must have a board of directors, the board will have management responsibilities only to the extent permitted by the investors.

Among the important advantages of the corporate form is that the owners' liability generally is limited to the amounts of their investments. Also, a corporation has a greater ability to attract new capital by selling more stock, and generally it has a higher credit-worthiness than other business forms by virtue of its size and perpetual existence. From the viewpoint of the owners (shareholders), their investments in a corporation usually are more liquid than those in a sole proprietorship or a partnership. All or any portion of their shares can be sold, and often it can be done quickly through an organized stock exchange. Generally, however, corporations may suffer the disadvantage of double taxation. The entity's profits are taxed under one set of provisions of the income-tax laws, and then any profits distributed to shareholders are again taxed under another set of provisions, because the money is now part of the personal income of the investors.

In order to avoid the problem of double taxation, it is possible to form a "Small Business Corporation," sometimes called a **Subchapter S corporation.** If the requirements are met, corporate profits are taxed as they are in partnerships. That is, there is no corporate income tax, and the profits are taxed to the shareholders as a part of their personal incomes.

OTHER TYPES OF BUSINESS ORGANIZATION

Joint Venture

A **joint venture** is basically the same as a partnership, but it is created for the purpose of conducting either a single transaction or a limited activity. In all respects, the law relating to a partnership is applicable to a joint venture. Generally speaking, less formality surrounds a joint ven-

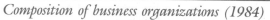
Composition of business organizations (1984)

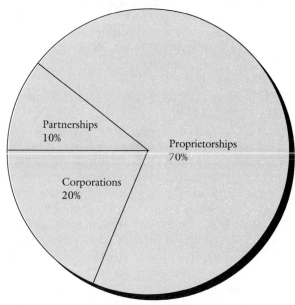

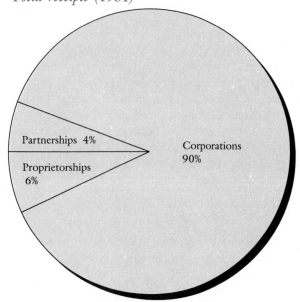
Total receipts (1984)

Source: Statistical Abstract of the U.S. (1988), Table 823.

ture's creation than is involved with the formation of a partnership. Joint ventures frequently are used to finance research and exploration projects. For example, a group of investors may form a joint venture to explore for oil. Regular investors in such projects sometimes are called *venture capitalists*.

Syndicate

A **syndicate** is another type of association created for a limited business purpose, usually the financing of a project such as a building, a shopping center, or the acquisition of certain property to be held for investment purposes only. For example, a syndicate might be formed to finance the exploration of an area of the ocean where a treasure ship is believed to have sunk. The precise organizational forms of syndicates differ, but commonly the members become joint owners of the particular property financed. In general, *joint venture* and *syndicate* are considered interchangeable terms.

Joint Stock Company

A **joint stock company,** little known today, is an association of owners into what is essentially a partnership. Partnership law normally is applied for such purposes as unlimited personal liability and taxation. The business is not chartered as a corporation, and bears no resemblance to a corporation other than in the sense that the interests of the owners are represented by shares of stock that are transferable.

Business Trust

Another of the business forms that has become virtually extinct is the **business trust,** although it is commonly used in Massachusetts. It is a "trust" in the legal meaning of the term, as governed by the principles discussed in Chapter 29. A business trust is an association of persons coming together to contribute their individual property to be managed by a trustee. The owners then become the beneficiaries of the trust and receive certificates of beneficial interest similar to stock certificates. Legal title rests with the trustee and beneficial title with the beneficiaries. The original intent behind the creation of business trusts was to achieve limited liability without the problems of the corporate form, including double taxation. This plan did not succeed as the states began either allowing the limited liability and applying the double corporate tax, or taxing the owners as partners with unlimited liability. The effects of antitrust laws also took their toll.

Holding Company

A holding company is not actually a distinct form of business organization. Although it normally is operated under the corporate form, it could be a partnership or a sole proprietorship. The **holding company** is distinguished only in that its business is the ownership of interests in other businesses, typically corporate stock, and its profits are derived from the profits of the businesses in which it has invested. Perhaps anyone who owns interests in two or more businesses, and earns a living from the profits of these investments, technically can be called a holding company.

CHOICE OF A BUSINESS FORM

The particular form of business organization chosen in a given situation will depend on an analysis of a number of factors. Among the most important are (1) ease and expense of formation, (2) potential liability of the owners, (3) tax considerations, (4) need for capital, and (5) desirability of continuity.

The sole proprietorship is the simplest and least expensive to form, although a very simple partnership might run a close second, at least if the partners are willing to be governed by the general partnership law of the state. A small corporation may be formed relatively inexpensively, but it must be granted corporate existence by the state, and there are some complexities involved in preparing a corporate charter and bylaws and seeing to the requirements of filing.

From the perspective of risk, the corporate form allows the owners to limit their personal liability, and so does a limited partnership. General partnerships and sole proprietorships, however, have the disadvantage of unlimited liability.

Tax considerations are complex and are best left to a professional trained in the intricacies of the subject. However, it may be understood that the profits of a proprietorship, a partnership, and a Subchapter S Corporation (discussed in Chapter 40) are taxed as personal income of the owners. The profits of the ordinary corporation are taxed at a separate corporate rate when earned, and again as personal income of the owners on distribution. Many tax implications beyond the rate of taxation and who is taxed on what merit consideration, however.

SUMMARY

The choice of the form of organization for a particular business depends on many factors. Among them are the objectives of the business, availability of resources, relationship of investors and the nature of their contributions, and applicable state laws, in addition to tax law. In forming any kind of serious business venture, the planning talents of a tax specialist and a lawyer are almost indispensable.

KEY TERMS AND CONCEPTS

business organization
sole proprietorship
partnership
general partnership
limited partnership
corporation
Subchapter S corporation
joint venture
syndicate
joint stock company
business trust
holding company

PROBLEMS

1. William Lyons died as a result of a defective heater on premises owned by the American Legion Post No. 650 Realty Co. He suffocated because of the escape of carbon monoxide. His wife, Martha, as executrix of his estate, sued the post and its individual members. The members contended they were not liable individually because, by statute, the post, and therefore the Realty Co., was recognized as a legal person. Are they correct?

2. Brenner operated a business and began experiencing financial difficulties. Plitt agreed to help him by advancing money as needed, and began doing so on an almost daily basis. The money was to be repaid when merchandise was sold. When it became obvious that the business was going to fail, Plitt demanded payment in full, and Brenner defended on the ground that the parties were joint venturers in the business, and therefore Plitt should suffer his share of losses. Is Brenner correct?

3. Repass and Sharp were partners in a racing stable. As part of the business, they also placed illegal bets on horses, and shared profits and losses equally. When Sharp died, Repass sought an accounting, seeking his share of the business, together with a $4000 gambling fund held by Sharp and Sharp's share of some $10,000 in winnings not yet placed in the partnership account. Is he entitled to the relief requested?

4. Hodge and Voller were partners in a drive-in theater. Voller was the managing partner. Without Hodge's knowledge or consent, Voller sold some land adjoining the drive-in to Garrett, who purchased it in good faith. The land had been held in the partnership name. Upon discovering the sale, Hodge sued Garrett for return of the land to the partnership. Is Hodge entitled to the relief?

5. Harris and Zajac operated a junkyard. Zajac provided everything, and Harris managed the business. Harris received expenses plus one-half of profits. There was no other agreement. Harris sued for an accounting as a partner; Zajac contended Harris was only an employee, and moved for summary judgment. The court granted the motion on the ground that with no further agreement, no partnership could exist. Was the court's ruling correct?

6. Fletcher leased certain land to Bramble, on which Bramble operated a fruit farm and orchard. Fletcher took no part in this business or its profits, and received only the rental due on the land. However, to the knowledge of Fletcher, advertisements in newspapers carried the name "F & B Enterprises." When Bramble died, Pullen, who had supplied fruit trees to the farm, sued Fletcher,

as a partner, for the unpaid price of trees delivered. Fletcher defended on the ground that he was not a partner. Should Fletcher be liable?

7. A partnership was formed, of which a corporation was a general partner. First Bank lent money to the partnership at an interest rate allowed on loans to a corporation, but in excess of that allowed on loans to an individual. A partner sued First Bank to recover the amount of the excess interest on behalf of the partnership. Is she entitled to judgment?

8. A partnership operating a hospital was indicted for allowing an unauthorized person to participate in surgical procedure on an uninformed, nonconsenting patient. Thereafter, some of the records were falsified in an attempt to cover up the crime. The partnership appealed its conviction on the ground that because it was not an entity, it could not be charged with a crime. Is the contention correct?

Partnerships: Nature and Formation

INTRODUCTION

This chapter sets out the basic nature and legal requirements for the formation of a partnership and discuss the general nature of a partnership. It is suggested strongly that you review Chapters 31 through 34 on agency law at this time. In addition to the Uniform Partnership Act and the general law of contracts, it is the body of the law of agency that most profoundly impacts the law of partnerships. A thorough understanding of agency law is an enormous help in achieving a good grasp of partnership operation.

NATURE OF A PARTNERSHIP

The partnership form of business organization is an ancient concept, having originated well before the birth of Christ. It has many of the legal characteristics of a proprietorship, especially in terms of ownership of property, extent of liability of the owners, and taxation. The main difference, of course, is that it is owned by two or more persons. The **Uniform Partnership Act (UPA)** defines a **partnership** as "an association of two or more persons to carry on as co-owners a business for profit." In fact, a partnership is much like the coming together of two or more sole proprietorships under a contractual agreement. Because two or more individuals are involved, and each is both the principal and the agent of the other, the law of partnership borrows heavily from the law of agency.

A partnership may arise by express contractual agreement or by implication from the surrounding facts and circumstances, or even by operation of law. Generally, there are no strict formalities required, as there are for the creation of a corporation. However, an express contract creating a partnership for a stated term longer than one year must be in writing to satisfy the Statute of Frauds.

Theories of the Organization

Historically, there have been conflicting theories concerning the nature of the partnership form of organization. Early in the history of our law, there was considerable sympathy for the *entity* **theory,** which regarded a partnership as a separate legal entity (person) independent of the partners. This was the approach taken in the first draft of the

Uniform Partnership Act, but that was changed prior to its final form, which was completed in 1914.

The *aggregate* **theory** is more descriptive of the partnership form. Under this theory, the partnership itself has no existence separate and apart from the partners. It cannot own property in its own name, nor can it sue or be sued. A partnership, therefore, is only a relationship or descriptive term; it is not a "thing."

The Uniform Partnership Act adopts somewhat of a *hybrid* position between these competing entity and aggregate theories, but is aligned primarily with the former. Subsections (3) and (4) of Section 8 of the act state that property may be conveyed to, and held by, a partnership in the partnership name. Section 10(1) provides that real property can be conveyed in the partnership name. Section 2 defines the term *person* as including a partnership. In addition, other references in the act allude to the partnership as a person. The Bankruptcy Act allows for the bankruptcy of a partnership apart from that of the partners. State law also may provide for "person" status of a partnership for certain purposes, such as suing and being sued. The following case considers the entity and aggregate theories in deciding whether a partnership may sue in its own name.

MARVIL PROPERTIES v. FRIPP ISLAND DEVELOPMENT CORPORATION
273 S.C. 619, 258 S.E.2d 106 (1979)

This was an action by Marvil Properties, a general partnership (Plaintiff/Respondent) against Fripp Island Development Corporation (Defendant/Appellant) for specific performance of a sales agreement. Plaintiff sued in the name of the partnership without joining the individual partners as plaintiffs. The question before the court was whether a partnership, alone, could sue in its own name.

Defendant filed a demurrer to the complaint for want of a proper party plaintiff. The trial court overruled the demurrer and Defendant appealed. Reversed.

LEWIS, Chief Justice.

The dispositive question to be decided is whether a general partnership has the capacity to sue in its name.

South Carolina has long adopted the rule that a partnership is not such a legal entity as to authorize it to sue or be sued as such. . . .

The foregoing rule was confirmed in the 1969 decision of White v. Jackson . . . and no decision of this Court has been found, or cited, to sustain the conclusion that a partnership may sue or be sued in the partnership name alone.

The statement in Chitwood v. McMillan, . . . that "A partnership under the law is an entity, separate and distinct from the persons who compose it," does not, as argued, support the conclusion that a partnership may sue in its name. This principle has been applied solely in determining the legal relationships and liabilities of the partners, and has never been construed in this State as permitting a suit only in the partnership name.

Neither have legislative enactments in this State changed the principle that a partnership may not sue or be sued as such. On the contrary, the Uniform Partnership Act is not only silent on the subject, but leaves the foregoing rule in effect by specifically providing that, in any case not covered by the Act, "the rules of law and equity, including the law merchant, shall govern." Section 33–41–50, 1976 Code of Laws. The lower court should have sustained the demurrer. Judgment is accordingly reversed.

Questions

1. What are the relative merits and demerits of the entity and aggregate theories of partnership?

2. What is the effect of the court's ruling in this case on the course of this lawsuit?

Sources of Law

The law concerning partnerships is found primarily in the law of *contracts* and the law of *agency*. For the most part, the rights and obligations of the partners, among themselves, can be regulated by agreement. Relations between the partnership and third persons, however, are controlled largely by the law of agency. In addition, the Uniform Partnership Act has been adopted by most states (except Georgia, Louisiana, and Mississippi). This act establishes the general structure for partnership law, and fills in when there is no agreement to the contrary. Also, the act provides for each state's power to pass *additional*, although presumably not contradictory, laws. Limited partnerships, discussed in Chapter 39, also are affected by the *Uniform Limited Partnership Act* and the *Revised Uniform Limited Partnership Act*.

CREATION OF A PARTNERSHIP

No particular legal formalities are required for the formation of a partnership. Since the question of whether a partnership has been created is one of fact, the UPA establishes some rules for guidance.

Rules for Determining Existence

Section 6 of the UPA provides that, with the exception of circumstances that would require the application of the doctrine of estoppel, "persons who are not partners as to each other are not partners as to third persons." That is, the existence of a partnership requires that the parties objectively intended to be partners. One person would not be able to bind another person to a third party unless the other person voluntarily has granted him authority to do so. This is a basic tenet of agency law.

Second, the existence of a partnership is not established by the fact that two or more people are co-owners of property. This is true even though they may share in the profits from the property. A partnership is created only if the co-owners intend to operate a *business* for profit. Something more than co-ownership and the sharing of profits from property must appear in order to satisfy this requirement.

Third, receipt by a person of a share of the profits of a business is *prima facie* evidence that she is a partner, except when the share is received in payment: (1) of a debt, (2) as wages or rent, (3) as an annuity to a window or representative of a deceased partner, (4) as interest on a loan, or (5) as consideration for the sale of good-will or other property to the business. These, standing alone or in combination, would not be indicative of a continuing intent to join together to conduct business. The following case addresses the question of whether a particular transaction created a partnership.

P & M CATTLE CO. v. HOLLER
559 P.2d 1019 (Wyo. 1977)

This was an action by P & M Cattle Co., a partnership (Plaintiff/Appellant) against Rusty Holler (Defendant/Appellee) to recover reimbursement for a share of losses sustained by a joint venture of the parties. Plaintiff contended their relationship should be treated as a partnership, and entered into evidence the following written agreement:

2-23-1971

Contract-Rusty Holler (60 Bar Ranch)—L. W. Maxfield and Bill Poage
Rusty to furnish grass for est 1000 yr st and 21 heifers
—"Maxfield & Poage to furnish money for cattle plus trucking & salt—and max of $300.00 per month for labor
Rusty to take cattle around May 1st and cattle to be sold at a time this fall agreed upon by all parties involved
Cost of cattle plus freight—salt and labor to be first cost
Net money from sale of cattle less first cost to be split 50–50 between Rusty (1/2) and Maxfield and Poage (1/2) (death loss to be part of first cost)

/s/ L. W. Maxfield
/s/ Bill Poage
LM
/s/ Rusty Holler

This contract had been renewed for the years 1972, 1973, and 1974. In 1974, losses were sustained in the amount of $89,000. Plaintiff sued to require Defendant to pay one half, or $44,500.

The trial court entered judgment for Defendant, and Plaintiff appealed. Affirmed.

RAPER, Justice.

In Wyoming, a joint adventure partakes of the nature of a partnership and is governed substantially by the same rules of law, the principal distinction being that a joint adventure usually relates to a single transaction, though it may be continued over a period of years. . . .

Since joint adventures, also frequently referred to as joint ventures, are a species of and governed by the law of partnerships, we must go to the Uniform Partnership Act, Section 17-195, et seq. . . . Section 17-200(1) . . . defines a partnership as follows: "A partnership is an association of two or more persons to carry on as co-owners a business for profit." . . . Section 17-201, . . . lays out the criteria for resolving the question as to whether a partnership obtains:

> In determining whether a partnership exists, these rules shall apply:
>
> **(1)** Except as provided by section 16 [Section 17-210] persons who are not partners as to each other are not partners as to third persons;
> **(2)** Joint tenancy, tenancy in common, tenancy by the entireties, joint property, common property, or part ownership does not of itself establish a partnership, whether such co-owners do or do not share any profits made by the use of the property;
> **(3)** The sharing of gross returns does not of itself establish a partnership, whether or not the person sharing them have a joint or common right or interest in any property from which the returns are derived;
> **(4)** The receipt by a person of a share of the profits of a business is prima facie evidence that he is a partner in the business, but no such inference shall be drawn if such profits were received in payment:
>   (a) As a debt by installments or otherwise,
>   (b) As wages of an employee or rent to a landlord,
>   (c) As an annuity to a widow or representative of a deceased partner,
>   (d) As an interest on a loan, though the amount of payment vary with the profits of the business,
>   (e) As the consideration for sale of the good-will of a business or other property by installments or otherwise.

As can be seen from Section 17-201, an agreement to share profits is far from decisive that a partnership is intended.

As in any contractual relationship, the intent of the parties is controlling. The parties must intend to create the relationship of joint adventure or partnership. . . . Superimposed upon the rule of intent, it is frequently held that where there is no express agreement to form a partnership, the question of whether such a relation exists must be gathered from the conduct, surrounding circumstances and the transactions between the parties. . . .

Since we cannot look at the face of the instrument here and determine whether there is a partnership, it is necessary that we examine into the complete relationship between plaintiff and defendant. . . .

In the first place, the agreement is not labeled a "partnership agreement" nor is the term "partnership" anywhere mentioned within its terms. The plaintiff was itself a partnership made up of two ranchers well acquainted with that arrangement, one of whom drew the contract. From its inception, then, none of the parties ever identified it as such. The pact was conceived in an atmosphere created by defendant's desire to sell grass. The division of losses was never discussed between the parties until the plaintiff delivered the bad news to the defendant following fall cattle sales in 1974. No partnership federal income tax return in any of the years 1971–74 was prepared and submitted to the Internal Revenue Service of the United States. On the income tax returns made by the plaintiff during the period in question, the part of profits paid to the defendant was carried as a business expense listed as "contract feeding." The defendant included such payments on his individual income tax return as a sale of "crops," nor were the cattle grazed on his place by the defendant carried on defendant's income tax return livestock inventory. The livestock were carried on plaintiff's partnership income tax returns. On the check given by plaintiff to defendant in 1973, for defendant's share of profits at the end of the season, it was shown as being for "pasture."

Within the framework of the Uniform Partnership Act, we find rules available to the trial judge to determine that there was no partnership. The division of profits was only a measure—a standard of payment by plaintiff to defendant in discharge of a debt for services and grass under Section 17-201(4)(a) or in payment to defendant for wages of an employee in caring for the cattle while on his ranch and rent to him as landlord for his pasture under Section 17-201(4)(b) or sale of grass as personal property under Section 17-201(4)(e) or through a combination of those lettered subsections for wages and rent or sale of property. We need not determine precisely what it was as long it was as outside the pale of partnership. We are satisfied that no partnership was intended. The agreement was only an apparatus to pay defendant for his grass and services and we return to its terms after reconnoitering the outer regions.

Questions

1. Do you agree with the court's interpretation of the transaction? Why or why not?
2. What kinds of facts would have to be present to convince the court that a partnership had been formed?

INTENT (CONSENT). As alluded to in the case, the intent to be partners is *the* critical factor in the creation of any partnership. This is true primarily because every partnership creates an agency relationship. Each partner is both the principal and the agent of the other partners. The act of each binds himself, and binds the others under agency law. In most cases the law will not impose this vicarious liability without the consent of the person to be bound. The required consent may be manifested in writing, orally, by implication, or by some combination of these, but it *must* be present. This is implicit in the definition of a partnership as "an association."

CARRYING ON BUSINESS. The term *business* is defined in Section 2 of the UPA as including "every trade, occupation, or profession." The requirement that the association be for the purpose of carrying on business may include a broad range of activities, including manufacturing, wholesaling, retailing, and the sale of services. However, if

Requirements for creation of a partnership

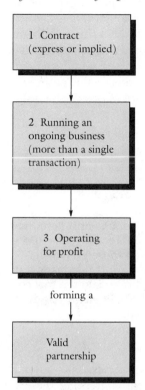

two or more people join together for the purpose of combining their purchasing power, acquiring property for the purpose of investment only, or conducting a single transaction, the association is unlikely to be found to be a partnership. More likely these would be considered joint ventures or syndicates. For example, suppose the independent grocers in an area combined to form a cooperative association for the purpose of acquiring stock in trade in bulk, at a lower price. Presumably this would not be considered a partnership. However, it might become one if they began to market this "buying-power service" to other grocers. Two individuals who combined their assets to build a shopping center probably would not be a partnership if their objective was to sell the completed property, either as a package or unit by unit.

However, it probably would become a partnership if they continued their association to manage the property.

FOR PROFIT.   Very simply, a not-for-profit association is *not* considered to be a partnership. The requirement that the association be for the purpose of conducting a "business" seems to connote "for profit." Moreover, the drafters of the UPA clearly intended that its provisions apply only to commercial ventures. Perhaps it was felt that the characteristics of the not-for-profit sector might be unique. In any case, it is certain that the need for uniform regulation in the for-profit sector was much greater. Two or more persons still can join together for the purpose of operating a not-for-profit venture. The fact that probably the association is not technically a "partnership" is of no real legal importance to the venture or to its associates.

Partnership by Estoppel

The question whether someone who is not actually a partner can be held liable for partnership transactions has been the subject of doubt and conflicting case decisions for some time. Generally, courts were somewhat liberal in finding liability on the basis of "ostensible" agency. This liability frequently was extended to situations in which a person was represented to be a partner by a member of the partnership and took no steps to correct the impression in the mind of the third person to whom the representation was made.

The Uniform Partnership Act limits the circumstances in which this liability may be found. Section 7(1) states that "persons who are not partners as to each other are not partners as to third persons." However, there is a proviso. Section 16 provides that if a person *consents* to being held out as a partner, she may be liable as a **partner by estoppel.** This liability may extend to third persons to whom the representation was made and who, in reliance, dealt with the partnership. It also can extend to persons to whom the representation was not communicated if there has been consent to a *public* representation. Further, any partners making a representation or *consenting* to it may be bound by the acts of the person held out to be a partner.

The key to liability, in addition to there being a representation, is the factor of consent. Thus, liability has been extended to cover public representations. However, it apparently no longer covers situations in which a representation has been made and, although this is known to the person represented to be a partner, that person takes no action to correct the problem. Under these circumstances, the required consent seems to be lacking, and this is the position taken in cases under the UPA. Consider the following case.

MONTANTA FARM SERVICE CO. v. MARQUART
176 Mont. 357, 578 P.2d 315 (1978)

This was an action by Montana Farm Service Co. (Plaintiff/Respondent) against Leo Marquart and Larry Roth dba Southside Tire and Clinic (Defendants/Appellants) for the price of merchandise delivered to Defendants.

The facts were in dispute, and on appeal the court first made a statement of the findings upon which the trial decision had rested. In the trial court, Plaintiff had been awarded judgment in the sum of $5301.27 plus attorney fees of $1500 and costs. Defendants then appealed. Affirmed.

HASWELL, Chief Justice.

[Finding a partnership by estoppel.] We recount the evidence supporting the findings: the testimony of Plaintiff's agent, Burwell, concerning the execution of the agreements; his testimony that defendant Marquart stated that he and defendant Roth were going into a joint venture as the service agent for plaintiff; the agreements themselves which both defendants signed on the same signature line and next to each other's signature; and defendant Marquart's testimony that he had taken over the property owned by defendant Roth, which indicates some business dealing between the two men. The only evidence presented by defendants against the court's findings was their own testimony and a calendar which was introduced into evidence. The calendar read that defendant Roth was the owner and manager of Southside Tire and Clinic.

In making its findings, the District Court must have chosen to believe plaintiff's version of the facts concerning the execution of the agreements, rather than the version presented by defendants. The weight of the evidence and credibility of witnesses, where the evidence is conflicting, is a matter for the trial court's determination in a nonjury case. . . . Therefore, we cannot readjudicate defendants' version of the facts.

In our view the evidence indicates that a partnership existed between the defendants as far as their relationship with the plaintiff is concerned. One may become a partner of a firm, as to third persons, without intending to, by words spoken or written or by conduct, and thereby become liable to those who have, on the faith thereof, given credit to the actual or apparent partnership. . . . We hold then that defendant Marquart, by signing the service agency agreement and never having his name removed from it, is liable to plaintiff for the merchandise delivered to Southside Tire and Clinic.

Question

1. Do you think sufficient consent existed in this case to find a partnership by estoppel?
2. What evil does the rule of partnership by estoppel seek to prevent?

CAPACITY TO BE A PARTNER

Assuming other requirements are met, there is no requirement that partners possess any particular degree of capacity. This is because, for most purposes, a partnership is considered to be an agency relationship among the partners, and no particular capacity is required to be either a principal or an agent. Of course, a partner, regardless of his *own* capacity, can bind another partner to an authorized transaction only to the extent that the other partner's own capacity would allow her to bind herself. Thus, a partnership transaction may be void or voidable as to a particular partner, depending on that partner's own capacity, but regardless of the capacity of the partner who acted as her agent. For example, suppose a minor and an adult form a partnership, and the minor acts, with authority, on behalf of the partnership. Her act will bind the adult partner, but not herself.

Incompetent Partners

An incompetent partner may bind his partners to an authorized transaction, but cannot bind himself or be bound by even the "authorized" acts of his partners. The acts of incompetent persons, either directly or through an agent, generally are declared void by statute. Also, Section 32(1)(a) of the Uniform Partnership Act provides that a court shall decree a dissolution of a partnership on application of a partner who has been declared incompetent by a court. Until that adjudication, although the partner may be insane, his liability is not governed by the principles applicable to incompetency.

Insane Partners

Texts treating the liabilities of partners are conspicuously silent on the subject of partners who are insane but have not yet been adjudicated incompetent. By analogy to the theory of liability in cases involving an insane person who becomes a party to a contract, the best rules seem to be as follows:

1. As to transactions directly and individually negotiated or authorized by an insane partner, they should be voidable by that partner but not by the other partners.
2. If the insane partner was dealt with fairly and in good faith, or if the transaction actually was negotiated by a sane partner, the insane partner's right to avoid should be conditioned on his ability to do so without injury to the the rights of the other party to the contract.

Minor Partners

Although the law has spoken more directly and frequently on the liability of minor partners, the decisions have not been consistent. There is agreement that, absent a statute to the contrary (such a statute would be permitted by the UPA), a minor partner is allowed to avoid partnership contracts. Some courts have ruled that this right is absolute, but most place conditions on its exercise. For example, there is general agreement that a minor partner, upon withdrawing from the partnership, can withdraw her capital contributions only to the extent that the rights of third-party creditors will not be injured. Otherwise, most courts allow the minor to withdraw her investment, sharing proportionately in the profits of the partnership to the date of withdrawal, without sharing in the losses.

Corporate Partners

Whether a corporation can be a partner is a prime subject for theoretical discussion. Although most states permit corporate partners, a few prohibit them, but such a prohibition usually is of little or no consequence. Courts in those jurisdictions typically characterize the corporations as members of joint ventures. Even when there is no general bar

to corporate partners, there is a further question of whether the powers of the individual corporation as set out in its charter and by the state's corporation law permit the corporation to be a partner. The Model Business Corporation Act generally empowers corporations to enter into contracts and to incur liability. This presumably would authorize a corporation to incur partnership liability in the absence of specific provisions to the contrary in the articles of incorporation. Also, under the UPA, the term *person* in Section 2 includes corporations. Section 6(1) of the act then defines a partnership as "an association of two or more *persons* [emphasis added]."

In addition to natural persons and business corporations, other entities may qualify as partners. Consider the following case in which the court was faced with the question of whether the state of New Jersey and the city of Atlantic City were partners concerning a federal funds grant.

STATE v. ATLANTIC CITY
23 N.J. 337, 129 A.2d 293 (1957)

This was an action by the state of New Jersey (Plaintiff/Appellant) against the city of Atlantic City, New Jersey (Defendant/Appellee) to require the city to share federal funds it had received.

Through a series of statutes, Plaintiff determined to provide funds to Defendant to combat beach erosion. The statutes provided that Plaintiff would pay not more than 50 percent, and Defendant would pay the remaining 50 percent of the costs of the projects. Defendant applied for federal funds for its project and was granted $580,213.94—approximately one-third of the total cost. Plaintiff contended that part of the federal funds should be shared with it, and Defendant refused.

The trial court granted judgment for Defendant, and Plaintiff appealed. Reversed.

VANDERBILT, C. J.

A review of the relations between the State and Atlantic City (especially in the light of the earlier statutes which cast the entire responsibility for protection against beach erosion on the municipality) reveals very clearly that the Legislature never intended that the State would become responsible for more than one-half of the cost of the improvement. Nor did the Legislature ever intend that Atlantic City should pay less than one-half of the cost of the improvement. There is no indication of ambiguity in the statutes under review on this fundamental point.

Moreover, if the parties to the arrangement had been private parties, and not the State and one of its political subdivisions, they would clearly have been treated as partners, with an obligation on the part of the city of Atlantic City to account to the State for the proportion of the fund received by it from the Federal Government, which would otherwise reduce its payment below the 50% it had obligated itself to pay to the State. A partner cannot be permitted to enrich himself at the expense of his partner; citation of authority on such an elementary point is unnecessary.

There is no need to catalogue all the principles of partnership law. It need only be pointed out that in every such relationship the act of one of the parties in the course of and in furtherance of the joint undertaking is an act for the benefit of all the parties to the relationship. Neither party will be permitted to use the joint enterprise to benefit himself to the exclusion of his partner except by consent of the latter.

The doctrine of accountability applies with even greater force here, first, because parties to the transaction are not merely private parties, but a sovereign state on the one side and, on the other, one of its political subdivisions which owes not only its life but its continued existence and the terms on which it shall live to the State. Secondly, the State has here assumed as a grant or gratuity a limited obligation of 50% of the cost to particular beach protection projects conditioned on a like payment toward the cost by Atlantic City. As between the sovereign state and one of its political subdivisions, any doubt should be construed in favor of the sovereign state. Where the payment by the sovereign state to its political subdivision is a mere gratuity, that construction should be adopted which does not extend the scope of the gratuity beyond its obvious intent. Atlantic City cannot be permitted by any maneuver against its partner, the sovereign state, to reduce its liability for these improvements from one-half to one-sixth of the cost thereof. . . .

The State of New Jersey, like the city of Atlantic City, was one of the class of parties to be benefited by the federal grants, and there is no indication of any intention on the part of the Federal Government to favor one interest as against the other. The federal grant-in-aid was to the total project, leaving the balance to be provided for by State and for local interests. Thus, when the city applied for all the federal aid which was available to both, it precluded the State from obtaining any of the federal aid on the same project.

Questions

1. Do you agree with the decision of the court in this case? Why or why not?
2. Is the finding that the state should share in the grant really founded on the law of partnership, or is partnership law used only as an analogy?

GENERAL LIABILITY OF PARTNERS

The authorized transactions of any partner render all partners jointly liable. Although the partnership may not be treated as an entity for liability purposes, the partners are treated as a unit, rather than as individuals, in assessing responsibility. Joint liability means that a plaintiff may take judgment against all of the partners. This liability generally extends to their personal assets as well as their business assets. However, a partner may assume complete liability to perform partnership contracts, as by a separate collateral contract or contract of guarantee. Also, a partner may be liable, both jointly *and severally,* in situations in which the partnership is bound by the wrongful act, or a breach of trust, by one of the partners. Several liability means that a plaintiff may take judgment against only one of the partners, and not the other.

Partner's Wrongful Act

A partner who, while in the course and scope of transacting the partnership's authorized business, commits a tort, such as committing fraud or negligently causing physical injury to someone, renders himself and the other partners both jointly and severally liable to the injured third party, except when the injured party is also a member of the same partnership. That means the injured party may recover for her injuries against the partners jointly or against any one of them. This is consistent with the general principles of agency law and with the conclusive presumption that each partner has the right to control the details of the performance of partnership duties by the other partners.

Criminal acts of one partner, even in the course and scope of the performance of partnership business, usually will not impose vicarious criminal liability on his partners. There are, however, some statutory exceptions, and currently there is increasing pressure to impose vicarious criminal liability on partnerships and corporations. For example, in *United States v. Park,* Acme Markets, Inc. was charged with a criminal violation of the Food, Drug and Cosmetics Act for maintaining an unsanitary food-storage warehouse. Acme pleaded guilty. Its president, Park, who also was charged, contested his conviction on appeal. The Supreme Court's opinion discussed corporate criminal liability as a new trend. Many modern criminal codes define the term *person* to include

both partnerships and corporations, so the possibility already exists in these jurisdictions. Courts continue to be hesitant, however, to find that the requisite *mens rea* (criminal intent) exists vicariously. For example, when Ford Motor Company was charged criminally for the deaths of passengers of a Pinto when the car burst into flames upon being hit in the rear, an Indiana court dismissed the charge after some two weeks of argument. The judge found no basis for imparting the criminal intent of agents and employees to their corporations. The requirement of criminal intent is discussed more fully in Chapter 4.

Partner's Breach of Trust

If a third party pays over money or property to a partner who is acting in the course and scope of her apparently authorized duties for the partnership, the partners are jointly and severally liable if it is misappropriated by that partner. In other words, the liability of the third party concerning the underlying transaction is discharged. The same is true if the money or property is paid into the custody of the partnership and later is misappropriated by one of the partners. Again, this is consistent with general principles of agency law.

Partner's Liability for Admissions

An admission or representation of one of the partners concerning partnership affairs may be used as evidence against both himself and other partners, so long as he was acting within the scope of his authority. However, this rule does not apply to a statement that the speaker is a partner, or is authorized to conduct particular business. It pertains only when a partner actually is acting within the course and scope of some existing authority.

Knowledge or Notice to a Partner

Notice to a partner relating to partnership affairs, and the knowledge of a partner acting in regard to that particular matter, will operate as notice or knowledge to the entire partnership. This is true even of knowledge acquired before becoming a partner if it is still in the mind of the partner. The same is true of notice or knowledge of any matters that reasonably could be expected to be communicated to the partnership. The only exception to this rule is in situations involving fraud on the partnership committed by or with the consent of the partner. This exception is based on the reality that a partner committing fraud on the partnership is not going to communicate that fact to the partnership. Consider the following case.

HENRY v. UNITED STATES
424 F.2d 677 (5th Cir. 1970)

This was an action by the United States government (Plaintiff/Appellee) against Dennis A. Henry and Anne Durrah, individually and as partners of Arawak Chemical Company (Defendants/Appellants), to recover under the False Claims Act for fraudulent sales of disinfectant to the General Services Administration.

Henry ran the business of the partnership, and Durrah was inactive. During the course of selling pine oil disinfectant to the General Services Administration, Henry knowingly and fraudulently shipped some inferior product. This was done without the knowledge or participation of Durrah.

The trial court awarded Plaintiff $20,166.58 (twice the amount fraudulently billed and $2000 for each of the five invoices). The judgment was against Defendant partnership and each of the partners individually. Defendant Durrah appealed, contending she should not be held individually liable. Affirmed in part and reversed in part.

SIMPSON, Circuit Judge.

The troublesome aspect of this appeal is the question of whether the False Claims Act can be properly applied to an inactive partner who had no knowledge of and did not participate in the fraudulent scheme, as was the case with Anne Durrah. The reported cases supply no definitive answer to the proposition.

The False Claims Act is confined to those persons who make or cause to be made a claim "knowing such claim to be false, fictitious, or fraudulent" or who knowingly "enters into any agreement combination, or conspiracy to defraud the Government . . . by obtaining . . . the payment . . . of any false or fraudulent claim." Knowledge of the fraud then is an essential element of the statute.

The penalty provisions of the statute are harsh. As a result, this Circuit has been reluctant to impute knowledge of fraud to unknowing participants. In United States v. Priola, . . . the Court refused to impute guilty knowledge to an unknowing partner and found that the inactive partner could not be held to be individually liable for the government's claim brought under the False Claims Act. In that case, the government brought suit against the appellant individually and not against the partnership, as is the situation in our case. In United States v. Ridglea State Bank, . . . this Court, in a False Claims Act case, refused to impute the fraud of a corporate employee to an innocent and unsuspecting corporation. The refusal to impute was based on the conclusion that the corporation did not benefit from the fraud.

We conclude that the partnership assets can be reached because the fraud was perpetrated by one of the partners on behalf of the partnership. Anne Durrah's personal assets may not be used to satisfy the judgment under the False Claims Act because she in no way contributed to the fraud and had no knowledge of it.

The United States urges that if False Claims Act claim fails, the pleadings asserted a common law action for fraud and that under the common law, both Georgia and federal, an inactive partner is individually liable for the actual damages sustained. . . . The point is well taken. The district court found, as above set forth, the actual damages amounted to $5083.29. The proof was sufficient to support common law action for fraud, and this relief should be granted to the government, regardless of consistency, Rule 8(e) (2), F.R.Civ.P, and even though not specifically demanded by the pleadings, Rule 54(c), F.R.Civ.P.

The case is affirmed in part and reversed and remanded in part. Upon remand the district court is directed to vacate the judgment against Anne Durrah individually except for actual damages in the amount of $5083.29. The judgment against the partnership and against Dennis A. Henry is affirmed.

Questions

1. Why did the court treat Durrah differently under the False Claims Act than it did under the common law?

2. Is it fair to hold a partner liable for the wrongful act of another partner when the former had no knowledge of, and therefore no ability to stop, the latter's conduct? What is your reasoning?

Liability of an Incoming Partner

An incoming partner assumes liability for all partnership obligations, even those incurred by the partnership prior to her admission as a partner. However, her liability for prior obligations is limited to the amount of her investment in the partnership. This liability cannot be altered as to third persons by any agreement among the partners. However, the incoming partner's liability can be altered by such agreement in terms of redistributing liability, as among the partners. For example, the existing partners, or any of them, may agree to indemnify the incoming partner concerning prior obligations to third persons.

PROPERTY OF THE PARTNERSHIP

Sometimes it is necessary to determine which property used in connection with, or for the bene-

fit of, a partnership is partnership property. This may be important especially upon dissolution of the partnership, when the remaining partnership property is divided by the partners.

Section 8 of the Uniform Partnership Act provides that **partnership property** includes all property originally brought into the partnership stock or subsequently acquired, by purchase or otherwise, on account of the partnership. Whether or not a particular piece of property is partnership property is a question of fact. The extent to which it is identified as partnership property, as by representations of its status or the extent of its use for partnership purposes, is very relevant to the determination. For example, a vehicle with the partnership name painted on the side, or painted with unusual designs or colors and used primarily on partnership business—especially if used first by one partner, then by another—is likely to be classified as partnership property. The fact that title to the property was taken or held in the partnership name, or was purchased with partnership funds, obviously is very persuasive.

The effect of conveyance of partnership property is controlled by Sections 9(1) and 10 of the Uniform Partnership Act. The former provides that each partner is an agent of the partnership and, among other things, when a partner conveys partnership property for apparently carrying on partnership business in the usual way, the partnership is bound by the transfer unless the partner had no authority and this fact was known to the person with whom the partner was dealing.

In the case of real property, the partnership is bound by a conveyance, as provided in Section 9(1), if it is:

1. held in the partnership name and the con-

veyance is by a partner either in the name of the partnership or in his own name; or

2. held in the names of one or more but not all of the partners, the record does not disclose the partnership interest, and the conveyance is in the names of the partner in whose name the title stands; or

3. held in the names of one or more or all of the partners, or the name of a third person in trust for the partnership, and the conveyance is by a partner in his own name or the name of the partnership.

Further, the partnership is bound by a conveyance of real estate held in the partnership name and conveyed by a partner in the partnership name, and by any conveyance as in (2) above, if the property subsequently is transferred to a person who takes it for value and without notice that the transferring partner was without authority. Consider the following case.

GAULDIN v. CORN
595 S.W.2d 329 (Mo.App. 1980)

This was an action by Claude Gauldin (Plaintiff/Appellant) against Joe Corn (Defendant/Respondent) for dissolution and accounting of a partnership. For a period the parties had operated a business as a partnership, raising hogs and cattle on 25 acres of an 83-acre tract owned by Defendant. During that time, they expended substantial sums of partnership money in maintaining and improving the land, including building a machine shed at a cost of $2487.50 and adding a cargill (hog house) at a cost of $8000. Upon dissolution of the partnership they settled the distribution of "movable assets." The shed and cargill were not movable. Defendant contended they became his property, as improvements to his land, upon dissolution of the partnership. Plaintiff contended they were partnership property, and that he was entitled to one-half of their value. There was no partnership agreement.

The trial court entered judgment for Defendant, and Plaintiff appealed. Reversed and remanded with directions.

GREENE, Justice.

We agree with the court in Re Condemnation of Land for Spring Valley Park, . . . that the rule is "well-established" that improvements made upon lands owned by one partner, if made with partnership funds for purposes of partnership business, are the personal property of the partnership, and the non-landowning partner is entitled to his proportionate share of their value. In so doing, we reject, as inappropriate, the reasoning set out in Knauss. Grissom, Flint, and the cases following them, reflect a more fair and equitable rule which is consistent with the language contained in Missouri's Uniform Partnership Law, Section 358.010 et seq., RSMo 1978. Section 358.080, RSMo 1978, states, in part:

1. *All property* originally brought into the partnership stock or *subsequently acquired by purchase or otherwise, on account of the partnership is partnership property.*
2. *Unless the contrary intention appears,* property acquired with partnership funds is partnership property. (emphasis added)

It is clear from the cases, which we have cited, that the general rule, governing the disposition of improvements upon dissolution of a partnership, is activated only where, as here, there is no agreement between the partners which controls such disposition. It matters not that the landowning partner contributed the use of his land to the partnership, that the non-landowning partner knew that the improvements, when made, could not be removed from the land, or that a joint owner with the landowning partner was not joined in the suit for dissolution and accounting of the partnership. Thus the trial court, after finding that the partners had no agreement regarding the disposition of fixed assets upon dissolution of the partnership, should have applied the rule, that we have approved here, and should have awarded plaintiff his proportionate share of the value of the improvements at the time of dissolution of the partnership.

We therefore reverse the judgment of the trial court awarding plaintiff nothing, and remand with directions to the trial court to determine, from the record, the value of the Cargill unit and the barn at the time of dissolution of the partnership, that the trial court reopen the record for the purpose of hearing testimony on that issue only, and to thereafter enter a judgment awarding plaintiff his proportionate share (one-half) of their value.

Questions

1. Do you think the result in this case is fair? Does it recognize the contribution given by the defendant in the form of the use of his land? If not, how could that be done?
2. Are there other forms of "property" that should be valued upon dissolution and that might cause difficulty?

DURATION OF A PARTNERSHIP

For the purpose of continuing in business, a partnership generally is not considered a separate legal entity. Its existence depends on the continuation of its individual partners, so the death or the withdrawal of any partner will cause the partnership to terminate. The same is true if a new partner is admitted. However, Section 27(1) of the Uniform Partnership Act provides that the assignment by a partner of his or her interest in the partnership does not, of itself, cause termination. The theory is that an assignment neither bestows partnership rights in management to the assignee, nor relieves the assignor of his or her obligations to either the partnership or to third persons dealing with the partnership. The only thing it achieves is that the assignee becomes entitled to the assignor's share of profits and, upon dissolution, to that share of partnership property.

Partnerships very frequently are formed for specific periods of time fixed by the partnership agreement. But if the partners choose to do so, they may continue the partnership beyond the end of the term. This may be done without express agreement, and the partnership simply becomes one at will. Under these circumstances, the partners remain liable to the same extent as they were at the end of the term. The continuation of the partnership's business, without settlement or liquidation of its affairs, is *prima facie* evidence of the continuation of the partnership.

SUMMARY

A partnership is "an association of two or more persons to carry on a business for profit." Its creation requires no formalities, and may be found to exist by implication. In effect, a partnership is much like the joinder of two or more individual proprietorships to carry out a single business. For most purposes, a partnership is considered to exist only through its partners, not being an entity itself; however, under the Uniform Partnership Act, a partnership can hold title to and transfer real estate under the partnership name.

Partnership law is derived primarily from the law of contracts and the law of agency. In addition, most states have enacted special legislation to govern partnerships, including the Uniform Partnership Act, the Uniform Limited Partnership Act, and the Revised Uniform Limited Partnership Act.

Generally, three factors are required to bring a partnership into existence. First, the parties must intend to form a partnership. Intent is measured objectively, however, and will be found to exist any time the parties—by words, conduct, or a combination of these—objectively manifest their consent to the formation of a partnership. Second, they must intend to carry on a business. That is, they have joined together to operate a continuing business, not just to consummate one or a few transactions, or to hold property for investment. Third, the venture must be one for profit. A nonprofit association cannot be a partnership.

No particular requirement exists concerning a person's capacity to be a partner. General rules of agency and contract law govern. Therefore, a person's capacity to do business is neither increased nor decreased by the fact that he is a partner. The contractual obligations of a minor partner still are voidable, and those of an incompetent partner are void. However, a few jurisdictions have special rules governing these liabilities.

General rules of agency law govern a partnership's tort and criminal liability. Partners generally are liable, jointly and severally, for any torts committed by a partner in the course and scope of her duties for the partnership. With few exceptions, however, partners are not liable vicariously for crimes committed by their partners, although there is a trend toward the creation of more such liability by statute.

Partnership property includes all property brought into partnership stock, and all property thereafter acquired on account of the partnership. The property may be held in the partnership name, in the names of the partners as co-owners, or in the name of one of the partners individually. Exactly what property is included as partnership property is a question of fact, and individual property may become partnership property if it is represented as such by the nature of its use and, sometimes, even by its appearance.

The duration of a partnership normally is contingent on the continued existence of all of the partners and their consent to continue as partners. Many times the partnership agreement specifies a fixed period of time for the partnership to exist. Even in the face of a term, however, intent remains the major factor, and a partnership may continue to exist beyond the time agreed upon. The only requirement is that the partners continue to operate the business as it was before.

KEY TERMS AND CONCEPTS

Uniform Limited Partnership Act (UPA)
partnership
entity theory
aggregate theory
partner by estoppel
partnership property

PROBLEMS

1. Bill Harris and his son, Don, owned a feed store operated as a partnership, Harris & Son. In 1961 they incorporated under the name Harris & Son, Inc. They failed to publish notice of the incorporation in the newspaper, as required by statute. The statute provided that until notice was published, there would be no change in the liabilities of the owners. In 1964, they purchased $963.98 worth of feed from Gay and, when the account was not paid, Gay sought to hold them liable as partners. Should Gay be successful?

2. Herbst and Parzych entered into an agreement concerning a farm owned by Herbst. It provided that Parzych would lease the farm and operate it, and in return Herbst would receive $6000 payable without interest and one-half of net profits. It expressly stated that the parties were not partners. Rosenberger sold large quantities of grain, feed, and fertilizer to the farm, and when the account was not paid he sought to charge Herbst as a partner on the basis that he shared in the profits. Should Herbst be considered a partner?

3. Under what circumstances may a partnership be treated as an entity to sue in its own name?

4. Jenkins operated 30 trucks for the purpose of hauling cattle. Some of the trucks were leased from Lewis, under an agreement providing that Lewis was to receive a share of gross profits. Should Jenkins and Lewis be considered partners?

5. After obtaining a judgment against a number of partners of a partnership, Port Richey Shopping Center, the plaintiff instructed the sheriff to seize certain property of the partnership to pay the judgment. Port Richey resisted the levy as improper. Is Port Richey correct?

6. Hogan, a member of a partnership together with Ward and Cipullo, padded the payrolls of certain ships for the purpose of reducing the federal tax liability of the partners. Charges of defrauding the government were filed against the partnership, and upon conviction the partnership was assessed a substantial fine. Ward and Cipullo appealed, contending that since they did not know of Hogan's activities, the partnership should not have been charged. Are they correct?

7. W. A. McMichaels Construction Company D & W Properties, Inc. were partners in a land development company. At one point, D & W obtained a profitable sublease on certain property. Without revealing this, D & W purchased McMichaels's interest. When McMichaels learned of this, he sued to recover additional compensation for his one-half interest. Is McMichaels entitled to recover?

8. Davis and Emery formed a partnership, each agreeing to put in $5000 for partnership capital. Emery, a minor, contributed $1500 before she gave notice that she was withdrawing, while still a minor. In the meantime, however, the partnership had accumulated debt of $9000 to Phillips. Phillips sued the partnership and the partners individually. To what extent is Emery liable?

9. Birch, a member of a partnership, appropriated partnership funds for his own use. He was charged with embezzlement. Birch defended on the ground that a partner cannot be guilty of embezzling the funds of his partnership. Was Birch correct?

10. In order to collect a debt owed by a partnership, Horn's Crane Service filed suit against Prior, one of the partners, to hold her liable individually. Prior contended she should be liable individually only if partnership assets were inadequate to pay the debt. Is Prior correct?

Chapter | 37

Partnerships: Operation

PARTNERS AS AGENTS OF A PARTNERSHIP

A partnership is not a natural person and usually is considered to have no existence independent of the partners who own and operate it. The functioning of a partnership comes under agency principles, as discussed in Chapters 31 and 32.

General Agency Powers

Section 9(1) of the Uniform Partnership Act provides that each partner is the agent of the partnership for the purpose of its business. In other words, each partner is the agent of all of the other partners. The fact that she is a partner makes her a general (as opposed to a special) agent, and thereby she is vested with **apparent authority** to carry on the business of the partnership as long as it is done in the usual way. So acting, she binds the partnership, which means herself and the other partners. This authority may be exercised by executing agreements with third parties in the partnership name, or even in her own name. All that is necessary is a determination that the third person reasonably understood that the transaction was entered into on behalf of the partnership. This is true even though the partner may have had no actual (express or implied) authority to bind the partnership, as long as the third party had no knowledge of the lack of authorization. However, a partner's act that is not *apparently* in furtherance of the partnership business, or is not undertaken in the organization's usual way, does not bind the partnership unless it actually is authorized by the other partners. The question of apparent authority is considered in the following case.

HODGE v. GARRETT
101 Idaho 397, 614 P.2d 420 (1980)

This was an action by Bill Hodge (Plaintiff/Respondent) against Louise A. Garrett and others individually and as partners of Pay-Ont Drive-in Theater (Defendants/ Appellants) for specific performance of a contract to sell land. Plaintiff and Rex E. Voeller, managing partner of Defendant partnership, entered into a contract under the terms of which Voeller agreed, on behalf of the partnership, to sell a tract of partnership land to Plaintiff. The contract was signed in the name of the partnership. Defendants contended that Voeller was not authorized, and thus the contract was not binding on the partnership or its other partners.

The trial court found for Plaintiff, and Defendants appealed. Reversed.

BISTLINE, Justice.

At common law one partner could not, "without the concurrence of his copartners, convey away the real estate of the partnership, bind his partners by a deed, or transfer the title and interest of his copartners in the firm real estate." 60 Am.Jur. 2d Partnership Section 149 (1972) (footnotes omitted). This rule was changed by the adoption of the Uniform Partnership Act. The relevant provisions are currently embodied in I.C. Subsection 53-309(1) and 53-310(1) as follows:

I.C. Section 53-310(1): Where title to real property is in the partnership name, any partner may convey title to such property by a conveyance executed in the partnership name; but the partnership may recover such property unless the partner's act binds the partnership under the provisions of paragraph 1 of section 53-309, unless such property has been conveyed by the grantee or a person claiming through such grantee to a holder for value without knowledge that the partner, in making the conveyance, has exceeded his authority.

I.C. Section 53-309(1): Every partner is an agent of the partnership for the purpose of its business, and the act of every partner, including the execution in the partnership name of any instrument, for apparently carrying on in the usual way the business of the partnership of which he is a member binds the partnership, unless the partner so acting has in fact no authority to act for the partnership in the particular matter, and the person with whom he is dealing has knowledge of the fact that he has no such authority.

The meaning of these provisions was stated in one text as follows:

If record title is in the partnership and a partner conveys in the partnership name, legal title passes. But the partnership may recover the property (except from a bona fide purchaser from the grantee) if it can show (A) that the conveying partner was not apparently carrying on business in the usual way or (B) that he had in fact no authority and the grantee had knowledge of the fact. The burden of proof with respect to authority is thus on the partnership. Crane and Bromburg on Partnership Section 50A (1968) (footnotes omitted).

Thus this contract is enforceable if Voeller had the actual authority to sell the property, or, even if Voeller did not have such authority, the contract is still enforceable if the sale was in the usual way of carrying on the business and Hodge did not know that Voeller did not have this authority.

As to the question of actual authority, such authority must affirmatively appear, "for the authority of one partner to make and acknowledge a deed for the firm will not be presumed. . . . 60 Am.Jur.2d Partnership Section 151 (1972). Although such authority may be implied from the nature of the business, id., or from similar past transactions, Smith v. Dixon, . . . nothing in the record in this case indicates that Voeller had express or implied authority to sell real property belonging to the partnership. There is no evidence that Voeller had sold property belonging to the partnership in the past, and obviously the partnership was not engaged in the business of buying and selling real estate.

The next question, since actual authority has not been shown, is whether Voeller was conducting the partnership business in the usual way in selling this parcel of land such that the contract is binding under I.C. Subsection 53-310(1) and 309(1), i.e., whether Voeller had apparent authority. Here the evidence showed, and the trial court found:

> That the defendant, Rex E. Voeller, was one of the original partners of the Pay-Ont Drive-In Theatre; that the other defendants obtained their partnership interest by inheritance upon the death of other original partners; that upon the death of a partner the partnership affairs were not wound up, but instead, the partnership merely continued as before, with the heirs of the deceased partner owning their proportionate share of the partnership interest.
>
> That at the inception of the partnership, and at all times thereafter, Rex E. Voeller was the exclusive, managing partner of the partnership and had the full authority to make all decisions pertaining to the partnership affairs, including paying the bills, preparing profit and loss statements, income tax returns and the ordering of any goods or services necessary to the operation of the business.

The court made no finding that it was customary for Voeller to sell real property, or even personal property, belonging to the partnership. Nor was there any evidence to this effect. Nor did the court discuss whether it was in the usual course of business for the managing partner of a theater to sell real property. Yet the trial court found that Voeller had apparent authority to sell the property. From this it must be inferred that the trial court believed it to be in the usual course of business for a partner who has exclusive control of the partnership business to sell real property belonging to the partnership, where that property is not being used in the partnership business. We cannot agree with this conclusion. For a theater, "carrying on in the usual way the business of the partnership," I.C. Section 53-309(1), means running the operations of the theater; it does not mean selling a parcel of property adjacent to the theater. Here the contract of sale stated that the land belonged to the partnership, and, even if Hodge believed that Voeller as the exclusive manager had authority to transact all business for the firm, Voeller still could not bind the partnership through a unilateral act which was not in the usual business of the partnership. We therefore hold that the trial court erred in holding that this contract was binding on the partnership.

Questions

1. Did the court take too narrow a view of what is "in the usual way" for purposes of binding the partnership?

2. What is the purpose of the "usual way" requirement?

Limitation of a Partner's Authority

Because apparent authority is bestowed on every partner by virtue of Section 9(1) of the UPA, it is necessary that any agreed-upon limitations on that power be communicated to third persons who otherwise would not know of them. For example, one partner may be designated as the sole purchasing agent for the partnership; but anyone selling to any of the other partners, without knowledge of this limitation, is entitled to believe that all partners are authorized to make purchases on behalf of the partnership, and the organization will be bound by the transaction. The same is true in any other case in which the partners wish to place limitations on their usual powers.

TRADING AND NON-TRADING PARTNER-SHIPS. The common law drew an important distinction between trading and non-trading partnerships. A **trading partnership** is one that has the purchase and sale of property as its primary business. The typical retail partnership would be an example. A **non-trading partnership** is one that has the sale of a service as its primary business, such as a professional partnership (law, medicine, or accounting), a real estate agency, or a partnership that operates a theater. Common law courts generally found the apparent authority of partners of a non-trading partnership more limited than that of partners of a trading partnership, particularly regarding the execution of negotiable instruments.

Because of the rise of modern creative financing methods, it is questionable whether a majority of courts today would continue to draw this distinction, at least as completely as the earlier courts

did. But the will of history is a strong one, and even though the matter is nowhere addressed by the UPA, a number of modern cases under the act have recognized the distinction. This seems unsound, because it is not really clear that there is any logical connection between the business of a partnership and its borrowing.

ADDITIONAL LIMITATIONS. The broad grant of apparent authority specifically is limited by Section 9(3) of the UPA, which provides that unless the other partners have agreed, or unless they have abandoned the business, no partner is authorized to enter into certain unusual transactions. These include: (1) assignment of partnership property for certain purposes stated in the act; (2) disposal of the partnership's goodwill; (3) doing any act that would make it impossible to carry on the ordinary business of the partnership; (4) confession of a judgment against the partnership; and (5) the submission of a partnership claim to arbitration or reference. These specific limitations merit consideration especially because they provide some perspective on the tremendous breadth of the grant of apparent authority under Section 9(1).

RIGHTS AND DUTIES AMONG PARTNERS

The rights and duties among the partners are established by the Uniform Partnership Act, but the provisions of the act are subject to any contrary agreement by the partners. As to relations among themselves, the partners are free to agree to almost anything they see fit. Of course, the same is not true when the rights of third parties may be affected.

Because the liability of partners for obligations of the partnership generally is unlimited, and each partner had broad power to bind the partnership, the UPA provides that the unanimous consent of all existing partners is required for the admission of a new partner. Although consent usually is manifested by a vote on the question, formality is not required. Silent acquiescence is sufficient as long as it is unambiguous. Section 18 of the act provides for partnership by estoppel.

Property Rights of the Partners

The property rights of partners fall into three general categories. (1) Each may have rights in specific partnership property, as opposed to (2) an interest in the partnership as a whole. A general partner also has (3) a right (whether or not it is exercised) to participate in the management of the partnership. Of course, this most pointedly distinguishes the general partner from the limited partner, a matter discussed in Chapter 39. The nature and extent of a partner's actual management participation is governed completely by the partnership agreement, and if there is no agreement, then by provisions of the UPA.

The partners hold title to specific partnership property as **tenants in partnership.** This is a hybrid form of tenancy, but is most like a joint tenancy (discussed in Chapter 26) tailored to suit the needs of the partnership form of organization. Each partner has an equal right to possess specific partnership property for partnership purposes, but may not use it for his individual—or any other—purposes without the consent of the other partners. A partner's right in specific property is not assignable, and cannot be taken by attachment or execution, except as part of an assignment by all of the partners or an attachment or levy of execution for partnership debts. Also, neither homestead nor exemption laws apply to partnership property. Finally, partnership property is not subject to any type of family interest such as dower, curtesy, or spousal allowance. No interests attach to this property except those of all of the partners, and upon the death of a partner, title to his interest in partnership property vests in the remaining partners. The only interest a partner has that is freely alienable by assignment, attachment, or levy of execution, and which is taken by his personal representative upon death, is his share of the profits and surplus of the partnership, except that the deceased partner's representative also is entitled to his contribution to the partnership. Consider the following case concerning property rights of partners.

BOHONUS v. AMERCO
124 Ariz. 88, 602 P.2d 469 (1979)

This was an action by Amerco (a corporation) and others (Plaintiffs/Appellees) against Jerry R. Bohonus (Defendant/Appellant) to collect a debt.

After judgment was granted for Plaintiffs, they sought to attach Defendant's interest in a partnership and have the partnership property sold to pay the judgment. The trial court ordered the sale and that part of the judgment was appealed by defendant. Reversed and remanded.

HAYS, Justice.

The appellee, Amerco, after it secured a judgment against the appellant, Bohonus, sought a charging order from the court pursuant to A.R.S. [Arizona Revised Statutes] Section 19-118, a provision embodied in the Uniform Partnership Act. The court granted the request for a charging order and as a part of that order mandated the sale of appellant's interest in the assets and property of the partnership business, including a spiritous liquor license. The sheriff proceeded with the sale and filed his return.

We now look at the partnership statute. A.R.S. Section 29-225(B) (3) says:

> A partner's right in specific partnership property is not subject to attachment or execution, except on a claim against the partnership. . . .

A.R.S. Section 29-224 sets forth the extent of the property rights of the partner:

> The property rights of a partner are:

1. His rights in specific partnership property.

2. His interest in the partnership.

3. His right to participate in the management.

A.R.S. Section 29-226 defines "a partner's interest":

> A partner's interest in the partnership is his share of the profits and surplus, and the same is personal property.

A.R.S. Section 29-228 reads, in pertinent part, as follows:

> A. On due application to a competent court by any judgment creditor of a partner, the court which entered the judgment, order, or decree, or any other court, may charge the interest of the debtor partner with payment of the unsatisfied amount of such judgment debt with interest thereon; and may then or later appoint a receiver of his share of the profits, and of any other money due or to fall due to him in respect of the partnership, and make all other orders, directions, accounts and inquiries which the debtor partner might have made, or which the circumstances of the case may require.

With the foregoing statutes in mind, we note that it is only a partner's interest in the partnership which may be charged and, in some jurisdictions, sold. It cannot be overemphasized that "interest in the partnership" has a special limited meaning in the context of the Uniform Partnership Act and hence in the Arizona statutes.

The appellee urges that somehow A.R.S. Section 29-228(A), supra, authorizes the sale of partnership assets and property. We note that the record reflects that pursuant to the provisions of the same statute a receiver was appointed in this case. The fact of the receivership provision enforces the conclusion that only the "interest in the partnership" may be charged and we find no provision therein for sale of assets or property of the partnership. Appellee seeks aid and comfort in the language of A.R.S. Section 29-232(B) which provides for dissolution of the partnership upon application of the purchaser of a partner's interest under Subsection 29-227 or 29-228. No decree of dissolution however has been asked for here.

We concur with appellee's position that the charged interest of a debtor-partner can be sold, but further enforcement of the creditor's rights must be pursuant to statute. . . . However, this in nowise makes the sale of the partnership assets valid.

Questions

1. What is the difference between partnership property and a partner's interest in a partnership?
2. How can you sell someone's interest in a partnership? What does the buyer get?

A Partner's Contributions

In addition to the rights already described, a partner retains a general property right in all property contributions made to the partnership. This includes all money and other property contributed by her as capital, and any authorized advances made by her on behalf of the partnership. The partner is entitled to their return upon the termination of the partnership, by her withdrawal or otherwise. This right, of course, is subject to reduction to pay her share of any partnership losses. Unless the partnership agreement specifies to the contrary, each partner is presumed to share in losses in the same proportion as she is entitled to share in gains. If there is no agreement to the contrary, gains and losses are shared equally. Upon repayment of her capital contribution, a partner is entitled to interest on that contribution only from the date that it became payable—not from the time of the contribution.

A Partner's Right to Indemnity and Reimbursement

During the course of conducting partnership affairs, a partner may incur liability of various kinds. The extent to which he is entitled to be indemnified is governed by the general principles of agency law. His rights, in large part, will depend on the nature of the liability.

Liability for torts and criminal acts usually is not subject to the rules requiring indemnity, even if the act was authorized expressly by the other partners. This is true even if the partnership agreement provides to the contrary. The exception would be for some forms of negligence, as long as the partners, in authorizing (if they did so) and committing the negligent act, proceeded in good faith. To allow reimbursement would be in conflict with public policy, which seeks to promote lawful and careful conduct. Of course, insurance usually can be obtained to cover negligent wrongdoing. Also, in a suit by a third party in circumstances in which the tort was authorized by the partners, the partner being sued is entitled to join the other partners as defendants, thereby causing any judgment to be enforceable against all the partners. A court also has the power, in a separate suit by a partner against whom judgment has been entered, to order contribution by the other partners. For the most part, however, a partner should not expect to be reimbursed for his torts or crimes, even if the partnership agreement provides for it.

A partner who is sued individually on an authorized contract entered into on behalf of the partnership, or who makes authorized advances for the benefit of the partnership, is entitled to reimbursement by the partnership less his share of partnership expenses and losses. In addition, he is entitled to interest on any advances from the date he paid the advance. All of this, of course, depends on the partner's having acted on behalf of the partnership, as authorized. He is strictly on his own for any liability incurred for unauthorized acts. Consider the following case.

WHITE v. BROWN
292 F.2d 725 (D.C.Cir. 1961)

This was an action by William A. Brown (Plaintiff/Appellee) against John J. White, Jr. (Defendant/Appellant), a retired partner, to recover the amount allegedly owed by the partnership.

Defendant was a member of a partnership that dissolved upon his retirement in January 1957. The remaining partners agreed to assume all partnership debts and to indemnify Defendant against any liability for them. Plaintiff was notified of this in April 1957. In September 1957, Plaintiff accepted certain promissory notes from the continuing partners to secure existing partnership debts. These partners became insolvent and the notes were not paid. The question before the court was whether Defendant was liable on partnership debts.

The trial court found for Plaintiff and Defendant appealed. Reversed and remanded.

FAHY, Circuit Judge.

While the indemnity agreement could not in itself alter the rights of creditors, yet, whether or not the creditor is a party to the agreement, it constitutes a promise made for his benefit and one of which he as at liberty to take advantage. . . . If appellee assented to the arrangement and adopted the remaining partners as his debtors, then the liability of appellant is at an end. Appellant was discharged from his liability if there was an agreement to that effect between himself, the remaining partners and appellee; and such agreement may be inferred from the course of dealing between the remaining partners and the creditor who has knowledge of the dissolution agreement. . . .

We come to appellant's further contention that he became a surety for the indebtedness to appellee, and that the latter's conduct brought about appellant's discharge from his obligation as surety. . . .

Where a partner withdraws from a partnership under an agreement with his former partners who continue the business that they assume the partnership obligations and will indemnify him, and notice of these arrangements is given a creditor, who acquiesces in the situation, the rule derived from a majority of the decisions appears to be that the withdrawing partner becomes a surety for the payment of the obligation. This occurs by operation of law, that is, by equitable implication, rather than by express agreement between the creditor and the withdrawing partner. . . .

We adopt the rule which appears to have the support of the weight of authority, with a qualification now to be noted. A compensated surety is not discharged by an extension by the creditor of a definite period of time for payment, except to the extent that the surety is harmed by the extension. . . . We think appellant's position is analogous to that of a compensated surety. Before he retired and when the indebtedness was incurred, appellant was personally liable, jointly and severally with his partners. On his retirement he could not fairly be said to have acquired the status of a gratuitous surety, that is, one who obligingly lends his credit to another; so to consider the matter would be to disregard entirely the fact that before his retirement the partnership relation had imposed upon appellant a primary obligation. If he were in the position of a gratuitous surety he would be released by a definite extension of time by the creditor for payment, granted to the principals without his consent, if supported by a consideration. Prejudice need not be shown. But appellant is not in a like position. . . .

On his defense of release first above considered appellant conceded no prejudice, taking the position, we think correctly, that prejudice need not be shown as a condition to that defense. But this concession was not made with respect to his defense of discharge as a surety. In view of the rule we now adopt based on the suretyship relation appellant should be given an opportunity to prove the extent, if any, of prejudice. Otherwise stated on this branch of the case the jury would be entitled to consider on the evidence whether or not the giving of the notes, in terms for value received, was intended to and did constitute a definite extension of time for the payment of the original indebtedness, and, if so, the court should also instruct the jury that this would release the retired partner from obligation to the appellee to the extent, if any, that appellant could show he was prejudiced by the extension.

Questions

1. Why does the court conclude that the defendant has the status of a compensated surety?

2. When the case returns to the trial court, what kind of prejudice might the retired partner be able to show?

A Partner's Rights in Management

One of the fundamental rights of a partner is to share in partnership management. This right is considered of greater importance to a partner than to a shareholder of a corporation because of the unlimited personal liability of partners for partnership obligations. The importance of this position also affects the law concerning limited partnerships, which will be discussed in Chapter 39. Because a limited partner does not have a general partner's unlimited liability, neither can she have a right to participate actively in management decisions.

Section 18(r) of the Uniform Partnership Act provides that all partners have equal rights in the management of a partnership. This, however, is one of the provisions of the UPA that frequently is altered by the partnership agreement. A partner's right to share in management decisions often is limited to the proportion of her investment to the total capital of the partnership, or to her proportionate share of profits and losses. Also, partnership agreements sometimes provide that certain management decisions are within the exclusive domain of one particular partner, or are made under different "voting" rules than are other management decisions. In addition, the UPA provides that certain important decisions may be made, and certain actions taken, only by unanimous consent of all the partners. They are: (1) to do any act that is contrary to the provisions of the partnership agreement; (2) to admit a new partner; (3) to enter a completely new business; (4) to dispose of the partnership's goodwill; (5) to assign partnership property in trust for the benefit of partnership creditors; (6) to confess judgment against the partnership; (7) to submit any partnership claim to binding arbitration; and (8) to undertake any other act that would render the conduct of further partnership business impossible.

A Partner's Right to Compensation

A partner's right to compensation for his personal labors on behalf of a partnership is limited to his right to share in profits. This is true even if he renders services "above and beyond" those anticipated or agreed on among the partners. In this respect, a partner is viewed as an owner, not an employee of the partnership. Of course, as noted, a partner may be entitled to indemnity or reimbursement of expenses incurred in conducting authorized partnership business.

The question of "extra compensation" is another subject frequently provided for in partnership agreements. Many times one partner may take on specific "extra" duties for the partnership. For example, one doctor in a medical partnership may take on responsibility for presenting patient education programs or overseeing the partnership library. Frequently one partner in a law firm may function as "office manager." Sometimes partnerships are formed in which one or more of the partners are investors only and do not participate in management. In these cases, it is not uncommon that profits are shared in proportion to each partner's investment in capital, and the managing partners receive specified salaries in addition to their shares of the profits.

A Partner's Right to an Accounting

A partner's right to an accounting of partnership income, expenses, and assets involves more than the ordinary "keeping of books" by a person assigned to that task. It also involves the right of a partner to receive an explanation of any of the financial affairs of the partnership. This right must be exercised, however, within the limits established by Section 22 of the UPA. In addition to the right of a partner to an accounting upon dissolution of the partnership, this section provides for a right to an accounting (1) if the right exists under the terms of any agreement, (2) if she is excluded wrongfully from the partnership business or possession of its property by her copartners, (3) if any partner is withholding any property or other benefit rightfully belonging to the partnership, in breach of her fiduciary duty, and (4) any other time the circumstances render it just and reasonable. The accounting may be formal or informal depending on what is reasonable under the circumstances, from a complete audit by an outside auditor to the simple production of documents.

A Partner's Fiduciary Duty

Each partner owes a fiduciary duty to his copartners. This is true of any agent, and is required by general principles of agency law. The duty is owed to each copartner unless the copartner is placed on notice to the contrary and, with full knowledge of all relevant facts, has consented to waive the duty.

A partner's fiduciary duty may be defined as "the highest duty of trust and confidence one person can owe to another." The person to whom it is owed is entitled to presume that the party owing it will do nothing to harm him unreasonably. This duty requires that the fiduciary not only will be honest and loyal, but will do nothing that reasonably could raise a suspicion that he *might* be violating his duty. In effect, the existence of the fiduciary duty negates the normal presumption that the relationship of the parties is one at arm's length as prescribed by the adversary nature of ordinary relationships. This duty is breached by the acquiring of any "secret benefit" by a partner during the conduct of partnership affairs. Consider the following case on the fiduciary duty of a partner.

HUFFINGTON v. UPCHURCH
532 S.W.2d 516 (Tex. 1976)

This was an action by Haden J. Upchurch (Plaintiff/Respondent) against Roy M. Huffington and others (Defendants/Petitioners) to impress a constructive trust on a partnership opportunity that he claimed had been misappropriated by Defendant (the managing partner) for his own use.

Defendant was the sole owner of Roy Huffington, Inc. The business of the corporation was to seek investors in oil and gas properties, taking small interests in any resulting leases as a fee for its services. Defendant also entered into a partnership with three of the corporation's employees, Upchurch, Warren, and Scott. The business of the partnership was "to acquire, own, develop and operate oil, gas and mineral leases. . . ." Defendant was the managing partner. In 1968, Defendant negotiated, and eventually acquired for Huffington, Inc., an interest in a highly profitable Indonesian oil and gas project. Plaintiff claimed the interest should belong to the partnership, and Defendant contended it was the property of the corporation.

The trial court granted judgment for Plaintiff, awarding him a 14.285-percent share. The Court of Civil Appeals modified the share to 20 percent and affirmed, and Defendant appealed. The Supreme Court severed the judgment, affirming the judgment for Plaintiff and reversing to consider the percentage share to which he was entitled.

POPE, Justice.

The partnership contract obligated Roy Huffington to "give his attendance to, and to the utmost of his skill and power shall exert himself for, the joint interest, benefit and advantage of said partnership business." In a case of this kind, where the partner who has misappropriated a particular opportunity is also the partner who is primarily responsible for finding financial backing, the burden of proving financial incapability should be on him so as to encourage the exertion of his best efforts. Judge Swan spoke of this aspect of the financial capability defense in Irving Trust Co. v. Deutsch. . . .

> If directors are permitted to justify their conduct on such a theory, there will be a temptation to refrain from exerting their strongest efforts on behalf of the corporation since, if it does not meet the obligations, an opportunity of profit will be open to them personally. . . . Indeed, in the present suit it is at least open to question whether a stronger effort might not have been made on the part of the management to procure for Acoustic the necessary funds or credit.

As managing partner of Huffington Associates, Roy Huffington owed to his copartners one of the highest fiduciary duties recognized in the law. In Smith v. Bolin, . . . this court quoted at length from Justice Cardozo's opinion in Meinhard v. Salmon, 249 N.Y. 458, 164 N.E. 545 (1928) concerning the fiduciary duties of managing partners.

> As managing partner of their partnership entreprise, respondent owed his partners even a greater duty of loyalty than is normally required. In the Meinhard v. Salmon case, supra, the

court said: 'Salmon had put himself in a position in which thought of self was to be renounced, however hard the abnegation. He was much more than a coadventurer. He was a managing coadventurer. . . . For him, and for those like him the rule of undivided loyalty is relentless and supreme.'

Questions

1. Why did the defendant have a greater fiduciary duty to the partnership than to the corporation?

2. Should a managing partner's fiduciary duty be any greater than that of any other partner?

A Partner's Duty to Render Information

Every partner, as an agent of the partnership, has a duty to provide the partnership any information she has relevant to the affairs entrusted to her. This is critically important because, under Section 12 of the UPA, a partnership may be charged with knowing anything of which any partner has knowledge or notice. This even includes information a partner acquired before entering the partnership that is still present in her mind at the time of the transaction in question. The only circumstance in which a partnership is not charged with a partner's notice or knowledge is when a fraud on the partnership is committed by, or with the consent of, the partner having such knowledge.

The question of what constitutes knowledge or notice is discussed in Section 3 of the act. Subsection 1 provides: "A person has 'knowledge' of a fact within the meaning of this act not only when he has actual knowledge thereof, but also when he has knowledge of such other facts as in the circumstances shows bad faith." Subsection 2 provides: "A person has 'notice' of a fact within the meaning of this act when the person who claims the benefit of the notice (a) states the fact to such person, or (b) delivers through the mail, or by any other means of communication, a written statement of the fact to such a person or to a proper person at his place of business or residence." The provisions, taken together, impose a substantial obligation on each partner.

Partnership Records

The partners are under a duty to render, on demand or as provided by the partnership agreement, information of all things affecting the partnership (UPA Sec. 20). In addition, the partnership ordinarily will keep books concerning the details of its day-to-day business. This information is required to be kept at the partnership's principal place of business. Each partner has a right to reasonable access to the books and other information, and may inspect and copy any of them for legitimate purposes. The representative of a deceased partner or one under a legal disability has the same right as a partner. The reasons for providing these rights, of course, is to give each partner the ability to keep track of the business, to protect his investment, and to monitor his potential liability.

Dispute Resolution

The Uniform Partnership Act provides little guidance on the subject of resolving disagreements among the partners. As noted earlier, in the absence of an agreement to the contrary, unanimous consent of the partners is required to take certain specified actions, such as altering the capital structure of the partnership, admitting a new partner, and encumbering partnership property for the benefit of creditors. Section 18(h) of the act provides that other differences arising as to ordinary matters connected with partnership business may be decided by a majority vote of the partners. The method of resolving disputes should be among the most important provisions of any partnership agreement. Unnecessary expenses and delay resulting from lengthy litigation may be avoided by carefully drafted provisions, perhaps including an agreement to arbitrate or even a "buy-sell" provision. The possibilities for avoiding conflict in this regard are virtually unlimited, but should be carefully thought out at the time the partnership is formed.

SUMMARY

Because a partnership is not a natural person or, for most purposes, even a legal entity, each partner, according to common law principles and Section 9(1) of the UPA, is a general agent of the partnership. Thus the principle of apparent authority allows each member to bind herself and her partners in contract. This power applies to the conduct of any matter that *appears* to be in the ordinary course of partnership affairs, even if the partner has an agreement with her partners to the contrary, as long as the third party with whom she deals is not on notice of the limitation. Potentially this power may be even broader in the case of trading, as opposed to non-trading, partnerships.

The UPA limits a partner's apparent authority in certain types of transactions, including those listed in Sections 9(3) and 18(h). Of course, these limitations, as is true of most limitations in the UPA, are subject to modification by agreement among the partners. However, modifications are not binding on third parties who have no notice of them.

The property rights of each partner include (1) the general rights in partnership property, (2) the right to share in profits and the obligation to share in partnership losses, and (3) the right to participate in the partnership's management. The partners hold title to specific partnership property as tenants in partnership. This is a hybrid form of tenancy, much like joint tenancy with the addition of limitations on the use, assignment, and encumbrance of the property.

Each partner retains a general property right in all contributions made to the partnership capital, and has an equal vote in partnership affairs. Each partner also is presumed to share in partnership losses in proportion to his right to share in partnership profits.

The Uniform Partnership Act provides for certain additional rights of partners. They include the right to indemnity in the event that a partner is held individually liable in an authorized partnership transaction, and the right to reimbursement of reasonable expenses incurred in the conduct of authorized partnership affairs. The presumption is that a partner is not entitled to any compensation other than her share of the profits. This presumption is overcome if the partnership agreement expressly provides to the contrary. In order to assure that each partner is getting her agreed-upon share, the UPA provides that she is entitled to reasonable access to partnership records, and to an accounting of partnership affairs if reasonably necessary.

Each partner is considered a fiduciary of the partnership and, as such, is under a duty to act only in the best interests of the partnership while conducting its business, to avoid taking any position adverse to the partnership, and to avoid any conduct that reasonably might appear to be improper. A partner's duty to render to the partnership all information he has knowledge or notice of affecting the affairs of partnership in any way is of special importance, because that notice and knowledge are imputed to the partnership by law.

Disputes arising during the course of the partnership association may be resolved in any manner agreeable to the partners. If there is no agreement, ordinary disputes are expected to be resolved by majority vote.

KEY TERMS AND CONCEPTS

apparent authority
trading partnership
non-trading partnership
tenants in partnership

PROBLEMS

1. Liggett and Lester formed a partnership to operate a service station. At the time, Lester was a distributor for an oil company and could get a discount on gasoline and oil products, which was used for the benefit of the partnership. Later, he purchased a bulk plant and became entitled to a second discount, which he did not mention or share. When Liggett discovered this, he sued Lester, claiming he was entitled to share the second discount. Is Liggett correct?

2. Acri and her husband were partners in a tavern business. While working as the bartender, Mr. Acri shot and injured Vrabel, a customer. Vrabel sought to hold Mrs. Acri liable as a partner in the business. Should Mrs. Acri be liable?

3. Picone and Cox were partners. Cox contracted for certain goods in the partnership's name, and then had them delivered to his own store. Commercial Paste, the seller, sought to charge the partnership, and Picone contended neither she nor the partnership should be liable because the partnership agreement provided that neither partner could contract for the partnership without the consent of the others, Cox had no authority, and the goods were not for the benefit of the partnership. Should the partnership and Picone be liable?

4. While in Michigan, Lyle, a partner in the Cherokee Box and Handle Co. of Tennessee, purported to sell lumber to Boles. Boles sent a check to the company, and it was intercepted and cashed by Lyle, who then used the money for her own

benefit. When Boles did not receive the lumber, he contacted Cherokee. Cherokee denied any knowledge of the transaction and refused to perform. Is Cherokee liable on the contract?

5. Phillips was involved in a collision with an automobile driven by Cook. At the time, Phillips was operating an automobile owned by a partnership of which he was a member. The collision occurred because of the negligence of Phillips. Is the partnership liable for Cook's injuries?

6. On October 4, 1929, Ellingson rented certain property to the partnership Walsh & O'Connor. The lease was for a period of ten years, at a total rental of $60,000. On April 28, 1931, Barneson became a member of the partnership. Thereafter, Ellingson sued for rent due during the period of March 1, 1932, to January 25, 1933. Barneson contended he should not be liable for the rent because it was due pursuant to a lease signed before he became a partner. Is Barneson correct?

7. Michele and Roth were partners in a business for a number of years. Michele took very little active part, and the day-to-day affairs of the business were handled primarily by Roth. Michele became concerned about the share she was receiving and, upon examining the books, learned that for some time Roth had been grossly mismanaging the business, causing a considerable loss of profits. Immediately Michele filed suit against Roth, asking for damages in the amount of her share of the profits lost. Is Michele entitled to a judgment?

8. Vann and Nash decided to terminate their partnership. During the process of winding up, Vann, a licensed real estate broker, sold the partnership's real estate, and then sought payment to herself of a commission from partnership funds. Is she entitled to a commission?

9. Summers and Dooley were partners in a trash collection business. When Dooley became disabled, he hired a substitute to do his part of the collection route, paying him out of his own pocket, as provided in the partnership agreement. Thereafter, Summers hired a second employee to help, over the objections of Dooley. He paid the employee $12,000 out of partnership funds. Dooley sued Summers for the return of his share of the $12,000. Summers defended on the ground that the work had become too much for two people. Is Dooley entitled to a judgment?

10. Brown and Padgett were partners in a business, Alabama Cabinet Workers. Contrary to an express provision of the partnership agreement, Brown executed promissory notes to the Benson Hardware Co. in payment for materials purchased for the business. When Benson sued for payment of the notes, Padgett defended on the ground that Brown was not authorized. Is Padgett's defense good?

Chapter | 38

Partnerships: Termination

INTRODUCTION

Every partnership, like every proprietorship, eventually must come to an end. The continuation of both business forms depends on at least the physical existence of their owners. This is one of the major features, and perhaps drawbacks, distinguishing these forms of business organization from the corporate form. Corporations may be chartered in perpetuity. Death of a stock owner, and other changes in ownership, do not affect corporate existence.

Discontinuation of a partnership may involve three possible steps: (1) dissolution, (2) winding up, and (3) termination. Often the partnership will end, perhaps because of the death of a partner, but the business will continue. In such situations, only a dissolution is involved. Sometimes, there will be both an end to the partnership (dissolution) and a discontinuation of business (termination), in which event the process will involve all three steps—a dissolution, a winding up of partnership affairs, and a termination of the partnership.

DISSOLUTION

Dissolution is defined in Section 29 of the Uniform Partnership Act as: "the change in relation of the partners caused by any partner ceasing to be associated in the carrying on as distinguished

Steps in discontinuing a partnership

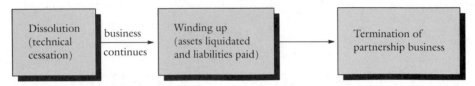

from the winding up of the business." It is important to note that dissolution may occur without a termination; *termination* occurs only after a winding up.

Causes of Dissolution

Dissolution of a partnership may come about for a variety of reasons, which may be grouped into three general classifications: (1) dissolution by acts of the partners, (2) dissolution by operation of law, and (3) dissolution by court order. No matter what the cause, however, dissolution always causes a partnership to cease as a going concern, although it continues to exist for the purpose of either reorganization or winding up.

Dissolution by Acts of the Partners

A partnership arises by the voluntary consent of the partners. Therefore, the partners also have the right to stipulate the period during which the partnership will continue. This time period may be a stated one (for example, ten years); it may be for the duration of a particular activity; or it may run until the occurrence of a specific future event. At the end of the stated period, dissolution may occur, although the partners then will have the right to extend the period by modification of their partnership agreement, if they see fit.

In keeping with the principle that a partnership is a voluntary association, the partners also have the right to dissolve the partnership at any time they choose to do so. Neither the public nor any member of the public has any interest in any

private partnership that would entitle him to compel its continuance. However, any dissolution contrary to the terms of a partnership is rightful only if all partners agree. If the partners have not agreed to a stated term, the partnership is considered to be one "at will," and it can be terminated rightfully by the express will of any partner.

Any change in the composition of the partners will cause dissolution. Either the admission of a new partner or the expulsion of an existing partner constitutes such a change. Every partnership depends on the peculiar composition of its partners for its identification. No two partnerships are alike. Each is unique. Therefore, upon the admission of a new partner or the expulsion of an existing partner, the result is the dissolution of the original partnership and the formation of a new, different, partnership.

A PARTNER'S POWER TO CAUSE DISSOLUTION.   No one can be compelled against his will to remain a partner. Therefore, each partner has the *power* although perhaps not the *right* to cause the dissolution of the partnership at will. If his withdrawal is in contravention of the partnership agreement, although he has the power to withdraw and end the partnership, he does not have the right, and he is subject to suit by the other partners for any damages that result. Under these circumstances, the withdrawal is simply a matter of breach of contract.

ASSIGNMENT OF A PARTNER'S INTEREST.   Section 27 of the Uniform Partnership Act provides that the simple conveyance, by a partner, of her interest in the partnership does not itself dissolve the partnership. The assignee is presumed entitled only to the assigning partner's share of profits and, upon dissolution, the assigning partner's interest in the distribution. The assignee is not considered to be a new partner, and is not entitled to share in the management of the business.

Dissolution by Operation of Law

The death of any partner is another type of change in the composition of partners, and, just as with the others, causes dissolution of the partnership. Again, business may continue as usual, and the partnership among the remaining partners may be reformed, but the association is a new partnership.

Bankruptcy of a partner also causes dissolution by operation of law, as does the bankruptcy of the partnership itself. Because of the unlimited liability of partners and the nonentity character of a partnership, each partner's personal credit is necessary to maintain the credit configuration of the partnership. The continuing credit of all of the partners is considered as important as their physical existence. Therefore, the "death" of a partner's personal credit will cause dissolution.

Dissolution also will occur if the object or purpose of a partnership becomes illegal. This might occur because of a change in the law that forbids the type of business in which the partnership is involved or the product it sells. For example, a partnership might be formed to sell fireworks at retail. Subsequently, the state legislature passes a statute forbidding the retail sale of fireworks. The purpose of the partnership having become illegal, the partnership would be dissolved. Of course, had the purpose of the partnership been to sell fireworks at retail in a number of states, some of which still allow their sale, the partnership would not dissolve, but would lose only part of its market. In addition, remember that a partnership, once dissolved, may be reformed for another (legal) purpose.

Another type of intervening illegality occurs when one or more of the partners loses his professional or business qualification. For example, suppose Smith and Smith form a partnership, the purpose of which is to conduct business as certified public accountants. If either Smith loses his certification, the partnership would dissolve. If a CPA employed by the firm, but not a partner, lost his certification, a dissolution would not occur.

Dissolution by Court Order

Section 32 of the UPA provides that on application by or for a partner a court *shall* decree a dissolution under certain circumstances. If any of the grounds discussed here is alleged, the court sits only as a trier of fact to determine whether the circumstances are as alleged. If they are, the court *must* decree dissolution.

The first of these grounds is that a partner has been adjudicated incompetent. *Incompetence* should not be confused with *insanity*. The former is the result of a judicial decree; the latter is a question of fact. The reason a partnership must be dissolved if one of the partners is incompetent is that the law, by statute in most states, considers acts of incompetent persons to be *void*. In essence, an incompetent is considered a "non-person" for most purposes.

If a partner becomes incapable of performing her part of the partnership agreement in any significant way, dissolution must be decreed according to Section 32. This includes insanity and any other disability. (This determination involves questions of fact, rather than whether a judicial decree of incompetency exists.) It is a catch-all category and is intended to fill in the gaps between other, specific, circumstances.

Dissolution will be ordered by a court if it is shown that a partner has been guilty of misconduct that tends to affect the carrying on of business prejudicially. For example, a partner's misconduct might make his reputation so unsavory that continued relations between the partnership and its customers becomes impossible or unreasonably burdensome. Or, because of a change in appearance or lifestyle, a partner no longer may be a proper representative for the partnership. Perhaps, even a partner's personal dress or hygiene may become so unacceptable as to cause his partners to petition for dissolution. A related ground for dissolution by court order exists if a partner persistently violates provisions of the partnership agreement or otherwise conducts himself in such a manner that it no longer really is practicable to carry on partnership business with him as a partner.

Dissolution will be decreed by a court if the evidence establishes that the business of a partnership can be carried on only at a loss. Business partnerships always are formed for the purpose of profit, and the definition of a partnership under Section 6 of the UPA includes "for profit." In addition, because of the unlimited liability of partners for partnership debts, they should not be required to continue a partnership that only will continue to generate losses. Of course, all of this assumes there is no significant chance of a business turn-around.

Finally, courts are given the authority to grant dissolution under any other circumstances that would render dissolution equitable. In spite of the fact that Section 32 of the UPA provides that the court *shall* decree dissolution upon finding these facts, the application of this provision involves equitable principles, and therefore a court has great latitude in deciding whether to grant relief based on any given set of facts. Of course, this provision is intended to be another catch-all, which is premised on the application of judicial flexibility. Consider the following case.

COOPER v. ISAACS
448 F.2d 1202 (D.C.Cir. 1971)

This was an action by Burton M. Cooper (Plaintiff/Appellee) against Leslie A. Isaacs (Defendant/Appellant) for dissolution of a partnership.

The parties were partners in the partnership of Lesco Associates, engaged in the sale of janitorial supplies. They commenced business in 1962 and entered into an agreement in 1965. Plaintiff filed for and was granted dissolution, and a receiver was appointed until the business was wound up. Defendant counterclaimed for wrongful dissolution under Section 41-330 of the D.C. Uniform Partnership Act. This counterclaim was rejected by the trial court and Defendant appealed. Affirmed.

TAMM, Circuit Judge.

Section 41-330 of the Act provides: Dissolution is caused: . . .

(6) By *decree of court* under section 44-331. (Emphasis added.)

Turning to section 44-331, we find the following provisions:

(1) On application by or for a partner the court shall decree a dissolution whenever— . . .
    (c) a partner has been guilty of such conduct as tends to affect prejudicially the carrying on of the business;
    (d) a partner willfully or persistently commits a breach of the partnership agreement, or otherwise so conducts himself in matters relating to the

partnership business that it is not reasonably practicable to carry on the business in partnership with him, . . .

(f) other circumstances render a dissolution equitable.

Courts interpreting these provisions have consistently held that serious and irreconcilable differences between the parties are proper grounds for dissolution by decree of court. . . . Since the Act provides for dissolution for cause by decree of court and Cooper has alleged facts which would entitle him to a dissolution on this ground if proven, his filing of his complaint cannot be said to effect a dissolution, wrongful or otherwise, under the Act; dissolution would occur only when decreed by the court or brought about by other actions.

A partnership agreement can presumably change this result, but the terms of the agreement must be quite specific to effect such a change. This is so because the provisions of the Act regarding dissolution by decree of court were clearly designed to allow partners to extricate themselves from business relationships which they felt had become intolerable without exposing themselves to liability in the process, and this sound policy should apply unless expressly negated, and perhaps even then.

We do not believe it can be said at this time, with the case in its present posture, that the partnership agreement involved here was clearly meant to exclude the possibility of dissolution of the partnership by decree of court under section 41-331. True, the partnership agreement does discuss certain ways by which the partnership can be terminated and states that the partnership "shall continue until terminated as herein provided." . . . However, it may well be that the parties did not consider the possibility that serious disagreements would arise at the time they made the agreement; the language limiting the methods of terminating the partnership may have been intended only to prevent a partner from dissolving the partnership voluntarily and without good cause. We thus conclude that without further inquiry into the partnership and the claims made by the parties, it is impossible to say that the mere filing of the complaint by Cooper constituted a wrongful dissolution.

Questions

1. Do you think the court is interpreting the partnership agreement properly? How would it have to be drafted to overcome the statutory language?

2. What facts of conduct would constitute irreconcilable differences for purposes of dissolution?

Effects of Dissolution

One point concerning dissolution bears repeating at this time. It is that dissolution does not, of itself, cause a winding up of a partnership's affairs. The discontinuation of the quasi-legal entity has nothing to do with the operation of the business. In fact, in reviewing the causes of dissolution discussed before, it is clear that most of them ordinarily will result in only a technical change in the partnership, with no effect at all on daily operations. This point is illustrated by the following case.

ROSS v. WALSH

629 S.W.2d 823 (Tex.App. 1982)

This was an action by Dorothy A. Ross (Plaintiff/Appellant) against Linda M. Walsh (Defendant/Appellee) to dissolve a partnership and determine the shares of the partners.

The parties entered into an agreement on August 17, 1977, to operate a business to sell real estate as a partnership. The agreement provided for the giving of 90-days notice if either partner wished to withdraw from the partnership, and that upon dissolution business would be concluded, the assets liquidated, and any surplus divided equally after the payment of debts. Plaintiff gave notice on May 24, 1978, and continued to occupy the premises and to operate under the partnership name.

The court granted dissolution and determined the value of the shares of the partners as of August 24, 1978. Plaintiff appealed contending the date of dissolution was May 24, 1978. Affirmed.

PAUL PRESSLER, Justice.

In her first point of error, appellant claims the trial court erred as a matter of law in holding that the partnership was dissolved on August 24, 1978. Appellant maintains that every partnership can be terminated at the will of any partner, and, that therefore, the court erred in finding the dissolution was effective on August 24 rather than on May 24. It is unnecessary for us to consider appellant's argument because the date of dissolution was immaterial in settling the affairs of the partnership. The basic common law rule adopted by this State is that the act of dissolution does not terminate a partnership relationship. Section 30 of the Texas Uniform Partnership Act, Article 6132b provides:

> On dissolution the partnership is not terminated, but continues until the winding up of partnership affairs is completed.

Therefore, a partnership continues through the winding up and accounting periods. . . . Dissolution is only one step in the process of concluding a partnership agreement; winding up, termination and accounting are the other necessary steps. . . . Even the case relied on by appellant, Woodruff v. Bryant, . . . affirms this proposition:

> [D]issolution does not necessarily terminate the partnership business. Even if the partnership is to be discontinued, the partnership continues to exist, at least for the limited purpose of winding up. (citations omitted) It is only upon termination that the final partnership relationship ceases to exist.

Appellee, as the ousted partner, continued to have an interest in the partnership business conducted during the winding up process and in all outstanding accounts after the appellant's notice on May 24. That appellant may have mistakenly operated the business for her own benefit "as an individual, not as a partner" during this period makes no difference. Appellant owed a fiduciary duty to appellee for the business conducted during this period.

> Dissolution does not terminate a partnership. The relationship continues during the winding up period. This is especially true when one of the parties is still in charge of the business. He occupies a fiduciary relationship to the other partner until the winding up of the partnership affairs is complete.

> Section 21 specifically extends the fiduciary duties owed by one partner to another to transactions connected with the partnership business during the period of winding up the partnership business and liquidating the partnership assets. . . .

If the trial court erred in finding the date of dissolution to be August 24, 1978, such error was harmless. This point is overruled.

Questions

1. If dissolution does not end the operation of the partnership, what is its legal significance?
2. Can a partner of a dissolved but operating partnership be held liable for debts incurred after dissolution?

Upon dissolution of a partnership, (1) if the cause is other than the conduct, bankruptcy, or death of a partner, all authority of any partner is terminated. However, (2) if dissolution was caused by the act, bankruptcy, or death of a partner, a partner's authority is terminated only when she has *knowledge* of the dissolution when it is by act of the partner, or *notice* of the partner's bankruptcy or death. *As among the partners,* if a partner acts after the termination of her authority, the partnership is not bound by her act. Therefore, she is not entitled to contribution by her co-partners on the obligation incurred. Otherwise, she is.

The rule is different concerning the rights of third parties. Matters that affect liability among the partners are not necessarily binding on third parties who may be dealing with partners on the basis of their apparent authority. Although a partner no longer has the *right* to bind the partnership after his authority has terminated, he still may have the power to do so. Therefore, he may bind the partnership to innocent third parties, but the partnership (other partners) then will be entitled

to reimbursement from him. Granting a third party rights against the partnership under these circumstances is not intended to be an ultimate resolution of the liability. It is intended only as an intermediate step. Ultimately, liability should rest with the partner who acted without authority. Section 35 of the Uniform Partnership Act sets certain limits on this power, however, and should be carefully reviewed.

The dissolution of a partnership does not itself discharge a partner's liability that existed at the time of the dissolution. Her liability may be discharged, however, by an express or implied novation agreement to which she, a person or partnership continuing the business, and an affected partnership creditor consent. The partnership creditor's consent may be inferred from a course of dealing between the creditor and the person or partnership continuing the business, or from the creditor's consent to a material alteration in the nature or time of payment of the obligations involved. Consent will be implied, however, only if the creditor receives knowledge of the dissolution and the business continues during the course of dealing, or learns of the assumption of liability by the person or partnership continuing the business at the time of the alteration. If the dissolution of the partnership is caused by the death of a partner, however, her individual property is subject to the payment of her share of partnership debts only after all of her separate debts have been paid. Separate creditors have a prior claim to a partner's separate property, just as partnership creditors have a prior claim to her partnership property.

WINDING UP

Because of Section 37 of the Uniform Partnership Act, every partner is on notice of the possibility that sometime in the future, the business of the partnership may wind up, unless otherwise agreed by the parties. Any partner, or representative of a deceased partner, who has not dissolved the partnership wrongfully and is not bankrupt has a right to wind up the partnership affairs. Also, any partner, or the representative of a deceased partner, may obtain a winding up by a court for good cause, regardless of the reason for the dissolution.

Just as dissolution terminated the quasi-legal entity of the partnership, **winding up** terminates the business of the partnership. After winding up is completed, the other partners may form a new partnership and begin a new business, even if it is the same as the previous partnership's business. However, this action does not constitute a continuation of the previous partnership's business, as it did when a partnership was dissolved without a winding up. The distinction is important because it relates to the rights of third parties, their rights to immediate payment of obligations owed to them, and the question of the assumption of existing liabilities by the new partnership.

In the process of winding up a partnership, the partners are entitled to a final accounting, and the assets of the partnership may be liquidated. A **final accounting** is a statement of the assets and the liabilities of the partnership. **Liquidation** means that the assets of the partnership are con-

verted to cash. Creditors will be paid, and the remaining cash will be distributed to the partners in proportion to their shares in the partnership, assuming there is cash left after the creditors have been paid. The liquidation may be partial or complete. That is, only enough assets may be sold to pay creditors and the remaining assets may be distributed to the partners if they agree to such a distribution.

Rights of Partners to the Application of Partnership Property

When a partnership is dissolved for any reason other than an act in contravention of the partnership agreement, each owner has the right to have the **partnership property** applied to pay the liabilities of the business, and to have the remainder paid in cash to the partners according to their proportionate shares. If the cause of dissolution was the expulsion of a partner as permitted by the partnership agreement, however, the expelled partner can require only that he receive, in cash, the net amount of *his* proportionate share. The remaining partners then may continue the partnership business as a new partnership.

When dissolution is caused by a violation of the partnership agreement, each partner who has not caused the dissolution has the rights already mentioned and, in addition, the right to damages from the wrongful partners for breach of the partnership agreement. If they choose, they also may elect to continue the partnership business, and may retain possession of the partnership property for that purpose. If they do so, however, they must indemnify the wrongful partner against liability for all present and future partnership liabilities, and secure, by a bond, payment of her proportionate net interest in the partnership property less the damages adjudged against her for the wrongful dissolution. Her interest, however, will not include any share of the partnership goodwill. Also, the partner who acted wrongfully is entitled to have her net interest paid in cash rather than secured by bond.

A Partner's Rights when Dissolution is for Fraud or Misrepresentation

When a partner has been induced to enter into a partnership by fraud or misrepresentation, he is entitled to rescission of the agreement. The agreement to be a partner, under those circumstances, is voidable the same as any other contract. Upon rescission, he also is entitled to be returned to the position he was in prior to entering into the agreement. In order to accomplish this, he is entitled to a lien on, or possession of, partnership property, after partnership liabilities are paid, in order to secure payment to him of the amount of his capital and other contributions to the partnership. Further, he is entitled to be subrogated to the claims of any creditors to whom he personally paid partnership liabilities. Finally, he is entitled to be indemnified against all partnership debts and liabilities by the person guilty of the fraud or misrepresentation.

The right to rescission specifically is provided for in the Uniform Partnership Act. However, the act is not intended to be the exclusive remedy of partners. Therefore, if a partner was induced to form a partnership by fraud, he may waive his right to rescind under the UPA, and may elect to recover damages in an action for deceit and to proceed with dissolution to recover his interest in the partnership.

The Distribution of Assets

For purposes of distribution, the assets of a partnership include its property and any personal contributions by the partners that are necessary to pay partnership liabilities. Those liabilities, *in order of highest to lowest priority,* are (1) debts to partnership creditors who are not partners, (2) obligations to partners other than for capital or profits, (3) repayments to partners of their capital contributions, and (4) obligations to partners for their shares of profits. Upon distribution, partnership liabilities, in rank order, are paid out of partnership assets, beginning with partnership property, and then by contribution of the partners if necessary.

When contributions are necessary to pay partnership liabilities, all partners are expected to pay in their proportionate shares. If any partner is either unable or unwilling to contribute, her share must be provided by the other partners in proportion to their respective rights to share in partnership profits. This reflects a partner's unlimited personal liability, and is not subject to modification by the partnership agreement. Ultimately, it is possible that one partner might be responsible for the entire contribution. Of course, the contributing partners have claims against any partner who failed to contribute to the payment of the partnership's liabilities.

If, at the time of distribution, a partner is bankrupt or his estate is insolvent, available individual property is taken in order of priorities established by Section 40(i) of the UPA. The order of payment is: (1) to his individual creditors, (2) to partnership creditors who are not partners, and (3) amounts owing to partners by way of contribution (not personal debts to those who also happen to be partners). This provision will take precedence over any inconsistent provision of state law, except state laws concerning exempt property. However, it will not take precedence over any inconsistent aspect of federal bankruptcy law.

CONTINUING BUSINESS

As indicated earlier, when an existing partnership merely is dissolved, or is dissolved with only a partial winding up, the business of the partnership may be continued. **Termination** (discontinuation of business) need not take place.

The Right to Continue Business

Continuing the business of a partnership may be done by one or more of those already partners, or by one or more previous partners and one or more new partners. A new partnership is formed, the remaining assets of the dissolved partnership are taken as capital, and its existing liabilities are assumed. In some cases, prior partners who do not join will become creditors of the new partnership to the extent of their interests in the dissolved partnership. Sometimes they are paid their interests in the assets of the dissolved partnership and are indemnified, by the new partnership, against existing and future partnership liabilities. If possible, it is probably the wisest choice to have their interests paid completely and to enter into a novation including themselves, the partners of the new partnership, and existing partnership creditors. The following case considers the ability of partners to provide in the partnership agreement for the continuation of business.

McCLENNEN et al. v. COMMISSIONER OF INTERNAL REVENUE
131 F.2d 165 (1st Cir. 1942)

George R. McNutter was a partner in a law firm, and died on February 21, 1937. The partnership continued in business under the terms of the partnership agreement, which stated, in part:

> On the retirement of a partner or on his death—the others continuing the business—the retiring partner or his estate in the case of his death shall, in addition to his percentage of net profits of the Firm received by it in cash up to the date of such death or retirement, also receive the same percentage of net profits of the Firm received by it in cash until the expiration of the eighteen (18) calendar months next after such retirement, or death, and this shall be in full of the retiring or deceasing member's interest in the capital, the assets, the receivables, the possibilities and the good will of the Firm. . . .

McClennen, the personal representative of McNutter's estate, elected to value the estate as of the end of the year, 1937. In the valuation, he accounted for none of the income for the 18-month period specified in the partnership agreement, since it was not to be paid until the end of the period. The Internal Revenue Service issued a deficiency in the amount of the tax due on the future value of the income during the period. (When paid, the estate received $34,069.99.) The Commissioner agreed with the assessment of the deficiency and the estate appealed. Affirmed.

MAGRUDER, Circuit Judge.

This chose in action [right to receive payment of a debt] to which the representative of the deceased partner succeeds, the right to receive payment of a sum of money shown to be due upon a liquidation and accounting, is of course a part of the deceased partner's wealth, and includable in the decedent's gross estate for purposes of computing the estate tax by virtue of the comprehensive definition in Section 302 of the Revenue Act of 1926. . . . This is none the less true even though the net amount thus shown to be due to the estate is derived in whole or in part from past earnings or profits of the partnership resulting from personal services—profits which the decedent, if he had lived, would have had to report as income. The valuation of this chose in action might be a matter of difficulty, especially in the case of a partnership which cannot be speedily liquidated and whose accounts are complicated. Nevertheless, for estate tax purposes, the valuation must be made by the legal representatives of the deceased partner, on the basis of the best evidence available at the applicable valuation date. . . .

To obviate the necessity of a liquidation, or to eliminate accounting difficulties in determining the value of the deceased partner's interest, partners often make specific provision in the partnership articles.

Sometimes the partnership agreement merely provides for the postponement of liquidation, say, to the end of the term for which the partnership was created. Thus, a partnership agreement between A, B, and C might provide that "should any partner die during the term of said co-partnership the firm shall not be dissolved thereupon, but the business shall be continued by the survivors until the expiration of said partnership term, the estate of the deceased partner to bear the same share in profits and losses as would have been received and borne by the deceased partner had he lived." Under such an agreement, if A dies, B and C do not buy out A's interest in the partnership. Unless more appears, A's executor does not become personally liable as a general partner. . . . Nor is A's general estate in the executor's hands liable as a partner for new debts created by B and C in continuing the business. . . . For the remainder of the term, A's share already embarked in the business remains in, subject to the risks of the business. It would seem not improper to describe the continuing business as now being owned by B and C as general partners, with A's estate (or A's executor as trustee under the will of A) as a limited partner therein, sharing in the profits, but not liable beyond the amount or interest already embarked in the business. . . .

We have spoken of a common type of arrangement whereby liquidation of the partnership is merely postponed, the deceased partner's estate sharing in the profits meanwhile. The payment to the estate of a share of the intervening profits could in no sense be described as the purchase price for the deceased partner's interest, for the value of that interest is ultimately to be paid over to the legal representative upon a final liquidation and accounting at the end of the partnership term.

In the case at bar the partnership agreement contains another familiar arrangement, whereby no liquidation and final accounting will ever be necessary in order to satisfy the claim of the deceased partner. In place of the chose in action to which Mr. McNutter's executor would have succeeded in the absence of specific provision in the partnership articles, that is, a right to receive payment in cash of the amount shown to be due the deceased partner upon a complete liquidation and accounting, a different right is substituted, a right of the estate to receive a share of the net profits of the firm for 18 calendar months after the partner's death.

The language of the partnership agreement in the present case is couched in terms of a purchase of the deceased partner's interest. What the estate is to receive "shall be in full of the retiring or deceasing member's interest in the capital, the assets, the receivables, the possibilities and the good will of the Firm". There is to be an extinguishment of the decedent's interest in the totality of the firm assets, tangible and intangible, as they stood at the moment of death, and the interests therein of the surviving partners are to be correspondingly augmented. Decision in the estate tax case now before us does not turn on the question whether the effect of the partnership agreement may be characterized with entire accuracy as a "purchase" and "sale" of the deceased partner's interest in the partnership.

Questions

1. Under what circumstances is it desirable for the partnership agreement to provide for the continuation of business without any time limitation?

2. When would it be desirable for the agreement to limit post-dissolution business to a fixed time period?

3. When should the agreement call for winding up immediately upon dissolution?

Liabilities of Persons Continuing Business

When one or more of the partners of a dissolved partnership continue the business, the creditors of the dissolved partnership also are creditors of the new partnership if business goes on without liquidation. If only one person continues the business, he assumes all of the existing liabilities. This is true regardless of the cause of the dissolution. If the person continuing the business was not a partner of the dissolved partnership, or a new partner is admitted to the new partnership, his liability to creditors of the dissolved partnership is limited to his interest in the partnership property.

If a partnership is dissolved because of the retirement or death of a partner, partnership creditors have a prior claim, over that of her individual creditors, to her interest in the dissolved partnership's property. That is, her proportionate share of partnership liabilities must be paid, or arranged for, before she is paid her interest or it is taken by her individual creditors. With respect to a deceased partner, this is the reciprocal to the rights of her individual creditors to priority over partnership creditors concerning that partner's obligation of contribution to pay partnership debts, as discussed previously. The circumstances of, and the reasons for, these priorities and their relationship to state exempt-property laws and the federal bankruptcy laws should be understood. They help to put the unlimited liability of partners in perspective. An unsecured partnership creditor and an unsecured general creditor are not treated the same when the partnership or the individual partners experience financial problems. They have different rights in different property. To the extent that these creditors are secured, however, their rights are the same.

Rights of a Retiring or Deceased Partner

A retiring partner, or a deceased partner through his personal representative, is entitled to a settlement of his interest in the partnership upon dissolution, unless another arrangement is made in the partnership agreement. This may be paid in cash or other partnership property. If the partnership business is continued, and no settlement of the deceased or retiring partner's interest has been made, he is a creditor of the person or partnership continuing the business. Under these circumstances, the retiring partner or representative of the deceased partner has two choices. He is entitled to an amount equal to the value of his interest in the dissolved partnership together with interest. He may elect, however, to take the profits earned by the new business which are attributable to its use of his right. If interest is paid on either amount, it will be at either a rate established specifically by state law, or, if no rate specifically is established, at the judgment rate existing during the period the property was used after his retirement or death. The judgment rate is the rate of interest established by state law to be paid on

judgments between the time they are entered by a court and the time they are paid. This rate, of course, varies from state to state. Consider the following case discussing the rights of a deceased partner's personal representative.

BOHN v. BOHN IMPLEMENT CO.
325 N.W.2d 281 (N.D. 1982)

This was an action by JoAnn Bohn, as personal representative of the estate of Clyde M. Bohn, deceased (Plaintiff/Appellee) against the Bohn Implement Co., a partnership, and Graydon J. Bohn, Sr. (Defendants/Appellants) to determine the validity and meaning of a partnership agreement.

Clyde M. Bohn and Graydon J. Bohn were the sole partners in a farming partnership. Upon Clyde's death, Graydon gave notice of his intent to buy Clyde's interest under the terms of the partnership agreement. His tender of $134,497.96 was refused by Plaintiff, and this action was filed.

The trial court determined that the partnership agreement was ambiguous and that the provision for "buying out" was unconscionable, awarding Plaintiff a judgment for one-half the net value of the partnership as appraised ($750,000) with payment of 15 percent in cash and the remainder in equal annual installments at 6-percent interest. Defendants appealed. Affirmed.

VANDE WALLE, Justice.

The trial court concluded and the parties admitted the partnership agreement is ambiguous. According to paragraph 15 the value of a partner's interest for the purpose of a buy-out is "the capital amount." However, accountant Harris Widmer testified at trial that the term "capital amount" has no known definition in the accounting profession. The buy-out value cannot be ascertained from the agreement. Because of this ambiguity, we must look to other evidence to understand the agreement between Clyde and Graydon. When the intent of the parties cannot be determined from the agreement alone, the issue of the parties' intent is a question of fact. . . .

JoAnn argues that in the case at hand the purchase price of Clyde's partnership interest should be based upon the fair market value. JoAnn relies upon Anderson v. Wadena Silo Co. . . . In Anderson administrators of the estate of a deceased partner in Wadena Silo Company brought an action for a declaratory judgment providing that they could sell the deceased partner's interest at fair market value. The partnership agreement stated that the purchase price in this situation was "the seller's interest as determined by the examination of the partnership affairs by a certified public accountant." . . . The general rule in Minnesota is that "the estate of a deceased partner is entitled to the actual fair market value of that partner's interest unless the partners have agreed otherwise." . . . In Anderson the surviving partners urged that the partnership agreement revealed the partners had agreed the buy-out price was the book value of the deceased partner's interest. The estate administrators contended that the partnership agreement was ambiguous.

The Minnesota court examined Arizona, Kentucky, and Wisconsin decisions involving the issue of whether the purchase price of a deceased partner's interest should be book value or fair market value. . . . Each of the three State courts determined that the deceased partner's selling interest should be priced at the fair market value. The Anderson court concluded its analysis of these cases as follows:

> These opinions clearly demonstrate a judicial hostility to the use of book value as a measure of a partner's interest. We believe that the reason for this hostility is simply the well-recognized fact that book value does not reflect the true value of a partner's interest. Thus, it would be inequitable to require a partner to sell his interest in a partnership for a price which does not reflect its true value unless it is clear that the partner explicitly agreed to do so. . . .

In Anderson the court found that the partnership agreement did not explicitly establish the book value as the selling price upon a partner's death. Therefore, the estate administrators were entitled to the fair market value of the deceased's interest from the surviving partners. The Minnesota court noted the adoption of the Uniform Partnership Act by that State and quoted Minn.St. 323.41. North Dakota also has adopted the Uniform Partnership Act. Section 45-09-14, N.D.C.C., which contains wording nearly identical to that of Minnesota, provides, in part:

> When any partner . . . dies, and the business is continued . . . without any settlement of accounts as between his estate and the person or partnership continuing the business, unless otherwise agreed, his legal representative as against such persons or partnership may have the value of his interest at the date of dissolution ascertained, and shall receive as an ordinary creditor an amount equal to the value of his interest. . . .

The Minnesota court concluded that unless the agreement explicitly establishes the buy-out price, the Uniform Partnership Act statutory provision that the price will be the actual value of the interest will prevail.

Neither Anderson nor In re Randall's Estate varies the general rule. If the partnership agreement clearly and specifically states the price the surviving partners must pay for a deceased partner's interest, the agreement will be upheld in the absence of fraud. However, if the partnership agreement is ambiguous, the surviving partners must pay the fair market value for the interest. In the instant case the trial court concluded the 1979 Bohn Implement partnership agreement is ambiguous. Graydon needed to prove by clear and convincing evidence that he and Clyde had agreed to a buy-out price less than the fair market value. He did not do so. Because the partnership agreement in this case does not explicitly establish the value of Clyde's interest, pursuant to Section 45-09-14, N.D.C.C., Clyde's estate is entitled to fair market value as of the date of Clyde's death.

The trial court correctly determined Graydon Bohn must pay JoAnn Bohn one-half of the net fair market value, or $750,000, if he elects to purchase Clyde's interest. The new terms of payment determined by the trial court, 14 percent down and the balance in equal installments over 20 years, are fair. The trial judge has the equitable authority to devise terms of payment when the terms in the agreement are deemed unconscionable.

Questions

1. How can the problem that arose in this case be avoided?
2. Is there any argument that a retiring or deceased partner's share should be valued at *less* than fair market value?
3. Why did the court allow the payment of the deceased's share to be stretched over 20 years? Isn't immediate payment more appropriate?

SUMMARY

The three steps in discontinuing a partnership are (1) dissolution, (2) winding up, and (3) termination. *Dissolution* is defined as any change in the relations of the partners caused by any partner, for any reason, ceasing to be associated with the partnership. This results only in a technical cessation of the partnership as an organization. Dissolution of a partnership may be caused by some act of the parties, such as a term of the partnership agreement, by the withdrawal of a partner, or by the admission of a new partner. A partner even has the power to cause dissolution at will, contrary to the partnership agreement and for no particular reason at all. Dissolution also may be caused by the operation of some law, as with the death or bankruptcy of a partner or by some intervening illegality concerning the association or business of the partnership. Finally, dissolution may be caused by a decree of a court under a variety of specific circumstances, and generally whenever it is determined that dissolution is equitable.

The business of the partnership will continue after dissolution until there has been a winding up of partnership business. The process of winding up may be total or partial. When total, the assets of the partnership are liquidated, and partnership liabilities are paid first to partnership creditors who are not partners, then to the partners—first with respect to their contributions to partnership capital, and then with respect to their shares of partnership profits. If the property is not suffici-

ent to pay the partnership creditors who are not partners, the partners are liable for contributions in the same proportion as their rights to share partnership property and in an amount sufficient to satisfy the creditors' claims. When the winding up is partial, the net interest of the departing partner is paid, and he or she is indemnified against further liability to partnership creditors. Upon dissolution and any necessary winding up, the partnership is terminated. Any person or partnership continuing the business of the terminated partnership is a new and separate business. Its only connection with the terminated partnership is that it continues to be liable to all partnership creditors.

KEY TERMS AND CONCEPTS

dissolution
winding up
final accounting
liquidation
partnership property
termination

PROBLEMS

1. At various times, Farmer's Bank made loans to a partnership called Ed Cox and Son. Of the

total $108,492.42, some of the loans were made after the death of Ed Cox and were used by his son to pay partnership obligations. The personal representative of Cox's estate contended Cox's interest in the partnership was not chargeable with the loans made after Cox's death because the death of a partner terminates the partnership. Is the personal representative correct?

2.   Donald and William Petersen formed a partnership, with William contributing the capital and Donald furnishing the labor. The business operated for 19 years, with all taxes, upkeep, and expenses paid out of partnership funds. Upon dissolution, William claimed he was entitled to all of the partnership property since he had contributed the full capital in the beginning. Is William correct?

3.   Laddon and Whittlesey were partners in a salvage business and determined that it was floundering. Whittlesey devoted little time to the business, which upset Laddon. Eventually Laddon suffered a heart attack, and Whittlesey refused to put more money in the business. Finally, Whittlesey sued to dissolve the partnership and to enjoin Laddon from contracting any more partnership debts, although Laddon wanted to continue the business. The trial court granted the relief requested, and Laddon appealed. Should the judgment be reversed?

4.   Michelle and Chris Belfos, sisters, were partners in a shoe repair business. Some of the property used in the business was held in Michelle's name, some in Chris's name, and the real estate was held jointly. Upon Michelle's death, she sought to transfer the portion held in her name by her will. May she do that?

5.   Upon dissolution of their partnership, Jackson sued his partner, Cadwell, asking for an accounting. He asked that good will of the business be considered in arriving at his share of partnership assets. Cadwell objected, stating that good will never had been recognized and never was carried on the books as an asset. Should an amount for good will be included in the statement?

6.   Mary and Nick, sister and brother, inherited the family business, as partners, upon the death of their father. Disputes arose, along with accusations of misappropriation of assets and other wrongdoings, and continued for six years, until Mary filed for dissolution. After a hearing, the referee found irreconcilable differences and called for the two to bid on the partnership, which had total assets of $95,000 at the time. Nick bid $65,000 and Mary didn't bid, so the referee ordered sale to Nick. Thereafter, Mary wanted to offer additional evidence concerning the appraisal, but the referee refused to reopen the matter. Mary contended that in doing so, the referee exceeded his authority. Is Mary correct?

7.   Two partners, acting together, froze out the third by refusing to allow her to participate in management decisions, and then bought out the business after an accounting. Was it proper for the court to allow the purchase?

8.   Burrus and Williams were partners in a restaurant business. The business and a liquor license had been purchased in Burrus's name because Williams was unacceptable to the liquor commission. Williams later sued Burrus for dissolution and an accounting. Under the circumstances, should the court grant the relief?

9.   Jebeles and Costello were partners under an oral partnership agreement. They were also sisters-in-law, and operated Dino's Hot Dogs. Difficulties mounted between them and, at the time Jebeles was divorced from Costello's brother, things got hostile. Costello ceased to contribute to the business; finally, Jebeles asked the court for dissolution. The court refused the petition, stating it was doing so to preserve the business's future profits and its interest in a valuable lease.

Instead, it ordered that the business continue, with Jebeles as the sole active partner. Was the order proper?

10. Sta-Rite had been selling to the partnership of Taylor and Hood for a number of years. Taylor bought out Hood's interest and began operating as sole owner in March 1968. On October 28, 1968, he incurred indebtedness on a note to Sta-Rite. At the time, the sales manager knew that the partnership had been undergoing dissolution since early in the year, but had received no notice of termination. The note was signed by Taylor as sole maker, but when it wasn't paid Sta-Rite sued both Taylor and Hood. Should Hood be liable?

Limited Partnerships

THE ROLE OF THE LIMITED PARTNERSHIP

To be precise, the type of partnership association discussed in the previous four chapters should be referred to as a *general partnership*. A general partnership is characterized by the facts that it is not considered an entity for most purposes, it may be formed with little or nothing in the way of mandatory formalities, and the liability of each of its partners for partnership obligations is unlimited. Although this business form is perfectly adequate for many business purposes, it suffers in two major respects. First, it is not suited to large organizations because of the right of each partner to participate fully in management (unless the partnership agreement specifies to the contrary) and because of the power to bind the partnership to obligations to third parties who deal with any partner in good faith (regardless of provisions of the partnership agreement to the contrary). Second, it is difficult for a general partnership to acquire new capital other than by contributions from existing partners.

The **limited partnership** emerged primarily to overcome these limitations. This modified form of partnership retains many of the benefits of the general partnership, such as simplicity in formation and operation, and tax benefits in some circumstances (depending on the other personal income of the partners). However, it also provides for the acquisition of new capital by allowing people to become investors in the business with neither the right to (nor burden of) participating in management, the power to bind the partnership to general obligations, or the unlimited liability assumed by the partners of a general partnership.

Limited partnerships are creatures of state statute and, today, all states have statutes authorizing their creation. Their provisions are fairly uniform because all states except Louisiana have adopted the **Uniform Limited Partnership Act (ULPA).** This act, first promulgated in 1916 by the National Conference of Commissioners on Uniform State Laws, provides uniformity of treatment. Although states may modify its provisions, most of them chose not to do so when they promulgated

the act. Moreover, Section 3 of the act invites the states to limit the kinds of businesses that are allowed to be carried on as limited partnerships. In addition, many states now have adopted the *Revised* Uniform Limited Partnership Act, which makes some changes in the provisions of the ULPA. These changes will be discussed in detail later in this chapter.

A limited partnership is formed by two or more persons. Of these, at least one must be a general partner with the same general rights and liabilities discussed with regard to general partnerships. If the statutory requirements are met, limited partners are not bound personally by the obligations of the partnership. Their liability is limited to their capital investments in the partnership. However, there must be strict compliance with the statute authorizing the creation of limited partnerships. In the following case, the court considered whether a limited partnership had been formed.

KLINE v. WEISS et al.
284 Md. 36, 395 A.2d 126 (1978)

This was an action by Gerald S. Kline, as receiver of a limited partnership (Plaintiff/Appellant), against Frederick K. Weiss and other limited partners (Defendants/Appellees) to recover on behalf of creditors certain amounts due creditors in excess of Defendants' contributions paid into the partnership. One of the many questions before the court was whether a limited partnership had been formed. On this point, the trial court ruled "Yes," and Plaintiff appealed. Remanded without affirmance or reversal for findings of fact.

MURPHY, Chief Judge.

Limited partnerships were unknown at common law; they are exclusively a creature of statute, their main purpose being to permit a form of business enterprise, other than a corporation, in which persons could invest money without becoming liable as general partners for all debts of the partnership. . . . "The general purpose of [limited partnership] acts was not to assist creditors, but was to enable persons to invest their money in partnerships and share in the profits without being liable for more than the amount of money they had contributed. The reason for this was to encourage investing." Gilman Paint & Varnish Co. v. Legum, 197 Md. 665, 670, 80 A.2d 906, 908 (1951).

The first limited partnership statute in the United States was enacted by New York in 1822; Maryland adopted a similar statute by ch. 97 of the Acts of 1836. These early statutes required the recording of a partnership certificate giving notice to the public of the exact terms of the partnership, including the amount of the capital contributions of the limited partners, so that the public could deal with the partnership "advisedly." . . . Strict compliance with all statutory provisions was deemed essential to create a limited partnership under these early statutes, since they were in derogation of the common law. As a consequence, even minor or trivial infractions of the statute were held by some courts to subject the limited partners to unlimited liability as general partners. Rowley, supra, at Section 53.0; A. Bromberg, Crane and Bromberg on Partnership Subsection 26, 32 (1968). Because the strict construction of these statutes inhibited the effective accomplishment of the purpose for which they were intended, the National Conference of Commissioners on Uniform State Laws proposed the adoption in 1916 of a Uniform Limited Partnership Act. Maryland enacted the Uniform Act by ch. 280 of the Acts of 1918, and the statute with minor modifications is now in effect in every state in the country except Louisiana. The Act's provisions are intended to govern the determination of essentially all questions arising out of the formation and operation of limited partnerships. The rule that statutes in derogation of the common law are to be strictly construed is expressly made inapplicable to the Uniform Act.

Decisions interpreting the Uniform Act recognize that a limited partnership consists of general partners who conduct the business and who have unlimited liability to creditors for its obligations, and of limited partners who have no right to participate in the management of the business, and whose liability is limited to the amount of their capital contribution. . . .

The creation of a limited partnership is not a mere private, informal, voluntary agreement as in the case of a general partnership, but is a public and formal proceeding which must follow the statutory requirements of the Uniform Act. . . . The Act prescribes, Section 10-102(b) of the Corporations Article, that a limited partnership is formed "if there has been substantial compliance in good faith" with the requirements contained in Section 10-102(a). That subsection mandates that a certificate of partnership be signed by the parties, acknowledged, and recorded with the clerk of the court. It requires that the certificate set forth 14 designated partnership details, including the name of the partnership, the character and location of the business, the identity of the general and limited partners, the term of the partnership, the cash contributions made by the limited partners, and such addition contributions, if any, which the limited partners have agreed to make in the future. The certificate is a statutory prerequisite to creation of a limited partnership and until it is filed, the partnership is not formed as a limited partnership. The principal function of the certificate is to give third persons notice of the essential features of the limited partnership. Of course, whether a limited partnership has been formed is of particular importance in determining whether a person has achieved the status of a limited partner with the attendant limitation of his liability to third persons dealing with the partnership.

Questions

1. Is there any reason today to demand strict compliance with the limited partnership statute?

2. What limited partnership prerequisites *always* should be insisted upon by the courts?

FORMATION

Unlike a general partnership, a limited partnership may be formed only be meeting certain statutory requirements. These include filing a certificate, which becomes a public record.

Filing of a Certificate

Parties wishing to form a limited partnership must swear to and sign a **certificate of limited partnership**, and must place it on public record. In this regard, the ULPA imposes a formality on the formation of a qualifying partnership that is similar in form and purpose to that required by incorporation acts in order to establish a corporation. As noted, the place of filing was provided by each state upon the adoption of the Uniform Act. Typically, the certificate must be filed with a designated official in the county in which the partnership has its principal place of business. In addition, state filing is common, and sometimes it is required that a copy be filed in each county in which the partnership does business.

The certificate is required to contain the name of the partnership, the character of the business, the location of the principal place of business, the name and residence address of each partner—with each designated as general or limited, the term the partnership is to exist, the amount of cash and agreed-upon value of other property contributed by each limited partner, the additional contributions agreed to be made in the future by the limited partners and the times or events upon which they will be made, the time, if agreed, when the contribution of each limited

Formation of a limited partnership

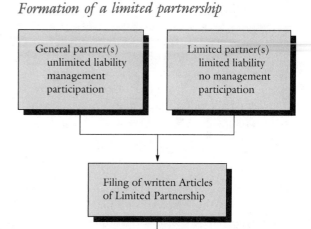

partner will be returned, and the share of profits or other compensation that each limited partner is to receive in return for his or her contribution. Other matters also *may* be included. They are: the right, if any, of a limited partner to substitute an assignee as contributor in his place, and the terms and conditions of the substitution; the right, if any, of the partners to admit additional partners; the right of any of the limited partners to have priority over any of the other limited partners as to compensation by way of income, and the nature of that priority; the right, if any, of a remaining general partner to continue business upon the death, retirement, or insanity of any other general partner; and the right, if any, of a limited partner to receive property other than cash in return for his contribution.

Partnership Name

The name of the partnership cannot contain the surname of any limited partner, unless it is also the surname of a general partner or the business was carried on under that surname prior to becoming a limited partnership. If this provision is violated, the limited partner whose name is used is liable as a general partner concerning any creditor who extended credit without actual knowledge that she was not a general partner. No degree of reliance on the part of the creditor need be shown, and even notice will not relieve the limited partner of this change in her liability.

A Limited Partner's Contribution to Capital

All contributions to capital by any limited partner must be stated in the certificate filed to form the partnership. These contributions may be made in any form of cash of other property—but not services—and their amount must be stated. Even agreed-upon future contributions must be stated, together with a declaration of what times or conditions will cause them to be made. A limited partner is liable personally for the amount that his or her contribution falls short of the amount stated in the certificate. This is very similar to the liability of those who are supposed to furnish the stated capital of a corporation.

Defective Formation

As we learned in the *Kline* case, in order to take advantage of the benefits of the Uniform Limited Partnership Act it is necessary that the requirements of the act be met. However, *strict* compliance is not always required. Section 2(2) of the ULPA provides that if there has been substantial compliance, in good faith, meeting the requirements of signing, swearing, and filing a proper certificate, a limited partnership is formed. Apparently, however, acceptance of substantial compliance does *not* mean that the partnership name can contain the surname of a limited partner. The benefits of the limited partnership under these circumstances may be lost by the limited partner whose name is used. Also, according to Section 6, if the certificate contains false statements, any party who knew of the false statement, either when she signed it or thereafter (if she learned of it in sufficient time to see to it that the certificate was amended or cancelled before it was relied on), is liable to anyone who is injured by the false statement.

If a person has contributed to the capital of a business, erroneously believing that he has become a limited partner of a limited partnership, he will not be held liable as a general partner if certain requirements are met. Most importantly, he must have acted only as a limited partner. That is, he must not have participated in management, sought to bind the partnership with regard to third parties by virtue of his ownership, or otherwise held himself out to be a general partner. Also, upon learning of the mistake, he must have renounced his interest in the profits, or other compensation by way of income, immediately. A failure to comply, of course, will cause him to be liable as a general partner. In the following case, the court deals with the problem of a defectively formed limited partnership in a special setting.

GARRETT v. KOEPEKE
569 S.W.2d 568 (Tex.App. 1978)

This was an action by James R. Garrett and Efton M. Henson (Plaintiffs/Appellants) against Edwin E. Koepeke and other limited partners (Defendants/Appellees) to establish personal liability for the breach of a lease by their limited partnership. Plaintiffs' theory was that Defendants were not entitled to the shield of the Uniform Limited Partnership Act because they had not filed a certificate of limited partnership with the Secretary of State as required under the act. Defendants contended the failure to file should not deprive them of limited liability because Plaintiffs, at the time of the lease transaction, actually knew Defendants were limited partners.

From the granting of a summary judgment in favor of Defendants, Plaintiffs appealed. Affirmed.

AKIN, Justice.

Appellees admit that they had failed to file a certificate of limited partnership as required by Tex.Rev.Civ. Stat.Ann. art. 6132a (Vernon 1970). Appellants contend, therefore, that appellees are liable for the debt sued upon as general partners. We cannot agree with this contention. We see no logical reason to strip appellees of their limited liability under their partnership agreement merely because they failed to comply with art. 6132a. The purpose of the filing requirements under the act is to provide notice to third persons dealing with the partnership of the essential features of the partnership arrangement. . . . Since appellants knew that the entity with which they were dealing was a limited partnership, as well as the consequences of dealing with such an entity, they were in no way prejudiced by the failure to comply with the statute. We see no compelling policy reason here for holding that appellees became general partners by requiring technical compliance with these notice provisions. Indeed, such was not the intent of the legislature in enacting the statute; instead, its' [*sic*] intent was to provide notice of limited liability of certain partners to third parties dealing with a partnership. . . . The nature and legal existence of a partnership does not depend upon any filing required by a statute. . . . We hold, therefore, that where a party has knowledge that the entity with which he is dealing is a limited partnership, that status is not changed by failing to file under art. 6132a.

Questions

1.   Is this decision fair to the plaintiffs? to the defendants?
2.   Is this decision consistent with the policies underlying the ULPA? Is it consistent with the *Kline* case?

OPERATION

Business that May Be Carried On

The ULPA places no limitations on the kind of business that may be carried on by a limited partnership. However, Section 3 specifically invites adopting states to impose restrictions. This ability to control the availability of the limited part-nership form probably has become less important as states have begun to allow professional associations, such as those involving doctors, lawyers, and dentists, to become incorporated. Today there is somewhat less public policy opposition to limited liability for professionals, but the states still clearly are permitted to prevent them from being involved in limited partnerships.

Partners' Rights

General partners in a limited partnership have the same rights and powers as general partners in a general partnership, with certain limitations intended to accommodate the limited partnership form of association. Some acts of the general partners require the written consent or ratification of all of the limited partners. Only to this extent are limited partners allowed a voice in the management of the partnership. The following conduct by a general partner is wrongful unless consent or ratification has been obtained from the partners: (1) any act in contravention of the certificate; (2) any act that would make it impossible to carry on the ordinary business of the partnership; (3) possession of partnership property, or assignment of the partners' rights in specific partnership property, for other than a partnership purpose; (4) confession of a judgment against the partnership; (5) admission of another person as a general partner; (6) admission of another person as a limited partner, unless this right is granted in the certificate; and (7) continuation of the business with partnership property after the death, retirement, or insanity of a general partner, unless that is provided for in the certificate.

Limited partners have the same rights as general partners to have the books kept at the principal place of business and to inspect them; to have, on demand, information of things relating to the partnership and, if reasonable, a full accounting; and to have dissolution and a winding up on decree of a court. A limited partner also has a right to share in profits, or to receive other income in recognition of her contribution to capital, and to have a return of her contribution upon termination of her interest in the partnership. The details of this financial interest are spelled out in the partnership agreement. The principal right she does *not* have, of course, is the right to share

in the management of the partnership business. Exactly what acts might constitute a breach of this limitation are not spelled out precisely by the ULPA.

Assignment of a Limited Partner's Interest

Consistent with the view of a limited partner as an investor only, similar to a stockholder in a corporation, the interest of a limited partner is fully assignable. This may be done without the consent of the other partners, and even contrary to the express will of any or all of them. By assignment, the transferee becomes entitled to share in the profits or other income, and to receive return of the assigning partner's contribution to the partnership. He has none of the other rights of a limited partner unless, in addition to the assignment, he is admitted as a substituted limited partner.

An assignee of a limited partner's interest may become entitled to admission as a substituted limited partner if all partners (other than the assigning partner) consent, or if he is given that right because the assigning partner was empowered to do so by the limited partnership certificate. The assignee becomes a substituted limited partner when the certificate is amended to reflect the fact. He then has the same rights, powers, and limitations as the assigning partner except with regard to liabilities of which he was ignorant at the time he became a partner and that could not be ascertained from the certificate.

The substitution of an assignee as a limited partner only bestows rights on the assignee. According to the ULPA, it does not relieve the assigning partner of her liability. The assigning partner remains liable for any false statements in the certificate (Sec. 6) and for her general liability to the partnership (Sec. 17). The latter includes her liability (1) for any agreed-upon contributions to capital that remain unpaid, (2) for any partnership money or other partnership property in her possession, (3) to partnership creditors who extended credit prior to the return to her of any of her capital contribution, if there was such a return. Of course, this liability is limited to the amount of capital returned to her. Any or all of these liabilities may be discharged by waiver, compromise, or a composition agreement with all of the partners. However, a waiver, compromise, or composition agreement is not binding on third parties, including creditors, who do not participate in it.

A Limited Partner's Rights to the Return of Contribution

The most typical reason for the return of a limited partner's contribution to a partnership is dissolution. It also may occur upon his voluntary or involuntary withdrawal. However, the ULPA places conditions upon the partner's right to receive it. First, all liabilities to third-party (non-

partner) creditors of the partnership must be paid or sufficient property must remain in the partnership to pay them after the return of the partner's contribution. The consent of all members of the partnership must be obtained unless the withdrawing partner has a right to demand the return. Finally, the certificate must have been either cancelled or amended to reflect the withdrawal.

A limited partner has a right to demand the return of his contribution without seeking the consent of the other partners, upon dissolution, when this is provided specifically by the certificate, or upon giving six months' notice if there is no provision in the certificate. Unless agreed to the contrary, the withdrawing partner may demand to be paid in cash. The following case addresses the question of whether a partner can secure the risk of return of his capital contribution.

KRAMER v. McDONALD'S SYSTEM, INC.
77 Ill.2d 323, 33 Ill.Dec. 115, 396 N.E.2d 504 (1979)

This was an action by Arnold I. Kramer (Plaintiff/Appellant) against McDonald's System, Inc. and the Bank of River Oaks (Defendants/Appellees) for conversion of certain restaurant equipment.

Plaintiff was a limited partner in a restaurant business that was a franchisee of McDonald's System, Inc. At the time of the agreement, Plaintiff contributed capital of $90,000 and took a security interest in certain equipment to secure the contribution. Later, the franchisee restaurant business borrowed money from Defendant bank, giving a security interest in the same equipment. When the loan was not repaid, the bank foreclosed on the equipment and sold it to the franchisor. The question before the court was whether Plaintiff's security interest was enforceable.

The trial court held in favor of Plaintiff. Defendant appealed, and the decision reversed by the Illinois Court of Appeals. Plaintiff appealed. Affirmed.

CLARK, Justice.

We think that the pleadings, depositions, affidavits and documents on record clearly evince that the $90,000 was intended as a contribution to the capital of the limited partnership. The word "contributions" as it is used in the ULPA is limited to the contribution made by a limited partner at the time of the formation of the partnership for the benefit of the partnership's creditors. . . .

Kramer's transfer to Baker of $90,000 was made at the time of the formation of the limited partnership. This is revealed in the limited partnership agreement executed on January 17, 1975, the certificate of limited partnership, as well as in the mutual agreement indemnifying the limited partners, signed on January 22, 1975.

The important distinction between the initial capital contribution and subsequent transfers of funds to the partnership has been noted elsewhere by courts which have been asked to decide whether limited partners may take collateral security for loans made to the partnership. Those courts had been careful to note that the initial contribution had been made previously, and that it was subsequent advances of money over which issue was joined. . . .

A limited partnership interest is in the nature of an investment. . . . Through his contribution, the limited partner becomes entitled to share in the profits and losses of the partnership, though his share of the losses will not exceed the amount of capital initially contributed to the enterprise. . . . However, when the limited partner makes the contribution, he is placing that amount at risk. He is not permitted to insure that risk or to guarantee a return to himself by taking some form of security. He may not vie with creditors for the assets available to pay the partnership's obligations. "[The ULPA] was designed to prevent illegal competition between the limited partner and creditors of the partnership for the assets of the partnership." . . . It would therefore defeat the purpose of the ULPA to permit Kramer to enforce a security interest against the property purchased by the partnership to operate the restaurant.

We therefore hold that Kramer is prohibited by the express provisions of section 16 of the ULPA from accepting collateral as security for his capital contribution. The legal effect of the holding accords with the holding of the appellate court only to the extent that it held that Kramer was not a secured creditor, that he possesses no enforceable interest in the collateral, and that, therefore, Kramer may not maintain an action for conversion of the collateral.

Questions

1. What are the policies that support the court's result?
2. Is there any way that a limited partner can protect his or her investment in a venture in light of this court's holding?

Liability of a Limited Partner

The liability of a limited partner to the partnership is noted under assignment. The limited partner is responsible for unpaid contributions, the return of partnership property then in her possession, and for her share of liabilities to third-party creditors of the partnership, up to the amount of her contribution. Section 7 of the ULPA provides that she will not be liable as a general partner unless she takes part in the control (management) of the business. Consider the following case.

HOLZMAN v. deESCAMILLA et al.
86 Cal.App.2d 858, 195 P.2d 833 (1948)

This was an action by Lawrence Holzman, as trustee in bankruptcy of Hacienda Farms, Limited, a limited partnership (Plaintiff/Appellee) against Ricardo deEscamilla, general partner (Defendant) and James L. Russell and H. W. Andrews, limited partners (Defendants/Appellants) for a determination that Russell and Andrews were liable as general partners for partnership debts. Plaintiff's contention was that they exercised control over the business of the partnership. The evidence established that Defendants Russell and Andrews were consulted, and helped determine, what crops were to be planted each season. On October 15, 1943, they requested Defendant Escamilla to resign as manager of the farm, which he did, and appointed Henry Miller in his place. Also, checks drawn on the partnership bank account required the signatures of at least two partners—the two limited partners, or the general partner and one of the limited partners. All checks were signed in this manner.

The trial court found Russell and Andrews liable as general partners and they appealed. Affirmed.

MARKS, Justice.

Section 2483 of the Civil Code provides as follows:

A limited partner shall not become liable as a general partner, unless, in addition to the exercise of his rights and powers as a limited partner, he takes part in the control of the business.

The foregoing illustrations sufficiently show that Russell and Andrews both took "part in the control of the business." The manner of withdrawing money from the bank accounts is particularly illuminating. The two men had absolute power to withdraw all the partnership funds in the banks without the knowledge or consent of the general partner. Either Russell or Andrews could take control of the business from de Escamilla by refusing to sign checks for bills contracted by him and thus limited his activities in the management of the business. They required him to resign as manager and selected his successor. They were active in dictating the crops to be planted, some of them against the wish of Escamilla. This clearly shows they took part in the control of the business of the partnership and thus became liable as general partners.

Questions

1. Would limited partners be treated as general partners if their views were solicited by the general partner but were not considered binding?

2. What if the general partner always followed the views of limited partners but there was no evidence that he was required to do so?

The partnership interest of a limited partner is subject to garnishment and levy of execution by a judgment creditor as is any other property. It also may be subject to attachment if the state, under Section 22 of the ULPA, has elected to provide for that right. In any such proceeding, state exemption laws will apply. Also, property taken by any of these processes may be redeemed with the separate property of any general partner, but not with partnership property. Although the interest of a limited partner is considered individual personal property of that partner, the ULPA recognizes that, in some circumstances, some specific property included in the limited partner's interest may be important, or even necessary, to the continuation of the business. Therefore, this property can be redeemed by a general partner for partnership use. However, whenever a limited partner's interest is withdrawn or reduced by any of these legal processes, the certificate must be amended to reflect the change.

Amendment or Cancellation of the Certificate

The certificate of limited partnership is intended to reflect the current status of the partnership and, in particular, financial information concerning the involvement of each limited partner. Its importance, and the importance of keeping it current, cannot be overstated. Whenever the partnership is dissolved, or when all limited partners withdraw, it must be cancelled. In addition, it must be amended in the event of any material change in the status of the limited partners.

Section 24 of the ULPA provides for the certificate's amendment in specific circumstances. These occur when there has been a change in the name of the partnership or in the amount or character of the contribution of any limited partner. However, no amendment is required for a change in a limited partner's contribution if the change was planned in advance and was to occur at a stated future time, and this information was set out in the certificate in advance. Other changes that require an amendment are: there is substitution of a person as a limited partner after assignment of a limited partner's interest; an additional partner, either general or limited, is admitted to the partnership; a general partner retires, dies, or becomes insane and the business is continued; there is a material change in the character of the business; there is a time stated in the certificate for dissolution or a return of a contribution, and the time is changed, or if a time not previously stated is established; or any other change is deemed necessary to reflect the agreement of the partners accurately. The last provision is intended as a catch-all and would include any material factor that should be made known to the public. For example, if the partners establish a future time for further contributions by a limited partner or change an existing time, the certificate should be amended. The partners of a limited partnership are expected to know when a change has occurred that is so important as to require an amendment.

DISSOLUTION

Unlike a general partnership, not every change in the composition of the partners of a limited partnership will cause dissolution. The admission of a new limited partner will not, because the contribution of a limited partner is considered only an investment, much the same as if the partnership had borrowed from a lender. The difference is primarily a bookkeeping matter, with the investment of a limited partner being recorded as part of the capital structure rather than as a debt; it is also a matter of the method of paying a return to the investor, in that the return is not fixed, but ordinarily is based only on the partnership's profits. For the same reason, the retirement, death, insanity, or any other change in the status of a limited partner will not cause dissolution. These changes only require an amendment to the certificate.

Causes

The causes of dissolution of a limited partnership are the same as those that will cause dissolution of a general partnership, such as illegality, bankruptcy of the partnership, the expulsion of a general partner, or the desire of any general partner to dissolve the partnership, even in contravention of the partnership agreement. The retirement, death, or insanity of a general partner also will cause dissolution unless the business can be continued by the remaining general partners either under a right to do so stated in the certificate or with the consent of all members of the partnership. In addition, a limited partner has the power to cause dissolution if he rightfully has demanded the return of his contribution, and that has not been done.

Although there is no dissolution upon the death of a limited partner, his executor or administrator takes all of the deceased's rights and assumes all of his liabilities for the purpose of settling the partner's estate. This will include the right to be a substitute limited partner, if the right was granted in the certificate or later is bestowed by consent of the remaining members of the partnership. The difference between being a simple assignee and being a substitute limited partner was discussed in the section concerning assignment.

Distribution of Assets

Section 23 of the ULPA establishes the order in which assets are to be distributed to settle partnership accounts after dissolution. First, creditors of the partnership, other than general partners or limited partners in respect to their contributions, are paid. The priority of payment to these creditors is to be the priority established by portions of state law other than the ULPA. Thereafter, the order of distribution to partners is: (1) limited partners in respect to their shares of profits and other income or their contributions; (2) limited partners in respect to capital contributions; (3)

Hierarchy of distribution of assets upon dissolution

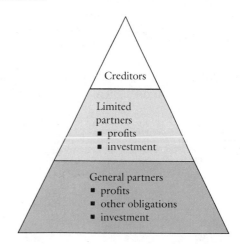

general partners other than for capital and profits; (4) general partners in respect to profits; and (5) general partners in respect to capital. Thus, in the overall distribution of assets, general creditors rank over limited partners, who rank over general partners.

THE REVISED UNIFORM LIMITED PARTNERSHIP ACT

Changes under RULPA

The **Revised Uniform Limited Partnership Act (RULPA)** was promulgated by the National Conference of Commissioners on Uniform State Laws in 1976. It is intended to replace the original Uniform Limited Partnership Act and includes many of the ULPA provisions, but also adds a number of new provisions and discusses others in more detail than did the earlier act. Also, the RULPA altered some ULPA provisions in order to treat limited partnerships more like corporations.

With regard to the name of the partnership, the RULPA requires that it contain the words "limited partnership" in full, and it cannot contain anything indicating it is organized for any purpose other than one stated in its certificate. Thus, in preparation for registration of the name, the act requires that it be sufficiently distinctive so as not to be confused with that of other limited partnerships or corporations. Finally the name may be reserved for the benefit of the partnership, so no one else may use it, by filing with, and securing the approval of, the secretary of state. Registration is available for both existing and future limited partnerships, foreign or organized within that state, doing business or intending to do business in the state.

A partnership with no place of business in the state is required to have a registered agent located in the state for the purpose of receiving service of process should anyone wish to sue the partnership. Certain records must be kept at a specified place of business or at the location of the registered agent.

What constitutes participation in control of the business, to cause a limited partner to be liable as a general partner, is discussed in Section 303(b) of the RULPA; it was not addressed in the ULPA. The RULPA lists activities that are *not* to be construed as participating in control, but the list is not intended to indicate that other activities *do* evidence control. Those listed include acting as a contractor, agent, or employee of the partnership or as a consultant to advise the general partners, acting as a surety for the partnership, approving or disapproving an amendment to the partnership agreement, or voting on certain specified extraordinary acts by the partnership.

Article 4 of the RULPA is devoted to general partners, who were not addressed separately in the ULPA, and to circumstances that may cause a general partner to cease being a general partner of a limited partnership. The grounds for losing general-partner status are increased to include more types of financial difficulty, such as the filing of a petition for reorganization, arrangement, composition, and dissolution. These grounds are tailored to suit general partners who are corporations or other partnerships, as well as natural persons.

Foreign Limited Partnerships

Because of the growth both in size and number of partnerships, and particularly limited partnerships, their business activities have ceased to be as confined and localized as they once were. We see more and more multistate limited partnerships. Just as the RULPA altered the ULPA provisions in order to treat limited partnerships more like corporations, provision also has been made concerning foreign limited partnerships. A **foreign limited partnership** is one formed under the laws of another state. Basically, foreign limited partnerships may reserve a partnership name and, in doing so, must comply with the same requirements as a domestic limited partnership, including using the words "limited partnership" in its name. This name may or may not be the one under which the partnership does business in any other state. Compliance by the foreign organization with the other prerequisites for limited partnerships also is required.

If properly registered, a foreign limited partnership will have the same rights and obligations as a domestic limited partnership. The transaction of business within the state *without* registration will prevent a nonregistered partnership from maintaining any lawsuit or other action or proceeding in a court of the state, and causes the secretary of state to become its agent for the purpose of receiving service of process with respect to claims arising in connection with the partnership's transacting business without registration. However, a nonregistered limited partnership may appear and defend any lawsuit, or other action or proceeding, filed against it. Also, failure to register does not render the limited partners liable as general partners.

SUMMARY

As the partnership came to be used more and more, even in connection with larger businesses, the limitations of the general partnership form became more inhibiting. The open-ended liability of the partners and the fragile existence of the partnership, dissolving any time there was any change in the composition of the partners, and the general partnership's inability to attract new capital conveniently, gave rise to the limited partnership. This organizational form is created by meeting the requirements of state enabling legislation, particularly the Uniform Limited Partnership Act (ULPA) and the Revised Uniform Limited Partnership Act (RULPA). This includes the filing of a certificate containing information about the partnership and having at least one general partner and one limited partner.

A limited partner is liable for partnership debts only to the extent of her contribution to the capital of the partnership, unlike the unlimited liability of the general partner. However, a limited partner is not allowed to participate in control (management) of the business, or she will become liable as a general partner.

The limited partner is treated more like an investor than partner. His interest in the partnership is considered personal property, and it is assignable freely without the consent of the partners. No change in the status of this type of partner, even his death or withdrawal, causes dissolution of the limited partnership. The rights and duties of the general partners of a limited partnership, and the circumstances that will cause dissolution of the partnership, usually are the same as those governing general partnerships. General partners are considered "true partners," not simply investors.

The Revised Uniform Limited Partnership Act of 1976 made a number of changes in the ULPA. It is more specific in some of its provisions, such as those relating to what constitutes "participation in control." The RULPA covers matters only implied under the previous act. For example, it provides some details concerning the rights and duties of a general partner. It also provides for registration of limited partnership names, much the same as has been done regarding corporations; registration of foreign limited partnerships; and penalties for doing business without registration.

Overall, a limited partnership is a hybrid form of organization, falling somewhere between the general partnership and the corporation. The policies of the Uniform Limited Partnership Act have been carried forward by the 1976 RULPA, moving the limited partnership a little further toward the corporate form, and clarifying and firming up prior law in a number of important respects.

KEY TERMS AND CONCEPTS

limited partnership
Uniform Limited Partnership Act (ULPA)
certificate of limited partnership
Revised Uniform Limited Partnership Act (RULPA)
foreign limited partnership

PROBLEMS

1. Micheli brought an action against Fairwood, the only general partner, and all the limited partners of Fairwood Associates, for labor and materials on an apartment project. Micheli contended all were liable individually because, although a certificate of limited partnership had been executed and filed in the office of the Albany County Clerk, no proof of publication of notice had been filed as required by statute. Should the limited partners be liable individually?

2. Define the steps necessary for the formation of a limited partnership under the ULPA.

3. Davis was a limited partner in Phillips & Associates, a real estate investment firm. She assigned her rights in the partnership to Norton, who gave notice of the assignment to the partnership. Several months later, a partnership meeting was held, and the partners voted on some matters of importance to Norton, but he was not notified until after the meeting. Was the action valid?

4. Khoury and Martin each were to contribute a total of $83,000 to the capital of Columbia-Heather, Ltd., a limited partnership. Their contributions were payable in installments. Martin made the first payment and two more, then refused to contribute further, charging Khoury with a breach of the partnership agreement and mismanagement. If Martin's charges are true, is he relieved of his obligation to pay the remainder of the installments?

5. Snow became a limited partner in a business created to develop a special-purpose incinerator. In the first year there were no profits, and she sought to deduct her share of the loss from ordinary income, under a statute allowing a deduction for "experimental expenditures." The Commissioner of Internal Revenue disallowed the deduction, stating it was not a loss from a "business or profession" but a loss on an investment. Was the commissioner correct?

6. Vidricksen agreed to become a limited partner with Thom and Thom Chevrolet. After operating for a time, Vidricksen learned that the papers to form the partnership might not have been filed. Six months later, Vidricksen filed a renunciation of profits, eight days after the business went into bankruptcy. Grover, a creditor, claimed Vidricksen still should be held liable as a general partner, in spite of the renunciation. Is Grover correct?

7. Woods Mill was a limited partnership, owning an apartment building under construction. When the contractor was not paid, he sought to hold the limited partners liable as general partners, because they had participated in management by attending two meetings after seeing the project was in financial difficulty, about which a presentation was made by the general partner, and had engaged in discussions to correct the problem. In addition, one of the limited partners went to the supervisor on the job and complained about how the work was being performed. Should this result in liability as general partners?

8. Filisi, a limited partner in Jolly Tavern, was sued to establish individual liability for assessments and penalties because the tavern did not obtain a cabaret license, as required by law. During the time in question, Filisi had wanted out, but her partner lacked the money to purchase her share and induced her to stay. As security, Filisi managed the business for a salary, and took 50 percent of profits as her share. Filisi contends she should not be liable since she was managing the business only to secure repayment of her investment, and on salary rather than as a partner. Is Filisi correct?

9. Brown, a limited partner, was "frozen out" of partnership affairs. As a result, he formally requested the return of his contribution. Did Brown's request constitute dissolution of the partnership?

Corporations: Nature and Formation

INTRODUCTION

The corporate form of business organization obviously is extremely important today. One of the major reasons for this is because a corporation is particularly suited to the needs of large enterprises. It provides many potential advantages over the proprietorship and the partnership, but at the same time suffers from some disadvantages. The choice of the best form of organization for any particular business can be made only by evaluating the advantages and disadvantages as they apply to the circumstances of the particular venture being considered.

Advantages and Disadvantages of the Corporation

Among the major advantages of a corporation is its stability as an entity. It may have a virtually perpetual existence. It does not experience dissolution upon the death—or any other change in the status—of any of its owners. As a result, shares of ownership in a corporation are transferable freely, subject to possible agreement among the owners to the contrary. Transfer usually is facilitated by ownership's being represented by divisible shares, which is the second major advantage. An owner of shares in a corporation normally may transfer all or some portion of this interest at any time. Frequently this is done on an organized stock exchange. The third advantage, related to the first two, is that it generally is easier for a corporation than for other business forms to acquire new capital contributions. It simply may issue new shares of stock, if that is approved by the shareholders and the board of directors. Finally, investment of capital is made attractive by the fact that the liability of shareholders for corporate obligations generally is limited to their individual investments.

Among the disadvantages, a corporation is somewhat more cumbersome to form, requiring registration and the meeting of certain formal statutory requirements. Also, the sale of shares often is subject to an elaborate set of statutory and regulatory requirements. Finally, depending on the income of a corporation, and the income of an owner of its shares, the taxation of both corporate profits and the distributions to owners frequently proves to be a disadvantage.

History of Corporations

Corporations date back at least as far as the Roman Empire, although they did not exist at that time in their modern form. Separate entities were created by express grant from the emperors, and generally were authorized for public purposes such as governance or education, and sometimes for religious objectives. Having been created by the emperor's authority, they also were subject to his control, and depended for their existence on his continued good will. By the fourteenth century, corporate organizations had developed for a wider variety of purposes, and came to be recog-

nized by the Common Law. The recognition of corporate entities under the Roman Law and the Common Law then gave rise to codification by statute throughout Europe.

More closely related to the modern business corporation were the English trading companies, such as the Virginia Company and the British East India Company. They were organized, and given royal charters, for purposes of exploration and colonization, in addition to general trading. (The Virginia Company, of course, was prominent in American history as the founder of the Virginia Colony.) These were the foundations for the emergence of the corporation in the United States. As had been true in other parts of the world, the first corporations in this country were formed by extraordinary governmental action in the form of special legislation. Today, incorporation generally is accomplished by complying with incorporation statutes. Both the federal government and each of the state governments may authorize the formation of corporations within the limits of their individual jurisdictions.

Types of Corporations

Corporations may be classified according to (1) purpose, (2) characteristics of ownership, and (3) method of taxation. The basic reasons for these categories are to develop common terminology, and to provide groupings of corporations that share common legal characteristics. Corporations also may be classified as *public* or *private*. A public corporation is one that is created to administer governmental or quasi-governmental affairs. For example, a city may be incorporated by a state as a municipal corporation, and the Tennessee Valley Authority (TVA) was incorporated by the federal government to provide electrical power to areas in the Tennessee Valley that could not be served economically by other utility companies. All other corporations may be broadly classified as private, and include the hundreds of manufacturers and service providers familiar to all of us. Some of these however, are sub-classified as *quasi-public* or *public-service* corporations. These are private corporations that are created for the purpose of supplying services to customers, such as electricity, telephone, and railroad service. They are granted monopolies to operate within certain specified areas, and in return are subject to additional governmental regulation of such matters as rates and quality of service.

Private corporations also may be classified further as *for profit* and *nonprofit*. The former, as the name implies, are organized to pursue some type of business venture for the purpose of earning profits to be shared by stockholders. General Motors, IBM, and the New York Yankees are examples. Nonprofit corporations are organized for various charitable, religious, and educational purposes. Harvard University, the American Red Cross, and the Mayo Clinic fall into this category. Their main source of income is generally from contributions. If a nonprofit corporation meets certain Internal Revenue Service requirements, these contributions are deductible by donors for income-tax purposes.

Corporations also may be classified as domestic, foreign, or alien. A corporation is a **domestic corporation** in the state under the laws of which it was created and granted its charter. In all other states, it is a **foreign corporation.** In other countries, it is an **alien corporation.** For example, Chrysler Corporation is incorporated in the state of Delaware, where it is a domestic corporation, and has its headquarters and some manufacturing facilities in the state of Michigan, where it is classified as a foreign corporation. When it does business in foreign countries, such as Japan, it is classified as an alien corporation. Foreign and alien corporations doing business in a state are required to register and to designate a resident agent authorized to receive service of process. Failure to meet these requirements may subject the corporation to some penalty, the most common of which is that, although the corporation may be sued and obliged to defend a lawsuit in

the state's courts, it is not allowed to sue or to make any other use of the local courts on its own initiative.

Until relatively recently, professionals such as doctors, lawyers, dentists, and certified public accountants were not allowed to incorporate their businesses. Today, all states allow **professional corporations (PCs).** Professionals, by incorporating, may gain some tax advantages. Because they become employees of the corporation, they may participate in certain tax-sheltered pension plans and other fringe benefits, the costs of which are deductible as business expenses of the corporation. They also enjoy limited liability for wrongdoings of other corporate employees, although they are fully liable for their own malpractice.

A corporation whose stock is held by a small group of investors, frequently a family, and is not offered for sale to the public, often is referred to as a **close corporation.** This is as opposed to a **publicly held corporation.** Generally, close corporations are kept closed to public ownership by agreements that effectively prevent the free sale of shares to "outsiders," such as an agreement to give the corporation a first right of refusal if the stock is to be sold.

Corporations also may become *Subchapter S* corporations. This means that they have qualified for special treatment for federal income-tax purposes. Qualifying corporations do not pay a corporate income tax. Rather, the corporation's income is taxed directly to its shareholders as if it were a partnership. This avoids the double taxation of profits, which may be desirable.

The Model Business Corporation Act

Corporate law primarily is statutory, although the corporation itself is regarded as a "person" and is subject to most of the same contract and tort rules that apply to a natural person. Each state has its own statute, or statutes, governing the formation of a corporation, its operation, its unique obligations (not shared by natural persons), and its termination. These usually consist of one general corporation code and a number of special statutes dealing with certain types of corporations such as banks, insurance companies, and professional corporations.

The main elements of these laws are similar and have many common characteristics. Although no uniform law has been promulgated by the National Conference of Commissioners on Uniform State Laws, such as the Uniform Partnership Act or the Uniform Commercial Code, the **Model Business Corporations Act (MBCA)** has provided a structure for corporation statutes that has been followed by a substantial number of states.

The MBCA was first drafted in 1946 under the auspices of the American Bar Association. It went through a comprehensive revision in 1969, and another in 1983. Its original draft followed the pattern of the Illinois Act. No state has adopted it completely, as states typically do with a "Uniform" act, and the MBCA encourages that approach. However, it does serve as a model, and will be followed in our discussion of corporate law.

THE NATURE OF CORPORATIONS

As compared with proprietorships and general partnerships, the corporation is a truly unique form of business organization. Its uniqueness flows directly from its status as a separate legal entity.

The Corporate Entity

As mentioned above, a **corporation** is considered a legal entity, or "fictitious legal person." It has substantially the same rights and obligations as any "natural person." It may own property in its own name, and it may transfer property in its own name. It may sue and be sued; it may be liable for the commission of torts; it is liable on its separate contracts; it is liable for the commission of certain crimes when statutes so provide; and it more or less has the same constitutional rights, and is entitled to the same constitutional protections, as any other citizen. The fact that a corporation is a separate legal **entity,** or legal person, is the foun-

Classification of corporations

Type	Definition/Meaning	Example
Public	created to administer governmental affairs	city of New York
Private	created for private benefit	IBM
Public service	heavily regulated private corporation that provides services to the public	Amtrack
For profit	profit is of primary concern	General Motors
Non-profit	profit is not allowed	United Way
Domestic	domestic when operating in the state in which incorporation took place	Chrysler in Delaware (its state of incorporation)
Foreign	foreign when operating in any state other than the state of incorporation	Chrysler in Michigan
Alien	alien when operating in another country	Chrysler in West Germany
Closely held	stock not offered for sale to the public	Ma and Pa Inc. (a small family corporation)
Publicly held	stock held by public at large	Exxon
Professional	composed of professionals, usually for tax and liability considerations (but a professional who is negligent is liable for his or her own malpractice)	Teeth, P.C. (a corporation of dentists)
Subchapter S	special corporations in which only shareholders are taxed, not the corporation itself	Smalltime Inc. (a small business corporation)

dation of other characteristics of a corporation. A corporation generally is subject to income tax, as is any other citizen. The owners of a corporation have limited liability for obligations of the corporation because it, as a person, should be responsible for itself. Changes in the status, or the composition, of the owners do not cause dissolution, because these matters do not change the character of the corporation itself.

Transferable Interests

The interests of each owner of a private business corporation are represented by **shares,** usually in the form of stock evidenced by a certificate. The shares represented may be transferred, either all at one time or in smaller units. In order to keep track of ownership, especially for purposes of paying dividends and determining voting rights, when shares of stock are sold, the sale must be registered with the corporation, which will then issue a new certificate (or new certificates) evidencing the rights of the transferor, if any are left, and of the transferee.

The fact that the ownership interests in a corporation may be broken into many small units is one of the major advantages of the corporate form. Not only is it easier for an owner to sell part of his interest, but it is easy for a corporation to appeal to a larger group of potential investors by issuing more shares of stock at a lower market price per share. This ability of a corporation to divide its stock into any number of transferable shares is one of the factors leading to the popularity of the corporate form of business organization. Millions of citizens now own a portion of corporate America, either directly or through mutual funds and pensions. In some cases, the ownership may be little more than a fraction of a share.

Shareholder Liability

Since a corporation is considered a distinct legal person, separate from the individual identities of its owners, it usually is solely liable for its own obligations. Therefore, **shareholders** are not personally responsible, but have at risk only their individual contributions to the capital of the corporation. This includes the amount paid as the purchase price of the stock, together with any undistributed profits retained by the corporation. Other circumstances occasionally may impose further liability on shareholders, such as fraud in the creation and operation of the corporation, which may cause a court to **pierce the corporate veil** (to disregard the fact that the corporation is a separate legal entity and hold the owners liable as though they were general partners or proprietors), and subscriptions to the stated capital of the corporation remaining unpaid. These situations, however, occur only infrequently. The following case illustrates the principle.

WALKOVSZKY v. CARLTON et al.
18 N.Y.2d 414, 223 N.E.2d 6 (1966)

This was an action by John Walkovszky (Plaintiff/Respondent) against William Carlton and others (Defendants/Appellants) to recover damages for personal injuries.

Plaintiff was injured when run down by a cab driven by Defendant Marchese. The cab was registered to Defendant Seon Cab Corporation. Defendant Carlton was alleged to be the owner of ten corporations, one of which was Seon. Each corporation owned only two cabs and carried a $10,000 liability insurance policy—the minimum permitted by law. It was alleged that they were operated as a "single entity, unit and enterprise," sharing financing, supplies, employees, repairs, and garages. Plaintiff contended that the arrangement was devised to defraud the general public and, therefore, that all of the corporations, and their owners individually, should be liable for his injuries.

The trial court found for Defendants. On appeal, the decision was reversed and remanded, and Defendants appealed. Reversed, with the trial court decision reinstated with leave to serve an amended complaint.

FULD, Judge.

The law permits the incorporation of a business for the very purpose of enabling its proprietors to escape personal liability . . . but, manifestly, the privilege is not without its limits. Broadly speaking, the courts will disregard the corporate form, or, to use accepted terminology, "pierce the corporate veil", whenever necessary "to prevent fraud or to achieve equity". . . . In determining whether liability should be extended to reach assets beyond those belonging to the corporation, we are guided, as Judge Cardozo noted, by "general rules of agency". . . . In other words, whenever anyone uses control of the corporation to further his own rather than the corporation's business, he will be liable for the corporation's acts "upon the principle of respondeat superior applicable even where the agent is a natural person". . . . Such liability, moreover, extends not only to the corporation's commercial dealing . . . but to its negligent acts as well. . . .

In the case before us, the plaintiff has explicitly alleged that none of the corporations "had a separate existence of their own" and, as indicated above, all are named as defendants. However, it is one thing to assert that a corporation is a fragment of a larger corporate combine which actually conducts the business. . . . It is quite another to claim that the corporation is a "dummy" for its individual stockholders who are in reality carrying on the business in their personal capacities for purely personal rather than corporate ends. . . . Either circumstance would justify treating the corporation as an agent and piercing the corporate veil to reach the principal but a different result would follow in each case. In the first, only a larger corporate entity would be held financially responsible . . . while, in the other the stockholder would be personally liable. . . . Either the stockholder is conducting the business in his individual capacity or he is not. If he is, he will be liable; if he is not, then, it does not matter—insofar as his personal liability is concerned—that the enterprise is actually being carried on by a larger "enterprise entity". . . .

The individual defendant is charged with having "organized, managed, dominated and controlled" a fragmented corporate entity but there are no allegations that he was conducting business in his individual capacity. Had the taxicab fleet been owned by a single corporation, it would be readily apparent that the plaintiff would face formidable barriers in attempting to establish personal liability on the part of the corporation's stockholders. The fact that the fleet ownership has been deliberately split up among many corporations does not ease the plaintiff's burden in that respect. The corporate form may not be disregarded merely because the assets of the corporation, together with the mandatory insurance coverage of the vehicle which struck the plaintiff, are insufficient to assure him the recovery sought. If Carlton were to be held individually liable on those facts alone, the decision would apply equally to the thousands of cabs which are owned by their individual drivers who conduct their businesses through corporations organized pursuant to section 401 of the Business Corporation Law, . . . and carry the minimum insurance required. . . .

These taxi owner-operators are entitled to form such corporations . . . and we agree with the court at Special Term that, if the insurance coverage required by statute "is inadequate for the protection of the public, the remedy lies not with the courts but with the Legislature." . . .

In point of fact, the principle relied upon in the complaint to sustain the imposition of personal liability is not agency but fraud. Such a cause of action cannot withstand analysis. If it is not fraudulent for the owner-operator of a single cab corporation to take out only the minimum required liability insurance, the enterprise does not become either illicit or fraudulent merely because it consists of many such corporations. The plaintiff's injuries are the same regardless of whether the cab which strikes him is owned by a single corporation or part of a fleet with ownership fragmented among many corporations. Whatever rights he may be able to assert against parties other than the registered owner of the vehicle come into being not because he has been defrauded but because, under the principle of respondeat superior, he is entitled to hold the whole enterprise responsible for the acts of its agents.

In sum, then, the complaint falls short of adequately stating a cause of action against the defendant Carlton in his individual capacity.

Questions

1. Can you explain why the court refuses to allow the plaintiff to pursue a fraud theory?

2. Can you formulate the arguments that the plaintiff will have to present successfully when he returns to the trial court to prevail based on an agency theory?

Taxation

As a separate legal person, a corporation is subject to federal income-tax law. It must file a return and pay income tax on its profits in much the same manner as any other person. This gives rise to the problem of **double taxation** that has been mentioned before. The corporation's earnings are taxed once when earned, and again to the individual shareholders when paid out in dividends. Attempts to avoid this result by having the corporation retain large amounts of earnings have been met with a tax on excessive retained earnings. However, a method that may be used successfully in suitable circumstances is the formation of a Subchapter S corporation.

A **Subchapter S corporation** also is called a "small business corporation." It is formed under the provisions of Sections 1371 through 1377 of Title 26 of the United States Code, as amended by the 1982 Subchapter S Revision Act. To be eligible, a corporation must meet certain requirements:

1. it may have no more than 35 shareholders;
2. only one class of voting and non-voting stock is permitted;
3. all shareholders owning stock at the time of election to become a Subchapter S corporation must consent;

4. the corporation is restricted as to the amount of passive investment income (such as royalties or rental income) it can have (the limit is 25 percent of gross receipts for corporations that have accumulated earnings and profits at the end of the taxable year; income in excess of 25 percent is taxed at a corporate rate of 46 percent), and if the corporation has excess passive investment income for three consecutive years, its election will be terminated;

5. the election of Subchapter S treatment may be terminated by a vote of the majority of voting shares; and

6. profits must be passed on to the shareholders on a per-share basis.

When these requirements are met, the corporation is not taxed. It is considered only a conduit through which income flows to the shareholders. The corporation will file only an information return, disclosing data on its earnings and distributions.

FORMATION

In order to form a corporation, a number of preliminary steps must be taken. Perhaps the most important is that the amount to be shown as stated capital on the articles of incorporation must be subscribed. This is one of the jobs of a *promoter*. The promoter operates independently, because the corporation is not yet in existence.

Promoters

The **promoter,** who is the person seeking to form the corporation, first must decide on the general limits of the business to be conducted and how much initial capital will be needed. In order to raise the capital, the promoter will sell **stock subscriptions.** These are contracts binding each prospective investor **(subscriber)** to purchase a certain number of shares of stock, at a stated price per share, when the corporation comes into existence. Subscribers who fail to meet this obligation are subject to suit for breach of contract. The promoter also may enter into other contracts in anticipation of incorporation. These may include the purchase and rental of property to be used by the corporation. In some cases, for example, forming a corporation that will operate a shopping center, the promoter's contracts may include commitments to lease out property, such as store space, that will belong to the corporation. In addition, some financing by way of borrowing, as opposed to selling shares of stock, may be arranged.

In the absence of statutory authority, a promoter has no power to bind the corporation. The contracts she enters into and her expenses in promoting the corporation, however, will be taken over by the corporation once it is formed. (Although the new corporation has no legal obligation to assume these liabilities, in practice the failure to do so would be rare.) This may be done by assignment, novation, or simple assumption. It is not correct to say that the corporation "ratifies," because ratification requires that the person doing it—the corporation—existed at the time of the unauthorized act.

Although a promoter is not an agent of the corporation, since the corporation is nonexistent during the promotion period, it has been held that she owes a fiduciary duty to it once it comes into existence and takes over her liabilities, and that the duty dates back to acts during the promotion period. Therefore, a promoter who has dealt for herself, profited secretly, or otherwise acted contrary to the corporation's best interests is guilty of a breach of duty, and is subject to pay damages to it.

Torts committed by the promoter during the promotion period are her own responsibility, and are not assumed by the corporation unless it does so expressly, or it accepts the benefits of a transaction with knowledge or notice of fraud committed by the promoter in securing the transaction.

Contract liability, when assumed, will render the corporation liable to the third party, but this does not relieve the promoter of individual liability, unless agreed to by the third party, as could be accomplished with an exculpatory clause in the original agreement or by novation.

The following case considers promoters' liability on subscription contracts.

MOLINA v. LARGOSA
465 P.2d 293 (Haw. 1970)

This was an action by Henry Molina (Plaintiff/Appellant) against Rudy Largosa (Defendant/Appellee) to recover from Defendant, the promoter of a corporation, his investment in the corporation.

On April 15, 1963, Plaintiff signed a subscription contract to purchase $2000 worth of stock (40 shares) in a proposed corporation being promoted by Defendant. The corporation was formed, properly filing its articles of incorporation and meeting other requirements of state law. Thereafter, the corporation failed. The question before the court was whether Defendant could be held liable for the loss to Plaintiff, who contended the subscription contract was invalid because it did not set out the total capital of the corporation and his proportionate interest in it.

The trial court found for Defendant, and Plaintiff appealed. Affirmed.

WONG, Circuit Judge.

Plaintiff contends that because the subscription form did not set out the total capital of the proposed corporation and his proportionate interest in it, there was no valid subscription contract. As a general proposition, in the absence of any statutory requirement (and the Hawaii statute is silent in this respect), no particular form is required if the intent of the parties can be collected from the writing. As one court put it in Draper v. Chicago Horseshoe Co.: "The real question is, Was such paper intended and accepted as a subscription?"

In this case the trial court reached an affirmative answer to that question, which conclusion is supported by the record. Although the subscription form did not state the total capital and Molina's interest, these were ascertainable by merely adding up the investments of all subscribers. This information is also obtainable from the affidavit filed with the corporation's Articles, which listed all subscribers and the respective amounts invested. The interest of any subscriber would then be the amount of his investment divided by the total investment in the corporation.

Upon filing of the said Articles and affidavit, the corporation came into existence. . . . In this jurisdiction, however, the mere fact of incorporation does not amount to an acceptance by the corporation of a subscriber's offer. There must be an expressed or implied acceptance of that offer. . . . After payment of the subscription price by Molina, not only was his name listed as a stockholder in the affidavit filed with the corporation's Articles, but Molina himself on different occasions made inquiries concerning his stock certificate, and from time to time requested Largosa to sell his shares of stock. The acceptance by the corporation of Molina's offer and Molina's acknowledgment of such acceptance are, therefore, clearly supported by the record.

Molina may not now rescind his contract. In Buffalo & J.R.R. v. Gifford, . . . a subscriber made two installment payments pursuant to a subscription agreement, the corporation was formed and his name was placed on the corporation's stock ledger. It was held that the corporation could enforce the stock subscription agreement, recovering the balance due thereunder. *A fortiori* [because of the foregoing fact, the last statement must be true] Molina, who has paid the full amount provided in his stock subscription agreement, has no right to get his money back. . . . It should be noted, in passing, that even if he were entitled to rescission, his action should be against the corporation and not the promoter.

The promoter may be discharged from liability to a third party (creditor) on a preincorporation contract by a novation, if the corporation assumes the contract, and the other contracting party assents to the substitution of the corporation for the promoter. . . .

In the case of a subscription contract, however, the objective is a valid incorporation pursuant to the terms of the contract. Once that is accomplished, the contract has been performed. There is no need for a discharge by novation of the promoter from liability as the promoter is liable only if there is failure of such incorporation. . . .

Largosa promised to form a corporation, and he performed this promise. Plaintiff Molina got just what he paid for: stock in a corporation. There was no failure of consideration in the contract; only a failure of a corporation in which Molina had purchased stock. Clearly, if the corporation had succeeded, Molina would have been entitled to his share of the stock appreciation and any dividends declared.

Molina complains that shareholders' meetings were not held, and that his certificate of 40 shares was never delivered. A certificate is not necessary to make him a stockholder. . . . His remedy for this complaint was to compel such meetings and delivery. These are not adequate grounds to support his claim that there was no contract with the corporation.

Questions

1. Do you agree with the court's decision? Why or why not?
2. Was the investor prejudiced by the promoter's failure to state total capital or his share? How important do you think that was to the court?

Subscribers' Liability

As noted previously, a subscription is an agreement to purchase shares of corporate stock, the subscription price to be paid later. If the agreement is entered into prior to incorporation, Section 6.20(a) of the Model Business Corporation Act provides that it is irrevocable for a period of six months. If entered into after incorporation, it is simply a contract between the subscriber and the corporation.

Payment terms for shares may be established in

the subscription agreement and, if they are not, the terms may be established by the board of directors of the corporation. If established by the board, the terms must be uniform within each class or issue of stock.

If a subscriber defaults on payment, the corporation is entitled to proceed to collect the amount due as a debt. The corporate bylaws also may prescribe reasonable penalties for nonpayment. However, the corporation may not require forfeiture of payments already made unless it first gives a written notice, and the obligation remains unpaid for a period of twenty days after the effective date of the notice. If the subscription is then forfeited, the shares subscribed may be sold by the corporation. Any amount by which the proceeds exceed the amount due on the subscription, together with reasonable expenses of the sale, must be paid to the subscriber, and the subscriber remains liable to the corporation for any deficiency.

A subscriber may transfer his shares to a third party before they are paid fully. If he does so, he remains liable to the corporation for the unpaid amount, but the purchaser is not liable in the absence of a novation.

Incorporation

One of the first decisions to be made after there has been a decision to incorporate is to select a state in which to do it. Although state incorporation acts follow a similar pattern, specific provisions may vary widely, as may the attitudes of the courts in the various states. For example, for both of these reasons, Delaware has been considered a favorable state, from the viewpoint of corporate management, for some time. As a result, it has become the state of incorporation for many of the major corporations whose headquarters are all over the United States.

Each state has a provision concerning how many incorporators are required to form a corporation. (**Incorporators** are the people who will see to the preparation and filing of the documents

necessary for incorporation. Often they also are the promoters.) Section 2.01 of the MBCA suggests "one or more." Historically, three was a common requirement, but more and more states have reduced that number to one. This has been encouraged by a tendency toward the incorporation of smaller businesses.

ARTICLES OF INCORPORATION

The incorporators must file **articles of incorporation** to be approved by the state. Under the MBCA, the articles *must* include: (1) the name of the proposed corporation; (2) the number of shares the corporation is authorized to issue; (3) the address of the corporation's registered office; (4) the name of its registered agent; and (5) the names and addresses of the incorporators. In addition, the articles *may* include: (1) names and addresses of the members of the first board of directors; (2) provisions regarding the purposes of the corporation, management of its affairs, limitations on its powers, its directors, its shareholders, and the par value of authorized shares; and (3) its bylaws. Based on these documents, the state will issue a **certificate of incorporation (charter)**, which officially brings the corporation into existence.

Name

Rules concerning the name of a corporation usually are very simple. Generally, the name may be any designation that clearly indicates that the business is a corporation and is not deceptive or easily confused with the name of another corporate name registered or reserved in that state. (In many states, a corporate name may be reserved in advance of incorporation, if approved, and will be held for a time—120 days under the MBCA.)

In order for the business to be identified clearly as a corporation, state acts typically require that the name include one of a list of specific designations such as "Incorporated," "Corporation," or

"Company," or "Inc.," "Corp.," or "Ltd." These designations are specific, and a corporation is not entitled to use them interchangeably. For example, "ABC Incorporated" is not the same entity as "ABC, Inc." or "ABC Corporation."

Prior to approving a corporate name, the secretary of state will examine the corporate records to determine whether the requested name is in use or has been reserved, or if it is "not distinguishable on the records" from such a name. If everything is in order, the name will be approved. Frequently, the articles of incorporation will list three or more names in order of preference. This may avoid an amendment and refiling of the papers in the event that the most desireable name is not available. The following case considers the question of whether a corporate name is too close to the name of another corporation.

FIRST NATIONAL BANK OF LANDER v. FIRST WYOMING SAVINGS AND LOAN ASSOCIATION
592 P.2d 697 (Wyo. 1979)

This was an action by First Wyoming Savings and Loan Association (Plaintiff/Appellee) against First National Bank of Lander (Defendant/Appellant) to enjoin Defendant from changing the name of a subsidiary bank to First Wyoming Bank. Plaintiff contended the name would be confused with its own.

The trial court granted a permanent injunction, and Defendant appealed. Affirmed in the part material here.

ROSE, Justice.

The general rule is that a national bank can adopt any name approved by the Federal Comptroller of Currency; and it cannot be interfered with by any other authority, except where its use constitutes a tortious infringement on the name of another existing bank. 9 C.J.S. Banks and Banking Section 561 (1938). Generally, administrative rulings on whether the name of a proposed corporation is so similar to that of an existing corporation as to be calculated to deceive are not conclusive as to the right to use the name. . . .

The defendants contend that the trial court's finding—that the words "First Wyoming" had taken on a secondary meaning and had been appropriated by plaintiff as a common-law trade name in Fremont County—is not supported by the law and the evidence. In addition, they urge that this court should more stringently review the decision in this case, based on an allegation that the trial court adopted, without change, findings prepared by the plaintiff. . . .

As stated in Wyoming National Bank v. Security Bank & Trust Co., . . . questions regarding trade-name infringement are largely factual determinations to be made by the trier-of-fact and, therefore, we will not disturb a trial court's findings thereon unless they are clearly erroneous or contrary to the great weight of the evidence. We also set forth the applicable standard of law as follows:

> . . . Unless a trade name is confusing and deceptive on its face, those seeking such protection must take the burden of proving that they have given to their trade names a secondary meaning through years of usage and if in this case defendant was to be allowed to use its new

name, the public would be confused by its similarity to the trade names of plaintiffs. This confusion, in turn, must be such as to warrant issuance of an injunction. This is, potential customers must be confused or deceived into patronizing one bank in the mistaken belief that they are dealing with another bank. . . .

A secondary meaning is supplied to geographic or generic words—like those at issue here—when by the process of association the words become distinctive and distinguish the producer of a particular service and the name of that producer. . . . With regard to the likelihood of confusion, the consumer bears some responsibility for using reasonable care. . . .

A review of the record discloses that, in Fremont County, questions of fact were present with respect to the likelihood of confusion and the acquisition of a secondary meaning by plaintiff in the words "First Wyoming." The plaintiff presented evidence of one of its signs located in Lander on which the words "First Wyoming" were predominant. It presented various radio announcements—covering the period from March 1975 to August 1976—in which the words "First Wyoming" were emphasized. Five witnesses testified that they commonly referred to plaintiff as "First Wyoming." Finally, a portion of a study—entitled "The Effect of a Proposed Name Change in Lander, Wyoming"—prepared for the plaintiff was admitted into evidence. The study concludes that "the proposed name change would likely create an awkward and confusing situation in Lander." The study contains data which, if believed by the trial court, would support the trial court's findings. We noted in the Wyoming National Bank decision that the technical adequacy of a survey is a matter of the weight to be attached to it and that its validity may be rebutted. . . . Apparently in this case the trial court was satisfied with the survey's validity, and we are in no position to say otherwise.

We hold that the trial court did not clearly err in finding that the defendants' proposed name-change would infringe upon the secondary meaning acquired by plaintiff in the words "First Wyoming" and that injunctive relief in Fremont County was necessary to avoid confusion and deception.

Questions

1. In picking a corporate name, what are the arguments for picking one that is descriptive of what the company does—for example, International Business Machines—and one that is fanciful—for example, Kodak?

2. In determining whether a name is confusingly similar to another, should the court ask people on the street? actual customers of the two companies? who else?

Authorized Shares

The articles of incorporation must state the number of shares authorized initially. This may be changed later by amendment. However, most incorporators state sufficient shares at the outset to take care of an initial offering and to provide a buffer for the foreseeable future. Simply having a number of shares authorized does not commit the corporation to issuing them.

The shares to be authorized may be all of one class, which will give all shareholders the same rights. However, the articles of incorporation may provide for different classes of stock, such as common and preferred, and even may specify different classes of common stock and different classes of preferred stock. The various classes may represent different rights, such as preferences in dividends and upon liquidation, voting rights, rights to redemption, and rights regarding conversion to another class of stock. Sometimes, stock in one class may be issued in more than one series, each series giving its owners different rights. In the event that more than one class or series is authorized, the different rights must be spelled out in the articles of incorporation.

Registered Agent

The name and the address of a **registered agent** of the proposed corporation must be included in the articles of incorporation. Since the corporation is a fictitious person, some natural person must be designated for the purpose of official contact with the corporation. The primary reasons, of course, are for sending official notifications and serving process. In the event of any change in the registered agent or his address, the secretary of state must be notified. Failure to maintain an accessible registered agent within the state of incorporation results in the automatic appointment of the secretary of state as an agent of the corporation.

Incorporators

The names and addresses of at least the required minimum number of incorporators must be included in the articles of incorporation. An incorporator may be any "person," including a natural person, corporation, partnership, or other association as provided in the corporation laws of the state. It is the job of the incorporators to see to the filing of the articles of incorporation. After a corporation comes into being and begins to operate, the identity of the incorporators, and their locations, is of very little significance. The corporation is then represented by its board of directors. Therefore, the secretary of state need not be notified of changes in the status of incorporators, such as by death or moving to a new address. The incorporators, as such, no longer have powers or obligations regarding the corporation.

Other Matters

A number of other matters *may* be included in the articles of incorporation, such as the names and addresses of the first board of directors and the initial bylaws. Any matter not inconsistent with the corporation laws of the state may be included in the articles.

Bylaws should be formulated to provide how the business is to be managed and how corporate affairs are to be regulated. Their formulation should not be done hurriedly; they require considerable thought. However, the initial bylaws of the proposed corporation frequently are adopted by the incorporators and included in the articles of incorporation. This is a good policy for two reasons. It helps to assure that the corporation, at least in the beginning, will be operated as intended by the incorporators. Also, it avoids having a total absence of operating procedures at the beginning of the corporation's life. If bylaws are not adopted by the incorporators, they must be adopted by the initial board of directors.

DEFECTIVE FORMATIONS

Upon the approval of the articles of incorporation by the secretary of state and the issuance of a certificate of incorporation, the corporation comes into being. This is true even if there have been defects in the incorporation procedures. The existence of the corporation is not subject to either direct or collateral attack, except by the state.

A corporation is considered a *de jure* **corporation** if it either has complied fully with all requirements for incorporation or has complied substantially, and has done so in good faith. *De* *jure* simply means "as a matter of law." The company has all of the rights and obligations prescribed by law, although the secretary of state may require that the articles of incorporation be amended in cases in which compliance with incorporation law has not been complete.

If the defects in complying with the requirements for incorporation have been substantial, even though the corporation has not acquired *de jure* status it will be considered a ***de facto* corporation.** *De facto* means "as a matter of fact." Again, even though the noncompliance is substantial, if the certificate of incorporation has been issued, a corporation is formed, even if only *de facto*. This assumes that the corporation could have been formed legally under the laws of the state, and there was a good-faith attempt to comply.

If no certificate of incorporation has been issued by the state, no corporation comes into existence, either *de jure* or *de facto*. However, persons who have dealt with others, and in doing so have represented that they were doing so on behalf of a corporation, may become liable to the third parties under the theory of **corporation by estoppel** or under the tort theory of deceit (if the misrepresentation of authority was intentional), or under the contract theory of breach of warranty of authority. In any event, a person acting on behalf of the enterprise will be liable personally without limitation. Consider the following two cases.

BUKACEK v. PELL CITY FARMS, INC. et al.
286 Ala. 141, 237 So.2d 851 (1970)

This was an action by James Bukacek (Complainant/Appellant) against Pell City Farms, Inc. and other (Respondents/Appellees) to quiet title to land. Respondents filed a cross-complaint asking the court to vest title in the name of the corporation.

Complainant was having financial difficulties and, in January 1968, met with individual Respondents Burtram, Kelly, and Wyatt to see about saving "my farm" (300 acres and an option on another 180 acres). The four agreed to form a corporation, Pell City Farms, Inc. Complainant then transferred title to the 300 acres and assigned the option to the corporation. The corporation paid all taxes and assessments up to date, and assumed liability on two mortages on the land. Complainant's principal contention was that Pell City Farms, Inc. could not take title because its articles of incorporation had not been filed with the Judge of Probate, as required by Alabama corporate law.

The trial court found for Respondents and Complainant appealed. Modified and affirmed.

MADDOX, Justice.

Assuming, without deciding, that we would subscribe to the broad view that no corporation was here formed prior to the filing of the Articles of Incorporation, we think the fact situation here presented shows that while Pell City Farms, Inc., may not have been a corporation de jure—or perhaps even de facto—insofar as the transaction here is concerned, it should be regarded practically as a corporation, being recognized as such by the parties themselves. In other words, the incidents of corporate existence may exist as between the parties by virtue of an estoppel. Thus, besides corporations de jure and de facto, there can be a recognition of a third class known as "Corporations by estoppel." Corporations by estoppel are not based upon the same principles as corporations de facto. The doctrine of de facto corporations has nothing to do with the principle of estoppel. In fact, a corporation de facto cannot be created by estoppel, the only effect of an estoppel being to prevent the raising of the question of the existence of a corporation.

Bukacek was one of the incorporators; he dealt with the corporation as a corporation both before and after the Articles of Incorporation were filed. Under such facts, Bukacek is estopped to deny the existence of the corporation at the time he voluntarily executed a deed transferring property to the corporation even though the Articles of Incorporation had not been filed at that time.

Our ruling here is limited. It is based on equitable grounds which preclude the complainant here from denying corporate existence. As against the state, of course, a corporation cannot be created by agreement of the parties—the statutes make certain prerequisites—but as between themselves and in connection with their own private litigations as here involved they may, by their agreements or their conduct estop themselves from denying the fact of the existence of the corporation. We hold, therefore, that Bukacek is estopped to deny the existence of Pell City Farms, Inc., even though it may have been neither de facto nor de jure at the time he executed the deed making the corporation, *by its corporate name,* the grantee.

Questions

1. To what extent is the concept of a corporation by estoppel likely to produce uncertainty in the law?

2. Is the court's ruling in this case really limited as suggested in the opinion?

3. Can you identify the factual elements in this case that gave rise to the estoppel?

ROBERTSON v. LEVY
197 A.2d 443 (D.C.App. 1964)

This was an action by Martin G. Robertson (Plaintiff/Appellant) against Eugene M. Levy (Defendant/Appellee) to hold Defendant personally liable on a note executed in the name of a corporation of which Defendant purported to be president.

Plaintiff and Defendant entered into an agreement under which Defendant was to form a corporation, Penn Ave. Record Shack, Inc., which was to purchase Plaintiff's business. Defendant submitted articles of incorporation on December 24, 1961, and commenced business under the corporate name on January 2, 1962. Plaintiff executed a bill of sale, transferring his business to the "corporation" and took a note for the sale price, signed in the name of Penn Ave. Record Shack, Inc. by Defendant as president. A certificate of incorporation was issued later, on January 17, 1962.

The trial court entered judgment for Defendant, and Plaintiff appealed. Reversed with instruction to enter judgment for Plaintiff.

HOOD, Chief Justice.

For a full understanding of the problems raised, some historical grounding is not only illuminative but necessary. In early common law time private corporations were looked upon with distrust and disfavor. This distrust of the corporate form for private enterprise was eventually overcome by the enactment of statutes which set forth certain prerequisites before the status was achieved, and by court decisions which eliminated other stumbling blocks. Problems soon arose, however, where there was substantial compliance with the prerequisites of the statute, but not complete formal compliance. Thus the concepts of de jure corporations, de facto corporations, and of "corporations by estoppel" came into being.

Taking each of these in turn, a de jure corporation results when there has been conformity with the mandatory conditions precedent (as opposed to merely directive conditions) established by the statute. A de jure corporation is not subject to direct or collateral attack either by the state in a quo warranto proceeding [a lawsuit to require the corporation to explain *by what right* it claims to be a corporation] or by any other person.

A de facto corporation is one which has been defectively incorporated and thus is not de jure. The Supreme Court has stated that the requisites for a corporation de facto are: (1) A valid law under which such a corporation can be lawfully organized; (2) An attempt to organize thereunder; (3) Actual user of the corporate franchise. Good faith in claiming to be and in doing business as a corporation is often added as a further condition. A de facto corporation is recognized for all purposes except where there is a direct attack by the state in a quo warranto proceeding. The concept of de facto corporation has been roundly criticized.

Cases continued to arise, however where the corporation was not de jure, where it was not de facto because of failure to comply with one of the four requirements above, but where the courts, lacking some clear standard or guideline, were willing to decide on the equities of the case. Thus another concept arose, the so-called "corporation by estoppel." This term was a complete misnomer. There was no corporation, the acts of the associates having failed even to colorably fulfill the statutory requirements; there was no estoppel in the pure sense of the word because generally there was no holding out followed by reliance on the part of the other party. Apparently estoppel can arise whether or not a de facto corporation has come into existence. Estoppel problems arose where the certificate of incorporation had been issued as well as where it had not been issued, and under the following general conditions: where the "association" sues a third party and the third party is estopped from denying that the plaintiff is a corporation; where a third party sues the "association" as a corporation and the "association" is precluded from denying that it was a corporation; where a third party sues the "association" and the members of that association cannot deny its existence as a corporation where they participated in holding it out as a corporation; where a third party sues the individuals behind the "association" but is estopped from denying the existence of the "corporation"; where either a third party, or the "association" is estopped from denying the corporate existence because of prior pleadings.

One of the reasons for enacting modern corporation statutes was to eliminate problems inherent in the de jure, de facto and estoppel concepts. Thus sections 29-921c and 950 were enacted as follows:

> Section 29-921c. Effect of issuance of incorporation. Upon the issuance of the certificate of incorporation, the corporate existence shall begin, and such certificate of incorporation shall be conclusive evidence that all conditions precedent required to be performed by the incorporators have been complied with and that the corporation has been incorporated under this chapter, except as against the District of Columbia in a proceeding to cancel or revoke the certificate of incorporation.
>
> Section 29-950. Unauthorized assumption of corporate powers.
>
> All persons who assume to act as a corporation without authority so to do shall be jointly and severally liable for all debts and liabilities incurred or arising as a result thereof.

The first portion of section 29-921c sets forth a sine qua non regarding compliance. No longer must the courts inquire into the equities of a case to determine whether there has been "colorable compliance" with the statute. The corporation comes into existence only when the certificate has been issued. Before the certificate issues, there is no corporation de jure, de facto or by estoppel. After the certificate is issued under section 921c, the de jure corporate existence commences. Only after such existence has begun can the corporation commence business through compliance with section 29-921ld, by paying into the corporation the minimum capital and with section 921a(f), which requires that the capitalization be no less than $1,000. These latter two sections are given further force and effect by section 29-918(a)(2) which declares that directors of a corporation are jointly and severally liable for any assets distributed or any dividends paid to shareholders which renders the corporation insolvent or reduces its net assets below its stated capital. (See also, Code 1961, Section 29-917).

The authorities which have considered the problem are unanimous in their belief that . . . [These provisions] have put to rest de facto corporations and corporations by estoppel. . . .

Turning to the facts of this case, Penn Ave. Record Shack, Inc. was not a corporation when the original agreement was entered into, when the lease was assigned, when Levy took over Robertson's business, when operations began under the Penn Ave. Record Shack, Inc. name, or when the bill of sale was executed. Only on January 17 did Penn Ave. Record Shack, Inc. become a corporation. Levy is subject to personal liability because, before this date, he assumed to act as a corporation without any authority so to do. Nor is Robertson estopped from denying the existence of the corporation because after the certificate was issued he accepted one payment on the note. An individual who incurs statutory liability on an obligation under section 29-950 because he has acted without authority, is not relieved of that liability where, at a later time, the corporation does come into existence by complying with section 29-921c. Subsequent partial payment by the corporation does not remove this liability.

Questions

1. Does the statute really simplify matters by eliminating the prior distinctions and categories?

2. Is this case different in attitude or result from *Bukacek*? Why or why not?

ORGANIZATION OF THE CORPORATION

After incorporation, an organizational meeting must be held. If the first board of directors was named in the articles of incorporation, a majority of the directors must call this meeting. The purpose of the initial meeting is to complete the organization by appointing officers, adopting bylaws, and handling any other business that may be brought before the meeting. If the directors were not named, it is the duty of the incorporators either to conduct the organizational meeting, or to elect a board of directors to do so.

The organizational meeting conducted by the incorporators may be handled anywhere, either within or outside of the state. Matters to be handled at this meeting even may be determined without a meeting, as long as all incorporators consent and sign a written memorandum approving the action taken. The primary concern is that the operations of the corporation begin.

PURPOSES AND POWERS OF THE CORPORATION

As an artificial person, a corporation exists only for the purposes, and with the powers, stated in its articles of incorporation. Therefore, it is important that its activities remain within the bounds of those stated purposes and powers. Otherwise, the validity of its actions may be questioned.

The Purpose of the Corporation

As a general rule, a corporation may be formed for any legal purpose and will be entitled to conduct business as would any other person. However, the purposes of any corporation may be limited by including a restrictive statement in the articles of incorporation. Such a provision is not mandatory, but is permissable. In most cases, a limitation or corporate purpose is of no particular benefit, and even may be undesirable in the event that there is a need or a desire to expand the activities of the corporation. If the purposes are limited, the name of the corporation should not imply a purpose for which the business was not organized; for example, "ABC Abstract and Title Assurance Company" seems inappropriate when the business of the corporation is preparing abstracts and certifying their accuracy, but not issuing title-insurance policies. Sometimes the stated purposes of a corporation must be very specific. For example, a bank must meet the requirements of banking statutes in addition to the general incorporation statute.

The Powers of the Corporation

The basic powers of a corporation are set out in the general incorporation statute, and in other statutes for corporations having special purposes. The general statutes normally grant to corporations the same powers as a natural person to conduct its stated business and to do all things reasonably necessary to that end. In addition, the statutes usually include some express powers, such as the power to exist perpetually, to sue and be sued, to use a corporate seal, and to make and amend its bylaws. These powers, of course, are subject to limitation by a provision of the articles of incorporation.

In the past, corporate powers granted by general incorporation statutes were much more limited than they have been in recent years. Corporations now generally are granted broad implied powers by the statutes, and are permitted to include broad grants of power in the articles of incorporation. Since the possession of broad powers usually is convenient and provides greater flexibility of action for the corporation, these grants are common now. As a result, the incidence of corporations acting beyond their powers has lessened considerably.

Ultra Vires Acts

An act that is beyond the legal powers of a corporation is call an ***ultra vires*** act. In the past, *ultra vires* acts generally were held to be void. Then, the law began to support the notion that a corporation might be bound by an *ultra vires* act if it elected to ratify it. Today, the trend is toward limiting the legal significance of the *ultra vires* principle. Section 3.04 of the Model Business Corporation Act provides that acts of a corporation cannot be challenged on the ground that they were *ultra vires* except in a proceeding (1) by the shareholders to enjoin the act, (2) by the corporation against an incumbent or former director, officer, employee, or agent of the corporation, or (3) by the state attorney general. Thus, the corporation normally cannot use the defense of *ultra vires* to escape obligations to parties with whom it has dealt, except that some states still allow it in cases involving wholly executory contracts. Overall, the doctrine of *ultra vires* is far less important today than it was in the past. Consider the following case.

A.P. SMITH MFG. CO. v. BARLOW et al.
13 N.J. 145, 98 A.2d 581 (1953)

This was an action by A. P. Smith Mfg. Co. (Plaintiff/Appellee) against one Barlow and other stockholders (Defendants/Appellants) for a judgment declaring its contribution to a private educational institution to be within its corporate powers. Defendant contended it was *ultra vires*.

For many years, Plaintiff had made contributions for various charitable and educational purposes. The contribution in this case was one of $1500 to Princeton University. Defendants claimed this act was *ultra vires* because it was based on no power expressed in Plaintiff's articles of incorporation.

The trial court found for Plaintiff, holding the contribution to be *intra vires*, and Defendants appealed. Affirmed.

JACOBS, J.

During the first world war corporations loaned their personnel and contributed substantial corporate funds in order to insure survival; during the depression of the '30s they made contributions to alleviate the desperate hardships of the millions of unemployed; and during the second world war they again contributed to insure survival. They now recognize that we are faced with other, though nonetheless vicious, threats from abroad which must be withstood without impairing the vigor of our democratic institutions at home and that otherwise victory will be pyrrhic indeed. More and more they have come to recognize that their salvation rests upon sound economic and social environment which in turn rests in no insignificant part upon free and vigorous nongovernmental institutions of learning. It seems to us that just as the conditions prevailing when corporations were originally created required that they serve public as well as private interests, modern conditions require that corporations acknowledge and discharge social as well as private responsibilities as members of the communities within which they operate. Within this broad concept there is no difficulty in sustaining, as incidental to their proper objects and in aid of the public welfare, the power of corporations to contribute corporate funds within reasonable limits in support of academic institutions. But even if we confine ourselves to the terms of the common-law rule in its application to current conditions, such expenditures may likewise readily be justified as being for the benefit of the corporation; indeed, if need be the matter may be viewed strictly in terms of actual survival of the corporation in a free enterprise system. The genius of our common law has been its capacity for growth and its adaptability to the needs of the times. Generally courts have accomplished the desired result indirectly through the molding of old forms. Occasionally they have done it directly through frank rejection of the old and recognition of the new. But whichever path the common law has taken it has not been found wanting as the proper tool for the advancement of the general good. . . .

In 1930 a statute was enacted in our State which expressly provided that any corporation could cooperate with other corporations and natural persons in the creation and maintenance of community funds and charitable, philanthropic or benevolent instrumentalities conducive to public welfare, and could for such purposes expend such corporate sums as the directors "deem expedient and as in their judgment will contribute to the protection of the corporate interests." . . . In this enactment the Legislature declared that it shall be the public policy of our State and in furtherance of the public interest and welfare that encouragement be given to the creation and maintenance of institutions engaged in community fund, hospital, charitable, philanthropic, educational, scientific or benevolent activities or patriotic or civic activities conducive to the betterment of social and economic conditions; and it expressly empowered corporations acting singly or with others to contribute reasonable sums to such institutions, provided, however, that the contribution shall not be permissible if the donee institution owns more than 10% of the voting stock of the donor and provided, further, that the contribution shall not exceed 1% of capital and surplus unless the excess is authorized by the stockholders at a regular or special meeting. . . .

The appellants contend that the foregoing New Jersey statutes may not be applied to corporations created before their passage. Fifty years before the incorporation of the A. P. Smith manufacturing Company our Legislature provided that every corporate charter thereafter granted "shall be subject to alteration, suspension and repeal, in the discretion of the legislature." . . . A similar reserved power was placed into our State Constitution in 1875 (Art. IV, Sec. VII, par. 11), and is found in our present Constitution. . . .

In the light of all of the foregoing we have no hesitancy in sustaining the validity of the donation by the plaintiff. There is no suggestion that it was made indiscriminately or to a pet charity of the corporate directors in furtherance of personal rather than corporate ends. On the contrary, it was made to a preeminent institution of higher learning, was modest in amount and well within the limitations imposed by the statutory enactments, and was voluntarily made in the reasonable belief that it would aid the public welfare and advance the interests of the plaintiff as a private corporation and as part of the community in which it operates. We find that it was a lawful exercise of the corporation's implied and incidental powers under common-law principles and that it came within the express authority of the pertinent state legislation.

Questions

1. Would the result be the same if the president of the company and many members of the board of directors were graduates of Princeton?

2. Could the donation be made to a political party or to a candidate for public office?

SUMMARY

The corporation is a legal concept of ancient origin, dating back at least to the Roman Empire. In its more contemporary use as a business form, it has been in existence since the fourteenth century.

The corporation has been popular as a form of business organization primarily because it is well adapted to the needs of large businesses. Its existence, in theory, may be perpetual since it does not depend on the continuity or composition of its owners. Its ownership can be represented by divisible shares that usually are freely transferable. Also, it is easier for a corporation to attract new capital, both for the reasons stated and because the liability of investors is limited to the amount of their investments only. However, the formality required for creation of a corporation, and double taxation of corporation profits, frequently are considered distinct disadvantages of this business form.

Corporations may be classified according to certain characteristics. They may be public or private, depending on the purposes for which they are organized; for profit or charitable; domestic or foreign (or alien, if organized under the laws of another country); and publicly held or close, depending on the breadth of their ownership. In addition, some corporations are organized for the purpose of supplying professional services. These professional corporations frequently are governed by special rules concerning liability. Finally, corporations qualifying for taxation similar to that for partnerships often are referred to as Subchapter S corporations.

The most distinguishing characteristics of the corporate form are its existence as a separate legal entity and the limited liability of its owners. In effect, if proper procedures are complied with in its formation, a corporation is recognized as a fictitious legal person, and is responsible, out of capital, for its own obligations. The precise requirements for formation depend on state law. There is no uniform corporate law, although the Model Business Corporation Act provides much guidance that has been closely followed by many states.

In order to form a corporation, capital must be raised or subscribed, articles of incorporation must be filed, and a certificate of incorporation must be issued by the secretary of state of the state of incorporation. The articles of incorporation usually must state the name of the proposed corporation and give information concerning authorized shares of stock. The name of the registered agent for the corporation and his or her address must be included, as well as the names and addresses of the incorporators. Other matters, such as names of directors, bylaws, and limitations on the powers of the corporation also may be included. If all requirements are met, the result is a *de jure* corporation. If a certificate is issued but some material requirements are not met, the result is a *de facto* corporation. A *de facto* corporation ordinarily has the same rights and obligations as a *de jure* corporation. A corporation by estoppel also has been recognized by the court when equitable principles would be served.

Unless limited by the articles of incorporation, a corporation will have specific express powers provided for in the state's incorporation statute. In addition, it ordinarily will have the implied power to do all things reasonably necessary to carry on the business for which it was incorporated. Any acts in excess of these powers are considered *ultra vires*. However, the modern trend is to hold a corporation liable for *ultra vires* actions much the same as if they had been done within its powers. Thus, the doctrine of *ultra vires* has far less impact today than it once did.

KEY TERMS AND CONCEPTS

domestic corporation

foreign corporation

alien corporation

professional corporation (PC)

close corporation

publicly held corporation
Model Business Corporations Act (MBCA)
corporation
entity
shares of stock
shareholder
pierce the corporate veil
double taxation
Subchapter S corporation
promoter
stock subscription
subscriber
incorporator
articles of incorporation
certificate of incorporation (charter)
registered agent
bylaws
de jure corporation
de facto corporation
corporation by estoppel
ultra vires act

PROBLEMS

1.   Cohen was the sole shareholder in Mobile Roofing and Construction Co. The corporation had existed for twenty-five years, subcontracting work to various contractors and paying them by assignments of claims under the primary contracts. There had been no meetings of shareholders or directors during the past ten years; Cohen had drawn freely from the corporation's profits; and, upon its dissolution, Cohen paid its debts out of his own pocket, except for one owing to Burrell. The reason the corporation was dissolved is because Burrell had obtained an $11,000 judgment against it. Should Burrell be allowed to collect the judgment from Cohen individually?

2.   Conway entered into a contract with Trend Steel Corp. The contract was signed on behalf of Trend by Samet. Conway claimed breach, and in the process of filing suit discovered that Trend was not incorporated properly. Conway then sought to hold Samet liable as an individual. At the time of the supposed incorporation, the attorney had completed all of the papers and given Samet a corporate seal, stating the papers would be filed immediately. Samet contended that she was entitled to assume everything was taken care of and had no notice to the contrary. Should Samet be held liable?

3.   Phillips and Triplett were promoters, selling subscriptions in Acme Corp. When the corporation was formed, Triplett became a director and Phillips took a position as sales representative. Eighteen months after incorporation, the State of Kansas filed suit to recover employment taxes the corporation had failed to pay. The state sought to hold Phillips and Triplett liable personally. Should they be liable?

4.   Graziano was a promoter and, in that capacity, entered into a contract agreeing to purchase a theater from RKO. The contract was on behalf of the corporation Graziano was forming. After a series of delays in getting the corporation started, RKO sued Graziano for breach of contract. Graziano contended he should not be liable because it was to be the corporation's contract. Is Graziano correct?

5.   Bujosa was injured by the negligence of the Long Island Railroad Company, which was a wholly owned subsidiary of Metropolitan Transit Authority. Bujosa sued MTA for the injury, contending Long Island really was part of MTA, since MTA owned all of its stock. Is Bujosa correct?

6.   Emmick suggested to Oahe that she should incorporate, and acted as promoter for the new corporation. Oahe was incorporated on October 26, 1966, with Emmick as president. Emmick transferred, as his share of capital, 6315 shares of CM stock having an apparent value of $19 per share. However, Emmick, as a board member of CM, knew that the board of CM had voted at its

September meeting to reduce the value of the shares to $9.50. When this was discovered, Golden, a shareholder of Oahe's corporations brought a derivative suit, charging Emmick had breached his duty to the corporation. Emmick denied the charge on the ground that a promoter owes no duty to the corporation. Is Emmick correct?

7.   Whiting was in default on a substantial loan from the Bank of Douglass. Emery, a vice-president of the bank, asked Moore if he would give a note to secure Whiting's loan "in order to fool the bank examiners." Moore agreed and, in return, Emery gave Moore a written agreement, on behalf of the bank, that the bank would not attempt to collect the note. When Whiting didn't pay, the bank demanded payment from Moore, who defended on the ground that the commitment signed by Emery was binding on the bank. Is Moore correct?

8.   The Free Baptist College leased liquor dispensing equipment from Southeastern Beverage, and began running an establishment called Soul on Top of Peachtree. The college fell behind in paying on the lease and Southeastern sued for the balance due. The college defended on the ground that the lease was beyond its powers as a corporation and, therefore, void as to the college. Is the contention correct?

9.   Cranston, acting as the president of a corporation, entered into a contract to purchase typewriters from IBM. At the time, the company's articles of incorporation had not been filed, but they were shortly thereafter. Sometime later, when the corporation did not pay, IBM, learning the facts, sought to hold Cranston liable individually. Should Cranston be liable?

10.   Ratner, as promoter of Stereo Center, Inc., signed a contract with Central Bank. The agreement was for Mastercharge services, and under the agreement the merchant guaranteed payment of all sales drafts. Although Ratner signed as president of Stereo Center, she made no effort to incorporate until eight months later. During that time some employees of Stereo Center had forged several sales drafts. Ratner defended on the ground that Stereo Center, Inc. had adopted the liability on the contract when it came into existence and, therefore, she no longer was liable. Is Ratner correct?

Corporations: Financing and Operation

FINANCING

One of the major advantages of the corporate form of business organization is the ability of a corporation to attract investment capital and, to a lesser extent, other financing. This financing, for the most part, is evidenced by the issuing of long-term securities. Financing also is done by issuing short-term securities and an open credit account.

Types of Securities

The two broad categories of corporate securities are equity and debt. **Equity securities** are those that evidence a corporation's indebtedness to stockholders with regard to their stock ownership. **Debt securities** evidence forms of financing other than through the sale of ownership interests.

EQUITY SECURITIES. Equity securities may be sold in such types, classes, and issues, in such denominations, and with such rights and limitations as the individual corporation sees fit. The only characteristic that they always have in common is that all evidence ownership interests in the issuing corporation. Ownership interests are the rights (1) to participate in the control of the corporation, (2) to share in the profits of the corporation, and (3) to share in any residual assets upon the dissolution or termination of the corporation.

The two general *types* of stock issued are preferred and common. **Preferred stock,** as the name implies, carries some priority advantage (preference) over common stock. The preference is in relation to dividends, or to the distribution of assets on dissolution, or both. Preferred shareholders may be entitled to receive dividends in a specified amount before dividends may be paid to the holders of common stock. For example, "5-percent preferred stock" carries the right to a dividend of 5 percent of the value of the stock appearing on the face of the certificate. If earnings available for distribution in a particular year are sufficient to pay only the full amount of preferred dividends, or less, common stockholders receive no dividend.

There are a number of variations possible in issuing preferred stock. There may be two or more issues carrying relative preferences among themselves, such as "Class A," "Class B," and "Class C." Any or all of these may be "cumulative," "participating," "convertible," or some combination of these. Shareholders of *cumulative* preferred stock are entitled not only to dividends for the current year before distributions to other shareholders, but also to any dividends that were not paid in previous years. Sometimes the accumulation of unpaid dividends is limited to the amount of earnings in each year during which they were not paid. Shareholders of *participating* **preferred stock** are entitled to receive the required preferred dividend, and also to share in any excess dividends, either proportionately with the common stock or after the payment of a specified dividend on the common stock. *Convertible* **preferred stock** entitles the owner to convert his or her shares to some other type of security according to an established formula. Ordinarily, the privilege allows conversion to common stock, which owners of preferred stock are likely to do if there is a significant market rise in the common stock price. However, in recent years, some bank corporations have issued stock convertible to debt securities as a method of lessening the chances of an unfriendly takeover by another company. When the threat is posed, shareholders may convert their shares to short-term debt securities. This reduces the invested capital of the company and increases its debt, probably to such a degree as to make the corporation an unattractive takeover target.

Common stock is the more basic type of stock issued by a corporation. Frequently it is the only stock issued and, if not, it certainly will represent the greatest proportion of outstanding stock. As its name suggests, it has no preferences over other types of stock and it carries no right to any partic-

---

Types of securities

Equity
1. Preferred stocks
   - Cumulative
   - Participating
   - Convertible
2. Common stock

and

Debt
1. Commercial paper
2. Bonds
   - Secured
     Convertible
     Callable
   - Unsecured (debentures)
     Convertible
     Callable

ular amount of declared dividends. When dividends are declared, common stockholders share proportionally, as they do in the company's residual assets upon liquidation, after the payment of debts and the satisfaction of the rights of preferred stockholders.

DEBT SECURITIES.   Most corporations are financed, in part, by the assumption of debt obligations, in addition to issuing equity securities. These debts may be short term, either on open account or evidenced by various forms of commercial paper such as promissory notes. In addition, corporations frequently secure long-term debt financing by issuing bonds. The only characteristic common to these methods of debt financing is that with all of them, the corporation ordinarily becomes obligated to pay the stated debt, either on demand of the creditor or at a definite future time, plus interest at a rate set forth in the debt instrument.

Bonds may be issued carrying specific rights or

New York Stock Exchange Securities (1986)

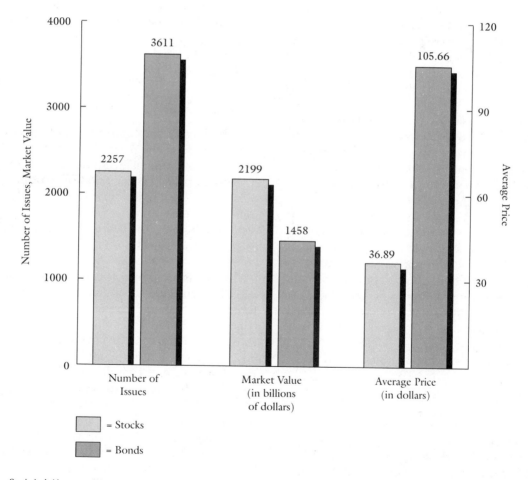

Source: Statistical Abstract of the U.S. (1988), Table 809.

obligations in addition to those generally provide for all debt securities. They may be secured or unsecured. When secured, a contract called the **indenture** sets out the lender's security rights. The security may be in specific property held and used by the corporation, or it may be in specific property transferred in trust to a "trustee under the indenture." Although the corporation ordinarily has the use of the trust property, its condition is monitored by the trustee, and it may be sold only with the trustee's permission. Unsecured bonds sometimes are called **debentures.** When issued under an indenture, the indenture does not include a security provision.

Although bonds typically carry the right to interest at a stated rate, a corporation may issue *income bonds*. The payment of interest on these bonds may be conditional, either wholly or in part, on the issuing corporation's level of earnings. Unpaid interest on the bonds may or may not accumulate.

As with stock, bonds may be convertible. They may be exchanged for other securities of the corporation (frequently stock) at a stated rate. This is attractive from an investor's perspective since it gives him an opportunity to participate in any rise in the value of the company's stock. Bonds also may be *callable*. If so, the corporation is entitled to redeem them prior to the date fixed for maturity. In order to exercise its right to redeem, the corporation will pay the redemption price (usually the face value of the bond) plus a declining premium. For example, the premium after the first year might be five points above the face of the bond, declining to zero points at maturity. This may be an attractive feature for a corporation, especially if the bonds are issued at a high rate of interest.

The Choice of Debt or Equity Financing

The precise mix of debt and equity is largely a matter of individual choice for each corporation. Debt financing is advantageous in that the interest paid on debt is deductible, for income-tax purposes, as an operating expense. Dividends paid on stock are not. However, debts also represent fixed obligations, payable regardless of earnings and profits, and interest owed on those obligations usually is part of the debt. This is not true of equity capital, particularly common stock.

Corporations, however, may be limited as to the ratio of debt to equity capital. For example, regulators may require banks to maintain 3- or 5-percent equity as a percentage of total assets. Also, the Internal Revenue Service has brought suit to compel corporations to pay additional tax on the ground of an excessive debt to capital ratio. Although the courts have recognized the principle that excessive interest on debt should not be deductible, they have considered situations on a case-by-case basis, and have not yet established firm guidelines for what constitutes an excessive accumulation of debt.

Distributions to Shareholders

Distributions of corporate assets to shareholders may be made in the form of ordinary dividends (distributing earnings), **liquidating dividends** (returning capital), redemption of shares, or the purchase of outstanding shares. The corporation usually is under no obligation to make any such distribution unless the board of directors decides to do so and passes a valid resolution to that effect.

Dividends are the most common form of distribution. The assets distributed are usually in the form of cash, but a corporation also may distribute other property, even stock. Although all three are recognized as dividends, cash and property dividends reduce the assets of the corporation, but stock dividends do not. The net effect of a stock dividend is a restructuring of the corporation's capital. Increasing the number of outstanding shares does not affect the amount of net assets. As a result, the total value of each shareholder's interest in the company remains the same and only the value of each share is reduced proportionately. This type of dividend, therefore, is not taxable as income unless the shareholder has an option to accept either stock or cash (or other property).

Most states place some restrictions on the right of directors to declare and pay dividends. Under Section 6.40 of the Model Business Corporation Act, distributions are prohibited (1) if they would cause the corporation to be unable to pay its debts as they come due in the ordinary course of business, or (2) if following the distribution, total assets of the corporation would be less than total debt plus the maximum amount payable to shareholders having preferential rights on liquidation (unless the articles of incorporation provide to the contrary). These restrictions, of course, are for the purpose of preventing the owners from "milking" the corporation to defraud creditors. Consider the following case in which the court found debenture bonds to be, in fact, stock.

CHAMPAIGN REALTY CO. v. UNITED STATES
342 F.Supp. 922 (S.D.Ohio, 1971)

This was an action by Champaign Realty Co. (Plaintiff) against the United States (Defendant) for a refund of corporate income taxes.

Plaintiff was an Ohio corporation organized in 1958 by a group of eight doctors for the purpose of constructing and maintaining a medical building in which they would lease space. The project was financed, in part, by the issuance of certain debenture bonds to seven of the doctor-shareholders and to Mr. N. N. Sams, the father-in-law of the other doctor-shareholder. No interest was paid on the debentures, but each year Plaintiff deducted the interest due on its corporate income tax form as an accrual-basis taxpayer. Because of circumstances discussed in the court's opinion, the Internal Revenue Service assessed a deficiency for the years 1962, 1963, and 1964, contending the amounts advanced to the corporation evidenced by the debentures were really investments of capital rather than loans and the "interest" accrued was, therefore, not deductible. Plaintiff's complaint was dismissed.

WEINMAN, Chief Justice.

The sole question raised by this action is whether the advances to the plaintiff corporation as evidenced by the alleged debentures are legitimate loans for federal tax purposes. In order to recover, plaintiff has the burden of showing that a legitimate debtor-creditor relationship existed between the corporation and the holders of the alleged debentures. . . .

In resolving this issue the Court must evaluate the evidence as stipulated by the parties to see if the objective criteria normally associated with legitimate debts are present in this case. . . .

In summary the controlling objective factors establishing the existence of a legitimate loan for federal tax purposes are (1) a fixed maturity date and interest rates (2) an unconditional promise to repay the loan (3) a fixed schedule of payments (4) normal security (5) a sinking fund to provide funds for repayment of the loan and (6) lack of subordination of the loans to the rights of other creditors.

An analysis of the facts of the present case in terms of these controlling objective factors demonstrates that the alleged debentures lack the characteristics of legitimate loans.

The debentures have some of the formal characteristics of legitimate loans. The alleged debentures state a fixed maturity date of December 14, 1973 and provide for the payment of interest at a rate of 5% per annum. However, the restrictions imposed upon the right of an individual debenture holder to enforce the "obligation" to pay interest or to repay principal on the maturity date as a practical matter nullifies the former obligation to pay interest and repay principal.

Each debenture provides that "No holder or holders of less than seventy five (75%) percent in the principal amount of the debentures shall have the right to commence suit or obtain judgment thereon." A suit can only be brought if interest is in arrears for two or more years and then in that event only upon the consent of seventy-five (75%) percent or more of the holders in the principal amount of the debentures. Thus an individual debenture holder possesses no right to compel payment of interest, to accelerate the repayment of principal upon default or to compel repayment of the principal on the maturity date. . . .

It is also significant that the percentage of holders required to enforce the "obligation" created by the debentures necessarily includes a majority or more of the corporate shareholders. There is an identity of interest between the debenture holders whose consent is required to enforce the debentures and the corporate shareholders which dispels the existence of a legitimate debtor-creditor relationship.

Plaintiff relies upon the fact that one debenture holder, Mr. N. N. Sams is not a corporate shareholder. This fact is not significant because Mr. Sams, the father-in-law of a shareholder-doctor, purchased debentures to enable his son-in-law to carry his share of the load. Mr. Sams as an individual debenture holder has no right to compel payment of interest or to compel repayment of principal on the maturity date without the consent of other debenture holders who are also shareholders of the corporation. Furthermore, assuming Mr. Sams possessed an individual right to commence suit to enforce the debenture "obligations" it is highly unlikely that he would exercise this right against the interest of his shareholder son-in-law. . . .

The alleged debentures lack other characteristics of legitimate loans. The absence of an individual right by a holder to enforce his debentures and conditioning enforcement upon the consent of a group of holders consisting of a majority of corporate stockholders negates the existence of an unconditional promise to repay principal. None of the individual holders possessed a right to demand payment unconditionally at a fixed time. Furthermore, no sinking fund is maintained by the plaintiff corporation to provide funds for the repayment of principal and unlike a legitimate loan, the debentures are unsecured and subordinated to the rights of all corporate creditors including those who advanced credit after the issuance of the debentures.

The conclusion of this Court that the alleged debentures are not legitimate loans is further supported when the alleged debentures are compared with the loans made to the plaintiff by the four financial institutions. The loans from the financial institutions were evidenced by notes which provided for the current amortization of principal, contained the right to accelerate repayment of principal upon default on interest payments and contained a confession of judgment clause. The notes were secured by a real estate mortgage on the real property of the corporation and by the assignment to the financial institutions of ten year leases signed by the shareholder-doctors. In addition the plaintiff was required by the financial institutions to maintain mortgage redemption insurance on the life of each shareholder-doctor and to maintain fire and extended coverage insurance for the benefit of the financial institutions.

In contrast the debentures do not afford the holders with normal creditor safeguards. There is no provision for the current amortization of principal. A holder possesses no individual right to compel interest payments upon default or to compel repayment on the maturity date. Enforcement as a practical matter is contingent upon the consent of a group of holders which includes a majority of the corporate shareholders. The debentures are unsecured and subordinated to the rights of all corporate creditors. Thus the debentures in fact resemble a capital contribution in that the debentures are subject to the primary risks of the corporate enterprise. Repayment is solely dependent upon the future earnings of the corporation.

It is also significant that the sum of $57,000.00 advanced to the corporation by the purchase of the alleged debentures was essential to the acquisition of the corporation's primary capital asset, the medical building.

. . . According, The Court concludes that the Commissioner correctly disallowed a deduction for accrued interest on plaintiff's corporation income tax returns for the years 1962, 1963, and 1964.

Questions

1.   Is the result in this case fair to the investors? Did they have a legitimate expectation of being able to take a tax deduction?
2.   Which of the factors mentioned by the court do you think are critical to the court's conclusion that the instrument was stock and not bonds?

THE ROLE OF THE BOARD OF DIRECTORS

In most cases a corporation is required, by law, to have a board of directors. All of the powers of the corporation are vested in the board, either to be exercised by it, or under its management and direction. In essence, the **board of directors** constitutes a collective, natural, alter ego of the corporation's fictitious "legal persona." In addition to some specific duties prescribed by state statutes and some provided for in the articles of incorporation, the board of directors has the general duty to set broad corporate policy within which day-to-day management decisions will be made by the corporate officers.

Duties

Some specific duties with which the board of directors normally is charged are calling meetings of the board and meetings of the shareholders; selecting corporate officers; declaring dividends; approving any consolidation, merger, or dissolution; and adopting amendments to the articles of incorporation and the bylaws.

Section 8.01(c) of the MBCA allows corporations having fifty or fewer shareholders to dispense with the requirement of a board of directors, or to permit the shareholders to perform some or all of the duties of the board. This often is practical for smaller corporations, although there ordinarily is nothing wrong with having a small number of shareholders who also are the incorporators and the board of directors. Under these circumstances, having a board of directors may be nothing more than an empty formality.

Qualifications of Directors

There usually are no statutory qualifications that must be met for a person to be able to serve as a director. Certainly an understanding of business generally and of the activities of the particular corporation is desirable. Sometimes the articles of incorporation establish qualifications, most commonly that a director also must be a shareholder. Frequently, boards have a structure, either formal or informal, with seats assigned to directors with certain backgrounds or areas of expertise, such as a representative from labor, one from banking or some other financial institution, an attorney, and a director with a marketing background. The logic of this is that a board composed of directors with diversified backgrounds, interests, and experience may well improve the efficiency of the decision-making process.

Election and Removal of Directors

State statutes fix a minimum number of directors for a corporation. Traditionally, the most common provision was for three. However, with the increase in the number of states allowing corporations to have only one incorporator and one shareholder, the trend has been toward also allowing a board to consist of one director. As noted before, Section 8.01(c) of the MBCA even allows a corporation with fifty or fewer shareholder to dispense with an authorized board entirely.

A corporation may choose to have a number of directors greater than the statutory minimum, or a range (for example, between nine and twelve). This may be done in either the articles of incorporation or the bylaws. If the number is fixed by the articles of incorporation, it can be changed only by the shareholders, because a shareholder's vote is required to amend the articles. If fixed by the bylaws, it can be changed by the directors themselves, unless the articles of incorporation provide to the contrary.

The first board of directors may be appointed by incorporators, and it will serve until the first shareholders' meeting. Thereafter, directors are elected by the shareholders at the annual meeting. Under Section 8.06 of the MBCA, if the corporation has nine or more directors, they may serve staggered terms. For example, if the corporation has nine directors, the first board might include three directors who will serve for one year, three who will serve for two years, and three who will serve for three years. After the first two years, all directors will serve three-year terms, with three elected each year. This obviously ensures that at least two-thirds of every board will have some experience.

Ordinarily, each shareholder is entitled to one vote for each share of stock owned. However, because directors normally are elected by receiving a majority of the votes cast, this leaves minority shareholders with no power, because any shareholder with more than 50 percent of the voting shares can elect the entire board. To prevent this, the articles of incorporation or the bylaws may provide for **cumulative voting**. Under this system, each shareholder is entitled to the number of votes equal to the number of shares she owns multiplied by the number of directors to be elected. Then, she may distribute these total votes over a number of candidates or cast all of them for one. Suppose, for example, the corporation has three shareholders, and Mo owns 60 shares, Larry owns 30, and Curly owns 10 (a total of 100 shares). Three directors are to be elected. Mo would be entitled to distribute 180 votes, Larry

90 votes, and Curly 30 votes. Therefore, although Mo can elect at least two of the three directors, Larry can elect at least one. Curly's share is too small, however, to ensure electing even one. Cumulative voting is permitted by the Model Business Corporation Act, and by the statutes of most states.

Removal of directors ordinarily follows the same procedures as the election of directors. Of course, a director can be removed by not being reelected upon the expiration of his term. At common law, a director could be removed only for cause. Under the MBCA—and there is a trend to the same effect among the states—directors may be removed either with or without cause. This marks a change in attitude from the view that a corporation (represented by its board) was a creature of the state and, and as such, was not to be interfered with except for good cause. Today the attitude is that the directors are agents of the shareholders and should serve only with their continuing consent.

Most states permit vacancies on a board of directors to be filled either by a vote of a majority of the remaining directors or by a vote of the shareholders. Some states, however, require that this be done by the shareholders only. Also, when the statutes allow either procedure, as does the MBCA, the articles of incorporation or the bylaws may specify the procedure to be used. Normally, if a vacancy is filled by the vote of the remaining directors, the person filling the vacancy will serve only until the next meeting of the shareholders at which directors are elected.

Consider the following case addressing the question of the right to remove directors.

GRACE v. GRACE INSTITUTE
19 N.Y.2d 307, 226 N.E.2d 531 (1967)

This was an action by Michael P. Grace, II (Petitioner/Respondent) against Grace Institute (Respondent/Appellant) seeking annulment of a decision of life members and trustees of Respondent to remove him as a life member and trustee.

Grace Institute was incorporated in 1897 by an act of the New York Legislature. By family succession, Petitioner became a life member and trustee. During his tenure, among other things, he commenced several actions against the Institute. In none of these did the courts find a triable issue. Finally, after a hearing, at which Petitioner was represented by an attorney, his life membership and position as trustee of the Institute were terminated. Petitioner contended that the Institute was without power to remove him.

The trial court refused to grant a summary judgment in favor of the Institute and the Institute appealed. Reversed and remanded.

KEATING, Judge.

While the Institute disputes the Appellate Division's interpretation of the law of trusts as it existed at the time the Institute was created, it is clear that a corporation and not a trust was created and, regardless of what the law as to trusts was at the time, corporate law and not trust law should govern.

The law is settled that a corporation possesses the inherent power to remove a member, officer or director for cause, regardless of the presence of a provision in the charter or by-laws providing for such removal. . . .

The question with which we are presented in this case is whether there exists any triable issues [*sic*] relating to the manner in which this petitioner was removed from his position as a life member and trustee.

It has been the consistent policy of the courts of this State to avoid interference with the internal management and operation of corporations. . . . Although we are dealing here with a charitable corporation over which the Supreme Court is vested with supervisory powers the Legislature in creating it set up a governing board of trustees and vested in them the power and authority necessary for the management and operation of the Institute. That body, after hearings and deliberation, has decided that the petitioner's conduct was so inimical to the corporate interests as to require his removal. In reaching that conclusion, the trustees had before them evidence of a series of lawsuits commenced by the petitioner against the corporation in each of which he was unsuccessful and in none of which did any of the 13 jurists who took part find even so much as a single triable issue.

After reviewing each of these actions and after studying the entire record in this case, we have reached the conclusion that the evidence clearly supported the finding of the trustees that Michael had embarked on a course of conduct designed to involve the Institute in endless and costly litigation and that the suits were undertaken for the purpose of harassing the Institute and its members. Under these circumstances, courts should not substitute their judgment for the judgment of those charged by the Legislature with the responsibility of running the corporation and seeing to it that it fulfills the purposes for which it was created.

In addition, we have examined the procedure by which the petitioner was removed and we have concluded there is no question but that he was given a reasonable opportunity to be heard and to answer the charges leveled against him. At the hearing during which the charges were aired, he was represented by three attorneys and a law assistant. His attorneys were permitted to cross-examine one of the parties who had been instrumental in preparing the charges against Michael and they could have exercised their right to examine others. Yet despite this opportunity to be heard and to present evidence, Michael never took the stand and never even attempted to answer the charges. The objections of Michael to the hearings we find to be without merit. The things to which he objects in no way detracted from his opportunity to be heard or the validity of his removal.

Michael argues, however, that the position of life member was created by the Legislature and "only the Legislature has the power to change the rights and privileges specifically granted by the act of incorporation." Michael obviously misapprehends the nature of the rights and privileges accorded to him. The Legislature surely could not have intended that a life member retain his position regardless of the manner in which he acted and regardless of the manner in which he abused his trust. The petitioner may not be removed so long as he adheres to what must be regarded as an implied condition of his position—that is so long as he faithfully serves the Institute. Once he breaches that condition and engages in activities that obstruct and interfere with the operation of the corporation and the purposes for which the Legislature created it, he may be removed. Indeed, the statute creating the corporation appears to recognize that a member may leave his position through ways other than death or voluntary resignation. Section 4 provides that a member may designate a successor "who shall take the place made vacant by the death, resignation or otherwise of the person making such nomination."

Questions

1. Should courts exercise significantly more supervision over the removal of board members of charitable corporations than business corporations? Why or why not?
2. Was it necessary for the Grace Institute to give the petitioner a hearing and the right to have a lawyer present? Would the result have been different if the Institute had not provided those procedures?

Meetings of the Board of Directors

Unless the governing statute or the articles of incorporation specify to the contrary, a meeting of the board of directors may be held anywhere, either within or outside of the state of incorporation. A meeting even may be conducted through some means of communication, such as by telephone, closed-circuit television, or a computer network. A board of directors also may conduct business without a meeting, as long as all members consent to the action. Often the necessary consent must be evidenced by a signed writing, and the action taken becomes effective at the moment and place of the last director's signature.

Regular meetings of the board ordinarily may be held without the requirement of a special notice as long as the time, date, and place of the meetings is set out in the articles of incorporation or the bylaws of the corporation. Special meetings, however, may be held only after a notice, which must be given to the shareholders no less than a specified time before the meeting (two days under the MBCA). A director may waive any required notice, either before or after the required time, and is considered to have done so if she attends and participates at the meeting, or just attends without objecting to the lack of notice.

Quorum requirements are set by statute, and may be changed by the articles of incorporation or the bylaws. The minimum requirement, however, ordinarily is that action may be taken by a major-ity vote of the directors present if those at the meeting constitute a majority of the directors (**quorum**). The MBCA further provides that any or all of the duties of a board of directors may be delegated to one or more committees, in which case the quorum and voting requirements for the entire board are adjusted to the size of the committee.

Standards of Conduct for Directors

Each director owes a *fiduciary* duty to the corporation and its shareholders. This requires that each director act with total loyalty, in good faith, and only in the best interests of the corporation and its shareholders. In other words, a director, in all actions taken on behalf of the corporation, must act only as he reasonably, and in good faith, believes the company (the shareholders collectively) would act under the same circumstances. If a particular director has special skill or knowledge not common to the shareholders, he is expected to exercise it in all actions taken.

Specifically, each director is expected to act with *obedience* to his duty as a director, within the authority granted to him, and with due diligence in exercising that authority. For example, a director must not vote to permit the corporation to enter into a transaction outside of the purposes stated in its articles of incorporation. Exactly what constitutes due diligence has not been settled entirely by judicial precedent. A few courts have held that due diligence requires that a director conduct corporate affairs in the manner in which he would conduct his own. The MBCA, and most courts, however, have adopted the position that due diligence requires a director to exercise only that degree of care that would be employed by an ordinary, prudent person under similar circumstances. The latter standard generally is supported as being more objective.

The so-called **business judgment rule** usually is recognized as insulating a director from liability as long as he has exercised his own judgment, in good faith, and has taken action accordingly. Under those circumstances, a court will refuse to substitute its judgment for that of the director. Of course, a director still may be liable for negligence in failing to keep himself reasonably informed about the state of corporate affairs prior to making decisions, or if the facts show he acted in bad faith. However, a director is permitted to rely on information, opinions, reports, and statements made or prepared by corporate officers and employees, or legal counsel or other experts, unless he has reason to believe that the data may not be accurate or otherwise reliable. A director ordinarily need not gather all information himself in order to avoid liability. Because there has been an increased willingness to hold directors liable in recent years, many companies provide liability insurance for their board members.

Although a director may make mistakes in the conduct of the corporation's affairs, as long as he acts reasonably and in good faith he normally will incur no liability for his actions. This is true even though he may act in a transaction in which he has a personal interest. Propriety is presumed unless a complaining party produces a preponderance of evidence to the contrary, and the existence of such a conflict of interest alone does not affect the validity of the action taken. Consider the following case concerning the right of shareholders to have decisions of the board of directors set aside.

SCHLENSKY v. WRIGLEY
95 Ill.App.2d 173, 237 N.E.2d 776 (1968)

This was a stockholders' derivative action by William Schlensky on behalf of and as representative of Chicago National League Ball Club, Inc. (Plaintiff/Appellant) against Phillip K. Wrigley and others (Defendants/Appellees) for negligence and mismanagement and for an order that Defendants install lights in their stadium for night baseball games. Plaintiff's contention was that the decision of Defendants, directors of the club, was based on Defendant Wrigley's personal belief that baseball was a daytime game and his personal concern for inconvenience to the neighborhood surrounding the stadium. It was alleged that the decision was in disregard of the revenue to be derived from playing night baseball, and that the stadiums of all other clubs in the league were lighted.

The trial court dismissed the complaint for failure to state a cause of action, and Plaintiff appealed. Affirmed.

SULLIVAN, Justice.

The question on appeal is whether plaintiff's amended complaint states a cause of action. It is plaintiff's position that fraud, illegality and conflict of interest are not the only bases for a stockholder's derivative action against the directors. Contrariwise, defendants argue that the courts will not step in and interfere with honest business judgment of the directors unless there is a showing of fraud, illegality or conflict of interest. . . .

Plaintiff in the instant case argues that the directors are acting for reasons unrelated to the financial interest and welfare of the Cubs. However, we are not satisfied that the motives assigned to Philip K. Wrigley, and through him to the other directors, are contrary to the best interests of the corporation and the stockholders. For example, it appears to us that the effect on the surrounding neighborhood might well be considered by a director who was considering the patrons who would or would not attend the games if the park were in a poor neighborhood. Futhermore, the long run interest of the corporation in its property value at Wrigley Field might demand all efforts to keep the neighborhood from deteriorating. By these thoughts we do not mean to say that we have decided that the decision of the directors was a correct one. That is beyond our jurisdiction and ability. We are merely saying that the decision is one properly before directors and the motives alleged in the amended complaint showed no fraud, illegality or conflict of interest in their making of that decision.

While all the courts do not insist that one or more of the three elements must be present for a stockholder's derivative action to lie, nevertheless we feel that unless the conduct of the defendants at least borders on one of the elements, the courts should not interfere. . . .

Finally, we do not agree with plaintiff's contention that failure to follow the example of the other major league clubs in scheduling night games constituted negligence. Plaintiff made no allegation that these teams' night schedules were profitable or that the purpose for which night baseball had been undertaken was fulfilled. Furthermore, it cannot be said that directors, even those of corporations that are losing money, must follow the lead of the other corporations in the field. Directors are elected for their business capabilities and judgment and the courts cannot require them to forego their judgment because of the decisions of directors of other companies. Courts may not decide these questions in the absence of a clear showing of dereliction of duty on the part of the specific directors and mere failure to "follow the crowd" is not such a dereliction.

For the foregoing reasons the order of dismissal entered by the trial court is affirmed.

Questions

1. Does this court's "hands-off" attitude make sense? Is it fair to the other shareholders of the Cubs?

2. Are the court's reasons for accepting the directors' judgment persuasive? Do they seem realistic in the modern day?

Amendments to Articles and Bylaws

Amendments to the articles of incorporation ordinarily are made by a vote of the shareholders, and amendments to the bylaws are made by the board of directors. However, the power of the directors to amend the bylaws does not prohibit the shareholders from doing so. In addition, the

MBCA sets aside certain amendments to the articles that can be adopted by the directors, unless the articles provide to the contrary. These include extending the duration of the corporation; "housekeeping" changes, such as deleting the names and addresses of initial directors or the initial registered agent who no longer is serving in that capacity; changes of the corporate name; and changing the par value of authorized shares that have been split.

Extraordinary Transactions

The board of directors generally is responsible for the conduct of the corporation's *ordinary* business. Extraordinary transactions usually require a majority vote of the shareholders. These include most transactions involving the sale or lease of most or all of the assets of the corporation (not in the ordinary course of business), or the merger or consolidation of the corporation with another corporation. If one corporation purchases the outstanding shares of another, the transaction ordinarily requires no action by either the board of directors, or the collective vote of the shareholders of the acquired corporation, since it occurs by action of the shareholders individually.

THE ROLE OF THE OFFICERS

The officers of a corporation are appointed for the purpose of representing and operating the corporation in its day-to-day activities. They are appointed by the board of directors and, for the most part, derive their power and authority from that board.

Duties

The power and authority of officers usually is delegated in the corporate bylaws, but also may be granted in the articles of incorporation or by special resolution of the board of directors or a committee of the board. In effect, the board of directors sets broad corporate policy within limits established by the law and the shareholders.

Within that broad policy, the **corporate officers** are responsible for executing the details of administration, either personally or through other agents and employees of the corporation.

Requirements for Officers

A corporation may be represented by as many officers as is deemed desirable to the shareholders and the board of directors. States usually set some minimum number, but not a maximum. The Revised Model Business Corporation Act (RMBCA) provides for the appointment of a secretary, and specifies that the duties of the secretary are to prepare minutes of meetings of the board of directors and of the shareholders, and to authenticate records of the corporation. Usually, the secretary also is responsible for keeping and using the corporate seal, if the corporation has one.

Other officers commonly appointed for a corporation are a president, one or more vice-presidents, and a treasurer. One person may serve in any or all of these offices, although many states require that the office of secretary be held separately from the others.

Standards of Conduct for Officers

The standards of conduct applied to officers of a corporation are the same as those applied to directors. Each officer is a fiduciary of the corporation. As such, she owes the corporation and its shareholders the duties of loyalty, honesty, and good faith in the conduct of all affairs relating to the corporation. This duty may be of more significance to an officer than to a director, however, in that an officer is ordinarily a full-time employee of the corporation, and has more opportunities to violate it.

As was true of directors, officers owe a duty of obedience and a responsibility to act with due diligence. In doing so, an officer is entitled to act in good faith reliance on information, opinions, reports, and statements of other officers or employees of the corporation, legal counsel, or other experts, such as accountants. However, these rights, and the protections afforded to directors by the business judgment rule, may be of more limited application in an officer's case than a director's. The nature of the officer's duties place her in closer contact with the detailed affairs of the corporation. Activities that she does not execute personally she is expected to oversee. Thus, an officer is expected to know far more than a director. This view is supported by the comment to Section 8.42 of the RMBCA.

Resignation and Removal of Officers

As previously noted, the officers of a corporation are appointed by the board of directors and receive their power and authority by delegation from the directors. Therefore, most state statutes provide that officers serve at the pleasure of the board, and may be removed with or without cause. This view is supported by Section 8.42 of the RMBCA, and by the general rule of agency law that an agent's authority may exist only with the continued consent of the principal. Of course, assuming the officer has a valid contract of employment with the corporation, his dismissal without cause may constitute a breach of that contract for which the corporation may be required to respond in damages.

An officer may resign his position at any time by giving written notice to the board of directors. The resignation may be effective when notice is given, or at some specified future date if accepted by the corporation. Again, however, in the face of a valid employment contract, a resignation without cause may constitute a breach of that agreement. In any case, upon receipt of a notice of resignation, the board of directors may proceed to fill the vacancy, effective at the time the vacancy occurs.

LIABILITY OF DIRECTORS AND OFFICERS

The liability of directors and officers of a corporation is substantially the same as the liability of any other agent. Liability may be found in the areas of contract law, tort law, or criminal law, and may result from a breach of duty that arises under either state or federal law; that duty may be owed to the corporation, third parties, or the public. The sources of possible liability for directors and officers may be greater than for other agents, of course, because of the provisions of the many statutes specifically regulating corporations.

Defective Incorporation

A director or officer may be liable for transacting business on behalf of a corporation that has not come into existence because of some defect in the incorporation. Agency law renders her liable as an agent for a nonexistent principal. This position was continued under Section 146 of the earlier Model Business Corporation Act, which stated: "All persons who assume to act as a corporation without authority so to do shall be jointly and severally liable for all debts and liabilities incurred or arising as a result thereof." The rule is softened, however, under Section 2.04 of the 1983 RMBCA, which imposes liability only if the action was taken "knowing there was no incorporation under this Act." This, in conjunction with the increasing use of the doctrine of *de facto* incorporation, discussed in the preceding chapter, signals a substantial trend away from liability in this area.

Breach of Duty to the Corporation

A breach of duty to the corporation may involve a contract duty, a general agency duty, or a fiduciary duty. The breach of any of these may result in the discharge of the director or the officer for cause. In addition, the corporation is entitled to any damages from the director or officer that flow proximately as a result of the breach. The breach of the fiduciary duty may give rise to additional remedies, such as loss of compensation for the unfaithful agent, the recovery of any secret profits he received, and possibly rescission of the contract with the third party, if the third party either knew or should have known of the breach. Consider the following case.

WILSHIRE OIL COMPANY OF TEXAS v. RIFFE
406 F.2d 1061 (10th Cir. 1969)

This was an action by Wilshire Oil Company of Texas (Plaintiff/Appellant) against L. E. Riffe (Defendant/Appellee) to recover from a former corporate officer profits he made by participating in competitive enterprises and personally receiving commissions for corporate work, and for compensation paid to him as a corporate officer during the priod of these breachs. The trial court refused to grant relief, Plaintiff appealed, the Court of Appeals reversed and remanded, the trial court granted relief in part, and Plaintiff again appealed. Reversed and remanded again.

SETH, Circuit Judge.

When a corporate officer engages in activities which constitute a breach of his duty of loyalty, or if it is a wilful breach of his contract of employment, he is not entitled to compensation for services during such a period of time although part of his services may have been properly performed. In the Restatement (Second), Agency Section 469 the above doctrine is set forth, and this is followed by the comment which states in part:

> An agent, who, without the acquiescence of his principal, acts for his own benefit or for the benefit of another in antagonism to or in competition with the principal in a transaction is not entitled to compensation which otherwise be due him.

The comment continues and states that the agent is not entitled to compensation although the acts may not actually harm his principal and even if he thinks his actions will benefit the principal or he is otherwise "justified" in "so acting."

This rule is applicable to the case before us, and it is not necessary to again describe the several breaches of duty involved which were clearly established in the record. The record shows, as to one of the principal events, that the failure commenced on or before May 31, 1962, and continued to the end of the year when the officer's employment terminated. It was then also that the particular division which he was responsible for was sold by the corporation. The record thus sets out the period of this violation, and this is sufficient to apply the above doctrine. Thus we hold that the appellee was not entitled to compensation of any kind from May 31, 1962, to December 31, 1962.

The appellee argues that the corporate division he was responsible for made money during the period in question, and that the division was itself sold at a profit to appellant corporation. However, under the authorities or on any other basis, this is no answer to the established violation of duty. The fact that the division may have made money does not prove that no breach took place nor does it excuse one any more than a failure to make money demonstrates a breach of duty. The same may be said about whether the officer considered that he was acting properly or in good faith.

The case is reversed and remanded to the trial court with directions to enter judgment for appellant against appellee in an amount equal to seven-twelfths of all compensation (both salary and bonus) paid to appellee for services during the calendar year 1962.

Questions

1. Should the defendant be denied all compensation for the period if he spent much of his time working effectively for the corporation?

2. If a disloyal officer gives information to a competitor, who knows that it should not have the information, can the officer's corporation recover damages if the competitor profits from the information? If you think the answer is yes, will the recovery be from the disloyal officer, the competitor, or both? How much should the recovery be?

Corporate Opportunity Doctrine

A special subdivision of the duty of loyalty owed by directors, officers, and other agents of a corporation is the **corporate opportunity doctrine.** This doctrine prohibits these corporate personnel from taking for themselves any opportunity in which the corporation has a right, property interest, or expectancy, or which justice requires should belong to the corporation. Thus, if the corporation has been seeking the opportunity or it has been offered to the corporation, or its funds, facilities, or personnel have been used in developing the opportunity, the opportunity belongs to the corporation. It is available to corporate agents only if the corporation is unable to accept it (for example, doing so would be *ultra vires*), or is unable to finance it, or the corporation rejects it with full knowledge of the facts. If an opportunity unexpectedly appears, and it is offered to one who happens to be a director, officer, or other agent of the corporation, and it was not developed with the use of corporate funds, facilities, or personnel, it is not regarded as corporate property. For the usurpation of a corporate opportunity, the corporation may recover damages or profits realized by the corporate agent, or may attach a constructive trust for its benefit on the subject matter of the opportunity.

Contract and Tort Liability

An officer who assumes to bind the corporation, but has no authority to do so or is acting in excess of her authority, is liable to the third party for the breach of her implied warranty of authority. In addition, she is liable to the corporation for any losses it suffers as a result of the transaction. If an officer commits a tort against a third party while in the course and scope of her duties for the corporation, she becomes personally liable to the third party, and also renders the corporation liable under the doctrine of *respondeat superior*. If, as a result, the corporation is required to pay damages to the third party, it is entitled to recover the amount of the loss from the officer. A corporation ordinarily is not vicariously liable for most torts of its directors because the company usually is not in a position to exercise detailed control over the activities of the directors.

Statutory Violations

Directors and officers may be liable for violations of duties prescribed by the incorporation statutes, such as the duty to keep records, to file reports, and to permit inspection of the corporate books by shareholders. Additional potential liability may be found in a failure to comply with securities regulations or other administrative rules. Antitrust laws provide other possibilities for a director or officer to incur liability, either civil or criminal. Directors also may be liable for unlawful distributions to shareholders, such as those made while the corporation was insolvent, or when the distribution renders it insolvent.

SEC Rule 10b-5

Securities and Exchange Commission Rule 10b-5 has been the basis for many shareholder lawsuits against corporate officers, directors, and controlling shareholders for various kinds of unfaithful, fraudulent activity. Although in many cases the same lawsuits could have been founded on the breach of the duty of loyalty, a suit under Rule 10b-5 may have some substantive and procedural advantages.

In general, Rule 10b-5 prohibits the use of any device, scheme, or artifice to defraud, particularly in connection with the purchase or sale of securities. The rule has been invoked by minority shareholders against abuse by corporate management or controlling shareholders in connection with the sale of controlling shares at a premium, in connection with mergers that attempt to freeze out minority shareholders, in connection with registration materials and proxy statements, and especially in situations involving insider trading.

Until 1977 there was disagreement among the courts as to whether Rule 10b-5 covered only actual fraud (deceit) or deception, or included constructive fraud (breach of fiduciary duty) as well. In that year, the Supreme Court held, in *Santa Fe Industries v. Green,* that the rule covered only actual fraud, not mismanagement absent deception.

Two general areas of misconduct apparently not foreclosed by the *Santa Fe Industries* case are (1) sale (by issue or otherwise) or purchase (by redemption or otherwise) of securities (whether issued by the corporation or another), in a transaction authorized by corporate personnel with conflicting interests, and not in the best interests of the corporation; and (2) failure to comply with applicable federal securities laws or regulations in the sale or purchase of securities. Rule 10b-5 is discussed more fully in Chapter 47.

SUMMARY

A wider variety of financing methods is available to a corporation than to other types of business organizations. These fall into two major categories—debt and equity. Of the two types of financing methods, equity financing is probably the more important. This is done by issuing shares of ownership, usually in the form of readily marketable shares of stock. The only characteristic shares of stock necessarily must have in common is that they will all evidence ownership in the issuing corporation. Some may have preferences over other classes of stock, either in the right of the shareholder to dividends, or upon dissolution, or both. Although shares ordinarily carry with them voting rights, non-voting shares may be issued. Shares may be issued in different classes, or in different series within a class. Preferred stock may carry the right to declared dividends at a stated percentage, with a right to accumulate unpaid dividends, and with the right to participate in dividends along with common stock after first receiving dividends at a prescribed rate. Preferred stock may be convertible to other classes or types of securities, and may be redeemable by the corporation. Common stockholders, then, share in dividends after preferred stockholders have been paid. Common stockholders also ordinarily share in liquidation distributions only after preferred stockholders have received theirs.

Debt financing may be accomplished in the normal way, by the issuance of notes and the use of open-account credit. In addition, however, a corporation may issue readily salable corporate bonds. These bonds may be either secured or unsecured; they may pay interest at a stated rate or a rate based on the income of the issuing corporation; they may be convertible into other types of securities at the option of the bond-holder; and they may bind the corporation for a stated time or be callable at the corporation's option. A corporation may be limited by statute, however, as to the percentage of its financing that it can accomplish by debt as compared to its total capital.

Dividend distributions to shareholders may be of many types. Although they normally are made in cash, they also may be made in other corporate property, including more stock. Dividends ordinarily are not required to be paid, and do not become an obligation of the corporation until they are declared.

Management of a corporation consists of a board of directors and officers appointed by them. The directors are elected by the shareholders at annual meetings. Officers, in turn, are appointed by the board. Control of a corporation rests with the directors. They are responsible to oversee the operation of the corporation, and to establish policy within which it is to operate. The day-to-day management functions are the responsibility of the corporation's officers.

Directors and officers are fiduciaries of the corporation. As such, they owe to the corporation the duties of loyalty, honesty, and good faith in the conduct of corporate affairs. Directors and officers are entitled to exercise their judgments, as long as they do so in good faith. The failure to meet any of their obligations may render them liable to the corporation and its shareholders, and sometimes to third parties, for any damages that result. They also are liable for any failure to meet obligations imposed by state incorporation statutes, and for any torts they may commit. They even have some potential criminal liability imposed by statutes, such as antitrust statutes.

KEY TERMS AND CONCEPTS

equity securities
debt securities
preferred stock
cumulative preferred stock
participating preferred stock
convertible preferred stock
common stock
indenture
debenture
liquidating dividends
dividend
board of directors
cumulative voting
quorum
business judgment rule
corporate officer
Corporate Opportunity Doctrine

PROBLEMS

1. Morad and Thompson, while officers and directors of Bio-Lab, Inc., formed Med-Lab, Inc. and began business in the same line as Bio-Lab, but served another, adjoining geographical area. When this was discovered, Coupounas filed a shareholder derivative suit claiming that the formation of Med-Lab by Morad and Thompson was a violation of their duties to Bio-Lab. Is Coupounas correct?

2. The shareholders of United States Steel, and the corporation, brought action against Hurt and Grifitts for cancellation of 5000 and 4000 shares of stock, respectively. The 5000 shares issued to Hurt were issued in payment of C.P.A. services, part of which had been performed and part of which were to be performed in the future. The 4000 shares to Grifitts were in return for land he was to transfer in the future. Should the shareholders succeed?

3. An action was brought by Francis, trustee in bankruptcy of Baird Corp., against the administrator of the estate of Charles Prichard and his mother for breach of their duties as directors of the corporation. Prichard had used $10 million in corporate funds to make loans to family members, and the loans were not repaid. The practice had continued for a number of years and Prichard's mother, who paid little attention to the business, had not discovered the misappropriations. Should Prichard's mother be liable?

4. The board of directors of Pacific Gas & Electric Co. contributed funds to help defeat Proposition T. If passed, Proposition T would have prohibited construction in San Francisco of a building over 72 feet tall without prior voter approval. The board argued that it would raise the company's tax rate, interfere with construction of new corporate facilities, reduce construction jobs available to the public, and prove costly for everyone. Was the contribution improper?

5. A statute required that a provision for greater-than-majority voting requirements for a corporation's board of directors must be in the articles of incorporation. One corporation had such a provision in a shareholder agreement, but not in its articles. The shareholders sued to cancel the provision, and the corporation counter-sued to be permitted to amend its articles to include it. Which suit should prevail?

6. Certain employees of Allis-Chalmers Manufacturing Company were involved with illegal price-fixing. As a result, the board of directors, on behalf of the corporation, pleaded guilty to eight counts of antitrust violation. The directors then were sued by the shareholders for negligence and mismanagement. They defended on the ground that they were not aware of the violations because the employees involved had submitted false information concerning their activities. Is the defense appropriate?

7. Rachel Stone, widow of Harold Stone, who had been chairman of the board of directors of the American Lacquer Solvents Co., sued American for pension benefits. The board had adopted a resolution granting Stone a pension of $8000 per year, the pension to be continued to Rachel upon her husband's death. After a marital dispute, Harold sent a letter to Shaw, another director, asking for cancellation of the resolution. Shaw convened a meeting for that purpose, but notified only five of the seven directors of the meeting. At that meeting, the board unanimously agreed to cancel the resolution. Was the action valid?

8. The president of Hessler, Inc. owned 80 percent of its stock and was allowed to manage the corporate business with great independence. Over the course of several years, in order to keep Ferrell, one of the employees, from seeking another job, he repeatedly promised her that she would have retirement benefits when she retired. The matter never was presented to the board of directors and, after the president died and Ferrell retired, she was given no benefits. When Ferrell sued, the corporation defended on the ground that only the board of directors had the power to grant retirement benefits. Should the corporation be bound by the president's promises?

9. The board of directors of Apex Corp. failed to declare a dividend during five successive years. In each year, some $40,000,000 was added to surplus. Dodge, a shareholder, brought an action to compel the declaration of a dividend. The board defended on the ground that only the board of directors may declare that a dividend is to be distributed, and cannot be compelled to do so contrary to its discretion. Is the board correct?

Chapter 42

Corporations: Shareholders' Rights and Liabilities

THE ROLE OF SHAREHOLDERS

Although the shareholders are the owners of the corporation and are the ultimate beneficiaries of all of its business activities, they play only a limited role in the actual conduct of its affairs. Shareholders usually function only in two major ways —they elect directors and they vote on certain ex-traordinary matters involving the corporation, such as the sale of corporate assets outside the ordinary course of business, plans for merger or consolidation, and proposals concerning dissolution. The primary control exercised by shareholders is in staying informed about the policies and activities of the corporation and voting to elect directors and to approve major corporate plans that will best promote the policies they favor.

Shareholders Meetings

Most states require every corporation to hold one **shareholder meeting** annually, at a time (and sometimes place) provided for in the bylaws. The shareholders have their principal opportunity for input at this meeting, which ordinarily may be held anywhere, inside or outside of the state of incorporation. Some large corporations rotate their meeting places in order to invite the largest shareholder participation.

A corporation also may hold special shareholder meetings as they become necessary. These ordinarily are called by the board of directors, but also may be called by a petition of the shareholders holding at least a specified percentage of the stock entitled to vote at the meeting (5 percent under the Revised Model Business Corporation Act).

Notice of Meetings

Most state statutes require that notice of all meetings be given to the shareholders entitled to vote.

The notice must be in writing, and must state the time, place, and the purpose of the meeting. Ordinarily any matter may be brought before a regular annual meeting. However, the business conducted at special meetings often is restricted to that set out in the notice. Under the Model Business Corporation Act and the Revised Model Business Corporation Act, the required notice must be given not more than 50 days nor less than 10 days prior to the meeting. Any action taken in violation of the notice requirement is voidable at the demand of any shareholder. The policy of the law is to promote the participation of shareholders, and particularly to protect minority shareholders. Consider the following case.

DARVIN v. BELMONT INDUSTRIES, INC.
40 Mich.App. 672, 199 N.W.2d 542 (1972)

This was an action by Frank Darvin (Plaintiff/Appellant) against Belmont Industries, Inc. and V & F Investment Company (Defendant/Appellees) for a writ of *mandamus* (a special appeal procedure seeking immediate action) to order Defendant corporations to set aside actions taken at shareholders' and directors' meetings.

Plaintiff was one of five shareholders and four directors of Defendants, both of which were closely held corporations. After a dispute over management, the other four shareholders, three of whom were directors, decided to get rid of Plaintiff by reducing the four directorships to three. Plaintiff received notice of the meetings one day before they were scheduled. He attended them with his attorney, objected to insufficient notice at the beginning and, although the evidence was conflicting, apparently did not vote his shares at the shareholder meetings. Plaintiff contended that all of the actions taken at the meetings were invalid.

The trial court denied relief, and Plaintiff appealed. Reversed and remanded.

LESINSKI, Chief Justice.

A purpose of the time-notice requirement is, of course, to allow a shareholder sufficient time to arrange to attend the meeting. If the shareholder did, in fact, attend the meeting, despite a failure by the corporation to comply with the time-notice requirement, courts have reasoned that he has suffered no harm because he was still able to be present. The purpose-notice requirement serves another function, however. It provides a shareholder with sufficient opportunity to study contemplated action at the meeting and the legality thereof. When the shareholder possesses knowledge of the purpose of a special meeting, he can study the proposal, arrive at a position, and either oppose it or support it. . . .

There has been a recognition by the courts of this State, . . . that the notice requirement has other functions besides that of insuring a shareholder's or director's attendance at a meeting. Courts in other jurisdictions have ruled specifically on the issue at hand, holding that attendance at a meeting, without participation, does not constitute waiver of defective notice. . . .

Although the notice given to plaintiff Darvin in the instant case was sufficient to obtain his physical presence at the meeting, it is plain that it was not sufficient to allow him to ascertain what action was to be taken at the special meeting of defendant corporations, and to determine what steps could be taken to protect his position. The weight of the evidence at trial, although it was contradicted, revealed that plaintiff had not voted his shares at the meeting. He specifically refused the opportunity to do so. If he had voted his shares, he could have made use of the protection afforded him by M.C.L.A. Section 450.13(3); M.S.A. Section 21.13(3), which governs reduction of members of the board of directors in this State. With sufficient notice, plaintiff Darvin and his attorney could have had the opportunity to apprise themselves of the existence of this provision which has been recognized as supplying special protection to the minority shareholder in the close corporation. . . .

Defendants maintain that their by-law provision, providing for waiver of notice "whenever all the shareholders shall meet," should control in this situation, however. The statutory provision concerning notice does give corporations flexibility in setting notice requirements to meet their individual needs. However, to interpret the statutory notice requirement in the manner which defendants urge would vitiate in large part the purposes thereof. This provision of the by-laws must be read to require consent of all shareholders to the meeting or participation therein.

Corporations can determine, under the statute, how much notice will be given of shareholders' meetings. Defendants in this case chose ten days. Yet, a corporation can neither eliminate notice altogether, nor interpret its notice provision in such a way that the protection it provides shareholders is virtually eliminated, for such action would contravene statutory and public policy in this State. . . .

Plaintiff lacked proper notice of the shareholders' meetings in this case. He did not waive that notice by attending the meetings, objecting to the lack of notice, and refusing to vote his shares. Therefore, the actions of defendant corporations at those shareholders' meetings of September 12, 1969, in reducing the board of directors from four to three, and electing a new board, are invalid.

Questions

1. Is the court simply being technical in this case, since the shareholders probably will reduce the board at the next meeting?

2. Do you think the notice requirement is as important as the court suggests?

3. What if the notice was improper but all shareholders or directors attended anyway?

Section 7.04 of the RMBCA, and the statutes in many states, allow action to be taken by the shareholders without a meeting, if all consent. This is, of course, in recognition of the fact that the shareholders of smaller corporations often can meet or otherwise communicate informally.

SHAREHOLDER VOTING

The shareholders are the owners of the corporation. A fundamental right of owners is to run their business. In the corporate context, this is done by voting at shareholder meetings.

Shareholder Voting Rights

Each share ordinarily is entitled to one vote on each issue at a shareholder's meeting. This rule, however, is subject to a number of possible exceptions. The articles of incorporation or the bylaws may establish a different rule, such as cumulative voting (discussed in the previous chapter), or some shares may carry voting rights (non-voting shares). State statutes also may place restrictions on voting. Section 7.21(b) of the RMBCA provides that unless there are special circumstances, shares of one corporation that are owned by a second corporation may not be voted if the first corporation owns a majority of the voting shares of the second corporation.

In order to be entitled to vote or to take other action at a meeting of shareholders, a shareholder must have owned the shares, and had his name on the books of the corporation as a shareholder, no later than the **record date** for the particular meeting. This date may be fixed by the bylaws, or the bylaws may provide a method by which it is to be determined. In the absence of a provision in the bylaws, it may be fixed by the board of directors. Section 7.07 of the RMBCA sets certain minimum requirements for a valid record date. It must be no later than 60 days before the meeting, and if a meeting is adjourned, other than by court order, for a period of longer than 120 days after the record date of the adjourned meeting, a new date must be fixed. Thus, intervening shareholders who have held their shares for 60 to 120 days would be entitled to vote when the adjourned meeting is resumed. If the meeting is one called by the shareholders rather than the board of directors, the RMBCA establishes a record date in terms of the first shareholder's demand, unless the bylaws provide to the contrary. A list of the names of all shareholders entitled to vote ordinarily must be made available for inspection prior to the meeting and at the meeting itself.

Quorum Requirements

Voting at a meeting is valid only if a quorum is present. Ordinarily, a quorum is constituted by the presence of a majority of the shares entitled to vote. The shareholders may be present either personally, or through a representative in the case of shares being voted by proxy or a voting trust. However, quorum requirements higher than a majority may be established by the articles of incorporation or the bylaws.

It should be noted that quorum requirements are established according to the number of shares entitled to vote, not according to the number of shareholders. Also, voting on some matters may be restricted to a particular class of shares, in which case the quorum requirement will be established according to the shares in that class.

In the event a quorum is not present at a regular or special meeting, a new meeting time may be established, or the meeting may be adjourned to a later date. Any action taken at a meeting attended by less than a quorum may be declared void at the insistence of any shareholder entitled to vote at that meeting. In the alternative, the shareholders may ratify the action, but by unanimous consent only. Ordinarily, that consent must be in writing.

Class Voting

Voting by class of shares was not provided for specifically in the Model Business Corporation Act, but was added by the RMBCA in 1983.

However, prior to 1983, many state statutes permitted such voting. **Class voting** recognizes that some matters affect only one class of stock, and only that class should have a say on the subject. For example, a particular class of shares may be divided into two or more issues, with rights varying among the issues, such as rights concerning distributions. Any action concerning a change in relative rights between those two issues legitimately is a concern only of the class including those issues, and could be voted on only by those shareholders. Another situation that invites class voting, and is widely recognized, is class voting for directors. This is sometimes done to ensure that each class will be able to elect one or more directors to represent their unique interests.

Cumulative Voting

The concept of cumulative voting was briefly mentioned in Chapter 41. General corporation law provides that each share is entitled to one vote unless the articles of incorporation or bylaws provide to the contrary. Therefore, cumulative voting must be provided for expressly. This means a formula must be established by which each share is entitled to more than one vote in electing directors. The most common formula is "number of shares × number of directors to be elected = number of votes." In most cases, this ensures that one majority shareholder cannot elect the entire board of directors.

Proxy Voting

A **proxy** is a grant of authority given by an owner of registered securities to someone else authorizing that person to cast the owner's votes at a shareholder's meeting. The person holding the proxy acts as agent for the shareholder. A proxy ordinarily must be in writing and becomes effective when received by the secretary of the corporation. A proxy may be given only because the shareholder is not going to be present at a meeting, or because it is solicited by someone who has

an interest in the outcome of a director's election or a vote on a proposal. Proxies frequently are solicited by incumbent management as a method of keeping themselves and their policies in control.

Proxy solicitation sometimes is regulated by the Securities Exchange Act and the rules of the Securities and Exchange Commission. Then proxy statements must be filed with the SEC prior to being mailed to shareholders, and the SEC must be given an opportunity to comment and to suggest changes. All material information concerning matters to be voted on must be given to the shareholders. Each shareholder also must be furnished with a form on which he may indicate his agreement or disagreement with the proposals to be voted on. If the vote concerns the election of directors, each shareholder also must be furnished with an annual report.

Proxy grants ordinarily are effective for a certain period of time. Under Section 7.22 of the RMBCA, the period is eleven months unless a longer time is provided in the proxy. In spite of this, however, a grant of authority under a proxy ordinarily is revocable at the option of the shareholder, just as is any other grant of agency authority. The exception to this rule is a proxy "coupled with an interest" (also sometimes called a proxy "given as security"). That is, the proxy holder somehow is entitled to the proxy, having given up something in reliance on receiving it. Under Section 7.22 of the RMBCA, a proxy right coupled with an interest includes the appointment of: "(1) a [holder of] pledge[d stock]; (2) a person who purchased or agreed to purchase the shares; (3) a creditor of the corporation who extended it credit under terms requiring the appointment; (4) an employee of the corporation whose employment contract requires the appointment; or (5) a party to a voting trust agreement under Section 7.31."

Voting Trusts

In order to obtain increased influence in voting, shareholders may pool their shares. These pooling arrangements may be quite informal, as by an agreement between two or more shareholders to vote their shares in a particular way. Whether such an agreement is binding legally depends on whether the shareholders enter into a binding contract according to general principles of contract law. At the other end of the spectrum, the statutes of most states and the RMBCA permit the creation of voting trusts. A **voting trust** is an arrangement under which the rights that accompany shares of stock (and the title to those shares) are split. Legal title, and the right to vote the shares, will be vested in a trustee, and the equitable title, and the rights to dividends and distributions upon liquidation, will rest in the "shareholder/beneficiaries" of the trust. A trust may be arranged at the time the corporation issues shares, or after acquisition by the shareholders through their subsequent transfer of the shares to a trustee. The trustee will be shown, on the books of the corporation, as the owner of the shares. The obligations of the trustee, and the extent of the interest of the beneficiaries, will be spelled out in a trust agreement. Such arrangements, although permitted by most states, usually are limited as to duration—commonly ten years.

The Corporation's Acceptance of Votes

A corporation is obligated to accept all valid votes cast in an election. Difficulty sometimes arises, however, when shares are to be voted by someone other than the registered owner of the shares, such as by proxy or by a trustee. Signatures also may come into question because the shareholder's signature on a proxy or other document relating to voting appears different than on the records of the corporation. Also, shares may be owned by another corporation and the person authorized by that other corporation to vote the shares has changed. A corporation may adopt rules of voting that alleviate some of these problems. However, in doing so, care must be taken to avoid rules that would unreasonably infringe on the rights of shareholders to vote. In general, as long as the secretary, or other person in charge of the decision, elects either to accept or to reject a signature, does so in good faith, and it does not affect the outcome of an election or other result, neither he nor the corporation will be liable in the event a mistake is made.

SHAREHOLDERS' INSPECTION OF BOOKS

Shareholders, as owners of the corporation, have the right to inspect the corporation's books and records. This right, however, is limited to inspections at reasonable times, and reasonable places, for proper purposes. Although seldom exercised, this right is supported both by the theory that each shareholder should be able to protect her investment and be in a position to make shareholder decisions in an informed way. Of course, ultimately, all corporate authority is derived from the collective will of the shareholders, and it is the investment of the shareholders that is at stake in every corporate decision.

Normally, regular business hours are considered a reasonable time for an inspection. Corporate officers and their delegates, however, may refuse to grant an inspection even during regular business hours if it would create an unreasonable burden on operations. What constitutes a reasonable place of inspection ordinarily depends on where the relevant books and records are kept. Reasonable time and place, of course, may be altered by a showing of some emergency. Also, they may be fixed by court order. That is, the books might be seized in the middle of the night and inspected at a place wholly separate from the corporate offices if a court so ordered.

A proper purpose for inspection generally means a purpose that reasonably is relevant to the furtherance of some legitimate interest of the shareholders in the corporation. For example, a shareholder may wish to inspect the books in order to discover evidence of fraud or mismanagement, or perhaps to compile a list of all shareholders. That list might be used to communicate with other shareholders on any matter of corporate business, or to aid her in acquiring proxies. A purpose of compiling a mailing list to be used or sold, for individual profit, would not be proper. The right to inspect a company's books is illustrated by the following case.

IN RE APPLICATION OF LOPEZ
71 A.D.2d 976, 420 N.Y.S.2d 225 (1979)

This was an action by Jose J. Lopez (Petitioner/Appellant) against SCM Corporation (Respondent/Respondent) seeking a court order allowing him access to the shareholder records of Respondent.

Respondent was involved in a lawsuit brought against it by one Muller. Muller also had formed a committee of shareholders to challenge Respondent's position in the matter. Petitioner, also a shareholder of Respondent, founded the committee and, on the same day, requested of Respondent a list of its shareholders' names and addresses, and daily transfer sheets showing those eligible to vote in the next election. The stated purpose was to solicit proxies from shareholders in support of the committee's nominees for directors. Respondent refused this request.

The trial court refused Petitioner's application, and Petitioner appealed. Reversed and petition granted.

MEMORANDUM DECISION.

The purpose of petitioner's demand was clearly set forth in his letter of August 6, so there is no procedural basis for respondent's rejection. . . . Further, the inspection of shareholder lists to facilitate a proxy challenge to incumbent directors is a valid purpose. . . . The burden is on respondent to show an improper purpose for the demand. . . . Petitioner's association with Muller is certainly no indication of impropriety, in light of the otherwise valid stated purpose of the demand. Petitioner alleges without challenge that he has independently concluded that changes in the management of SCM in the interest of its shareholders is [*sic*] warranted, and that in this respect his views and those of the committee are similar. Where the demand is facially valid, good faith is assumed, obviating the necessity for a hearing on this issue. . . . The mere fact that Muller and his companies are engaged in litigation with SCM does not demonstrate lack of good faith. Nor would there be an improper purpose or bad faith if communications with shareholders discussed such litigation. . . .

Petitioner is entitled to access to available transfer sheets, at his expense, showing the daily status of record and beneficial ownership throught September 7, 1979. . . .

Questions

1. How can a corporation protect itself against shareholders who would misuse their right to inspection?

2. Can you think of any improper reasons a shareholder might have for wanting to inspect a company's books?

The right to inspect may be limited by the articles of incorporation or the bylaws, as long as the limitation is reasonable. Also, a number of states limit this right by statute. The MBCA provided that this right was limited to shareholders (including a trustee of a voting trust) of shares held for at least six months or which represent 5 percent or more of the total outstanding shares. This limitation was not included in the RMBCA, and the RMBCA also provides that the right to inspect cannot be abolished by the articles of incorporation or the bylaws. Also, under Section 52 of the MBCA, the right to inspect included the right to "make extracts therefrom." This has been expanded by Section 16.03 of the RMBCA to include the right to make copies by photographic or other means.

SHAREHOLDERS' RIGHTS TO DISTRIBUTION

As noted in Chapter 40, distributions to shareholders may be made in many forms. Some may be made because they were provided for in the articles of incorporation, others by vote of the board of directors, and still others because they are mandated by law. Most frequently, they come as a result of a declaration by the board of directors, and are in the form of cash dividends.

Dividends

The directors of a corporation determine whether dividends should be distributed. The shareholders ordinarily have no right to dividends until they are declared. When declared, however, dividends become obligations of the corporation to the same extent as obligations to creditors.

In determining whether to declare dividends, the board of directors is obligated to make its decision in the best interests of the shareholders, to whom it owes a fiduciary duty. Sometimes this may require that dividends be paid out in cash, or in stock or other property of the corporation. However, sometimes the interests of the shareholders are served better by "plowing back" accumulated earnings into the corporation to finance its operations, or to retire some of the corporation's debt. The former might be true when funds are needed to develop and market an exciting new product. The latter is true especially in times of declining interest rates. The earnings of a corporation ultimately will flow to the shareholders anyway, either through the payment of dividends, in the form of higher market value of their shares, or by distribution upon liquidation. Earnings left with the corporation simply change the nature of the risks taken. Reinvested earnings present the opportunity for profits and losses on those earnings, depending upon the general success of the corporation. The following case considers the question of what circumstances may justify a court's requiring a distribution of dividends upon suit by the shareholders.

GUTTMANN v. ILLINOIS CENTRAL R. CO.
189 F.2d 927 A.L.R.2d 1066 (2nd Cir. 1951)

This was an action by Alexander Guttmann (Plaintiff/Appellant) against the Illinois Central Railroad Company (Defendant/Appellee) for a judgment decreeing that dividends on noncumulative preferred stock had been earned and should have been declared for the years 1937 to 1947 inclusive. The trial court refused relief on the ground that the evidence did not establish that the board of directors had abused its discretion by withholding dividends during those years, and Plaintiff appealed. Affirmed.

FRANK, Circuit Judge.

Our lode-star is Wabash Railway Co. v. Barclay, 280 U.S. 197, 50 S.Ct. 106, 74 L.Ed. 368, which dealt with the non-cumulative preferred stock of an Indiana railroad corporation. There were no controlling Indiana decisions or statutes on that subject. The United States Supreme Court was therefore obliged to interpret the contract according to its own notions of what the contract meant. We have a similar problem here, since there are no Illinois decisions or statutory provisions which control or guide us. Absent such decisions and statutes, we must take the Wabash opinion as expressing the correct interpretation of the rights of non-cumulative preferred stockholders of this Illinois company. For the difference between the language of the preferred stock here and that in Wabash seems to us to be of no moment. [*sic*]

In the Wabash case, plaintiffs, holders of non-cumulative preferred stock, sought an injunction preventing the defendant railroad company from paying dividends on the common stock unless it first paid dividends on the non-cumulative preferred to the extent that the company, in previous years, had net earnings available for that payment and that such dividends remained unpaid. The Court decided against the plaintiffs. It spoke of the fact that, in earlier years, "net earnings that could have been used for the payment were expended upon improvements and additions to the property and equipment of the road"; it held that the contract with the preferred meant that "if those profits are justifiably applied by the directors to capital improvements and no dividend is declared within the year, the claim for that year is gone and cannot be asserted at a later date." We take that as a ruling that the directors were left with no discretion ever to pay any such dividend. For if they had had that discretion, it would surely have been an "abuse" to pay dividends on the common while disregarding the asserted claim of the non-cumulative preferred to back dividends. Indeed, the plaintiff in the instant case contends that a payment of common dividends, whenever there is such a discretion, constitutes an unlawful "diversion"; and such a "diversion" would be an "abuse" of discretion.

Plaintiff, however, seeks to limit the effect of the Wabash ruling to instances where the net earnings, for a given year, which could have been paid to the non-cumulative preferred, have once been expended justifiably for "capital improvements" or "additions to the property or equipment." He would have us treat the words "non-cumulative" as if they read "cumulative if earned except only when the earnings are paid out for capital additions." He argues that the Wabash ruling has no application when net earnings for a given year are legitimately retained for any one of a variety of other corporate purposes, and when in a subsequent year it develops that such retention was not necessary. We think the attempted distinction untenable. It ascribes to the Supreme Court a naive over-estimation of the importance of tangibles (because they can be touched and seen) as contrasted with intangibles. Suppose the directors of a corporation justifiably invested the retained earnings for the year 1945 in land which, at the time, seemed essential or highly desirable for the company's future welfare. Suppose that, in 1948, it turned out that the land so purchased was not necessary or useful, and that the directors thereupon caused it to be sold. Plaintiff's position compels the implied concession that the proceeds of such a sale would never be available for payment of so-called arrears of unpaid non-cumulative preferred dividends, and that the directors would forever lack all discretion to pay them. We fail to see any intelligible difference between (1) such a situation and (2) one where annual earnings are properly retained for any appropriate corporate purpose, and where in a later year the retention proves wholly unnecessary. There is no sensible ground for singling out legitimate capital outlays, once made, as the sole cause of the irrevocable destruction of the claims of the preferred. We do not believe that the Supreme Court gave the contract with the preferred such an irrational interpretation. It simply happened that in the Wabash case the earnings had been used for capital additions, and that, accordingly, the court happened to mention that particular purpose. Consequently, we think that the Court, in referring to that fact, did not intend it to have any significance. We disregard the decisions of the New Jersey courts, and the decision of the Ninth Circuit, since we think they are at odds with the rationale of the Wabash decision.

Questions

1. Why are courts, as illustrated by this case, so reluctant to look behind a decision by a corporate board of directors?
2. When would a refusal to pay dividends be such an abuse of discretion that a court might intervene and order them paid?

Share Exchanges, Stock Dividends, and Splits

Distributions to shareholders may come in the form of share exchanges, stock dividends, and stock splits. All are regarded as distributions, just as are cash dividends. The major differences are in terms of type of risk, accounting procedures, and tax consequences.

Generally, distributions of the corporation's shares are not taxable as income, but may change the *basis* (net cost to be deducted from sale price in determining taxable gain) of the shares when later sold. For example, in a **share exchange** an equal number of shares of a different class or issue are exchanged for a shareholder's stock, or in conversion of the shares, the shareholder's investment in the corporation remains the same, and his interest is represented by the same number of shares. Therefore, the distribution is not taxable as income, and the basis of his shares remains the same. The same is true of stock dividends. As discussed in the previous chapter, the net effect of a **stock dividend** is only a restructuring of the capital section of the corporation's balance sheet.

The major effect of a **stock split** is to divide the capital of the corporation over a larger number of shares, and to reduce the value of the stock proportionately. Therefore, a "4-for-1" stock split of shares valued at $60 per share, would quadruple the number of shares outstanding and reduce the value per share to $15. This does not mean, however, that the market value will be cut to one-fourth of its former value. A stock split may cause the market value to be more than one-fourth because the new lower price may make the shares marketable to more investors.

Options and Warrants

A corporation may issue to shareholders the right to purchase additional shares in the corporation. These rights may be a part of the original issue of stock, or may be issued at times, and for prices, established later by the board of directors. When created and issued later, these rights, of course, are considered distributions.

The rights may be in the form of a simple **option** to purchase, which is personal to the shareholder, or in the form of a **warrant,** which the shareholder may transfer. Warrants very frequently have a published price and are bought and sold on stock exchanges much like shares themselves.

Typically, options and warrants are given to directors, officers, or employees of the corporation as a part of their compensation packages. Also, they may be issued to shareholders in order to prevent the dilution of ownership. The value of options and warrants is established by the board of directors. As long as the directors do so in good faith, their valuation is conclusive under the RMBCA.

Shareholders' Preemptive Rights

Depending on the provisions of a particular state's corporation laws and the articles of incorporation, shareholders may have preemptive rights in new issues of corporate shares. A **preemptive right** is a right to purchase additional shares, and is binding on the corporation and others who may purchase its stock. That is, if shares are sold by the corporation in violation of a shareholder's preemptive right, the shareholder is entitled to recover the shares sold. The corporation is then liable to the purchaser of the stock for the breach of its implied warranty of title.

A majority of the states provide by statute that shareholders do not have preemptive rights unless they are provided for in the articles of incorporation. This is also the position of Section 6.30 of the RMBCA. The MBCA adopted this position in Section 26, but provided an alternative (Section 26A), which gave each shareholder automatic preemptive rights in the absence of a provision of the articles of incorporation to the contrary. A substantial minority of states have the latter provision. Preemptive rights are accorded to shareholders to prevent the dilution of a shareholder's interest without his or her consent. The

split among the states on this subject, therefore, is one of philosophy. In either case, the matter may be controlled by an appropriate provision of the articles of incorporation.

Preemptive rights, when granted, always are subject to some limitations. Overall, for example, they apply only to new issues, and not to shares issued pursuant to an existing plan, or to shares issued and then reacquired, though not cancelled, by the issuing corporation *(treasury shares)*. The RMBCA, in Section 6.30(e), provides: "There is no preemptive right: (1) to acquire shares issued as incentives to directors, officers, or employees. . . . (2) to acquire shares issued to satisfy conversion or option rights; (3) to acquire shares authorized by the articles of incorporation that are issued within six months from the effective date of incorporation; (4) to acquire shares sold otherwise than for money; (5) for holders of shares of any class preferred or limited as to its entitlement to dividends or assets; [or] (6) for holders of common shares to acquire shares of any class preferred or limited as to obligations or entitlement to dividends or assets unless the shares are convertible into common shares or carry a right to subscribe for or acquire common shares."

SHAREHOLDER SUITS

Shareholder suits may be classified into two broad categories—direct suits by individuals and derivative suits. In the first, the shareholders are suing on behalf of themselves, individually. In the latter, they are suing on behalf of the corporation.

Individual Suits

Individual suits may be brought by one or more shareholders. In the case of more than one, a number of shareholders actually may join together as plaintiffs, or one may bring action on behalf of herself and "all other shareholders similarly situated" (known as a class action). All these suits are brought to enforce rights belonging to the shareholders by virtue of their ownership of shares in the defendant corporation. For example, a shareholder may wish to bring a suit to enforce her right to vote, her right to reasonable inspection of corporate books and records, or, within limitations, the right to force the payment of dividends. The first two are more often causes for an individual suit by one shareholder, and the third more appropriately may be brought as a class action.

Class-action suits may be brought only under circumstances narrowly defined by statute, by court rule, or by case law. They ordinarily are appropriate only: (1) when the class of plaintiffs is so large as to make actual joinder of the parties impracticable; (2) after all who will be affected have been notified directly, when that is possible, or have been notified by publication when actual notice is not possible; (3) when each party has been given the opportunity to consent to participate in the action or be eliminated as a party; and (4) when the court has approved the proceeding as a class action. In shareholder class actions, because the names and addresses of all shareholders can be determined from the records of the corporation, each would have to be actually notified, by mail or otherwise. The expense of actual notification may not be possible to fund in order to get started, and it may well exceed the value of the ultimate benefits to be derived from the suit. When this is true, a lawsuit becomes impractical and the right of shareholders to bring one really is only theoretical.

Derivative Suits

Shareholder derivative suits differ from individual suits primarily as to procedure, although they do, in some respects, resemble class actions. In an individual suit, a shareholder seeks to vindicate his individual rights. In a derivative suit, a shareholder seeks to vindicate some right of the corporation (that is, of all the shareholders). Ordinarily, the rights of a corporation are enforced by its board of directors. A derivative suit, then, is necessary only when the board of directors is either unable or unwilling to act.

In many instances the board will be unwilling to act because it is the conduct of some or all of its members that is being challenged. Shareholders might bring a derivative suit against some or all of the directors to recover damages for *ultra vires* acts, or for illegal actions, such as illegal distributions or self-dealing. Under appropriate circumstances, shareholders even may sue to require directors to declare and pay dividends, or to pay dividends that have been declared. Such a suit also might be brought against the officers of the corporation if they have failed to meet their management responsibilities.

Under Section 7.40 of the RMBCA, a shareholder wishing to bring a derivative action must first request that the board of directors pursue the matter and receive a refusal, or he must be able to establish a good reason for not making the request. If the derivative action is allowed by the court, it cannot be settled, or otherwise disposed of, without the court's approval. The reason for having the court monitor the disposition of derivative suits is the same as it is in class-action litigation. When one person acts as representative of a group, the court wants to be sure that the best interests of that group are not sacrificed by the representative choosing to pursue his own best interests.

In cases in which a derivative suit is for money damages, the net proceeds, after court-approved costs and attorney fees are paid, are put into the corporation's treasury, which will benefit the shareholders in proportion to their relative interests. In other cases, typically those involving nonmonetary remedies, the shareholder bringing the suit, if successful, ordinarily is reimbursed by the corporation for the expenses incurred. Even if unsuccessful, the representative may be reimbursed if the suit was processed diligently and in good faith, and involved something that should have been pursued by the board of directors.

Can any shareholder bring a derivative suit? Consider the following case.

VISTA FUND v. GARIS
277 N.W.2d 19 (Minn. 1979)

This was a stockholders' derivative action by Vista Fund and other stockholders (Plaintiffs/Appellants) against Gordon O. Garis, Deltak Corporation and others (Defendants/Respondents). The question before the court was whether Plaintiffs were entitled to bring a derivative suit.

Vista Fund acquired shares in RayGo Corporation in 1967. In 1972, Defendants, all of them officers and directors of RayGo, formed a new corporation, Deltak. Shortly thereafter RayGo conveyed one of its divisions to Deltak. In May 1974, RayGo merged with Foster Wheeler, and RayGo stockholders exchanged their stock for Foster Wheeler stock. In October 1974 Vista Fund sold its Foster Wheeler stock. In August 1977 Vista Fund purchased 100 shares of Foster Wheeler stock, and then instituted this action, complaining of the 1972 sale of the division of RayGo to Deltak, which it contended was fraudulent, negligent, and in breach of fiduciary duties by the officers and directors of RayGo.

The trial court found that Vista Fund was not a proper party plaintiff in a stockholders' derivative suit, and Vista Fund appealed. That portion of the trial court judgment was affirmed.

SCOTT, Justice.

The trial court interpreted Rule 23.06 as requiring a plaintiff, in order to have standing to maintain a derivative action, to continuously and uninterruptedly own stock in the corporation from the time of the alleged wrongs through the time suit is commenced. Since Vista sold its stock before it commenced suit (although it purchased 100 shares of Foster Wheeler stock shortly before bringing this action), the district court ruled that it lacked standing to maintain the instant derivative action. Vista argues that the trial court's ruling is erroneous because even if it must be a shareholder at the time of suit, uninterrupted ownership of the stock from the time of the alleged wrongs until commencement of suit is not required. It claims that it owned RayGo stock at the time of the alleged wrongs and owned Foster Wheeler stock at the time suit was brought, and thus satisfied Rule 23.06. Again, this contention is without merit.

It is consistent with the policy underlying Rule 23.06 to require continuous stock ownership. The purpose of the stockholding requirements of the rule is "to prevent persons from purchasing stock solely for purposes of maintaining shareholders' derivative actions." Rule 23.06, Advisory Committee Note. In other words, the share ownership requirement is intended to prevent the litigating of purchased grievances or speculating in wrongs done to corporations. . . . Once a shareholder has sold his stock he is in the same position as any other non-shareholder. Accordingly, when he reacquires stock and brings suit based on a corporate wrong occurring during his prior ownership he is, in effect, purchasing a grievance or speculating in corporate wrongs. Indeed, this is what occurred here. . . .

Before the district court, and on appeal, plaintiff relies primarily on the case of Bateson v. Magna Oil Corp., . . . to support its contention that continuous stock ownership is not required by Rule 23.06. Vista's reliance on that decision is misplaced. In Bateson, the plaintiff sought to enforce a right of the Magna Corporation in a derivative action. The plaintiff owned Magna stock continuously from 1956 until May 5, 1967, when he sold all his Magna shares. Plaintiff stated in a deposition that he intended to retain 100 or 200 shares of Magna stock because he had long planned the derivative action. On July 21, 1967, plaintiff purchased 100 Magna shares for the purpose of bringing suit. The derivative action was filed on September 21, 1967. The district court dismissed the suit on the ground that the stockholding requirements of Rule 23.1, Rules of Federal Civil Procedure, had not been complied with. The circuit court reversed. . . . The essence of the Bateson holding was that most of the alleged wrongs were continuing in nature and therefore occurred at the time the plaintiff owned the repurchased Magna stock. Consequently, plaintiff complied with Federal Rule 23,1 because he owned stock at the time of these alleged wrongs. It is evident that the Bateson case does not support plaintiff's position, but instead supports the decision reached herein. . . .

In Bateson, the court acknowledged that continuing wrongs existed where the defendant caused the corporation to purchase an airplane which was used more for the benefit of the defendant than the company and where the defendant caused company property to be mortgaged in order to secure the payment of the defendant's personal debt. These wrongs are, arguably, analogous to the alleged wrongs in this case. However, the Bateson decision is a very liberal application of the continuing wrong theory and its views are not shared by most courts. See, 7A Wright and Miller, Federal Practice and Procedure, Section 1828, pp. 346, 48 (1972). If the alleged wrongs in this case were construed to be "continuing," the contemporaneous ownership requirement of Rule 23.06 would be substantially subverted. For this reason, we reject Vista's "continuing wrong" theory.

Questions

1. Are you persuaded by the way the court distinguishes the decision in the *Bateson* case?

2. Is it true that the policies underlying the ownership rule would be subverted if people in the plaintiffs' postion were permitted to sue?

LIABILITIES OF SHAREHOLDERS

Shareholders usually are liable for the debts of the corporation only to the extent of their individual investments. This, of course, includes liability for any unpaid portion of the subscription price in the case of subscribers, and any unpaid portion of the purchase price in the case of other purchasers of shares from the issuing corporation. Although obligations to pay in the future, such as promissory notes, are not considered payment, payment for shares may be made in services or property, as long as the services actually are performed or the property actually is transferred to the corporation. In the absence of fraud, a good-faith evaluation of the worth of the services or property by the board of directors ordinarily is taken as conclusive.

Watered Shares

Share of stock issued by a corporation in return for non-cash payments must be fully paid, just as if issued for cash. A share is considered fully paid when par value shares are issued at par value, or when no-par shares are paid in an amount established by the board of directors, to be allocated to capital, rather than surplus. When issued for less, the shares are called "watered," the capital of the corporation is overstated, creditors are less secure

than the books of the corporation would indicate, and the real value of all shares is reduced proportionately. This may result from a bad-faith or fraudulent evaluation of the property or services received by the board of directors. Some examples of watered shares include: (1) shares issued for cash, before the cash price is fully paid; (2) shares issued in return for property having a fair market value less than the stated value; and (3) shares issued in return for services never rendered.

When **stock watering** is discovered, the shares may be treated as void, voidable, assessable, or subject to liability for creditor claims. Commonly, the corporation will recover the difference from the offending purchaser. The following case considers the question of watering stock.

HASELBUSH v. ALSCO OF COLORADO, INC.
161 Colo. 138, 421 P.2d 113 (1967)

This was an action by Willard C. Haselbush (Plaintiff/Plaintiff In Error) against Alsco of Colorado, Inc. (Defendant/Defendant In Error) to cancel a promissory note given to Defendant to purchase its stock. Defendant counterclaimed for payment of the note together with interest. Plaintiff claimed that issuance of the stock in return for the note was illegal and void under the Colorado Constitution, which provided:

> No corporation shall issue stocks or bonds, except for labor done, services performed, or money or property actually received, and all fictitious increase of stock or indebtedness shall be void. . . .

C.R.S. 1963, 31-4-5(2) reads as follows:

> Neither promissory notes nor future services shall constitute payment or part payment, for shares of a corporation.

The trial court found for Defendant on both the complaint and the counterclaim, and Plaintiff appealed. Affirmed.

PRINGLE, Justice.

In Boldt v. Motor Securities Co. . . . we held that Article XV, Sec. 9 of the Colorado Constitution is not a defense to an action (in this case a counterclaim) brought on a promissory note given for the stock of a corporation. The statute does not affect that holding and we adhere to the rule in that case.

The statute does not forbid the corporation from taking a note or obligation from a prospective stockholder. On the contrary, it impliedly recognizes the right to do so, but declares that no such note shall be considered as payment, and no certificate shall issued until the note is paid. . . . The issuance of the certificate, if in fact there was such here, does not affect the enforceability of the note.

Both the constitutional provision and the statute are aimed at preventing the watering of corporate stock. Their purpose is to prevent corporations from issuing stock without receiving full value, and so to prevent the diluting of the holdings of innocent stockholders, and the reliance by creditors on false or non-existent capital resulting from the issuance of watered stock. This purpose would not be served by holding, as Haselbush asks us to hold, that these provisions may be used to defeat an action by the corporation seeking to enforce payment on a promissory note given for the issuance of stock when the transaction has been made in good faith.

Questions

1. To what extent is the result in this case simply a function of the fact that the plaintiff was trying to get away with something, and to what extent is it based on sound policy?

2. What should the result be under the Colorado Constitution and its statutes if stock is given for future services but those services subsequently are not performed? Should the stock be cancelled?

Defective Incorporation

As discussed previously in Chapter 40, shareholders may be liable personally, without limitation, for debts of a purported corporation that failed to meet the formation requirements of the state's incorporation statute. The liability, when imposed, will be joint and several. In order for liability to arise, however, the attempt to incorporate must be so defective that it fails to qualify as either a *de jure* or a *de facto* corporation, and the circumstances do not qualify for the application of the doctrine of estoppel. Under the MBCA, such liability was imposed on all who "presume to act as a corporation without authority so to do." The RMBCA, however, requires that, in addition, the person do so "knowing there was no incorporation under this act." The rule of the RMBCA seems the better reasoned, especially in cases involving larger, publicly held, corporations.

Piercing the Corporate Veil

A business may be incorporated to secure the advantages of limited liability for its owners. This is within both the letter and the spirit of corporation law. However, when a business is incorporated for the purpose of committing fraud or other wrongdoing, or it is operated for improper purposes, a court may elect to disregard the corporate entity. In other words, if fairness requires, a court may treat the owner or owners as if they have done business as a sole proprietorship or a partnership, and refuse to extend the advantages of limited liability to them.

The causes for **piercing the corporate veil** range from operating an undercapitalized corporation (capital is insufficient to meet the reasonably anticipated obligations of the business) to operating in a manner not consistent with a separate corporate entity. The latter may include the failure to observe corporate formalities, to hold regular meetings of shareholders and directors, to keep corporate funds separate from those of shareholders, to keep corporate books, or to operate independently of a dominant parent corporation. These circumstances arise more frequently with regard to closely held corporations and those that are established as subsidiaries of parent corporations. Courts use their power to pierce the corporate veil sparingly, however, in order to avoid creating too much doubt about the stability of this business form.

Illegal Distributions

Distributions by a corporation, in the form of cash dividends or otherwise, ordinarily are made at the discretion of its board of directors. In unusual situations, however, the shareholders may force the payment of dividends. Any dividend paid while the corporation is insolvent, or that will cause it to become insolvent, is illegal. Also illegal are dividends paid out of trust or other accounts set aside for other purposes. If directors pay illegal dividends, they are liable personally for the amounts of the payments. In addition, shareholders are liable if they receive dividends knowing that they are illegal.

Whether a corporation is insolvent may be determined either by the balance-sheet or the cash-flow test. Under the *balance sheet test,* a corporation is insolvent if its liabilities (including any amount of the dividends payable to shareholders having preference upon liquidation) exceed assets. Under the *cash-flow test,* a corporation is insolvent if it is not able to pay its debts as they become due in the ordinary course of business. A particular state, under its corporation statute, may use either or both of these tests. The cash-flow approach is the position of Section 6.40 of the RMBCA and Section 45 of the MBCA.

Controlling Shareholders

Shareholders, in voting and other acts of participation in corporate affairs, ordinarily may act in their own self-interest. They are considered "at arm's length" with respect to each other. However, this may not be true concerning controlling shareholders. Someone may be considered a **controlling shareholder** if her ownership interest effectively enables her to dominate the affairs and the destiny of the corporation.

The law may impose something in the nature of a fiduciary duty on a controlling shareholder. In most cases, the duty imposed on a controlling shareholder is unlike the fiduciary duty imposed on directors, officers, and other agents in that it does not require that she sacrifice herself for the good of other shareholders. However, it does require that she exercise her power reasonably and that she not set out to harm other shareholders maliciously. The degree to which this duty is imposed will depend on the circumstances. Many courts treat all shareholders of a closely held corporation as having the same duty as directors. Otherwise, the duty of the controlling shareholder is less comprehensive.

Although even a controlling shareholder is free to transfer her shares at any price agreeable to the purchaser, if a premium is received over and above the reasonable market value of the shares, and the premium is paid in recognition that the shares constitute a controlling interest, a court may require that it be shared proportionately with other shareholders. Another aspect of this duty is considered by the court in the following case.

DeBAUN v. FIRST WESTERN BANK AND TRUST COMPANY
46 Cal.App.3d 686, 120 Cal.Rptr. 354 (1975)

This was a stockholders' derivative action brought by James DeBaun and Walter H. Stephens (Plaintiffs/Respondents) against First Western Bank and Trust Company (Defendant/Appellant) for damages for breach of its duty as a majority shareholder.

Plaintiff owned 20 of 100 shares outstanding in Alfred S. Johnson Incorporated (the Corporation). Defendant held 70 shares in a trust it managed. Defendant sold the 70 shares to S.O.F. Fund, an *inter vivos* revocable trust, of which Raymond J. Mattison was both settlor and trustee. At the time of the sale, Defendant knew of an outstanding judgment against Mattison for fraud. Defendant also had begun an investigation of Mattison prior to the sale, but discontinued it without finding, on public record, 38 unsatisfied judgments against Mattison or his entities totalling $330,886.27, and 54 pending actions claiming a total of $373,588.67 from them. After Mattison acquired control of the Corporation by the sale in question, he systematically "looted" it, and it went from a successful, growing company to a state of insolvency, its liabilities exceeding its assets by more than $200,000. Plaintiff contended Defendant breached its duty as majority stockholder. Defendant contended it had no such duty.

The trial court found for Plaintiff, and Defendant appealed. Affirmed and remanded with directions.

THOMPSON, Associate Justice.

Early case law held that a controlling shareholder owed no duty to minority shareholders or to the controlled corporation in the sale of his stock. . . . Decisional law, however, has since recognized the fact of financial life that corporate control by ownership of a majority of shares may be misused. Thus the applicable proposition now is that "In any transaction where the control of the corporation is material," the controlling majority shareholder must exercise good faith and fairness "from the viewpoint of the corporation and those interested therein." . . . That duty of good faith and fairness encompasses an obligation of the controlling shareholder in possession of facts "[s]uch as to awaken suspicion and put a prudent man on his guard [that a potential buyer of his shares may loot the corporation of its assets to pay for the shares purchased] . . . to conduct a reasonable adequate investigation [of the buyer]." . . .

Here Bank was the controlling majority shareholder of Corporation. As it was negotiating with Mattison, it became directly aware of facts that would have alerted a prudent person that Mattison was likely to loot the corporation. Bank knew from the Dun & Bradstreet report that Mattison's financial record was notable by the failure of entities controlled by him. Bank knew that the only source of funds available to Mattison to pay it for the shares he was purchasing lay in the assets of the corporation. The after-tax net income from the date of the sale would not be sufficient to permit the payment of dividends to him which would permit the making of payments. An officer of Bank possessed personal knowledge that Mattison, on at least one occasion, had been guilty of a fraud perpetrated on Bank's predecessor in interest and had not satisfied a judgment Bank held against him for damages flowing from that conduct.

Armed with knowledge of those facts, Bank owed a duty to Corporation and its minority shareholders to act reasonably with respect to its dealings in the controlling shares with Mattison. It breached that duty. . . . Had Bank investigated, as any prudent man would have done, it would have discovered from the public records the additional detail of Mattison's long, long trail of financial failure that would have precluded its dealings with him except under circumstances where his obligation was secured beyond question and his ability to loot Corporation precluded.

Bank, however, elected to deal with Mattison in a fashion that invited rather than tended to prevent his looting of Corporation's assets. It agreed to a payment schedule that virtually required Mattison to do so. By fraudulently concealing its nature from DeBaun and Stephens, Bank obtained corporate approval of a security agreement which hypothecated corporate assets to secure Mattison's obligation to it. Thus, to permit it to sell its majority shares to Mattison, Bank placed the assets and business of Corporation in peril. Not content with so doing, Bank used its control for still another purpose of its own by requiring Mattison to agree to cause Corporation to give its major banking business to Bank.

Thus the record establishes the duty of Bank and its breach. Appellant Bank seeks to avoid responsibility for its action by reversing the position taken by it in its demurrer to the complaint filed by DeBaun and Stephens individually for injury to their minority stock position by now claiming that its duty ran only to the minority shareholders and not to the controlled corporation. California precedent is to the contrary, holding that the duty runs to both.

Questions

1. Was the bank's breach of duty in this case that (1) it sold the shares to someone it knew might loot the corporation, (2) it acted in its self-interest by selling the shares to someone who would give the bank business, or (3) both of these factors? Would the result in the case have been the same if only one of these elements had been present? both?

2. What are the differences between a controlling shareholder's duty to the minority shareholders and the duty of the controlled corporation?

SUMMARY

The shareholders of a corporation are its owners, but they have very little to do with the control and operation of the business. They are entitled to vote on certain extraordinary matters, and to elect the members of the board of directors. The members of the board of directors then control the business, executing their policies and decisions through officers they appoint to take care of day-to-day operations.

Most states require at least one annual meeting of the shareholders, called by the board of directors. Additional special meetings may be called as needed, but no meeting may be conducted properly unless adequate notice is sent to shareholders of record on a date fixed by the directors.

Unless otherwise provided, as by a provision for cumulative voting or the issuance of non-voting shares, each share is entitled to one vote on all matters brought before the shareholders. Decisions ordinarily are made by a majority of the shares voted, with a quorum present. The majority rule may be changed by a provision in the article of incorporation or the bylaws, as may the quorum requirements. Any action taken in violation of these rules may be ratified later by the shareholders, or may be declared void in the absence of ratification.

Voting may be done in person by each shareholder; most states also allow proxy voting and voting by a trustee. A proxy is a grant of authority by a shareholder to an agent (for example, incumbent management) to vote his or her shares. This differs from a voting trust in that in the voting trust, the shares are issued in the name of a trustee who holds them for the benefit of certain beneficiaries under a trust agreement. The trustee, as owner of the legal title to the shares, then votes them for the benefit of the beneficiaries, who are owners of the beneficial (equitable) title to the shares. Most state statutes and federal law impose some limitations on the soliciting of proxies and upon the operation of voting trusts.

Shareholders are entitled to inspect the books of the corporation as long as the request is reasonable. The request may be required to be in writing, and the inspection must take place at a reasonable time, at a reasonable place, and for reasonable purposes. If necessary, a shareholder may secure a court order to enforce this right. Inspections normally are conducted during business hours at the location where the books are kept. The purpose must have some relationship to the business of the corporation, and not be solely for personal reasons. Under the RMBCA, a shareholder, as a part of the inspection, may copy records by any of a variety of means.

Shareholders are entitled to distributions from the corporation. These ordinarily are in the form of cash dividends, voted by the board of directors, but may be stock or other property, stock splits, or liquidating dividends (discussed in the next chapter). Although normally declared by the board of directors, the payment of dividends may be ordered by a court if the board unreasonably refuses to declare and distribute them. Shareholders also may be entitled to purchase additional shares issued by the corporation because of preemptive rights, an option, or by the ownership of warrants.

Shareholders, if necessary, may enforce their rights by bringing lawsuits, which may be either individual or derivative. Individual suits are those brought to enforce individual rights, and may be filed with one or more shareholders as plaintiffs, or by one shareholder as representative of a class of shareholders. Shareholder derivative suits are those brought on behalf of the corporation, to enforce the rights of all the shareholders as owners of the corporation. As with class-action suits, shareholder derivative suits are monitored carefully by the court in order to protect the rights of shareholders who do not directly participate but whose rights are being adjudicated.

Shareholders ordinarily enjoy limited liability concerning the corporation's obligations. They are liable, however, for any unpaid portion of stock subscriptions, for any unpaid portion of the price of shares issued to them, and for deficiencies in the case of watered stock. Beyond these obligations, shareholders also may be liable prsonally for the debts of a corporation that is so defectively formed that they must be considered as doing business as individuals, or when a court finds that a corporation has been set up for the purpose of fraud or other wrongdoing and, as a result, orders that the corporate entity be ignored in the interest of justice.

Shareholders usually are not responsible to each other to exercise their powers for the benefit of anyone other than themselves. However, a controlling shareholder, under certain circumstances, may be considered to owe a fiduciary duty to other shareholders. The imposition of this duty is more likely with regard to the shareholders of a closely held corporation.

KEY TERMS AND CONCEPTS

shareholder meeting
record date
class voting
proxy
voting trust
share exchange
stock dividend
stock split

option
warrant
preemptive right
class-action suit
shareholder derivative suit
stock watering
piercing the corporate veil
controlling shareholder

PROBLEMS

1. August, Robert, and Edward Marien together owned one-half of the stock in a corporation of which they were directors. Schwartz, who owned the other one-half of the stock, was the fourth director. Shortly after Edward came on the board to fill a vacancy caused by the death of Dietrich, the Mariens voted to sell five shares of treasury stock (see p.887), one share to each of themselves and the other two shares to two long-time employees. Schwartz contended that the action, without offering treasury stock to him in proportion to his interest, constituted a breach of the Marien's duties as directors. Is Schwartz correct?

2. Pillsbury purchased shares of stock in Honeywell Inc. because she had heard the company manufactured bombs for the military and wanted to verify this by looking at the corporation's books. Her demand to inspect the books was refused, however. She contended that because she was a shareholder, she was legally entitled to inspect them. Is Pillsbury correct?

3. The directors of the St. Louis & Southwestern Railway Company voted a $1.00-per-share dividend on its stock. After it was declared, the directors sought to rescind the action. May they do so?

4. The minority shareholders of Banker's Security Corporation brought an action against the board of directors to compel the payment of a $3 million arrearage in dividends. The shareholders contended the dividend was being withheld in order to benefit the majority shareholders and that surplus was more than adequate to pay the arrearage. The court granted summary judgment for the directors on the ground that the declaration of dividends was within the discretion of the board. Should the judgment be overruled?

5. A meeting of Levisa Oil Corporation was called and was attended by the holder of a majority of shares, as was necessary for a quorum. During the meeting, in protest over a proposal under consideration, two shareholders left. Between them, they owned a majority of the shares in Levisa. Thereafter, a vote was taken and the proposal was passed. Was the action valid?

6. Inland Printing Company owed a debt to Equitable Insurance Company, evidenced by a note and secured by a mortgage. Because of gross mismanagement, Inland was not able to pay the note, and Equitable sued to foreclose the mortgage and to collect any dificiency from the officers and directors. If gross mismanagement is proven, should the officers and directors be liable for the deficiency?

7. Goldstein filed a shareholder derivative actionsagainst the corporation asking for the appointment of receiver to operate the business for the benefit of the shareholders. The eight-member board of directors had voted four-to-four on most issues presented to it and had been deadlocked for a substantial period of time. Should the relief be granted?

8. Four shareholders of a corporation each owned 25 percent of its stock. One of the shareholders, Wolfson, wanted money for improvement to existing facilities rather than paying dividends. The others refused. The by-laws provided that action could be taken by shareholders only with an 80-percent vote. In retaliation, Wolfson refused to vote his shares for the next seven years. During the time he was warned repeatedly of the danger that the corporation might be assessed penalties for excessive accumulation of earnings. When a penalty finally was assessed, the three shareholders sued Wolfson for the amount of the penalty. Should Wolfson be liable?

9. Levin, a shareholder in Metro-Goldwyn-Mayer, Inc., brought an action against the board of directors charging improper proxy solicitation. The board had hired a public relations firm, lawyers, and an advertising firm, and had used company employees on working time, all to give out information and solicit proxies. Was the board's action improper?

10. Upon the death of her husband, Emma Galler sued for an accounting and for specific performance of a shareholder's agreement. The business was Galler Drugs, and it was owned by Emma Galler, her husband, Isadore Galler, and his wife. The agreement provided that the salaries of the two men would be continued after their deaths, payable to their wives, and that an annual dividend of $50,000 would be paid as long as an earned surplus of $500,000 or more was maintained. The defendants contended the agreement deprived the directors (the four Gallers) of their discretion in paying dividends and, therefore, was void. Is the defense valid?

Chapter 43

Corporations: Acquisition, Merger, and Dissolution

INTRODUCTION

Although a corporation ordinarily may be incorporated in perpetuity (for an unlimited term of life), it is highly unlikely that any corporation will exist forever. As business conditions change, a corporation may be able to alter its operation to meet the challenge of those changes for a time. Thus, at the turn of the century, buggy-whip and horse-drawn-carriage manufacturers had to modify their product lines or be rendered obsolete as a result of the development of the automobile. Eventually however, most corporations will terminate as independent operating entities. This may come as a result of acquisition by another business, by merger or consolidation with another corporation, or by dissolution and a winding up of the company's affairs.

The Merger Phenomenon

The principal motives underlying most mergers, consolidations, and acquisitions are efficiency and diversification of the company's line of business. Other motives may include the desire to acquire new technology and know-how, and even the elimination of competition.

Whether a combination of two businesses will result in greater efficiency is primarily a question of economic theory. Economists discuss this question in terms of "economies of scale." It appears that combining two businesses can result in a lower cost per unit of product or service sold. This may be particularly true in industries involving high fixed production costs or elaborate and expensive distribution networks. The automobile business exemplifies both of these characteristics, which led to Chrysler Corporation's purchase of American Motors and General Motors's joint marketing venture with Nissan. In other industries, such as the banking industry, economists argue that either economies of scale do not exist, or are not a strong factor in determining efficiency.

Diversification of a company's line of business has given rise to many conglomerate mergers (between companies in different lines of business). For example, R.J. Reynolds began as a tobacco company, and later diversified into many other lines of business. In 1989, RJR was purchased by Nabisco, another conglomerate that began as a food-product manufacturer (National Biscuit Company). That merger was the largest ever in the United States.

In addition to economic and financial considerations, merger activity gives rise to questions of legality, especially under antitrust law, discussed in Chapters 48 and 49. Particularly suspect are horizontal mergers (those between two competing companies on the same level, such as two shoe manufacturers). Somewhat less suspect are vertical mergers (those on different levels of the same product line, such as a shoe manufacturer and a leather supply company or a retail shoe outlet). Least suspicious are conglomerate mergers.

Whether a merger will be challenged under the antitrust laws is controlled to a great extent by regulatory policy. During the 1980s merger activity hit an all-time high because of the Reagan administration's policy of deregulation. Many mergers that would have been challenged during previous administrations took place with official sanction. This was true especially in the banking industry as a result of new laws permitting interstate banking (a bank holding company is allowed to own banks in more than one state). Such giants as Citicorp and Hanover Trust bear witness to this phenomenon.

When any of these events occurs, certain procedures required by law must be followed to safeguard the rights of those having interests in the affected company. For example, shareholders must vote on all extraordinary business or fundamental structural changes in the corporation. Similarly, dissenting shareholders have rights and creditors of the corporation must be protected.

Voting on Fundamental Changes

Fundamental changes include any corporate action that is outside the limits of its regular course of business. Shareholders are entitled to vote on all fundamental changes. A vote of the corporation's board of directors also ordinarily is required, except in the case of a voluntary dissolution upon the *unanimous* vote of the shareholders.

In addition to amendments to the articles of incorporation, fundamental changes may involve the sale or lease of all or substantially all of the corporation's assets, as long as the sale is not in the regular course of business. Merger or consolidation with another, separate business involve a fundamental change, and the shareholders are entitled to vote. However, a decision to merge a subsidiary, 90 percent or more of whose shares are owned by the parent corporation, does not require a vote by the shareholders. A voluntary dissolution is a fundamental change.

The acquisition by one corporation of shares voluntarily sold by the shareholders of another corporation is not subject to a vote of the shareholders of either corporation. In effect then, one corporation actually may purchase another without collective intervention of the shareholders of either corporation. However, the acquisition of shares through a *compulsory share exchange* requires a vote by the shareholders of the corporation to be acquired, but not by the shareholders of the acquiring corporation. A **compulsory share exchange** involves the purchase of 100 percent of the shares of the acquired corporation, which then becomes a wholly owned subsidiary. This, therefore, is a fundamental change in the management structure of that corporation, but not of the parent.

ACQUISITIONS

Purchase or Lease of Assets

The purchase or lease of all, or substantially all, of the assets of one corporation by another does not affect the corporate persona of either. Both corporations continue to exist as separate entities, and the same control and management is maintained as before the acquisition. Only the settlor/lessor corporation's asset structure has been changed by the transaction. For example, it may have converted its assets from buildings, equipment, and inventory to cash. As previously noted, this constitutes a fundamental change for the seller, and therefore requires shareholder approval, but no such change has taken place for the purchaser.

Ordinarily, a **purchase of assets** does not impose new liabilities on the purchaser. That is, the seller's liabilities are not assumed, as long as the transaction was in good faith and based upon sufficient and adequate consideration. However, a sale or lease of assets for the purpose of defrauding creditors or shareholders may give rise to obligations. The purchaser of the assets of a business also may assume liability for products previously sold by the seller under modern theories of product liability, and may assume some liability under a state's employment laws, such as for making up deficiencies in the seller's unemployment compensation payments. Finally, it should be noted that the merger guidelines of the United States Department of Justice may be applied to acquisitions of this type, which means that the effects of the transaction on competition must be considered to see if the purchase violates the antitrust or any other regulatory statutes.

The following case considers the liability of the purchaser of assets for products liability claims arising before the purchase.

ORTIZ v. SOUTH BEND LATHE
46 Cal.App.3d 842, 120 Cal.Rptr. 556 (1975)

This was an action by Refugio Ortiz (Plaintiff/Respondent) against South Bend Lathe, a subsidiary of Amsted Industries, Inc. (Defendant/Appellant) and Meyer Sheet Metal Machinery Company (Defendant/Respondent) to recover damages for injuries caused by a punch press that admittedly was defective, manufactured by the Johnson Machine and Press Company.

The machine, manufactured by Johnson sometime prior to August of 1955, was sold by Meyer (the sole distributor for Johnson in the area) to Western Lighting Company. Western continued to use the press until 1967 when Plaintiff, an employee of Western, was injured. There was no question that Plaintiff was entitled to compensation. However, Johnson was no longer in existence. In 1956, its assets had been acquired by Bontrager Corporation, and Johnson became a mere "shell," transacting no business on its own, continuing only to preserve the Johnson trade name. In 1962, the principal assets of Bontrager were acquired by

Amsted, and Bontrager ultimately was liquidated. Amsted continued to manufacture the Johnson press through its subsidiary, South Bend Lathe. In August 1965, Johnson was dissolved. There were no assets to distribute since they had been purchased earlier by Bontrager.

The question before the court was whether South Bend Lathe and its parent corporation, Amsted, could be held responsible for the agreed-upon liability of Johnson. Among other theories, Amsted and South Bend Lathe contended that liability did not pass to them because the agreement under which Amsted purchased Bontrager expressly provided that Amsted would not assume any liabilities of Bontrager "arising prior to or subsequent to the closing."

The trial court found for Plaintiff and Defendant South Bend Lathe (Amsted), appealed. Reversed.

COMPTON, Associate Justice.

The general rule is where one corporation sells or transfers all of its assets to another corporation, the latter is not liable for the debts and liabilities of the former unless (1) the purchaser expressly or impliedly agrees to such assumption, (2) the transaction amounts to a consolidation or merger of the two corporation, (3) the purchasing corporation is merely a continuation of the selling corporation, or (4) the transaction is entered into fraudulently to escape liability for debts. . . .

By the terms of the purchase agreement between Amsted and Bontrager there was no express or implied assumption of liability. There was, as noted, no fraud in the transaction and the consideration flowing to Bontrager was ample. Bontrager and Amsted dealt at arms-length, there was no mixture of officers or stockholders. The two corporate entities were completely separate and distinct both before and after the sale. Under these facts there was neither a consolidation or merger nor a continuation or reincarnation of Bontrager, the old corporation. Before one corporation can be said to be a mere continuation or reincarnation of another it is required that there be insufficient consideration running from the new company to the old. . . .

Amsted did not assume the liabilities of Bontrager either by agreement, express or implied, or involuntarily by operation of law. Nor does it make any difference that the assets which were acquired consisted of trade names, customer lists or business good will. . . .

The evidence of the history of these corporate acquisitions was not in dispute, nor was the purchase agreement between Amsted and Bontrager ambiguous so as to require any factual resolution of extrinsic evidence in interpreting its meaning. Thus it was improper for the trial court to submit the question of Amsted's liability to the jury.

Questions

1. From whom is Ortiz supposed to recover damages for his injuries now?
2. Doesn't the court in this case merely glorify the form of the transaction? Why should the plaintiff's rights turn on that?

Purchase of Individual Shares

Another method of acquiring a corporation is to purchase all of its outstanding shares, or a sufficient number of shares to constitute a controlling interest. Although a **purchase of shares** may be just as effective in acquiring a corporation as the purchase or lease of its assets, because shareholders sell the shares there is no need for the "acquired" corporation's shareholders, as a body, to meet and approve the sale. The acquired corporation will continue as before, and its capital structure will remain unchanged. Nothing really has happened except that the business has come under new ownership.

Although no formalities are required, except for action by the board of directors of the purchasing corporation to authorize buying the stock, acquisition by this method may involve much time and many transactions. Also, as it becomes apparent that a corporation is being "bought up," the value of its shares may be inflated temporarily, making this method of acquisition more costly and more uncertain than others. Finally, it should be kept in mind that the purchase of individual shares does not circumvent the operation of antitrust laws.

Compulsory Share Exchange

An alternative method of acquiring shares of another corporation is by a compulsory share exchange. As previously discussed, this involves the purchase of all of the outstanding shares of one or more classes of stock of the corporation being acquired. It also constitutes a fundamental change for that corporation, and may be done only with the approval of its shareholders and its board of directors. However, approval of the shareholders of the acquiring corporation is not required.

Although called a "share exchange," the shares to be acquired are not necessarily paid for in shares of the acquiring corporation. The Model Business Corporation Act and the Revised Model Business Corporation Act both provide that the shares may be purchased in return for cash, other obligations, or other consideration. The sale of the shares by all of the shareholders of the class or classes specified is compulsory. Any affected shareholder who is dissatisfied is entitled to the remedy of appraisal, which is discussed later in this chapter.

Following a compulsory exchange of shares, the corporation acquired remains in existence and may continue business much the same as before, except that it will do so as a subsidiary of the acquiring corporation. The effect is similar to a merger. This method of acquisition may be chosen instead of a merger, however, in order to preserve the separate identity. This might be important especially when the acquired corporation has an established name, steeped in tradition, or if it is acquired by a holding company or a corporation forming a holding company.

Upon completion of the required procedures, **articles of exchange** are sent to the secretary of state. This is done for the purpose of updating the state's incorporation records concerning the acquired corporation. When approved by the secretary of state, a copy of the articles of exchange is returned to the acquiring corporation.

MERGER

Merger involves the combination of two or more corporations so that one continues to exist and the other ceases to exist. The corporation that remains assumes all of the assets and the liabilities of the other, and is called the **surviving corporation.** The other is called the **merged corporation.** The shareholders of the merged corporation ordinarily receive stock in the surviving corporation in return for their shares, but they may be paid in other securities, other obligations, cash, or any other consideration.

Number of merger and acquisition transactions for selected industries (1986)

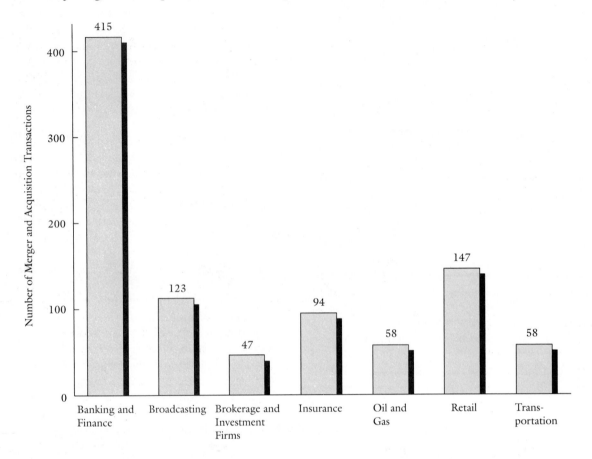

Source: Statistical Abstract of the U.S. (1988), Table 843.

A merger is achieved through the approval of a merger plan by the boards of directors of both corporations and by the shareholders of the corporation to be merged. Approval by the shareholders of the corporation to survive is not always required. Both the MBCA (Section 73(d) and the RMBCA (Section 11.30) provide that this share-holder approval is not necessary if: (1) there will be no change in the articles of incorporation of the surviving corporation, other than its name; (2) the number of shares of each shareholder, and the rights accompanying the shares, will remain unchanged; (3) the number of voting shares will not be increased more than 20 percent; and (4)

Value of merger and acquisition transactions for selected industries (1986) (in billions of dollars)

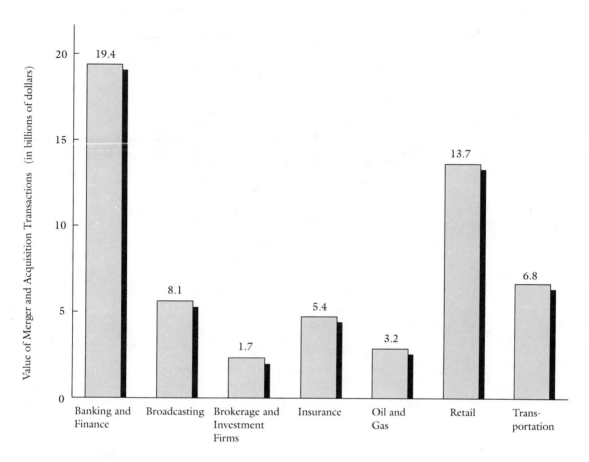

Source: Statistical Abstract of the U.S. (1988), Table 843.

the number of shares will not be increased more than **20** percent. Dissenting shareholders of the merged corporation, and those of the surviving corporation if their vote was required, are entitled to the remedy of appraisal.

Upon completing these procedures, **articles of merger** are filed with the secretary of state. These are handled just like the articles of exchange in an acquisition, and a copy of the articles of merger is returned to the surviving corporation.

After merger, does the surviving corporation stand in the shoes of the merged corporation concerning rights of action that arose prior to the merger, or are such rights extinguished? Consider the following case.

Typical steps in a merger

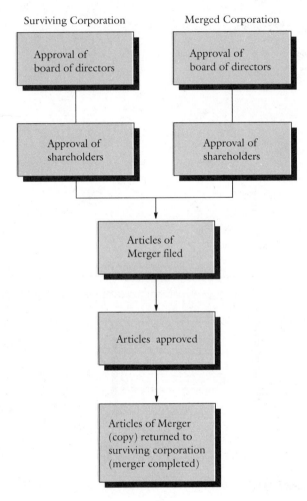

SUN PIPE LINE COMPANY v. ALTES
511 F.2d 280 (8th Cir. 1975)

This was an action by Sun Pipe Line Company (Plaintiff/Appellant) against Robert Altes, dba A & A Materials and Landfill Company (Defendant/Appellee) to recover damages for negligent injury to a pipeline. At the time of the incident in question, the pipeline was owned by OMR, Inc. In August 1972, OMR was merged with Plaintiff, and Plaintiff was the surviving corporation. The question before the court was whether Plaintiff, by virtue of the merger, acquired OMR, Inc.'s rights against Defendant.

The trial court found for Defendant and Plaintiff appealed. Reversed and remanded.

ROSS, Circuit Judge.

Fed.R.Civ.P. 17(b) states that "[t]he capacity of a corporation to sue or be sued shall be determined by the law under which it was organized." Sun is a Pennsylvania corporation, so the law of that state determines whether it can sue to recover premerger damages to OMR.

Pa.Stat.Ann. tit. 15, Section 1907 (1974 Suppl.) deals with the effect of a merger or consolidation of corporations and provides:

> All the property, real, personal, and mixed and franchises of each of the corporations parties to the plan of merger or consolidation, *and all debts due on whatever account to any of them, including subscriptions to shares and other choses in action belonging to any of them,* shall be taken and deemed to be transferred to and vested in the surviving or new corporation, as the case may be, without further act or deed. (Emphasis supplied.)

This statute makes it explicitly clear that Sun, the surviving corporation, was vested with OMR's chose in action against Altes and could bring this lawsuit to recover for OMR's damages. See In re Penn Central Securities Litigation, 335 F.Supp. 1026, 1034 (E.D.Pa.1971). In addition, we note that the merger agreement itself conformed to the Pennsylvania statute by providing that Sun would be vested with "all property, real, personal and mixed, and all debts due to each" of the corporations.

Finally, this Court has stated that statutes, such as Pennsylvania's, which provide that a successor corporation inherits a chose in action from a merging corporation as a matter of law merely serve to codify the common law rule "which recognizes that a chose in action to enforce a property right upon merger vests in the successor corporation and no right of action remains in the merging corporation."

Questions

1. Is the result of this case fair to the defendant? Why or why not?
2. Should the surviving corporation succeed to the claims of the merged corporation no matter what their nature might be?

CONSOLIDATION

Consolidation is similar, in effect, to merger. Two or more corporations combine into one. The difference is that none of the participating corporations continues to exist. All are combined into a completely new entity. The shareholders of each corporation receive shares in the new corporation according to the approved consolidation plan. The ratio of new shares to old and the rights accompanying the new shares will depend on the relative values of the constituent corporations, the number of shares outstanding from each, and the mix of rights accompanying the outstanding shares of each.

Action on consolidation proposals is taken by the boards of directors and shareholders of all corporations that participate. Dissenting shareholders are entitled to the appraisal remedy, and **articles of consolidation** are filed, as in the cases of exchange and merger.

The similarity between merger and consolidation may raise a question of why one might be chosen over the other as a method of combination. From a legal standpoint, the differences are no more than academic. In fact, consolidation has fallen into disuse in modern corporate affairs. Modern combinations most frequently are between two corporations of widely disparate power and influence. Almost always it is to the advantage of one of the corporations to survive. Today, combinations seem to be inspired most frequently by one corporation seeking business power and advantage while the other acquiesces. This can be seen clearly in the acquisition of small- and medium-size companies by huge conglomerate corporations, and the gobbling up of individual banks and small- and medium-size bank holding companies by large bank holding companies.

RIGHTS OF DISSENTING SHAREHOLDERS

The rights of dissenting shareholders have been alluded to in the discussion of acquisitions, mergers, and consolidations. In any of these circumstances, if the shareholders are entitled by law to vote on the action to be taken, the law seeks to protect the ownership rights of those who are dissatisfied to the extent possible. The most important of the remedies available to a dissenting shareholder is the right to an appraisal.

Sections 80 and 81 of the MBCA, and Sections 13.01–13.31 of the RMBCA establish the right to dissent, and the procedures for dissenting. The **appraisal remedy** ordinarily is provided for by state law, because shareholders who feel their interests are injured by extraordinary corporate action become, in a sense, involuntary owners of a corporation unlike the one they previously owned. Therefore, it only is equitable that they should be given an opportunity to surrender their shares to the corporation and receive the fair market value of those shares.

The procedures for effecting this appraisal right usually are complicated, and the job of determining the fair market value of shares may spawn ready disagreement. State statutes ordinarily require that a dissenting shareholder give notice of dissent to the corporation within a prescribed time. Thereafter, the corporation decides on the fair market value of the shares. If the shareholder is not satisfied with the corporation's evaluation, he may submit his own and demand payment. If agreement cannot be reached, the value of the shares may be determined by a court. An appraisal action may proceed concerning the shares of only one shareholder, or the statute or the court may require the joinder of all shareholders' properly dissenting from the same action by the corporation.

The following case illustrates the process.

SWANSON v. AMERICAN CONSUMERS INDUSTRIES, INC.
475 F.2d 516 (7th Cir. 1973)

This was a stockholder derivative action by Knute Swanson on his own behalf and on behalf of Peoria Service Company (Plaintiff/Appellant) against American Consumers Industries, Inc. and others (Defendants/Appellees) challenging a merger.

In 1965, Peoria Service Company entered into an agreement with American Consumers Industries, Inc. under which American purchased substantially all of the assets of Peoria in exchange for American stock. Plaintiff contended this was accomplished by the use of fraudulent and deceptive proxy statements, and by manipulation devices. Defendants contended that they should be found to have met their obligations to minority stockholders because the value received by all stockholders was a fair return for their stock.

The trial court found for Defendants, and upon remand from the Court of Appeals, again found for Defendants after trial, and Plaintiff appealed. Reversed and remanded for further proceedings.

CUMMINGS, Circuit Judge.

When the case was before us previously, the defendants contended that no injury could be shown because any corporate opportunities or going concern value of which Peoria shareholders might have been deprived are retained by them by virtue of their continuing equity position in ACI. We responded that "if the allegations of the complaint are proved, the Peoria shareholders were entitled to a more favorable exchange ratio than they were granted and may have had their equity position unfairly diluted." 415 F.2d at 1332. But the allegations of unfairness in the complaint were not proved. . . . The lower court having concluded that the terms of the merger were fair and reasonable at the time of the transaction, and we having concurred with that conclusion, the plaintiffs are not entitled to a retrospective revision of the merger terms.

Whether or not causation should be taken as established between the deceptive proxy statement and consummation of the merger, causation between the proxy statement and other injury claimed to have been suffered stands on an entirely different footing. As we said in our prior opinion, "The power to effect a given result certainly does not negative [*sic*] all possibility of injury resulting from the fraudulent or manipulative use of that power." . . . Particularizing the possibility of injury, we stated "[i]t may well be that the misstatements and omissions contained in the proxy statements caused some Peoria shareholders to approve the sale, thus losing their statutory appraisal remedies." . . . Operating under this Court's decision in Mills v. Electric Auto-Lite Co., . . . we remanded the case for a factual determination of whether a causal relationship existed between the deficiency in the proxy statement and the loss of statutory appraisal rights. Under the Supreme Court's decision in Mills, causation and reliance are no longer factually-to-be-proven predicates to recovery. As most recently stated by a unanimous Supreme Court in Affiliated Ute Citizens v. United States, . . .

Under the circumstances of this case, involving primarily a failure to disclose, positive proof of reliance is not a prerequisite to recovery. All that is necessary is that the facts withheld be material in the sense that a reasonable investor might have considered them important in the making of this decision. . . . This obligation to disclose and this withholding of a material fact establish the requisite element of causation in fact.

Thus the plaintiff sellers who were defrauded in that case were entitled to damages measured by the difference between the fair value of what they would have received had there been no fraudulent conduct. . . .

Consequently, it is inescapable that plaintiff shareholders have proven all the elements required to impress liability on defendants under Section 10(b) of the Securities and Exchange Act and the Commission's Rule 10b-5 for loss of their informed ability to exercise their statutory appraisal rights. In such a posture the appropriate remedy is to restore to the plaintiff shareholders the opportunity to receive cash rather than ACI shares. Therefore, ACI must offer to each Peoria shareholder $3.55, the market value attributed to Peoria stock in the reorganization plan, for each share of Peoria stock held by such shareholder on March 31, 1965, together with legal interest from that date to the date judgment is entered by the district court. Any minority shareholders who exchanged Peoria shares must, of course, return an equivalent number of ACI shares exchanged in order to receive the cash. Plaintiff is also entitled to reimbursement of reasonable attorneys' fees in an amount to be fixed by the district court, of course taking into consideration the modest recovery achieved, but cognizant that pecuniary benefit is not the sole criterion for the award of attorneys' fees.

Questions

1. Why should the plaintiff have his attorney fees paid for him?
2. Why is it important that shareholders have the right too receive cash rather than ACI stock?

DISSOLUTION

At some time, the lives of all, or at least most, corporations will come to an end. **Dissolution** may come about for any number of reasons. For example, business or social circumstances may change, making the continued operation of the business unwise or even illegal, or mismanagement may take its toll. Two corporations may find it mutually beneficial to combine by the transfer of assets, merger, or consolidation. Sometimes corporations fall victim to unfriendly takeovers. It even is possible that the shareholders simply may decide that they do not want to continue business for a variety of personal reasons. Dissolutions, however they may occur, may be classified as voluntary or involuntary, and judicial or non-judicial.

Non-Judicial Dissolution

A basic cause of voluntary non-judicial dissolution is the expiration of a specific term of existence stated in the articles of incorporation, although such termination is uncommon. Ordinarily, a corporation having a stated term is dissolved before the end of the period or its articles of incorporation are amended to continue its life. A corporation that is merged, and those that consolidate, are dissolved without the involvement of a court.

A corporation that has obtained its charter but has not begun to do business may be dissolved by its incorporators. This action may be taken simply by filing articles of dissolution and securing approval of the secretary of state of the state of incorporation. Once business has been commenced, however, voluntary dissolution may result only upon a vote of the board of directors and the shareholders, or a unanimous vote of all of the shareholders alone.

Involuntary non-judicial dissolution may occur if the stated purpose of the corporation becomes illegal. For example, the legislature of the state of incorporation might enact a statute prohibiting certain types of businesses from being incorporated. Also, the legislature may prohibit the manufacture or sale of a product of the type that is the sole purpose of a corporation. Without an amendment to the articles of incorporation, the company would go out of business and, of necessity, be dissolved.

Judicial Dissolution

Under Section 99 of the MBCA, the attorney general of the state of incorporation is authorized to seek judicial dissolution of a corporation on any of six grounds. They are: (1) failure of the corporation to file an annual report as required; (2) failure to pay the required franchise tax; (3) failure, for 30 days, to appoint a registered agent; (4) failure, for 30 days, to notify the secretary of state of a change in the location of the registered office, or of a change of registered agent; (5) if the corporation continues to exceed or abuse its authority granted by law; and (6) fraud in procuring

the articles of incorporation. Under Section 14.20 of the RMBCA, the first four of these are changed from judicial to administrative proceedings, and the relevant time limits are changed to 60 days. The last two are continued as judicial proceedings under Section 14.30.

Shareholders also may seek judicial dissolution. Under Section 14.30 of the RMBCA, the bases for doing so are: (1) a deadlock of the board of directors that cannot be broken by the shareholders and prevents the business from being run to the shareholders' advantage; (2) the directors or those in control of the corporation are acting in a manner that is illegal, oppressive, or fraudulent; (3) the shareholders are deadlocked and have not been able to fill vacancies on the board of directors for two successive annual meetings; and (4) the corporate assets are being misapplied or wasted.

Also, under Section 14.30, creditors are allowed to seek dissolution if an execution on a judgment has been returned unsatisfied, or the corporation admits in writing that it is unable to pay a valid debt because it is insolvent. Additionally, under Section 14.30, the corporation itself can request judicial dissolution.

The following case considers whether a court should grant dissolution.

CALLIER v. CALLIER
61 Ill.App.3d 1011, 378 N.E.2d 405 (1978)

This was an action by Leo Callier (Plaintiff/Appellee) against Scott Callier, Felix Callier, and All Steel Pipe and Tube, Inc. (Defendants/Appellants) for liquidation of assets and dissolution of the corporation.

After the formation of the corporation, a successful and growing business, differences developed between Leo Callier and Scott Callier, the two equal shareholders. Leo informed Scott that he did not want to be associated with him any more, and negotiations began for Leo to buy out Scott. The negotiations, although diligent, were not successful. Neither were negotiations toward dissolution. On May 5, 1975, Leo formed a new corporation, doing the same business as All Steel, and All Steel ceased operations on May 30. On June 2, the new corporation opened for business, employing about 40 percent of All Steel's previous employees. On June 11, this action was filed.

The trial court granted liquidation and dissolution and Defendants appealed. Reversed and remanded.

WINELAND, Justice.

The issue on this appeal is whether the plaintiff sustained his burden of proof under Section 86(a)(1) of the Business Corporation Act. The defendants contend that there was insufficient proof of either a deadlock or irreparable injury within the meaning of the Act to justify dissolution and liquidation of the corporation.

Corporations, which are creatures of statute, can only be dissolved according to statute. . . . As our Supreme court said in the Davis case, "Corporate dissolution is a drastic remedy, and the teachings of generations of chancellors admonish us that it must not be lightly invoked." . . .

The statute at issue here is as follows:

> Circuit courts have full power to liquidate the assets and business of a corporation:
> (a) In an action by a shareholder when it appears:
> (1) That the directors are deadlocked in the management of the corporate affairs and the shareholders are unable to break the deadlock, and that irreparable injury to the corporation is suffered or threatened by reason thereof. . . . (Ill.Rev.Stat. 1975, ch. 32, par. 157-86(a)(1).)

Section 86(a)(1) has not been a frequently used basis for dissolution, presumably because of the "substantial problems of interpretation" connected with its provisions. . . . The terms deadlock and irreparable injury are both undefined and troublesome. It has been said that mere dissension among stockholders is not a ground for dissolution unless it is of such serious proportions as to defeat the end for which the corporation is organized. . . .

After a careful review of the entire record, we have concluded that plaintiff's proof was insufficient to show either deadlock in the management of corporate affairs or the threat of irreparable injury to the corporation. What the evidence shows, instead, is two equal shareholders who were unable to get along and unable to reach agreement within a four-month period as to the redemption of one's shares by the other or to the terms of voluntary dissolution. This is not equivalent to an inability of the corporation to perform the functions for which it was created. Without adopting the position of defendants that the threat of irreparable injury can never be shown under this statute so long as a corporation is making a profit, we must agree with defendants that such a threat was not proved here.

It appears to us that Leo Callier simply decided that he was not going to have anything more to do with Scott Callier, and when their redemption-liquidation negotiations stalled, he made a unilateral decision—without consulting the other director or shareholder—to shut down the corporation. On the day that he informed the employees of the closing of the corporation, corporate affairs were being managed, and quite successfully. In fact, the company appeared on its way to the second best year of its history, despite a general downturn in the pipe industry. Neither Scott nor Felix Callier was interfering with the management of the corporation; Scott has in fact intentionally stayed away from the company and allowed Leo to run things alone while the redemption discussions were going on.

Thus, absent sufficient proof of the jurisdictional facts of deadlock and irreparable injury, the court below erred in ordering liquidation of the corporate assets.

A further consideration impels us towards reversal of the trial court's decision. At the time that he was winding down the affairs of All Steel, Leo Callier was in the process of forming another company to carry on the same kind of business, with many of the same employees and the same customers. That company is now doing business; All Steel is not. Should we sanction what appears to be a flagrant breach of Leo's fiduciary duty as a director of All Steel, we would be permitting him to siphon off the going-concern value of All Steel, leaving the 50 per cent shareholder who was opposed to dissolution with only half of whatever assets are in the control of the receiver. This, we think, would be manifestly unfair. . . .

We realize, of course, that merely by reversing the order of the court below we cannot revivify All Steel Pipe and Tube in this appeal. We cannot, however, sustain a judgment which is not founded on proof of the statutory requirements for dissolution and which permits one owner of a corporation to deprive . . . an equal owner of his equal share of the corporate assets by means of self-help.

Questions

1. Why is the court resisting the obvious fact that the Calliers cannot get along and they probably will not be able to operate the corporation effectively? Isn't that "deadlock"?

2. Is there anything the court can do that will restore the business values Leo Callier has siphoned off to the other company?

BANKRUPTCY

Under federal law, a corporation that is insolvent, or unable to pay its debts as they fall due, ordinarily is entitled to petition for bankruptcy; also, creditors may bring a bankruptcy proceeding against a corporation. The action ordinarily can be filed under Chapter 7 of the Bankruptcy Act for liquidation, or under Chapter 11 for reorganization. If it is under Chapter 7, the creditors will be paid, and any remaining assets will be distributed to the shareholders. If under Chapter 11, the corporation may be placed in the hands of a receiver, who will operate the corporation in an attempt to salvage it. No dissolution will take place if the reorganization plan is successful. Bankruptcy is covered in detail in Chapter 24.

SUMMARY

Along with normal operations, a corporation reasonably may be expected either to terminate its existence or to change materially in composition. It may be acquired by another corporation by a sale or lease of its assets, sale of its stock, or by the sale of the stock of most or all of its shareholders. It may combine with another corporation by way of merger or consolidation. Finally, it may be dissolved, either voluntarily or involuntarily, by judicial or non-judicial procedures.

In the event that a corporation is acquired, either by sale or lease of assets or by the sale of stock—or if a corporation combines with another corporation by merging the other into itself—the corporation will continue in existence. If it consolidates with another corporation, is merged, or is dissolved, its existence will terminate.

Shareholders and creditors are protected by procedural safeguards in the event the corporation takes any action that may be outside the ordinary course of business or constitute a material change in the nature of their investment. In the event the corporation makes a change that requires a vote of the shareholders and any shareholder is dissatisfied, he may exercise his right to appraisal, requiring the corporation to buy his shares at their fair value.

Dissolution may occur as a result of a unanimous vote of the shareholders, or by vote of the majority of the shareholders and the majority of the board of directors. It also may occur as a result of judicial action brought by a shareholder, a creditor, the attorney general of the state of incorporation, or upon the request of the corporation.

Dissolution of a corporation results in a discontinuation of the corporate entity. After dissolution, the corporation's assets will be liquidated. Creditors are paid first, and the remaining assets are distributed to the shareholders according to their shares. The process of liquidation ordinarily is handled by the board of directors in voluntary cases, and by a receiver or trustee in involuntary cases and those involving bankruptcy.

KEY TERMS AND CONCEPTS

fundamental changes
compulsory share exchange
purchase of assets
purchase of shares
articles of exchange
merger
surviving corporation
merged corporation
articles of merger
consolidation
appraisal remedy
dissolution

PROBLEMS

1. The New York, Chicago & St. Louis Railway Company was merged into the Norfolk & Western Railway Company in October. In December, the Nationwide Insurance Company filed suit against New York, Chicago & St. Louis on a claim that had arisen before the merger. Although the suit was permitted by statute, Norfolk & Western challenged the validity of the statute on the ground that the defendant corporation had ceased to exist at the moment of the merger. What should be the result?

2. The bylaws of United Board required shareholder approval of any merger or consolidation. The board agreed to transfer 40 percent of its stock in return for all of the stock in another corporation, owned by a sole shareholder. The minority shareholders of United sued, contending the agreement required shareholder approval. Are they correct?

3. Johnston owned 50 percent, and her sister owned 49 percent, of the Livingston Nursing Home. After operating for four years, their constant unpleasantness and bickering became so bad that Johnston sued to have a receiver appointed and for dissolution. Should the relief be granted?

4. An Oklahoma statute provided that minority shareholders had the right to dissent and have their shares redeemed in the event of the sale of all or substantially all of the assets of their corporation. Kirby Corporation created a subsidiary and sold all of its assets to it. In return, it took all of the stock of the subsidiary. Then, a director of Kirby obtained a loan from the subsidiary. Minority shareholders of Kirby filed suit claiming the transaction entitled them to the rights of dissent and redemption. Are they correct?

5. Bellanka Corporation purchased every share of the stock of seven California corporations, all of which were involved in the egg business. Then Bellanka went through a "short-form merger" and changed its name to Olson Bros., Inc. The minority shareholders of Olson Bros. then sued, claiming the transaction was a merger and that they were entitled to dissent and appraisal rights. Are they correct?

6.   National Trust Association filed suit against the officers and directors of a corporation who had entered into a contract for the corporation after its right to do business had been suspended by the state for non-payment of its taxes. At the time the contract was entered into, the officers and directors had not been notified of the suspension. Should they be liable?

7.   The Martin Trucking Company, owned by Thornbury, Cook, and Edwards, obtained a certificate of public convenience and necessity from the Alabama Public Service Commission on July 13, 1950. The certificate was necessary to operate as a public carrier in the state. In June 1952, Houghland and Page purchased all of the stock in Martin, and began operating under Martin's certificate. Alabama Truck Lines filed suit, contending that Houghland and Page were not entitled to operate under the certificate by simply buying Martin's stock. Is the contention correct?

8.   Morejon was injured by the negligence of the Ajax Corporation, and obtained judgment against the company in the amount of $375,000. The corporation paid all but $50,000 of the judgment and then was dissolved. Morejon then sought to hold the sole shareholder liable for the deficiency. The evidence showed that the shareholder had received all of the corporation's assets upon dissolution. Should he be liable to Morejon?

9.   Gervin, a minority shareholder, sought dissolution of Capitol Toyota, Inc. on the ground of oppression. She had been fired as manager because of inadequate management. Should the court grant dissolution?

10.   Harff sued the directors of Bell Corporation to recover a dividend that had been declared, on the ground that it unreasonably injured the corporation's capital position. The directors moved to dismiss the derivative action because Harff was not a shareholder. Harff owned no stock in Bell, but held debentures that were convertible to common shares at the option of the holder. Should the court dismiss the suit?

Chapter | 44

Foreign Corporations

INTRODUCTION

Within limits, each state is entitled to determine what kinds of business may operate within its boundaries. However, its ability to determine who legally can operate any permitted business is limited in one important respect. Although the state may prohibit the conduct of certain kinds of business, it has no power to exclude the corporation itself if the corporation conducts business that is involved in or affects interstate commerce. In fact, most businesses today either are "involved in" or "affect" interstate commerce. This concept is more fully discussed in Chapter 5.

Although a state may not be entitled to exclude most corporations from doing business within its borders, it clearly has the power to impose reasonable, nondiscriminatory regulations on their activities. The state may prohibit certain types of business, such as gambling and prostitution. It may require licensing, and the payment of license fees, in order to conduct various businesses and to practice particular professions or trades. It may require every corporation to register and meet certain requirements, to pay a franchise fee (a fee to register), to pay taxes, and to comply with other reasonable state laws.

A *domestic* corporation is one that has been incorporated in the state in which it is doing business. A corporation is **foreign** with respect to any state in which it does business when it was incorporated under the laws of any other state, territory, or country. The term **alien corporation** frequently is used to refer to a foreign corporation that is doing business in the United States or its territories but was incorporated under the laws of another country.

A state is entitled to require that a foreign or alien corporation doing business within its territory register, maintain a registered office and a registered agent, and pay certain taxes. These requirements are very similar to those imposed on domestic corporations. Failure to meet these obligations makes a corporation subject to penalties ranging from fines to restrictions concerning the use of state courts. Provisions relating to foreign corporations are included in Sections 106 to 124 of the Model Business Corporation Act and Sections 15.01 to 15.32 of the Revised Model Business Corporation Act.

THE BASIS FOR REGULATION OF FOREIGN CORPORATIONS

Section 106 of the MBCA provides: "No foreign corporation shall have the right to transact business in this state until it shall have procured a certificate of authority so to do from the Secretary of State." The language of this general provision

is typical of that contained in the corporation laws of the states, and is repeated in Section 15.01 of the RMBCA.

Transacting Business

Although the importance of the registration requirement is clear, precisely what activities may constitute **transacting business** is not. There is only general agreement from state to state, and the definition may vary depending on what action the state intends to take.

In order for a state to be entitled to require a foreign corporation to register and submit to comprehensive local regulation, the corporation ordinarily must conduct substantial business within the state. To be subject to state income tax, however, only one sale of property or services, entered into within the state, may be sufficient for at least some degree of taxation. Going further, a state court may acquire jurisdiction over a foreign corporation for purposes of a lawsuit by virtue of a minimal contract, including the execution of a contract or the manufacture of a product within the state, regardless of when the breach or injury caused by the product takes place. Therefore, a higher level of "transacting business" is necessary for regulation, than for taxation, and taxation requires a higher level than state court jurisdiction. Consider the following case.

REISMAN v. MARTORI, MEYER, HENDRICKS, & VICTOR
155 Ga.App. 551, 271 S.E.2d 685 (1980)

This was an action by Martori and others (Plaintiff/Appellee) against Dr. Reisman (Defendant/Appellant) to recover legal fees. Plaintiff was an Arizona association of lawyers and Defendant was a doctor and general surgeon practicing in Georgia. Defendant contacted Hendricks, a member of Plaintiff's association, for help in resolving the legal problem with the Floyd County (Georgia) Medical Center (Hospital). Hendricks flew to Atlanta and associated with local counsel, who was hired with Defendant's consent and paid directly by Defendant. Hendricks represented Defendant in hearings held by the hospital, the commencement of injunction proceedings in federal court, and final negotiations to settlement with the hospital. Of Plaintiff's charges of $21,438.14, Defendant had advanced $15,000, but refused to pay the balance. Defendant's principal defense was that Plaintiff had failed to register as a foreign corporation.

The trial court found for Plaintiff, and Defendant appealed. Affirmed.

BANKE, Judge.

Dr. Reisman urges that the trial court erred in denying his motion for directed verdict based upon appellee's failure to register as a foreign corporation in accordance with Code Ann. Section 22-1421(b) for the purpose of maintaining this suit. We do not agree. Assuming, without deciding, that the appellee professional association was required under Code Ann. Section 22-1421(a) to procure a certificate of authority from the Secretary of State in order to transact business in Georgia, its activities in this state have not been sufficiently extensive to invoke the statute here. "'In most jurisdictions it has been held that single or isolated transactions do not constitute doing business within the meaning of such statutes, although they are a part of the very business for [*sic*] which the corporation is organized to transact, if the action of the corporation in engaging therein indicated no purpose of continuity of conduct in that respect.' [Cit.]" Winston Corp. v. Park Elec. Co., 126 Ga.App. 489, 493, 191 S.E.2d 340,344, 90 A.L.R.3d 929 (1972).

Winston held that "the question of 'doing business' is to be considered a matter of fact to be resolved on an ad hoc or case-by-case basis . . . [and] . . . the meaning of 'isolated transaction' in our corporation code is to be determined in the same way as the term 'doing business.'" . . . Winston also makes it clear that the purpose of Code Ann. Section 22-1401 is to require registration of foreign corporations which intend to conduct business in Georgia on a continuous basis, not as a temporary matter. Activity related to a single transaction or contract is thus not contemplated.

The evidence here showed that the appellee's activities were concentrated in Arizona, although various attorneys in the firm had handled litigation (or "transacted business") outside the state of incorporation. Hendricks had represented clients in Georgia on two prior occasions, but these had nothing to do with his representation of Dr. Reisman. Under these circumstances, there is ample basis for the court's conclusion that the appellee had neither extended its business into Georgia on a continuous basis nor engaged "in the course of a number of repeated transactions of like nature" within the state. . . . The trial court correctly held that the appellee's representation of Dr. Reisman amounted to an isolated transaction and therefore properly denied the motion for directed verdict.

Questions

1. Is the result in this case sound?
2. To what degree do you think the court was simply unwilling to let the defendant get away with something?
3. What if the law firm did work for a single Georgia client on an ongoing basis?

Jurisdiction for Litigation

In order to acquire jurisdiction over a person, including a corporation, it usually is necessary that the person be found within the state so that process may be served within state boundaries. Similarly, jurisdiction over property may be exercised concerning any property located within the state. Any expansion of state court jurisdiction beyond these limits must be supported by some legitimate state concern, and must be within the limits of the due process and fairness that are imposed on state courts by the Fourteenth Amendment to the United States Constitution.

Until 1945, the limits of state court jurisdiction were rather narrowly prescribed. In that year, the Supreme Court of the United States, in *International Shoe Company v. State of Washington*, interpreted the requirements of due process more liberally than ever before, giving the state courts much greater authority to assert jurisdiction over defendants in other parts of the country. As a result, most states have now passed special **long-arm jurisdiction** statutes granting jurisdiction to state courts in cases involving foreign corporations having rather limited contact with the state. These statutes are not uniform. Some list certain specific activities that will confer jurisdiction; others impose jurisdiction whenever business is done in the state. But in all cases, some minimum contact between the foreign company and the state is required. A state cannot simply assume jurisdiction over "anyone for any reason."

Power to Tax

The right of a state to impose taxes on a foreign corporation arises under the same circumstances as with any other person. A foreign corporation, even one doing business solely in interstate commerce, acquires no unique protection from local taxation by virtue of its status.

The power of a state to levy taxes on real and personal property located within its boundaries is clear. It makes no difference that the property is owned by a foreign corporation, or even by a corporation not registered, or required to be registered, in the taxing state. Nor does it matter that the property is used in doing interstate business. The only requirement is that the tax must be valid, and must apply so as not to discriminate.

What is not so clear is the power of a state to tax personal property that moves in and out of its borders during a year—for example, a truck, a railroad train, or an airplane. The problem is one of determining whether the transient property may be said to have a "situs" (to be located, for legal purposes) in a state in which it does not remain on a relatively permanent basis. The presence of an appropriate tax situs ordinarily is determined by examining whether the tax bears any reasonable relationship to the privileges or benefits bestowed on the company by the taxing state. If that question is resolved in favor of the state, the remaining questions are whether the due process guarantee has been met, and whether the imposition of the proposed tax would place an undue restriction, or an unreasonable burden, on interstate commerce.

Much more controversial is the right of a state to tax the income of a foreign corporation, at least one that neither is registered nor required to be registered in the taxing state. In the beginning, the right to impose a tax on income was determined to require some substantial relationship between the state and the person (company) to be taxed. Although it was clear that the company's residence within the state should not be the only sufficient relationship, at least it should be established that the income had been earned within the state. Therefore, income from a contract entered into within the state is a sufficient basis for taxation. However, what about the next logical extension—income from a contract partially executed within the state, or perhaps from orders solicited within the state, regardless of which state's law governed the contract itself?

In 1959, in *Northwestern States Portland Cement Co. v. State of Minnesota*, the Supreme Court of the United States upheld a state income tax imposed on the net income of a corporation. The tax was based on the proportion its total sales assignable to the state bore to its total sales, and the proportion its payroll in the state bore to its total payroll, among other factors. Northwestern States Portland's allegations that such taxation violated the Commerce Clause and the Fourteenth Amendment's Due Process Clause were rejected by the Court. However, Congress acted immediately to register its disapproval of the Court's holding by passing the Federal Interstate Income Law of 1959. The statute provided that income derived from transactions in interstate commerce was not subject to net income taxation by a state or its subdivisions if the only connection between the company and the taxing jurisdiction was that orders were solicited from within that state, but were accepted and shipped from outside. The act also provided that the fact that a foreign corporation employed an independent contractor to solicit orders, even if he had an office within the jurisdiction, would not subject the corporation to income tax. Congress thus effectively returned the theory of taxing a foreign corporation's income derived from interstate commerce to the question of where the underlying contract was accepted.

The following case considers the power of a state to tax foreign corporations.

COMPLETE AUTO TRANSIT, INC. v. BRADY
430 U.S. 274, 97 S.Ct. 1076, 51 L.Ed.2d 326 (1977)

This was an action by Complete Auto Transit, Inc. (Plaintiff/Appellant) against the Mississippi State Tax Commission, headed by Brady (Defendant/Appellee), for a refund of state sales taxes.

Plaintiff was a Michigan corporation engaged in transporting motor vehicles for General Motors Corporation. The motor vehicles were manufactured outside of Mississippi and shipped by rail to Jackson, Mississippi. They were then loaded on Plaintiff's motor carriers and driven to dealers in Mississippi. The state of Mississippi assessed a sales tax of 5 percent gross income derived from doing business within the state, including the business of transporting property. Plaintiff contended the state was without power to assess the tax because doing so would violate the constitutional prohibition against state burdens on interstate commerce.

The trial court upheld the assessment and the Supreme Court of Mississippi affirmed. Plaintiff then appealed to the Supreme Court of the United States. Affirmed.

BLACKMUN, Justice.

Appellant, in its complaint in Chancery Court, did not allege that its activity which Mississippi taxes does not have a sufficient nexus with the State; or that the tax discriminates against interstate commerce; or that the tax is unfairly apportioned; or that it is unrelated to services provided by the State. No such claims were made before the Mississippi Supreme Court, and although appellant argues here that a tax on "the privilege of engaging in interstate commerce" creates an unacceptable risk of discrimination and undue burdens, Brief for Appellant 20-27, it does not claim that discrimination or undue burdens exist in fact.

Appellant's attack is based solely on decisions of this Court holding that a tax on the "privilege" of engaging in an activity in the State may not be applied to an activity that is part of the interstate commerce. See e.g., Spector Motor Service v. O'Connor, 340 U.S. 602, 71 S.Ct. 508, 95 L.Ed. 573 (1951); Freeman v. Hewit, 329 U.S. 249, 67 S.Ct. 274, 91 L.Ed. 265 (1946). This rule looks only to the fact that the incidence of the tax is the "privilege of doing business"; it deems irrelevant any consideration of the practical effect of the tax. The rule reflects an underlying philosophy that interstate commerce should enjoy a sort of "free trade" immunity from state taxation.

Appellee, in its turn, relies on decisions of this Court stating that "[i]t was not the purpose of the commerce clause to relieve those engaged in interstate commerce from their just share of state tax burden even though it increases the cost of doing the business." Western Live Stock v. Bureau of Revenue, 303 U.S. 250, 254 58 S.Ct. 546, 548, 82 L.Ed. 823 (1938). These decisions have considered not the formal language of the tax statute but rather its practical effect, and have sustained a tax against Commerce Clause challenge when the tax is applied to an activity with a substantial nexus with the taxing State, is fairly apportioned, does not discriminate against interstate commerce, and is fairly related to the services provided by the State.

Over the years, the Court has applied this practical analysis in approving many types of tax that avoided running afoul of the prohibition against taxing the "privilege of doing business," but in each instance it has refused to overrule the prohibition. Under the present state of the law, the Spector rule, as it has come to be known, has no relationship to economic realities. Rather it stands only as a trap for the unwary draftsman. . . .

The unsatisfactory operation of the Spector rule is well demonstrated by our recent case of Colonial Pipeline Co. v. Traigle, 421 U.S. 100, 95 S. Ct. 1538, 44 L.Ed.2d 1 (1975). Colonial was a Delaware corporation with an interstate pipeline running through Louisiana for approximately 258 miles. It maintained a work force and pumping stations in Louisiana to keep the pipeline flowing, but it did no intrastate business in that State. . . . In 1962, Louisiana imposed on Colonial a franchise tax for "the privilege of carrying on or doing business" in the State. The Louisiana Court of Appeal invalidated the tax as violative of the rule of Spector. . . . The Supreme Court of Louisiana refused review. . . . The Louisiana Legislature, perhaps recognizing that it had run afoul of a rule of words rather than a rule of substance, then redrafted the statute to levy the tax, as an alternative incident, on the "qualification to carry on or do business in this state or the actual doing of business within this state in a corporate form." Again, the Court of Appeal held the tax unconstitutional as applied to the appellant. Colonial Pipeline Co. v. Agerton, 275 So.2d 834 (La.App. 1973). But this time the Louisiana Supreme Court upheld the new tax. 289 So.2d 93 (La. 1974).

By a 7-to-1 vote, this Court affirmed. No question had been raised as to the propriety of the apportionment of the tax, and no claim was made that the tax was discriminatory. 421 U.S., at 101, 95 S.Ct., at 1539. The Court noted that the tax was imposed on that aspect of interstate commerce to which the State bore a special relation, and that the State bestowed powers, privileges, and benefits sufficient to support a tax on doing business in the corporate form in Louisiana. . . . Accordingly, on the authority of Memphis Gas, the tax was held to be constitutional. The Court distinguished Spector on the familiar ground that it involved a tax on the privilege of carrying on interstate commerce, while the Louisiana Legislature, in contrast, had worded the statute at issue "narrowly to confine the impost to one related to appellant's activities within the State in the corporate form." . . .

While refraining from overruling Spector, the Court noted:

> [D]ecisions of this Court, particularly during recent decades, have sustained non-discriminatory, properly apportioned state corporate taxes upon foreign corporations doing an exclusively interstate business when the tax is related to a corporation's local activities and the State has provided benefits and protections for those activities for which it is justified in asking a fair and reasonable return. . . .

One commentator concluded: "After reading Colonial, only the most sanguine tax-payer would conclude that the Court maintains a serious belief in the doctrine that the privilege of doing interstate business is immune from state taxation." . . .

In this case, of course, we are confronted with a situation like that presented in Spector. The tax is labeled a privilege tax "for the privilege of . . . doing business" in Mississippi, Section 10105 of the State's 1942 Code, as amended, and the activity taxed is, or has assumed to be, interstate commerce. We note again that no claim is made that the activity is not sufficiently connected to the State to justify a tax, or that the tax is not fairly related to benefits provided the taxpayer, or that the tax discriminates against interstate commerce, or that the tax is not fairly apportioned.

The view of the Commerce Clause that gave rise to the rule of Spector perhaps was not without some substance. Nonetheless, the possibility of defending it in the abstract does not alter the fact that the Court has rejected the proposition that interstate commerce is immune from state taxation:

> It is a truism that the mere act of carrying on business in interstate commerce does not exempt a corporation from state taxation. 'It was not the purpose of the commerce clause to relieve those engaged in interstate commerce from their just share of state tax burden even though it increases the cost of doing business.' Western Live Stock v. Bureau of Revenue. . . .

Not only has the philosophy underlying the rule been rejected, but the rule itself has been stripped of any practical significance. If Mississippi had called its tax one on "net income" or on the "going concern value" of appellant's business, the Spector rule could not invalidate it. There is no economic consequence that follows necessarily from the use of the particular words, "privilege of doing business," and a focus on that formalism merely obscures the question whether the tax produces a forbidden effect. Simply put, the Spector rule does not address the problems with which the Commerce Clause is concerned. Accordingly, we now reject the rule of Spector Motor Service, Inc. v. O'Connor, that a state tax on the "privilege of doing business" is per se unconstitutional when it is applied to interstate commerce, and that case is overruled.

There being no objection to Mississippi's tax on appellant except that it was imposed on nothing other than the "privilege of doing business" that is interstate, the judgment of the Supreme Court of Mississippi is affirmed.

Questions

1. Can you articulate the reasons the court chose to abandon the ruling in the *Spector* case?

2. What is it about the Mississippi tax that enables it to pass constitutional muster?

Requiring Registration

As mentioned previously in this chapter, it is not entirely clear what degree of connection is necessary to entitle a state to require a foreign corporation to register. It generally is agreed only that the connection must be substantial. Accordingly, under Section 106 of the MBCA, a foreign corporation must register first if it intends to "transact business" in the state. The section proceeds, then, to enumerate activities that may be carried on lawfully without registration. These include maintaining or defending any action or suit and any administrative or arbitration proceeding; holding any meeting of its directors or shareholders, or carrying on other internal activities; maintaining bank accounts; conducting activities relating to its own securities; effecting sales through independent contractors; soliciting orders to be accepted outside the state; creating evidences of debt, mortgages, or liens on property; securing or collecting debts, or enforcing any rights in property that secures some debt; transacting any business in interstate commerce; and conducting certain isolated transactions. Section 15.01 of the RMBCA repeats this language, and adds simple ownership of real or personal property. Both acts also clearly provide that the list of exclusive activities is not exhaustive. Therefore, a state is free to waive registration if a foreign corporation is engaged only in these or other activities that it believes do not constitute some substantial "transacting business."

In enumerating the excluded activities, both acts seem not only to list activities that have proven insufficient to provide a basis for requiring registration, but to provide a margin for error.

This is done by providing for additional discretion to be exercised by the states, excluding *all* transactions in interstate commerce, and also excluding "isolated" transactions "not in the course of a number of repeated transactions of like nature." It seems these exclusions are considerably more than would be required by the Supreme Court.

Registration involves most of the same requirements as does forming a new incorporation. An application must be filed with the secretary of state. This application will include information such as the corporate name, powers, names of directors, and the name and address of the corporation's registered agent, among other matters. Thereafter, the corporation must file regular reports with the secretary of state, just like a domestic corporation.

Penalties for Failure to Register

Although the failure of a foreign corporation to register when required may subject it to a fine or other sanction by the state, the most frequent penalty imposed is a restriction on its right to maintain an action, suit, or proceeding in the courts of the offended state. Section 124 of the MBCA provides that, in addition, no successor of such a corporation can maintain an action, suit, or proceeding on any claim that arose during the period its predecessor was not registered. This section further provides for the payment of all back fees, franchise taxes, and penalties imposed by the act.

Consider the following case involving the right of an unregistered foreign corporation.

ELI LILLY AND COMPANY v. SAV-ON-DRUGS, INC.
366 U.S. 276, 81 S.Ct. 1316, 6 L.Ed.2d 288 (1961)

This was an action by Eli Lilly and Company (Plaintiff/Appellant) against Sav-On-Drugs, Inc. (Defendant/Appellee) to enjoin Defendant from selling Plaintiff's products below agreed-upon (Fair Trade) prices.

Plaintiff was an Indiana corporation. It maintained an office in Newark, New Jersey, from which some eighteen "detailmen" (sales representatives) operated. Their job was to visit retail drugstores, physicians, and hospitals in the state, acquainting them with Plaintiff's products with the object of encouraging them to sell or use those products. They did not directly solicit orders, but took them "as a service to the retailers."

Defendant moved to dismiss Plaintiff's complaint because Plaintiff was not registered to do business in New Jersey. Plaintiff opposed the motion on the grounds that (1) it was not "doing business" in New Jersey, within the meaning of the statute requiring registration, and even if it was, (2) its business in New Jersey was entirely interstate, and thus not constitutionally subject to the registration statute.

The judgment of the trial court dismissing the complaint was affirmed by the New Jersey Supreme Court, and Plaintiff appealed. Affirmed.

BLACK, Justice.

We agree with the trial court that "[t]o hold under the facts above recited that plaintiff [Lilly] is not doing business in New Jersey is to completely ignore reality." Eighteen "detailmen," working out of a big office in Newark, New Jersey, with Lilly's name on the door and in the lobby of the building, and with Lilly's district manager and secretary in charge, have been regularly engaged in work for Lilly which relates directly to the intrastate aspects of the sale of Lilly's products. These eighteen "detailmen" have been traveling throughout the State of New Jersey promoting the sales of Lilly's products, not to the wholesalers, Lilly's interstate customers, but to the physicians, hospitals and retailers who buy those products in intrastate commerce from the wholesalers. To this end, they have provided these hospitals, physicians and retailers with up-to-date knowledge of Lilly's products and with free advertising and promotional material designed to encourage the general public to make more intrastate purchases of Lilly's products. And they sometimes even directly participate in the intrastate sales themselves by transmitting orders from the hospitals, physicians and drugstores they service to the New Jersey wholesalers.

This Court had a somewhat similar problem before in Cheney Brothers Co. v. Comm. of Massachusetts. In that case, the Northwestern Consolidated Milling Company of Minnesota had been conducting business in Massachusetts in a manner quite similar to that being used by Lilly in New Jersey—a number of wholesalers were buying Northwestern's flour in interstate commerce and selling it to retail stores in Massachusetts in intrastate commerce. Northwestern had in Massachusetts, in addition to any force of drummers it may have had to promote its interstate sales to the wholesalers, a group of salesmen who traveled the State promoting the sale of flour by

Massachusetts wholesalers to Massachusetts retailers. These salesmen also solicited orders from the retail dealers and turned them over to the nearest Massachusetts wholesaler. Despite this substantial connection with the intrastate business in Massachusetts, Northwestern contended that its business was wholly in interstate commerce—a contention that this Court disposed of summarily in the following words: "Of course this is a domestic business—inducing one local merchant to buy a particular class of goods from another."

Lilly attempts to distinguish the holding in the Cheney case on the ground that here its detailmen are not engaged in a systematic solicitation of orders from the retailers. It is true that the record in the Cheney case shows a more regular solicitation of orders than does the record here. But that difference is not enough to distinguish the cases. . . .

Lilly also contends that even if it is engaged in intrastate commerce in New Jersey and can by virtue of that fact be required to get a license to do business in that State, New Jersey cannot properly deny it access to the courts in this case because the suit is one arising out of the interstate aspects of its business. In this regard, Lilly relies upon such cases as International Textbook Co. v. Pigg, holding that a State cannot condition the right of a foreign corporation to sue upon a contract for the interstate sale of goods. We do not think that those cases are applicable here, however, for the present suit is not of that kind. Here, Lilly is suing upon a contract entirely separable from any particular interstate sale and the power of the State is consequently not limited by cases involving such contracts.

What we have said would be enough to dispose of this case were it not for the contention that the question whether Lilly is engaged in intrastate commerce in New Jersey is not properly before us. This contention is based upon Lilly's interpretation of the decision of the New Jersey court as resting upon the assumption that Lilly has been engaged in interstate commerce only. We cannot accept that contention because, in the first place, it rests upon a completely erroneous interpretation of the New Jersey court's opinion. That court was called upon to decide whether appellant was "transacting business" in New Jersey within the meaning of the statute which requires the registration of foreign corporations. In deciding that question, the court relied upon the facts set out in the affidavits with regard to the various local activities of Lilly as summarized in the findings quoted above. The only reasonable inference from these findings is that the trial court interpreted the phrase "transacting business" in the New Jersey statute to mean transacting local intrastate business and concluded from the facts it found that Lilly was transacting such business. This conclusion is reinforced by a subsequent New Jersey opinion that distinguishes the decision in this case on precisely that ground.

Questions

1. To what degree do you think denying access to the local courts is an effective way to induce foreign corporations to register?

2. What are the objectives of a scheme for registering foreign corporations? Are they worth the effort?

Although an unregistered foreign corporation that violates a state's corporation code cannot bring an action, suit, or other proceeding, it usually is allowed to defend itself. In addition, contracts and other transactions entered into are valid as against the corporation, even though it may not bring an action to enforce its rights. The logic of these points should be obvious. If a corporation were allowed to deny liability based on its failure to register, this would allow a corporation to use the state's law to reward it for its own wrongdoing.

An even harsher penalty is imposed by some states. In addition to preventing an unregistered corporation from bringing an action, suit, or proceeding in the state's courts, they disallow the corporation from defending the merits of the claim. Although these provisions have been upheld as within the powers of the states, they generally are viewed as unnecessary and, perhaps, overzealous. The object of the law requiring registration is the protection of the public, not the simple vindication of state power.

SUMMARY

Corporations may be classified as domestic, foreign, and alien. A domestic corporation is one doing business in its state of incorporation. A foreign corporation is one that is doing business in a state other than its state of incorporation. An alien corporation is a foreign corporation incorporated outside of the United States or its territories.

A state has the right to exercise certain powers over foreign corporations that transact business within the state. The power may take the form of the jurisdiction of its state courts, taxation, or registration. The right to require registration ordinarily demands a more substantial relationship between the corporation and the state than does the imposition of court jurisdiction or taxes.

When a foreign corporation must register, the requirements are very similar to those for the incorporation of a domestic corporation. An application must be filed and approved, a name must be accepted, a registered office and a registered agent must be designated, and reports must be filed. The failure of a foreign corporation to register as required subjects the corporation to a variety of possible penalties. The most common penalty is that of preventing the corporation from bringing suit in a state court. A few states even disallow the corporation from defending a suit.

KEY TERMS AND CONCEPTS

foreign corporation
alien corporation
transacting business
long-arm jurisdiction

PROBLEMS

1. Sinwellan Corporation sued Farmer's Bank in Delaware for alleged wrongful dishonor of checks. The bank moved to dismiss the suit on the ground that Sinwellan, a foreign corporation, was doing business in Delaware without having registered as required by statute. The evidence showed Sinwellan maintained a Delaware bank account, advertised in two Delaware newspapers, stored financial records in Delaware, executed contracts in Delaware with Delaware residents and entered into credit transactions with them, and provided taxi services to and from Delaware. The trial court denied the motion on the ground that these activities were incidental only to the running of Sinwellan's Great Oaks Lodge in Maryland. Should that decision be affirmed on appeal?

2. Allenberg Cotton Company, a Tennessee Corporation, purchased cotton through a broker in Mississippi. The broker received the cotton at its warehouses, sorted it, obtained signatures on contracts for Allenberg, and shipped cotton to Allenberg's customers. When Allenberg sued a farmer for breach of contract in a Mississippi court, the defendant moved to dismiss because Allenberg was not registered to do business in Mississippi. Allenberg responded that it could not be required to register because requiring it to do so would be unconstitutional state interference with interstate commence. What should be the result?

3. Aldens, Inc., an Illinois corporation, sold goods by mail order. It received orders in Illinois, and shipped the goods from Illinois. Charges on an order sent to Packel, in Pennsylvania, remained unpaid. Alden sued on the account, and the customer contended that the interest rate Alden charged on accounts was in excess of the rate permitted by Pennsylvania law, and therefore Alden was not entitled to collect any interest. Alden contended it was not subject to the Pennsylvania statute concerning interest rates since it had no physical presence in the state. Therefore, to apply the statute to its operation would be an unconstitutional state interference with interstate commerce. Is Aldens correct?

4. Zielinski was injured by a defective electric grill manufactured in Missouri by Zippo Industries, a Missouri corporation. The electric grill had been sold by Zippo to a wholesaler in Missouri, which resold it to the Gadget Company in New Mexico, where Zielinski bought it. Zielinski filed suit against Zippo by serving process on the secretary of state of New Mexico, since Zippo was not registered to do business in the state. Zippo moved to dismiss on the ground of improper service, claiming it did not do business in New Mexico. Is Zippo correct?

5. Norfolk was injured when a fork lift arm fell on him. The injury occurred in Florida; the fork lift was manufactured by J. I. Case Company, a Wisconsin corporation; and the defective part had been manufactured by Harlo, a Michigan corporation, and sold to Case in Wisconsin. Norfolk sued Case, which in turn filed a third-party complaint against Harlo. Both complaints were filed in a Florida court. Under these facts, does the Florida court have jurisdiction over Harlo?

6. Action was brought in a Tennessee court by Rochester Capital Leasing Corporation, a lessor of postage-stamp vending machines, against Shilling, a lessee, for nonpayment of agreed-upon rental on 15 machines. Rochester was a New York corporation; the machines were leased to Schilling in Tennessee through Hilsum Sales, a Florida corporation; and rental was to be paid to Rochester at its New York office. All the arrangements had been transacted by correspondence. Schilling moved to dismiss the complaint because Rochester had not registered to do business in Tennessee. Under the facts, should the motion be granted?

7. Burke Construction Company, a foreign corporation, filed suit challenging an Arkansas statute requiring registration of foreign corporations doing business in the state. The statute provided that a corporation could register only if it agreed that if it was sued in a state court it would not remove the action to a federal court. Should Burke's challenge be upheld?

8. Golden Dawn Foods, Inc., a Pennsylvania corporation, sued Cekuta, an Ohio resident, in an Ohio court for failure to pay a note. The note was to secure payment for food supplied to Cekuta's store in Ohio by Golden Dawn. Cekuta moved to dismiss the complaint because Golden Dawn was not registered to do business in Ohio. The evidence showed that Golden Dawn operated in Pennsylvania, and sold wholesale groceries to some 100 independent retail grocery stores in Pennsylvania and to 50 in Ohio. Golden Dawn owned no real estate in Ohio, did no advertising in Ohio, gave no assistance to Ohio stores, and sales were made by salespeople dispatched from its Pennsylvania facility. Should Cekuta's motion be granted?

Franchising and Cooperatives

INTRODUCTION

In the preceding chapters, discussion has focused on types of business organizations, particularly general partnerships, limited partnerships, and corporations, and on the various laws concerning their formation and operation. Franchises and cooperatives, the subjects of this chapter, are not distinct forms of business organization but, perhaps, are better characterized as methods of doing business. Usually, the businesses involved are organized as corporations, but the corporate form is not necessary to doing business as either a franchise or a cooperative.

FRANCHISING: AN OVERVIEW

The History and Development of the Modern Franchise

Franchising has a relatively short history in the United States, beginning at around the turn of this century. Early franchises were found mostly in the automobile, petroleum, and soft-drink industries. Beginning in about 1950, franchising became accepted on a much broader scale, and today franchises account for some 25 percent of retail sales and almost 15 percent of the gross national product. The growth of franchising during the past 40 years nowhere is more evident than in the fast-food industry, which boasts such mega-franchises as McDonald's, Burger King, and Big Boy, to mention only three.

The modern acceptance of franchising probably is the result of two primary advantages it offers over other types of business operations. First, franchising allows many small investors to become entrepreneurs in spite of their limited financial resources and perhaps limited knowledge of business management. Second, it makes it possible for the public to purchase uniform products and services, in many cases throughout the nation and even internationally. In effect, everyone may benefit from this business method.

Definition

The term *franchise* has a variety of meanings depending upon the context in which it is used. Broadly, a franchise is a grant of a special right or privilege. In the public context, the right to vote is a franchise granted by a government to its citizens, and the right of a public utility, such as a power company or a telephone company, to an exclusive service area is a franchise granted by a government for business purposes. However, the discussion in this chapter will be limited to private franchises.

In the private context, franchising involves an arrangement between someone holding the right to a product or service (the franchisor) and someone who will market the product or service (the franchisee). More precisely, the International Franchise Association (IFA) has defined **franchise** as "a continuing relationship in which the franchisor provides a licensed privilege to do business, plus assistance in organizing, training, mer-

chandising and management in return for a consideration from the franchisee." In contrast to this business-oriented definition, the Federal Trade Commission (FTC) has provided a more legalistic definition, stating that a franchise is "an arrangement in which the owner of a trademark, trade name, or a copyright licenses others, under specific conditions or limitations, to use the trademark, trade name, or copyright in purveying goods or services." Both of these definitions are useful in understanding franchising, because each emphasizes different aspects of the practice. In any case, however, private franchising involves a private grant of a special right by the franchisor to the franchisee. The franchisee may be an individual retailer, one who is part of a chain-type operation, or a merchant-middleman such as a "wholesaler" or a "jobber." The latter differ from the retailer only in that they are authorized by a manufacturer to sell primarily to retailers, other merchants, or to commercial users rather than to consumers.

The Franchise Relationship

In the simplest form of franchising, the franchisor merely permits the franchisee to market the product or service independently as the franchisee sees fit. More often, however, the franchisee is required to give up much of his or her independence and to follow numerous standards and practices established by the franchisor. The previously noted IFA definition of a franchise suggests that assistance in organizing, training, merchandising, and management are made available to the franchisee. In fact, the acceptance of those and other services usually is demanded by the franchisor as a condition of the franchise grant.

THE LAW OF FRANCHISING

The relationship between a franchisor and a franchisee is governed almost entirely by state law. For the most part, franchise law is derivative of the common law of contracts and agency (includ-

Domestic franchise sales (1987)

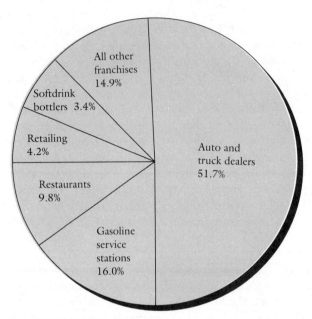

Source: Statistical Abstract of the U.S. (1988), Table 1312.

ing employment law). Approximately 40 percent of the states have enacted statutes specifically addressing the subject of franchising. Although the contents of these statutes are not uniform, most were enacted for the purpose of regulating the right of a franchisor to terminate a franchise. The power of termination clearly has been perceived as presenting the greatest chance for unfairness in any franchise relationship.

Federal Regulation

Federal law includes a number of statutes and regulations affecting franchising. Some were promulgated with franchising in mind, and others have been adapted to franchise law. Specific federal statutes include the **Automobile Dealers' Franchise Act,** also known as the Automobile Dealers' Day In Court Act, and the **Petroleum Marketing Practices Act.** (It may be interesting to note that these two acts involve two of the industries that have been involved in franchising the longest.) In addition, the Federal Trade Commission Act prohibits unfair or deceptive acts or practices in interstate commerce. Pursuant to its authority granted under this act, the Federal Trade Commission adopted rules requiring certain disclosures by franchisors and franchise brokers in connection with the sale of a franchise. These rules are intended to ensure that every prospective franchise purchaser is provided with sufficient truthful and relevant information to enable him to make an enlightened decision about entering into a franchise agreement.

Federal law also includes other provisions that significantly affect franchising, although they are not specifically designed to do so. These include the Mail Fraud Act, prohibiting the use of the mails in any scheme to defraud, and to a lesser extent the federal securities laws. Attempts to use the securities laws have met with only limited success, however, because of the difficulty in establishing that a franchise is an investment under those statutes. Determining what constitutes an "investment" is discussed more fully in Chapter 47.

State Regulation

As previously noted, state regulation of franchising is accomplished primarily by the application of common law principles rather than statutory provisions. State statutes, where they exist, are not uniform. One important reason for this lack of uniformity is that there is a great deal of disagreement as to the definition of a "franchise." A few state statutes are patterned after the federal Automobile Dealers' Franchise Act, and deal with the problems of franchises head-on. Others function much in the manner of the federal securities acts and require a franchisor to register and to disclose certain information that may be used by a prospective franchise purchaser in making a decision about buying the franchise. Overall, this latter approach is thought by many to be the most effective, and the least intrusive, approach to dealing with franchise abuses.

THE FRANCHISE AGREEMENT

The **franchise agreement** is an enforceable contract between the franchisor and the franchisee. As such, it forms the fundamental basis of the relationship between the parties. Most importantly, it sets the limits of the extent to which each party may expect performance from the other during the period of the agreement. Thus, in addition to federal and state regulation, franchise agreements always are subject to the common law of contracts. To the extent that they involve the sale of goods by the franchisor to the franchisee, they also may be subject to the provisions of Article 2 of the Uniform Commercial Code.

Provisions of the Agreement

The specific provisions of franchise agreements are not uniform, either among industries or even among agreements within the same industry. However, some generalizations can be made concerning some of the more common provisions. These include promises concerning: (1) the payment of a franchise fee and royalties by the franchisee; (2) the location and territory of a franchise; (3) the duty to furnish facilities and equipment; (4) the franchisor's obligation to provide training and supervision to the franchisee and her employees; (5) advertising and who pays for it; (6) supplies; (7) standards of price and quality control; and (8) the duration of the franchise and the grounds for its termination.

In order to receive a franchise, it is customary for the prospective franchisee to pay a franchise fee to the franchisor. The amount of this fee will vary in relation to the anticipated value of the franchise, and it may be payable in a lump sum or in installments over an agreed-upon period of time, as determined by the parties. This franchise fee is paid in addition to the royalty fees the franchisee will pay to the franchisor. The latter usually are established as a percentage of sales, and continue for the life of the franchise agreement.

The location and territory of the franchise usually are determined by the franchisor, because the franchisor ordinarily has researched the market and has the expertise to select the most effective service area that may be covered by an individual franchisee. In addition, it may be of special concern to the franchisor to make sure that each new franchise fits into its present and projected comprehensive marketing plans.

Although great variation is possible in arrangements concerning who will provide the business premises and equipment, these frequently are provided to the franchisee by the franchisor under a leasing clause in the franchise agreement. The reasons for this are that uniformity in appearance is important to both parties, and often the equipment involved is somewhat specialized. In some cases that uniformity is achieved to the extent that the franchisor even supplies a restaurant's signs, menus, and napkins. Nevertheless, it is not uncommon that at least the building and land are provided by the franchisee, sometimes with money borrowed from the franchisor, and then are leased back to the franchisor.

One of the significant benefits to the franchisee is the training and supervision that often is provided by the franchisor. Many franchise businesses are highly specialized, so that even a franchisee who is schooled and experienced in business management may be ill equipped to begin operating the particular franchise business.

The benefits of training and supervision, of course, are even more significant to a franchisee who is new to the business world. In reality, effective training is to the advantage of both parties to the franchise. The degree to which training and supervision are provided depends heavily on the nature of the business and the education and experience of the franchisee. It generally is understood that in the absence of agreement to the contrary, the franchisor is obligated to make a reasonable assessment of the franchisee's needs and to provide the training and supervision necessary to meet those needs. A failure to do so constitutes a breach of the franchise agreement, as the following case illustrates.

ABERLE v. NORTH DAKOTA B & B PERMANENT AND TEMPORARY PERSONNEL SYSTEMS, INC.
186 N.W.2d 446 (N.D. 1971)

This was an action by a franchisee, Francis Aberle (Plaintiff/Respondent) against the franchisor, North Dakota Permanent and Temporary Personnel Systems, Inc. (Defendant/Appellant) for damages for breach of contract. Under the franchise agreement, Defendant had promised to furnish Plaintiff "A complete training program for the Franchisee which includes training in Permanent Personnel System management at B & B's Training Center or in Franchisee's office (B & B's option)." The agreement stated that the training program included instruction in:

    A. Selection of office site and layout.
    B. Selection of equipment.
    C. Recruiting of personnel.
    D. Advertising, marketing procedure.
    E. Recruiting of accounts.
    F. Recruiting of applicants.
    G. Credit and collections.
    H. Financing program and procedure.
    I. Recruiting of both continuing accounts and applicants.

The agreement also provided that B & B was "under a continuing obligation to render advice, training and guidance . . . ." Thereafter, Defendant furnished Plaintiff with training manuals, letters, three and a half days' training, and one day of instruction at another office.

Plaintiff, who had limited educational background and experience in the operation of such a business, became disenchanted with the operation and closed the office. He claimed that he failed because of a lack of training and

supervision by Defendant. Defendant claimed the training provided met its obligation under the franchise agreement.
From a judgment for Plaintiff, Defendant appealed. Affirmed.

TEIGEN, Judge.

On the basis of the testimony, the trial court found "that the defendant must have foreseen that with the plaintiff's educational background and experience and his intellectual and emotional endowments . . . he could not succeed without a thorough training program and constant advice and counsel, particularly in the initial stages of this admittedly complex enterprise." Giving appreciable weight to the findings of the trial court, we find the evidence sustains this finding. Under the circumstances, the training program furnished did not comply with the contract provision that B & B furnish "a complete training program. . . ." The trial court was in a much better position to evaluate the intellectual and emotional endowments of Aberle, and to determine the amount and kind of training necessary to carry out the terms of the contract, than we are from the cold record, and we accept the trial court's findings.

Questions

1. Why should the franchisor in this case be obligated to become an expert in determining the training needs of each franchisee? Wasn't it the responsibility of the franchisee to inform the franchisor if he felt additional training was needed rather than simply complaining after it was too late?
2. If the manuals provided by the franchisor cover the subject matter spelled out in the agreement, hasn't the franchisor met his duty under the training clause?

Advertising clauses usually cover both the obligation to advertise and the question of which party will pay the costs; in most cases, the franchisor retains either total or almost-total control over these matters. The advertising clause may require that a specified amount be spent on advertising, although more commonly the amount is established by some variable such as a percentage of gross sales. The selection of advertising media and layout ordinarily are determined by the franchisor, who even may provide advertising mats for printed media, tapes and films for radio and television, and mailing fliers. Payment for advertising runs the gamut from full payment by the franchisor to some contribution (but usually not full payment) by the franchisee. When a franchisee contribution is required, the amount frequently is established, as noted previously, by some variable, such as a percentage of gross sales. In most cases it would not be in an experienced franchisee's best interest to agree to pay a fixed percentage or flat amount for advertising, particularly in the beginning of a new franchise's operation.

In the interest of uniform appearance, but also as a method of controlling quality and price, the franchise agreement usually provides that the franchisee will purchase some of his stock-in-trade and supplies from the franchisor. The price may be fixed during a specified period of time; it may vary according to rising and falling market prices; or the parties even may agree that the franchisor will provide these things at a "reasonable" price. The latter two arrangements are permitted by Section 2-305 of the Uniform Commercial Code when the stock-in-trade and supplies are "goods," which usually is the case.

Also in the interest of uniformity, the franchisor is especially interested in establishing and enforcing quality standards for the goods sold under the franchise name. Established standards then may be monitored by the franchisor by reasonable inspections to ensure that the standards are being met. There is no disagreement over the general right of the franchisor to do this. However, the franchisor cannot establish the price at which the franchisee will resell the goods. To do so would violate state and federal antitrust laws, as discussed in more detail later in this chapter. The franchisor, however, may establish a "suggested price," which the franchisee may adopt voluntarily.

Franchise agreements usually specify the duration of the agreement (for example, ten years) and also contain provisions for renewal. In addition, they ordinarily provide a list of causes for termination, and may require that some notice be given of a party's intent to terminate.

The problem of terminating franchise agreements has been foremost in the minds of lawmakers, including legislators and judges who have been involved in decisions concerning franchising regulation. Most states with franchising statutes require some notice (for example, 90 days) along with other regulatory provisions. In the absence of specific laws and franchise provisions governing notice and termination without cause, it is agreed generally that terminations should not be arbitrary or unfair. This position clearly is appropriate, because most franchise agreements are drafted by the franchisor with little or no involvement by the franchisee, and many are presented to the prospective franchisee on a take-it-or-leave-it basis. These contracts, called contracts of adhesion, historically have been subject to close scrutiny and flexible interpretation by the courts. In enforcing such agreements, courts are likely to find that the franchisor has protected herself effectively and, thus, are likely to emphasize the need to safeguard the interests of the franchisee, under the reasonable assumption that the parties intended (or should have intended) a good-faith agreement. To the extent to which the Uniform Commercial Code may govern these agreements, Section 1-203 imposes the general obligation of good faith on both parties. The following case illustrates that requirement.

KOWATCH v. ATLANTIC RICHFIELD COMPANY
480 Pa. 388, 390 A.2d 747 (1978)

This was an action by Robert S. Kowatch (Plaintiff/Appellant) against Atlantic Richfield Company (Defendant/Appellee) seeking a preliminary injunction prohibiting Defendant from terminating the business relationship between the parties.

On May 1, 1974, the parties signed a document captioned "Service Station Lease" under the terms of which Plaintiff was to operate an Arco (Atlantic Richfield Company) service station for one year. Thereafter Plaintiff operated the station as provided, complying with all provisions except one that required that the station operate from 6:00 A.M. until 11:00 P.M. Plaintiff reduced the hours, operating from 9:00 A.M. until 9:00 P.M. He stated the reason for this was in recognition of the national policy of conserving energy and the economic realities. Plaintiff alleges that he was then harassed by Defendant. On March 24, 1975, he was served with a "Notice of Default," and the next day was sent a "Notice of Lease Termination" effective at the end of the lease.

The trial court found that the relationship of the parties was one of lessor-lessee, and that Atlantic Richfield had an absolute right to repossession of the premises at the termination of the existing lease. As a result, the court dismissed Plaintiff's complaint, and Plaintiff appealed. Reversed and remanded.

ROBERTS, Justice.

In *Atlantic Richfield Co. v. Razumic* . . . we held that a printed form "DEALER LEASE" containing provisions requiring a gasoline dealer to operate a petroleum supplier's service station in a manner reflecting favorably on the supplier's public image and displaying the supplier's trademarks and products as prescribed by the supplier, and authorizing the supplier to inspect the service station and the dealer's financial records periodically to assure continued compliance with the terms of the writing, embodied a franchise agreement. We reached this conclusion even though the parties captioned the writing in a manner suggesting a landlord and tenant relationship. The form writing in this case contains provisions substantially identical to the writing in *Razumic*. Based on *Razumic*, we agree with Kowatch that the writing he and Arco signed embodies a franchise.

In *Razumic*, the form writing was silent concerning the petroleum supplier's right to terminate the franchise agreement without cause. After considering the relationship between parties to a contract nearly identical to the present one and their reasonable expectations, we concluded that the supplier owed its dealer an obligation to act in a commercially reasonable manner, which precluded arbitrary termination of the franchise agreement based solely upon expiration of the term of occupancy.

Here, too, the writing does not expressly provide for Arco's termination of the franchise agreement without cause. Here, as in *Razumic*, we hold that Arco cannot arbitrarily terminate its franchise agreement with Kowatch.

Questions

1. Why was the termination arbitrary?

2. When the parties have characterized their agreement as one of landlord-tenant, is it proper for the court to change that? Why shouldn't the written intention of the parties be controlling?

3. Even if the relationship of the parties is determined to be franchisor-franchisee, the agreement was for one year. Is it proper for the court to say, in effect, that the relationship must continue beyond the agreed-upon one year unless there is cause for termination? Is such liberty taken by courts in any other context?

Remedies for Breach

Breach of a franchise agreement may arise from a failure to abide by any of the provisions of the termination clause, in whole or in part, or failure to honor the other provisions of the general agreement. The usual remedies for breach are money damages, restitution, accounting, and rescission. However, the Uniform Commercial Code also provides for reformation in cases of unconscionable provisions (Section 2-302).

Damages is the most common relief sought for

breach of a franchise agreement. The right of the franchisor or the franchisee to collect damages rests on the general principles of damages applicable to breach of contract. Therefore, the prevailing party is entitled only to be placed in the position he would have occupied had the breaching party performed in accordance with the agreement. However, the award may include an amount for consequential damages, so a franchisee may recover the costs of training, office expense, and a amount for lost income. Damages also may be awarded incidental to other relief in cases involving the breach of a covenant, such as an injunction in a case of breach of a covenant not to compete upon termination of the franchise. However, a franchisee is not entitled to an award of damages for an unsuccessful business venture as such. That is, an additional amount will not be added for the loss of speculative profits.

Because the law always will seek to prevent one person from enriching herself unjustly at the expense of another, the remedy of restitution may be appropriate in cases of breach of a franchise agreement. In granting restitution, a court will require the breaching party to return or to pay for benefits or property wrongfully received, retained, or appropriated. Thus, if a franchisee has purchased and paid for a franchise, and the franchisor immediately breaches the franchise agreement in some material respect, the franchisee may be entitled to the return of the sum paid. If the breaching franchisor had refused to transfer the franchise in the first place and had sold it to a third party, the first franchisee may be permitted to elect between either the return of his fee or receiving the amount received by the franchisor from the third party.

An accounting also has been held to be an appropriate remedy for the breach of a franchise agreement. For example, if a franchisor permitted a second franchisee to do business within a territory previously set aside for another franchisee, the first franchisee may be entitled to a refund of royalties paid for the exclusive right to use the franchise name.

Under the principles of general contract law, rescission is an appropriate remedy whenever there has been fraud, failure of consideration, or a material breach or default in the performance of any of the provisions of a franchise agreement. When this remedy is granted, the franchise agreement is terminated and the parties are discharged of further obligation to each other. Rescission is not an alternative remedy, however. This means that it may be requested in conjunction with an action for damages or restitution. Its effect is only to discontinue the relationship of the parties and to discharge them of their mutual obligations of further performance.

To the extent that a franchise agreement involves a sale of goods, it may be governed by Article 2 of the Uniform Commercial Code. If the Code applies, and a court determines that any provision of a franchise agreement is unconscionable, Section 2-302 empowers the court to refuse to enforce the provision, or to rewrite the agreement to avoid any unconscionable result. The difficulty with obtaining relief under this section comes in establishing that the Code is applicable and then proving that the provision in question is unconscionable. The latter, in particular, may be troublesome because the term *unconscionable* is not defined in the Code itself, but has been defined only through judicial interpretation. In a general way, the term may be considered applicable to provisions that are grossly one-sided in favor of a party who has imposed the provision by the exercise of a greatly disproportionate bargaining position. Clearly, franchise agreements are prime candidates for falling within this general definition.

FRANCHISOR'S LIABILITY FOR ACTS OF THE FRANCHISEE

The liability of a franchisor for the acts of a franchisee are governed by the principles of agency law, discussed at length in Chapters 31–34. The franchisor's liability may be founded on contract law, tort law, or criminal law. Vicarious liability may arise under a franchise agreement for the simple reason that every such agreement involves the establishment of some form of agency relationship between the franchisor and the franchisee. This is true because every franchise agreement contemplates that the franchisee will perform services in part for the benefit of the franchisor, or even will act directly in the franchisor's behalf. However, in spite of the fact that some agency relation is established in every franchise, it may be stated, as a broad principle, that a franchisor ordinarily has no vicarious liability for a franchisee's acts.

Franchisee's Contracts

In order for a franchisor to be bound as a party to a contract entered into by a franchisee, it is necessary for the third party to prove that the franchisor authorized the franchisee to act on her (the franchisor's) behalf. Express authority may be found in the franchise agreement or under a separate agreement but, as noted previously, most franchise agreements confer no such authority on the franchisee. Nor does the fact that the franchisee uses the franchisor's trade name create that authority ostensibly or by implication. However, in cases in which third parties are misled by the use of the franchisor's name in advertisements, billings, telephone calls from the franchisor, trade literature, or the like, courts may find that authority existed, and the franchisor may be bound. Further, a franchisor may control the franchisee to such a degree that the court concludes that the franchisee is acting as an agent for the franchisor, as the following case illustrates.

NICHOLS v. ARTHUR MURRAY, INC.
248 Cal.2d 610, 56 Cal.Rptr. 728 (1967)

Gertrude Nichols (Plaintiff/Respondent) entered into prepaid contracts for dancing lessons with the "Arthur Murray School of Dancing" of San Diego, operated by Burkin, Inc. When the contracts were not fulfilled, Plaintiff sued the franchisor, Arthur Murray, Inc. (Defendant/Appellant) for breach of contract on the theory that Defendant was an undisclosed principal of the franchisee-dance studio. Defendant contended that it was only the licensor of its trade name, and its contract with the dance studio so provided.

The trial court found that the agreement between Defendant and the dance studio conferred upon Defendant the right to control the employment of all employees of the dance studio, to fix tuition, to select financial institutions and financial arrangements, and to do other things. In effect, Defendant controlled almost every aspect of the dance studio's operations.

The court found for Plaintiff on the theory that Defendant was an undisclosed principal, and Defendant appealed. Affirmed.

COUGHLIN, Associate Justice.

Many of the controls conferred were not related anywise to the protection of defendant's trade name, including its dancing and teaching methods, good will and business image. Other controls, although related to the protection of the trade name, because the exercise thereof was not limited to effecting such purpose, enabled defendant to impose its will upon the franchise holder in areas wholly unrelated to that purpose.

Defendant directs attention to provisions in the agreement which it claims expressly declare the intention of the parties that no agency relationship is intended; refers to the established principle that agency is a consensual relationship; and contends these circumstances dictate the conclusion no agency was created by the subject agreement. This contention disregards the fact that the agreement, as such, was consensual; both parties consented to the provisions imposing controls; and the agency relationship was created by the legal effect of those provisions.

. . . Our conclusion is that the controls imposed upon the franchise holder by defendant completely deprived the former of any independence in the business operation subject to the agreement. . . .

The evidence adequately supports the conclusion that in executing the subject contract and receiving the prepayments thereon, Burkin, Inc. was acting as agent for defendant.

Questions

1. Is it correct to visit contractual liability on the franchisor in this case simply because it closely controlled the franchisee, when the franchise agreement clearly states that the franchisee is *not* an agent of the franchisor (so is not authorized to bind the franchisor contractually)?

2. When the plaintiff contracted with the dance studio, didn't she know the dance studio was the other party to her contract? Was it not the intention of the parties to have a contract between themselves only?

3. Is there any way to define the amount of control the franchisor can exercise without the franchisee becoming its agent? Can you state that standard?

Franchisee's Torts

The franchisor's vicarious tort liability depends on whether the franchisor maintained a sufficient right to control the operation of the franchised business. If a significant right to control exists, either because of the terms of the franchise agreement or as evidenced by direction, supervision, and other control actually exercised by the franchisor, a franchisor may be liable for the franchisee's torts. Whether a sufficient right to control exists is a question of fact that sometimes is difficult for a court to resolve. Again, in the ordinary situation, the franchisor-franchisee relationship does not involve sufficient control (the franchisee is an independent contractor rather than a servant), and the franchisor is not vicariously liable in tort. A clear exception to this general position probably would be found in cases in which the franchise business involved ultrahazardous under-takings, such as the use of explosives, the demolition of buildings, the keeping of wild animals, or the use of hazardous chemicals.

Franchisee's Crimes

There is very little basis for finding a franchisor liable for a franchisee's crimes, since the imposition of criminal liability requires a showing that the defendant acted with criminal intent. For the most part, courts have held that one person cannot be assumed to have criminal intent vicariously. It simply is unrealistic to assume that a franchisor has an evil mind just because the franchisee does. In recent years the courts have found some exception to this almost-universal principle in cases involving the violation of regulatory laws promulgated for the public's safety.

ANTITRUST IMPLICATIONS OF FRANCHISING

Franchising presents a fertile field for possible antitrust violations. Many franchises involve the granting of the right to serve a particular territory, with an express or implied agreement by the franchisee not to do business beyond the established territorial boundary. This may be viewed as a violation of state or federal antitrust laws, particularly when territorial restrictions are intended to insulate one franchisee from competition by another franchisee.

A second characteristic of franchise agreements that raises antitrust questions is the tendency of franchisors to influence the price at which products and services are sold by franchisees. This tendency stems from the desire to maintain uniformity among franchises. Although uniformity is one of the most attractive features of a franchise operation, antitrust law does not permit a franchisor to impose and enforce mandatory pricing. However, it does permit a franchisor to "suggest" a price, as long as the franchisee's compliance is voluntary and his failure to comply will not result in the franchise's termination or other sanctions imposed by the franchisor.

Antitrust implications also most be considered in deciding the extent to which a franchisor may require the franchisee to purchase her stock-in-trade and supplies from the franchisor, and the extent to which a franchisor may require that the franchisee not sell other goods or services outside of those included in the franchise. Whether these arrangements constitute antitrust violations is determined by the courts under the so-called rule of reason. In other words, they are not violations *per se* (automatically), but are prohibited only if they have a substantial anticompetitive effect. Each case is decided on its own facts.

In providing goods and services to its franchisees, a franchisor must also be conscious to avoid price discrimination. Charging different franchisees different prices has a potential anticompetitive effect, and unless the price differentials are based on some acceptable (exempt) grounds, they may constitute an antitrust violation under the Robinson-Patman Act. Exemptions include changing market conditions, passing along actual savings to the franchisee, and meeting competition.

Because of the complexity of the subject, antitrust law is only touched on here. A more in-depth discussion can be found in Chapters 48 and 49.

COOPERATIVES: AN OVERVIEW

The term *cooperative* has an almost infinite variety of meanings. In a broad sense, any binding together of people for their mutual benefit may be characterized as a cooperative. Therefore, any governmental unit, federal, state, or local, may fit into that definition. More to the point here, *Black's Law Dictionary* (Rev. 4th Edition) defines a **cooperative** as "A union of individuals, commonly laborers, farmers, or small capitalists, formed for the prosecution in common of some prospective enterprise, the profits being shared in accordance with the capital or labor contributed by each." This definition, although broad, alludes to some important characteristics of a cooperative, as the term will be used in this discussion. Its inclusion of a reference to the types of individuals who may be involved, and the sharing of profits according to labor, as well as to capital, contributed are meaningful. In many cooperatives, labor is the principal thing contributed by members. In others it is capital, patronage, or some other use that is made of the cooperative's facilities.

The Cooperative Distinguished from Other Businesses

Although most cooperatives are formed as corporations, the corporate character is neither necessary to their creation nor a distinctive feature of cooperatives. When organized as a corporation, however, a cooperative is governed by a state's general corporation law, and it is considered a separate person (an entity) for the purposes of holding and transferring property, and suing and being sued. When a cooperative is not organized as a corporation, the common law rule that property must be held and transferred, and lawsuits must be processed, in the names of the individual owners (members) applies. Of course, this may be changed by state statutes. Also, an unincorporated cooperative or other association may sue or be sued in its common name in federal courts in any case involving the enforcement of rights under the Constitution or laws of the United States.

Features that do distinguish a cooperative from other business forms include (1) democratic control and voting by members; (2) one vote per member rather than one vote per share; (3) the distribution of profits and other benefits to members, usually in relation to their relative contributions of capital or labor, their use of the association's facilities, or some combination of these; (4) limited return on capital; and (5) the fact that most of its business is done with its members. These features sometimes are altered by the association's charter or bylaws (particularly voting rights), or by statute. For example, federal legislation affecting agricultural cooperatives limits the amount of dividends that may be paid on capital, and requires these cooperatives to do no more than 50 percent of their business with nonmembers.

The distinction between a cooperative and an ordinary business corporation results in some differences in the treatment of cooperatives under the law. This especially is true regarding the relationship between a cooperative and its members, as the following case illustrates.

LAMBERT v. FISHERMAN'S DOCK COOPERATIVE, INC.
115 N.J.Super. 424, 280 A.2d 193 (1971)

This was an action by William M. Lambert (Plaintiff/Respondent), a former member of Fisherman's Dock Cooperative, Inc. (Defendant/Appellant) against the cooperative to recover the fair book value of his shares, which he was required to surrender to Defendant upon termination of his membership. At the time he purchased the shares in question, the bylaws of the cooperative provided that upon termination a member would receive the "fair book value" of his shares. Thereafter, and prior to Plaintiff's termination, the bylaws were amended to provide that a terminated member would receive the price he paid for his shares instead of their fair book value. At the time of Plaintiff's termination, the fair book value of his shares was greater than the price paid. Plaintiff argued that he had purchased the shares as "growth" stock, and that by changing the bylaws the association destroyed the "growth potential" of his shares, thus breaching its contract with him as a shareholder.

The trial court found for Plaintiff, and Defendant appealed. Reversed and remanded.

LABRECQUE, J.A.D.

The court below appears to have accepted plaintiff's theory as to the nature of his relationship with the association. It held that the provision in the bylaws fixing the amount to be paid an expelled member for his stock constituted a contract between plaintiff and defendant and vested in plaintiff certain rights that could not be altered without his assent. . . . He ruled that it made no difference whether the corporation was one formed [as a cooperative]; that the association's stock bore all of the essential characteristics of stock issued by corporations formed primarily for profit. We find ourselves in disagreement.

A cooperative association is a unique institution, differing in many of its essentials from a corporation organized for profit. The relationship between such an association and one of its members is in many respects the antithesis of that which exists between a corporation organized under the General Corporation Act and its stockholders. The latter exists for the purpose of making a profit for its stockholders and its activities are geared to the accomplishment of that end. The amount of dividends paid each stockholder, as well as the number of votes he may cast, depend upon the number of shares held by him. One may be a stockholder though he has never purchased the corporation's product or availed himself of its services—and never intends to. With certain exceptions not here relevant, the stock of such a corporation may be purchased, held and transferred without restriction and without the necessity of corporate approval.

A cooperative association, on the other hand, has been defined as a democratic association of persons organized to furnish themselves an economic service under a plan that eliminates entrepreneur profit and that provides for substantial equality of ownership and control. . . . In general, each shareholder has equal ownership and exercises an equal share in the control of the association, regardless of the number of shares of stock he holds. . . . By its very nature a cooperative is not designed to make a profit, and the return on capital, if authorized, is limited. . . . Usually, such profits as may be realized from the association's activities are proportionately divided among the shareholders on the basis of the amount of their patronage during the period the profit was earned. . . .

A significant characteristic of a cooperative is the right of the association to restrict ownership of its shares to those availing themselves of its services, to restrict the number of shares held by a member and to prohibit or limit transfers of stock. . . .

A cooperative may also specify how members may withdraw or otherwise be separated from membership, and the amount to be paid them upon such withdrawal or separation. . . .

From the foregoing it is clear that a cooperative association exists primarily for the purpose of furnishing services for its members. It is intended to continue to function, notwithstanding the withdrawal or expulsion of individual members. Unless and until liquidation takes place, individual members have no present possessory interest in the association's assets and may be required to surrender their shares to the association upon receipt of such consideration as may be fixed by the bylaws. A growth stock would be a rank misnomer for such a security.

Questions

1. What kind of a contract can there be between a cooperative and its members if the cooperative is permitted to change the terms unilaterally? Would an ordinary business corporation be permitted to do the same thing? Why or why not?

2. What does the court mean when it says that the members of a cooperative "have no present possessory interest" in the assets of the cooperative? Is this also true for the shareholders of an ordinary business corporation?

Why Cooperatives Are Organized

As previously noted, the primary purpose served by a cooperative is to pursue the mutual benefit of its members. Broadly speaking, then, cooperatives may be formed for the purposes of purchasing, marketing, or securing any of a myriad of financial services for their members. Their memberships may include consumers, businesses, or both, and their services may be available directly to members only, as in the case of a credit union, or to non-members as well, as in the case of many farmers' cooperatives. Regardless of the details of their operations, the purpose of cooperatives is to secure lower purchase prices and higher selling prices or other economic advantage by using the combined market power of their members.

Regulation of Cooperatives

There are numerous statutes, both state and federal, regulating cooperatives either directly or indirectly. Many of them deal with establishing cooperatives, others deal with cooperative operation, and several grant privileges, immunities, and exemptions to cooperatives that are not enjoyed by other business associations.

Almost all states have adopted legislation permitting the formation of cooperatives. State statutes usually permit both newly organized cooperatives and the conversion of other existing businesses to the cooperative form. Most of these laws are designed particularly to encourage formation of agricultural associations of growers and producers, and the cooperative marketing of agricultural and horticultural products.

Federal efforts directed at encouraging cooperatives abound. Within certain limits, federal law grants them exemptions from the application of antimonopoly, anticonspiracy, and antitrust regulations. Also, Congress has created the Division of Cooperative Marketing under the direction and supervision of the Secretary of Agriculture. The division's function is to render assistance to associations of producers of agricultural products and their federations and subsidiaries. In addition, Congress has authorized the creation of a bank in each farm credit district, and of a central bank for cooperatives. These banks are authorized to make loans for some purposes and to render technical and financial assistance to qualified cooperatives. Finally, Congress also has created the National Consumer Cooperative Bank to encourage the growth of consumer cooperatives by making and guaranteeing loans and rendering a number of other types of financial services. These include purchasing and discounting member obligations, and aiding members in obtaining private funds through the sale of bonds, notes, and other obligations.

As previously noted, because most cooperatives are organized as corporations, they are subject to a state's general corporation law. Thus the same rules applicable to other corporations apply equally to cooperatives. The same is true of general business laws. Cooperatives are accorded generally the same treatment as other businesses under statutes relating to workers' compensation, unemployment compensation, and other employment legislation. However, court interpretation of the common law of contracts often is more favorable to cooperatives involving contracts with members.

ORGANIZING A COOPERATIVE

The form of business organization under which a cooperative may be established frequently is provided by the statute authorizing that particular kind of cooperative. Otherwise, the organizers may adopt any of the possible business forms. As discussed earlier, the most commonly adopted is the corporate form.

Basic Organization

To form a corporation, it is necessary to apply for a charter under the laws of the state in which the cooperative intends to have its principal office. After the corporate charter is granted, the cooperative should register in other states in which it intends to do business.

The process by which a charter may be obtained, and the registration requirement, are discussed more fully in Chapter 40. Briefly, however, the following should be considered in drafting the articles of incorporation of a cooperative:

1. The state in which to incorporate;
2. names and addresses of the incorporators;
3. name of the cooperative;
4. purpose of the business;
5. powers;
6. compensation and terms of the board of directors, and names and addresses of the initial board;
7. requirements for membership;
8. voting rights of members;
9. stated capital;
10. number of shares to be authorized and their par value;
11. duration of the corporation;
12. disposition of assets upon dissolution; and
13. the process for amending the articles of incorporation.

Bylaws

The bylaws of an organization constitute a very important part of the charter application. The bylaws should contain the rules governing the operation of the cooperative, which either are to be temporary or which the members may wish to change in the future. Bylaws are just as binding on the organization as rules stated in the charter it-

self, but bylaws ordinarily are easier to amend. Some matters to consider for inclusion in the bylaws are:

1. Membership eligibility, fees, voting rights, and suspension;
2. membership meeting time and place, notification, quorum, parliamentary procedures, and limitations on business to be discussed;
3. director and officer qualifications, numbers, details of election, terms of office, powers, duties, responsibilities, compensation, and filling vacancies;
4. details concerning distributions;
5. rules governing dissolution; and
6. process for amending the bylaws.

Although amendment of the bylaws may be less complicated to achieve than a charter amendment, this should not be taken as encouraging sloppy drafting of bylaws. It should not be a simple process to amend the bylaws either.

DIRECTORS AND OFFICERS

The owners of a cooperative have the job of managing and operating the organization. To do so through a democratic process is unwieldy. Therefore, these functions are executed by delegating them to directors and officers.

Functions

The inherent power of members to manage their cooperative usually is vested in a board of directors. The directors, then, have control over the organization, including the general powers of management and supervision. The board manages the organization by establishing broad policy within which the day-to-day operating decisions are made. The latter usually are the work of the officers, who are appointed by the board. Having established policy and appointed officers, the duty of the directors becomes supervision. In some cases, the specific powers of cooperative boards of directors are provided by statute.

Liabilities

Because directors ordinarily are not expected to monitor every aspect of a cooperative's day-to-day operations, they naturally are insulated to some extent from liability for acts of officers and employees, who are liable for their own wrongdoings, as frequently is true of the cooperative itself. However, directors may become liable for a failure to meet their obligations of supervision and reasonable decision making. A director also may be liable for acting in his own interest and contrary to the interests of the membership (a breach of fiduciary duty to the organization and its members) and to some extent for the wrongdoings of co-directors.

Whether a director is liable for negligent decision making usually is determined by the application of the so-called **business judgment rule,** which is discussed more fully in Chapter 41. This principle provides an objective standard by which the reasonableness of directors' decisions may be judged. It provides that as long as a director has exercised independent and informed judgment, in good faith, and has taken action accordingly, she will not be liable even if the decision she has made

Cooperative membership (1985)

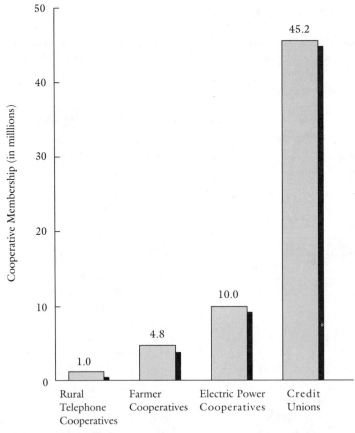

Source: Statistical Abstract of the U.S. (1988), Tables 833 and 1084.

proves wrong. Good faith by a director is presumed, even when making decisions in transactions in which she has a personal interest.

In most situations, a director is not liable for the wrongdoing of a co-director unless the director has failed to stay reasonably informed, or he has notice or knowledge of the wrongdoing and fails to act reasonably on that information. Of course, directors may be liable for any acts that are beyond the cooperative's articles of incorporation and bylaws.

MEMBERSHIP AND MEMBERS

The prerequisites for membership in a cooperative usually are prescribed by the statute authorizing its establishment. In most cases these qualifications may be further restricted, but may not be expanded, by the association's articles of incorporation and bylaws. In the absence of an expressed restriction on membership eligibility, a cooperative has the inherent power to do what reasonably is necessary to accomplish its legitimate purposes. This includes determining membership eligibility.

Membership normally is effected through application by a prospective member and approval of that application by the association. Membership is personal to each member and is not assignable, although certain rights of members may be, such as the right to participate in periodic distributions and to share assets upon dissolution.

Members' Rights

Members' rights may be established by statute, the association's articles of incorporation and bylaws, and by an agreement between the association and its members. Otherwise, members' rights are governed by the rules applicable to business organizations generally in the jurisdiction in which the association is organized. However, a fundamental right of all members is the right to proper notice of membership meetings and a reasonable opportunity to vote.

Among the other fundamental rights of members is their entitlement to have reasonable inspection of the cooperative's books and records. *Reasonable*, in this context, means that the request must be for inspection at a reasonable time and place, and for legitimate reasons that are not in conflict with the well-being of the association. Acting within these limits, a member also is entitled to make copies of the books and records.

Members may require periodic distributions of association profits. Ordinarily these distributions are in the form of patronage rebates of some portion of the prices paid on their purchases from the association, or in the form of patronage dividends that are proportionate to the use each member makes of the facilities. The manner in which payments are determined often is established by statute. As is true of distributions by ordinary business corporations, however, profits of a cooperative association belong to the association and not to its members until the board of directors, in its discretion, decides to distribute them. Also, any distributions, even after declared by the board of directors, are subject to the claims of association creditors in spite of the fact that distributions then belong to the members and not to the association. In effect, distributions may be claimed by association creditors until they actually are placed in the hands of the members, and members who have received advances in anticipation of a later distribution may be required to refund the money to pay creditor claims.

By retaining some portion of the profits of the association, a cooperative's board of directors creates a fund comparable to the earned-surplus or retained-earnings account held by an ordinary business corporation. This is an important method by which a cooperative may raise capital, and it has been held to be the most equitable of the options available because it is proportionate to the contributions of all members. Each member's share in the fund is evidence by equity credits on the association's books. These are not considered indebtedness of the association, and do not necessarily vest at a member's death. Instead, they may be distributed only at a time determined by the board of directors, or along with other assets upon dissolution of the association.

Members' Liability for Association Obligations

Members' liability for association obligations may arise out of specific constitutional or statutory provisions defining liability, the association's articles of incorporation or bylaws, the application for membership, an agreement between the members and the association, or a resolution adopted by the stockholder-members of a corporate cooperative. Otherwise, members of a corporate cooperative are insulated from liability to a great extent, and members of an unincorporated association have broad personal liability for association obligations.

Member liability for operating losses of an association depends on the association's right to assess members in order to increase working capital, and also may vary according to the nature of the relationship between the association and its members. The great weight of judicial opinion is that a cooperative has no inherent power to assess its members to cover operating losses, but that power may be granted in the articles of incorporation or bylaws, or by specific statutory provision. Further, courts in several states have held that a cooperative that has no capital stock may not assess members for losses even when the power to do so has been provided for in the articles of incorporation. This judicial viewpoint is based on the belief that in the absence of capital stock there is no fair way to assess members.

An association's right to recover losses from its members also may depend on whether the court finds, in the particular case before it, that the association was acting as an agent or a principal in its relationship with its members. If acting as an agent in disposing of members' produce, liability ordinarily may be imposed on the members. If the association was acting as a principal, purchasing produce from its members and re-selling it, there is no general member liability, although limited liability sometimes is imposed by statute. Usually, however, a cooperative association is considered an agent of its members in the absence of specific statutory or any other clear indication to the contrary.

There is little question concerning members' liability to association creditors. Members are liable for their *pro rata* shares of association debts, and a lawsuit to enforce that liability may be brought by a creditor, the association, association members, a receiver, or a trustee in bankruptcy. Liability may remain even after a member has terminated her membership to the extent that debts were generated while she was a member, and a compromise, or accord and satisfaction, between the departing member and the association has been held ineffective as against the rights of third-party creditors. In these respects, the liability of a member of a corporate cooperative is broader than that of a shareholder of an ordinary business corporation.

ANTITRUST EXEMPTIONS

Cooperatives enjoy limited exemptions from the antitrust laws by virtue of specific statutory provisions, such as those found in the Clayton Act and the **Capper-Volstead Act,** which authorizes agricultural cooperatives. The purpose of granting these exemptions is to enable members of cooperatives to reap the competitive advantages available to businesses acting through corporations. However, it is important to understand that these exemptions are not complete. For example, Section 2 of the Capper-Volstead Act empowers the Secretary of Agriculture to take action against an agricultural cooperative if he has reason to believe that the cooperative monopolizes or restrains interstate or foreign commerce "to such an extent that the price of any agricultural product is unduly enhanced by reason thereof."

In determining whether a particular cooperative qualifies for antitrust exemption, it is necessary to determine, first, that it is organized and is operating within the requirements of the statute under which it seeks exemption. These statutes usually specify the types of individuals and organizations that may be members, place limitations on voting rights of members (for example, one vote per member regardless of the size of that member's share in the association), stipulate the degree to which the cooperative may deal with nonmembers, and also may spell out other requirements. All of these must be followed scrupulously, and any failure to comply, no matter how small, may disqualify the cooperative for exemption, as the following case illustrates.

NATIONAL BROILER MARKETING ASSOCIATION v. UNITED STATES
436 U.S. 816, 56 L.Ed.2d 728, 98 S.Ct. 2122 (1978)

This was an action by the United States (Plaintiff/Respondent) against the National Broiler Marketing Association (NBMA) (Defendant/Petitioner) for antitrust violations. The activities of Defendant were of a nature that, if Defendant was a cooperative within the Capper-Volstead Act, Defendant was exempt from antitrust prosecution, as provided in the act. The United States contended that Defendant was not exempt because some of its members, who were packers and processors sometimes in addition to being producers, were ineligible because they were not "farmers" within the meaning of Capper-Volstead.

The district court dismissed the action, holding that Defendant was exempt, and the government appealed. The Court of Appeals reversed, and *certiorari* was granted. Affirmed.

BLACKMUN, Justice.

The Capper-Volstead Act removed from the proscription of the antitrust laws cooperatives formed by certain agricultural producers that otherwise would be directly competing with each other in efforts to bring their goods to market. But if the cooperative includes among its members those not so privileged under the statute to act collectively, it is not entitled to the protection of the act. . . . Thus, in order for NBMA to enjoy the limited exemption of the Capper-Volstead Act, and, as a consequence, to avoid liability under the antitrust laws for its collective activity, *all* its members must be qualified to act collectively. It is not enough that a typical member qualify, or even that most of NBMA's members qualify. We therefore must determine not whether the typical integrated broiler producer is qualified under the Act, but whether all the integrated producers who are members of NBMA are entitled to the Act's protection.

The Act protects "[p]ersons engaged in the production of agricultural products *as farmers, planters, ranchmen, dairymen, nut or fruit growers*" (emphasis added). A common-sense reading of this language clearly leads one to conclude that not all persons engaged in the production of agricultural products are entitled to join together and to obtain and enjoy the Act's benefits: The italicized phrase restricts and limits the broader preceding phrase "[p]ersons engaged in the production of agricultural products . . . ."

NBMA argues that [the history of the Act] demonstrates that the Act was meant to protect all those that must bear the costs and risks of a fluctuating market, and that all its members, because they are exposed to those costs and risks and must make decisions affected thereby, are eligible to organize in exempt cooperative associations. The legislative history indicates, however, and does it clearly, that it is not simply exposure to those costs and risks, but the inability of the individual farmer to respond effectively, that led to the passage of the Act. . . . Clearly, Congress did not intend to extend the benefits of the Act to the processors and packers to whom the farmers sold their goods, even when the relationship was such that the processor and packer bore a part of the risk.

Questions

1. As long as the cooperative was acting in good faith regarding membership, why should the fact that one of its members was an ineligible person cancel the entire cooperative's protection under the act? Isn't that unduly harsh?
2. The people Congress sought to benefit under the act were farmers. Why should the fact that a farmer also is a processor or packer cause the protection to be removed? Would it make any difference if integrating operations was shown to be a widespread practice among broiler farmers, and was necessary to remain financially sound?

Second, antitrust exemptions do not extend to contracts, combinations, or conspiracies with outsiders. These exemptions were granted so that cooperatives might contract freely with their members without risking violation, and might reap the fruits of these contracts even if the result was the creation of large, monopolistic power in a particular market. In effect, any concerted action with competitors, including other exempt cooperatives or other nonmembers, may be considered a violation if it otherwise would violate the antitrust laws.

Third, antitrust exemptions also do not extend to activities that may be considered predatory. For example, a cooperative may not lawfully fix prices at which its products will be bought or sold, control production and supply of products, or attempt to force eligible non-members to join the cooperative by force or threats of force. The purpose of the exemptions is to enable cooperative members to compete fairly, not to provide them with unfair competitive advantages or the power to force unwilling competitors to join.

Finally, it is important to remember that stat-

utory antitrust exemptions are in derogation of both existing antitrust statutes and the common law. As such, they are construed very strictly by the courts. Conflicting legislative purposes must be balanced, and courts will construe these exemptions no more broadly than is necessary to comply with legislative intent and other public policy.

SUMMARY

Franchising has been known in this country since the turn of the twentieth century, but has become widely accepted only in the last 40 years or so. It is popular as a method of doing business because it makes uniform products and services available to consumers on a nationwide basis, and permits aspiring entrepreneurs to go into business with limited financial and educational resources.

The simplest form of franchise is one in which a franchisor licenses a franchisee to market a product or service using the franchisor's trademark, trade name, or copyright, and the franchisee sees to the organization and operation of her own business as she sees fit. Most franchises are much more involved than this, however. Some obligations and limitations are placed on the parties by law. Most franchise law enforced by the states is the common law with the addition of some specialized statutes. Applicable federal law is primarily statutory, with provisions found in special franchise statutes and other statutes adapted to accommodate franchising.

The franchise relationship generally is entered into by means of a contract called a franchise agreement. Although franchise agreements are not uniform in their provisions, most include some provisions in common, such as those covering the payment of fees, the location and territory of the franchise, who has the duty to furnish facilities and equipment, the franchisor's obligation to provide such services as training and supervision, some provision concerning advertising, and the very important matters of duration of the agreement and causes for termination. The normal remedies for breach of the agreement are money damages and rescission, although other less-frequently used remedies also are available, such as restitution and reformation. In general, the rules of contract law are applied in cases of breach.

In most cases, a franchisee is considered an independent contractor in his relationship to the franchisor. As such, he seldom renders the franchisor liable on contracts with third parties (such as his customers), and rarely is there a basis for holding the franchisor liable for the franchisee's torts or crimes.

Franchising presents possible conflicts with antitrust law. Some of the laws that might be affected are those dealing with price fixing, territorial and customer allocations, and price discrimination. Franchises have no exemption from antitrust laws, and special attention should be given to areas of possible conflict both in the formulation of the franchise agreement and in the relationship between the franchisor and the franchisee.

A cooperative is a special form of business operation heavily regulated by statute, particularly on the federal level. Cooperatives usually are organized as corporations, although they may assume any other business form, such as a partnership. When organized as a corporation, a cooperative is regulated by general corporation law except to the extent that there are statutory provisions to the contrary. However, cooperatives are distinguished from ordinary business corporations by a variety of characteristics, including the voting rights of members, the distribution of profits, and the fact that most of the business transacted by a cooperative is with its members, for whose exclusive benefit it was organized.

Cooperatives enjoy limited exemptions from antitrust laws, as provided by various statutes, including the Capper-Volstead Act and specific statutes authorizing their organization. These exemptions apply to contracts between a cooperative and its members, but not to agreements with outside parties or to actions that would be considered predatory and violative of the antitrust laws if done by non-cooperative businesses. In order to be permitted to take advantage of these exemptions, a cooperative must be sure that it has complied with the membership and other requirements of the statute under which it seeks the exemption. Courts permit little if any variation from the statutes, and construe exemptions strictly.

KEY TERMS AND CONCEPTS

franchise
Automobile Dealers' Franchise Act
Petroleum Marketing Practices Act
franchise agreement
cooperative
business judgment rule
Capper-Volstead Act

PROBLEMS

1. In 1976 Imperial Motors entered into Direct Dealer Agreements for Chrysler and Plymouth dealerships with Chrysler Corporation. Although the agreements provided that Imperial would have the "non-exclusive rights" to sell Chryslers and Plymouths, Imperial was told, orally, by Chrysler's Area District Manager that it would have the only dealership in the surrounding towns of Myrtle Beach, Murrell's Inlet, North Myrtle Beach, and Little River. In August 1976 Chrysler allowed another dealership to move within the described territory. Imperial sued Chrysler under the Automobile Dealers' Day In Court Act for breach of the franchise agreement. Is Imperial entitled to judgment?

2.   In June 1963 Taute entered into a franchise agreement with Econo-Car International, Inc. to operate a car-rental business. In August of the same year Taute learned that certain material statements of Econo-Car's agent were false. However, she accepted her first delivery of rental automobiles in October, and continued in business for 16 months. During that period she said nothing about the misrepresentations and negotiated several changes to the franchise agreement. When she went out of business she sued Econo-Car for fraud in inducing the agreement. Is Taute entitled to judgment?

3.   In 1970 Quirk entered into an agreement with Atlanta Stove Works under which Quirk was to sell stoves in an exclusive territory. He was to be compensated on a commission basis determined by the volume of each product sold and shipped by Atlanta to Quirk's customers. Quirk was given a $1000 (later $1500) draw to pay expenses, and the amount drawn was deducted from commissions. Quirk also was given a car. When Atlanta terminated the relationship, Quirk charged a breach of state franchise law. Was the relationship between Quirk and Atlanta one of franchisor-franchisee?

4.   Cullen sued BMW of North America, Inc., when the owner of one of its franchises stole money from her—receiving a check for $18,245 from her and then failing to deliver the car. The plaintiff's claim was grounded on the negligence of the defendant in selecting its franchisee, particularly someone who was in shaky financial condition when that fact was known to the defendant. Is Cullen entitled to judgment?

5.   The Waverly Creamery Association was organized as a cooperative association. Its business was the purchase of milk from its members, which it processed into a number of products and sold to various purchasers. The bylaws of the association provided that members would be paid a fixed price each month based on the quantity of butterfat delivered. The price was subject to change upon agreement of the parties. When the association was declared bankrupt, the trustee in bankruptcy sued members to recover the difference between what they had been paid and the net of association gross receipts less expenses. In the trustee entitled to judgment?

6.   The Rockingham Co-operative Farm Bureau, Inc. was organized as a cooperative association under the Virginia Co-operative Marketing Act. It was authorized to sell agricultural products and supplies. The act provided, "The term 'agricultural products' shall consist of horticultural, viticultural, forestry, dairy, livestock, poultry, bee, and any other farm products; and the term 'supplies' shall include seed, feed, fertilizer, equipment and other products used in the production of crops and livestock and in the operation of farms and farm houses." The association sold gasoline, oil, hardware (heavy and light), salt, dry goods, groceries, crockery, glassware, boots, shoes, toilet articles, cosmetics, drugs, floor covering and carpeting, paint, automobile tires and tubes, and a variety of other products. Under the act, cooperatives were exempt from all license fees. However, the city of Harrisonburg sought to charge the Rockingham Co-operative with a substantial city tax. Is the cooperative entitled to exemption in light of the goods it sold?

7.   The Arizona Citrus Growers was an agricultural cooperative organized under the agricultural cooperatives law of Arizona. Twelve of its employees who were engaged in the manual work

of grading, sorting, cleaning, wrapping, and boxing fresh citrus fruits claimed unemployment compensation under the Arizona Unemployment Compensation Act. The association never had contributed to Arizona's unemployment compensation fund for these employees, because under the act "agricultural labor" was exempt. Were these employees exempt employees?

Government

Regulation

Part I of this book dealt with the legal environment—those aspects of our legal system within which all of us must live and work on a daily basis. This part addresses the regulatory environment, which is particularly important to business students. Much of the paperwork generated in business today is necessary in order to comply with regulations created by the federal, state, and local governments. Many of the rules by which business is conducted are those that are handed down, policed, and enforced by various administrative agencies. Chapter 46 looks at the nature of administrative agencies and their creation, procedures, and operation. Chapters 47 through 52 address the substantive law in some of the various regulatory areas—securities regulation, antitrust, and labor and employment.

Chapter | 46

Administrative Agencies

INTRODUCTION

One of the most distinctive characteristics of our country's structure of government is that power is divided among three branches: executive, legislative, and judicial. This principle is called the separation of powers; it is set out in the United States Constitution and the constitutions of the various states. How these three branches of government function on a day-to-day basis has a dramatic impact on businesses and individual citizens. But in today's world, we cannot begin to understand the actual workings of government without looking at what some writers and political commentators have called the "fourth branch" of government—administrative agencies. This is a "branch" that is not even mentioned in the United States Constitution.

THE RISE OF ADMINISTRATIVE AGENCIES

Administrative agencies are governmental agencies charged with the enforcement of particular legislation. They have existed in this country since our beginning as an independent nation. Until the end of the nineteenth century, most agencies were creations of state or local governments. This reflected the localized nature of the country's early economic and social life. As the nation's industrial and technological advances spread rapidly, however, it became obvious that action on the federal level was necessary in order to control what by then had become large-scale and far-reaching economic and industrial development.

All federal administrative agencies created prior to 1887 were "line" agencies. That is, they were sub-units of cabinet offices. For example, the Internal Revenue Service is a sub-unit of the Treasury Department, as is the Secret Service. The Federal Bureau of Investigation (FBI) is a sub-unit of the Department of Justice. The other type of administrative agency, the **independent administrative agency,** is not attached to a cabinet office. Instead, these agencies operate as independent governmental units, and frequently are designated as boards or commissions, such as the National Labor Relations Board and the Interstate Commerce Commission.

In 1887, Congress created the Interstate Commerce Commission (ICC) as the first independent federal agency. The ICC was established to regulate the railroad industry, and was followed by agencies such as the Federal Trade Commission (FTC), which was created in 1914 to control unfair and deceptive trade practices. These independent regulatory agencies represented Congress's first attempts to investigate and stop potentially monopolistic and improper business practices that were contrary to the free enterprise system. Today, in one way or another, administrative agencies regulate the food we eat, the air we breathe, and the water we drink; our drugs, housing, transportation, safety on the job, entertainment, health care, and television programs; how the products we buy are manufactured and marketed, how personnel are employed, how capital is secured, and much more. To understand this better, stop reading for just a few minutes and think about what you have done so far today, or even what you did yesterday. The meat in the

hamburger you ate had to meet standards that were established and enforced by administrative agencies, and the compact discs or tapes you played are copyright protected, with fees for their use established by a congressional body, the Copyright Royalty Tribunal. The radio station you listened to is careful to make sure that it meets all the requirements set out by the Federal Communications Commission, otherwise it might not have its license renewed, and of course you remembered to carry your driver's license when you drove to work or school as required by your state's motor vehicle department. Most of the things you do on any given day are affected to some degree by administrative agencies. And that is true whether we are talking about your business life or your personal life.

The division of law that concerns itself with the operation of regulatory agencies is known as **administrative law.** Understanding administrative law is extremely important in our modern business world. Without some knowledge of how and why agencies function as they do, it is very difficult to deal with the many forms, rules, and regulations that so significantly affect today's business environment.

This chapter will focus on federal agencies and the laws and regulations under which they operate. It is important to recognize, however, that administrative agencies also are found on the state and local levels. Many of those agencies follow the federal model, and some even regulate activities in the same general subject area, although usually they are responsible for implementing state and local law, not federal law. Areas in which there may be both federal and state or local agency activity include securities and banking, the environment, education, hospitals and health care, and consumer protection. Exclusive state or local authority usually is exercised in fields such as highway safety, pensions of public employees, unemployment insurance benefits, workers' compensation laws, zoning, and building construction.

Federal administrative agencies are created by Congress. Some of them are independent bodies, however, and operate separate and apart from any branch of government. At the federal level, the members of these agencies usually are called commissioners, and they are appointed by the president and confirmed by the Senate. Commissioners are removable from office only for cause. Other agencies are part of one of the branches of government, although most are executive-branch agencies. The administrators of these agencies also are appointed by the president and confirmed by the Senate, but they are removable at the president's discretion.

GROWTH AND DEVELOPMENT OF ADMINISTRATIVE AGENCIES

The Great Depression of the 1930s spurred tremendous growth in regulatory agencies, as New Deal legislation attempted to respond to the devastating economic situation of that period. Congress created agencies such as the Securities and Exchange Commission, the Federal Deposit Insurance Corporation, the Civil Aeronautics Board, the Tennessee Valley Authority, and the National Labor Relations Board with powers to regulate activities within their respective areas of authority. National attention became focused on business and economic regulation, and the role of administrative agencies grew and was established firmly during the next decades.

In the 1960s, the focus of regulation expanded to include social issues as well as economic matters. Concern over national problems of discrimination, poverty, and injustice led Congress to enact legislation to remedy those ills. Among the agencies Congress established to implement its programs were the Equal Employment Opportunity Commission and the Department of Housing and Urban Development. Emphasis on social concerns continued into the 1970s, and grew to encompass environmental policy, occupational safety and health issues, consumer protection, and energy development. The Environmental Protection Administration, Occupational Safety and Health Administration, Nuclear Regulatory Commission, Department of Energy, and Consumer Product Safety Commission were among the agencies created during that decade.

These agencies came into existence as a result of concerns for social justice and they have had, and continue to have, a dramatic effect on business. One consequence of that impact is a growing debate over whether economic regulation helps or hurts our ability to have an efficient and effective business environment. Partially as a result of concern over the cost of regulation and its impact on the ability of American business to compete in the world marketplace, there has been a definite trend since the late 1970s toward *deregulation* of business and industry. **Deregulation** occurs when government cuts back on or eliminates its economic regulation of a particular industry. In 1978, for example, the Civil Aeronautics Board (CAB) deregulated the airlines industry when it opened up competition in airline routes and allowed airlines to charge rates that were lower than those the CAB had set. Eventually, Congress acted to eliminate all agency control over both the setting of rates in this industry and the entry into new routes.

Despite criticism of the administrative structure, these agencies have enabled government to deal with complex economic, social, and technological issues. They bring flexibility to the regulatory process, allow decisions to be based on analysis of individual problems, and add considerable expertise to the decision-making equation. They accomplish all of this as a result of a delegation of power from the legislature to each agency, either when the agency is created or as part of a statute the agency is given responsibility for implementing. Congress may grant the agency **quasi-legislative power** in the form of **rulemaking** authority, **quasi-judicial power** through requirements that the agency hold hearings to determine whether a business or an individual has complied with the law (known as adjudication), and **executive power** by virtue of the agency's ability to investigate actions taken pursuant to statutory and agency rules and regulations. An agency may be given any combination of these forms of authority. The Internal Revenue Service and the Securities and Exchange Commission are examples of agencies to which all three powers have been delegated.

Now that the agencies are established as watchdogs over business and industry, is anyone watching the agencies? The answer is *yes*—no regulatory agency is left uncontrolled. There are judicial, legislative, and executive restraints on agency actions.

Judicial Controls

Under the delegation doctrine, a statute conferring power on an agency may be invalidated if a court believes that the legislature cannot delegate its regulatory power in that area, or the delegation is too broad. Delegations of power by Congress have been declared unconstitutional by the United States Supreme Court in only two cases, both of which occurred in 1935 and involved congressional attempts to deal with the Great Depression (review the *A.L.A. Schechter Poultry Corporation* case in Chapter 5). Since then, judicial emphasis has been on controlling the way an agency exercises its discretion rather than on striking down particular legislation.

When an administrative program is challenged, the court's main concern is to make certain that the fundamental characteristics of representative government are maintained. The judge generally will seek to determine if the statute contains sufficiently explicit standards to ensure that fundamental policy decisions are being made by elected representatives and not by the agency, and that there are procedural protections that will ensure representation during administrative rulemaking and adjudicatory proceedings. Probably the most important recent Supreme Court case raising the traditional delegation doctrine stemmed from Congress's passing the Gramm-Rudman balanced-budget bill in late 1985. A year later the Supreme Court concluded that it unconstitu-

tionally gave to nonelected administrators the hard policy choices that legislators must make when deciding which federal programs to fund.

Courts also exercise control through their powers of judicial review of agency actions, both in terms of rulemaking and administration. That subject will be discussed later in this chapter.

Legislative Controls

The legislature exercises control over administrative agencies through statutory provisions dealing with the appropriation of funds, appointment powers, and general oversight of government. For example, Congress can forbid an agency to spend money on a particular program, or may approve reduced appropriations for a given enactment; through its standing committees it oversees governmental functions and programs, and investigates agency actions; it participates in the appointment process by voting to confirm, or to deny confirmation to, presidential appointments; and it exercises a legislative veto over agency actions in some regulatory areas by requiring that final agency rules be submitted for its approval.

Executive Controls

Powers of the executive office relating to administrative law include the appointment and removal of agency officials, control of agency requests to Congress, direct participation in administrative decisions, and control of agency rulemaking. Involvement in agency rulemaking has become especially important since the implementation of Executive Order (EO) 12291 early in President Reagan's administration. This order, which applies to executive-branch agencies only, requires that for each rule it proposes, the agency must prepare an impact analysis that weighs the costs and benefits of the rule. This report is then submitted to the Office of Management and Budget, which must approve it before the agency can implement the rule.

Regulatory agency controls/restraints

Judicial Controls	Legislative Controls	Executive Controls
1. agency power may be invalidated (delegation doctrine) 2. judicial review of agency actions	1. control of agency funding 2. aproval of presidential appointments 3. ability to investigate agency actions 4. veto power over some regulatory areas	1. appointment and removal of agency officials 2. control of agency requests to Congress 3. direct participation in administration decisions 4. agencies must submit an impact analysis for each proposed rule, which is subject to OMB approval

THE BASIS OF AGENCY ACTION

Administrative agencies are created to implement the laws Congress has enacted. Because of this, their powers usually are defined specifically in the particular laws they are administering. In general, however, an agency will have both rulemaking and adjudicatory powers, as well as the ability to conduct investigations to carry out those powers. Federal agencies are required to follow practices mandated by the **Administrative Procedure Act (APA).** This act was passed in 1946 to ensure that all federal agencies act uniformly with regard to their basic procedures. The APA contains provisions that govern such matters as what an agency must do to promulgate rules, when a hearing is required, the mechanics of the hearing, who makes decisions and under what circumstances, and how judicial review of agency decisions is obtained.

Rulemaking

Rulemaking can be thought of as quasi-legislative action by the agency. That is, the agency is acting in a manner that will affect people in the future, and its conduct is based on policy considerations found in the particular law being implemented. The agency does this by adopting rules. For example, a rule might establish future rates in an industry, describe how a corporate or financial reorganization of a company will take place, or fix standards for permissible levels for the disposal of environmental pollutants.

Under the APA, rules are developed through either a very formal procedure consisting of a hearing and decision based on the material presented—**formal,** or **on-the-record, rulemaking**—or by a more informal procedure in which interested parties can present their views to the agency—**informal,** or **notice-and-comment, rulemaking.** Usually, informal rulemaking is used unless formal rulemaking is required. Rulemaking proceedings are initiated when the agency publishes a notice in the *Federal Register* (the federal government's medium for giving official notices) announcing its intention to issue a regulation. This notice must give the terms or substance of the proposed provision. The rule that is promulgated may be reviewed by a court if someone challenges it. The following case provides an illustration of court scrutiny of a rule adopted by informal rulemaking.

COMMUNITY NUTRITION INSTITUTE v. BERGLAND
493 F.Supp. 488 (D.C.D.C. 1980)

In 1977, Congress passed an amendment to the National School Lunch and Breakfast programs authorizing Bergland, the Secretary of Agriculture (Defendant), to regulate the sale to school children during school hours of non-nutritious food that was in competition with nutritious food. The secretary issued a regulation prohibiting the sale of certain non-nutritious foods on school premises until after lunch hours. The regulation was challenged by the Community Nutrition Institute (CNI) (Plaintiff), which criticized it for allowing the sale of non-nutritious food that is fortified and that contains saccharin, and by the National Soft Drink Association (NSDA) (another Plaintiff), which sought to prevent all aspects of the rule from being implemented.

GESSELL, District Judge.

For more than 30 years, Congress has recognized the desirability of providing school children with nutritious foods during the school day . . . It has long been recognized that foods sold in competition with the school lunch and school breakfast programs might impede the nutritional objectives of such programs, promote waste and confuse children as to the relative nutritional value of different foods [footnote omitted]. In 1977, Congress authorized the Secretary of Agriculture to regulate the sale of such competitive foods. . . . In conferring this authority on the Secretary, Congress expected and intended that new affirmative steps would be taken to restrict access by school children to foods of low nutritional value. . . . The legislative debates convey an unmistakable concern that "junk foods," notably various types of candy bars, chewing gum and soft drinks, not be allowed to compete in participating schools. [Citations omitted.]

The Secretary issued the regulation here under attack after two years of thorough examination and analysis. He had the benefit of elaborate input from representatives of state government, school systems, parents, students, citizens-at-large, and the potentially affected industries, as well as assorted health and nutrition experts. [Footnote omitted]. . . .

The supporting preambles [footnote omitted] are lucid and often persuasive. They reflect the exercise of judgment, a willingness to weigh alternatives, an appreciation of complexity inherent in the undertaking and an absence of preconception. The regulation is accompanied by explanations discussing with clarity and common sense many issues raised in the comments. Such supporting evidence reinforces the Court's overall view that the promulgation of the challenged regulation was done responsibly and rationally. In most instances, the claims of arbitrary and capricious action are wholly lacking in merit. . . .

The competitive food regulation was promulgated under informal rulemaking procedures of the Administrative Procedure Act. . . . It is established that such agency action deserves considerable deference when tested in the context of the rulemaking process. The regulation is to be set aside, wholly or in part, only if found to be "arbitrary, capricious, an abuse of discretion, or otherwise not in accordance with law." 5 U.S.C. s.706(2)(A). (citations omitted) Where as here, the interests at stake are not merely economic but include the health and well-being of children, thorough scrutiny of administrative action is both appropriate and desirable. . . . But in assuring itself that full consideration has been given to all significant factors, the Court need not find that the administrator's choice was optimal. So long as the decision has a reasoned basis and support in the record, the Court may not substitute its own judgment for that of the agency. . . .

[The court then reviewed whether the Secretary had acted arbitrarily in both his approach to the problem and his failure to address various criticisms or alternative proposals, and concluded that he had not. The court did, however, find that the Secretary failed to deal adequately with the issue of food products that contain saccharin.]

CNI expressed concern that the regulation authorizes sale to children of products containing saccharin. . . . Many children cannot read the statutorily required warning; others would ignore it. The proof before the Secretary was strongly opposed to the sale of such products.

The Secretary failed to deal adequately with the problem. He placed reliance on the fact that the Federal Drug Administration has not banned such products and ignored the congressionally mandated warning. . . .

In any event, the record is incomplete. The Secretary must make further analysis of this aspect. Evidence at hand suggests that the vast majority of saccharin consumed by school-age children is contained in artificially sweetened soft drinks. . . . On remand, the Secretary must justify, in health and nutrition terms, the continuing availability to school children of any competitive foods containing saccharin. His study must be completed and announced within one year from this date.

[The court dismissed both cases, denying NSDA's request for a preliminary injunction against implementation of the rule, and granting CNI's motion only with respect to requiring the Secretary to study the saccharin issue.]

Questions

1. What purpose is served by having a generalist judge review and sometimes reject an agency decision that presumably reflects the wisdom of experts?
2. Is it fair to say that this federal court is regulating the regulators? Who should regulate the court?

Adjudication

Just as rulemaking may be thought of as quasi-legislative action, adjudication may be thought of as quasi-judicial action. In adjudication, the agency is making a decision about a particular problem that has arisen under the statute. The decision then is applied retroactively to the parties involved in the proceeding. In accordance with the APA, the agency must conduct a trial-type hearing in which the affected parties participate. This is *adjudication* (also called *formal rulemaking*), and applies when a statute requires that the agency make its determination "on the record."

Sometimes agencies reach decisions through a process called *informal rulemaking*, which occurs when the agency's decision is not based "on the record" of a hearing. Unlike formal rulemaking, there is no APA provision governing this procedure.

The agency may base its decisions on material in the record or on information obtained outside of the hearing. This type of rulemaking, involving a combination of formal and informal procedures, has been called *hybrid rulemaking*. It breaks the overall process into two components—matters directly related to the individual charge (questions of fact) and those generally applicable to the type of circumstance involved (questions of law). The former are adjudicated formally, and the latter informally. For example, suppose the operator of a nursing home is charged with violating regulations established by the Department of Health. The existence of the rules and questions as to their interpretation, wisdom, and constitutionality might be adjudicated informally. The circumstances of the particular alleged violations, however, would be subject to formal procedures.

Most statutes provide agencies with both rulemaking and adjudicatory powers. The choice of which one to use in a given situation is made by the agency, and that decision can have significant consequences. Because rulemaking is more general, applies to everyone, and is prospective in nature, it enables the agency to establish greater uniformity in its decisions because it clarifies the law in advance. However, it also is a more time-consuming process and has more procedural requirements than adjudication, so that many agencies end up making policy through adjudication rather than rulemaking. But if an agency does that, there occasionally is a serious question of whether the action is fair to the parties affected by the agency's adjudication, either directly or indirectly. Because an agency's adjudication is applied to a past event, there may be situations in which a business is penalized for something it did at a time when the action did not appear to violate any rule or regulation. The issue of whether an agency can act by adjudication rather than by rulemaking was raised in the following case.

FORD MOTOR COMPANY v. FTC
673 F.2d 1008 (9th Cir. 1981)

The Federal Trade Commission (FTC) had taken action against a car dealer for giving credit to purchasers of cars it later repossessed. The FTC was opposed to this practice and used this adjudicatory proceeding to prohibit its use. The problem arose nationwide, because this was a standard credit practice throughout the car dealership industry. Ford Motor Company appealed the FTC decision to the Ninth Circuit Court of Appeals, which reversed the FTC's decision.

GOODWIN, Circuit Judge.

The narrow issue presented here is whether the F.T.C. should have proceeded by rulemaking in this case rather than by adjudication. The Supreme Court has said that an administrative agency, such as the F.T.C., "is not precluded from announcing new principles in the adjudicative proceeding and that the choice between rulemaking and adjudication lies in the first instance within the [agency's] discretion." *NLRB v. Bell Aerospace Co.*, 416 U.S. 267, 294 S.Ct. 1757, 1771, 40 L.Ed.2d 134 (1974). But like all grants of discretion, "there may be situations where the [agency's] reliance on adjudication would amount to an abuse of discretion. . . ." *Bell Aerospace Co.*, 416

U.S. at 294, 94 S.Ct. at 1771. The problem is one of drawing the line. On that score the Supreme Court has avoided black-letter rules. *See id.* at 294, 94 S.Ct. at 1772 ("[i]t is doubtful whether any generalized standard could be framed which would have more than marginal utility. . . ."). Lower courts have been left, therefore, with the task of dealing with the problem on a case-by-case basis. . . .

In the present case, the F.T.C., by its order, has established a rule that would require a secured creditor to credit the debtor with the "best possible" value of the repossessed vehicle, and forbid the creditor from charging the debtor with overhead and lost profits. The administrative decision below so holds. . . . [T]he precise issue therefore is whether this adjudication changes existing law, and has widespread application. It does, and the matter should be addressed by rulemaking.

The F.T.C. admits that industry practice has been to do what Francis Ford does— credit the debtor with the wholesale value and charge the debtor for indirect expenses. But the F.T.C. contends that Francis Ford's particular practice violates state law (ORS 79.5040); that the violation will not be reached by the proposed trade rule on credit practices; and that this adjudication will have only local application. The arguments are not persuasive. . . .

[W]e are persuaded to set aside this order because the rule of the case made below will have general application. It will not apply just to Francis Ford. Credit practices similar to those of Francis Ford are widespread in the car dealership industry; and the U.C.C. section the F.T.C. wishes us to interpret exists in 49 states. The F.T.C. is aware of this. It has already appended a "Synopsis of Determination" to the order, apparently for the purpose of advising other automobile dealerships of the results of this adjudication. To allow the order to stand as presently written would do far more than remedy a discrete violation of a singular Oregon law as the F.T.C. contends; it would create a national interpretation of U.C.C. s.9-504 and in effect enact the precise rule the F.T.C. has proposed, but not yet promulgated.

Under these circumstances, the F.T.C. has exceeded its authority by proceeding to create new law by adjudication rather than by rulemaking.

The order is vacated.

Questions

1. Why would the F.T.C. prefer adjudication to rulemaking as a means of establishing the principle involved in this case?

2. The court seems to be concerned about others in the car dealership industry who will be affected by this adjudication. How are their rights affected any differently if the principle is established by adjudication rather than rulemaking?

Investigation and Enforcement

Administrative agencies are powerful entities, owing in no small part to their ability to conduct investigations into individual or business actions and to force compliance with a regulatory scheme. An agency's investigatory power enables it to obtain information to be used in establishing rules or rate structures, or in documenting actions that are the subject of adjudicatory proceedings. In addition, many statutes give agencies the authority to require businesses to keep records of their activities in a prescribed form and to make those records available to the agency upon request. If a business fails to do so, most agencies have subpoena power and can order the business to turn over the desired information.

The Occupational Safety and Health Administration (OSHA) is an example of an agency that has extensive investigatory and enforcement powers. OSHA has issued detailed regulations concerning the records of workplace exposure and employee health that a business must keep. In addition, OSHA employees may make physical inspections of a workplace to determine if the business complies with OSHA regulations, and may order remedial action if necessary. Companies are protected against certain OSHA activity, however, since in most cases the agency must obtain a search warrant to conduct an investigation, and provisions exist for protecting "trade secrets." Other safeguards for businesses and individuals stem from the requirement that due process of law must be honored by the agency.

DUE PROCESS IN ADMINISTRATIVE AGENCY PROCEEDINGS

Due process guarantees that an individual has a right to be given notice of a proposed action and to have an opportunity to be heard whenever governmental action is proposed that affects that person's "liberty or property" interests. A "liberty" interest is one that involves not only a threat to personal freedom, but also action that may damage a person's reputation and make it difficult for that person to obtain employment or operate a business. For example, a restaurant owner who is charged with maintaining unsanitary conditions or serving adulterated food should be entitled to a hearing to clear his or her name.

A "property" interest exists when an individual has a legitimate claim of entitlement to something, such as to a job, or to a government benefit such as welfare or social security. If there is a liberty or property interest involved, the individual or company is entitled to a hearing. This would occur, for example, if an injured police officer had been receiving disability benefits, and those in charge of the disability fund determined that he no longer was disabled.

The type of notice and hearing depends on the interest that is affected, the risk to that interest if existing procedures are inadequate, and the burden additional procedures might impose on government. A decision of a high-school principal to impose a ten-day suspension on a student may be handled more casually than a decision of the Nuclear Regulatory Commission to close a nuclear generating plant permanently.

AGENCY DECISION MAKING

Knowledge of how an agency operates is of central importance in understanding what can and cannot be done within the administrative structure. The process by which an agency makes a determination in a particular adjudication or rulemaking proceeding usually begins with a notice of proposed action and a hearing before an **administrative law judge (ALJ).** The ALJ is an employee of the agency, but is expected to act independently in the conduct of the hearings and the issuance of his or her decision. Under the Administrative Procedure Act, an ALJ's powers include issuing subpoenas, ruling on evidence, taking depositions, administering oaths, and otherwise regulating the hearing.

In a hearing that is part of a formal adjudication, the ALJ who presides must make the initial recommendation on what action the agency should take. In rulemaking, a responsible officer of the agency makes this recommendation. In both adjudication and rulemaking, if the report made by the ALJ is not appealed by any of the parties, it becomes the agency's decision. Agency officials can overrule the ALJ, but the report must be part of the evidence the agency considers in making its final decision.

Most agencies have many functions and employ a staff that is competent to conduct investigations, pursue enforcement measures, and provide expertise on scientific and technological matters. For example, the Environmental Protection Agency employs physicists and toxicologists to evaluate suspected environmental pollution. One problem that agencies face is the various roles these different staff members play in the agency's decision-making process. In adjudicatory proceedings, there are sharp lines separating the ALJ, employees performing investigatory or informational functions, and those who act as prosecutors. In rulemaking, however, these distinctions are blurred, raising serious questions about when an agency can act like a judge, jury, and prosecutor. Courts distinguish among (1) agency staff who act as prosecutors, (2) those who help evaluate the record because of their expertise, and (3) those who perform the agency's investigatory functions. They assume the agency is discharging its duties honestly and with integrity, so a business or industry that believes the agency has not acted fairly because of this combination of functions has a strong burden to overcome in trying to prove its case. A more common situation that industry faces is the agency's attempt to use its own experts to supply scientific or technological information missing from the record. This generally is prohibited when the statute requires a decision "on the record," unless all parties have had an opportunity to see and comment on the information supplied by the agency's staff.

The idea that "on the record" means everyone knows what information formed the basis for the agency's decision, and is given a chance to respond to possibly detrimental material, also is behind the prohibition against *"ex parte"* decisions in formal proceedings. These contacts occur when only one side in a dispute provides material or information to the agency. *Ex parte* communications also may be an issue in informal proceedings, but they are not prohibited in that context. Agencies often find themselves involved in these contacts in the informal setting when the White House or particular congressional representatives have an interest in a proceeding and express concern or voice their opinions about what the agency is proposing. Agencies also find themselves besieged by industry lobbyists whose job it is to make sure that regulatory steps are not taken against their interests.

As long as the statute does not prohibit this type of contact, a court will not interfere with the agency's action. But this is not a blanket approval for a legislator to exercise political influence and pressure an agency to ensure a decision she desires personally or supports on behalf of a constituent. Particularly in the context of an adjudication, a court will overturn an agency decision if it appears that the agency considered political factors that Congress did not intend to be given weight when it passed the statute under which the action has been taken. In one informal adjudication in the early 1970s, a congressman threatened to withhold mass transit funds from Washington, D.C., unless the Department of Transportation reconsidered its decision to halt construction of a bridge the representative wanted built. The agency approved plans reviving construction, but a federal court ordered a rehearing to determine the factual basis on which the agency made its decision.

A very different kind of influence that administrative agencies confront stems from the role these agencies play in the functioning of government. As indicated at the beginning of this chapter, high-level agency personnel are appointed by the president, and generally reflect the administration's point of view on particular subjects. However, agencies also are responsible for implementing regulations that may have been put into effect under an earlier administration with a different attitude toward various problems. The following case provides an example of a change in agency direction concerning automobile safety.

MOTOR VEHICLE MANUFACTURERS ASSOCIATION v. STATE FARM MUTUAL AUTOMOBILE INSURANCE CO.

463 U.S. 29, 103 S.Ct. 2856, 77 L.Ed.2d 443 (1983)

In 1981, the Department of Transportation (DOT) reversed a previous agency regulation mandating that air bags be put into new automobiles beginning with model year 1982. The earlier regulation had been written to comply with the National Traffic and Motor Vehicle Safety Act of 1966, which required DOT to issue standards to ensure motor vehicle safety. The secretary of transportation reopened rulemaking on this issue due to what the agency considered to be changed economic circumstances in general, and due to the automobile industry's difficulties in particular. The agency eventually determined that air bags would not produce significant safety benefits, and that the plans of the industry to install seat belts in 99 percent of new cars would protect the public adequately.

State Farm Mutual Automobile Insurance Co. petitioned the Circuit Court of Appeals for the District of Columbia for review of the agency's decision. That court held that the agency's rescission of its previous rule was arbitrary and capricious, and therefore reversed the agency's decision. The Supreme Court, upon petition by the Automobile Manufacturer's Association, affirmed the Circuit Court's decision. A large part of the Supreme Court's decision contains an analysis of the appropriate standard of judicial review applicable in this case, followed by the Court's decision that the agency failed to provide a reasonable analysis of why the regulation should be changed. The portion of the Court's opinion excerpted here concerns its review of the Department of Transportation's power to revoke the regulation.

WHITE, Justice.

. . . [T]he revocation of an extant regulation is substantially different than a failure to act. Revocation constitutes a reversal of the agency's former views as to the proper course. A "settled course of behavior embodies the agency's informed judgment that, by pursuing that course, it will carry out the policies committed to it by Congress. There is, then, at least a presumption that those policies will be carried out best if the settled rule is adhered to." *Atchison, T. & S.F.R. Co. v. Wichita Bd. of Trade,* 412 U.S. 800, 807-808. 93 S.Ct. 2367, 2374-2375, 37 L.E.2d 350 (1973). Accordingly, an agency changing its course by rescinding a rule is obligated to supply a reasoned analysis for the change beyond that which may be required when an agency does not act in the first instance.

In so holding, we fully recognize that "regulatory agencies do not establish rules of conduct to last forever," *American Trucking Ass'n. Inc. v. Atchison, T. & S.F.R. Co.,* 387 U.S. 397, 416, 87 S.Ct. 1608, 1618, 18 L.Ed.2d 847 (1967), and that an agency must be given ample latitude to "adapt their [*sic*] rules and policies to the demands of changing circumstances." *Permian Basin Area Rate Cases,* 390 U.S. 747, 784, 88 S.Ct. 1344, 1368-1369, 20 L.Ed.2d 312 (1968). But the forces of change do not always or necessarily point in the direction of deregulation. In the abstract, there is no more reason to presume that changing circumstances require the rescission of prior action, instead of a revision in or even the extension of current regulation. If Congress established a presumption from which judicial review should start, that presumption—contrary to petitioners' views—is not *against* [emphasis in original] safety regulation, but *against* [emphasis in original] changes in current policy that are not justified by the rulemaking record. While the removal of a regulation may not entail the monetary expenditures and other costs of enacting a new standard, and accordingly, it may be easier for an agency to justify a deregulatory action, the direction in which an agency chooses to move does not alter the standard of judicial review established by law. . . .

"An agency's view of what is in the public interest may change, either with or without a change in circumstances. But an agency changing its course must supply a reasoned analysis. . . ." *Greater Boston Television Corp. v. FCC*, 444 F.2d 841, 852 (CADC), cert. denied, 403 U.S. 923, 91 S.Ct. 2233, 29 L.Ed.2d 701 (1971). We do not accept all of the reasoning of the Court of Appeals but we do conclude that the agency has failed to supply the requisite "reasoned analysis" in this case. Accordingly, we vacate the judgment of the Court of Appeals and remand the case to that court with directions to remand the matter to the NHTSA for further consideration consistent with this opinion. *So ordered.*

Questions

1. How "independent" are administrative agencies if federal courts are looking over their shoulders this way all of the time?

2. Is the Court telling the agency it cannot withdraw the regulation, or can the agency do something at this point to achieve its objectives? What can it do?

JUDICIAL REVIEW

Judicial review represents an important independent control on agency action by the courts. The statute that the agency is implementing may contain specific provisions covering the scope of a court's review powers, such as those found in the Clean Air Act, or review may be governed by the general provisions of the APA. In a few instances judicial review of some agency decisions may be precluded entirely. When agency action may be challenged in court, however, certain requirements always must be met.

Standing

Only those parties who can show that they will suffer harm as a result of the agency's action have a right to seek judicial review—**standing to sue.** This typically means that he must (1) suffer an injury in fact, and (2) arguably be within the interests the applicable statute sought to protect. For example, low-income families may be very interested in a lawsuit challenging a zoning ordinance that prohibits multiple-dwelling housing in certain parts of a community. Whether representatives of these families are allowed to join the lawsuit will depend on the court's determination of their interest in the litigation and the injury they might suffer as a result of a decision in the case. Some statutes specifically grant certain groups that have a close relationship to the subject matter of the agency's action "specific standing to sue."

Exhaustion of Administrative Remedies

Most statutes do not state at what point in the administrative process judicial review becomes appropriate. Courts usually are hesitant about intervening in agency proceedings and will not do so unless all administrative remedies have been exhausted. The factors that a court considers in this circumstance include the gravity of the harm that may occur without review, whether the question raised is factual or legal in nature (the latter being more appropriate for a judicial determination), the obviousness of the agency's error, and the impact of judicial intervention on agency functioning.

Ripeness

Ripeness is very similar to exhaustion of administrative remedies, but it focuses primarily on whether the disputed issue has been defined clearly enough for judicial review. In determining **ripeness,** the court looks at factors such as the nature of the issue and the harm to the parties that would result from denying judicial review. In general, a court will review an agency's rules before it has taken any enforcement action if the agency's action is considered final, if there is an interpretation of law involved, and if a party can show that compliance with the rule will cause hardship (as when large sums of money would have to be spent to comply).

Scope of Review

Once the court determines that judicial review is available in a particular circumstance, the question becomes one of the proper scope of that review. A court is given the greatest latitude when it is reviewing an agency's determination of an issue of law, particularly the statute the agency is empowered to administer. When the matter at issue concerns the findings of fact that an agency has made, however, a court usually will defer to the agency as long as the agency's decision is supported by at least **substantial evidence,** which means the agency had some rational basis for its decision or, as the Supreme Court has stated, "more than a scintilla but less than a preponderance." However, a court's decision on this question still may entail consideration of the relevant factors the agency looked at and of whether a clear error of judgment was made. When the court is reviewing an agency decision that was required to be "on the record," the standard of review may be more stringent and require that the record provide substantial evidence supporting the agency's action. This creates some problems in the context of informal rulemaking, when there may be only a very limited record, especially because courts are not permitted to add procedures to those that an agency already follows or conduct additional hearings. This restriction resulted from the Supreme Court's decision in the following case.

VERMONT YANKEE NUCLEAR POWER CORP. v. NATURAL RESOURCES DEFENSE COUNCIL, INC.
435 U.S. 519, 98 S.Ct. 1197, 55 L.Ed.2d 460 (1978)

The Atomic Energy Commission (now the Nuclear Regulatory Commission) instituted rulemaking on whether to include fuel reprocessing when considering the environmental effects of a nuclear power plant. The hearing held by the agency met the requirements for informal rulemaking under Section 553 of the APA.

The Natural Resources Defense Council, Inc. sought review of this rule by the circuit court of appeals, contending that the agency should have made the rule through the use of formal procedures in individual licensing hearings, and that the rule should have been applied to its previous decision to license nuclear reactors to be used by the Vermont Yankee Nuclear Power Corp. The court of appeals overturned the rule requiring consideration of the environmental effects of nuclear fuel reprocessing when considering nuclear reactor licensing, determining that the commission should have been dealing with this issue through individual licensing proceedings. Vermont Yankee appealed this circuit court decision to the Supreme Court. Reversed and remanded.

REHNQUIST, Mr. Justice.

. . . [A]bsent constitutional constraints or extremely compelling circumstances the "administrative agencies 'should be free to fashion their own rule of procedure and to pursue methods of inquiry capable of permitting them to discharge their multitudinous duties.'" FCC v. Schreiber, 381 U.S., at 290, quoting from FCC v. Pottsville Broadcasting Co., 309 U.S., at 143.

We have continually repeated this theme through the years . . . [I]n determining the proper scope of judicial review of agency action under the Natural Gas Act, we held that while a court may have occasion to remand an agency decision because of the inadequacy of the record, the agency should normally be allowed to "exercise its administrative discretion in deciding how, in light of internal organization considerations, it may best proceed to develop the needed evidence and how its prior decision should be modified in light of such evidence as develops." We went on to emphasize: "At least in the absence of substantial justification for doing otherwise, a reviewing court may not, after determining that additional evidence is requisite for adequate review, proceed by dictating to the agency the methods, procedures, and time dimension of the needed inquiry and ordering the results to be reported to the court without opportunity for further consideration on the basis of the new evidence by the agency. Such a procedure clearly runs the risk of propel[ling] the court into the domain which Congress has set aside exclusively for the administrative agency." . . .

Respondent NRDC argues that Section 4 of the Administrative Procedure Act merely establishes lower procedural bounds and that a court may routinely require more than the minimum when an agency's proposed rule addresses complex or technical factual issues or "Issues of Great Public Import." We have, however, previously shown that our decisions reject this view. . . . We also think the legislative history, even the part which it cites, does not bear out its contention. . . .

[T]his sort of review fundamentally misconceives the nature of the standard for judicial review of an agency rule. The court below uncritically assumed that additional procedures will automatically result in a more adequate record because it will give interested parties more of an opportunity to participate and contribute to the proceedings. But informal rulemaking need not be based solely on the transcript of a hearing held before an agency. Indeed, the agency need not even hold a formal hearing. . . . Thus, the adequacy of the "record" in this type of proceeding is not correlated directly to the type of procedural devices employed, but rather turns on whether the agency has followed the statutory mandate of the Administrative Procedure Act or other relevant statutes. If the agency is compelled to support the rule which it ultimately adopts with the type of record produced only after a full adjudicatory hearing, it simply will have no choice but to conduct a full adjudicatory hearing prior to promulgating every rule. In sum, this sort of unwarranted judicial examination of perceived procedural shortcomings of a rulemaking proceeding can do nothing but seriously interfere with the process prescribed by Congress.

Questions

1. Why does a court defer to an agency's fact findings?
2. Why is the Supreme Court so concerned about judicial proceedings that will supplement an agency's procedures?

THE FREEDOM OF INFORMATION ACT

On July 4, 1966, President Lyndon B. Johnson signed into law a bill that had passed the House of Representatives by a vote of 307–0. It was called the **Freedom of Information Act (FOIA).** The moving force behind passage of the act was the press, which believed that the information gathered by agencies should be available to the public. Journalists also were instrumental in getting twenty-eight states to adopt open-records laws during the 1960s. Among the earliest beneficiaries of the FOIA were consumer and environmental advocacy groups, which used the statute to obtain information about agency activities of importance to them.

The FOIA requires an agency to make available for copying and public inspection its records, opinions, statements of policy and interpretations, and administrative manuals or instructions to staff that affect members of the public. Every federal agency is covered by the act and is required to have regulations detailing the procedures to be followed by someone requesting information under the FOIA. An agency has ten days to respond to requests, and compliance may be enforced by the federal courts.

Most lawsuits under the FOIA are for the purpose of obtaining information from a recalcitrant agency. However, sometimes an individual or business seeks to prevent an agency from disclosing documents by bringing an action under the act. Some have been successful. The act does contain exceptions to disclosure, which include materials relating to national defense, law enforcement

actions, internal memoranda, reports on financial institutions, personal privacy, and confidential commercial or financial data of non-governmental persons and businesses. This last exemption grows out of a major fear of business leaders that the act will be used by competitors to obtain data otherwise inaccessible to them. The likelihood of competitive injury can justify an agency's granting confidential status to particular commercial or financial information, especially when sought by another business in the same industry.

SUMMARY

Administrative, or regulatory, agencies are created by the legislature to implement the laws it has passed. They exist on the federal, state, and local levels, and in many respects are the day-to-day functioning arm of contemporary government.

Agencies have both rulemaking and adjudicatory powers. In rulemaking, the agency adopts regulations that will affect people in the future and that are based on policy considerations found in the law being implemented. In adjudication, the agency makes a decision about a particular problem that has arisen under the law. Rulemaking may be thought of as quasi-legislative power, and adjudication as quasi-judicial power.

In addition to these powers, agencies also may have broad authority to investigate whether business is complying with a particular law, and to halt any noncompliance. OSHA is an example of an agency with extensive investigatory and enforcement powers.

Agencies usually make their determinations after a hearing by an administrative law judge (ALJ), who listens to all parties and presents a recommendation to agency officials for their implementation. There are other requirements that an ALJ or other agency staff may have to follow if the statute requires that a decision be made "on the record."

Agency staffs are subject to political and industry pressures, although this generally is not considered improper unless it results in the agency making a decision based on political factors that Congress did not intend it to consider. In addition, since agencies act to administer laws that Congress has passed, changes in presidential administrations may affect how agencies interpret and apply the statutes they are responsible for implementing. Agencies must be careful to act within appropriate bounds of the legislation being administered.

Judicial review is an important control over agency action and helps ensure that an agency does not become a captive of industry and political forces. A court may overturn an agency determination that it finds to be "arbitrary and capricious," and may require an agency to provide substantial evidence justifying its actions.

Finally, the Freedom of Information Act (FOIA) gives the press and members of the public who are affected by agency action the right to see agency records, opinions, statements of policy, and administrative manuals or instructions issued to its agency's staff. This is an important protection against arbitrary and abusive action by administrative agencies.

KEY TERMS AND CONCEPTS

administrative agency
independent administrative agency
administrative law
deregulation
quasi-legislative power
rulemaking
quasi-judicial power
executive power
Administrative Procedure Act (APA)
formal (on-the-record) rulemaking
informal (notice-and-comment) rulemaking
Federal Register
administrative law judge (ALJ)
standing to sue
exhaustion of administrative remedies
ripeness
substantial evidence
Freedom of Information Act (FOIA)

PROBLEMS

1. The Occupational Safety and Health Act authorizes Department of Labor officials to conduct inspections of business premises without notice. There is no express requirement for a search warrant. Pursuant to that authority, officials sought to inspect the premises of Barlow's, Inc., an electrical and plumbing installation business. Mr. Barlow refused to allow the inspection without a search warrant. Was Mr. Barlow within his rights?

2. The Economic Stabilization Act of 1970 gave President Nixon broad powers to freeze prices, rents, wages, and salaries to aid in the fight against runaway inflation. The act provided that freezes could not be set at levels lower than those on the date of the act, and all freezes were to be across-the-board unless it could be demonstrated that levels for particular industries were disproportionately high. When the president exercised his power concerning wages, a meat cutter's union objected and sought a judgment declaring the act unconstitutional as an impermissible delegation of legislative power. Should the union be given a judgment to that effect?

3. The Illinois legislature enacted the Currency Exchange Act, empowering the Director of Financial Institutions to set maximum fees chargeable for check cashing and writing money orders by currency exchanges in the state. This was the substance of the act, and it was challenged as an unconstitutional delegation of legislative power. What should be the result?

4. An Ohio statute provided that principals of Ohio public schools could suspend a student for up to ten days, or expel her, for misconduct. The statute provided for a hearing and appeal to the local school board in cases of expulsion, but made no similar provisions for cases of suspension. Lopez was suspended summarily, without notice or a hearing, under the authority of the statute. Lopez contended the statute was unconstitutional on the ground of lack of due process. School authorities contended Lopez had no right to due process, because attending public school was a privilege, not a right granted by the Constitution. What result would you recommend?

5. The Board of Zoning Appeals granted preliminary approval of an application for special exception to develop a mobile home park in an agriculture zone. Land owners in the area objected and filed suit in state circuit court for an injunction to prevent the approval from being finalized. The board contended the court had no jurisdiction to hear the suit until a final order was issued. Is the board correct?

6. Collins, an employee of MBPXL Corp., brought an action for fraud and outrage against his employer and a supervisor. The charges arose in connection with his firing, allegedly in violation of a collective bargaining agreement. The defendants contended the suit should be dismissed because it should have been brought before the National Labor Relations Board, and not the court. Is this contention correct?

7. The federal Black Bass Act forbids the transportation of black bass and certain other fish from a state if it is contrary to that state's "law."

Howard was convicted of violation of the act as a result of transporting fish from Florida, contrary to a regulation of the Florida Game and Fresh Water Fish Commission. Howard challenged the conviction on the ground that a regulation of the state agency was not a "law" of the state within the meaning of the federal statute. Is Howard correct?

8. Provisions of the Price Control Act required that each business under the act maintain certain records. Authorities examined Shapiro's records and, on the basis of information found there, charged her with violation of the act. Shapiro contended the information should not be used against her because it would be contrary to her constitutional right not to give evidence against herself. Is Shapiro correct?

9. A regulation of the Federal Communications Commission forbidding cable television broadcasters to air certain first-run movies until after they had been released for a specified period of time was challenged. The FCC justified its regulation on the ground that it was necessary to prevent "siphoning" of the movies. It reasoned that cable broadcasters would obtain exclusive rights to certain films, and they then would not be available for showing in local theaters. Is the FCC's justification sufficient as a proper reason for the regulation?

10. The National Parks and Conservation Association, a private organization, sought to examine records of audits on the bonds of companies operating concessions in national parks. The records were held by the Department of the Interior, which refused to allow the examination. The association sued for an injunction to permit the examination, grounding its request on the Freedom of Information Act. Department officials contended the information was within an exception to the FOIA for confidential commercial or financial information. The court granted summary judgment for the department and the association appealed. Should the judgment be affirmed?

Chapter 47

Securities Regulation

OUTLINE

INTRODUCTION

Early in the twentieth century, the large number of fraudulent sales of securities to unsophisticated purchasers prompted state legislatures to protect investors. In every state, laws were enacted to prevent fraud in connection with sales of debt and equity instruments in fly-by-night companies, completely speculative oil wells, and unexplored gold and silver mines. These laws focused on high-risk schemes and eventually became known as **blue sky laws.** That term came into general use after Kansas adopted legislation against promoters who would go so far as to attempt to "sell building lots in the blue sky."

Federal regulation of stocks and bonds began only after the stock market crash in 1929. The federal government concluded the public had to be protected against questionable and undesirable practices that had been uncovered by congressional studies. A series of federal regulatory statutes was enacted to provide investors with information so they could make informed decisions. The statutes also were designed to prohibit unfair, deceptive, and manipulative practices in the marketing of securities.

Securities regulation is a complex and highly technical area of law, much of which is far beyond the compass of this course. This chapter, therefore, merely will attempt to sketch the essential aspects of the subject to provide a background for understanding securities regulation and the impact it has on the business world.

FEDERAL SECURITIES REGULATION

The two most important federal statutes regulating securities transactions are the **Securities Act of 1933** and the **Securities Exchange Act of 1934.** The 1933 act primarily regulates the initial issuance of securities; the 1934 act primarily regulates the trading of securities after their issuance. Some other federal laws that regulate securities are the Investment Company Act of 1940, the Investment Advisors Act of 1940, and the more recent Securities Investor Protection Act of 1970. The **Securities and Exchange Commission (SEC)** was established under the 1934 act to administer the various federal securities laws.

As the titles of the 1933 and 1934 acts suggest, the object of the federal regulation is "securities." Corporate stocks and bonds are the types of instruments that normally come to mind when people speak of securities, but they are not the only types of instruments or contracts covered by the federal securities statutes. Section 2(1) of the Securities Act of 1933 defines a **security** in the following broad language: "any note, stock, treasury stock, bond, debenture, evidence of indebtedness, certificate of interest or participation in any profit sharing agreement, . . . investment contract, voting trust certificate, . . . fractional undivided interest in oil, gas or other mineral rights, . . . or in general, any interest or instrument commonly known as a security." The language used to define a security in the 1934 act is similar to that in the 1933 act. Many of the state regulatory statutes define the term *security* equally broadly.

This definition of a security has been interpreted by the SEC and the Supreme Court to include "investment contracts." If a contract involves an investment of money in participation with others in a common enterprise, and the profits therefrom are expected to accrue solely from the efforts of third parties, the contract is an **investment contract** within the meaning of the statutes. Examples of the many transactions that have been subject to regulation as investment contracts include sales of limited partnership interests, scotch whiskey receipts, franchises, live animals in conjuction with contracts to care for them, and, as is described in the following case, even citrus groves.

SECURITIES & EXCHANGE COMMISSION v. W. J. HOWEY CO.
328 U.S. 293, 66 S.Ct. 1100, 90 L.Ed. 1244 (1946)

The SEC (Plaintiff/Petitioner) brought suit to restrain W. J. Howey Company and Howey-in-the-Hills Service, Inc. (Defendants/Respondents) from using the mails and instrumentalities of interstate commerce to offer and sell units of a citrus grove development in conjunction with a contract for cultivation and marketing in violation of the registration provisions of the Securities Act of 1933. The District Court denied the injunction and the Fifth Circuit Court of Appeals affirmed the lower court's judgment. The Supreme Court reversed.

MURPHY, Justice.

W. J. Howey Company and Howey-in-the-Hills Service, Inc., are Florida corporations under direct common control and management. The Howey Company owns several large tracts of citrus acreage in Lake County, Florida. During the past several years it has planted about 500 acres annually, keeping half of the groves itself and offering the other half to the public "to help us finance additional development." Howey-in-the-Hills Service, Inc., is a service company engaged in cultivating and developing many of these groves, including the harvesting and marketing of the crops.

Each prospective customer is offered both a land sales contract and a service contract, after having been told that it is not feasible to invest in a grove unless service arrangements are made. While the purchaser is free to make arrangements with other service companies, the superiority of Howey-in-the-Hills Service, Inc., is stressed. Indeed, 85% of the acreage sold during the 3-year period ending May 31, 1943, was covered by service contracts with Howey-in-the-Hills Service, Inc. . . .

The service contract, generally of a 10 year duration without option of cancellation, gives Howey-in-the-Hills Service, Inc., a leasehold interest and "full and complete" possession of the acreage. For a specified fee plus the cost of labor and materials, the company is given full discretion and authority over cultivation of the groves and the harvest and marketing of the crops. Without the consent of the company, the landowner or purchaser has no right of entry to market the crop, thus there is no right to specific fruit. The company is accountable only for an allocation of the net profits based upon a check made at the time of picking. All of the produce is pooled by the respondent companies, which do business under their own names.

The purchasers for the most part are non-residents of Florida. They are predominantly business and professional people who lack the knowledge, skill and equipment necessary for the care and cultivation of citrus trees. They are attracted by the expectation of substantial profits.

Section 2(1) of the Act defines the term "security" to include the commonly known documents traded for speculation or investment. This definition also includes "securities" of a more variable character, designated by such descriptive terms as "certificate of interest or participation in any profit sharing agreement," "investment contract" and "in general, any interest or instrument commonly known as a 'security.'" The legal issue in this case turns upon a determination of whether, under the circumstances, the land sales contract, the warranty deed and the service contract together constitute an "investment contract" within the meaning of S. 2(1). The lower courts, in reaching a negative answer to this problem, treated the contracts and deed as separate transactions involving no more than an ordinary real estate sale and an agreement by the seller to manage the property for the buyer.

The term "investment contract" is undefined by the Securities Act or by relevant legislative reports. But the term was common in many "blue sky" laws in existence prior to the adoption of the federal statute and, although the term was also undefined by state laws, it had been broadly construed by state courts so as to afford the investing public a full measure of protection. Form was disregarded for substance and emphasis was placed upon economic reality.

By including an investment contract within the scope of S. 2(1) of the Securities Act, Congress was using a term the meaning of which had been crystallized by this prior judicial interpretation. It is therefore reasonable to attach that meaning to the term as was used by Congress. In other words, an investment contract for purposes of the Securities Act means a contract, transaction or scheme whereby a person invests his money in a common enterprise and is led to expect profits solely from the efforts of the promoter or a third party, it being immaterial whether shares in the enterprise are evidenced by formal certificates or by nominal interests in the physical assets employed in the enterprise. Such a definition . . . permits the fulfillment of the statutory purpose of compelling full and fair disclosure relative to the issuance of "the many types of instruments that in our commercial world fall within the ordinary concept of a security." [Citation to the House Report deleted.] It embodies a flexible rather than a static principle, one that is capable of adaption to meet the countless and variable schemes devised by those who seek the use of the money of others on the promise of profits.

The transactions in this case clearly involve investment contracts as so defined. The respondent companies are offering something more than fee simple interests in land, something different from a farm or orchard coupled with management services. They are offering an opportunity to contribute money and to share in the profits of a large citrus fruit enterprise managed and partly owned by respondents. They are offering this opportunity to persons who reside in distant localities and who lack the equipment and expertise requisite to the cultivation, harvesting and marketing of the citrus products. Such persons have no desire to occupy the land or develop it themselves; they are attracted solely by the prospects of a return on their investment. The resulting transfer of rights in land is purely incidental.

Thus all elements of a profit-seeking business venture are present here. The investors provide the capital and share in the earnings and profits; the promoters manage, control and operate the enterprise. It follows that the arrangements whereby the investors' interests are made manifest involve investment contracts, regardless of the legal terminology in which such contracts are clothed.

This conclusion is unaffected by the fact that some purchasers choose not to accept the full offer of an investment contract by declining to enter into a service contract with the respondents. The Securities Act prohibits the offer as well as the sale of unregistered, non-exempt securities. Hence it is enough that the respondents merely offer the essential ingredients of an investment contract.

Questions

1. Do you think the Supreme Court's decision in this case is sound?

2. Do you think Congress intended these types of investments to be regulated by the SEC?

3. What objectives and policies are served by federal regulation of investments as in this case?

THE SECURITIES AND EXCHANGE COMMISSION

As previously noted, the Securities and Exchange Commission was established by the 1934 act. This federal agency is composed of five commissioners appointed by the president with the approval of the Senate. The SEC administers the various federal securities acts, including three not discussed further in this chapter—the Public Utility Holding Company Act of 1935, the Trust Indenture Act of 1939, and certain aspects of the Bankruptcy Act. (The Public Utility Holding Company Act of 1935 regulates electric and gas holding companies and their subsidiaries and affiliates, to ensure compliance with certain geographic and corporate structural standards. The Trust Indenture Act of 1939 supplements the 1933 Act with certain additional statutory requirements whenever a distribution consisting of debt instruments is made. Under the Bankruptcy Act, which is discussed in Chapter 24, the SEC plays an advisory role in corporate reorganizations.)

The SEC's functions include adopting administrative rules to implement the federal securities laws, interpreting the securities laws by way of disseminating public information on general policy and issuing private **no-action letters** (in response to a private inquiry about a proposed transaction, a letter is sent stating that the staff will recommend that the commission take no action opposing the transaction), investigating securities law violations, and initiating formal proceedings when necessary. The major responsibilities of the SEC include: (1) requiring the disclosure of all material facts in offerings of securities that are listed on national securities exchanges and on certain securities traded over the counter; (2) regulating the trading of securities in the national and regional securities markets and in the over-the-counter market; (3) regulating and registering brokers, dealers, and investment advisors; (4) overseeing mutual funds; (5) investigating securities frauds; and (6) enforcing the

securities laws against violators by administrative sanctions and by seeking injunctions and criminal prosecution.

THE SECURITIES ACT OF 1933

The Securities Act of 1933 has two basic objectives. The first is to provide investors with a complete disclosure of all material investment information concerning the original issuance of a security to the public. The second objective is to prevent misrepresentation and fraud in the sale of securities to the public. The basic technique of the 1933 act is to require disclosure prior to investment.

The provisions of the 1933 act apply to all transactions made in interstate commerce. The SEC and the federal courts have given a broad interpretation to the concept of interstate commerce. Anyone using an instrumentality of interstate commerce, such as the mails or the telephone, as any part of a securities transaction, even if only for intrastate contracts, is subject to regulation under the Securities Act.

Basic Terms

The term **issuer** means any person who distributes or intends to distribute any security. For example, a corporation that plans to raise money by selling a series of bonds is referred to as the issuer of the bonds. Note that the term *person* in this context can refer both to natural and to artificial persons such as corporations, including corporations in the process of being formed.

An **underwriter** is a firm that contracts with the original issuer to distribute the securities once they are issued. The process by which the securities are marketed by the issuer to the retail investor is known as underwriting. Firms that buy from underwriters to resell to the general public are **dealers.** A dealer is "engaged in the business of buying and selling securities for *his own account.*" A **broker** is "engaged in the business of effecting transactions in securities for the accounts

Typical distribution of securities

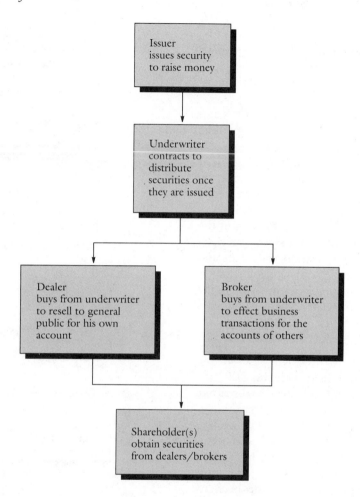

of *others.*" In practice, the same firms often act as both brokers and dealers.

Registration

The **disclosure requirement** of the Securities Act requires that before a security is issued, the issuer must file a registration statement with the SEC containing information about the security itself, the issuer, and the underwriter. The **registration statement** should contain, first, a description of the security that is being issued, including its relationship to the registrant's other capital securities. Second, the registrant must disclose the use to which it intends to put the proceeds of the sale of the securities. Third, the statement must be signed by the issuer, its chief executive officer, its chief financial officer, and a majority of the issuer's directors. The statement also must be signed by any expert who renders an opinion or provides information that is used to prepare the registration statement. Fourth, the statement must contain a description of the registrant that should include information about its business and assets as well as a description of the managers and their respective interests in the company. Material transactions of the directors and officers with the company also must be disclosed. Fifth, the registration statement should describe any pending litigation involving the issuer. Finally, the registration statement must contain a certified financial statement.

The public has access to the registration statements filed with the SEC, but the investing public typically acquires this disclosed information in the form of a **prospectus** made available by the underwriter on behalf of the issuer. It contains the most important information included in the registration statement. Under the 1933 act, a prospectus must be given to all investors before or at the time of sale or delivery of the newly issued security. In theory, the registration statement and prospectus should provide sufficient information for the investor to evaluate the risk involved in the security transaction. In reality, these documents are lengthy and complex, making them incomprehensible to most people.

HOW REGISTRATION WORKS. Before the registration statement is filed with the SEC, the issuer may obtain an underwriter to distribute the securities when they are issued. After the registration is filed there is a twenty-day waiting period before sales of the new securities can occur. Once the registration has been filed, but before the waiting period is over, oral offers for purchases of the securities may be made between investors and the issuer or the underwriter. During this period only very limited written advertising about the securities is allowed. A "red herring" prospectus may be distributed to potential investors during the waiting period. This type of prospectus takes its name from the red legend stamped across it stating that the filed registration statement has not yet become effective. In most cases, the red herring prospectus is complete except for inclusion of the actual price of the securities.

Once the waiting period is over, the registered securities may be bought and sold. "Tombstone"

Registration of securities

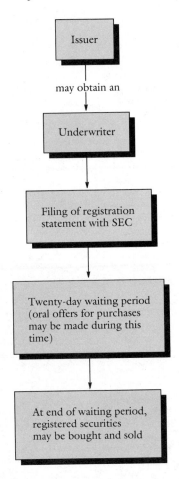

ads telling the investor where and how to obtain a prospectus generally are the only type of advertising allowed with regard to the registered securities. These ads, which take their name from their peculiar form, most often are found in business journals like *The Wall Street Journal*.

THE POWER OF THE SEC. The SEC does not have the power to approve or disapprove what securities may be sold to the public. The SEC's responsibility is to see that the requisite disclosures are made before the securities are distributed. However, if the disclosure requirements are not met, the SEC can prevent or suspend the effectiveness of the issuer's registration statement. Moreover, material omissions or misstatements on the registration statement or prospectus can subject the issuer to civil and criminal penalties.

The SEC has the power to reduce the twenty-day waiting period after the filing of the registration statement or any amendment thereto. Amendments, such as a last-minute inclusion of the offering price of the securities, normally will start the twenty-day period running again. Once a price is determined, a securities offering must be quickly brought on the market. This is necessary to enable the underwriter and the issuer to avoid major price fluctuations that could occur over the twenty-day waiting period. Thus, SEC approval usually is sought to get the waiting period reduced. This may not occur, however, because the commission can demand that additional requirements be satisfied. The SEC usually requires further changes or clarifications in the issuer's registration statement and prospectus, and the distribution of a preliminary prospectus to all underwriters and dealers involved in the offering, before it will shorten the waiting period and allow the registration to become effective.

The price of the securities usually will be added to the registration statement by an amendment just before the securities are publicly offered. If the SEC's additional requirements have been met, the registration will be accelerated and become effective immediately thereafter.

EXEMPTIONS.   There are two types of exemptions from the registration procedure required by the 1933 act. The first is for specific kinds of securities; the second is for certain types of transactions. Because of the time and expense involved in complying with the registration requirements, an issuer will attempt to distribute securities under an exemption if it is possible to do so.

Securities that are exempt include: (1) securities issued by banks, (2) securities issued or guaranteed by governments or governmental units, (3) securities of nonprofit charitable institutions, (4) commercial paper (notes or drafts) arising out of

current transactions if the maturity date does not exceed nine months, (5) securities issued by federally regulated common carriers, and (6) insurance, annuity, and endowment policies and contracts.

Also, transactions are exempt if they do not involve a public offering. Thus, transactions between individual investors generally are exempt from the registration requirements of the Securities Act. On the other hand, issuers, underwriters, dealers, and those who are in control of issuers are not exempt and may not be able to sell their securities without complying with the registration requirements. Whether a particular transaction is a public offering is a question of fact. A court will look at a number of factors to determine the character of the offer in question. For example, the court will examine the way in which the offer was made, the number of offerees, the size of the offer, the availability of material information about the securities being offered, the need to protect the investors involved, and the marketability of the securities.

There are three types of exempt transactions that are of special importance—private offerings, small offerings, and intrastate offerings. If a transaction meets the guidelines established by the SEC for any of these types of offers, the commission will not challenge the distribution.

Private Offerings.   A private offering following the guidelines set forth in SEC Rule 506 will be exempt from the registration disclosure procedures. The requirements for a **private offering** are that: (1) no offer can be made to the public; (2) the offer is open to any number of "accredited" investors but is limited to thirty-five other "sophisticated" purchasers; (3) the same information that would be contained in a registration statement must be available to any of the offerees; and (4) the seller must exercise reasonable care to protect against purchases of the securities for resale rather than for investment.

Basically, *accredited investors* are those that meet defined standards indicating investment experience and ability to assume economic risk. The *sophisticated investor* standard is defined less stringently, but still requires a knowledgeable purchaser. There are two different methods by which the seller assures that the buyer is purchasing the securities as an investment rather than for resale. The first is to require a letter from the purchaser stating that the purpose of purchase is for investment only (an investment letter). The second method is to place a restrictive legend on the stock certificate indicating that it is a restricted security.

Small Offerings. There are several SEC rules under which a small issue of securities may be sold without complying with registration requirements. Under the SEC's Regulation D there are two **small-issue exemptions.** Rule 504 provides an exemption for offers and sales of up to $5 million worth of securities during any one-year period. This exemption is not available to companies that report under the 1934 act. Rule 505 provides an exemption for offers and sales of up to $5 million worth of securities to an unlimited number of accredited investors and up to thirty-five non-accredited purchasers during any one year period.

Intrastate Offerings. The **intrastate offering exemption** is available only on securities offered and sold to residents of a single state when the issuer also resides in and does business in that state. SEC Rule 147 provides criteria to ensure that an offer qualifies for this exemption. No part of the securities issue may be offered or sold to nonresidents within nine months from the date of the original distribution. The issuer must be incorporated in the selling state if it is a corporation. For an issuer to be doing business in a state, 80 percent of its proceeds must be used within the state. This exemption is applied strictly; if even a single offeree is a nonresident, the exemption is lost. As is the case with many private offerings, issuers often require an investment letter or place a legend indicating a restriction on the stock certificate.

Restricted Securities. Securities that are not registered but are obtained through exempt offerings are considered **restricted securities.** They may not be bought and sold in the same manner as registered securities. Thus, if an investor is ever to realize a profit on her investment, there must be some means to dispose of the securities. That is provided by SEC Rule 144, which permits restricted securities to be resold if they have been held for two years, adequate public information about the issuer is available, and the volume of sales is limited.

Anti-fraud Provisions. Even though a security or certain types of transactions may be exempt from the registration requirements of the 1933 act, there is no exemption from the anti-fraud provisions contained in Section 12 of the statute. In addition, state regulatory requirements still must be honored.

The principal **anti-fraud provision** of the Securities Act is Section 12. Section 12(1) provides that anyone who offers or sells a security in violation of the registration provisions is strictly liable to the person who purchases that security. Section 12(2) is a general anti-fraud civil liability provision under which any person who offers to sell or sells a security by means of a written or oral communication that contains any untrue statement of material fact, or that omits or fails to state a material fact, may be held civilly liable for damages. Section 12 applies to offers or sales only; it does not apply to statements by purchasers.

Section 11 of the act imposes civil liability for material misstatements or omissions in the registration statement or prospectus. Every person who signed the registration statement, all directors of the issuer, and the underwriters are subject to liability for materially false statements or omissions. Any defendant except the issuer may assert as a defense that he exercised due diligence. If the defendant shows that after reasonable investigation he believed, and had reasonable grounds to believe, that the material contained in the registration statement was correct and without material omissions, that defendant has shown due diligence and is excused from liability. How heavy a burden of proof is required varies with the defendant and type of material at issue.

Section 17 of the act makes it unlawful, in the offer or sale of securities in interstate commerce, for anyone (1) to employ any device or scheme to defraud, (2) to obtain property by an untrue statement or omission of material fact, or (3) to engage in a practice or course of business to defraud purchasers. This section is enforced through injunctions and criminal penalties, and some courts have permitted private damage actions.

THE SECURITIES EXCHANGE ACT OF 1934

The Securities Exchange Act of 1934 was enacted to regulate securities transactions after the original issuance. The 1934 act provides for the regulation of brokers and dealers and the securities exchanges and markets. Through self-regulatory organizations, disclosure procedures, and the Securities Exchange Commission's oversight of the marketplace, Congress hoped to prevent fraud and manipulation in securities trading.

To distinguish the two key federal statutes, the 1933 act provides for disclosure by the registration of transactions involving the initial issuance of securities, and the 1934 act requires the registration of all of a company's securities that are traded in the securities markets. The 1934 act focuses on the companies that issued the securities under its disclosure requirements and requires periodic reports from these companies. The 1934 act also regulates corporate proxy statements, proxy contests, and tender offers. Finally, the act seeks to prevent insider trading, by which people close to the corporation use information gained from their positions for financial gain to the detriment of other security holders.

Registration

The Securities Exchange Act requires all brokers and dealers in securities to register with the SEC unless exempted by the commission. Stock exchanges also must register with the SEC. Much of the actual policing of these two groups is done by self-regulatory organizations such as the National Association of Securities Dealers (NASD) and the stock exchanges themselves. The SEC maintains a surpervisory or oversight role over these national securities associations and stock exchanges. To enforce the 1934 act, the SEC has been given the authority to suspend brokers or dealers or to force rules changes on the securities exchanges.

Section 12 of the 1934 act requires corporations having total assets exceeding $3 million and a class of equity securities held by more than 500 persons to register these securities. Registered securities may be traded freely by investors. The information that is provided in the registration statement is similar to that provided under the 1933 act. Companies with securities that are listed on a stock exchange also must register with the SEC. Finally, companies that have securities traded on the over-the-counter market must comply with the registration requirements if the issuer has gross assets greater than $1 million and more than 500 shareholders. These registrants must provide the SEC with current information by filing periodic reports.

Periodic Reports

Issuers who must register their securities under the 1934 act also must file periodic reports with the SEC. The different reports include an annual report (Form 10-K), a quarterly report (Form 10-Q), and, when applicable, a current report (Form 8-K). The information from these reports is intended to keep the registration statement up to date.

The **Form 10-K** must contain audited financial statements on the present fiscal year and current information concerning the corporation, its operations, legal proceedings, and the condition of its securities. The Form 10-K also should contain a summary of the last five fiscal years of operation and a listing of affiliated companies. This report, like the registration statement, must be signed by a majority of the board of directors.

The Form 10-Q report requires only a quarterly summary of operations and an unaudited operating statement. This report also must contain figures on the corporation's capitalization. The Form 8-K is required within ten days of the end of the month in which certain specified, materially important events occur, such as a merger or a settlement of a major lawsuit.

Annual Shareholder Report

The 1934 act requires that an **annual report** be sent to shareholders by every corporation registered under the act. This report also must be filed with the SEC. The purpose of these requirements is to provide a greater disclosure of the company's financial position to its shareholders. Annual reports include information about the last two fiscal years, and reflect the results of business operations and the corporation's financial picture. The reports include much of the same information found in the Form 10-K, but in a more summary form. Corporations also are required to list the names of corporate directors and executive officers and their positions and occupations. The report also must state the annual range of trading prices for the company's shares, the amount of dividends paid, and an offer to provide a copy of the Form 10-K filed with the SEC upon request.

Proxy Statements

Section 14 of the 1934 act requires a corporation registered under the act to furnish a **proxy statement** along with any request for a proxy it solicits for a shareholder meeting. If the corporation does not solicit proxies it must send an "information statement" containing much the same informa-

tion to all shareholders entitled to vote at the meeting. The proxy or information statement must be filed with the SEC at least ten days before it is sent to shareholders. If the statement is in connection with an annual meeting of shareholders at which directors are to be elected, an annual report must be sent to the shareholders before the statement is sent.

The SEC requires certain disclosures to be made in proxy solicitation materials to permit shareholders to make informed choices in voting on resolutions or for directors. They must indicate in whose behalf the proxy is being solicited. The shareholder must be able to vote for, against, or to abstain from voting on any resolution on the meeting agenda by means of the proxy. If there are material misstatements or omissions in the proxy solicitation materials, a court can enjoin the meeting or cancel any action taken at it.

Proxy Contests

A **proxy contest** occurs when a shareholder decides to solicit votes in competition with the current management's position. This type of solicitation is regulated by the SEC, as are corporate management's solicitation efforts. In order to assist these contests and to make sure they are conducted fairly, the SEC requires the corporation either to mail the competing proxy material or to furnish a shareholder list to those shareholders attempting to wage a proxy contest. Management generally is reimbursed by the corporation for proxy expenses. Insurgents are reimbursed for the costs of proxy solicitations only if they are successful.

Other Proxy Considerations

Shareholder resolutions provide another means by which shareholders may propose a course of action to the rest of the corporation's shareholders. A resolution, and a short statement by the resolution's proponent, may be required to be included in management's proxy statement under highly detailed SEC rules.

The courts have permitted private lawsuits under Section 14(a) for violations of the 1934 act's proxy requirements. SEC Rule 14a-9 is a general anti-fraud provision similar to Rule 10b-5 (dis-

cussed later in the chapter). Fraud, manipulation, and material misrepresentations or omissions in proxy materials may be remedied in civil suits brought by private plaintiffs. The following case details this type of action.

TSC INDUSTRIES, INC. v. NORTHWAY, INC.
426 U.S. 438, 96 S.Ct. 2126, 48 L.Ed.2d 757 (1976)

The facts of this case are stated in the Court's opinion.

MARSHALL, Justice.

. . . We are called upon to consider the definition of a material fact under those rules, and the appropriateness of resolving the question of materiality by summary judgment in this case.

The dispute in this case centers on the acquisition of petitioner TSC Industries, Inc., by petitioner National Industries, Inc. . . . On October 16, 1969, the TSC board . . . approved a proposal to liquidate and sell all of TSC's assets to National. The proposal in substance provided for the exchange of TSC common and Series 1 preferred stock for National Series B preferred stock and warrants. On November 12, 1969, TSC and National issued a joint proxy statement to their shareholders, recommending approval of the proposal. The proxy solicitation was successful, TSC was placed in liquidation and dissolution, and the exchange of shares was effected.

This is an action brought by respondent Northway, a TSC shareholder, against TSC and National, claiming that their joint proxy statement was incomplete and materially misleading in violation of Section 14(a) of the Securities Exchange Act of 1934. . . . The basis of Northway's claim under Rule 14a-3 is that TSC and National failed to state in the proxy statement that [a previous] transfer of the Schmidt interests in TSC to National had given National control of TSC. The Rule 14a-9 claim, insofar as it concerns us, is that TSC and National omitted from the proxy statement material facts relating to the degree of National's control over TSC and the favorability of the terms of the proposal to TSC shareholders. . . .

. . . We now have noted on more than one occasion, Section 14(a) of the Securities Exchange Act "was intended to promote 'the free exercise of the voting rights of stockholders' by ensuring that proxies would be solicited with 'explanation to the stockholder of the real nature of the questions for which authority to cast his vote is sought.'" Mills v. Electric Auto-Lite Co., 396 U.S. 375, 381 (1970). . . . In a suit challenging the sufficiency under Section 14(a) and Rule 14a-9 of a proxy statement soliciting votes in favor of a merger, we held [in Mills] that there was no need to demonstrate that the alleged defect in the proxy statement actually had a decisive effect on the voting. So long as the misstatement or omission was material, the causal relation between violation and injury is sufficiently established, we concluded, if "the proxy solicitation itself . . . was an essential link in the accomplishment of the transaction." . . .

The question of materiality, it is universally agreed, is an objective one, involving the significance of an omitted or misrepresented fact to a reasonable investor. Variations in the formulation of a general test of materiality occur in the articulation of just how significant a fact must be or, put another way, how certain it must be that the fact would affect a reasonable investor's judgment.

. . . In formulating a standard of materiality under Rule 14a-9, we are guided, of course, by . . . the Rule's broad remedial purpose. That purpose is not merely to ensure by judicial means that the transaction, when judged by its real terms, is fair and otherwise adequate, but to ensure disclosures by corporate management in order to enable the shareholders to make an informed choice. . . . As an abstract proposition, the most desirable role for a court in a suit of this sort, coming after the consummation of the proposed transaction, would perhaps be to determine whether in fact the proposal would have been favored by the shareholders and consummated in the absence of any misstatement or omission. But . . . such matters are not subject to determination with certainty. Doubts as to the critical nature of information misstated or omitted will be commonplace. And particularly in view of the prophylactic purpose of the Rule and the fact that the content of the proxy statement is within management's control, it is appropriate that these doubts be resolved in favor of those the statute is designed to protect. . . .

The general standard of materiality that we think best comports with the policies of Rule 14a-9 is as follows: An omitted fact is material if there is a substantial likelihood that a reasonable shareholder would consider it important in deciding how to vote. . . . It does not require proof of a substantial likelihood that disclosure of the omitted fact would have caused the reasonable investor to change his vote. What the standard does contemplate is a showing of a substantial likelihood that, under all the circumstances, the omitted fact would have assumed actual significance in the deliberations of the reasonable shareholder. Put another way, there must be a substantial likelihood that the disclosure of the omitted fact would have been viewed by the reasonable investor as having significantly altered the "total mix" of information made available.

[The Court went on to hold that the omissions concerning the degree of National's control over TSC and the favorability of the terms of the proposed transaction to TSC shareholders were not materially misleading "as a matter of law," which made the granting of summary judgment improper. The Court reversed so the case could be tried before a jury.]

Questions

1. What is the purpose of allowing private lawsuits under Section 14(a) if the SEC is supervising the enforcement of the proxy provisions?

2. How significant to the average investor is the availability of all of the intricate information that the statute requires be furnished? Is the cost of complying with the information requirement of the act and their enforcement worthwhile?

Insider Trading

In recent years there has been enormous attention paid to many of the practices of the wheeler-dealer types in the investment community. One of the most commented-upon practices has been the making of vast sums of money by purchasing and selling stocks based on corporate information not known by the general public. Thus, the media paid special attention to Ivan Boesky, one of Wall Street's most successful investors, when the federal government prosecuted him for **insider trading.** Boesky eventually plea bargained, gave information on other illegal traders, and was sent to prison.

There are two basic methods preventing people from trading on inside information under the 1934 act—Section 16(b) and Rule 10b-5. Section 16(b) operates automatically and applies only to corporate insiders to eliminate short-swing profits. Rule 10b-5, on the other hand, is a flexible, general anti-fraud provision that applies to anyone having access to or receiving material inside information from someone having access to it.

SECTION 16.   **Section 16** of the Securities Exchange Act is designed to prevent abuse of inside information in stock trading by corporate insiders, officers, and other informed corporate employees. The provision seeks to prevent profits being made by insiders on short-term trading, called *short-swing* transactions. Section 16(a) applies to all officers, directors, and beneficial owners of ten percent or more of any class of equity securities of companies with securities registered under Section 12 of the 1934 act. It requires them to report transactions in the company's securities to the SEC within ten days of the end of the month in which these transactions occurred.

Section 16(b) provides that any profit made by an insider (a director, officer, or ten-percent-beneficial owner) belongs to the corporation if the profit was made by either a purchase or sale of the corporation's securities within a time period of less than six months. There is no defense to this action; the statute applies mechanically to every transaction within its definition. In other words, it does not matter if the insider actually had access to inside information or not. Since the provision is designed to remove the temptation to use inside information to make short-term profits, the insider's intent is ignored. Under this section, either the corporation or a security holder of the corporation (derivative suit) may sue to recover the profits for the corporation.

RULE 10b-5.   Section 10 is the general anti-fraud provision contained in the 1934 act. However, this section is not self-implementing. Thus, the SEC has issued regulations to carry out the purpose of Section 10(b). The broadest and most important rule issued by the SEC under Section 10 is **Rule 10b-5,** which makes three types of activities unlawful: (1) using any device, artifice, or scheme to defraud, (2) making any untrue statement of material fact or omitting any statement of material fact, and (3) engaging in any course of conduct that operates as a fraud or deceit. The rule is applicable to all types of securities transactions, including transactions in nonregistered securities. The courts have interpreted Rule 10b-5 broadly and, since 1946, have recognized that the actual buyers and seller of the stock have a right to sue for damages. As a result, there has been considerable private litigation under the rule.

The rule has been used to attack both deceptive practices and the lack of adequate information for the investor. False or misleading statements, or a failure to file or provide information as required by the SEC and the federal statutes, may be violations of Rule 10b-5. To recover under the rule there must be a deceptive or defrauding action relating to the sale or purchase of securities, it must be shown that an omitted or misstated fact is material, and that at least one person actually sought to deceive or to manipulate another.

Trading on inside information commonly is attacked under Rule 10b-5. Many cases have involved concealment or failure to disclose material information in a transaction between an insider and another. Others have involved trading that did not involve face-to-face transactions, but rather consisted of trading on an exchange by insiders in possession of material, non-disclosed information. Under Rule 10b-5 persons having access to material information that has not been made public are *insiders*. Persons to whom this material is communicated are called *tippees*. Both insiders and tippees are liable under Rule 10b-5 if they trade in securities that they have inside information about without disclosing that information. The SEC has broad power to seek civil remedies and criminal sanctions against someone who violates the anti-fraud provisions of the law. The following case addressed the question of just who owes a duty to disclose before trading.

CHIARELLA v. UNITED STATES
445 U.S. 222, 100 S.Ct. 1108, 63 L.Ed.2d 348 (1980)

[The facts of this case are stated in the Court's opinion.]

POWELL, Justice.

The question in this case is whether a person who learns from the confidential documents of one corporation that it is planning an attempt to secure control of a second corporation violates Section 10(b) of the Securities Exchange Act of 1934 if he fails to disclose the impending takeover before trading the target company's securities.

Petitioner is a printer by trade. In 1975 and 1976, he worked as a "markup man" in the New York composing room of Pandick Press, a financial printer. Among documents that petitioner handled were five announcements of corporate takeover bids. When these documents were delivered to the printer, the identities of the acquiring and target corporations were concealed by blank spaces or false names. The true names were sent to the printer on the night of the final printing.

The petitioner, however, was able to deduce the names of the target companies before the final printing from other information contained in the documents. Without disclosing his knowledge, petitioner purchased stock in the target companies and sold the shares immediately after the takeover attempts were made public. By this method, petitioner realized a gain of slightly more than $30,000 in the course of 14 months. Subsequently, the Securities and Exchange Commission (Commission or SEC) began an investigation of his trading activities. In May 1977, petitioner entered into a consent decree with the Commission in which he agreed to return his profits to the sellers of the shares. On the same day, he was discharged by Pandick Press.

In January 1978, petitioner was indicted on 17 counts of violating Section 10(b) of the Securities Exchange Act of 1934 (1934 Act) and SEC Rule 10b-5. After petitioner unsuccessfully moved to dismiss the indictment, he was brought to trial and convicted on all counts.

The Court of Appeals for the Second Circuit affirmed petitioner's conviction . . . and we now reverse.

In this case, the petitioner was convicted of violating Section 10(b) although he was not a corporate insider and he received no confidential information from the target company. Moreover, the "market information" upon which he relied did not concern the earning power or operations of the target company, but only the plans of the acquiring company. Petitioner's use of that information was not a fraud under Section 10(b) unless he was subject to an affirmative duty to disclose it before trading. . . . The Court of Appeals affirmed the conviction by holding that "[a]nyone—corporate insider or not—who regularly receives material nonpublic information may not use that information to trade in securities without incurring an affirmative duty to disclose." . . . Although the court said that its test would include only persons who regularly receive material, nonpublic information, its rationale for that limitation is unrelated to the existence of a duty to disclose. The Court of Appeals, like the trial court, failed to identify a relationship between petitioner and the sellers that could give rise to a duty. Its decision thus rested solely upon its belief that the federal securities laws have "created a system providing equal access to information necessary for reasoned and intelligent investment decisions." . . . The use by anyone of material information not generally available is fraudulent, this theory suggests, because such information gives certain buyers or sellers an unfair advantage over less informed buyers and sellers.

This reasoning suffers from two defects. First, not every instance of financial unfairness constitutes fraudulent activity under Section 10(b). . . . Second, the element required to make silence fraudulent—a duty to disclose—is absent in this case. No duty could arise from petitioner's relationship with the sellers of the target company's securities, for petitioner had no prior dealings with them. He was not their agent, he was not a fiduciary, he was not a person in whom the sellers had placed their trust and confidence. He was, in fact, a complete stranger who dealt with the sellers only through impersonal market transactions.

We cannot affirm petitioner's conviction without recognizing a general duty between all participants in market transactions to forgo actions based on material, nonpublic information. Formulation of such a broad duty, which departs radically from the established doctrine that duty arises from a specific relationship between two parties . . . should not be undertaken absent some explicit evidence of congressional intent.

As we have seen, no such evidence emerges from the language or legislative history of Section 10(b). Moreover neither the Congress nor the Commission ever has adopted a parity-of-information rule. Instead the problems caused by misuse of market information have been addressed by detailed and sophisticated regulation that recognizes when use of market information may not harm operation of the securities markets. For example, the Williams Act limits but does not completely prohibit a tender offeror's purchases of target corporation stock before public announcement of the offer. Congress' careful action in this and other areas contrasts, and is in some tension, with the broad rule of liability we are asked to adopt in this case.

We see no basis for applying such a new and different theory of liability in this case. . . . Section 10(b) is aptly described as a catchall provision, but what it catches must be fraud. When an allegation of fraud is based upon nondisclosure, there can be no fraud absent a duty to speak. We hold that a duty to disclose under Section 10(b) does not arise from the mere possession of nonpublic market information. . . .

Questions

1. Do you agree with the Court's decision? Why isn't there a special relationship between a financial printer and the parties involved in corporate takeovers, when the printer knows the confidential nature of the transaction?

2. Should someone in Chiarella's position—a printer—be subject to civil liability even though he cannot be convicted of a crime? Why should there be a difference?

3. Would the result be the same if Chiarella had been a lawyer employed to draft the documents? Why or why not?

MATERIAL INFORMATION. Only material omissions and misstatements in connection with the purchase or sale of securities must be disclosed so as not to violate Rule 10b-5. One difficult aspect of applying the rule has been determining exactly what is considered material information. In essence, material information may be defined as any information that is likely to have a market-price impact on a security. The SEC has stated that a fact is material if disclosing it reasonably would be expected to cause a prospective buyer to buy, sell, or delay such action, or if it otherwise would affect the market price of a security.

Courts also have struggled with the issue of when material inside information has become public information so that insiders may trade without being subject to Rule 10b-5 liability. The current standard suggests refraining from trading for a "reasonable waiting period," if release of the information to the public is not immediately translated into investment action.

Tender Offers

Takeovers are common in the corporate world today, and the tender offer is the favorite technique used in this aggressive strategy. Beginning in the 1960s, the tender offer rose to prominence as the preeminent means of effecting unfriendly corporate mergers. A **tender offer** is a public offer, made directly to the shareholders of the target corporation, to purchase the target company's equity securities at a set price for a certain period of time. The price generally is set well above market price and the amount of the securities sought usually is enough to gain control of the target corporation. Typically, the latter responds with a counteroffer designed to attract shareholders away from the "corporate raider" and leave control with existing mangement. The process continues until one side is exhausted or a shareholder vote actually is taken to determine who will control the company. In many instances, a deal is struck between the company and the raider to bring peace, which usually results in the group seeking control receiving a handsome profit on its stock. This has led cynics to brand this modern phenomenon *greenmail*. There is tremendous debate over the desirability of this activity, some believing it is purely predatory and others taking the view that it is a healthy way of shaking up a sleepy management and increasing stock prices to their full value.

THE WILLIAMS ACT. In 1968 the **Williams Act** was added to the Securities Exchange Act. The purpose of the statute is to provide investors with more information and a greater time in which to make an informed decision on tender-offer bids, by establishing reporting and procedural requirements for tender offers. However, these provisions apply only if the target corporation's securities are registered under the Securities Exchange Act.

Only public tender offers are subject to regulation under the Williams Act. There is a minimum offer size for a public offer. The bidder must intend to attain at least a five-percent stake in the target corporation for the act to apply. Even though the act does not define a public offer, anyone purchasing shares from a number of shareholders runs the risk that a court could determine that action to be a public tender offer. It is clearly a private offer when the purchase is made by a single face-to-face transaction for a block of stock or by the purchase of shares on an exchange. The more public the offer is, the more shareholders will be involved, and the less sophisticated the investors to whom the offer is made, the more likely a court will conclude it was a public offer.

In general, courts have held that actions for violation of the Williams Act can be brought only by the SEC. That is, the act does not create a private right for an unsuccessful bidder to sue its opponent for damages. However, the Supreme Court held, in a 1977 case, that suits by private individuals seeking to protect interests of the shareholders of the target corporation (those the act sought to safeguard) might be permitted. Since that time some lower federal courts have allowed suits seeking protection.

REPORTING REQUIREMENTS. Anyone who makes a non-public tender offer must file a statement with the SEC and send a copy to the target company within ten days of becoming a five-percent shareholder in the target corporation. A filing is not required if no more than two percent of the shares were purchased within the last year.

A person who makes a public tender offer must file with the SEC before the offer is made. Certain information must be included in this public tender offer statement: the terms of the tender offer; information about the bidder; past dealings of the bidder, the target corporation, and its management; and the purpose of the offer.

TENDER-OFFER REGULATIONS. The public tender offer must be kept open for at least twenty business days. Tendering shareholders may back out and withdraw their shares during part of this open period. All tendering shareholders, no matter when they tendered their shares during the offer period, must be paid the highest bid price paid by the bidder. If too many shares are offered, the bidder must prorate among the shares offered. The target company's management is required to respond to its shareholders and tell them its position on the tender offer and the reasons therefor. A number of states have different types of statutes regulating tender offers. Some of these have been held unconstitutional as preempted by the federal Williams Act. Finally, the Williams Act contains anti-fraud provisions covering a broad range of fraudulent and manipulative activities that might occur in connection with a tender offer.

REGULATION OF INVESTMENT COMPANIES

An **investment company** is defined as a business that (1) is engaged primarily in investing or trading in securities, or (2) is engaged in that business and more than 40 percent of the assets of the company are investment securities. Investment companies began to grow rapidly in the late 1940s. Today a large part of the country's wealth is handled by these concerns, including mutual funds, and they are regulated by the Investment Company Act of 1940. This act provides for SEC control over the activities of these investment firms. Persons or companies that operate as professional investment advisors are regulated separately under the Investment Advisors Act of 1940.

The Investment Company Act requires every investment company to register with the SEC and to follow strict guidelines. Each year registered companies file reports with the commission. The range of activities these companies may engage in is regulated by the SEC. Certain institutions are excluded from coverage under the act, such as banks, insurance companies, finance companies, charitable foundations, tax-exempt pension funds, and closely held corporations.

STATE SECURITIES REGULATION

Blue Sky Laws

State securities statutes, called blue sky laws, are based on the premise that the public-at-large lacks sophisticated knowledge of securities investments. The purpose of these laws, therefore, is to protect the public form fraud and deceit in securities transactions by unscrupulous promoters. Not surprisingly, these laws generally are paternalistic in character because the states have adopted them to protect their citizens from fraudulent stock promotions.

The federal and state statutes overlap and operate concurrently. Both the Securities Act and Securities Exchange Act specifically acknowledge that they do not supercede or displace the possible state regulation. However, a number of states exempt from state registration those securities that have been registered with the SEC under the provisions of the 1933 act.

The form of blue sky regulation varies from state to state. Most states incorporate one or more of three basic types of regulatory schemes. The first scheme adopted by almost all states involves anti-fraud provisions that apply to all securities transactions. These provisions often are modeled after Federal Rule 10b-5, discussed earlier in this chapter. The second scheme adopted by a majority of states requires the registration of securities that are to be sold or distributed in that state. The third requires the registration of brokers and deal-ers who trade in securities in that state. The registration of securities, brokers, and dealers is accomplished by filing with a state official, usually the secretary of corporations or the corporate commissioner. The power to enfore the anti-fraud provisions usually is vested either in the same state official or in the state attorney general.

The underlying philosophies of the states' statutes differ. Some are similar to the Securities Act of 1933 and require only certain disclosures for an effective registration. Once the required disclosures are made in the registration application, the filing party is allowed to issue and sell the registered securities. Other states require that the terms of the securities and the manner in which they will be offered to the public meet a fairness standard before the securities can be offered or sold in that state. In addition, a few states regulate the selling price of securities and the fees charged by brokers and dealers. Finally, some states have adopted other components of the federal statutes, such as the regulation of takeover bids.

Uniform Securities Act

Slightly over half of the states have adopted, in whole or part, the **Uniform Securities Act.** The act consists of four parts. The first three parts set forth the three basic schemes, described previously, that historically have been used by the states to regulate securities. The fourth contains administrative and enforcement provisions. The act is structured so that a state may enact any one or more of these sections as it sees fit. This flexible form of drafting has made the act acceptable to states with different regulatory philosophies.

SUMMARY

The process of providing corporate capital is accomplished primarily by the sale of securities. The federal securities laws regulate the original issuance and subsequent trade in *securities,* a term that has been given a very broad interpretation by the courts. Securities regulation proceeds both through required disclosures and through anti-fraud provisions. The SEC oversees the disclosure process and seeks injunctions and criminal sanctions to ensure compliance with the statutes. Enforcement of securities regulation by self-regulatory organizations and private actions for civil liability allows the securities markets to function consistently with the regulations promulgated under federal law.

The Securities Act of 1933 is designed to give investors complete investment information and to prevent misrepresentation and fraud. The statute operates by requiring disclosure through the registration of securities before they are issued. The SEC makes certain that the required information is supplied. A wide range of securities are exempted from the registration requirement, as are private offerings, small issues of securities, and intrastate offerings. Securities obtained through private placements are restricted, and their purchase and sale is regulated.

The Securities Exchange Act of 1934 regulates brokers and dealers of securities, and securities exchanges and markets, in order to prevent fraud and market manipulation. The act requires registration of these people and entities, as well as registration of company securities that are traded in the marketplace. The issuers of the securities that must be registered must file a variety of periodic reports. The act also regulates proxy contests by requiring disclosures so that shareholders can vote intelligently.

The 1934 act tries to prevent people from trading on inside information by forcing persons who profit from those transactions to disgorge their ill-gotten gains. Insider trading and a variety of fraudulent activities are remedied by the SEC, or in private lawsuits under Rule 10b-5. A final element of the 1934 act is the regulation of tender offers. This is done under a 1968 amendment to a federal statute, known as the Williams Act, which provides investors with information and procedural protections in the context of public tender offers.

The states also engage in significant securities regulation through statutes known as blue sky laws. Some states focus on anti-fraud activity, others on registration of securities or brokers and dealers, and others on disclosure. More than half the states have now adopted the Uniform Securities Act. There is considerable overlap between the federal and state statutes; compliance with both is necessary.

KEY TERMS AND CONCEPTS

blue sky laws
Securities Act of 1933
Securities Exchange Act of 1934
Securities and Exchange Commission (SEC)
security
investment contract
no-action letter
issuer
underwriter
dealer
broker
disclosure requirement
registration statement
prospectus
private offering
small-issue exemptions
intrastate offering exemption
restricted securities
anti-fraud provision
Form 10-K
annual report
proxy statement
proxy
proxy contest
insider trading
Section 16
Rule 10b-5
tender offer
Williams Act
investment company
Uniform Securities Act

PROBLEMS

1. Ralston Purina Company sold $2 million of its stock to key employees (shop and dock foremen, stenographers, clerical assistants, copywriters, and veterinarians). When the sale was challenged by the SEC because of Ralston Purina's failure to register, Ralston Purina defended on the ground that the sale was a "private sale" rather than public and, therefore, registration was not required. The district court found for Ralston Purina and the circuit court of appeals affirmed. Should these decisions be reversed by the Supreme Court?

2. Minority shareholders of Kirby Lumber sued, contending that the merger of Kirby with Santa Fe Industries involved a fraudulent appraisal of the fair value of Kirby Stock instigated by the majority shareholders. They contended the appraisal was designed to "freeze out" minority shareholders, and that this breach of fiduciary duty by majority shareholders constituted a violation of Section 10(b) of the 1934 act and Rule 10b-5. The section and rule prohibited the use of any manipulative or deceptive device or contrivance in contravention of SEC rules, the use of any artifice to defraud, and any act that would operate as a fraud or deceit. Is the contention of these shareholders correct?

3. A limited partnership was formed to develop residential property amounting to 100 acres. The limited partners were required to make periodic payments as the project progressed. They were called upon to contribute an additional $500,000. At the time, unknown to them, the general partners had reached a disagreement and had abandoned the project. The limited partners sued to recover their contributions under the antifraud provisions of the 1934 act. The defendants defended on the ground that the transaction was not covered by the act because it did not involve a "sale of securities." Is the defendants' contention correct?

4. Ross, vice-president of Mapco, purchased Mapco warrants on the open market and held them for more than six months. She then surrendered them to Mapco; in return for each warrant plus $9.00 cash, she received Mapco stock (1100 shares), and immediately sold the stock at a profit. Morales brought a shareholder derivative suit to recover the short-swing profits, alleging illegal insider trading under Section 16(b) of the 1934 act. Ross defended on the ground that the transaction was not covered because the stock sold was related to the purchase of warrants more than six months previously. Is the defense good?

5. Fredericksen and Emerald City Corporation (ECC) purchased the assets and stock of North Shore Marina (NSM) from Poloway. Later, Fredericksen and ECC alleged that certain aspects of the sale involved violations of the federal securities laws. Poloway contended the transaction was not covered by federal securities laws because it did not involve a "security" within the meaning of these laws. Is Poloway correct?

6. The Teamsters Union negotiated a pension plan with Chicago-area trucking companies. The plan called for contributions by employers, with none from employees. Danial, an employee of one of the trucking companies, was denied benefits on retirement, and he charged fraud in violation of Section 10 and Rule 10b-5. The union contended the section and rule were not applicable to this plan. The district court disagreed, holding the plan to be an "investment contract" and a security under the test announced in the *Howey* case (abstracted on pp. 973–75). Was the court correct?

7. After an unsuccessful takeover bid for Piper Aircraft, Chris-Craft sued Piper and the unsuccessful bidder, Bangor Punta, alleging that misleading statements were made by Bangor Punta in violation of Section 16 of the Williams Act. The defendants contended the Williams Act did not create a right in private parties to sue for its violation. Are the defendants correct?

8. After purchasing all of the stock in a timber company owned by Landreth and her two sons, the purchasers sued for rescission when the business failed. Among other grounds for rescission, they contended the sellers had failed to register as required by the 1933 act. Defendants countered that registration is not required for the sale of all of the stock in a closely held corporation. Are defendants correct?

9. Koscot was a vendor of cosmetics using a multilevel network of distributorship. Individual distributors could earn bonuses of up to $3000 by recruiting new salespeople into the plan. Distributors, after buying in, would introduce the plan to recruits at "opportunity meetings," at which Koscot representatives would use films, speeches, and high-pressure sales tactics in an effort to get the recruits to sign up. When it was charged with the sale of unregistered securities, Koscot defended on the ground that the bonuses to the distributors were not earned "solely from the efforts of others," so there was no sale of securities. Is Koscot correct?

10. Small and Avard were charged with insider trading in violation of Section 16(b) of the 1934 act. Although both were senior executive vice-presidents of the corporation involved, they contended they should not be considered officers under the act because they did not have access to material inside information about the corporation. If, in fact, they had no access, should that constitute a defense?

Antitrust: Introduction and the Sherman Act

INTRODUCTION

Antitrust law is a complex subject that strikes to the core of the legitimacy of a wide range of business activities and economic relationships. Today, this area of law is governed mainly by federal statutes. However, there is a rich heritage based on the early common law.

The common law developed several legal theories that could be used to attack contracts in restraint of trade, which in general terms were defined as agreements used solely for the purpose of limiting competition. A contract or agreement containing ancillary restraints that were limited in time and place usually were considered acceptable. For example, a contract in which a baker sold his small-town bakery to another person might contain restrictions prohibiting the baker from starting another bakery in the same town for a period of five years. Unfortunately, the true purpose of any restraint is not always easy to determine. Thus, the distinction between acceptable restraints and unacceptable ones often was elusive and ill-defined, subject to fluctuation and uncertainty in the hands of the courts. Under these circumstances, the common law varied from state to state and provided no guarantee against overreaching by someone with great economic power.

Antitrust law in the United States began with Congress's enactment of the **Sherman Antitrust Act** in 1890. During the last quarter of the nineteenth century, large corporate organizations, known in common parlance as **trusts,** were accused of abusive practices. The term *trust* was used loosely to apply to business combinations of many different types. The standard organization of one of these trusts would be an arrangement by which the owners of stock in the major companies in a certain industry would transfer their stock to trustees. In return, the owners would receive a specified share of the pooled earnings of the jointly managed companies. These trusts took many different forms and existed in many industries, including oil, sugar, whiskey, and cotton.

The trusts' activities were condemned as predatory. Many commentators of the time suggested that the consolidation process of the trusts succeeded by threatening to drive competitors out of business. The trusts were accused of creating a situation in which their competitors either joined or were forced out of the industry. Any trust that dominated an industry could dictate prices, determine what products would be produced, and allocate markets among the participants. The Sherman Act was Congress's response to these accusations, and was designed to protect the public from the power of large business enterprises. On a functional level, the antitrust laws are meant to preserve competition in the marketplace, and their actual effectiveness should be measured against that goal.

Antitrust law has several unique characteristics. For example, the statutes are written in very general terms. This means that the broad, and sometimes vague, language can be understood only with reference to court opinions and the facts of the individual cases. Antitrust lawsuits often present complex factual situations involving large numbers of individuals or companies and numerous instances of alleged restraints of trade (hindrances to free competition). Judges often are forced to engage in difficult statistical and economic analysis to resolve these cases.

Moreover, the antitrust laws are designed somewhat differently than most other business regulations. The general approach of most laws is to specify what the industry being regulated should do. In contrast, antitrust law specifies what businesses cannot do.

It is important that businesspeople know about potential antitrust problems, not only because they are possible defendants, but because they may be plaintiffs if they are subjected to anticompetitive practices. This potential for being involved in a lawsuit is important today because antitrust litigation in this country, itself, has become a large business.

In this chapter we will explore Sections 1 and 2 of the Sherman Act, which concern monopolistic and oligopolistic practices, and we will also discuss the concept of exclusionary practices under the **Clayton Act** Section 3. The next chapter will cover the Clayton Act Section 7 dealing with mergers, the Robinson-Patmann Act on price discrimination, unfair competition under Section 5 of the Federal Trade Commission Act, the major enforcement mechanisms and the remedies available under the various statutes, and exemptions from the antitrust laws.

The core concept of antitrust law is the preservation of competition. This idea can be introduced through the study of monopolies under Section 2 of the Sherman Act more easily than through the material in Section 1, which involves more complex oligopolistic relationships. Furthermore, almost by definition, when there is monopolization, competition is threatened or no longer exists. Finally, most significant challenges to antitrust policies are presented by bigness and anticompetitive activities. Because monopolies generally are big and pose a great threat to competition, we will begin our discussion of the Sherman Act with that subject.

THE SHERMAN ACT

Section 1 of the Sherman Act deals with agreements in **restraint of trade** (often characterized as oligopolistic behavior). It states: "Every contract, combination in the form of trust or otherwise, or conspiracy, in restraint of trade or commerce among the several states, or with foreign nations, is declared to be illegal." Section 2 covers monopoly, attempts to monopolize, and conspiracy to monopolize. It reads: "Every person who shall monopolize, or attempt to monopolize, or combine or conspire with any other person or persons, to monopolize any part of the trade or commerce among the several states, or with foreign nations shall be deemed to be guilty of a felony."

For several years after it was enacted, the Sherman Act was limited by narrow court interpretations. The Supreme Court soon shifted to the other extreme by interpreting the extremely broad language of the statute literally. In *United States v. Trans-Missouri Freight Association,* the Court held that the Sherman Act condemned every restraint of trade. This rule was too broad to last and, bowing to practical business necessities (under the *Trans-Missouri* standard any contract would be illegal), the Court reinterpreted the act. Beginning in 1911 with *Standard Oil Co. of New Jersey v. United States,* which is presented later in this chapter, the Court determined that reasonable restraints were not made illegal by the Sherman Act.

MONOPOLIZATION UNDER SECTION 2

A **monopoly** exists when a single firm has the power to exclude competitors from a market or to control prices in a market. Under the statute, having a monopoly is not itself illegal. It is the act of monopolizing, as in trying to gain or keep such power, that is the essence of illegal activity under Section 2. Intent to exercise monopoly power is a requisite element of the offense of monopolizing. Thus, the mere possession of monopoly power is not an antitrust offense because it may be an absolutely natural consequence of legitimate competitive activity. Rather, it is the monopolist's purpose and intent in exerting its monopoly power that will be scrutinized under Section 2. If a firm has achieved monopoly power by lawful means—for example, because it owns a patented process—it is not in violation of Section 2, but an intent to exercise that power unreasonably is.

Some Economic Considerations

Monopoly power is feared because of the impact it can have on competition. In a general sense, the possession of monopoly power allows a company to restrict output, thereby causing an increase in prices and enabling the monopolist to receive a larger (or monopoly) profit. An element of interference with the market is involved. A monopolist can succeed in raising prices, and thereby increase its profits, only if it is able to exclude competitors from the market. Remember, the goal of the antitrust laws is to maintain competition. Thus monopolizing is dangerous not simply because it may increase prices to consumers, nor because it may cause the inappropriate expenditure of economic resources (although it may do both), but because it impinges on competition that Congress has determined is to be protected.

The Relevant Market

To determine if a company has monopoly power, the concept of *market power* must be understood. The first step in determining a company's market power is to determine the relevant market. The courts have divided the definition of **relevant**

market into two separate components: the **relevant product market** (for example, sneakers, all leisure footwear, or all footwear) and the **relevant geographic market** (for example, a state, a region, or the country).

Disagreements among the opposing parties on what constitutes the relevant market often form the main ingredient of a Section-2 monopoly case. A narrowing or a broadening of the relevant market will enlarge or shrink the alleged monopolist's market share, and will have a dramatic effect on the outcome of the lawsuit. It is important to note that a company's relevant market is not definable with any real precision. The concept is very fuzzy.

THE PRODUCT MARKET. The method for determining the relevant product market was set out in *United States v. E. I. DuPont De Nemours & Co.,* (referred to as the Cellophane Case). DuPont controlled approximately 75 percent of the cellophane market. In defending an antitrust suit brought against it, DuPont claimed that the product market in which cellophane competed included all flexible wrapping materials. If the product market as defined by DuPont were used, the company's market share figure was reduced to around 20 percent. The Supreme Court held that commodities that reasonably could be used interchangeably by consumers for the same purpose were products with enough "cross-elasticity" to be treated as a single product market for antitrust purposes. **Cross-elasticity** means that products overlap and may be used to perform the same function at the edges of their respective product markets, depending on price. The Court, applying the standards of quality, end use, and price responsiveness to sales, decided that flexible wrapping paper was the relevant market.

Quality and *end use* are fairly easily understood standards, but *price responsiveness to sales* is a standard that compares the interchangeability of demand for two products to decide if the products are in the same market. If a slight decrease in the price of product A causes buyers of product B to buy product A in place of B, the price responsiveness suggests that products A and B are competitors in a single market.

For example, in *United States v. Grinell Corp.,* the quality and end-use tests were used to determine that central station alarm systems were a separate product market from other alarm and protective systems. In this case, the price responsiveness-to-sales standard, a hard element to measure, was deleted as a component in the relevant-product-market analysis. It is not yet clear whether the price responsiveness standard will be applied in future cases.

THE GEOGRAPHIC MARKET. Compared with the complexities of determining the relevant product market, determining the geographic market typically is much simpler. When products are sold throughout the nation, courts generally will decide that the relevant market is the entire country. On the other hand, when a company and its rivals operate in a limited geographic area and their customers have no external source of supply, the area so covered usually is determined to be the relevant geographic market.

Market Share

Once the court has decided what constitutes the product and geographic markets, it is relatively easy to determine a firm's market share. Generally, a company with a market share greater than 75 percent will be considered to have monopoly power. However, a violation of Section 2 requires more than just monopoly power; it requires an element of intent to restrain trade. The monopoly power must be connected with the illegal use of the power in predatory ways. The following case represents perhaps the high point in the development of antitrust law under Section 2 of the Sherman Act.

UNITED STATES v. ALUMINUM COMPANY OF AMERICA
148 F.2d 416 (2d Cir. 1945)

The Antitrust Division of the United States Justice Department (Plaintiff/Appellee) brought suit against the Aluminum Company of America (Alcoa) (Defendant/Appellant) in 1937, seeking to have the company dissolved. The district court rendered judgement for Defendant and the government appealed. This appeal was heard by a special three-judge panel of the United States Second Circuit Court of Appeals because a quorum of six disinterested justices of the Supreme Court was not available to hear the case. The appellate court considered four issues in the case. The most important discussion concerned whether Alcoa had monopolized the market in aluminum.

L. HAND, Circuit Judge.

. . . It is undisputed that throughout this period "Alcoa" continued to be the single producer of "virgin" ingot in the United States; and the plaintiff argues that this without more was enough to make it an unlawful monopoly. It also takes an alternative position: that in any event during this period "Alcoa" consistently pursued unlawful exclusionary practices, which made its dominant position certainly unlawful, even though it would not have been, had it been retained only by "natural growth." Finally, it asserts that many of these practices were of themselves unlawful, as contracts in restraint of trade under Section 1 of the Act. "Alcoa's" position is that the fact that it alone continued to make "virgin" ingot in the country did not, and does not, give it a monopoly of the market; that it was always subject to the competition of imported "virgin" ingot, and of what is called "secondary" ingot; and that even if it had not been its monopoly would not have been retained by unlawful means, but would have been the result of a growth which the Act does not forbid, even when it results in a monopoly. We shall first consider the amount and character of this competition; next, how far it established a monopoly; and finally, if it did, whether that monopoly was unlawful under Section 2 of the Act. . . .

[Alcoa's] control over the ingot market must be reckoned at over ninety per cent; that being the proportion which its production bears to imported "virgin" ingot. If the fraction which it did not supply were the produce of domestic manufacture, there could be no doubt that this percentage gave it a monopoly—lawful or unlawful, as the case might be. The producer of so large a proportion of the supply has complete control within certain limits. . . .

[I]t might have been thought adequate to condemn only those monopolies which could not show that they had exercised the highest possible ingenuity, had adopted every possible economy, had anticipated every conceivable improvement, stimulated every possible demand [*sic*]. No doubt, that would be one way of dealing with the matter, although it would imply constant scrutiny and constant supervision, such as courts are unable to provide. Be that as it may, that was not the way that Congress chose; it did not condone "good trusts" and condemn "bad" ones; it forbade all.

Moreover, in so doing it was not necessarily actuated by economic motives alone. It is possible, because of its indirect social or moral effect, to prefer a system of small producers, each dependent for his success upon his own skill and character, to one in which the great mass of those engaged must accept the direction of a few. These considerations, which we have suggested only as possible purposes of the Act, we think the decisions prove to have been in fact its purposes. . . .

. . . Starting, however, with the authoritative premise that all contracts fixing prices are unconditionally prohibited, the only possible difference between them and a monopoly is that while a monopoly necessarily involves an equal, or even greater, power to fix prices, its mere existence might be thought not to constitute an exercise of that power. That distinction is nevertheless purely formal; it would be valid only so long as the monopoly remained wholly inert; it would disappear as soon as the monopoly began to operate; for, when it did—that is, as soon as it began to sell at all—it must sell at some price and the only price at which it could sell is a price which it itself fixed. Thereafter the power and its exercise must needs coalesce. Indeed it would be absurd to condemn such contracts unconditionally, and not to extend the condemnation to monopolies; for the contracts are only steps toward that entire control which monopoly confers: they are really partial monopolies.

It does not follow because "Alcoa" had such a monopoly, that it "monopolized" the ingot market: it may not have achieved monopoly; monopoly may have been thrust upon it. . . .

It would completely misconstrue "Alcoa's" position in 1940 to hold that it was the passive beneficiary of a monopoly, following upon an involuntary elimination of competitors by automatically operative economic forces. Already in 1909, when its last lawful monopoly ended, it sought to strengthen its position by unlawful practices, and these concededly continued until 1912. In that year it had two plants in New York, at which its produced less than 42 million pounds of ingot; in 1934 it had five plants . . . and its production had risen to about 327 million pounds, an increase of almost eightfold. Meanwhile not a pound of ingot had been produced by anyone else in the United States. This increase and this continued and undisturbed control did not fall undesigned into "Alcoa's" lap; obviously it could not have done so. It could have resulted, as it did result, from a persistent determination to maintain the control, with which it found itself vested in 1912. There were at least one or two abortive attempts to enter the industry, but "Alcoa" effectively anticipated and forestalled all competition, and succeeded in holding the field alone. True, it stimulated demand and opened new uses for the metal, but not without making sure that it could supply what it had evoked. There is no dispute as to this; "Alcoa" avows it as evidence of the skill, energy and initiative with which it has always conducted its business; as a reason why, having won its way by fair means, it should be commended, and not dismembered. We need charge it with no moral derelictions after 1912; we may assume that all it claims for itself is true. The only question is whether it falls within the exception established in favor of those who do not seek, but cannot avoid, the control of a market. It seems to us that question scarcely survives its statement. It was not inevitable that it should always anticipate increases in the demand for ingot and be prepared to supply them. Nothing compelled it to keep doubling and redoubling its capacity before others entered the field. It insists that it never excluded competitors; but we can think of no more effective exclusion than progressively to embrace each new opportunity as it opened, and to face every newcomer with new capacity already geared into a great organization, having the advantage of experience, trade connections and the elite of personnel. Only in case we interpret "exclusion" as limited to maneuvers not honestly industrial, but actuated solely by a desire to prevent competition, can such a course, indefatigably pursued, be deemed not "exclusionary." So to limit it would in our judgment emasculate the Act; would permit just such consolidations as it was designed to prevent.

[The court required Alcoa to divest itself of its Canadian subsidiary. During World War II the United States government had subsidized two other companies to enter the aluminum market as major producers. The court also required Alcoa to turn over plants it had built and operated for the government during the war to these two new companies. The aluminum market had changed enough in the intervening years since the suit was initiated that the dissolution of Alcoa was not required.]

Questions

1. Can you describe the conduct that led the court to brand Alcoa a monopolist? What differentiates these activities from good, aggressive business conduct?

2. Is the result in this case inconsistent with traditional American values such as the work ethic, seizing upon opportunities, playing to win, seeking success, and others?

3. Do you think it was proper for the court to order that two of Alcoa's plants be turned over to competitors?

Attempts and Conspiracy to Monopolize

Attempts to monopolize are recognized as violations under Section 2 of the Sherman Act, but there are not many reported cases dealing with this offense. There is a twofold test to determine if a firm is guilty of attempted monopoly: (1) there must be specific intent to attain a monopoly and (2) there must be a substantive probability of success. Because a violation of the "attempt to monopolize" provision has been held to require a probability of success—without actually monopolizing—it has tended to merge into the "monopolization" provision. Similarly, conspiracy to monopolize significantly overlaps with the general Section 1 conspiracy element, which is discussed below, and there are few cases under this provision as well.

OLIGOPOLISTIC RESTRAINTS

There are a number of differences between violations of Section 1 and violations of Section 2 of the Sherman Act. Section 1 prohibits every **contract, combination, or conspiracy** in restraint of trade. The element of agreement (contract, combination, or conspiracy) is an essential part of Section 1. This means there must be more than one company, or one person, involved in the illegal conduct. Thus, two divisions of the same company could not violate Section 1, although it is possible that a company and its subsidiaries could act together to violate the statute. The phrase "restraint of trade" has been interpreted to mean restraint of competition. Agreements between companies may be unlawful not only if they restrain the trade of other companies, but also if they affect competition among themselves.

Oligopoly Theory

At the heart of the antitrust notions in the Sherman Act Section 1 and the Clayton Act Section 3 is the theory of **oligopoly** (shared monopoly). This theory is based on the principle that in a market with only a few major competitors, all of them realize that they are interdependent. Thus, when making pricing and output decisions, competitors take into account the reactions of their rivals.

Oligopolistic restraints can be either horizontal or vertical. Horizontal restraints involve agreements between competitors on the same business level, for example, two manufacturers. Vertical restraints are caused by agreements between companies on different levels, for example, a whole-saler and a retailer. Either type may violate Section 1. Some exclusionary practices, including tying arrangements in which two distinct products are sold as a single unit, are oligopolistic practices that involve the Clayton Act Section 3, which will be discussed later.

The Rule of Reason

There are two basic methods of legal analysis to determine whether conduct is illegal under Section 1 of the Sherman Act. The first method is the **rule of reason,** under which a court may permit certain activity that restrains trade if it finds the restraint reasonable and consistent with public policy, as described in the following case.

STANDARD OIL CO. OF NEW JERSEY v. UNITED STATES
221 U.S. 1, 31 S.Ct. 502, 55 L.Ed. 619 (1911)

This case involved a suit brought by the United States (Plaintiff/Appellee) to dissolve the Standard Oil Company of New Jersey (Defendant/Appellant) for participation in illegal combinations under the Sherman Act. The suit alleged that John D. Rockefeller used a holding company structure to restrain interstate commerce in petroleum and its products. The district court gave judgment for Plaintiff and the company was ordered dissolved. Affirmed.

WHITE, Chief Justice.

. . . The statute under this view evidenced the intent not to restrain the right to make and enforce contracts, whether resulting from combinations or otherwise, which did not unduly restrain interstate or foreign commerce, but to protect that commerce from being restrained by methods, whether old or new which would constitute an interference,—that is, an undue restraint.

And as the contracts or acts embraced in the provision were not expressly defined, since the enumeration addressed itself simply to classes of acts, those classes being broad enough to embrace every conceivable contract or combination which could be made concerning trade or commerce, and thus caused any act done by any of the enumerated methods anywhere in the whole field of human activity to be illegal if in restraint of trade, it inevitably follows that the provision necessarily called for the exercise of judgment which required that some standard should be resorted to for the purpose of determining whether the prohibition contained in the statute had or had not in any given case been violated. Thus not specifying, but indubitably contemplating and requiring a standard, it follows that it was intended that the standard of reason which had been applied at the common law and in this country in dealing with subjects of the character embraced by the statute was intended to be the measure used for the purpose of determining whether, in a given case, a particular act had or had not brought about the wrong against which the statute provided.

If the criterion by which it is to be determined in all cases whether every contract, combination, etc., is a restraint of trade within the intendment of the law, is the direct of indirect effect of the acts involved, then of course the rule of reason becomes the guide, and the construction which we have given the statute, instead of being refuted by the cases relied upon, is by those cases demonstrated to be correct. This is true, because the construction which we have deduced from the history of the act and the analysis of its text is simply that in every case where it is claimed that an act or acts are in violation of the statute, the rule of reason, in the light of the principles of law and the public policy which the act embodies, must be applied.

[The dissolution of the company was affirmed because Standard Oil's actions were found to be unreasonable restraints of trade.]

Questions

1. What was wrong with the judicial standard in force before the Supreme Court replaced it with the rule of reason in this case?

2. On the basis of the *Standard Oil* case, what is meant by the rule of reason? Can you define its scope of application?

The *Per Se* Illegal Rule

The second method of analysis is the ***per se* illegal rule,** under which certain types of conduct have been declared unreasonable as such. This means these business activities have been deemed inherently anticompetitive as a matter of law. The most important examples of conduct that constitute *per se* violations under Section 1 are price fixing and the division of market territories or customers between competitors. Other exclusionary practices such as refusals to deal, group boycotts, and tying also are treated as *per se* violations and are discussed later in this section.

The rationale for the *per se* illegal rule usually is that, over time, the courts have become familiar with various business practices and agree on whether or not they violate the antitrust laws. Certain techniques or arrangements whose primary thrust and effect were likely to be anticompetitive and that were without any redeeming pro-competitive virtues became classified as *per se*

violations. An example of an arrangement that is treated as *per se* illegal is one by which competitors agree to fix a price at which they will sell a product they all produce. Roughly speaking, the *per se* analysis is used in cases that are not worthy of extensive judicial consideration because past court experience with similar business practices shows that they should be condemned.

Horizontal Restraints

As mentioned earlier, oligopolistic restraints may be either horizontal or vertical. **Horizontal restraints** are those between competitors within an industry, and can be divided into four categories: price fixing, information dissemination, refusals to deal, and reasonable restraints. Underlying this division is the "conspiracy" element of Section 1. Businesspeople seldom openly enter into agreements to restrain competition. Thus, in most cases the courts must determine if the parties acted together with an implicit agreement to violate antitrust laws.

CONCERTED ACTIVITY.   Direct evidence of concerted action is difficult to find. Therefore, the courts often are forced to rely on circumstantial evidence to establish antitrust violations. Should **conscious parallelism** of business behavior, without finding an explicit agreement, be enough to infer interdependent actions and a violation of Section 1? The courts have wavered on this issue. The problem is that seemingly interdependent conduct that might imply a conspiracy also could be actions undertaken by several entities for independent business reasons. Interdependence can be a difficult element to prove or disprove in a Section 1 antitrust case. Thus, whether this inference will be accepted by a court is a major factor in these suits.

Today the courts seem to look to certain "plus

factors" to decide if they should find implicit agreement. If one or more of these factors are present, the court may infer that an agreement exists. Some examples are: (1) conduct against self-interest; (2) a company's unexplained departure from past practices; (3) uniform action by competitors in a complex situation; and (4) opportunities to agree or past agreements among competitors. The weight to be given by the court to the presence or absence of any of these plus factors is unclear.

PRICE FIXING.   **Price fixing** is the agreement between or among competitors to raise, depress, or otherwise fix the price of goods. A large number of antitrust cases brought by the government under Section 1 involve this type of violation. Price fixing is *per se* illegal, and no justification or defense is recognized by the courts. The classic statement of the courts on price fixing appears in the following case.

UNITED STATES v. SOCONY-VACUUM OIL COMPANY
310 U.S. 150, 60 S.Ct. 811, 84 L.Ed. 1129 (1940)

Numerous oil companies and individuals were charged with violating Section 1 of the Sherman Act by conspiring to raise and maintain the spot-market prices of gasoline. Defendants were accused of buying up surplus gasoline so as to eliminate it as a market factor. Defendants were convicted in the District Court. The Circuit Court of Appeals for the Seventh Circuit reversed and remaned for a new trial. Reversed and convictions reinstated.

DOUGLAS, Justice.

Scope and Purpose of the Alleged Conspiracy

As a result of these buying programs it was hoped and intended that both the tank car and the retail markets would improve. The conclusion is irresistible that defendants' purpose was not merely to raise the spot market prices but, as the real and ultimate end, to raise the price of gasoline in their sales to jobbers and consumers in the Mid-Western area. Their agreement or plan embraced not only buying on the spot markets but also, at least by clear implication, an understanding to maintain such improvements in Mid-Western prices as would result from those purchases of distress gasoline. The latter obviously would be achieved by selling at the increased prices, not by price cutting. Any other understanding would have been wholly inconsistent with and contrary to the philosophy of the broad stabilization efforts which were underway. In essence the raising and maintenance of the spot market prices were but the means adopted for raising and maintaining prices to jobbers and consumers.

The elimination of so-called competitive evils is no legal justification for such buying programs. The elimination of such conditions was sought primarily for its effect on the price structures. Fairer competitive prices, it is claimed, resulted when distress gasoline was removed from the market. But such defense is typical of the protestations usually made in price-fixing cases. Ruinous competition, financial disaster, evils of price cutting and the like appear throughout our history as ostensible justifications for price-fixing. If the so-called competitive abuses were to be appraised here, the reasonableness of prices would necessarily become an issue in every price-fixing case. In that event the Sherman Act would soon be emasculated; its philosophy would be supplanted by one which is wholly alien to a system of free competition; it would not be the charter of freedom which its framers intended. The reasonableness of prices has no constancy due to the dynamic quality of business facts underlying price structures. Those who fixed reasonable prices today would perpetuate unreasonable prices tomorrow, since those prices would not be subject to continuous administrative supervision and readjustment in light of changed conditions. Those who controlled the prices would control or effectively dominate the market. And those who were in the strategic position would have it in their power to destroy or drastically impair the competitive system. But the thrust of the rule is deeper and reaches more than monopoly power. Any combination which tampers with price structures is engaged in an unlawful activity. Even though the members of the price-fixing group were in no position to control the market, to the extent that they raised, lowered, or stabilized prices they would be directly interfering with the free play of market forces. The Act places all such schemes beyond the pale and protects that vital part of our economy against any degree of interference. Congress has not left with us the determination of whether or not particular price-fixing schemes are wise or unwise, healthy or destructive. It has not permitted the age-old cry of ruinous competition and competitive evils to be a defense to price-fixing conspiracies. It has no more allowed genuine or fancied competitive abuses as a legal justification for such schemes than it has the good intentions of the members of the combination. If such a shift is to be made, it must be done by the Congress. Certainly Congress has not left us with any such choice. Nor has the Act created or authorized the creation of any special exception in favor of the oil industry. Whatever may be its peculiar problems and characteristics, the Sherman Act, so far as price-fixing agreements are concerned, establishes one uniform rule applicable to all industries alike.

Questions

1.   Do you agree with the *per se* illegal approach to certain activities? Does it have any disadvantages?

2.   Can you think of any situations in which price fixing can be justified and, thus, the *per se* doctrine should not be used?

3.   Why is Justice Douglas so cynical about the oil companies' explanations? Is his opinion anti-business?

MARKET DIVISION. All **market (territorial) divisions** (agreements between competitors to divide a geographical area, each staying out of the other's part of the area) also are the illegal *per se*. However, there are two minor exceptions to this principle. First, if, as at common law, the restraint merely is ancillary to a proper business purpose, for example, protecting the goodwill in a recently purchased business, and the restraint is only for a reasonable period of time and in a limited area, the market division is not necessarily treated as a *per se* violation. Second, if the market division is a result of a joint venture, then it probably will be judged under a rule-of-reason analysis for purposes of the antitrust laws.

INFORMATION DISSEMINATION. Market-perfecting techniques that involve the exchange of price information have been condemned as horizontal restraints of trade. The problem is that oligopolists can use **information-dissemination** techniques to engage in illicit price coordination, which is one of the evils condemned under price-fixing arrangements. At a minimum, competitors' access to each other's pricing structures tends to stabilize prices. This can lead to interdependent pricing because all the competitors in a market will know and react to other competitors' price concessions.

A rule-of-reason analysis generally will be applied to exchanges of non-price information, but, as noted above, any exchange of price information will be suspect as price fixing and receive *per se* illegal treatment.

REFUSALS TO DEAL. Group boycotts, or **refusals to deal,** also are treated as *per se* illegal. This type of restraint involves joint activities by a group of competitors that tries to foreclose another competitor's access to a source of supply or to a market in which to sell. In *Fashion Originators' Guild of America, Inc. v. Federal Trade Commission,* dress manufacturers joined together to attempt to prevent retail stores from buying from other manufacturers who were pirating guild members' designs. Even though it might seem that the guild members were acting only to protect their legitimate creations and to preserve competition, the Court concluded that the conduct was a violation of Section 1 of the Sherman Act. The dress manufacturers acted as if they represented a private government, but private parties cannot violate the antitrust laws to protect competition. It is the federal government's job to protect competition by enforcing the antitrust laws. In a later case the Court extended this line of reasoning and held that a chill on commerce in a refusal-to-deal situation may be enough to violate Section 1, even if the power to affect competition and an actual impact on competition are lacking.

REASONABLE RESTRAINTS. Not all horizontal restraints are dealt with under a *per se* analysis. Some restraints have been held to be reasonable under a rule-of-reason approach. One Supreme Court case involved rules of a grain exchange constraining sales of wheat when the exchange was closed. This was held to be a **reasonable restraint.** As a general standard, if there is a competition-promoting virtue involved (for example, a new product that will vie for market share), the restraint is minor, and there is no way to secure the benefit except with the restraint, the courts may find it reasonable.

THE QUICK-LOOK APPROACH. In more recent years, the courts often have used a "quick-look" approach. (This also applies to vertical restraints.) In any case that does not clearly fall within a defined *per se* category—and even in some cases in which a restraint does but there are countervailing, redeeming virtues to the conduct—the court may take a "quick look" to examine the behavior and the restraint. The court will determine if the conduct was positive or negative and whether the restraint might be considered as reasonable based on this quick look; then the court will classify the case as *per se* or rule of reason and proceed with a full analysis. Thus, in attempting to determine into which pigeonhole

Restraints of trade

Restraint	Legal Analysis Used by Courts
Horizontal Restraints	
Price fixing	*per se* illegal
Market division	*per se* illegal
Information dissemination	
non-price information	rule of reason
price information	*per se* illegal
Refusals to deal	*per se* illegal
Reasonable restraints	rule of reason
Vertical Restraints	
Distribution restrictions	
resale price maintenance	*per se* illegal
consignment agreements	rule of reason
customer and territorial restrictions	rule of reason
Refusals to deal	*per se* illegal
Tying arrangements	*per se* illegal
Exclusive dealing	rule of reason

to classify the restraint, the court may manage to find a redeeming virtue in the arrangement that might allow rule-of-reason treatment.

Vertical Restraints

Vertical restraints are another form of oligopolistic activity. In contrast to horizontal restraints, **vertical restraints** involve firms operating at different levels, for example, a manufacturer-supplier or a retailer-distributor. Vertical restraints that are subject only to Section 1 of the Sherman Act involve distribution restrictions and refusals to deal. Vertical restraints prohibited by both the Sherman Act Section 1 and the Clayton Act Section 3 include tying arrangements and exclusive dealing. As with horizontal restraints, vertical restraints may receive either *per se* illegal or rule-of-reason treatment.

DISTRIBUTION RESTRICTIONS. **Distribution restrictions** can be grouped into three types of restrictions: resale price maintenance, consignment agreements, and customer and territorial restrictions. Resale price maintenance is *per se* illegal. This restriction involves manufacturers setting the price at which their product must be sold by retailers to consumers. Both maximum and minimum resale price restrictions are considered unlawful, for the same reasons as were discussed under horizontal restraints involving information dissemination, because these so-called maximum or minimum prices may be used to peg a fixed price. However, suggested retail prices or consignment arrangements may be used to achieve substantially the same result indirectly, without being treated as *per se* illegal. Manufacturers who retain title and market their goods through consignment arrangements are allowed to specify the terms of sale, including setting the price, as long as they bear the risks associated with ownership.

Manufacturers who have a network of dealers through which they distribute their products may wish to protect these dealers from competition by granting them exclusive territories. The Supreme Court, as is illustrated in the following case, has allowed customer or territorial restrictions unless they unreasonably restrict trade.

CONTINENTAL T.V., INC. v. GTE SYLVANIA INC.
433 U.S. 36, 97 S.Ct. 2549, 53 L.Ed.2d 568 (1977)

In an attempt to improve its market position by attracting better and more aggressive retailers, Sylvania limited the number of retail franchises in any specific area and required each retailer to sell Sylvania's televisions from only the single franchise location. Continental (Plaintiff/Appellee), a disgruntled Sylvania retailer, brought suit against Sylvania (Defendant/Appelant) claiming this location restriction violated Section 1 of the Sherman Act. The District Court awarded damages to Continental using a *per-se* method of analysis. The United States Court of Appeals for the Ninth Circuit reversed, holding that this case should be interpreted using a rule-of-reason standard. The Supreme Court affirmed the Ninth Circuit's decision.

POWELL, Justice.

Per se rules . . . require the Court to make broad generalizations about the social utility of particular commercial practices. The probability that anticompetitive consequences will result from a practice and the severity of those consequences must be balanced against its procompetitive consequences. Cases that do not fit the generalization may arise, but a per se rule reflects the judgment that such cases are not sufficiently common or important to justify the time and expense necessary to identify them. Once established, per se rules tend to provide guidance to the business community and to minimize the burdens on litigants and the judicial system of the more complex rule-of-reason trials, . . . but those advantages are not sufficient in themselves to justify the creation of per se rules. If it were otherwise, all of antitrust law would be reduced to per se rules, thus introducing an unintended and undesirable rigidity in the law.

Interbrand competition is the competition among the manufacturers of the same generic product—television sets in this case—and is the primary concern of antitrust law. The extreme example of a deficiency of interbrand competition is monopoly, where there is only one manufacturer. In contrast, intrabrand competition is the competition between the distributors—wholesale or retail—of the product of a particular manufacturer.

The degree of intrabrand competition is wholly independent of the level of interbrand competition confronting the manufacturer. Thus, there may be fierce intrabrand competition among the distributors of a product produced by a monopolist and no intrabrand competition among the distributors of a product produced by a firm in a highly competitive industry. But when interbrand competition exists, as it does among television manufacturers, it provides a significant check on the exploitation of intrabrand market power because of the ability of consumers to substitute a different brand of the same product. Vertical restrictions reduce intrabrand competition by limiting the number of sellers of a particular product competing for the business of a given group of buyers. Location restrictions have this effect because of practical constraints on the effective marketing area of retail outlets. Although intrabrand competition may be reduced, the ability of retailers to exploit the resulting market may be limited both by the ability of consumers to travel to other franchised locations and, perhaps more importantly, to purchase the competing products of other manufacturers. None of these key variables, however, is affected by the form of the transaction by which a manufacturer conveys his products to the retailers.

Vertical restrictions promote interbrand competition by allowing the manufacturer to achieve certain efficiencies in the distribution of his products. These "redeeming virtues" are implicit in every decision sustaining vertical restrictions under the rule of reason. Economists have identified a number of ways in which manufacturers can use such restrictions to compete more effectively against other manufacturers. . . . For example, new manufacturers and manufacturers entering new markets can use the restrictions in order to induce competent and aggressive retailers to make the kind of investment of capital and labor that is often required in the distribution of products unknown to the consumer. Established manufacturers can use them to induce retailers to engage in promotional activities or to provide service and repair facilities necessary to the efficient marketing of their products. Service and repair are vital for many products, such as automobiles and major household appliances. The availability and quality of such services affect a manufacturer's goodwill and the competitiveness of his product. Because of market imperfections such as the so-called "free rider" effect, these services might not be provided by retailers in a purely competitive situation, despite the fact that each retailer's benefit would be greater if all provided the services than if none did.

Certainly, there has been no showing in this case, either generally or with respect to Sylvania's agreements, that vertical restrictions have or are likely to have a "pernicious effect on competition" or that they "lack . . . any redeeming virtue." Accordingly, we conclude that the per se rule stated in Schwinn must be overruled. . . . Sylvania was faltering, if not failing, and we think it would be unduly artificial to deny it the use of valuable competitive tools.

In sum, we conclude that the appropriate decision is to return to the rule of reason that governed vertical restrictions prior to Schwinn. When anticompetitive effects are shown to result from particular vertical restrictions they can be adequately policed under the rule of reason, the standard traditionally applied for the majority of anticompetitive practices challenged under [Section] 1 of the Act.

Questions

1. Is the court's reasoning persuasive? Why or why not?

2. Is the approach of Justice Powell in this case inconsistent with that of Justice Douglas in *Socony-Vacuum*, or are the two cases sufficiently distinguishable? What is your reasoning?

TYING ARRANGEMENTS. Tying exists when a seller refuses to sell or lease a desired product to a buyer unless they buyer also purchases or leases another undesired product. Section 3 of the Clayton Act and Section 1 of the Sherman Act prohibit tie-ins when the effect may be to lessen competition substantially.

Tying arrangements are analyzed under a qualified *per se* standard. Several requirements must be met to prove a violation. First, two separate and distinct products must be shown to exist—a tying product and a tied product. Second,

the producer of the tying product must be shown to have market power. If there is market power in the tying product, a company could foreclose a significant amount of commerce in the tied product. For example, imagine a company has two products, electric razors (the tying product) and razor blades (the tied product). If that company has an 80-percent share of the electric razor market, it could force anyone that wanted to sell its electric razors also to sell its razor blades, thereby restricting competition in the tied product market. A defendant legally may justify a tying arrangement by proving the tying and tied items are a single product (like left and right shoes) or that the defendant does not have sufficient market power, or that the tie does not affect a substantial amount of commerce.

In addition, *reciprocal agreements* may be attacked as vertical restraints because they, like tying arrangements, give firms economic leverage that may produce effects that restrain trade. Consider the following case.

FORTNER ENTERPRISES, INC. v. UNITED STATES STEEL CORPORATION

394 U.S. 495, 89 S.Ct. 1252, 22 L.Ed.2d 495 (1969)

Fortner Enterprises (Plaintiff/Appellee) brought suit against United States Steel Corporation and its wholly owned subsidiary, United States Steel Homes Credit Corporation (Defendants/Appellants), charging that Defendants had engaged in activities to restrain trade and monopolize the prefabricated homes industry. Fortner claimed that in order to receive loans from Homes Credit Corporation to purchase and develop land, it had been forced to agree to purchase, at artificially high prices, prefabricated houses manufactured by United States Steel. The District Court granted summary judgment for Defendant. The United States Court of Appeals for the Sixth Circuit affirmed. The Supreme Court decided that the question of power in the credit market was a substantial issue, and reversed and remanded the case for further consideration.

BLACK, Justice.

We agree with the District Court that the conduct challenged here primarily involves a tying arrangement of the traditional kind. The Credit Corp. sold its credit only on the condition that petitioner purchase a certain number of prefabricated houses from the Homes Division of U.S. Steel. Our cases have made clear that, at least when certain prerequisites are met, arrangements of this kind are illegal in and of themselves, and no specific showing of unreasonable competitive effect is required.

The standard of "sufficient economic power" does not, as the District Court held, require that the defendant have a monopoly or even a dominant position throughout the market for the tying product. Our tie-in cases have made unmistakably clear that the economic power over the tying product can be sufficient even though the power falls far short of dominance and even though that power exists only with respect to some of the buyers in the market. . . . As we said in the Loew's case, 371 U.S., at 45: "Even absent a showing of market dominance, the crucial economic power may be inferred from the tying product's desirability to consumers or from uniqueness in its attributes." These decisions rejecting the need for proof of truly dominant power over the tying product have all been based on a recognition that because tying arrangements generally serve no legitimate business purpose that cannot be achieved in some less restrictive way, the presence of any appreciable restraint on competition provides a sufficient reason for invalidating the tie. Such appreciable restraint results whenever the seller can exert some power over them [some buyers] and over all other buyers in the market.

Nor does anything in respondents' arguments serve to distinguish credit from other kinds of goods and services, all of which may, when used as tying products, extend the seller's economic power to new markets and foreclose competition in the tied product. The asserted business justifications for a tie of credit are not essentially different from the justifications that can be advanced when the tying product is some other service or commodity. Although advantageous credit terms may be viewed as a form of price competition in the tied product, so is the offer of any other tying product on advantageous terms. In both instances, the seller can achieve his alleged purpose, without extending his economic power, by simply reducing the price of the tied product itself.

Where price reductions on the tied product are made difficult in practice by the structure of that market, the seller can still achieve his alleged objective by offering other kinds of fringe benefits over which he has no economic power.

The potential harm is also essentially the same when the tying product is credit. The buyer may have the choice of buying the tangible commodity separately, but as in other cases the seller can use his power over the tying product to win customers that would otherwise have constituted a market available to competing producers of the tied product. "[Competition] on the merits with respect to the tied product is inevitably curbed." . . . Nor can it be assumed that because the product involved is money needed to finance a purchase, the buyer would not have been able to purchase from anyone else without the seller's attractive credit. A buyer might have a strong preference for a seller's credit because it would eliminate the need for him to lay out personal funds, borrow from relatives, put up additional collateral, or obtain guarantors, but any of these expedients might have been chosen to finance a purchase from a competing producer if the seller had not captured the sale by means of his tying arrangement.

Questions

1. Should the Supreme Court have reversed the two lower federal courts? Why or why not?

2. What issue must the trial court decide when the case returns to it on remand?

EXCLUSIVE DEALING. **Exclusive dealing** exists when a firm agrees to purchase all of a particular product it needs from a seller for a specified period of time. The restraint on competition arises when these agreements have a substantial foreclosure effect on competing sellers, which presupposes a fairly long period of time. These agreements, although similar to tying arrangements, are scrutinized under the rule-of-reason standard. The exclusive dealing test of "substantiality" has involved both quantitative analysis (the foreclosure of a considerable share of the market) and qualitative analysis (the foreclosure of a significant product) in determining the impact on the affected market.

SUMMARY

At common law there were several legal actions that could be instituted to attack restraints of trade. By the end of the nineteenth century, large amounts of economic power had become concentrated in the hands of large entities. The Sherman Act was passed in response to a perceived threat to competition from this economic concentration.

Section 2 of the act forbids monopolization, which is a single company's action to attain an unacceptable amount of market power. The concept of market power is analyzed in the case law to mean control in the relevant product and geographic markets. A company must be exercising this power in both delineated markets to be monopolizing.

Section 1 of the Sherman Act prohibits agreements between competitors to restrain trade. Restraints of trade can be either horizontal or vertical in form. Courts analyze Section 1 cases under either the *per se* illegal or rule-of-reason standard. Certain types of agreements, including price fixing, market divisions, refusals to deal, and tying arrangements are dealt with by the courts as *per se* violations of Section 1 because these restraints have no redeeming competitive virtues. Other restrictions of trade are dealt with under the rule-of-reason approach, which requires the court to look for redeeming competitive virtues and balance them against the restraint on trade to determine if there is an antitrust violation. Recently, courts have initiated a "quick look" approach to cases to determine if they are to be analyzed under the *per se* illegal standard or the rule-of-reason approach.

The antitrust laws studied to this point, the Sherman Act Sections 1 and 2 and the Clayton Act Section 3, represent the American legal system's attempt to deal with the perceived problems of monopoly and oligopoly. The basic principle is that a firm engaging in monopolization or in other anticompetitive practices presents a threat to competition.

Large aggregations of economic power also bring out a latent anti-bigness element of the antitrust laws. Bigness, in the context of the market, is seen as a potential threat to competition. As was noted in the *Alcoa* case, and as will be seen more clearly in the next chapter, economic concentration may be viewed as a danger to competition as much as predatory activities are. The antitrust laws are designed to deal with these dangers. Congress enacted antitrust laws and the courts attempt to interpret them to preserve the natural competition in a free market.

KEY TERMS AND CONCEPTS

antitrust law
trust
Sherman Antitrust Act
Clayton Act
restraint of trade
monopoly
relevant market
relevant product market
relevant geographic market
cross-elasticity
contract, combination, or conspiracy
oligopoly
rule of reason
per se illegal rule
horizontal restraints
price fixing
conscious parallelism
market (territorial) divisions
information dissemination
refusals to deal
reasonable restraint
vertical restraints
distribution restrictions
tying arrangements
exclusive dealing

PROBLEMS

1. Executives from a group of railroad companies hired a public relations firm to create an atmosphere that was favorable to railroads and adverse to trucking companies. The campaign was to be carried out by advertising and persuasion, including influencing legislation. Noerr Motor Freight charged a conspiracy in violation of Section 1 of the Sherman Act. Should the charge be upheld?

2. Catalano, Inc., and other beer retailers in the Fresno, California, area brought suit against Target Sales, Inc., and other area beer wholesalers, charging violation of Section 1 of the Sherman Act. The wholesalers had agreed among themselves that credit no longer would be extended to the retailers. They contended their action in no way constituted a restraint of trade. Are they correct?

3. Topco Associates manufactured a line of household items sold under the Topco name. They were distributed primarily by grocery stores and supermarkets, which were granted exclusive selling territories. A new store could distribute Topco products in an existing dealer's territory only with permission of that dealer. When charged with a violation of the Sherman Act, Topco defended on the ground that the territorial restriction was reasonable, and was designed to stimulate competition between the smaller stores handling Topco and the big chains. Should the defense be permitted?

4. Telex Corporation filed suit against IBM on the ground that IBM controlled too large a share of the market of peripheral devices to be used with its computers. These devices included disk drives, communications adapters (modems), and printers. The trial court held that the relevant market should be restricted to those devices that worked with the IBM computer's unique central processing unit, and IBM appealed, contending the relevant market should be all similar peripheral devices. Should the trial court be reversed?

5. Tampa Electric Company entered into a contract to purchase its entire coal requirements for the next twenty years from West Kentucky Coal Company. Nashville Coal Company sued, contending the contract was a violation of Section 3 of the Clayton Act because it involved too large a percentage of the coal production for peninsular Florida. Tampa defended on the ground that the relevant market should not be restricted to peninsular Florida. What should be the result?

6. A group owned theaters in 85 towns. In 45 of those, there were no other theaters. The group used the power derived from ownership of the 45 noncompeting theaters to get exclusive first- and second-run privileges in the other 35 towns. When charged with antitrust violations, the group defended on the ground that its monopoly in the 45 towns was a natural one, which they were not responsible for creating. Thus, their use of their position should not be considered a violation. Is the defense good?

7. An action was filed by suburban theater owners against a number of movie producers and distributors alleging a violation of Section 1 of the Sherman Act. The evidence showed that the defendants uniformly supplied first-run movies to downtown theaters only, shutting out suburban theaters. The plaintiffs requested, but were refused, a directed verdict that such action was in violation of the Sherman Act, and the plaintiffs appealed. Should the trial court decision be reversed?

8. Suit was brought against an association of container manufacturers, charging violation of Section 1 of the Sherman Act. The defendants, by agreement, freely exchanged pricing information concerning their products. They defended on the ground that they had not agreed to fix price, and had done nothing more than exchange price information. Should the defendants be granted dismissal if only an exchange of pricing information is proven?

9. East Jefferson Hospital, in New Orleans, had an agreement with a group of anesthesiologists. It provided that only they could practice anesthesiology in the hospital. Hyde, another area hospital, brought an action challenging that the agreement was an illegal tying agreement under the Clayton Act. East Jefferson defended on the ground that since there were twenty hospitals in Jefferson Parish, the agreement was not a violation. Is East Jefferson correct?

10. The New York Stock Exchange was charged with perpetrating a concerted refusal to deal when it withdrew the private wire connection of Silver, a broker. Silver could not effectively conduct his business without the direct wire to the exchange, which enabled him to keep track of stock sales and prices as the transactions were completed. No reason was given for the action, which was taken without notice to Silver. The exchange defended on the ground that it was entitled to regulate wire connections to its members. Should the defense be allowed?

Chapter 49

Antitrust: Mergers, Enforcement, and Exemptions

OUTLINE

INTRODUCTION

This chapter continues the discussion of antitrust regulation begun in the last chapter, which con-

sidered the common law origins and abusive industry practices regarding competition that led to the enactment of the first United States antitrust statute, the Sherman Act. In this chapter we will explore Section 7 of the Clayton Act, regulating merger activity; the Robinson-Patman Act, which prohibits price discrimination; Section 8 of the Clayton Act, which prohibits interlocking directorates among certain companies; and Section 5 of the Federal Trade Commission Act, which regulates unfair methods of competition. The other substantive section of the Clayton Act, Section 3, which deals with exclusive dealing contracts and tying arrangements, was covered in the last chapter in the discussion of vertical restraints and will not be examined further. In this chapter we will study the jurisdictional reach of the different statutes; the available remedies for antitrust violations, and who can enforce those remedies; and finally, we will briefly survey some exemptions to the antitrust laws.

MERGERS

A **merger** occurs when one company acquires all the assets or stock of another company, and takes over the control of and combines with that company. Mergers may leave only a handful of companies in an industry and can result in an increased concentration of market power. When there are only a few companies in an industry, the danger of undetectable collusion among them increases. This is one reason concentration is feared. Another is that mergers sometimes squeeze small and local concerns out of the marketplace. Because of their potential anti-competitive impact, mergers are subject to regulation under Section 7 of the Clayton Act.

Mergers are classified into three groups. First, there are **horizontal mergers,** those between two companies within the same industry. Second, there are **vertical mergers,** which occur between companies at different levels of production. Finally, there are **conglomerate mergers,** which have been described as mergers that are neither vertical nor horizontal, and there usually is no functional link between the two companies. When a shoe manufacturer merges with another shoe manufacturer, it is a horizontal merger. If the resulting shoe company then acquired a leather supply company it would be engaging in a vertical merger. If the shoe company were taken over by a grocery store chain, that probably would constitute a conglomerate merger unless the chain was planning to sell shoes in their stores along with groceries.

History

The government had difficulties in controlling mergers under Section 1 of the Sherman Act be-

cause the statute was interpreted by the courts under a rule-of-reason approach after 1911. This standard did not prohibit a proposed merger unless the merger was intended to create a monopoly and actually succeeded in doing so. In *United States v. United States Steel,* even though a merger had been planned to gain monopoly control of the steel industry, the Supreme Court concluded that United States Steel had not achieved monopoly power. By the time the merger was completed, the company had abandoned the goal of monopolization but possessed between 80 and 90 percent of capacity in the steel industry. The Court decided that the merger did not violate the Sherman Act.

Clayton Act Section 7

Because the Supreme Court's permissive standard of judging mergers failed to prevent anti-competitive acquisitions, Section 7 of the Clayton Act was adopted by Congress in 1914. However, because the original section's language applied only to stock purchases, its usefulness was limited. Congress rewrote the statute in 1950 (as part of the Celler-Kefauver Amendment) to make it apply to asset acquisitions as well.

As amended, Section 7 states that no person engaged "in any activity affecting commerce shall acquire" any of the "stock" or "assets" of another person engaged in the same "line of commerce" in the same "section of the country" when "the effect of such acquisition" may be to "substantially lessen competition," or "tend to create a monopoly." The section covers vertical and conglomerate as well as horizontal mergers. The standard of proof also was altered so that, under the current statute, all that need be shown is that there are probable anti-competitive effects from the merger. The purposes of Section 7 are: (1) to prohibit increased market concentration that might create less competitive markets (it is believed this will ensure better market performance); (2) to ensure that small and local businesses can survive as independent business entities in the marketplace; and (3) to encourage internal growth and investment by companies to promote competition in place of the external expansive growth through mergers.

MERGER GUIDELINES. The Justice Department follows written policy guidelines in deciding whether to challenge mergers. The first set of **merger guidelines** were issued in 1968, and they were revamped thoroughly in 1982. The basic policy detailed in the guidelines states that mergers should not be allowed to create or increase a company's market power or to increase the company's ability to exercise that power.

The government's guidelines look at the same market-definition standards that the courts do. The Antitrust Division of the Justice Department has drafted the guidelines to take into consideration various factors, including product and geographic markets. The guidelines also review factors such as product and geographic substitutability, the relative sizes of the two merging firms, and the merging companies' market shares. The focus is on the after-merger impact in the relevant market.

The decision on whether to challenge often is based on the relative size of the after-merged firm in relation to the other companies in the industry. When evaluating horizontal mergers, the government may use the **Herfindahl-Hirsham Index (HHI),** which measures the degree of market concentration in an industry. Regardless of the HHI factor, the Antitrust Division is likely to challenge the merger of any significant firm with the leading firm in any market when the leader has a 35-percent or greater market share.

PRE-MERGER NOTIFICATION. In 1976, Clayton Act Section 7A was enacted requiring advance notice to the government of large mergers. When the acquiring company's total assets or annual sales are at least $100 million, and the acquired company has assets or sales of $10 million or more, notice must be given. A waiting period of thirty days is required after the notice is given before the merger may be completed. Rules governing mergers subject to Section 7A are promulgated by the FTC in conjunction with the Justice Department's Antitrust Division. In addition, certain other government agencies must approve mergers of regulated companies before they can be consummated. For example, mergers between railroads are subject to the Department of Transportation's approval.

JUDICIAL INTERPRETATION. In applying Section 7 the federal courts have focused on three key phrases in the statute. The "line of commerce" language refers to a type of product-market analysis similar to the discussion courts engage in to determine if there has been a Sherman Act Section-2 monopolization. The "section of the country" provision requires the geographic market to be determined. The Supreme Court has recognized that submarkets may exist in both the product and geographic markets. Finally, the court must look into whether the proposed merger "may substantially lessen competition." Under Section 7, there needs to be only a reasonable probability that the merger under examination will cause anti-competitive effects for the courts to prohibit it.

Merger Defenses

Because the standards under Section 7 may prohibit mergers that have only a slight impact on competition, judicial doctrines have arisen that may justify allowing an otherwise-prohibited merger. One general technique for attempting to justify a merger is to defend it on the ground that it will enhance competition. An argument that might be asserted is that two or more small companies should be allowed to merge to compete with larger companies that dominate the market. However, this justification was rejected, or at least strongly limited, by the following case.

UNITED STATES v. VON'S GROCERY CO.
384 U.S. 270, 86 S.Ct. 1478, 16 L.Ed.2d 555 (1966)

The United States (Plaintiff/Appellant) brought an action charging that the acquisition by Von's Grocery of its direct competitor, Shopping Bag Food Stores (Defendants/Appellees), violated Section 7 of the Clayton Act. The District Court concluded that there was "not a reasonable probability" that the merger would tend "substantially to lessen competition" or "create a monopoly" in violation of Section 7, and entered judgment for Defendants. The government appealed directly to the Supreme Court as authorized by an Expediting Act, and the Supreme Court reversed and ordered divestiture.

BLACK, Justice.

. . . The market involved here is the retail grocery market in the Los Angeles area. In 1958, Von's retail sales ranked third in the area and Shopping Bag's ranked sixth. In 1960, their sales together were 7.5% of the total two and one-half billion dollars of retail groceries sold in the Los Angeles market each year. For many years before the merger, both companies had enjoyed great success as rapidly growing companies. [From 1948 to 1958] . . . Von's sales increased fourfold and its share of the market almost doubled while Shopping Bag's sales multiplied seven times and its share of the market tripled. The merger of these two highly successful, expanding and aggressive competitors created the second largest grocery chain in Los Angeles with sales of almost $172,488,000 annually. . . . While the grocery business was being concentrated into the hands of fewer and fewer owners, the small companies were continually being absorbed by the larger firms through mergers. . . . [A]cquisitions and mergers in the Los Angeles retail grocery market have continued at a rapid rate since the merger. These facts alone are enough to cause us to conclude contrary to the District Court that the Von's-Shopping Bag merger did violate S.7.

. . . [T]he basic purpose of the 1950 Celler-Kefauver Act [which amended the Clayton Act to apply to asset acquisitions] was to prevent economic concentration in the American economy by keeping a large number of small competitors in business. In stating the purposes of their bill, both sponsors, Representatives Celler and Kefauver, emphasized their fear, widely shared by other members of Congress, that this concentration was rapidly driving the small businessman out of the market. To arrest this "rising tide" toward concentration into too few hands and to halt the gradual demise of the small businessman, Congress decided to clamp down with vigor on mergers. It both revitalized S.7 of the Clayton Act by "plugging its loophole" and broadened its scope as not only to prohibit mergers between competitors, the effect of which "may be substantially to lessen competition, or to tend to create a monopoly" but to prohibit all mergers having that effect. By using these terms in S.7 which look not merely to the actual present effect of a merger but instead to its effect upon future competition, Congress sought to preserve competition among many small businesses by arresting a trend toward concentration in its incipiency before that trend developed to the point that a market was left in the grip of a few big companies. Thus, where concentration is gaining momentum in a market, we must be alert to carry out Congress' intent to protect competition against ever-increasing concentration through mergers. The facts of this case present exactly the threatening trend toward concentration which Congress wanted to halt. The number of small grocery companies in the Los Angeles retail grocery market had been declining rapidly before the merger and continued to decline rapidly afterwards. This rapid decline in the number of grocery store owners moved hand in hand with a large number of significant absorptions of the small companies by the larger ones. In the midst of this steadfast trend toward concentration, Von's and Shopping Bag, two of the most successful and largest companies in the area, jointly owning 66 grocery stores merged to become the second largest chain in Los Angeles. This merger cannot be defended on the ground that one of the companies was about to fail or that the two had to merge to save themselves from destruction by some larger and more powerful competitor. What we have on the contrary is simply the case of two already powerful companies merging in a way which makes them even more powerful than they were before. If ever such a merger would not violate S.7, certainly it does when it takes place in a market characterized by a long and continuous trend toward fewer and fewer owner-competitors which is exactly the sort of trend which Congress, with power to do so, declared must be arrested.

Appellees' primary argument is that the merger between Von's and Shopping Bag is not prohibited by S.7 because the Los Angeles grocery market was competitive before the merger, has been since, and may continue to be in the future. Even so, S.7 "requires not merely an appraisal of the immediate impact of the merger upon competition, but a prediction of its impact upon competitive conditions in the future; this is what is meant when it is said that the amended S.7 was intended to arrest anticompetitive tendencies in their 'incipiency.'"

[Note: Since the adoption of the 1968 Merger Guidelines, this merger probably would be approved.]

Questions

1. How far in the future must a court look to see if there are potential anti-competitive consequences from a merger?
2. Given the difficulties of foretelling the future, isn't the process described by the Supreme Court something like gazing into a crystal ball?
3. Would the result in this case have been the same had there been no clear trend in the Los Angeles grocery market?

A second merger justification is the **failing company doctrine.** When a company will go out of business unless it is allowed to merge with a competitor, the merger may be allowed. The Supreme Court has narrowed this defense by insisting that there be no other alternative open to the company and no other purchasers interested in the failing company before it will allow the merger.

A third defense suggested by commentators probably would justify mergers; this is when economic efficiencies are produced by the combination of two relatively small and inefficient firms. The courts have not adopted this position, however, arguing that Congress already has decided by law when mergers are to be prohibited. Congress prefers that efficiencies enhancing competition be achieved by internal growth, as opposed to external growth through mergers.

Horizontal Mergers

In the case of a merger of two companies in the same industry, the Federal Trade Commission, the Department of Justice, and the courts will look at the degree of concentration in the relevant market and at the market shares of the two firms. To determine the legality of an acquisition that

Major merger movements (number of manufacturing and mining firms acquired, 1895–1986)

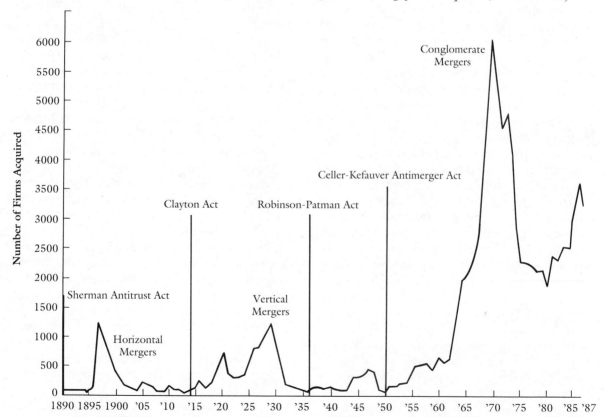

Source: Data for 1895–1968 from F. M. Scherer, *Industrial Market Structure and Economic Performance*, (Chicago: Rand McNally & Company, 1980), p. 120. Data for 1963–1988 from *Economic Report of the President*, 1985. Data for 1986–1987 from *Mergers and Acquisitions*, Vol. 22, April 1988. *Economics* 4th ed. by Ralph T. Burns and Gerald W. Stone. Copyright © 1989, 1987, 1984, 1981 Scott, Foresman and Company.

has been challenged, the court first must determine the "line of commerce"—the product. The second step is to determine the "section of the country" affected—the relevant geography. The court then must look at the probable impact of the proposed merger. If a merger increases the chances of horizontal collusion and does not produce distribution or market efficiencies, it will be declared invalid. On the other hand, if a merger will increase distribution or production efficiency, and will not facilitate collusion among horizontal competitors, it probably will be permitted.

Vertical Mergers

The first step again is to determine the relevant product and geographic markets. The court then must determine if the merger will lessen competition. Vertical mergers often are examined by the courts as a problem of vertical integration. This integration may impede competition by keeping competitors of either the acquirer or the acquired company from a part of the market in which the competitors otherwise might compete. For example, if a supplier of raw materials is acquired by a company that uses those raw materials, competitors of the supplier no longer will be able to sell to the user company if it deals solely with its acquired company for raw materials. Similarly, the acquiring company's competitors may be less able to compete with the acquiring company if the acquired company was the major source of supply for the acquirer's competitors and the raw materials no longer are available to them after the merger. Vertical mergers are prohibited when there is a substantial likelihood that they could create barriers to entry to a potential competitor.

It should be noted that the acquiring company that expands internally, in the example above, by developing its own source of supply of raw materials, may cause the same market foreclosure. Although it might have the same net effect, internal growth is not challengeable under the antitrust laws.

Conglomerate Mergers

A merger between companies in different industries may be viewed as anti-competitive for a number of reasons. The possibility exists that reciprocal trading privileges between the merged companies may foreclose competitors from a significant market. For example, a hotel chain that acquires a car rental agency might swap discounts, allowing people who rent cars from the merged firm a discount on using the hotel chain and viceversa.

Even when there is no perceivable business link between the companies, a conglomerate merger might damage competition by eliminating a plausible potential market entrant. This is called the loss of the "wings effect." The merger eliminates a competitor "waiting in the wings." (See the following *Procter & Gamble* case.) A merger could give an already powerful firm an unfair advantage, because it may increase the barriers to entry in a particular market or because it may increase the opportunity for the powerful company to engage in practices that cause price rigidity. A merger may give a company enough market power to set, or at least to influence, prices in an industry.

Another element of the conglomerate merger situation that is subject to abuse is the potential for a large firm to run amuck in a market of small firms. This concern about market dominance also is present in the following case.

Finally, there is a degree of danger of a "future deconcentration effect." The government has attempted to apply Section 7 to mergers that eliminate the possibility of future competitors entering and deconcentrating a market. The argument runs as follows: But for the merger the acquiring company would have entered the market on its own, thus increasing, as opposed to decreasing, competition, as the acquirer did through the merger. The courts have examined this argument as the Supreme Court does in the following case, but have not yet either accepted or rejected it, generally finding other grounds for liability under Section 7.

FEDERAL TRADE COMMISSION v.
PROCTER & GAMBLE CO.
368 U.S. 568, 87 S.Ct. 1224, 18 L.Ed.2d 303 (1967)

The FTC initiated a proceeding asserting that Procter & Gamble had acquired the assets of Clorox Chemical Company in violation of Section 7 of the Clayton Act. After a hearing the FTC Examiner held the acquisition unlawful and ordered divestiture. The Commission affirmed. The Court of Appeals for the Sixth Circuit reversed and dismissed the FTC's complaint. The Supreme Court reversed the appeals court and affirmed the FTC order of divestiture.

DOUGLAS, Justice.

. . . At the time of the merger, in 1957, Clorox was the leading manufacturer in the heavily concentrated household liquid bleach industry. It is agreed that household liquid bleach is the relevant line of commerce. It is a distinctive product with no close substitutes. Liquid bleach is a low-price, high-turnover consumer product sold mainly through grocery stores and supermarkets. Because of high shipping costs and low sales price, it is not feasible to ship the product more than 300 miles from its point of manufacture. Most manufacturers are limited to competition within a single region since they have but one plant. Clorox is the only firm selling nationally; it has 13 plants distributed throughout the Nation. Purex, Clorox's closest competitor in size, does not distribute its bleach in the northeast or mid-Atlantic States. . . .

At the time of the acquisition, Clorox was the leading manufacturer of household liquid bleach, with 48.8% of the national sales. Its nearest rival was Purex, which accounted for 15.7% of the household liquid bleach market. The industry is highly concentrated; in 1957, Clorox and Purex accounted for almost 65% of the Nation's household liquid bleach sales, and together with four other firms, for almost 80%. . . .

Since all liquid bleach is chemically identical, advertising and sales promotion are vital. In 1957, Clorox spent almost $3,700,000 on advertising, imprinting the value of its bleach in the mind of the consumer. In addition it spent $1,700,000 for other promotional activities. The Commission found that these heavy expenditures went far to explain why Clorox maintained so high a market share despite the fact that its brand, though chemically indistinguishable from rival brands, retailed for a price equal to or, in many instances, higher than its competitors.

Procter is a large, diversified manufacturer of low-price, high-turnover household products sold through grocery, drug and department stores. Prior to its acquisition of Clorox, it did not produce household bleach. . . . Its primary activity is in the general area of soaps, detergents, and cleansers; in 1957, of total domestic sales, more than one-half (over $500,000,000) were in this field. Procter was the dominant factor in this area. It accounted for 54.4% of all packaged detergent sales. The industry is heavily concentrated—Procter and its nearest competitors, Colgate-Palmolive and Lever Brothers, account for 80% of the market.

In 1957, Procter was the Nation's largest advertiser, spending more than $80,000,000 on advertising and an additional $47,000,000 on sales promotion. Due to its tremendous volume, Procter receives substantial discounts from the media. As a multiproduct producer, Procter enjoys substantial advantages in advertising and sales promotion. Thus, it can and does feature several products in its promotions, reducing the printing, mailing, and other costs for each product. It also purchases network programs on behalf of several products, enabling it to give each product network exposure at a fraction of the cost per product that a firm with only one product to advertise would incur. . . .

The decision to acquire Clorox was the result of a study conducted by Procter's promotion department designed to determine the advisability of entering the liquid bleach industry. [The report] recommended that Procter purchase Clorox rather than enter independently. Since a large investment would be needed to obtain a satisfactory market share, acquisition of the industry's leading firm was attractive. . . . The final report confirmed the conclusions of the initial report and emphasized that Procter could make more effective use of Clorox's advertising budget and that the merger would facilitate advertising economies. . . .

The Commission found that the substitution of Procter with its huge assets and advertising advantages for the already dominant Clorox would dissuade new entrants and discourage active competition from the firms already in the industry due to fear of retaliation by Procter. . . . Further, the merger would seriously diminish potential competition by eliminating Procter as a potential entrant into the industry. Prior to the merger, the Commission found, Procter was the most likely prospective entrant, and absent the merger would have remained on the periphery, restraining Clorox from exercising its market power. If Procter had actually entered, Clorox's dominant position would have been eroded and the concentration of the industry reduced. . . .

Section 7 of the Clayton Act was intended to arrest the anticompetitive effects of market power in their incipiency. The core question is whether a merger may substantially lessen competition, and necessarily requires a prediction of the merger's impact on competition, present and future. . . .

The anticompetitive effects with which this product-extension merger is fraught can easily be seen: (1) the substitution of the powerful acquiring firm for the smaller, but already dominant, firm may substantially reduce the competitive structure of the industry by raising entry barriers and by dissuading the smaller firms from aggressively competing; (2) the acquisition eliminates the potential competition of the acquiring firm.

The liquid bleach industry was already oligopolistic before the acquisition, and price competition was certainly not as vigorous as it would have been if the industry were competitive. The interjection of Procter into the market considerably changed the situation. . . . There is every reason to assume that the smaller firms would become more cautious in competing due to their fear of retaliation by Procter. It is probable that Procter would become the price leader and the oligopoly would become more rigid.

The acquisition may also have the tendency of raising the barriers to new entry. The major competitive weapon in the successful marketing of bleach is advertising. Thus, a new entrant would be much more reluctant to face giant Procter than it would the smaller Clorox. . . .

It is clear that the existence of Procter at the edge of the industry exerted considerable influence on the market. First, the market behavior of the liquid bleach industry was influenced by each firm's predictions of the market behavior of its competitors, actual and potential. Second, the barriers to entry by a firm of Procter's size and with its advantages were not significant. Third, the number of potential entrants was not so large that the elimination of one would be insignificant. Fourth, Procter was found by the Commission to be the most likely entrant.

Questions

1. Is Procter & Gamble being punished for failing to enter the liquid bleach industry itself?

2. After this decision, is Procter & Gamble free to acquire Purex? Would its entry into the liquid bleach field in any manner pose any antitrust problems?

INTERLOCKING DIRECTORATES

Section 8 of the Clayton Act prohibits a person from holding directorships in two or more competing corporations. The purpose behind this statute is to remove one temptation for directors to enter into illegal agreements between competitors. The section applies only when at least one of the corporations "has capital, surplus and undivided profits" of more than $1 million. **Interlocking directorates** are forbidden when the elimination of competition between the companies with such directorates would violate the antitrust laws. Section 8 also has provisions, supplemented by Section 10 of the Clayton Act, that deal with banks and trust companies and allow certain regulatory agencies to approve interlocks on firms under their regulatory jurisdiction.

For many years Section 8 was not enforced. Even when an illegal interlock was found, the offending director often was allowed to resign, resolving the problem. More recently, however, the FTC frequently has taken action by issuing a formal order dissolving the interlock and placing restrictions on director elections.

THE ROBINSON-PATMAN ACT

Section 2 of the Clayton Act was amended by Congress in 1936 in response to a concern for small retailers endangered by competition from the growth of chain stores. The act, known as the **Robinson-Patman Act,** was passed in the midst of the Great Depression when many "mom-and-pop" stores were being forced out of business. The act's intention was to limit the price concessions granted to powerful buyers. Section 2, as amended, is designed to prohibit price discrimination unless that discrimination is necessary to meet a competitor's price or is a true reflection of cost savings in the sale.

The primary objectives of the Robinson-Patman Act are (1) to prevent suppliers from gaining an unfair advantage over their competitors by discriminating among buyers through price discounts, or by varying allowances or services to buyers, and (2) to prevent buyers from gaining an edge on their competitors by using their own market power to receive discriminatory prices from suppliers.

The Robinson-Patman Act is a striking example of a statute containing complex and indefinite language. Indeed, Supreme Court Justice Jackson described the statute as "complicated and vague in itself and even more so in its context." One result of the lack of clarity in drafting the legislation has been its negative effect in application. Some commentators have attacked the statute as being anticompetitive in practice, criticizing it for encouraging price uniformity and discouraging price competition.

Clayton Act Section 2(a)

Section 2(a) makes it unlawful "for any person engaged in commerce" . . . "to discriminate in price between different purchasers of commodities of like grade and quality," when the discrimination may "substantially lessen competition or tend to create a monopoly," or "injure, destroy, or prevent competition with any person."

VIOLATION OF THE STATUTE. Section 2(a) sets forth the conditions that must be met before a violation will be found. If they are met, there is a *prima facie* violation of Section 2(a), which means that the plaintiff or the prosecution has met its burden of proof. The defendant then must successfully rebut the case put forward by the other side, provide an acceptable justification for the violation, or lose.

In Commerce. The "in commerce" provision has been interpreted by the courts as a narrow jurisdictional provision (see the discussion of jurisdiction). One of the two compared sales must have been across a state line for the Robinson-Patman Act to apply.

Discrimination in Price. There must be a price difference in two or more sales to different purchasers under Section 2(a). The sales must be fairly close in time and there must be an actual sale at a discriminatory price. Quoting prices or making a discriminatory leasing arrangement does not violate the act.

Commodities. The sale must be of commodities of like grade and quality. Section 2(a) applies only to goods. Price discrimination in services and intangibles is not prohibited. For example, advertising sales, and heat and power provided by utilities, are not subject to Section 2(a) because they are not commodities. In determining products of like grade and quality, different brands or labels are not a sufficient distinction. There must be actual physical differences between the two products to escape the Section 2(a) prohibition.

Injury to Competition. Section 2(a) prohibits discrimination that has the reasonable probability of lessening or injuring competition. There are several types or levels of injury to competition. The lessening of competition between sellers is a primary-line injury. If the injury is to competition between buyers, it is a secondary-line injury. An example of secondary-line injury to competition might be when a wholesaler sells at one price to a small, single retail store and at a lower price to a chain of retail stores. Of course, in that case the price discrimination may cause injury at both levels—to both competitors of the favored buyer and competitors of the discriminating seller.

Finally, competitive injury can occur at a third level—the tertiary line. This injury may occur when the discrimination affects competition between customers of the customers of the seller who discriminates in price. For example, tertiary-line injury would occur when a wholesaler passes his price-favored savings from a manufacturer on to his retail customers. Persons who may bring suit for tertiary-line injuries are limited by the Supreme Court's rule that a remote purchaser cannot sue a remote supplier, because of complicated problems involved in the tracing and apportioning of damages.

It also should be noted, however, that functional discounts are not dealt with by the act. A wholesaler may pay a different price than a retailer for the same goods. These differences in price may result from a difference in the quantity of goods purchased or the different natures and functions of the purchasers. Retailers perform a different function, and operate in the market differently, than wholesalers.

Defenses

Once the listed conditions are satisfied, the defendant will attempt to defend the price discrimination. Under the Robinson-Patman Act, a successful defense completely absolves the defendant. There are three defenses a seller might use to justify a price differential.

The first defense is to show that a price difference is justified on the basis of cost differences to the seller in the sale, delivery, or manufacture to specific customers. If there are differences in the delivery costs or quantities sold, this may cause differences in the seller's costs. Cost differences can justify a price differential. For example, Buyer A, who purchases the seller's product in bulk lots or from the seller's nearby warehouse, will incur less costs to the seller than Buyer B, who purchases the seller's product in small quantities or is a great distance from seller's warehouse. The cost savings may be passed on by the seller to the buyer. However, the expense and difficulties involved in assessing the actual cost savings have hindered the use of this defense. Consider the following case.

UNITED STATES v. BORDEN COMPANY
370 U.S. 460, 82 S.Ct. 1309, 8 L.Ed.2d 627 (1962)

The government (Plaintiff/Appellant) brought this suit to enjoin Appellees, the Borden Company and Bowman Dairy Company (Defendants/Appellees), from selling milk in the Chicago area at prices that discriminated between independently owned stores and chain stores, in violation of Section 2(a) of the Clayton Act—Robinson-Patman. The District Court found a *prima facie* violation, but concluded that the discriminatory prices were justified as a price differential that made "due allowance for differences in the cost of manufacture, sale, or delivery." The government appealed directly to the Supreme Court under the Expediting Act, and the Court reversed and remanded the case.

CLARK, Justice.

There was no dispute as to the existence of price discrimination; the sole question was whether the differences in price reflected permissible allowances for variances in cost.

Both appellees are major distributors of fluid milk products in metropolitan Chicago. The sales of both dairies to retail stores during the period in question were handled under plans which gave most of their customers—the independently owned stores—percentage discounts off list price which increased with the volume of their purchases to a specified maximum while granting a few customers—the grocery store chains—a flat discount without reference to volume and substantially greater than the maximum discount available under the volume plan offered independent stores. These discounts were made effective through schedules which appeared to cover all stores; however, the schedules were modified by private letters to the grocery chains confirming their higher discounts.

To support their defense that the disparities in price between independents and chains were attributable to differences in the cost of dealing with the two types of customers, the appellees introduced cost studies.

The Borden pricing system produced two classes of customers. The two chains, A&P and Jewel, with their combined total of 254 stores constituted one class. The 1,322 independent stores, grouped in four brackets based on the volume of their purchases, made up the other. Borden's cost justification was built on comparisons of its average cost of similar sales to each of the four groups of independents. The costs considered were personnel (including routemen, clerical and sales employees), truck expenses, and losses on bad debts and returned milk.

Bowman's cost justification was based on differences in volume and methods of delivery. It relied heavily upon a study of the cost per minute of its routemen's time. It determined that substantial portions of this time were devoted to three operations, none of which were ever performed for the 163 stores operated by its two major chain customers. These added work steps arose from the method of collection, i.e., cash on delivery and the delayed collections connected therewith, and the performance of "optional customer services." In essence, the Bowman justification was merely a comparison of the costs of these services in relation to the disparity between the chain and independent prices.

On these facts, stated here in rather summary fashion, the trial court held that appellees had met the requirement of the proviso of S.2(a) on the theory that the general cost differences between chain stores as a class and independents as a class justified the disparities in price reflected in appellees' schedules. It noted the "seemingly arbitrary" nature of a classification resulting "in percentage discounts which do not bear a direct ratio to differences in volume of sales." But it found "this mode of classification is not wholly arbitrary." We believe it was erroneous for the trial court to permit cost justifications based upon such classifications.

The burden, of course, was upon the appellees to prove that the illegal price discrimination, which the Government claimed and the trial court found present, was immunized by the cost justification proviso of S.2(a). Such is the mandate of S.2(b). The only question before us is how accurate this showing must be in relation to each particular purchaser.

. . . [T]he practice of grouping customers for pricing purposes has long had the approval of the Federal Trade Commission. . . . [T]o completely renounce class pricing as justified by class accounting would be to eliminate in practical effect the cost justification proviso as to sellers having a large number of purchasers, thereby preventing such sellers from passing on economies to their customers. It seems hardly necessary to say that such a result is at war with Congress' language and purpose.

But this is not to say that price differentials can be justified on the basis of arbitrary classifications or even classifications which are representative of a numerical majority of the individual members. At some point practical considerations shade into a circumvention of the proviso. A balance is struck by the use of classes for cost justification which are composed of members of such selfsameness as to make the averaging of the cost of dealing with the group a valid and reasonable indicium of the cost of dealing with any specific member. High on the list of "musts" in the average cost of customer groupings under the proviso of S.2(a) is a close resemblance of the individual members of each group on the essential point or points which determine the costs considered.

In this regard we do not find the classifications submitted by the appellees to have been shown to be of sufficient homogeneity. Certainly, the cost factors considered were not necessarily encompassed within the manner in which a customer is owned. Turning first to Borden's justification, we note that it not only failed to show that the economics relied upon were isolated within the favored class but affirmatively revealed that members of the classes utilized were substantially unalike in the cost savings aspects considered. Likewise the details of Bowman's cost study show a failure in classification.

In sum, the record here shows that price discriminations have been permitted on the basis of cost differences between broad customer groupings, apparently based on the nature of ownership but in any event not shown to be so homogeneous as to permit the joining together of these purchasers for cost allocations purposes.

Questions

1.   What will the Borden Company have to do on the remand if it hopes to have its defense of cost differences prevail?

2.   Does the theory advanced by Borden Company seem implausible? Why or why not?

As a second defense, a defendant might be able to prove that the lower price of a commodity was altered to respond to changing market conditions. The last proviso in Section 2(a) provides for this defense, but it will be allowed only in rare cases when temporary conditions brought about by the physical nature of the commodity cause drastic shifts in the value. For example, imminent deterioration of perishable goods might be a circumstance in which this defense would be recognized. A price discount on seasonal goods—like Christmas decorations—that have become obsolete also may be a changing condition permitting this defense to be asserted successfully.

Finally, Section 2(b) provides that a seller may rebut a *prima facie* violation by proving that the lower price was made in good faith to match a competitor's low price. This defense has been interpreted strictly by the FTC, which has persuaded the courts to limit it. The seller can only meet, not undercut, the price offered by a competitor. The good-faith standard requires the seller to have reasonable grounds to believe it is meeting a competitor's lower price; the word of a customer or salesperson may not be sufficient. Exactly what evidence would be sufficient is not entirely clear.

The Robinson-Patman Act's other provisions, Sections 2(c), (d), and (e), forbid indirect price discrimination in the form of commissions, services, or facilities supplied by the seller or other payments to buyers. Violations of these sections are *per se* illegal and there are no defenses comparable to Sections 2(a) or (b) to rebut the violations.

THE FEDERAL TRADE COMMISSION ACT

Section 5 of the **Federal Trade Commission Act** declares that "unfair methods of competition" and "unfair or deceptive acts or practices," in or affecting commerce, are unlawful. This broad language gives the FTC the power to enforce "the spirit" of the antitrust laws. The commission is not limited to enforcing the statutory prohibitions or attacking common-law restraints of trade. Section 5 authorizes the FTC to act before an actual violation occurs. The FTC can intervene to stop conduct in its incipiency that has the potential to violate the antitrust laws. In addition, the gaps left in the antitrust statutes may be filled by orders and interpretations of the commission. Finally, the FTC may find that conduct, although it does not violate the letter or spirit of the other antitrust statutes, is an **unfair method of competition.** In practice, this gives the FTC powers similar to a court of equity. With a quasi-legislative power to determine what is "unfair" in business competition, the commission may consider public values beyond those expressed in the antitrust laws. The FTC has expressed its standards of unfairness as those actions offensive to public policy—immoral, unethical, oppressive, and unscrupulous acts—or those actions that cause substantial injury to competitors or others in business. This certainly is not an exact or fixed standard; it is more of a golden rule.

The Magnuson-Moss Warranty Act of 1975 added a new Section 18 to the FTC Act authorizing the commission to issue substantive rules of business conduct. The FTC has used this power to prescribe consumer-protection rules in an attempt to define what is and what is not unfair business conduct in the eyeglass industry, and has proposed rules in other areas such as the funeral industry and advertising directed primarily toward children. The FTC also used this power to eliminate the holder in due course doctrine in consumer transactions, as discussed in Chapter 18.

JURISDICTION OF COURTS

The Sherman Act, covered in the last chapter, the Clayton Act, and Section 5 of the FTC Act all give United States courts the power to enforce the antitrust laws whenever interstate commerce is affected. The Supreme Court has adopted a very broad view of what affects interstate commerce. Today, almost all business activity would be considered to have an interstate impact, so the antitrust laws extend to all commerce that is not completely local. Even if a particular restraint of trade is purely local—if the restraint and its effect are contained entirely within a single state—it will not escape regulation. In virtually every state there are unfair-competition and trade-regulation statutes that contain many of the same provisions as the federal antitrust laws.

Only the Robinson-Patman Act has a narrower jurisdictional scope, because it only applies to acts that occur "in commerce," in contrast to the standard of "affecting commerce." For a transaction to be within the reach of this act, it must involve two or more states directly. For example, a seller in Iowa who discriminates in the price of a product between buyers from Iowa and buyers from Arizona would be acting "in commerce." A seller in Iowa who sold a product in Iowa that indirectly caused a price discrimination in that product in Arizona would not be acting "in commerce." The statute also is restricted to American companies and sales within the United States.

Foreign commerce may lie within the bounds of the federal antitrust laws. Sherman Act Sections 1 and 2 apply also to persons who act under an agreement to restrain trade or who act to monopolize trade with foreign nations. The foreign commerce provision of the Sherman Act may be enforced against foreign companies or American companies acting outside the United States. Situations in which the Sherman Act is applied to foreign trade are subtle and complex. It is sufficient to note that the crucial element in determining if the Sherman Act covers an activity is the impact it has on the United States. International concerns and the reach of the laws of other nations also restrict the exercise of jurisdiction under the Sherman Act when dealing with foreign nations.

ENFORCEMENT AND REMEDIES

The United States Department of Justice and the Federal Trade Commission are the federal agencies responsible for enforcing the antitrust laws.

The Justice Department has the basic power to enforce the Sherman Act and the Clayton Act. The FTC has exclusive authority under Section 5 of the FTC Act to pursue unfair methods of competition affecting commerce. The FTC also has overlapping responsibility with the Justice Department in enforcing the Clayton Act Sections 2, 3, 7, and 8. In practice, the commission is most concerned with unfair competition involving the Clayton and Robinson-Patman acts. Thus, in most cases the FTC investigates reported abuses, but actual prosecutions for antitrust violations usually are carried out by the Justice Department.

The Justice Department

Under the Sherman Act, the Antitrust Division of the Department of Justice can seek either criminal or civil sanctions for violations of the statute. The act provides for criminal felony prosecution. Any person convicted under the statute is subject to a fine of up to $100,000 or imprisonment of up to three years, or both. A corporation can be fined up to $1 million. The Clayton Act provides for only civil proceedings to enforce its provisions.

Under either act, the Antitrust Division may institute civil proceedings to restrain conduct in violation of the antitrust statutes. The division may request various remedies, including injunctions prohibiting the continuance of the activity violating the acts and decrees of divorcement, divestiture, or dissolution. *Divorcement* may force a company to stop a certain aspect of its activity. For example, a manufacturer may be ordered to stop the retail part of its business. *Divestiture* is an order for a company to dispose of certain assets— often a subsidiary corporation or stock in another company—ownership of which is causing an antitrust violation. *Dissolution* is the most drastic remedy. It requires a company to liquidate its assets and go out of business.

The division also may settle a controversy with an antitrust defendant by means of an agreement known as a *consent decree*. In this type of decree, both parties agree to the remedy or relief that the court should order, but the defendant does not acknowledge guilt of any antitrust violation. In the criminal context, an antitrust defendant may plead *nolo contendere* (no contest) and pay a fine or comply with the course of action ordered in the court's decree. The government uses these decrees to secure enforcement of the antitrust statutes without the expense and time-consuming aspects involved in a full trial. Defendants often agree to meet the conditions of a decree in order to avoid private lawsuits for civil liability based on an antitrust conviction.

Before a consent decree can be entered, the federal court must determine that the decree satisfies the "public interest." Thus, the final responsibility for enforcing the provisions of the antitrust laws rests with the courts. Consent decrees and pleas of *nolo contendere* cannot be used against a defendant in subsequent private lawsuits. Section 5(a) of the Clayton Act provides that convictions for antitrust violations may be used in private treble-damage lawsuits as proof that an antitrust act was violated.

The Federal Trade Commission

The FTC was created by Section 1 of the Federal Trade Commission Act of 1914. It is an independent administrative agency composed of five commissioners appointed by the president. The FTC has the authority to investigate and report on violations of the antitrust laws. The agency usually acts on complaints from businesses or the general public that unfair or deceptive practices are occurring. Section 5 of the FTC Act also empowers the FTC to promulgate rules and regulations to reduce unfair methods of competition.

The FTC's main enforcement mechanism is the **cease and desist order,** which tells the persons engaging in activitites or practices in violation of the act to stop them. The cease and desist order acts much like a court injunction, and is reviewable by a court. Anyone who violates a cease and desist order is subject to a fine of up to $10,000 per day for as long as the violation continues.

Other Administrative Agencies

Certain administrative agencies that regulate specific industries have been authorized by federal statutes to control competition in those industries. For example, the Federal Aviation Administration is authorized to control competition on air routes, and the Federal Communications Commission is authorized to regulate radio and television licenses. Some of these specific statutes provide for exemptions from certain antitrust statutes for the regulated industry. In recent years, there has been an enormous movement to deregulate various industries, which has reduced the activity of these agencies considerably.

Private Enforcement

Individuals and companies injured by antitrust violations may bring private damage suits against the violators. In order to have standing to bring a damage suit (or to seek any other remedy), the plaintiff must prove that there is a direct connection between her injury and the defendant's actions. As noted earlier, the Supreme Court has restricted suits for damages to those directly injured. Anyone who suffers indirect injury through a distributional chain does not have standing to sue under the Clayton Act Section 4. This section provides relief for a private party suing under either the Sherman Act or the Clayton Act only if (1) the antitrust violation caused or was a substantial factor in bringing about the injury suffered, and (2) the defendant's illegal acts affected business activities of the plaintiff that the antitrust laws were designed to protect.

In damage suits brought under either the Sherman Act or Clayton Act, a successful plaintiff can collect treble damages—three times the actual damages awarded. In addition, a successful plaintiff may be able to collect reasonable attorneys' fees. The possibility of treble damage awards and attorneys' fees provides an incentive for private parties to help enforce the antitrust laws. Sometimes, however, the motivation for private antitrust actions seems to be some type of competitive advantage or an attempt to punish another business. There has been such a large amount of litigation by private plaintiffs in recent years that the Justice Department and congressional committees

Summary of antitrust laws

Statute	Major Provisions
Sherman Antitrust Act (1890)	Prohibits contracts, combinations, and conspiracies in retraint of trade and forbids monopolization or attempts to monopolize
Clayton Act (1914)	Prohibits certain forms of price discrimination, contracts that prevent buyers from dealing with sellers' competitors, acquisition of one corporation's shares by another if the effect will be to substantially lessen competition, and interlocking directorates between competing corporations
Federal Trade Commission Act (1914)	Established the FTC to investigate unfair and deceptive business practices
Robinson-Patman Act (1936)	Amended the Clayton Act (Section 2) to prohibit discounts and other special price concessions. Price discrimination is permissible only where it is (1) based on differences in cost, (2) a good-faith effort to meet competition, and (3) based on differences in marketability of product
Celler-Kefauver Antimerger Act (1950)	Amended Section 7 of the Clayton Act to plug the loopholes that permitted merger via acquisition of assets. In addition, the law prohibited mergers where there was a trend toward concentration

have considered eliminating the treble-damage provision, but it is unlikely that this will happen.

EXEMPTIONS

The antitrust statutes are subject to certain limitations, exceptions, and exemptions. As noted above, activities that are totally intrastate are beyond the reach of the federal statutes, as are certain aspects of foreign trade. There are several areas of the economy that have been completely shielded from antitrust scrutiny by statutory exemptions, including labor unions, agricultural and fishing cooperatives, exporting associations, and the insurance industry. There also are limited exceptions to the antitrust laws covering certain industries, such as banking, public utilities, transportation, and communications, that "affect the public interest" and are regulated by state and federal agencies. Finally, certain constitutional rights limit the application of the antitrust laws.

Statutory Exemptions

One of the most extensive exemptions has been granted to labor unions and collective bargaining agreements. In 1914, the Clayton Act first established the labor union exemption, which was further strengthened under the Norris-LaGuardia Act of 1932. With the establishment of the National Labor Relations Act in 1935, unions and their activities became almost completely protected from antitrust legislation. Unions, however, cannot combine with non-labor groups— for example, businesses—for the purpose of illegally restraining competition.

Agricultural cooperatives are exempt from antitrust regulation under Section 6 of the Clayton Act. The fishing industry also is allowed to form marketing cooperatives exempt from the antitrust laws. Monopoly prices charged by organizations in these two industries may be restrained by cease and desist orders issued by the appropriate cabinet member, the secretary of agriculture, or the secretary of the interior.

Trade associations of exporters involved in foreign trade are exempted from the antitrust laws by the Webb-Pomerene Act. The activities of exporters are exempt to the extent they do not "artificially or intentionally enhance or depress prices within the United States." This statute is designed to allow American companies to compete in world markets with foreign cartels.

Finally, the patent and copyright laws provide for a statutorily approved monopoly awarded for invention and artistic creativity. Thus certain activities relating to patents and copyrights are exempt from the antitrust laws.

Regulated Industries

Industries that already are regulated by state and federal authorities are exempt from certain aspects of the antitrust laws. Under the McCarran-Ferguson Act, the insurance business is exempt from the antitrust laws if it is regulated by state law. Today, all fifty states individually regulate the insurance industry, and thus it is not subject to federal regulation. Bank mergers are exempt from Section 1 of the Sherman Act and Section 7 of the Clayton Act under special legislation.

Common carriers are regulated by the Interstate Commerce Commission (ICC). Mergers, acquisitions of properties, and pooling agreements concerning routes or revenues, if approved by the commission, are exempt from the antitrust laws. The ICC is charged with reviewing arrangements that affect competition in order to protect the public interest.

The airline industry is regulated by the Federal Aviation Administration (FAA). Agreements among airlines involving competitive practices must be approved by that agency. The FAA maintains a cease and desist order power to regulate unfair or deceptive practices by air carriers. Because of the Airline Deregulation Act of 1978, certain practices that previously were regulated by the FAA now may be subject to antitrust regulation.

Sports and Professional Organizations

Ever since the 1920s, a judicially created exemption has protected professional baseball from the antitrust laws. The Supreme Court determined that baseball was a sport and was not "commerce." No other professional sport has been exempt from the antitrust statutes, as was well illustrated in the recent suit by the United States Football League against the National Football League. They all have been determined to be operating in interstate commerce, creating an historical anomaly for baseball.

At one time professional organizations were not regulated under the antitrust laws. This is no longer the case. Lawyers, doctors, and other professionals have been sued under the antitrust laws for setting fees and restricting competitive bidding. The old argument supporting these anti-competitive restrictions, which was that they were necessary to maintain professional standards and high quality of services for the client, no longer prevents antitrust regulation of professionals.

NATIONAL SOCIETY OF PROFESSIONAL ENGINEERS v. UNITED STATES
435 U.S. 679, 98 S.Ct. 1355, 55 L.Ed.2d 637 (1978)

The United States brought a civil antitrust suit against the National Society of Professional Engineers alleging that the society's canon of ethics, prohibiting competitive bidding by its members, suppressed competition in violation of Section 1 of the Sherman Act. The District Court opinion, as modified by the Court of Appeals, prohibited the society from adopting any official guidelines implying that competition was unethical. The Supreme Court affirmed.

STEVENS, Justice.

. . . The question is whether the canon may be justified under the Sherman Act, because it was adopted by members of a learned profession for the purpose of minimizing the risk that competition would produce inferior engineering work endangering the public safety. . . .

This case involves a charge that the members of the society have unlawfully agreed to refuse to negotiate or even to discuss the question of fees until after a prospective client has selected the engineer for a particular project. Evidence of this agreement is found in S.11(c) of the Society's Code of Ethics, adopted in July 1964.

. . . [T]he Society averred that the standard set out in the Code of Ethics was reasonable because competition among professional engineers was contrary to the public interest. It was averred that it would be cheaper and easier for an engineer "to design and specify inefficient and unnecessarily expensive structures and methods of construction." Accordingly, competitive pressure to offer engineering services at the lowest possible price would adversely affect the quality of engineering. Moreover, the practice of awarding engineering contracts to the lowest bidder, regardless of quality, would be dangerous to the public health, safety, and welfare. For these reasons, the Society claimed that its Code of Ethics was not an "unreasonable restraint of interstate trade or commerce." . . .

In *Goldfarb v. Virginia State Bar,* the Court held that a bar association's rule prescribing minimum fees for legal services violated S.1 of the Sherman Act. In that opinion the Court noted that certain practices by members of a learned profession might survive scrutiny under the Rule of Reason even though they would be viewed as a violation of the Sherman Act in another context. The Court said:

> The fact that a restraint operates upon a profession as distinguished from a business is, of course, relevant in determining whether that particular restraint violates the Sherman Act. It would be unrealistic to view the practice of professions as interchangeable with other business activities, and automatically to apply to the professions antitrust concepts which originated in other areas. The public service aspect, and other features of the professions may require that a particular practice, which could properly be viewed as a violation of the Sherman Act in another context be treated differently. . . .

In this case we are presented with an agreement among competitors to refuse to discuss prices with potential customers until after negotiations have resulted in a selection of an engineer. While this is not price fixing as such, no elaborate industry analysis is required to demonstrate the anticompetitive character of such an agreement. It operates as an absolute ban on competitive bidding, applying with equal force to both complicated and simple projects and to both inexperienced and sophisticated customers. As the District Court found, the ban "impedes the ordinary give and take of the marketplace," and substantially deprives this customer of the "ability to utilize and compare prices in selecting engineering services." On its face, this agreement restrains trade within the meaning of S.1 of the Sherman Act.

The Society's affirmative defense confirms rather than refutes the anticompetitive purpose and effect of its agreement. The Society argues that the restraint is justified because bidding on engineering services is inherently imprecise, would lead to deceptively low bids, and would thereby tempt individual engineers to do inferior work with consequent risk to public safety and health. The logic of this argument will tend to maintain the price level; if it had no such effect, it would not serve its intended purpose. . . .

Petitioner's ban on competitive bidding prevents all customers from making price comparisons in the initial selection of an engineer, and imposes the Society's views of the costs and benefits of competition on the entire marketplace. It is this restraint that must be justified under the Rule of Reason, and petitioner's attempts to do so on the basis of the potential threat that competition poses to the public safety and the ethics of its profession is nothing less than a frontal assault on the basic policy of the Sherman Act.

The Sherman Act reflects a legislative judgment that ultimately competition will produce not only lower prices, but also better goods and services. . . . [T]he statutory policy precludes inquiry into the question whether competition is good or bad.

The fact that engineers are often involved in large-scale projects significantly affecting public safety does not alter our analysis. Exceptions to the Sherman Act for potentially dangerous goods and services would be tantamount to a repeal of the statute. . . .

We are faced with a contention that a total ban on competitive bidding is necessary because otherwise engineers will be tempted to submit deceptively low bids. Certainly, the problem of professional deception is a proper subject of an ethical cannon. But, once again, the equation of competition with deception, like the similar equation with safety hazards, is simply too broad; we may assume that competition is not entirely conducive to ethical behavior, but that is not a reason, cognizable under the Sherman Act, for doing away with competition.

In sum, the Rule of Reason does not support a defense based on the assumption that competition itself is unreasonable. . . .

Questions

1. In what ways would it be appropriate to treat members of a learned profession differently under the antitrust laws?

2. Are there any arguments that the notion of price competition for professional services is *not* an essential ingredient of the antitrust laws?

Protected Activities

Government actions, and activities by state administrative agencies, are immune from the antitrust laws. According to the Supreme Court, if there is adequate public supervision and the state has a clear purpose to displace competition, the antitrust laws are not applicable. Examples of subject matters determined to be immune under this doctrine are state-authorized preferences for small businesses, minority employment, and state professional-license boards.

The Supreme Court also has stated that the Sherman Act does not prohibit two or more persons from associating together in an attempt to persuade the legislature or government from taking a specific action with regard to laws involving competitive restraints or monopolization. However, this First Amendment right to associate and to petition the government for redress is limited. Conduct that really is a sham attempt to engage in protected activity is not shielded from the antitrust laws.

SUMMARY

Mergers may present a threat to competition. The greater the concentration in an industry and the larger the size of the merger, the more there is a danger to competition. Because of the potential impact on competition, all three types of mergers—horizontal, vertical, and conglomerate—are scrutinized and are subject to Section 7 of the Clayton Act. The Justice Department has a set of guidelines that establish standards for mergers. When reviewing mergers, courts analyze market power in ways similar to the analysis under Section 2 of the Sherman Act. There are several defenses to a violation of Section 7, but the judiciary has construed these merger justifications narrowly. Different types of mergers may have different anticompetitive impacts.

Section 7A of the Clayton Act requires that corporations involved in certain large mergers notify the government. This gives the government a chance to review and, if necessary, act to prevent the merger before it is completed.

Section 8 of the Clayton Act prohibits interlocking directorates. This is intended to remove the temptation of illegal collusion from corporate boardrooms.

The Robinson-Patman Act is designed to prevent abuses of economic power by businesses that buy and sell products in commerce. The act was designed to forestall price discrimination, in order to bring an equality of economic bargaining power to the selling-buying business relationship. The statute's technical language requires certain specific conditions to be met before a violation occurs. There are, in response, certain defenses that may justify price discrimination. However, the statute does not address all of the potential injuries to competition.

The technical and complex nature of the act makes it difficult to apply, and it has been criticized for inducing rather than reducing anti-competitive effects. The defenses are construed strictly and the requirements often are hard for a defendant to meet. Overall, it is not clear that competition is enhanced by this act, but it remains an important component of antitrust law.

Section 5 of the FTC Act fills the gaps in the other statutes and helps to enforce the spirit as well as the letter of the antitrust laws, especially by trying to reach potentially anti-competitive behavior before it matures. It is enforced exclusively by the FTC.

The jurisdiction of most antitrust laws extends to all activities affecting commerce. This covers most significant business activity. The Robinson-Patman Act has a more limited, "in commerce" jurisdictional standard. Legal tools available to enforce the antitrust laws include civil fines, criminal charges, administrative cease and desist orders, and a variety of court orders. Treble damages are available to private plaintiffs.

There are a number of exemptions to the antitrust acts, some complete, some partial. Generally, these exemptions have been granted because another government agency has been delegated the task of regulating competitive practices in a particular industry. Government activities are immune from the antitrust laws.

KEY TERMS AND CONCEPTS

merger
horizontal merger
vertical merger
conglomerate merger
merger guidelines
Herfindahl-Hirsham Index (HHI)
failing company doctrine
line of commerce
interlocking directorate
Robinson-Patman Act
Federal Trade Commission Act
unfair method of competition
cease and desist order

PROBLEMS

1. Reynolds Metals, a producer of aluminum products and the world's largest producer of aluminum foil, purchased all of the assets and stock of Arrow Brands, Incorporated, a company engaged in converting aluminum foil into decorative foil used by the florist trade. The FTC challenged the acquisition as a violation of Section 7 of the Clayton Act. The district court ordered divestiture, and Reynolds appealed, contending the relevant product market should be the sale of decorative foil generally rather than the sale of decorative foil only to the florist trade (the standard used by the district court). Of approximately 9.7 million pounds of decorative foil produced each year by some 200 firms, only 1.5 million was sold to the florist trade. The latter was produced by eight firms, and was sold at a lower price than other decorative foil. Should the relevant product market be redefined on appeal?

2. Continental Can, the nation's second-largest producer of metal containers, acquired all of the assets and business of Hazel-Atlas Glass Company, the nation's third-largest producer of glass containers. This merger was challenged by the government. After a hearing, the district court dismissed the complaint, holding that metal containers and glass containers made up separate product markets. Should the dismissal be reversed?

3. Ford Motor Company acquired all of the assets of Autolite. At the time of acquisition, there were two independent manufacturers of spark plugs, Autolite and Champion, and a third company, AC, which was owned by General Motors. The court found the acquisition to be in violation of Section 7 of the Clayton Act, reasoning that it foreclosed ten percent of the market for independent spark-plug producers, and ordered divestiture, an injunction prohibiting Ford from manufacturing its own spark plugs for a period of ten years, and that Ford should buy half of its requirements from Autolite for the next five years. Ford challenged the second and third parts of the order as unreasonable and in excess of the court's remedial powers. Should those parts of the order be set aside?

4. The government challenged a merger of Phillipsburg National Bank and Second National Bank, even though the merger had been approved by the comptroller of the currency. There were seven banks in the area served, but only two in Phillipsburg after the merger. The merging banks drew 85 percent of their business from the Phillipsburg-Easton area, and only about 10 percent from the Easton area. The government contended that the relevant geographical market was Phillipsburg, and the banks contended it should be the entire area served. Which is correct?

5. Paragraph 1, Section 8 of the Clayton Act prohibits interlocking directorates between certain banks. Paragraph 4 prohibits interlocking directorates between any two or more corporations under certain circumstances, but says "other than banks, banking associations . . . ." Crocker National [banking] Corporation shared three directors with some large life insurance companies that competed with Crocker in the real-estate loan market. Crocker claimed that the exemption in Paragraph 4 of Section 8 excepted the directorates in question. Is Crocker correct?

6. The Shipping Act of 1916 authorizes the Federal Maritime Commission to approve cooperative working agreements between shipping companies, including agreements not to compete. It further provides that approved agreements will be exempt from the antitrust laws. The commission approved the acquisition of two of the world's largest containership companies by a third corporation. They were to be subsidiaries of the parent, and the commission required that they be operated independently. This was challenged as in excess of the commission's powers under the act. The commission contended that the arrangement was an ongoing one, with independent operation, and was within its powers. Should the commission's order be affirmed or vacated?

7. May a merger between two noncompeting companies involved in the same line of commerce, but in different geographical locations, be considered an antitrust violation under the Clayton Act?

8. A working agreement between the corporate publishers of a city's only evening newspaper and its only morning and Sunday paper was challenged under the Sherman and Clayton acts. The publishers defended on the ground that one of the newspapers, *(The Citizen)* was in danger of failing if the agreement was not approved. The evidence showed that, indeed, *The Citizen* had been operating at a loss while the other newspaper, *The Star,* was profitable. On this evidence, should the agreement, involving agreements not to compete, be exempt from the antitrust laws?

9. A consolidation of two Philadelphia banks was held anti-competitive in the Philadelphia market and, thus, in violation of the Clayton Act. The banks, however, sought an exemption from the act on the ground that the resulting larger bank would increase competition in the area of larger commercial loans, a disproportionate number of which were being taken by large out-of-state banks, particularly New York banks. If the evidence shows that the effect contended would result, should the exemption be granted?

10. In the previous case, the banks also argued that the transaction actually constituted only an acquisition of assets, since the resulting stock given to the seller in exchange would be distributed to the seller's shareholders. Therefore, the transaction would not be covered by the Clayton Act, since banks are not subject to regulation by the Federal Trade Commission. Are the banks correct?

Labor-Management Relations

AN OVERVIEW OF LABOR LAW

Labor law, in the broadest sense of the term, contemplates a wide variety of federal and state law. Much of it is statutory, but it also includes a considerable amount of case law. In addition, labor law derives from some other general areas of law, specifically agency and contracts.

Today, labor law and policy are set primarily on the federal level, although state law also is important in four principal circumstances. First, federal laws does not govern labor relations concerning state and local public employees. Second, even in the public sector, federal law governs disputes involving only certain employers and certain employees who are involved in or affect interstate commerce, and usually only when the business of the employer is above a certain specified size limit. Third, some aspects of federal law defer to the states to set policy, such as whether to permit certain provisions—for example, "union shop" or "agency shop" (discussed in Chapter 51)—in collective bargaining agreements. Finally, state law tends to control the portion of labor law generally called *employment law,* which embraces workers' compensation and aspects of the workplace such as privacy, safety, and discrimination. Employment law is the subject of Chapter 52. Most state legislation in the labor law field tends to follow the general outline of major federal labor enactments, especially the National Labor Relations Act.

The **National Labor Relations Act** is the major piece of federal legislation in the labor law area. Actually, it is not one act, but a combination of three. They are the *Wagner Act* of 1935, the *Taft-Hartley Act* of 1947, and the *Landrum-Griffin Act* of 1959. Each of these separate statutes marks a distinct turning point in United States labor policy, and they are best understood when studied against a backdrop of the labor movement's history.

Early History through 1842

During the eleventh, twelfth, and thirteenth centuries, English society was dominated by a *feudal system*. Labor was performed primarily by *serfs*, who were akin to slaves except that they were bound to the land rather than being the property of a master. Because of this, there was no significant notion of labor rights. However, during the same time, the Crusades were being fought, and this decimated the noble class. Also, the bubonic plague (Black Death) swept Europe in the fourteenth century, creating an acute shortage of labor. Serfs and villains defected from the manors to the towns and cities, and trade routes were reopened to the East. With these events, labor became independent and its bargaining position began to improve.

In an effort to curb the effects of this change, the *First Statute of Laborers* was enacted by Parliament in 1351. One of its provisions made every "conspiracy" to raise the wages for labor a criminal offense. A conspiracy, of course, involved collusion by two or more persons. Therefore, in effect, any kind of effective organization by labor was held to be illegal, the common law adopting this so-called *criminal conspiracy doctrine.* This was bolstered and expanded in 1562 by the passage of the *Second Statute of Laborers.* With the approach of the nineteenth century and the beginning of the Industrial Revolution, the criminal

conspiracy doctrine began to lose support, and finally was disposed of by the *Conspiracy and Protection Act* of 1875.

To replace the faltering criminal conspiracy doctrine, two other concepts were established by the English courts and accepted in America—the *contractual interference doctrine,* first arising in the case of *Lumley v. Gye* in 1853, and the *civil conspiracy doctrine,* in *Quinn v. Leathem,* in 1901. These replaced labor's criminal liability with tort liability. Plainly, the mood of both English and American law remained anti-labor.

The first, although isolated, prolabor case of consequence to be decided in America was *Commonwealth v. Hunt* in 1842, in which the Massachusetts court held that organized labor activity was not unlawful *per se,* as long as it sought to accomplish legal ends by legal means. Since the birth of this so-called Ends and Means Doctrine, the right of labor to *organize* (although not necessarily to act) has not been questioned seriously in either courts or legislatures in the United States.

The Antitrust Years

Although the decision in *Commonwealth v. Hunt* was a significant victory for labor, the flush of success was to be short lived. Congress passed the Sherman Act of 1890, declaring "Every contract, combination . . . or conspiracy, in restraint of trade or commerce . . ." to be illegal. Whether Congress intended that this act apply to labor or only to big business combinations such as Standard Oil has been debated since its enactment. What is clear, however, is that the courts applied its prohibitions to all combinations, including labor. Labor activity, beyond mere organization, was subject to injunction upon petition by the attorney general, and business took full advantage.

The passage of the Clayton Act of 1914 appeared to manifest Congress's intent that labor be relieved of the constraints of the Sherman Act. Among its provisions was Section 6, which stated: "That the labor of a human being is not a commodity or article of commerce. Nothing contained in the antitrust laws shall be construed to forbid the existence and operation of a labor . . . organization . . . instituted for the purposes of mutual help . . . or to forbid or restrain individual members of such organizations from lawfully carrying out the legitimate objects thereof, nor shall such organizations, or the members thereof, be held or construed to be illegal combinations or conspiracies in restraint of trade, under the antitrust laws." Although Congress's intent seems clear, by the process of convoluted reasoning the courts interpreted the act against labor's interests.

They held that the Clayton Act only restated previous principles. In addition, the labor movement was placed in a position even worse than before, because the act provided for the issuance of restraining orders at the instance of private individuals and businesses, instead of only the attorney general. Suits for labor injunctions multiplied, and the apparent philosophical split between Congress and the courts continued for the next eighteen years. The following case illustrates the Supreme Court's adverse interpretation of the Clayton Act.

AMERICAN STEEL FOUNDRIES v. TRI-CITY CENTRAL TRADES COUNCIL
257 U.S. 184, 42 S.Ct. 72, 66 L.Ed. 189 (1921)

This was an action by American Steel Foundries (Plaintiff/Petitioner) against Tri-City Central Trades Council (Defendant/Respondent) seeking an injunction. The purpose was to have Defendant enjoined from picketing Plaintiff's business in conjunction with a strike called by Defendant.

The District Court granted a comprehensive injunction under the terms of which Defendant was "perpetually restrained and enjoined from in any way or manner whatsoever by the use of persuasion . . . interfering with, hindering, obstructing or stopping any person engaged in the employ of American Steel Foundries. . . ." On appeal, the Circuit Court of Appeals modified the decree, striking out the word *persuasion* and inserting "in a threatening or intimidating manner." Plaintiff appealed. Reversed in part and affirmed in part and remanded to the District Court.

TAFT, J.

The first question in the case is whether section 20 of the Clayton Act of October 15, 1914 . . . is to be applied in this case. . . .

Section 20 is as follows:

> That no restraining order or injunction shall be granted by any court of the United States, or a judge or the judges thereof, in any case between an employer and employees, or between employers and employees or between employees, or between persons employed and persons seeking employment, involving, or growing out of, a dispute concerning terms or conditions of employment, unless necessary to prevent irreparable injury to property, or to a property right, of the party making the application, for which injury there is no adequate remedy at law, and such property or property right must be described with particularity in the application, which must be in writing and sworn to by the applicant or by his agent or attorney.

And no such restraining order or injunction shall prohibit any person or persons, whether singly or in concert, from terminating any relation of employment, or from ceasing to perform any work or labor, or from recommending, advising, or persuading others by peaceful means to do so; or from attending at any place where any such person or persons may lawfully be, for the purpose of peacefully obtaining or communicating information, or from peacefully persuading any person to work or to abstain from working; or from ceasing to patronize or to employ any party to such dispute, or from recommending, advising, or persuading others by peaceful and lawful means so to do; or from paying or giving to, or withholding from, any person engaged in such dispute, any strike benefits or other moneys or things of value; or from peaceably assembling in a lawful manner, and for lawful purposes; or from doing any act or thing which might lawfully be done in the absence of such dispute by any party thereto; nor shall any of the acts specified in this paragraph be considered or held to be violations of any law of the United States. . . .

The prohibitions of Section 20, material here, are those which forbid an injunction against, first, recommending, advising or persuading others by peaceful means to cease employment and labor; second, attending at any place where such person or persons may lawfully be for the purpose of peacefully obtaining or communicating information, or peacefully persuading any person to work or to abstain from working; third, peaceably assembling in a lawful manner and for lawful purposes. This court has already called attention in the Duplex Case to the emphasis upon the words "peaceable" and "lawful" in this section. . . .

How far may men go in persuasion and communication and still not violate the right of those whom they would influence? In going to and from work, men have a right to as free a passage without obstruction as the streets afford, consistent with the rights of others to enjoy the same privilege. We are a social people and the accosting by one of another in an inoffensive way and an offer by one to communicate and discuss information with a view to influencing the other's actions are not regarded as aggression or a violation of that other's rights. If, however, the offer is declined, as it may rightfully be, then persistence, importunity, following and dogging become unjustifiable annoyance and obstruction which is likely soon to savor of intimidation. From all of this the person sought to be influenced has a right to have him free.

The nearer this importunate intercepting of employees or would-be employees is to the place of business, the greater the obstruction and interference with the business and especially with the property right of access of the employer. Attempted discussion and argument of this kind in such proximity is certain to attract attention and congregation of the curious, or, it may be, interested bystanders, and thus to increase the obstruction as well as the aspect of intimidation which the situation quickly assumes. . . .

A restraining order against picketing will advise earnest advocates of labor's cause that the law does not look with favor on an enforced discussion of the merits of the issue between individuals who wish to work, and groups of those who do not, under conditions which subject the individuals who wish to work to a severe test of their nerve and physical strength and courage. But while this is so, we must have every regard to the congressional intention manifested in the act and to the principle of existing law which it declared, that ex-employees and others properly acting with them shall have an opportunity, so far as is consistent with peace and law, to observe who are still working for the employer, to communicate with them and to persuade them to join the ranks of his opponents in a lawful economic struggle. . . .

Each case must turn on its own circumstances. It is a case for the flexible remedial power of a court of equity which may try one mode of restraint, and if it fails or proves to be too drastic, may change it. We think that the strikers and their sympathizers engaged in the economic struggle should be limited to one representative for each point of ingress and egress in the plant or place of business and that all others be enjoined from congregating or loitering at the plant or in the neighboring streets by which access is had to the plant, that such representatives should have the right of observation, communication and persuasion, but with special admonition that their communication, arguments and appeals shall not be abusive libelous or threatening, and that they shall not approach individuals together but singly, and shall not in their single efforts at communication or persuasion obstruct an unwilling listener by importunate following or dogging his steps. . . . With these views, it is apparent that we can not sustain the qualification of the order of the District Court which the Circuit Court of Appeals made. That court followed the case of Iron Moulders Union v. Allis-Chalmers Co., 166 Fed. 45, 91 C. C. A. 631, 20 L. R. A. (N. S.) 315, and modified the order of the District Court which enjoined defendants "from picketing or maintaining at or near the premises of the complainant or on the streets leading to the premises of said complainant, any pickets and pickets" by adding the words "in a threatening manner." This qualification seems to us to be inadequate. In actual result, it leaves compliance largely to the discretion of the pickets. It ignores the necessary element of intimidation in the presence of groups as pickets. It does not secure practically that which the court must secure and to which the complainant and his workmen are entitled. The phrase really recognizes as legal that which bears the sinister name of "picketing" which it is to be observed Congress carefully refrained from using in section 20.

Questions

1. To what extent is the Supreme Court's decision consistent or inconsistent with your understanding of freedom of speech, freedom of petition and assembly, and freedom of dissent?

2. What would happen to someone who chose to picket in violation of the court order?

In 1932, Congress passed the **Norris-Laguardia** (Federal Anti-Injunction) **Act.** Congress's determination to rescue the labor movement from antitrust law no longer could be ignored by the courts. Among the most important provisions of the act were those explicitly setting out the rights of labor organizations. Section 1 divested federal courts of injunctive powers in labor cases, except as set forth in Section 7; Section 7 stated very restrictive rules for granting injunctions, including proof that police are unable or unwilling to furnish adequate protection to the complainant's property. As a result, the use of labor injunctions markedly declined.

The First Labor Relations Acts

In 1926, Congress passed the *Railway Labor Act*. This was the first important attempt by Congress to regulate labor relations. Drawing on its experience from disputes surrounding early railway labor statutes, Congress strengthened provisions for peaceful arbitration and mediation, continued the emphasis on voluntary dispute settlement without resort to the mandatory provisions of the act, and eliminated the criminal penalties for noncompliance. The Railway Labor Act was held constitutional and laid the foundation for future labor legislation.

One of the effects of the Great Depression of the early 1930s was an increase in the fervor of sentiment to protect labor. A notable manifestation of this was the passage of the *National Industrial Recovery Act* of 1933, which included broad and far-reaching regulations concerning the obligations of employers and employment relations. Because of its great scope, it was declared unconstitutional by the Supreme Court in 1935, in *Schechter Poultry Corporation v. United States,* which appears in Chapter 5. The Court found that the powers assumed by Congress in the act were beyond those granted to the federal government by the Constitution.

The National Labor Relations Act

In passing the **Wagner Act** in 1935, Congress drew heavily on its experience with the Railway Labor Act, and on the lesson it had learned only recently concerning constitutional limitations on its powers. The basic framework of the Railway Labor Act was incorporated in the Wagner Act, and it scope was limited to labor relations involving interstate commerce. Administration of the act was placed in the hands of the *National Labor Relations Board* (NLRB), which originally had been created under the then-defunct National Industrial Recovery Act.

The Wagner Act was born of Congress's desire to protect labor from the seemingly unlimited power of business. Section 7 of the act spelled out the rights of labor to organize and to use such weapons as strike, picket, and boycott activity, particularly in pursuit of collective bargaining. Section 8 then set out five unfair labor practices that management was forbidden to use against labor.

Twelve years of experience under the Wagner Act proved productive for labor. However, not only had the act placed unions in parity with business; it appeared that it had placed them in a position of dominance. Fears of a new, postwar inflation were kindled, and Congress responded with the **Taft-Hartley Act** of 1947. Most notably, the new act sought to bolster management's position by prohibiting unions from engaging in specified unfair labor practices. Satisfied with the new balance of power, Congress continued to monitor labor relations over the next twelve years. During that period it discovered that, although labor had now been protected from management and management from unions, one major flaw remained. It became apparent that members needed protection from their own unions. To meet this need, Congress passed the **Landrum-Griffin Act** in 1959, including provisions sometimes called "Labor's Bill of Rights." Landrum-Griffin marked a complete departure from Congress's previous policy of noninterference with the internal operation of labor organizations. It provided detailed regulations concerning financial and reporting requirements, the right of members to sue the union, standards for internal disciplinary proceedings, rules of conduct for the union as a trustee, and rules of conduct for its officers and many others.

COVERAGE OF THE NATIONAL LABOR RELATIONS ACT

The jurisdiction of the National Labor Relations Board and the scope of the act are limited to prescribed matters that "affect commerce." *Commerce* means commerce among the states and with foreign countries (interstate and international commerce). **Affecting commerce** is defined in

Section 2(7) to mean "in commerce, or burdening or obstructing commerce or the free flow of commerce, or having led or tending to lead to a labor dispute burdening or obstructing commerce or the free flow of commerce." This restriction, of course, is imposed in keeping with the need for the federal government to assume only powers granted to it in the Constitution, a lesson learned from the *Schechter* case previously noted. The following case left no doubt that the National Labor Relations Act is constitutional. It also made clear that the powers granted were not restricted only to those businesses that were involved directly in interstate commerce, but included enterprises that merely "affected" interstate commerce as well.

NATIONAL LABOR RELATIONS BOARD v. JONES & LAUGHLIN STEEL CORPORATION
310 U.S. 1, 57 S.Ct. 615, 81 L.Ed. 893 (1937)

This was an action by the National Labor Relations Board (Petitioner) against Jones & Laughlin Steel Corporation (Respondent) to enforce its order in which it found Respondent had violated the National Labor Relations Act of 1935. Respondent contended the order was unenforceable because the act was unconstitutional.

The Circuit Court of Appeals denied the petition on the ground that the act was unconstitutional and Petitioner appealed. Reversed and remanded.

HUGHES, Justice.

The act is challenged in its entirety as an attempt to regulate all industry, thus invading the reserved powers of the States over their local concerns. It is asserted that the references in the act to interstate and foreign commerce are colorable at best; that the act is not a true regulation of such commerce or of matters which directly affect it, but on the contrary has the fundamental object of placing under the compulsory supervision of the federal government all industrial labor relations within the nation. The argument seeks support in the broad words of the preamble (Section 1) and in the sweep of the provisions of the act, and it is further insisted that its legislative history shows an essential universal purpose in the light of which its scope cannot be limited by either construction or by the application of the separability clause.

If this conception of terms, intent and consequent inseparability were sound, the act would necessarily fall by reason of the limitation upon the federal power which inheres in the constitutional grant, as well as because of the explicit reservation of the Tenth Amendment. Schechter Corporation v. United States. . . . The authority of the federal government may not be pushed to such an extreme as to destroy the distinction, which the commerce clause itself establishes, between commerce "among the several States" and the internal concerns of a state. That distinction between what is national and what is local in the activities of commerce is vital to the maintenance of our federal system. Id. . . .

We think it clear that the National Labor Relations Act may be construed so as to operate within the sphere of constitutional authority. The jurisdiction conferred upon the Board, and invoked in this instance, is found in section 10(a), 29 U.S.C.A. Section 160(a), which provides:

> Sec. 10(a). The Board is empowered, as hereinafter provided, to prevent any person from engaging in any unfair labor practice (listed in section 8 [section 158]) affecting commerce.

The critical words of this provision, prescribing the limits of the Board's authority in dealing with the labor practices, are "affecting commerce." The act specifically defines the "commerce" to which it refers (section 2(6), 29 U.S.C.A. Section 152(6)):

> The term 'commerce' means trade, traffic, commerce, transportation, or communication among the several States, or between the District of Columbia or any Territory of the United States and any State or other Territory, or between any foreign country and any State, Territory, or the District of Columbia, or within the District of Columbia or any Territory, or between points in the same State but through any other State or any Territory or the District of Columbia or any foreign country.

There can be no question that the commerce thus contemplated by the act (aside from that within a Territory or the District of Columbia) is interstate and foreign commerce in the constitutional sense. The act also defines the term "affecting commerce" section 2(7), 29 U.S.C.A. Section 152(7):

> The term 'affecting commerce' means in commerce, or burdening or obstructing commerce or the free flow of commerce, or having led or tending to lead to a labor dispute burdening or obstructing commerce or the free flow of commerce.

This definition is one of exclusion as well as inclusion. The grant of authority to the Board does not purport to extend to the relationship between all industrial employees and employers. Its terms do not impose collective bargaining upon all industry regardless of effects upon interstate or foreign commerce. It purports to reach only what may be deemed to burden or obstruct that commerce and, thus qualified, it must be construed as contemplating the exercise of control within constitutional bounds. It is a familiar principle that acts which directly burden or obstruct interstate or foreign commerce, or its free flow, are within the reach of the congressional power. Acts having that effect are not rendered immune because they grow out of labor disputes. . . . It is the effect upon commerce, not the source of the injury, which is the criterion. . . . Whether or not particular action does affect commerce in such a close and intimate fashion as to be subject to federal control, and hence to lie within the authority conferred upon the Board, is left by the statute to be determined as individual cases arise. We are thus to inquire whether in the instant case the constitutional boundary has been passed.

Questions

1. Why does the Court work so hard to limit the act's construction so that it applies only to labor matters affecting commerce?

2. Is it sound, given the constitutional commitment to states' rights in the Tenth Amendment, to allow the federal government so much power over labor relations?

Definition of "Employer"

The second restriction in the application of the National Labor Relations Act is that it applies to labor disputes only when they involve a covered employer. Section 2(2) defines **employer** by exclusion. In addition to employers whose operations do not "affect commerce," the act exempts: (1) the federal government, every wholly owned government corporation, and federal reserve banks; (2) the state governments and their political subdivisions (such as counties and cities); (3) employers subject to the Railway Labor Act; and (4) labor organizations, except when they act as employers. Therefore, most private employers are covered by the act as long as their businesses affect interstate commerce in some way.

Definition of "Employee"

The general definition of **employee** in Section 2(3) of the act is quite broad. It includes not only employees currently on the payroll, but also those whose work ceased because of an unfair labor practice committed by the employer, or because of any current labor dispute, and who have not obtained any other regular and substantially equivalent employment. However, excluded from coverage are: (1) agricultural laborers; (2) domestic-service laborers employed in the service of a family or person at home; (3) independent contractors; and (4) persons employed by employers subject to the Railway Labor Act. Most of these exclusions involve persons whose labor disputes are likely to be infrequent and would have an insubstantial effect on interstate commerce, and those who are not in a close employment relationship, or are "management" rather than "labor." The following case involves a question concerning one of these exemptions.

NATIONAL LABOR RELATIONS BOARD v. BAYSIDE ENTERPRISES, INC.

429 U.S. 298, 97 S.Ct. 576, 50 L.Ed.2d 494 (1977)

Bayside Enterprises, Inc. (Petitioner) brought this appeal, on *certiorari,* for review of a decision of the National Labor Relations Board (Respondent) ordering Petitioner to negotiate with certain truck drivers.

Petitioner operated a large, vertically integrated poultry business. The truck drivers in question hauled feed from Petitioner's feed mill to 119 farms to feed the Petitioner's chickens. When the drivers sought to bargain collectively, Petitioner refused, contending the drivers were "agricultural workers" and, as such, were not covered by the National Labor Relations Act.

The National Labor Relations Board found that Petitioner had violated Section 8(a)(5) of the act and ordered bargaining, and that order was affirmed by the Court of Appeals. Affirmed.

STEVENS, Justice.

Section 3(f) provides, in relevant part:

'Agriculture' includes farming in all its branches [including] the raising of . . . poultry, and any practices . . . performed by a farmer or on a farm as an incident to or in conjunction with such farming operations . . . .

This statutory definition includes farming in both a primary and a secondary sense. The raising of poultry is primary farming, but hauling products to or from a farm is not primary farming. Such hauling may, however, be secondary farming if it is work performed "by a farmer or on a farm as an incident to or in conjunction with such farming operations. . . ." Since there is no claim that these drivers work "on a farm," the question is whether their activities should be regarded as work performed "by a farmer." The answer depends on the character of their employer's activities.

An employer's business may include both agricultural and nonagricultural activities. Thus, even though most of the operations on a sugar plantation are agricultural, persons employed in the plantation's sugar-processing plant are not "agricultural employees." . . .

The Labor Board has squarely and consistently rejected the argument that all of the activity on a contract farm should be regarded as agricultural activity of an integrated farmer such as Bayside. This conclusion by the Board is one we must respect even if the issue might "with nearly equal reason be resolved one way rather than another."

Even if we should regard a contract farm as a hybrid operation where some of the agricultural activity is performed by Bayside and some by the owner of the farm, we would nevertheless be compelled to sustain the Board's order. For the activity of storing poultry feed and then using it to feed the chicks is work performed by the contract farmer rather than by Bayside. Since the status of the drivers is determined by the character of the work which they perform for their own employer, the work of the contract farmer cannot make the drivers agricultural laborers. And their employer's operation of the feedmill is a nonagricultural activity. Thus, the Board properly concluded that the work of the truck drivers on behalf of their employer is not work performed "by a farmer" whether attention is focused on the origin or the destination of the feed delivery.

Questions

1. Why did Congress exempt agricultural workers from the act?
2. Does the Court's narrow construction of the exemptions undermine Congress's intentions?
3. Why is the Court so deferential to the National Labor Relations Board's decision?

Jurisdictional Yardsticks

The NLRB refuses to assume jurisdiction over some labor disputes that, although covered under the act's language, the board believes are not likely to burden interstate commerce substantially. Therefore, these disputes are excluded from coverage by regulation. Fifteen separate standards have been set, basing assumption of jurisdiction on dollar volume of business, by industry. For example, (1) a nonretail business is covered only if its outflow of goods, sold directly or indirectly to consumers, or its inflow of goods, directly or indirectly from others, across state lines is at least $50,000; (2) a retail business is covered if its total volume of business is at least $500,000; and (3) a radio, telegraph, television, or telephone business is covered if it has at least $100,000 total annual volume of business.

The 1959 Landrum-Griffin Act provides that the NLRB may not refuse jurisdiction over any case not excluded under its guidelines on the effective date of the act. Therefore, since that time, the guidelines could not be made more restrictive. However, the NLRB is entitled to assume broader jurisdiction. It did this in 1969 concerning organized baseball, and in 1974 concerning charitable hospitals. Other industries also have been included within its jurisdiction.

KEY PROVISIONS OF THE ACT

Section 7

Section 7 of the 1935 Wagner Act established the basic rights of labor to form and assist in the organization of unions, to bargain collectively, and to exert economic pressures such as strike, picket, and boycott activities in furtherance of these rights. In the 1947 Taft-Hartley Act, language was added to Section 7 to provide employees with the right to *refrain* from such activities. (See Appendix M for the text of the present Section 7.)

Section 8

Section 8 of the act sets out the kinds of activities the employer and the union are not allowed to participate in as part of the labor-management dynamic. This section represents the keystone of the statute's attempt to regulate the behavior of labor and management. Most litigation under the act involves allegations of violation of one or more of the provisions of Section 8. Therefore, a thorough understanding of the scope of Section 8 provisions is necessary to an understanding of the effect of the act itself.

SECTION 8(a). This is the **unfair labor practice** section of the Act. It governs employers, and was part of the 1935 act. Later, by provision in the 1947 act, Subsection (b) was added, governing unions.

Section 8(a)(1) makes it an unfair labor practice for an employer to "interfere with, restrain, or coerce employees in the exercise of the rights granted in section 7." Although the statement of this principle is not difficult, its application to some factual situations is. Consider the following examples:

1. Ordinarily, an employer may prohibit the distribution of literature and solicitation by non-employee (outside) union organizers as long as (a) employees reasonably may be reached otherwise, and (b) the employer's ban does not unlawfully discriminate against the union. Qualification "(a)" is a question of fact, and union access to employees outside of work has been promoted by requiring employers to give the union the names and addresses of all employees once the union has given notice to the employer of its desire to solicit those employees. Qualification "(b)" may be violated, for example, by prohibiting union solicitation while allowing solicitation and distribution by others on company premises. Generally, the defense of "safety considerations" is not available if even outsiders such as salespersons are allowed into the offices, or if plant tours are conducted for outsiders. However, the rights of employers have been interpreted more broadly in cases brought under the act than in those brought under the First Amendment (freedom of speech). Also, the rights of states to impose reasonable restrictions on employers has been affirmed by the Supreme Court.

2. Solicitation during working hours, even by employees, may be prohibited, if done non-discriminatorily. The courts have determined that "working time is for working."

3. Solicitation by employees in nonworking

areas during nonworking time may not be prohibited.

4. Solicitation by employees in working areas during nonworking time may be prohibited only if the maintenance of production or discipline require. For example, prohibiting solicitation at any time in the sales area of a retail store has been upheld uniformly.

5. If a retail store enforces a prohibition on employee solicitation on the selling floor during both working and nonworking time, it is not permitted to use company time to give speeches against unions. These are known as "captive audience" speeches. In any case, speeches to employees within 24 hours of an election are not permitted unless all contending unions are invited to speak.

6. One-on-one discussions with employees in areas usually recognized as "management areas," such as the office of a manager or supervisor, are prohibited if any part of the discussion involves anti-union propaganda.

7. Threats of punishment if a union is elected are prohibited, such as a threat to move the plant, to cut wages, or to cancel any other benefits. Promises of reward if the union is defeated also are prohibited.

8. The use of espionage or surveillance, or even the appearance of such, is prohibited.

Section 8(a)(2) prohibits employer domination of a labor organization, or favoring one union over another. Because of this, a "company union"—an "in-house" union of employees—is viewed with suspicion. In the past, employers have suggested that employees should form their own union rather than become affiliated with an "outside" union. This is a violation of Section 8(a)(2). So is employer propaganda favoring one union over another, or giving aid and support such as financial support, to one and not another, or allowing the use of plant premises or working time for discriminatory union solicitation. The statutory proscriptions reflect the fear that a union is less likely to represent members effectively against the interests of a "friendly" employer.

Section 8(a)(3) prohibits an employer from discriminating in making decisions about hiring, tenure, or any term or condition of employment as a way of encouraging or discouraging membership in any labor organization. In other words, the employer must allow the employee a free choice as to whether to join or support a union. This section does have a proviso, however. An employer must abide by any enforceable union security clauses in the collective bargaining contract, such as a "union-shop" or "agency-shop" clause. This topic will be discussed in more detail later in connection with collective bargaining. It should be noted that this statutory provision is applicable not only to present employees, but also to job applicants. A refusal to hire an applicant on the ground of union preference is a violation, just as is discrimination after a worker is hired.

Section 8(a)(4) prohibits discharge or other discrimination against an employee for filing charges or giving testimony under the act. This protects the ability of the NLRB to obtain assistance from employees in properly administering the act's provisions and purposes.

Section 8(a)(5) requires the employer to **bargain in good faith** with collective bargaining agents selected by the employees. This section does not require that the employer agree to any proposal advanced by the union, but only that the employer *bargain* and do so in *good faith*. It requires that the parties meet and discuss the issues. It is violated only when the employer declares or indicates that further discussion is cut off. For example, a "take-it-or-leave-it" proposal is considered an 8(a)(5) violation. Although the duty of an employer to bargain with a union generally is of concern only after an election to determine who is to serve as **collective bargaining agent,** as the following case illustrates, the duty may arise without an election.

NATIONAL LABOR RELATIONS BOARD v. GISSEL PACKING CO.
395 U.S. 575, 89 S.Ct. 1918, 23 L.Ed.2d 547 (1969)

This was an action by the National Labor Relations Board (Petitioner) for enforcement of its order against Gissel Packing Co. (Respondent). Upon a complaint filed by Food Store Employees Union, Local No. 347, Petitioner had ordered Respondent to bargain with the union based on the union's showing of authorization cards signed by a majority of Respondent's employees in the bargaining unit the union sought to represent. Respondent contended it was not required to bargain until the union had been certified after an NLRB-supervised election.

The NLRB's petition for enforcement was denied by the Fourth Circuit Court of Appeals, and Petitioner appealed. Reversed and remanded.

WARREN, Chief Justice.

The first issue facing us is whether a union can establish a bargaining obligation by means other than a Board election and whether the validity of alternate routes to majority status, such as cards, was affected by the 1947 Taft-Hartley amendments. The most commonly traveled route for a union to obtain recognition as the exclusive bargaining representative of an unorganized group of employees is through the Board's election and certification procedures under Section 9(c) of the Act . . . it is also, from the Board's point of view, the preferred route. A union is not limited to a Board election, however, for, in addition to Section 9, the present Act provides in Section 8(a)(5) . . . as did the Wagner Act in Section 8(5), that "[i]t shall be an unfair labor practice for an employer . . . to refuse to bargain collectively with the representatives of his employees, subject to the provisions of section 9(a)." Since Section 9(a), in both the Wagner Act and the present Act, refers to the representative as the one "designated or selected" by a majority of the employees without specifying precisely how that representative is to be chosen, it was early recognized that an employer had a duty to bargain whenever the union representative presented "convincing evidence of majority support." Almost from the inception of the Act, then, it was recognized that a union did not have to be certified as the winner of a Board election to invoke a bargaining obligation; it could establish majority status by other means under the unfair labor practice provision of Section 8(a)(5)—by showing convincing support, for instance, by a union-called strike or strike vote, or, as here, by possession of cards signed by a majority of the employees authorizing the union to represent them for collective bargaining purposes.

We have consistently accepted this interpretation of the Wagner Act and the present Act, particularly as to the use of authorization cards. . . . Thus, in United Mine Workers, . . . we noted that a "Board election is not the only method by which an employer may satisfy itself as to the union's majority status," . . . since Section 9(a), "which deals expressly with employee representation, says nothing as to how the employees' representative shall be chosen." . . . We therefore pointed out in that case, where the union had obtained signed authorization cards from a majority of the employees, that "[i]n the absence of any bona fide dispute as to the existence of the required majority of eligible employees, the employer's denial of recognition of the union would have violated Section 8(a)(5) of the Act." . . . We see no reason to reject this approach to bargaining obligations now, and we find unpersuasive the Fourth Circuit's view that the 1947 Taft-Hartley amendments, enacted some nine years before our decision in United Mine Workers, supra, require us to disregard that case. Indeed, the 1947 amendments weaken rather than strengthen the position taken by the employers here and the Fourth Circuit below. . . .

The employers rely finally on the addition to Section 9(c) of subparagraph (B), which allows an employer to petition for an election whenever "one or more individuals or labor organizations have presented to him a claim to be recognized as the representative defined in section 9(a)." That provision was not added, as the employers assert, to give them an absolute right to an election at any time; rather, it was intended, as the legislative history indicates, to allow them, after being asked to bargain, to test out their doubts as to a union's majority in a secret election which they would then presumably not cause to be set aside by illegal antiunion activity. We agree with the Board's assertion here that there is no suggestion that Congress intended Section 9(c)(1)(B) to relieve any employer of his Section 8(a)(5) bargaining obligation where, without good faith, he engaged in unfair labor practices disruptive of the Board's election machinery. And we agree that the policies reflected in Section 9(c)(1)(B) fully support the Board's present administration of the Act . . . for an employer can insist on a secret ballot election, unless in the words of the Board, he engages "in contemporaneous unfair labor practices likely to destroy the union's majority and seriously impede the election." . . .

In short, we hold that the 1947 amendments did not restrict an employer's duty to bargain under Section 8(a)(5) solely to those unions whose representative status is certified after a Board election.

Questions

1. What arguments can be advanced for a contrary result—namely that an employer need bargain only after a formal election?
2. Is there a breach of good faith if the employer refuses to talk on the ground that some of the authorization cards are invalid?

SECTION 8(b). This subsection describes unfair labor practices that may be committed by a union. Some are corollary to those concerning employers; others are uniquely applicable to unions.

Section 8(b)(1) is similar to Section 8(a)(1). It prohibits a union from restraining or coercing employees in the exercise of their rights under Section 7. Notably missing is the prohibition, imposed under 8(a)(1), of "interference." Therefore, unlike the employer, a union may interfere, but not restrain or coerce. The reason Section 8(b)(1) does not contain that prohibition is that, by its very nature, a union campaign will be an "interference." It is intended that a union be free to interfere, within limits, but not an employer.

Section 8(b)(3) is a corollary to Section 8(a)(5). The duty to bargain in good faith is imposed on the union to the same extent as it is imposed on the employer. Again, the purpose is to require that the parties meet and discuss in the hope of resolving their difficulties.

Section 8(b)(4) is the broadest and most complicated of the provisions dealing with union unfair labor practices. It generally prohibits the union from applying economic pressures, such as strikes, picketing, and boycott activity, when the objective is illegal. The circumstances to which this section applies are when the objective is: (1) to force an owner-worker (employer or self-employed person) to join any labor organization or employer organization; (2) to require any employer to agree not to deal in the products of another employer (called a **hot cargo agreement**), if the hot cargo agreement would be prohibited by Section 8(e); (3) to force an employer to refuse to deal with another employer in an effort to make the second employer agree to union demands (participate in a secondary boycott); (4) to coerce an employer to deal with one union when another union has been certified as collective bargaining agent of the employees involved; or (5) to force an employer to assign particular work to its members (work assignment dispute), since disputes between unions as to which is to receive a particular work assignment are required to be submitted to the NLRB for resolution.

There are two important provisos to Section 8(b)(4). *First* nothing in this section, or anything else in the act, makes it illegal for an employee to refuse to cross a *proper, authorized* picket line set up by even another union. However, if an employee exercises this right, the employer is entitled to have *this particular work* done by someone who will cross the picket line, but not to discharge or permanently replace the employee who refuses to cross the line. In addition, a union is entitled to levy a reasonable, uniform fine against members who cross a duly constituted picket line. *Second*, nothing in this section, or any other provision in the act, prohibits pure *publicity* picketing (picketing for the sole purpose of advertising that a dispute exists), unless it has the *effect* of inducing employees of another employer (not the one picketed) to refuse to pick up, deliver, or transport goods, or to perform services, for the employer picketed.

Section 8(b)(5) prohibits the union from charging excessive or discriminatory initiation fees or dues to membership if payment is required as a condition of employment—for example, if the collective bargaining contract contains an enforceable union-shop or agency-shop clause. Presumably, if membership in the union is totally voluntary, initiation fees and dues need not be reasonable, just as they need not be reasonable for joining any other purely private organization. Of course, discriminatory dues may be attacked for other reasons, such as a violation of a federal or state civil rights law.

Section 8(b)(6) concerns **featherbedding.** It prohibits the union from requiring an employer to pay for work not performed or intended to be performed. Notice that the standard is not whether the work is *needed* but whether it is, or is intended to be, *performed*. A union may require payment to an employee who performs, or stands ready, willing, and able to perform, even though the employer neither needs or wants the service nor allows it to be performed. This distinction is illustrated by the following case.

AMERICAN NEWSPAPER PUBLISHER ASSOCIATION v. NATIONAL LABOR RELATIONS BOARD
193 F.2d 782 (7th Cir. 1951)

This was an action by the American Newspaper Publisher Association (Petitioner) against the International Typographical Union (one of the respondents), by way of filing unfair labor practices with the National Labor Relations Board (Respondent). One of the charges was that the union had caused or attempted to cause publishers to pay money "in the nature of an exaction, for services which were not performed or not to be performed," in violation of Section 8(b)(6) of the National Labor Relations Act.

The union claimed the right to "reproduction" or "setting bogus." When advertisers submitted a "mat" ready for printing, the union required that its members be allowed to make another mat, which would be discarded. In other words, it required that they be allowed to do the same work as if the advertiser had submitted flat copy rather than a ready-to-print mat. Petitioner contended this would be featherbedding in violation of the act.

The board found that the facts did not constitute featherbedding in violation of the act and Petitioner appealed. Affirmed on this point.

SWAIM, Circuit Judge.

In . . . [S]ection 8(b)(6) of the Act we are again confronted with a situation where Congress could have outlawed all so-called "feather-bedding" but apparently did not see fit to do so. Instead Congress declared in Section 8(b)(6): "It shall be an unfair labor practice for a labor organization or its agents . . . to cause or attempt to cause an employer to pay or deliver or agree to pay or deliver any money or other thing of value, in the nature of an exaction, for services which are not performed or not to be performed.

The ANPA insists that this language is sufficient to cover the reproduction or "setting bogus" practice which had prevailed in composing rooms for many years and which the ITU insisted be continued.

With this contention we cannot agree. The legislative history of the Act clearly indicates that Congress did not intend by this section to cover all types of "feather-bedding." While the ANPA contends that Congress, by using the words "exaction" and "services," has made this section so clear that it is not subject to interpretation, we note that there was much discussion and some disagreement in Congress as to its correct interpretation and that the parties here are in sharp disagreement as to what the section means.

While this question was before Congress, the House Bill defined several practices as feather-bedding and prohibited strike activity to compel an employer to accede to any such practices. The Senate Bill contained no such prohibition. The Conference Committee compromised the matter by agreeing on Section 8(b)(6) in its present form. Senator Taft in explaining this provision to the Senate said: "The House had rather elaborate provisions prohibiting so-called feather-bedding practices and making them unlawful labor practices. The Senate conferees, while not approving of feather-bedding practices, felt that it was impracticable to give to a board or a court the power to say that so many men are all right and so many men are too many. It would require a practical application of the law by the courts in hundreds of different industries, and a determination of facts which it seemed to me would be almost impossible. So we declined to adopt the provisions which are now in the Petrillo (Lea) Act. . . . We thought that probably we had better wait and see what happened, in any event, even though we are in favor of prohibiting all feather-bedding practices. *However, we did accept one provision which makes it an unlawful labor practice for a union to accept money for people who do not work. That seemed to be a fairly clear case, easy to determine.* . . . (Emphasis supplied.) 93 Cong.Rec. 6441, Leg.Hist. p. 1535.

Senator Taft by this statement clearly indicated that in his opinion the only practice covered by Section 8(b)(6) was the practice of demanding money where no *work* had been done. He explained further, however, that the section did not even cover all cases where employees were paid for time during which they did not work, such as rest periods, time for lunch and vacation periods; that such periods were merely incidental to the work for which the employee was hired and paid. Examples of practices covered by the section were explained by Senator Taft as follows: ". . . it seems to me that it is perfectly clear what is intended. It is intended to make it an unfair labor practice for a man to say, 'You must have 10 musicians, and if you insist that there is room for only 6, you must pay the other 4 anyway.' That is in the nature of an exaction from the employer for services which he does not want, does not need, and is not even willing to accept." (93 Cong.Rec. 6603).

Senator Ball in speaking in favor of this section also said that it applied to a situation where an employer is required to pay for a stand-by orchestra, "which does no work at all." (93 Cong.Rec. 7683).

In the instant case the pay for "setting bogus" was only for the time the employees actually worked in setting the "bogus," amounting to approximately five per cent of and his total working time. He was a regular employee, not hired merely to set "bogus," but hired to do composition work which the employer required. While the "bogus" was not ordinarily used by the employer, the necessary work to compose it was actually done by the employee. Requiring that the employer pay for such work was not a violation of Section 8(b)(6).

We conclude that the actions and order of the Board in this case were correct with the exception of the Board's failure to make a finding and an appropriate order on the allegation of the complaint that the ITU and its agents had failed to bargain collectively in good faith. That part of the case is, therefore, remanded to the Board for the purpose of making a finding on this charge and an appropriate supplementary order based thereon.

Questions

1. Are you persuaded that Congress should *not* have banned all forms of featherbedding?

2. Are you persuaded by the court's explanation of why Congress did not ban all forms of featherbedding?

3. How can the legal system approve of the "setting bogus" practice, since it requires an employer to pay for absolutely worthless work? Review Chapter 1, and consider whether the result in this case is consistent with notions of ethics.

Section 8(b)(7) prohibits a union from picketing or causing an employer to be picketed, or threatening to do either, in certain circumstances. It applies if the union is not the certified representative of the employees of the picketed employer, and the objective is causing the employer to recognize the union as representative of the employees or causing the employees to accept it as their representative. The circumstances under which this activity is prohibited are if: (1) the employer already has a contract with another union concerning the affected employees, and the contract is allowed as a bar to consideration of another representative under section 9(c), which allows a valid contract as a bar during its term, up to three years; (2) a valid election has been held concerning representation within the previous twelve months; or (3) the union has picketed for a reasonable time (one month has been NLRB policy) without calling for an election. Again, however, a proviso excepts pure publicity picketing, as it does in Section 8(b)(4).

OPERATION OF THE NATIONAL LABOR RELATIONS ACT

Administration of the National Labor Relations Act is vested in the **National Labor Relations Board,** which consists of five members appointed by the president of the United States. They serve five-year terms and may be reappointed at the end of each term. The president also appoints a **general counsel** of the board, who serves a four-year term.

Under the Wagner Act, the three major administrative functions—rulemaking, policing of compliance, and adjudication of violations—all were vested in the whole board. Under the Taft-Hartley Act, the policing function, including investigation and prosecution, was placed with the general counsel, who is to act independently of the board. The general counsel is responsible to the president, not to the board.

NLRB Functions

By virtue of the independence of the general counsel since 1947, the remaining functions of the board primarily are rulemaking and adjudication. These functions are discussed more fully in Chapter 46. In broad outline, however, the functions of the board are as follows:

1. Preventing unfair labor practices. The board sits as a quasi-judicial body, deciding whether unfair labor practices have been committed based on investigation and prosecution by the general counsel.

2. Conducting representation proceedings, including entertaining petitions for certification or decertification of a union, determining appropriate bargaining units, and conducting elections.

3. Seeking enforcement of its orders in the courts.
4. Conducting a poll among employees about to be involved in a National Emergency Strike (Section 209) to determine whether they wish to accept the employer's final offer.
5. Determining work assignments when two or more unions are involved in a jurisdictional dispute, discussed under Section 8(b)(4).
6. Securing injunctions against unlawful activities when necessary and provided for under the act.
7. Making substantive and procedural rules necessary to administration, within limits prescribed by the act.

Procedure in Unfair Labor Practice Cases

Unfair labor practice proceedings are initiated by filing charges in the district office of the National Labor Relations Board. This may be done by an employee, or by an applicant for employment claiming to have suffered because of an unfair labor practice on the part of a union or employer.

Following the filing of charges, an investigation is conducted by the district director. A **field examiner** then may be sent to make an on-site investigation, and may make recommendations concerning possible prosecution to the district director. The district director, as delegate of the general counsel, determines whether to prosecute. If this decision is in the affirmative, a complaint is issued.

Upon issuance of a complaint, a formal hearing is held before an administrative law judge. Proceedings are much the same as in a court. Witnesses are heard, and are subject to cross-examination. Other evidence is presented. The administrative law judge passes on the admissability of all evidence, determines questions of fact, and reaches conclusions of law.

The decision of an administrative law judge may be appealed to the full board in Washington, D.C. If no appeal is taken within twenty days, the decision is final. If appealed, the decision of the full board may be appealed further to a federal circuit court of appeals. Any further appeal is to the Supreme Court of the United States. However, that appeal cannot be taken as a matter of right, but only by permission of the Court by its granting of a writ of *certiorari*.

When the decision of the board has become final, if the party against whom it is rendered refuses to comply, the board seeks an **enforcement order** in the federal appellate court. The board has no power to enforce its own orders. If the enforcement order of the court is not complied with, the party refusing to comply is subject to contempt of court. It might be noted that the validity of a board order may be tested judicially either by appeal or during the hearing on the enforcement order. Usually, the latter is less desirable because it indicates a certain lack of good faith.

Remedies Under the Act

The NLRB has no power to assess fines or other criminal penalties for violations of the act. The only criminal sanctions that may be imposed come by way of punishment in criminal contempt proceedings for violation of a court order enforcing an NLRB decision or an injunction. NLRB remedies are of two general types—cease and desist orders and "make-whole" remedies.

Cease and desist orders may be issued for any unfair labor practice violation, but it is most common, and is the usual remedy, in cases involving a refusal to bargain in good faith. Employers often have used the time lag attendant to a cease and desist order, and ultimate enforcement by a court, as a tactic to buy time. During the delay, the employer may be successful in eroding the union's majority position with employees, or at least in eroding the fervor of the members' support for

Procedure in unfair labor practice cases

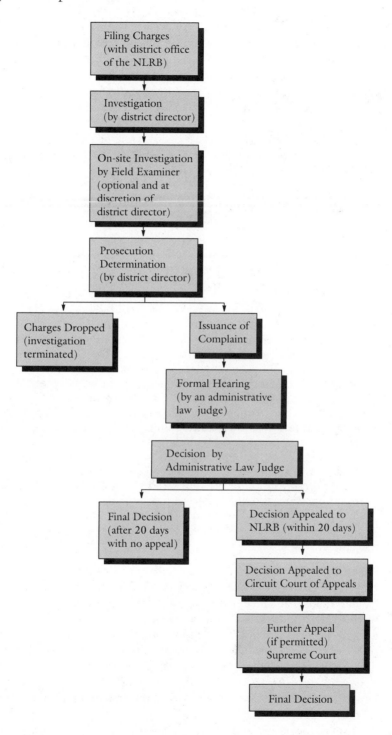

the union's position on certain negotiation subjects. For this reason, it also may be necessary for the board to issue a make-whole order. For example, an employer found to have used this tactic may be ordered to pay employees what it would have paid them if there had been no refusal to bargain. The amount typically would be determined by the length of the delay and what the parties ultimately agree is appropriate. Make-whole orders also may be issued to remedy other violations. For example, for a discriminatory refusal to hire, an employer may be ordered to hire

the aggrieved applicant and to pay back wages lost during the refusal, less any amount earned by the applicant in other employment during the period; reinstatement with back pay may be ordered for improper discharge; or a union may be ordered to rebate the excessive or discriminatory amount of dues in a case of a Section 8(b)(5) violation. The board, in appropriate cases, even may order the payment of costs and expenses generated by an unfair labor practice. In sum, the board has the power to order whatever reasonably is necessary to remedy the violation. Consider the following case.

NATIONAL LABOR RELATIONS BOARD v. FOOD STORE EMPLOYEES, LOCAL 347
417 U.S. 1, 94 S.Ct. 2074, 40 L.Ed.2d 612 (1974)

The Food Store Employees, Local 347 (Respondent) filed unfair labor practice charges against Heck's, Inc. concerning the latter's actions during an organization campaign. The National Labor Relations Board (Petitioner) found that Heck's had violated Sections 8(a)(1) and (5) of the National Labor Relations Act, and also that Heck's had a long history of the same kinds of activities at its other stores. The board ordered Heck's to bargain with the union but refused the union's request that it be granted litigation expenses and excess organizational costs.

The union, in enforcement and review proceedings before the court of appeals for the District of Columbia, succeeded, and the court of appeals expanded the board's order to include the requested expenses and costs and remanded. After reconsideration, the board declined to change its order and appealed the court of appeals's decision. Reversed and remanded with direction.

BRENNAN, J.

[The Court first noted the Board's decision in Tidee Products, Inc., 194 N.L.R.B. 1234 (1972) in which the Board ordered reimbursement of litigation expenses, having found that Tidee had engaged in "frivolous litigations."] In the circumstances of this case, the Court of Appeals, in our view, improperly exercised its authority under Section 10(e) and (f) to modify Board orders, and the case must therefore be returned to the Board. Congress has invested the Board, not the courts, with broad discretion to order a violator "to take such affirmative action . . . as will effectuate the policies of [the Act]." . . . This case does not present the exceptional situation in which crystal-clear Board error renders a remand an unnecessary formality. . . . For it cannot be gainsaid that the finding here that Heck's asserted at least "debatable" defenses to the unfair labor practice charges, whereas objections to the representation election in Tidee were "patently frivolous," might have been viewed by the Board as putting the question of remedy in a different light. We cannot say that the Board in performing its appointed function of balancing conflicting interests, could not reasonably decide that where "debatable" defenses are asserted, the public and private interests in affording the employer a determination of his "debatable" defenses, unfettered by the prospect of bearing his adversary's litigation costs, outweigh the public interest in uncrowded dockets.

. . . The integrity of the administrative process demands no less than that the Board, not its legal representative, exercise the discretionary judgment which Congress has entrusted to it. But since a plausible reconciliation by the Board of the seeming inconsistency was reasonably possible, it was "incompatible with the orderly function of the process of judicial review," NLRB v. Metropolitan Life Ins. Co., supra, 380 U.S. at 444, 85 S.Ct. at 1064, for the Court of Appeals to enlarge the Heck's order without first affording the Board an opportunity to clarify the inconsistencies.

It is a guiding principle of administrative law, long recognized by this Court, that "an administrative determination in which is imbedded a legal question open to judicial review does not impliedly foreclose the administrative agency, after its error has been corrected, from enforcing the legislative policy committed to its charge." . . . Thus, when a reviewing court concludes that an agency invested with broad discretion to fashion remedies has apparently abused that discretion by omitting a remedy justified in the court's view by the factual circumstances, remand to the agency for reconsideration, and not enlargement of the agency order, is ordinarily the reviewing court's proper course. Application of that general principle in this case best respects the congressional scheme investing the Board and not the courts with broad powers to fashion remedies that will effectuate national labor policy. It also affords the Board the opportunity, through additional evidence or findings, to reframe its order better to effectuate that policy. . . . Moreover, in this case, if the Court of Appeals correctly read Tidee as having signaled a change of policy in respect of reimbursement, a remand was necessary, because the Board should be given the first opportunity to determine whether the new policy should be applied retroactively.

Questions

1. What is the objective of limiting the court of appeals in its review of the board's decision?

2. What happens next in this proceeding?

SUMMARY

Early in the history of management-labor relations, most labor was performed by serfs (who effectively were slaves), so labor was completely subservient to management and there were few problems. Even when labor became more independent, the law was anti-labor, and efforts to organize, bargain collectively, and exert economic pressure were thwarted to a great extent.

In 1935, Congress passed the Wagner Act to aid labor in achieving its objectives. The Wagner Act provided for the right of labor to organize, bargain collectively, and use economic pressure to support its efforts. The act also listed five unfair labor practices that could be committed by an employer. In 1947, Congress passed the Taft-Hartley Act, trying to equalize power between management and labor, listing unfair labor practices that could be committed by unions. In 1959, Congress passed the Landrum-Griffin Act, imposing a number of management and reporting requirements on unions and declaring the rights of union members against their unions. These three acts, together, now are known as the National Labor Relations Act.

The key sections of the National Labor Relations Act are Sections 7 and 8. Section 7 states the rights of labor concerning organization, collective bargaining, and concerted action. Section 8 sets out unfair labor practices. These sections should be studied in detail.

The National Labor Relations Board is the agency charged with administration of the act. It consists of a five-member board that is responsible for rulemaking and adjudication, and a general counsel who is responsible for investigating and prosecuting violations. All are appointed by the president for five- and four-year terms, respectively. The responsibilities of the board and the general counsel have been kept entirely separate since 1972, each reporting directly to the president.

Upon the filing of an unfair labor practices complaint, sometimes following an examination by a field examiner, a formal quasi-judicial hearing is held before an administrative law judge. The decision of the administrative law judge may be appealed within twenty days to the NLRB in Washington, D.C. If it is not, it becomes final. Appeals of final decisions are appealable further to a United States Court of Appeals. Also, since the board has no power to enforce its own orders, an action for an enforcement order by the board also is taken to a court of appeals. In either case, any further appeal is upon petition to the Supreme Court of the United States. The Court is not required to hear the appeal.

Remedies under the National Labor Relations Act are of two general types—cease and desist orders and make-whole orders. The former seek to prevent the commission, or further commission, of unfair labor practices. The latter seek to compensate injured parties for a wrong already done. Examples of make-whole orders are those requiring an employer to hire or to reinstate, orders for payment of back wages, and orders to pay costs and expenses. The board has no authority to impose criminal sanctions.

KEY TERMS AND CONCEPTS

labor law
National Labor Relations Act
criminal conspiracy doctrine
contractual interference doctrine
civil conspiracy doctrine
Norris-Laguardia Act
Wagner Act
Landrum-Griffin Act
Taft-Hartley Act
affecting commerce
employer
employee
jurisdictional yardsticks
unfair labor practice
bargain in good faith
collective bargaining agent
hot cargo agreement
publicity picketing
featherbedding
National Labor Relations Board (NLRB)
General Counsel
field examiner
enforcement order

PROBLEMS

1. After a petition for an election was filed, and a hearing was held, a representation election was ordered on February 19, to be held on March 18 for the employees of Exchange Parts Co. A few days prior to the election, Exchange Parts announced that, beginning the current year, the employees would be given a "floating vacation day," and they were invited to a dinner at the home of the company's vice-president. At the dinner they would decide which day would be designated. The union contended that this was an unfair labor practice, and Exchange Parts contended it was only announcing a decision it already had made that had no relationship to the election. Was an unfair labor practice committed?

2. Darlington Manufacturing Company was organized by the Textile Workers of America. Immediately following the election of the union by Darlington employees, the board of directors of Darlington voted to shut down operations. This was done for the expressed reason that Darlington chose not to continue business with unionized employees. Did Darlington commit an unfair labor practice?

3. Without consulting the union representing its employees, Pittsburgh Plate Glass changed the benefits of its retired employees. Rather than paying for its previous group health plan, it changed to provide Medicare supplement coverage, which enabled it to reduce the amount of its health insurance contribution substantially. The union charged this was a violation of the company's duty to bargain under Section 8(a)(5). Is the union correct?

4. After a union announced its intention to organize the employees of a store belonging to Montgomery Ward, the head of store security solicited the help of some of the employees to report on certain activities at the store. In addition to reporting on thefts and other such matters, he also asked them to report on any conversations among employees concerning their attitudes about the union. The union learned of this when a sympathetic employee was solicited with promises of extra pay and other benefits, and charged the company with unfair labor practices. Should the charge be sustained?

5. First National Maintenance Corp. lost a cleaning contract with one of its largest customers. It then announced that, because of this, it was discharging the thirty-five employees who were working on that job. The union representing its employees charged the company with violating

Sections 8(a)(1) and 8(a)(5). Is the union correct on either count?

6. The owner of a shopping center prevented employees of one of the tenant stores from picketing the store on the premises of the shopping center. The picketing was being carried on peacefully, and was protesting employment practices. The employees charged a violation of their First Amendment right of free speech. What should be the decision?

7. Mary Weatherman was personal secretary to the General Manager and Chief Executive Officer of the Hendricks County R.E.M.C. (Rural Electric Membership Corporation). She signed a petition seeking reinstatement of an employee who had been discharged after he was injured on the job, losing his hand. As a result, she also was discharged. She charged a violation of Section 8(a)(1), and the employer contended she was not covered by the National Labor Relations Act because she was a confidential secretary in the management area. Is the employer correct?

8. An employee of Eastex, Inc. sought to distribute a union newsletter to other employees in a nonworking area (the employee lounge) during nonworking time. The newsletter asked workers to write to legislators to stop passage of a right-to-work law. The employer ordered him to stop, threatening disciplinary action if he persisted. The employer was charged with a violation of Section 8(a)(1). What should be the decision?

9. Producers, directors, and story editors continued to work during a strike called by their union. They did supervisory tasks, including adjustment of grievances. At the conclusion of the strike, the union fined them in amounts ranging from $10,000 to $50,000. The employer filed unfair labor practices charges, alleging a violation of Section 8(b)(1). Is the employer correct?

10. Ford Motor Co. was charged with violating Section 8(a)(5) when it unilaterally changed the prices of vending-machine food in the employees' cafeteria of one of its plants, and then refused to bargain concerning the changes. Should the charge be sustained? Why or why not?

Chapter | 51

Collective Bargaining and Concerted Action

THE THEORY OF COLLECTIVE BARGAINING

The concept of collective bargaining often is thought of in too-narrow terms by laypeople and the media. The word raises visions of adversarial and hostile parties in shirt-sleeves arguing across a bargaining table, each seeking to impose outrageous demands on the other. Certainly this is an aspect of collective bargaining, but not the whole picture. Ideally, **collective bargaining** involves a *continuing relationship* between an employer and a defined group of employees. It involves not only contract negotiation, but contract administration while the agreement is in force. It is at the time agreement is reached that the real work of collective bargaining should begin, not end.

Collective bargaining began as a method of putting employers and employees on a more equal footing. Employers were powerful and individual employees were not. However, there is strength in numbers, so employees first sought to bargain as a group. Today, collective bargaining through representatives is common. Although it ordinarily is thought of as a massing of employees under one bargaining agent, employers also may join together in associations under one bargaining agent. Up to a point, larger bargaining units are desirable because when agreement is reached more parties are affected, and the opportunities for labor problems are reduced.

Who Can Be a Collective Bargaining Agent?

Almost anyone. A **collective bargaining agent** is just that—an agent. On the employee side, the job usually is entrusted to an organized union—perhaps a national union affiliated with the AFL-CIO. However, it may be an "in-house" union or even an individual. In fact, the job often is undertaken by labor attorneys.

Duties of the Bargaining Agent

A collective bargaining agent is empowered by law to act as the representative for a defined group of employees, legally binding them on matters of contract negotiation and administration. A bargaining agent becomes the *exclusive* voice of *all* employees within the unit represented. For example, suppose a union is selected as the bargaining agent for clerical employees of a particular employer. The union will bargain with the employer on all matters concerning wages, hours, and terms and conditions of employment. The employer no longer is permitted to bargain on these matters with individual employees in the clerical unit. In addition, this applies to *all* employees in the bargaining unit, regardless of whether they are union members.

All matters that must be decided in the operation of a business may be classified into three categories: (1) mandatory bargaining issues, (2) permissive bargaining issues, and (3) management prerogatives. The first category, **mandatory bargaining issues,** usually is defined as those involving "wages, hours, and terms and conditions of employment." Precisely what this comprehends has been the subject of some debate.

Wages may include any conceivable remuneration for work performed, such as basic hourly rates of pay, piece rates, shift differentials, severance pay, paid vacations and holidays, and any other fringe benefits including insurance, personal use of the employer's vehicles, and furnishing meals and uniforms. Bonuses are included if they are paid in relation to work done, such as according to quantity, quality, or length of service, but not if they are gifts.

Hours are considered to include *all* time worked. The most common disputes in this area arise concerning whether employees may be required to work more than an established number of hours, at what times these hours must be worked, and what is to be thought of as "working time." For example, suppose employees driving to work must park in a remote parking lot and take a shuttle bus to the workplace, punch in on a time clock, and then walk ten minutes to their work stations. At what point do "working hours" begin and end?

Terms and conditions of employment may comprehend a wide variety of issues. These may relate to lighting, ventilation, work rules, grievance procedures, break periods, or any number of other matters. Most disagreements concerning whether particular issues are mandatory arise in this context. A refusal to negotiate on a mandatory bargaining issues is an unfair labor practice—a violation of Section 8(a)(5) or Section 8(b)(3).

The second class of bargainable issues, **permissive bargaining issues,** is optional. A refusal to bargain with respect to them is not an unfair labor practice. Even if a permissive subject is included in a collective bargaining agreement, a refusal to bargain with respect to it in negotiations on the next contract is not a violation. Permissive issues are those that do not directly touch on wages, hours, or terms and conditions of employment, but regard the relationship between the employer and the union. These may be matters such as internal union affairs, arbitration clauses, and union security clauses—for example, the matter of whether to have a union-shop clause in the contract. (Security clauses, such as union-shop provisions, are discussed later in this chapter.) Disagreement may arise whether a particular issue is mandatory or permissive.

The final category of issues is classified as **management prerogatives.** Although the employer may bargain voluntarily with respect to them, a refusal to do so is not an unfair labor practice, but *insistence* on bargaining about them by the union *is*. These are internal management issues that the employer must be free to decide for itself—for example, qualifications, training, and compensation of management personnel, management reporting procedures, matters relating to stockholders, the company logo, and even whether to open a new plant (except for effects the decision to expand may have on present employees). The choice of what products to manufacture ordinarily is a matter of management prerogative. Of course, if the decision was to switch production from toys to gunpowder, it would be a mandatory issue because the change would involve at least a change in the conditions of employment.

REPRESENTATION ELECTIONS

At the heart of the National Labor Relations Act, the Railway Labor Act, and labor regulation in general, is the objective of providing for collective bargaining. By this process, the relative power of management and labor may approach equality. The process begins by the employees electing a collective bargaining representative.

Pre-election Campaign

A campaign begins with some contact between employees and a potential representative (usually a union). It may be at the instance of either. A union may seek to represent certain employees; that is its business. On the other hand, employees may become disturbed about the conditions of their employment and seek a union to represent them as a group. In either situation, the union will seek to determine what percentage of employees is interested in being represented, and also may try to sway those who are neutral or opposed. In the latter case, a campaign will be involved.

Early in the campaign, the interested union often will contact the employer, either giving notice of its intention to campaign or demanding to be recognized as the representative of the employees without an election. It typically is to the advantage of both to have an NLRB-monitored election, but that is not required. (See *National Labor Relations Board v. Gissel Packing Co.*, which was set out in the previous chapter.) When an employer is notified of the union's intention to campaign, it is required to furnish the union with the names and addresses of all employees for whom the union seeks to bargain. As discussed in the previous chapter, the right of nonemployee recruiters to campaign on company property is very limited. Even the distribution of literature at plant gates may be prohibited if it unreasonably interferes with traffic or presents a hazard to safety. Therefore, a list of names and addresses is necessary to allow the union to contact employees away from work. Consider the following case, in which the disagreement is about the union's access to solicit employees.

NATIONAL LABOR RELATIONS BOARD v. BABCOCK AND WILCOX COMPANY
351 U.S. 105, 76 S.Ct. 679, 100 L.Ed. 975 (1956)

This case began with a charge of unfair labor practices against Babcock and Wilcox Company (Respondent), filed with the National Labor Relations Board.

Respondent's plant was located on a 100-acre tract about one mile from a community of 21,000 people. Approximately 40 percent of its 500 employees lived there, and the remainder lived within a 30-mile radius. More than 90 percent drove to work in private automobiles and parked in Respondent's parking lot adjacent to the plant. The parking lot could be reached only by a driveway 100 yards long, entirely on company property.

The union charging the unfair labor practices when it was prohibited by Respondent from distributing leaflets in its parking lot. The union contended there was no other reasonable means of reaching the employees, so the prohibition constituted interference with the employee's right to organize. Respondent contended it applied the same no-distribution rule to everyone to prevent littering of the premises.

The board found Respondent in violation of Section 8(a)(1) of the National Labor Relations Act and ordered that the union be allowed to distribute its pamphlets in the parking lot. The Fifth Circuit Court of Appeals refused enforcement and the board appealed. Affirmed.

REED, J.

In these present cases the Board has set out the facts that support its conclusions as to the necessity for allowing nonemployee union organizers to distribute union literature on the company's property. In essence they are that nonemployee union representatives, if barred, would have to use personal contacts on streets or at home, telephones, letters or advertised meetings to get in touch with the employees. The force of this position in respect to employees isolated from normal contacts has been recognized by this Court and by others. . . .

It is our judgment, however, that an employer may validly post his property against nonemployee distribution of union literature if reasonable efforts by the union through other available channels of communication will enable it to reach the employees with its message and if the employer's notice or order does not discriminate against the union by allowing other distribution. In these circumstances the employer may not be compelled to allow distribution even under such reasonable regulations as the orders in these cases permit.

This is not a problem of always open or always closed doors for union organization on company property. Organization rights are granted to workers by the same authority, the National Government, that preserves property rights. Accommodation between the two must be obtained with as little destruction of one as is consistent with the maintenance of the other. The employer may not affirmatively interfere with organization; the union may not always insist that the employer aid organization. But when the inaccessibility of employees makes ineffective the reasonable attempts by nonemployees to communicate with them through the usual channels, the right to exclude from property has been required to yield to the extent needed to permit communication of information on the right to organize.

The determination of the proper adjustments rests with the Board. Its rulings, when reached on findings of fact supported by substantial evidence on the record as a whole, should be sustained by the courts unless its conclusions rest on erroneous legal foundations. Here the Board failed to make a distinction between rule of law applicable to employees and those applicable to nonemployees.

The distinction is one of substance. No restriction may be placed on the employees' right to discuss self-organization among themselves, unless the employer can demonstrate that a restriction is necessary to maintain production or discipline. . . . But no such obligation is owed nonemployee organizers. Their access to company property is governed by a different consideration. The right of self-organization depends in some measure on the ability of employees to learn the advantages of self-organization from others. Consequently, if the location of a plant and the living quarters of the employees place the employees beyond the reach of reasonable union efforts to communicate with them, the employer must allow the union to approach his employees on his property. No such conditions are shown in these records.

The plants are close to small well-settled communities where a large percentage of the employees live. The usual methods of imparting information are available. . . . The various instruments of publicity are at hand. Though the quarters of the employees are scattered they are in reasonable reach. The Act requires only that the employer refrain from interference, discrimination, restraint or coercion in the employees' exercise of their own rights. It does not require that the employer permit the use of its facilities for organization when other means are readily available.

Questions

1. When would an employer's denial of access to its property be unreasonable? Is there a magic distance the union organizers would have to travel?

2. Would you characterize this decision as fair, pro-union, or anti-union? What is your reasoning?

During campaign time, the employer must be especially careful to avoid committing unfair labor practices, particularly Section 8(a)(1) and (2) violations. Of course, this does not mean that the employer may not campaign fairly and truthfully against union representation. However, the use of such tactics as threats of reprisal, giving benefits or promising them if the union is defeated, "captive audience" speeches (for example, requiring that employees come to an anti-union address by management during working time), and showing favoritism for one union over others especially are to be avoided. The commission of any unfair labor practice may be grounds for setting aside an election if the union is defeated.

The extent to which false and fraudulent statements by either side may be grounds for setting aside an election has been a volatile subject. The board's (NLRB) decisions have varied between finding such statements as cause if they are material, and finding them to be cause only if they *also* are made so near to election time that the other party has insufficient time to counteract them. The latter most nearly is the board's present position.

One final observation is in order. Speeches by the employer to assembled groups of employees, on working time, within 24 hours of the election *always* must be avoided unless the union or unions campaigning also are invited and are given an opportunity to present the other side. NLRB rules on this are enforced very strictly.

Appropriate Unit

The **bargaining unit** is the group of employees the union seeks to represent. This may be all employees of the employer or any discrete group of employees, such as line workers, custodians, secretarial/clerical staff, or grounds and maintenance workers. The unit may be selected employees of a single plant, or two or more plants of the same employer. The NLRB will certify "any appropriate" unit. Whether the unit is the *most* appropriate does not matter, if it is *an* appropriate unit. The board generally favors the broadest, or most comprehensive, unit. The fewer the bargaining units, the smaller the overall chance of strife. However, the most desirable unit is one agreeable to the parties, especially if there has been a favorable history of bargaining regarding that unit.

If the unit selected includes professional or craft employees with others, the professional and craft employees must be given an opportunity to vote on whether to remain part of the unit. **Professional employees** typically are white-collar employees and are distinguished by educational requirements. **Craft employees** normally are distinguished by their skill, and frequently have begun in apprentice programs. This is done prior to certifying the unit and holding the general election. The procedure is called a **severance vote.**

Security personnel *must* be excluded from any unit including nonsecurity employees. Although they may organize, they may not be represented by a union that bargains with their employer on behalf of nonsecurity employees. The rationale for this restriction is that in the event of a strike or other concerted activity, security personnel must be faithful to the employer and protect the employer's premises against striking employees.

Time and Place of the Election

In addition to selecting an appropriate unit, the NLRB must determine an appropriate time and place for the election. Time must take account of work schedules. If the employer runs three shifts, the voting must be held for a reasonable period during each shift. If employees work different days, a two-day election may be necessary. For example, consider a vote by college teachers. Classes may be held during the day from 8 A.M.

until 5 P.M., and night classes from 6:00 P.M. until 9:00 P.M. In addition, some may teach on only Mondays, Wednesdays, and Fridays, and others on only Tuesdays and Thursdays. In this case, the election might be scheduled from 9:00 A.M. until 9:00 P.M. on two successive days, such as Wednesday and Thursday.

The place of the election may be anywhere that gives employees reasonable access to the polls. It may be on the employer's premises, at the union hall, or on neutral grounds. In some cases, such as those involving multi-plant units, voting may be held in more than one location. Voting by mail may be allowed either as to the entire unit or as to some employees only, such as those who are disabled or who are on vacation.

The time and location of voting are two very important aspects of every election. The objective is to give the employees reasonable access to the polls. In keeping with this objective, the employer is required to allow employees to vote during working time if necessary. If the employer and the union agree to an election, to the appropriate unit, and to the time, place, and method of voting, the election is said to be a *consent election*.

The Ballot

The ballot in all NLRB elections must provide a space for voting for each union participating. A union may call for an election by showing an interest on the part of 30 percent of the employees in the prospective unit. Generally, this is done by having employees sign *authorization cards*, but may be done by petition or otherwise. Thereafter, any other union may be placed on the ballot by a showing of 10-percent interest.

In addition to providing a space for each union, a space also must be provided for a "no-union" vote. In NLRB elections, anyone not voting is considered as approving the results of the vote by those who do. This is the same as with political elections. The rule is different for elections conducted by the National Mediation Board under the Railway Labor Act, in which a "no-union"

Union membership in total and as a percentage of the nonfarm work force

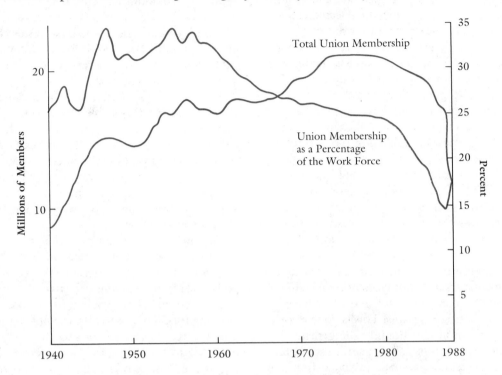

Total Union Membership

Union Membership
as a Percentage
of the Work Force

Source: *Economics* 4th ed. by Ralph T. Burns and Gerald W. Stone. Copyright © 1989, 1987, 1984, 1981 Scott, Foresman and Company.

space is not required because anyone not voting is considered as voting against representation.

NLRB Certification

The results of an election will be validated (called **certification**) by the board only if a substantial number of eligible employees participate. Generally, the board has considered 30 percent substantial. In addition, the results will be certified only if a majority of those voting have agreed on a choice. If there is a tie, or if more than one union appears on the ballot and none of the choices receives a majority, then a run-off election must be held. For example, suppose the ballot provided for three unions, A, B, and C, and a "no-union" choice, and the results were Union A—20 per-

cent, Union B—15 percent, Union C—30 percent, and No-Union—35 percent. A run-off election would be held between the two most popular choices—Union C and No Union. Note that if the unit was made up to 100 employees, only 30 voted, and 16 agreed on a union, the union could be certified and would represent all 100 employees.

If a substantial vote was cast (30 percent), the board will certify the election upon finishing the election process. A winning union will be certified, or the board will certify that a proper election was held and that the employees elected not to be represented. Once an election has been certified, another election concerning that unit ordinarily will not be permitted for twelve months. An exception to this rule is that the board may permit a **decertification election** at the request of employees (but not the employer). This may be done if a union has been certified but has ceased to represent the employees because it has ceased to exist, has lost interest, or has become incapable of adequately representing them because of a schism in its ranks. Otherwise, if the employees have voted against representation, the employer should be free of further demands for twelve months (called the **certification bar**), and if a union has been certified it should be allowed that period to secure a contract without having to fend off competing unions. Consider the following case, in which the employees "changed their minds" about being represented.

BROOKS v. NATIONAL LABOR RELATIONS BOARD
348 U.S. 96, 75 S.Ct. 176, 99 L.Ed. 125 (1954)

This was an action by the National Labor Relations Board (Respondent) against Ray Brooks (Petitioner) to enforce its bargaining order.

District Lodge No. 727, International Association of Machinists, by a vote of eight to five in a Board-conducted election, was certified as collective bargaining agent for Petitioner's employees. A few days later a petition was presented to Petitioner, signed by nine of the thirteen employees in the bargaining unit, stating: "We, the undersigned majority of employees . . . are not in favor of being represented by Union Local No. 727 as a bargaining agent." Relying on the statements, Petitioner refused to bargain.

The board found Petitioner in violation of Section 8(a)(5) of the National Labor Relations Act, and ordered bargaining. The Court of Appeals for the Ninth Circuit enforced the board's order, and Petitioner appealed. Affirmed.

FRANKFURTER, J.

The issue before us is the duty of an employer toward a duly certified bargaining agent if, shortly after the election which resulted in the certification, the union has lost, without the employer's fault, a majority of the employees from its membership.

Under the original Wagner Act, the Labor Board was given the power to certify a union as the exclusive representative of the employees in a bargaining unit when it had determined by election or "any other suitable method", that the union commanded majority support. Section 9(c), 49 Stat. 453. In exercising this authority the Board evolved a number of working rules, of which the following are relevant to our purpose:

(a) A certification, if based on a Board-conducted election, must be honored for a "reasonable" period, ordinarily "one year," in the absence of "unusual circumstances."

(b) "Unusual circumstances" were found in at least three situations: (1) the certified union dissolved or became defunct; (2) as a result of a schism, substantially all the members and officers of the certified union transferred their affiliation to a new local or international; (3) the size of the bargaining unit fluctuated radically within a short time.

(c)   Loss of majority support after the "reasonable" period could be questioned in two ways: (1) employer's refusal to bargain, or (2) petition by a rival union for a new election.

(d)   If the initial election resulted in a majority for "no union," the election—unlike a certification—did not bar a second election within a year. . . .

Petitioner contends that whenever an employer is presented with evidence that his employees have deserted their certified union, he may forthwith refuse to bargain. In effect, he seeks to vindicate the rights of his employees to select their bargaining representative. If the employees are dissatisfied with their chosen union, they may submit their own grievance to the Board. If an employer had doubts about his duty to continue bargaining, it is his responsibility to petition the Board for relief, while continuing to bargain in good faith at least until the Board has given some indication that his claim has merit. Although the Board may, if the facts warrant, revoke a certification or agree not to pursue a charge of an unfair labor practice, these are matters for the Board; they do not justify employer self-help or judicial intervention. The underlying purpose of this statute is industrial peace. To allow employers to rely on employees' rights in refusing to bargain with the formally designated union is not conducive to that end, it is inimical to it. Congress has devised a formal mode for selection and rejection of bargaining agents and has fixed the spacing of elections, with a view of furthering industrial stability and with due regard to administrative prudence.

Questions

1.   Hasn't this decision made bargaining unduly complicated for an employer who has been given clear evidence that the workers have abandoned the union?

2.   What is the court worried about?

3.   Couldn't the circumstances in this case fall within one of the "unusual circumstances" set out in the court's opinion?

If during the campaign or the voting the union has committed unfair labor practices, making a fair election impossible, the board may refuse to certify the election (if that union is elected). If the employer has done so, and the union has been defeated, the board has the power to certify the union as representative of the employees anyway. Of course, these circumstances are unusual, but in most cases if the union was defeated, the union will file unfair labor practice charges against the employer as a matter of course. This establishes grounds to challenge the election if the results are unfavorable. This is done less frequently by an employer.

The Contract

When a union has been certified, negotiations for a contract will begin almost immediately. As previously noted, the elected union is protected from interference by competing unions for twelve months by the so-called certification bar. However, the negotiating process, especially concerning the first contract, often takes a long time.

When a contract has been agreed upon by the negotiators and has been ratified by both the employer and the employees, it becomes binding. During the period of the contract, but only up to a maximum of three years, a new election in the unit is prohibited. This is called the **contract ban.** A contract for less than three years bans an election during its term; a contract for a longer term is a ban for only three years; and a contract for an indefinite term does not act as a ban at all.

A new election may be called at the end of a contract's term. However, certain procedures must be followed. An election may be requested by filing with the NLRB not more than ninety days or less than sixty days prior to the end of the term of an existing contract. Earlier filing will be rejected by the board as premature. Filing during the last sixty days of a contract is not permitted because this is the **cooling-off period** when the employer and the existing union should be negotiating without the distractions of outside demands for an election.

If a contract terminates without agreement on a new one, two things occur. The old contract is considered in force as between the parties. Also, a new election becomes possible. A new election may be called based on a petition filed either during the thirty-day period noted above, or during the gap between contracts. If the parties have agreed to a new contract before terminating the old one, no election will be held. The reason is that the objective of labor harmony is best achieved by continuing the relationship between an employer and a particular union.

UNION SECURITY CLAUSES

In the negotiation of a collective bargaining contract, the union usually will seek to include some provision concerning union membership and the payment of fees by members of the bargaining unit. These **union security clauses** vary in terms of benefit to the union, depending on their content. Because they are so highly sought after by

the unions, employers generally agree to them only in return for some substantial concession by the unions, and they are seldom negotiated as part of the first contract between the two.

Types of Clauses

In rank order of desirability from the union's viewpoint, the most common security clauses are: (1) closed shop, (2) union shop, (3) agency shop, (4) maintenance of membership, and (5) checkoff.

A **closed (or close)-shop** clause provides that an applicant for employment must be a union member before he or she can be hired. The closed shop is illegal under the National Labor Relations Act and the law of most states. Thus, it is permitted in only a few states in cases not governed by the NLRA.

A **union-shop** clause provides that an applicant may be hired regardless of union membership, but must become a union member within a stated time. The applicable period is established by the collective bargaining agreement. The act provides that it may be no less than thirty days, except in the construction industry it may be no less than seven days. The reason for the exception is that the construction industry is characterized by relatively high wages, and the majority of its work is highly seasonal and therefore short term. In particular, the rule is intended to lessen the chance of temporary employment, for substantial wages, without union membership, by students on summer vacation from school. If this could be done repeatedly, the union would be deprived of a substantial portion of its potential power base.

An **agency-shop** clause provides that no employee is required to be a union member, but those who are not must pay a *service fee* to support the work of the union regarding collective bargaining and contract administration. This is seen as fair because the union must bargain for all employees in the unit, regardless of union membership. Therefore all should contribute to its costs. As a general rule, the service fee (sometimes referred to as an "affiliation fee") is the same, or close to, union dues (which average between one and three percent of wages). Sometimes agency-shop clauses provide for "conscientious objection" to the payment of these fees. The agreement may provide for the payment of equivalent amounts to an agreed-upon charity in these cases.

A **maintenance of membership** clause provides that employees who are union members on the date of the contract must remain union members to be employed. Those who are not need not join. However, if a non-member joins during the contract period, he or she also must continue to be a member. Membership may be terminated only during a period of either no contract or a contract without a maintenance-membership clause. This kind of provision, as well as agency shop, may be of benefit to an employer as well as the union because it encourages the union not to allow a gap between the end of one contract and the beginning of the next.

A **checkoff** clause provides that union dues and service fees may be deducted from each employee's paycheck by the employer and forwarded to the union. The employer becomes the collecting agent of the union. Some argue that the checkoff really is not a security clause. Many unions feel this clause is not desirable because having dues and fees collected by a shop steward adds to the spirit of solidarity. When a checkoff clause is in force, dues and fees may be deducted by the employer only from the pay of employees who voluntarily authorize it. The act requires that the authority must be renewed each year. Therefore, the provision for checkoff is permissive, not mandatory.

Right-to-Work Laws

The Taft-Hartley Act of 1947 authorizes states to pass **right-to-work** legislation that invalidates some or all union security clauses for employers in those states. This affects even employers subject to the National Labor Relations Act. Approximately twenty states today have passed right-to-work legislation. Some prohibit all union security clauses, including maintenance of membership. Others are less comprehensive. For example, Indiana law prohibits the closed shop and union shop, but permits the agency shop. This right-to-work legislation is fought bitterly by unions, as is the Taft-Hartley provision permitting it.

STRIKES

Of all concerted activities that a union may use in improving its bargaining position and defending itself from assault, the one most commonly associated with unions is the strike. Although strikes are most frequent during collective bargaining negotiations, collective bargaining and serious disagreement may proceed without a strike, and employees may vote to strike for reasons not connected with collective bargaining.

The term **strike** is defined as "a concerted withdrawal of services by two or more employees who retain contingent interests in their employment." Thus, an employee cannot strike alone—he or she only can refuse to work. A strike requires that two or more employees act in concert. Also, employees on strike remain employees for the purpose of bargaining and protection under the National Labor Relations Act, until they have been discharged properly or have obtained substantially equivalent permanent employment elsewhere and, therefore, have abandoned their previous employment.

Whether employees have a right to strike is a matter of statute. There is no constitutional or inherent right to do so. The right to strike is created by Section 7 of the National Labor Relations Act, and by equivalent provisions of state law concerning private-sector employees. Employees of the federal government, and those of most states and their subdivisions (public-sector

Number of major strikes and the percentage of labor time lost, 1947–1987

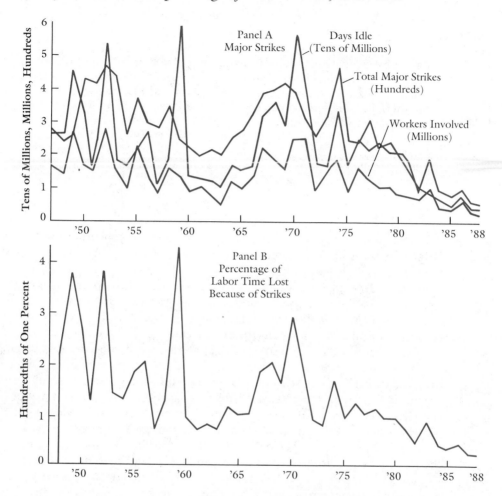

Source: *Economics* 4th ed. by Ralph T. Burns and Gerald W. Stone. Copyright © 1989, 1987, 1984, 1981 Scott, Foresman and Company.

employees) have no such right. Public employees, especially public school teachers, do strike, but these usually are not legal strikes and create special problems for courts asked to enjoin an illegal walkout.

Roughly comparable to employees' right to strike is employers' right to lockout. A **lockout** occurs when an employer refuses to allow the employees to work. Although comparable to a strike, the right to lockout is considerably more restricted. Generally, a lockout is legal only for defensive purposes rather than to improve the employer's bargaining position. Consider the following case.

NATIONAL LABOR RELATIONS BOARD v. BROWN, et al.
380 U.S. 278, 85 S.Ct. 980, 13 L.Ed.2d 839 (1965)

Respondents, including John Brown, were members of a multi-employer bargaining unit that had bargained with Local 462 of the Retail Clerks International Union. Faced with a "whipsaw strike" (a strike of first one employer and then another), Respondents locked out their employees and continued business with temporary replacements.

The National Labor Relations Board (Petitioner) found that the respondents' lockouts violated Sections 8(a)(1) and (3) of the National Labor Relations Act. The Tenth Circuit Court of Appeals disagreed and refused enforcement of the board's order, and the board appealed. Affirmed.

BRENNAN, J.

We begin with the proposition that the Act does not constitute the Board as an "arbiter of the sort of economic weapons the parties can use in seeking to gain acceptance of their bargaining demands." . . . In the absence of proof of unlawful motivation, there are many economic weapons which an employer may use that either interfere in some measure with concerted employee activities, or which are in some degree discriminatory and discourage union membership, and yet the use of such economic weapons does not constitute conduct that is within the prohibition of either Section 8(a)(1) or Section 8(a)(3). . . . Even the Board concedes that an employer may legitimately blunt the effectiveness of an anticipated strike by stockpiling inventories, readjusting contract schedules, or transferring work from one plant to another, even if he thereby makes himself "virtually strikeproof." As a general matter he may completely liquidate his business without violating either Section 8(a)(1) or Section 8(a)(3), whatever the impact of his action on concerted employee activities. Textile Workers v. Darlington Mfg. Co. . . . Specifically, he may in various circumstances use the lockout as a legitimate economic weapon. . . . And in American Ship Building Co. v. Labor Board, . . . we held that a lockout is not an unfair labor practice simply because used by an employer to bring pressure to bear in support of his bargaining position after an impasse in bargaining negotiations has been reached.

In the circumstances of this case, we do not see how the continued operations of respondents and their use of temporary replacements imply hostile motivation any more than the lockout itself; nor do we see how they are inherently more destructive of employee rights. Rather, the compelling inference is that this was all part and parcel of respondents' defensive measure to preserve the multiemployer group in the face of the whipsaw strike. . . .

The Board's finding of a Section 8(a)(1) violation emphasized the impact of respondents' conduct upon the effectiveness of the whipsaw strike. It is no doubt true that the collective strength of the stores to resist that strike is maintained, and even increased, when all stores stay open with temporary replacements. The pressures on the employees are necessarily greater when none of the union employees is working and the stores remain open. But these pressures are no more than the result of the Local's inability to make effective use of the whipsaw tactic. Moreover, these effects are no different from those that result from the legitimate use of any economic weapon by an employer. Continued operations with the use of temporary replacements may result in the failure of the whipsaw strike, but this does not mean that the employers' conduct is demonstrably so destructive of employee rights and so devoid of significant service to any legitimate business and that it cannot be tolerated consistently with the Act. Certainly then, in the absence of evidentiary findings of hostile motive, there is no support for the conclusion that respondents violated Section 8(a)(1).

Nor does the record show any basis for concluding that respondents violated Section 8(a)(3). Under that section both discrimination and a resulting discouragement of union membership are necessary, but the added element of unlawful intent is also required. In Buffalo Linen itself the employers treated the locked-out employees less favorably because of their union membership, and this may have tended to discourage continued membership, but we rejected the notion that the use of the lockout violated the statute. The discriminatory act is not by itself unlawful unless intended to prejudice the employees' position because of their membership in the union; some element of anti-union animus is necessary.

Questions

1. Isn't the Court being disingenuous or naive in not simply presuming that a lockout *always* has "anti-union animus"?
2. Is this decision fair, anti-union, or pro-union?
3. How would a union prove a company's anti-union motivation?

No-Strike Clauses

A collective bargaining contract may include a clause forbidding strikes by employees. **No-strike clauses** usually also forbid lockouts by the employer, and include provisions for dispute settlement, such as arbitration. Although a part of only a minority of contracts, these clauses are not uncommon today. The degree to which they meet their intended objective is largely a matter of good faith by the employer and the employees alike. Frequently these clauses are not enforced effectively by the courts, as with the problem of illegal strikes in the public sector. Also, they apply only to strikes for the purpose of supporting collective bargaining efforts, and not to those against an employer's unfair labor practices. Most strikes involve allegations of employer unfair labor practices, and the fear that that these charges may be upheld often keep employers from pursuing their rights in cases of illegal strikes. This will become clearer after strikes are discussed further. The following case discusses the enforceability of no-strike clauses in collective bargaining contracts.

BOY'S MARKET, INC. v. RETAIL CLERK'S UNION, LOCAL 770
398 U.S. 235, 90 S.Ct. 1583, 26 L.Ed.2d 199 (1970)

This was an action by Boy's Market, Inc. (Plaintiff/Petitioner) against Retail Clerk's Union, Local, 770 (Defendant/Respondent) to enjoin a strike by Defendant in violation of a no-strike clause in a collective bargaining contract. The District Court granted the injunction, and its decision was reversed by the Court of Appeals for the Ninth Circuit. Plaintiff appealed. Reversed and remanded.

BRENNAN, Justice.

In this case we re-examine the holding of Sinclair Refining Co. v. Atkinson, . . . (1962), that the anti-injunction provisions of the Norris-LaGuardia Act preclude a federal district court from enjoining a strike in breach of a no-strike obligation under a collective bargaining agreement, even though that agreement contains provisions, enforceable under Section 301(a) of the Labor Management Relations Act, 1947, for binding arbitration of the grievance dispute concerning which the strike was called. The Court of Appeals for the Ninth Circuit, considering itself bound by Sinclair reversed the grant by the District Court for the Central District of California of petitioner's prayer for injunctive relief. . . . Having concluded that Sinclair was erroneously decided and that subsequent events have undermined its continuing validity, we overrule that decision and reverse the judgment of the Court of Appeals. . . .

As we have previously indicated, a no-strike obligation, express or implied, is the quid pro quo for an undertaking by the employer to submit grievance disputes to the process of arbitration. See Textile Workers Union of America v. Lincoln Mills, supra, 353 U.S., at 455, 77 S.Ct. at 917. Any incentive for employers to enter into such an arrangement is necessarily dissipated if the principal and most expeditious method by which the no-strike obligation can be enforced is eliminated. While it is of course true, as respondent contends, that other avenues of redress, such as an action for damages, would remain open to an aggrieved employer, an award of damages after a dispute has been settled is no substitute for an immediate halt to an illegal strike. Furthermore, an action for damages prosecuted during or after a labor dispute would only tend to aggravate industrial strife and delay an early resolution of the difficulties between employer and union.

Even if management is not encouraged by the unavailability of the injunction remedy to resist arbitration agreements, the fact remains that the effectiveness of such agreements would be greatly reduced if injunctive relief were withheld. Indeed, the very purpose of arbitration procedures is to provide a mechanism for the expeditious settlement of industrial disputes without resort to strikes, lockouts, or other self-help measures. This basic purpose is obviously largely undercut if there is no immediate, effective remedy for those very tactics that arbitration is designed to obviate. . . .

The literal terms of Section 4 of the Norris-LaGuardia Act must be accommodated to the subsequently enacted provisions of Section 301(a) of the Labor Management

Relations Act and the purposes of arbitration. Statutory interpretation requires more than concentration upon isolated words; rather, consideration must be given to the total corpus of pertinent law and the policies that inspired ostensibly inconsistent provisions.

Questions

1. Is the basic policy of industrial peace really furthered by permitting federal courts to enjoin strikes?

2. Is this decision fair, pro-union, or anti-union?

3. What has happened that led the Court to reconsider and overrule the *Sinclair Refining* decision?

Classification of Strikes

All strikes are classified by the NLRB into three general categories—unfair labor practice, economic, and unprotected. The rights of the employer and affected employees differ depending on which type of strike is involved. Sometimes a single strike may include the elements of more than one category. In these instances, called dual-motive cases, difficult problems of classification often must be faced. It is not useful to classify a strike as "partially this and partially that," because the rights of the parties must be determined, and that requires more precision.

An **unfair labor practice strike** is one brought about or perpetuated by a violation of Section 8(a) of the National Labor Relations Act—employer unfair labor practices. Employees on strike because of an unfair labor practice retain absolute job rights. When the strike is over, they are entitled to reinstatement in their previous jobs, and often are entitled to back wages and time toward seniority, promotion, and other benefits during the period of the strike.

An **economic strike** is one intended to support collective bargaining demands by the employees. Pressure is put on the employer to improve wages, hours, or terms and conditions of employment. During these strikes, employees retain only contingent job rights. They may not be fired for striking, but may be replaced permanently. That

is, they may not be fired and then replaced *later*, and they are entitled to reinstatement after the strike only if permanent replacements have not been hired in the meantime.

An **unprotected strike** is one involving illegal action. This category includes sitdown strikes, slowdowns, key-man strikes, those in violation of a no-strike clause, wildcat strikes, strikes for purposes defined as union unfair labor practices, and strikes to pressure the employer to act in violation of the law. As the name implies, employees involved in strikes in this category forfeit protection of job rights. They may be dismissed summarily by the employer. Unlike the rule regarding economic strikes, there is no requirement that the employee's job must be permanently filled before dismissal. The employee may be discharged immediately and the job filled later.

In **dual-motive cases,** the NLRB must place the strike in one of these three categories. Usually this is done by determining which set of circumstances was the principal cause of the strike and contributed most to its continuation. It should be noted that a strike may begin in one category and be continued for reasons related to a second, and the classification of the entire strike may be changed. For example, a strike may begin to support economic demands, and be continued and lengthened by employer unfair labor practices. In that case, its classification might be switched, dramatically affecting the rights of the parties. Any question of which category is appropriate ordinarily is resolved against the employer, in order to promote the important policy of protecting the employees' right to use concerted action to enforce their bargaining position. Therefore, when faced with a strike, it is particularly important that the employer be careful of conduct or appearances that might be construed as an unfair labor practice.

Previously it was noted that in the process of collective bargaining it is common, and perhaps routine, that the union will file unfair labor practice charges against the employer. This particularly is true when bargaining is accompanied by an economic strike. The reason for this practice now should be clear—an employer faced with unfair labor practice charges during an economic strike is less likely to hire permanent replacements for striking employees. Instead, the employer is likely to hire only temporary replacements.

PICKETING

Although picketing usually accompanies every strike, it may occur independent of a strike. **Picketing** is the dissemination of information, such as employee dissatisfaction with treatment by an employer. The term generally conjures up an image of employees milling around their place of employment carrying angrily-worded placards. More accurately, picketing is the process of informing others of the grievance, and the physical presence of employees on the picket line is called **patrolling.** Most picketing involves patrolling, but may be done without it, for example by mail, signs, handing out information sheets, or placing them under windshield wipers in a parking lot. With increasing frequency today, it even is done by the use of electronic media, such as advertisements on television.

Because the crux of picketing is the dissemination of information, unlike striking, it has constitutional protection. It is embraced by the First Amendment's provision concerning freedom of speech. As with other freedoms, however, the right to free speech is not absolute. It may be lost if carried on for purposes not permitted by the National Labor Relations Act, if abused, or if carried on in such a manner as to infringe unreasonably on other constitutionally protected rights. Consider the following case, in which the court was required to weigh and balance two competing rights.

THORNHILL v. STATE OF ALABAMA
310 U.S. 88, 60 S.Ct. 736, 84 L.Ed. 1093 (1940)

This case involved the conviction of Byron Thornhill (Petitioner) for violation of an Alabama state statute prohibiting "loitering or picketing near or about the premises or place of business of any other person . . . for the purpose, or with the intent of influencing, or inducing other persons not to trade with, buy from, sell to, have business dealings with . . . such person. . . ." Petitioner was among a group of six or eight other men who were on the picket line as a result of a strike called against the Brown Wood Preserving Company by a union, and was arrested and convicted of violating the statute in question. This conviction was upheld through the Alabama state courts, and came to the Supreme Court on *certiorari.* Reversed.

MURPHY, J.

The freedom of speech and of the press, which are secured by the First Amendment against abridgment by the United States, are among the fundamental personal rights and liberties which are secured to all persons by the Fourteenth Amendment against abridgment by a state.

The safeguarding of these rights to the ends that men may speak as they think on matters vital to them and that falsehoods may be exposed through the processes of education and discussion is essential to free government. . . .

Section 3448 has been applied by the State courts so as to prohibit a single individual from walking slowly and peacefully back and forth on the public sidewalk in front of the premises of an employer, without speaking to anyone, carrying a sign or placard on a staff above his head stating only the fact that the employer did not employ union men affiliated with the American Federation of Labor; the purpose of the described activity was concededly to advise customers and prospective customers of the relationship existing between the employer and its employees and thereby to induce such customers not to patronize the employer. . . . The statute as thus authoritatively construed and applied leaves room for no exceptions based upon either the number of persons engaged in the proscribed activity, the peaceful character of their demeanor, the nature of their dispute with an employer, or the restrained character and the accurateness of the terminology used in notifying the public of the facts of the dispute.

The numerous forms of conduct proscribed by Section 3448 are subsumed under two offenses: the first embraces the activities of all who "without a just cause or legal excuse" "go near to or loiter about the premises" of any person engaged in a lawful business for the purpose of influencing or inducing others to adopt any of certain enumerated courses of action; the second, all who "picket" the place of business of any such person "for the purpose of hindering, delaying, or interfering with or injuring any lawful business or enterprise of another." It is apparent that one or the other of the offenses comprehends every practicable method whereby the facts of a labor dispute may be publicized in the vicinity of the place of business of an employer. The phrase "without a just cause or legal excuse" does not in any effective manner restrict the breadth of the regulation; the words themselves have no ascertainable meaning either inherent or historical. . . .

The courses of action, listed under the first offense, which an accused—including an employee—may not urge others to take, comprehends those which in many instances would normally result from merely publicizing, without annoyance or threat of any kind, the facts of a labor dispute. An intention to hinder, delay or interfere with a lawful business, which is an element of the second offense, likewise can be proved merely by showing that others reacted in a way normally expectable of some upon learning the facts of a dispute. The vague contours of the term "picket" are nowhere delineated. Employees or others, accordingly, may be found to be within the purview of the term and convicted for engaging in activities identical with those proscribed by the first offense. In sum, whatever the means used to publicize the facts of a labor dispute, whether by printed sign, by pamphlet, by word of mouth or otherwise, all such activity without exception is within the inclusive prohibition of the statute so long as it occurs in the vicinity of the scene of the dispute. . . .

The freedom of speech and of the press guaranteed by the Constitution embraces at the least the liberty to discuss publicly and truthfully all matters of public concern without previous restraint or fear of subsequent punishment. The exigencies of the colonial period and the efforts to secure freedom from oppressive adminstration developed a broadened conception of these liberties as adequate to supply the public need for information and education with respect to the significant issues of the times. . . .

In the circumstances of our times the dissemination of information concerning the facts of a labor dispute must be regarded as within that area of free discussion that is guaranteed by the Constitution.

Questions

1. Did the Court ban all state law restrictions on picketing? If you think not, describe the elements of the Alabama statute the Court found constitutionally offensive.

2. Would the Court strike down a statute that prohibited picketing an employer's premises under any circumstances?

Restrictions Under the National Labor Relations Act

In some cases, picketing may be an unfair labor practice. Section 8(b) of the act prohibits picketing for any of the following purposes:

1. To restrain or coerce employees in the exercise of their rights under Section 7. For example, a union cannot picket employees, or the premises of their employer, for the purpose of forcing those employees to join a union or attend an organizational meeting, or to force the employer to cause them to do so (Section 8(b)(1) and (3)).

2. To force an employer or a self-employed person to join any labor organization or employer organization. Although infrequent, this violation has occurred most frequently in connection with attempting to cause an employer to join a multi-employer bargaining association (Section 8(b) (4) (A)).

3. To force an employer to enter into a hot-cargo agreement in violation of Section 8(e). (A *hot-cargo agreement* is one in which an employer agrees not to handle the products of another employer or, in particular, not to require that employees work with these products. This is an illegal tactic, coming under the broad term *secondary boycott*, as discussed later in this chapter.) Section 8(e) allows hot-cargo agreements only in the construction and garment industries. In these, subcontracting is so common that a comprehensive ban on hot-cargo agreements would be too great a burden on unions in enforcing employee rights under Section 7 (Section 8(b)(4)(A)).

4. To force an employer to participate in a boycott of another employer. Again, this is part of the general position against secondary boycott activity (Section 8(b)(4)(B)).

5. To force an employer to recognize the union as collective bargaining agent of his or her employees when another union has been certified by the National Labor Relations Board (Section 8(b)(4)(C)).

6. To force an employer to assign work to employees who are members of a particular union. This was discussed previously with regard to conflicts between two or more unions as to the "jurisdiction" over certain work of a common employer. Under the act, these so-called **jurisdictional disputes** must be presented to the NLRB for resolution (Section 8(b)(4)(D)).

7. To force an employer to recognize the union as collective bargaining agent: (a) when the employer has a contract with another union representing the same employees, during the term of the contract up to a reasonable time, not exceeding three years; (b) when the union is not certified and a representation election has been held in the unit within the previous twelve months; or (c) when the union is not certified and has picketed for more than a reasonable time not exceeding thirty days, without requesting an election. (Section 8(b)(7)). In addition, extortionate picketing is prohibited under Section 602 of the Landrum-Griffin Act of 1959.

Abusive Picketing

When picketing is carried on in such a manner that its main purpose of giving information becomes overshadowed by other effects, it may be restricted or prohibited. Some examples are:

1. Massed picketing, which involves the presence of an unreasonable number of participants at a particular location. The purpose of such massing is seen as intimidation rather than education. As one judge stated the principle, a court may limit the number of participants at a location and the free right to picket may be restricted when "a picket line becomes a picket fence."

2. Fraudulent picketing, which involves the giving out of information so false that it goes beyond the statement of an opinion, and is calculated to cause unreasonable harm to the employer being picketed. For example, picketing was held to be illegal in one case involving a jewelry store when picketing employees were telling customers that during the strike they were not required to pay on their accounts with the store.

3. Picketing accompanied by violence. Although isolated and infrequent incidents usually will not cause picketing to be held illegal, at some point further picketing may be prohibited.

4. Picketing to cause the employer to violate other laws—for example, to cause the employer to enforce a policy of racial or other discimination prohibited by the Civil Rights Act of 1964.

These are only some examples of abuses of the right to picket.

Generally, any picketing may be prohibited when it becomes inconsistent with public policy, especially when it unreasonably infringes on the constitutional rights of others. This may result from the use of language so offensive that its offensiveness outweighs its value as a means of communication. It also may result when picketing involves an invasion of privacy, as by the publication of private information about an individual. Most frequently, it involves a conflict between the right to picket and the rights of an owner of private property. This topic was discussed in some detail in Chapter 5, along with other topics in constitutional law. A re-examination of that portion of Chapter 5 is recommended at this point.

BOYCOTTS

A **boycott** is a refusal to deal. This may be a consumer refusing to buy the products of a seller, a customer refusing to buy from a supplier, a supplier refusing to service a customer, or employees refusing to deal with an employer concerning their services. A boycott of the last kind, of course, is called a strike. An objective of picketing, in addition to providing information, often is to create a boycott. It is hoped that when third parties are made aware of the "wrongdoings" of a particular employer, they will, by refusing to patronize that employer, encourage it to make concessions to the union.

All boycotts may be categorized as primary, secondary, or tertiary. Classification is made according to the relationship between the point of the boycott and the employer or other person it is intended ultimately to pressure.

A **primary boycott** is one against the person or employer with whom the dispute exists. For example, in an effort to pressure Employer A to agree to certain demands, suppose the employees of Employer A picket, asking customers and suppliers not to deal with A. The attempt is to create a primary boycott—one against the employer with whom the dispute exists. Primary boycotts generally are legal. Their legality is determined by application of the "ends and means doctrine" announced in 1842 in the case of *Commonwealth v. Hunt*, discussed early in the preceding chapter. As long as legal ends are sought by legal means, the boycott is legal.

A **secondary boycott** is one step more remote than a primary boycott. It is one applied against a customer or supplier of the employer with whom the dispute exists. The purpose is to apply pressure against the customer or supplier, in turn, to apply pressure against the "unfair" employer. For example, suppose that in the dispute with Employer A, the employees picketed A's Customer B, asking that B's customers or suppliers not deal with B in order to pressure B to pressure A. This would be an attempt to create an illegal secondary boycott.

Generally, secondary boycotts are illegal. One exception, however, applies in situations involving a **unity of interest** between the primary and secondary parties. A unity of interest exists if the secondary party will be affected materially by the decision of the primary party. For example, suppose in the previous example Employer A is a producer of kosher meat products, and Customer B is a delicatessen that sells A's products almost exclusively. Sales of these products represents a substantial part of B's income. Under these circumstances, A and B may be held to have a unity of interest, making the attempt to establish a boycott against patronizing B legal.

Courts also permit picketing of a secondary party for the purpose of asking the secondary party's customers to refuse to buy the primary party's products there. Continuing the previous example, suppose A's employees picketed B's premises asking that B's customers refuse to purchase A's products from B. Without regard to a unity of interest, this activity would be lawful. Note that the purpose is not to encourage customers not to deal at all with B, but only to refuse to purchase A's products. The products of the primary party usually may be followed by picketing through the channels of commerce. However, the exemption would not apply in a case in which the primary party's product was an insignificant part of the object of the boycott. For example, suppose Employer A was a manufacturer of windshield wiper blades used by General Motors on their Buick automobiles. A's employees would not be permitted to picket a Buick dealer's showroom because the connection would be insignificant.

Of principal importance in the definition of secondary boycott is that the effect is to cause a secondary employer to cease to do business with the primary employer. Consider the following case.

NATIONAL LABOR RELATIONS BOARD v. LOCAL 825, INTERNATIONAL UNION OF OPERATING ENGINEERS

400 U.S. 297, 91 S.Ct. 402, 27 L.Ed.2d 398 (1971)

A general contractor (Burns) subcontracted construction work to three sub-contractors, all of which employed members of Local 825, International Union of Operating Engineers (Respondent). Burns assigned certain work involving a welding machine to White, who employed members of another labor organization, and immediately was advised that unless he assigned the work to members of Respondent union, all members of that union would go on strike. Burns submitted the question to an arbitrator, who ruled there was no reason to change the assignment. When Burns refused to change the assignment, Respondent union physically prevented operation of the welding machine.

The National Labor Relations Board (Petitioner) found that Respondent had violated Section 8(b)(4)(B) of the National Labor Relations Act by exerting coercive pressures on a neutral employer to cause him "to cease doing business with any other person." (In addition, a violation of Section 8(b)(4)(D) was found.) On the board's petition for enforcement, the Circuit Court of Appeals for the Third Circuit refused enforcement of the part of the board's order concerning Section 8(b)(4)(B) (although it granted enforcement concerning Section 8(b)(4)(D)), and both the board and the union appealed. Reversed as to the Court of Appeals' refusal to enforce on Section 8(b)(4)(B).

MARSHALL, J.

Local 825's coercive activity was aimed directly at Burns and the subcontractors that were not involved in the dispute. The union engaged in a strike against these neutral employers for the specific, overt purpose of forcing them to put pressure on White to assign the job of operating the welding machine to operating engineers. Local 825 was not attempting to apply the full force of primary action by directing its efforts at all phases of Burns' normal operation as was the case in United Steelworkers of America, AFL-CIO (Carrier) v. NLRB . . . , and Local 761, International Union of Electrical, Radio and Machine Workers, AFL-CIO (General Electric) v. NLRB. . . . It was instead using a sort of pressure that was unmistakably and flagrantly secondary. . . .

The more difficult task is to determine whether one of Local 825's objectives was to force Burns and the other neutrals to "cease doing business" with White as Section 8(b)(4)(B) requires. The Court of Appeals concluded that the union's objective was to force Burns "to use its influence with the subcontractor to change the subcontractor's conduct, not to terminate their relationship" and that was not enough. . . . That court read the statute as requiring that the union demand nothing short of a complete termination of the business relationship between the neutral and the primary employer. Such a reading is too narrow.

Some disruption of business relationships is the necessary consequence of the purest form of primary activity. These foreseeable disruptions are, however, clearly protected. . . . Likewise, secondary activity could have such a limited goal and the foreseeable result of the conduct could be, while disruptive, so slight that the "cease doing business" requirement is not met. Local 825's goal was not so limited nor were the foreseeable consequences of its secondary pressure slight. The operating engineers sought to force Burns to bind all the subcontractors on the project to a particular form of job assignments. The clear implication of the demands was that Burns would be required either to force a change in White's policy or to terminate White's contract. The strikes shut down the whole project. If Burns was unable to obtain White's consent, Local 825 was apparently willing to continue disruptive conduct that would bring all the employers to their knees.

Certainly, the union would have preferred to have the employers capitulate to its demands; it wanted to take the job of operating the welding machines away from the Ironworkers. It was willing, however, to try to obtain this capitulation by forcing neutrals to compel White to meet union demands. To hold that this flagrant secondary conduct with these most serious disruptive effects was not prohibited by Section 8(b)(4)(B) would be largely to ignore the original congressional concern. . . .

Questions

1. What would Local 825 be permitted to do under the Court's ruling?
2. Do the limitations on secondary boycotts tip the balance of power too much in favor of management?

At any point beyond the boycott of a secondary party, a boycott becomes **tertiary.** This may be a boycott sought against a customer or supplier of a customer or supplier of the primary party. It also may be a boycott sought against a party having no connection to the primary party in the chain of commerce. For example, suppose in the previous example, Employer A owned a business that manufactured automobile parts, and also owned a golf course in a nearby town. If employees of the automobile parts plant sought a boycott of the golf course, the action would be tertiary. The two businesses have no connection other than common ownership. In these circumstances, a boycott would be permitted only if the policies of one business affected policies of the other to a substantial degree—for example, if the primary employer was a bank holding company that also owned a mortgage company. In this situation there might be a sufficient connection, if their commercial policies were the same. For the most part, tertiary boycotts are illegal.

DISPUTE RESOLUTION

Disputes between employers and unions may be resolved by any of a number of processes other than agreement. A dispute concerning jurisdiction over a work assignment must be presented to the NLRB for a decision, and the same is true of questions of unfair labor practices. Other matters, such as discrimination and wage and hour questions, may be referred to various administrative agencies. Many disputes in contract administration may be settled by a court in a lawsuit for breach of contract. However, mediation and arbitration also may be used. Frequently these techniques are less expensive and time consuming than the other approaches.

Mediation

Mediation involves the use of a third party as an interface between the two contending parties. The mediator attempts to reconcile the parties or to induce them to agree on a settlement. Sometimes this may amount to carrying proposals and counter-proposals back and forth. In other cases, the mediator may make recommendations for settlement. However, a mediator has no authority to make a final decision in any case.

It should not be assumed that the parties to a labor dispute will approach the bargaining table in an objective frame of mind. In fact, reality usually is to the contrary. Collective bargaining is an adversarial process and should proceed with each party advocating its own best interests. For this reason, the mediator's services may be of great benefit. A mediator provides a neutral "sounding board" to add objectivity to negotiations. As already noted, a mediator may function only as a messenger, as an advisor, or also may render opinions as to the proper resolution of matters in dispute.

Mediation may be entirely voluntary. The parties may agree in advance, in a collective bargaining agreement, that all disputes, or particular disputes, will be resolved by mediation. Also, they may agree to mediation at the time a dispute arises. In these cases, the mediator may be anyone—either a professional mediator or any other person in whom the parties have confidence. In some cases, mediation may be required under the National Labor Relations Act.

Section 8(d) of the act, which defines the obligation to bargain in good faith, provides that if one party wishes to terminate or modify an existing contract, certain procedures must be followed. The same procedures also must be complied with to negotiate a new, different contract upon ex-

piration of the existing one. Notice must be given to the other party sixty days prior to the expiration date of the existing contract, or sixty days prior to the effective date of the termination or modification of a contract having no expiration date. This is the cooling-off period discussed earlier in this chapter. Then, if no agreement has been reached within thirty days after the notice, the party seeking the termination or modification must give notice to both the National Mediation and Conciliation Service (NMCS) and the state or territorial agency responsible for mediation and conciliation of such disputes.

The NMCS also functions in every case involving a national-emergency strike. A *national-emergency strike* is one that, in the opinion of the president, would "imperil the national health or safety." Sections 206 through 210 of the National Labor Relations Act provide for elaborate procedures in these cases, among which is the intervention of the NMCS.

Under Section 213, the NMCS may intervene in any case of a labor dispute in the health care industry. Procedures are initiated at the discretion of the Director of the Service, and include the use of a board of inquiry to make findings and recommendations for settlement.

Arbitration

Arbitration involves the submission of a dispute to a third party who makes a final decision, much as a judge does in a court case. Procedure in an arbitration hearing is similar to that of a court, but often is less formal and more flexible. When procedures are followed properly, the effect of an arbitration award is much the same as that of a court judgment.

Arbitration of labor disputes is less common than mediation, but is a very effective method of dispute resolution. With rare exceptions, arbitration must be voluntary, although occasionally it is mandated by statute (such as in time of war), and then it is referred to as *compulsory arbitration*. As with mediation, arbitration may cover all or only selected subjects of dispute, and consent to arbitration may be included in a collective bargaining agreement or may be obtained after a dispute arises. Usually, no-strike clauses in contracts also provide for arbitration.

The person to act as the arbitrator is chosen by the parties. He or she is ordinarily someone with expertise concerning labor problems in the particular industry, or concerning the particular matter involved in the dispute. Individuals often serve as private arbitrators, and names of qualified persons are supplied on request by the American Arbitration Association.

Because an arbitrator acts much like a judge and makes a final decision binding on the parties, the authority of arbitrators is founded on statute. Acts on the federal level, and in each state, permit the process and dictate basic procedural requirements. Commonly, the decision of an arbitrator becomes legally enforceable by being filed with an appropriate court, and sometimes by being read into the record in open court. The decision, called an *award*, then has the effect of a court judgment.

SUMMARY

The entire process of collective bargaining involves a continuing relationship between an employer and a defined group of employees, and includes contract negotiation and administration. Originally it was intended to equalize the relative power of the employer and employees by uniting the latter under one bargaining head—the collective bargaining agent. It often is thought of as a means of maximizing the chance of achieving industrial peace.

Although frequently a collective bargaining representative is a union, the duties may be performed by an individual. Once elected by the employees to be represented (called a bargaining unit), the agent bargains for all employees in the unit. The employer must deal with the bargaining agent exclusively on all bargainable issues, and not with individual employees.

Three general categories of labor-management issues are mandatory issues, permissive issues, and management prerogatives. The first category involves all matters concerning wages, hours, and terms and conditions of employment. A refusal of either party to bargain on these mandatory issues is an unfair labor practice. The second category includes matters involving the relationship between the employer and the union, such as internal union affairs, dispute settlement, and union security clauses. Bargaining concerning permissive issues is allowed, but a refusal to bargain concerning them is not an unfair labor practice. The last category includes internal management issues, such as compensation of management personnel, product mix, and whether to open a new office or plant. It is an unfair labor practice for a union to insist on bargaining concerning issues of management prerogative.

A bargaining agent may become the representative of employees by their choice and recognition by their employer. This usually is determined by an election conducted by the National Labor Relations Board, but it may be accomplished without an election. If an election is held, the NLRB will certify its results, if the election was participated in by a substantial member of employees in the unit eligible to vote. This usually is considered to be thirty percent. An agent will be certified only if approved by a majority of those voting. Prior to the election, professional and craft employees must be allowed to vote as to whether to be included in a unit with other employees. Security personnel may not be included, although they may form a separate unit.

After an election is certified, another cannot be held in the same unit for twelve months. If a bargaining agent was certified, the collective bargaining process will begin. When a contract is signed, a new election is barred for the term of the contract, up to a maximum of three years.

Collective bargaining contracts frequently include union security clauses requiring the employees in the unit to become members, or sometimes only to pay service fees to support the bargaining effort by the union. These have been prohibited by a number of states that have enacted right-to-work legislation.

A strike is a concerted withdrawal of services by two or more employees who retain contingent interests in their employment. Strikes are classified as unfair labor practice strikes, economic strikes, and unprotected strikes. Employees participating in a strike aimed at an employer's unfair labor practice are guaranteed rights in their jobs when the strike is over. Those participating in an economic strike may not have their jobs when the strike is over, if they have been replaced permanently in the meantime. Those participating in an unprotected strike may be discharged and replaced later.

Picketing is the dissemination of information concerning a dispute. It typically is accompanied by patrolling, but may be done by mail, handing out literature, or otherwise. Unlike the right to strike, which exists only if granted by statute, the right to picket is protected by the First Amendment of the United States Constitution. It may be restrained only as prohibited under the National Labor Relations Act, when the right is abused, or when it unreasonably infringes on other constitutionally protected rights.

A boycott is a refusal to deal. The legality of a boycott is judged according to the "ends and means doctrine." It is upheld if it seeks legal ends by legal means. As a general rule, most primary boycotts are legal, most secondary boycotts are illegal, and all tertiary boycotts are illegal. These classifications refer to the remoteness of the boycott from the party it ultimately is intended to affect.

Disputes between management and labor may be settled in several ways. Most commonly, the NLRB or the courts are used. However, some settlements are achieved through the services of a mediator. This person operates as an intermediary between the parties, carrying proposals between them, sometimes giving advise, and sometimes even suggesting solutions. Mediation may be mandated under the NLRA in some cases. Otherwise it may be sought voluntarily by the parties.

Another possible method of dispute resolution is arbitration. Usually, arbitration may not be compelled, but may come about only by the parties' voluntary consent. An arbitrator functions much like a judge. Unlike the mediator, an arbitrator is empowered to hand down an award that is binding on the parties, as is a court judgment. Arbitration is possible only by statutory authority granted by federal and state statutes. Each statute establishes procedures that must be followed to make arbitration valid.

KEY TERMS AND CONCEPTS

collective bargaining
collective bargaining agent
mandatory bargaining issues
permissive bargaining issues
management prerogatives
bargaining unit
professional employees
craft employees
severance vote
certification
decertification election
certification bar
contract ban
cooling-off period
union security clause
closed shop
union shop
agency shop
maintenance of membership

checkoff

right to work law

strike

lockout

no-strike clause

unfair labor practice strike

economic strike

unprotected strike

dual-motive case

picketing

patrolling

jurisdictional dispute

boycott

primary boycott

secondary boycott

unity of interest doctrine

tertiary boycott

mediation

arbitration

PROBLEMS

1. American Ship Building made its business repairing ships that navigated the Great Lakes. Usually the ships were brought in when the lakes froze, to be ready for work again when the water thawed, a period of approximately three months. Negotiations between American and its union began in late June, on a contract dated August 1. Bargaining reached an impasse and, fearing the union would wait to call a strike until the first ship came in, American locked out its employees. The union charged that doing so was a violation of Section 8(a)(1). Is the union correct?

2. The union obtained authorization cards from a majority of Linden Lumber's employees, but Linden refused to bargain without first having an election. Did Linden's refusal constitute a violation of Section 8(a)(5)?

3. In its collective bargaining contract with Matro Plastics Corp., the union agreed "to refrain from engaging in any strike or work stoppage during the term of this agreement." However, during the sixty days prior to the end of the contract, the employees struck because of unfair labor practices. Was the strike legal?

4. The Fruit and Vegetable Packers union, during a dispute with an employer, caused employees to picket grocery stores selling the employer's produce. They asked that customers of the stores not purchase the employer's produce. Was this an illegal secondary boycott in violation of Section 8(b)(4)?

5. Striking technicians of a radio station picketed. They distributed leaflets charging that the station had substandard programming and didn't care about the needs of the community it was supposed to be serving, along with other such statements. The employer contended such picketing tactics were improper, and discharged those involved. Was the employer within its rights?

6. W & I Blumenthal, a manufacturer of kosher meat products, paid its employees wages 25 percent lower than its competitors. Its employees struck for higher wages and, in the process, picketed a store owned by one of Blumenthal's customers. The picket signs read: "This store sells delicatessen that is made in a non-union factory— Please buy union-made delicatessen only." Of the store's total sales, 80 to 90 percent were derived from the sale of Blumenthal's meat. Did the employees' picketing constitute an illegal attempt to create a secondary boycott?

7. The longshoremen's union ordered a boycott of Russian goods, protesting the invasion of Afghanistan. It instructed its members not to unload or load cargo coming from or going to the Soviet Union. The union was charged with illegal secondary boycott activity. The union defended on the grounds that it was exercising its constitutional right to express its opinion, and its activities were political, not labor-oriented. Should the secondary-boycott charge stand?

8. When a union sought to organize the employees of Daylight Grocery, Daylight actively resisted, and campaigned against union involvement. Daylight, however, did support collective bargaining by its employees through the use of an employee committee. Daylight was charged with violating Section 8(a)(2). Daylight contended the charge was false—it was not seeking to dominate a union, but only to support collective bargaining by its employees without the involvement of a union. Is Daylight correct?

9. During an organizing campaign of Fishman's employees, Fishman stated, on several occasions, that she felt she could not operate a unionized plant, and that if the union was voted in, the adverse economic impact would cause her to close down. The union charged that such statements violated Section 8(a)(1). Was the union correct?

10. Rutherford Freight Lines operated under a collective bargaining contract with its employees. Overnight Transportation Co. purchased the business, and immediately made unilateral changes in pay and benefits. The union contended Overnight was bound to the terms of the contract with Rutherford, and that it committed unfair labor practices by making unilateral changes. Is the union correct?

Chapter | 52

Employment Law

_____

_____

_____

_____

OUTLINE

INTRODUCTION

Prior to the second half of the nineteenth century, employment regulation was virtually unknown. Most people were self-employed in farming or local trading, and there was little need for legal intervention in the few employment relationships that did exist.

With the Industrial Revolution came the growth of the large factories using heavy machinery and the employment of large numbers of workers, creating the workforce and the workplace as we know it today. Despite the increased concentration and interaction of workers and employers, the law remained much the same as it had been in earlier times. State and federal governments maintained a hands-off approach in order to encourage the growth of business, which gave employers tremendous freedom to set the terms and conditions of employment. The courts simply enforced the basic rules of contract law and property law, which left workers, who had virtually no bargaining power, basically unprotected. Unfortunately, the law's failure to adapt to changes in the employment environment eventually exacerbated the inevitable occupational hazards and workplace tensions.

By the beginning of this century, it became clear that unrestrained industrial growth exacted too high a toll on workers' lives. Workplace dangers and oppressive conditions abounded, and workers frequently had no avenue of redress. It was theoretically possible for workers to bargain for acceptable working conditions, but in reality they often had to agree to the terms dictated by large and powerful organizations.

The modern era has been marked by increased government regulation of industry, including the labor-management relationship. The idea of unrestrained business growth has been tempered by the need to provide workers with safe and decent working conditions. Moreover, the entry of new waves of immigrants and women into the workforce posed new issues in the area of employment relations.

This chapter traces the evolution of employment law from a policy of governmental abstention to one of government involvement. Presented below are the major statutory responses to the problems of workplace injury, wrongful discharge, worker privacy, and employment discrimination.

WORKERS' COMPENSATION

During the nineteenth century, employers frequently included clauses in employment contracts excusing them from liability to their workers in case of accidental injury. These disclaimers usually were upheld by courts, because it was presumed that the contracts were bargained for and that the workers had received benefits in return for assuming the risk of injury. In truth, however, the employees' inferior bargaining positions often forced them to engage in dangerous occupations without adequate compensation. Since they were protected by contractual disclaimers of liability, em-

ployers had little incentive to improve the safety of the workplace. This condition was exacerbated by the judicially created **fellow-servant rule,** which meant that a plaintiff could not recover against his or her employer for acts of negligence committed by a fellow worker, and by the **contributory negligence rule,** which denied the plaintiff all recovery if he or she contributed to the injury in even the smallest way.

In the 1880s, the first comprehensive workers' compensation legislation was developed in Germany to help alleviate this injustice. The idea quickly spread throughout Europe, and in the early 1900s, the United States government began experimenting with a compensation program for federal employees. By 1920, most states had enacted some form of workers' compensation legislation that usually extended coverage to all employees, regardless of the hazards of their employment.

Workers' Compensation as a No-Fault Scheme

Unlike the typical tort lawsuit in which the plaintiff's recovery depends upon a determination of the defendant's negligence, in a **workers' compensation** proceeding, fault is irrelevant. The employee may recover regardless of his or her own negligent or reckless behavior (absent intentional conduct or intoxication) and despite diligent efforts by the employer to create and maintain safe working conditions. The workers' compensation system avoids having to determine who was at fault in order to preserve good will between employers and employees and to limit administrative delay and expense in processing claims. Furthermore, without the costly fault determination required in a typical lawsuit, 70 percent of the money used to resolve claims goes directly to the compensation of injured workers. This is in marked contrast to the mere 35 percent of total costs that actually is received by the plaintiffs in ordinary personal injury lawsuits.

Since there is no appraisal of fault, workers' compensation is essentially an insurance plan financed by employers. However, rather than permitting each employer to decide on its own whether to provide the insurance, what level of coverage to provide, or whether to allow its policy to lapse, the workers' compensation system makes insurance a mandatory requirement. In some states, the insurance may be provided by a state fund; in others, employers must seek private insurance. A small number of employers are permitted to self-insure if they can demonstrate their financial strength and ability to maintain the compensation program.

The rationale behind the insurance program is that society as a whole should pay for workplace injuries indirectly through increased prices for goods and services, rather than have the entire burden fall on the individual worker. Furthermore, if a product's price reflects the cost of injuries caused by producing it, employers will have

an incentive to reduce the dangers of their activities in order to be competitive.

Injuries Covered

Despite the broad coverage of workers' compensation, not all accidents are compensable. Only those injuries that arise out of the course of employment are covered by the insurance. Furthermore, it is not enough that the injury merely occurs at the workplace; it must be related causally to the employment site in some manner. Therefore, an employee who suffers a heart attack due to high cholesterol may not recover merely because it strikes while on the job.

Other questions of coverage arise when the accident occurs while the employee is on the way to or from work. Although there is no consensus among the states on how to treat this situation, courts often consider who was paying the transportation costs and whether the employee was on a work assignment, rather than merely commuting, at the time of the incident.

The most troublesome issue confronting workers' compensation at the present time, however, is the problem of distinguishing occupational diseases caused by workplace hazards from those caused by everyday exposure to toxic substances. For instance, it often is impossible to determine whether the respiratory disease of an asbestos worker is attributable to contact with asbestos dust on the job or to the consumption of two packs of cigarettes a day. Obviously the workplace is not responsible for every plight of all asbestos workers, but how can a compensation system accurately identify the claims that should fail under the insurance program?

Amount of Compensation

Because workers' compensation is a no-fault system based entirely on employer insurance programs and is available to all workers for all work-related accidents, workers are not compensated at the same level as in tort actions in the

Workers' compensation, annual benefits paid (1985)

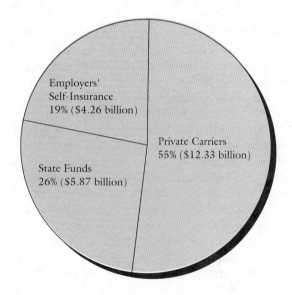

Employers'
Self-Insurance
19% ($4.26 billion)

State Funds
26% ($5.87 billion)

Private Carriers
55% ($12.33 billion)

Source: Statistical Abstract of the U.S. 1988, Table 583.

courts requiring proof of negligence. In fact, the fundamental premise of the compensation system is that the expansion of benefits to all those injured in the course of employment, whether as a result of negligence or not, justifies the reduction in actual payments to individual employees.

Accordingly, workers' compensation covers only financial harm—no relief may be sought for pain and suffering or emotional distress. Full recovery is guaranteed only for medical costs; wage losses must be shared by employer and employee. Generally, most states require that the employee absorb the entire loss during a waiting period of three or four days. After that point, the employer will begin to make payments to the worker for 60 to 80 percent of his or her earnings. Since workers' compensation benefits are not taxable, however, the employee really receives closer to 90 percent of his or her earnings. But the size of the payment usually may not exceed that state's average weekly wage (SAWW)—the average salary of all workers in the state as calculated by the compensation board. Therefore, no lost earnings above the SAWW may be recovered. For example, if Sarah Worker, who earns $900 a week, breaks her leg on the job, she will receive no compensation for the first three days she misses work. After that point, she will begin to receive weekly payments as prescribed by the state's law, say two-thirds of her salary. Although two-thirds of her $900 a week salary is $600, she will receive only $500 a week if that is the state's average weekly wage.

Exclusive Remedy

Once it is determined that an employee's injury arose out of the course of employment, workers' compensation is his or her sole remedy against an employer; no civil lawsuit for damages may be filed. This prohibition stems from the belief that the efficiency and fairness gains of workers' compensation would be lost if workers dissatisfied with their reward levels merely could bring their claims to the court system. Furthermore, emo-tionally traumatic and expensive litigation would be likely to foster ill will between employers and employees and threaten industrial peace. Thus, employers are given immunity against litigation in exchange for their funding the insurance plan.

Types of Disabilities Covered

TEMPORARY DISABILITIES. Most claimants under the workers' compensation system suffer only temporary disabilities. These injuries may be total, leaving the worker incapacitated for a time, or partial, merely reducing his or her work capacity. In either case, the worker will be able to function normally again once the injury has healed, and compensation will be paid only until then.

The system is most successful in compensating these types of injuries. The worker will be reimbursed for all of his or her medical costs and will receive payments almost immediately for 60 to 80 percent of lost wages, which will cover living expenses during the disability. Also, in many cases of this type, there is relatively little pain and suffering, the administrative proceeding is quick and efficient, and there is rarely any need for a lawyer.

PERMANENT TOTAL DISABILITIES. A small fraction of claimants suffer from permanent total disabilities or death (in that case, the worker's dependents will receive the benefits). These long-term injuries are the most expensive for the system, consuming up to 60 percent of its resources. Some states, in an effort to limit the sheer size of the payments, have placed caps either on total benefits that can be received by a worker or the number of weeks that payments may be collected. These restrictions have been sharply criticized because they arbitrarily cut off benefits without regard to the condition of the worker or the availability of other sources of income. As a result, some states have abolished these caps.

Another problem that faces those afflicted with permanent total disabilities is the effect of inflation on the real worth of their benefits. Compensation payments are based on the employee's wage at the time of the injury, and rarely are adjusted to meet the rate of inflation. This has little impact on a worker with a temporary injury, because he or she only misses seventeen days of work on the average. To the worker with a long-term disability, however, the effect can be devastating, given that the real value of his earnings may be cut to one-third in some cases. There is no clear rationale for the lack of adjustment, especially since employees with permanent total disabilities are arguably the most deserving and needy of meaningful benefits. Perhaps the reason is that it is politically more advantageous to channel benefits to larger groups of claimants, such as those with temporary injuries.

PERMANENT PARTIAL DISABILITIES. The most difficult type of injury to deal with effectively under the workers' compensation program is that of permanent partial disabilities—injuries that are lifetime in character but do not completely incapacitate the worker. Generally, there is little objection to abolishing recovery for pain and suffering in the case of a temporary injury, yet a great deal of injustice results when compensation is denied to someone who still is able to work but whose enjoyment of life is impaired permanently. For instance, an employee who has suffered a disfiguring burn may not miss any days from work once healed, but she will endure a great deal of pain and humiliation on a long-term basis that will not be compensated.

Another problem with permanent partial disability claims is that, by compensating medical bills and lost wages, the workers' compensation system tends to encourage employees to stay home and collect payments rather than return to work. Some states have responded to this concern by granting the employee a lump-sum payment *ex ante* (in advance). This system, however, still does not substantially reduce the potential disincentive effect, and does not help at all those employees whose injuries have little to do with their working lives. Other states have taken a more sophisticated approach than the lump-sum payment, combining a schedule for lost wages that will be awarded in periodic installments, with a lump-sum *ex ante* payment based on the calculated "worth" of the physical impairment.

Third-Party Suits

As was mentioned earlier, workers' compensation is the employee's exclusive remedy against the employer for workplace injuries. The worker, however, is not barred from bringing a lawsuit against a third-party manufacturer who may be responsible for a defect in the machinery or product that caused the job-related injury. Third-party suits became increasingly popular in the 1970s, due to the inadequate levels of workers' compensation benefits at the time and the development of strict-liability tort theories in some states that eliminated any need for a finding of fault against the manufacturer. Thus, most claims by workers for asbestos-related injuries have been against the manufacturers of the product rather than their employers.

If an employee is successful in a lawsuit against the manufacturer, he or she must reimburse the employer for any compensation benefits paid. Therefore, the employee, in real terms, only will recover wages and nonfinancial damages, such as pain and suffering or emotional harm, from the third-party lawsuit that exceed the workers' compensation award.

Need for Additional Protection

Although workers' compensation does provide employers with some incentive to reduce dangerous workplace conditions because they must finance the systems' insurance, there are several reasons to believe that these incentives are inadequate to ensure worker safety. First, since the compensation paid to workers is less than the full accident cost (this especially was true before the 1970s), it is likely that employers are not deterred sufficiently from creating and maintaining hazardous conditions. Second, workers' compensation only assesses a financial cost on the employer after an accident has taken place. An additional system always has been needed to formulate safety rules and regulations *before* any harm is done. Finally, workers' compensation will not deter employers who already have factored the cost of worker injury into their cost-benefit calculus. For example, a manufacturer may decide that even after paying out workers' compensation benefits to injured employees, it still is profitable to manufacture products that require the handling of toxic substances or engaging in other dangerous activities. The Occupational Safety and Health Act was passed by Congress in 1970 to address these important issues of employee safety.

OCCUPATIONAL SAFETY AND HEALTH ACT

Although workplace dangers have been commonplace for hundreds of years, it was not until the latter part of the nineteenth century that any positive step was taken to eliminate occupational hazards. Even then, the first efforts, such as the federal Mine Safety Act, were of limited effect since they were directed at regulating specialized industrial areas rather than the workplace as a whole. Most states had developed more comprehensive laws by the 1920s, but even the broadest statutes left substantial gaps in protection. Furthermore, the efforts of the more vigorous states frequently were undermined by the short-sightedness of others, thereby enabling many corporations simply to do business in the state with the least restrictive safety laws.

By the 1960s, occupational hazards had reached critical proportions and the evidence of a need for legislation had become clear. Ancient industrial substances such as coal, mercury, and lead posed a constant threat. In addition, scientific knowledge emerging at the time revealed unsuspected cause-and-effect relationships between exposure to toxins, such as asbestos and pesticides, and many chronic diseases including cancer, respiratory ailments, allergies, and heart disease. Furthermore, given the demands of advanced technology, it was estimated that every twenty minutes a new and potentially toxic chemical was being introduced into industry. A 1967 Surgeon General's Report, based on a study of 1700 industrial plants, concluded that 65 percent of workers potentially were exposed to harmful physical agents—to noise or vibration—or to toxic materials.

The statistics presented to a committee of the United States Senate in 1970 were staggering, and left little doubt of the critical need for a uniform, national standard for occupational safety. It was reported that 14,500 people were killed annually as a result of industrial accidents and that, between 1966 and 1970, more Americans were killed in the workplace than in the Vietnam war. Moreover, the evidence indicated that over two million people were disabled on the job each year resulting in a total of 250 million lost work days a year. In terms of the economic effect, industrial accidents were responsible for $1.5 billion in lost wages and an $8 billion drop in the Gross National Product annually. Furthermore, the Senate report recognized that one company or industry simply could not make the necessary investment in health and safety and survive competitively, unless all were compelled to do so.

In December of 1970, the **Occupational Safety and Health Act (OSHA)** was signed into law by President Nixon. Its express purpose was to "assure so far as possible every working man and woman in the Nation safe and healthful working conditions." The act, which is administered by the Department of Labor, has been controversial throughout its history, some claiming it is not effective enough and others believing it is far too burdensome for American business.

Scope of the Act

OSHA expressly applies to all employers engaged in a business "affecting interstate commerce."

This provision is read very broadly in order to extend coverage of the act to the greatest extent possible. As a result, the act currently applies to over 5 million workplaces and 75 million employees. To achieve OSHA's objective, even a small, local retail business is considered to affect interstate commerce since its goods might be carried into another state. Nonetheless, some employers are exempted from certain requirements of the act that would prove too onerous for them—these include businesses with ten employees or less, farmers, and state and federal employers.

Duties Under the Act

All employers must comply with OSHA's voluminous and detailed workplace regulations covering noise levels, ventilation, labelling, parts per million of toxicity permitted, and other factors. The Department of Labor uses standards already developed by well-recognized and respected private groups, such as the American National Standards Institute (ANSI), so as to cause as little disruption as possible to industries already observing appropriate safety rules. Furthermore, the National Institute for Occupational Safety and Health (NIOSH) was created within the Department of Health and Human Services (HHS) to conduct research and make recommendations. Its primary focus in recent years has been on studying asbestosis, mesothelioma (a fatal condition caused by asbestos), and other occupational diseases.

Beyond the specific administrative regulations, however, employers have a general duty under Section 5(a) of the act to provide employees with working conditions and a place of employment free from recognized hazards to their health and safety. The provision was included to reflect the fact that precise standards to cover every conceivable dangerous situation typically do not exist. Therefore, Section 5(a) is meant to augment specific directives, and generally is used only if no precise standard applies.

RECORDKEEPING AND REPORTING.   Since the Department of Labor can employ only a few thousand inspectors nationwide, the OSHA system relies primarily upon voluntary compliance by business. Therefore, employers are required to maintain accurate records of, and make periodic reports on, work-related deaths, illnesses, and injuries. They also must keep records of employee exposure to certain toxic or otherwise hazardous materials such as asbestos, pesticides, or radiation. Finally, any employee exposed to these materials must be notified by his or her employer.

WORKER "RIGHT-TO-KNOW" LAWS.   The OSHA requirement of giving notice of toxic substance exposure has prompted a heated debate between workers and employers over the extent of the latter's obligation to inform. Employees argue that they have an absolute right to know what substances they are exposed to, and therefore demand elaborate labelling requirements, training programs, material safety data sheets (MSDS), and lists of hazardous chemicals in each work area. Employers, on the other hand, believe that this imposes too onerous a burden, especially for industries not regularly engaged in hazardous activities, and would prefer that workers simply be able to seek out the information.

Many states have developed **worker right-to-know laws** specifying the degree of disclosure required of employers. On November 25, 1983, OSHA promulgated its final **Hazard Communication Standard (HCS).** Its effect is to preempt the state laws. The federal standard required chemical manufacturers and importers to assess the hazards of substances they produced or imported, and ordered employers to provide information to their employees regarding dangerous materials. The standard, however, came under serious attack and court challenges because it only applied to chemical manufacturers and importers, was limited in scope to only 600 substances, and excluded hazardous wastes, foods, drugs, and pesticides. Furthermore, trade secrets did not have to be disclosed under the HCS, with an exception giving access to treating physicians.

As a result of these attacks on the HCS, in 1986 OSHA amended the regulation, which now contains a new definition of trade secrets and new rules related to the disclosure of secret information. Access no longer is limited to health professionals, but all those seeking the information now must file a written request and sign a confidentiality agreement.

In August of 1987, pursuant to a court order, another amendment to the HCS was published expanding its coverage to all workers in all industries. Special exemptions were made, however, for food, drugs, cosmetics, consumer products, certain pharmaceuticals, and alcoholic beverages that were packaged for retail sale and were sold in a retail establishment.

RELATIONSHIP BETWEEN THE HCS AND STATE RIGHT-TO-KNOW LAWS.   The HCS was promulgated by OSHA with the express purpose of preempting state right-to-know laws. Therefore, any state law that conflicts with the HCS theoretically is invalid. Questions arise, however, when the state law coverage is broader than that of the HCS. Is that a conflict or can the two co-exist? For instance, the New Jersey Worker and Community Right-to-Know Act is one of the most comprehensive standards in the country. Under the New Jersey law, information about toxic chemicals must be disclosed to public safety officers, workers, New Jersey residents, and environmental control officials. In 1985, a federal appeals court concluded that because OSHA standards by definition only govern occupational safety and health issues, they do not preempt state laws that promulgate standards regulating other concerns.

Enforcement of the Act

OSHA officials are empowered to inspect all places of employment that are subject to the act's regulations. An inspection can be initiated by OSHA, by NIOSH to further its research, or by an employee concerned about health hazards in the workplace. In the last case, employees are granted protection against retaliation for exercising their statutory rights (these include filing a complaint and testifying at trial, as well as initiating an inspection). If the employer so desires, he or she may insist on a search warrant before the inspection takes place.

A postinspection conference will be held with the employer to discuss violations and the means of eliminating them. Any citations must be issued promptly, at least within six months of the inspection. In addition to imposing penalties under the act, the citation will set a date by which the violations must be abated. The employer is given fifteen work days to contest the citation before it becomes final. If it is challenged, the Occupational Safety and Health Review Commission (OSHRC) will reevaluate the violation. Further appeal may be sought within OSHRC, or in special circumstances, a federal court may be available to review the proceedings.

Penalties

OSHA provides for mandatory penalties of at least $1000 for serious violations, which means that there is a substantial probability that death or serious harm could result from a workplace condition, unless the employer did not, or could not with reasonable diligence, know of the violation. Fines of up to $1000 may be assessed for "non-serious" violations such as improper ventilation or noise levels. Willful or repeated infractions that demonstrate a "plain indifference" to statutory requirements may be penalized up to $10,000. Furthermore, if willful or repeated behavior in violation of OSHA leads to an employee's death, criminal prosecution of those responsible may be available. Finally, the secretary of labor, in extreme circumstances, may exercise injunctive power to order that a company's operations cease if the hazard presents an imminent threat of death or physical harm to the workers. For example, if abnormally high levels of radiation that place workers in imminent danger are detected in a factory, it may be justifiable to close the facility until the radiation is reduced to an acceptable amount.

States' Role in Occupational Health and Safety

As discussed earlier, a movement for a national health and safety standard arose in the 1960s because most states had failed to take adequate measures to protect workers from occupational hazards. Despite the passage of OSHA in 1970, however, there still was pressure within Congress to allow states to develop their own plans, subject to OSHA approval. It was argued that state plans would be better adapted to local industries, whether they be agricultural or industrial, and that a local plan could be administered more efficiently than a federal plan. Organized labor, however, contended that state plans would be underfunded, susceptible to local political influence, and would lead to uneven enforcement standards among states.

The federal act is a compromise between the two positions. It allows a state to assert jurisdiction over job safety and health matters, but only after it has submitted a plan to the agency that is sufficient to meet OSHA's approval. The plan must go through a development stage, during which time the state works closely with OSHA to formulate standards. States are precluded from enacting or enforcing any law that would soften the national regulations. Next, the plan is put into effect with OSHA closely monitoring its progress. During this time, OSHA will exercise loose concurrent jurisdiction over the health and safety standards. It is only after the state plan has withstood this rigorous scrutiny that OSHA will grant approval. If the plan is not approved, or if no plan is submitted, the state may not enforce its own regulations regarding health and safety, except when OSHA has not addressed the issue.

Generous federal grants of up to 90 percent of the costs made it very attractive for a state to formulate its own plan in the 1970s. In recent years, however, with federal grants often covering less than 50 percent of costs, interest among the states in developing their own plans has waned.

WRONGFUL DISCHARGE

For the great majority of the workforce not represented by unions (about 80 percent according to the 1987 Labor Bureau figures), individuals must do their own bargaining, to the extent that is possible. Not surprisingly, most individual employment contracts do not contain the explicit "just-cause" requirement for employee termination that unions collectively bargain for and receive. This means that, unless they have obtained contractual protection indicating otherwise, employees face the possibility that their job security is only what their employers say it is.

The historical basis for this is the notion that everyone should be free to contract as he or she pleases. In the employment context, contracts that did not provide they were for a definite period were considered to be **at will,** which meant they were terminable at any time by either party for any reason. As early as 1877 a famous scholar wrote: "The rule [in America] is inflexible that a general or indefinite hiring is prima facie a hiring at will, and if the servant seeks to make it a yearly hiring, the burden is on him to establish it by proof." Modern commentators have questioned the case precedents the writer used to support this statement of the law, but this passage remained the dominant American sentiment about employment well into this century.

Needless to say, individual workers generally are in no position to bargain for job security, because anyone who demands it usually can be replaced easily by another worker who is more desperate for the job. In recent years, however, the law has begun to lessen the severity of the employment-at-will doctrine. The process began when various forms of discrimination were prohibited by state and federal law, and employers were banned by the National Labor Relations Act from discharging employees who attempted to form a union (see Chapters 50 and 51). But these provisions cover only instances in which an employer breaks a law. They do not apply to the large number of cases in which employees who thought they had some measure of job security find themselves suddenly unemployed, but their firing does not violate a specific law. Three judicially developed methods to counter the notion of employment at will have become increasingly influential in the past twenty years. As a result, many discharges that would have been accepted without question in the past now may be classified as wrongful and give rise to civil liability under at least one of the judicial methods.

Implied-in-Fact or Implied-in-Law Contracts

As mentioned previously, most employment contracts do not contain language promising that a discharge will be "for good/just cause only," but many contemporary courts are willing to infer that promise from certain actions of the employer. A common practice of companies is to prepare an employee manual or handbook, often distributed to employees upon hiring, that describes the employer's expectations of its workers, rules of behavior, and procedures. There is usually a section on termination, which outlines the procedure the employer follows when an employee breaks the rules, or lists causes for which termination is the disciplinary result. Courts increasingly are examining these handbooks and finding that many of them, in effect, create a right to be discharged for cause only, either because they explicitly state that right or implicitly create it by providing an apparently exclusive list of causes for discharge. Similarly, if an employer has an established procedure for terminating employees (for example, an impartial hearing), an employee fired without following the procedure can claim breach of the implied contract. Even when an employee's entire contract is oral, a court can look to statements made by the employer to the employee before or during the hiring process, such as "you can work here so long as you do your job," as assurances

that give the employee a reasonable expectation of being discharged only for cause.

Some courts still adhere to the traditional standards of contract, however, and are unwilling to find a promise of termination only for "good cause" in the circumstances of a particular situation. In addition, they consider any such promise one-sided and reject it for want of consideration or lack of mutuality, and insist that the employee either offer something in return for guaranteed "good-cause" employment (above and beyond the worker's services to the employer, since those already are reimbursed by his pay) or at least get a more definite promise in writing from the employer.

Implied-in-law contracts are more difficult to establish than the various forms of express agreements, but some courts will accept evidence of the employee's length of employment or record of satisfactory performance as indication that the employer has bound itself to the "just-cause" standard. At the other end of the spectrum is the employee who gave up other acceptable opportunities, traveled a great distance to take the job, or otherwise relied upon an employer's assurances of an ongoing position, only to be denied any employment security. The doctrine of promissory estoppel, which you examined in Chapter 6, is an appropriate, although not always successful, legal principle that can be invoked in such cases.

Public Policy

A second limitation on the ability of employers to discharge employees is the principle that terminations without cause that violate fundamental notions of public policy are unjust and—at least occasionally—actionable. Four overlapping subcategories form a useful way of thinking about this method. First, if an employee is exercising a statutory right, such as the right to file a workers' compensation claim or to refuse to take a polygraph test, the employer can be prevented from forcing the employee to choose between losing her job and foregoing a right that state or federal law has granted workers. Second, and in a similar vein, an employee may not be discharged for refusing to engage in activities that are illegal, such as committing perjury, participating in a price-fixing scheme, or tampering with pollution-control reports. Third, in order to encourage an employee to fulfill a legal obligation, such as jury duty or, more recently, "whistleblowing," the worker must be safeguarded by preventing discharge when she performs them. Finally, some employers engage in activities that, although they may not be illegal, nevertheless may be repugnant to general notions of public policy or fair play. A situation that unfortunately arises all to frequently is that of the employee who refuses the sexual advances of his or her boss and is discharged or not promoted. Even if no discrimination claim under the federal statute were possible for some reason, some courts will recognize a wrongful discharge claim under the rubric of public policy. Some courts, however, are more restrained in their use of the public policy limitation on the employment-at-will doctrine and will intervene in a discharge on the basis of public policy only when an employer's actions clearly violate a statute or law.

Implied Covenant of Good Faith

The last and most narrowly applied of the exceptions to the employment-at-will principle is the implied covenant of good faith and fair dealing. As we saw in Chapter 13, the Uniform Commercial Code imposes this standard on all contracts for sale of goods, but employment contracts, which are for services, are not included. Nonetheless, some courts have extended this principle to employment contracts, particularly when an employer behaves so outrageously as to indicate bad faith or intentional ill will. An example is the employee who works for many years for a single employer, only to be dismissed months before he is entitled to collect his pension or just before the right to be paid certain sales commissions comes due.

Often it is very difficult to determine what an employer's true purpose is because the termination is accompanied by charges of misconduct or substandard performance against the employee. In courts that are willing to take into account an implied covenant of good faith and fair dealing, juries are permitted in these "mixed" motive cases to determine the employer's primary motivation for discharging the employee. The failure of an employer to use an existing company procedure, such as a worker's right to an impartial hearing, often is persuasive evidence that the discharge was not for good cause.

Despite the growth of these doctrines, the prevailing notion in the United States, absent any indication of employer-employee agreement, continues to be at-will employment, even though the example of union bargaining (the one situation in which both sides stand on approximately even ground) suggests that the rule should be changed to permit discharge for cause only, unless the employer can prove that the contract intended otherwise. Perhaps the influence of these judge-created exceptions in the long run will be to effect that change. Consider the following illustrative case.

TOUSSAINT v. BLUE CROSS & BLUE SHIELD OF MICHIGAN
408 Mich. 579, 292 N.W.2d 880 (1980)

Charles Toussaint (Plaintiff/Appellant) was employed in a middle-management position with Blue Cross (Defendant/Appellee). After five years with Blue Cross,

Toussaint was discharged. He was not told of any cause for his discharge, nor were any of the procedures outlined in the *Blue Cross Supervisory Manual* followed. He sued for wrongful discharge and obtained a jury verdict for $72,835.52. The Michigan Court of Appeals reversed. Toussaint appealed to the Supreme Court of Michigan, which reversed the Court of Appeals. In this opinion, the court also reviews the companion case of *Ebling v. Masco Corp.*, in which a jury verdict of $300,000 was affirmed by the Court of Appeals, and affirms it because of its similar factual situation to *Toussaint.*

LEVIN, Justice.

. . . Ebling testified that he was told that if he was "doing the job" he would not be discharged. . . . Toussaint testified that he had been interviewed by and, on the date of his hire, met with an officer of Blue Cross who "indicated to me that as long as I did my job that I would be with the company" until mandatory retirement at age 65. The officer gave him a Supervisory Manual. Toussaint asked "how secure a job it was and [the officer] said that if I came to Blue Cross, I wouldn't have to look for another job because he knew of no one ever being discharged." Toussaint's case is, if anything, stronger because he was handed a manual of Blue Cross personnel policies which reinforced the oral assurances of job security. It stated that the disciplinary procedures applied to all Blue Cross employees who had completed their probationary period and that it was the "policy" of the company to release employees "for just cause only." . . . We hold that:

1) a provision of an employment contract providing that an employee shall not be discharged except for cause is legally enforceable although the contract is not for a definite term—the term is "indefinite," and

2) such a provision may become part of the contract either by express agreement, oral or written, or as a result of an employee's legitimate expectations grounded in an employer's policy statements.

3) In *Toussaint,* as in *Ebling,* there was sufficient evidence of an express agreement to justify submission to the jury.

4) A jury could also find for Toussaint based on legitimate expectations grounded in his employer's written policy statements set forth in the manual of personnel policies. . . .

In light of the jury verdicts we proceed on the basis that the contracts provided that the employee would not be discharged except for good cause.

We see no reason why an employment contract which does not have a definite term . . . cannot legally provide job security. When a prospective employee inquires about job security and the employer agrees that the employee shall be employed as long as he does the job, a fair construction is that the employer has agreed to give up his right to discharge at will without assigning cause and may discharge only for cause (good or just cause). . . . [T]he employee, if discharged without good or just cause, may maintain an action for wrongful discharge. . . . No pre-employment negotiations need take place and the parties' minds need not meet on the subject; nor does it matter that the employee knows nothing of the particulars of the employer's policies and practices or that the employer may change them unilaterally. It is enough that the employer chooses . . . to create an environment in which the employee believes that, whatever the personnel policies and practices, they are established and official at any given time, . . . and are applied consistently and uniformly to each employee. The employer has then created a situation "instinct with an obligation."

Blue Cross offered no evidence that the manual and guidelines are not what they purport to be—statements of company policy on the subjects there addressed, including discipline and termination.

The jury could properly conclude that the statements of policy on those subjects were applicable to Toussaint although the manual did not explicitly refer to him. . . . The inference that the policies and procedures applied to Toussaint is supported by his testimony that he was handed the manual in the course of a conversation in which he inquired about job security. . . .

[W]here an employer has agreed to discharge an employee for cause only, its declaration that the employee was discharged for unsatisfactory work is subject to judicial review. The jury as trier of facts decides whether the employee was, in fact, discharged for unsatisfactory work. . . .

Where the employer alleges that the employee was discharged for one reason . . . and the employee presents evidence that he was really discharged for another reason . . . the question is also one of fact for the jury. The jury is always permitted to determine the employer's true reason for discharging the employee. . . .

In addition to deciding questions of fact and determining the employer's true motive for discharge, the jury should, where such a promise was made, decide whether the reason for discharge amounts to good cause: is it the kind of thing that justifies terminating the employment relationship? Does it demonstrate that the employee was no longer doing the job? . . .

We affirm *EBLING* and remand *TOUSSAINT* to the trial court with instructions to reinstate the [jury] verdict.

Questions

1. Which of the legal theories outlined in this section do you think Toussaint argued in claiming that his discharge was wrongful? Which of them does the court accept and what is their order of importance?

2. What would the result be if, after Blue Cross had hired Toussaint, it had changed the manual by removing the promise of just cause release and adding this sentence: "Employer retains the right to discharge any employee whenever it deems this to be appropriate"?

3. What are the arguments for keeping the historic employment-at-will principle in force?

WORKPLACE PRIVACY

A subject that has come to the foreground in employment law in recent years is that of workplace privacy. The rights of employers to keep their factories and stores safe and productive often can conflict with the rights of individual employees to be free from unreasonable searches and unwarranted intrusions on their privacy, obliging courts to weigh the conflicting interests to determine the standard that is most appropriate. The discussion that follows will examine, briefly, several situations in which the balancing of the competing interests is extremely important. Because the subject is a relatively new one, the law regarding most of them has not been clarified as yet.

Drugs and Alcohol

Drug and alcohol abuse significantly reduces the effectiveness of this country's workforce every year. Employers feel this in six different ways:

1. lost productivity: this includes reduced efficiency of workers, greater absenteeism, increased sick leave and medical insurance, and early turnover of employees—in 1986, the total loss in productivity was estimated at $99 billion;
2. more frequent accidents and injuries: employee impairment because of drugs and alcohol results in increases in workplace deaths and accidents;
3. higher insurance costs: increased medical insurance payments and workers' compensation claims seem to accompany drug and alcohol use;
4. more theft and other crimes: although this is not supported by empirical evidence, it is feared by employers nonetheless, and appears to be a logical concern because there is so much drug- and alcohol-related crime in our society;
5. damage to employee relations: morale suffers and resentment builds when workers have to cover for abusers and perform extra tasks; and
6. increased legal liability: workers' compensation claims by abusers and other workers they injure, and lawsuits brought by innocent workers and third persons hurt by an impaired employee, appear to be on the rise.

The devastating impact of drug and alcohol abuse on the workforce has made employers increasingly concerned, and some have turned to testing employees for these substances in order to protect others and to deter potential abusers. The major impetus for drug testing has been at the federal level. This is somewhat surprising, because federal workers have more legal protection for their privacy than private employees. In large part this is because the Fourth Amendment of the Constitution requires that official searches and seizures be reasonable, and this provision applies to searches by the government, not by private organizations. Nonetheless, testing of military personnel was begun in 1981, and in 1986 President Reagan signed an executive order that allows testing of federal agency members in "sensitive positions," which are defined to include presidential appointees, law-enforcement officers, people who deal with classified information, national security, protection of life, property, public health and safety, and anyone in a position of high trust or confidence. The testing may occur when the employee is under "reasonable suspicion" of drug abuse, after an accident, or as part of a drug-rehabilitation program. In addition, all applicants for "sensitive positions" may be tested.

The federal courts have tended to uphold most drug-testing programs that have been challenged, and in 1989 the Supreme Court upheld testing programs involving public safety and highly sensitive jobs. However, both federal and state courts have begun to strike down testing when the work is nonsafety specific or when employers present no evidence suggesting the existence of widespread drug abuse in the company. In general, the more extensive or indiscriminate the drug testing, the more likely that a court will declare it an invasion of worker privacy.

Among private employers, there seems to be a correlation between the size of the company and the prevalence of drug testing—larger companies tend to test more frequently. As one might suspect, testing also is more common in higher-risk industries such as the airlines, power plants, and railroads. However, larger employers also seem to have the resources to test effectively and to refer the employee to an Employee Assistance Program rather than dismiss him. This care in testing procedures and follow-up is important, because it makes the program appear fair and because drug tests do not indicate addiction or even present impairment; they only reflect the presence of certain substances in the body. Thus, it is possible for an individual to test positive for a substance days after using it, raising serious legal questions about an employer's right to control an employee's use of substances when not working, especially when it does not appear to reduce her job performance—at least not in the short term. It is for this reason, as well as the possibility of false positives, that many courts require the employer to have a "reasonable suspicion" before testing an employee, and the quality of the testing procedures is given great scrutiny. But there is no doubt that the practice is growing, particularly in connection with the hiring process.

Polygraphs and Other Searches

Another method traditionally used by employers to monitor their employees is to administer polygraphs or lie-detector tests. The effectiveness of these devices always has been under serious scrutiny (the results never have been permitted to be used in court to indicate guilt, for example). As a result, and because of their inherent intrusiveness, some states have passed legislation limiting the use of lie detectors. In particular, employers can be prohibited from asking questions about political or religious affiliation or about an applicant's arrest record (questions about convictions, on the other hand, generally are permitted).

At the federal level, the **Employee Polygraph Protection Act** became effective in December of 1988. It bans, with certain exceptions, the use of lie detectors for preemployment screening and random employee testing. But the act does not ban the use of polygraphs when there is "reasonable suspicion" of wrongdoing and the employee is notified of his rights. A worker cannot be discharged solely on the basis of a lie-detector test, however. Many people believe that this federal

statute will eliminate virtually all workplace polygraph use, except in the security-guard industry and when controlled substances are handled by the company doing the testing.

Regarding other forms of employer searches, courts tend to look to the purpose of the inquiry. For example, if a search of an employee's work area is conducted as part of a criminal investigation, it will be permitted, but all of the protections of the Fourth Amendment to the Constitution apply, the most important of which is the requirement of securing a search warrant from a court. However, if the search is merely for the employer's own knowledge about the employee, many courts will not allow it. Any search of an employee's person should be reasonable (for example, a pat down for drugs in a prison or rehabilitation clinic) or the employer runs the risk of an assault and battery charge. Some courts allow employees to establish an expectation of privary—for instance, by allowing them to place a lock on a company locker—but if the employer distributes the locks or posts a notice that lockers are subject to search, an employee's unreasonable-search claim is likely to fail.

ACQUIRED IMMUNE DEFICIENCY SYNDROME

Few subjects generate as much controversy today as that of Acquired Immune Deficiency Syndrome, or AIDS. This disease, for which no cure or vaccine has been found as yet, destroys the lives of those who contract it by taking away the ability to fight off infection. Perhaps just as catastrophic as the disease itself is the fear of contracting it that has spread throughout the country, including in workplaces.

As with drugs and alcohol, some employers have decided that the appropriate response to AIDS is testing. Like the test for drugs, however, the test for AIDS can give false positives and does not reveal the disease but only the presence of the antibodies to the virus, which may not develop into the full disease in any particular individual for years or, possibly, ever. The legal implications of AIDS testing are just being perceived, and policies on the subject are only being formulated. A few states have prohibited the testing of job applicants, but because current medical opinion is to the effect that AIDS cannot be spread by casual contact, the dismissal of an employee (or even the rejection of a job applicant) for a positive test result may well be considered unreasonable. And at least one court has concluded that AIDS is a handicap under the federal Rehabilitation Act of 1973, which prohibits discrimination against anyone who is handicapped. As a result, firing someone because of AIDS might well be branded as a form of illegal discrimination by a court and create liability for an employer.

EMPLOYMENT DISCRIMINATION

The law of employment discrimination is of recent origin. Until the 1960s and 1970s, an employer's decisions with respect to hiring, firing, promotions, and conditions of employment were considered a private matter, governed only by the law of contract. An employer could set wage levels or reject employment applicants on any basis whatsoever, no matter how arbitrary or subjective the reasons. Given that many modern employers are large, powerful organizations whose employment decisions affect significant numbers of people, the potential social consequences of unbridled discrimination are substantial. Nonetheless, significant pressure against employment discrimination did not build up until the rise of the civil rights movement of the 1960s. Changing social attitudes brought about a commitment to equal opportunity in many of the fundamental areas of life such as housing, work, education, and criminal justice. In the employment environment, several important statutes, regulations, and executive orders were adopted to prohibit differential treatment of employees on the basis of personal characteristics other than job performance or ability.

The Civil Rights Act of 1964

Title VII of the Civil Rights Act of 1964 is the most comprehensive federal enactment regulating employment discrimination. As amended by the **Equal Employment Opportunity Act** of 1972, Title VII prohibits employers, labor unions, and employment agencies from discriminating in employment-related decisions on the basis of five specific classifications: race, color, religion, sex, and national origin. An *employer* includes any individual, private organization, or government entity that engages in an industry affecting interstate commerce and employs more than fifteen people. Labor unions also are prohibited from discriminating with respect to membership if they represent over fifteen workers.

Categories of Discrimination

Racial and "color" discrimination includes discrimination against all racial minorities, such as blacks, Asians, and American Indians. It also includes discrimination against whites in the so-called reverse discrimination context. However, an affirmative action program may not be illegal. (See the following discussion.) *National origin* refers to discrimination based on the country of one's ancestry. Most national-origin cases involve discrimination on the basis of Spanish or other ethnic surnames. Covert discrimination of this kind usually focuses on characteristics peculiar to an individual's heritage, such as refusing to hire on the basis of the applicant's height or accented speech. Title VII also may bar an employer from banning the use of a worker's native language on the job and may require the employer to prevent its employees from making derogatory remarks or engaging in other forms of harassment. The Supreme Court has held that discrimination based solely on someone's lack of United States citizenship is *not* prohibited by Title VII.

Title VII's prohibition of *religious* discrimination means that an employer must make "reasonable accommodation" for the employee's religious beliefs and practices. To be deemed religious, an employee's beliefs must be deeply and sincerely held. For example, belief in a Supreme Being and observance of a weekly holy day would be considered religious for Title VII purposes and cannot be the basis of refusing to hire or promote someone. However, observance of a religious holiday for the sake of convenience would not be protected under Title VII. Reasonable accommodation might mean that an employer must allow employees to wear religious garb and to observe religious holidays. An employer is excused from the obligation of accommodating an employee when doing so would cause undue hardship to the business.

Sex discrimination most often involves the perpetuation of sexual stereotypes in hiring and job assignments, resulting in the denial of equal opportunity for women. Some states' so-called *protective laws* (for example, setting maximum hours or weight-lifting restrictions for women workers) have been found to violate Title VII as not being legitimate employment criteria. Title VII applies equally to discrimination against males as well as females. It does not, however, protect against discrimination based on sexual preference, such as homosexuality.

"Sex-plus" discrimination refers to discrimination against a subcategory of women, such as married or pregnant women, rather than all women. The federal Pregnancy Discrimination Act of 1978 amended Title VII to prohibit differential treatment of pregnant women for all employment-related purposes. Primarily, it requires employers to treat pregnancy and childbirth as they would any disability; they must provide the same benefits, leave, and reinstatement rights as they do for other impairments.

Types of Discrimination

An employer's refusal to hire a qualified applicant solely on the basis of race is a clear example of illegal discrimination. Suppose, however, that the refusal was based, not on race, but on the applicant's failure to achieve a certain score on a standardized aptitude test. Suppose further that certain minorities tend to do poorly on this test and that the test, or a substantial portion of it, is unrelated to the job sought by the applicant. If minority-group members consistently are rejected for employment as a result of their test performance, does this constitute actionable discrimination? Would it be actionable even if the employer actually hires minority applicants who do score well on the test? These questions illustrate two theories of employment discrimination recognized by the Supreme Court: *disparate treatment,* or intentional discrimination, and *disparate impact,* or discriminatory effects. These principles serve as the foundation for most Title VII actions.

Disparate treatment occurs when an employer's actions or policies explicitly differentiate among employees or applicants on one of the federal statute's prohibited grounds. Recruiting, hiring, and promotion decisions may reflect disparate treatment of certain individuals or groups. Obvious examples are not hiring women, restricting blacks to menial positions, or paying Hispanics substantially less than other workers. Similarly, maintaining segregated facilities or failing to protect employees from racial or sexual intimidation can support charges of discrimination.

What a plaintiff must prove in an action under the federal statute varies according to the type of discriminatory treatment alleged. Someone seeking to prove discrimination in hiring must show: (1) that he belongs to one of Title VII's five protected classes; (2) that he applied and was qualified for a job for which the employer was seeking applicants; (3) that despite his qualifications, he was rejected; and (4) that, after his rejection, the position remained open and the employer continued to seek applicants. By meeting this burden of proof, the plaintiff establishes what is known as a *prima facie* case—one that will prevail unless contradicted by other evidence. The burden then shifts to the defendant to show that it had a legitimate, nondiscriminatory reason for denying employment. The plaintiff then may overcome the employer's defense by proving that the stated reason is merely a pretext for illegal discrimination.

Disparate treatment also may occur on a class-wide basis. Rather than a specific instance of discrimination, the plaintiff may allege a general pattern or practice of discrimination over a period of time by an employer. To support this type of case, the plaintiff may provide statistical evidence demonstrating that a particular protected group is under-represented in the employer's workforce, perhaps by showing that the percentage of that group in the employer's workforce is significantly less than the percentage of that group in the local labor market. This evidence would establish a rebuttable presumption of disparate treatment.

Disparate impact describes the situation when employment decisions are based on standards that appear neutral, but they actually operate to exclude a particular protected class. Height requirements, for example, often exclude women and certain ethnic groups. Regardless of the employer's intentions, the practice violates Title VII when its consequences are discriminatory. Neutral standards also may perpetuate the effects of past discrimination. For example, testing or educational requirements may exclude those traditionally denied equal educational opportunities. To establish discriminatory effect, a plaintiff must provide statistical data of the kind used in class-wide disparate-treatment cases. Once a *prima facie* case is established, the employer must show that the challenged practice is job related or justified by business necessity. The plaintiff then will be given an opportunity to overcome this defense by showing there are other nondiscriminatory selection methods that can serve the employer's legitimate business needs adequately.

Special Defenses

An employer may defend against charges of discrimination under Title VII by demonstrating that an employment decision was based on employee merit, a valid and ongoing seniority system, or a *bona fide* occupational qualification (BFOQ). The merit defense may be used when an employee challenges a testing or selection procedure. As already noted, this defense requires a demonstration that the procedure is job related—that it actually measures the applicant's ability to perform.

The seniority defense typically arises when an employment decision based on length of service to the business has the effect of perpetuating past discrimination. For example, in a situation in which the number of employees must be reduced temporarily or permanently, an employer typically lays off the most recently hired workers first. Groups historically discriminated against are likely to be among the most recently hired workers and thus will be affected disproportionately by the layoff. The seniority defense shields the employer from liability when the seniority system is pre-existing and formalized, and when there is no evidence of discriminatory intent.

Finally, the **bona fide occupational qualification** defense excuses certain kinds of discrimination deemed reasonably necessary to the employer's business. The defense applies only to hiring (or referral) decisions based on religion, sex, or national origin, but not to racial discrimination. Generally, the defense has been construed narrowly by the courts. Discrimination based on stereotypes or customer preferences, as once was claimed as a justification for the airlines hiring only young, attractive, female flight attendants, is not permitted. On the other hand, an applicant's ability to fulfill an essential job requirement or a need for authenticity may qualify as a BFOQ precluding liability. Hiring a French cook for a French restaurant or an actress for a female role are examples.

Procedure and Remedies

Before an aggrieved worker may bring suit under Title VII, he first must file a claim with certain state and federal administrative agencies. States having fair-employment laws and antidiscrimination commissions take exclusive jurisdiction over the claim for sixty days. Afterward, the employee is free to file a claim with the **Equal Employment Opportunity Commission (EEOC),** a federal agency established by the Civil Rights Act of 1964 to administer and interpret Title VII. It also enforces some of the other federal statutes discussed here. The EEOC may investigate a charge, attempt conciliation or settlement of the claim, institute a lawsuit against the offending employer, or issue a right-to-sue letter to the claimant, enabling the worker to bring a lawsuit on his own behalf.

A variety of remedies may be available to a successful claimant. Monetary damages often include an award of back pay for a period up to two years prior to the filing of the claim, and also may include attorney's fees. Courts are divided as to whether an employee may recover general compensatory damages. Punitive damages rarely are awarded. Nonmonetary or equitable remedies are designed to eliminate and make amends for the discriminatory situation. A court may enjoin the unlawful employment practice and order that the claimant be hired or reinstated or promoted. In addition, the court may provide retroactive seniority for the period during which the claimant should have been employed. These and other highly controversial remedies will be discussed separately in this chapter.

DOTHARD v. RAWLINSON
433 U.S. 321, 97 S.Ct. 2720, 53 L.Ed.2d 786 (1977)

Plaintiff (Appellee), a female applicant who was denied a guard position at an Alabama state prison, brought a class-action suit against the prison system (Appellant) under Title VII claiming that her rejection was based on gender discrimination. The action challenged the validity of Alabama's hiring provisions, which included (1) a stature specifying minimum height and weight requirements of 5'2" and 120 lbs. and (2) a regulation prohibiting the hiring of women as prison guards at the state's maximum-security male prisons in "contact positions" that require close physical proximity to inmates. A three-judge federal trial court held that the statute and regulation violated Title VII and thus were invalid. On direct review from the three-judge court, the United States Supreme Court affirmed in part and reversed in part.

STEWART, Justice.

. . . The gist of the claim that the statutory height and weight requirements discriminate against women does not involve an assertion of purposeful discriminatory motive. It is asserted, rather, that these facially neutral qualification standards work in fact disproportionately to exclude women from eligibility for employment by the Alabama Board of Corrections. . . .

Although women 14 years of age or older comprise 52.75% of the Alabama population and 36.89% of its total labor force, they hold only 12.9% of its correctional counselor positions. In considering the effect of the minimum height and weight standards on this disparity in rate of hiring between the sexes, the District Court found that . . . Alabama's statutory standards would exclude 41.13% of the female population while excluding less than 1% of the male population. Accordingly, the District Court found that Rawlinson had made out a prima facie case of unlawful sex discrimination. . . .

. . . The appellants argu[e] that they have rebutted the prima facie case of discrimination by showing that the height and weight requirements are job related. These requirements, they say, have a relationship to strength, a sufficient but unspecified amount of which is essential to effective job performance as a correctional counselor. . . . If the job-related quality that the appellants identify is bona fide, their purpose could be achieved by adopting and validating a test for applicants that measures strength directly. . . . But nothing in the present record even approaches such a measurement. . . . The District Court was not in error in holding that Title VII prohibits application of the statutory height and weight requirements to Rawlinson and the class she represents.

Unlike the statutory height and weight requirements, Regulation 204 explicitly discriminates against women on the basis of their sex. In defense of this overt discrimination, the appellants rely on §703(e) of [Title VII], which permits sex-based discrimination "in those certain instances where [sex] is a bona fide occupational qualification reasonably necessary to the normal operation of that particular business or enterprise." . . .

. . . The bfoq exception was in fact meant to be an extremely narrow exception to the general prohibition of discrimination on the basis of sex. In the particular factual circumstances of this case, however, we conclude that the District Court erred in rejecting the State's contention that Regulation 204 falls within the narrow ambit of the bfoq exception.

The environment in Alabama's penitentiaries is a peculiarly inhospitable one for human beings of whatever sex. . . . [N]o attempt is made in the four maximum security male penitentiaries to classify or segregate inmates according to their offense or level of dangerousness. . . . Consequently, the estimated 20% of the male prisoners who are sex offenders are scattered throughout the penitentiaries' dormitory facilities.

In this environment of violence and disorganization, . . . [m]ore is at stake . . . than an individual woman's decision to weigh and accept the risks of employment. . . .

The essence of a correctional counselor's job is to maintain prison security. A woman's relative ability to maintain order in a male, maximum-security, unclassified penitentiary of the type Alabama now runs could be directly reduced by her womanhood. There is a basis in fact for expecting that sex offenders who have criminally assaulted women in the past would be moved to do so again if access to women were established within the prison. There would also be a real risk that other inmates, deprived of a normal heterosexual environment, would assault women guards because they were women. . . .

The judgment is accordingly affirmed in part and reversed in part, and the case is remanded to the District Court for further proceedings consistent with this opinion.

Questions

1. How might you argue that height and weight requirements for prison guards are job-related and should be a BFOQ? One judge has reasoned that an *appearance* of strength might be necessary to maintain psychological control over inmates. Do you agree? Does a 5'2", 120 lbs. requirement appropriately measure the appearance of strength? How could a plaintiff overcome this defense?

2.   The Court accepted the argument that the job of prison guard in a male maximum-security prison is too dangerous for a woman. Do you think that a high level of job danger is an acceptable basis for excluding women? Why or why not?

3.   Do you agree that the sexuality of female guards is a threat to prison discipline? If so, are there ways to minimize that threat other than refusing to hire women?

The Equal Pay Act

The **Equal Pay Act of 1963,** an amendment to the **Fair Labor Standards Act** of 1938 (regulating wages and hours), prohibits wage discrimination on the basis of sex. It is applicable when substantially equal jobs are compensated unequally. Under the Equal Pay Act, jobs are substantially equal if they require equal effort, skill, and responsibility and if they are performed under similar working conditions in the same establishment. Factors relating to working conditions may include indoor/outdoor job performance, workplace temperature, toxic conditions, or risk of injury. The law provides an exception for wage differentials based on seniority, merit, quantity or quality of production, or any factor other than sex. This exception applies only when wages are determined according to a pre-existing and organized rating system communicated to employees and applied equally to both sexes.

The Equal Pay Act is enforced by the EEOC, but an employee does not have to file charges with the commission prior to instituting his or her own lawsuit, as is necessary in the case of a claim of discrimination under Title VII. The prescribed remedy is increased wages. An employer is not permitted to reduce the wages of higher-paid employees in order to resolve inequities. In addition to a salary adjustment, a successful claimant may recover back pay plus an equal amount in liquidated damages.

The Comparable Worth Doctrine

Title VII of the Civil Rights Act of 1964 overlaps with the Equal Pay Act in that it also prohibits wage discrimination on the basis of sex. Under either statute, courts may apply the same standard of equal pay for equal work. Because Title VII does not explicitly incorporate the equal-work concept, and therefore is not expressly limited to it, a question has arisen whether claims also may be based on a broader notion: that employees should receive equal pay for *comparable* work. Comparable work is not necessarily similar in kind, but has the same inherent worth or a comparable worth to the employer. This doctrine has emerged because of a belief that less obvious forms of wage discrimination are not revealed simply by comparing equal jobs. Whole classes of jobs dominated by members of one of the groups historically discriminated against may be undervalued equally. Thus a subtler and more pervasive discrimination than unequal pay for the same work may be seen by comparing those jobs traditionally held by women with different but comparable jobs held by men. According to the theory, discrepancies in their respective salaries would reflect a longstanding pattern of inequality in the market values of traditionally segregated skills. That might be true, for example, by comparing telephone operators (traditionally women), and telephone installers (traditionally men) or truck drivers (men) and secretaries (women).

Ratio of women to men (number and earnings) in selected job categories

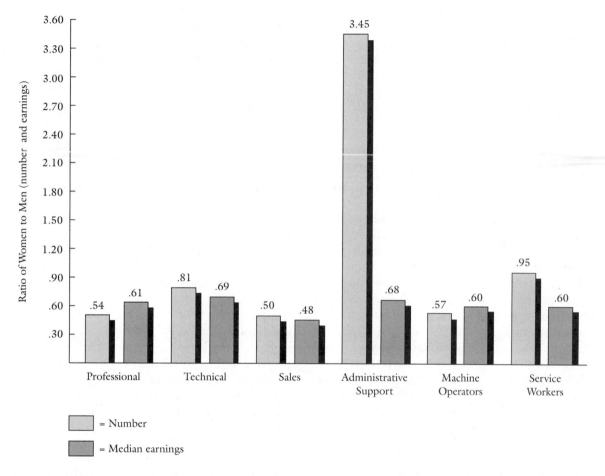

= Number

= Median earnings

Source: Statistical Abstract of the U.S. 1988, Table 653.

Thus, to remedy wage discrimination, salaries should be adjusted to reflect a job's inherent worth, measured not by its current market value but by its value to the employer or to society.

The **comparable-worth doctrine** is highly controversial. Critics charge that any assessment of the inherent worth of services is inevitably subjective and unlikely to provide a meaningful or consistent basis of comparison. They also point to the economic consequences to the business community of ignoring the market value accorded different forms of labor and the potential flood of litigation that a comparable-worth system might produce.

The courts' treatment of comparable worth cases has been varied. Although the Supreme Court has held that sex-based wage discrimination claims under Title VII are not limited by the equal-work standard of the Equal Pay Act, thus far it has explicitly refrained from endorsing any alternative standard, such as comparable worth. Recent state and federal court decisions have been divided, with a predominant number rejecting comparable-worth claims. Nonetheless, some states have enacted equal-pay statutes that incorporate the notion of comparable worth. Further legal developments on this subject are inevitable.

Age Discrimination in Employment Act

The **Age Discrimination in Employment Act** of 1967 (ADEA), as amended, prohibits job discrimination against workers who are forty to seventy years of age. Any employer or employment agency engaged in interstate commerce and employing twenty or more workers is subject to ADEA regulation. Labor unions meeting the same criteria are covered by the act with respect to their own employment practices. With respect to their membership practices, unions are covered if they have twenty-five or more members.

The ADEA protects workers over forty from discrimination in hiring, firing, compensation, and other conditions and privileges of employment. The act's hiring provision bars the publication of help-wanted advertisements that indicate a preference or limitation based on age. Pursuant to a very important 1986 amendment to the statute, the ADEA also prohibits mandatory retirement at any protected age, subject to limited exceptions. Like Title VII, the ADEA is administered by the EEOC, and ADEA remedies resemble those available under Title VII of the Civil Rights Act and the Equal Pay Act.

DEFENSES. An employer will not incur liability when age discrimination is based on a *bona fide* occupational qualification. For example, this defense would apply when a young actor is hired for a youthful role and an older one is not. Differential treatment also may be based on reasonable factors other than age, such as physical or mental

fitness for particular jobs. An employer, however, may not make assumptions as to an employee's fitness based solely on age. The act provides that any employee may be disciplined or discharged for good cause. In addition, employment decisions may be based on a *bona fide* seniority system, as long as it was not created to evade the purposes of the act. Finally, ADEA permits some differential in the amount of pension or insurance benefits provided under an otherwise valid employee benefit plan. Generally, if an employer spends an equal amount on benefits for each employee, the benefit plan is lawful even if it yields fewer benefits for older employees than for younger ones.

Vocational Rehabilitation Act

Sections 503 and 504 of the federal **Vocational Rehabilitation Act** provide important protections for the handicapped. Section 503 requires all contractors with the federal government with contracts over $2500 to take affirmative action measures and to make reasonable accommodations in hiring handicapped persons. Section 504 prohibits discrimination against the handicapped in programs receiving federal financial assistance.

For purposes of both sections, a handicapped individual is someone who has a physical or mental impairment that substantially limits one or more major life activities. Handicaps include epilepsy, cancer, amputation, blindness, or emotional disorders. The Vocational Rehabilitation Act may become increasingly important as a statutory basis for AIDS discrimination cases since, as noted earlier, at least one federal court has held that contagious diseases are covered by the act. The Vocational Rehabilitation Act also deems handicapped those individuals who have no current disability but have a record of impairment or are regarded as impaired. In any case, only those employees capable of fulfilling their job requirements are protected. An employer may refuse to accommodate an individual whose handicap prevents her from performing her job.

Enforcement of the Vocational Rehabilitation

Act is delegated to the Office of Federal Contract Compliance Programs (OFCCP) of the Labor Department. Generally, no private right of action exists under Section 503, which means that an aggrieved worker cannot go to court to seek damages and other remedies in a civil lawsuit.

Other Applicable Law

FEDERAL CONTRACTORS. Companies doing business with the federal government are subject to regulation by Title VII. In addition, a number of laws enforceable by the Office of Federal Contract Compliance Programs are addressed specifically to federal contractors. Executive orders by the president and statutes like the Vocational Rehabilitation Act require contractors to take affirmative action measures and, in some cases, to protect groups not covered by Title VII. One executive order issued by the president applies to contractors whose business with the federal government exceeds $10,000 per year. Failure to comply with the order's antidiscrimination and affirmative-action provisions can expose a contractor to sanctions or cancellation of the contract. The Vietnam Era Veterans' Readjustment Assistance Act of 1974 requires federal contractors to hire and promote disabled and qualified veterans of the Vietnam War era.

SECTION 1981 OF THE CIVIL RIGHTS ACT. Enacted during the Reconstruction period following the Civil War, Section 1981 of the Civil Rights Act of 1866 gives all persons the same contractual rights as white citizens. In recent years, this section has been used in employment-discrimination actions based on race, alienage, and national origin.

STATE LAW. Fair employment practices laws are found in most states. These laws often are patterned after federal legislation, but the coverage and administrative and substantive provisions of state statutes vary widely, as does the construction given them by state courts. State laws frequently extend farther than their federal counterparts. For example, some of these state statutes prohibit discrimination based on marital status, sexual preference, or political affiliation. As a result, employers have to satisfy the combined requirements of state and federal law.

Affirmative Action

For two decades, courts and scholars have grappled with the question of **affirmative action.** At issue is whether an organization that employs a low percentage of minorities or women may remedy the imbalance by giving preferences to these groups in hiring or other employment decisions. Preferences may be implemented by having different employment criteria, by introducing quota systems, or by modifying layoff procedures and seniority systems. Proponents of affirmative action argue that society must compensate for years of past discrimination against certain groups: When purely neutral criteria are applied, they claim, discrepancies in experience and educational opportunity will operate to perpetuate the imbalances of the past. Critics of affirmative action argue that these preferences amount to reverse discrimination and thus violate Title VII. This problem especially is acute in the layoff situation, when a newly-hired woman or minority employee's rights under affirmative action conflict with a long-term white male employee's rights under a *bona fide* seniority system.

The courts generally have upheld carefully designed affirmative action programs against Title VII and constitutional challenges. The Supreme Court has held that preferences may be used to remedy egregious and longstanding discrimination. Recently, the Court decided that an employer need not point to its own past discriminatory practices, but may rely on the reality of past discrimination in the industry or business community in general in order to justify the adoption of an affirmative action plan. However it arises, a conspicuous imbalance reflecting under representation of women or minorities in traditionally segregated job categories apparently will warrant the remedy of affirmative action. Case law suggests that an affirmative action plan must be narrowly tailored to serve its purposes in order to do the least damage to the rights of groups disfavored by the plan. The degree of protection or relief afforded minorities and women thus far has been defined on a case-by-case basis, and is likely to remain a major source of contention and litigation in the years to come.

SEXUAL HARASSMENT

Although Title VII of the Civil Rights Act of 1964 provides that "it shall be an unlawful employment practice for an employer . . . to discriminate against any individual with respect to his . . . terms, conditions or privileges of employment, because of such individual's . . . sex," it would take another thirteen years before an action for sexual harassment would be recognized by the courts. Early cases ruled that disadvantaging an employee for refusal to engage in sexual activities was not a form of sex discrimination. Instead, the alleged sexual harassment was seen merely as a matter of "personal proclivity" of male supervisors that was not actionable under Title VII. These courts apparently failed to recognize the pervasiveness of the practice and the degree to which such "personal" actions could alter the workplace environment. Thus, it was not until 1977 that sexual harassment finally was acknowledged as a form of sex discrimination.

EEOC Guidelines

In 1980, The Equal Employment Opportunity Commission (EEOC) published its *Sexual Harassment Guidelines* to help shape the law. Although the commission's interpretations of the law have no legal effect in and of themselves, they are regarded as very important by the courts and are accorded a great deal of deference.

Sexual harassment, under the guidelines, is defined as "unwelcome sexual advances, requests for sexual favors, and other verbal or physical conduct of a sexual nature." This behavior is said to violate Title VII when (1) submission to sexual advances is made, either implicitly or explicitly, a term or condition of an individual's employment; (2) submission to or rejection of the conduct is used as the basis for any significant employment decision affecting an individual; or (3) the conduct has the purpose or effect of unreasonably interfering with an individual's work performance or creating an intimidating, hostile, or offensive work environment.

The first two factors are referred to as *quid pro quo* sexual harassment, since specific employment benefits are withheld as a means of compelling sexual favors. The plaintiff has a Title VII claim for relief if the party in the superior position uses his or her apparent authority to hire, fire, discipline, or promote. The third factor is referred to as hostile-environment sexual harassment, and it occurs when continued and pervasive touchings, comments, inquiries, jokes, and any form of abusive treatment make the workplace intolerable for the employee. Isolated incidents, social invitations, or minor flirtation generally are not sufficient to maintain a Title VII claim.

Elements of a *Prima Facie* Case

In order to support a Title VII claim for sexual harassment, a plaintiff must prove five elements to establish his or her case. First, the plaintiff must state that he or she is a member of a protected group under Title VII of the Civil Rights Act, and, second, that he or she has been subject to "unwelcomed" sexual harassment. The fact that the plaintiff may have acceded "voluntarily" to the sexual demands is irrelevant, since courts have recognized that employees often feel coerced to participate in the conduct in order to maintain their jobs. Sexual harassment may be shown by evidence of uninvited pressure for sexual favors, uninvited and deliberate touching, leaning over, cornering or pinching, as well as other objectionable conduct. As mentioned earlier, the behavior generally must be of a continuing and pervasive nature.

Third, the plaintiff must show that the sexual harassment was based on the complaining worker's gender. An interesting question has been raised over whether this requirement would be satisfied if a bisexual supervisor were to make sexual advances to both genders, or if the conduct complained of was offensive to men and women equally. So far no case has arisen specifically addressing the issue, but several courts have speculated that there still would be a claim for sex discrimination by either the male or the female.

Fourth, the sexual harassment or the employee's response to the harassment must affect the worker's "terms, conditions or privileges" of employment. The altered "terms, conditions or privileges" need not be tangible; evidence of serious emotional harm affecting work performance usually will be sufficient to satisfy the requirement.

Fifth, since a Title VII suit cannot be brought against an individual employee, the plaintiff must show that the employer is liable for the acts of his or her employee. This is the most difficult element of the *prima facie* case to prove, and will be considered separately in the next section.

If all five elements are satisfied by the employee, the burden shifts to the employer to articulate some legitimate, nondiscriminatory reasons for his or her actions. The plaintiff then may show that the excuses offered are mere pretexts for the employer's sexual harassments. As you can see, a sexual harassment case is very similar in structure to any other Title VII action.

Employer Liability

Under the 1980 EEOC Guidelines, "an employer . . . is responsible for its acts and those of its agents and supervisory employees with respect to sexual harassment regardless of whether the specific acts complained of were authorized or even forbidden by the employer."

In cases involving sexual harassment by a supervisor, the EEOC suggests a strict liability approach in both *quid pro quo* and hostile-environment situations. Therefore, the employer should be held liable under Title VII regardless of whether it knew or should have known of the offensive behavior. Although courts generally have followed the EEOC guidelines regarding *quid pro quo* cases, some courts have been reluctant to extend liability in hostile-environment cases to employers who either had no knowledge of the abusive conduct or who took immediate corrective measures once they learned of it.

In cases involving sexual harassment by a coworker, the EEOC guidelines suggest that an employer be held responsible for the acts of the complaining worker's fellow employees when the employer (or its agents or supervisory employees) knows or should have known of the conduct, unless it can demonstrate that it took immediate corrective action. This standard has been applied by most courts, although proof of what the employer knew or should have known often is difficult.

In a few cases, an employer has been held liable for sexual harassment by a nonemployee if the employer was aware of the offensive conduct or could anticipate it, and had the power to remedy the situation. For example, a female receptionist was successful in maintaining a sexual harassment suit against her employer for the lewd comments and gestures she received from patrons of the company. The employer had required her to wear a very revealing uniform—portions of her thighs and buttocks were exposed. When the plaintiff complained to the employer, however, she was told that is she did not wear the outfit, she would be fired. The court found the employer responsible for the harassment since he was aware of the abusive conduct, yet still required the plaintiff to sport the offensive uniform.

SUMMARY

Prior to the nineteenth century, regulation by the law of the employment relationship virtually was unknown. By the turn of the century, however, it became clear that unrestrained industrial growth exacted too high a toll on workers' lives. The need to provide workers with safe and decent working conditions inspired the development of governmental regulation of various aspects of the terms and conditions of employment.

By 1920, most states had enacted some form of workers' compensation legislation to guarantee compensation to employees injured on the job, irrespective of fault. The system functions as a mandatory insurance plan financed by employers. But only injuries that arise out of the course of employment are covered. Furthermore, workers' compensation will recompense only financial harm—not pain and suffering or emotional distress. Four types of disabilities emerge in workers' compensation cases—temporary partial, temporary total, permanent partial, and permanent total. Of these, temporary disabilities are the most effectively handled by the system, since the employees are reimbursed for all medical costs and there is often little pain and suffering. Permanent partial disabilities are the most difficult to deal with effectively, because compensation is denied to someone who still is able to work but whose enjoyment of life is impaired permanently.

The Occupational Safety and Health Act (OSHA) was passed by Congress in 1970 to address the overwhelming problems of workplace hazards. OSHA expressly requires most employers to maintain accurate records of, and make periodic reports on, work-related deaths, illnesses, and injuries. Furthermore, employers are required to inform and educate employees about occupational hazards in the workplace. OSHA officials are empowered to inspect all places of employment subject to the act's regulations. Penalties may be assessed for violations. Certain states assert their own jurisdiction over job safety and health matters, but may do so only after they have submitted a plan that meets OSHA's approval.

Until relatively recently, the presumption as to individual employment contracts that were not for a definite term was that the job was at will (meaning terminable at any time by either party for any reason). But the courts have begun to lessen the severity of the employment-at-will doctrine by developing exceptions to it.

First, many courts now are willing to infer a promise that employees will be discharged "for good/just cause only" from certain actions of the employer. Employers may create implied-in-fact contracts by establishing procedures for discharging employees or by promising job security during the employment interview or in the employee manual. A second limitation on employers' discharge of employees is the principle that terminations that violate any important public policy are unjust and—under certain circumstances—actionable. The last and most narrowly applied of the exceptions to employment at will is the development of a covenant of good faith and fair dealing by the courts.

An area that recently has come to the foreground in employment law is that of workplace privacy. Drug and alcohol abuse significantly reduce the effectiveness of this country's workforce every year, and many concerned employers have turned to testing employees for these substances in order to deter potential abusers, protect others, and restore the lost productivity. The federal courts have tended to uphold most drug-testing programs, but more recently both they and state courts have begun to strike down testing when the work is not specifically related to safety or when employers present no evidence suggesting the existence of wide-spread drug abuse.

Another method used by employers to monitor their employees is to administer polygraphs or lie-detector tests. Some states prohibit employers from using these devices to ask questions about employees' religious or political affiliations, and a few limit the questions to those that bear directly on the employment position being offered. A 1988 federal statute prohibits pre-employment and random use of polygraphs by employers, and may have the effect of virtually ending their use by the business community.

Regarding other forms of employer searches, such as of lockers and workspace, courts tend to look to the purpose of the intrusion. A workplace search for criminal-investigation purposes will be permitted, but it must provide the employee with his or her protections under the Fourth Amendment to the Constitution. A search that is for the employer's own knowledge occasionally can be challenged successfully.

Few subjects generate as much controversy as the disease known as Acquired Immune Deficiency Syndrome, or AIDS. As with drugs and alcohol, some employers have decided the appropriate response is testing. Like the test for drugs, however, the test for AIDS can give false positives and does not reveal the disease (addiction) but only the presence of the antibodies to the virus (controlled substance). Only a few states have prohibited testing, but because current medical opinion is that AIDS cannot be spread by casual contact, the dismissal of an employee (or even the rejection of a job applicant) for a positive test result may well be considered unreasonable.

The law of employment discrimination developed primarily during the 1960s and 1970s with the rise of the civil rights movement. Title VII of the federal Civil Rights Act of 1964 is the most important federal or state law on the subject. It prohibits employers, labor unions, and employment agencies from discriminating in employment-related decisions on the basis of five specific classifications—race, color, religion, sex, and national origin. Some states statutes prohibit discrimination against other groups.

Two theories of discrimination serve as the foundation for most Title VII actions: (1) disparate treatment or intentional discrimination, and (2) disparate impact or discriminatory effects. Discriminatory practices do not violate Title VII if they are job-related or justified by business necessity, unless there are other nondiscriminatory selection methods that can serve the employer's business needs adequately, or unless it appears that the employer's justification for the practice is merely a pretext. Title VII also provides special exceptions for employment decisions based on employee merit, a valid seniority system, or a *bona fide* occupational qualification. Claims under Title VII may be enforced by the Equal Employment Opportunity Commission (a federal agency that administers and interprets Title VII and other federal antidiscrimination statutes) or taken to court.

Like Title VII, the Equal Pay Act of 1963 prohibits wage discrimination on the basis of sex and requires that substantially equal jobs be compensated equally. Title VII, however, may go beyond the Equal Pay Act to permit actions based on the notion of equal pay for comparable work—tasks that are not necessarily similar in kind, but have the same inherent worth or a comparable worth to the employer. The issue is in the courts.

The Age Discrimination in Employment Act of 1967 protects workers forty to seventy years old from discrimination in hiring, firing, compensation, and other conditions and privileges of employment. It also prohibits mandatory retirement at any protected age, subject to limited exceptions.

Important protections for the handicapped are guaranteed by Sections 503 and 504 of the Vocational Rehabilitation Act. The act provides that certain federal contractors and all programs receiving federal financial assistance may not discriminate against the handicapped and must take affirmative-action measures and make reasonable accommodations in hiring handicapped persons.

Among the various legal remedies for discrimination, affirmative action plans have generated the most controversy during the last two decades. Critics argue that special preferences in employment decisions favoring minorities or women amount to reverse discrimination and thus violate Title VII. The courts generally have upheld carefully constructed affirmative-action programs, but the precise balance between the rights of beneficiaries and the rights of those disfavored by affirmative action is likely to remain a major source of contention in the years to come.

Sexual harassment, another recognized type of Title VII discrimination, is defined as unwelcome sexual advances, requests for sexual favors, and other verbal or physical conduct of a sexual nature. A plaintiff may have either a claim for *quid pro quo* sexual harassment (when specific employment benefits are withheld as a means of compelling sexual favors) or hostile-environment harassment (when pervasive offensive conduct makes the workplace environment intolerable). In order to maintain a claim for sexual harassment, the employer's responsibility for the conduct of the offending employee must be established.

KEY TERMS AND CONCEPTS

fellow-servant rule
contributory negligence rule
workers' compensation
Occupational Safety and Health Act (OSHA)
worker right-to-know law
Hazard Communication Standard (HCS)
hiring at will
whistleblowing
Employee Polygraph Protection Act
Title VII of the Civil Rights Act of 1964
Equal Employment Opportunity Act
disparate treatment
disparate impact
bona fide occupational qualification
Equal Employment Opportunity Commission (EEOC)
Equal Pay Act of 1963
Fair Labor Standards Act
comparable-worth doctrine
Age Discrimination in Employment Act
Vocational Rehabilitation Act

Office of Federal Contract Compliance Programs
affirmative action
sexual harassment

PROBLEMS

1. Sarah works in an asbestos-manufacturing plant and is concerned about the effect asbestos dust may have on her health. What type of procedures are available for her to gather information on this subject? Does she have any recourse if she suspects that her employer may be violating some of OSHA's regulations?

2. Joe Worker is injured when a forklift he is operating overturns. What workers' compensation benefits will he receive if he incurs $10,000 in medical costs and misses twenty days of work (assume that his weekly wage is $500, the waiting period is three days, and that the state average weekly wage (SAWW) is $400)? Would it make any difference if Joe had been negligent in handling the forklift? What if he had been intoxicated at the time of the accident? Is there any way he can recover for his pain and suffering?

3. Pete has been working for Smith Company for four years. He has no written contract but at the time of his hiring he was told, "keep doing your job and you'll keep working here." He was also handed an employee manual that explained the sanctions to be imposed when an employee violates the rules: a first offense receives a six-month salary reduction and a second offense means termination. On March 20, Pete's boss called him into his office and said, "Pete, local elections are tomorrow. I certainly hope you intend to vote for candidate Shannon, who will support causes beneficial to this company." Pete thought about it and said, "I can't promise to vote for this man." Two days later, Pete was fired. What are the various arguments that he might make against his employer in a wrongful-discharge action?

4. Mary had been working for the First Credit Bank for fifteen years, and each year she received a highly favorable rating from her superiors. Then she discovered that some bank employees were overcharging customers for certain bank services, and she informed the bank's vice-president. He promised to look into the matter, but the overcharging continued. She then informed the bank's president of the situation. Several days later she was discharged for "poor work performance." On what grounds might she bring a wrongful-discharge suit?

5. Traynor Institute, a federally funded company, never had tested any of its employees for drugs or alcohol. On September 23, an employee was observed behaving very strangely, and upon questioning, he admitted to smoking marijuana on the job. The next day, the company ordered all employees to submit to urine testing to determine the presence of drugs and alcohol in their systems. Those who refused were discharged immediately. Under current guidelines, would a court be likely to uphold such a drug-testing program in a suit by one of the fired employees?

6. Menn & Boise, a large national law firm, adopted a firm-wide rule against hiring female associates with preschool-aged children. The hiring partner believed that child-care responsibilities would prevent a woman from concentrating fully and devoting the long hours required of a lawyer in a large firm. Janet Momm, a qualified law-school graduate with a two-year-old daughter in a full-time day-care program, was refused a position because of the rule. Janet brought a Title VII action based on sex discrimination. Can Janet establish a *prima facie* case? Can Menn & Boise invoke the BFOQ defense? What if the percentage of men and women employed by the firm as associates in recent years is approximately equal? Does it make a difference that the firm has no comparable rule for male associates with preschool-aged children?

7. (a) If the BFOQ defense is not applicable to racial discrimination, can a white actor sue under Title VII if he is denied a role as a black character? (b) Can a Catholic woman who is denied admission to the priesthood institute a lawsuit under Title VII with any possible hope of being successful?

8. Joe Spry is eighty years old. Hearing that Lacy's Department Store was seeking applicants for its management-training program, he rushed over on his bicycle, dashed up the stairs to the employment office, and filled out the application. Lacy's told him that he was ineligible for the program because it involved a mandatory three-year commitment. What rights does Joe have? What defense might Lacy's make?

9. Jennifer is one of only two female warehouse employees at Stor-it, Inc. Her supervisor and her co-workers often make suggestive comments about her appearance, post sexually oriented drawings in the warehouse referring to her in derogatory terms, and tell her lewd stories. Several of the workers have propositioned her on various occasions. Does Jennifer have a cause of action for sexual harassment against Stor-it, Inc? If yes, what kind of action can she bring? Assume that the employer is on notice of Jennifer's working conditions but takes no action. May it be held liable? To what extent? What if the company's president verbally reprimands the supervisor and the co-workers? What if the president is unaware of the offensive conduct?

PART X

Other Legal

Considerations

This part of the book includes independent topics that seem to stand alone rather than to fit in as necessary divisions of any of the other general categories of law. Chapter 53 discusses insurance law. This is an important topic as it relates to both our personal and our business lives. The availability of insurance enables each of us to spread many of the risks unavoidably involved in life and the operation of a business. Chapter 54 presents information of special importance to accountants. However, many of the principles discussed there apply equally to other professions. Finally, Chapter 55 presents a broad overview of international law. Although the advent of international agreements has rapidly brought international law to a position of considerable relevance in the business world, its content is not a part of American law per se, and it differs from traditional law greatly, especially in terms of the means by which it may be enforced.

Chapter | 53

Insurance

INTRODUCTION

Insurance has become a major phenomenon of modern business and personal life. It has become the basic way of financially surviving some of the catastrophic risks that threaten our health, safety, and economic viability. Because of its importance and the needs of people—both the wealthy and those of modest means—to have access to it and to be safeguarded against policies that are too favorable to the insurance company and com-

panies that are insufficiently funded to stand behind their policies, the law has regulated the industry heavily. As a result of a federal statute, the **McCarran-Ferguson Act,** regulation of the insurance industry has been left to the states, which has led to a significant amount of variation in the law. This has led in turn to some dissatisfaction, and there has been a movement in recent years to repeal the statute and develop a more uniform national policy.

Questions concerning the availability and cost of insurance are a source of constant controversy. For years the medical profession has complained bitterly about the escalating cost of malpractice insurance, claiming it is driving practitioners in certain specialties, such as neurosurgery and obstetrics, away from the profession. A similar rise in automobile insurance has raised the ire of consumer organizations. More recently, the emergence of Acquired Immune Deficiency Syndrome (AIDS) has raised questions about the coverage provided by existing policies and the right of insurance companies to exclude people with the disease from future policies or to test all applicants for health and life policies for the related HIV virus.

THE NATURE OF INSURANCE

Insurance involves a contract between two parties under which one, in return for the payment of consideration, agrees to indemnify the other for losses from certain specified existing risks. Of particular importance in this definition is that the risk insured must be an existing one. This differentiates insurance from *gambling,* which may be defined as the creation of a risk for the purpose of assuming it. Insurance contracts generally are legal, but gambling contracts generally are not.

Insurance contracts are important because they make possible the "pooling of risks." The operation of any business inevitably involves the assumption of certain existing risks, such as general liability for injuries to others, loss of or injury to business property, and even the loss of life. The financial loss that can be occasioned by these risks can be substantial and easily beyond the ability of a single entrepreneur to bear. Insurance contracts make it possible to spread these risks of loss over a substantial pool of policy holders. Then when a loss occurs, each policyholder theoretically pays a modest share to the one who sustained the loss, and no one suffers to any significant degree. The insurance company makes its profit by setting insurance rates to include profit, and by earning money by investing the premiums. However, not all plans providing for such risk sharing are insurance plans, governed by insurance law. Consider the following case.

FEINSTEIN v. ATTORNEY GENERAL
36 N.Y.2d 199, 326 N.E. 2d 288 (1975)

This was an action by Barry Feinstein (Applicant/Appellant) as trustee of an employees union, and the New York Country Lawyers Association, seeking approval of two prepaid legal services plans. The action was opposed by the attorney general of the state of New York (Respondent) on behalf of the state. The plan had not been submitted to the Insurance Commission for approval. The question before the court was whether it was an "insurance" plan.

The Appellate Division of the Supreme Court denied the application, and the applicant appealed. Reversed and remitted.

BREITEL, Chief Judge.

Despite the Appellate Division's proper concern with the possible proliferation of prepaid legal services plans without adequate assessment of their fiscal implications by an agency capable of making that assessment, it lacked the power to withhold approval on that ground. Nor are prepaid legal services plans properly encompassed by the statutes regulating insurance. At least this is true, if one were to consider the essential purpose and scope of those statutes, although to be sure, there are elements of contingency and reimbursement in any such plan which bear a similarity to certain kinds of insurance or indemnity. On this view, the two plans were improperly excluded from approval, and the applications should be remitted to the Appellate Division for reconsideration. . . .

The Insurance Law is designed to prohibit the business of insurance and related activities, except as licensed and regulated by the Department of Insurance or exempted from such licensure and regulation (see Insurance Law, Section 40, subd.1). The threshold issue arises from the definition of insurance. Section 41 provides that an insurance contract "include[s] any agreement or other transaction whereby one party, herein called the insurer, is obligated to confer benefit of pecuniary value upon another party, herein called the insured or the beneficiary, dependent upon the happening of a fortuitous event in which the insured or beneficiary has, or is expected to have at the time of such happening, a material interest which will be adversely affected by the happening of such event. A fortuitous event is any occurrence or failure to occur which is, or is assumed by the parties to be a substantial extent beyond the control of either party."

A reading of the statute for its sense and purpose does not suggest that the instant plans for prepaid legal services are insurance schemes. A literal reading of the statute, disregarding its sense and purpose, would of course take in some of the prepaid or reimbursable fees for legal services, to the extent that the legal services would not be required until a "fortuitous event" had occurred. As for many of the legal services involved, however, there is no fortuitousness, in any ordinary sense of the word, in the event which precipitates the retention of a lawyer, such as the drafting of a will, a separation agreement, the purchase of a house, and many others of the same kind.

Terms like fortuitousness of event in the law, as with the word accident, have always caused conceptual difficulties. . . . The statute, in circumscribing the term to mean that which is to a substantial extent beyond the control of either party, is useful in relating regulation to insurance schemes as they have been known (see Insurance Law, Section 46), but it is not exact in the consideration of agreements to provide services of various kinds. In this area it is easy to slip into metaphysical, even validly metaphysical, distinctions.

But metaphysics is not the concern of section 41 of the Insurance Law; instead the licensure and regulation of insurance activity is. The proposed prepaid legal services plans are not insurance businesses or insurance contracts, although it may be that, in the Appellate Division's judgment and in the future possibly that of the Legislature, they merit the same degree of regulation and supervision from their fiscal aspects and perhaps even from other aspects.

Viewed as a provider of professional services, sought as a matter of choice, at flat fees rather than as reimbursement for material losses or expenses precipitated by fortuitous events, the proposed plans do not pose the dangers that the Insurance Law was designed to obviate. Those dangers embrace inadequate coverage of determinable actuarial risks, excessive premiums on an actuarial basis, and fiscal irresponsibility. . . .

That hospital, medical and dental indemnity contracts have been covered in detailed and close regulation in the Insurance Law is not contradictory of what has been said thus far. As the Bar Association argues: "All that the enactment of [article IX-C of the Insurance Law] demonstrates is that the legislature believed that such contracts . . . should be regulated by a statute especially tailored to those services and deemed the Insurance Department the most appropriate agency in which to vest the supervision of such corporations." That the same may become true of organizations providing for prepaid legal services is evidenced by legislation proposed last year, and now pending this year in the Legislature. . . .

Questions

1. Can you see any real difference between medical insurance and prepaid legal services? If so, what is it?

2. What about an employee pension plan? What are the arguments for and against treating it as insurance?

Definitions

The field of insurance incorporates some terms not shared with other areas of law. To understand insurance law, an understanding of the meanings of some of these is helpful.

1. *Assured.* This is the person for whose benefit a policy of insurance is issued, and to whom any covered loss ordinarily is payable. The assured may be the same person as the "insured," but not necessarily. For example, a parent may buy an insurance policy on the life of a child. The parent would be the assured, and the child the insured.

2. *Beneficiary.* This is the person who will receive the proceeds of an insurance policy. In the previous example, if the parent made the insurance policy payable to a third person (such as a guardian), the third person would be the beneficiary.

3. *Hazard.* This is the circumstance or condition that creates or increases a risk. In general, it is that which is insured against, such as fire, theft, or death.

4. *Insured.* This is the person upon whose life or property (including liability) a policy of insurance is obtained. In the example, the child is the insured. Commonly the assured, the beneficiary, and the insured are the same person, especially in the context of property and liability insurance.

5. *Insurer.* This is the person (ordinarily a company) who issues an insurance policy agreeing, in return for a premium, to assume the risks of loss or losses specified in the policy.

6. *Policy.* This is the contract of insurance. Technically, a formal policy of insurance must be in writing, but substantially the same purpose may be achieved by oral indemnity agreements.

Types of Insurance

Insurance may be obtained to insure against almost any risk imaginable, within the limits of public policy. Of primary importance to a business person, perhaps, are policies covering liability, fire and other property loss, marine, life, key man, and title insurance. Others, such as fidelity and security bonding, health insurance, and pension endowments, are beyond the scope of this chapter. Examples of risks generally not insurable are wagering losses and the assured's intentional tort liability.

Liability insurance may be obtained to cover risks of business or professional activity, personal liability for a wide variety of torts, or risks imposed under modern "no-fault statutes." Perhaps the most widely discussed of these today is malpractice insurance, which covers risks of errors in judgment or in the execution of professional work. For example, an accountant may obtain a malpractice policy to insure against liability for errors in gathering information during an audit, errors in calculating and entering figures on a financial statement, and errors in judgment, such as how items should be reflected on a financial statement. Although liability policies generally do not cover liability for injuries intentionally inflicted, the following case presents an exception.

HARTFORD FIRE INSURANCE CO. v. SPREEN, et al.
343 So.2d 649 (Fla.App. 1977)

This is an action on a cross-complaint by Donald Spreen et al. (Cross-Complainants/Appellees) against Hartford Fire Insurance Co. and St. Paul Fire and Marine Insurance Co. (Cross-Defendants/Appellants). Spreen was sued by William and Edna King in an action for assault and battery. At a party, Spreen had struck William King because of an allegedly crude remark by King concerning Spreen's wife. Spreen cross-complained against Appellants, claiming coverage under insurance policies issued by Appellants.

The trial court entered summary judgment for Spreen against Appellants, and Appellants appealed. Affirmed in part and reversed in part.

HUBBARD, Judge.

The Florida courts in a line of cases have consistently held that insurance policies covering liability for an "accident" apply to any bodily injury or property damage inflicted by the insured on a third party where the insured does not intend to cause any harm to the third party; this result obtains even though damages are caused by the insured's intentional acts and were reasonably foreseeable by the insured. Insurance coverage has accordingly been found under such policies where an insured unintentionally shoots himself while playing "Russian Roulette" . . . or unintentionally shoots himself while attempting to disarm a person in a fight in which the insured is the aggressor . . . or unintentionally shoots a bystander during a family quarrel . . . or unintentionally hits a person in a crowd of people with a car while slowly driving into the edge of the crowd intending to disperse them . . . or unintentionally injures a person in a car while intentionally pushing the car which was blocking a driveway. . . . Running through all of these cases is an act of negligence by the insured, sometimes gross or even culpable negligence. But never has coverage been found under such policies where the insured's act was deliberately designed to cause harm to the injured party.

Indeed the law is well-settled that there can be no coverage under an insurance policy which insures against an "accident" where "the [insured's] wrongful act complained of is intentionally directed specifically toward the person injured by such act. . . . Early on it became the overwhelming consensus in those cases that since such a policy was in essence an indemnification contract public policy mandated that an intentional tort was not an 'accident' within the coverage for the reason that one ought not to be permitted to indemnify himself against his intentional [torts]." . . . Accordingly, an assault and battery committed by the insured has been held to be an intentional tort which is not covered by insurance policies which insure against an "accident."

In the instant case, the insured Donald Spreen committed an assault and battery upon William King. He reacted to deliberately hit King for a crude and insulting remark about his wife. In no sense, can this assault and battery be considered an "accident" which is covered under the Hartford policy.

The appellees argue that while Spreen intended to hit King he did so on the spur of the moment, did not foresee the extent of King's injuries, and therefore did not intend them. The argument is unpersuasive. It is a subtle method of introducing the tort rule of reasonable foreseeability into insurance contract cases through the back door. Such a notion has been repeatedly rejected by the Florida courts. . . . The fact that Spreen did not foresee the extent of King's injuries when he swung at King can no more provide coverage under the Hartford policy than can be coverage be denied by the fact that Spreen should have foreseen such injury. Foreseeability is irrelevant to the coverage issue. The sole issue is whether Spreen intended to inflict any harm on King. This he clearly intended to do and the fact that he did not foresee or intend the extent of the harm inflicted does not convert the admitted assault and battery into an accident. . . .

The St. Paul policy is a personal catastrophe insurance policy which covers the insured's legal obligation to pay damages for "personal injuries." "Personal injuries" are defined as including but not limited to "bodily injury" as well as a number of intentional torts which do not include assault and battery.

As to this policy, the issue presented for review is whether bodily injury inflicted by the insured in an assault and battery is covered by a personal catastrophe policy which insures against "personal injuries," or "bodily injury" but does not specifically mention the tort of assault and battery. We conclude that the assault and battery in the instant case is covered by the St. Paul policy and affirm.

Unlike Hartford, the St. Paul policy is not limited to coverage for damages arising from an "accident." It broadly covers damages which the insured is liable to pay on account of "personal injuries," or "bodily injury." There is no limitation in the coverage section of the policy which refers to an "accident." Nor is there a specific exclusion in the policy for damages which are intentionally cause by the insured.

The law is well-settled that "[a] contract of insurance, prepared and phrased by the insurer is to be construed liberally in favor of the insured and strictly against the insurer, where the meaning of the language is doubtful, uncertain or ambiguous." . . . In view of this canon of construction, we think the coverage of the St. Paul policy for "personal injuries" defined inter alia as a "bodily injury" is broad enough to cover damages caused by an intentional assault and battery.

Questions

1. If there is a public policy against allowing someone to be indemnified against her intentional torts, why does the St. Paul policy apply?

2. Should an automobile policy indemnify the insured for injuries caused by his drunk driving? What about a manufacturer's intentional environmental pollution?

Personal liability policies of particular importance are those regarding the operation of a motor vehicle and the ownership or control of property, such as one's home or business. Most states, today, require anyone operating a motor vehicle to first obtain a policy covering, at least, liability for personal injury and property damage to others.

No-fault insurance, although not entirely a new area, has received increased attention during the past decade and a half. The two types of **no-fault liability** are liability *to* others, such as worker's compensation, and elimination of tort liability in some cases involving injuries *by* others, such as no-fault automobile insurance. In the latter, each party in an accident must provide coverage for his or her own injuries rather than suing the other in tort.

Fire and property insurance generally covers losses to property sustained as a result of fire and theft. Frequently, fire insurance also may cover losses occasioned by other perils such as wind, lightning, and flood. Property insurance also may cover additional perils such as damage, perhaps by dropping a camera into sand, or simple breakage while in use.

A basic theft policy ordinarily covers some property only at a specific location. Therefore, it is necessary to purchase separate *off-premises coverage*. Also, recovery under a theft policy requires proof of theft, such as evidence of forcible entry.

Property and liability insurance, premiums written (1986)

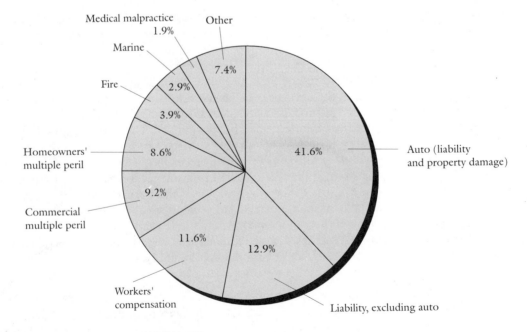

Source: Statistical Abstract of the U.S. 1988, Table 819.

An alternative is an additional premium to cover **mysterious disappearance,** which requires only proof that the item was placed somewhere and then disappeared. For example, the policyholder placed his ring by the washbasin of a public restroom, left it, and upon returning found it gone. This is more than simply "losing" it. Finally, fire and property policies generally provide for exclusion of some items, or limitations on liability for them. Firearms, antiques, silverware, jewelry, and cash are among the most common. Specific provision must be made for such property in the policy. Sometimes this is accomplished merely by supplying the insurer with a specific inventory, although sometimes an additional premium also is required.

Fire insurance policies commonly include some standard limitations, such as those concerning vacant premises, friendly fires, and increases of hazard. A vacancy clause relieves the insurer of liability after the insured premises have been vacant or unoccupied for a particular stated period of time. **Friendly fires** ordinarily are exempt from coverage. These are fires that are set intentionally by the insured and do some damage, although they remain contained as intended. For example, a fire in a fireplace may be too hot and cause damage to the structure, or to adjoining structures if the fireplace is not installed properly. However, if the fire escapes, as in the case of sparks igniting living-room furnishings, it is covered because the fire became unfriendly or hostile. Finally, if the insured does something that materially increases the hazard, the insurer may be relieved of liability. For example, the owner of a single-family dwelling converts the space in the furnace area to a storage room for newspapers and other flammables, or begins taking in roomers. Consider the following case involving the question of a friendly fire.

SCHULZE AND BURCH BISCUIT CO. v. AMERICAN PROTECTION INSURANCE COMPANY
96 Ill.App.3d 350, 421 N.E.2d 331 (1981)

This was an action by Schulze and Burch Biscuit Co. (Plaintiff/Appellee) against American Protection Insurance Company (Defendant/Appellant) to recover under a fire insurance policy.

Plaintiff's business was covered under the terms of a fire insurance policy issued by Defendant. At the end of one working shift, one of Plaintiff's ovens was inadvertently left on. With no product to absorb the heat, the temperature of the oven rose to 1600 degrees Fahrenheit, damaging the oven. The cost of repair was $149,836.93. Defendant refused to pay under the policy, contending the damages were caused by a "friendly fire."

The trial court found for Plaintiff, and Defendant appealed. Affirmed.

JOHNSON, Justice.

We are well aware of the case Gibbons v. German Insurance & Savings Institute (1889). . . . However, the facts in Gibbons are inapposite to those existing before this court. Here, the problem does not involve the third agency of steam as in Gibbons. Rather, it is the direct heat from the fire contained in an insured oven. Absent an express exclusion by the insurer, any unanticipated loss or damage caused by fire emanating from such a vessel should be indemnified. Insurers have more than ample opportunity to limit their liability by way of the contract of insurance. In most instances, as is the circumstance here, the terms and conditions of insurance contracts are not negotiable. Without express provision, it is our view that it is improper to allow liability to turn on the location of the fire causing damage apart from the damage itself. When one purchases standard fire insurance he does so with the idea in mind of protecting himself and his property from loss or damage. Our decision conserves that expectation. The trial court was, therefore, correct in reaching its decision in favor of the insured.

Questions

1. Why, in this case, as was true in the *Hartford Fire* case, is the policy construed so favorably to the insured?
2. Don't results like this one simply encourage people to be negligent?

Marine insurance, in general, is intended to cover losses involving marine navigation, other than those resulting from normal wear to a vessel or equipment, and those resulting from delays. This type of insurance is of particular importance to businesspeople who own vessels for shipping goods in connection with their businesses. However, someone who owns a pleasure boat, outboard motor, and other boating equipment also must be aware that these items ordinarily are not covered under a household policy. Depending on the state, the same may be true of some recreational equipment, such as snowmobiles.

Life insurance covers the risk of the insured's death. Its objectives ordinarily are to provide maintenance and support for dependents of the insured, and to guard against financial loss and expenses attending the death. In the latter context, life insurance may be purchased to cover a mortgage and other indebtedness of the insured, or in the commercial context, to relieve the loss to a business caused by the death of a critically important owner or employer, giving rise to the name **key-man insurance.**

A life insurance policy may be either a *term* policy or *straight or whole life*. **Term life insurance** is pure insurance. It involves the payment of a premium for a stated period, and proceeds are payable only if the insured dies during that period. Because the risk of death increases with age, a progressively higher premium is required as the insured gets older. Therefore, a term policy may provide that the premium will increase year by year, or in blocks of five years or so; it may provide that a level premium will be paid, which would be higher in the beginning years and lower in the later years than otherwise would be charged; or it may provide for a level premium, with benefits decreasing year by year or in blocks.

A **straight or whole life** policy is, in essence, a pure insurance policy plus a savings feature, called "reserve." After a time, ordinarily three years or so, the policy is worth something, and the insured may "cash it in" or borrow against the accumulating cash value. This type of policy, of course, requires the payment of a higher premium than does a term policy. The premium may be paid in a lump sum or by installments, as the parties may arrange.

The typical life insurance policy is a third-party beneficiary contract. That is, the beneficiary is someone other than the insured, and is usually a donee beneficiary rather than a creditor beneficiary. As such, the rights of the beneficiary vest at the time the contract is entered into. Therefore, unless the assured reserves the right to change beneficiaries, she has no such power. Nor would the assured have the power to cancel the policy without the consent of the beneficiary. For these reasons, a policy should contain a provision ex-

Average life insurance policy size in force (1986)

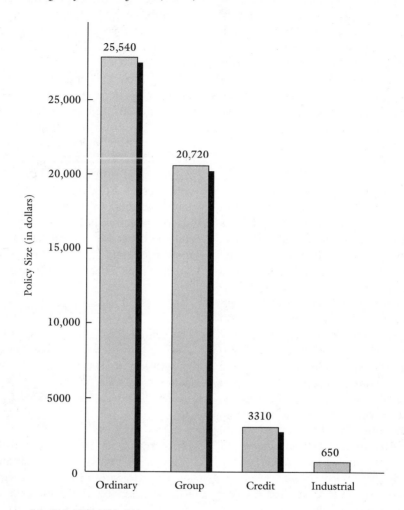

Source: Statistical Abstract of the U.S. 1988, Table 816.

pressly reserving these rights. Third-party beneficiary contracts are discussed more fully in Chapter 11.

Title **insurance** covers losses arising from any defect in the title to real estate. Prior to its use, a potential purchaser of real estate relied on an attorney to examine the title and render an opinion as to the existence of defects before he agreed to buy. If the title later proved defective, and the

defect had not been revealed by the attorney, the attorney might be liable for professional negligence (malpractice). When title insurance is obtained, the insurer will have had its own attorney render a title opinion, and on that basis will issue a title insurance policy. This policy guarantees against all defects other than those excluded by the policy. Excluded defects ordinarily include particular defects listed on the policy and any that do not appear on the records. A purchaser still must examine the property physically for the existence of possible defects apparent on the property itself, such as a third party in possession, or paths or other evidence of adverse use. Ordinarily, a one-time premium is paid by the seller of the land in lieu of furnishing an abstract (a history of the title to the property). A title policy may have as its beneficiary the purchaser, a mortgagee or other security holder, or both.

Indemnity

The principle of **indemnity** is that an insurer will pay only to the extent that a loss has been suffered, and not more. Therefore, someone who has a fire insurance policy of $80,000 and sustains a loss of $50,000 may collect only $50,000. If the loss had been $90,000, she could collect only $80,000—the face amount of the policy. Suppose, however, she had two fire insurance policies, both for $80,000. In the case of the $50,000 loss, she still would be entitled to only $50,000 of proceeds. Whether she would collect $25,000 from each insurer, the entire $50,000 from one and nothing from the other, or some combination of the two would depend on state law and the provisions of the policies. The same is true in the case of the $90,000 loss. The assured would be allowed only $80,000 in some combination of benefits from the two policies. Recovery of the policy maximum is also the rule.

The principle of indemnity is applied for reasons of public policy. First, to allow the assured to collect more than the loss sustained would convert an insurance contract into a gambling contract; that result is not consistent with the concept of insurance and would be illegal in most states. Second, the policy discourages intentional destruction. A person with a house for which he paid $80,000 that was insured for $160,000 might be tempted to pray for a fire, or worse, might assist it in happening.

These problems do not arise in connection with life insurance contracts. No one can place a value on human life. Therefore, life insurance is not considered indemnity insurance. Neither is health insurance, and for that reason almost all policies issued have a specific provision, called an "other insurance clause," that limits recovery in cases of multiple policies.

Finally, two insurance policies may complement each other in the case of *co-insurance.* This means the insured has a "primary" policy, and another (co-insurance) policy that pays other expenses, such as deductibles not paid by the primary policy. For example, benefits under a primary health insurance policy may pay benefits only after a flat deductible, such as $500, and then pay 80 percent of the rest up to a stated maximum. The co-insurance policy, then, would pay the $500 and the other 20 percent, and possibly amounts above the limits of the primary policy. A common example is a medicare-supplement policy.

THE INSURANCE CONTRACT

The validity and enforceability of insurance policies are governed by the law of contracts. This is in addition to specific law that relates only to insurance contracts.

General Requirements

There must be an *offer.* Usually this is extended by an applicant in seeking the insurance by completing the company's forms. The *acceptance* is then accomplished by the insurance company's issuance of a policy to the applicant. The company's selling agent usually has no power to bind the insurer to a permanent policy, but frequently is empowered to bind it for a temporary period between the tender of the application and a decision whether a policy will be issued. When the insurance company issues the policy, it contains the terms of the contract. The *consideration* paid by the applicant is in the form of a promise to pay a premium, and that of the insurer is the promise to insure. Notice that an insurance contract is bilateral, resting not on the payment of a premium but on the promise to do so. State law generally provides a period, such as thirty days, during which an insurance contract will remain in force even though the premium is past due and unpaid.

Capacity of the parties (the assured and insurer) is required in order to make the insurance policy binding. The assured (but not necessarily the insured) must be of legal age and sound mind. The insurer must be authorized under state law, and by its articles of incorporation, bylaws, or other grant of authority by its owners, to issue insurance policies of the type involved.

The policy must involve a *legal subject matter*. For example, a policy insuring against losses from an illegal activity, such as gambling, is unenforceable. The same would be true of a policy indemnifying the insured against criminal penalties such as fines or confiscation of property used in the commission of a crime. Also, public policy generally prohibits the issuance of insurance policies indemnifying someone against liability for intentional torts and punitive damage awards. (However, note the *Hartford Fire* case presented earlier in this chapter.)

Special state legislation ordinarily requires insurance contracts to be in *writing*. In fact, this requirement is included in the definition of an insurance policy. However, statutes of frauds usually do not include insurance contracts within their provisions, and either insurance, or something comparable to insurance, may be accomplished orally in many cases.

Insurance contracts are *voidable* under the same circumstances as other contracts, most commonly when they are induced by actionable misrepresentation or fraud, particularly on the part of the applicant. Also, however, they are voidable when material factors leading to the issuance of a policy are changed by an act of the assured or the insured. For example, this would be true if the use of an insured's premises is changed in a manner that increases the risk to the insurer materially, or the insured does some "amateur rewiring" of the premises in violation of building code requirements. As to disagreements arising concerning the meanings of the terms of an insurance policy, any *ambiguities* ordinarily will be resolved against the insurer, as the party who drafted the terms.

Insurable Interest

Indemnity insurance, such as fire and property insurance, requires that an assured (1) must have a legal interest in the property that is the subject of the policy and (2) must stand to suffer a financial loss by its being damaged, destroyed, or otherwise lost. The legal **insurable interest** may involve title, the right to possession, the right to nonpossessory use, or a security interest. The risk of financial loss is required, because insurance pays only money and is not payable to compensate for such intangible interests as loss of happiness, beauty, or sentimental value. These cannot be reduced to economic terms. The following case illustrates the general concept of insurable interest in an unusual context.

BUTLER v. FARMERS INSURANCE COMPANY OF ARIZONA
126 Ariz. 371, 616 P.2d 46 (1980)

This was an action by James Butler (Plaintiff/Appellant) against Farmers Insurance Company of Arizona (Defendant/Appellee) to recover benefits under an automobile insurance policy.

Plaintiff purchased an insurance policy covering loss to an Austin-Healy he purchased for $3500. Unknown to Plaintiff, the car had been stolen, and approximately two years later, it was repossessed by its true owner. Defendant refused to pay the loss under the policy, contending Plaintiff did not have an insurable interest.

The trial court found for Plaintiff (the insured) and its decision was reversed by the court of appeals. Plaintiff appealed this reversal. Vacated and remanded.

HAYS, Justice.

The facts as indicated previously reveal that appellee based its refusal to reimburse upon a lack of insurable interest. Although the question of whether a bona fide purchaser of stolen commodities may claim this relationship is one of first impression in Arizona, we note that the appellate courts of several jurisdictions have considered this issue and are in disagreement. Some courts, relying upon, inter alia, the inability of a seller of stolen property to transfer valid title, deny the innocent purchaser an interest of insurable quality. . . . Other jurisdictions, however, cite principles of real property or public policy in finding the existence of the requisite relationship. . . . Intending no disrespect to those courts holding otherwise, it is the considered opinion of this court that a bona fide purchaser of a stolen automobile has an interest sufficient to qualify as insurable.

Any analysis of the insurable interest principle in Arizona must focus initially upon the language of our statutes. The governing standard is set forth in A.R.S. Section 20-1105(B):

> "Insurable interest" . . . means any actual, lawful and substantial economic interest in the safety or preservation of the subject of the insurance free from loss, destruction or pecuniary damage or impairment.

We believe that the innocent purchaser of stolen property falls within this protection and reject any construction to the contrary.

Initially, examination of identical circumstances reveals that appellant's interest in conservation of the vehicle was both "lawful" and "substantial." The law is clear that a bona fide purchaser of stolen commodities inherits title defeasible by none other than the rightful owner. . . . S/he possesses a valid legal claim to the property which will be given full force and effect in a court of law. Even as against the true owner, moreover, the innocent purchaser may, upon loss or destruction of the illicit merchandise, be held liable in tort for conversion, and therefore has an interest in maintaining the property in an undamaged condition. . . .

In addition, the rule above-stated is not only sustained by the authorities, but is in accord with justice and common sense. Among the vices sought to be discouraged by the insurable interest requirement is the intentional destruction of the covered property in order to profit from the insurance proceeds. We believe this purpose will be furthered where the insured has a financial investment in the property and believes him or herself to be in lawful possession. We see no greater risk of illicit activity under these circumstances than where the insured is, in actuality, the rightful owner.

Questions

1. Since some courts have reached the opposite conclusion, there must be reasons for concluding there is no insurable interest. What are they?

2. If an insurance company already had paid the true owner of the car (at the time it was stolen), who now owns the repossessed car—the original owner or the insurance company?

Because life insurance is not indemnity insurance, different rules apply. The assured is required to have an insurable interest, but not the beneficiary. Generally, an assured has an insurable interest in his or her own life and in the lives of those related by blood or marriage, those who are dependents of the assured or upon whom the assured is dependent, and those in whom the assured has a special investment or business interest. For example, a corporation has insurable interests in its officers and directors, and partners have insurable interests in each other. Additionally, a creditor always has an insurable interest in the debtor, whether the creditor's claim is secured or unsecured.

In the case of an indemnity policy, the assured's insurable interest must exist at the time the policy is acquired, and must continue to exist until the time of the loss. In the case of life insurance, however, or any other nonindemnity policy, the insurable interest need exist only at the time of the casualty, such as death.

Effective Time

When application is made for an insurance policy, it is important, and sometimes critical, to know at what time coverage becomes effective. Without a stipulation in the application and the policy, some general principles may be applied. First, insurance ordinarily is purchased through an agent of the insurer. As already briefly noted, the agent typically is empowered to bind the insurer to insure for a temporary period between the tender of the application and the actual issuance of the permanent policy. This commitment is called a **binder.** Generally, a binder may be oral, and usually is followed by a signed, written memorandum issued by the agent.

Second, rather than purchasing a policy through an agent of the insurer, an applicant may apply through an independent broker, who is then an agent of the applicant rather than the insurer. The insurer has no obligation until it agrees to issue a policy. However, upon receiving the application the broker may make independent commitments to the applicant and be personally liable for any loss either before acceptance by an insurer, or resulting from the failure to obtain insurance for the applicant.

Third, it generally is understood that actual delivery of a policy is not necessary to an insurer's commitment. It is necessary only to prove that the insurer has agreed to accept the application. Of course the decision to accept the application may be difficult to prove without a binder in any case of a loss occurring after the submission of the application and before delivery of the policy.

Fourth, in cases involving indemnity insurance such as fire or property insurance, coverage usually begins even though the required premium has not been paid. Life insurance policies, however, ordinarily become binding only when they are delivered, and after the payment of the required premium.

Finally, some policies require a waiting period after issuance of the policy. For example, a health policy may not cover dental expenses or expenses of pregnancy until a stated period, such as six months, after the effective time of other coverage.

These provisions are commonly used to discourage persons from waiting until a loss is imminent to buy applicable insurance.

Interpretation

Insurance policies are interpreted according to the same rules used in interpreting other kinds of contracts. Words are given their ordinarily, generally understood meanings unless it is clear that a word is intended to have a technical meaning (the latter is known as a *term of art*). Usually, terms of art are defined in the policy. Also, as noted in two of the cases in this chapter, ambiguities normally are resolved against the insurer, who drafted the policy.

In recent years courts have become increasingly more aware that applicants for insurance are not conversant with technical legal terminology, particularly that used in specialized fields such as insurance. As a result, courts have tended more toward interpreting policy language broadly, in favor of the policyholder. Because of this, insurance companies have begun to draft policies in language more readily understandable by the average person, and have begun to supply more supplemental information, such as summary statements, to policyholders. The purpose is to lessen the time in litigation concerning policy coverage.

Incontestability Clauses

Most states require by statute that life insurance policies contain **incontestability clauses** that prohibit the insurance company from refusing to pay benefits because of misrepresentation or concealment of material facts in the application for insurance. They take effect at a certain time, commonly one year, after a policy is issued. The primary purpose for requiring such clauses is to prevent the insurer from raising questions of misrepresentation or concealment long after the policy was issued and, particularly, after the death of the insured who ordinarily would have been in the best position to present evidence to defend against the challenge. Consider the following case.

HULME v. SPRINGFIELD LIFE INSURANCE COMPANY
565 P.2d 666 (Okla. 1977)

This was an action by Homer H. Hulme and Chickasha Transit Mixed Concrete (Plaintiffs/Appellees) against Springfield Life Insurance Company, Inc. (Defendant/Appellant) to recover, on behalf of one Richard L. Kamm, benefits under a group life insurance policy.

Kamm died on January 6, 1974. He was named as an insured, by a certificate issued by Defendant, under a group life insurance policy covering Plaintiff's employees. The evidence showed that Kamm was not an employee of Plaintiff, but was the owner of another concrete company. There was no agency relationship of any kind between Kamm and Plaintiff, nor was Kamm a partner in Plaintiff's business. Because of this Defendant refused to pay benefits to Kamm. Plaintiff contended the benefits were payable because Defendant's right to contest Kamm's eligibility had been foreclosed by a two-year incontestability clause in the policy.

The trial court sustained a motion for summary judgment in favor of Plaintiff, and Defendant appealed. Affirmed.

LAVENDER, V.C.J.

We reach, first, the issue of precluding the defense, that the deceased was not in fact an employee, by the operation of the incontestability clause. Insurer says there was no contract of insurance on the life of Kamm for Kamm did not qualify as a member of the eligible group. An attack on validity is admitted to be precluded by the incontestable clause. It is argued that this is not an attack on the original validity of the contract. This court has rejected that position in Baum v. Massachusetts Mutual Life Insurance Co. . . . That opinion approved the line of reasoning advanced in the quoted case of Equitable Life Assurance Society v. Florence. . . . This Georgia opinion finds the incontestable clause estops the insurer from denying that the insured was an employee at the time of the issuance of the policy. In Baum, supra, the deceased regularly did tax work for the employer but the evidence failed to show he was, in a technical sense, an employee and as such a member of the class covered under the group policy. On the purpose of the incontestable clause, the opinion quotes from Metropolitan Life Ins. Co. v. Peeler . . . saying:

> . . . The meaning of the provision is that, if the premiums are paid, the liability shall be absolute under the policy, and that no question shall be made of its original validity. The language admits of no reasonable construction other than that the company reserves to itself the right to ascertain all the matter and facts material to its risk and the validity of its contract for one (present case, two) year; and that if within that time it does not ascertain all the facts, and does not cancel and rescind the contract, it may not do so afterwards upon any ground then in existence.' (Citing cases.) . . .

Here, whether Kamm qualified as a member of the eligible group goes to the question of original validity. Under the incontestable clause, the insurer reserved the right to ascertain all facts material to the validity of its contract, including the eligibility of Kamm to enroll as a member of the covered group. If within that two year time period, the insurer did not cancel or rescind the contract, it may not do so afterwards upon grounds then in existence.

The insurer would distinguish present case from Baum, supra, on (1) bad faith misrepresentation of Kamm being an employee. . . .

According to the affidavit of Nelson, the insurance agent, he was aware of Kamm's relations with the policyholder and believed there was justification to include Kamm as a member of the group to whom insurance was offered. Baum, supra, . . . We find no bad faith in the inclusion of Kamm in the group that would prevent the application of Baum, supra, to this case.

Questions

1. Given the result in this case, what is to prevent an employer from listing anyone as an insured under a group policy?

2. To what extent does the result in this case depend on the fact that the proceeds are payable to the deceased's estate rather than to the assured?

Even after the incontestability period has expired, an insurer still may raise certain challenges. These, however, involve matters not peculiarly within the assured's knowledge. They include lack of insurable interest, failure to pay premiums, failure to file proof of death as required by the policy terms, and proof that the risk leading to death was excluded from coverage under the policy. For example, an applicant for life insurance who has an aircraft pilot's license may be required to pay an additional premium for an "aviation rider" in order to be covered when piloting an aircraft. The same is true of applicants who are involved in other kinds of "hazardous" pursuits, such as race-car driving.

Two other matters are accorded special treatment concerning the contestability of a life insurance policy. They are misrepresentation of age and suicide. Age is a material factor in establishing the rate of premium the insured will pay, but ordinarily not in whether a policy will be issued. Therefore, if it is discovered that the insured's age has been misrepresented, the policy is not voided, and the insurer is required to pay benefits, but only in an amount that the premiums would have purchased given the correct age of the insured. Suicide is excluded from coverage because no risk would be involved, in the sense of defining the insurable risks as the intervention of an outside force against the will of the insured. However, most policies contain a **suicide clause** providing for coverage of death by suicide after a certain period of time elapses, commonly one or two years after the policy issues. The theory is that the passage of that length of time indicates that the insured is unlikely to have contemplated suicide seriously at the time of application, or at least would have changed his or her mind in the intervening period. Thereafter, suicide may be classified as an insurable casualty.

Cancellation

Usually, an insurance policy may not be cancelled during its stated term for reasons other than breach by the other party or some change in conditions that would excuse performance. However, because an insurance policy is a contract, either party ordinarily may elect not to renew for another period. It should be noted, however, that insurance law, particularly state insurance commission regulations, often restrict the insurer's freedom in this respect. For example, an insurance company may be prevented from cancelling arbitrarily, or arbitrarily raising a premium to force a policyholder to cancel. Instead, the company must state good cause. In addition, cancellation is not permitted for reasons that would offend public policy—for example, because a policyholder filed suit against the company over a benefit determination that the policyholder contested in good faith, or because of the insured's race, color, or membership in any other protected classification.

Assignment

The term *assignment* commonly is used in two contexts—to refer to the transfer of rights under a contract or, more broadly, to refer to the transfer of both rights and duties. Assignments are covered more fully in Chapter 11. However, some rules may be stated that relate specifically to insurance contracts.

The right of an insurer to premiums owed generally is freely assignable. Also, the duty to pay claims may be delegated, as may the duty of the assured to pay premiums. Of course, when a duty is delegated the party delegating remains liable on the policy should the delegate fail to perform. The only exception to this is in a case involving a *novation,* in which the person to whom the duty is owed agrees to discharge the party delegating and to look only to the delegate for performance.

The rules of assignment of rights by an assured are more complex. An insurance policy typically is considered a personal contract, and the assured's rights may not be assigned without the consent of the insurer, who is entitled to withhold consent, even without a reason. However, this does not prohibit an assignment of the right to proceeds *after a loss,* or to the assignment of the rights to the proceeds of a life insurance policy even during the lifetime of the insured. Also, an assignment of proceeds *as collateral,* even prior to loss, is recognized widely. For example, an owner of real estate ordinarily may assign the right to proceeds under a fire or property insurance policy to a mortgager of the property. In that case the risk of loss is not increased materially, if at all, because the policyholder remains the owner of the property.

Subrogation means that, upon payment of a loss under the policy, the insurer is entitled to have the rights of the assured against any third person who caused the loss. In essence, the insurer is an automatic assignee of the assured's rights. For example, if the insurance company pays a claim to its policyholder, Foote, resulting from an automobile accident caused by the negligence of Arms, upon payment of the claim the company is vested with Foote's rights against Arms, and may sue Arms and recover. However, the insurance company's rights are limited by the amount paid to Foote.

Two points concerning subrogation should be kept in mind. First, the proceeds of an insurance policy may not completely compensate the assured for the injury sustained. In that case, the insurer may have only an interest in any recovery from the wrongdoer, not the right to any portion of the claim in excess of the policy limits. Moreover, the wrongdoer is entitled to have the rights of both the assured and the insurer adjudicated in one lawsuit. Since the person injured is "the real party in interest" according to the law, the action probably would be brought in his name for the entire amount claimed. Second, if the assured releases the wrongdoer of liability, the assured is not entitled to proceeds under an applicable insurance policy, having thereby impaired the insurance company's rights against the wrongdoer.

DEFENSES OF THE INSURER

Because an insurance policy is a contract, an insurer has available the same defenses available to any other party in a contract action. These usually fall into two general classifications: (1) those that

make an insurance policy voidable by the insurer and (2) those that excuse the insurer's performance.

Grounds for Rescission

The first class of defenses relates to wrongs committed by the applicant, including misrepresentation, fraud, duress, undue influence, and mistake. These problems involve inducing the insurer to issue the policy in the first place. Proof of any of these entitles the insurer to rescind the contract. The most common of these, of course, are misrepresentation and fraud, followed at some distance by mistake. For example, an applicant for life or health insurance may misrepresent his or her state of health. An applicant for automobile insurance may misrepresent his or her driving record. These misrepresentations would entitle the insurer to cancel the policy—that is, to rescind the contract. If the misrepresentation was fraudulent (made knowingly, with intent to defraud, and an injury resulted to the insurer), the insurer would be entitled to elect to bring an action for money damages based on the tort of deceit instead of seeking rescission under the law of contracts.

There are two important limitations on an insurer's right to rescind. First, as was discussed previously in this chapter, most states require that life insurance policies include an incontestability clause providing that the insurer's right to rescind for problems terminates after a stated period, commonly two years. Second, in all cases of rescission by the insurer, the assured is entitled to return of the premiums paid.

Grounds for Nonperformance

The second class of defenses involve warranties by the assured. A *warranty* is a contractual promise. In the context of insurance law, a warranty is a statement or promise by the assured that becomes part of the contract itself instead of simply being a factor that induced the contract. If an applicant for life insurance misstated her state of health, that would be considered a misrepresentation only. The question would be, had the insurer known the applicant's true state of health, would the policy have been issued in the first place? If the applicant had misstated her age instead, the error would constitute a warranty that was breached immediately. The question would not be whether the insurer would have issued the policy, but what the premium would have been if the truth had been known.

There are two general types of warranties—affirmative warranties and continuing, or promissory, warranties. *Affirmative warranties* relate to facts existing at the time of the application. They either warrant that a fact exists or that a fact does not exist. For example, an applicant for life insurance may warrant that he is not, at the time, a licensed pilot. Although the applicant thereafter may become a licensed pilot, the affirmative warranty is not breached as long as it was true at the time of the application. *Continuing,* or *promissory warranties* relate to facts that must continue to exist during the life of the policy. For example, a fire insurance policy may provide that the insured premises is covered only as long as it is equipped with approved smoke detectors and a sprinkling system. If these were in place at the time of the application but later were removed or disabled, the warranty would be breached when the promised condition no longer existed.

In the event of a breach of either type of warranty, the insurer would not be liable to perform if a casualty occurred during the breach. One important exception to this rule was noted previously in this chapter: Most life insurance policies provide that if the insured's age is misstated, resulting in a material breach of warranty of age, the insurer will not be relieved of the obligation to pay on the policy, but payment will be in an amount that the premiums actually paid would have purchased at the correct age.

Waiver of Defenses

In addition to these limitations, an insurer may waive the right to assert defenses under some circumstances. These involve cases in which the insurer knows or has reason to know that a misrepresentation has been made, or that a mistake or a breach of warranty has occurred. If the insurer issues a policy with such knowledge or notice, or allows a policy to remain in effect, the insurer is not entitled to assert the defense and must perform. This may result from a waiver of a right by the insurer, an election among possible options by the insurer, or from the application of the principle of equitable estoppel. The first two result from affirmative steps by the insurer, and the last from operation of law in order to prevent injustice. For example, an insurer affirmatively may *waive* rating (charging a higher premium to) an applicant with a bad driving record or, upon later learning of the driving record, affirmatively may *elect* not to rate the assured, or may do nothing for more than a reasonable period of time, causing a court to *estop* the insurer from exercising its rights at a later time because it would be unfair for the insurer to do so.

The question of whether an insurer's defense is valid is not always as clear as it may seem. Consider the following case.

RYAN v. MFA MUTUAL INSURANCE COMPANY
610 S.W.2d 428 (Tenn. 1980)

This was an action by James Ryan (Plaintiff/Appellant) against MFA Mutual Insurance Company (Defendant/Appellee) to collect benefits under a fire insurance policy.

Plaintiff and his wife were co-insureds under a fire insurance policy issued on their house and its contents by Defendant. Plaintiff's wife set fire to the house.

She did so intentionally, without Plaintiff's consent or participation. Defendant refused to pay under the policy. Plaintiff contended that he should be paid benefits to the extent of his individual interest. The loss was $20,000 to the house and $10,000 to contents.

The trial court granted Defendant's motion to dismiss the complaint and Plaintiff appealed. Reversed and remanded.

DROWOTA, Justice.

Our research, along with that of the appellant, has brought to light ten jurisdictions, including Alabama, Michigan, and California, which would allow recovery under a policy such as the one herein at issue to an innocent co-insured whose interest in property, the loss of which was wrongfully caused by another co-insured, is severable from that of the other co-insured. In some of these jurisdictions, recovery would be allowed whether the property interest were several or joint, but we need not go so far in this case, as that issue is not before us. We find it sufficient to note that, as to the issue which is before us, a new "dominant line of authority" has emerged in the last two years, at least six of the cases in this line having been decided since 1978.

The earliest case in this new line is the Hoyt case . . . from New Hampshire, decided in 1942. In Hoyt one of three tenants in common intentionally burned the insured property. In holding that the two innocent co-insureds might recover under insurance policies each issued in all three names, the court considered how to construe the language in the policy:

> The mere fact that the language employed may be sufficient to "express a joint covenant" is not conclusive . . . whether the rights of obligees are joint or several is a question of construction . . . , and in construing an insurance contract the test is not what the insurance company intended the words of the policy to mean but what a reasonable person in the position of the insured would have understood them to mean. . . .
>
> The ordinary person owning an undivided interest in property, not versed in the nice distinctions of insurance law, would naturally suppose that his individual interest in the property was covered by a policy which named him without qualification as one of the persons insured. And the fact that under such circumstances the insurance company may have had good reasons for preferring to issue a joint policy . . . is unimportant unless those reasons were disclosed. . . .

Although, as we have indicated, this Court has stated that in a case such as this it would follow the "dominant line of authority," we have herein illustrated that a new "dominant line" has emerged since our decision in Cox, supra. We find this new majority rule to be better reasoned, and to produce a more equitable result.

We find that a reasonable person, reading the provisions in the policy at issue here which refer to fraud of "the insured," and neglect of "the insured," etc. would conclude that if an insured was guilty of fraud or neglect or increasing of hazard to property, then he or she may not recover under the policy. If the company wanted to assure its position, i.e. that misconduct of any insured would bar recovery by any other insured, it might have made it clear and unambiguous in the policy and it might have informed the prospective applicants for insurance of this position from the start.

It did not do so in this case and it is bound by the language it unilaterally drafted into the "contract" of insurance between the parties.

The law in Tennessee is that an insurance policy is construed more strongly against an insurer who has prepared it, and in favor of the insured. . . .

This being so, it necessarily results in this case that appellant Ryan should not be barred from recovery because of the misconduct of his wife in setting fire to their house, at least as to those items of contents in which he can show he had the sole or major and separable interest. As we have stated, we need go no further in our holding in regard to this case, since appellant seeks recovery only for items he claims belong to him.

Questions

1. What are the risks that are created by a rule that permits a co-insured to recover for conduct like that in the *Ryan* case? Is there any way to be fair to an innocent co-insured and, at the same time, reduce these risks?

2. Draft an insurance policy clause that would protect an insurance company against having to pay for a loss of the type incurred in *Ryan*. Would it be valid?

SUMMARY

Insurance involves a contract between two parties, under the terms of which an *insurer* promises an *assured* to indemnify the assured against specific, existing risks concerning an *insured* or his property. The assured and the insured usually are the same person. Among the common types of insurance are liability, fire, property, marine, life, and title insurance. Many principles of insurance law apply to all, and some are peculiar to particular types of policies.

Most types of insurance, other than life and health, are indemnity policies. The principle of indemnity is that insurance will pay no more than the amount of the loss. This seeks to prevent the use of insurance policies for purposes of gambling that money can be made on certain risks, and to lessen temptation to destroy property intentionally in order to collect the insurance.

Insurance contracts are governed by the same rules that apply to other kinds of contracts. The usual sequence of events is that a person applying for insurance will make an offer to purchase, an insurance company will accept by issuing the pol-

icy, and the consideration is in the form of a premium paid by the assured. The contract must be between parties having contractual capacity, or it will be voidable. It must be for a legal purpose, or it will be unenforceable. In addition, individual state statutes may require insurance contracts to be in writing, but not the general Statute of Frauds.

An assured must have an insurable interest in the life or property covered by the insurance policy. In the case of indemnity insurance, this requires both a legal interest and the possibility of financial loss from the stated risk. Life and health insurance require only the latter. Indemnity insurance also requires that the insurable interest exist both at the time the policy is issued and at the time of the casualty. Nonindemnity insurance requires only the latter.

As a general rule, an insurance policy becomes effective at the moment the insurer manifests a willingness to issue the policy. Frequently this is when the policy is delivered, but it may be before then, and even before the payment of a premium.

By policy provision, however, life insurance typically becomes effective only upon payment of the premium. In addition, if an applicant applies for insurance through an agent of the insurer rather than an independent broker, the agent usually is empowered to issue a binder covering the applicant between the time of application and the decision to issue a permanent policy.

Questions involving the interpretation of an insurance policy's language usually are dealt with as with other contracts, and ambiguities generally are resolved against the insurer. In addition, in recent years courts have shown a marked tendency to construe all language more in favor of the assured, because policies are drafted by the company and the purchaser really has no practical ability to negotiate a change in language. This has led many insurance companies to revise their policies, stating provisions in more commonly understood language.

Insurers typically are more restricted in their rights to cancel policies than parties to other kinds of contracts. These restrictions come from statutes and regulations of the state insurance commissions and are designed to protect the consumer of insurance. Good cause usually must be shown and notice is required.

Insurance contracts may be assigned, but any assignment that would change the obligation of the other party materially or increase the risk to that party is prohibited unless the other party consents. The right to receive proceeds after a loss has occurred normally is assignable, but the right to be insured is not. One type of assignment is permitted, and even occurs by operation of law. That is subrogation, which means that when an insurer pays a claim that has arisen as a result of wrongdoing by a third party, the insurer is entitled to any rights the assured had against that third party that relate to the claim.

An insurer has the same rights to avoid a contract, or to refuse to perform, as any other party to a contract, unless limited by state statute or regulation. Grounds for rescission include misrepresentation, fraud, duress, undue influence, and mistake. If fraud is involved, the insurer may elect money damages instead of rescission. Breach of warranty entitles the insurer to refuse to perform. Warranties are facts or conditions that must exist, or not exist, as terms of the policy in question. An insurer, however, may be deprived of this right by waiver, election, the application of the principles of equitable estoppel, or by the terms of an incontestable clause. Incontestable clauses ordinarily are required in life insurance contracts by state law.

KEY TERMS AND CONCEPTS

McCarren-Ferguson Act
insurance
gambling
assured
beneficiary
hazard
insured
insurer
policy
liability insurance
no-fault liability
fire and property insurance
mysterious disappearance
friendly fire
marine insurance
life insurance
key-man insurance
term life insurance
straight or whole life insurance
title insurance
indemnity
co-insurance
insurable interest
binder
incontestability clause
suicide clause
subrogation

PROBLEMS

1. D'Alassandro owned an automobile insured by Bulldog Insurance. After the automobile was stolen, he assigned his claim under the policy to Ginsburg. The insurance company refused to pay the proceeds to Ginsburg because of a policy provision that stated: "No assignment of interest under this policy shall be binding upon the association unless the written consent of the attorney is indorsed thereon and an additional membership fee paid." Was the company within its rights?

2. Youse was carrying her diamond ring in her handkerchief one day. When she arrived at home, she placed the handkerchief and kleenex on her dresser. The maid picked it up, placed it along with trash in a trash burner, and set fire to the accumulation. The ring was damaged to the extent of $900. The insurance company refused to pay under a fire insurance policy on the ground that the damage resulted from a friendly fire. Should the insurance company pay the claim?

3. Roy was injured in an accident. He was unable to work for a year. He went back to work and five months later he had surgery to remove a traumatic cataract caused by the accident. Thereafter, he was unable to wear a special contact lens. As a result he had almost no vision in one eye. He claimed benefits under an insurance policy providing payment for "total and irrevocable loss of the entire sight of one eye." The company refused to pay, contending the loss of sight was not complete, and the eye would be usable if it wasn't for Roy's inability to wear the contact lens. Should the claim be paid?

4. David Noah purchased three life insurance policies on his brother, William—one for $1500 plus double indemnity in the case of accidental death, one for $1000 plus double indemnity, and a burial policy providing for the payment of certain funeral expenses. William was killed in an automobile accident, but the insurance company refused to pay on the ground that David did not have an insurable interest in William's life. Is the company correct? Why or why not?

5. Edwards sold his car, but later found the check received in payment was worthless. He sought to collect on his insurance policy claiming theft of the car. The insurance company refused to pay on the ground that although the term *theft* was not defined in the policy, the transaction in question certainly never was intended to be included in the definition. Should the claim be paid?

6. Mrs. Moore made application for an accidental death policy for her husband and paid a premium. Three weeks later she inquired about the policy, but the agent had heard nothing. Two or three weeks before her husband was killed, she inquired again and was told, by the agent, that he thought it had come in, and he would let her know in a few days. She heard nothing more, but several days after her husband was killed she was notified that her application had been rejected. Should the company be required to pay on the policy anyway?

7. Pioneer employed Secor. The company purchased a $50,000 key-man policy on his life. Secor continued the employment for nine years, and within a year after he left for another job he died. Mrs. Secor sued to have the proceeds of the policy paid to her instead of Pioneer on the ground that, at the time of death, Pioneer no longer had an insurable interest in Secor's life. Is Mrs. Secor correct?

8. Scarola purchased a car he did not know was stolen. When it was recovered by its owner, he filed a claim on his insurance policy for the loss. The insurance company refused to pay on the ground that since the car was stolen, Scarola did not have an insurable interest. Is the company correct?

9. Mattson purchased an automobile insurance policy, falsely stating that he had no prior cancellations. Six-and-one-half months later, his son was involved in an accident. The other party, who was injured, claimed against her own policy and assigned to the company (Hawkeye Ins.) her rights against Mattson. After the claim was filed with Mattson's insurance company, it refused to pay, having discovered the misrepresentation, and tendered return of Mattson's premium. Mattson and Hawkeye contended that the policy could not be voided, saying the misrepresentation was harmless because Mattson's son had the accident. Is this contention correct?

10. Lewis owned a home on Dixwell Avenue in New Haven, which she insured with Michigan Millers Insurance Company. She had purchased the policy through Cahn, an insurance broker. When she moved to a new home on Read Street, without selling the other one, she asked Cahn to send new premium notices to her new address. Cahn misunderstood, and had the insurance policy on her Dixwell Avenue home switched to cover her Read Street home. Her Dixwell Avenue home burned, and when the insurance company refused the claim, Lewis first learned of the mixup. Her Read Street home was insured by another company. Is Lewis entitled to recover from Michigan Millers for her loss anyway?

Chapter | 54

Accountants' Professional Liability

_____

_____

_____

_____

OUTLINE

INTRODUCTION

The liability of an accountant is generally the same as that of any other employee, which is discussed broadly in Chapters 32 and 33. A review of those chapters, therefore, is recommended. This chapter will focus primarily on the liability of accountants as independent contractors, applying the important general concepts discussed earlier.

An accountant's liability may be both criminal and civil, and the latter may flow to the accountant's employer or to some third party, such as a stockholder or a lender who relied on the accuracy of financial statements or other work and opinions of the accountant. The primary source of civil liability is the common law of contracts and torts. However, significant liability also may arise from state statutes, and particularly the federal Securities Act of 1933, Securities Exchange Act of 1934, and Internal Revenue Code. Criminal liability, similarly, may be founded on either state or federal statutes, especially the securities acts and the Internal Revenue Code.

Because of the nature of the accountant-client relationship, additional considerations that usually are not present in other employment relationships merit special attention. These involve the handling of clients' records, the treatment of the accountant's working papers, the extent of the confidential relationship between the accountant and client, and the limits of disclosure of communications.

THE RELATIONSHIP BETWEEN ACCOUNTANT AND CLIENT

The relationship between an accountant and his or her client is normally one of *independent contractor* and employer. This means that an accountant ordinarily works for more than one client, and the details of the performance of the work undertaken are not subject to detailed control by the client. Instead, an accountant usually is asked to produce an end product, and the details of performance are left to his professional judgment. The work may involve establishing an accounting system, conducting an audit of financial records, or rendering an opinion concerning financial data or statements.

In exercising professional judgment in the conduct of each task assigned, an accountant is bound to act within the limits of **generally accepted accounting principles.** These standards, however, are only parameters. Acting outside their limits raises a presumption of malpractice, but acting within them does not assure an accountant that she is free of liability. The circumstances of each case must be considered, and an accountant is expected to act appropriately. The two primary sources of accepted standards are the American Institute of Certified Public Accountants (AICPA) and the Financial Accounting Standards Board (FASB).

Duty Not to Practice Law

Accountants frequently find themselves walking a thin, and often blurred, line between the practice of accounting and the practice of law, particularly in the contexts of tax and securities law. An accountant must have some knowledge of the legal significance of the activities of his client, and of particular transactions, in order to reflect their nature and materiality properly in all accounting services rendered to a client. An accountant also may apply legal knowledge and answer questions in connection with his ordinary work as an accountant. However, an accountant must be careful to avoid giving legal advice or rendering legal opinions disassociated with that work, because that would be practicing law without a license.

Communications to Client

An accountant is obligated to make a *fair and complete disclosure* to each client of all facts and matters relevant to the duties assigned. Precisely what this entails depends on each client's unique characteristics and the circumstances of each engagement. It may not be sufficient simply to comply with generally accepted accounting principles and **generally accepted auditing standards.** A full disclosure in technical terms not understandable to a client does not fulfill this obligation. Today, more than in the past, courts tend to evaluate the fullness and fairness of disclosures in terms of what actually has been communicated in each case. That is, they consider whether the information was meaningful to the particular client.

Confidential Information

In the ordinary course of completing an audit or other accounting service, an accountant may come into possession of confidential information concerning a client or the client's business. This may involve information about purely personal business, or may be information constituting a trade secret. The communication of either to others by the accountant may result in personal tort liability.

Communication of personal, nonpublic information may constitute the tort of defamation, or of invasion of the client's privacy. These companion torts generally are distinguished on two grounds: (1) defamation usually relates to a person's reputation, and privacy to a person's peace of mind and solitude; and (2) truth ordinarily is a complete defense to an action for defamation, but not to an invasion of privacy action. Information concerning the personal finances of an officer of a corporate client, or her personal or domestic life, are examples of the type of information that can get an accountant into trouble. These torts are covered more fully in Chapter 4.

A trade secret is any information about a client's business operation that is not generally known, and that gives the client a competitive advantage over others who do not use or know the information. This advantage may include a method of doing business, a process, a formula, or a list of names of customers with whom the client does business. Wrongful disclosure of this information by an accountant constitutes an independent tort.

Contract Liability

Typically, a contract forms the basis of an accountant-client relationship, although the relationship may be formed without a contract. When the latter is true, the obligations of the accountant are prescribed primarily by agency and tort law. However, the absence of a formal written agreement does not mean a contract does not exist.

The duties under an accountant-client contract may be either express or implied. The vast majority are implied. When a contract exists, ordinarily there is no requirement that it be in writing unless the services of the accountant are to extend over a stated period of more than one year, which brings the Statute of Frauds into operation. However, if a written contract is signed, it is important that it fully and accurately reflects the agreement of the parties. Later oral testimony concerning any incompleteness or inaccuracy of the writing often would be prohibited by the Parol Evidence Rule. The need for a writing under the Statute of Frauds and admissibility of oral evidence under the Parol Evidence Rule are discussed more fully in Chapter 10.

An accountant's failure properly to discharge his duties under a contract, whether express or implied, constitutes a breach of the contract, subjecting the accountant to liability and the payment of damages. If the accountant is a partnership, which is very common, the obligations under the contract frequently will be delegated to an employee. However, the partnership will remain liable to the client if the services are not performed properly by the employee. Of course, the same is true of any delegation of performance by a professional corporation or even a sole proprietor.

The following factors are considered in determining whether an accountant has fulfilled his contract. *First,* specific obligations must be performed. For example, an audit must be completed, and specific reports must be made. *Second,* accounting services performed must comply with generally accepted accounting standards and practices. For example, an accountant is required to study and evaluate the internal control procedures of the client in order to determine what procedures and tests are necessary for the proper conduct of an audit. Uniformed reliance on information and data supplied by the client is a breach of this standard. *Third,* within prescribed standards and practices, an accountant must perform all duties with the degree of care, skill, and knowledge that reasonably can be expected of members of the profession. For example, data gathered during an audit may be contradictory, indicating a need for a different or closer examination. Failure to notice the contradiction, to understand its significance, or to pursue other lines of inquiry may render the accountant liable for breach of contract. Although an acountant may be liable for mistakes, he is not a guarantor of the financial statements.

An accountant's failure to perform any part of a contract may constitute breach. However, two general types of duties may arise under a contract—those that can be performed with precision, and those that can be performed only within general limits. For example, an accountant can do data transfers, and mathematical and statistical calculations precisely. However, the duty accurately to reflect relevant information in a clear and understandable way in the client's financial statements, by definition, is subjective, and given to some variation within reasonable limits. Therefore the two possible types of duties require different proofs of breach.

A breach of contract may be either material or insubstantial. A material breach occurs when the client receives no real benefit from the accountant's performance. For example, the accountant may fail to complete an audit, or fail to report the results on time when time is of the essence. When an accountant commits a material breach, he is not entitled to compensation, and is liable to pay damages for any injuries to the client that result either directly or consequentially from the breach. If the breach is an insubstantial one, such as a slight inaccuracy in completing the audit or report, the accountant is entitled to compensation but also is liable for any resulting damage.

Professional Tort Liability

The professional tort liability of an accountant to a client is based on the general principles of **negligence** (malpractice) or fraud. The majority of cases, of course, involve negligence.

The duty of care of a professional, such as an accountant, is not measured by the general "reasonable person" standard applied in ordinary cases, as discussed in Chapter 4. Instead, the standard is the degree of care that would be exercised by the average accountant under like circumstances. The question is not one of intent, but one of quality, accuracy, and completeness of the accountant's work. Even honest inaccuracies and simple errors in judgment may violate the standard. For example, the failure to notice that certain major assets of a client are overvalued slightly may not constitute negligence, but the failure to notice that it is greatly overvalued or that the claimed assets do not exist probably would. The accountant's liability for damages resulting from her negligence is generally the same as that for breach of contract. That would be damages to compensate the client for all losses that flow directly or consequentially from the negligence. Consider the following case involving negligence by an accountant.

1136 TENANTS' CORPORATION v. MAX ROTHENBERG & COMPANY
36 App. Div. 2d 804, 319 N.Y.S. 2d 1007 (1971)

This was an action by 1136 Tenants' Corporation (Plaintiff/Respondent) against Max Rothenberg & Company (Defendant/Appellant) to recover damages for negligence in performing accounting services.

Plaintiff, the owner of an apartment house, hired Defendant, a certified public accounting firm, to perform accounting services in connection with its apartment building. The building was managed by Riker & Co., which had collected maintenance fees from tenants and had not paid certain bills of Plaintiff as it was supposed to do. Each month, Riker submitted a statement to Defendant listing all collections and payments. Substantial amounts of alleged payments were not supported by invoices, and this fact was never disclosed by Defendant to Plaintiff. The parties disagreed as to whether Defendant was employed to audit the management of the business, or only to "write up" receipts and disbursements.

The trial court found for Plaintiff in the amount of $237,278.83 and Defendant appealed. Affirmed.

PER CURIAM.

The record amply supports the Trial Court's findings that defendant was engaged to audit and not merely "write-up" plaintiff's books and records and that the procedures performed by defendant were "incomplete, inadequate and improperly employed". One of defendant's senior partners admitted at the trial that defendant performed services for plaintiff which went beyond the scope of a "write-up" and that it actually performed some auditing procedures for plaintiff. Defendant's worksheets indicate that defendant did examine plaintiff's bank statement, invoices and bills and, in fact, one of the worksheets is entitled "Missing Invoices 1/1/63–12/31/63" (plaintiff's exhibit 16-B-6). That sheet alone indicates invoices missing from the records of Riker & Co. which totalled more than $44,000.

Utilization of the simplest audit procedures would have revealed Riker's defalcations. Moreover, even if defendant were hired to perform only "writeup" services, it is clear, beyond dispute, that it did become aware that material invoices purportedly paid by Riker were missing, and, accordingly, had a duty to at least inform plaintiff of this. But even this it failed to do. Defendant was not free to consider these and other suspicious circumstances as being of no significance and prepare its financial reports as if same did not exist.

Questions

1. Is there any reason why an accountant's conduct should be judged more stringently than the performance of any other employee for purposes of determining negligence?

2. Is the burden of inquiry on an accountant so heavy that, as a practical matter, she is being held strictly liable for her errors? Does this case so hold? Should the law hold a professional, such as an accountant, strictly liable?

An accountant's tort liability for fraud rests on intent. As in other contexts, **fraud** involves: (1) a misrepresentation, (2) of material fact, (3) knowingly made, (4) with intent to defraud, (5) justifiable reliance by the client, and (6) a resulting injury to the client.

A misrepresentation ordinarily is a direct misstatement. However, a concealment of the truth also may be actionable. For example, leaving facts or data out of a report may constitute misrepresentation as well as misstating a result or the significance of particular findings.

The misrepresentation must be of fact. Ordinarily, that means a past or present fact, and not merely speculation about the future. However, forecasts by one who holds herself out as being capable of accurately forcasting may be considered statements of fact. Therefore, an accountant should avoid speculating as to the future. In addition, the fact misrepresented must be material.

That is, it must be of sufficient importance that someone relying on the statement might have chosen a different course of action had the truth been known.

The misrepresentation must be knowingly made. The accountant must either know that the statement is not true, or make it recklessly. For example, an accountant might report that the client owns 500 tons of a particular grain in storage unit, but has made no effort to verify the fact. If the fact is materially untrue, liability for fraud may result.

The single element most distinguishing fraud from negligence and simple breach of contract is that of *intent* to defraud. The motive must be one to cause the client to rely on the accountant to his or her detriment. Simply relying on information given by an employee of the client, with no attempt to verify it, may constitute negligence or recklessness, and breach of contract if the information is incorrect, but it would not constitute active fraud.

As to justifiable reliance, the fifth element, a client ordinarily is entitled to rely on the audit and report of an accountant. However, reliance is not justified if the client either knows, or has reason to know, that data or a statement is inaccurate. This may be because the client knows or should suspect the source of the information, or because the results appear to be inaccurate.

Finally, the client must be injured by the misrepresentation, which means suffering a financial loss or damage to the client's business or commerical reputation. Fraud in the abstract is not actionable.

When these elements have been met, the accountant is liable for damages to the same extent as in an action for breach of contract or negligence. However, in addition, the accountant also may be required to pay *punitive (or exemplary) damages.* These are damages in addition to the normal *compensatory damages,* and are awarded to punish a wrongdoer and to deter her, and others by example, from committing fraud in the future.

They are awarded at the discretion of the court or jury, and in an amount considered necessary in each particular case, and only in cases involving *scienter* (an evil mind).

Compensation for Services

Compensation for an accountant's services usually is provided for in the contract of employment. If not, he is entitled to reasonable compensation, unless the services were performed under circumstances that led the client reasonably to believe that the services were being rendered as a gift. Those, of course, would be unusual circumstances. Note, however, that the accountant has no unilateral power to impose an amount for a fee. The compensation must be agreed upon between the parties or established by a court in the event of a dispute. The accountant does not have a common law lien on a client's materials he has in possession, but may have a statutory lien by virtue of improvements to the client's books. This varies from state to state.

THE RELATIONSHIP TO THIRD PARTIES

An accountant performing services for a client usually has no legal relationship to third parties. Therefore the accountant has no obligation to third parties and, as a result, no liability. However, liability may arise from any of four sources, under appropriate circumstances: (1) a third-party beneficiary contract, (2) fraud, (3) negligence, or (4) federal statute.

Contract

The usual contract of employment entered into between an accountant and a client is for the benefit of them only. However, under some circumstances, a contract may be in part for the benefit of a particular third person or third persons. For example, an accountant may be employed for the purpose of preparing financial statements to be presented with a loan application at a particular bank. In this case, the bank is a third-party beneficiary of the contract between the accountant and the client and, as such, is a party to the contract. Any breach of the contract that causes injury to the bank will entitle it to recover damages from the accountant. Essentially, a third-party beneficiary is treated the same as any other party to a contract. Third-party beneficiary contracts are discussed more fully in Chapter 11.

Fraud

The elements of fraud, already discussed relative to the liability of an accountant to a client, apply equally to liability to third parties. The duty to perform accounting services without fraud is owed to the general public. A third party who has relied reasonably on the accountant's work is entitled to compensatory damages for any resulting injuries, and possibly punitive damages, regardless of whether the work product was intended primarily for that party's use.

Negligence

The extent to which an accountant may be liable to third parties for ordinary negligence is not entirely settled. Disagreement focuses on whether *privity* is necessary to entitle third parties to sue an accountant for negligence in the performance of an audit and the preparation of resulting financial statements. **Privity** means that parties are contractually related. That is, the person suing the accountant must be a direct party, an assignee, or a third-party beneficiary of a contract with the accountant. In the 1931 landmark decision in Ultramares Corp. v. Touche, the New York Court of Appeals, that state's highest court, held that privity was necessary. Today, a majority of the states still follow the reasoning of that decision. However, some have expanded an auditor's liability, allowing recovery by parties not in privity, such as lenders who relied on statements in extending loans, even though the statements were not prepared for the purpose of obtaining those particular loans. Three courts to date (New Jersey, Wisconsin, and California) have found liability on an even broader scale, rendering auditors liable to all foreseeable parties. As the next two cases graphically demonstrate, the law on the point is unsettled, and there is considerable doubt as to what the trend is. Keep in mind that the following cases involve an accountant's liability for negligence, even though fraud is alleged in both of them.

H. ROSENBLUM, INC. v. ADLER
93 N.J. 324, 461 A.2d 138 (1983)

This was an action by H. Rosenblum, Inc. and its owners (Plaintiffs/Appellants) against Jack F. Adler and 426 others, partners in the accounting firm, Touche Ross & Co. (Defendants/Respondents) for negligence and fraud in the preparation of financial statements.

Defendants were employed to complete an audit and prepare financial statements for Giant Stores Corporation. Relying on these statements, Plaintiffs acquired common stock in Giant in conjunction with the sale of their business to Giant. The stock proved to be worthless and the financial statements fraudulent. Plaintiff alleged Defendants were negligent in the conduct of the audit upon which the statements were based. The question before the court was whether a third party could maintain a suit for negligence of Defendants in the conduct of an audit for their client.

The trial court granted Defendants' motion for a summary judgment on the negligence claim. This decision was affirmed by the Superior Court, Appellate Division, and Plaintiff appealed. Reversed and remanded.

SCHREIBER, J.

Recovery of economic loss, due to negligent misrepresentation by one furnishing a service, has long been permitted when there existed a direct contractual relationship between the parties or when the injured third party was a known beneficiary of the defendant's undertaking. . . .

Our case law, however, has been split on whether privity or a similar relationship is necessary in a suit against the supplier of a service for negligent misrepresentation causing economic loss.

Kahl v. Love, 37 N.J.L. 5 (Sup.Ct.1873), is probably the first reported New Jersey negligent misrepresentation case concerned with a service resulting in economic loss. Defendant was the Jersey City collector of taxes. Upon receiving the check of a landowner in payment of taxes, defendant gave the landowner a receipt in full. The land, the subject of these taxes, was sold to the plaintiff, who relied on the receipt as proof of payment of the taxes. The check was later dishonored and taxes were levied on the lands after the plaintiff acquired title. The plaintiff sued the collector for the damages suffered and obtained a judgment. The Supreme Court reversed, citing both the absence of a duty and the unreasonableness of the plaintiff's reliance. The Court assumed that the defendant knew that these receipts were used on the sale of land to establish that taxes were paid up. It held that a duty, arising from contract or otherwise, had to exist before liability could ensue. Chief Justice Beasley, writing on behalf of the Court, stated:

> Such a restriction on the right to sue for a want of care in the exercise of employments or the transaction of business, is plainly necessary to restrain the remedy from being pushed to an impracticable extreme. There would be no bounds to actions and litigious intricacies, if the ill effects of the negligence of men could be followed down the chain of results to the final effect.

A more recent lower court decision has held to the contrary. In Immerman v. Ostertag, 83 N.J. Super. 364, 199 A.2d 869 (Law Div. 1964), the court stated that a notary public owes a duty to third persons who rely on his acknowledgment to refrain from acts or omissions that constitute negligence. Immerman accepted the proposition that "an acknowledgment-taking officer has a duty to refrain from acts or omissions which constitute negligence, a duty which he owes not only to persons with whom he has privity, but also to any member of the public who, in reasonable contemplation, might rely upon the officer's certification." . . . This Court has approvingly cited Immerman as articulating the general rule with respect to notaries. . . .

Similarly, lack of privity has been held not to bar the liability of an independent contractor engaged to perform services for his negligent nonfeasance. . . .

We have never passed upon the problem of an accountant's liability to third persons who have relied on negligently audited statements to their economic detriment. Many other jurisdictions have limited an accountant's liability to those with whom the accountant is in privity. The earliest decision in the United States our research has uncovered is Landell v. Lybrand, 264 Pa. 406, 107 A. 783 (1919), holding that an accountant was not liable for misstatements in a company's financial statements to a third person who had relied upon the financials and had purchased the company's stock. The leading opinion is that of Chief Judge Cardozo in Ultramares v. Touche. . . . In rejecting a claim against an accounting firm for a negligent audit relied upon by a third person who advanced credit to the firm's client he wrote:

> If liability for negligence exists, a thoughtless slip or blunder, the failure to detect a theft or forgery beneath the cover of deceptive entries, may expose accountants to a liability in an indeterminate amount for an indeterminate time to an indeterminate class. The hazards of a business conducted on these terms are so extreme as to enkindle doubt whether a flaw may not exist in the implication of a duty that exposes to these consequences. . . .

Chief Judge Cardozo, like Chief Justice Beasley in Kahl, believed that imposition of this type of exposure would be an undue burden upon the declarants, when balanced against the functions they performed. . . .

> Many commentators have questioned the wisdom of Ultramares and Glanzer. . . . Criticism of the primary benefit rule led in part to the adoption of Section 552 of the Restatement (Second) of Torts, which limited liability for negligent misrepresentation to the loss suffered (a) by the person or one of a limited group of persons for whose benefit and guidance he intends to supply the information or knows that the recipient intends to supply it; and (b) through reliance upon it in a transaction that he [the auditor] intends the information to influence or knows that the recipient so intends or in a substantially similar transaction.

When applied to an auditor, the Restatement limits the persons to whom he owes a duty to his client, to intended identifiable beneficiaries and to any unidentified member of the intended class of beneficiaries. The only extension in the Restatement beyond Ultramares and Glanzer appears to be that the auditor need not know the identity of the beneficiaries if they belong to an identifiable group for whom the information was intended to be furnished. There is a substantial split of authority among the courts, some following Ultramares and others adopting the Restatement. See Annot., "Liability of public accountant to third parties," 46 A.L.R.3d 979, 989 (1972). . . .

There remains to be considered whether the public interest will be served by a proposition holding an auditor responsible for negligence to those persons who the auditor should reasonably foresee will be given the audit to rely upon and do in fact place such reliance on the audit to their detriment. Should there be such a duty imposed? Chief Justice Weintraub in Goldberg v. Housing Auth. of Newark, 38 N.J. 578, 583, 186 A.2d 291, (1962), explained the judicial analysis that must be made:

> Whether a duty exists is ultimately a question of fairness. The inquiry involves a weighing of the relationship of the parties, the nature of the risk, and the public interest in the proposed solution. . . .

When the independent auditor furnishes an opinion with no limitation in the certificate as to whom the company may disseminate the financial statements, he has a duty to all those whom that auditor should reasonably foresee as recipients from the company of the statements for its proper business purposes, provided that the recipients rely on the statements pursuant to those business purposes. The principle that we have adopted applies by its terms only to those foreseeable users who receive the audited statements from the business entity for a proper business purpose to influence a business decision of the user, the audit having been made for that business entity. Thus, for example, an institutional investor or portfolio manager who does not obtain audited statements from the company would not come within the stated principle. Nor would stockholders who purchased the stock after a negligent audit be covered in the absence of demonstrating the necessary conditions precedent. Those and similar cases beyond the stated rule are not before us and we express no opinion with respect to such situations.

Certified financial statements have become the benchmark for various reasonably foreseeable business purposes and accountants have been engaged to satisfy those ends. In those circumstances accounting firms should no longer be permitted to hide within the citadel of privity and avoid liability for their malpractice. The public interest will be served by the rule we promulgate this day. . . .

Irrespective of whether the defendants had actual knowledge of Giant's proposed use of the 1972 audit in connection with the merger, it was reasonably foreseeable that Giant would use the audited statement in connection with the merger and its consummation. This is particularly so since the defendants were familiar with the merger agreement and had been engaged by Giant to audit the books and records of the plaintiffs' enterprises for the purpose of the merger. . . .

Questions

1. As a practical matter, does this case impose any real limitations on an accountant's liability to third persons for economic loss? Can you describe these limitations?
2. Who, if anyone, among the general public would be excluded as being a foreseeable third person? Why?

In the following case, the New York Court of Appeals reconsidered its decision in *Ultramares* in light of modern developments. In doing so, the court determined that the public policy underlying its decision in *Ultramares* remained valid.

CREDIT ALLIANCE CORPORATION et al. v. ARTHUR ANDERSON & CO.
493 N.Y.S.2d 435, 483 N.E.2d 110 (1985)

This was an action by Credit Alliance Corporation (Plaintiff/Respondent) against Arthur Anderson & Co. (Defendant/Appellant) for negligence and fraud in the preparation of financial statements.

Plaintiff extended major financing to L. B. Smith of Virginia during 1978 and 1979. A condition of the financing, during both years, was that Smith provide Plaintiff with audited financial statements. Smith submitted consolidated statements that had been prepared for the company (Smith) by Defendant, a national accounting firm. It was alleged that these statements overstated Smith's assets, net worth, and general financial condition, resulting because of Defendant's failure to follow proper procedures in the conduct of the audits.

The trial court found for Plaintiff on both counts (negligence and fraud). The Appellate Division affirmed on both counts, and Defendant appealed. Reversed.

JASEN, Judge.

In the seminal case of Ultramares Corp. v. Touche & Co. (255 N.Y. 170), this court, speaking through the opinion of Chief Judge Cardozo more than fifty years ago, disallowed a cause of action in negligence against a public accounting firm for inaccurately prepared financial statements which were relied upon by a plaintiff having no contractual privity with the accountants. This court distinguished its holding from Glanzer v. Shepard (233 N.Y. 236), a case decided in an opinion also written by Cardozo nine years earlier. We explained that in Glanzer, an action in negligence against public weighers had been permitted, despite the absence of a contract between the parties, because the plaintiff's intended reliance, on the information directly transmitted by the weighers, created a bond so closely approaching privity that it was, in practical effect, virtually indistinguishable therefrom. This court has subsequently reaffirmed its holding in Ultramares which has been, and continues to be, much discussed and analyzed by the commentators and by the courts of other jurisdictions. These appeals now provide us with the opportunity to reexamine and delineate the principles enunciated in both Ultramares and Glanzer. Inasmuch as we believe that a relationship "so close as to approach that of privity" (255 N.Y., at pp. 182–183) remains valid as the predicate for imposing liability upon accountants to non-contractual parties for the negligent preparation of financial reports, we restate and elaborate upon our adherence to that standard today. . . .

[In *Ultramares* we] acknowledged that inroads had been made, for example, where third party beneficiaries or dangerous instrumentalities were involved. (Id, at p. 181.) Indeed, we referred to this court's holding in MacPherson v. Buick Motor Co. (217 N.Y. 382) where it was decided that the manufacturer of a defective chattel—there an automobile—may be liable in negligence for the resulting injuries sustained by a user regardless of the absence of privity—a belated rejection of the doctrine of privity as applied to the facts in Winterbottom. Nevertheless, regarding an accountant's liability to unknown parties with whom he had not contracted, the considerations were deemed sufficiently dissimilar to justify different treatment. . . .

The critical distinctions between [Ultramares and Glanzer] were highlighted in Ultramares, where we explained:

> In Glanzer v. Shepard, . . . [the certificate of weight], which was made out in duplicate, one copy to the seller and the other to the buyer, recites that it was made by order of the former for the use of the latter. . . . Here was something more than the rendition of a service in the expectation that the one who ordered the certificate to another was not merely one possibility among many, but the end and aim of the transaction, as certain and immediate and deliberately willed as if a husband were to order a gown to be delivered to his wife, or a telegraph company, contracting with the sender of a message, were to telegraph it wrongly

to the damage of the person expected to receive it. . . . The intimacy of the resulting nexus is attested by the fact that after stating the case in terms of legal duty, we went on to point out that . . . we could reach the same result by stating it in terms of contract. . . .

Several years subsequent to the decision in Ultramares, this court reiterated the requirement for a "contractual relationship or its equivalent" (State Street Trust Co. v. Ernst, 278 N.Y. 104, 111), and more recently, in White v. Guarente (43 N.Y. 2d 356), such an equivalent was presented for our consideration. There, the accountants had contracted with a limited partnership to perform an audit and prepare the partnership's tax returns. The nature and purpose of the contract, to satisfy the requirement in the partnership agreement for an audit, made it clear that the accountants' services were obtained to benefit the members of the partnership who, like plaintiff, a limited partner, were necessarily dependent upon the audit to prepare their own tax returns. After outlining the principles articulated in Ultramares and Glanzer, this court observed that:

> The plaintiff seeks redress, not as a mere member of the public, but as one of a settled and particularized class among the members of which the report would be circulated for the specific purpose of fulfilling the limited partnership agreed upon arrangement. . . .
>
> Because the accountants knew that a limited partner would have to rely upon the audit and tax returns of the partnership, and inasmuch as this was within the specific contemplation of the accounting retainer, we held that, "at least on the facts here, and accountant's liability may be so imposed." . . . The resulting relationship between the accountants and the limited partner was clearly one "approach[ing] that of privity, if not completely one with it. . . .

Upon examination of Ultramares and Glanzer and our recent affirmation of their holdings in White, certain criteria may be gleaned. Before accountants may be held liable in negligence to noncontractual parties who rely to their detriment on inaccurate financial reports, certain prerequisites must be satisfied: (1) the accountants must have been aware that the financial reports were to be used for a particular purpose or purposes; (2) in the furtherance of which a known party or parties was intended to rely; and (3) some conduct on the part of the accountants linking them to that party or parties, which evinces the accountants' understanding of that party or parties' reliance. While these criteria permit some flexibility in the application of the doctrine of privity to accountants' liability, they do not represent a departure from the principles articulated in Ultramares, Glanzer and White, but, rather, they are intended to preserve the wisdom and policy set forth therein.

We are aware that the courts throughout this country are divided as to the continued validity of the holding in Ultramares. Some courts continue to insist that a rather strict application of the privity requirement governs the law of accountants' liability except, perhaps, where special circumstances compel a different result. . . . On the other hand, an increasing number of courts have adopted what they deem to be a more flexible approach then that permitted under this court's past decisions. . . .

In all of the foregoing cases, the courts found the facts amenable to the imposition of accountants' liability under the principles of Ultramares-Glanzer or extended those principles to permit a more liberalized application. To the extent that the holdings in those cases are predicated upon certain criteria—to wit, a particular purpose for the accountants' report, a known relying party, and some conduct on the part of the accountants linking them to that party—they are consonant with the principles reaffirmed in this decision. To the extent, however, that those cases were decided upon the ground that Ultramares should not be followed and, instead, a rule permitting recovery by any foreseeable plaintiff should be adopted, the law in this State, as reiterated today, is clearly distinguishable.

[Another case on similar facts, *European American Bank and Trust Company v. Strauhs & Kaye,* was joined with *Ultramares Credit Alliance* for decision. In that case, however, the evidence demonstrated that the defendant accounting firm knew that the primary, if not exclusive, purpose of the audit of its client, Majestic Electro, was to produce financial statements that were required by the plaintiff, European American Bank. Because of that fact, the court held that the defendant could be liable to the plaintiff for negligence in the preparation of the financial statements involved.]

Questions

1. Reading the language of the court in this case very, very carefully, is it clear that the court is simply reaffirming its decision in *Ultramares?*
2. Can you tell the difference between the rule in the *Rosenblum* case and the rule in this case?
3. Why is the New York court afraid to expand the rule in *Ultramares?* Is it simply a matter of blind adherence to a precedent?
4. Is there any other standard that might be used to measure an accountant's liability to third persons for negligence?

The Securities Act of 1933

This act, also known as the "Truth In Securities Act," seeks to ensure that the public is provided with complete and accurate information concerning securities that are offered for sale to the public through the mails or in interstate commerce, as discussed more fully in Chapter 47. The registration statement that must be filed with the Securities and Exchange Commission (SEC) prior to the offering must be accompanied by financial statements certified by an independent public accountant. Although the certifying accountant need not be a CPA, invariably a CPA is used. The act places upon the certifying accountant a duty to make a full and accurate disclosure of all material facts relevant to the offering. Any failure to com-ply with this duty will render the accountant liable to anyone who purchases securities that are part of the offering.

The basis for a claim under the act is that the financial statements accompanying the registration statement for the securities the plaintiff purchased contained either false statements or omissions that were material. The plaintiff need not establish reliance on the statements in purchasing the securities. Also, the plaintiff is not required to prove that the statements were materially misleading. Rather, the accountant must prove that they were *not*. Thus, the plaintiff's mere allegation of a material misstatement or omission, along with proof of the purchase, establishes a *prima facie* case, and the burden of proof switches to the accountant to prove the accuracy or immateriality of the statements. The burden is switched for reasons similar to those underlying the common law doctrine of *res ipsa loquitur,* as discussed in Chapter 4, and has a similar effect. The primary basis is that evidence concerning the completeness and accuracy of the statements is more available to the accountant than to the third party. In addition, public policy requires a higher degree of performance from an accountant in the context of registering securities.

An accountant sued under the act may defend on the basis of due care or, as specifically provided in the act, on the ground of "due diligence." The defense of **due diligence** requires the accountant to prove that she used reasonable procedures, in making a reasonable examination, and had a reasonable basis for believing (and did believe) that the statements she certified fully and fairly disclosed all material facts concerning the client's financial position, and that this was done in meaningful and understandable terms. The fact that the accountant complied with generally accepted standards and principles is strongly persuasive of due diligence, but it is not determinative. Any conflict between these standards and full and fair disclosure must be resolved in favor of the disclosure requirements. Beyond due diligence, a second defense available to the accountant is that the plaintiff's loss actually was caused by factors other than misstatements or omissions in the financial statements.

All lawsuits under the Securities Act must be brought within periods of limitations prescribed in the statute. A lawsuit must be brought within *one year* after the misstatement or omission was discovered or should have been discovered with the exercise of reasonable diligence. Also, in every case, it must be brought within *three years* of the time the affected securities were first offered to the public. A failure to comply with these limitations will bar the action.

The Securities Exchange Act of 1934

This act was designed to control national exchanges and the securities sold on them. It is unlike the 1933 act, which controls initial offerings of securities regardless of whether they are sold on an exchange. The 1934 act requires the filing of an annual report, called a "10-K form," which must be accompanied by financial statements certified by an independent public accountant. The act applies to the securities of companies that own more than $5 million in assets and have stock held by 500 or more shareholders as of the last day of the fiscal year.

As under the 1933 act, an accountant's primary liability under the 1934 act results from misstatements or omissions of material facts in the required statements. However, unlike the 1933 act, the burden of proof rests entirely with the plaintiff, and fraud must be established. That is, the plaintiff must prove: (1) that a misstatement or omission of material fact was made by the accountant, (2) knowingly, (3) with intent to defraud, (4) that the plaintiff purchased the securities in justifiable reliance on the statements, (5) and was injured as a result. The periods of limitations are the same as under the 1933 act. Consider the following case.

BERKOWITZ et al. v. BARON et al.
428 F.Supp. 1190 (S.D.N.Y., 1977)

This was an action by Nathaniel Berkowitz, Edward Yates, and Howard Hoffman (Plaintiffs) against Gail and Joel Baron and S. Markowe & Company (Defendants) for violation of Section 10(b) of the Securities Exchange Act and New York State fraud law.

Plaintiffs purchased all of the stock in two companies owned by Defendants Gail and Joel Baron. They did so in reliance on financial statements, prepared at the request of the Barons, by Defendant S. Markowe & Company, an accounting firm. Evidence indicated that the statements were prepared in a manner contrary to generally accepted accounting principles, and that they overstated net profit. The court found for Plaintiffs.

CANNELLA, District Judge.

Given these conditions, a finding that the financial statement is "materially misleading" is fully supported. Stated generally, the traditional test of materiality in 10b-5 suits is whether the fact is such that a reasonable investor would have considered it important in making the decision or might have acted otherwise had it not been misleadingly represented. . . . Whether this standard survives the definition of materiality recently enunciated by the Supreme Court with respect to misleading proxy statements—a fact is material "if there is a substantial likelihood that a reasonable shareholder would consider it important" in reaching a decision, . . . or has been replaced by it, the net income/net loss and inventory value entries on a corporate financial statement are of material importance to parties interested in purchasing all of the outstanding shares of the company. This is especially true where, as here, little other information about the business is transmitted to the purchasers prior to the consummation of the sale.

Similarly, the Court finds that plaintiffs have established reliance on the misrepresentations; they have proved that the misrepresentations were in fact substantial factors in the securities transactions involved. . . . Plaintiffs' testimony, though it established little else, established that they relied exclusively on the representations contained in the financial statement and the fact that the factory was in operation when the transaction took place. Moreover, the fact that plaintiffs demanded and received assurance that the net worth of the companies had not changed by more than $30,000 between April 30, the effective date of the financial statement, and the August 26 signing of the contract indicates that the financial picture of the companies as reflected in the financial statement was a substantial factor in plaintiffs' decision to purchase. In sum, plaintiffs were induced to purchase a business that was worth less than they had been led to believe.

Furthermore, the Court is convinced that the Barons acted with the intent—scienter—required for a Rule 10b-5 violation. . . . Given the rapidly deteriorating health of both Joel Baron and the companies, the Barons' consequent strong desire to dispose of the business and the unexplained change in presentation between 1969 and 1970 of the items discussed above, the Court concludes that the financial statements were purposely prepared to give a false impression of the companies' value as a going concern and thus foster the Barons' sale of the business. The Court also concludes that this was done with the knowledge of the Barons, if not at their direction. The Barons, having caused the issuance of a materially misleading financial statement on which plaintiffs have relied, thereby violated Section 10(b) of the Securities Exchange Act of 1934, . . . and Rule 10b-5 of the SEC, . . . promulgated thereunder.

Questions

1. Why are the investors entitled to rely on the accountant's statements?

2. Why shouldn't the purchaser be obliged to do its own analysis? What ever happened to "let the buyer beware"?

Two important differences between the two federal acts are apparent. First, the 1933 act is more comprehensive in its coverage. Second, the 1933 act imposes on the accountant something just short of absolute liability for errors and the burden of proving innocence; the 1934 act requires proof of *scienter* (evil intent) and the burden of proof is on the plaintiff.

ACCOUNTANTS' CRIMINAL LIABILITY

Criminal liability may be imposed on an accountant under either federal statute or state statute. (There is no "common law" of crimes.) Federal statutes of primary importance are the Securities Act of 1933, the Securities Exchange Act of 1934, and the Internal Revenue Code. On the state level, of principal importance are statutes governing false certification, criminal fraud, and criminal conversion (or theft).

The Securities Acts

Any willful violation of the Securities Act of 1933 or the Securities Exchange Act of 1934, or any regulation under either, subjects the accountant to a fine of not more than $100,000, imprisonment for not more than five years, or both. Punishable violations include falsification of any material fact in a registration statement and willful omission of any material fact required to be stated in a registration statement or necessary to keep any statement from being misleading. As was true in determining civil liability under these acts, compliance with generally accepted accounting standards and practices is persuasive of innocence, but it is not dispositive of the question of criminal liability. Consider the following case involving criminal liability. Note, particularly, the effect of the defendant's defense that he had followed generally accepted accounting principles.

UNITED STATES v. SIMON
425 F.2d 796 (2d Cir. 1969)

This action involved a criminal prosecution of Carl Simon, Robert Kaiser, and Melvin Fishman, partners and an associate in the accounting firm of Lybrand, Ross Brothers & Montgomery (Defendants/Appellants), for violations of Section 32 of the Securities Exchange Act of 1934 and Sections 1001 and 1341 of the federal mail fraud statute. It was charged that they knowingly overstated the value of certain receivables on a statement required to be filed under the Securities Exchange Act, and used the mails to further the fraud. The question before the court was what proof was necessary to constitute these offenses.

Defendants were convicted and appealed, challenging instructions to the jury. Affirmed.

FRIENDLY, Circuit Judge.

Defendants asked for two instructions which, in substance, would have told the jury that a defendant could be found guilty only if, according to generally accepted accounting principles, the financial statements as a whole did not fairly present the financial condition of Continental at September 30, 1962, and then only if his departure from accepted standards was due to willful disregard of those standards with knowledge of the falsity of the statements and an intent to deceive. The judge declined to give these instructions. Dealing with the subject in the course of his charge, he said that the "critical test" was whether the financial statements as a whole "fairly presented the financial position of Continental as of September 30, 1962, and whether it accurately reported the operations for fiscal 1962." If they did not, the basic issue became whether defendants acted in good faith. Proof of compliance with generally accepted standards was "evidence which may be very persuasive but not necessarily conclusive that he acted in good faith, and that the facts as certified were not materially false or misleading." "The weight and credibility to be extended by you to such proof, and its persuasiveness, must depend, among other things, on how authoritative you find the precedents and the teachings relied upon by the parties to be, the extent to which they contemplate, deal with, and apply to the type of circumstances found by you to have existed here, and the weight you give to expert opinion evidence offered by the parties. Those may depend on the credibility extended by you to expert witnesses, the definiteness with which they testified, the reasons given for their opinions, and all the other facts affecting credibility. . . ."

Defendants contend that the charge and refusal to charge constituted error. We think the judge was right in refusing to make the accountant's testimony so nearly a complete defense. The critical test according to the charge was the same as that which the accountants testified was critical. We do not think the jury was also required to accept the accountants' evaluation whether a given fact was material to overall fair presentation, at least not when the accountants' testimony was not based on specific rules or prohibitions to which they could point, but only on the need of the auditor to make an honest judgment and their conclusion that nothing in the financial statements themselves negated the conclusion that an honest judgment had been made. Such evidence may be highly persuasive, but it is not conclusive, and so the trial judge correctly charged. . . .

Even if there were no satisfactory showing of motive, we think the Government produced sufficient evidence of criminal intent. Its burden was not to show that defendants were wicked men with designs on anyone's purse, which they obviously were not, but rather that they had certified a statement knowing it to be false. As Judge Hough said for us long ago, "while there is no allowable inference of knowledge from the mere fact of falsity, there are many cases where from the actor's special situation and continuity of conduct an inference that he did know the untruth of what he said or wrote may legitimately be drawn."

Questions

1. Why shouldn't following generally accepted accounting principles be a defense to a criminal charge? Doesn't compliance show a lack of criminal intent?

2. What policies are served by imposing such an extensive threat of criminal liability on accountants?

The Internal Revenue Code

The Internal Revenue Code primarily provides for criminal penalties on an accountant involved in the preparation of tax returns for a client. The only civil actions brought under the code are those for injunction, by which the Internal Revenue Service seeks to prevent a violation of code provisions. Violations that may be enjoined include: (1) misrepresentation of the accountant's eligibility to practice before the Internal Revenue Service, or his education or experience as a tax preparer; (2) guaranteeing payment of a tax refund or the allowance of any tax credit; (3) using or disclosing confidential information provided by the taxpayer for any purpose other than the preparation of the taxpayer's tax return; (4) negligent or intentional disregard of tax rules or regulations that result in an understatement of tax liability; (5) conduct subject to criminal penalties under the code; and (6) any other fraudulent or deceptive act that substantially interferes with the proper administration of internal revenue laws. An injunction may seek to prohibit, or to mandate, particular acts, or it may seek to prohibit the accountant from preparing tax returns at all, either temporarily or permanently. Violation of an injunction subjects the accountant to criminal penalties for contempt of court.

Penalties directly provided for by the code include: (1) a $500 penalty for willful (intentional) understatement of the client's tax liability, or a $100 penalty if the understatement is due to a negligent or intentional disregard of tax rules or regulations; (2) a $25 penalty for failure to sign a return for which the accountant was compensated, to furnish an identifying number, or to furnish the taxpayer with a copy of the return; (3) a $50 penalty for failure to retain a copy of any compensated return prepared; (4) a $100 penalty for failure to file an annual information return, or $5 per item omitted on an incomplete return; and (5) a $500 penalty for wrongfully endorsing or negotiating a client's tax refund check. In addition, criminal penalties also may be assessed for wrongful communication of confidential information supplied by the client for the purpose of preparing a tax return. Of course, any criminal violation under the code also may result in civil liability to a client who is injured as a result of the misconduct.

Other Federal Statutes

In addition to the particular federal statutes just discussed, criminal sanctions are imposed by others, although the provisions are not specifically directed toward accountants. Among the other violations to which an accountant is most vulnerable are any conspiracy to violate federal law, the use of the mail to defraud, and perjury.

State Statutes

State laws proscribe a variety of acts in which an accountant may become involved—for example, state licensing regulations, and particularly those regarding the preparation of public documents, and those involving fraud and obtaining property by false pretenses. In fact, a particular activity may involve multiple violations on both the state and federal levels, and punishment for one ordinarily does not preclude punishment for others, although a single activity is the basis for all. Also, even a single violation, if moral turpitude or incompetence is involved, may result in the suspension or revocation of an accountant's license to practice.

OTHER CONSIDERATIONS

In addition to the common-law and statutory duties of care and statutory compliance, two other matters are important to the accountant. First, who owns the accountant's working papers? Second, to what extent does a client have a privilege with respect to audit information communicated to the auditor?

Accountants' Working Papers

An accountant's **working papers** generally are the written records of procedures and materials used in the process of an audit, upon which significant decisions and conclusions are based. This may include reviews of entire systems, internal controls, testing procedures used, and summaries and excerpts from clients' records and other documents.

At common law, and by statute in roughly half of the states, working papers are the property of the accountant who produced them. However, the accountant's ownership is primarily a matter of custody. Each client holds an interest in the contents of working papers, and the accountant is required to treat that material as confidential. The contents should not be communicated by the accountant to any third party without the permission of the client. However, the papers must be handed over if properly subpoenaed, and may be used by the accountant as the basis for, and corroboration of, testimony in court concerning matters relating to the audit during which they were produced. They are not property that can be sold or given away by the accountant, inherited, or transferred by will. When the accountant dies or no longer wants them, they should be given to the client or, preferably, physically destroyed.

Privileged Client Information

As previously discussed, information given by a client to an accountant for the purpose of conducting an audit or performing other accounting services is considered confidential. However, this means only that it ordinarily should not be communicated by the accountant to a third party without permission from the client. At common law, these *confidential* communications were not considered *privileged*. That is, if testimony concerning them was required in court, the **defense of privilege** was not available as a ground for refusing to testify. However, today, in some states, the status of privilege has been accorded these communications by statute. The majority of states, and federal law, have retained the common law rule. When provided for, the privilege may be asserted or waived only by the client. It is granted for his or her protection alone, not the accountant's.

In summary, confidential client communications properly may be disclosed only in circumstances *specifically* required or permitted by law. There is no *general* right to do so. Such circumstances include: (1) when the client consents; (2) when a court requires, as by the issuance of a valid subpoena or by court-ordered testimony; (3) when required by statute, such as the Securities Act of 1933; (4) when necessary to comply with generally accepted accounting standards or practices; (5) when it appears reasonably necessary to defend a civil lawsuit filed against the accountant by the client, or to defend against a criminal charge; and (6) when necessary to defend charges before a licensing or other regulatory agency, or a certifying body such as the American Insitute of Certified Public Accountants.

SUMMARY

An accountant may encounter both civil and criminal liability arising out of services performed for a client. The civil liability may be to the client or to a third party such as shareholders or a lender. Most civil liability arises under the common law, but it also may arise under state or federal statute. Of particular importance on the federal level are the Securities Act of 1933, the Securities Exchange Act of 1934, and the Internal Revenue Code.

An accountant basically is an independent contractor. As such, he owes a duty to a client to act with reasonable care, skill, and diligence. Ordinarily this means services must be performed according to generally accepted accounting standards and practices, and also according to the terms of the contract with each client. Although acting beyond the limits of generally accepted accounting standards raises a presumption of malpractice, compliance with them does not automatically insulate an accountant from liability. Each case must be judged according to its merits.

An accountant must take care not to stray from rendering accounting services into the practice of law, unless she is also a licensed attorney. In communicating to the client material information, facts, and conclusions concerning the services rendered, the accountant is obligated to make a full and complete disclosure in a form reasonably understandable by the client.

The principal duties of an accountant are contractual. Compliance requires that the accountant fully and completely discharge all express and implied obligations, within generally accepted accounting standards and practices, with a degree of care and skill reasonably expected of members of the accounting profession. Any breach of these duties renders the accountant liable for damages resulting to the client, and if the breach is material, the accountant is not entitled to compensation. Tort liability also may result from the accountant's failure to exercise due care. Negligence is the basis of these tort damages. If the failure to meet required standards is intentional, and the elements of fraud can be established, damages may be recovered, including an amount for the purpose of punishing the wrongdoer (punitive damages).

Civil liability to third parties may arise in cases of fraud or negligence, by virtue of a third-party beneficiary contract, or under federal statute. The federal Securities Act of 1933 generally provides for damages for failure to make a full and complete disclosure in required financial statements involving new issues of securities. The federal Securities Exchange Act of 1934 has similar provisions relating to financial statements, but allows recovery only if fraud is proven. Of course fraud

not related to these statutes also is actionable. Third parties ordinarily may not recover on the ground of simple negligence. However, an action is allowed in some states when the third party's reliance is foreseeable, as would be true of a lender.

Criminal liability is possible under a variety of state and federal statutes. Most important are those relating to fraud, obtaining property by false pretenses, mail fraud, perjury, conspiracy, the federal Internal Revenue Code, and the 1933 and 1934 securities acts.

Other legal matters to be considered by an accountant are ownership and disposition of working papers, the confidentiality of client information and communications, the privilege accorded these regarding testimony in court, and the duties of nondisclosure.

KEY TERMS AND CONCEPTS

independent contractor
generally accepted accounting principles
generally accepted auditing standards
negligence
fraud
privity
Securities Act of 1933
defense of "due diligence"
Securities Exchange Act of 1934
working papers
defense of privilege

PROBLEMS

1. Bancroft presented to his accountant (a CPA) a plan to distribute shares in SFK Corp. to members of his family, asking what the federal tax implications would be. After examining the plan, the accountant rendered her opinion that the transactions would not be taxable. This advice turned out to be incorrect, and Bancroft sued the accountant and her malpractice insurer for the

$35,419.74 paid in taxes, penalties, and interest. The insurance company defended on the ground that the advice constituted the illegal practice of law, and, therefore, was not covered under the malpractice policy. Is the defense good? Why or why not?

2. Chase, the president of Shatterproof Glass, contacted Paschal to see if four corporations controlled by Paschal would be interested in acting as distributors for Shatterproof. Paschal then requested James, a CPA, to prepare certified audits of the four corporations, and authorized the release of the information to Shatterproof. Chase contacted James, who gave him some preliminary information, knowing Shatterproof was to receive the audits. If James is negligent in the preparation of the audits, and Shatterproof is injured by the negligence, would James be liable to Shatterproof for its injuries, assuming the transaction is in a nonprivity state?

3. The shareholders of Thor Power Tools sued Peat, Marwick, Mitchell, & Co., a CPA firm, for negligence in the certification of an audit. The audit had been prepared for Thor, which distributed it to the shareholders. The suit was filed under Section 10(b) of the Securities Exchange Act of 1934. Peat, Marwick defended on the ground that only criminal liability existed under the act, and that there was no privity between themselves and the shareholders. May either, or both, of these defenses be sustained?

4. Discuss the basic obligations of an accountant under the Securities Act of 1933.

5. What changes were brought about by the Securities Exchange Act of 1934?

6. Peat, Marwick, Mitchell, & Co. were employed to audit Yale Express for Yale's 1963 *Annual Report* to its shareholders. The audit was certified in March 1964 and the report was sent to shareholders on April 9. On June 29, a 10-K report containing the same figures was filed with the SEC. Shortly thereafter, Yale engaged Peat, Marwick to do some management studies. During their investigation, Peat, Marwick discovered errors in the previous audit. The errors were not disclosed to the SEC, the New York Stock Exchange, or the general public until the studies were released in May 1965. A group of investors who had purchased Yale stock in the interim sued Peat, Marwick. Should Peat, Marwick be liable? Why or why not?

7. Herzfeld invested in the stock of FGL, a real estate investment firm. Originally, she was interested in FGL through some friends. Prior to investing, she had examined financial statements of FGL prepared by Laventhal, a CPA. The statements were false and misleading, as was FGL's cover letter accompanying the statements, which was sent by FGL. Both of these facts were known to Laventhal, who defended on the ground that Herzfeld's decision to invest was influenced mostly by her friends, and not the statements. Should this defense be sustained? Why or why not?

8. Gross, trustee in bankruptcy for the Hawaii Corporation, sought damages of $22 million allegedly suffered as a result of reliance on an audit by Peat, Marwick, Mitchell, & Co. in connection with reorganizing the company and another corporation. The evidence demonstrated that Peat, Marwick had failed to follow generally accepted accounting principles and generally accepted auditing standards. The defendant offered proof that the methods used were "just as" clear and accurate. Should the defense be permitted?

9. A seller of a car rental business employed an accountant to prepare an audit. He instructed the accountant not to do a full audit, and, particularly, not to adjust accounts receivable for uncollectible accounts. The absence of the adjustment was disclosed in the opinion accompanying the audit. Does the disclosure immunize the accountant from liability for misrepresentation in the audit?

10. Discuss what constitutes negligent conduct, particularly as it relates to accountants.

International Law

INTRODUCTION

Nations today do not exist in isolation; they are tied together by the cord of economic interdependence. The march of history, although it has been a journey with many detours, has been toward the integration of national economies into one world economy. With ever-greater frequency, businesses have been reaching across national frontiers to acquire new markets, secure raw materials, and increase labor resources. Although both international and domestic transactions generally are motivated by similar considerations and are comparable in many other ways, the legal climate of international business has many unique characteristics. In order to give you some sense of the world market, this chapter will illustrate some of the basic principles that govern international transactions. In doing so, the discussion also should provide an illuminating comparative perspective on the domestic side of the legal system.

The contemporary international arena has been shaped in the years following the Second World War. Abandoning its long-standing policy of isolationism, the United States became the architect of postwar institutions of international cooperation. In July 1944, only a month after the allied armies landed in Normandy to liberate Europe, the United States and other nations met in Bretton Woods, New Hampshire to devise the postwar monetary system. The Bretton Woods Agreement, signed by forty-four nations, created the International Monetary Fund and the World Bank. The United Nations was formed in 1945. By 1947, the concern for free trade among nations culminated in the *General Agreement on Tariffs and Trade (GATT),* which was joined in at that time by twenty-two nations and has grown into an institution of enormous significance. Today, multi-national organizations and treaties regulate many aspects of international commerce, including aviation, shipping, communications, atomic energy, agriculture, banking, education, science, and culture. Private international trade has multiplied in the postwar years under the protection and encouragement of these, and other, agreements and institutions of cooperation. The American business community has benefitted from the development of relatively stable international markets, but it also has been hurt by the competition facilitated by the network of regulation that now comes from so many other countries in the world.

DIRECT SALE ABROAD

One way in which an American company can exploit foreign markets is to sell its products abroad directly. Suppose Acme Oddments, Inc., an American manufacturer of wooden picture frames, contracts to sell its product to a customer within the United States. That transaction poses no special difficulties; the sales contract will be governed by the Uniform Commercial Code, and any disputes can be resolved in the American courts, typically a court selected in the contract itself. But suppose the sale is to be made to a customer in France, with delivery to be made in that country. The principal problem is that if a dispute arises, no convenient mechanism for enforcing the contract exists. The French buyer might turn out to be insolvent, or quibble over whether the goods conform to the contract, or simply refuse to honor his promise to buy. Even if Acme successfully sues the French company for breach of contract in an American court, if the delinquent buyer has no assets in the United States there is no way to enforce the judgment of that American court and collect damages in this country. Realizing that, Acme may decide to bring a suit in the French courts, but the complexity and the cost of litigating in a foreign court, not to mention the inhospitality some foreign tribunals exhibit towards American businesses, may well prove overwhelming. For these reasons, Acme may chose not to risk shipping its product abroad without a greater guarantee of payment than the buyer's naked promise to pay for the picture frames.

These problems can be solved if the sale is structured as a **documentary irrevocable letter of credit transaction.** In addition to Acme and its foreign customer, this technique involves an "issuing bank" located in the buyer's home country and a "confirming bank" in the United States that is well known to the seller. The **letter of credit** is a promise by the issuing bank in France to pay the stated amount upon proof that the goods have been shipped. The bank in this country confirms the letter of credit, and agrees to pay it to Acme. This is necessary because the American seller may know as little about the solvency of the foreign bank as it knows about the foreign customer. The

Typical letter of credit transaction

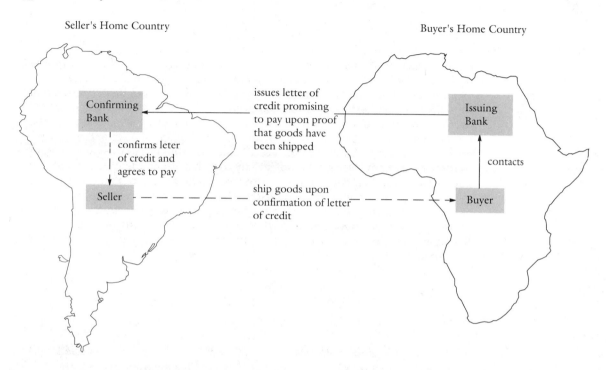

Seller's Home Country

Buyer's Home Country

Confirming Bank

issues letter of credit promising to pay upon proof that goods have been shipped

Issuing Bank

confirms leter of credit and agrees to pay

contacts

Seller

ship goods upon confirmation of letter of credit

Buyer

chief advantage of this arrangement is that the seller secures the promise of immediate payment from a local bank that it knows is reliable.

The contract between the buyer and seller typically incorporates the applicable provisions of the Uniform Customs and Practices for Documentary Credits and the Uniform Commercial Code. The **Uniform Customs and Practices for Documentary Credits,** published by the International Chamber of Commerce, essentially codifies international practices with respect to letter of credit transactions. Both the UCC and the Uniform Customs and Practices provide that the promise by the confirming (local) bank is independent of the underlying sales contract. Thus, if the seller were forced to sue the confirming bank for payment under the letter of credit, the only issue is

whether the designated goods were shipped by the seller; the bank cannot refuse to pay on the ground that the goods are defective or did not arrive in proper condition.

In practice, therefore, international contractual risks are assumed—for a fee, naturally—by the two certifying banks. The value of this technique is that the banks are able to narrow the lack of information buyers and sellers in the international marketplace have about each other and promote their doing business. Each bank is familiar with its client and is better able to judge the risks of the transaction. A loss, moreover, will not crush the banks; in reality, the cost of transactions that fail will be incorporated into the fee the banks charge for issuing letters of credit. The following case illustrates the letter-of-credit practice.

MARINO INDUSTRIES CORP. v.
CHASE MANHATTAN BANK, N.A.
686 F.2d 112 (2d Cir. 1982)

Marino (Plaintiff/Appellant), an American manufacturer of construction materials, agreed with Bautechnik, a German company, to ship material to a job site in Saudi Arabia. Marino was to be paid by the Chase Manhattan Bank (Defendant/ Appellee) on two letters of credit issued by Chase. One letter provided for 40-percent payment upon shipment; the other authorized the payment of the remaining 60 percent upon arrival of the material in Saudi Arabia. Both letters obligated Marino to present various certificates of shipment to the bank in order to receive payment. Marino did not strictly comply with all the requirements set out in the letters, and the bank refused payment on them. Plaintiff sued to recover the payment, and the United States District Court ruled for Defendant on all three claims. The Court of Appeals affirmed the judgment that the bank was justified in refusing payment on two of the claims. (The Court reversed on the third claim and remanded to the trial court for further proceedings, for reasons not important here.)

FRIEDMAN, Chief Judge.

United States Court of Claims (sitting by designation): . . .

II.

"[T]he essential requirements of a letter of credit must be strictly complied with by the party entitled to draw against the letter of credit, which means that the papers, documents, and shipping descriptions must be as stated in the letter." *Veniezelos, S.A. v. Chase Manhattan Bank,* 425 F.2d 461, 465 (2d Cir. 1970). . . .

The rule of strict compliance reflects the fact that a letter of credit is a contract between the bank and the beneficiary of the letter that is separate and distinct from the commercial contract between the beneficiary (usually the seller) and the bank's customer (usually the buyer). The letter of credit is not tied to or dependent upon the underlying commercial transaction. . . . In determining whether to pay, the bank looks solely at the letter and the documentation the beneficiary presents, to determine whether the documentation meets the requirements in the letter. . . .

III.

[The court's discussion of the first and third claims is omitted.] . . .

Marino's second claim is for $46,388 under the 40 percent provision of the second letter of credit. Under that provision Marino was entitled to payment upon shipment of the goods.

The magistrate upheld Chase's refusal to pay this claim because of four deficiencies he found in the supporting documentation Marino submitted. Since we conclude that one of these deficiencies is fatal to Marino's claim, we need not consider the other three.

Paragraph b) of Chase's confirmation of the letter required Marino to submit to Chase in order to obtain payment under the 40 percent provision copy of telex confirmation . . . addressed to Dietrich Garski [one of the principles of Bauthechnik] . . . , showing that 1/2 original clean on board ocean liner bills of lading, 1 legalized commercial invoice, 1 legalized packing list, and 1 legalized certificate of origin have been sent to both: 1) Bauthechnik, Riyadh and 2) custom agent at port of destination.

Legalization apparently is a process by which a document is stamped by the consulate of the country of destination—here Saudi Arabia.

The telex to Dietrich Garski, a copy of which Marino submitted to Chase, did not show that a "legalized" packing list had been sent but referred only to a [plain] packing list.

Under the rule of strict compliance, this defect justified Chase in refusing payment. The language is clear and unambiguous. Marino was required to submit a copy of telex showing that a "legalized" packing list had been sent. It did not do so. "'There is no room for documents which are almost the same, or which will do just as well.'" H. Harfield, *Bank Credits & Acceptances* 73 (5th ed. 1974) (citation omitted), *quoted in Eximetals,* 73 A.D.2d at 527, 422 N.Y.S.2d at 686. . . .

The portion of the judgment dismissing the $46,000 claim is affirmed.

Questions

1. Do you agree with the court's decision? Why or why not? Could Marino have argued that it was entitled to be paid by the bank because Bautechnik had promised to pay Marino for the material?

2. In this case, the plaintiff in fact did not "legalize" the packing list. Would the court view the case differently if the list actually had been legalized but the telex still omitted any mention of legalization?

3. Unlike the attitude of the court in the *Marino* case, many areas of the law do not rely on sharply drawn rules but instead look to the totality of circumstances in each case. Are there special reasons that justify rigid application of the rules relating to letters of credit in the context of international trade? Should every slip be fatal?

THE GENERAL AGREEMENT ON TARIFFS AND TRADE

It is not enough for private parties to agree to buy and sell in the international arena. Their transaction must be approved by the trading nations; the seller must have permission to export, and the buyer must be able to import the product into the country. For example, certain sensitive military technology may not be exported from the United States. Also, it is unlikely that Congress would allow an American oil company to sell its oil abroad during a domestic energy crisis. Short of a national emergency, however, a government normally has no incentive to curb exports, especially something as noncritical as Acme's wooden picture frames.

Every government, including that of the United States, strives to bolster its exports in order to enhance the position of its nationals in the world market and to improve its balance of payments. The reason is simple—sales abroad protect jobs at home and contribute to the profitability of American businesses. With expanded sales abroad, American companies can expand their operations, employ more people, pay higher wages, and earn higher profits. The result theoretically is lower unemployment and a higher standard of living in the United States. Of course, other countries are trying to achieve the same result, and they encourage their companies to roam the globe in search of customers. Consequently, this competition among governments focuses on the ability to introduce products manufactured at home into a foreign market.

Historically, nations traded with one another on the basis of bilateral treaties that accorded each country more or less favorable trading status as compared with that given nontreaty countries. These special arrangements between some countries, high import tariffs imposed on the goods of nontreaty nations, and various nontariff barriers to trade combined to hold international trade in a restrictive vise before World War II. The postwar decade was characterized by a determined effort on the part of the United States and other countries to create a world of relatively free circulation of goods and services unconstrained by national frontiers. The **General Agreement on Tariffs and Trade (GATT)** embodies the efforts of over eighty-four nations to reduce restrictions on international trade. It clearly is the most important multinational treaty on the subject currently in existence.

GATT takes a broad and strong position against all nontariff restrictions on trade, such as quotas and import licenses. The long-standing practice of one nation according most-favored-nation status to one or more of its special trading partners is extended by GATT to all nations that are members of the agreement. Article I provides that any privilege granted one member country immediately and unconditionally must be accorded to every GATT member. The agreement does have its limitations, however, one of which is of enormous significance. Although trade in services accounts for two-thirds of the United States' Gross National Product and one third of its trade abroad, GATT does not apply to international trade in services. GATT, like the Uniform Commercial Code, applies only to the buying and selling of goods.

Despite GATT's prohibition against nontariff import barriers, the agreement recognizes that it could cause serious economic dislocations within a member state and therefore provides a number of exceptions. The most important of these are: (1) the right to impose antidumping duties when one nation seeks to introduce one or more of its products into another country at less than their normal value; (2) the right to impose restrictions when there is a threat to important national interests such as domestic security, monetary reserves, health, plant and animal life, or morality; and (3) the ability to suspend the agreement's obligations when conditions "threaten serious injury to domestic producers."

Over the years, many countries have imposed a variety of trading restrictions despite their commitment to GATT. For example, Syria in 1981 banned all importation of air conditioners and cosmetics. A less blatant restriction than an outright ban on a category of products is the imposition of manufacturing standards on imported products. For example, all motor vehicles imported into the United States must comply with federal safety standards. Although many types of product standards are justifiable and well-intentioned, they obviously can be manipulated and imposed by member governments to achieve a partial or total exclusion of foreign products, thereby favoring domestic manufacturers. Unfortunately, even when restrictive trade measures do not qualify for one of the exceptions set out in the agreement and are inconsistent with a country's obligations under GATT, they are enforced as a matter of domestic law. These import restrictions, therefore, are of enormous concern to anyone seeking to invest in a foreign market. When a disagreement under GATT arises as to whether a particular country is complying with the agreement, it generally is dealt with at a meeting of the member nations. The process of resolving a dispute often involves seeking advice from one or more of the international organizations having specialized knowledge of the contested matter.

CUSTOMS DUTIES

If an item complies with all applicable product standards and other import regulations, it is eligible to be admitted into the country. At this point, the product will be assessed a customs duty, the amount of which depends on the item's value and classification. The classification can pose a particularly vexing problem. Suppose Acme, the United States manufacturer, and its French customer successfully enter into a purchase and sales contract, and Acme ships the agreed-upon number of wooden picture frames to the buyer. When the shipment arrives in France, it will be assessed a customs duty at the border. The amount charged may depend on the form in which the product is sent, because that may determine how it is classified. If the shipment is of finished picture frames it may be assessed one duty, but if the shipment is of the wooden pieces for later assembly by the buyer in France, the amount of the duty may be entirely different because the customs classification for each of these shipments may be entirely different. What is the product in each case? Is it "wooden picture frames" or "simply strips of wood molding"? Perhaps it will be treated as an "art object" or a "forest product." The answer to these questions, and many more that arise in connection with other products, is by no means clear.

Most countries, the United States and Canada excluded, adhere to the Brussels Tariff Nomenclature, which identifies items along a developmental progression from raw materials to finished products. The customs duties for goods entering the United States are set out in a federal statute. Disputes between the importer and United States custom officials are resolved in a highly specialized federal tribunal called the Court of International Trade, which has exclusive jurisdiction over such matters.

APPOINTING A FOREIGN DISTRIBUTOR

An American manufacturing company may find that there is a substantial demand for its products abroad. The cumbersome procedure for direct sales abroad is not well suited for large-volume export. Moreover, a United States firm may want to establish a permanent presence abroad and build a following for its products in the foreign market. Direct sales to other countries are unlikely to accomplish that goal. Appointing a distributor that already does business in the country of sale or creating a local company to promote and sell products often are more effective means of exploiting the foreign market. The product to be distributed, of course, must pass through customs and comply with all of the other laws of the nation in which it is to be marketed.

A distribution agreement for a foreign market will closely parallel a comparable domestic agreement. It will specify various contractual terms for marketing the product—prices, dates of delivery, minimum purchase requirements, guarantees of supply, and the like. Additionally, an international distribution agreement is likely to include several provisions for resolving any disputes that might arise, as would a distribution contract for handling a product in the United States. The contracting parties, for example, may provide that all disputes must be resolved under the laws of the United States and of the State of California and be heard by a court in that state. Inasmuch as the substantive law of contracts in this country and that of the country of the distributor may be different, the choice of governing law and a forum for hearing disputes are critical provisions in the contract. Alternatively, the parties may choose to submit all their disputes to arbitration. The **London Court of Arbitration,** a private institution founded in 1892, provides a convenient arbitration forum for international trade disputes. (See the discussions of international dispute resolution later in this chapter.)

It is common for a United States firm to seek an *exclusive-dealing* provision in its agreement with the distributor, under which the latter promises not to sell competing products. For example, an American appliance manufacturer will not want its distributor in Germany to handle comparable appliances manufactured by other American companies. Exclusivity serves as a guarantee to the American firm that the distributor will devote its full time and effort to the promotion of its products.

An exclusive-dealing provision, however, may raise questions under our antitrust laws and quite possibly the antitrust laws of the distributorship country. These arrangements are a restraint on inter-brand competition and often violate the law. Section 1 of the Sherman Antitrust Act pointedly prohibits anticompetitive practices in dealing with foreign nations, because they deny other American firms access to the foreign marketplace. (See the discussion in Chapters 48 and 49 on the United States antitrust laws.) An exclusive-dealing arrangement is not an automatic or *per se* violation of the Sherman Act; instead, it is scrutinized under the rule of reason created by the federal courts. Whether a particular distributorship arrangement will be found to be an unreasonable restraint on trade depends on the factual scenario of each situation. Thus, an exclusive-dealing agreement will survive judicial scrutiny if it is limited in scope and duration and is designed to gain a foothold in a foreign market rather than to dominate it.

The foreign distributor also will want to be protected and typically will seek an exclusive-appointment provision from the United States firm. An exclusive appointment leaves inter-brand competition intact, but it protects the distributor from intra-brand competition by eliminating other sellers of the same product in the foreign country. The provision excludes, in effect, other foreign distributors from marketing a particular American product. (No other American firms or distributors handling a similar product are excluded from participating in the foreign marketplace by such a provision, however.) This arrangement does not violate our antitrust laws because it does not have any anticompetitive impact in the United States. A problem may arise, however, under the antitrust laws of the host country. Most industrialized nations prohibit—although none as strictly as the United States—the artificial exclusion of competitors from the marketplace.

THE EUROPEAN ECONOMIC COMMUNITY

The **European Economic Community (EEC),** often referred to as the Common Market, is a multinational legal regime established by the EEC treaty. Several of these entities have come into being in different parts of the world since the Second World War, but the EEC has been the most successful and certainly is the most significant to the United States both geopolitically and commercially. The goals of the EEC are, among others, the abolition of tariffs and quotas within the Community and the application of a common customs tariff and commercial policy toward other countries. All major European trading partners of the United States are members of the EEC; it represents a formidable economic bloc.

The EEC is more than a multinational treaty; it is an international body in its own right with powers to enact laws and conclude international agreements on its own behalf. The sovereign powers of the EEC extend to areas of "competence" that have been delegated to the Community by the member states. These are very considerable and embrace virtually all aspects of business activity within the EEC. The Community's laws operate as an umbrella above the legal systems of the member states. Thus, in many ways the structural scheme of the EEC is similar to the principle of federalism embodied in the United States Constitution, by which the national government exercises powers delegated to it by the states. Within the scope of its competence, the EEC can enact

European Economic Community (EEC)

Countries in EEC:

1	Belgium	7	Italy
2	Denmark	8	Luxemburg
3	France	9	Netherlands
4	West Germany	10	Portugal
5	Greece	11	Spain
6	Ireland	12	United Kingdom

laws that are enforced directly in the courts of member states without any intervention by national legislatures. In case of conflict, moreover, Community law supersedes the domestic law of its members. Again, to draw a direct analogy to the superior status of federal law over state law in the United States, the law of the EEC is the supreme law within the European community. The following case illustrates this.

DEFRENNE v. SABENA

Court of Justice of the European Communities 1976 E.C.R. 455,
CCH C.M.R. 8346 (1976)

The *Cour* [court] *du travail* in Brussels, Belgium referred to the Court of Justice under Article 177 of the EEC Treaty two questions concerning the effect and implementation of Article 119 of the Treaty regarding the principle that men and women should receive equal pay for equal work. The questions arose in an action between an air hostess and her employer, Sabena S.A., concerning compensation claimed by the applicant on the ground that, between February 15, 1963 and February 1, 1966, she suffered discrimination as a female worker in terms of her pay as compared with that received by male colleagues who were doing the same work as "cabin stewards." The parties agreed that the work of an air hostess is identical to that of a cabin steward, and therefore the existence of discrimination in pay to the detriment of the air hostess was not disputed.

OPINION.

The first question asks whether Article 119 of the Treaty introduces "directly into the national law of each Member State of the European Community the principle that men and women should receive equal pay for equal work and does it therefore, independently of any national provision, entitle workers to institute proceedings before national courts in order to ensure its observance?" . . .

If the answer to this question is in the affirmative, the question further enquires as from what date this effect must be recognized. . . .

Article 119 pursues a double aim.

First, in the light of the different stages of the development of social legislation in the various Member States, the aim of Article 119 is to avoid a situation in which undertakings established in States which have actually implemented the principle of equal pay suffer a competitive disadvantage in intra-Community competition as compared with undertakings established in States which have not yet eliminated discrimination against women workers as regards pay.

Secondly, this provision forms part of the social objectives of the Community, which is not merely an economic union, but is at the same time intended, by common action, to ensure social progress and seek the constant improvement of the living and working conditions of their peoples, as is emphasized by the Preamble to the Treaty.

This aim is accentuated by the insertion of Article 119 into the body of a chapter devoted to social policy whose preliminary provision, Article 117, marks "the need to promote improved working conditions and an improved standard of living for workers, so as to make possible their harmonization while the improvement is being maintained."

This double aim, which is at once economic and social, shows that the principle of equal pay forms part of the foundations of the Community. . . .

It is impossible not to recognize that the complete implementation of the aim pursued by Article 119, by means of the elimination of all discrimination, direct or indirect, between men and women workers, not only as regards individual undertakings but also entire branches of industry and even of the economic system as a whole, may in certain cases involve the elaboration of criteria whose implementation necessitates the taking of appropriate measures at Community and national level. . . .

Although Article 119 is expressly addressed to the Member States in that it imposes on them a duty to ensure, within a given period, and subsequently to maintain the application of the principle of equal pay, that duty assumed by the State does not exclude competence in this matter on the part of the Community.

On the contrary, the existence of competence on the part of the Community is shown by the fact that Article 119 sets out one of the "social policy" objectives of the Treaty which form the subject of Title III, which itself appears in Part Three of the Treaty dealing with the "Policy of the Community."

As has been shown in the reply to the first question, no implementing provision, whether adopted by the institutions of the Community or by the national authorities, could adversely affect the direct effect of Article 119. . . .

Even in the areas in which Article 119 has no direct effect, that provision cannot be interpreted as reserving to the national legislature exclusive power to implement the principle of equal pay since, to the extent to which such implementation is necessary, it may be relieved by a combination of Community and national measures. . . .

The Governments of Ireland and the United Kingdom have drawn the Court's attention to the possible economic consequences of attributing direct effect to the provisions of Article 119, on the ground that such a decision might, in many branches of economic life, result in the introduction of claims dating back to the time at which such effect came into existence.

In view of the large number of people concerned [by the] claims, [retroactive application of the court's order] might seriously affect the financial situation of [the affected companies] and even drive some of them to bankruptcy. . . .

Therefore, the direct effect of Article 119 cannot be relied on in order to support claims concerning pay periods prior to the date of this judgment, except as regards those workers who have already brought legal proceedings or made an equivalent claim. . . .

Questions

1. How would the issue of "equal pay" be decided by the United States Supreme Court in a comparable case in this country? (Review the material on discrimination in Chapter 52.)

2. Do you think the Court of Justice of the European Communities has more or less power under the EEC Treaty than the United States Supreme Court has under our Constitution? Why or why not?

3. Do you think it was proper for the court to give its decision only prospective effect?

The EEC is the institutionalization of the free market. The **Treaty of Rome,** which is the backbone of the Community, fully embraces the American model of free competition undistorted by restrictive trade practices. Articles 85 and 86 of the treaty contain broad antitrust provisions. Paragraph 1 of Article 85, for example, prohibits "all agreements . . . which may affect trade between member states and which have as their object or effect the prevention, restriction or distortion of competition." Agreements in violation of this article anywhere in the Community are void.

As a consequence of the Treaty of Rome, if Acme, our United States manufacturer of wooden picture frames, wishes to conclude some form of distribution agreement with a French company, the EEC's antitrust laws directly apply. France is a member of the EEC, and Community laws are binding on the French courts. Thus, if Acme established the type of exclusive distribution agreement discussed earlier, it probably would violate the antitrust laws of the Common Market. As is typical of most laws, the all-embracive language of Article 85 contains several escape valves. Acme's distributorship agreement, for instance, may be so confined in its geography and volume of frames as not to "effect trade between member states." Even the broad sweep of Article 85 does not reach agreements that are too insubstantial to be concerned about. Another escape valve is the possibility of an administrative waiver of the application of Article 85. Paragraph 3 of the article gives the Commission of European Communities, which functions more or less like the EEC's Executive Branch, the power to declare the provisions of paragraph 1 inapplicable to any agreement

which contributes to improving the production or distribution of goods or to promoting technical or economic progress, while allowing consumers a fair share of the resulting benefit, and which does not . . . (b) afford [the parties] the possibility of eliminating competition in respect of a substantial part of the products in question.

By properly "notifying" the commission of its proposed distributorship agreement, Acme may obtain the needed exemption. In practice, the commission enjoys great discretion in deciding waiver cases, and its analysis is similar to the rule-of-reason test employed by American courts in deciding antitrust cases under the Sherman Act. Accordingly, if Acme's agreement is not a predatory tactic to corner the market and does not otherwise pose a threat to the Community's marketplace, but simply is an effort to introduce its products into the EEC, the agreement probably will be viewed sympathetically. Not surprisingly, the Community is concerned primarily with the economic health of its own members and thus carefully scrutinizes the activities of major American companies, like IBM and Xerox, that compete directly with companies that are indigenous to the EEC. This has led many American businesses to manufacture their products within the Community in the hope of being treated, to some degree, as if they were local enterprises.

DIRECT INVESTMENT IN MANUFACTURING FACILITIES ABROAD

There are many advantages to establishing a manufacturing facility in a foreign market rather than shipping goods or working through a local distributor. American firms often can find cheaper labor and natural resources abroad; an overseas facility also gives the United States firm ready access to the host country's market, thereby by-passing some of the import restrictions. This last consideration prompted several Japanese car makers to open manufacturing plants in the United States in recent years. Local manufacturing also can help overcome prejudice against foreign products.

The legal problems of an overseas venture, however, are manifold. Perhaps most fundamental is the problem of ownership of the foreign operation. Some countries, like the Soviet Union, do not permit foreign ownership of domestic enterprises; others, like Mexico and India, limit foreign ownership to a minority (up to a 49-percent) interest. The **Andean Common Market Group,** which includes most countries in South America and functions somewhat like the EEC, abides by a "fade-out" provision under which foreign ownership reduces and then disappears over a period of fifteen to twenty years. Thus, American-owned enterprises in South America have a maximum life span of that number of years (tourism enterprises are exempt). Most developing countries also prohibit foreign ownership of vital domestic industries such as communications and transportation. In addition, the labor laws of many nations impose long-term obligations on the employer; as a result, a United States firm must be prepared for a lengthy commitment to its venture in those countries.

Limitations on the ability of an American company to bring its foreign earnings to the United States are among the most important problems associated with direct investment abroad. In many cases, a foreign venture's profits must be convertible into United States dollars, and an American investor must be able to take those profits (or liquidation proceeds when the business venture is ended) out of the host country and bring them to the United States—a process called **repatriation**—in order to make the investment attractive. Numerous countries, particularly in the developing world, impose strict rules on the conversion of

their currency into the hard currency of another country, such as the United States dollar. These nations usually have minimal foreign-currency reserves and have a keen interest in conserving those reserves (and therefore United States dollars) for vital domestic uses. Instead of facilitating conversion, therefore, the host country encourages reinvestment of profits within its borders. As a consequence, American firms operating in countries having these controls cannot convert their earnings into United States dollars and repatriate the money without permission from local currency-control authorities. Some countries place an absolute limit, stated as a percentage of total investment, on the amount that may be repatriated each year. Others levy a graduated "withholding tax" on repatriated earnings. The tax increases with the amount of earnings to be repatriated; at its high end, the tax can wipe out the earnings, destroying any incentive to repatriate the funds. Attempts to liquidate a foreign investment in these nations also may encounter many difficulties. All sales proceeds above the original investment will be considered profit, and the repatriation of those funds will be restricted or taxed accordingly.

EXPROPRIATION

The most crushing blow to a United States firm that has invested in a foreign country is the possibility that its facilities will be **expropriated** by the host government. In many foreign countries the official policy on foreign investment fluctuates with each change in political regime, and revolutions frequently lead to a reversal of pre-existing policies. After the Castro revolution in Cuba, for example, the new laws of that country gave the Cuban president full discretion to nationalize property in which Americans had an interest. Castro exercised that discretion to expropriate American-owned sugar-cane plantations. Thus, the political stability and orientation of the host country is an integral factor in assessing the risks of a foreign venture. Even an orderly transfer of power in some countries can lead to a change in policy and the expropriation of foreign assets.

The dangers are highest in the young nations of the developing world, but in the 1970s even mature countries like Canada and Great Britain evidenced a willingness to nationalize commercial enterprises. A 1979 comparative rating of 57 countries indicated that 13 countries pose *less* of a takeover risk than the United States. It should be understood that the nation-state's power of expropriation or nationalization is recognized internationally. A United Nations General Assembly Resolution supports the

> *Full permanent sovereignty of every State over its natural resources and all economic activities. In order to safeguard these resources, each State is entitled to exercise effective control over them including the right to nationalization or transfer of ownership to its nationals.*

Confiscation

Although expropriation obviously is an unsettling experience, it is not ruinous if it is followed by fair and speedy compensation for the assets taken by the nationalizing country. In that sense, expropriation must be distinguished from **confiscation** without compensation. If the laws of the host country do not provide for compensation, the foreign investor must turn to the limited protections provided by international law and diplomacy. In the United States, the power of eminent domain permits the government—either state or federal—to take (expropriate) private property for public use, but the investor is protected by the constitutional requirement of "just compensation." The Fifth and the Fourteenth Amendments to the United States Constitution do not bar government takings; they only require that due process of law and just compensation be provided to the owner.

The point of contention in international law is whether there should be a requirement of compensation that accompanies a nation's right of expropriation. The absence of universal recognition of such a requirement is the real fear of American investors, because history has demonstrated that foreign governments rarely compensate for what they take. The United States espouses the view that international law requires fair and prompt compensation. This position is shared by most developed Western nations. The long-standing view of the Soviet Union and other communist states is that there is no international obligation to make any payment in connection with the taking of a foreign investor's property. Despite this attitude, the Soviet Union eventually settled the claims arising from the Bolshevik Revolution of 1917. Mexico and other developing nations take the position that a foreign investor may not be treated differently from a domestic investor. Expropriation is legitimate, under Mexico's view, as long as the government does not intentionally discriminate against foreign investors. In practice, this position denies compensation to domestic and foreign investors alike. Thus, if a United States firm decides to bring a lawsuit to recover compensation for a confiscation by a foreign state, such as the Soviet Union or Mexico, the action probably will be dismissed by the courts of that country.

Moreover, the picture is bleak for seeking judicial relief in the United States from a confiscation in another country—for example, by attempting to get a court order to seize some of that nation's property in the United States. Although the sympathies of a court in this country undoubtedly will be with the American firm wrongfully deprived of its investment, the judge will be powerless to help. The *sovereign-immunity* and *act-of-state* doctrines shield foreign states from suits in our courts. Looking for an open courthouse door in some other country also is futile. Other nations have no connection with and no interest in the dispute, and their courts are likely to abide by the same doctrines of sovereign immunity and act of state as our courts. Thus, in practical effect, there is no forum for presenting a challenge to a confiscation by a foreign government.

Non-Judicial Remedies

Insurance is one way an American company can protect itself against expropriation. The United States government operates the **Overseas Private Investment Corporation (OPIC),** which provides low-cost expropriation insurance for eligible investments in designated countries. OPIC is an outgrowth of the Marshall Plan, which helped rebuild Europe following World War II and aims to encourage private investment in less-developed, friendly nations.

In the event of an uninsured takeover of an American company by a foreign country, the general policy of the United States is to pursue compensation for the business through diplomatic channels. Unlike the attempt to secure a judicial remedy, which will fail because of sovereign immunity or the act-of-state doctrine, diplomatic pressure usually succeeds in securing at least partial satisfaction of the claim. In 1974, for example, the Soviet Union offered a lump-sum payment in satisfaction of all claims arising out of the Russian Revolution of 1917; in 1979, the People's Republic of China offered to pay $131 million in satisfaction of investor claims arising out of its 1949 revolution. These amounts are less than the claims, of course. Only Italy ever has offered to pay the full value of documented claims. The funds recovered through diplomacy are distributed to investors by the **Foreign Claims Settlement Commission,** a federal agency. Investors apply to the commission for compensation and present documents to support their claims. The decision of the commission is final and not reviewable by any court, except for claims that the methodology of the tribunal has violated the United States Constitution.

THE SOVEREIGN IMMUNITY DOCTRINE

The doctrine of **sovereign immunity** completely bars an action against a foreign state. The defense is embedded in the jurisprudence of communist, socialist, capitalist, and developing nations alike. The origins of the doctrine can be traced to the classical notion that all sovereigns are equal, and to the satellite principle that the sovereign can do no wrong. For one nation's courts to assert jurisdiction over another sovereign state is to deny its equality, to affront its dignity, and, in practice, to create friction between the nations. A sovereign state, therefore, when it exercises one of its official functions, is immune from the jurisdiction of the courts of other countries.

However, this immunity does not extend to everything a sovereign does. With the expansion of international trade in recent years, governments increasingly have engaged in purely commercial, as opposed to governmental, activity, and the doctrine of sovereign immunity has been restricted to noncommercial activity. The theory of this is simple. When a sovereign state enters the marketplace, it should be treated on the same basis as other traders. In other words, the doctrine of sovereign immunity has become limited so that it only protects a nation's political acts.

In the United States, the doctrine is codified in the **Foreign Sovereign Immunities Act (FSIA),** which enables foreign states to claim immunity, with some exceptions, from suits in the federal courts of the United States. One of the exceptions in the act is for a foreign government's purely commercial activities. These can take many forms. The government of Egypt, for example, might contract with Acme to purchase wooden picture frames for its national art galleries. If any disputes under this contract arise, Egypt will not be shielded by FSIA. In general, a government's contracts for the purchase or sale of goods rarely are viewed as *sovereign* acts. The expropriation of foreign investment, by way of contrast, is recognized widely as the paradigm of a sovereign act that is entitled to immunity.

Private persons of foreign citizenship cannot invoke sovereign immunity; only foreign states and their official agents and entities are shielded by FSIA. Thus, a corporation that is wholly owned by a foreign government, such as a national airline, is a "foreign state" for purposes of the FSIA. In many parts of the world, the state-owned commercial enterprise is an important concept. In the Soviet Union, for example, every enterprise is controlled by the government. Consequently, Soviet banks, trading companies, manufacturers, and ballet companies all are entitled to assert sovereign immunity (although the immunity defense still may fail because of the commercial-activity exception). In many nations comparable entities would be owned partially by the government. The distinction between public and private blurs when the government is only part owner of the enterprise, making the application of sovereign immunity more difficult.

THE ACT-OF-STATE DOCTRINE

A complement to sovereign immunity is the **act-of-state doctrine,** which also bars the adjudication of a claim against a foreign sovereign. This defense prevents a court in one country from questioning the legitimacy of the conduct of another country. Thus, United States courts will not examine the validity of an expropriation by a foreign government of property within its own territory, even if the taking violates international law. As long as the state expropriates on its own soil, the American investor will find her lawsuit blocked in a court in this country because the taking falls within the act-of-state doctrine.

The underpinnings of this doctrine in the United States lie in the constitutional principle of separation of powers among the three branches of our government. An American court cannot question the acts of a foreign government, let alone seize its property in the United States, without engendering that nation's hostility for interfering with its activities. If an American court could second guess the acts of another state and refuse to honor them, in effect a judge would be shaping or influencing United States foreign policy from the bench. Under our Constitution, this role is reserved for the president and other members of the executive branch of the national government.

LICENSING TECHNOLOGY ABROAD

As an alternative to direct investment abroad, a United States firm can license its technology or know-how to a foreign manufacturer. A licensing agreement permits an American firm to tap overseas labor and sales markets without establishing overseas facilities and encountering all of the difficulties and risks that might present. Although licensing agreements avoid the threat of expropriation of physical property, they do have their disadvantages because they compromise the integrity and secrecy of "industrial" or "intellectual" property, which can prove very damaging to the American firm.

Patents are the chief legal vehicle for protecting industrial creativity. The laws on what constitutes patentable technology are peculiar to each country, but usually a patent is available for "useful innovations"—those not known to the general public. A patent may be based on a creative improvement in a product, giving it superior features, or may be based on an innovation in the manufacturing process, perhaps by lowering the cost of production. A valid patent permits its holder to prohibit others from use of the patented invention for a period of years that varies from country to country; in the United States a patent's life is seventeen years. American patent law is discussed at greater length in Chapter 28.

There is no worldwide legal system for regulating patents. As a result, a patent secured under our laws offers no protection from infringements abroad, because patents are not recognized outside of their country of origin—an American patent has no application beyond the territorial borders of the United States. American firms must rely on the laws of any country in which their patents are licensed to protect their industrial innovations.

It should be kept in mind that not all useful innovations are patentable. When unpatented technology is to be licensed, companies must rely on the secrecy of their operations and pledges of confidentiality to safeguard valuable information and innovation. Thus, when trade secrets are to be licensed abroad it is imperative to include a non-disclosure clause in the contract. Unfortunately, these provisions are difficult to enforce for the reasons outlined at the beginning of this chapter. Moreover, because licensing abroad reveals the secrets to new parties and subjects them to pressures by foreign governments to disclose, the potential for information leaks and loss of secrecy multiplies. That is why American companies are not likely ever to part with the core of their technology and rarely license their entire operations in foreign countries. Instead, licensing agreements typically are limited to a few specific, patentable innovations.

In order to protect a patent when it is to be used abroad, a United States firm can apply for a parallel patent in any country that maintains a patent system. Once an American firm obtains a parallel patent, it can license its exclusive technology to a manufacturer in the country that granted it in exchange for royalty payments without fear that it will be stolen. Similarly, if the American firm chooses to market its locally patented product directly, it is not necessary to rely on pledges of secrecy because the novelty embedded in the product is protected from duplication by that nation's law.

Success in obtaining a parallel patent is not automatic, however. Since the law in each nation is entirely controlling within that country as to what is protectable, the existence of an American patent is irrelevant. A given innovation may be patentable in one country but not in another. Efforts to create a uniform international patent law have been frustrated by deep divisions separating industrialized from developing nations. Aggressive industrialization campaigns launched by the developing countries often are accompanied by demands for access to protected information held by persons from highly industrialized nations. The United States balance of payments in this area illustrates the nature of the problem. In 1987, companies in the United States paid $565

million in royalties for the use of technology from abroad but received $5 billion, or ten times as much, in royalty payments from technology sent abroad. Despite the many obstacles to agreement on uniform treatment, 85 countries have joined the International Convention for the Protection of Industrial Property Rights. The convention brings some harmony, although not uniformity, into the field. It recognizes, among other things, the date of the first filing for patent protection in any of the signatory countries as the filing date in all of them.

Some countries, particularly in the developing world, require that all licensing agreements with their nationals be registered with a government agency. That agency typically has broad discretion to prohibit licensing agreements considered out of step with the national program for economic development. The other objective of this type of government involvement is to enhance the bargaining power of local manufacturers. Japan, for example, often uses its regulatory scheme to handicap foreign licensors in favor of domestic manufacturers.

THE INTERNATIONAL MONETARY SYSTEM

One of the reasons international business is much more complicated than domestic business is because each country has its own currency and pursues its own monetary policies. Since there is no worldwide authority that controls the movement of currency, the system is decentralized. Nonetheless, money must cross national boundaries and, not surprisingly, extensive arrangements exist to facilitate this. Perhaps the most important of these is the **International Monetary Fund,** which, along with the World Bank, is designed to stabilize the world's money market, promote international trade, and eliminate foreign-exchange restrictions that hamper trade. A number of regional institutions, such as the European Monetary System and the Asian Development Bank, also exist to facilitate the movement of money and promote trade. In the United States, the **Export-Import Bank,** a federal agency, performs comparable services by providing loans and making loan guarantees to foreign purchasers for goods to be exported from this country.

Buying and selling across national boundaries usually involves people who want to trade in their own currencies. Acme, the American manufacturer of wooden picture frames, will want to be paid in United States dollars; its French customer, however, will want to pay in French francs. These conflicting desires can be accommodated because the monetary system permits the conversion of one currency into another through a worldwide network of money brokers and dealers, with the funds actually changing hands through entries in accounts in commercial banks, often electronically.

However, private transactions, like the one between Acme and the French buyer, are governed by national financial institutions that determine what fiscal policy would best serve the country's interest. In the United States, it is the Department of the Treasury. The actual implementation of the government's policy is carried out by the central bank of the country, which in the United States is the Federal Reserve Bank. It is these governmental instrumentalities that control the conduct of the commercial banks, many of which have branches in foreign countries, and make certain that the nation's financial policy is carried out. The demands of this policy can have a significant impact on the international marketplace.

Despite all of this superstructure, the execution of a purchase and sale can be accomplished relatively simply in most instances. Assuming no letter of credit is being used, when the French buyer of Acme's frames is ready to pay for them it will go to a French bank and ask that the appropriate amount of its funds be transferred, in dollars, to Acme's account in an American bank. The French bank will ask an American bank with which it has established relations to do so, and will permit the American bank to reimburse itself out of an account in dollars that the French bank has opened

with the American bank. The transfer can work in reverse, because the American bank will have opened an account in francs with the French bank.

INTERNATIONAL DISPUTE SETTLEMENT

As has been seen throughout this chapter, doing business in the international marketplace entails a number of special risks, such as expropriation and import and monetary controls. In addition, even normal commercial risks, such as breach of contract, are accompanied by hazards that are made more difficult to deal with by language, custom, and national boundaries. In the case of purely commerical disputes between businesses, like Acme and its French customer, the courts of both the seller's and the buyer's nation are available to hear the matter. Issues such as sovereign immunity and the act-of-state doctrine do not arise. Nonetheless, a national of one country often is loathe to submit his fortunes to a tribunal in his adversary's country. This is particularly true, for example, when an American merchant has a disagreement with a company in a communist or third-world country. Even when the American can bring suit in a United States court, there always is a question of whether the courts in the opposing party's nation will enforce the American judgment. Because of these difficulties, other dispute-resolution techniques are necessary.

If an investor believes that another nation has caused him damage in violation of international law, he can try to persuade his country to bring a lawsuit against the other nation in the **International Court of Justice,** which is part of the United Nations. The court, which sits in The Hague, Netherlands, has fifteen judges from all over the world and has been instrumental since its creation in developing a body of international law. But only nations may appear before the International Court, so the investor will have to convince his government to proceed. Even when one nation decides to go forward, the other nation may decline to accept the court's jurisdiction on the ground that the matter is "domestic." For these reasons, resort to the International Court is rare.

Because of the great uncertainties associated with international business transactions, many companies have turned to arbitration as the preferred mechanism for handling disputes. Most nations in the world now recognize and have enacted legislation authorizing the use of this procedure. Indeed, there are now a number of international agreements designed to facilitate and effectuate arbitration. The most important of these is the United Nations Convention on the Recognition and Enforcement of Foreign Arbitral Awards, which seeks to support the use of arbitration by providing some assurance that arbitration agreements will be honored and arbitration awards will be enforced. Courts in the United States generally have carried out the intention of the convention and have interpreted its limitations narrowly. Thus, for example, parties who have agreed to arbitration in their contract cannot bring a lawsuit instead. The decision to submit all disputes arising out of an international trade agreement to arbitration must be made carefully, and the terms and conditions of the arbitration must be spelled out very carefully in the contract.

SUMMARY

Since the Second World War, international business has played an increasingly important role in American commercial life. In the decades following the war the United States was instrumental in promoting the creation of an integrated world market unconstrained by national boundaries. Although many problems still remain regarding international trade, the situation is far better than it was during the age of national isolationism that preceded the war.

American firms can participate in international business by selling their products directly abroad, appointing a foreign distributor, establishing manufacturing facilities abroad, or licensing their technology to a foreign manufacturer. Whatever the mode of participation, the legal environment for international business can be quite different abroad than in the United States.

Direct international sales are fraught with pitfalls for the buyer and the seller, because there is no convenient mechanism for enforcing their purchase and sales agreement. The buyer will not risk paying for the goods until she receives them, and the seller will not risk shipping the goods without some assurance of fairly immediate payment. The gap between the trading partners is closed by a documentary irrevocable letter of credit issued by a bank in the buyer's country and confirmed by another bank in the seller's country. This transaction gives the seller a promise of payment upon shipment, from a local bank. Agreements between the bank and the seller usually are subject to the Uniform Customs and Practices for Documentary Credits, a publication of the International Chamber of Commerce. (If the seller is in the United States, the Uniform Commercial Code also applies.) The Uniform Customs and Practices for Documentary Credits provides that the agreement between the bank and the seller is independent of the underlying sales agreement. Once the designated goods are shipped properly, the seller is entitled to immediate payment by the bank.

Every private international sale has to be approved by the trading countries. The seller must have the right to export and the buyer to import the product into the country. For example, sensitive military technology may not be exported from the United States. A customs tariff is imposed on imported items based on each item's value and classification.

Restrictions on imports are governed by the General Agreement on Tariffs and Trade, which has been agreed to by 84 nations. GATT prohibits all nontariff restrictions on international trade. Despite this agreement, before an item can be imported into the country it must comply with all applicable customs regulations and a number of other legal requirements, such as product standards. For example, motor vehicles imported into the United States must comply with federal safety statutes. Compliance with a nation's restrictions is necessary whether or not they are in violation of a country's obligation under GATT.

Appointing a distributor abroad is an effective way to gain a foothold in a foreign market. A distribution agreement often will include a promise by the distributor not to sell competing products. A United States firm the includes an exclusive-dealing provision may be in violation of Section 1 of the Sherman Antitrust Act. Appointing an exclusive distributor in a foreign country, however, does not raise problems under the American antitrust laws, although the practice may violate the antitrust laws of the host country. For example, anticompetitive trade is restricted in the European Economic Community by Article 85 of the Treaty of Rome. A United States firm is likely to escape the sanction of EEC and American antitrust laws if its exclusive distribution agreement is limited in scope and duration.

Several multinational legal regimes have emerged since World War II. Perhaps the most important of these, from the perspective of the United States, is the European Economic Community (EEC), which ties most of our European trading partners together. The goals of the EEC are to abolish tariffs and quotas within the Community and develop common customs tariff and commerical policy toward other nations. The EEC has the power to enact laws and enter into treaties that bind the member states. An American business entering the EEC must comply with all of its laws and regulations.

A United States firm may open a manufacturing facility in a foreign country to take advantage of an abundant labor supply or a profitable market abroad. That frequently is not easy to accomplish, and is accompanied by many dangers. The laws of the host nation may require a long-term commitment from foreign investors. Additionally, an American firm faces the problem of limitations on its ability to convert its profits from the local currency into United States dollars and repatriate the funds. Many countries do not want a foreign company's earnings to leave their economy, especially in the form of a hard currency like the dollar.

The most disquieting fear of investment in another country is the threat of outright government expropriation of assets, especially because it typically is not accompanied by compensation for the seized property. An American investor can protect itself against this type of loss by buying expropriation insurance from the Overseas Private Investment Corporation, an insurance fund managed by the United States government. When an American company's loss is uninsured, our government has a policy of applying measured diplomatic pressure to obtain compensation from the expropriating country, but little else is possible.

The two doctrines of sovereign immunity and act of state usually preclude any judicial remedy in this country for an investor whose property has been expropriated or who has been injured in any other way by a foreign nation. The doctrine of sovereign immunity reflects the unwillingness of nations to subject another sovereign or any of its instrumentalities to suit in a foreign court. An important distinction is drawn between sovereign acts and purely commerical activity by foreign governments. Within the exception for purely commerical activity, immunity from suit is not available to a sovereign defendant or any entity it owns or controls, such as a national airline. Expropriation always has been deemed a sovereign act; hence, there is no judicial remedy for an investor either in our courts or in the courts of any other country that follows the immunity doctrine. Similarly, a government taking of private property on its own soil is considered an act of state. The act-of-state doctrine recognizes that judges should not shape United States foreign policy from the bench by adjudicating the propriety of domestic actions of foreign governments. Our relations with foreign governments are to be left to the executive branch.

A United States firm may choose to license its technology to a foreign manufacturer in exchange for royalty payments. Patents are the chief vehicle for protecting industrial innovations, but there is no worldwide recognition of patents, and to be protected an American firm must obtain parallel patents under the laws of other countries. Trade secrets often are licensed to foreign companies under agreements containing nondisclosure clauses. This is risky because of the serious likelihood that the agreement will be violated. In addition, some countries require registration of all licensing agreements involving technology. The usual goal of such registration is to enhance the bargaining power of local businesses.

Because each nation has its own currency, the payment of international transactions can become complicated. Stability is achieved with the aid of the International Monetary Fund, the World Bank, and a number of regional institutions. Because buyers and sellers wish to trade in their own currencies, the international monetary system must arrange the conversion of one monetary unit into another. Private international transactions are governed by the fiscal policies of the parties' countries, which are established by government agencies.

Doing business in the international environment is full of risks that require special attention to determining how to resolve any disputes that might arise between the parties. Although each nation's courts are open to hear commerical disputes, many businesspeople understandably are reluctant to have their rights determined by a foreign tribunal or to run the risk that a judgment from their own courts will not be enforced by the courts in the opponent's country. On some occasions, the matter can be taken to the International Court of Justice by the nations whose citizens are involved. The commerical dispute-settlement technique that has become very common is an agreement to submit all disagreements to arbitration under terms specified in the basic contract.

KEY TERMS AND CONCEPTS

documentary irrevocable letter of credit
letter of credit
Uniform Customs and Practices for Documentary Credits
General Agreement on Tariffs and Trade (GATT)
customs duty
London Court of Arbitration
European Economic Community (EEC)
Treaty of Rome
Andean Common Market Group
repatriation
expropriation
confiscation
Overseas Private Investment Corporation (OPIC)
Foreign Claims Settlement Commission
sovereign immunity
Foreign Sovereign Immunities Act (FSIA)
act-of-state doctrine
International Monetary Fund
Export-Import Bank
International Court of Justice

PROBLEMS

1. Chips Unlimited, an American company, contracted to sell one million computer chips to Informatique, a French company. A letter of credit was issued by a French bank and confirmed by the Big Apple Bank in New York City. Two days after the chips had been shipped to France, Informatique declared bankruptcy under French law. What are the Big Apple Bank's obligations under the letter of credit?

2. International Shoe Corporation, located in the state of Washington, decided to expand its sales into Japan by signing a distribution agreement with Oshinko, a Japanese shoe distributor. Under the agreement, Oshinko was to buy at least 5,000 pairs of shoes a year from International Shoe at a price highly favorable to Oshinko. Oshinko also agreed not to sell any other brands of American-made shoes. The agreement was to last for three years. What are the potential legal problems of this transaction? How are they likely to be resolved?

3. World-wide Volkswagen, an automobile distributor in Cos Cob, Connecticut, imports Volkswagen automobiles into the United States. The latest shipment is awaiting customs clearance on a New York dock. This year, customs regulations imposed a limit on the number of convertibles that can be brought into the country. Volkswagen's new model, a sporty T-roof compact, has been classified by the customs officials as a convertible, and only a part of World-wide's shipment has been allowed to enter the country. What recourse is available to World-wide Volkswagen? What is the relevance of the fact that the United States is a member of GATT?

4. An American company, Endicott Copper, established copper-mining facilities in Chile in 1940. Over the years the government of that country placed ever-greater restrictions on Endicott's profits. Then, in 1980, the Chilean government nationalized the entire copper-mining industry. Endicott sued for compensation through all levels of the Chilean court system but was unsuccessful because the courts declined to hear claims challenging the government's actions. Endicott now wants to sue Chile in the courts of another country for violations of international law. In what types of countries would it make or not make sense to bring suit? How would a court in the United States resolve this case?

5. Ever since 1935, Canadian Fibres, Inc. has sold asbestos to companies in the United States. In 1978, the Canadian government purchased a controlling interest in the company. In 1985, a group of workers at a plant in Tyler, Texas, who had handled products manufactured with Canadian's asbestos over the years and who are now suffering from asbestosis and mesothelioma brought suit for damages against Canadian Fibres in a federal court in Texas. Should the American court hear the lawsuit?

6. The nation of Utopia, a hypothetical member of GATT, has just unilaterally imposed a ten-percent surcharge on imports, justifying its action on the ground that it had a serious imbalance in its international balance of payments. Several other member states disagree with Utopia's action. Is Utopia justified in imposing the surcharge, or is it in violation of its obligations under GATT? By what procedure will the dispute be resolved?

APPENDIX

Appendix A

How to Read and Brief a Case

_____

_____

_____

_____

The study of American law, and the legal system through which it is administered, involves the study of three primary sources of law—constitutional provisions, statutes, and court cases. Written constitutions, both federal and state, embody the authority from the people to the federal and state governments to make and enforce laws, and provide the limits within which governmental powers may be exercised. Statutes, then, are enacted by legislative bodies, including Congress and the various state legislatures, and are regarded generally as positive law. Courts hand down decisions in cases. Some of these decisions interpret constitutional provisions, some determine the validity of statutes, and some make positive law involving matters not addressed by statutes. Therefore, it is essential that a student of law be thoroughly familiar with reading and understanding cases.

Case briefing involves summarizing, or abstracting, cases. The entire process requires the student to read a case carefully, to extract the important points, and to set those points down in a form that enables him to read the brief later and refresh his memory as to the essentials of the case. The precise form used is a matter of personal taste. However, the following is a list of elements generally recognized as important for a complete brief:

1) Case name
2) Citation
3) Summary of important facts
4) Issue(s) before the court
5) The court's decision on each issue
6) The reason(s) for each decision
7) Dissenting and concurring opinions

8) Dictum

9) Comments

Of these, the first six are essential, and the last three are optional and may be important in only some cases.

Case Name

The name of the case is important as a reference. It serves the same purpose as a person's name—as a means of identification. It should be understood that the order of the names of the parties, as they appear in the case name, are of no significance unless the student is familiar with the procedure of the jurisdiction in which the particular case was decided. That is, the party whose name appears first is not always the plaintiff. In the original trial court, the plaintiff's name does appear first. Thereafter, some jurisdictions continue to use the same name throughout the appeal process. Others follow the practice of putting the name of the appellant first. In the latter, a case may begin in the trial court "Smith v. Jones," and if Jones appeals, the name will be changed to "Jones v. Smith." If the original decision is reversed on appeal and Smith appeals further, the name will again be changed to "Smith v. Jones." (Incidentally, the "v." between the names of the parties stands for "versus," which is Latin for "against.") One further matter should be noted concerning case names. Many cases have multiple plaintiffs and multiple defendants. Then, the usual practice is to entitle the case using the names of only the first plaintiff and the first defendant listed on the complaint.

Citation

A case citation usually is found directly below the case name. A complete citation will reveal four important points about the case: (1) where a report of the case may be found, (2) the jurisdiction in which it was decided, (3) the level of the court handing down the decision, and (4) the date of the decision. Consider, for example, the first case in Chapter 2:

FLAGIELLO v. PENNSYLVANIA HOSPITAL
417 Pa. 486, 208 A.2d 193 (1965)

A report of this case can be found in two places—volume 417 of the Pennsylvania Reporter, beginning on page 486, and volume 208 of the Atlantic Reporter, Second Series, beginning on page 193. The case was decided in Pennsylvania by the highest state court which, in Pennsylvania, is the Pennsylvania Supreme Court. (If it had been decided in the intermediate court

of appeals, the first half of the citation would have been "417 Pa.*App.* 486.") The case was decided by the supreme court in 1965.

The reason the case is reported in two places is that, at the time of the decision, the state of Pennsylvania published the decisions of its supreme court in an "official reporter," Pennsylvania Reports, and a private publisher, West Publishing Company, reported cases decided on appeal in all states. Pennsylvania cases appear in the Atlantic Reporter, which also reports cases decided in Connecticut, Delaware, District of Columbia, Maine, Maryland, New Hampshire, New Jersey, Rhode Island, and Vermont. The following is a list of the state "regional reporters" and the states covered in each:

Atlantic Reporter (A)—Connecticut, Delaware, District of Columbia, Maine, Maryland, New Hampshire, New Jersey, Pennsylvania, Rhode Island, and Vermont

North Eastern Reporter (NE)—Illinois, Indiana, Massachusetts, New York, and Ohio

North Western Reporter (NW)—Iowa, Michigan, Minnesota, Nebraska, North Dakota, South Dakota, and Wisconsin

Pacific Reporter (P)—Alaska, Arizona, California, Colorado, Hawaii, Idaho, Kansas, Montana, Nevada, New Mexico, Oklahoma, Oregon, Utah, Washington, and Wyoming

Southern Reporter (S)—Alabama, Florida, Louisiana, and Mississippi

South Eastern Reporter (SE)—Georgia, North Carolina, South Carolina, Virginia, and West Virginia

South Western Reporter (SW)—Arkansas, Kentucky, Missouri, Tennessee, and Texas

After each of these reporters reaches a certain point in volume numbering (200 in the case of the Atlantic Reporter), a Second Series is begun. This is indicated by a "2d" following the name. Thus, "200 A.2d" means volume 200 in the second series of the Atlantic Reporter, which is different than "200 A.," and contains more recent cases.

Some states do not publish a separate official reporter. Instead, the regional reporter is *de facto*, or by adoption, the official reporter. Note that the first case in Chapter 1, *Eaton v. Sontag*, is cited "387 A.2d 333 (Me, 1978)." The jurisdiction and the level of court are included next to the date—here, the Supreme Court of Maine.

In addition to the state regional reporters, West Publishing Company also publishes federal reporters as follows:

Supreme Court Reporter (S.Ct.)—United States Supreme Court

Supreme Court Reporter, Lawyers Edition (L.Ed.)—United States Supreme Court

Federal Reporter (F.)—United States circuit courts of appeals

Federal Supplement (F.Supp.)—Selected United States district court cases

Of these, the Federal Supplement is unique. It reports selected trial decisions of the federal district courts. Ordinarily trial court decisions are not reported since they are not binding as legal precedent. (The concept of precedent is discussed in Chapter 2 under the heading *"Stare Decisis."*)

Facts

One of the most difficult tasks in briefing is properly summarizing the facts. One is tempted to say "the shorter the better" and, although the idea has merit, care must be taken to state all of the facts necessary to developing an understanding of the decision and reasoning. The detail also must be sufficient to permit the reader to refresh his memory as to the case's background, and who was plaintiff and who was defendant, by a quick reading.

Issue(s)

This section of the brief states the legal question or questions presented to the appeals court. Generally, issues are the questions of law to be decided, although in some cases questions of fact may be presented, such as whether the evidence was sufficient for a court to find that the defendant was negligent.

Holding(s)

A holding is the court's decision on an issue. Reference to the parties may be either plaintiff/defendant, as they appeared in the trial court, or appellant/appellee (or other appropriate titles), as they appeared on appeal.

Reasoning

This part of the brief is used for the statements by the court as to why it decided the issues as it did. It is here that the important rules of law are found. This section often is difficult to formulate, but it is perhaps the most important part of any brief. The statements found in the reasoning set precedent for future court decisions.

Dissenting and Concurring Opinions

This is the first of the optional sections. The decision of the court is found in the majority opinion, written by one of the justices. In addition, one or more of the justices may wish to write a separate opinion embodying other observations about the case. A justice who agrees with the majority of the court may write a separate concurring opinion, and one who disagrees with the majority may write a dissenting opinion. These opinions do not set precedent, but they may contain information you consider important.

Dictum

Not all statements of rules of law in a court's decision relate to the facts of the case. Sometimes justices also express their opinions as to the attitude the court might have in the event that the facts of the case were different in some respect. Also, justices sometimes state rules of law that have no relationship whatsoever to the case before them. All such statements are considered dicta. Although they are not considered binding precedent, they may be of value in predicting future court decisions.

Comments

You may wish to include notes as to your feelings or opinion concerning the outcome of a case, particularly important portions of the court's reasoning, or any other matter involving the case. In fact, you should never hesitate to disagree with a court's decision just because it was handed down by justices who, we may assume, know more about the law than you do. Because judges are human, they are subject to human error. At the very least, questions and disagreements concerning cases provide a basis for discussion of principles of law, sometimes even those not directly involved in the case under consideration. Such discussion can be extremely valuable in the study of law.

Now it is time to try your hand at briefing a case. Read and study the first case in Chapter 1, *Eaton v. Sontag*. You may find you will want to read through the case once, just as you read other kinds of material, to get a general idea of what the case is about, and then go through it a second time paying close attention to the details you want to include in your brief, beginning with the essential facts. Construct your brief section by section.

When you have finished your brief, compare it to the one presented here. Keep in mind that you may be referring to your brief weeks, months, or even years later. Which brief better meets your needs—yours or the one here? Why? Maybe you will find that neither really satisfies you. If so, perhaps a rewrite is in order.

EATON v. SONTAG
387 A.2d 33 (Me. 1978)

FACTS: Plaintiffs (Eatons) sued the Sontags to recover money due on a note given by Defendants to secure the purchase price of property they purchased from Plaintiffs. Defendants counter-claimed for fraud, contending that because they had been close friends of Plaintiffs for fifteen years, Plaintiffs owed to them a higher duty of disclosure of facts than would be owed by an ordinary seller to an ordinary purchaser. The trial court held for Plaintiffs on both the complaint and the counter-claim. Affirmed.

ISSUE: Does a long-time friendship between a buyer and a seller impose additional duties of disclosure on the seller?

HOLDING: No—for Plaintiffs

REASONING: Generally the relationship of vendor-vendee does not give rise to an imposition of special duties imposed in confidential relationships. The fact that the parties had been friends for a long time does not change this. Here, there was no indication that Defendants were dependent on Plaintiff's judgement—they rejected the first offer Plaintiffs made. In addition, there was no indication that Defendants acted without first fully considering the facts.

Appendix | B

The Constitution of the United States

PREAMBLE

We the People of the United States, in Order to form a more perfect Union, establish Justice, insure domestic Tranquility, provide for the common defence, promote the general Welfare, and secure the Blessings of Liberty to ourselves and our Posterity, do ordain and establish this Constitution for the United States of America.

Article I

Section 1. All legislative Powers herein granted shall be vested in a Congress of the United States, which shall consist of a Senate and House of Representatives.

Section 2. [1] The House of Representatives shall be composed of Members chosen every second Year by the People of the several States, and the Electors in each State shall have the Qualifications requisite for Electors of the most numerous Branch of the State Legislature.

[2] No Person shall be a Representative who shall not have attained to the Age of twenty five Years, and been seven Years a Citizen of the United States, and who shall not, when elected, be an Inhabitant of that State in which he shall be chosen.

[3] Representatives and direct Taxes shall be apportioned among the several States which may be included within this Union, according to their respective Numbers, which shall be determined by adding to the whole Number of free Persons, including those bound to Service for a Term of Years, and excluding Indians not taxed, three fifths of all other Persons. The actual Enumeration shall be made within three Years after the first Meeting of the Congress of the United States, and within every subsequent Term of ten Years, in such Manner as they shall by Law direct. The Number of Representatives shall not exceed one for every thirty Thousand, but each State shall have at Least one Repre-

sentative; and until such enumeration shall be made, the State of New Hampshire shall be entitled to chuse three, Massachusetts eight, Rhode Island and Providence Plantations one, Connecticut five, New York six, New Jersey four, Pennsylvania eight, Delaware one, Maryland six, Virginia ten, North Carolina five, South Carolina five, and Georgia three.

[4] When vacancies happen in the Representation from any State, the Executive Authority thereof shall issue Writs of Election to fill such Vacancies.

[5] The House of Representation shall chuse their Speaker and other Officers; and shall have the sole Power of Impeachment.

Section 3. [1] The Senate of the United States shall be composed of two Senators from each State, chosen by the Legislature thereof, for six Years; and each Senator shall have one Vote.

[2] Immediately after they shall be assembled in Consequence of the first Election, they shall be divided as equally as may be into three Classes. The Seats of the Senators of the first Class shall be vacated at the Expiration of the Second Year, of the second Class at the Expiration of the fourth Year, and of the third Class at the Expiration of the sixth Year, so that one third may be chosen every second Year; and if Vacancies happen by Resignation, or otherwise, during the Recess of the Legislature of any State, the Executive thereof may make temporary Appointments until the next Meeting of the Legislature, which shall then fill such Vacancies.

[3] No Person shall be a Senator who shall not have attained to the Age of thirty Years, and been nine Years a Citizen of the United States, and who shall not, when elected, be an Inhabitant of that State for which he shall be chosen.

[4] The Vice President of the United States shall be President of the Senate, but shall have no Vote, unless they be equally divided.

[5] The Senate shall chuse their other Officers, and also a President pro tempore, in the Absence of the Vice President, or when he shall exercise the Office of President of the United States.

[6] The Senate shall have the sole Power to try all Impeachments. When sitting for that Purpose, they shall be on Oath or Affirmation. When the President of the United States is tried, the Chief Justice shall preside: And no Person shall be convicted without the Concurrence of two thirds of the Members present.

[7] Judgment in Cases of Impeachment shall not extend further than to removal from Office, and dis-

qualification to hold and enjoy any Office of honor, Trust, or Profit under the United States: but the Party convicted shall nevertheless be liable and subject to Indictment, Trial, Judgment, and Punishment, according to Law.

Section 4. [1] The Times, Places and Manner of holding Elections for Senators and Representatives, shall be prescribed in each State by the Legislature thereof; but the Congress may at any time by Law make or alter such Regulations, except as to the Places of chusing Senators.

[2] The Congress shall assemble at least once in every Year, and such Meeting shall be on the first Monday in December, unless they shall by Law appoint a different Day.

Section 5. [1] Each House shall be the Judge of the Elections, Returns, and Qualifications of its own Members, and a Majority of each shall constitute a Quorum to do Business; but a smaller Number may adjourn from day to day, and may be authorized to compel the Attendance of absent Members, in such Manner, and under such Penalties as each House may provide.

[2] Each House may determine the Rules of its Proceedings, punish its Members for disorderly Behavior, and, with the Concurrence of two thirds, expel a Member.

[3] Each House shall keep a Journal of its Proceedings, and from time to time publish the same, excepting such Parts as may in their Judgment require Secrecy; and the Yeas and Nays of the Members of either House on any question shall, at the Desire of one fifth of those Present, be entered on the Journal.

[4] Neither House, during the Session of Congress, shall, without the Consent of the other, adjourn for more than three days, nor to any other Place than that in which the two Houses shall be sitting.

Section 6. [1] The Senators and Representatives shall receive a Compensation for their Services, to be ascertained by Law, and paid out of the Treasury of the United States. They shall in all Cases, except Treason, Felony and Breach of the Peace, be privileged from Arrest during their Attendance at the Session of their respective Houses, and in going to and returning from the same; and for any Speech or Debate in either House, they shall not be questioned in any other Place.

[2] No Senator or Representative shall, during the Time for which he was elected, be appointed to any civil Office under the Authority of the United States, which shall have been created, or the Emoluments

whereof shall have been encreased during such time; and no Person holding any Office under the United States, shall be a Member of either House during his Continuance in Office.

Section 7. [1] All Bills for raising Revenue shall originate in the House of Representatives; but the Senate may propose or concur with Amendments as on other Bills.

[2] Every Bill which shall have passed the House of Representatives and the Senate, shall, before it become a Law, be presented to the President of the United States; If he approve he shall sign it, but if not he shall return it, with his Objections to the House in which it shall have originated, who shall enter the Objections at large on their Journal, and proceed to reconsider it. If after such Reconsideration two thirds of that House shall agree to pass the Bill, it shall be sent together with the Objections, to the other House, by which it shall likewise be reconsidered, and if approved by two thirds of that House, it shall become a Law. But in all such Cases the Votes of both Houses shall be determined by yeas and Nays, and the Names of the Persons voting for and against the Bill shall be entered on the Journal of each House respectively. If any Bill shall not be returned by the President within ten Days (Sundays excepted) after it shall have been presented to him, the Same shall be a Law, in like Manner as if he had signed it, unless the Congress by their Adjournment prevent its Return in which Case it shall not be a Law.

[3] Every Order, Resolution, or Vote, to Which the Concurrence of the Senate and House of Representatives may be necessary (except on a question of Adjournment) shall be presented to the President of the United States; and before the Same shall take Effect, shall be approved by him, or being disapproved by him, shall be repassed by two thirds of the Senate and House of Representatives, according to the Rules and Limitations prescribed in the Case of a Bill.

Section 8. [1] The Congress shall have Power To lay and collect Taxes, Duties, Imposts and Excises, to pay the Debts and provide for the common Defence and general Welfare of the United States; but all Duties, Imposts and Excises shall be uniform throughout the United States;

[2] To borrow money on the credit of the United States;

[3] To regulate Commerce with foreign Nations, and among the several States, and with the Indian Tribes;

[4] To establish an uniform Rule of Naturalization, and uniform Laws on the subject of Bankruptcies throughout the United States;

[5] To coin Money, regulate the Value thereof, and of foreign Coin, and fix the Standard of Weights and Measures;

[6] To provide for the Punishment of counterfeiting the Securities and current Coin of the United States;

[7] To Establish Post Offices and Post Roads;

[8] To promote the Progress of Science and useful Arts, by securing for limited Times to Authors and Inventors the exclusive Right to their respective Writings and Discoveries;

[9] To constitute Tribunals inferior to the supreme Court;

[10] To define and punish Piracies and Felonies committed on the high Seas, and Offenses against the Law of Nations:

[11] To declare War, grant Letters of Marque and Reprisal, and make Rules concerning Captures on Land and Water;

[12] To raise and support Armies, but no Appropriation of Money to that Use shall be for a longer Term than two Years;

[13] To provide and maintain a Navy;

[14] To make Rules for the Government and Regulation of the land and naval Forces;

[15] To provide for calling forth the Militia to execute the Laws of the Union, suppress Insurrections and repel Invasions;

[16] To provide for organizing, arming, and disciplining, the Militia, and for governing such Part of them as may be employed in the Service of the United States, reserving to the States respectively, the Appointment of the Officers, and the Authority of training the Militia according to the discipline prescribed by Congress;

[17] To exercise exclusive Legislation in all Cases whatsoever, over such District (not exceeding ten Miles square) as may, by Cession of particular States, and the Acceptance of Congress, become the Seat of the Government of the United States, and to exercise like Authority over all Places purchased by the Consent of the Legislature of the State in which the Same shall be, for the Erection of Forts, Magazines, Arsenals, dockYards, and other needful Buildings;—And

[18] To make all Laws which shall be necessary and proper for carrying into Execution the foregoing

Powers, and all other Powers vested by this Constitution in the Government of the United States, or in any Department or Officer thereof.

Section 9. [1] The Migration or Importation of Such Persons as any of the States now existing shall think proper to admit, shall not be prohibited by the Congress prior to the Year one thousand eight hundred and eight, but a Tax or duty may be imposed on such Importation, not exceeding ten dollars for each Person.

[2] The privilege of the Writ of Habeas Corpus shall not be suspended, unless when in Cases of Rebellion or Invasion the public Safety may require it.

[3] No Bill of Attainder or ex post facto Law shall be passed.

[4] No Capitation, or other direct, Tax shall be laid, unless in Proportion to the Census or Enumeration herein before directed to be taken.

[5] No Tax or Duty shall be laid on Articles exported from any State.

[6] No Preference shall be given by any Regulation of Commerce or Revenue to the Ports of one State over those of another: nor shall Vessels bound to, or from, one State be obliged to enter, clear, or pay Duties in another.

[7] No money shall be drawn from the Treasury, but in Consequence of Appropriations made by Law; and a regular Statement and Account of Receipts and Expenditures of all public Money shall be published from time to time.

[8] No Title of Nobility shall be granted by the United States: And no Person holding any Office of Profit or Trust under them, shall, without the Consent of the Congress, accept of any present, Emolument, Office, or Title, of any kind whatever, from any King, Prince, or foreign State.

Section 10. [1] No State shall enter into any Treaty, Alliance, or Confederation; grant Letters of Marque and Reprisal; coin Money; emit Bills of Credit; make any Thing but gold and silver Coin a Tender in Payment of Debts; pass any Bill of Attainder, ex post facto Law, or Law impairing the Obligation of Contracts, or grant any Title of Nobility.

[2] No State shall, without the Consent of the Congress, lay any Imposts or Duties on Imports or Exports, except what may be absolutely necessary for executing it's inspection Laws: and the net Produce of all Duties and Imposts, laid by any State on Imports or Exports, shall be for the Use of the Treasury of the United States; and all such Laws shall be subject to the Revision and Controul of the Congress.

[3] No State shall, without the Consent of Congress, lay any Duty of Tonnage, keep Troops, or Ships of War in time of Peace, enter into any Agreement or Compact with another State, or with a foreign Power, or engage in War, unless actually invaded, or in such imminent Danger as will not admit of delay.

Article II

Section 1. [1] The executive Power shall be vested in a President of the United States of America. He shall hold his Office during the Term of four Years, and, together with the Vice President, chosen for the same Term, be elected, as follows:

[2] Each State shall appoint, in such Manner as the Legislature thereof may direct, a Number of Electors, equal to the whole Number of Senators and Representatives to which the State may be entitled in the Congress; but no Senator or Representative, or Person holding an Office of Trust or Profit under the United States, shall be appointed an Elector.

[3] The Electors shall meet in their respective States, and vote by Ballot for two Persons, of whom one at least shall not be an Inhabitant of the same State with themselves. And they shall make a List of all the Persons voted for, and of the Number of Votes for each; which List they shall sign and certify, and transmit sealed to the Seat of the Government of the United States, directed to the President of the Senate. The President of the Senate shall, in the Presence of the Senate and House of Representatives, open all the Certificates, and the Votes shall then be counted. The Person having the greatest Number of Votes shall be the President, if such Number be a Majority of the whole Number of Electors appointed; and if there be more than one who have such Majority, and have an equal Number of Votes, then the House of Representatives shall immediately chuse by Ballot one of them for President; and if no Person have a Majority, then from the five highest on the List the said House shall in like Manner chuse the President. But in chusing the President, the Votes shall be taken by States, the Representation from each State having one Vote; A quorum for this Purpose shall consist of a Member or Members from two thirds of the States, and a Majority of all the States shall be necessary to a Choice. In every Case, after the Choice of the

President, the Person having the greater Number of Votes of the Electors shall be the Vice President. But if there should remain two or more who have equal Votes, the Senate shall chuse from them by Ballot the Vice President.

[4] The Congress may determine the Time of chusing the Electors, and the Day on which they shall give their Votes; which Day shall be the same throughout the United States.

[5] No person except a natural born Citizen, or a Citizen of the United States, at the time of the Adoption of this Constitution, shall be eligible to the Office of President; neither shall any Person be eligible to that Office who shall not have attained to the Age of thirty five Years, and been fourteen Years a Resident within the United States.

[6] In case of the removal of the President from Office, or of his Death, Resignation or Inability to discharge the Powers and Duties of the said Office, the Same shall devolve on the Vice President, and the Congress may by Law provide for the Case of Removal, Death, Resignation or Inability, both of the President and Vice President, declaring what Officer shall then act as President, and such Officer shall act accordingly, until the Disability be removed, or a President shall be elected.

[7] The President shall, at stated Times, receive for his Services, a Compensation, which shall neither be encreased nor diminished during the Period for which he shall have been elected, and he shall not receive within that Period any other Emolument from the United States, or any of them.

[8] Before he enter on the Execution of his Office, he shall take the following Oath or Affirmation: "I do solemnly swear (or affirm) that I will faithfully execute the Office of President of the United States, and will to the best of my Ability, preserve, protect and defend the Constitution of the United States."

Section 2. [1] The President shall be Commander in Chief of the Army and Navy of the United States, and of the militia of the several States, when called into the actual Service of the United States; he may require the Opinion, in writing, of the principal Officer in each of the executive Departments, upon any Subject relating to the Duties of their respective Offices, and he shall have Power to grant Reprieves and Pardons for Offenses against the United States, except in Cases of Impeachment.

[2] He shall have Power, by and with the Advice and Consent of the Senate, to make Treaties, provided two thirds of the Senators present concur; and he shall nominate, and by and with the Advice and Consent of the Senate, shall appoint Ambassadors, other public Ministers and Consuls, Judges of the supreme Court, and all other Officers of the United States, whose Appointments are not herein otherwise provided for, and which shall be established by Law; but the Congress may by Law vest the Appointment of such inferior Officers, as they think proper, in the President alone, in the Courts of Law, or in the Heads of Departments.

[3] The President shall have Power to fill up all Vacancies that may happen during the Recess of the Senate, by granting Commissions which shall expire at the End of their next Session.

Section 3. He shall from time to time give to the Congress Information of the State of the Union, and recommend to their Consideration such Measures as he shall judge necessary and expedient; he may, on extraordinary Occasions, convene both Houses, or either of them, and in Case of Disagreement between them, with Respect to the Time of Adjournment, he may adjourn them to such Time as he shall think proper; he shall receive Ambassadors and other public Ministers; he shall take Care that the Laws be faithfully executed, and shall Commission all the Officers of the United States.

Section 4. The President, Vice President and all civil Officers of the United States, shall be removed from Office on Impeachment for, and Conviction of, Treason, Bribery, or other high Crimes and Misdemeanors.

Article III

Section 1. The judicial Power of the United States, shall be vested in one supreme Court, and in such inferior Courts as the Congress may from time to time ordain and establish. The Judges, both of the supreme and inferior Courts, shall hold their Offices during good Behaviour, and shall, at stated Times, receive for their Services a Compensation, which shall not be diminished during their Continuance in Office.

Section 2. [1] The judicial Power shall extend to all Cases, in Law and Equity, arising under this Constitution, the Laws of the United States, and Treaties made, or which shall be made, under their Authority;—to all Cases affecting Ambassadors, other public Ministers and Consuls;—to all Cases of admiralty and maritime Jurisdiction;—to Controversies to which the United States shall be a Party;—to Controversies between two or more States;—between a State and Citizens of another State;—between Citizens of different States;—between Citizens of the same State claiming Lands under the Grants of different States, and between a State, or the Citizens thereof, and foreign States, Citizens or Subjects.

[2] In all Cases affecting Ambassadors, other public Ministers and Consuls, and those in which a State shall be a Party, the supreme Court shall have original Jurisdiction. In all the other Cases before mentioned, the supreme Court shall have appellate Jurisdiction, both as to Law and Fact, with such Exceptions, and under such Regulations as the Congress shall make.

[3] The trial of all Crimes, except in Cases of Impeachment, shall be by Jury; and such Trial shall be held in the State where the said Crimes shall have been committed; but when not committed within any State, the Trial shall be at such Place or Places as the Congress may by Law have directed.

Section 3. [1] Treason against the United States, shall consist only in levying War against them, or, in adhering to their Enemies, giving them Aid and Comfort. No Person shall be convicted of Treason unless on the Testimony of two Witnesses to the same overt Act, or on Confession in open Court.

[2] The Congress shall have Power to declare the Punishment of Treason, but no Attainder of Treason shall work Corruption of Blood, or Forfeiture except during the Life of the Person attainted.

Article IV

Section 1. Full Faith and Credit shall be given in each State to the public Acts, Records, and judicial Proceedings of every other State. And the Congress may by general Laws prescribe the Manner in which such Acts, Records and Proceedings shall be proved, and the Effect thereof.

Section 2. [1] The Citizens of each State shall be entitled to all Privileges and Immunities of Citizens in the several States.

[2] A Person charged in any State with Treason, Felony, or other Crime, who shall flee from Justice, and be found in another State, shall on demand of the executive Authority of the State from which he fled, be delivered up, to be removed to the State having Jurisdiction of the Crime.

[3] No Person held to Service or Labour in one State, under the Laws thereof, escaping into another, shall, in Consequence of any Law or Regulation therein, be discharged from such Service or Labour, but shall be delivered up on Claim of the Party to whom such Service or Labour may be due.

Section 3. [1] New States may be admitted by the Congress into this Union; but no new State shall be formed or erected within the Jurisdiction of any other State; nor any State be formed by the Junction of two or more States, or Parts of States, without the Consent of the Legislatures of the States concerned as well as of the Congress.

[2] The Congress shall have Power to dispose of and make all needful Rules and Regulations respecting the Territory or other Property belonging to the United States; and nothing in this Constitution shall be so construed as to Prejudice any Claims of the United States, or of any particular State.

Section 4. The United States shall guarantee to every State in this Union a Republican Form of Government, and shall protect each of them against Invasion; and on Application of the Legislature, or of the Executive (when the Legislature cannot be convened) against domestic Violence.

Article V

The Congress, whenever two thirds of both Houses shall deem it necessary, shall propose Amendments to this Constitution, or, on the Application of the Legislatures of two thirds of the several States, shall call a Convention for proposing Amendments, which, in either Case, shall be valid to all Intents and Purposes, as part of this Constitution, when ratified by the Legislatures of three fourths of the several States, or by Conventions in three fourths thereof, as the one or the other Mode of Ratification may be proposed by the Congress; Provided that no Amendment which may be made prior to the Year One thousand eight hundred and eight shall in any Manner affect the first and fourth Clauses in the Ninth Section of the first Article; and that no State, without its Consent, shall be deprived of its equal Suffrage in the Senate.

Article VI

[1] All Debts contracted and Engagements entered into, before the Adoption of this Constitution shall be as valid against the United States under this Constitution, as under the Confederation.

[2] This Constitution, and the Laws of the United States which shall be made in Pursuance thereof; and all Treaties made, or which shall be made, under the Authority of the United States, shall be the supreme Law of the Land; and the Judges in every State shall be bound thereby, any Thing in the Constitution or Laws of any State to the Contrary notwithstanding.

[3] The Senators and Representatives before mentioned, and the Members of the several State Legislatures, and all executive and judicial Officers, both of the United States and of the several States, shall be bound by Oath or Affirmation, to support this Constitution; but no religious Test shall ever be required as a Qualification to any Office or public Trust under the United States.

Article VII

The Ratification of the Conventions of nine States shall be sufficient for the Establishment of this Constitution between the States so ratifying the Same.

ARTICLES IN ADDITION TO, AND AMENDMENT OF, THE CONSTITUTION OF THE UNITED STATES OF AMERICA, PROPOSED BY CONGRESS, AND RATIFIED BY THE LEGISLATURES OF THE SEVERAL STATES PURSUANT TO THE FIFTH ARTICLE OF THE ORIGINAL CONSTITUTION.

Amendment I [1791]

Congress shall make no law respecting an establishment of religion, or prohibiting the free exercise thereof; or abridging the freedom of speech, or of the press; or the right of the people peaceably to assemble, and to petition the Government for a redress of grievances.

Amendment II [1791]

A well regulated Militia, being necessary to the security of a free State, the right of the people to keep and bear Arms, shall not be infringed.

Amendment III [1791]

No Soldier shall, in time of peace be quartered in any house, without the consent of the Owner, nor in time of war, but in a manner to be prescribed by law.

Amendment IV [1791]

The right of the people to be secure in their persons, houses, papers, and effects, against unreasonable searches and seizures, shall not be violated, and no Warrants shall issue, but upon probable cause, supported by Oath or affirmation, and particularly describing the place to be searched, and the persons or things to be seized.

Amendment V [1791]

No person shall be held to answer for a capital, or otherwise infamous crime, unless on a presentment or indictment of a Grand Jury, except in cases arising in the land or naval forces, or in the Militia, when in actual service in time of War or public danger; nor shall any person be subject for the same offence to be twice put in jeopardy of life or limb; nor shall be compelled in any criminal case to be a witness against himself, nor be deprived of life, liberty, or property, without due process of law; nor shall private property be taken for public use, without just compensation.

Amendment VI [1791]

In all criminal prosecutions, the accused shall enjoy the right to a speedy and public trial, by an impartial jury of the State and district wherein the crime shall have been committed, which district shall have been previously ascertained by law, and to be informed of the nature and cause of the accusation; to be confronted with the witnesses against him; to have compulsory process for obtaining witnesses in his favor, and to have the Assistance of Counsel for his defence.

Amendment VII [1791]

In Suits at common law, where the value in controversy shall exceed twenty dollars, the right of trial by jury shall be preserved, and no fact tried by jury, shall be otherwise re-examined in any Court of the United States, than according to the rules of the common law.

Amendment VIII [1791]

Excessive bail shall not be required, nor excessive fines imposed, nor cruel and unusual punishments inflicted.

Amendment IX [1791]

The enumeration in the Constitution, of certain rights, shall not be construed to deny or disparage others retained by the people.

Amendment X [1791]

The powers not delegated to the United States by the Constitution, nor prohibited by it to the States, are reserved to the States respectively, or to the people.

Amendment XI [1798]

The Judicial power of the United States shall not be construed to extend to any suit in law or equity, commenced or prosecuted against one of the United States by Citizens of another State, or by Citizens or Subjects of any Foreign State.

Amendment XII [1804]

The Electors shall meet in their respective states and vote by ballot for President and Vice-President, one of whom, at least, shall not be an inhabitant of the same state with themselves; they shall name in their ballots the person voted for as President, and in distinct ballots the person voted for as Vice-President, and they shall make distinct lists of all persons voted for as President, and of all persons voted for as Vice-President, and of the number of votes for each, which lists they shall sign and certify, and transmit sealed to the seat of the government of the United States, directed to the President of the Senate;—The President of the Senate shall, in the presence of the Senate and House of Representatives, open all the certificates and the votes shall then be counted;—The person having the greatest number of votes for President, shall be the President, if such number be a majority of the whole number of Electors appointed; and if no person have such majority, then from the persons having the highest numbers not exceeding three on the list of those voted for as President, the House of Representatives shall choose immediately, by ballot, the President. But in choosing the President, the votes shall be taken by states, the representation from each state having one vote; a quorum for this purpose shall consist of a member or members from two-thirds of the states, and a majority of all the states shall be necessary to a choice. And if the House of Representatives shall not choose a President whenever the right of choice shall devolve upon them before the fourth day of March next following, then the Vice-President shall act as President, as in the case of the death or other constitutional disability of the President.—The person having the greatest number of votes as Vice-President, shall be the Vice-President, if such number be a majority of the whole number of Electors appointed, and if no person have a majority, then from the two highest numbers on the list, the Senate shall choose the Vice-President; a quorum for the purpose shall consist of two-thirds of the whole number of Senators, and a majority of the whole number shall be necessary to a choice. But no person constitutionally ineligible to the office of President shall be eligible to that of Vice-President of the United States.

Amendment XIII [1865]

Section 1. Neither slavery nor involuntary servitude, except as a punishment for crime whereof the party shall have been duly convicted, shall exist within the United States, or any place subject to their jurisdiction.

Section 2. Congress shall have power to enforce this article by appropriate legislation.

Amendment XIV [1868]

Section 1. All persons born or naturalized in the United States, and subject to the jurisdiction thereof, are citizens of the United States and of the State wherein they reside. No State shall make or enforce any law which shall abridge the privileges or immunities of citizens of the United States; nor shall any State deprive any person of life, liberty, or property, without due process of law; nor deny to any person within its jurisdiction the equal protection of the laws.

Section 2. Representatives shall be apportioned among the several States according to their respective numbers, counting the whole number of persons in each State, excluding Indians not taxed. But when the right to vote at any election for the choice of electors for President and Vice President of the United States, Representatives in Congress, the Executive and Judicial officers of a State, or the members of the Legislature thereof, is denied to any of the male inhabitants of such State, being twenty-one years of age, and citizens of the United States, or in any way abridged, except for participation in rebellion, or other crime, the basis of representation therein shall be reduced in the proportion which the number of such male citizens shall bear to the whole number of male citizens twenty-one years of age in such State.

Section 3. No person shall be a Senator or Representative in Congress, or elector of President and Vice President, or hold any office, civil or military, under the United States, or under any State, who having previously taken an oath, as a member of Congress, or as an officer of the United States, or as a member of any State legislature, or as an executive or judicial officer of any State, to support the Constitution of the United States, shall have engaged in insurrection of rebellion against the same, or given aid or comfort to the enemies thereof. But Congress may by a vote of two-thirds of each House, remove such disability.

Section 4. The validity of the public debt of the United States, authorized by law, including debts incurred for payment of pensions and bounties for services in suppressing insurrection or rebellion, shall not be questioned. But neither the United States nor any State shall assume or pay any debt or obligation incurred in aid of insurrection or rebellion against the United States, or any claim for the loss or emancipation of any slave; but all such debts, obligations and claims shall be held illegal and void.

Section 5. The Congress shall have power to enforce, by appropriate legislation, the provisions of this article.

Amendment XV [1870]

Section 1. The right of citizens of the United States to vote shall not be denied or abridged by the United States or by any State on account of race, color, or previous condition of servitude.

Section 2. The Congress shall have power to enforce this article by appropriate legislation.

Amendment XVI [1913]

The Congress shall have power to lay and collect taxes on incomes, from whatever source derived, without apportionment among the several States, and without regard to any census or enumeration.

Amendment XVII [1913]

[1] The Senate of the United States shall be composed of two Senators from each State, elected by the people thereof, for six years; and each Senator shall have one vote. The electors in each State shall have the qualifications requisite for electors of the most numerous branch of the State legislatures.

[2] When vacancies happen in the representation of any State in the Senate, the executive authority of such State shall issue writs of election to fill such vacancies: *Provided,* That the legislature of any State may empower the executive thereof to make temporary appointments until the people fill the vacancies by election as the legislature may direct.

[3] This amendment shall not be so construed as to affect the election or term of any Senator chosen before it becomes valid as part of the Constitution.

Amendment XVIII [1919]

Section 1. After one year from the ratification of this article the manufacture, sale, or transportation of intoxicating liquors within, the importation thereof into, or the exportation thereof from the United States and all territory subject to the jurisdiction thereof for beverage purposes is hereby prohibited.

Section 2. The Congress and the several States shall have concurrent power to enforce this article by appropriate legislation.

Section 3. This article shall be inoperative unless it shall have been ratified as an amendment to the Constitution by the legislatures of the several States, as provided in the Constitution, within seven years from the date of the submission hereof to the States by the Congress.

Amendment XIX [1920]

[1] The right of citizens of the United States to vote shall not be denied or abridged by the United States or by any State on account of sex.

[2] Congress shall have power to enforce this article by appropriate legislation.

Amendment XX [1933]

Section 1. The terms of the President and Vice President shall end at noon on the 20th day of January, and the terms of Senators and Representatives at noon on the 3d day of January, of the years in which such terms would have ended if this article had not been ratified; and the terms of their successors shall then begin.

Section 2. The Congress shall assemble at least once in every year, and such meeting shall begin at noon on the 3d day of January, unless they shall by law appoint a different day.

Section 3. If, at the time fixed for the beginning of the term of the President, the President elect shall have died, the Vice President elect shall become President. If the President shall not have been chosen before the time fixed for the beginning of his term, or if the President elect shall have failed to qualify, then the Vice President elect shall act as President until a President shall have qualified; and the Congress may by law provide for the case wherein neither a President elect nor a Vice President elect shall have qualified, declaring who shall then act as President, or the manner in which one who is to act shall be selected, and such person shall act accordingly until a President or Vice President shall have qualified.

Section 4. The Congress may by law provide for the case of the death of any of the persons from whom the House of Representatives may choose a President whenever the right of choice shall have devolved upon them, and for the case of the death of any of the persons from whom the Senate may choose a Vice President whenever the right of choice shall have devolved upon them.

Section 5. Sections 1 and 2 shall take effect on the 15th day of October following the ratification of this article.

Section 6. This article shall be inoperative unless it shall have been ratified as an amendment to the Constitution by the legislatures of three-fourths of the several States within seven years from the date of its submission.

Amendment XXI [1933]

Section 1. The eighteenth article of amendment to the Constitution of the United States is hereby repealed.

Section 2. The transportation or importation into any State, Territory, or possession of the United States for delivery or use therein of intoxicating liquors, in violation of the laws thereof, is hereby prohibited.

Section 3. This article shall be inoperative unless it shall have been ratified as an amendment to the Constitution by conventions in the several States, as provided in the Constitution, within seven years from the date of the submission hereof to the States by the Congress.

Amendment XXII [1951]

Section 1. No person shall be elected to the office of the President more than twice, and no person who has held the office of President, or acted as President, for more than two years of a term to which some other person was elected President shall be elected to the office of President more than once. But this Article shall not apply to any person holding the office of President when this Article was proposed by the Congress, and shall not prevent any person who may be holding the office of President, or acting as President, during the term within which this Article becomes operative from holding the office of President or acting as President during the remainder of such term.

Section 2. This article shall be inoperative unless it shall have been ratified as an amendment to the Constitution by the legislatures of three-fourths of the several States within seven years from the date of its submission to the States by the Congress.

Amendment XXIII [1961]

Section 1. The District constituting the seat of Government of the United States shall appoint in such manner as the Congress may direct:

A number of electors of President and Vice President equal to the whole number of Senators and Representatives in Congress in which the District would be entitled if it were a State, but in no event more than the least populous state; they shall be in addition to those appointed by the states, but they shall be considered, for the purposes of the election of President and Vice President, to be electors appointed by a state; and they shall meet in the District and perform such duties as provided by the twelfth article of amendment.

Section 2. The Congress shall have power to enforce this article by appropriate legislation.

Amendment XXIV [1964]

Section 1. The right of citizens of the United States to vote in any primary or other election for President or Vice President, for electors for President or Vice President, or for Senator or Representative in Congress, shall not be denied or abridged by the United States or any State by reason of failure to pay any poll tax or other tax.

Section 2. The Congress shall have power to enforce this article by appropriate legislation.

Amendment XXV [1967]

Section 1. In case of the removal of the President from office or of his death or resignation, the Vice President shall become President.

Sec. 2. Whenever there is a vacancy in the office of the Vice President, the President shall nominate a Vice President who shall take office upon confirmation by a majority vote of both Houses of Congress.

Sec. 3. Whenever the President transmits to the President pro tempore of the Senate and the Speaker of the House of Representatives his written declaration that he is unable to discharge the powers and duties of his office, and until he transmits to them a written declaration to the contrary, such powers and duties shall be discharged by the Vice President as Acting President.

Sec. 4. Whenever the Vice President and a majority of either the principal officers of the executive departments or of such other body as Congress may by law provide, transmit to the President pro tempore of the Senate and the Speaker of the House of Representatives their written declaration that the President is unable to discharge the powers and duties of his office, the Vice President shall immediately assume the powers and duties of the office as Acting President.

Thereafter, when the President transmits to the President pro tempore of the Senate and the Speaker of the House of Representatives his written declaration that no inability exists, he shall resume the powers and duties of his office unless the Vice President and a majority of either the principal officers of the executive department or of such other body as Congress may by law provide, transmit within four days to the President pro tempore of the Senate and the Speaker of the House of Representatives their written declaration that the President is unable to discharge the powers and duties of his office. Thereupon Congress shall decide the issue, assembling within forty-eight hours for that purpose if not in session. If the Congress, within twenty-one days after receipt of the latter written declaration, or, if Congress is not in session, within twenty-one days after Congress is required to assemble, determines by two-thirds vote of both Houses that the President is unable to discharge the powers and duties of his office, the Vice President shall continue to discharge the same as Acting President; otherwise, the President shall resume the powers and duties of his office.

Amendment XXVI [1971]

Section 1. The right of citizens of the United States, who are eighteen years of age or older, to vote shall not be denied or abridged by the United States or by any State on account of age.

Section 2. The Congress shall have power to enforce this article by appropriate legislation.

Appendix C

Uniform Commercial Code (1978 Official Text)

ARTICLE 1.   General Provisions

PART 1. *Short Title, Construction, Application and Subject Matter of the Act*

ARTICLE 1.   General Provisions

PART 1. *Short Title, Construction, Application and Subject Matter of the Act*

§ 1-101.   Short Title

This Act shall be know and may be cited as Uniform Commercial Code.

§ 1-102.   Purposes; Rules of Construction; Variation by Agreement

(1) This Act shall be liberally construed and applied to promote its underlying purposes and policies.

(2) Underlying purposes and policies of this Act are

(a) to simplify, clarify and modernize the law governing commercial transactions;

(b) to permit the continued expansion of commercial practices through custom, usage and agreement of the parties;

(c) to make uniform the law among the various jurisdictions.

(3) The effect of provisions of this Act may be varied by agreement, except as otherwise provided in this Act and except that the obligations of good faith, diligence, reasonableness and care prescribed by this Act may not be disclaimed by agreement but the parties may by agreement determine the standards by which the performance of such obligations is to be measured if such standards are not manifestly unreasonable.

(4) The presence in certain provisions of this Act of the words "unless otherwise agreed" or words of similar import does not imply that the effect of other provisions may not be varied by agreement under subsection (3).

(5) In this Act unless the context otherwise requires

(a) words in the singular number include the plural, and in the plural include the singular;

(b) words of the masculine gender include the feminine and the neuter, and when the sense so indicates words of the neuter gender may refer to any gender.

§ 1-103.   Supplementary General Principles of Law Applicable

Unless displaced by the particular provisions of this Act, the principles of law and equity, including the law merchant and the law relative to capacity to contract, principal and agent, estoppel, fraud, misrepresentation, duress, coercion, mistake, bankruptcy, or other validating or invalidating cause shall supplement its provisions.

§ 1-104.   Construction Against Implicit Repeal

This Act being a general act intended as a unified coverage of its subject matter, no part of it shall be deemed to be impliedly repealed by subsequent legislation if such construction can reasonably be avoided.

§ 1-105.   Territorial Application of the Act; Parties' Power to Choose Applicable Law

(1) Except as provided hereafter in this section, when a transaction bears a reasonable relation to this state and also to another state or nation the parties may agree that the law either of this state or of such other state or nation shall govern their rights and duties. Failing such agreement this Act applies to transactions bearing an appropriate relation to this state.

(2) Where one of the following provisions of this Act specifies the applicable law, that provision governs and a contrary agreement is effective only to the extent permitted by the law (including the conflict of laws rules) so specified:

Rights of creditors against sold goods. Section 2-402.

Applicability of the Article on Bank Deposits and collections. Section 4-102.

Bulk transfers subject to the Article on Bulk Transfers. Section 6-102.

Applicability of the Article on Investment Securities. Section 8-106.

Perfection provisions of the Article on Secured Transactions. Section 9-103.

As amended 1972.

§ 1-106.   Remedies to Be Liberally Administered

(1) The remedies provided by this Act shall be liberally administered to the end that the aggrieved party may be put in as good a position as if the other party had fully performed but neither consequential or special nor penal damages may be had except as specifically provided in this Act or by other rule of law.

(2) Any right or obligation declared by this Act is enforceable by action unless the provision declaring it specifies a different and limited effect.

§ 1-107.   Waiver or Renunciation of Claim or Right After Breach

Any claim or right arising out of an alleged breach can be discharged in whole or in part without consideration by a written waiver or renunciation signed and delivered by the aggrieved party.

§ 1-108.   Severability

If any provision or clause of this Act or application thereof to any person or circumstances is held invalid, such invalidity shall not affect other provisions or applications of the Act which can be given effect without the invalid provision or application, and to this end the provisions of this Act are declared to be severable.

§ 1-109.   Section Captions

Section captions are parts of this Act.

PART 2. General Definitions and Principles of Interpretation

§ 1-201.   General Definitions

Subject to additional definitions contained in the subsequent Articles of this Act which are applicable to specific Articles or Parts thereof, and unless the context otherwise requires, in this Act:

(1) "Action" in the sense of a judicial proceeding includes recoupment, counterclaim, set-off, suit in equity and any other proceedings in which rights are determined.

(2) "Aggrieved party" means a party entitled to resort to a remedy.

(3) "Agreement" means the bargain of the parties in fact as found in their language or by implication from other circumstances including course of dealing or usage of trade or course of performance as provided in this Act (Sections 1-205 and 2-208). Whether an agreement has legal consequences is determined by the provisions of this Act, if applicable; otherwise by the law of contracts (Section 1-103). (Compare "Contract".)

(4) "Bank" means any person engaged in the business of banking.

(5) "Bearer" means the person in possession of an instrument, document of title, or certificated security payable to bearer or indorsed in blank.

(6) "Bill of lading" means a document evidencing the receipt of goods for shipment issued by a person engaged in the business of transporting or forwarding goods, and includes an airbill. "Airbill" means a document serving for air transportation as a bill of lading does for marine or rail transportation, and includes an air consignment note or air waybill.

(7) "Branch" includes a separately incorporated foreign branch of a bank.

(8) "Burden of establishing" a fact means the burden of persuading the triers of fact that the existence of the fact is more probable than its non-existence.

(9) "Buyer in ordinary course of business" means a person who in good faith and without knowledge that the sale to him is in violation of the ownership rights or security interest of a third party in the goods buys in ordinary course from a person in the business of selling goods of that kind but does not include a pawnbroker. All persons who sell minerals or the like (including oil and gas) at wellhead or minehead shall be deemed to be persons in the business of selling goods of that kind. "Buying" may be for cash or by exchange of other property or on secured or unsecured credit and includes receiving goods or documents of title under a pre-existing contract for sale but does not include a transfer in bulk or as security for or in total or partial satisfaction of a money debt.

(10) "Conspicuous": A term or clause is conspicuous when it is so written that a reasonable person against whom it is to operate ought to have noticed it. A printed heading in capitals (as: NON-NEGOTIABLE BILL OF LADING) is conspicuous. Language in the body of a form is "conspicuous" if it is in larger or other contrasting type or color. But in a telegram any stated term is "conspicuous". Whether a term or clause is "conspicuous" or not is for decision by the court.

(11) "Contract" means the total legal obligation which results from the parties' agreement as affected by this Act and any other applicable rules of law. (Compare "Agreement".)

(12) "Creditor" includes a general creditor, a secured creditor, a lien creditor and any representative of creditors, including an assignee for the benefit of creditors, a trustee in bankruptcy, a receiver in equity and an executor or administrator of an insolvent debtor's or assignor's estate.

(13) "Defendant" includes a person in the position of defendant in a cross-action or counterclaim.

(14) "Delivery" with respect to instruments, documents of title, chattel paper, or certificated securities means voluntary transfer of possession.

(15) "Document of title" includes bill of lading, dock warrant, dock receipt, warehouse receipt or order for the delivery of goods, and also any other document which in the regular course of business or financing is treated as adequately evidencing that the person in possession of it is entitled to receive, hold and dispose of the document and the goods it covers. To be a document of title a document must purport to be issued by or addressed to a bailee and purport to cover goods in the bailee's possession which are either identified or are fungible portions of an identified mass.

(16) "Fault" means wrongful act, omission or breach.

(17) "Fungible" with respect to goods or securities means goods or securities of which any unit is, by nature or usage of trade, the equivalent of any other like unit. Goods which are not fungible shall be deemed fungible for the purposes of this Act to the extent that under a particular agreement or document unlike units are treated as equivalents.

(18) "Genuine" means free of forgery or counterfeiting.

(19) "Good faith" means honesty in fact in the conduct or transaction concerned.

(20) "Holder" means a person who is in possession of a document of title or an instrument or a certificated investment security drawn, issued, or indorsed to him or his order or to bearer or in blank.

(21) To "honor" is to pay or to accept and pay, or where a credit so engages to purchase or discount a draft complying with the terms of the credit.

(22) "Insolvency proceedings" includes any assignment for the benefit of creditors or other proceedings intended to liquidate or rehabilitate the estate of the person involved.

(23) A person is "insolvent" who either has ceased to pay his debts in the ordinary course of business or cannot pay his debts as they become due or is insolvent within the meaning of the federal bankruptcy law.

(24) "Money" means a medium of exchange authorized or adopted by a domestic or foreign government as a part of its currency.

(25) A person has "notice" of a fact when

(a) he has actual knowledge of it; or

(b) he has received a notice or notification of it; or

(c) from all the facts and circumstances known to him at the time in question he has reason to know that it exists.

A person "knows" or has "knowledge" of a fact when he has actual knowledge of it. "Discover" or "learn" or a word or phrase of similar import refers to knowledge rather than to reason to know. The time and circumstances under which a notice or notification may cease to be effective are not determined by this Act.

(26) A person "notifies" or "gives" a notice or notification to another by taking such steps as may be reasonably required to inform the other in ordinary course whether or not such other actually comes to know of it. A person "receives" a notice or notification when

(a) it comes to his attention; or

(b) it is duly delivered at the place of business through which the contract was made or at any other place held out by him as the place for receipt of such communications.

(27) Notice, knowledge or a notice or notification received by an organization is effective for a particular transaction from the time when it is brought to the attention of the individual conducting that transaction, and in any event from the time when it would have been brought to his attention if the organization had exercised due diligence. An organization exercises due diligence if it maintains reasonable routines for communicating significant information to the person conducting the transaction and there is reasonable compliance with the routines. Due diligence does not require an

individual acting for the organization to communicate information unless such communication is part of his regular duties or unless he has reason to know of the transaction and that the transaction would be materially affected by the information.

(28) "Organization" includes a corporation, government or governmental subdivision or agency, business trust, estate, trust, partnership or association, two or more persons having a joint or common interest, or any other legal or commercial entity.

(29) "Party", as distinct from "third party", means a person who has engaged in a transaction or made an agreement within this Act.

(30) "Person" includes an individual or an organization (See Section I-102).

(31) "Presumption" or "presumed" means that the trier of fact must find the existence of the fact presumed unless and until evidence is introduced which would support a finding of its non-existence.

(32) "Purchase" includes taking by sale, discount, negotiation, mortgage, pledge, lien, issue or re-issue, gift or any other voluntary transaction creating an interest in property.

(33) "Purchaser" means a person who takes by purchase.

(34) "Remedy" means any remedial right to which an aggrieved party is entitled with or without resort to a tribunal.

(35) "Representative" includes an agent, an officer of a corporation or association, and a trustee, executor or administrator of an estate, or any other person empowered to act for another.

(36) "Rights" includes remedies.

(37) "Security interest" means an interest in personal property or fixtures which secures payment or performance of an obligation. The retention or reservation of title by a seller of goods notwithstanding shipment or delivery to the buyer (Section 2-401) is limited in effect to a reservation of a "security interest". The term also includes any interest of a buyer of accounts or chattel paper which is subject to Article 9. The special property interest of a buyer of goods on identification of such goods to a contract for sale under Section 2-401 is not a "security interest", but a buyer may also acquire a "security interest" by complying with Article 9. Unless a lease or consignment is intended as security, reservation of title thereunder is not a "security interest" but a consignment is in any event subject to the provisions on consignment sales (Section 2-326). Whether a lease is intended as security is to be determined by the facts of each case; however, (a) the inclusion of an option to purchase does not of itself make the lease one intended for security, and (b) an agreement that upon compliance with the terms of the lease the lessee shall become or has the option to become the owner of the property for no additional consideration or for a nominal consideration does make the lease one intended for security.

(38) "Send" in connection with any writing or notice means to deposit in the mail or deliver for transmission by any other usual means of communication with postage or cost of transmission provided for and properly addressed and in the case of an instrument to an address specified thereon or otherwise agreed, or if there be none to any address reasonable under the circumstances. The receipt of any writing or notice within the time at which it would have arrived if properly sent has the effect of a proper sending.

(39) "Signed" includes any symbol executed or adopted by a party with present intention to authenticate a writing.

(40) "Surety" includes guarantor.

(41) "Telegram" includes a message transmitted by radio, teletype, cable, any mechanical method of transmission, or the like.

(42) "Term" means that portion of an agreement which relates to a particular matter.

(43) "Unauthorized" signature or indorsement means one made without actual, implied or apparent authority and includes a forgery.

(44) "Value". Except as otherwise provided with respect to negotiable instruments and bank collections (Sections 3-303, 4-208 and 4-209) a person gives "value" for rights if he acquires them

(a) in return for a binding commitment to extend credit or for the extension of immediately available credit whether or not drawn upon and whether or not a charge-back is provided for in the event of difficulties in collection; or

(b) as security for or in total or partial satisfaction of a pre-existing claim; or

(c) by accepting delivery pursuant to a pre-existing contract for purchase; or

(d) generally, in return for any consideration sufficient to support a simple contract.

(45) "Warehouse receipt" means a receipt issued by a person engaged in the business of storing goods for hire.

(46) "Written" or "writing" includes printing, typewriting or any other intentional reduction to tangible form. Amended in 1962, 1972 and 1977.

§ 1-202. Prima Facie Evidence by Third Party Documents

A document in due form purporting to be a bill of lading, policy or certificate of insurance, official weigher's or inspector's certificate, consular invoice, or any other document authorized or required by the contract to be issued by a third party shall be prima facie evidence of its own authenticity and genuineness and of the facts stated in the document by the third party.

§ 1-203. Obligation of Good Faith

Every contract or duty within this Act imposes an obligation of good faith in its performance or enforcement.

§ 1-204. Time; Reasonable Time; "Seasonably"

(1) Whenever this Act requires any action to be taken within a reasonable time, any time which is not manifestly unreasonable may be fixed by agreement.

(2) What is a reasonable time for taking any action depends on the nature, purpose and circumstances of such action.

(3) An action is taken "seasonably" when it is taken at or within the time agreed or if no time is agreed at or within a reasonable time.

§ 1-205. Course of Dealing and Usage of Trade

(1) A course of dealing is a sequence of previous conduct between the parties to a particular transaction which is fairly to be regarded as establishing a common basis of understanding for interpreting their expressions and other conduct.

(2) A usage of trade is any practice or method of dealing having such regularity of observance in a place, vocation or trade as to justify an expectation that it will be observed with respect to the transaction in question. The existence and scope of such a usage are to be proved as facts. If it is established that such a usage is embodied in a written trade code or similar writing the interpretation of the writing is for the court.

(3) A course of dealing between parties and any usage of trade in the vocation or trade in which they are engaged or of which they are or should be aware give particular meaning to and supplement or qualify terms of an agreement.

(4) The express terms of an agreement and an applicable course of dealing or usage of trade shall be construed wherever reasonable as consistent with each other; but when such construction is unreasonable express terms control both course of dealing and usage of trade and course of dealing controls usage of trade.

(5) An applicable usage of trade in the place where any part of performance is to occur shall be used in interpreting the agreement as to that part of the performance.

(6) Evidence of a relevant usage of trade offered by one party is not admissible unless and until he has given the other party such notice as the court finds sufficient to prevent unfair surprise to the latter.

§ 1-206. Statute of Frauds for Kinds of Personal Property Not Otherwise Covered

(1) Except in the cases described in subsection (2) of this section a contract for the sale of personal property is not enforceable by way of action or defense beyond five thousand dollars in amount or value of remedy unless there is some writing which indicates that a contract for sale has been made between the parties at a defined or stated price, reasonably identifies the subject matter, and is signed by the party against whom enforcement is sought or by his authorized agent.

(2) Subsection (1) of this section does not apply to contracts for the sale of goods (Section 2-201) nor of securities (Section 8-319) nor to security agreements (Section 9-203).

§ 1-207. Performance or Acceptance Under Reservation of Rights

A party who with explicit reservation of rights performs or promises performance or assents to performance in a manner demanded or offered by the other party does not thereby prejudice the rights reserved. Such words as "without prejudice", "under protest" or the like are sufficient.

§ 1-208. Option to Accelerate at Will

A term providing that one party or his successor in interest may accelerate payment or performance or require collateral or additional collateral "at will" or "when he deems himself insecure" or in words of similar import shall be construed to mean that he shall have power to do so only if he in good faith believes that the prospect of payment or performance is impaired. The burden of establishing lack of good faith is on the party against whom the power has been exercised.

§ 1-209.   Subordinated Obligations

An obligation may be issued as subordinated to payment of another obligation of the person obligated, or a creditor may subordinate his right to payment of an obligation by agreement with either the person obligated or another creditor of the person obligated. Such a subordination does not create a security interest as against either the common debtor or a subordinated creditor. This section shall be construed as declaring the law as it existed prior to the enactment of this section and not as modifying it. Added 1966.

Note: This new section is proposed as an optional provision to make it clear that a subordination agreement does not create a security interest unless so intended.

ARTICLE 2.   Sales

PART 1. *Short Title, General Construction and Subject Matter*

Section

PART 2. *Form, Formation and Readjustment of Contract*

PART 3. *General Obligation and Construction of Contract*

2-721. Remedies for Fraud.

2-722. Who Can Sue Third Parties for Injury to Goods.

2-723. Proof of Market Price: Time and Place.

2-724. Admissibility of Market Quotations.

2-725. Statute of Limitations in Contracts for Sale.

ARTICLE 2.   Sales

PART 1. *Short Title, General Construction and Subject Matter*

§ 2-101.   Short Title

This Article shall be known and may be cited as Uniform Commercial Code—Sales.

§ 2-102.   Scope; Certain Security and Other Transactions Excluded From This Article

Unless the context otherwise requires, this Article applies to transactions in goods; it does not apply to any transaction which although in the form of an unconditional contract to sell or present sale is intended to operate only as a security transaction nor does this Article impair or repeal any statue regulating sales to consumers, farmers or other specified classes of buyers.

§ 2-103.   Definitions and Index of Definitions

(1) In this Article unless the context otherwise requires

(a) "Buyer" means a person who buys or contracts to buy goods.

(b) "Good faith" in the case of a merchant means honesty in fact and the observance of reasonable commercial standards of fair dealing in the trade.

(c) "Receipt" of goods means taking physical possession of them.

(d) "Seller" means a person who sells or contracts to sell goods.

(2) Other definitions applying to this Article or to specified Parts thereof, and the sections in which they appear are:

"Acceptance". Section 2-606.

"Banker's credit". Section 2-325.

"Between merchants". Section 2-104.

"Cancellation". Section 2-106(4).

"Commercial unit". Section 2-105.

"Confirmed credit". Section 2-325.

"Conforming to contract". Section 2-106.

"Contract for sale". Section 2-106.

"Cover". Section 2-712.

"Entrusting". Section 2-403.

"Financing agency". Section 2-104.

"Future goods". Section 2-105.

"Goods". Section 2-105.

"Identification". Section 2-501.

"Installment contract". Section 2-612.

"Letter of Credit". Section 2-325.

"Lot". Section 2-105.

"Merchant". Section 2-104.

"Overseas". Section 2-323.

"Person in position of seller". Section 2-707.

"Present sale". Section 2-106.

"Sale". Section 2-106.

"Sale on approval". Section 2-326.

"Sale or return". Section 2-326.

"Termination". Section 2-106.

(3) The following definitions in other Articles apply to this Article:

"Check". Section 3-104.

"Consignee". Section 7-102.

"Consignor". Section 7-102.

"Consumer goods". Section 9-109.

"Dishonor". Section 3-507.

"Draft". Section 3-104.

(4) In addition Article 1 contains general definitions and principles of construction and interpretation applicable throughout this Article.

§ 2-104.   Definitions: "Merchant"; "Between Merchants"; "Financing Agency"

(1) "Merchant" means a person who deals in goods of the kind or otherwise by his occupation holds himself out as having knowledge or skill peculiar to the practices or goods involved in the transaction or to whom such knowledge or skill may be attributed by his employment of an agent or broker or other intermediary who by his occupation holds himself out as having such knowledge or skill.

(2) "Financing agency" means a bank, finance company or other person who in the ordinary course of business makes advances against goods or documents of title or who by arrangement with either the seller or the buyer intervenes in ordinary course to make or collect payment due or claimed under the contract for sale, as by purchasing or paying the seller's draft or making

advances against it or by merely taking it for collection whether or not documents of title accompany the draft. "Financing agency" includes also a bank or other person who similarly intervenes between persons who are in the position of seller and buyer in respect to the goods (Section 2-707).

(3) "Between merchants" means in any transaction with respect to which both parties are chargeable with the knowledge or skill of merchants.

§ 2-105.   Definitions: Transferability; "Goods"; "Future" Goods; "Lot"; "Commercial Unit"

(1) "Goods" means all things (including specially manufactured goods) which are movable at the time of identification to the contract for sale other than the money in which the price is to be paid, investment securities (Article 8) and things in action. "Goods" also includes the unborn young of animals and growing crops and other identified things attached to realty as described in the section on goods to be served from realty (Section 2-107).

(2) Goods must be both existing and identified before any interest in them can pass. Goods which are not both existing and identified are "future" goods. A purported present sale of future goods or of any interest therein operates as a contract to sell.

(3) There may be a sale of a part interest in existing identified goods.

(4) An undivided share in an identified bulk of fungible goods is sufficiently identified to be sold although the quantity of the bulk is not determined. Any agreed proportion of such a bulk or any quantity thereof agreed upon by number, weight or other measure may to the extent of the seller's interest in the bulk be sold to the buyer who then becomes an owner in common.

(5) "Lot" means a parcel or a single article which is the subject matter of a separate sale or delivery, whether or not it is sufficient to perform the contract.

(6) "Commercial unit" means such a unit of goods as by commercial usage is a single whole for purposes of sale and division of which materially impairs its character or value on the market or in use. A commercial unit may be a single article (as a machine) or a set of articles (as a suite of furniture or an assortment of sizes) or a quantity (as a bale, gross, or carload) or any other unit treated in use or in the relevant market as a single whole.

§ 2-106.   Definitions: "Contract"; "Agreement"; "Contract for Sale"; "Sale"; "Present Sale"; "Conforming" to Contract; "Termination"; "Cancellation"

(1) In this Article unless the context otherwise requires "contract" and "agreement" are limited to those relating to the present or future sale of goods. "Contract for sale" includes both a present sale of goods and a contract to sell goods at a future time. A "sale" consists in the passing of title from the seller to the buyer for a price (Section 2-401). A "present sale" means a sale which is accomplished by the making of the contract.

(2) Goods or conduct including any part of a performance are "conforming" or conform to the contract when they are in accordance with the obligations under the contract.

(3) "Termination" occurs when either party pursuant to a power created by agreement or law puts an end to the contract otherwise than for its breach. On "termination" all obligations which are still executory on both sides are discharged but any right based on prior breach or performance survives.

(4) "Cancellation" occurs when either party puts an end to the contract for breach by the other and its effect is the same as that of "termination" except that the cancelling party also retains any remedy for breach of the whole contract or any unperformed balance.

§ 2-107.   Goods to Be Severed From Realty: Recording

(1) A contract for the sale of minerals or the like (including oil and gas) or a structure or its materials to be removed from realty is a contract for the sale of goods within this Article if they are to be severed by the seller but until severance a purported present sale thereof which is not effective as a transfer of an interest in land is effective only as a contract to sell.

(2) A contract for the sale apart from the land of growing crops or other things attached to realty and capable of severance without material harm thereto but not described in subsection (1) or of timber to be cut is a contract for the sale of goods within this Article whether the subject matter is to be severed by the buyer or by the seller even though it forms part of the realty at the time of contracting, and the parties can by identification effect a present sale before severance.

(3) The provisions of this section are subject to any third party rights provided by the law relating to realty

records, and the contract for sale may be executed and recorded as a document transferring an interest in land and shall then constitute notice to third parties of the buyer's rights under the contract for sale. As amended 1972.

PART 2. *Form, Formation and Readjustment of Contract*

§ 2-201.   Formal Requirements; Statute of Frauds

(1) Except as otherwise provided in this section a contract for the sale of goods for the price of $500 or more is not enforceable by way of action or defense unless there is some writing sufficient to indicate that a contract for sale has been made between the parties and signed by the party against whom enforcement is sought or by his authorized agent or broker. A writing is not insufficient because it omits or incorrectly states a term agreed upon but the contract is not enforceable under this paragraph beyond the quantity of goods shown in such writing.

(2) Between merchants if within a reasonable time a writing in confirmation of the contract and sufficient against the sender is received and the party receiving it has reason to know its contents, it satisfies the requirements of subsection (1) against such party unless written notice of objection to its contents is given within 10 days after it is received.

(3) A contract which does not satisfy the requirements of subsection (1) but which is valid in other respects is enforceable

(a) if the goods are to be specially manufactured for the buyer and are not suitable for sale to others in the ordinary course of the seller's business and the seller, before notice of repudiation is received and under circumstances which reasonably indicate that the goods are for the buyer, has made either a substantial beginning of their manufacture or commitments for their procurement; or

(b) if the party against whom enforcement is sought admits in his pleading, testimony or otherwise in court that a contract for sale was made, but the contract is not enforceable under this provision beyond the quantity of goods admitted; or

(c) with respect to goods for which payment has been made and accepted or which have been received and accepted (Sec. 2-606).

§ 2-202.   Final Written Expression: Parol or Extrinsic Evidence

Terms with respect to which the confirmatory memoranda of the parties agree or which are otherwise set forth in a writing intended by the parties as a final expression of their agreement with respect to such terms as are included therein may not be contradicted by evidence of any prior agreement or of a contemporaneous oral agreement but may be explained or supplemented

(a) by course of dealing or usage of trade (Section 1-205) or by course of performance (Section 2-208); and

(b) by evidence of consistent additional terms unless the court finds the writing to have been intended also as a complete and exclusive statement of the terms of the agreement.

§ 2-203.   Seals Inoperative

The affixing of a seal to a writing evidencing a contract for sale or an offer to buy or sell goods does not constitute the writing a sealed instrument and the law with respect to sealed instruments does not apply to such a contract or offer.

§ 2-204.   Formation in General

(1) A contract for sale of goods may be made in any manner sufficient to show agreement, including conduct by both parties which recognizes the existence of such a contract.

(2) An agreement sufficient to constitute a contract for sale may be found even though the moment of its making is undetermined.

(3) Even though one or more terms are left open a contract for sale does not fail for indefiniteness if the parties have intended to make a contract and there is a reasonably certain basis for giving an appropriate remedy.

§ 2-205.   Firm Offers

An offer by a merchant to buy or sell goods in a signed writing which by its terms gives assurance that it will be held open is not revocable, for lack of consideration, during the time stated or if no time is stated for a reasonable time, but in no event may such period of irrevocability exceed three months; but any such term of assurance on a form supplied by the offeree must be separately signed by the offeror.

§ 2-206. Offer and Acceptance in Formation of Contract

(1) Unless otherwise unambiguously indicated by the language or circumstances

(a) an offer to make a contract shall be construed as inviting acceptance in any manner and by any medium reasonable in the circumstances;

(b) an order or other offer to buy goods for prompt or current shipment shall be construed as inviting acceptance either by a prompt promise to ship or by the prompt or current shipment of conforming or nonconforming goods, but such a shipment of non-conforming goods does not constitute an acceptance if the seller seasonably notifies the buyer that the shipment is offered only as an accommodation to the buyer.

(2) Where the beginning of a requested performance is a reasonable mode of acceptance an offeror who is not notified of acceptance within a reasonable time may treat the offer as having lapsed before acceptance.

§ 2-207. Additional Terms in Acceptance or Confirmation

(1) A definite and seasonable expression of acceptance or a written confirmation which is sent within a reasonable time operates as an acceptance even though it states terms additional to or different from those offered or agreed upon, unless acceptance is expressly made conditional on assent to the additional or different terms.

(2) The additional terms are to be construed as proposals for addition to the contract. Between merchants such terms become part of the contract unless:

(a) the offer expressly limits acceptance to the terms of the offer;

(b) they materially alter it; or

(c) notification of objection to them has already been given or is given within a reasonable time after notice of them is received.

(3) Conduct by both parties which recognizes the existence of a contract is sufficient to establish a contract for sale although the writings of the parties do not otherwise establish a contract. In such case the terms of the particular contract consist of those terms on which the writings of the parties agree, together with any supplementary terms incorporated under any other provisions of this Act.

§ 2-208. Course of Performance or Practical Construction

(1) Where the contract for sale involves repeated occasions for performance by either party with knowledge of the nature of the performance and opportunity for objection to it by the other, any course of performance accepted or acquiesced in without objection shall be relevant to determine the meaning of the agreement.

(2) The express terms of the agreement and any such course of performance, as well as any course of dealing and usage of trade, shall be construed whenever reasonable as consistent with each other; but when such construction is unreasonable, express terms shall control course of performance and course of performance shall control both course of dealing and usage of trade (Section 1-205).

(3) Subject to the provisions of the next section on modification and waiver, such course of performance shall be relevant to show a waiver or modification of any term inconsistent with such course of performance.

§ 2-209. Modification, Rescission and Waiver

(1) An agreement modifying a contract within this Article needs no consideration to be binding.

(2) A signed agreement which excludes modification or rescission except by a signed writing cannot be otherwise modified or rescinded, but except as between merchants such a requirement on a form supplied by the merchant must be separately signed by the other party.

(3) The requirements of the statute of frauds section of this Article (Section 2-201) must be satisfied if the contract as modified is within its provisions.

(4) Although an attempt at modification or rescission does not satisfy the requirements of subsection (2) or (3) it can operate as a waiver.

(5) A party who has made a waiver affecting an executory portion of the contract may retract the waiver by reasonable notification received by the other party that strict performance will be required of any term waived, unless the retraction would be unjust in view of a material change of position in reliance on the waiver.

§ 2-210. Delegation of Performance; Assignment of Rights

(1) A party may perform his duty through a delegate unless otherwise agreed or unless the other party has a

substantial interest in having his original promisor perform or control the acts required by the contract. No delegation of performance relieves the party delegating of any duty to perform or any liability for breach.

(2) Unless otherwise agreed all rights of either seller or buyer can be assigned except where the assignment would materially change the duty of the other party, or increase materially the burden or risk imposed on him by his contract, or impair materially his chance of obtaining return performance. A right to damages for breach of the whole contract or a right arising out of the assignor's due performance of his entire obligation can be assigned despite agreement otherwise.

(3) Unless the circumstances indicate the contrary a prohibition of assignment of "the contract" is to be construed as barring only the delegation to the assignee of the assignor's performance.

(4) An assignment of "the contract" or of "all my rights under the contract" or an assignment in similar general terms is an assignment of rights and unless the language or the circumstances (as in an assignment for security) indicate the contrary, it is a delegation of performance of the duties of the assignor and its acceptance by the assignee constitutes a promise by him to perform those duties. This promise is enforceable by either the assignor or the other party to the original contract.

(5) The other party may treat any assignment which delegates performance as creating reasonable grounds for insecurity and may without prejudice to his rights against the assignor demand assurances from the assignee (Section 2-609).

PART 3. *General Obligation and Construction of Contract*

§ 2-301.   **General Obligations of Parties**

The obligation of the seller is to transfer and deliver and that of the buyer is to accept and pay in accordance with the contract.

§ 2-302.   **Unconscionable Contract or Clause**

(1) If the court as a matter of law finds the contract or any clause of the contract to have been unconscionable at the time it was made the court may refuse to enforce the contract, or it may enforce the remainder of the

contract without the unconscionable clause, or it may so limit the application to any unconscionable clause as to avoid any unconscionable result.

(2) When it is claimed or appears to the court that the contract or any clause thereof may be unconscionable the parties shall be afforded a reasonable opportunity to present evidence as to its commercial setting, purpose and effect to aid the court in making the determination.

§ 2-303.   **Allocation or Division of Risks**

Where this Article allocates a risk or a burden as between the parties "unless otherwise agreed", the agreement may not only shift the allocation but may also divide the risk or burden.

§ 2-304.   **Price Payable in Money, Goods, Realty, or Otherwise**

(1) The price can be made payable in money or otherwise. If it is payable in whole or in part in goods each party is a seller of the goods which he is to transfer.

(2) Even though all or part of the price is payable in an interest in realty the transfer of the goods and the seller's obligations with reference to them are subject to this Article, but not the transfer of the interest in realty or the transferor's obligations in connection therewith.

§ 2-305.   **Open Price Term**

(1) The parties if they so intend can conclude a contract for sale even though the price is not settled. In such a case the price is a reasonable price at the time for delivery if

(a) nothing is said as to price; or

(b) the price is left to be agreed by the parties and they fail to agree; or

(c) the price is to be fixed in terms of some agreed market or other standard as set or recorded by a third person or agency and it is not so set or recorded.

(2) A price to be fixed by the seller or by the buyer means a price for him to fix in good faith.

(3) When a price left to be fixed otherwise than by agreement of the parties fails to be fixed through fault of one party the other may at his option treat the contract as cancelled or himself fix a reasonable price.

(4) Where, however, the parties intend not to be bound unless the price be fixed or agreed and it is not fixed or agreed there is no contract. In such a case the buyer must return any goods already received or if

unable so to do must pay their reasonable value at the time of delivery and the seller must return any portion of the price paid on account.

§ 2-306. Output, Requirements and Exclusive Dealings

(1) A term which measures the quantity by the output of the seller or the requirements of the buyer means such actual output or requirements as may occur in good faith, except that no quantity unreasonably disproportionate to any stated estimate or in the absence of a stated estimate to any normal or otherwise comparable prior output or requirements may be tendered or demanded.

(2) A lawful agreement by either the seller or tne buyer for exclusive dealing in the kind of goods concerned imposes unless otherwise agreed an obligation by the seller to use best efforts to supply the goods and by the buyer to use best efforts to promote their sale.

§ 2-307. Delivery in Single Lot or Several Lots

Unless otherwise agreed all goods called for by a contract for sale must be tendered in a single delivery and payment is due only on such tender but where the circumstances give either party the right to make or demand delivery in lots the price if it can be apportioned may be demanded for each lot.

§ 2-308. Absence of Specified Place for Delivery

Unless otherwise agreed

(a) the place for delivery of goods is the seller's place of business or if he has none his residence; but

(b) in a contract for sale of identified goods which to the knowledge of the parties at the time of contracting are in some other place, that place is the place for their delivery; and

(c) documents of title may be delivered through customary banking channels.

§ 2-309. Absence of Specific Time Provisions; Notice of Termination

(1) The time for shipment or delivery or any other action under a contract if not provided in this Article or agreed upon shall be a reasonable time.

(2) Where the contract provides for successive performances but is indefinite in duration it is valid for a reasonable time but unless otherwise agreed may be terminated at any time by either party.

(3) Termination of a contract by one party except on the happening of an agreed event requires that reasonable notification be received by the other party and an agreement dispensing with notification is invalid if its operation would be unconscionable.

§ 2-310. Open Time for Payment or Running of Credit; Authority to Ship Under Reservation

Unless otherwise agreed

(a) payment is due at the time and place at which the buyer is to receive the goods even though the place of shipment is the place of delivery; and

(b) if the seller is authorized to send the goods he may ship them under reservation, and may tender the documents of title, but the buyer may inspect the goods after their arrival before payment is due unless such inspection is inconsistent with the terms of the contract (Section 2-513); and

(c) if delivery is authorized and made by way of documents of title otherwise than by subsection (b) then payment is due at the time and place at which the buyer is to receive the documents regardless of where the goods are to be received; and

(d) where the seller is required or authorized to ship the goods on credit the credit period runs from the time of shipment but post-dating the invoice or delaying its dispatch will correspondingly delay the starting of the credit period.

§ 2-311. Options and Cooperation Respecting Performance

(1) An agreement for sale which is otherwise sufficiently definite (subsection (3) of Section 2-204) to be a contract is not made invalid by the fact that it leaves particulars of performance to be specified by one of the parties. Any such specification must be made in good faith and within limits set by commercial reasonableness.

(2) Unless otherwise agreed specifications relating to assortment of the goods are at the buyer's option and except as otherwise provided in subsections (1) (c) and (3) of Section 2-319 specifications or arrangements relating to shipment are at the seller's option.

(3) Where such specification would materially affect the other party's performance but is not seasonally

made or where one party's cooperation is necessary to the agreed performance of the other but is not seasonably forthcoming, the other party in addition to all other remedies

(a) is excused for any resulting delay in his own performance; and

(b) may also either proceed to perform in any reasonable manner or after the time for a material part of his own performance treat the failure to specify or to cooperate as a breach by failure to deliver or accept the goods.

§ 2-312. Warranty of Title and Against Infringement; Buyer's Obligation Against Infringement

(1) Subject to subsection (2) there is in a contract for sale a warranty by the seller that

(a) the title conveyed shall be good, and its transfer rightful; and

(b) the goods shall be delivered free from any security interest or other lien or encumbrance of which the buyer at the time of contracting has no knowledge.

(2) A warranty under subsection (1) will be excluded or modified only by specific language or by circumstances which give the buyer reason to know that the person selling does not claim title in himself or that he is purporting to sell only such right or title as he or a third person may have.

(3) Unless otherwise agreed a seller who is a merchant regularly dealing in goods of the kind warrants that the goods shall be delivered free of the rightful claim of any third person by way of infringement or the like but a buyer who furnishes specifications to the seller must hold the seller harmless against any such claim which arises out of compliance with the specifications.

§ 2-313. Express Warranties by Affirmation, Promise, Description, Sample

(1) Express warranties by the seller are created as follows:

(a) Any affirmation of fact or promise made by the seller to the buyer which relates to the goods and becomes part of the basis of the bargain creates an express warranty that the goods shall conform to the affirmation or promise.

(b) Any description of the goods which is made part of the basis of the bargain creates an express warranty that the goods shall conform to the description.

(c) Any sample or model which is made part of the basis of the bargain creates an express warranty that the whole of the goods shall conform to the sample or model.

(2) It is not necessary to the creation of an express warranty that the seller use formal words such as "warrant" or "guarantee" or that he have a specific intention to make a warranty, but an affirmation merely of the value of the goods or a statement purporting to be merely the seller's opinion or commendation of the goods does not create a warranty.

§ 2-314. Implied Warranty: Merchantability; Usage of Trade

(1) Unless excluded or modified (Section 2-316), a warranty that the goods shall be merchantable is implied in a contract for their sale if the seller is a merchant with respect to goods of that kind. Under this section the serving for value for food or drink to be consumed either on the premises or elsewhere is a sale.

(2) Goods to be merchantable must be at least such as

(a) pass without objection in the trade under the contract description; and

(b) in the case of fungible goods, are of fair average quality within the description; and

(c) are fit for the ordinary purposes for which such goods are used; and

(d) run, within the variations permitted by the agreement, of even kind, quality and quantity within each unit and among all units involved; and

(e) are adequately contained, packaged, and labeled as the agreement may require; and

(f) conform to the promises or affirmations of fact made on the container or label if any.

(3) Unless excluded or modified (Section 2-316) other implied warranties may arise from course of dealing or usage of trade.

§ 2-315. Implied Warranty: Fitness for Particular Purpose

Where the seller at the time of contracting has reason to know any particular purpose for which the goods are required and that the buyer is relying on the seller's skill or judgment to select or furnish suitable goods, there is unless excluded or modified under the next section an implied warranty that the goods shall be fit for such purpose.

§ 2-316. Exclusion or Modification of Warranties

(1) Words or conduct relevant to the creation of an express warranty and words or conduct tending to negate or limit warranty shall be construed wherever reasonable as consistent with each other; but subject to the provisions of this Article on parol or extrinsic evidence (Section 2-202) negation or limitation is inoperative to the extent that such construction is unreasonable.

(2) Subject to subsection (3), to exclude or modify the implied warranty of merchantability or any part of it the language must mention merchantability and in case of a writing must be conspicuous, and to exclude or modify any implied warranty of fitness the exclusion must be by a writing and conspicuous. Language to exclude all implied warranties of fitness is sufficient if it states, for example, that "There are no warranties which extend beyond the description of the face hereof."

(3) Notwithstanding subsection (2)

(a) unless the circumstances indicate otherwise, all implied warranties are excluded by expressions like "as is", "with all faults" or other language which in common understanding calls the buyer's attention to the exclusion of warranties and makes plain that there is no implied warranty; and

(b) when the buyer before entering into the contract has examined the goods or the sample or model as fully as he desired or has refused to examine the goods there is no implied warranty with regard to defects which an examination ought in the circumstances to have revealed to him; and

(c) an implied warranty can also be excluded or modified by course of dealing or course of performance or usage of trade.

(4) Remedies for breach of warranty can be limited in accordance with the provisions of this Article on liquidation or limitation of damages and on contractual modification of remedy (Sections 2-718 and 2-719).

§ 2-317. Cumulation and Conflict of Warranties Express or Implied

Warranties whether express or implied shall be construed as consistent with each other and as cumulative, but if such construction is unreasonable the intention of the parties shall determine which warranty is dominant. In ascertaining that intention the following rules apply:

(a) Exact or technical specifications displace an inconsistent sample or model or general language of description.

(b) A sample from an existing bulk displaces inconsistent general language of description.

(c) Express warranties displace inconsistent implied warranties other than an implied warranty of fitness for a particular purpose.

§ 2-318. Third Party Beneficiaries of Warranties Express or Implied

Note: If this Act is introduced in the Congress of the United States this section should be omitted. (States to select one alternative.)

Alternative A. A seller's warranty whether express or implied extends to any natural person who is in the family or household of his buyer or who is a guest in his home if it is reasonable to expect that such person may use, consume or be affected by the goods and who is injured in person by breach of the warranty. A seller may not exclude or limit the operation of this section.

Alternative B. A seller's warranty whether express or implied extends to any natural person who may reasonably be expected to use, consume or be affected by the goods and who is injured in person by breach of the warranty. A seller may not exclude or limit the operation of this section.

Alternative C. A seller's warranty whether express or implied extends to any person who may reasonably be expected to use, consume or be affected by the goods and who is injured by breach of the warranty. A seller may not exclude or limit the operation of this section with respect to injury to the person of an individual to whom the warranty extends. As amended 1966.

§ 2-319. F.O.B. and F.A.S. Terms

(1) Unless otherwise agreed the term F.O.B. (which means "free on board") at a named place, even though used only in connection with the stated price, is a delivery term under which

(a) when the term is F.O.B. the place of shipment, the seller must at that place ship the goods in the manner provided in this Article (Section 2-504) and bear the expense and risk of putting them into the possession of the carrier; or

(b) when the term is F.O.B. the place of destination, the seller must at his own expense and risk transport the goods to that place and there tender delivery of them in the manner provided in this Article (Section 2-503);

(c) when under either (a) or (b) the term is also F.O.B. vessel, car or other vehicle, the seller must in addition at his own expense and risk load the goods on board. If the term is F.O.B. vessel the buyer must name the vessel and in an appropriate case the seller must comply with the provisions of this Article on the form of bill of lading (Section 2-323).

(2) Unless otherwise agreed the term F.A.S. vessel (which means "free alongside") at a named port, even though used only in connection with the stated price, is a delivery term under which the seller must

(a) at his own expense and risk deliver the goods alongside the vessel in the manner usual in that port or on a dock designated and provided by the buyer; and

(b) obtain and tender a receipt for the goods in exchange for which the carrier is under a duty to issue a bill of lading.

(3) Unless otherwise agreed in any case falling within subsection (1) (a) or (c) or subsection (2) the buyer must seasonably give any needed instructions for making delivery, including when the term is F.A.S. or F.O.B. the loading berth of the vessel and in an appropriate case its name and sailing date. The seller may treat the failure of needed instructions as a failure of cooperation under this Article (Section 2-311). He may also at his option move the goods in any reasonable manner preparatory to delivery or shipment.

(4) Under the term F.O.B. vessel or F.A.S. unless otherwise agreed the buyer must make payment against tender of the required documents and the seller may not tender nor the buyer demand delivery of the goods in substitution for the documents.

§ 2-320. C.I.F. and C. & F. Terms

(1) The term C.I.F. means that the price includes in a lump sum the cost of the goods and the insurance and freight to the named destination. The term C. & F. or C.F. means that the price so includes cost and freight to the named destination.

(2) Unless otherwise agreed and even though used only in connection with the stated price and destination, the term C.I.F. destination or its equivalent requires the seller at his own expense and risk to

(a) put the goods into the possession of a carrier at the port for shipment and obtain a negotiable bill or

bills of lading covering the entire transportation to the named destination; and

(b) load the goods and obtain a receipt from the carrier (which may be contained in the bill of lading) showing that the freight has been paid or provided for; and

(c) obtain a policy or certificate of insurance, including any war risk insurance, of a kind and on terms then current at the port of shipment in the usual amount, in the currency of the contract, shown to cover the same goods covered by the bill of lading and providing for payment of loss to the order of the buyer or for the account of whom it may concern; but the seller may add to the price the amount of the premium for any such war risk insurance; and

(d) prepare an invoice of the goods and procure any other documents required to effect shipment or to comply with the contract; and

(e) forward and tender with commercial promptness all the documents in due form and with any indorsement necessary to perfect the buyer's rights.

(3) Unless otherwise agreed the term C. & F. or its equivalent has the same effect and imposes upon the seller the same obligations and risks as a C.I.F. term except the obligation as to insurance.

(4) Under the term C.I.F. or C. & F. unless otherwise agreed the buyer must make payment against tender of the required documents and the seller may not tender nor the buyer demand delivery of the goods in substitution for the documents.

§ 2-321. C.I.F. or C. & F.: "Net Landed Weights"; "Payment on Arrival"; Warranty of Condition on Arrival

Under a contract containing a term C.I.F. or C. & F.

(1) Where the price is based on or is to be adjusted according to "net landed weights", "delivered weights", "out turn" quantity or quality or the like, unless otherwise agreed the seller must reasonably estimate the price. The payment due on tender of the documents called for by the contract is the amount so estimated, but after final adjustment of the price a settlement must be made with commercial promptness.

(2) An agreement described in subsection (1) or any warranty of quality or condition of the goods on arrival places upon the seller the risk of ordinary deterioration, shrinkage and the like in transportation but has no

effect on the place or time of identification to the contract for sale or delivery or on the passing of the risk of loss.

(3) Unless otherwise agreed where the contract provides for payment on or after arrival of the goods the seller must before payment allow such preliminary inspection as is feasible; but if the goods are lost delivery of the documents and payment are due when the goods should have arrived.

§ 2-322. Delivery "Ex-Ship"

(1) Unless otherwise agreed a term for delivery of goods "ex-ship" (which means from the carrying vessel) or in equivalent language is not restricted to a particular ship and requires delivery from a ship which has reached a place at the named port of destination where goods of the kind are usually discharged.

(2) Under such a term unless otherwise agreed

(a) the seller must discharge all liens arising out of the carriage and furnish the buyer with a direction which puts the carrier under a duty to deliver the goods; and

(b) the risk of loss does not pass to the buyer until the goods leave the ship's tackle or are otherwise properly unloaded.

§ 2-323. Form of Bill of Lading Required in Overseas Shipment; "Overseas"

(1) Where the contract contemplates overseas shipment and contains a term C.I.F. or C. & F. or F.O.B. vessel, the seller unless otherwise agreed must obtain a negotiable bill of lading stating that the goods have been loaded on board or, in the case of a term C.I.F. or C. & F., received for shipment.

(2) Where in a case within subsection (1) a bill of lading has been issued in a set of parts, unless otherwise agreed if the documents are not to be sent from abroad the buyer may demand tender of the full set; otherwise only one part of the bill of lading need be tendered. Even if the agreement expressly requires a full set

(a) due tender of a single part is acceptable within the provisions of this Article on cure of improper delivery (subsection (1) of Section 2-508); and

(b) even though the full set is demanded, if the documents are sent from abroad the person tendering an incomplete set may nevertheless require payment upon furnishing an indemnity which the buyer in good faith deems adequate.

(3) A shipment by water or by air or a contract contemplating such shipment is "overseas" insofar as by usage of trade or agreement it is subject to the commerical, financing or shipping practices characteristic of international deep water commerce.

§ 2-324. "No Arrival, No Sale" Term

Under a term "no arrival, no sale" or terms of like meaning, unless otherwise agreed,

(a) the seller must properly ship conforming goods and if they arrive by any means he must tender them on arrival but he assumes no obligation that the goods will arrive unless he has caused the non-arrival; and

(b) where without fault of the seller the goods are in part lost or have so deteriorated as no longer to conform to the contract or arrive after the contract time, the buyer may proceed as if there had been casualty to identified goods (Section 2-613).

§ 2-325. "Letter of Credit" Term; "Confirmed Credit"

(1) Failure of the buyer seasonably to furnish an agreed letter of credit is a breach of the contract for sale.

(2) The delivery to seller of a proper letter of credit suspends the buyer's obligation to pay. If the letter of credit is dishonored, the seller may on seasonable notification to the buyer require payment directly from him.

(3) Unless otherwise agreed the term "letter of credit" or "banker's credit" in a contract for sale means an irrevocable credit issued by a financing agency of good repute and, where the shipment is overseas, of good international repute. The term "confirmed credit" means that the credit must also carry the direct obligation of such an agency which does business in the seller's financial market.

§ 2-326. Sale on Approval and Sale or Return; Consignment Sales and Rights of Creditors

(1) Unless otherwise agreed, if delivered goods may be returned by the buyer even though they conform to the contract, the transaction is

(a) a "sale on approval" if the goods are delivered primarily for use, and

(b) a "sale or return" if the goods are delivered primarily for resale.

(2) Except as provided in subsection (3), goods held on approval are not subject to the claims of the buyer's creditors until acceptance; goods held on sale or return are subject to such claims while in the buyer's possession.

(3) Where goods are delivered to a person for sale and such person maintains a place of business at which he deals in goods of the kind involved, under a name other than the name of the person making delivery, then with respect to claims of creditors of the person conducting the business the goods are deemed to be on sale or return. The provisions of this subsection are applicable even though an agreement purports to reserve title to the person making delivery until payment or resale or uses such words as "on consignment" or "on memorandum". However, this subsection is not applicable if the person making delivery

(a) complies with an applicable law providing for a consignor's interest or the like to be evidenced by a sign, or

(b) establishes that the person conducting the business is generally known by his creditors to be substantially engaged in selling the goods of others, or

(c) complies with the filing provisions of the Article on Secured Transactions (Article 9).

(4) Any "or return" term of a contract for sale is to be treated as a separate contract for sale within the statute of frauds section of this Article (Section 2-201) and as contradicting the sale aspect of the contract within the provisions of this Article on parol or extrinsic evidence (Section 2-202).

§ 2-327. Special Incidents of Sale on Approval and Sale or Return

(1) Under a sale on approval unless otherwise agreed

(a) although the goods are identified to the contract the risk of loss and the title do not pass to the buyer until acceptance; and

(b) use of the goods consistent with the purpose of trial is not acceptance but failure seasonably to notify the seller of election to return the goods is acceptance, and if the goods conform to the contract acceptance of any part is acceptance of the whole; and

(c) after due notification of election to return, the return is at the seller's risk and expense but a merchant buyer must follow any reasonable instructions.

(2) Under a sale or return unless otherwise agreed

(a) the option to return extends to the whole or any commercial unit of the goods while in substantially

their original condition, but must be exercised seasonably; and

(b) the return is at the buyer's risk and expense.

§ 2-328.   Sale by Auction

(1) In a sale by auction if goods are put up in lots each lot is the subject of a separate sale.

(2) A sale by auction is complete when the auctioneer so announces by the fall of the hammer or in other customary manner. Where a bid is made while the hammer is falling in acceptance of a prior bid the auctioneer may in his discretion reopen the bidding or declare the goods sold under the bid on which the hammer was falling.

(3) Such a sale is with reserve unless the goods are in explicit terms put up without reserve. In an auction with reserve the auctioneer may withdraw the goods at any time until he announces completion of the sale. In an auction without reserve, after the auctioneer calls for bids on an article or lot, that article or lot cannot be withdrawn unless no bid is made within a reasonable time. In either case a bidder may retract his bid until the auctioneer's announcement of completion of the sale, but a bidder's retraction does not revive any previous bid.

(4) If the auctioneer knowingly receives a bid on the seller's behalf or the seller makes or procures such a bid, and notice has not been given that liberty for such bidding is reserved, the buyer may at his option avoid the sale or take the goods at the price of last good faith bid prior to the completion of the sale. This subsection shall not apply to any bid at a forced sale.

PART 4. *Title, Creditors and Good Faith Purchasers*

§ 2-401.   Passing of Title; Reservation for Security; Limited Application of This Section

Each provision of this Article with regard to the rights, obligations and remedies of the seller, the buyer, purchasers or other third parties applies irrespective of title to the goods except where the provision refers to such title. Insofar as situations are not covered by the other provisions of this Article and matters concerning title become material the following rules apply:

(1) Title to goods cannot pass under a contract for sale prior to their identification to the contract (Section 2-501), and unless otherwise explicitly agreed the buyer acquires by their identification a special property as

limited by this Act. Any retention or reservation by the seller of the title (property) in goods shipped or delivered to the buyer is limited in effect to a reservation of a security interest. Subject to these provisions and to the provisions of the Article on Secured Transactions (Article 9), title to goods passes from the seller to the buyer in any manner and on any conditions explicitly agreed on by the parties.

(2) Unless otherwise explicitly agreed title passes to the buyer at the time and place at which the seller completes his performance with reference to the physical delivery of the goods, despite any reservation of a security interest and even though a document of title is to be delivered at a different time or place; and in particular and despite any reservation of a security interest by the bill of lading

(a) if the contract requires or authorizes the seller to send the goods to the buyer but does not require him to deliver them at destination, title passes to the buyer at the time and place of shipment; but

(b) if the contract requires delivery at destination, title passes on tender there.

(3) Unless otherwise explicitly agreed where delivery is to be made without moving the goods,

(a) if the seller is to deliver a document of title, title passes at the time when and the place where he delivers such documents; or

(b) if the goods are at the time of contracting already identified and no documents are to be delivered, title passes at the time and place of contracting.

(4) A rejection or other refusal by the buyer to receive or retain the goods, whether or not justified, or a justified revocation of acceptance revests title to the goods in the seller. Such revesting occurs by operation of law and is not a "sale".

§ 2-402. Rights of Seller's Creditors Against Sold Goods

(1) Except as provided in subsections (2) and (3), rights of unsecured creditors of the seller with respect to goods which have been identified to a contract for sale are subject to the buyer's rights to recover the goods under this Article (Sections 2-502 and 2-716).

(2) A creditor of the seller may treat a sale or an identification of goods to a contract for sale as void if as against him a retention of possession by the seller is fraudulent under any rule of law of the state where the goods are situated, except that retention of possession in good faith and current course of trade by a merchant-seller for a commercially reasonable time after a sale or identification is not fraudulent.

(3) Nothing in this Article shall be deemed to impair the rights of creditors of the seller

(a) under the provisions of the Article on Secured Transactions (Article 9); or

(b) where identification to the contract or delivery is made not in current course of trade but in satisfaction of or as security for a pre-existing claim for money, security or the like and is made under circumstances which under any rule of law of the state where the goods are situated would apart from this Article constitute the transaction a fraudulent transfer or voidable preference.

§ 2-403. Power to Transfer; Good Faith Purchase of Goods; "Entrusting"

(1) A purchaser of goods acquires all title which his transferor had or had power to transfer except that a purchaser of a limited interest acquires rights only to the extent of the interest purchased. A person with voidable title has power to transfer a good title to a good faith purchaser for value. When goods have been delivered under a transaction of purchase the purchaser has such power even though

(a) the transferor was deceived as to the identity of the purchaser, or

(b) the delivery was in exchange for a check which is later dishonored, or

(c) it was agreed that the transaction was to be a "cash sale", or

(d) the delivery was procured through fraud punishable as larcenous under the criminal law.

(2) Any entrusting of possession of goods to a merchant who deals in goods of that kind gives him power to transfer all rights of the entruster to a buyer in ordinary course of business.

(3) "Entrusting" includes any delivery and any acquiescence in retention of possession regardless of any condition expressed between the parties to the delivery or acquiescence and regardless of whether the procurement of the entrusting or the possessor's disposition of the goods have been such as to be larcenous under the criminal law.

(4) The rights of other purchasers of goods and of lien creditors are governed by the Articles on Secured

Transactions (Article 9), Bulk Transfers (Article 6) and Documents of Title (Article 7).

PART 5. *Performance*

§ 2-501.   Insurable Interest in Goods; Manner of Identification of Goods

(1) The buyer obtains a special property and an insurable interest in goods by identification of existing goods as goods to which the contract refers even though the goods so identified are non-conforming and he has an option to return or reject them. Such identification can be made at any time and in any manner explicitly agreed to by the parties. In the absence of explicit agreement identification occurs

(a) when the contract is made if it is for the sale of goods already existing and identified;

(b) if the contract is for the sale of future goods other than those described in paragraph (c), when goods are shipped, marked or otherwise designated by the seller as goods to which the contract refers;

(c) when the crops are planted or otherwise become growing crops or the young are conceived if the contract is for the sale of unborn young to be born within twelve months after contracting or for the sale of crops to be harvested within twelve months or the next normal harvest season after contracting whichever is longer.

(2) The seller retains an insurable interest in goods so long as title to or any security interest in the goods remains in him and where the identification is by the seller alone he may until default or insolvency or notification to the buyer that the identification is final substitute other goods for those identified.

(3) Nothing in this section impairs any insurable interest recognized under any other statute or rule of law.

§ 2-502.   Buyer's Right to Goods on Seller's Insolvency

(1) Subject to subsection (2) and even though the goods have not been shipped a buyer who has paid a part or all of the price of goods in which he has a special property under the provisions of the immediately preceding section may on making and keeping good a tender of any unpaid portion of their price recover them from the seller if the seller becomes insolvent within ten days after receipt of the first installment on their price.

(2) If the identification creating his special property has been made by the buyer he acquires the right to recover the goods only if they conform to the contract for sale.

§ 2-503.   Manner of Seller's Tender of Delivery

(1) Tender of delivery requires that the seller put and hold conforming goods at the buyer's disposition and give the buyer any notification reasonably necessary to enable him to take delivery. The manner, time and place for tender are determined by the agreement and this Article, and in particular.

(a) tender must be at a reasonable hour, and if it is of goods they must be kept available for the period reasonably necessary to enable the buyer to take possession; but

(b) unless otherwise agreed the buyer must furnish facilities reasonably suited to the receipt of the goods.

(2) Where the case is within the next section respecting shipment tender requires that the seller comply with its provisions.

(3) Where the seller is required to deliver at a particular destination tender requires that he comply with subsection (1) and also in any appropriate case tender documents as described in subsections (4) and (5) of this section.

(4) Where goods are in the possession of a bailee and are to be delivered without being moved

(a) tender requires that the seller either tender a negotiable document of title covering such goods or procure acknowledgment by the bailee of the buyer's right to possession of the goods; but

(b) tender to the buyer of a non-negotiable document of title or of a written direction to the bailee to deliver is sufficient tender unless the buyer seasonably objects, and receipt by the bailee of notification of the buyer's rights fixes those rights as against the bailee and all third persons; but risk of loss of the goods and of any failure by the bailee to honor the non-negotiable document of title or to obey the direction remains on the seller until the buyer has had a reasonable time to present the document or direction, and a refusal by the bailee to honor the document or to obey the direction defeats the tender.

(5) Where the contract requires the seller to deliver documents

(a) he must tender all such documents in correct form, except as provided in this Article with respect to bills of lading in a set (subsection (2) of Section 2-323); and

(b) tender through customary banking channels is sufficient and dishonor of a draft accompanying the documents constitutes non-acceptance or rejection.

§ 2-504.   Shipment by Seller

Where the seller is required or authorized to send the goods to the buyer and the contract does not require him to deliver them at a particular destination, then unless otherwise agreed he must

(a) put the goods in the possession of such a carrier and make such a contract for their transportation as may be reasonable having regard to the nature of the goods and other circumstances of the case; and

(b) obtain and promptly deliver or tender in due form any document necessary to enable the buyer to obtain possession of the goods or otherwise required by the agreement or by usage of trade; and

(c) promptly notify the buyer of the shipment.

Failure to notify the buyer under paragraph (c) or to make a proper contract under paragraph (a) is a ground for rejection only if material delay or loss ensues.

§ 2-505.   Seller's Shipment Under Reservation

(1) Where the seller has identified goods to the contract by or before shipment:

(a) his procurement of a negotiable bill of lading to his own order or otherwise reserves in him a security interest in the goods. His procurement of the bill to the order of a financing agency or of the buyer indicates in addition only the seller's expectation of transferring that interest to the person named.

(b) a non-negotiable bill of lading to himself or his nominee reserves possession of the goods as security but except in a case of conditional delivery (subsection (2) of Section 2-507) a non-negotiable bill of lading naming the buyer as consignee reserves no security interest even though the seller retains possession of the bill of lading.

(2) When shipment by the seller with reservation of a security interest is in violation of the contract for sale it constitutes an improper contract for transportation within the preceding section but impairs neither the rights given to the buyer by shipment and identification of the goods to the contract nor the seller's powers as a holder of a negotiable document.

§ 2-506.   Rights of Financing Agency

(1) A financing agency by paying or purchasing for value a draft which relates to a shipment of goods acquires to the extent of the payment or purchase and in addition to its own rights under the draft and any document of title securing it any rights of the shipper in the goods including the right to stop delivery and the shipper's right to have the draft honored by the buyer.

(2) The right to reimbursement of a financing agency which has in good faith honored or purchased the draft under commitment to or authority from the buyer is not impaired by subsequent discovery of defect with reference to any relevant document which was apparently regular on its face.

§ 2-507.   Effect of Seller's Tender; Delivery on Condition

(1) Tender of delivery is a condition to the buyer's duty to accept the goods and, unless otherwise agreed, to his duty to pay for them. Tender entitles the seller to acceptance of the goods and to payment according to the contract.

(2) Where payment is due and demanded on the delivery to the buyer of goods or documents of title, his right as against the seller to retain or dispose of them is conditional upon his making the payment due.

§ 2-508.   Cure by Seller of Improper Tender or Delivery; Replacement

(1) Where any tender or delivery by the seller is rejected because non-conforming and the time for performance has not yet expired, the seller may seasonably notify the buyer of his intention to cure and may then within the contract time make a conforming delivery.

(2) Where the buyer rejects a non-conforming tender which the seller had reasonable grounds to believe would be acceptable with or without money allowance the seller may if he seasonably notifies the buyer have a further reasonable time to substitute a conforming tender.

§ 2-509.   Risk of Loss in the Absence of Breach

(1) Where the contract requires or authorizes the seller to ship the goods by carrier

(a) if it does not require him to deliver them at a particular destination, the risk of loss passes to the buyer when the goods are duly delivered to the carrier even though the shipment is under reservation (Section 2-505); but

(b) if it does require him to deliver them at a particular destination and the goods are there duly tendered while in the possession of the carrier, the risk of loss passes to the buyer when the goods are there duly so tendered as to enable the buyer to take delivery.

(2) Where the goods are held by a bailee to be delivered without being moved, the risk of loss passes to the buyer

(a) on his receipt of a negotiable document of title covering the goods; or

(b) on acknowledgment by the bailee of the buyer's right to possession of the goods; or

(c) after his receipt of a non-negotiable document of title or other written direction to deliver, as provided in subsection (4) (b) of Section 2-503.

(3) In any case not within subsection (1) or (2), the risk of loss passes to the buyer on his receipt of the goods if the seller is a merchant; otherwise the risk passes to the buyer on tender of delivery.

(4) The provisions of this section are subject to contrary agreement of the parties and to the provisions of this Article on sale on approval (Section 2-327) and on effect of breach on risk of loss (Section 2-510).

§ 2-510.   Effect of Breach on Risk of Loss

(1) Where a tender or delivery of goods so fails to conform to the contract as to give a right of rejection the risk of their loss remains on the seller until cure of acceptance.

(2) Where the buyer rightfully revokes acceptance he may to the extent of any deficiency in his effective insurance coverage treat the risk of loss as having rested on the seller from the beginning.

(3) Where the buyer as to conforming goods already identified to the contract for sale repudiates or is otherwise in breach before risk of their loss has passed to him, the seller may to the extent of any deficiency in his effective insurance coverage treat the risk of loss as resting on the buyer for a commerically reasonable time.

§ 2-511.   Tender of Payment by Buyer; Payment by Check

(1) Unless otherwise agreed tender of payment is a condition to the seller's duty to tender and complete any delivery.

(2) Tender of payment is sufficient when made by any means or in any manner current in the ordinary course of business unless the seller demands payment in legal tender and gives any extension of time reasonably necessary to procure it.

(3) Subject to the provisions of this Act on the effect of an instrument on an obligation (Section 3-802), payment by check is conditional and is defeated as between the parties by dishonor of the check on due presentment.

§ 2-512.   Payment by Buyer Before Inspection

(1) Where the contract requires payment before inspection non-conformity of the goods does not excuse the buyer from so making payment unless

(a) the non-conformity appears without inspection; or

(b) despite tender of the required documents the circumstances would justify injunction against honor under the provisions of this Act (Section 5-114.)

(2) Payment pursuant to subsection (1) does not constitute an acceptance of goods or impair the buyer's right to inspect or any of his remedies.

§ 2-513.   Buyer's Right to Inspection of Goods

(1) Unless otherwise agreed and subject to subsection (3), where goods are tendered or delivered or identified to the contract for sale, the buyer has a right before payment or acceptance to inspect them at any reasonable place and time and in any reasonable manner. When the seller is required or authorized to send the goods to the buyer, the inspection may be after their arrival.

(2) Expenses of inspection must be borne by the buyer but may be recovered from the seller if the goods do not conform and are rejected.

(3) Unless otherwise agreed and subject to the provisions of this Article on C.I.F. contracts (subsection (3) of Section 2-321), the buyer is not entitled to inspect the goods before payment of the price when the contract provides

(a) for delivery "C.O.D." or on other like terms; or

(b) for payment against documents of title, except where such payment is due only after the goods are to become available for inspection.

(4) A place or method of inspection fixed by the parties is presumed to be exclusive but unless otherwise expressly agreed it does not postpone identification or shift the place for delivery or for passing the risk of loss. If compliance becomes impossible, inspection shall be as provided in this section unless the place or method fixed was clearly intended as an indispensable condition failure of which avoids the contract.

§ 2-514.   When Documents Deliverable on Acceptance; When on Payment

Unless otherwise agreed documents against which a draft is drawn are to be delivered to the drawee on acceptance of the draft if it is payable more than three days after presentment; otherwise, only on payment.

§ 2-515.   Preserving Evidence of Goods in Dispute

In furtherance of the adjustment of any claim or dispute

(a) either party on reasonable notification to the other and for the purpose of ascertaining the facts and preserving evidence has the right to inspect, test and sample the goods including such of them as may be in the possession or control of the other; and

(b) the parties may agree to a third party inspection or survey to determine the conformity or condition of the goods and may agree that the findings shall be binding upon them in any subsequent litigation or adjustment.

PART 6. *Breach, Repudiation and Excuse*

§ 2-601.   Buyer's Rights on Improper Delivery

Subject to the provisions of this Article on breach in installment contracts (Section 2-612) and unless otherwise agreed under the sections on contractual limitations of remedy (Sections 2-718 and 2-719), if the goods or the tender of delivery fail in any respect to conform to the contract, the buyer may

(a) reject the whole; or

(b) accept the whole; or

(c) accept any commercial unit or units and reject the rest.

§ 2-602.   Manner and Effect of Rightful Rejection

(1) Rejection of goods must be within a reasonable time after their delivery or tender. It is ineffective unless the buyer seasonably notifies the seller.

(2) Subject to the provisions of the two following sections on rejected goods (Sections 2-603 and 2-604),

(a) after rejection any exercise of ownership by the buyer with respect to any commercial unit is wrongful as against the seller; and

(b) if the buyer has before rejection taken physical possession of goods in which he does not have a security interest under the provisions of this Article (subsection (3) of Section 2-711), he is under a duty after rejection to hold them with reasonable care at the seller's disposition for a time sufficient to permit the seller to remove them; but

(c) the buyer has no further obligations with regard to goods rightfully rejected.

(3) The seller's rights with respect to goods wrongfully rejected are governed by the provisions of this Article on Seller's remedies in general (Section 2-703).

§ 2-603.   Merchant Buyer's Duties as to Rightfully Rejected Goods

(1) Subject to any security interest in the buyer (subsection (3) of Section 2-711), when the seller has no agent or place of business at the market of rejection a merchant buyer is under a duty after rejection of goods in his possession or control to follow any reasonable instruction received from the seller with respect to the goods and in the absence of such instructions to make reasonable efforts to sell them for the seller's account if they are perishable or threaten to decline in value speedily. Instructions are not reasonable if on demand indemnity for expenses is not forthcoming.

(2) When the buyer sells goods under subsection (1), he is entitled to reimbursement from the seller or out of the proceeds for reasonable expenses of caring for and selling them, and if the expenses include no selling commission then to such commission as is usual in the trade or if there is none to a reasonable sum not exceeding ten per cent on the gross proceeds.

(3) In complying with this section the buyer is held only to good faith and good faith conduct hereunder is neither acceptance nor conversion nor the basis of an action for damages.

§ 2-604. Buyer's Options as to Salvage of Rightfully Rejected Goods

Subject to the provisions of the immediately preceding section on perishables if the seller gives no instructions within a reasonable time after notification of rejection the buyer may store the rejected goods for the seller's account or reship them to him or resell them for the seller's account with reimbursement as provided in the preceding section. Such action is not acceptance or conversion.

§ 2-605. Waiver of Buyer's Objections by Failure to Particularize

(1) The buyer's failure to state in connection with rejection a particular defect which is ascertainable by reasonable inspection precludes him from relying on the unstated defect to justify rejection or to establish breach

(a) where the seller could have cured it if stated seasonably; or

(b) between merchants when the seller has after rejection made a request in writing for a full and final written statement of all defects on which the buyer proposes to rely.

(2) Payment against documents made without reservation of rights precludes recovery of the payment for defects apparent on the face of the documents.

§ 2-606. What Constitutes Acceptance of Goods

(1) Acceptance of goods occurs when the buyer

(a) after a reasonable opportunity to inspect the goods signifies to the seller that the goods are conforming or that he will take or retain them in spite of their non-conformity; or

(b) fails to make an effective rejection (subsection (1) of Section 2-602), but such acceptance does not occur until the buyer has had a reasonable opportunity to inspect them; or

(c) does any act inconsistent with the seller's ownership; but if such act is wrongful as against the seller it is an acceptance only if ratified by him.

(2) Acceptance of a part of any commercial unit is acceptance of that entire unit.

§ 2-607. Effect of Acceptance; Notice of Breach; Burden of Establishing Breach After Acceptance; Notice of Claim or Litigation to Person Answerable Over

(1) The The buyer must pay at the contract rate for any goods accepted.

(2) Acceptance of goods by the buyer precludes rejection of the goods accepted and if made with knowledge of a non-conformity cannot be revoked because of it unless the acceptance was on the reasonable assumption that the non-conformity would be seasonably cured but acceptance does not of itself impair any other remedy provided by this Article for non-conformity.

(3) Where a tender has been accepted

(a) the buyer must within a reasonable time after he discovers or should have discovered any breach notify the seller of breach or be barred from any remedy; and

(b) if the claim is one for infringement or the like (subsection (3) of Section 2-312) and the buyer is sued as a result of such a breach he must so notify the seller within a reasonable time after he receives notice of the litigation or be barred from any remedy over for liability established by the litigation.

(4) The burden is on the buyer to establish any breach with respect to the goods accepted.

(5) Where the buyer is sued for breach of a warranty or other obligation for which his seller is answerable over

(a) he may give his seller written notice of the litigation. If the notice states that the seller may come in and defend and that if the seller does not do so he will be bound in any action against him by his buyer by any determination of fact common to the two litigations, then unless the seller after seasonable receipt of the notice does come in and defend he is so bound.

(b) if the claim is one for infringement or the like (subsection (3) of Section 2-312) the original seller may demand in writing that his buyer turn over to him control of the litigation including settlement or else be barred from any remedy over and if he also agrees to bear all expense and to satisfy any adverse judgment, then unless the buyer after seasonable receipt of the demand does turn over control the buyer is so barred.

(6) The provisions of subsections (3), (4) and (5) apply to any obligation of a buyer to hold the seller

harmless against infringement or the like (subsection (3) of Section 2-312).

§ 2-608. Revocation of Acceptance in Whole or in Part

(1) The buyer may revoke his acceptance of a lot or commercial unit whose non-conformity substantially impairs its value to him if he has accepted it

(a) on the reasonable assumption that its non-conformity would be cured and it has not been seasonally cured; or

(b) without discovery of such non-conformity if his acceptance was reasonably induced either by the difficulty of discovery before acceptance or by the seller's assurances.

(2) Revocation of acceptance must occur within a reasonable time after the buyer discovers or should have discovered the ground for it and before any substantial change in condition of the goods which is not caused by their own defects. It is not effective until the buyer notifies the seller of it.

(3) A buyer who so revokes has the same rights and duties with regard to the goods involved as if he had rejected them.

§ 2-609. Right to Adequate Assurance of Performance

(1) A contract for sale imposes an obligation on each party that the other's expectation of receiving due performance will not be impaired. When reasonable grounds for insecurity arise with respect to the performance of either party the other may in writing demand adequate assurance of due performance and until he receives such assurance may if commercially reasonable suspend any performance for which he has not already received the agreed return.

(2) Between merchants the reasonableness of grounds for insecurity and the adequacy of any assurance offered shall be determined according to commercial standards.

(3) Acceptance of any improper delivery or payment does not prejudice the aggrieved party's right to demand adequate assurance of future performance.

(4) After receipt of a justified demand failure to provide within a reasonable time not exceeding thirty days such assurance of due performance as is adequate under the circumstances of the particular case is a repudiation of the contract.

§ 2-610. Anticipatory Repudiation

When either party repudiates the contract with respect to a performance not yet due the loss of which will substantially impair the value of the contract to the other, the aggrieved party may

(a) for a commercially reasonable time await performance by the repudiating party; or

(b) resort to any remedy for breach (Section 2-703 or Section 2-711), even though he has notified the repudiating party that he would await the latter's performance and has urged retraction; and

(c) in either case suspend his own performance or proceed in accordance with the provisions of this Article on the seller's right to identify goods to the contract not withstanding breach or to salvage unfinished goods (Section 2-704).

§ 6-611. Retraction of Anticipatory Repudiation

(1) Until the repudiating party's next performance is due he can retract his repudiation unless the aggrieved party has since the repudiation cancelled or materially changed his position or otherwise indicated that he considers the repudiation final.

(2) Retraction may be any method which clearly indicates to the aggrieved party that the repudiating party intends to perform, but must include any assurance justifiably demanded under the provisions of this Article (Section 2-609).

(3) Retraction reinstates the repudiating party's rights under the contract with due excuse and allowance to the aggrieved party for any delay occasioned by the repudiation.

§ 2-612. "Installment Contract"; Breach

(1) An "installment contract" is one which requires or authorizes the delivery of goods in separate lots to be separately accepted, even though the contract contains a clause "each delivery is a separate contract" or its equivalent.

(2) The buyer may reject any installment which is non-conforming if the non-conformity substantially impairs the value of that installment and cannot be cured or if the non-conformity is a defect in the required documents; but if the non-conformity does not fall within subsection (3) and the seller gives adequate assurance of its cure the buyer must accept that installment.

(3) Whenever non-conformity or default with respect to one or more installments substantially impairs the value of the whole contract there is a breach of the whole. But the aggrieved party reinstates the contract if he accepts a nonconforming installment without seasonably notifying of cancellation or if he brings an action with respect only to past installments or demands performance as to future installments.

§ 2-613.   Casualty to Identified Goods

Where the contract requires for its performance goods identified when the contract is made, and the goods suffer casualty without fault of either party before the risk of loss passes to the buyer, or in a proper case under a "no arrival, no sale" term (Section 2-324) then

(a) if the loss is total the contract is avoided; and

(b) if the loss is partial or the goods have so deteriorated as no longer to conform to the contract the buyer may nevertheless demand inspection and at his option either treat the contract as avoided or accept the goods with due allowance from the contract price for the deterioration or the deficiency in quantity but without further right against the seller.

§ 2-614.   Substituted Performance

(1) Where without fault of either party the agreed berthing, loading, or unloading facilities fail or an agreed type of carrier becomes unavailable or the agreed manner of delivery otherwise becomes commercially impracticable but a commercially reasonable substitute is available, such substitute performance must be tendered and accepted.

(2) If the agreed means or manner of payment fails because of domestic or foreign governmental regulation, the seller may withhold or stop delivery unless the buyer provides a means or manner of payment which is commercially a substantial equivalent. If delivery has already been taken, payment by the means or in the manner provided by the regulation discharges the buyers obligation unless the regulation is discriminatory, oppressive or predatory.

§ 2-615.   Excuse by Failure of Presupposed Conditions

Except so far as a seller may have assumed a greater obligation and subject to the preceding section on substituted performance:

(a) Delay in delivery or non-delivery in whole or in part by a seller who complies with paragraphs (b) and

(c) is not a breach of his duty under a contract for sale if performance as agreed has been made impracticable by the occurrence of a contingency the non-occurrence of which was a basic assumption on which the contract was made or by compliance in good faith with any applicable foreign or domestic governmental regulation or order whether or not it later proves to be invalid.

(b) Where the causes mentioned in paragraph (a) affect only a part of the seller's capacity to perform, he must allocate production and deliveries among his customers but may at his option include regular customers not then under contract as well as his own requirements for further manufacture. He may so allocate in any manner which is fair and reasonable.

(c) The seller must notify the buyer seasonably that there will be delay or non-delivery and, when allocation is required under paragraph (b), of the estimated quota thus made available for the buyer.

§ 2-616.   Procedure on Notice Claiming Excuse

(1) Where the buyer receives notification of a material or indefinite delay or an allocation justified under the preceding section he may by written notification to the seller as to any delivery concerned, and where the prospective deficiency substantially impairs the value of the whole contract under the provisions of this Article relating to breach of installment contracts (Section 2-612), then also as to the whole,

(a) terminate and thereby discharge any unexecuted portion of the contract; or

(b) modify the contract by agreeing to take his available quota in substitution.

(2) If after receipt of such notification from the seller the buyer fails so to modify the contract within a reasonable time not exceeding thirty days the contract lapses with respect to any deliveries affected.

(3) The provisions of this section may not be negated by agreement except in so far as the seller has assumed a greater obligation under the preceding section.

PART 7. Remedies

§ 2—701.   Remedies for Breach of Collateral Contracts Not Impaired

Remedies for breach of any obligation or promise collateral or ancillary to a contract for sale are not impaired by the provisions of this Article.

§ 2-702. Seller's Remedies on Discovery of Buyer's Insolvency

(1) Where the seller discovers the buyer to be insolvent he may refuse delivery except for cash including payment for all goods theretofore delivered under the contract, and stop delivery under this Article (Section 2-705).

(2) Where the seller discovers that the buyer has received goods on credit while insolvent he may reclaim the goods upon demand made within ten days after the receipt, but if misrepresentation of solvency has been made to the particular seller in writing within three months before delivery the ten day limitation does not apply. Except as provided in this subsection the seller may not base a right to reclaim goods on the buyer's fraudulent or innocent misrepresentation of solvency or of intent to pay.

(3) The seller's right to reclaim under subsection (2) is subject to the rights of a buyer in ordinary course or other good faith purchaser under this Article (Section 2-403). Successful reclamation of goods excludes all other remedies with respect to them. As amended 1966.

§ 2-703. Seller's Remedies in General

Where the buyer wrongfully rejects or revokes acceptance of goods or fails to make a payment due on or before delivery or repudiates with respect to a part or the whole, then with respect to any goods directly affected and, if the breach is of the whole contract (Section 2-612), then also with respect to the whole undelivered balance, the aggrieved seller may

(a) withhold delivery of such goods;

(b) stop delivery by any bailee as hereafter provided (Section 2-705);

(c) proceed under the next section respecting goods still unidentified to the contract;

(d) resell and recover damages as hereafter provided (Section 2-706);

(e) recover damages for non-acceptance (Section 2-708) or in a proper case the price (Section 2-709);

(f) cancel.

§ 2-704. Seller's Right to Identify Goods to the Contract Notwithstanding Breach or to Salvage Unfinished Goods

(1) An aggrieved seller under the preceding section may

(a) identify to the contract conforming goods not already identified if at the time he learned of the breach they are in his possession or control;

(b) treat as the subject of resale goods which have demonstrably been intended for the particular contract even though those goods are unfinished.

(2) Where the goods are unfinished an aggrieved seller may in the exercise of reasonable commercial judgment for the purposes of avoiding loss and of effective realization either complete the manufacture and wholly identify the goods to the contract or cease manufacture and resell for scrap or salvage value or proceed in any other reasonable manner.

§ 2-705. Seller's Stoppage of Delivery in Transit or Otherwise

(1) The seller may stop delivery of goods in the possession of a carrier or other bailee when he discovers the buyer to be insolvent (Section 2-702) and may stop delivery of carload, truckload, planeload or larger shipments of express or freight when the buyer repudiates or fails to make a payment due before delivery or if for any other reason the seller has a right to withhold or reclaim the goods.

(2) As against such buyer the seller may stop delivery until

(a) receipt of the goods by the buyer; or

(b) acknowledgment to the buyer by any bailee of the goods except a carrier that the bailee holds the goods for the buyer; or

(c) such acknowledgment to the buyer by a carrier by reshipment or as warehouseman; or

(d) negotiation to the buyer of any negotiable document of title covering the goods.

(3) (a) To stop delivery the seller must so notify as to enable the bailee by reasonable diligence to prevent delivery of the goods.

(b) After such notification the bailee must hold and deliver the goods according to the directions of the seller but the seller is liable to the bailee for any ensuing charges or damages.

(c) If a negotiable document of title has been issued for goods the bailee is not obliged to obey a notification to stop until surrender of the document.

(d) A carrier who has issued a non-negotiable bill of lading is not obliged to obey a notification to stop received from a person other than the consignor.

§ 2-706. Seller's Resale Including Contract for Resale

(1) Under the conditions stated in Section 2-703 on seller's remedies, the seller may resell the goods concerned or the undelivered balance thereof. Where the resale is made in good faith and in a commercially reasonable manner the seller may recover the difference between the resale price and the contract price together with any incidental damages allowed under the provisions of this Article (Section 2-710), but less expenses saved in consequence of the buyer's breach.

(2) Except as otherwise provided in subsection (3) or unless otherwise agreed resale may be at public or private sale including sale by way of one or more contracts to sell or of identification to an existing contract of the seller. Sale may be as a unit or in parcels and at any time and place and on any terms but every aspect of the sale including the method, manner, time, place and terms must be commercially reasonable. The resale must be reasonably identified as referring to the broken contract, but it is not necessary that the goods be in existence or that any or all of them have been identified to the contract before the breach.

(3) Where the resale is at private sale the seller must give the buyer reasonable notification of his intention to resell.

(4) Where the resale is at public sale

(a) only identified goods can be sold except where there is a recognized market for a public sale of futures in goods of the kind; and

(b) it must be made at a usual place or market for public sale if one is reasonably available and except in the case of goods which are perishable or threaten to decline in value speedily the seller must give the buyer reasonable notice of the time and place of the resale; and

(c) if the goods are not to be within the view of those attending the sale the notification of sale must state the place where the goods are located and provide for their reasonable inspection by prospective bidders; and

(d) the seller may buy.

(5) A purchaser who buys in good faith at a resale takes the goods free of any rights of the original buyer even though the seller fails to comply with one or more of the requirements of this section.

(6) The seller is not accountable to the buyer for any profit made on any resale. A person in the position of a seller (Section 2-707) or a buyer who has rightfully rejected or justifiably revoked acceptance must account for any excess over the amount of his security interest, as hereinafter defined (subsection (3) of Section 2-711).

§ 2-707. "Person in the Position of a Seller"

(1) A "person in the position of a seller" includes as against a principal an agent who has paid or become responsible for the price of goods on behalf of his principal or anyone who otherwise holds a security interest or other right in goods similar to that of a seller.

(2) A person in the position of a seller may as provided in this Article withhold or stop delivery (Section 2-705) and resell (Section 2-706) and recover incidental damages (Section 2-710).

§ 2-708. Seller's Damages for Non-acceptance or Repudiation

(1) Subject to subsection (2) and to the provisions of this Article with respect to proof of market price (Section 2-723), the measure of damages for non-acceptance or repudiation by the buyer is the difference between the market price at the time and place for tender and the unpaid contract price together with any incidental damages provided in this Article (Section 2-710), but less expenses saved in consequence of the buyer's breach.

(2) If the measure of damages provided in subsection (1) is inadequate to put the seller in as good a position as performance would have done then the measure of damages is the profit (including reasonable overhead) which the seller would have made from full performance by the buyer, together with any incidental damages provided in this Article (Section 2-710), due allowance for costs reasonably incurred and due credit for payments or proceeds of resale.

§ 2-709. Action for the Price

(1) When the buyer fails to pay the price as it becomes due the seller may recover, together with any incidental damages under the next section, the price

(a) of goods accepted or of conforming goods lost or damaged within a commercially reasonable time after risk of their loss has passed to the buyer; and

(b) of goods identified to the contract if the seller is unable after reasonable effort to resell them at a reasonable price or the circumstances reasonably indicate that such effort will be unavailing.

(2) Where the seller sues for the price he must hold for the buyer any goods which have been identified to the contract and are still in his control except that if resale becomes possible he may resell them at any time prior to the collection of the judgment. The net proceeds of any such resale must be credited to the buyer and payment of the judgment entitles him to any goods not resold.

(3) After the buyer has wrongfully rejected or revoked acceptance of the goods or has failed to make a payment due or has repudiated (Section 2-610), a seller who is held not entitled to the price under this section shall nevertheless be awarded damages for a non-acceptance under the preceding section.

§ 2-710.   Seller's Incidental Damages

Incidental damages to an aggrieved seller include any commercially reasonable charges, expenses or commissions incurred in stopping delivery, in the transportation, care and custody of goods after the buyer's breach, in connection with return or resale of the goods or otherwise resulting from the breach.

§ 2-711.   Buyer's Remedies in General; Buyer's Security Interest in Rejected Goods

(1) Where the seller fails to make delivery or repudiates or the buyer rightfully rejects or justifiably revokes acceptance then with respect to any goods involved, and with respect to the whole if the breach goes to the whole contract (Section 2-612), the buyer may cancel and whether or not he has done so may in addition to recovering so much of the price as has been paid

(a) "cover" and have damages under the next section as to all the goods affected whether or not they have been identified to the contract; or

(b) recover damages for non-delivery as provided in this Article (Section 2-713).

(2) Where the seller fails to deliver or repudiates the buyer may also

(a) if the goods have been identified recover them as provided in this Article (Section 2-502); or

(b) in a proper case obtain specific performance or replevy the goods as provided in this Article (Section 2-716).

(3) On rightful rejection or justifiable revocation of acceptance a buyer has a security interest in goods in his possession or control for any payments made on their price and any expenses reasonably incurred in their inspection, receipt, transportation, care and custody and may hold such goods and resell them in like manner as an aggrieved seller (Section 2-706).

§ 2-712.   "Cover"; Buyer's Procurement of Substitute Goods

(1) After a breach within the preceding section the buyer may "cover" by making in good faith and without unreasonable delay any reasonable purchase of or contract to purchase goods in substitution for those due from the seller.

(2) The buyer may recover from the seller as damages the difference between the cost of cover and the contract price together with any incidental or consequential damages as hereinafter defined (Section 2-715), but less expenses saved in consequence of the seller's breach.

(3) Failure of the buyer to effect cover within this section does not bar him from any other remedy.

§ 2-713.   Buyer's Damages for Non-Delivery or Repudiation

(1) Subject to the provisions of this Article with respect to proof of market price (Section 2-723), the measure of damages for non-delivery or repudiation by the seller is the difference between the market price at the time when the buyer learned of the breach and the contract price together with any incidental and consequential damages provided in this Article (Section 2-715), but less expenses saved in consequence of the seller's breach.

(2) Market price is to be determined as of the place for tender or, in cases of rejection after arrival or revocation of acceptance, as of the place of arrival.

§ 2-714.   Buyer's Damages for Breach in Regard to Accepted Goods

(1) Where the buyer has accepted goods and given notification (subsection (3) of Section 2-607) he may recover as damages for any non-conformity of tender the loss resulting in the ordinary course of events from the seller's breach as determined in any manner which is reasonable.

(2) The measure of damages for breach of warranty is the difference at the time and place of acceptance between the value of the goods accepted and the value they would have had if they had been as warranted, unless special circumstances show proximate damages of a different amount.

(3) In a proper case any incidental and consequential damages under the next section may also be recovered.

§ 2-715. Buyer's Incidental and Consequential Damages

(1) Incidental damages resulting from the seller's breach include expenses reasonably incurred in inspection, receipt, transportation and care and custody of goods rightfully rejected, any commercially reasonable charges, expenses or commissions in connection with effecting cover and any other reasonable expenses incident to the delay or other breach.

(2) Consequential damages resulting from the seller's breach include

(a) any loss resulting from general or particular requirements and needs of which the seller at the time of contracting had reason to know and which could not reasonably be prevented by cover or otherwise; and

(b) injury to person or property proximately resulting from any breach of warranty.

§ 2-716. Buyer's Right to Specific Performance or Replevin

(1) Specific performance may be decreed where the goods are unique or in other proper circumstances.

(2) The decree for specific performance may include such terms and conditions as to payment of the price, damages, or other relief as the court may deem just.

(3) The buyer has a right of replevin for goods identified to the contract if after reasonable effort he is unable to effect cover for such goods or the circumstances reasonably indicate that such effort will be unavailing or if the goods have been shipped under reservation and satisfaction of the security interest in them has been made or tendered.

§ 2-717. Deduction of Damages From the Price

The buyer on notifying the seller of his intention to do so may deduct all or any part of the damages resulting from any breach of the contract from any part of the price still due under the same contract.

§ 2-718. Liquidation or Limitation of Damages; Deposits

(1) Damages for breach by either party may be liquidated in the agreement but only at an amount which is reasonable in the light of the anticipated or actual harm caused by the breach, the difficulties of proof of loss, and the inconvenience of nonfeasibility of otherwise obtaining an adequate remedy. A term fixing unreasonably large liquidated damages is void as a penalty.

(2) Where the seller justifiably withholds delivery of goods because of the buyer's breach, the buyer is entitled to restitution of any amount by which the sum of his payments exceeds

(a) the amount to which the seller is entitled by virtue of terms liquidating the seller's damages in accordance with subsection (1), or

(b) in the absence of such terms, twenty per cent of the value of the total performance for which the buyer is obligated under the contract of $500, whichever is smaller.

(3) The buyer's right to restitution under subsection (2) is subject to offset to the extent that the seller establishes

(a) a right to recover damages under the provisions of this Article other than subsection (1), and

(b) the amount or value of any benefits received by the buyer directly or indirectly by reason of the contract.

(4) Where a seller has received payment in goods their reasonable value or the proceeds of their resale shall be treated as payments for the purposes of subsection (2); but if the seller has notice of the buyer's breach before reselling goods received in part performance, his resale is subject to the conditions laid down in this Article on resale by an aggrieved seller (Section 2-706).

§ 2-719. Contractual Modification or Limitation of Remedy

(1) Subject to the provisions of subsections (2) and (3) of this section and of the preceding section on liquidation and limitation of damages,

(a) the agreement may provide for remedies in addition to or in substitution for those provided in this Article and may limit or alter the measure of damages recoverable under this Article, as by limiting the buyer's remedies to return of the goods and repayment of the price or to repair and replacement of non-conforming goods or parts; and

(b) resort to a remedy as provided is optional unless the remedy is expressly agreed to be exclusive, in which case it is the sole remedy.

(2) Where circumstances cause an exclusive or limited remedy to fail of its essential purpose, remedy may be had as provided in this Act.

(3) Consequential damages may be limited or excluded unless the limitation or exclusion is unconscionable. Limitation of consequential damages for injury to the person in the case of consumer goods is prima facie unconscionable but limitation of damages where the loss is commercial is not.

§ 2-720. Effect of "Cancellation" or "Rescission" on Claims for Antecedent Breach

Unless the contrary intention clearly appears, expressions of "cancellation" or "rescission" of the contract or the like shall not be construed as a renunciation or discharge of any claim in damages for an antecedent breach.

§ 2-721. Remedies for Fraud

Remedies for material misrepresentation or fraud include all remedies available under this Article for non-fraudulent breach. Neither rescission or a claim for rescission of the contract for sale nor rejection or return of the goods shall bar or be deemed inconsistent with a claim for damages or other remedy.

§ 2-722. Who Can Sue Third Parties for Injury to Goods

Where a third party so deals with goods which have been identified to a contract for sale as to cause actionable injury to a party to that contract

(a) a right of action against the third party is in either party to the contract for sale who has title to or a security interest or a special property or an insurable interest in the goods; and if the goods have been destroyed or converted a right of action is also in the party who either bore the risk of loss under the contract for sale or has since the injury assumed that risk as against the other;

(b) if at the time of the injury the party plaintiff did not bear the risk of loss as against the other party to the contract for sale and there is no arrangement between them for disposition of the recovery, his suit or settle-

ment is, subject to his own interest, as a fiduciary for the other party to the contract.

(c) either party may with the consent of the other sue for the benefit of whom it may concern.

§ 2-723. Proof of Market Price: Time and Place

(1) If an action based on anticipatory repudiation comes to trial before the time for performance with respect to some or all of the goods, any damages based on market price (Section 2-708 or Section 2-713) shall be determined according to the price of such goods prevailing at the time when the aggrieved party learned of the repudiation.

(2) If evidence of a price prevailing at the times or places described in this Article is not readily available the price prevailing within any reasonable time before or after the time described or at any other place which in commercial judgment or under usage of trade would serve as a reasonable substitute for the one described may be used, making any proper allowance for the cost of transporting the goods to or from such other place.

(3) Evidence of a relevant price prevailing at a time or place other than the one described in this Article offered by one party is not admissible unless and until he has given the other party such notice as the court finds sufficient to prevent unfair surprise.

§ 2-724. Admissibility of Market Quotations

Whenever the prevailing price or value of any goods regularly bought and sold in any established commodity market is in issue, reports in official publications or trade journals or in newspapers or periodicals of general circulation published as the reports of such market shall be admissible in evidence. The circumstances of the preparation of such a report may be shown to affect its weight but not its admissibility.

§ 2-725. Statute of Limitations in Contracts for Sale

(1) An action for breach of any contract for sale must be commenced within four years after the cause of action has accrued. By the original agreement the parties may reduce the period of limitation to not less than one year but may not extend it.

(2) A cause of action accrues when the breach occurs, regardless of the aggrieved party's lack of knowledge of

the breach. A breach of warranty occurs when tender of delivery is made, except that where a warranty explicitly extends to future performance of the goods and discovery of the breach must await the time of such performance the cause of action accrues when the breach is or should have been discovered.

(3) Where an action commenced within the time limited by subsection (1) is so terminated as to leave available a remedy by another action for the same breach such other action may be commenced after the expiration of the time limited and within six months after the termination of the first action unless the termination resulted from voluntary discontinuance or from dismissal for failure or neglect to prosecute.

(4) This section does not alter the law on tolling of the statute of limitations nor does it apply to causes of action which have accrued before this Act becomes effective.

ARTICLE 3.   Commercial Paper

PART 1. *Short Title, Form and Interpretation*

PART 5. *Presentment, Notice of Dishonor and Protest*

PART 6. *Discharge*

PART 7. *Advice of International Sight Draft*

PART 8. *Miscellaneous*

ARTICLE 3. Commercial Paper

PART 1. *Short Title, Form and Interpretation*

§ 3-101. **Short Title**

This Article shall be known and may be cited as Uniform Commercial Code—Commercial Paper.

§ 3-102. **Definitions and Index of Definitions**

(1) In this Article unless the context otherwise requires

(a) "Issue" means the first delivery of an instrument to a holder or a remitter.

(b) An "order" is a direction to pay and must be more than an authorization or request. It must identify the person to pay with reasonable certainty. It may be addressed to one or more such persons jointly or in the alternative but not in succession.

(c) A "promise" is an undertaking to pay and must be more than an acknowledgment of an obligation.

(d) "Secondary party" means a drawer or endorser.

(e) "Instrument" means a negotiable instrument.

(2) Other definitions applying to this Article and the sections in which they appear are:

"Acceptance". Section 3-410.
"Accommodation party". Section 3-415.
"Alteration". Section 3-407.
"Certificate of deposit". Section 3-104.
"Certification". Section 3-411.
"Check". Section 3-104.
"Definite time". Section 3-109.
"Dishonor". Section 3-507.
"Draft". Section 3-104.
"Holder in due course". Section 3-302.
"Negotiation". Section 3-202.
"Note". Section 3-104.
"Notice of dishonor". Section 3-508.
"On demand". Section 3-108.
"Presentment". Section 3-504.
"Protest". Section 3-509.
"Restrictive Indorsement". Section 3-205.
"Signature". Section 3-401.

(3) The following definitions in other Articles apply to this Article:

"Account". Section 4-104.
"Banking Day". Section 4-104.
"Clearing house". Section 4-104.
"Collecting bank". Section 4-105.
"Customer". Section 4-104.
"Depositary Bank". Section 4-105.
"Documentary Draft". Section 4-104.
"Intermediary Bank". Section 4-105.
"Item". Section 4-104.
"Midnight deadline". Section 4-104.
"Payor bank". Section 4-105.

(4) In addition Article 1 contains general definitions and principles of construction and interpretation applicable throughout this Article.

§ 3-103.   Limitations on Scope of Article

(1) This Article does not apply to money, documents of title or investment securities.

(2) The provisions of this Article are subject to the provisions of the Article on Bank Deposits and Collections (Article 4) and Secured Transactions (Article 9).

§ 3-104.   Form of Negotiable Instruments; "Draft"; "Check"; "Certificate of Deposit"; "Note"

(1) Any writing to be a negotiable instrument within this Article must

(a) be signed by the maker or drawer; and

(b) contain an unconditional promise or order to pay a sum certain in money and no other promise, order, obligation or power given by the maker or drawer except as authorized by this Article; and

(c) be payable on demand or at a definite time; and

(d) be payable to order or to bearer.

(2) A writing which complies with the requirements of this section is

(a) a "draft" ("bill of exchange") if it is an order;

(b) a "check" if it is a draft drawn on a bank and payable on demand;

(c) a "certificate of deposit" if it is an acknowledgment by a bank of receipt of money with an engagement to repay it;

(d) a "note" if it is a promise other than a certificate of deposit.

(3) As used in other Articles of this Act, and as the context may require, the terms "draft", "check", "certificate of deposit" and "note" may refer to instruments which are not negotiable within this Article as well as to instruments which are so negotiable.

§ 3-105.   When Promise or Order Unconditional

(1) A promise or order otherwise unconditional is not made conditional by the fact that the instrument

(a) is subject to implied or constructive conditions; or

(b) states its consideration, whether performed or promised, or the transaction which gave rise to the instrument, or that the promise or order is made or the instrument matures in accordance with or "as per" such transaction; or

(c) refers to or states that it arises out of a separate agreement or refers to a separate agreement for rights as to prepayment or acceleration; or

(d) states that it is drawn under a letter of credit; or

(e) states that it is secured, whether by mortgage, reservation of title or otherwise; or

(f) indicates a particular account to be debited or any other fund or source from which reimbursement is expected; or

(g) is limited to payment out of a particular fund or the proceeds of a particular source, if the instrument is issued by a government or governmental agency or unit; or

(h) is limited to payment out of the entire assets of a partnership, unincorporated association, trust or estate by or on behalf of which the instrument is issued.

(2) A promise or order is not unconditional if the instrument

(a) states that it is subject to or governed by any other agreement; or

(b) states that it is to be paid only out of a particular fund or source except as provided in this section. As amended 1962.

§ 3-106.   Sum Certain

(1) The sum payable is a sum certain even though it is to be paid

(a) with stated interest or by stated installments; or

(b) with stated different rates of interest before and after default or a specified date; or

(c) with a stated discount or addition if paid before or after the date fixed for payment; or

(d) with exchange or less exchange, whether at a fixed rate or at the current rate; or

(e) with costs of collection or an attorney's fee or both upon default.

(2) Nothing in this section shall validate any term which is otherwise illegal.

§ 3-107.   Money

(1) An instrument is payable in money if the medium of exchange in which it is payable is money at the time the instrument is made. An instrument payable in "currency" or "current funds" is payable in money.

(2) A promise or order to pay a sum stated in a foreign currency is for a sum certain in money and, unless a different medium of payment is specified in the instrument, may be satisfied by payment of that number of dollars which the stated foreign currency will purchase at the buying sight rate for that currency on the day on which the instrument is payable or, if payable on demand, on the day of demand. If such an instrument specifies a foreign currency as the medium of payment the instrument is payable in that currency.

§ 3-108. Payable on Demand
Instruments payable on demand include those payable at sight or on presentation and those in which no time for payment is stated.

§ 3-109. Definite Time
(1) An instrument is payable at a definite time if by its terms it is payable

(a) on or before a stated date or at a fixed period after a stated date; or

(b) at a fixed period after sight; or

(c) at a definite time subject to any acceleration; or

(d) at a definite time subject to extension at the option of the holder, or to extension to a further definite time at the option of the maker or acceptor or automatically upon or after a specified act or event.

(2) An instrument which by its terms is otherwise payable only upon an act or event uncertain as to time of occurrence is not payable at a definite time even though the act or event has occurred.

§ 3-110. Payable to Order
(1) An instrument is payable to order when by its terms it is payable to the order or assigns of any person therein specified with reasonable certainty, or to him or his order, or when it is conspicuously designated on its face as "exchange" or the like and names a payee. It may be payable to the order of

(a) the maker or drawer; or

(b) the drawee; or

(c) a payee who is not maker, drawer or drawee; or

(d) two or more payees together or in the alternative; or

(e) an estate, trust or fund, in which case it is payable to the order of the representative of such estate, trust or fund or his successors; or

(f) an office, or an officer by his title as such in which case it is payable to the principal but the incumbent of the office or his successors may act as if he or they were the holder; or

(g) a partnership or unincorporated association, in which case it is payable to the partnership or association and may be indorsed or transferred by any person thereto authorized.

(2) An instrument not payable to order is not made so payable by such words as "payable upon return of this instrument properly indorsed."

(3) An instrument made payable both to order and to bearer is payable to order unless the bearer words are handwritten or typewritten.

§ 3-111. Payable to Bearer
An instrument is payable to bearer when by its terms it is payable to

(a) bearer or the order of bearer; or

(b) a specified person or bearer; or

(c) "cash" or the order of "cash", or any other indication which does not purport to designate a specific payee.

§ 3-112. Terms and Omissions Not Affecting Negotiability
(1) The negotiability of an instrument is not affected by

(a) the omission of a statement of any consideration or of the place where the instrument is drawn or payable; or

(b) a statement that collateral has been given to secure obligations either on the instrument or otherwise of an obligor on the instrument or that in case of default on those obligations the holder may realize on or dispose of the collateral; or

(c) a promise or power to maintain or protect collateral or to give additional collateral; or

(d) a term authorizing a confession of judgment on the instrument if it is not paid when due; or

(e) a term purporting to waive the benefit of any law intended for the advantage or protection of any obligor; or

(f) a term in a draft providing that the payee by indorsing or cashing it acknowledges full satisfaction of an obligation of the drawer; or

(g) a statement in a draft drawn in a set of parts (Section 3-801) to the effect that the order is effective only if no other part has been honored.

(2) Nothing in this section shall validate any term which is otherwise illegal. As amended 1962.

§ 3-113.   Seal

An instrument otherwise negotiable is within this Article even though it is under a seal.

§ 3-114.   Date, Antedating, Postdating

(1) The negotiability of an instrument is not affected by the fact that it is undated, antedated or postdated.

(2) Where an instrument is antedated or postdated the time when it is payable is determined by the stated date if the instrument is payable on demand or at a fixed period after date.

(3) Where the instrument or any signature thereon is dated, the date is presumed to be correct.

§ 3-115.   Incomplete Instruments

(1) When a paper whose contents at the time of signing show that it is intended to become an instrument is signed while still incomplete in any necessary respect it cannot be enforced until completed, but when it is completed in accordance with authority given it is effective as completed.

(2) If the completion is unauthorized the rules as to material alteration apply (Section 3-407), even though the paper was not delivered by the maker or drawer; but the burden of establishing that any completion is unauthorized is on the party so asserting.

§ 3-116.   Instruments Payable to Two or More Persons

An instrument payable to the order of two or more persons

(a) if in the alternative is payable to any one of them and may be negotiated, discharged or enforced by any of them who has possession of it;

(b) if not in the alternative is payable to all of them and may be negotiated, discharged or enforced only by all of them.

§ 3-117.   Instruments Payable With Words of Description

An instrument made payable to a named person with the addition of words describing him

(a) as agent or officer of a specified person is payable to his principal but the agent or officer may act as if he were the holder;

(b) as any other fiduciary for a specified person or purpose is payable to the payee and may be negotiated, discharged or enforced by him;

(c) in any other manner is payable to the payee unconditionally and the additional words are without effect on subsequent parties.

§ 3-118.   Ambiguous Terms and Rules of Construction

The following rules apply to every instrument:

(a) Where there is doubt whether the instrument is a draft or a note the holder may treat it as either. A draft drawn on the drawer is effective as a note.

(b) Handwritten terms control typewritten and printed terms, and typewritten control printed.

(c) Words control figures except that if the words are ambiguous figures control.

(d) Unless otherwise specified a provision for interest means interest at the judgment rate at the place of payment from the date of the instrument, or if it is undated from the date of issue.

(e) Unless the instrument otherwise specifies two or more persons who sign as maker, acceptor or drawer or indorser and as a part of the same transaction are jointly and severally liable even though the instrument contains such words as "I promise to pay."

(f) Unless otherwise specified consent to extension authorizes a single extension for not longer than the original period. A consent to extension, expressed in the instrument, is binding on secondary parties and accommodation makers. A holder may not exercise his option to extend an instrument over the objection of a maker or acceptor or other party who in accordance with Section 3-604 tenders full payment when the instrument is due.

§ 3-119.   Other Writings Affecting Instrument

(1) As between the obligor and his immediate obligee or any transferee the terms of an instrument may be modified or affected by any other written agreement executed as a part of the same transaction, except that a holder in due course is not affected by any limitation of his rights arising out of the separate written agreement if he had no notice of the limitation when he took the instrument.

(2) A separate agreement does not affect the negotiability of an instrument.

§ 3-120. Instruments "Payable Through" Bank

An instrument which states that it is "payable through" a bank or the like designates that bank as a collecting bank to make presentment but does not of itself authorize the bank to pay the instrument.

§ 3-121. Instruments Payable at Bank

Note: If this Act is introduced in the Congress of the United States this section should be omitted. (States to select either alternative)

Alternative A. A note or acceptance which states that it is payable at a bank is the equivalent of a draft drawn on the bank payable when it falls due out of any funds of the maker or acceptor in current account or otherwise available for such payment.

Alternative B. A note or acceptance which states that it is payable at a bank is not of itself an order or authorization to the bank to pay it.

§ 3-122. Accrual of Cause of Action

(1) A cause of action against a maker or an acceptor accrues

(a) in the case of a time instrument on the day after maturity;

(b) in the case of a demand instrument upon its date or, if no date is stated, on the date of issue.

(2) A cause of action against the obligor of a demand or time certificate of deposit accrues upon demand, but demand on a time certificate may not be made until on or after the date of maturity.

(3) A cause of action against a drawer of a draft or an indorser of any instrument accrues upon demand following dishonor of the instrument. Notice of dishonor is a demand.

(4) Unless an instrument provides otherwise, interest runs at the rate provided by law for a judgment

(a) in the case of a maker, acceptor or other primary obligor of a demand instrument, from the date of demand;

(b) in all other cases from the date of accrual of the cause of action. As amended 1962.

PART 2. *Transfer and Negotiation*

§ 3-201. Transfer: Right to Indorsement

(1) Transfer of an instrument vests in the transferee such rights as the transferor has therein, except that a transferee who has himself been a party to any fraud or illegality affecting the instrument or who as a prior holder had notice of a defense or claim against it cannot improve his position by taking from a later holder in due course.

(2) A transfer of a security interest in an instrument vests the foregoing rights in the transferee to the extent of the interest transferred.

(3) Unless otherwise agreed any transfer for value of an instrument not then payable to bearer gives the transferee the specifically enforceable right to have the unqualified indorsement of the transferor. Negotiation takes effect only when the indorsement is made and until that time there is no presumption that the transferee is the owner.

§ 3-202. Negotiation

(1) Negotiation is the transfer of an instrument in such form that the transferee becomes a holder. If the instrument is payable to order it is negotiated by delivery with any necessary indorsement; if payable to bearer it is negotiated by delivery.

(2) An indorsement must be written by or on behalf of the holder and on the instrument or on a paper so firmly affixed thereto as to become a part thereof.

(3) An indorsement is effective for negotiation only when it conveys the entire instrument or any unpaid residue. If it purports to be of less it operates only as a partial assignment.

(4) Words of assignment, condition, waiver, guaranty, limitation or disclaimer of liability and the like accompanying an indorsement do not affect its character as an indorsement.

§ 3-203. Wrong or Mispelled Name

Where an instrument is made payable to a person under a misspelled name or one other than his own he may indorse in that name or his own or both; but signature in both names may be required by a person paying or giving value for the instrument.

§ 3-204. Special Indorsement; Blank Indorsement

(1) A special indorsement specifies the person to whom or to whose order it makes the instrument payable. Any instrument specially indorsed becomes payable to the order of the special indorsee and may be further negotiated only by his indorsement.

(2) An indorsement in blank specifies no particular indorsee and may consist of a mere signature. An instrument payable to order and indorsed in blank becomes payable to bearer and may be negotiated by delivery alone until specially indorsed.

(3) The holder may convert a blank indorsement into a special indorsement by writing over the signature of the indorser in blank any contract consistent with the character of the indorsement.

§ 3-205.   Restrictive Indorsements

An indorsement is restrictive which either

(a) is conditional; or

(b) purports to prohibit further transfer of the instrument; or

(c) includes the words "for collection," "for deposit," "pay any bank," or like terms signifying a purpose of deposit or collection; or

(d) otherwise states that it is for the benefit or use of the indorser or of another person.

§ 3-206.   Effect of Restrictive Indorsement

(1) No restrictive indorsement prevents further transfer or negotiation of the instrument.

(2) An intermediary bank, or a payor bank which is not the depositary bank, is neither given notice nor otherwise affected by a restrictive indorsement of any person except the bank's immediate transferor or the person presenting for payment.

(3) Except for an intermediary bank, any transferee under an indorsement which is conditional or includes the words "for collection," "for deposit," "pay any bank," or like terms (subparagraphs (a) and (c) of Section 3-205) must pay or apply any value given by him for or on the security of the instrument consistently with the indorsement and to the extent that he does so he becomes a holder for value. In addition such transferee is a holder in due course if he otherwise complies with the requirements of Section 3-302 on what constitutes a holder in due course.

(4) The first taker under an indorsement for the benefit of the indorser or another person (subparagraph (d) of Section 3-205) must pay or apply any value given by him for or on the security of the instrument consistently with the indorsement and to the extent that he does so he becomes a holder for value. In addition such taker is a holder in due course if he otherwise complies with the requirements of Section

3-302 on what constitutes a holder in due course. A later holder for value is neither given notice nor otherwise affected by such restrictive indorsement unless he has knowledge that a fiduciary or other person has negotiated the instrument in any transaction for his own benefit or otherwise in breach of duty (subsection (2) of Section 3-304).

§ 3-207.   Negotiation Effective Although It May Be Rescinded

(1) Negotiation is effective to transfer the instrument although the negotiation is

(a) made by an infant, a corporation exceeding its powers, or any other person without capacity; or

(b) obtained by fraud, duress or mistake of any kind; or

(c) part of an illegal transaction; or

(d) made in breach of duty.

(2) Except as against a subsequent holder in due course such negotiation is in an appropriate case subject to rescission, the declaration of a constructive trust or any other remedy permitted by law.

§ 3-208.   Reacquisition

Where an instrument is returned to or reacquired by a prior party he may cancel any indorsement which is not necessary to his title and reissue or further negotiate the instrument, but any intervening party is discharged as against the reacquiring party and subsequent holders not in due course and if his indorsement has been cancelled is discharged as against subsequent holders in due course as well.

PART 3. *Rights of a Holder*

§ 3-301.   Rights of a Holder

The holder of an instrument whether or not he is the owner may transfer or negotiate it and, except as otherwise provided in Section 3-603 on payment or satisfaction, discharge it or enforce payment in his own name.

§ 3-302.   Holder in Due Course

(1) A holder in due course is a holder who takes the instrument

(a) for value; and

(b) in good faith; and

(c) without notice that it is overdue or has been dishonored or of any defense against or claim to it on the part of any person.

(2) A payee may be a holder in due course.

(3) A holder does not become a holder in due course of an instrument:

    (a) by purchase of it at judicial sale or by taking it under legal process; or

    (b) by acquiring it in taking over an estate; or

    (c) by purchasing it as part of a bulk transaction not in regular course of business of the transferor.

(4) A purchaser of a limited interest can be a holder in due course only to the extent of the interest purchased.

§ 3-303.   Taking for Value

A holder takes the instrument for value

    (a) to the extent that the agreed consideration has been performed or that he acquires a security interest in or a lien on the instrument otherwise than by legal process; or

    (b) when he takes the instrument in payment of or as security for an antecedent claim against any person whether or not the claim is due; or

    (c) when he gives a negotiable instrument for it or makes an irrevocable commitment to a third person.

§ 3-304.   Notice to Purchaser

(1) The purchaser has notice of a claim or defense if

    (a) the instrument is so incomplete, bears such visible evidence of forgery or alteration, or is otherwise so irregular as to call into question its validity, terms or ownership or to create an ambiguity as to the party to pay; or

    (b) the purchaser has notice that the obligation of any party is voidable in whole or in part, of that all parties have been discharged.

(2) The purchaser has notice of a claim against the instrument when he has knowledge that a fiduciary has negotiated the instrument in payment of or as security for his own debt or in any transaction for his own benefit or otherwise in breach of duty.

(3) The purchaser has notice that an instrument is overdue if he has reason to know

    (a) that any part of the principal amount is overdue or that there is an uncured default in payment of another instrument of the same series; or

    (b) that acceleration of the instrument has been made; or

    (c) that he is taking a demand instrument after demand has been made or more than a reasonable length of time after its issue. A reasonable time for a check drawn and payable within the states and territories of the United States and the District of Columbia is presumed to be thirty days.

(4) Knowledge of the following facts does not of itself give the purchaser notice of a defense or claim

    (a) that the instrument is antedated or postdated;

    (b) that it was issued or negotiated in return for an executory promise or accompanied by a separate agreement, unless the purchaser has notice that a defense or claim has arisen from the terms thereof;

    (c) that any party has signed for accommodation;

    (d) that an incomplete instrument has been completed, unless the purchaser has notice of any improper completion;

    (e) that any person negotiating the instrument is or was a fiduciary;

    (f) that there has been default in payment of interest on the instrument or in payment of any other instrument, except one of the same series.

(5) The filing or recording of a document does not of itself constitute notice within the provisions of this Article to a person who would otherwise be a holder in due course.

(6) To be effective notice must be received at such time and in such manner as to give a reasonable opportunity to act on it.

§ 3-305.   Rights of a Holder in Due Course

To the extent that a holder is a holder in due course he takes the instrument free from

(1) all claims to it on the part of any person; and

(2) all defenses of any party to the instrument with whom the holder has not dealt except

    (a) infancy, to the extent that it is a defense to a simple contract; and

    (b) such other incapacity, or duress, or illegality of the transaction, as renders the obligation of the party a nullity; and

    (c) such misrepresentation as has induced the party to sign the instrument with neither knowledge nor reasonable opportunity to obtain knowledge of its character or its essential terms; and

    (d) discharge in insolvency proceedings; and

    (e) any other discharge of which the holder has notice when he takes the instrument.

§ 3-306.   Rights of One Not Holder in Due Course

Unless he has the rights of a holder in due course any person takes the instrument subject to

(a) all valid claims to it on the part of any person; and

(b) all defenses of any party which would be available in an action on a simple contract; and

(c) the defenses of want or failure of consideration, non-performance of any condition precedent, non-delivery, or delivery for a special purpose (Section 3-408); and

(d) the defense that he or a person through whom he holds the instrument acquired it by theft, or that payment or satisfaction to such holder would be inconsistent with the terms of a restrictive indorsement. The claim of any third person to the instrument is not otherwise available as a defense to any party liable thereon unless the third person himself defends the action for such party.

§ 3-307. Burden of Establishing Signatures, Defenses and Due Course

(1) Unless specifically denied in the pleadings each signature on an instrument is admitted. When the effectiveness of a signature is put in issue

(a) the burden of establishing it is on the party claiming under the signature; but

(b) the signature is presumed to be genuine or authorized except where the action is to enforce the obligation of a purported signer who has died or become incompetent before proof is required.

(2) When signatures are admitted or established, production of the instrument entitles a holder to recover on it unless the defendant establishes a defense.

(3) After it is shown that a defense exists a person claiming the rights of a holder in due course has the burden of establishing that he or some person under whom he claims is in all respects a holder in due course.

PART 4. *Liability of Parties*

§ 3-401. Signature

(1) No person is liable on an instrument unless his signature appears thereon.

(2) A signature is made by use of any name, including any trade or assumed name, upon an instrument, or by any word or mark used in lieu of a written signature.

§ 3-402. Signature in Ambiguous Capacity

Unless the instrument clearly indicates that a signature is made in some other capacity it is an indorsement.

§ 3-403. Signature by Authorized Representative

(1) A signature may be made by an agent or other representative, and his authority to make it may be established as in other cases of representation. No particular form of appointment is necessary to establish such authority.

(2) An authorized representative who signs his own name to an instrument

(a) is personally obligated if the instrument neither names the person represented nor shows that the representative signed in a representative capacity;

(b) except as otherwise established between the immediate parties, is personally obligated if the instrument names the person represented but does not show that the representative signed in a representative capacity, or if the instrument does not name the person represented but does show that the representative signed in a representative capacity.

(3) Except as otherwise established the name of an organization preceded or followed by the name and office of an authorized individual is a signature made in a representative capacity.

§ 3-404. Unauthorized Signatures

(1) Any unauthorized signature is wholly inoperative as that of the person whose name is signed unless he ratifies it or is precluded from denying it; but it operates as the signature of the unauthorized signer in favor of any person who in good faith pays the instrument or takes it for value.

(2) Any unauthorized signature may be ratified for all purposes of this Article. Such ratification does not of itself affect any rights of the person ratifying against the actual signer.

§ 3-405. Impostors; Signature in Name of Payee

(1) An indorsement by any person in the name of a named payee is effective if

(a) an impostor by use of the mails or otherwise has induced the maker or drawer to issue the instrument to him or his confederate in the name of the payee; or

(b) a person signing as or on behalf of a maker or drawer intends the payee to have no interest in the instrument; or

(c) an agent or employee of the maker or drawer has supplied him with the name of the payee intending the latter to have no such interest.

(2) Nothing in this section shall affect the criminal or civil liability of the person so indorsing.

§ 3-406.   Negligence Contributing to Alteration or Unauthorized Signature

Any person who by his negligence substantially contributes to a material alteration of the instrument or to the making of an unauthorized signature is precluded from asserting the alteration or lack of authority against a holder in due course or against a drawee or other payor who pays the instrument in good faith and in accordance with the reasonable commercial standards of the drawee's or payor's business.

§ 3-407.   Alteration

(1) Any alteration of an instrument is material which changes the contract of any party thereto in any respect, including any such change in

(a) the number or relations of the parties; or

(b) an incomplete instrument, by completing it otherwise than as authorized; or

(c) the writing as signed, by adding to it or by removing any part of it.

(2) As against any person other than a subsequent holder in due course

(a) alteration by the holder which is both fraudulent and material discharges any party whose contract is thereby changed unless that party assents or is precluded from asserting the defense;

(b) no other alteration discharges any party and the instrument may be enforced according to its original tenor, or as to incomplete instruments according to the authority given.

(3) A subsequent holder in due course may in all cases enforce the instrument according to its original tenor, and when an incomplete instrument has been completed, he may enforce it as completed.

§ 3-408.   Consideration

Want or failure of consideration is a defense as against any person not having the rights of a holder in due course (Section 3-305), except that no consideration is necessary for an instrument or obligation thereon given in payment of or as security for an antecedent obligation of any kind. Nothing in this section shall be taken to displace any statute outside this Act under which a promise is enforceable notwithstanding lack or failure of consideration. Partial failure of consideration is a

defense pro tanto whether or not the failure is in an ascertained or liquidated amount.

§ 3-409.   Draft Not an Assignment

(1) A check or other draft does not of itself operate as an assignment of any funds in the hands of the drawee available for its payment, and the drawee is not liable on the instrument until he accepts it.

(2) Nothing in this section shall affect any liability in contract, tort or otherwise arising from any letter of credit or other obligation or representation which is not an acceptance.

§ 3-410.   Definition and Operation of Acceptance

(1) Acceptance is the drawee's signed engagement to honor the draft as presented. It must be written on the draft, and may consist of his signature alone. It becomes operative when completed by delivery of notification.

(2) A draft may be accepted although it has not been signed by the drawer or is otherwise incomplete or is overdue or has been dishonored.

(3) Where the draft is payable at a fixed period after sight and the acceptor fails to date his acceptance the holder may complete it by supplying a date in good faith.

§ 3-411.   Certification of a Check

(1) Certification of a check is acceptance. Where a holder procures certification the drawer and all prior indorsers are discharged.

(2) Unless otherwise agreed a bank has no obligation to certify a check.

(3) A bank may certify a check before returning it for lack of proper indorsement. If it does so the drawer is discharged.

§ 3-412.   Acceptance Varying Draft

(1) Where the drawee's proffered acceptance in any manner varies the draft as presented he holder may refuse the acceptance and treat the draft as dishonored in which case the drawee is entitled to have his acceptance cancelled.

(2) The terms of the draft are not varied by an acceptance to pay at any particular bank or place in the United States, unless the acceptance states that the draft is to be paid only at such bank or place.

(3) Where the holder assents to an acceptance varying the terms of the draft each drawer and indorser who does not affirmatively assent is discharged. As amended 1962.

§ 3-413.   Contract of Maker, Drawer and Acceptor

(1) The maker or acceptor engages that he will pay the instrument according to its tenor at the time of his engagement or as completed pursuant to Section 3-115 on incomplete instruments.

(2) The drawer engages that upon dishonor of the draft and any necessary notice of dishonor or protest he will pay the amount of the draft to the holder or to any indorser who takes it up. The drawer may disclaim this liability by drawing without recourse.

(3) By making, drawing or accepting the party admits as against all subsequent parties including the drawee the existence of the payee and his then capacity to indorse.

§ 3-414.   Contract of Indorser; Order of Liability

(1) Unless the indorsement otherwise specifies (as by such words as "without recourse") every indorser engages that upon dishonor and any necessary notice of dishonor and protest he will pay the instrument according to its tenor at the time of his indorsement to the holder or to any subsequent indorser who takes it up, even though the indorser who takes it up was not obligated to do so.

(2) Unless they otherwise agree indorsers are liable to one another in the order in which they indorse, which is presumed to be the order in which their signatures appear on the instrument.

§ 3-415.   Contract of Accommodation Party

(1) An accommodation party is one who signs the instrument in any capacity for the purpose of lending his name to another party to it.

(2) When the instrument has been taken for value before it is due the accommodation party is liable in the capacity in which he has signed even though the taker knows of the accommodation.

(3) As against a holder in due course and without notice of the accommodation oral proof of the accommodation is not admissible to give the accommodation party the benefit of discharges dependent on his char-

acter as such. In other cases the accommodation character may be shown by oral proof.

(4) An indorsement which shows that it is not in the chain of title is notice of its accommodation character.

(5) An accommodation party is not liable to the party accommodated, and if he pays the instrument has a right of recourse on the instrument against such party.

§ 3-416.   Contract of Guarantor

(1) "Payment guaranteed" or equivalent words added to a signature mean that the signer engages that if the instrument is not paid when due he will pay it according to its tenor without resort by the holder to any other party.

(2) "Collection guaranteed" or equivalent words added to a signature mean that the signer engages that if the instrument is not paid when due he will pay it according to its tenor, but only after the holder has reduced his claim against the maker or acceptor to judgment and execution has been returned unsatisfied, or after the maker or acceptor has become insolvent or it is otherwise apparent that it is useless to proceed against him.

(3) Words of guaranty which do not otherwise specify guarantee payment.

(4) No words of guaranty added to the signature of a sole maker or acceptor affect his liability on the instrument. Such words added to the signature of one of two or more makers or acceptors create a presumption that the signature is for the accommodation of the others.

(5) When words of guaranty are used presentment, notice of dishonor and protest are not necessary to charge the user.

(6) Any guaranty written on the instrument is enforceable notwithstanding any statute of frauds.

§ 3-417.   Warranties on Presentment and Transfer

(1) Any person who obtains payment or acceptance and any prior transferor warrants to a person who in good faith pays or accepts that

(a) he has a good title to the instrument or is authorized to obtain payment or acceptance on behalf of one who has a good title; and

(b) he has no knowledge that the signature of the maker or drawer is unauthorized, except that this warranty is not given by a holder in due course acting in good faith

(i) to a maker with respect to the maker's own signature; or

(ii) to a drawer with respect to the drawer's own signature, whether or not the drawer is also the drawee; or

(iii) to an acceptor of a draft if the holder in due course took the draft after the acceptance or obtained the acceptance without knowledge that the drawer's signature was unauthorized; and

(c) the instrument has not been materially altered, except that this warranty is not given by a holder in due course acting in good faith

(i) to the maker of a note; or

(ii) to the drawer of a draft whether or not the drawer is also the drawee; or

(iii) to the acceptor of a draft with respect to an alteration made prior to the acceptance if the holder in due course took the draft after the acceptance, even though the acceptance provided "payable as originally drawn" or equivalent terms; or

(iv) to the acceptor of a draft with respect to an alteration made after the acceptance.

(2) Any person who transfers an instrument and receives consideration warrants to his transferee and if the transfer is by indorsement to any subsequent holder who takes the instrument in good faith that

(a) he has a good title to the instrument or is authorized to obtain payment or acceptance on behalf of one who has a good title and the transfer is otherwise rightful; and

(b) all signatures are genuine or authorized; and

(c) the instrument has not been materially altered; and

(d) no defense of any party is good against him; and

(e) he has no knowledge of any insolvency proceeding instituted with respect to the maker or acceptor or the drawer of an unaccepted instrument.

(3) By transferring "without recourse" the transferor limits the obligation stated in subsection (2) (d) to a warranty that he has no knowledge of such a defense.

(4) A selling agent or broker who does not disclose the fact that he is acting only as such gives the warranties provided in this section, but if he makes such disclosure warrants only his good faith and authority.

§ 3-418. Finality of Payment or Acceptance

Except for recovery of bank payments as provided in the Article on Bank Deposits and Collections (Article 4) and except for liability for breach of warranty on presentment under the preceding section, payment or acceptance of any instrument is final in favor of a holder in due course, or a person who has in good faith changed his position in reliance on the payment.

§ 3-419. Conversion of Instrument; Innocent Representative

(1) An instrument is converted when

(a) a drawee to whom it is delivered for acceptance refuses to return it on demand; or

(b) any person to whom it is delivered for payment refuses on demand either to pay or to return it; or

(c) it is paid on a forged indorsement.

(2) In an action against a drawee under subsection (1) the measure of the drawee's liability is the face amount of the instrument. In any other action under subsection (1) the measure of liability is presumed to be the face amount of the instrument.

(3) Subject to the provisions of this Act concerning restrictive indorsements a representative, including a depositary or a collecting bank, who has in good faith and in accordance with the reasonable commercial standards applicable to the business of such representative dealt with an instrument or its proceeds on behalf of one who was not the true owner is not liable in conversion or otherwise to the true owner beyond the amount of any proceeds remaining in his hands.

(4) An intermediary bank or payor bank which is not a depositary bank is not liable in conversion solely by reason of the fact that proceeds of an item indorsed restrictively (Sections 3-205 and 3-206) are not paid or applied consistently with the restrictive indorsement of an indorser other than its immediate transferor.

PART 5. Presentment, Notice of Dishonor and Protest

§ 3-501. When Presentment, Notice of Dishonor, and Protest Necessary or Permissible

(1) Unless excused (Section 3-511) presentment is necessary to charge secondary parties as follows:

(a) presentment for acceptance is necessary to charge the drawer and indorsers of a draft where the draft so provides, or is payable elsewhere than at the residence or place of business of the drawee, or its date of payment depends upon such presentment. The holder may at his option present for acceptance any other draft payable at a stated date;

(b) presentment for payment is necessary to charge any indorser;

(c) in the case of any drawer, the acceptor of a draft payable at a bank or the maker of a note payable at a bank, presentment for payment is necessary, but failure to make presentment discharges such drawer, acceptor or maker only as stated in Section 3-502(1) (b).

(2) Unless excused (Section 3-511)

(a) notice of any dishonor is necessary to charge any indorser;

(b) in the case of any drawer, the acceptor of a draft payable at a bank or the maker of a note payable at a bank, notice of any dishonor is necessary, but failure to give such notice discharges such drawer, acceptor or maker only as stated in Section 3-502(1) (b).

(3) Unless excused (Section 3-511) protest of any dishonor is necessary to charge the drawer and indorsers of any draft which on its face appears to be drawn or payable outside of the states, territories, dependencies and possessions of the United States, the District of Columbia and the Commonwealth of Puerto Rico. The holder may at his option make protest of any dishonor of any other instrument and in the case of a foreign draft may on insolvency of the acceptor before maturity make protest for better security.

(4) Notwithstanding any provision of this section, neither presentment nor notice of dishonor nor protest is necessary to charge an indorser who has indorsed an instrument after maturity. As amended 1966.

§ 3-502. Unexcused Delay; Discharge

(1) Where without excuse any necessary presentment or notice of dishonor is delayed beyond the time when it is due

(a) any indorser is discharged; and

(b) any drawer or the acceptor of a draft payable at a bank or the maker of a note payable at a bank who because the drawee or payor bank becomes insolvent during the delay is deprived of funds maintained with the drawee or payor bank to cover the instrument may discharge his liability by written assignment to the holder of his rights agaist the drawee or payor bank in respect of such funds, but such drawer, acceptor or maker is not otherwise discharged.

(2) Where without excuse a necessary protest is delayed beyond the time when it is due any drawer or indorser is discharged.

§ 3-503. Time of Presentment

(1) Unless a different time is expressed in the instrument the time for any presentment is determined as follows:

(a) where an instrument is payable at or a fixed period after a stated date any presentment for acceptance must be made on or before the date it is payable;

(b) where an instrument is payable after sight it must either be presented for acceptance or negotiated within a reasonable time after date of issue whichever is later;

(c) where an instrument shows the date on which it is payable presentment for payment is due on that date;

(d) where an instrument is accelerated presentment for payment is due within a reasonable time after the acceleration;

(e) with respect to the liability of any secondary party presentment for acceptance or payment of any other instrument is due within a reasonable time after such party becomes liable thereon.

(2) A reasonable time for presentment is determined by the nature of the instrument, any usage of banking or trade and the facts of the particular case. In the case of an uncertified check which is drawn and payable within the United States and which is not a draft drawn by a bank the following are presumed to be reasonable periods within which to present for payment or to initiate bank collection:

(a) with respect to the liability of the drawer, thirty days after date or issue whichever is later; and

(b) with respect to the liability of an indorser, seven days after his indorsement.

(3) Where any presentment is due on a day which is not a full business day for either the person making presentment or the party to pay or accept, presentment is due on the next following day which is a full business day for both parties.

(4) Presentment to be sufficient must be made at a reasonable hour, and if at a bank during its banking day.

§ 3-504. How Presentment Made

(1) Presentment is a demand for acceptance or payment made upon the maker, acceptor, drawee or other payor by or on behalf of the holder.

(2) Presentment may be made

(a) by mail, in which event the time of presentment is determined by the time of receipt of the mail; or

(b) through a clearing house; or

(c) at the place of acceptance or payment specified in the instrument or if there be none at the place of business or residence of the party to accept or pay. If neither the party to accept or pay nor anyone authorized to act for him is present or accessible at such place presentment is excused.

(3) It may be made

(a) to any one of two or more makers, acceptors, drawees or other payors; or

(b) to any person who has authority to make or refuse the acceptance or payment.

(4) A draft accepted or a note made payable at a bank in the United States must be presented at such bank.

(5) In the cases described in Section 4-210 presentment may be made in the manner and with the result stated in that section. As amended 1962.

§ 3-505. Rights of Party to Whom Presentment Is Made

(1) The party to whom presentment is made may without dishonor require

(a) exhibition of the instrument; and

(b) reasonable identification of the person making presentment and evidence of his authority to make it if made for another; and

(c) that the instrument be produced for acceptance or payment at a place specified in it, or if there be none at any place reasonable in the circumstances; and

(d) a signed receipt on the instrument for any partial or full payment and its surrender upon full payment.

(2) Failure to comply with any such requirement invalidates the presentment but the person presenting has a reasonable time in which to comply and the time for acceptance or payment runs from the time of compliance.

§ 3-506. Time Allowed for Acceptance or Payment

(1) Acceptance may be deferred without dishonor until the close of the next business day following presentment. The holder may also in a good faith effort to obtain acceptance and without either dishonor of the instrument or discharge of secondary parties allow postponement of acceptance for an additional business day.

(2) Except as a longer time is allowed in the case of documentary drafts drawn under a letter of credit, and unless an earlier time is agreed to by the party to pay, payment of an instrument may be deferred without dishonor pending reasonable examination to determine whether it is properly payable, but payment must be made in any event before the close of business on the day of presentment.

§ 3-507. Dishonor; Holder's Right of Recourse; Term Allowing Re-Presentment

(1) An instrument is dishonored when

(a) a necessary or optional presentment is duly made and due acceptance or payment is refused or cannot be obtained within the prescribed time or in case of bank collections the instrument is seasonably returned by the midnight deadline (Section 4-301); or

(b) presentment is excused and the instrument is not duly accepted or paid.

(2) Subject to any necessary notice of dishonor and protest, the holder has upon dishonor an immediate right of recourse against the drawers and indorsers.

(3) Return of an instrument for lack of proper indorsement is not dishonor.

(4) A term in a draft or an indorsement thereof allowing a stated time for re-presentment in the event of any dishonor of the draft by nonacceptance if a time draft or by nonpayment if a sight draft gives the holder as against any secondary party bound by the term an option to waive the dishonor without affecting the liability of the secondary party and he may present again up to the end of the stated time.

§ 3-508. Notice of Dishonor

(1) Notice of dishonor may be given to any person who may be liable on the instrument by or on behalf of the holder or any party who has himself received notice, or any other party who can be compelled to pay the instrument. In addition an agent or bank in whose hands the instrument is dishonored may give notice to his principal or customer or to another agent or bank from which the instrument was received.

(2) Any necessary notice must be given by a bank before its midnight deadline and by any other person before midnight of the third business day after dishonor or receipt of notice of dishonor.

(3) Notice may be given in any reasonable manner. It may be oral or written and in any terms which identify the instrument and state that it has been dishonored. A misdescription which does not mislead the party notified does not vitiate the notice. Sending the instrument bearing a stamp, ticket or writing stating that acceptance or payment has been refused or sending a notice of debit with respect to the instrument is sufficient.

(4) Written notice is given when sent although it is not received.

(5) Notice to one partner is notice to each although the firm has been dissolved.

(6) When any party is in insolvency proceedings instituted after the issue of the instrument notice may be given either to the party or to the representative of his estate.

(7) When any party is dead or incompetent notice may be sent to his last known address or given to his personal representative.

(8) Notice operates for the benefit of all parties who have rights on the instrument against the party notified.

§ 3-509. Protest; Noting for Protest

(1) A protest is a certificate of dishonor made under the hand and seal of a United States consul or vice consul or a notary public or other person authorized to certify dishonor by the law of the place where dishonor occurs. It may be made upon information satisfactory to such person.

(2) The protest must identify the instrument and certify either that due presentment has been made or the reason why it is excused and that the instrument has been dishonored by nonacceptance or nonpayment.

(3) The protest may also certify that notice of dishonor has been given to all parties or to specified parties.

(4) Subject to subsection (5) any necessary protest is due by the time that notice of dishonor is due.

(5) If, before protest is due, an instrument has been noted for protest by the officer to make protest, the protest may be made at any time thereafter as of the date of the noting.

§ 3-510. Evidence of Dishonor and Notice of Dishonor

The following are admissible as evidence and create a presumption of dishonor and of any notice of dishonor therein shown:

(a) a document regular in form as provided in the preceding section which purports to be a protest;

(b) the purported stamp or writing of the drawee, payor bank or presenting bank on the instrument or accompanying it stating that acceptance or payment has been refused for reasons consistent with dishonor;

(c) any book or record of the drawee, payor bank, or any collecting bank kept in the usual course of business which shows dishonor, even though there is no evidence of who made the entry.

§ 3-511. Waived or Excused Presentment, Protest or Notice of Dishonor or Delay Therein

(1) Delay in presentment, protest or notice of dishonor is excused when the party is without notice that it is due or when the delay is caused by circumstances beyond his control and he exercises reasonable diligence after the cause of the delay ceases to operate.

(2) Presentment or notice or protest as the case may be is entirely excused when

(a) the party to be charged has waived it expressly or by implication either before or after it is due; or

(b) such party has himself dishonored the instrument or has countermanded payment or otherwise has no reason to expect or right to require that the instrument be accepted or paid; or

(c) by reasonable diligence the presentment or protest cannot be made or the notice given.

(3) Presentment is also entirely excused when

(a) the maker, acceptor or drawee of any instrument except a documentary draft is dead or in insolvency proceedings instituted after the issue of the instrument; or

(b) acceptance or payment is refused but not for want of proper presentment.

(4) Where a draft has been dishonored by nonacceptance a later presentment for payment and any notice of dishonor and protest for nonpayment are excused unless in the meantime the instrument has been accepted.

(5) A waiver of protest is also a waiver of presentment and of notice of dishonor even though protest is not required.

(6) Where a waiver of presentment or notice or protest is embodied in the instrument itself it is binding upon all parties; but where it is written above the signature of an indorser it binds him only.

PART 6. *Discharge*

§ 3-601. Discharge of Parties

(1) The extent of the discharge of any party from liability on an instrument is governed by the sections on

(a) payment or satisfaction (Section 3-603); or

(b) tender of payment (Section 3-604); or

(c) cancellation or renunciation (Section 3-605); or

(d) impairment or right of recourse or of collateral (Section 3-606); or

(e) reacquisition of the instrument by a prior party (Section 3-208); or

(f) fraudulent and material alteration (Section 3-407); or

(g) certification of a check (Section 3-411); or

(h) acceptance varying a draft (Section 3-412); or

(i) unexcused delay in presentment or notice of dishonor or protest (Section 3-502).

(2) Any party is also discharged from his liability on an instrument to another party by any other act or agreement with such party which would discharge his simple contract for the payment of money.

(3) The liability of all parties is discharged when any party who has himself no right of action or recourse on the instrument

(a) reacquires the instrument in his own right; or

(b) is discharged under any provision of this Article, except as otherwise provided with respect to discharge for impairment of recourse or of collateral (Section 3-606).

§ 3-602. Effect of Discharge Against Holder in Due Course

No discharge of any party provided by this Article is effective against a subsequent holder in due course unless he has notice thereof when he takes the instrument.

§ 3-603. Payment or Satisfaction

(1) The liability of any party is discharged to the extent of his payment or satisfaction to the holder even though it is made with knowledge of a claim of another person to the instrument unless prior to such payment or satisfaction the person making the claim either supplies indemnity deemed adequate by the party seeking the discharge or enjoins payment or satisfaction by order of a court of competent jurisdiction in an action in which the adverse claimant and the holder are par-

ties. This subsection does not, however, result in the discharge of the liability

(a) of a party who in bad faith pays or satisfies a holder who acquired the instrument by theft or who (unless having the rights of a holder in due course) holds through one who so acquired it; or

(b) of a party (other than an intermediary bank or a payor bank which is not a depositary bank) who pays or satisfies the holder of an instrument which has been restrictively indorsed in a manner not consistent with the terms of such restrictive indorsement.

(2) Payment or satisfaction may be made with the consent of the holder by any person including a stranger to the instrument. Surrender of the instrument to such a person gives him the rights of a transferee (Section 3-201).

§ 3-604. Tender of Payment

(1) Any party making tender of full payment to a holder when or after it is due is discharged to the extent of all subsequent liability for interest, costs and attorney's fees.

(2) The holder's refusal of such tender wholly discharges any party who has a right of recourse against the party making the tender.

(3) Where the maker or acceptor of an instrument payable otherwise than on demand is able and ready to pay at every place of payment specified in the instrument when it is due, it is equivalent to tender.

§ 3-605. Cancellation and Renunciation

(1) The holder of an instrument may even without consideration discharge any party

(a) in any manner apparent on the face of the instrument or the indorsement, as by intentionally cancelling the instrument or the party's signature by destruction or mutilation, or by striking out the party's signature; or

(b) by renouncing his rights by a writing signed and delivered or by surrender of the instrument to the party to be discharged.

(2) Neither cancellation nor renunciation without surrender of the instrument affects the title thereto.

§ 3-606. Impairment of Recourse or of Collateral

(1) The holder discharges any party to the instrument to the extent that without such party's consent the holder

(a) without express reservation of rights releases or agrees not to sue any person against who the party has to the knowledge of the holder a right of recourse or agrees to suspend the right to enforce against such person the instrument or collateral or otherwise discharges such person, except that failure or delay in effecting any required presentment, protest or notice of dishonor with respect to any such person does not discharge any party as to whom presentment, protest or notice of dishonor is effective or unnecessary; or

(b) unjustifiably impairs any collateral for the instrument given by or on behalf of the party or any person against whom he has a right of recourse.

(2) By express reservation of rights against a party with a right of recourse the holder preserves

(a) all his rights against such party as of the time when the instrument was originally due; and

(b) the right of the party to pay the instrument as of that time; and

(c) all rights of such party to recourse against others.

PART 7. Advice of International Sight Draft

§ 3-701. Letter of Advice of International Sight Draft

(1) A "letter of advice" is a drawer's communication to the drawee that a described draft has been drawn.

(2) Unless otherwise agreed when a bank receives from another bank a letter of advice of an international sight draft the drawee bank may immediately debit the drawer's account and stop the running of interest pro tanto. Such a debit and any resulting credit to any account covering outstanding drafts leaves in the drawer full power to stop payment or otherwise dispose of the amount and creates no trust or interest in favor of the holder.

(3) Unless otherwise agreed and except where a draft is drawn under a credit issued by the drawee, the drawee of an international sight draft owes the drawer no duty to pay an unadvised draft but if it does so and the draft is genuine, may appropriately debit the drawer's account.

PART 8. Miscellaneous

§ 3-801. Drafts in a Set

(1) Where a draft is drawn in a set of parts, each of which is numbered and expressed to be an order only if no other part has been honored, the whole of the parts constitutes one draft but a taker of any part may become a holder in due course of the draft.

(2) Any person who negotiates, indorses or accepts a single part of a draft drawn in a set thereby becomes liable to any holder in due course of that part as if it were the whole set, but as between different holders in due course to whom different parts have been negotiated the holder whose title first accrues has all rights to the draft and its proceeds.

(3) As against the drawee the first presented part of a draft drawn in a set is the part entitled to payment, or if a time draft to acceptance and payment. Acceptance of any subsequently presented part renders the drawee liable thereon under subsection (2). With respect both to a holder and to the drawer payment of a subsequently presented part of a draft payable at sight has the same effect as payment of a check notwithstanding an effective stop order (Section 4-407).

(4) Except as otherwise provided in this section, where any part of a draft in a set is discharged by payment or otherwise the whole draft is discharged.

§ 3-802. Effect of Instrument on Obligation for Which It Is Given

(1) Unless otherwise agreed where an instrument is taken for an underlying obligation

(a) the obligation is pro tanto discharged if a bank is drawer, maker or acceptor of the instrument and there is no recourse on the instrument against the underlying obligor; and

(b) in any other case the obligation is suspended pro tanto until the instrument is due or if it is payable on demand until its presentment. If the instrument is dishonored action may be maintained on either the instrument or the obligation; discharge of the underlying obligor on the instrument also discharges him on the obligation.

(2) The taking in good faith of a check which is not postdated does not of itself so extend the time on the original obligation as to discharge a surety.

§ 3-803. Notice to Third Party

Where a defendant is sued for breach of an obligation for which a third person is answerable over under this Article he may give the third person written notice of the litigation, and the person notified may then give similar notice to any other person who is answerable over to him under this Article. If the notice states that the person notified may come in and defend and if the person notified does not do so he will in any action against him by the person giving the notice be bound by any determination of fact common to the two litigations, then unless after seasonable receipt of the notice the person notified does come in and defend he is so bound.

§ 3-804.   Lost, Destroyed or Stolen Instruments

The owner of an instrument which is lost, whether by destruction, theft or otherwise, may maintain an action in his own name and recover from any party liable thereon upon due proof of his ownership, the facts which prevent his production of the instrument and its terms. The court may require security indemnifying the defendant against loss by reason of further claims on the instrument.

§ 3-805.   Instruments Not Payable to Order or to Bearer

This Article applies to any instrument whose terms do not preclude transfer and which is otherwise negotiable within this Article but which is not payable to order or to bearer, except that there can be no holder in due course of such an instrument.

ARTICLE 4.   Bank Deposits and Collections

PART 1. General Provisions and Definitions

PART 2. Collection of Items: Depositary and Collecting Banks

PART 3. Collection of Items: Payor Banks

PART 4. Relationship Between Payor Bank and Its Customer

4-403. Customer's Right to Stop Payment; Burden of Proof of Loss.

4-404. Bank Not Obligated to Pay Check More Than Six Months Old.

4-405. Death or Incompetence of Customer.

4-406. Customer's Duty to Discover and Report Unauthorized Signature or Alteration.

4-407. Payor Bank's Right to Subrogation on Improper Payment.

PART 5. *Collection of Documentary Drafts*

4-501. Handling of Documentary Drafts; Duty to Send for Presentment and to Notify Customer of Dishonor.

4-502. Presentment of "On Arrival" Drafts.

4-503. Responsibility of Presenting Bank for Documents and Goods; Report of Reasons for Dishonor; Referee in Case of Need.

4-504. Privilege of Presenting Bank to Deal With Goods; Security Interest for Expenses.

ARTICLE 4. Bank Deposits and Collections

PART 1. *General Provisions and Definitions*

§ 4-101. Short Title

This Article shall be known and may be cited as Uniform Commercial Code—Bank Deposits and Collections.

§ 4-102. Applicability

(1) To the extent that items within this Article are also within the scope of Articles 3 and 8, they are subject to the provisions of those Articles. In the event of conflict to the provisions of this Article govern those of Article 3 but the provisions of Article 8 govern those of this Article.

(2) The liability of a bank for action or non-action with respect to any item handled by it for purposes of presentment, payment or collection is governed by the law of the place where the bank is located. In the case of action or non-action by or at a branch or separate office of a bank, its liability is governed by the law of the place where the branch or separate office is located.

§ 4-103. Variation by Agreement; Measure of Damages; Certain Action Constituting Ordinary Care

(1) The effect of the provisions of this Article may be varied by agreement except that no agreement can disclaim a bank's responsibility for its own lack of good faith or failure to exercise ordinary care or can limit the measure of damages for such lack or failure; but the parties may by agreement determine the standards by which such responsibility is to be measured if such standards are not manifestly unreasonable.

(2) Federal Reserve regulations and operating letters, clearing house rules, and the like, have the effect of agreements under subsection (1), whether or not specifically assented to by all parties interested in items handled.

(3) Action or non-action approved by this Article or pursuant to Federal Reserve regulations or operating letters constitutes the exercise of ordinary care and, in the absence of special instructions, action or non-action consistent with clearing house rules and the like or with a general banking usage not disapproved by this Article, prima facie constitutes the exercise of ordinary care.

(4) The specification or approval of certain procedures by this Article does not constitute disapproval of other procedures which may be reasonable under the circumstances.

(5) The measure of damages for failure to exercise ordinary care in handling an item is the amount of the item reduced by an amount which could not have been realized by the use of ordinary care, and where there is bad faith it includes other damages, if any, suffered by the party as a proximate consequence.

§ 4-104. Definitions and Index of Definitions

(1) In this Article unless the context otherwise requires

　(a) "Account" means any account with a bank and includes a checking, time, interest or savings account;

　(b) "Afternoon" means the period of a day between noon and midnight;

　(c) "Banking day" means that part of any day on which a bank is open to the public for carrying on substantially all of its banking functions;

　(d) "Clearing house" means any association of banks or other payors regularly clearing items;

　(e) "Customer" means any person having an account with a bank or for whom a bank has agreed to collect items and includes a bank carrying an account with another bank;

(f) "Documentary draft" means any negotiable or non-negotiable draft with accompanying documents, securities or other papers to be delivered against honor of the draft;

(g) "Item" means any instrument for the payment of money even though it is not negotiable but does not include money;

(h) "Midnight deadline" with respect to a bank is midnight on its next banking day following the banking day on which it receives the relevant item or notice or from which the time for taking action commences to run, whichever is later;

(i) "Properly payable" includes the availability of funds for payment at the time of decision to pay or dishonor;

(j) "Settle" means to pay in cash, by clearing house settlement, in a charge or credit or by remittance, or otherwise as instructed. A settlement may be either provisional or final;

(k) "Suspends payments" with respect to a bank means that it has been closed by order of the supervisory authorities, that a public officer has been appointed to take it over or that it ceases or refuses to make payments in the ordinary course of business.

(2) Other definitions applying to this Article and the sections in which they appear are:

"Collecting bank"	Section 4-105.
"Depositary bank"	Section 4-105.
"Intermediary bank"	Section 4-105.
"Payor bank"	Section 4-105.
"Presenting bank"	Section 4-105.
"Remitting bank"	Section 4-105.

(3) The following definitions in other Articles apply to this Article:

"Acceptance"	Section 3-410.
"Certificate of deposit"	Section 3-104.
"Certification"	Section 3-411.
"Check"	Section 3-104.
"Draft"	Section 3-104.
"Holder in due course"	Section 3-302.
"Notice of dishonor"	Section 3-508.
"Presentment"	Section 3-504.
"Protest"	Section 3-509.
"Secondary party"	Section 3-102.

(4) In addition Article 1 contains general definitions and principles of construction and interpretation applicable throughout this Article.

§ 4-105.   "Depositary Bank"; "Intermediary Bank"; "Collecting Bank"; "Payor Bank"; "Presenting Bank"; "Remitting Bank"

In this Article unless the context otherwise requires:

(a) "Depositary bank" means the first bank to which an item is transferred for collection even though it is also the payor bank;

(b) "Payor bank" means a bank by which an item is payable as drawn or accepted;

(c) "Intermediary bank" means any bank to which an item is transferred in course of collection except the depositary or payor bank;

(d) "Collecting bank" means any bank handling the item for collection except the payor bank;

(e) "Presenting bank" means any bank presenting an item except a payor bank;

(f) "Remitting bank" means any payor or intermediary bank remitting for an item.

§ 4-106.   Separate Office of a Bank

A branch or separate office of a bank [maintaining its own deposit ledgers] is a separate bank for the purpose of computing the time within which and determining the place at or to which action may be taken or notices or orders shall be given under this Article and under Article 3. As amended 1962.

Note: The brackets are to make it optional with the several states whether to require a branch to maintain its own deposit ledgers in order to be considered to be a separate bank for certain purposes under Article 4. In some states "maintaining its own deposit ledgers" is a satisfactory test. In others branch banking practices are such that this test would not be suitable.

§ 4-107.   Time of Receipt of Items

(1) For the purpose of allowing time to process items, prove balances and make the necessary entries on its books to determine its position for the day, a bank may fix an afternoon hour of 2 P.M. or later as a cut-off hour for the handling of money and items and the making of entries on its books.

(2) Any item or deposit of money received on any day after a cut-off hour so fixed or after the close of the banking day may be treated as being received at the opening of the next banking day.

§ 4-108.   Delays

(1) Unless otherwise instructed, a collecting bank in a good faith effort to secure payment may, in the case of specific items and with or without the approval of any person involved, waive, modify or extend time limits imposed or permitted by this Act for a period not in excess of an additional banking day without discharge of secondary parties and without liability to its transferor or any prior party.

(2) Delay by a collecting bank or payor bank beyond time limits prescribed or permitted by this Act or by instructions is excused if caused by interruption of communication facilities, suspension of payments by another bank, war, emergency conditions or other circumstances beyond the control of the bank provided it exercises such diligence as the circumstances require.

§ 4-109.   Process of Posting

The "process of posting" means the usual procedure followed by a payor bank in determining to pay an item and in recording the payment including one or more of the following or other steps as determined by the bank:

(a) verification of any signature;

(b) ascertaining that sufficient funds are available;

(c) affixing a "paid" or other stamp;

(d) entering a charge or entry to a customer's account;

(e) correcting or reversing an entry or erroneous action with respect to the item. Added 1962.

PART 2. Collection of Items: Depositary and Collecting Banks

§ 4-201.   Presumption and Duration of Agency Status of Collecting Banks and Provisional Status of Credits; Applicability of Article; Item Indorsed "Pay Any Bank"

(1) Unless a contrary intent clearly appears and prior to the time that a settlement given by a collecting bank for an item is or becomes final (subsection (3) of Section 4-211 and Sections 4-212 and 4-213) the bank is an agent or sub-agent of the owner of the item and any settlement given for the item is provisional. This provision applies regardless of the form of indorsement or lack of indorsement and even though credit given for the item is subject to immediate withdrawal as of right or is in fact withdrawn; but the continuance of ownership of an item by its owner and any rights of the owner to proceeds of the item are subject to rights of a collecting bank such as those resulting from outstanding advances on the item and valid rights of setoff. When an item is handled by banks for purposes of presentment, payment and collection, the relevant provisions of this Article apply even though action of parties clearly establishes that a particular bank has purchased the item and is the owner of it.

(2) After an item has been indorsed with the words "pay any bank" or the like, only a bank may acquire the rights of a holder

(a) until the item has been returned to the customer initiating collection; or

(b) until the item has been specially indorsed by a bank to a person who is not a bank.

§ 4-202.   Responsibility for Collection; When Action Seasonable

(1) A collecting bank must use ordinary care in

(a) presenting an item or sending it for presentment; and

(b) sending notice of dishonor or non-payment or returning an item other than a documentary draft to the bank's transferor [or directly to the depositary bank under subsection (2) of Section 4-212] (see note to Section 4-212) after learning that the item has not been paid or accepted, as the case may be; and

(c) settling for an item when the bank receives final settlement; and

(d) making or providing for any necessary protest; and

(e) notifying its tranferor of any loss or delay in transit within a reasonable time after discovery thereof.

(2) A collecting bank taking proper action before its midnight deadline following receipt of an item, notice or payment acts seasonably; taking proper action within a reasonably longer time may be seasonable but the bank has the burden of so establishing.

(3) Subject to subsection (1) (a), a bank is not liable for the insolvency, neglect, misconduct, mistake or default of another bank or person or for loss or destruction of an item in transit or in the possession of others.

§ 4-203.   Effect of Instructions

Subject to the provisions of Article 3 concerning conversion of instruments (Section 3-419) and the provisions of both Article 3 and this Article concerning restrictive indorsements only a collecting bank's transferor can give instructions which affect the bank or constitute notice to it and a collecting bank is not liable to prior parties for any action taken pursuant to such instructions or in accordance with any agreement with its transferor.

§ 4-204. Methods of Sending and Presenting; Sending Direct to Payor Bank

(1) A collecting bank must send items by reasonably prompt method taking into consideration any relevant instructions, the nature of the item, the number of such items on hand, and the cost of collection involved and the method generally used by it or others to present such items.

(2) A collecting bank may send

(a) any item direct to the payor bank;

(b) any item to any non-bank payor if authorized by its transferor; and

(c) any item other than documentary drafts to any non-bank payor, if authorized by Federal Reserve regulation or operating letter, clearing house rule or the like.

(3) Presentment may be made by a presenting bank at a place where the payor bank has requested that presentment be made. As amended 1962.

§ 4-205. Supplying Missing Indorsement; No Notice from Prior Indorsement

(1) A depositary bank which has taken an item for collection may supply any indorsement of the customer which is necessary to title unless the item contains the words "payee's indorsement required" or the like. In the absence of such a requirement a statement placed on the item by the depositary bank to the effect that the item was deposited by a customer or credited to his account is effective as the customer's indorsement.

(2) An intermediary bank, or payor bank which is not a depositary bank, is neither given notice nor otherwise affected by a restrictive indorsement of any person except the bank's immediate transferor.

§ 4-206. Transfer Between Banks

Any agreed method which identifies the transferor bank is sufficient for the item's further transfer to another bank.

§ 4-207. Warranties of Customer and Collecting Bank on Transfer or Presentment of Items; Time for Claims

(1) Each customer or collecting bank who obtains payment or acceptance of an item and each prior customer and collecting bank warrants to the payor bank or other payor who in good faith pays or accepts the item that

(a) he has a good title to the item or is authorized to obtain payment or acceptance on behalf of one who has a good title; and

(b) he has no knowledge that the signature of the maker or drawer is unauthorized, except that this warranty is not given by any customer or collecting bank that is a holder in due course and acts in good faith

(i) to a maker with respect to the maker's own signature; or

(ii) to a drawer with respect to the drawer's own signature, whether or not the drawer is also the drawee; or

(iii) to an acceptor of an item if the holder in due course took the item after the acceptance or obtained the acceptance without knowledge that the drawer's signature was unauthorized; and

(c) the item has not been materially altered, except that this warranty is not given by any customer or collecting bank that is a holder in due course and acts in good faith

(i) to the maker of a note; or

(ii) to the drawer of a draft whether or not the drawer is also the drawee; or

(iii) to the acceptor of an item with respect to an alteration made prior to the acceptance if the holder in due course took the item after the acceptance, even though the acceptance provided "payable as originally drawn" or equivalent terms; or

(iv) to the acceptor of an item with respect to an alteration made after the acceptance.

(2) Each customer and collecting bank who transfers an item and receives a settlement or other consideration for it warrants to his transferee and to any subsequent collecting bank who takes the item in good faith that

(a) he has a good title to the item or is authorized to obtain payment or acceptance on behalf of one who has a good title and the transfer is otherwise rightful; and

(b) all signatures are genuine or authorized; and

(c) the item has not been materially altered; and

(d) no defense of any party is good against him; and

(e) he has no knowledge of any insolvency proceeding instituted with respect to the maker or acceptor or the drawer of an unaccepted item.

In addition each customer and collecting bank so transferring an item and receiving a settlement or other consideration engages that upon dishonor and any necessary notice of dishonor and protest he will take up the item.

(3) The warranties and the engagement to honor set forth in the two preceding subsections arise notwithstanding the absence of indorsement or words of guaranty or warranty in the transfer or presentment and a collecting bank remains liable for their breach despite remittance to its transferor. Damages for breach of such warranties or engagement to honor shall not exceed the consideration received by the customer or collecting bank responsible plus finance charges and expenses related to the item, if any.

(4) Unless a claim for breach of warranty under this section is made within a reasonable time after the person claiming learns of the breach, the person liable is discharged to the extent of any loss caused by the delay in making claim.

§ 4-208. Security Interest of Collecting Bank in Items, Accompanying Documents and Proceeds

(1) A bank has a security interest in an item and any accompanying documents or the proceeds of either

(a) in case of an item deposited in an account to the extent to which credit given for the item has been withdrawn or applied;

(b) in case of an item for which it has given credit available for withdrawal as of right, to the extent of the credit given whether or not the credit is drawn upon and whether or not there is a right of charge-back; or

(c) if it makes an advance on or against the item.

(2) When credit which has been given for several items received at one time or pursuant to a single agreement is withdrawn or applied in part the security interest remains upon all the items, any accompanying documents or the proceeds of either. For the purpose of this section, credits first given are first withdrawn.

(3) Receipt by a collecting bank of a final settlement for an item is a realization on its security interest in the item, accompanying documents and proceeds. To the extent and so long as the bank does not receive final settlement for the item or give up possession of the item

or accompanying documents for purposes other than collection, the security interest continues and is subject to the provisions of Article 9 except that

(a) no security agreement is necessary to make the security interest enforceable (subsection (1)(a) of Section 9-203); and

(b) no filing is required to perfect the security interest; and

(c) the security interest has priority over conflicting perfected security interests in the item, accompanying documents or proceeds.

§ 4-209. When Bank Gives Value for Purposes of Holder in Due Course

For purposes of determining its status as a holder in due course, the bank has given value to the extent that it has a security interest in an item provided that the bank otherwise complies with the requirements of Section 3-302 on what constitutes a holder in due course.

§ 4-210. Presentment by Notice of Item Not Payable by, Through or at a Bank; Liability of Secondary Parties

(1) Unless otherwise instructed, a collecting bank may present an item not payable by, through or at a bank by sending to the party to accept or pay a written notice that the bank holds the item for acceptance or payment. The notice must be sent in time to be received on or before the day when presentment is due and the bank must meet any requirement of the party to accept or pay under Section 3-505 by the close of the bank's next banking day after it knows of the requirement.

(2) Where presentment is made by notice and neither honor nor request for compliance with a requirement under Section 3-505 is received by the close of business on the day after maturity or in the case of demand items by the close of business on the third banking day after notice was sent, the presenting bank may treat the item as dishonored and charge any secondary party by sending him notice of the facts.

§ 4-211. Media of Remittance; Provisional and Final Settlement in Remittance Cases

(1) A collecting bank may take in settlement of an item

(a) a check of the remitting bank or of another bank on any bank except the remitting bank; or

(b) a cashier's check or similar primary obligation of a remitting bank which is a member of or clears through a member of the same clearing house or group as the collecting bank; or

(c) appropriate authority to charge an account of the remitting bank or of another bank with the collecting bank; or

(d) if the item is drawn upon or payable by a person other than a bank, a cashier's check, certified check or other bank check or obligation.

(2) If before its midnight deadline the collecting bank properly dishonors a remittance check or authorization to charge on itself or presents or forwards for collection a remittance instrument of or on another bank which is of a kind approved by subsection (1) or has not been authorized by it, the collecting bank is not liable to prior parties in the event of the dishonor of such check, instrument or authorization.

(3) A settlement for an item by means of a remittance instrument or authorization to charge is or becomes a final settlement as to both the person making and the person receiving the settlement

(a) if the remittance instrument or authorization to charge is of a kind approved by subsection (1) or has not been authorized by the person receiving the settlement and in either case the person receiving the settlement acts seasonably before its midnight deadline in presenting, forwarding for collection or paying the instrument or authorization,—at the time the remittance instrument or authorization is finally paid by the payor by which it is payable;

(b) if the person receiving the settlement has authorized remittance by a non-bank check or obligation or by a cashier's check or similar primary obligation of or a check upon the payor or other remitting bank which is not of a kind approved by subsection (1) (b),—at the time of the receipt of such remittance check or obligation; or

(c) if in a case not covered by sub-paragraphs (a) or (b) the person receiving the settlement fails to seasonably present, forward for collection, pay or return a remittance instrument or authorization to it to charge before its midnight deadline,—at such midnight deadline.

§ 4-212.   Right of Charge-Back or Refund

(1) If a collecting bank has made provisional settlement with its customer for an item and itself fails by reason of dishonor, suspension of payments by a bank or otherwise to receive a settlement for the item which is or becomes final, the bank may revoke the settlement given by it, charge back the amount of any credit given for the item to its customer's account or obtain refund from its customer whether or not it is able to return the items if by its midnight deadline or within a longer reasonable time after it learns the facts it returns the item or sends notification of the facts. These rights to revoke, charge-back and obtain refund terminate if and when a settlement for the item received by the bank is or becomes final (subsection (3) of Section 4-211 and subsections (2) and (3) of Section 4-213).

[(2) Within the time and manner prescribed by this section and Section 4-301, an intermediary or payor bank, as the case may be, may return an unpaid item directly to the depositary bank and may send for collection a draft on the depositary bank and obtain reimbursement. In such case, if the depositary bank has received provisional settlement for the item, it must reimburse the bank drawing the draft and any provisional credits for the item between banks shall become and remain final.]

Note: Direct returns is recognized as an innovation that is not yet established bank practice, and therefore, Paragraph 2 has been bracketed. Some lawyers have doubts whether it should be included in legislation or left to development by agreement.

(3) A depositary bank which is also the payor may charge-back the amount of an item to its customer's account or obtain refund in accordance with the section governing return of an item received by a payor bank for credit on its books. (Section 4-301).

(4) The right to charge-back is not affected by

(a) prior use of the credit given for the item; or

(b) failure by any bank to exercise ordinary care with respect to the item but any bank so failing remains liable.

(5) A failure to charge-back or claim refund does not affect other rights of the bank against the customer or any other party.

(6) If credit is given in dollars as the equivalent of the value of an item payable in a foreign currency the dollar amount of any charge-back or refund shall be calculated on the basis of the buying sight rate for the foreign currency prevailing on the day when the person entitled to the charge-back or refund learns that it will not receive payment in ordinary course.

§ 4-213. Final Payment of Item by Payor Bank; When Provisional Debits and Credits Become Final; When Certain Credits Become Available for Withdrawal

(1) An item is finally paid by a payor bank when the bank has done any of the following, whichever happens first:

(a) paid the item in cash; or

(b) settled for the item without reserving a right to revoke the settlement and without having such right under statue, clearing house rule or agreement; or

(c) completed the process of posting the item to the indicated account of the drawer, maker or other person to be charged therewith; or

(d) made a provisional settlement for the item and failed to revoke the settlement in the time and manner permitted by statute, clearing house rule or agreement.

Upon a final payment under subparagraphs (b), (c) or (d) the payor bank shall be accountable for the amount of the item.

(2) If provisional settlement for an item between the presenting and payor banks is made through a clearing house or by debits or credits in an account between them, then to the extent that provisional debits or credits for the item are entered in accounts between the presenting and payor banks or between the presenting and successive prior collecting banks seriatim, they become final upon final payment of the item by the payor bank.

(3) If a collecting bank receives a settlement for an item which is or becomes final (subsection (3) of Section 4-211, subsection (2) of Section 4-213) the bank is accountable to its customer for the amount of the item and any provisional credit given for the item in an account with its customer becomes final.

(4) Subject to any right of the bank to apply the credit to an obligation of the customer, credit given by a bank for an item in an account with its customer becomes available for withdrawal as of right

(a) in any case where the bank has received a provisional settlement for the item,—when such settlement becomes final and the bank has had a reasonable time to learn that the settlement is final;

(b) in any case where the bank is both a depositary bank and a payor bank and the item is finally paid,—at the opening of the bank's second banking day following receipt of the item.

(5) A deposit of money in a bank is final when made

but, subject to any right of the bank to apply the deposit to an obligation of the customer, the deposit becomes available for withdrawal as of right at the opening of the bank's next banking day following receipt of the deposit.

§ 4-214. Insolvency and Preference

(1) Any item in or coming into the possession of a payor or collecting bank which suspends payment and which item is not finally paid shall be returned by the receiver, trustee or agent in charge of the closed bank to the presenting bank or the closed bank's customer.

(2) If a payor bank finally pays an item and suspends payments without making a settlement for the item with its customer or the presenting bank which settlement is or becomes final, the owner of the item has a preferred claim against the payor bank.

(3) If a payor bank gives or a collecing bank gives or receives a provisional settlement for an item and thereafter suspends payments, the suspension does not prevent or interfere with the settlement becoming final if such finality occurs automatically up on the lapse of certain time or the happening of certain events (subsection (3) of Section 4-211, subsections (1) (d), (2) and (3) of Section 4-213).

(4) If a collecting bank receives from subsequent parties settlement for an item which settlement is or becomes final and suspends payments without making a settlement for the item with its customer which is or becomes final, the owner of the item has a preferred claim against such collecting bank.

PART 3. Collections of Items: Payor Banks

§ 4-301. Deferred Posting; Recovery of Payment by Return of Items; Time of Dishonor

(1) Where an authorized settlement for a demand item (other than a documentary draft) received by a payor bank otherwise than for immediate payment over the counter has been made before midnight of the banking day of receipt the payor bank may revoke the settlement and recover any payment if before it has made final payment (subsection (1) of Section 4-213) and before its midnight deadline it

(a) returns the item; or

(b) sends written notice of dishonor or nonpayment if the item is held for protest or is otherwise unavailable for return.

(2) If a demand item is received by a payor bank for credit on its books it may return such item or send notice of dishonor and may revoke any credit given or recover the amount thereof withdrawn by its customer, if it acts within the time limit and in the manner specified in the preceding subsection.

(3) Unless previous notice of dishonor has been sent an item is dishonored at the time when for purposes of dishonor it is returned or notice sent in accordance with this section.

(4) An item is returned:

(a) as to an item received through a clearing house, when it is delivered to the presenting or last collecting bank or to the clearing house or is sent or delivered in accordance with its rules; or

(b) in all other cases, when it is sent or delivered to the bank's customer or transferor or pursuant to his instructions.

§ 4-302.   Payor Bank's Responsibility for Late Return of Item

In the absence of a valid defense such as breach of a presentment warranty (subsection (1) of Section 4-207), settlement effected or the like, if an item is presented on and received by a payor bank the bank is accountable for the amount of

(a) a demand item other than a documentary draft whether properly payable or not if the bank, in any case where it is not also the depositary bank, retains the item beyond midnight of the banking day of receipt without settling for it or, regardless of whether it is also the depositary bank, does not pay or return the item or send notice of dishonor until after its midnight deadline; or

(b) any other properly payable item unless within the time allowed for acceptance or payment of that item the bank either accepts or pays the item or returns it and accompanying documents.

§ 4-303.   When Items Subject to Notice, Stop-Order, Legal Process or Setoff; Order in Which Items May Be Charged or Certified

(1) Any knowledge, notice or stop-order received by, legal process served upon or setoff exercised by a payor bank, whether or not effective under other rules of law to terminate, suspend or modify the bank's right or duty to pay an item or to charge its customer's account for the item, comes too late to so terminate, suspend or modify such right or duty if the knowledge, notice, stop-order or legal process is received or served and a reasonable time for the bank to act thereon expires or the setoff is exercised after the bank has done any of the following:

(a) accepted or certified the item;

(b) paid the item in cash;

(c) settled for the item without reserving a right to revoke the settlement and without having such right under statute, clearing house rule or agreement;

(d) completed the process of posting the item to the indicated account of the drawer, maker or other person to be charged therewith or otherwise has evidenced by examination of such indicated account and by action its decision to pay the item; or

(e) become accountable for the amount of the item under subsection (1)(d) of Section 4-213 and Section 4-302 dealing with the payor bank's responsibility for late return of items.

(2) Subject to the provisions of subsection (1) items may be accepted, paid, certified or charged to the indicated account of its customer in any order convenient to the bank.

PART 4. *Relationship Between Payor Bank and Its Customer*

§ 4-401.   When Bank May Charge Customer's Account

(1) As against its customer, a bank may charge against his account any item which is otherwise properly payable from that account even though the charge creates an overdraft.

(2) A bank which in good faith makes payment to a holder may charge the indicated account of its customer according to

(a) the original tenor of his altered item; or

(b) the tenor of his completed item, even though the bank knows the item has been completed unless the bank has notice that the completion was improper.

§ 4-402.   Bank's Liability to Customer for Wrongful Dishonor

A payor bank is liable to its customer for damages proximately caused by the wrongful dishonor of an item. When the dishonor occurs through mistake liability is limited to actual damages proved. If so proximately caused and proved damages may include damages for an arrest or prosecution of the customer or other consequential damages. Whether any consequential damages are proximately caused by the wrongful dishonor is a question of fact to be determined in each case.

§ 4-403. Customer's Right to Stop Payment; Burden of Proof of Loss

(1) A customer may by order to his bank stop payment of any item payable for his account but the order must be received at such time and in such manner as to afford the bank a reasonable opportunity to act on it prior to any action by the bank with respect to the item described in Section 4-303.

(2) An oral order is binding upon the bank only for fourteen calendar days unless confirmed in writing within that period. A written order is effective for only six months unless renewed in writing.

(3) The burden of establishing the fact and amount of loss resulting from the payment of an item contrary to a binding stop payment order is on the customer.

§ 4-404. Bank Not Obligated to Pay Check More Than Six Months Old

A bank is under no obligation to a customer having a checking account to pay a check, other than a certified check, which is presented more than six months after its date, but it may charge its customer's account for a payment made thereafter in good faith.

§ 4-405. Death or Incompetence of Customer

(1) A payor or collecting bank's authority to accept, pay or collect an item or to account for proceeds of its collection if otherwise effective is not rendered ineffective by incompetence of a customer of either bank existing at the time the item is issued or its collection is undertaken if the bank does not know of an adjudication of incompetence. Neither death nor incompetence of a customer revokes such authority to accept, pay, collect or account until the bank knows of the fact of death or of an adjudication of incompetence and has reasonable opportunity to act on it.

(2) Even with knowledge a bank may for 10 days after the date of death pay or certify checks drawn on or prior to that date unless ordered to stop payment by a person claiming an interest in the account.

§ 4-406. Customer's Duty to Discover and Report Unauthorized Signature or Alteration

(1) When a bank sends to its customer a statement of account accompanied by items paid in good faith in support of the debit entries or holds the statement and items pursuant to a request for instructions of its customer or otherwise in a reasonable manner makes the statement and items available to the customer, the customer must exercise reasonable care and promptness to examine the statement and items to discover his unauthorized signature or any alteration on an item and must notify the bank promptly after discovery thereof.

(2) If the bank establishes that the customer failed with respect to an item to comply with the duties imposed on the customer by subsection (1) customer is precluded from asserting against the bank

(a) his unauthorized signature or any alteration on the item if the bank also establishes that it suffered a loss by reason of such failure; and

(b) an unauthorized signature or alteration by the same wrongdoer on any other item paid in good faith by the bank after the first item and statement was available to the customer for a reasonable period not exceeding fourteen calendar days and before the bank receives notification from the customer of any such unauthorized signature or alteration.

(3) The preclusion under subsection (2) does not apply if the customer establishes lack of ordinary care on the part of the bank in paying the item(s).

(4) Without regard to care or lack of care of either the customer or the bank a customer who does not within one year from the time the statement and items are made available to the customer (subsection (1)) discover and report his unauthorized signature or any alteration on the face or back of the item or does not within 3 years from that time discover and report any unauthorized indorsement is precluded from asserting against the bank such unauthorized signature or indorsement or such alteration.

(5) If under this section a payor bank has a valid defense against a claim of a customer upon or resulting from payment of an item and waives or fails upon request to assert the defense the bank may not assert against any collecting bank or other prior party presenting or transferring the item a claim based upon the

unauthorized signature or alteration giving rise to the customer's claim.

§ 4-407.   Payor Bank's Right to Subrogation on Improper Payment

If a payor bank has paid an item over the stop payment order of the drawer or maker or otherwise under circumstances giving a basis for objection by the drawer or maker, to prevent unjust enrichment and only to the extent necessary to prevent loss to the bank by reason of its payment of the item, the payor bank shall be subrogated to the rights

(a) of any holder in due course on the item against the drawer or maker; and

(b) of the payee or any other holder of the item against the drawer or maker either on the item or under the transaction out of which the item arose; and

(c) of the drawer or maker against the payee or any other holder of the item with respect to the transaction out of which the item arose.

PART 5.   Collection of Documentary Drafts

§ 4-501.   Handling of Documentary Drafts; Duty to Send for Presentment and to Notify Customer of Dishonor

A bank which takes a documentary draft for collection must present or send the draft and accompanying documents for presentment and upon learning that the draft has not been paid or accepted in due course must seasonably notify its customer of such fact even though it may have discounted or bought the draft or extended credit available for withdrawal as of right.

§ 4-502.   Presentment of "On Arrival" Drafts

When a draft or the relevant instructions require presentment "on arrival", "when goods arrive" or the like, the collecting bank need not present until in its judgment a reasonable time for arrival of the goods has expired. Refusal to pay or accept because the goods have not arrived is not dishonor; the bank must notify its transferor of such refusal but need not present the draft again until it is instructed to do so or learns of the arrival of the goods.

§ 4-503.   Responsibility of Presenting Bank for Documents and Goods; Report of Reasons for Dishonor; Referee in Case of Need

Unless otherwise instructed and except as provided in Article 5 a bank presenting a documentary draft

(a) must deliver the documents to the drawee on acceptance of the draft if it is payable more than three days after presentment; otherwise, only on payment; and

(b) upon dishonor, either in the case of presentment for acceptance or presentment for payment, may seek and follow instructions from any referee in case of need designated in the draft or if the presenting bank does not choose to utilize his services it must use diligence and good faith to ascertain the reason for dishonor, must notify its transferor of the dishonor and of the results of its effort to ascertain the reasons therefor and must request instructions.

But the presenting bank is under no obligation with respect to goods represented by the documents except to follow any reasonable instructions seasonably received; it has a right to reimbursement for any expense incurred in following instructions and to prepayment of or indemnity for such expenses.

§ 4-504.   Privilege of Presenting Bank to Deal With Goods; Security Interest for Expenses

(1) A presenting bank which, following the dishonor of a documentary draft, has seasonably requested instructions but does not receive them within a reasonable time may store, sell, or otherwise deal with the goods in any reasonable manner.

(2) For its reasonable expenses incurred by action under subsection (1) the presenting bank has a lien upon the goods or their proceeds, which may be foreclosed in the same manner as an unpaid seller's lien.

ARTICLE 5.   Letters of Credit

ARTICLE 5.   Letters of Credit

§ 5-101.   Short Title

This Article shall be known and may be cited as Uniform Commercial Code—Letters of Credit.

§ 5-102.   Scope

(1) This Article applies

(a) to a credit issued by a bank if the credit requires a documentary draft or a documentary demand for payment; and

(b) to a credit issued by a person other than a bank if the credit requires that the draft or demand for payment be accompanied by a document of title; and

(c) to a credit issued by a bank or other person if the credit is not within subparagraphs (a) or (b) but conspicuously state that it is a letter of credit or is conspicuously so entitled.

(2) Unless the engagement meets the requirements of subsection (1), this Article does not apply to engagements to make advances or to honor drafts or demands for payment, to authorities to pay or purchase, to guarantees or to general agreements.

(3) This Article deals with some but not all of the rules and concepts of letters of credit as such rules or concepts have developed prior to this act or may hereafter develop. The fact that this Article states a rule does not by itself require, imply or negate application of the same or a converse rule to a situation not provided for or to a person not specified by this Article.

§ 5-103.   Definitions

(1) In this Article unless the context otherwise requires

(a) "Credit" or "letter of credit" means an engagement by a bank or other person made at the request of a customer and of a kind within the scope of this Article (Section 5-102) that the issuer will honor drafts or other demands for payment upon compliance with the conditions specified in the credit. A credit may be either revocable or irrevocable. The engagement may be either an agreement to honor or a statement that the bank or other person is authorized to honor.

(b) A "documentary draft" or a "documentary demand for payment" is one honor of which is conditioned upon the presentation of a document or documents. "Document" means any paper including document of title, security, invoice, certificate, notice of default and the like.

(c) An "issuer" is a bank or other person issuing a credit.

(d) A "beneficiary" of a credit is a person who is entitled under its terms to draw or demand payment.

(e) An "advising bank" is a bank which gives notification of the issuance of a credit by another bank.

(f) A "confirming bank" is a bank which engages either that it will itself honor a credit already issued by another bank or that such a credit will be honored by the issuer or a third bank.

(g) A "customer" is a buyer or other person who causes an issuer to issue a credit. The term also includes a bank which procures issuance or confirmation on behalf of that bank's customer.

(2) Other definitions applying to this Article and the sections in which they appear are:

"Notation of Credit".   Section 5-108.

"Presenter".   Section 5-112(3).

(3) Definitions in other Articles applying to this Article and the sections in which they appear are:

"Accept" or "Acceptance".   Section 3-410.

"Contract for sale".   Section 2-106.

"Draft".   Section 3-104.

"Holder in due course".   Section 3-302.

"Midnight deadline".   Section 4-104.

"Security".   Section 8-102.

(4) In addition, Article 1 contains general definitions and principles of construction and interpretation applicable throughout this Article.

§ 5-104.   Formal Requirements; Signing

(1) Except as otherwise required in subsection (1) (c) of Section 5-102 on scope, no particular form of phrasing is required for a credit. A credit must be in writing and signed by the confirming bank. A modification of the terms of a credit or confirmation must be signed by the issuer or confirming bank.

(2) A telegram may be a sufficient signed writing if it identifies its sender by an authorized authentication. The authentication may be in code and the authorized naming of the issuer in an advice of credit is a sufficient signing.

§ 5-105.   Consideration

No consideration is necessary to establish a credit or to enlarge or otherwise modify its terms.

§ 5-106.   Time and Effect of Establishment of Credit

(1) Unless otherwise agreed a credit is established

(a) as regards the customer as soon as a letter of credit is sent to him or the letter of credit or an authorized written advice of its issuance is sent to the beneficiary; and

(b) as regards the beneficiary when he receives a letter of credit or an authorized written advice of its issuance.

(2) Unless otherwise agreed once an irrevocable credit is established as regards the customer it can be modified or revoked only with the consent of the customer and once it is established as regards the beneficiary it can be modified or revoked only with his consent.

(3) Unless otherwise agreed after a revocable credit is established it may be modified or revoked by the issuer without notice to or consent from the customer or beneficiary.

(4) Notwithstanding any modification or revocation of a revocable credit any person authorized to honor or negotiate under the terms of the original credit is entitled to reimbursement for or honor of any draft or demand for payment duly honored or negotiated before receipt of notice of the modification or revocation

and the issuer in turn is entitled to reimbursement from its customer.

§ 5-107.   Advice of Credit; Confirmation; Error in Statement of Terms

(1) Unless otherwise specified an advising bank by advising a credit issued by another bank does not assume any obligation to honor drafts drawn or demands for payment made under the credit but it does assume obligation for the accuracy of its own statement.

(2) A confirming bank by confirming a credit becomes directly obligated on the credit to the extent of its confirmation as though it were its issuer and acquires the rights of an issuer.

(3) Even though an advising bank incorrectly advises the terms of a credit it has been authorized to advise the credit is established as against the issuer to the extent of its original terms.

(4) Unless otherwise specified the customer bears as against the issuer all risks of transmission and reasonable translation or interpretation of any message relating to a credit.

§ 5-108.   "Notation Credit"; Exhaustion of Credit

(1) A credit which specifies that any person purchasing or paying drafts drawn or demands for payment made under it must note the amount of the draft or demand on the letter or advice of credit is a "notation credit".

(2) Under a notation credit

(a) a person paying the beneficiary or purchasing a draft or demand for payment from him acquires a right to honor only if the appropriate notation is made and by transferring or forwarding for honor the documents under the credit such a person warrants to the issuer that the notation has been made; and

(b) unless the credit or a signed statement that an appropriate notation has been made accompanies the draft or demand for payment the issuer may delay honor until evidence of notation has been procured which is satisfactory to it but its obligation and that of its customer continue for a reasonable time not exceeding thirty days to obtain such evidence.

(3) If the credit is not a notation credit

(a) the issuer may honor complying drafts or demands for payment presented to it in the order in which they are presented and is discharged pro tanto by honor of any such draft or demand;

(b) as between competing good faith purchasers of complying drafts or demands the person first purchasing has priority over a subsequent purchaser even though the later purchased draft or demand has been first honored.

§ 5-109.   Issuer's Obligation to Its Customer

(1) An issuer's obligation to its customer includes good faith and observance of any general banking usage but unless otherwise agreed does not include liability or responsibility

(a) for performance of the underlying contract for sale or other transaction between the customer and the beneficiary; or

(b) for any act or omission of any person other than itself or its own branch or for loss or destruction of a draft, demand or document in transit or in the possession of others; or

(c) based on knowledge or lack of knowledge of any usage of any particular trade.

(2) An issuer must examine documents with care so as to ascertain that on their face they appear to comply wth the terms of the credit but unless otherwise agreed assumes no liability or responsibility for the genuineness, falsification or effect of any document which appears on such examination to be regular on its face.

(3) A non-bank issuer is not bound by any banking usage of which it has no knowledge.

§ 5-110.   Availability of Credit in Portions; Presenter's Reservation of Lien or Claim

(1) Unless otherwise specified a credit may be used in portions in the discretion of the beneficiary.

(2) Unless otherwise specified a person by presenting a documentary draft or demand for payment under a credit relinquishes upon its honor all claims to the documents and a person by transferring such draft or demand or causing such presentment authorizes such relinquishment. An explicit reservation of claim makes the draft or demand non-complying.

§ 5-111.   Warranties on Transfer and Presentment

(1) Unless otherwise agreed the beneficiary by transferring or presenting a documentary draft or demand

for payment warrants to all interested parties that the necessary conditions of the credit have been complied with. This is in addition to any warranties arising under Articles 3, 4, 7 and 8.

(2) Unless otherwise agreed a negotiating, advising, confirming, collecting or issuing bank presenting or tranferring a draft or demand for payment under a credit warrants only the matters warranted by a collecting bank under Article 4 and any such bank transferring a document warrants only the matters warranted by an intermediary under Articles 7 and 8.

§ 5-112.   Time Allowed for Honor or Rejection; Withholding Honor or Rejection by Consent; "Presenter"

(1) A bank to which a documentary draft or demand for payment is presented under a credit may without dishonor of the draft, demand or credit

(a) defer honor until the close of the third banking day following receipt of the documents; and

(b) further defer honor if the presenter has expressly or impliedly consented thereto.

Failure to honor within the time here specified constitutes dishonor of the draft or demand and of the credit [except as otherwise provided in subsection (4) of Section 5-114 on conditional payment].

Note: The bracketed language in the last sentence of subsection (1) should be included only if the optional provisions of Section 5-114(4) and (5) are included.

(2) Upon dishonor the bank may unless otherwise instructed fulfill its duty to return the draft or demand and the documents by holding them at the disposal of the presenter and sending him an advice to that effect.

(3) "Presenter" means any person presenting a draft or demand for payment for honor under a credit even though that person is a confirming bank or other correspondent which is acting under an issuer's authorization.

§ 5-113.   Indemnities

(1) A bank seeking to obtain (whether for itself or another) honor, negotiation or reimbursement under a credit may give an indemnity to induce such honor, negotiation or reimbursement.

(2) An indemnity agreement inducing honor, negotiation or reimbursement

(a) unless otherwise explicitly agreed applies to defects in the documents but not in the goods; and

(b) unless a longer time is explicitly agreed expires at the end of ten business days following receipt of the documents by the ultimate customer unless notice of objection is sent before such expiration date. The ultimate customer may send notice of objection to the person from whom he received the documents and any bank receiving such notice is under a duty to send notice to its tranferor before its midnight deadline.

§ 5-114. Issuer's Duty and Privilege to Honor; Right to Reimbursement

(1) An issuer must honor a draft or demand for payment which complies with the terms of the relevant credit regardless of whether the goods or documents conform to the underlying contract for sale or other contract between the customer and the beneficiary. The issuer is not excused from honor of such a draft or demand by reason of an additional general term that all documents must be satisfactory to the issuer, but an issuer may require that specified documents must be satisfactory to it.

(2) Unless otherwise agreed when documents appear on their face to comply with the terms of a credit but a required document does not in fact conform to the warranties made on negotiation or transfer of a document of title (Section 7-507) or of a certificated security (Section 8-306) or is forged or fraudulent or there is fraud in the transaction:

(a) the issuer must honor the draft or demand for payment if honor is demanded by a negotiating bank or other holder of the draft or demand which has taken the draft or demand under the credit and under circumstances which would make it a holder in due course (Section 3-302) and in an appropriate case would make it a person to whom a document of title has been duly negotiated (Section 7-502) or a bona fide purchaser of a certificated security (Section 8-302); and

(b) in all other cases as against its customer, an issuer acting in good faith may honor the draft or demand for payment despite notification from the customer of fraud, forgery or other defect not apparent on the face of the documents but a court of appropriate jurisdiction may enjoin such honor.

(3) Unless otherwise agreed an issuer which has duly honored a draft or demand for payment is entitled to immediate reimbursement of any payment made under

the credit and to be put in effectively available funds not later than the day before maturity of any acceptance made under the credit.

[(4) When a credit provides for payment by the issuer on receipt of notice that the required documents are in the possession of a correspondent or other agent of the issuer

(a) any payment made on receipt of such notice is conditional; and

(b) the issuer may reject documents which do not comply with the credit if it does so within three banking days following its receipt of the documents; and

(c) in the event of such rejection, the issuer is entitled by charge back or otherwise to return of the payment made.]

[(5) In the case covered by subsection (4) failure to reject documents within the time specified in sub-paragraph (b) constitutes acceptance of the documents and makes the payment final in favor of the beneficiary.] Amended in 1977.

Note: Subsections (4) and (5) are bracketed as optional. If they are included the bracketed language in the last sentence of Section 5-112(1) should also be included.

§ 5-115. Remedy for Improper Dishonor or Anticipatory Repudiation

(1) When an issuer wrongfully dishonors a draft or demand for payment presented under a credit the person entitled to honor has with respect to any documents the rights of a person in the position of a seller (Section 2-707) and may recover from the issuer the face amount of the draft or demand together with incidental damages under Section 2-710 on seller's incidental damages and interest but less any amount realized by resale or other use or disposition of the subject matter of the transaction. In the event no resale or other utilization is made the documents, goods or other subject matter involved in the transaction must be turned over to the issuer on payment of judgment.

(2) When an issuer wrongfully cancels or otherwise repudiates a credit before presentment of a draft or demand for payment drawn under it the beneficiary has the rights of a seller after anticipatory repudiation by the buyer under Section 2-610 if he learns of the repudiation in time reasonably to avoid procurement of the required documents. Otherwise the beneficiary has an immediate right of action for wrongful dishonor.

§ 5-116. Transfer and Assignment

(1) The right to draw under a credit can be transferred or assigned only when the credit is expressly designated as transferable or assignable.

(2) Even though the credit specifically states that it is nontransferable or nonassignable the beneficiary may before performance of the conditions of the credit assign his right to proceeds. Such an assignment is an assignment of an account under Article 9 on Secured Transactions and is governed by that Article except that

(a) the assignment is ineffective until the letter of credit or advice of credit is delivered to the assignee which delivery constitutes perfection of the security interest under Article 9; and

(b) the issuer may honor drafts or demands for payment drawn under the credit until it receives a notification of the assignment signed by the beneficiary which reasonably identifies the credit involved in the assignment and contains a request to pay the assignee; and

(c) after what reasonably appears to be such a notification has been received the issuer may without dishonor refuse to accept or pay even to a person otherwise entitled to honor until the letter of credit or advice of credit is exhibited to the issuer.

(3) Except where the beneficiary has effectively assigned his right to draw or his right to proceeds, nothing in this section limits his right to transfer or negotiate drafts or demands drawn under the credit. Amended in 1972.

§ 5-117. Insolvency of Bank Holding Funds for Documentary Credit

(1) Where an issuer or an advising or confirming bank or a bank which has for a customer procured issuance of a credit by another bank becomes insolvent before final payment under the credit and the credit is one to which this Article is made applicable by paragraphs (a) or (b) of Section 5-102(1) on scope, the receipt or allocation of funds or collateral to secure or meet obligations under the credit shall have the following results:

(a) to the extent of any funds or collateral turned over after or before the insolvency as indemnity against or specifically for the purpose of payment of drafts or demands for payment drawn under the designated credit, the drafts or demands are entitled to payment in preference over depositors or other general creditors of the issuer or bank; and

(b) on expiration of the credit or surrender of the beneficiary's rights under it unused any person who has given such funds or collateral is similarly entitled to return thereof; and

(c) a charge to a general or current account with a bank if specifically consented to for the purpose of indemnity against or payment of drafts or demands for payment drawn under the designated credit falls under the same rules as if the funds had been drawn out in cash and then turned over with specific instructions.

(2) After honor or reimbursement under this section the customer or other person for whose account the insolvent bank has acted is entitled to receive the documents involved.

ARTICLE 6. Bulk Transfers

Section

6-101. Short Title.

6-102. "Bulk Transfer"; Transfers of Equipment; Enterprises Subject to This Article; Bulk Transfers Subject to This Article.

6-103. Transfers Excepted From This Article.

6-104. Schedule of Property, List of Creditors.

6-105. Notice to Creditors.

6-106. Application of the Proceeds.

6-107. The Notice.

6-108. Auction Sales; "Auctioneer".

6-109. What Creditors Protected; [Credit for Payment to Particular Creditors].

6-110. Subsequent Transfers.

6-111. Limitation of Actions and Levies.

ARTICLE 6. Bulk Transfers

§ 6-101. Short Title

This Article shall be known and may be cited as Uniform Commerical Code—Bulk Transfers.

§ 6-102. "Bulk Transfers"; Transfers of Equipment; Enterprises Subject to This Article; Bulk Transfers Subject to This Article

(1) A "bulk transfer" is any transfer in bulk and not in the ordinary course of the tranferor's business of a major part of the materials, supplies, merchandise or other inventory (Section 9-109) of an enterprise subject to this Article.

(2) A transfer of a substantial part of the equipment (Section 9-109) of such an enterprise is a bulk transfer if it is made in connection with a bulk transfer of inventory, but not otherwise.

(3) The enterprises subject to this Article are all those whose principal business is the sale of merchandise from stock, including those who manufacture what they sell.

(4) Except as limited by the following section all bulk transfers of goods located within this state are subject to this Article.

§ 6-103. Transfers Excepted From This Article

The following transfers are not subject to this Article:

(1) Those made to give security for the performance of an obligation;

(2) General assignments for the benefit of all the creditors of the transferor, and subsequent transfers by the assignee thereunder;

(3) Transfers in settlement or realization of a lien or other security interests;

(4) Sales by executors, administrators, receivers, trustees in bankruptcy, or any public officer under judicial process;

(5) Sales made in the course of judicial or administrative proceedings for the dissolution or reorganization of a corporation and of which notice is sent to the creditors of the corporation pursuant to order of the court or administrative agency;

(6) Transfers to a person maintaining a known place of business in this State who becomes bound to pay the debts of the transferor in full and gives public notice of that fact, and who is solvent after becoming so bound;

(7) A transfer to a new business enterprise organized to take over and continue the business, if public notice of the transaction is given and the new enterprise assumes the debts of the transferor and he receives nothing from the transaction except an interest in the new enterprise junior to the claims of creditors;

(8) Transfers of property which is exempt from execution.

Public notice under subsection (6) or subsection (7) may be given by publishing once a week for two consecutive weeks in a newspaper of general circulation where the transferor had its principal place of business in this state an advertisement including the names and addresses of the transferor and transferee and the effective date of the transfer. As amended 1962.

§ 6-104. Schedule of Property, List of Creditors

(1) Except as provided with respect to auction sales (Section 6-108), a bulk transfer subject to this Article is ineffective against any creditor of the transferor unless:

(a) The transferee requires the transferor to furnish a list of his existing creditors prepared as stated in this section; and

(b) The parties prepare a schedule of the property transferred sufficient to identify it; and

(c) The transferee preserves the list and schedule for six months next following the transfer and permits inspection of either or both and copying therefrom at all reasonable hours by any creditor of the transferor, or files the list and schedule in (a public office to be here identified).

(2) The list of creditors must be signed and sworn to or affirmed by the transferor or his agent. It must contain the names and business addresses of all creditors of the transferor, with the amounts when known, and also the names of all persons who are known to the transferor to assert claims against him even though such claims are disputed. If the transferor is the obligor of an outstanding issue of bonds, debentures or the like as to which there is an indenture trustee, the list of creditors need include only the name and address of the indenture trustee and the aggregate outstanding principal amount of the issue.

(3) Responsibility for the completeness and accuracy of the list of creditors rests on the transferor, and the transfer is not rendered ineffective by errors or omissions therein unless the transferee is shown to have had knowledge. As amended 1962.

§ 6-105. Notice to Creditors

In addition to the requirements of the preceding section, any bulk transfer subject to this Article except one made by auction sale (Section 6-108) is ineffective against any creditor of the transferor unless at least ten days before he takes possession of the goods or pays for them, whichever happens first, the transferee gives notice of the transfer in the manner and to the persons hereafter provided (Section 6-107).

§ 6-106. Application of the Proceeds

In addition to the requirements of the two preceding sections:

(1) Upon every bulk transfer subject to this Article for which new consideration becomes payable except

those made by sale at auction it is the duty of the transferee to assure that such consideration is applied so far as necessary to pay those debts of the transferor which are either shown on the list furnished by the transferor (Section 6-104) or filed in writing in the place stated in the notice (Section 6-107) within thirty days after the mailing of such notice. This duty of the transferee runs to all the holders of such debts, and may be enforced by any of them for the benefit of all.

(2) If any of said debts are in dispute the necessary sum may be withheld from distribution until the dispute is settled or adjudicated.

(3) If the consideration payable is not enough to pay all of the said debts in full distribution shall be made pro rata.]

Note: This section is bracketed to indicate division of opinion as to whether or not it is a wise provision, and to suggest that this is a point on which State enactments may differ without serious damage to the principle of uniformity.

In any State where this section is omitted, the following parts of sections, also bracketed in the text, should also be omitted, namely:

Section 6-107(2)(e).
        6-108(3)(c).
        6-109(2).

In any State where this section is enacted, these other provisons should be also.

OPTIONAL SUBSECTION (4). [(4) The transferee may within ten days after he takes possession of the goods pay the consideration into the (specify court) in the county where the transferor had its principal place of business in this state and thereafter may discharge his duty under this section by giving notice by registered or certified mail to all the persons to whom the duty runs that the consideration has been paid into that court and that they should file their claims there. On motion of any interested party, the court may order the distribution of the consideration to the persons entitled to it.] As amended 1962.

Note: Optional subsection (4) is recommended for those states which do not have a general statute providing for payment of money into court.

§ 6-107. The Notice

(1) The notice to creditors (Section 6-105) shall state:

(a) that a bulk transfer is about to be made; and

(b) the names and business addresses of the transferor and transferee, and all other business names and addresses used by the transferor within three years last past so far as known to the transferee; and

(c) whether or not all the debts of the transferor are to be paid in full as they fall due as a result of the transaction, and if so, the address to which creditors should send their bills.

(2) If the debts of the transferor are not to be paid in full as they fall due or if the transferee is in doubt on that point then the notice shall state further:

(a) the location and general description of the property to be transferred and the estimated total of the transferor's debts;

(b) the address where the schedule of property and list of creditors (Section 6-104) may be inspected;

(c) whether the transfer is to pay existing debts and if so the amount of such debts and to whom owing;

(d) whether the transfer is for new consideration and if so the amount of such consideration and the time and place of payment; [and]

[(e) if for new consideration the time and place where creditors of the transferor are to file their claims.]

(3) The notice in any case shall be delivered personally or sent by registered or certified mail to all persons shown on the list of creditors furnished by the transferor (Section 6-104) and to all other persons who are known to the transferee to hold or assert claims against the transferor. As amended 1962.

Note: The words in brackets are optional. See note under §6-106.

§ 6-108. Auction Sales; "Auctioneer"

(1) A bulk transfer is subject to this Article even though it is by sale at auction, but only in the manner and with the results stated in this section.

(2) The transferor shall furnish a list of his creditors and assist in the preparation of a schedule of the property to be sold, both prepared as before stated (Section 6-104).

(3) The person or persons other than the transferor who direct, control or are responsible for the auction are collectively called the "auctioneer". The auctioneer shall:

(a) receive and retain the list of creditors and prepare and retain the schedule of property for the period stated in this Article (Section 6-104);

(b) give notice of the auction personally or by registered or certified mail at least ten days before it occurs to all persons shown on the list of creditors and to all other persons who are known to him to hold or assert claims against the transferor; [and]

[(c) assure that the net proceeds of the auction are applied as provided in this Article (Section 6-106).]

(4) Failure of the auctioneer to perform any of these duties does not affect the validity of the sale or the title of the purchasers, but if the auctioneer knows that the auction constitutes a bulk transfer such failure renders the auctioneer liable to the creditors of the transferor as a class for the sums owing to them from the transferor up to but not exceeding the net proceeds of the auction. If the auctioneer consists of several persons their liability is joint and several. As amended 1962.

Note: The words in brackets are optional. See Note under §6-106.

§ 6-109.   What Creditors Protected; [Credit for Payment to Particular Creditors]

(1) The creditors of the transferor mentioned in this Article are those holding claims based on transactions or events occurring before the bulk transfer, but creditors who become such after notice of creditors is given (Section 6-105 and 6-107) are entitled to notice.

[(2) Against the aggregate obligation imposed by the provisions of this Article concerning the application of the proceeds (Section 6-106 and subsection (3) (c) of 6-108) the transferee or auctioneer is entitled to credit for sums paid to particular creditors of the transferor, not exceeding the sums believed in good faith at the time of the payment to be properly payable to such creditors.]

Note: The words in brackets are optional. See Note under §6-106.

§ 6-110.   Subsequent Transfers

When the title of a transferee to property is subject to a defect by reason of his non-compliance with the requirements of this Article, then:

(1) a purchaser of any of such property from such transferee who pays no value or who takes with notice of such non-compliance takes subject to such defect, but

(2) a purchaser for value in good faith and without such notice takes free of such defect.

§ 6-111.   Limitation of Actions and Levies

No action under this Article shall be brought nor levy made more than six months after the date on which the transferee took possession of the goods unless the transfer has been concealed. If the transfer has been concealed, actions may be brought or levies made within six months after its discovery.

ARTICLE 7.   Warehouse Receipts, Bills of Lading and Other Documents of Title

PART 1. General

PART 2. Warehouse Receipts: Special Provisions

PART 3. Bills of Lading: Special Provisions

ARTICLE 7. Warehouse Receipts, Bills of Lading and Other Documents of Title

PART 1. *General*

§ 7-101. Short Title

This Article shall be known and may be cited as Uniform Commercial Code—Documents of Title.

§ 7-102. Definitions and Index of Definitions

(1) In this Article, unless the context otherwise requires:

(a) "Bailee" means the person who by a warehouse receipt, bill of lading or other document of title acknowledges possession of goods and contracts to deliver them.

(b) "Consignee" means the person named in a bill to whom or to whose order the bill promises delivery.

(c) "Consignor" means the person named in a bill as the person from whom the goods have been received for shipment.

(d) "Delivery order" means a written order to deliver goods directed to a warehouseman, carrier or other person who in the ordinary course of business issues warehouse receipts or bills of lading.

(e) "Document" means document of title as defined in the general definitions in Article 1 (Section 1-201).

(f) "Goods" means all things which are treated as movable for the purposes of a contract of storage or transportation.

(g) "Issuer" means a bailee who issues a document except that in relation to an unaccepted delivery order it means the person who orders the possessor of goods to deliver. Issuer includes any person for whom an agent or employee purports to act in issuing a document if the agent or employee has real or apparent authority to issue documents, notwithstanding that the issuer received no goods or that the goods were misdescribed or that in any other respect the agent or employee violated his instructions.

(h) "Warehouseman" is a person engaged in the business of storing goods for hire.

(2) Other definitions applying to this Article or to specified Parts thereof, and the sections in which they appear are:

"Duly negotiate".	Section 7-501.
"Person entitled under the document".	Section 7-403(4).

(3) Definitions in other Articles applying to this Article and the sections in which they appear are:

"Contract for sale".   Section 2-106.
"Overseas".   Section 2-323.
"Receipt" of goods.   Section 2-103.

(4) In addition Article 1 contains general definitions and principles of construction and interpretation applicable throughout this Article.

§ 7-103. Relation of Article to Treaty, Statute, Tariff, Classification or Regulation

To the extent that any treaty or statute of the United States, regulatory statute of this State or tariff, classification or regulation filed or issued pursuant thereto is applicable, the provisions of this Article are subject thereto.

§ 7-104. Negotiable and Non-Negotiable Warehouse Receipt, Bill of Lading or Other Document of Title

(1) A warehouse receipt, bill of lading or other document of title is negotiable

(a) if by its terms the goods are to be delivered to bearer or to the order of a named person; or

(b) where recognized in overseas trade, if it runs to a named person or assigns.

(2) Any other document is non-negotiable. A bill of lading in which it is stated that the goods are consigned to a named person is not made negotiable by a provision that the goods are to be delivered only against a written order signed by the same or another named person.

PART 2. *Warehouse Receipts: Special Provisions*

§ 7-201. Who May Issue a Warehouse Receipt; Storage Under Government Bond

(1) A warehouse receipt may be issued by any warehouseman.

(2) Where goods including distilled spirits and agricultural commodities are stored under a statute requiring a bond against withdrawal or a license for the issuance of receipts in the nature of warehouse receipts, a receipt issued for the goods has like effect as a warehouse receipt even though issued by a person who is the owner of the goods and is not a warehouseman.

§ 7-202. Form of Warehouse Receipt; Essential Terms; Optional Terms

(1) A warehouse receipt need not be in any particular form.

(2) Unless a warehouse receipt embodies within its written or printed terms each of the following, the warehouseman is liable for damages caused by the omission to a person injured thereby:

(a) the location of the warehouse where the goods are stored;

(b) the date of issue of the receipt;

(c) the consecutive number of the receipt;

(d) a statement whether the goods received will be delivered to the bearer, to a specified person, or to a specified person or his order;

(e) the rate of storage and handling charges, except that where goods are stored under a field warehousing arrangement a state of that fact is sufficient on a non-negotiable receipt;

(f) a description of the goods or of the packages containing them;

(g) the signature of the warehouseman, which may be made by his authorized agent;

(h) if the receipt is issued for goods of which the warehouseman is owner, either solely or jointly or in common with others, the fact of such ownership; and

(i) a statement of the amount of advances made and of liabilities incurred for which the warehouseman claims a lien or security interest (Section 7-209). If the precise amount of such advances made or of such liabilities incurred is, at the time of the issue of the receipt, unknown to the warehouseman or to his agent who issues it, a statement of the fact that advances have been made or liabilities incurred and the purpose thereof is sufficient.

(3) A warehouseman may insert in his receipt any other terms which are not contrary to the provisions of this Act and do not impair his obligation of delivery (Section 7-403) or his duty of care (Section 7-204). Any contrary provisions shall be ineffective.

§ 7-203. Liability for Non-Receipt or Misdescription

A party to or purchaser for value in good faith of a document of title other than a bill of lading relying in either case upon the description therein of the goods may recover from the issuer damages caused by the non-receipt or misdescription of the goods, except to the extent that the document conspicuously indicates that the issuer does not know whether any part or all of the goods in fact were received or conform to the description, as where the description is in terms of marks or labels or kind, quantity or condition, or the receipt or description is qualified by "contents, condition and quality unknown", "said to contain" or the like, if such indication be true, or the party or purchaser otherwise has notice.

§ 7-204.   Duty of Care; Contractual Limitation of Warehouseman's Liability

(1) A warehouseman is liable for damages for loss of or injury to the goods caused by his failure to exercise such care in regard to them as a reasonably careful man would exercise under like circumstances but unless otherwise agreed he is not liable for damages which could not have been avoided by the exercise of such care.

(2) Damages may be limited by a term in the warehouse receipt or storage agreement limiting the amount of liability in case of loss or damage, and setting forth a specific liability per article or item, or value per unit of weight, beyond which the warehouseman shall not be liable; provided, however, that such liability may on written request of the bailor at the time of signing such storage agreement or within a reasonable time after receipt of the warehouse receipt be increased on part or all of the goods thereunder, in which event increased rates may be charged based on such increased valuation, but that no such increase shall be permitted contrary to a lawful limitation of liability contained in the warehouseman's tariff, if any. No such limitation is effective with respect to the warehouseman's liability for conversion to his own use.

(3) Reasonable provisions as to the time and manner of presenting claims and instituting actions based on the bailment may be included in the warehouse receipt or tariff.

(4) This section does not impair or repeal . . .

Note: Insert in subsection (4) a reference to any statute which imposes a higher responsibility upon the warehouseman or invalidates contractual limitations which would be permissible under this Article.

§ 7-205.   Title Under Warehouse Receipt Defeated in Certain Cases

A buyer in the ordinary course of business of fungible goods sold and delivered by a warehouseman who is also in the business of buying and selling such goods takes free of any claim under a warehouse receipt even though it has been duly negotiated.

§ 7-206.   Termination of Storage at Warehouseman's Option

(1) A warehouseman may on notifying the person on whose account the goods are held and any other person known to claim an interest in the goods require payment of any charges and removal of the goods from the warehouse at the termination of the period of storage fixed by the document, or, if no period is fixed, within a stated period not less than thirty days after the notification. If the goods are not removed before the date specified in the notification, the warehouseman may sell them in accordance with the provisions of the section on enforcement of a warehouseman's lien (Section 7-210).

(2) If a warehouseman in good faith believes that the goods are about to deteriorate or decline in value to less than the amount of his lien within the time prescribed in subsection (1) for notification, advertisement and sale, the warehouseman may specify in the notification any reasonable shorter time for removal of the goods and in case the goods are not removed, may sell them at public sale held not less than one week after a single advertisement or posting.

(3) If as a result of a quality or condition of the goods of which the warehouseman had no notice at the time of deposit the goods are a hazard to other property or to the warehouse or to persons, the warehouseman may sell the goods at public or private sale without advertisement on reasonable notification to all persons known to claim an interest in the goods. If the warehouseman after a reasonable effort is unable to sell the goods he may dispose of them in any lawful manner and shall incur no liability by reason of such disposition.

(4) The warehouseman must deliver the goods to any person entitled to them under this Article upon due demand made at any time prior to sale or other disposition under this section.

(5) The warehouseman may satisfy his lien from the proceeds of any sale or disposition under this section but must hold the balance for delivery on the demand of any person to whom he would have been bound to deliver the goods.

§ 7-207. Goods Must Be Kept Separate; Fungible Goods

(1) Unless the warehouse receipt otherwise provides, a warehouseman must keep separate the goods covered by each receipt so as to permit at all times identification and delivery of those goods except that different lots of fungible goods may be commingled.

(2) Fungible goods so commingled are owned in common by the persons entitled thereto and the warehouseman is severally liable to each owner for that owner's share. Where because of overissue a mass of fungible goods is insufficient to meet all the receipts which the warehouseman has issued against it, the persons entitled include all holders to whom overissued receipts have been duly negotiated.

§ 7-208. Altered Warehouse Receipts

Where a blank in a negotiable warehouse receipt has been filled in without authority, a purchaser for value and without notice of the want of authority may treat the insertion as authorized. Any other unauthorized alteration leaves any receipt enforceable against the issuer according to its original tenor.

§ 7-209. Lien of Warehouseman

(1) A warehouseman has a lien against the bailor on the goods covered by a warehouse receipt or on the proceeds thereof in his possession for charges for storage or transportation (including demurrage and terminal charges), insurance, labor, or charges present or future in relation to the goods, and for expenses necessary for preservation of the goods or reasonably incurred in their sale pursuant to law. If the person on whose account the goods are held is liable for like charges or expenses in relation to other goods whenever deposited and it is stated in the receipt that a lien is claimed for charges and expenses in relation to other goods, the warehouseman also has a lien against him for such charges and expenses whether or not the other goods have been delivered by the warehouseman. But against a person to whom a negotiable warehouse receipt is duly negotiated a warehouseman's lien is limited to charges in an amount or at a rate specified on the receipt or if no charges are so specified then to a reasonable charge for storage of the goods covered by the receipt subsequent to the date of the receipt.

(2) The warehouseman may also reserve a security interest against the bailor for a maximum amount specified on the receipt for charges other than those specified in subsection (1), such as for money advanced and interest. Such a security interest is governed by the Article on Secured Transactions (Article 9).

(3) (a) A warehouseman's lien for charges and expenses under subsection (1) or a security interest under subsection (2) is also effective against any person who so entrusted the bailor with possession of the goods that a pledge of them by him to a good faith purchaser for value would have been valid but is not effective against a person as to whom the document confers no right in the goods covered by it under Section 7-503.

(b) A warehouseman's lien on household goods for charges and expenses in relation to the goods under subsection (1) is also effective against all persons if the depositor was the legal possessor of the goods at the time of deposit. "Household goods" means furniture, furnishings and personal effects used by the depositor in a dwelling.

(4) A warehouseman loses his lien on any goods which he voluntarily delivers or which he unjustifiably refuses to deliver. As amended in 1966.

§ 7-210. Enforcement of Warehouseman's Lien

(1) Except as provided in subsection (2), a warehouseman's lien may be enforced by public or private sale of the goods in block or in parcels, at any time or place and on any terms which are commercially reasonable, after notifying all persons known to claim an interest in the goods. Such notification must include a statement of the amount due, the nature of the proposed sale and the time and place of any public sale. The fact that a better price could have been obtained by a sale at a different time or in a different method from that selected by the warehouseman is not of itself sufficient to establish that the sale was not made in a commercially reasonable manner. If the warehouseman either sells the goods in the usual manner in any recognized market therefore, or if he sells at the price current in such market at the time of his sale, or if he has otherwise sold in conformity with commercially reasonable practices among dealers in the type of goods sold, he has sold in a commercially reasonable manner. A sale of more goods than apparently necessary to be offered to insure satisfaction of the obligation is not commercially reasonable except in cases covered by the preceding sentence.

(2) A warehouseman's lien on goods other than goods stored by a merchant in the course of his business may be enforced only as follows:

(a) All persons known to claim an interest in the goods must be notified.

(b) The notification must be delivered in person or sent by registered or certified letter to the last known address of any person to be notified.

(c) The notification must include an itemized statement of the claim, a description of the goods subject to the lien, a demand for payment within a specified time not less than ten days after receipt of the notification, and a conspicuous statement that unless the claim is paid within that time the goods will be advertised for sale and sold by auction at a specified time and place.

(d) The sale must conform to the terms of the notification.

(e) The sale must be held at the nearest suitable place to that where the goods are held or stored.

(f) After the expiration of the time given in the notification, an advertisement of the sale must be published once a week for two weeks consecutively in a newspaper of general circulation where the sale is to be held. The advertisement must include a description of the goods, the name of the person on whose account they are being held, and the time and place of the sale. The sale must take place at least fifteen days after the first publication. If there is no newspaper of general circulation where the sale is to be held, the advertisement must be posted at least ten days before the sale in not less than six conspicious places in the neighborhood of the proposed sale.

(3) Before any sale pursuant to this section any person claiming a right in the goods may pay the amount necessary to satisfy the lien and the reasonable expenses incurred under this section. In that event the goods must not be sold, but must be retained by the warehouseman subject to the terms of the receipt and this Article.

(4) The warehouseman may buy at any public sale pursuant to this section.

(5) A purchaser in good faith of goods sold to enforce a warehouseman's lien takes the goods free of any rights of persons against whom the lien was valid, despite noncompliance by the warehouseman with the requirements of this section.

(6) The warehouseman may satisfy his lien from the proceeds of any sale pursuant to this section but must hold the balance, if any, for delivery on demand to any person to whom he would have been bound to deliver the goods.

(7) The rights provided by this section shall be in addition to all other rights allowed by law to a creditor against his debtor.

(8) Where a lien is on goods stored by a merchant in the course of his business the lien may be enforced in accordance with either subsection (1) or (2).

(9) The warehouseman is liable for damages caused by failure to comply with the requirements for sale under this section and in case of willful violation is liable for conversion. As amended in 1962.

PART 3. *Bills of Lading: Special Provisions*

§ 7-301.   Liability for Non-Receipt or Misdescription; "Said to Contain"; "Shipper's Load and Count"; Improper Handling

(1) A consignee of a non-negotiable bill who has given value in good faith or a holder to whom a negotiable bill has been duly negotiated relying in either case upon the description therein of the goods, or upon the date therein shown, may recover from the issuer damages caused by the misdating of the bill or the nonreceipt or misdescription of the goods, except to the extent that the document indicates that the issuer does not know whether any part or all of the goods in fact were received or conform to the description, as where the description is in terms of marks or labels or kind, quantity, or condition or the receipt or description is qualified by "contents or condition of contents of packages unknown", "said to contain", "shipper's weight, load and count" or the like, if such indication be true.

(2) When goods are loaded by an issuer who is a common carrier, the issuer must count the packages of goods if package freight and ascertain the kind and quantity if bulk freight. In such cases "shipper's weight, load and count" or other words indicating that the description was made by the shipper are ineffective except as to freight concealed by packages.

(3) When bulk freight is loaded by a shipper who makes available to the issuer adequate facilities for weighing such freight, an issuer who is a common carrier must ascertain the kind and quantity within a reasonable time after receiving the written request of the shipper to do so. In such cases "shipper's weight" or other words of like purport are ineffective.

(4) The issuer may by inserting in the bill the words "shipper's weight, load and count" or other words of like purport indicate that the goods are loaded by the

shipper; and if such statement be true the issuer shall not be liable for damages caused by the improper loading. But their omission does not imply liability for such damages.

(5) The shipper shall be deemed to have guaranteed to the issuer the accuracy at the time of shipment of the description, marks, labels, number, kind, quantity, condition and weight, as furnished by him; and the shipper shall indemnify the issuer against damage caused by inaccuracies in such particulars. The right of the issuer to such indemnity shall in no way limit his responsibility and liability under the contract of carriage to any person other than the shipper.

§ 7-302. Through Bills of Lading and Similar Documents

(1) The issuer of a through bill of lading or other document embodying an undertaking to be performed in part by persons acting as its agents or by connecting carriers is liable to anyone entitled to recover on the document for any breach by such other persons or by a connecting carrier of its obligation under the document but to the extent that the bill covers an undertaking to be performed overseas or in territory not contiguous to the continental United States or an undertaking including matters other than transportation this liability may be varied by agreement of the parties.

(2) Where goods coverd by a through bill of lading or other document embodying an undertaking to be performed in part by persons other than the issuer are received by any such person, he is subject with respect to his own performance while the goods are in his possession to the obligation of the issuer. His obligation is discharged by delivery of the goods to another such person pursuant to the document, and does not include liability for breach by any other such persons or by the issuer.

(3) The issuer of such through bill of lading or other document shall be entitled to recover from the connecting carrier or such other person in possession of the goods when the breach of the obligation under the document occurred, the amount it may be required to pay to anyone entitled to recover on the document therefor, as may be evidenced by any receipt, judgment, or transcript thereof, and the amount of any expense reasonably incurred by it in defending any action brought by anyone entitled to recover on the document therefor.

§ 7-303. Diversion; Reconsignment; Change of Instructions

(1) Unless the bill of lading otherwise provides, the carrier may deliver the goods to a person or destination other than that stated in the bill or may otherwise dispose of the goods on instructions from

(a) the holder of a negotiable bill; or

(b) the consignor on a non-negotiable bill notwithstanding contrary instructions from the consignee; or

(c) the consignee on a non-negotiable bill in the absence of contrary instructions from the consignor, if the goods have arrived at the billed destination or if the consignee is in possession of the bill; or

(d) the consignee on a non-negotiable bill if he is entitled as against the consignor to dispose of them.

(2) Unless such instructions are noted on a negotiable bill of lading, a person to whom the bill is duly negotiated can hold the bailee according to the original terms.

§ 7-304. Bills of Lading in a Set

(1) Except where customary in overseas transportation, a bill of lading must not be issued in a set of parts. The issuer is liable for damages caused by violation of this subsection.

(2) Where a bill of lading is lawfully drawn in a set of parts, each of which is numbered and expressed to be valid only if the goods have not been delivered against any other part, the whole of the parts constitute one bill.

(3) Where a bill of lading is lawfully issued in a set of parts and different parts are negotiated to different persons, the title of the holder to whom the first due negotiation is made prevails as to both the document and the goods even though any later holder may have received the goods from the carrier in good faith and discharged the carrier's obligation by surrender of his part.

(4) Any person who negotiates or transfers a single part of a bill of lading drawn in a set is liable to holders of that part as if it were the whole set.

(5) The bailee is obliged to deliver in accordance with Part 4 of this Article against the first presented part of a bill of lading lawfully drawn in a set. Such delivery discharges the bailee's obligation on the whole bill.

§ 7-305. Destination Bills

(1) Instead of issuing a bill of lading to the consignor at the place of shipment a carrier may at the request of

the consignor procure the bill to be issued at destination or at any other place designated in the request.

(2) Upon request of anyone entitled as against the carrier to control the goods while in transit and on surrender of any outstanding bill of lading or other receipt covering such goods, the issuer may procure a substitute bill to be issued at any place designated in the request.

§ 7-306.   Altered Bills of Lading

An unauthorized alteration or filling in of a blank in a bill of lading leaves the bill enforceable according to its original tenor.

§ 7-307.   Lien of Carrier

(1) A carrier has a lien on the goods covered by a bill of lading for charges subsequent to the date of its receipt of the goods for storage or transportation (including demurrage and terminal charges) and for expenses necessary for preservation of the goods incident to their transportation or reasonably incurred in their sale pursuant to law. But against a purchaser for value of a negotiable bill of lading a carrier's lien is limited to charges stated in the bill or the applicable tariffs, or if no charges are stated then to a reasonable charge.

(2) A lien for charges and expenses under subsection (1) on goods which the carrier was required by law to receive for transportation is effective against the consignor or any person entitled to the goods unless the carrier had notice that the consignor lacked authority to subject the goods to such charges and expenses. Any other lien under subsection (1) is effective against the consignor and any person who permitted the bailor to have control or possession of the goods unless the carrier had notice that the bailor lacked such authority.

(3) A carrier loses his lien on any goods which he voluntarily delivers or which he unjustifiably refuses to deliver.

§ 7-308.   Enforcement of Carrier's Lien

(1) A carrier's lien may be enforced by public or private sale of the goods, in block or in parcels, at any time or place and on any terms which are commercially reasonable, after notifying all persons known to claim an interest in the goods. Such notification must include a statement of the amount due, the nature of the proposed sale and the time and place of any public sale. The fact that a better price could have been obtained by a sale at a different time or in a different method from that selected by the carrier is not of itself sufficient to establish that the sale was not made in a commercially reasonable manner. If the carrier either sells the goods in the usual manner in any recognized market therefor or if he sells at the price current in such market at the time of his sale or if he has otherwise sold in conformity with commercially reasonable practices among dealers in the type of goods sold he has sold in a commercially reasonable manner. A sale of more goods than apparently necessary to be offered to ensure satisfaction of the obligation is not commercially reasonable except in cases covered by the preceding sentence.

(2) Before any sale pursuant to this section any person claiming a right in the goods may pay the amount necessary to satisfy the lien and the reasonable expenses incurred under this section. In that event the goods must not be sold, but must be retained by the carrier subject to the terms of the bill and this Article.

(3) The carrier may buy at any public sale pursuant to this section.

(4) A purchaser in good faith of goods sold to enforce a carrier's lien takes the goods free of any rights of persons against whom the lien was valid, despite noncompliance by the carrier with the requirements of this section.

(5) The carrier may satisfy his lien from the proceeds of any sale pursuant to this section but must hold the balance, if any, for delivery on demand to any person to whom he would have been bound to deliver the goods.

(6) The rights provided by this section shall be in addition to all other rights allowed by law to a creditor against his debtor.

(7) A carrier's lien may be enforced in accordance with either subsection (1) or the procedure set forth in subsection (2) of Section 7-210.

(8) The carrier is liable for damages caused by failure to comply with the requirements for sale under this section and in case of willful violation is liable for conversion.

§ 7-309.   Duty of Care; Contractual Limitation of Carrier's Liability

(1) A carrier who issues a bill of lading whether negotiable or non-negotiable must exercise the degree of care in relation to the goods which a reasonably careful man would exercise under like circumstances. Ths subsection does not repeal or change any law or rule of law

which imposes liability upon a common carrier for damages not caused by its negligence.

(2) Damages may be limited by a provision that the carrier's liability shall not exceed a value stated in the document if the carrier's rates are dependent upon value and the consignor by the carrier's tariff is afforded an opportunity to declare a higher value or a value as lawfully provided in the tariff, or where no tariff is filed he is otherwise advised of such opportunity; but no such limitation is effective with respect to the carrier's liability for conversion to its own use.

(3) Reasonable provisions as to the time and manner of presenting claims and instituting actions based on the shipment may be included in a bill of lading or tariff.

PART 4. *Warehouse Receipts and Bills of Lading: General Obligations*

§ 7-401. Irregularities in Issue of Receipt or Bill or Conduct of Issuer

The obligations imposed by this Article on an issuer apply to a document of title regardless of the fact that

(a) the documents may not comply with the requirements of this Article or of any other law or regulation regarding its issue, form or content; or

(b) the issuer may have violated laws regulating the conduct of his business; or

(c) the goods covered by the document were owned by the bailee at the time the document was issued; or

(d) the person issuing the document does not come within the definition of warehouseman if it purports to be a warehouse receipt.

§ 7-402. Duplicate Receipt or Bill; Overissue

Neither a duplicate nor any other document of title purporting to cover goods already represented by an outstanding document of the same issuer confers any right in the goods, except as provided in the case of bills in a set, overissue of documents for fungible goods and substitutes for lost, stolen or destroyed documents. But the issuer is liable for damages caused by his overissue or failure to identify a duplicate document as such by conspicuous notation on its face.

§ 7-403. Obligation of Warehouseman or Carrier to Deliver; Excuse

(1) The bailee must deliver the goods to a person entitled under the document who complies with sub-sections (2) and (3), unless and to the extent that the bailee establishes any of the following:

(a) delivery of the goods to a person whose receipt was rightful as against the claimant;

(b) damage to or delay, loss or destruction of the goods for which the bailee is not liable [, but the burden of establishing negligence in such cases is on the person entitled under the document];

Note: The brackets in (1) (b) indicate that State enactments may differ on this point without serious damage to the principle of uniformity.

(c) previous sale or other disposition of the goods in lawful enforcement of a lien or on warehouseman's lawful termination of storage;

(d) the exercise by a seller of his right to stop delivery pursuant to the provisions of the Article on Sales (Section 2-705);

(e) a diversion, reconsignment or other disposition pursuant to the provisions of this Article (Section 7-303) or tariff regulating such right;

(f) release, satisfaction or any other fact affording personal defense against the claimant;

(g) any other lawful excuse.

(2) A person claiming goods covered by a document of title must satisfy the bailee's lien where the bailee so requests or where the bailee is prohibited by law from delivering the goods until the charges are paid.

(3) Unless the person claiming is one against whom the document confers no right under Sec. 7-503(1), he must surrender for cancellation or notation of partial deliveries any outstanding negotiable document covering the goods, and the bailee must cancel the document or conspicuously note the partial delivery thereon or be liable to any person to whom the document is duly negotiated.

(4) "Person entitled under the document" means holder in the case of a negotiable document, or the person to whom delivery is to be made by the terms of or pursuant to written instructions under a non-negotiable document.

§ 7-404. No Liability for Good Faith Delivery Pursuant to Receipt or Bill

A bailee who in good faith including observance of reasonable commercial standards has received goods and delivered or otherwise disposed of them according to the terms of the document of title or pursuant to this Article is not liable therefor. This rule applies even though the person from whom he received the goods had no authority to procure the document or to dispose of the goods and even though the person to whom he delivered the goods had no authority to receive them.

PART 5. *Warehouse Receipts and Bills of Lading: Negotiation and Transfer*

§ 7-501. Form of Negotiation and Requirements of "Due Negotiation"

(1) A negotiable document of title running to the order of a named person is negotiated by his indorsement and delivery. After his indorsement in blank or to bearer any person can negotiate it by delivery alone.

(2) (a) A negotiable document of title is also negotiated by delivery alone when by its original terms it runs to bearer.

(b) When a document running to the order of a named person is delivered to him the effect is the same as if the document had been negotiated.

(3) Negotiation of a negotiable document of title after it has been indorsed to a specified person requires indorsement by the special indorsee as well as delivery.

(4) A negotiable document of title is "duly negotiated" when it is negotiated in the manner stated in this section to a holder who purchases it in good faith without notice of any defense against or claim to it on the part of any person and for value, unless it is established that the negotiation is not in the regular course of business or financing or involves receiving the document in settlement or payment of a money obligation.

(5) Indorsement of a non-negotiable document neither makes it negotiable nor adds to the transferee's rights.

(6) The naming in a negotiable bill of a person to be notified of the arrival of the goods does not limit the negotiability of the bill nor constitute notice to a purchaser thereof of any interest of such person in the goods.

§ 7-502. Rights Acquired by Due Negotiation

(1) Subject to the following section and to the provisions of Section 7-205 on fungible goods, a holder to whom a negotiable document of title has been duly negotiated acquires thereby:

(a) title to the document;

(b) title to the goods;

(c) all rights accruing under the law of agency or estoppel, including rights to goods delivered to the bailee after the document was issued; and

(d) the direct obligation of the issuer to hold or deliver the goods according to the terms of the document free of any defense or claim by him except those arising under the terms of the document or under this Article. In the case of a delivery order the bailee's obligation accrues only upon acceptance and the obligation acquired by the holder is that the issuer and any indorser will procure the acceptance of the bailee.

(2) Subject to the following section, title and rights so acquired are not defeated by any stoppage of the goods represented by the document or by surrender of such goods by the bailee, and are not impaired even though the negotiation or any prior negotiation constituted a breach of duty or even though any person has been deprived of possession of the document by misrepresentation, fraud, accident, mistake, duress, loss, theft or conversion, or even though a previous sale or other transfer of the goods or document has been made to a third person.

§ 7-503. Document of Title to Goods Defeated in Certain Cases

(1) A document of title confers no right in goods against a person who before issuance of the document had a legal interest or a perfected security interest in them and who neither

(a) delivered or entrusted them or any document of title covering them to the bailor or his nominee with actual or apparent authority to ship, store or sell or with power to obtain delivery under this Article (Section 7-403) or with power of disposition under this Act (Sections 2-403 and 9-307) or other statute or rule of law; nor

(b) acquiesced in the procurement by the bailor or his nominee of any document of title.

(2) Title to goods based upon an unaccepted delivery order is subject to the rights of anyone to whom a negotiable warehouse receipt or bill of lading covering the goods has been duly negotiated. Such a title may be defeated under the next section to the same extent as the rights of the issuer or a transferee from the issuer.

(3) Title to goods based upon a bill of lading issued to a freight forwarder is subject to the rights of anyone to whom a bill issued by the freight forwarder is duly negotiated; but delivery by the carrier in accordance

with Part 4 of this Article pursuant to its own bill of lading discharges the carrier's obligation to deliver.

§ 7-504. Rights Acquired in the Absence of Due Negotiation; Effect of Diversion; Seller's Stoppage of Delivery

(1) A transferee of a document, whether negotiable or nonnegotiable, to whom the document has been delivered but not duly negotiated, acquires the title and rights which his transferor had or had actual authority to convey.

(2) In the case of a non-negotiable document, until but not after the bailee receives notification of the transfer, the rights of the transferee may be defeated

(a) by those creditors of the transferor who could treat the sale as void under Section 2-402; or

(b) by a buyer from the transferor in ordinary course of business if the bailee has delivered the goods to the buyer or received notification of his rights; or

(c) as against the bailee by good faith dealings of the bailee with the transferor.

(3) A diversion or other change of shipping instructions by the consignor in a non-negotiable bill of lading which causes the bailee not to deliver to the consignee defeats the consignee's title to the goods if they have been delivered to a buyer in ordinary course of business and in any event defeats the consignee's rights against the bailee.

(4) Delivery pursuant to a non-negotiable document may be stopped by a seller under Section 2-705, and subject to the requirement of due notification there provided. A bailee honoring the seller's instructions is entitled to be indemnified by the seller against any resulting loss or expense.

§ 7-505. Indorser Not a Guarantor for Other Parties

The indorsement of a document of title issued by a bailee does not make the indorser liable for any default by the bailee or by previous indorsers.

§ 7-506. Delivery Without Indorsement: Right to Compel Indorsement

The transferee of a negotiable document of title has a specifically enforceable right to have his transferor supply any necessary indorsement but the transfer becomes a negotiation only as of the time the indorsement is supplied.

§ 7-507. Warranties on Negotiation or Transfer of Receipt or Bill

Where a person negotiates or transfers a document of title for value otherwise than a mere intermediary under the next following section, then unless otherwise agreed he warrants to his immediate purchaser only in addition to any warranty made in selling the goods

(a) that the document is genuine; and

(b) that he has no knowledge of any fact which would impair its validity or worth; and

(c) that his negotiation or transfer is rightful and fully effective with respect to the title to the document and the goods it represents.

§ 7-508. Warranties of Collecting Bank as to Documents

A collecting bank or other intermediary known to be entrusted with documents on behalf of another or with collection of a draft or other claim against delivery of documents warrants by such delivery of the documents only its own good faith and authority. This rule applies even though the intermediary has purchased or made advances against the claim or draft to be collected.

§ 7-509. Receipt or Bill: When Adequate Compliance With Commercial Contract

The question whether a document is adequate to fulfill the obligations of a contract for sale or the conditions of a credit is governed by the Articles on Sales (Article 2) and on Letters of Credit (Article 5).

PART 6. *Warehouse Receipts and Bills of Lading: Miscellaneous Provisions*

§ 7-601. Lost and Missing Documents

(1) If a document has been lost, stolen or destroyed, a court may order delivery of the goods or issuance of a substitute document and the bailee may without liability to any person comply with such order. If the document was negotiable the claimant must post security approved by the court to indemnify any person who may suffer loss as a result of non-surrender of the document. If the document was not negotiable, such security may be required at the discretion of the court.

The court may also in its discretion order payment of the bailee's reasonable costs and counsel fees.

(2) A bailee who without court order delivers goods to a person claiming under a missing negotiable document is liable to any person injured thereby, and if the delivery is not in good faith becomes liable for conversion. Delivery in good faith is not conversion if made in accordance with a filed classification or tariff or, where no classification or tariff is filed, if the claimant posts security with the bailee in an amount at least double the value of the goods at the time of posting to indemnify any person injured by the delivery who files a notice of claim within one year after the delivery.

§ 7-602. Attachment of Goods Covered by a Negotiable Document

Except where the document was originally issued upon delivery of the goods by a person who had no power to dispose of them, no lien attaches by virtue of any judicial process to goods in the possession of a bailee for which a negotiable document of title is outstanding unless the document be first surrendered to the bailee or its negotiation enjoined, and the bailee shall not be compelled to deliver the goods pursuant to process until the document is surrendered to him or impounded by the court. One who purchases the document for value without notice of the process or injunction takes free of the lien imposed by judicial process.

§ 7-603. Conflicting Claims; Interpleader

If more than one person claims title or possession of the goods, the bailee is excused from delivery until he has had a reasonable time to ascertain the validity of the adverse claims or to bring an action to compel all claimants to interplead and may compel such interpleader, either in defending an action for non-delivery of the goods, or by original action, whichever is appropriate.

ARTICLE 8. Investment Securities

PART 1. *Short Title and General Matters*

Section

PART 2. *Issue-Issuer*

PART 3. *Transfer*

PART 4. *Registration*

ARTICLE 8. Investment Securities

PART 1. *Short Title and General Matters*

§ 8-101. Short Title

This Article shall be known and may be cited as Uniform Commercial Code—Investment Securities.

§ 8-102. Definitions and Index of Definitions

(1) In this Article, unless the context otherwise requires:

(a) A "certificated security" is a share, participation, or other interest in property of or an enterprise of the issuer or an obligation of the issuer which is

(i) represented by an instrument issued in bearer or registered form;

(ii) of a type commonly dealt in on securities exchanges or markets or commonly recognized in any area in which it is issued or dealt in as a medium for investment; and

(iii) either one of a class or series or by its terms divisible into a class or series of shares, participations, interests, or obligations.

(b) An "uncertificated security" is a share, participation, or other interest in property or an enterprise of the issuer or an obligation of the issuer which is

(i) not represented by an instrument and the transfer of which is registered upon books maintained for that purpose by or on behalf of the issuer;

(ii) of a type commonly dealt in on securities exchanges or markets; and

(iii) either one of a class or series or by its terms divisible into a class or series of shares, participations, interests, or obligations.

(c) A "security" is either a certificated or an uncertificated security. If a security is certificated, the terms "security" and "certificated security" may mean either the intangible interest, the instrument representing that interest, or both, as the context requires. A writing that is a certificated security is governed by this Article and not by Article 3, even though it also meets the requirements of that Article. This Article does not apply to money. If a certificated security has been retained by or surrendered to the issuer or its transfer agent for reasons other than registration of transfer, other temporary purpose, payment, exchange, or acquisition by the issuer, that security shall be treated as an uncertificated security for purposes of this Article.

(d) A certificated security is in "registered form" if

(i) it specifies a person entitled to the security of the rights it represents; and

(ii) its transfer may be registered upon books maintained for that purpose by or on behalf of the issuer, or the security so states.

(e) A certificated security is in "bearer form" if it runs to bearer according to its terms and not by reason of any indorsement.

(2) A "subsequent purchaser" is a person who takes other than by original issue.

(3) A "clearing corporation" is a corporation registered as a "clearing agency" under the federal securities laws or a corporation:

(a) at least 90 percent of whose capital stock is held by or for one or more organizations, none of which, other than a national securities exchange or association, holds in excess of 20 percent of the capital stock of the corporation, and each of which is

(i) subject to supervision or regulation pursuant to

the provisions of federal or state banking laws or state insurance laws,

(ii) a broker or dealer or investment company registered under the federal securities laws, or

(iii) a national securities exchange or association registered under the federal securities laws; and

(b) any remaining capital stock of which is held by individuals who have purchased it at or prior to the time of their taking office as directors of the corporation and who have purchased only so much of the capital stock as is necessary to permit them to qualify as directors.

(4) A "custodian bank" is a bank or trust company that is supervised and examined by state or federal authority having supervision over banks and is acting as custodian for a clearing corporation.

(5) Other definitions applying to this Article or to specified Parts thereof and the sections in which they appear are:

"Adverse claim".	Section 8-302.
"Bona fide purchaser".	Section 8-302.
"Broker".	Section 8-303.
"Debtor".	Section 9-105.
"Financial intermediary".	Section 8-313.
"Guarantee of the signature".	Section 8-402.
"Initial transaction statement".	Section 8-408.
"Instruction".	Section 8-308.
"Intermediary bank".	Section 4-105.
"Issuer".	Section 8-201.
"Overissue".	Section 8-104.
"Secured Party".	Section 9-105.
"Security Agreement".	Section 9-105.

(6) In addition, Article 1 contains general definitions and principles of construction and interpretation applicable throughout this Article. Amended in 1962, 1973 and 1977.

§ 8-103. Issuer's Lien

A lien upon a security in favor of an issuer thereof is valid against a purchaser only if:

(a) the security is certificated and the right of the issuer to the lien is noted conspicuously thereon; or

(b) the security is uncertificated and a notation of the right of the issuer to the lien is contained in the initial transaction statement sent to the purchaser or, if his interest is transferred to him other than by registration of transfer, pledge, or release, the initial transaction statement sent to the registered owner or the registered pledgee. Amended in 1977.

§ 8-104. Effect of Overissue; "Overissue"

(1) The provisions of this Article which validate a security or compel its issue or reissue do not apply to the extent that validation, issue, or reissue would result in overissue; but if:

(a) an identical security which does not constitute an overissue is reasonably available for purchase, the person entitled to issue or validation may compel the issuer to purchase the security for him and either to deliver a certificated security or to register the transfer of an uncertificated security to him, against surrender of any certificated security he holds; or

(b) a security is not so available for purchase, the person entitled to issue or validation may recover from the issuer the price he or the last purchaser for value paid for it with interest from the date of his demand.

(2) "Overissue" means the issue of securities in excess of the amount the issuer has corporate power to issue. Amended in 1977.

§ 8-105. Certificated Securities Negotiable; Statements and Instructions Not Negotiable; Presumptions

(1) Certificated securities governed by this Article are negotiable instruments.

(2) Statements (Section 8-408), notices, or the like, sent by the issuer of uncertificated securities and instructions (Section 8-308) are neither negotiable instruments nor certificated securities.

(3) In any action on a security:

(a) unless specifically denied in the pleadings, each signature on a certificated security, in a necessary indorsement, on an initial transaction statement, or on an instruction, is admitted;

(b) if the effectiveness of a signature is put in issue, the burden of establishing it is on the party claiming under the signature, but the signature is presumed to be genuine or authorized;

(c) if signatures on a certificated security are admitted or established, production of the security entitles a holder to recover on it unless the defendant establishes a defense or a defect going to the validity of the security;

(d) if signatures on an initial transaction statement are admitted or established, the facts stated in the statement are presumed to be true as of the time of its issuance; and

(e) after it is shown that a defense or defect exists, the plaintiff has the burden of establishing that he or some person under whom he claims is a person against whom the defense or defect is ineffective (Section 8-202). Amended in 1977.

§ 8-106. Applicability

The law (including the conflict of laws rules) of the jurisdiction of organization of the issuer governs the validity of a security, the effectiveness of registration by the issuer, and the rights and duties of the issuer with respect to:

(a) registration of transfer of a certificated security;

(b) registration of transfer, pledge, or release of an uncertificated security; and

(c) sending of statements of uncertificated securities. Amended in 1977.

§ 8-107. Securities Transferable; Action for Price

(1) Unless otherwise agreed and subject to any applicable law or regulation respecting short sales, a person obligated to transfer securities may transfer any certificated security of the specified issue in bearer form or registered in the name of the transferee, or indorsed to him or in blank, or he may transfer an equivalent uncertified security to the transferee or a person designated by the transferee.

(2) If the buyer fails to pay the price as it comes due under a contract of sale, the seller may recover the price of:

(a) certificated securities accepted by the buyer;

(b) uncertificated securites that have been transferred to the buyer or a person designated by the buyer; and

(c) other securities if efforts at their resale would be unduly burdensome or if there is no readily available market for their resale. Amended in 1977.

§ 8-108. Registration of Pledge and Release of Uncertificated Securities

A security interest in an uncertificated security may be evidenced by the registration of pledge to the secured party or a person designated by him. There can be no more than one registered pledge of an uncertificated security at any time. The registered owner of an uncertificated security is the person in whose name the security is registered, even if the security is subject to a registered pledge. The rights of a registered pledgee of an uncertificated security under this Article are terminated by the registration of release. Added in 1977.

PART 2. *Issue-Issuer*

§ 8-201. "Issuer"

(1) With respect to obligations on or defenses to a security, "issuer" includes a person who:

(a) places or authorizes the placing of his name on a certificated security (otherwise than as authenticating trustee, registrar, transfer agent, or the like) to evidence that it represents a share, participation, or other interest in his property or in an enterprise, or to evidence his duty to perform an obligation represented by the certificated security;

(b) creates shares, participations, or other interests in his property or in an enterprise or undertakes obligations, which shares, participations, interests, or obligations are uncertificated securities;

(c) directly or indirectly creates fractional interests in his rights or property, which fractional interests are represented by certificated securities; or

(d) becomes responsible for or in place of any other person described as an issuer in this section.

(2) With respect to obligations on or defenses to a security, a guarantor is an issuer to the extent of his guaranty, whether or not his obligation is noted on a certificated security or on statements of uncertificated securities sent pursuant to Section 8-408.

(3) With respect to registration of transfer, pledge, or release (Part 4 of this Article), "issuer" means a person on whose behalf transfer books are maintained. Amended in 1977.

§ 8-202. Issuer's Responsibility and Defenses; Notice of Defect or Defense

(1) Even against a purchaser for value and without notice, the terms of a security include:

(a) if the security is certificated, those stated on the security;

(b) if the security is uncertificated, those contained in the initial transaction statement sent to such purchaser or, if his interest is transferred to him other than by registration of transfer, pledge, or release, the initial transaction statement sent to the registered owner or registered pledgee; and

(c) those made part of the security by reference, on the certificated security or in the initial transaction statement, to another instrument, indenture, or document or to a constitution, statute, ordinance, rule, regulation, order or the like, to the extent that the terms referred to do not conflict with the terms stated on the certificated security or contained in the statement. A reference under this paragraph does not of itself charge a purchaser for value with notice of a defect going to the validity of the security, even though the certificated security or statement expressly states that a person accepting it admits notice.

(2) A certificated security in the hands of a purchaser for value or an uncertificated security as to which an initial transaction statement has been sent to a purchaser for value, other than a security issued by a government or governmental agency or unit, even though issued with a defect going to its validity, is valid with respect to the purchaser if he is without notice of the particular defect unless the defect involves a violation of constitutional provisions, in which case the security is valid with respect to a subsequent purchaser for value and without notice of the defect. This subsection applies to an issuer that is a government or governmental agency or unit only if either there has been substantial compliance with the legal requirements governing the issue or the issuer has received a substantial consideration for the issue as a whole or for the particular security and a stated purpose of the issue is one for which the issuer has power to borrow money or issue the security.

(3) Except as provided in the case of certain unauthorized signatures (Section 8-205), lack of genuineness of a certificated security or an initial transaction statement is a complete defense, even against a purchaser for value and without notice.

(4) All other defenses of the issuer of a certificated or uncertificated security, including nondelivery and conditional delivery of a certificated security, are ineffective against a purchaser for value who has taken without notice of the particular defense.

(5) Nothing in this section shall be construed to affect the right of a party to a "when, as and if issued" or a "when distributed" contract to cancel the contract in the event of a material change in the character of the security that is the subject of the contract or in the plan or arrangement pursuant to which the security is to be issued or distributed. Amended in 1977.

§ 8-203. Staleness as Notice of Defects or Defenses

(1) After an act or event creating a right to immediate performance of the principal obligation represented by a certificated security or that sets a date on or after which the security is to be presented or surrendered for redemption or exchange, a purchaser is charged with notice of any defect in its issue or defense of the issuer if:

(a) the act or event is one requiring the payment of money, the delivery of certificated securities, the registration of transfer of uncertificated securities, or any of these on presentation or surrender of the certificated security, the funds or securities are available on the date set for payment or exchange, and he takes the security more than one year after that date; and

(b) the act or event is not covered by paragraph (a) and he takes the security more than 2 years after the date set for surrender or presentation or the date on which performance became due.

(2) A call that has been revoked is not within subsection (1). Amended in 1977.

§ 8-204. Effect of Issuer's Restrictions on Transfer

A restriction on transfer of a security imposed by the issuer, even if otherwise lawful, is ineffective against any person without actual knowledge of it unless:

(a) the security is certificated and the restriction is noted conspicuously thereon; or

(b) the security is uncertificated and a notation of the restriction is contained in the initial transaction statement sent to the person or, if his interest is transferred to him other than by registration of transfer, pledge, or release, the initial transaction statement sent to the registered owner or the registered pledgee. Amended in 1977.

§ 8-205. Effect of Unauthorized Signature on Certificated Security or Initial Transaction Statement

An unauthorized signature placed on a certificated security prior to or in the course of issue or placed on an initial transaction statement is ineffective, but the signature is effective in favor of a purchaser for value of the certified security or a purchaser for value of an uncertificated security to whom the initial transaction statement has been sent, if the purchaser is without notice of the lack of authority and the signing has been done by:

(a) an authenticating trustee, registrar, transfer agent, or other person entrusted by the issuer with the signing of the security, of similar securities, or of initial transaction statements or the immediate preparation for signing of any of them; or

(b) an employee of the issuer, or of any of the foregoing, entrusted with responsible handling of the security or initial transaction statement. Amended in 1977.

§ 8-206. Completion or Alteration of Certificated Security or Initial Transaction Statement

(1) If a certificated security contains the signatures necessary to its issue or transfer but is incomplete in any other respect:

(a) any person may complete it by filling in the blanks as authorized; and

(b) even though the blanks are incorrectly filled in, the security as completed is enforceable by a purchaser who took it for value and without notice of the incorrectness.

(2) A complete certificated security that has been improperly altered, even though fraudulently, remains enforceable, but only according to its original terms.

(3) If an initial transaction statement contains the signatures necessary to its validity, but is incomplete in any other respect:

(a) any person may complete it by filling in the blanks as authorized; and

(b) even though the blanks are incorrectly filled in, the statement as completed is effective in favor of the person to whom it is sent if he purchased the security referred to therein for value and without notice of the incorrectness.

(4) A complete initial transaction statement that has been improperly altered, even though fraudulently, is effective in favor of a purchaser to whom it has been sent, but only according to its original terms. Amended in 1977.

§ 8-207. Rights and Duties of Issuer With Respect to Registered Owners and Registered Pledgees

(1) Prior to due presentment for registration of transfer of a certificated security in registered form, the issuer or indenture trustee may treat the registered owner as the person exclusively entitled to vote, to receive notifications, and otherwise to exercise all the rights and powers of an owner.

(2) Subject to the provisions of subsections (3), (4), and (6), the issuer or indenture trustee may treat the registered owner of an uncertificated security as the person exclusively entitled to vote, to receive notifications, and otherwise to exercise all the rights and powers of an owner.

(3) The registered owner of an uncertificated security that is subject to a registered pledge is not entitled to registration of transfer prior to the due presentment to the issuer of a release instruction. The exercise of conversion rights with respect to a convertible uncertificated security is a transfer within the meaning of this section.

(4) Upon due presentment of a transfer instruction from the registered pledgee of an uncertificated security, the issuer shall:

(a) register the transfer of the security to the new owner free of pledge, if the instruction specifies a new owner (who may be the registered pledgee) and does not specify a pledgee;

(b) register the transfer of the security to the new owner subject to the interest of the existing pledgee, if the instruction specifies a new owner and the existing pledgee; or

(c) register the release of the security from the existing pledge and register the pledge of the security to the other pledgee, if the instruction specifies the existing owner and another pledgee.

(5) Continuity of perfection of a security interest is not broken by registration of transfer under subsection (4)(b) or by registration of release and pledge under subsection (4)(c), if the security interest is assigned.

(6) If an uncertificated security is subject to a registered pledge:

(a) any uncertificated securities issued in exchange for or distributed with respect to the pledged security shall be registered subject to the pledge;

(b) any certificated securities issued in exchange for or distributed with respect to the pledged security shall be delivered to the registered pledgee; and

(c) any money paid in exchange for or in redemption of part or all of the security shall be paid to the registered pledgee.

(7) Nothing in this Article shall be construed to affect the liability of the registered owner of a security for calls, assessments, or the like. Amended in 1977.

§ 8-208. Effect of Signature of Authenticating Trustee, Registrar, or Transfer Agent

(1) A person placing his signature upon a certificated security or an initial transaction statement as authenticating trustee, registrar, transfer agent, or the like, warrants to a purchaser for value of the certificated security or a purchaser for value of an uncertificated security to whom the initial transaction statement has been sent, if the purchaser is without notice of the particular defect, that:

(a) the certificated security or initial transaction statement is genuine;

(b) his own participation in the issue or registration of the transfer, pledge, or release of the security is within his capacity and within the scope of the authority received by him from the issuer; and

(c) he has reasonable grounds to believe the security is in the form and within the amount the issuer is authorized to issue.

(2) Unless otherwise agreed, a person by so placing his signature does not assume responsibility for the validity of the security in other respects. Amended in 1962 and 1977.

PART 3. Transfer

§ 8-301. Rights Acquired by Purchaser

(1) Upon transfer of a security to a purchaser (Section 8-313), the purchaser acquires the rights in the security which his transferor had or had actual authority to convey unless the purchaser's rights are limited by Section 8-302(4).

(2) A transferee of a limited interest acquires rights only to the extent of the interest transferred. The creation or release of a security interest in a security is the transfer of a limited interest in that security. Amended in 1977.

§ 8-302. "Bona Fide Purchaser"; "Adverse Claim"; Title Acquired by Bona Fide Purchaser

(1) A "bona fide purchaser" is a purchaser for value in good faith and without notice of any adverse claim:

(a) who takes delivery of a certificated security in bearer form or in registered form, issued or indorsed to him or in blank;

(b) to whom the transfer, pledge, or release of an uncertificated security is registered on the books of the issuer; or

(c) to whom a security is transferred under the provisions of paragraph (c), (d)(i), or (g) of Section 8-313(1).

(2) "Adverse claim" includes a claim that a transfer was or would be wrongful or that a particular adverse person is the owner of or has an interest in the security.

(3) A bona fide purchaser in addition to acquiring the rights of a purchaser (Section 8-301) also acquires his interest in the security free of any adverse claim.

(4) Notwithstanding Section 8-301(1), the transferee of a particular certificated security who has been a party to any fraud or illegality affecting the security, or who as a prior holder of that certificated security had notice of an adverse claim, cannot improve his position by taking from a bona fide purchaser. Amended in 1977.

§ 8-303. "Broker"

"Broker" means a person engaged for all or part of his time in the business of buying and selling securities, who in the transaction concerned acts for, buys a security from, or sells a security to, a customer. Nothing in this Article determines the capacity in which a person acts for purposes of any other statute or rule to which the person is subject.

§ 8-304. Notice to Purchaser of Adverse Claims

(1) A purchaser (including a broker for the seller or buyer, but excluding an intermediary bank) of a certifi-

cated security is charged with notice of adverse claims if:

(a) the security, whether in bearer or registered form, has been indorsed "for collection" or "for surrender" or for some other purpose not involving transfer; or

(b) the security is in bearer form and has on it an unambiguous statement that it is the property of a person other than the transferor. The mere writing of a name on a security is not such a statement.

(2) A purchaser (including a broker for the seller or buyer, but excluding an intermediary bank) to whom the transfer, pledge, or release of an uncertificated security is registered is charged with notice of adverse claims as to which the issuer has a duty under Section 8-403(4) at the time of registration and which are noted in the initial transaction statement sent to the purchaser or, if his interest is transferred to him other than by registration of transfer, pledge, or release, the initial transaction statement sent to the registered owner or the registered pledgee.

(3) The fact that the purchaser (including a broker for the seller or buyer) of a certificated or uncertificated security has notice that the security is held for a third person or is registered in the name of or indorsed by a fiduciary does not create a duty of inquiry into the rightfulness of the transfer or constitute constructive notice of adverse claims. However, if the purchaser (excluding an intermediary bank) has knowledge that the proceeds are being used or that the transaction is for the individual benefit of the fiduciary or otherwise in breach of duty, the purchaser is charged with notice of adverse claims. Amended in 1977.

§ 8-305. Staleness as Notice of Adverse Claims

An act or event that creates a right to immediate performance of the principal obligation represented by a certificated security or sets a date on or after which a certificated security is to be presented or surrendered for redemption or exchange does not itself constitute any notice of adverse claims except in the case of a transfer:

(a) after one year from any date set for presentment or surrender for redemption or exchange; or

(b) after 6 months from any date set for payment of money against presentation or surrender of the security

if funds are available for payment on that date. Amended in 1977.

§ 8-306. Warranties on Presentment and Transfer of Certificated Securites; Warranties of Originators of Instructions

(1) A person who presents a certificated security for registration of transfer or for payment or exchange warrants to the issuer that he is entitled to the registration, payment, or exchange. But, a purchaser for value and without notice of adverse claims who receives a new, reissued, or re-registered certificated security on registration of transfer or receives an initial transaction statement confirming the registration of transfer of an equivalent uncertificated security to him warrants only that he has no knowledge of any unauthorized signature (Section 8-311) in a necessary indorsement.

(2) A person by transferring a certificated security to a purchaser for value warrants only that:

(a) his transfer is effective and rightful;

(b) the security is genuine and has not been materially altered; and

(c) he knows of no fact which might impair the validity of the security.

(3) If a certificated security is delivered by an intermediary known to be entrusted with delivery of the security on behalf of another or with collection of a draft or other claim against delivery, the intermediary by delivery warrants only his own good faith and authority, even though he has purchased or made advances against the claim to be collected against the delivery.

(4) A pledgee or other holder for security who redelivers a certificated security received, or after payment and on order of the debtor delivers that security to a third person, makes only the warranties of an intermediary under subsection (3).

(5) A person who originates an instruction warrants to the issuer that:

(a) he is an appropriate person to originate the instruction; and

(b) at the time the instruction is presented to the issuer he will be entitled to the registration of transfer, pledge, or release.

(6) A person who originates an instruction warrants to any person specially guaranteeing his signature (subsection 8-312 (3)) that:

(a) he is an appropriate person to originate the instruction; and

(b) at the time the instruction is presented to the issuer

(i) he will be entitled to the registration of transfer, pledge, or release; and

(ii) the transfer, pledge, or release requested in the instruction will be registered by the issuer free from all liens, security interests, restrictions, and claims other than those specified in the instruction.

(7) A person who originates an instruction warrants to a purchaser for value and to any person guaranteeing the instruction (Section 8-312(6)) that:

(a) he is an appropriate person to originate the instruction;

(b) the uncertificated security referred to therein is valid; and

(c) at the time the instruction is presented to the issuer

(i) the transferor will be entitled to the registration of transfer, pledge, or release;

(ii) the transfer, pledge, or release requested in the instruction will be registered by the issuer free from all liens, security interests, restrictions, and claims other than those specified in the instruction; and

(iii) the requested transfer, pledge, or release will be rightful.

(8) If a secured party is the registered pledgee or the registered owner of an uncertificated security, a person who originates an instruction of release or transfer to the debtor or, after payment and on order of the debtor, a transfer instruction to a third person, warrants to the debtor or the third person only that he is an appropriate person to originate the instruction and, at the time the instruction is presented to the issuer, the transferor will be entitled to the registration of release or transfer. If a transfer instruction to a third person who is a purchaser for value is originated on order of the debtor, the debtor makes to the purchaser the warranties of paragraphs (b), (c)(ii) and (c)(iii) of subsection (7).

(9) A person who transfers an uncertificated security to a purchaser for value and does not originate an instruction in connection with the transfer warrants only that:

(a) his transfer is effective and rightful; and

(b) the uncertificated security is valid.

(10) A broker gives to his customer and to the issuer and a purchaser the applicable warranties provided in this section and has the rights and privileges of a purchaser under this section. The warranties of and in favor of the broker, acting as an agent are in addition to applicable warranties given by and in favor of his customer. Amended in 1962 and 1977.

§ 8-307. Effect of Delivery Without Indorsement; Right to Compel Indorsement

If a certificated security in registered form has been delivered to a purchaser without a necessary indorsement he may become a bona fide purchaser only as of the time the indorsement is supplied; but against the transferor, the transfer is complete upon delivery and the purchaser has a specifically enforceable right to have any necessary indorsement supplied. Amended in 1977.

§ 8-308. Indorsements; Instructions

(1) An indorsement of a certificated security in registered form is made when an appropriate person signs on it or on a separate document an assignment or transfer of the security or a power to assign or transfer it or his signature is written without more upon the back of the security.

(2) An indorsement may be in blank or special. An indorsement in blank includes an indorsement to bearer. A special indorsement specifies to whom the security is to be transferred, or who has power to transfer it. A holder may convert a blank indorsement into a special indorsement.

(3) An indorsement purporting to be only a part of a certificated security representing units intended by the issuer to be separately transferable is effective to the extent of the indorsement.

(4) An "instruction" is an order to the issuer of an uncertificated security requesting that the transfer, pledge, or release from pledge of the uncertificated security specified therein be registered.

(5) An instruction originated by an appropriate person is:

(a) a writing signed by an appropriate person; or

(b) a communication to the issuer in any form agreed upon in a writing signed by the issuer and an appropriate person.

If an instruction has been originated by an appropriate person but is incomplete in any other respect, any person may complete it as authorized and the issuer may rely on it as completed even though it has been completed incorrectly.

(6) "An appropriate person" in subsection (1) means the person specified by the certificated security or by special indorsement to be entitled to the security.

(7) "An appropriate person" in subsection (5) means:

(a) for an instruction to transfer or pledge an uncertificated security which is then not subject to a registered pledge, the registered owner; or

(b) for an instruction to transfer or release an uncertificated security which is then subject to a registered pledge, the registered pledgee.

(8) In addition to the persons designated in subsections (6) and (7), "an appropriate person" in subsections (1) and (5) includes:

(a) if the person designated is described as a fiduciary but is no longer serving in the described capacity, either that person or his successor;

(b) if the persons designated are described as more than one person as fiduciaries and one or more are no longer serving in the described capacity, the remaining fiduciary or fiduciaries, whether or not a successor has been appointed or qualified;

(c) if the person designated is an individual and is without capacity to act by virtue of death, incompetence, infancy, or otherwise, his executor, administrator, guardian, or like fiduciary;

(d) if the persons designated are described as more than one person as tenants by the entirety or with right of survivorship and by reason of death all cannot sign, the survivor or survivors;

(e) a person having power to sign under applicable law or controlling instrument; and

(f) to the extent that the person designated or any of the foregoing persons may act through an agent, his authorized agent.

(9) Unless otherwise agreed, the indorser of a certificated security by his indorsement or the originator of an instruction by his origination assumes no obligation that the security will be honored by the issuer but only the obligations provided in Section 8-306.

(10) Whether the person signing is appropriate is determined as of the date of signing and an indorsement made by or an instruction originated by him does not become unauthorized for the purposes of this Article by virtue of any subsequent change of circumstances.

(11) Failure of a fiduciary to comply with a controlling instrument or with the law of the state having jurisdiction of the fiduciary to obtain court approval of the transfer, pledge, or release, does not render his indorsement or an instruction originated by him unauthorized for the purposes of this Article. Amended in 1962 and 1977.

§ 8-309. Effect of Indorsement Without Delivery

An indorsement of a certificated security, whether special or in blank, does not constitute a transfer until delivery of the certificated security on which it appears or, if the indorsement is on a separate document, until delivery of both the document and the certificated security. Amended in 1977.

§ 8-310. Indorsement of Certificated Security in Bearer Form

An indorsement of a certificated security in bearer form may give notice of adverse claims (Section 8-304) but does not otherwise affect any right to registration the holder possesses. Amended in 1977.

§ 8-311. Effect of Unauthorized Indorsement or Instruction

Unless the owner or pledgee has ratified an unauthorized indorsement or instruction or is otherwise precluded from asserting its ineffectiveness:

(a) he may assert its ineffectiveness against the issuer or any purchaser, other than a purchaser for value and without notice of adverse claims, who has in good faith received a new, reissued, or re-registered certificated security on registration of transfer or received an initial transaction statement confirming the registration of transfer, pledge, or release of an equivalent uncertificated security to him; and

(b) an issuer who registers the transfer of a certificated security upon the unauthorized indorsement or who registers the transfer, pledge, or release of an uncertificated security upon the unauthorized instruction is subject to liability for improper registration (Section 8-404). Amended in 1977.

§ 8-312. Effect of Guaranteeing Signature, Indorsement or Instruction

(1) Any person guaranteeing a signature of an indorser of a certificated security warrants that at the time of signing:

(a) the signature was genuine;

(b) the signer was an appropriate person to indorse (Section 8-308); and

(c) the signer had legal capacity to sign.

(2) Any person guaranteeing a signature of the originator of an instruction warrants that at the time of signing:

(a) the signature was genuine;

(b) the signer was an appropriate person to originate the instruction (Section 8-308) if the person specified in the instruction as the registered owner or registered pledgee of the uncertificated security was, in fact, the registered owner or registered pledgee of the security, as to which fact the signature guarantor makes no warranty;

(c) the signer had legal capacity to sign; and

(d) the taxpayer identification number, if any, appearing on the instruction as that of the registered owner or registered pledgee was the taxpayer identification number of the signer or of the owner or pledgee for whom the signer was acting.

(3) Any person specially guaranteeing the signature of the originator of an instruction makes not only the warranties of a signature guarantor (subsection (2)) but also warrants that at the time the instruction is presented to the issuer:

(a) the person specified in the instruction as the registered owner or registered pledgee of the uncertificated security will be the registered owner or registered pledgee; and

(b) the transfer, pledge, or release of the uncertificated security requested in the instruction will be registered by the issuer free from all liens, security interests, restrictions, and claims other than those specified in the instruction.

(4) The guarantor under subsections (1) and (2) or the special guarantor under subsection (3) does not otherwise warrant the rightfulness of the particular transfer, pledge, or release.

(5) Any person guaranteeing an indorsement of a certificated security makes not only the warranties of a signature guarantor under subsection (1) but also warrants the rightfulness of the particular transfer in all respects.

(6) Any person guaranteeing an instruction requesting the transfer, pledge, or release of an uncertificated security makes not only the warranties of a special signature guarantor under subsection (3) but also warrants the rightfulness of the particular transfer, pledge, or release in all respects.

(7) No issuer may require a special guarantee of signature (subsection (3)), a guarantee of indorsement (subsection (5)), or a guarantee of instruction (subsection (6)) as a condition to registration to transfer, pledge, or release.

(8) The foregoing warranties are made to any person taking or dealing with the security in reliance on the guarantee, and the guarantor is liable to the person for any loss resulting from breach of the warranties. Amended in 1977.

§ 8-313. When Transfer to Purchaser Occurs; Financial Intermediary as Bona Fide Purchaser; "Financial Intermediary"

(1) Transfer of a security or a limited interest (including a security interest) therein to a purchaser occurs only:

(a) at the time he or a person designated by him acquires possession of a certificated security;

(b) at the time the transfer, pledge, or release of an uncertificated security is registered to him or a person designated by him;

(c) at the time his financial intermediary acquires possession of a certificated security specially indorsed to or issued in the name of the purchaser;

(d) at the time a financial intermediary, not a clearing corporation, sends him confirmation of the purchase and also by book entry or otherwise identifies as belonging to the purchaser

(i) a specific certificated security in the financial intermediary's possession;

(ii) a quantity of securities that constitute or are part of a fungible bulk of certificated securities in the financial intermediary's possession or of uncertificatd securities registered in the name of the financial intermediary; or

(iii) a quantity of securities that constitute or are part of a fungible bulk of securities shown on the account of the financial intermediary on the books of another financial intermediary;

(e) with respect to an identified certificated security to be delivered while still in the possession of a third person, not a financial intermediary, at the time that person acknowledges that he holds for the purchaser;

(f) with respect to a specific uncertificated security the pledge or transfer of which has been registered to a third person, not a financial intermediary, at the time that person acknowledges that he holds for the purchaser;

(g) at the time appropriate entries to the account of the purchaser or a person designated by him on the books of a clearing corporation are made under Section 8-320;

(h) with respect to the transfer of a security interest where the debtor has signed a security agreement containing a description of the security, at the time a written notification, which, in the case of the creation of the security interest, is signed by the debtor (which may be a copy of the security agreement) or which, in the case of the release or assignment of the security interest created pursuant to this paragraph, is signed by the secured party, is received by

(i) a financial intermediary on whose books the interest of the transferor in the security appears;

(ii) a third person, not a financial intermediary, in possession of the security, if it is certificated;

(iii) a third person, not a financial intermediary, who is the registered owner of the security, if it is uncertificated and not subject to a registered pledge; or

(iv) a third person, not a financial intermediary, who is the registered pledgee of the security, if it is uncertificated and subject to a registered pledge;

(i) with respect to the transfer of a security interest where the transferor has signed a security agreement containing a description of the security, at the time new value is given by the secured party; or

(j) with respect to the transfer of a security interest where the secured party is a financial intermediary and the security has already been transferred to the financial intermediary under paragraphs (a), (b), (c), (d), or (g), at the time the transferor has signed a security agreement containing a description of the security and value is given by the secured party.

(2) The purchaser is the owner of a security held for him by a financial intermediary, but cannot be a bona fide purchaser of a security so held except in the circumstances specified in paragraphs (c), (d) (i), and (g) of subsection (1). If a security so held is part of a fungible bulk, as in the circumstances specified in paragraphs (d) (ii) and (d) (iii) of subsection (1), the purchaser is the owner of a proportionate property interest in the fungible bulk.

(3) Notice of an adverse claim received by the financial intermediary or by the purchaser after the financial intermediary takes delivery of a certificated security as a holder for value or after the transfer, pledge, or release of an uncertificated security has been registered free of the claim to a financial intermediary who has given value is not effective either as to the financial intermediary or as to the purchaser. However, as between the financial intermediary and the purchaser the purchaser may demand transfer of an equivalent security as to which no notice of adverse claim has been received.

(4) A "financial intermediary" is a bank, broker, clearing corporation, or other person (or the nominee of any of them) which in the ordinary course of its business maintains security accounts for its customers and is acting in that capacity. A financial intermediary may have a security interest in securities held in account for its customer. Amended in 1962 and 1977.

§ 8-314. Duty to Transfer, When Completed

(1) Unless otherwise agreed, if a sale of a security is made on an exchange or otherwise through brokers:

(a) the selling customer fulfills his duty to transfer at the time he:

(i) places a certificated security in the possession of the selling broker or a person designated by the broker;

(ii) causes an uncertificated security to be registered in the name of the selling broker or a person designated by the broker;

(iii) if requested, causes an acknowledgment to be made to the selling broker that a certificated or uncertificated security is held for the broker; or

(iv) places in the possession of the selling broker or of a person designated by the broker a transfer instruction for an uncertificated security, providing the issuer does not refuse to register the requested transfer if the instruction is presented to the issuer for registration within 30 days thereafter; and

(b) the selling broker, including a correspondent broker acting for a selling customer, fulfills his duty to transfer at the time he:

(i) places a certificated security in the possession of the buying broker or a person designated by the buying broker;

(ii) causes an uncertificated security to be registered in the name of the buying broker or a person designated by the buying broker;

(iii) places in the possession of the buying broker or a person designated by the buying broker a transfer instruction for an uncertificated security, providing the issuer does not refuse to register the requested transfer if the instruction is presented to the issuer for registration within 30 days thereafter; or

(iv) effects clearance of the sale in accordance with the rules of the exchange on which the transaction took place.

(2) Except as provided in this section or unless otherwise agreed, a transferor's duty to transfer a security under a contract of purchase is not fulfilled until he:

(a) places a certificated security in form to be negotiated by the purchaser in the possession of the purchaser or of a person designated by the purchaser;

(b) causes an uncertificated security to be registered in the name of the purchaser or a person designated by the purchaser; or

(c) if the purchaser requests, causes an acknowledgment to be made to the purchaser that a certificated or uncertificated security is held for the purchaser.

(3) Unless made on an exchange, a sale to a broker purchasing for his own account is within subsection (2) and not within subsection (1). Amended in 1977.

§ 8-315. Action Against Transferee Based Upon Wrongful Transfer

(1) Any person against whom the transfer of a security is wrongful for any reason, including his incapacity, as against anyone except a bona fide purchaser, may:

(a) reclaim possession of the certificated security wrongfully transferred;

(b) obtain possession of any new certificated security representing all or part of the same rights;

(c) compel the origination of an instruction to transfer to him or a person designated by him an uncertificated security constituting all or part of the same rights; or

(d) have damages.

(2) If the transfer is wrongful because of an unauthorized indorsement of a certificated security, the owner may also reclaim or obtain possession of the security or a new certificated security, even from a bona fide purchaser, if the ineffectiveness of the purported indorsement can be asserted against him under the provisions of this Article on unauthorized indorsements (Section 8-311).

(3) The right to obtain or reclaim possession of a certificated security or to compel the origination of a transfer instruction may be specifically enforced and the transfer of a certificated or uncertificated security enjoined and a certificated security impounded pending the litigation. Amended in 1977.

§ 8-316. Purchaser's Right to Requisites for Registration of Transfer, Pledge, or Release on Books

Unless otherwise agreed, the transferor of a certificated security or the transferor, pledgor, or pledgee of an uncertificated security on due demand must supply his purchaser with any proof of his authority to transfer, pledge, or release or with any other requisite necessary to obtain registration of the transfer, pledge, or release of the security; but if the transfer, pledge or release is not for value, a transferor, pledgor, or pledgee need not do so unless the purchaser furnishes the necessary expenses. Failure within a reasonable time to comply with a demand made gives the purchaser the right to reject or rescind the transfer, pledge, or release. Amended in 1977.

§ 8-317. Creditor's Rights

(1) Subject to the exceptions in subsections (3) and (4), no attachment or levy upon a certificated security or any share or other interest represented thereby which is outstanding is valid until the security is actually seized by the officer making the attachment or levy, but a certificated security which has been surrendered to the issuer may be reached by a creditor by legal process at the issuer's chief executive office in the United States.

(2) An uncertificated security registered in the name of the debtor may not be reached by a creditor except by legal process at the issuer's chief executive office in the United States.

(3) The interest of a debtor in a certificated security that is in the possession of a secured party not a financial intermediary or in an uncertificated security registered in the name of a secured party not a financial intermediary (or in the name of a nominee of the secured party) may be reached by a creditor by legal process upon the secured party.

(4) The interest of a debtor in a certificated security that is in the possession of or registered in the name of a financial intermediary or in an uncertificated security registered in the name of a financial intermediary may be reached by a creditor by legal process upon the financial intermediary on whose books the interest of the debtor appears.

(5) Unless otherwise provided by law, a creditor's lien upon the interest of a debtor in a security obtained pursuant to subsection (3) or (4) is not a restraint on the transfer of the security, free of the lien, to a third

party for new value; but in the event of a tranfer, the lien applies to the proceeds of the transfer in the hands of the secured party or financial intermediary, subject to any claims having priority.

(6) A creditor whose debtor is the owner of a security is entitled to aid from courts of appropriate jurisdiction, by injunction or otherwise, in reaching the security or in satisfying the claim by means allowed at law or in equity in regard to property that cannot readily be reached by ordinary legal process. Amended in 1977.

§ 8-318. No Conversion by Good Faith Conduct

An agent or bailee who in good faith (including observance of reasonable commercial standards if he is in the business of buying, selling, or otherwise dealing with securities) has received certificated securities and sold, pledged, or delivered them or has sold or caused the transfer or pledge of uncertificated securities over which he had control according to the instructions of his principal, is not liable for conversion or for participation in breach of fiduciary duty although the principal had no right so to deal with the securities. Amended in 1977.

§ 8-319. Statute of Frauds

A contract for the sale of securities is not enforceable by way of action or defense unless:

(a) there is some writing signed by the party against whom enforcement is sought or by his authorized agent or broker, sufficient to indicate that a contract has been made for sale of a stated quantity of described securities at a defined or stated price;

(b) delivery of a certificated security or transfer of an uncertificated security has been registered and the transferee has failed to send written objection to the issuer within 10 days after receipt of the initial transaction statement confirming the registration, or payment has been made, but the contract is enforceable under this provision only to the extent of the delivery, registration, or payment;

(c) within a reasonable time a writing in confirmation of the sale or purchase and sufficient against the sender under paragraph (a) has been received by the party against whom enforcement is sought and he has failed to send written objection to its contents within 10 days after its receipt; or

(d) the party against whom enforcement is sought admits in his pleading, testimony, or otherwise in court that a contract was made for the sale of a stated quantity of described securities at a defined or stated price. Amended in 1977.

§ 8-320. Transfer or Pledge Within Central Depository System

(1) In addition to other methods, a transfer, pledge, or release of a security or any interest therein may be effected by the making of appropriate entries on the books of a clearing corporation reducing the account of the transferor, pledgor, or pledgee and increasing the account of the transferee, pledgee, or pledgor by the amount of the obligation of the number of shares or rights transferred, pledged, or released, if the security is shown on the account of a transferor, pledgor, or pledgee on the books of the clearing corporation; is subject to the control of the clearing corporation; and

(a) if certificated,

(i) is in the custody of the clearing corporation, another clearing corporation, a custodian bank, or a nominee of any of them; and

(ii) is in bearer form or indorsed in blank by an appropriate person or registered in the name of the clearing corporation, a custodian bank, or a nominee of any of them; or

(b) if uncertificated, is registered in the name of the clearing corporation, another clearing corporation, a custodian bank, or a nominee of any of them.

(2) Under this section entries may be made with respect to like securities or interests therein as a part of a fungible bulk and may refer merely to a quantity of a particular security without reference to the name of the registered owner, certificate or bond number, or the like, and, in appropriate cases, may be on a net basis taking into account other tranfers, pledges, or releases of the same security.

(3) A transfer under this section is effective (Section 8-313) and the purchaser acquires the rights of the transferor (Section 8-301). A pledge or release under this section is the transfer of a limited interest. If a pledge or the creation of a security interest is intended, the security interest is perfected at the time when both value is given by the pledgee and the appropriate entries are made (Section 8-321). A transferee or pledgee under this section may be a bona fide purchaser (Section 8-302).

(4) A transfer or pledge under this section is not a registration of transfer under Part 4.

(5) That entries made on the books of the clearing corporation as provided in subsection (1) are not appropriate does not affect the validity or effect of the entries or the liabilities or obligations of the clearing corporation to any person adversely affected thereby. Added in 1962; amended in 1977.

§ 8-321. Enforceability, Attachment, Perfection and Termination of Security Interests

(1) A security interest in a security is enforceable and can attach only if it is transferred to the secured party or a person designated by him pursuant to a provision of Section 8-313(1).

(2) A security interest so transferred pursuant to agreement by a tranferor who has rights in the security to a transferee who has given value is a perfected security interest, but a security interest that has been transferred solely under paragraph (i) of Section 8-313(1) becomes unperfected after 21 days unless, within that time, the requirements for transfer under any other provision of Section 8-313(1) are satisfied.

(3) A security interest in a security is subject to the provisions of Article 9, but:

(a) no filing is required to perfect the security interest; and

(b) no written security agreement signed by the debtor is necessary to make the security interest enforceable, except as provided in paragraph (h), (i), or (j) of Section 8-313(1). The secured party has the rights and duties provided under Section 9-207, to the extent they are applicable, whether or not the security is certificated, and, if certificated, whether or not it is in his possession.

(4) Unless otherwise agreed, a security interest in a security is terminated by transfer to the debtor or a person designated by him pursuant to a provision of Section 8-313(1). If a security is thus transferred, the security interest, if not terminated, becomes unperfected unless the security is certificated and is delivered to the debtor for the purpose of ultimate sale or exchange or presentation, collection, renewal, or registration of transfer. In that case, the security interest becomes unperfected after 21 days unless, within that time, the security (or securities for which it has been exchanged) is transferred to the secured party or a person designated by him pursuant to a provision of Section 8-313(1). Added in 1977.

PART 4. *Registration*

§ 8-401. Duty of Issuer to Register Transfer, Pledge, or Release

(1) If a certificated security in registered form is presented to the issuer with a request to register transfer or an instruction is presented to the issuer with a request to register transfer, pledge, or release, the issuer shall register the transfer, pledge, or release as requested if:

(a) the security is indorsed or the instruction was originated by the appropriate person or persons (Section 8-308);

(b) reasonable assurance is given that those indorsements or instructions are genuine and effective (Section 8-402);

(c) the issuer has no duty as to adverse claims or has discharged the duty (Section 8-403);

(d) any applicable law relating to the collection of taxes has been complied with; and

(e) the transfer, pledge, or release is in fact rightful or is to a bona fide purchaser.

(2) If an issuer is under a duty to register a transfer, pledge, or release of a security, the issuer is also liable to the person presenting a certificated security or an instruction for registration or his principal for loss resulting from any unreasonable delay in registration or from failure or refusal to register the transfer, pledge, or release. Amended in 1977.

§ 8-402. Assurance that Indorsements and Instructions Are Effective

(1) The issuer may require the following assurance that each necessary indorsement of a certificated security or each instruction (Section 8-308) is genuine and effective:

(a) in all cases, a guarantee of the signature (Section 8-312(1) or (2)) of the person indorsing a certificated security or originating an instruction including, in the case of an instruction, a warranty of the taxpayer identification number or, in the absence thereof, other reasonable assurance of identity;

(b) if the indorsement is made or the instruction is originated by an agent, appropriate assurance of authority to sign;

(c) if the indorsement is made or the instruction is originated by a fiduciary, appropriate evidence of appointment or incumbency;

(d) if there is more than one fiduciary, reasonable assurance that all who are required to sign have done so; and

(e) if the indorsement is made or the instruction is originated by a person not covered by any of the foregoing, assurance appropriate to the case corresponding as nearly as may be to the foregoing.

(2) A "guarantee of the signature" in subsection (1) means a guarantee signed by or on behalf of a person reasonably believed by the issuer to be responsible. The issuer may adopt standards with respect to responsibility if they are not manifestly unreasonable.

(3) "Appropriate evidence of appointment or incumbency" in subsection (1) means:

(a) in the case of a fiduciary appointed or qualified by a court, a certificate issued by or under the direction or supervision of that court or an officer thereof and dated within 60 days before the date of presentation for transfer, pledge, or release; or

(b) in any other case, a copy of a document showing the appointment or a certificate issued by or on behalf of a person reasonably believed by the issuer to be responsible or, in the absence of that document or certificate, other evidence reasonably deemed by the issuer to be appropriate. The issuer may adopt standards with respect to the evidence if they are not manifestly unreasonable. The issuer is not charged with notice of the contents of any document obtained pursuant to this paragraph (b) except to the extent that the contents relate directly to the appointment or incumbency.

(4) The issuer may elect to require reasonable assurance beyond that specified in this section, but if it does so and, for a purpose other than that specified in subsection (3) (b), both requires and obtains a copy of a will, trust, indenture, articles of co-partnership, by-laws, or other controlling instrument, it is charged with notice of all matters contained therein affecting the transfer, pledge, or release. Amended in 1977.

§ 8-403.   Issuer's Duty as to Adverse Claims

(1) An issuer to whom a certificated security is presented for registration shall inquire into adverse claims if:

(a) a written notification of an adverse claim is received at a time and in a manner affording the issuer a reasonable opportunity to act on it prior to the issuance of a new, reissued, or re-registered certificated security, and the notification identifies the claimant, the registered owner, and the issue of which the security is a part, and provides an address for communications directed to the claimant; or

(b) the issuer is charged with notice of an adverse claim from a controlling instrument it has elected to require under Section 8-402(4).

(2) The issuer may discharge any duty of inquiry by any reasonable means, including notifying an adverse claimant by registered or certified mail at the address furnished by him or, if there be no such address, at his residence or regular place of business that the certificated security has been presented for registration of transfer by a named person, and that the transfer will be registered unless within 30 days from the date of mailing the notification, either:

(a) an appropriate restraining order, injunction, or other process issues from a court of competent jurisdiction; or

(b) there is filed with the issuer an idemnity bond, sufficient in the issuer's judgment to protect the issuer and any transfer agent, registrar, or other agent of the issuer involved from any loss it or they may suffer by complying with the adverse claim.

(3) Unless an issuer is charged with notice of an adverse claim from a controlling instrument which it has elected to require under Section 8-402(4) or receives notification of an adverse claim under subsection (1), if a certificated security presented for registration is indorsed by the appropriate person or persons the issuer is under no duty to inquire into adverse claims. In particular:

(a) an issuer registering a certificated security in the name of a person who is a fiduciary or who is described as a fiduciary is not bound to inquire into the existence, extent, or correct description of the fiduciary relationship; and thereafter the issuer may assume without inquiry that the newly registered owner continues to be the fiduciary until the issuer receives written notice that the fiduciary is no longer acting as such with respect to the particular security;

(b) an issuer registering transfer on an indorsement by a fiduciary is not bound to inquire whether the transfer is made in compliance with a controlling instrument or with the law of the state having jurisdiction of the fiduciary relationship, including any law requiring the fiduciary to obtain court approval of the transfer; and

(c) the issuer is not charged with notice of the contents of any court record or file or other recorded or unrecorded document even though the document is in its possession and even though the transfer is made on the indorsement of a fiduciary to the fiduciary himself or to his nominee.

(4) An issuer is under no duty as to adverse claims with respect to an uncertificated security except:

(a) claims embodied in a restraining order, injunction, or other legal process served upon the issuer if the process was served at a time and in a manner affording the issuer a reasonable opportunity to act on it in accordance with the requirements of subsection (5);

(b) claims of which the issuer has received a written notification from the registered owner or the registered pledgee if the notification was received at a time and in a manner affording the issuer a reasonable opportunity to act on it in accordance with the requirements of subsection (5);

(c) claims (including restrictions on transfer not imposed by the issuer) to which the registration of transfer to the present registered owner was subject and were so noted in the initial transaction statement sent to him; and

(d) claims as to which an issuer is charged with notice from a controlling instrument it has elected to require under Section 8-402(4).

(5) If the issuer of an uncertificated security is under a duty as to an adverse claim, he discharges that duty by:

(a) including a notation of the claim in any statement sent with respect to the security under Sections 8-408 (3), (6), and (7); and

(b) refusing to register the transfer or pledge of the security unless the nature of the claim does not preclude transfer or pledge subject thereto.

(6) If the transfer or pledge of the security is registered subject to an adverse claim, a notation of the claim must be included in the initial transaction statement and all subsequent statements sent to the transferee and pledgee under Section 8-408.

(7) Notwithstanding subsections (4) and (5), if an uncertificated security was subject to a registered pledge at the time the issuer first came under a duty as

to a particular adverse claim, the issuer has no duty as to that claim if transfer of the security is requested by the registered pledgee or an appropriate person acting for the registered pledgee unless:

(a) the claim was embodied in legal process which expressly provides otherwise;

(b) the claim was asserted in a written notification from the registered pledgee;

(c) the claim was one as to which the issuer was charged with notice from a controlling instrument it required under Section 8-402(4) in connection with the pledgee's request for transfer; or

(d) the transfer requested is to be registered owner. Amended in 1977.

§ 8-404. Liability and Non-Liability for Registration

(1) Except as provided in any law relating to the collection of taxes, the issuer is not liable to the owner, pledgee, or any other person suffering loss as a result of the registration of a transfer, pledge, or release of a security if:

(a) there were on or with a certificated security the necessary indorsements or the issuer had received an instruction originated by an appropriate person (Section 8-308); and

(b) the issuer had no duty as to adverse claims or has discharged the duty (Section 8-403).

(2) If an issuer has registered a transfer of a certificated security to a person not entitled to it, the issuer on demand shall deliver a like security to the true owner unless:

(a) the registration was pursuant to subsection (1);

(b) the owner is precluded from asserting any claim for registering the transfer under Section 8-405(1); or

(c) the delivery would result in overissue, in which case the issuer's liability is governed by Section 8-104.

(3) If an issuer has improperly registered a transfer, pledge, or release of an uncertificated security, the issuer on demand from the injured party shall restore the records as to the injured party to the condition that would have obtained if the improper registration had not been made unless:

(a) the registration was pursuant to subsection (1); or

(b) the registration would result in overissue, in which case the issuer's liability is governed by Section 8-104. Amended in 1977.

§ 8-405. Lost, Destroyed, and Stolen Certificated Securities

(1) If a certificated security has been lost, apparently destroyed, or wrongfully taken, and the owner fails to notify the issuer of that fact within a reasonable time after he has notice of it and the issuer registers a transfer of the security before receiving notification, the owner is precluded from asserting against the issuer any claim for registering the transfer under Section 8-404 or any claim to a new security under this section.

(2) If the owner of a certificated security claims that the security has been lost, destroyed, or wrongfully taken, the issuer shall issue a new certificated security or, at the option of the issuer, an equivalent uncertificated security in place of the original security if the owner:

(a) so requests before the issuer has notice that the security has been acquired by a bona fide purchaser;

(b) files with the issuer a sufficient indemnity bond; and

(c) satisfies any other reasonable requirements imposed by the issuer.

(3) If, after the issue of a new certificated or uncertificated security, a bona fide purchaser or the original certificated security presents it for registration of transfer, the issuer shall register the transfer unless registration would result in overissue, in which event the issuer's liability is governed by Section 8-104. In addition to any rights on the indemnity bond, the issuer may recover the new certificated security from the person to whom it was issued or any person taking under him except a bona fide purchaser or may cancel the uncertificated security unless a bona fide purchaser or any person taking under a bona fide purchaser is then the registered owner or registered pledgee thereof. Amended in 1977.

§ 8-406. Duty of Authenticating Trustee, Transfer Agent, or Registrar

(1) If a person acts as authenticating trustee, transfer agent, registrar, or other agent for an issuer in the registration of transfers of its certificated securities or in the registration of transfers, pledges, and releases of its uncertificated securities, in the issue of new securities, or in the cancellation of surrendered securities:

(a) he is under a duty to the issuer to exercise good faith and due diligence in performing his functions; and

(b) with regard to the particular functions he performs, he has the same obligation to the holder or owner of a certificated security or to the owner or pledgee of an uncertificated security and has the same rights and privileges as the issuer has in regard to those functions.

(2) Notice to an authenticating trustee, transfer agent, registrar or other agent is notice to the issuer with respect to the functions performed by the agent. Amended in 1977.

§ 8-407. Exchangeability of Securities

(1) No issuer is subject to the requirements of this section unless it regularly maintains a system for issuing the class of securities involved under which both certificated and uncertificated securities are regularly issued to the category of owners, which includes the person in whose name the new security is to be registered.

(2) Upon surrender of a certificated security with all necessary indorsements and presentation of a written request by the person surrendering the security, the issuer, if he has no duty as to adverse claims or has discharged the duty (Section 8-403), shall issue to the person or a person designated by him an equivalent uncertificated security subject to all liens, restrictions, and claims that were noted on the certificated security.

(3) Upon receipt of a transfer instruction originated by an appropriate person who so requests, the issuer of an uncertificated security shall cancel the uncertificated security and issue an equivalent certificated security on which must be noted conspicuously any liens and restrictions of the issuer and any adverse claims (as to which the issuer has a duty under Section 8-403 (4)) to which the uncertificated security was subject. The certificated security shall be registered in the name of and delivered to:

(a) the registered owner, if the uncertificated security was not subject to a registered pledge; or

(b) the registered pledgee, if the uncertificated security was subject to a registered pledge. Added in 1977.

§ 8-408. Statements of Uncertificated Securities

(1) Within 2 business days after the transfer of an uncertificated security has been registered, the issuer shall send to the new registered owner and, if the security has been transferred subject to a registered

pledge, to the registered pledgee a written statement containing:

(a) a description of the issue of which the uncertificated security is a part;

(b) the number of shares or units transferred;

(c) the name and address and any taxpayer identification number of the new registered owner and, if the security has been transferred subject to a registered pledge, the name and address and any taxpayer identification number of the registered pledgee;

(d) a notation of any liens and restrictions of the issuer and any adverse claims (as to which the issuer has a duty under Section 8-403(4)) to which the uncertificated security is or may be subject at the time of registration or a statement that there are none of those liens, restrictions, or adverse claims; and

(e) the date the transfer was registered.

(2) Within 2 business days after the pledge of an uncertificated security has been registered, the issuer shall send to the registered owner and the registered pledgee a written statement containing:

(a) a description of the issue of which the uncertificated security is a part;

(b) the number of shares or units pledged;

(c) the name and address and any taxpayer identification number of the registered owner and the registered pledgee;

(d) a notation of any liens and restrictions of the issuer and any adverse claims (as to which the issuer has a duty under Section 8-403(4)) to which the uncertificated security is or may be subject at the time of registration or a statement that there are none of those liens, restrictions, or adverse claims; and

(e) the date the pledge was registered.

(3) Within 2 business days after the release from pledge of an uncertificated security has been registered, the issuer shall send to the registered owner and the pledge whose interest was released a written statement containing:

(a) a description of the issue of which the uncertificated security is a part;

(b) the number of shares or units released from pledge;

(c) the name and address and any taxpayer identification number of the registered owner and the pledgee whose interest was released;

(d) a notation of any liens and restrictions of the issuer and any adverse claims (as to which the issuer has a duty under Section 8-403(4)) to which the uncertificated security is or may be subject at the time of registration or a statement that there are none of those liens, restrictions, or adverse claims; and

(e) the date the release was registered.

(4) An "initial transaction statement" is the statement sent to:

(a) the new registered owner and, if applicable, to the registered pledgee pursuant to subsection (1);

(b) the registered pledgee pursuant to subsection (2); or

(c) the registered owner pursuant to subsection (3). Each initial transaction statement shall be signed by or on behalf of the issuer and must be identified as "Initial Transaction Statement."

(5) Within 2 business days after the transfer of an uncertificated security has been registered, the issuer shall send to the former registered owner and the former registered pledgee, if any, a written statement containing:

(a) a description of the issue of which the uncertificated security is a part;

(b) the number of shares or units transferred;

(c) the name and address and any taxpayer identification number of the former registered owner and of any former registered pledgee; and

(d) the date the transfer was registered.

(6) At periodic intervals no less frequent than annually and at any time upon the reasonable written request of the registered owner, the issuer shall send to the registered owner of each uncertificated security a dated written statement containing:

(a) a description of the issue of which the uncertificated security is a part;

(b) the name and address and any taxpayer identification number of the registered owner;

(c) the number of shares or units of the uncertificated security registered in the name of the registered owner on the date of the statement;

(d) the name and address and any taxpayer identification number of any registered pledgee and the number of shares or units subject to the pledge; and

(e) a notation of any liens and retrictions of the issuer and any adverse claims (as to which the issuer has a duty under Section 8-403(4)) to which the uncertificated security is or may be subject or a statement that there are none of those liens, restrictions, or adverse claims.

(7) At periodic intervals no less frequent than annually and at any time upon the reasonable written request of the registered pledgee, the issuer shall send to the registered pledgee of each uncertificated security a dated written statement containing:

(a) a description of the issue of which the uncertificated security is a part;

(b) the name and address and any taxpayer identification number of the registered owner;

(c) the name and address and any taxpayer identification number of the registered pledgee;

(d) the number of shares or units subject to the pledge; and

(e) a notation of any liens and restrictions of the issuer and any adverse claims (as to which the issuer has a duty under Section 8-403(4)) to which the uncertificated security is or may be subject or a statement that there are none of those liens, restrictions, or adverse claims.

(8) If the issuer sends the statements described in subsections (6) and (7) at periodic intervals no less frequent than quarterly, the issuer is not obliged to send additional statements upon request unless the owner or pledgee requesting them pays to the issuer the reasonable cost of furnishing them.

(9) Each statement sent pursuant to this section must bear a conspicuous legend reading substantially as follows: "This statement is merely a record of the rights of the addressee as of the time of its issuance. Delivery of this statement, of itself, confers no rights on the recipient. This statement is neither a negotiable instrument nor a security." Added in 1977.

ARTICLE 9.   Secured Transactions; Sales of Accounts and Chattel Paper

PART 1. *Short Title, Applicability and Definitions*

PART 2. *Validity of Security Agreement and Rights of Parties Thereto*

PART 3. *Rights of Third Parties; Perfected and Unperfected Security Interests; Rules of Priority*

ARTICLE 9.   Secured Transactions; Sales of Accounts and Chattel Paper

PART 1. *Short Title, Applicability and Definitions*

§ 9-101.   Short Title

This Article shall be known and may be cited as Uniform Commercial Code-Secured Transactions.

§ 9-102.   Policy and Subject Matter of Article

(1) Except as otherwise provided in Section 9-104 on excluded transactions, this Article applies

(a) to any transaction (regardless of its form) which is intended to create a security interest in personal property or fixtures including goods, documents, instruments, general intangibles, chattel paper or accounts; and also

(b) to any sale of accounts or chattel paper.

(2) This Article applies to security interests created by contract including pledge, assignment, chattel mortgage, chattel trust, trust deed, factor's lien, equipment trust, conditional sale, trust receipt, other lien or title retention contract and lease or consignment intended as security. This Article does not apply to statutory liens except as provided in Section 9-310.

(3) The application of this Article to a security interest in a secured obligation is not affected by the fact that the obligation is itself secured by a transaction or interest to which this Article does not apply. Amended in 1972.

Note: The adoption of this Article should be accompanied by the repeal of existing statutes dealing with conditional sales, trust receipts, factors liens where the factor is given a non-possessory lien, chattel mortgages, crop mortgages, mortgages on railroad equipment, assignment of accounts and generally statutes regulating security interests in personal property.

Where the state has a retail installment selling act or small loan act, that legislation should be carefully examined to determine what changes in those acts are needed to conform them to this Article. This Article primarily sets out rules defining rights of a secured party against persons dealing with the debtor; it does not prescribe regulations and controls which may be necessary to curb abuses arising in the small loan business or in the financing of consumer purchases on credit. Accordingly there is no intention to repeal existing regulatory acts in those fields by enactment or re-enactment of Article 9. See Section 9-203(4) and the Note thereto.

§ 9-103. Perfection of Security Interest in Multiple State Transactions

(1) Documents, instruments and ordinary goods.

(a) This subsection applies to documents and instruments and to goods other than those covered by a certificate of title described in subsection (2), mobile goods described in subsection (3), and minerals described in subsection (5).

(b) Except as otherwise provided in this subsection, perfection and the effect of perfection or non-perfection of a security interest in collateral are governed by the law of the jurisdiction where the collateral is when the last event occurs on which is based the assertion that the security interest is perfected or unperfected.

(c) If the parties to a transaction creating a purchase money security interest in goods in one jurisdiction understand at the time that the security interest attaches that the goods will be kept in another jurisdiction, then the law of the other jurisdiction governs the perfection and the effect of perfection or non-perfection of the security interest from the time it attaches until thirty days after the debtor receives possession of the goods and thereafter if the goods are taken to the other jurisdiction before the end of the thirty-day period.

(d) When collateral is brought into and kept in this state while subject to a security interest perfected under the law of the jurisdiction from which the collateral was removed, the security interest remains perfected, but if action is required by Part 3 of this Article to perfect the security interest,

(i) if the action is not taken before the expiration of the period of perfection in the other jurisdiction or the end of four months after the collateral is brought into this state, whichever period first expires, the security interest becomes unperfected at the end of that period and is thereafter deemed to have been unperfected as against a person who became a purchaser after removal;

(ii) if the action is taken before the expiration of the period specified in subparagraph (i), the security interest continues perfected thereafter;

(iii) for the purpose of priority over a buyer of consumer goods (subsection (2) of Section 9-307), the period of the effectiveness of a filing in the jurisdiction from which the collateral is removed is governed by the rules with respect to the perfection in subparagraphs (i) and (ii).

(2) Certificate of title.

(a) This subsection applies to goods covered by a certificate of title issued under a statute of this state or of another jurisdiction under the law of which indication of a security interest on the certificate is required as a condition of perfection.

(b) Except as otherwise provided in this subsection, perfection and the effect of perfection or non-perfection of the security interest are governed by the law (including the conflict of laws rules) of the jurisdiction issuing the certificate until four months after the goods are removed from that jurisdiction and thereafter until the goods are registered in another jurisdiction, but in any event not beyond surrender of the certificate. After the expiration of that period, the goods are not covered by the certificate of title within the meaning of this section.

(c) Except with respect to the rights of a buyer described in the next paragraph, a security interest, perfected in another jurisdiction otherwise than by notation on a certificate of title, in goods brought into this state and thereafter covered by a certificate of title issued by this state is subject to the rules stated in paragraph (d) of subsection (1).

(d) If goods are brought into this state while a security interest therein is perfected in any manner under the law of the jurisdiction from which the goods are removed and a certificate of title is issued by this state and the certificate does not show that the goods are subject to the security interest or that they may be subject to security interests not shown on the certificate, the security interest is subordinate to the rights of a buyer of the goods who is not in the business of selling goods of that kind to the extent that he gives value and receives delivery of the goods after issuance of the certificate and without knowledge of the security interest.

(3) Accounts, general intangibles and mobile goods.

(a) This subsection applies to accounts (other than an account described in subsection (5) on minerals) and general intangibles (other than uncertificated securities) and to goods which are mobile and which are of a type normally used in more than one jurisdiction, such as motor vehicles, trailers, rolling stock, airplanes, shipping containers, road building and construction machinery and commercial harvesting machinery and the like, if the goods are equipment or are inventory leased or held for lease by the debtor to others, and are not covered by a certificate of title described in subsection (2).

(b) The law (including the conflict of laws rules) of the jurisdiction in which the debtor is located governs the perfection and the effect of perfection or non-perfection of the security interest.

(c) If, however, the debtor is located in a jurisdiction which is not a part of the United States, and which does not provide for perfection of the security interest by filing or recording in that jurisdiction, the law of the jurisdiction in the United States in which the debtor has its major executive office in the United States governs the perfection and the effect of perfection or non-perfection of the security interest through filing. In the alternative, if the debtor is located in a jurisdiction which is not a part of the United States or Canada and the collateral is accounts or general intangibles for money due or to become due, the security interest may be perfected by notification to the account debtor. As used in this paragraph, "United States" includes its territories and possessions and the Commonwealth of Puerto Rico.

(d) A debtor shall be deemed located at his place of business if he has one, at his chief executive office if he has more than one place of business, otherwise at his residence. If, however, the debtor is a foreign air carrier under the Federal Aviation Act of 1958, as amended, it shall be deemed located at the designated office of the agent upon whom service of process may be made on behalf of the foreign air carrier.

(e) A security interest perfected under the law of the jurisdiction of the location of the debtor is perfected until the expiration of four months after a change of the debtor's location to another jurisdiction, or until perfection would have ceased by the law of the first jurisdiction, whichever period first expires. Unless perfected in the new jurisdiction before the end of that period, it becomes unperfected thereafter and is deemed to have been unperfected as against a person who became a purchaser after the change.

(4) Chattel paper.

The rules stated for goods in subsection (1) apply to a possessory security interest in chattel paper. The rules stated for accounts in subsection (3) apply to a non-possessory security interest in chattel paper, but the security interest may not be perfected by notification to the account debtor.

(5) Minerals.

Perfection and the effect of perfection or non-perfection of a security interest which is created by a debtor who has an interest in minerals or the like (including oil and gas) before extraction and which attaches thereto as extracted, or which attaches to an account resulting from the sale thereof at the wellhead or minehead are governed by the law (including the conflict of laws rules) of the jurisdiction wherein the wellhead or minehead is located.

(6) Uncertificated securities.

The law (including the conflict of laws rules) of the jurisdiction of organization of the issuer governs the perfection and the effect of perfection or non-perfection of a security interest in uncertificated securities. Amended in 1972 and 1977.

§ 9-104.   Transactions Excluded From Article

This Article does not apply

(a) to a security interest subject to any statute of the United States, to the extent that such statute governs the rights of parties to and third parties affected by transactions in particular types of property; or

(b) to a landlord's lien; or

(c) to a lien given by statute or other rule of law for services or materials except as provided in Section 9-310 on priority of such liens; or

(d) to a transfer of a claim for wages, salary or other compensation of an employee; or

(e) to a transfer by a government or governmental subdivision or agency; or

(f) to a sale of accounts or chattel paper as part of a sale of the business out of which they arose, or an assignment of accounts or chattel paper which is for the purpose of collection only, or a transfer of a right to payment under a contract to an assignee who is also to do the performance under the contract or a transfer of a single account to an assignee in whole or partial satisfaction of a preexisting indebtedness; or

(g) to a transfer of an interest in or claim in or under any policy of insurance, except as provided with respect to proceeds (Section 9-306) and priorities in proceeds (Section 9-312); or

(h) to a right represented by a judgment (other than a judgment taken on a right to payment which was collateral); or

(i) to any right of set-off; or

(j) except to the extent that provision is made for

fixtures in Section 9-313, to the creation or transfer of an interest in or lien on real estate, including a lease or rents thereunder; or

(k) to a transfer in whole or in part of any claim arising out of tort; or

(l) to a transfer of an interest in any deposit account (subsection (1) of Section 9-105), except as provided with respect to proceeds (Section 9-306) and priorities in proceeds (Section 9-312).

Amended in 1972.

§ 9-105. Definitions and Index of Definitions

(1) In this Article unless the context otherwise requires:

(a) "Account debtor" means the person who is obligated on an account, chattel paper or general intangible;

(b) "Chattel paper" means a writing or writings which evidence both a monetary obligation and a security interest in or a lease of specific goods, but a charter or other contract involving the use or hire of a vessel is not chattel paper. When a transaction is evidenced both by such a security agreement or a lease and by an instrument or a series of instruments, the group of writings taken together constitutes chattel paper;

(c) "Collateral" means the property subject to a security interest, and includes accounts and chattel paper which have been sold;

(d) "Debtor" means the person who owes payment or other performance of the obligation secured, whether or not he owns or has rights in the collateral, and includes the seller of accounts or chattel paper. Where the debtor and the owner of the collateral are not the same person, the term "debtor" means the owner of the collateral in any provision of the Article dealing with the collateral, the obligor in any provision dealing with the obligation, and may include both where the context so requires;

(e) "Deposit account" means a demand, time, savings, passbook or like account maintained with a bank, savings and loan association, credit union or like organization, other than an account evidenced by a certificate of deposit;

(f) "Document" means document of title as defined in the general definitions of Article 1 (Section 1-201), and a receipt of the kind described in subsection (2) of Section 7-201;

(g) "Encumbrance" includes real estate mortgages and other liens on real estate and all other rights in real estate that are not ownership interests;

(h) "Goods" includes all things which are movable at the time the security interest attaches or which are fixtures (Section 9-313), but does not include money, documents, instruments, accounts, chattel paper, general intangibles, or minerals or the like (including oil and gas) before extraction. "Goods" also includes standing timber which is to be cut and removed under a conveyance or contract for sale, the unborn young of animals, and growing crops;

(i) "Instrument" means a negotiable instrument (defined in Section 3-104), or a certificated security (defined in Section 8-102) or any other writing which evidences a right to the payment of money and is not itself a security agreement or lease and is of a type which is in ordinary course of business transferred by delivery with any necessary indorsement or assignment;

(j) "Mortgage" means a consensual interest created by a real estate mortgage, a trust deed on real estate, or the like;

(k) An advance is made "pursuant to commitment" if the secured party has bound himself to make it, whether or not a subsequent event of default or other event not within his control has relieved or may relieve him from his obligation;

(l) "Security agreement" means an agreement which creates or provides for a security interest;

(m) "Secured party" means a lender, seller or other person in whose favor there is a security interest, including a person to whom accounts or chattel paper have been sold. When the holders of obligations issued under an indenture of trust, equipment trust agreement or the like are represented by a trustee or other person, the representative is the secured party;

(n) "Transmitting utility" means any person primarily engaged in the railroad, street railway or trolley bus business, the electric or electronics communications transmission business, the transmission of goods by pipeline, or the transmission of the production and transmission of electricity, steam, gas or water, or the provision of sewer service.

(2) Other definitions applying to this Article and the sections in which they appear are:

"Account".	Section 9-106.
"Attach".	Section 9-203.
"Construction mortgage".	Section 9-313(1).

"Consumer goods".   Section 9-109(1).
"Equipment".   Section 9-109(2).
"Farm products".   Section 9-109(3).
"Fixture".   Section 9-313(1).
"Fixture filing".   Section 9-313(1).
"General intangibles".   Section 9-106.
"Inventory".   Section 9-109(4).
"Lien creditor".   Section 9-301(3).
"Proceeds".   Section 9-306(1).
"Purchase money security interest". Section 9-107.
"United States".   Section 9-103.

(3) The following definitions in other Articles apply to this Article:

"Check".   Section 3-104.
"Contract for sale".   Section 2-106.
"Holder in due course".   Section 3-302.
"Note".   Section 3-104.
"Sale".   Section 2-106.

(4) In addition Article 1 contains general definitions and principles of construction and interpretation applicable throughout this Article. Amended in 1966, 1972 and 1977.

§ 9-106. Definitions: "Account"; "General Intangibles"

"Account" means any right to payment for goods sold or leased or for services rendered which is not evidenced by an instrument or chattel paper, whether or not it has been earned by performance. "General intangibles" means any personal property (including things in action) other than goods, accounts, chattel paper, documents, instruments, and money. All rights to payment earned or unearned under a charter or other contract involving the use of hire of a vessel and all rights incident to the charter or contract are accounts. Amended in 1966, 1972.

§ 9-107. Definitions: "Purchase Money Security Interest"

A security interest is a "purchase money security interest" to the extent that it is

(a) taken or retained by the seller of the collateral to secure all or part of its price; or

(b) taken by a person who by making advances or incurring an obligation gives value to enable the debtor to acquire rights in or the use of collateral if such value is in fact so used.

§ 9-108. When After-Acquired Collateral Not Security for Antecedent Debt

Where a secured party makes an advance, incurs an obligation, releases a perfected security interest, or otherwise gives new value which is to be secured in whole or in part by after-acquired property his security interest in the after-acquired collateral shall be deemed to be taken for new value and not as security for an antecedent debt if the debtor acquires his rights in such collateral either in the ordinary course of his business or under a contract of purchase made pursuant to the security agreement within a reasonable time after new value is given.

§ 9-109. Classification of Goods; "Consumer Goods"; "Equipment"; "Farm Products"; "Inventory"

Goods are

(1) "consumer goods" if they are used or bought for use primarily for personal, family or household purposes:

(2) "equipment" if they are used or bought for use primarily in business (including farming or a profession) or by a debtor who is a non-profit organization or a governmental subdivision or agency or if the goods are not included in the definitions of inventory, farm products or consumer goods;

(3) "farm products" if they are crops or livestock or supplies used or produced in farming operations or if they are products of crops or livestock in their unmanufactured states (such as ginned cotton, wool-clip, maple syrup, milk and eggs), and if they are in the possession of a debtor engaged in raising, fattening, grazing or other farming operations. If goods are farm products they are neither equipment nor inventory;

(4) "inventory" if they are held by a person who holds them for sale or lease or to be furnished under contracts of service or if he has so furnished them, or if they are raw materials, work in process or materials used or consumed in a business. Inventory of a person is not to be classified as his equipment.

§ 9-110. Sufficiency of Description

For the purposes of this Article any description of personal property or real estate is sufficient whether or not it is specific if it reasonably identifies what is described.

§ 9-111. Applicability of Bulk Transfer Laws

The creation of a security interest is not a bulk transfer under Article 6 (see Section 6-102).

§ 9-112. Where Collateral Is Not Owned by Debtor

Unless otherwise agreed, when a secured party knows that collateral is owned by a person who is not the debtor, the owner of the collateral is entitled to receive from the secured party any surplus under Section 9-502(2) or under Section 9-504(1), and is not liable for the debt or for any deficiency after resale, and he has the same right as the debtor

(a) to receive statements under Section 9-208;

(b) to receive notice of and to object to a secured party's proposal to retain the collateral in satisfaction of the indebtedness under Section 9-505;

(c) to redeem the collateral under Section 9-506;

(d) to obtain injunctive or other relief under Section 9-507(1); and

(e) to recover losses caused to him under Section 9-208(2).

§ 9-113. Security Interest Arising Under Article on Sales

A security interest arising solely under the Article on Sales (Article 2) is subject to the provisions of this Article except that to the extent that and so long as the debtor does not have or does not lawfully obtain possession of the goods

(a) no security agreement is necessary to make the security interest enforceable; and

(b) no filing is required to perfect the security interest; and

(c) the rights of the secured party on default by the debtor are governed by the Article on Sales (Article 2).

§ 9-114. Consignment

(1) A person who delivers goods under a consignment which is not a security interest and who would be required to file under this Article by paragraph (3) (c) of Section 2-326 has priority over a secured party who is or becomes a creditor of the consignee and who would have a perfected security interest in the goods if they were the property of the consignee, and also has priority with respect to identifiable cash proceeds received on or before delivery of the goods to a buyer, if

(a) the consignor complies with the filing provision of the Article on Sales with respect to consignments (paragraph (3) (c) of Section 2-326) before the consignee receives possession of the goods; and

(b) the consignor gives notification in writing to the holder of the security interest if the holder has filed a financing statement covering the same types of goods before the date of the filing made by the consignor; and

(c) the holder of the security interest receives the notification within five years before the consignee receives possession of the goods; and

(d) the notification states that the consignor expects to deliver goods on consignment to the consignee, describing the goods by item or type.

(2) In the case of a consignment which is not a security interest and in which the requirements of the preceding subsection have not been met, a person who delivers goods to another is subordinate to a person who would have a perfected security interest in the goods if they were the property of the debtor. Added in 1972.

PART 2. *Validity of Security Agreement and Rights of Parties Thereto*

§ 9-201. General Validity of Security Agreement

Except as otherwise provided by this Act a security agreement is effective according to its terms between the parties, against purchasers of the collateral and against creditors. Nothing in this Article validates any charge or practice illegal under any statute or regulation thereunder governing usury, small loans, retail installment sales, or the like, or extends the application of any such statute or regulation to any transaction not otherwise subject thereto.

§ 9-202. Title to Collateral Immaterial

Each provision of this Article with regard to rights, obligations and remedies applies whether title to collateral is in the secured party or in the debtor.

§ 9-203. Attachment and Enforceability of Security Interest; Proceeds; Formal Requisites

(1) Subject to the provisions of Section 4-208 on the security interest of a collecting bank, Section 8-321 on security interests in securities and Section 9-113 on a

security interest arising under the Article on Sales, a security interest is not enforceable against the debtor or third parties with respect to the collateral and does not attach unless:

(a) the collateral is in the possession of the secured party pursuant to agreement, or the debtor has signed a security agreement which contains a description of the collateral and in addition, when the security interest covers crops growing or to be grown or timber to be cut, a description of the land concerned;

(b) value has been given; and

(c) the debtor has rights in the collateral.

(2) A security interest attaches when it becomes enforceable against the debtor with respect to the collateral. Attachment occurs as soon as all of the events specified in subsection (1) have taken place unless explicit agreement postpones the time of attaching.

(3) Unless otherwise agreed a security agreement gives the secured party the rights to proceeds provided by Section 9-306.

(4) A transaction, although subject to this Article, is also subject to . . . .*, and in the case of conflict between the provisions of this Article and any such statute, the provisions of such statute control. Failure to comply with any applicable statute has only the effect which is specified therein. Amended in 1972 and 1977.

Note: At* in subsection (4) insert reference to any local statute regulating small loans, retail installment sales and the like.

The foregoing subsection (4) is designed to make it clear that certain transactions, although subject to this Article, must also comply with other applicable legislation.

This Article is designed to regulate all the "security" aspects of transactions within its scope. There is, however, much regulatory legislation, particularly in the consumer field, which supplements this Article and should not be repealed by its enactment. Examples are small loan acts, retail installment selling acts and the like. Such acts may provide for licensing and rate regulation and may prescribe particular forms of contract. Such provisions should remain in force despite the enactment of this Article. On the other hand if a retail installment selling act contains provisions on filing, rights on default, etc., such provisions should be repealed as inconsistent with this Article except that inconsistent provisions as to deficiencies,

penalties, etc., in the Uniform Consumer Credit Code and other recent related legislation should remain because those statutes were drafted after the substantial enactment of the Article and with the intention of modifying certain provisions of this Article as to consumer credit.

§ 9-204. After-Acquired Property; Future Advances

(1) Except as provided in subsection (2), a security agreement may provide that any or all obligations covered by the security agreement are to be secured by after-acquired collateral.

(2) No security interest attaches under an after-acquired property clause to consumer goods other than accessions (Section 9-314) when given as additional security unless the debtor acquires rights in them within ten days after the secured party gives value.

(3) Obligations covered by a security agreement may include future advances or other value whether or not the advances or value are given pursuant to commitment (subsection (1) of Section 9-105). Amended in 1972.

§ 9-205. Use or Disposition of Collateral Without Accounting Permissible

A security interest is not invalid or fraudulent against creditors by reason of liberty in the debtor to use, commingle or dispose of all or part of the collateral (including returned or repossessed goods) or to collect or compromise accounts or chattel paper, or to accept the return of goods or make repossessions, or to use, commingle or dispose of proceeds, or by reason of the failure of the secured party to require the debtor to account for proceeds or replace collateral. This section does not relax the requirements of possession where perfection of a security interest depends upon possession of the collateral by the secured party or by a bailee. Amended in 1972.

§ 9-206. Agreement Not to Assert Defenses Against Assignee; Modification of Sales Warranties Where Security Agreement Exists

(1) Subject to any statute or decision which establishes a different rule for buyers or lessees of consumer goods, an agreement by a buyer or lessee that he will not assert against an assignee any claim or defense which he may have against the seller or lessor is enforce-

able by an assignee who takes his assignment for value, in good faith and without notice of a claim or defense, except as to defenses of a type which may be asserted against a holder in due course of a negotiable instrument under the Article on Commercial Paper (Article 3). A buyer who as part of one transaction signs both a negotiable instrument and a security agreement makes such an agreement.

(2) When a seller retains a purchase money security interest in goods the Article on Sales (Article 2) governs the sale and any disclaimer, limitation or modification of the seller's warranties. Amended in 1962.

§ 9-207. Rights and Duties When Collateral Is in Secured Party's Possession

(1) A secured party must use reasonable care in the custody and preservation of collateral in his possession. In the case of an instrument or chattel paper reasonable care includes taking necessary steps to preserve rights against prior parties unless otherwise agreed.

(2) Unless otherwise agreed, when collateral is in the secured party's possession

(a) reasonable expenses (including the cost of any insurance and payment of taxes or other charges) incurred in the custody, preservation, use or operation of the collateral are chargeable to the debtor and are secured by the collateral;

(b) the risk of accidental loss or damage is on the debtor to the extent of any deficiency in any effective insurance coverage;

(c) the secured party may hold as additional security any increase or profits (except money) received from the collateral, but money so received, unless remitted to the debtor, shall be applied in reduction of the secured obligation;

(d) the secured party must keep the collateral identifiable but fungible collateral may be commingled;

(e) the secured party may repledge the collateral upon terms which do not impair the debtor's right to redeem it.

(3) A secured party is liable for any loss caused by his failure to meet any obligation imposed by the preceding subsections but does not lose his security interest.

(4) A secured party may use or operate the collateral for the purpose of preserving the collateral or its value or pursuant to the order of a court of appropriate jurisdiction or, except in the case of consumer goods, in the manner and to the extent provided in the security agreement.

§ 9-208. Request for Statement of Account or List of Collateral

(1) A debtor may sign a statement indicating what he believes to be the aggregate amount of unpaid indebtedness as of a specified date and may send it to the secured party with a request that the statement be approved or corrected and returned to the debtor. When the security agreement or any other record kept by the secured party identifies the collateral a debtor may similarly request the secured party to approve or correct a list of the collateral.

(2) The secured party must comply with such a request within two weeks after receipt by sending a written correction or approval. If the secured party claims a security interest in all of a particular type of collateral owned by the debtor he may indicate that fact in his reply and need not approve or correct an itemized list of such collateral. If the secured party without reasonable excuse fails to comply he is liable for any loss caused to the debtor thereby; and if the debtor has properly included in his request a good faith statement of the obligation or a list of the collateral or both the secured party may claim a security interest only as shown in the statement against persons misled by his failure to comply. If he no longer has an interest in the obligation or collateral at the time the request is received he must disclose the name and address of any successor in interest known to him and he is liable for any loss caused to the debtor as a result of failure to disclose. A successor in interest is not subject to this section until a request is received by him.

(3) A debtor is entitled to such a statement once every six months without charge. The secured party may require payment of a charge not exceeding $10 for each additional statement furnished.

PART 3. Rights of Third Parties; Perfected and Unperfected Security Interests; Rules of Priority

§ 9-301. Persons Who Take Priority Over Unperfected Security Interests; Rights of "Lien Creditor"

(1) Except as otherwise provided in subsection (2), an unperfected security interest is subordinate to the rights of

(a) persons entitled to priority under Section 9-312;

(b) a person who becomes a lien creditor before the security interest is perfected;

(c) in the case of goods, instruments, documents, and chattel paper, a person who is not a secured party and who is a transferee in bulk or other buyer not in ordinary course of business or is a buyer of farm products in ordinary course of business, to the extent that he gives value and receives delivery of the collateral without knowledge of the security interest and before it is perfected;

(d) in the case of accounts and general intangibles, a person who is not a secured party and who is a transferee to the extent that he gives value without knowledge of the security interest and before it is perfected.

(2) If the secured party files with respect to a purchase money security interest before or within ten days after the debtor receives possession of the collateral, he takes priority over the rights of a transferee in bulk or of a lien creditor which arise between the time the security interest attaches and the time of filing.

(3) A "lien creditor" means a creditor who has acquired a lien on the property involved by attachment, levy or the like and includes an assignee for benefit of creditors from the time of assignment, and a trustee in bankruptcy from the date of the filing of the petition or a receiver in equity from the time of appointment.

(4) A person who becomes a lien creditor while a security interest is perfected takes subject to the security interest only to the extent that it secures advances made before he becomes a lien creditor or within 45 days thereafter or made without knowledge of the lien or pursuant to a commitment entered into without knowledge of the lien. Amended in 1972.

§ 9-302. When Filing Is Required to Perfect Security Interest; Security Interests to Which Filing Provisions of This Article Do Not Apply

(1) A financing statement must be filed to perfect all security interests except the following:

(a) a security interest in collateral in possession of the secured party under Section 9-305;

(b) a security interest temporarily perfected in instruments or documents without delivery under Section 9-304 or in proceeds for a 10 day period under Section 9-306;

(c) a security interest created by an assignment of a beneficial interest in a trust or a decedent's estate;

(d) a purchase money security interest in consumer goods; but filing is required for a motor vehicle required to be registered; and fixture filing is required for

priority over conflicting interests in fixtures to the extent provided in Section 9-313;

(e) an assignment of accounts which does not alone or in conjunction with other assignments to the same assignee transfer a significant part of the outstanding accounts of the assignor;

(f) a security interest of a collecting bank (Section 4-208) or in securities (Section 8-321) or arising under Article on Sales (see Section 9-113) or covered in subsection (3) of this section;

(g) an assignment for the benefit of all the creditors of the transferor, and subsequent transfers by the assignee thereunder.

(2) If a secured party assigns a perfected security interest, no filing under this Article is required in order to continue the perfected status of the security interest against creditors of and transferees from the original debtor.

(3) The filing of a financing statement otherwise required by this Article is not necessry or effective to perfect a security interest in property subject to

(a) a statute or treaty of the United States which provides for a national or international registration or a national or international certificate of title or which specifies a place of filing different from that specified in this Article for filing of the security interest; or

(b) the following statutes of this state; [list any certificate of title statute covering automobiles, trailers, mobile homes, boats, farm tractors, or the like, and any central filing statute *.]; but during any period in which collateral is inventory held for sale by a person who is in the business of selling goods of that kind, the filing provisions of this Article (Part 4) apply to a security interest in that collateral created by him as debtor; or

(c) a certificate of title statute of another jurisdiction under the law of which indication of a security interest on the certificate is required as a condition of perfection (subsection (2) of Section 9-103).

(4) Compliance with a statute or treaty described in subsection (3) is equivalent to the filing of a financing statement under this Article, and a security interest in property subject to the statute or treaty can be perfected only by compliance therewith except as provided in Section 9-103 on multiple state transactions. Duration and renewal of perfection of a security interest perfected by compliance with the statute or treaty are governed by the provisions of the statute or treaty; in other respects the security interest is subject to this Article. Amended in 1972 and 1977.

*Note: It is recommended that the provisions of certificate of title acts for perfection of security interests by notation on the certificates should be amended to exclude coverage of inventory held for sale.

§ 9-303. When Security Interest Is Perfected; Continuity of Perfection

(1) A security interest is perfected when it has attached and when all of the applicable steps required for perfection have been taken. Such steps are specified in Sections 9-302, 9-304, 9-305 and 9-306. If such steps are taken before the security interest attaches, it is perfected at the time when it attaches.

(2) If a security interest is originally perfected in any way permitted under this Article and is subsequently perfected in some other way under this Article, without an intermediate period when it was unperfected, the security interest shall be deemed to be perfected continuously for the purposes of this Article.

§ 9-304. Perfection of Security Interest in Instruments, Documents, and Goods Covered by Documents; Perfection by Permissive Filing; Temporary Perfection Without Filing or Transfer of Possession

(1) A security interest in chattel paper or negotiable documents may be perfected by filing. A security interest in money or instruments (other than certificated securities or instruments which constitute part of chattel paper) can be perfected only by the secured party's taking possession, except as provided in subsections (4) and (5) of this section and subsections (2) and (3) of Section 9-306 on proceeds.

(2) During the period that goods are in the possession of the issuer of a negotiable document therefor, a security interest in the goods is perfected by perfecting a security interest in the document, and any security interest in the goods otherwise perfected during such period is subject thereto.

(3) A security interest in goods in the possession of a bailee other than one who has issued a negotiable document therefor is perfected by issuance of a document in the name of the secured party or by the bailee's receipt of notification of the secured party's interest or by filing as to the goods.

(4) A security interest in instruments (other than certificated securities) or negotiable documents is per-

fected without filing or the taking of possession for a period of 21 days from the time it attaches to the extent that it arises for new value given under a written security agreement.

(5) A security interest remains perfected for a period of 21 days without filing where a secured party having a perfected security interest in an instrument (other than a certificated security), a negotiable document or goods in possession of a bailee other than one who has issued a negotiable document therefor

(a) makes available to the debtor the goods or documents representing the goods for the purpose of ultimate sale or exchange or for the purpose of loading, unloading, storing, shipping, transshipping, manufacturing, processing or otherwise dealing with them in a manner preliminary to their sale or exchange, but priority between conflicting security interests in the goods is subject to subsection (3) of Section 9-312; or

(b) delivers the instrument to the debtor for the purpose of ultimate sale or exchange or of presentation, collection, renewal or registration of transfer.

(6) After the 21 day period in subsections (4) and (5) perfection depends upon compliance with applicable provisions of this Article. Amended in 1972 and 1977.

§ 9-305. When Possession by Secured Party Perfects Security Interest Without Filing

A security interest in letters of credit and advices of credit (subsection (2) (a) of Section 5-116) goods instruments (other than certificated securities), money negotiable documents, or chattel paper may be perfected by the secured party's taking possession of the collateral. If such collateral other than goods covered by a negotiable document is held by a bailee, the secured party is deemed to have possession from the time the bailee receives notification of the secured party's interest. A security interest is perfected by possession from the time possession is taken without relation back and continues only so long as possession is retained, unless otherwise specified in this Article. The security interest may be otherwise perfected as provided in this Article before or after the period of possession by the secured party. Amended in 1972 and 1977.

§ 9-306. "Proceeds"; Secured Party's Rights on Disposition of Collateral

(1) "Proceeds" includes whatever is received upon the sale, exchange, collection or other disposition of collat-

eral or proceeds. Insurance payable by reason of loss or damage to the collateral is proceeds, except to the extent that it is payable to a person other than a party to the security agreement. Money, checks, deposit accounts, and the like are "cash proceeds". All other proceeds are "non-cash proceeds".

(2) Except where this Article otherwise provides, a security interest continues in collateral notwithstanding sale, exchange or other disposition thereof unless the disposition was authorized by the secured party in the security agreement or otherwise, and also continues in any identifiable proceeds including collections received by the debtor.

(3) The security interest in proceeds is a continuously perfected security interest if the interest in the original collateral was perfected but it ceases to be a perfected security interest and becomes unperfected ten days after receipt of the proceeds by the debtor unless

(a) a filed financing statement covers the original collateral and the proceeds are collateral in which a security interest may be perfected by filing in the office or offices where the financing statement has been filed and, if the proceeds are acquired with cash proceeds, the description of collateral in the financing statement indicates the types of property constituting the proceeds; or

(b) a filed financing statement covers the original collateral and the proceeds are identifiable cash proceeds; or

(c) the security interest in the proceeds is perfected before the expiration of the ten day period.

Except as provided in this section, a security interest in proceeds can be perfected only by the methods or under the circumstances permitted in this Article for original collateral of the same type.

(4) In the event of insolvency proceedings instituted by or against a debtor, a secured party with a perfected security interest in proceeds has a perfected security interest only in the following proceeds:

(a) in identifiable non-cash proceeds and in separate deposit accounts containing only proceeds;

(b) in identifiable cash proceeds in the form of money which is neither commingled with other money nor deposited in a deposit account prior to the insolvency proceedings;

(c) in identifiable cash proceeds in the form of checks and the like which are not deposited in a deposit account prior to the insolvency proceedings; and

(d) in all cash and deposit accounts of the debtor in which proceeds have been commingled with other funds, but the perfected security interest under this paragraph (d) is

(i) subject to any right to set-off; and

(ii) limited to an amount not greater than the amount of any cash proceeds received by the debtor within ten days before the institution of the insolvency proceedings less the sum of (I) the payments to the secured party on account of cash proceeds received by the debtor during such period and (II) the cash proceeds received by the debtor during such period to which the secured party is entitled under paragraphs (a) through (c) of this subsection (4).

(5) If a sale of goods results in an account or chattel paper which is transferred by the seller to a secured party, and if the goods are returned to or are repossessed by the seller or the secured party, the following rules determine priorities:

(a) If the goods were collateral at the time of sale, for an indebtedness of the seller which is still unpaid, the original security interest attaches again to the goods and continues as a perfected security interest if it was perfected at the time when the goods were sold. If the security interest was originally perfected by a filing which is still effective, nothing further is required to continue the perfected status; in any other case, the secured party must take possession of the returned or repossessed goods or must file.

(b) An unpaid transferee of the chattel paper has a security interest in the goods against the transferor. Such security interest is prior to a security interest asserted under paragraph (a) to the extent that the transferee of the chattel paper was entitled to priority under Section 9-308.

(c) An unpaid transferee of the account has a security interest in the goods against the transferor. Such security interest is subordinate to a security interest asserted under paragraph (a).

(d) A security interest of an unpaid transferee asserted under paragraph (b) or (c) must be perfected for protection against creditors of the transferor and purchasers of the returned or repossessed goods. Amended in 1972.

§ 9-307. Protection of Buyers of Goods

(1) A buyer in ordinary course of business (subsection (9) of Section 1-201) other than a person buying farm products from a person engaged in farming opera-

tions takes free of a security interest created by his seller even though the security interest is perfected and even though the buyer knows of its existence.

(2) In the case of consumer goods, a buyer takes free of a security interest even though perfected if he buys without knowledge of the security interest, for value and for his own personal, family or household purpose unless prior to the purchase the secured party has filed a financing statement covering such goods.

(3) A buyer other than a buyer in ordinary course of business (subsection (1) of this section) takes free of a security interest to the extent that it secures future advances made after the secured party acquires knowledge of the purchase, or more than 45 days after the purchase, whichever first occurs, unless made pursuant to a commitment entered into without knowledge of the purchase and before the expiration of the 45 day period. Amended in 1972.

§ 9-308. Purchase of Chattel Paper and Instruments

A purchaser of chattel paper or an instrument who gives new value and takes possession of it in the ordinary course of his business has priority over a security interest in the chattel paper or instrument

(a) which is perfected under Section 9-304 (permissive filing and temporary perfection) or under Section 9-306 (perfection as to proceeds) if he acts without knowledge that the specific paper or instrument is subject to a security interest; or

(b) which is claimed merely as proceeds of inventory subject to a security interest (Section 9-306) even though he knows that the specific paper or instrument is subject to the security interest. Amended in 1972.

§ 9-309. Protection of Purchasers of Instruments, Documents and Securities

Nothing in this Article limits the rights of a holder in due course of a negotiable instrument (Section 3-302) or a holder to whom a negotiable document of title has been duly negotiated (Section 7-501) or a bona fide purchaser of a security (Section 8-302) and such holders or purchasers take priority over an earlier security interest even though perfected. Filing under this Article does not constitute notice of the security interest to such holders or purchasers. Amended in 1977.

§ 9-310. Priority of Certain Liens Arising by Operation of Law

When a person in the ordinary course of his business furnishes services or materials with respect to goods subject to a security interest, a lien upon goods in the possession of such person given by statute or rule of law for such materials or services takes priority over a perfected security interest unless the lien is statutory and the statute expressly provides otherwise.

§ 9-311. Alienability of Debtor's Rights: Judicial Process

The debtor's rights in collateral may be voluntarily or involuntarily transferred (by way of sale, creation of a security interest, attachment, levy, garnishment or other judicial process) notwithstanding a provision in the security agreement prohibiting any transfer or making the transfer constitute a default.

§ 9-312. Priorities Among Conflicting Security Interests in the Same Collateral

(1) The rules of priority stated in other sections of this Part and in the following sections shall govern when applicable: Section 4-208 with respect to the security interests of collecting banks in items being collected, accompanying documents and proceeds; Section 9-103 on security interests related to other jurisdictions; Section 9-114 on consignments.

(2) A perfected security interest in crops for new value given to enable the debtor to produce the crops during the production season and given not more than three months before the crops become growing crops by planting or otherwise takes priority over an earlier perfected security interest to the extent that such earlier interest secures obligations due more than six months before the crops become growing crops by planting or otherwise, even though the person giving new value had knowledge of the earlier security interest.

(3) A perfected purchase money security interest in inventory has priority over a conflicting security interest in the same inventory and also has priority in identifiable cash proceeds received on or before the delivery of the inventory to a buyer if

(a) the purchase money security interest is perfected at the time the debtor receives possession of the inventory; and

(b) the purchase money secured party gives notification in writing to the holder of the conflicting security interest if the holder had filed a financing statement covering the same types of inventory (i) before the date of the filing made by the purchase money secured party, or (ii) before the beginning of the 21 day period where the purchase money security interest is temporarily perfected without filing or possession (subsection (5) of Section 9-304); and

(c) the holder of the conflicting security interest receives the notification within five years before the debtor receives possession of the inventory; and

(d) the notification states that the person giving the notice has or expects to acquire a purchase money security interest in inventory of the debtor, describing such inventory by item or type.

(4) A purchase money security interest in collateral other than inventory has priority over a conflicting security interest in the same collateral or its proceeds if the purchase money security interest is perfected at the time the debtor receives possession of the collateral or within ten days thereafter.

(5) In all cases not governed by other rules stated in this section (including cases of purchase money security interests which do not qualify for the special priorities set forth in subsections (3) and (4) of this section), priority between conflicting security interests in the same collateral shall be determined according to the following rules:

(a) Conflicting security interests rank according to priority in time of filing or perfection. Priority dates from the time a filing is first made covering the collateral or the time the security interest is first perfected, whichever is earlier, provided that there is no period thereafter when there is neither filing nor perfection.

(b) So long as conflicting security interests are unperfected, the first to attach has priority.

(6) For the purposes of subsection (5) a date of filing or perfection as to collateral is also a date of filing or perfection as to proceeds.

(7) If future advances are made while a security interest is perfected by filing, the taking of possession, or under Section 8-321 on securities, the security interest has the same priority for the purposes of subsection (5) with respect to the future advances as it does with respect to the first advance. If a commitment is made before or while the security interest is so perfected, the security interest has the same priority with respect to advances made pursuant thereto. In other cases a perfected security interest has priority from the date the advance is made. Amended in 1972 and 1977.

§ 9-313. Priority of Security Interests in Fixtures

(1) In this section and in the provisions of Part 4 of this Article referring to fixture filing, unless the context otherwise requires

(a) goods are "fixtures" when they become so related to particular real estate that an interest in them arises under real estate law

(b) a "fixture filing" is the filing in the office where a mortgage on the real estate would be filed or recorded of a financing statement covering goods which are or are to become fixtures and conforming to the requirements of subsection (5) of Section 9-402

(c) a mortgage is a "construction mortgage" to the extent that it secures an obligation incurred for the construction of an improvement on land including the acquisition cost of the land, if the recorded writing so indicates.

(2) A security interest under this Article may be created in goods which are fixtures or may continue in goods which become fixtures, but no security interest exists under this Article in ordinary building materials incorporated into an improvement on land.

(3) This Article does not prevent creation of an encumbrance upon fixtures pursuant to real estate law.

(4) A perfected security interest in fixtures has priority over the conflicting interest of an encumbrancer or owner of the real estate where

(a) the security interest is a purchase money security interest, the interest of the encumbrancer or owner arises before the goods become fixtures, the security interest is perfected by a fixture filing before the goods become fixtures or within ten days thereafter, and the debtor has an interest of record in the real estate or is in possession of the real estate; or

(b) the security interest is perfected by a fixture filing before the interest of the encumbrancer or owner is of record, the security interest has priority over any conflicting interest of a predecessor in title of the encumbrancer or owner, and the debtor has an interest of record in the real estate or is in possession of the real estate; or

(c) the fixtures are readily removable factory or office machines or readily removable replacements of domestic appliances which are consumer goods, and before the goods become fixtures the security interest is perfected by any method permitted by this Article; or

(d) the conflicting interest is a lien on the real estate obtained by legal or equitable proceedings after the security interest was perfected by any method permitted by this Article.

(5) A security interest in fixtures, whether or not perfected, has priority over the conflicting interest of an encumbrancer or owner of the real estate where

(a) the encumbrancer or owner has consented in writing to the security interest or has disclaimed an interest in the goods as fixtures; or

(b) the debtor has a right to remove the goods as against the encumbrancer or owner. If the debtor's right terminates, the priority of the security interest continues for a reasonable time.

(6) Notwithstanding paragraph (a) of subsection (4) but otherwise subject to subsections (4) and (5), a security interest in fixtures is subordinate to a construction mortgage recorded before the goods become fixtures if the goods become fixtures before the completion of the construction. To the extent that it is given to refinance a construction mortgage, a mortgage has this priority to the same extent as the construction mortgage.

(7) In cases not within the preceding subsections, a security interest in fixtures is subordinate to the conflicting interest of an encumbrancer or owner of the related real estate who is not the debtor.

(8) When the secured party has priority over all owners and encumbrancers of the real estate, he may, on default, subject to the provisions of Part 5, remove his collateral from the real estate but he must reimburse any encumbrancer or owner of the real estate who is not the debtor and who has not otherwise agreed for the cost of repair of any physical injury, but not for any diminution in value of the real estate caused by the absence of the goods removed or by any necessity of replacing them. A person entitled to reimbursement may refuse permission to remove until the secured party gives adequate security for the performance of this obligation. Amended in 1972.

§ 9-314.   Accessions

(1) A security interest in goods which attaches before they are installed in or affixed to other goods takes priority as to the goods installed or affixed (called in this section "accessions") over the claims of all persons to the whole except as stated in subsection (3) and subject to Section 9-315(1).

(2) A security interest which attaches to goods after they become part of a whole is valid against all persons subsequently acquiring interests in the whole except as

stated in subsection (3) but is invalid against any person with an interest in the whole at the time the security interest attaches to the goods who has not in writing consented to the security interest or disclaimed an interest in the goods as part of the whole.

(3) The security interests described in subsections (1) and (2) do not take priority over

(a) a subsequent purchaser for value of any interest in the whole; or

(b) a creditor with a lien on the whole subsequently obtained by judicial proceedings; or

(c) a creditor with a prior perfected security interest in the whole to the extent that he makes subsequent advances

if the subsequent purchase is made, the lien by judicial proceedings obtained or the subsequent advance under the prior perfected security interest is made or contracted for without knowledge of the security interest and before it is perfected. A purchaser of the whole at a foreclosure sale other than the holder of a perfected security interest purchasing at his own foreclosure sale is a subsequent purchaser within this section.

(4) When under subsections (1) or (2) and (3) a secured party has an interest in accessions which has priority over the claims of all persons who have interests in the whole, he may on default subject to the provisions of Part 5 remove his collateral from the whole but he must reimburse any encumbrancer or owner of the whole who is not the debtor and who has not otherwise agreed for the cost of repair of any physical injury but not for any diminution in value of the whole caused by the absence of the goods removed or by any necessity for replacing them. A person entitled to reimbursement may refuse permission to remove until the secured party gives adequate security for the performance of this obligation.

§ 9-315.   Priority When Goods Are Commingled or Processed

(1) If a security interest in goods was perfected and subsequently the goods or a part thereof have become part of a product or mass, the security interest continues in the product or mass if

(a) the goods are so manufactured, processed, assembled or commingled that their identity is lost in the product or mass; or

(b) a financing statement covering the original goods also covers the product into which the goods have been manufactured, processed or assembled.

In a case to which paragraph (b) applies, no separate security interest in that part of the original goods which has been manufactured, processed or assembled into the product may be claimed under Section 9-314.

(2) When under subsection (1) more than one security interest attaches to the product or mass, they rank equally according to the ratio that the cost of the goods to which each interest originally attached bears to the cost of the total product or mass.

§ 9-316.   Priority Subject to Subordination

Nothing in this Article prevents subordination by agreement by any person entitled to priority.

§ 9-317.   Secured Party Not Obligated on Contract of Debtor

The mere existence of a security interest or authority given to the debtor to dispose of or use collateral does not impose contract or tort liability upon the secured party for the debtor's acts or omissions.

§ 9-318.   Defenses Against Assignee; Modification of Contract After Notification of Assignment; Term Prohibiting Assignment Ineffective; Identification and Proof of Assignment

(1) Unless an account debtor has made an enforceable agreement not to assert defenses or claims arising out of a sale as provided in Section 9-206 the rights of an assignee are subject to

(a) all the terms of the contract between the account debtor and assignor and any defense or claim arising therefrom; and

(b) any other defense or claim of the account debtor against the assignor which accrues before the account debtor receives notification of the assignment.

(2) So far as the right to payment or a part thereof under an assigned contract has not been fully earned by performance, and notwithstanding notification of the assignment, any modification of or substitution for the contract made in good faith and in accordance with reasonable commercial standards is effective against an assignee unless the account debtor has otherwise agreed but the assignee acquires corresponding rights under the modified or substituted contract. The assignment may provide that such modification or substitution is a breach by the assignor.

(3) The account debtor is authorized to pay the as-signor until the account debtor receives notification that the amount due or to become due has been assigned and that payment is to be made to the assignee. A notification which does not reasonably identify the rights assigned is ineffective. If requested by the account debtor, the assignee must seasonably furnish reasonable proof that the assignment has been made and unless he does so the account debtor may pay the assignor.

(4) A term in any contract between an account debtor and an assignor is ineffective if it prohibits assignment of an account or prohibits creation of a security interest in a general intangible for money due or to become due or requires the account debtor's consent to such assignment or security interest. Amended in 1972.

PART 4. *Filing*

§ 9-401.   Place of Filing; Erroneous Filing; Removal of Collateral

FIRST ALTERNATIVE SUBSECTION (1). (1) The proper place to file in order to perfect a security interest is as follows:

(a) when the collateral is timber to be cut or is minerals or the like (including oil and gas) or accounts subject to subsection (5) of Section 9-103, or when the financing statement is filed as a fixture filing (Section 9-313) and the collateral is goods which are or are to become fixtures, then in the office where a mortgage on the real estate would be filed or recorded;

(b) in all other cases, in the office of the [Secretary of State].

SECOND ALTERNATIVE SUBSECTION (1). (1) The proper place to file in order to perfect a security interest is as follows:

(a) when the collateral is equipment used in farming operations, or farm products, or accounts or general intangibles arising from or relating to the sale of farm products by a farmer, or consumer goods, then in the office of the . . . . . . in the county of the debtor's residence or if the debtor is not a resident of this state then in the office of the . . . . . . in the county where the goods are kept, and in addition when the collateral is crops growing or to be grown in the office of the . . . . . . in the county where the land is located;

(b) when the collateral is timber to be cut or is minerals or the like (including oil and gas) or accounts subject to subsection (5) of Section 9-103, or when the financing statement is filed as a fixture filing (Section

9-313) and the collateral is goods which are or are to become fixtures, then in the office where a mortgage on the real estate would be filed or recorded;

(c) in all other cases, in the office of the [Secretary of State].

THIRD ALTERNATIVE SUBSECTION (1). (1) The proper place to file in order to perfect a security interest is as follows:

(a) when the collateral is equipment used in farming operations, or farm products, or accounts or general intangibles arising from or relating to the sale of farm products by a farmer, or consumer goods, then in the office of the . . . . . . in the county of the debtor's residence or if the debtor is not a resident of this state then in the office of the . . . . . . in the county where the goods are kept, and in addition when the collateral is crops growing or to be grown in the office of the . . . . . . in the county where the land is located;

(b) when the collateral is timber to be cut or is minerals or the like (including oil and gas) or accounts subject to subsection (5) of Section 9-103, or when the financing statement is filed as a fixture filing (Section 9-313) and the collateral is goods which are or are to become fixtures, then in the office where a mortgage on the real estate would be filed or recorded;

(c) in all other cases, in the office of the [Secretary of State] and in addition, if the debtor has a place of business in only one county of this state, also in the office of . . . . . . of such county, or, if the debtor has no place of business in this state, but resides in the state, also in the office of . . . . . . of the county in which he resides.

Note: One of the three alternatives should be selected as subsection (1).

(2) A filing which is made in good faith in an improper place or not in all of the places required by this section is nevertheless effective with regard to any collateral as to which the filing complied with the requirements of this Article and is also effective with regard to collateral covered by the financing statement against any person who has knowledge of the contents of such financing statement.

(3) A filing which is made in the proper place in this state continues effective even though the debtor's residence or place of business or the location of the collateral or its use, whichever controlled the original filing, is thereafter changed.

ALTERNATIVE SUBSECTION [(3).

(3) A filing which is made in the proper county continues effective for four months after a change to another county of the debtor's residence or place of business or the location of the collateral, whichever controlled the original filing. It becomes ineffective thereafter unless a copy of the financing statement signed by the secured party is filed in the new county within said period. The security interest may also be perfected in the new county after the expiration of the four-month period; in such case perfection dates from the time of perfection in the new county. A change in the use of the collateral does not impair the effectiveness of the original filing.]

(4) The rules stated in Section 9-103 determine whether filing is necessary in this state.

(5) Notwithstanding the preceding subsections, and subject to subsection (3) of Section 9-302, the proper place to file in order to perfect a security interest in collateral, including fixtures, of a transmitting utility is the office of the [Secretary of State]. This filing constitutes a fixture filing (Section 9-313) as to the collateral described therein which is or is to become fixtures.

(6) For the purposes of this section, the residence of an organization is its place of business if it has one or its chief executive office if it has more than one place of business. Amended in 1962 and 1972.

Note: Subsection (6) should be used only if the state chooses the Second or Third Alternative Subsection (1).

§ 9-402. Formal Requisites of Financing Statement; Amendments; Mortgage as Financing Statement

(1) A financing statement is sufficient if it gives the names of the debtor and the secured party, is signed by the debtor, gives an address of the secured party from which information concerning the security interest may be obtained, gives a mailing address of the debtor and contains a statement indicating the types, or describing the items, of collateral. A financing statement may be filed before a security agreement is made or a security interest otherwise attaches. When the financing statement covers crops growing or to be grown, the statement must also contain a description of the real estate concerned. When the financing statement covers timber to be cut or covers minerals or the like (including oil

and gas) or accounts subject to subsection (5) of Section 9-103, or when the financing statement is filed as a fixture filing (Section 9-313) and the collateral is goods which are or are to become fixtures, the statement must also comply with subsection (5). A copy of the security agreement is sufficient as a financing statement if it contains the above information and is signed by the debtor. A carbon, photographic or other reproduction of a security agreement or a financing statement is sufficient as a financing statement if the security agreement so provides or if the original has been filed in this state.

(2) A financing statement which otherwise complies with subsection (1) is sufficient when it is signed by the secured party instead of the debtor if it is filed to perfect a security interest in

(a) collateral already subject to a security interest in another jurisdiction when it is brought into this state, or when the debtor's location is changed to this state. Such a financing statement must state that the collateral was brought into this state or that the debtor's location was changed to this state under such circumstances; or

(b) proceeds under Section 9-306 if the security interest in the original collateral was perfected. Such a financing statement must describe the original collateral; or

(c) collateral as to which the filing has lapsed; or

(d) collateral acquired after a change of name, identity or corporate structure of the debtor (subsection (7)).

(3) A form substantially as follows is sufficient to comply with subsection (1):

Name of debtor (or assignor) ....
Address ....
Name of secured party (or assignee) ....
Address ....

1. This financing statement covers the following types (or items) of property:
   (Describe) ....
2. (If collateral is crops) The above described crops are growing or are to be grown on:
   (Describe Real Estate) ....
3. (If applicable) The above goods are to become fixtures on *
   (Describe Real Estate) .... and this financing statement is to be filed [for record] in the real estate records. (If the debtor does not

have an interest of record) The name of a record owner is ....
4. (If products of collateral are claimed) Products of the collateral are also covered.

(use ....
whichever Signature of Debtor (or Assignor)
is ....
applicable) Signature of Secured Party (or Assignee)

(4) A financing statement may be amended by filing a writing signed by both the debtor and the secured party. An amendment does not extend the period of effectiveness of a financing statement. If any amendment adds collateral, it is effective as to the added collateral only from the filing date of the amendment. In this Article, unless the context otherwise requires, the term "financing statement" means the original financing statement and any amendments.

(5) A financing statement covering timber to be cut or covering minerals or the like (including oil and gas) or accounts subject to subsection (5) of Section 9-103, or a financing statement filed as a fixture filing (Section 9-313) where the debtor is not a transmitting utility, must show that it covers this type of collateral, must recite that it is to be filed [for record] in the real estate records, and the financing statement must contain a description of the real estate [sufficient if it were contained in a mortgage of the real estate to give constructive notice of the mortgage under the law of this state]. If the debtor does not have an interest of record in the real estate, the financing statement must show the name of a record owner.

(6) A mortgage is effective as a financing statement filed as a fixture filing from the date of its recording if

(a) the goods are described in the mortgage by item or type; and

(b) the goods are or are to become fixtures related to the real estate described in the mortgage; and

(c) the mortgage complies with the requirements for a financing statement in this section other than a recital that it is to be filed in the real estate records; and

(d) the mortgage is duly recorded.

No fee with reference to the financing statement is required

*Where appropriate substitute either "The above timber is standing on . . . ." or "The above minerals or the like (including oil and gas) or accounts will be financed

at the wellhead or minehead of the well or mine located on . . . ." other than the regular recording and satisfaction fees with respect to the mortgage.

(7) A financing statement sufficiently shows the name of the debtor if it gives the individual, partnership or corporate name of the debtor, whether or not it adds other trade names or names of partners. Where the debtor so changes his name or in the case of an organization its name, identity or corporate structure that a filed financing statement becomes seriously misleading, the filing is not effective to perfect a security interest in collateral acquired by the debtor more than four months after the change, unless a new appropriate financing statement is filed before the expiration of that time. A filed financing statement remains effective with respect to collateral transferred by the debtor even though the secured party knows of or consents to the transfer.

(8) A financing statement substantially complying with the requirements of this section is effective even though it contains minor errors which are not seriously misleading. Amended in 1972.

Note: Language in brackets is optional.

Note: Where the state has any special recording system for real estate other than the usual grantor-grantee index (as, for instance, a tract system or a title registration or Torrens system) local adaptations of subsection (5) and Section 9-403(7) may be necessary. See Mass.Gen.Laws Chapter 106, Section 9-409.

§ 9-403. What Constitutes Filing; Duration of Filing; Effect of Lapsed Filing; Duties of Filing Officer

(1) Presentation for filing of a financing statement and tender of the filing fee or acceptance of the statement by the filing officer constitutes filing under this Article.

(2) Except as provided in subsection (6) a filed financing statement is effective for a period of five years from the date of filing. The effectiveness of a filed financing statement lapses on the expiration of the five year period unless a continuation statement is filed prior to the lapse. If a security interest perfected by filing exists at the time insolvency proceedings are commenced by or against the debtor, the security interest remains perfected until termination of the insolvency proceedings and thereafter for a period of sixty days or until expira-

tion of the five year period, whichever occurs later. Upon lapse the security interest becomes unperfected, unless it is perfected without filing. If the security interest becomes unperfected upon lapse, it is deemed to have been unperfected as against a person who became a purchaser or lien creditor before lapse.

(3) A continuation statement may be filed by the secured party within six months prior to the expiration of the five year period specified in subsection (2). Any such continuation statement must be signed by the secured party, identify the original statement by file number and state that the original statement is still effective. A continuation statement signed by a person other than the secured party of record must be accompanied by a separate written statement of assignment signed by the secured party of record and complying with subsection (2) of Section 9-405, including payment of the required fee. Upon timely filing of the continuation statement, the effectiveness of the original statement is continued for five years after the last date to which the filing was effective whereupon it lapses in the same manner as provided in subsection (2) unless another continuation statement is filed prior to such lapse. Succeeding continuation statements may be filed in the same manner to continue the effectiveness of the original statement. Unless a statute on disposition of public records provides otherwise, the filing officer may remove a lapsed statement from the files and destroy it immediately if he has retained a microfilm or other photographic record, or in other cases after one year after the lapse. The filing officer shall so arrange matters by physical annexation of financing statements to continuation statements or other related filings, or by other means, that if he physically destroys the financing statements of a period more than five years past, those which have been continued by a continuation statement or which are still effective under subsection (6) shall be retained.

(4) Except as provided in subsection (7) a filing officer shall mark each statement with a file number and with the date and hour of filing and shall hold the statement or a microfilm or other photographic copy thereof for public inspection. In addition the filing officer shall index the statement according to the name of the debtor and shall note in the index the file number and the address of the debtor given in the statement.

(5) The uniform fee for filing and indexing and for stamping a copy furnished by the secured party to show the date and place of filing for an original financing

statement or for a continuation statement shall be $. . . . . if the statement is in the standard form prescribed by the [Secretary of State] and otherwise shall be $. . . . . , plus in each case, if the financing statement is subject to subsection (5) of Section 9-402, $. . . . . The uniform fee for each name more than one required to be indexed shall be $. . . . . The secured party may at his option show a trade name for any person and an extra uniform indexing fee of $. . . . . shall be paid with respect thereto.

(6) If the debtor is a transmitting utility (subsection (5) of Section 9-401) and a filed financing statement so states, it is effective until a termination statement is filed. A real estate mortgage which is effective as a fixture filing under subsection (6) of Section 9-402 remains effective as a fixture filing until the mortgage is released or satisfied of record or its effectiveness otherwise terminates as to the real estate.

(7) When a financing statement covers timber to be cut or covers minerals or the like (including oil and gas) or accounts subject to subsection (5) of Section 9-103, or is filed as a fixture filing, [it shall be filed for record and] the filing officer shall index it under the names of the debtor and any owner of record shown on the financing statement in the same fashion as if they were the mortgagors in a mortgage of the real estate described, and, to the extent that the law of this state provides for indexing of mortgages under the name of the mortgagee, under the name of the secured party as if he were the mortgagee thereunder, or where indexing is by description in the same fashion as if the financing statement were a mortgage of the real estate described. Amended in 1972.

Note: In states in which writings will not appear in the real estate records and indices unless actually recorded the bracketed language in subsection (7) should be used.

§ 9-404.   Termination Statement

(1) If a financing statement covering consumer goods is filed on or after. . . . . , then within one month or within ten days following written demand by the debtor after there is no outstanding secured obligation and no commitment to make advances, incur obligations or otherwise give value, the secured party must file with each filing officer with whom the financing statement was filed, a termination statement to the effect that he no longer claims a security interest under the financing statement, which shall be identified by file number. In other cases whenever there is no outstanding secured obligation and no commitment to make advances, incur obligations or otherwise give value, the secured party must on written demand by the debtor send the debtor, for each filing officer with whom the financing statement was filed, a termination statement to the effect that he no longer claims a security interest under the financing statement, which shall be identified by file number. A termination statement signed by a person other than the secured party of record must be accompanied by a separate written statement of assignment signed by the secured party of record complying with subsection (2) of Section 9-405, including payment of the required fee. If the affected secured party fails to file such a termination statement as required by this subsection, or to send such a termination statement within ten days after proper demand therefor, he shall be liable to the debtor for one hundred dollars, and in addition for any loss caused to the debtor by such failure.

(2) On presentation to the filing officer of such a termination statement he must note it in the index. If he has received the termination statement in duplicate, he shall return one copy of the termination statement to the secured party stamped to show the time of receipt thereof. If the filing officer has a microfilm or other photographic record of the financing statement, and of any related continuation statement, statement of assignment and statement of release, he may remove the originals from the files at any time after receipt of the termination statement, or if he has no such record, he may remove them from the files at any time after one year after receipt of the termination statement.

(3) If the termination statement is in the standard form prescribed by the [Secretary of State], the uniform fee for filing and indexing the termination statement shall be $. . . . . , and otherwise shall be $. . . . . , plus in each case an additional fee of $. . . . . , for each name more than one against which the termination statement is required to be indexed. Amended in 1972.

Note: The date to be inserted should be the effective date of the revised Article 9.

§ 9-405.   Assignment of Security Interest; Duties of Filing Officer; Fees

(1) A financing statement may disclose an assignment of a security interest in the collateral described in the

financing statement by indication in the financing statement of the name and address of the assignee or by an assignment itself or a copy thereof on the face or back of the statment. On presentation to the fiing officer of such a financing statement the filing officer shall mark the same as provided in Section 9-403(4). The uniform fee for filing, indexing and furnishing filing data for a financing statement so indicating an assignment shall be $ . . . . . . if the statement is in the standard form prescribed by the [Secretary of State] and otherwise shall be $. . . . . . , plus in each case an additional fee of $. . . . . . , for each name more than one against which the financing statement is required to be indexed.

(2) A secured party may assign or record all or part of his rights under a financing statement by the filing in the place where the original financing statement was filed of a separate written statement of assignment signed by the secured party of record and setting forth the name of the secured party of record and the debtor, the file number and the date of filing of the financing statement and the name and address of the assignee and containing a description of the collateral assigned. A copy of the assignment is sufficient as a separate statement if it complies with the preceding sentence. On presentation to the filing officer of such a separate statement, the filing officer shall mark such separate statement with the date and hour of the filing. He shall note the assignment on the index of the financing statement, or in the case of a fixture filing, or a filing covering timber to be cut, or covering minerals or the like (including oil and gas) or accounts subject to subsection (5) of Section 9-103, he shall index the assignment under the name of the assignor as grantor and, to the extent that the law of this state provides for indexing the assignment of a mortgage under the name of the assignee, he shall index the assignment of the financing statement under the name of the assignee. The uniform fee for filing, indexing and furnishing filing data about such a separate statement of assignment shall be $. . . . . . , if the statement is in the standard form prescribed by the [Secretary of State] and otherwise shall be $. . . . . . , plus in each case an additional fee of $. . . . . for each name more than one against which the statement of assignment is required to be indexed. Notwithstanding the provisions of this subsection, an assignment of record of a security interest in a fixture contained in a mortgage effective as a fixture filing (subsection (6) of Section 9-402) may be made only by an assignment of the mortgage in the manner provided by the law of this state other than this Act.

(3) After the disclosure or filing of an assignment under this section, the assignee is the secured party of record. Amended in 1972.

§ 9-406.   Release of Collateral; Duties of Filing Officer; Fees

A secured party of record may by his signed statement release all or a part of any collateral described in a filed financing statement. The statement of release is sufficient if it contains a description of the collateral being released, the name and address of the debtor, the name and address of the secured party, and the file number of the financing statement. A statement of release signed by a person other than a secured party of record must be accompanied by a separate written statement of assignment signed by the secured party of record and complying with subsection (2) of Section 9-405, including payment of the required fee. Upon presentation of such a statement of release to the filing officer he shall mark the statement with the hour and date of filing and shall note the same upon the margin of the index of the filing of the financing statement. The uniform fee for filing and noting such a statement of release shall be $. . . . . if the statement is in the standard form prescribed by the [Secretary of State] and otherwise shall be $. . . . . for each name more than one against which the statement of release is required to be indexed. Amended in 1972.

[§ 9-407.   Information From Filing Officer]

[(1) If the person filing any financing statement, termination statement, statement of assignment, or statement of release, furnishes the filing officer a copy thereof, the filing officer shall upon request note upon the copy the file number and date and hour of the filing of the original and deliver or send the copy to such person.]

[(2) Upon request of any person, the filing officer shall issue his certificate showing whether there is on file on the date and hour stated therein, any presently effective financing statement naming a particular debtor and any statement of assignment thereof and if there is, giving the date and hour of filing of each such statement and the names and addresses of each secured party thereon. The uniform fee for such a certificate shall be $. . . . . if the request for the certificate is in the standard form prescribed by the [Secretary of State] and otherwise shall be $. . . . . Upon request the filing officer shall furnish a copy of any filed financing statement or statement of assignment for a uniform fee of $. . . . . per page.] Amended in 1972.

Note: This section is proposed as an optional provision to require filing officers to furnish certificates. Local law and practices should be consulted with regard to the advisability of adoption.

§ 9-408. Financing Statements Covering Consigned or Leased Goods

A consignor or lessor of goods may file a financing statement using the terms "consignor," "consignee," "lessor," "lessee" or the like instead of the terms specified in Section 9-402. The provisions of this Part shall apply as appropriate to such a financing statement but its filing shall not of itself be a factor in determining whether or not the consignment or lease is intended as security (Section 1-201(37)). However, if it is determined for other reasons that the consignment or lease is so intended, a security interest of the consignor or lessor which attaches to the consigned or leased goods is perfected by such filing. Added in 1972.

PART 5. Default

§ 9-501. Default; Procedure When Security Agreement Covers Both Real and Personal Property

(1) When a debtor is in default under a security agreement, a secured party has the rights and remedies provided in this Part and except as limited by subsection (3) those provided in the security agreement. He may reduce his claim to judgment, foreclose or otherwise enforce the security interest by any available judicial procedure. If the collateral is documents the secured party may proceed either as to the documents or as to the goods covered thereby. A secured party in possession has the rights, remedies and duties provided in Section 9-207. The rights and remedies referred to in this subsection are cumulative.

(2) After default, the debtor has the rights and remedies provided in this Part, those provided in the security agreement and those provided in Section 9-207.

(3) To the extent that they give rights to the debtor and impose duties on the secured party, the rules stated in the subsections referred to below may not be waived or varied except as provided with respect to compulsory disposition of collateral (subsection (3) of Section

9-504 and Section 9-505) and with respect to redemption of collateral (Section 9-506) but the parties may by agreement determine the standards by which the fulfillment of these rights and duties is to be measured if such standards are not manifestly unreasonable:

(a) subsection (2) of Section 9-502 and subsection (2) of Section 9-504 insofar as they require accounting for surplus proceeds of collateral;

(b) subsection (3) of Section 9-504 and subsection (1) of Section 9-505 which deal with disposition of collateral;

(c) subsection (2) of Section 9-505 which deals with acceptance of collateral as discharge of obligation;

(d) Section 9-506 which deals with redemption of collateral; and

(e) subsection (1) of Section 9-507 which deals with the secured party's liability for failure to comply with this Part.

(4) If the security agreement covers both real and personal property, the secured party may proceed under this Part as to the personal property or he may proceed as to both the real and the personal property in accordance with his rights and remedies in respect of the real property in which case the provisions of this Part do not apply.

(5) When a secured party has reduced his claim to judgment the lien or any levy which may be made upon his collateral by virtue of any execution based upon the judgment shall relate back to the date of the perfection of the security interest in such collateral. A judicial sale, pursuant to such execution, is a foreclosure of the security interest by judicial procedure within the meaning of this section, and the secured party may purchase at the sale and thereafter hold the collateral free of any other requirements of this Article. Amended in 1972.

§ 9-502. Collection Rights of Secured Party

(1) When so agreed and in any event on default the secured party is entitled to notify an account debtor or the obligor on an instrument to make payment to him whether or not the assignor was theretofore making collections on the collateral, and also to take control of any proceeds to which he is entitled under Section 9-306.

(2) A secured party who by agreement is entitled to charge back uncollected collateral or otherwise to full or limited recourse against the debtor and who undertakes to collect from the account debtors or obligors must proceed in a commercially reasonable manner and may

deduct his reasonable expenses of realization from the collections. If the security agreement secures an indebtedness, the secured party must account to the debtor for any surplus, and unless otherwise agreed, the debtor is liable for any deficiency. But, if the underlying transaction was a sale of accounts or chattel paper, the debtor is entitled to any surplus or is liable for any deficiency only if the security agreement so provides. Amended in 1972.

§ 9-503. Secured Party's Right to Take Possession After Default

Unless otherwise agreed a secured party has on default the right to take possession of the collateral. In taking possession a secured party may proceed without judicial process if this can be done without breach of the peace or may proceed by action. If the security agreement so provides the secured party may require the debtor to assemble the collateral and make it available to the secured party at a place to be designated by the secured party which is reasonably convenient to both parties. Without removal a secured party may render equipment unusable, and may dispose of collateral on the debtor's premises under Section 9-504.

§ 9-504. Secured Party's Right to Dispose of Collateral After Default; Effect of Disposition

(1) A secured party after default may sell, lease or otherwise dispose of any or all of the collateral in its then condition or following any commercially reasonable preparation or processing. Any sale of goods is subject to the Article on Sales (Article 2). The proceeds of disposition shall be applied in the order following to

(a) the reasonable expenses of retaking, holding, preparing for sale or lease, selling, leasing and the like and, to the extent provided for in the agreement and not prohibited by law, the reasonable attorneys' fees and legal expenses incurred by the secured party;

(b) the satisfaction of indebtedness secured by the security interest under which the disposition is made;

(c) the satisfaction of indebtedness secured by any subordinate security interest in the collateral if written notification of demand therefor is received before distribution of the proceeds is completed. If requested by the secured party, the holder of a subordinate security interest must seasonably furnish reasonable proof of his interest, and unless he does so, the secured party need not comply with his demand.

(2) If the security interest secures an indebtedness, the secured party must account to the debtor for any surplus, and, unless otherwise agreed, the debtor is liable for any deficiency. But if the underlying transaction was a sale of accounts or chattel paper, the debtor is entitled to any surplus or is liable for any deficiency only if the security agreement so provides.

(3) Disposition of the collateral may be by public or private proceedings and may be made by way of one or more contracts. Sale or other disposition may be as a unit or in parcels and at any time and place and on any terms but every aspect of the disposition including the method, manner, time, place and terms must be commercially reasonable. Unless collateral is perishable or threatens to decline speedily in value or is of a type customarily sold on a recognized market, reasonable notification of the time and place of any public sale or reasonable notification of the time after which any private sale or other intended disposition is to be made shall be sent by the secured party to the debtor, if he has not signed after default a statement renouncing or modifying his right to notification of sale. In the case of consumer goods no other notification need be sent. In other cases notification shall be sent to any other secured party from whom the secured party has received (before sending his notification to the debtor or before the debtor's renunciation of his rights) written notice of a claim of an interest in the collateral. The secured party may buy at any public sale and if the collateral is of a type customarily sold in a recognized market or is of a type which is the subject of widely distributed standard price quotations he may buy at private sale.

(4) When collateral is disposed of by a secured party after default, the disposition transfers to a purchaser for value all of the debtor rights therein, discharges the security interest under which it is made and any security interest or lien subordinate thereto. The purchaser takes free of all such rights and interests even though the secured party fails to comply with the requirements of this Part or of any judicial proceedings

(a) in the case of a public sale, if the purchaser has no knowledge of any defects in the sale and if he does not buy in collusion with the secured party, other bidders or the person conducting the sale; or

(b) in any other case, if the purchaser acts in good faith.

(5) A person who is liable to a secured party under a guaranty, indorsement, repurchase agreement or the like and who receives a transfer of collateral from the secured party or is subrogated to his rights has there-

after the rights and duties of the secured party. Such a transfer of collateral is not a sale or disposition of the collateral under this Article. Amended in 1972.

§ 9-505. Compulsory Disposition of Collateral; Acceptance of the Collateral as Discharge of Obligation

(1) If the debtor has paid sixty percent of the cash price in the case of a purchase money security interest in consumer goods or sixty percent of the loan in the case of another security interest in consumer goods, and has not signed after default a statement renouncing or modifying his rights under this Part a secured party who has taken possession of collateral must dispose of it under Section 9-504 and if he fails to do so within ninety days after he takes possession the debtor at his option may recover in conversion or under Section 9-507(1) on secured party's liability.

(2) In any other case involving consumer goods or any other collateral a secured party in possession may, after default, propose to retain the collateral in satisfaction of the obligation. Written notice of such proposal shall be sent to the debtor if he has not signed after default a statement renouncing or modifying his rights under this subsection. In the case of consumer goods no other notice need be given. In other cases notice shall be sent to any other secured party from whom the secured party has received (before sending his notice to the debtor or before the debtor's renunciation of his rights) written notice of a claim of an interest in the collateral. If the secured party receives objection in writing from a person entitled to receive notification within twenty-one days after the notice was sent, the secured party must dispose of the collateral under Section 9-504. In the absence of such written objection the secured party may retain the collateral in satisfaction of the debtor's obligation. Amended in 1972.

§ 9-506. Debtor's Right to Redeem Collateral

At any time before the secured party has disposed of collateral or entered into a contract for its disposition under Section 9-504 or before the obligation has been discharged under Section 9-505(2) the debtor or any other secured party may unless otherwise agreed in writing after default redeem the collateral by tendering fulfillment of all obligations secured by the collateral as well as the expenses reasonably incurred by the secured party in retaking, holding and preparing the collateral

for disposition, in arranging for the sale, and to the extent provided in the agreement and not prohibited by law, his reasonable attorney's fees and legal expenses.

§ 9-507. Secured Party's Liability for Failure to Comply With This Part

(1) If it is established that the secured party is not proceeding in accordance with the provisions of this Part disposition may be ordered or restrained on appropriate terms and conditions. If the disposition has occurred the debtor or any person entitled to notification or whose security interest has been made known to the secured party prior to the disposition has a right to recover from the secured party any loss caused by a failure to comply with the provisions of this Part. If the collateral is consumer goods, the debtor has a right to recover in any event an amount not less than the credit service charge plus ten percent of the principal amount of the debt or the time price differential plus 10 percent of the cash price.

(2) The fact that a better price could have been obtained by a sale at a different time or in a different method from that selected by the secured party is not of itself sufficient to establish that the sale was not made in a commercially reasonable manner. If the secured party either sells the collateral in the usual manner in any recognized market therefore or if he sells at the price current in such market at the time of his sale or if he has otherwise sold in conformity with reasonable commercial practices among dealers in the type of property sold he has sold in a commercially reasonable manner. The principles stated in the two preceding sentences with respect to sales also apply as may be appropriate to other types of disposition. A disposition which has been approved in any judicial proceeding or by any bona fide creditors' committee or representative of creditors shall conclusively be deemed to be commercially reasonable, but this sentence does not indicate that any such approval must be obtained in any case nor does it indicate that any disposition not so approved is not commercially reasonable.

§ ARTICLE 10. Effective Date and Repealer
[Text omitted.]

§ ARTICLE 11. Effective Date and Transition Provisions
[Text omitted.]

Appendix | D

Uniform Partnership Act

PART I

Preliminary Provisions

§ 1. Name of Act

This act may be cited as Uniform Parntership Act.

§ 2. Definition of Terms

In this act, "Court" includes every court and judge having jurisdiction in the case.

"Business" includes every trade, occupation, or profession.

"Person" includes individuals, partnerships, corporations, and other associations.

"Bankrupt" includes bankrupt under the Federal Bankruptcy Act or insolvent under any state insolvent act.

"Conveyance" includes every assignment, lease, mortgage, or encumbrance.

"Real property" includes land and any interst or estate in land.

§ 3. Interpretation of Knowledge and Notice

(1) A person has "knowledge" of a fact within the meaning of this act not only when he has actual knowledge thereof, but also when he has knowledge of such other facts as in the circumstances shows bad faith.

(2) A person has "notice" of a fact within the meaning of this act when the person who claims the benefit of the notice:

(a) States the fact to such person, or

(b) Delivers through the mail, or by other means of communication, a written statement of the fact to such person or to a proper person at his place of business or residence.

§ 4. Rules Construction

(1) The rule that statutes in derogation of the common law are to be strictly construed shall have no application to this act.

(2) The law of estoppel shall apply under this act.

(3) The law of agency shall apply under this act.

(4) This act shall be so interpreted and construed as to effect its general purpose to make uniform the law of those states which enact it.

(5) This act shall not be construed so as to impair the obligations of any contract existing when the act goes into effect, not to affect any action or proceedings begun or right accrued before this act takes effect.

§ 5. Rules for Cases Not Provided for in This Act

In any case not provided for in this act the rules of law and equity, including the law merchant, shall govern.

PART II

Nature of a Partnership

§ 6. Partnership Defined

(1) A partnership is an association of two or more persons to carry on as co-owners a business for profit.

(2) But any association formed under any other statute of this state, or any statute adopted by authority, other than the authority of this state, is not a partnership under this act, unless such association would have been a partnership in this state prior to the adoption of this act; but this act shall apply to limited partnerships except in so far as the statutes relating to such partnerships are inconsistent herewith.

§ 7. Rules for Determining the Existence of a Partnership

In determining whether a partnership exists, these rules shall apply:

(1) Except as provided by section 16 persons who are not partners as to each other are not partners as to third persons.

(2) Joint tenancy, tenancy in common, tenancy by the entireties, joint property, common property, or part ownership does not of itself establish a partnership, whether such co-owners do or do not share any profits made by the use of the property.

(3) The sharing of gross returns does not of itself establish a partnership, whether or not the persons sharing them have a joint or common right or interest in any property from which the returns are derived.

(4) The receipt by a person of a share of the profits of a business is prima facie evidence that he is a partner in the business, but no such inference shall be drawn if such profits were received in payment:

(a) As a debt by installments or otherwise,

(b) As wages of an employee or rent to a landlord,

(c) As an annuity to a widow or representative of a deceased partner,

(d) As interest on a loan, though the amount of payment vary with the profits of the business,

(e) As the consideration for the sale of a good-will of a business or other property by installments or otherwise.

§ 8. Partnership Property

(1) All property originally brought into the partnership stock or subsequently acquired by purchase or otherwise, on account of the partnership, is partnership property.

(2) Unless the contrary intention appears, property acquired with partnership funds is partnership property.

(3) Any estate in real property may be acquired in the partnership name. Title so acquired can be conveyed only in the partnership name.

(4) A conveyance to a partnership in the partnership name, though without words of inheritance, passes the entire estate of the grantor unless a contrary intent appears.

PART III

Relations Of Partners To Persons Dealing With The Partnership

§ 9. Partner Agent of Partnership as to Partnership Business

(1) Every partner is an agent of the partnership for the purpose of its business, and the act of every partner, including the execution in the partnership name of any instrument, for apparently carrying on in the usual way the business of the partnership of which he is a member binds the partnership, unless the partner so acting has in fact no authority to act for the partnership in the particular matter, and the person with whom he is dealing has knowledge of the fact that he has no such authority.

(2) An act of a partner which is not apparently for the carrying on of the business of the partnership in the

usual way does not bind the partnership unless authorized by the other partners.

(3) Unless authorized by the other partners or unless they have abandoned the business, one or more but less than all the partners have no authority to:

(a) Assign the partnership property in trust for creditors or on the assignee's promise to pay the debts of the partnership,

(b) Dispose of the good-will of the business,

(c) Do any other act which would make it impossible to carry on the ordinary business of a partnership,

(d) Confess a judgment,

(e) Submit a partnership claim or liability to arbitration or reference.

(4) No act of a partner in contravention of a restriction on authority shall bind the partnership to persons having knowledge of the restriction.

§ 10. Conveyance of Real Property of the Partnership

(1) Where title to real property is in the partnership name, any partner may convey title to such property by a conveyance executed in the partnership name; but the partnership may recover such property unless the partner's act binds the partnership under the provisions of paragraph (1) of section 9, or unless such property has been conveyed by the grantee or a person claiming through such grantee to a holder for value without knowledge that the partner, in making the conveyance, has exceeded his authority.

(2) Where title to real property is in the name of the partnership, a conveyance executed by a partner, in his own name, passes the equitable interest of the partnership, provided the act is one within the authority of the partner under the provisions of paragraph (1) of section 9.

(3) Where title to real property is in the name of one or more but not all the partners, and the record does not disclose the right of the partnership, the partners in whose name the title stands may convey title to such property, but the partnership may recover such property if the partners' act does not bind the partnership under the provisions of paragraph (1) of section 9, unless the purchaser or his assignee, is a holder for value, without knowledge.

(4) Where the title to real property is in the name of one or more or all the partners, or in a third person in trust for the partnership, a conveyance executed by a partner in the partnership name, or in his own name, passes the equitable interest of the partnership, provided the act is one within the authority of the partner under the provisions of paragraph (1) of section 9.

(5) Where the title to real property is in the names of all the partners a conveyance executed by all the partners passes all their rights in such property.

§ 11. Partnership Bound by Admission of Partner

An admission or representation made by any partner concerning partnership affairs within the scope of his authority as conferred by this act is evidence against the partnership.

§ 12. Partnership Charged with Knowledge of or Notice to Partner

Notice to any partner of any matter relating to partnership affairs, and the knowledge of the partner acting in the particular matter, acquired while a partner or then present to his mind, and the knowledge of any other partner who reasonably could and should have communicated it to the acting partner, operate as notice to or knowledge of the partnership, except in the case of a fraud on the partnership committed by or with the consent of that partner.

§ 13. Partnership Bound by Partner's Wrongful Act

Where, by any wrongful act or omission of any partner acting in the ordinary course of the business of the partnership or with the authority of his co-partners, loss or injury is caused to any person, not being a partner in the partnership, or any penalty is incurred, the partnership is liable therefor to the same extent as the partner so acting or omitting to act.

§ 14. Partnership Bound by Partner's Breach of Trust

The partnership is bound to make good the loss:

(a) Where one partner acting within the scope of his apparent authority receives money or property of a third person and misapplies it; and

(b) Where the partnership in the course of its business receives money or property of a third person and the money or property so received is misapplied by any partner while it is in the custody of the partnership.

§ 15.   Nature of Partner's Liability

All partners are liable

(a) Jointly and severally for everything chargeable to the partnership under sections 13 and 14.

(b) Jointly for all other debts and obligations of the partnership; but any partner may enter into a separate obligation to perform a partnership contract.

§ 16.   Partner by Estoppel

(1) When a person, by words spoken or written or by conduct, represents himself, or consents to another representing him to any one, as a partner in an existing partnership or with one or more persons not actual partners, he is liable to any such person to whom such representation has been made, who has, on the faith of such representation, given credit to the actual or apparent partnership, and if he has made such representation or consented to its being made in a public manner he is liable to such person, whether the representation has or has not been made or communicated to such person so giving credit by or with the knowledge of the apparent partner making the representation or consenting to its being made.

(a) When a partnership liability results, he is liable as though he were an actual member of the partnership.

(b) When no partnership liability results, he is liable jointly with the other persons, if any, so consenting to the contract or representation as to incur liability, otherwise separately.

(2) When a person has been thus represented to be a partner in an existing partnership, or with one or more persons not actual partners, he is an agent of the persons consenting to such representation to bind them to the same extent and in the same manner as though he were a partner in fact, with respect to persons who rely upon the representation. Where all the members of the existing partnership consent to the representation, a partnership act or obligation results; but in all other cases it is the joint act or obligation of the person acting and the persons consenting to the representation.

§ 17.   Liability of Incoming Partner

A person admitted as a partner into an existing partnership is liable for all the obligations of the partnership arising before his admission as though he had been a partner when such obligations were incurred, except that this liability shall be satisfied only out of partnership property.

PART IV

Relations of Partners to One Another

§ 18.   Rules Determining Rights and Duties of Partners

The rights and duties of the partners in relation to the partnership shall be determined, subject to any agreement between them, by the following rules:

(a) Each partner shall be repaid his contributions, whether by way of capital or advances to the partnership property and share equally in the profits and surplus remaining after all liabilities, including those to partners, are satisfied; and must contribute towards the losses, whether of capital or otherwise, sustained by the partnership according to his share in the profits.

(b) The partnership must indemnify every partner in respect of payments made and person liabilities reasonably incurred by him in the ordinary and proper conduct of its business, or for the preservation of its business or property.

(c) A partner, who in aid of the partnership makes any payment or advance beyond the amount of capital which he agreed to contribute, shall be paid interest from the date of payment or advance.

(d) A partner shall receive interest on the capital contributed by him only from the date when repayment should be made.

(e) All partners have equal rights in the management and conduct of the partnership business.

(f) No partner is entitled to remuneration for acting in the partnership business, except that a surviving partner is entitled to reasonable compensation for his services in winding up the partnership affairs.

(g) No person can become a member of a partnership without the consent of all the partners.

(h) Any difference arising as to ordinary matters connected with the partnership business may be decided by a majority of the partners; but no act in contravention of any agreement between the partners may be done rightfully without the consent of all the partners.

§ 19.   Partnership Books

The partnership books shall be kept, subject to any agreement between the partners, at the principal place of business of the partnership, and every partner shall at all times have access to and may inspect and copy any of them.

§ 20. Duty of Partners to Render Information

Partners shall render on demand true and full information of all things affecting the partnership to any partner or the legal representative of any deceased partner or partner under legal disability.

§ 21. Partner Accountable as a Fiduciary

(1) Every partner must account to the partnership for any benefit, and hold as trustee for it any profits derived by him without the consent of the other partners from any transaction connected with the formation, conduct, or liquidation of the partnership or from any use by him of its property.

(2) This section applies also to the representatives of a deceased partner engaged in the liquidation of the affairs of the partnership as the personal representatives of the last surviving partner.

§ 22. Right to an Account

Any partner shall have the right to a formal account as to partnership affairs:

(a) If he is wrongfully excluded from the partnership business or possession of its property by his co-partners,

(b) If the right exists under the terms of any agreement,

(c) As provided by section 21,

(d) Whenever other circumstances render it just and reasonable.

§ 23. Continuation of Partnership Beyond Fixed Term

(1) When a partnership for a fixed term or particular undertaking is continued after the termination of such term or particular undertaking without any express agreement, the rights and duties of the partners remain the same as they were at such termination, so far as is consistent with a partnership at will.

(2) A continuation of the business by the partners or such of them as habitually acted therein during the term, without any settlement or liquidation of the partnership affairs, is prima facie evidence of a continuation of the partnership.

PART V

Property Rights of a Partner

§ 24. Extent of Property Rights of a Partner

The property rights of a partner are (1) his rights in specific partnership property, (2) his interest in the partnership, and (3) his right to participate in the management.

§ 25. Nature of a Partner's Right in Specific Partnership Property

(1) A partner is co-owner with his partners of specific partnership property holding as a tenant in partnership.

(2) The incidents of this tenancy are such that:

(a) A partner, subject to the provisions of this act and to any agreement between the partners, has an equal right with his partners to possess specific partnership property for partnership purposes; but he has no right to possess such property for any other purpose without the consent of his partners.

(b) A partner's right in specific partnership property is not assignable except in connection with the assignment of rights of all the partners in the same property.

(c) A partner's right in specific partnership property is not subject to attachment or execution, except on a claim against the partnership. When partnership property is attached for a partnership debt the partners, or any of them, or the representatives of a deceased partner, cannot claim any right under the homestead or exemption laws.

(d) On the death of a partner his right in specific partnership property vests in the surviving partner or partners, except where the deceased was the last surviving partner, when his right in such property vests in his legal representative. Such surviving partner or partners, or the legal representative of the last surviving partner, has no right to possess the partnership property for any but a partnership purpose.

(e) A partner's right in specific partnership property is not subject to dower, curtesy, or allowances to widows, heirs, or next of kin.

§ 26. Nature of Partner's Interest in the Partnership

A partner's interest in the partnership is his share of the profits and surplus, and the same is personal property.

§ 27. Assignment of Partner's Interest

(1) A conveyance by a partner of his interest in the partnership does not of itself dissolve the partnership, nor, as against the other partners in the absence of agreement, entitle the assignee, during the continuance of the partnership, to interfere in the management or administration of the partnership business or affairs, or to require any information or account of partnership transactions, or to inspect the partnership books; but it merely entitles the assignee to receive in accordance with his contract the profits to which the assigning partner would otherwise be entitled.

(2) In case of a dissolution of the partnership, the assignee is entitled to receive his assignor's interest and may require an account from the date only of the last account agreed to by all the partners.

§ 28. Partner's Interest Subject to Charging Order

(1) On due application to a competent court by any judgment creditor of a partner, the court which entered the judgment, order, or decree, or any other court, may charge the interest of the debtor partner with payment of the unsatisfied amount of such judgment debt with interest thereon; and may then or later appoint a receiver of his share of the profits, and of any other money due or to fall due to him in respect of the partnership, and make all other orders, directions, accounts and inquiries which the debtor partner might have made, or which the circumstances of the case may require.

(2) The interest charged may be redeemed at any time before foreclosure, or in case of a sale being directed by the court may be purchased without thereby causing a dissolution:

(a) With separate property, by any one or more of the partners, or

(b) With partnership property, by any one or more of the partners with the consent of all the partners whose interests are not so charged or sold.

(3) Nothing in this act shall be held to deprive a partner of his right, if any, under the exemption laws, as regards his interest in the partnership.

PART VI

Dissolution and Winding Up

§ 29. Dissolution Defined

The dissolution of a partnership is the change in the relation of the partners caused by any partner ceasing to be associated in the carrying on as distinguished from the winding up of the business.

§ 30. Partnership not Terminated by Dissolution

On dissolution the partnership is not terminated, but continues until the winding up of partnership affairs is completed.

§ 31. Causes of Dissolution

Dissolution is caused:

(1) Without violation of the agreement between the partners,

(a) By the termination of the definite term or particular undertaking specified in the agreement,

(b) By the express will of any partner when no definite term or particular undertaking is specified,

(c) By the express will of all the partners who have not assigned their interests or suffered them to be charged for their separate debts, either before or after the termination of any specified term or particular undertaking,

(d) by the expulsion of any partner from the business bona fide in accordance with such a power conferred by the agreement between the partners;

(2) In contravention of the agreement between the partners, where the circumstances do not permit a dissolution under any other provision of this section, by the express will of any partner at any time;

(3) By any event which makes it unlawful for the business of the partnership to be carried on or for the members to carry it on in partnership;

(4) By the death of any partner;

(5) By the bankruptcy of any partner or the partnership;

(6) By decree of court under section 32.

§ 32. Dissolution by Decree of Court

(1) On application by or for a partner the court shall decree a dissolution whenever:

(a) A partner has been declared a lunatic in any judicial proceeding or is shown to be of unsound mind,

(b) A partner becomes in any other way incapable of performing his part of the partnership contract,

(c) A partner has been guilty of such conduct as tends to affect prejudicially the carrying on of the business,

(d) A partner wilfully or persistently commits a breach of the partnership agreement, or otherwise so conducts himself in matters relating to the partnership business that it is not reasonably practicable to carry on the business in partnership with him,

(e) The business of the partnership can only be carried on at a loss,

(f) Other circumstances render a dissolution equitable.

(2) On the application of the purchaser of a partner's interest under sections 28 or 29:

(a) After the termination of the specified term or particular undertaking,

(b) At any time if the partnership was a partnership at will when the interest was assigned or when the charging order was isssued.

§ 33.   General Effect of Dissolution on Authority of Partner

Except so far as may be necessary to wind up partnership affairs or to complete transactions begun but not then finished, dissolution terminates all authority of any partner to act for the partnership,

(1) With respect to the partners,

(a) When the dissolution is not by the act, bankruptcy or death of a partner; or

(b) When the dissolution is by such act, bankruptcy or death of a partner, in cases where section 34 so requires.

(2) With respect to persons not partners, as declared in section 35.

§ 34.   Right of Partner to Contribution from Co-partners after Dissolution

Where the dissolution is caused by the act, death or bankruptcy of a partner, each partner is liable to his co-partners for his share of any liability created by any partner acting for the partnership as if the partnership had not been dissolved unless

(a) The dissolution being by act of any partner, the partner acting for the partnership had knowledge of the dissolution, or

(b) The dissolution being by the death or bankruptcy of a partner, the partner acting for the partnership had knowledge or notice of the death or bankruptcy.

§ 35.   Power of Partner to Bind Partnership to Third Persons after Dissolution

(1) After dissolution a partner can bind the partnership except as provided in Paragraph (3).

(a) By any act appropriate for winding up partnership affairs or completing transactions unfinished at dissolution;

(b) By any transaction which would bind the partnership if dissolution had not taken place, provided the other party to the transaction

(I) Had extended credit to the partnership prior to dissolution and had no knowledge or notice of the dissolution; or

(II) Though he had not so extended credit, had nevertheless known of the partnership prior to dissolution, and, having no knowledge or notice of dissolution, the fact of dissolution had not been advertised in a newspaper of general circulation in the place (or in each place if more than one) at which the partnership business was regularly carried on.

(2) The liability of a partner under Paragraph (1b) shall be satisfied out of partnership assets alone when such partner had been prior to dissolution

(a) Unknown as a partner to the person with whom the contract is made; and

(b) So far unknown and inactive in partnership affairs that the business reputation of the partnership could not be said to have been in any degree due to his connection with it.

(3) The partnership is in no case bound by any act of a partner after dissolution

(a) Where the partnership is dissolved because it is unlawful to carry on the business, unless the act is appropriate for winding up partnership affairs; or

(b) Where the partner has become bankrupt; or

(c) Where the partner has no authority to wind up partnership affairs; except by a transaction with one who

(I) Had extended credit to the partnership prior to dissolution and had no knowledge or notice of his want of authority; or

(II) Had not extended credit to the partnership prior to dissolution, and, having no knowledge or notice of his want of authority, the fact of his want of authority has not been advertised in the manner provided for advertising the fact of dissolution in Paragraph (1b II).

(4) Nothing in this section shall affect the liability under Section 16 of any person who after dissolution represents himself or consents to another representing him as a partner in a partnership engaged in carrying on business.

§ 36. Effect of Dissolution on Partner's Existing Liability

(1) The dissolution of the partnership does not of itself discharge the existing liability of any partner.

(2) A partner is discharged from any existing liability upon dissolution of the partnership by an agreement to that effect between himself, the partnership creditor and the person or partnership continuing the business; and such agreement may be inferred from the course of dealing between the creditor having knowledge of the dissolution and the person or partnership continuing the business.

(3) Where a person agrees to assume the existing obligations of a dissolved partnership, the partners whose obligations have been assumed shall be discharged from any liability to any creditor of the partnership who, knowing of the agreement, consents to a material alteration in the nature or time of payment of such obligations.

(4) The individual property of a deceased partner shall be liable for all obligations of the partnership incurred while he was a partner but subject to the prior payment of his separate debts.

§ 37. Right to Wind Up

Unless otherwise agreed the partners who have not wrongfully dissolved the partnership or the legal representative of the last surving partner, not bankrupt, has the right to wind up the partnership affairs; provided, however, that any partner, his legal representative or his assignee, upon cause shown, may obtain winding up by the court.

§ 38. Rights of Partners to Application of Partnership Property

(1) When dissolution is caused in any way, except in contravention of the partnership agreement, each partner, as against his co-partners and all persons claiming through them in respect of their interests in the partnership, unless otherwise agreed, may have the partnership property applied to discharge its liabilities, and the surplus applied to pay in cash the net amount owing to the respective partners. But if dissolution is caused by expulsion of a partner, bona fide under the partnership agreement and if the expelled partner is discharged from all partnership liabilities, either by payment or agreement under section 36(2), he shall receive in cash only the net amount due him from the partnership.

(2) When dissolution is caused in contravention of the partnership agreement the rights of the partners shall be as follows:

(a) Each partner who has not caused dissolution wrongfully shall have,

I. All the rights specified in paragraph (1) of this section, and

II. The right, as against each partner who has caused the dissolution wrongfully, to damages for breach of the agreement.

(b) The partners who have not caused the dissolution wrongfully, if they all desire to continue the business in the same name, either by themselves or jointly with others, may do so, during the agreed term for the partnership and for that purpose may possess the partnership property, provided they secure the payment by bond approved by the court, or pay to any partner who has caused the dissolution wrongfully, the value of his interest in the partnership at the dissolution, less any damages recoverable under clause (2a II) of this section, and in like manner indemnify him against all present or future partnership liabilities.

(c) A partner who has caused the dissolution wrongfully shall have:

I. If the business is not continued under the provisions of paragraph (2b) all the rights of a partner under paragraph (1), subject to clause (2a II), of this section,

II. If the business is continued under paragraph (2b) of this section the right as against his co-partners and all claiming through them in respect of their interests in the partnership, to have the value of his interest in the partnership, less any damages caused to his co-partners by the dissolution, ascertained and paid to him in cash, or the payment secured by bond approved by the court, and to be released from all existing liabilities of the partnership; but in ascertaining the value of the partner's interest the value of the good-will of the business shall not be considered.

§ 39. Rights Where Partnership is Dissolved for Fraud or Misrepresentation

Where a partnership contract is rescinded on the ground of the fraud or misrepresentation of one of the parties thereto, the party entitled to rescind is, without prejudice to any other right, entitled,

(a) To a lien on, or a right of retention of, the surplus of the partnership property after satisfying the partnership liabilities to third persons for any sum of money paid by him for the purchase of an interest in the partnership and for any capital or advances contributed by him; and

(b) To stand, after all liabilities to third persons have been satisfied, in the place of the creditors of the partnership for any payments made by him in respect of the partnership liabilities; and

(c) To be indemnified by the person guilty of the fraud or making the representation against all debts and liabilities of the partnership.

§ 40. Rules for Distribution

In settling accounts between the partners after dissolution, the following rules shall be observed, subject to any agreement to the contrary:

(a) The assets of the partnership are:

I. The partnership property,

II. The contributions of the partners necessary for the payment of all the liabilities specified in clause (b) of this paragraph.

(b) The liabilities of the partnership shall rank in order of payment, as follows:

I. Those owing to creditors other than partners,

II. Those owing to partners other than for capital and profits,

III. Those owing to partners in respect of capital,

IV. Those owing to partners in respect of profits.

(c) The assets shall be applied in the order of their declaration in clause (a) of this paragraph to the satisfaction of the liabilities.

(d) The partners shall contribute, as provided by section 18 (a) the amount necessary to satisfy the liabilities; but if any, but not all, of the partners are insolvent, or, not being subject to process, refuse to contribute, the other partners shall contribute their share of the liabilities, and, in the relative proportions in which they share the profits, the additional amount necessary to pay the liabilities.

(e) An assignee for the benefit of creditors or any person appointed by the court shall have the right to enforce the contributions specified in clause (d) of this paragraph.

(f) Any partner or his legal representative shall have the right to enforce the contributions specified in clause (d) of this paragraph, to the extent of the amount which he has paid in excess of his share of the liability.

(g) The individual property of a deceased partner shall be liable for the contributions specified in clause (d) of this paragraph.

(h) When partnership property and the individual properties of the partners are in possession of a court for distribution, partnership creditors shall have priority on partnership property and separate creditors on individual property, saving the rights of lien or secured creditors as heretofore.

(i) Where a partner has become bankrupt or his estate is insolvent the claims against his separate property shall rank in the following order:

I. Those owing to separate creditors,

II. Those owing to partnership creditors,

III. Those owing to partners by way of contribution.

§ 41. Liability of Persons Continuing the Business in Certain Cases

(1) When any new partner is admitted into an existing partnership, or when any partner retires and assigns (or the representative of the deceased partner assigns) his rights in partnership property to two or more of the partners, or to one or more of the partners and one or more third persons, if the business is continued without liquidation of the partnership affairs, creditors of the first or dissolved partnership are also creditors of the partnership so continuing the business.

(2) When all but one partner retire and assign (or the representative of a deceased partner assigns) their rights in partnership property to the remaining partner, who continues the business without liquidation of partnership affairs, either alone or with others, creditors of the dissolved partnership are also creditors of the person or partnership so continuing the business.

(3) When any partner retires or dies and the business of the dissolved partnership is continued as set forth in paragraphs (1) and (2) of this section, with the consent of the retired partners or the representative of the deceased partner, but without any assignment of his right in partnership property, rights of creditors of the dissolved partnership and of the creditors of the person or partnership continuing the business shall be as if such assignment had been made.

(4) When all the partners or their representatives assign their rights in partnership property to one or more third persons who promise to pay the debts and who continue the business of the dissolved partnership, creditors of the dissolved partnership are also creditors of the person or partnership continuing the business.

(5) When any partner wrongfully causes a dissolution and the remaining partners continue the business under the provisions of section 38(2b), either alone or with others, and without liquidation of the partnership affairs, creditors of the dissolved partnership are also creditors of the person or partnership continuing the business.

(6) When a partner is expelled and the remaining partners continue the business either alone or with others, without liquidation of the partnership affairs, creditors of the dissolved partnership are also creditors of the person or partnership continuing the business.

(7) The liability of a third person becoming a partner in the partnership continuing the business, under this section, to the creditors of the dissolved partnership shall be satisfied out of partnership property only.

(8) When the business of a partnership after dissolution is continued under any conditions set forth in this section the creditors of the dissolved partnership, as against the separate creditors of the retiring or deceased partner or the representative of the deceased partner, have a prior right to any claim of the retired partner or the representative of the deceased partner against the person or partnership continuing the business, on account of the retired or deceased partner's interest in the dissolved partnership or on account of any consideration promised for such interest or for his right in partnership property.

(9) Nothing in this section shall be held to modify any right of creditors to set aside any assignment on the ground of fraud.

(10) The use by the person or partnership continuing the business of the partnership name, or the name of a deceased partner as part thereof, shall not of itself make the individual property of the deceased partner liable for any debts contracted by such person or partnership.

§ 42. Rights of Retiring or Estate of Deceased Partner When the Business Is Continued

When any partner retires or dies, and the business is continued under any of the conditions set forth in section 41(1, 2, 3, 5, 6), or section 38(2b) without any settlement of accounts as between him or his estate and the person or partnership continuing the business, unless otherwise agreed, he or his legal representative as against such persons or partnership may have the value of his interest at the date of dissolution ascertained, and shall receive as an ordinary creditor an amount equal to the value of his interest in the dissolved partnership with interest, or, at his option or at the option of his legal representative, in lieu of interest, the profits attributable to the use of his right in the property of the dissolved partnership; provided that the creditors of the dissolved partnership as against the separate creditors, or the representative of the retired or deceased partner, shall have priority on any claim arising under this section, as provided by section 41(8) of this act.

§ 43. Accrual of Actions

The right to an account of his interest shall accrue to any partner, or his legal representative, as against the winding up partners or the surviving partners or the person or partnership continuing the business, at the date of dissolution, in the absence of any agreement to the contrary.

PART VII

Miscellaneous Provisions

§ 44. When Act Takes Effect

This act shall take effect on the . . . . day of . . . . . . one thousand nine hundred and . . . .

§ 45. Legislation Repealed

All acts or parts of acts inconsistent with this act are hereby repealed.

Appendix E

Uniform Limited Partnership Act

Approved by the National Conference of Commissioners on Uniform State Laws, August 28, 1916, and adopted in the following jurisdictions: Alabama (1972), Alaska (1917), Arizona (1943), Arkansas (1953), California (1949), Colorado (1931), Connecticut (1961), Delaware (1973), District of Columbia (1962), Florida (1943), Georgia (1952), Hawaii (1943), Idaho (1920), Illinois (1917), Indiana (1949), Iowa (1924), Kansas (1967), Kentucky (1970), Maine (1969), Maryland (1918), Massachusetts (1924), Michigan (1921), Minnesota (1919), Mississippi (1964), Missouri (1947), Montana (1947), Nebraska (1939), Nevada (1931), New Hampshire (1937), New Jersey (1919), New Mexico (1947), New York (1922), North Carolina (1941), North Dakota (1959), Ohio (1957), Oklahoma (1951), Oregon (1971), Pennsylvania (1917), Rhode Island (1930), South Carolina (1960), South Dakota (1925), Tennessee (1920), Texas (1955), Utah (1921), Vermont (1941), Virgin Islands (1957), Virginia (1918), Washington (1945), West Virginia (1953), Wisconsin (1919), and Wyoming (1971).

Louisiana is the only state not included.

§ 1. Limited Partnership defined

A limited partnership is a partnership formed by two or more persons under the provisions of Section 2, having as members one or more general partners and one or more limited partners. The limited partners as such shall not be bound by the obligations of the partnership.

Official Comment

The business reason for the adoption of acts making provisions for limited or special partners is that men in business often desire to secure capital from others.

There are at least three classes of contracts which can be made with those from whom the capital is secured: One, the ordinary loan on interest; another, the loan where the lender, in lieu of interest, takes a share in the profits of the business; third, those cases in which the person advancing the capital secures, besides a share in the profits, some measure of control over the business.

At first, in the absence of statutes the courts, both in this country and in England, assumed that one who is interested in a business is bound by its obligations, carrying the application of this principle so far, that a contract where the only evidence of interest was a share in the profits made one who supposed himself a lender, and who was probably unknown to the creditors at the times they extended their credits, unlimitedly liable as a partner for the obligations of those actually conducting the business.

Later decisions have much modified the earlier cases. The lender who takes a share in the profits, except possibly in one or two of our jurisdictions, does not by reason of that fact run a risk of being held as a partner. If, however, his contract falls within the third class mentioned, and he has any measure of control over the business, he at once runs serious risk of being held liable for the debts of the business as a partner; the risk increasing as he increases the amount of his control.

The first Limited Partnership Act was adopted by New York in 1822; the other commercial states, during the ensuing 30 years, following her example. Most of the statutes follow the language of the New York statute with little material alteration. These statutes were adopted, and to a considerable degree interpreted by the courts, during that period when it was generally held that any interest in a business should make the person holding the interest liable for its obligations. As a result the courts usually assume in the interpretation of these statutes two principles as fundamental.

First: That a limited (or as he is also called a special) partner is a partner in all respects like any other partner, except that to obtain the privilege of a limitation on his liability, he has conformed to the statutory requirements in respect to filing a certificate and refraining from participation in the conduct of the business.

Second: The limited partner, on any failure to follow the requirements in regard to the certificate or any participation in the conduct of his business, loses his privilege of limited liability and becomes, as far as those dealing with the business are concerned, in all respects a partner.

The courts in thus interpreting the statutes, although they made an American partnership with limited members something very different from the French Societe en Commandite from which the idea of the original statutes was derived, unquestionably carried out the intent of those responsible for their adoption. This is shown by the very wording of the statutes themselves. For instance, all the statutes require that all partners, limited and general, shall sign the certificate, and nearly all state that: "If any false statement be made in such certificate all the persons interested in such partnership shall be liable for all the engagements thereof as general partners."

The practical result of the spirit shown in the language and in the interpretation of existing statutes, coupled with the fact that a man may now lend money to a partnership and take a share in the profits in lieu of interest without running serious danger of becoming bound for partnership obligations, has, to a very great extent, deprived the existing statutory provisions for limited partners of any practical usefulness. Indeed, apparently their use is largely confined to associations in which those who conduct the business have not more than one limited partner.

One of the causes forcing business into the corporate form, in spite of the fact that the corporate form is ill suited to many business conditions, is the failure of the existing limited partnership acts to meet the desire of the owners of a business to secure necessary capital under the existing limited partnership form of business association.

The draft herewith submitted proceeds on the following assumptions:

First: No public policy requires a person who contributes to the capital of a business, acquires an interest in the profits, and some degree of control over the conduct of the business, to become bound for the obligations of the business; provided creditors have no reason to believe at the times their credits were extended that such person was so bound.

Second: That persons in business should be able, while remaining themselves liable without limit for the obligations contracted in its conduct to associate with themselves other who contribute to the capital and acquire rights of ownership, provided that such contributors do not compete with creditors for the assets of the partnership.

The attempt to carry out these ideas has led to the incorporation into the draft submitted of certain features, not found in, or differing from, existing limited partnership acts.

First: In the draft the person who contributes the capital, though in accordance with custom called a limited partner, is not in any sense a partner. He is, however, a member of the association (see Sec. 1).

Second: As limited partners are not partners securing limited liability by filing a certificate, the association is formed when substantial compliance, in good faith, is had with the requirements for a certificate (Sec.2(2)). This provision eliminates the difficulties which arise from the recognition of de facto associations, made necessary by the assumption that the association is not formed unless a strict compliance with the requirements of the act is had.

Third: The limited partner not being in any sense a principal in the business, failure to comply with the requirements of the act in respect to the certificate, while it may result in the nonformation of the association, does not make him a partner or liable as such. The exact nature of his ability in such cases is set forth in Sec. 11.

Fourth: The limited partner, while not as such in any sense a partner, may become a partner as any person not a member of the association may become a partner; and, becoming a partner, may nevertheless retain his rights as limited partner; this last provision enabling the entire capital embraced in the business to be divided between the limited partners, all the general partners being also limited partners (Sec. 12).

Fifth: The limited partner is not debarred from loaning money or transacting other business with the partnership as any other non-member; provided he does not, in respect to such transactions, accept from the partnership collateral security, or receive from any partner or the partnership any payment, conveyance, or release from liability, if at the time the assets of the partnership are not sufficient to discharge its obligations to persons not general or limited partners. (Sec. 13).

Sixth: The substitution of a person as limited partner in place of an existing limited partner, or the withdrawal of a limited partner, or the addition of new limited partners, does not necessarily dissolve the association (Secs. 8, 16(2b)); no limited partner, however, can withdraw his contribution until all liabilities to creditors are paid (Sec. 16(1a)).

Seventh: As limited partners are not principals in transactions of the partnership, their liability, except for known false statements in the certificate (Sec. 6), is to the partnership, not to creditors of the partnership (Sec. 17). The general partners cannot, however, waive any liability of the limited partners to the prejudice of such creditors. (Sec. 17(3)).

§ 2.   Formation

(1) Two or more persons desiring to form a limited partnership shall

(a) Sign and swear to a certificate, which shall state

I. The name of the partnership,

II. The character of the business,

III. The location of the principal place of business,

IV. The name and place of residence of each member; general and limited partners being respectively designated,

V. The term for which the partnership is to exist,

VI. The amount of cash and a description of and the agreed value of the other property contributed by each limited partner,

VII. The additional contributions, if any, agreed to be made by each limited partner and the times at which or events on the happening of which they shall be made,

VIII. The time, if agreed upon, when the contribution of each limited partner is to be returned,

IX. The share of the profits or the other compensation by way of income which each limited partner shall receive by reason of his contribution,

X. The right, if given, of a limited partner to substitute an assignee as contributor in his place, and the terms and conditions of the substitution,

XI. The right, if given, of the partners to admit additional limited partners,

XII. The right, if given, of one or more of the limited partners to priority over other limited partners, as to contributions or as to compensation by way of income, and the nature of such priority,

XIII. The right, if given, of the remaining general partner or partners to continue the business on the death, retirement or insanity of a general partner, and

XIV. The right, if given, of a limited partner to demand and receive property other than cash in return for his contribution.

(b) File for record the certificate in the office of [here designate the proper office].

(2) A limited partnership is formed if there has been substantial compliance in good faith with the requirements of paragraph (1).

§ 3. Business Which May Be Carried On

A limited partnership may carry on any business which a partnership without limited partners may carry on, except [here designate the business to be prohibited].

§ 4. Character of Limited Partner's Contribution

The contributions of a limited partner may be cash or other property, but not services.

§ 5. A Name Not to Contain Surname of Limited Partner; Exceptions

(1) The surname of a limited partner shall not appear in the partnership name, unless

(a) It is also the surname of a general partner, or

(b) Prior to the time when the limited partner became such the business had been carried on under a name in which his surname appeared.

(2) A limited partner whose name appears in a partnership name contrary to the provisions of paragraph (1) is liable as a general partner to partnership creditors who extend credit to the partnership without actual knowledge that he is not a general partner.

§ 6. Liability for False Statements in Certificate

If the certificate contains a false statement, one who suffers loss by reliance on such statement may hold liable any party to the certificate who knew the statement to be false.

(a) At the time he signed the certificate, or

(b) Subsequently, but within a sufficient time before the statement was relied upon to enable him to cancel or amend the certificate, or to file a petition for its cancellation or amendment as provided in Section 25(3).

§ 7. Limited Partner Not Liable to Creditors

A limited partner shall not become liable as a general partner unless, in addition to the exercise of his rights and powers as a limited partner, he takes part in the control of the business.

§ 8. Admission of Additional Limited Partners

After the formation of a limited partnership, additional limited partners may be admitted upon filing an amendment to the original certificate in accordance with the requirements of Section 25.

§ 9. Rights, Powers and Liabilities of a General Partner

(1) A general partner shall have all the rights and powers and be subject to all the restrictions and liabilities of a partner in a partnership without limited partners, except that without the written consent or ratification of the specific act by all the limited partners, a general partner or all of the general partners have no authority to

(a) Do any act in contravention of the certificate,

(b) Do any act which would make it impossible to carry on the ordinary business of the partnership,

(c) Confess a judgment against the partnership,

(d) Possess partnership property, or assign their rights in specific partnership property, for other than a partnership purpose,

(e) Admit a person as a general partner,

(f) Admit a person as a limited partner, unless the right so to do is given in the certificate,

(g) Continue the business with partnership property on the death, retirement or insanity of a general partner, unless the right so to do is given in the certificate.

§ 10. Rights of a Limited Partner

(1) A limited partner shall have the same rights as a general partner to

(a) Have the partnership books kept at the principal place of business of the partnership, and at all times to inspect and copy any of them.

(b) Have on demand true and full information of all things affecting the partnership, and a formal account of partnership affairs whenever circumstances render it just and reasonable, and

(c) Have dissolution and winding up by decree of court.

(2) A limited partner shall have the right to receive a share of the profits or other compensation by way of income, and to the return of his contribution as provided in Sections 15 and 16.

§ 11. Status of Person Erroneously Believing Himself a Limited Partner

A person who has contributed to the capital of a business conducted by a person or partnership erroneously believing that he has become a limited partner in a limited partnership, is not, by reason of his exercise of the rights of a limited partner, a general partner with the person or in the partnership carrying on the business, or bound by the obligations of such person or partnership; provided that on ascertaining the mistake he promptly renounces his interest in the profits of the business, or other compensation by way of income.

§ 12. One Person Both General and Limited Partner

(1) A person may be a general partner and a limited partner in the same partnership at the same time.

(2) A person who is a general, and also at the same time a limited partner, shall have all the rights and powers and be subject to all the restrictions of a general partner; except that, in respect to his contribution, he shall have the rights against the other members which he would have had if he were not also a general partner.

§ 13. Loans and Other Business Transactions with Limited Partner

(1) A limited partner also may loan money to and transact other business with the partnership, and, unless he is also a general partner, receive on account of resulting claims against the partnership, with general creditors, a pro rata share of the assets. No limited partner shall in respect to any such claim

(a) Receive or hold as collateral security any partnership property, or

(b) Receive from a general partner or the partnership any payment, conveyance, or release from liability, if at the time the assets of the partnership are not sufficient to discharge partnership liabilities to persons not claiming as general or limited partners,

(2) The receiving of collateral security, or a payment, conveyance, or release in violation of the provisions of paragraph (1) is a fraud on the creditors of the partnership.

§ 14. Relation of Limited Partners Inter Se

Where there are several limited partners the members may agree that one or more of the limited partners shall have a priority over other limited partners as to the return of their contributions, as to their compensation by way of income, or as to any other matter. If such an agreement is made it shall be stated in the certificate, and in the absence of such a statement all the limited partners shall stand upon equal footing.

§ 15. Compensation of Limited Partner

A limited partner may receive from the partnership the share of the profits or the compensation by way of income stipulated for in the certificate; provided, that after such payment is made, whether from the property of the partnership or that of a general partner, the partnership assets are in excess of all liabilities of the partnership except liabilities to limited partners on account of their contributions and to general partners.

§ 16. Withdrawal or Reduction of Limited Partner's Contribution

(1) A limited partner shall not receive from a general partner or out of partnership property any part of his contribution until

(a) All liabilities of the partnership, except liabilities to general partners and to limited partners on account of their contributions, have been paid or there remains property of the partnership sufficient to pay them,

(b) The consent of all members is had, unless the return of the contribution may be rightfully demanded under the provisions of paragraph (2), and

(c) The certificate is cancelled or so amended as to set forth the withdrawal or reduction.

(2) Subject to the provisions of paragraph (1) a limited partner may rightfully demand the return of his contribution

(a) On the dissolution of a partnership, or

(b) When the date specified in the certificate for its return has arrived, or

(c) After he has given six months' notice in writing to all other members, if no time is specified in the certificate either for the return of the contribution or for the dissolution of the partnership,

(3) In the absence of any statement in the certificate to the contrary or the consent of all members, a limited partner, irrespective of the nature of his contribution, has only the right to demand and receive cash in return for his contribution.

(4) A limited partner may have the partnership dissolved and its affairs wound up when

(a) He rightfully but unsuccessfully demands the return of his contribution, or

(b) The other liabilities of the partnership have not been paid, or the partnership property is insufficient for their payment as required by paragraph (1a) and the limited partner would otherwise be entitled to the return of his contribution.

§ 17.   Liability of Limited Partner to Partnership

(1) A limited partner is liable to the partnership

(a) For the difference between his contribution as actually made and that stated in the certificate as having been made, and

(b) For any unpaid contribution which he agreed in the certificate to make in the future at the time and on the conditions stated in the certificate.

(2) A limited partner holds as trustee for the partnership

(a) Specific property stated in the certificate as contributed by him, but which was not contributed or which has been wrongfully returned, and

(b) Money or other property wrongfully paid or conveyed to him on account of his contribution.

(3) The liabilities of a limited partner as set forth in this section can be waived or compromised only by the consent of all members; but a waiver or compromise shall not affect the right of a creditor of a partnership who extended credit or whose claim arose after the filing and before a cancellation or amendment of the certificate, to enforce such liabilities.

(4) When a contributor has rightfully received the return in whole or in part of the capital of his contribution, he is nevertheless liable to the partnership for any sum, not in excess of such return with interest, necessary to discharge its liabilities to all creditors who extended credit or whose claims arose before such return.

§ 18.   Nature of Limited Partner's Interest in Partnership

A limited partner's interest in the partnership is personal property.

§ 19.   Assignment of Limited Partner's Interest

(1) A limited partner's interest is assignable.

(2) A substituted limited partner is a person admitted to all the rights of a limited partner who has died or has assigned his interest in a partnership.

(3) An assignee, who does not become a substituted limited partner, has no right to require any information or account of the partnership transactions or to inspect the partnership books; he is only entitled to receive the share of the profits or other compensation by way of income, or the return of his contribution, to which his assignor would otherwise be entitled.

(4) An assignee shall have the right to become a substituted limited partner if all the members (except the assignor) consent thereto or if the assignor, being thereunto empowered by the certificate, gives the assignee that right.

(5) An assignee becomes a substituted limited partner when the certificate is appropriately amended in accordance with Section 25.

(6) The substituted limited partner has all the rights and powers, and is subject to all the restrictions and liabilities of his assignor, except those liabilities of which he was ignorant at the time he became a limited partner and which could not be ascertained from the certificate.

(7) The substitution of the assignee as a limited partner does not release the assignor from liability to the partnership under Sections 6 and 17.

§ 20.   Effect of Retirement, Death or Insanity of a General Partner

The retirement, death or insanity of a general partner dissolves the partnership, unless the business is continued by the remaining general partners.

(a) Under a right so to do stated in the certificate, or

(b) With the consent of all members.

§ 21.   Death of Limited Partner

(1) On the death of a limited partner his executor or administrator shall have all the rights of a limited partner for the purpose of settling his estate, and such power as the deceased had to constitute his assignee a substituted limited partner.

(2) The estate of a deceased limited partner shall be liable for all his liabilities as a limited partner.

§ 22.   Rights of Creditors of Limited Partner

(1) On due application to a court of competent jurisdiction by any judgment creditor of a limited partner, the court may charge the interest of the indebted limited partner with payment of the unsatisfied amount of the judgment debt; and may appoint a receiver, and make all other orders, directions, and inquiries which the circumstances of the case may require.

In those states where a creditor on beginning an action can attach debts due the defendant before he has obtained a judgment against the defendant it is recommended that paragraph (1) of this section read as follows:

On due application to a court of competent jurisdiction by any creditor of a limited partner, the court may charge the interest of the indebted limited partner with payment of the unsatisfied amount of such claim; and may appoint a receiver, and make all other orders, directions, and inquiries which the circumstances of the case may require.

(2) The interest may be redeemed with the separate property of any general partner, but may not be redeemed with partnership property.

(3) The remedies conferred by paragraph (1) shall not be deemed exclusive of others which may exist.

(4) Nothing in this act shall be held to deprive a limited partner of his statutory exemption.

§ 23. Distribution of Assets

(1) In settling accounts after dissolution the liabilities of the partnership shall be entitled to payment in the following order:

(a) Those to creditors, in the order of priority as provided by law, except those to limited partners on account of their contributions, and to general partners,

(b) Those to limited partners in respect to their share of the profits and other compensation by way of income on their contributions,

(c) Those to limited partners in respect to the capital of their contributions,

(d) Those to general partners other than for capital and profits,

(e) Those to general partners in respect to profits,

(f) Those to general partners in respect to capital.

(2) Subject to any statement in the certificate or to subsequent agreement, limited partners share in the partnership assets in respect to their claims for capital, and in respect to their claims for profits or for compensation by way of income on their contributions respectively, in proportion to the respective amounts of such claims.

§ 24. When Certificate Shall be Cancelled or Amended

(1) The certificate shall be cancelled when the partnership is dissolved or all limited partners cease to be such.

(2) A certificate shall be amended when

(a) There is a change in the name of the partnership or in the amount or character of the contribution of any limited partner,

(b) A person is substituted as a limited partner,

(c) An additional limited partner is admitted,

(d) A person is admitted as a general partner,

(e) A general partner retires, dies or becomes insane, and the business is continued under Section 20,

(f) There is a change in the character of the business of the partnership,

(g) There is a false or erroneous statement in the certificate,

(h) There is a change in the time as stated in the certificate for the dissolution of the partnership or for the return of a contribution,

(i) A time is fixed for the dissolution of the partnership, or the return of a contribution, no time having been specified in the certificate, or

(j) The members desire to make a change in any other statement in the certificate in order that it shall accurately represent the agreement between them.

§ 25. Requirements for Amendment and for Cancellation of Certificate

(1) The writing to amend a certificate shall

(a) Conform to the requirements of Section 2 (1a) as far as necessary to set forth clearly the change in the certificate which it is desired to make, and

(b) Be signed and sworn to by all members, and an amendment substituting a limited partner or adding a limited or general partner shall be signed also by the member to be substituted or added, and when a limited partner is to be substituted, the amendment shall also be signed by the assigning limited partner.

(2) The writing to cancel a certificate shall be signed by all members.

(3) A person desiring the cancellation or amendment of a certificate, if any person designated in paragraphs (1) and (2) as a person who must execute the writing refuses to do so, may petition the [here designate the proper court] to direct a cancellation or amendment thereof.

(4) If the court finds that the petitioner has a right to have the writing executed by a person who refuses to do so, it shall order the [here designate the responsible official in the office designated in Section 2] in the office where the certificate is recorded to record the cancellation or amendment of the certificate; and where

the certificate is to be amended, the court shall also cause to be filed for record in said office a certified copy of its decree setting forth the amendment.

(5) A certificate is amended or cancelled when there is filed for record in the office [here designate the office designated in Section 2] where the certificate is recorded

(a) A writing in accordance with the provisions of paragraph (1), or (2) or

(b) A certified copy of the order of court in accordance with the provisions of paragraph (4).

(6) After the certificate is duly amended in accordance with this section, the amended certificate shall thereafter be for all purposes the certificate provided for by this act.

§ 26.   Parties to Actions

A contributor, unless he is a general partner, is not a proper party to proceedings by or against a partnership, except where the object is to enforce a limited partner's right against or liability to the partnership.

§ 27.   Name of Act

This act may be cited as The Uniform Limited Partnership Act.

§ 28.   Rules of Construction

(1) The rule that statutes in derogation of the common law are to be strictly construed shall have no application to this act.

(2) This act shall be so interpreted and construed as to effect its general purpose to make uniform the law of those states which enact it.

(3) This act shall not be so construed as to impair the obligations of any contract existing when the act goes into effect, nor to affect any action or proceedings begun or right accrued before this act takes effect.

§ 29.   Rules for Cases Not Provided for in This Act

In any case not provided for in this act the rules of law and equity, including the law merchant, shall govern.

§ 30.   Provisions for Existing Limited Partnerships

(1) A limited partnership formed under any statute of this state prior to the adoption of this act, may become a limited partnership under this act by complying with the provisions of Section 2; provided the certificate sets forth

(a) The amount of the original contribution of each limited partner, and the time when the contribution was made, and

(b) That the property of the partnership exceeds the amount sufficient to discharge its liabilities to persons not claiming as general or limited partners by an amount greater than the sum of the contributions of its limited partners.

(2) A limited partnership formed under any statute of this state prior to the adoption of this act, until or unless it becomes a limited partnership under this act, shall continue to be governed by the provisions of [here insert proper reference to the existing limited partnership act or acts], except that such partnership shall not be renewed unless so provided in the original agreement.

§ 31.   Act (acts) Repealed

Except as affecting existing limited partnerships to the extent set forth in Section 30, the act (acts) of [here designate the existing limited partnership act or acts] is (are) hereby repealed.

Appendix F

Revised Uniform Limited Partnership Act

ARTICLE 1

General Provisions

Section 101. [Definitions.]

As used in this Act, unless the context otherwise requires:

(1) "Certificate of limited partnership" means the certificate referred to in Section 201, and the certificate as amended.

(2) "Contribution" means any cash, property, services rendered, or a promissory note or other binding obligation to contribute cash or property or to perform services, which a partner contributes to a limited partnership in his capacity as a partner.

(3) "Event of withdrawal of a general partner" means an event that causes a person to cease to be a general partner as provided in Section 402.

(4) "Foreign limited partnership" means a part-nership formed under the laws of any State other than this State and having as partners one or more general partners and one or more limited partners.

(5) "General partner" means a person who has been admitted to a limited partnership as a general partner in accordance with the partnership agreement and named in the certificate of limited partnership as a general partner.

(6) "Limited partner" means a person who has been admitted to a limited partnership as a limited partner in accordance with the partnership agreement and named in the certificate of limited partnership as a limited partner.

(7) "Limited partnership" and "domestic limited partnership" mean a partnership formed by 2 or more persons under the laws of this State and having one or more general partners and one or more limited partners.

(8) "Partner" means a limited or general partner.

(9) "Partnership agreement" means any valid agreement, written or oral, of the partners as to the affairs of a limited partnership and the conduct of its business.

(10) "Partnership interest" means a partner's share of the profits and losses of a limited partnership and the right to receive distributions of partnership assets.

(11) "Person" means a natural person, partnership, limited partnership (domestic or foreign), trust, estate, association, or corporation.

(12) "State" means a state, territory, or possession of the United States, the District of Columbia, or the Commonwealth of Puerto Rico.

Section 102.   [Name.]

The name of each limited partnership as set forth in its certificate of limited partnership:

(1) shall contain without abbreviation the words "limited partnership";

(2) may not contain the name of a limited partner unless (i) it is also the name of a general partner or the corporate name of a corporate general partner, or (ii) the business of the limited partnership had been carried on under that name before the admission of that limited partner;

(3) may not contain any word or phrase indicating or implying that it is organized other than for a purpose stated in its certificate of limited partnership;

(4) may not be the same as, or deceptively similar to, the name of any corporation or limited partnership organized under the laws of this State or licensed or registered as a foreign corporation or limited partnership in this State; and

(5) may not contain the following words [here insert prohibited words].

Section 103.   [Reservation of Name.]

(a) The exclusive right to the use of a name may be reserved by:

(1) any person intending to organize a limited partnership under this Act and to adopt that name;

(2) any domestic limited partnership or any foreign limited partnership registered in this State which, in either case, intends to adopt that name;

(3) any foreign limited partnership intending to register in this State and adopt that name; and

(4) any person intending to organize a foreign limited partnership and intending to have it register in this State and adopt that name.

(b) The reservation shall be made by filing with the Secretary of State an application, executed by the applicant, to reserve a specified name. If the Secretary of State finds that the name is available for use by a domestic or foreign limited partnership, he shall reserve the name for the exclusive use of the applicant for a period of 120 days. Once having so reserved a name, the same applicant may not again reserve the same name until more than 60 days after the expiration of the last 120-day period for which that applicant reserved that name. The right to the exclusive use of a reserved name may be transferred to any other person by filing in the office of the Secretary of State a notice of the transfer, executed by the applicant for whom the name was reserved and specifying the name and address of the transferee.

Section 104.   [Specified Office and Agent.]

Each limited partnership shall continuously maintain in this State:

(1) an office, which may but need not be a place of its business in this State, at which shall be kept the records required by Section 105 to be maintained; and

(2) an agent for service of process on the limited partnership, which agent must be an individual resident of the State, a domestic corporation, or a foreign corporation authorized to do business in this State.

Section 105.   [Records to Be Kept.]

Each limited partnership shall keep at the office referred to in Section 104(1) the following: (1) a current list of the full name and last known business address of each partner set forth in alphabetical order, (2) a copy of the certificate of limited partnership and all certificates of amendment thereto, together with executed copies of any powers of attorney pursuant to which any certificate has been executed, (3) copies of the limited partnership's federal, state and local income tax returns and reports, if any, for the 3 most recent years, and (4) copies of any then effective written partnership agreements and of any financial statements of the limited partnership for the 3 most recent years. Those records are subject to inspection and copying at the reasonable request, and at the expense, of any partner during ordinary business hours.

Section 106.   [Nature of Business.]

A limited partnership may carry on any business that a partnership without limited partners may carry on except [here designate prohibited activities].

Section 107. [Business Transactions of Partner with Partnership.]

Except as provided in the partnership agreement, a partner may lend money to and transact other business with the limited partnership and, subject to other applicable law, has the same rights and obligations with respect thereto as a person who is not a partner.

ARTICLE 2

Formation: Certificate of Limited Partnership

Section 201. [Certificate of Limited Partnership.]

(a) In order to form a limited partnership two or more persons must execute a certificate of limited partnership. The certificate shall be filed in the office of the Secretary of State and set forth:

(1) the name of the limited partnership;

(2) the general character of its business;

(3) the address of the office and the name and address of the agent for service of process required to be maintained by Section 104;

(4) the name and the business address of each partner (specifying separately the general partners and limited partners);

(5) the amount of cash and a description and statement of the agreed value of the other property or services contributed by each partner and which each partner has agreed to contribute in the future;

(6) the times at which or events on the happening of which any additional contributions agreed to be made by each partner are to be made;

(7) any power of a limited partner to grant the right to become a limited partner to an assignee of any part of his partnership interest, and the terms and conditions of the power;

(8) if agreed upon, the time at which or the events on the happening of which a partner may terminate his membership in the limited partnership and the amount of, or the method of determining, the distribution to which he may be entitled respecting his partnership interest, and the terms and conditions of the termination and distribution;

(9) any right of a partner to receive distributions of property, including cash from the limited partnership;

(10) any right of a partner to receive, or of a general partner to make, distributions to a partner which include a return of all or any part of the partner's contribution;

(11) any time at which or events upon the happening of which the limited partnership is to be dissolved and its affairs wound up;

(12) any right of the remaining general partners to continue the business on the happening of an event of withdrawal of a general partner; and

(13) any other matters the partners determine to include therein.

(b) A limited partnership is formed at the time of the filing of the certificate of limited partnership in the office of the Secretary of State or at any later time specified in the certificate of limited partnership if, in either case, there has been substantial compliance with the requirements of this section.

Section 202. [Amendment to Certificate.]

(a) A certificate of limited partnership is amended by filing a certificate of amendment thereto in the office of the Secretary of State. The certificate shall set forth:

(1) the name of the limited partnership;

(2) the date of filing the certificate; and

(3) the amendment to the certificate.

(b) Within 30 days after the happening of any of the following events, an amendment to a certificate of limited partnership reflecting the occurrence of the event or events shall be filed:

(1) a change in the amount or character of the contribution of any partner, or in any partner's obligation to make a contribution;

(2) the admission of a new partner;

(3) the withdrawal of a partner; or

(4) the continuation of the business under Section 801 after an event of withdrawal of a general partner.

(c) A general partner who becomes aware that any statement in a certificate of limited partnership was false when made or that any arrangements or other facts described have changed, making the certificate inaccurate in any respect, shall promptly amend the certificate, but an amendment to show a change of address of a limited partner need be filed only once every 12 months.

(d) A certificate of limited partnership may be amended at any time for any other proper purpose the general partners determine.

(e) No person has any liability because an amendment to a certificate of limited partnership has not been filed to reflect the occurrence of any event referred to in subsection (b) of this Section if the amendment is filed within the 30-day period specified in subsection (b).

Section 203.   [Cancellation of Certificate.]

A certificate of limited partnership shall be cancelled upon the dissolution and the commencement of winding up of the partnership or at any other time there are no limited partners. A certificate of cancellation shall be filed in the office of the Secretary of State and set forth:

(1) the name of the limited partnership;

(2) the date of filing of its certificate of limited partnership;

(3) the reason for filing the certificate of cancellation;

(4) the effective date (which shall be a date certain) of cancellation if it is not to be effective upon the filing of the certificate; and

(5) any other information the general partners filing the certificate determine.

Section 204.   [Executive of Certificates.]

(a) Each certificate required by this Article to be filed in the office of the Secretary of State shall be executed in the following manner:

(1) an original certificate of limited partnership must be signed by all partners named therein;

(2) a certificate of amendment must be signed by at least one general partner and by each other partner designated in the certificate as a new partner or whose contribution is described as having been increased; and

(3) a certificate of cancellation must be signed by all general partners.

(b) Any person may sign a certificate by an attorney-in-fact, but a power of attorney to sign a certificate relating to the admission, or increased contribution, of a partner must specifically describe the admission or increase.

(c) The execution of a certificate by a general partner constitutes an affirmation under the penalties of perjury that the facts stated therein are true.

Section 205.   [Amendment or Cancellation by Judicial Act.]

If a person required by Section 204 to execute a certificate of amendment or cancellation fails or refuses to do so, any other partner, and any assignee of a partnership interest, who is adversely affected by the failure or refusal, may petition the [here designate the proper court] to direct the amendment or cancellation. If the court finds that the amendment or cancellation is proper and that any person so designated has failed or refused to execute the certificate, it shall order the Secretary of State to record an appropriate certificate of amendment or cancellation.

Section 206.   [Filing in Office of Secretary of State.]

(a) Two signed copies of the certificate of limited partnership and of any certificates of amendment or cancellation (or of any judicial decree of amendment or cancellation) shall be delivered to the Secretary of State. A person who executes a certificate as an agent or fiduciary need not exhibit evidence of his authority as a prerequisite to filing. Unless the Secretary of State finds that any certificate does not conform to law, upon receipt of all filing fees required by law he shall:

(1) endorse on each duplicate original the word "Filed" and the day, month and year of the filing thereof;

(2) file one duplicate original in his office; and

(3) return the other duplicate original to the person who filed it or his representative.

(b) Upon the filing of a certificate of amendment (or judicial decree of amendment) in the office of the Secretary of State, the certificate of limited partnership shall be amended as set forth therein, and upon the effective date of a certificate of cancellation (or a judicial decree thereof), the certificate of limited partnership is cancelled.

Section 207.   [Liability for False Statement in Certificate.]

If any certificate of limited partnership or certificate of amendment or cancellation contains a false statement, one who suffers loss by reliance on the statement may recover damages for the loss from:

(1) any person who executes the certificate, or causes another to execute it on his behalf, and knew, and any general partner who knew or should have known, the statement to be false at the time the certificate was executed; and

(2) any general partner who thereafter knows or should have known that any arrangement or other fact described in the certificate has changed, making the

statement inaccurate in any respect within a sufficient time before the statement was relied upon reasonably to have enabled that general partner to cancel or amend the certificate, or to file a petition for its cancellation or amendment under Section 205.

Section 208.   [Notice.]

The fact that a certificate of limited partnership is on file in the office of the Secretary of State is notice that the partnership is a limited partnership and the persons designated therein as limited partners are limited partners, but it is not notice of any other fact.

Section 209.   [Delivery of Certificates to Limited Partners.]

Upon the return by the Secretary of State pursuant to Section 206 of a certificate marked "Filed", the general partners shall promptly deliver or mail a copy of the certificate of limited partnership and each certificate to each limited partner unless the partnership agreement provides otherwise.

ARTICLE 3

Limited Partners

Section 301.   [Admission of Additional Limited Partners.]

(a) After the filing of a limited partnership's original certificate of limited partnership, a person may be admitted as an additional limited partner:

(1) in the case of a person acquiring a partnership interest directly from the limited partnership, upon the compliance with the partnership agreement or, if the partnership agreement does not so provide, upon the written consent of all partners; and

(2) in the case of an assignee of a partnership interest of a partner who has the power, as provided in Section 704, to grant the assignee the right to become a limited partner, upon the exercise of that power and compliance with any conditions limiting the grant or exercise of the power.

(b) In each case under subsection (a), the person acquiring the partnership interest becomes a limited partner only upon amendment of the certificate of limited partnership reflecting that fact.

Section 302.   [Voting.]

Subject to Section 303, the partnership agreement may grant to all or a specified group of the limited partners the right to vote (on a per capita or other basis) upon any matter.

Section 303.   [Liability to Third Parties.]

(a) Except as provided in subsection (d), a limited partner is not liable for the obligations of a limited partnership unless he is also a general partner or, in addition to the exercise of his rights and powers as a limited partner, he takes part in the control of the business. However, if the limited partner's participation in the control of the business is not substantially the same as the exercise of the powers of a general partner, he is liable only to persons who transact business with the limited partnership with actual knowledge of his participation in control.

(b) A limited partner does not participate in the control of the business within the meaning of subsection (a) solely by doing one or more of the following:

(1) being a contractor for or an agent or employee of the limited partnership or of a general partner;

(2) consulting with and advising a general partner with respect to the business of the limited partnership;

(3) acting as surety for the limited partnership;

(4) approving or disapproving an amendment to the partnership agreement; or

(5) voting on one or more of the following matters:

(i) the dissolution and winding up of the limited partnership;

(ii) the sale, exchange, lease, mortgage, pledge, or other transfer of all or substantially all of the assets of the limited partnership other than in the ordinary course of its business;

(iii) the incurrence of indebtedness by the limited partnership other than in the ordinary course of its business;

(iv) a change in the nature of the business; or

(v) the removal of a general partner.

(c) The enumeration in subsection (b) does not mean that the possession or exercise of any other powers by a limited partner constitutes participation by him in the business of the limited partnership.

(d) A limited partner who knowingly permits his name to be used in the name of the limited partnership, except under circumstances permitted by Section

102(2)(i), is liable to creditors who extend credit to the limited partnership without actual knowledge that the limited partner is not a general partner.

Section 304.   [Person Erroneously Believing Himself Limited Partner.]

(a) Except as provided in subsection (b), a person who makes a contribution to a business enterprise and erroneously but in good faith believes that he has become a limited partner in the enterprise is not a general partner in the enterprise and is not bound by its obligations by reason of making the contribution, receiving distributions from the enterprise, or exercising any rights of a limited partner, if, on ascertaining the mistake, he:

(1) causes an appropriate certificate of limited partnership or a certificate of amendment to be executed and filed; or

(2) withdraws from future equity participation in the enterprise.

(b) A person who makes a contribution of the kind described in subsection (a) is liable as a general partner to any third party who transacts business with the enterprise (i) before the person withdraws and an appropriate certificate is filed to show withdrawal, or (ii) before an appropriate certificate is filed to show his status as a limited partner and, in the case of an amendment, after expiration of the 30-day period for filing an amendment relating to the person as a limited partner under Section 202, but in either case only if the third party actually believed in good faith that the person was a general partner at the time of the transaction.

Section 305.   [Information.]

Each limited partner has the right to:

(1) inspect and copy any of the partnership records required to be maintained by Section 105; and

(2) obtain from the general partners from time to time upon reasonable demand (i) true and full information regarding the state of the business and financial condition of the limited partnership, (ii) promptly after becoming available, a copy of the limited partnership's federal, state and local income tax returns for each year, and (iii) other information regarding the affairs of the limited partnership as is just and reasonable.

ARTICLE 4

General Partners

Section 401.   [Admission of Additional General Partners.]

After the filing of a limited partnership's original certificate of limited partnership, additional general partners may be admitted only with the specific written consent of each partner.

Section 402.   [Events of Withdrawal.]

Except as approved by the specific written consent of all partners at the time, a person ceases to be a general partner of a limited partnership upon the happening of any of the following events:

(1) the general partner withdraws from the limited partnership as provided in Section 602;

(2) the general partner ceases to be a member of the limited partnership as provided in Section 702;

(3) the general partner is removed as a general partner in accordance with the partnership agreement;

(4) unless otherwise provided in the certificate of limited partnership, the general partner: (i) makes an assignment for the benefit of creditors; (ii) files a voluntary petition in bankruptcy; (iii) is adjudicated a bankrupt or insolvent; (iv) files a petition or answer seeking for himself any reorganization, arrangement, composition, readjustment, liquidation, dissolution or similar relief under any statute, law, or regulation; (v) files an answer or other pleading admitting or failing to contest the material allegations of a petition filed against him in any proceeding of this nature; or (vi) seeks, consents to, or acquiesces in the appointment of a trustee, receiver, or liquidator of the general partner or of all or any substantial part of his properties;

(5) unless otherwise provided in the certificate of limited partnership, [120] days after the commencement of any proceeding against the general partner seeking reorganization, arrangement, composition, readjustment, liquidation, dissolution or similar relief under any statute, law, or regulation, the proceeding has not been dismissed, or if within [90] days after the appointment without his consent or acquiescence of a trustee, receiver, or liquidator of the general partner or of all or any substantial part of his properties, the appointment is not vacated or stayed or within [90] days after the

expiration of any such stay, the appointment is not vacated;

(6) in the case of a general partner who is a natural person,

(i) his death; or

(ii) the entry by a court of competent jurisdiction adjudicating him incompetent to manage his person or his estate;

(7) in the case of a general partner who is acting as a general partner by virtue of being a trustee of a trust, the termination of the trust (but not merely the substitution of a new trustee);

(8) in the case of a general partner that is a separate partnership, the dissolution and commencement of winding up of the separate partnership;

(9) in the case of a general partner that is a corporation, the filing of a certificate of dissolution, or its equivalent, for the corporation or the revocation of its charter; or

(10) in the case of an estate, the distribution by the fiduciary of the estate's entire interest in the partnership.

Section 403.   [General Powers and Liabilities.]

Except as provided in this Act or in the partnership agreement, a general partner of a limited partnership has the rights and powers and is subject to the restrictions and liabilities of a partner in a partnership without limited partners.

Section 404.   [Contributions by General Partner.]

A general partner of a limited partnership may make contributions to the partnership and share in the profits and losses of, and in distributions from, the limited partnership as a general partner. A general partner also may make contributions to and share in profits, losses, and distributions as a limited partner. A person who is both a general partner and a limited partner has the rights and powers, and is subject to the restrictions and liabilities, of a general partner and, except as provided in the partnership agreement, also has the powers, and is subject to the restrictions, of a limited partner to the extent of his participation in the partnership as a limited partner.

Section 405.   [Voting.]

The partnership agreement may grant to all or certain identified general partners the right to vote (on a per capita or any other basis), separately or with all or any class of the limited partners, on any matter.

ARTICLE 5

Finance

Section 501.   [Form of Contribution.]

The contribution of a partner may be in cash, property, or services rendered, or a promissory note or other obligation to contribute cash or property or to perform services.

Section 502.   [Liability for Contribution.]

(a) Except as provided in the certificate of limited partnership, a partner is obligated to the limited partnership to perform any promise to contribute cash or property or to perform services, even if he is unable to perform because of death, disability or any other reason. If a partner does not make the required contribution of property or services, he is obligated at the option of the limited partnership to contribute cash equal to that portion of the value (as stated in the certificate of limited partnership) of the stated contribution that has not been made.

(b) Unless otherwise provided in the partnership agreement, the obligation of a partner to make a contribution or return money or other property paid or distributed in violation of this Act may be compromised only by consent of all the partners. Notwithstanding the compromise, a creditor of a limited partnership who extends credit, or whose claim arises, after the filing of the certificate of limited partnership or an amendment thereto which, in either case, reflects the obligation, and before the amendment or cancellation thereof to reflect the compromise, may enforce the original obligation.

Section 503.   [Sharing of Profits and Losses.]

The profits and losses of a limited partnership shall be allocated among the partners, and among classes of partners, in the manner provided in the partnership agreement. If the partnership agreement does not so provide, profits and losses shall be allocated on the basis of the value (as stated in the certificate of limited partnership) of the contributions made by each partner to the extent they have been received by the partnership and have not been returned.

Section 504.   [Sharing of Distributions.]

Distributions of cash or other assets of a limited partnership shall be allocated among the partners, and among classes of partners, in the manner provided in the partnership agreement. If the partnership agreement does not so provide, distributions shall be made on the basis of the value (as stated in the certificate of limited partnership) of the contributions made by each partner to the extent they have been received by the partnership and have not been returned.

ARTICLE 6

Distributions and Withdrawal

Section 601.   [Interim Distributions.]

Except as provided in this Article, a partner is entitled to receive distributions from a limited partnership before his withdrawal from the limited partnership and before the dissolution and winding up thereof:

  (1) to the extent and at the times or upon the happening of the events specified in the partnership agreement; and

  (2) if any distribution constitutes a return of any part of his contribution under Section 608(c), to the extent and at the times or upon the happening of the events specified in the certificate of limited partnership.

Section 602.   [Withdrawal of General Partner.]

A general partner may withdraw from a limited partnership at any time by giving written notice to the other partners, but if the withdrawal violates the partnership agreement, the limited partnership may recover from the withdrawing general partner damages for breach of the partnership agreement and offset the damages against the amount otherwise distributable to him.

Section 603.   [Withdrawal of Limited Partner.]

A limited partner may withdraw from a limited partnership at the time or upon the happening of events specified in the certificate of limited partnership and in accordance with the partnership agreement. If the certificate does not specify the time or the events upon the happening of which a limited partner may withdraw or a definite time for the dissolution and winding up of the limited partnership, a limited partner may withdraw upon not less than 6 months' prior written notice to each general partner at his address on the books of the limited partnership at its office in this State.

Section 604.   [Distribution Upon Withdrawal.]

Except as provided in this Article, upon withdrawal any withdrawing partner is entitled to receive any distribution to which he is entitled under the partnership agreement and, if not otherwise provided in the agreement, he is entitled to receive, within a reasonable time after withdrawal, the fair value of his interest in the limited partnership as of the date of withdrawal based upon his right to share in distributions from the limited partnership.

Section 605.   [Distribution in Kind.]

Except as provided in the certificate of limited partnership, a partner, regardless of the nature of his contribution, has no right to demand and receive any distribution from a limited partnership in any form other than cash. Except as provided in the partnership agreement, a partner may not be compelled to accept a distribution of any asset in kind from a limited partnership to the extent that the percentage of the asset distributed to him exceeds a percentage of that asset which is equal to the percentage in which he shares in distributions from the limited partnership.

Section 606.   [Right to Distribution.]

At the time a partner becomes entitled to receive a distribution, he has the status of, and is entitled to all remedies available to, a creditor of the limited partnership with respect to the distribution.

Section 607.   [Limitations on Distribution.]

A partner may not receive a distribution from a limited partnership to the extent that, after giving effect to the distribution, all liabilities of the limited partnership, other than liabilities to partners on account of their partnership interests, exceed the fair value of the partnership assets.

Section 608. [Liability Upon Return of Contribution.]

(a) If a partner has received the return of any part of his contribution without violation of the partnership agreement or this Act, he is liable to the limited partnership for a period of one year thereafter for the amount of the returned contribution, but only to the extent necessary to discharge the limited partnership's liabilities to creditors who extended credit to the limited partnership during the period the contribution was held by the partnership.

(b) If a partner has received the return of any part of his contribution in violation of the partnership agreement or this Act, he is liable to the limited partnership for a period of 6 years thereafter for the amount of the contribution wrongfully returned.

(c) A partner receives a return of his contribution to the extent that a distribution to him reduces his share of the fair value of the net assets of the limited partnership below the value (as set forth in the certificate of limited partnership) of his contribution which has not been distributed to him.

ARTICLE 7

Assignment of Partnership Interests

Section 701. [Nature of Partnership Interest.]

A partnership interest is personal property.

Section 702. [Assignment of Partnership Interest.]

Except as provided in the partnership agreement, a partnership interest is assignable in whole or in part. An assignment of a partnership interest does not dissolve a limited partnership or entitle the assignee to become or to exercise any rights of a partner. An assignment entitles the assignee to receive, to the extent assigned, only the distribution to which the assignor would be entitled. Except as provided in the partnership agreement, a partner ceases to be a partner upon assignment of all his partnership interest.

Section 703. [Rights of Creditor.]

On application to a court of competent jurisdiction by any judgment creditor of a partner, the court may charge the partnership interest of the partner with payment of the unsatisfied amount of the judgment with interest. To the extent so charged, the judgment creditor has only the rights of an assignee of the partnership interest. This act does not deprive any partner of the benefit of any exemption laws applicable to his partnership interest.

Section 704. [Right of Assignee to Become Limited Partner.]

(a) An assignee of a partnership interest, including an assignee of a general partner, may become a limited partner if and to the extent that (1) the assignor gives the assignee that right in accordance with authority described in the certificate of limited partnership, or (2) all other partners consent.

(b) An assignee who has become a limited partner has, to the extent assigned, the rights and powers, and is subject to the restrictions and liabilities, of a limited partner under the partnership agreement and this Act. An assignee who becomes a limited partner also is liable for the obligations of his assignor to make and return contributions as provided in Article 6. However, the assignee is not obligated for liabilities unknown to the assignee at the time he became a limited partner and which could not be ascertained from the certificate of limited partnership.

(c) If an assignee of a partnership interest becomes a limited partner, the assignor is not released from his liability to the limited partnership under Sections 207 and 502.

Section 705. [Power of Estate of Deceased or Incompetent Partner.]

If a partner who is an individual dies or a court of competent jurisdiction adjudges him to be incompetent to manage his person or his property, the partner's executor, administrator guardian, conservator, or other legal representative may exercise all the partner's rights for the purpose of settling his estate or administering his property, including any power the partner had to give an assignee the right to become a limited partner. If a partner is a corporation, trust, or other entity and is dissolved or terminated, the powers of that partner may be exercised by its legal representative or successor.

ARTICLE 8

Dissolution

Section 801.   [Nonjudicial Dissolution.]

A limited partnership is dissolved and its affairs shall be wound up upon the happening of the first to occur of the following:

(1) at the time or upon the happening of events specified in the certificate of limited partnership;

(2) written consent of all partners;

(3) an event of withdrawal of a general partner unless at the time there is at least one other general partner and the certificate of limited partnership permits the business of the limited partnership to be carried on by the remaining general partner and that partner does so, but the limited partnership is not dissolved and is not required to be wound up by reason of any event of withdrawal, if, within 90 days after the withdrawal, all partners agree in writing to continue the business of the limited partnership and to the appointment of one or more additional general partners if necessary or desired; or

(4) entry of a decree of judicial dissolution under Section 802.

Section 802.   [Judicial Dissolution.]

On application by or for a partner the [here designate the proper court] court may decree dissolution of a limited partnership whenever it is not reasonably practicable to carry on the business in conformity with the partnership agreement.

Section 803.   [Winding Up.]

Except as provided in the partnership agreement, the general partners who have not wrongfully dissolved a limited partnership or, if none, the limited partners, may wind up the limited partnership's affairs; but the [here designate the proper court] court may wind up the limited partnership's affairs upon application of any partner, his legal representative, or assignee.

Section 804.   [Distribution of Assets.]

Upon the winding up of a limited partnership, the assets shall be distributed as follows:

(1) to creditors, including partners who are creditors, to the extent permitted by law, in satisfaction of liabilities of the limited partnership other than liabilities for distributions to partners under Section 601 or 604;

(2) except as provided in the partnership agreement, to partners and former partners in satisfaction of liabilities for distributions under Section 601 or 604; and

(3) except as provided in the partnership agreement, to partners *first* for the return of their contributions and *secondly* respecting their partnership interests, in the proportions in which the partners share in distributions.

ARTICLE 9

Foreign Limited Partnerships

Section 901.   [Law Governing.]

Subject to the Constitution of this State, (1) the laws of the state under which a foreign limited partnership is organized govern its organization and internal affairs and the liability of its limited partners, and (2) a foreign limited partnership may not be denied registration by reason of any difference between those laws and the laws of this State.

Section 902.   [Registration.]

Before transacting business in this State, a foreign limited partnership shall register with the Secretary of State. In order to register, a foreign limited partnership shall submit to the Secretary of State, in duplicate, an application for registration as a foreign limited partnership, signed and sworn to by a general partner and setting forth:

(1) the name of the foreign limited partnership and, if different, the name under which it proposes to register and transact business in this State;

(2) the state and date of its formation;

(3) the general character of the business it proposes to transact in this State;

(4) the name and address of any agent for service of process on the foreign limited partnership whom the foreign limited partnership elects to appoint; the agent must be an individual resident of this state, a domestic corporation, or a foreign corporation having a place of business in, and authorized to do business in, this State;

(5) a statement that the Secretary of State is appointed the agent of the foreign limited partnership for service of process if no agent has been appointed under paragraph (4) or, if appointed, the agent's authority has been revoked or if the agent cannot be found or served with the exercise of reasonable diligence;

(6) the address of the office required to be maintained in the State of its organization by the laws of that State or, if not so required, of the principal office of the foreign limited partnership; and

(7) if the certificate of limited partnership filed in the foreign limited partnership's state of organization is not required to include the names and business addresses of the partners, a list of the names and addresses.

Section 903.   [Issuance of Registration.]

(a) If the Secretary of State finds that an application for registration conforms to law and all requisite fees have been paid, he shall:

(1) endorse on the application the word "Filed", and the month, day and year of the filing thereof;

(2) file in his office a duplicate original of the application; and

(3) issue a certificate of registration to transact business in this State.

(b) The certificate of registration, together with a duplicate original of the application, shall be returned to the person who filed the application or his representative.

Section 904.   [Name.]

A foreign limited partnership may register with the Secretary of State under any name (whether or not it is the name under which it is registered in its state of organization) that includes without abbreviation the words "limited partnership" and that could be registered by a domestic limited partnership.

Section 905.   [Changes and Amendments.]

If any statement in the application for registration of a foreign limited partnership was false when made or any arrangements or other facts described have changed, making the application inaccurate in any respect, the foreign limited partnership shall promptly file in the office of the Secretary of State a certificate, signed and sworn to by a general partner, correcting such statement.

Section 906.   [Cancellation of Registration.]

A foreign limited partnership may cancel its registration by filing with the Secretary of State a certificate of cancellation signed and sworn to by a general partner. A cancellation does not terminate the authority of the Secretary of State to accept service of process on the foreign limited partnership with respect to [claims for relief] [causes of action] arising out of the transactions of business in this State.

Section 907.   [Transaction of Business Without Registration.]

(a) A foreign limited partnership transacting business in this State may not maintain any action, suit, or proceeding in any court of this State until it has registered in this State.

(b) The failure of a foreign limited partnership to register in this State does not impair the validity of any contract or act of the foreign limited partnership or prevent the foreign limited partnership from defending any action, suit, or proceeding in any court of this State.

(c) A limited partner of a foreign limited partnership is not liable as a general partner of the foreign limited partnership solely by reason of having transacted business in this State without registration.

(d) A foreign limited partnership, by transacting business in this State without registration, appoints the Secretary of State as its agent for service of process with respect to [claims for relief] [causes of action] arising out of the transaction of business in this State.

Section 908.   [Action by Appropriate Official.]

The [appropriate official] may bring an action to restrain a foreign limited partnership from transacting business in this State in violation of this Article.

ARTICLE 10

Derivative Actions

Section 1001.   [Right of Action.]

A limited partner may bring an action in the right of a limited partnership to recover a judgment in its favor if general partners with authority to do so have refused to bring the action or if an effort to cause those general partners to bring the action is not likely to succeed.

Section 1002.   [Proper Plaintiff.]

In a derivative action, the plaintiff must be a partner at the time of bringing the action and (1) at the time of the transaction of which he complains or (2) his status as a partner had devolved upon him by operation of law or pursuant to the terms of the partnership agreement from a person who was a partner at the time of the transaction.

Section 1003.   [Pleading.]

In a derivative action, the complaint shall set forth with particularity the effort of the plaintiff to secure initiation of the action by a general partner or the reasons for not making the effort.

Section 1004.   [Expenses.]

If a derivative action is successful, in whole or in part, or if anything is received by the plaintiff as a result of a judgment, compromise or settlement of an action or claim, the court may award the plaintiff reasonable expenses, including reasonable attorney's fees, and shall direct him to remit to the limited partnership the remainder of those proceeds received by him.

ARTICLE 11

Miscellaneous

Section 1101.   [Construction and Application.]

This Act shall be so applied and construed to effectuate its general purpose to make uniform the law with respect to the subject of this Act among states enacting it.

Section 1102.   [Short Title.]

This Act may be cited as the Uniform Limited Partnership Act.

Section 1103.   [Severability.]

If any provision of this Act or its application to any person or circumstance is held invalid, the invalidity does not affect other provisions or applications of the Act which can be given effect without the invalid provision or application, and to this end the provisions of this Act are severable.

Section 1104.   [Effective Date, Extended Effective Date and Repeal.]

Except as set forth below, the effective date of this Act is and the following Acts [list prior limited partnership acts] are hereby repealed:

(1) The existing provisions for execution and filing of certificates of limited partnerships and amendments thereunder and cancellations thereof continue in effect until [specify time required to create central filing system], the extended effective date, and Sections 102, 103, 104, 105, 201, 202, 203, 204 and 206 are not effective until the extended effective date.

(2) Section 402, specifying the conditions under which a general partner ceases to be a member of a limited partnership, is not effective until the extended effective date, and the applicable provisions of existing law continue to govern until the extended effective date.

(3) Sections 501, 502 and 608 apply only to contributions and distributions made after the effective date of this Act.

(4) Section 704 applies only to assignments made after the effective date of this Act.

(5) Article 9, dealing with registration of foreign limited partnerships, is not effective until the extended effective date.

Section 1105.   [Rules for Cases Not Provided for in This Act.]

In any case not provided for in this Act the provisions of the Uniform Partnership Act govern.

Appendix | G

Model Business Corporation Act

_____

_____

_____

_____

CHAPTER 1. General Provisions

SUBCHAPTER A. *Short Title and Reservation of Power*

§ 1.01 Short Title

This Act shall be known and may be cited as the "[name of state] Business Corporation Act."

§ 1.02 Reservation of Power to Amend or Repeal

The [name of state legislature] has power to amend or repeal all or part of this Act at any time and all domestic and foreign corporations subject to this Act are governed by the amendment or repeal.

SUBCHAPTER B. *Filing Documents*

§ 1.20 Filing Requirements

(a) A document must satisfy the requirements of this section, and of any other section that adds to or varies these requirements, to be entitled to filing by the secretary of state.

(b) This Act must require or permit filing the document in the office of the secretary of state.

(c) The document must contain the information required by this Act. It may contain other information as well.

(d) The document must be typewritten or printed.

(e) The document must be in the English language. A corporate name need not be in English if written in English letters or Arabic or Roman numerals, and the certificate of existence required of foreign corporations need not be in English if accompanied by a reasonably authenticated English translation.

(f) The document must be executed:

(1) by the chairman of the board of directors of a domestic or foreign corporation, by its president, or by another of its officers;

(2) if directors have not been selected or the corporation has not been formed, by an incorporator; or

(3) if the corporation is in the hands of a receiver, trustee, or other court-appointed fiduciary, by that fiduciary.

(g) The person executing the document shall sign it and state beneath or opposite his signature his name and the capacity in which he signs. The document may but need not contain: (1) the corporate seal, (2) an attestation by the secretary or an assistant secretary, (3) an acknowledgement, verification, or proof.

(h) If the secretary of state has prescribed a mandatory form for the document under section 1.21, the document must be in or on the prescribed form.

(i) The document must be delivered to the office of the secretary of state for filing and must be accompanied by one exact or conformed copy (except as provided in sections 5.03 and 15.09), the correct filing fee, and any franchise tax, license fee, or penalty required by this Act or other law.

§ 1.21   Forms

(a) The secretary of state may prescribe and furnish on request forms for: (1) an application for a certificate of existence, (2) a foreign corporation's application for a certificate of authority to transact business in this state, (3) a foreign corporation's application for a certificate of withdrawal, and (4) the annual report. If the secretary of state so requires, use of these forms is mandatory.

(b) The secretary of state may prescribe and furnish on request forms for other documents required or permitted to be filed by this Act but their use is not mandatory.

§ 1.22   Filing, Service and Copying Fees

(a) The secretary of state shall collect the following fees when the documents described in this subsection are delivered to him for filing:

Document	Fee
(1) Articles of incorporation	$_____.
(2) Application for use of indistinguishable name	$_____.
(3) Application for reserved name	$_____.
(4) Notice of transfer of reserved name	$_____.
(5) Application for registered name	$_____.
(6) Application for renewal of registered name	$_____.
(7) Corporation's statement of change of registered agent or registered office or both	$_____.
(8) Agent's statement of change of registered office for each affected corporation	$_____.
not to exceed a total of	$_____.
(9) Agent's statement of resignation	No fee.
(10) Amendment of articles of incorporation	$_____.
(11) Restatement of articles of incorporation	$_____.
with amendment of articles	$_____.
(12) Articles of merger or share exchange	$_____.
(13) Articles of dissolution	$_____.
(14) Articles of revocation of dissolution	$_____.
(15) Certificate of administrative dissolution	No fee.
(16) Application for reinstatement following administrative dissolution	$_____.
(17) Certificate of reinstatement	No fee.
(18) Certificate of judicial dissolution	No fee.
(19) Application for certificate of authority	$_____.
(20) Application for amended certificate of authority	$_____.
(21) Application for certificate of withdrawal	$_____.
(22) Certificate of revocation of authority to transact business	No fee.
(23) Annual report	$_____.
(24) Articles of correction	$_____.
(25) Application for certificate of existence or authorization	$_____.
(26) Any other document required or permitted to be filed by this Act.	$_____.

(b) The secretary of state shall collect a fee of $_____ each time process is served on him under this Act. The party to a proceeding causing service of process is entitled to recover this fee as costs if he prevails in the proceeding.

(c) The secretary of state shall collect the following fees for copying and certifying the copy of any filed document relating to a domestic or foreign corporation:

(1) $_____ a page for copying; and

(2) $_____ for the certificate.

§ 1.23 Effective Time and Date of Document

(a) Except as provided in subsection (b) and section 1.24(c), a document accepted for filing is effective:

(1) at the time of filing on the date it is filed, as evidenced by the secretary of state's date and time endorsement on the original document; or

(2) at the time specified in the document as its effective time on the date it is filed.

(b) A document may specify a delayed effective time and date, and if it does so the document becomes effective at the time and date specified. If a delayed effective date but no time is specified, the document is effective at the close of business on that date. A delayed effective date for a document may not be later than the 90th day after the date it is filed.

§ 1.24 Correcting Filed Document

(a) A domestic or foreign corporation may correct a document filed by the secretary of state if the document (1) contains an incorrect statement or (2) was defectively executed, attested, sealed, verified, or acknowledged.

(b) A document is corrected:

(1) by preparing articles of correction that (i) describe the document (including its filing date) or attach a copy of it to the articles, (ii) specify the incorrect statement and the reason it is incorrect or the manner in which the execution was defective, and (iii) correct the incorrect statement or defective execution; and

(2) by delivering the articles to the secretary of state for filing.

(c) Articles of correction are effective on the effective date of the document they correct except as to persons relying on the uncorrected document and adversely affected by the correction. As to those persons, articles of correction are effective when filed.

§ 1.25 Filing Duty of Secretary of State

(a) If a document delivered to the office of the secretary of state for filing satisfies the requirements of section 1.20, the secretary of state shall file it.

(b) The secretary of state files a document by stamping or otherwise endorsing "Filed," together with his name and official title and the date and time of receipt, on both the original and the document copy and on the receipt for the filing fee. After filing a document, except as provided in sections 5.03 and 15.10, the secretary of state shall deliver the document copy, with the filing fee receipt (or acknowledgement of receipt if no fee is required) attached, to the domestic or foreign corporation or its representative.

(c) If the secretary of state refuses to file a document, he shall return it to the domestic or foreign corporation or its representative within five days after the document was delivered, together with a brief, written explanation of the reason for his refusal.

(d) The secretary of state's duty to file documents under this section is ministerial. His filing or refusing to file a document does not:

(1) affect the validity or invalidity of the document in whole or part;

(2) relate to the correctness or incorrectness of information contained in the document;

(3) create a presumption that the document is valid or invalid or that information contained in the document is correct or incorrect.

§ 1.26 Appeal From Secretary of State's Refusal to File Document

(a) If the secretary of state refuses to file a document delivered to his office for filing, the domestic or foreign corporation may appeal the refusal to the [name or describe] court [of the county where the corporation's principal office (or, if none in this state, its registered office) is or will be located] [of $_____ county]. The appeal is commenced by petitioning the court to compel filing the document and by attaching to the petition the document and the secretary of state's explanation of his refusal to file.

(b) The court may summarily order the secretary of state to file the document or take other action the court considers appropriate.

(c) The court's final decision may be appealed as in other civil proceedings.

§ 1.27 Evidentiary Effect of Copy of Filed Document

A certificate attached to a copy of the document filed by the secretary of state, bearing his signature (which may be in facsimile) and the seal of this state, is conclusive evidence that the original document is on file with the secretary of state.

§ 1.28 Certificate of Existence

(a) Anyone may apply to the secretary of state to furnish a certificate of existence for a domestic corporation or a certificate of authorization for a foreign corporation.

(b) A certificate of existence or authorization sets forth:

(1) the domestic corporation's corporate name or the foreign corporation's corporate name used in this state;

(2) that (i) the domestic corporation is duly incorporated under the law of this state, the date of its incorporation, and the period of its duration if less than perpetual; or (ii) that the foreign corporation is authorized to transact business in this state;

(3) that all fees, taxes, and penalties owed to this state have been paid, if (i) payment is reflected in the records of the secretary of state and (ii) nonpayment affects the existence or authorization of the domestic or foreign corporation;

(4) that its most recent annual report required by section 16.22 has been delivered to the secretary of state;

(5) that articles of dissolution have not been filed; and

(6) other facts of record in the office of the secretary of state that may be requested by the applicant.

(c) Subject to any qualification stated in the certificate, a certificate of existence or authorization issued by the secretary of state may be relied upon as conclusive evidence that the domestic or foreign corporation is in existence or is authorized to transact business in this state.

§ 1.29 Penalty for Signing False Document

(a) A person commits an offense if he signs a document he knows is false in any material respect with intent that the document be delivered to the secretary of state for filing.

(b) An offense under this section is a [_____] misdemeanor [punishable by a fine of not to exceed $_____].

SUBCHAPTER C. *Secretary of State*

§ 1.30 Powers

The secretary of state has the power reasonably necessary to perform the duties required of him by this Act.

SUBCHAPTER D. *Definitions*

§ 1.40 Act Definitions

In this Act:

(1) "Articles of incorporation" include amended and restated articles of incorporation and articles of merger.

(2) "Authorized shares" means the shares of all classes a domestic or foreign corporation is authorized to issue.

(3) "Conspicuous" means so written that a reasonable person against whom the writing is to operate should have noticed it. For example, printing in italics or boldface or contrasting color, or typing in capitals or underlined, is conspicuous.

(4) "Corporation" or "domestic corporation" means a corporation for profit, which is not a foreign corporation, incorporated under or subject to the provisions of this Act.

(5) "Deliver" includes mail.

(6) "Distribution" means a direct or indirect transfer of money or other property (except its own shares) or incurrence of indebtedness by a corporation to or for the benefit of its shareholders in respect of any of its shares. A distribution may be in the form of a declaration or payment of a dividend; a purchase, redemption, or other acquisition of shares; a distribution of indebtedness; or otherwise.

(7) "Effective date of notice" is defined in section 1.41.

(8) "Employee" includes an officer but not a director. A director may accept duties that make him also an employee.

(9) "Entity" includes corporation and foreign corporation; not-for-profit corporation; profit and not-for-profit unincorporated association; business trust, estate, partnership, trust, and two or more persons having a joint or common economic interest; and state, United States, and foreign government.

(10) "Foreign corporation" means a corporation for profit incorporated under a law other than the law of this state.

(11) "Governmental subdivision" includes authority, county, district, and municipality.

(12) "Includes" denotes a partial definition.

(13) "Individual" includes the estate of an incompetent or deceased individual.

(14) "Means" denotes an exhaustive definition.

(15) "Notice" is defined in section 1.41.

(16) "Person" includes individual and entity.

(17) "Principal office" means the office (in or out of this state) so designated in the annual report where the principal executive offices of a domestic or foreign corporation are located.

(18) "Proceeding" includes civil suit and criminal, administrative, and investigatory action.

(19) "Record date" means the date established under chapter 6 or 7 on which a corporation determines the identity of its shareholders for purposes of this Act.

(20) "Secretary" means the corporate officer to whom the board of directors has delegated responsibility under section 8.40(c) for custody of the minutes of the meetings of the board of directors and of the shareholders and for authenticating records of the corporation.

(21) "Shares" mean the unit into which the proprietary interests in a corporation are divided.

(22) "Shareholder" means the person in whose name shares are registered in the records of a corporation or the beneficial owner of shares to the extent of the rights granted by a nominee certificate on file with a corporation.

(23) "State," when referring to a part of the United States, includes a state and commonwealth (and their agencies and governmental subdivisions) and a territory, and insular possession (and their agencies and governmental subdivisions) of the United States.

(24) "Subscriber" means a person who subscribes for shares in a corporation, whether before or after incorporation.

(25) "United States" includes district, authority, bureau, commission, department, and any other agency of the United States.

(26) "Voting group" means all shares of one or more classes or series that under the articles of incorporation or this Act are entitled to vote and be counted together collectively on a matter at a meeting of shareholders. All shares entitled by the articles of incorporation or this Act to vote generally on the matter are for that purpose a single voting group.

§ 1.41   Notice

(a) Notice under this Act shall be in writing unless oral notice is reasonable under the circumstances.

(b) Notice may be communicated in person; by telephone, telegraph, teletype, or other form of wire or wireless communication; or by mail or private carrier. If these forms of personal notice are impracticable, notice may be communicated by a newspaper of general circulation in the area where published; or by radio, television, or other form of public broadcast communication.

(c) Written notice by a domestic or foreign corporation to its shareholder, if in a comprehensible form, is effective when mailed, if mailed postpaid and correctly addressed to the shareholder's address shown in the corporation's current record of shareholders.

(d) Written notice to a domestic or foreign corporation (authorized to transact business in this state) may be addressed to its registered agent at its registered office or to the corporation or its secretary at its principal office shown in its most recent annual report or, in the case of a foreign corporation that has not yet delivered an annual report, in its application for a certificate of authority.

(e) Except as provided in subsections (c) and (d), written notice, if in a comprehensible form, is effective at the earliest of the following:

(1) when received;

(2) five days after its deposit in the United States Mail, as evidenced by the postmark, if mailed postpaid and correctly addressed;

(3) on the date shown on the return receipt, if sent by registered or certified mail, return receipt requested, and the receipt is signed by or on behalf of the addressee.

(f) Oral notice is effective when communicated if communicated in a comprehensible manner.

(g) If this Act prescribes notice requirements for particular circumstances, those requirements govern. If articles of incorporation or bylaws prescribe notice requirements, not inconsistent with this section or other provisions of this Act, those requirements govern.

§ 1.42   Number of Shareholders

(a) For purposes of this Act, the following identified as a shareholder in a corporation's current record of shareholders constitutes one shareholder:

(1) three or fewer co-owners;

(2) a corporation, partnership, trust, estate, or other entity;

(3) the trustees, guardians, custodians, or other fiduciaries of a single trust, estate, or account.

(b) For purposes of this Act, shareholdings registered in substantially similar names constitute one shareholder if it is reasonable to believe that the names represent the same person.

CHAPTER 2. Incorporation

§ 2.01 Incorporators

One or more persons may act as the incorporator or incorporators of a corporation by delivering articles of incorporation to the secretary of state for filing.

§ 2.02 Articles of Incorporation

(a) The articles of incorporation must set forth:

(1) a corporate name for the corporation that satisfies the requirements of section 4.01;

(2) the number of shares the corporation is authorized to issue;

(3) the street address of the corporation's initial registered office and the name of its initial registered agent at the office; and

(4) the name and address of each incorporator.

(b) The articles of incorporation may set forth:

(1) the names and addresses of the individuals who are to serve as the initial directors;

(2) provisions not inconsistent with law regarding:

(i) the purpose or purposes for which the corporation is organized;

(ii) managing the business and regulating the affairs of the corporation;

(iii) defining, limiting, and regulating the powers of the corporation, its board of directors, and shareholders;

(iv) a par value for authorized shares or classes of shares;

(v) the imposition of personal liability on shareholders for the debts of the corporation to a specified extent and upon specified conditions; and

(3) any provision that under this Act is required or permitted to be set forth in the bylaws.

(c) The articles of incorporation need not set forth any of the corporate powers enumerated in this Act.

§ 2.03 Incorporation

(a) Unless a delayed effective date is specified, the corporate existence begins when the articles of incorporation are filed.

(b) The secretary of state's filing of the articles of incorporation is conclusive proof that the incorporators satisfied all conditions precedent to incorporation except in a proceeding by the state to cancel or revoke the incorporation or involuntarily dissolve the corporation.

§ 2.04 Liability for Preincorporation Transactions

All persons purporting to act as or on behalf of a corporation, knowing there was no incorporation under this Act, are jointly and severally liable for all liabilities created while so acting.

§ 2.05 Organization of Corporation

(a) After incorporation:

(1) if initial directors are named in the articles of incorporation, the initial directors shall hold an organizational meeting, at the call of a majority of the directors, to complete the organization of the corporation by appointing officers, adopting bylaws, and carrying on any other business brought before the meeting;

(2) if initial directors are not named in the articles, the incorporator or incorporators shall hold an organizational meeting at the call of a majority of the incorporators:

(i) to elect directors and complete the organization of the corporation; or

(ii) to elect a board of directors who shall complete the organization of the corporation.

(b) Action required or permitted by this Act to be taken by incorporators at an organizational meeting may be taken without a meeting if the action taken is evidenced by one or more written consents describing the action taken and signed by each incorporator.

(c) An organizational meeting may be held in or out of this state.

§ 2.06 Bylaws

(a) The incorporators or board of directors of a corporation shall adopt initial bylaws for the corporation.

(b) The bylaws of a corporation may contain any provision for managing the business and regulating the affairs of the corporation that is not inconsistent with law or the articles of incorporation.

§ 2.07   Emergency Bylaws

(a) Unless the articles of incorporation provide otherwise, the board of directors of a corporation may adopt bylaws to be effective only in an emergency defined in subsection (d). The emergency bylaws, which are subject to amendment or repeal by the shareholders, may make all provisions necessary for managing the corporation during the emergency, including:

(1) procedures for calling a meeting of the board of directors;

(2) quorum requirements for the meeting; and

(3) designation of additional or substitute directors.

(b) All provisions of the regular bylaws consistent with the emergency bylaws remain effective during the emergency. The emergency bylaws are not effective after the emergency ends.

(c) Corporate action taken in goods faith in accordance with the emergency bylaws:

(1) binds the corporation; and

(2) may not be used to impose liability on a corporate director, officer, employee, or agent.

(d) An emergency exists for purposes of this section if a quorum of the corporation's directors cannot readily be assembled because of some catastrophic event.

CHAPTER 3.   Purposes and Powers

§ 3.01   Purposes

(a) Every corporation incorporated under this Act has the purpose of engaging in any lawful business unless a more limited purpose is set forth in the articles of incorporation.

(b) A corporation engaging in a business that is subject to regulation under another statute of this state may incorporate under this Act only if permitted by, and subject to all limitations of, the other statute.

§ 3.02   General Powers

Unless its articles of incorporation provide otherwise, every corporation has perpetual duration and succession in its corporate name and has the same powers as an individual to do all things necessary or convenient to carry out its business and affairs, including without limitation power:

(1) to sue and be sued, complain and defend in its corporate name;

(2) to have a corporate seal, which may be altered at will, and to use it, or a facsimile of it, by impressing or affixing it or in any other manner reproducing it;

(3) to make and amend bylaws, not inconsistent with its articles of incorporation or with the laws of this state, for managing the business and regulating the affiars of the corporation;

(4) to purchase, receive, lease, or otherwise acquire, and own, hold, improve, use, and otherwise deal with, real or personal property, or any legal or equitable interest in property, wherever located;

(5) to sell, convey, mortgage, pledge, lease, exchange, and otherwise dispose of all or any part of its property;

(6) to purchase, receive, subscribe for, or otherwise acquire; own, hold, vote, use, sell, mortgage, lend, pledge, or otherwise dispose of; and deal in and with shares or other interests in, or obligations of, any other entity;

(7) to make contracts and guarantees, incur liabilities, borrow money, issue its notes, bonds, and other obligations, (which may be convertible into or include the option to purchase other securities of the corporation), and secure any of its obligations by mortgage or pledge of any of its property, franchises, or income;

(8) to lend money, invest and reinvest its funds, and receive and hold real and personal property as security for repayment;

(9) to be a promoter, partner, member, associate, or manager of any partnership, joint venture, trust, or other entity;

(10) to conduct its business, locate offices, and exercise the powers granted by this Act within or without this state;

(11) to elect directors and appoint officers, employees, and agents of the corporation, define their duties, fix their compensation, and lend them money and credit;

(12) to pay pensions and establish pension plans, pension trusts, profit sharing plans, share bonus plans, share option plans, and benefit or incentive plans for any or all of its current or former directors, officers, employees, and agents;

(13) to make donations for the public welfare or for charitable, scientific, or educational purposes;

(14) to transact any lawful business that will aid governmental policy;

(15) to make payments or donations, or do any other act, not inconsistent with law, that furthers the business and affairs of the corporation.

§ 3.03   Emergency Powers

(a) In anticipation of or during an emergency defined in subsection (d), the board of directors of a corporation may:

(1) modify lines of succession to accommodate the incapacity of any director, officer, employee, or agent; and

(2) relocate the principal office, designate alternative principal offices or regional offices, or authorize the officers to do so.

(b) During an emergency defined in subsection (d), unless emergency bylaws provide otherwise:

(1) notice of a meeting of the board of directors need be given only to those directors whom it is practicable to reach and may be given in any practicable manner, including by publication and radio; and

(2) one or more officers of the corporation present at a meeting of the board of directors may be deemed to be directors for the meeting, in order of rank and within the same rank in order of seniority, as necessary to achieve a quorum.

(c) Corporate action taken in good faith during an emergency under this section to further the ordinary business affairs of the corporation:

(1) binds the corporation; and

(2) may not be used to impose liability on a corporate director, officer, employee, or agent.

(d) An emergency exists for purposes of this section if a quorum of the corporation's directors cannot readily be assembled because of some catastrophic event.

§ 3.04   Ultra Vires

(a) Except as provided in subsection (b), the validity of corporate action may not be challenged on the ground that the corporation lacks or lacked power to act.

(b) A corporation's power to act may be challenged:

(1) in a proceeding by a shareholder against the corporation to enjoin the act;

(2) in a proceeding by the corporation, directly, derivatively, or through a receiver, trustee, or other legal representative, against an incumbent or former director, officer, employee, or agent of the corporation; or

(3) in a proceeding by the Attorney General under section 14.30.

(c) In a shareholder's proceeding under subsection (b)(1) to enjoin an unauthorized corporate act, the court may enjoin or set aside the act, if equitable and if all affected persons are parties to the proceeding, and may award damages for loss (other than anticipated profits) suffered by the corporation or another party because of enjoining the unauthorized act.

CHAPTER 4.   Name

§ 4.01   Corporate Name

(a) A corporate name:

(1) must contain the word "corporation," "incorporated," "company," or "limited," or the abbreviation "corp.," "inc.," "co.," or "ltd.", or words or abbreviations of like import in another language; and

(2) may not contain language stating or implying that the corporation is organized for a purpose other than that permitted by section 3.01 and its articles of incorporation.

(b) Except as authorized by subsections (c) and (d), a corporate name must be distinguishable upon the records of the secretary of state from:

(1) the corporate name of a corporation incorporated or authorized to transact business in this state;

(2) a corporate name reserved or registered under section 4.02 or 4.03;

(3) the fictitious name adopted by a foreign corporation authorized to transact business in this state because its real name is unavailable; and

(4) the corporate name of a not-for-profit corporation incorporated or authorized to transact business in this state.

(c) A corporation may apply to the secretary of state for authorization to use a name that is not distinguishable upon his records from one or more of the names described in subsection (b). The secretary of state shall authorize use of the name applied for if:

(1) the other corporation consents to the use in writing and submits an undertaking in form satisfactory to the secretary of state to change its name to a name that is distinguishable upon the records of the secretary of state from the name of the applying corporation; or

(2) the applicant delivers to the secretary of state a certified copy of the final judgment of a court of competent jurisdiction establishing the applicant's right to use the name applied for in this state.

(d) A corporation may use the name (including the fictitious name) of another domestic or foreign corporation that is used in this state if the other corporation is incorporated or authorized to transact business in this state and the proposed user corporation:

(1) has merged with the other corporation;

(2) has been formed by reorganization of the other corporation; or

(3) has acquired all or substantially all of the assets, including the corporate name, of the other corporation.

(e) This Act does not control the use of fictitious names.

§ 4.02   Reserved Name

(a) A person may reserve the exclusive use of a corporate name, including a fictitious name for a foreign corporation whose corporate name is not available, by delivering an application to the secretary of state for filing. The application must set forth the name and address of the applicant and the name proposed to be reserved. If the secretary of state finds that the corporate name applied for is available, he shall reserve the name for the applicant's exclusive use for a nonrenewable 120-day period.

(b) The owner of a reserved corporate name may transfer the reservation to another person by delivering to the secretary of state a signed notice of the transfer that states the name and address of the transferee.

§ 4.03   Registered Name

(a) A foreign corporation may register its corporate name, or its corporate name with any addition required by section 15.06, if the name is distinguishable upon the records of the secretary of state from the corporate names that are not available under section 4.01(b)(3).

(b) A foreign corporation registers its corporate name, or its corporate name with any addition required by section 15.06, by delivering to the secretary of state for filing an application:

(1) setting forth its corporate name, or its corporate name with any addition required by section 15.06, the state or country and date of its incorporation, and a brief description of the nature of the business in which it is engaged; and

(2) accompanied by a certificate of existence (or a document of similar import) from the state or country of incorporation.

(c) The name is registered for the applicant's exclusive use upon the effective date of the application.

(d) A foreign corporation whose registration is effective may renew it for successive years by delivering to the secretary of state for filing a renewal application, which complies with the requirements of subsection (b), between October 1 and December 31 of the preceding year. The renewal application renews the registration for the following calendar year.

(e) A foreign corporation whose registration is effective may thereafter qualify as a foreign corporation under that name or consent in writing to the use of that name by a corporation thereafter incorporated under this Act or by another foreign corporation thereafter authorized to transact business in this state. The registration terminates when the domestic corporation is incorporated or the foreign corporation qualifies or consents to the qualification of another foreign corporation under the registered name.

CHAPTER 5.   Office and Agent

§ 5.01   Registered Office and Registered Agent

Each corporation must continuously maintain in this state:

(1) a registered office that may be the same as any of its places of business; and

(2) a registered agent, who may be:

(i) an individual who resides in this state and whose business office is identical with the registered office;

(ii) a domestic corporation or not-for-profit domestic corporation whose business office is identical with the registered office; or

(iii) a foreign corporation or not-for-profit foreign corporation authorized to transact business in this state whose business office is identical with the registered office.

§ 5.02   Change of Registered Office or Registered Agent

(a) A corporation may change its registered office or registered agent by delivering to the secretary of state for filing a statement of change that sets forth:

(1) the name of the corporation;

(2) the street address of its current registered office;

(3) if the current registered office is to be changed, the street address of the new registered office;

(4) the name of its current registered agent;

(5) if the current registered agent is to be changed, the name of the new registered agent and the new agent's written consent (either on the statement or attached to it) to the appointment; and

(6) that after the change or changes are made, the street addresses of its registered office and the business office of its registered agent will be identical.

(b) If a registered agent changes the street address of his business office, he may change the street address of the registered office of any corporation for which he is the registered agent by notifying the corporation in writing of the change and signing (either manually or in facsimile) and delivering to the secretary of state for filing a statement that complies with the requirements of subsection (a) and recites that the corporation has been notified of the change.

§ 5.03   Resignation of Registered Agent

(a) A registered agent may resign his agency appointment by signing and delivering to the secretary of state for filing the signed original and two exact or conformed copies of a statement of resignation. The statement may include a statement that the registered office is also discontinued.

(b) After filing the statement the secretary of state shall mail one copy to the registered office (if not discontinued) and the other copy to the corporation at its principal office.

(c) The agency appointment is terminated, and the registered office discontinued if so provided, on the 31st day after the date on which the statement was filed.

§ 5.04   Service on Corporation

(a) A corporation's registered agent is the corporation's agent for service of process, notice, or demand required or permitted by law to be served on the corporation.

(b) If a corporation has no registered agent, or the agent cannot with reasonable diligence be served, the corporation may be served by registered or certified mail, return receipt requested, addressed to the secretary of the corporation at its principal office. Service is perfected under this subsection at the earliest of:

(1) the date the corporation receives the mail;

(2) the date shown on the return receipt, if signed on behalf of the corporation; or

(3) five days after its deposit in the United States Mail, if mailed postpaid and correctly addressed.

(c) This section does not prescribe the only means, or necessarily the required means, of serving a corporation.

CHAPTER 6.   Shares and Distributions
SUBCHAPTER A. *Shares*

§ 6.01   Authorized Shares

(a) The articles of incorporation must prescribe the classes of shares and the number of shares of each class that the corporation is authorized to issue. If more than one class of shares is authorized, the articles of incorporation must prescribe a distinguishing designation for each class, and prior to the issuance of shares of a class the preferences, limitations, and relative rights of that class must be described in the articles of incorporation. All shares of a class must have preferences, limitations, and relative rights identical with those of other shares of the same class except to the extent otherwise permitted by section 6.02.

(b) The articles of incorporation must authorize (1) one or more classes of shares that together have unlimited voting rights, and (2) one or more classes of shares (which may be the same class or classes as those with voting rights) that together are entitled to receive the net assets of the corporation upon dissolution.

(c) The articles of incorporation may authorize one or more classes of shares that:

(1) have special, conditional, or limited voting rights, or no right to vote, except to the extent prohibited by this Act;

(2) are redeemable or convertible as specified in the articles of incorporation (i) at the option of the corporation, the shareholder, or another person or upon the occurrence or a designated event; (ii) for cash, indebtedness, securities, or other property; (iii) in a designated amount or in an amount determined in accordance with a designated formula or by reference to extrinsic data or events;

(3) entitle the holders to distributions calculated in any manner, including dividends that may be cumulative, noncumulative, or partially cumulative;

(4) have preference over any other class of shares with respect to distributions, including dividends and distributions upon the dissolution of the corporation.

(d) The description of the designations, preferences, limitations, and relative rights of share classes in subsection (c) is not exhaustive.

§ 6.02   Terms of Class or Series Determined by Board of Directors

(a) If the articles of incorporation so provide, the board of directors may determine, in whole or in part, the preferences, limitations, and relative rights (within the limits set forth in section 6.01) of (1) any class of shares before the issuance of any shares of that class or (2) one or more series within a class before the issuance of any shares of that series.

(b) Each series of a class must be given a distinguishing designation.

(c) All shares of a series must have preferences, limitations, and relative rights identical with those of other shares of the same series and, except to the extent otherwise provided in the description of the series, of those of other series of the same class.

(d) Before issuing any shares of a class or series created under this section, the corporation must deliver to the secretary of state for filing articles of amendment, which are effective without shareholder action, that set forth:

   (1) the name of the corporation;

   (2) the text of the amendment determining the terms of the class or series of shares;

   (3) the date it was adopted; and

   (4) a statement that the amendment was duly adopted by the board of directors.

§ 6.03   Issued and Outstanding Shares

(a) A corporation may issue the number of shares of each class or series authorized by the articles of incorporation. Shares that are issued are outstanding shares until they are reacquired, redeemed, converted, or cancelled.

(b) The reacquisition, redemption, or conversion of outstanding shares is subject to the limitations of subsection (c) of this section and to section 6.40.

(c) At all times that shares of the corporation are outstanding, one or more shares that together have unlimited voting rights and one or more shares that together are entitled to receive the net assets of the corporation upon dissolution must be outstanding.

§ 6.04   Fractional Shares

(a) A corporation may:

   (1) issue fractions of a share or pay in money the value of fractions of a share;

   (2) arrange for disposition of fractional shares by the shareholders;

   (3) issue scrip in registered or bearer form entitling the holder to receive a full share upon surrendering enough scrip to equal a full share.

(b) Each certificate representing scrip must be conspicuously labeled "scrip" and must contain the information required by section 6.25(b).

(c) The holder of a fractional share is entitled to exercise the rights of a shareholder, including the right to vote, to receive dividends, and to participate in the assets of the corporation upon liquidation. The holder of scrip is not entitled to any of these rights unless the scrip provides for them.

(d) The board of directors may authorize the issuance of scrip subject to any condition considered desirable, including:

   (1) that the scrip will become void if not exchanged for full shares before a specified date; and

   (2) that the shares for which the scrip is exchangeable may be sold and the proceeds paid to the scripholders.

SUBCHAPTER B. *Issuance of Shares*

§ 6.20   Subscription for Shares Before Incorporation

(a) A subscription for shares entered into before incorporation is irrevocable for six months unless the subscription agreement provides a longer or shorter period or all the subscribers agree to revocation.

(b) The board of directors may determine the payment terms of subscriptions for shares that were entered into before incorporation, unless the subscription agreement specifies them. A call for payment by the board of directors must be uniform so far as practicable as to all shares of the same class or series, unless the subscription agreement specifies otherwise.

(c) Shares issued pursuant to subscriptions entered into before incorporation are fully paid and nonassessable when the corporation receives the consideration specified in the subscription agreement.

(d) If a subscriber defaults in payment of money or property under a subscription agreement entered into before incorporation, the corporation may collect the amount owed as any other debt. Alternatively, unless the subscription agreement provides otherwise, the corporation may rescind the agreement and may sell the shares if the debt remains unpaid more than 20 days after the corporation sends written demand for payment to the subscriber.

(e) A subscription agreement entered into after incorporation is a contract between the subscriber and the corporation subject to section 6.21.

§ 6.21   Issuance of Shares

(a) The powers granted in this section to the board of directors may be reserved to the shareholders by the articles of incorporation.

(b) The board of directors may authorize shares to be issued for consideration consisting of any tangible or intangible property or benefit to the corporation, including cash, promissory notes, services performed, contracts for services to be performed, or other securities of the corporation.

(c) Before the corporation issues shares, the board of directors must determine that the consideration received or to be received for shares to be issued is adequate. That determination by the board of directors is conclusive insofar as the adequacy of consideration for the issuance of shares relates to whether the shares are validly issued, fully paid, and nonassessable.

(d) When the corporation receives the consideration for which the board of directors authorized the issuance of shares, the shares issued therefor are fully paid and nonassessable.

(e) The corporation may place in escrow shares issued for a contract for future services or benefits or a promissory note, or make other arrangements to restrict the transfer of the shares, and may credit distributions in respect of the shares against their purchase price, until the services are performed, the note is paid, or the benefits received. If the services are not performed, the note is not paid, or the benefits are not received, the shares escrowed or restricted and the distributions credited may be cancelled in whole or part.

§ 6.22   Liability of Shareholders

(a) A purchaser from a corporation of its own shares is not liable to the corporation or its creditors with respect to the shares except to pay the consideration for which the shares were authorized to be issued (section 6.21) or specified in the subscription agreement (section 6.20).

(b) Unless otherwise provided in the articles of incorporation, a shareholder of a corporation is not personally liable for the acts or debts of the corporation except that he may become personally liable by reason of his own acts or conduct.

§ 6.23   Share Dividends

(a) Unless the articles of incorporation provide otherwise, shares may be issued pro rata and without consideration to the corporation's shareholders or to the shareholders of one or more classes or series. An issuance of shares under this subsection is a share dividend.

(b) Shares of one class or series may not be issued as a share dividend in respect of shares of another class or series unless (1) the articles of incorporation so authorize, (2) a majority of the votes entitled to be cast by the class or series to be issued approve the issue, or (3) there are no outstanding shares of the class or series to be issued.

(c) If the board of directors does not fix the record date for determining shareholders entitled to a share dividend, it is the date the board of directors authorizes the share dividend.

§ 6.24   Share Options

A corporation may issue rights, options, or warrants for the purchase of shares of the corporation. The board of directors shall determine the terms upon which the rights, options, or warrants are issued, their form and content, and the consideration for which the shares are to be issued.

§ 6.25   Form and Content of Certificates

(a) Shares may but need not be represented by certificates. Unless this Act or another statute expressly provides otherwise, the rights and obligations of shareholders are identical whether or not their shares are represented by certificates.

(b) At a minimum each share certificate must state on its face:

(1) the name of the issuing corporation and that it is organized under the law of this state;

(2) the name of the person to whom issued; and

(3) the number and class of shares and the designation of the series, if any, the certificate represents.

(c) If the issuing corporation is authorized to issue different classes of shares or different series within a class, the designations, relative rights, preferences, and limitations applicable to each class and the variations in rights, preferences, and limitations determined for each series (and the authority of the board of directors to determine variations for future series) must be summarized on the front or back of each certificate. Alternatively, each certificate may state conspicuously on its front or back that the corporation will furnish the shareholder this information on request in writing and without charge.

(d) Each share certificate (1) must be signed (either manually or in facsimile) by two officers designated in the bylaws or by the board of directors and (2) may bear the corporate seal or its facsimile.

(e) If the person who signed (either manually or in facsimile) a share certificate no longer holds office when the certificate is issued, the certificate is nevertheless valid.

§ 6.26   Shares Without Certificates

(a) Unless the articles of incorporation or bylaws provide otherwise, the boad of directors of a corporation may authorize the issue of some or all of the shares of any or all of its classes or series without certificates. The authorization does not affect shares already represented by certificates until they are surrendered to the corporation.

(b) Within a reasonable time after the issue or transfer of shares without certificates, the corporation shall send the shareholder a written statement of the information required on certificates by section 6.25(b) and (c), and, if applicable, section 6.27.

§ 6.27   Restriction on Transfer of Shares and Other Securities

(a) The articles of incorporation, bylaws, an agreement among shareholders, or an agreement between shareholders and the corporation may impose restrictions on the transfer or registration of transfer of shares of the corporation. A restriction does not affect shares issued before the restriction was adopted unless the holders of the shares are parties to the restriction agreement or voted in favor of the restriction.

(b) A restriction on the transfer or registration of transfer of shares is valid and enforceable against the holder or a transferee of the holder if the restriction is authorized by this section and its existence is noted conspicuously on the front or back of the certificate or is contained in the information statement required by section 6.26(b). Unless so noted, a restriction is not enforceable against a person without knowledge of the restriction.

(c) A restriction on the transfer or registration of transfer of shares is authorized:

(1) to maintain the corporation's status when it is dependent on the number or identity of its shareholders;

(2) to preserve exemptions under federal or state securities law;

(3) for any other reasonable purpose.

(d) A restriction on the transfer or registration of transfer of shares may:

(1) obligate the shareholder first to offer the corporation or other persons (separately, consecutively, or simultaneously) an opportunity to acquire the restricted shares;

(2) obligate the corporation or other persons (separately, consecutively, or simultaneously) to acquire the restricted shares;

(3) require the corporation, the holders of any class of its shares, or another person to approve the transfer of the restricted shares, if the requirement is not manifestly unreasonable;

(4) prohibit the transfer of the restricted shares to designated persons or classes of persons, if the prohibition is not manifestly unreasonable.

(e) For purposes of this section, "shares" includes a security convertible into or carrying a right to subscribe for or acquire shares.

§ 6.28   Expense of Issue

A corporation may pay the expenses of selling or underwriting its shares, and of organizing or reorganizing the corporation, from the consideration received for shares.

SUBCHAPTER C. *Subsequent Acquisition of Shares by Shareholders and Corporation*

§ 6.30   Shareholders' Preemptive Rights

(a) The shareholders of a corporation do not have a preemptive right to acquire the corporations unissued shares except to the extent the articles of incorporation so provide.

(b) A statement included in the articles of incorporation that "the corporation elects to have preemptive rights" (or words of similar import) means that the following principles apply except to the extent the articles of incorporation expressly provide otherwise:

(1) The shareholders of the corporation have a preemptive right, granted on uniform terms and conditions prescribed by the board of directors to provide a fair and reasonable opportunity to exercise the right, to acquire proportional amounts of the corporation's unissued shares upon the decision of the board of directors to issue them.

(2) A shareholder may waive his preemptive right. A waiver evidenced by a writing is irrevocable even though it is not supported by consideration.

(3) There is no preemptive right with respect to:

(i) shares issued as compensation to directors, officers, agents, or employees of the corporation, its subsidiaries or affiliates;

(ii) shares issued to satisfy conversion or option rights created to provide compensation to directors, officers, agents, or employees of the corporation, its subsidiaries or affiliates;

(iii) shares authorized in articles of incorporation that are issued within six months from the effective date of incorporation;

(iv) shares sold otherwise than for money.

(4) Holders of shares of any class without general voting rights but with preferential rights to distributions or assets have no preemptive rights with respect to shares of any class.

(5) Holders of shares of any class with general voting rights but without preferential rights to distributions or assets have no preemptive rights with respect to shares of any class with preferential rights to distributions or assets unless the shares with preferential rights are convertible into or carry a right to subscribe for or acquire shares without preferential rights.

(6) Shares subject to preemptive rights that are not acquired by shareholders may be issued to any person for a period of one year after being offered to shareholders at a consideration set by the board of directors that is not lower than the consideration set for the exercise of preemptive rights. An offer at a lower consideration or after the expiration of one year is subject to the shareholders' preemptive rights.

(c) For purposes of this section, "shares" includes a security convertible into or carrying a right to subscribe for or acquire shares.

§ 6.31 Corporation's Acquisition of Its Own Shares

(a) A corporation may acquire its own shares and shares so acquired constitute authorized but unissued shares.

(b) If the articles of incorporation prohibit the reissue of acquired shares, the number of authorized shares is reduced by the number of shares acquired, effective upon amendment of the articles of incorporation.

(c) Articles of amendment may be adopted by the board of directors without shareholder action, shall be delivered to the secretary of state for filing, and shall set forth:

(1) the name of the corporation;

(2) the reduction in the number of authorized shares, itemized by class and series; and

(3) the total number of authorized shares, itemized by class and series, remaining after reduction of the shares.

SUBCHAPTER D. *Distributions*

§ 6.40 Distributions to Shareholders

(a) A board of directors may authorize and the corporation may make distributions to its shareholders subject to restriction by the articles of incorporation and the limitation in subsection (c).

(b) If the board of directors does not fix the record date for determining shareholders entitled to a distribution (other than one involving a repurchase or reacquisition of shares), it is the date the board of directors authorizes the distribution.

(c) No distribution may be made if, after giving it effect:

(1) the corporation would not be able to pay its debts as they become due in the usual course of business; or

(2) the corporation's total assets would be less than the sum of its total liabilities plus (unless the articles of incorporation permit otherwise) the amount that would be needed, if the corporation were to be dissolved at the time of the distribution, to satisfy the preferential rights upon dissolution of shareholders

whose preferential rights are superior to those receiving the distribution.

(d) The board of directors may base a determination that a distribution is not prohibited under subsection (c) either on financial statements prepared on the basis of accounting practices and principles that are reasonable in the circumstances or on a fair valuation or other method that is reasonable in the circumstances.

(e) The effect of a distribution under subsection (c) is measured:

(1) in the case of distribution by purchase, redemption, or other acquisition of the corporation's shares, as of the earlier of (i) the date money or other property is transferred or debt incurred by the corporation or (ii) the date the shareholder ceases to be a shareholder with respect to the acquired shares;

(2) in the case of any other distribution of indebtedness, as of the date the indebtedness is distributed;

(3) in all other cases, as of (i) the date the distribution is authorized if the payment occurs within 120 days after the date of authorization or (ii) the date the payment is made if it occurs more than 120 days after the date of authorization.

(f) A corporation's indebtedness to a shareholder incurred by reason of a distribution made in accordance with this section is at parity with the corporation's indebtedness to its general, unsecured creditors except to the extent subordinated by agreement.

CHAPTER 7. Shareholders

SUBCHAPTER A. *Meetings*

§ 7.01 Annual Meeting

(a) A corporation shall hold annually at a time stated in or fixed in accordance with the bylaws a meeting of shareholders.

(b) Annual shareholders' meetings may be held in or out of this state at the place stated in or fixed in accordance with the bylaws. If no place is stated in or fixed in accordance with the bylaws, annual meetings shall be held at the corporation's principal office.

(c) The failure to hold an annual meeting at the time stated in or fixed in accordance with a corporation's bylaws does not affect the validity of any corporate action.

§ 7.02 Special Meeting

(a) A corporation shall hold a special meeting of shareholders:

(1) on call of its board of directors or the person or persons authorized to do so by the articles of incorporation or bylaws; or

(2) if the holders of at least 10 percent of all the votes entitled to be cast on any issue proposed to be considered at the proposed special meeting sign, date, and deliver to the corporation's secretary one or more written demands for the meeting describing the purpose or purposes for which it is to be held.

(b) If not otherwise fixed under sections 7.03 or 7.07, the record date for determining shareholders entitled to demand a special meeting is the date the first shareholder signs the demand.

(c) Special shareholders' meetings may be held in or out of this state at the place stated in or fixed in accordance with the bylaws. If no place is stated or fixed in accordance with the bylaws, special meetings shall be held at the corporation's principal office,

(d) Only business within the purpose or purposes described in the meeting notice required by section 7.05(c) may be conducted at a special shareholders' meeting.

§ 7.03 Court-Ordered Meeting

(a) The [name or describe] court of the county where a corporation's principal office (or, if none in this state, its registered office) is located may summarily order a meeting to be held:

(1) on application of any shareholder of the corporation entitled to participate in an annual meeting if an annual meeting was not held within the earlier of 6 months after the end of the corporation's fiscal year or 15 months after its last annual meeting; or

(2) on application of a shareholder who signed a demand for a special meeting valid under section 7.02 if:

(i) notice of the special meeting was not given within 30 days after the date the demand was delivered to the corporation's secretary; or

(ii) the special meeting was not held in accordance with the notice.

(b) The court may fix the time and place of the meeting, determine the shares entitled to participate in the meeting, specify a record date for determining shareholders entitled to notice of and to vote at the meeting, prescribe the form and content of the meeting notice, fix the quorum required for specific matters to be considered at the meeting (or direct that the votes represented at the meeting constitute a quorum for action on those matters), and enter other orders necessary to accomplish the purpose or purposes of the meeting.

§ 7.04   Action Without Meeting

(a) Action required or permitted by this Act to be taken at a shareholders' meeting may be taken without a meeting if the action is taken by all the shareholders entitled to vote on the action. The action must be evidenced by one or more written consents describing the action taken, signed by all the shareholders entitled to vote on the action, and delivered to the corporation for inclusion in the minutes or filing with the corporate records.

(b) If not otherwise determined under sections 7.03 or 7.07, the record date for determining shareholders entitled to take action without a meeting is the date the first shareholder signs the consent under subsection (a).

(c) A consent signed under this section has the effect of a meeting vote and may be described as such in any document.

(d) If this Act requires that notice of proposed action be given to nonvoting shareholders and the action is to be taken by unanimous consent of the voting shareholders, the corporation must give its nonvoting shareholders written notice of the proposed action at least 10 days before the action is taken. The notice must contain or be accompanied by the same material that, under this Act, would have been required to be sent to nonvoting shareholders in a notice of meeting at which the proposed action would have been submitted to the shareholders for action.

§ 7.05   Notice of Meeting

(a) A corporation shall notify shareholders of the date, time, and place of each annual and special shareholders' meeting no fewer than 10 nor more than 60 days before the meeting date. Unless this Act or the articles of incorporation require otherwise, the corporation is required to give notice only to shareholders entitled to vote at the meeting.

(b) Unless this Act or the articles of incorporation require otherwise, notice of an annual meeting need not include a description of the purpose or purposes for which the meeting is called.

(c) Notice of a special meeting must include a description of the purpose or purposes for which the meeting is called.

(d) If not otherwise fixed under sections 7.03 or 7.07, the record date for determining shareholders entitled to

notice of and to vote at an annual or special shareholders' meeting is the close of business on the day before the first notice is delivered to shareholders.

(e) Unless the bylaws require otherwise, if an annual or special, shareholders' meeting is adjourned to a different date, time, or place, notice need not be given of the new date, time, or place if the new date, time, or place is announced at the meeting before adjournment. If a new record date for the adjourned meeting is or must be fixed under section 7.07, however, notice of the adjourned meeting must be given under this section to persons who are shareholders as of the new record date.

§ 7.06   Waiver of Notice

(a) A shareholder may waive any notice required by this Act, the articles of incorporation, or bylaws before or after the date and time stated in the notice. The waiver must be in writing, be signed by the shareholder entitled to the notice, and be delivered to the corporation for inclusion in the minutes or filing with the corporate records.

(b) A shareholder's attendance at a meeting:

(1) waives objection to lack of notice or defective notice of the meeting, unless the shareholder at the beginning of the meeting objects to holding the meeting or transacting business at the meeting;

(2) waives objection to consideration of a particular matter at the meeting that is not within the purpose or purposes described in the meeting notice, unless the shareholder objects to considering the matter when it is presented.

§ 7.07   Record Date

(a) The bylaws may fix or provide the manner of fixing the record date for one or more voting groups in order to determine the shareholders entitled to notice of a shareholders' meeting, to demand a special meeting, to vote, or to take any other action. If the bylaws do not fix or provide for fixing a record date, the board of directors of the corporation may fix a future date as the record date.

(b) A record date fixed under this section may not be more than 70 days before the meeting or action requiring a determination of shareholders.

(c) A determination of shareholders entitled to notice of or to vote at a shareholders' meeting is effective for any adjournment of the meeting unless the board of directors fixes a new record date, which it must do if the meeting is adjourned to a date more than 120 days after the date fixed for the original meeting.

(d) If a court orders a meeting adjourned to a date more than 120 days after the date fixed for the original meeting, it may provide that the original record date continues in effect or it may fix a new record date.

SUBCHAPTER B. *Voting*

§ 7.20 Shareholders' List for Meeting

(a) After fixing a record date for a meeting, a corporation shall prepare an alphabetical list of the names of all its shareholders who are entitled to notice of a shareholders' meeting. The list must be arranged by voting group (and within each voting group by class or series of shares) and show the address of and number of shares held by each shareholder.

(b) The shareholders' list must be available for inspection by any shareholder, beginning two business days after notice of the meeting is given for which the list was prepared and continuing through the meeting, at the corporation's principal office or at a place identified in the meeting notice in the city where the meeting will be held. A shareholder, his agent, or attorney is entitled on written demand to inspect and, subject to the requirements of section 16.02(c), to copy the list, during regular business hours and at his expense, during the period it is available for inspection.

(c) The corporation shall make the shareholders' list available at the meeting, and any shareholder, his agent, or attorney is entitled to inspect the list at any time during the meeting or any adjournment.

(d) If the corporation refuses to allow a shareholder, his agent, or attorney to inspect the shareholders' list before or at the meeting (or copy the list as permitted by subsection (b)), the [name or describe] court of the county where a corporation's principal office (or, if none in this state, its registered office) is located, on application of the shareholder, may summarily order the inspection or copying at the corporation's expense and may postpone the meeting for which the list was prepared until the inspection or copying is complete.

(e) Refusal or failure to prepare or make available the shareholders' list does not affect the validity of action taken at the meeting.

§ 7.21 Voting Entitlement of Shares

(a) Except as provided in subsections (b) and (c) or unless the articles of incorporation provide otherwise, each outstanding share, regardless of class, is entitled to one vote on each matter voted on at a shareholders' meeting. Only shares are entitled to vote.

(b) Absent special circumstances, the shares of a corporation are not entitled to vote if they are owned, directly or indirectly, by a second corporation, domestic or foreign, and the first corporation owns, directly or indirectly, a majority of the shares entitled to vote for directors of the second corporation.

(c) Subsection (b) does not limit the power of a corporation to vote any shares, including its own shares, held by it in a fiduciary capacity.

(d) Redeemable shares are not entitled to vote after notice of redemption is mailed to the holders and a sum sufficient to redeem the shares has been deposited with a bank, trust company, or other financial institution under an irrevocable obligation to pay the holders the redemption price on surrender of the shares.

§ 7.22 Proxies

(a) A shareholder may vote his shares in person or by proxy.

(b) A shareholder may appoint a proxy to vote or otherwise act for him by signing an appointment form, either personally or by his attorney-in-fact.

(c) An appointment of a proxy is effective when received by the secretary or other officer or agent authorized to tabulate votes. An appointment is valid for 11 months unless a longer period is expressly provided in the appointment form.

(d) An appointment of a proxy is revocable by the shareholder unless the appointment form conspicuously states that it is irrevocable and the appointment is coupled with an interest. Appointments coupled with an interest include the appointment of:

(1) a pledgee;

(2) a person who purchased or agreed to purchase the shares;

(3) a creditor of the corporation who extended it credit under terms requiring the appointment;

(4) an employee of the corporation whose employment contract requires the appointment; or

(5) a party to a voting agreement created under section 7.31.

(e) The death or incapacity of the shareholder appointing a proxy does not affect the right of the corporation to accept the proxy's authority unless notice of the death or incapacity is received by the secretary or other officer or agent authorized to tabulate votes before the proxy exercises his authority under the appointment.

(f) An appointment made irrevocable under subsection (d) is revoked when the interest with which it is coupled is extinguished.

(g) A transferee for value of shares subject to an irrevocable appointment may revoke the appointment if he did not know of its existence when he acquired the shares and the existence of the irrevocable appointment was not noted conspicuously on the certificate representing the shares or on the information statement for shares without certificates.

(h) Subject to section 7.24 and to any express limitation on the proxy's authority appearing on the face of the appointment form, a corporation is entitled to accept the proxy's vote or other action as that of the shareholder making the appointment.

§ 7.23   Shares Held by Nominees

(a) A corporation may establish a procedure by which the beneficial owner of shares that are registered in the name of a nominee is recognized by the corporation as the shareholder. The extent of this recognition may be determined in the procedure.

(b) The procedure may set forth:

(1) the types of nominees to which it applies;

(2) the rights of privileges that the corporation recognizes in a beneficial owner;

(3) the manner in which the procedure is selected by the nominee;

(4) the information that must be provided when the procedure is selected;

(5) the period for which selection of the procedure is effective; and

(6) other aspects of the rights and duties created.

§ 7.24   Corporation's Acceptance of Votes

(a) If the name signed on a vote, consent, waiver, or proxy appointment corresponds to the name of a shareholder, the corporation if acting in good faith is entitled to accept the vote, consent, waiver, or proxy appointment and give it effect as the act of the shareholder.

(b) If the name signed on a vote, consent, waiver, or proxy appointment does not correspond to the name of its shareholder, the corporation if acting in good faith is nevertheless entitled to accept the vote, consent, waiver, or proxy appointment and give it effect as the act of the shareholder if:

(1) the shareholder is an entity and the name signed purports to be that of an officer or agent of the entity;

(2) the name signed purports to be that of an administrator, executor, guardian, or conservator representing the shareholder and, if the corporation requests, evidence of fiduciary status acceptable to the corporation has been presented with respect to the vote, consent, waiver, or proxy appointment;

(3) the name signed purports to be that of a receiver or trustee in bankruptcy of the shareholder and, if the corporation requests, evidence of this status acceptable to the corporation has been presented with respect to the vote, consent, waiver, or proxy appointment;

(4) the name signed purports to be that of a pledgee, beneficial owner, or attorney-in-fact of the shareholder and, if the corporation requests, evidence acceptable to the corporation of the signatory's authority to sign for the shareholder has been presented with respect to the vote, consent, waiver, or proxy appointment;

(5) two or more persons are the shareholder as cotenants or fiduciaries and the name signed purports to be the name of at least one of the coowners and the person signing appears to be acting on behalf of all the coowners.

(c) The corporation is entitled to reject a vote, consent, waiver, or proxy appointment if the secretary or other officer or agent authorized to tabulate votes, acting in good faith, has reasonable basis for doubt about the validity of the signature on it or about the signatory's authority to sign for the shareholder.

(d) The corporation and its officer or agent who accepts or rejects a vote, consent, waiver, or proxy appointment in good faith and in accordance with the standards of this section are not liable in damages to the shareholder for the consequences of the acceptance or rejection.

(e) Corporate action based on the acceptance or rejection of a vote, consent, waiver, or proxy appointment under this section is valid unless a court of competent jurisdiction determines otherwise.

§ 7.25   Quorum and Voting Requirements for Voting Groups

(a) Shares entitled to vote as a separate voting group may take action on a matter at a meeting only if a quorum of those shares exists with respect to that matter. Unless the articles of incorporation or this Act provide otherwise, a majority of the votes entitled to be cast on the matter by the voting group constitutes a quorum of that voting group for action on that matter.

(b) Once a share is represented for any purpose at a meeting, it is deemed present for quorum purposes for the remainder of the meeting and for any adjournment of that meeting unless a new record date is or must be set for that adjourned meeting.

(c) If a quorum exists, action on a matter (other than the election of directors) by a voting group is approved if the votes cast within the voting group favoring the action exceed the votes cast opposing the action, unless the articles of incorporation or this Act require a greater number of affirmative votes.

(d) An amendment of articles of incorporation adding, changing, or deleting a quorum or voting requirement for a voting group greater than specified in subsection (b) or (c) is governed by section 7.27.

(e) The election of directors is governed by section 7.28.

§ 7.26   Action by Single and Multiple Voting Groups

(a) If the articles of incorporation or this Act provide for voting by a single voting group on a matter, action on that matter is taken when voted upon by that voting group as provided in section 7.25.

(b) If the articles of incorporation or this Act provide for voting by two or more voting groups on a matter, action on that matter is taken only when voted upon by each of those voting groups counted separately as provided in section 7.25. Action may be taken by one voting group on a matter even though no action is taken by another voting group entitled to vote on the matter.

§ 7.27   Greater Quorum or Voting Requirements

(a) The articles of incorporation may provide for a greater quorum or voting requirement for shareholders (or voting groups of shareholders) than is provided for by this Act.

(b) An amendment to the articles of incorporation that adds, changes, or deletes a greater quorum or voting requirement must meet the same quorum requirement and be adopted by the same vote and voting groups required to take action under the quorum and voting requirements then in effect or proposed to be adopted, whichever is greater.

§ 7.28   Voting for Directors; Cumulative Voting

(a) Unless otherwise provided in the articles of incorporation, directors are elected by a plurality of the votes cast by the shares entitled to vote in the election at a meeting at which a quorum is present.

(b) Shareholders do not have a right to cumulate their votes for directors unless the articles of incorporation so provide.

(c) A statement included in the articles of incorporation that "[all] [a designated voting group of] shareholders are entitled to cumulate their votes for directors" (or words of similar import) means that the shareholders designated are entitled to multiply the number of votes they are entitled to cast by the number of directors for whom they are entitled to vote and cast the product for a single candidate or distribute the product among two or more candidates.

(d) Shares otherwise entitled to vote cumulatively may not be voted cumulatively at a particular meeting unless:

(1) the meeting notice or proxy statement accompanying the notice states conspicuously that cumulative voting is authorized; or

(2) a shareholder who has the right to cumulate his votes gives notice to the corporation not less than 48 hours before the time set for the meeting of his intent to cumulate his votes during the meeting, and if one shareholder gives this notice all other shareholders in the same voting group participating in the election are entitled to cumulate their votes without giving further notice.

SUBCHAPTER C. Voting Trusts and Agreements

§ 7.30   Voting Trusts

(a) One or more shareholders may create a voting trust, conferring on a trustee the right to vote or otherwise act for them, by signing an agreement setting out the provisions of the trust (which may include anything consistent with its purpose) and transferring their shares to the trustee. When a voting trust agreement is signed, the trustee shall prepare a list of the names and addresses of all owners of beneficial interests in the trust, together with the number and class of shares each transferred to the trust, and deliver copies of the list and agreement to the corporation's principal office.

(b) A voting trust becomes effective on the date the first shares subject to the trust are registered in the trustee's name. A voting trust is valid for not more than 10 years after its effective date unless extended under subsection (c).

(c) All or some of the parties to a voting trust may extend it for additional terms of not more than 10 years each by signing an extension agreement and obtaining the voting trustee's written consent to the extension. An extension is valid for 10 years from the date the first shareholder signs the extension agreement. The voting trustee must deliver copies of the extension agreement and list of beneficial owners to the corporation's principal office. An extension agreement binds only those parties signing it.

§ 7.31 Voting Agreements

(a) Two or more shareholders may provide for the manner in which they will vote their shares by signing an agreement for that purpose. A voting agreement created under this section is not subject to the provisions of section 7.30.

(b) A voting agreement created under this section is specifically enforceable.

SUBCHAPTER D. *Derivative Proceedings*

§ 7.40 Procedure in Derivative Proceedings

(a) A person may not commence a proceeding in the right of a domestic or foreign corporation unless he was a shareholder of the corporation when the transaction complained of occurred or unless he became a shareholder through transfer by operation of law from one who was a shareholder at that time.

(b) A complaint in a proceeding brought in the right of a corporation must be verified and allege with particularity the demand made, if any, to obtain action by the board of directors and either that the demand was refused or ignored or why he did not make the demand. Whether or not a demand for action was made, if the corporation commences an investigation of the changes made in the demand or complaint, the court may stay any proceeding until the investigation is completed.

(c) A proceeding commenced under this section may not be discontinued or settled without the court's approval. If the court determines that a proposed discontinuance or settlement will substantially affect the interest of the corporation's shareholders or a class of

shareholders, the court shall direct that notice be given the shareholders affected.

(d) On termination of the proceeding the court may require the plaintiff to pay any defendant's reasonable expenses (including counsel fees) incurred in defending the proceeding if it finds that the proceeding was commenced without reasonable cause.

(e) For purposes of this section, "shareholder" includes a beneficial owner whose shares are held in a voting trust or held by a nominee on his behalf.

CHAPTER 8. Directors and Officers

SUBCHAPTER A. *Board of Directors*

§ 8.01 Requirement for and Duties of Board of Directors

(a) Except as provided in subsection (c), each corporation must have a board of directors.

(b) All corporate powers shall be exercised by or under the authority of, and the business and affairs of the corporation managed under the direction of, its board of directors, subject to any limitation set forth in the articles of incorporation.

(c) A corporation having 50 or fewer shareholders may dispense with or limit the authority of a board of directors by describing in its articles of incorporation who will perform some or all of the duties of a board of directors.

§ 8.02 Qualifications of Directors

The articles of incorporation or bylaws may prescribe qualifications for directors. A director need not be a resident of this state or a shareholder of the corporation unless the articles of incorporation or bylaws so prescribe.

§ 8.03 Number and Election of Directors

(a) A board of directors must consist of one or more individuals, with the number specified in or fixed in accordance with the articles of incorporation or bylaws.

(b) If a board of directors has power to fix or change the number of directors, the board may increase or decrease by 30 percent or less the number of directors last approved by the shareholders, but only the shareholders may increase or decrease by more than 30 percent the number of directors last approved by the shareholders.

(c) The articles of incorporation or bylaws may establish a variable range for the size of the board of directors by fixing a minimum and maximum number of directors. If a variable range is established, the number of directors may be fixed or changed from time to time, within the minimum and maximum, by the shareholders or the board of directors. After shares are issued, only the shareholders may change the range for the size of the board or change from a fixed to a variable-range size board or vice versa.

(d) Directors are elected at the first annual shareholders' meeting and at each annual meeting thereafter unless their terms are staggered under section 8.06.

§ 8.04   Election of Directors by Certain Classes of Shareholders

If the articles of incorporation authorize dividing the shares into classes, the articles may also authorize the election of all or a specified number of directors by the holders of one or more authorized classes of shares. Each class (or classes) of shares entitled to elect one or more directors is a separate voting group for purposes of the election of directors.

§ 8.05   Terms of Directors Generally

(a) The terms of the initial directors of a corporation expire at the first shareholders' meeting at which directors are elected.

(b) The terms of all other directors expire at the next annual shareholders' meeting following their election unless their terms are staggered under section 8.06.

(c) A decrease in the number of directors does not shorten an incumbent director's term.

(d) The term of a director elected to fill a vacancy expires at the next shareholders' meeting at which directors are elected.

(e) Despite the expiration of a director's term, he continues to serve until his successor is elected and qualifies or until there is a decrease in the number of directors.

§ 8.06   Staggered Terms for Directors

If there are nine or more directors, the articles of incorporation may provide for staggering their terms by dividing the total number of directors into two or three groups, with each group containing one-half or one-third of the total, as near as may be. In that event, the terms of directors in the first group expire at the first

annual shareholders' meeting after their election, the terms of the second group expire at the second annual shareholders' meeting after their election, and the terms of the third group, if any, expire at the third annual shareholders' meeting after their election. At each annual shareholders' meeting held thereafter, directors shall be chosen for a term of two years or three years, as the case may be, to succeed those whose terms expire.

§ 8.07   Resignation of Directors

(a) A director may resign at any time by delivering written notice to the board of directors, its chairman, or to the corporation.

(b) A resignation is effective when the notice is delivered unless the notice specifies a later effective date.

§ 8.08   Removal of Directors by Shareholders

(a) The shareholders may remove one or more directors with or without cause unless the articles of incorporation provide that directors may be removed only for cause.

(b) If a director is elected by a voting group of shareholders, only the shareholders of that voting group may participate in the vote to remove him.

(c) If cumulative voting is authorized, a director may not be removed if the number of votes sufficient to elect him under cumulative voting is voted against his removal. If cumulative voting is not authorized, a director may be removed only if the number of votes cast to remove him exceeds the number of votes cast not to remove him.

(d) A director may be removed by the shareholders only at a meeting called for the purpose of removing him and the meeting notice must state that the purpose, or one of the purposes, of the meeting is removal of the director.

§ 8.09   Removal of Directors by Judicial Proceeding

(a) The [name or describe] court of the county where a corporation's principal office (or, if none in this state, its registered office) is located may remove a director of the corporation from office in a proceeding commenced either by the corporation or by its shareholders holding at least 10 percent of the outstanding shares of any class if the court finds that (1) the director engaged in fraudulent or dishonest conduct, or gross abuse of authority or discretion, with respect to the corporation and (2) removal is in the best interest of the corporation.

(b) The court that removes a director may bar the director from reelection for a period prescribed by the court.

(c) If shareholders commence a proceeding under subsection (a), they shall make the corporation a party defendant.

§ 8.10   Vacancy on Board

(a) Unless the articles of incorporation provide otherwise, if a vacancy occurs on a board of directors, including a vacancy resulting from an increase in the number of directors:

(1) the shareholders may fill the vacancy;

(2) the board of directors may fill the vacancy; or

(3) if the directors remaining in office constitute fewer than a quorum of the board, they may fill the vacancy by the affirmative vote of a majority of all the directors remaining in office.

(b) If the vacant office was held by a director elected by a voting group of shareholders, only the holders of shares of that voting group are entitled to vote to fill the vacancy if it is filled by the shareholders.

(c) A vacancy that will occur at a specific later date (by reason of a resignation effective at a later date under section 8.07(b) or otherwise) may be filled before the vacancy occurs but the new director may not take office until the vacancy occurs.

§ 8.11   Compensation of Directors

Unless the articles of incorporation or bylaws provide otherwise, the board of directors may fix the compensation of directors.

SUBCHAPTER B. *Meetings and Action of the Board*

§ 8.20   Meetings

(a) The board of directors may hold irregular or special meetings in or out of this state.

(b) Unless the articles of incorporation or bylaws provide otherwise, the board of directors may permit any or all directors to participate in a regular or special meeting by, or conduct the meeting through the use of, any means of communication by which all directors participating may simultaneously hear each other during the meeting. A director participating in a meeting

by this means is deemed to be present in person at the meeting.

§ 8.21   Action Without Meeting

(a) Unless the articles of incorporation or bylaws provide otherwise, action required or permitted by this Act to be taken at a board of directors' meeting may be taken without a meeting if the action is taken by all members of the board. The action must be evidenced by one or more written consents describing the action taken, signed by each director, and included in the minutes or filed with the corporate records reflecting the action taken.

(b) Action taken under this section is effective when the last director signs the consent, unless the consent specifies a different effective date.

(c) A consent signed under this section has the effect of a meeting vote and may be described as such in any document.

§ 8.22   Notice of Meeting

(a) Unless the articles of incorporation or bylaws provide otherwise, regular meetings of the board of directors may be held without notice of the date, time, place, or purpose of the meeting.

(b) Unless the articles of incorporation or bylaws provide for a longer or shorter period, special meetings of the board of directors must be preceded by at least two days' notice of the date, time, and place of the meeting. The notice need not describe the purpose of the special meeting unless required by the articles of incorporation or bylaws.

§ 8.23   Waiver of Notice

(a) A director may waive any notice required by this Act, the articles of incorporation, or bylaws before or after the date and time stated in the notice. Except as provided by subsection (b), the waiver must be in writing, signed by the director entitled to the notice, and filed with the minutes or corporate records.

(b) A director's attendance at or participation in a meeting waives any required notice to him of the meeting unless the director at the beginning of the meeting (or promptly upon his arrival) objects to holding the meeting or transacting business at the meeting and does not thereafter vote for or assent to action taken at the meeting.

§ 8.24 Quorum and Voting

(a) Unless the articles of incorporation or bylaws require a greater number, a quorum of a board of directors consists of:

(1) a majority of the fixed number of directors if the corporation has a fixed board size; or

(2) a majority of the number of directors prescribed, or if no number is prescribed the number in office immediately before the meeting begins, if the corporation has a variable-range size board.

(b) The articles of incorporation or bylaws may authorize a quorum of a board of directors to consist of no fewer than one-third of the fixed or prescribed number of directors determined under subsection (a).

(c) If a quorum is present when a vote is taken, the affirmative vote of a majority of directors present is the act of the board of directors unless the articles of incorporation or bylaws require the vote of a greater number of directors.

(d) A director who is present at a meeting of the board of directors or a committee of the board of directors when corporate action is taken is deemed to have assented to the action taken unless: (1) he objects at the beginning of the meeting (or promptly upon his arrival) to holding it or transacting business at the meeting; (2) his dissent or abstention from the action taken is entered in the minutes of the meeting; or (3) he delivers written notice of his dissent or abstention to the presiding officer of the meeting before its adjournment or to the corporation immediately after adjournment of the meeting. The right of dissent or abstention is not available to a director who votes in favor of the action taken.

§ 8.25 Committees

(a) Unless the articles of incorporation or bylaws provide otherwise, a board of directors may create one or more committees and appoint members of the board of directors to serve on them. Each committee must have two or more members, who serve at the pleasure of the board of directors.

(b) The creation of a committee and appointment of members to it must be approved by the greater of (1) a majority of all the directors in office when the action is taken or (2) the number of directors required by the articles of incorporation or bylaws to take action under section 8.24.

(c) Sections 8.20 through 8.24, which govern meetings, action without meetings, notice and waiver of notice, and quorum and voting requirements of the board of directors, apply to committees and their members as well.

(d) To the extent specified by the board of directors or in the articles of incorporation or bylaws, each committee may exercise the authority of the board of directors under section 8.01.

(e) A committee may not, however:

(1) authorize distributions;

(2) approve or propose to shareholders action that this Act requires to be approved by shareholders;

(3) fill vacancies on the board of directors or on any of its committees;

(4) amend articles of incorporation pursuant to section 10.02;

(5) adopt, amend, or repeal bylaws;

(6) approve a plan of merger not requiring shareholder approval;

(7) authorize or approve reacquisition of shares, except according to a formula or method prescribed by the board of directors; or

(8) authorize or approve the issuance or sale or contract for sale of shares, or determine the designation and relative rights, preferences, and limitations of a class or series of shares, except that the board of directors may authorize a committee (or a senior executive officer of the corporation) to do so within limits specifically prescribed by the board of directors.

(f) The creation of, delegation of authority to, or action by a committee does not alone constitute compliance by a director with the standards of conduct described in section 8.30.

SUBCHAPTER C. Standards of Conduct

§ 8.30 General Standards for Directors

(a) A director shall discharge his duties as a director, including his duties as a member of a committee:

(1) in good faith;

(2) with the care an ordinarily prudent person in a like position would exercise under similar circumstances; and

(3) in a manner he reasonably believes to be in the best interests of the corporation.

(b) In discharging his duties a director is entitled to rely on information, opinions, reports, or statements, including financial statements and other financial data, if prepared or presented by:

(1) one or more officers or employees of the corpo-

ration whom the director reasonably believes to be reliable and competent in the matters presented;

(2) legal counsel, public accountants, or other persons as to matters the director reasonably believes are within the person's professional or expert competence; or

(3) a committee of the board of directors of which he is not a member if the director reasonably believes the committee merits confidence.

(c) A director is not acting in good faith if he has knowledge concerning the matter in question that makes reliance otherwise permitted by subsection (b) unwarranted.

(d) A director is not liable for any action taken as a director, or any failure to take any action, if he performed the duties of his office in compliance with this section.

§ 8.31 Director Conflict of Interest

(a) A conflict of interest transaction is a transaction with the corporation in which a director of the corporation has a direct or indirect interest. A conflict of interest transaction is not voidable by the corporation solely because of the director's interest in the transaction if any one of the following is true:

(1) the material facts of the transaction and the director's interest were disclosed or known to the board of directors or a committee of the board of directors and the board of directors or committee authorized, approved, or ratified the transaction;

(2) the material facts of the transaction and the director's interest were disclosed or known to the shareholders entitled to vote and they authorized, approved, or ratified the transaction; or

(3) the transaction was fair to the corporation.

(b) For purposes of this section, a director of the corporation has an indirect interest in a transaction if (1) another entity in which he has a material financial interest or in which he is a general partner is a party to the transaction or (2) another entity of which he is a director, officer, or trustee is a party to the transaction and the transaction is or should be considered by the board of directors of the corporation.

(c) For purposes of subsection (a)(1), a conflict of interest transaction is authorized, approved, or ratified if it receives the affirmative vote of a majority of the directors on the board of directors (or on the committee) who have no direct or indirect interest in the transaction, but a transaction may not be authorized, approved, or ratified under this section by a single director. If a majority of the directors who have no direct or indirect interest in the transaction vote to authorize, approve, or ratify the transaction, a quorum is present for the purpose of taking action under this section. The presence of, or a vote cast by, a director with a direct or indirect interest in the transaction does not affect the validity of any action taken under subsection (a)(1) if the transaction is otherwise authorized, approved, or ratified as provided in that subsection.

(d) For purposes of subsection (a)(2), a conflict of interest transaction is authorized, approved, or ratified if it receives the vote of a majority of the shares entitled to be counted under this subsection. Shares owned by or voted under the control of a director who has a direct or indirect interest in the transaction, and shares owned by or voted under the control of an entity described in subsection (b)(1), may not be counted in a vote of shareholders to determine whether to authorize, approve, or ratify a conflict of interest transaction under subsection (a)(2). The vote of those shares, however, shall be counted in determining whether the transaction is approved under other sections of this Act. A majority of the shares, whether or not present, that are entitled to be counted in a vote on the transaction under this subsection constitutes a quorum for the purpose of taking action under this section.

§ 8.32 Loans to Directors

(a) Except as provided by subsection (c), a corporation may not lend money to or guarantee the obligation of a director of the corporation unless:

(1) the particular loan or guarantee is approved by a majority of the votes represented by the outstanding voting shares of all classes, voting as a single voting group, except the votes of shares owned by or voted under the control of the benefited director; or

(2) the corporation's board of directors determines that the loan or guarantee benefits the corporation and either approves the specific loan or guarantee or a general plan authorizing loans and guarantees.

(b) The fact that a loan or guarantee is made in violation of this section does not affect the borrower's liability on the loan.

(c) This section does not apply to loans and guarantees authorized by statute regulating any special class of corporations.

§ 8.33 Liability for Unlawful Distributions

(a) Unless he complies with the applicable standards of conduct described in section 8.30, a director who votes for or assents to a distribution made in violation of this Act or the articles of incorporation is personally liable to the corporation for the amount of the distribution that exceeds what could have been distributed without violating this Act or the articles of incorporation.

(b) A director held liable for an unlawful distribution under subsection (a) is entitled to contribution:

(1) from every other director who voted for or assented to the distribution without complying with the applicable standards of conduct described in section 8.30; and

(2) from each shareholder for the amount the shareholder accepted knowing the distribution was made in violation of this Act or the articles of incorporation.

SUBCHAPTER D. *Officers*

§ 8.40 Required Officers

(a) A corporation has the officers described in its bylaws or appointed by the board of directors in accordance with the bylaws.

(b) A duly appointed officer may appoint one or more officers or assistant officers if authorized by the bylaws or the board of directors.

(c) The bylaws or the board of directors shall delegate to one of the officers responsibility for preparing minutes of the directors' and shareholders' meetings and for authenticating records of the corporation.

(d) The same individual may simultaneously hold more than one office in a corporation.

§ 8.41 Duties of Officers

Each officer has the authority and shall perform the duties set forth in the bylaws or, to the extent consistent with the bylaws, the duties prescribed by the board of directors or by direction of an officer authorized by the board of directors to prescribe the duties of other officers.

§ 8.42 Standards of Conduct for Officers

(a) An officer with discretionary authority shall discharge his duties under that authority:

(1) in good faith;

(2) with the care an ordinarily prudent person in a like position would exercise under similar circumstances; and

(3) in a manner he reasonably believes to be in the best interests of the corporation.

(b) In discharging his duties an officer is entitled to rely on information, opinions, reports, or statements, including financial statements and other financial data, if prepared or presented by:

(1) one or more officers or employees of the corporation whom the officer reasonably believes to be reliable and competent in the matters presented; or

(2) legal counsel, public accountants, or other persons as to matters the officer reasonably believes are within the person's professional or expert competence.

(c) An officer is not acting in good faith if he has knowledge concerning the matter in question that makes reliance otherwise permitted by subsection (b) unwarranted.

(d) An officer is not liable for any action taken as an officer, or any failure to take any action, if he performed the duties of his office in compliance with this section.

§ 8.43 Resignation and Removal of Officers

(a) An officer may resign at any time by delivering notice to the corporation. A resignation is effective when the notice is delivered unless the notice specifies a later effective date. If a resignation is made effective at a later date and the corporation accepts the future effective date, its board of directors may fill the pending vacancy before the effective date if the board of directors provides that the successor does not take office until the effective date.

(b) A board of directors may remove any officer at any time with or without cause.

§ 8.44 Contract Rights of Officers

(a) The appointment of an officer does not itself create contract rights.

(b) An officer's removal does not affect the officer's contract rights, if any, with the corporation. An officer's resignation does not affect the corporation's contract rights, if any, with the officer.

SUBCHAPTER E. *Indemnification*

§ 8.50 Subchapter Definitions

In this subchapter:

(1) "Corporation" includes any domestic or foreign predecessor entity of a corporation in a merger or other transaction in which the predecessor's existence ceased upon consummation of the transaction.

(2) "Director" means an individual who is or was a director of a corporation or an individual who, while a director of a corporation, is or was serving at the corporation's request as a director, officer, partner, trustee, employee, or agent of another foreign or domestic corporation, partnership, joint venture, trust, employee benefit plan, or other enterprise. A director is considered to be serving an employee benefit plan at the corporation's request if his duties to the corporation also impose duties on, or otherwise involve services by, him to the plan or to participants in or beneficiaries of the plan. "Director" includes, unless the context requires otherwise, the estate or personal representative of a director.

(3) "Expenses" include counsel fees.

(4) "Liability" means the obligation to pay a judgment, settlement, penalty, fine (including an excise tax assessed with respect to an employee benefit plan), or reasonable expenses incurred with respect to a proceeding.

(5) "Official capacity" means: (i) when used with respect to a director, the office of director in a corporation; and (ii) when used with respect to an individual other than a director, as contemplated in section 8.56, the office in a corporation held by the officer or the employment or agency relationship undertaken by the employee or agent on behalf of the corporation. "Official capacity" does not include service for any other foreign or domestic corporation or any partnership, joint venture, trust, employee benefit plan, or other enterprise.

(6) "Party" includes an individual who was, is, or is threatened to be made a named defendant or respondent in a proceeding.

(7) "Proceeding" means any threatened, pending, or completed action, suit, or proceeding, whether civil, criminal, administrative, or investigative and whether formal or informal.

§ 8.51   Authority to Indemnify

(a) Except as provided in subsection (d), a corporation may indemnify an individual made a party to a proceeding because he is or was a director against liability incurred in the proceeding if:

(1) he conducted himself in good faith; and

(2) he reasonably believed:

(i) in the case of conduct in his official capacity with the corporation, that his conduct was in its best interests; and

(ii) in all other cases, that his conduct was at least not opposed to its best interests; and

(3) in the case of any criminal proceeding, he has no reasonable cause to believe his conduct was unlawful.

(b) A director's conduct with respect to an employee benefit plan for a purpose he reasonably believed to be in the interests of the participants in and beneficiaries of the plan is conduct that satisfies the requirement of subsection (a)(2)(ii).

(c) The termination of a proceeding by judgment, order, settlement, conviction, or upon a plea of nolo contendere or its equivalent is not, of itself, determinative that the director did not meet the standard of conduct described in this section.

(d) A corporation may not indemnify a director under this section:

(1) in connection with a proceeding by or in the right of the corporation in which the director was adjudged liable to the corporation; or

(2) in connection with any other proceeding charging improper personal benefit to him, whether or not involving action in his official capacity, in which he was adjudged liable on the basis that personal benefit was improperly received by him.

(e) Indemnification permitted under this section in connection with a proceeding by or in the right of the corporation is limited to reasonable expenses incurred in connection with the proceeding.

§ 8.52   Mandatory Indemnification

Unless limited by its articles of incorporation, a corporation shall indemnify a director who was wholly successful, on the merits or otherwise, in the defense of any proceeding to which he was a party because he is or was a director of the corporation against reasonable expenses incurred by him in connection with the proceeding.

§ 8.53   Advance for Expenses

(a) A corporation may pay for or reimburse the reasonable expenses incurred by a director who is a party to a proceeding in advance of final disposition of the proceeding if:

(1) the director furnishes the corporation a written affirmation of his good faith belief that he has met the standard of conduct described in section 8.51;

(2) the director furnishes the corporation a written undertaking, executed personally or on his behalf, to

repay the advance if it is ultimately determined that he did not meet the standard of conduct; and

(3) a determination is made that the facts then known to those making the determination would not preclude indemnification under this subchapter.

(b) The undertaking required by subsection (a)(2) must be an unlimited general obligation of the director but need not be secured and may be accepted without reference to financial ability to make repayment.

(c) Determinations and authorizations of payments under this section shall be made in the manner specified in section 8.55.

§ 8.54 Court-Ordered Indemnification

Unless a corporation's articles of incorporation provide otherwise, a director of the corporation who is a party to a proceeding may apply for indemnification to the court conducting the proceeding or to another court of competent jurisdiction. On receipt of an application, the court after giving any notice the court considers necessary may order indemnification if it determines:

(1) the director is entitled to mandatory indemnification under section 8.52, in which case the court shall also order the corporation to pay the director's reasonable expenses incurred to obtain court-ordered indemnification; or

(2) the director is fairly and reasonably entitled to indemnification in view of all the relevant circumstances, whether or not he met the standard of conduct set forth in section 8.51 or was adjudged liable as described in section 8.51(d), but if he was adjudged so liable his indemnification is limited to reasonable expenses incurred.

§ 8.55 Determination and Authorization of Indemnification

(a) A corporation may not indemnify a director under section 8.51 unless authorized in the specific case after a determination has been made that indemnification of the director is permissible in the circumstances because he has met the standard of conduct set forth in section 8.51.

(b) The determination shall be made:

(1) by the board of directors by majority vote of a quorum consisting of directors not at the time parties to the proceeding;

(2) if a quorum cannot be obtained under subdivision (1), by majority vote of a committee duly designated by the board of directors (in which designation directors who are parties may participate), consisting solely of two or more directors not at the time parties to the proceeding;

(3) by special legal counsel:

(i) selected by the board of directors or its committee in the manner prescribed in subdivision (1) or (2); or

(ii) if a quorum of the board of directors cannot be obtained under subdivision (1) and a committee cannot be designated under subdivision (2), selected by majority vote of the full board of directors (in which selection directors who are parties may participate); or

(4) by the shareholders, but shares owned by or voted under the control of directors who are at the time parties to the proceeding may not be voted on the determination.

(c) Authorization of indemnification and evaluation as to reasonableness of expenses shall be made in the same manner as the determination that indemnification is permissible, except that if the determination is made by special legal counsel, authorization of indemnification and evaluation as to reasonableness of expenses shall be made by those entitled under subsection (b)(3) to select counsel.

§ 8.56 Indemnification of Officers, Employees, and Agents

Unless a corporation's articles of incorporation provide otherwise:

(1) an officer of the corporation who is not a director is entitled to mandatory indemnification under section 8.52, and is entitled to apply for court-ordered indemnification under section 8.54, in each case to the same extent as a director;

(2) the corporation may indemnify and advance expenses under this subchapter to an officer, employee, or agent of the corporation who is not a director to the same extent as to a director; and

(3) a corporation may also indemnify and advance expenses to an officer, employee, or agent who is not a director to the extent, consistent with public policy, that may be provided by its articles of incorporation, bylaws, general or specific action of its board of directors, or contract.

§ 8.57 Insurance

A corporation may purchase and maintain insurance on behalf of an individual who is or was a director, officer, employee, or agent of the corporation, or who, while a director, officer, employee, or agent of the corporation, is or was serving at the request of the corporation as a director, officer, partner, trustee, employee, or agent of another foreign or domestic corporation, partnership, joint venture, trust, employee benefit plan, or other enterprise, against liability asserted against or incurred by him in that capacity or arising from his status as a director, officer, employee, or agent, whether or not the corporation would have power to indemnify him against the same liability under section 8.51 or 8.52.

§ 8.58   Application of Subchapter

(a) A provision treating a corporation's indemnification of or advance for expenses to directors that is contained in its articles of incorporation, bylaws, a resolution of its shareholders or board of directors, or in a contract or otherwise, is valid only if and to the extent the provision is consistent with this subchapter. If articles of incorporation limit indemnification or advance for expenses, indemnification and advance for expenses are valid only to the extent consistent with the articles.

(b) This subchapter does not limit a corporation's power to pay or reimburse expenses incurred by a director in connection with his appearance as a witness in a proceeding at a time when he has not been made a named defendant or respondent to the proceeding.

CHAPTER 9.   [Reserved]

CHAPTER 10.   Amendment of Articles of Incorporation and Bylaws

SUBCHAPTER A. *Amendment of Articles of Incorporation*

§ 10.01   Authority to Amend

(a) A corporation may amend its articles of incorporation at any time to add or change a provision that is required or permitted in the articles of incorporation or to delete a provision not required in the articles of incorporation. Whether a provision is required or permitted in the articles of incorporation is determined as of the effective date of the amendment.

(b) A shareholder of the corporation does not have a vested property right resulting from any provision in the articles of incorporation, including provisions relat-

ing to management, control, capital structure, dividend entitlement, or purpose or duration of the corporation.

§ 10.02   Amendment by Board of Directors

Unless the articles of incorporation provide otherwise, a corporation's board of directors may adopt one or more amendments to the corporation's articles of incorporation without shareholder action:

(1) to extend the duration of the corporation if it was incorporated at a time when limited duration was required by law;

(2) to delete the names and addresses of the initial directors;

(3) to delete the name and address of the initial registered agent or registered office, if a statement of change is on file with the secretary of state;

(4) to change each issued and unissued authorized share of an outstanding class into a greater number of whole shares if the corporation has only shares of that class outstanding;

(5) to change the corporate name by substituting the word "corporation," "incorporated," "company," "limited," or the abbreviation "corp.," "inc.," "co.," or "ltd.," for a similar word or abbreviation in the name, or by adding, deleting, or changing a geographical attribution for the name; or

(6) to make any other change expressly permitted by this Act to be made without shareholder action.

§ 10.03   Amendment by Board of Directors and Shareholders

(a) A corporation's board of directors may propose one or more amendments to the articles of incorporation for submission to the shareholders.

(b) For the amendment to be adopted:

(1) the board of directors must recommend the amendment to the shareholders unless the board of directors determines that because of conflict of interest or other special circumstances it should make no recommendation and communicates the basis for its determination to the shareholders with the amendment; and

(2) the shareholders entitled to vote on the amendment must approve the amendment as provided in subsection (e).

(c) The board of directors may condition its submission of the proposed amendment on any basis.

(d) The corporation shall notify each shareholder, whether or not entitled to vote, of the proposed shareholders' meeting in accordance with section 7.05. The notice of meeting must also state that the purpose, or one of the purposes, of the meeting is to consider the proposed amendment and contain or be accompanied by a copy or summary of the amendment.

(e) Unless this Act, the articles of incorporation, or the board of directors (acting pursuant to subsection (c)) require a greater vote or a vote by voting groups, the amendment to be adopted must be approved by:

(1) a majority of the votes entitled to be cast on the amendment by any voting group with respect to which the amendment would create dissenters' rights; and

(2) the votes required by sections 7.25 and 7.26 by every other voting group entitled to vote on the amendment.

§ 10.04   Voting on Amendments by Voting Groups

(a) The holders of the outstanding shares of a class are entitled to vote as a separate voting group (if shareholder voting is otherwise required by this Act) on a proposed amendment if the amendment would:

(1) increase or decrease the aggregate number of authorized shares of the class;

(2) effect an exchange or reclassification of all or part of the shares of the class into shares of another class;

(3) effect an exchange or reclassification, or create the right of exchange, of all or part of the shares of another class into shares of the class;

(4) change the designation, rights, preferences, or limitations of all or part of the shares of the class;

(5) change the shares of all or part of the class into a different number of shares of the same class;

(6) create a new class of shares having rights or preferences with respect to distributions or to dissolution that are prior, superior, or substantially equal to the shares of the class;

(7) increase the rights, preferences, or number of authorized shares of any class that, after giving effect to the amendment, have rights or preferences with respect to distributions or to dissolution that are prior, superior, or substantially equal to the shares of the class;

(8) limit or deny an existing preemptive right of all or part of the shares of the class; or

(9) cancel or otherwise affect rights to distributions or dividends that have accumulated but not yet been declared on all or part of the shares of the class.

(b) If a proposed amendment would affect a series of a class of shares in one or more of the ways described in subsection (a), the shares of that series are entitled to vote as a separate voting group on the proposed amendent.

(c) If a proposed amendment that entitles two or more series of shares to vote as separate voting groups under this section would affect those two or more series in the same or a substantially similar way, the shares of all the series so affected must vote together as a single voting group on the proposed amendment.

(d) A class or series of shares is entitled to the voting rights granted by this section although the articles of incorporation provide that the shares are nonvoting shares.

§ 10.05   Amendment Before Issuance of Shares

If a corporation has not yet issued shares, its incorporators or board of directors may adopt one or more amendments to the corporation's articles of incorporation.

§ 10.06   Articles of Amendment

A corporation amending its articles of incorporation shall deliver to the secretary of state for filing articles of amendment setting forth:

(1) the name of the corporation;

(2) the text of each amendment adopted;

(3) if an amendment provides for an exchange, reclassification, or cancellation of issued shares, provisions for implementing the amendment if not contained in the amendment itself;

(4) the date of each amendment's adoption;

(5) if an amendment was adopted by the incorporators or board of directors without shareholder action, a statement to that effect and that shareholder action was not required;

(6) if an amendment was approved by the shareholders:

(i) the designation, number of outstanding shares, number of votes entitled to be cast by each voting group entitled to vote separately on the amendment, and number of votes of each voting group indisputably represented at the meeting;

(ii) either the total number of votes cast for and against the amendment by each voting group entitled to vote separately on the amendment or the total number of undisputed votes cast for the amendment by each voting group and a statement that the number cast for the amendment by each voting group was sufficient for approval by that voting group.

§ 10.07   Restated Articles of Incorporation

(a) A corporation's board of directors may restate its articles of incorporation at any time with or without shareholder action.

(b) The restatement may include one or more amendments to the articles. If the restatement includes an amendment requiring shareholder approval, it must be adopted as provided in section 10.03.

(c) If the board of directors submits a restatement for shareholder action, the corporation shall notify each shareholder, whether or not entitled to vote, of the proposed shareholders' meeting in accordance with section 7.05. The notice must also state that the purpose, or one of the purposes, of the meeting is to consider the proposed restatement and contain or be accompanied by a copy of the restatement that identifies any amendment or other change it would make in the articles.

(d) A corporation restating its articles of incorporation shall deliver to the secretary of state for filing articles of restatement setting forth the name of the corporation and the text of the restated articles of incorporation together with a certificate setting forth:

(1) whether the restatement contains an amendment to the articles requiring shareholder approval and, if it does not, that the board of directors adopted the restatement; or

(2) if the restatement contains an amendment to the articles requiring shareholder approval, the information required by section 10.06.

(e) Duly adopted restated articles of incorporation supersede the original articles of incorporation and all amendments to them.

(f) The secretary of state may certify restated articles of incorporation, as the articles of incorporation currently in effect, without including the certificate information required by subsection (d).

§ 10.08   Amendment Pursuant to Reorganization

(a) A corporation's articles of incorporation may be amended without action by the board of directors or shareholders to carry out a plan of reorganization ordered or decreed by a court of competent jurisdiction under federal statute if the articles of incorporation

after amendment contain only provisions required or permitted by section 2.02.

(b) The individual or individuals designated by the court shall deliver to the secretary of state for filing articles of amendment setting forth:

(1) the name of the corporation;

(2) the text of each amendment approved by the court;

(3) the date of the court's order or decree approving the articles of amendment;

(4) the title of the reorganization proceeding in which the order or decree was entered; and

(5) a statement that the court had jurisdiction of the proceeding under federal statute.

(c) Shareholders of a corporation undergoing reorganization do not have dissenters' rights except as and to the extent provided in the reorganization plan.

(d) This section does not apply after entry of a final decree in the reorganization proceeding even though the court retains jurisdiction of the proceeding for limited purposes unrelated to consummation of the reorganization plan.

§ 10.09   Effect of Amendment

An amendment to articles of incorporation does not affect a cause of action existing against or in favor of the corporation, a proceeding to which the corporation is a party, or the existing rights of persons other than shareholders of the corporation. An amendment changing a corporation's name does not abate a proceeding brought by or against the corporation in its former name.

SUBCHAPTER B. *Amendment of Bylaws*

§ 10.20   Amendment by Board of Directors or Shareholders

(a) A corporation's board of directors may amend or repeal the corporation's bylaws unless:

(1) the articles of incorporation or this Act reserve this power exclusively to the shareholders in whole or part; or

(2) the shareholders in amending or repealing a particular bylaw provide expressly that the board of directors may not amend or repeal that bylaw.

(b) A corporation's shareholders may amend or repeal the corporation's bylaws even though the bylaws may also be amended or repealed by its board of directors.

§ 10.21 Bylaw Increasing Quorum or Voting Requirement for Shareholders

(a) If expressly authorized by the articles of incorporation, the shareholders may adopt or amend a bylaw that fixes a greater quorum or voting requirement for shareholders (or voting groups of shareholders) than is required by this Act. The adoption or amendment of a bylaw that adds, changes, or deletes a greater quorum or voting requirement for shareholders must meet the same quorum requirement and be adopted by the same vote and voting groups required to take action under the quorum and voting requirement then in effect or proposed to be adopted, whichever is greater.

(b) A bylaw that fixes a greater quorum or voting requirement for shareholders under subsection (a) may not be adopted, amended, or repealed by the board of directors.

§ 10.22 Bylaw Increasing Quorum or Voting Requirement for Directors

(a) A bylaw that fixes a greater quorum or voting requirement for the board of directors may be amended or repealed:

(1) if originally adopted by the shareholders, only by the shareholders;

(2) if originally adopted by the board of directors, either by the shareholders or by the board of directors.

(b) A bylaw adopted or amended by the shareholders that fixes a greater quorum or voting requirement for the board of directors may provide that it may be amended or repealed only by a specified vote of either the shareholders or the board of directors.

(c) Action by the board of directors under subsection (a)(2) to adopt or amend a bylaw that changes the quorum or voting requirement for the board of directors must meet the same quorum requirement and be adopted by the same vote required to take action under the quorum and voting requirement then in effect or proposed to be adopted, whichever is greater.

CHAPTER 11. Merger and Share Exchange

§ 11.01 Merger

(a) One or more corporations may merge into another corporation if the board of directors of each corporation adopts and its shareholders (if required by section 11.03) approve a plan of merger.

(b) The plan of merger must set forth:

(1) the name of each corporation planning to merge and the name of the surviving corporation into which each other corporation plans to merge;

(2) the terms and conditions of the merger; and

(3) the manner and basis of converting the shares of each corporation into shares, obligations, or other securities of the surviving or any other corporation or into cash or other property in whole or part.

(c) The plan of merger may set forth:

(1) amendments to the articles of incorporation of the surviving corporation; and

(2) other provisions relating to the merger.

§ 11.02 Share Exchange

(a) A corporation may acquire all of the outstanding shares of one or more classes or series of another corporation if the board of directors of each corporation adopts and its shareholders (if required by section 11.03) approve the exchange.

(b) The plan of exchange must set forth:

(1) the name of the corporation whose shares will be acquired and the name of the acquiring corporation;

(2) the terms and conditions of the exchange;

(3) the manner and basis of exchanging the shares to be acquired for shares, obligations, or other securities of the acquiring or any other corporation or for cash or other property in whole or part.

(c) The plan of exchange may set forth other provisions relating to the exchange.

(d) This section does not limit the power of a corporation to acquire all or part of the shares of one or more classes or series of another corporation through a voluntary exchange or otherwise.

§ 11.03 Action on Plan

(a) After adopting a plan of merger or share exchange, the board of directors of each corporation party to the merger, and the board of directors of the corporation whose shares will be acquired in the share exchange, shall submit the plan of merger (except as provided in subsection (g)) or share exchange for approval by its shareholders.

(b) For a plan of merger or share exchange to be approved:

(1) the board of directors must recommend the plan of merger or share exchange to the shareholders, unless the board of directors determines that because of conflict of interest or other special circumstances it should

make no recommendation and communicates the basis for its determination to the shareholders with the plan; and

(2) the shareholders entitled to vote must approve the plan.

(c) The board of directors may condition its submission of the proposed merger or share exchange on any basis.

(d) The corporation shall notify each shareholder, whether or not entitled to vote, of the proposed shareholders' meeting in accordance with section 7.05. The notice must also state that the purpose, or one of the purposes, of the meeting is to consider the plan of merger or share exchange and contain or be accompanied by a copy or summary of the plan

(e) Unless this Act, the articles of incorporation, or the board of directors (acting pursuant to subsection (c)) require a greater vote or a vote by voting groups, the plan of merger or share exchange to be authorized must be approved by each voting group entitled to vote separately on the plan by a majority of all the votes entitled to be cast on the plan by that voting group.

(f) Separate voting by voting groups is required:

(1) on a plan of merger if the plan contains a provision that, if contained in a proposed amendment to articles of incorporation, would require action by one or more separate voting groups on the proposed amendment under section 10.04;

(2) on a plan of share exchange by each class or series of shares included in the exchange, with each class or series constituting a separate voting group.

(g) Action by the shareholders of the surviving corporation on a plan of merger is not required if:

(1) the articles of incorporation of the surviving corporation will not differ (except for amendments enumerated in section 10.02) from its articles before the merger;

(2) each shareholder of the surviving corporation whose shares were outstanding immediately before the effective date of the merger will hold the same number of shares, with identical designations, preferences, limitations, and relative rights, immediately after;

(3) the number of voting shares outstanding immediately after the merger, plus the number of voting shares issuable as a result of the merger (either by the conversion of securities issued pursuant to the merger or the exercise of rights and warrants issued pursuant to the merger), will not exceed by more than 20 percent the total number of voting shares of the surviving cor-

poration outstanding immediately before the merger; and

(4) the number of participating shares outstanding immediately after the merger, plus the number of participating shares issuable as a result of the merger (either by the conversion of securities issued pursuant to the merger or the exercise of rights and warrants issued pursuant to the merger), will not exceed by more than 20 percent the total number of participating shares outstanding immediately before the merger.

(h) As used in subsection (g):

(1) "Participating shares" means shares that entitle their holders to participate without limitation in distributions.

(2) "Voting shares" means shares that entitle their holders to vote unconditionally in elections of directors.

(i) After a merger or share exchange is authorized, and at any time before articles of merger or share exchange are filed, the planned merger or share exchange may be abandoned (subject to any contractual rights), without further shareholder action, in accordance with the procedure set forth in the plan of merger or share exchange or, if none is set forth, in the manner determined by the board of directors.

§ 11.04 Merger of Subsidiary

(a) A parent corporation owning at least 90 percent of the outstanding shares of each class of a subsidiary corporation may merge the subsidiary into itself without approval of the shareholders of the parent or subsidiary.

(b) The board of directors of the parent shall adopt a plan of merger that sets forth:

(1) the names of the parent and subsidiary; and

(2) the manner and basis of converting the shares of the subsidiary into shares, obligations, or other securities of the parent or any other corporation or into cash or other property in whole or part.

(c) The parent shall mail a copy or summary of the plan of merger to each shareholder of the subsidiary who does not waive the mailing requirement in writing.

(d) The parent may not deliver articles of merger to the secretary of state for filing until at least 30 days after the date it mailed a copy of the plan of merge to each shareholder of the subsidiary who did not waive the mailing requirement.

(e) Articles of merger under this section may not contain amendments to the articles of incorporation of the parent corporation (except for amendments enumerated in section 10.02).

§ 11.05   Articles of Merger or Share Exchange

(a) After a plan of merger or share exchange is approved by the shareholders, or adopted by the board of directors if shareholder approval is not required, the surviving or acquiring corporation shall deliver to the secretary of state for filing articles of merger or share exchange setting forth:

(1) the plan of merger or share exchange;

(2) if shareholder approval was not required, a statement to that effect;

(3) if approval of the shareholders of one or more corporations party to the merger or share exchange was required:

(i) the designation, number of outstanding shares, and number of votes entitled to be cast by each voting group entitled to vote separately on the plan as to each corporation; and

(ii) either the total number of votes cast for and against the plan by each voting group entitled to vote separately on the plan or the total number of undisputed votes cast for the plan separately by each voting group and a statement that the number cast for the plan by each voting group was sufficient for approval by that voting group.

(b) Unless a delayed effective date is specified, a merger or share exchange takes effect when the articles of merger or share exchange are filed.

§ 11.06   Effect of Merger or Share Exchange

(a) When a merger takes effect:

(1) every other corporation party to the merger merges into the surviving corporation and the separate existence of every corporation except the surviving corporation ceases;

(2) the title to all real estate and other property owned by each corporation party to the merger is vested in the surviving corporation without reversion or impairment;

(3) the surviving corporation has all liabilities of each corporation party to the merger;

(4) a proceeding pending against any corporation party to the merger may be continued as if the merger did not occur or the surviving corporation may be substituted in the proceeding for the corporation whose existence ceased;

(5) the articles of incorporation of the surviving corporation are amended to the extent provided in the plan of merger; and

(6) the shares of each corporation party to the merger that are to be converted into shares, obligations, or other securities of the surviving or any other corporation or into cash or other property are converted and the former holders of the shares are entitled only to the rights provided in the articles of merger or to their rights under chapter 13.

(b) When a share exchange takes effect, the shares of each acquired corporation are exchanged as provided in the plan, and the former holders of the shares are entitled only to the exchange rights provided in the articles of share exchange or to their rights under chapter 13.

§ 11.07   Merger or Share Exchange With Foreign Corporation

(a) One or more foreign corporations may merge or enter into a share exchange with one or more domestic corporations if:

(1) in a merger, the merger is permitted by the law of the state or country under whose law each foreign corporation is incorporated and each foreign corporation complies with that law in effecting the merger;

(2) in a share exchange, the corporation whose shares will be acquired is a domestic corporation, whether or not a share exchange is permitted by the law of the state or country under whose law the acquiring corporation is incorporated;

(3) the foreign corporation complies with section 11.05 if it is the surviving corporation of the merger or acquiring corporation of the share exchange; and

(4) each domestic corporation complies with the applicable provisions of sections 11.01 through 11.04 and, if it is the surviving corporation of the merger or acquiring corporation of the share exchange, with section 11.05.

(b) Upon the merger or share exchange taking effect, the surviving foreign corporation of a merger and the acquiring foreign corporation of a share exchange is deemed:

(1) to appoint the secretary of state as its agent for service of process in a proceeding to enforce any obligation or the rights of dissenting shareholders of each domestic corporation party to the merger or share exchange; and

(2) to agree that it will promptly pay to the dissent-

ing shareholders of each domestic corporation party to the merger or share exchange the amount, if any, to which they are entitled under chapter 13.

(c) This section does not limit the power of a foreign corporation to acquire all or part of the shares of one or more classes or series of a domestic corporation through a voluntary exchange or otherwise.

CHAPTER 12. Sale of Assets

§ 12.01 Sale of Assets in Regular Course of Business and Mortgage of Assets

(a) A corporation may, on the terms and conditions and for the consideration determined by the board of directors:

(1) sell, lease, exchange, or otherwise dispose of all, or substantially all, of its property in the usual and regular course of business,

(2) mortgage, pledge, dedicate to the repayment of indebtedness (whether with or without recourse), or otherwise encumber any or all of its property whether or not in the usual and regular course of business, or

(3) transfer any or all of its property to a corporation all the shares of which are owned by the corporation.

(b) Unless the articles of incorporation require it, approval by the shareholders of a transaction described in subsection (a) is not required.

§ 12.02 Sale of Assets Other Than in Regular Course of Business

(a) A corporation may sell, lease, exchange, or otherwise dispose of all, or substantially all, of its property (with or without the goods will), otherwise than in the usual and regular course of business, on the terms and conditions and for the consideration determined by the corporation's board of directors, if the board of directors proposes and its shareholders approve the proposed transaction.

(b) For a transaction to be authorized:

(1) the board of directors must recommend the proposed transaction to the shareholders unless the board of directors determines that because of conflict of interest or other special circumstances it should make no recommendation and communicates the basis for its determination to the shareholders with the submission of the proposed transaction; and

(2) the shareholders entitled to vote must approve the transaction.

(c) The board of directors may condition its submission of the proposed transaction on any basis.

(d) The corporation shall notify each shareholder, whether or not entitled to vote, of the proposed shareholders' meeting in accordance with section 7.05. The notice must also state that the purpose, or one of the purposes, of the meeting is to consider the sale, lease, exchange, or other disposition of all, or substantially all, the property of the corporation and contain or be accompanied by a description of the transaction.

(e) Unless the articles of incorporation or the board of directors (acting pursuant to subsection (c)) require a greater vote or a vote by voting groups, the transaction to be authorized must be approved by a majority of all the votes entitled to be cast on the transaction.

(f) After a sale, lease, exchange, or other disposition of property is authorized, the transaction may be abandoned (subject to any contractual rights) without further shareholder action.

(g) A transaction that constitutes a distribution is governed by section 6.40 and not by this section.

CHAPTER 13. Dissenters' Rights

SUBCHAPTER A. *Right to Dissent and Obtain Payment for Shares*

§ 13.01 Definitions

In this chapter:

(1) "Corporation" means the issuer of the shares held by a dissenter before the corporate action, or the surviving or acquiring corporation by merger of share exchange of that issuer.

(2) "Dissenter" means a shareholder who is entitled to dissent from corporate action under section 13.02 and who exercises that right when and in the manner required by sections 13.20 through 13.28.

(3) "Fair value," with respect to a dissenter's shares, means the value of the shares immediately before the effectuation of the corporate action to which the dissenter objects, excluding any appreciation or depreciation in anticipation of the corporate action unless exclusion would be inequitable.

(4) "Interest" means interest from the effective date of the corporate action until the date of payment, at the average rate currently paid by the corporation on its principal bank loans or, if none, at a rate that is fair and equitable under all the circumstances.

(5) "Record shareholder" means the person in whose name shares are registered in the records of a corporation or the beneficial owner of shares to the

extent of the rights granted by a nominee certificate on file with a corporation.

(6) "Beneficial shareholder" means the person who is a beneficial owner of shares held by a nominee as the record shareholder.

(7) "Shareholder" means the record shareholder or the beneficial shareholder.

§ 13.02   Right to Dissent

(a) A shareholder is entitled to dissent from, and obtain payment of the fair value of his shares in the event of, any of the following corporate actions:

(1) consummation of a plan of merger to which the corporation is a party (i) if shareholder approval is required for the merger by section 11.03 or the articles of incorporation and the shareholder is entitled to vote on the merger or (ii) if the corporation is a subsidiary that is merged with its parent under section 11.04;

(2) consummation of a plan of share exchange to which the corporation is a party as the corporation whose shares will be acquired, if the shareholder is entitled to vote on the plan;

(3) consummation of a sale or exchange of all, or substantially all, of the property of the corporation other than in the usual and regular course of business, if the shareholder is entitled to vote on the sale or exchange, including a sale in dissolution, but not including a sale pursuant to court order or a sale for cash pursuant to a plan by which all or substantially all of the net proceeds of the sale will be distributed to the shareholders within one year after the date of sale;

(4) an amendment of the articles of incorporation that materially and adversely affects rights in respect of a dissenter's shares because it:

(i) alters or abolishes a preferential right of the shares;

(ii) creates, alters, or abolishes a right in respect of redemption, including a provision respecting a sinking fund for the redemption or repurchase, of the shares;

(iii) alters or abolishes a preemptive right of the holder of the shares to acquire shares or other securities;

(iv) excludes or limits the right of the shares to vote on any matter, or to cumulate votes, other than a limitation by dilution through issuance of shares or other securities with similar voting rights; or

(v) reduces the number of shares owned by the shareholder to a fraction of a share if the fractional share so created is to be acquired for cash under section 6.04; or

(5) any corporate action taken pursuant to a shareholder vote to the extent the articles of incorporation, bylaws, or a resolution of the board of directors provides that voting or nonvoting shareholders are entitled to dissent and obtain payment for their shares.

(b) A shareholder entitled to dissent and obtain payment for his shares under this chapter may not challenge the corporate action creating his entitlement unless the action is unlawful or fraudulent with respect to the shareholder or the corporation.

§ 13.03   Dissent by Nominees and Beneficial Owners

(a) A record shareholder may assert dissenters' rights as to fewer than all the shares registered in his name only if he dissents with respect to all shares beneficially owned by any one person and notifies the corporation in writing of the name and address of each person on whose behalf he asserts dissenters' rights. The rights of a partial dissenter under this subsection are determined as if the shares as to which he dissents and his other shares were registered in the names of different shareholders.

(b) A beneficial shareholder may assert dissenters' rights as to shares held on his behalf only if:

(1) he submits to the corporation the record shareholder's written consent to the dissent not later than the time the beneficial shareholder asserts dissenters' rights; and

(2) he does so with respect to all shares of which he is the beneficial shareholder or over which he has power to direct the vote.

SUBCHAPTER B. *Procedure for Exercise of Dissenters' Rights*

§ 13.20   Notice of Dissenters' Rights

(a) If proposed corporate action creating dissenters' rights under section 13.02 is submitted to vote at a shareholders' meeting, the meeting notice must state that shareholders are or may be entitled to assert dissenters' rights under this chapter and be accompanied by a copy of this chapter.

(b) If corporate action creating dissenters' rights under section 13.02 is taken without a vote of shareholders, the corporation shall notify in writing all shareholders entitled to assert dissenters' rights that the action was taken and send them the dissenters' notice described in section 13.22.

§ 13.21   Notice of Intent to Demand Payment

(a) If proposed corporate action creating dissenters' rights under section 13.02 is submitted to a vote at a shareholders' meeting, a shareholder who wishes to assert dissenters' rights (1) must deliver to the corporation before the vote is taken written notice of his intent to demand payment for his shares if the proposed action is effectuated and (2) must not vote his shares in favor of the proposed action.

(b) A shareholder who does not satisfy the requirements of subsection (a) is not entitled to payment for his shares under this chapter.

§ 13.22   Dissenters' Notice

(a) If proposed corporate action creating dissenters' rights under section 13.02 is authorized at a shareholders' meeting, the corporation shall deliver a written dissenters' notice to all shareholders who satisfied the requirements of section 13.21.

(b) The dissenters' notice must be sent no later than 10 days after the corporate action was taken, and must:

(1) state where the payment demand must be sent and where and when certificates for certificated shares must be deposited;

(2) inform holders of uncertificated shares to what extent transfer of the shares will be restricted after the payment demand is received:

(3) supply a form for demanding payment that includes the date of the first announcement to news media or to shareholders of the terms of the proposed corporate action and requires that the person asserting dissenters' rights certify whether or not he acquired beneficial ownership of the shares before that date;

(4) set a date by which the corporation must receive the payment demand, which date may not be fewer than 30 nor more than 60 days after the date the subsection (1) notice is delivered; and

(5) be accompanied by a copy of this chapter.

§ 13.23   Duty to Demand Payment

(a) A shareholder sent a dissenters' notice described in section 13.22 must demand payment, certify whether he acquired beneficial ownership of the shares before the date required to be set forth in the dissenter's notice pursuant to section 13.22(b)(3), and deposit his certificates in accordance with the terms of the notice.

(b) The shareholder who demands payment and deposits his shares under section (a) retains all other rights of a shareholder until these rights are cancelled or modified by the taking of the proposed corporate action.

(c) A shareholder who does not demand payment or deposit his share certificates where required, each by the date set in the dissenters' notice, is not entitled to payment for his shares under this chapter.

§ 13.24   Share Restrictions

(a) The corporation may restrict the transfer of uncertificated shares from the date the demand for their payment is received until the proposed corporate action is taken or the restrictions released under section 13.26.

(b) The person for whom dissenters' rights are asserted as to uncertificated shares retains all other rights of a shareholder until these rights are cancelled or modified by the taking of the proposed corporate action.

§ 13.25   Payment

(a) Except as provided in section 13.27, as soon as the proposed corporate action is taken, or upon receipt of a payment demand, the corporation shall pay each dissenter who complied with section 13.23 the amount the corporation estimates to be the fair value of his shares, plus accrued interest.

(b) The payment must be accompanied by:

(1) the corporation's balance sheet as of the end of a fiscal year ending not more than 16 months before the date of payment, an income statement for that year, a statement of changes in shareholders' equity for that year, and the latest available interim financial statements, if any;

(2) a statement of the corporation's estimate of the fair value of the shares;

(3) an explanation of how the interest was calculated;

(4) a statement of the dissenter's right to demand payment under section 13.28; and

(5) a copy of this chapter.

§ 13.26   Failure to Take Action

(a) If the corporation does not take the proposed action within 60 days after the date set for demanding payment and depositing share certificates, the corporation shall return the deposited certificates and release the transfer restrictions imposed on uncertificated shares.

(b) If after returning deposited certificates and releasing transfer restrictions, the corporation takes the proposed action, it must send a new dissenters' notice under section 13.22 and repeat the payment demand procedure.

§ 13.27   After-Acquired Shares

(a) A corporation may elect to withhold payment required by section 13.25 from a dissenter unless he was the beneficial owner of the shares before the date set forth in the dissenters' notice as the date of the first announcement to new media or to shareholders of the terms of the proposed corporate action.

(b) To the extent the corporation elects to withhold payment under subsection (a), after taking the proposed corporate action, it shall estimate the fair value of the shares, plus accrued interest, and shall pay this amount to each dissenter who agrees to accept it in full satisfaction of his demand. The corporation shall send with its offer a statement of its estimate of the fair value of the shares, an explanation of how the interest was calculated, and a statement of the dissenter's right to demand payment under section 13.28.

§ 13.28   Procedure if Shareholder Dissatisfied With Payment or Offer

(a) A dissenter may notify the corporation in writing of his own estimate of the fair value of his shares and amount of interest due, and demand payment of his estimate (less any payment under section 13.25), or reject the corporation's offer under section 13.27 and demand payment of the fair value of his shares and interest due, if:

(1) the dissenter believes that the amount paid under section 13.25 or offered under section 13.27 is less than the fair value of his shares or that the interest due is incorrectly calculated;

(2) the corporation fails to make payment under section 13.25 within 60 days after the date set for demanding payment; or

(3) the corporation, having failed to take the proposed action, does not return the deposited certificates or release the transfer restrictions imposed on uncertificated shares within 60 days after the date set for demanding payment.

(b) A dissenter waives his right to demand payment under this section unless he notifies the corporation of his demand in writing under subsection (a) within 30 days after the corporation made or offered payment for his shares.

SUBCHAPTER C. *Judicial Appraisal of Shares*

§ 13.30   Court Action

(a) If a demand for payment under section 13.28 remains unsettled, the corporation shall commence a proceeding within 60 days after receiving the payment demand and petition the court to determine the fair value of the shares and accrued interest. If the corporation does not commence the proceeding within the 60-day period, it shall pay each dissenter whose demand remains unsettled the amount demanded.

(b) The corporation shall commence the proceeding in the [name or describe] court of the county where a corporation's principal office (or, if none in this state, its registered office) is located. If the corporation is a foreign corporation without a registered office in this state, it shall commence the proceeding in the county in this state where the registered office of the domestic corporation merged with or whose shares were acquired by the foreign corporation was located.

(c) The corporation shall make all dissenters (whether or not residents of this state) whose demands remain unsettled parties to the proceeding as in an action against their shares and all parties must be served with a copy of the petition. Nonresidents may be served by registered or certified mail or by publication as provided by law.

(d) The jurisdiction of the court in which the proceeding is commenced under subsection (b) is plenary and exclusive. The court may appoint one or more persons as appraisers to receive evidence and recommend decision on the question of fair value. The appraisers have the powers described in the order appointing them, or in any amendment to it. The dissenters are entitled to the same discovery rights as parties in other civil proceedings.

(e) Each dissenter made a party to the proceeding is entitled to judgment (1) for the amount, if any, by which the court finds the fair value of his shares, plus interest, exceeds the amount paid by the corporation or (2) for the fair value, plus accrued interest, of his after-acquired shares for which the corporation elected to withhold payment under section 13.27.

§ 13.31   Court Costs and Counsel Fees

(a) The court in an appraisal proceeding commenced under section 13.30 shall determine all costs of the proceeding, including the reasonable compensation and expenses of appraisers appointed by the court. The court shall assess the costs against the corporation, except that the court may assess costs against all or some of the dissenters, in amounts the court finds equitable, to the extent the court finds the dissenters acted arbitrarily vexatiously, or not in good faith in demanding payment under section 13.28.

(b) The court may also assess the fees and expenses of counsel and experts for the respective parties, in amounts the court finds equitable:

(1) against the corporation and in favor of any or all dissenters if the court finds the corporation did not substantially comply with the requirements of sections 13.20 through 13.28; or

(2) against either the corporation or a dissenter, in favor of any other party, if the court finds that the party against whom the fees and expenses are assessed acted arbitrarily, vexatiously, or not in good faith with respect to the rights provided by this chapter.

(c) If the court finds that the services of counsel for any dissenter were of substantial benefit to other dissenters similarly situated, and that the fees for those services should not be assessed against the corporation, the court may award to these counsel reasonable fees to be paid out of the amounts awarded the dissenters who were benefited.

CHAPTER 14. Dissolution

SUBCHAPTER A. *Voluntary Dissolution*

§ 14.01 Dissolution by Incorporators or Initial Directors

A majority of the incorporators or initial directors of a corporation that has not issued shares or has not commenced business may dissolve the corporation by delivering to the secretary of state for filing articles of dissolution that set forth:

(1) the name of the corporation;

(2) the date of its incorporation;

(3) either (i) that none of the corporation's shares has been issued or (ii) that the corporation has not commenced business;

(4) that no debt of the corporation remains unpaid;

(5) that the net assets of the corporation remaining after winding up have been distributed to the shareholders, if shares were issued; and

(6) that a majority of the incorporators or initial directors authorized the dissolution.

§ 14.02 Dissolution by Board of Directors and Shareholders

(a) A corporation's board of directors may propose dissolution for submission to the shareholders.

(b) For a proposal to dissolve to be adopted:

(1) the board of directors must recommend dissolution to the shareholders unless the board of directors determines that because of conflict of interest or other special circumstances it should make no recommendation and communicates the basis for its determination to the shareholders; and

(2) the shareholders entitled to vote must approve the proposal to dissolve as provided in subsection (e).

(c) The board of directors may condition its submission of the proposal for dissolution on any basis.

(d) The corporation shall notify each shareholder, whether or not entitled to vote, of the proposed shareholders' meeting in accordance with section 7.05. The notice must also state that the purpose, or one of the purposes, of the meeting is to consider dissolving the corporation.

(e) Unless the articles of incorporation or the board of directors (acting pursuant to subsection (c)) require a greater vote or a vote by voting groups, the proposal to dissolve to be adopted must be approved by a majority of all the votes entitled to be cast on that proposal.

§ 14.03 Articles of Dissolution

(a) At any time after dissolution is authorized, the corporation may dissolve by delivering to the secretary of state for filing articles of dissolution setting forth:

(1) the name of the corporation;

(2) the date dissolution was authorized;

(3) if dissolution was approved by the shareholders:

(i) the number of votes entitled to be cast on the proposal to dissolve; and

(ii) either the total number of votes cast for and against dissolution or the total number of undisputed votes cast for dissolution and a statement that the number cast for dissolution was sufficient for approval.

(4) If voting by voting groups is required, the information required by subparagraph (3) shall be separately provided for each voting group entitled to vote separately on the plan to dissolve.

(b) A corporation is dissolved upon the effective date of its articles of dissolution.

§ 14.04 Revocation of Dissolution

(a) A corporation may revoke its dissolution within 120 days of its effective date.

(b) Revocation of dissolution must be authorized in the same manner as the dissolution was authorized unless that authorization permitted revocation by action by the board of directors alone, in which event the board of directors may revoke the dissolution without shareholder action.

(c) After the revocation of dissolution is authorized, the corporation may revoke the dissolution by delivering to the secretary of state for filing articles of revocation of dissolution, together with a copy of its articles of dissolution, that set forth:

(1) the name of the corporation;

(2) the effective date of the dissolution that was revoked;

(3) the date that the revocation of dissolution was authorized;

(4) if the corporation's board of directors (or incorporators) revoked the dissolution, a statement to that effect;

(5) if the corporation's board of directors revoked a dissolution authorized by the shareholders, a statement that revocation was permitted by action by the board of directors alone pursuant to that authorization; and

(6) if shareholder action was required to revoke the dissolution, the information required by section 14.03(3) or (4).

(d) Unless a delayed effective date is specified, revocation of dissolution is effective when articles of revocation of dissolution are filed.

(e) When the revocation of dissolution is effective, it relates back to and takes effect as of the effective date of the dissolution and the corporation resumes carrying on its business as if dissolution had never occurred.

§ 14.05 Effect of Dissolution

(a) A dissolved corporation continues its corporate existence but may not carry on any business except that appropriate to wind up and liquidate its business and affairs, including:

(1) collecting its assets;

(2) disposing of its properties that will not be distributed in kind to its shareholders;

(3) discharging or making provision for discharging its liabilities;

(4) distributing its remaining property among its shareholders according to their interests; and

(5) doing every other act necessary to wind up and liquidate its business and affairs.

(b) Dissolution of a corporation does not:

(1) transfer title to the corporation's property;

(2) prevent transfer of its shares or securities, although the authorization to dissolve may provide for closing the corporation's share transfer records;

(3) subject its directors or officers to standards of conduct different from those prescribed in chapter 8;

(4) change quorum or voting requirements for its board of directors or shareholders; change provisions for selection, resignation, or removal of its directors or officers or both; or change provisions for amending its bylaws;

(5) prevent commencement of a proceeding by or against the corporation in its corporate name;

(6) abate or suspend a proceeding pending by or against the corporation on the effective date of dissolution; or

(7) terminate the authority of the registered agent of the corporation.

§ 14.06 Known Claims Against Dissolved Corporation

(a) A dissolved corporation may dispose of the known claims against it by following the procedure described in this section.

(b) The dissolved corporation shall notify its known claimants in writing of the dissolution at any time after its effective date. The written notice must:

(1) describe information that must be included in a claim;

(2) provide a mailing address where a claim may be sent;

(3) state the deadline, which may not be fewer than 120 days from the effective date of the written notice, by which the dissolved corporation must receive the claim; and

(4) state that the claim will be barred if not received by the deadline.

(c) A claim against the dissolved corporation is barred:

(1) if a claimant who was given written notice under subsection (b) does not deliver the claim to the dissolved corporation by the deadline;

(2) if a claimant whose claim was rejected by the dissolved corporation does not commence a proceeding to enforce the claim within 90 days from the effective date of the rejection notice.

(d) For purposes of this section, "claim" does not include a contingent liability or a claim based on an event occurring after the effective date of dissolution.

§ 14.07   Unknown Claims Against Dissolved Corporation

(a) A dissolved corporation may also publish notice of its dissolution and request that persons with claims against the corporation present them in accordance with the notice.

(b) The notice must:

(1) be published one time in a newspaper of general circulation in the county where the dissolved corporation's principal office (or, if none in this state, its registered office) is or was last located;

(2) describe the information that must be included in a claim and provide a mailing address where the claim may be sent; and

(3) state that a claim against the corporation will be barred unless a proceeding to enforce the claim is commenced within five years after the publication of the notice.

(c) If the dissolved corporation publishes a newspaper notice in accordance with subsection (b), the claim of each of the following claimants is barred unless the claimant commences a proceeding to enforce the claim against the dissolved corporation within five years after the publication date of the newspaper notice:

(1) a claimant who did not receive written notice under section 14.06;

(2) a claimant whose claim was timely sent to the dissolved corporation but not acted on;

(3) a claimant whose claim is contingent or based on an event occurring after the effective date of dissolution.

(d) A claim may be enforced under this section:

(1) against the dissolved corporation, to the extent of its undistributed assets; or

(2) if the assets have been distributed in liquidation, against a shareholder of the dissolved corporation to the extent of his pro rata share of the claim or the corporate assets distributed to him in liquidation, whichever is less, but a shareholder's total liability for all claims under this section may not exceed the total amount of assets distributed to him.

SUBCHAPTER B. *Administrative Dissolution*

§ 14.20   Grounds for Administrative Dissolution

The secretary of state may commence a proceeding under section 14.21 to administratively dissolve a corporation if:

(1) the corporation does not pay within 60 days after they are due any franchise taxes or penalties imposed by this Act or other law;

(2) the corporation does not deliver its annual report to the secretary of state within 60 days after it is due;

(3) the corporation is without a registered agent or registered office in this state for 60 days or more;

(4) the corporation does not notify the secretary of state within 60 days that its registered agent or registered office has been changed, that its registered agent has resigned, or that its registered office has been discontinued; or

(5) the corporation's period of duration stated in its articles of incorporation expires.

§ 14.21   Procedure for and Effect of Administrative Dissolution

(a) If the secretary of state determines that one or more grounds exist under section 14.20 for dissolving a corporation, he shall serve the corporation with written notice of his determination under section 5.04.

(b) If the corporation does not correct each ground for dissolution or demonstrate to the reasonable satisfaction of the secretary of state that each ground determined by the secretary of state does not exist within 60 days after service of the notice is perfected under section 5.04, the secretary of state shall administratively dissolve the corporation by signing a certificate of dissolution that recites the ground or grounds for dissolution and its effective date. The secretary of state shall file the original of the certificate and serve a copy on the corporation under section 5.04.

(c) A corporation administratively dissolved continues its corporate existence but may not carry on any business except that necessary to wind up and liquidate its business and affairs under section 14.05 and notify claimants under sections 14.06 and 14.07.

(d) The administrative dissolution of a corporation does not terminate the authority of its registered agent.

§ 14.22   Reinstatement Following Administrative Dissolution

(a) A corporation administratively dissolved under section 14.21 may apply to the secretary of state for reinstatement within two years after the effective date of dissolution. The application must:

(1) recite the name of the corporation and the effective date of its administrative dissolution;

(2) state that the ground or grounds for dissolution either did not exist or have been eliminated;

(3) state that the corporation's name satisfies the requirements of section 4.01; and

(4) contain a certificate from the [taxing authority] reciting that all taxes owed by the corporation have been paid.

(b) If the secretary of state determines that the application contains the information required by subsection (a) and that the information is correct, he shall cancel the certificate of dissolution and prepare a certificate of reinstatement that recites his determination and the effective date of reinstatement, file the original of the certificate, and serve a copy on the corporation under section 5.04.

(c) When the reinstatement is effective, it relates back to and takes effect as of the effective date of the administrative dissolution and the corporation resumes carrying on its business as if the administrative dissolution had never occurred.

§ 14.23   Appeal From Denial of Reinstatement

(a) If the secretary of state denies a corporation's application for reinstatement following administrative dissolution, he shall serve the corporation under section 5.04 with a written notice that explains the reason or reasons for denial.

(b) The corporation may appeal the denial of reinstatement to the [name or describe] court within 30 days after service of the notice of denial is perfected. The corporation appeals by petitioning the court to set aside the dissolution and attaching to the petition copies of the secretary of state's certificate of dissolution, the corporation's application for reinstatement, and the secretary of state's notice of denial.

(c) The court may summarily order the secretary of state to reinstate the dissolved corporation or may take other action the court considers appropriate.

(d) The court's final decision may be appealed as in other civil proceedings.

SUBCHAPTER C. *Judicial Dissolution*

§ 14.30   Grounds for Judicial Dissolution

The [name or describe court or courts] may dissolve a corporation:

(1) in a proceeding by the attorney general if it is established that:

(i) the corporation obtained its articles of incorporation through fraud; or

(ii) the corporation has continued to exceed or abuse the authority conferred upon it by law;

(2) in a proceeding by a shareholder if it is established that:

(i) the directors are deadlocked in the management of the corporate affairs, the shareholders are unable to break the deadlock, and irreparable injury to the corporation is threatened or being suffered, or the business and affairs of the corporation can no longer be conducted to the advantage of the shareholders generally, because of the deadlock;

(ii) the directors or those in control of the corporation have acted, are acting, or will act in a manner that is illegal, oppressive, or fraudulent;

(iii) the shareholders are deadlocked in voting power and have failed, for a period that includes at least two consecutive annual meeting dates, to elect successors to directors whose terms have expired; or

(iv) the corporate assets are being misapplied or wasted;

(3) in a proceeding by a creditor if it is established that:

(i) the creditor's claim has been reduced to judgment, the execution on the judgment returned unsatisfied, and the corporation is insolvent; or

(ii) the corporation has admitted in writing that the creditor's claim is due and owing and the corporation is insolvent; or

(4) in a proceeding by the corporation to have its voluntary dissolution continued under court supervision.

§ 14.31   Procedure for Judicial Dissolution

(a) Venue for a proceeding by the attorney general to dissolve a corporation lies in [name the county or counties]. Venue for a proceeding brought by any other party named in section 14.30 lies in the county where a corporation's principal office (or, if none in this state, its registered office) is or was last located.

(b) It is not necessary to make shareholders parties to

a proceeding to dissolve a corporation unless relief is sought against them individually.

(c) A court in a proceeding brought to dissolve a corporation may issue injunctions, appoint a receiver or custodian pendente lite with all powers and duties the court directs, take other action required to preserve the corporate assets wherever located, and carry on the business of the corporation until a full hearing can be held.

§ 14.32   Receivership or Custodianship

(a) A court in a judicial proceeding brought to dissolve a corporation may appoint one or more receivers to wind up and liquidate, or one or more custodians to manage, the business and affairs of the corporation. The court shall hold a hearing, after notifying all parties to the proceeding and any interested persons designated by the court, before appointing a receiver or custodian. The court appointing a receiver or custodian has exclusive jurisdiction over the corporation and all its property wherever located.

(b) The court may appoint an individual or a domestic or foreign corporation (authorized to transact business in this state) as a receiver or custodian. The court may require the receiver or custodian to post bond, with or without sureties, in an amount the court directs.

(c) The court shall describe the powers and duties of the receiver or custodian in its appointing order, which may be amended from time to time. Among other powers:

(1) the receiver (i) may dispose of all or any part of the assets of the corporation wherever located, at a public or private sale, if authorized by the court; and (ii) may sue and defend in his own name as receiver of the corporation in all courts of this state;

(2) the custodian may exercise all of the powers of the corporation, through or in place of its board of directors or officers, to the extent necessary to manage the affairs of the corporation in the best interests of its shareholders and creditors.

(d) The court during a receivership may redesignate the receiver a custodian, and during a custodianship may redesignate the custodian a receiver, if doing so is in the best interests of the corporation, its shareholders, and creditors.

(e) The court from time to time during the receivership or custodianship may order compensation paid and expense disbursements or reimbursements made to the receiver or custodian and his counsel from the assets of the corporation or proceeds from the sale of the assets.

§ 14.33   Decree of Dissolution

(a) If after a hearing the court determines that one or more grounds for judicial dissolution described in section 14.30 exist, it may enter a decree dissolving the corporation and specifying the effective date of the dissolution, and the clerk of the court shall deliver a certified copy of the decree to the secretary of state, who shall file it.

(b) After entering the decree of dissolution, the court shall direct the winding up and liquidation of the corporation's business and affairs in accordance with section 14.05 and the notification of claimants in accordance with sections 14.06 and 14.07.

SUBCHAPTER D. *Miscellaneous*

§ 14.40   Deposit With State Treasurer

Assets of a dissolved corporation that should be transferred to a creditor, claimant, or shareholder of the corporation who cannot be found or who is not competent to receive them shall be reduced to cash and deposited with the state treasurer or other appropriate state official for safekeeping. When the creditor, claimant, or shareholder furnishes satisfactory proof of entitlement to the amount deposited, the state treasurer or other appropriate state official shall pay him or his representative that amount.

CHAPTER 15. Foreign Corporations

SUBCHAPTER A. *Certificate of Authority*

§ 15.01   Authority to Transact Business Required

(a) A foreign corporation may not transact business in this state until it obtains a certificate of authority from the secretary of state.

(b) The following activities, among others, do not constitute transacting business within the meaning of subsection (a):

(1) maintaining, defending, or settling any proceeding;

(2) holding meetings of the board of directors or

shareholders or carrying on other activities concerning internal corporate affairs;

(3) maintaining bank accounts;

(4) maintaining offices or agencies for the transfer, exchange, and registration of the corporation's own securities or maintaining trustees or depositaries with respect to those securities;

(5) selling through independent contractors;

(6) soliciting or obtaining orders, whether by mail or through employees or agents or otherwise, if the orders require acceptance outside this state before they become contracts;

(7) creating or acquiring indebtedness, mortgages, and security interests in real or personal property;

(8) securing or collecting debts or enforcing mortgages and security interests in property securing the debts;

(9) owning, without more, real or personal property;

(10) conducting an isolated transaction that is completed within 30 days and that is not one in the course of repeated transactions of a like nature;

(11) transacting business in interstate commerce.

(c) The list of activities in subsection (b) is not exhaustive.

§ 15.02 Consequences of Transacting Business Without Authority

(a) A foreign corporation transacting business in this state without a certificate of authority may not maintain a proceeding in any court in this state until it obtains a certificate of authority.

(b) The successor to a foreign corporation that transacted business in this state without a certificate of authority and the assignee of a cause of action arising out of that business may not maintain a proceeding based on that cause of action in any court in this state until the foreign corporation or its successor obtains a certificate of authority.

(c) A court may stay a proceeding commenced by a foreign corporation, its successor, or assignee until it determines whether the foreign corporation or its successor requires a certificate of authority. If it so determines, the court may further stay the proceeding until the foreign corporation or its successor obtains the certificate.

(d) A foreign corporation is liable for a civil penalty of $_____ for each day, but not to exceed a total of $_____ for each year, it transacts business in this state

without a certificate of authority. The attorney general may collect all penalties due under this subsection.

(e) Notwithstanding subsections (a) and (b), the failure of a foreign corporation to obtain a certificate of authority does not impair the validity of its corporate acts or prevent it from defending any proceeding in this state.

§ 15.03 Application for Certificate of Authority

(a) A foreign corporation may apply for a certificate of authority to transact business in this state by delivering an application to the secretary of state for filing. The application must set forth:

(1) the name of the foreign corporation or, if its name is unavailable for use in this state, a corporate name that satisfies the requirements of section 15.06;

(2) the name of the state or country under whose law it is incorporated;

(3) its date of incorporation and period of duration;

(4) the street address of its principal office;

(5) the address of its registered office in this state and the name of its registered agent at that office; and

(6) the names and usual business addresses of its current directors and officers.

(b) The foreign corporation shall deliver with the completed application a certificate of existence (or a document of similar import) duly authenticated by the secretary of state or other official having custody of corporate records in the state or country under whose law it is incorporated.

§ 15.04 Amended Certificate of Authority

(a) A foreign corporation authorized to transact business in this state must obtain an amended certificate of authority from the secretary of state if it changes:

(1) its corporate name;

(2) the period of its duration; or

(3) the state or country of its incorporation.

(b) The requirements of section 15.03 for obtaining an original certificate of authority apply to obtaining an amended certificate under this section.

§ 15.05 Effect of Certificate of Authority

(a) A certificate of authority authorizes the foreign corporation to which it is issued to transact business in this state subject, however, to the right of the state to revoke the certificate as provided in this Act.

(b) A foreign corporation with a valid certificate of authority has the same but no greater rights and has the same but no greater privileges as, and except as otherwise provided by this Act is subject to the same duties, restrictions, penalties, and liabilities now or later imposed on, a domestic corporation of like character.

(c) This Act does not authorize this state to regulate the organization or internal affairs of a foreign corporation authorized to transact business in this state.

§ 15.06 Corporate Name of Foreign Corporation

(a) If the corporate name of a foreign corporation does not satisfy the requirements of section 4.01, the foreign corporation to obtain or maintain a certificate of authority to transact business in this state:

(1) may add the word "corporation," "incorporated," "company," or "limited," or the abbreviation "corp.," "inc.," "co.," or "ltd.," to its corporate name for use in this state; or

(2) may use a fictitious name to transact business in this state if its real name is unavailable and it delivers to the secretary of state for filing a copy of the resolution of its board of directors, certified by its secretary, adopting the fictitious name.

(b) Except as authorized by subsections (c) and (d), the corporate name (including a fictitious name) of a foreign corporation must be distinguishable upon the records of the secretary of state from:

(1) the corporate name of a corporation incorporated or authorized to transact business in this state;

(2) a corporate name reserved or registered under section 4.02 or 4.03;

(3) the fictitious name of another foreign corporation authorized to transact business in this state; and

(4) the corporate name of a not-for-profit corporation incorporated or authorized to transact business in this state.

(c) A foreign corporation may apply to the secretary of state for authorization to use in this state the name of another corporation (incorporated or authorized to transact business in this state) that is not distinguishable upon his records from the name applied for. The secretary of state shall authorize use of the name applied for if:

(1) the other corporation consents to the use in writing and submits an undertaking in form satisfactory to the secretary of state to change its name to a name that is distinguishable upon the records of the secretary of state from the name of the applying corporation; or

(2) the applicant delivers to the secretary of state a certified copy of a final judgment of a court of competent jurisdiction establishing the applicant's right to use the name applied for in this state.

(d) A foreign corporation may use in this state the name (including the fictitious name) of another domestic or foreign corporation that is used in this state if the other corporation is incorporated or authorized to transact business in this state and the foreign corporation:

(1) has merged with the other corporation;

(2) has been formed by reorganization of the other corporation; or

(3) has acquired all or substantially all of the assets, including the corporate name, of the other corporation.

(e) If a foreign corporation authorized to transact business in this state changes its corporate name to one that does not satisfy the requirements of section 4.01, it may not transact business in this state under the changed name until it adopts a name satisfying the requirements of section 4.01 and obtains an amended certificate of authority under section 15.04.

§ 15.07 Registered Office and Registered Agent of Foreign Corporation

Each foreign corporation authorized to transact business in this state must continuously maintain in this state:

(1) a registered office that may be the same as any of its places of business; and

(2) a registered agent, who may be:

(i) an individual who resides in this state and whose business office is identical with the registered office;

(ii) a domestic corporation or not-for-profit domestic corporation whose business office is identical with the registered office; or

(iii) a foreign corporation or foreign not-for-profit corporation authorized to transact business in this state whose business office is identical with the registered office.

§ 15.08 Change of Registered Office or Registered Agent of Foreign Corporation

(a) A foreign corporation authorized to transact business in this state may change its registered office or registered agent by delivering to the secretary of state for filing a statement of change that sets forth:

(1) its name;

(2) the street address of its current registered office;

(3) if the current registered office is to be changed, the street address of its new registered office;

(4) the name of its current registered agent;

(5) if the current registered agent is to be changed, the name of its new registered agent and the new agent's written consent (either on the statement or attached to it) to the appointment; and

(6) that after the change or changes are made, the street addresses of its registered office and the business office of its registered agent will be identical.

(b) If a registered agent changes the street address of his business office, he may change the street address of the registered office of any foreign corporation for which he is the registered agent by notifying the corporation in writing of the change and signing (either manually or in facsimile) and delivering to the secretary of state for filing a statement of change that complies with the requirements of subsection (a) and recites that the corporation has been notified of the change.

§ 15.09 Resignation of Registered Agent of Foreign Corporation

(a) The registered agent of a foreign corporation may resign his agency appointment by signing and delivering to the secretary of state for filing the original and two exact or conformed copies of a statement of resignation. The statement of resignation may include a statement that the registered office is also discontinued.

(b) After filing the statement, the secretary of state shall attach the filing receipt to one copy and mail the copy and receipt to the registered office if not discontinued. The secretary of state shall mail the other copy to the foreign corporation at its principal office address shown in its most recent annual report.

(c) The agency appointment is terminated, and the registered office discontinued if so provided, on the 31st day after the date on which the statement was filed.

§ 15.10 Service on Foreign Corporation

(a) The registered agent of a foreign corporation authorized to transact business in this state is the corporation's agent for service of process, notice, or demand required or permitted by law to be served on the foreign corporation.

(b) A foreign corporation may be served by registered or certified mail, return receipt requested, addressed to the secretary of the foreign corporation at its principal office shown in its application for a certificate of authority or in its most recent annual report if the foreign corporation:

(1) has no registered agent or its registered agent cannot with reasonable diligence be served;

(2) has withdrawn from transacting business in this state under section 15.20; or

(3) has had its certificate of authority revoked under section 15.31.

(c) Service is perfected under subsection (b) at the earliest of:

(1) the date the foreign corporation receives the mail;

(2) the date shown on the return receipt, if signed on behalf of the foreign corporation; or

(3) five days after its deposit in the United States Mail, if mailed postpaid and correctly addressed.

(d) This section does not prescribe the only means, or necessarily the required means, of serving a foreign corporation.

SUBCHAPTER B. Withdrawal

§ 15.20 Withdrawal of Foreign Corporation

(a) A foreign corporation authorized to transact business in this state may not withdraw from this state until it obtains a certificate of withdrawal from the secretary of state.

(b) A foreign corporation authorized to transact business in this state may apply for a certificate of withdrawal by delivering an application to the secretary of state for filing. The application must set forth:

(1) the name of the foreign corporation and the name of the state or country under whose law it is incorporated;

(2) that it is not transacting business in this state and that it surrenders its authority to transact business in this state;

(3) that it revokes the authority of its registered agent to accept service on its behalf and appoints the secretary of state as its agent for service of process in any proceeding based on a cause of action arising during the time it was authorized to transact business in this state;

(4) a mailing address to which the secretary of state may mail a copy of any process served on him under subdivision (3); and

(5) a commitment to notify the secretary of state in the future of any change in its mailing address.

(c) After the withdrawal of the corporation is effective, service of process on the secretary of state under this section is service on the foreign corporation. Upon receipt of process, the secretary of state shall mail a copy of the process to the foreign corporation at the mailing address set forth in its application for withdrawal.

SUBCHAPTER C. *Revocation of Certificate of Authority*

§ 15.30   Grounds for Revocation

The secretary of state may commence a proceeding under section 15.31 to revoke the certificate of authority of a foreign corporation authorized to transact business in this state if:

(1) the foreign corporation does not deliver its annual report to the secretary of state within 60 days after it is due;

(2) the foreign corporation does not pay within 60 days after they are due any franchise taxes or penalties imposed by this Act or other law;

(3) the foreign corporation is without a registered agent or registered office in this state for 60 days or more;

(4) the foreign corporation does not inform the secretary of state under section 15.08 or 15.09 that its registered agent or registered office has changed, that its registered agent has resigned, or that its registered office has been discontinued within 60 days of the change, resignation, or discontinuance;

(5) an incorporator, director, officer, or agent of the foreign corporation signed a document he knew was false in any material respect with intent that the document be delivered to the secretary of state for filing;

(6) the secretary of state receives a duly authenticated certificate from the secretary of state or other official having custody of corporate records in the state or country under whose law the foreign corporation is incorporated stating that it has been dissolved or disappeared as the result of a merger.

§ 15.31   Procedure for and Effect of Revocation

(a) If the secretary of state determines that one or more grounds exist under section 15.30 for revocation of a certificate of authority, he shall serve the foreign corporation with written notice of his determination under section 15.10.

(b) If the foreign corporation does not correct each ground for revocation or demonstrate to the reasonable satisfaction of the secretary of state that each ground determined by the secretary of state does not exist within 60 days after service of the notice is perfected under section 15.10, the secretary of state may revoke the foreign corporation's certificate of authority by signing a certificate of revocation that recites the ground or grounds for revocation and its effective date. The secretary of state shall file the original of the certificate and serve a copy on the foreign corporation under section 15.10.

(c) The authority of a foreign corporation to transact business in this state ceases on the date shown on the certificate revoking its certificate of authority.

(d) The secretary of state's revocation of a foreign corporation's certificate of authority appoints the secretary of state the foreign corporation's agent for service of process in any proceeding based on a cause of action which arose during the time the foreign corporation was authorized to transact business in this state. Service of process on the secretary of state under this subsection is service on the foreign corporation. Upon receipt of process, the secretary of state shall mail a copy of the process to the secretary of the foreign corporation at its principal office shown in its most recent annual report or in any subsequent communication received from the corporation stating the current mailing address of its principal office, or, if none are on file, in its application for a certificate of authority.

(e) Revocation of a foreign corporation's certificate of authority does not terminate the authority of the registered agent of the corporation.

§ 15.32   Appeal From Revocation

(a) A foreign corporation may appeal the secretary of state's revocation of its certificate of authority to the [name or describe] court within 30 days after service of the certificate of revocation is perfected under section 15.10. The foreign corporation appeals by petitioning the court to set aside the revocation and attaching to the petition copies of its certificate of authority and the secretary of state's certificate of revocation.

(b) The court may summarily order the secretary of state to reinstate the certificate of authority or may take any other action the court considers appropriate.

(c) The court's final decision may be appealed as in other civil proceedings.

CHAPTER 16. Records and Reports

SUBCHAPTER A. *Records*

§ 16.01 Corporate Records

(a) A corporation shall keep as permanent records minutes of all meetings of its shareholders and board of directors, a record of all actions taken by the shareholders or board of directors without a meeting, and a record of all actions taken by a committee of the board of directors in place of the board of directors on behalf of the corporation.

(b) A corporation shall maintain appropriate accounting records.

(c) A corporation or its agent shall maintain a record of its shareholders, in a form that permits preparation of a list of the names and addresses of all shareholders, in alphabetical order by class of shares showing the number and class of shares held by each.

(d) A corporation shall maintain its records in written form or in another form capable of conversion into written form within a reasonable time.

(e) A corporation shall keep a copy of the following records at its principal office:

(1) its articles or restated articles of incorporation and all amendments to them currently in effect;

(2) its bylaws or restated bylaws and all amendments to them currently in effect;

(3) resolutions adopted by its board of directors creating one or more classes or series of shares, and fixing their relative rights, preferences, and limitations, if shares issued pursuant to those resolutions are outstanding;

(4) the minutes of all shareholders' meetings, and records of all action taken by shareholders without a meeting, for the past three years;

(5) all written communications to shareholders generally within the past three years, including the financial statements furnished for the past three years under section 16.20;

(6) a list of the names and business addresses of its current directors and officers; and

(7) its most recent annual report delivered to the secretary of state under section 16.22.

§ 16.02 Inspection of Records by Shareholders

(a) Subject to section 16.03(c), a shareholder of a corporation is entitled to inspect and copy, during regular business hours at the corporation's principal office, any of the records of the corporation described in section 16.01(e) if he gives the corporation written notice of his demand at least five business days before the date on which he wishes to inspect and copy.

(b) A shareholder of a corporation is entitled to inspect and copy, during regular business hours at a reasonable location specified by the corporation, any of the following records of the corporation if the shareholder meets the requirements of subsection (c) and gives the corporation written notice of his demand at least five business days before the date on which he wishes to inspect and copy:

(1) excerpts from minutes of any meeting of the board of directors, records of any action of a committee of the board of directors while acting in place of the board of directors on behalf of the corporation, minutes of any meeting of the shareholders, and records of action taken by the shareholders or board of directors without a meeting, to the extent not subject to inspection under section 16.02(a);

(2) accounting records of the corporation; and

(3) the record of shareholders.

(c) A shareholder may inspect and copy the records identified in subsection (b) only if:

(1) his demand is made in good faith and for a proper purpose;

(2) he describes with reasonable particularity his purpose and the records he desires to inspect; and

(3) the records are directly connected with his purpose.

(d) The right of inspection granted by this section may not be abolished or limited by a corporation's articles of incorporation or bylaws.

(e) This section does not affect:

(1) the right of a shareholder to inspect records under section 7.20 or, if the shareholder is in litigation with the corporation, to the same extent as any other litigant;

(2) the power of a court, independently of this Act, to compel the production of corporate records for examination.

§ 16.03 Scope of Inspection Right

(a) A shareholder's agent or attorney has the same inspection and copying rights as the shareholder he represents.

(b) The right to copy records under section 16.02 includes, if reasonable, the right to receive copies made by photographic, xerographic, or other means.

(c) The corporation may impose a reasonable charge,

covering the costs of labor and material, for copies of any documents provided to the shareholder. The charge may not exceed the estimated cost of production or reproduction of the records.

(d) The corporation may comply with a shareholder's demand to inspect the record of shareholders under section 16.02(b)(3) by providing him with a list of its shareholders that was complied no earlier than the date of the shareholder's demand.

§ 16.04   Court-Ordered Inspection

(a) If a corporation does not allow a shareholder who complies with section 16.02(a) to inspect and copy any records required by that subsection to be available for inspection, the [name or describe court] of the county where the corporation's principal office (or, if none in this state, its registered office) is located may summarily order inspection and copying of the records demanded at the corporation's expense upon application of the shareholder.

(b) If a corporation does not within a reasonable time allow a shareholder to inspect and copy any other record, the shareholder who complies with section 16.02(b) and (c) may apply to the [name or describe court] in the county where the corporation's principal office (or, if none in this state, its registered office) is located for an order to permit inspection and copying of the records demanded. The court shall dispose of an application under this subsection on an expedited basis.

(c) If the court orders inspection and copying of the records demanded, it shall also order the corporation to pay the shareholder's costs (including reasonable counsel fees) incurred to obtain the order unless the corporation proves that it refused inspection in good faith because it had a reasonable basis for doubt about the right of the shareholder to inspect the records demanded.

(d) If the court orders inspection and copying of the records demanded, it may impose reasonable restrictions on the use or distribution of the records by the demanding shareholder.

SUBCHAPTER B. Reports

§ 16.20   Financial Statements for Shareholders

(a) A corporation shall furnish its shareholders annual financial statements, which may be consolidated or combined statements of the corporation and one or more of its subsidiaries, as appropriate, that include a balance sheet as of the end of the fiscal year, an income statement for that year, and a statement of changes in shareholders' equity for the year unless that information appears elsewhere in the financial statements. If financial statements are prepared for the corporation on the basis of generally accepted accounting principles, the annual financial statements must also be prepared on that basis.

(b) If the annual financial statements are reported upon by a public accountant, his report must accompany them. If not, the statements must be accompanied by a statement of the president or the person responsible for the corporation's accounting records:

(1) stating his reasonable belief whether the statements were prepared on the basis of generally accepted accounting principles and, if not, describing the basis of preparation; and

(2) describing any respects in which the statements were not prepared on a basis of accounting consistent with the statements prepared for the preceding year.

(c) A corporation shall mail the annual financial statements to each shareholder within 120 days after the close of each fiscal year. Thereafter, on written request from a shareholder who was not mailed the statements, the corporation shall mail him the latest financial statements.

§ 16.21   Other Reports to Shareholders

(a) If a corporation indemnifies or advances expenses to a director under section 8.51, 8.52, 8.53, or 8.54 in connection with a proceeding by or in the right of the corporation, the corporation shall report the indemnification or advance in writing to the shareholders with or before the notice of the next shareholders' meeting.

(b) If a corporation issues or authorizes the issuance of shares for promissory notes or for promises to render services in the future, the corporation shall report in writing to the shareholders the number of shares authorized or issued, and the consideration received by the corporation, with or before the notice of the next shareholders' meeting.

§ 16.22   Annual Report for Secretary of State

(a) Each domestic corporation, and each foreign corporation authorized to transact business in this state, shall deliver to the secretary of state for filing an annual report that sets forth:

(1) the name of the corporation and the state or country under whose law it is incorporated;

(2) the address of its registered office and the name of its registered agent at that office in this state;

(3) the address of its principal office;

(4) the names and business addresses of its directors and principal officers;

(5) a brief description of the nature of its business;

(6) the total number of authorized shares, itemized by class and series, if any, within each class; and

(7) the total number of issued and outstanding shares, itemized by class and series, if any, within each class.

(b) Information in the annual report must be current as of the date the annual report is executed on behalf of the corporation.

(c) The first annual report must be delivered to the secretary of state between January 1 and April 1 of the year following the calendar year in which a domestic corporation was incorporated or a foreign corporation was authorized to transact business. Subsequent annual reports must be delivered to the secretary of state between January 1 and April 1 of the following calendar years.

(d) If an annual report does not contain the information required by this section, the secretary of state shall promptly notify the reporting domestic or foreign corporation in writing and return the report to it for correction. If the report is corrected to contain the information required by this section and delivered to the secretary of state within 30 days after the effective date of notice, it is deemed to be timely filed.

CHAPTER 17. Transition Provisions

§ 17.01 Application to Existing Domestic Corporations

This Act applies to all domestic corporations in existence on its effective date that were incorporated under any general statute of this state providing for incorporation of corporations for profit if power to amend or repeal the statute under which the corporation was incorporated was reserved.

§ 17.02 Application to Qualified Foreign Corporations

A foreign corporation authorized to transact business in this state on the effective date of this Act is subject to this Act but is not required to obtain a new certificate of authority to transact business under this Act.

§ 17.03 Saving Provisions

(a) Except as provided in subsection (b), the repeal of a statute by this Act does not affect:

(1) the operation of the statute or any action taken under it before its repeal;

(2) any ratification, right, remedy, privilege, obligation, or liability acquired, accrued, or incurred under the statute before its repeal;

(3) any violation of the statute, or any penalty, forfeiture, or punishment incurred because of the violation, before its repeal;

(4) any proceeding, reorganization, or dissolution commenced under the statute before its repeal, and the proceeding, reorganization, or dissolution may be completed in accordance with the statute as if it had not been repealed.

(b) If a penalty or punishment imposed for violation of a statute repealed by this Act is reduced by this Act, the penalty or punishment if not already imposed shall be imposed in accordance with this Act.

§ 17.04 Severability

If any provision of this Act or its application to any person or circumstance is held invalid by a court of competent jurisdiction, the invalidity does not affect other provisions or applications of the Act that can be given effect without the invalid provision or application, and to this end the provisions of the Act are severable.

§ 17.05 Repeal

The following laws and parts of laws are repealed: [to be inserted].

§ 17.06 Effective Date

This Act takes effect _____.

The Sherman Act (As Amended) (excerpts)

Section 1. Every contract, combination in the form of trust or otherwise, or conspiracy, in restraint of trade or commerce among the several States, or with foreign nations, is declared to be illegal. Every person who shall make any contract or engage in any combination or conspiracy hereby declared to be illegal shall be deemed guilty of a felony, and, on conviction thereof, shall be punished by fine not exceeding one million dollars if a corporation, or, if any other person, one hundred thousand dollars or by imprisonment not exceeding three years, or by both said punishments, in the discretion of the court.

Section 2. Every person who shall monopolize, or attempt to monopolize, or combine or conspire with any other person or persons, to monopolize any part of the trade or commerce among the several States, or with foreign nations, shall be deemed guilty of a felony, and, on conviction thereof, shall be punished by fine not exceeding one million dollars if a corporation, or, if any other person, one hundred thousand dollars or by imprisonment not exceeding three years, or by both said punishments, in the discretion of the court.

Appendix | I

The Clayton Act (As Amended) (excerpts)

Section 3. It shall be unlawful for any person engaged in commerce, in the course of such commerce, to lease or make a sale or contract for sale of goods, wares, merchandise, machinery, supplies, or other commodities, whether patented or unpatented, for use, consumption, or resale within the United States or any Territory thereof or the District of Columbia or any insular possession or other place under the jurisdiction of the United States, or fix a price charged therefor, or discount from, or rebate upon, such price, on the condition, agreement, or understanding that the lessee or purchaser thereof shall not use or deal in the goods, wares, merchandise, machinery, supplies, or other commodities of a competitor or competitors of the lessor of seller, where the effect of such lease, sale, or contract for sale or such condition, agreement, or understanding may be to substantially lessen competition or tend to create a monopoly in any line of commerce.

Section 4. Any person who shall be injured in his business or property by reason of anything forbidden in the antitrust laws may sue therefor in any district court of the United States in the district in which the defendant resides or is found or has an agent, without respect to the amount in controversy, and shall recover threefold the damages by him sustained, and the cost of suit, including a reasonable attorney's fee. . . .

Section 6. The labor of a human being is not a commodity or article of commerce. Nothing contained in the antitrust laws shall be construed to forbid the existence and operation of labor, agricultural, or horticultural organizations, instituted for the purposes of mutual help, and not having capital stock or conducted for profit, or to forbid or restrain individual members of such organizations from lawfully carrying out the legitimate objects thereof; nor shall such organizations, or the members thereof, be held or construed to be illegal combinations or conspiracies in restraint of trade, under the antitrust laws.

Section 7. No person engaged in commerce or in any activity affecting commerce shall acquire, directly or indirectly, the whole or any part of the stock or other share capital and no person subject to the jurisdiction of the Federal Trade Commission shall acquire the whole or any part of the assets of another person engaged also in commerce or in any activity affecting commerce, where in any line of commerce in any section of the country, the effect of such acquisition may be substantially to lessen competition, or to tend to create a monopoly.

No person shall acquire, directly or indirectly, the whole or any part of the stock or other share capital and no person subject to the jurisdiction of the Federal Trade Commission shall acquire the whole or any part of the assets of one or more persons engaged in commerce or in any activity affecting commerce, where in any line of commerce in any section of the country, the effect of such acquisition, of such stocks or assets, or of the use of such stock by the voting or granting of proxies or otherwise, may be substantially to lessen competition, or to tend to create a monopoly.

This section shall not apply to persons purchasing such stock solely for investment and not using the same by voting or otherwise to bring about, or in attempting to bring about, the substantial lessening of competition. . . .

Section 8. . . . [N]o person at the same time shall be a director in any two or more corporations, any one of which has capital, surplus, and undivided profits aggregating more than $1,000,000, engaged in whole or in part in commerce, . . . if such corporations are or shall have been theretofore, by virtue of their business and location of operation, competitors, so that the elimination of competition by agreement between them would constitute a violation of any of the provisions of any of the antitrust laws. . . .

Appendix | J

The Federal Trade Commission Act (excerpts)

§ Section 5

(a) (1) Unfair methods of competition in or affecting commerce, and unfair or deceptive acts or practices in or affecting commerce, are declared unlawful.

* * *

(1) Any person, partnership, or corporation who violates an order of the Commission after it has become final, and while such order is in effect, shall forfeit and pay to the United States a civil penalty of not more than $10,000 for each violation, which shall accrue to the United States and may be recovered in a civil action brought by the Attorney General of the United States. Each separate violation of such an order shall be a separate offense, except that in the case of a violation through continuing failure to obey or neglect to obey a final order of the Commission, each day of continuance of such failure or neglect shall be deemed a separate offense. In such actions, the United States district courts are empowered to grant mandatory injunctions and such other and further equitable relief as they deem appropriate in the enforcement of such final orders of the Commission.

Appendix | K

The Robinson-Patman Act (excerpts)

Section 2. (a) It shall be unlawful for any person engaged in commerce, in the course of such commerce, either directly or indirectly, to discriminate in price between different purchasers of commodities of like grade and quality, where either or any of the purchases involved in such discrimination are in commerce, where such commodities are sold for use, consumption, or resale within the United States or any Territory thereof or the District of Columbia or any insular possession or other place under the jurisdiction of the United States, and where the effect of such discrimination may be substantially to lessen competition or tend to create a monopoly in any line of commerce, or to injure, destroy, or prevent competition with any person who either grants or knowingly receives the benefit of such discrimination, or with customers of either of them: *Provided,* That nothing herein contained shall prevent differentials which make only due allowance for differences in the cost of manufacture, sale, or delivery resulting from the differing methods or quantities in which such commodities are to such purchasers sold or delivered: *Provided, however,* That the Federal Trade Commission may, after due investigation and hearing to all interested parties, fix and establish quantity limits, and revise the same as it finds necessary, as to particular commodities or classes of commodities, where it finds that available purchasers in greater quantities are so few as to render differentials on account thereof unjustly discriminatory or promotive of monopoly in any line of commerce; and the foregoing shall then not be construed to permit differentials based on differences in quantities greater than those so fixed and established: *And provided further,* That nothing herein contained shall prevent persons engaged in selling goods, wares, or merchandise in commerce from selecting their own customers in bona fide transactions and not in restraint of trade: *And provided further,* That nothing herein contained shall prevent price changes from time to time where in response to changing conditions affecting the market for or the marketability of the goods concerned, such as but not limited to actual or imminent deterioration of perishable goods, obsolescence of seasonal goods, distress sales under court process, or sales in good faith in discontinuance of business in the goods concerned.

(b) Upon proof being made, at any hearing on a complaint under this section, that there has been discrimination in price or services or facilities furnished, the burden of rebutting the prima-facie case thus made by showing justification shall be upon the person charged with a violation of this section, and unless justification shall be affirmatively shown, the Commission is authorized to issue an order terminating the discrimination: *Provided, however,* That nothing herein contained shall prevent a seller rebutting the prima-facie case thus made by showing that his lower price or the furnishing of services or facilities to any purchaser or purchasers was made in good faith to meet an equally low price of a competitor, or the services or facilities furnished by a competitor.

(c) It shall be unlawful for any person engaged in commerce, in the course of such commerce, to pay or grant, or to receive or accept, anything of value as a commission, brokerage, or other compensation, or any allowance or discount in lieu thereof, except for services rendered in connection with the sale or purchase of goods, wares, or merchandise, either to the other party to such transaction or to an agent, representative, or other intermediary therein where such intermediary is acting in fact for or in behalf, or is subject to the direct or indirect control, of any party to such transaction other than the person by whom such compensation is so granted or paid.

(d) It shall be unlawful for any person engaged in commerce to pay or contract for the payment of anything of value to or for the benefit of a customer of such person in the course of such commerce as compensation or in consideration for any services or facilities furnished by or through such customer in connection with the processing, handling, sale, or offering for sale of any products or commodities manufactured, sold, or offered for sale by such person, unless such payment or consideration is available on proportionally equal terms to all other customers competing in the distribution of such products or commodities.

(e) It shall be unlawful for any person to discriminate in favor of one purchaser against another purchaser or purchasers of a commodity bought for resale, with or without processing, by contracting to furnish or furnishing, or by contributing to the furnishing of, any services or facilities connected with the processing, handling, sale, or offering for sale of such commodity so purchased upon terms not accorded to all purchasers on proportionally equal terms.

(f) It shall be unlawful for any person engaged in commerce, in the course of such commerce, knowingly to induce or receive a discrimination in price which is prohibited by this section.

Appendix L

The Foreign Corrupt Practices Act

An Act to amend the Securities Exchange Act of 1934 to make it unlawful for an issuer of securities registered pursuant to section 12 of such Act or an issuer required to file reports pursuant to section 15(d) of such Act to make certain payments to foreign officials and other foreign persons, to require such issuers to maintain accurate records, and for other purposes.

Be it enacted by the Senate and House of Representatives of the United States of America in Congress assembled,

TITLE I—FOREIGN CORRUPT PRACTICES

Short Title

Sec. 101. This title may be cited as the "Foreign Corrupt Practices Act of 1977".

Accounting Standards

Sec. 102. Section 13(b) of the Securities Exchange Act of 1934 (15 U.S.C. 78q(b)) is amended by inserting "(1)" after "(b)" and by adding at the end thereof the following:

"(2) Every issuer which has a class of securities registered pursuant to section 12 of this title and every issuer which is required to file reports pursuant to section 15(d) of this title shall—

"(A) make and keep books, records, and accounts, which, in reasonable detail, accurately and fairly reflect the transactions and dispositions of the assets of the issuer; and

"(B) devise and maintain a system of internal accounting controls sufficient to provide reasonable assurances that—

"(i) transactions are executed in accordance with management's general or specific authorization;

"(ii) transactions are recorded as necessary (I) to permit preparation of financial statements in conformity with generally accepted accounting principles or any other criteria applicable to such statements, and (II) to maintain accountability for assets;

"(iii) access to assets is permitted only in accordance with management's general or specific authorization; and

"(iv) the recorded accountability for assets is compared with the existing assets at reasonable intervals and appropriate action is taken with respect to any differences.

"(3)(A) With respect to matters concerning the national security of the United States, no duty or liability under paragraph (2) of this subsection shall be imposed upon any person acting in cooperation with the head of any Federal department or agency responsible for such matters if such act in cooperation with such head of a department or agency was done upon the specific, written directive of the head of such department or agency pursuant to Presidential authority to issue such directives. Each directive issued under this paragraph shall set forth the specific facts and circumstances with respect to which the provisions of this paragraph are to be invoked. Each such directive shall, unless renewed in writing, expire one year after the date of issuance.

"(B) Each head of a Federal department or agency of the United States who issues a directive pursuant to this paragraph shall maintain a complete file of all such directives and shall, on October 1 of each year, transmit a summary of matters covered by such directives in force at any time during the previous year to the Permanent Select Committee on Intelligence of the House of Representatives and the Select Committee on Intelligence of the Senate.".

Foreign Corrupt Practices By Issuers

Sec. 103. (a) The Securities Exchange Act of 1934 is amended by inserting after section 30 the following new section:

"Foreign Corrupt Practices By Issuers

"Sec. 30A. (a) It shall be unlawful for any issuer which has a class of securities registered pursuant to section 12 of this title or which is required to file reports under section 15(d) of this title, or for any officer, director, employee, or agent of such issuer or any stockholder thereof acting on behalf of such issuer, to make use of the mails or any means or instrumentality of interstate commerce corruptly in furtherance of an offer, payment, promise to pay, or authorization of the payment of any money, or offer, gift, promise to give, or authorization of the giving of anything of value to—

"(1) any foreign official for purposes of—

"(A) influencing any act or decision of such foreign official in his official capacity, including a decision to fail to perform his official functions; or

"(B) inducing such foreign official to use his influence with a foreign government or instrumentality thereof to affect or influence any act or decision of such government or instrumentality,

in order to assist such issuer in obtaining or retaining business for or with, or directing business to, any person;

"(2) any foreign political party or official thereof or any candidate for foreign political office for purposes of—

"(A) influencing any act or decision of such party, official, or candidate in its or his official capacity, including a decision to fail to perform its or his official functions: or

"(B) inducing such party, official, or candidate to use its or his influence with a foreign government or instrumentality thereof to affect or influence any act or decision of such government or instrumentality,

in order to assist such issuer in obtaining or retaining business for or with, or directing business to, any person; or

"(3) any person, while knowing or having reason to know that all or a portion of such money or thing of value will be offered, given, or promised, directly or indirectly, to any foreign official, to any foreign political paty or official thereof, or to any candidate for foreign political office, for purposes of—

"(A) influencing any act or decision of such foreign official, political party, party official, or candidate in his or its official capacity, including a decision to fail to perform his or its official functions; or

"(B) inducing such foreign official, political party, party official, or candidate to use his or its influence with a foreign government or instrumentality thereof to affect or influence any act or decision of such government or instrumentality, in order to assist such issuer in obtaining or retaining business for or with, or directing business to, any person.

"(b) As used in this section, the term 'foreign official' means any officer or employee of a foreign government or any department, agency, or instrumentality thereof, or any person acting in an official capacity for or on behalf of such government or department, agency, or instrumentality. Such term does not include any employee of a foreign government or any department, agency, or instrumentality thereof whose duties are essentially ministerial or clerical.".

(b)(1) Section 32(a) of the Securities Exchange Act of 1934 (15 U.S.C. 78ff(a)) is amended by inserting "(other than section 30A)" immediately after "title" the first place it appears.

(2) Section 32 of the Securities Exchange Act of 1934 (15 U.S.C. 78ff) is amended by adding at the end thereof the following new subsection:

"(c)(1) Any issuer which violates section 30A(a) of this title shall, upon conviction, be fined not more than $1,000,000.

"(2) Any officer or director of an issuer, or any stockholder acting on behalf of such issuer, who willfully violates section 30A(a) of this title shall, upon conviction, be fined not more than $10,000, or imprisoned not more than five years, or both.

"(3) Whenever an issuer is found to have violated section 30A(a) of this title, any employee or agent of such issuer who is a United States citizen, national, or resident or is otherwise subject to the jurisdiction of the United States (other than an officer, director, or stockholder of such issuer), and who willfully carried out the act or practice constituting such violation shall, upon conviction, be fined not more than $10,000, or imprisoned not more than five years, or both.

"(4) Whenever a fine is imposed under paragraph (2) or (3) of this subsection upon any officer, director, stockholder, employee, or agent of an issuer, such fine shall not be paid, directly or indirectly by such issuer".

Foreign Corrupt Practices By Domestic Concerns

Sec. 104. (a) It shall be unlawful for any domestic concern, other than an issuer which is subject to section 30A of the Securities Exchange Act of 1934, or any officer, director, employee, or agent of such domestic concern or any stockholder thereof acting on behalf of such domestic concern, to make use of the mails or any means or instrumentality of interstate commerce corruptly in furtherance of an offer, payment, promise to pay, or authorization of the payment of any money, or offer, gift, promise to give, or authorization of the giving of anything of value to—

(1) any foreign official for purposes of—

(A) influencing any act or decision of such foreign official in his official capacity, including a decision to fail to perform his official functions; or

(B) inducing such foreign official to use his influence with a foreign government or instrumentality thereof to affect or influence any act or decision of such government or instrumentality,

in order to assist such domestic concern in obtaining or retaining business for or with, or directing business to, any person;

(2) any foreign political party or official thereof or any candidate for foreign political office for purposes of—

(A) influencing any act or decision of such party, official, or candidate in its or his official capacity, including a decision to fail to perform its or his official functions; or

(B) inducing such party, official, or candidate to use its or his influence with a foreign government or instrumentality thereof to affect or influence any act or decision of such government or instrumentality,

in order to assist such domestic concern in obtaining or retaining business for or with, or directing business to, any person; or

(3) any person, while knowing or having reason to know that all or a portion of such money or thing of value will be offered, given, or promised, directly or indirectly, to any foreign official, to any foreign political party or official thereof, or to any candidate for foreign political office, for purposes of—

(A) influencing any act or decision of such foreign official, political party, party official, or candidate in his or its official capacity, including a decision to fail to perform his or its official functions; or

(B) inducing such foreign official, political party, party official, or candidate to use his or its influence with a foreign government or instrumentality thereof to affect or influence any act or decision of such government or instrumentality,

in order to assist such domestic concern in obtaining or retaining business for or with, or directing business to, any person.

(b)(1)(A) Except as provided in subparagraph (B), any domestic concern which violates subsection (a) shall, upon conviction, be fined not more than $1,000,000.

(B) Any individual who is a domestic concern and who willfully violates subsection (a) shall, upon conviction, be fined not more than $10,000, or imprisoned not more than five years, or both.

(2) Any officer or director of a domestic concern, or stockholder acting on behalf of such domestic concern, who willfully violates subsection (a) shall, upon conviction, be fined not more than $10,000, or imprisoned not more than five years, or both.

(3) Whenever a domestic concern is found to have violated subsection (a) of this section, any employee or agent of such domestic concern who is a United States citizen, national, or resident or is otherwise subject to the jurisdiction of the United States (other than an officer, director, or stockholder acting on behalf of such domestic concern), and who willfully carried out the act or practice constituting such violation shall, upon conviction, be fined not more than $10,000, or imprisoned not more than five years, or both.

(4) Whenever a fine is imposed under paragraph (2) or (3) of this subsection upon any officer, director, stockholder, employee, or agent of a domestic concern, such fine shall not be paid, directly or indirectly, by such domestic concern.

(c) Whenever it appears to the Attorney General that any domestic concern, or officer, director, employee, agent, or stockholder thereof, is engaged, or is about to engage, in any act or practice constituting a violation of subsection (a) of this section, the Attorney General may, in his discretion, bring a civil action in an appropriate district court of the United States to enjoin such act or practice, and upon a proper showing a permanent or temporary injunction or a temporary restraining order shall be granted without bond.

(d) As used in this section:

(1) The term "domestic concern" means (A) any individual who is a citizen, national, or resident of the United States; or (B) any corporation, partnership, association, joint-stock company, business trust, unincorporated organization, or sole proprietorship which has its principal place of business in the United States, or which is organized under the laws of a State of the United States or a territory, possession, or commonwealth of the United States.

(2) The term "foreign official" means any officer or employee of a foreign government or any department, agency, or instrumentality thereof, or any person acting in an official capacity for or on behalf of any such government or department, agency, or instrumentality. Such term does not include any employee of a foreign government or any department, agency, or instrumen-

tality thereof whose duties are essentially ministerial or clerical.

(3) The term "interstate commerce" means trade, commerce, transportation, or communication among the several States, or between any foreign country and any State or between any State and any place or ship outside thereof. Such term includes the intrastate use of (A) a telephone or other interstate means of communication, or (B) any other interstate instrumentality.

TITLE II—DISCLOSURE

Sec. 201. This title may be cited as the "Domestic and Foreign Investment Improved Disclosure Act of 1977".

Sec. 202. Section 13(d)(1) of the Securities Exchange Act of 1934 (15 U.S.C. 78m) is amended to read as follows:

"(d)(1) Any person who, after acquiring directly or indirectly the beneficial ownership of any equity security of a class which is registered pursuant to section 12 of this title, or any equity security of an insurance company which would have been required to be so registered except for the exemption contained in section 12(g)(2)(G) of this title, or any equity security issued by a closed-end investment company registered under the Investment Company Act of 1940, is directly or indirectly the beneficial owner of more than 5 per centum of such class shall, within ten days after such acquisition, send to the issuer of the security at its principal executive office, by registered or certified mail, send to each exchange where the security is traded, and file with the Commission, a statement containing such of the following information, and such additional information, as the Commission may by rules and regulations, prescribe as necessary or appropriate in the public interest or for the protection of investors—

"(A) the background, and identity, residence, and citizenship of, and the nature of such beneficial ownership by, such person and all other persons by whom or on whose behalf the purchases have been or are to be effected;

"(B) the source and amount of the funds or other consideration used or to be used in making the purchases, and if any part of the purchase price is represented or is to be represented by funds or other consideration borrowed or otherwise obtained for the purpose of acquiring, holding, or trading such security, a description of the transaction and the names of the parties thereto, except that where a source of funds is a loan made in the ordinary course of business by a bank, as defined in section 3(a)(6) of this title, if the person filing such statement so requests, the name of the bank shall not be made available to the public;

"(C) if the purpose of the purchases or prospective purchases is to acquire control of the business of the issuer of the securities, any plans or proposals which such persons may have to liquidate such issuer, to sell its assets to or merge it with any other persons, or to make any other major change in its business or corporate structure;

"(D) the number of shares of such security which are beneficially owned, and the number of shares concerning which there is a right to acquire, directly or indirectly, by (i) such person, and (ii) by each associate of such person, giving the background, identity, residence, and citizenship of each such associate; and

"(E) information as to any contracts, arrangements, or understandings with any person with respect to any securities of the issuer, including but not limited to transfer of any of the securities, joint ventures, loan or option arrangements, puts or calls, guaranties of loans, guaranties against loss or guaranties of profits, division of losses or profits, or the giving or withholding of proxies, naming the persons with whom such contracts, arrangements, or understandings have been entered into, and giving the details thereof.".

Sec. 203. Section 13 of the Securities Exchange Act of 1934, as amended (15 U.S.C. 78m), is amended by adding at the end thereof the following new subsection:

"(g)(1) Any person who is directly or indirectly the beneficial owner of more than 5 per centum of any security of a class described in subsection (d)(1) of this section shall send to the issuer of the security and shall file with the Commission a statement setting forth, in such form and at such time as the Commission may, by rule, prescribe—

"(A) such person's identity, residence, and citizenship; and

"(B) the number and description of the shares in which such person has an interest and the nature of such interest.

"(2) If any material change occurs in the facts set forth in the statement sent to the issuer and filed with the Commission, an amendment shall be transmitted to the issuer and shall be filed with the Commission, in accordance with such rules and regulations as the Com-

mission may prescribe as necessary or appropriate in the public interest or for the protection of investors.

"(3) When two or more persons act as a partnership, limited partnership, syndicate, or other group for the purpose of acquiring, holding, or disposing of securities of an issuer, such syndicate or group shall be deemed a 'person' for the purposes of this subsection.

"(4) In determining, for purposes of this subsection, any percentage of a class of any security, such class shall be deemed to consist of the amount of the outstanding securities of such class, exclusive of any securities of such class held by or for the account of the issuer or a subsidiary of the issuer.

"(5) In exercising its authority under this subsection, the Commission shall take such steps as it deems necessary or appropriate in the public interest or for the protection of investors (A) to achieve centralized reporting of information regarding ownership, (B) to avoid unnecessarily duplicative reporting by and minimize the compliance burden on persons required to report, and (C) to tabulate and promptly make available the information contained in any report filed pursuant to this subsection in a manner which will, in the view of the Commission, maximize the usefulness of the information to other Federal and State agencies and the public.

"(6) The Commission may, by rule or order, exempt, in whole or in part, any person or class of persons from any or all of the reporting requirements of this subsection as it deems necessary or appropriate in the public interest or for the protection of investors.

"(h) The Commission shall report to the Congress within thirty months of the date of enactment of this subsection with respect to (1) the effectiveness of the ownership reporting requirements contained in this title, and (2) the desirability and the feasibility of reducing or otherwise modifying the 5 per centum threshold used in subsections (d)(1) and (g)(1) of this section, giving appropriate consideration to—

"(A) the incidence of avoidance of reporting by beneficial owners using multiple holders of record;

"(B) the cost of compliance to persons required to report;

"(C) the cost to issuers and others of processing and disseminating the reported information;

"(D) the effect of such action on the securities markets, including the system for the clearance and settlement of securities transactions;

"(E) the benefits to investors and to the public;

"(F) any bona fide interests of individuals in the privacy of their financial affairs;

"(G) the extent to which such reported information gives or would give any person an undue advantage in connection with activities subject to sections 13(d) and 14(d) of this title:

"(H) the need for such information in connection with the administration and enforcement of this title; and

"(I) such other matters as the Commission may deem relevant, including the information obtained pursuant to section 13(f) of this title.".

Sec. 204. Section 15(d) of the Securities Exchange Act of 1934 is amended by inserting immediately before the last sentence the following new sentence: "The Commission may, for the purpose of this subsection, define by rules and regulations the term 'held of record' as it deems necessary or appropriate in the public interest or for the protection of investors in order to prevent circumvention of the provisions of this subsection.".

Approved December 19, 1977.

The National Labor Relations Act (As Amended) (excerpts)

Section 7. Employees shall have the right to self-organization, to form, join, or assist labor organizations, to bargain collectively through representatives of their own choosing, and to engage in other concerted activities for the purpose of collective bargaining or other mutual aid or protection, and shall also have the right to refrain from any or all of such activities except to the extent that such right may be affected by an agreement requiring membership in a labor organization as a condition of employment as authorized in section 8(a)(3).

Section 8. (a) It shall be an unfair labor practice for an employer—

(1) to interfere with, restrain, or coerce employees in the exercise of the rights guaranteed in section 7;

(2) to dominate or interfere with the formation or administration of any labor organization or contribute financial or other support to it: *Provided,* That subject to rules and regulations made and published by the Board pursuant to section 6, an employer shall not be prohibited from permitting employees to confer with him during working hours without loss of time or pay;

(3) by discrimination in regard to hire or tenure of employment or any term or condition of employment to encourage or discourage membership in any labor organization: *Provided,* That nothing in this Act, or in any other statute of the United States, shall preclude an employer from making an agreement with a labor organization (not established, maintained, or assisted by any action defined in section 8(a) of this Act as an unfair labor practice) to require as a condition of employment membership therein on or after the thirtieth day following the beginning of such employment or the effective date of such agreement, whichever is the later, (i) if such labor organization is the representative of the employees as provided in section 9(a), in the appropriate collective-bargaining unit covered by such agree-

ment when made, and (ii) unless following an election held as provided in section 9(e) within one year preceding the effective date of such agreement, the Board shall have certified that at least a majority of the employees eligible to vote in such election have voted to rescind the authority of such labor organization to make such an agreement: *Provided further,* That no employer shall justify any discrimination against an employee for non-membership in a labor organization (A) if he has reasonable grounds for believing that such membership was not available to the employee on the same terms and conditions generally applicable to other members, or (B) if he has reasonable grounds for believing that membership was denied or terminated for reasons other than the failure of the employee to tender the periodic dues and the initiation fees uniformly required as a condition of acquiring or retaining membership;

(4) to discharge or otherwise discriminate against an employee because he has filed charges or given testimony under this Act;

(5) to refuse to bargain collectively with the representatives of his employees, subject to the provisions of section 9(a).

(b) It shall be an unfair labor practice for a labor organization or its agents—

(1) to restrain or coerce (A) employees in the exercise of the rights guaranteed in section 7: *Provided,* That this paragraph shall not impair the right of a labor organization to prescribe its own rules with respect to the acquisition or retention of membership therein; or (B) an employer in the selection of his representatives for the purposes of collective bargaining or the adjustment of grievances;

(2) to cause or attempt to cause an employer to discriminate against an employee in violation of subsection (a)(3) or to discriminate against an employee with respect to whom membership in such organization has been denied or terminated on some ground other than his failure to tender the periodic dues and the initiation fees uniformerly required as a condition of acquiring or retaining membership;

(3) to refuse to bargain collectively with an employer, provided it is the representative of his employees subject to the provisions of section 9(a);

(4)(i) to engage in, or to induce or encourage any individual employed by any person engaged in commerce or in an industry affecting commerce to engage in, a strike or a refusal in the course of his employment to use, manufacture, process, transport, or otherwise handle or work on any goods, articles, materials, or commodities or to perform any services; or (ii) to threaten, coerce, or restrain any person engaged in commerce or in an industry affecting commerce, where in either case an object thereof is:

(A) forcing or requiring any employer or self-employed person to join any labor or employer organization or to enter into any agreement which is prohibited by section 8(e);

(B) forcing or requiring any person to cease using, selling, handling, transporting, or otherwise dealing in the products of any other producer, processor, or manufacturer, to cease doing business with any other person, or forcing or requiring any other employer to recognize or bargain with a labor organization as the representative of his employees unless such labor organization has been certified as the representative of such employees under the provisions of section 9: *Provided,* That nothing contained in this clause (B) shall be construed to make unlawful, where not otherwise unlawful, any primary strike or primary picketing;

(C) forcing or requiring any employer to recognize or bargain with a particular labor organization as the representative of his employees if another labor organization has been certified as the representative of such employees under the provisions of section 9;

(D) forcing or requiring any employer to assign particular work to employees in a particular labor organization or in a particular trade, craft, or class rather than to employees in another labor organization or in another trade, craft, or class, unless such employer is failing to conform to an order or certification of the Board determining the bargaining representative for employees performing such work:
Provided, That nothing contained in this subsection (b) shall be construed to make unlawful a refusal by any person to enter upon the premises of any employer (other than his own employer), if the employees of such employer are engaged in a strike ratified or approved by a representative of such employees whom such employer is required to recognize under this Act: *Provided further,* That for the purposes of this paragraph (4) only, nothing contained in such paragraph shall be construed to prohibit publicity, other than picketing, for the purpose of truthfully advising the public, including consumers and members of a labor organization, that a product or products are produced by an employer with whom the labor organization has a primary dispute and are distributed by another employer,

as long as such publicity does not have an effect of inducing any individual employed by any person other than the primary employer in the course of his employment to refuse to pick up, deliver, or transport any goods, or not to perform any services, at the establishment of the employer engaged in such distribution;

(5) to require of employees covered by an agreement authorized under subsection (a)(3) the payment, as a condition precedent to becoming a member of such organization, of a fee in an amount which the Board finds excessive or discriminatory under all the circumstances. In making such a finding, the Board shall consider, among other relevant factors, the practices and customs of labor organizations in the particular industry, and the wages currently paid to the employees affected;

(6) to cause or attempt to cause an employer to pay or deliver or agree to pay or deliver any money or other thing of value, in the nature of an exaction, for services which are not performed or not to be performed; and

(7) to picket or cause to be picketed, or threaten to picket or cause to be picketed, any employer where an object thereof is forcing or requiring an employer to recognize or bargain with a labor organization as the representative of his employees, or forcing or requiring the employees of an employer to accept or select such labor organization as their collective bargaining representative, unless such labor organization is currently certified as the representative of such employees:

(A) where the employer has lawfully recognized in accordance with this Act any other labor organization and a question concerning representation may not appropriately be raised under section 9(c) of this Act,

(B) where within the preceding twelve months a valid election under section 9(c) of this Act has been conducted, or

(C) where such picketing has been conducted without a petition under section 9(c) being filed within a reasonable period of time not to exceed thirty days from the commencement of such picketing: *Provided,* That when such a petition has been filed the Board shall forthwith, without regard to the provisions of section 9(c)(1) or the absence of a showing of a substantial interest on the part of the labor organization, direct an election in such unit as the Board finds to be appropriate and shall certify the results thereof: *Provided further,* That nothing in this subparagraph (C) shall be construed to prohibit any picketing or other publicity for the purpose of truthfully advising the public (including

consumers) that an employer does not employ members of, or have a contract with, a labor organization, unless an effect of such picketing is to induce any individual employed by any other person in the course of his employment, not to pick up, deliver or transport any goods or not to perform any services.

Nothing in this paragraph (7) shall be construed to permit any act which would otherwise be an unfair labor practice under this section 8(b).

(c) The expressing of any views, argument, or opinion, or the dissemination thereof, whether in written, printed, graphic, or visual form, shall not constitute or be evidence of an unfair labor practice under any of the provisions of this Act, if such expression contains no threat of reprisal or force or promise of benefit.

(d) For the purposes of this section, to bargain collectively is the performance of the mutual obligation of the employer and the representative of the employees to meet at reasonable times and confer in good faith with respect to wages, hours, and other terms and conditions of employment, or the negotiation of an agreement, or any question arising thereunder, and the execution of a written contract incorporating any agreement reached if requested by either party, but such obligation does not compel either party to agree to a proposal or require the making of a concession: *Provided,* That where there is in effect a collective-bargaining contract covering employees in an industry affecting commerce, the duty to bargain collectively shall also mean that no party to such contract shall terminate or modify such contract, unless the party desiring such termination or modification—

(1) serves a written notice upon the other party to the contract of the proposed termination or modification sixty days prior to the expiration date thereof, or in the event such contract contains no expiration date, sixty days prior to the time it is proposed to make such termination or modification;

(2) offers to meet and confer with the other party for the purpose of negotiating a new contract or a contract containing the proposed modifications;

(3) notifies the Federal Mediation and Conciliation Service within thirty days after such notice of the existence of a dispute, and simultaneously therewith notifies any State or Territorial agency established to mediate and conciliate disputes within the State or Territory where the dispute occurred, provided no agreement has been reached by that time; and

(4) continues in full force and effect, without resort-

ing to strike or lockout, all the terms and conditions of the existing contract for a period of sixty days after such notice is given or until the expiration date of such contract, whichever occurs later:

The duties imposed upon employers, employees, and labor organizations by paragraphs (2), (3), and (4) shall become inapplicable upon an intervening certification of the Board, under which the labor organization or individual, which is a party to the contract, has been superseded as or ceased to be the representative of the employees subject to the provisions of section 9(a), and the duties so imposed shall not be construed as requiring either party to discuss or agree to any modification of the terms and conditions contained in a contract for a fixed period, if such modification is to become effective before such terms and conditions can be reopened under the provisions of the contract. Any employee who engages in a strike within any notice period specified in this subsection, or who engages in any strike within the appropriate period specified in subsection (g) of this section shall lose his status as an employee of the employer engaged in the particular labor dispute, for the purposes of sections 8, 9, and 10 of this Act, as amended, but such loss of status for such employee shall terminate if and when he is reemployed by such employer. Whenever the collective bargaining involves employees of a health care institution, the provisions of this section 8(d) shall be modified as follows:

(A) The notice of section 8(d)(1) shall be ninety days; the notice of section 8(d)(3) shall be sixty days; and the contract period of section 8(d)(4) shall be ninety days;

(B) Where the bargaining is for an initial agreement following certification or recognition, at least thirty days' notice of the existence of a dispute shall be given by the labor organization to the agencies set forth in section 8(d)(3).

(C) After notice is given to the Federal Mediation and Conciliation Service under either clause (A) or (B) of this sentence, the Service shall promptly communicate with the parties and use its best efforts, by mediation and conciliation, to bring them to agreement. The parties shall participate fully and promptly in such meetings as may be undertaken by the Service for the purpose of aiding in a settlement of the dispute.

(e) It shall be an unfair labor practice for any labor organization and any employer to enter into any contract or agreement, express or implied, whereby such employer ceases or refrains or agrees to cease or refrain from handling, using, selling, transporting or otherwise dealing in any of the products of any other employer, or to cease doing business with any other person, and any contract or agreement entered into heretofore or hereafter containing such an agreement shall be to such extent unenforceable and void: *Provided,* That nothing in this subsection (e) shall apply to an agreement between a labor organization and an employer in the construction industry relating to the contracting or subcontracting of work to be done at the site of the construction, alteration, painting, or repair of a building, structure, or other work: *Provided further,* That for the purposes of this subsection (e) and section 8(b)(4)(B) the terms "any employer", "any person engaged in commerce or in industry affecting commerce", and "any person" when used in relation to the terms "any other producer, processor, or manufacturer", "any other employer", or "any other person" shall not include persons in the relation of a jobber, manufacturer, contractor, or subcontractor working on the goods or premises of the jobber or manufacturer or performing parts of an integrated process of production in the apparel and clothing industry: *Provided further,* That nothing in this Act shall prohibit the enforcement of any agreement which is within the foregoing exception.

(f) It shall not be unfair labor practice under subsections (a) and (b) of this section for an employer engaged primarily in the building and construction industry to make an agreement covering employees engaged (or who, upon their employment, will be engaged) in the building and construction industry with a labor organization of which building and construction employees are members (not established, maintained, or assisted by any action defined in section 8(a) of this Act as an unfair labor practice) because (1) the majority status of such labor organization has not been established under the provisions of section 9 of this Act prior to the making of such agreement, or (2) such agreement requires as a condition of employment, membership in such labor organization after the seventh day following the beginning of such employment or the effective date of the agreement, whichever is later, or (3) such agreement requires the employer to notify such labor organization of opportunities for employment with such employer, or gives such labor organization an opportunity to refer qualified applicants for such employment, or (4) such agreement specifies minimum training or experience qualifications for employment or provides for priority in opportunities for employment based upon length of service with such employer, in the industry or in the particular geographical area: *Provided,* That nothing in this subsection shall set aside the final proviso to section 8(a)(3) of this Act: *Provided further,* That any agreement which would be invalid, but for clause (1) of this subsection, shall not be a bar to a petition filed pursuant to section 9(c) or 9(e).

(g) A labor organization before engaging in any strike, picketing, or other concerted refusal to work at any health care institution shall, not less than ten days prior to such action, notify the institution in writing and the Federal Mediation and Conciliation Service of that intention, except that in the case of bargaining for an initial agreement following certification or recognition the notice required by this subsection shall not be given until the expiration of the period specified in clause (B) of the last sentence of section 8(d) of this Act. The notice shall state the date and time that such action will commence. The notice, once given, may be extended by the written agreement of both parties.

Section 9. (a) Representatives designated or selected for the purposes of collective bargaining by the majority of the employees in a unit appropriate for such purposes, shall be the exclusive representatives of all the employees in such unit for the purposes of collective bargaining in respect to rates of pay, wages, hours of employment, or other conditions of employment: *Provided,* That any individual employee or a group of employees shall have the right at any time to present grievances to their employer and to have such grievances adjusted, without the intervention of the bargaining representative, as long as the adjustment is not inconsistent with the terms of a collective-bargaining contract or agreement then in effect: *Provided further,* That the bargaining representative has been given opportunity to be present at such adjustment.

(b) The Board shall decide in each case whether, in order to assure to employees the fullest freedom in exercising the rights guaranteed by this Act, the unit appropriate for the purposes of collective bargaining shall be the employer unit, craft unit, plant unit, or subdivision thereof: *Provided,* That the Board shall not (1) decide that any unit is appropriate for such purposes if such unit includes both professional employees and employees who are not professional employees unless a majority of such professional employees vote for inclusion in such unit; or (2) decide that any craft unit is inappropriate for such purposes on the ground that a different unit has been established by a prior Board

determination, unless a majority of the employees in the proposed craft unit vote against separate representation or (3) decide that any unit is appropriate for such purposes if it includes, together with other employees, any individual employed as a guard to enforce against employees and other persons rules to protect property of the employer or to protect the safety of persons on the employer's premises; but no labor organization shall be certified as the representative of employees in a bargaining unit of guards if such organization admits to membership, or is affiliated directly or indirectly with an organization which admits to membership, employees other than guards.

(c)(1) Wherever a petition shall have been filed, in accordance with such regulations as may be prescribed by the Board—

(A) by an employee or group of employees or an individual or labor organization acting in their behalf alleging that a substantial number of employees (i) wish to be represented for collective bargaining and that their employer declines to recognize their representative as the representative defined in section 9(a), or (ii) assert that the individual or labor organization, which has been certified or is being currently recognized by their employer as the bargaining representative, is no longer a representative as defined in section 9(a); or

(B) by an employer, alleging that one or more individuals or labor organizations have presented to him a claim to be recognized as the representative defined in section 9(a);

the Board shall investigate such petition and if it has reasonable cause to believe that a question of representation affecting commerce exists shall provide for an appropriate hearing upon due notice. Such hearing may be conducted by an officer or employee of the regional office, who shall not make any recommendations with respect thereto. If the Board finds upon the record of such hearing that such a question of representation exists, it shall direct an election by secret ballot and shall certify the results thereof.

(2) In determining whether or not a question of representation affecting commerce exists, the same regulations and rules of decision shall apply irrespective of the identity of the persons filing the petition or the kind of relief sought and in no case shall the Board deny a labor organization a place on the ballot by reason of an order with respect to such labor organization or its predecessor not issued in conformity with section 10(c).

(3) No election shall be directed in any bargaining unit or any subdivision within which, in the preceding twelve-month period, a valid election shall have been held. Employees engaged in an economic strike who are not entitled to reinstatement shall be eligible to vote under such regulations as the Board shall find are consistent with the purposes and provisions of this Act in any election conducted within twelve months after the commencement of the strike. In any election where none of the choices on the ballot receives a majority, a run-off shall be conducted, the ballot providing for a selection between the two choices receiving the largest and second largest number of valid votes cast in the election.

(4) Nothing in this section shall be construed to prohibit the waiving of hearings by stipulation for the purpose of a consent election in conformity with regulations and rules of decision of the Board.

(5) In determining whether a unit is appropriate for the purposes specified in subsection (b) the extent to which the employees have organized shall not be controlling.

(d) Whenever an order of the Board made pursuant to section 10(c) is based in whole or in part upon facts certified following an investigation pursuant to subsection (c) of this section and there is a petition for the enforcement or review of such order, such certification and the record of such investigation shall be included in the transcript of the entire record required to be filed under section 10(e) or 10(f), and thereupon the decree of the court enforcing, modifying, or setting aside in whole or in part the order of the Board shall be made and entered upon the pleadings, testimony, and proceedings set forth in such transcript.

(e)(1) Upon the filing with the Board, by 30 per centum or more of the employees in a bargaining unit covered by an agreement between their employer and a labor organization made pursuant to section 8(a)(3), of a petition alleging they desire that such authority be rescinded, the Board shall take a secret ballot of the employees in such unit and certify the results thereof to such labor organization and to the employer.

(2) No election shall be conducted pursuant to this subsection in any bargaining unit or any subdivision within which, in the preceding twelve-month period, a valid election shall have been held.

Section 14. . . . (b) Nothing in this Act shall be construed as authorizing the execution or application of agreements requiring membership in a labor organization as a condition of employment in any State or Territory in which such execution or application is prohibited by State or Territorial law.

Glossary

administrative agency. An organ of government, usually created by statute, sometimes by constitutional provision or executive order, charged with the administration of particular legislation or some other administrative function.

administrative law judge (ALJ). The presiding officer at initial hearings involving litigation in administrative agencies; a quasi-judge presiding at quasi-judicial hearings before an agency.

administrative rule. Similar to a statute, but promulgated by an administrative agency functioning in its quasi-legislative capacity.

administrator. Broadly, an officer of the executive branch of government, particularly an administrative agency. In probate law, a man selected by a court to carry out the wishes of a testator under a will.

administratrix. A female administrator.

adversary system. A concept underlying the American legal system that opposing parties in a transaction or litigation will look out for their own best interests, and not those of the other party.

adverse possession. A method of acquiring title to property by possessing it for a certain statutory period as a trespasser, and meeting certain other conditions.

affidavit. A written statement sworn to and signed before a person authorized to swear a person to an oath.

affirmative action. In civil rights law, going beyond providing equal opportunity, and including actively seeking women and minorities for employment or other opportunities.

affirmative defense. A new defense asserted by a defendant in a lawsuit in addition to a denial of facts stated in the complaint, such as contributory negligence of the plaintiff in a negligence action.

affirmative easement. An easement or non-possessory right, granted by the owner of property to another, permitting the other to use the property of the grantor for specific purposes, such as walking across it.

after-acquired property. Property subject to a security interest although acquired by the debtor after the security interest was granted, but provided for in the granting of the security interest.

agency coupled with an interest. Agency power granted by a principal to an agent to secure some obligation owed by the principal, such as the power granted by a debtor to a creditor to sell property pledged to secure a loan if the loan is not paid when due.

agency shop. A union security clause providing that all members of a bargaining unit must pay a set fee for representation, either by way of membership dues or an affiliation fee in the case of a non-member.

agent. Broadly, one who provides services to another in an agency relationship. More specifically, one employed by a principal to alter the principal's contractual affairs with third parties.

aggregate theory. In business organizations law, the theory that a business has no independent existence separate from its owners, as opposed to the entity theory.

aleatory promise. A promise conditioned on an uncertain event other than performance by the other party (e.g., a promise to pay an insurance premium is not conditioned on performance of an act by the insurance company).

alien corporation. A corporation incorporated under the laws of a foreign country.

allonge. A second document, executed in testamentary form, amending a previous will.

answer. In civil pleading, the defendant's response to a complaint, admitting and denying certain allegations in the complaint, and stating that the defendant is without information as to others.

anticipatory breach. Words or conduct by a promisor that evidence the promisor will breach his obligation in the future when performance of the obligation becomes due.

antitrust law.   A body of law seeking to preserve free and open competition in the marketplace by prohibiting and controlling concentrations of market power.

apparent (ostensible) authority.   Authority that a principal, by words or conduct, leads a third party to believe his agent has.

appeal.   A review, by an upper court, of a decision of a lower court or an administrative agency. This type of review extends to decisions of both law and fact.

appellate jurisdiction.   Jurisdiction to review the decision of a lower court or an administrative agency (as opposed to original jurisdiction).

appraisal remedy.   A remedy available to a dissenting shareholder in circumstances of a forced sale of his shares, ordering that the value of the shares to be sold will be determined by disinterested persons.

arbitration.   A private means of resolving a dispute under which the parties select a neutral person to hear and decide the controversy much in the manner of a court. The decision of the arbitrator is binding on the parties when they have so agreed.

Articles of Exchange.   Similar to articles of incorporation, but filed by an acquiring corporation upon the purchase of one or more classes of shares in an acquired corporation (called a "share exchange") for the purpose of updating the records of the secretary of state concerning the acquired corporation.

Articles of Merger.   Similar to articles of incorporation, but filed by a merging corporation for the purpose of updating the records of the secretary of state concerning the merged corporation.

assault.   An intentional and unlawful placing of another person in fear of an impending battery by one apparently able to inflict it.

assignment.   The transfer of rights under an existing contract to a third person.

assumption of risk.   A doctrine in negligence law providing that one who enters into a course of action knowing of the risk of injury, whether through the negligence of the defendant, a third person, or the fault of no one, is not permitted to maintain an action for such an injury; a complete defense to a negligence action.

assured.   The person for whose benefit a policy of insurance is issued, and to whom any covered loss ordinarily is payable (may or may not be the insured).

at will employment.   Non-contractual employment for an indefinite period of time.

attachment.   In the law of procedure, to seize property by court order, generally for the purpose of acquiring jurisdiction over the property or to secure the payment of a judgment in an action pending against the property owner. In the law of secured transactions, the process of making a security agreement binding as between the debtor and the secured party. (See also, *perfection.*)

attractive nuisance doctrine.   Provides that when one maintains on his property something that is calculated to lure young children (generally under fourteen years of age) to their injury, he will be liable for such injuries as may occur without proof of other fault.

authority by estoppel.   A legal fiction in agency law, that one person was acting as the agent of another when the latter has misled third parties into acting. Frequently associated with an owner's denial of title to goods and a purchase of those goods from a thief.

authority by operation of law.   Agency authority granted by statute in certain circumstances (e.g., the secretary of state as agent for unregistered foreign corporations doing business in the state).

authority by ratification.   Agency authority created after the fact by the principal's manifestation of willingness to be bound to a previous transaction done in his name without authority.

automatic perfection.   The perfection of a security interest by attachment only.

automatic stay.   A moratorium or stay against all other proceedings to collect debts by creditors against a bankrupt upon the granting of an order for relief by a bankruptcy court.

bailment.   A relationship created whenever an owner entrusts property to another who agrees to return or dispose of the property according to the directions of the owner.

bankruptcy estate.   The non-exempt assets of a person undergoing bankruptcy.

bargained for.   In the law of contracts, the concept that, in order to constitute consideration, a promisee's detriment or promisor's benefit must have been what the promisor wanted to achieve by making the promise.

bargaining unit. Homogenous group of employees represented by a union as bargaining agent.

battery. An unpermitted and unprivileged touching of the body of another.

bearer. One in possession of commercial paper drawn, issued, or indorsed to no particular person (e.g., to cash).

bearer instrument. In commercial paper law, an instrument not made payable to a particular person. (See also, *order instrument*.)

beneficiary. Generally, one who owns beneficial or equitable (as opposed to legal) title to property; one who is to benefit from property held by another. In insurance law, the person to receive the proceeds of an insurance policy upon the occurrence of the risk specified.

bilateral contract. A contract resulting when the offer is a promise and the acceptance is a promise in return.

bill of exchange. In commercial paper law, a three-party instrument under which a drawer orders a drawee to pay money to a payee; bills of exchange include checks and drafts.

Bill of Rights. The collective name given to the first ten amendments to the United States Constitution.

binder. In insurance law, a commitment, by an insurer or its agent, to insure a risk during the period between tender of the insurance application and the issuance of the permanent policy.

blank indorsement. An indorsement that does not name the indorsee; may be the signature only of the indorser.

blue sky laws. A popular name given to state laws regulating and supervising investment companies for the purpose of protecting potential investors from investing in fraudulent schemes.

board of directors. A body of persons elected by the owners of a corporation to oversee corporate operations, and to set policies to be executed by the operating corporate officers.

bona fide occupational qualification (BFOQ). In employment law, a qualification permitting the employment of persons with certain characteristics as an exception to the ordinary rules governing equal employment opportunity and nondiscrimination against protected classes.

bonding. The process by which one person (usually an insurance company) agrees to be responsible for the debt, default, or miscarriage of another upon payment of a bonding fee or premium.

boycott. A concerted (two or more participants) refusal to deal with another person by selling or purchasing property or services (e.g., a strike).

breach of trust. An act contrary to a fiduciary duty.

bribery. The illegal giving or receiving of something of value to influence an official action or to discharge a debt owed to the public.

brief. A short summary, or abstract, of a court case. Also, a document setting out legal authority supporting a party's position upon the appeal of a decision to an appellate court.

broker. An agent or intermediary employed to bring together a buyer and a seller of property or services (e.g., a stock broker or real estate broker).

bulk transfer. A transfer in bulk, and not in the ordinary course of the transferor's business, of a major part of the materials, supplies, merchandise, or other inventory. Governed by UCC Article 6.

burden of proof. The margin of evidence necessary to prove an alleged fact in court—a preponderance in civil actions, and beyond a reasonable doubt in criminal actions.

business invitee. A person on property belonging to another for the mutual benefit of the parties or the sole benefit of the property owner.

business judgment rule. A rule in corporation law by which the decisions of the directors and officers of a corporation may be judged. The rule requires that these parties act reasonably in corporate affairs, in a manner in which they would conduct their own business affairs.

business trust (Massachusetts trust). A type of business organization similar to a corporation, and treated as such in many respects, but involving property being placed in the hands of trustees who manage it for the benefit of the owners.

bylaws. In corporation law, the rules adopted by the corporation for its governance, in addition to those stated in its articles of incorporation.

C. & F. A shipping term (cost and freight) meaning that the purchase price of goods includes the cost of the goods and freight costs to some destination.

C.I.F.   A shipping term (cost, insurance, and freight) meaning that the purchase price of goods includes the cost of the goods, and insurance and freight costs to some destination.

case of first impression.   A court case raising an issue of law for which there is no statutory or case precedent in the jurisdiction.

cash-flow test.   In bankruptcy law, a qualification for being declared bankrupt—that a debtor is unable to pay his debts currently as they become due.

***causa mortis* gift.**   A gift given in contemplation of death, or on the condition of the donor's death by a feared peril. A gift *causa mortis* becomes vested if the donor dies of the peril feared.

caveat emptor.   Let the buyer beware. A summary of the rule that a purchaser must examine the subject matter of a transaction, test it, and judge for himself without help from the seller.

cease and desist order.   Similar to a mandatory injunction—that a person stop doing something—except that it is issued by a governmental agency other than a court of equity.

certificate of deposit (CD).   A type of commercial paper (note) involving a deposit of money, and a promise by the depository to repay the money at a future time, usually with interest.

certificate of limited partnership.   A document similar to articles of incorporation, necessary to establish a limited partnership. The certificate ordinarily is filed on public record in the county (rather than the state) of organization. In general, it states the name of the partnership, the nature of its business, its location, membership, powers of members, and limitations on liability.

certification (NLRB).   In labor law, occurs when the National Labor Relations Board, in writing, makes the results of a representation election or other selection of a collective bargaining agent official.

certification bar.   In labor law, once the results of a representation election has been certified by the National Labor Relations Board, a representation election cannot be held in the same bargaining unit for one year.

certified check.   A check accepted by the drawee (acceptor) for payment.

charge to the jury.   The process by which the judge in a court case instructs the jury concerning the rules of law involved in the case.

charitable trust.   A trust established for charitable, educational, or other eleemosynary purposes (as opposed to a private trust).

charter.   In corporation law, a grant by a government creating a corporation, generally based on the filing of articles of incorporation, and pursuant to a general incorporation statute.

chattel mortgage.   A mortgage granted in personal property.

check.   A type of commercial paper (bill of exchange or draft) in which a drawer orders a bank to pay money to a payee on demand. The essence of a check is that the drawee must be a bank and it must be payable on demand.

checkoff.   In labor law, a union member authorizes his employer to deduct union dues or other fees from his pay and remit them to the union.

checks and balances.   Constitutional provisions granting each of the three branches of government some limited power to control the activities of the other two. For example, federal judges (judicial branch) are nominated by the president (executive branch) and approved by the Senate (legislative branch).

chose in action (thing in action).   Any property that must be converted into something else in order to be used, commonly accounts receivable and other obligations owned by a debtor.

civil conspiracy doctrine.   An antilabor doctrine of early English Law holding concerted action by two or more laborers to improve their bargaining position with their employer to be a ground for a civil suit by the employer.

civil law.   One of the three modern legal systems, based on roman law, with statutes as its primary source of law. Also, a classification of law (as opposed to criminal law) that has as its object the creation and protection of individual rights (as opposed to rights of the general public).

class voting.   Voting on corporate issues affecting only one, or less than all, classes of stock, is restricted to holders of the affected class or classes only.

class-action suit.   A lawsuit commenced on behalf of a group of persons by a court-approved representative; rules of procedure require that actual joinder of the persons affected must be impossible or impracticable, and that all have causes of action based on the same, or substantially the same, issues of law and fact.

close corporation. A corporation whose stock is held by a small group of investors, frequently a family, and is not offered for sale to the public.

closed shop. In labor law, a type of union security agreement requiring membership in the union as a condition of becoming employed.

closing statement. A review of the evidence at the close of a jury trial, made by both parties, from their respective points of view, suggesting how the jury should weigh certain evidence and resolve specific issues of fact.

co-insurance. The division of risk of loss under an insurance policy between the insurer and another (co-) insurer, the co-insurer paying all or part of the loss to the insured that exceeds the payment by the insurer, but remains within the limits of the policy.

co-sign. A signed assumption of primary liability on an obligation along with the principal debtor.

code. Generally, a written compilation of laws; a written compilation of laws in which laws governing each discreet area or subject matter are placed together.

codicil. A testamentary addition to an earlier will. A codicil must meet the same testamentary form as a will.

collateral. In the law of secured transactions, property rights given to secure the payment of an obligation.

collateral promise. A promise to assume secondary liability to pay for the debt, default, or miscarriage of another person.

collective bargaining. The act of a group of employees in bargaining with their employer concerning matters relating to their employment, the results of which become legally binding on all members of the group.

collective bargaining agent. A person (usually a union) authorized by a unit of employees to act as their agent in negotiating with their employer on matters relating to their employment.

commerce clause. Article I, Section 8, Clause 3 of the Constitution of the United States providing that Congress has the power to regulate commerce among the states (interstate commerce), with foreign nations, and with Indian tribes.

commercial impracticability. Not impossible of performance, but unreasonably burdensome from a business standpoint.

commercial paper. A type of formal contract calling for the payment of money, and governed by Article 3 of the Uniform Commercial Code.

commercial reasonableness. Reasonableness in a commercial setting.

common law. One of the three modern legal systems, originating in England, having judicial cases as its primary source of law; law based on previous cases, as opposed to statutes; that part of law administered by law courts, as opposed to equity courts.

common stock. Evidence of ownership rights in a corporation, and entitled to the payment of dividends only after dividends owing to preferred stockholders have been paid.

community ethics. The rules set down as minimum requirements for ethical conduct by members of society. (See also, *individual ethics*.)

community property. A system of spousal ownership of property under which all property acquired during the marriage by the efforts of either party belongs one-half to each spouse. It does not apply to property brought into the marriage by either party, or to property acquired during the marriage by gift, inheritance, or under a will. Upon the death of one spouse, that spouse's one-half interest may be disposed of by will.

comparable worth doctrine. A doctrine adopted by courts in hearing cases involving gender discrimination, providing that employees should receive equal pay for *comparable* work.

comparative negligence. A defense in negligence cases, replacing the defense of contributory negligence, providing that each party should pay for the costs of an injury in proportion to the degree to which his negligence contributed to that injury.

compensatory damage. Amount of money, awarded in civil lawsuits, intended to compensate an injured plaintiff for injuries caused by the defendant.

complaint. A document filed by a plaintiff in order to commence a civil lawsuit, asserting the court's jurisdiction to hear the case, asserting facts sufficient to showing that the plaintiff has a legal grievance and is entitled to a remedy, and identifying the remedy the plaintiff is seeking.

complete and satisfactory performance. Performance to a degree that would meet the reasonable expectation of the purchaser, when performance to perfection is not possible.

composition. A contractual method of discharging liquidated obligations by payment of less than the agreed sum, involving a contract between the debtor and two or more creditors.

compromise. *See* accord and satisfaction.

condemnation. A public taking or destruction of private property in the public interest. Often confused with eminent domain, which is a taking for public use.

condition. An uncertain act or event in the future.

condition precedent. A condition that gives rise to a duty to perform an obligation.

condition subsequent. A condition that excuses further performance of an obligation.

conditional acceptance. A response to a contractual offer indicating the offeree's unwillingness to accept the offer unless the offeror is willing to accept certain express conditions.

conditional sales contract. A secured transaction in which a vendor sells goods and retains title to them as security for payment of their price, agreeing to pass title to the purchaser when full payment is received.

conditions concurrent. Two obligations that are dependent upon each other for performance. For example, a buyer is entitled to receive goods when payment for them is made, and the seller is entitled to be paid when the goods are delivered.

condominium. A type of concurrent ownership of real estate under which the owners hold fee simple title in their separate units, with common parts, such as hallways, stairs, any lounge area or club facilities, and surrounding land being held in common. Condominium owners then pay a maintenance fee for the upkeep of these common areas.

confederation. The form of government adopted in the United States by the first Constitution, with strong state governments and relatively weaker central government, as opposed to a federation.

conglomerate merger. A merger of two businesses having dissimilar lines of products or services.

conscious parallelism. In antitrust law, two competitors conduct business alike, one raising and lowering prices as the other raises and lowers prices, and otherwise operating as the other operates, with no agreement or conspiracy to do so.

consequential damages. Damages awarded to compensate for losses that do not flow as a normal result of a breach of the type being considered, but have been suffered by the plaintiff in the particular circumstances.

consideration. In contract law, that which is paid to bind a promisor to a simple contract promise; a legal benefit to the promisor or a legal detriment to the promisee, bargained for and given in exchange for a promise.

consignment. A form of bailment in which the owner of goods (consignor) retains title, and gives possession to a consignee who attempts to sell them.

consolidation. Two corporations are combined to create a new third corporation.

conspiracy. The agreement of two or more persons to commit an unlawful act (usually a crime) in the future.

constitution. A document establishing, and conferring powers on, a government as a grant from the people.

constructive possession. The owner of legal title to property is considered to have constructive possession even when he does not have actual possession.

constructive trust. A trust imposed on property by operation of law to redress a wrong, or to prevent an unjust enrichment.

consumer product. A product produced or distributed for use by consumers in the home, at school, or for recreation.

Consumer Product Safety Act. A federal statute, administered by the Consumer Product Safety Council, regulating the safety of consumer products.

Consumer Product Safety Council. A federal administrative agency created by the Consumer Product Safety Act, and charged with administration of the act.

continuation statement. A document, signed by a debtor and filed in the manner of a financing statement, giving notice that a previous security interest is being continued. In order to be effective, this statement must be filed within six months prior to the lapse of the financing statement to which it refers.

contract. A promise or set of promises, given in return for consideration, and creating an apparent legal obligation.

contract ban. In labor law, a rule under which the National Labor Relations Board will refuse to grant a certification election during the effective period of a valid collective bargaining contract, up to three years.

contract of guaranty. A contract rendering a guarantor secondarily liable on an obligation owed by another; the contract of a collateral promisor.

contractual interference doctrine. A doctrine of English labor law, first handed down in 1853, and adopted by courts in the United States, providing that when two or more employees conspired (joined together) to raise wages or to bargain for other benefits of employment, their act constituted the tort of contractual interference.

contribution. The payment of a proportionate share of liability by co-sureties.

contributory negligence. A defense in negligence cases providing that when a plaintiff injured by the defendant's negligence also was negligent, and that negligence contributed to his injuries, his cause of action against the defendant is totally defeated.

controlling shareholder. A shareholder whose ownership interest enables him effectively to dominate the affairs and the destiny of the corporation.

conversion. In tort law, the unlawful exercise of dominion and control over the property of another. Conversion also is the basis for the crime of theft.

convertible stock. A type of corporate stock that entitles the owner to convert his shares to some other type of security according to an established formula.

cooling-off period. In labor law, a sixty-day period beginning not more than ninety days, nor less than sixty days, prior to the end of the term of an existing contract, during which a union other that the certified union may not petition the National Labor Relations Board for a representation election.

cooperative. A cooperative may take the form of a trust or corporation that purchases the land and constructs the building that is then divided into apartment units. The trust or corporation holds title, and then lets apartments to the owners by long-term proprietary leases. In the trust form, the tenants acquire their rights to occupancy by the trust issuance of certificates of beneficial interest.

copyright. Rights under the common law, and by statute, granted to the creator of an artistic expression, to use and profit from his creation, continuing for a period commencing at the time of creation, and continuing for fifty years after the death of the last of the creators.

corporate opportunity doctrine. In corporation law, a doctrine that prohibits corporate personnel from diverting to themselves opportunities in which the corporation has a right, property interest, or expectancy, or that in justice should belong to the corporation.

corporate reorganization. A type of bankruptcy under Chapter 11 of the federal bankruptcy act, involving the filing of a repayment plan for all or some portion of a corporation's debts. If the plan is approved, the corporation will continue operation under the direction of the bankruptcy court. Debts of corporate creditors will be paid according to the terms set out in the plan and, if all goes well, the corporation will be discharged of its debts and resume functioning independently.

corporation. An artificial legal person created pursuant to state (or federal) corporation law. A corporation generally is managed by a board of directors, elected by shareholders, who establish operating policies and delegate day-to-day operating decisions to appointed officers. A corporation is an entity (a person) existing separate and apart from its shareholders.

counter-offer. A response to an offer that indicates the offeree's unwillingness to comply with the terms of the original offer and offers back different terms.

counterclaim. In effect, a complaint filed by a defendant in a civil lawsuit, as a part of his answer to the plaintiff's complaint.

course and scope of employment. An agent or employee is in the course and scope of employment when he is properly pursuing the interests of his principal or employer, usually with the permission of the principal or employer.

course of dealing. The conduct of the parties in previous transactions between them. Used in interpreting later contracts between the same parties.

course of performance. The conduct of the parties in performing a present contract. Used in interpreting the obligations under that contract in cases of disagreement.

covenant not to compete.   A contractual promise by an employee, in an employment contract, or the seller of a business, as part of the contract of sale, not to enter business in competition with the employer or purchaser in the future, generally for a stated time and within stated geographical limits.

cover.   The purchase of substitute goods by the buyer to replace those the seller has failed to tender. Cover is one of the buyer's methods of mitigating damages.

craft employee.   An employee, other than a professional or unskilled employee, whose employment generally is distinguished by a training (particularly an apprenticeship) requirement.

creditor beneficiary.   A third-party beneficiary intended by the parties to benefit as a means of paying an obligation one of the parties owes to that person. (See also *donee beneficiary* and *incidental beneficiary*.)

crime.   A breach of duty to society, grounded on statute in American law.

criminal conspiracy doctrine.   A doctrine of early English labor law providing that when two or more employees conspired (joined together) to raise wages or to bargain for other benefits of employment, their act constituted a crime.

criminal law.   Law involving duties owed by individuals to society, as opposed to other individuals. (See also, *crime*.)

cross examination.   Examination of a witness by the opposing party during a court trial or other legal hearing.

cross-elasticity.   In antitrust law, cross-elasticity of demand between two products is determined the extent to which a rise in the price of one will cause purchasers to switch to the other. The more readily this will happen, the greater the cross-elasticity of the products.

cumulative preferred stock.   Preferred stock entitling its owner not only to dividends for the current year prior to distributions to other shareholders, but also to any dividends that were not paid in previous years.

cumulative voting.   In corporation law, a system of voting under which each shareholder is entitled to the number of votes equal to the number of shares he owns multiplied by the number of directors to be elected.

curtesy.   The common law right of a surviving husband to a life estate in 1/3 of all of the real property owned by his wife during their marriage. (See also, *dower*.)

customs duty.   A tax charged on goods that are imported.

cy pres doctrine.   Translated "as near as possible," this doctrine states that when a charitable trust is involved, and the class of beneficiaries stated in the trust document ceases to exist, or the application of the corpus as stated would be illegal, or the language is so vague or uncertain that the settlor's intent must be ascertained by construction, the courts will seek to apply the trust as nearly as possible to what it determines the settlor's intent to have been.

***de facto* corporation.**   A corporation "in fact," established by the issuance of a certificate of incorporation, in spite of the fact that it has failed to comply substantially, and in good faith, with legal requirements for incorporation.

***de jure* corporation.**   A corporation "as a matter of law," established by fully complying with all requirements for incorporation, or substantially complying, in good faith.

debenture.   A corporate debt security that is unsecured; debenture holders are general creditors of the corporation.

debt security.   A corporate security evidencing an obligation to pay money, but carrying no ownership interest in the issuing corporation.

deceit.   Fraud in tort (as opposed to contract) law.

decertification election.   In labor law, an election conducted by the National Labor Relations Board to determine whether a certified union should be terminated as collective bargaining agent.

deed.   An instrument by which title to real estate is transferred.

default.   A failure to meet an obligation.

default judgment.   A judgment granted to the plaintiff in a civil lawsuit, based on his complaint and, usually, the presentation of enough evidence to establish a *prima facie* case, granted for failure of the defendant to appear as summoned.

defendant. The party against whom a lawsuit or criminal charges have been filed.

definite future time. In commercial paper law, a definite moment in the future beyond which a maturity date for payment cannot be extended without the permission of the holder.

***del credere* agent.** An agent who guarantees the credit of his principal's customers.

delegation. The transfer of an obligation.

demurrer. A motion to dismiss the complaint in a civil lawsuit for its failure to state a cause of action against the defendant.

deposition. Testimony by a witness, given before trial, in the presence of both parties and a reporter authorized to swear witnesses and to report testimony. In appropriate circumstances a deposition may be entered into evidence during a trial.

deregulation. A lessening or cessation of businesses regulation by regulatory administrative agencies.

direct examination. The examination of a witness by the party who called him to a criminal or civil trial to testify.

disaffirmance. Cancellation of a contract or other duty by the party owning it.

discharge. Termination of an obligation, usually by complete performance.

disclosed principal. A principal whose existence and identity is known to a third party, other than the principal and the agent.

discovery. A procedure in civil lawsuits permitting each of the parties to obtain information from the other party or his witnesses prior to trial, concerning evidence to be given at the trial.

dishonor. A refusal to perform a contractual obligation.

dissolution. In the law of business organizations, the cessation of existence of a business organization.

diversity of citizenship. A federal court may decide a civil case involving state law when the parties are residents of different states or a state and a foreign country when the value of the controversy exceeds $50,000 exclusive of interest and costs.

dividend. A distribution of corporate profits to a shareholder.

document of title. A written document evidencing title to goods. (See also, *bill of lading* and *warehouse receipt.*)

domestic corporation. A corporation doing business in the state in which it was incorporated.

donee beneficiary. A third-party beneficiary intended by the parties to benefit as a means of giving a gift to that person. (See also *creditor beneficiary* and *incidental beneficiary.*)

double taxation. The method of taxing corporate profits, which are subject to income tax when earned, and then they are taxed a second time when they are distributed to the shareholders in the form of dividends.

dower. The common law right of a surviving wife to a life estate in 1/3 of all of the real property owned by her husband during their marriage. (See also, *curtesy.*)

draft. In commercial paper law, a three-party instrument containing an order by a drawer, to a drawee, to pay money to a payee. (See also, *check.*)

drawee. In commercial paper law, the party to a bill of exchange ordered by the drawer to pay the payee.

drawer. In commercial paper law, the party to a bill of exchange ordering the drawee to pay the payee.

dual court structure. A reference to the fact that the jurisdiction of courts in the United States is divided between federal courts and state courts.

dual-motive case. In labor law, a strike that may be classified partly in one NLRB classification and partly in another, the classifications being (1) illegal, (2) economic, and (3) unfair labor practice.

due diligence. In the law of accountants' liability, an accountant sued for negligence under the federal securities acts may defend by proving that he used reasonable procedures, in making a reasonable examination, and had a reasonable basis for believing, and did believe, that the statements he or she certified fully and fairly disclosed all material facts concerning the client's financial position, and that this was done in meaningful and understandable terms.

duress. Unlawful pressure or coercion exercised over the will of another, usually by force or threats of force, causing him to do something he would not otherwise have done.

easement. An irrevocable right to use, but not to possess, land belonging to another, granted in writing.

easement appurtenant. An easement requiring for its ownership the ownership of an estate in a particular piece of land for the benefit of which the easement was given.

easement in gross. A personal easement not requiring ownership of any estate in land, as opposed to an easement appurtenant.

economic strike. In labor law, a strike motivated by an intention to improve the employees' bargaining position with their employer.

Electronic Fund Transfers Act. A federal statute regulating any means of transfer of funds by the use of an electronic terminal, telephone, or computer, or magnetic tape. These means include point-of-sale transfers, automated teller machine transactions, direct deposits or withdrawals of funds, and transfers initiated by telephone.

emancipation. A condition of a minor whose parents have given up their common law rights to his earnings and services, as a result of which the minor becomes self-supporting.

embezzlement. The conversion of property by one in whom lawful custody has been entrusted by the owner, who owes a fiduciary duty to the owner.

eminent domain. The power of government to take private property for public use upon the payment of fair compensation to the owner.

employee. A person who is requested or permitted to perform manual or mental labor for another. (See also, *agent.*)

employer. One who requests or permits another to perform manual or mental labor for him. (See also, *principal.*)

entity. A person or being; having an existence discrete and apart from its owners or property, such as natural persons, corporations, and constitutional entities (e.g., a state).

entity theory. In the law of business organizations, a theory applied to corporations, and to partnerships in limited respects, that they are separate legal persons for such purposes as owning and transferring property, and suing and being sued.

entrusting. A bailment of goods by the owner, or with the owner's authority, with a merchant who ordinarily deals in goods of that kind.

enumerated powers. In the Constitution of the United States, the powers specifically granted to the federal government, as opposed to reserved powers, which were to be retained by the states or the people.

Equal Employment Opportunity Commission. A federal agency established by the Civil Rights Act of 1964 to administer and interpret Title VII.

equipment. Goods held primarily for use (not sale) in a business.

equitable (beneficial) title. Ownership of property in the sense of having the right to the benefits derived from the property, as opposed to legal title.

equity. A system of courts, under the Common Law of England, having jurisdiction to grant special relief when the courts of law had no remedy or the remedy available was inadequate; remedies granted by a court of equity. The ownership interest in a business derived from subtracting liabilities from assets.

equity security. A corporate security evidencing an ownership interest in the issuing corporation.

estate. The interest that anyone has in property; the property itself.

estate planning. A process of planning for the accumulation and the distribution of a person's property upon death.

estoppel. A general principal of equity by which a person may be stopped from exercising certain legal rights in the interest of justice. Estoppel generally is based on some wrongdoing of the person estopped, but may be based on a need to vindicate public policy contrary to the rights of the person estopped.

ethics. A branch of philosophy that addresses each person's relationships with every other person, as opposed to a person's relationship to God.

ex parte. Without participation by the defendant.

ex ship. "From the ship or carrier." Expense and risk do not pass to the buyer until the goods have been unloaded at their destination.

exclusive dealing. An arrangement between a supplier of goods or services and a customer under which the parties agree to deal only with each other, and not with a competitor of the other.

exculpatory clause. A contract clause taking away blame or liability from someone.

executed contract. A contract that has been performed completely on both sides.

executive order. A source of law involving orders promulgated by the chief governmental executive—the president of the United States or the governor of a state.

executive power. In administrative law, the power of an administrative agency to police compliance with its regulations and orders.

executor. A man named in a will to administer its provisions.

executory contract. A contract under which one or more obligations are yet to be performed.

executrix. A female executor.

exempt property. In bankruptcy law, property that by state law, or under the bankruptcy act, cannot be taken by operation of law to pay the debts of a debtor.

exhaustion of administrative remedies. In administrative law, a part of the concept of ripeness, requiring that before judicial review of an administrative agency decision will be granted, all appeals rights within the agency must be exhausted.

express authority. Authority granted by a principal by words, written or spoken, communicated by the principal to an agent.

express contract. A contract, the material terms of which have been agreed to by words, written or spoken. (See also, *implied contract*.)

express warranty. A warranty communicated by written or spoken words.

F.A.S. "Free alongside ship." This term is the maritime equivalent of F.O.B. and means that the seller bears the expense and risk of loss until the goods are delivered to the place of the carrier.

F.O.B. "Free on board." The seller bears the expense and the risk of loss until delivery to the specified location.

fact. Anything observable by the use of one or more of the five human senses—sight, hearing, smell, taste, and touch.

fact finding. A determination of fact issues in a case from conflicting evidence.

factor. An agent entrusted with possession and control of the principal's property consigned to him or her for sale.

Federal Register. In administrative law, a publication of the federal government in which notices of proposed rulemaking, and final rules promulgated by federal administrative agencies, are required to be published. Later, these rules are republished in the Code of Federal Regulation (CFR).

federalism. The form of government adopted in the United States by the second Constitution, with a strong central government and relatively weaker state governments, as opposed to a confederation.

fee simple. An estate an owner has in land that is given to him and his heirs forever, without condition; absolute ownership of land.

fee simple determinable. A fee simple, the continuance of which is conditioned on the occurrence of some uncertain event occurring or not occurring in the future.

fellow-servant rule. In workers' compensation law, a defense available to employers sued for employee injuries prior to the enactment of workers' compensation statutes, freeing an employer from liability when an employee's injury was caused by the fault of another employee working in the general proximity of the injured employee.

felony. A crime other than treason or a misdemeanor; a crime involving possible punishment by imprisonment in a state or federal penitentiary.

fiduciary duty. The highest duty of trust and confidence one person may owe to another. It is an exception to the adversary principal of American law.

fiduciary relationship. A relationship of trust and confidence of the highest sort.

financing statement. A document filed in the appropriate public office by a secured party giving notice of a security interest in personal property or fixtures.

firm offer. A contract offer that cannot be revoked if made as specified in Section 2-205 of the Uniform Commercial Code.

fixture. Personal property attached to real estate in such a manner as to become real estate, itself.

floating lien.   A lien that does not remain attached to a single piece of property at a fixed location, but adjusts to accommodate three common changes: 1) after-acquired property, 2) future advances, and 3) the conversion of the secured property to proceeds.

foreclosure.   A legal process by which property subject to a security interest is sold to pay the debt underlying the security interest.

foreign corporation.   A corporation doing business in a state other than its state of incorporation.

Foreign Corrupt Practices Act.   A 1977 federal statute, jointly enforced by the SEC and the Department of Justice, proscribing bribery of foreign officials by United States domestic corporations.

form 10-K.   An annual report required by federal securities law that must contain audited financial statements on the present fiscal year and current information concerning the corporation, its operations, legal proceedings, and the condition of its securities, and should contain a summary of the last five fiscal years of operation and a listing of affiliated companies.

formal contract.   A contract that takes its validity from being placed in a prescribed form, as opposed to a simple contract.

formal rulemaking.   Rulemaking by administrative agencies, generally only when required by the Administrative Procedure Act (APA), through trial-type proceedings, involving the presentation of evidence and examination and cross-examination of witnesses. Also called "on the record" rulemaking.

four unities.   In real estate law, the doctrine that concurrent owners of real estate with the right of survivorship (joint tenants, tenants by the entireties, and tenants in partnership) must receive their titles at the same time, by the same instrument of transfer, must acquire equal interests, and must have equal rights to possession.

franchise.   An arrangement between someone holding the right to a product or service (the franchisor) and someone who will market the product or service (the franchisee).

franchise agreement.   A contract between the franchisor and the franchisee establishing a franchise.

fraud.   In contract law, an intentional misrepresentation, for the purpose of defrauding, resulting in an injury to the person defrauded; deceit in tort law.

fraud in the execution.   A fraud causing a person to sign a document, the nature of which is unknown to him without his own fault.

fraud in the inducement.   A fraud causing a person to undertake a known obligation.

fraudulent conveyance.   In bankruptcy law, transfers or obligations made by a debtor with actual intent to hinder, delay, or defraud a creditor.

Freedom of Information Act.   A federal statute requiring administrative agencies to release public information upon proper application or request from an interested person.

freehold estate.   In real estate law, an estate for an indefinite time into the future, such as a fee simple or a life estate.

friendly fire.   In insurance law, fires that are set intentionally by the insured and do some damage although they remain contained as intended. Friendly fires usually are excluded from coverage under fire insurance policies.

fundamental change.   In the law of business organizations, any corporate action that is outside the limits of its regular course of business.

future advance.   Credit given subsequent to the giving of a security interest, but secured by that interest if it expressly provides for future advances.

future interest.   A present non-possessory interest in real estate to become possessory in the future.

garnishment.   A method of collecting a debt by a court order directing some third party (commonly a bank or an employer) to pay to the court money or other property belonging to the debtor.

general agent.   An agent having authority to conduct a relatively broad range of duties for his principal. (See also, *special agent.*)

general jurisdiction.   Court jurisdiction over a broad variety of types of cases; broad subject-matter jurisdiction; the opposite of special jurisdiction.

general partnership.   A form of business organization involving a combination of two or more persons as co-owners to operate an ongoing business for profit, and the assumption of unlimited personal liability by all owners.

general warranty deed.   A deed containing warranties (contractual promises) concerning the real estate transferred, commonly title, right to convey, against encumbrances, quiet and peaceful enjoyment, and further assurances.

gift.   Property given without consideration paid for the grant.

good faith.   Fundamental fairness in the conduct of a transaction.

goods.   Generally personal property, excluding purchase-price money, investment security, and things (choses) in action, and including certain other items of property as set out in Section 2-107 of the Uniform Commercial Code.

hearsay.   Testimony by a witness of what he has been told by another person when the truth of the other person's statement is in controversy.

heir.   A relative by blood of a deceased person. Heirs also may be created by statute (e.g., a spouse or adopted child).

Herfindahl-Hirsham Index (HHI).   An index used by the United States Department of Justice to measure the degree of market concentration in an industry.

holder.   In commercial paper law, a person who is in possession of an instrument drawn, issued or indorsed to him, or to his order, or to bearer, or in blank; a person in possesion of a negotiable instrument that has been negotiated to him.

holder in due course.   In commercial paper law, a holder, who takes the instrument for value, with no notice of defenses, in good faith, and in the ordinary course of business.

holding company.   An organization having as its principal business the ownership of stock in one or more corporations.

holdover tenant.   A real estate tenant who continues in possession, as a trespasser, after the term of a lease.

holographic will.   A will written entirely in the hand of the testator and is valid in spite of the absence of witnesses.

horizontal merger.   A merger between two companies within the same industry, and on the same production level, such as retail or wholesale. (See also, *vertical merger*.)

horizontal restraint.   A restraint of trade involving agreements between competitors on the same business level, such as two manufacturers or two retailers.

identified to the contract.   Goods are identified to a particular contract when the specific goods relating to the contract are in existence and known, whether by marking them, setting them aside, or shipping them.

illusory promise.   An unreal promise (only an illusion of a promise); a promise based on a condition the occurrence of which is within the control of the promisor.

impairment of recourse.   In suretyship, an act interfering with the right of a surety to go back against a principal liable to him on a transaction.

implied authority.   Authority an agent has to do all things reasonably necessary to the performance of his express authority.

implied contract.   A contract found to exist by an examination of the facts and circumstances surrounding a transaction. (See also, *express contract*.)

implied warranty.   A warranty the existence of which is derived from the conduct of the parties in light of surrounding facts and circumstances; also implied warranties are established by Article 2 of the Uniform Commercial Code.

imposter rule.   A rule in the law of commercial paper, providing that one who makes commercial paper payable to a particular payee, but gives the instrument to another, is prevented from using the forgery of the payee's indorsement as a defense to liability if the instrument falls into the hands of a good-faith holder.

incidental beneficiary.   A person who will benefit from the performance of a contract between two other persons, but it was not the intent of the parties or the purpose of the contract to confer that benefit. (See also, *creditor beneficiary* and *donee beneficiary*.)

incidental damages.   Damages in additional to ordinary compensatory damages awarded to reimburse a plaintiff for additional costs and expenses that flowed from the breach of a contract.

incompetence.   A status acquired by a person when a court, after a full and fair hearing, has determined that the person represents a danger to himself or to others. (See also, *insanity*.)

incontestability clause. A clause in an insurance policy prohibiting the insurance company from refusing to pay benefits because of misrepresentation or concealment of material facts in the application for insurance.

indemnity. In insurance law, the principle that an insurer will pay only to the extent that a loss has been suffered, and not more; generally, an obligation to pay debts or losses of another.

indenture. A contract between a corporation and bondholders, usually in the form of a trust, under which the bonds are issued and administered.

independent administrative agency. Administrative agency that is not part of a larger agency, but operates as an independent entity in the governmental structure. Generally, these agencies may be distinguished by the designation "board," such as the National Labor Relations Board, or "commission," such as the Federal Trade Commission.

independent (professional) agent. An agent over whom the principal has no right of control.

independent contractor. An employee over whose duties the employer has no right to control. (See also, *servant*.)

indorsement. A signature on an instrument, or on a separate piece of paper firmly attached to the instrument, made by or on behalf of the indorser, for the purpose of transferring an interest in the instrument to another.

infant. A minor, or person under legal age to conduct contractual or certain other transactions.

informal rulemaking. Rulemaking by administrative agencies, generally when not required to use formal rulemaking, involving only publication of a notice of proposed rulemaking, and an opportunity for the public to comment orally, in writing, or both. Also called "notice and comment" rulemaking.

injunction. A court order either requiring that something be done, or that something not be done, after a hearing and an opportunity for the defendant to appear and defend. (See also, *temporary restraining order*.)

insanity. In contract law, the condition of a person who is incapable of comprehending the nature of the business at hand at some moment in time. (See also, *incompetence*.)

insider trading. Trading in the securities of a corporation by people close to the corporation, who use information gained from their positions for financial gain to the detriment of other security holders.

insurable interest. In insurance law, the requirement that an assured have a legal interest in the property that is the subject of the policy, and stand to suffer a financial loss by its being damaged, destroyed, or otherwise lost.

insurance. A type of contract under which an insurer, for compensation, agrees to compensate a person for specified losses from specified perils.

insured. The person upon whose life or property (including liability) a policy of insurance is obtained.

insurer. The party assuming liability under an insurance policy.

intangible property. Property that has no tangible or corporeal existence, although it may be evidenced by a writing, such as an account receivable.

intellectual property. A catch-all phrase that encompasses the four legal areas of patents, trademarks, copyrights, and trade secrets.

intent. In contract law, a manifest willingness of a party as measured by the objective standard of "a reasonable person familiar with the surrounding facts and circumstances." In tort law, to intend an injury or the act that caused the injury.

intentional tort. A tort committed for the purpose of causing an injury or intending the act that causes an injury.

inter vivos **trust.** A trust created, and to be effective, during the life of the settlor, and may continue to be effective after the settlor's death.

inter vivos **gift.** A gift made, and to be effective, during the life of the grantor, and usually thereafter.

interlocking directorate. Two or more corporations sharing common members of their boards of directors.

interrogatories. Questions; a list of questions submitted by a party to a civil lawsuit, to be answered under oath; a list of questions to be submitted to a deponent during a deposition.

intestate succession. A process of determining who shall be entitled to receive property of a deceased in the absence of a will, established by statute.

intoxication. Temporary insanity caused by the voluntary use of alcohol or other drugs.

intrastate-offering exemption. An exemption from the registration requirement of the 1933 Federal Securities Act for securities offered and sold to residents of a single state when the issuer also resides in and does business in that state.

inventory. Goods held for resale in the ordinary course of business.

investment contract. A contract that involves an investment of money in participation with others in a common enterprise and the profits therefrom are expected to accrue solely from the efforts of others.

involuntary bailment. A relationship of bailment created when the bailee takes or retains possession of the property of another in order to preserve it while it is out of the control of its owner (e.g., when one takes possession of lost or mislaid property).

involuntary bankruptcy. A bankruptcy proceeding initiated by creditors without the petition of the debtor.

issuer. In securities law, any person who distributes or intends to distribute any security. In commercial paper law, the maker or drawer of commercial paper.

joint and several liability. Liability such that a plaintiff in a lawsuit is permitted to take judgment against either both, or either, of two parties at the plaintiff's option.

joint liability. Liability such that a plaintiff in a lawsuit is permitted to take judgment against both of two parties to a transaction. (See also, *several liability*.)

joint stock company. An association of owners into what is essentially a partnership, and generally is governed by partnership law, except that the interests of the owners are represented by shares of transferable stock.

joint tenancy. A method of concurrent ownership of property with a right of survivorship (deceased tenant's interest passes to the surviving tenant(s)).

joint venture. An association of two or more owners to operate in what is essentially a partnership, and generally is governed by partnership law, differing from a partnership in that it is organized for one, or a limited number of, transactions, rather than to operate an ongoing business.

judgment. The decision of a court in final resolution of a lawsuit or criminal trial.

judgment lien. An automatic, statutory security interest in real estate owned by a judgment debtor to secure the payment of the judgment. This lien applies to real estate located in the county in which the judgment was granted or is recorded.

judgment N.O.V. Judgment *non obstante verdicto* or judgment notwithstanding the verdict; a request to the court, submitted following the announcement of the jury's verdict, requesting the judge to grant a judgment contrary to the jury's verdict.

jurisdictional disputes. A dispute between two unions, each claiming rights of its members to perform a particular task for an employer.

justice. Fundamental fairness with respect to the rights and obligations of all parties involved.

key-man insurance. Insurance obtained to relieve the loss to a business caused by the death of a critically-important owner or employee.

laches. A principle of equity jurisprudence, comparable to the running of a statute of limitations in actions at common law; the running of a reasonable time allowed for bringing a suit in equity.

land. The earth's crust; often held to mean real estate.

land contract. A contract for the sale of real estate under which the seller takes a security interest in the real estate to secure the sale price by retaining title until the debt is paid.

law. Various definitions, but used in this book to mean "a set of norms conceived by society for its own regulation."

leasehold estate. An estate in land for a definite term.

legal benefit. In contract law, something acquired to which the acquiring party was not previously entitled.

legal detriment. An act the party suffering the detriment was under no previous obligation to suffer.

legal realism. A school of jurisprudence combining the basic tenants of the historical school and the school of legal positivism, believing that law is given by society acting through the power of a government.

legal title. Title to property recognized by a court of law, carrying the apparent ownership and right to possession of the property, but not the right to benefit from the property. (See also, *equitable title*.)

letter of credit. A promise by an issuing bank to pay a stated amount upon proof that certain credit has been extended to the holder under its terms and the holder has defaulted.

letters testamentary. Written grant from a probate (or similar) court to a personal representative of the estate of a deceased person, granting legal authority to administer the estate.

libel. Written defamation.

license. A revocable, nonpossessory right to use real estate of another. (See also, *easement*.)

licensee. One who has a license to use property belonging to another.

lien. An interest in property held to secure payment or the meeting of some other obligation; a security interest.

life estate. A freehold estate in land that terminates upon the death of a specified person, ordinarily the owner of the life estate.

limited partnership. A partnership having one or more partners with limited personal liability.

liquidated debt. A debt agreed to between two parties both as to its existence and its exact amount.

liquidated damages. Damages for breach of contract that have been agreed between the parties prior to the breach.

liquidating dividends. Dividends distributed to shareholders representing a return of capital rather than a distribution of profits.

liquidation. The process of reducing property to a form (usually money) to be distributed to creditors and, thereafter, owners; also, the process under Chapter 7 of the federal bankruptcy act.

loaned-servant doctrine. A doctrine of agency law stating that if one person borrows an agent or servant of another, and has the right of control over the details of the performance to be rendered for him, the borrower also assumes *respondeat superior* liability for any torts committed by the agent or servant during the course and scope of performing duties for him.

lockout. A refusal of an employer to accept the services of employees; generally comparable to a strike by employees.

long-arm jurisdiction. Jurisdiction of a state court to serve process on a defendant located in another state, granted by statute.

lost property. Property that has separated from its owner without the owner's knowledge.

Magnuson-Moss Warranty Act. A federal statute, passed as an amendment to the Federal Trade Commission Act, seeking to improve the quality of warranties given by manufacturers.

main purpose doctrine. An exception to the Statute of Frauds requirement that collateral contracts must be in writing to be legally enforceable, and involves a collateral promise made by a promisor who has selfish reasons for making the promise.

maintenance of membership. A type of union security agreement in a collective bargaining agreement requiring that employees who were members of the union on a particular date (usually the effective date of the contract) remain members as a condition to continuing employment with the employer.

maker. In commercial paper law, the party on a note making a promise to pay the payee.

malfeasance. Evil doing or ill conduct. The doing of something one ought not do. (See also, *misfeasance* and *non-feasance*.)

malum in se. A wrong considered wrong even in the absence of positive law; a wrong under natural law.

malum prohibitum. A wrong made so by positive law.

management prerogative. In labor law, a collective bargaining issue on which an employer may bargain voluntarily. A refusal to do so is not an unfair labor practice, but insistence on bargaining about one by the union is.

mandatory bargaining issue. In labor law, a collective bargaining issue involving wages, hours, or terms and conditions of employment. A refusal by the employer or the union to bargain on these issues is an unfair labor practice.

marine insurance. Insurance obtained to cover losses involving marine navigation, other than those resulting from normal wear to a vessel or equipment, and those resulting from delays.

marketable title. In real estate law, a title to real estate that would be expected to pass without reasonable objection.

master. One who employs a servant.

material breach. A breach of contract resulting when performance is so defective as to impair the value of the contract and make it substantially worthless so that the obligation of the non-breaching party is discharged.

material term. In contract law, a term sufficiently important that a court is unwilling to establish it for the parties; the parties must actually agree on it themselves.

mechanic's lien. A security interest to secure the price of services or materials furnished in the construction, repair, or improvement of property.

mediation. An alternative (to litigation) method of dispute resolution involving a private person who acts as a go-between in the negotiation of rights and duties between two parties. A mediator is not empowered to decide these questions for the parties, but often is empowered to make suggestions for resolving disputes.

mens rea. Criminal intent.

merchant. Defined in UCC Section 2-104(1) as: "a person who deals in goods of the kind or otherwise by his occupation holds himself out as having knowledge or skill peculiar to the practices or goods involved in the transaction or to whom such knowledge or skill may be attributed by his employment of an agent or broker or other intermediary who by his occupation holds himself out as having such knowledge or skill."

merchantability. A concept in property and sales law describing property as of at least average quality, and such as ordinarily would pass without objection in business.

merged corporation. In a merger of corporations, the corporation that loses its identity. (See also, *surviving corporation*.)

merger. The combination of two corporations so that one continues to exist (the surviving corporation) and the other (merged corporation) ceases to exist.

merger of law and equity. The concept in American law that the powers of the historic courts of law and courts of equity have been combined into a single court.

merger guidelines. Standards issued by the United States Department of Justice and used in determining whether particular business acquisitions should be challenged as in violation of federal antitrust laws.

mini probate. An abbreviated probate process permitted by statute in cases of certain small decedents' estates.

minor. *See* infant.

minority shareholder. *See* controlling shareholder.

misdemeanor. The least serious class of crimes, as opposed to treason or felony, punishable by a maximum penalty of fine and imprisonment in a jail, as opposed to a state or federal penitentiary, usually for one year or less.

misfeasance. Doing something one had a right or duty to do, but doing it improperly or poorly. (See also, *malfeasance* and *non-feasance*.)

mislaid property. Property placed somewhere by its owner, who unintentionally left it there.

misrepresentation. A misstatement of fact by words or conduct.

mitigation of damages. An obligation of a plaintiff in a breach of contract case to do whatever is reasonable to lessen his losses resulting from the breach.

money. In commercial paper law, the currency of the United States or any foreign government.

monopoly. In antitrust law, a circumstance under which a single firm has the power to exclude competitors from a market or to control prices in a market.

mortgage. A nonpossessory security interest in property, real or personal (chattel), involving a transfer of title by the owner to the secured party, who promises to re-convey title when the debt it secures is paid.

mortgagee. A lender who secures the debt by taking a mortgage on property owned by the debtor.

mortgagor. A borrower who secures the debt by giving a mortgage on property he owns.

motion to dismiss. A motion directed to the court in a civil or criminal case asking the court to dismiss a complaint or other request for relief, or a criminal charge, for some failure by the other party to comply with procedural rules for obtaining relief.

mutual assent.   In contract law, the manifest willingness of the offeror and the offeree to enter into a contract with each other on agreed terms.

mutual (bilateral) mistake.   A mistake of both parties to a contract or other transaction.

mutual-benefit bailment.   A bailment for the benefit of both the bailor and the bailee (e.g., a rental or property for consideration).

mysterious disappearance.   A clause in an insurance policy providing for payment of a loss incurred when property has been placed in a known location and then disappears. This is similar to theft except that it does not require proof of unauthorized entry.

natural law.   A school of jurisprudence believing that law is given by god, and humankind only seek to discover it.

necessaries.   Goods and services reasonably necessary for continued health and well-being.

negative easement.   An easement permitting the holder to prohibit certain kinds of uses of land belonging to another.

negligence.   An unreasonable act; an act that would not be committed by a reasonable person of ordinary prudence under the same or similar circumstances.

negotiation.   In commercial paper law, the transfer of a negotiable instrument in a manner that constitutes the transferee a holder; indorsement and delivery of an order instrument or delivery of a bearer instrument.

no arrival, no sale.   The seller promises to ship conforming goods but does not guarantee their delivery to the destination. The seller pays the expense of shipping, the buyer assumes the risk of loss, destruction, and deterioration, unless the seller is at fault.

no-fault insurance.   A type of insurance providing for the payment of benefits to the assured regardless of who was at fault in causing them, or whether fault was involved at all.

no-strike clause.   In labor law, a clause in a collective bargaining contract providing that employees will not strike to increase their bargaining position. These clauses often are accompanied by an agreement to arbitrate.

nominal consideration.   Consideration "in name only"; usually a recital of consideration in a contract that the parties do not intended to be paid, in attempting to make a gift promise appear contractual.

nominal damages.   Damages "in name only," commonly one dollar, awarded in cases of technical breach of an obligation when no real injury has been suffered as a consequence.

non-conforming goods.   Goods that do not meet the precise specifications of the contract of sale.

non-conforming use.   In zoning law, property within a particular zone that, by structure, architecture, or use, does not meet the requirements of the ordinance.

non-delegable duty.   A duty fixed by law on a particular person who cannot escape that liability by delegating performance to an independent contractor.

non-dischargeable debt.   A debt that cannot be discharged under the applicable chapter of the federal bankruptcy act.

non-feasance.   Not doing. A failure to perform a duty. (See also, *malfeasance* and *misfeasance*.)

non-obviousness.   In patent law, this term means that someone skilled in the relevant field of technology and familiar with its subject matter could not have invented it with comparative ease had he tried.

nonpossessory interest.   A right to use property but not to possess it, such as an easement, or any right to become possessory in the future, called a future interest.

note.   In commercial paper law, a two-party instrument in which a maker promises to pay money to a payee.

notice.   In general, information such that a person either knew or should have known of the existence of a certain fact.

notice-and-comment rulemaking.   *See* informal rulemaking.

novation.   A process by which a contractual duty is delegated and the creditor agrees to look only to the delegate for performance, thereby discharging the original debtor.

novelty.   In patent law, this term means that an invention must be something new. An invention that already has been patented, that already is in public use, or that has been described in detail in publications is not "novel."

nuisance.   In tort law, a wrong recognized by courts of equity, involving an unreasonable invasion of the property interests of another. The typical remedy for nuisance is an injunction.

nuncupative will.   An oral will.

obstruction of justice.   Interference with governmental investigations or other proceedings.

offer.   In contract law, the manifestation of the offeror's willingness to enter into a contract with the offeree on certain terms.

offeree.   In contract law, one to whom an offer is directed.

offeror.   In contract law, one who directs an offer to an offeree.

Office of Federal Contract Compliance Programs.   A subdivision of the United States Department of Labor charged with administration of certain executive orders, statutes such as the Vocational Rehabilitation Act, and general compliance with civil rights legislation by holders of federal contracts.

officer.   A person, such as a president, appointed by the owners of a business, or the directors of a corporation, who is charged with day-to-day business management responsibilities.

oligopoly.   In antitrust law, a circumstance under which only a few major firms have the power to exclude competitors from a market or to control prices in a market. Sometimes called a "shared monopoly."

on-the-record rulemaking.   *See* formal rulemaking.

opening statement.   A statement by each party in a civil lawsuit, made prior to offering evidence, stating to the jury what that party intends to prove during the evidentiary portion of the trial.

option.   The right of a person, paid for in advance, to purchase certain services, goods, or a certain quantity of investment securities at an established price during an established future time.

order.   In commercial paper law, a mandate or directive, as contrasted to a promise.

order instrument.   In commercial paper law, an instrument made payable to a particular payee, as opposed to a bearer instrument.

order for relief.   The acceptance of a case by a bankruptcy court.

ordinance.   A legislative enactment by a state subdivision, such as a county or a municipality.

original jurisdiction.   The jurisdiction of a court to act as a trial court, as opposed to appellate jurisdiction.

ostensible authority.   Also called apparent authority, that authority a principal leads third parties reasonably to believe his agent possesses.

pari delicto.   Around or in the area of wrong doing; used in contract law to designate parties to an illegal contract.

parol evidence rule.   An exclusionary rule of evidence providing, in general, that the terms of a written contract may not be altered, varied, or modified by oral evidence (or any other evidence outside the four corners of the writing).

partially disclosed principal.   A principal whose existence, but not whose identity, is known to a third party who is not the principal or the agent.

partner by estoppel.   One who is not an actual partner, but consents to being held out as a partner. A partner by estoppel may be held liable as a partner concerning partnership obligations to persons who were misled.

partnership.   An association of two or more owners to operate an ongoing business for profit. (See also, *general partnership* and *limited partnership*.)

partnership property.   All property originally brought into the partnership stock, or subsequently acquired, by purchase or otherwise, on account of the partnership.

past consideration.   A legal benefit to a promisor or a legal detriment to a promisee that was performed prior to the making of the promise.

patent.   An exclusive right granted by federal statute to an inventor to determine who, if anyone, will be permitted to use, make, or sell the patented item for a period of seventeen years after the patent is granted.

patrolling.   In labor law, the physical presence of employees and sympathizers at a picketing location.

payee.   In commercial paper law, the party to be paid.

per se **violation.**   In antitrust law, a violation of the law that always is a violation; there are no circumstances that can justify the activity. (See aso, *rule of reason*.)

peremptory challenge. A challenge other than a challenge for cause, seeking to prevent that prospective juror from acting as a juror during the trial of a civil lawsuit or a criminal action.

perfection. The process by which a lien on property becomes protected against claims of third persons to the collateral.

period of redemption. The right of a mortgagor to reclaim the property from the purchaser at a foreclosure sale upon payment to the latter of the sale price any time during a period set by law.

permissive bargaining issue. In labor law, a collective bargaining issue that may be voluntarily negotiated, but the refusal of either party to negotiate is not considered an unfair labor practice.

personal defense. In commercial paper law, defenses that cannot be asserted against a holder in due course. (See also, *real (absolute) defenses.*)

personal ethics. Conduct that aspires to a higher standard of behavior than the minimums established by community ethics.

personal jurisdiction. A court's jurisdiction over the person, or sometimes the property of a person, involved in a civil lawsuit, necessary to summon that person to court.

personal property. All property other than real estate.

personal representative. A person authorized to administer a decedent's estate; historically termed executor/rix or administrator/rix.

picketing. In labor law, the dissemination of information concerning a dispute with an employer (or, rarely, employees), usually accompanied by patrolling.

pierce the corporate veil. A doctrine that when a corporation is established to take advantage of limited liability, but is underfunded so as to perpetuate a fraud on creditors, a court may make the owners personally liable for corporate obligations.

plaintiff. The party commencing a civil lawsuit.

pleadings. The complaint(s) and the answer(s) in a civil lawsuit.

pledge. A method of perfecting a security interest by the secured party's taking possession of the collateral.

possession. The right to control property (See also, *actual possession* and *constructive possession.*)

possibility of reverter. A future interest in real estate held by a grantor and his heirs when he has granted a fee simple on a condition. Unlike the right of entry, a possibility of reverter automatically vests a possessory right upon the occurrence of the condition.

power of attorney. A written grant of agency authority.

pre-existing obligation. In contract law, a benefit to a promisor or a detriment to a promisee to which the promisor already was entitled prior to the making of a second promise.

precedent. In the Common Law system, a judicial case decision that establishes law to be followed by lower courts in deciding subsequent cases based on the same or similar fact situations.

preemptive right. In corporation law, a right of shareholders to purchase additional shares, when issued, before those shares are offered to the public or other shareholders.

preference. In bankruptcy law, a transfer by an insolvent debtor, prior to bankruptcy, that prefers (places in a better position) one creditor over others.

preferred stock. A class of stock having preference over other classes of stock in the distribution of dividends, or on liquidation, or both.

prenuptial (antenuptial) contract. A contract providing for a division of property rights upon the death of one or both partners to a marriage, or in the event of their divorce, given by the promisor in consideration of the marriage or a promise to marry.

prescriptive easement. A right to use real estate belonging to another by having trespassed on it for a prescribed period of time, meeting all other legal requirements for a prescriptive easement.

present sale. A transaction by which the title to specified goods passes from a seller to a buyer, as opposed to a contract for sale.

presentment. The act of a holder requesting payment from a party liable on commercial paper.

pretrial conference. A conference involving the judge and the parties to a civil lawsuit, held prior to the trial, during which the judge seeks to identify the disputed issues, to structure the course of the trial so that it runs smoothly and without surprises, to obtain stipulations of fact from the parties, and to encourage settlement negotiations.

price fixing. In antitrust law, the conduct of two firms agreeing to establish the price of goods or services at a level agreeable to both.

prima facie. "On its face"; a *prima facie* case is one sufficient that if all of the facts (during the pleading stage of a trial) or evidence (during trial) is believed and not countered by the other party, it would merit a judgement by the court.

primary liability. Unconditional liability; liability not dependent upon failure of another to perform an obligation. (See also, *secondary liability*.)

principal. One who employs an agent.

prior acquisition. A system of ownership of water rights providing that water belongs to the first person who takes it. (See also, *riparian rights*.)

private offering. An offering of securities meeting the following requirements: (1) no offer can be made to the public; (2) the offer is open to any number of "accredited" investors but is limited to 35 other "sophisticated" purchasers; (3) the same information that would be contained in a registration statement must be available to any of the offerees; and (4) the seller must exercise reasonable care to protect against purchases of the securities for resale rather than for investment.

privilege. A basis for refusing to disclose certain client information during an official investigation or a judicial proceeding, based on the public policy to preserve the secrecy or confidentiality of certain information communicated between two persons, such as a lawyer, doctor, or accountant and his client.

privity of contract. A contractual relationship between two parties.

probate. A body of law governing the administration of decedents' estates; in modern terminology, probate also includes other areas of jurisdiction of probate courts.

procedural due process. Requires that for any governmental action that involves a taking of private property for public use, or the deprivation of any other individual right, is constitutional only if the means of taking insures an opportunity for the rights of the individual to be fairly considered.

procedural law. The body of law governing the process by which legal rights are to be vindicated in courts or quasi-judicial bodies, and the remedies or penalties to be handed down in each case.

procedure. The process or rules by which civil or criminal rights are vindicated.

proceeds. Money or other things of value received from the sale of property.

professional employee. An employee, as distinguished from craft or unskilled employees, whose employment generally is distinguished by an educational requirement.

professional ethics. Ethical standards promulgated and enforced by professional associations concerning the conduct of their members.

profit a prendre. A right to take the produce of land belonging to another.

promise. A commitment to do something in the future.

promissory estoppel. A doctrine of equity that enforces some promises even though they have not been supported by the payment of consideration.

property. A bundle of rights, including the rights to use, to possess, to enjoy, and to dispose of things of value.

protest. In commercial paper law, a formal, written notice of dishonor witnessed by a notary public, a consul or a vice consul, or any other public official authorized to certify dishonors.

proxy. In corporation law, agency authority from a shareholder to another, to vote his shares at a shareholder meeting.

proxy contest. A contest between management and a shareholder who has decided to solicit votes in competition with the current management's position on one or more issues to be voted on at a shareholder meeting.

public policy. Generally, a concept of promoting the greatest good for society.

publicly held corporation. A corporation whose stock is sold to the public. (See also, *close corporation*.)

punitive (exemplary) damages. Damages awarded in addition to compensatory damages in order to punish the defendant for evil conduct, and to provide a deterrent to such conduct in the future.

purchase money security interest. A security interest taken by the seller of goods, or a lender who financed the purchase of the property, to secure the purchase price.

qualified indorsement. In commercial paper law, any indorsement that includes the words "Without Recourse," or words of similar import.

quasi (implied in law) contract. A doctrine derived from the Civil Law, and applied under equitable principles, that provides for the payment of the reasonable value of an unjust enrichment conferred on one party at the expense of another.

quasi-judicial power. In administrative law, the power of an agency to conduct hearings before an administrative law judge to determine whether its rules have been violated in a trial-type proceeding.

quasi-legislative power. In administrative law, the power of an agency to make rules that have the same force and effect as statutes.

quiet title action. A legal action by which a person claiming an interest in certain real estate challenges others also claiming an interest to come before a court, which will decide the validity of any conflicting claims.

quitclaim. The basic form of a deed. It transfers the interest, if any, held by the grantor, with no promises (warranties).

quorum. Percentage of voters, established by-laws or other organization rules, needed at a meeting in order to conduct business legally.

race recording statute. A real estate recording statute that gives priority to the first interest to be recorded.

race-notice recording statute. A real estate recording statute that gives priority to first good faith interestholder to record.

ratification. Authorization, or manifestation of the intent to become bound to a previous transaction that was not binding at the time it occurred.

real (absolute) defense. In commercial paper law, a defense that may be asserted even against a holder in due course. (See also, *personal defense.*)

real estate. All property other than personal property, generally including the earth's crust together with all things attached thereto in a permanent fashion or peculiarly adapted for use with other real estate.

real property. Real estate.

rebuttal. A statement or evidence offered during legal proceedings to challenge the statement or evidence offered by the opposing party.

record date. In corporation law, a date established by a board of directors upon which a shareholder must be the registered owner of corporate shares in order to vote at a shareholder meeting.

reformation. In contract law, a judicial alteration of a writing to conform to the agreement of the parties.

registered agent. An agent of a foreign or alien corporation, registered in a state in which such a corporation has registered to do business, who is authorized to receive communications, and particularly service of process, on behalf of the corporation.

registration statement. A statement required to be filed by the 1933 federal securities act prior to the issuance of stock, containing information about the security itself, the issuer, and the underwriter.

relevant market. In antitrust law, the market (product or geographic) in which two firms are considered competitors.

remainder. A future interest in real estate belonging to someone other than the grantor, when there has been a grant of land less than a fee simple.

remand. The act of an appellate court sending a case back to a previous court for reconsideration in accord with the opinion of the appellate court.

replevin. An action by an owner to reclaim his property being wrongfully withheld.

republic. The form of government adopted for the United States, in which the citizens exercise control over the government through elected representatives, as opposed to a democracy in which citizens vote personally on all issues; sometimes called "representative democracy."

repudiation. The act of expressly or impliedly refusing to meet a contractual obligation.

rescission. Cancellation of a contractual or other obligation.

***respondeat superior*.** Liability of a principal or employer for torts committed by his agents or employees.

responsible share doctrine. The rule that corporate employees who have played a part the furtherance of a transaction that a regulatory statute outlaws are subject to the criminal provisions of the act.

restitution. A remedy requiring a person to restore to the plaintiff certain property he owns, being withheld by the defendant, or proceeds derived from the sale of the property.

restraint of trade. Anything that restricts the free flow of property or services in trade.

restricted securities. Securities that are not registered but are obtained through private placements.

restrictive covenant. A covenant (contractual promise) in a grant of real estate creating a restriction on the rights that otherwise would be held by the grantee.

restrictive indorsement. In commercial paper law, an indorsement that either (1) places a condition on the transfer of the instrument, or (2) *purports* to prohibit further negotiation.

resulting trust. When the owner of property has transferred legal title to another, but it appears from the conduct of the parties, or other facts and circumstances surrounding the transfer, that the transferor did not intend to transfer the equitable title (beneficial interest), or has done so imperfectly, a trust will "result" in favor of the transferor.

revenue-raising statute. A statute, the purpose of which is to raise revenue for the government, contrasted to safety statutes, which seek to protect the public from injury.

reverse. The act of an appellate court disagreeing with the decision of a prior court whose decision was appealed. A reversal frequently is accompanied by a remand.

reversion. A future interest in real estate involving a right of the grantor and his heirs to the property upon the termination of a previous estate.

revocable trust. A trust that may be canceled by the settlor at will.

revocation. A cancellation of a contractual offer by the offeror.

right of entry. A future interest in real estate similar to a possibility of reverter, differing only in that a possibility of reverter vests possession automatically, and a right of entry must be affirmatively exercised by its owner, usually by way of a lawsuit to take title.

right of redemption. A statutory right of a debtor to recover title to property that has been sold in a foreclosure sale by the payment of the purchase price and costs.

right of survivorship. The right of a surviving co-tenant of property to receive the share, or some part of the share, of his deceased co-tenant.

right to work law. In labor law, a state statute forbidding certain union security clauses, such as "union shop" or "agency shop." These laws are permitted by a provision of the 1947 Taft-Hartley Act.

riparian rights. A system of ownership of water rights under which owners of land abutting streams are entitled to use the water to the extent that they do not unreasonably diminish the flow down stream. See also, prior acquisition.

ripeness. In administrative law, a decision of an administrative agency is ripe (ready) for judicial review only when all appeals within the agency have been exhausted and the agency has made a final decision.

rule of reason. In antitrust law, a method by which conduct is determined to violate the law by considering that conduct, but also the surrounding facts and circumstances, as opposed to a per se violation.

rule 10b-5. A flexible general anti-fraud rule promulgated and enforced by the SEC that applies to anyone having access to or receiving material inside information from someone having access to it.

rule against perpetuities. A rule of law concerning future interests in real estate that prevents a grantor from controlling the title to the property for too long a time in the future. The rule provides that future interests must become possessory within a life in being plus 21 years in order to be valid.

sale on approval. Both title and risk of loss remain with the seller until the buyer accepts the goods.

sale or return. Title and risk pass according to the rules for a normal sale, but if the buyer elects to return the goods, the return is then treated as a separate contract of sale, and title and risk again shift as under a regular contract.

sales talk (puffing). General misrepresentations by a seller that one reasonably might expect a seller to make in bragging about his wares. These are not considered actionable misrepresentations in and of themselves.

scienter. Evil, tortious, intent.

secondary boycott. A boycott, or refusal to deal, directed toward a customer or supplier of an employer involved in a labor dispute.

secondary liability. Liability of a party that depends upon a failure of a party primarily liable to discharge a duty.

Securities and Exchange Commission (SEC). An administrative agency established under the 1934 Act to administer the various federal securities laws.

securities dealer. One engaged in the business of buying and selling securities for his own account.

securities underwriter. A person or firm that contracts with the original issuer to distribute the securities once they are issued.

security. Defined by the 1933 federal securities act as "any note, stock, treasury stock, bond, debenture, evidence of indebtedness, certificate of interest or participation in any profit sharing agreement, . . . investment contract, voting trust certificate, . . . fractional undivided interest in oil, gas or other mineral rights, . . . or in general, any interest or instrument commonly known as a security."

security interest. An interest in property of a debtor, taken by a creditor to secure the payment of an obligation.

self-proving will. A formal will that may be proved in the absence of signatures of ordinary witnesses. Self-proving wills are provided for by statute, and usually replace the ordinary witness requirement with a requirement that the testator swear and sign the will before a notary public or other official authorized to administer oaths.

separation of powers. A principle of the Constitution of the United States that the legislative, executive, and judicial powers of the United States government are divided among three branches of government, each with its own head, rather than resting with one individual.

servant. An employee over whom an employer maintains a right of control.

service of process. The act of legally summoning to court, generally by service of a summons or a subpoena.

servient tenement. In real estate law, land that is encumbered by an easement appurtenant.

settlor (trustor). The creator of a trust, who owns or controls the property later placed in the trust.

several liability. Liability such that a plaintiff in a lawsuit against two defendants, after a jury verdict or judicial determination of liability, must choose to hold one or the other to a judgment, but not both. (See also, *joint liability.*)

severance. In property law, a method of converting real estate to personal property by severing, or detaching, it from the real estate to which it is attached (e.g., cutting a tree).

severance vote. In labor law, if the collective bargaining unit selected for a representation election includes professional or craft employees with others, the professional and craft employees must be given an opportunity to vote on whether to remain part of the unit. This is done prior to certifying the unit and holding the general election.

sexual harassment. In employment law, defined by EEOC guidelines as unwelcome sexual advances, requests for sexual favors, and other verbal or physical conduct of a sexual nature.

share exchange. The exchange of a shareholder's shares for shares of a different class as a method of distribution, or for shares in another corporation as a method of reorganization.

shareholder. An owner of a corporation, the ownership interest being evidenced by shares of stock.

shareholder derivative suit. A lawsuit brought by a representative on behalf of shareholders, seeking to vindicate some right of the corporation, when the board of directors has failed or refused to seek enforcement on behalf of the corporation.

shelter rule. In commercial paper law, a rule that a person who takes an instrument after it has fallen into the hands of a holder in due course ordinarily is entitled to the rights of that holder in due course.

sheriff's deed. The type of deed received by a purchaser of real estate at a judicially-ordered sale.

sign. To place a mark on an instrument for the purpose of authentication.

simple contract. A contract deriving its validity from the presence of an offer, an acceptance, and consideration. (See also, *formal contract.*)

slander. Spoken defamation.

small issue exemption. An exemption for registration requirements under the 1933 Federal Securities Act for offers and sales of up to an amount of

$5,000,000 worth of securities during any one year period.

sole proprietorship.   A form of business organization having one owner/manager who has unlimited personal liability for business obligations.

sovereign immunity.   A doctrine that a government cannot be sued in tort without its permission.

sovereignty.   The supreme, ultimate, and uncontrollable power enjoyed by an independent government. (Under our system of government in the United States, the United States government is a sovereignty, but state governments, being controlled to some extent by the federal government, are not.)

special agent.   An agent possessing authority to conduct only one or a few transactions.

special damages.   *See* consequential damages.

special indorsement.   In commercial paper law, any indorsement that specifies (names) the indorsee.

special jurisdiction.   A court's jurisdiction over only a specific type of case, or limited types of cases, as opposed to general jurisdiction.

special warranty (trustee's) deed.   Like a general warranty deed except that the warranties apply only to the period during which the grantor has held the property granted.

specific performance.   A remedy granted by a court of equity, requiring the defendant to perform as promised rather than pay damages for breach of a contract.

spendthrift trust.   A trust for the purpose of seeing that the person is supported and has no power to dispose of the res (property), thus preventing the property from being squandered.

stale check.   A domestic check that has been outstanding for an unreasonable period (presumed under the UCC to be more than 30 days) after the date of execution.

standing to sue.   In administrative law, a person has standing to sue (is a proper person) for judicial review of an agency decision only if the decision affects him in some manner.

stare decisis.   The principal of Common Law providing that a judicial case decision establishes law to be followed by lower courts in deciding subsequent cases based on the same or similar fact situations.

statute.   The legislative enactment of Congress or a state legislature.

Statute of Frauds.   A statute generally requiring that certain kinds of contracts be evidenced by a proper writing in order to be legally enforceable.

stock.   Ownership of an interest in a corporation, evidenced by a stock certificate.

stock dividend.   A distribution to shareholders of corporate profits in the form of additional stock rather than cash.

stock split.   A share of stock in a corporation is split into a larger number of shares with no allocation of surplus to capital. The ownership interest of the affected shareholders remains the same, but is represented by a larger number of shares. (Note: Reverse stock splits combine shares of stock into a smaller number of shares.)

stop-payment order.   An order by a depositor to his bank withdrawing the bank's authority to pay a particular check out of the stated account.

strict (absolute) liability.   Civil liability without fault.

strict foreclosure.   In the law of secured transactions, a process by which a secured party, upon default by the debtor, may elect to take the collateral in full satisfaction of the debt rather than to undergo court-administered foreclosure proceedings.

strike.   In labor law, a concerted withdrawal of services by employees instituted against their employer.

subchapter s corporation.   A corporation approved by the Internal Revenue Service to be taxed as a partnership.

subject-matter jurisdiction.   The power of a court to hear cases involving certain types of subject matter or claims.

sublease.   A lease granted to a third party by a lessee of property.

subpoena.   A writ of process issued by a court to compel the attendance of witnesses, or jurors, or for the production of certain tangible evidence (subpoena duces tecum), at the trial of a civil lawsuit or a criminal action.

subrogation.   Under insurance law, upon payment of a loss under the policy, the insurer is entitled to have the rights of the assured against any third person who caused the loss.

substantial evidence. In administrative law, an agency's decisions on questions of fact will not be set aside by a court if they are supported by substantial evidence. In general, the term means only "some credible evidence" or, as one federal court stated, "more than a scintilla, but less than a preponderance."

substantial performance. Defective performance of a contract obligation to a degree less than material breach, but substantial enough to require the payment of damages. (See also, *material breach*.)

substantive due process. A requirement that any governmental action that involves a taking of private property for public use, or the deprivation of any other individual right, is constitutional only if it is fair for the government to take that action.

substantive law. The body of law establishing rights and imposing duties.

sufficient consideration. Consideration that meets the legal definition of consideration.

suicide clause. In insurance law, a provision in a life insurance policy covering death by suicide after a certain period of time elapses, commonly one or two years after the policy issues.

sum certain. In commercial paper laws, an agreed, or fixed, sum.

summary judgment. A judgment in a civil lawsuit, granted prior to trial, based on the pleadings and other evidence, such as affidavits or evidence obtained during discovery, demonstrating that an issue that is decisive of the case can be resolved without a trial.

summons. A writ of process issued by a court compelling the attendance of the defendant in a civil or a criminal action.

Sunday-closing statute. A statute requiring that most kinds of business remain closed on Sundays.

supremacy clause. Article VI, Clause 2 of the United States Constitution, which provides: "This constituion, and the laws of the United States which shall be made in pursuance thereof, and all treaties made, or which shall be made, under the authority of the United States, shall be the supreme law of the land; and the judges in every state shall be bound thereby, anything in the constitution or laws of any state to the contrary notwithstanding."

suretyship. A body of law involving contracts by which one person agrees to be liable for the debt, default, or miscarriage of another.

surviving corporation. In a merger of corporations, the corporation surviving as an entity. (See also, *merged corporation*.)

syndicates. *See* joint venture.

tangible property. Property that has a physical existence.

tax lien. A lien to secure the payment of taxes.

temporary restraining order (tro). Similar to an injunction, but granted by a court without prior notice to the affected persons defendant.

tenancy by the entireties. A type of concurrent ownership of real estate by a husband and wife. Such property can be taken by creditors only for joint debts of the husband and wife, and it is held with a right of survivorship.

tenancy in common. A type of concurrent ownership of property in which the owners own an undivided interest in the whole property. Such property can be taken by creditors of the individual owners, who hold the property without a right of survivorship.

tenancy in partnership. A type of concurrent ownership of partnership property by the partners. Such property can be taken only by creditors of the partnership, and it is held by the partners with a right of survivorship.

tenant. In real estate law, a lessee or holder of a leasehold interest; a concurrent owner of real estate.

tenant at sufferance. A tenant continuing in possession of property after termination of the lease (holdover tenant), who continues in possession "at the sufferance" of the landlord under terms specified by state law, usually month to month or for a specified period.

tender. An offer to perform by one ready, willing, and able to do so.

tender offer. A public offer, made directly to the shareholders of the target corporation (a corporation the tender offeror wishes to take over), to purchase the target company's equity securities at a set price for a certain period of time.

term life insurance.   Life insurance paying benefits only upon the death of the insured, with no savings feature, as opposed to whole life insurance.

termination.   In the law of business organizations, a ceasing to do business following the distribution of assets.

termination statement.   In the law of secured transaction, a document signed by a secured creditor releasing his claim to the collateral.

tertiary boycott.   A boycott, or refusal to deal, against a person more remote than a customer or supplier of the employer with whom a dispute exists. This may be a disassociated person or a customer or supplier of a customer or supplier of the "unfair" employer.

testamentary trust.   A trust created by a will.

testator.   A man disposing of property by will.

testatrix.   A female testator.

thing in action.   Chose in action.

third-party beneficiary.   One who will benefit from the performance of a contract entered into between two other persons. (See also, *creditor beneficiary, donee beneficiary,* and *incidental beneficiary.*)

time is of the essence.   When the parties to a contract have agreed expressly that time is of the essence of performance, late performance constitutes a material breach.

title.   The rights associated with the ownership of property.

title insurance.   Insurance issued covering losses resulting from defects in the title to real estate.

torrens recording statute.   A real estate recording statute that provides for interests to be recorded on a certificate, called a "torrens certificate," rather than on another public record.

tort.   A civil wrong arising out of the breach of a duty that has been imposed by society; a civil wrong other than a breach of contract.

totten trust.   A trust created by the deposit by one person of his own property in his own name as trustee for another.

trade acceptance.   In commercial paper law, a draft drawn by a seller of goods, ordering the buyer to pay the purchase price.

trade fixture.   A fixture that is attached for the purpose of conducting a trade or business, and ordinarily is attached by a tenant rather than an owner of the premises.

trade secret.   Any formula, pattern, device, or compilation of information that is used in one's business, and that gives him an opportunity to gain an advantage over competitors who do not know or use it.

trademark.   A symbol used to identify a product as that of a particular producer.

trading partnership.   A partnership that has the purchase and sale of property as its primary business.

treason.   Defined in Article 3, Section 3, clause 1, as follows: "Treason against the United States, shall consist only in levying war against them, or in adhering to their enemies, giving them aid and comfort."

trespass.   Entering or causing something to enter the property of another without permission or privilege; a civil action at law, as opposed to equity, generally resulting in the payment of money damages.

trespasser.   One who commits a trespass.

trust.   In the law of trusts, a separation of legal and equitable title in property so that one person, called the trustee, holds the legal title for the benefit of another, who holds the equitable title, called the beneficiary, and is entitled to the benefits flowing from the use of the property; in antitrust law, a business combination in which the shareholders of two or more corporations place their shares in trust, to be voted by the trustee in the best interests of the shareholders.

trust deed.   A real estate security device under which the debtor (settlor or trustor) will transfer title to a trustee, who will hold legal title in trust to secure fulfillment of the debtor's obligations to the creditor.

trustee.   The person holding legal title to trust property, to administer it for the benefit of the beneficiary.

trustor.   *See* settlor.

tying.   In antitrust law, a requirement of a seller that a purchaser must also purchase other specified goods or services in order to be qualified to purchase the goods or services he wants.

***ultra vires* act.**   An act by a corporation outside of its lawful powers.

ultrahazardous activity. An activity that is so dangerous to the public that the public cannot be adequately protected by the actor's exercise of ordinary care. Such activities give rise to strict (absolute) liability.

unconscionable contract. A contract so disproportionately favoring one party over the other that enforcing it would shock the conscience of an ordinary person, and generally entered into by parties who have grossly disproportionate bargaining power.

undisclosed principal. A principal whose existence and identity are not known to a third party who is not the principal or the agent.

undue influence. The use of a relationship of trust and confidence in order to extract from another promises or acts that would not have been given in the absence of the relationship.

unenforceable contract. A contract that, although valid, a court of law will not enforce. This differs from a void contract in that the court will not order the parties returned to status quo as of the time the contract was entered into.

unfair labor practice. An act proscribed by Section 8 of the National Labor Relations Act.

unfair labor practice strike. A strike by employees that is motivated by an unfair labor practice (in violation of Section 8(a) of the National Labor Relations Act) alleged to have been committed by their employer.

unforeseeable difficulty. A difficulty that could not have been foreseen through the exercise of reasonable care.

Uniform Commercial Code (UCC). A proposed statute governing commercial transactions, promulgated by the Commissioners on Uniform State Laws, and given to state legislatures for their adoption.

Uniform Consumer Credit Code (UCCC) A uniform act that prohibited a seller in a consumer transaction from taking a UCC Article 3 instrument, other than a check, as evidence of the purchaser's indebtedness.

unilateral contract. A contract formed by an act in return for a promise. (See also, *bilateral contract.*)

union security clause. In labor law, a clause in a collective bargaining contract that enhances the power of a union as collective bargaining agent, including closed shop, union ship, agency shop, maintenance of membership, and (in the opinions of some) checkoff.

union shop. In labor law, a union security clause in a collective bargaining contract providing that employees must become members of the union within a certain time after becoming employed as a condition of continued employment.

unprotected strike. In labor law, a strike contrary to a no-strike clause in a collective bargaining strike or involving a union unfair labor practice in violation of Section 8(b) of the National Labor Relations Act.

usage of trade. Any practice commonly observed in a place, vocation, or trade.

usury. Charging on a loan or forbearance interest in excess of the maximum rate established by law for that type of obligation.

valid contract. A simple contract that involves offer, acceptance, and consideration, or a formal contract that complies with the prescribed form.

value. In the law of secured transactions, anything that would be valid consideration for a contract as well as security interests or the satisfaction of all or part of a preexisting obligation. In the law of commercial paper, generally the same, but not including executory promises.

venue. The geographic place where a court's jurisdiction properly should be exercised.

verdict. The decision of a jury following the trial of a civil or a criminal case.

vertical merger. A merger between two businesses in an industry but on different levels of production, such as retail or wholesale. (See also, *horizontal mergers.*)

vertical restraint. In antitrust law, a restraint of trade involving agreements between firms on the different business levels, such as a manufacturer and a retailer, in the same line of business.

vested right. A right that cannot be taken away by others without the consent of the person holding the right.

void contract. An agreement that is not a valid contract.

voidable contract. A valid contract subject to being declared void at the request of one or more of the parties.

voluntary bankruptcy. Bankruptcy proceedings initiated by a debtor.

voting trust. Shareholders transfer their voting rights to a trustee who votes them at shareholder meetings on behalf of the shareholders, who are beneficiaries of the trust.

wage-earner bankruptcy. A proceeding under Chapter 13 of the federal bankruptcy act involving the filing of a plan for the payment of some or all of the debts of a person with regular income, leading to the discharge of the debts.

wagering. The creation of a risk for the purpose of assuming it; generally contrasted to insurance.

warrant. A certificate issued to shareholders evidencing option rights.

warranty. A contractual promise.

warranty deed. *See* general warranty deed and special warranty deed.

watered stock. Stock issued by a corporation for which the holder has paid less than his proportionate share of stated capital.

whole life insurance. A life insurance policy providing a savings feature, under which benefits are payable upon lapse or termination of the policy, as opposed to term life insurance.

will. A document disposing of property upon the death of the owner.

winding up. In the law of business organizations, the liquidation and distribution of assets.

worker right-to-know law. Originally state statutes, now supplemented by federal legislation, requiring employers to assess hazards in the workplace and to inform employees of them.

workers' compensation. A no-fault statutory system of compensating employees for injuries arising out of, and in the course and scope of, employment, and replacing the previous tort (fault) system of compensation.

working papers. In general, the written records of procedures and materials used in the process of an audit, upon which significant decisions and conclusions are based. This may include reviews of entire systems, internal controls, testing procedures used, and summaries and excerpts from clients' records and other documents.

writ. In the law of judicial procedure, an order or precept issued by a court.

writ of *certiorari*. An order by an upper court directing a lower court to send up the records of a case for its review.

writ of execution. An order of a court after a civil lawsuit ordering that certain non-exempt property of the defendant be seized and sold to pay a judgment.

writing. In commercial paper law, the reduction of thought to tangible form.

zoning. A process involving a local ordinance by which a city or other state subdivision restricts structural and architectural designs, and also the uses to which property may be subject. The affected city, township, or county is divided into districts (zones), each controlled by a different set of restrictions.

Case Index

Subject Index